The
National Electrical Code®
Handbook

The
National Electrical Code® Handbook

Based on the 1984 Edition of the *National Electrical Code*

PETER J. SCHRAM, Editor

JOHN M. CALOGGERO, Associate Editor
JOSEPH A. TEDESCO, Associate Editor

Third Edition

National Fire Protection Association
Quincy, Massachusetts

This is the third edition of *The National Electrical Code® Handbook* published by the National Fire Protection Association. The National Fire Protection Association formerly sponsored a handbook which was published by the McGraw-Hill Book Company and based on the *National Electrical Code.®* This publication, *The National Electrical Code® Handbook,* does not emanate from and is not in any way connected with or associated with the McGraw-Hill Book Company.

®Registered trademarks of the National Fire Protection Association
Life Safety Code® is a registered trademark of the National Fire Protection Association.

Copyright © 1983
National Fire Protection Association
All rights reserved

NFPA No. SPP-6D
ISBN 0-87765-250-3
Library of Congress No. 77-93950
Printed in the United States of America

First Printing, October 1983
Second Printing, January 1984

Contents

CONTENTS

CONTENTS

CONTENTS

CONTENTS

CONTENTS

CONTENTS

CONTENTS

CONTENTS

Preface

The *National Electrical Code* is the most widely adopted code in the world. The combined sales of the 1978 and 1981 editions totaled over 1.7 million copies. The *National Electrical Code* is a nationally accepted guide for the safe installation of electrical conductors and equipment and is, in fact, the basis for all electrical codes used in the United States. It is also used extensively outside of the United States, particularly where American-made equipment is installed.

The *National Electrical Code Handbook* is published by the National Fire Protection Association in order to assist those concerned with electrical safety in understanding the intent of the 1984 edition of the *Code*. A verbatim reproduction of the 1984 *National Electrical Code* is included, and added where necessary are comments, diagrams, and illustrations that are intended to clarify further some of the intricate requirements of the *National Electrical Code*.

The editor has worked very closely with members of the National Electrical Code Committee in discussions that have led to the various revisions that have been incorporated in the 1984 Edition of the *Code*. The assistance and cooperation of the Code-Making Panel Chairmen and various Committee members are herein gratefully acknowledged.

The editor acknowledges with thanks the manufacturers and their representatives who generously supplied photographs, drawings, and data upon request. Special thanks, too, go to the editors and contributors to past editions, in particular past editors Wilford I. Summers and Joseph A. Ross.

Appreciation is expressed to the NFPA staff members who attended to the countless details that went into the preparation of this *Handbook,* and especially to Mary Strother and Cassandra Goldwater, editing and proofreading; Elizabeth Carmichael, Louise Grant, and Peggy Travers, composition; Jim L. Linville, editorial liaison; Carmen Johnson, art coordinator; Shirley (Lee) Letta, technical material coordination; Gloria Levine, typing; and Donald McGonagle, production.

Finally, the editor wishes to express his sincere appreciation to Paul Duks and Charles B. Schram of UL for their special help on specific articles.

Peter J. Schram, *Editor*

Concise History of the
National Electrical Code

In 1881, the National Association of Fire Engineers met in Richmond, Virginia. From this meeting came a proposal that served as a basis for the first *National Electrical Code,* covering items such as the use of insulated conduit, the use of single disconnect devices, and the identification of the white wire. The first nationally recommended electrical code was published by the National Board of Fire Underwriters (now the American Insurance Association) in 1895. (The National Board of Fire Underwriters continued to publish the *National Electrical Code* until 1962, thus contributing greatly to its current universality.) With this 1895 code as a basis, in 1897 the *National Electrical Code* was drafted, the product of the combined labors of architectural, electrical, insurance, and allied interests which, through the National Conference on Standard Electrical Rules, composed of delegates from various national associations, unanimously voted to recommend it to their respective associations for approval or adoption.

In 1911, the National Fire Protection Association (NFPA) assumed sponsorship and control of the *National Electrical Code,* the National Conference on Standard Electrical Rules having disbanded in that very same year. Since 1920, the *National Electrical Code* has also been officially endorsed by the American National Standards Institute (formerly the United States of America Standards Institute and the American Standards Association), and the NFPA has maintained its capacity as Administrative Sponsor. Since that date, the Committee has been identified as "ANSI Standards Committee C1" (formerly "USAS C1" or "ASA C1").

In 1923, the *National Electrical Code* was rearranged and rewritten; in 1937 it was editorially revised so that all of the general rules would appear in the first chapters followed by supplementary rules in the following chapters; and, in 1959, it was editorially revised again, this time in order to incorporate a new numbering system under which each section of each article is identified by the article number preceding the section number. The National Fire Protection Association has been publishing and distributing the *National Electrical Code* since 1951. It does so through its own office and through the American National Standards Institute. In addition, the *National Electrical Code* is found in Volume Six of the NFPA's annual *National Fire Codes®.* The *National Electrical Code* is acknowledged to be the most widely adopted code of standard practices in the U.S.A.

1984 Edition of the *National Electrical Code*

This 1984 Edition of the *National Electrical Code* (NFPA 70-1984) was adopted by the National Fire Protection Association on May 18, at its 1983 Annual Meeting held in Kansas City, MO. It was approved by the American National Standards Institute on August 5, 1983, and it will be known as ANSI/NFPA 70-1984. It supersedes all previous editions of the *National Electrical Code,* the most recent previous edition being 1981.

This *Code* is purely advisory as far as the NFPA and ANSI are concerned but is offered for use in law and for regulatory purposes in the interest of life and property protection. Anyone noticing any errors should please notify the NFPA Executive Office, the Chairman and the Secretary of the Committee.

CONCISE HISTORY OF THE NATIONAL ELECTRICAL CODE

Development of the *National Electrical Code*

In accordance with the provisions of the NFPA Regulations Governing Committee Projects, a National Electrical Code Committee Report containing proposed amendments to the 1981 *National Electrical Code* was published by the NFPA in June 1982. This report recorded the actions of the various Code-Making Panels and the Correlating Committee of the National Electrical Code Committee on each proposal that had been made to revise the 1981 *Code*. The report was circulated to all members of the National Electrical Code Committee, and was made available to other interested NFPA members and to the public for review and comment. Following the close of the public comment period, the Code-Making Panels met, acted on each comment and reported their action to the Correlating Committee. The NFPA published the National Electrical Code Technical Committee Documentation in April, 1983, which recorded the actions of the Code-Making Panels and the Correlating Committee on each public comment to the National Electrical Code Technical Committee Report. The NFPA also published the Advanced Printing of the Proposed 1984 *National Electrical Code* in April 1983 to permit the study and evaluation by those interested, prior to formal action on the Committee Report by the 1983 NFPA Annual Meeting. The National Electrical Code Committee Report and National Electrical Code Committee Documentation were presented to the 1983 NFPA Annual Meeting for adoption. The proceedings of that adoption are published in the September 1983 issue of the NFPA *Fire Journal*®.

Coincident with the above processing procedures, each of the Code-Making Panels and the Chairman of the Correlating Committee reported their recommendations to meetings of the Electrical Section at the 1983 NFPA Annual Meeting. The Electrical Section thus had opportunity to discuss and review the report of the National Electrical Code Committee prior to the adoption of this edition of the *Code* by the Association.

The *Electrical Code for One- and Two-Family Dwellings*, NFPA 70A-1984, is an abridged version of the 1984 text, edited only as dictated to eliminate extraneous material not of concern to this type of occupancy, and to place in the text only the more popular types of wiring methods, not to exclude any other type authorized by the complete *Code*.

Summary of Code Changes

Art. 90 — Introduction
New. 90-2(a)(4); 90-4 3rd paragraph; 90-5 Fine Print Note; Titles, 90-7(a); 90-7(b).
Revised. 90-5.

Art. 100 — Definitions
New. Ground-Fault Protection of Equipment; Solar Photovoltaic System.
Revised. Accessible (As applied to Equipment); Ampacity; Interrupting Rating; Fine Print Note, Raceway; Readily Accessible (See "Accessible Readily").
Deleted. Communication Circuit.

Art. 110 — Requirements for Electrical Installations
New. 110-14, Fine Print Note; 110-16(c), Exception Nos. 1 and 2; Titles, 110-17(a); 110-17(b); 110-17(c); 110-33(a), Exception Nos. 1 and 2; Title, 110-33(b).
Revised. 110-1; 110-16(c); 110-31(b)(1), Fine Print Note; 110-33(a).

Art. 200 — Use and Identification of Grounded Conductors
New. Reference to 690-41, Exception, 200-2.

Art. 210 — Branch Circuits
New. 210-3, Exception; 210-6(a), Exception No. 5; 210-6(b)(2), Fine Print Note; 210-7, Exception No. 2; 210-8(b); 210-20, Exception No. 2; 210-23(d).
Revised. 210-4; 210-6(a), Exception No. 1 a., b., Exception No. 2; Exception No. 2 c.; 210-6(c)(2); 210-7(b), Exception No. 2; 210-7(d), Exception; 210-19(a); 210-20, Exception Nos. 1 and 2; 210-21(b)(3); 210-23(a); 210-23(b); 210-23(c); 210-24; Table 210-24 single asterisk (*) Note; 210-52(d); 210-60; 210-70(a).
Deleted. 210-8(b), Exception Nos. 1 and 2 (See Art. 305); reference to 210-8(a)(4) in 210-52(f).

Art. 215 — Feeders
Revised. 215-2; 215-9.

Art. 220 — Branch-Circuit and Feeder Calculations
New. Second paragraph, 220-1; 220-3(b)(1), Exception Nos. 1 and 2; Table 220-19, Note 5, Fine Print Note.
Revised. 220-2(c), Exception Nos. 1 and 3; Table 220-2(b); 220-3(b)(2); 220-3(d); Fine Print Note, 220-3(d); Table 220-11; 220-12; Table 220-13; 220-15; 220-16(a); 220-16(b); Title, 220-17; 220-18; 220-19; 220-20; 220-22; Fine Print Note, 220-22; 220-30(b)(1)(2)(3); Table 220-30; 220-31; 220-32(c)(1) and (2); Table 220-34.
Deleted. 220-2, Exception No. 2.

Art. 225 — Outside Branch-Circuits and Feeders
New. Reference to Solar Photovoltaic Systems, 225-2.
Revised. Fine Print Note, 225-1; 225-6(b), Definition of Festoon Lighting to full size print; 225-7(d); 225-18; 225-19(a); 225-19(a), Exception No. 5; 225-19(d), last sentence to Exception; 225-19(e); Fine Print Note.

Art. 230 — Services
New. 230-40; Exception No. 6, 230-82; Exception No. 1, 230-83; Exception Nos. 1 and 2, 230-84(a); 230-205(a) and Exception.
Revised. 230-2, Exception No. 2; 230-2, Exception No. 3; 230-2, Exception No. 7; 230-4, Third Fine Print Note; 230-5, reference to service-entrance conductors; 230-24(c), Exception; 230-40 renumbered 230-41; 230-41 renumbered 230-42; 230-70; 230-71(a); 230-72(a); 230-72(d) renumbered 230-72(c); 230-74; 230-76; 230-77; 230-83, Exception, renumbered Exception No. 2; 230-84(a); reference in Exception No. 5, 230-90, 230-95(c); Fine Print Note reference 230-200; 230-202(b); 230-205(a); 230-205(b); Fine Print Note 230-208.
Deleted. Exception No. 1, 230-72(a); 230-72(c); 230-96.

Art. 240 — Overcurrent Protection
New. Reference to Solar Photovoltaic Systems, 240-2; Exception Nos. 1, 2 and 3, 240-4; Exception No. 10 g., 240-21; Exception, 240-33; Second paragraph, 240-100.
Revised. Exception Nos. 1 and 2, 240-3; 240-4; Exception, 240-20; Exception No. 3, 240-21; Exception No. 2, 240-22; 240-23; Exception No. 2, 240-24(a) renumbered to Exception No. 1; Exception No. 3, 240-24(a) renumbered to Exception No. 2; 240-33; 240-61; 240-81; 240-83(a); 240-83(d).
Deleted. Exception No. 1, 240-24(a); Exception Nos. 1 and 2, 240-61.

Art. 250 — Grounding
New. Reference to Solar Photovoltaic Systems, 690-41, 690-42, 690-43, 690-44, 250-2; Exception

SUMMARY OF CODE CHANGES

Nos. 1 and 2, 250-24; Fine Print Note, 250-74; Exception, 250-76; 250-76(c); Exception, 250-79(d); Exception, 250-80(a); Second paragraph, 250-81(a); Exception No. 1 b. and c., 250-94; Exception No. 2 b. and c., 250-94.

Revised. References from 675-8, 675-9, 675-10, 675-11 to 675-11(c), 675-12, 675-13, 675-14, 675-15, Electrically Driven or Controlled Irrigation Machines; Titles, Metalworking Machine Tools to Metalworking Machine Tools and Plastic Machinery; Outlet, Switch and Junction Boxes, and Fittings to Outlet, Device, Pull and Junction Boxes, Conduit Bodies and Fittings, 250-2; 250-24(a); 250-24(b); Exception, 250-26(a); Exception, 250-26(b); Exception No. 1, 250-45(d); Fine Print Note, 250-45(d); Reference Fine Print Note, 250-46; Exception, 250-50(a)(b); Exception No. 1, 250-57(b); 250-60; 250-60(c); 250-71(a)(3); 250-71(b)(1); 250-72(c); 250-72(d); Exception Nos. 1 and 4, 250-74; 250-76(a); 250-76(b); 250-79(c); 250-79(d); 250-80(a); 250-81(a); 250-91; Exception No. 2, 250-91(b); Third paragraph, 250-95; Exception, 250-112; 250-114.

Art. 280 — Surge Arresters
Revised. 280-4(b), Fine Print Note.

Art. 300 — Wiring Methods
New. Exception Nos. 3 and 5, 300-1(a); Exception, 300-1(c); Exception, 300-3(a); Exception, 300-4(a)(1); Exception, 300-4(a)(2); 300-4(c); Exception Nos. 1 and 2, 300-5(i); Second paragraph and Exception, 300-11; Exception No. 7, 300-15(b); Fine Print Note, 300-21.

Revised. Exception No. 3 renumbered Exception No. 4, 300-1(a); 300-3(a); 300-3(b); 300-1(a)(1); 300-1(a)(2); Exception No. 1, 300-5(a); 300-5(b); 300-5(d); Exception Nos. 4 and 5, 300-15(b); Fine Print Note, 300-17; 300-21.

Deleted. 300-18; 300-33.

Art. 305 — Temporary Wiring
New. 305-4 [relocated from 210-8(b)].

Art. 310 — Conductors for General Wiring
New. Fine Print Note, Exception No. 2, 310-4; Fine Print Notes, 310-15(b); Obelisk Notes, Table 310-13; Type SA, Table 310-13; Exception No. 4, Note 8 to Tables 310-16 through 310-19; Tables 310-20, 310-20A, 310-21, 310-22, 310-23, 310-24, 310-25, 310-26, 310-27, 310-28, 310-29, 310-30; Figure 310-1.

Revised. 310-4; Second and fourth paragraphs, Exception No. 2, 310-4; Fine Print Note, Table 310-5; 310-6; Fine Print Note, 310-10; Exception No. 1, 310-12(b); 310-13; 310-15(a); Table 310-13 arranged in alphabetical order and Types AVA, AVB and AVL reference from Table 310-37 to Table 310-67; Types FEP or FEPB; MI; PFA; RHH; RHW; Z; ZW; Type V, Reference from Table 310-35 or 310-36 to Table 310-65 or 310-66; Titles, Tables 310-16, 310-17, 310-18, 310-19; Notes following Tables 310-16 and 310-17; Note 8 to Tables 310-16 through 310-19; Table 310-31 renumbered to 310-61; Table 310-32 renumbered to 310-62; Table 310-33 renumbered to 310-63; Table 310-34 renumbered to 310-64; Table 310-35 renumbered to 310-65; Table 310-36 renumbered to 310-66; Table 310-37 renumbered to 310-67; Title and Table 310-39 renumbered to 310-69; Title and Table 310-40 renumbered to 310-70; Title and Table 310-41 renumbered to 310-71; Title and Table 310-42 renumbered to 310-72;

Title and Table 310-43 renumbered to 310-73; Title and Table 310-44 renumbered to 310-74; Title and Table 310-45 renumbered to 310-75; Title and Table 310-46 renumbered to 310-76; Title and Table 310-47 renumbered to 310-77; Title and Table 310-48 renumbered to 310-78; Title and Table 310-49 renumbered to 310-79; Title and Table 310-50 renumbered to 310-80; Title and Table 310-51 renumbered to 310-81; Title and Table 310-52 renumbered to 310-82; Title and Table 310-53 renumbered to 310-83; Title and Table 310-54 renumbered to 310-84; Title, Notes to Tables 310-39 through 310-54 renumbered to Notes to Tables 310-69 through 310-84; Notes 2 and 3 to Tables 310-69 through 310-84.

Deleted. Reference to 680-20(b)(1), Exception No. 2, 310-3; Notes 2 and 12 to Tables 310-16 through 310-19.

Art. 318 — Cable Trays
Revised. 318-1; 318-2(b)(1); 318-4(c); Title 318-5(d); 318-5(d); Exception No. 1, 318-5(d); Exception Nos. 1 and 2, 318-12(a); 318-12(b)(1) and (2).

Art. 320 — Open Wiring on Insulators
No Changes.

Art. 321 — Messenger Supported Wiring
New. 321-3(b) (1) and (2).
Revised. 321-3(b); 321-5.

Art. 324 — Concealed Knob-and-Tube Wiring No Changes.

Art. 325 — Integrated Gas Spacer Cable Type IGS *New.* Complete Article.

Art. 326 — Medium Voltage Cable
Revised. 326-3; 326-5.

Art. 328 — Flat Conductor Cable Type FCC *Revised.* 328-10.

Art. 330 — Mineral-Insulated, Metal-Sheathed Cable No Changes.

Art. 331 — Electrical Nonmetallic Tubing
New. Complete Article.

Art. 333 — Armored Cable
New. Titles 333-6(a) and (b).

Art. 334 — Metal-Clad Cable
No Changes.

Art. 336 — Nonmetallic-Sheathed Cable
Revised. 336-2; 336-3; 336-6(b).

Art. 337 — Shielded Nonmetallic-Sheathed Cable No Changes.

Art. 338 — Service-Entrance Cable
Revised. 338-1(a) and (b).

Art. 339 — Underground Feeder and Branch-Circuit Cable *New.* Exception, 339-3(a)(2).
Revised. Exception, 339-3(a)(4).

Art. 340 — Power and Control Tray Cable *Revised.* 340-3; 340-7.

Art. 342 — Nonmetallic Extensions
Revised. 342-3(c).

Art. 344 — Underplaster Extensions
No Changes.

Art. 345 — Intermediate Metal Conduit
New. Exception Nos. 1 and 2, 345-12.
Revised. 345-14.

Art. 346 — Rigid Metal Conduit
New. Fine Print Note, 346-6.
Revised. Table 346-10; Table 346-10 Exception; 346-14; 346-15(a).
Deleted. 346-15(d).

Art. 347 — Rigid Nonmetallic Conduit
New. Fine Print Note, 347-11.
Revised. 347-16.
Deleted. 347-17(b).

Art. 348 — Electrical Metallic Tubing
New. Fine Print Note, 348-6.
Revised. 348-14.

Art. 349 — Flexible Metallic Tubing
New. Fine Print Note, 349-12(b).

Art. 350 — Flexible Metal Conduit
Revised. 305-2.

Art. 351 — Liquidtight Flexible Conduit
New. Exception No. 3, 351-8; Exception No. 2, 351-9; Fine Print Note, 351-9; Exception, 351-24.
Revised. 351-4(a); Exception No. 2, 351-8; Exception, 351-9 to Exception No. 1, 351-22; 351-24.

Art. 352 — Surface Raceways
New. Fine Print Note, 352-4.
Revised. 352-1; 352-22.

Art. 353 — Multioutlet Assembly
No Changes.

Art. 354 — Underfloor Raceways
New. Fine Print Note, 354-5.
Revised. 354-15.

Art. 356 — Cellular Metal Floor Raceways
New. Fine Print Note, 356-5.
Revised. 356-11.

Art. 358 — Cellular Concrete Floor Raceways
No Changes.

Art. 362 — Wireways
New. Fine Print Note, 362-5.
Revised. 362-2; 362-10.

Art. 363 — Flat Cable Assemblies
No Changes.

Art. 364 — Busways
Revised. 364-4.

Art. 365 — Cablebus
No Changes.

Art. 366 — Electrical Floor Assemblies
No Changes.

Art. 370 — Outlet, Device, Pull and Junction Boxes, Conduit Bodies and Fittings
New. Exception, 370-7(c); Fine Print Note, 370-22.
Revised. Title; 370-1; 370-4; 370-5; 370-6; 370-6(a); 370-7; 370-7(b); 370-7(c); 370-8; 370-13; Fine Print Note, 370-15(a); 370-15(c); 370-18(a)(2); 370-18(c); Title, 370-20; 370-20(a); 370-20(b); 370-20(c); 370-22.

Art. 373 — Cabinets and Cutout Boxes
New. Exception, 373-6(c).
Revised. Table 373-6(b); 373-6(c); 373-10(b).

Art. 374 — Auxiliary Gutters
New. Fine Print Note, 374-5.
Revised. 374-9(d); 374-9(e).

Art. 380 — Switches
Revised. 380-11.

Art. 384 — Switchboards and Panelboards
New. Exception, 384-3(f); Exception Nos. 3 and 4, 384-25.
Revised. 384-2; 384-3(e); 384-6; 384-7; Exception No. 1, 384-7.

Art. 400 — Flexible Cords and Cables
New. Fine Print Note, 400-10.
Revised. 400-4; Table 400-4; 400-5; 400-7(a); 400-7(b); 400-9; 400-10; 400-36.

Art. 402 — Fixture Wires
Revised. 402-3; Table 402-3.

Art. 410 — Lighting Fixtures, Lampholders, Lamps, Receptacles, and Rosettes
New. Fine Print Note, 410-4(c)(4); Exception, 410-14(a); Exception, 410-56(b); Part S, Lighting Track.
Revised. 410-4(a); 410-4(b); 410-4(c)(4); 410-4(d); 410-16(d); 410-16(f); 410-25(a); 410-25(b); 410-27(c); 410-29(b); Exception No. 1, 410-31; 410-36; 410-56(g) renumbered 410-56(b); 410-56(b) renumbered 410-56(c); 410-56(c) renumbered 410-56(d); 410-56(e) renumbered 410-56(f); 410-56(f) renumbered 410-56(g); 410-66 to 410-66(a), (b) and Exception; 410-73(e); 410-73(f); 410-82; 410-84.

Art. 422 — Appliances
Revised. 422-8(d)(1); 422-8(d)(2); 422-27(a).

Art. 424 — Fixed Electric Space Heating Equipment
New. Part I, Electric Radiant Heating Panels and Heating Panel Sets.
Revised. 424-3(b); 424-22(a); 424-22(b); Title Part E; 424-34; 424-35; 424-37; 424-38(a); 424-38(b); 424-38(c); 424-39; Title 424-43; 424-43(a); Title 424-44; 424-44(a); 424-59; Fine Print Note, 424-59; 424-61; 424-62; 424-66; 424-82.

Art. 426 — Fixed Outdoor Electric De-Icing and Snow-Melting Equipment
New. 426-50(b).
Revised. 426-3; 426-50 renumbered 426-50(a); 426-52.

Art. 427 — Fixed Electric Heating Equipment for Pipelines and Vessels
New. 427-30.

Art. 430 — Motors, Motor Circuits, and Controllers
New. Fine Print Note, 430-16; Exception, 430-28; 430-29; Second Fine Print Note, 430-31; Exception, 430-35(b); Fine Print Note, 430-51; Fine Print Note, 430-61; Table 430-72(b); Exception No. 1, 430-72(c); 430-91; Table 430-91.
Revised. 430-5; Table 430-12(b) for Direct Current Motors; Table 430-23(c); 430-27; Fine Print Note, 430-31; 430-32; 430-32(a)(3); 430-32(b)(1); 430-32(c)(3); 430-32(d); 430-33; 430-51; 430-52; 430-53(c), (c)(1), (c)(2) and (c)(3); 430-72(b) and Exception Nos. 1, 2, 3 and 4; 430-72(c) Exceptions renumbered; 430-81(a); 430-109; 430-111; 430-123; 430-145(a).
Deleted. 430-4.

Art. 440 — Air-Conditioning and Refrigerating Equipment
New. 440-12(d); Exception, 440-22(a).
Revised. 440-2(d); 440-12(d) renumbered to 440-12(e); 440-22(a); Exception No. 1, 440-22(b)(2); 440-41(a); 440-52(b).

Art. 445 — Generators
Revised. 445-6.

Art. 450 — Transformers and Transformer Vaults

New. Fine Print Note, 450-3(c); 450-4; First Fine Print Note, 450-23; 450-28.

Revised. Fine Print Note, 450-2; 450-4 renumbered to 450-5; 450-5 renumbered to 450-6; 450-6 renumbered to 450-7; 450-7 renumbered to 450-8; 450-8 renumbered to 450-9; Fine Print Note, 450-9; 450-9 renumbered to 450-10; 450-10 renumbered to 450-11; 450-11 renumbered to 450-12; 450-21(b); 450-23; 450-27.

Art. 460 — Capacitors

Revised. Exception, 460-8(b); 460-9.
Deleted. 460-7.

Art. 470 — Resistors and Reactors

No Changes.

Art. 480 — Storage Batteries

Revised. 480-6.

Art. 500 — Hazardous (Classified) Locations

New. 3rd and 5th through 12th Fine Print Notes, 500-2; 16th and 19th Fine Print Notes, 500-2; 3rd and 4th paragraphs, 500-2(a); 4th paragraph, 500-2(b); 500-2(d); Fine Print Notes, 500-5(b).

Revised. 3rd and 6th Fine Print Notes 500-1; 500-2; 2nd and 13th through 15th Fine Print Notes, 500-2; 500-2(a); Exception No. 2 and Fine Print Note, 500-2(b); 500-2(c); Fine Print Note, 500-2(c); 500-5(a); 500-5(b); Fine Print Notes, 500-6(a).

Deleted. 5th Fine Print Note, 500-1; 4th Fine Print Note, 500-2; 6th Fine Print Note, 500-2; Table 500-2.

Art. 501 — Class I Locations

New. Fine Print Note, 501-8(b); Exception, 501-9(b)(1); 501-17.

Revised. 501-3(a); 501-3(b)(5); 501-4(b); Fine Print Note, 501-5; Exception, 501-5(a)(1); 501-5(a)(2); Fine Print Note, 501-5(a)(2); 501-5(a)(4); 501-5(b)(2); Exception, 501-5(b)(2); 501-5(e)(1); 501-5(e)(3); 501-5(f)(3); Fine Print Note, 501-5(f)(3); 501-6(b)(2); 501-6(b)(5); 501-8(b); 501-9(b)(1); 501-11; 501-16; 501-16(a); 501-16(b).

Deleted. 501-16(c), (d), and (e).

Art. 502 — Class II Locations

New. 502-17.

Revised. Last paragraph, 502-1; 502-11(b)(1); Fine Print Note, 502-14; 502-16; 502-16(a); 502-16(b).

Deleted. Table 502-1; 502-3; 502-16(c) and (d).

Art. 503 — Class III Locations

New. Exception, 503-11; 503-16(a); 503-16(b).

Revised. Fine Print Note, 503-1; 503-3(a); 503-6; 503-9(c); 503-9(d); 503-10; 503-11; 503-12; 503-13(a); 503-16.

Art. 510 — Hazardous (Classified) Locations — Specific

No Changes.

Art. 511 — Commercial Garages, Repair and Storage

Revised. 511-2(f); 511-5(a).

Art. 513 — Aircraft Hangars

Revised. 513-5(c).

Art. 514 — Gasoline Dispensing and Service Stations

New. Exception No. 2, 514-8.

Revised. Fine Print Note, 514-1; 514-8 and Exceptions.

Art. 515 — Bulk Storage Plants

No Changes.

Art. 516 — Spray Application, Dipping and Coating Processes

Revised. Article rewritten to correlate with NFPA 33 and NFPA 34.

Art. 517 — Health Care Facilities

New. Two Fine Print Notes, 517-1; 517-2, Psychiatric Hospital; 517-6; Fine Print Note, 517-13; 517-14(c); Fine Print Note, Part E; Fine Print Note, 517-58; Fine Print Note, Part F; 517-82; 517-83(b), Exception; 517-84(c)(4); 517-101(b)(2), Exception; 517-101(c)(1), Exception; Fine Print Note, 517-143(a)(2).

Revised. 517-1; 517-2, Anesthetizing Location, Flammable Anesthetizing Location, Health Care Facilities, Nurses' Station, Patient Vicinity, Reference Grounding Point, Residential Custodial Care Facility; Title, 517-11; Fine Print Note, Part C; 517-44(c); 517-47(d) renumbered 517-47(c); 517-47(e) changed to Fine Print Note, 517-47(c); Fine Print Note, Part E; 517-58; 517-60(a)(5) renumbered 517-60(a)(4); 517-61(a) renumbered 517-61; 517-65(d) renumbered 517-65(c); 517-65(e) changed to Fine Print Note, 517-65(c); Fine Print Note, 517-80; 517-84(a); 517-84(c)(4) renumbered to 517-84(c)(2); 517-84(c)(5) renumbered to 517-84(c)(3); 517-84(d); 517-90(b); 517-100(b); 517-101(b)(5); 517-101(c)(1); 517-104(a)(2); 517-104(a)(3); 517-141(b); 517-143(a)(2); 517-143(b).

Deleted. 517-2, Anesthetizing Location Receptacle, Immediate Restoration of Service; 517-11(b); 517-31; 517-43; 517-47(c); 517-59; 517-60(a)(4); 517-61(b); 517-65(c); 517-83(c); 517-84(c)(2); 517-84(c)(3); 517-106; 517-122(c); 517, Part J; 517-144; 517-147.

Art. 518 — Places of Assembly

New. 518-2(c).
Revised. Fine Print Note, 518-1; 518-3.

Art. 520 — Theaters and Similar Locations

New. 520-7; Exception Nos. 1 and 2, 520-53(h); 520-53(j), (k), (l), (n); 520-62(d).

Revised. 520-45; 520-51; 520-53(f); 520-53(j) to 520-53(m); 520-67; 520-81.

Art. 530 — Motion Picture and Television Studios and Similar Locations

New. 530-21.
Revised. Fine Print Note, 530-1; 530-18(a).

Art. 540 — Motion Picture Projectors

New. 540-11(c).
Revised. Fine Print Note, 540-1; Fine Print Note, 540-10.

Art. 545 — Manufactured Building

No Changes.

Art. 547 — Agricultural Buildings

New. Fine Print Note, 547-7.

Art. 550 — Mobile Homes and Mobile Home Parks

New. Second Fine Print Note, 550-3(i); Fine Print Note, 550-12(b); 550-24.

Revised. 550-1(b); 550-8(e); 550-10(b)(1); 550-10(b)(3); 550-11(a); 550-11(b)(6); 550-12; 550-12(a) and (b); Fine Print Note, 550-12(b); 550-21; 550-22(a); Table 550-22; 550-22(b); 550-23(c) and (d).

Art. 551 — Recreational Vehicles and Recreational Vehicle Parks

New. 551-5(f); 551-14(p); 551-14(q); Fine Print Note, 551-44(c).

Revised. Fine Print Note, 551-1; 551-3(d); 551-5(b);

551-8; 551-8(a), (b), (c), and (d); 551-9(b) and (c); 551-10(a), (b), (c), and (d); 551-12(b); 551-13(b); 551-20(a); 551-24; 551-42; 551-44(a); Table 551-44; 551-44(c).

Art. 555 — Marinas and Boatyards
New. Second Fine Print Note, 555-3.
Revised. Fine Print Note, 555-2; 555-3; 555-4; 555-22.

Art. 600 — Electric Signs and Outline Lighting *Revised.* 600-8(g); 600-11; 600-21(b).

Art. 604 — Manufactured Wiring Systems *Revised.* 604-6(a).

Art. 605 — Office Furnishings
New. Complete Article.

Art. 610 — Cranes and Hoists
Revised. 610-12(b); 610-14(g); 610-42; 610-43; 610-43(2); 610-43(3); Exception Nos. 1, 2 and 3, 610-43.

Art. 620 — Elevators, Dumbwaiters, Escalators, and Moving Walks *New.* 620-11(b); Exception No. 5, 620-21; 620-44; 620-51(b)(3); 620-52.
Revised. Fine Print Note, 620-1; 620-2(a) and (b); 620-11(b) to (c); 620-11(c) to (d); 620-11(d) to (e); Exception No. 3, 620-21; 620-41; 620-51; 620-71 and Exception; 620-72 and Exception.

Art. 630 — Electric Welders
No Changes.

Art. 640 — Sound-Recording and Similar Equipment No Changes.

Art. 645 — Data Processing Systems
New. Fine Print Note, 645-1.
Revised. 645-2(b); 645-2(c); Fine Print Note, 645-2(c)(1); 645-3.
Deleted. Paragraph following title Article 645.

Art. 650 — Organs
No Changes.

Art. 660 — X-Ray Equipment
Revised. Second Fine Print Note, 660-1; Fine Print Note, 660-6.

Art. 665 — Induction and Dielectric Heating Equipment No Changes.

Art. 668 — Electrolytic Cells
Revised. 668-30(c); 668-30(c)(2).

Art. 670 — Metalworking Machine Tools and Plastics Machinery *Revised.* Title; 670-1; 670-2; 670-3(a) and (b); 670-4(a); 670-4(b).

Art. 675 — Electrically Driven or Controlled Irrigation Machines *New.* 675-7; 675-11(d).
Revised. 675-23 renumbered 675-8 and revised; 675-24 renumbered 675-9 and revised; 675-25 renumbered 675-10 and revised; 675-26 renumbered 675-11 and revised; 675-8 renumbered 675-12; 675-9 renumbered 675-13 and revised; 675-10 renumbered 675-14; 675-11 renumbered 675-15; 675-12 renumbered 675-16; 675-13 renumbered 675-17.
Deleted. 675-7; 675-8.

Art. 680 — Swimming Pools, Fountains and Similar Installations *New.* Definitions of Hydromassage Bathtub, Pool Cover, Electri-

cally Operated, 680-4; 680-6(b)(1), Exception No. 2; 680-6(c); Fine Print Note, 680-22; 680-22(a)(5); 680-25(c); 680-26; Exception, 680-41(a)(1); Exception, 680-41(b); Exception, 680-41(c).
Revised. 680-6; 680-6(a)(1), Exception; 680-6(a)(2); 680-6(a)(3); 680-6(b)(1), Exception renumbered to Exception No. 1; 680-11; 680-20(b)(1); 680-22(a)(5) renumbered to 680-22(a)(6); 680-25(a); 680-25(c) renumbered to 680-25(d); 680-25(d) renumbered to 680-25(f); 680-27(c); Title, Part D; 680-41(a)(2); 680-41(b)(1); 680-50; 680-55(a).

Art. 685 — Integrated Electrical Systems
Revised. 685-2.

Art. 690 — Solar Photovoltaic Systems
New. Complete Article.

Art. 700 — Emergency Systems
New. Last paragraph, 700-6; 700-6(e); 700-8; Last paragraph and Exception, 700-21.
Revised. 700-1; Fine Print Note, 700-1; 700-4(e); 700-5(a); 700-12; 700-16.

Art. 701 — Legally Required Standby Systems *New.* Second paragraph, 701-7; 701-9.
Revised. 701-1.

Art. 702 — Optional Standby Systems
New. Fine Print Note, 702-5.

Art. 710 — Over 600 Volts, Nominal General *New.* 710-21(e)(1), (e)(2), (e)(3), (e)(4), (e)(5), (e)(6), and Exception; 710-41(d).
Revised. 710-2; 710-9; 710-21(b)(1).

Art. 720 — Circuits and Equipment Operating at Less than 50 Volts No Changes.

Art. 725 — Class 1, Class 2, and Class 3 Remote-Control, Signaling, and Power-Limited Circuits *New.* Two Fine Print Notes, 725-2(b); Fine Print Note, 725-11; Fine Print Note, 725-12; Exception, 725-15.
Revised. 725-2(b) and Exception; 725-11(a)(2); 725-12; Exception Nos. 1, 2, and 3, 725-12; 725-16(b); Table 725-31(a); Table 725-31(b); 725-37; 725-38(a), 725-38(a)(1) and Exception No. 1; 725-38(a)(2); 725-38(a)(3) and Exception Nos. 1 and 2; Exception, 725-40(a); 725-41.
Deleted. 725-12(b).

Art. 760 — Fire Protective Signaling Systems *New.* Fine Print Note, 760-2; Fine Print Note, 760-4(d); 760-16(c) and Exception Nos. 1, 2, and Exception to (b) and (c); Exception No. 2, 760-30(a).
Revised. 760-2; 760-4(d) and Exception; 760-12 and Exception; 760-16(a) and (b); 760-22; Fine Print Note, 760-22; 760-29(a) and Exception No. 1; 760-29(a)(2), (a)(3), and Exception Nos. 1 and 2; Exception No. 1, 760-30(a).
Deleted. 760-12(a); 760-12(b).

Art. 770 — Optical Fiber Cables
New. Complete Article.

Art. 800 — Communication Circuits
New. Fine Print Note, 800-3(d); 800-11(a)(4); Exception No. 2, 800-11(b).
Revised. 800-1; 800-3(a)(1) and Exception No. 1; 800-3(a)(2); 800-3(a)(3) and Exception No. 2; 800-3(b) and Exception; Fine Print Note, 800-3(c); 800-3(d) and Exception to (d); 800-11(a); 800-11(a)(1); 800-11(c)(3); 800-31(b)(5), paragraphs a, b and c; 800-31(b)(6).

SUMMARY OF CODE CHANGES

Art. 810 — Radio and Television Equipment *New.* 810-21(j).
Revised. 810-2; 810-21(f)(1), (f)(2), and (f)(3).

Art. 820 — Community Antenna Television and Radio Distribution Systems *New.* Exception Nos. 1 and 2, 820-11(c); Fine Print Note, 820-15.
Revised. 820-1; 820-11(a); 820-11(c); 820-11(e)(1); 820-13(a), (b), and (c); Exception No. 2, 820-13(c); 820-15 and Exception; 820-22(f)(1), (f)(2), and (f)(3).

Chapter 9, Tables
Revised. Table 5; Table 8; Table 9.

Deleted. 4½ in. Trade Size Conduit from Tables 3A, 3B, 3C, 4.

Chapter 9, Examples
New. Examples 5(a) and 5(b).
Revised. Part B, second and third paragraphs; Examples revised and renumbered as follows: Renumbered No. 1 to No. 1(a); No. 1(a) to No. 1(b); No. 1(b) to No. 2(a); No. 1(c) to No. 2(b); No. 4 to No. 4(a); No. 4(a) to No. 4(b). Revised Example Nos. 1(a), 1(b), 2(a), 2(b), 3, 4(a), 4(b), 8.
Deleted. Example Nos. 2 and 7.

The
National Electrical Code®
Handbook

National Electrical Code

NFPA 70

ARTICLE 90 — INTRODUCTION

Contents

90-1. Purpose.

(a) Practical Safeguarding. The purpose of this Code is the practical safeguarding of persons and property from hazards arising from the use of electricity.

The *National Electrical Code* (*NEC*) is the most widely adopted set of electrical safety requirements in the world and is offered for use in law and for regulatory purposes in the interest of life and property protection. NFPA 70L, Model State Law Providing for Inspection of Electrical Installations, provides information on adopting the *NEC*.

(b) Adequacy. This Code contains provisions considered necessary for safety. Compliance therewith and proper maintenance will result in an installation essentially free from hazard, but not necessarily efficient, convenient, or adequate for good service or future expansion of electrical use.

(FPN): Hazards often occur because of overloading of wiring systems by methods or usage not in conformity with this Code. This occurs because initial wiring did not provide for increases in the use of electricity. An initial adequate installation and reasonable provisions for system changes will provide for future increases in the use of electricity.

Consideration should always be given to future expansion of electrical uses, i.e., plan an initial installation comprising service-entrance conductors and equipment, feeder conductors, and panelboards that will allow for future additions, alterations, designs, etc.

(c) Intention. This Code is not intended as a design specification nor an instruction manual for untrained persons.

The *National Electrical Code* is intended for use by capable engineers and electrical contractors for the basic design and/or installation of electrical equipment; by inspection authorities exercising legal jurisdiction over electrical

1

installations; by property insurance inspectors; by qualified industrial, commercial, and residential electricians; and by instructors teaching electrical apprentices or students.

90-2. Scope.

(a) Covered. This Code covers:

(1) Installations of electric conductors and equipment within or on public and private buildings or other structures, including mobile homes, recreational vehicles, and floating dwelling units; and other premises such as yards, carnival, parking and other lots, and industrial substations.

(2) Installations of conductors that connect to the supply of electricity.

(3) Installations of other outside conductors on the premises.

(4) Installations of optical fiber cable.

Section 90-2(a)(4) is new in the 1984 *NEC*. See new Article 770 for the requirements for optical fiber cable installations.

(b) Not Covered. This Code does not cover:

(1) Installations in ships, watercraft other than floating dwelling units, railway rolling stock, aircraft, or automotive vehicles other than mobile homes and recreational vehicles.

(2) Installations underground in mines.

(3) Installations of railways for generation, transformation, transmission, or distribution of power used exclusively for operation of rolling stock or installations used exclusively for signaling and communication purposes.

(4) Installations of communication equipment under the exclusive control of communication utilities, located outdoors or in building spaces used exclusively for such installations.

(5) Installations under the exclusive control of electric utilities for the purpose of communication, or metering; or for the generation, control, transformation, transmission, and distribution of electric energy located in buildings used exclusively by utilities for such purposes or located outdoors on property owned or leased by the utility or on public highways, streets, roads, etc., or outdoors by established rights on private property.

(FPN): It is the intent of this section that this Code covers all premises' wiring or wiring other than utility owned metering equipment, on the load side of the service point of buildings, structures, or any other premises not owned or leased by the utility. Also, it is the intent that this Code cover installations in buildings used by the utility for purposes other than listed in (b)(5) above, such as office buildings, warehouses, garages, machine shops, and recreational buildings which are not an integral part of a generating plant, substation, or control center.

See Figure 90-1.

(c) Special Permission. The authority having jurisdiction for enforcing this Code may grant exception for the installation of conductors and equipment, not under the exclusive control of the electric utilities and used to connect the electric utility supply system to the service-entrance conductors of the premises served, provided such installations are outside a building or terminate immediately inside a building wall.

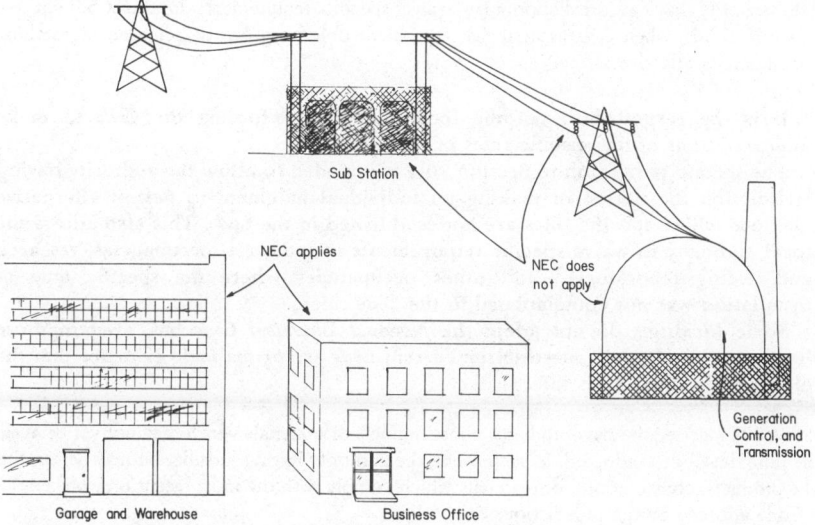

Figure 90-1. A typical electric utility complex indicating those facilities subject to the provisions of the *NEC*.

90-3. Code Arrangement. This Code is divided into the Introduction and nine chapters. Chapters 1, 2, 3, and 4 apply generally; Chapters 5, 6, and 7 apply to special occupancies, special equipment, or other special conditions. These latter chapters supplement or modify the general rules. Chapters 1 through 4 apply except as amended by Chapters 5, 6, and 7 for the particular conditions.

Chapter 8 covers communications systems and is independent of the other chapters except where they are specifically referenced therein.

Chapter 9 consists of tables and examples.

The reference to the "Introduction" and "Tables and Examples" is made with the intention that Article 90 and Chapter 9 be included in the application of this *Code*.

Chapters 1 through 4 apply generally, except "as amended" or "specifically referenced therein." For example, Section 300-22 (Chapter 3) is modified by Sections 725-2 and 760-4 (Chapter 7) and specifically referenced in Section 800-3 (Chapter 8).

90-4. Enforcement. This Code is intended to be suitable for mandatory application by governmental bodies exercising legal jurisdiction over electrical installations and for use by insurance inspectors. The authority having jurisdiction of enforcement of the Code will have the responsibility for making interpretations of the rules, for deciding upon the approval of equipment and materials, and for granting the special permission contemplated in a number of the rules.

Section 90-4 advises that an authority must grant approval for all materials and equipment used under the requirements of the *Code* in its area of jurisdiction. The texts of Sections 90-6, 110-2, and 110-3, along with the definitions of "Approved," "Identified," "Listed," and "Labeled," are intended to provide a basis for the authority having jurisdiction to make necessary judgments that are its responsibility.

The authority having jurisdiction may waive specific requirements in this Code or permit alternate methods, where it is assured that equivalent objectives can be achieved by establishing and maintaining effective safety.

It is the responsibility of the local authority enforcing the *Code* to make interpretations of the specific rules of the *Code*.

The second paragraph to Section 90-4 is included to allow the authority having jurisdiction the option of making an individual judgment to permit alternative methods where specific rules are not established in the *Code*. This also allows the local authority to waive specific requirements in industrial occupancies, research and testing laboratories, and other occupancies where the specific type of installation was not contemplated in the *Code* rules.

Some localities do not adopt the *National Electrical Code* but, even in those localities, installations meeting the current *Code* are prima facie evidence that the electrical installation is safe.

This Code may require new products, constructions, or materials which may not yet be available at the time the Code is adopted. In such event, the authority having jurisdiction may permit the use of the products, constructions, or materials which comply with the most recent previous edition of this Code adopted by the jurisdiction.

The third paragraph of Section 90-4 is new in the 1984 *NEC*. The second paragraph permits the authority having jurisdiction to waive specific requirements on the basis of equivalent safety. However, until the 1984 *NEC* there was no provision to permit the authority to waive a new *Code* requirement during the interim period between the acceptance of a new edition of the *NEC* and the availability of the new product, construction, or material redesigned to comply with the increased safety required by the new *Code* edition. It was difficult to establish a viable future effective date in the *NEC* because the time needed to change existing products and standards, and to develop new materials and test methods, was not usually known at the time of adoption of the new requirement in the *NEC*.

90-5. Formal Interpretations. To promote uniformity of interpretation and application of the provisions of this Code, Formal Interpretation procedures have been established.

(FPN): These procedures may be found in the "NFPA Regulations Governing Committee Projects."

The procedures for formal interpretations of the provisions of the *National Electrical Code* are outlined in the Regulations Governing Committee Projects that may be obtained from the V.P.-Standards of the National Fire Protection Association. The formal interpretations procedure can be found in Section 16 and has been reprinted in its entirety in the appendix to this Handbook.

The Interpretations Subcommittee is made up of five or more members or alternates of the Code Panel(s) having primary jurisdiction over the part(s) of the *Code* covering the subject under consideration. The members are selected by the Chairman of the Correlating Committee or the V.P.-Standards if the Chairman is not available. No member or alternate is eligible for appointment to an Interpretations Subcommittee if he or she is directly involved in the particular case prompting the request for the Interpretation. The personnel of NEC Interpretations Subcommittees are varied for each request.

The National Electrical Code Committee cannot be responsible for subsequent actions by authorities enforcing the *NEC* as to whether they accept or reject the findings. The authority having jurisdiction has the responsibility of interpreting the *Code* rules and should attempt to resolve all disagreements at the local level.

Two general forms of Formal Interpretations are recognized: (1) those making an interpretation of the literal text and (2) those making an interpretation of the intent of the Committee when the particular text was adopted.

Interpretations of the NEC not subject to processing are those that (1) involve a determination of compliance of a design, installation, or product or equivalency of protection, including the suitability of isolation or guarding, (2) involve a review of plans or specifications or require judgment or knowledge that can only be acquired as a result of on-site inspection, including the degree and extent of a hazardous (classified) location, and (3) involve text that clearly and decisively provides the requested information.

Formal Interpretations of *Code* rules are published in the NFPA *Fire News*, the NFPA Electrical Section News Bulletin, NFPA's Standards Information Service, and sent to interested trade publications.

Most interpretations of the *NEC* are rendered as the personal opinion of NFPA Electrical Department staff, or of the involved member of the National Electrical Code Committee, because the request does not qualify for processing as a Formal Interpretation. Such opinions are rendered in writing only in response to written requests. They are identified as personal opinions and the response indicates that the opinion shall not be considered the official position of the NFPA or of the National Electrical Code Committee, and shall not be considered to be, nor be relied upon as, a Formal Interpretation.

90-6. Examination of Equipment for Safety. For specific items of equipment and materials referred to in this Code, examinations for safety made under standard conditions will provide a basis for approval where the record is made generally available through promulgation by organizations properly equipped and qualified for experimental testing, inspections of the run of goods at factories, and service-value determination through field inspections. This avoids the necessity for repetition of examinations by different examiners, frequently with inadequate facilities for such work, and the confusion that would result from conflicting reports as to the suitability of devices and materials examined for a given purpose.

It is the intent of this Code that factory-installed internal wiring or the construction of equipment need not be inspected at the time of installation of the equipment, except to detect alterations or damage, if the equipment has been listed by a qualified electrical testing laboratory which is recognized as having the facilities described above and which requires suitability for installation in accordance with this Code.

(FPN): See Examination of Equipment, Section 110-3.

(FPN): See definition of "Listed," Article 100.

Qualified testing laboratories, inspection agencies, or other organizations concerned with product evaluation publish lists of equipment or materials that have been tested and meet nationally recognized standards or that have been found suitable for use in a specified manner. The *Code* does not contain detailed information on equipment or materials, but refers to the products as "Listed," "Labeled," or "Identified." See Article 100, "Definitions," for explanation of these terms.

The National Fire Protection Association does not approve, inspect or certify any installations, procedures, equipment or materials nor does it approve or evaluate testing laboratories. In determining the acceptability of installations or procedures, equipment or materials, the "authority having jurisdiction" may base acceptance on compliance with NFPA or other appropriate standards. In the absence of such standards, said authority may require evidence of proper installation, procedure, or use. The "authority having jurisdiction" may also refer to the listings or labeling practices of an organization concerned with product

5

evaluations which is in a position to determine compliance with appropriate standards for the current production of listed items.

It is not the intent of the *Code* to apply to the internal factory-installed wiring, or to the construction of listed equipment at the time of installation, unless damage or alterations are detected.

90-7. Wiring Planning.

(a) Future Expansion and Convenience. Plans and specifications that provide ample space in raceways, spare raceways, and additional spaces will allow for future increases in the use of electricity. Distribution centers located in readily accessible locations will provide convenience and safety of operation. See Sections 110-16 and 240-24 for clearances and accessibility.

(b) Number of Circuits in Enclosures. It is elsewhere provided in this Code that the number of wires and circuits confined in a single enclosure be varyingly restricted. Limiting the number of circuits in a single enclosure will minimize the effects from a short-circuit or ground fault in one circuit.

Distribution centers should contain additional spaces and capacity for future additions and should be conveniently located for accessibility.

Where easy access is not achieved, a spare raceway(s) or "pull line(s)" should be run to specific areas. See Figure 90-2.

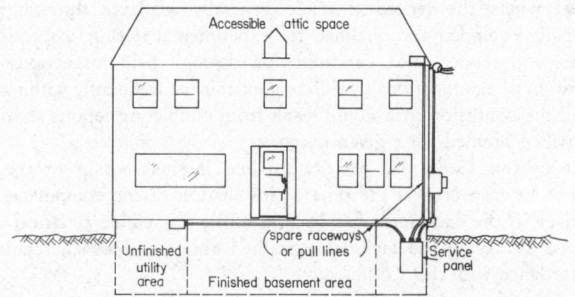

Figure 90-2. Spare raceways or pull lines provide additional capacity for future additions to the distribution system.

90-8. Metric Units of Measurement.
For the purpose of this Code metric units of measurement are in accordance with the modernized metric system known as the International System of Units (SI).

Values of measurement in the Code text will be followed by an approximate equivalent value in SI units. Tables will have a footnote for SI conversion units used in the table.

Conduit size, wire size, horsepower designation for motors, and trade sizes that do not reflect actual measurements, e.g., box sizes, will not be assigned dual designation SI units.

(FPN): For metric conversion practices, see ANSI Z210.1-1976, Standard for Metric Practice.

In addition, warning signs stating specific clearances, such as in Section 513-11(a), do not include metric equivalents.

An example of an application of SI conversion units as used in Table 110-16(a) is as follows:

3 ft = 36 in. × 25.4 mm = 914 mm
3½ ft × 0.3048 m   = 1.07 m
4 ft × 0.3048 m   = 1.22 m

Generally, dimensions up to 36 inches are expressed in millimeters, and those over 36 inches are expressed in meters. Footnotes to tables involving dimensions in feet are expressed as "one foot = 0.3048 meter"; however, throughout the text the metric equivalent has been converted to millimeters and rounded off to 305 millimeters.

1 GENERAL

ARTICLE 100 — DEFINITIONS

Scope. Only definitions of terms peculiar to and essential to the proper use of this Code are included. In general, only those terms used in two or more articles are defined in Article 100. Other definitions are included in the article in which they are used but may be referenced in Article 100.

Other definitions are included in the following sections:

9

ARTICLE 100—DEFINITIONS

Part A of this article contains definitions intended to apply wherever the terms are used throughout this Code. Part B contains definitions applicable only to the parts of articles covering specifically installations and equipment operating at over 600 volts, nominal.

Contents

A. General

B. Over 600 Volts, Nominal

A. General

AC General-Use Snap Switch: See under "Switches."

AC-DC General-Use Snap Switch: See under "Switches."

Accessible: (As applied to wiring methods.) Capable of being removed or exposed without damaging the building structure or finish, or not permanently closed in by the structure or finish of the building. (See "Concealed" and "Exposed.")

Wiring methods located behind removable panels designed to allow access are not considered permanently enclosed. See Figure 100-1.

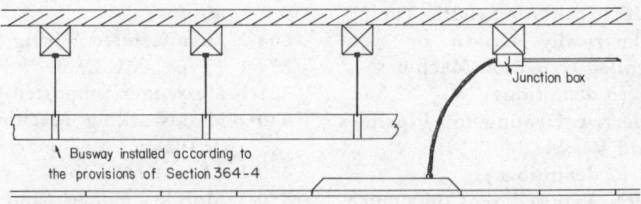

Figure 100-1. Busways and junction boxes are considered accessible when located above hung ceilings having lift-out panels.

Accessible: (As applied to Equipment.) Admitting close approach: not guarded by locked doors, elevation, or other effective means. (See "Accessible, Readily.")

Accessible, Readily: (Readily Accessible.) Capable of being reached quickly for operation, renewal, or inspections, without requiring those to whom ready access is requisite to climb over or remove obstacles or to resort to portable ladders, chairs, etc. (See "Accessible.")

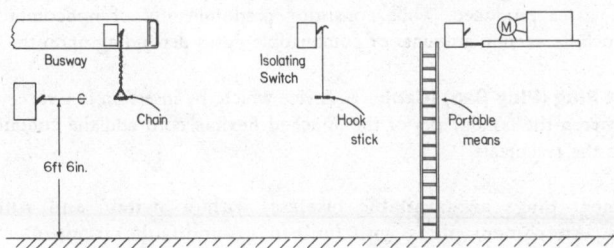

Figure 100-2. This figure illustrates the provisions of Section 380-8. Section 364-12 permits ropes, chains, or hook sticks as suitable for operating disconnecting means mounted on busways.

Ampacity: The current in amperes a conductor can carry continuously under the conditions of use without exceeding its temperature rating.

The definition of "ampacity" has been revised in the 1984 *NEC* to recognize that the maximum current a conductor can carry varies with the conditions of use as well as with the temperature rating of the conductor insulation. For example, ambient temperature is a condition of use. A conductor with 60°C insulation installed near a furnace so that the ambient temperature is 60°C continuously has no current-carrying capacity. Any current flowing through the conductor will raise its temperature, and thus raise the temperature of the conductor insulation to a value over its rated 60°C. The ampacity of this conductor, regardless of its size, is therefore zero. See the ampacity correction factors following Tables 310-16 through 310-19.

Another condition of use is the number of conductors in a raceway or cable. See Note 8 to Tables 310-16 through 310-19.

Anesthetizing Location: See Section 517-2.

Appliance: Utilization equipment, generally other than industrial, normally built in standardized sizes or types, which is installed or connected as a unit to perform one or more functions such as clothes washing, air conditioning, food mixing, deep frying, etc.

Appliance Branch Circuit: See "Branch Circuit, Appliance."

Approved: Acceptable to the authority having jurisdiction.

The phrase "authority having jurisdiction" is used in NFPA documents in a broad manner since jurisdiction and "approval" agencies vary as do their responsibilities. Where public safety is primary, the "authority having jurisdiction" may be a federal, state, local, or other regional department or individual such as a fire chief, fire marshal, chief of a fire prevention bureau, labor department, health department, building official, electrical inspector, or others having statutory authority. For insurance purposes, an insurance inspection department, rating bureau, or other insurance company representative may be the "authority having jurisdiction." In many circumstances the property owner or his designated agent assumes the role of the "authority having jurisdiction"; at government installations, the commanding officer or departmental official may be the "authority having jurisdiction."

Askarel: A generic term for a group of nonflammable synthetic chlorinated hydrocarbons used as electrical insulating media. Askarels of various compositional types are used. Under arcing conditions the gases produced, while consisting predominantly of noncombustible hydrogen chloride, can include varying amounts of combustible gases depending upon the askarel type.

Attachment Plug (Plug Cap) (Cap): A device which, by insertion in a receptacle, establishes connection between the conductors of the attached flexible cord and the conductors connected permanently to the receptacle.

Attachment plugs are available fuseless, with a switch, and with overload protection. Attachment plugs with built-in ground-fault circuit-interrupters are also available.

Automatic: Self-acting, operating by its own mechanism when actuated by some impersonal influence, as for example, a change in current strength, pressure, temperature, or mechanical configuration. (See "Nonautomatic.")

Bare Conductor: See under "Conductor."

Block (City, Town, or Village): See Section 800-2.

Bonding: The permanent joining of metallic parts to form an electrically conductive path which will assure electrical continuity and the capacity to conduct safely any current likely to be imposed.

Bonding Jumper: A reliable conductor to assure the required electrical conductivity between metal parts required to be electrically connected.

See Figure 100-3.

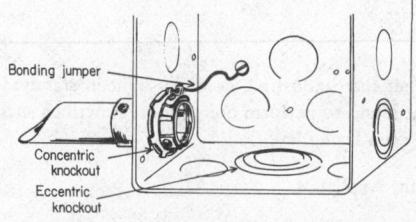

Bonding jumper

Concentric knockout

Eccentric knockout

Figure 100-3. A bonding jumper around a concentric or eccentric knockout is required by Section 250-72(d) for servicing equipment.

Bonding Jumper, Circuit: The connection between portions of a conductor in a circuit to maintain required ampacity of the circuit.

Bonding Jumper, Equipment: The connection between two or more portions of the equipment grounding conductor.

Bonding Jumper, Main: The connection between the grounded circuit conductor and the equipment grounding conductor at the service.

See Figure 100-4.

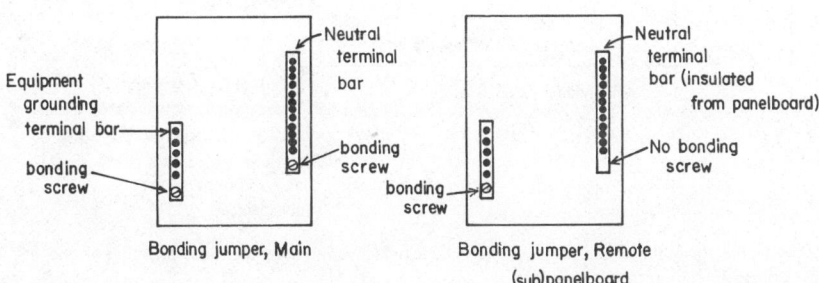

Figure 100-4. The equipment grounding terminal bar is to be bonded to the panelboard (or cabinet) frame and is not to be connected to the neutral bar in other than service equipment. Bonding method may be by bonding screws or bonding jumpers.

Branch Circuit: The circuit conductors between the final overcurrent device protecting the circuit and the outlet(s).

(FPN): See Section 240-9 for thermal cutouts, thermal relays, and other devices.

See Figure 100-5.

Figure 100-5. Conductors between the overcurrent device in the panelboard and the duplex receptacle are branch-circuit conductors.

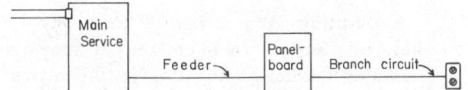

Branch Circuit, Appliance: A branch circuit supplying energy to one or more outlets to which appliances are to be connected; such circuits to have no permanently connected lighting fixtures not a part of an appliance.

> Receptacle outlets as required in Section 220-3(b) for the kitchen, pantry, etc. and Section 220-3(c) for laundry areas are not to have any other outlets or permanently connected lighting fixtures connected to them. See comments following Section 220-3(b).

Branch Circuit, General Purpose: A branch circuit that supplies a number of outlets for lighting and appliances.

Branch Circuit, Individual: A branch circuit that supplies only one utilization equipment.

> An individual branch circuit is a circuit that supplies "only" one utilization equipment, that is, one range, or one space heater, or one motor. See Section 210-23.
> It may supply "only" one single receptacle for the connection of a single attachment plug. See Section 210-21(b).
> A branch circuit may be installed to supply one duplex receptacle which can accommodate two cord- and plug-connected appliances or similar equipment and therefore this circuit would not be considered an individual branch circuit. See Figure 100-6.

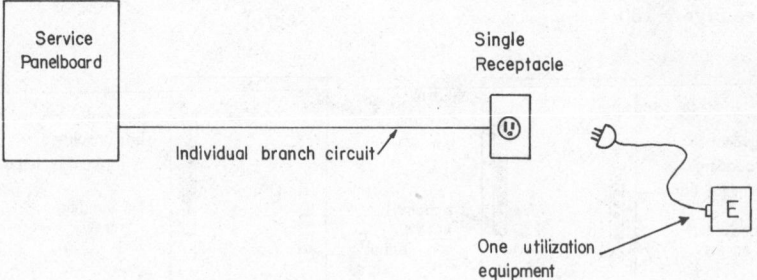

Figure 100-6. Illustrated is a single receptacle, which is intended for the connection of one utilization equipment.

Branch Circuit, Multiwire: A branch circuit consisting of two or more ungrounded conductors having a potential difference between them, and a grounded conductor having equal potential difference between it and each ungrounded conductor of the circuit and which is connected to the neutral conductor of the system.

See Sections 210-4, 210-6(c), and 240-20(b).

Branch-Circuit Selection Current: See Section 440-3(c), Definition.

Building: A structure which stands alone or which is cut off from adjoining structures by fire walls with all openings therein protected by approved fire doors.

A building is a structure that may be used or intended for supporting or sheltering any use or occupancy. It may also be a separate structure such as a pole or water tower. Definitions of the terms "fire walls" and "fire doors" are the responsibility of the municipal and/or state building codes and interpretations of "building terms" have been avoided by *NEC* committees. Fire-resistance rating is defined as the time, in minutes or hours, that materials or assemblies have withstood a fire exposure.

Cabinet: An enclosure designed either for surface or flush mounting and provided with a frame, mat, or trim in which a swinging door or doors are or may be hung.

Both cabinets and cutout boxes are covered in Article 373. Cabinets are designed for surface or flush mounting with a trim to which a swinging door(s) is hung. Cutout boxes are designed for surface mounting with a swinging door(s) secured directly to the box.

Cell (As applied to Raceways): See Sections 356-1 and 358-1.

Circuit Breaker: A device designed to open and close a circuit by nonautomatic means and to open the circuit automatically on a predetermined overcurrent without injury to itself when properly applied within its rating.

(FPN): The automatic opening means can be integral, direct acting with the circuit breaker or remote from the circuit breaker. See definition of "Switching Devices" in Part B of this article for definition applying to circuits and equipment over 600 volts, nominal.

Adjustable: (As applied to Circuit Breakers.) A qualifying term indicating that the circuit breaker can be set to trip at various values of current and/or time within a predetermined range.

Instantaneous Trip: (As applied to Circuit Breakers.) A qualifying term indicating that no delay is purposely introduced in the tripping action of the circuit breaker.

Inverse Time: (As applied to Circuit Breakers.) A qualifying term indicating there is purposely introduced a delay in the tripping action of the circuit breaker, which delay decreases as the magnitude of the current increases.

Nonadjustable: (As applied to Circuit Breakers.) A qualifying term indicating that the circuit breaker does not have any adjustment to alter the value of current at which it will trip or the time required for its operation.

Setting: (of Circuit Breaker.) The value of current and/or time at which an adjustable circuit breaker is set to trip.

Concealed: Rendered inaccessible by the structure or finish of the building. Wires in concealed raceways are considered concealed, even though they may become accessible by withdrawing them. [See "Accessible — (As applied to wiring methods)."]

Raceways and cables supported within the hollow frames or permanently closed in by the finish of buildings are considered "concealed." Open-type work, such as raceways and cables in open areas, for example, in unfinished basements, in accessible underfloor areas or attics, or attached to the surface of finished areas, which may be removed without damage to the building structure or finish is not considered "concealed." See definition of "Exposed (as applied to wiring methods)."

Conductor:

Bare: A conductor having no covering or electrical insulation whatsoever. (See "Conductor, Covered.")

Covered: A conductor encased within material of composition or thickness that is not recognized by this Code as electrical insulation. (See "Conductor, Bare.")

A covered conductor should be treated as a bare conductor for working clearances, etc.

Insulated: A conductor encased within material of composition and thickness that is recognized by this Code as electrical insulation.

Conduit Body: A separate portion of a conduit or tubing system that provides access through a removable cover(s) to the interior of the system at a junction of two or more sections of the system or at a terminal point of the system.
Boxes such as FS and FD or larger cast or sheet metal boxes are not classified as conduit bodies. See Table 370-6(a).

This definition is intended to clarify that conduit bodies are a portion of a raceway system with removable covers to allow access to the interior of the system.
Conduit bodies are referred to in the trade as "condulets" and include the LB, LL, LR, C, T, and X designs. Sections 300-15, 331-13, 345-14, 346-14, 347-16, and 348-14, and Article 370 may be referred to for the rules on the usage of conduit bodies.
Type FS or FD boxes are not classified as conduit bodies; they are listed with boxes in Table 370-6(a).

Connector, Pressure (Solderless): A device that establishes a connection between two or more conductors or between one or more conductors and a terminal by means of mechanical pressure and without the use of solder.

Continuous Duty: See under "Duty."

Continuous Load: A load where the maximum current is expected to continue for three hours or more.

Control Circuit: See Section 430-71.

Controller: A device or group of devices that serves to govern, in some predetermined manner, the electric power delivered to the apparatus to which it is connected. See also Section 430-81(a).

A "controller" may be a switch, circuit breaker, or device normally used to start and stop motors and other apparatus and, in the case of motors, is to be capable of interrupting the stalled-rotor current of the motor.

Cooking Unit, Counter-Mounted: A cooking appliance designed for mounting in or on a counter and consisting of one or more heating elements, internal wiring, and built-in or separately mountable controls. (See "Oven, Wall-Mounted.")

Copper-Clad Aluminum Conductors: Conductors drawn from a copper-clad aluminum rod with the copper metallurgically bonded to an aluminum core. The copper forms a minimum of 10 percent of the cross-sectional area of a solid conductor or each strand of a stranded conductor.

Covered Conductor: See under "Conductor."

Current-Limiting Overcurrent Protective Device: See Section 240-11.

Cutout Box: An enclosure designed for surface mounting and having swinging doors or covers secured directly to and telescoping with the walls of the box proper. (See "Cabinet.")

Damp Location: See under "Location."

Dead Front: Without live parts exposed to a person on the operating side of the equipment.

Demand Factor: The ratio of the maximum demand of a system, or part of a system, to the total connected load of a system or the part of the system under consideration.

Device: A unit of an electrical system which is intended to carry but not utilize electric energy.

Units, such as switches, circuit breakers, fuseholders, receptacles, and lampholders, that distribute or control but do not consume electricity are termed devices.

Disconnecting Means: A device, or group of devices, or other means by which the conductors of a circuit can be disconnected from their source of supply.

For disconnecting means for service equipment, see Part H of Article 230; for fuses and thermal cutouts, see Part D of Article 240; for circuit breakers, see Part G of Article 240; for appliances, see Part D of Article 422; for space heating equipment, see Part C of Article 424; for motors and controllers, see Part H of Article 430; and for air-conditioning and refrigerating equipment, see Part B of Article 440. See also references for "Disconnecting Means" in Index.

(FPN): See definition in Part B of this article for definition applying to circuits and equipment over 600 volts, nominal.

Dry Location: See under "Location."

Dust-Ignitionproof: See Section 502-1.

Dustproof: So constructed or protected that dust will not interfere with its successful operation.

Dusttight: So constructed that dust will not enter the enclosing case under specified test conditions.

(FPN): For test conditions other than for rotating equipment, see ANSI/NEMA ICS6-1978, Enclosures for Industrial Controls and Systems, Paragraph ICS6-110.54.

Reference to the ANSI/NEMA Standard will permit the user to evaluate the enclosure with regard to actual conditions of use. See Section 430-91 for motor controller enclosure types.

Duty:

Continuous Duty: Operation at a substantially constant load for an indefinitely long time.

Intermittent Duty: Operation for alternate intervals of (1) load and no load; or (2) load and rest; or (3) load, no load, and rest.

Periodic Duty: Intermittent operation in which the load conditions are regularly recurrent.

Short-Time Duty: Operation at a substantially constant load for a short and definitely specified time.

Varying Duty: Operation at loads, and for intervals of time, both of which may be subject to wide variation.

(FPN): See Table 430-22(a), Exception for illustration of various types of duty.

For the protection of intermittent, periodic, short-time, and varying-duty motors against overload, see Section 430-33.

Duty Cycle (Welding): See Section 630-31(b), Fine Print Note.

Dwelling:

Dwelling Unit: One or more rooms for the use of one or more persons as a housekeeping unit with space for eating, living, and sleeping, and permanent provisions for cooking and sanitation.

Where dwelling units are referenced throughout the *Code*, it is important to note that rooms of motels, hotels, and similar occupancies may be classified as dwelling units. See Figure 100-7.

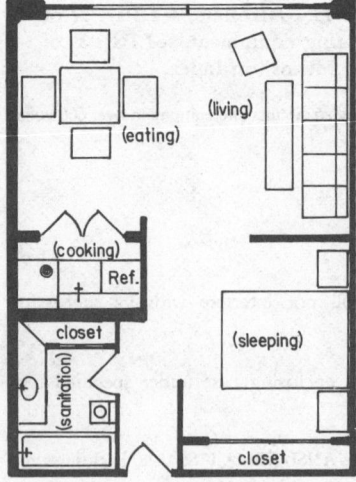

Figure 100-7. A motel or hotel room with eating, living, and sleeping areas and areas having permanent provisions for cooking and sanitation meets the definition of a "dwelling unit."

Multifamily Dwelling: A building containing three or more dwelling units.

One-Family Dwelling: A building consisting solely of one dwelling unit.

Two-Family Dwelling: A building consisting solely of two dwelling units.

Electric Sign: A fixed, stationary, or portable self-contained, electrically illuminated utilization equipment with words or symbols designed to convey information or attract attention.

Enclosed: Surrounded by a case, housing, fence, or walls which will prevent persons from accidentally contacting energized parts.

Enclosure: The case or housing of apparatus, or the fence or walls surrounding an installation to prevent personnel from accidentally contacting energized parts, or to protect the equipment from physical damage.

Equipment: A general term including material, fittings, devices, appliances, fixtures, apparatus, and the like used as a part of, or in connection with, an electrical installation.

Equipment Grounding Conductor: See "Grounding Conductor, Equipment."

See Section 250-91(b) for types of equipment grounding conductors.

Explosionproof Apparatus: Apparatus enclosed in a case that is capable of withstanding an explosion of a specified gas or vapor which may occur within it and of preventing the ignition of a specified gas or vapor surrounding the enclosure by sparks, flashes, or explosion of the gas or vapor within, and which operates at such an external temperature that a surrounding flammable atmosphere will not be ignited thereby.

Exposed: (As applied to live parts.) Capable of being inadvertently touched or approached nearer than a safe distance by a person. It is applied to parts not suitably guarded, isolated, or insulated. (See "Accessible" and "Concealed.")

See Section 110-17. See also comments following definition of "Guarded."

Exposed: (As applied to wiring methods.) On or attached to the surface or behind panels designed to allow access. [See "Accessible — (As applied to wiring methods)."]

See Figure 100-1.

Externally Operable: Capable of being operated without exposing the operator to contact with live parts.

Feeder: All circuit conductors between the service equipment, or the generator switchboard of an isolated plant, and the final branch-circuit overcurrent device.

See Figure 100-5.

Festoon Lighting: See Section 225-6(b).

Fitting: An accessory such as a locknut, bushing, or other part of a wiring system that is intended primarily to perform a mechanical rather than an electrical function.

Garage: A building or portion of a building in which one or more self-propelled vehicles carrying volatile flammable liquid for fuel or power are kept for use, sale, storage, rental, repair, exhibition, or demonstrating purposes, and all that portion of a building which is on or below the floor or floors in which such vehicles are kept and which is not separated therefrom by suitable cutoffs.

(FPN): See Section 511-1.

General-Purpose Branch Circuit: See "Branch Circuit, General Purpose."

General-Use Snap Switch: See under "Switches."

General-Use Switch: See under "Switches."

Ground: A conducting connection, whether intentional or accidental, between an electrical circuit or equipment and the earth, or to some conducting body that serves in place of the earth.

Grounded: Connected to earth or to some conducting body that serves in place of the earth.

Grounded (Effectively Grounded Communication System): See Section 800-2(c)(1).

Grounded Conductor: A system or circuit conductor that is intentionally grounded.

Grounding Conductor: A conductor used to connect equipment or the grounded circuit of a wiring system to a grounding electrode or electrodes.

Grounding Conductor, Equipment: The conductor used to connect the noncurrent-carrying metal parts of equipment, raceways, and other enclosures to the system grounded conductor and/or the grounding electrode conductor at the service equipment or at the source of a separately derived system.

Grounding Electrode Conductor: The conductor used to connect the grounding electrode to the equipment grounding conductor and/or to the grounded conductor of the circuit at the service equipment or at the source of a separately derived system.

The grounding electrode conductor is to be of copper, aluminum, or copper-clad aluminum and is used to connect the equipment grounding conductor and/or the grounded conductor (at the service equipment or at the separately derived system) to the grounding electrode for either grounded or ungrounded systems.

It is sized by using Table 250-94. See also Article 250, Parts H and J.

Ground-Fault Circuit-Interrupter: A device intended for the protection of personnel that functions to de-energize a circuit or portion thereof within an established period of time when a current to ground exceeds some predetermined value that is less than that required to operate the overcurrent protective device of the supply circuit.

See Figures 210-11, 210-12, and 210-13.

Ground-Fault Protection of Equipment: A system intended to provide protection of equipment from damaging line-to-ground fault currents by operating to cause a disconnecting means to open all ungrounded conductors of the faulted circuit. This protection is provided at current levels less than those required to protect conductors from damage through the operation of a supply circuit overcurrent device.

This definition is new in the 1984 *NEC*. See commentary on Section 230-95.

Guarded: Covered, shielded, fenced, enclosed, or otherwise protected by means of suitable covers, casings, barriers, rails, screens, mats, or platforms to remove the likelihood of approach or contact by persons or objects to a point of danger.

Hazardous (Classified) Locations: See Article 500.

Header: See Sections 356-1 and 358-1.

Hermetic Refrigerant Motor-Compressor: See Section 440-1.

Hoistway: Any shaftway, hatchway, well hole, or other vertical opening or space in which an elevator or dumbwaiter is designed to operate.

See Article 620 for the installation of electric equipment and wiring methods in hoistways.

Identified: (As applied to Equipment.) Recognizable as suitable for the specific purpose, function, use, environment, application, etc., where described in a particular Code requirement. (See "Equipment.")

(FPN): Suitability of equipment for a specific purpose, environment, or application may be determined by a qualified testing laboratory, inspection agency, or other organization concerned with product evaluation. Such identification may include labeling or listing: see "Labeled," "Listed," and Section 90-6.

Individual Branch Circuit: See "Branch Circuit, Individual."

In Sight From (Within Sight From, Within Sight.): Where this Code specifies that one equipment shall be "in sight from," "within sight from," or "within sight," etc., of another equipment, one of the equipments specified shall be visible and not more than 50 feet (15.24 m) distant from the other.

See Figures 430-18, 430-19, and 430-20, and Figure 600-1.

Insulated Conductor: See under "Conductor."

Intermittent Duty: See under "Duty."

Interrupting Rating: The highest current at rated voltage that an overcurrent protective device is intended to interrupt under standard test conditions.

(FPN): Equipment intended to break current at other than fault levels may have its interrupting rating implied in other ratings, such as horsepower or locked rotor current.

Interrupting ratings are essential to coordinating electrical systems so that available fault currents can be properly controlled.

Isolated: Not readily accessible to persons unless special means for access are used.

See definition of "Isolating Switch " under "Switches" in Article 100.

Labeled: Equipment or materials to which has been attached a label, symbol, or other identifying mark of an organization acceptable to the authority having jurisdiction and concerned with product evaluation, that maintains periodic inspection of production of labeled equipment or materials and by whose labeling the manufacturer indicates compliance with appropriate standards or performance in a specified manner.

Equipment and conductors required or permitted by this *Code* are acceptable only when approved for a specific environment or application by the authority having jurisdiction. See Section 110-2.
"Listing" or "Labeling" by a qualified testing laboratory will provide a basis for approval. See Section 90-6.

Lighting Outlet: An outlet intended for the direct connection of a lampholder, a lighting fixture, or a pendant cord terminating in a lampholder.

Listed: Equipment or materials included in a list published by an organization acceptable to the authority having jurisdiction and concerned with product evaluation, that maintains periodic inspection of production of listed equipment or materials, and whose listing states either that the equipment or material meets appropriate standards or has been tested and found suitable for use in a specified manner.

(FPN): The means for identifying listed equipment may vary for each organization concerned with product evaluation, some of which do not recognize equipment as listed unless it is also labeled. The authority having jurisdiction should utilize the system employed by the listing organization to identify a listed product.

See comments that follow the definition of "Labeled."

Location:

Damp Location: Partially protected locations under canopies, marquees, roofed open porches, and like locations, and interior locations subject to moderate degrees of moisture, such as some basements, some barns, and some cold-storage warehouses.

Dry Location: A location not normally subject to dampness or wetness. A location classified as dry may be temporarily subject to dampness or wetness, as in the case of a building under construction.

Wet Location: Installations underground or in concrete slabs or masonry in direct contact with the earth, and locations subject to saturation with water or other liquids, such as vehicle washing areas, and locations exposed to weather and unprotected.

ARTICLE 100—DEFINITIONS

See Sections 300-6(c) and 410-4.

Low-Energy Power Circuit: A circuit that is not a remote-control or signaling circuit but has its power supply limited in accordance with the requirements of Class 2 and Class 3 circuits. (See Article 725.)

Multioutlet Assembly: A type of surface or flush raceway designed to hold conductors and receptacles, assembled in the field or at the factory.

In dry locations, metallic and nonmetallic multioutlet assemblies are permitted; however, they are not to be installed where concealed. See Article 353 for details on recessing these assemblies.

Multiwire Branch Circuit: See "Branch Circuit, Multiwire."

Neutral Conductor: See Note 10 to Tables 310-16 through 310-19.

Nonautomatic: Action requiring personal intervention for its control. (See "Automatic.")

(FPN): As applied to an electric controller, nonautomatic control does not necessarily imply a manual controller, but only that personal intervention is necessary.

Outlet: A point on the wiring system at which current is taken to supply utilization equipment.

For example, a lighting outlet or a receptacle outlet.

Outline Lighting: An arrangement of incandescent lamps or electric discharge tubing to outline or call attention to certain features such as the shape of a building or the decoration of a window.

See Article 600, Part B (600 Volts, Nominal, or Less) and Part C (Over 600 Volts, Nominal).

Oven, Wall-Mounted: An oven for cooking purposes designed for mounting in or on a wall or other surface and consisting of one or more heating elements, internal wiring, and built-in or separately mountable controls. (See "Cooking Unit, Counter-Mounted.")

Overcurrent: Any current in excess of the rated current of equipment or the ampacity of a conductor. It may result from overload (see definition), short circuit, or ground fault.

(FPN): A current in excess of rating may be accommodated by certain equipment and conductors for a given set of conditions. Hence the rules for overcurrent protection are specific for particular situations.

Overload: Operation of equipment in excess of normal, full-load rating, or of a conductor in excess of rated ampacity which, when it persists for a sufficient length of time, would cause damage or dangerous overheating. A fault, such as a short circuit or ground fault, is not an overload. (See "Overcurrent.")

(FPN): For motor apparatus applications, see Section 430-31.

Panelboard: A single panel or group of panel units designed for assembly in the form of a single panel; including buses, automatic overcurrent devices, and with or without switches for the control of light, heat, or power circuits; designed to be placed in a cabinet or cutout box placed in or against a wall or partition and accessible only from the front. (See "Switchboard.")

See Article 384.

Periodic Duty: See under "Duty."

Power Outlet: An enclosed assembly which may include receptacles, circuit breakers, fuseholders, fused switches, buses, and watt-hour meter mounting means; intended to supply and control power to mobile homes, recreational vehicles, or boats; or to serve as a means for distributing power required to operate mobile or temporarily installed equipment.

See Figures 305-1 and 550-1.

Premises Wiring (System): That interior and exterior wiring, including power, lighting, control, and signal circuit wiring together with all of its associated hardware, fittings, and wiring devices, both permanently and temporarily installed, which extends from the load end of the service drop, or load end of the service lateral conductors to the outlet(s). Such wiring does not include wiring internal to appliances, fixtures, motors, controllers, motor control centers, and similar equipment.

Projector, Nonprofessional: See Section 540-3.

Projector, Professional: See Section 540-2.

Qualified Person: One familiar with the construction and operation of the equipment and the hazards involved.

Raceway: An enclosed channel designed expressly for holding wires, cables, or busbars, with additional functions as permitted in this Code.

(FPN): Raceways may be of metal or insulating material, and the term includes rigid metal conduit, rigid nonmetallic conduit, intermediate metal conduit, liquidtight flexible metal conduit, flexible metallic tubing, flexible metal conduit, electrical nonmetallic tubing, electrical metallic tubing, underfloor raceways, cellular concrete floor raceways, cellular metal floor raceways, surface raceways, wireways, and busways.

Cable trays (see Article 318) are not considered raceways in the *NEC*.

Rainproof: So constructed, protected, or treated as to prevent rain from interfering with the successful operation of the apparatus under specified test conditions.

Testing laboratories perform tests which are used to evaluate equipment under specified test conditions. These tests are well known to manufacturers of electrical products as well as to users of this type of equipment. Descriptions of the tests are available from the testing laboratories. Users of the *NEC* should be alerted to the existence of these tests.

Raintight: So constructed or protected that exposure to a beating rain will not result in the entrance of water under specified test conditions.

Raceways on exterior surfaces of buildings are to be made raintight. See Sections 225-22 and 230-53.
For boxes and cabinets, see Section 300-6.
See comments following definition of "Rainproof."

Rated-Load Current: See Section 440-3(a), Definition.

Readily Accessible: (See "Accessible, Readily.")

Overcurrent devices are to be readily accessible. See Section 240-24(a). There is considered to be a high degree of safety when switches or circuit breakers can be disconnected quickly without being hindered by obstacles. See Section 230-72(c) for services. See also the exceptions to this rule for busways, Section 364-12; and for supplementary overcurrent protection, Section 240-10.

Receptacle: A receptacle is a contact device installed at the outlet for the connection of a single attachment plug.

(FPN): A single receptacle is a single contact device with no other contact device on the same yoke. A multiple receptacle is a single device containing two or more receptacles.

The basic receptacle is a single contact device for the connection of a single attachment plug. A multiple receptacle is a contact device containing two or more receptacles for the connection of two or more attachment plugs. A duplex receptacle is a multiple receptacle. See Figure 100-8.

Receptacle Outlet: An outlet where one or more receptacles are installed.

See Figure 100-8.

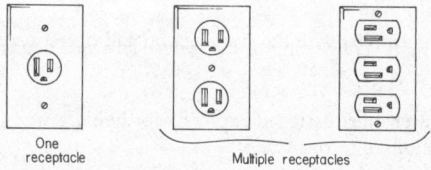

One receptacle

Multiple receptacles

Figure 100-8. When calculating other loads — all occupancies [Section 220-2(c)], loads for additions to existing dwelling units [Section 220-2(d)(1)], and other dwelling units [Section 220-2(d)(2)] each single or multiple receptacle is to be considered at not less than 180 VA.

Remote-Control Circuit: Any electric circuit that controls any other circuit through a relay or an equivalent device.

See Figure 100-9.

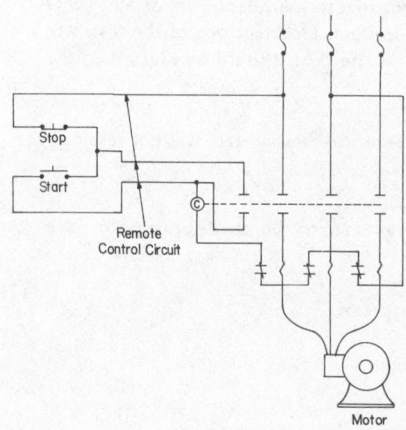

Stop

Start

Remote Control Circuit

Motor

Figure 100-9. A remote control circuit for starting and stopping an electric motor.

Sealable Equipment: Equipment enclosed in a case or cabinet that is provided with a means of sealing or locking so that live parts cannot be made accessible without opening the enclosure. The equipment may or may not be operable without opening the enclosure.

Service: The conductors and equipment for delivering energy from the electricity supply system to the wiring system of the premises served.

Service Cable: Service conductors made up in the form of a cable.

Service Conductors: The supply conductors that extend from the street main or from transformers to the service equipment of the premises supplied.

Service conductors from an overhead distribution system originate at the utility pole, or wires attached to it, and terminate at the service equipment.

Service conductors from an underground distribution system originate at the utility manhole and terminate at the service equipment. When primary conductors are extended to outdoor pad-mounted or underground transformers on private property, the service conductors originate at the secondary connections of the transformers.

See Article 230, Part K for service conductors exceeding 600 V.

Service Drop: The overhead service conductors from the last pole or other aerial support to and including the splices, if any, connecting to the service-entrance conductors at the building or other structure.

See Figure 100-10.

Service-Entrance Conductors, Overhead System: The service conductors between the terminals of the service equipment and a point usually outside the building, clear of building walls, where joined by tap or splice to the service drop.

See Figure 100-10.

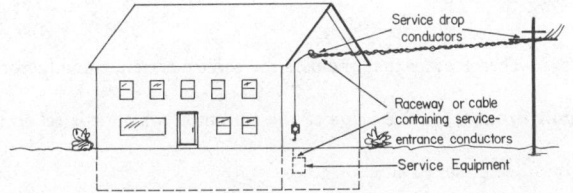

Figure 100-10. Illustration of an overhead system showing a service drop from a utility pole to attachment on the house and service-entrance conductors from point of attachment (spliced to service drop conductors), down the side of the house, through the meter socket, and terminating within the service equipment.

Service-Entrance Conductors, Underground System: The service conductors between the terminals of the service equipment and the point of connection to the service lateral.

See Figure 100-11.

(FPN): Where service equipment is located outside the building walls, there may be no service-entrance conductors, or they may be entirely outside the building.

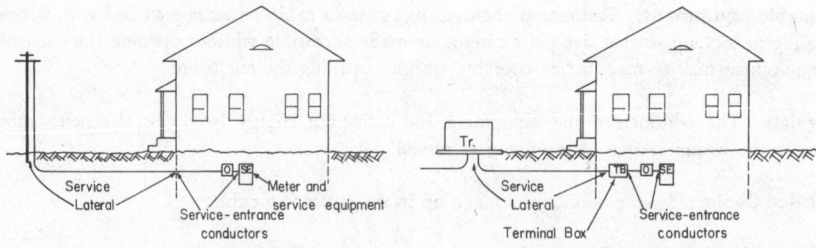

Figure 100-11. Service laterals (underground systems) may be run from poles or from transformers and with or without terminal boxes.

Service Equipment: The necessary equipment, usually consisting of a circuit breaker or switch and fuses, and their accessories, located near the point of entrance of supply conductors to a building or other structure, or an otherwise defined area, and intended to constitute the main control and means of cutoff of the supply.

Service equipment consists of a circuit breaker or a fused switch provided to disconnect all conductors in a building or other structure from the service-entrance conductors.

The disconnecting means is to consist of not more than six circuit breakers or six switches and is to be readily accessible, either inside or outside the building or structure nearest the point of entrance of the service-entrance conductors.

See Article 230, Part H.

Service Lateral: The underground service conductors between the street main, including any risers at a pole or other structure or from transformers, and the first point of connection to the service-entrance conductors in a terminal box or meter or other enclosure with adequate space, inside or outside the building wall. Where there is no terminal box, meter, or other enclosure with adequate space, the point of connection shall be considered to be the point of entrance of the service conductors into the building.

See Figure 100-11.

Service Raceway: The raceway that encloses the service-entrance conductors.

Setting (of Circuit Breaker): The value of the current at which it is set to trip.

Short-Time Duty: See under "Duty."

Show Window: Any window used or designed to be used for the display of goods or advertising material, whether it is fully or partly enclosed or entirely open at the rear and whether or not it has a platform raised higher than the street floor level.

See Figure 220-5.

Sign: See "Electric Sign."

Signaling Circuit: Any electric circuit that energizes signaling equipment.

Solar Photovoltaic System: The total components and subsystems which in combination convert solar energy into electrical energy suitable for connection to a utilization load.

See Article 690 for requirements for solar photovoltaic systems.

Special Permission: The written consent of the authority having jurisdiction.

The authority having jurisdiction for enforcement of the *Code* has responsibility for making interpretations and granting special permission contemplated in a number of the rules. Examples: see Section 110-16(a), Exception No. 2; Section 230-2, Exception Nos. 3 and 5; and Section 426-14.

Switchboard: A large single panel, frame, or assembly of panels on which are mounted, on the face or back or both, switches, overcurrent and other protective devices, buses, and usually instruments. Switchboards are generally accessible from the rear as well as from the front and are not intended to be installed in cabinets. (See "Panelboard.")

Busbars are to be arranged to avoid inductive overheating.

Service busbars are to be isolated by barriers from the remainder of the switchboard.

Most modern switchboards are totally enclosed to reduce to a minimum the probability of communicating fire to adjacent combustible materials and to guard live parts.

Switches:

General-Use Switch: A switch intended for use in general distribution and branch circuits. It is rated in amperes, and it is capable of interrupting its rated current at its rated voltage.

General-Use Snap Switch: A form of general-use switch so constructed that it can be installed in flush device boxes or on outlet box covers, or otherwise used in conjunction with wiring systems recognized by this Code.

AC General-Use Snap Switch: See Section 380-14(a).

AC-DC General-Use Snap Switch: See Section 380-14(b).

Isolating Switch: A switch intended for isolating an electric circuit from the source of power. It has no interrupting rating, and it is intended to be operated only after the circuit has been opened by some other means.

Motor-Circuit Switch: A switch, rated in horsepower, capable of interrupting the maximum operating overload current of a motor of the same horsepower rating as the switch at the rated voltage.

Thermal Cutout: An overcurrent protective device that contains a heater element in addition to and affecting a renewable fusible member which opens the circuit. It is not designed to interrupt short-circuit currents.

Thermally Protected: (As applied to motors.) The words "Thermally Protected" appearing on the nameplate of a motor or motor-compressor indicate that the motor is provided with a thermal protector.

Thermal Protector: (As applied to motors.) A protective device for assembly as an integral part of a motor or motor-compressor and which, when properly applied, protects the motor against dangerous overheating due to overload and failure to start.

(FPN): The thermal protector may consist of one or more sensing elements integral with the motor or motor-compressor and an external control device.

Utilization Equipment: Equipment which utilizes electric energy for mechanical, chemical, heating, lighting, or similar purposes.

ARTICLE 100—DEFINITIONS

Varying Duty: See under "Duty."

Ventilated: Provided with a means to permit circulation of air sufficient to remove an excess of heat, fumes, or vapors.

See commentary following Section 110-13(b).

Volatile Flammable Liquid: A flammable liquid having a flash point below 38°C (100°F), or a flammable liquid whose temperature is above its flash point, or a Class II combustible liquid having a vapor pressure not exceeding 40 psia (276 kPa) at 38°C (100°F) whose temperature is above its flash point.

The flash point of a liquid is the minimum temperature at which it gives off sufficient vapor to form an ignitible mixture with the air near the surface of the liquid or within the vessel used. An "ignitible mixture" is a mixture within the explosive or flammable range (between upper and lower limits) that is capable of the propagation of flame away from the source of ignition when ignited. Some emission of vapors takes place below the flash point but not in sufficient quantities to form an ignitible mixture.

Voltage (of a Circuit): The greatest root-mean-square (effective) difference of potential between any two conductors of the circuit concerned.

(FPN): Some systems, such as 3-phase 4-wire, single-phase 3-wire, and 3-wire direct-current may have various circuits of various voltages.

A 3-phase, 4-wire wye system has two voltages (for example, 277/480 or 120/208). The "voltage of the circuit" is the highest voltage between any two conductors, that is, 480 V and 208 V. The "voltage of the circuit" of a 2-wire feeder or branch circuit (one phase and the grounded conductor) derived from the above systems would be the voltage between the two conductors at the lower voltage, that is, 277 V and 120 V.
The same applies to dc or single-phase, 3-wire systems where there are two voltages.

Voltage, Nominal: A nominal value assigned to a circuit or system for the purpose of conveniently designating its voltage class (as 120/240, 480Y/277, 600, etc.).
The actual voltage at which a circuit operates can vary from the nominal within a range that permits satisfactory operation of equipment.

(FPN): See "Voltage Ratings for Electric Power Systems and Equipment (60 Hz)," ANSI C84.1-1977.

Voltage to Ground: For grounded circuits, the voltage between the given conductor and that point or conductor of the circuit that is grounded; for ungrounded circuits, the greatest voltage between the given conductor and any other conductor of the circuit.

The "voltage to ground" of a 277/480 V wye system would be 277 V; of a 120/208 V wye system, 120 V; and of a 3-phase, 3-wire ungrounded 480 V system, 480 V.

Watertight: So constructed that moisture will not enter the enclosure under specified test conditions.

(FPN): For test conditions other than for rotating equipment, see ANSI/NEMA, ICS6-1978, Enclosures for Industrial Controls and Systems, Paragraph ICS6-110.56.

Unless the enclosure is hermetically sealed, it is possible for moisture to enter the enclosure. The ANSI/NEMA Standard alerts the user to the possibility of condensation in the enclosure and contains widely used testing procedures for enclosures for electrical equipment.

Weatherproof: So constructed or protected that exposure to the weather will not interfere with successful operation.

(FPN): Rainproof, raintight, or watertight equipment can fulfill the requirements for weatherproof where varying weather conditions other than wetness, such as snow, ice, dust, or temperature extremes, are not a factor.

Welder, Electric:

Actual Primary Current: See Section 630-31(b).

Rated Primary Current: See Section 630-31(b).

Wet Location: See under "Location."

X-ray:

Long-Time Rating: See Sections 517-140 and 660-2.

Momentary Rating: See Sections 517-140 and 660-2.

B. Over 600 Volts, Nominal

Whereas the preceding definitions are intended to apply wherever the terms are used throughout this Code, the following ones are applicable only to the parts of articles specifically covering installations and equipment operating at over 600 volts, nominal.

Circuit Breaker: See under "Switching Devices."

Cutout: See under "Switching Devices."

Disconnect (Isolator): See under "Switching Devices."

Disconnecting Means: See under "Switching Devices."

Fuse: An overcurrent protective device with a circuit opening fusible part that is heated and severed by the passage of overcurrent through it.

(FPN): A fuse comprises all the parts that form a unit capable of performing the prescribed functions. It may or may not be the complete device necessary to connect it into an electrical circuit.

Expulsion Fuse Unit (Expulsion Fuse): A vented fuse unit in which the expulsion effect of gases produced by the arc and lining of the fuseholder, either alone or aided by a spring, extinguishes the arc.

Power Fuse Unit: A vented, nonvented or controlled vented fuse unit in which the arc is extinguished by being drawn through solid material, granular material, or liquid, either alone or aided by a spring.

Vented Power Fuse: A fuse with provision for the escape of arc gases, liquids, or solid particles to the surrounding atmosphere during circuit interruption.

Nonvented Power Fuse: A fuse without intentional provision for the escape of arc gases, liquids, or solid particles to the atmosphere during circuit interruption.

Controlled Vented Power Fuse: A fuse with provision for controlling discharge circuit interruption such that no solid material may be exhausted into the surrounding atmosphere. The discharge gases shall not ignite or damage insulation in the path of the discharge, nor shall these gases propagate a flashover to or between grounded members or conduction members in the path of the discharge when the distance between the vent and such insulation or conduction members conforms to manufacturer's recommendations.

Grounded, Effectively: Permanently connected to earth through a ground connection of sufficiently low impedance and having sufficient ampacity that ground-fault current which may occur cannot build up to voltages dangerous to personnel.

Interrupter Switch: See under "Switching Devices."

Multiple Fuse: An assembly of two or more single-pole fuses.

Oil (Filled) Cutout: See under "Switching Devices."

Power Fuse: See under "Fuse."

Regulator Bypass Switch: See under "Switching Devices."

Switching Device: A device designed to close and/or open one or more electric circuits.

Switching Devices:

Circuit Breaker: A switching device capable of making, carrying, and breaking currents under normal circuit conditions, and also making, carrying for a specified time, and breaking currents under specified abnormal circuit conditions, such as those of short circuit.

Cutout: An assembly of a fuse support with either a fuseholder, fuse carrier, or disconnecting blade. The fuseholder or fuse carrier may include a conducting element (fuse link), or may act as the disconnecting blade by the inclusion of a nonfusible member.

Disconnecting (or Isolating) Switch (Disconnector, Isolator): A mechanical switching device used for isolating a circuit or equipment from a source of power.

Disconnecting Means: A device, group of devices, or other means whereby the conductors of a circuit can be disconnected from their source of supply.

Interrupter Switch: A switch capable of making, carrying, and interrupting specified currents.

Oil Cutout (Oil-Filled Cutout): A cutout in which all or part of the fuse support and its fuse link or disconnecting blade are mounted in oil with complete immersion of the contacts and the fusible portion of the conducting element (fuse link), so that arc interruption by severing of the fuse link or by opening of the contacts will occur under oil.

Oil Switch: An oil switch is a switch having contacts which operate under oil (or askarel or other suitable liquid).

Regulator Bypass Switch: A specific device or combination of devices designed to bypass a regulator.

ARTICLE 110 — REQUIREMENTS FOR
ELECTRICAL INSTALLATIONS

Contents

A. General

110-1. Mandatory Rules and Explanatory Material. Mandatory rules of this Code are characterized by the use of the word "shall." Explanatory material is in the form of Fine Print Notes (FPN).

In addition to printing explanatory material in fine print (small type), the material is further identified in the 1984 *NEC* by the term "(FPN)" preceding the paragraph. Footnotes to tables, although also in fine print, are not explanatory material; the footnotes are part of the tables and are necessary for the proper use of the tables. For example, see the footnotes to Table 310-16.

ARTICLE 110—REQUIREMENTS FOR ELECTRICAL INSTALLATIONS

110-2. Approval. The conductors and equipment required or permitted by this Code shall be acceptable only if approved.

(FPN): See Examination of Equipment for Safety, Section 90-6 and Examination, Identification, Installation, and Use of Equipment, Section 110-3. See definitions of "Approved," "Identified," "Labeled," and "Listed."

Section 110-2 of the *Code* requires that all equipment be approved and, as such, be acceptable to the authority having jurisdiction. Section 110-3 provides guidance for the judging of equipment and recognizes listing or labeling as a means of establishing suitability.

Approval of equipment is the responsibility of the electrical inspection authority and many such "approvals" are based on tests and listings of testing laboratories such as Underwriters Laboratories Inc. (UL) or Factory Mutual (FM), etc.

110-3. Examination, Identification, Installation, and Use of Equipment.

(a) Examination. In judging equipment, considerations such as the following shall be evaluated:

(1) Suitability for installation and use in conformity with the provisions of this Code. Suitability of equipment use may be identified by a description marked on or provided with a product to identify the suitability of the product for a specific purpose, environment, or application. Suitability of equipment may be evidenced by listing or labeling.

(2) Mechanical strength and durability, including, for parts designed to enclose and protect other equipment, the adequacy of the protection thus provided.

(3) Wire-bending and connection space.

(4) Electrical insulation.

(5) Heating effects under normal conditions of use and also under abnormal conditions likely to arise in service.

(6) Arcing effects.

(7) Classification by type, size, voltage, current capacity, specific use.

(8) Other factors which contribute to the practical safeguarding of persons using or likely to come in contact with the equipment.

For wire-bending and connection space in cabinets and cutout boxes, see Section 373-6, Tables 373-6(a) and 373-6(b), and Sections 373-7, 373-9, and 373-11. For wire-bending and connection space in other equipment, see the appropriate *NEC* article and section. For example, see Section 370-18 for outlet, device, pull and junction boxes and conduit bodies; Section 380-3 for switches; Section 384-3(g) for switchboards and panelboards; and Section 430-10 for motors and motor controllers.

(b) Installation and Use. Listed or labeled equipment shall be used or installed in accordance with any instructions included in the listing or labeling.

Installation instructions are usually supplied with equipment by the manufacturer for use by the general contractor, erector, electrical contractor, electrical inspector, and others concerned with the installation. It is very important to consider the listing or labeling installation instructions. For example, Section

210-52(a), Exception permits permanently installed electric baseboard heaters to be equipped with receptacle outlets that are the required receptacle outlets for the wall space utilized by such heaters. Installation instructions for such permanent baseboard heaters indicate that these heaters should not be mounted beneath a receptacle. In dwelling units, it is very common to use low-density heat units which may measure in excess of 12 ft in length; therefore, to meet the provisions of Section 210-52(a) first paragraph and also the installation instructions, a receptacle must either be part of the heating unit or be installed in the floor close to the wall as it should not be placed above the heating unit. See Figures 210-24 and 210-25.

110-4. Voltages. Throughout this Code the voltage considered shall be that at which the circuit operates.

See definitions of "Voltage (of a Circuit)," "Voltage, Nominal," and "Voltage to Ground" in Article 100.
See also Sections 300-2 and 300-3.

110-5. Conductors. Conductors normally used to carry current shall be of copper unless otherwise provided in this Code. Where the conductor material is not specified, the sizes given in this Code shall apply to copper conductors. Where other materials are used, the size shall be changed accordingly.

(FPN): For aluminum and copper-clad aluminum conductors, see Tables 310-16 through 310-19.

See Section 310-14 for aluminum conductor material.

110-6. Conductor Sizes. Conductor sizes are expressed in American Wire Gage (AWG) or in circular mils.

For copper, aluminum, or copper-clad aluminum conductors up to size No. 0000 (4/0), this *Code* uses the American Wire Gage (AWG) for size identification, which is the same as the Brown and Sharpe Gage (BS).
Conductors larger than 4/0 are sized in circular mils, beginning with 250,000 circular mils (or 250 MCM). See Tables 310-16 through 310-19.
The circular mil (CM) area of a conductor is equal to its diameter, in mils, squared (1 in. equals 1,000 mils).

Example: The diameter of a No. 8 solid conductor is 0.1285 in.

$$0.1285 \text{ in.} \times 1,000 = 128.5 \text{ mils}$$
$$128.5 \times 128.5 \quad = 16512.25 \text{ CM}$$

or 16510 CM, as rounded off by Table 8 of Chapter 9.
This represents the circular mil area for one conductor. Where stranded conductors are used, the resulting figure must be multiplied by the number of strands (see Table 8 of Chapter 9).

110-7. Insulation Integrity. All wiring shall be so installed that when completed the system will be free from short circuits and from grounds other than as permitted in Article 250.

Insulation is the material between points of different potential in an electrical system preventing the flow of electricity between those points. Failure of the insulation system is one of the most common causes of problems in electrical installations. This is true on both high-voltage and low-voltage systems.

Insulation tests are performed on new or existing installations to determine the quality or condition of the insulation of conductors and/or equipment.

The principal causes of insulation failures are heat, moisture, and dirt. Insulation can also fail due to chemical attack, mechanical damage, sunlight, and excessive voltage stresses.

In an insulation resistance test, an applied voltage from 100 to 5,000 V (usually 500 to 1,000 V for systems of 600 V or less), supplied from a source of constant potential, is applied across the insulation. A hand-generated megohmmeter is the usual potential source, and it indicates the insulation resistance directly on a scale calibrated in megohms. The quality of the insulation is evaluated based on the level of the insulation resistance.

The insulation resistance of many types of insulation is quite variable with temperature, so the data obtained should be corrected to the standard temperature for the class of equipment under test.

The megohm value of insulation resistance obtained will be inversely proportional to the volume of insulation being tested. As an example, a cable 1,000 ft long would be expected to have one-tenth the insulation resistance of a cable 100 ft long if all other conditions were identical.

The insulation resistance test is relatively easy to perform and is useful on all types and classes of electrical equipment. Its main value lies in the charting of data from periodic tests, corrected for temperature, over the life of the equipment so that deteriorative trends might be detected.

Excellent manuals on this subject are available from instrument manufacturers. Thorough knowledge in the use of insulation testers is essential if the test results are to be meaningful.

See Figure 110-1 for a typical megohmmeter insulation tester.

110-8. Wiring Methods. Only wiring methods recognized as suitable are included in this Code. The recognized methods of wiring shall be permitted to be installed in any type of building or occupancy, except as otherwise provided in this Code.

The scope of Article 300 applies generally to all wiring methods, except as amended, modified, or supplemented by Chapter 5 (Special Occupancies), Chapter 6 (Special Equipment), and Chapter 7 (Special Conditions).

Chapter 8 (Communications Systems) is independent of the other chapters except where some other section is specifically referenced in Chapter 8 of the *Code*. For example, see Section 800-3(d).

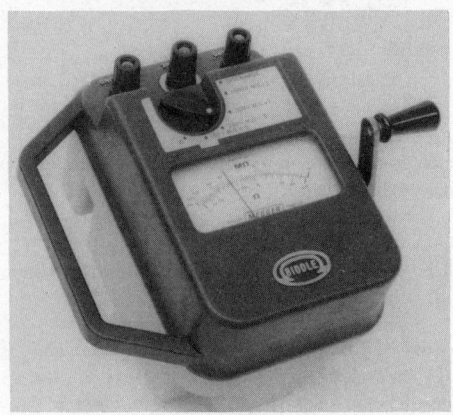

Figure 110-1. Multivoltage multirange insulation tester. (*James G. Biddle Co.*)

110-9. Interrupting Rating. Equipment intended to break current at fault levels shall have an interrupting rating sufficient for the system voltage and the current which is available at the line terminals of the equipment.

Equipment intended to break current at other than fault levels shall have an interrupting rating at system voltage sufficient for the current that must be interrupted.

Section 110-9 states that all fuses and circuit breakers intended to break the circuit at fault levels must have an adequate interrupting rating wherever they are used in the electrical system. Fuses or circuit breakers which do not have adequate interrupting ratings could rupture while attempting to clear a short circuit.

Instructions for calculating available short-circuit currents are provided in ANSI/IEEE Std. C37.010-1982, Application Guide for AC High-Voltage Circuit Breakers Rated on a Symmetrical Current Basis. Additional details are provided in IEEE Std. 141-1976, Recommended Practice for Electric Power Distribution for Industrial Plants, Chapter 4; and IEEE Std. 241-1974, Recommended Practice for Electric Power Systems in Commercial Buildings, Chapter 9.

110-10. Circuit Impedance and Other Characteristics. The overcurrent protective devices, the total impedance, the component short-circuit withstand ratings, and other characteristics of the circuit to be protected shall be so selected and coordinated as to permit the circuit protective devices used to clear a fault without the occurrence of extensive damage to the electrical components of the circuit. This fault shall be assumed to be either between two or more of the circuit conductors, or between any circuit conductor and the grounding conductor or enclosing metal raceway.

The basic purpose of overcurrent protection is to open the circuit before conductors or conductor insulation are damaged when an overcurrent condition exists. An overcurrent condition can be the result of an overload or a short circuit and must be removed before the conductor insulation damage point is reached.

Overcurrent protective devices (such as fuses and circuit breakers) should be selected in such a manner that the short-circuit rating of the system components will not be exceeded should a short circuit occur. System components include wire, bus structures, starters, etc., all of which have limited short-circuit ratings and would be damaged or destroyed if these short-circuit ratings are exceeded. Merely providing overcurrent protective devices with sufficient interrupting capacity will not assure short-circuit protection for the system components to be protected. When the available short-circuit current exceeds the withstand rating of an electrical component, the overcurrent protective device must limit the let-through energy to within the rating of that electrical component.

Utility companies usually determine and provide information on available short-circuit current at the service equipment. Literature on calculating short-circuit currents can be obtained by contacting representatives of manufacturers of overcurrent protective devices.

The following information on cartridge fuses has been extracted from the UL Electrical Construction Materials List:

Fuses designated as Class K1, K5, and K9 (0-600 A, 250 V, ac or 600 V, ac) are classified as to interrupting capacity and in terms of maximum clearing ampere squared seconds and maximum peak let-through current. They incorporate dimensional features equivalent to, and are interchangeable with, other nonrenewable cartridge fuses intended for installation in conventional designs of equipment recognized by the *Code* for branch circuit, service, and motor overload use. They are not marked "Current Limiting."

Fuses designated as Class RK1 and RK5 (0-600 A, 250 V, ac or 600 V, ac) are high interrupting capacity types and are marked "Current Limiting." They are classified in terms of maximum clearing ampere squared seconds and maximum peak let-through currents at 50,000, 100,000, and 200,000 rms symmetrical amperes.

They incorporate features that permit their insertion into holders for other nonrenewable cartridge fuses intended for installation in conventional designs of equipment recognized by the *NEC* for branch circuit, service, and motor overload use. They are provided with a feature that allows their insertion into rejection-type fuseholders designed to accept only Class RK1 or RK5 fuses.

The rejection-type fuseholders are used in equipment as covered in the *NEC*.

Fuses designated as Class CC (0-30 A, 600 V, ac) are high interrupting capacity types and are marked "Current Limiting." They are not interchangeable with fuses of higher voltage or interrupting rating or lower current rating.

Fuses designated as Class G (0-60 A, 300 V, ac) are high interrupting capacity types and are marked "Current Limiting." They are not interchangeable with other fuses mentioned above and below.

Fuses designated as Class J (0-600 A, 600 V, ac) or Class L (601-6000 A, 600 V, ac) are high interrupting capacity types and are marked "Current Limiting." They are not interchangeable with other fuses such as those mentioned above and below.

Fuses designated as Class T (0-600 A, 300 and 600 V, ac) are high interrupting capacity types and are marked "Current Limiting." They are not interchangeable with other fuses mentioned above.

The term "Current Limiting" indicates that a fuse, when tested on a circuit capable of delivering a specific short-circuit current (rms amperes symmetrical) at rated voltage, will start to melt within 90 electrical degrees and will clear the circuit within 180 electrical degrees (1/2 cycle).

Because the time required for a fuse to melt is dependent on the available current of the circuit, a fuse which may be current limiting when subjected to a specific short-circuit current (rms amperes symmetrical) may not be current limiting on a circuit of lower maximum available current.

The performance of a fuse, as it is determined by the ability of the fuse to open and clear a circuit, is indicated by the following maximum permissible let-through values which are obtained when fuses of the Class K designs are connected to circuits having an available current of up to 100,000 A maximum (rms symmetrical) but not greater than the marked interrupting rating of the fuse if it is less than 100,000 A, when fuses of the Class G design are connected to circuits having an available current of 100,000 A maximum (rms symmetrical), and when fuses of the Class CC, J, L, RK, and T designs are connected to circuits having available currents of 50,000, 100,000 and 200,000 A maximum (rms symmetrical). (See UL List for tabulated values.)

Class K1, K5, and K9 fuses are marked, in addition to their regular voltage and current ratings, with an interrupting rating of 200,000, 100,000, or 50,000 A (rms symmetrical).

Class CC, RK1, RK5, J, L, and T fuses are marked, in addition to their regular voltage and current ratings, with an interrupting rating of 200,000 A (rms symmetrical).

Class G fuses are marked, in addition to their regular voltage and current ratings, with an interrupting rating of 100,000 A (rms symmetrical).

Equipment (switches, motor starters, panelboards, etc.) which has been investigated and found suitable for use with these fuses is marked with the class of fuse intended to be used in the equipment and an available current rating applicable to that piece of equipment.

The equipment, when so marked, with these fuses installed, is considered to be suitable for use on circuits which can deliver currents under short-circuit conditions up to the available current rating of the equipment, or the interrupting rating of the fuse, whichever is lower.

An interrupting rating on a fuse included in a piece of equipment does not automatically qualify the equipment in which the fuses are installed for use on circuits with higher available currents than the rating of the equipment itself.

Class L fuses are designed for use in equipment to which line and load connections are made by means of solid busbars. For this reason temperature rises on Class L fuse blades may exceed those observed in connection with other cartridge fuse designs. Terminal connections for wires in such equipment must be designed to avoid excessive temperatures on the wire insulation.

Class CC, G, H, J, K, L and RK fuses may be marked as having a time delay characteristic. For Class CC, G, H, J, K and RK fuses, this characteristic (a minimum clearing time under a particular overcurrent condition) has been investigated. Class G or CC fuses which can carry 200 percent of rated current for 12 seconds or more, and Class H, J, K or RK fuses which can carry 500 percent of rated current for 10 seconds or more may be marked with "D," "Time Delay," "Dual Element," or some equivalent designation. Class L fuses are permitted to be marked "Time Delay," but have not been evaluated for such performance. Class T fuses are not permitted to be marked "Time Delay."

110-11. Deteriorating Agents. Unless identified for use in the operating environment, no conductors or equipment shall be located in damp or wet locations; where exposed to gases, fumes, vapors, liquids, or other agents having a deteriorating effect on the conductors or equipment; nor where exposed to excessive temperatures.

Listed wire pulling compounds are available for use as lubricants in raceways. The use of grease, soap, or wax should be avoided as these materials may damage the insulation.

(FPN): See Section 300-6 for protection against corrosion.

Control equipment, utilization equipment, and busways approved for use in dry locations only shall be protected against permanent damage from the weather during building construction.

110-12. Mechanical Execution of Work. Electric equipment shall be installed in a neat and workmanlike manner.

Unused openings in boxes, raceways, auxiliary gutters, cabinets, equipment cases or housings shall be effectively closed to afford protection substantially equivalent to the wall of the equipment.

Many *Code* conflicts or violations have been cited by the authority having jurisdiction based on the authority's interpretation of "neat and workmanlike manner."

Many electrical inspection authorities use their own experience or precedents in their local areas as the basis for their judgments but they should realize that any ruling should be based on uniformity as intended by the National Electrical Code Committee.

Examples of installations that are considered not to be "neat and in a workmanlike manner" are exposed runs of cables or raceways that are improperly supported, that is, sagging between supports or using unapproved methods for supports; field-bent and kinked, flattened, or poorly measured raceways; or cabinets, cutout boxes, and enclosures that are not plumb or that are not properly secured.

ARTICLE 110—REQUIREMENTS FOR ELECTRICAL INSTALLATIONS

110-13. Mounting and Cooling of Equipment.

(a) Mounting. Electric equipment shall be firmly secured to the surface on which it is mounted. Wooden plugs driven into holes in masonry, concrete, plaster, or similar materials shall not be used.

(b) Cooling. Electrical equipment which depends upon the natural circulation of air and convection principles for cooling of exposed surfaces shall be installed so that room air flow over such surfaces is not prevented by walls or by adjacent installed equipment. For equipment designed for floor mounting, clearance between top surfaces and adjacent surfaces shall be provided to dissipate rising warm air.

See Sections 430-14(a) and 430-16 for motor locations, and Sections 450-9 and 450-45 for transformer locations.

Electrical equipment provided with ventilating openings shall be installed so that walls or other obstructions do not prevent the free circulation of air through the equipment.

For example, a ventilated busway must be located where there are no walls or other objects that might interfere with the natural circulation of air and convection principles for cooling. See definition of "Ventilated" in Article 100.

Some types of equipment, such as panelboards and transformers, are adversely effected if enclosure surfaces normally exposed to room air are covered or tightly enclosed. Ventilating openings in equipment are provided to allow the circulation of room air around internal components of the equipment and the blocking of such openings can cause dangerous overheating.

110-14. Electrical Connections.

Because of different characteristics of copper and aluminum, devices such as pressure terminal or pressure splicing connectors and soldering lugs shall be suitable for the material of the conductor and shall be properly installed and used. Conductors of dissimilar metals shall not be intermixed in a terminal or splicing connector where physical contact occurs between dissimilar conductors (such as copper and aluminum, copper and copper-clad aluminum, or aluminum and copper-clad aluminum), unless the device is suitable for the purpose and conditions of use. Materials such as solder, fluxes, inhibitors, and compounds, where employed, shall be suitable for the use and shall be of a type which will not adversely affect the conductors, installation, or equipment.

(FPN): Many terminations and equipment are marked with a tightening torque.

Tightening Torques

Figures 110-2, 110-3, 110-4, and 110-5 provide information on the tightening torques used by Underwriters Laboratories Inc. when testing wire connectors unless the manufacturer assigns another value appropriate for the design. This information should be used for guidance only where no tightening information on the specific wire connector is available. It should not be used to replace manufacturer's instructions which should always be followed. This information was taken from the edition of UL Standard 486B that was in effect at the time of the printing of this Handbook. Similar information can be found in UL 486A.

Tightening Torques for Screws—Pound Inches[a]

Wire Size	Slotted Head No. 10 and Larger				Hexagonal Head—External Drive Socket Wrench	
	Slot Width— Inches[b]		Slot Length— Inches[b]		Split-Bolt Connectors	Other Connectors
	to 3/64	over 3/64	to 1/4	over 1/4		
18-10 AWG	20	35	20	35	80	75
8	25	40	25	40	80	75
6	35	45	35	45	165	110
4	35	45	35	45	165	110
3	35	50	35	50	275	150
2	40	50	40	50	275	150
1	—	50	—	50	275	150
1/0	—	50	—	50	385	180
2/0	—	50	—	50	385	180
3/0	—	50	—	50	500	250
4/0	—	50	—	50	500	250
250 MCM	—	50	—	50	650	325
300	—	50	—	50	650	325
350	—	50	—	50	650	325
400	—	50	—	50	825	325
500	—	50	—	50	825	375
600	—	50	—	50	1000	375
700	—	50	—	50	1000	375
750	—	50	—	50	1000	375
800	—	50	—	50	1100	500
900	—	50	—	50	1100	500
1000	—	50	—	50	1100	500
1250	—	—	—	—	1100	600
1500	—	—	—	—	1100	600
1750	—	—	—	—	1100	600
2000	—	—	—	—	1100	600

a. Clamping screws with multiple tightening means: for example, for a slotted hexagonal head screw, use the torque value associated with the tool used in the installation. UL uses both values when testing.

b. For values of slot width or length other than those specified, select the largest torque value associated with conductor size.

Figure 110-2. Tightening torques for screws in pound-inches. (*Underwriters Laboratories Inc.*)

Torques in Pound-Inches for Slotted Head Screws[a] Smaller than No. 10, for Use with No. 8 AWG or Smaller Conductors

Screw-Slot Length in Inches[b]	Screw-Slot Width Less than 3/64 in.	Screw-Slot Width 3/64 in. and Larger
to 5/32	7	9
5/32	7	12
3/16	7	12
7/32	7	12
1/4	9	12
9/32	—	15
above 9/32	—	20

a. Clamping screws with multiple tightening means: for example, for a slotted hexagonal head screw, use the torque value associated with the tool used in the installation. UL uses both values when testing.

b. For slot lengths of intermediate values, select torques pertaining to next shorter slot length.

Figure 110-3. Tightening torques for slotted head screws in pound-inches. (*Underwriters Laboratories Inc.*)

Torques for Socket Head Screws[a]

Socket Size Across Flats—Inches	Torque, Pound-Inches
⅛	45
5/32	100
3/16	120
7/32	150
¼	200
5/16	275
⅜	375
½	500
9/16	600

a. Clamping screws with multiple tightening means: for example, for a slotted hexagonal head screw, use the torque value associated with the tool used in the installation. UL uses both values when testing.

Figure 110-4. Tightening torques for socket head screws in pound-inches. (*Underwriters Laboratories Inc.*)

Lug Bolting Torques for Connection of Wire Connectors to Busbars, etc.

Bolt Diameter— Inches	Tightening Torque Pound-Feet
No. 8	1.5
No. 10	2.0
¼ or less	6
5/16	11
⅜	19
7/16	30
½	40
⅝ or more	55

Figure 110-5. Lug bolting torques in pound-feet for connection of wire connectors to busbars, etc. (*Underwriters Laboratories Inc.*)

(a) Terminals. Connection of conductors to terminal parts shall ensure a thoroughly good connection without damaging the conductors and shall be made by means of pressure connectors (including set-screw type), solder lugs, or splices to flexible leads.

Exception: Connection by means of wire binding screws or studs and nuts having upturned lugs or equivalent shall be permitted for No. 10 or smaller conductors.

Terminals for more than one conductor and terminals used to connect aluminum shall be so identified.

(b) Splices. Conductors shall be spliced or joined with splicing devices suitable for the use or by brazing, welding, or soldering with a fusible metal or alloy. Soldered splices shall first be so spliced or joined as to be mechanically and electrically secure without solder and then soldered. All splices and joints and the free ends of conductors shall be covered with an insulation equivalent to that of the conductors or with an insulating device suitable for the purpose.

Field observations and trade magazine articles indicate that failures of electrical connections are the cause of many equipment burnouts and fires. Many of these failures are attributable to improper terminations, poor workmanship, different characteristics of dissimilar metals, and improper binding screws or splicing devices.

Recent revisions in Underwriters Laboratories Inc. requirements for listing solid aluminum conductors in sizes No. 12 and No. 10 AWG and for listing snap switches and receptacles for use on 15- and 20-A branch circuits incorporate stringent tests which take the factors listed in the previous paragraph into account. See Sections 380-14(c) and 410-56(b).

Screwless pressure terminal connectors of the conductor push-in type are for use with copper and copper-clad aluminum conductors only.

Instructions describing proper installation techniques and emphasizing the need to follow these techniques and practice good workmanship are required to be included with each coil of No. 12 and No. 10 AWG insulated aluminum wire or cable. Also, see commentary on tightening torque under Section 110-14, FPN.

New product and material designs which provide for increased levels of safety of aluminum wire terminations have been developed by the electrical industry.

To assist all concerned parties in the proper and safe use of solid aluminum wire in making connections to wiring devices used on 15- and 20-A branch circuits, the following information is presented. Understanding and utilizing this information is essential to proper application of materials and devices now available.

For New Installations

The following was prepared by the Ad Hoc Committee on Aluminum Terminations: Comply with Section 110-14(a) of the 1984 *NEC* when aluminum wire is used in new installations.

New Materials and Devices
 a. For direct connection use only 15- and 20-A receptacles and switches marked "CO/ALR" and connected as described under "Installation Method."

The "CO/ALR" marking is on the device mounting strap. The "CO/ALR" marking means the devices have been tested to stringent heat cycling requirements to determine their suitability for use with UL-labeled aluminum, copper, or copper-clad aluminum wire.

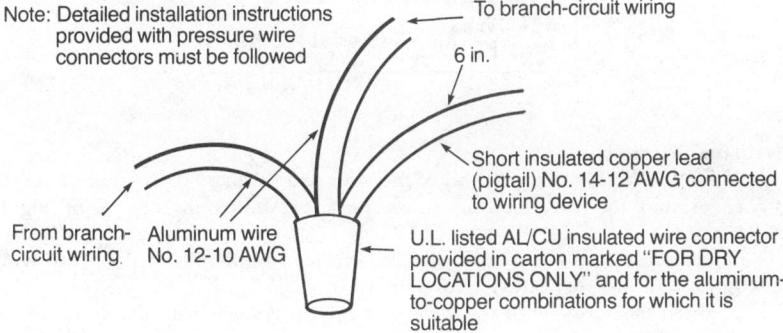

Note: Detailed installation instructions provided with pressure wire connectors must be followed

To branch-circuit wiring

6 in.

Short insulated copper lead (pigtail) No. 14-12 AWG connected to wiring device

From branch-circuit wiring

Aluminum wire No. 12-10 AWG

U.L. listed AL/CU insulated wire connector provided in carton marked "FOR DRY LOCATIONS ONLY" and for the aluminum-to-copper combinations for which it is suitable

Figure 110-6. Pigtailing copper to aluminum conductor. (*Underwriters Laboratories Inc.*)

Note. Pigtailing, either field- or factory-wired, as illustrated in Figure 110-6, is recognized by the *NEC*.
 b. Use solid aluminum wire, No. 12 or No. 10 AWG, marked with the Underwriters Laboratories' new aluminum insulated wire label, as shown in Figure 110-7. Follow the installation instructions packaged with the wire.

1. Strip wires ⅜" 2. Pretwisting unnecessary. Hold stripped wires together with ends even. 　(Lead stranded wires slightly.) 3. Screw on connector—push wires firmly into connector when starting. COPPER TO COPPER ALUMINUM TO ALUMINUM	Typical connector carton marking

COPPER TO ALUMINUM (dry locations only)

Temperature rating: 150°C. (302°F.) Max.
Listed as a PRESSURE TYPE wire connector on the following solid and/or stranded wire combinations.

2 or 3 #8	3 #10 with 1 or 2 #14
2 #8 with 1 or 2 #10	→2 #10 with 1,2,3, or 4 #12
2 #8 with 1,2, or 3 #12	2 #10 with 1,2, or 3 #14
1 #8 with 1,2,3, or 4 #10	1 #10 with 1,2,3,4, or 5 #12
1 #8 with 1,2,3,4, or 5 #12	1 #10 with 1,2,3, or 4 #14
3 #8 with 1 #12	2,3,4,5, or 6 #12
2,3,4, or 5 #10	4 #12 with 1 or 2 #14
5 #10 with 1 #12	3 #12 with 1,2, or 3 #14
4 #10 with 1 or 2 #12	→2 #12 with 1,2, or 3 #14
4 #10 with 1 #14	1 #12 with 2,3, or 4 #14
3 #10 with 1,2, or 3 #12	

Conductor bearing this UL label is judged under the requirements for the chemistry, physical properties, and processing of the conductor which became effective September 20, 1972.

Installation Method

1. Wrap the freshly stripped end of the wire two-thirds to three-quarters of the distance around the wire-binding screw post, as shown in Step A of Figure 110-7.

The loop is made so that rotation of the screw in tightening will tend to wrap the wire around the post rather than unwrap it.

2. Tighten the screw until the wire is snugly in contact with the underside of the screw head and with the contact plate on the wiring device, as shown in Step B of Figure 110-7.

3. Tighten the screw an additional one-half turn, thereby providing a firm connection. Where torque screwdrivers are used, tighten to 12 pound-inches. See Step C of Figure 110-7.

4. Position the wires behind the wiring device so as to decrease the likelihood of the terminal screws loosening when the device is positioned into the outlet box.

Correct method of terminating
aluminum wire at wire-binding-
screw terminals of receptacles
and snap switches

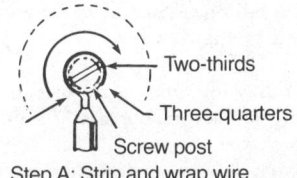

Two-thirds

Three-quarters

Screw post

Step A: Strip and wrap wire

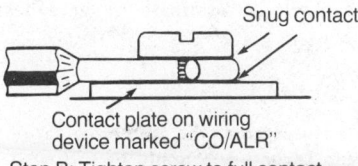

Snug contact

Contact plate on wiring
device marked "CO/ALR"

Step B: Tighten screw to full contact

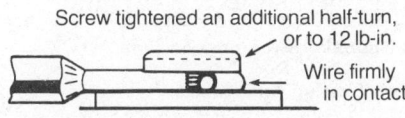

Screw tightened an additional half-turn,
or to 12 lb-in.

Wire firmly
in contact

Step C: Complete connection

Figure 110-7. Correct method of terminating aluminum wire at wire-binding screw terminals of receptacles and snap switches. (*Underwriters Laboratories Inc.*)

Figure 110-8 illustrates incorrect methods for connection and should not be used.

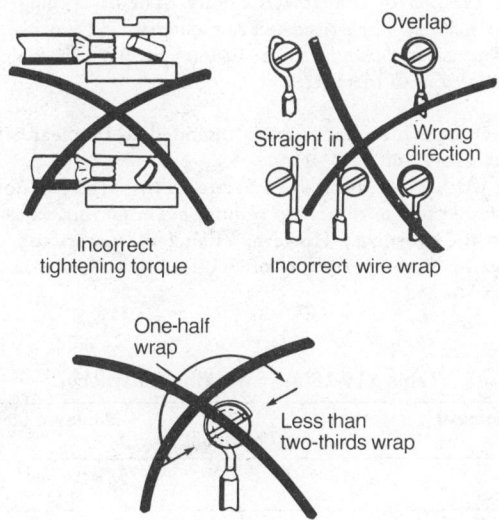

Incorrect
tightening torque

Overlap

Straight in

Wrong
direction

Incorrect wire wrap

One-half
wrap

Less than
two-thirds wrap

Figure 110-8. Incorrect methods of terminating aluminum wire at wire-binding screw terminals of receptacles and snap switches. (*Underwriters Laboratories Inc.*)

Existing Inventory

When UL-labeled solid aluminum wire No. 12 and No. 10 AWG not bearing the new aluminum wire label is used, it should be used with wiring devices marked "CO/ALR" and connected as described in "Installation Method." This is the preferred and recommended method for using such wire.

Note. Pigtailing, either field- or factory-wired, as illustrated in Figure 110-6, is recognized by the *NEC*.

In the following types of devices the terminals shall not be directly connected to aluminum conductors but may be used with UL-labeled copper or copper-clad conductors:

Receptacles and snap switches marked "AL-CU";

Receptacles and snap switches having no conductor marking;

Receptacles and snap switches having backwired terminals or screwless terminals of the push-in type.

For Existing Installations

If examination discloses overheating or loose connections the recommendations described under "For New Installations Existing Inventory" should be followed.

110-16. Working Space About Electric Equipment (600 Volts, Nominal, or Less). Sufficient access and working space shall be provided and maintained about all electric equipment to permit ready and safe operation and maintenance of such equipment.

(a) Working Clearances. Except as elsewhere required or permitted in this Code, the dimension of the working space in the direction of access to live parts operating at 600 volts, nominal, or less and likely to require examination, adjustment, servicing, or maintenance while energized shall not be less than indicated in Table 110-16(a). Distances shall be measured from the live parts if such are exposed or from the enclosure front or opening if such are enclosed. Concrete, brick, or tile walls shall be considered as grounded.
In addition to the dimensions shown in Table 110-16(a), the work space shall not be less than 30 inches (762 mm) wide in front of the electric equipment.

Note that the 30-in. wide dimension is intended to be clear all the way to the floor. See Figures 110-9 and 110-10.
The minimum working clearances of Section 110-16(a) are not required if the equipment is such that it is not likely to require examination, adjustment, servicing, or maintenance while energized. However "sufficient" access and working space is still required by the first paragraph of Section 110-16. Also, see commentary following Section 384-2.

Table 110-16(a). Working Clearances

Voltage to Ground, Nominal	Minimum Clear Distance (feet)		
Condition:	1	2	3
0-150	3	3	3
151-600	3	3½	4

For SI units: one inch = 25.4 millimeters; one foot = 0.3048 meter.

Where the "Conditions" are as follows:

1. Exposed live parts on one side and no live or grounded parts on the other side of the working space, or exposed live parts on both sides effectively guarded by suitable wood or other insulating materials. Insulated wire or insulated busbars operating at not over 300 volts shall not be considered live parts.

2. Exposed live parts on one side and grounded parts on the other side.

3. Exposed live parts on both sides of the work space (not guarded as provided in Condition 1) with the operator between.

Exception No. 1: Working space shall not be required in back of assemblies such as dead-front switchboards, or motor control centers where there are no renewable or adjustable parts such as fuses or switches on the back and where all connections are accessible from locations other than the back.

Exception No. 2: By special permission smaller spaces may be permitted (1) where it is judged that the particular arrangement of the installation will provide adequate accessibility, or (2) where all uninsulated parts are at a voltage no greater than 30 volts RMS or 42V dc.

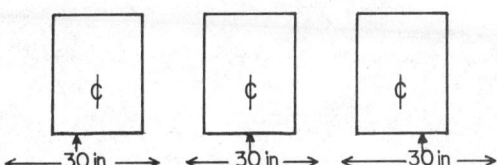

Figure 110-9. The 30-in. wide front work space need not be directly centered on the electrical equipment where it is assured that the space is sufficient for safe operation and maintenance of such equipment.

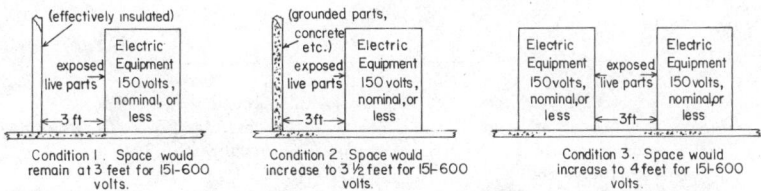

Figure 110-10. Distances are measured from the live parts if such are exposed or from the enclosure front if live parts are enclosed. If any assemblies, such as switchboards or motor-control centers, are accessible from the back and expose live parts, the working clearance dimensions would be required at the rear of the equipment as illustrated above.

(b) Clear Spaces. Working space required by this section shall not be used for storage. When normally enclosed live parts are exposed for inspection or servicing, the working space, if in a passageway or general open space, shall be suitably guarded.

(c) Access and Entrance to Working Space. At least one entrance of sufficient area shall be provided to give access to the working space about electric equipment. For switchboards and control panels rated 1200 amperes or more and over 6 feet (1.83 m) wide, there shall be one entrance not less than 24 inches (610 mm) wide and 6½ feet (1.98 m) high at each end.

Section 110-16(c) has been revised for the 1984 *NEC*. For switchboards and control panels over 6 ft wide and rated 1200 amperes or more, the requirement has been revised to be more specific. See Figures 110-11, 110-12, and 110-13.

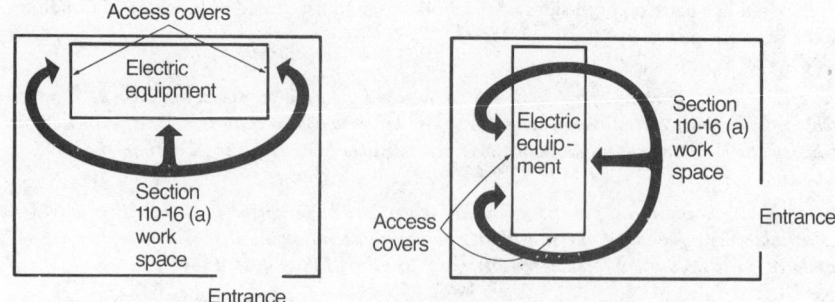

Figure 110-11. Section 110-16(c), Basic Rule, first sentence. At least one entrance is required to provide access to the working space around electric equipment. The installation shown in the sketch on the right would not be acceptable if the electric equipment was a switchboard or panelboard over 6 ft wide and rated 1200 A or more.

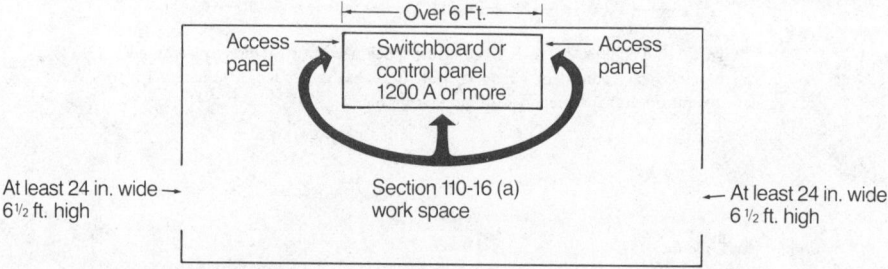

Figure 110-12. Section 110-16(c), Basic Rule, second sentence. For switchboards and control panels rated 1200 A or more, and over 6 ft wide, there shall be one entrance not less than 24 in. wide and 6½ ft high at each end.

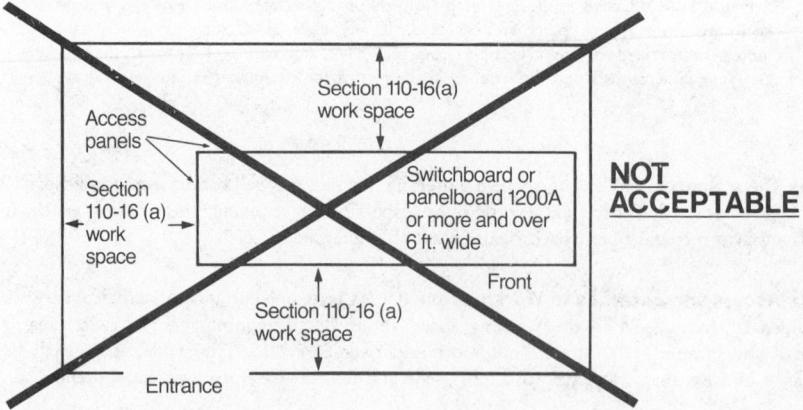

Figure 110-13. Unacceptable arrangement of large switchboard or panelboard. A person could be trapped behind arcing electric equipment.

Exception No. 1: Where the equipment location permits a continuous and unobstructed way of exit travel.

See Figure 110-14.

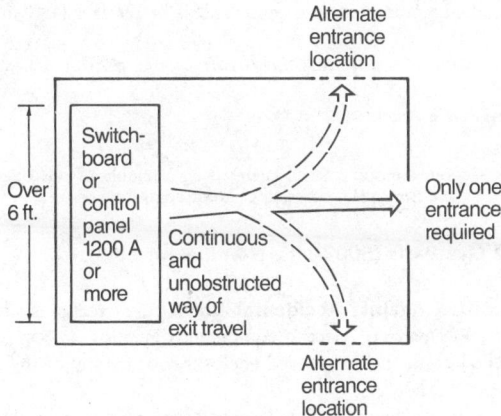

Figure 110-14. Section 110-16(c), Exception No. 1. Where the equipment location permits a continuous and unobstructed way of exit travel.

Exception No. 2: Where the work space required by Section 110-16(a) is doubled.

See Figure 110-15.

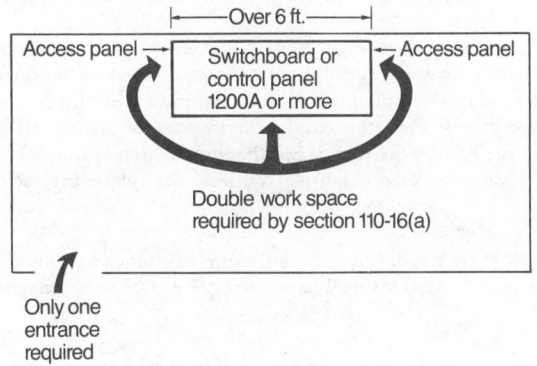

Figure 110-15. Section 110-16(c), Exception No. 2. Where the work space required by Section 110-16(a) is doubled.

(d) Front Working Space. In all cases where there are live parts normally exposed on the front of switchboards or motor control centers, the working space in front of such equipment shall not be less than 3 feet (914 mm).

(e) Illumination. Illumination shall be provided for all working spaces about service equipment, switchboards, panelboards, or motor control centers installed indoors.

Exception: Service equipment or panelboards, in dwelling units, that do not exceed 200 amperes.

(f) Headroom. The minimum headroom of working spaces about service equipment, switchboards, panelboards, or motor control centers shall be 6¼ feet (1.91 m).

Exception: Service equipment or panelboards, in dwelling units, that do not exceed 200 amperes.

(FPN): For higher voltages, see Article 710.

(FPN): As used in this section, a motor control center is an assembly of one or more enclosed sections having a common power bus and principally containing motor control units.

110-17. Guarding of Live Parts (600 Volts, Nominal, or Less).

(a) Live Parts Guarded Against Accidental Contact. Except as elsewhere required or permitted by this Code, live parts of electric equipment operating at 50 volts or more shall be guarded against accidental contact by approved enclosures or by any of the following:

(1) By location in a room, vault, or similar enclosure that is accessible only to qualified persons.

(2) By suitable permanent, substantial partitions or screens so arranged that only qualified persons will have access to the space within reach of the live parts. Any openings in such partitions or screens shall be so sized and located that persons are not likely to come into accidental contact with the live parts or to bring conducting objects into contact with them.

(3) By location on a suitable balcony, gallery, or platform so elevated and arranged as to exclude unqualified persons.

(4) By elevation of 8 feet (2.44 m) or more above the floor or other working surface.

For example, see the requirements of Sections 610-13, Exception No. 2 and 610-21(a). Although contact conductors obviously need to be bare in order for contact shoes on the moving member to make contact with the conductor, it is also possible to place guards near the conductor to prevent accidental contact with it by persons and yet have slots or spaces through which the moving contacts can operate. Note that the *Code* also recognizes the guarding of live parts by elevation.

(b) Prevent Physical Damage. In locations where electric equipment would be exposed to physical damage, enclosures or guards shall be so arranged and of such strength as to prevent such damage.

(c) Warning Signs. Entrances to rooms and other guarded locations containing exposed live parts shall be marked with conspicuous warning signs forbidding unqualified persons to enter.

(FPN): For motors, see Sections 430-132 and 430-133. For over 600 volts, see Section 110-34.

Live parts of electric equipment should be covered, shielded, enclosed, or otherwise protected by covers, barriers, mats, or platforms to remove the likelihood of contact by persons or objects. See definitions for "Dead Front," "Guarded," and "Isolated" in Article 100.

110-18. Arcing Parts. Parts of electric equipment which in ordinary operation produce arcs, sparks, flames, or molten metal shall be enclosed or separated and isolated from all combustible material.

(FPN): For hazardous (classified) locations, see Articles 500 through 517. For motors, see Section 430-14.

An example of electric equipment that in "ordinary" operation produces sparks is an open motor having commutators or collector rings. Adequate separation from combustible material is necessary where open motors are used.

110-19. Light and Power from Railway Conductors. Circuits for lighting and power shall not be connected to any system containing trolley wires with a ground return.

Exception: Car houses, power houses, or passenger and freight stations operated in connection with electric railways.

110-21. Marking. The manufacturer's name, trademark, or other descriptive marking by which the organization responsible for the product may be identified shall be placed on all electric equipment. Other markings shall be provided giving voltage, current, wattage, or other ratings as are specified elsewhere in this Code. The marking shall be of sufficient durability to withstand the environment involved.

The *Code* requires that the rating of equipment be marked on the equipment and that such markings be located so as to be visible or easily accessible, during or after installation.

110-22. Identification of Disconnecting Means. Each disconnecting means required by this Code for motors and appliances, and each service, feeder, or branch circuit at the point where it originates shall be legibly marked to indicate its purpose unless located and arranged so the purpose is evident. The marking shall be of sufficient durability to withstand the environment involved.

Note that proper identification is to be specific. For example, it is not merely to indicate "motor," but rather "motor, water pump"; not merely "lights," but rather "lights, front lobby."

B. Over 600 Volts, Nominal

110-30. General. Conductors and equipment used on circuits over 600 volts, nominal, shall comply with all applicable provisions of the preceding sections of this article and with the following sections, which supplement or modify the preceding sections. In no case shall the provisions of this part apply to equipment on the supply side of the service conductors.

See "Over 600 Volts" in Index for various articles and sections that include requirements for installations over 600 volts.

110-31. Enclosure for Electrical Installations. Electrical installations in a vault, room, or closet or in an area surrounded by a wall, screen, or fence, access to which is controlled by lock and key or other approved means, shall be considered to be accessible to qualified persons only. The type of enclosure used in a given case shall be designed and constructed according to the nature and degree of the hazard(s) associated with the installation.

A wall, screen, or fence less than 8 feet (2.44 m) in height shall not be considered as preventing access unless it has other features that provide a degree of isolation equivalent to an 8-foot (2.44-m) fence.

ARTICLE 110—REQUIREMENTS FOR ELECTRICAL INSTALLATIONS

(FPN): Article 450 covers minimum construction requirements for transformer vaults.

(FPN): Isolation by elevation is covered in paragraph (b) of this section and in Section 110-34.

(a) Indoor Installations.

(1) In Places Accessible to Unqualified Persons. Indoor electrical installations that are open to unqualified persons shall be made with metal-enclosed equipment or shall be enclosed in a vault or in an area access to which is controlled by a lock. Metal-enclosed switchgear, unit substations, transformers, pull boxes, connection boxes, and other similar associated equipment shall be marked with appropriate caution signs. Openings in ventilated dry-type transformers or similar openings in other equipment shall be designed so that foreign objects inserted through these openings will be deflected from energized parts.

(2) In Places Accessible to Qualified Persons Only. Indoor electrical installations considered accessible to qualified persons only in accordance with this section shall comply with Sections 110-34, 710-32, and 710-33.

(b) Outdoor Installations.

(1) In Places Accessible to Unqualified Persons. Outdoor electrical installations that are open to unqualified persons shall comply with Article 225.

(FPN): For clearances of conductors for system voltages over 600 volts, nominal, see National Electrical Safety Code (ANSI C2-1981).

(2) In Places Accessible to Qualified Persons Only. Outdoor electrical installations having exposed live parts shall be accessible to qualified persons only in accordance with the first paragraph of this section and shall comply with Sections 110-34, 710-32, and 710-33.

(c) Metal-Enclosed Equipment Accessible to Unqualified Persons. Ventilating or similar openings in equipment shall be so designed that foreign objects inserted through these openings will be deflected from energized parts. When exposed to physical damage from vehicular traffic suitable guards shall be provided. Metal-enclosed equipment located outdoors accessible to the general public shall be designed so that exposed nuts or bolts cannot be readily removed, permitting access to live parts. Where metal-enclosed equipment is accessible to the general public and the bottom of the enclosure is less than 8 feet (2.44 m) above the floor or grade level, the enclosure door or hinged cover shall be kept locked.

110-32. Work Space about Equipment. Sufficient space shall be provided and maintained about electric equipment to permit ready and safe operation and maintenance of such equipment. Where energized parts are exposed, the minimum clear work space shall not be less than 6½ feet (1.98 m) high (measured vertically from the floor or platform), or less than 3 feet (914 mm) wide (measured parallel to the equipment). The depth shall be as required in Section 110-34(a). In all cases, the work space shall be adequate to permit at least a 90-degree opening of doors or hinged panels.

110-33. Entrance and Access to Work Space.

(a) Entrance. At least one entrance not less than 24 inches (610 mm) wide and 6½ feet (1.98 m) high shall be provided to give access to the working space about electric equipment. On switchboard and control panels exceeding 6 feet (1.83 m) in width, there shall be one entrance at each end of such board.

Section 110-33(a) has been revised for the 1984 *NEC* to coordinate with changes in Section 110-16(c). See commentary following Section 110-16(c). However, because of the high voltages involved, Section 110-33(a) includes minimum work space entrance dimensions, even for boards 6 ft or less in width.

Exception No. 1: Where the equipment location permits a continuous and unobstructed way of exit travel.

See commentary following Section 110-16(c), Exception No. 1.

Exception No. 2: Where the work space required in Section 110-34(a) is doubled.

See commentary following Section 110-16(c), Exception No. 2.

Where bare energized parts at any voltage or insulated energized parts above 600 volts, nominal, are located adjacent to such entrance, they shall be suitably guarded.

(b) Access. Permanent ladders or stairways shall be provided to give safe access to the working space around electric equipment installed on platforms, balconies, mezzanine floors, or in attic or roof rooms or spaces.

110-34. Work Space and Guarding.

(a) Working Space. The minimum clear working space in front of electric equipment such as switchboards, control panels, switches, circuit breakers, motor controllers, relays, and similar equipment shall not be less than specified in Table 110-34(a) unless otherwise specified in this Code. Distances shall be measured from the live parts if such are exposed, or from the enclosure front or opening if such are enclosed.

Table 110-34(a)
Minimum Depth of Clear Working Space in Front of Electric Equipment

Nominal	Conditions		
Voltage to Ground	1	2	3
	(Feet)	(Feet)	(Feet)
601-2500	3	4	5
2501-9000	4	5	6
9001-25,000	5	6	9
25,001-75 kV	6	8	10
Above 75 kV	8	10	12

For SI units: one foot = 0.3048 meter.

Where the "Conditions" are as follows:

1. Exposed live parts on one side and no live or grounded parts on the other side of the working space or exposed live parts on both sides effectively guarded by suitable wood or other insulating materials. Insulated wire or insulated busbars operating at not over 300 volts shall not be considered live parts.

2. Exposed live parts on one side and grounded parts on the other side. Concrete, brick, or tile walls will be considered as grounded surfaces.

3. Exposed live parts on both sides of the work space (not guarded as provided in Condition 1) with the operator between.

Exception: Working space is not required in back of equipment such as dead-front switchboards or control assemblies where there are no renewable or adjustable parts (such as fuses or switches) on the back and where all connections are accessible from locations other than the back. Where rear access is required to work on de-energized parts on the back of enclosed equipment, a minimum working space of 30 inches (762 mm) horizontally shall be provided.

(b) Separation from Low-Potential Equipment. Where switches, cutouts, or other equipment operating at 600 volts, nominal, or less, are installed in a room or enclosure where there are exposed live parts or exposed wiring operating at over 600 volts, nominal, the high-potential equipment shall be effectively separated from the space occupied by the low-potential equipment by a suitable partition, fence, or screen.

Exception: Switches or other equipment operating at 600 volts, nominal, or less, and serving only equipment within the high-voltage vault, room, or enclosure may be installed in the high-voltage enclosure, room, or vault if accessible to qualified persons only.

(c) Locked Rooms or Enclosures. The entrances to all buildings, rooms, or enclosures containing exposed live parts or exposed conductors operating at over 600 volts, nominal, shall be kept locked.

Exception: Where such entrances are under the observation of a qualified person at all times.

Equipment used on circuits over 600 volts, nominal, containing exposed live parts or exposed conductors is to be located in a locked room or enclosure. The provisions for locking are not required where the location is under observation at all times such as some engine rooms.

Where the voltage exceeds 600 volts, nominal, permanent and conspicuous warning signs shall be provided, reading substantially as follows: "Warning—High Voltage—Keep Out."

(d) Illumination. Adequate illumination shall be provided for all working spaces about electrical equipment. The lighting outlets shall be so arranged that persons changing lamps or making repairs on the lighting system will not be endangered by live parts or other equipment.

The points of control shall be so located that persons are not likely to come in contact with any live part or moving part of the equipment while turning on the lights.

(e) Elevation of Unguarded Live Parts. Unguarded live parts above working space shall be maintained at elevations not less than required by Table 110-34(e).

Table 110-34(e)
Elevation of Unguarded Live Parts above Working Space

Nominal Voltage Between Phases	Elevation
601-7500	8'6"
7501-35000	9'
Over 35kV	9' +0.37" per kV above 35

For SI units: one inch = 25.4 millimeters; one foot = 0.3048 meter.

2 WIRING DESIGN AND PROTECTION

ARTICLE 200 — USE AND IDENTIFICATION
OF GROUNDED CONDUCTORS

Contents

200-1. Scope. This article provides requirements for: (1) identification of terminals; (2) grounded conductors in premises wiring systems; and (3) identification of grounded conductors.

(FPN): See Article 100 for definitions of "Grounded Conductor" and "Grounding Conductor."

200-2. General. All premises wiring systems shall have a grounded conductor that is identified in accordance with Section 200-6.

Exception: Circuits and systems exempted or prohibited by Sections 210-10, 215-7, 250-3, 250-5, 250-7, 503-13, 517-104, and 690-41 Exception.

Isolated circuits are required in hazardous areas of hospital anesthetizing locations. The ungrounded conductors of these circuits are colored orange and brown (for 3-phase systems, the third conductor is yellow) and are provided with a continually operating "Line Isolation Monitor." See Section 517-104 and NFPA 56A, Standard for the Use of Inhalation Anesthetics.

The grounded conductor, when insulated, shall have insulation: (1) which is suitable, other than color, for any ungrounded conductor of the same circuit on circuits of less than 1000 volts, or (2) rated not less than 600 volts for solidly grounded neutral systems of 1 kV and over as described in Section 250-152(a).

This paragraph is intended to correlate Section 200-2, which requires full system voltage rating for neutral conductor insulation, and Section 250-152, which only requires 600-volt rating on the insulation of high-voltage solidly grounded neutral conductors.

200-3. Connection to Grounded System. Premises wiring shall not be electrically connected to a supply system unless the latter contains, for any grounded conductor of the interior system, a corresponding conductor which is grounded.

For the purpose of this section, "electrically connected" shall mean connection capable of carrying current as distinguished from connection through electromagnetic induction.

Grounded conductors of premises wiring are to be connected to the supply system grounded conductor to assure a common, continuous grounded system.

200-6. Means of Identifying Grounded Conductors.

(a) Sizes No. 6 or Smaller. An insulated grounded conductor of No. 6 or smaller shall be identified by a continuous white or natural gray outer finish along its entire length.

Exception No. 1: The grounded conductor of a mineral-insulated, metal-sheathed cable shall be identified at the time of installation by distinctive marking at its terminations.

See Figure 330-1.

Exception No. 2: Where the conditions of maintenance and supervision assure that only qualified persons will service the installation, grounded conductors in multiconductor cables shall be permitted to be permanently identified at their terminations at the time of installation by a distinctive white marking or other equally effective means.

See Figure 200-1.

(b) Sizes Larger than No. 6. An insulated grounded conductor larger than No. 6 shall be identified either by a continuous white or natural gray outer finish along its entire length or at the time of installation by a distinctive white marking at its terminations.

See Figure 200-2.

Exception: Where the conditions of maintenance and supervision assure that only qualified persons will service the installation, grounded conductors in multiconductor cables shall be permitted to be permanently identified at their terminations at the time of installation by a distinctive white marking or other equally effective means.

(c) Flexible Cords. An insulated conductor intended for use as a grounded conductor, where contained within a flexible cord, shall be identified by a white or natural gray outer finish or by methods permitted by Section 400-22.

Article 200 contains the grounded circuit identification requirements. The grounded circuit conductor is referred to throughout the *Code* as the grounded conductor. It is often, but not always (as in corner-grounded delta systems), also the neutral conductor. The *NEC* formerly made recommendations for identification of ungrounded circuit conductors for branch circuits. Section 210-5, however, no longer requires or recommends an identification scheme for ungrounded branch-circuit conductors.

Section 215-8, covering 3-phase, 4-wire delta-connected systems with the midpoint of one phase grounded, requires that the conductor with the higher phase-to-ground voltage be identified by the color orange, by tagging, or by some other effective means at every point of connection where the neutral is also present. The high leg of 120/240 4-wire, 3-phase delta systems is 208 V to ground (120 V x 1.73).

Both Sections 200-6(a) and (b) contain exceptions introducing a concept for identifying grounded conductors of multiconductor cables. These exceptions allow the identification of conductors at the time of installation by a distinctive white marking or other equally effective means. A variety of other schemes, equally effective, include numbering, lettering, or tagging. These exceptions are intended to apply in locations where a regulated system of maintenance and supervision assures that only qualified persons will service the installation.

For the identification of branch-circuit conductors, see Section 210-5. For the identification of the high leg (delta-system) conductor, see Section 215-8. See Section 384-3(f) for the phase arrangement of 3-phase buses on switchboards and panelboards.

200-7. Use of White or Natural Gray Color. A continuous white or natural gray covering on a conductor or a termination marking of white or natural gray color shall be used only for the grounded conductor.

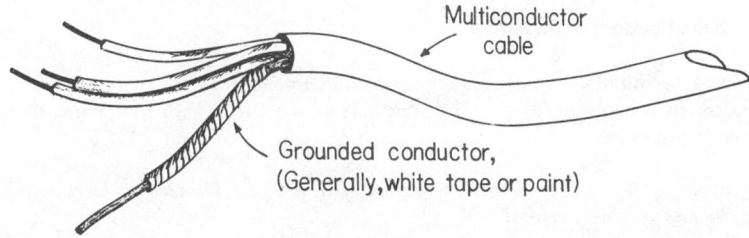

Figure 200-1. The grounded conductor of multiconductor cable is identified at the time of installation by qualified persons, generally in commercial or industrial locations, where supervision and maintenance are assured. This method is permitted for all sizes of conductors of multiconductor cables.

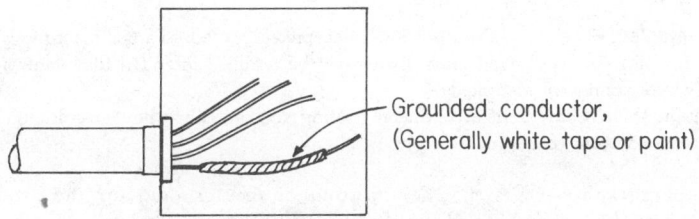

Figure 200-2. The "larger than No. 6" in Section 200-6(b) applies to all conductor materials.

Exception No. 1: An insulated conductor with a white or natural gray finish shall be permitted as an ungrounded conductor where permanently reidentified to indicate its use, by painting or other effective means at its termination, and at each outlet where the conductor is visible and accessible.

Exception No. 2: A cable containing an insulated conductor with a white or natural gray outer finish shall be permitted for single-pole, 3-way, or 4-way switch loops where the white or natural gray conductor is used for the supply to the switch, but not as a return conductor from the switch to the switched outlet. In these applications, reidentification of the white or natural gray conductor shall not be required.

Exception No. 3: A flexible cord for connecting an appliance having one conductor identified with a white or natural gray outer finish, or by any other means permitted by Section 400-22, shall be permitted whether or not the outlet to which it is connected is supplied by a circuit having a grounded conductor.

Exception No. 4: A white or natural gray conductor of circuits of less than 50 volts shall be required to be grounded only as required by Section 250-5(a).

200-9. Means of Identification of Terminals. The identification of terminals to which a grounded conductor is to be connected shall be substantially white in color. The identification of other terminals shall be of a readily distinguishable different color.

Exception: Where the conditions of maintenance and supervision assure that only qualified persons will service the installations, terminals for grounded conductors shall be permitted to be permanently identified at the time of installation by a distinctive white marking or other equally effective means.

See the comments following Section 200-6.

200-10. Identification of Terminals.

(a) Device Terminals. All devices provided with terminals for the attachment of conductors and intended for connection to more than one side of the circuit shall have terminals properly marked for identification.

Exception No. 1: Where the electrical connection of a terminal intended to be connected to the grounded conductor is clearly evident.

Exception No. 2: Single-pole devices to which only one side of the line is connected.

Exception No. 3: The terminals of lighting and appliance branch-circuit panelboards.

Exception No. 4: Devices having a normal current rating of over 30 amperes other than polarized attachment plugs and polarized receptacles for attachment plugs as required in (b) below.

(b) Receptacles, Plugs, and Connectors. Receptacles, polarized attachment plugs and cord connectors for plugs and polarized plugs shall have the terminal intended for connection to the grounded (white) conductor identified.
Identification shall be by a metal or metal coating substantially white in color or the word "white" located adjacent to the identified terminal.

> This paragraph permits the identification of the terminal for the grounded conductor to be accomplished by the use of the word "white" or otherwise identified by a distinctive white color on all devices including those with binding head screws. These permitted methods would allow plating of all screws and terminals to meet requirements of specific applications, such as corrosion-resistant devices.

If the terminal is not visible, the conductor entrance hole for the connection shall be colored white or marked with the word "white."
The terminal for the connection of the equipment grounding conductor shall be identified by: (1) a green-colored, not readily removable terminal screw with a hexagonal head; (2) a green-colored, hexagonal, not readily removable terminal nut; or (3) a green-colored pressure wire connector. If the terminal for the grounding conductor is not visible, the conductor entrance hole shall be marked with the word "green" or otherwise identified by a distinctive green color.

Exception: Terminal identification shall not be required for 2-wire nonpolarized attachment plugs.

This exception coordinates with Section 410-42(a) and makes it clear that two-wire "polarized" attachment plugs are to have the grounded terminal identified.

(c) Screw Shells. For devices with screw shells, the terminal for the grounded conductor shall be the one connected to the screw shell.

(d) Screw-Shell Devices with Leads. For screw-shell devices with attached leads, the conductor attached to the screw shell shall have a white or natural gray finish. The outer finish of the other conductor shall be of a solid color that will not be confused with the white or natural gray finish used to identify the grounded conductor.

(e) Appliances. Appliances that have a single-pole switch or a single-pole overcurrent device in the line or any line-connected screw-shell lampholders, and that are to be connected (1) by permanent wiring methods or (2) by field-installed attachment plugs and cords with three or more wires (including the equipment grounding conductor) shall have means to identify the terminal for the grounded circuit conductor (if any).

The "means" for identifying the terminal for the grounded conductor may be by a metal, or metal coating, substantially white in color or by the word "white" located adjacent to the terminal to be so identified.

200-11. Polarity of Connections. No grounded conductor shall be attached to any terminal or lead so as to reverse designated polarity.

ARTICLE 210 — BRANCH CIRCUITS

Contents

ARTICLE 210—BRANCH CIRCUITS

A. General Provisions

210-1. Scope. The provisions of this article apply to branch circuits supplying lighting or appliance loads or combinations of both. Where motors or motor-operated appliances are connected to any branch circuit that also supplies lighting or other appliance loads, the provisions of both this article and Article 430 shall apply. Article 430 applies where a branch circuit supplies motor loads only.

Exception: See Section 668-3(c), Exceptions No. 1 and No. 4 for electrolytic cells.

Section 668-3(c), Exception Nos. 1 and 4 indicate that electrolytic cell line conductors, cells, cell line attachments, and the wiring of auxiliary equipment and devices within the cell line working zone are not required to comply with the provisions of Article 210.

210-2. Other Articles for Specific-Purpose Branch Circuits. Branch circuits shall comply with this article and also with the applicable provisions of other articles of this Code. The provisions for branch circuits supplying equipment in the following list amend or supplement the provisions in this article and shall apply to branch circuits referred to therein:

	Article	Section
Air-Conditioning and Refrigerating Equipment		440-5
		440-31
		440-32
Busways		364-9
Class 1, Class 2, and Class 3 Remote Control, Signaling, and Power-Limited Circuits	725	
Cranes and Hoists		610-42
Data Processing Systems		645-2
Electrical Floor Assemblies	366	
Electric Signs and Outline Lighting		600-6
Electric Welders	630	
Elevators, Dumbwaiters, Escalators, and Moving Walks		620-61
Fire Protective Signaling Systems	760	
Fixed Electric Space Heating Equipment		424-3
Fixed Outdoor Electric De-icing and Snow-Melting Equipment		426-4
Infrared Lamp Industrial Heating Equipment		422-15
		424-3

210-3. Classifications. Branch circuits recognized by this article shall be classified in accordance with the maximum permitted ampere rating or setting of the overcurrent device. The classification for other than individual branch circuits shall be: 15, 20, 30, 40, and 50 amperes. Where conductors of higher ampacity are used for any reason, the ampere rating or setting of the specified overcurrent device shall determine the circuit classification.

Conductors of higher ampacity may be necessary to compensate for voltage drop. For example, a branch circuit of No. 10 AWG Type THW copper conductors with a 30-ampere ampacity protected by a 20-ampere overcurrent device would be classified as a 20-ampere branch circuit.

Exception: Multioutlet branch circuits greater than 50 amperes shall be permitted on industrial premises where maintenance and supervision indicate that qualified persons will service equipment.

This exception is new in the 1984 *NEC*. It is common in industrial establishments to provide several single receptacles of 50-ampere or higher rating on a single branch circuit to allow quick relocation of equipment for production and/or maintenance use, such as electric welders. Generally, only one piece of equipment is operated at a time. The type of receptacles used are generally of the non-NEMA type configuration, known as a pin-and-sleeve receptacle, although the *Code* does not so limit the design. These may or may not be horsepower rated.

210-4. Multiwire Branch Circuits. Branch circuits recognized by this article shall be permitted as multiwire circuits. A multiwire branch circuit shall be permitted to be considered as multiple circuits. All conductors shall originate from the same panelboard.

This section was revised in the 1984 *NEC* to make it clear that it is acceptable to use a multiwire branch circuit as the two small appliance branch circuits required in Section 220-3(b)(1).

In dwelling units a multiwire branch circuit supplying more than one device on the same yoke shall be provided with a means to disconnect simultaneously all ungrounded conductors at the panelboard where the branch circuit originated.

A "Device" is defined in Article 100 as a unit of an electrical system which is intended to carry but not utilize electric energy. The term device, therefore, includes receptacles, switches, and lampholders, — the three types of "devices" normally used on dwelling unit switch and receptacle yokes.

Many 125-volt, 15- and 20-ampere duplex receptacles have a break-off feature that permits each of the two receptacles to be supplied from a different polarity and the single grounded conductor of a three-wire (multiwire) branch circuit. This is commonly called a "split-wired" receptacle, i.e., one-half of the duplex receptacle on one circuit and the other half on another circuit. The simultaneous opening of both "hot" conductors at the panelboard will effectively protect personnel from inadvertent contact with an energized conductor or device terminal. The simultaneous disconnection can be secured by a 2-pole circuit breaker or by two single-pole circuit breakers with a handle tie. Where fuses are used, a 2-pole disconnect switch is required. See Figure 210-1.

Where the duplex receptacle or other devices on the same yoke are supplied from a single (2-wire) branch circuit and all devices are connected to the same "hot" conductor, a switched lower half and unswitched upper half duplex receptacle, for example, the requirement for simultaneous disconnection does not apply.

Some "amateur electricians" have attempted to replace "split-wired" receptacles and were not aware that the break-off link must first be removed. Failure to remove this link results in a short circuit when the multiwire branch circuit is energized. It is necessary to break off the link connection between the ungrounded conductor terminals, leaving the link on the grounded side in place. The link is removed by prying and bending with a thin screwdriver and/or long-nose pliers. See Figure 210-2.

Break–off link removed.

Double–pole circuit breaker or two single–pole circuit breakers with a "handle-tie" or a two–pole switch.

Figure 210-1. A multiwire branch circuit supplying a split-wired receptacle, i.e., a duplex receptacle with the break-off link removed.

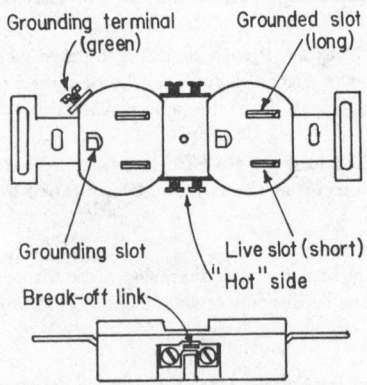

Grounding terminal (green)

Grounded slot (long)

Grounding slot

Live slot (short) "Hot" side

Break-off link

Figure 210-2. A grounding-type of duplex receptacle is illustrated with the break-off link in place.

Multiwire branch circuits shall supply only line to neutral load.

Exception No. 1: A multiwire branch circuit that supplies only one utilization equipment.

Exception No. 2: Where all ungrounded conductors of the multiwire branch circuit are opened simultaneously by the branch-circuit overcurrent device.

Article 100 defines "Branch Circuit, Multiwire" as two or more ungrounded conductors having a potential difference between them, and a grounded conductor having an equal potential difference between it and each ungrounded conductor.

The circuit generally used as a multiwire branch circuit consists of two ungrounded conductors and one grounded conductor supplied from a single-phase, 3-wire system. Multiwire branch circuits have many advantages, such as three wires doing the work of four (in place of two 2-wire circuits), less conduit fill, easier balancing and phasing of a system, and less voltage drop (see comments following Section 215-2).

Other multiwire branch circuits are 3-phase, 4-wire; 2-phase, 3-wire; and 2-phase, 5-wire. It is always advisable to properly balance all multiwire branch circuits. See Section 220-3(d). In a 3-phase, 4-wire circuit the neutral could be called upon to carry a current equal to that carried by each of the three phase conductors and should, therefore, be sized the same. The neutral for a 2-phase, 3-wire or 2-phase, 5-wire circuit must be sized to carry 140 percent of the ampere rating of the circuit. See Section 220-22.

Where loads are connected "line-to-line" (utilization equipment connected between two or three phases), it requires 2-pole or 3-pole circuit breakers or switches to disconnect all ungrounded conductors simultaneously. There have been cases of multiwire branch circuits supplying a "line-to-line" load (240 V) and a "line-to-neutral" load (120 V) causing a hazard where two single-pole circuit breakers are used and the opening of one could cause the two loads (240 V and 120 V) to create a 120-V series circuit. In testing 240-V equipment, it is quite possible not to realize that the circuit is still energized with 120 V if one overcurrent device is open. See Sections 210-10 and 240-20(b).

210-5. Color Code for Branch Circuits.

(a) Grounded Conductor. The grounded conductor of a branch circuit shall be identified by a continuous white or natural gray color. Where conductors of different systems are installed in the same raceway, box, auxiliary gutter, or other types of enclosures, one system neutral, if required, shall have an outer covering of white or natural gray. Each other system neutral, if required, shall have an outer covering of white with an identifiable colored stripe (not green) running along the insulation or other and different means of identification.

See Figure 210-3.

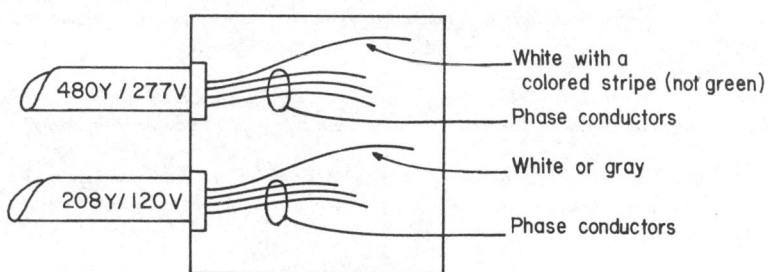

480Y / 277V — White with a colored stripe (not green) — Phase conductors

208Y / 120V — White or gray — Phase conductors

Figure 210-3. Illustrated are conductors of different systems in the same enclosure. Phase conductors may be any color other than white, gray, or green.

Exception No. 1: The grounded conductors of mineral-insulated, metal-sheathed cable shall be identified by distinctive marking at the terminals during the process of installation.

See Figure 330-1.

Exception No. 2: As permitted in Exception No. 2 of Section 200-6(a) and the Exception to Section 200-6(b).

See Figure 200-1.

(b) Equipment Grounding Conductor. The equipment grounding conductor of a branch circuit shall be identified by a continuous green color or a continuous green color with one or more yellow stripes unless it is bare.

Exception No. 1: As permitted in Section 250-57(b), Exceptions No. 1 and 3 and Section 310-12(b), Exceptions No. 1 and 2.

Exception No. 2: The use of conductor insulation having a continuous green color or a continuous green color with one or more yellow stripes shall be permitted for internal wiring of equipment if such wiring does not serve as the lead wires for connection to branch-circuit conductors.

The color-coding requirements for grounded and grounding conductors are given in Section 210-5. Section 210-5(a) covers installations where more than one grounded conductor is carried in a raceway, box, or other enclosure. It requires one grounded conductor to have an outer covering of white or natural gray, and each other system neutral in the raceway, etc., where required, is to have an outer coloring of white with an identifiable colored stripe (not green) to provide a means of identifying the grounded conductors of each different system.

Although the *Code* no longer recommends the use of black, red, and blue for phase conductors of a circuit, it is extremely important that multiwire branch circuits and their grounded circuit conductors (neutral) be identified in the course of installation to assure that the phase conductors are connected to the proper circuit breakers so that the grounded circuit conductors (neutral) will not be overloaded.

210-6. Maximum Voltage.

(a) Voltage to Ground. Branch circuits supplying lampholders, fixtures, or standard receptacles rated 15 amperes or less shall not exceed 150 volts to ground.

Exception No. 1: The voltage shall be permitted to exceed 150 volts to ground but shall not exceed 300 volts to ground on branch circuits within the confines of industrial premises where all of the following conditions are met:

a. The conditions of maintenance and supervision indicate that only qualified persons will service the system(s).

b. The branch circuits supply only lighting fixtures that are equipped with mogul-base screw-shell lampholders or with lampholders other than the screw shell type applied within their voltage rating.

c. Incandescent lamp fixtures, if used, shall be mounted not less than 8 feet (2.44 m) above the floor. Where conditions do not permit 8 feet (2.44 m), the incandescent fixtures shall be permitted at the available height.

(FPN): See Section 110-17.

d. Integral lighting switch, if used, shall not be readily accessible.

The provisions of Exception No. 1 permit the connection of lighting fixtures within the confines of an industrial premises line-to-line on a 4-wire, 3-phase neutral grounded system of 480Y/277 volts or 240 V delta, grounded or ungrounded, with conditions that need to be met in order to apply this exception. The judgment of the local authority having jurisdiction of enforcement of the *Code* is involved in determining the conditions of maintenance and supervision. See Figure 210-4.

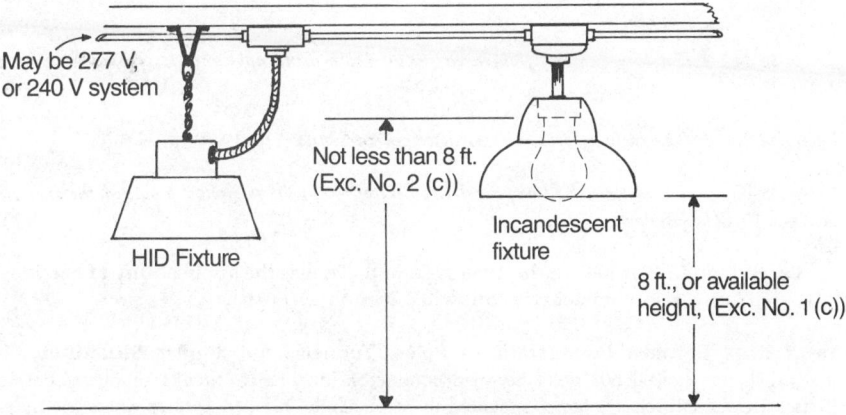

Figure 210-4. Cord-and-plug connected high-intensity discharge fixtures or incandescent fixtures (mogul-base screw-shell lampholders) at over 150 V but not to exceed 300 V to ground are permitted in industrial locations only. Permanently installed HID fixtures are permitted in other locations. See Exception No. 2 and comments for Exception No. 2.

Exception No. 2: The voltage shall be permitted to exceed 150 volts to ground but shall not exceed 300 volts to ground on branch circuits on premises other than within dwelling units where all of the following are met:

a. The branch circuits only supply the ballasts for permanently installed electric-discharge lamp fixtures.

b. Integral lighting switch, if used, shall not be readily accessible.

c. Electric-discharge lampholders of the screw shell type, if used, shall be mounted not less than 8 feet (2.44 m) from the floor.

Exception No. 2 is applicable to all occupancies other than dwelling units. Industrial occupancies are therefore included in both Exception No. 1 and Exception No. 2. Ballasts for electric-discharge lamps may be supplied by voltages not exceeding 300 V to ground. Where lampholders of the screw shell type are used, they are to be mounted not less than 8 ft from the floor, and where integral lighting switches are provided, they are not to be readily accessible. See Figure 210-5.

ARTICLE 210—BRANCH CIRCUITS

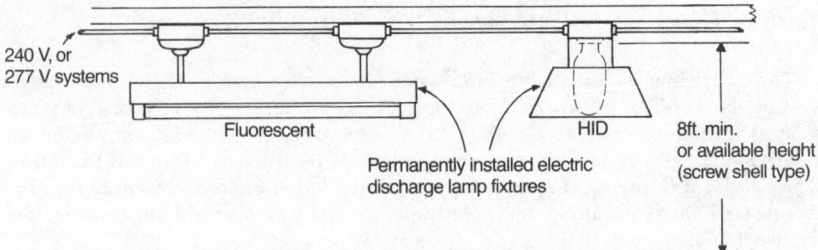

240 V, or
277 V systems

Fluorescent

HID

8ft. min.
or available height
(screw shell type)

Permanently installed electric
discharge lamp fixtures

Figure 210-5. Permanently installed electric-discharge lamp fixtures not exceeding 300 V to ground are permitted in stores, health care facilities, office buildings, schools, etc.

Exception No. 3: For lampholders of infrared industrial heating appliances as provided in Section 422-15(c).

Exception No. 4: The railway properties as described in Section 110-19.

Exception No. 5: The voltage shall be permitted to exceed 300 volts to ground provided the conditions of Section 210-6(b) are met.

Exception No. 5 is new in the 1984 *NEC* and clarifies the applicability of Section 210-6(b). See also commentary following Section 210-6(b).

(b) Voltage Between Conductors — Poles, Tunnels, and Similar Structures. The voltage shall not exceed 600 volts between conductors on branch circuits supplying only the ballasts for electric-discharge lamps mounted in permanently installed fixtures where the fixtures are mounted as follows:

(1) Not less than a height of 22 feet (6.71 m) on poles or similar structures for the illumination of outdoor areas, such as highways, roads, bridges, athletic fields, or parking lots.

(2) Not less than a height of 18 feet (5.49 m) on other structures, such as tunnels.

(FPN): See Section 410-78.

Formal Interpretation 78-2 was released in October 1979 as follows:
Statement: The 1971 *National Electrical Code* in Sections 210-6(a), Exception No. 5, and 730-7(c) established mounting heights for lighting fixtures mounted outside of buildings or on poles or other structures and used for area illumination. These sections contained the requirements for mounting heights of lighting fixtures for branch circuits of 150 volts to ground, 300 volts to ground, and 500 volts between conductors.
In the editorial rewrite of the 1971 *National Electrical Code*, the literal wording of the text seems to have changed the intent of the rules.
Question: Is the intent of Sections 210-6(b) and 225-7 of the 1978 *National Electrical Code* to require electric-discharge lighting fixtures, supplied by branch circuits of 150 volts to ground or 300 volts to ground, to be mounted no less than 22 feet on poles or similar structures?
Answer: No.

(c) Voltage Between Conductors.

(1) The voltage shall not exceed 150 volts between conductors on branch circuits supplying screw-shell lampholder(s), receptacle(s), or appliance(s) in dwelling unit(s) and guest rooms in hotels, motels, and similar occupancies.

See comments following the second paragraph of Section 210-4.

Exception No. 1: Permanently connected appliances.

Exception No. 2: Cord- and plug-connected loads of more than 1380 watts or ¼ horsepower or greater rating.

(FPN): See Article 100 for definition of Receptacle.

(2) The voltage shall not exceed 150 volts between conductors on branch circuits supplying one or more medium-base screw-shell lampholders in occupancies other than those specified in (c)(1).

In dwelling units, 240-V circuits may supply permanently connected appliances (such as water heaters and baseboard electric heaters), cord- and plug-connected appliances of more than 1380 W (such as electric ranges or clothes dryers), or lampholders for fluorescent lamps as they are not of the screw shell type. In occupancies other than dwelling units and guest rooms in hotels, motels, and similar occupancies, 240-V circuits may supply admedium and mogul-base screw-shell lampholders.

210-7. Receptacles and Cord Connectors.

(a) Grounding Type. Receptacles installed on 15- and 20-ampere branch circuits shall be of the grounding type. Grounding-type receptacles shall be installed only on circuits of the voltage class and current for which they are rated, except as provided in Tables 210-21(b)(2) and (b)(3).

A single receptacle installed on an individual branch circuit is to have an ampere rating of not less than that of the branch circuit. That is, a single receptacle on a 20-ampere circuit must be rated at 20 amperes; however, two or more 15-ampere receptacles would be permitted on a 20-ampere circuit.

Exception No. 1: Grounding-type receptacles of the type that reject nongrounding-type attachment plugs or which are of the locking type shall be permitted for specific purposes or in special locations. Receptacles required in Sections 517-101(a)(3) and 517-101(c) shall be considered as meeting the requirements of this section.

Exception No. 2: Nongrounding-type receptacles installed in accordance with Section 210-7(d), Exception.

(b) To Be Grounded. Receptacles and cord connectors having grounding contacts shall have those contacts effectively grounded.

Requiring grounding-type receptacles and grounding-type cord connectors came about because of the work of a technical subcommittee representing all the major affected interests using the *National Electrical Code.* The subcommittee concluded that the proper grounding of portable hand-held tools and appliances was necessary for safety.

Grounding is not required on all cord- and plug-connected equipment, such as toasters and other types of heating appliances having exposed or nonsheathed elements. These appliances are subject to physical contact of the heating elements by insertion of knives, forks, or other objects. It is a common occurrence for a householder to insert a fork in a toaster to remove a slice of toast, and additional hazards are thereby introduced by grounding such appliances.

Exception No. 1: Receptacles mounted on portable and vehicle-mounted generators in accordance with Section 250-6.

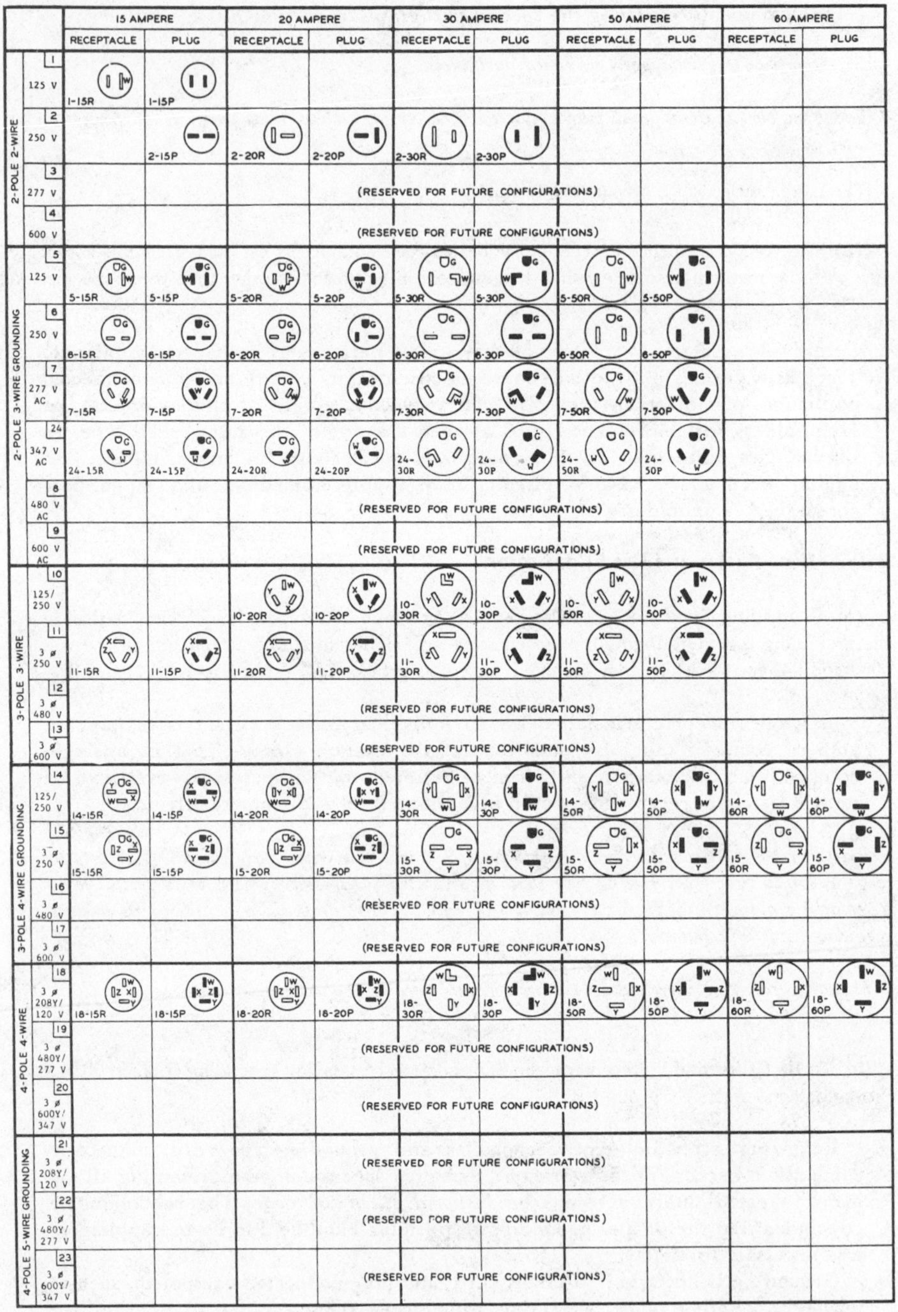

ARTICLE 210—BRANCH CIRCUITS

Figure 210-6. Configuration chart for general-purpose nonlocking plugs and receptacles; taken from ANSI C73 Standard.

Exception No. 2: Ground-fault circuit-interrupter replacement receptacles as permitted by Section 210-7(d), Exception.

See commentary following Section 210-7(d), Exception.

(c) Methods of Grounding. The grounding contacts of receptacles and cord connectors shall be grounded by connection to the equipment grounding conductor of the circuit supplying the receptacle or cord connector.

(FPN): For installation requirements for the reduction of electrical noise, see Section 250-74, Exception No. 4.

The branch circuit or branch-circuit raceway shall include or provide a grounding conductor to which the grounding contacts of the receptacle or cord connector shall be connected.

(FPN): Section 250-91(b) describes acceptable grounding means.

(FPN): For extensions of existing branch circuits, see Section 250-50.

(d) Replacements. Grounding-type receptacles shall be used as replacements for existing nongrounding types and shall be connected to a grounding conductor installed in accordance with (c) above.

Exception: Where a grounding means does not exist in the receptacle enclosure either a nongrounding or a ground-fault circuit-interrupter type of receptacle shall be used, provided the ground-fault circuit-interrupter does not supply other receptacles.

When existing nongrounding-type receptacles are replaced, it is necessary to use only grounding-type receptacles where a grounding means exists in the receptacle enclosure. Where a grounding means does not exist, there are three choices. A nongrounding-type receptacle can be used, thereby indicating to the user that a grounding means for an appliance is not available. A grounding type receptacle can be used. See Section 250-50, Exception. The third choice is a ground-fault circuit-interrupter type of receptacle. If the ground-fault circuit-interrupter type of receptacle is used it shall not supply other receptacles. It can either be the nonfeed-through type, or a feed-through type wired so that the feed-through feature is not used. For example, the down stream receptacles can be connected on the line side of the ground-fault circuit-interrupter receptacle. Permission to use a ground-fault circuit-interrupter type of receptacle for a nongrounding type of receptacle where no grounding means exists in the box is new in the 1984 *NEC*. It is based on the ability of the GFCI to provide shock hazard protection whether or not the tool, appliance, etc., connected to it is grounded. A GFCI type of receptacle therefore provides better protection than a nongrounding type of receptacle.

If the GFCI type of receptacle is used, care should be exercised in the installation to be sure the grounding lead of the receptacle is insulated or otherwise kept from contacting uninsulated live parts in the box. Since the box is not grounded in this type of installation, Section 250-74 does not require bonding the grounding lead to the box.

See also Section 250-50, Exception.

(e) Cord- and Plug-Connected Equipment. The installation of grounding-type receptacles shall not be used as a requirement that all cord- and plug-connected equipment be of the grounded type.

			15 AMPERE		20 AMPERE		30 AMPERE	
			RECEPTACLE	PLUG	RECEPTACLE	PLUG	RECEPTACLE	PLUG
2-pole 2-wire	125 V	L1	L1-15R	L1-15P				
	250 V	L2			L2-20R	L2-20P		
	277 V AC	L3	F	U	T	U	R	E
	600 V	L4	F	U	T	U	R	E
2-pole 3-wire grounding	125 V	L5	L5-15R	L5-15P	L5-20R	L5-20P	L5-30R	L5-30P
	250 V	L6	L6-15R	L6-15P	L6-20R	L6-20P	L6-30R	L6-30P
	277 V AC	L7	L7-15R	L7-15P	L7-20R	L7-20P	L7-30R	L7-30P
	480 V AC	L8			L8-20R	L8-20P	L8-30R	L8-30P
	600 V AC	L9			L9-20R	L9-20P	L9-30R	L9-30P
3-pole 3-wire	125/250 V	L10			L10-20R	L10-20P	L10-30R	L10-30P
	3 phase 250 V	L11	L11-15R	L11-15P	L11-20R	L11-20P	L11-30R	L11-30P
	3 phase 480 V	L12			L12-20R	L12-20P	L12-30R	L12-30P
	3 phase 600 V	L13			L13-20R	L13-20P	L13-30R	L13-30P
3-pole 4-wire grounding	125/250 V	L14			L14-20R	L14-20P	L14-30R	L14-30P
	3 phase 250 V	L15			L15-20R	L15-20P	L15-30R	L15-30P
	3 phase 480 V	L16			L16-20R	L16-20P	L16-30R	L16-30P
	3 phase 600 V	L17					L17-30R	L17-30P
4-pole 4-wire	3 phase 208Y/120 V	L18			L18-20R	L18-20P	L18-30R	L18-30P
	3 phase 480Y/277 V	L19			L19-20R	L19-20P	L19-30R	L19-30P
	3 phase 600Y/347 V	L20			L20-20R	L20-20P	L20-30R	L20-30P
4-pole 5-wire grounding	3 phase 208Y/120V	L21			L21-20R	L21-20P	L21-30R	L21-30P
	3 phase 480Y/277 V	L22			L22-20R	L22-20P	L22-30R	L22-30P
	3 phase 600Y/347 V	L23			L23-20R	L23-20P	L23-30R	L23-30P

Figure 210-7. Configuration chart for specific-purpose locking plugs and receptacles; taken from ANSI C73 Standard.

(FPN): See Section 250-45 for type of cord- and plug-connected equipment to be grounded.

Over the years there has been a requirement that grounding-type receptacles be used as replacements for nongrounding types. See Section 210-7(d). It is intended that grounding-type receptacles be conveniently located for use with utilization equipment that is required to be grounded. For cord- and plug-connected equipment that is required to be grounded, see Section 250-45.

Many appliances are not required to be grounded, for example, toasters, flat irons, and some heating equipment [see commentary following Section 210-7(b)] and there are many nongrounding-type receptacles in use. The use of an adapter or other approved means is necessary where grounding is required. Distinctively marked, listed, double-insulated tools and appliances are not required to be grounded.

(f) Noninterchangeable Types. Receptacles connected to circuits having different voltages, frequencies, or types of current (ac or dc) on the same premises shall be of such design that the attachment plugs used on these circuits are not interchangeable.

210-8. Ground-Fault Protection for Personnel.

(a) Dwelling Units.

(1) All 125-volt, single-phase, 15- and 20-ampere receptacles installed in bathrooms shall have ground-fault circuit-interrupter protection for personnel.

The requirement for ground-fault circuit-interrupters for receptacles in bathrooms was originally inserted in the *Code* because data supplied with the *Code* proposal for GFCIs indicated that a number of accidents occurring in bathrooms could be prevented by GFCIs. See Figure 210-8.

(2) All 125-volt, single-phase, 15- or 20-ampere receptacles installed in garages shall have ground-fault circuit-interrupter protection for personnel.

Exception No. 1 to (a)(2): Receptacles which are not readily accessible.

Exception No. 2 to (a)(2): Receptacles for appliances occupying dedicated space which are cord- and plug-connected in accordance with Section 400-7(a)(6), (a)(7), or (a)(8).

Receptacles installed under Exceptions to Section 210-8(a)(2) shall not be considered as meeting the requirements of Section 210-52(f).

The purpose of GFCIs in garages is to provide a degree of safety for persons using portable hand-held tools, gardening appliances, and snow blowers, which might be connected in the garage because it is the closest receptacle. GFCIs are not needed for appliances such as freezers or refrigerators, and these appliances should not be subjected to power loss due to tripping caused by other appliances. See Figure 210-9.

(3) All 125-volt, single-phase, 15- and 20-ampere receptacles installed outdoors where there is direct grade level access to the dwelling unit and to the receptacles shall have ground-fault circuit-interrupter protection for personnel.

See commentary following Section 210-52(d) and Section 410-57. See also Figure 210-10.

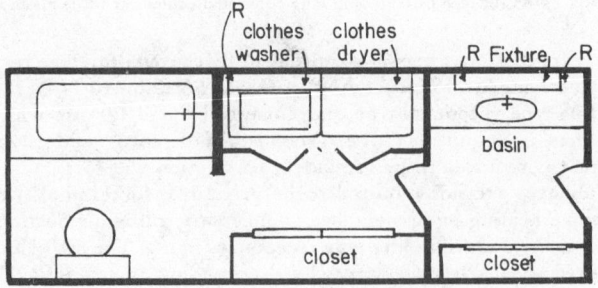

R = 125-V, 15-A or 20-A Receptacle

Figure 210-8. Section 210-8(a)(1) indicates that all receptacles in bathrooms are to have GFCI protection for personnel including any located for a clothes washer, clothes dryer (gas), or integral with the lighting fixture, and, of course, the one wall-mounted adjacent to the basin. The definition of bathroom refers to an area that includes the entire area shown above, whether a separating door (as illustrated) is present or not.

Such ground-fault circuit-interrupter protection may be provided for other circuits, locations, and occupancies, and, where used, will provide additional protection against line-to-ground shock hazard.

(FPN): See Section 215-9 for feeder protection.

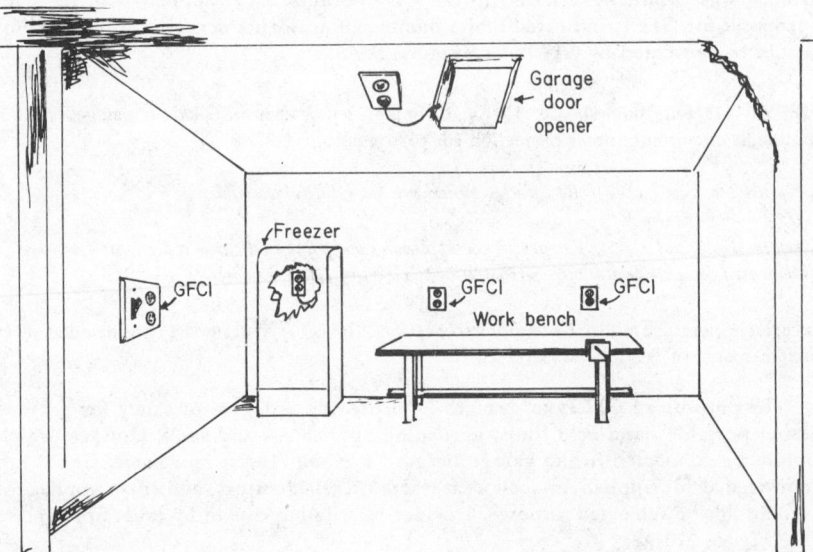

Figure 210-9. Receptacles that are not readily accessible (door opener) or are located for appliances occupying dedicated space (food freezer) are not required to have GFCI protection for personnel.

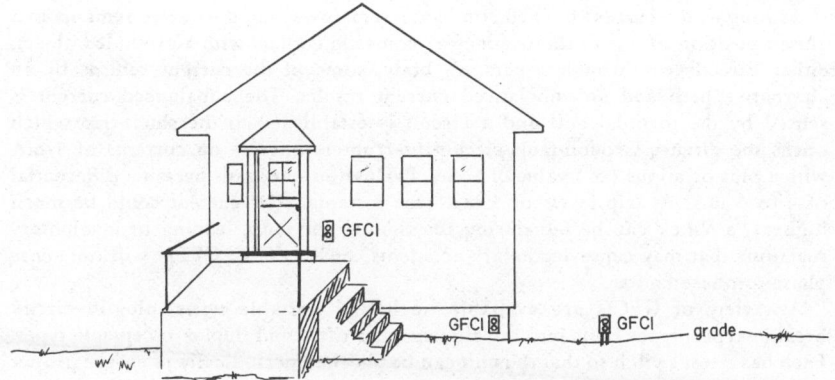

Figure 210-10. The three receptacles located outdoors at a dwelling unit are considered to be at direct grade level access and must have GFCI protection for personnel.

(b) Hotels and Motels. All 125-volt, single-phase, 15- and 20-ampere receptacles installed in bathrooms of guest rooms in hotels and motels shall have ground-fault circuit-interrupter protection for personnel.

The requirement of Section 210-8(b) is new in the 1984 *NEC*. It extends the requirement of Section 210-8(a)(1) to receptacles in all hotel and motel bathrooms. See commentary following Section 210-8(a)(1).

The requirement for ground-fault circuit-interrupter protection for receptacles on construction sites appearing as Section 210-8(b) in previous *Code* editions has been relocated as Section 305-4 in the 1984 *NEC*.

Bathroom: A bathroom is an area including a basin with one or more of the following: a toilet, a tub, or a shower.

Figure 210-11 shows a typical circuit arrangement of a GFCI for personnel protection. The line conductors are passed through a toroidal coil and connected to a shunt-trip device.

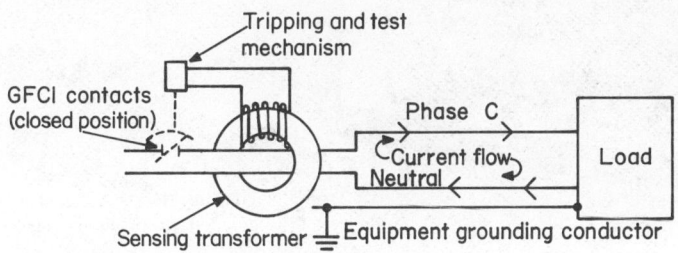

Figure 210-11. The circuitry and components for a typical ground-fault circuit-interrupter.

As long as the current in each conductor remains equal, the device remains in a closed position. If one of the conductors comes in contact with a grounded object, either directly or through a person's body, some of the current returns by an alternative path and an unbalanced current results. The unbalanced current is sensed by the toroidal coil and a circuit is established to the shunt-trip which opens the circuit. Ground-fault circuit-interrupters operate on currents of 5 mA with a plus or minus ($\pm$) value of 1 mA. Evaluation standards permit a differential of 4 to 6 mA. At trip levels of 5 mA (the instantaneous current could be much higher), a shock can be felt during the time of the fault, leading to involuntary reactions that may cause secondary accidents, such as falls. GFCIs will not sense phase-to-phase faults.

A variety of GFCIs are available, including portable types, plug-in circuit breaker types, types built into attachment plug caps, and duplex receptacle types. Each has a test switch so that the unit can be checked periodically to ensure proper operation.

Figure 210-12. A portable plug-in-type ground-fault circuit-interrupter. (*Square D Co.*)

210-9. Circuits Derived from Autotransformers. Branch circuits shall not be supplied by autotransformers.

Exception No. 1: Where the system supplied has a grounded conductor that is electrically connected to a grounded conductor of the system supplying the autotransformer.

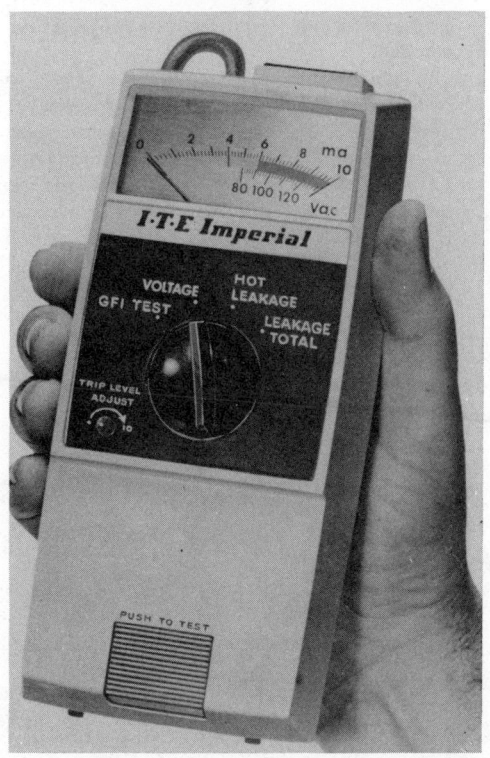

Figure 210-13. A 15-A duplex receptacle with integral ground-fault circuit-interrupter, which also protects downstream loads. (*Pass & Seymour, Inc.*)

Figure 210-14. Leakage of the neutral conductor to ground and ground-fault leakage current from the hot conductor can be measured by this GFI tester. (*Gould Inc.*)

Exception No. 2: An autotransformer used to extend or add an individual branch circuit in an existing installation for an equipment load without the connection to a similar grounded conductor when transforming from a nominal 208 volts to a nominal 240-volt supply or similarly from 240 volts to 208 volts.

(FPN): An autotransformer is a transformer in which a part of the winding is common to both primary and secondary circuits.

Figures 210-15 and 210-16 illustrate autotransformers used to derive 120-V and 240-V systems from 240-V and 208-V systems. In Figure 210-15 the grounded conductor of the primary system is electrically connected to the grounded conductor of the secondary system.

Exception No. 2 allows an autotransformer (without an electrical connection to a grounded conductor) to extend or add an individual branch circuit in an existing installation when, for example, transforming (boosting) 208 V to 240 V as shown in Figure 210-16, or transforming (bucking) 240 V to 208 V for use with appliances, for example, ranges, air conditioners, heating elements, and motors. It is also possible to increase 240 V to 277 V for lighting systems, and 440 V to 550 V for power equipment. A single unit is used to boost or buck single-phase voltage, but two or three units are used to boost or buck 3-phase voltage. An autotransformer requires little physical space, is economical, and, above all, efficient.

A buck-boost transformer is a means of raising or lowering (boosting or bucking) a supply line voltage by a small amount—usually no more than ± 20 percent. It is an insulating transformer with two primary (input) windings, both rated at 120 V or 240 V and two secondary (output) windings, both rated at either 12 V, 16 V, or 24 V. Its primary and secondary windings can be connected together so that the electrical characteristics are changed from an insulating transformer to those of a "boosting" or "bucking" autotransformer correcting voltage up to ± 20 percent.

Literature is available from manufacturers containing diagrams for connection and application of autotransformers.

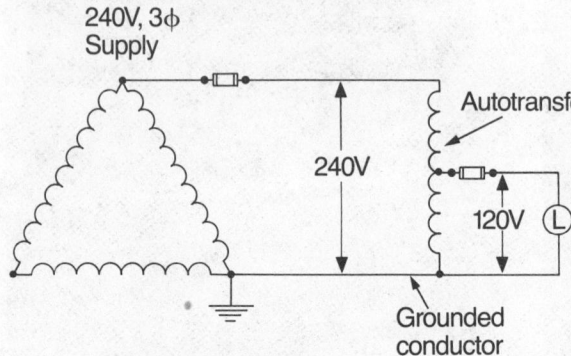

Figure 210-15. The circuitry for an autotransformer used to derive a 2-wire, 120-V system for lighting from a 240-V corner-grounded delta power system.

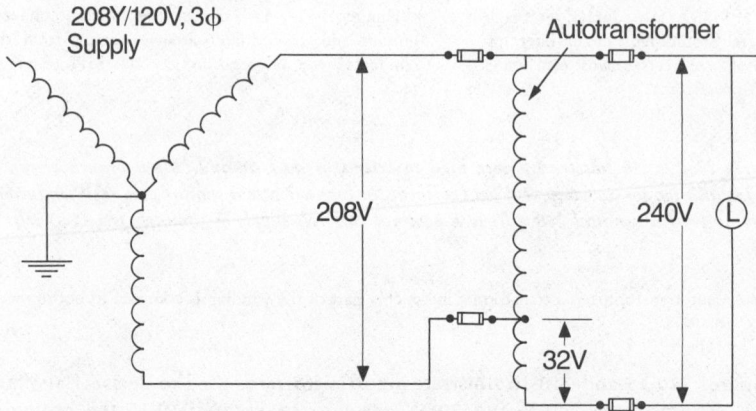

Figure 210-16. The circuitry for an autotransformer used to derive a 240-V system from a 208-V supply.

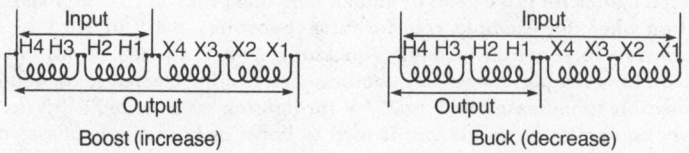

Figure 210-17. Typical hookups for buck or boost transformers connected as autotransformers to change 240 V single-phase to 208 V or vice versa.

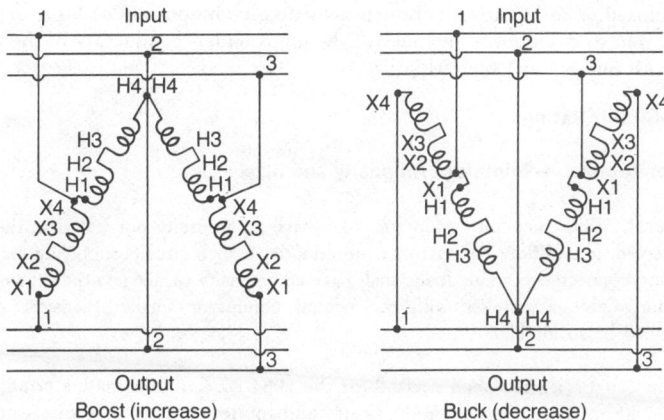

Figure 210-18. Typical hookups for buck or boost transformers connected in 3-phase open delta as autotransformers to change 240 V to 208 V or vice versa.

210-10. Ungrounded Conductors Tapped from Grounded Systems. Two-wire dc circuits and ac circuits of two or more ungrounded conductors shall be permitted to be tapped from the ungrounded conductors of circuits having a grounded neutral conductor. Switching devices in each tapped circuit shall have a pole in each ungrounded conductor. All poles of multipole switching devices shall manually switch together where such switching devices also serve as a disconnecting means as required by Section 422-21(b) for an appliance; Section 424-20 for a fixed electric space heating unit; Section 426-51 for electric de-icing and snow-melting equipment; Section 430-85 for a motor controller; and Section 430-103 for a motor.

Two-wire ungrounded branch circuits may be tapped from ac or dc circuits of two or more ungrounded conductors having a grounded neutral conductor. Figure 210-19 (on the left) illustrates ungrounded 2-wire branch circuits tapped from the ungrounded conductors of a dc or single-phase system to supply a small motor. Figure 210-20 illustrates a 3-phase, 4-wire wye system.

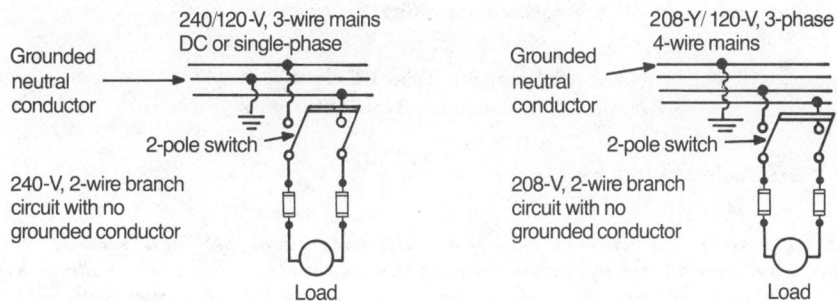

Figures 210-19 and 210-20. Branch circuits tapped from ungrounded conductors of multiwire systems.

Circuit breakers or switches used as the disconnecting means for a branch circuit are to open all poles simultaneously. This requirement involves only the manual operation of the disconnecting means; thus, where switches and fuses are used and one fuse blows, or where circuit breakers (two single-pole circuit breakers with a "handle-tie") are used and one breaker trips, one pole could remain closed. The intention is not to provide a common trip of fuses or circuit breakers, but to disconnect "manually" the ungrounded conductors of the branch circuit with one manual operation.

B. Branch-Circuit Ratings

210-19. Conductors — Minimum Ampacity and Size.

(a) General. Branch-circuit conductors shall have an ampacity not less than the maximum load to be served. In addition, conductors of multioutlet branch circuits supplying receptacles for cord- and plug-connected portable loads shall have an ampacity of not less than the rating of the branch circuit. Cable assemblies with the neutral conductor smaller than the ungrounded conductors shall be so marked.

Section 210-19(a) has been revised for the 1984 *NEC* to eliminate a conflict with Section 240-3, Exception No. 1. Only multioutlet branch circuits supplying receptacles for cord- and plug-connected portable loads are required to have an ampacity not less than the rating of the circuit (the rating of the overcurrent device per Section 210-3) because the loading of such circuits is unpredictable.

(FPN): See Tables 310-16 through 310-19 for ampacity ratings of conductors.

(FPN): See Part B of Article 430 for minimum rating of motor branch-circuit conductors.

(FPN): Conductors for branch circuits as defined in Article 100, sized to prevent a voltage drop exceeding 3 percent at the farthest outlet of power, heating, and lighting loads, or combinations of such loads and where the maximum total voltage drop on both feeders and branch circuits to the farthest outlet does not exceed 5 percent, will provide reasonable efficiency of operation. See Section 215-2 for voltage drop on feeder conductors.

(b) Household Ranges and Cooking Appliances. Branch-circuit conductors supplying household ranges, wall-mounted ovens, counter-mounted cooking units, and other household cooking appliances shall have an ampacity not less than the rating of the branch circuit and not less than the maximum load to be served. For ranges of 8¾ kW or more rating, the minimum branch-circuit rating shall be 40 amperes.

For a minimum 40-A branch-circuit rating, for example:

No. 8 AWG copper, Type TW   = 40 A.
No. 6 AWG aluminum, Type TW = 40 A.

See Table 310-16 for other applications.

Exception No. 1: The neutral conductor of a 3-wire branch circuit supplying a household electric range, a wall-mounted oven, or a counter-mounted cooking unit shall be permitted to be smaller than the ungrounded conductors where the maximum demand of a range of 8¾ kW or more rating has been computed according to Column A of Table 220-19, but shall have an ampacity of not less than 70 percent of the ampacity of the ungrounded conductors and shall not be smaller than No. 10.

Column A of Table 220-19 and Section 220-19 indicate that the maximum demand for one range (not over 12 kW rating) is 8 kVA (8 kW = 8000 watts = 8000 volt-amperes; 8000 volt-amperes divided by 240 V = 33.3 A). The allowable ampacity of a No. 8 TW copper conductor is 40 A (see Table 310-16) and may be used for the range branch circuit. According to this computation, the neutral of this 3-wire circuit can be smaller than No. 8 but not smaller than No. 10 which has an allowable ampacity of 30 A (30 A is more than 70 percent of 40 A, as per the exception). The maximum demand for a neutral of an 8 kW range circuit seldom exceeds 25 A since current is drawn from the neutral only for lights, clocks, timers, and heating elements when in the low-heating position.

Exception No. 2: Tap conductors supplying electric ranges, wall-mounted electric ovens, and counter-mounted electric cooking units from a 50-ampere branch circuit shall have an ampacity of not less than 20 and shall be sufficient for the load to be served. The taps shall be no longer than necessary for servicing the appliance.

This exception permits a 20-A tap conductor from a range, oven, or cooking unit to be connected to a 50-A branch circuit provided: the taps are no longer than necessary for servicing or to allow accessibility to the junction box; the taps to each unit are properly spliced; the junction box is adjacent to each unit; and the taps are of sufficient size for the load to be served. See Figure 210-21.

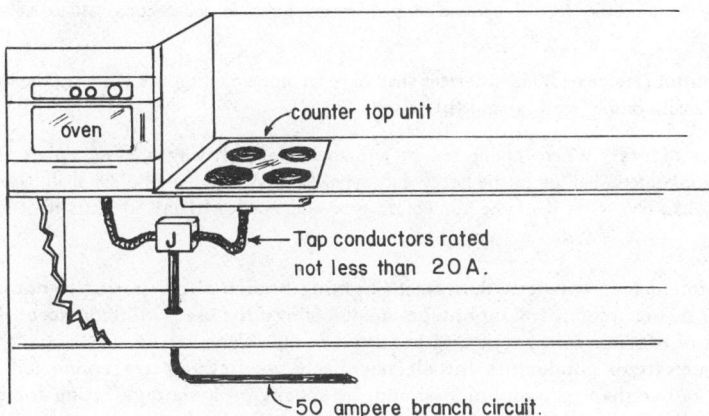

counter top unit

oven

Tap conductors rated not less than 20 A.

50 ampere branch circuit.

Figure 210-21. Tap conductors are permitted to be sized smaller than the branch-circuit conductors, but they are to be no longer than necessary for servicing.

(c) Other Loads. Branch-circuit conductors supplying loads other than cooking appliances as covered in (b) above and as listed in Section 210-2 shall have an ampacity sufficient for the loads served and shall not be smaller than No. 14.

Exception No. 1: Tap conductors for such loads shall have an ampacity not less than 15 for circuits rated less than 40 amperes and not less than 20 for circuits rated at 40 or 50 amperes and only where these tap conductors supply any of the following loads:

a. Individual lampholders or fixtures with taps extending not longer than 18 inches (457 mm) beyond any portion of the lampholder or fixture.

b. A fixture having tap conductors as provided in Section 410-67.

c. Individual outlets with taps not over 18 inches (457 mm) long.

d. Infrared lamp industrial heating appliances.

e. Nonheating leads of de-icing and snow-melting cables and mats.

Exception No. 2: Fixture wires and cords as permitted in Section 240-4.

Tap conductors are to be suitable for the temperature encountered and, where the conductors supply loads as specified in subparts a. through e. of Exception No. 1, they are to have an ampacity of 15 A or more (No. 14 AWG copper conductors) for circuits rated less than 40 A, and an ampacity of 20 A or more (No. 12 AWG copper conductors) for circuits rated 40 or 50 A.

210-20. Overcurrent Protection. Branch-circuit conductors and equipment shall be protected by overcurrent protective devices having a rating or setting (1) not exceeding that specified in Section 240-3 for conductors; (2) not exceeding that specified in the applicable articles referenced in Section 240-2 for equipment; and (3) as provided for outlet devices in Section 210-21.

Exception No. 1: Tap conductors as permitted in Section 210-19(c) shall be permitted to be protected by the branch-circuit overcurrent device.

Exception No. 2: Fixture wire and cords as permitted in Section 240-4.

(FPN): See Section 240-1 for the purpose of overcurrent protection and Sections 210-22 and 220-2 for continuous loads.

210-21. Outlet Devices. Outlet devices shall have an ampere rating not less than the load to be served and shall comply with (a) and (b) below.

(a) Lampholders. Where connected to a branch circuit having a rating in excess of 20 amperes, lampholders shall be of the heavy-duty type. A heavy-duty lampholder shall have a rating of not less than 660 watts if of the admedium type and not less than 750 watts if of any other type.

The intent is to restrict a fluorescent lighting branch-circuit rating to not more than 20 A, because most lampholders manufactured for use with fluorescent lights are not of the heavy-duty type and are rated at 660 W or 250 W.
Branch-circuit conductors for electric-discharge lighting are connected to a ballast rather than to lampholders, and, by specifying a wattage rating for these lampholders, a limit of 20 A is applied to ballast circuits.
It is only the admedium-base lampholder that is recognized as heavy duty at the rating of 660 W. The medium-base lampholder (usually rated 250 W or 660 W) is required to have a rating of not less than 750 watts to be recognized as heavy duty. The requirement stated in Section 210-21(a) prohibits the use of medium-base lampholders on branch circuits in excess of 20 amperes.

(b) Receptacles.

(1) A single receptacle installed on an individual branch circuit shall have an ampere rating of not less than that of the branch circuit.

See comment following Section 210-7(a).

(FPN): See definition of Receptacle in Article 100.

(2) Where connected to a branch circuit supplying two or more receptacles or outlets, a receptacle shall not supply a total cord- and plug-connected load in excess of the maximum specified in Table 210-21(b)(2).

(3) Where connected to a branch circuit supplying two or more receptacles or outlets, receptacle ratings shall conform to the values listed in Table 210-21(b)(3) or where larger than 50 amperes, the receptacle rating shall not be less than the branch-circuit rating.

See comment following Section 210-7(a).

(4) It shall be acceptable to base the ampere rating of a range receptacle on a single range demand load specified in Table 220-19.

Table 210-21(b)(2)
Maximum Cord- and Plug-Connected Load to Receptacle

Circuit Rating Amperes	Receptacle Rating Amperes	Maximum Load Amperes
15 or 20	15	12
20	20	16
30	30	24

Table 210-21(b)(3)
Receptacle Ratings for Various Size Circuits

Circuit Rating Amperes	Receptacle Rating Amperes
15	Not over 15
20	15 or 20
30	30
40	40 or 50
50	50

210-22. Maximum Loads. The total load shall not exceed the rating of the branch circuit, and it shall not exceed the maximum loads specified in (a) through (c) below under the conditions specified therein.

(a) Motor-Operated and Combination Loads. Where a circuit supplies only motor-operated loads, Article 430 shall apply. Where a circuit supplies only air-conditioning and/or refrigerating equipment, Article 440 shall apply. For circuits supplying loads consisting of motor-operated utilization equipment that is fastened in place and that has a motor larger than ⅛ horsepower in combination with other loads, the total computed load shall be based on 125 percent of the largest motor load plus the sum of the other loads.

(b) Inductive Lighting Loads. For circuits supplying lighting units having ballasts, transformers, or autotransformers, the computed load shall be based on the total ampere ratings of such units and not on the total watts of the lamps.

(c) Other Loads. Continuous loads, such as store lighting and similar loads, shall not exceed 80 percent of the rating of the branch circuit.

Exception No. 1: Motor loads having demand factors computed in accordance with Article 430.

Exception No. 2: Circuits supplied by an assembly together with its overcurrent devices that is listed for continuous operation at 100 percent of its rating.

It shall be acceptable to apply demand factors for range loads in accordance with Table 220-19, including Note 4.

Article 100 defines a "Continuous Load" as a load where the maximum current is expected to continue for three hours or more. Continuous loads, such as lighting in mercantile occupancies, restaurants, etc., must not exceed 80 percent of the branch-circuit rating. Exception No. 1 prevents a "double" derating of circuits.

Exception No. 2 provides for a 100 percent rating of a circuit if supplied by an overcurrent device and assembly listed by a qualified testing laboratory for continuous operation.

210-23. Permissible Loads. In no case shall the load exceed the branch-circuit ampere rating. It shall be acceptable for an individual branch circuit to supply any load for which it is rated. A branch circuit supplying two or more outlets shall supply only the loads specified according to its size in (a) through (c) below and summarized in Section 210-24 and Table 210-24.

(a) 15- and 20-Ampere Branch Circuits. A 15- or 20-ampere branch circuit shall be permitted to supply lighting units, other utilization equipment, or a combination of both. The rating of any one cord- and plug-connected utilization equipment shall not exceed 80 percent of the branch-circuit ampere rating. The total rating of utilization equipment fastened in place shall not exceed 50 percent of the branch-circuit ampere rating where lighting units, cord- and plug-connected utilization equipment not fastened in place, or both, are also supplied.

Exception: The small appliance branch circuits required in a dwelling unit(s) by Section 220-3(b) shall supply only the receptacle outlets specified in that section.

This permits a 15- or 20-A branch circuit for lighting to also supply utilization equipment fastened in place, such as an air conditioner rated not to exceed 50 percent of the branch-circuit ampere rating, that is, 7.5 A on a 15-A circuit and 10 A on a 20-A circuit. Such equipment, fastened in place, is not to be installed on the small-appliance branch circuits required in the kitchen, dining room, etc., as per Section 220-3(b).

(b) 30-Ampere Branch Circuits. A 30-ampere branch circuit shall be permitted to supply fixed lighting units with heavy-duty lampholders in other than dwelling unit(s) or utilization equipment in any occupancy. A rating of any one cord- and plug-connected utilization equipment shall not exceed 80 percent of the branch-circuit ampere rating.

(c) 40- and 50-Ampere Branch Circuits. A 40- or 50-ampere branch circuit shall be permitted to supply cooking appliances that are fastened in place in any occupancy. In other than dwelling units, such circuits shall be permitted to supply fixed lighting units with heavy-duty lampholders, infrared heating units or other utilization equipment.

A branch circuit supplying two or more outlets is to supply only the loads specified according to its size as per Section 210-23(a) through (c) and summarized in Section 210-24 and Table 210-24. Any other circuit is not permitted to have more than one outlet and would be an individual branch circuit. However, individual branch circuits are not required for portable, mobile, and transportable medical X-ray equipment requiring a capacity of not over 60 A [see Sections 517-141(b) and 660-4].

(d) Branch Circuits Larger than 50 Amperes. Branch circuits larger than 50 amperes shall supply only nonlighting outlet loads.

Section 210-23(d) is new in the 1984 *NEC*. It correlates with the new exception to Section 210-3.

210-24. Branch-Circuit Requirements — Summary. The requirements for circuits having two or more outlets, other than the receptacle circuits of Section 220-3(b) as specifically provided for above, are summarized in Table 210-24. Branch circuits in dwelling units shall not be connected to serve more than one dwelling unit.

The last sentence of Section 210-24 is new for the 1984 *NEC*. It is intended to prevent overloading of branch circuits. Table 210-24 summarizes branch-circuit requirements of conductors, overcurrent protection, outlet devices, maximum load, and permissible loads where two or more outlets are supplied.

Where the branch circuit serves a fixture load and supplies two or more fixture outlets, Section 210-23 requires the branch circuit to have a specific ampere rating which is also the rating of the overcurrent device as stated in Section 210-3. Thus, if the circuit breaker protecting the branch circuit is rated 20 A, the conductors supplying this circuit must have a 20-A ampacity. Note that in accordance with the new definition of ampacity in the 1984 *NEC*, the ampacity is determined after applying all derating factors, such as those in Note 8 to Tables 310-16 through 310-19. Where 7 to 24 such conductors are in one conduit, a No. 12 AWG THHN copper conductor (30 A per Table 310-16) derated to 70 percent per Note 8 would have an ampacity of 21 A and would be suitable for a load of 20 A. It would thus be acceptable for use on the 20-A multioutlet branch circuit.

Table 210-24
Summary of Branch-Circuit Requirements

(Type FEP, FEPB, RUW, SA, T, TW, RH, RUH, RHW, RHH, THHN, THW, THWN, and XHHW conductors in raceway or cable.)

CIRCUIT RATING	15 Amp	20 Amp	30 Amp	40 Amp	50 Amp
CONDUCTORS (Min. Size)					
Circuit Wires*	14	12	10	8	6
Taps	14	14	14	12	12
Fixture Wires and Cords			Refer to Section 240-4		
OVERCURRENT PROTECTION	15 Amp	20 Amp	30 Amp	40 Amp	50 Amp
OUTLET DEVICES:					
Lampholders Permitted	Any Type	Any Type	Heavy Duty	Heavy Duty	Heavy Duty
Receptacle Rating**	15 Max. Amp	15 or 20 Amp	30 Amp	40 or 50 Amp	50 Amp
MAXIMUM LOAD	15 Amp	20 Amp	30 Amp	40 Amp	50 Amp
PERMISSIBLE LOAD	Refer to Section 210-23(a)	Refer to Section 210-23(a)	Refer to Section 210-23(b)	Refer to Section 210-23(c)	Refer to Section 210-23(c)

* These gages are for copper conductors.
** For receptacle rating of cord-connected electric-discharge lighting fixtures, see Section 410-30(c).

C. Required Outlets

210-50. General. Receptacle outlets shall be installed as specified in Sections 210-52 through 210-62.

(a) Cord Pendants. A cord connector that is supported by a permanently installed cord pendant shall be considered a receptacle outlet.

(b) Cord Connections. A receptacle outlet shall be installed wherever flexible cords with attachment plugs are used. Where flexible cords are permitted to be permanently connected, it shall be permitted to omit receptacles for such cords.

Flexible cords may be permitted to be permanently connected to boxes or fittings where specifically permitted by the *Code*. However, plugging a cord into a lampholder by inserting a screw-plug adapter is not permissible (see Section 410-47).

(c) Laundry Outlet. Appliance outlets installed in a dwelling unit for specific appliances, such as laundry equipment, shall be installed within 6 feet (1.83 m) of the intended location of the appliance.

See Sections 210-52(e) and (f) and 220-3(c).

210-52. Dwelling Unit Receptacle Outlets.

(a) General Provisions. In every kitchen, family room, dining room, living room, parlor, library, den, sun room, bedroom, recreation room, or similar rooms of dwelling units, receptacle outlets shall be installed so that no point along the floor line in any wall space is more than 6 feet (1.83 m), measured horizontally, from an outlet in that space, including any wall space 2 feet (610 mm) or more in width and the wall space occupied by sliding panels in exterior walls. The wall space afforded by fixed room dividers, such as free-standing bar-type counters, shall be included in the 6-foot (1.83-m) measurement.

See Figure 210-22.

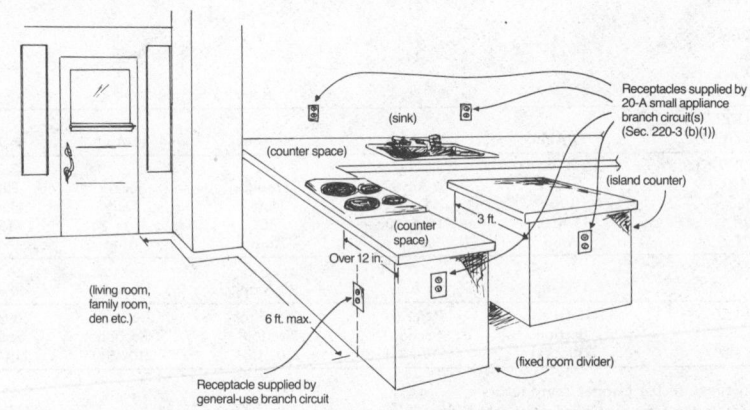

Figure 210-22. Section 210-52(a) requires the wall space afforded by fixed room dividers to be included in the 6-ft measurement. Section 210-52(b) requires a receptacle at each counter space wider than 12 in.

As used in this section a "wall space" shall be considered a wall unbroken along the floor line by doorways, fireplaces, and similar openings. Each wall space 2 or more feet (610 mm or more) wide shall be treated individually and separately from other wall spaces within the room. A wall space shall be permitted to include two or more walls of a room (around corners) where unbroken at the floor line.

(FPN): The purpose of this requirement is to minimize the use of cords across doorways, fireplaces, and similar openings.

Receptacle outlets shall, insofar as practicable, be spaced equal distances apart. Receptacle outlets in floors shall not be counted as part of the required number of receptacle outlets unless located close to the wall.

Receptacles are to be located so that no "point" in any wall space is more than 6 ft from a receptacle. This rule intends that an appliance or lamp with a flexible cord attached may be placed anywhere in the room and be within 6 ft of a receptacle, thus eliminating the need for extension cords.

A "wallspace" is a wall unbroken along the floor line by doorways, fireplaces, archways and similar openings, and may include two or more walls of a room (around corners, as illustrated in Figure 210-23).

Fixed room dividers, including bar-type counters, are to be included in the 6-ft measurement. Isolated, individual wall spaces 2 ft or more in width are considered usable for the location of a lamp or appliance and a receptacle outlet must be provided. This also applies to counter spaces wider than 12 in. in kitchen or dining areas. Receptacles are required to be located at these spaces, thereby eliminating probable hazards caused by running cords across doorways or passageways or across sinks or range tops, etc. Sliding panels in exterior walls are counted as regular wall space, and a floor-type receptacle can be used to meet the required spacing.

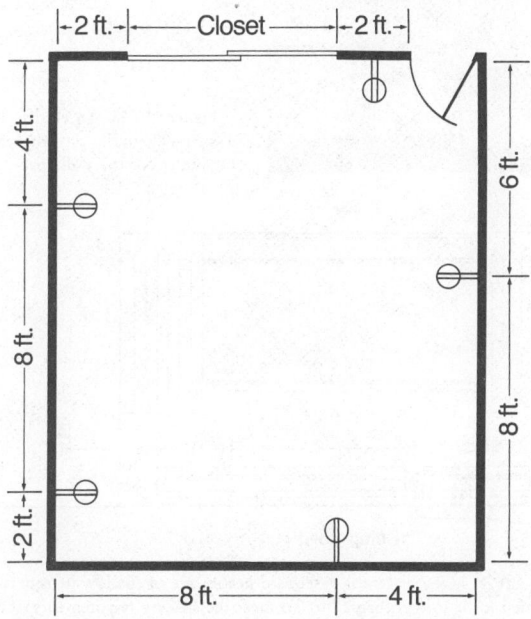

Figure 210-23. Plan view of the location of receptacles in a typical room. Receptacles are spaced to permit a lamp or appliance equipped with 6-ft cords to be located anywhere in the room.

The receptacle outlets required by this section shall be in addition to any receptacle that is part of any lighting fixture or appliance, located within cabinets or cupboards, or located over 5½ feet (1.68 m) above the floor.

Exception: Permanently installed electric baseboard heaters equipped with factory-installed receptacle outlets or outlets provided as a separate assembly by the manufacturer shall be permitted as the required outlet or outlets for the wall space utilized by such permanently installed heaters. Such receptacle outlets shall not be connected to the heater circuits.

According to listing instructions [see Section 110-3(b)], permanent electric baseboard heaters are not to be located beneath wall receptacles. Where the receptacle is a part of the heater, cords of appliances or lamps are less apt to be exposed to the heating elements, such as falling into convector slots. See Figures 210-24 and 210-25.

Figure 210-24. An electric baseboard heater with a receptacle outlet provided as the required receptacle outlet for the wall space. (*Square D Co.*)

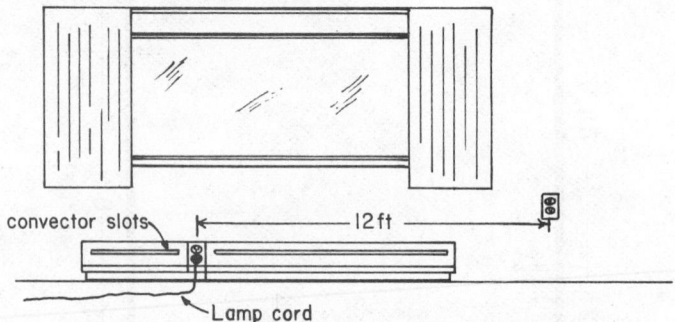

Figure 210-25. Many electrical baseboard heaters are of the low-density type and are designed to be longer than 12 ft. To meet the spacing requirements of Section 210-52(a), it is necessary that the required receptacle be located as a part of the heater unit.

(b) Counter Tops. In kitchen and dining areas of dwelling units a receptacle outlet shall be installed at each counter space wider than 12 inches (305 mm). Counter top spaces separated by range tops, refrigerators, or sinks shall be considered as separate counter top spaces. Receptacles rendered inaccessible by appliances fastened in place or appliances occupying dedicated space shall not be considered as these required outlets.

Receptacles rendered inaccessible by appliances fastened in place or by appliances occupying dedicated space, such as dishwashers, garbage disposal units, built-in gas ovens, waste compactors, etc., are not to be considered as the required receptacles.

(c) Bathrooms. In dwelling units at least one wall receptacle outlet shall be installed in the bathroom adjacent to the basin location. See Section 210-8(a)(1).

In bathrooms of a dwelling unit, one wall receptacle is to be installed adjacent to the wash basin and this receptacle is required in addition to any receptacle that may be part of any lighting fixture or medicine cabinet. All 125-V single-phase, 15- and 20-A receptacles installed in bathroom areas are to have ground-fault circuit-interrupter protection for personnel.

(d) Outdoor Outlets. For a one-family dwelling at least one receptacle outlet accessible at grade level shall be installed outdoors. For a two-family dwelling at least one receptacle outlet accessible at grade level shall be installed outdoors for each dwelling unit which is at grade level. See Section 210-8(a)(3).

Section 210-52(d) has been revised for the 1984 *NEC* to require two receptacle outlets, one for each dwelling unit, for a two-family dwelling such as shown in Figure 210-26. If the two dwelling units were one over the other rather than side by side, only a single receptacle outlet would be required.

Installation of outdoor receptacles requires that care be taken to assure that the receptacle faceplate rests securely on the supporting surface to prevent moisture from entering the enclosure. Where uneven surfaces such as brick, stone, or stucco are encountered, it may be necessary to close openings with caulking compound or mastic.

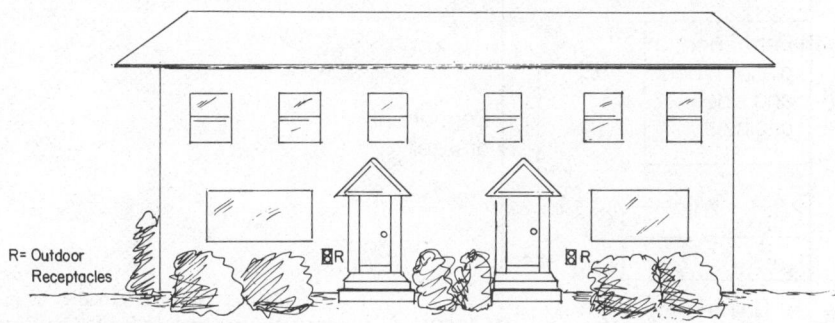

R= Outdoor Receptacles

Figure 210-26. Illustration of the intended number of outdoor receptacles for a two-family dwelling with dwelling units at grade level.

(e) Laundry Areas. In dwelling units at least one receptacle outlet shall be installed for the laundry.

Exception No. 1: In a dwelling unit that is an apartment or living area in a multifamily building where laundry facilities are provided on the premises that are available to all building occupants, a laundry receptacle shall not be required.

Exception No. 2: In other than one-family dwellings where laundry facilities are not to be installed or permitted, a laundry receptacle shall not be required.

(f) Basements and Garages. For a one-family dwelling at least one receptacle outlet in addition to any provided for laundry equipment shall be installed in each basement and in each attached garage. See Section 210-8(a)(2).

It is mandatory in a one-family dwelling to install a receptacle in each basement (in addition to the laundry receptacle, which is also mandatory), and in each attached garage. The *Code* intends that it is not mandatory to install a receptacle in unattached garages. However, if receptacles are installed in this location, GFCIs must be provided in accordance with Section 210-8(a)(2).

210-60. Guest Rooms. Guest rooms in hotels, motels, and similar occupancies shall have receptacle outlets installed in accordance with Section 210-52. See Section 210-8(b).

Exception: In rooms of hotels and motels, receptacle outlets may be located convenient for the permanent furniture layout.

It is the intent of the exception to Section 210-60 that the location (and therefore the minimum number) of receptacle outlets be determined after the location of any permanent furniture which may make wall space unusable has been established. This also makes it unnecessary to locate receptacles where they are not readily accessible. See Figure 210-27.

Bathrooms for guest rooms of hotels and motels are required to be provided with a receptacle outlet adjacent to the basin location in accordance with Section 210-52(c), protected by a GFCI in accordance with Section 210-8(b).

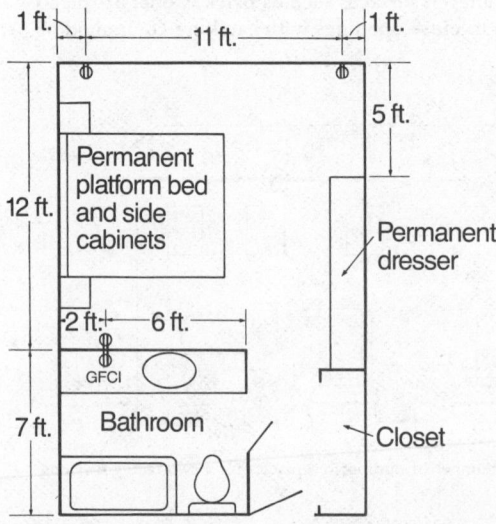

Figure 210-27. Receptacle outlets in guest rooms of hotels may be located convenient for the permanent furniture layout. If the furniture was not permanent at least one more receptacle would be required.

210-62. Show Windows. At least one receptacle outlet shall be installed directly above a show window for each 12 linear feet (3.66 m) or major fraction thereof of show window area measured horizontally at its maximum width.

Show windows are usually designed from floor to ceiling for maximum display. To discourage floor receptacles and unsightly extension cords likely to cause physical injury, receptacles must be installed "directly above" a show window and one receptacle is required for every 12 linear feet or "major (more than 6 ft) fraction" thereof.

210-70. Lighting Outlets Required. Lighting outlets shall be installed where specified in (a) and (b) below.

(a) Dwelling Unit(s). At least one wall switch-controlled lighting outlet shall be installed in every habitable room; in bathrooms, hallways, stairways, and attached garages; and at outdoor entrances.

(FPN): A vehicle door in an attached garage is not considered as an outdoor entrance.

At least one lighting outlet shall be installed in an attic, underfloor space, utility room and basement only where these spaces are used for storage or contain equipment requiring servicing.

Exception No. 1: In habitable rooms, other than kitchens, one or more receptacles controlled by a wall switch shall be permitted in lieu of lighting outlets.

Exception No. 2: In hallways, stairways, and at outdoor entrances remote, central, or automatic control of lighting shall be permitted.

(b) Guest Rooms. At least one wall switch-controlled lighting outlet or wall switch-controlled receptacle shall be installed in guest rooms in hotels, motels, or similar occupancies.

This section points out that adequate lighting and proper control and location of switching is as essential to the safety of occupants of dwelling units(s), hotels, motels, etc., as are proper wiring requirements. Proper illumination assures safe movement for persons of all ages and many accidents are avoided.

Installation of lighting outlets in attics, under floor space or crawl areas, utility rooms or basements are required "only" where these spaces are used for storage (Christmas decorations, luggage, etc.) or where such spaces contain equipment requiring servicing (air-handling units, cooling and heating equipment, water pumps, sump pumps, etc.).

Remote, central, or automatic control of lighting for hallways, stairways, and outdoor entrances is practical in multifamily dwellings where it is desirable to use time clocks or to locate switches where they may not be intentionally or inadvertently turned "off."

Although the requirement calls for a lighting outlet at outdoor entrances, it does not prohibit a single lighting outlet, if suitably located, from serving more than one door.

A wall switch controlled lighting outlet is required in the kitchen and bathroom.

ARTICLE 215 — FEEDERS

Contents

215-1. Scope. This article covers the installation requirements and minimum size and ampacity of conductors for feeders supplying branch-circuit loads as computed in accordance with Article 220. The requirements of Section 215-8 shall apply to feeders and other applications where identification is equally necessary.

Exception: See Section 668-3(c), Exceptions No. 1 and No. 4 for electrolytic cells.

A thorough calculation of the total connected load to be supplied by the feeder is required to determine accurately feeder conductor ampacity. The sum of the computed and connected loads supplied by a feeder is multiplied by the "demand factor" to determine the load which the feeder conductors must be sized to serve. (See Article 100 for definition of "Demand Factor.")

When the total connected load is operated simultaneously, the demand factor is 100 percent; that is, the maximum demand is equal to the total connected load. Due to diversity, the maximum operating load ever carried may be ¾ of the total connected load; the demand factor is thus 75 percent.

On a new installation, a minimum value for the demand factor can be determined by applying the requirements and tables of Article 220 (Branch Circuit and Feeder Calculations).

Feeder conductor sizes are determined by calculating the total volt-amperes of the feeder load at the nominal voltage of the feeder circuit:

$$\text{Single Phase} \qquad\qquad \text{Three Phase}$$

$$I = \frac{\text{volt-amperes load}}{E} \qquad\qquad I = \frac{\text{volt-amperes load}}{E \times 1.73}$$

$$\text{where } I = \text{current in amperes}$$
$$E = \text{volts}$$

See Tables of Article 310 for allowable ampacities and sizes of insulated conductors.

Feeder circuits are to have sufficient ampacity for safety. Overloading of a wiring system that does not provide for increases in the use of electricity often creates hazards. It is good practice to allow for future increases.

215-2. Minimum Rating and Size. Feeder conductors shall have an ampacity not lower than required to supply the load as computed in Parts B, C, and D of Article 220. The minimum sizes shall be as specified in (a) and (b) below under the conditions stipulated. Feeder conductors for a dwelling unit or a mobile home need not be larger than service-entrance conductors. Note 3 of Table 310-16 shall be permitted to be used for conductor size.

This section correlates with Note 3 of Table 310-16. For example, Table 310-16 allows 200 amperes for a No. 3/0 THW copper wire. But for a 3-wire, single-phase dwelling service, Note 3 permits 200 amperes for a 2/0 AWG copper THW conductor or 200 amperes for a 4/0 AWG aluminum THW conductor. It stands to reason that feeder conductors carrying the total load supplied by the service-entrance conductors should not be required to be sized larger than the service-entrance conductors. See Figure 215-1.

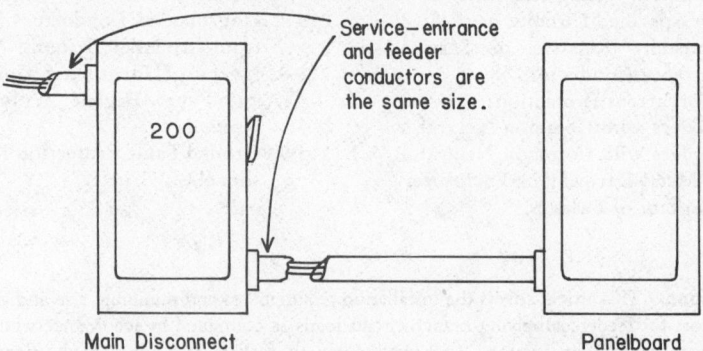

Service—entrance and feeder conductors are the same size.

200

Main Disconnect   Panelboard

Figure 215-1. For a 3-wire, single-phase dwelling service, Note 3 permits an ampacity of 200 A for 2/0 copper conductors for use as service-entrance conductors and for feeder conductors.

(a) For Specified Circuits. The ampacity of feeder conductors shall not be less than 30 where the load supplied consists of the following number and types of circuits: (1) two or more 2-wire branch circuits supplied by a 2-wire feeder; (2) more than two 2-wire branch circuits supplied by a 3-wire feeder; and (3) two or more 3-wire branch circuits supplied by a 3-wire feeder.

(b) Ampacity Relative to Service-Entrance Conductors. The feeder conductor ampacity shall not be lower than that of the service-entrance conductors where the feeder conductors carry the total load supplied by service-entrance conductors with an ampacity of 55 or less.

(FPN): See Examples 1 through 8 in Chapter 9.

(FPN): Conductors for feeders as defined in Article 100, sized to prevent a voltage drop exceeding 3 percent at the farthest outlet of power, heating, and lighting loads, or combinations of such loads and where the maximum total voltage drop on both feeders and branch circuits to the farthest outlet does not exceed 5 percent, will provide reasonable efficiency of operation.

(FPN): See Section 210-19(a) for voltage drop for branch circuits.

Total voltage drop consists of the voltage drop in the feeder plus the voltage drop in the branch circuit. Reasonable operating efficiency will be achieved where the maximum voltage drop of a feeder and a branch circuit does not exceed 5 percent. Conductors of a feeder should be sized to prevent a voltage drop exceeding 3 percent and conductors of a branch circuit should be sized to prevent a voltage drop exceeding 2 percent. See Article 100 for definition of "Feeder" and "Branch Circuit."

The 5 percent voltage drop value is a recommended practice, and, as such, it appears as a Fine Print Note. Fine Print Notes are explanatory and not mandatory (see Section 110-1).

The resistance or impedance of conductors may cause a substantial difference between voltage values at service equipment and voltage values at the point of utilization equipment. Excessive voltage drop impairs the starting and operation of electrical equipment. In addition to resistance or impedance, length, size, and type of conductor; type of raceway or cable enclosure; type of circuit, ac, dc, single-phase, 3-phase; and power factor are to be considered to determine voltage drop.

The basic formula for determining voltage drop in a 2-wire dc circuit, a 2-wire ac circuit, or a 3-wire ac single-phase circuit with a balanced load at 100 percent power factor and where reactance can be neglected is:

$$VD = \frac{2 \times L \times R \times I}{1000}$$

where VD = voltage drop (based on conductor temperature of 75°F)

L = One-way length of circuit (feet)

R = Conductor resistance in ohms per thousand feet (from Chapter 9, Table 8)

I = Load current (amperes)

For 3-phase circuits (at 100 percent power factor) the voltage drop between any two phase conductors is 0.866 times the voltage drop calculated by this formula.

Example: 240-V 2-wire heating circuit. Load is 50 A. Circuit size is No. 6 AWG THHN copper and the one-way circuit length is 100 ft.

$$VD = \frac{2 \times L \times R \times I}{1000} = \frac{2 \times 100 \times 0.491 \times 50}{1000}$$

$$VD = \frac{4910}{1000} = 4.91\text{-V drop}$$

A 12-V drop on a 240-V circuit is a 5 percent drop; therefore, a 4.91-V drop falls within this percentage.

Should the voltage drop exceed 5 percent then a larger size conductor should be used, or the circuit length shortened, or the circuit load should be reduced.

Voltage drop tables and calculations are available from various manufacturers.

215-3. Overcurrent Protection. Feeders shall be protected against overcurrent in accordance with the provisions of Part A of Article 240.

215-4. Feeders with Common Neutral.

(a) Feeders with Common Neutral. Feeders containing a common neutral shall be permitted to supply two or three sets of 3-wire feeders, or two sets of 4-wire or 5-wire feeders.

(b) In Metal Raceway or Enclosure. Where installed in a metal raceway or other metal enclosure, all conductors of all feeders using a common neutral shall be enclosed within the same raceway or other enclosure as required in Section 300-20.

Where feeder conductors carrying ac current, including the neutral, are installed in metal raceways, they are to be grouped together to avoid induction heating of the surrounding metal.

A 3-phase, 4-wire (208 wye/120-V, 480 wye/277-V) system is often used to supply both lighting and motor loads. The 3-phase motor loads will cause no current to flow in the neutral conductor. Therefore, the maximum current on the neutral is due to lighting loads, or circuits where the neutral is used. On this type of system (3-phase, 4-wire), a demand factor of 70 percent is to be permitted for that portion of the neutral load in excess of 200 A. See Section 220-22. Thus, if the maximum possible load is 500 A, the neutral would need to be large enough to carry 200 A plus 70 percent of 300 A, or 410 A. There is to be no reduction of the neutral capacity for that portion of the load consisting of electric-discharge lighting. See Note 10(c) to Tables 310-16 through 310-19. See Section 220-22 for other systems to which the 70 percent demand factor may be applied. The maximum unbalanced load for feeders supplying clothes dryers, household ranges, wall-mounted ovens, and counter-mounted cooking units is to be considered as 70 percent of the load of the ungrounded conductors. See Example Nos. 1 through 5(b) of Chapter 9.

See new Examples 5(a) and 5(b) of Chapter 9 for a multifamily dwelling served at 208Y/120 volts, three phase.

215-5. Diagrams of Feeders. If required by the authority having jurisdiction, a diagram showing feeder details shall be provided prior to the installation of the feeders. Such a diagram shall show the area in square feet of the building or other structure supplied by each feeder, the total connected load before applying demand factors, the demand factors used, the computed load after applying demand factors, and the size and type of conductors to be used.

215-6. Feeder Conductor Grounding Means. Where a feeder supplies branch circuits in which equipment grounding conductors are required, the feeder shall include or provide a grounding means in accordance with the provisions of Section 250-57 to which the equipment grounding conductors of the branch circuits shall be connected.

215-7. Ungrounded Conductors Tapped from Grounded Systems. Two-wire dc circuits and ac circuits of two or more ungrounded conductors may be tapped from the ungrounded conductors of circuits having a grounded neutral conductor. Switching devices in each tapped circuit shall have a pole in each ungrounded conductor.

It is not intended to provide a common trip of fuses or circuit breakers but to disconnect "manually" the ungrounded conductors of the feeder. See Section 210-10.

215-8. Means of Identifying Conductor with the Higher Voltage to Ground. On a 4-wire, delta-connected secondary where the midpoint of one phase is grounded to supply lighting and similar loads, the phase conductor having the higher voltage to ground shall be identified by an outer finish that is orange in color or by tagging or other effective means. Such identification shall be placed at each point where a connection is made if the neutral conductor is also present.

It is permitted to ground the midpoint of one phase to supply (120 V) lighting and similar loads from a delta-connected secondary. This results in one phase conductor having a higher voltage to ground and it is identified by an orange finish at any point, such as junction or pull boxes, panelboards, etc., where connections may be made and the neutral is also present. The orange high-leg of a 3-phase, 4-wire (120/240-V) delta system is 208 V to ground (120 V × 1.73 = 208 V) and should obviously not be used for 120-V circuits. See Sections 230-56, and 384-3(e) and (f). See Figure 215-2.

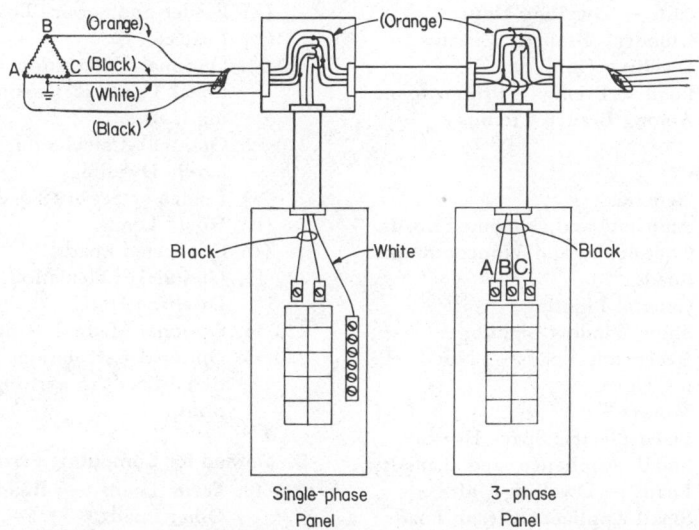

Figure 215-2. With a 4-wire, delta-connected secondary in which the midpoint of one phase is grounded, one phase conductor has a higher voltage to ground than the other two. It is identified in this illustration as having an "orange" finish. The identification must be visible at every point where a connection is made if a neutral is present.

215-9. Ground-Fault Protection for Personnel. Feeders supplying 15- and 20-ampere receptacle branch circuits shall be permitted to be protected by a ground-fault circuit-interrupter in lieu of the provisions for such interrupters as specified in Section 210-8 and Article 305.

Several manufacturers offer double-pole 120/240-V ground-fault circuit-interrupters for application to a feeder, thereby protecting all branch circuits supplied by that feeder. This installation is in lieu of provisions of Section 210-8 for outdoor, bathroom, garage, and construction-site receptacles.

It may be more economical or convenient to install ground-fault circuit-interrupters for feeders. However, it will be monitoring several branch circuits and, in response to a line-to-ground fault from one branch circuit, it will de-energize all of the branch circuits.

ARTICLE 220 — BRANCH-CIRCUIT AND FEEDER CALCULATIONS

Contents

A. General

220-1. Scope. This article provides requirements for determining the number of branch circuits required and for computing branch-circuit and feeder loads.

Unless other voltages are specified, for purposes of computing branch-circuit and feeder loads, nominal system voltages of 120, 120/240, 208Y/120, 240, 480Y/277, 480, and 600 volts shall be used.

For uniform application of the provisions of Articles 210, 215 and 220, a nominal voltage of 120, 208 and 240 volts is to be used in computing the ampere load on the conductor.

See Chapter 9, Examples 1 through 5(b). The results of these examples are generally expressed in amperes. Except where the computations result in a major fraction of an ampere (0.5 or larger), such fractions may be dropped.

To select conductor sizes, refer to Tables 310-16 through 310-19 and the notes that pertain to these tables.

There are two changes in the 1984 *NEC* that relate to all calculations of load. One of these is that the ampere load of conductors on 120-V and 240-V, nominal, circuits is computed using the nominal circuit voltage of 120 and 240, rather than 115 and 230 as in previous editions of the *Code*. The calculations for 120-V and 240-V circuits are therefore now consistent with the calculations for 208-V, 277-V, 480-V, and 600-V circuits. See Section 220-1 above.

The second change is that loads are computed on the basis of volt-amperes (VA) or kVA rather than watts or kW. However, the rating of equipment is still given in watts or kW. Such ratings are considered the equivalent of the same rating in volt-amperes or kVA. See, for example, Section 220-19. This change recognizes that load calculations are to determine conductor and circuit sizes, that the power-factor of the load is often unknown, and that the conductor "sees" the circuit volt-amperes only, not the circuit power (watts).

Exception: See Section 668-3(c), Exceptions No. 1 and No. 4 for electrolytic cells.

This exception also appears after Sections 210-1, 215-1, and 225-1.

220-2. Computation of Branch Circuits. Branch-circuit loads shall be computed as shown in (a) through (d) below.

(a) Continuous Loads. The continuous load supplied by a branch circuit shall not exceed 80 percent of the branch-circuit rating.

See Figure 220-1.

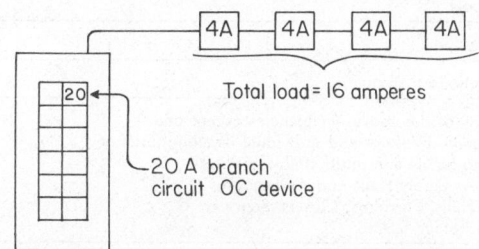

Figure 220-1. Continuous loads, such as store lighting, must not exceed 80 percent of the branch-circuit rating.

Exception: Where the assembly, including overcurrent devices, is listed for continuous operation of 100 percent of its rating.

Where branch-circuit conductors have been derated according to the provisions of Note 8 to Tables 310-16 through 310-19 because of the number of conductors in a raceway, cable, or stacked bundle, it is not necessary to apply the derating provisions of Section 220-2(a), i.e., "double-derating" is not required.

(b) Lighting Load for Listed Occupancies. A unit load of not less than that specified in Table 220-2(b) for occupancies listed therein shall constitute the minimum lighting load for each square foot (0.093 sq m) of floor area. The floor area for each floor shall be computed from the outside dimensions of the building, apartment, or other area involved. For dwelling unit(s), the computed floor area shall not include open porches, garages, or unused or unfinished spaces not adaptable for future use.

ARTICLE 220—BRANCH-CIRCUIT AND FEEDER CALCULATIONS

Examples of "unused or unfinished" spaces are some attics or some crawl spaces.

(FPN): The unit values herein are based on minimum load conditions and 100 percent power factor, and may not provide sufficient capacity for the installation contemplated.

Table 220-2(b).   General Lighting Loads by Occupancies

Type of Occupancy	Unit Load per Sq. Ft. (Volt-Amperes)
Armories and Auditoriums	1
Banks	3½**
Barber Shops and Beauty Parlors	3
Churches	1
Clubs	2
Court Rooms	2
*Dwelling Units	3
Garages — Commercial (storage)	½
Hospitals	2
*Hotels and Motels, including apartment houses without provisions for cooking by tenants	2
Industrial Commercial (Loft) Buildings	2
Lodge Rooms	1½
Office Buildings	3½**
Restaurants	2
Schools	3
Stores	3
Warehouses (storage)	¼
In any of the above occupancies except one-family dwellings and individual dwelling units of two-family and multifamily dwellings:	
Assembly Halls and Auditoriums	1
Halls, Corridors, Closets, Stairways	½
Storage Spaces	¼

For SI units: one square foot = 0.093 square meter.

* All receptacle outlets of 20-ampere or less rating in one-family, two-family and multifamily dwellings and in guest rooms of hotels and motels [except those connected to the receptacle circuits specified in Section 220-3(b)] shall be considered as outlets for general illumination, and no additional load calculations shall be required for such outlets.

** In addition a unit load of 1 volt-ampere per square foot shall be included for general purpose receptacle outlets when the actual number of general purpose receptacle outlets is unknown.

(c) Other Loads — All Occupancies. In all occupancies the minimum load for each outlet for general-use receptacles and outlets not used for general illumination shall be not less than the following, the loads shown being based on nominal branch-circuit voltages.

A load of 180 VA is not required to be considered for outlets supplying recessed lighting fixtures, outlets for general illumination, and small appliance branch circuits. To apply the 180-VA requirement, in this case, would be unrealistic as it would restrict the number of lighting or receptacle outlets on a branch circuit unnecessarily.

(1) Outlet for a specific appliance or other load except for a motor load .... ampere rating of appliance or load served.

(2) Outlet for motor load .... See Sections 430-22 and 430-24 and Article 440.

(3) An outlet supplying recessed lighting fixture(s) shall be the maximum volt-ampere rating of the equipment and lamps for which the fixture(s) is rated.

(4) Outlet for heavy-duty lampholder .... 600 volt-amperes.

(5) *Other outlets .... 180 volt-amperes per outlet.

For receptacle outlets, each single or multiple receptacle shall be considered at not less than 180 volt-amperes.

* This provision shall not be applicable to receptacle outlets connected to the circuit specified in Section 220-3(b) nor to receptacle outlets provided for the connection of cord- and plug-connected equipment as provided for in Section 400-7.

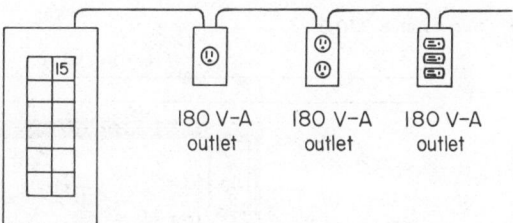

Figure 220-2. The 180-VA rating is applied to the outlet, regardless of whether a single, duplex, or triplex receptacle is connected to that outlet.

180 V-A outlet   180 V-A outlet   180 V-A outlet

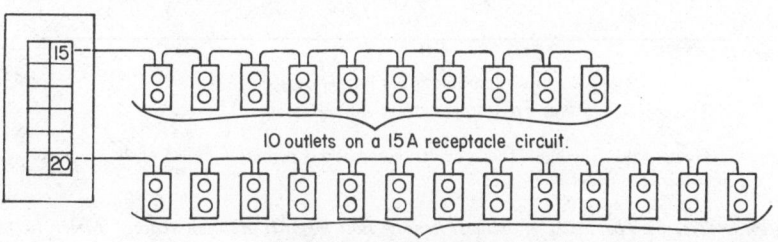

10 outlets on a 15A receptacle circuit.

13 outlets on a 20A receptacle circuit.

15 amperes x 120 volts = 1800 VA ÷ 180 VA = 10 receptacle outlets
20 amperes x 120 volts = 2400 VA ÷ 180 VA = 13 receptacle outlets

Figure 220-3. Computation of the maximum number of outlets permitted on 15- and 20-A branch circuits. This is not applicable to outlets connected to a general lighting or small appliance branch circuit.

Exception No. 1: Where fixed multioutlet assemblies are employed, each 5 feet (1.52 m) or fraction thereof of each separate and continuous length shall be considered as one outlet of not less than 180 volt-amperes capacity, except in locations where a number of appliances are likely to be used simultaneously, when each 1 foot (305 mm) or fraction thereof shall be considered as an outlet of not less than 180 volt-amperes. The requirements of this section shall not apply to dwelling unit(s) or the guest rooms of hotels or motels.

See Figure 220-4.

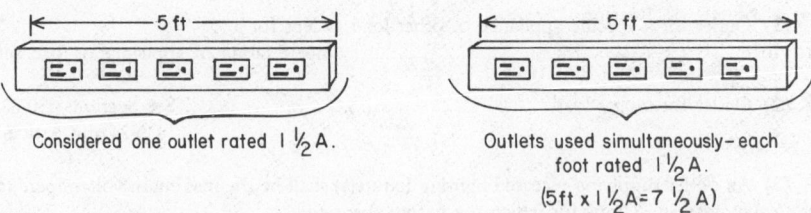

Considered one outlet rated 1½ A.

Outlets used simultaneously–each foot rated 1½ A.

(5ft x 1½A=7½ A)

Figure 220-4. Fixed multi-outlet assemblies are commonly used in commercial or industrial locations and may have been selected for a number of receptacles along a given work area (light use) or for the simultaneous connection and use of a number of appliances (heavy use).

Exception No. 2: Table 220-19 shall be considered as an acceptable method of computing the load for a household electric range.

Exception No. 3: A load of not less than 200 volt-amperes per linear foot (305 mm) of show window, measured horizontally along its base, shall be permitted instead of the specified unit load per outlet.

See Figure 220-5.

200 volt-amperes per linear foot

200 V A x 10 ft = 2000 volt-amperes

Figure 220-5. The linear foot calculation method is permitted in lieu of the specified unit load per outlet.

Exception No. 4: The loads of outlets serving switchboards and switching frames in telephone exchanges shall be waived from the computations.

(d) Loads for Additions to Existing Installations.

(1) Dwelling Units. Loads for structural additions to an existing dwelling unit or to a previously unwired portion of an existing dwelling unit, either of which exceeds 500 square feet (46.5 sq m), shall be computed in accordance with (b) above. Loads for new circuits or extended circuits in previously wired dwelling units shall be computed in accordance with either (b) or (c) above.

(2) Other than Dwelling Units. Loads for new circuits or extended circuits in other than dwelling units shall be computed in accordance with either (b) or (c) above.

220-3. Branch Circuits Required. Branch circuits for lighting and for appliances, including motor-operated appliances, shall be provided to supply the loads computed in accordance with Section 220-2. In addition, branch circuits shall be provided for specific loads not covered by Section 220-2 where required elsewhere in this Code; for small appliance loads as specified in (b) below; and for laundry loads as specified in (c) below.

(a) Number of Branch Circuits. The minimum number of branch circuits shall be determined from the total computed load and the size or rating of the circuits used. In all installations the number of circuits shall be sufficient to supply the load served. In no case shall the load on any circuit exceed the maximum specified by Section 210-22.

(b) Small Appliance Branch Circuits — Dwelling Unit.

(1) In addition to the number of branch circuits determined in accordance with (a) above, two or more 20-ampere small appliance branch circuits shall be provided for all receptacle outlets specified by Section 210-52 for the small appliance loads, including refrigeration equipment, in the kitchen, pantry, breakfast room, and dining room of a dwelling unit. Such circuits, whether two or more are used, shall have no other outlets.

See Figure 220-6.

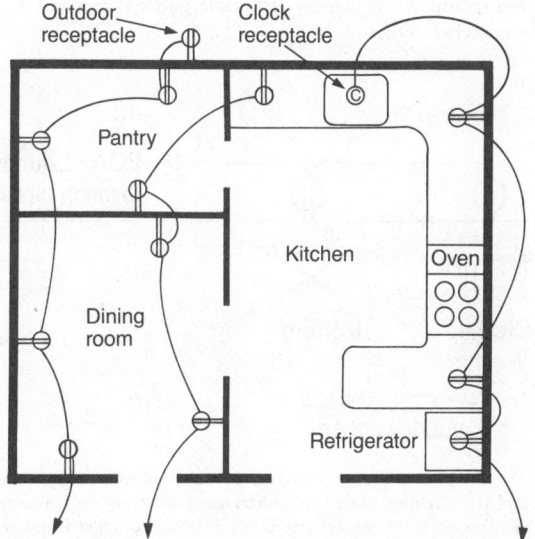

Figure 220-6. This figure illustrates the requirements of Section 220-3(b)(1) and (2). Though these small appliance branch circuits may serve certain outlets in other specified areas, they are not permitted to serve any other outlets such as might be connected to exhaust hoods or fans, disposal units, or dishwashers.

Exception No. 1: A receptacle installed solely for the electric supply to and support of an electric clock in any of the rooms specified above.

Exception No. 2: Outdoor receptacles.

(2) Countertop receptacle outlets installed in the kitchen shall be supplied by not less than two small appliance branch circuits, either or both of which shall also be permitted to supply receptacle outlets in kitchen and other rooms specified in (b)(1) above. Additional small appliance branch circuits shall be permitted to supply receptacle outlets in kitchen and other rooms specified in (b)(1) above.

Two or more 20-A circuits are to be provided for all receptacle outlets for the small appliance loads, including refrigeration equipment, in the kitchen, dining room, pantry, and breakfast room of a dwelling unit. Countertop receptacle outlets in kitchens are to be supplied by no fewer than two small appliance branch circuits. These circuits may also supply receptacle outlets in the pantry, dining room, and breakfast room as well as an electric clock receptacle or outdoor receptacles, but are to have no other outlets.

At least one additional 20-A branch circuit is to be provided to supply the laundry receptacle outlet(s) required, and this circuit is to have no other outlets. See Figures 220-6 and 220-7.

There is no restriction placed on the number of outlets connected to a general lighting or small appliance branch circuit. The number of receptacle outlets in a room is determined by Section 210-52(a). It is desirable to provide more than the minimum number of receptacle outlets required, thereby further reducing the need for use of extension cords.

(c) Laundry Branch Circuits — Dwelling Unit. In addition to the number of branch circuits determined in accordance with (a) and (b) above, at least one additional 20-ampere branch circuit shall be provided to supply the laundry receptacle outlet(s) required by Section 210-52(e). This circuit shall have no other outlets.

See Figure 220-7.

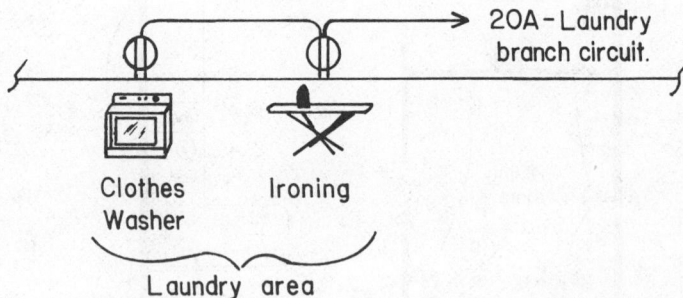

Figure 220-7. At least one 20-A branch circuit is required to supply the laundry receptacle outlet(s). Lighting outlets in laundry areas must not be connected to the laundry branch circuit. If the laundry area is in a basement or an attached garage, this receptacle outlet is not to be considered as that required by Section 210-52(f).

(d) Load Evenly Proportioned Among Branch Circuits. Where the load is computed on a volt-amperes-per-square-foot (0.093 sq m) basis, the wiring system up to and including the branch-circuit panelboard(s) shall be provided to serve not less than the calculated load. This load shall be evenly proportioned among multioutlet branch circuits within the panelboard(s). Branch-circuit overcurrent devices and circuits need only be installed to serve the connected load.

(FPN): See Examples 1(a), 1(b), 2(b) and 4(a), Chapter 9.

B. Feeders

220-10. General.

(a) Ampacity and Computed Loads. Feeder conductors shall have sufficient ampacity to supply the load served. In no case shall the computed load of a feeder be less than the sum of the loads on the branch circuits supplied as determined by Part A of this article after any applicable demand factors permitted by Parts B, C, or D have been applied.

See Figure 220-8.

(FPN): See Examples 1 through 8, Chapter 9. See Section 210-22(b) for maximum load in amperes permitted for lighting units operating at less than 100 percent power factor.

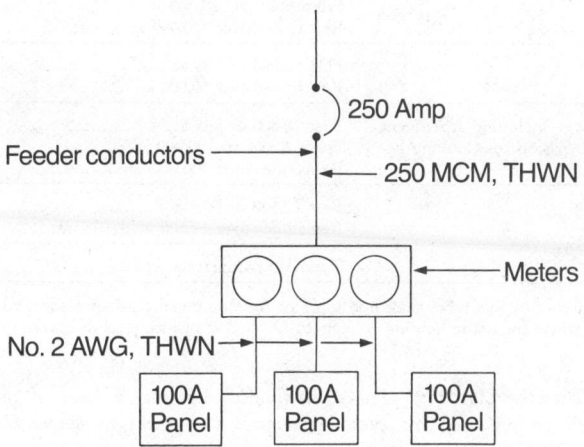

Figure 220-8. Each panel serves an 80-A load. The feeder size is based on the sum of the computed and connected loads served by each panel not on the sum of the panel or overcurrent device rating.

(b) Continuous and Noncontinuous Loads. Where a feeder supplies continuous loads or any combination of continuous and noncontinuous load, neither the ampere rating of the overcurrent device nor the ampacity of the feeder conductors shall be less than the noncontinuous load plus 125 percent of the continuous load.

Exception: Where the assembly including the overcurrent devices protecting the feeder(s) are listed for operation at 100 percent of their rating, neither the ampere rating of the overcurrent device nor the ampacity of the feeder conductors shall be less than the sum of the continuous load plus the noncontinuous load.

Sections 220-10 through 220-22, which are included in Part B, give the requirements for calculating feeder loads. Sections 220-30 and 220-32 give optional methods for calculating feeder loads in dwelling units and multifamily dwellings.

220-11. General Lighting. The demand factors listed in Table 220-11 shall apply to that portion of the total branch-circuit load computed for general illumination. They shall not be applied in determining the number of branch circuits for general illumination.

(FPN): See Section 220-16 for application of demand factors to small appliance and laundry loads in dwellings.

Table 220-11.   Lighting Load Feeder Demand Factors

Type of Occupancy	Portion of Lighting Load to Which Demand Factor Applies (volt-amperes)	Demand Factor Percent
Dwelling Units	First 3000 or less at	100
	From 3001 to 120,000 at..................................	35
	Remainder over 120,000 at	25
*Hospitals	First 50,000 or less at....................................	40
	Remainder over 50,000 at	20
*Hotels and Motels — Including Apartment Houses without Provision for Cooking by Tenants	First 20,000 or less at....................................	50
	From 20,001 to 100,000 at	40
	Remainder over 100,000 at	30
Warehouses (Storage)	First 12,500 or less at....................................	100
	Remainder over 12,500 at...............................	50
All Others	Total Volt-amperes	100

* The demand factors of this table shall not apply to the computed load of feeders to areas in hospitals, hotels, and motels where the entire lighting is likely to be used at one time, as in operating rooms, ballrooms, or dining rooms.

220-12. Show-Window Lighting. For show-window lighting, a load of not less than 200 volt-amperes shall be included for each linear foot (305 mm) of show window, measured horizontally along its base.

(FPN): See Section 220-2(c), Exception No. 3, for branch circuits supplying show windows.

See Figure 220-5.

220-13. Receptacle Loads — Nondwelling Units. In other than dwelling units, the use of the demand factors for lighting loads in Table 220-11 or those shown in Table 220-13 shall be permitted for receptacle loads computed at not more than 180 volt-amperes per outlet in accordance with Section 220-2(c)(5).

Table 220-13
Demand Factors for Nondwelling Receptacle Loads

Portion of Receptacle Load to which demand factor applies (volt-amperes)	Demand Factor Percent
First 10 kVA or less	100
Remainder over 10 kVA at	50

220-14. Motors. Motor loads shall be computed in accordance with Sections 430-24, 430-25, and 430-26.

220-15. Fixed Electric Space Heating. Fixed electric space heating loads shall be computed at 100 percent of the total connected load; however in no case shall a feeder load current rating be less than the rating of the largest branch circuit supplied.

Exception No. 1: Where reduced loading of the conductors results from units operating on duty-cycle, intermittently, or from all units not operating at one time, the authority having jurisdiction may grant permission for feeder conductors to have an ampacity less than 100 percent, provided the conductors have an ampacity for the load so determined.

Exception No. 2: The use of the optional calculations in Sections 220-30 and 220-31 shall be permitted for fixed electric space heating loads in a dwelling unit. In a multifamily dwelling the use of the optional calculation in Section 220-32 shall be permitted.

220-16. Small Appliance and Laundry Loads — Dwelling Unit.

(a) Small Appliance Circuit Load. In each dwelling unit the feeder load shall be computed at 1500 volt-amperes for each 2-wire small appliance branch circuit required by Section 220-3(b) for small appliances supplied by 15- or 20-ampere receptacles on 20-ampere branch circuits in the kitchen, pantry, dining room, and breakfast room. Where the load is subdivided through two or more feeders, the computed load for each shall include not less than 1500 volt-amperes for each 2-wire branch circuit for small appliances. These loads shall be permitted to be included with the general lighting load and subjected to the demand factors permitted in Table 220-11 for the general lighting load.

(b) Laundry Circuit Load. A feeder load of not less than 1500 volt-amperes shall be included for each 2-wire laundry branch circuit installed as required by Section 220-3(c). It shall be permissible to include this load with the general lighting load and subject it to the demand factors provided in Section 220-11.

In each dwelling unit, the feeder load is to be calculated at 1500 VA for each of the two or more (2-wire) small appliance branch circuits and 1500 VA for each (2-wire) laundry branch circuit. It is permissible to total these loads and add them to the general lighting load and subject the total load (small appliance, laundry, plus general lighting) to the demand factors provided in Table 220-11.

220-17. Appliance Load — Dwelling Unit(s). It shall be permissible to apply a demand factor of 75 percent to the nameplate-rating load of four or more appliances fastened in place served by the same feeder in a one-family, two-family, or multifamily dwelling.

Exception: This demand factor shall not be applied to electric ranges, clothes dryers, space heating equipment, or air-conditioning equipment.

Example: 120/240 V Fastened in place appliance load — Dwelling unit(s)

water heater	4,000 W	240 V		4000 VA
kitchen disposal	½ hp	120 V		1176 VA
dishwasher	1,200 W	120 V		1200 VA
furnace motor	¼ hp	120 V		696 VA
attic fan	¼ hp	120 V		696 VA
water pump	½ hp	240 V		1176 VA
			Total	8944 VA

For appliances fastened in place (other than ranges, clothes dryers, space heating equipment, and air-conditioning equipment), feeder capacity must be provided for the sum of these loads, and the total load of four or more such appliances may be reduced by a demand factor of 75 percent.

Seventy-five percent of 8944 VA = 6708 VA, which is the load to be added to the other determined loads for calculating the size of service and/or feeder conductors.

See Table 430-148 for the full-load current in amperes of single-phase ac motors.

220-18. Electric Clothes Dryers — Dwelling Unit(s). The load for household electric clothes dryers in a dwelling unit(s) shall be 5000 watts (volt-amperes) or the nameplate rating, whichever is larger, for each dryer served. The use of the demand factors in Table 220-18 shall be permitted.

This requirement provides a minimum demand of 5 kVA for the calculation of feeder conductors to compute the load of household electric dryers. Where the nameplate rating is known and exceeds 5 kW, the larger rating is to be applied.

Table 220-18
Demand Factors for Household Electric Clothes Dryers

Number of Dryers	Demand Factor Percent
1	100
2	100
3	100
4	100
5	80
6	70
7	65
8	60
9	55
10	50
11-13	45
14-19	40
20-24	35
25-29	32.5
30-34	30
35-39	27.5
40 & over	25

220-19. Electric Ranges and Other Cooking Appliances — Dwelling Unit(s). The feeder demand load for household electric ranges, wall-mounted ovens, counter-mounted cooking units, and other household cooking appliances individually rated in excess of 1¾ kW shall be permitted to be computed in accordance with Table 220-19. Where two or more single-phase ranges are supplied by a 3-phase, 4-wire feeder, the total load shall be computed on the basis of twice the maximum number connected between any two phases. kVA shall be considered equivalent to kW for loads computed under this section.

(FPN): See Example 5(b), Chapter 9.

It is permissible to add the nameplate ratings of all household cooking appliances rated more than 1¾ kW, but not more than 8¾ kW, and multiply the sum by the demand factors specified in Column B or C for the given number of appliances.

For feeder demand factors other than for dwelling unit(s), that is, commercial electric cooking equipment, dishwasher booster heaters, water heaters, etc., see Table 220-20.

Demand factors of this *Code* are based on the diversified use of appliances since it is unlikely that all appliances will be energized simultaneously or that all cooking units and the oven of a range will be at maximum heat for any length of time.

Table 220-19. Demand Loads for Household Electric Ranges, Wall-Mounted Ovens, Counter-Mounted Cooking Units, and Other Household Cooking Appliances over 1¾ kW Rating.
Column A to be used in all cases except as otherwise permitted in Note 3 below.

NUMBER OF APPLIANCES	Maximum Demand (See Notes)	Demand Factors Percent (See Note 3)	
	COLUMN A (Not over 12 kW Rating)	COLUMN B (Less than 3½ kW Rating)	COLUMN C (3½ kW to 8¾ kW Rating)
1	8 kW	80%	80%
2	11 kW	75%	65%
3	14 kW	70%	55%
4	17 kW	66%	50%
5	20 kW	62%	45%
6	21 kW	59%	43%
7	22 kW	56%	40%
8	23 kW	53%	36%
9	24 kW	51%	35%
10	25 kW	49%	34%
11	26 kW	47%	32%
12	27 kW	45%	32%
13	28 kW	43%	32%
14	29 kW	41%	32%
15	30 kW	40%	32%
16	31 kW	39%	28%
17	32 kW	38%	28%
18	33 kW	37%	28%
19	34 kW	36%	28%
20	35 kW	35%	28%
21	36 kW	34%	26%
22	37 kW	33%	26%
23	38 kW	32%	26%
24	39 kW	31%	26%
25	40 kW	30%	26%
26-30	15 kW plus 1 kW for each range	30%	24%
31-40		30%	22%
41-50	25 kW plus ¾ kW for each range	30%	20%
51-60		30%	18%
61 & over		30%	16%

Note 1. Over 12 kW through 27 kW ranges all of same rating. For ranges individually rated more than 12 kW but not more than 27 kW, the maximum demand in Column A shall be increased 5 percent for each additional kW of rating or major fraction thereof by which the rating of individual ranges exceeds 12 kW.

The size of the conductors is to be determined by the rating of the range. By referring to Table 220-19, it can be seen that for a range not over 12 kW the demand load is 8 kW (8 kVA per Section 220-19) and a No. 8 AWG copper conductor, with 60°C insulation, would suffice.

Note 2. Over 12 kW through 27 kW ranges of unequal ratings. For ranges individually rated more than 12 kW and of different ratings but none exceeding 27 kW, an average value of rating shall be computed by adding together the ratings of all ranges to obtain the total connected load (using 12 kW for any range rated less than 12 kW) and dividing by the total number of ranges; and then the maximum demand in Column A shall be increased 5 percent for each kW or major fraction thereof by which this average value exceeds 12 kW.

Note 2 provides for ranges larger than 12 kW, and Note 4 covers situations in which the range consists of several components.

Note 3.   Over 1¾ kW through 8¾ kW. In lieu of the method provided in Column A, it shall be permissible to add the nameplate ratings of all ranges rated more than 1¾ kW but not more than 8¾ kW and multiply the sum by the demand factors specified in Column B or C for the given number of appliances.

Note 4.   Branch-Circuit Load. It shall be permissible to compute the branch-circuit load for one range in accordance with Table 220-19. The branch-circuit load for one wall-mounted oven or one counter-mounted cooking unit shall be the nameplate rating of the appliance. The branch-circuit load for a counter-mounted cooking unit and not more than two wall-mounted ovens, all supplied from a single branch circuit and located in the same room, shall be computed by adding the nameplate rating of the individual appliances and treating this total as equivalent to one range.

It is permissible to compute the branch-circuit load for one range by the nameplate rating of the appliance or in accordance with Table 220-19. Where a single branch circuit supplies a counter-mounted cooking unit and not more than two wall-mounted ovens, all of which are located in the same room, it is permissible to add the nameplate ratings of these appliances and treat this total as equivalent to one range.

Example: a single branch circuit for

one counter-mounted cooking unit	8 kW
one wall-mounted oven	7 kW
one wall-mounted oven	6 kW
Total	21 kW

The maximum demand from Column A of Table 220-19 for one range not over 12 kW is 8 kW.

21 kW is less than 27 kW and exceeds 12 kW by 9 kW (see Note 1). The maximum demand in Column A (8 kW) is to be increased 5 percent for each additional kW exceeding 12 kW (9 kW).

$$5 \text{ percent} \times 8 \text{ kW} = 0.40 \text{ kW}$$
$$0.40 \text{ kW} \times 9 \text{ percent} = 3.6 \text{ kW increase}$$
$$8 \text{ kW} + 3.6 \text{ kW} = 11.6 \text{ kW load}$$
$$11,600 \text{ watts} = 11,600 \text{ volt-amperes} \div 240 \text{ V} = 48.3 \text{ A}$$

Note 5.   This table also applies to household cooking appliances rated over 1¾ kW and used in instructional programs.

(FPN): See Table 220-20 for commercial cooking equipment.

(FPN): See Examples, Chapter 9.

220-20. Kitchen Equipment — Other than Dwelling Unit(s). It shall be permissible to compute the load for commercial electric cooking equipment, dishwasher booster heaters, water heaters, and other kitchen equipment in accordance with Table 220-20. These demand factors shall be applied to all equipment which has either thermostatic control or intermittent use as kitchen equipment. They shall not apply to space heating, ventilating or air-conditioning equipment.

Table 220-20
Feeder Demand Factors for Kitchen Equipment — Other than Dwelling Unit(s)

Number of Units of Equipment	Demand Factors Percent
1	100
2	100
3	90
4	80
5	70
6 & over	65

However, in no case shall the feeder demand be less than the sum of the largest two kitchen equipment loads.

220-21. Noncoincident Loads. Where it is unlikely that two dissimilar loads will be in use simultaneously, it shall be permissible to omit the smaller of the two in computing the total load of a feeder.

220-22. Feeder Neutral Load. The feeder neutral load shall be the maximum unbalance of the load determined by this article. The maximum unbalanced load shall be the maximum net computed load between the neutral and any one ungrounded conductor, except that the load thus obtained shall be multiplied by 140 percent for 5-wire, 2-phase systems. For a feeder supplying household electric ranges, wall-mounted ovens, counter-mounted cooking units, and electric dryers the maximum unbalanced load shall be considered as 70 percent of the load on the ungrounded conductors, as determined in accordance with Table 220-19 for ranges and Table 220-18 for dryers. For 3-wire dc or single-phase ac, 4-wire, 3-phase, and 5-wire, 2-phase systems, a further demand factor of 70 percent shall be permitted for that portion of the unbalanced load in excess of 200 amperes. There shall be no reduction of the neutral capacity for that portion of the load which consists of electric-discharge lighting.

(FPN): See Examples 1(a), 1(b), 2(b), 4, and 5(a), Chapter 9.

Section 220-22 of the *Code* describes the basis for calculating the neutral load as the maximum unbalanced load that can occur between the neutral and any other ungrounded conductor. In the 1984 *NEC*, electric dryers (such as electric clothes dryers) were added as introducing a neutral load of 70 percent of the load on ungrounded conductors.

For a household electric range or clothes dryer, the maximum unbalanced load may be assumed at 70 percent so the neutral may be sized on this basis. Section 250-60 of the *Code* allows the grounded circuit conductor of not less than No. 10 AWG to ground the frame of a range, except for ranges in mobile homes and travel trailers. The supply cable to the range or electric clothes dryer may be service-entrance cable with an uninsulated grounded conductor, if the branch circuit originates at the service equipment. If the range or dryer is supplied with a three-conductor branch circuit, a receptacle and attachment plug, if used, may be of the three-pole type without an equipment ground. If nonmetallic-sheathed cable is used to supply the range, the conductor provided for equipment grounding purposes cannot be used for the grounded circuit conductor, as stated in Section 336-2.

Where the system supplies electric discharge lighting, such as fluorescent or HID, the neutral is considered to be a current-carrying conductor if the electric discharge lighting load on the feeder neutral consists of more than half of the total load. Electric discharge lighting will have harmonic current in the neutral which may approximate the load current, and it would be appropriate to require a full-size feeder neutral conductor.

C. Optional Calculations for Computing Feeder and Service Loads

220-30. Optional Calculation — Dwelling Unit.

(a) Feeder and Service Load. For a dwelling unit having the total connected load served by a single 3-wire, 120/240-volt or 208Y/120-volt set of service-entrance or feeder conductors with an ampacity of 100 or greater, it shall be permissible to compute the feeder and service loads in accordance with Table 220-30 instead of the method specified in Part B of this article. Feeder and service-entrance conductors whose demand load is determined by this optional calculation shall be permitted to have the neutral load determined by Section 220-22.

The optional method given in Section 220-30 is applicable to a single-dwelling unit, whether it is a separate building or located in a multifamily dwelling. The optional calculation permitted by Section 220-30 may be used only where the service-entrance or feeder conductors have an ampacity of at least 100 amperes.

Examples of the optional calculation for a dwelling unit are given in Chapter 9, Example Nos. 2(a), 2(b), and 4(b).

See Article 100 for definition of "Dwelling Unit."

(b) Loads. The loads identified in Table 220-30 as "other load" and as "remainder of other load" shall include the following:

(1) 1500 volt-amperes for each 2-wire, 20-ampere small appliance branch circuit and each laundry branch circuit specified in Section 220-16.

(2) 3 volt-amperes per square foot (0.093 sq m) for general lighting and general-use receptacles.

(3) The nameplate rating of all fastened in place appliances, ranges, wall-mounted ovens, and counter-top cooking units.

(4) The nameplate ampere or kVA rating of all motors and of all low-power-factor loads.

Table 220-30
Optional Calculation for Dwelling Unit
Load in kVA

Largest of the following four selections.

(1) 100 percent of the nameplate rating(s) of the air conditioning and cooling, including heat pump compressors.

(2) 65 percent of the nameplate rating(s) of the central electric space heating including integral supplemental heating in heat pumps.

(3) 65 percent of the nameplate rating(s) of electric space heating if less than four separately controlled units.

(4) 40 percent of the nameplate rating(s) of electric space heating of four or more separately controlled units.

Plus: 100 percent of the first 10 kVA of all other load. 40 percent of the remainder of all other load.

Section 220-21 states that when considering noncoincident loads you are to use the largest of those being considered. While the air-conditioning load is considered at 100 percent, the central electric space heating load is considered at 65 percent including supplemental heaters. If the air-conditioning equipment is also a heat pump, it is added to the heating load at 100 percent.

220-31. Optional Calculation for Additional Loads in Existing Dwelling Unit. For an existing dwelling unit presently being served by an existing 120/240 volt or 208Y/120, 3-wire service, it shall be permissible to compute load calculations as follows:

Load (in kVA)	Percent of Load
First 8 kVA of load at	100%
Remainder of load at	40%

Load calculation shall include lighting at 3 volt-amperes per square foot (0.093 sq m); 1500 volt-amperes for each 20-ampere appliance circuit; range or wall-mounted oven and counter-mounted cooking unit, and other appliances that are permanently connected or fastened in place, at nameplate rating.

If air-conditioning equipment or electric space heating equipment is to be installed the following formula shall be applied to determine if the existing service is of sufficient size.

Air-conditioning equipment* 100%
Central electric space heating* 100%
Less than four separately controlled space heating units* 100%
First 8 kVA of all other load 100%
Remainder of all other load 40%

Other loads shall include:

1500 volt-amperes for each 20-ampere appliance circuit.

Lighting and portable appliances at 3 volt-amperes per square foot (0.093 sq m)

Household range or wall-mounted oven and counter-mounted cooking unit.

All other appliances fastened in place, including four or more separately controlled space heating units, at nameplate rating.

* Use larger connected load of air conditioning and space heating, but not both.

This optional method allows an additional load to be supplied by an existing service.

Example: An existing dwelling unit is served by a 100-A service. An additional load of 5 kVA, 240-V air conditioning is to be installed. The existing load consists of the following:

general lighting 24 ft × 40 ft = 960 sq ft × 3 VA/sq ft	=	2880 VA
small appliance circuits 3 × 1500 VA	=	4500 VA
laundry circuit at 1500 VA	=	1500 VA
electric range rated 10.5 kW	=	10,500 VA
electric water heater rated 3.0 kW	=	3000 VA
existing other load		
	Total	22,380

Computation of existing load plus additional load		
air conditioning 5 kVA at 100%	=	5000 VA
first 8 kVA of all other load at 100%	=	8000 VA
remainder of other load at 40%		
22,380 − 8000 = 14,380 × 0.40	=	5752 VA
	Total	18,752 VA

18,752 ÷ 240 = 78.1 amperes

The additional load contributed by the 5 kVA air conditioning does not exceed the allowable load permitted on a 100-A service.

220-32. Optional Calculation — Multifamily Dwelling.

(a) Feeder or Service Load. It shall be permissible to compute the feeder or service load of a multifamily dwelling in accordance with Table 220-32 instead of Part B of this article where all the following conditions are met:

(1) No dwelling unit is supplied by more than one feeder.

(2) Each dwelling unit is equipped with electric cooking equipment.

It should be recognized that the method of calculation of load under Section 220-32 is optional and only applies where one feeder supplies all of the load of a dwelling unit and has the other limitations that are intended to provide appropriate diversity. It should be understood that where all of the stated conditions prevail, it is intended that the optional calculations in Section 220-32 may be used instead of those in Part B of Article 220 and this is stated in paragraph (a).

ARTICLE 220—BRANCH-CIRCUIT AND FEEDER CALCULATIONS

Exception: When the computed load for multifamily dwellings without electric cooking in Part B of this article exceeds that computed under Part C for the identical load plus electric cooking (based on 8 kW per unit), the lesser of the two loads may be used.

Section 220-32(a)(2) requires each dwelling unit to be equipped with electric cooking in order to use this method of calculation. This exception permits calculation under this section for dwelling units which do not have electric cooking.

(3) Each dwelling unit is equipped with either electric space heating or air conditioning or both.

Feeders and service-entrance conductors whose demand load is determined by this optional calculation shall be permitted to have the neutral load determined by Section 220-22.

(b) House Loads. House loads shall be computed in accordance with Part B of this article and shall be in addition to the dwelling unit loads computed in accordance with Table 220-32.

(c) Connected Loads. The connected load to which the demand factors of Table 220-32 apply shall include the following:

(1) 1500 volt-amperes for each 2-wire, 20-ampere small appliance branch circuit and each laundry branch circuit specified in Section 220-16.

(2) 3 volt-amperes per square foot (0.093 sq m) for general lighting and general-use receptacles.

(3) The nameplate rating of all appliances that are fastened in place, permanently connected or located to be on a specific circuit, ranges, wall-mounted ovens, counter-mounted cooking units, clothes dryers, water heaters, and space heaters.

Table 220-32
Optional Calculation — Demand Factors for Three or More Multifamily Dwelling Units

Number of Dwelling Units	Demand Factor Percent
3–5	45
6–7	44
8–10	43
11	42
12–13	41
14–15	40
16–17	39
18–20	38
21	37
22–23	36
24–25	35
26–27	34
28–30	33
31	32
32–33	31
34–36	30
37–38	29
39–42	28
43–45	27
46–50	26
51–55	25
56–61	24
62 & over	23

If water heater elements are so interlocked that all elements cannot be used at the same time, the maximum possible load shall be considered the nameplate load.

(4) The nameplate ampere or kVA rating of all motors and of all low-power-factor loads.

(5) The larger of the air-conditioning load or the space heating load.

220-33. Optional Calculation — Two Dwelling Units. Where two dwelling units are supplied by a single feeder and the computed load under Part B of this article exceeds that for three identical units computed under Section 220-32, the lesser of the two loads shall be permitted to be used.

220-34. Optional Method — Schools. The calculation of a feeder or service load for schools shall be permitted in accordance with Table 220-34 in lieu of Part B of this article where equipped with electric space heating, or air conditioning, or both. The connected load to which the demand factors of Table 220-34 apply shall include all of the interior and exterior lighting, power, water heating, cooking, other loads, and the larger of the air-conditioning load or space heating load within the building or structure.

Feeders and service-entrance conductors whose demand load is determined by this optional calculation shall be permitted to have the neutral load determined by Section 220-22. Where the building or structure load is calculated by this optional method, feeders within the building or structure shall have ampacity as permitted in Part B of this article; however, the ampacity of an individual feeder need not be larger than the ampacity for the entire building.

This section shall not apply to portable classroom buildings.

Many schools add small portable classroom buildings. The air-conditioning load is to comply with Article 440 and the lighting load is to be considered as continuous. To allow the demand factors of Table 220-34 to be applied to a portable classroom would decrease the feeder or service size to below that required for the connected continuous load.

Table 220-34

**Optional Method — Demand Factors for Feeders
and Service-Entrance Conductors for Schools**

Connected Load Volt-Amperes per Square Foot	Demand Factors Percent
Connected load up to and including 3, plus	100
Connected load over 3 and including 20, plus	75
Connected load over 20 at	25

For SI units: one square foot = 0.093 square meter.

220-35. Optional Calculations for Additional Loads to Existing Installations. For the purpose of allowing additional loads to be connected to existing feeders and services, it shall be permitted to use actual maximum kVA demand figures to determine the existing load on a service or feeder when all the following conditions are met:

(1) The maximum demand data is available in kVA for a minimum of a one-year period.

(2) The existing demand at 125 percent plus the new load does not exceed the ampacity of the feeder or rating of the service.

(3) The feeder or service has overcurrent protection in accordance with Sections 230-90 and 240-3.

ARTICLE 220—BRANCH-CIRCUIT AND FEEDER CALCULATIONS

Where existing installations have been checked and the maximum demand kVA data for a minimum of a one-year period is available and the installation complies with (2) and (3), it is to be permitted to connect additional loads to existing services and feeders.

D. Method for Computing Farm Loads

220-40. Farm Loads — Buildings and Other Loads.

(a) Dwelling Unit. The feeder or service load of a farm dwelling unit shall be computed in accordance with the provisions for dwellings in Part B or C of this article.

(b) Other than Dwelling Unit. For each farm building or load supplied by two or more branch circuits the load for feeders, service-entrance conductors, and service equipment shall be computed in accordance with demand factors not less than indicated in Table 220-40.

(FPN): See Section 230-21 for overhead conductors from a pole to a building or other structure.

Section 230-21 requires such overhead conductors to be considered as a service drop and installed accordingly.

Table 220-40
Method for Computing Farm Loads for Other Than Dwelling Unit

Ampere Load at 240 Volts	Demand Factor Percent
Loads expected to operate without diversity, but not less than 125 percent full-load current of the largest motor and not less than the first 60 amperes of load	100
Next 60 amperes of all other loads	50
Remainder of other load	25

220-41. Farm Loads — Total.
The total load of the farm for service-entrance conductors and service equipment shall be computed in accordance with the farm dwelling unit load and demand factors specified in Table 220-41. Where there is equipment in two or more farm equipment buildings or for loads having the same function, such loads shall be computed in accordance with Table 220-40 and may be combined as a single load in Table 220-41 for computing the total load.

(FPN): See Section 230-21 for overhead conductors from a pole to a building or other structure.

Table 220-41
Method for Computing Total Farm Load

Individual Loads Computed in Accordance with Table 220-40	Demand Factor Percent
Largest load	100
Second largest load	75
Third largest load	65
Remaining loads	50

To this total load, add the load of the farm dwelling unit computed in accordance with Part B or C of this article.

ARTICLE 225 — OUTSIDE BRANCH CIRCUITS AND FEEDERS

Contents

225-1. Scope. This article covers electric equipment and wiring for the supply of utilization equipment located on or attached to the outside of public and private buildings, or run between buildings, other structures or poles on other premises served.

Exception: See Section 668-3(c), Exceptions No. 1 and No. 4 for electrolytic cells.

(FPN): For additional information on wiring over 600 volts, see the National Electrical Safety Code (ANSI C2-1981).

225-2. Other Articles. Application of other articles, including additional requirements to specific cases of equipment and conductors, is as follows:

	Article
Branch Circuits	210
Class 1, Class 2, and Class 3 Remote Control, Signaling, and Power-Limited Circuits	725
Communication Circuits	800
Community Antenna Television and Radio Distribution Systems	820
Conductors	310
Electrically Driven or Controlled Irrigation Machines	675
Electric Signs and Outline Lighting	600
Feeders	215

ARTICLE 225—OUTSIDE BRANCH CIRCUITS AND FEEDERS

225-3. Calculation of Load.

(a) Branch Circuits. The load on outdoor branch circuits shall be as determined by Section 220-2.

(b) Feeders. The load on outdoor feeders shall be as determined by Part B of Article 220.

225-4. Conductor Covering. Where within 10 feet (3.05 m) of any building or other structure, open wiring on insulators shall be insulated or covered. Conductors in cables or raceways, except Type MI cable, shall be of the rubber-covered type or thermoplastic type and in wet locations shall comply with Section 310-8. Conductors for festoon lighting shall be of the rubber-covered or thermoplastic type.

225-5. Size of Conductors. The ampacity of outdoor branch-circuit and feeder conductors shall be in accordance with Tables 310-16 through 310-19 based on loads as determined under Section 220-2 and Part B of Article 220.

225-6. Minimum Size of Conductor.

(a) Overhead Spans. Overhead conductors shall not be smaller than the following:

(1) For 600 volts, nominal, or less, No. 10 copper or No. 8 aluminum for spans up to 50 feet (15.2 m) in length and No. 8 copper or No. 6 aluminum for a longer span.

(2) For over 600 volts, nominal, No. 6 copper or No. 4 aluminum where open individual conductors and No. 8 copper or No. 6 aluminum where in cable.

The size limitation of copper or aluminum conductors is based upon an adequate mechanical strength. See Figure 225-1.

(b) Festoon Lighting. Overhead conductors for festoon lighting shall not be smaller than No. 12.

Exception: Where supported by messenger wires.

(FPN): See Section 225-24 for outdoor lampholders.

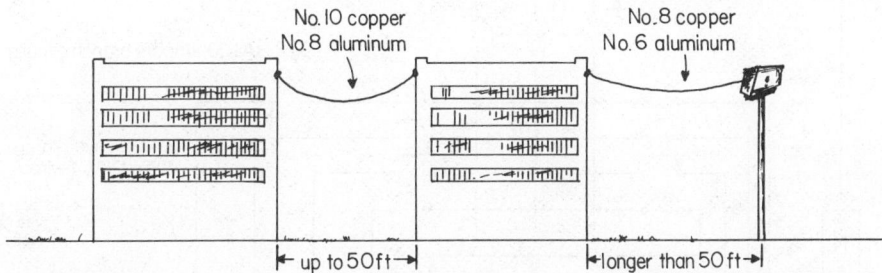

Figure 225-1. Overhead spans run between buildings, structures, or poles for 600 V or less.

Definition: Festoon lighting is a string of outdoor lights suspended between two points more than 15 feet (4.57 m) apart.

See Figure 225-5.

225-7. Lighting Equipment on Poles or Other Structures.

(a) **General.** For the supply of lighting equipment installed on a single pole or structure, the branch circuits shall comply with Article 210 and (c) below.

(b) **Common Neutral.** It shall be permissible to use a multiwire branch circuit consisting of the neutral and not more than eight ungrounded conductors. The ampacity of the neutral conductor shall not be less than the calculated sum of the currents in all ungrounded conductors connected to any one phase of the circuit.

See Figures 225-2 and 225-3.

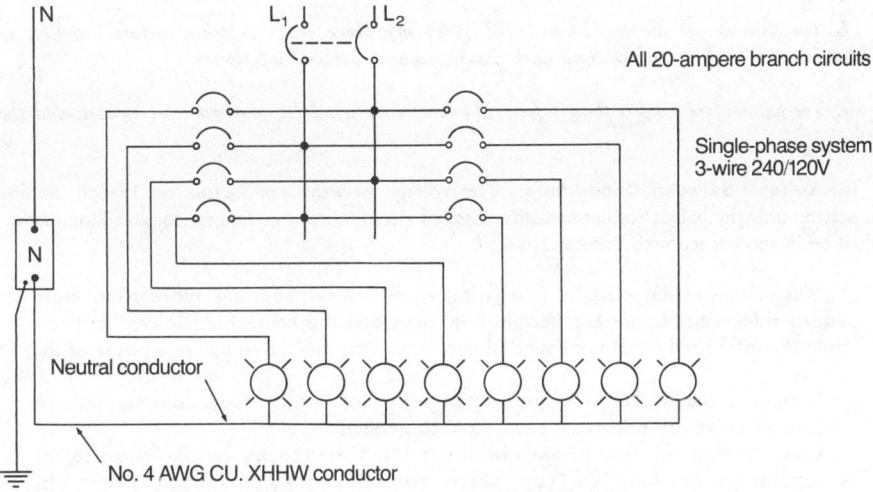

Figure 225-2. The maximum unbalance current that can occur will be four times 20 A which is 80 A.

113

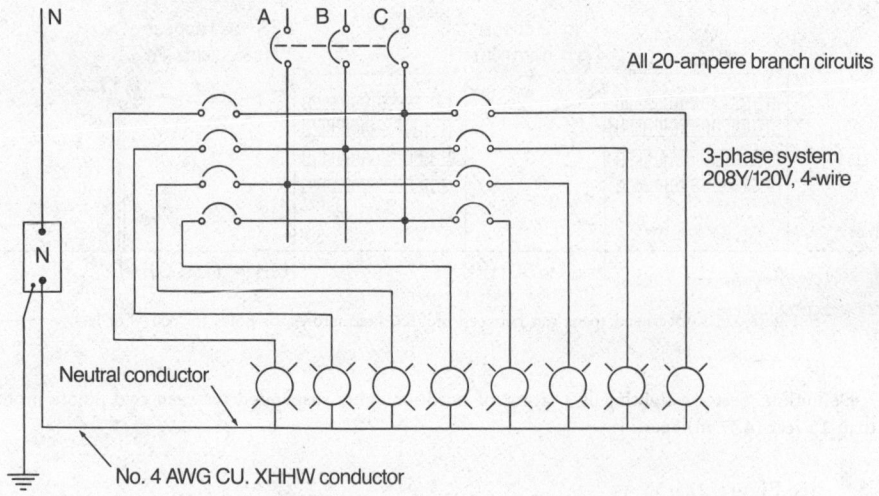

All 20-ampere branch circuits

3-phase system
208Y/120V, 4-wire

Neutral conductor

No. 4 AWG CU. XHHW conductor

Figure 225-3. The maximum unbalance current that can occur on a 3-phase system with the load connected as shown will be 80 A due to the load on phase C.

(c) Voltage to Ground. Branch circuits supplying lampholders or lighting fixtures mounted on the outside of buildings or on poles or structures for area illumination of residential, commercial, or industrial property shall not exceed 150 volts to ground.

Exception: The voltage shall not exceed 300 volts to ground on branch circuits supplying lighting fixtures for illumination of outdoor areas of industrial establishments, office buildings, schools, stores, and other commercial or public buildings where all of the following conditions are met:

a. The fixtures are mounted on the outside of buildings or out-of-doors on poles or other structures.

b. The fixtures are not less than 8 feet (2.44 m) above grade or other surface accessible to individuals other than those charged with fixture maintenance and supervision.

c. The fixtures are not less than 3 feet (914 mm) from windows, platforms, fire escapes, and the like.

(d) Voltage Between Conductors. The voltage between conductors on branch circuits supplying only the ballast for permanently installed electric-discharge fixtures for area illumination shall be in accordance with Section 210-6(b).

Multiwire branch circuits consisting of a neutral and not more than eight ungrounded conductors are permissible, provided the neutral capacity is not less than the total load of all ungrounded conductors connected to any one phase of the circuit.

Branch circuits for outdoor illumination of residential, commercial, or industrial areas are not to exceed 150 V to ground.

Exceptions to the rule of not exceeding 150 V to ground can be found in the exception to Section 225-7(c) which allows 300 V to ground where the installation requirements of the exception are met and, also, Section 225-7(d) which allows 600 V between branch-circuit conductors mounted at the heights required by Section 210-6(b) and supplying only the ballasts of electric-discharge lamps.

Operating a 120-V circuit at approximately 10 percent over voltage will provide increased light intensity. Many designers of outdoor light installations on poles, however, prefer a nominal 10 percent under voltage (130-V rated lamps on nominal 120-V circuits) thereby decreasing the light intensity, prolonging the life of the lamps, and minimizing pole lamp maintenance, which can be difficult, because longer periods of time elapse between relamping.

225-8. Disconnection. The disconnecting means for branch-circuit and feeder fuses shall be in accordance with Section 240-40.

225-9. Overcurrent Protection. Overcurrent protection shall be in accordance with Section 210-20 for branch circuits and Part A of Article 240 for feeders.

225-10. Wiring on Buildings. The installation of outside wiring on surfaces of buildings shall be permitted for circuits of not over 600 volts, nominal, as open wiring on insulators, as multiconductor cable, as Type MC cable, as Type MI cable, in rigid metal conduit, in intermediate metal conduit, in rigid nonmetallic conduit as provided in Section 347-2, in busways as provided in Article 364, or in electrical metallic tubing. Circuits of over 600 volts, nominal, shall be installed as provided for services in Section 230-202. Circuits for sign and outline lighting shall be installed in accordance with Article 600.

225-11. Circuit Exits and Entrances. Where outside branch and feeder circuits leave or enter a building, the requirements of Sections 230-43, 230-52, and 230-54 shall apply.

See Figure 225-4.

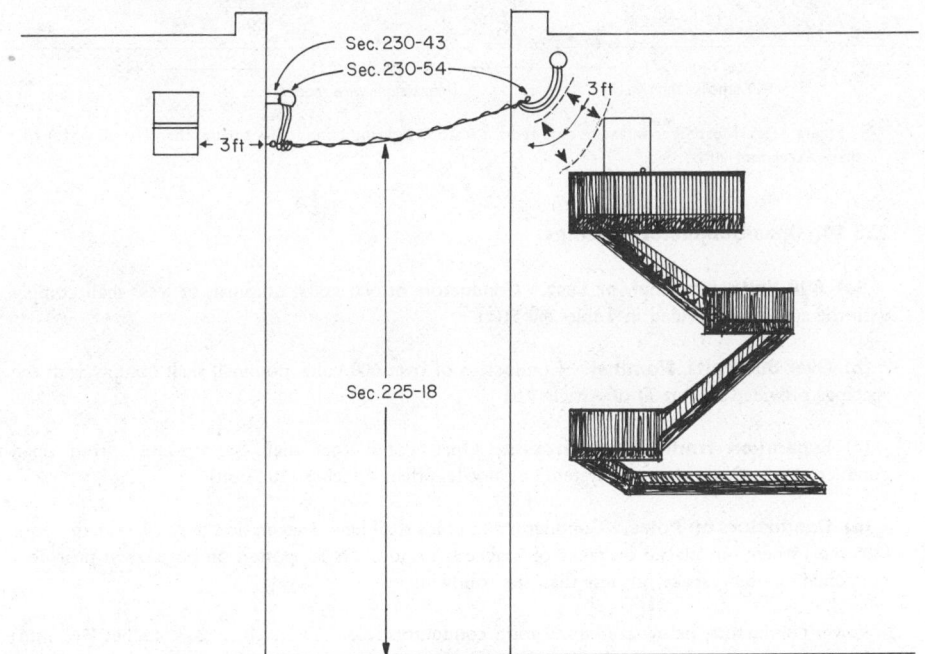

Figure 225-4. Section 225-11 references Sections 230-43 (wiring methods) and 230-54 (weather service heads, points of attachment, and drip loops). Section 225-18 covers the requirements for clearances from ground (not over 600 V), and Section 225-19 covers the requirements for clearances from buildings (not over 600 V). See Section 225-19(d) for clearances from windows, doors, fire escapes, etc.

ARTICLE 225—OUTSIDE BRANCH CIRCUITS AND FEEDERS

225-12. Open-Conductor Supports. Open conductors shall be supported on glass or porcelain-knobs, racks, brackets, or strain insulators.

225-13. Festoon Supports. In spans exceeding 40 feet (12.2 m), the conductors shall be supported by a messenger wire; and the messenger wire shall be supported by strain insulators. Conductors or messenger wires shall not be attached to any fire escape, downspout, or plumbing equipment.

Festoon lighting consists of a string of outdoor lights suspended between two points more than 15 ft apart. The conductors are not to be smaller than No. 12 unless they are supported by a messenger wire. On all spans of festoon lighting exceeding 40 ft, messenger wire is required and is to be supported by strain insulators. Where no messenger wire is required, the No. 12 or larger conductors are to be supported by strain insulators. See Figure 225-3.

Attachment to fire escapes, plumbing equipment, or drainspouts is prohibited since they could provide a path to ground. Moreover, such methods of attachment could not be relied upon for permanent or secure means of support.

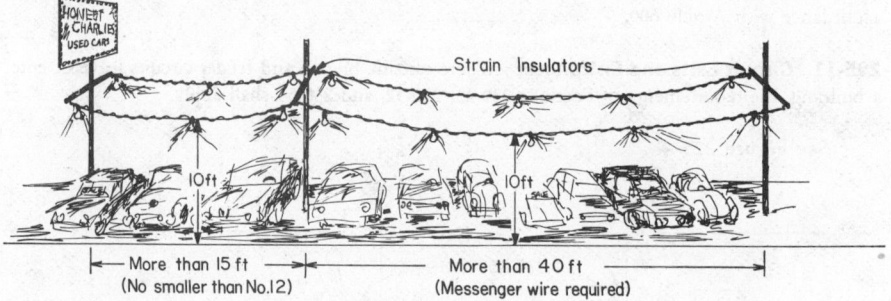

Figure 225-5. Messenger wires are required for festoon lighting conductors smaller than No. 12 or for spans exceeding 40 ft.

225-14. Open-Conductor Spacings.

(a) 600 Volts, Nominal, or Less. Conductors of 600 volts, nominal, or less, shall comply with the spacings provided in Table 230-51(c).

(b) Over 600 Volts, Nominal. Conductors of over 600 volts, nominal, shall comply with the spacings provided in Part D of Article 710.

(c) Separation from Other Circuits. Open conductors shall be separated from open conductors of other circuits or systems by not less than 4 inches (102 mm).

(d) Conductors on Poles. Conductors on poles shall have a separation of not less than 1 foot (305 mm) where not placed on racks or brackets. Conductors supported on poles shall provide a horizontal climbing space not less than the following:

Power conductors, below communication conductors .... 30 inches (762 mm)
Power conductors alone or above communication conductors:
    300 volts or less .... 24 inches (610 mm)
    Over 300 volts .... 30 inches (762 mm)
Communication conductors below power
    conductors .... same as power conductors
Communication conductors alone .... no requirement

Ample space is required to enable linemen to climb over or through conductors to safely service conductors on the pole.

225-15. Supports Over Buildings. Supports over a building shall be in accordance with Section 230-29.

225-16. Point of Attachment to Buildings. The point of attachment to a building shall be in accordance with Section 230-26.

225-17. Means of Attachment to Buildings. The means of attachment to a building shall be in accordance with Section 230-27.

225-18. Clearance from Ground. Open conductors of not over 600 volts, nominal, shall conform to the following:

10 feet (3.05 m) — above finished grade, sidewalks, or from any platform or projection from which they might be reached where the supply conductors are limited to 150 volts to ground and accessible to pedestrians only.

12 feet (3.66 m) — for those areas listed in the 15-foot (4.57-m) classification when the voltage is limited to 300 volts to ground.

15 feet (4.57 m) — over residential property and driveways, and those commercial areas not subject to truck traffic.

18 feet (5.49 m) — over public streets, alleys, roads, parking areas subject to truck traffic, driveways on other than residential property, and other land traversed by vehicles such as cultivated, grazing, forest, and orchard.

The clearances from ground, as given, coordinate with the National Electrical Safety Code. See Section 230-24 and Figure 225-4.

(FPN): Note: For clearances of conductors of over 600 volts, see National Electrical Safety Code (ANSI C2-1981).

225-19. Clearances from Buildings for Conductors of Not Over 600 Volts, Nominal.

(a) Above Roofs. Conductors not fully insulated for the operating voltage shall have a vertical or diagonal clearance of not less than 10 feet (3.05 m) from the roof surface.

Exception No. 1: Fully insulated conductors shall be permitted to have vertical or diagonal clearance of 3 feet (914 mm) or more.

Exception No. 2: Above roof space accessible to pedestrians. Vertical clearance shall be not less than 15 feet (4.57 m) for uninsulated, 8 feet (2.44 m) for insulated conductors.

Exception No. 3: Above roof space accessible to vehicular traffic, vertical clearance shall be not less than 18 feet (5.49 m).

Exception No. 4: Where the voltage between conductors does not exceed 300 and the roof has a slope of not less than 4 inches (102 mm) in 12 inches (305 mm), a reduction in clearance to 3 feet (914 mm) shall be permitted.

Exception No. 5: Where the voltage between conductors does not exceed 300, a reduction in clearance above only the overhanging portion of the roof to not less than 18 inches (457 mm) shall be permitted if (1) not more than 4 feet (1.22 m) of the conductors pass above the roof overhang, and (2) they are terminated at a through-the-roof raceway or approved support.

(b) From Nonbuilding or Nonbridge Structures. From signs, chimneys, radio and television antennas, tanks, other nonbuilding or nonbridge structures, clearances, vertical, diagonal and horizontal, shall be not less than 5 feet (1.52 m) for uninsulated conductors, 3 feet (914 mm) for insulated conductors.

(c) **Horizontal Clearances.** Clearances shall be not less than 5 feet (1.52 m) for uninsulated conductors, 3 feet (914 mm) for insulated conductors.

(d) **Final Spans.** Final spans of feeders or branch circuits to a building they supply or from which they are fed shall be permitted to be attached to the building, but they shall be kept 3 feet (914 mm) from windows, doors, porches, fire escapes, or similar locations.

Exception: Conductors run above the top level of a window shall be permitted to be less than the 3 feet (914 mm) requirement above.

See Figure 225-4.

(e) **Zone for Fire Ladders.** Where buildings exceed three stories or 50 feet (15.2 m) in height, overhead lines shall be arranged, where practicable, so that a clear space (or zone) at least 6 feet (1.83 m) wide will be left either adjacent to the buildings or beginning not over 8 feet (2.44 m) from them to facilitate the raising of ladders when necessary for fire fighting.

(FPN): Note: For clearance of conductors over 600 volts, see National Electrical Safety Code (ANSI C2-1981).

225-20. Mechanical Protection of Conductors. Mechanical protection of conductors on buildings, structures, or poles shall be as provided for services in Section 230-50.

225-21. Multiconductor Cables on Exterior Surfaces of Buildings. Multiconductor cables on exterior surfaces of buildings shall be as provided for service cable in Section 230-51.

225-22. Raceways on Exterior Surfaces of Buildings. Raceways on exterior surfaces of buildings shall be made raintight and suitably drained.

Raintight is defined as "so constructed or protected that exposure to a beating rain will not result in the entrance of water." To assure this, all conduit bodies, fittings, and boxes used in wet locations are to be provided with threaded hubs or other approved means. Threadless couplings and connectors used with metal conduit or electrical metallic tubing are required to be of the raintight type (see Sections 345-9, 346-9, and 348-8).

Where exposed to weather or rain through weatherhead openings, condensation is likely to occur, causing moisture to accumulate within raceways at low points of the installation and in junction boxes. Raceways should thus be installed to permit drainage through drain holes at appropriate locations.

225-23. Underground Circuits. Underground circuits shall meet the requirements of Section 300-5.

225-24. Outdoor Lampholders. Where outdoor lampholders are attached as pendants, the connections to the circuit wires shall be staggered. Where such lampholders have terminals of a type that puncture the insulation and make contact with the conductors, they shall be attached only to conductors of the stranded type.

Splices to branch-circuit conductors for outdoor lampholders of the Edison-base type or "pig-tail sockets" are to be staggered so as not to place splices in close proximity to each other.

"Pin-type" terminal sockets are to be attached to stranded conductors only and are intended for installations for temporary lighting or decorations, signs, or specifically approved applications. See Figure 225-6.

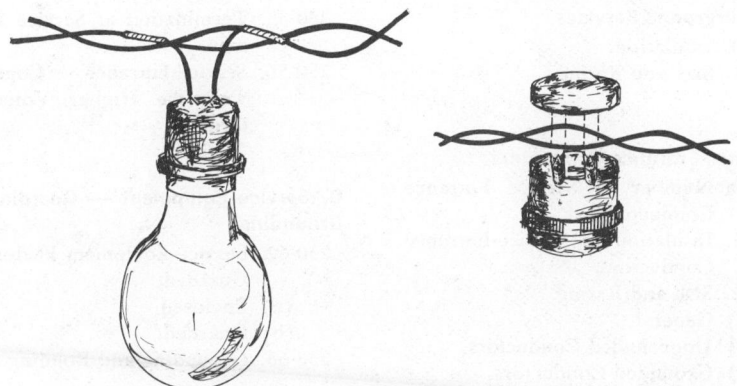

Figure 225-6. Outdoor lampholders attached as pendants showing staggered connections and pin- or puncture-type for use with standard conductors.

225-25. Location of Outdoor Lamps. Locations of lamps for outdoor lighting shall be below all live conductors, transformers, or other electric equipment.

Exception No. 1: Where clearances or other safeguards are provided for relamping operations.

Exception No. 2: Where equipment is controlled by a disconnecting means that can be locked in the open position.

Since Section 225-18 requires a minimum clearance for open conductors of 10 ft above grade or platforms, it would be difficult to keep all electrical equipment above the lamps. Exception No. 1, therefore, allows other clearances or safeguards to permit safe relamping, and Exception No. 2 permits the use of a disconnecting means to de-energize the circuit. It may be assumed that metal raceways would not be considered as "other electrical equipment," according to this section.

ARTICLE 230 — SERVICES

Contents

ARTICLE 230—SERVICES

A. General

230-1. Scope. This article covers service conductors and equipment for control and protection of services; the number, types, and sizes of services and service equipment; and the installation requirements.

230-2. Number of Services. A building or other structure served shall be supplied by only one service.

Where more than one service is permitted by any of the following exceptions, a permanent plaque or directory shall be installed at each service drop or lateral or at each service-equipment location denoting all other services on or in that building or structure and the area served by each.

    The basic requirement of this section is that a building or other structure can be supplied by only one service. A permanent plaque or directory is required to be installed at each service drop or lateral or at each service-equipment location denoting all of the other services on or in that building or structure and the area served by each. This plaque or directory should be constructed of sufficient durability to withstand the environment where it is located. See Figure 230-1.

ARTICLE 230—SERVICES

The service disconnecting means for each service or for each set of service-entrance conductors permitted by Section 230-2, Exception No. 3 shall consist of not more than six switches or six circuit breakers, at any one location, mounted in a single enclosure, in a group of separate enclosures, or in or on a switchboard. See Sections 230-71 and 230-72.

The *Code* permits a separate service for each occupancy in multiple-occupancy buildings, provided the service-entrance conductors are installed outside of the building, or encased in concrete, to a point where the conductors enter the individual occupancy. See Section 230-44 and Figure 230-9.

Exception No. 1: For fire pumps where a separate service is required.

Exception No. 2: For emergency, legally required standby, optional standby, or parallel power production systems where a separate service is required.

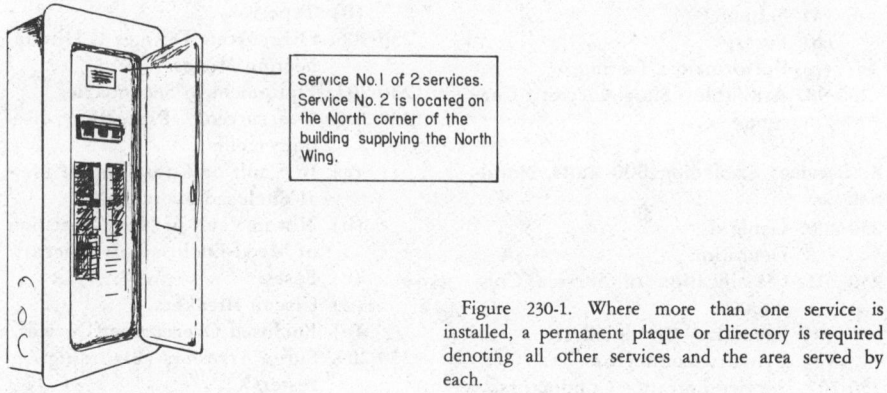

Service No.1 of 2 services. Service No. 2 is located on the North corner of the building supplying the North Wing.

Figure 230-1. Where more than one service is installed, a permanent plaque or directory is required denoting all other services and the area served by each.

Exception No. 3: Multiple-Occupancy Buildings. By special permission, in multiple-occupancy buildings where there is no available space for service equipment accessible to all the occupants.

Exception No. 4: Capacity Requirements. Two or more services shall be permitted:

a. Where the capacity requirements are in excess of 3000 amperes at a supply voltage of 600 volts or less; or

b. Where the load requirements of a single-phase installation are greater than the serving agency normally supplies through one service; or

c. By special permission.

Exception No. 5: Buildings of Large Area. By special permission, for a single building or other structure sufficiently large to make two or more services necessary.

Exception No. 6: For different characteristics, such as for different voltages, frequencies, or phases, or for different uses, such as for different rate schedules.

Exception No. 7: For the purpose of Section 230-45 only, underground sets of conductors, size 1/0 and larger, running to the same location and connected together at their supply end but not connected together at their load end shall be considered to be one service lateral.

The basic rule is that a building or other structure is to be supplied by only one service. There are, however, several exceptions.

Exception Nos. 1 and 2 permit separate services where necessary for fire pumps (with one to six switches or circuit breakers) or emergency, legally required standby, optional standby electrical systems, or parallel power production systems (with one to six switches or circuit breakers) in addition to the regular building service (with one to six switches or circuit breakers). The intent here is that a disruption of the main building service should not disconnect fire pump equipment or emergency, legally required standby, optional standby, or parallel power production systems. Exception No. 2 was revised for the 1984 *Code* to permit a solar photovoltaic system as covered in (new) Article 690. See Section 230-72(b).

Exception No. 3 permits a separate service in multiple-occupancy buildings:

(a) By special permission [the written consent of the authority having jurisdiction (see Definitions, Article 100)], where there is no space available for service equipment accessible to all occupants as permitted by the exception to Section 240-24(b).

(b) Multiple-occupancy buildings are permitted to have service-entrance conductors run to each occupancy, but there is no requirement indicating that the service-entrance conductors must terminate within the individual occupancy. See Section 230-72(c).

Exception No. 4 permits two or more services where capacity requirements are in excess of 3,000 A, where supplied by 600 V or less, or for lesser loads by special permission.

Many electric power companies have specifications and have adopted special regulations covering certain types of electrical loads and service equipment that may be energized from their lines. It is advisable to consult with the serving utility to determine line capacities before designing electrical services for large buildings.

Exception No. 5 requires special permission for the installation of more than one service to a sufficiently large building. Expansion of buildings, shopping centers, or industrial plants would often necessitate the addition of two or more services. It would, for example, be impossible to install one service for an industrial plant with capacity requirements to compensate for any and all future load requirements. It is also impractical to run feeders extremely long distances due to high costs and voltage drop problems. Again, it is advisable to consult with the serving utility and the authority having jurisdiction before contemplating use of this exception.

Exception No. 6 allows the installation of more than one service for different characteristics, such as different voltages, frequencies, single-phase and 3-phase, or different utility rate schedules for different uses. For example, different service characteristics exist between a 3-wire, 120/240-V single-phase service and a 3-phase, 4-wire, 480Y/277-V service. For different uses, such as different rate schedules, it is intended to allow a second service for supplying a second meter for equipment such as an electric water heater on a different rate.

Exception No. 7 allows from two to six sets of service lateral conductors to serve up to six service disconnecting means, provided the service lateral conductors are 1/0 AWG or larger and are connected together at their supply end, which is normally at the transformer secondary terminals. This exception is included in the *Code* to increase the cable impedance by not paralleling the conductors, thereby lowering the available short-circuit current at the building. See Sections 110-9 and 110-10. Also, Exception No. 7 does not require that each set of service lateral conductors be of the same size, provided that each set of service lateral conductors are 1/0 AWG or larger. The Code-Making Panel added the word "lateral" to the 1984 *Code* at the end of Exception No. 7 for clarification. See Figure 230-2.

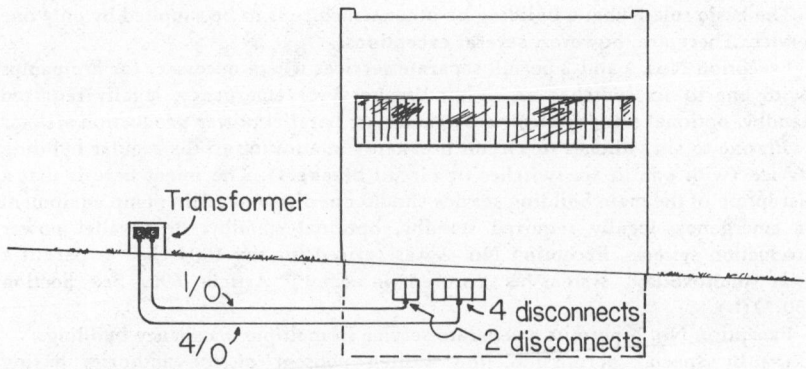

Figure 230-2. Illustrated are two sets of underground conductors, size 1/0 and larger (4/0), connected at their supply and running to the same location, not connected together at their supply end, and not more than six disconnects. It is permissible to run six such sets of conductors to six individual service disconnects.

230-3. One Building or Other Structure Not to Be Supplied Through Another. Service conductors supplying a building or other structure shall not pass through the interior of another building or other structure.

Exception: Where the buildings or other structures served are under single occupancy or management.

(FPN): See Section 230-44 for masonry-encased conductors considered outside of a building.

It is permissible for service conductors to be installed along the "exterior" of one building to supply another building. However, service conductors supplying a building are not to pass through the "interior" of a building *unless* the buildings being served are under a single occupancy or single management. Each building served in this manner is required to be provided with a disconnecting means for all ungrounded conductors as required by Section 230-84(a). See Figure 230-3.

Service-entrance conductors are considered to be outside of a building where they are installed beneath the building under not less than 2 in. of concrete or concealed in a raceway within the building and enclosed by not less than 2 in. of concrete or brick. See Section 230-44 and Figure 230-9.

Figure 230-3. Service conductors may pass through the interior of Building No. 1 to supply Building No. 2 where both buildings are under single occupancy or management. A disconnecting means suitable for use as service equipment is to be provided for each building. For overhead service conductors, it is common to run the service conductors along the outside of Building No. 1. See Figure 230-5.

B. Insulation and Size of Service Conductors

230-4. Insulation of Service Conductors. Service conductors shall normally withstand exposure to atmospheric and other conditions of use without detrimental leakage of current.

(FPN): For Service Drops — See Section 230-22.

(FPN): For Underground Services — See Section 230-30.

(FPN): For Service-Entrance Conductors — See Section 230-41.

230-5. Size of Service Conductors. Service conductors shall have adequate ampacity to conduct safely the current for the loads supplied without a temperature rise detrimental to the insulation or covering of the conductors, and shall have adequate mechanical strength.

(FPN): Minimum sizes are given in the following references:
For Service Drops — See Section 230-23.
For Underground Service Conductors — See Section 230-31.
For Service-Entrance Conductors — See Section 230-42.
For Farmstead Service Conductors — See Part D of Article 220.

C. Overhead Services

230-21. Overhead Supply. Overhead conductors to a building or other structure from another building or other structure (such as a pole) on which a meter or disconnecting means is installed shall be considered as a service drop and installed accordingly.

(FPN): Example: Farm loads in Part D of Article 220.

230-22. Insulation or Covering. Individual conductors shall be insulated or covered with an extruded thermoplastic or thermosetting insulating material.

The intent of this section is to prevent problems that are created by covered cable or covered open wiring, which over a period of years is subjected to weather, abrasion, and other deleterious effects that reduce the nonconductive properties of the covering.

Exception: The grounded conductor of a multiconductor cable shall be permitted to be bare.

(FPN): Service-drop conductors in cable or open wiring and covered with an extruded thermoplastic or thermosetting insulating material have an ampacity equal to that of bare conductors of the same size as listed in Table 310-19.

230-23. Size and Rating. Conductors shall have sufficient ampacity to carry the load. They shall have adequate mechanical strength and shall not be smaller than No. 8 copper, No. 6 aluminum or copper-clad aluminum.

Exception: For installations to supply only limited loads of a single branch circuit such as small polyphase power, controlled water heaters and the like, they shall not be smaller than No. 12 hard-drawn copper or equivalent.

The grounded conductor shall not be less than the minimum size required by Section 250-23(b).

230-24. Clearances. The vertical clearances of all service-drop conductors shall be based on conductor temperature of 60°F (15°C), no wind, with final unloaded sag in the wire, conductor, or cable.

Service-drop conductors shall not be readily accessible and shall comply with (a) through (d) below for services not over 600 volts, nominal.

(a) Above Roofs. Conductors shall have a vertical clearance of not less than 8 feet (2.44 m) from all points of roofs above which they pass.

Exception No. 1: Where the voltage between conductors does not exceed 300 and the roof has a slope of not less than 4 inches (102 mm) in 12 inches (305 mm), a reduction in clearance to 3 feet (914 mm) shall be permitted.

Service-drop conductors are not permitted to be readily accessible and, where passing over roofs and not over 600 V, are to have a clearance of 8 ft. Exception No. 1 permits a clearance of 3 ft where the voltage between conductors does not exceed 300 and the roof is sloped at not less than 4 in. in 12 in. It is difficult to walk upon a sloped roof of this angle or pitch. See Figure 230-4.

Exception No. 2: Where the voltage between conductors does not exceed 300, a reduction in clearance above only the overhanging portion of the roof to not less than 18 inches (457 mm) shall be permitted if (1) not more than 4 feet (1.22 m) of service-drop conductors pass above the roof overhang, and (2) they are terminated at a through-the-roof raceway or approved support.

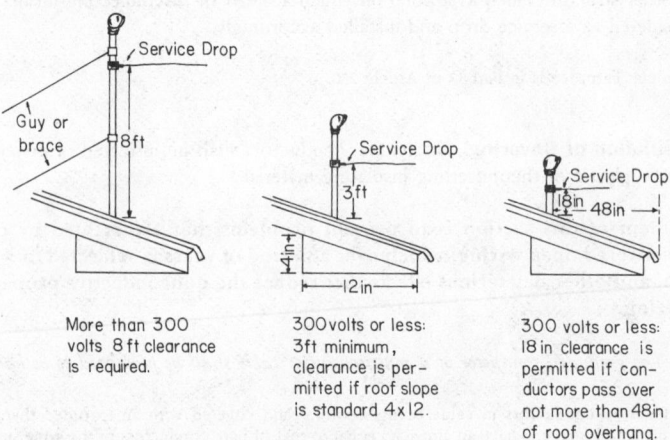

More than 300 volts 8 ft clearance is required.

300 volts or less: 3ft minimum, clearance is permitted if roof slope is standard 4x12.

300 volts or less: 18 in clearance is permitted if conductors pass over not more than 48in of roof overhang.

Figure 230-4. Clearances for service-drop conductors passing over the overhanging portion of a roof and minimum angle of roof slope permitting a 3-ft clearance for service-drop conductors.

(FPN): See Section 230-28 for mast supports.

A further reduction of service-drop conductor clearances to 18 in. is permitted by Exception No. 2 for service-mast (through-the-roof) installations where the voltage between conductors does not exceed 300 and the mast is located within 4 ft of the edge of the roof. See Figure 230-4. This exception applies to either sloped or flat roofs. Many electric utility companies will not permit a coupling between the service head and the point where a service raceway extends through the roof.

(b) Vertical Clearance from Ground. Service-drop conductors where not in excess of 600 volts, nominal, shall have the following minimum clearance from final grade.

10 feet (3.05 m) — at the electric service entrance to buildings, or at the drip loop of the building electric entrance, measured from final grade or other accessible surface only for service-drop cables supported on and cabled together with a grounded bare messenger and limited to 150 volts to ground.

12 feet (3.66 m) — for those areas listed in the 15 foot (4.57 m) classification when the voltage is limited to 300 volts to ground.

15 feet (4.57 m) — over residential property and driveways, and those commercial areas not subject to truck traffic.

18 feet (5.49 m) — over public streets, alleys, roads, parking areas subject to truck traffic, driveways on other than residential property, and other land traversed by vehicles such as cultivated, grazing, forest, and orchard.

See Figure 230-5.

(c) Clearance from Building Openings. Service conductors shall have a clearance of not less than 3 feet (914 mm) from windows, doors, porches, fire escapes, or similar locations.

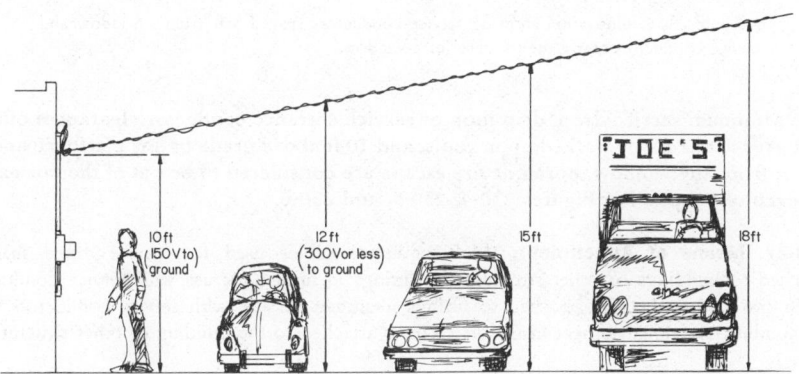

Figure 230-5. Illustrated clearances are coordinated with the National Electrical Safety Code (ANSI C2.)

Exception: Conductors run above the top level of a window shall be permitted to be less than the 3 feet (914 mm) requirement above.

The clearance of 3 ft is applicable to the conductors and not to a raceway or cable assembly approved for use as service conductors. The intent is to protect the conductors from physical damage and/or accidental contact. The last sentence of subsection (c) was revised and converted into an exception for the 1984 *Code*. This exception permits service conductors, including drip loops and service-drop conductors, to be located just above window openings, because they are considered to be "out of reach." See Figure 230-6.

(d) Clearance from Swimming Pools. See Section 680-8.

230-26. Point of Attachment. The point of attachment of conductors to a building or other structure shall provide the minimum clearances as specified in Section 230-24. In no case shall this point of attachment be less than 10 feet (3.05 m) above finished grade.

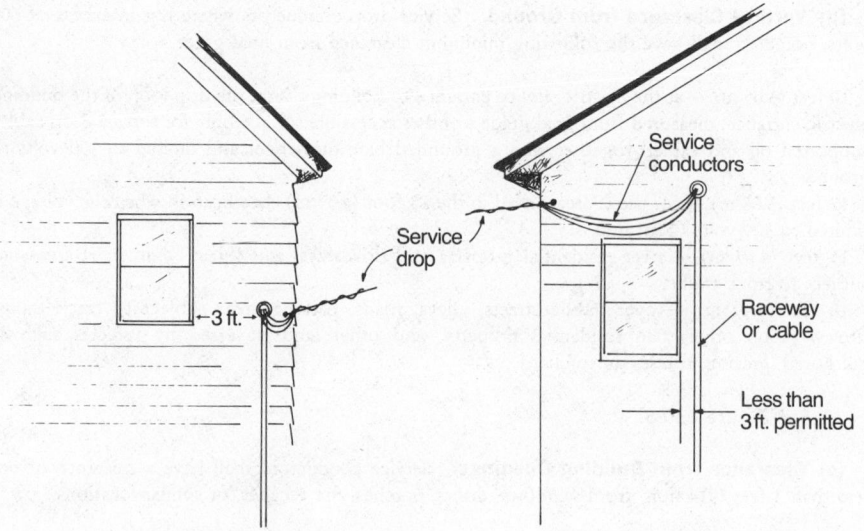

Figure 230-6. Illustration showing service conductors spaced 3 ft from a window and service conductors above the top level of a window.

Minimum service-drop, drip loop or service-entrance conductor clearances of 8 ft over flat or easily walked-upon roofs, and 10 ft above grade or any platform, and 3 ft from any window, porch or fire escape are considered to be out of the normal reach of people. See Figures 230-4, 230-5, and 230-6.

230-27. Means of Attachment. Multiconductor cables used for service drops shall be attached to buildings or other structures by fittings identified for use with service conductors. Open conductors shall be attached to fittings identified for use with service conductors or to noncombustible, nonabsorbent insulators securely attached to the building or other structure.

See Section 230-51 for mounting and supporting of service cables or individual open service conductors and Section 230-54 for connections at service heads.

230-28. Service Masts as Supports. Where a service mast is used for the support of service-drop conductors, it shall be of adequate strength or be supported by braces or guys to withstand safely the strain imposed by the service drop. Where raceway-type service masts are used, all raceway fittings shall be identified for use with service masts.

See Figure 230-4.

230-29. Supports Over Buildings. Service-drop conductors passing over a roof shall be securely supported by substantial structures. Where practicable, such supports shall be independent of the building.

D. Underground Services

230-30. Insulation. Service lateral conductors shall be insulated for the applied voltage.

Exception: A grounded conductor shall be permitted to be uninsulated as follows:

a. Bare copper used in a raceway.

b. Bare copper for direct burial where bare copper is judged to be suitable for the soil conditions.

c. Bare copper for direct burial without regard to soil conditions when part of a cable assembly identified for underground use.

d. Aluminum or copper-clad aluminum without individual insulation or covering when part of a cable assembly identified for underground use in a raceway or for direct burial.

See Figure 230-7.

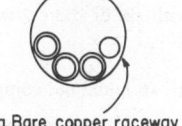
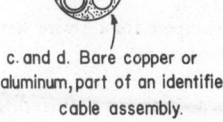

a.Bare copper, raceway   b.Bare copper direct   c. and d. Bare copper or
buried, suitable for   aluminum, part of an identified
soil conditions.   cable assembly.

Figure 230-7. Various applications of bare grounded conductors for underground locations. Aluminum or copper-clad aluminum conductors must be insulated where run in a raceway or direct-buried.

230-31. Size and Rating. Conductors shall have sufficient ampacity to carry the load. They shall not be smaller than No. 8 copper or No. 6 aluminum or copper-clad aluminum. The grounded conductor shall not be less than the minimum size required by Section 250-23(b).

Exception: For installations to supply only limited loads of a single branch circuit such as small polyphase power, controlled water heaters and the like, they shall not be smaller than No. 12 copper or No. 10 aluminum or copper-clad aluminum.

E. Service-Entrance Conductors

230-40. Number of Service-Entrance Conductor Sets. Each service drop or lateral shall supply only one set of service-entrance conductors.

Exception No. 1: Buildings of multiple occupancy shall be permitted to have one set of service-entrance conductors run to each occupancy or to a group of occupancies.

Exception No. 2: As permitted in Section 230-45.

This is new in the 1984 *Code* and is intended to correlate with Section 230-71(a).

230-41. Insulation of Service-Entrance Conductors. Service-entrance conductors entering or on the exterior of buildings or other structures shall be insulated.

Exception: A grounded conductor shall be permitted to be uninsulated as follows:

a. Bare copper used in a raceway or part of a service cable assembly.

b. Bare copper for direct burial where bare copper is judged to be suitable for the soil conditions.

c. Bare copper for direct burial without regard to soil conditions when part of a cable assembly identified for underground use.

d. Aluminum or copper-clad aluminum without individual insulation or covering when part of a cable assembly or identified for underground use in a raceway or for direct burial.

230-42. Size and Rating.

(a) General. Conductors shall be of sufficient size to carry the loads as computed in accordance with Article 220. Ampacity shall be determined from Tables 310-16 through 310-19 and all applicable notes to these tables.

(b) Ungrounded Conductors. Ungrounded conductors shall have an ampacity of not less than:

(1) 100 ampere for a 3-wire service to a one-family dwelling with six or more 2-wire branch circuits.

(2) 100 ampere for a 3-wire service to a one-family dwelling with an initial net computed load of 10 kVA or more.

This section was revised for the 1984 *Code*. The intent is to require that only the ungrounded (hot) conductors be sized to conform with Sections 230-42(b)(1) and 230-42(b)(2), and to permit a smaller neutral conductor in accordance with Section 220-22.

(3) 60 amperes for other loads.

See Figure 230-8.

Exception No. 1: For loads consisting of not more than two 2-wire branch circuits, No. 8 copper or No. 6 aluminum or copper-clad aluminum.

Exception No. 2: By special permission, for loads limited by demand or by the source of supply, No. 8 copper or No. 6 aluminum or copper-clad aluminum.

Exception No. 3: For limited loads of a single branch circuit, No. 12 copper or No. 10 aluminum or copper-clad aluminum, but in no case smaller than the branch-circuit conductors.

(c) Grounded Conductors. The grounded (neutral) conductor shall not be less than the minimum size as required by Section 250-23(b).

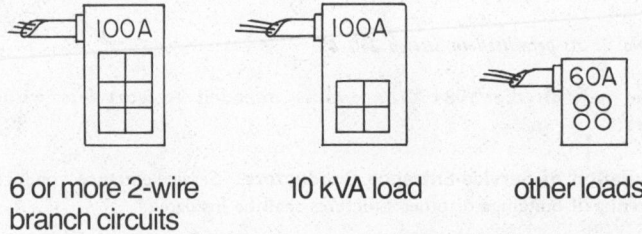

6 or more 2-wire branch circuits   10 kVA load   other loads

Figure 230-8. Ungrounded service-entrance conductors are to have an ampacity of at least 100 A for a 3-wire service to a one-family dwelling if it has six or more 2-wire branch circuits or a computed load of 10 kVA or more. Sixty A would be permissible for a one-family dwelling with four branch circuits and a computed load of less than 10 kVA.

F. Installation of Service Conductors

230-43. Wiring Methods for 600 Volts, Nominal, or Less. Service-entrance conductors shall be installed in accordance with the applicable requirements of this Code covering the type of wiring method used and limited to the following methods: (1) open wiring on insulators; (2) rigid metal conduit; (3) intermediate metal conduit; (4) electrical metallic tubing; (5) service-entrance cables; (6) wireways; (7) busways; (8) auxiliary gutters; (9) rigid nonmetallic conduit; (10) cablebus; (11) Type MC cable; or (12) mineral-insulated, metal-sheathed cable.

Approved cable tray systems shall be permitted to support cables approved for use as service-entrance conductors. See Article 318.

230-44. Conductors Considered Outside of Building. Conductors shall be considered outside of a building or other structure under any of the following conditions: (1) where installed under not less than 2 inches (50.8 mm) of concrete beneath a building or other structure, or (2) where installed within a building or other structure in a raceway that is enclosed by concrete or brick not less than 2 inches (50.8 mm) thick.

See Figure 230-9.

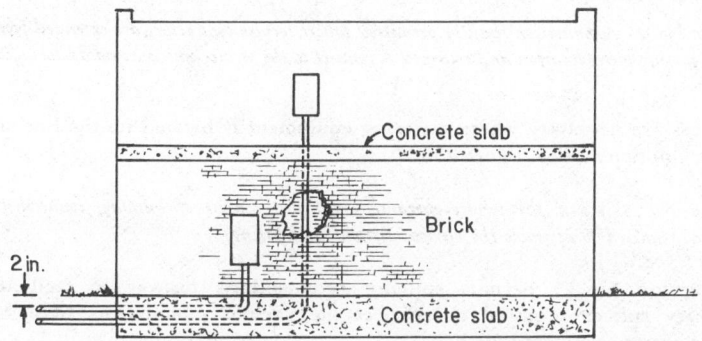

Figure 230-9. Conductors are considered outside of a building where installed under not less than 2 in. of concrete beneath a building or in a raceway enclosed by 2 in. of concrete or brick within a building.

230-45. Separate Enclosures. Where two to six service disconnecting means in separate enclosures supply separate loads from one service drop or lateral, one set of service-entrance conductors shall be permitted to supply each or several such service equipment enclosures.

One set of service-entrance conductors, either overhead or underground, is permitted to supply two to six service disconnecting means in lieu of a single main disconnect. A single-occupancy or multiple-occupancy building (either residential or other than residential) may have one main service disconnect or up to six main disconnects supplying separate loads.

An installation where the main service disconnecting means is rated 1200 A, 480 Y/277-V (see Section 230-95) would require ground-fault protection of equipment. However, this same installation with two service disconnects rated at 600 A each, three service disconnects rated at 400 A each, or six rated at 200 A each would not require ground-fault protection.

Where two to six sets of fuses or circuit breakers are used, the total rating of the multiple overcurrent devices are not required to match the ampacities of the service-entrance conductors. The combined ratings of all switches or circuit breakers are not required to be less than the rating required for a single overcurrent device and may exceed the ampacity of the service-entrance conductors.

See Section 230-2, Exception No. 7 for (underground) sets of service lateral conductors.

ARTICLE 230—SERVICES

230-46. Unspliced Conductors. Service-entrance conductors shall not be spliced.

Exception No. 1: Clamped or bolted connections in metering equipment enclosures shall be permitted.

Exception No. 2: Where service-entrance conductors are tapped to supply two to six disconnecting means grouped at a common location.

Exception No. 3: At a properly enclosed junction point where an underground wiring method is changed to another type of wiring method.

Where a building has a basement, an underground service raceway usually terminates at a terminal box. At this point service conductors may be spliced or run directly to the service equipment. Splices are permitted where, for example, conduit enters a terminal box and a different wiring method, such as service cable, continues to the service equipment. See Section 230-43 for wiring methods for service conductors for 600 V, nominal, or less.

Exception No. 4: A connection shall be permitted where service conductors are extended from a service drop to an outside meter location and returned to connect to the service-entrance conductors of an existing installation.

Splices are necessary where metering equipment is located on the line side of service equipment. See Figure 230-10.

Exception No. 5: When the service-entrance conductors consist of busway, connections shall be permitted as required to assemble the various sections and fittings.

Exception No. 5 permits splicing (connecting) busway to facilitate the necessary splices required to connect the various components of a busway service-entrance system together.

230-47. Other Conductors in Raceway or Cable. Conductors other than service conductors shall not be installed in the same service raceway or service-entrance cable.

Exception No. 1: Grounding conductors.

Exception No. 2: Time switch conductors having overcurrent protection.

Time switch conductors are control circuit or switch leg conductors for use with special rate meters, usually for water heater circuits. Electric utility companies usually refer to these special rate meters as "Off Peak." See Figure 230-10.

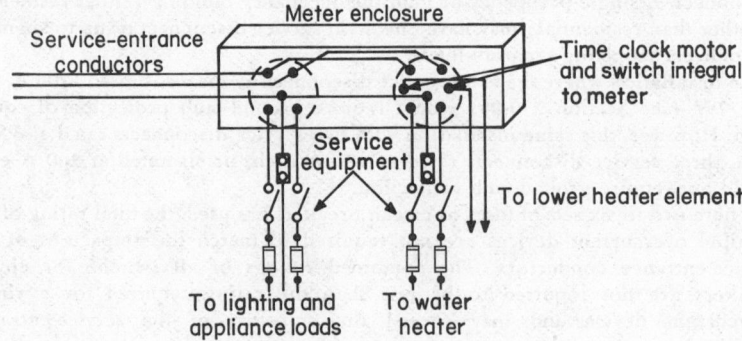

Figure 230-10. Time clock and control switch integral to a meter for use, generally, with water heaters.

230-48. Raceway Seal. Where a service raceway enters from an underground distribution system, it shall be sealed in accordance with Section 300-5. Spare or unused raceways shall also be sealed. Sealants shall be identified for use with the cable insulation, shield, or other components.

Sealing, such as duct seal or a bushing incorporating the physical characteristics of a seal, is required to be used to seal the ends of service raceways. The intent of this requirement is to prevent water, usually the result of condensation, from entering the service equipment via the raceway. See Figure 300-5. Some sealants are known to have deleterious effects on insulations, extruded semiconducting layers, etc.

230-49. Protection Against Damage — Underground. Underground service conductors shall be protected against physical damage in accordance with Section 300-5.

230-50. Protection of Open Conductors and Cables Against Damage — Above-ground. Service-entrance conductors installed aboveground shall be protected against physical damage as specified in (a) or (b) below.

(a) Service-Entrance Cables. Service-entrance cables, where subject to physical damage, such as where installed in exposed places near driveways or coal chutes, or where subject to contact with awnings, shutters, swinging signs, or similar objects, shall be protected in any of the following ways: (1) by rigid metal conduit; (2) by intermediate metal conduit; (3) by rigid nonmetallic conduit suitable for the location; (4) by electrical metallic tubing; (5) by Type MC cable; or (6) by other approved means.

(b) Other than Service-Entrance Cable. Individual open conductors and cables other than service-entrance cables shall not be installed within 10 feet (3.05 m) of grade level or where exposed to physical damage.

230-51. Mounting Supports. Cables or individual open service conductors shall be supported as specified in (a), (b), or (c) below.

(a) Service-Entrance Cables. Service-entrance cables shall be supported by straps or other approved means within 12 inches (305 mm) of every service head, gooseneck, or connection to a raceway or enclosure and at intervals not exceeding 4½ feet (1.37 m).

(b) Other Cables. Cables that are not approved for mounting in contact with a building or other structure shall be mounted on insulating supports installed at intervals not exceeding 15 feet (4.57 m) and in a manner that will maintain a clearance of not less than 2 inches (50.8 mm) from the surface over which they pass.

(c) Individual Open Conductors. Individual open conductors shall be installed in accordance with Table 230-51(c). Where exposed to the weather, the conductors shall be mounted on insulators or on insulating supports attached to racks, brackets, or other approved means. Where not exposed to the weather, the conductors shall be mounted on glass or porcelain knobs.

Table 230-51(c). Supports and Clearances for Individual Open Service Conductors

Maximum Volts	Maximum Distance In Feet Between Supports	Minimum Clearances In Inches	
		Between Conductors	From Surface
600	9	6	2
600	15	12	2
300	4½	3	2
600*	4½*	2½*	1*

For SI units: one inch = 25.4 millimeters; one foot = 0.3048 meter.
* Where not exposed to weather.

230-52. Individual Conductors Entering Buildings or Other Structures. Where individual open conductors enter a building or other structure, they shall enter through roof bushings or through the wall in an upward slant through individual, noncombustible, nonabsorbent insulating tubes. Drip loops shall be formed on the conductors before they enter the tubes.

230-53. Raceways to Drain. Where exposed to the weather, raceways enclosing service-entrance conductors shall be raintight and arranged to drain. Where embedded in masonry, raceways shall be arranged to drain.

Service raceways exposed to the weather are required to have raintight fittings and drainholes. During installation of raceways in masonry, it is nearly impossible to prevent the entrance of surface water, rain, or water from poured concrete.

230-54. Connections at Service Head.

(a) Raintight Service Head. Service raceways shall be equipped with a raintight service head.

(b) Service Cable Equipped with Raintight Service Head or Gooseneck. Service cables, either (1) unless continuous from pole to service equipment or meter, shall be equipped with a raintight service head, or (2) formed in a gooseneck and taped and painted or taped with a self-sealing, weather-resistant thermoplastic.

(c) Service Heads Above Service-Drop Attachment. Service heads and goosenecks in service-entrance cables shall be located above the point of attachment of the service-drop conductors to the building or other structure.

Exception: Where it is impracticable to locate the service head above the point of attachment, the service head location shall be permitted not farther than 24 inches (610 mm) from the point of attachment.

(d) Secured. Service cables shall be held securely in place.

(e) Opposite Polarity Through Separately Bushed Holes. Service heads shall have conductors of opposite polarity brought out through separately bushed holes.

(f) Drip Loops. Drip loops shall be formed on individual conductors. To prevent the entrance of moisture, service-entrance conductors shall be connected to the service-drop conductors either (1) below the level of the service head, or (2) below the level of the termination of the service-entrance cable sheath.

(g) Arranged that Water Will Not Enter Service Raceway or Equipment. Service-drop conductors and service-entrance conductors shall be arranged so that water will not enter service raceway or equipment.

Many areas throughout the country require that service raceways and service cables be equipped with a raintight service (weather) head. Type (SE) service-entrance cables, however, may be run continuous from a utility pole to metering or service equipment or, where shaped in a downward direction or "gooseneck" and sealed by taping and painting, may be installed without a service head. See Figure 230-11.

Wherever practical, service heads and goosenecks are required to be located above the service-drop attachment. Individual conductors should extend in a downward direction, as shown in Figure 230-11, or drip loops are required to be formed.

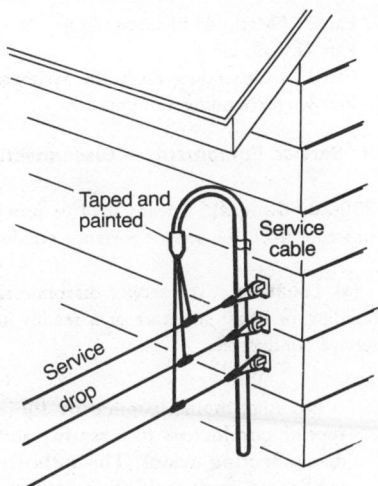

Figure 230-11. A service-entrance cable that terminates in a "gooseneck" without a raintight service weather head.

230-55. Termination at Service Equipment. Any service raceway or cable shall terminate at the inner end in a box, cabinet, or equivalent fitting that effectively encloses all live metal parts.

Exception: Where the service disconnecting means is mounted on a switchboard having exposed busbars on the back, a raceway shall be permitted to terminate at a bushing.

230-56. Service-Entrance Conductor with the Higher Voltage-to-Ground. On a 4-wire delta-connected service where the midpoint of one phase is grounded, the service-entrance conductor having the higher phase voltage-to-ground shall be durably and permanently marked by an outer finish that is orange in color or by other effective means.

Proper service connections cannot be made without durably marking the service conductor having the higher voltage-to-ground by an outer finish of orange, by tagging, etc. Marking should be both at the point of connection to the service-entrance conductors and the point of connection to the service disconnect. See Figure 215-2. See Sections 215-8 and 384-3(e) and (f).

G. Service Equipment — Guarding and Grounding

230-62. Service Equipment — Enclosed or Guarded. Live parts of service equipment shall be enclosed as specified in (a) below, or guarded as specified in (b) below.

(a) Enclosed. Live parts shall be enclosed so that they will not be exposed to accidental contact or guarded as in (b) below.

(b) Guarded. Live parts that are not enclosed shall be installed on a switchboard, panelboard, or control board and guarded in accordance with Sections 110-17 and 110-18. Such an enclosure shall be provided with means for locking or sealing doors giving access to live parts.

230-63. Grounding and Bonding. Service equipment, raceways, cable armor, cable sheaths, etc., and any service conductor that is to be grounded shall be grounded in accordance with the following parts of Article 250.

Part B.   Circuit and System Grounding.
Part C.   Location of System Grounding Connections.
Part D.   Enclosure Grounding.

ARTICLE 230—SERVICES

Part F. Methods of Grounding.
Part G. Bonding.
Part H. Grounding Electrode Systems.
Part J. Grounding Conductors.

H. Service Equipment — Disconnecting Means

230-70. General. Means shall be provided to disconnect all conductors in a building or other structure from the service-entrance conductors.

(a) Location. The service disconnecting means shall be installed either inside or outside of a building or other structure at a readily accessible location nearest the point of entrance of the service conductors.

No maximum distance or footage is specified from the point of entrance of service conductors to a readily accessible location for the installation of a service disconnecting means. The authority enforcing this *Code* has the responsibility and is charged with making interpretations related to specific individual installations. The length of service-entrance conductors should be kept to a minimum inside buildings since power utilities provide limited overcurrent protection and, in the event of a "fault," the service conductors could ignite nearby combustible materials.

The authority having jurisdiction may permit service conductors to bypass coal bins, oil barrels, or gas meters, etc., permitting the service disconnecting means to be located in a readily accessible location. However, if the authority judges the distance as being excessive, the disconnecting means may be required to be located outside, according to this section. See also Section 230-44 and Figure 230-9 for conductors considered to be outside of a building.

(b) Marking. Each service disconnecting means shall be permanently marked to identify it as a service disconnecting means and shall be of the type that is suitable for use as service equipment.

(c) Suitable For Use. Each service disconnecting means shall be suitable for the prevailing conditions. Service equipment installed in hazardous (classified) locations shall comply with the requirements of Articles 500 through 517.

This section was revised for the 1984 *Code*. Some of the important rules were restructured to the present form to avoid misinterpretation and enhance compliance with the *Code*.

230-71. Maximum Number of Disconnects.

(a) General. The service disconnecting means for each service permitted by Section 230-2, or for each set of service-entrance conductors permitted by Section 230-40, shall consist of not more than six switches or six circuit breakers mounted in a single enclosure, in a group of separate enclosures, or in or on a switchboard. There shall be no more than six disconnects per service grouped in any one location.

The intent of this section is to recognize up to six disconnecting means for each service. Each service, permitted by Section 230-2, must be disconnected with not more than six operations of the hand in any one location.

Figure 230-12. An enclosure for grouping service equipment, consisting of six circuit breakers or six fused-switches. This arrangement does not require a main switch. Six separate enclosures would also be permitted as the service equipment. (*Anchor Electric*)

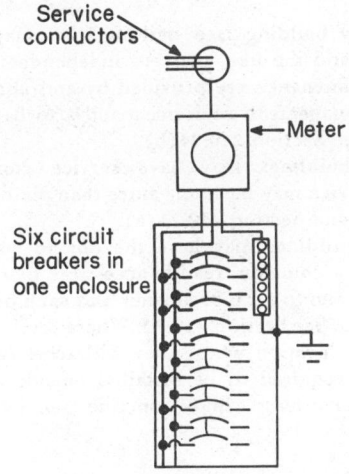

Figure 230-13. Six circuit breakers in one service equipment enclosure.

(b) Single-Pole Units. Two or three single-pole switches or breakers, capable of individual operation, shall be permitted on multiwire circuits, one pole for each ungrounded conductor, as one multipole disconnect provided they are equipped with "handle ties" or a "master handle" to disconnect all conductors of the service with no more than six operations of the hand.

(FPN): See Section 384-16(a) for service equipment in panelboards.

230-72. Grouping of Disconnects.

(a) General. The two to six disconnects as permitted in Section 230-71 shall be grouped. Each disconnect shall be marked to indicate the load served.

Exception: One of the two to six service disconnecting means permitted in Section 230-71, when used only for a water pump also intended to provide fire protection, shall be permitted to be located remote from the other disconnecting means.

(b) Additional Service Disconnecting Means. The one or more additional service disconnecting means for fire pumps or for emergency, legally required standby, or optional standby services permitted by Section 230-2 shall be installed sufficiently remote from the one to six service disconnecting means for normal service to minimize the possibility of simultaneous interruption of supply.

The intent of Section 230-2, Exception Nos. 1 and 2, is to permit separate services where necessary for fire pumps (with one to six disconnects) or emergency systems (with one to six disconnects) in addition to the one to six disconnects for the normal building service. Article 230 recognizes that a disruption of the normal building service should not disconnect the fire pump or emergency systems.

(FPN): See Section 700-12(d) and (e) for emergency system services.

(c) Access to Occupants. In a multiple-occupancy building, each occupant shall have access to his service disconnecting means.

A multiple-occupancy building is a building that may have any number of dwelling units, offices, and the like, that are independent of each other. Unless electric service and maintenance are provided by and under continuous supervision of the building management, each occupant is to have access to his or her disconnecting means. See Section 240-24(b).

Multiple-occupancy buildings may have service conductors run to each occupancy and each service may have not more than six disconnects. See Section 230-2, Exception No. 3 and Section 230-71(a).

Multiple-occupancy buildings may have the one to six disconnecting means located and grouped in a common, readily accessible place, or it is permitted to have service conductors run to each occupancy and each occupancy may have one to six service disconnects. See Section 230-72. Where service conductors are run to each occupancy or to a location where they will serve several occupancies, the service conductors are required to be installed outside of the building or are required to be encased in at least 2 in. of concrete (see Section 230-44 and Figure 230-9).

230-73. Working Space.
Sufficient working space shall be provided in the vicinity of the service disconnecting means to permit safe operation, inspection, and repairs. In no case shall this be less than that specified by Section 110-16.

230-74. Simultaneous Opening of Poles. Each service disconnecting means shall simultaneously disconnect all ungrounded service conductors from the premises wiring system.

230-75. Disconnection of Grounded Conductor. Where the service disconnecting means does not disconnect the grounded conductor from the premises wiring, other means shall be provided for this purpose in the service equipment. A terminal or bus to which all grounded conductors can be attached by means of pressure connectors shall be permitted for this purpose.

At the service equipment, provisions are to be made to disconnect the grounded conductor from the premises wiring. This disconnection need not be by operation of the service disconnecting means. Disconnection can be, and most commonly is, accomplished by "manually" removing it from the bus or terminal bar to which it is lugged or bolted. This is often referred to as the "Neutral Disconnect Link."

Manufacturers design neutral terminal bars for service equipment so that grounded conductors must be cut to be attached, that is, the grounded conductor cannot be run straight through the service equipment without means of disconnection from the premises wiring.

230-76. Manually or Power Operable. The service disconnecting means for ungrounded service conductors shall consist of either (1) a manually operable switch or circuit breaker equipped with a handle or other suitable operating means, or (2) a power-operated switch or circuit breaker provided the switch or circuit breaker can be opened by hand in the event of a power supply failure.

230-77. Indicating. The service disconnecting means shall plainly indicate whether it is in the open or closed position.

230-78. Externally Operable. An enclosed service disconnecting means shall be externally operable without exposing the operator to contact with live parts.

Exception: A power-operated switch or circuit breaker shall not be required to be externally operable by hand to a closed position.

A service disconnecting means must be capable of being operated to the "On" or "Off" position without exposing unqualified persons to live parts. See Article 100 for definition of "Dead Front."

230-79. Rating of Disconnect. The service disconnecting means shall have a rating not less than the load to be carried, determined in accordance with Article 220. In no case shall the rating be lower than specified in (a), (b), (c), or (d) below.

(a) One-Circuit Installation. For installations to supply only limited loads of a single branch circuit, the service disconnecting means shall have a rating of not less than 15 amperes.

(b) Two-Circuit Installations. For installations consisting of not more than two 2-wire branch circuits, the service disconnecting means shall have a rating of not less than 30 amperes.

(c) One-Family Dwelling. For a one-family dwelling, the service disconnecting means shall have a rating of not less than 100 amperes, 3-wire under either of the following conditions: (1) where the initial computed load is 10 kVA or more, or (2) where the initial installation consists of six or more 2-wire branch circuits.

A service disconnecting means is required to have a rating of not less than the load to be carried. See Example 2(a) in Chapter 9 and Figure 230-8.

(d) All Others. For all other installations the service disconnecting means shall have a rating of not less than 60 amperes.

230-80. Combined Rating of Disconnects. Where the service disconnecting means consists of more than one switch or circuit breaker, as permitted by Section 230-71, the combined ratings of all the switches or circuit breakers used shall not be less than the rating required for a single switch or circuit breaker.

Section 230-71(a) permits up to six individual switches or circuit breakers, mounted in a single enclosure or in a group of separate enclosures or in or on a switchboard, to serve as the required service disconnecting means at any one location. Section 230-80 refers to where more than one switch or circuit breaker is used and indicates that the combined rating of all the switches or circuit breakers used shall not be less than the rating required for a single switch or circuit breaker. Section 230-90 requires that overcurrent protection be provided in each ungrounded service conductor. This overcurrent protection must have a rating or setting not higher than the allowable ampacity of the service conductors. Exception No. 3 to Section 230-90 allows not more than six circuit breakers or six sets of fuses to be considered as the overcurrent device. None of these individual overcurrent devices can have a rating or setting higher than the ampacity of the service conductors.

In complying with these rules, it is possible for the total of the six overcurrent devices to be larger than the rating of the service-entrance conductors. However, the size of the service-entrance conductors is required to be adequate for the connected load and each individual service disconnecting means is required to be large enough for the individual loads supplied.

230-81. Connection to Terminals. The service conductors shall be connected to the service disconnecting means by pressure connectors, clamps, or other approved means. Connections that depend upon solder shall not be used.

230-82. Equipment Connected to the Supply Side of Service Disconnect. Equipment shall not be connected to the supply side of the service disconnecting means.

Exception No. 1: Cable limiters or other current-limiting devices.

Section 230-91 does not permit service overcurrent devices to be located at the point of connection to the service drop or service lateral where joined to the service-entrance conductors. The requirement is that the overcurrent device be an integral part of the service disconnecting means. See Figures 230-12 and 230-13. The safest practice is to disconnect the service before replacing an overcurrent device.

Exception No. 2: Fuses and disconnecting means or circuit breakers suitable for use as service equipment, in meter pedestals or otherwise provided and connected in series with the ungrounded service conductors and located away from the building supplied.

Exception No. 3: Meters nominally rated not in excess of 600 volts, provided all metal housings and service enclosures are grounded in accordance with Article 250.

Exception No. 4: Instrument transformers (current and potential), high-impedance shunts, surge-protective devices identified for use on the supply side of the service disconnect, time switches, and surge arresters.

Exception No. 5: Taps used only to supply time switches, circuits for emergency systems, stand-by power systems, fire pump equipment, and fire and sprinkler alarms if provided with service equipment and installed in accordance with requirements for service-entrance conductors.

Systems such as emergency lighting, fire alarms, fire pumps, stand-by power, and sprinkler alarms are permitted to be connected ahead of the normal service disconnecting means where such systems are provided with a separate disconnecting means and overcurrent protection. See Section 700-12(e).

Exception No. 6: Interconnected electric power production sources. See Article 690.

This exception is new in the 1984 *Code*. It permits another electric power production source to be connected to the supply side of a service disconnecting means.

230-83. Transfer Equipment. Transfer equipment shall operate such that all ungrounded conductors of one source of supply are disconnected before any ungrounded conductors of the second source are connected.

Exception No. 1: Where manual equipment identified for the purpose, or suitable automatic equipment is utilized, two or more sources shall be permitted to be connected in parallel through transfer equipment.

Exception No. 1 is new in the 1984 *Code*. Suitable transfer equipment is required to assure that successful shifting of loads from normal power to emergency power will occur without back-feeding into utility power lines.

Exception No. 2: Where parallel operation is used and suitable automatic or manual control equipment is provided.

230-84. More than One Building or Other Structure.

(a) Disconnect Required for Each. Where more than one building or other structure is on the same property and under single management, each building or other structure served shall be provided with means for disconnecting all ungrounded conductors.
Location shall be in accordance with Section 230-70.

Exception No. 1: For large capacity multibuilding industrial installations under single management, where it is assured that the disconnecting can be accomplished by establishing and maintaining safe switching procedures, the disconnecting means shall be permitted to be located elsewhere on the premises. See Section 230-90(c).

Exception No. 2: Buildings or other structures qualifying under the provisions of Article 685.

(b) Suitable for Service Equipment. The disconnecting means specified in (a) above shall be suitable for use as service equipment.

Exception: For garages and outbuildings on residential property, a snap switch or a set of 3-way or 4-way snap switches suitable for use on branch circuits shall be permitted as the disconnecting means.

The reference to Section 230-70 and Exceptions No. 1 and 2 are new in the 1984 *Code*.
Section 230-70 provides for the service equipment disconnecting means, specifying its location, marking, and suitability for use under the prevailing conditions.
Exception No. 1 is applicable to industrial installations. The reference to Section 230-90(c) was added to clarify that ungrounded conductors, where run to each building, are to be provided with overcurrent protection.
Exception No. 2 was added to correlate with Article 685, allowing for a safe and orderly shutdown.

141

The requirements for applying the rule of a disconnect for each building, for two buildings under single management, and for three buildings under single management are shown in Figures 230-14 and 230-15. The garage circuits for a detached garage supplied from a dwelling unit are required to be controlled by a switch and this is normally done by either single-pole or 3-way snap switches. All farm buildings are required to be provided with a disconnecting means to disconnect the wiring in each building.

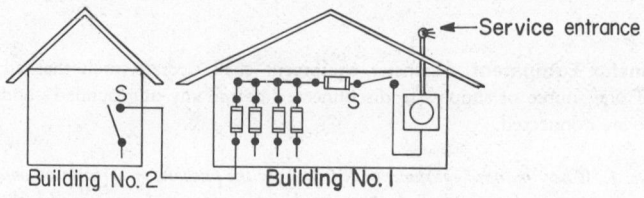

Figure 230-14. A switch (S) is required in Building No. 2.

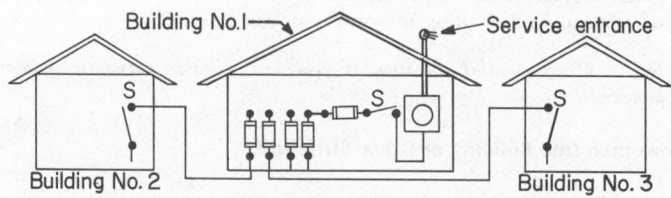

Figure 230-15. Switches are required in Buildings Nos. 2 and 3.

J. Service Equipment — Overcurrent Protection

230-90. Where Required. Each ungrounded service-entrance conductor shall have overcurrent protection.

Service-entrance conductors, overhead or underground, are the supply conductors from the point of connection of service drop or service lateral conductors to the service equipment. Service equipment is intended to constitute the main control and means of cutoff of the supply to the premises wiring system. At this point an overcurrent device, which usually consists of circuit breakers or a set of fuses, is required to be installed in series with each ungrounded service conductor. This will protect "loadside" conductors and will prevent an overload on service-entrance conductors.

The basic purpose of overcurrent protection is to open the circuit before conductors are damaged by an overcurrent condition, such as a short circuit or ground fault.

(a) Ungrounded Conductor. Such protection shall be provided by an overcurrent device in series with each ungrounded service conductor having a rating or setting not higher than the allowable ampacity of the conductor.

Exception No. 1: For motor-starting currents, ratings in conformity with Sections 430-52, 430-62, and 430-63 shall be permitted.

Where a service supplies a motor load as well as lighting or a lighting and appliance load, the overcurrent protective device is required to have a rating sufficient for the lighting and/or appliance load as determined in accordance with Articles 210 and 220 plus, for an individual motor, the rating permitted by Section 430-52 and, for two or more motors, the rating permitted by Section 430-62.

Example: A service consisting of a 100-A, lighting and appliance load, one 25-hp squirrel cage induction motor (full-voltage starting, service factor 1.15, Code letter F), and two 30-hp wound rotor induction motors (40°C rise) on a 240-V, 3-phase system is to have the service conductors and service disconnecting means calculated as follows:

Conductor Loads

The full-load current of the 25-hp motor is 68 A (Table 430-150). The full-load current of the 30-hp motor is 80 A (Table 430-150). The service-entrance conductors are calculated at 125 percent of 80 A (100 A), plus 80 A, plus 68 A, for a total of 248 A (Section 430-24).

$$
\begin{array}{ll}
& \text{248-A motors} \\
& \underline{\text{100-A lighting and appliance}} \\
\text{Total} & \text{348 A}
\end{array}
$$

Therefore, the service-entrance conductors would have to be, for example, 500 MCM Type THW copper or 700 MCM Type THW aluminum or copper-clad aluminum conductors (Table 310-16).

Overcurrent Protection

The maximum rating of the service overcurrent protective device is based on the sum of the largest branch-circuit overcurrent device [300 percent for the 25-hp motor using a nontime delay fuse (Table 430-152) = 68 × 3 = 204 A, therefore the next larger size 225 A] plus the sum of the full-load currents of the other motors plus the lighting and appliance load (see Section 430-63).

$$
\begin{array}{ll}
& \text{225-A 25-hp motor} \\
& \text{80-A 30-hp motor} \\
& \text{80-A 30-hp motor} \\
& \underline{\text{100-A lighting and appliance load}} \\
\text{Total} & \text{485 A}
\end{array}
$$

The nearest standard fuse that does not exceed this total value is 450 A.

Exception No. 2: Fuses and circuit breakers with a rating or setting in conformity with Section 240-3, Exception No. 1, and Section 240-6.

Exception No. 3: Not more than six circuit breakers or six sets of fuses shall be considered as the overcurrent device.

Circuit-breaker or fuse-ampere ratings are not permitted to be greater than the ampacity of the service conductor (except for motor-starting currents), unless such conductor rating does not correspond to the standard ampere rating of a circuit breaker or fuse, whereupon the next larger size circuit breaker or fuse may be used, provided its rating does not exceed 800 A as permitted in Section 240-3, Exception No. 1. See Section 240-6 for standard ampere ratings of fuses and circuit breakers.

Example: The ampacity of a 500 MCM THW copper conductor is 380 A (Table 310-16) and may be protected by a 400-A fuse or circuit breaker. The rating of the fuse or circuit breaker is based on the ampacity of the service conductor and not the rating of the service disconnect switch.

As shown in the Example, a 400-A fuse or circuit breaker may be considered as properly sized for the protection of 500 MCM THW copper service conductors. If the service disconnecting means (see Exception No. 3) consists of six circuit breakers or six sets of fuses, the total rating of the six disconnecting means should be as near as practicable to the ampacity of the service-entrance conductors, that is, six disconnects at 100 A each with a total rating of 600 A would not be unreasonable where the calculated load did not exceed the ampacity of the service conductors. See Section 230-80.

Exception No. 4: In a multiple-occupancy building each occupant shall have access to his overcurrent protective devices.

Exception No. 5: Fire Pumps. Where the service to the fire pump room is judged to be outside of buildings, these provisions shall not apply. Overcurrent protection for fire pump services shall be selected or set to carry locked-rotor current of the motor(s) indefinitely [see NFPA 20-1983 (ANSI), Standard for Centrifugal Fire Pumps].

Section 230-90(a), Exception No. 5, permits service-entrance conductors connected ahead of the main service disconnect for a service to a fire pump room and one permitted to be installed without overload protection for the conductors. Two methods of installation are considered as meeting the intent of this section. They are (1) where the service conductors to the pump room are installed outside the building; or (2) where the conductors are installed under not less than 2 in. of concrete or concealed in a raceway enclosed by concrete or brick not less than 2 in. thick (see Section 230-44 and Figure 230-9) that terminates in a fire-resistant pump room.

Section 430-31 of the *Code* indicates that provisions for motor and branch circuit running overcurrent and overload protection are not to be interpreted as requiring overload protection in cases where it might introduce additional or increased hazards. Fire pump motors are a case in point; they are allowed much larger overcurrent protection than other motors, recognizing that fire pumps should be allowed to operate to failure rather than be removed from the line in order to prolong their usefulness under adverse fire conditions. See Section 230-95, Exception No. 2.

Figure 230-16 is a diagram of the wiring and components of a fire pump circuit designed to comply with requirements of the *NEC* and NFPA 20, Standard for the Installation of Centrifugal Fire Pumps. The pump motor represented is a 100-hp, 460-V, 3-phase, squirrel-cage induction type, and its full-load current, taken from Table 430-150, is 124 A.

The service conductors, feeder conductors, and branch-circuit conductors are sized at 125 percent of the motor full-load current rating (124 A x 125 percent = 155 A). According to Table 310-16, the next closest copper wire size for 155 A is a 3/0 AWG TW conductor with an allowable ampacity of 165 A; therefore, all the conductors would be sized at 3/0 AWG TW copper. (See Sections 430-22 and 430-23 for sizing of conductors.) Other conductors with an ampacity of 155 A or more would also be permitted in this instance.

The locked-rotor current of the motor in the installation illustrated is 744 A, as

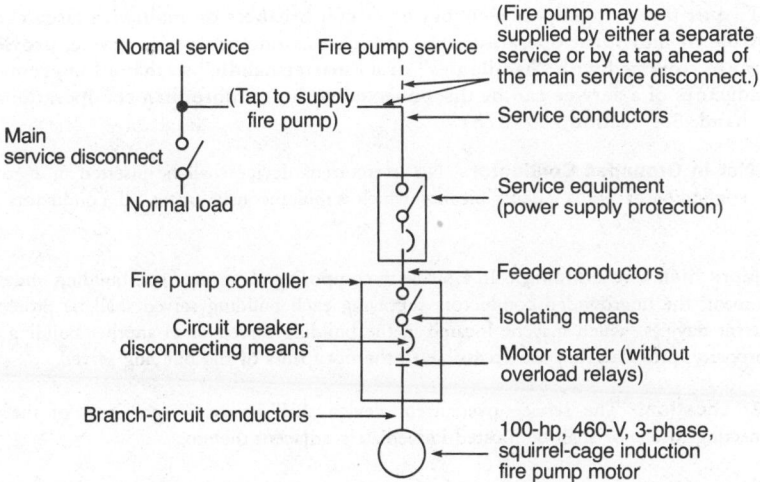

Figure 230-16. A typical fire pump installation.

derived from Table 430-151, and the power supply protection may consist of either fuses or circuit breakers sized so that they will not open at locked-rotor current. In either case, the next standard ampere rating for fuses or circuit breakers is 800 A. (See Section 240-6.) This protection complies with the intent of the requirements of Section 6-3.4 of NFPA 20 and also of Section 430-31 of the *NEC.*

The isolating means in the illustrated pump's controller could be a motor circuit switch rated in horsepower (see Section 430-109) or a suitable nonautomatic circuit breaker (molded case switch), as required by Section 7-4.1 of NFPA 20.

If a motor circuit switch were used for the isolating means, it would be horsepower rated at 100 hp and have an ampere rating of at least 115 percent of the full-load current rating of the motor, that is, 124 A x 115 percent = 142.6 A, to meet requirements of Section 430-110(a) of the *NEC* and Subsection 7-4.1.2 of NFPA 20.

The circuit breaker used to protect the branch circuit to the squirrel-cage induction motor would be a magnetic trip type having a time delay of not over 20 seconds at locked-rotor current, and it would be calibrated up to and set at 300 percent of the motor's full-load current (see Section 7-4.3 of NFPA 20). In this particular instance it would be calibrated at 372 A (124 A x 300 percent).

Circuit breakers for dc and wound-rotor ac motors for fire pumps are of the instantaneous type, calibrated up to and set at 400 percent of the motor's full-load current. See Section 7-4.3 of NFPA 20.

UL-listed pump controllers are investigated for their ability to meet the requirements of the *NEC* and NFPA 20 for the time-current characteristics of the magnetic circuit breakers to assure the 20-second delay at locked-rotor current and 300 percent or 400 percent trip setting, depending on the type of motor used.

The motor starter (without overload relays) is of a magnetic type with a contact in each ungrounded conductor, in accordance with Section 7-4.4 of NFPA 20.

A set of fuses shall be considered all the fuses required to protect all the ungrounded conductors of a circuit. Single-pole circuit breakers, grouped in accordance with Section 230-71(b), shall be considered as one protective device.

Two or three single-pole switches or circuit breakers on multiwire circuits and capable of individual operation are permitted as one protective device, provided they are equipped with "handle ties" or a "master handle" so that all ungrounded conductors of a service can be disconnected with not more than six operations of the hand. See Section 230-71(b).

(b) Not in Grounded Conductor. No overcurrent device shall be inserted in a grounded service conductor except a circuit breaker which simultaneously opens all conductors of the circuit.

(c) More than One Building. In a property comprising more than one building under single management, the ungrounded conductors supplying each building served shall be protected by overcurrent devices, which may be located in the building served or in another building on the same property, provided they are accessible to the occupants of the building served.

230-91. Location. The service overcurrent device shall be an integral part of the service disconnecting means or shall be located immediately adjacent thereto.

Service overcurrent protective devices (fuses or circuit breakers), where within a building, are required to be located at a readily accessible location nearest to the entrance of the service conductors. If there is no readily accessible area, or if the available readily accessible area is not near the entrance of the service conductors, and the distance is judged by the authority having jurisdiction to be a potential hazard, the overcurrent devices are permitted to be located outside of the building.

230-92. Location of Branch-Circuit Overcurrent Devices. Where the service overcurrent devices are locked or sealed, or otherwise not readily accessible, branch-circuit overcurrent devices shall be installed on the load side, shall be mounted in an accessible location, and shall be of lower rating than the service overcurrent device.

230-93. Protection of Specific Circuits. Where necessary to prevent tampering, an automatic overcurrent device protecting service conductors supplying only a specific load, such as a water heater, shall be permitted to be locked or sealed where located so as to be accessible.

230-94. Relative Location of Overcurrent Device and Other Service Equipment. The overcurrent device shall protect all circuits and devices.

Exception No. 1: The service switch shall be permitted on the supply side.

Exception No. 2: High-impedance shunt circuits, lightning arresters, surge protective capacitors, and instrument transformers (current and potential) shall be permitted to be connected and installed on the supply side of the service disconnecting means as permitted in Section 230-82.

Exception No. 3: Circuits for emergency supply and time switches shall be permitted to be connected on the supply side of the service overcurrent device where separately provided with overcurrent protection.

Exception No. 4: Circuits used only for the operation of fire alarm, other protective signaling systems, or the supply to fire pump equipment shall be permitted to be connected on the supply side of the service overcurrent device where separately provided with overcurrent protection.

Exception No. 5: Meters nominally rated not in excess of 600 volts, provided all metal housings and service enclosures are grounded in accordance with Article 250.

Exception No. 6: Where service equipment is power operable, the control circuit shall be permitted to be connected ahead of the service equipment if suitable overcurrent protection and disconnecting means are provided.

230-95. Ground-Fault Protection of Equipment. Ground-fault protection of equipment shall be provided for solidly grounded wye electrical services of more than 150 volts to ground, but not exceeding 600 volts phase-to-phase for each service disconnecting means rated 1000 amperes or more.

See definition of "Ground-Fault Protection of Equipment" in Article 100.

The reason for requiring ground-fault protection of equipment on services rated 480Y/277 V was the unusually high number of burndowns that were reported on this type of service. Ground-fault protection of services will not protect the conductors on the supply side of the service disconnecting means but is designed to provide protection from line-to-ground faults that occur on the load side of the service disconnecting means rated 1,000 A or more. Rather than installing ground-fault protection, it may be desirable to provide multiple disconnects rated less than 1,000 A. For instance, six 800-A disconnecting means may be used and, in this case, ground-fault protection would not be necessary. The second Fine Print Note in Section 230-95 recognizes that ground-fault protection may be desirable at lesser amperages on solidly grounded systems for voltages exceeding 150 V to ground, but not exceeding 600 V phase-to-phase.

In addition to providing ground-fault protection, engineering studies should be made to determine the circuit impedance and the short-circuit currents that would be available at the supply terminals so that equipment and overcurrent protection of the proper interrupting rating is used. See Sections 110-9 and 110-10.

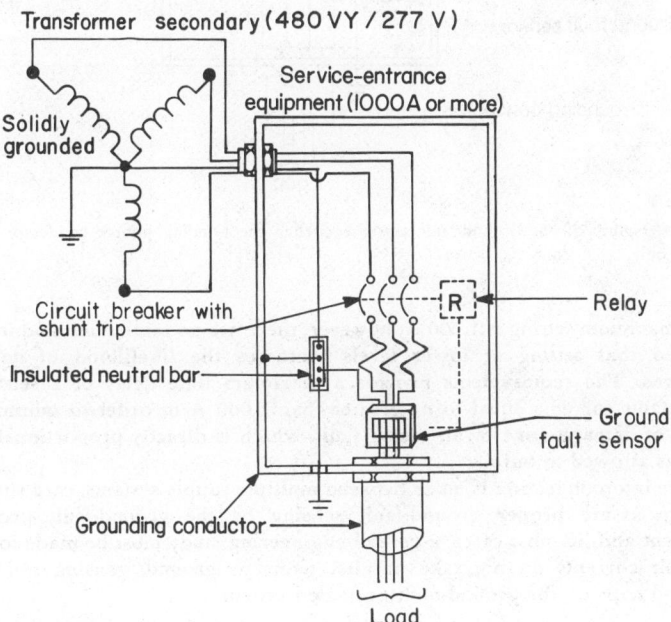

Figure 230-17. Ground-fault sensor encircling all circuit conductors, including the neutral.

There are two basic types of ground-fault equipment protectors. They are illustrated in Figures 230-17 and 230-18. In Figure 230-17, the ground-fault sensor is installed around all the circuit conductors, and a stray current on a line-to-ground fault will set up an unbalance of the currents flowing in individual

147

conductors installed through the ground-fault sensor. When this current exceeds the setting of the ground-fault sensor, the shunt trip will operate and remove the circuit breakers from the line.

The ground-fault sensor illustrated in Figure 230-18 is installed around the bonding jumper only, and when an unbalanced current from a line-to-ground fault occurs, the current will flow through the bonding jumper and the shunt trip will cause the circuit breaker to operate and remove the load from the line.

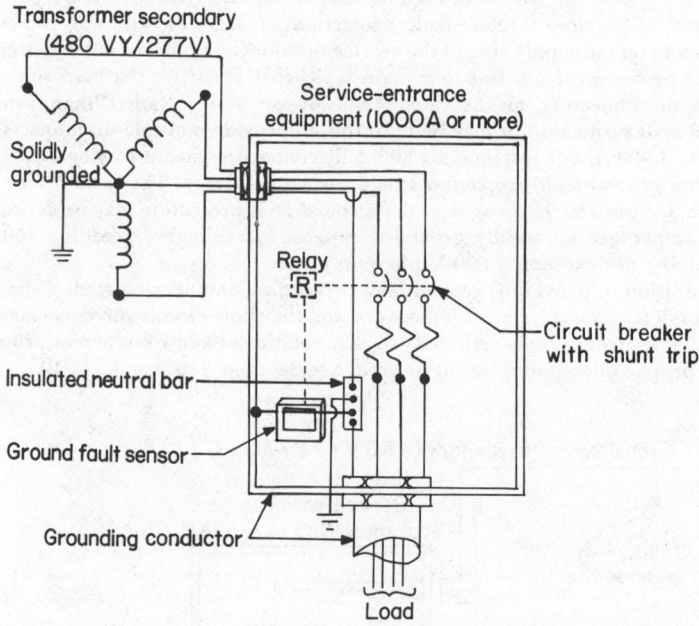

Figure 230-18. Ground-fault sensor encircling the bonding jumper conductor only.

The maximum setting is 1,200 A; however, there are no minimums, and it should be noted that setting at lower levels increases the likelihood of unwanted shutdowns. The requirements provide a maximum time delay of 1 second for ground-fault currents equal to or greater than 3,000 A in order to minimize the amount of damage done by an arcing fault, which is directly proportional to the time it is allowed to burn.

Where interconnection is made between multiple supply systems, care should be taken to assure proper ground-fault sensing by the ground-fault protection equipment and, in most cases, a careful engineering study must be made to assure that fault currents do not take parallel paths to ground, causing no trip or unwanted trips on the ground-fault protected system.

(a) Setting. The ground-fault protection system shall operate to cause the service disconnecting means to open all ungrounded conductors of the faulted circuit. The maximum setting of the ground-fault protection shall be 1200 amperes and the maximum time delay shall be one second for ground-fault currents equal to or greater than 3000 amperes.

Exception No. 1: The provisions of this section shall not apply to a service disconnecting means for a continuous industrial process where a nonorderly shutdown will introduce additional or increased hazards.

Exception No. 2: The provisions of this section shall not apply to fire pumps.

Most fire pumps rated 100 hp and over would require a disconnecting means rated at 1000 A or more; however, due to the nature of their use, fire pumps are exempt from the provisions of Section 230-95.

(b) Fuses. If a switch and fuse combination is used, the fuses employed shall be capable of interrupting any current higher than the interrupting capacity of the switch during a time when the ground-fault protective system will not cause the switch to open.

(FPN): As used in this section, the rating of the Service Disconnecting Means is considered to be the rating of the largest fuse that can be installed or the highest trip setting for which the actual overcurrent device installed in a circuit breaker is rated or can be adjusted.

(FPN): It is recognized that ground-fault protection may be desirable for service disconnecting means rated less than 1000 amperes on solidly grounded systems having more than 150 volts to ground, not exceeding 600 volts phase-to-phase.

(FPN): As used in this section, solidly grounded means that the grounded conductor (neutral) is grounded without inserting any resistor or impedance device.

(FPN): Ground-fault protection that functions to open the service disconnecting means will afford no protection from faults on the line side of the protective element. It serves only to limit damage to conductors and equipment on the load side in the event of an arcing ground fault on the load side of the protective element.

(FPN): This added protective equipment at the service equipment will make it necessary to review the overall wiring system for proper selective overcurrent protection coordination. Additional installations of ground-fault protective equipment will be needed on feeders and branch circuits where maximum continuity of electrical service is necessary.

(FPN): Where ground-fault protection is provided for the service disconnecting means and interconnection is made with another supply system by a transfer device, means or devices may be needed to assure proper ground-fault sensing by the ground-fault protection equipment.

(c) Performance Testing. The ground-fault protection system shall be performance tested when first installed on site. The test shall be conducted in accordance with instructions which shall be provided with the equipment. A written record of this test shall be made and shall be available to the authority having jurisdiction.

The requirement for ground-fault protection system "performance testing" is a result of numerous reports of ground-fault systems that were improperly wired and that could not or did not perform the function for which they were intended. The *Code* and qualified testing laboratories require a set of performance testing instructions to be supplied with the equipment in accordance with Section 110-3(b), for installation and use of listed and labeled equipment. Elimination of the word "approved" for the 1984 *Code* intends that the responsibility evaluation and listing of the instructions will fall under those qualified to make such judgments, the "Qualified Testing Laboratory." See Section 90-6. Addition of the words "on site" is intended to clarify where the test is to be conducted.

230-98. Available Short-Circuit Current. Service equipment shall be suitable for the short-circuit current available at its supply terminals.

K. Services Exceeding 600 Volts, Nominal

230-200. General. Service conductors and equipment used on circuits exceeding 600 volts, nominal, shall comply with all applicable provisions of the preceding sections of this article and with the following sections, which supplement or modify the preceding sections. In no case shall the provisions of this article apply to equipment on the supply side of the service-point.

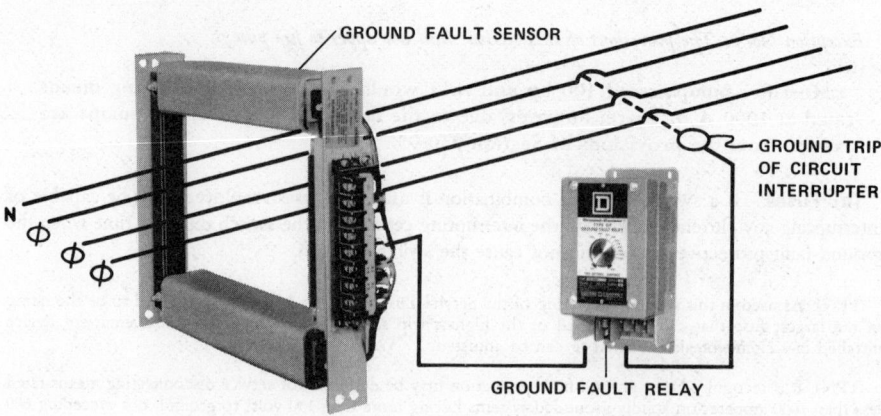

GROUND FAULT SENSOR

GROUND TRIP OF CIRCUIT INTERRUPTER

N Φ Φ Φ

GROUND FAULT RELAY

Figure 230-19. Ground-fault protection system. (*Square D Co.*)

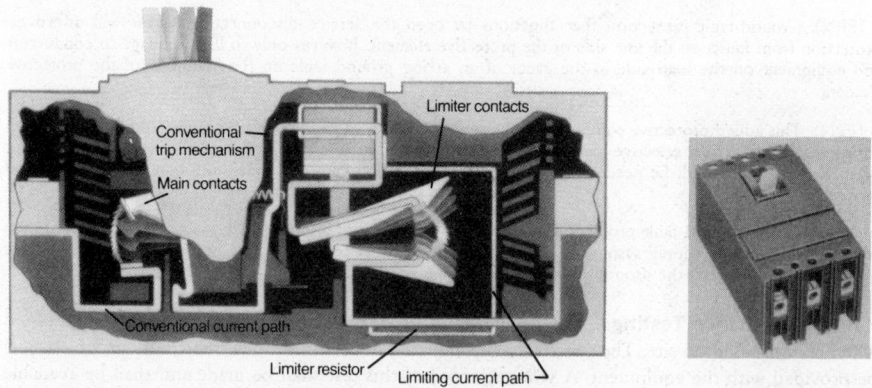

Conventional trip mechanism

Limiter contacts

Main contacts

Conventional current path

Limiter resistor   Limiting current path

Figure 230-20. Current-limiting circuit breaker within UL Class R fuse levels and former Class K-5 levels. (*Square D Co.*)

Definition: Service-point is the point of connection between the facilities of the serving utility and the premises' wiring.

(FPN): For clearances of conductors of over 600 volts, nominal, see National Electrical Safety Code (ANSI C2-1981).

230-201. Classification of Service Conductors.

(a) **Secondary Conductors.** The secondary conductors shall constitute the service conductors where the step-down transformers are located as follows: (1) outdoors; (2) in a separate building from the building or other structure served; (3) inside the building or other structure served where in a vault complying with Part C of Article 450; (4) inside the building or other structure served where in a locked room or other locked enclosure and accessible to qualified persons only; or (5) inside the building or other structure where in metal-enclosed gear.

(b) **Primary Conductors.** In all cases not specified in (a) above, the primary conductors shall be considered the service conductors.

Exception: Either the primary or the secondary conductors shall be permitted to constitute the service conductors for an industrial complex where both the primary and secondary voltages are over 600 volts, nominal.

For a transformer having a secondary voltage of 600 V or less, the secondary conductors are considered the service conductors. For a transformer where both the primary and secondary voltages are over 600 V, nominal, in an industrial complex, then either the primary or the secondary conductors are permitted to be the service conductors.

The design and installation of electrical distribution systems for large industrial complexes are engineered by persons who are highly trained in all aspects of the electrical power field. The type of distribution system, voltages selected, and installation practices have been proven by many successful years of experience. The intent here is not to restrict system designers with "hard to define and interpret" code requirements but to allow an industrial design to be viewed as a whole instead of many individual small concepts.

230-202. Service-Entrance Conductors. Service-entrance conductors to buildings or enclosures shall be installed to conform to the following:

(a) Conductor Size. Service conductors shall be not smaller than No. 6 unless in cable. Conductors in cable shall not be smaller than No. 8.

(b) Wiring Methods. Service-entrance conductors shall be installed by means of one of the following wiring methods: (1) in rigid metal conduit; (2) in intermediate metal conduit; (3) in rigid nonmetallic conduit; (4) as multiconductor cable identified as service cable; (5) as open conductors where supported on insulators and where either accessible only to qualified persons or where effectively guarded against accidental contact; (6) in cablebus; or (7) in busways.

Concrete encasement of rigid nonmetallic conduit is no longer required because of tests performed which showed that Schedule 40 PVC is suitable for applications where the potential exceeds 600 V.

Underground service-entrance conductors shall conform to Section 710-3(b).
Cable tray systems shall be permitted to support cables identified as service-entrance conductors. See Article 318.

(FPN): See Section 310-6 for shielding of solid dielectric insulated conductors.

(c) Open Work. Open wire services over 600 volts, nominal, shall be installed in accordance with the provisions of Article 710, Part D.

(d) Supports. Service conductors and their supports, including insulators, shall have strength and stability sufficient to ensure maintenance of adequate clearance with abnormal currents in case of short circuits.

(e) Guarding. Open wires shall be guarded to make them accessible only to qualified persons.

(f) Service Cable. Where cable conductors emerge from a metal sheath or raceway, the insulation of the conductors shall be protected from moisture and physical damage by a pothead or other approved means.

(g) Draining Raceways. Unless conductors identified for use in wet locations are used, raceways embedded in masonry or exposed to the weather shall be arranged to drain.

(h) Over 15,000 Volts. Where the voltage exceeds 15,000 volts between conductors they shall enter either metal-enclosed switchgear or a transformer vault conforming to the requirements of Sections 450-41 through 450-48.

(i) Conductor Considered Outside Building. Conductors placed under at least 2 inches (50.8 mm) of concrete beneath a building, or conductors within a building in conduit or raceway and enclosed by concrete or brick not less than 2 inches (50.8 mm) thick shall be considered outside the building.

230-203. Warning Signs. High voltage signs with the words "High Voltage" shall be posted where unauthorized persons might come in contact with live parts.

230-204. Isolating Switches.

(a) Where Required. Where oil switches or air or oil circuit breakers constitute the service disconnecting means, an air-break isolating switch shall be installed on the supply side of the disconnecting means and all associated service equipment.

Exception: Where such equipment is mounted on removable truck panels or metal-enclosed switchgear units, which cannot be opened unless the circuit is disconnected, and which, when removed from the normal operating position, automatically disconnect the circuit breaker or switch from all live parts.

(b) Fuses as Isolating Switch. Where fuses are of the type that can be operated as a disconnecting switch, a set of such fuses shall be permitted as the isolating switch where: (1) the oil disconnecting means is a nonautomatic switch, and (2) the set of fuses disconnect the oil switch and all associated service equipment from the service-entrance conductors.

(c) Accessible to Qualified Persons Only. The isolating switch shall be accessible to qualified persons only.

(d) Grounding Connection. Isolating switches shall be provided with a means for readily connecting the load side conductors to ground when disconnected from the source of supply.
A means for grounding the load side conductors need not be provided for any duplicate isolating switch installed and maintained by the electric supply company.

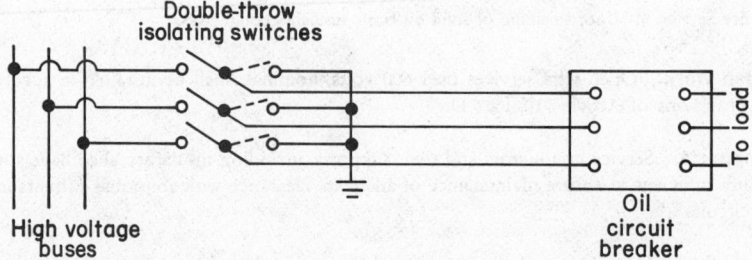

Figure 230-21. A two-position switch grounds load-side conductors when disconnected from high voltage line buses.

230-205. Disconnecting Means.

(a) Location. The service disconnecting means shall be located in accordance with Section 230-70 or Section 230-208(b).

Exception: Where under single management, the service disconnecting means shall be permitted to be located in a separate building or structure on the same premises. In such case the service disconnecting means shall be capable of being electrically opened by a readily accessible control device located as near as practicable to where the service conductors enter the building served. The control device shall be permanently marked to identify its function and shall provide visual indication of the On or Off status of the remote service disconnect.

(FPN): See Sections 230-3, 230-44, 230-70, 230-71(a) and 230-200.

(b) Type. The service disconnecting means shall simultaneously disconnect all ungrounded conductors and shall be capable of being closed on a fault equal to or greater than the maximum available short-circuit current in the circuit at its supply terminals.

Where fused switches or separately mounted fuses are installed, the fuse characteristics shall be permitted to contribute to the fault-closing rating of the disconnecting means.

230-206. Overcurrent Devices as Disconnecting Means. Where the circuit breaker or alternative for it specified in Section 230-208 for service overcurrent devices meets the requirements specified in Section 230-205, they shall constitute the service disconnecting means.

230-207. Equipment in Secondaries. Where the primary service equipment supplies one or more transformers whose secondary windings connect to a common bus of bars or wires, and the primary load-interrupter switch or circuit breaker is capable of being opened and closed from a point outside the transformer vault, the disconnecting means and overcurrent protection shall not be required in the secondary circuit if the primary fuse or circuit breaker is rated or set to protect the secondary circuit.

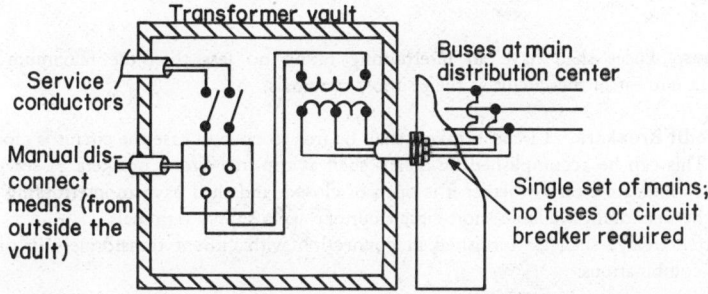

Figure 230-22. In installations where a transformer supplies a single set of secondary mains, the mains may be connected directly to the buses at the distribution center without a switch or overload protection; however, the primary breaker must be set to protect the secondary circuit.

230-208. Overcurrent Protection Requirements. Service-entrance conductors shall have a short-circuit protective device in each ungrounded conductor, on the load side of, or as an integral part of, the service-entrance switch. The protective device shall be capable of detecting and interrupting all values of current in excess of its trip setting or melting point, which can occur at its location. A fuse rated in continuous amperes not to exceed three times the ampacity of the conductor, or a circuit breaker with a trip setting of not more than six times the ampacity of the conductors shall be considered as providing the required short-circuit protection.

(FPN): See Tables 310-69 through 310-84 for ampacity of high-voltage conductors.

Overcurrent devices shall conform to the following:

ARTICLE 230—SERVICES

(a) In Vault or Consisting of Metal-Enclosed Switchgear. Where the service equipment is installed in a transformer vault meeting the provisions of Sections 450-41 through 450-48, or consists of metal-enclosed switchgear, the overcurrent protection and disconnecting means shall be one of the following:

(1) A nonautomatic oil switch, oil fuse cutout, or air load-interrupter switch shall be permitted with fuses. The interrupting rating of this switch shall equal or exceed the continuous current rating of the fuse.

(2) An automatic trip circuit breaker of suitable current-carrying and interrupting capacity.

(3) A switch capable of interrupting the no-load current of the transformer supplied through the switch and suitable fuses shall be permitted provided the switch is interlocked with a single switch or circuit breaker on the secondary circuit of the transformer so that the primary switch cannot be opened when the secondary circuit is closed.

(b) Not in Vault or Not Consisting of Metal-Enclosed Switchgear. Where the service equipment is not in a vault or metal-enclosed switchgear, the overcurrent protection and disconnecting means shall be either of the following:

(1) An air load-interrupter switch or other switch capable of interrupting the rated circuit load shall be permitted with fuses on a pole or elevated structure outside the building provided the switch is operable by persons using the building.

(2) An automatic-trip circuit breaker of suitable ampacity and interrupting capacity. The circuit breaker shall be located outside the building as near as practicable to where the service conductors enter the building. The location shall be permitted on a pole, roof, foundation, or other structure.

(c) Fuses. Fuses shall have an interrupting rating no less than the maximum available short-circuit current in the circuit at their supply terminals.

(d) Circuit Breakers. Circuit breakers shall be free to open in case the circuit is closed on an overload. This can be accomplished by means such as trip-free circuit breakers. A service circuit breaker shall indicate clearly whether it is open or closed, and shall have an interrupting rating no less than the maximum available short-circuit current at its supply terminals.

Overcurrent relays shall be furnished in connection with current transformers in one of the following combinations:

(1) Three overcurrent relays operated from current transformers in each phase.

(2) Two overcurrent relays operated by current from current transformers in any two phases and one overcurrent relay sensitive to ground-fault current that is operated by the sum of the currents from current transformers in each phase.

(3) Two overcurrent relays operated by current from current transformers in any two phases and one overcurrent relay sensitive to ground-fault current that is operated from a current transformer which links all three phase conductors and the grounded circuit conductor (neutral), if provided.

(e) Enclosed Overcurrent Devices. The restriction to 80 percent of rating for an enclosed overcurrent device on continuous loads shall not apply to overcurrent devices installed in services operating at over 600 volts.

230-209. Surge Arresters (Lightning Arresters). Surge arresters installed in accordance with the requirements of Article 280 shall be placed on each ungrounded overhead service conductor on the supply side of the service equipment, when called for by the authority having jurisdiction.

230-210. Service Equipment-General Provisions. Service equipment including instrument transformers shall conform to Article 710, Part B.

230-211. Metal-Enclosed Switchgear. Metal-enclosed switchgear shall consist of a substantial metal structure and a sheet metal enclosure. Where installed over a wood floor, suitable protection thereto shall be provided.

Figure 230-23. An assembly of metal-enclosed switchgear. (*Federal Pacific Electric Co.*)

ARTICLE 240 — OVERCURRENT PROTECTION

240-1. Scope. Parts A through G of this article provide the general requirements for overcurrent protection and overcurrent protective devices not more than 600 volts, nominal. Part H covers overcurrent protection over 600 volts, nominal.

(FPN): Overcurrent protection for conductors and equipment is provided to open the circuit if the current reaches a value that will cause an excessive or dangerous temperature in conductors or conductor insulation. See also Sections 110-9 and 110-10 for requirements for interrupting capacity and protection against fault currents.

Contents

240-12. Electrical System Coordination.

B. Location

240-20. Ungrounded Conductors.
 (a) Overcurrent Device Required.
 (b) Circuit Breaker as Overcurrent Device.
240-21. Location in Circuit.
240-22. Grounded Conductors.
240-23. Change in Size of Grounded Conductor.
240-24. Location in or on Premises.
 (a) Readily Accessible.
 (b) Occupant to Have Ready Access.
 (c) Not Exposed to Physical Damage.
 (d) Not in Vicinity of Easily Ignitible Material.

C. Enclosures

240-30. General.
240-32. Damp or Wet Locations.
240-33. Vertical Position.

D. Disconnecting and Guarding

240-40. Disconnecting Means for Fuses and Thermal Cutouts.
240-41. Arcing or Suddenly Moving Parts.
 (a) Location.
 (b) Suddenly Moving Parts.

E. Plug Fuses, Fuseholders, and Adapters

240-50. General.
 (a) Maximum Voltage.
 (b) Marking.
 (c) Hexagonal Configuration.
 (d) No Live Parts.
 (e) Screw Shell.

240-51. Edison-Base Fuses.
 (a) Classification.
 (b) Replacement Only.
240-52. Edison-Base Fuseholders.
240-53. Type S Fuses.
 (a) Classification.
 (b) Noninterchangeable.
240-54. Type S Fuses, Adapters, and Fuseholders.
 (a) To Fit Edison-Base Fuseholders.
 (b) To Fit Type S Fuses Only.
 (c) Nonremovable.
 (d) Nontamperable.
 (e) Interchangeability.

F. Cartridge Fuses and Fuseholders

240-60. General.
 (a) Maximum Voltage—300-Volt Type.
 (b) Noninterchangeable—0-6000 Ampere Cartridge Fuseholders.
 (c) Marking.
240-61. Classification.

G. Circuit Breakers

240-80. Method of Operation.
240-81. Indicating.
240-82. Nontamperable.
240-83. Marking.
 (a) Durable and Visible.
 (b) Location.
 (c) Interrupting Rating.
 (d) Circuit Breakers Used as Switches.

H. Overcurrent Protection Over 600 Volts, Nominal

240-100. Feeders.
240-101. Branch Circuits.

A. General

240-2. Protection of Equipment. Equipment shall be protected against overcurrent in accordance with the article in this Code covering the type of equipment as specified in the following list.

	Article
Air-Conditioning and Refrigerating Equipment	440
Appliances	422
Branch Circuits	210
Capacitors	460

240-3. Protection of Conductors — Other than Flexible Cords and Fixture Wires. Conductors, other than flexible cords and fixture wires, shall be protected against overcurrent in accordance with their ampacities as specified in Tables 310-16 through 310-19 and all applicable notes to these tables.

Exception No. 1: Next Higher Overcurrent Protective Device Rating. Where the ampacity of the conductor does not correspond with the standard ampere rating of a fuse or a circuit breaker without overload trip adjustment above its rating (but which may have other trip or rating adjustments), the next higher standard device rating shall be permitted only if this rating does not exceed 800 amperes and the conductor is not part of a multioutlet branch circuit supplying receptacles for cord- and plug-connected portable loads.

Table 210-24 summarizes the requirements for the size of conductors where two or more outlets are required. The first footnote also indicates that these ampacities are for copper conductors where derating is not required. Section 210-3 indicates that branch-circuit conductors rated 15, 20, 30, 40, and 50 A, with two or more outlets, must be protected at their ratings. Section 210-19(a) requires that branch-circuit conductors are to have an ampacity of not less than the rating of the branch circuit and not less than the maximum load to be served.

These are specific requirements and take precedence over Section 240-3, Exception No. 1 which applies generally. Where the conductor is not part of a multioutlet branch circuit supplying receptacles for cord- and plug-connected portable loads and the conductor ampacities do not correspond to standard ampere ratings of fuses or circuit breakers, the next standard device rating is permitted if this rating does not exceed 800 A.

Exception No. 2: Tap Conductors. Tap conductors as permitted in Sections 210-19(c); 240-21, Exceptions No. 2, 3, 5, 8, 9 and 10; 364-10 and 364-11; and Part D of Article 430.

Exception No. 3: Motor and Motor-Control Circuits. Motor and motor-control circuit conductors protected in accordance with Parts C, D, E, and F of Article 430. Motor-operated appliance circuit conductors protected in accordance with Parts B and D of Article 422. Air-conditioning and refrigerating equipment circuit conductors protected in accordance with Parts C and F of Article 440.

Exception No. 4: Remote Control Circuits. Remote-control circuits shall comply with Article 725.

See Section 725-12 and Exception Nos. 1, 2, and 3.

Exception No. 5: Transformer Secondary Conductors. Conductors supplied by the secondary side of a single-phase transformer having a 2-wire (single-voltage) secondary shall be considered as protected by overcurrent protection provided on the primary (supply) side of the transformer, provided this protection is in accordance with Section 450-3 and does not exceed the value determined by multiplying the secondary conductor ampacity by the secondary-to-primary transformer voltage ratio. Transformer secondary conductors (other than 2 wire) are not considered to be protected by the primary overcurrent protection.

The main rule of Section 240-3 requires that conductors be protected against overcurrent in accordance with their ampacity. Exception No. 5 permits the secondary circuit conductors from a transformer to be protected by overcurrent devices in the primary circuit conductors of the transformer, provided the transformer consists of a 2-wire primary and a 2-wire secondary and is protected in accordance with Section 450-3.

For example, a transformer that has a 2-wire, 480-V primary and a 2-wire, 240-V secondary with overcurrent protection in the primary rated at 50 A is considered to be protection for the secondary circuit conductors whose ampacity is not less than 100 A.

The secondary to primary ratio of the above transformer is 1:2 or 0.5. Multiplying the secondary conductor ampacity by the secondary to primary ratio results in the maximum rating of the overcurrent device permitted in the primary conductors to protect the secondary conductors. Therefore, the length of the secondary conductors is not limited and no overcurrent protection is required on the secondary side.

If the secondary consists of a 3-wire, 240/120-V system, a line to neutral load (120 V) could draw up to 200 A before the overcurrent device in the primary actuates. This is the result of the 1:4 secondary to primary voltage ratio of the 120-V section of the transformer secondary, thereby causing dangerous overloading of the secondary conductors.

Also, in analyzing the current ratios for a 3-phase transformer, unbalanced loading of the secondary circuit must be considered. Power to a single-phase secondary load will be delivered by all three transformers but the load is not shared equally. The ratio of the currents in the primary and secondary feeder conductors will not be in accordance with the transformer turns ratio.

Exception No. 6: Capacitor circuits which comply with Article 460.

Exception No. 7: Welders circuits which comply with Article 630.

Exception No. 8: Power Loss Hazard. Conductor overload protection shall not be required where the interruption of the circuit would create a hazard, such as in a material handling magnet circuit. Short-circuit protection shall be provided.

240-4. Protection of Fixture Wires and Cords. Flexible cord, including tinsel cord and extension cords, shall be protected against overcurrent in accordance with their ampacities as specified in Table 400-5. Fixture wire shall be protected against overcurrent in accordance with its ampacity as specified in Table 402-5. Supplementary overcurrent protection as in Section 240-10 shall be permitted to be an acceptable means for providing this protection.

Exception No. 1: When a flexible cord or a tinsel cord approved for and used with a specific listed appliance or portable lamps is connected to a branch circuit of Article 210 in accordance with the following:
20-ampere circuits, tinsel cord or No. 18 cord and larger.
30-ampere circuits, No. 16 cord and larger.
40-ampere circuits, cord of 20-ampere capacity and over.
50-ampere circuits, cord of 20-ampere capacity and over.

Exception No. 2: When fixture wire is connected to 120-volt or higher branch circuit of Article 210 in accordance with the following:
20-ampere circuits, No. 18 up to 50 feet (15.2 m) of run length.
20-ampere circuits, No. 16 up to 100 feet (30.5 m) of run length.
20-ampere circuits, No. 14 and larger.
30-ampere circuits, No. 14 and larger.
40-ampere circuits, No. 12 and larger.
50-ampere circuits, No. 12 and larger.

Exception No. 3: Flexible cord used in listed extension cord sets in lengths of 25 feet (7.62 m) or less and having No. 16 AWG conductors, or any length of larger conductors, shall be considered to be protected by 20-ampere branch-circuit overcurrent protection.

Section 240-4 clarifies the requirements for overcurrent protection of flexible cords and fixture wire by referencing Table 400-5 for flexible cords and Table 402-5 for fixture wire ampacity.

Exceptions are provided to permit smaller conductors to be connected to branch circuits of a greater rating where the smaller conductors are approved for and used with a specific listed appliance, portable lamp, or extension cord.

240-6. Standard Ampere Ratings. The standard ampere ratings for fuses and inverse time circuit breakers shall be considered 15, 20, 25, 30, 35, 40, 45, 50, 60, 70, 80, 90, 100, 110, 125, 150, 175, 200, 225, 250, 300, 350, 400, 450, 500, 600, 700, 800, 1000, 1200, 1600, 2000, 2500, 3000, 4000, 5000, and 6000.

Exception: Additional standard ratings for fuses shall be considered 1, 3, 6, 10, and 601.

240-8. Fuses or Circuit Breakers in Parallel. Fuses, circuit breakers, or combinations thereof shall not be connected in parallel.

Exception: Circuit breakers or fuses, factory assembled in parallel, and approved as a unit.

Section 240-8 prohibits the use of fuses or circuit breakers in parallel, and Section 380-17 prohibits the use of fuses in parallel in fused switches.

It is not the intent of this exception to restore the use of standard fuses in parallel in disconnect switches. However, this exception gives recognition to parallel low-voltage circuit breakers or fuses and parallel high-voltage circuit breakers or fuses where tested and factory-assembled in parallel and approved as a unit.

High-voltage fuses have long been recognized in parallel where assembled in an identified common mounting as per Section 710-21(b)(1).

240-9. Thermal Devices. Thermal cutouts, thermal relays, and other devices not designed to open short circuits shall not be used for the protection of conductors against overcurrent due to short circuits or grounds but the use of such devices shall be permitted to protect motor-branch-circuit conductors from overload if protected in accordance with Section 430-40.

Thermal cutouts are overcurrent protective devices consisting of a heater element that senses overloads on motors or motor branch-circuit conductors and opens the circuit by actuating a renewable fusible member. They are not designed to interrupt short-circuit currents.

240-10. Supplementary Overcurrent Protection. Where supplementary overcurrent protection is used for lighting fixtures, appliances, and other equipment or for internal circuits and components of equipment, it shall not be used as a substitute for branch-circuit overcurrent devices or in place of the branch-circuit protection specified in Article 210. Supplementary overcurrent devices shall not be required to be readily accessible.

240-11. Definition of Current-Limiting Overcurrent Protective Device. A current-limiting overcurrent protective device is a device which, when interrupting currents in its current-limiting range, will reduce the current flowing in the faulted circuit to a magnitude substantially less than that obtainable in the same circuit if the device were replaced with a solid conductor having comparable impedance.

Most electrical distribution systems can deliver large short-circuit currents to components, such as conductors, service equipment, etc. These components are

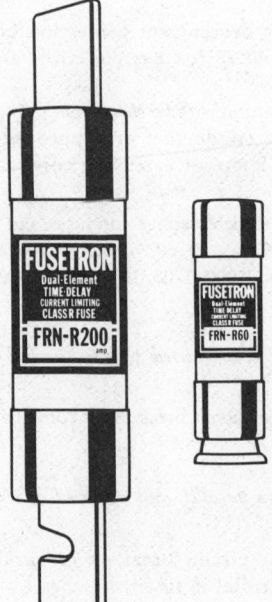

Figure 240-1. Class R current-limiting fuse with rejection feature to prohibit the installation of noncurrent-limiting fuses. (*Bussman Mfg. Co.*)

not generally able to handle short-circuit currents; they can be damaged or destroyed and serious "burndowns" and fires could result. Properly selected current-limiting overcurrent protective devices will limit the let-through energy to within the rating of the components in spite of high available short-circuit currents.

See Sections 110-9 and 110-10 for interrupting ratings, circuit impedance, and other characteristics requirements.

240-12. Electrical System Coordination. In industrial locations where an orderly shutdown is required to minimize hazard(s) to personnel and equipment, a system of coordination based on the following two conditions shall be permitted:

(1) Coordinated short-circuit protection.

(2) Overload indication based on monitoring systems or devices.

(FPN): Coordination is defined as properly localizing a fault condition to restrict outages to the equipment affected, accomplished by choice of selective fault-protective devices. The monitoring system may cause the condition to go to alarm allowing corrective action or an orderly shutdown thereby minimizing personnel hazard and equipment damage.

B. Location

240-20. Ungrounded Conductors.

(a) Overcurrent Device Required. A fuse or an overcurrent trip unit of a circuit breaker shall be connected in series with each ungrounded conductor. A combination of a current transformer and overcurrent relay shall be considered equivalent to an overcurrent trip unit.

(FPN): For motor circuits, see Parts C, D, F, and J of Article 430.

(b) Circuit Breaker as Overcurrent Device. Circuit breakers shall open all ungrounded conductors of the circuit.

Exception: Individual single-pole circuit breakers shall be acceptable as the protection for each ungrounded conductor of 3-wire direct-current or single-phase circuits, or for each ungrounded conductor of lighting or appliance branch circuits connected to 4-wire, 3-phase systems or 5-wire, 2-phase systems, provided such lighting or appliance circuits are supplied from a system having a grounded neutral and no conductor in such circuits operates at a voltage greater than permitted in Section 210-6.

240-21. Location in Circuit. An overcurrent device shall be connected at the point where the conductor to be protected receives its supply.

Exception No. 1: Smaller Conductor Protected. Where the overcurrent device protecting the larger conductor also protects the smaller conductor in accordance with Tables 310-16 through 310-19.

Exception No. 1 is illustrated by Figure 240-2. A smaller 1/0 THW conductor (150 A) is tapped from a larger 3/0 THW feeder conductor (200 A) which is in turn protected by a 150-A circuit breaker that is equal to the ampacity of the 1/0 tap conductor. The circuit breaker protecting the feeder conductors is rated to protect the tap conductors.

ARTICLE 240—OVERCURRENT PROTECTION

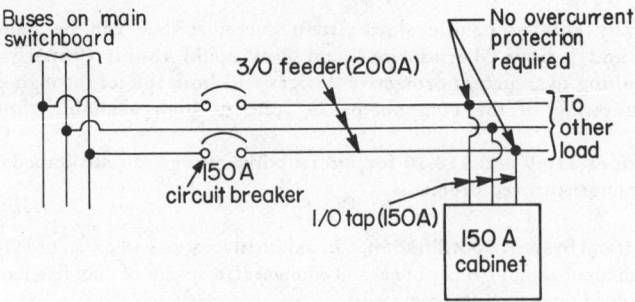

Figure 240-2. The circuit breaker protecting the feeder conductors also protects the tap conductors to the cabinet, in this case.

Exception No. 2: Feeder Taps Not Over 10 Feet (3.05 m) Long. For conductors tapped to a feeder or transformer secondary where all the following conditions are met:

a. The length of the tap conductors does not exceed 10 feet (3.05 m).

b. The ampacity of the tap conductors is:

(1) not less than the combined computed loads on the circuits supplied by the tap conductors, and

(2a) not less than the rating of the device supplied by the tap conductors, or

(2b) not less than the rating of the overcurrent protective device at the termination of the tap conductors.

c. The tap conductors do not extend beyond the switchboard, panelboard, or control devices they supply.

d. Except at the point of connection to the feeder, the tap conductors are enclosed in a raceway, which shall extend from the tap to the enclosure of an enclosed switchboard, panelboard, or control devices, or to the back of an open switchboard.

(FPN): See Section 384-16(a) for lighting and appliance branch-circuit panelboards.

Exception No. 2 permits a tap from a feeder or from a transformer secondary without requiring overcurrent protection at the point where the tap conductor receives its supply, provided the tap conductor (1) is not more than 10 ft long, (2) is enclosed in a raceway, (3) does not extend beyond the switchboard, panelboard, or control devices that it supplies, and (4) has an ampacity not less than the combined computed loads supplied and not less than the ampere rating of the switchboard, panelboard, or control devices supplied, except where the tap conductor terminates in an overcurrent protective device which does not exceed the ampacity of the tap conductor.

Exception No. 3: Feeder Taps Not Over 25 Feet (7.62 m) Long. For conductors tapped to a feeder where all of the following conditions are met:

a. The length of the tap conductors does not exceed 25 feet (7.62 m).

b. The ampacity of the tap conductors is not less than ⅓ that of the feeder conductors or overcurrent protection from which they are tapped.

c. The tap conductors terminate with a single circuit breaker or a single set of fuses that will limit the load to the ampacity of the tap conductors. This single overcurrent device shall be permitted to supply any number of additional overcurrent devices on its load side.

d. The tap conductors are suitably protected from physical damage and are enclosed in a raceway.

Exception No. 3 is illustrated in Figure 240-3. Three No. 3/0 THW copper tap conductors are protected from physical damage in a raceway. The lengths of the tap conductors are not more than 25 ft between terminations. They are tapped from a 500 MCM feeder and terminate in a circuit breaker.

Note: A No. 3/0 THW copper conductor (200 A) is more than ⅓ the ampacity of a 500 MCM THW (380 A) copper conductor. See Table 310-16 for ampacity of copper conductors in conduit.

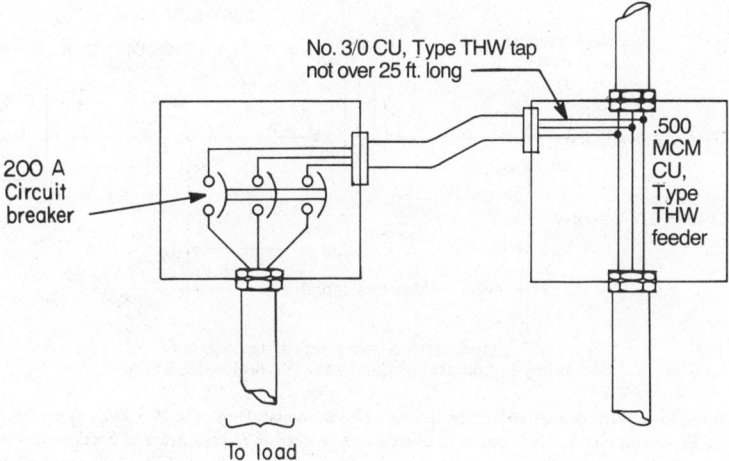

No. 3/0 CU, Type THW tap
not over 25 ft. long

.500 MCM CU, Type THW feeder

200 A Circuit breaker

To load

Figure 240-3. Feeder taps terminating in a single circuit breaker. See Exception No. 3.

Exception No. 4: Service Conductors. For service-entrance conductors where protected in accordance with Section 230-91.

Exception No. 5: Branch-Circuit Taps. Taps to individual outlets and circuit conductors supplying a single household electric range shall be considered as protected by the branch-circuit overcurrent devices when in accordance with the requirements of Sections 210-19, 210-20, and 210-24.

Exception No. 6: Motor Circuit Taps. For motor-branch-circuit conductors where protected in accordance with Sections 430-28 and 430-53.

Exception No. 7: Busway Taps. For busways where protected in accordance with Sections 364-10 through 364-14.

Exception No. 8: Transformer Feeder Taps with Primary Plus Secondary Not Over 25 Feet (7.62 m) Long. Where all of the following conditions are met:

a. The conductors supplying the primary of a transformer have an ampacity at least ⅓ that of the conductors or overcurrent protection from which they are tapped.

b. The conductors supplied by the secondary of the transformer have an ampacity that, when multiplied by the ratio of the secondary-to-primary voltage, is at least ⅓ the ampacity of the conductors or overcurrent protection from which the primary conductors are tapped.

c. The total length of one primary plus one secondary conductor, excluding any portion of the primary conductor that is protected at its ampacity, is not over 25 feet (7.62 m).

d. The primary and secondary conductors are suitably protected from physical damage.

e. The secondary conductors terminate in a single circuit breaker or set of fuses which will limit the load to that allowed in Tables 310-16 through 310-19.

Exception No. 8 is illustrated in Figure 240-4.

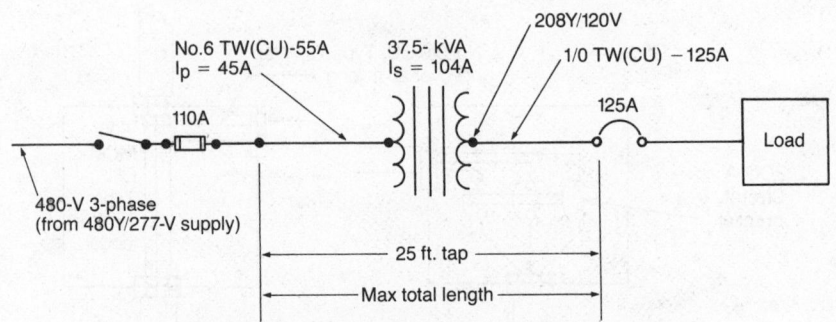

Figure 240-4. Transformer feeder taps (primary plus secondary) not over 25 ft long, as per Section 240-21, Exception No. 8. Also applies to overcurrent protection requirements of Sections 384-16(a) and 450-3(b).

Exception No. 9: Conductors from generator terminals to the first overcurrent device as covered in Section 445-5.

Exception No. 10: Feeder Taps Over 25 Feet (7.62 m) Long. In high bay manufacturing buildings [over 35 feet (10.67 m) high at walls], where conditions of maintenance and supervision assure that only qualified persons will service the systems, conductors tapped to a feeder shall be permitted to be not over 25 feet (7.62 m) long horizontally and not over 100 feet (30.5 m) total length where all of the following conditions are met.

a. The ampacity of the tap conductors is not less than ⅓ that of the overcurrent device from which they are supplied.

b. The tap conductors terminate with a single circuit breaker or a single set of fuses that will limit the load to the ampacity of the tap conductors. This single overcurrent device shall be permitted to supply any number of additional overcurrent devices on its load side.

c. The tap conductors are suitably protected from physical damage and are installed in raceways.

d. The tap conductors are continuous from end-to-end and contain no splices.

e. The tap conductors shall be No. 6 AWG copper or No. 4 AWG aluminum or larger.

f. The tap conductors shall not penetrate walls, floors, or ceilings.

g. The tap shall be made no less than 30 feet (9.14 m) from the floor.

See Figure 240-5.

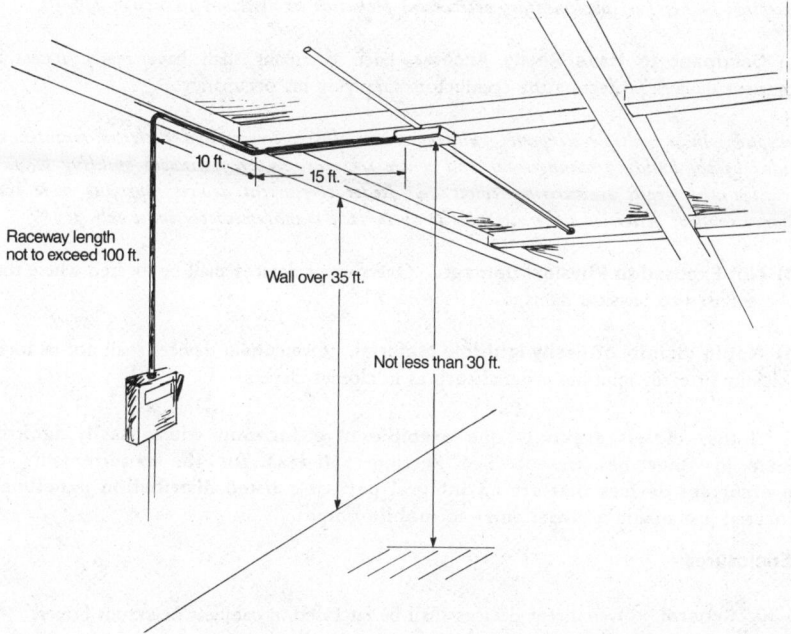

Figure 240-5. Section 240-21, Exception No. 9 permits a tap rule of 100 ft for manufacturing buildings with walls over 35 ft high. The tap connection is not less than 30 ft from the floor and conditions of maintenance and supervision must ensure that only qualified persons will service these systems.

240-22. Grounded Conductors. No overcurrent device shall be connected in series with any conductor that is intentionally grounded.

Exception No. 1: Where the overcurrent device opens all conductors of the circuit, including the grounded conductor, and is so designed that no pole can operate independently.

Exception No. 2: Where required by Sections 430-36 and 430-37 for motor overload protection.

240-23. Change in Size of Grounded Conductor. Where a change occurs in the size of the ungrounded conductor, a similar change shall be permitted to be made in the size of the grounded conductor.

This section acknowledges that the size of a grounded conductor may be increased or reduced to correspond to a change made in the size of an ungrounded conductor, such as in tap conductors, where all are of the same circuit.

240-24. Location in or on Premises.

(a) Readily Accessible. Overcurrent devices shall be readily accessible.

Exception No. 1: For busways as provided in Section 364-12.

This section is intended to correlate with Section 230-91, i.e., the service overcurrent device shall be an integral part of the service disconnecting means or shall be located immediately adjacent thereto. See comments following Section 230-91.

Exception No. 2: For supplementary overcurrent protection as described in Section 240-10.

(b) Occupant to Have Ready Access. Each occupant shall have ready access to all overcurrent devices protecting the conductors supplying his occupancy.

Exception: In a multiple-occupancy building where electric service and electrical maintenance are provided by the building management and where these are under continuous building management supervision, the service overcurrent devices and feeder overcurrent devices supplying more than one occupancy shall be permitted to be accessible to authorized management personnel only.

(c) Not Exposed to Physical Damage. Overcurrent devices shall be located where they will not be exposed to physical damage.

(d) Not in Vicinity of Easily Ignitible Material. Overcurrent devices shall not be located in the vicinity of easily ignitible material such as in clothes closets.

Clothes closets are only one example of a location where easily ignitible materials may be present. See Section 550-4(a) for the requirements for overcurrent devices that are an integral part of a listed distribution panelboard located just inside a closet entry in mobile homes.

C. Enclosures

240-30. General. Overcurrent devices shall be enclosed in cabinets or cutout boxes.

Exception No. 1: Where a part of an assembly that provides equivalent protection.

Exception No. 2: Where mounted on open-type switchboards, panelboards, or control boards that are in rooms or enclosures free from dampness and easily ignitible material and accessible only to qualified personnel.

Exception No. 3: The operating handle of a circuit breaker shall be permitted to be accessible without opening a door or cover.

Properly selected overcurrent protective devices are designed to open a circuit before an overcurrent condition can seriously damage conductor insulation, and requirements that overcurrent devices be enclosed in cabinets or cutout boxes are to ensure that electrical disturbances in the vicinity will be kept to a minimum. Overcurrent devices mounted on open-type switchboards, panelboards, or controlboards and having exposed live parts are to be located where accessible only to qualified persons.

240-32. Damp or Wet Locations. Enclosures for overcurrent devices in damp or wet locations shall be identified for use in such locations and shall be mounted so there is at least ¼-inch (6.35-mm) air space between the enclosure and the wall or other supporting surface.

240-33. Vertical Position. Enclosures for overcurrent devices shall be mounted in a vertical position.

Exception: Where this is shown to be impracticable and complies with Section 240-81.

This section indicates that a wall-mounted, vertical position is desirable to achieve easier access, natural hand-operation, normal swing or closing of doors or covers, and legibility of manufacturer's markings.

D. Disconnecting and Guarding

240-40. Disconnecting Means for Fuses and Thermal Cutouts. Disconnecting means shall be provided on the supply side of all fuses or thermal cutouts in circuits of over 150 volts to ground and cartridge fuses in circuits of any voltage, where accessible to other than qualified persons, so that each individual circuit containing fuses or thermal cutouts can be independently disconnected from the source of electric energy.

Exception No. 1: A device provided for current limiting on the supply side of the service disconnecting means as permitted by Section 230-82.

Exception No. 2: A single disconnecting means shall be permitted on the supply side of more than one set of fuses as provided by Section 430-112 for group operation of motors and in Section 424-22 for fixed electric space heating equipment.

Plug fuses are classified at not more than 125 V and 0 to 30 A (Section 240-51).

Cartridge fuses of the nonrenewable type are classified 0-600 A at not more than 250 V, 0-600 A at not more than 300 V, and 0-6000 A at not more than 600 V (Section 240-61). A disconnecting means must be provided whenever cartridge fuses are accessible to other than qualified persons.

Note: Cartridge fuseholders have live parts openly exposed to personnel during replacement of fuses.

240-41. Arcing or Suddenly Moving Parts. Arcing or suddenly moving parts shall comply with (a) and (b) below.

(a) Location. Fuses and circuit breakers shall be so located or shielded that persons will not be burned or otherwise injured by their operation.

(b) Suddenly Moving Parts. Handles or levers of circuit breakers, and similar parts which may move suddenly in such a way that persons in the vicinity are likely to be injured by being struck by them, shall be guarded or isolated.

Arcing or suddenly moving parts are usually associated with switchboards or controlboards which may be of the open type and which should be under competent supervision and accessible only to qualified persons. Fuses or circuit breakers are to be so located or shielded that under an abnormal condition the subsequent arc across the opened device will not injure persons in the vicinity.

Guardrails may be provided in the vicinity of disconnecting means. Modern switchboards, etc., are equipped with removable handles but these sudden-moving handles may be capable of causing injury.

See Article 100 for definition of "Guarded." See also Section 110-17.

E. Plug Fuses, Fuseholders, and Adapters

240-50. General.

(a) Maximum Voltage. Plug fuses and fuseholders shall not be used in circuits exceeding 125 volts between conductors.

Exception: In circuits supplied by a system having a grounded neutral and having no conductor at over 150 volts to ground.

(b) Marking. Each fuse, fuseholder, and adapter shall be marked with its ampere rating.

(c) Hexagonal Configuration. Plug fuses of 15-ampere and lower rating shall be identified by a hexagonal configuration of the window, cap, or other prominent part to distinguish them from fuses of higher ampere ratings.

(d) No Live Parts. Plug fuses, fuseholders, and adapters shall have no exposed live parts after fuses or fuses and adapters have been installed.

(e) Screw Shell. The screw shell of a plug-type fuseholder shall be connected to the load side of the circuit.

240-51. Edison-Base Fuses.

(a) Classification. Plug fuses of the Edison-base type shall be classified at not over 125 volts and 0 to 30 amperes.

(b) Replacement Only. Plug fuses of the Edison-base type shall be used only for replacements in existing installations where there is no evidence of overfusing or tampering.

240-52. Edison-Base Fuseholders. Fuseholders of the Edison-base type shall be installed only where they are made to accept Type S fuses by the use of adapters.

240-53. Type S Fuses. Type S fuses shall be of the plug type and shall comply with (a) and (b) below.

(a) Classification. Type S fuses shall be classified at not over 125 volts and 0 to 15 amperes, 16 to 20 amperes, and 21 to 30 amperes.

(b) Noninterchangeable. Type S fuses of an ampere classification as specified in (a) above shall not be interchangeable with a lower ampere classification. They shall be so designed that they cannot be used in any fuseholder other than a Type S fuseholder or a fuseholder with a Type S adapter inserted.

240-54. Type S Fuses, Adapters, and Fuseholders.

(a) To Fit Edison-Base Fuseholders. Type S adapters shall fit Edison-base fuseholders.

(b) To Fit Type S Fuses Only. Type S fuseholders and adapters shall be so designed that either the fuseholder itself or the fuseholder with a Type S adapter inserted cannot be used for any fuse other than a Type S fuse.

(c) Nonremovable. Type S adapters shall be so designed that once inserted in a fuseholder, they cannot be removed.

(d) Nontamperable. Type S fuses, fuseholders, and adapters shall be so designed that tampering or shunting (bridging) would be difficult.

(e) Interchangeability. Dimensions of Type S fuses, fuseholders, and adapters shall be standardized to permit interchangeability regardless of the manufacturer.

F. Cartridge Fuses and Fuseholders

240-60. General.

(a) Maximum Voltage — 300-Volt Type. Cartridge fuses and fuseholders of the 300-volt type shall not be used in circuits of over 300 volts between conductors.

Exception: In circuits supplied by a system having a grounded neutral and having no conductor at over 300 volts to ground.

(b) Noninterchangeable — 0-6000 Ampere Cartridge Fuseholders. Fuseholders shall be so designed that it will be difficult to put a fuse of any given class into a fuseholder that is designed for a current lower, or voltage higher, than that of the class to which it belongs. Fuseholders for current-limiting fuses shall not permit insertion of fuses that are not current limiting.

(c) Marking. Fuses shall be plainly marked, either by printing on the fuse barrel or by a label attached to the barrel, showing the following: (1) ampere rating; (2) voltage rating; (3) interrupting rating where other than 10,000 amperes; (4) "current limiting" where applicable; (5) the name or trademark of the manufacturer.

Exception: Interrupting rating marking shall not be required on fuses used for supplementary protection.

240-61. Classification. Cartridge fuses and fuseholders shall be classified according to voltage and amperage ranges. Fuses rated 600 volts, nominal, or less, shall be permitted to be used for voltages at or below their ratings.

See Section 710-21(b)(3) for application of high-voltage fuses.

G. Circuit Breakers

240-80. Method of Operation. Circuit breakers shall be trip free and capable of being closed and opened by manual operation. Their normal method of operation by other than manual means such as electrical or pneumatic shall be permitted if means for manual operation is also provided.

240-81. Indicating. Circuit breakers shall clearly indicate whether they are in the open "off" or closed "on" position.
Where circuit breaker handles on switchboards or in panelboards are operated vertically rather than rotationally or horizontally, the "up" position of the handle shall be the "on" position.

240-82. Nontamperable. A circuit breaker shall be of such design that any alteration of its trip point (calibration) or the time required for its operation will require dismantling of the device or breaking of a seal for other than intended adjustments.

240-83. Marking.

(a) Durable and Visible. Circuit breakers shall be marked with their ampere rating in a manner that will be durable and visible after installation. Such marking shall be required to be visible after removal of a trim or cover.

(b) Location. Circuit breakers rated at 100 amperes or less and 600 volts or less shall have the ampere rating molded, stamped, etched, or similarly marked into their handles or escutcheon areas.

(c) Interrupting Rating. Every circuit breaker having an interrupting rating other than 5000 amperes shall have its interrupting rating shown on the circuit breaker.

Exception: Interrupting rating marking shall not be required on circuit breakers used for supplementary protection.

(d) Circuit Breakers Used as Switches. Where used as switches in 120-volt and 277-volt fluorescent lighting circuits, circuit breakers shall be approved for such switching duty and shall be marked "SWD."

The marking of cartridge fuses, as per Section 240-60(c), with regard to interrupting capacity (IC) requires that the rating for other than 10,000 A be plainly marked on the fuse barrel. Class H-type cartridge fuses have a rating (IC) of 10,000 A, and this rating need not be marked on the fuse. However, Class G, J, K, L, R, and T cartridge fuses have over a 10,000 A interrupting rating (IC) and must be marked.

The marking of circuit breakers, as shown in Section 240-83(c), with regard to interrupting capacity (IC) requires that the rating for other than 5,000 A be indicated on the circuit breaker.

Fuses or circuit breakers used for supplementary protection of fluorescent fixtures, semiconductor rectifiers, motor-operated appliances, etc., need not be marked for IC.

Switching duty circuit breakers (SWD) are required where the breakers are used as switches for 120-V and 277-V fluorescent lighting. Switching duty circuit breakers generally have heavier-duty contacts.

H. Overcurrent Protection Over 600 Volts, Nominal

240-100. Feeders. Feeders shall have a short-circuit protective device in each ungrounded conductor or comply with Section 230-208(d)(2) or (d)(3). The protective device(s) shall be capable of detecting and interrupting all values of current which can occur at their location in excess of their trip setting or melting point. In no case shall the fuse rating in continuous amperes exceed three times, or the long-time trip element setting of a breaker six times, the ampacity of the conductor.

Conductors tapped to a feeder shall be permitted to be protected by the feeder overcurrent device where that overcurrent device also protects the tap conductors.

(FPN): The operating time of the protective device, the available short-circuit current, and the conductor used will need to be coordinated to prevent damaging or dangerous temperatures in conductors or conductor insulation under short-circuit conditions.

240-101. Branch Circuits. Branch circuits shall have a short-circuit protective device in each ungrounded conductor or comply with Section 230-208(d)(2) or (d)(3). The protective device(s) shall be capable of detecting and interrupting all values of current which can occur at their location in excess of their trip setting or melting point.

ARTICLE 250 — GROUNDING

Contents

250-115. Connection to Electrodes.
    (a) An Approved Bolted Clamp.
    (b) Pipe Fitting, Pipe Plug, etc.
    (c) Sheet-Metal-Strap   Type Ground Clamp.
    (d) An Equally Substantial Approved Means.
250-117. Protection of Attachment.
    (a) Not Likely to Be Damaged.
    (b) Protective Covering.
250-118. Clean Surfaces.

L. Instrument Transformers, Relays, etc.

250-121. Instrument Transformer Circuits.
250-122. Instrument Transformer Cases.
250-123. Cases of Instruments, Meters, and Relays—Operating at Less than 1000 Volts.
    (a) Not on Switchboards.
    (b) On Dead-Front Switchboards.
    (c) On Live-Front Switchboards.
250-124. Cases of Instruments, Meters, and Relays—Operating Voltage 1 kV and Over.
250-125. Instrument Grounding Conductor.

M. Grounding of Systems and Circuits of 1 kV and Over (High Voltage)

250-150. General.
250-151. Derived Neutral Systems.
250-152. Solidly Grounded Neutral Systems.
    (a) Neutral Conductor.
    (b) Multiple Grounding.
250-153. Impedance Grounded Neutral Systems.
    (a) Location.
    (b) Identified and Insulated.
    (c) System Neutral Connection.
    (d) Equipment Grounding Conductors.
250-154. Grounding of Systems Supplying Portable or Mobile Equipment.
    (a) Portable or Mobile Equipment.
    (b) Exposed Noncurrent-Carrying Metal Parts.
    (c) Ground-Fault Current.
    (d) Ground-Fault Detection and Relaying.
    (e) Isolation.
    (f) Trailing Cable and Couplers.
250-155. Grounding of Equipment.

A. General

250-1. Scope. This article covers general requirements for grounding and bonding of electrical installations, and specific requirements in (a) through (f) below.

(a) Systems, circuits, and equipment required, permitted, or not permitted to be grounded.

(b) Circuit conductor to be grounded on grounded systems.

(c) Location of grounding connections.

(d) Types and sizes of grounding and bonding conductors and electrodes.

(e) Methods of grounding and bonding.

(f) Conditions under which guards, isolation, or insulation may be substituted for grounding.

(FPN): Systems and circuit conductors are grounded to limit voltages due to lightning, line surges, or unintentional contact with higher voltage lines, and to stabilize the voltage to ground during normal operation. Systems and circuit conductors are solidly grounded to facilitate overcurrent device operation in case of ground faults.

(FPN): Conductive materials enclosing electrical conductors or equipment, or forming part of such equipment, are grounded to limit the voltage to ground on these materials and to facilitate overcurrent device operation in case of ground faults. See Section 110-10.

250-2. Application of Other Articles. In other articles applying to particular cases of installation of conductors and equipment, there are requirements that are in addition to those of this article or are modifications of them:

ARTICLE 250—GROUNDING

B. Circuit and System Grounding

250-3. Direct-Current Systems.

(a) **Two-Wire Direct Current Systems.** Two-wire dc systems supplying premises wiring shall be grounded.

Exception No. 1: A system equipped with a ground detector and supplying only industrial equipment in limited areas.

Exception No. 2: A system operating at 50 volts or less between conductors.

Exception No. 3: A system operating at over 300 volts between conductors.

Exception No. 4: A rectifier-derived dc system supplied from an ac system complying with Section 250-5.

Exception No. 5: DC fire protective signaling circuits having a maximum current of 0.030 amperes as specified in Article 760, Part C.

(b) **Three-Wire Direct-Current Systems.** The neutral conductor of all 3-wire dc systems supplying premises wiring shall be grounded.

250-5. Alternating-Current Circuits and Systems to Be Grounded.
AC circuits and systems shall be grounded as provided for in (a), (b), (c), or (d) below. Other circuits and systems shall be permitted to be grounded.

(a) **Alternating-Current Circuits of Less than 50 Volts.** AC circuits of less than 50 volts shall be grounded under any of the following conditions:

(1) Where supplied by transformers if the transformer supply system exceeds 150 volts to ground.

(2) Where supplied by transformers if the transformer supply system is ungrounded.

(3) Where installed as overhead conductors outside of buildings.

(b) Alternating-Current Systems of 50 Volts to 1000 Volts. AC systems of 50 volts to 1000 volts supplying premises wiring and premises wiring systems shall be grounded under any of the following conditions:

(1) Where the system can be so grounded that the maximum voltage to ground on the ungrounded conductors does not exceed 150 volts.

(2) Where the system is nominally rated 480Y/277-volt, 3-phase, 4-wire in which the neutral is used as a circuit conductor.

(3) Where the system is nominally rated 240/120-volt, 3-phase, 4-wire in which the midpoint of one phase is used as a circuit conductor.

(4) Where a service conductor is uninsulated in accordance with Section 230-4.

Exception No. 1: Electric systems used exclusively to supply industrial electric furnaces for melting, refining, tempering, and the like.

Exception No. 2: Separately derived systems used exclusively for rectifiers supplying only adjustable speed industrial drives.

Exception No. 3: Separately derived systems supplied by transformers that have a primary voltage rating less than 1000 volts provided that all of the following conditions are met:

a. The system is used exclusively for control circuits.

b. The conditions of maintenance and supervision assure that only qualified persons will service the installation.

c. Continuity of control power is required.

d. Ground detectors are installed on the control system.

Exception No. 4: Isolated systems as permitted in Article 517.

(FPN): The proper use of suitable ground detectors on ungrounded systems can provide additional protection.

(c) Alternating-Current Systems of 1 kV and Over. AC systems of 1 kV and over supplying mobile or portable equipment shall be grounded as specified in Section 250-154. Where supplying other than portable equipment, such systems shall be permitted to be grounded. Where such systems are grounded, they shall comply with the applicable provisions of this article.

(d) Separately Derived Systems. A premises wiring system whose power is derived from generator, transformer, or converter windings and has no direct electrical connection, including a solidly connected grounded circuit conductor, to supply conductors originating in another system, if required to be grounded as in (a) or (b) above, shall be grounded as specified in Section 250-26.

Figures 250-1 (A) and (B) depict a 480Y/277-V electrical service supplying a service disconnecting means to a building. The load side (feeder) conductors are to a dry-type transformer that transforms the 480Y/277-V system to a 208Y/120-V system. The 208Y/120-V system is fed through a transfer switch that is connected to a generator intended to provide power for an emergency or standby system. Figure 250-1(A) does not have the neutral conductor connected to the 3-pole transfer switch; thus there is a direct electrical connection of the grounded circuit conductor (neutral) to the generator. Therefore, the system supplied by the generator is not a separately derived system, and there are no requirements for grounding the neutral at the generator. Under these conditions it is necessary to run an equipment grounding conductor from the dry-type transformer to the 3-pole transfer switch and from the 3-pole transfer switch to the generator.

Figure 250-1(B) shows the grounded conductor (neutral) connected to a 4-pole transfer switch. Therefore, the generator system does not have a direct electrical connection to the grounded circuit conductor (neutral), and the generator is a separately derived system grounded in accordance with Section 250-26.

Note that each of the dry-type transformers in Figures 250-1 (A) and (B) qualifies as a separately derived system since they have no direct electrical connections, including the solidly connected grounded circuit conductor (neutral) to the supply conductors originating from the service disconnecting means.

Section 250-26 requires that a bonding jumper be installed and connected from the generator frame to the grounded circuit conductor (neutral). The grounding electrode conductor from the generator is required to be connected to a grounding electrode. This conductor should be located as close to the generator as practical. The preferred grounding electrode is the nearest effectively grounded structural metal member or the nearest available effectively grounded metal water pipe if they are available. If neither of these preferred grounding electrodes is available, then other electrodes specified in Sections 250-81 and 250-83 are permitted to be used.

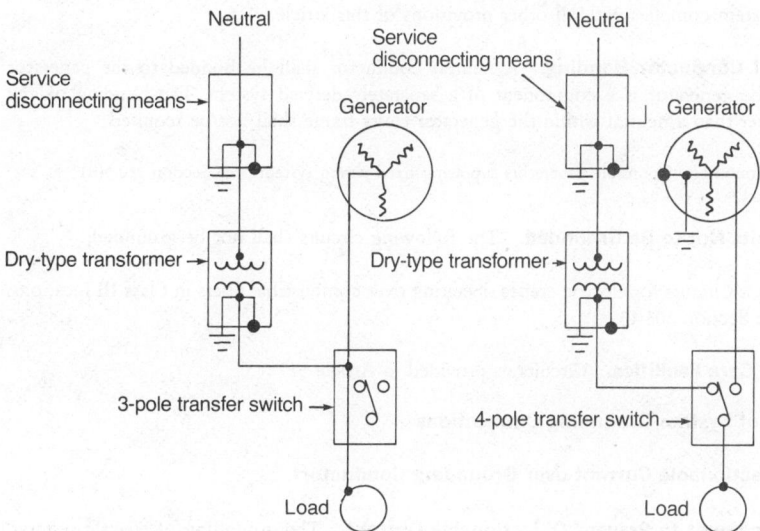

Figure 250-1. Installation A (left) has a direct electrical connection of the grounded circuit conductor (neutral) to the generator; therefore, the generator is not a separately derived system and there are no requirements for grounding the neutral. Installation B (right) does not have a direct electrical connection of the grounded circuit conductor (neutral); therefore, the generator is a separately derived system and is grounded in accordance with Section 250-26.

250-6. Portable and Vehicle-Mounted Generators.

(a) Portable Generators. Under the following conditions the frame of a portable generator shall not be required to be grounded and shall be permitted to serve as the grounding electrode for a system supplied by the generator:

(1) The generator supplies only equipment mounted on the generator and/or cord- and plug-connected equipment through receptacles mounted on the generator, and

(2) The noncurrent-carrying metal parts of equipment and the equipment grounding conductor terminals of the receptacles are bonded to the generator frame.

(b) Vehicle-Mounted Generators. Under the following conditions the frame of a vehicle shall be permitted to serve as the grounding electrode for a system supplied by a generator located on the vehicle:

(1) The frame of the generator is bonded to the vehicle frame, and

(2) The generator supplies only equipment located on the vehicle and/or cord- and plug-connected equipment through receptacles mounted on the vehicle or on the generator, and

(3) The noncurrent-carrying metal parts of equipment and the equipment grounding conductor terminals of the receptacles are bonded to the generator frame, and

(4) The system complies with all other provisions of this article.

(c) Neutral Conductor Bonding. A neutral conductor shall be bonded to the generator frame when the generator is a component of a separately derived system. The bonding of any conductor other than a neutral within the generator to its frame shall not be required.

(FPN): For grounding of portable generators supplying fixed wiring systems, see Section 250-5(d).

250-7. Circuits Not to Be Grounded. The following circuits shall not be grounded:

(a) Cranes. Circuits for electric cranes operating over combustible fibers in Class III locations, as provided in Section 503-13.

(b) Health Care Facilities. Circuits as provided in Article 517.

C. Location of System Grounding Connections

250-21. Objectionable Current over Grounding Conductors.

(a) Arrangement to Prevent Objectionable Current. The grounding of electric systems, circuit conductors, surge arresters, and conductive noncurrent-carrying materials and equipment shall be installed and arranged in a manner that will prevent an objectionable flow of current over the grounding conductors or grounding paths.

(b) Alterations to Stop Objectionable Current. If the use of multiple grounding connections results in an objectionable flow of current, one or more of the following alterations shall be made:

(1) Discontinue one or more such grounding connections.

(2) Change the locations of the grounding connections.

(3) Interrupt the continuity of the conductor or conductive path interconnecting the grounding connections.

(4) Take other suitable remedial action satisfactory to the authority having jurisdiction.

Section 250-21(b) is not intended to permit deletion of all grounding connections.

(c) Temporary Currents Not Classified as Objectionable Currents. Temporary currents resulting from accidental conditions, such as ground-fault currents, that occur only while the grounding conductors are performing their intended protective functions shall not be classified as objectionable current for the purposes specified in (a) and (b) above.

250-22. Point of Connection for Direct-Current Systems. DC systems to be grounded shall have the grounding connection made at one or more supply stations. A grounding connection shall not be made at individual services nor at any point on premises wiring.

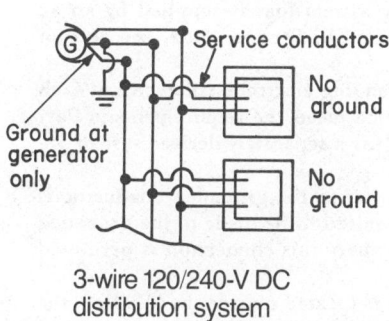

3-wire 120/240-V DC
distribution system

Figure 250-2. The neutral is shown grounded at the generator site in this 3-wire dc distribution system. Grounding of a 2-wire dc system would be accomplished in the same manner.

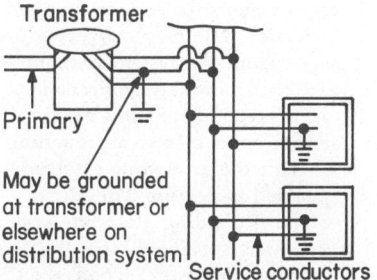

3-wire 120/240-V AC single-phase
secondary distribution system

Figure 250-3. On a 2-wire or 3-wire single-phase ac secondary distribution system, grounding connections are made on the secondary side of the transformer and on the supply side of the service disconnecting means.

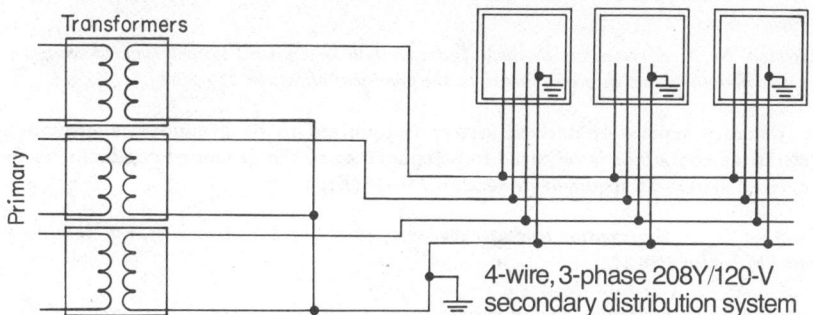

4-wire, 3-phase 208Y/120-V
secondary distribution system

Figure 250-4. The neutral is grounded at each service and also on the secondary side of the transformer on this 4-wire, 3-phase, 208Y/120-V secondary distribution system. When 3-wire, 3-phase service equipment is installed for power purposes on this type of ac system, the grounded (neutral) conductor is required to be run to the service equipment. See Section 250-23(b).

ARTICLE 250—GROUNDING

250-23. Grounding Service-Supplied Alternating-Current Systems.

(a) System Grounding Connections. A premises wiring system that is supplied by an ac service and is required to be grounded by Section 250-5 shall have at each service a grounding electrode conductor connected to a grounding electrode which complies with Part H of Article 250. The grounding electrode conductor shall be connected to the grounded service conductor at any accessible point from the load end of the service drop or service lateral to and including the terminal or bus to which the grounded service conductor is connected at the service disconnecting means. Where the transformer supplying the service is located outside the building, at least one additional grounding connection shall be made from the grounded service conductor to a grounding electrode, either at the transformer or elsewhere outside the building. A grounding connection shall not be made to any grounded circuit conductor on the load side of the service disconnecting means.

The power for ac premises wiring systems is either separately derived in accordance with Section 250-5(d), or is supplied by the service (see definition of "Service" in Article 100). Section 250-26 covers grounding requirements for separately derived ac systems. Section 250-23(a) covers system grounding requirements for service-supplied ac systems.

Section 250-23(a) covers a premises wiring system that is supplied by an ac service and the system is required to be grounded by Section 250-5. See Section 250-26 for similar requirements.

This type of system is required to have a grounding electrode conductor at each service connected to a grounding electrode which meets the requirements in Part H. Note the grounding electrode requirements for a separately derived system are specified in Section 250-26(c).

The grounding electrode conductor connection to the grounded conductor is accurately specified. First, the connection is required to be made to the grounded service conductor. Second, the *Code* describes where this connection is permitted to be made to the grounded service conductor.

Where the transformer supplying the service is located outside the building, the additional grounding connection to the grounded service conductor is required to be made outside the building. It is unnecessary to specify that this connection is to be made on the secondary side of the transformer because of the definition of "Service Conductors" in Article 100.

The main rule is that a grounding connection shall not be made to any grounded circuit conductor on the load side of the service disconnecting means. See Exception Nos. 1 through 5 below.

(FPN): See definition of Service Drop and Service Lateral; also Section 230-21.

Exception No. 1: A grounding electrode conductor shall be connected to the grounded conductor of a separately derived system in accordance with the provisions of Section 250-26(b).

Where a separately derived system is required to be grounded, a grounding electrode conductor is required to be connected to the grounded conductor of the derived system as specified in Section 250-26(b).

Exception No. 2: A grounding conductor connection shall be made at each separate building where required by Section 250-24.

Exception No. 3: For ranges, counter-mounted cooking units, wall-mounted ovens, clothes dryers, and meter enclosures as permitted by Section 250-61.

Exception No. 4: For services that are dual fed (double ended) in a common enclosure or grouped together in separate enclosures and employing a secondary tie, a single grounding electrode connection to the tie point of the grounded circuit conductors from each power source shall be permitted.

Exception No. 5: Where the main bonding jumper specified in Sections 250-53(b) and 250-79 is a wire or busbar, and is installed from the neutral bar or bus to the equipment grounding terminal bar or bus in the service equipment, the grounding electrode conductor shall be permitted to be connected to the equipment grounding terminal bar or bus to which the main bonding jumper is connected.

Where a ground-return type sensor is used for ground-fault protection of equipment (see Article 100 for definition of "Ground-Fault Protection of Equipment"), the sensor is required to be installed on the main bonding jumper and the grounding electrode conductor is required to be connected to the equipment grounding bus or terminal bar so that ground-fault current can be accurately sensed. Where the service equipment is power switchgear, it is often more practical to connect the grounding electrode conductor to the grounding bus inside the switchgear. See Figures 230-17 and 230-18.

(b) Grounded Conductor Brought to Service Equipment. Where an ac system operating at less than 1000 volts is grounded at any point, the grounded conductor shall be run to each service. This conductor shall be routed with the phase conductors and shall not be smaller than the required grounding electrode conductor specified in Table 250-94 and, in addition, for service phase conductors larger than 1100 MCM copper or 1750 MCM aluminum, the grounded conductor shall not be smaller than 12½ percent of the area of the largest phase conductor.

Exception: The grounded conductor shall not be required to be larger than the largest ungrounded service conductor.

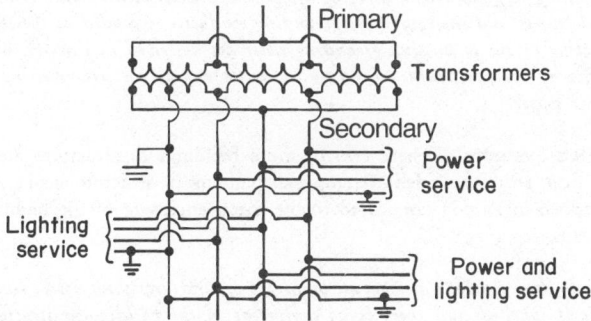

Figure 250-5. On a 4-wire, 3-phase, 240-V delta secondary system, a mid-phase tap is made at one transformer to provide a neutral for a 3-wire 120/240-V system for lighting and 125-V receptacles. This neutral is grounded at the transformer and at each individual service. This neutral is also required to be run to service equipment supplied from the above-mentioned secondary system, even though installed for 3-wire, 3-phase power purposes. Also, on a 3-wire, 3-phase, 240-V distribution system without a neutral, but with one phase conductor grounded, it is required to ground that phase conductor at each individual service.

250-24. Two or More Buildings or Structures Supplied from a Common Service.

(a) Grounded Systems. Where two or more buildings or structures are supplied from a common service, the grounded system in each building or structure shall have a grounding electrode as described in Part H connected to the metal enclosure of the building disconnecting means and to the ac system grounded circuit conductor on the supply side of the building or structure disconnecting means.

ARTICLE 250—GROUNDING

The following is a Formal Interpretation of Sections 250-23 and 250-24 of the 1978 edition of the *National Electrical Code*.

Statement: A building is supplied by an ac grounded system operating at less than 1,000 volts. It is intended to install electrical conductors within a grounded rigid metal conduit system from overcurrent protection located on the load side of the service-entrance equipment of this building and run to a second building, not containing livestock, on the same property and under the same management to supply a 3-phase motor load and/or other loads not requiring a grounded conductor. The second building is provided with a means for disconnecting all ungrounded conductors in accordance with Section 230-84.

Consider Sections 230-3, 230-40, 230-41(c), 230-84, 230-90(c), 250-23, 250-24, 250-91(b)(2), and any other pertinent parts of Articles 230 or 250. Also consider definitions in Article 100.

Question No. 1: Are the conductors to the second building defined as a feeder? Answer: Yes.

Question No. 2: Under the conditions specified in the statement, is a grounded conductor required from the first building to the second building? Answer: No.

Exception No. 1: A grounding electrode at separate buildings or structures shall not be required where only one branch circuit is supplied and there is no equipment in the building or structure that requires grounding.

Exception No. 2: A grounded circuit conductor connection to the grounding electrode shall not be required at the second building or structure if an equipment grounding conductor is run with the circuit conductors for grounding any noncurrent-carrying equipment, interior metal piping systems and building or structural metal frames and the equipment grounding conductor is bonded at the second building or structure disconnecting means to existing grounding electrodes described in Part H. Where livestock is housed, that portion of the equipment grounding conductor run to the disconnecting means shall be insulated or covered copper.

(b) Ungrounded Systems. Where two or more buildings or structures are supplied by a common service from an ungrounded system, each building or structure shall have a grounding electrode as described in Part H connected to the metal enclosure of the building or structure disconnecting means.

Exception: A grounding electrode at separate buildings or structures shall not be required where only one branch circuit is supplied and there is no equipment in the building or structure that requires grounding.

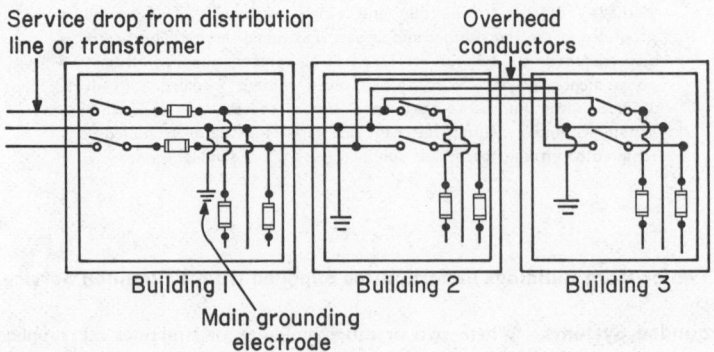

Figure 250-6. Where a single service (grounded system) supplies three buildings, each building is required to have a grounding electrode installed, unless conditions prevail as described in the exceptions to Section 250-24.

250-25. Conductor to Be Grounded — Alternating-Current Systems. For ac premises wiring systems, the conductor to be grounded shall be as specified in (1) through (5) below.

(1) Single-phase, 2-wire: one conductor.

(2) Single-phase, 3-wire: the neutral conductor.

(3) Multiphase systems having one wire common to all phases: the common conductor.

(4) Multiphase systems requiring one grounded phase: one phase conductor.

(5) Multiphase systems in which one phase is used as in (2) above: the neutral conductor. Grounded conductors shall be identified by the means specified in Article 200.

250-26. Grounding Separately Derived Alternating-Current Systems. A separately derived ac system that is required to be grounded by Section 250-5 shall be grounded as specified in (a) through (d) below.

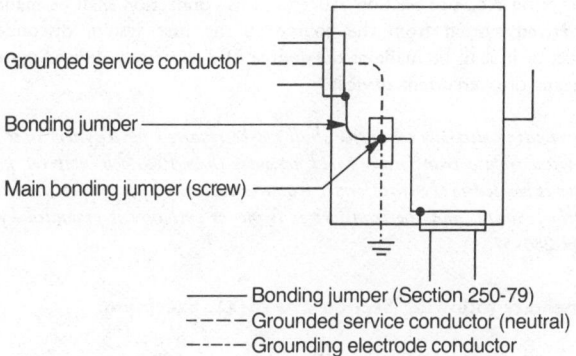

Grounded service conductor

Bonding jumper

Main bonding jumper (screw)

——— Bonding jumper (Section 250-79)
- - - - Grounded service conductor (neutral)
— — — Grounding electrode conductor

Figure 250-7. Grounding and bonding at an individual service.

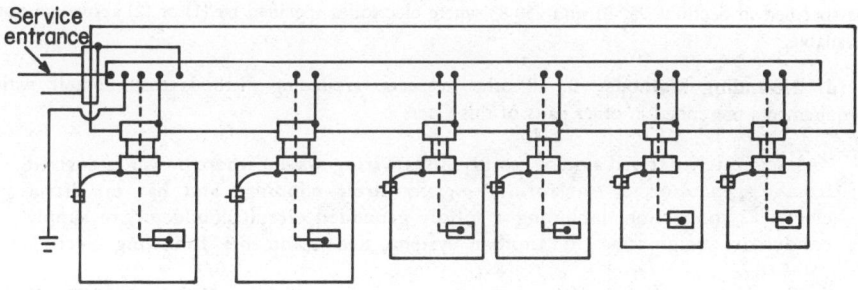

Service entrance

Figure 250-8. The grounding and bonding arrangement for six switches that serve as the service disconnecting means for an individual service.

(a) Bonding Jumper. A bonding jumper, sized in accordance with Section 250-79(c) for the derived phase conductors, shall be used to connect the equipment grounding conductors of the derived system to the grounded conductor. Except as permitted by Exception No. 4 of Section 250-23(a), this connection shall be made at any point on the separately derived system from the source to the first system disconnecting means or overcurrent device; or it shall be made at the source of a separately derived system which has no disconnecting means or overcurrent devices.

183

The intent here is to permit this connection at the transformer, etc., or at the first disconnecting means or overcurrent device where there is likely to be more standard arrangements incorporated (as in a panelboard suitable for service equipment).

Exception: The size of the bonding jumper for a system that supplies a Class 1 circuit, and is derived from a transformer rated not more than 1000 volt-amperes, shall not be smaller than the derived phase conductors and shall not be smaller than No. 14 copper or No. 12 aluminum.

Section 250-79(c) requires the bonding jumper to be not smaller than the sizes given in Table 250-94, e.g., not smaller than No. 8 AWG copper. This exception permits a bonding jumper for a Class 1 remote control or signaling circuit to be not smaller than No. 14 AWG copper.

(b) Grounding Electrode Conductor. A grounding electrode conductor, sized in accordance with Section 250-94 for the derived phase conductors, shall be used to connect the grounded conductor of the derived system to the grounding electrode as specified in (c) below. Except as permitted by Exception No. 4 of Section 250-23(a), this connection shall be made at any point on the separately derived system from the source to the first system disconnecting means or overcurrent device; or it shall be made at the source of a separately derived system which has no disconnecting means or overcurrent devices.

Exception: A grounding electrode conductor shall not be required for a system that supplies a Class 1 circuit, and is derived from a transformer rated not more than 1000 volt-amperes, provided the system grounded conductor is bonded to the transformer frame or enclosure by a jumper sized in accordance with the Exception for (a), above, and the transformer frame or enclosure is grounded by one of the means specified in Section 250-57.

See commentary following Section 250-26(a), Exception.

(c) Grounding Electrode. The grounding electrode shall be as near as practicable to and preferably in the same area as the grounding conductor connection to the system. The grounding electrode shall be: (1) the nearest available effectively grounded structural metal member of the structure; or (2) the nearest available effectively grounded metal water pipe; or (3) other electrodes as specified in Sections 250-81 and 250-83 where electrodes specified by (1) or (2) above are not available.

(d) Grounding Methods. In all other respects, grounding methods shall comply with requirements prescribed in other parts of this Code.

A separately derived system is a premises wiring system where power is derived from a generator, a transformer, or converter windings and has no direct electrical connection, including a solidly grounded circuit conductor, to supply conductors originating in another system. See comments following Section 250-5(d).

The requirements of Section 250-26 are most commonly applied to 480Y/277-V transformers which are used to transform a 480-V supply to a 208Y/120-V system to supply lighting and appliance loads.

These requirements provide for a low impedance path to ground so that line-to-ground faults from ungrounded conductors will create sufficient current to operate the overcurrent devices. These requirements also apply to generators or systems derived from converter windings, but do not have the same wide use as dry-type transformers.

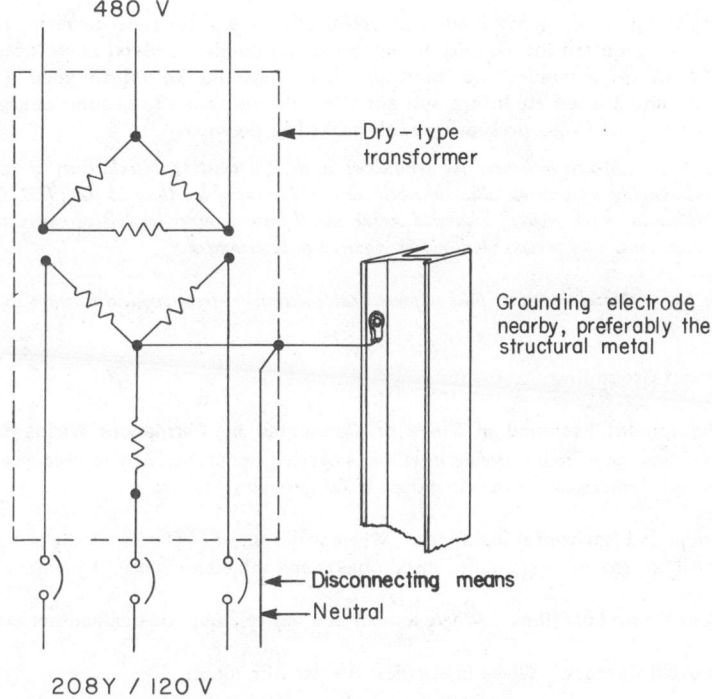

480 V

Dry – type
transformer

Grounding electrode
nearby, preferably the
structural metal

Disconnecting means

Neutral

208Y / 120 V

Figure 250-9. A grounding arrangement for a separately derived system. The bonding jumper connection is permitted at the transformer, as illustrated, or at the first system disconnecting means.

Figure 250-9 shows a typical diagram of a dry-type transformer supplied from a 480-V, 3-phase feeder to derive a 208Y/120-V secondary. As indicated in Section 250-26(a), the bonding jumper connection is required to be sized according to Section 250-79(c) and is to be made at the source of the separately derived system or the first system disconnecting means or overcurrent device and, as illustrated, would be at the transformer enclosure. With the grounding electrode conductor, the bonding jumper, and the bonding of the grounded circuit conductor (neutral) connected at the transformer enclosure, line-to-ground fault currents are permitted to return to the supply source rather than going through the earth. In this way, a path of low impedance is provided which facilitates the operation of overcurrent devices in accordance with Section 250-51(3).

The grounding electrode conductor from the secondary grounded circuit conductor is sized according to Section 250-94.

D. Enclosure Grounding

250-32. Service Raceways and Enclosures. Metal enclosures for service conductors and equipment shall be grounded.

250-33. Other Conductor Enclosures. Metal enclosures for other than service conductors shall be grounded.

This section requires bonding, grounding, and electrical continuity of metal raceways and thus requires connectors, couplings, or other fittings that provide bonding and grounding continuity between the fitting and the raceway metal (such as would be required for liquidtight flexible metal conduit). Metal enclosures are required to be grounded, so that any fault between an ungrounded (hot) conductor and a metal enclosure will not allow the enclosure to become energized and remain so and thus present a shock hazard to persons.

Exception No. 1: Metal enclosures for conductors added to existing installations of open wire, knob-and-tube wiring, and nonmetallic-sheathed cable, if in runs of less than 25 feet (7.62 m), if free from probable contact with ground, grounded metal, metal lath, or other conductive material, and if guarded against contact by persons shall not be required to be grounded.

Exception No. 2: Metal enclosures used to protect cable assemblies from physical damage shall not be required to be grounded.

E. Equipment Grounding

250-42. Equipment Fastened in Place or Connected by Permanent Wiring Methods (Fixed). Exposed noncurrent-carrying metal parts of fixed equipment likely to become energized shall be grounded under any of the conditions in (a) through (f) below.

(a) Vertical and Horizontal Distances. Where within 8 feet (2.44 m) vertically or 5 feet (1.52 m) horizontally of ground or grounded metal objects and subject to contact by persons.

(b) Wet or Damp Locations. Where located in a wet or damp location and not isolated.

(c) Electrical Contact. Where in electrical contact with metal.

(d) Hazardous (Classified) Locations. Where in a hazardous (classified) location as covered by Articles 500 through 517.

(e) Metallic Wiring Methods. Where supplied by a metal-clad, metal-sheathed, or metal-raceway wiring method, except as permitted by Section 250-33 for short sections of raceway.

(f) Over 150 Volts to Ground. Where equipment operates with any terminal at over 150 volts to ground.

Exception No. 1: Enclosures for switches or circuit breakers used for other than service equipment and accessible to qualified persons only.

Exception No. 2: Metal frames of electrically heated appliances, exempted by special permission, in which case the frames shall be permanently and effectively insulated from ground.

Exception No. 3: Distribution apparatus, such as transformer and capacitor cases, mounted on wooden poles, at a height exceeding 8 feet (2.44 m) above ground or grade level.

250-43. Fastened in Place or Connected by Permanent Wiring Methods (Fixed) — Specific. Exposed, noncurrent-carrying metal parts of the kinds of equipment described in (a) through (j) below, regardless of voltage, shall be grounded.

(a) Switchboard Frames and Structures. Switchboard frames and structures supporting switching equipment.

Exception: Frames of dc, single-polarity switchboards where effectively insulated.

(b) Organs. Generator and motor frames in an electrically operated organ.

Exception: Where the generator is effectively insulated from ground and from the motor driving it.

(c) Motor Frames. Motor frames, as provided by Section 430-142.

(d) Enclosures for Motor Controllers. Enclosures for motor controllers.

Exception: Lined covers of snap switches.

(e) Elevators and Cranes. Electric equipment for elevators and cranes.

(f) Garages, Theaters, and Motion Picture Studios. Electric equipment in garages, theaters, and motion picture studios.

Exception: Pendant lampholders supplied by circuits not over 150 volts to ground.

(g) Electric Signs. Electric signs and associated equipment.

Exception: Where insulated from ground and from other conductive objects and accessible only to qualified persons.

(h) Motion Picture Projection Equipment. Motion picture projection equipment.

(i) Class 1, Class 2, and Class 3 Circuits. Equipment supplied by Class 1, Class 2, and Class 3 remote-control and signaling circuits where required to be grounded by Part B of this article.

(j) Lighting Fixtures. Lighting fixtures as provided in Part E of Article 410.

250-44. Nonelectric Equipment. The metal parts of nonelectric equipment described in (a) through (e) below shall be grounded.

(a) Cranes. Frames and tracks of electrically operated cranes.

(b) Elevator Cars. Frames of nonelectrically driven elevator cars to which electric conductors are attached.

(c) Electric Elevators. Hand-operated metal shifting ropes or cables of electric elevators.

(d) Metal Partitions. Metal partitions, grill work, and similar metal enclosures around equipment of 1 kV and over between conductors except substations or vaults under the sole control of the supply company.

(e) Mobile Homes and Recreational Vehicles. Mobile homes and recreational vehicles as required in Articles 550 and 551.

(FPN): Where extensive metal in or on buildings may become energized and is subject to personal contact, adequate bonding and grounding will provide additional safety.

See Section 547-7 for grounding of agricultural buildings.

250-45. Equipment Connected by Cord and Plug. Under any of the conditions described in (a) through (d) below, exposed noncurrent-carrying metal parts of cord- and plug-connected equipment likely to become energized shall be grounded.

(a) In Hazardous (Classified) Locations. In hazardous (classified) locations (see Articles 500 through 517).

(b) Over 150 Volts to Ground. Where operated at over 150 volts to ground.

Exception No. 1: Motors, where guarded.

187

Exception No. 2: Metal frames of electrically heated appliances, exempted by special permission, in which case the frames shall be permanently and effectively insulated from ground.

See Section 422-16.

(c) In Residential Occupancies. In residential occupancies: (1) refrigerators, freezers, and air conditioners; (2) clothes-washing, clothes-drying, dish-washing machines, sump pumps, electrical aquarium equipment; (3) hand-held motor-operated tools; (4) motor-operated appliances of the following types: hedge clippers, lawn mowers, snow blowers, and wet scrubbers; (5) portable handlamps.

Exception: Listed tools and listed appliances protected by a system of double insulation, or its equivalent, shall not be required to be grounded. Where such a system is employed, the equipment shall be distinctively marked.

(d) In Other than Residential Occupancies. In other than residential occupancies: (1) refrigerators, freezers, and air conditioners; (2) clothes-washing, clothes-drying, dish-washing machines, sump pumps, electrical aquarium equipment; (3) hand-held motor-operated tools; (4) motor-operated appliances of the following types: hedge clippers, lawn mowers, snow blowers, and wet scrubbers; (5) cord- and plug-connected appliances used in damp or wet locations or by persons standing on the ground or on metal floors or working inside of metal tanks or boilers; (6) tools likely to be used in wet and conductive locations; and (7) portable handlamps.

Exception No. 1: Tools and portable handlamps likely to be used in wet and conductive locations shall not be required to be grounded where supplied through an isolating transformer with an ungrounded secondary of not over 50 volts.

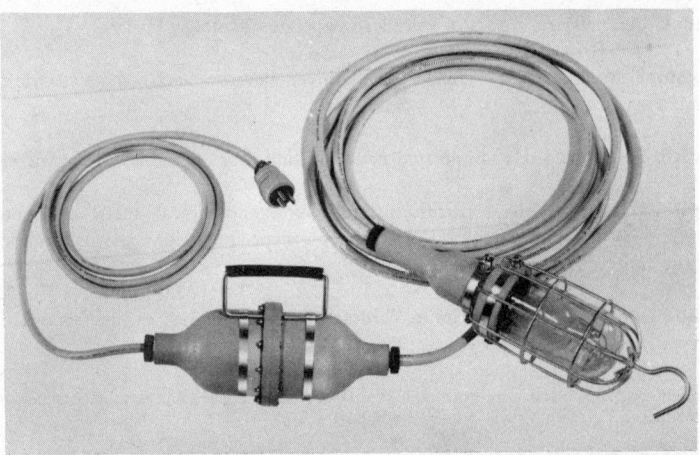

Figure 250-10. Lighting equipment supplied through an isolating transformer operating at 6 or 12 V provides safe illumination for work inside of boilers, tanks, and similar locations that may be metallic and/or wet. (*Daniel Woodhead Co.*)

Exception No. 2: Listed portable tools and listed appliances protected by an approved system of double insulation, or its equivalent, shall not be required to be grounded. Where such a system is employed, the equipment shall be distinctively marked.

(FPN): With reference to (c) and (d), portable tools or appliances are not intended to be used in damp, wet or conductive locations unless they are grounded, double insulated or supplied through an isolating transformer.

Tools are required to be grounded by an equipment grounding conductor in a cord or cable supplying the tool, except where supplied by an isolating transformer as permitted by Exception No. 1. Portable tools and appliances protected by an approved system of double insulation are required to be listed by a qualified electrical testing laboratory as being suitable for the purpose, and the equipment is required to be distinctively marked as double insulated.

Cord-connected portable tools or appliances are not intended to be used in damp, wet, or conductive locations unless supplied by an isolation transformer or protected by an approved system of double insulation.

250-46. Spacing from Lightning Rods. Metal raceways, enclosures, frames, and other noncurrent-carrying metal parts of electric equipment shall be kept at least 6 feet (1.83 m) away from lightning rod conductors, or they shall be bonded to the lightning rod conductors.

(FPN): See Sections 250-86 and 800-31(b)(5). For further information see the Lightning Protection Code, NFPA 78-1980 (ANSI), which contains detailed information on grounding lightning protection systems.

F. Methods of Grounding

250-50. Equipment Grounding Conductor Connections. Equipment grounding conductor connections at the source of separately derived systems shall be made in accordance with Section 250-26(a). Equipment grounding conductor connections at service equipment shall be made as indicated in (a) or (b) below.

(a) For Grounded System. The connection shall be made by bonding the equipment grounding conductor to the grounded service conductor and the grounding electrode conductor.

(b) For Ungrounded System. The connection shall be made by bonding the equipment grounding conductor to the grounding electrode conductor.

Exception for (a) and (b) above: For replacement of nongrounding-type receptacles with grounding-type receptacles and for branch-circuit extensions only in existing installations that do not have an equipment grounding conductor in the branch circuit, the grounding conductor of a grounding-type receptacle outlet shall be permitted to be grounded to a water pipe which is bonded in accordance with Section 250-80(a).

This exception was revised for the 1984 *Code.* It permits, under the specified conditions, the grounding of a grounding-type receptacle by a separate equipment grounding conductor run to a cold or hot water pipe when the provisions of Section 250-80(a) are met. See also the exception to Section 210-7(d).

250-51. Effective Grounding Path. The path to ground from circuits, equipment, and conductor enclosures shall: (1) be permanent and continuous; (2) have capacity to conduct safely any fault current likely to be imposed on it; and (3) have sufficiently low impedance to limit the voltage to ground and to facilitate the operation of the circuit protective devices in the circuit.

250-53. Grounding Path to Grounding Electrode at Services.

(a) Grounding Electrode Conductor. A grounding electrode conductor shall be used to connect the equipment grounding conductors, the service-equipment enclosures and, where the system is grounded, the grounded service conductor to the grounding electrode.

(FPN): See Section 250-23(a).

Reference to the Fine Print Note in Section 250-23(a) directs the reader to more detailed specifications for connecting the grounding electrode conductor.

(b) Main Bonding Jumper. For a grounded system, an unspliced main bonding jumper shall be used to connect the equipment grounding conductor and the service-equipment enclosure to the grounded conductor of the system within the service equipment or within the service conductor enclosure. A main bonding jumper shall be a wire, bus, screw, or similar suitable conductor.

250-54. Common Grounding Electrode. Where an ac system is connected to a grounding electrode in or at a building as specified in Sections 250-23 and 250-24, the same electrode shall be used to ground conductor enclosures and equipment in or on that building.

Two or more electrodes that are effectively bonded together shall be considered as a single electrode in this sense.

250-55. Underground Service Cable. Where served from a continuous underground metal-sheathed cable system, the sheath or armor of underground service cable metallically connected to the underground system, or underground service conduit containing a metal-sheathed cable bonded to the underground system, shall not be required to be grounded at the building and shall be permitted to be insulated from the interior conduit or piping.

250-56. Short Sections of Raceway. Isolated sections of metal raceway or cable armor, where required to be grounded, shall be grounded in accordance with Section 250-57.

250-57. Equipment Fastened in Place or Connected by Permanent Wiring Methods (Fixed) — Grounding. Noncurrent-carrying metal parts of equipment, raceways, and other enclosures, where required to be grounded, shall be grounded by one of the methods indicated in (a) or (b) below.

Exception: Where equipment, raceways, and enclosures are grounded by connection to the grounded circuit conductor as permitted by Sections 250-24, 250-60, and 250-61.

This exception eliminates any possible conflict between Section 250-57, which requires an equipment grounding conductor to be used for equipment grounding, and Sections 250-24, 250-60, and 250-61, which permit the grounded circuit conductor to be used for equipment grounding if certain specified conditions are met.

(a) Equipment Grounding Conductor Types. By any of the equipment grounding conductors permitted by Section 250-91(b).

(b) With Circuit Conductors. By an equipment grounding conductor contained within the same raceway, cable, or cord or otherwise run with the circuit conductors. Bare, covered or insulated equipment grounding conductors shall be permitted. Individually covered or insulated equipment grounding conductors shall have a continuous outer finish that is either green, or green with one or more yellow stripes.

Exception No. 1: An insulated or covered conductor larger than No. 6 copper or aluminum shall, at the time of installation, be permitted to be permanently identified as an equipment grounding conductor at each end and at every point where the conductor is accessible. Identification shall be accomplished by one of the following:

a. Stripping the insulation or covering from the entire exposed length,

b. Coloring the exposed insulation or covering green, or

c. Marking the exposed insulation or covering with green colored tape or green colored adhesive labels.

Exception No. 2: For direct-current circuits only, the equipment grounding conductor shall be permitted to be run separately from the circuit conductors.

Exception No. 3: Where the conditions of maintenance and supervision assure that only qualified persons will service the installation, an insulated conductor in a multiconductor cable shall, at the time of installation, be permitted to be permanently identified as an equipment grounding conductor at each end and at every point where the conductor is accessible by one of the following means:

a. Stripping the insulation from the entire exposed length,

b. Coloring the exposed insulation green, or

c. Marking the exposed insulation with green tape or green colored adhesive labels.

(FPN): See Section 250-79 for equipment bonding jumper requirements.

(FPN): See Section 400-7 for use of cords for fixed equipment.

250-58. Equipment Considered Effectively Grounded.   Under the conditions specified in (a) and (b) below, the noncurrent-carrying metal parts of the equipment shall be considered effectively grounded.

(a) Equipment Secured to Grounded Metal Supports.   Electric equipment secured to and in electrical contact with a metal rack or structure provided for its support and grounded by one of the means indicated in Section 250-57. The structural metal frame of a building shall not be used as the required equipment grounding conductor for ac equipment.

(b) Metal Car Frames.   Metal car frames supported by metal hoisting cables attached to or running over metal sheaves or drums of elevator machines which are grounded by one of the methods indicated in Section 250-57.

250-59. Cord- and Plug-Connected Equipment.   Noncurrent-carrying metal parts of cord- and plug-connected equipment, where required to be grounded, shall be grounded by one of the methods indicated in (a), (b), or (c) below.

(a) By Means of the Metal Enclosure.   By means of the metal enclosure of the conductors supplying such equipment if a grounding-type attachment plug with one fixed grounding contact is used for grounding the metal enclosure, and if the metal enclosure of the conductors is secured to the attachment plug and to equipment by approved connectors.

Exception: A self-restoring grounding contact shall be permitted on grounding-type attachment plugs used on the power supply cord of portable hand-held, hand-guided, or hand-supported tools or appliances.

(b) By Means of a Grounding Conductor.   By means of an equipment grounding conductor run with the power supply conductors in a cable assembly or flexible cord properly terminated in grounding-type attachment plug with one fixed grounding contact. An uninsulated equipment grounding conductor shall be permitted but, if individually covered, the covering shall have a continuous outer finish that is either green or green with one or more yellow stripes.

Exception: A self-restoring grounding contact shall be permitted on grounding-type attachment plugs used on the power supply cord of portable hand-held, hand-guided, or hand-supported tools or appliances.

(c) Separate Flexible Wire or Strap.   By means of a separate flexible wire or strap, insulated or bare, protected as well as practicable against physical damage, where part of equipment.

250-60. Frames of Ranges and Clothes Dryers. Frames of electric ranges, wall-mounted ovens, counter-mounted cooking units, clothes dryers, and outlet or junction boxes which are part of the circuit for these appliances shall be grounded in the manner specified by Section 250-57 or 250-59; or, except for mobile homes and recreational vehicles, shall be permitted to be grounded to the grounded circuit conductor if all of the conditions indicated in (a) through (d) below are met.

(a) The supply circuit is 120/240-volt, single-phase, 3-wire; or 208Y/120-volt derived from a 3-phase, 4-wire, wye-connected system.

(b) The grounded conductor is not smaller than No. 10 copper or No. 8 aluminum.

(c) The grounded conductor is insulated; or the grounded conductor is uninsulated and part of a Type SE service-entrance cable and the branch circuit originates at the service equipment.

(d) Grounding contacts of receptacles furnished as part of the equipment are bonded to the equipment.

The grounded circuit conductor (neutral) is permitted to be used to ground the frame of an electric range, wall-mounted oven, or counter-mounted cooking unit, provided all the conditions of (a) through (d) are met. The grounded circuit conductor is also permitted to be used to ground any junction boxes in the circuit supplying the appliance and a 3-wire pigtail and range receptacle is permitted to be used regardless of whether or not the circuit to the receptacle contains a separate equipment grounding conductor.

The use of the grounded circuit conductor for grounding purposes is contrary to other requirements of the *Code*; however, it has been allowed for many years because of the good safety record of appliances that are grounded through the grounded circuit conductor and because an open splice or break in the grounded circuit conductor would normally render the appliance inoperable. A subcommittee reevaluated this requirement for the 1984 *NEC* and verified the continued good safety record.

Where service-entrance cable with an uninsulated neutral is used, it is required that the circuit originate from the service equipment in order to avoid multiple grounding from downstream panelboards. Multiple grounding downstream would raise the potential of all exposed dead metal parts of equipment using this downstream grounding point for equipment grounding by an amount equal to the voltage drop along the neutral, a current-carrying conductor. Thus, under normal conditions adjacent exposed "dead metal" parts could be at a potential difference of several volts.

250-61. Use of Grounded Circuit Conductor for Grounding Equipment.

(a) **Supply-Side Equipment.** A grounded circuit conductor shall be permitted to ground noncurrent-carrying metal parts of equipment, raceways, and other enclosures on the supply side of the service disconnecting means, and on the supply side of the main disconnecting means for separate buildings as provided in Section 250-24.

(b) **Load-Side Equipment.** A grounded circuit conductor shall not be used for grounding noncurrent-carrying metal parts of equipment on the load side of the service disconnecting means or on the load side of a separately derived system disconnecting means or the overcurrent devices for a separately derived system not having a main disconnecting means.

Exception No. 1: The frames of ranges, wall-mounted ovens, counter-mounted cooking units, and clothes dryers under the conditions specified by Section 250-60.

Exception No. 2: As permitted in Section 250-24 for separate buildings.

Exception No. 3: It shall be permissible to ground meter enclosures by connection to the grounded circuit conductor on the load-side of the service disconnect if:

   a. No service ground-fault protection is installed; and

   b. All meter enclosures are located near the service disconnecting means.

250-62. Multiple Circuit Connections. Where equipment is required to be grounded, and is supplied by separate connection to more than one circuit or grounded premises wiring system, a means for grounding shall be provided for each such connection as specified in Sections 250-57 and 250-59.

G. Bonding

250-70. General. Bonding shall be provided where necessary to assure electrical continuity and the capacity to conduct safely any fault current likely to be imposed.

250-71. Service Equipment.

   (a) Bonding of Service Equipment. The noncurrent-carrying metal parts of equipment indicated in (1), (2) and (3) below shall be effectively bonded together.

   (1) Except as permitted in Section 250-55, the service raceways, cable trays, or service cable armor or sheath.

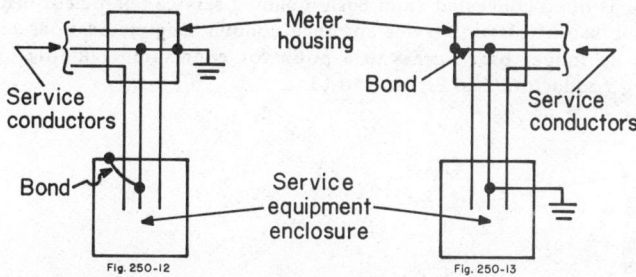

Figures 250-11 and 250-12. Two different types of grounding and bonding arrangements. Figure 250-11 shows a grounding electrode conductor at the meter housing with the service equipment enclosure bonded to the grounded service conductor. Figure 250-12 shows the grounding electrode conductor at the service equipment and the meter housing bonded to the grounded service conductor.

   (2) All service equipment enclosures containing service-entrance conductors, including meter fittings, boxes, or the like, interposed in the service raceway or armor.

   (3) Any metallic raceway or armor enclosing a grounding electrode conductor as permitted in Section 250-92(a).

   (b) Bonding to Other Systems. At dwellings, an accessible means external to enclosures for connecting intersystem bonding and grounding conductors shall be provided at the service by at least one of the following means:

   (1) Exposed metallic service raceways.

(2) Exposed grounding electrode conductor.

(3) Approved means for the external connection of a bonding, or grounding conductor to the service raceway or equipment.

(FPN): See Sections 800-31 and 820-22 for bonding and grounding requirements for communication and CATV circuits.

The *Code* requires that separate systems be bonded together to reduce differences of potentials between them, which can result from lightning or power contacts. Interconnection is required for lightning rod systems (Section 250-46), communications systems [Section 800-31(b)(5)], and CATV systems [Section 820-22(f)]. Lack of interconnection can result in a severe shock and fire hazard.

These rules are provided because of the difficulties encountered by communications and CATV installers in trying to comply with *Code* grounding and bonding requirements, particularly in residences, because of the increasing use of plastic for water pipe, fittings, water meters, and service conduit. In the past, bonding between communications, CATV, and power systems was usually achieved by connecting the communications protector grounds or cable shield to an interior metallic water pipe, because the pipe was often used as the power grounding electrode. Thus, the requirement that the power, communications, CATV cable shield, and metallic water piping systems be bonded together was easily satisfied. In the event that the power was grounded to one of the other electrodes permitted by the *Code*, usually by use of a made electrode such as a ground rod, the bond was connected to the power grounding electrode conductor or to a metallic service raceway, since at least one of these was usually accessible. With the growing proliferation of plastic water pipe, the increasing tendency for the service equipment to be installed in finished areas where the grounding electrode conductor is often concealed (and flush-mounted service equipment installed), as well as the use of plastic service-entrance conduit, communications and CATV installers no longer have access to a point for connecting bonding jumpers or grounding conductors. See Figure 250-13.

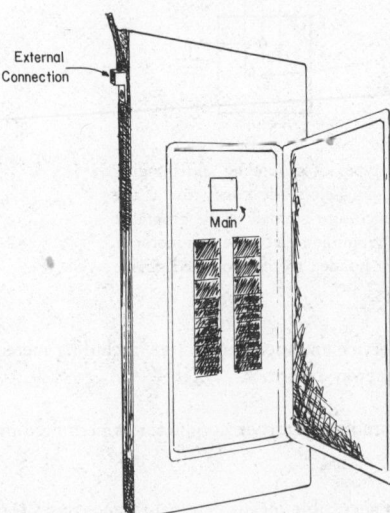

External
Connection

Main

Figure 250-13. An external accessible means for connecting intersystem bonding and grounding conductors for dwellings to provide a bonding point for such systems as communication and CATV circuits.

250-72. Method of Bonding Service Equipment. Electrical continuity at service equipment shall be assured by one of the methods specified in (a) through (e) below.

Figure 250-14. A grounding bushing used to connect a copper bonding or grounding wire to a conduit. (*The Thomas & Betts Co., Inc.*)

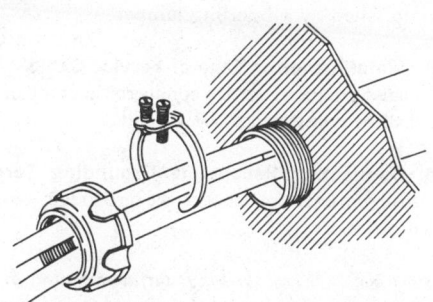

Figures 250-15 and 250-16. Figure 250-15 (left) shows a grounding wedge lug for providing an electrical connection between a conduit and a box. Figure 250-16 (right) shows the manner in which the lug is installed. (*The Thomas & Betts Co., Inc.*)

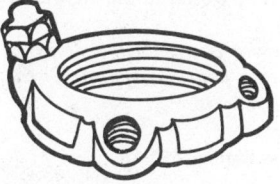

Figure 250-17. A threaded grounding bushing showing openings for set screws to assure electrical and mechanical connection. (*General Electric Co.*)

(a) Pressure Connectors, Clamps, etc. Bonding equipment to the grounded service conductor in a manner provided in Section 250-113.

(b) Threaded Couplings. Threaded couplings and threaded bosses on enclosures with joints shall be made up wrenchtight where rigid metal conduit and intermediate metal conduit are involved.

(c) Threadless Couplings and Connectors. Threadless couplings and connectors made up tight for rigid metal conduit, intermediate metal conduit and electrical metallic tubing.

(d) Bonding Jumpers. Bonding jumpers meeting the other requirements of this article shall be used around concentric or eccentric knockouts that are punched or otherwise formed so as to impair the electrical connection to ground.

(e) Other Devices. Other approved devices, such as bonding-type locknuts and bushings.

Note that paragraph (e) requires bonding-type locknuts. Standard locknuts or sealing locknuts are not acceptable for bonding at service equipment.

Bonding bushings for use with rigid or intermediate metal conduit are provided with means (usually one or more setscrews) for reliably bonding the bushing (and the conduit on which it is threaded) to the metal equipment enclosure or box. When means for connecting a grounding conductor or bonding jumper are not provided, and there is need for such a conductor, a grounding-type bushing is required to be used.

Grounding-type bushings used with rigid or intermediate metal conduit have provisions for the connection of a bonding jumper or have means for mounting a wire connector available from the manufacturer. This type of bushing may also have means (usually one or more setscrews) which are used for reliably bonding the bushing to the metal equipment enclosure or box in the same manner that is accomplished by a bonding jumper.

250-73. Metal Armor or Tape of Service Cable. The metal covering of service cable having an uninsulated grounded service conductor in continuous electrical contact with its metallic armor or tape shall be considered to be grounded.

250-74. Connecting Receptacle Grounding Terminal to Box. An equipment bonding jumper shall be used to connect the grounding terminal of a grounding-type receptacle to a grounded box.

Exception No. 1: Where the box is surface mounted, direct metal-to-metal contact between the device yoke and the box shall be permitted to ground the receptacle to the box. This Exception shall not apply to cover-mounted receptacles unless the box and cover combination are listed as providing satisfactory ground continuity between the box and the receptacle.

This exception was revised for the 1984 *Code.* Exception No. 1 had been misinterpreted to include outlet boxes with raised covers where only one 6-32 screw, which might be plastic, was used to secure a receptacle yoke to the cover.

Exception No. 2: Contact devices or yokes designed and listed for the purpose shall be permitted in conjunction with the supporting screws to establish the grounding circuit between the device yoke and flush-type boxes.

See Figure 250-18.

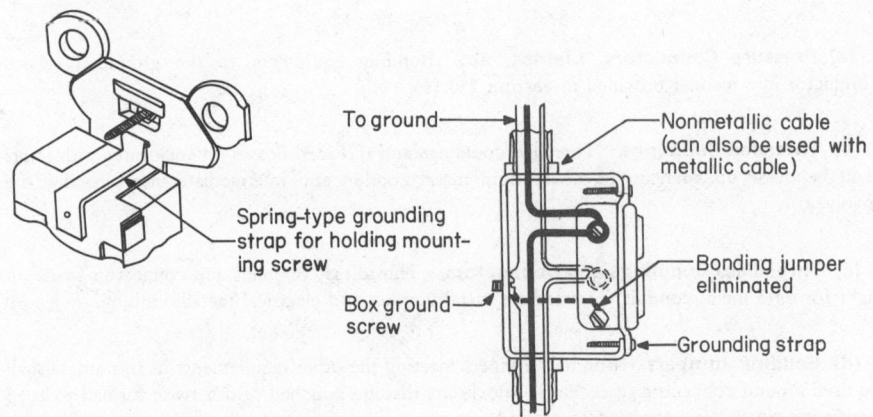

Figure 250-18. Receptacle designed with spring-type grounding strap which holds mounting screw captive and eliminates a bonding jumper to box in accordance with Exception No. 2 of Section 250-74.

Exception No. 3: Floor boxes designed for and listed as providing satisfactory ground continuity between the box and the device.

Exception No. 4: Where required for the reduction of electrical noise (electromagnetic interference) on the grounding circuit, a receptacle in which the grounding terminal is purposely insulated from the receptacle mounting means shall be permitted. The receptacle grounding terminal shall be grounded by an insulated equipment grounding conductor run with the circuit conductors. This grounding conductor shall be permitted to pass through one or more panelboards without connection to the panelboard grounding terminal as permitted in Section 384-27, Exception No. 1, so as to terminate directly at an equipment grounding conductor terminal of the applicable derived system or service.

(FPN): Use of an isolated equipment grounding conductor does not relieve the requirement for grounding the raceway system and outlet box.

This Fine Print Note, new in the 1984 *NEC*, was added as a reminder that metallic raceways and boxes are still required to be grounded in the usual manner. This could require a separate grounding conductor, for example, to ground a metal box in a nonmetallic raceway system, or to ground flexible metal conduit. Use of an existing equipment grounding conductor as the isolated receptacle grounding conductor when replacing an ordinary grounding-type receptacle with an isolated ground receptacle could effectively defeat or seriously compromise the required box or raceway ground.

250-75. Bonding Other Enclosures. Metal raceways, cable trays, cable armor, cable sheath, enclosures, frames, fittings, and other metal noncurrent-carrying parts that are to serve as grounding conductors shall be effectively bonded where necessary to assure electrical continuity and the capacity to conduct safely any fault current likely to be imposed on them. Any nonconductive paint, enamel, or similar coating shall be removed at threads, contact points, and contact surfaces or be connected by means of fittings so designed as to make such removal unnecessary.

250-76. Bonding for Over 250 Volts. For circuits of over 250 volts to ground, the electrical continuity of metal raceways and cables with metal sheaths that contain any conductor other than service conductors shall be assured by one or more of the methods specified for services in Section 250-72(b) through (e).

Exception: Where oversized, concentric, or eccentric knockouts are not encountered, the following methods shall be permitted:

a. Threadless couplings and connectors for cables with metal sheaths.

b. Two locknuts, on rigid metal conduit, or intermediate metal conduit, one inside and one outside of boxes and cabinets.

c. Fittings with shoulders that seat firmly against the box or cabinet, such as electrical metallic tubing connectors, flexible metallic conduit connectors and cable connectors, with one locknut on the inside of boxes and cabinets.

This section was revised for the 1984 *Code*. The intent here is that the methods in (a), (b), and (c) are permitted *only* where there are no oversize, concentric, or eccentric knockouts. Also, when these conditions are met, fittings, such as EMT connectors, cable connectors, etc., that have their shoulders firmly seated against the full metal of a box or cabinet need only one locknut located on the inside of the box.

250-77. Bonding Loosely Jointed Metal Raceways. Expansion joints and telescoping sections of raceways shall be made electrically continuous by equipment bonding jumpers or other means.

ARTICLE 250—GROUNDING

250-78. Bonding in Hazardous (Classified) Locations. Regardless of the voltage of the electrical system, the electrical continuity of noncurrent-carrying metal parts of equipment, raceways, and other enclosures in any hazardous (classified) location as defined in Article 500 shall be assured by any of the methods specified for services in Section 250-72(b) through (e) that are approved for the wiring method used.

250-79. Main and Equipment Bonding Jumpers.

(a) Material. Main and equipment bonding jumpers shall be of copper or other corrosion-resistant material.

(b) Attachment. Main and equipment bonding jumpers shall be attached in the manner specified by the applicable provisions of Section 250-113 for circuits and equipment and by Section 250-115 for grounding electrodes.

(c) Size — Equipment Bonding Jumper on Supply Side of Service and Main Bonding Jumper. The bonding jumper shall not be smaller than the sizes given in Table 250-94 for grounding electrode conductors. Where the service-entrance phase conductors are larger than 1100 MCM copper or 1750 MCM aluminum, the bonding jumper shall have an area not less than 12½ percent of the area of the largest phase conductor except that where the phase conductors and the bonding jumper are of different materials (copper or aluminum), the minimum size of the bonding jumper shall be based on the assumed use of phase conductors of the same material as the bonding jumper and with an ampacity equivalent to that of the installed phase conductors. Where the service-entrance conductors are paralleled in two or more raceways or cables, the size of the bonding jumper for each raceway or cable shall be based on the size of the service conductors in each raceway or cable.

The words "or cables" were added to paragraph (c) in the 1984 *Code.* This recognizes, for example, Types MI and MC cable since they are permitted to be used for services. See Section 230-43.

The size required for the equipment bonding jumper and the main bonding jumper on the supply side of a service is the same as the required size for the grounding electrode conductor taken from Table 250-94 (including the 12½ percent requirement for phase conductors larger than 1100 MCM copper or 1750 MCM aluminum).

Example: In applying the bonding requirements of Figure 250-8, if one of the switches is rated 100 A and the supply conductors are No. 2 AWG Type THW copper conductors, Table 250-94 requires a grounding electrode conductor sized at No. 8 AWG copper or No. 6 AWG aluminum or copper-clad aluminum. The bonding jumper would also be sized at No. 8 AWG copper or No. 6 AWG aluminum or copper-clad aluminum.

If another switch is rated at 200 A and the conductors supplying it are No. 3/0 AWG Type THW copper, the grounding electrode conductor and the bonding jumper are required to be sized at a minimum of No. 4 AWG copper or No. 2 AWG aluminum or copper-clad aluminum.

To apply the bonding jumper requirements, each switch should be treated as separate service equipment and Table 250-94 should be used to determine the size of the bonding jumper.

In some instances the bonding jumper may be required to be larger than the grounding electrode conductor. Section 250-79(c) indicates that, where the service-entrance conductors are larger than 1100 MCM copper or 1750 MCM aluminum, the bonding jumper is required to have a cross-sectional area of not less than 12½ percent of the cross-sectional area of the largest phase conductor. For example, if a service is supplied by four 500 MCM conductors in parallel for each phase, the minimum cross-sectional area of the bonding jumper is required to be 250 MCM (4 x 500 MCM = 2000 MCM x .125). See Table 8, Conductor Properties, in Chapter 9 for area in circular mils of AWG and MCM conductors.

(d) Size — Equipment Bonding Jumper on Load Side of Service. The equipment bonding jumper on the load side of the service overcurrent devices shall not be smaller than the sizes listed by Table 250-95 for equipment grounding conductors. A single common continuous equipment bonding jumper shall be permitted to bond two or more raceways or cables where the bonding jumper is sized in accordance with Table 250-95 for the largest overcurrent device supplying circuits therein.

Exception: The equipment bonding jumper shall not be required to be larger than the circuit conductors supplying the equipment, but shall not be smaller than No. 14 AWG.

(e) Installation — Equipment Bonding Jumper. The equipment bonding jumper shall be permitted to be installed inside or outside of a raceway or enclosure. Where installed on the outside, the length of the equipment bonding jumper shall not exceed 6 feet (1.83 m) and shall be routed with the raceway or enclosure.

In many applications it is necessary to install equipment bonding jumpers on the outside of metallic raceways and enclosures. For example, it would be impractical to install the bonding jumper for a conduit expansion joint on the inside of the conduit. For some metallic raceway and rigid conduit systems and conduit systems in hazardous (classified) locations, it is desirable to install the bonding jumper where it is visible and is accessible for inspection and maintenance. An external bonding jumper will have a higher impedance than an internal bonding jumper. However, by limiting the length to 6 ft and routing it with the raceway, there will not be a significant increase in the total impedance of the equipment grounding circuit. For example, this rule permits an exterior bonding jumper where run around a section of flexible metal conduit. Since the function of a bonding jumper is readily apparent, color identification is not necessary.

250-80. Bonding of Piping Systems.

(a) Metal Water Piping. The interior metal water piping system shall be bonded to the service equipment enclosure, the grounded conductor at the service, the grounding electrode conductor where of sufficient size, or to the one or more grounding electrodes used. The bonding jumper shall be sized in accordance with Table 250-94. The metal water piping bonding jumper shall be accessible.

This section requires a single connection to the metal water piping system. However, some judgment must be exercised in each specific case. Where it cannot reasonably be concluded that the hot and cold water pipes are reliably interconnected, then an electrical bonding jumper is required to assure that this connection is made.

Exception: In buildings of multiple occupancy, where the interior metal water piping system for the individual occupancies is metallically isolated from all other occupancies by use of nonmetallic water piping, the interior metal water piping system for each occupancy shall be permitted to be bonded to the panelboard or switchboard enclosure supplying that occupancy. The bonding jumper shall be sized in accordance with Table 250-95.

The exception is new in the 1984 *Code.* The intent here is to recognize the fact that increased use of nonmetallic water piping systems underground makes it virtually impossible to comply with the main rule of Section 250-80 in the circumstances described.

(b) Other Metal Piping. Interior metal piping which may become energized shall be bonded to the service equipment enclosure, the grounded conductor at the service, the grounding electrode conductor where of sufficient size, or to the one or more grounding electrodes used. The bonding jumper shall be sized in accordance with Table 250-95 using the rating of the circuit which may energize the piping.

The equipment grounding conductor for the circuit which may energize the piping shall be permitted to serve as the bonding means.

(FPN): Bonding all piping and metal air ducts within the premises will provide additional safety.

H. Grounding Electrode System

250-81. Grounding Electrode System. If available on the premises at each building or structure served, each item (a) through (d) below shall be bonded together to form the grounding electrode system. The bonding jumper shall be sized in accordance with Section 250-94 and shall be connected in the manner specified in Section 250-115. The unspliced grounding electrode conductor shall be permitted to run to any convenient grounding electrode available in the grounding electrode system. It shall be sized for the largest grounding electrode conductor required among all the available electrodes.

(a) Metal Underground Water Pipe. A metal underground water pipe in direct contact with the earth for 10 feet (3.05 m) or more (including any metal well casing effectively bonded to the pipe) and electrically continuous (or made electrically continuous by bonding around insulating joints or sections or insulating pipe) to the points of connection of the grounding electrode conductor and the bonding conductors. Continuity of the grounding path or the bonding connection to interior piping shall not rely on water meters. A metal underground water pipe shall be supplemented by an additional electrode of a type specified in Section 250-81 or in Section 250-83. The supplemental electrode shall be permitted to be bonded to the grounding electrode conductor, the grounded service-entrance conductor, the grounded service raceway, any grounded service enclosure, or the interior metal water piping at any convenient point.

> The addition of "any grounded service enclosure" to the last sentence is new in the 1984 *Code.* The connection of a supplemental grounding electrode conductor to "any service" enclosure on the supply side of the service disconnecting means is, in reality, connecting the grounding electrode conductor to the grounded service-entrance conductor.

Where the supplemental electrode is a made electrode as in Section 250-83(c) or (d), that portion of the bonding jumper which is the sole connection to the supplemental grounding electrode shall not be required to be larger than No. 6 copper wire or No. 4 aluminum wire.

> This paragraph is new in the 1984 *Code.* It was added to correlate with Section 250-83(c) or (d) and Section 250-94. If a "made electrode" is utilized, the size of the "sole" bonding jumper between the service equipment grounded conductor and, for example, a ground rod will not have to be larger than No. 6 AWG copper or No. 4 AWG aluminum.
>
> The requirement to supplement the metal water pipe is based on the practice of using a plastic pipe for replacement when the original metal water pipe fails from corrosion, which leaves the system without a grounding electrode where the supplementary electrode is not provided.

(b) Metal Frame of the Building. The metal frame of the building, where effectively grounded.

(c) Concrete-Encased Electrode. An electrode encased by at least 2 inches (50.8 mm) of concrete, located within and near the bottom of a concrete foundation or footing that is in direct contact with the earth, consisting of at least 20 feet (6.1 m) of one or more steel reinforcing bars or rods of not less than ½ inch (12.7 mm) diameter, or consisting of at least 20 feet (6.1 m) of bare copper conductor not smaller than No. 4 AWG.

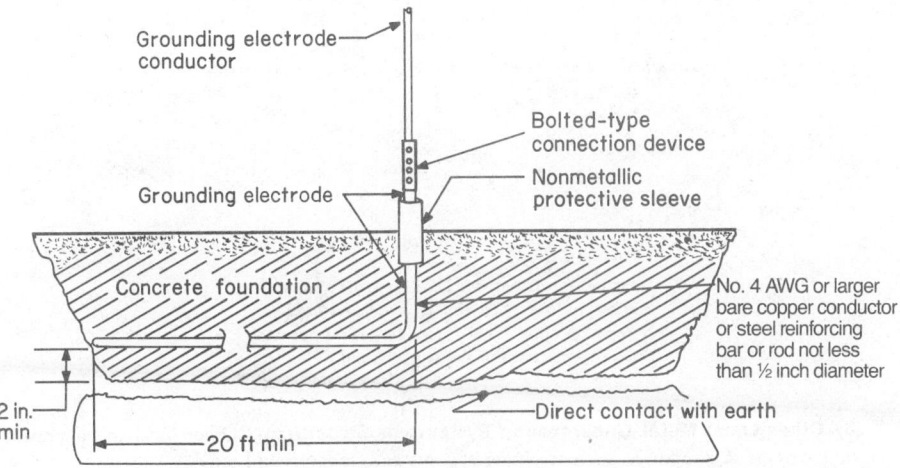

Figure 250-19. A concrete-encased electrode.

(d) Ground Ring. A ground ring encircling the building or structure, in direct contact with the earth at a depth below earth surface not less than 2½ feet (762 mm), consisting of at least 20 feet (6.1 m) of bare copper conductor not smaller than No. 2 AWG.

Section 250-81 requires the metal underground water pipe, the metal frame of the building, a concrete-encased electrode, and a ground ring type of electrode, only when they are available, to be bonded together to form the grounding electrode system. Where a metal underground water pipe is the only grounding electrode available, it must be supplemented by one of the grounding electrodes specified in Section 250-81 or Section 250-83.

There has always been a degree of misunderstanding as to whether metal water piping systems should be used as a grounding electrode, and a number of years ago the electrical industry and the water works industry formed a committee of all the affected interests to evaluate the use of metal underground water piping systems as the grounding electrode. Based on their findings, the committee issued an authoritative report on this subject. The International Association of Electrical Inspectors published the "Interim Report of the American Research Committee on Grounding" in January 1944 and had reprints made in March 1949.

The National Bureau of Standards in Washington, D.C., has monitored the electrolysis of metal systems because a flow of current at a grounding electrode on dc systems can cause displacement of metal. The results of this monitoring have shown that problems are minimal.

250-83. Made and Other Electrodes. Where none of the electrodes specified in Section 250-81 is available, one or more of the electrodes specified in (a) through (d) below shall be used. Where practicable, made electrodes shall be embedded below permanent moisture level. Made electrodes shall be free from nonconductive coatings, such as paint or enamel. Where more than one electrode system is used (including those used for lightning rods), each electrode of one system shall not be less than 6 feet (1.83 m) from any other electrode of another system.

(FPN): Two or more electrodes that are effectively bonded together are to be treated as a single electrode system in this sense.

(a) Metal Underground Gas Piping System. An electrically continuous metal underground gas piping system that is uninterrupted with insulating sections or joints and without an outer nonconductive coating, and then only if acceptable to and expressly permitted by both the serving gas supplier and the authority having jurisdiction.

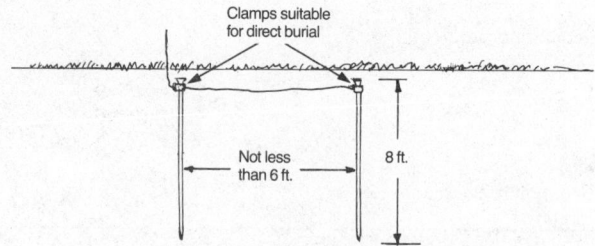

Figure 250-20. Section 250-83 presently requires a spacing of 6 ft between electrodes of different systems. Section 250-84 requires a 6-ft spacing between electrodes of the same system.

(b) Other Local Metal Underground Systems or Structures. Other local metal underground systems or structures, such as piping systems and underground tanks.

(c) Rod and Pipe Electrodes. Rod and pipe electrodes shall not be less than 8 feet (2.44 m) in length and shall consist of the following materials, and shall be installed in the following manner:

(1) Electrodes of pipe or conduit shall not be smaller than ¾-inch trade size and, where of iron or steel, shall have the outer surface galvanized or otherwise metal-coated for corrosion protection.

(2) Electrodes of rods of steel or iron shall be at least ⅝ inch (15.87 mm) in diameter. Nonferrous rods or their equivalent shall be listed and shall be not less than ½ inch (12.7 mm) in diameter.

(3) The electrode shall be installed such that at least 8 feet (2.44 m) of length is in contact with the soil. It shall be driven to a depth of not less than 8 feet (2.44 m) except that where rock bottom is encountered, the electrode shall be driven at an oblique angle not to exceed 45 degrees from the vertical or shall be buried in a trench that is at least 2½ feet (762 mm) deep. The upper end of the electrode shall be flush with or below ground level unless the aboveground end and the grounding electrode conductor attachment are protected against physical damage as specified in Section 250-117.

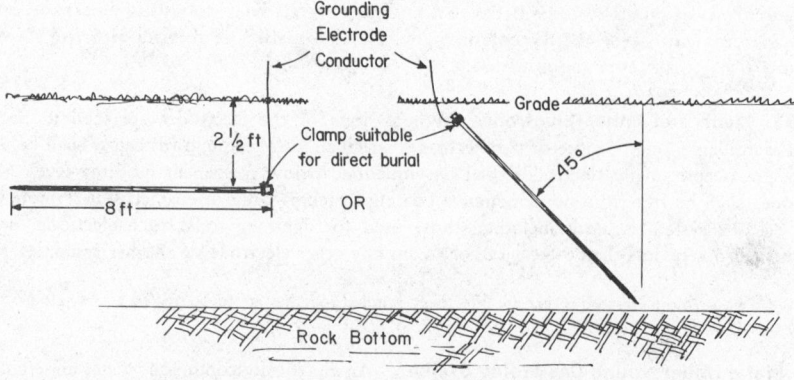

Figure 250-21. All pipe and rod electrodes must have 8 ft of length in contact with soil regardless of rock bottom and to provide that the upper end of the electrode be flush with or below ground level unless the above ground portion is protected against physical damage.

(d) Plate Electrodes. Each plate electrode shall expose not less than 2 square feet (0.186 sq m) of surface to exterior soil. Electrodes of iron or steel plates shall be at least ¼ inch (6.35 mm) in thickness. Electrodes of nonferrous metal shall be at least 0.06 inch (1.52 mm) in thickness.

250-84. Resistance of Made Electrodes. A single electrode consisting of a rod, pipe, or plate which does not have a resistance to ground of 25 ohms or less shall be augmented by one additional electrode of any of the types specified in Section 250-81 or 250-83. Where multiple rod, pipe, or plate electrodes are installed to meet the requirements of this section, they shall be not less than 6 feet (1.83 m) apart.

(FPN): The paralleling efficiency of rods longer than 8 feet (2.44 m) is improved by spacing greater than 6 feet (1.83 m).

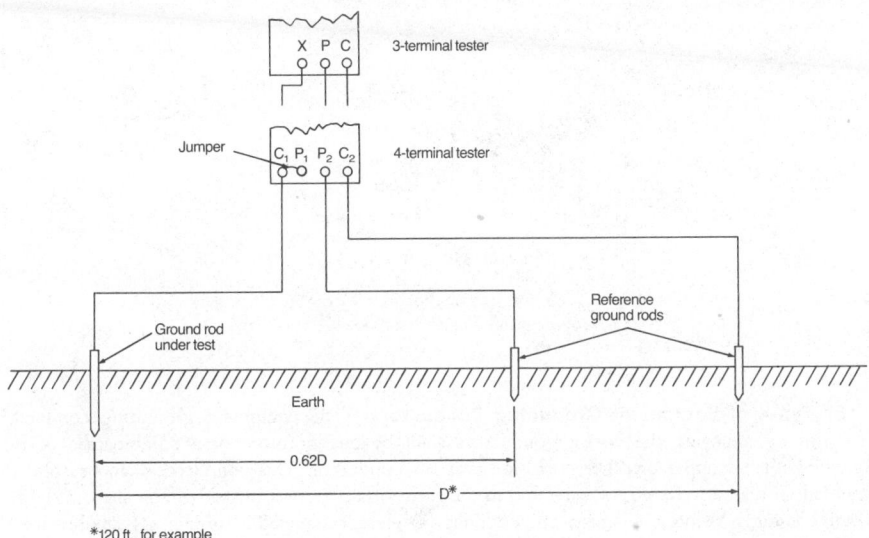

Figure 250-22. The resistance to ground of a driven grounding electrode can be measured by a ground tester used in this manner.

250-86. Use of Lightning Rods. Lightning rod conductors and driven pipes, rods, or other made electrodes used for grounding lightning rods shall not be used in lieu of the made grounding electrodes required by Section 250-83 for grounding wiring systems and equipment. This provision shall not prohibit the required bonding together of grounding electrodes of different systems.

(FPN): See Sections 250-46, 800-31(b)(7), and 820-22(h).

(FPN): Bonding together of all separate grounding electrode systems will limit potential differences between them and between their associated wiring systems.

J. Grounding Conductors

250-91. Material. The material for grounding conductors shall be as specified in (a), (b), and (c) below.

(a) Grounding Electrode Conductor. The grounding electrode conductor shall be of copper, aluminum, or copper-clad aluminum. The material selected shall be resistant to any corrosive condition existing at the installation or shall be suitably protected against corrosion. The conductor shall be solid or stranded, insulated, covered, or bare and shall be installed in one continuous length without a splice or joint.

Exception No. 1: Splices in busbars shall be permitted.

Exception No. 2: Where a service consists of more than a single enclosure as permitted in Section 230-45, it shall be permissible to connect taps to the grounding electrode conductor. Each such tap conductor shall extend to the inside of each such enclosure. The grounding electrode conductor shall be sized in accordance with Section 250-94, but the tap conductors shall be permitted to be sized in accordance with the grounding electrode conductors specified in Section 250-94 for the largest conductor serving the respective enclosures.

The grounding electrode (tap) conductors are required to be sized using Table 250-94 and are based on the size of the largest conductors serving each enclosure. The grounding electrode conductor is determined by the size of the largest service-entrance conductor or equivalent cross-sectional area for parallel conductors as per Table 250-94. See Figure 250-23.

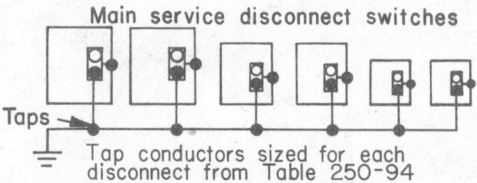

Figure 250-23. The tap method eliminates the difficulties found in looping grounding electrode conductors from one enclosure to another.

(b) Types of Equipment Grounding Conductors. The equipment grounding conductor run with or enclosing the circuit conductors shall be one or more or a combination of the following: (1) a copper or other corrosion-resistant conductor. This conductor shall be solid or stranded; insulated, covered, or bare; and in the form of a wire or a busbar of any shape; (2) rigid metal conduit; (3) intermediate metal conduit; (4) electrical metallic tubing; (5) flexible metal conduit where both the conduit and fittings are approved for grounding; (6) armor of Type AC cable; (7) the sheath of mineral-insulated, metal-sheathed cable; (8) the metallic sheath or the combined metallic sheath and grounding conductors of Type MC cable; (9) cable trays as permitted in Sections 318-2(c) and 318-6; (10) other electrically continuous metal raceways approved for grounding.

Exception No. 1: Flexible metal conduit and flexible metallic tubing shall be permitted for grounding if all the following conditions are met:

a. The length in any ground return path does not exceed 6 feet (1.83 m).

b. The circuit conductors contained therein are protected by overcurrent devices rated at 20 amperes or less.

c. The conduit or tubing is terminated in fittings approved for grounding.

Exception No. 2: Liquidtight flexible metal conduit shall be permitted as a grounding means in the 1¼-inch and smaller trade sizes if the total length of any ground return path is 6 feet (1.83 m) or less, the conduit is terminated in fittings approved for grounding, and the circuit conductors contained therein are protected by overcurrent devices rated at 20 amperes or less for ⅜-inch and ½-inch trade sizes and 60 amperes or less for ¾-inch through 1¼-inch trade sizes.

Exception No. 3: For direct-current circuits only, the equipment grounding conductor shall be permitted to be run separately from the circuit conductors.

The various types of conductors, armored or metal-sheathed cables, or metal raceways that are considered as suitable for use as equipment grounding conductors are described in Section 250-91(b).

Flexible metal conduit and flexible metallic tubing are recognized in Exception No. 1 as equipment grounding conductors, where termination fittings approved for grounding are used, if the total length is not over 6 ft in any ground return path, and the contained circuit conductors are protected by overcurrent devices rated at 20 A or less.

Liquidtight flexible metal conduit is recognized as an equipment grounding conductor by Exception No. 2 where used with termination fittings approved for grounding in sizes not over 1¼ in., and in lengths not over 6 ft in any ground return path.

Exception No. 2 has been revised for the 1984 *NEC* to add limitations on the overcurrent protection provided for the circuit conductors, thus providing overcurrent protection for the conduit when used as an equipment grounding conductor. Recent field experience and laboratory tests indicated that it was possible to overload the grounding path provided in the ⅜ in. through 1¼-in. trade sizes of UL-listed liquidtight flexible metal conduit under certain fault conditions, causing the liquidtight outer jacket to melt and emit smoke. This led to a study by UL and the electrical industry to determine the practical limits for the use of this type of conduit as a grounding conductor. Ground-fault current tests were conducted and it was determined that overcurrent protection as now specified would maintain the integrity of the outer jacket and the equipment grounding circuit.

The overcurrent protection limitations for the circuit conductors are not required if the conduit is not used as an equipment grounding conductor.

Termination fittings that are approved for grounding may be determined by a qualified testing laboratory, inspection agency, or other organization concerned with product evaluation as part of its listing and labeling program. See the definitions for "Approved," "Identified," "Listed," and "Labeled" in Article 100. For grounding requirements, see also Sections 349-16, 350-5, and 351-9.

(c) Supplementary Grounding. Supplementary grounding electrodes shall be permitted to augment the equipment grounding conductors specified in Section 250-91(b), but the earth shall not be used as the sole equipment grounding conductor.

The intent of this section is that grounding electrodes connected to equipment are not to be used in lieu of the equipment grounding conductor, but may be used for supplementary protection, for example for lightning protection or to equalize potentials in the area of the equipment.

250-92. Installation. Grounding conductors shall be installed as specified in (a) and (b) below.

(a) Grounding Electrode Conductor. A grounding electrode conductor or its enclosure shall be securely fastened to the surface on which it is carried. A No. 4, copper or aluminum, or larger conductor shall be protected if exposed to severe physical damage. A No. 6 grounding conductor that is free from exposure to physical damage shall be permitted to be run along the surface of the building construction without metal covering or protection where it is rigidly stapled to the construction; otherwise, it shall be in rigid metal conduit, intermediate metal conduit, rigid nonmetallic conduit, electrical metallic tubing, or cable armor. Grounding conductors smaller than No. 6 shall be in rigid metal conduit, intermediate metal conduit, rigid nonmetallic conduit, electrical metallic tubing, or cable armor.

Metal enclosures for grounding conductors shall be electrically continuous from the point of attachment to cabinets or equipment to the grounding electrode, and shall be securely fastened to the ground clamp or fitting. Metal enclosures that are not physically continuous from cabinet or equipment to the grounding electrode shall be made electrically continuous by bonding each end to the grounding conductor. Where intermediate metal conduit is used for protection for a grounding conductor, the installation shall comply with the requirements of Article 345. Where rigid metal conduit is used as protection for a grounding conductor, the installation shall comply with the requirements of Article 346. Where rigid nonmetallic conduit is used as protection for a grounding conductor, the installation shall comply with the requirements of Article 347. Where electrical metallic tubing is used, the installation shall comply with the requirements of Article 348.

Aluminum or copper-clad aluminum grounding conductors shall not be used where in direct contact with masonry or the earth or where subject to corrosive conditions. Where used outside, aluminum or copper-clad aluminum grounding conductors shall not be installed within 18 inches (457 mm) of the earth.

(b) Equipment Grounding Conductor. An equipment grounding conductor shall be installed as follows:

(1) Where it consists of a raceway, cable tray, cable armor, or cable sheath or where it is a wire within a raceway or cable, it shall be installed in accordance with the applicable provisions in this Code using fittings for joints and terminations approved for use with the type raceway or cable used. All connections, joints, and fittings shall be made tight using suitable tools.

(2) Where it is a separate grounding conductor as provided in the Exception for Section 250-50(a) and (b), it shall be installed in accordance with (a) above in regard to restrictions for aluminum and also in regard to protection from physical damage.

Exception: Sizes smaller than No. 6 shall not be required to be enclosed in a raceway or armor where run in the hollow spaces of a wall or partition or where otherwise installed so as not to be subject to physical damage.

250-93. Size of Direct-Current System Grounding Conductor. The size of the grounding conductor for a dc system shall be as specified in (a) through (c) below.

(a) Not Be Smaller than the Neutral Conductor. Where the dc system consists of a 3-wire balancer set or a balancer winding with overcurrent protection as provided in Section 445-4(d), the grounding conductor shall not be smaller than the neutral conductor.

(b) Not Be Smaller than the Largest Conductor. Where the dc system is other than as in (a) above, the grounding conductor shall not be smaller than the largest conductor supplied by the system.

(c) Not Be Smaller than No. 8. In no case shall the grounding conductor be smaller than No. 8 copper or No. 6 aluminum.

250-94. Size of Alternating-Current Grounding Electrode Conductor. The size of the grounding electrode conductor of a grounded or ungrounded ac system shall not be less than given in Table 250-94.

Exception No. 1: Grounded Systems.

a. Where connected to made electrodes as in Section 250-83 (c) or (d), that portion of the grounding electrode conductor which is the sole connection between the grounding electrode and the grounded system conductor shall not be required to be larger than No. 6 copper wire or No. 4 aluminum wire.

b. Where connected to a concrete-encased electrode as in Section 250-81(c), that portion of the grounding electrode conductor which is the sole connection between the grounding electrode and the grounded system conductor shall not be required to be larger than No. 4 copper wire.

c. Where connected to a ground ring as in Section 250-81(d), that portion of the grounding electrode conductor which is the sole connection between the grounding electrode and the grounded system conductor shall not be required to be larger than the conductor used for the ground ring.

Table 250-94
Grounding Electrode Conductor for AC Systems

Size of Largest Service-Entrance Conductor or Equivalent Area for Parallel Conductors		Size of Grounding Electrode Conductor	
Copper	Aluminum or Copper-Clad Aluminum	Copper	*Aluminum or Copper-Clad Aluminum
2 or smaller	0 or smaller	8	6
1 or 0	2/0 or 3/0	6	4
2/0 or 3/0	4/0 or 250 MCM	4	2
Over 3/0 thru 350 MCM	Over 250 MCM thru 500 MCM	2	0
Over 350 MCM thru 600 MCM	Over 500 MCM thru 900 MCM	0	3/0
Over 600 MCM thru 1100 MCM	Over 900 MCM thru 1750 MCM	2/0	4/0
Over 1100 MCM	Over 1750 MCM	3/0	250 MCM

Where there are no service-entrance conductors, the grounding electrode conductor size shall be determined by the equivalent size of the largest service-entrance conductor required for the load to be served.

* See installation restrictions in Section 250-92(a).

(FPN): See Section 250-23(b).

Exception No. 2: Ungrounded Systems.

a. Where connected to made electrodes as in Section 250-83 (c) or (d), that portion of the grounding electrode conductor which is the sole connection between the grounding electrode and the service equipment shall not be required to be larger than No. 6 copper wire or No. 4 aluminum wire.

b. Where connected to a concrete-encased electrode as in Section 250-81(c), that portion of the grounding electrode conductor which is the sole connection between the grounding electrode and the service equipment shall not be required to be larger than No. 4 copper wire.

c. Where connected to a ground ring as in Section 250-81(d), that portion of the grounding electrode conductor which is the sole connection between the grounding electrode and the service equipment shall not be required to be larger than the conductor used for the ground ring.

Exception Nos. 1 and 2, for both grounded and ungrounded systems, have been revised for the 1984 *Code.*

When a concrete-encased electrode is used per Section 250-81(c), the grounding electrode conductor which originates at the service equipment and is run to the concrete-encased electrode is not required to be any larger than a No. 4 AWG. This exception is applicable where there is only one connection between the grounding electrode and the grounded system conductor or the service equipment for ungrounded systems.

In the case of a ground ring type of electrode, required by Section 250-81(d) to be a bare copper conductor not smaller than No. 2 AWG, a similar rule is applicable. Again, this exception is applicable where there is only a single connection between the grounding electrode (ground ring) and the grounded system conductor or the service equipment for ungrounded systems. However, in this case, if the ground ring is sized at larger than No. 2 AWG then the actual size will determine the minimum size of the grounding electrode conductor.

250-95. Size of Equipment Grounding Conductors. The size of copper, aluminum, or copper-clad aluminum equipment grounding conductors shall not be less than given in Table 250-95.

Where conductors are run in parallel in multiple raceways, as permitted in Section 310-4, the equipment grounding conductor, where used, shall be run in parallel. Each parallel equipment grounding conductor shall be sized on the basis of the ampere rating of the overcurrent device protecting the circuit conductors in the raceway in accordance with Table 250-95.

When conductors are adjusted in size to compensate for voltage drop, equipment grounding conductors, where required, shall be adjusted proportionately according to circular mil area.

Where a single equipment grounding conductor is run with multiple circuits in the same raceway, it shall be sized for the largest overcurrent device protecting conductors in the raceway.

The words "according to circular mil area" are new in the 1984 *Code*.

A single equipment grounding conductor is required to be sized for the largest overcurrent device and is not required to be sized for the composite of all the circuits in the raceway. For example, three 3-phase circuits protected by overcurrent devices at 30, 60 and 100 A installed in the same raceway would require only one equipment grounding conductor sized according to the largest (100 A in this case) overcurrent device. Therefore, a No. 8 AWG copper or No. 6 AWG aluminum or copper-clad aluminum is required by Table 250-95.

Table 250-95. Minimum Size Equipment Grounding Conductors for Grounding Raceway and Equipment

Rating or Setting of Automatic Overcurrent Device in Circuit Ahead of Equipment, Conduit, etc., Not Exceeding (Amperes)	Size	
	Copper Wire No.	Aluminum or Copper-Clad Aluminum Wire No.*
15	14	12
20	12	10
30	10	8
40	10	8
60	10	8
100	8	6
200	6	4
300	4	2
400	3	1
500	2	1/0
600	1	2/0
800	0	3/0
1000	2/0	4/0
1200	3/0	250 MCM
1600	4/0	350 "
2000	250 MCM	400 "
2500	350 "	600 "
3000	400 "	600 "
4000	500 "	800 "
5000	700 "	1200 "
6000	800 "	1200 "

* See installation restrictions in Section 250-92(a).

Exception No. 1: An equipment grounding conductor not smaller than No. 18 copper and not smaller than the circuit conductors if an integral part of a listed flexible cord assembly shall be permitted for grounding cord-connected equipment where the equipment is protected by overcurrent devices not exceeding 20-ampere rating.

Exception No. 2: The equipment grounding conductor shall not be required to be larger than the circuit conductors supplying the equipment.

Exception No. 3: Where a raceway or a cable armor or sheath is used as the equipment grounding conductor, as provided in Sections 250-57(a) and 250-91(b).

250-97. Outline Lighting. Isolated noncurrent-carrying metal parts of outline lighting systems shall be permitted to be bonded together by a No. 14 copper or No. 12 aluminum conductor protected from physical damage, where a conductor complying with Section 250-95 is used to ground the group.

250-99. Equipment Grounding Conductor Continuity.

(a) Separable Connections. Separable connections such as those provided in draw-out equipment or attachment plugs and mating connectors and receptacles shall provide for first-make, last-break of the equipment grounding conductor.

Exception: Interlocked equipment, plugs, receptacles and connectors which preclude energization without grounding continuity.

(b) Switches. No automatic cutout or switch shall be placed in the equipment grounding conductor of a premises wiring system.

Exception: Where the opening of the cutout or switch disconnects all sources of energy.

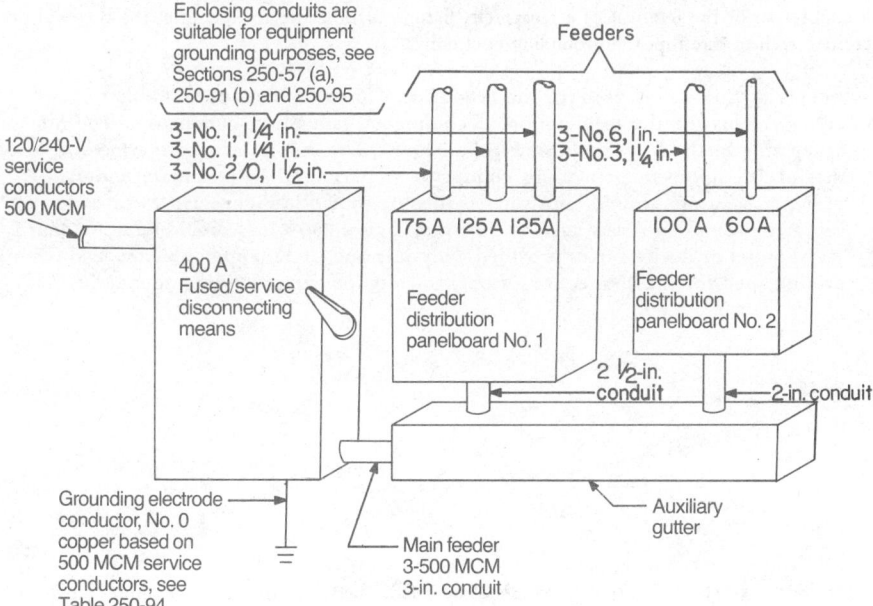

Figure 250-24. One example of the various sizes of enclosing metal conduits used as equipment grounding conductors are shown as they apply to a service and feeder system.

K. Grounding Conductor Connections

250-112. To Grounding Electrode. The connection of a grounding electrode conductor to a grounding electrode shall be accessible and made in a manner that will assure a permanent and effective ground. Where necessary to assure this for a metal piping system used as a grounding electrode, effective bonding shall be provided around insulated joints and sections and around any equipment that is likely to be disconnected for repairs or replacement.

Exception: An encased or buried connection to a concrete-encased, driven, or buried grounding electrode shall not be required to be accessible.

This exception was revised for the 1984 *Code* by adding the words "An encased or buried."

When the exposed portion of an encased, driven, or buried electrode is used for the termination of a grounding electrode conductor, the connection between them is required to be accessible. However, if the connection is buried or encased it is not required to be accessible. Note that ground clamps and other connectors which are suitable for use where buried in earth or embedded in concrete are identified for such use, either by a marking on the connector or by a tag attached to the connector.

See Figures 250-19 and 250-20.

250-113. To Conductors and Equipment. Required grounding conductors and bonding jumpers shall be connected by pressure connectors, clamps, or other approved means. Connection devices or fittings that depend on solder shall not be used.

250-114. Continuity and Attachment of Branch-Circuit Equipment Grounding Conductors to Boxes. Where more than one equipment grounding conductor enters a box all such conductors shall be spliced or joined within the box or to the box with devices suitable for the use. Connections depending on solder shall not be used and the arrangement shall be such that the disconnection or the removal of a receptacle, fixture, or other device fed from the box will not interfere with or interrupt the grounding continuity.

This section was revised for the 1984 *Code*. The intent is to permit either of two arrangements for the termination of equipment grounding conductors. The first acceptable method is shown in Figure 250-26. The second acceptable method is that each equipment grounding conductor is permitted to terminate under, for example, separate ground clips such as the one shown in Figure 250-25 or under a separate grounding screw such as shown in Figure 250-27. It should be noted that metal outlet or device boxes provided with only one 10-32 tapped hole marked GR are intended for the connection of only one equipment grounding conductor.

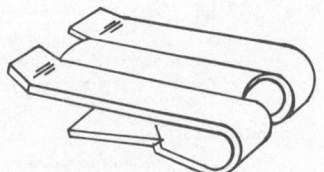

Figure 250-25. A clip used to connect a copper grounding conductor to a box.

(a) Metal Boxes. A connection shall be made between the one or more equipment grounding conductors and a metal box by means of a grounding screw which shall be used for no other purpose, or an approved grounding device.

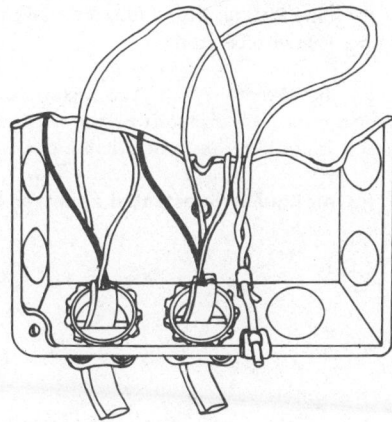

Figure 250-26. An application of a grounding clip.

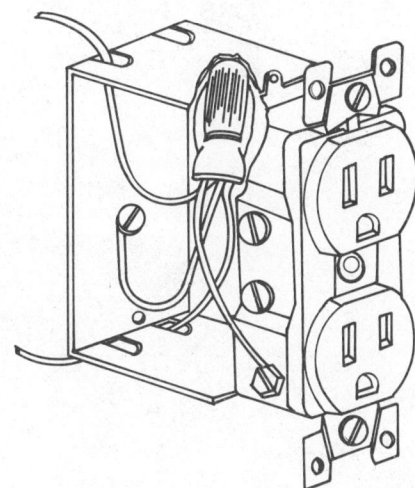

Figure 250-27. Grounding conductors may be attached to a box by a variety of methods, such as a screw, as show here, or with a grounding clip as shown in Figure 250-26.

(b) Nonmetallic Boxes. One or more equipment grounding conductors brought into a nonmetallic outlet box shall be so arranged that a connection can be made to any fitting or device in that box requiring grounding.

250-115. Connection to Electrodes. The grounding conductor shall be connected to the grounding fitting by suitable lugs, pressure connectors, clamps, or other approved means. Connections depending on solder shall not be used. Ground clamps shall be suitable for the materials of the grounding electrode and the grounding electrode conductor and where used on pipe, rod or other buried electrodes shall also be suitable for direct soil burial. Not more than one conductor shall be connected to the grounding electrode by a single clamp or fitting unless the clamp or fitting is approved for multiple conductors. One of the methods indicated in (a), (b), (c), or (d) below shall be used.

(a) An Approved Bolted Clamp. An approved bolted clamp of cast bronze or brass or plain or malleable iron.

(b) **Pipe Fitting, Pipe Plug, etc.** A pipe fitting, pipe plug, or other approved device screwed into a pipe or pipe fitting.

(c) **Sheet-Metal-Strap Type Ground Clamp.** A sheet-metal-strap type ground clamp having a rigid metal base that seats on the electrode and having a strap of such material and dimensions that it is not likely to stretch during or after installation.

(d) **An Equally Substantial Approved Means.** An equally substantial approved means.

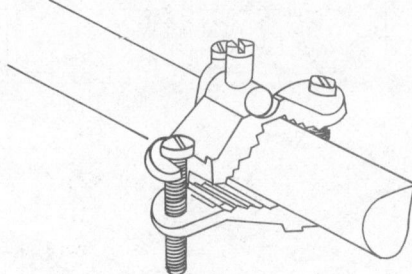

Figure 250-28. A ground clamp generally used with No. 8 through No. 4 grounding electrode conductors.

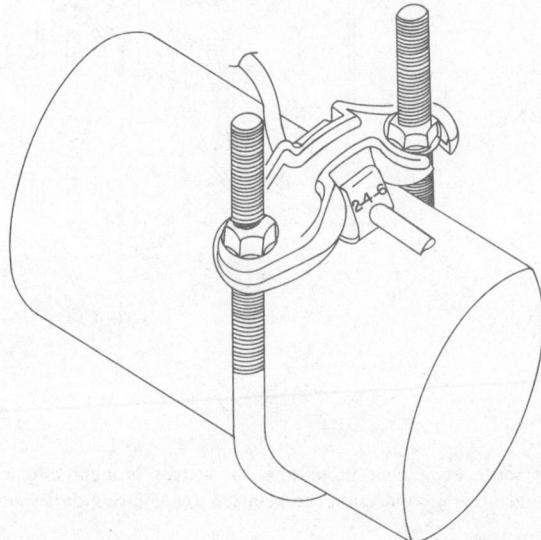

Figure 250-29. U-bolt ground clamps are available for all pipe sizes and all grounding electrode conductor sizes. Where grounding electrode conductors are run in conduits, conduit hubs may be bolted to the threaded portion of the U-bolt.

Consideration concerning the suitability of ground clamps for direct soil burial should be given when used on ground rod or pipe electrodes or other buried electrodes. Many of the ground clamps recognized for use on ground rods prior to the implementation of the requirements of the 1981 *NEC* were not suitable for direct soil burial since they were made of aluminum or steel or held together with steel screws. See commentary following Section 250-112, Exception.

When a ground clamp is used and terminates on, for example, a galvanized water pipe, it is required to be of material which is compatible with steel so as to prevent corrosion. The same type of compatability requirement applies to ground clamps on copper water pipe.

See Section 250-83(c)(3) for rod and pipe electrode installation requirements.

250-117. Protection of Attachment. Ground clamps or other fittings shall be approved for general use without protection or shall be protected from ordinary physical damage as indicated in (a) or (b) below.

(a) Not Likely to Be Damaged. Installations where they are not likely to be damaged.

(b) Protective Covering. Enclosing in metal, wood, or equivalent protective covering.

250-118. Clean Surfaces. Nonconductive coatings (such as paint, lacquer, and enamel) on equipment to be grounded shall be removed from threads and other contact surfaces to assure good electrical continuity.

L. Instrument Transformers, Relays, etc.

250-121. Instrument Transformer Circuits. Secondary circuits of current and potential instrument transformers shall be grounded where the primary windings are connected to circuits of 300 volts or more to ground, and where on switchboards, shall be grounded irrespective of voltage.

Exception: Circuits where the primary windings are connected to circuits of less than 1000 volts with no live parts or wiring exposed or accessible to other than qualified persons.

250-122. Instrument Transformer Cases. Cases or frames of instrument transformers shall be grounded where accessible to other than qualified persons.

Exception: Cases or frames of current transformers, the primaries of which are not over 150 volts to ground and which are used exclusively to supply current to meters.

250-123. Cases of Instruments, Meters, and Relays — Operating at Less than 1000 Volts. Instruments, meters, and relays operating with windings or working parts at less than 1000 volts shall be grounded as specified in (a), (b), or (c) below.

(a) Not on Switchboards. Instruments, meters, and relays not located on switchboards, operating with windings or working parts at 300 volts or more to ground, and accessible to other than qualified persons, shall have the cases and other exposed metal parts grounded.

(b) On Dead-Front Switchboards. Instruments, meters, and relays (whether operated from current and potential transformers, or connected directly in the circuit) on switchboards having no live parts on the front of the panels shall have the cases grounded.

(c) On Live-Front Switchboards. Instruments, meters, and relays (whether operated from current and potential transformers, or connected directly in the circuit) on switchboards having exposed live parts on the front of panels shall not have their cases grounded. Mats of insulating rubber or other suitable floor insulation shall be provided for the operator where the voltage to ground exceeds 150.

250-124. Cases of Instruments, Meters, and Relays — Operating Voltage 1 kV and Over. Where instruments, meters, and relays have current-carrying parts of 1 kV and over to ground, they shall be isolated by elevation or protected by suitable barriers, grounded metal or insulating covers or guards. Their cases shall not be grounded.

Exception: Cases of electrostatic ground detectors where the internal ground segments of the instrument are connected to the instrument case and grounded and the ground detector is isolated by elevation.

250-125. Instrument Grounding Conductor. The grounding conductor for secondary circuits of instrument transformers and for instrument cases shall not be smaller than No. 12 copper or No. 10 aluminum. Cases of instrument transformers, instruments, meters, and relays which are mounted directly on grounded metal surfaces of enclosures or grounded metal switchboard panels shall be considered to be grounded and no additional grounding conductor will be required.

M. Grounding of Systems and Circuits of 1 kV and Over (High Voltage)

250-150. General. Where high-voltage systems are grounded, they shall comply with all applicable provisions of the preceding sections of this article and with the following sections which supplement and modify the preceding sections.

250-151. Derived Neutral Systems. A system neutral derived from a grounding transformer shall be permitted to be used for grounding a high-voltage system.

250-152. Solidly Grounded Neutral Systems.

(a) Neutral Conductor. The neutral of a solidly grounded neutral system shall comply with (1) and (2) below.

(1) The minimum insulation level for neutral conductors of solidly grounded systems shall be 600 volts.

Exception No. 1: Bare copper conductors shall be permitted to be used for the neutral of service entrances and the neutral of direct buried portions of feeders.

Exception No. 2: Bare conductors shall be permitted for the neutral of overhead portions installed outdoors.

(2) The neutral grounding conductor shall be permitted to be a bare conductor if isolated from phase conductors and protected from physical damage.

(b) Multiple Grounding. The neutral of a solidly grounded neutral system shall be permitted to be grounded at more than one point for:

(1) Services.

(2) Direct buried portions of feeders employing a bare copper neutral.

(3) Overhead portion installed outdoors.

250-153. Impedance Grounded Neutral Systems. Impedance grounded neutral systems shall comply with the provisions of (a) through (d) below.

(a) Location. The grounding impedance shall be inserted in the grounding conductor between the grounding electrode of the supply system and the neutral point of the supply transformer or generator.

(b) Identified and Insulated. Where the neutral conductor of an impedance grounded neutral system is used, it shall be identified, as well as fully insulated with the same insulation as the phase conductors.

(c) System Neutral Connection. The system neutral shall not be connected to ground, except through the neutral grounding impedance.

(d) Equipment Grounding Conductors. Equipment grounding conductors shall be permitted to be bare and shall be connected to the ground bus and grounding electrode conductor at the service-entrance equipment and extended to the system ground.

250-154. Grounding of Systems Supplying Portable or Mobile Equipment. Systems supplying portable or mobile high-voltage equipment, other than substations installed on a temporary basis, shall comply with (a) through (e) below.

Portable means equipment that is easily carried, while mobile means equipment that is easily moved, as on wheels, treads, etc.

(a) Portable or Mobile Equipment. Portable or mobile high-voltage equipment shall be supplied from a system having its neutral grounded through an impedance. Where a delta-connected high-voltage system is used to supply portable or mobile equipment, a system neutral shall be derived.

(b) Exposed Noncurrent-Carrying Metal Parts. Exposed noncurrent-carrying metal parts of portable or mobile equipment shall be connected by an equipment grounding conductor to the point at which the system neutral impedance is grounded.

(c) Ground-Fault Current. The voltage developed between the portable or mobile equipment frame and ground by the flow of maximum ground-fault current shall not exceed 100 volts.

(d) Ground-Fault Detection and Relaying. Ground-fault detection and relaying shall be provided to automatically de-energize any high-voltage system component which has developed a ground fault. The continuity of the equipment grounding conductor shall be continuously monitored so as to de-energize automatically the high-voltage feeder to the portable or mobile equipment upon loss of continuity of the equipment grounding conductor.

(e) Isolation. The grounding electrode to which the portable or mobile equipment system neutral impedance is connected shall be isolated from and separated in the ground by at least 20 feet (6.1 m) from any other system or equipment grounding electrode, and there shall be no direct connection between the grounding electrodes, such as buried pipe, fence, etc.

(f) Trailing Cable and Couplers. High voltage trailing cable and couplers for interconnection of portable or mobile equipment shall meet the requirements of Part C of Article 400 for cables and Section 710-45 for couplers.

250-155. Grounding of Equipment. All noncurrent-carrying metal parts of fixed, portable, and mobile equipment and associated fences, housings, enclosures, and supporting structures shall be grounded.

Exception No. 1: Where isolated from ground and located so as to prevent any person who can make contact with ground from contacting such metal parts when the equipment is energized.

Exception No. 2: Pole-mounted distribution apparatus as provided in Section 250-42, Exception No. 3.

Grounding conductors not an integral part of a cable assembly shall not be smaller than No. 6 copper or No. 4 aluminum.

ARTICLE 280 — SURGE ARRESTERS

Contents

ARTICLE 280—SURGE ARRESTERS

Voltage surges with peaks of several thousand volts, even on 120-V circuits, are not uncommon. These surges occur because of induced voltages in power and transmission lines resulting from lightning strikes in the vicinity of the line. They also occur as a result of switching inductive circuits on the premises. Surge arresters for installation as part of an electric service and for use with cord- and plug-connected solid-state electronic equipment are commercially available. See Figures 280-1 and 280-2.

Figure 280-1. Lightning surge protector for service-entrance installation. This device is suitable for mounting in a panel knockout. (*General Electric Co.*)

Figure 280-2. Voltage spike protector suitable for use with 120-V cord- and plug-connected electronic equipment such as TV sets, small computers, medical equipment, and electronic organs. (*General Electric Co.*)

A. General

280-1. Scope. This article covers general requirements, installation requirements, and connection requirements for surge arresters installed on premises wiring systems.

280-2. Definition. A surge arrester is a protective device for limiting surge voltages by discharging or bypassing surge current, and it also prevents continued flow of follow current while remaining capable of repeating these functions.

280-3. Number Required. Where used at a point on a circuit, a surge arrester shall be connected to each ungrounded conductor. A single installation of such surge arresters shall be permitted to protect a number of interconnected circuits provided that no circuit is exposed to surges while disconnected from the surge arresters.

Means are required to be provided to protect circuits that may be disconnected from the generating station bus. A switch with double-throw action used to disconnect the outside circuits from the station generator and alternatively connect these circuits to ground would satisfy the condition of a single set of arresters protecting more than one circuit.

280-4. Surge Arrester Selection.

(a) On Circuits of Less than 1000 Volts. The rating of the surge arrester shall be equal to or greater than the maximum continuous phase-to-ground power frequency voltage available at the point of application.

(b) On Circuits of 1 kV and Over. The rating of the surge arrester shall be not less than 125 percent of the maximum continuous phase-to-ground voltage available at the point of application.

(FPN): For further information on selection of surge arresters, see Guide for the Application of Valve-Type Surge Arresters for Alternating-Current Systems (ANSI C62.2-1981).

B. Installation

280-11. Location. Surge arresters shall be permitted to be located indoors or outdoors and shall be made inaccessible to unqualified persons.

Exception: Surge arresters listed for installation in accessible locations.

280-12. Routing of Surge Arrester Connections. The conductor used to connect the surge arrester to line or bus and to ground shall not be any longer than necessary and shall avoid unnecessary bends.

Arrester conductors should be as short and run as straight as practicable, avoiding any sharp bends and turns which would increase the impedance to lightning discharges and tend to reduce the effectiveness of a grounding conductor.

C. Connecting Surge Arresters

280-21. Installed at Services of Less than 1000 Volts. Line and ground connecting conductors shall not be smaller than No. 14 copper or No. 12 aluminum. The arrester grounding conductor shall be connected to one of the following: (1) the grounded service conductor; (2) the grounding electrode conductor; (3) the grounding electrode for the service; or (4) the equipment grounding terminal in the service equipment.

ARTICLE 280—SURGE ARRESTERS

Single-phase or 3-phase grounded or ungrounded services are permitted to have the surge arrester grounded to the equipment grounding terminal in the service equipment. Figure 280-3 shows three methods of grounding the ground terminals of surge arresters at service entrances.

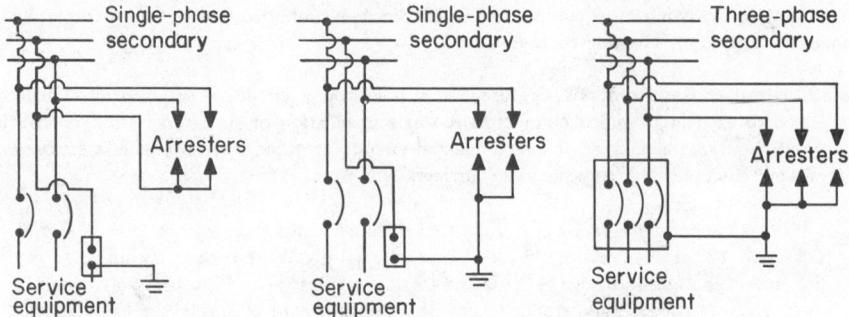

Figure 280-3. Three locations of grounding surge arresters at service entrances. Left, arrester connected to neutral service conductor; center, arrester connected to a grounding electrode conductor; and right, arrester connected to a grounding electrode conductor of an ungrounded system.

280-22. Installed on the Load Side of Services of Less than 1000 Volts. Line and ground connecting conductors shall not be smaller than No. 14 copper or No. 12 aluminum. A surge arrester shall be permitted to be connected between any two conductors (ungrounded conductor(s), grounded conductor, grounding conductor). The grounded conductor and the grounding conductor shall be interconnected only by the normal operation of the surge arrester during a surge.

280-23. Circuits of 1 kV and Over — Surge-Arrester Conductors. The conductor between the surge arrester and the line and surge arrester and the grounding connection shall not be smaller than No. 6 copper or aluminum.

280-24. Circuits of 1 kV and Over — Interconnections. The grounding conductor of a surge arrester protecting a transformer that supplies a secondary distribution system shall be permitted to be interconnected as specified in (a) and (b) below.

(a) Metallic Interconnections. A metallic interconnection shall be permitted to be made to the secondary neutral provided that, in addition to the direct grounding connection at the surge arrester:

(1) The grounded conductor of the secondary has elsewhere a grounding connection to a continuous metal underground water piping system. However, in urban water-pipe areas where there are at least four water-pipe connections on the neutral and not less than four such connections in each mile of neutral, the metallic interconnection shall be permitted to be made to the secondary neutral with omission of the direct grounding connection at the surge arrester.

(2) The grounded conductor of the secondary system is a part of a multiground neutral system of which the primary neutral has at least four ground connections in each mile of line in addition to a ground at each service.

(b) Through Spark Gap. Where the secondary is not grounded as in (a) above, but is otherwise grounded as in Sections 250-81 and 250-83, such interconnections, where made, shall be through a spark gap having a 60-hertz breakdown voltage of at least twice the primary circuit voltage but not necessarily more than 10 kV, and there shall be at least one other ground on the grounded conductor of the secondary not less than 20 feet (6.1 m) distant from the surge arrester grounding electrode.

(c) **By Special Permission.** An interconnection of the surge arrester ground and the secondary neutral, other than as provided in (a) or (b) above, shall be permitted to be made only by special permission.

280-25. Grounding. Except as indicated in this article, surge arrester grounding connections shall be made as specified in Article 250. Grounding conductors shall not be run in metal enclosures unless bonded to both ends of such enclosure.

3 WIRING METHODS AND MATERIALS

ARTICLE 300 — WIRING METHODS

Contents

ARTICLE 300—WIRING METHODS

300-32. Conductors of Different Systems.

300-34. Conductor Bending Radius.

300-35. Protection Against Induction Heating.

300-36. Grounding.

A. General Requirements

300-1. Scope.

(a) **All Wiring Installations.** The provisions of this article shall apply to all wiring installations.

Exception No. 1: Only those sections referenced in Article 725 shall apply to Class 1, Class 2, and Class 3 circuits.

Exception No. 2: Only those sections referenced in Article 760 shall apply to fire protective signaling circuits.

Exception No. 3: Only those sections referenced in Article 770 shall apply to optical fiber cables.

Exception No. 4: Only those sections referenced in Article 800 shall apply to communication systems.

Exception No. 5: Only those sections referenced in Article 820 shall apply to community antenna television and radio distribution systems.

The five exceptions clearly indicate that Article 300 is not applicable to Articles 725, 760, 770, 800, and 820. For example, the requirement of Section 300-15(a) is not applicable to a power-limited fire protective signaling system wired in accordance with Section 760-28(b)(1), so a box is not necessary at the "outlet" for a heat detector head on such a system. However, certain parts of Article 300 are applicable where they are referenced in Articles 725, 760, 770, 800, and 820. For example, see Sections 725-2(b), 760-4(d), 800-3(d), and 820-15, which reference Section 300-22. See also the exceptions to these sections.

(b) **Integral Parts of Equipment.** The provisions of this article are not intended to apply to the conductors which form an integral part of equipment, such as motors, controllers, motor control centers, or factory-assembled control equipment.

(c) **Single Conductors.** Single conductors specified in Table 310-13 shall only be permitted to be installed where part of a recognized wiring method of Chapter 3.

Exception: As permitted in Article 250.

This exception was added in the 1984 *NEC* to recognize that some types of grounding and bonding conductors can be run as single conductors. For example, see Sections 250-92 and 250-97.

300-2. Voltage Limitations.

Wiring methods specified in Chapter 3 shall be used for voltages 600 volts, nominal, or less where not specifically limited in some section of Chapter 3. They shall be permitted for voltages over 600 volts, nominal, where specifically permitted elsewhere in this Code.

300-3. Conductors of Different Systems.

(a) **600 Volts, Nominal, or Less.** Conductors of alternating current or direct current circuits, rated 600 volts, nominal, or less, shall be permitted to occupy the same equipment wiring enclosure, cable, or raceway. All conductors shall have an insulation voltage rating equal to at least the maximum nominal circuit voltage rating of any conductor within the enclosure, cable, or raceway.

> This section was revised for the 1984 *NEC* to make it clear that it is the maximum circuit voltage in the raceway, not the maximum insulation voltage rating of the conductors in the raceway, that determines the minimum voltage rating of conductors for 600 V or less systems.
>
> The conductors of a 3-phase, 4-wire, 208Y/120-V ac circuit; a 3-phase, 4-wire, 480Y/277-V ac circuit; and a 3-wire, 120/240-V dc circuit may occupy the same equipment wiring enclosure, cable, or raceway where all conductors are insulated for the maximum circuit voltage of any conductor. In this case the maximum circuit voltage would be 480 V, and 600-V insulation would be required for all of the conductors.
>
> Where a 2-wire, 120-V circuit is included in the same raceway with a 3-wire, 120/240-V circuit having 600-V conductors, the 2-wire, 120-V circuit conductors could utilize 300-V insulation.

Exception: For solar photovoltaic systems in accordance with Section 690-4(b).

> Section 690-4(b) prohibits solar photovoltaic circuits within the same enclosure as conductors of other systems unless the conductors are separated by a partition or are connected together.

(b) Over 600 Volts, Nominal. Conductors of circuits rated over 600 volts, nominal, shall not occupy the same equipment wiring enclosure, cable, or raceway with conductors of circuits rated 600 volts, nominal, or less.

(FPN): See Section 300-32, Conductors of Different Systems — over 600 volts, nominal.

Exception No. 1: Secondary wiring to electric-discharge lamps of 1000 volts or less, if insulated for the secondary voltage involved, shall be permitted to occupy the same fixture enclosure as the branch-circuit conductors.

Exception No. 2: Primary leads of electric-discharge lamp ballasts, insulated for the primary voltage of the ballast, when contained within the individual wiring enclosure, shall be permitted to occupy the same fixture enclosure as the branch-circuit conductors.

Exception No. 3: Excitation, control, relay, and ammeter conductors used in connection with any individual motor or starter shall be permitted to occupy the same enclosure as the motor circuit conductors.

300-4. Protection Against Physical Damage. Where subject to physical damage, conductors shall be adequately protected.

(a) Cables and Raceways Through Wood Members.

(1) Bored Holes. In both exposed and concealed locations, where a cable or raceway-type wiring method is installed through bored holes in joists, rafters, or wood members, holes shall be bored so that the edge of the hole is not less than 1¼ inches (31.8 mm) from the nearest edge of the wood member. Where this distance cannot be maintained the cable or raceway shall be protected from penetration by screws or nails by a steel plate or bushing, at least 1⁄16 inch (1.59 mm) thick, and of appropriate length and width installed to cover the area of the wiring.

Figure 300-1. Steel plate to protect nonmetallic-sheathed cables within 1¼ in. of the edge of a stud. (*RACO*)

The intent of this section is to prevent wallboard or drywall nails from being driven into cables. By keeping the edge of the drilled hole 1¼ in. from the nearest edge of the stud, nails would not be likely to penetrate the stud far enough to injure the cables. The model building codes provide maximum requirements for bored or notched holes in studs and Section 300-4(a)(2) indicates that consideration should be given to the size of notches in studs so as not to affect the strength of the structure. See Figure 300-1.

Exception: Raceways as covered in Articles 345, 346, 347, and 348.

This exception, new in the 1984 *NEC*, permits intermediate metal conduit, rigid metal conduit, rigid nonmetallic conduit, and EMT to be installed through bored holes less than 1¼ inch from the nearest edge of the stud without a steel plate or bushing.

(2) Notches in Wood. Where there is no objection because of weakening the building structure, in both exposed and concealed locations, cables or raceways shall be permitted to be laid in notches in wood studs, joists, rafters, or other wood members where the cable or raceway at those points is protected against nails or screws by a steel plate at least ¹⁄₁₆ inch (1.59 mm) thick installed before the building finish is applied.

Exception: Raceways as covered in Articles 345, 346, 347, and 348.

(b) Cables Through Metal Framing Members. In both exposed and concealed locations where nonmetallic-sheathed cables pass through either factory or field punched, cut or drilled slots or holes in metal members, the cable shall be protected by bushings or grommets securely fastened in the opening. Where nails or screws are likely to penetrate the cable, a steel sleeve, steel plate or steel clip not less than ¹⁄₁₆ inch (1.59 mm) in wall thickness shall be used to protect the nonmetallic cable.

Exception: When the slots or holes are so formed that no metal edge can cut or tear cable insulation, bushings or grommets shall not be required.

(c) Cables Through Spaces Behind Panels Designed to Allow Access. Cables, or raceway-type wiring methods, installed behind panels designed to allow access shall be supported according to their applicable articles.

Section 300-4(c) is new in the 1984 *NEC.* This new section makes it clear that cable or raceway wiring systems above suspended ceilings with lift-up panels cannot be laid on the suspended ceiling. They are required to be supported according to the requirements in the article applicable to the wiring method involved.

300-5. Underground Installations.

(a) Minimum Cover Requirements. Direct buried cable or conduit or other raceways shall be installed to meet the minimum cover requirements of Table 300-5.

Exception No. 1: The minimum cover requirements for other than rigid metal conduit and intermediate metal conduit shall be permitted to be reduced by 6 inches (152 mm) for installations where a 2-inch (50.8-mm) thick concrete pad or equivalent in physical protection is placed in the trench over the underground installation.

See Exception No. 2 for the exception to the Table 300-5 rule applicable to rigid metal conduit and intermediate metal conduit.

Exception No. 2: The minimum cover requirements shall not apply to conduits or other raceways which are located under a building or exterior concrete slab not less than 4 inches (102 mm) in thickness and extending not less than 6 inches (152 mm) beyond the underground installation.

Exception No. 3: Areas subject to heavy vehicular traffic, such as thoroughfares, shall have a minimum cover of 24 inches (610 mm).

Exception No. 3 applies to all wiring methods listed in Table 300-5, i.e., rigid metal conduit, intermediate metal conduit, rigid nonmetallic conduit, etc.

Exception No. 4: Residential branch circuits rated 300 volts or less and provided with overcurrent protection of not more than 30 amperes shall be permitted with a cover requirement of 12 inches (305 mm).

For example, a Type UF cable used for a 125-V, 15-A branch circuit for a lamp post on residential property is permitted to be buried 12 in. deep.

Exception No. 5: Lesser depths are permitted where cables and conductors rise for terminations or splices or where access is otherwise required.

See Section 300-5(d) and Figure 300-2.

Exception No. 6: In airport runways, including adjacent defined areas where trespass is prohibited, cable shall be permitted to be buried not less than 18 inches (457 mm) deep and without raceways, concrete encasement or equivalent.

Exception No. 7: Raceways installed in solid rock shall be permitted to be buried at a lesser depth when covered by 2 inches (50.8 mm) or more of concrete over the installation and extending down to the rock surface.

Exception No. 8: Circuits for the control of irrigation and landscape lighting systems which are limited to not more than 30 volts and are installed with Type UF or other approved cable shall be permitted with a minimum cover of 6 inches (152 mm).

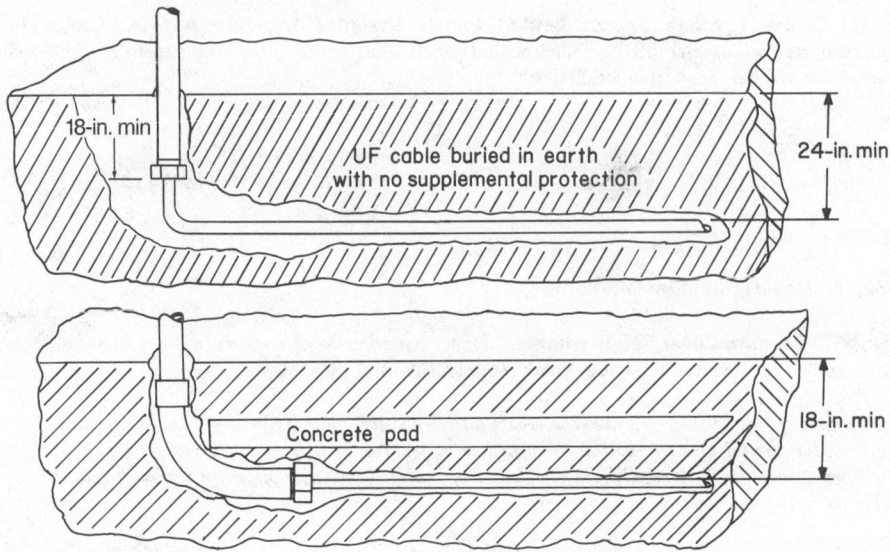

Figure 300-2. Type UF cable buried in compliance with Section 300-5. Note the protective bushing where the cable is used with metal conduit.

Table 300-5

Minimum Cover Requirements, 0 to 600 Volts, Nominal

(Cover is defined as the distance between the top surface of direct buried cable, conduit, or other raceways and the finished grade.)

Wiring Method	Minimum Burial (Inches)
Direct Buried Cables	24
Rigid Metal Conduit	6
Intermediate Metal Conduit	6
Rigid Nonmetallic Conduit Approved for Direct Burial without Concrete Encasement	18
Other Approved Raceways*	18

For SI units: one inch = 25.4 millimeters.

* Note: Raceways approved for burial only when concrete encased shall require a concrete envelope not less than 2 inches (50.8 mm) thick.

(b) Grounding. All underground installations shall be grounded and bonded in accordance with Article 250 of this Code.

(c) Underground Cables Under Buildings. Underground cable installed under a building shall be in a raceway that is extended beyond the outside walls of the building.

(d) Protection from Damage. Conductors emerging from the ground shall be protected by enclosures or raceways extending from a minimum of 18 inches (457 mm) below grade to a point at least 8 feet (2.44 m) above finished grade.

This section was revised in the 1984 *NEC* to specify that the protection is to extend at least 18 in. below grade.

Note that Section 230-50(b) requires service conductors and cables, other than service-entrance cables, to be protected to a height of 10 ft above grade level.

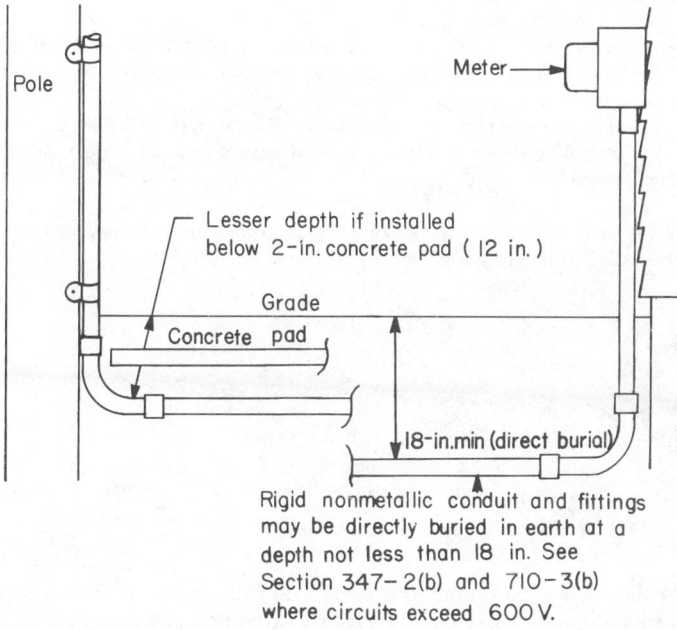

Figure 300-3. PVC rigid nonmetallic conduit buried in compliance with Section 300-5.

Conductors entering a building shall be protected to the point of entrance.

Where the enclosure or raceway is subject to physical damage the conductors shall be installed in rigid metal conduit, intermediate metal conduit, Schedule 80 rigid nonmetallic conduit or equivalent.

(e) Splices and Taps. Underground cables in trenches shall be permitted to be spliced or tapped without the use of splice boxes. The splices or taps shall be made by methods and with material identified for the purpose.

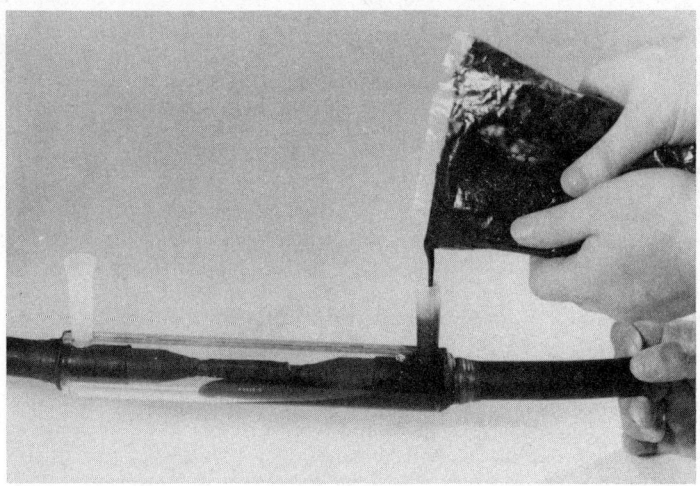

Figure 300-4. Electrical splicing kit for nonshielded single cables up to 5 kV and multiconductor cables up to 600 V. (*3M Company*)

(f) Backfill. Backfill containing large rock, paving materials, cinders, large or sharply angular substance, or corrosive material shall not be placed in an excavation where materials may damage raceways, cables, or other substructures or prevent adequate compaction of fill or contribute to corrosion of raceways, cables or other substructures.

Where necessary to prevent physical damage to the raceway or cable, protection shall be provided in the form of granular or selected material, suitable running boards, suitable sleeves, or other approved means.

(g) Raceway Seals. Conduits or raceways through which moisture may contact energized live parts shall be sealed or plugged at either or both ends.

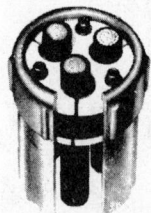

Figure 300-5. Conduit sealing bushing to prevent the entrance of gas or moisture. See Section 230-48 for sealing service raceways. (*O.Z./Gedney Co.*)

(h) Bushing. A bushing shall be used at the end of a conduit which terminates underground where cables leave the conduit as a direct burial wiring method. A seal incorporating the physical protection characteristics of a bushing shall be permitted to be used in lieu of a bushing.

See Figure 300-2.

(i) Single Conductors. All conductors of the same circuit including the grounding conductor where required shall be installed in the same raceway or shall be installed in close proximity in the same trench.

Exception No. 1: Conductors in parallel in raceways shall be permitted but each raceway shall contain all conductors of the same circuit including grounding conductors.

This exception, new in the 1984 *NEC*, makes it clear that paralleled conductors in different raceways are acceptable. See Section 310-4 for more information.

Exception No. 2: Isolated phase installations shall be permitted in nonmetallic raceways in close proximity where conductors are paralleled as permitted in Section 310-4 and the conditions of Section 300-20 are met.

Isolated phase installations are those in which there is only one phase per raceway. There may be some advantages to such an installation where there are many large conductors in parallel, as it avoids crossing conductors in the close quarters of the termination compartment of a switchboard, or in unit substation and transformer enclosures. The spacing between isolated phase raceways should be as small as possible and the length of the run limited, to avoid the increased circuit impedance and resulting increase in voltage drop inherent in an installation involving alternating-current circuits.

300-6. Protection Against Corrosion. Metal raceways, cable armor, boxes, cable sheathing, cabinets, elbows, couplings, fittings, supports, and support hardware shall be of materials suitable for the environment in which they are to be installed.

(a) General. Ferrous raceways, cable armor, boxes, cable sheathing, cabinets, metal elbows, couplings, fittings, supports, and support hardware shall be suitably protected against corrosion inside and outside (except threads at joints) by a coating of approved corrosion-resistant material such as zinc, cadmium, or enamel. Where protected from corrosion solely by enamel, they shall not be used out-of-doors or in wet locations as described in (c) below. When boxes or cabinets have an approved system of organic coatings and are marked "Raintight," "Rainproof" or "Outdoor Type," they shall be permitted out-of-doors.

(b) In Concrete or in Direct Contact with the Earth. Ferrous or nonferrous metal raceways, cable armor, boxes, cable sheathing, cabinets, elbows, couplings, fittings, supports, and support hardware shall be permitted to be installed in concrete or in direct contact with the earth, or in areas subject to severe corrosive influences when made of material judged suitable for the condition, or when provided with corrosion protection approved for the condition.

Section 300-6(a) and (b) applies generally. For specific applications, see the particular article covering the various cables, raceways, or enclosures, such as Sections 331-3, 333-6, 336-3(a), 345-3, 345-5, 346-1(c), 346-3, 346-4, 347-2, 348-1, 348-4, and 370-5.

(c) Indoor Wet Locations. In portions of dairies, laundries, canneries, and other indoor wet locations, and in locations where walls are frequently washed or where there are surfaces of absorbent materials, such as damp paper or wood, the entire wiring system, including all boxes, fittings, conduits, and cable used therewith, shall be mounted so that there is at least ¼-inch (6.35-mm) air space between it and the wall or supporting surface.

(FPN): In general, areas where acids and alkali chemicals are handled and stored may present such corrosive conditions, particularly when wet or damp. Severe corrosive conditions may also be present in portions of meat-packing plants, tanneries, glue houses, and some stables; installations immediately adjacent to a seashore and swimming pool areas; areas where chemical de-icers are used; and storage cellars or rooms for hides, casings, fertilizer, salt, and bulk chemicals.

Ferrous or nonferrous metal conduit may be installed in concrete, in contact with the earth, or in areas exposed to severe corrosive influences where protected by corrosion protection and judged suitable for the condition. Special precautions are normally necessary for installing aluminum conduits in concrete, and specific approval by the authority having jurisdiction may be necessary.

To help avoid deterioration, metal raceways installed in the earth can be coated with an asphalt compound, plastic sheath, or other equivalent protection. Galvanized rigid steel conduit and steel intermediate metal conduit do not generally require supplementary corrosion protection.

300-7. Raceways Exposed to Different Temperatures.

(a) Sealing. Where portions of an interior raceway system are exposed to widely different temperatures, as in refrigerating or cold-storage plants, circulation of air from a warmer to a colder section through the raceway shall be prevented.

Where a raceway is used to enclose the lighting and refrigeration branch-circuit conductors within a walk-in chest, for example, the circulation of air from a warmer to a colder section through the raceway would cause condensation within the raceway. This can be prevented by sealing the raceway with a suitable, pliable compound at a conduit body or junction box, usually installed in the raceway before it enters the colder section. Special sealing fittings, such as those used in hazardous (classified) locations, are not necessary.

(b) Expansion Joints. Raceways shall be provided with expansion joints where necessary to compensate for thermal expansion and contraction.

300-9. Grounding Metal Enclosures. Metal raceways, boxes, cabinets, cable armor, and fittings shall be grounded as required in Article 250.

ARTICLE 300—WIRING METHODS

300-10. Electrical Continuity of Metal Raceways and Enclosures. Metal raceways, cable armor, and other metal enclosures for conductors shall be metallically joined together into a continuous electric conductor, and shall be so connected to all boxes, fittings, and cabinets as to provide effective electrical continuity. Raceways and cable assemblies shall be mechanically secured to boxes, fittings, cabinets, and other enclosures, except as provided for nonmetallic boxes in Section 370-7(c).

Metal raceways, metal armor or sheaths of cable, metal outlet or junction boxes, and fittings, such as connectors, couplings, locknuts, bushings, etc., must form an effective low impedance path to ground to conduct safely any fault current and facilitate the operation of overcurrent devices protecting the enclosed circuit conductors.

300-11. Secured in Place. Raceways, cable assemblies, boxes, cabinets, and fittings shall be securely fastened in place, unless otherwise provided for specific purposes elsewhere in this Code.

(FPN): See Article 318 for cable trays.

Raceways shall not be used as a means of support for cables or nonelectric equipment.

Exception: As specifically permitted elsewhere in this Code.

The second paragraph of Section 300-11 and the exception are new in the 1984 *NEC.* They are intended to prevent the raceway from being used to support cables or nonelectric equipment such as drop ceilings, water pipe, etc., which could cause a mechanical failure of the raceway. Also, cables, such as telephone cables wrapped around the raceway, can prevent the dissipation of heat from the raceway and effect the temperature of the conductors in the raceway.

300-12. Mechanical Continuity — Raceways and Cables. Metal or nonmetallic raceways, cable armors, and cable sheaths shall be continuous between cabinets, boxes, fittings, or other enclosures or outlets.

300-13. Mechanical and Electrical Continuity — Conductors.

(a) General. Conductors shall be continuous between outlets, devices, etc., and there shall be no splice or tap within a raceway itself.

Exception No. 1: As provided in Section 374-8 for auxiliary gutters.

Exception No. 2: As provided in Section 362-6 for wireways.

Exception No. 3: As provided in Section 300-15(a), Exception No. 1 for boxes or fittings.

Exception No. 4: As provided in Section 352-7 for metal surface raceways.

Splices or taps are prohibited within a raceway, unless the raceways are equipped with hinged or removable covers according to the four exceptions.

(b) Device Removal. In multiwire circuits the continuity of a grounded conductor shall not be dependent upon device connections, such as lampholders, receptacles, etc., where the removal of such devices would interrupt the continuity.

Grounded (neutral) conductors of multiwire branch circuits supplying receptacles, lampholders, etc., are not to be dependent upon terminal connections for continuity. For such installations (3- or 4-wire circuits), a splice is made and a jumper is connected to the terminal unless "looped" (see comments to Section 300-14); that is, a receptacle or lampholder could be replaced without interrupting the continuity of energized downstream line-to-neutral loads. Opening the neutral could cause unbalanced voltages and a considerably higher voltage would be impressed on one part of a multiwire branch circuit, especially if the downstream line-to-neutral loads are appreciably unbalanced. This requirement does not apply to individual 2-wire circuits or to other circuits that do not contain a grounded neutral conductor. See Figure 370-1.

300-14. Length of Free Conductors at Outlets and Switch Points. At least 6 inches (152 mm) of free conductor shall be left at each outlet and switch point for splices or the connection of fixtures or devices.

Exception: Conductors that are not spliced or terminated at the outlet or switch point.

A conductor looping through an outlet box and intended for connection to receptacles, switches, lampholders, etc., requires enough slack so that terminal connections may be made easily.

Conductors running through a box should have sufficient slack to prevent physical injury from the insertion of devices or from the use of fixture studs, hickeys, or other fixture supports within the box.

300-15. Boxes or Fittings — Where Required.

(a) Box or Fitting. A box or fitting shall be installed at each conductor splice connection point, outlet, switch point, junction point, or pull point for the connection of conduit, electrical metallic tubing, surface raceway, or other raceways.

Exception No. 1: A box or fitting shall not be required for a conductor splice connection in surface raceways, wireways, header-ducts, multi-outlet assemblies, auxiliary gutters, cable trays, and conduit bodies having removable covers which are accessible after installation.

Conduit bodies (Types "T," "L," etc.) are a part of the conduit or tubing system and should not contain more conductors than permitted for the raceway. Conduit bodies having provisions for less than three conduit entries are not to contain splices, taps, or devices unless they are durably and legibly marked with their cubic inch capacity and the maximum number of conductors that are permitted to be enclosed is to be computed using the volume per conductor listed in Table 370-6(b). See Sections 370-6(b) and (c).

For the use of conductors No. 4 or larger, see Section 370-18(a).

Exception No. 2: As permitted in Section 410-31 where a fixture is used as a raceway.

(b) Box Only. A box shall be installed at each conductor splice connection point, outlet, switch point, junction point, or pull point for the connection of Type AC cable, Type MC cable, mineral-insulated, metal-sheathed cable, nonmetallic-sheathed cable, or other cables, at the connection point between any such cable system and a raceway system and at each outlet and switch point for concealed knob-and-tube wiring.

Exception No. 1: As permitted by Section 336-11 for insulated outlet devices supplied by nonmetallic-sheathed cable.

Exception No. 2: As permitted by Section 410-62 for rosettes.

Exception No. 3: Where accessible fittings are used for straight-through splices in mineral-insulated, metal-sheathed cable.

Exception No. 4: Where cables enter or exit from conduit or tubing which is used to provide cable support or protection against physical damage. A fitting shall be provided on the end(s) of the conduit or tubing, to protect the wires or cables from abrasion.

Exception No. 4 permits conduit or tubing to be used as support and protection against physical damage without terminating in a box at such places as boilers or furnaces where nonmetallic-sheathed cables would dangle in free air for 5 or 6 ft. This exception also permits conduit or tubing to be used as physical protection for underground cables exiting from buildings or outdoors on poles, without a box being required on the end of the conduit. A fitting to protect the wires or cables is required on the ends of the conduit or tubing used to provide protection against physical damage. See Figure 300-2.

Exception No. 5: A wiring device with integral enclosure identified for the use having brackets that securely fasten the device to walls or ceilings of conventional on-site frame construction for use with nonmetallic-sheathed cable shall be permitted without a separate box.

Exception No. 5 applies to a device with an integral enclosure (boxless device). This exception was revised in the 1984 *NEC* to delete the requirement for fastening to a structural member.

(FPN): See Sections 336-5, Exception No. 2; 545-10; 550-8(j); and 551-14(e), Exception No. 1.

Exception No. 6: Where metallic manufactured wiring systems are used.

See Article 604 — Manufactured Wiring Systems.

Exception No. 7: A conduit body shall be permitted in lieu of a box where installed to comply with Section 370-6(c) and Section 370-18.

300-16. Raceway or Cable to Open or Concealed Wiring.

(a) Box or Fitting. A box or terminal fitting having a separately bushed hole for each conductor shall be used wherever a change is made from conduit, electrical metallic tubing, nonmetallic-sheathed cable, Type AC cable, Type MC cable, or mineral-insulated, metal-sheathed cable and surface raceway wiring to open wiring or to concealed knob-and-tube wiring. A fitting used for this purpose shall contain no taps or splices and shall not be used at fixture outlets.

(b) Bushing. A bushing shall be permitted in lieu of a box or terminal fitting at the end of a conduit or electrical metallic tubing where the raceway terminates behind an open (unenclosed) switchboard or at an unenclosed control and similar equipment. The bushing shall be of the insulating type for other than lead-sheathed conductors.

300-17. Number and Size of Conductors in Raceway.
The number and size of conductors in any raceway shall not be more than will permit dissipation of the heat and ready installation or withdrawal of the conductors without damage to the conductors or to their insulation.

(FPN): See the following sections of this Code: electrical nonmetallic tubing, 331-6; conduit, 345-7 and 346-6; electrical metallic tubing, 348-6; rigid nonmetallic conduit, 347-11; flexible metallic tubing, 349-12; flexible metal conduit, 350-3; liquidtight flexible metal conduit, 351-6; liquidtight nonmetallic flexible conduit, 351-25; surface raceways, 352-4 and 352-25; underfloor raceways, 354-5; cellular metal floor raceways, 356-5; cellular concrete floor raceways, 358-9; wireways, 362-5; auxiliary gutters, 374-5; fixture wire, 402-7; theaters, 520-5; signs, 600-21(d); elevators, 620-33; sound recording, 640-3 and 640-4; Class 1, Class 2, and Class 3 circuits, Article 725; and fire protective signaling circuits, Article 760.

300-19. Supporting Conductors in Vertical Raceways.

(a) Spacing Intervals — Maximum. Conductors in vertical raceways shall be supported. One cable support shall be provided at the top of the vertical raceway or as close to the top as practical, plus a support for each additional interval of spacing as specified in Table 300-19(a).

Exception No. 1: If the total vertical riser is less than 25 percent of the spacing specified in Table 300-19(a), no cable support shall be required.

Exception No. 2: Steel wire armor cable shall be supported at the top of the riser with a cable support that clamps the steel wire armor. A safety device shall be permitted at the lower end of the riser to hold the cable in the event there is slippage of the cable in the wire armored cable support. Additional wedge-type supports shall be permitted to relieve the strain on the equipment terminals caused by expansion of the cable under load.

Table 300-19(a).   Spacings for Conductor Supports

Conductors		Aluminum or Copper-Clad Aluminum	Copper
No. 18	thru No. 8 ....Not greater than ....100 feet		100 feet
No. 6	thru No. 0........... " " " ....200 feet		100 feet
No. 00	thru No. 0000 .... " " " ....180 feet		80 feet
211,601 CM thru 350,000 CM .... " " " ....135 feet			60 feet
350,001 CM thru 500,000 CM .... " " " ....120 feet			50 feet
500,001 CM thru 750,000 CM .... " " " .... 95 feet			40 feet
Above 750,000 CM......... " " " .... 85 feet			35 feet

For SI units: one foot = 0.3048 meter.

(b) Support Methods. One of the following methods of support shall be used:

(1) By clamping devices constructed of or employing insulating wedges inserted in the ends of the conduits. Where clamping of insulation does not adequately support the cable, the conductor also shall be clamped.

(2) By inserting boxes at the required intervals in which insulating supports are installed and secured in a satisfactory manner to withstand the weight of the conductors attached thereto, the boxes being provided with covers.

(3) In junction boxes, by deflecting the cables not less than 90 degrees and carrying them horizontally to a distance not less than twice the diameter of the cable, the cables being carried on two or more insulating supports, and additionally secured thereto by tie wires if desired. When this method is used, cables shall be supported at intervals not greater than 20 percent of those mentioned in the preceding tabulation.

(4) By a method of equal effectiveness.

Conductors in long vertical runs are to be supported to prevent the weight of the conductors from damaging the insulation where leaving the conduit and to prevent the conductors from being pulled out of the terminals. Supports like those shown in Figures 300-6 and 300-7 may be used in addition to many other types of grips manufactured for this purpose.

Example: A vertical raceway contains 1/0 copper conductors. One cable support near the top of the run would be required if the vertical run is from 25 to 100 ft. If the vertical run in this example is less than 25 ft, no cable supports are required.

Figure 300-6. A support bushing located at the top of a vertical conduit at a cabinet or pull box, which prevents the weight of the conductors from damaging the insulation or placing a strain on termination points. (*O.Z./Gedney Co.*)

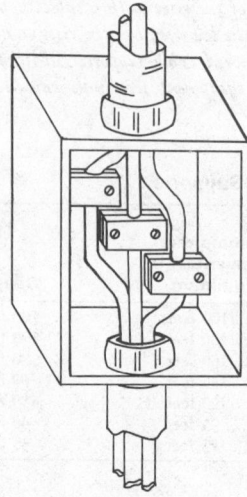

Figure 300-7. Vertical conductors supported by cleats in a pull box.

300-20. Induced Currents in Metal Enclosures or Metal Raceways.

(a) Conductors Grouped Together. Where conductors carrying alternating current are installed in metal enclosures or metal raceways, they shall be so arranged as to avoid heating the surrounding metal by induction. To accomplish this, all phase conductors and, where used, the neutral and all equipment grounding conductors shall be grouped together.

Exception No. 1: As permitted in Section 250-50, Exception for equipment grounding connections.

Exception No. 2: As permitted in Section 427-47 for skin effect heating.

By its very nature, skin effect heating uses induced currents in metal raceways to heat pipelines. Importantly, the temperature of the raceway is known and bears a definite relationship to the pipeline temperature and the overall thermal parameters of the system.

(b) Individual Conductors. When a single conductor of a circuit passes through metal with magnetic properties the inductive effect shall be minimized by: (1) cutting slots in the metal between the individual holes through which the individual conductors pass, or (2) passing all the conductors in the circuit through an insulating wall sufficiently large for all of the conductors of the circuit.

Exception: In the case of circuits supplying vacuum or electric-discharge lighting systems or signs, or X-ray apparatus, the currents carried by the conductors are so small that the inductive heating effect can be ignored where these conductors are placed in metal enclosures or pass through metal.

(FPN): Because aluminum is not a magnetic metal, there will be no heating due to hysteresis; however, induced currents will be present. They will not be of sufficient magnitude to require grouping of conductors or special treatment in passing conductors through aluminum wall sections.

300-21. Spread of Fire or Products of Combustion. Electrical installations in hollow spaces, vertical shafts, and ventilation or air-handling ducts shall be so made that the possible spread of fire or products of combustion will not be substantially increased. Openings around electrical penetrations through fire-resistance rated walls, partitions, floors, or ceilings shall be firestopped using approved methods to maintain the fire-resistance rating.

(FPN): Firestops may require decreasing the allowable load on the conductors.

It is the intent of this section that electrical equipment, raceways, cables, etc., be installed in such a manner that they will not contribute to the spread of fire or the products of combustion through the specified component parts of a building. In addition, the fire-stopping method used is required to effectively maintain the fire-resistance rating of the building component that is pierced. See Figures 300-8 and 300-9.

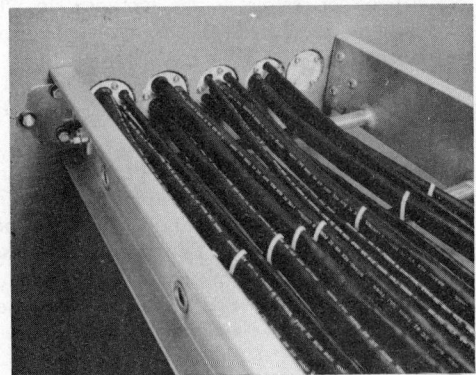

Figure 300-8. Fire seals used to maintain the integrity of fire-rated walls, floors, partitions, or ceilings as required by Section 300-21. (*O.Z./ Gedney Co.*)

Figure 300-9. Using approved caulking to meet the requirements of Section 300-21. (*Electro Products Div., 3M Co.*)

300-22. Wiring in Ducts, Plenums, and Other Air-Handling Spaces. The provisions of this section apply to the installation and uses of electric wiring and equipment in ducts, plenums, and other air-handling spaces.

(FPN): See Article 424, Part F for Electric Duct Heaters.

(a) Ducts for Dust, Loose Stock, or Vapor Removal. No wiring systems of any type shall be installed in ducts used to transport dust, loose stock, or flammable vapors. No wiring system of any type shall be installed in any duct, or shaft containing only such ducts, used for vapor removal or for ventilation of commercial-type cooking equipment.

(b) Ducts or Plenums Used for Environmental Air. Only wiring methods consisting of mineral-insulated, metal-sheathed cable, Type MC cable employing a smooth or corrugated impervious metal sheath without an overall nonmetallic covering, electrical metallic tubing, flexible metallic tubing, intermediate metal conduit, or rigid metal conduit shall be installed in ducts or plenums used for environmental air. Flexible metal conduit and liquidtight flexible metal conduit shall be permitted, in lengths not to exceed 4 feet (1.22 m), to connect physically adjustable equipment and devices permitted to be in these ducts and plenum chambers. The connectors used with flexible metal conduit shall effectively close any openings in the connection. Equipment and devices shall be permitted within such ducts or plenum chambers only if necessary for their direct action upon, or sensing of, the contained air. Where equipment or devices are installed and illumination is necessary to facilitate maintenance and repair, enclosed gasketed-type fixtures shall be permitted.

(FPN): The above applies to ducts and plenums specifically fabricated to transport environmental air.

The intent of this section is to limit the materials that would contribute smoke and products of combustion during a fire in an area that handles environmental air, and, in the case of paragraph (b), to provide an effective barrier against the excursion of products of combustion into the duct or plenum.

Paragraph (b) applies to ducts and plenums specifically constructed to transport environmental air, such as sheet metal ducts. Equipment and devices such as lighting fixtures and motors are not normally permitted in ducts or plenums and, for this reason, paragraph (b) wiring methods are different from the wiring methods permitted in paragraph (c).

(c) Other Space Used for Environmental Air. Only mineral-insulated, metal-sheathed cable, Type MC cable without an overall nonmetallic covering, and Type AC cable, and other factory-assembled multiconductor control or power cable which is specifically listed for the use shall be used for wiring in systems installed in other space used for environmental air. Other type cables and conductors shall be installed in electrical metallic tubing, flexible metallic tubing, intermediate metal conduit, rigid metal conduit, metal surface raceway or wireway with metal covers where accessible or flexible metal conduit. Electric equipment that is permitted within a building concealed space shall be permitted to be installed in other space used for environmental air if the associated wiring material and fixtures are suitable for the ambient temperature.

(FPN): The above applies to other spaces such as spaces over hung ceilings which are used for environmental air-handling purposes.

Paragraph (c) applies to other spaces used to transport environmental air that are not specifically manufactured as a duct or plenum, such as hung ceilings. Many hung ceilings are intended to transport return air. However, some are also used for supply air, but this use is not nearly so common as those used for return air. As the spaces above "hung-type" ceilings contain lighting fixtures, motors, and other equipment and devices, the wiring methods permitted in paragraph (c) are different from those contained in paragraph (b).

Exception No. 1: Liquidtight flexible metal conduit in single lengths not exceeding 6 feet (1.83 m).

Exception No. 2: Integral fan systems specifically identified for such use.

Exception No. 3: This section does not include habitable rooms or areas of buildings, the prime purpose of which is not air handling.

Exception No. 3 applies to rooms (such as electrical equipment rooms containing the air-handling equipment) and hallways being used as portions of air-return systems in buildings. It is not intended that the limitation of wiring methods be applied to these parts of a building.

Exception No. 4: Listed prefabricated cable assemblies of metallic manufactured wiring systems without nonmetallic sheath shall be permitted where listed for this use.

Note that the cable assembly must be listed for use in space used for environmental air. See Article 604.

Exception No. 5: This section does not include the joist or stud spaces in dwelling units when wiring or equipment passes through such spaces perpendicular to the long dimension of such spaces.

See Figure 300-10.

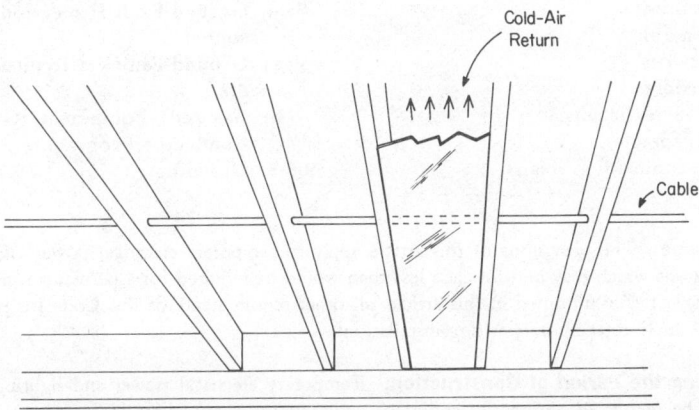

Figure 300-10. Illustrated is a cable passing through joist spaces of a dwelling unit. It is common to enclose a joist space with a sheet metal covering and use this space as a cold-air return for a forced warm-air central heating system.

(d) **Data Processing Systems.** Electric wiring in air-handling areas beneath raised floors for data processing systems shall comply with Article 645.

B. Requirements for Over 600 Volts, Nominal

300-31. Covers Required. Suitable covers shall be installed on all boxes, fittings, and similar enclosures to prevent accidental contact with energized parts or physical damage to parts or insulation.

300-32. Conductors of Different Systems. Conductors of high-voltage and low-voltage systems shall not occupy the same wiring enclosure or pull and junction boxes.

Exception No. 1: In motors, switchgear and control assemblies and similar equipment.

Exception No. 2: In manholes, if low-voltage conductors are separated from high-voltage conductors.

300-34. Conductor Bending Radius. The conductor shall not be bent to a radius less than eight times the overall diameter for nonshielded conductors or twelve times the diameter for shielded or lead-covered conductors during or after installation.

300-35. Protection Against Induction Heating. Metallic raceways and associated conductors shall be so arranged as to avoid heating of the raceway by induction.

300-36. Grounding. Wiring and equipment installations shall be grounded in accordance with the applicable provisions of Article 250.

ARTICLE 305 — TEMPORARY WIRING

Contents

305-1. Scope. The provisions of this article apply to temporary electrical power and lighting wiring methods which may be of a class less than would be required for a permanent installation. Except as specifically modified in this article, all other requirements of this Code for permanent wiring shall apply to temporary wiring installations.

(a) During the Period of Construction. Temporary electrical power and lighting installations shall be permitted during the period of construction, remodeling, maintenance, repair, or demolition of buildings, structures, equipment, or similar activities.

(b) 90 Days. Temporary electrical power and lighting installations shall be permitted for a period not to exceed 90 days for Christmas decorative lighting, carnivals, and similar purposes.

Note that the temporary wiring applications of paragraphs (a) and (c) are not restricted to 90 days.

(c) Emergencies and Tests. Temporary electrical power and lighting installations shall be permitted during emergencies and for tests, experiments, and developmental work.

(d) Removal. Temporary wiring shall be removed immediately upon completion of construction or purpose for which the wiring was installed.

305-2. General.

(a) Services. Services shall be installed in conformance with Article 230.

(b) Feeders. Feeders shall be protected as provided in Article 240. They shall originate in an approved distribution center. The conductors shall be permitted within multiconductor cord or cable assemblies or where not subject to physical damage; they shall be permitted to be run as open conductors on insulators not more than 10 feet (3.05 m) apart.

(c) Branch Circuits. All branch circuits shall originate in an approved power outlet or panelboard. Conductors shall be permitted within multiconductor cord or cable assemblies or as open conductors. All conductors shall be protected by overcurrent devices at their ampacity. Runs of open conductors shall be located where the conductors will not be subject to physical damage, and the conductors shall be fastened at intervals not exceeding 10 feet (3.05 m). No branch-circuit conductors shall be laid on the floor. Each branch circuit that supplies receptacles or fixed equipment shall contain a separate equipment grounding conductor when run as open conductors.

The basic requirement for safety is that temporary wiring is required to be located where it will not be subject to physical damage.
Note that extension cords are permitted to be laid on the floor.

(d) Receptacles. All receptacles shall be of the grounding type. Unless installed in a complete metallic raceway all branch circuits shall contain a separate equipment grounding conductor and all receptacles shall be electrically connected to the grounding conductor. Receptacles on construction sites shall not be installed on branch circuits which supply temporary lighting. Receptacles shall not be connected to the same ungrounded conductor of multiwire circuits which supply temporary lighting.

The intent of this paragraph is to require installations so that the operation of a fuse or circuit breaker or a ground-fault circuit-interrupter due to a fault or overload of equipment will not deenergize the lighting circuit.

(e) Disconnecting Means. Suitable disconnecting switches or plug connectors shall be installed to permit the disconnection of all ungrounded conductors of each temporary circuit.

(f) Lamp Protection. All lamps for general illumination shall be protected from accidental contact or breakage. Protection shall be provided by elevation of at least 7 feet (2.13 m) from normal working surface or by a suitable fixture or lampholder with a guard.
Brass shell, paper-lined sockets, or other metal-cased sockets shall not be used unless the shell is grounded.

(g) Splices. On construction sites a box shall not be required for splices or junction connections where the circuit conductors are multiconductor cord or cable assemblies or open conductors. See Sections 110-14(b) and 400-9. A box shall be used wherever a change is made to a raceway system or a cable system which is metal clad or metal sheathed.

(h) Protection from Accidental Damage. Flexible cords and cables shall be protected from accidental damage. Sharp corners and projections shall be avoided. When passing through doorways or other pinch points, protection shall be provided to avoid damage.

Note that, unlike Section 400-8, Section 305-2(h) permits flexible cords and cables, because of the nature of their use, to pass through doorways.

305-3. Grounding. All grounding shall conform with Article 250.

305-4. Ground-Fault Protection for Personnel. Ground-fault protection for personnel on construction sites shall be provided to comply with (a) or (b) below.

Section 305-4 is essentially the same as Section 210-8(b) of the 1971 through 1981 editions of the *Code*.

ARTICLE 305—TEMPORARY WIRING

(a) Ground-Fault Circuit-Interrupters. All 125-volt, single-phase, 15- and 20-ampere receptacle outlets which are not a part of the permanent wiring of the building or structure and which are in use by employees shall have ground-fault circuit-interrupter protection for personnel.

Exception: Receptacles on a 2-wire, single-phase portable or vehicle-mounted generator rated not more than 5 kW, where the circuit conductors of the generator are insulated from the generator frame and all other grounded surfaces.

Receptacle outlets that are a part of the permanent wiring of the building are not required to have GFCI protection. However, it is intended that they be used with portable GFCIs or meet the provisions of Section 305-4(b).

Ground-fault circuit-interrupters may be of the portable type (see Figure 210-12), receptacle type (see Figure 210-13), or circuit breaker type. A commonly used temporary power unit is shown in Figure 305-1.

See commentary on GFCIs following Section 210-8.

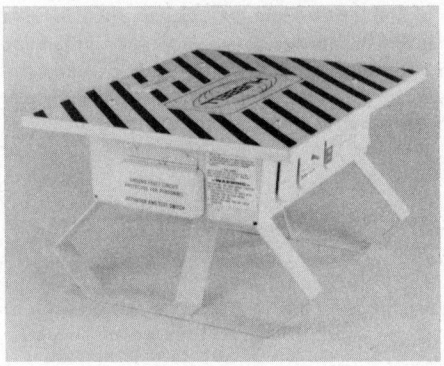

Figure 305-1. Temporary power outlet units commonly used on construction sites with a variety of configurations. Some are available with ground-fault interrupter protection. (*Hubbell*)

Figure 305-2. Nuisance tripping of ground-fault interrupter protective devices by wet or damp weather conditions can be avoided by using watertight plugs and connectors. (*Hubbell*)

(b) Assured Equipment Grounding Conductor Program. A written procedure shall be continuously enforced at the construction site by one or more designated persons to assure that equipment grounding conductors for all cord sets, receptacles which are not a part of the permanent wiring of the building or structure and equipment connected by cord and plug are installed and maintained in accordance with the applicable requirements of Sections 210-7(c), 250-45, 250-59, and 305-2(d).

(1) The following tests shall be performed on all cord sets, receptacles which are not part of the permanent wiring of the building or structure, and cord- and plug-connected equipment required to be grounded.

a. All equipment grounding conductors shall be tested for continuity and shall be electrically continuous.

b. Each receptacle and attachment plug shall be tested for correct attachment of the equipment grounding conductor. The equipment grounding conductor shall be connected to its proper terminal.

c. All required tests shall be performed:

1. Before first use on the construction site.

2. When there is evidence of damage.

3. Before equipment is returned to service following any repairs.

4. At intervals not exceeding 3 months.

(2) The tests required in (1) above shall be recorded and made available to the authority having jurisdiction.

305-5. Guarding. For temporary wiring over 600 volts, nominal, suitable fencing, barriers, or other effective means shall be provided to prevent access of other than authorized and qualified personnel.

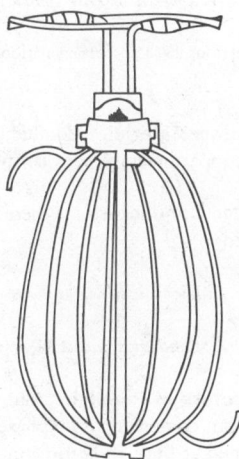

Figure 305-3. Temporary lighting can be supplied by factory-assembled lighting strings or by field-assembled units such as the type illustrated.

ARTICLE 310 — CONDUCTORS FOR GENERAL WIRING

Contents

ARTICLE 310—CONDUCTORS FOR GENERAL WIRING

310-13. Conductor Constructions and Applications.
310-14. Aluminum Conductor Material.
310-15. Ampacity.

(a) Applications Covered by Tables.
(b) Applications Not Covered by Tables.

310-1. Scope. This article covers general requirements for conductors and their type designations, insulations, markings, mechanical strengths, ampacity ratings, and uses. These requirements do not apply to conductors that form an integral part of equipment, such as motors, motor controllers, and similar equipment, or to conductors specifically provided for elsewhere in this Code.

(FPN): For flexible cords and cables, see Article 400. For fixture wires, see Article 402.

310-2. Conductors.

(a) Insulated. Conductors shall be insulated.

Exception: Where covered or bare conductors are specifically permitted elsewhere in this Code.

(FPN): See Section 250-152 for insulation of neutral conductors of a solidly grounded high-voltage system.

(b) Conductor Material. Conductors in this article shall be of aluminum, copper-clad aluminum, or copper unless otherwise specified.

310-3. Stranded Conductors. Where installed in raceways, conductors of size No. 8 and larger shall be stranded.

Exception No. 1: When used as busbars or in mineral-insulated, metal-sheathed cable.

Exception No. 2: Bonding conductors as required in Section 680-22(b).

310-4. Conductors in Parallel. Aluminum, copper-clad aluminum, or copper conductors of size 1/0 and larger, comprising each phase or neutral, shall be permitted to be connected in parallel (electrically joined at both ends to form a single conductor).
The paralleled conductors in each phase or neutral shall:

(1) Be the same length;

(2) Have the same conductor material;

(3) Be the same size in circular mil area;

(4) Have the same insulation type;

(5) Be terminated in the same manner.

Where run in separate raceways or cables the raceways or cables shall have the same physical characteristics.

Exception No. 1: As permitted in Section 620-12(a)(1), Exception.

Exception No. 2: Conductors in sizes smaller than No. 1/0 AWG shall be permitted to be run in parallel to supply control power to indicating instruments, contactors, relays, solenoids, and similar control devices provided: (a) they are contained within the same raceway or cable; (b) the ampacity of each individual conductor is sufficient to carry the entire load current shared by the parallel conductors; and (c) the overcurrent protection is such that the ampacity of each individual conductor will not be exceeded if one or more of the parallel conductors become inadvertently disconnected.

For example, in control work it is sometimes found necessary to reduce cable capacitance effect or voltage drop over long lengths of wire. If a No. 14 AWG conductor is more than enough to carry the load, yet two No. 14 conductors in parallel will reduce the voltage drop to acceptable limits, this should be permissible providing the safeguards indicated in Exception No. 2 are taken.

(FPN): Differences in inductive reactance and unequal division of current can be minimized by choice of materials, methods of construction and orientation of conductors. It is not the intent to require that conductors of one phase or neutral be the same as those of another phase or neutral to achieve balance.

For example, the conductors in Phases A and B may be copper, and those in Phase C aluminum.

When equipment grounding conductors are used with conductors in parallel, they shall comply with the requirements of this section except that they shall be sized as per Section 250-95.

When conductors are used in parallel, space in enclosures shall be given consideration (see Articles 370 and 373).

Conductors installed in parallel shall comply with the provisions of Note 8 to Tables 310-16 through 310-19.

This section permits a practical means of installing large capacity conductors for feeders or services. The paralleling of two or more conductors in place of one large conductor relies on a number of factors to ensure equal division of current; therefore, several conditions must be satisfied so as not to overload any of the individual paralleled conductors. Other than as permitted in Section 250-95 and the exceptions to Section 310-4, there does not appear to be any practical need to parallel conductors smaller than size 1/0.

To avoid excessive voltage drop and also to ensure equal division of current, it is essential that separate phase conductors be located close together and that each phase conductor and the neutral and grounding conductors, if used, be grouped together in each conduit. See Section 300-5(i), Exception No. 2 for an exception.

The impedance of a circuit in an aluminum raceway will be different from the impedance of the same circuit in a steel raceway, hence it is required that separate raceways have the same physical characteristics. See Section 300-20.

Note that all of the conductors of each phase are to be of the same conductor material. For example, if twelve conductors are to be paralleled for a 3-phase, 4-wire, 480Y/277-V ac circuit, four conductors could be installed in each of three raceways. The *Code* does not intend that all twelve conductors be of copper or all twelve conductors be of aluminum, but does intend that the three conductors in each phase be of the same material, insulation type, length, etc. Also, it is intended that the three raceways have the same physical characteristics, i.e., three rigid aluminum conduits or three steel IMC conduits or three EMTs or three nonmetallic conduits, i.e., not a mixture of two rigid aluminum conduits and one rigid steel conduit.

It is neither economical nor practical to use conductors larger than 1,000,000 CM in raceways unless the conductor size is governed by voltage drop. The ampacity of larger sizes would increase very little in proportion to the increase in the size of the conductor. Therefore, when the size of a conductor increases 50 percent, for example, from 1,000,000 to 1,500,000 CM, a Type THW conductor increases 80 A (less than 15 percent). An increase from 1,000,000 to 2,000,000 CM (100 percent increase) causes an increase of only 120 A (approximately 20 percent). Generally speaking, in situations that call for the use of single conductors larger than 500,000 CM, determining the cost of the entire installation using single conductors rather than two (or more) conductors in parallel is beneficial.

310-5. Minimum Size of Conductors. The minimum size of conductors shall be as given in Table 310-5.

Table 310-5

Voltage Rating of Conductor—Volts	Minimum Conductor Size—AWG
Up to 2000	14 Copper
	12 Aluminum or
	Copper-Clad Aluminum
2001 to 5000	8
5001 to 8000	6
8001 to 15000	2 100% Insulation Level*
	1 133% Insulation Level*
15001 to 28000	1
28001 to 35000	1/0

* See Table 310-64, Definitions.

Exception No. 1: For flexible cords as permitted by Section 400-12.

Exception No. 2: For fixture wire as permitted by Section 410-24.

Exception No. 3: For fractional horsepower motors as permitted by Section 430-22.

Exception No. 4: For cranes and hoists as permitted by Section 610-14.

Exception No. 5: For elevator control and signaling circuits as permitted by Section 620-12.

Exception No. 6: For Class 1, Class 2, and Class 3 circuits as permitted by Sections 725-16, 725-37, and 725-40.

Exception No. 7: For fire protective signaling circuits as permitted by Sections 760-16, 760-27, and 760-30.

Exception No. 8: For 2001-5000 volt for Types AVA, AVB, and AVL cables, the minimum conductor size is No. 14 AWG copper or No. 12 AWG aluminum or copper-clad aluminum.

Exception No. 9: For Type V cables, the minimum conductor sizes are: No. 12 AWG for 2000-volt rating, No. 10 AWG for 3000-volt rating, and No. 8 AWG for 4000-volt rating.

Exception No. 10: For motor control circuits as permitted by Section 430-72.

310-6. Shielding. Solid dielectric insulated conductors operated above 2000 volts in permanent installations shall have ozone-resistant insulation and shall be shielded. All metallic insulation shields shall be grounded through an effective grounding path meeting the requirements of Section 250-51. Shielding shall be for the purpose of confining the voltage stresses to the insulation.

Exception: Nonshielded insulated conductors listed by a qualified testing laboratory shall be permitted for use up to 8000 volts under the following conditions:

a. Conductors shall have insulation resistant to electric discharge and surface tracking, or the insulated conductor(s) shall be covered with a material resistant to ozone, electric discharge, and surface tracking.

b. Where used in wet locations the insulated conductor(s) shall have an overall nonmetallic jacket or a continuous metallic sheath.

c. Where operated at 5001 to 8000 volts, the insulated conductor(s) shall have a nonmetallic jacket over the insulation. The insulation shall have a specific inductive capacity no greater than 3.6 and the jacket shall have a specific inductive capacity no greater than 10 and no less than 6.

d. Insulation and jacket thicknesses shall be in accordance with Table 310-63.

Permanently installed solid dielectric insulated conductors operated above 2,000 V are to have ozone-resistant insulation and are to be shielded with a grounded metallic shield (note Exception).

Shielding is the application of a metallic tape or nonmetallic semiconducting tape around the conductor surface, which will prevent corona from forming and will reduce high-voltage stresses. Corona is a faint glow adjacent to the surface of the electrical conductor at high voltage. If there are high-voltage stresses and a charging current flowing between the conductor and ground (usually due to moisture), the surrounding atmosphere is ionized and ozone (which is generated by an electric discharge in ordinary oxygen or air) is formed, which will attack the conductor jacket and insulation and may eventually break them down. The shield is at ground potential; therefore, no voltage above ground is present on the jacket outside of the shield, thus preventing a discharge from the jacket and the subsequent formation of ozone.

Figure 310-1 shows a three-conductor cable of the shielded type.

Figure 310-2 illustrates a stress relief cone for an indoor cable terminator.

Figure 310-3 illustrates a stress cone on a single-conductor shielded cable terminating inside a pothead. Notice that a clamping ring provides a grounding connection between the copper shielding tape and shield to the metallic base of the pothead.

Specialized training and close adherence to manufacturer's instructions are absolutely essential for high-voltage cable installations.

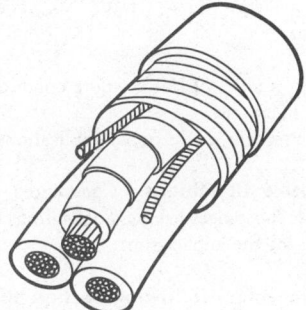

Figure 310-1. Three-conductor cable of the shielded type.

310-7. Direct Burial Conductors. Cables rated above 2000 volts shall be shielded. Conductors used for direct burial applications shall be of a type identified for such use.

Exception: Nonshielded multiconductor cables rated 2001-5000 volts shall be permitted if the cable has an overall metallic sheath or armor.

The metallic shield, sheath or armor shall be grounded through an effective grounding path meeting the requirements of Section 250-51.

(FPN): See Sections 300-5 and 710-3(b).

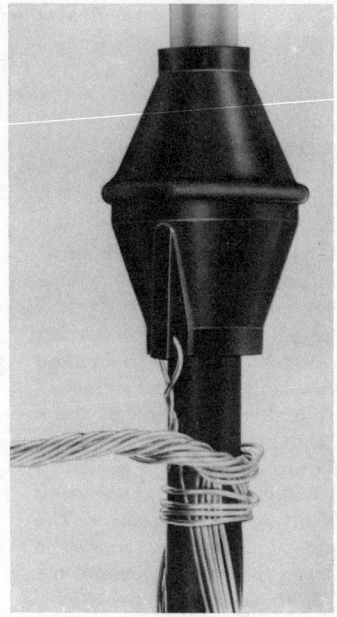

Figure 310-2. One-piece, premolded stress relief cone is for indoor cable terminations of up to 35 kV phase-to-phase. (*ITT Blackburn Co.*)

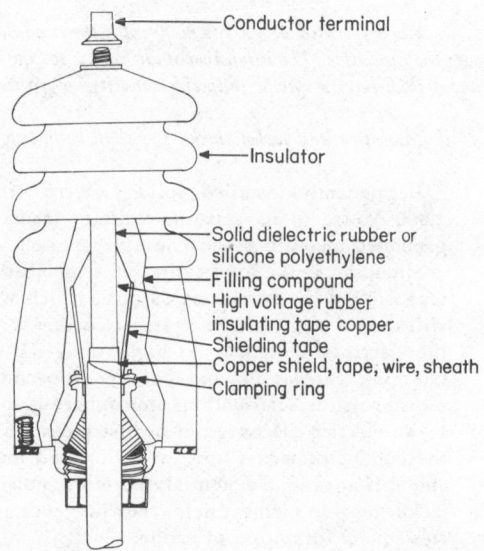

Conductor terminal

Insulator

Solid dielectric rubber or silicone polyethylene
Filling compound
High voltage rubber insulating tape copper
Shielding tape
Copper shield, tape, wire, sheath
Clamping ring

Figure 310-3. A stress cone on a single-conductor shielded cable terminating inside a pothead.

310-8. Wet Locations.

(a) Insulated Conductors. Insulated conductors used in wet locations shall be (1) lead-covered; (2) Types RHW, RUW, TW, THW, THWN, XHHW; or (3) of a type listed for use in wet locations.

(b) Cables. Cables of one or more conductors used in wet locations shall be of a type listed for use in wet locations.

Conductors used for direct burial applications shall be of a type listed for such use.

310-9. Corrosive Conditions. Conductors exposed to oils, greases, vapors, gases, fumes, liquids, or other substances having a deleterious effect upon the conductor or insulation shall be of a type suitable for the application.

See commentary following Section 501-13.

310-10. Temperature Limitation of Conductors. No conductor shall be used in such a manner that its operating temperature will exceed that designated for the type of insulated conductor involved. In no case shall conductors be associated together in such a way with respect to type of circuit, the wiring method employed, or the number of conductors that the limiting temperature of any conductor is exceeded.

Most terminations are designed only for 60°C (140°F) or 75°C (167°F) maximum temperatures; therefore, the higher rated ampacities for conductors of 90°C (194°F), 110°C (230°F), etc., cannot be utilized unless the terminations have comparable ratings.

Tables 310-16 through 310-19 have ampacity correction factor tables for ambient temperatures that exceed 30°C (86°F). To assign the proper ampacity to a conductor in an ambient above 30°C, the appropriate correction factors must be used. This correction factor is applied in addition to any derating factor, such as in Note 8 to Tables 310-16 through 310-19.

Example: No. 2 AWG TW copper conductors are to be installed in a raceway in an ambient temperature of 50°C (122°F). According to Table 310-16, the ampacity of the conductor at 30°C is 95 A which is multiplied by 0.58 (taken from the correction factors at the bottom of the table); thus the ampacity of the No. 2 conductor at 50°C is reduced to 55.1 A (95 A × 0.58 = 55.1 A).

If six of these conductors were run in a raceway, Note 8 to the tables would require the ampacity to be reduced to 80 percent, which, in this case, would be 55.1 A × 0.8 = 44.08 A. Under these conditions the No. 2 conductors would be suitable for a 40-A circuit.

The basis for determining the ampacities of conductors for Tables 310-16 through 310-19 was the "NEMA Report of Determination of Maximum Permissible Current-Carrying Capacity of Code Insulated Wires and Cables for Building Purposes" dated June 27, 1938.

The temperature rating of a conductor (see Table 310-13) is the maximum temperature, at any location along its length, that the conductor can withstand over a prolonged time period without serious degradation.

Conductors that have a rating above the anticipated maximum ambient temperature should be chosen. The operating temperature of conductors should be controlled at or below its rating by coordinating conductor size, number of associated conductors, and ampacity for the particular conductor rating and ambient temperature. Tables 310-17 and 310-19 give ampacities for isolated conductors (not in contact with other conductors). Tables 310-16 and 310-18 give ampacities where up to three conductors are closely associated (in contact). All tabulations are based on a 30°C (86°F) ambient temperature condition and should be corrected for the anticipated ambient using the ampacity correction factors at the bottom of the tables. Where more than three conductors are associated together, the additional correction given in Note 8 to the tables is to be applied.

(FPN): The temperature rating of a conductor (see Tables 310-13 and 310-61) is the maximum temperature, at any location along its length, that the conductor can withstand over a prolonged time period without serious degradation. Tables 310-16 through 310-19 and 310-69 through 310-84, the correction factors at the bottom of these tables, and the notes to the tables provide guidance for coordinating conductor sizes, types, ampacities, ambient temperatures, and number of associated conductors.

The Fine Print Note is intended to focus attention to the necessity for derating conductors where high ambient temperatures are encountered and to provide users with helpful information in coordinating ampacities, ambient temperatures, conductor size and number, etc., to assure operation at or below rating.

The principal determinants of operating temperature are:

1. Ambient temperature. Ambient temperature may vary along the conductor length as well as from time to time.

2. Heat generated internally in the conductor as the result of load current flow.

3. The rate at which generated heat dissipates into the ambient medium. Thermal insulation which covers or surrounds conductors will affect the rate of heat dissipation.

4. Adjacent load-carrying conductors. Adjacent conductors have the dual effect of raising the ambient temperature and impeding heat dissipation.

ARTICLE 310—CONDUCTORS FOR GENERAL WIRING

310-11. Marking.

(a) Required Information. All conductors and cables shall be marked to indicate the following information, using the applicable method described in (b) below.

(1) The maximum rated voltage for which the conductor was listed.

(2) The proper type letter or letters for the type of wire or cable as specified elsewhere in this article, in Tables 310-13 and 310-61, and in Articles 336, 337, 338, 339, 340, and Section 725-40(b)(3).

(3) The manufacturer's name, trademark, or other distinctive marking by which the organization responsible for the product can be readily identified.

(4) The AWG size or circular-mil area.

(b) Method of Marking.

(1) Surface Marking. The following conductors and cables shall be durably marked on the surface at intervals not exceeding 24 inches (610 mm):

(a) Single- and multiconductor rubber- and thermoplastic- insulated wire and cable.
(b) Nonmetallic-sheathed cable.
(c) Service-entrance cable.
(d) Underground feeder and branch-circuit cable.
(e) Tray cable.
(f) Irrigation cable.
(g) Power-limited tray cable.

(2) Marker Tape. Metal-covered multiconductor cables shall employ a marker tape located within the cable and running for its complete length.

Exception No. 1: Mineral-insulated, metal-sheathed cable.

Exception No. 2: Type AC cable.

Exception No. 3: The information required in Section 310-11(a)(1), (2), and (4) above shall be permitted to be durably marked on the outer nonmetallic covering of Type MC or Type PLTC cables at intervals not exceeding 24 inches (610 mm).

Exception No. 4: The information required in Section 310-11(a) shall be permitted to be durably marked on a nonmetallic covering under the metallic sheath of Type PLTC cable at intervals not exceeding 24 inches (610 mm).

Type PLTC cable is permitted to have a metallic sheath or armor over a nonmetallic jacketed cable. A second nonmetallic jacket is optional over the metallic sheath. Exception Nos. 2 and 3 will define the marking requirements for either case.

(FPN): Included in the group of metal-covered cables are: Type AC cable (Article 333), Type MC cable (Article 334) and lead-sheathed cable.

(3) Tag Marking. The following conductors and cables shall be marked by means of a printed tag attached to the coil, reel, or carton:

(a) Mineral-insulated, metal-sheathed cable.
(b) Switchboard wires.

(c) Metal-covered, single-conductor cables.

(d) Conductors having outer surface of asbestos.

(e) Type AC cable.

(4) Optional Marking of Wire Size. For the following multiconductor cables, the information required in (a) (4) above shall be permitted to be marked on the surface of the individual insulated conductors:

(a) Type MC cable.

(b) Tray cable.

(c) Irrigation cable.

(d) Power-limited tray cable.

(c) Suffixes to Designate Number of Conductors. A type letter or letters used alone shall indicate a single insulated conductor. The following letter suffixes shall indicate the following:

D—for two insulated conductors laid parallel within an outer nonmetallic covering.

M—for an assembly of two or more insulated conductors twisted spirally within an outer nonmetallic covering.

310-12. Conductor Identification.

(a) Grounded Conductors. Insulated conductors of No. 6 or smaller, intended for use as grounded conductors of circuits, shall have an outer identification of a white or natural gray color. Multiconductor flat cable No. 4 or larger shall be permitted to employ an external ridge on the grounded conductor.

Exception No. 1: Multiconductor varnished-cloth-insulated cables.

Exception No. 2: Fixture wires as outlined in Article 402.

Exception No. 3: Mineral-insulated, metal-sheathed cable.

Exception No. 4: A conductor identified as required by Section 210-5(a) for branch circuits.

Exception No. 5: Where the conditions of maintenance and supervision assure that only qualified persons will service the installation, grounded conductors in multiconductor cables shall be permitted to be permanently identified at their terminations at the time of installation by a distinctive white marking or other equally effective means.

For aerial cable the identification shall be as above, or by means of a ridge so located on the exterior of the cable as to identify it.

Wires having their outer covering finished to show a white or natural gray color but having colored tracer threads in the braid, identifying the source of manufacture, shall be considered as meeting the provisions of this section.

(FPN): For identification requirements for conductors larger than No. 6, see Section 200-6.

(b) Equipment Grounding Conductors. Bare, covered or insulated grounding conductors shall be permitted. Individually covered or insulated grounding conductors shall have a continuous outer finish that is either green, or green with one or more yellow stripes.

Exception No. 1: An insulated or covered conductor larger than No. 6 shall, at the time of installation, be permitted to be permanently identified as a grounding conductor at each end and at every point where the conductor is accessible. Identification shall be accomplished by one of the following means:

a. Stripping the insulation or covering from the entire exposed length;

b. Coloring the exposed insulation or covering green; or

c. Marking the exposed insulation or covering with green colored tape or green colored adhesive labels.

Exception No. 2: Where the conditions of maintenance and supervision assure that only qualified persons will service the installation, an insulated conductor in a multiconductor cable shall, at the time of installation, be permitted to be permanently identified as a grounding conductor at each end and at every point where the conductor is accessible by one of the following means:

a. Stripping the insulation from the entire exposed length;

b. Coloring the exposed insulation green; or

c. Marking the exposed insulation with green tape or green colored adhesive labels.

(c) Ungrounded Conductors. Conductors which are intended for use as ungrounded conductors, whether used as single conductors or in multiconductor cables, shall be finished to be clearly distinguishable from grounded and grounding conductors. Ungrounded conductors shall be distinguished by colors other than white, natural gray, or green; or by a combination of color plus distinguishing marking. Distinguishing markings shall also be in a color other than white, natural gray, or green, and shall consist of a stripe or stripes or a regularly spaced series of identical marks. Distinguishing markings shall not conflict in any manner with the surface markings required by Section 310-11(b)(1).

310-13. Conductor Constructions and Applications. Insulated conductors shall comply with the applicable provisions of one or more of the following: Tables 310-13, 310-61, 310-62, 310-63, 310-64, 310-65, 310-66, and 310-67.

These conductors shall be permitted for use in any of the wiring methods recognized in Chapter 3 and as specified in their respective tables.

(FPN): Thermoplastic insulation may stiffen at temperatures colder than minus 10°C (plus 14°F), requiring care be exercised during installation at such temperatures. Thermoplastic insulation may also be deformed at normal temperatures where subjected to pressure, requiring care be exercised during installation and at points of support.

Table 310-13 lists the various types of insulated conductors as covered by the requirements of this *Code*. More detailed wire classification information from sizes Nos. 14 AWG through 2,000 MCM may be obtained from standards or directories, such as those published by the Underwriters Laboratories Inc.

Table 310-13 also includes conductor applications and maximum operating temperatures. Some conductors have dual ratings, such as Type XHHW, rated 90°C (194°F) for dry locations and 75°C (167°F) for wet locations, or Type THW, 75°C (167°F) for dry and wet locations and 90°C (194°F) for special applications within electric-discharge lighting equipment. In no case are conductors to be associated together in such a way, with respect to type of circuit, the wiring method employed, or the number of conductors, that the limiting temperature of any conductor is exceeded (see Section 310-10). Most terminals of wiring devices, switches, and panelboards have not been tested for use with conductors whose maximum insulation temperature exceeds 75°C (167°F).

The maximum continuous ampacities for copper, copper-clad aluminum, and aluminum are listed in Tables 310-16 through 310-19 and accompanying Notes 1 through 11.

Receptacles and snap switches rated 20 A or less, not marked "CO/ALR," are for use with copper and copper-clad aluminum conductors only. Devices marked "CO/ALR" are for use with aluminum, copper, and copper-clad aluminum conductors. Screwless pressure terminal connectors of the conductor push-in type are for use only with copper and copper-clad aluminum conductors.

Receptacles rated 30 A or more and not marked "AL-CU" are for use with copper and copper-clad aluminum conductors only. Receptacles rated 30 A or more and marked "AL-CU" are for use with aluminum, copper, and copper-clad aluminum conductors.

Copper-clad aluminum conductors are drawn from a copper-clad aluminum rod with the copper metallurgically bonded to an aluminum core. The copper forms a minimum of 10 percent of the cross-sectional area of a solid conductor or each strand of a stranded conductor. See also comments following Section 110-14.

The following table compares the characteristics of copper-clad aluminum with copper and aluminum conductors.

Conductor Characteristics

	Copper	Cu/Al	Aluminum
Density lbs/in^3	0.323	0.121	0.098
Density gm/cm^3	8.91	3.34	2.71
Resistivity ohms/CMF	10.37	16.08	16.78
Resistivity Microhm-CM	1.724	2.673	2.790
Conductivity (IACS%)	100	61-63	61
Weight % Copper	100	26.8	. . . .
Tensile K psi-Hard	65.0	30.0	27.0
Tensile kg/mm^2-Hard	45.7	21.1	19.0
Tensile K psi-Annealed	35.0	17.0	17.0*
Tensile kg/mm^2-Annealed	24.6	12.0	12.0
Specific Gravity	8.91	3.34	2.71

*Semi-annealed

310-14. Aluminum Conductor Material.   Solid aluminum conductors No. 8, 10, and 12 AWG shall be made of an aluminum alloy conductor material.

As the *Code* recognizes CO/ALR devices, this section is to provide proper recognition of approved aluminum alloy conductor material.

310-15. Ampacity.

(a) Applications Covered by Tables.   Ampacities for conductors rated 0-2000 volts shall be as specified in Tables 310-16 through 310-19 and their accompanying notes. Effective January 1, 1987 ampacities for conductors rated 0-2000 volts shall be as specified in Tables 310-20 through 310-30 and their accompanying notes and figure. The ampacity for Types V, AVA, AVB, and AVL conductors rated 2001-5000 volts shall be the same as for those conductor types rated 0-2000 volts. The ampacities for solid dielectric insulated conductors rated 2001 to 35000 volts shall be as specified in Tables 310-69 through 310-84 and their accompanying notes.

It is the intent that in the next (1987) edition of the *Code* Tables 310-16 through 310-19, and the accompanying notes to these tables, be replaced by Tables 310-20 through 310-30 with appropriate notes similar to those presently shown for Tables 310-16 through 310-19. Tables 310-20 through 310-30 are published in the 1984 *NEC* to familiarize users of the *Code* with these new ampacity tables.

The ampacities in Tables 310-16 through 310-19 are based on a method of calculation developed by Sam J. Rosch and published in March 1938 in a paper entitled: "The Current-Carrying Capacity of Rubber-Insulated Conductors" which appeared in "Electrical Engineering," a monthly publication of the American

Institute of Electrical Engineers (predecessor of the Institute of Electrical and Electronic Engineers - IEEE). A copy of the paper was reprinted in the January/February 1981 issue of "IAEI News," a publication of the International Association of Electrical Inspectors.

The ampacities in Tables 310-20 through 310-30 are based on the Neher-McGrath method of calculating current-carrying capacity. This is the same method used for calculation of the ampacities of the high-voltage conductors in Tables 310-69 through 310-84. A description of this method of calculation was given in AIEE Paper No. 57-660, "The Calculation of the Temperature Rise and Load Capability of Cable Systems" by J. H. Neher and M. H. McGrath. This paper was presented to the AIEE General Meeting in Montreal, Quebec, Canada on June 24-28, 1956, and was published in "AIEE Transactions," Part III (Power Apparatus and Systems), Vol. 76, October 1957, pp. 752 through 772.

(b) Applications Not Covered by Tables. Ampacities for cable insulations, cable configurations, voltage levels, or thermal resistivities not included in the tables shall be permitted to be calculated, under engineering supervision, by means of the following general formula:

$$I = \sqrt{\frac{TC - (TA + DELTA\ TD)}{RDC\ (1 + YC)\ RCA}}$$

TC = Conductor temperature in degrees C

TA = Ambient temperature in degrees C

DELTA TD = Dielectric loss temperature rise

RDC = DC resistance of conductor at temperature TC

YC = Component AC resistance resulting from skin effect and proximity effect

RCA = Effective thermal resistance between conductor and surrounding ambient.

(FPN): The ampacities provided by this section are based on temperature alone and do not take voltage drop into consideration.

(FPN): Conductors of circuits as defined in Article 100, sized to prevent a voltage drop exceeding 5 percent, will provide reasonable efficiency of operation.

Table 310-13. Conductor Application and Insulations

Trade Name	Type Letter	Max. Operating Temp.	Application Provisions	Insulation	AWG or MCM	Thickness of Insulation		Mils	Outer Covering
Asbestos	A	200°C 392°F	Dry locations only. Only for leads within apparatus or within raceways connected to apparatus. Limited to 300 volts.	Asbestos	14 .... 12-8			30 40	Without asbestos braid
Asbestos	AA	200°C 392°F	Dry locations only. Only for leads within apparatus or within raceways connected to apparatus or as open wiring. Limited to 300 volts.	Asbestos	14 .... 12-8 .... 6-2 .... 1-4/0			30 30 40 60	With asbestos braid or glass
Asbestos	AI	125°C 257°F	Dry locations only. Only for leads within apparatus or within raceways connected to apparatus. Limited to 300 volts.	Impregnated Asbestos	14 .... 12-8			30 40	Without asbestos braid
Asbestos	AIA	125°C 257°F	Dry locations only. Only for leads within apparatus or within raceways connected to apparatus or as open wiring.	Impregnated Asbestos	14 .... 12-8 .... 6-2 .... 1-4/0 .... 213-500 .... 501-1000 ..	Sol. 30 30 40 60	Str. 30 40 60 75 90 105	With asbestos braid or glass

Table 310-13 (Continued)

Trade Name	Type Letter	Max. Operating Temp.	Application Provisions	Insulation	AWG or MCM	Thickness of Insulation — 1st Asb.	VC	Mils — AVA 2nd Asb.	Mils — AVL 2nd Asb.	Outer Covering
Asbestos and Varnished Cambric	AVA	110°C 230°F	Dry locations only.	Impregnated Asbestos and Varnished Cambric	14-8 (solid only)	—	30	25	25	AVA- asbestos braid or glass
					14-8	10	30	20	15	
					6-2	15	30	25	20	
					1-4/0	20	30	30	30	
					213-500	25	40	40	40	
					501-1000	30	40	40	40	
					1001-2000	30	50	50	50	
					For 1000-5000 volts, see Table 310-67.					

Trade Name	Type Letter	Max. Operating Temp.	Application Provisions	Insulation	AWG or MCM	Thickness of Insulation — Asb.	VC	Mils 2nd — VC	Mils 2nd — Asb.	Outer Covering
Asbestos and Varnished Cambric	AVB	90°C 194°F	Dry locations only.	Impregnated Asbestos and Varnished Cambric	18-8			30	20	Flame- retardant, cotton braid
					6-2			40	30	
					1-4/0			40	40	
					14-8	10	30	30	15	
					6-2	15	30	30	20	
					1-4/0	20	30	40	30	
					213-500	25	40	40	40	
					501-1000	30	40	40	40	
					1001-2000	30	50	50	50	
					For 1000-5000 volts, see Table 310-67.					

Note for AVA Outer Covering (switchboard wiring): Flame-retardant, cotton braid (switchboard wiring)

Table 310-13 (Continued)

Insulation (Trade Name)	Type	Max. Operating Temp.	Application Provisions	Insulation	Outer Covering
Asbestos and Varnished Cambric	AVL	110°C / 230°F	Dry and wet locations.	Impregnated Asbestos and Varnished Cambric	AVL-lead sheath
Fluorinated Ethylene Propylene	FEP or FEPB	90°C / 194°F; 200°C / 392°F	Dry locations. Dry locations—special applications.†	Fluorinated Ethylene Propylene; Fluorinated Ethylene Propylene	None; Glass braid; Asbestos braid
Mineral Insulation (Metal Sheathed)	MI	85°C / 185°F; 250°C / 482°F	Dry and wet locations. For special application.†	Magnesium Oxide	Copper
Moisture-, Heat- and Oil-Resistant Thermoplastic	MTW	60°C / 140°F; 90°C / 194°F	Machine tool wiring in wet locations as permitted in NFPA Standard No. 79. (See Article 670.) Machine tool wiring in dry locations as permitted in NFPA Standard No. 79. (See Article 670.)	Flame-Retardant, Moisture-, Heat- and Oil-Resistant Thermoplastic	(A) None; (B) Nylon jacket or equivalent

Thickness of Insulation (AVL):

AWG/kcmil	1st Asb.	VC	AVA 2nd Asb.	AVL 2nd Asb.
14-8 (solid only)	—	30	20	25
14-8	10	30	15	25
6-2	15	30	20	25
1-4/0	20	30	30	30
213-500	25	40	40	40
501-1000	30	40	40	40
1001-2000	30	50	50	50

For 1000-5000 volts, see Table 310-67.

Thickness of Insulation (FEP / FEPB):

AWG/kcmil	Mils
14-10	20
8-2	30
14-8	14
6-2	14

Thickness of Insulation (MI):

AWG/kcmil	Mils
16-10	36
9-4	50
3-250	55

Thickness of Insulation (MTW):

AWG/kcmil	(A)	(B)
22-12	30	15
10	30	20
8	45	30
6	60	30
4-2	60	40
1-4/0	80	50
213-500	95	60
501-1000	110	70

† Where environmental conditions require maximum conductor operating temperatures above 90°C.

Table 310-13 (Continued)

Trade Name	Type Letter	Max. Operating Temp.	Application Provisions	Insulation	AWG or MCM	Thickness of Insulation Mils	Outer Covering
Paper		85°C 185°F	For underground service conductors, or by special permission.	Paper			Lead sheath
Perfluoro-alkoxy	PFA	90°C 194°F 200°C 392°F	Dry locations. Dry locations—special applications.†	Perfluoro-alkoxy	14-10 8-2 1-4/0	20 30 45	None
Perfluoro-alkoxy	PFAH	250°C 482°F	Dry locations only. Only for leads within apparatus or within raceways connected to apparatus. (Nickel or nickel-coated copper only.)	Perfluoro-alkoxy	14-10 8-2 1-4/0	20 30 45	None
Heat-Resistant Rubber	RH	75°C 167°F	Dry locations.	Heat-Resistant Rubber	**14-12 10 8-2 1-4/0 213-500 501-1000 1001-2000 For 601-2000 volts, see Table 310-62.	30 45 60 80 95 110 125	*Moisture-resistant, flame-retardant, non-metallic covering
Heat-Resistant Rubber	RHH	90°C 194°F	Dry locations.				
Moisture- and Heat-Resistant Rubber	RHW	75°C 167°F	Dry and wet locations. For over 2000 volts insulation shall be ozone-resistant.	Moisture- and Heat-Resistant Rubber	14-10 8-2 1-4/0 213-500 501-1000 1001-2000 For 601-2000 volts, see Table 310-62.	45 60 80 95 110 125	*Moisture-resistant, flame-retardant, non-metallic covering

* Some rubber insulations do not require an outer covering.
** For 14-12 sizes RHH shall be 45 mils thickness insulation.
† Where environmental conditions require maximum conductor operating temperatures above 90°C.

Table 310-13 (Continued)

Heat-Resistant Latex Rubber	RUH	75°C 167°F	Dry locations.	90% Unmilled, Grainless Rubber	14-10 .... 18 8-2 25	Moisture-resistant, flame-retardant, non-metallic covering
Moisture-Resistant Latex Rubber	RUW	60°C 140°F	Dry and wet locations.	90% Unmilled, Grainless Rubber	14-10 .... 18 8-2 25	Moisture-resistant, flame-retardant, non-metallic covering
Silicone-Asbestos	SA	90°C 194°F 125°C 257°F	Dry locations. For special application.†	Silicone Rubber	14-10 .... 45 8-2 .... 60 1-4/0 .... 80 213-500 .... 95 501-1000 .... 110 1001-2000 125	Asbestos, glass or other suitable braid material
Synthetic Heat-Resistant	SIS	90°C 194°F	Switchboard wiring only.	Heat-Resistant Rubber	14-10 .... 30 8 .... 45 6-2 .... 60 1-4/0 80	None

† Where environmental conditions require maximum conductor operating temperatures above 90°C.

Table 310-13 (Continued)

Trade Name	Type Letter	Max. Operating Temp.	Application Provisions	Insulation	AWG or MCM	Thickness of Insulation (Mils)		Outer Covering
Thermoplastic	T	60°C 140°F	Dry locations.	Flame-Retardant, Thermoplastic Compound	14-10 8 6-2 1-4/0 213-500 501-1000 1001-2000	30 45 60 80 95 110 125		None
Thermoplastic and Asbestos	TA	90°C 194°F	Switchboard wiring only.	Thermoplastic and Asbestos	14-8 6-2 1-4/0	Th'pl'. 20 30 40	Asb. 20 25 30	Flame-retardant, nonmetallic covering
Thermoplastic and Fibrous Outer Braid	TBS	90°C 194°F	Switchboard wiring only.	Thermoplastic	14-10 8 6-2 1-4/0	30 45 60 80		Flame-retardant, nonmetallic covering
Extruded Polytetrafluoroethylene	TFE	250°C 482°F	Dry locations only. Only for leads within apparatus or within raceways connected to apparatus, or as open wiring. (Nickel or nickel-coated copper only.)	Extruded Polytetrafluoroethylene	14-10 8-2 1-4/0	20 30 45		None

Table 310-13 (Continued)

Trade Name	Type Letter	Max. Operating Temperature	Application Provisions	Insulation	AWG or MCM	Thickness of Insulation (Mils)	Outer Covering
Heat-Resistant Thermoplastic	THHN	90°C 194°F	Dry locations.	Flame-Retardant, Heat-Resistant Thermoplastic	14-12 .... 10 .... 8-6 .... 4-2 .... 1-4/0 .... 250-500 .... 501-1000	15 20 30 40 50 60 70	Nylon jacket or equivalent
Moisture- and Heat-Resistant Thermoplastic	THW	75°C 167°F 90°C 194°F	Dry and wet locations. Special applications within electric discharge lighting equipment. Limited to 1000 open-circuit volts or less. (Size 14-8 only as permitted in Section 410-31.)	Flame-Retardant, Moisture- and Heat-Resistant Thermoplastic	14-10 .... 8-2 .... 1-4/0 .... 213-500 .... 501-1000 .... 1001-2000	45 60 80 95 110 125	None
Moisture- and Heat-Resistant Thermoplastic	THWN	75°C 167°F	Dry and wet locations.	Flame-Retardant, Moisture- and Heat-Resistant Thermoplastic	14-12 .... 10 .... 8-6 .... 4-2 .... 1-4/0 .... 250-500 .... 501-1000	15 20 30 40 50 60 70	Nylon jacket or equivalent
Moisture-Resistant Thermoplastic	TW	60°C 140°F	Dry and wet locations.	Flame-Retardant, Moisture-Resistant Thermoplastic	14-10 .... 8 .... 6-2 .... 1-4/0 .... 213-500 .... 501-1000 .... 1001-2000	30 45 60 80 95 110 125	None

259

Table 310-13 (Continued)

Trade Name	Type Letter	Max. Operating Temp.	Application Provisions	Insulation	AWG or MCM	Thickness of Insulation Mils	Outer Covering
Underground Feeder & Branch-Circuit Cable-Single Conductor. (For Type UF cable employing more than one conductor, see Article 339.)	UF	60°C 140°F	See Article 339.	Moisture-Resistant	14-10 .... 8-2 .... 1-4/0	*60 *80 *95	Integral with insulation
		***75°C 167°F		Moisture-and Heat-Resistant			
Underground Service-Entrance Cable-Single Conductor. (For Type USE cable employing more than one conductor, see Article 338.)	USE	75°C 167°F	See Article 338.	Heat- and Moisture-Resistant	12-10 .... 8-2 .... 1-4/0 .... 213-500 .... 501-1000 .... 1001-2000	45 60 80 ***95 110 125	Moisture-resistant non-metallic covering [See 338-1 (2)]

* Includes integral jacket.
** For ampacity limitation, see Section 339-1(a).
*** Insulation thickness shall be permitted to be 80 mils for listed Type USE conductors that have been subjected to special investigations.

The nonmetallic covering over individual rubber-covered conductors of aluminum-sheathed cable and of lead-sheathed or multiconductor cable shall not be required to be flame retardant. For Type MC cable, see Section 334-20. For nonmetallic-sheathed cable, see Section 336-2. For Type UF cable, see Section 339-1.

Table 310-13 (Continued)

Trade Name	Type Letter	Max. Operating Temperature	Application Provisions	Insulation	Thickness of Insulation (Size AWG-MCM)	Outer Covering
Varnished Cambric	V	85°C 185°F	Dry locations only. Smaller than No. 6 by special permission.	Varnished Cambric	14-8.........45 6-2.........60 1-4/0.........80 213-500.........95 500-1000.........110 1001-2000.........125 For 1000-5000 volts, see Table 310-65 or 310-66.	Nonmetallic covering or lead sheath
Moisture- and Heat-Resistant Cross-Linked Synthetic Polymer	XHHW	90°C 194°F 75°C 167°F	Dry locations. Wet locations.	Flame-Retardant Cross-Linked Synthetic Polymer	14-10.........30 8-2.........45 1-4/0.........55 213-500.........65 501-1000.........80 1001-2000.........95	None
Modified Ethylene Tetrafluoroethylene	Z	90°C 194°F 150°C 302°F	Dry locations. Dry locations—special applications.†	Modified Ethylene Tetrafluoroethylene	14-12.........15 10.........20 8-4.........25 3-1.........35 1/0-4/0.........45	None
Modified Ethylene Tetrafluoroethylene	ZW	75°C 167°F 90°C 194°F 150°C 302°F	Wet locations. Dry locations. Dry locations—special applications.†	Modified Ethylene Tetrafluoroethylene	14-10.........30 8-2.........45	None

†Where environmental conditions require maximum conductor operating temperatures above 90°C.

Table 310-16. Ampacities of Insulated Conductors
Rated 0-2000 Volts, 60° to 90°C

Not More Than Three Conductors in Raceway or Cable or Earth
(Directly Buried), Based on Ambient Temperature of 30°C (86°F)

Size	Temperature Rating of Conductor, See Table 310-13								Size
	60°C (140°F)	75°C (167°F)	85°C (185°F)	90°C (194°F)	60°C (140°F)	75°C (167°F)	85°C (185°F)	90°C (194°F)	
AWG MCM	TYPES †RUW, †T, †TW, †UF	TYPES †FEPW, †RH, †RHW, †RUH, †THW, †THWN, †XHHW, †USE, †ZW	TYPES V, MI	TYPES TA, TBS, SA, AVB, SIS, †FEP, †FEPB, †RHH †THHN, †XHHW*	TYPES †RUW, †T, †TW, †UF	TYPES †RH, †RHW, †RUH, †THW †THWN, †XHHW, †USE	TYPES V, MI	TYPES TA, TBS, SA, AVB, SIS, †RHH, †THHN, †XHHW*	AWG MCM
	COPPER				ALUMINUM OR COPPER-CLAD ALUMINUM				
18	....	....	....	14	....	....	....	....	....
16	....	....	18	18	....	....	....	....	....
14	20†	20†	25	25†	....	....	....	....	....
12	25†	25†	30	30†	20†	20†	25	25†	12
10	30	35†	40	40†	25	30†	30	35†	10
8	40	50	55	55	30	40	40	45	8
6	55	65	70	75	40	50	55	60	6
4	70	85	95	95	55	65	75	75	4
3	85	100	110	110	65	75	85	85	3
2	95	115	125	130	75	90	100	100	2
1	110	130	145	150	85	100	110	115	1
0	125	150	165	170	100	120	130	135	0
00	145	175	190	195	115	135	145	150	00
000	165	200	215	225	130	155	170	175	000
0000	195	230	250	260	150	180	195	205	0000
250	215	255	275	290	170	205	220	230	250
300	240	285	310	320	190	230	250	255	300
350	260	310	340	350	210	250	270	280	350
400	280	335	365	380	225	270	295	305	400
500	320	380	415	430	260	310	335	350	500
600	355	420	460	475	285	340	370	385	600
700	385	460	500	520	310	375	405	420	700
750	400	475	515	535	320	385	420	435	750
800	410	490	535	555	330	395	430	450	800
900	435	520	565	585	355	425	465	480	900
1000	455	545	590	615	375	445	485	500	1000
1250	495	590	640	665	405	485	525	545	1250
1500	520	625	680	705	435	520	565	585	1500
1750	545	650	705	735	455	545	595	615	1750
2000	560	665	725	750	470	560	610	630	2000
AMPACITY CORRECTION FACTORS									
Ambient Temp. °C	For ambient temperatures other than 30°C, multiply the ampacities shown above by the appropriate factor shown below.								Ambient Temp. °F
31-40	.82	.88	.90	.91	.82	.88	.90	.91	87-104
41-45	.71	.82	.85	.87	.71	.82	.85	.87	105-113
46-50	.58	.75	.80	.82	.58	.75	.80	.82	114-122
51-60	....	.58	.67	.71	....	.58	.67	.71	123-141
61-70	....	.35	.52	.58	....	.35	.52	.58	142-158
71-80	....	....	.30	.41	....	....	.30	.41	159-176

† The overcurrent protection for conductor types marked with an obelisk (†) shall not exceed 15 amperes for 14 AWG, 20 amperes for 12 AWG, and 30 amperes for 10 AWG copper; or 15 amperes for 12 AWG and 25 amperes for 10 AWG aluminum and copper-clad aluminum after any correction factors for ambient temperature and number of conductors have been applied.

* For dry locations only. See 75°C column for wet locations.

Table 310-17. Ampacities of Insulated Conductors
Rated 0-2000 Volts, 60° to 90°C

Single conductors in free air, based on ambient temperature of 30°C (86°F).

Size	Temperature Rating of Conductor, See Table 310-13								Size
	60°C (140°F)	75°C (167°F)	85°C (185°F)	90°C (194°F)	60°C (140°F)	75°C (167°F)	85°C (185°F)	90°C (194°F)	
AWG MCM	TYPES †RUW, †T, †TW	TYPES †FEPW, †RH, †RHW, †RUH, †THW, †THWN, †XHHW, †ZW	TYPES V, MI	TYPES TA, TBS, SA, AVB, SIS, †FEP, †FEPB, †RHH †THHN, †XHHW*	TYPES †RUW, †T, †TW	TYPES †RH, †RHW, †RUH, †THW, †THWN, †XHHW	TYPES V, MI	TYPES TA, TBS, SA, AVB, SIS, †RHH, †THHN, †XHHW*	AWG MCM
	COPPER				ALUMINUM OR COPPER-CLAD ALUMINUM				
18	. . . .	. . . .	. . . .	18	. . . .	. . . .	. . . .	. . . .	. . . .
16	. . . .	. . . .	23	24	. . . .	. . . .	. . . .	. . . .	. . . .
14	25†	30†	30	35†	. . . .	. . . .	. . . .	. . . .	. . . .
12	30†	35†	40	40†	25†	30†	30	35†	12
10	40†	50†	55	55†	35†	40†	40	40†	10
8	60	70	75	80	45	55	60	60	8
6	80	95	100	105	60	75	80	80	6
4	105	125	135	140	80	100	105	110	4
3	120	145	160	165	95	115	125	130	3
2	140	170	185	190	110	135	145	150	2
1	165	195	215	220	130	155	165	175	1
0	195	230	250	260	150	180	195	205	0
00	225	265	290	300	175	210	225	235	00
000	260	310	335	350	200	240	265	275	000
0000	300	360	390	405	235	280	305	315	0000
250	340	405	440	455	265	315	345	355	250
300	375	445	485	505	290	350	380	395	300
350	420	505	550	570	330	395	430	445	350
400	455	545	595	615	355	425	465	480	400
500	515	620	675	700	405	485	525	545	500
600	575	690	750	780	455	540	595	615	600
700	630	755	825	855	500	595	650	675	700
750	655	785	855	885	515	620	675	700	750
800	680	815	885	920	535	645	700	725	800
900	730	870	950	985	580	700	760	785	900
1000	780	935	1020	1055	625	750	815	845	1000
1250	890	1065	1160	1200	710	855	930	960	1250
1500	980	1175	1275	1325	795	950	1035	1075	1500
1750	1070	1280	1395	1445	875	1050	1145	1185	1750
2000	1155	1385	1505	1560	960	1150	1250	1335	2000
AMPACITY CORRECTION FACTORS									
Ambient Temp. °C	For ambient temperatures other than 30°C, multiply the ampacities shown above by the appropriate factor shown below.								Ambient Temp. °F
31-40	.82	.88	.90	.91	.82	.88	.90	.91	87-104
41-45	.71	.82	.85	.87	.71	.82	.85	.87	105-113
46-50	.58	.75	.80	.82	.58	.75	.80	.82	114-122
51-60	. . . .	.58	.67	.71	. . . .	.58	.67	.71	123-141
61-70	. . . .	.35	.52	.58	. . . .	.35	.52	.58	142-158
71-80	. . . .	. . . .	.30	.41	. . . .	. . . .	.30	.41	159-176

† The overcurrent protection for conductor types marked with an obelisk (†) shall not exceed 20 amperes for 14 AWG, 25 amperes for 12 AWG, and 40 amperes for 10 AWG copper, or 20 amperes for 12 AWG and 30 amperes for 10 AWG aluminum and copper-clad aluminum after any correction factor for ambient has been applied.

* For dry locations only. See 75°C column for wet locations.

Table 310-18. Ampacities for Insulated Conductors Rated 0-2000 Volts, 110 to 250°C

Not More Than Three Conductors in Raceway or Cable
Based on Ambient Temperature of 30°C (86°F).

Size	Temperature Rating of Conductor. See Table 310-13								Size
	110°C (230°F)	125°C (257°F)	150°C (302°F)	200°C (392°F)	250°C (482°F)	110°C (230°F)	125°C (257°F)	200°C (392°F)	
AWG MCM	TYPES AVA, AVL	TYPES AI, AIA	TYPE Z	TYPES A, AA, FEP, FEPB, PFA	TYPES PFAH, TFE	TYPES AVA, AVL	TYPES AI, AIA	TYPES A, AA	AWG MCM
	COPPER				NICKEL OR NICKEL-COATED COPPER	ALUMINUM OR COPPER-CLAD ALUMINUM			
14	30	30	30	30	40	....	....	....	....
12	35	40	40	40	55	25	30	30	12
10	45	50	50	55	75	35	40	45	10
8	60	65	65	70	95	45	50	55	8
6	80	85	90	95	120	60	65	75	6
4	105	115	115	120	145	80	90	95	4
3	120	130	135	145	170	95	100	115	3
2	135	145	150	165	195	105	115	130	2
1	160	170	180	190	220	125	135	150	1
0	190	200	210	225	250	150	160	180	0
00	215	230	240	250	280	170	180	200	00
000	245	265	275	285	315	195	210	225	000
0000	275	310	325	340	370	215	245	270	0000
250	315	335	....	....	....	250	270	....	250
300	345	380	....	....	....	275	305	....	300
350	390	420	....	....	....	310	335	....	350
400	420	450	....	....	....	335	360	....	400
500	470	500	....	....	....	380	405	....	500
600	525	545	....	....	....	425	440	....	600
700	560	600	....	....	....	455	485	....	700
750	580	620	....	....	....	470	500	....	750
800	600	640	....	....	....	485	520	....	800
1000	680	730	....	....	....	560	600	....	1000
1500	785	....	....	....	....	650	....	....	1500
2000	840	....	....	....	....	705	....	....	2000

AMPACITY CORRECTION FACTORS

Ambient Temp. °C	For ambient temperatures other than 30°C, multiply the ampacities shown above by the appropriate factor shown below.								Ambient Temp. °F
31-40	.94	.95	.96	....	....	.94	.95	....	87-104
41-45	.90	.92	.94	....	....	.90	.92	....	105-113
46-50	.87	.89	.91	....	....	.87	.89	....	114-122
51-55	.83	.86	.89	....	....	.83	.86	....	123-131
56-60	.79	.83	.87	.91	.95	.79	.83	.91	132-141
61-70	.71	.76	.82	.87	.91	.71	.76	.87	142-158
71-75	.66	.72	.79	.86	.89	.66	.72	.86	159-167
76-80	.61	.68	.76	.84	.87	.61	.69	.84	168-176
81-90	.50	.61	.71	.80	.83	.50	.61	.80	177-194
91-100	....	.51	.65	.77	.80	....	.51	.77	195-212
101-120	....	....	.50	.69	.72	....	....	.69	213-248
121-140	....	....	.29	.59	.59	....	....	.59	249-284
141-160	....	....	....	....	.54	....	....	....	285-320
161-180	....	....	....	....	.50	....	....	....	321-356
181-200	....	....	....	....	.43	....	....	....	357-392
201-225	....	....	....	....	.30	....	....	....	393-437

Table 310-19. Ampacities for Insulated Conductors
Rated 0-2000 Volts, 110 to 250°C, and for Bare or Covered Conductors

Single Conductors in Free Air,
Based on Ambient Temperature of 30°C (86°F).

Size	Temperature Rating of Conductor. See Table 310-13.										Size
	110°C (230°F) TYPES AVA, AVL	125°C (257°F) TYPES AI, AIA	150°C (302°F) TYPE Z	200°C (392°F) TYPES A, AA, FEP, FEPB, PFA	Bare or covered conductors	250°C (482°F) TYPES PFAH, TFE	110°C (230°F) TYPES AVA, AVL	125°C (257°F) TYPES AI, AIA	200°C (392°F) TYPES A, AA	Bare or covered conductors	
AWG MCM	COPPER					NICKEL OR NICKEL-COATED COPPER	ALUMINUM OR COPPER-CLAD ALUMINUM				AWG MCM
14	40	40	40	45	30	60	....	....	....	....	....
12	50	50	50	55	40	80	40	40	45	30	12
10	65	70	70	75	55	110	50	55	60	45	10
8	85	90	95	100	70	145	65	70	80	55	8
6	120	125	130	135	100	210	95	100	105	80	6
4	160	170	175	180	130	285	125	135	140	100	4
3	180	195	200	210	150	335	140	150	165	115	3
2	210	225	230	240	175	390	165	175	185	135	2
1	245	265	270	280	205	450	190	205	220	160	1
0	285	305	310	325	235	545	220	240	255	185	0
00	330	355	360	370	275	605	255	275	290	215	00
000	385	410	415	430	320	725	300	320	335	250	000
0000	445	475	490	510	370	850	345	370	400	290	0000
250	495	530	....	....	410	....	385	415	320	320	250
300	555	590	....	....	460	....	435	460	360	360	300
350	610	655	....	....	510	....	475	510	400	400	350
400	665	710	....	....	555	....	520	555	435	435	400
500	765	815	....	....	630	....	595	635	490	490	500
600	855	910	....	....	710	....	675	720	....	560	600
700	940	1005	....	....	780	....	745	795	....	615	700
750	980	1045	....	....	810	....	775	825	....	640	750
800	1020	1085	....	....	845	....	805	855	....	670	800
900	....	....	....	....	905	....	....	....	....	725	900
1000	1165	1240	....	....	965	....	930	990	....	770	1000
1500	1450	....	....	....	1215	....	1175	....	....	985	1500
2000	1715	....	....	....	1405	....	1425	....	....	1165	2000

AMPACITY CORRECTION FACTORS

Ambient Temp. °C	For ambient temperatures other than 30°C, multiply the ampacities shown above by the appropriate factor shown below.								Ambient Temp. °F
31-40	.94	.95	.96	....		....	.94	.95	....	87-104
41-45	.90	.92	.94	....		....	.90	.92	....	105-113
46-50	.87	.89	.91	....		....	.87	.89	....	114-122
51-55	.83	.86	.89	....		....	.83	.86	....	123-131
56-60	.79	.83	.87	.91		.95	.79	.83	.91	132-141
61-70	.71	.76	.82	.87		.91	.71	.76	.87	142-158
71-75	.66	.72	.79	.86		.89	.66	.72	.86	159-167
76-80	.61	.68	.76	.84		.87	.61	.69	.84	168-176
81-90	.50	.61	.71	.80		.83	.50	.61	.80	177-194
91-100	....	.51	.65	.77		.80	....	.51	.77	195-212
101-120	....	....	.50	.69		.72	....	....	.69	213-248
121-140	....	....	.29	.59		.59	....	....	.59	249-284
141-160	....	....	....	....		.54	....	....	....	285-320
161-180	....	....	....	....		.50	....	....	....	321-356
181-200	....	....	....	....		.43	....	....	....	357-392
201-225	....	....	....	....		.30	....	....	....	393-437

Notes to Tables 310-16 through 310-19

1. Explanation of Tables. For explanation of Type Letters, and for recognized size of conductors for the various conductor insulations, see Section 310-13. For installation requirements, see Sections 310-1 through 310-10, and the various articles of this Code. For flexible cords, see Tables 400-4 and 400-5.

3. Three-Wire, Single-Phase Dwelling Services. In dwelling units, conductors, as listed below, shall be permitted to be utilized as three-wire, single-phase, service-entrance conductors and the three-wire, single-phase feeder that carries the total current supplied by that service.

Conductor Types and Sizes
RH-RHH-RHW-THW-THWN-THHN-XHHW

Copper	Aluminum and Copper-Clad AL	Service Rating in Amps
AWG	AWG	
4	2	100
3	1	110
2	1/0	125
1	2/0	150
1/0	3/0	175
2/0	4/0	200

If a single set of 3-wire, single-phase, service-entrance conductors supplies a one-family, two-family, or multifamily dwelling, the reduced conductor size permitted by Note 3 is applicable to the service-entrance conductors only. If there are panelboards on the load side of the main service-entrance equipment supplied by feeders, Note 3 does not permit a reduction in the conductor size for these feeders because they do carry the total current supplied by the service. See Figures 310-4 and 310-5.

See also Section 550-3(a) for a description of a feeder assembly that carries the total current supplied by the service and Section 215-2.

It is the intent that all conductors, including the neutral, be the same size when applying Note 3.

4. Type MC Cable. The ampacities of Type MC cables are determined by the temperature limitation of the insulated conductors incorporated within the cable. Hence the ampacities of Type MC cable may be determined from the columns in Tables 310-16 and 310-18 applicable to the type of insulated conductors employed within the cable.

5. Bare Conductors. Where bare conductors are used with insulated conductors, their allowable ampacities shall be limited to that permitted for the insulated conductors of the same size.

6. Mineral-Insulated, Metal-Sheathed Cable. The temperature limitation on which the ampacities of mineral-insulated, metal-sheathed cable are based is determined by the insulating materials used in the end seal. Termination fittings incorporating unimpregnated, organic, insulating materials are limited to 85°C operation.

7. Type MTW Machine Tool Wire. The ampacities of Type MTW wire are specified in Table 11-1(b) of the Standard for Electrical Metalworking Machine Tools and Plastics Machinery (NFPA 79-1980).

8. More than Three Conductors in a Raceway or Cable. Where the number of conductors in a raceway or cable exceeds three, the ampacities given in Table 310-16 or 310-18 shall be reduced as shown in the following table:

Number of Conductors	Percent of Values in Tables 310-16 and 310-18 as Adjusted for Ambient Temperature if Necessary
4 thru 6	80
7 thru 24	70
25 thru 42	60
43 and above	50

Where single conductors or multiconductor cables are stacked or bundled longer than 24 inches (610 mm) without maintaining spacing and are not installed in raceways, the ampacity of each conductor shall be reduced as shown in the above table.

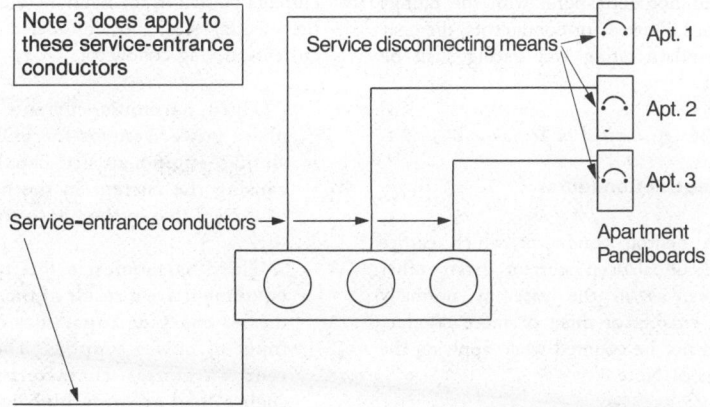

Figure 310-4. The reduced conductor size permitted in Note 3 to Tables 310-16 through 310-19 is applicable to the conductors going to each apartment from the meters.

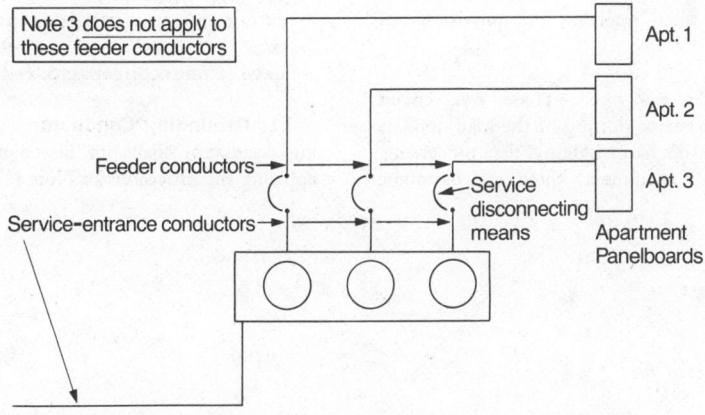

Figure 310-5. The reduced conductor size permitted in Note 3 to Tables 310-16 through 310-19 is not applicable to the conductors going to each apartment from the meters.

Exception No. 1: When conductors of different systems, as provided in Section 300-3, are installed in a common raceway the derating factors shown above shall apply to the number of power and lighting (Articles 210, 215, 220, and 230) conductors only.

Exception No. 2: The derating factors of Sections 210-22(c), 220-2(a) and 220-10(b) shall not apply when the above derating factors are also required.

Exception No. 2 is not applicable to motor circuit conductors because the so-called "derating

factor" for such conductors, as in Section 430-22(a), is not a derating factor. See commentary following Section 430-22(a).

Exception No. 3: For conductors installed in cable trays, the provisions of Section 318-10 shall apply.

Exception No. 4: Derating factors do not apply to conductors in nipples having a length not exceeding 24 inches (610 mm).

9. Overcurrent Protection. Where the standard ratings and settings of overcurrent devices do not correspond with the ratings and settings allowed for conductors, the next higher standard rating and setting shall be permitted.

Exception: As limited in Section 240-3.

10. Neutral Conductor.

(a) A neutral conductor which carries only the unbalanced current from other conductors, as in the case of normally balanced circuits of three or more conductors, shall not be counted when applying the provisions of Note 8.

(b) In a 3-wire circuit consisting of 2-phase wires and the neutral of a 4-wire, 3-phase wye-connected system, a common conductor carries approximately the same current as the other conductors and shall be counted when applying the provisions of Note 8.

(c) On a 4-wire, 3-phase wye circuit where the major portion of the load consists of electric-discharge lighting, data processing, or similar equipment, there are harmonic currents present in the neutral conductor and the neutral shall be considered to be a current-carrying conductor.

Third harmonic currents in 3-phase power systems for EDP and similar equipment are capable of causing the current in the neutral to exceed that in the phase conductor.

Third harmonics in this type of equipment are a result of the use of diodes charging capacitors on the input of power supplies. The current waveforms characteristic of such a load are very high in third harmonics. Third harmonics, in contrast to the fundamental, are not reduced by balancing the load. As a result, the neutral, in areas of concentrated electronic loads such as computer installations, production test areas, etc., should not have its current capacity reduced.

11. Grounding Conductor.
A grounding conductor shall not be counted when applying the provisions of Note 8.

**Table 310-20.   Ampacities for Bare and Covered Linewire
Based on 40°C Ambient, 80°C Total Conductor Temperature,
2 Feet per Second Wind Velocity**

Bare Copper Conductors		Weatherproofed Copper Linewire	
AWG MCM	AMPS	AWG MCM	AMPS
8	98	8	103
6	124	6	130
4	155	4	163
2	209	2	219
1/0	282	1/0	297
2/0	329	2/0	344
3/0	382	3/0	401
4/0	444	4/0	466
250	494	250	519
300	556	300	584
500	773	500	812
750	1000	750	1050
1000	1193	1000	1253

Bare AAC Aluminum Conductor		Weatherproofed AAC Aluminum	
AWG MCM	AMPS	AWG MCM	AMPS
8	76	8	80
6	96	6	101
4	121	4	127
2	163	2	171
1/0	220	1/0	231
2/0	255	2/0	268
3/0	297	3/0	312
4/0	346	4/0	364
266.8	403	266.8	423
336.4	468	336.4	492
397.5	522	397.5	548
477.0	588	477.0	617
556.5	650	556.5	682
636.0	709	636.0	744
795.0	819	795.0	860
954.0	920	1033.5	1017
1033.5	968	1272	1201
1272	1103	1590	1381
1590	1267	2000	1527
2000	1454		

Table 310-20A.   Ampacities of Multiconductor Cables with not more than Three Insulated Conductors, Rated 0-2000 Volts, in Free Air. Based on Ambient Air Temperature of 40°C (For NM, NMC, AC, TC, MC, MI and SNM cables)†

Size	Temperature Rating of Conductor. See Table 310-13.								Size
AWG	60°C	75°C	85°C	90°C	60°C	75°C	85°C	90°C	AWG
MCM	COPPER				ALUMINUM OR COPPER-CLAD ALUMINUM				MCM
18				11†					18
16				16†					16
14	18†	21†	24†	25†	....	....	....	....	14
12	21†	28†	30†	32†	18†	21†	24†	25†	12
10	28†	36†	41†	43†	21†	28†	30†	32†	10
8	39	50	56	59	30	39	44	46	8
6	52	68	75	79	41	53	59	61	6
4	69	89	100	104	54	70	78	81	4
3	81	104	116	121	63	81	91	95	3
2	92	118	132	138	72	92	103	108	2
1	107	138	154	161	84	108	120	126	1
0	124	160	178	186	97	125	139	145	0
00	143	184	206	215	111	144	160	168	00
000	165	213	238	249	129	166	185	194	000
0000	190	245	274	287	149	192	214	224	0000
250	212	274	305	320	166	214	239	250	250
300	237	306	341	357	186	240	268	280	300
350	261	337	377	394	205	265	296	309	350
400	281	363	406	425	222	287	317	334	400
500	321	416	465	487	255	330	368	385	500
600	354	459	513	538	284	368	410	429	600
700	387	502	562	589	306	405	462	473	700
750	404	523	586	615	328	424	473	495	750
800	415	539	604	633	339	439	490	513	800
900	438	570	639	670	362	469	514	548	900
1000	461	601	674	707	385	499	558	584	1000

Ambient Temp. °C	For ambient temperatures other than 40°C multiply the ampacities shown above by the appropriate factor shown below.								Ambient Temp.
21-25	1.32	1.20	1.15	1.14	1.32	1.20	1.15	1.14	21-25
26-30	1.22	1.13	1.11	1.10	1.22	1.13	1.11	1.10	26-30
31-35	1.12	1.07	1.05	1.05	1.12	1.07	1.05	1.05	31-35
36-40	1.00	1.00	1.00	1.00	1.00	1.00	1.00	1.00	36-40
41-45	.87	.93	.94	.95	.87	.93	.94	.95	41-45
46-50	.71	.85	.88	.89	.71	.85	.88	.89	46-50
51-55	.50	.76	.82	.84	.50	.76	.82	.84	51-55
56-60	....	.65	.75	.77	....	.65	.75	.77	56-60
61-70	....	.38	.58	.63	....	.38	.58	.63	61-70
71-80	....	....	.33	.44	....	....	.33	.44	71-80

The overcurrent protection for conductor types marked with an obelisk (†) shall not exceed 7 amperes for 18 AWG, 10 amperes for 16 AWG, and 15 amperes for 14 AWG, 20 amperes for 12 AWG, and 30 amperes for 10 AWG copper; or 15 amperes for 12 AWG and 25 amperes for 10 AWG aluminum and copper-clad aluminum.

Table 310-21. Ampacities of Single Insulated Conductors, Rated 0-2000 Volts, in Free Air Based on Ambient Air Temperature of 40°C

Size	Temperature Rating of Conductor. See Table 310-13.					
	60°C	75°C	90°C	60°C	75°C	90°C
AWG MCM	TYPES †T, †TW, †RUW	TYPES †RH, †RHW, †RUH, †THW, †THWN, †XHHW, †ZW	TYPES TA, TBS, SA, AVB, SIS, FEP, †FEPB, †RHH, †THHN, †XHHW*	TYPES †T, †TW, †RUW	TYPES †RH, †RHW, †RUH, †THW, †THWN, †XHHW	TYPES TA, TBS, SA, AVB, SIS, †RHH, †THHN, †XHHW*
	COPPER			ALUMINUM OR COPPER-CLAD ALUMINUM		
18			16†			
16			22†			
14	24†	30†	35†	. . . .	29†	. . . .
12	30†	39†	45†	24†	39†	36†
10	41†	51†	61†	30†	55	45†
8	55	71	83	43	55	64
6	73	94	109	57	73	85
4	96	124	145	75	97	113
3	112	145	169	88	113	132
2	128	165	192	100	128	150
1	148	191	223	115	149	174
0	171	221	258	133	172	201
00	198	255	298	154	199	232
000	229	295	345	178	230	269
0000	266	343	400	207	268	312
250	295	381	445	230	297	347
300	331	427	499	259	334	389
350	366	473	552	287	370	431
400	397	514	600	312	402	469
500	460	595	695	361	466	544
600	514	664	776	404	522	609
700	567	733	857	447	578	674
750	594	768	898	469	606	707
800	617	798	934	488	631	736
900	664	859	1005	527	680	795
1000	711	920	1076	566	730	853
1250	809	1048	1228	650	840	982
1500	898	1166	1367	730	944	1103
1750	978	1271	1493	803	1039	1216
2000	1051	1367	1606	871	1128	1321

Ambient Temp. °C	For ambient temperatures other than 40°C multiply the ampacities shown above by the appropriate factor shown below.					
21-25	1.32	1.20	1.14	1.32	1.20	1.14
26-30	1.22	1.13	1.10	1.22	1.13	1.10
31-35	1.12	1.07	1.05	1.12	1.07	1.05
36-40	1.00	1.00	1.00	1.00	1.00	1.00
41-45	.87	.93	.95	.87	.93	.95
46-50	.71	.85	.89	.71	.85	.89
51-55	.50	.76	.84	.50	.76	.84
56-60	. . . .	.65	.77	. . . .	.65	.77
61-70	. . . .	.38	.63	. . . .	.38	.63
71-80	. . . .	. . . .	.45	. . . .	. . . .	.45

The overcurrent protection for conductor types marked with an obelisk (†) shall not exceed 7 amperes for 18 AWG, 10 amperes for 16 AWG, 15 amperes for 14 AWG, 20 amperes for 12 AWG, and 30 amperes for 10 AWG copper, or 15 amperes for 12 AWG and 25 amperes for 10 AWG aluminum and copper-clad aluminum.

* For dry locations only. See 75° column for wet locations.

Table 310-22. Ampacities of Three Single Insulated Conductors, Rated 0-2000 Volts, Triplexed on a Messenger Based on Ambient Air Temperature of 40°C

Size	Temperature Rating of Conductor. See Table 310-13.			
	75°C	90°C	75°C	90°C
AWG MCM	TYPES RH, RHW, RUH, THW, THWN, XHHW, ZW	TYPES THHN, RHH, XHHW*	TYPES RH, RHW, RUH, THW, THWN, XHHW	TYPES THHN, RHH, XHHW*
	COPPER		ALUMINUM OR COPPER-CLAD ALUMINUM	
8	57	66	44	51
6	76	89	59	69
4	101	117	78	91
3	118	138	92	107
2	135	158	106	123
1	158	185	123	144
0	183	214	143	167
00	212	247	165	193
000	245	287	192	224
0000	287	335	224	262
250	320	374	251	292
300	359	419	282	328
350	397	464	312	364
400	430	503	339	395
500	496	580	392	458
600	553	647	440	514
700	610	714	488	570
750	638	747	512	598
800	660	773	532	622
900	704	826	572	669
1000	748	879	612	716

Ambient Temp. °C	For ambient temperatures other than 40°C multiply the ampacities shown above by the appropriate factor shown below.			
21-25	1.20	1.14	1.20	1.14
26-30	1.13	1.10	1.13	1.10
31-35	1.07	1.05	1.07	1.05
36-40	1.00	1.00	1.00	1.00
41-45	.93	.95	.93	.95
46-50	.85	.89	.85	.89
51-55	.76	.84	.76	.84
56-60	.65	.77	.65	.77
61-70	.38	.63	.38	.63
71-80	. . . .	.45	. . . .	.45

* For dry locations only. See 75° column for wet locations.

Table 310-23. Ampacities of Three Single Insulated Conductors, Rated 0-2000 Volts, in Conduit in Free Air Based on Ambient Air Temperature of 40°C

Size	Temperature Rating of Conductor. See Table 310-13.					
	60°C	75°C	90°C	60°C	75°C	90°C
AWG MCM	TYPES †RUW, †T, †TW, †UF	TYPES †RH, †RHW, †RUH, †THW, †THWN, †XHHW, †USE, †ZW	TYPES SA, AVB, †FEP, †FEPB, †THHN, †RHH, †XHHW*	TYPES †RUW, †T, †TW, †UF	TYPES †RH, †RHW, †RUH, †THW, †THWN, †XHHW, †USE	TYPES SA, AVB, †THHN, †RHH, †XHHW*
	COPPER			ALUMINUM OR COPPER-CLAD ALUMINUM		
14	18†	22†	25†	. . . .	. . . .	. . . .
12	23†	28†	32†	18†	22†	26†
10	29†	37†	42†	23†	29†	34†
8	36	48	55	28	37	43
6	50	64	75	37	50	58
4	65	83	97	50	65	76
3	76	98	114	59	76	89
2	87	112	130	68	87	102
1	104	134	156	81	104	122
0	119	153	179	93	119	139
00	135	175	204	106	137	159
000	160	207	242	125	162	189
0000	184	238	278	144	186	217
250	210	271	317	165	213	249
300	232	300	351	183	236	276
350	254	328	384	201	259	303
400	274	354	415	218	281	329
500	314	407	477	252	326	381
600	345	448	525	280	362	424
700	376	489	574	308	399	467
750	392	509	598	322	417	488
800	403	524	616	334	432	506
900	426	555	653	357	463	542
1000	499	585	689	380	493	578

Ambient Temp. °C	For ambient temperatures other than 40°C multiply the ampacities shown above by the appropriate factor shown below.					
21-25	1.32	1.20	1.14	1.32	1.20	1.14
26-30	1.22	1.13	1.10	1.22	1.13	1.10
31-35	1.12	1.07	1.05	1.12	1.07	1.05
36-40	1.00	1.00	1.00	1.00	1.00	1.00
41-45	.87	.93	.95	.87	.93	.95
46-50	.71	.85	.89	.71	.85	.89
51-55	.50	.76	.84	.50	.76	.84
56-60	. . . .	.65	.77	. . . .	.65	.77
61-70	. . . .	.38	.63	. . . .	.38	.63
71-80	. . . .	. . . .	.45	. . . .	. . . .	.45

The overcurrent protection for conductor types marked with an obelisk (†) shall not exceed 15 amperes for 14 AWG, 20 amperes for 12 AWG, and 30 amperes for 10 AWG copper; or 15 amperes for 12 AWG and 25 amperes for 10 AWG aluminum and copper-clad aluminum.

* For dry locations only. See 75° column for wet locations.

Table 310-24. Ampacities of Three Insulated Conductors, Rated 0-2000 Volts, Within an Overall Covering (Three Conductor Cable), in Conduit in Free Air Based on Ambient Air Temperature of 40°C

Size	Temperature Rating of Conductor. See Table 310-13.					
	60°C	75°C	90°C	60°C	75°C	90°C
AWG MCM	TYPES †RHW, †T, †TW	TYPES †RH, †RHW, †RUH, †THW, †THWN, †XHHW*, †ZW	TYPES †THHN, †RHH, †XHHW*	TYPES †RHH, †T, †TW	TYPES †RH, †RHW, †RUH, †THW, †THWN, †XHHW	TYPES †THHN, †RHH, †XHHW*
	COPPER			ALUMINUM OR COPPER-CLAD ALUMINUM		
14	16†	21†	24†	....	....	....
12	21†	27†	31†	17†	21†	24†
10	28†	35†	40†	21†	27†	30†
8	35	45	52	27	35	41
6	46	59	69	36	46	53
4	61	78	91	47	61	71
3	71	92	107	56	72	84
2	81	105	123	64	82	96
1	94	121	141	73	94	110
0	110	143	166	86	111	130
00	126	163	190	99	127	149
000	144	186	218	113	146	170
0000	169	219	255	133	171	200
250	187	241	282	147	189	221
300	209	269	315	165	212	248
350	230	297	348	182	235	274
400	247	319	374	197	254	296
500	280	363	425	226	291	341
600	305	396	465	250	322	377
700	330	429	504	273	353	414
750	342	445	524	285	369	432
800	350	456	537	294	381	446
900	365	477	564	313	405	475
1000	381	499	590	331	429	504

Ambient Temp. °C	For ambient temperatures other than 40°C multiply the ampacities shown above by the appropriate factor shown below.					
21-25	1.32	1.20	1.14	1.32	1.20	1.14
26-30	1.22	1.13	1.10	1.22	1.13	1.10
31-35	1.12	1.07	1.05	1.12	1.07	1.05
36-40	1.00	1.00	1.00	1.00	1.00	1.00
41-45	.87	.93	.95	.87	.93	.95
46-50	.71	.85	.89	.71	.85	.89
51-55	.50	.76	.84	.50	.76	.84
56-60	....	.65	.77	....	.65	.77
61-70	....	.38	.63	....	.38	.63
71-80	....	....	.45	....	....	.45

The overcurrent protection for conductor types marked with an obelisk (†) shall not exceed 15 amperes for 14 AWG, 20 amperes for 12 AWG, and 30 amperes for 10 AWG copper; or 15 amperes for 12 AWG and 25 amperes for 10 AWG aluminum and copper-clad aluminum.

* For dry locations only. See 75° column for wet locations.

Table 310-25. Ampacities of Single Insulated Conductors, Rated 0-2000 Volts, in Nonmagnetic Underground Raceways (One Conductor per Raceway) Based on Ambient Earth Temperature of 20°C, Raceway Arrangement as per Figure 310-1, 100 Percent Load Factor, Thermal Resistance (RHO) of 90, Conductor Temperature 75°C

Size	3 Raceways (Fig. 310-1 Detail 2)	6 Raceways (Fig. 310-1 Detail 3)	9 Raceways (Fig. 310-1 Detail 4)	3 Raceways (Fig. 310-1 Detail 2)	6 Raceways (Fig. 310-1 Detail 3)	9 Raceways (Fig. 310-1 Detail 4)
MCM	TYPES RHW, THW, THWN, XHHW, USE	TYPES RHW, THW, THWN, XHHW, USE	TYPES RHW, THW, THWN, XHHW, USE	TYPES RHW, THW, THWN, XHHW, USE	TYPES RHW, THW, THWN, XHHW, USE	TYPES RHW, THW, THWN, XHHW, USE
	COPPER			ALUMINUM OR COPPER-CLAD ALUMINUM		
250	344	295	273	269	230	213
350	418	355	328	327	277	256
500	511	431	397	401	337	311
750	640	534	490	505	421	387
1000	745	617	566	593	491	450
1250	832	686	628	668	551	504
1500	907	744	680	736	604	552
1750	970	793	723	796	651	594
2000	1027	836	762	850	693	631

Ambient Temp. °C	For ambient temperatures other than 20°C multiply the ampacities shown above by the appropriate factor shown below.					
6-10	1.09	1.09	1.09	1.09	1.09	1.09
11-15	1.04	1.04	1.04	1.04	1.04	1.04
16-20	1.00	1.00	1.00	1.00	1.00	1.00
21-25	.95	.95	.95	.95	.95	.95
26-30	.90	.90	.90	.90	.90	.90

**Table 310-26.   Ampacities of Three Insulated Conductors,
Rated 0-2000 Volts, Within an Overall Covering (Three Conductor Cable)
in Underground Raceways (One Cable per Raceway)
Based on Ambient Earth Temperature of 20°C,
Raceway Arrangement as per Figure 310-1, 100 Percent Load Factor,
Thermal Resistance (RHO) of 90, Conductor Temperature 75°C**

Size	1 Raceway (Fig. 310-1 Detail 1)	3 Raceways (Fig. 310-1 Detail 2)	6 Raceways (Fig. 310-1 Detail 3)	1 Raceway (Fig. 310-1 Detail 1)	3 Raceways (Fig. 310-1 Detail 2)	6 Raceways (Fig. 310-1 Detail 3)
AWG MCM	TYPES RHW, THW, THWN, XHHW, USE	TYPES RHW, THW, THWN, XHHW, USE	TYPES RHW, THW, THWN, XHHW, USE	TYPES RHW, THW, THWN, XHHW, USE	TYPES RHW, THW, THWN, XHHW, USE	TYPES RHW, THW, THWN, XHHW, USE
	COPPER			ALUMINUM OR COPPER-CLAD ALUMINUM		
8	54	48	42	42	37	32
6	71	63	54	55	49	42
4	93	81	69	72	63	54
2	121	105	89	94	82	70
1	140	121	102	109	94	79
0	160	137	116	125	107	90
00	183	156	131	143	122	102
000	210	178	148	164	139	116
0000	240	202	168	187	158	131
250	265	222	184	207	174	144
350	321	267	219	252	209	172
500	389	320	261	308	254	207
750	478	388	314	386	314	254
1000	539	435	351	447	361	291

Ambient Temp. °C	For ambient temperatures other than 20°C multiply the ampacities shown above by the appropriate factor shown below.					
6-10	1.09	1.09	1.09	1.09	1.09	1.09
11-15	1.04	1.04	1.04	1.04	1.04	1.04
16-20	1.00	1.00	1.00	1.00	1.00	1.00
21-25	.95	.95	.95	.95	.95	.95
26-30	.90	.90	.90	.90	.90	.90

Table 310-27. Ampacities of Three Single Insulated Conductors, Rated 0-2000 Volts, in Underground Raceways
(Three Conductors per Raceway)
Based on Ambient Earth Temperature of 20°C,
Raceway Arrangement per Figure 310-1, 100 Percent Load Factor,
Thermal Resistance (RHO) of 90, Conductor Temperature 75°C

Size	1 Raceway (Fig. 310-1 Detail 1)	3 Raceways (Fig. 310-1 Detail 2)	6 Raceways (Fig. 310-1 Detail 3)	1 Raceway (Fig. 310-1 Detail 1)	3 Raceways (Fig. 310-1 Detail 2)	6 Raceways (Fig. 310-1 Detail 3)
AWG / MCM	TYPES †RHW, †THW, †THWN, †XHHW, †USE	TYPES †RHW, †THW, †THWN, †XHHW, †USE	TYPES †RHW, †THW, †THWN, †XHHW, †USE	TYPES †RHW, †THW, †THWN, †XHHW, †USE	TYPES †RHW, †THW, †THWN, †XHHW, †USE	TYPES †RHW, †THW, †THWN, †XHHW, †USE
	COPPER			ALUMINUM OR COPPER-CLAD ALUMINUM		
12	36†	31†	24†	28†	22†	18†
10	46†	41†	32†	36†	31†	25†
8	58	51	44	45	40	34
6	77	67	56	60	52	44
4	100	86	73	78	67	57
3	116	99	83	91	77	65
2	132	112	93	103	87	73
1	153	128	106	119	100	83
0	175	146	121	136	114	94
00	200	166	136	156	130	106
000	228	189	154	178	147	121
0000	263	215	175	205	168	137
250	290	236	192	227	185	150
300	321	260	210	252	204	165
350	351	283	228	276	222	179
400	376	302	243	297	238	191
500	427	341	273	338	.270	216
600	468	371	296	373	296	236
700	509	402	319	408	321	255
750	529	417	330	425	334	265
800	544	428	338	439	344	273
900	575	450	355	466	365	288
1000	605	472	372	494	385	304

Ambient Temp. °C	For ambient temperatures other than 20°C multiply the ampacities shown above by the appropriate factor shown below.					
6-10	1.09	1.09	1.09	1.09	1.09	1.09
11-15	1.04	1.04	1.04	1.04	1.04	1.04
16-20	1.00	1.00	1.00	1.00	1.00	1.00
21-25	.95	.95	.95	.95	.95	.95
26-30	.90	.90	.90	.90	.90	.90

The overcurrent protection for conductor types marked with an obelisk (†) shall not exceed 20 amperes for 12 AWG and 30 amperes for 10 AWG copper; or 15 amperes for 12 AWG and 25 amperes for 10 AWG aluminum and copper-clad aluminum.

Table 310-28.   Ampacities of Two or Three Insulated Conductors,
Rated 0-2000 Volts, Cabled Within an Overall
(Two or Three Conductor) Covering Directly Buried in Earth
Based on Ambient Earth Temperature of 20°C,
Arrangement per Figure 310-1, 100 Percent Load Factor,
Thermal Resistance (RHO) of 90

Size	1 Cable (Fig. 310-1 Detail 5)		2 Cables (Fig. 310-1 Detail 6)		1 Cable (Fig. 310-1 Detail 5)		2 Cables (Fig. 310-1 Detail 3)	
	60°C	75°C	60°C	75°C	60°C	75°C	60°C	75°C
	TYPES		TYPES		TYPES		TYPES	
AWG MCM	†UF	†RHW, †THW, †THWN, †XHHW, †USE	†UF	†RHW, †THW, †THWN, †XHHW, †USE	†UF	†RHW, †THW, †THWN, †USE	†UF	†RHW, †THW, †THWN, †XHHW, †USE
	COPPER				ALUMINUM OR COPPER-CLAD ALUMINUM			
12	38†	43†	34†	41†	30†	34†	26†	32†
10	47†	56†	43†	52†	38†	45†	34†	41†
8	64	75	60	70	51	59	47	55
6	85	100	81	95	68	75	60	70
4	107	125	100	117	83	97	78	91
2	137	161	128	150	107	126	110	117
1	155	182	145	170	121	142	113	132
0	177	208	165	193	138	162	129	151
00	201	236	188	220	157	184	146	171
000	229	269	213	250	179	210	166	195
0000	259	304	241	282	203	238	188	220
250		333		308		261		241
350		401		370		315		290
500		481		442		381		350
750		585		535		473		433
1000		657		600		545		497

Ambient Temp. °C	For ambient temperatures other than 20°C multiply the ampacities shown above by the appropriate factor shown below.							
6-10	1.12	1.09	1.12	1.09	1.12	1.09	1.12	1.09
11-15	1.06	1.04	1.06	1.04	1.06	1.04	1.06	1.04
16-20	1.00	1.00	1.00	1.00	1.00	1.00	1.00	1.00
21-25	.94	.95	.94	.95	.94	.95	.94	.95
26-30	.87	.90	.87	.90	.87	.90	.87	.90

The overcurrent protection for conductor types marked with an obelisk (†) shall not exceed 20 amperes for 12 AWG and 30 amperes for 10 AWG copper; or 15 amperes for 12 AWG and 25 amperes for 10 AWG aluminum and copper-clad aluminum.

Table 310-29. Ampacities of Three Triplexed Single Insulated Conductors, Rated 0-2000 Volts, Directly Buried in Earth Based on Ambient Earth Temperature of 20°C, Arrangement per Figure 310-1, 100 Percent Load Factor, Thermal Resistance (RHO) of 90

Size	See Fig. 310-1 Detail 7		See Fig. 310-1 Detail 8		See Fig. 310-1 Detail 7		See Fig. 310-1 Detail 8	
	60°C	75°C	60°C	75°C	60°C	75°C	60°C	75°C
AWG	TYPES		TYPES		TYPES		TYPES	
MCM	†UF	†USE	†UF	†USE	†UF	†USE	†UF	†USE
	COPPER				ALUMINUM OR COPPER-CLAD ALUMINUM			
12	41†	48†	39†	46†	32†	38†	31†	36†
10	54†	63†	50†	59†	42†	49†	39†	46†
8	72	84	66	77	55	65	51	60
6	91	107	84	99	72	84	66	77
4	119	139	109	128	92	108	85	100
2	153	179	140	164	119	139	109	128
1	173	203	159	186	135	158	124	145
0	197	231	181	212	154	180	141	165
00	223	262	205	240	175	205	159	187
000	254	298	232	272	199	233	181	212
0000	289	339	263	308	226	265	206	241
250		370		336		289		263
350		445		403		349		316
500		536		483		424		382
750		654		587		525		471
1000		744		665		608		544

Ambient Temp. °C	For ambient temperatures other than 20°C multiply the ampacities shown above by the appropriate factor shown below.							
6-10	1.12	1.09	1.12	1.09	1.12	1.09	1.12	1.09
11-15	1.06	1.04	1.06	1.04	1.06	1.04	1.06	1.04
16-20	1.00	1.00	1.00	1.00	1.00	1.00	1.00	1.00
21-25	.94	.95	.94	.95	.94	.95	.94	.95
26-30	.87	.90	.87	.90	.87	.90	.87	.90

The overcurrent protection for conductor types marked with an obelisk (†) shall not exceed 20 amperes for 12 AWG and 30 amperes for 10 AWG copper; or 15 amperes for 12 AWG and 25 amperes for 10 AWG aluminum and copper-clad aluminum.

**Table 310-30.   Ampacities of Three Single Insulated Conductors,
Rated 0-2000 Volts, Directly Buried in Earth
Based on Ambient Earth Temperature of 20°C,
Arrangement per Figure 310-1, 100 Percent Load Factor,
Thermal Resistance (RHO) of 90**

Size	See Fig. 310-1 Detail 9		See Fig. 310-1 Detail 10		See Fig. 310-1 Detail 9		See Fig. 310-1 Detail 10	
	60°C	75°C	60°C	75°C	60°C	75°C	60°C	75°C
AWG MCM	TYPES		TYPES		TYPES		TYPES	
	UF	USE	UF	USE	UF	USE	UF	USE
	COPPER				ALUMINUM OR COPPER-CLAD ALUMINUM			
8	84		78		66		61	
6	107		101		84		78	
4	139		130		108		101	
2	178		165		139		129	
1	201		187		157		146	
0	230		212		179		165	
00	261		241		204		188	
000	297		274		232		213	
0000	336		309		262		241	
250		429		394		335		308
350		516		474		403		370
500		626		572		490		448
750		767		700		605		552
1000		887		808		706		642
1250		979		891		787		716
1500		1063		965		862		783
1750		1133		1027		930		843
2000		1195		1082		990		897

Ambient Temp. °C	For ambient temperatures other than 20°C multiply the ampacities shown above by the appropriate factor shown below.							
6-10	1.12	1.09	1.12	1.09	1.12	1.09	1.12	1.09
11-15	1.06	1.04	1.06	1.04	1.06	1.04	1.06	1.04
16-20	1.00	1.00	1.00	1.00	1.00	1.00	1.00	1.00
21-25	.94	.95	.94	.95	.94	.95	.94	.95
26-30	.87	.90	.87	.90	.87	.90	.87	.90

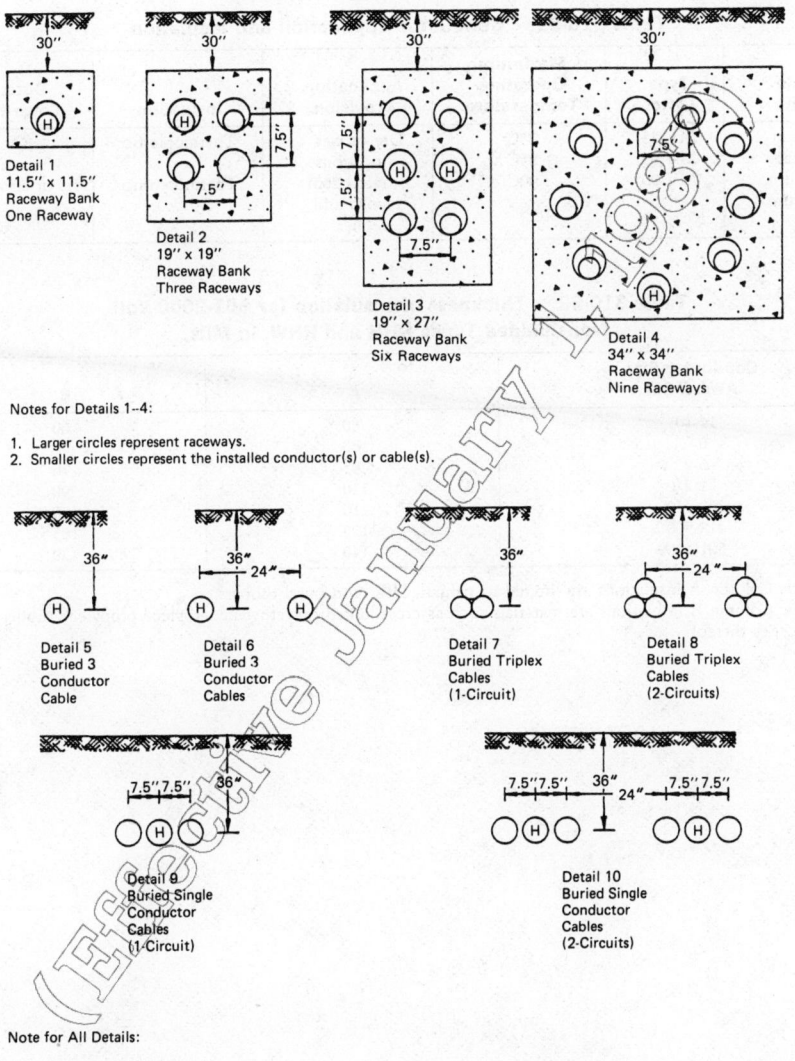

Detail 1
11.5″ x 11.5″
Raceway Bank
One Raceway

Detail 2
19″ x 19″
Raceway Bank
Three Raceways

Detail 3
19″ x 27″
Raceway Bank
Six Raceways

Detail 4
34″ x 34″
Raceway Bank
Nine Raceways

Notes for Details 1–4:

1. Larger circles represent raceways.
2. Smaller circles represent the installed conductor(s) or cable(s).

Detail 5
Buried 3
Conductor
Cable

Detail 6
Buried 3
Conductor
Cables

Detail 7
Buried Triplex
Cables
(1-Circuit)

Detail 8
Buried Triplex
Cables
(2-Circuits)

Detail 9
Buried Single
Conductor
Cables
(1-Circuit)

Detail 10
Buried Single
Conductor
Cables
(2-Circuits)

Note for All Details:

1. H indicates the hottest cable.

Figure 310-1 Cable Installation Dimensions

Table 310-61.   Conductor Application and Insulation

Trade Name	Type Letter	Maximum Operating Temperature	Application Provision	Insulation	Outer Covering
Medium voltage solid dielectric	MV-75 MV-85 MV-90	75C 85C 90C	Dry or wet locations rated 2001 volts and higher	Thermoplastic or Thermosetting	Jacket, Sheath or Armor

Table 310-62.   Thickness of Insulation for 601-2000 Volt Nonshielded Types RHH and RHW, in Mils

Conductor Size AWG-MCM	A	B
14-10	80	60
8	80	70
6-2	95	70
1-2/0	110	90
3/0-4/0	110	90
213-500	125	105
501-1000	140	120

Note: Column A insulations are limited to natural, SBR, and butyl rubbers.

Note: Column B insulations are materials such as cross-linked polyethylene, ethylene propylene rubber, and composites thereof.

Table 310-63. Thickness of Insulation and Jacket for Nonshielded Solid Dielectric Insulated Conductors Rated 2001 to 8000 Volts, in Mils

Conductor Size AWG-MCM	2001-5000 Volts						5001-8000 Volts 100 Percent Insulation Level Wet or Dry Locations		
	Dry Locations Single Conductor			Wet or Dry Locations					
	Without Jacket	With Jacket		Single Conductor		Multi-Conductor*	Single Conductor		Multi-Conductor*
	Insulation	Insulation	Jacket	Insulation	Jacket	Insulation	Insulation	Jacket	Insulation
8	110	90	30	125	80	90	180	80	180
6	110	90	30	125	80	90	180	80	180
4-2	110	90	45	125	80	90	180	95	180
1-2/0	110	90	45	125	80	90	180	95	180
3/0-4/0	110	90	65	125	95	90	180	110	180
213-500	120	90	65	140	110	90	210	110	210
501-750	130	90	65	155	125	90	235	125	235
751-1000	130	90	65	155	125	90	250	140	250

* Note: Under a common overall covering such as a jacket, sheath or armor.

Table 310-64. Thickness of Insulation for Shielded Solid Dielectric Insulated Conductors Rated 2001 to 35,000 Volts, in Mils

Conductor Size AWG-MCM	2001-5000 Volts	5001-8000		8001-15,000		15,001-25,000		25,001-28,000	28,001-35,000
		100* Per-cent Insulation level	133* Per-cent Insulation level	100* Per-cent insulation level	133* Per-cent insulation level	100* Per-cent insulation level	133* Per-cent insulation level	100* Per-cent insulation level	100* Per-cent insulation level
8	90	—	—	—	—	—	—	—	—
6-4	90	115	140	—	—	—	—	—	—
2	90	115	140	175	—	—	—	—	—
1	90	115	140	175	215	260	345	280	—
1/0-1000	90	115	140	175	215	260	345	280	345

*Definitions:

100 Percent Insulation Level. Cables in this category shall be permitted to be applied where the system is provided with relay protection such that ground faults will be cleared as rapidly as possible, but in any case within 1 minute. While these cables are applicable to the great majority of cable installations which are on grounded systems, they shall be permitted to be used also on other systems for which the application of cables is acceptable provided the above clearing requirements are met in completely de-energizing the faulted section.

133 Percent Insulation Level. This insulation level corresponds to that formerly designated for ungrounded systems. Cables in this category shall be permitted to be applied in situations where the clearing time requirements of the 100 percent level category cannot be met, and yet there is adequate assurance that the faulted section will be de-energized in a time not exceeding 1 hour. Also they shall be permitted to be used when additional insulation strength over the 100 percent level category is desirable.

Table 310-65. Thickness of Varnished-Cambric Insulation for Single-Conductor Cable, in Mils

Conductor Size AWG or MCM	For Voltages Not Exceeding				
	1000	2000	3000	4000	5000
14	60	—	—	—	—
12	60	80	—	—	—
10	60	80	95	—	—
8-2	60	80	95	110	140
1-4/0	80	95	95	110	140
213-500	95	95	110	125	155
501-1000	110	110	110	125	155
1001-2000	125	125	125	140	155

Table 310-66. Thickness of Varnished-Cambric Insulation for Multiconductor Cable, in Mils

Conductor Size AWG or MCM	For Voltages Not Exceeding									
	1000		2000		3000		4000		5000	
	C	B	C	B	C	B	C	B	C	B
14	60	0	—	—	—	—	—	—	—	—
12	60	0	80	0	—	—	—	—	—	—
10	60	0	80	0	80	30	—	—	—	—
8-2	60	0	80	0	80	30	95	45	95	60
1-4/0	80	0	95	0	95	30	95	45	95	60
213-500	95	0	95	0	95	30	95	45	110	60
501-1000	95	30	95	30	95	45	95	60	110	60
1001-2000	110	30	110	30	110	45	110	60	110	80

The thickness given in columns headed "C" are for the insulation on the individual conductors. Those given in the columns headed "B" are for the thickness of the overall belt of insulation.

Table 310-67

Thickness of Asbestos and Varnished-Cambric Insulation for Single-Conductor Cable, Types AVA, AVB, and AVL, in Mils

Conductor AWG or MCM	Asbestos 1st Wall	Varnished Cambric						Asbestos 2nd Wall
	1000-5000	For Voltages Not Exceeding						1000-5000
		1000	2000	3000	4000	5000		
14-2	15	45	60	80	100	120		25
1-4/0	20	45	60	80	100	120		30
213-500	25	45	60	80	100	120		40
501-1000	30	45	60	80	100	120		40
1001-2000	30	55	75	95	115	140		50

Table 310-69

Ampacities for Insulated Single Copper Conductor Isolated in Air

Based on Conductor Temperature of 90°C and Ambient Air Temperature of 40°C

Conductor Size AWG-MCM	2001-5000 Volts Ampacity	5001-15,000 Volts Ampacity	15,001-35,000 Volts Ampacity
8	83	—	—
6	110	110	—
4	145	150	—
2	190	195	—
1	225	225	225
1/0	260	260	260
2/0	300	300	300
3/0	345	345	345
4/0	400	400	395
250	445	445	440
350	550	550	545
500	695	685	680
750	900	885	870
1000	1075	1060	1040
1250	1230	1210	1185
1500	1365	1345	1315
1750	1495	1470	1430
2000	1605	1575	1535

Table 310-70
Ampacities for Insulated Single Aluminum Conductor Isolated in Air
Based on Conductor Temperature of 90°C and Ambient Air Temperature of 40°C

Conductor Size AWG-MCM	2001-5000 Volts Ampacity	5001-15,000 Volts Ampacity	15,001-35,000 Volts Ampacity
'8	64	—	—
6	85	87	—
4	115	115	—
2	150	150	—
1	175	175	175
1/0	200	200	200
2/0	230	235	230
3/0	270	270	270
4/0	310	310	310
250	345	345	345
350	430	430	430
500	545	535	530
750	710	700	685
1000	855	840	825
1250	980	970	950
1500	1105	1085	1060
1750	1215	1195	1165
2000	1320	1295	1265

Table 310-71
Ampacities of an Insulated Three Conductor Copper Cable Isolated in Air
Based on Conductor Temperature of 90°C and Ambient Air Temperature of 40°C

Conductor Size AWG-MCM	2001-5000 Volts Ampacity	5001-35,000 Volts Ampacity
8	59	—
6	79	93
4	105	120
2	140	165
1	160	185
1/0	185	215
2/0	215	245
3/0	250	285
4/0	285	325
250	320	360
350	395	435
500	485	535
750	615	670
1000	705	770

Table 310-72

Ampacities of an Insulated Three Conductor
Aluminum Cable Isolated in Air

Based on Conductor Temperature of 90°C and Ambient
Air Temperature of 40°C

Conductor Size AWG-MCM	2001-5000 Volts Ampacity	5001-35,000 Volts Ampacity
8	46	—
6	61	72
4	81	95
2	110	125
1	125	145
1/0	145	170
2/0	170	190
3/0	195	220
4/0	225	255
250	250	280
350	310	345
500	385	425
750	495	540
1000	585	635

Table 310-73

Ampacities of an Insulated Triplexed or Three Single
Conductor Copper Cables in Isolated Conduit in Air

Based on Conductor Temperature of 90°C and Ambient
Air Temperature of 40°C

Conductor Size AWG-MCM	2001-5000 Volts Ampacity	5001-35,000 Volts Ampacity
8	55	—
6	75	83
4	97	110
2	130	150
1	155	170
1/0	180	195
2/0	205	225
3/0	240	260
4/0	280	295
250	315	330
350	385	395
500	475	480
750	600	585
1000	690	675

Table 310-74

Ampacities of Insulated Triplexed or Three Single
Conductor Aluminum Cables in Isolated Conduit in Air

Based on Conductor Temperature of 90°C and Ambient
Air Temperature of 40°C

Conductor Size AWG-MCM	2001-5000 Volts Ampacity	5001-35,000 Volts Ampacity
8	43	—
6	58	65
4	76	84
2	100	115
1	120	130
1/0	140	150
2/0	160	175
3/0	190	200
4/0	215	230
250	250	255
350	305	310
500	380	385
750	490	485
1000	580	565

Table 310-75

Ampacities of an Insulated Three Conductor
Copper Cable in Isolated Conduit in Air

Based on Conductor Temperature of 90°C and Ambient
Air Temperature of 40°C

Conductor Size AWG-MCM	2001-5000 Volts Ampacity	5001-35,000 Volts Ampacity
8	52	—
6	69	83
4	91	105
2	125	145
1	140	165
1/0	165	195
2/0	190	220
3/0	220	250
4/0	255	290
250	280	315
350	350	385
500	425	470
750	525	570
1000	590	650

Table 310-76

**Ampacities of an Insulated Three Conductor
Aluminum Cable in Isolated Conduit in Air**

**Based on Conductor Temperature of 90°C and Ambient
Air Temperature of 40°C**

Conductor Size AWG-MCM	2001-5000 Volts Ampacity	5001-35,000 Volts Ampacity
8	41	—
6	53	64
4	71	84
2	96	115
1	110	130
1/0	130	150
2/0	150	170
3/0	170	195
4/0	200	225
250	220	250
350	275	305
500	340	380
750	430	470
1000	505	550

Table 310-77
Ampacities of an Insulated Triplexed or Three Single Conductor Copper Cables in Underground Raceways

Based on Conductor Temperature of 90°C, Ambient Earth Temperature of 20°C, 100% Load Factor and Thermal Resistance (RHO) of 90

One Circuit Size AWG-MCM	2001-5000 Volts Ampacity	5001-35,000 Volts Ampacity
8	64	—
6	85	90
4	110	115
2	145	155
1	170	175
1/0	195	200
2/0	220	230
3/0	250	260
4/0	290	295
250	320	325
350	385	390
500	470	465
750	585	565
1000	670	640
Three Circuit Size		
8	56	—
6	73	77
4	95	99
2	125	130
1	140	145
1/0	160	165
2/0	185	185
3/0	210	210
4/0	235	240
250	260	260
350	315	310
500	375	370
750	460	440
1000	525	495
Six Circuit Size		
8	48	—
6	62	64
4	80	82
2	105	105
1	115	120
1/0	135	135
2/0	150	150
3/0	170	170
4/0	195	190
250	210	210
350	250	245
500	300	290
750	365	350
1000	410	390

Table 310-78
Ampacities of an Insulated Triplexed or Three Single Conductor Aluminum Cables in Underground Raceways

Based on Conductor Temperature of 90°C, Ambient Earth Temperature of 20°C, 100% Load Factor and Thermal Resistance (RHO) of 90

One Circuit Size AWG-MCM	2001-5000 Volts Ampacity	5001-35,000 Volts Ampacity
8	50	—
6	66	70
4	86	91
2	115	120
1	130	135
1/0	150	155
2/0	170	175
3/0	195	200
4/0	225	230
250	250	250
350	305	305
500	370	370
750	470	455
1000	545	525
Three Circuit Size		
8	44	—
6	57	60
4	74	77
2	96	100
1	110	110
1/0	125	125
2/0	145	145
3/0	160	165
4/0	185	185
250	205	200
350	245	245
500	295	290
750	370	355
1000	425	405
Six Circuit Size		
8	38	—
6	48	50
4	62	64
2	80	80
1	91	90
1/0	105	105
2/0	115	115
3/0	135	130
4/0	150	150
250	165	165
350	195	195
500	240	230
750	290	280
1000	335	320

ARTICLE 310—CONDUCTORS FOR GENERAL WIRING

Table 310-79
Ampacities of an Insulated Three Conductor Copper Cable in Underground Raceways
Based on Conductor Temperature of 90°C, Ambient Earth Temperature of 20°C, 100% Load Factor and Thermal Resistance (RHO) of 90

One Circuit Size AWG-MCM	2001-5000 Volts Ampacity	5001-35,000 Volts Ampacity
8	59	—
6	78	88
4	100	115
2	135	150
1	155	170
1/0	175	195
2/0	200	220
3/0	230	250
4/0	265	285
250	290	310
350	355	375
500	430	450
750	530	545
1000	600	615
Three Circuit Size		
8	53	—
6	69	75
4	89	97
2	115	125
1	135	140
1/0	150	160
2/0	170	185
3/0	195	205
4/0	225	230
250	245	255
350	295	305
500	355	360
750	430	430
1000	485	485
Six Circuit Size		
8	46	—
6	60	63
4	77	81
2	98	105
1	110	115
1/0	125	130
2/0	145	150
3/0	165	170
4/0	185	190
250	200	205
350	240	245
500	290	290
750	350	340
1000	390	380

Table 310-80
Ampacities of an Insulated Three Conductor Aluminum Cable in Underground Raceways
Based on Conductor Temperature of 90°C, Ambient Earth Temperature of 20°C, 100% Load Factor and Thermal Resistance (RHO) of 90

One Circuit Size AWG-MCM	2001-5000 Volts Ampacity	5001-35,000 Volts Ampacity
8	46	—
6	61	69
4	80	89
2	105	115
1	120	135
1/0	140	150
2/0	160	170
3/0	180	195
4/0	205	220
250	230	245
350	280	295
500	340	355
750	425	440
1000	495	510
Three Circuit Size		
8	41	—
6	54	59
4	70	75
2	90	100
1	105	110
1/0	120	125
2/0	135	140
3/0	155	160
4/0	175	180
250	190	200
350	230	240
500	280	285
750	345	350
1000	400	400
Six Circuit Size		
8	36	—
6	46	49
4	60	63
2	77	80
1	87	90
1/0	99	105
2/0	110	115
3/0	130	130
4/0	145	150
250	160	160
350	190	190
500	230	230
750	280	275
1000	320	315

Table 310-81
Ampacities for an Insulated Single Copper Conductor, Direct Buried

Based on Conductor Temperature of 90°C, Ambient Earth
Temperature of 20°C, 100% Load Factor, Thermal Resistance (RHO)
of 90, and 7½ Inch Spacing Between Conductor Center Lines,
and 24 Inch Spacing Between Circuits

Conductor Size AWG-MCM	2001-5000 Volts Ampacity	5001-35,000 Volts Ampacity
One Circuit-3 Conductors		
8	110	—
6	140	130
4	180	170
2	230	210
1	260	240
1/0	295	275
2/0	335	310
3/0	385	355
4/0	435	405
250	470	440
350	570	535
500	690	650
750	845	805
1000	980	930
Two Circuits-6 Conductors		
8	100	—
6	130	120
4	165	160
2	215	195
1	240	225
1/0	275	255
2/0	310	290
3/0	355	330
4/0	400	375
250	435	410
350	520	495
500	630	600
750	775	740
1000	890	855

For SI units: one inch = 25.4 millimeters.

Table 310-82
Ampacities of an Insulated Single Aluminum Conductor, Direct Buried

Based on Conductor Temperature of 90°C, Ambient Earth
Temperature of 20°C, 100% Load Factor, Thermal Resistance (RHO)
of 90, and 7½ Inch Spacing Between Conductor Center Lines,
and 24 Inch Spacing Between Circuits

Conductor Size AWG-MCM	2001-5000 Volts Ampacity	5001-35,000 Volts Ampacity
One Circuit-3 Conductors		
8	85	—
6	110	100
4	140	130
2	180	165
1	205	185
1/0	230	215
2/0	265	245
3/0	300	275
4/0	340	315
250	370	345
350	445	415
500	540	510
750	665	635
1000	780	740
Two Circuits-6 Conductors		
8	80	—
6	100	95
4	130	125
2	165	155
1	190	175
1/0	215	200
2/0	245	225
3/0	275	255
4/0	310	290
250	340	320
350	410	385
500	495	470
750	610	580
1000	710	680

For SI units: one inch = 25.4 millimeters.

Table 310-83

Ampacities of an Insulated Three Conductor Copper Cable, Direct Buried

Based on Conductor Temperature of 90°C, Ambient Earth Temperature of 20°C, 100% Load Factor, Thermal Resistance (RHO) of 90, and 24 Inch Spacing Between Cable Center Lines

Conductor Size AWG-MCM	2001-5000 Volts Ampacity	5001-35,000 Volts Ampacity
One Circuit		
8	85	—
6	105	115
4	135	145
2	180	185
1	200	210
1/0	230	240
2/0	260	270
3/0	295	305
4/0	335	350
250	365	380
350	440	460
500	530	550
750	650	665
1000	730	750
Two Circuits		
8	80	—
6	100	105
4	130	135
2	165	170
1	185	195
1/0	215	220
2/0	240	250
3/0	275	280
4/0	310	320
250	340	350
350	410	420
500	490	500
750	595	605
1000	665	675

For SI units: one inch = 25.4 millimeters.

Table 310-84

Ampacities of an Insulated Three Conductor
Aluminum Cable, Direct Buried

Based on Conductor Temperature of 90°C, Ambient Earth
Temperature of 20°C, 100% Load Factor, Thermal Resistance (RHO)
of 90, and 24 Inch Spacing Between Cable Center Lines

Conductor Size AWG-MCM	2001-5000 Volts Ampacity	5001-35,000 Volts Ampacity
One Circuit		
8	65	—
6	80	90
4	105	115
2	140	145
1	155	165
1/0	180	185
2/0	205	210
3/0	230	240
4/0	260	270
250	285	300
350	345	360
500	420	435
750	520	540
1000	600	620
Two Circuits		
8	60	—
6	75	80
4	100	105
2	130	135
1	145	150
1/0	165	170
2/0	190	195
3/0	215	220
4/0	245	250
250	265	275
350	320	330
500	385	395
750	480	485
1000	550	560

For SI units: one inch = 25.4 millimeters.

Notes To Tables 310-69 Through 310-84

Ampacities calculated in accordance with the following Notes 1 and 2 will require reference to AIEE/IPCEA "Power Cable Ampacities" Vols. I and II (IPCEA Pub. No. P-46-426) and "The References" therein for availability of all factors and constants.

1. *Ambients Not in Tables.* Ampacities at ambient temperatures other than those shown in the tables shall be determined by means of the following formula:

$$I_2 = I_1 \sqrt{\frac{TC - TA_2 - DELTA\ TD}{TC - TA_1 - DELTA\ TD}}$$

Where,

I_1 = Ampacity from tables at ambient TA_1
I_2 = Ampacity at desired ambient TA_2
TC = Conductor temperature in degrees C
TA_1 = Surrounding ambient from tables in degrees C
TA_2 = Desired ambient in degrees C
DELTA TD = Dielectric loss temperature rise

2. *Grounded Shields.* Ampacities shown in Tables 310-69, 310-70, 310-81 and 310-82 are for cable with shields grounded at one point only. When shields are grounded at more than one point, ampacities shall be adjusted to take into consideration the heating due to shield currents.

3. *Duct Bank Configuration.* Ampacities shown in Tables 310-77, 310-78, 310-79 and 310-84 shall apply only when the cables are located in the outer ducts of the duct bank. Ampacities for cables located in the inner ducts of the duct bank will have to be determined by special calculations.

ARTICLE 318 — CABLE TRAYS

Contents

318-1. Scope. A cable tray system is a unit or assembly of units or sections, and associated fittings, made of metal forming a rigid structural system used to support cables. Flame-retardant nonmetallic materials shall be permitted in corrosive areas and in areas requiring voltage isolation. Cable tray systems include ladders, troughs, channels, solid bottom trays, and other similar structures.

It is not the intent of this article to require that cables be installed in cable tray systems or to recognize the use of all conductors described in Article 310 in cable tray systems for general wiring.

Glass fiber cable trays are often used to support cables between an energized cell in an electrochemical cell room (see Article 668) and the grounded frame of the cell room, to assure voltage isolation.

318-2. Uses Permitted.

(a) Wiring Methods. The following shall be permitted to be installed in cable tray systems under the conditions described in the article for each:

1. Mineral-insulated, metal-sheathed cable (Article 330); 2. armored cable (Article 333); 3. metal-clad cable (Article 334); 4. power-limited tray cable (Section 725-40); 5. nonmetallic-sheathed cable (Article 336); 6. shielded, nonmetallic-sheathed cable (Article 337); 7. multiconductor service-entrance cable (Article 338); 8. multiconductor underground feeder and branch-circuit cable (Article 339); 9. power and control tray cable (Article 340); 10. other factory-assembled, multiconductor control, signal, or power cables, which are specifically approved for installation in cable trays; or 11. any approved conduit or raceway with its contained conductors.

(b) In Industrial Establishments. In industrial establishments only, where conditions of maintenance and supervision assure that only qualified persons will service the installed cable tray system, any of the cables in (1) and (2) below shall be permitted to be installed in ladder, ventilated trough, or 4-inch (102-mm) ventilated channel-type cable trays.

(1) Single Conductor. Single conductor cables shall be 250 MCM or larger and shall be of a type listed for use in cable trays. Where exposed to direct rays of the sun, cables shall be sunlight-resistant.

(2) Multiconductor. Multiconductor cables Type MV (Article 326) where exposed to direct rays of the sun shall be sunlight-resistant.

(c) Equipment Grounding Conductors. Metal in cable trays, as defined in Table 318-6(b) (2), shall be permitted to be used as equipment grounding conductors in commercial and industrial establishments only, where continuous maintenance and supervision assure that only qualified persons will service the installed cable tray system.

The cross-sectional area of the grounding metal is marked on the outer surface of the sidewall of cable trays listed by UL.

(d) Hazardous (Classified) Locations. Cable trays in hazardous (classified) locations shall contain only the cable types permitted in Sections 501-4, 502-4, and 503-3.

318-3. Uses Not Permitted. Cable tray systems shall not be used in hoistways or where subjected to severe physical damage.

318-4. Construction Specifications. Cable trays shall comply with the following:

(a) Strength and Rigidity. Shall have suitable strength and rigidity to provide adequate support for all contained wiring.

(b) Smooth Edges. Shall not present sharp edges, burrs, or projections injurious to the insulation or jackets of the wiring.

(c) Corrosion Protection. Shall be made of corrosion-resistant material or, if made of metal, shall be adequately protected against corrosion.

See Section 318-1 for additional requirements if the material used is other than metal.

(d) Side Rails. Shall have side rails or equivalent structural members.

(e) Fittings. Shall include fittings or other suitable means for changes in direction and elevation of runs.

318-5. Installation.

(a) Complete System. Cable trays shall be installed as a complete system. Field bends or modifications shall be so made that the electrical continuity of the cable tray system and support for the cables shall be maintained.

ARTICLE 318—CABLE TRAYS

Cable tray is to be installed as a complete system, i.e., unconnected sections are not permitted to support conductors, cables, etc. Manufactured sections or field-adapted sections are to be used for angle turns or for changes in elevation.

(b) Completed Before Installation. Each run of cable tray shall be completed before the installation of cables.

(c) Supports. Supports shall be provided to prevent stress on cables where they enter another raceway or enclosure from cable tray systems.

(d) Covers. In portions of runs where additional protection is required, covers or enclosures providing the required protection shall be of a material compatible with the cable tray.

(e) Multiconductor Cables Rated 600 Volts or Less. Multiconductor cables rated 600 volts or less shall be permitted to be installed in the same cable tray.

(f) Cables Rated Over 600 Volts. Cables rated over 600 volts shall not be installed in the same cable tray with cables rated 600 volts or less.

Exception No. 1: Where separated by a solid fixed barrier of a material compatible with the cable tray.

Exception No. 2: Where cables are Type MC.

Figure 318-1. A cable tray installation. The trays are installed as complete systems; any field modifications made must not interfere with the electrical continuity of the system. (*Husky Trough and Ladder*)

(g) Through Partitions and Walls. Cable trays shall be permitted to extend transversely through partitions and walls or vertically through platforms and floors in wet or dry locations where the installations, complete with installed cables, are made in accordance with the requirements of Section 300-21.

See Figure 300-8.

(h) Exposed and Accessible. Cable trays shall be exposed and accessible except as permitted by Section 318-5(g).

(i) Adequate Access. Sufficient space shall be provided and maintained about cable trays to permit adequate access for installing and maintaining the cables.

> No specific clearance distance is given. Sufficient spacing is to be provided for cable installation and maintenance.

318-6. Grounding.

(a) Metallic Cable Trays. Metallic cable trays which support electrical conductors shall be grounded as required for conductor enclosures in Article 250.

> Much the same as the *Code* requires metal raceways and metal enclosures to be grounded, cable trays made of metal must also be grounded.

(b) Steel or Aluminum Cable Tray Systems. Where steel or aluminum cable tray systems are used as equipment grounding conductors, all of the following provisions shall be complied with:

(1) The cable tray sections and fittings shall be identified for grounding purposes.

(2) The minimum cross-sectional area of cable trays shall conform to the requirements in Table 318-6(b)(2).

(3) All cable tray sections and fittings shall be legibly and durably marked to show the cross-sectional area of metal in channel-type cable trays or cable trays of one-piece construction, and the total cross-sectional area of both side rails for ladder or trough-type cable trays.

(4) Cable tray sections, fittings, and connected raceways shall be bonded in accordance with. Section 250-75 using bolted mechanical connectors or bonding jumpers sized and installed in accordance with Section 250-79.

Table 318-6(b) (2)
Metal Area Requirements for Cable Trays
Used as Cable Trays Used as Equipment Grounding Conductors

Ampere Rating or Setting of Largest Automatic Overcurrent Device Protecting Any Circuit in the Cable Tray System	Minimum Cross-Sectional Area of Metal* in Square Inches	
	Steel Cable Trays	Aluminum Cable Trays
0— 60	0.20	0.20
61— 100	0.40	0.20
101— 200	0.70	0.20
201— 400	1.00	0.40
401— 600	1.50**	0.40
601— 1000	—	0.60
1001— 1200	—	1.00
1201— 1600	—	1.50
1601— 2000	—	2.00**

For SI units: one square inch = 645 square millimeters.

* Total cross-sectional area of both side rails for ladder or trough-type cable trays; or the minimum cross-sectional area of metal in channel-type cable trays or cable trays of one-piece construction.

** Steel cable trays shall not be used as equipment grounding conductors for circuits protected above 600 amperes. Aluminum cable trays shall not be used for equipment grounding conductors for circuits protected above 2000 amperes.

318-7. Cable Installation.

(a) Cable Splices. Cable splices made and insulated by approved methods shall be permitted to be located within a cable tray provided they are accessible and do not project above the side rails.

(b) Fastened Securely. In other than horizontal runs, the cables shall be fastened securely to transverse members of the cable trays.

(c) Bushed Conduit. A box shall not be required where cables or conductors are installed in bushed conduit used for support or for protection against physical damage.

(d) Connected in Parallel. Where single conductor cables comprising each phase or neutral of a circuit are connected in parallel as permitted in Section 310-4, the conductors shall be installed in groups consisting of not more than one conductor per phase or neutral, to prevent current unbalance in the paralleled conductors due to inductive reactance.

Single conductors shall be securely bound in circuit groups to prevent excessive movement due to fault-current magnetic forces.

Exception: Where single conductors are cabled together, such as triplexed assemblies.

318-8. Number of Multiconductor Cables, Rated 2000 Volts, Nominal, or Less, in Cable Trays.
The number of multiconductor cables, rated 2000 volts, nominal, or less, permitted in a single cable tray shall not exceed the requirements of this section. The conductor sizes herein apply to both aluminum and copper conductors.

(a) Any Mixture of Cables. Where ladder or ventilated trough cable trays contain multiconductor power or lighting cables, or any mixture of multiconductor power, lighting, control, and signal cables, the maximum number of cables shall conform to the following:

(1) Where all of the cables are 4/0 AWG or larger, the sum of the diameters of all cables shall not exceed the cable tray width, and the cables shall be installed in a single layer.

(2) Where all of the cables are smaller than 4/0 AWG, the sum of the cross-sectional areas of all cables shall not exceed the maximum allowable cable fill area in Column 1 of Table 318-8, for the appropriate cable tray width.

(3) Where 4/0 AWG or larger cables are installed in the same cable tray with cables smaller than 4/0 AWG, the sum of the cross-sectional areas of all cables smaller than 4/0 AWG shall not exceed the maximum allowable fill area resulting from the computation in Column 2 of Table 318-8, for the appropriate cable tray width. The 4/0 AWG and larger cables shall be installed in a single layer and no other cables shall be placed on them.

(b) Multiconductor Control and/or Signal Cables Only. Where a ladder or ventilated trough cable tray, having a usable inside depth of 6 inches (152 mm) or less, contains multiconductor control and/or signal cables only, the sum of the cross-sectional areas of all cables at any cross section shall not exceed 50 percent of the interior cross-sectional area of the cable tray. A depth of 6 inches (152 mm) shall be used to compute the allowable interior cross-sectional area of any cable tray which has a usable inside depth of more than 6 inches (152 mm).

(c) Solid Bottom Cable Trays Containing Any Mixture. Where solid bottom cable trays contain multiconductor power or lighting cables, or any mixture of multiconductor power, lighting, control, and signal cables, the maximum number of cables shall conform to the following:

(1) Where all of the cables are 4/0 AWG or larger, the sum of the diameters of all cables shall not exceed 90 percent of the cable tray width, and the cables shall be installed in a single layer.

(2) Where all of the cables are smaller than 4/0 AWG, the sum of the cross-sectional areas of all cables shall not exceed the maximum allowable cable fill area in Column 3 of Table 318-8, for the appropriate cable tray width.

(3) Where 4/0 AWG or larger cables are installed in the same cable tray with cables smaller than 4/0 AWG, the sum of the cross-sectional areas of all cables smaller than 4/0 AWG shall not exceed the maximum allowable fill area resulting from the computation in Column 4 of Table 318-8, for the appropriate cable tray width. The 4/0 AWG and larger cables shall be installed in a single layer and no other cables shall be placed on them.

(d) Solid Bottom Cable Tray Multiconductor Control and/or Signal Cables Only. Where a solid bottom cable tray, having a usable inside depth of 6 inches (152 mm) or less, contains multiconductor control and/or signal cables only, the sum of the cross-sectional areas of all cables at any cross section shall not exceed 40 percent of the interior cross-sectional area of the cable tray. A depth of 6 inches (152 mm) shall be used to compute the allowable interior cross-sectional area of any cable tray which has a usable inside depth of more than 6 inches (152 mm).

Table 318-8. Allowable Cable Fill Area for Multiconductor Cables in Ladder, Ventilated Trough, or Solid Bottom Cable Trays for Cables Rated 2000 Volts or Less

Inside Width of Cable Tray (Inches)	Maximum Allowable Fill Area in Square Inches for Multiconductor Cables			
	Ladder or Ventilated Trough Cable Trays, Section 318-8(a)		Solid Bottom Cable Trays, Section 318-8(c)	
	Column 1 Applicable for Section 318-8(a) (2) Only (Square Inches)	Column 2* Applicable for Section 318-8(a) (3) Only (Square Inches)	Column 3 Applicable for Section 318-8(c) (2) Only (Square Inches)	Column 4* Applicable for Section 318-8(c) (3) Only (Square Inches)
6	7	7—(1.2 Sd)**	5.5	5.5—Sd**
12	14	14—(1.2 Sd)	11.0	11.0—Sd
18	21	21—(1.2 Sd)	16.5	16.5—Sd
24	28	28—(1.2 Sd)	22.0	22.0—Sd
30	35	35—(1.2 Sd)	27.5	27.5—Sd
36	42	42—(1.2 Sd)	33.0	33.0—Sd

For SI units: one square inch = 645 square millimeters.
* The maximum allowable fill areas in Columns 2 and 4 shall be computed. For example, the maximum allowable fill, in square inches, for a 6-inch (152-mm) wide cable tray in Column 2 shall be: 7 minus (1.2 multiplied by Sd).
** The term Sd in Columns 2 and 4 is equal to the sum of the diameters, in inches, of all 4/0 AWG and larger multiconductor cables in the same cable tray with smaller cables.

(e) Ventilated Channel-type Cable Trays. Where ventilated channel-type cable trays contain multiconductor cables of any type, the combined cross-sectional area of all cables shall not exceed 1.3 square inches (839 sq mm) in 3-inch (76-mm) wide channel trays, or 2.5 square inches (1613 sq mm) in 4-inch (102-mm) wide channel trays.

Exception: Where only one multiconductor cable is installed in a ventilated channel-type tray the cross-sectional area of the cable shall not exceed 2.3 square inches (1484 sq mm) in a 3-inch (76-mm) wide channel tray, or 4.5 square inches (2903 sq mm) in a 4-inch (102-mm) wide channel tray.

Cable trays may be ladder or ventilated trough, solid bottom, ventilated channel type, unventilated, covered, etc., and of various widths and depths. Therefore, inspectors or contractors are not expected to compute the various combinations of cable tray fill in the field. Installation handbooks for cable tray applications are available from various manufacturers.

318-9. Number of Single Conductor Cables, Rated 2000 Volts or Less, in Cable Trays. The number of single conductor cables, nominally rated 2000 volts or less, permitted in a single cable tray section shall not exceed the requirements of this section. The single conductors, or conductor assemblies, shall be evenly distributed across the cable tray. The conductor sizes herein apply to both aluminum and copper conductors.

(a) Ladder or Ventilated Trough Cable Trays. Where ladder or ventilated trough cable trays contain single conductor cables, the maximum number of single conductors shall conform to the following:

(1) Where all of the cables are 1000 MCM or larger, the sum of the diameters of all single conductor cables shall not exceed the cable tray width.

Table 318-9. Allowable Cable Fill Area for Single Conductor Cables in Ladder or Ventilated Trough Cable Trays for Cables Rated 2000 Volts or Less

Inside Width of Cable Tray (Inches)	Maximum Allowable Fill Area in Square Inches for Single Conductor Cables in Ladder or Ventilated Trough Cable Trays	
	Column 1 Applicable for Section 318-9(a) (2) Only (Square Inches)	Column 2* Applicable for Section 318-9(a) (3) Only (Square Inches)
6	6.50	6.50—(1.1 Sd)**
12	13.0	13.0 —(1.1 Sd)
18	19.5	19.5 —(1.1 Sd)
24	26.0	26.0 —(1.1 Sd)
30	32.5	32.5 —(1.1 Sd)
36	39.0	39.0 —(1.1 Sd)

For SI units: one square inch = 645 square millimeters.
* The maximum allowable fill areas in Column 2 shall be computed. For example, the maximum allowable fill, in square inches, for a 6-inch (152-mm) wide cable tray shall be: 6.5 minus (1.1 multiplied by Sd).
** The term Sd in Column 2 is equal to the sum of the diameters, in inches, of all 1000 MCM and larger single conductor cables in the same ladder or ventilated trough cable tray with smaller cables.

(2) Where all of the cables are smaller than 1000 MCM, the sum of the cross-sectional areas of all single conductor cables shall not exceed the maximum allowable cable fill area in Column 1 of Table 318-9, for the appropriate cable tray width.

(3) Where 1000 MCM or larger single conductor cables are installed in the same cable tray with single conductor cables smaller than 1000 MCM, the sum of the cross-sectional areas of all cables smaller than 1000 MCM shall not exceed the maximum allowable fill area resulting from the computation in Column 2 of Table 318-9, for the appropriate cable tray width.

(b) 4-Inch (102-mm) Ventilated Channel-type Cable Trays. Where 4-inch (102-mm) wide ventilated channel-type cable trays contain single conductor cables, the sum of the diameters of all single conductors shall not exceed the inside width of the channel.

318-10. Ampacity of Cables Rated 2000 Volts or Less in Cable Trays. The derating factors of Note 8 to Tables 310-16 through 310-19 do not apply to the ampacity of cables in cable trays.

(a) Multiconductor Cables. The ampacity of multiconductor cables, nominally rated 2000 volts or less, installed according to the requirements of Section 318-8 shall comply with the allowable ampacities of Tables 310-16 and 310-18.

Exception: Where cable trays are continuously covered for more than 6 feet (1.83 m) with solid unventilated covers, not more than 95 percent of the allowable ampacities of Tables 310-16 and 310-18 shall be permitted for multiconductor cables.

(b) Single Conductor Cables. The ampacity of single conductor cables, or single conductors cabled together (triplexed, quadruplexed, etc.), nominally rated 2000 volts or less, shall comply with the following:

(1) Where installed according to the requirements of Section 318-9, the ampacities for 600 MCM and larger single conductor cables in uncovered cable trays shall not exceed 75 percent of the allowable ampacities in Tables 310-17 and 310-19. Where cable trays are continuously covered for more than 6 feet (1.83 m) with solid unventilated covers, the ampacities for 600 MCM and larger cables shall not exceed 70 percent of the allowable ampacities in Tables 310-17 and 310-19.

(2) Where installed according to the requirements of Section 318-9, the ampacities for 250 MCM through 500 MCM single conductor cables in uncovered cable trays shall not exceed 65 percent of the allowable ampacities in Tables 310-17 and 310-19. Where cable trays are continuously covered for more than 6 feet (1.83 m) with solid unventilated covers, the ampacities for 250 MCM through 500 MCM cables shall not exceed 60 percent of the allowable ampacities in Tables 310-17 and 310-19.

(3) Where single conductors are installed in a single layer in uncovered cable trays, with a maintained space of not less than one cable diameter between individual conductors, the ampacity of 250 MCM and larger cables shall not exceed the allowable ampacities in Tables 310-17 and 310-19.

318-11. Number of Type MV and Type MC Cables (2001 Volts or Over) in Cable Trays. The number of cables, nominally rated 2001 volts or over, permitted in a single cable tray shall not exceed the requirements of this section.

The sum of the diameters of single conductor and multiconductor cables shall not exceed the cable tray width, and the cables shall be installed in a single layer. Where single conductor cables are triplexed, quadruplexed, or bound together in circuit groups, the sum of the diameters of the single conductors shall not exceed the cable tray width, and these groups shall be installed in single layer arrangement.

318-12. Ampacity of Type MV and Type MC Cables (2001 Volts or Over) in Cable Trays. The ampacity of cables, rated 2001 volts, nominal, or over, installed according to Section 318-11 shall not exceed the requirements of this section.

(a) Multiconductor Cables (2001 Volts or Over). The ampacity of multiconductor cables shall comply with the allowable ampacities of Tables 310-75 and 310-76.

Exception No. 1: Where cable trays are continuously covered for more than 6 feet (1.83 m) with solid unventilated covers, not more than 95 percent of the allowable ampacities of Tables 310-75 and 310-76 shall be permitted for multiconductor cables.

Exception No. 2: Where multiconductor cables are installed in a single layer in uncovered cable trays, with a maintained spacing of not less than one cable diameter between cables, the ampacity shall not exceed the allowable ampacities of Tables 310-71 and 310-72.

(b) Single Conductor Cables (2001 Volts or Over). The ampacity of single conductor cables, or single conductors cabled together (triplexed, quadruplexed, etc.), shall comply with the following:

(1) The ampacities for 250 MCM and larger single conductor cables in uncovered cable trays shall not exceed 75 percent of the allowable ampacities in Tables 310-69 and 310-70. Where the cable trays are covered for more than 6 feet (1.83 m) with solid unventilated covers, the ampacities for 250 MCM and larger single conductor cables shall not exceed 70 percent of the allowable ampacities in Tables 310-69 and 310-70.

(2) Where single conductor cables are installed in a single layer in uncovered cable trays, with a maintained space of not less than one cable diameter between individual conductors, the ampacity of 250 MCM and larger cables shall not exceed the allowable ampacities in Tables 310-69 and 310-70.

ARTICLE 320 — OPEN WIRING ON INSULATORS

Contents

320-1. Definition. Open wiring on insulators is an exposed wiring method using cleats, knobs, tubes, and flexible tubing for the protection and support of single insulated conductors run in or on buildings, and not concealed by the building structure.

> Open wiring on insulators is an exposed wiring method and is not to be concealed by the structure or finish of the building. It is permitted indoors or outdoors, in dry or wet locations, and where subject to corrosive vapors. Open wiring may be any of the general-use conductors listed in Table 310-13, such as Types RH, T, TW, and XHHW; the selection, of course, is dependent upon whether the location is wet or dry, temperature considerations, ampacities, etc.
>
> This method of wiring may be used for temporary lighting and power circuits on construction sites, lighting and power circuits in agricultural buildings, and services, and is commonly used for feeders in industrial locations. See Sections 230-43, 305-2, and 547-3.

320-2. Other Articles. Open wiring on insulators shall comply with this article and also with the applicable provisions of other articles in this Code, especially Articles 225 and 300.

320-3. Uses Permitted. Open wiring on insulators shall be permitted on systems of 600 volts, nominal, or less, only for industrial or agricultural establishments, indoors or outdoors, in wet or dry locations, where subject to corrosive vapors, and for services.

320-5. Conductors.

(a) Type. Conductors shall be of a type specified by Article 310.

(b) Ampacity. The ampacity shall comply with Tables 310-17 and 310-19 and all applicable notes to those tables.

320-6. Conductor Supports. Conductors shall be rigidly supported on noncombustible, nonabsorbent insulating materials and shall not contact any other objects. Supports shall be installed as follows: (1) within 6 inches (152 mm) from a tap or splice; (2) within 12 inches (305 mm) of a dead-end connection to a rosette, lampholder, or receptacle; (3) at intervals not exceeding 4½ feet (1.37 m) and at closer intervals sufficient to provide adequate support where likely to be disturbed.

Exception No. 1: Supports for conductors No. 8 or larger installed across open spaces shall be permitted up to 15 feet (4.57 m) apart if noncombustible, nonabsorbent insulating spacers are used at least every 4½ feet (1.37 m) to maintain at least 2½ inches (64 mm) between conductors.

Exception No. 2: Where not likely to be disturbed in buildings of mill construction, No. 8 and larger conductors shall be permitted to be run across open spaces if supported from each wood cross member on approved insulators maintaining 6 inches (152 mm) between conductors.

Exception No. 3: In industrial establishments only, where conditions of maintenance and supervision assure that only qualified persons will service the system, conductors of size 250 MCM and larger shall be permitted to be run across open spaces where supported on intervals up to 30 feet (9.1 m) apart.

Mill construction is generally considered to be a building where the floors and ceilings are supported on wooden beams or wooden cross members spaced approximately 15 ft apart. No. 8 and larger conductors may safely span this distance, where the ceilings are high and the conductors are unlikely to contact other objects and are free from obstructions.

It is common practice in industrial buildings to install open feeders on insulators which are mounted on the bottom of roof trusses at every bay location. Many times bay locations are in excess of 15-ft spacing; therefore, Exception No. 3 permits size 250 MCM and larger conductors to be supported at 30-ft intervals where it is assured that qualified persons will service the system.

In addition to the ease and economy of installations or alterations of open wiring, it is to be noted that by close spacing of conductors the reactance of a circuit is reduced; hence, the voltage drop is reduced.

320-7. Mounting of Conductor Supports. Where nails are used to mount knobs, they shall not be smaller than 10 penny. Where screws are used to mount knobs, or where nails or screws are used to mount cleats, they shall be of a length sufficient to penetrate the wood to a depth equal to at least one-half the height of the knob and fully the thickness of the cleat. Cushion washers shall be used with nails.

320-8. Tie Wires. No. 8 or larger conductors supported on solid knobs shall be securely tied thereto by tie wires having an insulation equivalent to that of the conductor.

320-10. Flexible Nonmetallic Tubing. In dry locations where not exposed to severe physical damage, conductors shall be permitted to be separately enclosed in flexible nonmetallic tubing. The tubing shall be in continuous lengths not exceeding 15 feet (4.57 m) and secured to the surface by straps at intervals not exceeding 4½ feet (1.37 m).

320-11. Through Walls, Floors, Wood Cross Members, etc. Open conductors shall be separated from contact with walls, floors, wood cross members, or partitions through which they pass by tubes or bushings of noncombustible, nonabsorbent insulating material. Where the bushing is shorter than the hole, a waterproof sleeve of noninductive material shall be inserted in the hole and an insulating bushing slipped into the sleeve at each end in such a manner as to keep the conductors absolutely out of contact with the sleeve. Each conductor shall be carried through a separate tube or sleeve.

320-12. Clearance from Piping, Exposed Conductors, etc. Open conductors shall be separated at least 2 inches (50.8 mm) from metal conduit, piping, or other conducting material, and from any exposed lighting, power, or signaling conductor, or shall be separated therefrom by a continuous and firmly fixed nonconductor in addition to the insulation of the conductor. Where any insulating tube is used, it shall be secured at the ends. Where practicable, conductors shall pass over rather than under any piping subject to leakage or accumulations of moisture.

The provision for additional protective insulation on open wiring is to prevent contact with metal piping, metal objects, or exposed conductors of other circuits.

320-13. Entering Spaces Subject to Dampness, Wetness, or Corrosive Vapors. Conductors entering or leaving locations subject to dampness, wetness, or corrosive vapors shall have drip loops formed on them and shall then pass upward and inward from the outside of the buildings, or from the damp, wet, or corrosive location, through noncombustible, nonabsorbent insulating tubes.

(FPN): See also Section 230-52.

320-14. Protection from Physical Damage. Conductors within 7 feet (2.13 m) from the floor shall be considered exposed to physical damage. Where open conductors cross ceiling joists and wall studs and are exposed to physical damage, they shall be protected by one of the following methods: (1) by guard strips not less than ⅞ inch (22 mm) in thickness and at least as high as the insulating supports, placed on each side of and close to the wiring; (2) by a substantial running board at least ½ inch (12.7 mm) thick back of the conductors with side protections. Running boards shall extend at least 1 inch (25.4 mm) outside the conductors, but not more than 2 inches (50.8 mm), and the protecting sides shall be at least 2 inches (50.8 mm) high and at least ⅞ inch (22 mm) thick; (3) by boxing made as above and furnished with a cover kept at least 1 inch (25.4 mm) away from the conductors within. Where protecting vertical conductors on side walls, the boxing shall be closed at the top and the holes through which the conductors pass shall be bushed; (4) by rigid metal conduit, intermediate metal conduit, rigid nonmetallic conduit, or electrical metallic tubing, in which case the rules of Article 345, 346, 347, or 348 shall apply; or by metal piping, in which case the conductors shall be encased in continuous lengths of approved flexible tubing. The conductors passing through metal enclosures shall be so grouped that current in both directions is approximately equal.

320-15. Unfinished Attics and Roof Spaces. Conductors in unfinished attics and roof spaces shall comply with (a) or (b) below.

(a) Accessible by Stairway or Permanent Ladder. Conductors shall be installed along the side of or through bored holes in floor joists, studs, or rafters. Where run through bored holes, conductors in the joists and in studs or rafters to a height of not less than 7 feet (2.13 m) above the floor or floor joists shall be protected by substantial running boards extending not less than 1 inch (25.4 mm) on each side of the conductors. Running boards shall be securely fastened in place. Running boards and guard strips shall not be required for conductors installed along the sides of joists, studs, or rafters.

(b) Not Accessible by Stairway or Permanent Ladder. Conductors shall be installed along the sides of or through bored holes in floor joists, studs, or rafters.

Exception: In buildings completed before wiring is installed and having head room at all points of less than 3 feet (914 mm).

320-16. Switches. Surface-type snap switches shall be mounted in accordance with Section 380-10(a), and boxes shall not be required. Other type switches shall be installed in accordance with Section 380-4.

ARTICLE 321 — MESSENGER SUPPORTED WIRING

Contents

321-1. Definition. Messenger supported wiring is an exposed wiring support system using a messenger wire to support insulated conductors by any one of the following: (1) a messenger with rings and saddles for conductor support; (2) a messenger with a field-installed lashing material for conductor support; (3) factory-assembled aerial cable; (4) multiplex cables utilizing a bare conductor, factory assembled and twisted with one or more insulated conductors, such as duplex, triplex, or quadruplex type of construction.

Messenger supported wiring systems have been manufactured and have been used successfully for many years in industrial installations. They have also been used for many years as service drops by utilities for commercial and residential installations.

See reference to messenger supported wiring in Section 225-6, Exception.

321-2. Other Articles. Messenger supported wiring shall comply with this article and also with the applicable provisions of other articles in this Code, especially Articles 225 and 300.

321-3. Uses Permitted.

(a) Cable Types. The following shall be permitted to be installed in messenger supported wiring under the conditions described in the article for each: (1) mineral-insulated, metal-sheathed cable (Article 330); (2) metal-clad cable (Article 334); (3) multiconductor service-entrance cable (Article 338); (4) multiconductor underground feeder and branch-circuit cable (Article 339); (5) power and control tray cable (Article 340); (6) other factory-assembled, multiconductor control, signal, or power cables which are identified for the use.

(b) In Industrial Establishments. In industrial establishments only, where conditions of maintenance and supervision assure that only competent individuals will service the installed messenger supported wiring, the following shall be permitted:

(1) Any of the conductor types given in Table 310-13.

Some of the triplex and quadruplex used by utilities as service drop cable does not utilize conductors of the type covered in Table 310-13 and does not meet the requirements of Article 310. Such triplex and quadruplex would, therefore, not be acceptable in accordance with this section.

(2) MV Cable.

Where exposed to weather, conductors shall be listed for use in wet locations. Where exposed to direct rays of the sun, conductors or cables shall be sunlight-resistant.

(c) Hazardous (Classified) Locations. Messenger supported wiring shall be permitted to be used in hazardous (classified) locations where the contained cables are permitted for such use in Sections 501-4, 502-4, and 503-3.

321-4. Uses Not Permitted. Messenger supported wiring shall not be used in hoistways or where subjected to severe physical damage.

321-5. Ampacity. The ampacity shall be determined by Section 310-15.

321-6. Messenger Support. The messenger shall be supported at dead ends and at intermediate locations so as to eliminate tension on the conductors. The conductors shall not be permitted to come into contact with the messenger supports or any structural members, walls, or pipes.

321-7. Grounding. The messenger shall be grounded as required by Sections 250-32 and 250-33 for enclosure grounding.

321-8. Conductor Splices and Taps. Conductor splices and taps made and insulated by approved methods shall be permitted in messenger supported wiring.

ARTICLE 324 — CONCEALED
KNOB-AND-TUBE WIRING

Contents

324-1. Definition. Concealed knob-and-tube wiring is a wiring method using knobs, tubes, and flexible nonmetallic tubing for the protection and support of single insulated conductors concealed in hollow spaces of walls and ceilings of buildings.

Open wiring on insulators (Article 320) is an "exposed" wiring method, whereas knob-and-tube wiring is a "concealed" method. Conductors used for knob-and-tube work may be of any general-use type specified by Article 310.

324-2. Other Articles. Concealed knob-and-tube wiring shall comply with this article and also with the applicable provisions of other articles in this Code, especially Article 300.

324-3. Uses Permitted. Concealed knob-and-tube wiring shall be permitted to be used only for extensions of existing installations and elsewhere only by special permission under the following conditions:

(1) In the hollow spaces of walls and ceilings.

(2) In unfinished attic and roof spaces as provided in Section 324-11.

Knob-and-tube wiring is permitted to be installed "only" for extensions of existing installations and "only" if special permission is granted in writing by the authority having jurisdiction of enforcement of the *Code*. See definition of "Special Permission" in Article 100.

324-4. Uses Not Permitted. Concealed knob-and-tube wiring shall not be used in commercial garages, theaters and similar locations, motion picture studios, or hazardous (classified) locations.

324-5. Conductors.

(a) Type. Conductors shall be of a type specified by Article 310.

(b) Ampacity. The ampacity shall comply with Tables 310-17 and 310-19 and all applicable notes to those tables.

324-6. Conductor Supports. Conductors shall be rigidly supported on noncombustible, nonabsorbent insulating materials and shall not contact any other objects. Supports shall be installed as follows: (1) within 6 inches (152 mm) of each side of each tap or splice, and (2) at intervals not exceeding 4½ feet (1.37 m).

Exception: If it is not practicable to provide supports in dry locations it shall be permissible to fish conductors through hollow spaces if each conductor is individually enclosed in flexible nonmetallic tubing. The tubing shall be in continuous lengths between supports, between boxes, or between a support and a box.

324-7. Tie Wires. Where solid knobs are used, conductors shall be securely tied thereto by tie wires having insulation equivalent to that of the conductor.

324-8. Conductor Clearances. A clearance of not less than 3 inches (76 mm) shall be maintained between conductors and of not less than 1 inch (25.4 mm) between the conductor and the surface over which it passes.

Exception: Where space is too limited to provide the above minimum clearances, such as at meters, panelboards, outlets, and switch points, the conductors shall be individually enclosed in flexible nonmetallic tubing, which shall be in continuous lengths between the last support or box and the terminal point.

324-9. Through Walls, Floors, Wood Cross Members, etc. Conductors shall comply with Section 320-11 where passing through holes in structural members. Where passing through wood cross members in plastered partitions, conductors shall be protected by noncombustible, nonabsorbent, insulating tubes extending not less than 3 inches (76 mm) beyond the wood member.

The provision for insulated tubes for use with knob-and-tube wiring where passing through wood cross members in plastered partitions is to protect the wire from contact with plaster that is likely to accumulate on horizontal wood members.

324-10. Clearance from Piping, Exposed Conductors, etc. Conductors shall comply with Section 320-12 for clearances from other exposed conductors, piping, etc.

324-11. Unfinished Attics and Roof Spaces. Conductors in unfinished attics and roof spaces shall comply with (a) or (b) below.

(a) Accessible by Stairway or Permanent Ladder. Conductors shall be installed along the side of or through bored holes in floor joists, studs, or rafters. Where run through bored holes, conductors in the joists and in studs or rafters to a height of not less than 7 feet (2.13 m) above the floor or floor joists shall be protected by substantial running boards extending not less than 1 inch (25.4 mm) on each side of the conductors. Running boards shall be securely fastened in place. Running boards and guard strips shall not be required where conductors are installed along the sides of joists, studs, or rafters.

(b) Not Accessible by Stairway or Permanent Ladder. Conductors shall be installed along the sides of or through bored holes in floor joists, studs, or rafters.

Exception: In buildings completed before wiring is installed and having head room at all points of less than 3 feet (914 mm).

Figure 324-1 illustrates the "running board" method of protecting open-type conductors in an accessible attic. This method is applied in attics that are accessible by stairways or permanent ladders and where such spaces are generally used for storage.

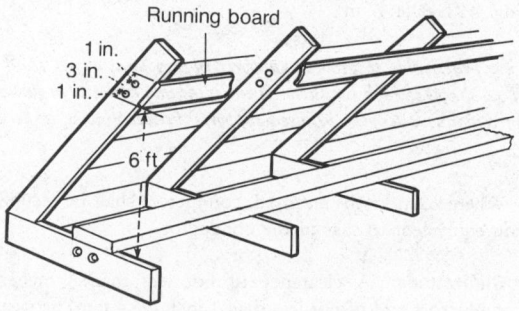

Figure 324-1. Open wiring in accessible attic. Wires run through rafters and through joists where there is no floor.

324-12. Splices. Splices shall be soldered unless approved splicing devices are used. In-line or strain splices shall not be used.

324-13. Boxes. Outlet boxes shall comply with Article 370.

324-14. Switches. Switches shall comply with Sections 380-4 and 380-10(b).

ARTICLE 325 — INTEGRATED GAS SPACER CABLE

Type IGS

Contents

A. General
325-1. Definition.
325-2. Other Articles.
325-3. Uses Permitted.
325-4. Uses Not Permitted.

B. Installation
325-11. Bending Radius.
325-12. Bends.
325-13. Fittings.
325-14. Ampacity.

C. Construction Specifications

325-20. Conductors.

325-21. Insulation.

325-22. Conduit.

325-23. Grounding.

325-24. Marking.

A. General

325-1. Definition. Type IGS cable is a factory assembly of one or more conductors, each individually insulated and enclosed in a loose fit nonmetallic flexible conduit as an integrated gas spacer cable rated 0-600 volts.

Article 325 is new in the 1984 *NEC*. The conductors consist of solid aluminum rods, 250 MCM minimum. These conductors are insulated with dry kraft paper and are factory-installed in a medium density polyethylene gas pipe, 2 in. minimum trade size, which is then filled with **sulfur hexafluoride gas** at a pressure of approximately 20 psi. See Figure 325-1.

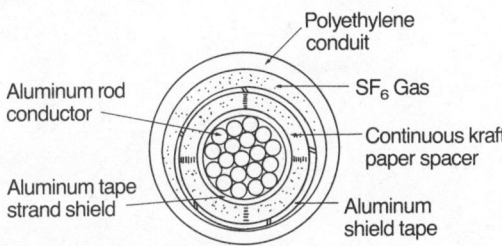

Figure 325-1. Cross section of single-conductor, 4,750 MCM, Type IGS cable.

325-2. Other Articles. The Type IGS cable shall comply with this article and also with the applicable provisions of other articles in this Code.

325-3. Uses Permitted. The Type IGS cable shall be permitted for use underground, including direct burial in the earth, as service-entrance conductors, or as feeder or branch-circuit conductors.

325-4. Uses Not Permitted. The Type IGS cable shall not be used as interior wiring or exposed in contact with buildings.

B. Installation

325-11. Bending Radius. Where the coilable nonmetallic conduit and cable is bent for installation purposes or is flexed or bent during shipment or installation, the radii of bends measured to the inside of the bend shall not be less than specified in Table 325-11.

Table 325-11.   Minimum Radii of Bends

Conduit Trade Size	Minimum Radii
2 Inch	24 Inches (610 mm)
3 Inch	35 Inches (889 mm)
4 Inch	45 Inches (1.14 m)

ARTICLE 325—INTEGRATED GAS SPACER CABLE

325-12. Bends. A run of Type IGS cable between pull boxes or terminations shall not contain more than the equivalent of four quarter bends (360 degrees, total), including those bends located immediately at the pull box or terminations.

325-13. Fittings. Terminations and splices for the Type IGS cable shall be identified as a type which is suitable for maintaining the gas pressure within the conduit. A valve and cap shall be provided for each length of the cable and conduit to check the gas pressure or to inject gas into the conduit.

325-14. Ampacity. The ampacity of the Type IGS-EC cable and conduit shall not exceed values shown in Table 325-14 for single conductor or multiconductor cable.

Table 325-14.   Ampacity Type IGS

Size MCM	Amperes
250	119
500	168
750	206
1000	238
1250	266
1500	292
1750	315
2000	336
2250	357
2500	376
3000	412
3250	429
3500	445
3750	461
4000	476
4250	491
4500	505
4750	519

C. Construction Specifications

325-20. Conductors. The conductors shall be solid aluminum rods, laid parallel, consisting of one to nineteen ½-inch (12.7-mm) diameter rods.

The minimum conductor size shall be 250 MCM and the maximum size shall be 4750 MCM.

325-21. Insulation. The insulation shall be dry kraft paper tapes and a pressurized sulfur hexafluoride gas (SF_6), both approved for electrical use. The nominal gas pressure shall be 20 pounds per square inch gage (psig) (138 kPa).

The thickness of the paper spacer shall be as specified in Table 325-21.

Table 325-21.   Paper Spacer Thickness

Size MCM	Thickness Inches (mm)
250-1000	.040 (1.02)
1250-4750	.060 (1.52)

325-22. Conduit. The conduit shall be an approved medium density polyethylene identified as suitable for use with natural gas rated pipe in 2 inches, 3 inches, 4 inches trade size. The percent fill dimensions for the conduit are given in Table 325-22.

The size of the conduit permitted for each conductor size shall be calculated for a percent fill not to exceed Table 1, Chapter 9.

Table 325-22.   Conduit Dimensions

Conduit Trade Size, Inches	Outside Diameter, Inches (mm)	Inside Diameter, Inches (mm)
2	2.375 (60)	1.947 (49.46)
3	3.500 (89)	2.886 (73.30)
4	4.500 (114)	3.710 (94.23)

325-23. Grounding.   The Type IGS cable shall comply with Article 250.

325-24. Marking.   The provisions of Section 310-11 shall apply for the Type IGS cable.

ARTICLE 326 — MEDIUM VOLTAGE CABLE

Type MV

Contents

326-1. Definition.
326-2. Other Articles.
326-3. Uses Permitted.
326-4. Uses Not Permitted.

326-5. Construction.
326-6. Ampacity.
326-7. Marking.

326-1. Definition.   Type MV is a single or multiconductor solid dielectric insulated cable rated 2001 volts or higher.

Medium voltage cables are rated 2001 to 35,000 V. Cables rated 2001 to 8000 V may be shielded or nonshielded. All insulated conductors 8001 V and higher have electrostatic shielding.

326-2. Other Articles.   In addition to the provisions of this article, Type MV cable shall comply with the applicable provisions of this Code, especially Articles 300, 305, 310, 318, 501, and 710.

326-3. Uses Permitted.   Type MV cables shall be permitted for use on power systems rated up to 35,000 volts, nominal, in wet or dry locations, in raceways, cable trays as specified in Section 318-2(b), or directly buried in accordance with Section 710-3(b) and in messenger supported wiring.

326-4. Uses Not Permitted.   Type MV cable shall not be used unless identified for the use (1) where exposed to direct sunlight, and (2) in cable trays.

Cables intended for installation in cable trays in accordance with Article 318 are marked "for CT Use" or "for use in cable trays."

326-5. Construction.   Type MV cables shall have copper, aluminum, or copper-clad aluminum conductors and shall be constructed in accordance with Article 310.

Cables with aluminum conductors are marked with the word "aluminum" or the letters "AL."

326-6. Ampacity. The ampacity of Type MV cable shall be in accordance with Section 310-15.

Exception: The ampacity of Type MV cable installed in cable tray shall be in accordance with Section 318-12.

This exception is required to provide the correct ampacities for conductors and multiconductor cables where installed in cable tray.

326-7. Marking. Medium voltage cable shall be marked as required in Section 310-11.

Cables are marked with their conductor size, voltage rating, and insulation level (100 percent or 133 percent).

ARTICLE 328 — FLAT CONDUCTOR CABLE TYPE FCC

Contents

A. General

328-1. Scope. This article covers a field-installed wiring system for branch circuits incorporating Type FCC cable and associated accessories as defined by the article. The wiring system is designed for installation under carpet squares.

The flat conductor cable system is designed to provide a completely accessible, flexible power system. It also provides an easy method for reworking obsolete wiring systems currently in use in many office facilities. See Figure 328-1.

The carpet squares are to be no larger than 30 in. by 30 in. See Section 328-10. This limitation was judged necessary to provide ready access to the cable by lifting a carpet square. It also reduced the likelihood of someone accessing the cable by cutting through the carpet over the cable with a knife or razor blade, and possibly penetrating the top shield of the cable in the process.

Figure 328-1. Installing flat conductor cable. (*AMP Products Corp.*)

328-2. Definitions.

Type FCC Cable. Type FCC cable consists of three or more flat copper conductors placed edge-to-edge and separated and enclosed within an insulating assembly.

FCC System. A complete wiring system for branch circuits that is designed for installation under carpet squares. The FCC system includes Type FCC cable and associated shielding, connectors, terminators, adapters, boxes, and receptacles.

Cable Connector. A connector designed to join Type FCC cables without using a junction box.

Insulating End. An insulator designed to electrically insulate the end of a Type FCC cable.

Top Shield. A grounded metal shield covering undercarpet components of the FCC system for the purposes of providing protection against physical damage.

Bottom Shield. A shield mounted on the floor under the FCC system to provide protection against physical damage.

Transition Assembly. An assembly to facilitate connection of the FCC system to other approved wiring systems, incorporating (1) a means of electrical interconnection, and (2) a suitable box or covering for providing electrical safety and protection against physical damage.

Metal Shield Connections. Means of connection designed to electrically and mechanically connect a metal shield to another metal shield, to a receptacle housing or self-contained device, or to a transition assembly.

328-3. Other Articles.
The FCC systems shall conform with applicable provisions of Articles 210, 220, 240, 250 and 300.

328-4. Uses Permitted.

(a) Branch Circuits. Use of FCC systems shall be permitted both for general-purpose and appliance branch circuits, and for individual branch circuits.

317

(b) Floors. Use of FCC systems shall be permitted on hard, sound, smooth, continuous floor surfaces made of concrete, ceramic, or composition flooring, wood, and similar materials.

(c) Walls. Use of FCC systems shall be permitted on wall surfaces in surface metal raceways.

(d) Damp Locations. Use of FCC systems in damp locations shall be permitted.

(e) Heated Floors. Materials used for floors heated in excess of 30°C (86°F) shall be identified as suitable for use at these temperatures.

328-5. Uses Not Permitted. FCC systems shall not be used: (1) outdoors or in wet locations; (2) where subject to corrosive vapors; (3) in any hazardous (classified) location; or (4) in residential, school, and hospital buildings.

328-6. Branch-Circuit Ratings.

(a) Voltage. Voltage between ungrounded conductors shall not exceed 300 volts. Voltage between ungrounded conductors and grounded conductor shall not exceed 150 volts.

(b) Current. General-purpose and appliance branch circuits shall have ratings not exceeding 20 amperes. Individual branch circuits shall have ratings not exceeding 30 amperes.

B. Installation

328-10. Coverings. Floor-mounted Type FCC cable, cable connectors, and insulating ends shall be covered with carpet squares no larger than 30 inches (762 mm) square. Those carpet squares that are adhered to the floor shall be attached with release-type adhesives.

328-11. Cable Connections and Insulating Ends. All Type FCC cable connections shall use connectors identified for their use, installed such that electrical continuity, insulation, and sealing against dampness and liquid spillage are provided. All bare cable ends shall be insulated and sealed against dampness and liquid spillage using listed insulating ends.

328-12. Shields.

(a) Top Shield. A metal top shield shall be installed over all floor-mounted Type FCC cable, connectors, and insulating ends. The top shield shall completely cover all cable runs, corners, connectors, and ends.

(b) Bottom Shield. A bottom shield shall be installed beneath all Type FCC cable, connectors, and insulating ends.

328-13. Enclosure and Shield Connections. All metal shields, boxes, receptacle housings, and self-contained devices shall be electrically continuous to the equipment grounding conductor of the supplying branch circuit. All such electrical connections shall be made with connectors identified for this use. The electrical resistivity of such shield system shall not be more than that of one conductor of the Type FCC cable used in the installation.

328-14. Receptacles. All receptacles, receptacle housings, and self-contained devices used with the FCC system shall be identified for this use and shall be connected to the Type FCC cable and metal shields. Connection from any grounding conductor of the Type FCC cable shall be made to the shield system at each receptacle.

328-15. Connection to Other Systems. Power feed, grounding connection, and shield system connection between the FCC system and other wiring systems shall be accomplished in a transition assembly identified for this use.

328-16. Anchoring. All FCC system components shall be firmly anchored to the floor or wall using an adhesive or mechanical anchoring system identified for this use. Floors shall be prepared to assure adherence of the FCC system to the floor until the carpet squares are placed.

328-17. Crossings. Crossings of two Type FCC cable runs shall be permitted. Crossings of a Type FCC cable over or under a flat telephone cable shall be permitted. In each case, a grounded layer of metal shielding shall separate the two cables.

328-18. System Height. Any portion of an FCC system with a height above floor level exceeding 0.090 inches (2.29 mm) shall be tapered or feathered at the edges to floor level.

328-19. FCC Systems Alterations. Alterations to FCC systems shall be permitted. New cable connectors shall be used at new connection points to make alterations. It shall be permitted to leave unused cable runs and associated cable connectors in place and energized. All cable ends shall be covered with insulating ends.

328-20. Polarization of Connections. All receptacles and connections shall be constructed and installed so as to maintain proper polarization of the system.

C. Construction

328-30. Type FCC Cable. Type FCC cable shall be approved for use with the FCC system and shall consist of three, four, or five flat copper conductors, one of which shall be an equipment grounding conductor. The insulating material of the cable shall be moisture-resistant and flame-retardant.

328-31. Markings. Type FCC cable shall be clearly and durably marked on both sides at intervals of not more than 24 inches (610 mm), with the information required by Section 310-11(a) and with the following additional information: (1) material of conductors; (2) maximum temperature rating; and (3) ampacity.

328-32. Conductor Identification.

(a) **Colors.** Conductors shall be clearly and durably marked on both sides throughout their length as specified in Section 310-12.

(b) **Order.** For a two-wire FCC system with grounding, the grounding conductor shall be central.

328-33. Corrosion Resistance. Metal components of the system shall be either: (1) corrosion-resistant; (2) coated with corrosion-resistant materials; or (3) insulated from contact with corrosive substances.

328-34. Insulation. All insulating materials in the FCC systems shall be identified for their use.

328-35. Shields.

(a) **Materials and Dimensions.** All top and bottom shields shall be of designs and materials identified for their use. Top shields shall be metal. Both metallic and nonmetallic materials shall be permitted for bottom shields.

(b) **Resistivity.** Metal shields have cross-sectional areas that provide for electrical resistivity of not more than that of one conductor of the Type FCC cable used in the installation.

(c) **Metal-Shield Connectors.** Metal shields shall be connected to each other and to boxes, receptacle housings, self-contained devices, and transition assemblies using metal-shield connectors.

328-36. Receptacles and Housings. Receptacle housings and self-contained devices designed either for floor mounting or for in- or on-wall mounting shall be permitted for use with the FCC system. Receptacle housings and self-contained devices shall incorporate means for facilitating entry and termination of Type FCC cable, and for electrically connecting the housing or device with the metal shield. Receptacles and self-contained devices shall comply with Section 210-7. Power and communications outlets installed together in common housing shall be permitted in accordance with Section 800-3(a)(2), Exception No. 1.

328-37. Transition Assemblies. All transition assemblies shall be identified for their use. Each assembly shall incorporate means for facilitating entry of the Type FCC cable into the assembly, for connecting the Type FCC cable to grounded conductors, and for electrically connecting the assembly to the metal cable shields and to equipment grounding conductors.

ARTICLE 330 — MINERAL-INSULATED, METAL-SHEATHED CABLE

Type MI

Contents

A. General
330-1. Definition.
330-2. Other Articles.
330-3. Uses Permitted.
330-4. Uses Not Permitted.

B. Installation
330-10. Wet Locations.
330-11. Through Joists, Studs, or Rafters.

330-12. Supports.
330-13. Bends.
330-14. Fittings.
330-15. Terminal Seals.

C. Construction Specifications
330-20. Conductors.
330-21. Insulation.
330-22. Outer Sheath.

A. General

330-1. Definition. Type MI mineral-insulated, metal-sheathed cable is a factory assembly of one or more conductors insulated with a highly compressed refractory mineral insulation and enclosed in a liquidtight and gastight continuous copper sheath.

330-2. Other Articles. Type MI cable shall comply with this article and also with the applicable provisions of other articles in this Code, especially Article 300.

Mineral-insulated, metal-sheathed cable consists of one or more solid copper conductors insulated with highly compressed magnesium oxide and enclosed in a continuous copper sheath. It is labeled by Underwriters Laboratories Inc. in sizes 16 AWG to 250 MCM one conductor, 16 to 4 AWG two and three conductor, 16 to 6 AWG four conductor, and 16 to 10 AWG seven conductor. The cable is rated 600 V.

Terminations especially investigated for use with this cable are listed by Underwriters Laboratories Inc. as Mineral Insulated Cable Fittings.

Supplementary nonmetallic coatings presently used have not been investigated for resistance to corrosion.

Fittings for use on mineral-insulated cable Type MI and small-diameter mineral-insulated cable are suitable for use at a maximum operating temperature of 85°C (185°F) in dry locations and 60°C (140°F) in wet locations. A complete box connector consists of a connector body and a screw-on potting fitting.

The screw-on potting fitting to be used with the connector may be used separately as an end fitting for change to open wiring. The screw-on potting fitting is to be assembled with a special tool and consists of a screw-on pot, insulating cap, insulating sleeving, anchoring bead, and sealing compound. See Figure 330-1.

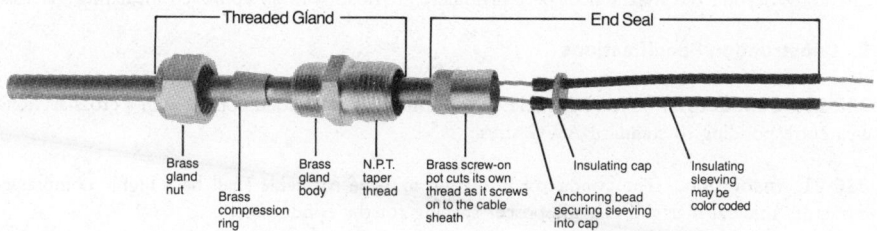

Figure 330-1. Type MI cable fitting used for terminating cable at box or equipment. (*Pyrotenaz USA, Inc.*)

330-3. Uses Permitted. Type MI cable shall be permitted as follows: (1) for services, feeders, and branch circuits; (2) in dry, wet, or continuously moist locations; (3) indoors or outdoors; (4) where exposed or concealed; (5) embedded in plaster, concrete, fill or other masonry, whether above or below grade; (6) in any hazardous (classified) location; (7) where exposed to oil and gasoline; (8) where exposed to corrosive conditions not deteriorating to its sheath; (9) in underground runs where suitably protected against physical damage and corrosive conditions.

Mineral-insulated, metal-sheathed cable (Type MI) is suitable for all power and control circuits up to 600 V and may be used for services, feeders, and branch circuits in exposed and concealed work; in dry and wet locations; for underplaster extensions and embedment in plaster; in masonry, concrete, or fill; for underground runs; or where exposed to weather, continuous moisture, oil in any hazardous (classified) location, or other conditions not having a deteriorating effect on the metallic sheath.

330-4. Uses Not Permitted. Type MI cable shall not be used where exposed to destructive corrosive conditions.

Exception: Where protected by materials suitable for the conditions.

B. Installation

330-10. Wet Locations. Where installed in wet locations, Type MI cable shall comply with Section 300-6(c).

330-11. Through Joists, Studs, or Rafters. Type MI cable shall comply with Section 300-4 where installed through studs, joists, rafters, or similar wood members.

330-12. Supports. Type MI cable shall be securely supported at intervals not exceeding 6 feet (1.83 m) by straps, staples, hangers, or similar fittings so designed and installed as not to damage the cable.

Exception: Where cable is fished in.

330-13. Bends. Bends in Type MI cable shall be so made as not to damage the cable. The radius of the inner edge of any bend shall not be less than five times the cable diameter.

330-14. Fittings. Fittings used for connecting Type MI cable to boxes, cabinets, or other equipment shall be identified for such use. Where single-conductor cables enter ferrous metal boxes or cabinets, the installation shall comply with Section 300-20 to prevent inductive heating.

330-15. Terminal Seals. Where Type MI cable terminates, an approved seal shall be provided immediately after stripping to prevent the entrance of moisture into the insulation. The conductors extending beyond the sheath shall be individually provided with an approved insulating material.

C. Construction Specifications

330-20. Conductors. Type MI cable conductors shall be of solid copper with a cross-sectional area corresponding to standard AWG sizes.

330-21. Insulation. The conductor insulation in Type MI cable shall be a highly compressed refractory mineral that will provide proper spacing for the conductors.

330-22. Outer Sheath. The outer sheath shall be of a continuous copper construction to provide mechanical protection, a moisture seal, and an adequate path for grounding purposes.

ARTICLE 331 — ELECTRICAL NONMETALLIC TUBING

Contents

A. General

331-1. Definition. Electrical nonmetallic tubing is a pliable corrugated raceway of circular cross-section with integral or associated couplings, connectors and fittings listed for the installation of electric conductors. It is composed of a material that is resistant to moisture, chemical atmospheres, and is flame-retardant.

Article 331 is new in the 1984 *NEC*. Electrical nonmetallic tubing (ENMT) is made of the same material (PVC) used for rigid nonmetallic conduit suitable for aboveground use (see Article 347). Because of the corrugations, the raceway can be bent by hand, but it is not intended for use where flexibility is necessary, as at motor terminations to prevent transmission of noise and vibration. See Figure 331-1.

A pliable raceway is a raceway which can be bent by hand with a reasonable force, but without other assistance.

Figure 331-1. Electrical nonmetallic tubing is permitted in ½-, ¾-, and 1-in. trade sizes only. (*Carlon, an Indian Head Co.*)

331-2. Other Articles. Installations for electrical nonmetallic tubing shall comply with the provisions of the applicable sections of Article 300. Where equipment grounding is required by Article 250, a separate equipment grounding conductor shall be installed in the raceway.

331-3. Uses Permitted. Electrical nonmetallic tubing and fittings shall be permitted to be used in one- and two-family dwellings, multifamily dwellings and other structures provided that such dwellings or structures do not exceed three floors above grade: (a) in walls, floors and ceilings; (b) in locations where subject to severe corrosive influences as covered in Section 300-6 and where subject to chemicals for which the materials are specifically approved; (c) in dry and damp locations not prohibited by Section 331-4; (d) for exposed work where not subject to physical damage; (e) where the potential is 600 volts or less.

For the purpose of this article, the first floor of a building shall be that floor which is designed for human habitation and which has 50 percent or more of its perimeter level with or above finished grade of the exterior wall line.

331-4. Uses Not Permitted. Electrical nonmetallic tubing shall not be used: (a) in hazardous (classified) locations; (b) for support of fixtures or other equipment; (c) where subject to physical damage; (d) where subject to ambient temperatures exceeding those for which the raceway is listed; (e) for conductors whose insulation temperature limitations exceed those for which the tubing is listed; (f) for direct earth burial; (g) embedded in poured concrete or aggregate; (h) where the potential is over 600 volts.

B. Installation

331-5. Size.

(a) **Minimum.** Tubing smaller than ½-inch electrical trade size shall not be used.

(b) **Maximum.** Tubing larger than 1-inch electrical trade size shall not be used.

331-6. Number of Conductors in Tubing. The number of conductors in a single tubing shall not exceed that permitted by the percentage fill in Table 1, Chapter 9.

331-7. Trimming. All cut ends of tubing shall be trimmed inside and outside to remove rough edges.

331-8. Joints. All joints between lengths of tubing and between tubing and couplings, fittings and boxes shall be by an approved method.

331-9. Bends — How Made. Bends of electrical nonmetallic tubing shall be so made that the tubing will not be damaged and that the internal diameter of the tubing will not be effectively reduced. Bends shall be permitted to be made manually without auxiliary equipment and the radius of the curve of the inner edge of such bends shall not be less than shown in Table 346-10.

331-10. Bends — Number in One Run. A run of tubing between outlet and outlet or outlet and fitting shall not contain more than the equivalent of four quarter bends (360 degrees, total) including those bends located immediately at the outlet or fitting.

331-11. Supports. Electrical nonmetallic tubing shall be installed as a complete system as provided in Article 300 and shall be securely fastened in place. Tubing shall be firmly fastened within 3 feet (914 mm) of each outlet box, junction box, cabinet or fitting. Tubing shall be secured at least every 3 feet (914 mm).

331-12. Boxes and Fittings. Boxes and fittings shall comply with the applicable provisions of Article 370.

331-13. Splices and Taps. Splices and taps shall be made only in junction boxes, outlet boxes or conduit bodies. See Article 370.

331-14. Bushings. Where a tubing enters a box or other fitting, a bushing or adapter shall be provided to protect the wire from abrasion unless the design of the box or fitting is such as to provide equivalent protection. See Section 370-6(c) for the protection of conductors at bushings.

C. Construction Specifications

331-15. General. Electrical nonmetallic tubing shall be clearly and durably marked at least every 10 feet (3.05 m) as required in the first sentence of Section 110-21. The type of material shall also be included in the marking.

ARTICLE 333 — ARMORED CABLE

Type AC Cable

Contents

333-1. Definition. Type AC cable is a fabricated assembly of insulated conductors in a flexible metallic enclosure. See Section 333-4.

Armored cable is listed by Underwriters Laboratories Inc. in sizes No. 14 through No. 1 AWG copper and No. 12 through No. 1 AWG aluminum or copper-clad aluminum and is rated at 600 V or less.

333-2. Other Articles. Type AC cable shall comply with this article and also with the applicable provisions of other articles in this Code, especially Article 300.

333-3. Marking. The provisions of Section 310-11 shall apply, except that Type AC cable shall have ready identification of the maker by distinctive external markers on the cable sheath throughout its entire length.

333-4. Construction. Type AC cable shall be an approved cable with acceptable metal covering. The insulated conductors shall conform with Section 333-5.

Type AC cables are branch-circuit and feeder cables with armor of flexible metal tape. Cables of the AC type, except ACL, shall have an internal bonding strip of copper or aluminum, in intimate contact with the armor for its entire length.

The armor of Type AC cable is recognized as an equipment grounding conductor by Section 250-91(b). The required internal bonding strip can be simply cut off at the termination of the armored cable or it can be bent back on the armor. It is not necessary to connect it to an equipment grounding terminal. Its use is to supplement the effectiveness of the spiral armor as an equipment grounding means.

333-5. Conductors. Insulated conductors shall be of a type listed in Table 310-13. In addition, the conductors shall have an overall moisture-resistant and fire-retardant fibrous covering. For Type ACT, a moisture-resistant fibrous covering shall be required only on the individual conductors.

UL data refers to the marking of cables as follows. ACT indicates an armored cable employing conductors having thermoplastic insulation. AC indicates an armored cable employing conductors having thermosetting insulation. No suffix indicates 60°C (140°F) rating. H indicates 75°C (167°F) rating. HH indicates 90°C (194°F) rating.

333-6. Use.

(a) Uses Permitted. Except where otherwise specified elsewhere in this Code, and where not subject to physical damage, Type AC cable shall be permitted for branch circuits and feeders in both exposed and concealed work.

Type AC cable shall be permitted in dry locations; for underplaster extensions as provided in Article 344; and embedded in plaster finish on brick or other masonry, except in damp or wet locations. It shall be permissible to run or fish this cable in the air voids of masonry block or tile walls; where such walls are exposed or subject to excessive moisture or dampness or are below grade line, Type ACL cable shall be used. This cable shall contain lead-covered conductors (Type ACL) if used where exposed to the weather or to continuous moisture; for underground runs in raceways and embedded in masonry, concrete, or fill in buildings in course of construction; or where exposed to oil, or other conditions having a deteriorating effect on the insulation.

(b) Uses Not Permitted. Type AC cable shall not be used where prohibited elsewhere in this Code, including (1) in theaters and similar locations, except as provided in Article 518, Places of Assembly; (2) in motion picture studios; (3) in any hazardous (classified) locations; (4) where exposed to corrosive fumes or vapors; (5) on cranes or hoists, except as provided in Section 610-11, Exception No. 3; (6) in storage battery rooms; (7) in hoistways or on elevators, except as provided in Section 620-21; or (8) in commercial garages where prohibited in Article 511.

Exception: See Section 501-4(b), Exception.

The exception permits Type AC cable and other wiring methods, including nonmetallic-sheathed cable, for the wiring of intrinsically safe and nonincendive circuits. See Sections 500-1 (4th paragraph) and 501-4(b), Exception.

Type ACL cable shall not be used for direct burial in the earth.

The designation "L" indicates that a lead covering has been applied over the conductor assembly.

333-7. Supports. Type AC cable shall be secured by approved staples, straps, hangers, or similar fittings so designed and installed as not to injure the cable at intervals not exceeding 4½ feet (1.37 m) and within 12 inches (305 mm) from every outlet box or fitting.

This section requires that the cable be SECURED. Simply draping the cable over air ducts, lower members of bar joists, pipes, and ceiling grid members is not adequate except as noted in Exception No. 1. See also Section 300-4(c).

Exception No. 1: Where cable is fished.

Exception No. 2: Lengths of not more than 2 feet (610 mm) at terminals where flexibility is necessary.

333-8. Bends. All bends shall be made so that the cable will not be injured, and the radius of the curve of the inner edge of any bend shall not be less than five times the diameter of the Type AC cable.

333-9. Boxes and Fittings. At all points where the armor of AC cable terminates, a fitting shall be provided to protect wires from abrasion, unless the design of the outlet boxes or fittings is such as to afford equivalent protection, and, in addition, an approved insulating bushing or its equivalent approved protection shall be provided between the conductors and the armor. The connector or clamp by which the Type AC cable is fastened to boxes or cabinets shall be of such design that the insulating bushing or its equivalent will be visible for inspection. This bushing shall not be required with lead-covered cables where so installed that the lead sheath will be visible for inspection. Where change is made from Type AC cable to other cable or raceway wiring methods, a box shall be installed at junction points as required in Section 300-15.

Armored cable connectors are considered suitable for grounding.

333-10. Through Studs, Joists, and Rafters. Type AC cable shall comply with Section 300-4 where installed through studs, joists, rafters, or similar wood members.

333-11. Exposed Work. Exposed runs of cable shall closely follow the surface of the building finish or of running boards.

Exception No. 1: Lengths of not more than 24 inches (610 mm) at terminals where flexibility is necessary.

Exception No. 2: On the underside of floor joists in basements where supported at each joist and so located as not to be subject to physical damage.

It is to be noted that this exception does not apply to Type NM or NMC cable.

333-12. In Accessible Attics. Type AC cables in accessible attics or roof spaces shall be installed as specified in (a) and (b) below.

(a) Where Run Across the Top of Floor Joists. Where run across the top of floor joists, or within 7 feet (2.13 m) of floor or floor joists across the face of rafters or studding, in attics and roof spaces which are accessible, the cable shall be protected by substantial guard strips which are at least as high as the cable. Where this space is not accessible by permanent stairs or ladders, protection shall only be required within 6 feet (1.83 m) of the nearest edge of the scuttle hole or attic entrance.

(b) Where Carried Along the Sides of Floor Joists. Where cable is carried along the sides of rafters, studs, or floor joists, neither guard strips nor running boards shall be required.

ARTICLE 334 — METAL-CLAD CABLE

Contents

A. General
334-1. Definition.
334-2. Other Articles.
334-3. Uses Permitted.
334-4. Uses Not Permitted.

B. Installation
334-10. Installation.
 (a) Support.
 (b) Cable Tray.
 (c) Direct Buried.
 (d) Installed as Service-Entrance Cable.
 (e) Installed Outside of Buildings or as Aerial Cable.
334-11. Bending Radius.

 (a) Smooth Sheath.
 (b) Interlocked-type Armor or Corrugated Sheath.
 (c) Shielded Conductors.
334-12. Fittings.
334-13. Ampacity.

C. Construction Specifications
334-20. Conductors.
334-21. Insulation.
 (a) 600 Volts.
 (b) Over 600 Volts.
334-22. Metallic Sheath.
334-23. Grounding.
334-24. Marking.

A. General

334-1. Definition. Type MC cable is a factory assembly of one or more conductors, each individually insulated and enclosed in a metallic sheath of interlocking tape, or a smooth or corrugated tube.

Type MC cable is of three designs: (1) interlocked metal tape, (2) corrugated tube, and (3) smooth tube, and all are intended for aboveground use, except when marked for direct burial. Cables which are suitable for use in cable trays, directly buried, or in direct sunlight are so marked. Type MC cables include Type CS (copper sheath) and Type ALS (aluminum sheath).

334-2. Other Articles. Metal-clad cable shall comply with this article and also with the applicable provisions of other articles in this Code, especially Article 300.
Type MC cable shall be permitted for systems in excess of 600 volts, nominal. See Section 300-2.

Type MC cable is rated for use up to 5000 V and listed in sizes No. 18 AWG and larger for copper and No. 12 AWG and larger for aluminum or copper-clad aluminum, and employs thermoset, thermoplastic, varnished cloth, or composite varnished cloth-thermoplastic insulated conductors. The latter is designated as Type VT and rated 85°C (185°F).

334-3. Uses Permitted. Except where otherwise specified in this Code and where not subject to physical damage, Type MC cables shall be permitted as follows: (1) for services, feeders, and branch circuits; (2) for power, lighting, control, and signal circuits; (3) indoors or outdoors; (4) where exposed or concealed; (5) direct buried; (6) in cable tray; (7) in any approved raceway; (8) as open runs of cable; (9) as aerial cable on a messenger; (10) in hazardous (classified) locations as permitted in Articles 501, 502, and 503; (11) in dry locations; and (12) in wet locations when any of the following conditions are met:

(1) The metallic covering is impervious to moisture.

327

(2) A lead sheath or moisture impervious jacket is provided under the metal covering.

(3) The insulated conductors under the metallic covering are approved for use in wet locations.

Exception: See Section 501-4(b), Exception.

(FPN): See Section 300-6 for protection against corrosion.

334-4. Uses Not Permitted. Type MC cable shall not be used where exposed to destructive corrosive conditions, such as direct burial in the earth, in concrete, or where exposed to cinder fills, strong chlorides, caustic alkalis, or vapors of chlorine or of hydrochloric acids.

Exception: Where the metallic sheath is suitable for the conditions or is protected by material suitable for the conditions.

B. Installation

334-10. Installation. Type MC cable shall be installed in compliance with Articles 300, 710, and 725 as applicable.

(a) Support. Type MC cable shall be supported and secured at intervals not exceeding 6 feet (1.83 m).

(b) Cable Tray. Type MC cable installed in cable tray shall comply with Article 318.

(c) Direct Buried. Direct buried cable shall comply with Section 300-5 or 710-3, as appropriate.

(d) Installed as Service-Entrance Cable. Type MC cable installed as service-entrance cable shall comply with Article 230.

(e) Installed Outside of Buildings or as Aerial Cable. Type MC cable installed outside of buildings or as aerial cable shall comply with Article 225.

334-11. Bending Radius. All bends shall be so made that the cable will not be injured, and the radius of the curve of the inner edge of any bend shall not be less than shown below.

(a) Smooth Sheath.

  (1) Ten times the external diameter of the metallic sheath for cable not more than ¾ inch (19 mm) in external diameter;

  (2) Twelve times the external diameter of the metallic sheath for cable more than ¾ inch (19 mm) but not more than 1½ inches (38 mm) in external diameter; and

  (3) Fifteen times the external diameter of the metallic sheath for cable more than 1½ inches (38 mm) in external diameter.

(b) Interlocked-type Armor or Corrugated Sheath. Seven times the external diameter of the metallic sheath.

(c) Shielded Conductors. Twelve times the overall diameter of one of the individual conductors or seven times the overall diameter of the multiconductor cable, whichever is greater.

The minimum bending radius of twelve times the overall diameter of a single shielded conductor is consistent with ICEA (formerly IPCEA) requirements and good engineering practice; however, the same minimum on a multiconductor cable would be excessive.

For example, consider 5000 MCM, 15 kV, 100 percent insulation level (0.175 in. insulation):

	O.D.	12 × O.D.	7 × O.D.
Single Conductor	1.50 in.	18 in.	—
Three Conductor	3.15—3.50 in.	38—42 in.	22—24 in.

334-12. Fittings. Fittings used for connecting Type MC cable to boxes, cabinets, or other equipment shall be identified for such use. Where single-conductor cables enter ferrous metal boxes or cabinets, the installation shall comply with Section 300-20 to prevent inductive heating.

Connectors should be selected in accordance with the size and type of cable for which they are designed. Bronze connectors are intended for use only with cable employing corrugated copper armor.

334-13. Ampacity. The ampacity of Type MC cable rated 2000 volts or less shall be determined from Tables 310-16 through 310-19 and their accompanying notes. The ampacities of Type MC cable rated over 2000 volts shall be determined from Section 310-15.

This section is required to correctly identify the allowable ampacities for Type MC cable depending on the installation, i.e., isolated in air, direct buried, in conduit, or in cable tray.

Exception: The ampacities for Type MC cable installed in cable tray shall be determined in accordance with Sections 318-10 and 318-12.

C. Construction Specifications

334-20. Conductors. The conductors shall be of copper, aluminum, or copper-clad aluminum, solid or stranded.

The minimum conductor size shall be No. 18 copper and No. 12 aluminum or copper-clad aluminum.

334-21. Insulation. The insulated conductors shall comply with (a) or (b) below.

(a) 600 Volts. Insulated conductors in sizes No. 18 and 16 shall be of a type listed in Table 402-3, with a maximum operating temperature not less than 90°C (194°F), and as permitted by Section 725-16. Conductors larger than No. 16 shall be of a type listed in Table 310-13 or of a type identified for use in MC cable.

(b) Over 600 Volts. Insulated conductors shall be of a type listed in Tables 310-61 through 310-67.

334-22. Metallic Sheath. The metallic covering shall be one of the following types: smooth metallic sheath, welded and corrugated metallic sheath, interlocking metal tape armor. The metallic sheath shall be continuous and close fitting.

Supplemental protection of an outer covering of corrosion-resistant material shall be permitted, and shall be required where such protection is needed. The sheath shall not be used as a current-carrying conductor.

(FPN): See Section 300-6 for protection against corrosion.

334-23. Grounding. Type MC cable shall provide an adequate path for equipment grounding as required by Article 250.

334-24. Marking. The provisions of Section 310-11 shall apply.

Type MC cable is required to be marked with the maximum working voltage, proper type letter or letters for the type of wire, and the AWG size or circular mil area. This marking may be on a marker tape located within the cable running for its complete length, or, if the metallic covering is of smooth construction which permits surface marking, the MC cable may be durably marked on the outer covering at intervals not exceeding 24 in. See Section 310-11 for marking requirements.

ARTICLE 336 — NONMETALLIC-SHEATHED CABLE

Types NM and NMC

Contents

336-1. Definition. Nonmetallic-sheathed cable is a factory assembly of two or more insulated conductors having an outer sheath of moisture-resistant, flame-retardant, nonmetallic material.

Nonmetallic-sheathed cable may be used for either exposed or concealed wiring and is a common substitute for concealed knob-and-tube wiring (Article 324) and open wiring on insulators (Article 320). The basic advantages of nonmetallic-sheathed cable (Type NM and Type NMC) are that the outer sheath provides continuous protection in addition to the rubber or thermoplastic insulation applied to the conductors; the cable is easily fished in partitions of finished buildings; no insulating supports are required; and only one hole need be bored which can accommodate more than one cable passing through a wooden cross member.

Where the cable passes through factory- or field-punched holes in metal studs or similar members, it is to be protected by bushings or grommets securely fastened in the opening. See Section 300-4(b).

336-2. Construction. Nonmetallic-sheathed cable shall be an approved Type NM or NMC in sizes No. 14 through 2 with copper conductors and in sizes No. 12 through 2 with aluminum or copper-clad aluminum conductors. In addition to the insulated conductors, the cable may have an approved size of insulated or bare conductor for equipment grounding purposes only.

Conductors of Types NM and NMC shall be one of the types listed in Table 310-13 which is suitable for branch-circuit wiring or one which is identified for use in these cables. Conductors shall be rated at 90°C (194°F). The ampacity of Types NM and NMC cable shall be that of 60°C (140°F) conductors in Table 310-16.

Prior to the 1984 *Code*, Types NM and NMC could have conductors rated 60°C (140°F), 75°C (167°F), or 90°C (194°F) for use in different ambient temperatures. Cables with conductors rated at 75°C (167°F) were designated Type NMA or NMC-A, and those with conductors rated 90°C (194°F) were designated Type NMB or NMC-B. The ampacities of nonmetallic-sheathed cable types, regardless of the conductor temperature rating, are those of 60°C (140°F) conductors.

(a) Type NM. The overall covering shall have a flame-retardant and moisture-resistant finish.

(b) Type NMC. The overall covering shall be flame-retardant, moisture-resistant, fungus-resistant, and corrosion-resistant.

(c) Marking. In addition to the provisions of Section 310-11, the cable shall have a distinctive marking on the exterior for its entire length specifying the cable type.

336-3. Uses Permitted or Not Permitted. Type NM and Type NMC cables shall be permitted to be used in one- and two-family dwellings, multifamily dwellings and other structures provided that such dwellings or structures do not exceed three floors above grade. For the purpose of this article, the first floor of a building shall be that floor which is designed for human habitation and which has 50 percent or more of its perimeter level with or above finished grade of the exterior wall line.

It is to be noted that Type NM and Type NMC cables are permitted for dwellings and other structures such as stores, professional offices, motels, etc., providing these dwellings or structures do not exceed three floors above grade. See Figure 336-1. The word "floor" as used in Section 336-3 means the entire "story" of the building, from floor to ceiling.

(a) Type NM. This type of nonmetallic-sheathed cable shall be permitted to be installed for both exposed and concealed work in normally dry locations. It shall be permissible to install or fish Type NM cable in air voids in masonry block or tile walls where such walls are not exposed or subject to excessive moisture or dampness.
Type NM cable shall not be installed where exposed to corrosive fumes or vapors; nor shall it be embedded in masonry, concrete, adobe, fill, or plaster; nor run in a shallow chase in masonry, concrete, or adobe and covered with plaster, adobe, or similar finish.

(b) Type NMC. Type NMC cable shall be permitted for both exposed and concealed work in dry, moist, damp, or corrosive locations, and in outside and inside walls of masonry block or tile.

(c) Uses Not Permitted for Either Type NM or NMC. Types NM and NMC cables shall not be used: (1) as service-entrance cable; (2) in commercial garages; (3) in theaters and similar locations, except as provided in Article 518, Places of Assembly; (4) in motion picture studios; (5) in storage battery rooms; (6) in hoistways; (7) in any hazardous (classified) location; or (8) embedded in poured cement, concrete, or aggregate.

Exception: See Section 501-4(b), Exception.

Type NMC (corrosion-resistant) cable has proven very beneficial for installations in dairy barns and similar farm buildings (see Article 547) where extremely cold temperatures are experienced and ordinary types of nonmetallic cables have in some cases deteriorated rapidly due to the growth of fungus or mold.

ARTICLE 336—NONMETALLIC-SHEATHED CABLE

In addition to the insulated conductors, nonmetallic-sheathed cable may have an approved size of covered, insulated, or bare conductor for equipment grounding purposes only. See Section 250-57 and Table 250-95.

336-4. Other Articles. In addition to the provisions of this article, installations of nonmetallic-sheathed cable shall comply with the other applicable provisions of this Code, especially Article 300 and Note 8 to Tables 310-16 through 310-19.

The second paragraph of Note 8 to Tables 310-16 through 310-19 states "Where single conductors or multiconductor cables are stacked or bundled longer than 24 inches (610 mm) without maintaining spacing and are not installed in raceways, the ampacity of each conductor shall be reduced as shown in the above table."

Failure to comply with the appropriate ampacity derating called for by Note 8, where Types NM and NMC cables may be stacked or bundled, can lead to overheating of conductors.

The requirements of Note 8 apply to other wiring methods as they do to nonmetallic-sheathed cables.

336-5. Supports. Nonmetallic-sheathed cable shall be secured by staples, straps, or similar fittings so designed and installed as not to injure the cable. Cable shall be secured in place at intervals not exceeding 4½ feet (1.37 m) and within 12 inches (305 mm) from every cabinet, box, or fitting.

This section requires that the cable be SECURED. Simply draping the cable over air ducts, lower members of bar joists, pipes, and ceiling grid members is not adequate except as noted in Exception No. 1. See also Section 300-4(c).

Exception No. 1: For concealed work in finished buildings, or finished panels for prefabricated buildings where such supporting is impracticable, it shall be permissible to fish the cable between access points.

Exception No. 2: A wiring device identified for the use, without a separate outlet box, incorporating an integral cable clamp shall be permitted when the cable is secured in place at intervals not exceeding

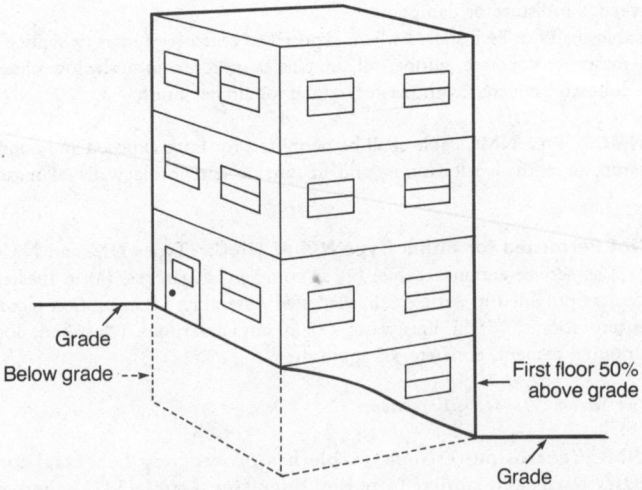

Figure 336-1. A representation of a first floor of a building which is level with or above finished grade of the exterior wall line of 50 percent or more of its perimeter.

4½ feet (1.37 m) and within 12 inches (305 mm) from the wiring device wall opening, and there shall be at least a 12-inch (305-mm) loop of unbroken cable or 6 inches (152 mm) of a cable end available on the interior side of the finished wall to permit replacement.

For concealed work, nonmetallic-sheathed cable should be installed in such a way as to be adequately protected from the physical damage that could be caused by nails or screws. Where practical, care should be taken to avoid areas where trim, door and window casings, baseboards, picture moldings, etc., may be nailed. See Section 300-4.

336-6. Exposed Work — General. In exposed work, except as provided in Sections 336-8 and 336-9, the cable shall be installed as specified in (a) and (b) below.

(a) To Follow Surface. The cable shall closely follow the surface of the building finish or of running boards.

(b) Protection from Physical Damage. The cable shall be protected from physical damage where necessary by conduit, electrical metallic tubing, pipe, guard strips, or other means. Where passing through a floor the cable shall be enclosed in rigid metal conduit, intermediate metal conduit, electrical metallic tubing, or other metal pipe extending at least 6 inches (152 mm) above the floor.

336-7. Through Studs, Joists, and Rafters. The cable shall comply with Section 300-4 where installed through studs, joists, rafters, and similar members.

336-8. In Unfinished Basements. Where the cable is run at angles with joists in unfinished basements, it shall be permissible to secure cables not smaller than two No. 6 or three No. 8 conductors directly to the lower edges of the joists. Smaller cables shall either be run through bored holes in joists or on running boards. Where run parallel to the joists, cable of any size shall be secured to the sides or faces of the joists.

336-9. In Accessible Attics. The installation of cable in accessible attics or roof spaces shall also comply with Section 333-12.

336-10. Bends. Bends in cable shall be so made, and other handling shall be such, that the protective coverings of the cable will not be injured, and no bend shall have a radius less than five times the diameter of the cable.

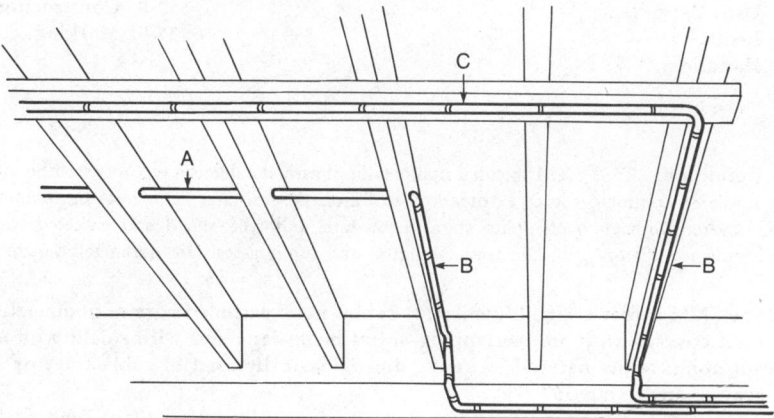

Figure 336-2. Nonmetallic-sheathed cable as installed in an unfinished basement. The cable can be run through joists (A), and attached to the side or face of joists or beams (B) and to the running boards (C).

336-11. Devices of Insulating Material. Switch, outlet, and tap devices of insulating material shall be permitted to be used without boxes in exposed cable wiring, and for rewiring in existing buildings where the cable is concealed and fished. Openings in such devices shall form a close fit around the outer covering of the cable, and the device shall fully enclose that part of the cable from which any part of the covering has been removed.

Where connections to conductors are by binding-screw terminals, there shall be available as many terminals as conductors.

Exception: Where cables are clamped within the structure, and terminals are of a type approved for multiconductors.

336-12. Boxes of Insulating Material. Nonmetallic outlet boxes shall be permitted as provided in Section 370-3.

Nonmetallic boxes and nonmetallic wiring systems are desired in corrosive atmospheres; however, nonmetallic boxes sized over 100 cu in. (for instance, 5 in. x 5 in. x 5 in. = 125 cu in.) with bonding means between all metal raceways and metal-enclosed cables are permitted. See Sections 370-3, 370-7(c), and Article 547.

336-13. Devices with Integral Enclosures. Wiring devices with integral enclosures identified for such use shall be permitted as provided in Section 300-15(b), Exception No. 5.

The *Code* recognizes wiring devices with integral enclosures in conventional on-site frame construction.

ARTICLE 337 — SHIELDED NONMETALLIC-SHEATHED CABLE

Type SNM

Contents

337-1. Definition. Type SNM shielded nonmetallic-sheathed cable is a factory assembly of two or more insulated conductors in an extruded core of moisture-resistant, flame-resistant nonmetallic material, covered with an overlapping spiral metal tape and wire shield and jacketed with an extruded moisture-, flame-, oil-, corrosion-, fungus-, and sunlight-resistant nonmetallic material.

Type SNM cables are multiconductor cables in an extruded core of nonmetallic material covered with an overlapping spiral metal tape and wire shield with an overall nonmetallic material jacketing and is basically used in cable trays or in raceways. See Section 337-3.

Figure 337-1 depicts a fragmentary perspective illustration of a Type SNM cable, and Figure 337-2 is a sectional view illustrating fittings for connecting such a cable to a rigid metal conduit or intermediate metal conduit.

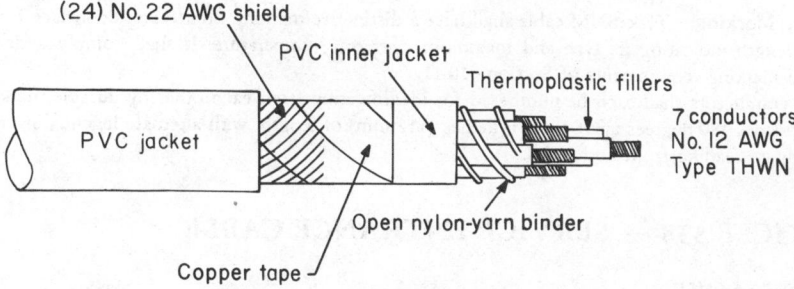

Figure 337-1. A 7-conductor No. 12 Type SNM cable typical for use in cable trays or raceways.

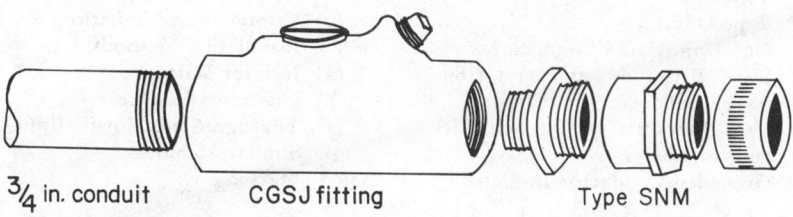

Figure 337-2. Connection-type fitting used where Type SNM cable enters a ¾-in. rigid metal conduit in Class I and Class II, Division 2 hazardous (classified) locations.

337-2. Other Articles. In addition to the provisions of this article, installation of Type SNM cable shall conform to other applicable provisions, such as Articles 300, 318, 501, and 502.

337-3. Uses Permitted. Type SNM cable shall be used only as follows: (1) where operating temperatures do not exceed the rating marked on the cable; (2) in cable trays or in raceways; or (3) in hazardous (classified) locations where permitted in Articles 500 through 516.

337-4. Bends. Bends in Type SNM cable shall be so made as not to damage the cable or its covering. The radius of the inner edge shall not be less than five times the cable diameter.

337-5. Handling. Type SNM cable shall be handled in such a manner as not to damage the cable or its covering.

337-6. Fittings. Fittings for connecting Type SNM cable to enclosures or equipment shall be identified for this use.

337-7. Bonding. The wire shield shall be bonded to the frame or enclosure of the utilization equipment and to the ground bus or connection at the power supply point. This bonding shall be accomplished using fittings (Section 337-6) or by other Code-approved bonding methods [Section 501-16(b)].

337-8. Construction. The conductors of Type SNM cable shall be Type TFN, TFFN, THHN or THWN in sizes No. 18 through No. 2 copper and No. 12 through No. 2 in aluminum or copper-clad aluminum. Conductor sizes may be mixed in individual cables. The flat overlapping metal tapes shall be spiraled with a long lay. The shield wires shall have a total cross-sectional area as required by Article 250 and not less than the largest circuit conductor in the cable.

The outer jacket shall be water-, oil-, flame-, corrosion-, fungus-, and sunlight-resistant, and suitable for installation in cable trays.

337-9. Marking. Type SNM cable shall have a distinctive marking on its exterior surface for its entire length indicating its type and maximum operating temperature. It shall comply with the general marking requirements of Section 310-11.

The conductors shall each be numbered for identification from each other by durable marking on two sides 180 degrees apart every 6 inches (152 mm) of length, with alternate legends inverted to facilitate reading from both sides.

ARTICLE 338 — SERVICE-ENTRANCE CABLE

Types SE and USE

Contents

338-1. Definition. Service-entrance cable is a single conductor or multiconductor assembly provided with or without an overall covering, primarily used for services and of the following types:

(a) Type SE. Type SE, having a flame-retardant, moisture-resistant covering.

(b) Type USE. Type USE, identified for underground use, having a moisture-resistant covering, but not required to have a flame-retardant covering.

Cabled single-conductor Type USE constructions recognized for underground use may have a bare copper conductor cabled with the assembly. Type USE single, parallel, or cabled conductor assemblies recognized for underground use may have a bare copper concentric conductor applied. These constructions do not require an outer overall covering.

(FPN): See Section 230-41, Exception b.

(c) One Uninsulated Conductor. If Type SE or USE cable consists of two or more conductors, one shall be permitted to be uninsulated.

Service-entrance cable is labeled in sizes No. 12 AWG and larger for copper and No. 10 AWG and larger for aluminum or copper-clad aluminum with Type RH, RHW, RHH or XHHW conductors. If the type designation for the conductors is marked on the outside surface of the cable, the temperature rating of the cable corresponds to the rating of the individual conductors. When this marking does not appear, the temperature of the cable is 75°C (167°F).

The cables are classified as follows:

Type SE—Cable for aboveground installation.

Type USE—Cable for underground installation including burial directly in the earth. Cable in sizes No. 4/0 AWG and smaller and having all conductors insulated is suitable for all of the underground uses for which Type UF cable is permitted.

338-2. Uses Permitted as Service-Entrance Conductors. Service-entrance cable used as service-entrance conductors shall be installed as required by Article 230.

338-3. Uses Permitted as Branch Circuits or Feeders.

(a) Grounded Conductor Insulated. Type SE service-entrance cables shall be permitted in interior wiring systems where all of the circuit conductors of the cable are of the rubber-covered or thermoplastic type.

(b) Grounded Conductor Not Insulated. Type SE service-entrance cables without individual insulation on the grounded circuit conductor shall not be used as a branch circuit or as a feeder within a building, except a cable that has a final nonmetallic outer covering and is supplied by alternating current at not over 150 volts to ground shall be permitted: (1) as a branch circuit to supply only a range, wall-mounted oven, counter-mounted cooking unit, or clothes dryer as covered in Section 250-60, or (2) as a feeder to supply only other buildings on the same premises.

Type SE service-entrance cable shall be permitted for interior use where the fully insulated conductors are used for circuit wiring and the uninsulated conductor is used for equipment grounding purposes.

According to the UL Electrical Construction Materials Directory, based upon tests which have been made involving the maximum heating that can be produced, an uninsulated conductor employed in a service cable assembly is considered to have the same current-carrying capacity as the insulated conductors even though it may be smaller in size.

(c) Temperature Limitations. Type SE service-entrance cable used to supply appliances shall not be subject to conductor temperatures in excess of the temperature specified for the type of insulation involved.

338-4. Installation Methods.

(a) Interior Wiring. In addition to the provisions of this article, Type SE service-entrance cable used for interior wiring shall comply with the applicable provisions of Article 300.

(b) Unarmored Cable. Unarmored cable shall be installed in accordance with the provisions of Article 336.

Section 336-3 prohibits the use of nonmetallic-sheathed cables in dwellings and other structures exceeding three floors above grade. Type SE cable (unarmored), which is similar in construction to Types NM and NMC, where used for interior branch circuits and feeders, should also meet the provisions of Section 336-3.

The same restriction is to be applied to Type UF where used for interior wiring. See Section 339-3(a)(4).

(c) Through Studs, Joists, Rafters, or Similar Members. Cables shall comply with Section 300-4 where installed through studs, joists, rafters, or similar members.

338-5. Marking. Service-entrance cable shall be marked as required in Section 310-11. Cable with the neutral conductor smaller than the ungrounded conductors shall be so marked.

ARTICLE 339 — UNDERGROUND FEEDER AND BRANCH-CIRCUIT CABLE

Type UF

Contents

339-1. Description and Marking.

(a) Description. Underground feeder and branch-circuit cable shall be an approved Type UF cable in sizes No. 14 copper or No. 12 aluminum or copper-clad aluminum through No. 4/0. The conductors of Type UF shall be one of the moisture-resistant types listed in Table 310-13 which is suitable for branch-circuit wiring or one which is identified for such use. The ampacity of Type UF cable shall be that of 60°C (140°F) conductors in Table 310-16. In addition to the insulated conductors, the cable shall be permitted to have an approved size of insulated or bare conductor for equipment grounding purposes only. The overall covering shall be flame-retardant, moisture-, fungus-, and corrosion-resistant, and suitable for direct burial in the earth.

(b) Marking. In addition to the provisions of Section 310-11, the cable shall have a distinctive marking on the exterior for its entire length specifying the cable type.

339-2. Other Articles. In addition to the provisions of this article, installations of underground feeder and branch-circuit cable (Type UF) shall comply with other applicable provisions of this Code, especially Article 300 and Section 310-13.

Underground feeder and branch-circuit cable is rated for use at 60°C (140°F), 600 V, and is labeled in sizes No. 14 to 4/0 AWG, copper, and No. 12 to 4/0 AWG, aluminum or copper-clad aluminum, for single and multiple conductor cables.

Submersible Water Pump Cable indicates a multiconductor cable in which 2, 3, or 4 single-conductor Type UF cables are twisted together without an outer covering. The cable is labeled in sizes from 14 AWG to 2 AWG, copper, and from 12 AWG to 2 AWG, aluminum or copper-clad aluminum. The cable is tag marked: For use within the well casing for wiring deep-well water pumps where the cable is not subject to repetitive handling caused by frequent servicing of the pump units. The insulation may also be surface-marked "Pump Cable."

This cable may employ copper, or aluminum, or copper-clad aluminum conductors. Cables with copper-clad aluminum conductors are surface-printed "AL (CU-CLAD)" or "Cu-Clad Al."

If single-conductor Type UF cable is terminated with a fitting not specifically recognized for use with single-conductor cable, special care should be taken to assure it is properly secured and not subject to damage.

339-3. Use.

(a) Uses Permitted.

(1) Type UF cable shall be permitted for use underground, including direct burial in the earth, as feeder or branch-circuit cable where provided with overcurrent protection of the rated ampacity as required in Section 339-4.

(2) Where single-conductor cables are installed, all cables of the feeder circuit, subfeeder circuit, or branch circuit, including the neutral conductor, if any, shall be run together in the same trench or raceway.

Exception: For solar photovoltaic systems in accordance with Section 690-31.

(3) For underground requirements, see Section 300-5.

(4) Type UF cable shall be permitted for interior wiring in wet, dry, or corrosive locations under the recognized wiring methods of this Code, and where installed as nonmetallic-sheathed cable, the installation shall comply with the provisions of Article 336 and shall be of the multiconductor type.

See commentary following Sections 336-3 and 338-4(b).

Exception: Single-conductor cables shall be permitted as the nonheating leads for heating cables as provided in Section 424-43 and in solar photovoltaic systems in accordance with Section 690-31.

Type UF cable supported by cable trays shall be of the multiconductor type.

(b) Uses Not Permitted. Type UF cable shall not be used: (1) as service-entrance cables; (2) in commercial garages; (3) in theaters; (4) in motion picture studios; (5) in storage battery rooms; (6) in hoistways; (7) in any hazardous (classified) location; (8) embedded in poured cement, concrete, or aggregate, except where embedded in plaster as nonheating leads as provided in Article 424; (9) where exposed to direct rays of the sun, unless identified as sunlight-resistant.

Exception: See Section 501-4(b), Exception.

Type UF cables suitable for exposure to the direct rays of the sun are indicated by tag marking and marking on the surface of the cable with the designation "Sunlight Resistant."

339-4. Overcurrent Protection. Overcurrent protection shall be provided in accordance with provisions of Section 240-3.

339-5. Rated Ampacity. The ampacities of conductors in Type UF cable shall be according to Table 310-16.

ARTICLE 340 — POWER AND CONTROL TRAY CABLE

Type TC

Contents

340-1. Definition. Type TC power and control tray cable is a factory assembly of two or more insulated conductors, with or without associated bare or covered grounding conductors under a nonmetallic sheath, approved for installation in cable trays, in raceways, or where supported by a messenger wire.

340-2. Other Articles. In addition to the provisions of this article, installations of Type TC tray cable shall comply with other applicable articles of this Code, especially Articles 300 and 318.

340-3. Construction. The insulated conductors of Type TC tray cable shall be in sizes 18 AWG through 1000 MCM copper and sizes 12 AWG through 1000 MCM aluminum or copper-clad aluminum. Insulated conductors of size 14 AWG and larger copper and size 12 AWG and larger aluminum or copper-clad aluminum shall be one of the types listed in Table 310-13 or 310-62, which is suitable for branch circuit and feeder circuits or one which is identified for such use. Insulated conductors of size No. 18 and No. 16 AWG copper shall be in accordance with Section 725-16. The outer sheath shall be a flame-retardant, nonmetallic material. A metallic sheath shall not be permitted either under or over the nonmetallic sheath. Where installed in wet locations, Type TC cable shall be resistant to moisture and corrosive agents.

The construction requirements were revised in the 1984 *NEC* to make it clear a metallic sheath is not permitted either under or over the nonmetallic sheath.

340-4. Use Permitted. Type TC tray cable shall be permitted to be used: (1) for power, lighting, control, signal, and communication circuits; (2) in cable trays, or in raceways, or where supported in outdoor locations by a messenger wire; (3) in cable trays in hazardous (classified) locations as permitted in Articles 318 and 501 in industrial establishments where the conditions of maintenance and supervision assure that only qualified persons will service the installation; (4) for Class 1 circuits as permitted in Article 725.

The restriction that requires the condition of maintenance and supervision to ensure that only qualified persons will service the installation of Type TC cable applies only where the cable is to be used in a hazardous (classified) location.

340-5. Uses Not Permitted. Type TC tray cable shall not be: (1) installed where they will be exposed to physical damage; (2) installed as open cable on brackets or cleats; (3) used where exposed to direct rays of the sun, unless identified as sunlight-resistant; (4) direct buried, unless identified for such use.

Where identified for the use, Type TC cable is permitted to be direct buried. See definition of "Identified" in Article 100.

340-6. Marking. The cable shall be marked in accordance with Section 310-11.

340-7. Ampacity. The ampacities of the conductors of Type TC tray cable shall be determined from Section 400-5 for conductors smaller than No. 14, and Section 318-10.

ARTICLE 342 — NONMETALLIC EXTENSIONS

Contents

342-1. Definition. Nonmetallic extensions are an assembly of two insulated conductors within a nonmetallic jacket or an extruded thermoplastic covering. The classification includes both surface extensions, intended for mounting directly on the surface of walls or ceilings, and aerial cable, containing a supporting messenger cable as an integral part of the cable assembly.

342-2. Other Articles. In addition to the provisions of this article, nonmetallic extensions shall be installed in accordance with the applicable provisions of this Code.

342-3. Uses Permitted. Nonmetallic extensions shall be permitted only where all of the following conditions are met:

(a) **From an Existing Outlet.** The extension is from an existing outlet on a 15- or 20-ampere branch circuit in conformity with the requirements of Article 210.

(b) **Exposed and in a Dry Location.** The extension is run exposed and in a dry location.

(c) **Nonmetallic Surface Extensions.** For nonmetallic surface extensions, the building is occupied for residential or office purposes, and does not exceed the height limitations specified in Section 336-3.

Nonmetallic surface extensions are limited to residential or office locations. However, it is permitted as an aerial cable in industrial occupancies where a highly flexible means for connecting equipment is necessary. See Sections 342-4(a) and 342-7(b).

(c1) **[Alternate to (c)]** For aerial cable, the building is occupied for industrial purposes, and the nature of the occupancy requires a highly flexible means for connecting equipment.

A nonmetallic extension is an assembly of two insulated circuit conductors with or without a grounding conductor within a nonmetallic jacket or extruded thermoplastic covering. Assemblies without a grounding conductor are marked "intended for replacement use only."

342-4. Uses Not Permitted. Nonmetallic extensions shall not be used:

(a) **Aerial Cable.** As aerial cable to substitute for one of the general wiring methods specified by this Code.

(b) **Unfinished Areas.** In unfinished basements, attics, or roof spaces.

(c) **Voltage Between Conductors.** Where the voltage between conductors exceeds 150 volts for nonmetallic surface extension and 300 volts for aerial cable.

(d) **Corrosive Vapors.** Where subject to corrosive vapors.

(e) **Through a Floor or Partition.** Where run through a floor or partition, or outside the room in which it originates.

342-5. Splices and Taps. Extensions shall consist of a continuous unbroken length of the assembly, without splices, and without exposed conductors between fittings. Taps shall be permitted where approved fittings completely covering the tap connections are used. Aerial cable and its tap connectors shall be provided with an approved means for polarization. Receptacle-type tap connectors shall be of the locking-type.

342-6. Fittings. Each run shall terminate in a fitting that covers the end of the assembly. All fittings and devices shall be of a type identified for the use.

342-7. Installation. Nonmetallic extensions shall be installed as specified in (a) and (b) below.

ARTICLE 344—UNDERPLASTER EXTENSIONS

(a) Nonmetallic Surface Extensions.

(1) One or more extensions shall be permitted to be run in any direction from an existing outlet, but not on the floor or within 2 inches (50.8 mm) from the floor.

(2) Nonmetallic surface extensions shall be secured in place by approved means at intervals not exceeding 8 inches (203 mm).

Exception: Where connection to the supplying outlet is made by means of an attachment plug, the first fastening shall be permitted 12 inches (305 mm) or less from the plug.

There shall be at least one fastening between each two adjacent outlets supplied. An extension shall be attached only to woodwork or plaster finish, and shall not be in contact with any metal work or other conductive material other than with metal plates on receptacles.

(3) A bend that reduces the normal spacing between the conductors shall be covered with a cap to protect the assembly from physical damage.

(b) Aerial Cable.

(1) Aerial cable shall be supported by its messenger cable, securely attached at each end with approved clamps and turnbuckles. Intermediate supports shall be provided at not more than 20-foot (6.1-m) intervals. Cable tension shall be adjusted to eliminate excessive sag. The cable shall have a clearance of not less than 2 inches (50.8 mm) from steel structural members or other conductive material.

(2) Aerial cable shall have a clearance of not less than 10 feet (3.05 m) above floor areas accessible to pedestrian traffic, and not less than 14 feet (4.27 m) above floor areas accessible to vehicular traffic.

(3) Cable suspended over work benches, not accessible to pedestrian traffic, shall have a clearance of not less than 8 feet (2.44 m) above the floor.

(4) Aerial cables shall be permitted as a means to support lighting fixtures when the total load on the supporting messenger cable does not exceed that for which the assembly is intended.

(5) The supporting messenger cable, when installed in conformity with the applicable provisions of Article 250 and when properly identified as an equipment grounding conductor, shall be permitted to ground equipment. The messenger cable shall not be used as a branch-circuit conductor.

342-8. Marking. Nonmetallic extensions shall be marked in accordance with Section 110-21.

ARTICLE 344 — UNDERPLASTER EXTENSIONS

Contents

344-1. Use. An underplaster extension installed as permitted by this article shall be permitted only for extending an existing branch circuit in a building of fire-resistive construction.

Many times workers have found it impossible to fish cables into voids or hollow spaces of fire-resistive construction, and in these instances underplaster extensions have been a suitable alternative. An underplaster extension, as specified in Sections 344-2 and 344-5, is buried in the plaster finish of ceilings and walls.

344-2. Materials. Such extension shall be run in rigid or flexible conduit, Type AC cable, intermediate metal conduit, rigid nonmetallic conduit, electrical metallic tubing, Type MI cable, or metal raceways. Standard sizes of conduit, cable, tubing, and raceways shall be used.

Exception: For a single conductor only, conduit or tubing having not less than ¾₁₆ inch inside diameter, single-conductor Type AC cable, or single-conductor Type MI cable shall be permitted.

344-3. Boxes and Fittings. Boxes and fittings shall comply with the applicable provisions of Article 370.

344-4. Installation. An underplaster extension shall be laid on the face of masonry or other material and buried in the plaster finish of ceilings or walls. The methods of installation of the raceway or cable for such extension shall be as specified elsewhere in this Code for the particular type of material used.

344-5. Extension to Another Floor. No such extension shall extend beyond the floor on which it originates unless installed in a standard size of rigid metal conduit, intermediate metal conduit, electrical metallic tubing, Type AC cable, or Type MI cable.

Underplaster extensions are permitted in buildings of fire-resistive construction, such as concrete and brick buildings, where fishing cables in hollow spaces is virtually impossible.

This type of installation is permitted only for extending an existing branch circuit and is limited to the wiring methods specified in Sections 344-2 and 344-5.

ARTICLE 345 — INTERMEDIATE METAL CONDUIT

Contents

A. General

345-1. Definition. Intermediate metal conduit is a metal raceway of circular cross section with integral or associated couplings, connectors and fittings approved for the installation of electrical conductors.

ARTICLE 345—INTERMEDIATE METAL CONDUIT

Intermediate metal conduit (IMC) is a thinner-walled rigid metal conduit and is satisfactory for use in all locations where rigid metal conduit may be used. Also, threaded and unthreaded fittings, couplings, connectors, etc., are interchangeable for either IMC or rigid metal conduit.

Galvanized IMC installed in concrete does not require supplementary corrosion protection. Wherever ferrous metal conduit runs directly from concrete encasement to soil burial, severe corrosive effects are likely to occur on the metal in contact with the soil. In the absence of specific local experience, soils producing severe corrosive effects are generally characterized by low resistivity, less than 2000 ohm-centimeters.

345-2. Other Articles. Installations for intermediate metal conduit shall comply with the provisions of the applicable sections of Article 300.

345-3. Uses Permitted.

(a) All Atmospheric Conditions and Occupancies. Use of intermediate metal conduit shall be permitted under all atmospheric conditions and occupancies. Where practicable, dissimilar metals in contact anywhere in the system shall be avoided to eliminate the possibility of galvanic action. Intermediate metal conduit shall be permitted as an equipment grounding conductor.

(FPN): See Section 250-91.

Exception: Aluminum fittings and enclosures shall be permitted to be used with steel intermediate metal conduit.

(b) Corrosion Protection. Intermediate metal conduit, elbows, couplings, and fittings shall be permitted to be installed in concrete, in direct contact with the earth, or in areas subject to severe corrosive influences when protected by corrosion protection and judged suitable for the condition.

(FPN): See Section 300-6.

(c) Cinder Fill. Intermediate metal conduit shall be permitted to be installed in or under cinder fill where subject to permanent moisture when protected on all sides by a layer of noncinder concrete not less than 2 inches (50.8 mm) thick; when the conduit is not less than 18 inches (457 mm) under the fill; or when protected by corrosion protection and judged suitable for the condition.

(FPN): See Section 300-6.

B. Installation

345-5. Wet Locations. All supports, bolts, straps, screws, etc., shall be of corrosion-resistant materials or protected against corrosion by corrosion-resistant materials.

(FPN): See Section 300-6 for protection against corrosion.

345-6. Size.

(a) Minimum. Conduit smaller than ½-inch electrical trade size shall not be used.

(b) Maximum. Conduit larger than 4-inch electrical trade size shall not be used.

345-7. Number of Conductors in Conduit. The number of conductors in a single conduit shall not exceed that permitted by the percentage fill specified in Table 1, Chapter 9, using the conduit dimensions of Table 4, Chapter 9.

345-8. Reaming and Threading. All cut ends of conduits shall be reamed or otherwise finished to remove rough edges. Where conduit is threaded in the field, an electrical conduit thread cutting die with a taper shall be used.

See commentary following Section 348-11.

345-9. Couplings and Connectors.

(a) Threadless. Threadless couplings and connectors used with conduit shall be made tight. Where buried in masonry or concrete, they shall be the concretetight type. Where installed in wet locations, they shall be the raintight type.

(b) Running Threads. Running threads shall not be used on conduit for connection at couplings.

See commentary following Section 346-9.

345-10. Bends — How Made. Bends of intermediate metal conduit shall be so made that the conduit will not be injured, and that the internal diameter of the conduit will not be effectively reduced. The radius of the curve of the inner edge of any field bend shall not be less than indicated in Table 346-10.

Exception: For field bends for conductors without lead sheath and made with a single operation (one shot) bending machine designed for the purpose, the minimum radius shall not be less than that indicated in Table 346-10 Exception.

See commentary following Section 346-10.

345-11. Bends — Number in One Run. A run of conduit between outlet and outlet, between fitting and fitting, or between outlet and fitting, shall not contain more than the equivalent of four quarter bends (360 degrees, total), including those bends located immediately at the outlet or fitting.

See commentary following 346-11.

345-12. Supports. Intermediate metal conduit shall be installed as a complete system as provided in Article 300 and shall be securely fastened in place. Conduit shall be firmly fastened within 3 feet (914 mm) of each outlet box, junction box, cabinet, or fitting. Conduit shall be supported at least every 10 feet (3.05 m).

Exception No. 1: If made up with threaded couplings, it shall be permissible to support straight runs of intermediate metal conduit in accordance with Table 346-12, provided such supports prevent transmission of stresses to termination where conduit is deflected between supports.

Exception No. 2: The distance between supports may be increased to 20 feet (6.1 m) for exposed vertical risers from machine tools and the like, provided the conduit is made up with threaded couplings firmly supported at the top and bottom of the riser, and no other means of intermediate support is readily available.

345-13. Boxes and Fittings. See Article 370.

345-14. Splices and Taps. Splices and taps shall be made only in junction boxes, outlet boxes or conduit bodies. See Article 370.

345-15. Bushings. Where a conduit enters a box or fitting, a bushing shall be provided to protect the wire from abrasion unless the design of the box or fitting is such as to afford equivalent protection. See Section 373-6(c) for the protection of conductors at bushings.

ARTICLE 346—RIGID METAL CONDUIT

See commentary following Section 373-6.

C. Construction Specifications

345-16. General. Intermediate metal conduit shall comply with (a) through (c) below.

(a) Standard Lengths. Intermediate metal conduit as shipped shall be in standard lengths of 10 feet (3.05 m) including coupling, one coupling to be furnished with each length. For specific applications or use, it shall be permissible to ship lengths shorter or longer than 10 feet (3.05 m), with or without couplings.

(b) Corrosion-Resistant Material. Nonferrous conduit of corrosion-resistant material shall have suitable markings.

(c) Marking. Each length shall be clearly and durably identified at 2½-foot (762-mm) intervals with the letters IMC. Each length shall be marked as required in the first sentence of Section 110-21.

ARTICLE 346 — RIGID METAL CONDUIT

Contents

346-1. Use. The use of rigid metal conduit shall be permitted under all atmospheric conditions and occupancies subject to the following:

(a) Protected by Enamel. Ferrous raceways and fittings protected from corrosion solely by enamel shall be permitted only indoors and in occupancies not subject to severe corrosive influences.

(b) Dissimilar Metals. Where practicable, dissimilar metals in contact anywhere in the system shall be avoided to eliminate the possibility of galvanic action.

Exception: Aluminum fittings and enclosures shall be permitted to be used with steel rigid metal conduit, and also, steel fittings and enclosures shall be permitted to be used with aluminum rigid metal conduit.

(c) Corrosion Protection. Ferrous or nonferrous metal conduit, elbows, couplings, and fittings shall be permitted to be installed in concrete, in direct contact with the earth, or in areas subject to severe corrosive influences where protected by corrosion protection and judged suitable for the condition.

(FPN): See Section 300-6.

This section indicates the permitted uses for ferrous and nonferrous conduit, including their use in concrete, in direct contact with the earth, and in corrosive areas. The Fine Print Note references Section 300-6 for additional information on protection against corrosion and specific types of corrosion-resistant materials.

The exception to Section 346-1(b) is intended to make it clear that aluminum rigid conduit can be used with steel fittings and enclosures as well as aluminum fittings and enclosures with steel rigid conduit. It has been shown by test that the galvanic corrosion at steel and aluminum interfaces is minor in comparison to the natural corrosion on the combination of steel and steel or aluminum and aluminum.

It is advisable to consult with the authority enforcing this *Code* for the approval of corrosion-resistant materials and/or for requirements prior to the installation of nonferrous metal (aluminum) conduit in concrete since chloride additives in the concrete mix have caused corrosion.

346-2. Other Articles. Installations of rigid metal conduit shall comply with the applicable provisions of Article 300.

A. Installation

346-3. Cinder Fill. Conduit shall not be used in or under cinder fill where subject to permanent moisture.

Exception No. 1: Where of corrosion-resistant material suitable for the purpose.

Exception No. 2: Where protected on all sides by a layer of noncinder concrete at least 2 inches (50.8 mm) thick.

Exception No. 3: Where the conduit is at least 18 inches (457 mm) under the fill.

Although cinder fill is not commonly used in modern construction, it is still encountered in older building basement slabs. Care should be taken to install rigid metal conduit as required by the exceptions because cinders contain sulphur, and sulfuric acid is formed which can corrode metal raceways.

346-4. Wet Locations. All supports, bolts, straps, screws, etc., shall be of corrosion-resistant materials or protected against corrosion by corrosion-resistant materials.

(FPN): See Section 300-6 for protection against corrosion.

346-5. Minimum Size. Conduit smaller than ½ inch electrical trade size shall not be used.

Exception No. 1: For underplaster extensions as permitted in Section 344-2.

Exception No. 2: For enclosing the leads of motors as permitted in Section 430-145(b).

346-6. Number of Conductors in Conduit. The number of conductors permitted in a single conduit shall not exceed the percentage fill specified in Table 1, Chapter 9.

(FPN): For conductor cross-sectional area see Tables 5, 6, 7, 8 and the applicable Notes to Tables at the beginning of Chapter 9.

Tables 3A, 3B, and 3C in Chapter 9 are based on the allowable percentages of Table 1, Chapter 9, for conduit or tubing fill, that is, 53 percent for 1 conductor,

31 percent for 2 conductors, and 40 percent for 3 or more conductors. Percentages for lead-covered conductors vary, somewhat, from other conductor types (see Table 1).

346-7. Reaming and Threading.

(a) Reamed. All cut ends of conduits shall be reamed or otherwise finished to remove rough edges.

See commentary following Section 348-11.

(b) Threaded. Where conduit is threaded in the field, a standard conduit cutting die with a ¾-inch (19-mm) taper per foot (305 mm) shall be used.

346-8. Bushings.
Where a conduit enters a box or other fitting, a bushing shall be provided to protect the wire from abrasion unless the design of the box or fitting is such as to afford equivalent protection.

(FPN): See Section 373-6(c) for the protection of conductors at bushings.

346-9. Couplings and Connectors.

(a) Threadless. Threadless couplings and connectors used with conduit shall be made tight. Where buried in masonry or concrete, they shall be of the concretetight type. Where installed in wet locations, they shall be of the raintight type.

(b) Running Threads. Running threads shall not be used on conduit for connection at couplings.

Figure 346-1 illustrates a threadless connection integral to a conduit body, FS box, etc. This type of connection may be separate from the conduit body or box as an individual fitting of the compression type (raintight) suitable for wet locations or of the set-screw type (concretetight).

Threadless connections are not intended for use over threads as the fitting will not properly seat. The threaded end of the conduit should be cut off before using at a threadless connection.

Figure 346-2 illustrates an Erickson coupling (the electrical equivalent of a pipe union) which is used to join two lengths of conduit where it is impossible to turn either length, such as in underground or concrete-slab construction. Bolted split

Figure 346-1. Conduit body with threadless connector. (*Appleton Electric Co.*)

Figure 346-2. Erickson or union-type coupling. (*Appleton Electric Co.*)

couplings may also be used. Running threads are not permitted to join two conduits, but may be permitted to join two boxes where electrical and mechanical connections are assured (locknuts and bushings).

346-10. Bends — How Made. Bends of rigid metal conduit shall be so made that the conduit will not be injured, and that the internal diameter of the conduit will not be effectively reduced. The radius of the curve of the inner edge of any field bend shall not be less than shown in Table 346-10.

Exception: For field bends for conductors without lead sheath and made with a single operation (one shot) bending machine designed for the purpose, the minimum radius shall not be less than indicated in Table 346-10 Exception.

The term "field bend" means any bend or offset made by installers, using proper tools and equipment, during the installation of conduit systems.

Table 346-10
Radius of Conduit Bends (Inches)

Size of Conduit (In.)	Conductors Without Lead Sheath (In.)	Conductors With Lead Sheath (In.)
½	4	6
¾	5	8
1	6	11
1¼	8	14
1½	10	16
2	12	21
2½	15	25
3	18	31
3½	21	36
4	24	40
5	30	50
6	36	61

For SI units: (Radius) one inch = 25.4 millimeters.

Table 346-10.   Exception
Radius of Conduit Bends (Inches)

Size of Conduit (In.)	Radius to Center of Conduit (In.)
½	4
¾	4½
1	5¾
1¼	7¼
1½	8¼
2	9½
2½	10½
3	13
3½	15
4	16
5	24
6	30

For SI units: (Radius) one inch = 25.4 millimeters.

346-11. Bends — Number in One Run. A run of conduit between outlet and outlet, fitting and fitting, or outlet and fitting shall not contain more than the equivalent of four quarter bends (360 degrees, total), including those bends located immediately at the outlet or fitting.

Limiting the number of bends in a conduit run eliminates pulling tension on conductors and ensures easy insertion or removal of conductors during later phases of construction when the conduit may be permanently enclosed by the finish of the building. Adjustments during that time are often impossible.

346-12. Supports. Rigid metal conduit shall be installed as a complete system as provided in Article 300 and shall be securely fastened in place. Conduit shall be firmly fastened within 3 feet (914 mm) of each outlet box, junction box, cabinet, or fitting. Conduit shall be supported at least every 10 feet (3.05 m).

Exception No. 1: If made up with threaded couplings, it shall be permissible to support straight runs of rigid metal conduit in accordance with Table 346-12, provided such supports prevent transmission of stresses to termination where conduit is deflected between supports.

Exception No. 2: The distance between supports may be increased to 20 feet (6.1 m) for exposed vertical risers from machine tools and the like, provided the conduit is made up with threaded couplings, is firmly supported at the top and bottom of the riser, and no other means of intermediate support is readily available.

Table 346-12.   Supports for Rigid Metal Conduit

Conduit Size (Inches)	Maximum Distance Between Rigid Metal Conduit Supports (Feet)
½–¾	10
1	12
1¼–1½	14
2–2½	16
3 and larger	20

For SI units: (Supports) one foot = 0.3048 meter.

346-13. Boxes and Fittings.   Boxes and fittings shall comply with the applicable provisions of Article 370.

346-14. Splices and Taps.   Splices and taps shall be made only in junction boxes, outlet boxes or conduit bodies. See Article 370.

B. Construction Specifications

346-15. General.   Rigid metal conduit shall comply with (a) through (d) below.

(a) Standard Lengths.   Rigid metal conduit as shipped shall be in standard lengths of 10 feet (3.05 m) including coupling, one coupling to be furnished with each length. Each length shall be reamed and threaded on each end. For specific applications or uses, it shall be permissible to ship standard lengths or lengths shorter or longer than 10 feet (3.05 m) with or without couplings and with or without threads.

(b) Corrosion-Resistant Material.   Nonferrous conduit of corrosion-resistant material shall have suitable markings.

(c) Durably Identified.   Each length shall be clearly and durably identified in every 10 feet (3.05 m) as required in the first sentence of Section 110-21.

ARTICLE 347 — RIGID NONMETALLIC CONDUIT

Contents

347-1. Description. This article shall apply to a type of conduit and fittings of suitable nonmetallic material that is resistant to moisture and chemical atmospheres. For use aboveground, it shall also be flame-retardant, resistant to impact and crushing, resistant to distortion from heat under conditions likely to be encountered in service, and resistant to low temperature and sunlight effects. For use underground, the material shall be acceptably resistant to moisture and corrosive agents and shall be of sufficient strength to withstand abuse, such as by impact and crushing, in handling and during installation. Where intended for direct burial, without encasement in concrete, the material shall also be capable of withstanding continued loading that is likely to be encountered after installation.

(FPN): Materials that have been recognized as having suitable physical characteristics when properly formed and treated include fiber, asbestos cement, soapstone, rigid polyvinyl chloride, fiberglass epoxy, and high-density polyethylene for underground use, and rigid polyvinyl chloride for use aboveground.

Unless marked for a higher temperature, rigid nonmetallic conduit (Schedule 40 and Schedule 80) in this category is intended for use with wires rated 75°C (167°F) or less (1) aboveground, (2) for direct burial underground, (3) where encased in concrete within buildings, and (4) where ambient temperature is 50°C (122°F) or less. When encased in concrete in trenches outside of buildings it is suitable for use with wire rated 90°C (194°F) or less.

Direct burial conduit is suitable for cables rated over 600 V when it is buried to a depth in accordance with Table 710-3(b). Rigid nonmetallic conduit is listed in sizes ½ to 6 in. inclusive.

Listed PVC conduit is inherently resistant to atmosphere containing common industrial corrosive agents and will also withstand vapors or mist of caustic, pickling acids, plating baths, and hydrofluoric and chromic acids.

PVC conduit is designed for connection to couplings, fittings, and boxes by the use of a suitable solvent-type cement. Instructions supplied by the manufacturer describe the method of assembly and precautions to be followed.

For use of Schedule 80, see Sections 300-5(d), 551-51(b), and 710-3(b)(1).

347-2. Uses Permitted. The use of rigid nonmetallic conduit and fittings shall be permitted under the following conditions:

ARTICLE 347—RIGID NONMETALLIC CONDUIT

(a) **Concealed.** In walls, floors, and ceilings.

(b) **Corrosive Influences.** In locations subject to severe corrosive influences as covered in Section 300-6 and where subject to chemicals for which the materials are specifically approved.

(c) **Cinders.** In cinder fill.

(d) **Wet Locations.** In portions of dairies, laundries, canneries, or other wet locations and in locations where walls are frequently washed, the entire conduit system including boxes and fittings used therewith shall be so installed and equipped as to prevent water from entering the conduit. All supports, bolts, straps, screws, etc., shall be of corrosion-resistant materials or be protected against corrosion by approved corrosion-resistant materials.

(e) **Dry and Damp Locations.** In dry and damp locations not prohibited by Section 347-3.

(f) **Exposed.** For exposed work where not subject to physical damage if identified for such use.

(g) **Underground Installations.** For underground installations, see Sections 300-5 and 710-3(b).

347-3. Uses Not Permitted. Rigid nonmetallic conduit shall not be used:

(a) **Hazardous (Classified) Locations.** In hazardous (classified) locations, except as covered in Sections 514-8 and 515-5; and Class I, Division 2 locations as permitted in the Exception to Section 501-4(b).

(b) **Support of Fixtures.** For the support of fixtures or other equipment.

(c) **Physical Damage.** Where subject to physical damage unless identified for such use.

(d) **Ambient Temperatures.** Where subject to ambient temperatures exceeding those for which the conduit is approved.

(e) **Insulation Temperature Limitations.** For conductors whose insulation temperature limitations would exceed those for which the conduit is approved.

Nonmetallic conduits are not permitted to be installed in ducts, plenums, and other air-handling spaces. See Section 300-22.

In addition, nonmetallic conduits should not be used where their use would substantially increase the possible spread of fire or products of combustion through fire-rated, fire-resistant or fire-stopped walls, partitions, ceilings and floors, hollow spaces, vertical shafts, and ventilating or air-handling ducts. See Section 300-21 for requirements covering the prevention of the spread of fire or products of combustion.

347-4. Other Articles. Installation of rigid nonmetallic conduit shall comply with the applicable provisions of Article 300. Where equipment grounding is required by Article 250, a separate equipment grounding conductor shall be installed in the conduit.

A. Installations

347-5. Trimming. All cut ends shall be trimmed inside and outside to remove rough edges.

See commentary following Section 348-11.

352

347-6. Joints. All joints between lengths of conduit, and between conduit and couplings, fittings, and boxes, shall be made by an approved method.

347-8. Supports. Rigid nonmetallic conduit shall be supported as required in Table 347-8. In addition, there shall be a support within 3 feet (914 mm) of each box, cabinet, or other conduit termination.

The requirement in Section 347-8 for a support within 3 ft of each conduit termination is consistent with the minimum support spacing in Table 347-8.

It is recognized that these requirements are fairly stringent because they are based on ambient temperatures much higher than normally encountered and utilize horizontal support tests only.

Table 347-8.   Support of Rigid Nonmetallic Conduit

Conduit Size (Inches)	Maximum Spacing Between Supports (Feet)
½-1	3
1¼-2	5
2½-3	6
3½-5	7
6	8

For SI units: (Supports) one foot = 0.3048 meter.

347-9. Expansion Joints. Expansion joints for rigid nonmetallic conduit shall be provided to compensate for thermal expansion and contraction.

Expansion joints or expansion couplings are generally provided in exposed runs of nonmetallic rigid conduit where (1) the run is long, (2) the run is subjected to large temperature variations, and (3) expansion and contraction measures are provided for the building structure. Rigid nonmetallic conduit exhibits a considerably greater change in length per degree change in temperature than metal raceway systems.

The normal expansion range of most larger sizes of rigid nonmetallic conduit expansion couplings is generally 6 in. Information concerning installation and application of this type of coupling may be obtained from manufacturer's instructions.

Expansion couplings are seldom used underground where temperatures are relatively constant. Where rigid nonmetallic conduit is buried or covered immediately, expansion and contraction are not a problem.

347-10. Minimum Size. No conduit smaller than ½-inch electrical trade size shall be used.

347-11. Number of Conductors. The number of conductors permitted in a single conduit shall not exceed the percentage fill specified in Table 1, Chapter 9.

(FPN): For conductor cross-sectional area see Tables 5, 6, 7, 8 and the applicable Notes to Tables at the beginning of Chapter 9.

See commentary following Section 346-6.

347-12. Bushings. Where a conduit enters a box or other fitting, a bushing or adapter shall be provided to protect the wire from abrasion unless the design of the box or fitting is such as to provide equivalent protection.

(FPN): See Section 373-6(c) for the protection of conductors at bushings.

347-13. Bends — How Made. Bends of rigid nonmetallic conduit shall be so made that the conduit will not be injured and that the internal diameter of the conduit will not be effectively reduced. Field bends shall be made only with bending equipment intended for the purpose, and the radius of the curve of the inner edge of such bends shall not be less than shown in Table 346-10.

See commentary following Section 346-10.

347-14. Bends — Number in One Run. A run of conduit between outlet and outlet, fitting and fitting, or outlet and fitting shall not contain more than the equivalent of four quarter bends (360 degrees, total), including those bends located immediately at the outlet or fitting.

347-15. Boxes and Fittings. Boxes and fittings shall comply with the applicable provisions of Article 370.

347-16. Splices and Taps. Splices and taps shall be made only in junction boxes, outlet boxes or conduit bodies. See Article 370.

B. Construction Specifications

347-17. General. Rigid nonmetallic conduit shall comply with the following:

Marking. Each length of nonmetallic conduit shall be clearly and durably marked at least every 10 feet (3.05 m) as required in the first sentence of Section 110-21. The type of material shall also be included in the marking unless it is visually identifiable. For conduit recognized for use aboveground these markings shall be permanent. For conduit limited to underground use only, these markings shall be sufficiently durable to remain legible until the material is installed.

ARTICLE 348 — ELECTRICAL METALLIC TUBING

Contents

348-1. Use. The use of electrical metallic tubing shall be permitted for both exposed and concealed work. Electrical metallic tubing shall not be used: (1) where, during installation or afterward, it will be subject to severe physical damage; (2) where protected from corrosion solely by enamel; (3) in cinder concrete or cinder fill where subject to permanent moisture unless protected on all sides by a layer of noncinder concrete at least 2 inches (50.8 mm) thick or unless the tubing is at least 18 inches (457 mm) under the fill. Where practicable, dissimilar metals in contact anywhere in the system shall be avoided to eliminate the possibility of galvanic action.

Exception: Aluminum fittings and enclosures shall be permitted to be used with steel electrical metallic tubing.

Ferrous or nonferrous electrical metallic tubing, elbows, couplings, and fittings shall be permitted to be installed in concrete, in direct contact with the earth, or in areas subject to severe corrosive influences when protected by corrosion protection and judged suitable for the condition.

Galvanized steel electrical metallic tubing installed in concrete on grade or above grade generally requires no supplementary corrosion protection. EMT installed in concrete below grade level or installed in contact with soil generally requires supplementary corrosion protection.

(FPN): See Section 300-6.

348-2. Other Articles. Installations of electrical metallic tubing shall comply with the applicable provisions of Article 300.

A. Installation

348-4. Wet Locations. All supports, bolts, straps, screws, etc., shall be of corrosion-resistant materials or protected against corrosion by corrosion-resistant materials.

(FPN): See Section 300-6 for protection from corrosion.

348-5. Size.

(a) Minimum. Tubing smaller than ½-inch electrical trade size shall not be used.

Exception No. 1: For underplaster extensions as permitted in Section 344-2.

Exception No. 2: For enclosing the leads of motors as permitted in Section 430-145(b).

(b) Maximum. The maximum size of tubing shall be the 4-inch electrical trade size.

348-6. Number of Conductors in Tubing. The number of conductors permitted in a single tubing shall not exceed the percentage fill specified in Table 1, Chapter 9.

(FPN): For conductor cross-sectional area see Tables 5, 6, 7, 8 and the applicable Notes to Tables at the beginning of Chapter 9.

348-7. Threads. Electrical metallic tubing shall not be threaded. Where integral couplings are utilized, such couplings shall be permitted to be factory threaded.

348-8. Couplings and Connectors. Couplings and connectors used with tubing shall be made up tight. Where buried in masonry or concrete, they shall be concretetight type. Where installed in wet locations, they shall be of the raintight type.

UL listed fittings that are suitable for use in poured concrete or where exposed to rain are so indicated on the fitting or carton. The term "raintight" or the equivalent on the carton indicates suitability for use where directly exposed to rain. The term "concretetight" or equivalent on the carton indicates suitability for use in poured concrete. See Sections 225-22 and 230-53.

Fittings have been tested for use only with steel tubing unless marked on the device or carton to indicate suitability for use with aluminum or other material.

Indentor-type fittings are for use with metallic-coated electrical metallic tubing only and require a special tool supplied by the manufacturer for proper installation. Diametrically opposed indentor-type tools require two sets of indentations nominally 90 degrees apart. Triple indent tools require one set of indentations.

348-9. Bends — How Made. Bends in the tubing shall be so made that the tubing will not be injured and that the internal diameter of the tubing will not be effectively reduced. The radius of the curve of the inner edge of any field bend shall not be less than shown in Table 346-10.

Exception: For field bends made with a bending machine designed for the purpose, the minimum radius shall not be less than indicated in Table 346-10 Exception.

348-10. Bends — Number in One Run. A run of electrical metallic tubing between outlet and outlet, fitting and fitting, or outlet and fitting shall not contain more than the equivalent of four quarter bends (360 degrees, total), including those bends located immediately at the outlet or fitting.

See commentary following Section 346-11.

348-11. Reaming. All cut ends of electrical metallic tubing shall be reamed or otherwise finished to remove rough edges.

In addition to a reamer, a half-round file has proven practical to remove rough edges with excellent results.

348-12. Supports. Electrical metallic tubing shall be installed as a complete system as provided in Article 300 and shall be securely fastened in place at least every 10 feet (3.05 m) and within 3 feet (914 mm) of each outlet box, junction box, cabinet, or fitting.

348-13. Boxes and Fittings. Boxes and fittings shall comply with the applicable provisions of Article 370.

348-14. Splices and Taps. Splices and taps shall be made only in junction boxes, outlet boxes or conduit bodies. See Article 370.

B. Construction Specifications

348-15. General. Electrical metallic tubing shall comply with (a) through (c) below.

(a) Cross Section. The tubing, and elbows and bends for use with the tubing, shall have a circular cross section.

(b) Finish. Tubing shall have such a finish or treatment of outer surfaces as will provide an approved durable means of readily distinguishing it, after installation, from rigid metal conduit.

(c) Connectors. Where the tubing is coupled together by threads, the connector shall be so designed as to prevent bending of the tubing at any part of the thread.

ARTICLE 349 — FLEXIBLE METALLIC TUBING

Contents

A. General

349-1. Scope. The provisions of this article apply to a raceway for electrical conductors which is circular in cross section, flexible, metallic, liquidtight without a nonmetallic jacket and intended for use where not subject to physical damage such as above suspended ceilings.

Flexible metallic tubing is a raceway used for certain specific applications, particularly for use under the requirements of Section 300-22(b) and (c) for wiring in ducts, plenums, and air-handling spaces. Flexible metallic tubing is a material that is readily flexed and is rarely affected by conditions of vibration or other movement. It is an effective barrier to gases and products of combustion when installed with matching fittings and is of adequate mechanical strength for use where not exposed to physical damage. Similarly, flexible metallic tubing has the necessary properties for use as required for tap conductors for lighting fixtures where outlet boxes are placed 1 ft from the fixture. Flexible metallic tubing has advantages over the use of liquidtight flexible metal conduit in ducts and plenums because it does not have a nonmetallic (PVC) outer sheath that would introduce a probable source of smoke and products of combustion into the ventilation system in the event of a fire situation.

349-2. Other Articles. Installations of flexible metallic tubing shall comply with the provisions of the applicable sections of Article 300.

349-3. Uses Permitted. Flexible metallic tubing shall be permitted to be used: (1) in dry locations; (2) in accessible locations when protected from physical damage or concealed; (3) for 1000 volts maximum; and (4) in branch circuits.

A common application of flexible metallic tubing is as a wiring method for equipment or lighting fixtures mounted on, or above, suspended ceilings.

349-4. Uses Not Permitted. Flexible metallic tubing shall not be used: (1) in hoistways; (2) in storage battery rooms; (3) in hazardous (classified) locations; (4) underground for direct earth burial, or embedded in poured concrete or aggregate; and (5) in lengths over 6 feet (1.83 m).

Unlike flexible metal conduit or liquidtight flexible metal conduit, flexible metallic tubing is limited to 6 ft in length.

B. Construction and Installation

349-10. Size.

(a) Minimum. Flexible metallic tubing smaller than ½-inch electrical trade size shall not be used.

Exception No. 1: ⅜-inch trade size shall be permitted to be installed in accordance with Section 300-22(b) and (c).

Exception No. 2: ⅜-inch trade size shall be permitted in lengths not in excess of 6 feet (1.83 m) as part of an approved assembly or for lighting fixtures. See Section 410-67(c).

(b) Maximum. The maximum size of flexible metallic tubing shall be the ¾-inch trade size.

349-12. Number of Conductors.

(a) ½-Inch and ¾-Inch Flexible Metallic Tubing. The number of conductors permitted in ½-inch and ¾-inch trade sizes of flexible metallic tubing shall not exceed the percentage of fill specified in Table 1, Chapter 9.

(b) ⅜-Inch Flexible Metallic Tubing. The number of conductors permitted in ⅜-inch trade size flexible metallic tubing shall not exceed that permitted in Table 350-3.

(FPN): For conductor cross-sectional area see Tables 5, 6, 7, 8 and the applicable Notes to Tables at the beginning of Chapter 9.

349-16. Grounding. See Section 250-91(b), Exception No. 1.

349-18. Fittings. Flexible metallic tubing shall be used only with approved terminal fittings. Fittings shall effectively close any openings in the connection.

(FPN): See Sections 300-22(b) and (c).

349-20. Bends.

(a) Infrequent Flexing Use. Where the flexible metallic tubing shall be infrequently flexed in service after installation, the radii of bends measured to the inside of the bend shall not be less than specified in Table 349-20(a).

(b) Fixed Bends. Where the flexible metallic tubing is bent for installation purposes and is not flexed or bent as required by use after installation, the radii of bends measured to the inside of the bend shall not be less than specified in Table 349-20(b).

Table 349-20(a). Minimum Radii for Flexing Use

Trade Size	Minimum Radii
⅜ inch	10 inches
½ inch	12½ inches
¾ inch	17½ inches

For SI units: (Radii) one inch = 25.4 millimeters.

Table 349-20(b). Minimum Radii for Fixed Bends

Trade Size	Minimum Radii
⅜ inch	3½ inches
½ inch	4 inches
¾ inch	5 inches

For SI units: (Radii) one inch = 25.4 millimeters.

ARTICLE 350 — FLEXIBLE METAL CONDUIT

Contents

350-1. Other Articles. Installations of flexible metal conduit shall comply with the applicable provisions of Articles 300, 333, and 346.

350-2. Use. Flexible metal conduit shall not be used: (1) in wet locations unless conductors are of lead-covered type or of other types approved for the specific conditions and the installation is such that water is not likely to enter other raceways or enclosures to which the conduit is connected; (2) in hoistways, other than provided in Section 620-21; (3) in storage-battery rooms; (4) in any hazardous (classified) location other than permitted in Section 501-4(b); (5) where rubber-covered conductors are exposed to oil, gasoline, or other materials having a deteriorating effect on rubber; nor (6) underground or embedded in poured concrete or aggregate.

This section was revised for the 1984 *NEC* to make it clear that flexible metal conduit is permitted for use in wet locations provided the completed installation prevents water from entering other raceways or enclosures to which the conduit is connected, and the conductors are suitable for wet locations. See Figure 350-1.

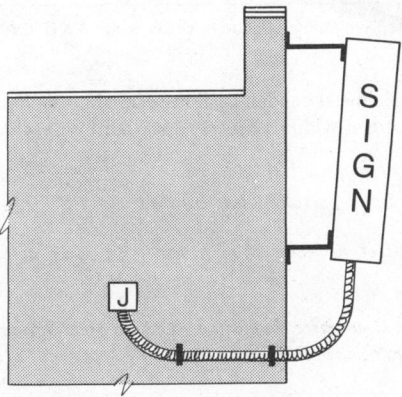

Figure 350-1. An example of one acceptable application of flexible metal conduit on the exterior of a building. The branch circuit supply conductors are suitable for use in a wet location and the junction box is listed for use in a wet location.

350-3. Minimum Size. Flexible metal conduit less than ½-inch electrical trade size shall not be used.

Exception No. 1: For underplaster extensions as permitted in Section 344-2.

Exception No. 2: For enclosing the leads of motors as permitted in Section 430-145(b).

Exception No. 3: Flexible metal conduit of ⅜-inch nominal trade size shall be permitted in lengths not in excess of 6 feet (1.83 m) as a part of an approved assembly, or for tap connections to lighting fixtures as required in Section 410-67(c), or for lighting fixtures.

This exception makes it clear that ⅜-in. flexible metal conduit is permitted to be used as the factory- or field-installed metal raceway (4 to 6 ft in length) to enclose tap conductors from the outlet box to the fixture terminal housing of recessed lighting fixtures.

Also, flexible metal conduit is permitted to be used, for example, as a 6-ft fixture "whip" from an outlet box to a lighting fixture supported on a suspended ceiling.

Table 350-3. Maximum Number of Insulated Conductors in ⅜-Inch Flexible Metal Conduit.*

Col. A = With fitting inside conduit.
Col. B = With fitting outside conduit.

Size AWG	Types RFH-2, SF-2		Types TF, T, XHHW, AF, TW, RUH, RUW		Types TFN, THHN, THWN		Types FEP, FEPB, PF, PGF	
	A	B	A	B	A	B	A	B
18	..	3	3	7	4	8	5	8
16	..	2	2	4	3	7	4	8
14	..	..	..	4	3	7	3	7
12	..	..	..	3	..	4	..	4
10	..	..	..	..	..	2	..	3

* In addition, one uninsulated grounding conductor of the same AWG size shall be permitted.

350-4. Supports. Flexible metal conduit shall be secured by an approved means at intervals not exceeding 4½ feet (1.37 m) and within 12 inches (305 mm) on each side of every outlet box or fitting.

Exception No. 1: Where flexible metal conduit is fished.

Exception No. 2: Lengths of not more than 3 feet (914 mm) at terminals where flexibility is necessary.

Exception No. 3: Lengths of not more than 6 feet (1.83 m) from a fixture terminal connection for tap connections to lighting fixtures as required in Section 410-67(c).

Flexible metal conduit is permitted to be concealed or rendered inaccessible by the finish of a building. However, unlike other raceways, such as rigid metal conduit, intermediate metal conduit, or electrical metallic tubing, which are required to be supported every 10 ft and within 3 ft of every box or fitting, flexible metal conduit is required to be supported at least every 4½ ft and within 12 in. of every box or fitting. See Sections 345-12, 346-12, and 348-12. Similar to other raceways, a run of flexible metal conduit installed between boxes, conduit bodies, etc., is not permitted to contain more than the equivalent of four quarter bends (360 degrees total). Adequate shaping and support of this flexible wiring method will assure that conductors can be easily installed or withdrawn at any time.

350-5. Grounding. Flexible metal conduit shall be permitted as a grounding means where both the conduit and the fittings are approved for grounding. Where an equipment bonding jumper is required around flexible metal conduit, it shall be installed in accordance with Section 250-79.

Where flexible metal conduit and fittings have not been specifically approved as a grounding means, a separate equipment grounding or bonding conductor (insulated or bare) is required to be run inside or outside the conduit. Where run outside as an equipment bonding jumper, the jumper is required to be 6 ft or less in length, routed with the raceway or enclosure, and bonded at each end of the flexible metal conduit to which it is connected.

When used in hazardous (classified) locations, a bonding jumper is required. See Sections 501-16(b), 502-16(b), and 503-16(b).

Exception: Flexible metal conduit shall be permitted as a grounding means if the total length in any ground return path is 6 feet (1.83 m) or less, the conduit is terminated in fittings approved for grounding, and the circuit conductors contained therein are protected by overcurrent devices rated at 20 amperes or less.

Flexible metal conduit is permitted as an equipment grounding means where it is installed in 6-ft lengths so that a ground fault anywhere in the circuit will not have to traverse through more than 6 ft of flexible metal conduit before the fault current returns to the overcurrent device protecting the circuit. When flexible metal conduit is not cut squarely, so as to provide a proper fit into fittings which clamp around the conduit or are screwed into the conduit, the effectiveness of the grounding path may be reduced. See the commentary following Section 250-91(b). See Figure 350-2.

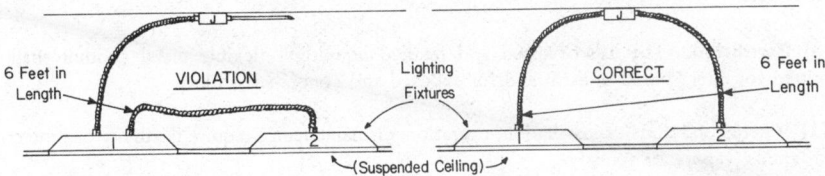

Figure 350-2. The sketch on the right shows the proper application of flexible metal conduit where the total length of any ground return path is limited to 6 ft. The sketch on the left shows an application that is in violation, as the ground return for fixture No. 2 is 12 ft.

350-6. Bends. A run of conduit between outlet and outlet, fitting and fitting, or outlet and fitting shall not contain more than the equivalent of four quarter bends (360 degrees, total), including those bends located immediately at the outlet or fitting.

Angle connectors shall not be used for concealed raceway installations.

ARTICLE 351 — LIQUIDTIGHT FLEXIBLE CONDUIT

Contents

A. Liquidtight Flexible Metal Conduit

351-1. Scope. Part A of this article covers use and installation requirements for liquidtight flexible metal conduit.

Liquidtight flexible metal conduit is intended for use in wet locations or where exposed to mineral oil, both at a maximum temperature of 60°C (140°F). It is not intended for use where exposed to gasoline or similar light petroleum solvents nor for use in hazardous (classified) locations unless so marked on the product.

ARTICLE 351—LIQUIDTIGHT FLEXIBLE CONDUIT

351-2. Definition. Liquidtight flexible metal conduit is a raceway of circular cross section having an outer liquidtight, nonmetallic, sunlight-resistant jacket over an inner flexible metal core with associated couplings, connectors, and fittings and approved for the installation of electric conductors.

351-3. Other Articles. Installations of liquidtight flexible metal conduit shall comply with the applicable provisions of Article 300 and with the specific sections of Articles 350, 501, 502, and 503 referenced below.

351-4. Use.

(a) Permitted. The use of listed and marked liquidtight flexible metal conduit shall be permitted for direct burial in earth and for exposed and concealed work:

(1) Where conditions of installation, operation, or maintenance require flexibility or protection from liquids, vapors, or solids.

(2) As permitted by Sections 501-4(b), 502-4, and 503-3, and in other hazardous (classified) locations where specifically approved.

This section was revised for the 1984 *Code.* "Listed and marked" liquidtight flexible metal conduit is permitted for direct burial in the earth. It should be noted that the requirements of Section 300-5 are now applicable to liquidtight flexible metal conduit where installed underground.

(b) Not Permitted. Liquidtight flexible metal conduit shall not be used:

(1) Where subject to physical damage.

(2) Where any combination of ambient and/or conductor temperature will produce an operating temperature in excess of that for which the material is approved.

351-5. Size.

(a) Minimum. Liquidtight flexible metal conduit smaller than ½-inch electrical trade size shall not be used.

Exception: ⅜-inch size shall be permitted as covered in Section 350-3.

(b) Maximum. The maximum size of liquidtight flexible metal conduit shall be the 4-inch trade size.

351-6. Number of Conductors.

(a) Single Conduit. The number of conductors permitted in a single conduit, ½- through 4-inch trade sizes, shall not exceed the percentage of fill specified in Table 1, Chapter 9.

(b) ⅜-Inch Liquidtight Flexible Metal Conduit. The number of conductors permitted in ⅜-inch liquidtight flexible metal conduit shall not exceed that permitted in Table 350-3.

351-7. Fittings. Liquidtight flexible metal conduit shall be used only with approved terminal fittings.

351-8. Supports. Where liquidtight flexible metal conduit is installed as a fixed raceway, it shall be secured at intervals not exceeding 4½ feet (1.37 m) and within 12 inches (305 mm) on each side of every outlet box or fitting.

Exception No. 1: Where liquidtight flexible metal conduit is fished.

Exception No. 2: Lengths of not more than 3 feet (914 mm) at terminals where flexibility is necessary.

Exception No. 3: Lengths of not more than 6 feet (1.83 m) from a fixture terminal connection for tap conductors to lighting fixtures as required in Section 410-67(c).

Exception No. 2 has been revised and Exception No. 3 is new in the 1984 *Code.*

Changing the word "desired" to "necessary" in Exception No. 2 is intended to require support of liquidtight flexible metal conduit to prevent possible damage or loosening where flexibility is not required.

Exception No. 3 was added to correlate with the exception to Section 351-5(a). See Figure 350-2.

351-9. Grounding. Liquidtight flexible metal conduit shall be permitted as a grounding conductor where both the conduit and the fittings are approved for grounding. Where an equipment bonding jumper is required around liquidtight flexible metal conduit, it shall be installed in accordance with Section 250-79.

Exception No. 1: Liquidtight flexible metal conduit shall be permitted as a grounding means in the 1¼-inch and smaller trade sizes if the total length of all liquidtight flexible metal conduit in any ground return path is 6 feet (1.83 m) or less, the conduit is terminated in fittings listed for grounding, and the circuit conductors contained therein are protected by overcurrent devices rated at 20 amperes or less for ⅜-inch and ½-inch trade sizes and 60 amperes or less for ¾-inch through 1¼-inch trade sizes.

See commentary following Section 250-91(b), Exception No. 2.

Exception No. 2: When used to connect equipment where flexibility is required, a grounding conductor shall be installed.

Exception No. 2 is new in the 1984 *NEC.* It is based on field experience with loose connections and lost equipment grounding.

(FPN): See Sections 501-16(b), 502-16(b), and 503-16.

When used in hazardous (classified) locations, a bonding jumper is required.

351-10. Bends. A run of conduit between outlet and outlet, fitting and fitting, or outlet and fitting shall not contain more than the equivalent of four quarter bends (360 degrees, total), including those bends located immediately at the outlet or fitting.

Angle connectors shall not be used for concealed raceway installations.

B. Liquidtight Flexible Nonmetallic Conduit

351-21. Scope. Part B of this article covers use and installation requirements for liquidtight flexible nonmetallic conduit for industrial application.

351-22. Definition. Liquidtight flexible nonmetallic conduit is a raceway of circular cross section having a smooth inner surface with integral reinforcement within the conduit wall. This conduit is flame-resistant and with fittings is approved for the installation of electrical conductors.

351-23. Use.

(a) Permitted. Liquidtight flexible nonmetallic conduit shall be permitted to be used in exposed locations:

(1) Where flexibility is required for installation, operation, or maintenance;

(2) Where protection of the contained conductors is required from vapors, liquids, or solids.

Liquidtight flexible nonmetallic conduit is used extensively in the machine tool and related industries. See Section 13-5 in NFPA 79-1980, Electrical Standard for Metalworking Machine Tools and Plastics Machinery.

(b) Not Permitted. Liquidtight flexible nonmetallic conduit shall not be used:

(1) Where subject to physical damage;

(2) Where any combination of ambient and conductor temperatures is in excess of that for which the liquidtight flexible nonmetallic conduit is approved;

(3) In lengths longer than 6 feet (1.83 m);

Exception: Where approved for special installations.

(4) Where voltage of the contained conductors is in excess of 600 volts, nominal.

351-24. Size. The sizes of liquidtight flexible nonmetallic conduit shall be electrical trade sizes ½ inch to 2 inch inclusive.

Exception: ⅜-inch size for enclosing the leads of motors as permitted in Section 430-145(b).

351-25. Number of Conductors. The number of conductors permitted in a single conduit shall be in accordance with the percentage fill specified in Table 1, Chapter 9.

351-26. Fittings. Liquidtight flexible nonmetallic conduit shall be used only with terminal fittings identified for such use.

351-27. Grounding. Where a grounding conductor is required for the circuits installed in liquidtight flexible nonmetallic conduit, it shall be contained in the conduit with the circuit conductors. Fittings and boxes shall be bonded or grounded in accordance with Article 250.

ARTICLE 352 — SURFACE RACEWAYS

Contents

A. Metal Surface Raceways

352-1. Use. The use of surface raceways shall be permitted in dry locations. They shall not be used: (1) where subject to severe physical damage unless otherwise approved; (2) where the voltage is 300 volts or more between conductors unless the metal has a thickness of not less than .040 inch (1.02 mm); (3) where subject to corrosive vapors; (4) in hoistways; (5) in any hazardous (classified) location except Class I, Division 2 locations as permitted in the Exception to Section 501-4(b); nor (6) concealed except as follows:

Exception No. 1: Metal surface raceways shall be permitted for underplaster extensions where identified for such use.

Exception No. 2: As permitted in Section 645-2(c)(2).

(FPN): See definition of "Exposed — (As applied to wiring methods)" in Article 100.

352-2. Other Articles. Metal surface raceways shall comply with the applicable provisions of Article 300.

The number, type, and size of conductors that are permitted to be installed in a listed raceway is marked on the raceway or on the package in which it is shipped.

Raceways, which have been listed for use with lighting fixtures and/or other devices, are marked to this effect on the raceway or on the package in which it is shipped.

The UL Listing Mark is applied to each length or package of complete raceway, raceway cover, or raceway base.

Some lighting fixtures covered under the UL categories of Fixtures and Recessed-Type Fixtures are suitable for use as raceways. See Section 250-91(b)(10).

352-3. Size of Conductors. No conductor larger than that for which the raceway is designed shall be installed in metal surface raceway.

See Figures 352-1 through 352-4.

352-4. Number of Conductors in Raceways. The number of conductors installed in any raceway shall be no greater than the number for which the raceway is designed.

The derating factors in Note 8 to Tables 310-16 through 310-19 shall not apply to conductors installed in surface raceways when all of the following conditions are met: (1) the cross-sectional area of the raceway exceeds 4 square inches (2580 sq mm); (2) the current-carrying conductors do not exceed thirty in number; (3) the sum of the cross-sectional area of all contained conductors does not exceed 20 percent of the interior cross-sectional area of the surface raceway.

(FPN): For conductor cross-sectional area see Tables 5, 6, 7, 8 and the applicable Notes to Tables at the beginning of Chapter 9.

352-5. Extension Through Walls and Floors. It shall be permissible to extend unbroken lengths of metal surface raceways through dry walls, dry partitions, and dry floors.

(FPN): See Section 353-3 for multioutlet assemblies.

352-6. Combination Raceways. Where combination metal surface raceways are used both for signaling and for lighting and power circuits, the different systems shall be run in separate compartments identified by sharply contrasting colors of the interior finish, and the same relative position of compartments shall be maintained throughout the premises.

Type of Raceway	Wire Size Gage No.	Number of Wires			
		Types RHH, RHW	Type THW	Type TW	Types THHN, THWN
No. 200 	12		2	3	3
	14		2	3	5
No. 500 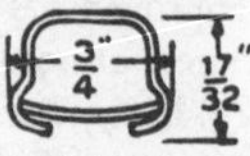	8			2	2
	10	2	2	3	4
	12	2	3	4	7
	14	2	4	6	9
No. 700 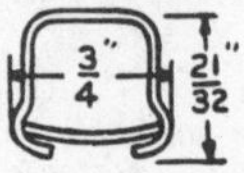	6				2
	8		2	2	3
	10	2	3	4	5
	12	2	4	6	8
	14	3	5	7	11
No. 1500 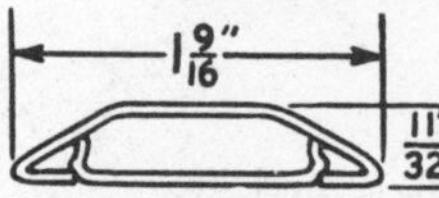	6				2
	8			2	3
	10	2	3	4	5
	12	2	3	5	7
	14	2	4	6	10
No. 2000† 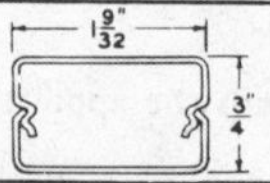	12			7	7
	14			7	7
No. 2100† 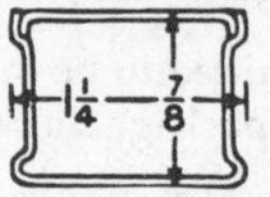	6	2	4	4	6
	8	4	6	8	10
	10	7	10	14	17
	12	8	13	19	28
	14	10	15	24	37
No. 2200† 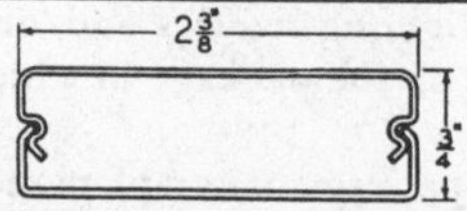	6	5	7	3* 7	11
	8	8	11	7* 14	19
	10	13	19	10* 26	32
	12	15	23	10* 34	51
	14	18	29	10* 44	69
No. 2600 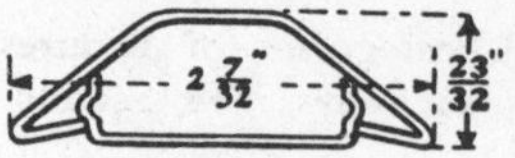	6	2	3	3	5
	8	4	5	7	9
	10	6	9	12	15
	12	7	11	16	24
	14	9	14	21	33
G-3000 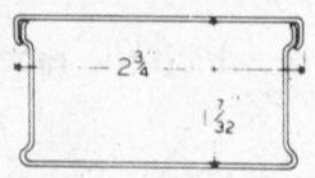	6	4* 11	6* 19	6* 17	6* 27
	8	6* 18	8* 26	8* 34	8* 44
	10	10* 30	10* 45	10* 62	10* 76
	12	14* 36	18* 55	18* 81	18* 119
	14	16* 42	26* 67	26* 103	26* 160
G-4000 — With Divider 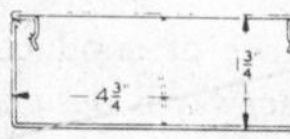	2	- 7	- 10	- 10	- 12
	3	- 8	- 11	- 11	- 15
	4	- 9	- 13	- 13	- 17
	6	4* 12	4* 18	4* 18	7* 28
	8	7* 19	7* 28	7* 36	8* 47
	10	11* 32	11* 48	11* 66	15* 81
	12	15* 39	15* 59	15* 86	24* 128
	14	17* 45	17* 72	17* 110	32* 171
Without Divider 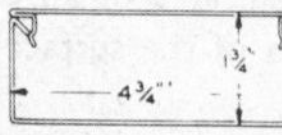	2	- 14	- 20	- 20	- 25
	3	- 16	- 23	- 23	- 30
	4	- 18	- 27	- 27	- 35
	6	8* 24	8* 36	8* 36	10* 57
	8	10* 39	10* 57	10* 78	15* 94
	10	15* 65	15* 96	12* 133	18* 163
	12	21* 78	21* 119	16* 174	34* 256
	14	21* 91	21* 145	17* 222	34* 344
G-6000 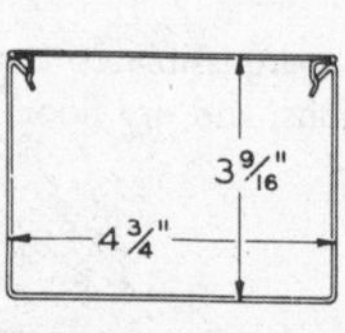	2/0	10* 17	12* 22	12* 22	15* 27
	1/0	11* 20	14* 26	14* 26	18* 33
	1	12* 23	17* 31	17* 31	21* 39
	2	16* 30	23* 43	23* 43	29* 53
	3	19* 34	27* 50	27* 50	34* 63
	4	21* 39	32* 58	32* 58	40* 74
	6	27* 51	42* 77	42* 77	66* 122
	8	40* 74	57* 106	73* 134	92* 169
	10	75* 137	111* 203	154* 282	187* 343
	12	90* 164	137* 252	200* 368	295* 540
	14	105* 193	167* 307	255* 469	396* 726

†Figures for Nos. 2000, 2100, 2200, G-3000, G-4000, and G-6000 are *without receptacles,* except where noted.
*With receptacles.

Figure 352-1. Wiremold metal surface raceway. (*The Wiremold Co.*)

Type of Raceway	Wire Size Gage No.	Types RHH, RHW		Type RH		Type THW		Types T, TW		Types THHN, THWN	
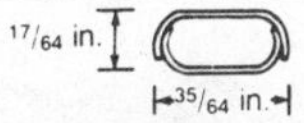 No. 111 (17/64 in. × 35/64 in.)	12							2		3	
	14							2		3	
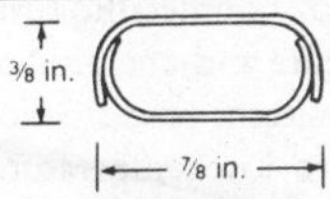 No. 222 (3/8 in. × 7/8 in.)	8							2		2	
	10	2				2		4		4	
	12	2				3		5		7	
	14	3				4		6		10	
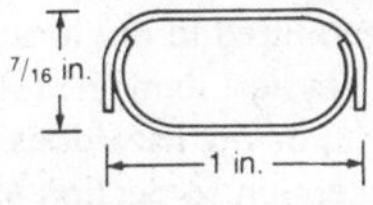 No. 333 (7/16 in. × 1 in.)	6									2	
	8					2		2		3	
	10	2		2		3		5		6	
	12	2		4		4		6		9	
	14	3		4		5		8		12	
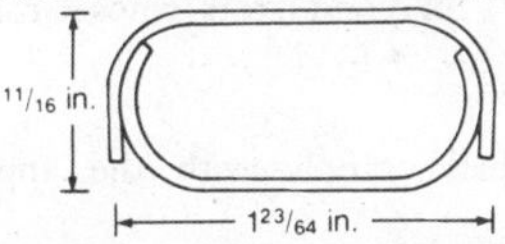 No. 888 (11/16 in. × 1 23/64 in.)	6	2		2		3		3		5	
	8	3		3		5		7		9	
	10	6		6		9		13		16	
	12	7		10		11		17		25	
	14	9		12		14		22		34	
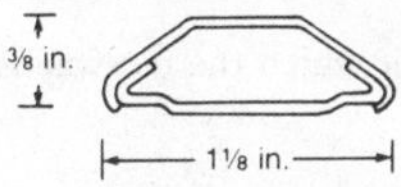 No. 711 (3/8 in. × 1 1/8 in.)	8							2		2	
	10					2		3		4	
	12	2		2		3		4		7	
	14	2		3		4		6		9	
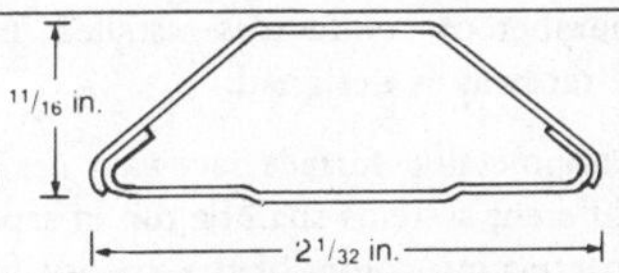 No. 733 (11/16 in. × 2 1/32 in.)	6	3		3		4		4		7	
	8	4		4		7		9		11	
	10	8		8		11		16		20	
	12	9		13		14		21		31	
	14	11		16		17		27		42	
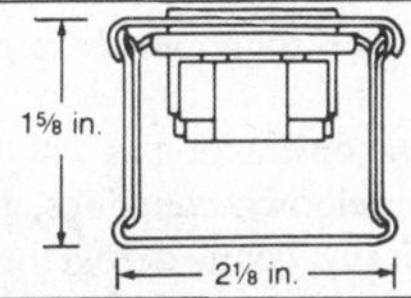 No. 1700† (1 5/8 in. × 2 1/8 in.)	6	3*	8	3*	8	5*	13	5*	13	8*	21
	8	5*	14	5*	14	8*	21	10*	27	13*	34
	10	9*	24	9*	24	13*	35	19*	49	23*	60
	12	11*	28	15*	39	17*	43	24*	64	36*	94
	14	13*	33	18*	48	20*	53	31*	81	49*	126
No. 3400	Catalog No. 3400 is a raceway consisting of two No. 1700 housings in a common cover. Each channel has the same wire fill as 1700.										
No. 5100	Catalog No. 5100 is a raceway consisting of three No. 1700 housings in a common cover. Each channel has the same wire fill at 1700.										

†Figures for No. 1700 are *without devices*, except where noted.
*With devices.

Figure 352-2. Types of metal surface raceways. (*Walker Div. of Butler Mfg. Co.*)

352-7. Splices and Taps. Splices and taps shall be permitted in metal surface raceway having a removable cover that is accessible after installation. The conductors, including splices and taps, shall not fill the raceway to more than 75 percent of its area at that point. Splices and taps in metal surface raceways without removable covers shall be made only in junction boxes. All splices and taps shall be made by approved methods.

352-8. Construction. Metal surface raceways shall be of such construction as will distinguish them from other raceways. Metal surface raceways and their elbows, couplings, and similar fittings shall be so designed that the sections can be electrically and mechanically coupled together without subjecting the wires to abrasion. Holes for screws or bolts inside the raceway shall be so designed that when screws or bolts are installed the heads will be flush with the metal surface.

Where covers and accessories of nonmetallic materials are used on metal raceways, they shall be identified for such use.

B. Nonmetallic Surface Raceways

352-21. Description. Part B of this article shall apply to a type of nonmetallic surface raceway and fittings of suitable nonmetallic material that is resistant to moisture and chemical atmospheres. It shall also be flame-retardant, resistant to impact and crushing, resistant to distortion from heat under conditions likely to be encountered in service, and resistant to low-temperature effects.

352-22. Use. The use of nonmetallic surface raceways shall be permitted in dry locations. They shall not be used: (1) where concealed; (2) where subject to severe physical damage; (3) where the voltage is 300 volts or more between conductors; (4) in hoistways; (5) in any hazardous (classified) location except Class I, Division 2 locations as permitted in the Exception to Section 501-4(b); (6) where subject to ambient temperature exceeding 50°C; nor (7) for conductors whose insulation temperature exceeds 75°C.

352-23. Other Articles. Nonmetallic surface raceways shall comply with the applicable provisions of Article 300.

352-24. Size of Conductors. No conductor larger than that for which the raceway is designed shall be installed in nonmetallic surface raceway.

352-25. Number of Conductors in Raceways. The number of conductors installed in any raceway shall be no greater than the number for which the raceway is designed.

352-26. Combination Raceways. Where combination nonmetallic surface raceways are used both for signaling and for lighting and power circuits, the different systems shall be run in separate compartments, identified by printed legend or by sharply contrasting colors of the interior finish, and the same relative position of compartments shall be maintained throughout the premises.

352-27. General. Nonmetallic surface raceways shall be of such construction as will distinguish them from other raceways. Nonmetallic surface raceways and their elbows, couplings, and similar fittings shall be so designed that the sections can be mechanically coupled together without subjecting the wires to abrasion. Holes for screws or bolts inside the raceway shall be so designed that when screws or bolts are installed the heads will be flush with the nonmetallic surface.

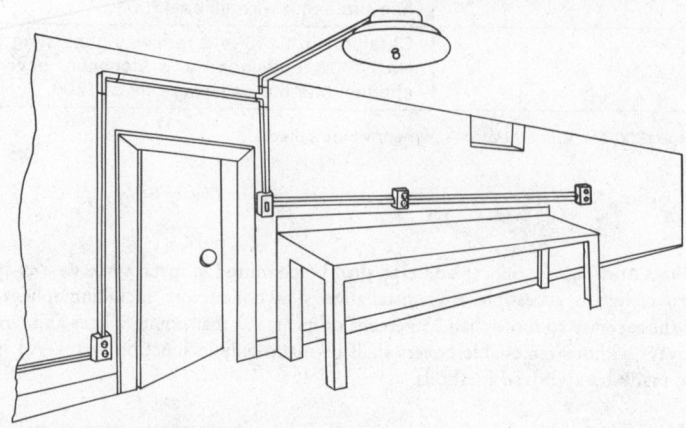

Figure 352-3. Metal surface raceway used as an extension from an existing receptacle. This installation is typical of how surface raceways can be used.

Figure 352-4. A shallow switch box used with a surface raceway.

ARTICLE 353 — MULTIOUTLET ASSEMBLY

Contents

353-1. Other Articles.
353-2. Use.

353-3. Metal Multioutlet Assembly Through Dry Partitions.

353-1. Other Articles. A multioutlet assembly shall comply with applicable provisions of Article 300.

(FPN): See definition in Article 100.

Multioutlet assemblies are metal raceways that are usually surface mounted and designed to contain branch-circuit conductors and receptacles. Receptacles may be spaced at desired intervals and may be assembled at the factory or in the field. See Section 220-2(c), Exception No. 1 and Figure 220-4.

353-2. Use. The use of multioutlet assembly shall be permitted in dry locations. It shall not be installed: (1) where concealed, except that it shall be permissible to surround the back and sides of a metal multioutlet assembly by the building finish or recess a nonmetallic multioutlet assembly in a baseboard; (2) where subject to severe physical damage; (3) where 300 volts or more between conductors unless the assembly is of metal having a thickness of not less than .040 inch (1.02 mm); (4) where subject to corrosive vapors; (5) in hoistways; nor (6) in any hazardous (classified) locations except Class I, Division 2 locations as permitted in the Exception to Section 501-4(b).

353-3. Metal Multioutlet Assembly Through Dry Partitions. It shall be permissible to extend a metal multioutlet assembly through (not run within) dry partitions, if arrangements are made for removing the cap or cover on all exposed portions and no outlet is located within the partitions.

ARTICLE 354 — UNDERFLOOR RACEWAYS

Contents

ARTICLE 354—UNDERFLOOR RACEWAYS

354-1. Other Articles. Underfloor raceways shall comply with the applicable provisions of Article 300.

354-2. Use. The installation of underfloor raceways shall be permitted beneath the surface of concrete or other flooring material or in office occupancies, where laid flush with the concrete floor and covered with linoleum or equivalent floor covering. Underfloor raceways shall not be installed (1) where subject to corrosive vapors, nor (2) in any hazardous (classified) location except Class I, Division 2 locations as permitted in the Exception to Section 501-4(b). Unless made of a material judged suitable for the condition or unless corrosion protection approved for the condition is provided, ferrous or nonferrous metal underfloor raceways, junction boxes, and fittings shall not be installed in concrete, or in areas subject to severe corrosive influences.

An underfloor raceway is a practical means of bringing light, power, and signal systems to desks or tables that are not located adjacent to wall space. This wiring method offers great flexibility in layout when used with movable partitions and is commonly used in large retail stores and office buildings to supply power at any desired location.

Underfloor raceways are permitted beneath the surface of concrete, wood, or other flooring material. The wiring method between cabinets, raceway junction boxes, and outlet boxes may be rigid metal conduit, rigid nonmetallic conduit, or EMT. Flexible metal conduit may be used when not installed in concrete.

354-3. Covering. Raceway coverings shall comply with (a) through (d) below.

(a) Raceways Not Over 4 Inches (102 mm) Wide. Half-round and flat-top raceways not over 4 inches (102 mm) in width shall have not less than ¾ inch (19 mm) of concrete or wood above the raceway.

Exception: As permitted in (c) below for flat-top raceways.

(b) Raceways Over 4 Inches (102 mm) Wide but Not Over 8 Inches (203 mm) Wide. Flat-top raceways over 4 inches (102 mm) but not over 8 inches (203 mm) wide with a minimum of 1 inch (25.4 mm) spacing between raceways shall be covered with concrete to a depth of not less than 1 inch (25.4 mm). Raceways spaced less than 1 inch (25.4 mm) apart shall be covered with concrete to a depth of 1½ inches (38 mm).

(c) Trench-type Raceways Flush with Concrete. Trench-type flush raceways with removable covers shall be permitted to be laid flush with the floor surface. Such approved raceways shall be so designed that the cover plates will provide adequate mechanical protection and rigidity equivalent to junction box covers.

Approved flush-type underfloor raceways may be installed flush with the floor surface provided they have reasonable covers at least equal to those of junction box covers. Coverings for underfloor raceways are illustrated in Figures 354-1, 354-2, and 354-3.

(d) Other Raceways Flush with Concrete. In office occupancies, approved metal flat-top raceways, if not over 4 inches (102 mm) in width, shall be permitted to be laid flush with the concrete floor surface provided they are covered with substantial linoleum not less than 1/16 inch

(1.59 mm) in thickness or with equivalent floor covering. Where more than one and not more than three single raceways are each installed flush with the concrete, they shall be contiguous with each other and joined to form a rigid assembly.

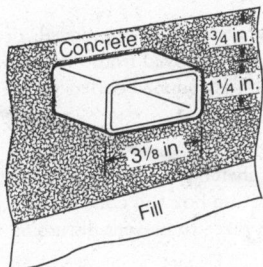 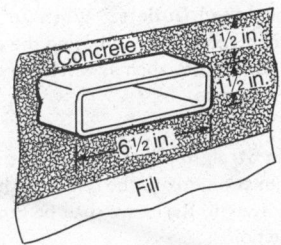

| Figure 354-1. A ¾-in. wood or concrete covering is required over underfloor raceways, except for trench-type flush raceways. See Section 354-3(a). (*Walker Div. of Butler Mfg. Co.*) | Figure 354-2. Flat-top underfloor raceways over 4 in. in width and spaced less than 1 in. apart must be covered with at least 1½ in. of concrete. See Section 354-3(b). (*Walker Div. of Butler Mfg. Co.*) |

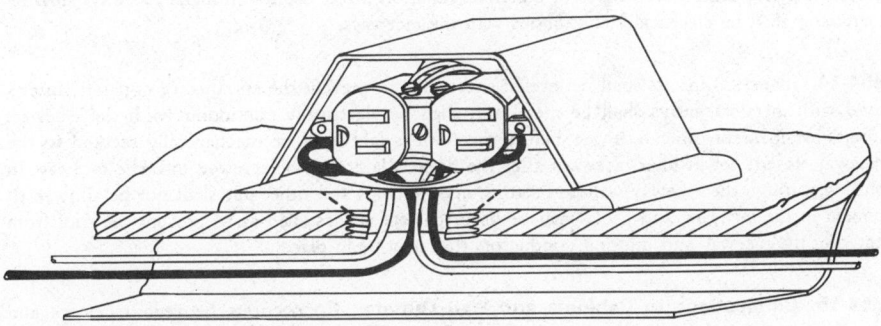

Figure 354-3. A receptacle outlet supplied from an underfloor raceway by the "loop" method of wiring.

354-4. Size of Conductors. No conductor larger than that for which the raceway is designed shall be installed in underfloor raceways.

354-5. Maximum Number of Conductors in Raceway. The combined cross-sectional area of all conductors or cables shall not exceed 40 percent of the interior cross-sectional area of the raceway.

(FPN): For conductor cross-sectional area see Tables 5, 6, 7, 8 and the applicable Notes to Tables at the beginning of Chapter 9.

354-6. Splices and Taps. Splices and taps shall be made only in junction boxes.
For the purposes of this section, so-called loop wiring (continuous, unbroken conductor connecting the individual outlets) shall not be considered to be a splice or tap.

Loop wiring (continuous, unbroken conductors) is recognized when it runs from the underfloor raceway up to the terminals of attached receptacles, back into the raceway, and then on to the next device. See Figure 354-3.

When an outlet is removed, the sections of conductors supplying the outlet must be removed from the raceway as well. As would be the case with abandoned outlets on loop wiring, reinsulated or spliced conductors are not allowed in the raceways. See Sections 300-15(a) and 354-7.

354-7. Discontinued Outlets. When an outlet is abandoned, discontinued, or removed, the sections of circuit conductors supplying the outlet shall be removed from the raceway. No splices or reinsulated conductors, such as would be the case with abandoned outlets on loop wiring, shall be allowed in raceways.

354-8. Laid in Straight Lines. Underfloor raceways shall be laid so that a straight line from the center of one junction box to the center of the next junction box will coincide with the center line of the raceway system. Raceways shall be firmly held in place to prevent disturbing this alignment during construction.

354-9. Markers at Ends. A suitable marker shall be installed at or near each end of each straight run of raceways to locate the last insert.

354-10. Dead Ends. Dead ends of raceways shall be closed.

354-13. Junction Boxes. Junction boxes shall be leveled to the floor grade and sealed to prevent the free entrance of water or concrete. Junction boxes used with metal raceways shall be metal and shall be electrically continuous with the raceways.

354-14. Inserts. Inserts shall be leveled and sealed to prevent the entrance of concrete. Inserts used with metal raceways shall be metal and shall be electrically continuous with the raceway. Inserts set in or on fiber raceways before the floor is laid shall be mechanically secured to the raceway. Inserts set in fiber raceways after the floor is laid shall be screwed into the raceway. In cutting through the raceway wall and setting inserts, chips and other dirt shall not be allowed to remain in the raceway, and tools shall be used that are so designed as to prevent the tool from entering the raceway and injuring conductors that may be in place.

354-15. Connections to Cabinets and Wall Outlets. Connections between raceways and distribution centers and wall outlets shall be made by means of flexible metal conduit when not installed in concrete, rigid metal conduit, intermediate metal conduit, electrical metallic tubing, or approved fittings. Where a metallic underfloor raceway system provides for the termination of an equipment grounding conductor, rigid nonmetallic conduit shall be permitted.

ARTICLE 356 — CELLULAR METAL FLOOR RACEWAYS

Contents

356-1. Definitions. For the purposes of this article, a "cellular metal floor raceway" shall be defined as the hollow spaces of cellular metal floors, together with suitable fittings, which may be approved as enclosures for electric conductors. A "cell" shall be defined as a single, enclosed tubular space in a cellular metal floor member, the axis of the cell being parallel to the axis of the metal floor member. A "header" shall be defined as a transverse raceway for electric conductors, providing access to predetermined cells of a cellular metal floor, thereby permitting the installation of electric conductors from a distribution center to the cells.

Cellular metal floor raceways are a form of metal floor deck construction, designed for use in steel frame buildings, and consist of sheet metal formed into shapes combining to form cells or raceways. The cells extend across the building and, depending on the structural strength required, can have various shapes and sizes.

A cross-sectional view of one type of cellular metal floor is illustrated in Figure 356-1. See Figure 356-2 for installation of header ducts (one for power conductors and one for telephone conductors) prior to the concrete being poured.

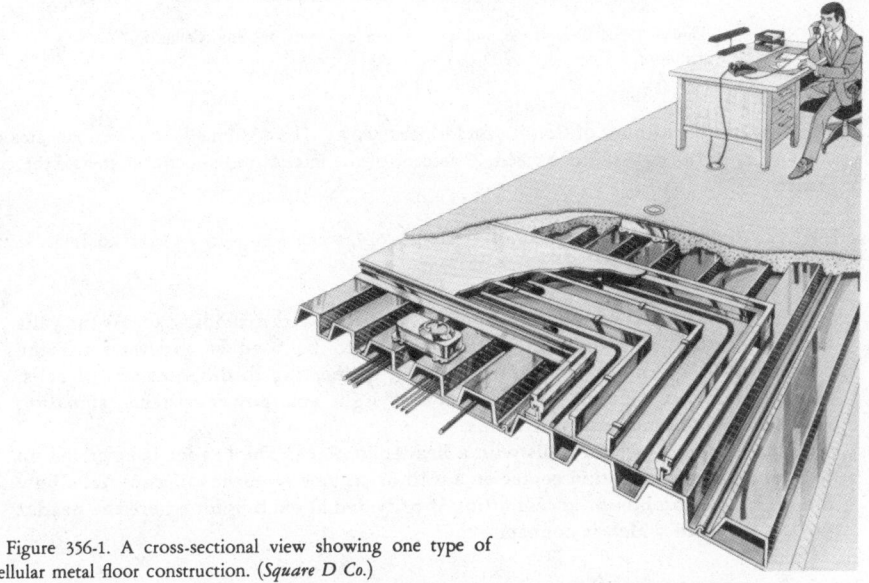

Figure 356-1. A cross-sectional view showing one type of cellular metal floor construction. (*Square D Co.*)

356-2. Use. Conductors shall not be installed in cellular metal floor raceways (1) where subject to corrosive vapor; (2) in any hazardous (classified) location except Class I, Division 2 locations as permitted in the Exception to Section 501-4(b); nor (3) in commercial garages, other than for supplying ceiling outlets or extensions to the area below the floor but not above. No electric conductors shall be installed in any cell or header that contains a pipe for steam, water, air, gas, drainage, or any service other than electrical.

356-3. Other Articles. Cellular metal floor raceways shall comply with the applicable provisions of Article 300.

A. Installation

356-4. Size of Conductors. No conductor larger than No. 1/0 shall be installed, except by special permission.

Figure 356-2. Telephone and power header ducts feeding Cellufloor distribution system. (*Square D Co.*)

356-5. Maximum Number of Conductors in Raceway. The combined cross-sectional area of all conductors or cables shall not exceed 40 percent of the interior cross-sectional area of the cell or header.

(FPN): For conductor cross-sectional area see Tables 5, 6, 7, 8 and the applicable Notes to Tables at the beginning of Chapter 9.

Connections to the cells are made by means of headers extending across the cells and connecting only to those cells that are to be used as raceways for the conductors. Two or three separate headers, connecting to different sets of cells, may be used for different systems, such as light and power systems, signaling systems, and communication systems.

Figure 356-3 shows the cells with a header in place. The header is extended up to a cabinet or distribution center on a wall or column by means of a special elbow fitting. A junction box or access fitting is provided at each point where the header crosses a cell to which it connects.

356-6. Splices and Taps. Splices and taps shall be made only in header access units or junction boxes.

For the purposes of this section, so-called loop wiring (continuous unbroken conductor connecting the individual outlets) shall not be considered to be a splice or tap.

See Figure 354-3 and commentary following Section 354-6.

356-7. Discontinued Outlets. When an outlet is abandoned, discontinued, or removed, the sections of circuit conductors supplying the outlet shall be removed from the raceway. No splices or reinsulated conductors, such as would be the case with abandoned outlets on loop wiring, shall be allowed in raceways.

356-8. Markers. A suitable number of markers shall be installed for the future locating of cells.

Figure 356-3. A typical cellular metal floor raceway installation showing cells, header ducts, junction boxes, and special elbow fittings. (*Square D Co.*)

Markers are brass flat-head screws set into the top side of the cells and so adjusted that their heads, flush with the floor finish, are exposed to locate cells for future installations.

356-9. Junction Boxes. Junction boxes shall be leveled to the floor grade and sealed against the free entrance of water or concrete. Junction boxes used with these raceways shall be of metal and shall be electrically continuous with the raceway.

356-10. Inserts. Inserts shall be leveled to the floor grade and sealed against the entrance of concrete. Inserts shall be of metal and shall be electrically continuous with the raceway. In cutting through the cell wall and setting inserts, chips and other dirt shall not be allowed to remain in the raceway, and tools shall be used that are designed to prevent the tool from entering the cell and injuring the conductors.

Figure 356-3 illustrates cells connected to "headers" with junction boxes for future access and a special elbow fitting for connecting the "header" to a cabinet. Connections to wall outlets are to be made with metal raceways (see Section 356-11).

Installation instructions are supplied by the manufacturer for the use of the general contractor, erector, electrical contractor, inspector, and others concerned with the installation.

Figure 356-4 illustrates a preset dual insert, installed prior to concrete being applied, used with cellular metal floor raceways. To install an insert after concrete has been applied, markers should be checked to locate a cell (see Section 356-8). Then a properly sized concrete-boring drill is used to cut through the concrete to expose the top of the cell. At this point a properly sized metal-cutting hole saw is used to cut through the cell wall. The saw depth is preset to prevent the tool from entering the cell and injuring the conductors. The metal insert threads into the hole providing an electrical, mechanical, and bushed connection.

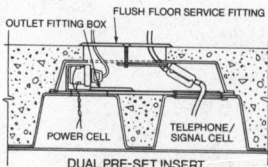

Figure 356-4. A preset dual insert used with a cellular metal floor raceway to provide access to the power and telephone/signal cells in the floor. Note separation. (*Square D Co.*)

356-11. Connection to Cabinets and Extensions from Cells. Connections between raceways and distribution centers and wall outlets shall be made by means of flexible metal conduit when not installed in concrete, rigid metal conduit, intermediate metal conduit, electrical metallic tubing, or approved fittings. Where there are provisions for the termination of an equipment grounding conductor, nonmetallic conduit shall be permitted.

B. Construction Specifications

356-12. General. Cellular metal floor raceways shall be so constructed that adequate electrical and mechanical continuity of the complete system will be secured. They shall provide a complete enclosure for the conductors. The interior surfaces shall be free from burrs and sharp edges, and surfaces over which conductors are drawn shall be smooth. Suitable bushings or fittings having smooth rounded edges shall be provided where conductors pass.

ARTICLE 358 — CELLULAR CONCRETE FLOOR RACEWAYS

Contents

358-1. Scope. Approved precast cellular concrete floor raceways shall comply with the applicable provisions of Article 300. For the purpose of this article, "precast cellular concrete floor raceways" shall be defined as the hollow spaces in floors constructed of precast cellular concrete slabs, together with suitable metal fittings designed to provide access to the floor cells in an approved manner. A "cell" shall be defined as a single, enclosed tubular space in a floor made of precast cellular concrete slabs, the direction of the cell being parallel to the direction of the floor member. A "header" shall be defined as transverse metal raceways for electric conductors, providing access to predetermined cells of a precast cellular concrete floor, thereby permitting the installation of electric conductors from a distribution center to the floor cells.

Cellular concrete floor raceways are a form of floor deck construction and are commonly used in high-rise office buildings. This method is very similar in design, application, and adaptation to cellular metal floor raceways.

Basically, this wiring method consists of floor cells (which are part of the structural floor system); header ducts, laid at right angles to the cells and which are used to carry conductors from cabinets to cells; and junction boxes as shown in Figure 358-1.

Figure 358-1. Standard underfloor duct used on precast cellular concrete floor raceway. (*Square D Co.*)

358-2. Use. Conductors shall not be installed in precast cellular concrete floor raceways (1) where subject to corrosive vapor; (2) in hazardous (classified) locations except Class I, Division 2 locations as permitted in the Exception to Section 501-4(b); nor (3) in commercial garages, other than for supplying ceiling outlets or extensions to the area below the floor but not above. No electric conductors shall be installed in any cell or header that contains a pipe for steam, water, air, gas, drainage, or any service other than electrical.

358-3. Header. The header shall be installed in a straight line, at right angles to the cells. The header shall be mechanically secured to the top of the precast cellular concrete floor. The end joints shall be closed by a metallic closure fitting and sealed against the entrance of concrete. The header shall be electrically continuous throughout its entire length and shall be electrically bonded to the enclosure of the distribution center.

358-4. Connection to Cabinets and Other Enclosures. Connections from headers to cabinets and other enclosures shall be made by means of metal raceways and approved fittings.

358-5. Junction Boxes. Junction boxes shall be leveled to the floor grade and sealed against the free entrance of water or concrete. Junction boxes shall be of metal and shall be mechanically and electrically continuous with the header.

Figure 358-2 illustrates a trench-type raceway with a rigid cover plate extending at a right angle across the cells, with access to predetermined cells.

358-6. Markers. A suitable number of markers shall be installed for the future location of cells.

358-7. Inserts. Inserts shall be leveled and sealed against the entrance of concrete. Inserts shall be of metal and shall be fitted with receptacles of the grounded type. A grounding conductor shall connect the insert receptacles to a positive ground connection provided on the header. In cutting through the cell wall for setting inserts or other purposes (such as providing access openings between header and cells), chips and other dirt shall not be allowed to remain in the raceway, and the tool used shall be so designed as to prevent the tool from entering the cell and injuring the conductors.

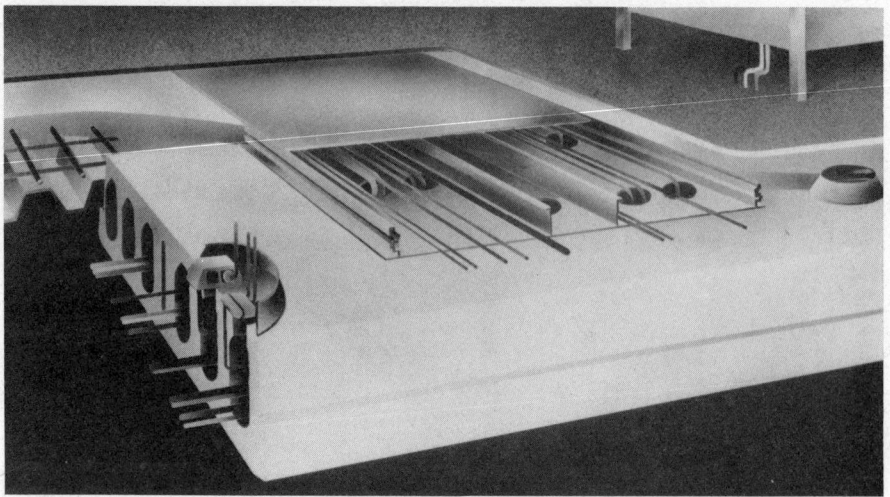

Figure 358-2. Trench-type raceway with removable cover shown extending at right angles across the cells of cellular concrete floor construction. (*Bargar Metal Fabricating Co.*)

358-8. Size of Conductors. No conductor larger than No. 1/0 shall be installed, except by special permission.

358-9. Maximum Number of Conductors. The combined cross-sectional area of all conductors or cables shall not exceed 40 percent of the cross-sectional area of the cell or header.

358-10. Splices and Taps. Splices and taps shall be made only in header access units or junction boxes.

For the purposes of this section, so-called loop wiring (continuous unbroken conductor connecting the individual outlets) shall not be considered to be a splice or tap.

358-11. Discontinued Outlets. When an outlet is abandoned, discontinued, or removed, the sections of circuit conductors supplying the outlet shall be removed from the raceway. No splices or reinsulated conductors, such as would be the case with abandoned outlets on loop wiring, shall be allowed in raceways.

ARTICLE 362 — WIREWAYS

Contents

362-1. Definition. Wireways are sheet-metal troughs with hinged or removable covers for housing and protecting electric wires and cable and in which conductors are laid in place after the wireway has been installed as a complete system.

Wireways are sheet-steel enclosures equipped with hinged or removable covers and are manufactured in lengths from 1 to 10 ft and various widths and depths. Couplings, elbows, end plates, and accessories, such as "T" and "X" fittings, are available.

Unlike auxiliary gutters, which are not permitted to extend more than 30 ft from the equipment they supplement, wireways may be run throughout an entire area, as shown in Figure 362-1.

The total of the cross-sectional areas of all conductors is not to exceed 20 percent of the interior cross-sectional area of the wireway. Where not more than thirty conductors are installed, the derating factors of Note 8 of Tables 310-16 to 310-19 are not applied.

Example: a wireway contains twenty-four TW conductors, eight No. 3/0 (8 × 0.3288 = 2.6304), three No. 6 (3 × 0.0819 = 0.2457), three No. 8 (3 × 0.0471 = 0.1413), and ten No. 12 (10 × 0.0172 = 0.172) which totals 3.1894 sq in. (dimensions of conductors are from Table 5, Chapter 9). Twenty percent of the cross-sectional area of the wireway is required to be 3.19 sq in. or greater. Therefore, 3.19 sq in. ÷ 0.20 = 15.95 sq in. A 4-in. × 4-in. wireway or greater is permitted to contain these conductors.

362-2. Use. Wireways shall be permitted only for exposed work. Wireways intended for outdoor use shall be of raintight construction. Wireways shall not be installed (1) where subject to severe physical damage or corrosive vapor, nor (2) in any hazardous (classified) location, except Class I, Division 2 and Class II, Division 2 locations as permitted in Sections 501-4(b) and 502-4(b).

Figure 362-1. A worker installing conductors in a sheet metal wireway after the complete wireway has been installed. (*Square D Co.*)

ARTICLE 362—WIREWAYS

362-3. Other Articles. Installations of wireways shall comply with the applicable provisions of Article 300.

362-4. Size of Conductors. No conductor larger than that for which the wireway is designed shall be installed in any wireway.

362-5. Number of Conductors. Wireways shall not contain more than thirty current-carrying conductors at any cross section. Conductors for signaling circuits or controller conductors between a motor and its starter and used only for starting duty shall not be considered as current-carrying conductors.

The sum of cross-sectional areas of all contained conductors at any cross section of the wireway shall not exceed 20 percent of the interior cross-sectional area of the wireway.

The derating factors specified in Note 8 to Tables 310-16 through 310-19 shall not be applicable to the thirty current-carrying conductors at 20 percent fill specified above.

Exception No. 1: Where the derating factors specified in Note 8 to Tables 310-16 through 310-19 are applied, the number of current-carrying conductors shall not be limited but the sum of the cross-sectional area of all contained conductors at any cross section of the wireway shall not exceed 20 percent of the interior cross-sectional area of the wireway.

Exception No. 2: As provided in Section 520-5, the thirty conductor limitation does not apply for theaters and similar locations.

Exception No. 3: As provided in Section 620-32, the 20 percent fill limitation does not apply for elevators and dumbwaiters.

(FPN): For conductor cross-sectional area see Tables 5, 6, 7, 8 and the applicable Notes to Tables at the beginning of Chapter 9.

362-6. Splices and Taps. Splices and taps shall be permitted within a wireway provided they are accessible. The conductors, including splices and taps, shall not fill the wireway to more than 75 percent of its area at that point.

Conductors in wireways are accessible through hinged or removable covers. Circuits, taps, or splices may be added or altered, if necessary.

See Section 362-5. See also Table 5 in Chapter 9 for the dimensions of all common sizes of conductors.

362-7. Supports. Wireways shall be securely supported at intervals not exceeding 5 feet (1.52 m), unless specially approved for supports at greater intervals, but in no case shall the distance between supports exceed 10 feet (3.05 m).

Exception: Vertical runs of wireways shall be securely supported at intervals not exceeding 15 feet (4.57 m) and shall have not more than one joint between supports. Adjoining wireway sections shall be securely fastened together to provide a rigid joint.

362-8. Extension Through Walls. Unbroken lengths of wireway shall be permitted to pass transversely through walls if in unbroken lengths where passing through.

362-9. Dead Ends. Dead ends of wireways shall be closed.

362-10. Extensions from Wireways. Extensions from wireways shall be made with rigid or flexible metal conduit, intermediate metal conduit, rigid nonmetallic conduit, electrical metallic tubing, metal surface raceway, Type MI cable, liquidtight flexible metal conduit, cord pendants, or metal-clad cable. Where rigid nonmetallic conduit is used, connection of equipment grounding conductors in the rigid nonmetallic conduit to the wireway shall comply with Sections 250-113 and 250-118.

Extensions are to be made from metal raceways or metal-clad cables through knockouts which are provided on the wireway or which may be field-punched. Rigid nonmetallic conduit may also be used. In this case, the equipment grounding conductor in the rigid nonmetallic conduit is to be connected to the metal wireway in accordance with Sections 250-113 and 250-118.

Sections of wireways, including accessory fittings (elbows, endplates, flanges, etc.) are bolted together assuring a rigid mechanical and electrical connection.

See Section 250-91(b)(10).

362-11. Marking. Wireways shall be marked so that their manufacturer's name or trademark will be visible after installation.

ARTICLE 363 — FLAT CABLE ASSEMBLIES

Type FC

Contents

363-1. Definition. Type FC, a flat cable assembly, is an assembly of parallel conductors formed integrally with an insulating material web specifically designed for field installation in metal surface raceway.

Type FC cable is an assembly of two, three, or four parallel No. 10 AWG special stranded copper wires formed integrally with an insulating material web. The cable is marked with the size of the maximum branch circuit to which it may be connected, the cable type designation, manufacturer's identification, maximum working voltage, conductor size, and temperature rating. A marking accompanying the cable on a tag or reel indicates the special metal raceways and specific type of FC cable fittings with which the cable is intended to be used.

Figures 363-1 and 363-2 show the basic components of this wiring method.

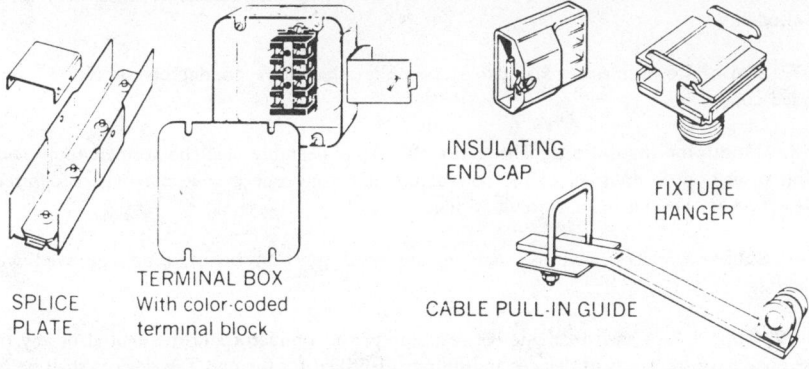

INSULATING
END CAP

FIXTURE
HANGER

SPLICE
PLATE

TERMINAL BOX
With color-coded
terminal block

CABLE PULL-IN GUIDE

Figure 363-1. The basic components and accessories used for an installation of Type FC (flat) cable assembly. (*The Wiremold Co.*)

ARTICLE 363—FLAT CABLE ASSEMBLIES

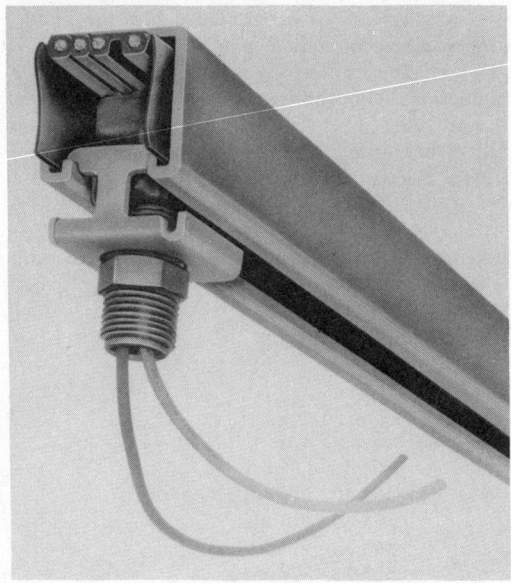

Figure 363-2. Fixture hanger used with Type FC cable assembly. (*The Wiremold Co.*)

363-2. Other Articles. In addition to the provisions of this article, installation of Type FC cable shall conform with the applicable provisions of Articles 210, 220, 250, 300, 310, and 352.

363-3. Uses Permitted. Flat cable assemblies shall be permitted only as branch circuits to supply suitable tap devices for lighting, small appliances, or small power loads. Flat cable assemblies shall be installed for exposed work only. Flat cable assemblies shall be installed in locations where they will not be subjected to severe physical damage.

363-4. Uses Not Permitted. Flat cable assemblies shall not be installed: (1) where subject to corrosive vapors unless suitable for the application; (2) in hoistways; (3) in any hazardous (classified) location; or (4) outdoors or in wet or damp locations unless identified for use in wet locations.

363-5. Installation. Flat cable assemblies shall be installed in the field only in metal surface raceways identified for the use. The channel portion of the metal surface raceway systems shall be installed as complete systems before the flat cable assemblies are pulled into the raceways.

363-6. Number of Conductors. The flat cable assemblies shall consist of either two, three, or four conductors.

363-7. Size of Conductors. Flat cable assemblies shall have conductors of No. 10 special stranded copper wires.

363-8. Conductor Insulation. The entire flat cable assembly shall be formed to provide a suitable insulation covering all of the conductors and using one of the materials recognized in Table 310-13 for general branch-circuit wiring.

363-9. Splices. Splices shall be made in approved junction boxes using approved wiring methods.

363-10. Taps. Taps shall be made between any phase conductor and the neutral or any other phase conductor by means of devices and fittings identified for the use. Tap devices shall be rated at not less than 15 amperes or more than 300 volts and they shall be color-coded in accordance with the requirements of Section 363-20.

363-11. Dead Ends. Each flat cable assembly dead end shall be terminated in an end-cap device identified for the use.

The dead-end fitting for the enclosing metal surface raceway shall be identified for the use.

363-12. Fixture Hangers. Fixture hangers installed with the flat cable assemblies shall be identified for the use.

363-13. Fittings. Fittings to be installed with flat cable assemblies shall be designed and installed to prevent physical damage to the cable assemblies.

363-14. Extensions. All extensions from flat cable assemblies shall be made by approved wiring methods, within the junction boxes, installed at either end of the flat cable assembly runs.

363-15. Supports. The flat cable assemblies shall be supported by means of their special design features, within the metal surface raceways.

The metal surface raceways shall be supported as required for the specific raceway to be installed.

363-16. Rating. The rating of the branch circuit shall not exceed 30 amperes.

363-17. Marking. In addition to the provisions of Section 310-11, Type FC cable shall have the temperature rating durably marked on the surface at intervals not exceeding 24 inches (610 mm).

363-18. Protective Covers. When a flat cable assembly is installed less than 8 feet (2.44 m) from the floor, it shall be protected by a metal cover identified for the use.

363-19. Identification. The neutral conductor shall be identified throughout its length by means of a distinctive and durable white or natural gray marking.

363-20. Terminal Block Identification. Terminal blocks identified for the use shall have distinctive and durable markings for color or word coding. The neutral section shall have a white marking or other suitable designation. The next adjacent section of the terminal block shall have a black marking or other suitable designation. The next section shall have a red marking or other suitable designation. The final or outer section, opposite the neutral section of the terminal block, shall have a blue marking or other suitable designation.

ARTICLE 364 — BUSWAYS

Contents

A. General Requirements

364-1. Scope. This article covers service-entrance, feeder, and branch-circuit busways and associated fittings.

364-2. Definition. For the purpose of this article a busway is considered to be a grounded metal enclosure containing factory mounted, bare or insulated conductors which are usually copper or aluminum bars, rods, or tubes.

(FPN): For cablebus, refer to Article 365.

The maximum rating of UL listed busway is 600 V.

A busway that has been investigated to determine its suitability for installation in a specified position, or for use in vertical runs, or for support at intervals greater than 5 ft, or for outdoor use is so marked.

A busway that is intended to supply and support industrial and commercial lighting fixtures is classified as "Lighting Busway" and is so marked. Trolley Busway is marked "Trolley Busway" and is additionally marked "Lighting Busway" if intended to supply and support industrial and commercial lighting fixtures. A busway with provision for insertion of plug-in devices at any point along the length of the busway and intended for general use is classified as "Continuous Plug-In Busway" and is so marked.

Short-Run Busways are marked to limit the run to 30 ft or less and no more than 10 ft vertically. They are intended primarily to feed switchboards. Except for transformer stubs, Short-Run Busways are not intended to have intermediate taps. Short-Run Busways are not ventilated and may be marked for outdoor use.

A busway marked "Lighting Busway" and protected by overcurrent devices rated in excess of 20 A is intended for use only with fixtures employing heavy-duty lampholders unless additional overcurrent protection is provided for the fixture in accordance with this *Code*.

A "Trolley Busway" should be installed out of the reach of persons or it should be otherwise installed to prevent accidental contact with exposed conductors. See Figures 364-1 and 364-2.

364-3. Other Articles. Installations of busways shall comply with the applicable provisions of Article 300.

364-4. Use.

(a) Use Permitted. Busways shall be installed only where located in the open and are visible.

Exception: Busways shall be permitted to be installed behind panels if means of access are provided and if all the following conditions are met.

a. No overcurrent devices are installed on the busway other than for an individual fixture.

b. The space behind the access panels is not used for air-handling purposes.

c. The busway is totally enclosed, nonventilating type.

d. Busway is so installed that the joints between sections and fittings are accessible for maintenance purposes.

See Figure 100-1.

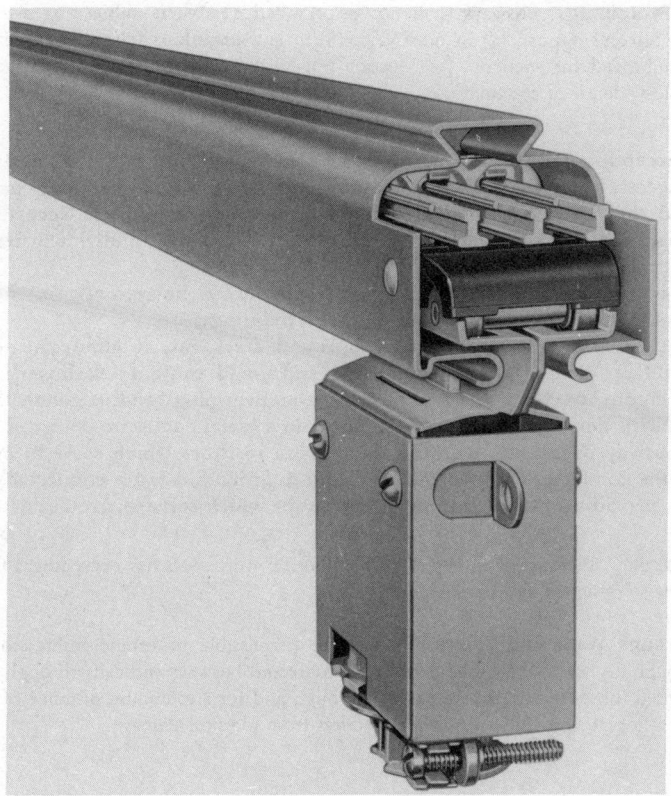

Figure 364-1. A trolley busway with the trolley in place. (*Midland Ross*)

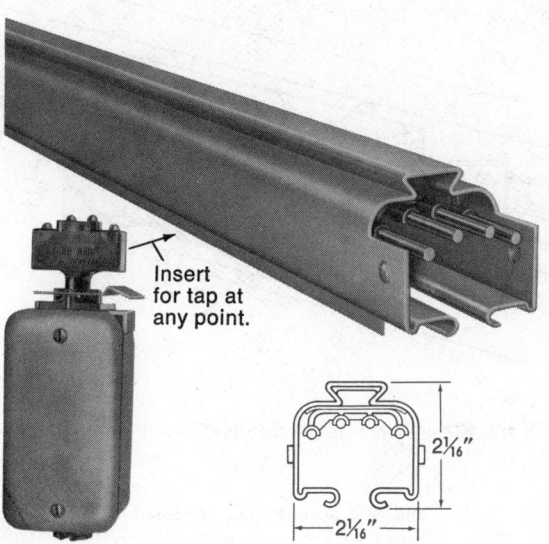

Insert for tap at any point.

2¼₆"

2¼₆"

Figure 364-2. A plug-in device for stationary use on a trolley busway. (*Midland Ross*)

ARTICLE 364—BUSWAYS

(b) Use Prohibited. Busways shall not be installed: (1) where subject to severe physical damage or corrosive vapors; (2) in hoistways; (3) in any hazardous (classified) location, unless specifically approved for such use [see Section 501-4(b)]; nor (4) outdoors or in wet or damp locations unless identified for such use.

The exception permits busways to be located behind panels that are designed to allow access, such as suspended ceilings not used for air-handling purposes, provided the busway is totally enclosed, joints and fittings are accessible for maintenance, and no overcurrent device (other than for an individual fixture) is installed.

Busways are commonly used as feeders, mounted horizontally in industrial buildings, or mounted vertically in high-rise buildings.

Where busways are employed for ungrounded systems, an abnormal potential may build up on one of the conductors and could cause a "flashover" on the system. Figure 364-3 is a diagram of a "potentializer plug" and its connection to a busway. This device is a complete assembly in a metal enclosure designed to plug into a busway. It consists of three 18,000-ohm resistors which serve to maintain each of the conductors at a normal potential to ground. A tap is connected to each resistor, providing 120 V to three 7.5-W lamps which serve as ground detectors.

364-5. Support. Busways shall be securely supported at intervals not exceeding 5 feet (1.52 m) unless otherwise designed and marked.

364-6. Through Walls and Floors. It shall be permissible to extend unbroken lengths of busway through dry walls. It shall be permissible to extend busways vertically through dry floors if totally enclosed (unventilated) where passing through and for a minimum distance of 6 feet (1.83 m) above the floor to provide adequate protection from physical damage.

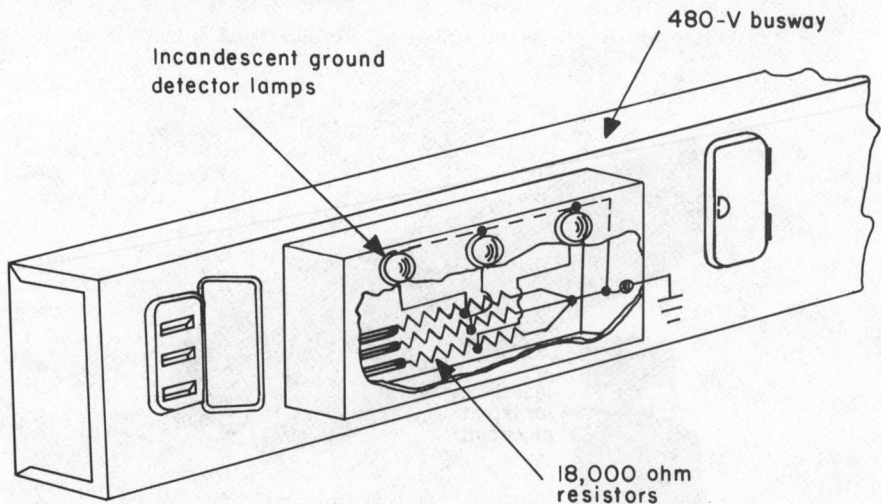

Figure 364-3. A schematic of a "potentializer plug" and its connections to a busway.

364-7. Dead Ends. A dead end of a busway shall be closed.

364-8. Branches from Busways. Branches from busways shall be made with busways, rigid metal conduit, intermediate metal conduit, rigid nonmetallic conduit, flexible metal conduit, electrical metallic tubing, metal surface raceway or metal-clad cable; or with suitable cord assemblies approved for hard usage for the connection of portable equipment or for the connection of stationary equipment to facilitate their interchange. Flexible cord assembly connections shall be permitted to be made directly to the load end terminals of a busway plug-in device, providing the connection includes a suitable tension take-up device on the cord. Where rigid nonmetallic conduit is used, connection of equipment grounding conductors in the rigid nonmetallic conduit to the busway shall comply with Sections 250-113 and 250-118.

364-9. Overcurrent Protection. Overcurrent protection shall be provided in accordance with Sections 364-10 through 364-14.

364-10. Rating of Overcurrent Protection — Feeders and Subfeeders. Where the allowable current rating of the busway does not correspond to a standard rating of the overcurrent device, the next higher rating shall be permitted.

> The rated ampacity of a busway is based on the allowable temperature rise of the conductors and can be determined in the field only by reference to the nameplate data.

364-11. Reduction in Size of Busway. Omission of overcurrent protection shall be permitted at points where busways are reduced in size, provided that the smaller busway does not extend more than 50 feet (15.2 m) and has a current rating at least equal to ⅓ the rating or setting of the overcurrent device next back on the line, and provided further that such busway is free from contact with combustible material.

> Where the smaller busway is kept within the specified limits, the additional cost of providing overcurrent protection at the point where the size is changed is not warranted. For example, busway protected by a 1200-A overcurrent device may be reduced in size, provided the smaller busway has a current rating of 400 A (⅓ of 1,200 A) and does not extend more than 50 ft. In this case overcurrent protection would be required if the smaller busway were rated less than 400 A, that is, 200 A, 300 A, etc.

364-12. Subfeeder or Branch Circuits. Where a busway is used as a feeder, devices or plug-in connections for tapping off subfeeder or branch circuits from the busway shall contain the overcurrent devices required for the protection of the subfeeder or branch circuits. The plug-in device shall consist of an externally operable circuit breaker or an externally operable fusible switch. Where such devices are mounted out of reach and contain disconnecting means, suitable means such as ropes, chains, or sticks shall be provided for operating the disconnecting means from the floor.

Exception No. 1: As permitted in Section 240-21 for taps.

Exception No. 2: For fixed or semi-fixed lighting fixtures, where the branch-circuit overcurrent device is part of the fixture cord plug on cord-connected fixtures.

Exception No. 3: Where fixtures without cords are plugged directly into the busway and the overcurrent device is mounted on the fixture.

> Externally operated fused switches and circuit breakers plugged into busways, which are mounted out of reach, are to be considered accessible when operated by means such as ropes, chains, or hooksticks.
> An appliance, without individual overcurrent protection, may be connected directly to a busway as permitted in Section 210-23; however, a motor-driven appliance must also meet all of the applicable requirements of Article 430.

364-13. Rating of Overcurrent Protection — Branch Circuits. A busway shall be permitted as a branch circuit of any one of the types described in Article 210. When so used, the rating or setting of the overcurrent device protecting the busway shall determine the ampere rating of the branch circuit, and the circuit shall in all respects conform with the requirements of Article 210 that apply to branch circuits of that rating.

364-14. Length of Busways Used as Branch Circuits. Busways which are used as branch circuits and which are so designed that loads can be connected at any point shall be limited to such lengths as will provide that in normal use the circuits will not be overloaded.

364-15. Marking. Busways shall be marked with the voltage and current rating for which they are designed, and with the manufacturer's name or trademark in such manner as to be visible after installation.

B. Requirements for Over 600 Volts, Nominal

364-21. Identification. Each bus run shall be provided with a permanent nameplate on which the following information shall be provided: (1) rated voltage; (2) rated continuous current; if bus is forced-cooled, both the normal forced-cooled rating and the self-cooled (not forced-cooled) rating for the same temperature rise shall be given; (3) rated frequency; (4) rated impulse withstand voltage; (5) rated 60-Hz withstand voltage (dry); (6) rated momentary current; and (7) manufacturer's name or trademark.

Metal-enclosed buses shall be constructed and tested in accordance with ANSI C37.20-1974, Switchgear Assemblies.

364-22. Grounding. Metal-enclosed bus shall be grounded in accordance with Article 250.

364-23. Adjacent and Supporting Structures. Metal-enclosed busways shall be installed so that temperature rise from induced circulating currents in any adjacent metallic parts will not be hazardous to personnel or constitute a fire hazard.

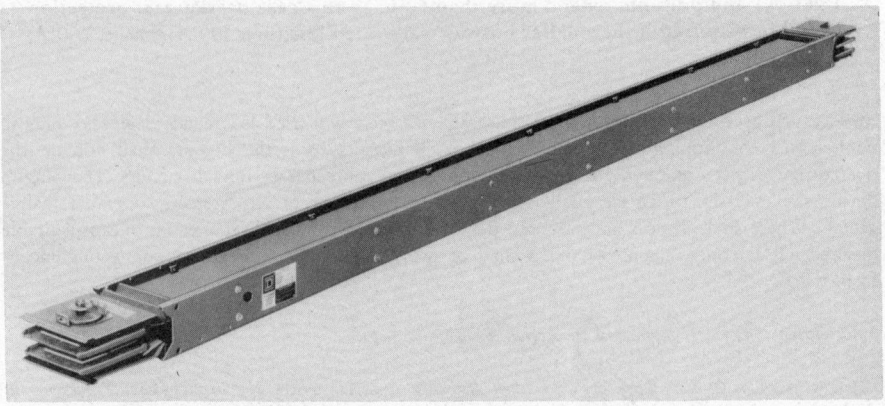

Figure 364-4. A 10-ft section of feeder busway. (*Square D Co.*)

364-24. Neutral. Neutral bus, where required, shall be sized to carry all neutral load current, including harmonic currents, and shall have adequate momentary and short-circuit rating consistent with system requirements.

364-25. Barriers and Seals. Bus runs having sections located both inside and outside of buildings shall have a vapor seal at the building wall to prevent interchange of air between indoor and outdoor sections.

Exception: Vapor seals not required in forced-cooled bus. Fire barriers shall be provided where fire walls, floors, or ceilings are penetrated.

364-26. Drain Facilities. Drain plugs, filter drains, or similar methods shall be provided to remove condensed moisture from low points in bus run.

364-27. Ventilated Bus Enclosures. Ventilated bus enclosures shall be installed in accordance with Article 710, Part D, unless designed so that foreign objects inserted through any opening will be deflected from energized parts.

364-28. Terminations and Connections. Where bus enclosures terminate at machines cooled by flammable gas, seal-off bushings, baffles, or other means shall be provided to prevent accumulation of flammable gas in the bus enclosures.

Flexible or expansion connections shall be provided in long, straight runs of bus to allow for temperature expansion or contraction, or where the bus run crosses building vibration insulation joints.

All conductor termination and connection hardware shall be accessible for installation, connection, and maintenance.

364-29. Switches. Switching devices or disconnecting links provided in the bus run shall have the same momentary rating as the bus. Disconnecting links shall be plainly marked to be removable only when bus is de-energized. Switching devices which are not load break shall be interlocked to prevent operation under load, and disconnecting link enclosures shall be interlocked to prevent access to energized parts.

364-30. Low-Voltage Wiring. Secondary control devices and wiring which are provided as part of the metal-enclosed bus run shall be insulated by fire-retardant barriers from all primary circuit elements with the exception of short lengths of wire, such as at instrument transformer terminals.

ARTICLE 365 — CABLEBUS

Contents

365-1. Definition. Cablebus is an approved assembly of insulated conductors with fittings and conductor terminations in a completely enclosed, ventilated protective metal housing. The assembly is designed to carry fault current and to withstand the magnetic forces of such current. Cablebus shall be permitted at any voltage or current for which the spaced conductors are rated.

Cablebus consists of a metal structure or framework which is installed in a manner similar to a cable tray support system. Insulated conductors, No. 1/0 or larger, are field-installed within the framework on special insulating blocks at specified intervals to provide controlled spacing between conductors. To completely enclose the conductors, a ventilated top cover is attached to the framework. See Figure 365-1.

ARTICLE 365—CABLEBUS

Figure 365-1. A section of cable-bus with conductors in place and the ventilated top cover ready to be attached to the busway frame. (*Husky Cabl-Bus*)

(FPN): Cablebus is ordinarily assembled at the point of installation from components furnished or specified by the manufacturer in accordance with instructions for the specific job.

365-2. Use. Cablebus shall be installed only for exposed work. Cablebus installed outdoors or in corrosive, wet, or damp locations shall be identified for such use. Cablebus shall not be installed in hoistways or in hazardous (classified) locations unless specifically approved for such use. Cablebus may be used for branch circuits, feeders, and services.

Cablebus framework, where adequately bonded, shall be permitted as the equipment grounding conductor for branch circuits and feeders.

365-3. Conductors.

(a) **Types of Conductors.** The current-carrying conductors in cablebus shall have an insulation rating of 75°C or higher of an approved type and suitable for the application in accordance with Articles 310 and 710.

(b) **Ampacity of Conductors.** The ampacity of conductors in cablebus shall be in accordance with Tables 310-17 and 310-19.

(c) **Size and Number of Conductors.** The size and number of conductors shall be that for which the cablebus is designed, and in no case smaller than No. 1/0.

(d) **Conductor Supports.** The insulated conductors shall be supported on blocks or other mounting means designed for the purpose.

The individual conductors in a cablebus shall be supported at intervals not greater than 3 feet (914 mm) for horizontal runs and 1½ feet (457 mm) for vertical runs. Vertical and horizontal spacing between supported conductors shall not be less than one conductor diameter at the points of support.

365-5. Overcurrent Protection. When the allowable ampacity of cablebus conductors does not correspond to a standard rating of an overcurrent device, the next higher ampere rated overcurrent device shall be permitted.

365-6. Support and Extension Through Walls and Floors.

(a) **Support.** Cablebus shall be securely supported at intervals not exceeding 12 feet (3.66 m).

390

Exception: Where spans longer than 12 feet (3.66 m) are required, the structure shall be specifically designed for the required span length.

(b) Transversely Routed. It shall be permissible to extend cablebus transversely through partitions or walls, other than fire walls, provided the section within the wall is continuous, protected against physical damage, and unventilated.

(c) Through Dry Floors and Platforms. Except where fire stops are required, it shall be permissible to extend cablebus vertically through dry floors and platforms, provided the cablebus is totally enclosed at the point where it passes through the floor or platform and for a distance of 6 feet (1.83 m) above the floor or platform.

(d) Through Floors and Platforms in Wet Locations. Except where fire stops are required, it shall be permissible to extend cablebus vertically through floors and platforms in wet locations where (1) there are curbs or other suitable means to prevent waterflow through the floor or platform opening, and (2) where the cablebus is totally enclosed at the point where it passes through the floor or platform and for a distance of 6 feet (1.83 m) above the floor or platform.

365-7. Fittings. A cablebus system shall include approved fittings for: (1) changes in horizontal or vertical direction of the run; (2) dead ends; (3) terminations in or on connected apparatus or equipment or the enclosures for such equipment; and (4) additional physical protection where required, such as guards for severe mechanical exposure.

365-8. Conductor Terminations. Approved terminating means shall be used for connections to cablebus conductors.

365-9. Grounding. Sections of cablebus shall be electrically bonded either by inherent design of the mechanical joints or by applied bonding means.

(FPN): See Section 250-75 for bonding of metal noncurrent-carrying parts.

A cablebus installation shall be grounded in accordance with Sections 250-32 and 250-33.

365-10. Marking. Each section of cablebus shall be marked with the manufacturer's name or trade designation and the maximum diameter, number, voltage rating, and ampacity of the conductors to be installed. Markings shall be so located as to be visible after installation.

ARTICLE 366 — ELECTRICAL FLOOR ASSEMBLIES

Contents

ARTICLE 366—ELECTRICAL FLOOR ASSEMBLIES

366-13. Receptacle Units.
366-14. Grounding.

C. Construction
366-20. Marking.

(a) Durable.
(b) Information.
366-21. Identification.
(a) Neutral.
(b) Grounding.

A. General

366-1. Scope. This article covers a field-installed wiring system using electrically conductive panels and receptacle housing units for branch circuits, signaling circuits, and communication circuits. The wiring system provides access into the panels and simultaneous conduction of power, signaling, and communication.

This article covers a field-installed wiring system using laminated panels containing sheets of electrical conducting material, separated by insulating material, that forms a modular panel (outside dimensions 1 5/16 in. thick x 4 ft wide x 8 ft long). These panels are located beneath the floor covering to carry both power and signal and contain four conductive planes: two ground planes, a neutral plane, and a phase (hot) plane, insulated from each other in the form of a "sandwich." The panels, sealed on all sides by a metallic, electrically grounded sheet, are connected to a standard 120-V, 20-A, 60-Hz branch-circuit panelboard power source through a panel input unit located at the start of the string of panels.

Panels are electrically interconnected to form "power areas." Each power area is protected by a standard 20-A fuse or circuit breaker. The power areas typically are from 200 to 1,000 sq ft each, depending on individual needs.

The features of this total system's package provide power (120 V, 20 A, 60 Hz) and signal (telephone, audio, data control) on a random basis, as required. Flexibility is the biggest advantage of this system since receptacle units can be installed or removed as desired, using special tools approved for the purpose.

366-2. Other Articles. In addition to the provisions of this article, installation of the assembly shall conform with the applicable provisions of Articles 210, 220, 250, and 310.

The signaling and communication circuits used in conjunction with this assembly shall also conform to Article 725 and to Article 800.

366-3. Definitions.

(a) Panels. Laminated panels containing sheets of electrical conducting material separated by insulating material(s).

(b) Receptacle Housing Unit. A special housing designed for insertion into the panels and containing power and/or signaling/communication outlets and filtering as required.

(c) Signaling/Communications Receptacle Outlet. An outlet whose use is specifically limited to signaling and/or communications circuits.

(d) Termination Unit. A special unit which presents the proper impedance to the high-frequency signaling and communication circuits within the electrical floor assemblies without affecting the 60-hertz power.

(e) Base Unit. That portion of the receptacle housing unit which contains terminal probes and means for terminating the various receptacle outlets.

(f) Terminal Probe. A special probe which makes contact only with the conductive sheet(s) with which it is designed to do so.

(g) **Inter-Panel Connector.** Connectors specifically designed with three conductors, one each for phase, neutral, and grounding connections to interconnect the panels, and/or panel input units to panels, and/or termination units to panels.

(h) **Panel Input Unit.** A unit specifically designed to permit connections between panels and the power branch circuit and the signaling/communication circuits or for only power branch circuits whenever signaling/communications circuits are not used.

(i) **Holddown Bar.** A bar designed specifically to secure the floor panels in place on the floor.

366-4. Uses Permitted. Electrical floor assemblies shall be used only: (1) as branch circuits to supply lighting, small appliances, and small power loads; (2) to supply signaling circuits; and (3) to supply communication circuits.

366-5. Uses Not Permitted. Electrical floor assemblies shall not be installed: (1) where subject to corrosive vapors; (2) outdoors or in a wet or damp location; or (3) in any hazardous (classified) location.

366-6. Branch Circuit. The rating of the branch circuit shall not exceed 20-amperes, 120-volts, nominal, 2-wire, single-phase.

B. Installation

366-10. Panels. The panels shall be installed on surfaces which are flat and smooth. The panels shall be installed in a secure fashion. The holddown bar shall be permitted for this purpose.

366-11. All Circuits.

(a) **From the Distribution Panelboards.** All 15- and 20-ampere branch circuits shall be extended from their respective branch-circuit panelboards.

(b) **From Signaling and/or Communication Equipment.** All circuits for signaling and/or communication shall be extended from Class 2 sources.

(c) **Wiring.** The branch-circuit conductors shall be installed in rigid metal conduit, intermediate metal conduit, or raceways specifically approved for grounding purposes.

(d) **Terminations.** Termination for combination of 15- or 20-ampere branch circuits and signaling and/or communications circuits shall be within a panel input unit.

366-12. Circuits.

(a) **Branch Circuits.** A maximum length of 200 feet (61 m) of panels shall be permitted to be connected in series. Any number of panels shall be permitted to be connected to form a single branch circuit provided the total area does not exceed 1024 square feet (95 sq m).

(b) **Signaling/Communication Circuits.** Signaling/communication circuits shall be permitted to feed any number of panels. A termination unit shall be permitted at the end of each series set of panels.

366-13. Receptacle Units. All receptacle units shall be installed or removed using suitable tools.

366-14. Grounding. The section of the branch circuit extended from the branch-circuit panelboard to the panel input unit shall have an equipment grounding conductor. This shall be a separate, continuous, copper equipment grounding conductor, not smaller than No. 12. This equipment grounding conductor shall be installed with the branch-circuit conductors in the approved metal raceway. The equipment grounding conductor shall be connected to a properly identified terminal screw in the panel input unit and in the branch-circuit panelboard.

C. Construction

366-20. Marking.

(a) Durable. All markings shall be durable and shall be placed on the surface of all components in a readily recognizable location.

(b) Information. All panels, receptacle housing units, base units, panel input units, and tools shall be marked to indicate the following information:

(1) The maximum working voltage and current.

(2) The manufacturer's name, trademark, or other distinctive marking by which the organization responsible for the component can be readily identified.

366-21. Identification.

(a) Neutral. All neutral connection points and terminations shall be identified by means of a distinctive, durable white or natural gray marking.

(b) Grounding. All grounding connection points and terminations shall be identified as required by Section 200-10.

ARTICLE 370 — OUTLET, DEVICE, PULL AND JUNCTION BOXES, CONDUIT BODIES AND FITTINGS

Contents

370-15. Covers and Canopies.
  (a) Nonmetallic or Metal Covers and Plates.
  (b) Exposed Combustible Wall or Ceiling Finish.
  (c) Flexible Cord Pendants.
370-16. Fastened to Gas Pipes.
370-17. Outlet Boxes.
  (a) Boxes at Lighting Fixture Outlets.
  (b) Floor Boxes.
370-18. Pull and Junction Boxes.
  (a) Minimum Size.
  (b) Conductors in Pull or Junction Boxes.
  (c) Covers.
  (d) Permanent Barriers.
370-19. Junction, Pull and Outlet Boxes to Be Accessible.

C. Construction Specifications
370-20. Metal Boxes, Conduit Bodies, and Fittings.
  (a) Corrosion-Resistant.

  (b) Thickness of Metal.
  (c) Metal Boxes Over 100 Cubic Inches.
  (d) Grounding Provisions.
370-21. Covers.
370-22. Bushings.
370-23. Nonmetallic Boxes.
370-24. Marking.

D. Pull and Junction Boxes for Use on Systems Over 600 Volts, Nominal
370-50. General.
370-51. Size of Pull and Junction Boxes.
  (a) For Straight Pulls.
  (b) For Angle or U Pulls.
  (c) Removable Sides.
370-52. Construction and Installation Requirements.
  (a) Corrosion Protection.
  (b) Passing Through Partitions.
  (c) Complete Enclosure.
  (d) Wiring Is Accessible.
  (e) Suitable Covers.
  (f) Suitable for Expected Handling.

A. Scope and General

370-1. Scope. This article covers the installation and use of all boxes, conduit bodies, and fittings as required by Section 300-15. Boxes, conduit bodies, and fittings referred to in Section 300-15 used as outlet, junction, or pull boxes shall conform with the provisions of this article depending on their use. Cast, sheet metal, nonmetallic, and other boxes such as FS, FD, and larger boxes are not classified as conduit bodies. Fittings, such as capped elbows and service entrance elbows, are not classified as conduit bodies and shall not contain splices, taps, or devices.

Installations in hazardous (classified) locations shall conform to Articles 500 through 517.

(FPN): For systems over 600 volts, nominal, see Part D of this article.

The title and scope of Article 370 have been revised for the 1984 *Code*. A device box is designed to accept the installation of a device such as a snap switch, receptacle, or dimmer. An outlet box requires the use of a plaster ring or special cover in order to be adapted for use as a device box.

Fittings such as capped elbows and service-entrance elbows are not classified as conduit bodies. Therefore, the rules covering the use of conduit bodies in this article are not applicable to these types of fittings. See the definitions of "Conduit Body," "Fitting," and "Outlet" in Article 100.

370-2. Round Boxes. Round boxes shall not be used where conduits or connectors requiring the use of locknuts or bushings are to be connected to the side of the box.

This rule requires the use of rectangular or octagonal boxes having a flat bearing surface at each knockout for locknuts and bushings to ensure an adequate mechanical connection and effective electrical continuity.

370-3. Nonmetallic Boxes. Nonmetallic boxes shall be permitted only with open wiring on insulators, concealed knob-and-tube wiring, nonmetallic-sheathed cable, and with rigid nonmetallic conduit.

In addition thereto, nonmetallic boxes over 100 cubic inches manufactured with bonding means between all raceway and cable entries shall also be permitted to be used with metal raceways and metal-sheathed cable.

370-4. Metal Boxes. All metal boxes shall be grounded in accordance with the provisions of Article 250.

B. Installation

370-5. Damp or Wet Locations. In damp or wet locations, boxes, conduit bodies, and fittings shall be so placed or equipped as to prevent moisture from entering or accumulating within the box, conduit body, or fitting. Boxes, conduit bodies, and fittings installed in wet locations shall be listed for use in wet locations.

(FPN): For boxes in floors, see Section 370-17(b).

(FPN): For protection against corrosion, see Section 300-6.

Article 100 defines "Weatherproof" as "So constructed or protected that exposure to the weather will not interfere with successful operation." Rainproof, raintight, or watertight equipment can fulfill the requirements for weatherproof where varying weather conditions other than wetness, such as snow, ice, dust, or temperature extremes, are not a factor.

A "weatherhead" fitting is considered to be weatherproof because the openings for the conductors are placed in a downward position so that rain or snow cannot enter the fitting.

See definitions of "Damp Location" and "Wet Location" under "Location" in Article 100.

370-6. Number of Conductors in Outlet, Device, and Junction Boxes, and Conduit Bodies. Boxes shall be of sufficient size to provide free space for all conductors enclosed in the box.

The provisions of this section shall not apply to terminal housings supplied with motors. See Section 430-12.

Boxes and conduit bodies containing conductors, size No. 4 or larger, shall also comply with the provisions of Section 370-18.

(a) Standard Boxes. The maximum number of conductors, not counting fixture wires smaller than No. 14, permitted in standard boxes shall be as is listed in Table 370-6(a). See Section 370-18 where boxes or conduit bodies are used as junction or pull boxes.

Fixture wires No. 14 AWG and larger are required to be counted for box fill when determining the number of conductors installed in a standard box. It should be noted that when conductors of different sizes terminate in a box, the requirements of Section 370-6(b) are applicable. For example, the size of a box without clamps, which contains two 3-wire, No. 12 AWG multiwire branch circuits installed in conduit, used to supply four fixtures with eight No. 14 AWG fixture tap conductors would require a box which is sized at 6 × 2.25 cu in. plus 8 × 2.0 cu in. = 29.5 cu in. minimum. Table 370-6(a) indicates that a 4 $^{11}/_{16}$ × 1½ square (29.5 cu in.), 4 x 2⅛ square (30.3 cu in.), or 4 $^{11}/_{16}$ × 2 ⅛ square (42.0 cu in.) box would satisfy this arrangement.

If the fixture tap conductors were No. 18 AWG or No. 16 AWG, the box would be sized at 6 × 2.25 cu in. = 13.5 cu in. minimum. However, in accordance with the basic requirement of Section 370-6, first paragraph, a larger box might be needed if the box was not of sufficient size to provide free space for all conductors in the box. Some judgment is needed to determine compliance with this requirement. The free space available will depend on the length and type of conductors, splicing method, and conductor arrangement in the box.

(1) Table 370-6(a) shall apply where no fittings or devices, such as fixture studs, cable clamps, hickeys, switches, or receptacles, are contained in the box and where no grounding conductors are part of the wiring within the box. Where one or more of these types of devices, such as fixture studs, cable clamps, or hickeys are contained in the box, the number of conductors shown in the table shall be reduced by one for each type of device; an additional deduction of one conductor shall be made for each strap containing one or more devices; and a further deduction of one conductor shall be made for one or more grounding conductors entering the box. A conductor running through the box shall be counted as one conductor, and each conductor originating outside of the box and terminating inside the box is counted as one conductor. Conductors, no part of which leaves the box, shall not be counted. The volume of a wiring enclosure (box) shall be the total volume of the assembled sections, and, where used, the space provided by plaster rings, domed covers, extension rings, etc., that are marked with their volume in cubic inches, or are made from boxes the dimensions of which are listed in Table 370-6(a).

(2) For combinations of conductor sizes shown in Table 370-6(a), the volume per conductor listed in Table 370-6(b) shall apply. The maximum number and size of conductors listed in Table 370-6(a) shall not be exceeded.

Table 370-6(a). Metal Boxes

Box Dimension, Inches Trade Size or Type	Min. Cu. In. Cap.	Maximum Number of Conductors				
		No. 14	No. 12	No. 10	No. 8	No. 6
4 x 1¼ Round or Octagonal	12.5	6	5	5	4	0
4 x 1½ Round or Octagonal	15.5	7	6	6	5	0
4 x 2⅛ Round or Octagonal	21.5	10	9	8	7	0
4 x 1¼ Square	18.0	9	8	7	6	0
4 x 1½ Square	21.0	10	9	8	7	0
4 x 2⅛ Square	30.3	15	13	12	10	6*
4¹¹⁄₁₆ x 1¼ Square	25.5	12	11	10	8	0
4¹¹⁄₁₆ x 1½ Square	29.5	14	13	11	9	0
4¹¹⁄₁₆ x 2⅛ Square	42.0	21	18	16	14	6
3 x 2 x 1½ Device	7.5	3	3	3	2	0
3 x 2 x 2 Device	10.0	5	4	4	3	0
3 x 2 x 2¼ Device	10.5	5	4	4	3	0
3 x 2 x 2½ Device	12.5	6	5	5	4	0
3 x 2 x 2¾ Device	14.0	7	6	5	4	0
3 x 2 x 3½ Device	18.0	9	8	7	6	0
4 x 2⅛ x 1½ Device	10.3	5	4	4	3	0
4 x 2⅛ x 1⅞ Device	13.0	6	5	5	4	0
4 x 2⅛ x 2⅛ Device	14.5	7	6	5	4	0
3¾ x 2 x 2½ Masonry Box/Gang	14.0	7	6	5	4	0
3¾ x 2 x 3½ Masonry Box/Gang	21.0	10	9	8	7	0
FS— Minimum Internal Depth 1¾ Single Cover/Gang	13.5	6	6	5	4	0
FD—Minimum Internal Depth 2⅜ Single Cover/Gang	18.0	9	8	7	6	3
FS— Minimum Internal Depth 1¾ Multiple Cover/Gang	18.0	9	8	7	6	0
FD—Minimum Internal Depth 2⅜ Multiple Cover/Gang	24.0	12	10	9	8	4

* Not to be used as a pull box. For termination only.

Table 370-6(a) lists the maximum number of conductors permitted in a "metal" box before the deductions provided for in Section 370-6(a)(1) are considered. Figure 370-1 illustrates one 14/2 and one 14/3 nonmetallic-sheathed cable, each with bare equipment grounding conductors installed in a device box. This arrangement would be counted as follows:

Two nonmetallic-sheathed cables (circuit conductors)	5
Two grounding conductors	1
Internal clamp(s) (hickeys or studs)	1
Receptacle (strap containing one or more devices)	1
Total	8

Column No. 1 in Table 370-6(a) lists a device box (3 × 2 × 3½ in.) which is adequate for nine No. 14 conductors. However, this box may be too deep for shallower partitions; thus, a smaller device box (3 × 2 × 2½ in.) is permitted with a domed side bracket (marked with its volume in cubic inches) and the maximum number of conductors is required to be computed as per Table 370-6(b). A 4 × 1¼ in. square box and plaster ring combination would also be permitted.

The phrase in the last sentence of Section 370-6(a)(1) "or are made from boxes the dimensions of which are listed in Table 370-6(a)" means that extension rings made from boxes having the dimensions tabulated in Table 370-6(a) do not have to be marked with their cubic inch volume to be considered as having volume.

Extension rings or boxes, domed covers or plaster rings, etc., that are marked with their volume in cubic inches are considered as having usable conductor space.

(b) Other Boxes. Boxes 100 cubic inches or less other than those described in Table 370-6(a), conduit bodies having provision for more than two conduit entries and nonmetallic boxes shall be durably and legibly marked by the manufacturer with their cubic inch capacity. The maximum number of conductors permitted shall be computed using the volume per conductor listed in Table 370-6(b) and the deductions provided for in Section 370-6(a)(1). Boxes described in Table 370-6(a) that have a larger cubic inch capacity than is designated in the table shall be permitted to have their cubic inch capacity marked as required by this section and the maximum number of conductors permitted shall be computed using the volume per conductor listed in Table 370-6(b).

Table 370-6(b).   Volume Required per Conductor

Size of Conductor	Free Space Within Box for Each Conductor
No. 14	2. cubic inches
No. 12	2.25 cubic inches
No. 10	2.5 cubic inches
No. 8	3. cubic inches
No. 6	5. cubic inches

Where No. 6 conductors are installed the minimum wire bending space required in Table 373-6(a) shall be provided.

Table 370-6(a) lists the cubic inch capacities and the maximum number of conductors (No. 14 through No. 6) permitted in most commonly used metal boxes.

Table 370-6(b) lists the volume that is required for conductors (No. 14 through No. 6) used in boxes less than 100 cu in., other than those described in Table 370-6(a). Such boxes are required to be marked with their cubic inch capacity. These provisions assure that free space for all conductors will be provided. A conductor running through a box without a splice or tap is counted as one conductor.

14/2 nonmetallic
with ground

14/3 nonmetallic
with ground

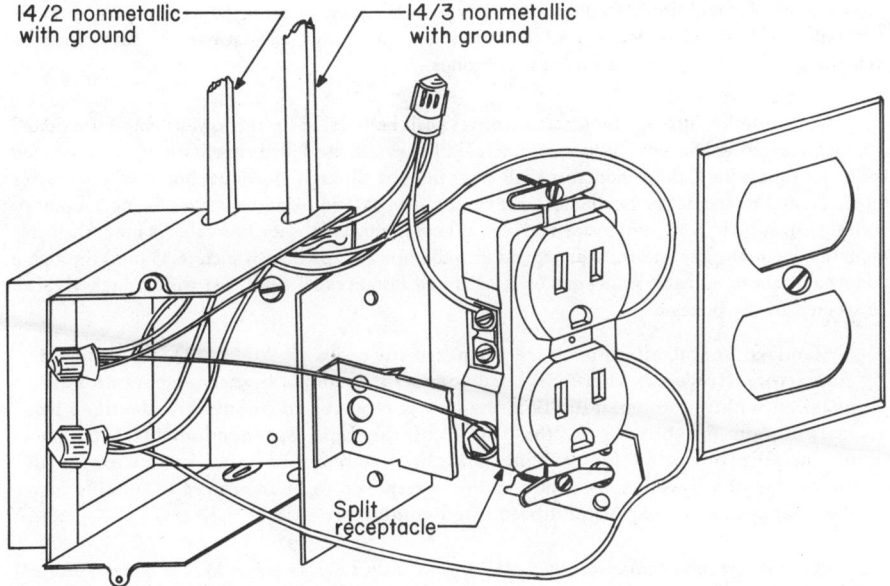

Figure 370-1. Device box, with a domed side, providing sufficient space for all conductors, clamp, and receptacle in compliance with Section 370-6(b).

(c) Conduit Bodies. Conduit bodies enclosing No. 6 conductors or smaller shall have a cross-sectional area not less than twice the cross-sectional area of the largest conduit to which it is attached. The maximum number of conductors permitted shall be the maximum number permitted by Table 1, Chapter 9, for the conduit to which it is attached.

Conduit bodies having provisions for less than three conduit entries shall not contain splices, taps, or devices unless they comply with the provisions of Section 370-6(b) and are supported in a rigid and secure manner.

> The intent of this section is to require that conduit bodies be supported in a rigid and secure manner so that they will not turn in place. See Section 370-13(g). Where conduit bodies have provisions for two or less conduit entries and contain splices, taps, or devices, they are required to be durably and legibly marked with their cubic inch capacity. The maximum number of conductors permitted in a conduit body is computed by using the volume for conductors listed in Table 370-6(b). See Section 370-18 for requirements when conduit bodies are used as pull and junction boxes.

370-7. Conductors Entering Boxes, Conduit Bodies, or Fittings. Conductors entering boxes, conduit bodies or fittings shall be protected from abrasion, and shall comply with (a) through (d) below.

(a) Openings to Be Closed. Openings through which conductors enter shall be adequately closed.

(b) Metal Boxes, Conduit Bodies, and Fittings. Where metal outlet boxes, conduit bodies or fittings are installed with open wiring or concealed knob-and-tube wiring, conductors shall enter through insulating bushings or, in dry places, through flexible tubing extending from the last insulating support and firmly secured to the box, conduit body or fitting. Where raceway or cable is installed with metal outlet boxes, conduit bodies or fittings, the raceway or cable shall be secured to such boxes, conduit bodies and fittings.

(c) Nonmetallic Boxes. Nonmetallic boxes shall be suitable for the lowest temperature rated conductor entering the box. Where nonmetallic boxes are used with open wiring or concealed knob-and-tube wiring, the conductors shall enter the box through individual holes. Where flexible tubing is used to encase the conductors, the tubing shall extend from the last insulating support to no less than ¼ inch (6.35 mm) inside the box. Where nonmetallic-sheathed cable is used, the cable assembly, including the sheath, shall extend into the box no less than ¼ inch (6.35 mm) through a nonmetallic-sheathed cable knockout opening. In all instances all permitted wiring methods shall be secured to the boxes.

Standard nonmetallic boxes are permitted for use with 90°C (194°F) insulated conductors. However, where insulated conductors rated at higher temperatures are installed within a nonmetallic box, the box is required to be suitably identified by marking on the box or in the listing of the box. See Section 110-3(b). A nonmetallic box used for splicing a higher temperature rated conductor to a conductor of a lower temperature rating is required to be identified as suitable for the temperature rating of the lower rated conductor.

Exception: Where nonmetallic-sheathed cable is used with boxes no larger than a nominal size 2¼ inch by 4 inch mounted in walls and where the cable is fastened within 8 inches (203 mm) of the box measured along the sheath and where the sheath extends into the box no less than ¼ inch (6.35 mm), securing the cable to the box shall not be required.

This exception is new in the 1984 *Code*. The next to the last sentence of Section 370-7(c) as it appeared in the 1981 *Code* was revised to become this exception. The words "single-gang box" were replaced with the words "no larger than a nominal size 2¼ in. by 4 in. mounted in walls," in order to make it clear that clamps are required in ceiling boxes and other boxes larger than 2¼ in. by 4 in. The requirement is based on the width of the box and the likelihood of the cable being pushed back out of the box when the conductors and device, if any, are folded back into the box during installation of receptacles, switches, etc.

(d) Conductors No. 4 AWG or Larger. Installation shall comply with Section 373-6(c).

370-8. Unused Openings. Unused openings in boxes, conduit bodies and fittings shall be effectively closed to afford protection substantially equivalent to that of the wall of the box, conduit body or fitting. Metal plugs or plates used with nonmetallic boxes, conduit bodies or fittings shall be recessed at least ¼ inch (6.35 mm) from the outer surface.

370-9. Boxes Enclosing Flush Devices. Boxes used to enclose flush devices shall be of such design that the devices will be completely enclosed on back and sides, and that substantial support for the devices will be provided. Screws for supporting the box shall not be used in attachment of the device contained therein.

370-10. In Wall or Ceiling. In walls or ceilings of concrete, tile, or other noncombustible material, boxes and fittings shall be so installed that the front edge of the box or fitting will not set back of the finished surface more than ¼ inch (6.35 mm). In walls and ceilings constructed of wood or other combustible material, outlet boxes and fittings shall be flush with the finished surface or project therefrom.

370-11. Repairing Plaster and Drywall or Plasterboard. Plaster, drywall or plasterboard surfaces that are broken or incomplete shall be repaired so there will be no gaps or open spaces at the edge of the box or fitting.

Exception: On walls or ceilings of concrete, tile, or other noncombustible material.

Sections 370-10 and 370-11 require that boxes installed in walls or ceilings of combustible materials be flush with the finished surface and any open spaces at the edge of the box be repaired.

Many inspection authorities require that "plaster rings" be installed on square or octagonal boxes for a proper installation.

370-12. Exposed Surface Extensions. In making an exposed surface extension from an existing outlet of concealed wiring, a box or an extension ring shall be mounted over the original box and electrically and mechanically secured to it.

Figure 370-2 illustrates an extension box that is mounted to an existing box, assuring mechanical and electrical continuity.

The use of a blank or "handy" box cover attached to an existing flush device, outlet or junction box, with a knockout in the cover used to connect a cable or flexible-type raceway, would not meet the requirements of this section. Also, grounding continuity would not be maintained if the cover were removed.

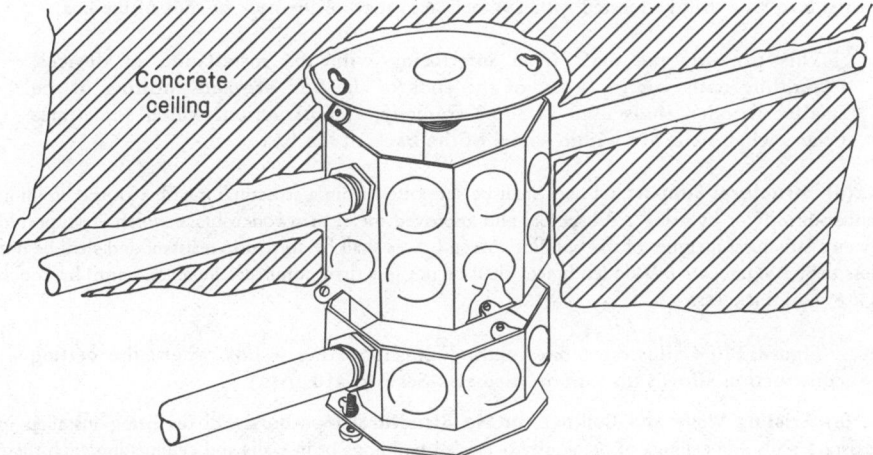

Concrete ceiling

Figure 370-2. Extension boxes are secured to existing boxes in concealed construction for additions or alterations to the wiring system.

370-13. Supports. In all cases boxes shall be rigidly and securely fastened in place as is defined in (a) through (g) below.

(a) Surface Mounting. They shall be fastened to the surface upon which they are mounted unless such surface does not provide adequate support in which case they shall be supported by some structural member.

Support of a box on a suspended-type ceiling is one example of where a rod or chain should be attached to the box and structural member.

(b) In Concrete or Masonry. They shall be embedded in either concrete or masonry.

Boxes are permitted to be embedded in masonry or concrete provided they are rigid and secure. See Figure 370-3.

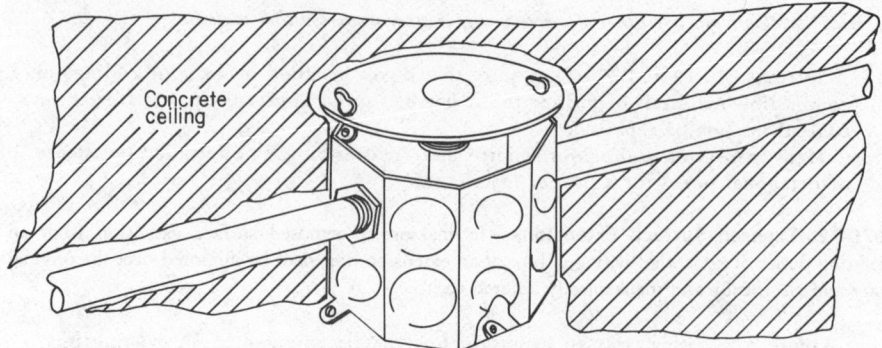

Figure 370-3. A "mud" box installed in a concrete ceiling. Additional support is not required.

(c) Nails. Where nails are used as a fastening means and where they pass through the interior of the box, they shall be located within ¼ inch (6.35 mm) of the back or ends of the box.

This prevents the nails from interfering with the installation of devices. Permitting nails within ¼ in. of the ends of the box prevents splitting of the smaller wooden studs used in some frame-type construction, which sometimes occurs when nails are within ¼ in. of the back of the box.

(d) Structural Support. Boxes shall be supported from a structural member of the building either directly or by using a substantial and approved metal or wooden brace which is supported from a structural member of the building. Metal braces shall be corrosion-resistant and shall be not less than .020 uncoated. Wooden braces shall be not less than nominal 1 inch (25.4 mm) by 2 inch (50.8 mm) thickness.

Figure 370-4 illustrates one method of supporting a box where the ceiling construction affords no support. See also Section 410-16(a).

(e) Existing Walls and Ceilings, or No Structural Members. Boxes being installed in existing walls and ceilings of previously occupied buildings or in walls and ceilings in which there are no structural members shall be supported by the use of devices, clamps or anchors which will provide the rigid and secure installation intended by this section of the Code.

Where there are no structural members, or where cut into existing walls, boxes are permitted to be secured by clamps or anchors. See Figure 370-5 for one example of an acceptable mounting method.

(f) Empty Threaded Boxes or Conduit Bodies. Threaded boxes or conduit bodies not over 100 cubic inches that do not contain devices, receptacles or switches and do not support fixtures shall be considered to be adequately supported if two or more conduits are threaded into the box wrenchtight and are supported within 3 feet (914 mm) of the box on two or more sides so as to provide the rigid and secure installation intended by this section of the Code.

Boxes are not permitted to be supported by rigid raceways using a connector or locknut and bushing connection, nor is a box permitted to be supported by a single raceway. See Figure 680-1 for an example of acceptable support.

(g) Other Threaded Boxes or Conduit Bodies. Threaded boxes or conduit bodies not over 100 cubic inches that contain devices, receptacles or switches shall be considered to be adequately supported if two or more conduits are threaded into the box wrenchtight and if each conduit is supported within 18 inches (457 mm) of the box so as to provide the rigid and secure installation intended by this section of the Code.

See commentary under (f) above.

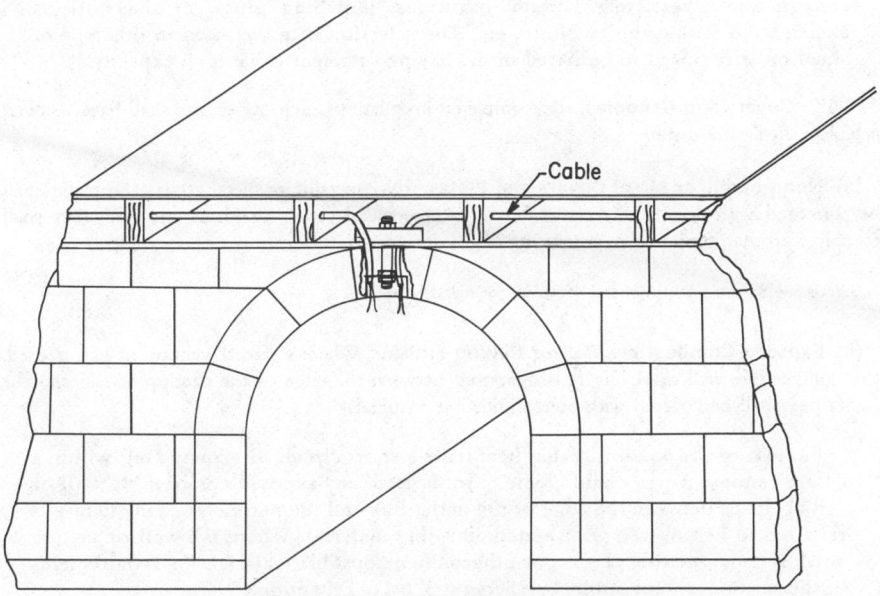

Box rod and plate hanger used when a fixture weighing more than 50 lbs. is to be installed, or when a box is installed in a large opening of a tile ceiling.

Figure 370-4. A plate and threaded-rod hanger used to support an outlet box in a tile arch ceiling.

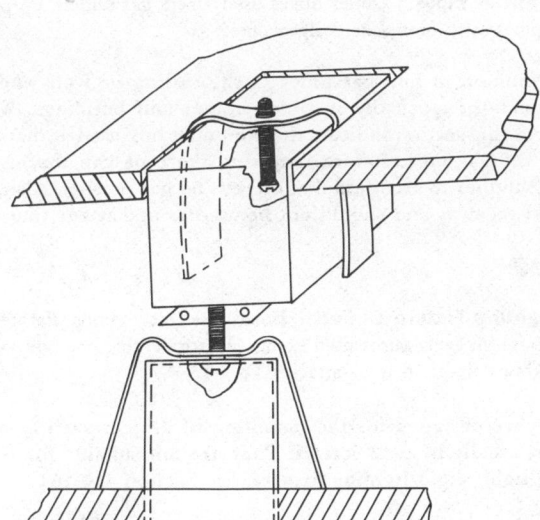

Figure 370-5. Top view of inserting and securing a box with a mounting bracket through an opening cut in an existing wall finish.

370-14. Depth of Outlet Boxes. No box shall have an internal depth of less than ½ inch (12.7 mm). Boxes intended to enclose flush devices shall have an internal depth of not less than 15/16 inch (23.8 mm).

The use of a shallow box may become necessary because of old work or existing construction where very narrow partitions, plumbing pipes, or ductwork is encountered within the partition, etc. The selection of a box used in this type of situation is required to be based on its having sufficient cubic inch capacity.

370-15. Covers and Canopies. In completed installations each outlet box shall have a cover, faceplate, or fixture canopy.

(a) Nonmetallic or Metal Covers and Plates. Nonmetallic or metal covers and plates shall be permitted with nonmetallic outlet boxes. Where metal covers or plates are used, they shall comply with the grounding requirements of Section 250-42.

(FPN): See Sections 410-18(a) and 410-56(c) for metal faceplates.

(b) Exposed Combustible Wall or Ceiling Finish. Where a fixture canopy or pan is used, any combustible wall or ceiling finish exposed between the edge of the canopy or pan and the outlet box shall be covered with noncombustible material.

Because of the possibility that heat from a short circuit or ground fault within a fixture canopy or pan could create a fire hazard, any exposed combustible wall or ceiling space between the edge of the outlet box and the perimeter of the fixture is required to be covered with noncombustible material. Where the wall or ceiling finish is concrete, tile, plaster, or other noncombustible material, the requirements of this section do not apply. See Section 370-11, Exception.

(c) Flexible Cord Pendants. Covers of outlet boxes and conduit bodies having holes through which flexible cord pendants pass shall be provided with bushings designed for the purpose or shall have smooth, well-rounded surfaces on which the cords may bear. So-called hard-rubber or composition bushings shall not be used.

370-16. Fastened to Gas Pipes. Outlet boxes used where gas outlets are present shall be so fastened to the gas pipes as to be mechanically secure.

It is not uncommon to find gas pipes in the ceiling or wall where they once provided illumination, especially in older homes and buildings. When encountered, the rules of this section indicate that an outlet box used at that location is to be attached to the gas pipe. Before removing the pipe cap the installer should contact the gas supplier to ascertain that there is no gas present. Also, a gas pipe is not an electrical raceway and should not be used as one at any time.

370-17. Outlet Boxes.

(a) Boxes at Lighting Fixture Outlets. Boxes used at lighting fixture outlets shall be designed for the purpose. At every outlet used exclusively for lighting, the box shall be so designed or installed that a lighting fixture may be attached.

Device boxes are designed for the mounting of devices such as snap-switches and receptacles, usually by 6-32 screws. They are not suitable for the support of other than very lightweight lighting fixtures. See Section 410-16.

(b) Floor Boxes. Boxes listed specifically for this application shall be used for receptacles located in the floor.

Exception: Boxes located in elevated floors of show windows and similar locations where the authority having jurisdiction judges them to be free from physical damage, moisture, and dirt.

370-18. Pull and Junction Boxes. Boxes and conduit bodies used as pull or junction boxes shall comply with (a) through (d) of this section.

(a) Minimum Size. For raceways ¾ inch trade size or larger, containing conductors of No. 4 or larger, and for cables containing conductors of No. 4 or larger, the minimum dimensions of pull or junction boxes installed in a raceway or cable run shall comply with the following:

(1) Straight Pulls. In straight pulls the length of the box shall not be less than eight times the trade diameter of the largest raceway.

(2) Angle or U Pulls. Where angle or U pulls are made, the distance between each raceway entry inside the box and the opposite wall of the box shall not be less than six times the trade diameter of the largest raceway. This distance shall be increased for additional entries by the amount of the sum of the diameters of all other raceway entries on the same wall of the box.

Exception: Where a conduit or cable entry is in the wall of a box or conduit body opposite to a removable cover and where the distance from that wall to the cover is in conformance with the column for one wire per terminal in Table 373-6(a).

The distance between raceway entries enclosing the same conductor shall not be less than six times the trade diameter of the larger raceway.

When transposing cable size into raceway size in (a)(1) and (a)(2) above, the minimum trade size raceway required for the number and size of conductors in the cable shall be used.

(3) Boxes of dimensions less than those required in (a)(1) and (a)(2) above shall be permitted for installations of combinations of conductors that are less than the maximum conduit fill (of conduits being used) permitted by Table 1, Chapter 9, provided the box has been approved for and is permanently marked with the maximum number and maximum size of conductors permitted.

Exception: Terminal housings supplied with motors which shall comply with the provisions of Section 430-12.

(b) Conductors in Pull or Junction Boxes. In pull boxes or junction boxes having any dimension over 6 feet (1.83 m), all conductors shall be cabled or racked up in an approved manner.

(FPN): See Section 373-6(c) for insulation of conductors at bushings.

(c) Covers. All pull boxes, junction boxes, conduit bodies, and fittings shall be provided with covers compatible with the box, conduit body or fitting construction and suitable for the conditions of use. Where metal covers are used, they shall comply with the grounding requirements of Section 250-42.

(d) Permanent Barriers. Where permanent barriers are installed in a box, each section shall be considered as a separate box.

This section applies to minimum dimensions of pull or junction boxes used with raceways (¾ in. or larger) or cables, where they contain conductors No. 4 AWG or larger.

For straight pulls, for example, a 2-in. conduit containing four 4/0 AWG conductors (see Table 3B in Chapter 9) requires a 16-in. long pull box [8 × 2 in. = 16 in. as per subparagraph (a)(1)]. It should be understood that 16 in. is the required minimum length; however, for maximum ease in handling this size of conductor, a longer length pull box may be desired.

For angle pulls or U pulls, subparagraph (a)(2) indicates two methods for computing the box dimensions. The largest dimension computed by either of the two methods is, of course, the one that should be used.

First method:

$$6 \times 4 \text{ in.} = 24 \text{ in.}$$
$$2 \times 3 \text{ in.} = 6$$
$$4 \times 2\frac{1}{2} \text{ in.} = \underline{10}$$
$$\text{Total } \overline{40} \text{ in.}$$

Second method:

Figure 370-6 illustrates a box in which the conduits enter and leave in the same order, that is, there is no crossover of conductors. The 2½-in. conduit in the top, left corner must be spaced not less than 15 in. (6 × 2½ in. = 15 in.) (dimension A, measured center to center). By calculation, or by sketching the layout of the box and conduits on paper, it is determined that distance C is approximately 10½ in. and, by practical installation methods for the spacing of conduits, distance B is approximately 32½ in. (10½ in. + 32½ in. = 43 in.); therefore, the second method determining the larger box would be applied in this case.

Larger sizes of conductors are generally formed in circuit groups and "tie wrapped" together, or sufficient space should be allowed to provide for insulated

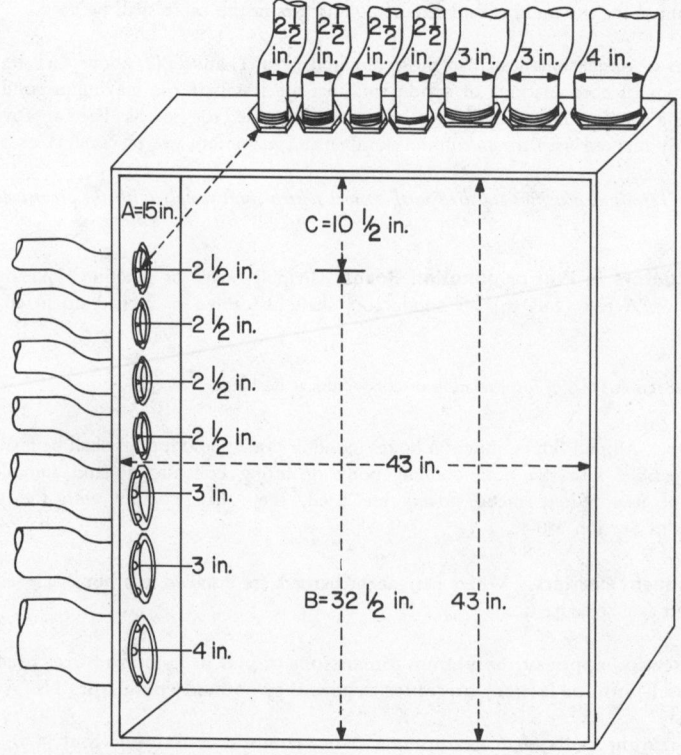

Figure 370-6. Raceways in a right-angle turn with no crossover of conductors within the pull box.

racks that will support conductors in an orderly manner. Conductors are required to be prevented from resting directly on metal inside the box and insulating bushings are required to be provided unless part of enclosures having an integral threaded hub or boss that provides a smoothly rounded or flared entry for conductors. See Section 373-6(c).

370-19. Junction, Pull and Outlet Boxes to Be Accessible. Junction, pull and outlet boxes shall be so installed that the wiring contained in them can be rendered accessible without removing any part of the building or in underground circuits without excavating sidewalks, paving, earth, or other substance that is to be used to establish the finished grade.

Exception: Listed boxes shall be permitted where covered by gravel, light aggregate, or noncohesive granulated soil if their location is effectively identified and accessible for excavation.

Consideration should also be given to the accessibility of junction boxes installed on a structural ceiling above a suspended ceiling. If an electrician has to stand on the top rung of a ladder to reach through a ceiling tile (2 ft × 4 ft) in order to gain access to splices in a box, safety may be reduced.

A covered box is permitted to be used at any point for the connection of conduit, tubing, or cable, provided it is not rendered inaccessible. See Article 100 for definition of "Accessible (as applied to wiring methods)." See also Section 300-15.

C. Construction Specifications

370-20. Metal Boxes, Conduit Bodies, and Fittings.

(a) Corrosion-Resistant. Metal boxes, conduit bodies, and fittings shall be corrosion-resistant or shall be well galvanized, enameled, or otherwise properly coated inside and out to prevent corrosion.

(FPN): See Section 300-6 for limitation in the use of boxes and fittings protected from corrosion solely by enamel.

(b) Thickness of Metal. Sheet steel boxes not over 100 cubic inches in size shall be made from steel not less than 0.0625 inch (1.59 mm) thick. The wall of a malleable iron box and a die-cast or permanent-mold cast aluminum, brass or bronze box shall not be less than 3/32 inch (2.38 mm) thick. Other cast metal boxes shall have a wall thickness not less than 1/8 inch (3.17 mm).

UL listed cast metal boxes suitable for field drilling and tapping of holes for conduit connections and mounting are marked to indicate the location and trade size of the openings.

(c) Metal Boxes Over 100 Cubic Inches. Metal boxes over 100 cubic inches in size shall be constructed so as to be of ample strength and rigidity. If of sheet steel the metal shall not be less than 0.053 inch (1.35 mm) uncoated.

(d) Grounding Provisions. A means shall be provided in each metal box, designed for use with nonmetallic raceways and nonmetallic cable systems, for the connection of an equipment grounding conductor.

The "means provided" by the box manufacturer is usually in the form of a 10-32 tapped hole marked "GR" or "GRD" or the equivalent, adjacent to the hole. It should be noted, however, that the "means provided" may not necessarily be utilized. See Figure 250-25 and the commentary following Section 250-114.

ARTICLE 370—OUTLET, DEVICE, BOXES AND FITTINGS

370-21. Covers. Metal covers shall be of a thickness not less than that specified for the walls of the box or fitting of the same material and with which they are designed to be used, or shall be lined with firmly attached insulating material not less than ½ inch (0.79 mm) in thickness. Covers of porcelain or other approved insulating material shall be permitted if of such form and thickness as to afford the required protection and strength.

370-22. Bushings. Covers of outlet boxes, conduit bodies and outlet fittings having holes through which flexible cord pendants may pass shall be provided with approved bushings or shall have smooth, well-rounded surfaces, upon which the cord may bear. Where conductors other than flexible cord may pass through a metal cover, a separate hole equipped with a bushing of suitable insulating material shall be provided for each conductor. Such separate holes shall be connected by a slot as required by Section 300-20.

(FPN): For alternating current conductors, see Section 300-20(b).

370-23. Nonmetallic Boxes. Provisions for supports or other mounting means for nonmetallic boxes shall be outside of the box, or the box shall be so constructed as to prevent contact between the conductors in the box and the supporting screws.

Nonmetallic boxes considered as being suitable for use with nonmetallic conduit are marked as per Section 110-3(b) and are usually intended for support by conduit. This type of box is not recognized for the support of fixtures or other equipment nor are they designed to accommodate heat-producing equipment.

370-24. Marking. All boxes and conduit bodies, covers, extension rings, plaster rings, and the like shall be durably and legibly marked with the manufacturer's name or trademark.

D. Pull and Junction Boxes for Use on Systems Over 600 Volts, Nominal

370-50. General. In addition to the generally applicable provisions of Article 370, the rules in Sections 370-51 and 370-52 shall apply.

370-51. Size of Pull and Junction Boxes. Pull and junction boxes shall provide adequate space and dimensions for the installation of conductors in accordance with the following:

(a) For Straight Pulls. The length of the box shall be not less than forty-eight times the outside diameter, over sheath, of the largest conductor or cable entering the box.

(b) For Angle or U Pulls. The distance between each cable or conductor entry inside the box and the opposite wall of the box shall not be less than thirty-six times the outside diameter, over sheath, of the largest cable or conductor. This distance shall be increased for additional entries by the amount of the sum of the outside diameters, over sheath, of all other cables or conductor entries through the same wall of the box.

The distance between a cable or conductor entry and its exit from the box shall be not less than thirty-six times the outside diameter, over sheath, of that cable or conductor.

Exception No. 1: Where a conductor or cable entry is in the wall of a box opposite to a removable cover and where the distance from that wall to the cover is in conformance with the provisions of Section 300-34.

Exception No. 2: Terminal housings supplied with motors which shall comply with the provisions of Section 430-12.

(c) Removable Sides. One or more sides of any pull box shall be removable.

370-52. Construction and Installation Requirements.

(a) Corrosion Protection. Boxes shall be made of material inherently resistant to corrosion or shall be suitably protected, both internally and externally, by enameling, galvanizing, plating, or other means.

(b) Passing Through Partitions. Suitable bushings, shields, or fittings having smooth rounded edges shall be provided where conductors or cables pass through partitions and at other locations where necessary.

(c) Complete Enclosure. Boxes shall provide a complete enclosure for the contained conductors or cables.

(d) Wiring Is Accessible. Boxes shall be so installed that the wiring is accessible without removing any part of the building. Working space shall be provided in accordance with Section 110-34.

(e) Suitable Covers. Boxes shall be closed by suitable covers securely fastened in place. Underground box covers that weigh over 100 pounds (43.6 kg) shall be considered as meeting this requirement. Covers for boxes shall be permanently marked "HIGH VOLTAGE." The marking shall be on the outside of the box cover and shall be readily visible. Letters shall be block type at least ½ inch (12.7 mm) in height.

(f) Suitable for Expected Handling. Boxes and their covers shall be capable of withstanding the handling to which they may be subjected.

ARTICLE 373 — CABINETS AND CUTOUT BOXES

Contents

373-1. Scope. This article covers the installation of cabinets and cutout boxes. Installations in hazardous (classified) locations shall comply with Articles 500 through 517.

See definitions of "Cabinet" and "Cutout Box" in Article 100. Cabinets and cutout boxes are designed with a swinging door(s) to enclose switches, overcurrent devices, or control equipment. Some panelboard cabinets for circuit breaker panelboards, "load centers," **do not** have doors as permitted by Exception

ARTICLE 373—CABINETS AND CUTOUT BOXES

No. 3 to Section 240-30. Cabinets and cutout boxes are required to be of sufficient size to accommodate all devices and conductors without overcrowding or jamming. This condition can be prevented by the use of auxiliary gutters (see Article 374).

A. Installation

373-2. Damp or Wet Locations. In damp or wet locations, cabinets and cutout boxes of the surface type shall be so placed or equipped as to prevent moisture or water from entering and accumulating within the cabinet or cutout box, and shall be mounted so there is at least ¼-inch (6.35-mm) air space between the enclosure and the wall or other supporting surface. Cabinets or cutout boxes installed in wet locations shall be weatherproof.

(FPN): For protection against corrosion, see Section 300-6.

See Section 430-91 for motor enclosure selection table for indoor and outdoor use and associated commentary.

373-3. Position in Wall. In walls of concrete, tile, or other noncombustible material, cabinets shall be so installed that the front edge of the cabinet will not set back of the finished surface more than ¼ inch (6.35 mm). In walls constructed of wood or other combustible material, cabinets shall be flush with the finished surface or project therefrom.

373-4. Unused Openings. Unused openings in cabinet or cutout boxes shall be effectively closed to afford protection substantially equivalent to that of the wall of the cabinet or cutout box. Where metal plugs or plates are used with nonmetallic cabinets or cutout boxes, they shall be recessed at least ¼ inch (6.35 mm) from the outer surface.

373-5. Conductors Entering Cabinets or Cutout Boxes. Conductors entering cabinets or cutout boxes shall be protected from abrasion and shall comply with (a) through (c) below.

See Section 373-6(c).

(a) Openings to Be Closed. Openings through which conductors enter shall be adequately closed.

(b) Metal Cabinets and Cutout Boxes. Where metal cabinets or cutout boxes are installed with open wiring or concealed knob-and-tube wiring, conductors shall enter through insulating bushings or, in dry places, through flexible tubing extending from the last insulating support and firmly secured to the cabinet or cutout box.

(c) Cables. Where cable is used, each cable shall be secured to the cabinet or cutout box.

This section prohibits the installation of several cables bunched together and run through a single hole or chase nipple. Individual cable clamps or connectors should be used with only one cable per clamp or connector unless the clamp or connector is approved for more than a single cable.

373-6. Deflection of Conductors. Conductors at terminals or conductors entering or leaving cabinets or cutout boxes and the like shall comply with (a) through (c) below.

(a) Width of Wiring Gutters. Conductors shall not be deflected within a cabinet or cutout box unless a gutter having a width in accordance with Table 373-6(a) is provided. Conductors in parallel in accordance with Section 310-4 shall be judged on the basis of the number of conductors in parallel.

Table 373-6(a).   Minimum Wire Bending Space at Terminals and
Minimum Width of Wiring Gutters in Inches

AWG or Circular-Mil Size of Wire	Wires per Terminal				
	1	2	3	4	5
14-10	Not Specified	—	—	—	—
8-6	1½	—	—	—	—
4-3	2	—	—	—	—
2	2½	—	—	—	—
1	3	—	—	—	—
0-00	3½	5	7	—	—
000-0000	4	6	8	—	—
250 MCM	4½	6	8	10	—
300-350 MCM	5	8	10	12	—
400-500 MCM	6	8	10	12	14
600-700 MCM	8	10	12	14	16
750-900 MCM	8	12	14	16	18
1,000-1,250 MCM	10	—	—	—	—
1,500-2,000 MCM	12	—	—	—	—

For SI units: one inch = 25.4 millimeters.
Bending space at terminals shall be measured in a straight line from the end of the lug or wire connector (in the direction that the wire leaves the terminal) to the wall, barrier, or obstruction.

(b) Wire Bending Space at Terminals. Wire bending space at each terminal shall be provided in accordance with (1) or (2) below:

(1) Table 373-6(a) shall apply where the conductor does not enter or leave the enclosure through the wall opposite its terminal.

Exception: A conductor shall be permitted to enter or leave an enclosure through the wall opposite its terminal provided the conductor enters or leaves the enclosure at a point where the wire bending space conforms to Table 373-6(b) for that conductor.

(2) Table 373-6(b) shall apply where the conductor enters or leaves the enclosure through the wall opposite its terminal.

Section 373-6(b)(2) and Table 373-6(b) provide the requirements for wire bending space where straight-in wiring or offset (double bends) are employed at terminals. Section 373-6(b)(1) is for use where only 90° bends are involved.

The revised second footnote and the last footnote under Table 373-6(b) are new in the 1984 *Code*. The footnotes are intended to permit a reduction in required bending space for removable wire terminals. These terminal wire connectors are required to be of the type that are intended for a single conductor (single barrel). To make wiring easier, it is intended that the terminal may be removed and placed on the stripped end of the conductor, which has been cut to the proper length. The terminal is then crimped or lightly torqued on the conductor as intended, and then remounted. If a mechanical screw connector is involved, the screw should then be torqued to the proper value. See commentary following the Fine Print Note under Section 110-14.

Note that in accordance with the footnotes to Tables 373-6(a) and 373-6(b), bending space is measured in the direction that the wire leaves the terminal when using Table 373-6(a) and in a direction perpendicular to the enclosure wall when using Table 373-6(b).

See Figure 373-1. See also Figure 430-1.

Table 373-6(b). Minimum Wire Bending Space at Terminals for Section 373-6(b)(2) in Inches

Wire Size	1		Wires per Terminal 2		3		4 or More	
14-10	Not Specified		—		—		—	
8	1½		—		—		—	
6	2		—		—		—	
4	3		—		—		—	
3	3		—		—		—	
2	3½		—		—		—	
1	4½		—		—		—	
0	5½		5½		7		—	
2/0	6		6		7½		—	
3/0	6½	(½)	6½	(½)	8		—	
4/0	7	(1)	7½	(1½)	8½	(½)	—	
250	8½	(2)	8½	(2)	9	(1)	10	
300	10	(3)	10	(2)	11	(1)	12	
350	12	(3)	12	(3)	13	(3)	14	(2)
400	13	(3)	13	(3)	14	(3)	15	(3)
500	14	(3)	14	(3)	15	(3)	16	(3)
600	15	(3)	16	(3)	18	(3)	19	(3)
700	16	(3)	18	(3)	20	(3)	22	(3)
750	17	(3)	19	(3)	22	(3)	24	(3)
800	18		20		22		24	
900	19		22		24		24	
1000	20		—		—		—	
1250	22		—		—		—	
1500	24		—		—		—	
1750	24		—		—		—	
2000	24		—		—		—	

For SI units: one inch = 25.4 millimeters.

Bending space at terminals shall be measured in a straight line from the end of the lug or wire connector in a direction perpendicular to the enclosure wall.

For removable wire terminals intended for only one wire, bending space shall be permitted to be reduced by the number of inches shown in parentheses.

(c) Insulated Bushings. Where ungrounded conductors of No. 4 or larger enter a raceway in a cabinet, pull box, junction box, or auxiliary gutter, the conductors shall be protected by a substantial bushing providing a smoothly rounded insulating surface, unless the conductors are separated from the raceway fitting by substantial insulating material securely fastened in place.

Where No. 4 or larger ungrounded (hot) conductors enter a cabinet or cutout box from metal raceways, subparagraph (c) requires a smoothly rounded insulating bushing to protect the conductors from abrasion. See Sections 345-15, 346-8, and 347-12.

Metal conduit bushings or fittings provided with insulated sleeves or linings are commonly used. It is also possible to use a separate insulating sleeve or lining to separate the conductors from the raceway fitting. See Figure 300-6.

UL listed insulating bushings provided either separately or as part of a fitting are suitable for a temperature of 150°C if they are colored black or brown, and for 90°C if of any other color unless specifically marked for a higher temperature. See Figure 373-2.

Exception: Where threaded hubs or bosses that are an integral part of an enclosure provide a smoothly rounded or flared entry for conductors.

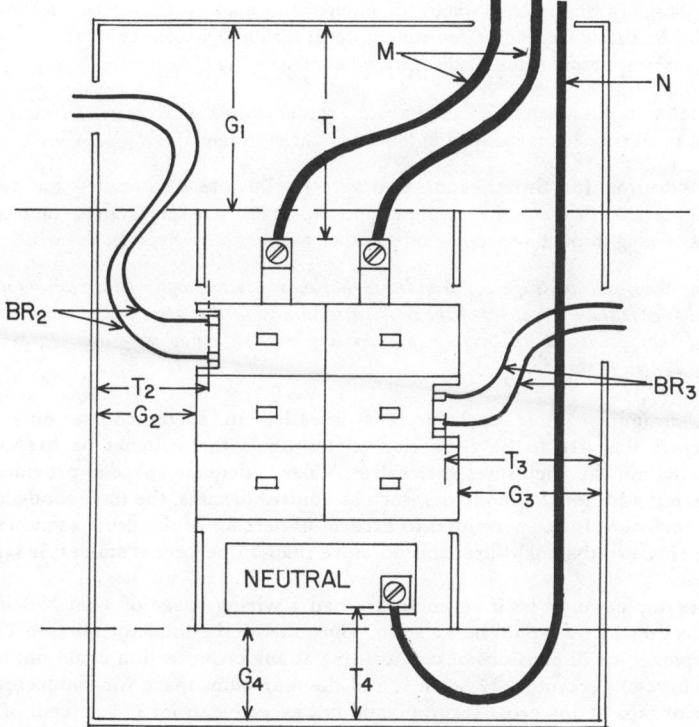

Figure 373-1. The following rules apply when wiring as shown.

T1, Section 373-6(b)(2): Table 373-6(b) applies for conductors M.

T2, Section 373-6(b)(2): Table 373-6(b) applies for conductors BR2 unless in accordance with Section 373-6(b)(1), Exception. Conductors enter a second wiring space G, conforming to Table 373-6(b) for conductors BR2.

T3, Section 373-6(b)(2): Table 373-6(b) applies for conductors BR3.

T4, Section 373-6(b)(1): Table 373-6(a) applies for conductor N.

G1, Section 373-6(a): Table 373-6(a) applies for conductors M. Table 373-6(b) applies for conductors BR2 when T2 does not comply with Table 373-6(b).

G2, Section 373-6(a): Table 373-6(a) applies for conductors BR2.

G3, Section 373-6(a): Table 373-6(a) applies for conductors BR3.

G4, Section 373-6(a): Table 373-6(a) applies for conductor N.

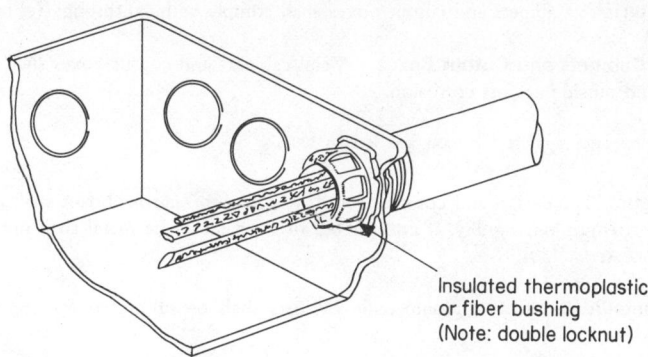

Insulated thermoplastic
or fiber bushing
(Note: double locknut)

Figure 373-2. An insulating bushing to protect conductors from chafing against a metal conduit fitting.

ARTICLE 373—CABINETS AND CUTOUT BOXES

Conduit bushings constructed wholly of insulating material shall not be used to secure a raceway. The insulating bushing or insulating material shall have a temperature rating not less than the insulation temperature rating of the installed conductors.

373-7. Space in Enclosures. Cabinets and cutout boxes shall have sufficient space to accommodate all conductors installed in them without crowding.

373-8. Enclosures for Switches or Overcurrent Devices. Enclosures for switches or overcurrent devices shall not be used as junction boxes, auxiliary gutters, or raceways for conductors feeding through or tapping off to other switches or overcurrent devices.

Exception: Where adequate space is provided so that the conductors do not fill the wiring space at any cross section to more than 40 percent of the cross-sectional area of the space, and so that the conductors, splices, and taps do not fill the wiring space at any cross section to more than 75 percent of the cross-sectional area of the space.

The design of most enclosures is intended to accommodate only those conductors that are to be connected to terminals for switches or overcurrent devices within the enclosures themselves. Where adequate space is provided that will permit additional conductors, such as control circuits, the total conductor fill in the enclosure is not permitted to exceed 40 percent of the cross section of the wiring space in the enclosure, and no more than 75 percent if splices or taps are necessary.

An example would be if an enclosure had a wiring space of 4 in. × 3 in., the cross-sectional area would be 12 sq in. Thus, the total conductor fill (see Table 5 in Chapter 9 for dimensions of conductors) at any cross section could not exceed 4.8 sq in. (40 percent of 12 sq in.), and the maximum space for conductors and splices or taps at any cross section could not exceed 9 sq in. (75 percent of 12 sq in.).

In general, the best way to avoid overcrowding enclosures is to use properly sized auxiliary gutters (Sections 374-5 and 374-8) or junction boxes (Sections 370-6 and 370-18). See Section 430-10 and commentary for wiring space in enclosures for motor controllers and disconnecting means. See also Section 710-59.

373-9. Side or Back Wiring Spaces or Gutters. Cabinets and cutout boxes shall be provided with back wiring spaces, gutters, or wiring compartments as required by Section 373-11(c) and (d).

B. Construction Specifications

373-10. Material. Cabinets and cutout boxes shall comply with (a) through (c) below.

(a) Metal Cabinets and Cutout Boxes. Metal cabinets and cutout boxes shall be protected both inside and outside against corrosion.

(FPN): For protection against corrosion, see Section 300-6.

(b) Strength. The design and construction of cabinets and cutout boxes shall be such as to secure ample strength and rigidity. If constructed of sheet steel, the metal shall not be less than 0.053 inch uncoated.

(c) Nonmetallic Cabinets. Nonmetallic cabinets shall be submitted for approval prior to installation.

373-11. Spacing. The spacing within cabinets and cutout boxes shall comply with (a) through (d) below.

(a) General. Spacing within cabinets and cutout boxes shall be sufficient to provide ample room for the distribution of wires and cables placed in them, and for a separation between metal parts of devices and apparatus mounted within them as follows:

(1) Base. Other than at points of support, there shall be an air space of at least ¹⁄₁₆ inch (1.59 mm) between the base of the device and the wall of any metal cabinet or cutout box in which the device is mounted.

(2) Doors. There shall be an air space of at least 1 inch (25.4 mm) between any live metal part, including live metal parts of enclosed fuses, and the door.

Exception: Where the door is lined with an approved insulating material or is of a thickness of metal not less than No. 12 MSG, the air space shall not be less than ½ inch (12.7 mm).

(3) Live Parts. There shall be an air space of at least ½ inch (12.7 mm) between the walls, back, gutter partition, if of metal, or door of any cabinet or cutout box and the nearest exposed current-carrying part of devices mounted within the cabinet where the voltage does not exceed 250. This spacing shall be increased to at least 1 inch (25.4 mm) for voltages 251 to 600, nominal.

Exception: As permitted in (2) above.

(b) Switch Clearance. Cabinets and cutout boxes shall be deep enough to allow the closing of the doors when 30-ampere branch-circuit panelboard switches are in any position; when combination cutout switches are in any position; or when other single-throw switches are opened as far as their construction will permit.

(c) Wiring Space. Cabinets and cutout boxes that contain devices or apparatus connected within the cabinet or box to more than eight conductors, including those of branch circuits, meter loops, subfeeder circuits, power circuits, and similar circuits, but not including the supply circuit or a continuation thereof, shall have back-wiring spaces or one or more side-wiring spaces, side gutters, or wiring compartments.

(d) Wiring Space — Enclosure. Side-wiring spaces, side gutters, or side-wiring compartments of cabinets and cutout boxes shall be made tight enclosures by means of covers, barriers, or partitions extending from the bases of the devices, contained in the cabinet to the door, frame, or sides of the cabinet.

Exception: Where the enclosure contains only those conductors that are led from the cabinet at points directly opposite their terminal connections to devices within the cabinet.

Partially enclosed back-wiring spaces shall be provided with covers to complete the enclosure. Wiring spaces that are required by (c) above, and that are exposed when doors are open, shall be provided with covers to complete the enclosure. Where adequate space is provided for feed-through conductors and for splices as required in Section 373-8, Exception, additional barriers shall not be required.

ARTICLE 374 — AUXILIARY GUTTERS

Contents

ARTICLE 374—AUXILIARY GUTTERS

374-9. Construction and Installation.
  (a) Electrical and Mechanical Continuity.
  (b) Substantial Construction.
  (c) Smooth Rounded Edges.
  (d) Deflected Insulated Conductors.
  (e) Outdoor Use.

374-1. Use. Auxiliary gutters shall be permitted to supplement wiring spaces at meter centers, distribution centers, switchboards, and similar points of wiring systems and may enclose conductors or busbars, but shall not be used to enclose switches, overcurrent devices, appliances, or other similar equipment.

Auxiliary gutter sections and associated fittings are identical to those of wireways, and each bears the single Underwriters Laboratories Inc. Listing Mark "Listed Wireway or Auxiliary Gutter." They differ only in their intended use. See commentary following Section 362-1. Gutters (and wireways) are required to be constructed and installed to assure adequate electrical and mechanical continuity of the complete system. See Section 250-91(b)(10).

Auxiliary gutters for outdoor use are required to be of "raintight" construction. See Section 620-35 for elevator uses and Section 640-4 for sound-recording equipment uses.

374-2. Extension Beyond Equipment. An auxiliary gutter shall not extend a greater distance than 30 feet (9.14 m) beyond the equipment which it supplements.

Exception: As provided in Section 620-35 for elevators.

(FPN): For wireways, see Article 362. For busways, see Article 364.

374-3. Supports. Gutters shall be supported throughout their entire length at intervals not exceeding 5 feet (1.52 m).

374-4. Covers. Covers shall be securely fastened to the gutter.

374-5. Number of Conductors. Auxiliary gutters shall not contain more than thirty current-carrying conductors at any cross section. The sum of the cross-sectional areas of all contained conductors at any cross section of an auxiliary gutter shall not exceed 20 percent of the interior cross-sectional area of the auxiliary gutter.

Exception No. 1: As provided in Section 620-35 for elevators.

Exception No. 2: Conductors for signaling circuits or controller conductors between a motor and its starter and used only for starting duty shall not be considered as current-carrying conductors.

Exception No. 3: Where the correction factors specified in Note 8 to Tables 310-16 through 310-19 are applied, there shall be no limit on the number of current-carrying conductors, but the sum of the cross-sectional area of all contained conductors at any cross section of the auxiliary gutter shall not exceed 20 percent of the interior cross-sectional area of the auxiliary gutter.

(FPN): For conductor cross-sectional area see Tables 5, 6, 7, 8 and the applicable Notes to Tables at the beginning of Chapter 9.

The dimensions of rubber-covered and thermoplastic-covered conductors given in Table 5 in Chapter 9 may be used to compute the size of gutters required to contain a given combination of such conductors.

Where auxiliary gutters contain thirty or fewer current-carrying conductors, the correction factors of Note 8 (Tables 310-16 through 310-19) do not apply. There is no limit on the number of current-carrying conductors if Note 8 is applied; however, the contained conductors are not permitted to exceed 20 percent of the interior cross-sectional area of the gutter. See example given in the commentary following Section 362-1 for method of calculating number of conductors within a wireway which is also applicable to auxiliary gutters.

No limit is placed on the size of conductors that may be installed in an auxiliary gutter; however, see Section 374-6 for limitations of bare copper or aluminum busbars enclosed in gutters.

374-6. Ampacity of Conductors. Where the number of current-carrying conductors contained in the auxiliary gutter is thirty or less, the correction factors specified in Note 8 to Tables 310-16 through 310-19 shall not apply. The current carried continuously in bare copper bars in auxiliary gutters shall not exceed 1000 amperes per square inch (645 sq mm) of cross section of the conductor. For aluminum bars, the current carried continuously shall not exceed 700 amperes per square inch (645 sq mm) of cross section of the conductor.

374-7. Clearance of Bare Live Parts. Bare conductors shall be securely and rigidly supported so that the minimum clearance between bare current-carrying metal parts of opposite polarities mounted on the same surface will not be less than 2 inches (50.8 mm), nor less than 1 inch (25.4 mm) for parts that are held free in the air. A clearance not less than 1 inch (25.4 mm) shall be secured between bare current-carrying metal parts and any metal surface. Adequate provisions shall be made for the expansion and contraction of busbars.

374-8. Splices and Taps. Splices and taps shall comply with (a) through (d) below.

(a) Within Gutters. Splices or taps shall be permitted within gutters when they are accessible by means of removable covers or doors. The conductors, including splices and taps, shall not fill the gutter to more than 75 percent of its area.

(b) Bare Conductors. Taps from bare conductors shall leave the gutter opposite their terminal connections and conductors shall not be brought in contact with uninsulated current-carrying parts of opposite polarity.

(c) Suitably Identified. All taps shall be suitably identified at the gutter as to the circuit or equipment which they supply.

(d) Overcurrent Protection. Tap connections from conductors in auxiliary gutters shall be provided with overcurrent protection as required in Section 240-21.

Precautions are required to be taken by providing suitable bushings, shields, etc., where conductors pass around bends, or between gutters and cabinets and other locations to prevent abrasion of the conductor insulation. Also, conductors are required to be shaped or formed in a permanent manner so that they are not in contact with bare busbars within the gutter.

Subparagraphs (c) and (d) provide rules indicating that all taps from gutters are required to be identified (as to circuits or equipment) and be protected with overcurrent devices per Section 240-21.

374-9. Construction and Installation. Auxiliary gutters shall comply with (a) through (e) below.

(a) Electrical and Mechanical Continuity. Gutters shall be so constructed and installed that adequate electrical and mechanical continuity of the complete system will be secured.

(b) Substantial Construction. Gutters shall be of substantial construction and shall provide a complete enclosure for the contained conductors. All surfaces, both interior and exterior, shall be suitably protected from corrosion. Corner joints shall be made tight and, where the assembly is held together by rivets or bolts, these shall be spaced not more than 12 inches (305 mm) apart.

(c) Smooth Rounded Edges. Suitable bushings, shields, or fittings having smooth rounded edges shall be provided where conductors pass between gutters, through partitions, around bends, between gutters and cabinets or junction boxes, and at other locations where necessary to prevent abrasion of the insulation of the conductors.

(d) Deflected Insulated Conductors. Where insulated conductors are deflected within an auxiliary gutter, either at the ends or where conduits, fittings, or other raceways or cables enter or leave the gutter, or where the direction of the gutter is deflected greater than 30 degrees, dimensions corresponding to Section 373-6 shall apply.

"Cables" were added to subparagraph (d) for the 1984 *Code*. This is intended to make it clear that cable-type wiring systems are to be considered when deflected in an auxiliary gutter.

(e) Outdoor Use. Auxiliary gutters installed in wet locations shall be of raintight construction.

This section was revised for the 1984 *Code* replacing the words "intended for outdoor use" with "installed in wet locations" and to correlate with Section 362-2. This change provides for auxiliary gutters which may be installed in locations which may not be outdoors, for example, in a vehicle car washing area inside of a building.

ARTICLE 380 — SWITCHES

Contents

A. Installation

380-1. Scope. The provisions of this article shall apply to all switches, switching devices, and circuit breakers where used as switches.

380-2. Switch Connections.

(a) Three-Way and Four-Way Switches. Three-way and four-way switches shall be so wired that all switching is done only in the ungrounded circuit conductor. Where in metal enclosures, wiring between switches and outlets shall be run with both polarities in the same enclosure.

Although the *NEC* does not specifically prohibit use of two 2-conductor nonmetallic-sheathed cables for wiring three-way and four-way switches instead of a single 3-conductor cable, use of two 2-conductor cables could easily result in a violation of Section 300-20 if steel boxes are used and the cables enter the box through separate knockouts. Use of the same clamp or section of a clamp for both cables would, in most cases, be in violation of Section 110-3(b) because clamps have been tested for only one cable per clamp or section of clamp.

(b) Grounded Conductors. Switches or circuit breakers shall not disconnect the grounded conductor of a circuit.

Exception No. 1: Where the switch or circuit breaker simultaneously disconnects all conductors of the circuit.

Exception No. 2: Where the switch or circuit breaker is so arranged that the grounded conductor cannot be disconnected until all the ungrounded conductors of the circuit have been disconnected.

380-3. Enclosure. Switches and circuit breakers shall be of the externally operable type mounted in an enclosure listed for the intended use. The minimum wire bending space at terminals and minimum gutter space provided in switch enclosures shall be as required in Section 373-6.

Exception: Pendant- and surface-type snap switches and knife switches mounted on an open-face switchboard or panelboard.

380-4. Wet Locations. A switch or circuit breaker in a wet location or outside of a building shall be enclosed in a weatherproof enclosure or cabinet that shall comply with Section 373-2.

380-5. Time Switches, Flashers, and Similar Devices. Time switches, flashers, and similar devices need not be of the externally operable type. They shall be enclosed in metal boxes or cabinets.

Exception No. 1: Where mounted in switchboards, control panels, or enclosures and so located that any live terminals, located within 6 inches (152 mm) of the manually adjustable clock dial or "on-off" switch, are covered by suitable barriers.

Exception No. 2: Where enclosed in approved individual housings with no live parts exposed to the operator.

Time-clock switches, flashers, etc., are required to be mounted in metal enclosures. Proper enclosures will prevent sparks or thermal energy from the natural operation of such automatic switching devices from contacting any combustible material in the area.

ARTICLE 380—SWITCHES

380-6. Position of Knife Switches.

(a) **Single-Throw Knife Switches.** Single-throw knife switches shall be so placed that gravity will not tend to close them. Single-throw knife switches, approved for use in the inverted position, shall be provided with a locking device that will ensure that the blades remain in the open position when so set.

(b) **Double-Throw Knife Switches.** Double-throw knife switches shall be permitted to be mounted so that the throw will be either vertical or horizontal. Where the throw is vertical, a locking device shall be provided to hold the blades in the open position when so set.

380-7. Connection of Knife Switches.
Single-throw knife switches shall be so connected that the blades are dead when the switch is in the open position.

380-8. Accessibility and Grouping.

(a) **Location.** All switches and circuit breakers used as switches shall be so located that they may be operated from a readily accessible place. They shall be so installed that the center of the grip of the operating handle of the switch or circuit breaker, when in its highest position, will not be more than 6½ feet (1.98 m) above the floor or working platform.

Exception No. 1: On busway installations, fused switches and circuit breakers shall be permitted to be located at the same level as the busway. Suitable means shall be provided to operate the handle of the device from the floor.

Exception No. 2: Switches installed adjacent to motors, appliances, or other equipment which they supply shall be permitted to be located higher than specified in the foregoing and to be accessible by portable means.

Exception No. 3: Hookstick operable isolating switches shall be permitted at heights of more than 6½ feet (1.98 m).

(b) **Voltage Between Adjacent Switches.** Snap switches shall not be grouped or ganged in outlet boxes unless they can be so arranged that the voltage between adjacent switches does not exceed 300, or unless they are installed in boxes equipped with permanently installed barriers between adjacent switches.

380-9. Faceplates for Flush-Mounted Snap Switches.
Flush snap switches, that are mounted in ungrounded metal boxes and located within reach of conducting floors or other conducting surfaces, shall be provided with faceplates of nonconducting, noncombustible material. Metal faceplates shall be of ferrous metal not less than 0.030 inch (0.762 mm) in thickness or of nonferrous metal not less than 0.040 inch (1.016 mm) in thickness. Faceplates of insulating material shall be noncombustible and not less than 0.10 inch (2.54 mm) in thickness but they shall be permitted to be less than 0.10 inch (2.54 mm) in thickness if formed or reinforced to provide adequate mechanical strength. Faceplates shall be installed so as to completely cover the wall opening and seat against the wall surface.

Switch plates attached to outlets supplied by a wiring method which does not provide a ready means for grounding are required to be made of insulating material and are required to have no exposed conductive parts.

380-10. Mounting of Snap Switches.

(a) **Surface-type.** Snap switches used with open wiring on insulators shall be mounted on insulating material that will separate the conductors at least ½ inch (12.7 mm) from the surface wired over.

(b) Box Mounted. Flush-type snap switches mounted in boxes that are set back of the wall surface as permitted in Section 370-10 shall be installed so that the extension plaster ears are seated against the surface of the wall. Flush-type snap switches mounted in boxes that are flush with the wall surface or project therefrom shall be so installed that the mounting yoke or strap of the switch is seated against the box.

Cooperation is necessary among the building trades (carpenters, dry-wall installers, plasterers, etc.) in order for electricians to properly set device boxes flush with the finish surface, thereby ensuring a secure seating of the switch yoke and permitting the maximum projection of switch handles through the installed switch plate.

380-11. Circuit Breakers as Switches. A hand-operable circuit breaker equipped with a lever or handle, or a power-operated circuit breaker capable of being opened by hand in the event of a power failure, shall be permitted to serve as a switch if it has the required number of poles. Note: See provisions contained in Section 240-81.

Circuit breakers capable of being hand-operated are required to clearly indicate whether they are in the open "off" or closed "on" position.
See Section 240-83(d) for marking (SWD) for circuit breakers used as switches for 120-V and 277-V fluorescent lighting circuits.

380-12. Grounding of Enclosures. Enclosures for switches or circuit breakers on circuits of over 150 volts to ground shall be grounded as specified in Article 250. Where nonmetallic enclosures are used with metal-sheathed cables or metallic conduits, provision shall be made for grounding continuity.

380-13. Knife Switches.

(a) Isolating Switches. Knife switches rated at over 1200 amperes at 250 volts or less, and at over 600 amperes at 251 to 600 volts, shall be used only as isolating switches and shall not be opened under load.

(b) To Interrupt Currents. To interrupt currents over 1200 amperes at 250 volts, nominal, or less, or over 600 amperes at 251 to 600 volts, nominal, a circuit breaker or a switch of special design listed for such purpose shall be used.

(c) General-Use Switches. Knife switches of ratings less than specified in (a) and (b) above shall be considered general-use switches.

(FPN): See definition of general-use switch in Article 100.

(d) Motor-Circuit Switches. Motor-circuit switches shall be permitted to be of the knife-switch type.

(FPN): See definition of a motor-circuit switch in Article 100.

380-14. Rating and Use of Snap Switches. Snap switches shall be used within their ratings and as follows:

(a) AC General-Use Snap Switch. A form of general-use snap switch suitable only for use on alternating-current circuits for controlling the following:

(1) Resistive and inductive loads, including electric-discharge lamps, not exceeding the ampere rating of the switch at the voltage involved.

(2) Tungsten-filament lamp loads not exceeding the ampere rating of the switch at 120 volts.

(3) Motor loads not exceeding 80 percent of the ampere rating of the switch at its rated voltage.

(b) AC-DC General-Use Snap Switch. A form of general-use snap switch suitable for use on either ac or dc circuits for controlling the following:

(1) Resistive loads not exceeding the ampere rating of the switch at the voltage applied.

(2) Inductive loads not exceeding 50 percent of the ampere rating of the switch at the applied voltage. Switches rated in horsepower are suitable for controlling motor loads within their rating at voltage applied.

(3) Tungsten-filament lamp loads not exceeding the ampere rating of the switch at the applied voltage if "T" rated.

(FPN): For switches on signs and outline lighting, see Section 600-2.

(FPN): For switches controlling motors, see Sections 430-83, 430-109, and 430-110.

(c) CO/ALR Snap Switches. Snap switches rated 20 amperes or less directly connected to aluminum conductors shall be listed and marked CO/ALR.

B. Construction Specifications

380-15. Marking. Switches shall be marked with the current and voltage and, if horsepower rated, the maximum rating for which they are designed.

380-16. 600-Volt Knife Switches. Auxiliary contacts of a renewable or quick-break type or the equivalent shall be provided on all knife switches rated 600 volts designed for use in breaking current over 200 amperes.

380-17. Fused Switches. A fused switch shall not have fuses in parallel.

(FPN): See Section 240-8, Exception.

380-18. Wire Bending Space. The wire bending space required by Section 380-3 shall meet Table 373-6(b) spacings to the enclosure wall opposite the line and load terminals.

ARTICLE 384 — SWITCHBOARDS AND PANELBOARDS

Contents

384-1. General.

(a) Scope. This article covers (1) all switchboards, panelboards, and distribution boards installed for the control of light and power circuits, and (2) battery-charging panels supplied from light or power circuits.

Exception: Switchboards or portions thereof used exclusively to control signaling circuits operated by batteries.

(b) Other Articles. Switches, circuit breakers, and overcurrent devices used on switchboards, panelboards, and distribution boards, and their enclosures, shall comply with the requirements of Articles 240, 250, 370, 380, and other articles that apply. Switchboards and panelboards in hazardous (classified) locations shall comply with the requirements of Articles 500 through 517.

See definitions of "Panelboard" and "Switchboard" in Article 100.

384-2. Installation. Equipment within the scope of Article 384 shall be located in rooms or spaces dedicated to such equipment. Such space shall include that space described in Section 110-16, and in addition shall include an exclusively dedicated space extending from floor to ceiling with a width and depth that of the equipment. No piping, ducts, or equipment foreign to the electrical equipment or architectural appurtenances shall be permitted to be installed in, enter or pass through such spaces or rooms.

Exception No. 1: Control equipment which by its very nature or because of other rules of this Code must be adjacent to or within sight of its operating machinery.

Exception No. 2: Ventilating, heating, or cooling equipment that serves the electrical rooms or spaces.

ARTICLE 384—SWITCHBOARDS AND PANELBOARDS

Exception No. 3: Equipment located throughout industrial plants which is isolated from foreign equipment by height or physical enclosures or covers which will afford adequate mechanical protection from vehicular traffic, accidental contact by unauthorized personnel, or accidental spillage or leakage from piping systems.

Exception No. 4: Outdoor electrical equipment located in weatherproof enclosures protected from accidental contact by unauthorized personnel or vehicular traffic or accidental spillage or leakage from piping systems.

This section has been revised for the 1984 *Code*. The word "exclusively" has been deleted from the first sentence to emphasize the following Formal Interpretation (because hallways are not used exclusively as spaces for panelboards), and to recognize the overlapping of working spaces required by Section 110-16.

The following Formal Interpretation No. 81-3 for Section 384-2 was issued in June, 1981 for the 1981 edition of the *National Electrical Code*.

Statement: A building has one or more closets located so as to feed electric and communication services to areas of the building. Each closet is entered by one door and it has no partitions. A portion of the closet is dedicated to a panelboard serving branch circuits for that area. Another portion of the closet is dedicated to telephone equipment. The telephone equipment and wiring does not encroach on the dedicated space for the panelboard.

Question: Is it the intent of Section 384-2 of the 1981 *National Electrical Code* to prohibit such an installation?

Answer: No.

Statement: It has been common practice to flush-mount panelboards in the walls of corridors and hallways in buildings and residences.

Question: Is it the intent of Section 384-2 of the 1981 *National Electrical Code* to prohibit such installation?

Answer: No.

The required space has been further defined to include the space described in Section 110-16 and an exclusively dedicated space extending to the ceiling over the equipment. It is intended that the "ceiling" be the structural ceiling. A suspended ceiling over the equipment would not be recognized as being a structural ceiling.

Many jurisdictions have permitted a hood or shield over equipment which provides a form of protection from possible leakage from water piping, building drains, sewer pipes, etc. Exception No. 3 specifically permits this for industrial plants.

Fire protective sprinkler systems are not considered foreign to the electrical equipment where their installation is in accordance with applicable building codes. This was ascertained by the following Formal Interpretation No. 81-5 issued in August, 1982, for the 1981 edition of the *National Electrical Code*.

Question: Is it the intent of Section 384-2 of the *National Electrical Code* to prohibit automatic sprinkler protection in rooms containing switchboards and panelboards?

Answer: No.

384-3. Support and Arrangement of Busbars and Conductors.

(a) Conductors and Busbars on a Switchboard, Panelboard, or Control Board. Conductors and busbars on a switchboard, panelboard, or control board shall be so located as to be free from physical damage and shall be held firmly in place. Other than the required interconnections and control wiring, only those conductors that are intended for termination in a vertical section of a switchboard shall be located in that section. Barriers shall be placed in all service switchboards that will isolate the service busbars and terminals from the remainder of the switchboard.

Exception: Conductors shall be permitted to travel horizontally through vertical sections of switchboards where such conductors are isolated from busbars by a barrier.

It is usually impractical to disconnect or deenergize the service conductors supplying a service switchboard. For this reason, it has been a universal practice for qualified electricians to work on these switchboards with the service bus electrically alive. Barriers are required in all UL listed service switchboards to isolate the service busbars and terminals from the remainder of the switchboard, thus providing some measure of safety against contact with line energized parts during maintenance and installation of new feeders or branch circuits. It must be remembered that deenergizing the load side of a switchboard, by operation of the disconnecting means, does not deenergize the ungrounded service conductors. Installers should also be careful to remove tools that may have been left on the inside of the gear in order to prevent serious ground faults or short circuits due to the tools coming in contact with busbars.

The exception permits conductors to travel horizontally through vertical sections of a switchboard where barriers are provided to isolate the conductors from the busbars.

(b) Overheating and Inductive Effects. The arrangement of busbars and conductors shall be such as to avoid overheating due to inductive effects.

(c) Used as Service Equipment. Each switchboard, switchboard section, or panelboard, if used as service equipment, shall be provided with a main bonding jumper sized in accordance with Section 250-79(c) or the equivalent placed within the service disconnect section for connecting the grounded service conductor on its supply side to the switchboard or panelboard frame. All sections of a switchboard shall be bonded together using an equipment grounding conductor sized in accordance with Table 250-95.

(d) Load Terminals. Load terminals in switchboards and panelboards shall be so located that it will be unnecessary to reach across or beyond an ungrounded line bus in order to make load connections.

(e) High-Leg Marking. On a switchboard or panelboard supplied from a 4-wire delta-connected system, where the midpoint of one phase is grounded, that phase busbar or conductor having the higher voltage to ground shall be durably and permanently marked by an outer finish that is orange in color, or by other effective means.

(f) Phase Arrangement. The phase arrangement on three-phase buses shall be A, B, C from front to back, top to bottom, or left to right, as viewed from the front of the switchboard or panelboard. The B phase shall be that phase having the higher voltage to ground on 3-phase, 4-wire delta-connected systems. Other busbar arrangements shall be permitted for additions to existing installations and shall be marked.

Exception: Equipment within the same switchboard or panelboard as the meter on 3-phase, 4-wire delta-connected systems shall be permitted to have the same phase configuration as the metering equipment.

ARTICLE 384—SWITCHBOARDS AND PANELBOARDS

Subparagraph (e) has been revised for the 1984 *Code* in order to correlate with Sections 215-8 and 230-56. The "high leg" marking covered by subparagraph (e) is intended to prevent problems due to the lack of complete standardization, where metered and nonmetered equipment are installed in the same installation. Electricians should always be cautious and test each phase to ground, with suitable equipment, in order to know exactly where this "high leg" is located in the system.

The exception to subparagraph (f) is new in the 1984 *Code*. The intent is that the phase leg having the higher voltage to ground (120 × 1.73 = 208 V on a 120/240-V, 3-phase, 4-wire delta-connected system) maintain the center position (B phase) in all panelboards or switchboards or at least maintain a standardized position in existing installations to avoid the hazards associated with running a 2-wire 208-V branch circuit when a 2-wire 120-V circuit is intended. The exception recognizes the fact that metering compartments have been standardized with the "high leg" at the right (C phase) position and the exception makes it unnecessary to transpose the busbar arrangement before and after a metering compartment.

(g) Minimum Wire Bending Space. The minimum wire bending space at terminals and minimum gutter space provided in panelboards and switchboards shall be as required in Section 373-6.

This section requires that installations in the field comply with Section 373-6. See also commentary following Section 384-25 which covers the size of the enclosure.

A. Switchboards

384-4. Location of Switchboards. Switchboards that have any exposed live parts shall be located in permanently dry locations and then only where under competent supervision and accessible only to qualified persons. Switchboards shall be so located that the probability of damage from equipment or processes is reduced to a minimum.

384-5. Wet Locations. Where a switchboard is in a wet location or outside of a building, it shall be enclosed in a weatherproof enclosure or cabinet installed to comply with Section 373-2.

384-6. Location Relative to Easily Ignitible Material. Switchboards shall be so placed as to reduce to a minimum the probability of communicating fire to adjacent combustible materials. Where installed over a combustible floor, suitable protection thereto shall be provided.

The second sentence is new in the 1984 *Code*. The intent is to prohibit the installation of switchboards on a combustible wooden floor. One method of compliance with this rule would be to form and set a piece of sheet steel or other suitable noncombustible material on the floor under the equipment.

384-7. Clearance from Ceiling. A space of 3 feet (914 mm) or more shall be provided between the top of any switchboard and any combustible ceiling.

Exception No. 1: Where a noncombustible shield is provided between the switchboard and the ceiling.

Exception No. 2: Totally enclosed switchboards.

This section was revised for the 1984 *Code* by replacing the word "nonfireproof" in the main rule and the word "fireproof" in Exception No. 1 with "combustible" and "noncombustible," respectively. The intent is to provide building designers with rules that are required to be considered when designing areas in which switchboards will be located.

384-8. Clearances Around Switchboards. Clearances around switchboards shall comply with the provisions of Section 110-16.

Sufficient access and working space is required to permit ready and safe operation and maintenance of such equipment. Table 110-16(a) indicates minimum working clearances from 0 to 600 V.

For work space clearances of switchboards operating at over 600 V, see Table 110-34(a).

384-9. Conductor Insulation. An insulated conductor used within a switchboard shall be listed, flame-retardant and shall be rated not less than the voltage applied to it and not less than the voltage applied to other conductors or busbars with which it may come in contact.

384-10. Clearance for Conductors Entering Bus Enclosures. Where conduits or other raceways enter a switchboard, floor standing panelboard, or similar enclosure at the bottom, sufficient space shall be provided to permit installation of conductors in the enclosure. The wiring space shall not be less than shown in the following table where the conduit or raceways enter or leave the enclosure below the busbars, their supports, or other obstructions. The conduit or raceways, including their end fittings, shall not rise more than 3 inches (76 mm) above the bottom of the enclosure.

Conductor	Minimum Spacing Between Bottom of Enclosure and Busbars, their Supports, or other Obstructions (Inches)
Insulated busbars, their supports, or other obstructions	8 (203mm)
Noninsulated busbars	10 (254mm)

This section should be carefully considered when installing underground conduit or raceways which will terminate in the bottom of an open switchboard. For example, if larger sizes of conduit are employed for service laterals or feeders and terminate where they extend more than 3 in. above the bottom of the enclosure, it will be difficult to cut them after it is discovered that they are too long. On the other hand, conduits or raceways should not be installed where flush with the finished floor under switchboards where located on the outside of buildings or in other locations where water could enter the raceways.

384-11. Grounding Switchboard Frames. Switchboard frames and structures supporting switching equipment shall be grounded.

Exception: Frames of direct-current, single-polarity switchboards shall not be required to be grounded if effectively insulated.

384-12. Grounding of Instruments, Relays, Meters, and Instrument Transformers on Switchboards. Instruments, relays, meters, and instrument transformers located on switchboards shall be grounded as specified in Sections 250-121 through 250-125.

ARTICLE 384—SWITCHBOARDS AND PANELBOARDS

B. Panelboards

384-13. General. All panelboards shall have a rating not less than the minimum feeder capacity required for the load computed in accordance with Article 220. Panelboards shall be durably marked by the manufacturer with the voltage and the current rating and the number of phases for which they are designed and with the manufacturer's name or trademark in such a manner as to be visible after installation, without disturbing the interior parts or wiring.

Some panelboards are suitable for use as service equipment and are so marked.

UL listed panelboards are for use with copper conductors unless marked to indicate which terminals are suitable for use with aluminum conductors. Such marking is required to be independent of any marking on terminal connectors and is required to be on a wiring diagram or other readily visible location. If all terminals are suitable for use with aluminum conductors as well as with copper conductors, the panelboard will be marked "Use Copper or Aluminum Wire." A panelboard employing terminals or main or branch-circuit units individually marked "AL-CU" will be marked as noted above or "Use Copper Wire Only." The latter marking indicates that wiring space or other factors make the panelboard unsuitable for aluminum conductors. See Section 110-14(a).

Panelboards to which units (circuit breakers, switches, etc.) may be added in the field are marked with the name or trademark of the manufacturer and the catalog number or equivalent of those units intended for installation in the field.

Unless the panelboard is marked to indicate otherwise, the termination provisions are based on the use of 60°C (140°F) ampacities for wire sizes No. 14-1 AWG, and 75°C (167°F) ampacities for wire sizes No. 1/0 AWG and larger.

384-14. Lighting and Appliance Branch-Circuit Panelboard. For the purposes of this article, a lighting and appliance branch-circuit panelboard is one having more than 10 percent of its overcurrent devices rated 30 amperes or less, for which neutral connections are provided.

A lighting and appliance branch-circuit panelboard is a panelboard having not more than 42 overcurrent devices (the maximum — see Section 384-15), where more than 10 percent of the installed overcurrent devices (10 percent of 42 = 4.2) [5 or more] are rated 30 A or less and for which circuit and neutral connections are provided. Lighting circuits rated 30 A or less without a neutral connection are not considered.

384-15. Number of Overcurrent Devices on One Panelboard. Not more than forty-two overcurrent devices (other than those provided for in the mains) of a lighting and appliance branch-circuit panelboard shall be installed in any one cabinet or cutout box.

A lighting and appliance branch-circuit panelboard shall be provided with physical means to prevent the installation of more overcurrent devices than that number for which the panelboard was designed, rated, and approved.

For the purposes of this article, a 2-pole circuit breaker shall be considered two overcurrent devices; a 3-pole breaker shall be considered three overcurrent devices.

Class CTL panelboards are identified by the words "Class CTL" on the Underwriters Laboratories Inc. "Listing Mark."

Class CTL panelboards incorporate physical features which, in conjunction with the physical size, configuration, or other means provided in Class CTL circuit breakers, fuseholders, or fusible switches, are designed to prevent the installation of more overcurrent protective poles than that number for which the device is designed and rated.

Class CTL is the Underwriters Laboratories Inc. designation for the *Code* requirement for circuit limitation within a lighting and appliance branch-circuit panelboard and means "circuit limiting."

Figure 384-1 shows a panelboard with a 200-A main circuit breaker. Figure 384-2 shows a panelboard without main overcurrent protection, but which may be protected by overcurrent protection as illustrated in Figure 384-3.

384-16. Overcurrent Protection.

(a) Lighting and Appliance Branch-Circuit Panelboard Individually Protected. Each lighting and appliance branch-circuit panelboard shall be individually protected on the supply side by not more than two main circuit breakers or two sets of fuses having a combined rating not greater than that of the panelboard.

Exception No. 1: Individual protection for a lighting and appliance panelboard shall not be required if the panelboard feeder has overcurrent protection not greater than that of the panelboard.

Main overcurrent protection may be an integral part of a panelboard or located remote from the panelboard. See Figures 384-1, 384-2, and 384-3. See also commentary following Section 384-15.

Figure 384-2. A panelboard with main lugs only. (*Square D Co.*)

Figure 384-1. A panelboard with main circuit breaker disconnect suitable for use as service equipment. (*Square D Co.*)

Exception No. 2: For existing installations, individual protection for lighting and appliance branch-circuit panelboards is not required where such panelboards are used as service equipment in supplying an individual residential occupancy.

ARTICLE 384—SWITCHBOARDS AND PANELBOARDS

The phrase "For existing installations" in Exception No. 2 means the existing panelboard. It is not intended that a split-bus panelboard used in an individual dwelling occupany be replaced if a circuit is added to the existing panelboard. However, it does mean that for installation of new panelboards in new or existing residential occupancies, a split-bus six disconnect panelboard (with more than two circuit breakers or sets of fuses protecting the panelboard) is not permitted for the service equipment.

An individual residential occupancy could be a dwelling unit in a multifamily dwelling where the panelboard is used as service equipment. See the definition of "Dwelling Unit" in Article 100.

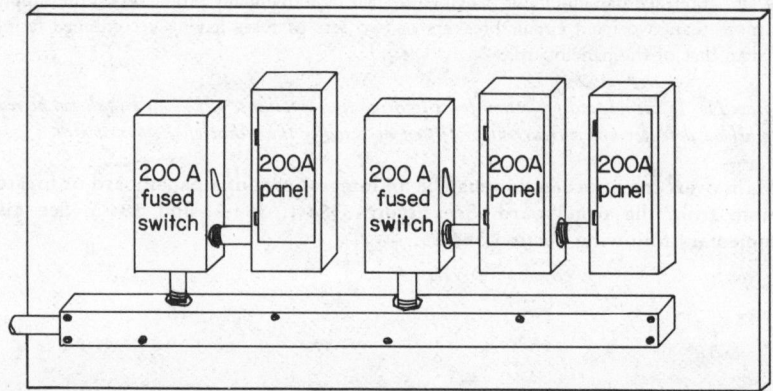

Figure 384-3. An arrangement of three individual lighting and appliance branch-circuit panelboards with main overcurrent protection remote from the panelboards. Note that the panelboard feeders have overcurrent protection not greater than the rating of the panelboard.

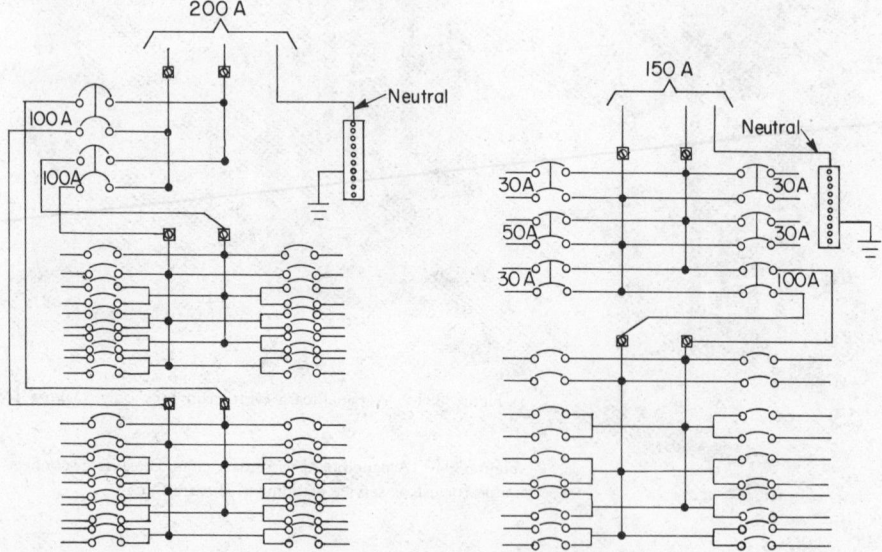

Figure 384-4. Panel on left has two 100-A main breakers installed as disconnecting means and 200-A main lugs. Panel on right is a split-bus panel with 150-A main lugs and six main breaker disconnecting means. The 150-A panelboard on the right is suitable for use as service equipment only if it is not a lighting and appliance panelboard or if it presently exists in an individual residential occupancy.

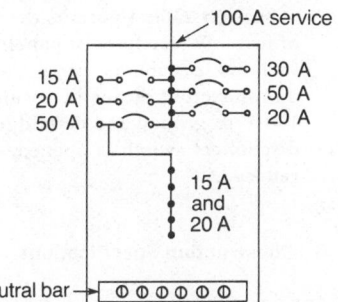

Figure 384-5. A split-bus lighting and appliance branch-circuit panelboard supplying an individual residential occupancy.

(b) Snap Switches Rated at 30 Amperes or Less. Panelboards equipped with snap switches rated at 30 amperes or less shall have overcurrent protection not in excess of 200 amperes.

This requirement is limited to snap switches; it does not apply to panelboards equipped with circuit breakers.

(c) Continuous Load. The total load on any overcurrent device located in a panelboard shall not exceed 80 percent of its rating where in normal operation the load will continue for 3 hours or more.

Exception: Where the assembly including the overcurrent device is approved for continuous duty at 100 percent of its rating.

(d) Supplied through a Transformer. Where a panelboard is supplied through a transformer, the overcurrent protection required in (a) and (b) above shall be located on the secondary side of the transformer.

Exception: A panelboard supplied by the secondary side of a single-phase transformer having a two-wire (single-voltage) secondary shall be considered as protected by overcurrent protection provided on the primary (supply) side of the transformer, provided this protection is in accordance with Section 450-3(b)(1) and does not exceed the value determined by multiplying the panelboard rating by the secondary-to-primary voltage ratio.

(e) Delta Breakers. A three-phase disconnect or overcurrent device shall not be connected to the bus of any panelboard that has less than three-phase buses.

(FPN): This is intended to prohibit the use of "delta breakers" in panelboards.

384-17. Panelboards in Damp or Wet Locations. Panelboards in damp or wet locations shall be installed to comply with Section 373-2.

384-18. Enclosure. Panelboards shall be mounted in cabinets, cutout boxes, or enclosures designed for the purpose and shall be dead front.

Exception: Panelboards other than of the dead front externally operable type shall be permitted where accessible only to qualified persons.

384-19. Relative Arrangement of Switches and Fuses. In panelboards, fuses of any type shall be installed on the load side of any switches.

Exception: As provided in Section 230-94 for use as service equipment.

ARTICLE 384—SWITCHBOARDS AND PANELBOARDS

Section 230-94 permits the service switch on either the supply side or load side of fuses. Where fuses of panelboards are accessible to other than qualified persons, such as occupants of a multifamily dwelling, Section 240-40 requires that disconnecting means be located on the supply side of all fuses in circuits of over 150 V to ground and cartridge-type fuses in circuits of any voltage. Thus, when the disconnect switch is opened, the fuses are deenergized and danger from shock is reduced.

C. Construction Specifications

384-20. Panels. The panels of switchboards shall be made of moisture-resistant, noncombustible material.

384-21. Busbars. Insulated or bare busbars shall be rigidly mounted.

384-22. Protection of Instrument Circuits. Instruments, pilot lights, potential transformers, and other switchboard devices with potential coils shall be supplied by a circuit that is protected by standard overcurrent devices rated 15 amperes or less.

Exception No. 1: Where the operation of the overcurrent device might introduce a hazard in the operation of devices.

Exception No. 2: For ratings of 2 amperes or less, special types of enclosed fuses shall be permitted.

384-23. Component Parts. Switches, fuses, and fuseholders used on panelboards shall comply with the applicable requirements of Articles 240 and 380.

384-24. Knife Switches. Exposed blades of knife switches shall be dead when open.

384-25. Wire Bending Space in Panelboards. The enclosure for a panelboard shall have the top and bottom wire bending space sized in accordance with Table 373-6(b) for the largest conductor entering or leaving the enclosure. Side wire bending space shall be in accordance with Table 373-6(a) for the largest conductor to be terminated in that space.

Exception No. 1: Either the top or bottom wire bending space shall be permitted to be sized in accordance with Table 373-6(a) for a lighting and appliance branch-circuit panelboard rated 225 amperes or less.

Exception No. 2: Either the top or bottom wire bending space for any panelboard shall be permitted to be sized in accordance with Table 373-6(a) where at least one side wire bending space is sized in accordance with Table 373-6(b) for the largest conductor to be terminated in any side wire bending space.

Exception No. 3: The top and bottom wire bending space shall be permitted to be sized in accordance with Table 373-6(a) spacings if the panelboard is designed and constructed for wiring using only one single 90 degree bend for each conductor including the neutral and the wiring diagram shows and specifies the method of wiring that must be used.

Exception No. 4: Either the top or the bottom wire bending space, but not both, shall be permitted to be sized in accordance with Table 373-6(a) where there are no conductors terminated in that space.

This section dictates the size of the enclosure for a panelboard. With reference to Figure 373-1 (see Section 373-6), the general rule calls for wire bending space T1 and T4 to be in accordance with Table 373-6(b) for conductors M (assuming these are the largest conductors entering the enclosure). Side wire bending space T2 shall be in accordance with Table 373-6(a) for the wire size to be used with the largest rated unit facing that side space and T3 shall be similarly sized for the largest rated unit facing the right side of the enclosure. Exception No. 1 permits either T1 or T4 (not both) to be reduced to the space required by Table 373-6(a) for size M conductors for a panelboard rated 225 A or less. Exception No. 2 permits either T1 or T4 (not both) to be reduced to the space required by Table 373-6(a) for size M conductors for *any* panelboard where either T2 or T3 (or both) is sized in accordance with Table 373-6(b) for the largest conductor to be terminated in either the left or right side spaces. Under the construction rules of Section 384-25 a panelboard enclosure might not be of adequate size for all manner of wiring and Section 373-6 must be considered when wiring is planned.

Exception Nos. 3 and 4 are new in the 1984 *Code*. Exception No. 3 permits both the top and bottom wire bending space to be reduced as noted. A single 90 degree bend, meaning one and only one 90 degree bend, is required to be present for the ungrounded conductors. A grounded conductor is permitted to be wired straight in if Table 373-6(b) spacing is provided for the grounded conductor.

Exception No. 4 permits reduction of the top or bottom space to Table 373-6(a) spacings where there are no terminals facing that space. In this case, the space is a gutter space and measurement is on a line perpendicular to the wall of the enclosure and to the closest barrier post or side of a switch, fuse, or circuit breaker unit that is, or may be, installed.

384-26. Minimum Spacings. The distance between bare metal parts, busbars, etc., shall not be less than specified in Table 384-26.

Exception No. 1: At switches or circuit breakers.

Exception No. 2: Inherent spacings in listed components.

Where close proximity does not cause excessive heating, parts of the same polarity at switches, enclosed fuses, etc., shall be permitted to be placed as close together as convenience in handling will allow.

Table 384-26.   Minimum Spacings Between Bare Metal Parts

	Opposite Polarity Where Mounted on the Same Surface	Opposite Polarity Where Held Free in Air	*Live Parts to Ground
Not over 125 volts, nominal	¾ inch	½ inch	½ inch
Not over 250 volts, nominal	1¼ inch	¾ inch	½ inch
Not over 600 volts, nominal	2 inches	1 inch	1 inch

For SI units: one inch = 25.4 millimeters.
* For spacing between live parts and doors of cabinets, see Section 373-11(a) (1), (2), and (3).

384-27. Grounding of Panelboards. Panelboard cabinets shall be grounded in the manner specified in Article 250 or Section 384-3(c). An approved terminal bar for equipment grounding conductors shall be provided and secured inside of the cabinet for the attachment of all the feeder and branch-circuit equipment grounding conductors, where the panelboard is used with nonmetallic raceway or cable, or where separate grounding conductors are provided. The terminal bar shall be bonded to the cabinet or panelboard frame and shall not be connected to the neutral bar in other than service equipment.

ARTICLE 384—SWITCHBOARDS AND PANELBOARDS

A separate equipment grounding conductor terminal bar is required to be installed and bonded to the panelboard for the termination of feeder and branch-circuit equipment grounding conductors. Where installed within service equipment, this terminal is permitted to be bonded to the neutral terminal bar. Any other connection between the equipment grounding terminal bar and the neutral bar, other than as permitted by Exception No. 2, would raise the potential of all exposed dead metal parts of equipment since current flow in the neutral or grounded conductor would allow a potential difference of several volts, and would also permit neutral current to take two paths back to the service equipment — one being through the equipment grounding conductor (the raceway, for example). This is important when subpanels are used, since arcing and/or loose connections at connectors, raceway fittings, etc., could serve to create a potential fire or shock hazard.

Exception No. 1: When an isolated ground conductor is provided as in Section 250-74, Exception No. 4, the insulated ground conductor which is run with the circuit conductors shall be permitted to pass through the panelboard without being connected to the panelboard grounding terminal bar.

Exception No. 2: The terminal bar for equipment grounding conductors shall be permitted to be connected to the neutral bar at separate buildings in accordance with the provisions of Section 250-24.

Electronic equipment, which is often used in data processing systems, hospitals laboratories, etc., may fail to perform properly due to electromagnetic interference present in the electrical supply.

Where required for the reduction of electrical noise (electromagnetic interference) on the grounding circuit, an isolated grounding terminal is permitted. This equipment grounding terminal is required to be grounded by an insulated equipment grounding conductor that is run with the circuit conductors. It is also permitted to pass through one or more panelboards (without connection to the panelboard grounding terminal) but it is very important that it terminate directly at the applicable derived system or service grounding terminal. Connection only to a separate grounding electrode places earth in the fault return path and may prevent sufficient current to open overcurrent protection when a ground fault occurs. See the Fine Print Note in Section 250-74 and the commentary that follows.

4 EQUIPMENT FOR GENERAL USE

ARTICLE 400 — FLEXIBLE CORDS AND CABLES

Contents

A. General

400-1. Scope. This article covers general requirements, applications, and construction specifications for flexible cords and flexible cables.

Flexible cords and cables as covered by Article 400 are not considered a wiring method. Wiring methods are covered in Chapter 3 of the *Code*.

400-2. Other Articles. Flexible cords and flexible cables shall comply with this article and with the applicable provisions of other articles of this Code.

400-3. Suitability. Flexible cords and cables and their associated fittings shall be suitable for the conditions of use and location.

400-4. Types. Flexible cords and flexible cables shall conform to the description in Table 400-4. Types of flexible cords and flexible cables other than those listed in the table shall be the subject of special investigation.

Table 400-4.   Flexible Cords and Cables
(See Section 400-4)

Trade Name	Type Letter	Size AWG	No. of Conductors	Insulation	Nominal *Insulation Thickness AWG	Mils	Braid on Each Conductor	Outer Covering	Use		
Asbestos-Covered Heat-Resistant Cord	AFC	18-10	2 or 3	Impregnated Asbestos	18-14	30	Cotton or Rayon	None	Pendant	Dry Locations	Not Hard Usage
	AFPD				12-10	45	None	Cotton, Rayon, or Saturated Asbestos			
Thermoset-Jacketed Heat-Resistant Cord	AFS	18-10	2 or 3	Impregnated Asbestos	18-14	30	None	Thermoset	Portable Heaters	Damp Locations	Extra Hard Usage
	AFSJ	18-16									Hard Usage
Lamp Cord	C	18-10	2 or more	Thermoset or Thermoplastic	18-16	30	Cotton	None	Pendant or Portable	Dry Locations	Not Hard Usage
Data Processing Cable	DP See Note 2.	32 Min.	2 or More	Thermoplastic, Thermoset or Cross-linked Synthetic Polymer	32-27 (50V) 26-23 (50V) 22-20 (50V) 32-16 (300V) 14-10 (300V) 8- 2 (300V)	8 12 16 20 30 60	None	Thermoplastic, Thermoset or Crosslinked Synthetic Polymer	Data Processing Systems	Dry Locations	Power and Signaling Circuits

See Notes 1 through 9.
* See Note 9.

Table 400-4 (Continued)

Trade Name	Type	AWG	Conductors	Insulation	AWG	Size	Braid	Outer Covering	Use	Location
Elevator Cable	E See Note 6.	20-14	2 or More	Thermoset	20-16	20	Cotton	Three Cotton, Outer one Flame-Retardant & Moisture-Resist. See Note 4.	Elevator Lighting and Control	Nonhazardous Locations
	EN See Note 6.				20-16	20	Flexible Nylon Jacket	One Cotton and a Neoprene or Thermoplastic Jacket See Note 4.	Elevator Lighting and Control	Hazardous (Classified) Locations
Elevator Cable	EO See Note 6.	20-14	2 or More	Thermoset	20-16	20	Cotton	Three Cotton, Outer one Flame-Retardant & Moisture-Resist. See Note 4.		Nonhazardous Locations
					14	30		One Cotton and a Neoprene Jacket See Note 4.	Elevator Lighting and Control	Hazardous (Classified) Locations
Elevator Cable	ET See Note 6.	20-14	2 or More	Thermoplastic	20-16	20	Rayon	Three Cotton, Outer one Flame-Retardant & Moisture-Resist. See Note 4.		Nonhazardous Locations
	ETLB See Note 6.				14	30	None			
	ETP See Note 6.			Thermoplastic			Rayon	Thermoplastic		
	ETT See Note 6.			Thermoplastic			None	One Cotton and a Thermoplastic jacket		Hazardous (Classified) Locations

See Notes 1 through 9.
* See Note 9.

Table 400-4 (Continued)

Trade Name	Type Letter	Size AWG	No. of Conductors	Insulation	*Insulation Thickness AWG	Mils	Braid on Each Conductor	Outer Covering	Use		
Heater Cord	HPD	18-12	2, 3, or 4	Thermoset with Asbestos or All Thermoset	Thermoset 18-16 / 14-12	15 / 30	None	Cotton or Rayon	Portable Heaters	Dry Locations	Not Hard Usage
Parallel Heater Cord	HPN See Note 7.	18-12	2 or 3	Thermosetting	18-16 / 14 / 12	45 / 80 / 95	None	Thermosetting	Portable	Damp Locations	Not Hard Usage
Jacketed Heater Cord Thermoset	HS	14-12	2, 3 or 4	Thermoset with Asbestos	14-12	30	None	Cotton and Thermoset	Portable	Damp Locations	Hard Usage
Jacketed Heater Cord	HSJ	18-12		All Thermoset	18-16 / 14-12	30 / 45			Portable Heaters		
Jacketed Heater Cord	HSJO	18-12	2, 3 or 4	Thermoset with Asbestos	18-16 / 14-12	15 / 30	None	Cotton and Oil-Resistant Compound	Portable		Hard Usage
	HSO	14-12		All Thermoset	18-16 / 14-12	30 / 45		Cotton and Oil-Resistant Compound	Portable	Damp Locations	Extra Hard Usage
Twisted Portable Cord	PD	18-10	2 or more	Thermoset or Thermoplastic	18-16 / 14-10	30 / 45	Cotton	Cotton or Rayon	Pendant or Portable	Dry Locations	Not Hard Usage

See Notes 1 through 9.
* See Note 9.

Table 400-4 (Continued)

Trade Name	Type Letter	Size AWG	No. of Conductors	Insulation	AWG	Nom. Thickness	Braid / Covering	Outer Covering	Pendant or Portable	Damp Locations	Use
Hard Service Cord	S See Note 5.	18-2	2 or more	Thermoset	18-16 (Thermoset)	30		Thermoset	Pendant or Portable	Damp Locations	Extra Hard Usage
					14-10 (Thermoset)	45					
					8-2 (Thermoset)	60					
	SE See Note 5.			Thermoplastic Elastomer			None	Thermoplastic Elastomer			
Junior Hard Service Cord	SJ	18-10	2, 3, or 4	Thermoset	10	45	None	Thermoset	Pendant or Portable	Damp Locations	Hard Usage
	SJE			Thermoplastic Elastomer	18-12	30		Thermoplastic Elastomer			
	SJO			Thermoset				Oil-Resistant Thermoset			
	SJOO			Oil-Resistant Thermoset				Oil-Resistant Thermoset			
	SJT			Thermoplastic or Thermoset	18-12	30		Thermoplastic			
					10	45					
	SJTO			Thermoset or Thermoplastic				Oil-Resistant Thermoplastic			
	SJTOO			Oil-Resistant Thermoplastic or Thermoset				Oil-Resistant Thermoplastic			

See Notes 1 through 9.

* See Note 9.

Table 400-4 (Continued)

Trade Name	Type Letter	Size AWG	No. of Conductors	Insulation	Nominal *Insulation Thickness AWG	Mils	Braid on Each Conductor	Outer Covering	Use		
Hard Service Cord	SO	18-2	2 or more	Thermoset	18-16 (Thermoset)	30		Oil-Resistant Thermoset	Pendant or Portable	Damp Locations	Extra Hard Usage
	SOO	18-2	2 or more	Oil-Resistant Thermoset	14-10 (Thermoset)	45		Oil-Resistant Thermoset			
					8-2 (Thermoset)	60					
All Thermoset Parallel Cord	SP-1 See Note 7.	18		Thermoset	18	30	None	Thermoset	Pendant or Portable	Damp Locations	Not Hard Usage
	SP-2 See Note 7.	18-16	2 or 3		18-16	45					
	SP-3 See Note 7.	18-12		Thermoset	18-16	60	None	Thermoset	Refrigerators, Room Air Conditioners and as permitted in Section 422-8(d)	Damp Locations	Not Hard Usage
					14	80					
					12	95					
					10	110					

See Notes 1 through 9.
*See Note 9.

Table 400-4 (Continued)

Trade Name	Type Letter	Size AWG	No. of Conductors	Insulation	AWG	Thickness	Braid	Outer Covering	Use		
All Elastomer (thermoplastic) Parallel Cord	SPE-1 See Note 7.	18	2 or 3	Thermoplastic Elastomer	18	30	None	Thermoplastic Elastomer	Pendant or Portable	Damp Locations	Not Hard Usage
	SPE-2 See Note 7.	18-16			18-16	45					
	SPE-3 See Note 7.	18-12			18-16 14 12 10	60 80 95 110	None	Thermoplastic Elastomer	Refrigerators, Room Air Conditioners and as permitted in Section 422-8(d)	Damp Locations	Not Hard Usage
All Plastic Parallel Cord	SPT-1 See Note 7.	18	2 or 3	Thermoplastic	18	30	None	Thermoplastic	Pendant or Portable	Damp Locations	Not Hard Usage
	SPT-2 See Note 7.	18-16			18-16	45					
	SPT-3 See Note 7.	18-10		Thermoplastic	18-16 14 12 10	60 80 95 110	None	Thermoplastic	Refrigerators, Room Air Conditioners and as permitted in Section 422-8(d)	Damp Locations	Not Hard Usage

See Notes 1 through 9.
* See Note 9.

441

Table 400-4 (Continued)

Trade Name	Type Letter	Size AWG	No. of Conductors	Insulation	Nominal *Insulation Thickness AWG	Mils	Braid on Each Conductor	Outer Covering		Use	
Range, Dryer Cable	SRD	10-4	3 or 4	Thermoset			None	Thermoset	Portable	Damp Locations	Ranges, Dryers
	SRDE	10-4	3 or 4	Thermoplastic Elastomer	10-4	45	None	Thermoplastic Elastomer	Portable	Damp Locations	Ranges, Dryers
	SRDT	10-4	3 or 4	Thermoplastic			None	Thermoplastic	Portable	Damp Locations	Ranges, Dryers
Hard Service Cord	ST	18-2	2 or more	Thermoplastic or Thermoset	18-16 14-10 8- 2	30 45 60	None	Thermoplastic	Pendant or Portable	Damp Locations	Extra Hard Usage
	STO							Oil-Resistant Thermoplastic			
	STOO			Oil-Resistant Thermoplastic or Thermoset							
Vacuum Cleaner Cord	SV See Note 7.	18-17	2 or 3	Thermoset	18-17	15	None	Thermoset	Pendant or Portable	Damp Locations	Not Hard Usage
	SVE See Note 7.			Thermoplastic Elastomer				Thermoplastic Elastomer			
	SVO			Thermoset				Oil-Resistant Thermoset			
	SVOO			Oil-Resistant Thermoset				Oil-Resistant Thermoset			

See Notes 1 through 9.
* See Note 9.

Table 400-4 (Continued)

Trade Name	Type Letter	18-17	2 or 3	Thermoset or Thermoplastic	18-17	15	None	Thermoplastic	Pendant or Portable	Damp Locations	Not Hard Usage
Vacuum Cleaner Cord	SVT See Note 7.	18-17	2 or 3	Thermoset or Thermoplastic				Thermoplastic			
	SVTO See Note 7.			Thermoset or Thermoplastic				Oil-Resistant Thermoplastic			
	SVTOO			Oil-Resistant Thermoplastic or Thermoset				Oil-Resistant Thermoplastic			
Parallel Tinsel Cord	TP See Note 3.	27	2	Thermoset	27		None	Thermoset	Attached to an Appliance	Damp Locations	Not Hard Usage
	TPT See Note 3.	27	2	Thermoplastic	27	30	None	Thermoplastic	Attached to an Appliance	Damp Locations	Not Hard Usage
Jacketed Tinsel Cord	TS See Note 3.	27	2	Thermoset	27		None	Thermoset	Attached to an Appliance	Damp Locations	Not Hard Usage
	TST See Note 3.	27	2	Thermoplastic	27	15	None	Thermoplastic	Attached to an Appliance	Damp Locations	Not Hard Usage

See Notes 1 through 9.
* See Note 9.

ARTICLE 400—FLEXIBLE CORDS AND CABLES

Notes to Table 400-4

1. Except for Types SP-1, SP-2, SP-3, SPT-1, SPT-2, SPT-3, HPN, TP, TPT, SRD (3-conductor) and SRDT (3-conductor), individual conductors are twisted together.

2. Cables constructed differently than specified herein and listed as component parts of a data processing system shall be permitted.

3. Types TP, TPT, TS, and TST shall be permitted in lengths not exceeding 8 feet (2.44 m) when attached directly, or by means of a special type of plug, to a portable appliance rated at 50 watts or less and of such nature that extreme flexibility of the cord is essential.

4. Rubber-filled or varnished cambric tapes shall be permitted as a substitute for the inner braids.

5. Types S, SO, ST, and STO shall be permitted for use on theater stages, in garages, and elsewhere where flexible cords are permitted by this Code.

6. Elevator traveling cables for operating control and signal circuits shall contain nonmetallic fillers as necessary to maintain concentricity. Cables exceeding 100 feet (30.5 m) between supports shall have steel supporting members. In locations subject to excessive moisture or corrosive vapors or gases, supporting members of other materials shall be permitted. Where steel supporting members are used, they shall run straight through the center of the cable assembly and shall not be cabled with the copper strands of any conductor.

In addition to conductors used for control and signaling circuits, Types E, EO, EN, ET, ETP, ETLB and ETT elevator cables shall be permitted to incorporate in the construction one or more No. 20 AWG telephone conductor pairs and/or one or more coaxial cables. The No. 20 AWG conductor pairs may be covered with suitable shielding for telephone, audio or higher frequency communication circuits; the coaxial cables consist of a center conductor, insulation and shield for use in video or other radio frequency communication circuits. The insulation of the conductors shall be rubber or thermoplastic of thickness not less than specified for the other conductors of the particular type of cable. Metallic shields shall have their own protective covering. Where used, these components shall be permitted to be incorporated in any layer of the cable assembly but shall not run straight through the center.

7. A third conductor in these cables is for grounding purposes only.

8. The individual conductors of all cords, except those of heat-resistant cords (Types AFC, AFPD, AFS, AFSJ, and CFPD), shall have a thermoset or thermoplastic insulation, except that the grounding conductor where used shall be in accordance with Section 400-23(b). Unvulcanized rubber compounds shall be permitted to be used for heater cords Types HPD, HSJ, HSJO, HS, and HSO.

9. Where the voltage between any two conductors exceeds 300, but does not exceed 600, flexible cord of No. 10 and smaller shall have thermoset or thermoplastic insulation on the individual conductors at least 45 mils in thickness, unless Type S, SO, ST, or STO cord is used.

400-5. Ampacity of Flexible Cords and Cables. Table 400-5 gives the allowable ampacity for not more than three current-carrying copper conductors in a cord. If the number of current-carrying conductors in a cord exceeds three, the ampacity of each conductor shall be reduced as shown in the following table:

Number of Conductors	Percent of Values in Table 400-5
4 through 6	80
7 through 24	70
25 through 42	60
43 and above	50

A conductor used for equipment grounding and a neutral conductor which carries only the unbalanced current from other conductors, as in the case of normally balanced circuits of three or more conductors, shall not be considered as current-carrying conductors.

Where a single conductor is used for both equipment grounding and to carry unbalanced current from other conductors, as provided for in Section 250-60 for electric ranges and electric clothes dryers, it shall not be considered as a current-carrying conductor.

Table 400-5.   Ampacity of Flexible Cords and Cables

[Based on Ambient Temperature of 30° C (86°F). See Section 400-13 and Table 400-4.]

Size AWG	Thermoset Types TP, TS / Thermoplastic Types TPT, TST	Thermoset Types C, PD, E, EO, EN, S SO, SRD, SJ, SJO, SV, SVO, SP / Thermoplastic Types ET, ETT, ETLB, ETP, ST, STO, SRDT, SJT, SJTO, SVT, SVTO, SPT		Types AFS, AFSJ, HPD, HSJ, HSJO, HS, HSO, HPN	Cotton Types CFPD* Asbestos Types AFC* AFPD*
		A†	B†		
27**	0.5	..	..	..	..
20	..	5***	7***	..	..
18	..	7	10	10	6
17	..	..	12	..	..
16	..	10	13	15	8
15	..	..	..	17	..
14	..	15	18	20	17
12	..	20	25	30	23
10	..	25	30	35	28
8	..	35	40	..	..
6	..	45	55	..	..
4	..	60	70	..	..
2	..	80	95	..	..

* These types are used almost exclusively in fixtures where they are exposed to high temperatures and ampere ratings are assigned accordingly.

** Tinsel cord.

*** Elevator cables only.

† The ampacities under sub-heading A apply to 3-conductor cords and other multiconductor cords connected to utilization equipment so that only 3 conductors are current carrying. The ampacities under sub-heading B apply to 2-conductor cords and other multiconductor cords connected to utilization equipment so that only 2 conductors are current carrying.

NOTE. Ultimate Insulation Temperature. In no case shall conductors be associated together in such a way with respect to the kind of circuit, the wiring method used, or the number of conductors that the limiting temperature of the conductors will be exceeded.

400-6. Marking. Flexible cords and cables shall be marked by means of a printed tag attached to the coil reel or carton. The tag shall contain the information required in Section 310-11(a).

Types SJ, SJO, SJT, SJTO, S, SO, ST, and STO flexible cords shall be durably marked on the surface at intervals not exceeding 24 inches (610 mm) with the type designation, size, and number of conductors.

400-7. Uses Permitted.

   (a) Uses. Flexible cords and cables shall be used only for (1) pendants; (2) wiring of fixtures; (3) connection of portable lamps or appliances; (4) elevator cables; (5) wiring of cranes and hoists; (6) connection of stationary equipment to facilitate their frequent interchange; (7) prevention of the transmission of noise or vibration; (8) appliances where the fastening means and mechanical connections are designed to permit removal for maintenance and repair; (9) data processing cables as permitted by Section 645-2; (10) connection of moving parts; or (11) temporary wiring as permitted in Sections 305-2(b) and 305-2(c).

(b) Attachment Plugs. Where used as permitted in subsections (a)(3), (a)(6), and (a)(8) of this section, each flexible cord shall be equipped with an attachment plug and shall be energized from a receptacle outlet.

The flexible cords and cables referred to in this article are not limited to use with portable equipment. However, they are not permitted to be used as a substitute for the fixed wiring of a structure or where concealed behind building walls, ceilings, or floors. See Section 400-8. Also see Section 240-4 Exception No. 3 and Article 305 for provisions covering extension cords.

400-8. Uses Not Permitted. Unless specifically permitted in Section 400-7 flexible cords and cables shall not be used (1) as a substitute for the fixed wiring of a structure; (2) where run through holes in walls, ceilings, or floors; (3) where run through doorways, windows, or similar openings; (4) where attached to building surfaces; or (5) where concealed behind building walls, ceilings, or floors.

400-9. Splices. Flexible cord shall be used only in continuous lengths without splice or tap when initially installed in applications permitted by Section 400-7(a). The repair of hard service cord (see Column 1, Table 400-4) No. 14 and larger shall be permitted if conductors are spliced in accordance with Section 110-14(b) and the completed splice retains the insulation, outer sheath properties, and usage characteristics of the cord being spliced.

400-10. Pull at Joints and Terminals. Flexible cords shall be so connected to devices and to fittings that tension will not be transmitted to joints or terminals.

(FPN): Some methods of preventing pull on a cord from being transmitted to joints or terminals are (1) knotting the cord, (2) winding with tape, and (3) fittings designed for the purpose.

400-11. In Show Windows and Show Cases. Flexible cords used in show windows and show cases shall be Type S, SO, SJ, SJO, ST, STO, SJT, SJTO, or AFS.

Exception No. 1: For the wiring of chain-supported lighting fixtures.

Exception No. 2: As supply cords for portable lamps and other merchandise being displayed or exhibited.

Flexible cords listed for "hard usage" or "extra hard usage" should be used in show windows and show cases and precautions should be taken to ensure that these cords are maintained in good condition because of possible contact with combustible materials usually present at these locations and because of the wear and tear they are exposed to by continuous housekeeping and display changes.

400-12. Minimum Size. The individual conductors of a flexible cord or cable shall not be smaller than the sizes in Table 400-4.

400-13. Overcurrent Protection. Flexible cords not smaller than No. 18, and tinsel cords or cords having equivalent characteristics of smaller size approved for use with specific appliances, shall be considered as protected against overcurrent by the overcurrent devices described in Section 240-4.

400-14. Protection from Damage. Flexible cords and cables shall be protected by bushings or fittings where passing through holes in covers, outlet boxes, or similar enclosures.

There are a variety of bushings and fittings available for this purpose, both insulated and noninsulated, some including strain relief means as required in Section 400-10. Many insulating bushings are listed by Underwriters Laboratories Inc. in the product categories Conduit Fittings (bushings and fittings for use on the ends of conduit in boxes, gutters, etc.); Insulating Devices and Materials, Bushings (bushings for the protection of cords where they pass through walls or barriers of metal); Outlet Bushings and Fittings (bushings and fittings for use on the ends of conduit, EMT, or armored cable where a change to open wiring is made).

B. Construction Specifications

400-20. Labels. Flexible cords shall be examined and tested at the factory and labeled before shipment.

See definition of "Labeled" in Article 100.

400-21. Nominal Insulation Thickness. The nominal thickness of insulation for conductors of flexible cords and cables shall not be less than specified in Table 400-4.

400-22. Grounded-Conductor Identification. One conductor of flexible cords which is intended to be used as a grounded circuit conductor shall have a continuous marker readily distinguishing it from the other conductor or conductors. The identification shall consist of one of the methods indicated in (a) through (f) below.

(a) Colored Braid. A braid finished to show a white or natural gray color and the braid on the other conductor or conductors finished to show a readily distinguishable solid color or colors.

(b) Tracer in Braid. A tracer in a braid of any color contrasting with that of the braid and no tracer in the braid of the other conductor or conductors. No tracer shall be used in the braid of any conductor of a flexible cord which contains a conductor having a braid finished to show white or natural gray.

Exception: In the case of Types C and PD, and cords having the braids on the individual conductors finished to show white or natural gray. In such cords the identifying marker shall be permitted to consist of the solid white or natural gray finish on one conductor, provided there is a colored tracer in the braid of each other conductor.

(c) Colored Insulation. A white or natural gray insulation on one conductor and insulation of a readily distinguishable color or colors on the other conductor or conductors for cords having no braids on the individual conductors.

For jacketed cords furnished with appliances, one conductor having its insulation colored light blue, with the other conductors having their insulation of a readily distinguishable color other than white or natural gray.

Exception: Cords which have insulation on the individual conductors integral with the jacket.

It shall be permissible to cover the insulation with an outer finish to provide the desired color.

(d) Colored Separator. A white or natural gray separator on one conductor and a separator of a readily distinguishable solid color on the other conductor or conductors of cords having insulation on the individual conductors integral with the jacket.

(e) Tinned Conductors. One conductor having the individual strands tinned and the other conductor or conductors having the individual strands untinned for cords having insulation on the individual conductors integral with the jacket.

(f) Surface Marking. One or more stripes, ridges, or grooves so located on the exterior of the cord as to identify one conductor for cords having insulation on the individual conductors integral with the jacket.

400-23. Grounding-Conductor Identification. A conductor intended to be used as a grounding conductor shall have a continuous identifying marker readily distinguishing it from the other conductor or conductors. Conductors having a continuous green color or a continuous green color with one or more yellow stripes shall not be used for other than grounding purposes. The identifying marker shall consist of one of the methods in (a) or (b) below.

(a) Colored Braid. A braid finished to show a continuous green color or a continuous green color with one or more yellow stripes.

(b) Colored Insulation or Covering. For cords having no braids on the individual conductors, an insulation of a continuous green color or a continuous green color with one or more yellow stripes.

400-24. Attachment Plugs. Where a flexible cord is provided with a grounding conductor and equipped with an attachment plug, the attachment plug shall comply with Section 250-59(a) and (b).

C. Portable Cables Over 600 Volts, Nominal

400-30. Scope. This part applies to multiconductor portable cables used to connect mobile equipment and machinery.

400-31. Construction.

(a) Conductors. The conductors shall be No. 8 AWG copper or larger and shall employ flexible stranding.

(b) Shields. Cables operated at over 2000 volts shall be shielded. Shielding shall be for the purpose of confining the voltage stresses to the insulation.

(c) Grounding Conductor(s). Grounding conductor(s) shall be provided. The total area shall be not less than that of the size of the conductor required in Section 250-95.

400-32. Shielding. All shields shall be grounded.

400-33. Grounding. Grounding conductors shall be connected in accordance with Part K of Article 250.

400-34. Minimum Bending Radii. The minimum bending radii for portable cables during installation and handling in service shall be adequate to prevent damage to the cable.

400-35. Fittings. Connectors used to connect lengths of cable in a run shall be of a type which lock firmly together. Provisions shall be made to prevent opening or closing these connectors while energized. Suitable means shall be used to eliminate tension at connectors and terminations.

400-36. Splices and Terminations. Portable cables shall not be operated with splices unless the splices are of the permanent molded, vulcanized types in accordance with Section 110-14(b). Terminations on high-voltage portable cables shall be accessible only to authorized and qualified personnel.

ARTICLE 402 — FIXTURE WIRES

Contents

402-1. Scope. This article covers general requirements and construction specifications for fixture wires.

402-2. Other Articles. Fixture wires shall comply with this article and also with the applicable provisions of other articles of this Code.

(FPN): For application in lighting fixtures, see Article 410.

402-3. Types. Fixture wires shall be of a type listed in Table 402-3, and they shall comply with all requirements of that table. The fixture wires listed in Table 402-3 are all suitable for service at 600 volts, nominal, unless otherwise specified.

(FPN): Thermoplastic insulation may stiffen at temperatures colder than minus 10°C (plus 14°F), requiring care be exercised during installation at such temperatures. Thermoplastic insulation may also be deformed at normal temperatures where subjected to pressure, requiring care be exercised during installation and at points of support.

402-5. Ampacity of Fixture Wires. The ampacity of fixture wire shall not exceed the following:

Table 402-5

Size (AWG)	Ampacity
18	6
16	8
14	17
12	23
10	28

No conductor shall be used under such conditions that its operating temperature will exceed the temperature specified in Table 402-3 for the type of insulation involved.

402-6. Minimum Size. Fixture wires shall not be smaller than No. 18.

402-7. Number of Conductors in Conduit. The number of fixture wires permitted in a single conduit shall be as given in Table 2 of Chapter 9.

402-8. Grounded-Conductor Identification. One conductor of fixture wires which is intended to be used as a grounded conductor shall be identified by means of stripes or by the means described in Section 400-22(a) through (e).

Table 402-3.   Fixture Wire

Trade Name	Type Letter	Insulation	AWG	Thickness of Insulation (Mils)	Outer Covering	Max. Operating Temp.	Application Provisions
Heat-Resistant Rubber-Covered Fixture Wire Solid or 7-Strand	RFH-1	Heat-Resistant Rubber	18	15	Nonmetallic Covering	75°C 167°F	Fixture wiring. Limited to 300 volts.
	RFH-2	Heat-Resistant Rubber	18-16	30	Nonmetallic Covering	75°C 167°F	Fixture wiring, and as permitted in Sections 725-16 and 760-16.
		Heat-Resistant Latex Rubber	18-16	18			
Heat-Resistant Cross-Linked Synthetic Polymer-Insulated Fixture Wire—Solid or Stranded	RFHH-2	Cross-Linked Synthetic Polymer	18-16	30	None or Nonmetallic Covering	90°C 194°F	Fixture wiring, and as permitted in Sections 725-16 and 760-16. Multiconductor cable as permitted in Sections 725-16 and 760-16.
	RFHH-3		18-16	45			
Heat-Resistant Rubber-Covered Fixture Wire Flexible Stranding	FFH-1	Heat-Resistant Rubber	18	15	Nonmetallic Covering	75°C 167°F	Fixture wiring. Limited to 300 volts.
	FFH-2	Heat-Resistant Rubber	18-16	30	Nonmetallic Covering	75°C 167°F	Fixture wiring, and as permitted in Section 725-16.
		Heat-Resistant Latex Rubber	18-16	18			

Table 402-3 (Continued)

	Type	Insulation	AWG	Outer Covering	Max. Temp.	Application
Thermoplastic-Covered Fixture Wire—Solid or 7-Strand	TF	Thermoplastic	18-16 30	None	60°C 140°F	Fixture wiring, and as permitted in Sections 725-16 and 760-16.
Thermoplastic-Covered Fixture Wire—Flexible Stranding	TFF	Thermoplastic	18-16 30	None	60°C 140°F	Fixture wiring, and as permitted in Section 725-16.
Heat-Resistant Thermoplastic-Covered Fixture Wire—Solid or 7-Strand	TFN	Thermoplastic	18-16 15	Nylon Jacketed or equivalent	90°C 194°F	Fixture wiring, and as permitted in Sections 725-16 and 760-16.
Heat-Resistant Thermoplastic-Covered Fixture Wire—Flexible Stranded	TFFN	Thermoplastic	18-16 15	Nylon Jacketed or equivalent	90°C 194°F	Fixture wiring, and as permitted in Section 725-16.
Cotton-Covered, Heat-Resistant, Fixture Wire	CF	Impregnated Cotton	18-14 30	None	90°C 194°F	Fixture wiring. Limited to 300 volts.

Table 402-3 (Continued)

Trade Name	Type Letter	Insulation	AWG	Thickness of Insulation		Outer Covering	Max. Operating Temp.	Application Provisions
				Thickness of Moisture-Resistant Insulation Mils	Thickness of Asbestos Mils			
Asbestos Covered Heat-Resistant Fixture Wire	AF	Impregnated Asbestos or Moisture-Resistant Insulation and Impregnated Asbestos	18-14 / 12-10	— 20 / — 25	30 10 / 45 20	None	150°C 302°F	Fixture wiring. Limited to 300 volts and indoor dry locations.
Silicone Insulated Fixture Wire Solid or 7-Strand	SF-1	Silicone Rubber	18............	15		Nonmetallic Covering	200°C 392°F	Fixture wiring. Limited to 300 volts.
	SF-2	Silicone Rubber	18-14............	30		Nonmetallic Covering	200°C 392°F	Fixture wiring, and as permitted in Sections 725-16 and 760-16.
Silicone Insulated Fixture Wire Flexible Stranding	SFF-1	Silicone Rubber	18............	15		Nonmetallic Covering	150°C 302°F	Fixture wiring. Limited to 300 volts.
	SFF-2	Silicone Rubber	18-14	30		Nonmetallic Covering	150°C 302°F	Fixture wiring, and as permitted in Section 725-16.

Table 402-3 (Continued)

Trade Name	Type Letter	Insulation	AWG	Outer Covering	Temperature	Application Provisions
Fluorinated Ethylene Propylene Fixture Wire Solid or 7-Strand	PF PGF	Fluorinated Ethylene Propylene	18-14 ......20 18-14 14	None Glass Braid	200°C 392°F	Fixture wiring, and as permitted in Sections 725-16 and 760-16.
Fluorinated Ethylene Propylene Fixture Wire Flexible Stranding	PFF PGFF	Fluorinated Ethylene Propylene	18-14 ......20 18-14 14	None Glass Braid	150°C 302°F	Fixture wiring, and as permitted in Section 725-16.
Tape Insulated Fixture Wire Solid or 7-Strand	KF-1	Aromatic Polyimide Tape	18-10 ......5.5	None	200°C 392°F	Fixture wiring. Limited to 300 volts.
	KF-2	Aromatic Polyimide Tape	18-10 ......8.4	None	200°C 392°F	Fixture wiring, and as permitted in Sections 725-16 and 760-16.
Tape Insulated Fixture Wire Flexible Stranding	KFF-1	Aromatic Polyimide Tape	18-10 ......5.5	None	200°C 392°F	Fixture wiring. Limited to 300 volts.
	KFF-2	Aromatic Polyimide Tape	18-10 ......8.4	None	200°C 392°F	Fixture wiring, and as permitted in Section 725-16.
ECTFE Solid or 7-Strand	HF	Ethylene Chloro Trifluoro Ethylene	18-14 15	None	150°C 302°F	Fixture wiring, and as permitted in Section 725-16.

Table 402-3 (Continued)

Trade Name	Type Letter	Insulation	AWG	Thickness of Insulation Mils	Outer Covering	Max. Operating Temp.	Application Provisions
ECTFE Flexible Stranding	HFF	Ethylene Chloro Trifluoro Ethylene	18-14	15	None	150°C 302°F	Fixture wiring, and as permitted in Section 725-16.
Crosslinked Polyolefin Insulated Fixture Wire Solid or 7-Strand	XF	Crosslinked Polyolefin	18-14 12-10	30 45	None	150°C 302°F	Fixture wiring. Limited to 300 volts.
Crosslinked Polyolefin Insulated Fixture Wire Flexible Stranded	XFF	Crosslinked Polyolefin	18-14 12-10	30 45	None	150°C 302°F	Fixture wiring. Limited to 300 volts.
Modified ETFE Solid or 7-Strand	ZF	Modified Ethylene Tetrafluoroethylene	18-14	15	None	150°C 302°F	Fixture wiring, and as permitted in Sections 725-16 and 760-16.
Flexible Stranding	ZFF	Modified Ethylene Tetrafluoroethylene	18-14	15	None	150°C 302°F	Fixture wiring, and as permitted in Section 725-16.

Table 402-3 (Continued)

Extruded Polytetrafluoroethylene Solid or 7-Strand (Nickel or Nickel-Coated Copper)	PTF	Extruded Polytetrafluoroethylene	18-14	None	250°C 482°F	Fixture wiring, and as permitted in Sections 725-16 and 760-16. (Nickel or nickel-coated copper)
Extruded Polytetrafluoroethylene Flexible Stranding (No. 26-36 AWG Silver or Nickel-Coated Copper)	PTFF	Extruded Polytetrafluoroethylene	18-14	None	150°C 302°F	Fixture wiring, and as permitted in Section 725-16. (Silver or nickel-coated copper)
Perfluoroalkoxy Solid or 7-Strand (Nickel or Nickel-Coated Copper)	PAF	Perfluoroalkoxy	18-14	None	250°C 482°F	Fixture wiring, and as permitted in Sections 725-16 and 760-16. (Nickel or nickel-coated copper)
Perfluoroalkoxy Flexible Stranding	PAFF	Perfluoroalkoxy	18-14	None	150°C 302°F	Fixture wiring, and as permitted in Section 725-16.

402-9. Marking.

(a) **Required Information.** All fixture wires shall be marked to indicate the information required in Section 310-11(a).

(b) **Method of Marking.** Thermoplastic-insulated fixture wire shall be durably marked on the surface at intervals not exceeding 24 inches (610 mm). All other fixture wire shall be marked by means of a printed tag attached to the coil, reel, or carton.

402-10. Uses Permitted. Fixture wires shall be permitted: (1) for installation in lighting fixtures and in similar equipment where enclosed or protected and not subject to bending or twisting in use, or (2) for connecting lighting fixtures to the branch-circuit conductors supplying the fixtures.

402-11. Uses Not Permitted. Fixture wires shall not be used as branch-circuit conductors.

Exception: As permitted by Section 725-16 for Class 1 circuits and Section 760-16 for fire protective signaling circuits.

402-12. Overcurrent Protection. Overcurrent protection for fixture wires shall be as specified in Section 240-4.

ARTICLE 410 — LIGHTING FIXTURES, LAMPHOLDERS, LAMPS, RECEPTACLES, AND ROSETTES

Contents

A. General

410-1. Scope. This article covers lighting fixtures, lampholders, pendants, receptacles, and rosettes, incandescent filament lamps, arc lamps, electric-discharge lamps, the wiring and equipment forming part of such lamps, fixtures and lighting installations which shall conform to the provisions of this article.

Exception: As otherwise provided in this Code.

410-2. Application to Other Articles. Equipment for use in hazardous (classified) locations shall conform to Articles 500 through 517.

410-3. Live Parts. Fixtures, lampholders, lamps, rosettes, and receptacles shall have no live parts normally exposed to contact. Exposed accessible terminals in lampholders, receptacles, and switches shall not be installed in metal fixture canopies or in open bases of portable table or floor lamps.

Exception: Cleat-type lampholders, receptacles, and rosettes located at least 8 feet (2.44 m) above the floor shall be permitted to have exposed contacts.

B. Fixture Locations

410-4. Fixtures in Specific Locations.

Underwriters Laboratories Inc. (UL) publishes a pamphlet titled: "Fixture Marking Guide." This pamphlet was developed to help electrical inspectors quickly determine whether common types of UL listed fluorescent and incandescent fixtures are installed correctly. It is available from UL.

(a) Wet and Damp Locations. Fixtures installed in wet or damp locations shall be so installed that water cannot enter or accumulate in wireways, lampholders, or other electrical parts. All fixtures installed in wet locations shall be marked, "Suitable for Wet Locations." All fixtures installed in damp locations shall be marked, "Suitable for Wet Locations" or "Suitable for Damp Locations."

Installations underground or in concrete slabs or masonry in direct contact with the earth, and locations subject to saturation with water or other liquids, such as locations exposed to weather and unprotected, vehicle washing areas, and like locations, shall be considered to be wet locations with respect to the above requirement.

Interior locations protected from weather but subject to moderate degrees of moisture, such as some basements, some barns, some cold-storage warehouses and the like, the partially protected locations under canopies, marquees, roofed open porches, and the like, shall be considered to be damp locations with respect to the above requirement.

(FPN): See Article 680 for lighting fixtures in swimming pools, fountains, and similar installations.

Fixtures marked "Suitable for Wet Locations" are to be used where exposed to the weather or where subject to water saturation. Construction, design, and installation are to be such as to prevent the entrance of rain, snow, ice, and dust. Outdoor parks and parking lots, outdoor recreational areas (tennis, golf, baseball, etc.), car wash areas, and building exteriors are areas which would be considered "wet locations."

Areas protected from the weather and not subject to water saturation, but exposed to moisture, such as the underside of store or gasoline station canopies, or theater marquees, some cold-storage warehouses, some agricultural buildings, some basements, and roofed open porches and carports may be considered "damp locations" and fixtures are to be marked "Suitable for Damp Locations." See definition of "Damp Location," "Dry Location," and "Wet Location," under "Location" in Article 100, Definitions.

(b) Corrosive Locations. Fixtures installed in corrosive locations shall be of a type suitable for such locations.

(FPN): See Section 210-7 for receptacles in fixtures.

(c) In Ducts or Hoods. Fixtures shall be permitted to be installed in cooking hoods of nonresidential occupancies where all of the following conditions are met:

(1) The fixture shall be identified for use within commercial cooking hoods and installed so that the temperature limits of the materials used are not exceeded.

(2) The fixture shall be so constructed that all exhaust vapors, grease, oil or cooking vapors are excluded from the lamp and wiring compartment. Diffusers shall be resistant to thermal shock.

(3) Parts of the fixture exposed within the hood shall be noncorrosive or protected against corrosion and the surface shall be smooth so as not to collect deposits and facilitate cleaning.

(4) Wiring methods and materials supplying the fixture(s) shall not be exposed within the cooking hood.

(FPN): See Section 110-11.

The requirements for this section were initially taken from NFPA 96, Removal of Smoke and Grease-Laden Vapors from Commercial Cooking Equipment. NFPA 96 covers the basic requirements for the design, installation, and use of exhaust system components including (1) hoods, (2) grease-removal devices, (3) exhaust ducts, (4) dampers, (5) air-moving devices, (6) auxiliary equipment, and (7) fire extinguishing equipment for the exhaust system and the cooking equipment used therewith in commercial, industrial, institutional, and similar cooking applications. This standard does not apply to installations for normal residential family use.

Grease can cause short circuits or grounds in wiring, hence the requirement prohibiting wiring methods and materials (raceways, cables, lampholders, etc.) within ducts or hoods. Conventional enclosed and gasketed fixtures located in the path of travel of exhaust products are not acceptable because a fire could result from the high temperatures on grease-coated glass bowls or globes enclosing the lamps. Recessed or surface fixtures intended for location within hoods are required to be identified as suitable for the specific purpose, and should be installed with the required clearances maintained.

(d) Pendants. No parts of hanging fixtures or pendants shall be located within a zone measured 3 feet (914 mm) horizontally and 8 feet (2.44 mm) vertically from the top of the bathtub rim. This zone is all encompassing and includes the zone directly over the tub.

Section 410-4(d) was revised for the 1984 *Code.* The intent is to keep the fixture out of reach of a person when standing on the bathtub. See Figure 410-1.

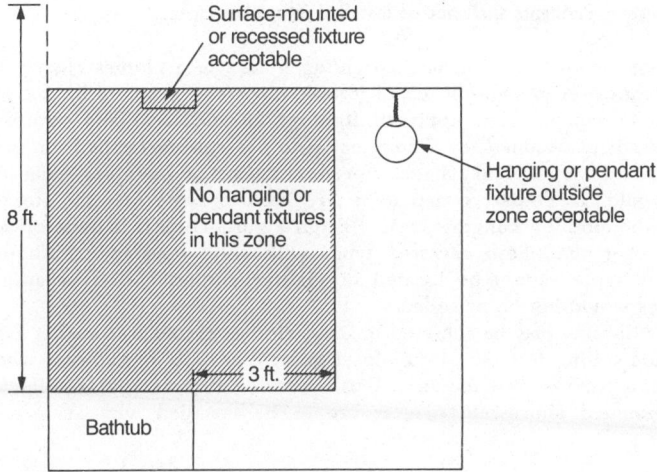

Figure 410-1. Fixtures located in bathrooms.

410-5. Fixtures Near Combustible Material. Fixtures shall be so constructed, or installed, or equipped with shades or guards that combustible material will not be subjected to temperatures in excess of 90°C (194°F).

410-6. Fixtures Over Combustible Material. Lampholders installed over highly combustible material shall be of the unswitched type. Unless an individual switch is provided for each fixture, lampholders shall be located at least 8 feet (2.44 m) above the floor, or shall be so located or guarded that the lamps cannot be readily removed or damaged.

This refers to pendants and fixed lighting equipment installed above highly combustible material. Where the lamp cannot be located out of reach, the requirement can be met by equipping the lamp with a suitable guard. This section does not refer to portable lamps.

410-7. Fixtures in Show Windows. Externally wired fixtures shall not be used in a show window.

Exception: Fixtures of the chain-supported type may be externally wired.

410-8. Fixtures in Clothes Closets.

(a) Location. A fixture in a clothes closet shall be permitted to be installed:

(1) On the wall above the closet door, provided the clearance between the fixture and a storage area where combustible material may be stored within the closet is not less than 18 inches (457 mm), or

(2) On the ceiling over an area which is unobstructed to the floor, maintaining an 18-inch (457-mm) clearance horizontally between the fixture and a storage area where combustible material may be stored within the closet.

A flush recessed fixture with a solid lens or a ceiling-mounted fluorescent fixture shall be permitted to be installed provided there is a 6-inch (152-mm) clearance, horizontally, between the fixture and the storage area.

ARTICLE 410—LIGHTING FIXTURES, ETC.

(b) Pendants. Pendants shall not be installed in clothes closets.

It is not mandatory to install a lighting fixture in a clothes closet; if one is installed, however, the conditions of installation are as required by this section.

The requirements here apply to lighting, incandescent and fluorescent, in various kinds of occupancies. The intent is to prevent hot lamps from coming in contact with cartons, blankets, etc., stored on shelves and clothing hung in closets which would, of course, constitute a fire hazard. Note that the storage area includes the clothing hanging area.   From Figure 410-2 it is quite obvious that fixtures other than flush recessed types with solid lens and ceiling-mounted fluorescent types cannot be located in shallow clothes closets because proper clearances would not be provided.

Proper lighting may be achieved in small clothes closets by locating fixtures on the outside ceiling in front of the closet door, especially in hallways where such fixtures can serve a dual function. Flush recessed fixtures with a solid lens and ceiling-mounted fluorescent fixtures are to be installed with at least a 6-in. clearance.

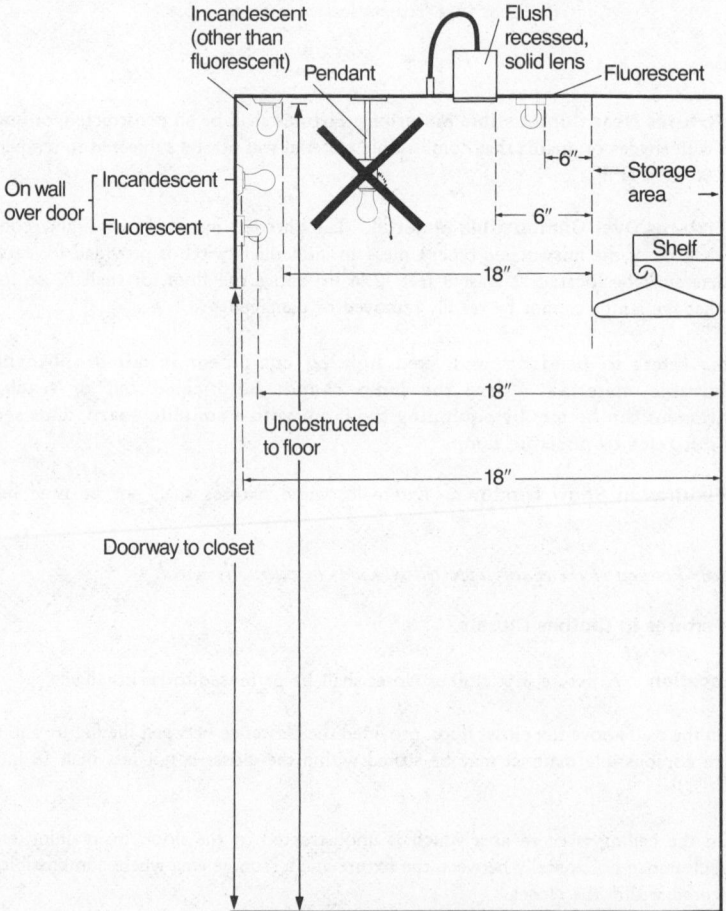

Figure 410-2. Lighting fixtures are required to be installed in clothes' closets so as to maintain the minimum clearances shown above. Pendants are prohibited.

410-9. Space for Cove Lighting. Coves shall have adequate space and shall be so located that lamps and equipment can be properly installed and maintained.

Adequate space permits easy access for relamping fixtures or replacing sockets, ballasts, etc., and also improves ventilation.

C. Provisions at Fixture Outlet Boxes, Canopies, and Pans

410-10. Space for Conductors. Canopies and outlet boxes taken together shall provide adequate space so that fixture conductors and their connecting devices can be properly installed.

410-11. Temperature Limit of Conductors in Outlet Boxes. Fixtures shall be of such construction or so installed that the conductors in outlet boxes shall not be subjected to temperatures greater than that for which the conductors are rated.

Branch-circuit wiring shall not be passed through an outlet box that is an integral part of an incandescent fixture unless the fixture is identified for through wiring.

Branch-circuit conductors run to a lighting outlet box are not to be subjected to greater temperatures than those for which they are rated. For example, conductors are rated 60°C (140°F) and are to supply a ceiling outlet box for the connection of a surface-mounted incandescent fixture or attached outlet box of a recessed fixture. The design and installation of the fixture should be such that the heat of the incandescent lamps does not subject the conductors to a greater temperature than 60°C (140°F). These types of fixtures are listed by Underwriters Laboratories Inc. based on the heat-contributing factor of the supply conductors at not more than the maximum permitted lamp wattage of the fixture.

Figure 410-3 illustrates a recessed fixture listed by UL for one set of supply conductors, and Figure 410-4 illustrates a fixture listed for a "feed through" installation.

The following paragraph is an excerpt from the Underwriters Laboratories Inc. Electrical Construction Materials List:

With the exception of fluorescent-lamp fixtures, recessed fixtures are marked with the required minimum temperature rating of wiring supplying the fixture. Unless marked in combination with the listing mark "Maximum of _____ No. _____ AWG branch-circuit conductors suitable for at least _____°C (_____°F) permitted in junction box," no allowance has been made for any heat contributed by branch-circuit conductors which pass through, or supply and pass through, an outlet box or other splice compartment which is part of the fixture.

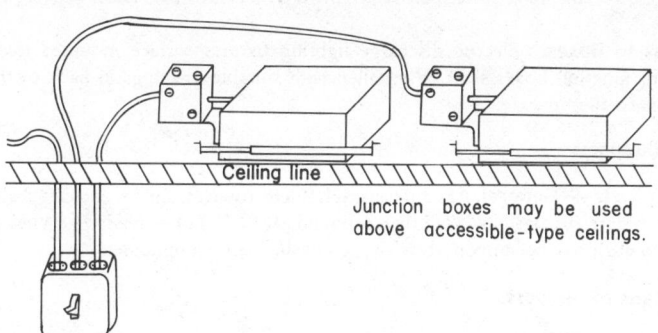

Junction boxes may be used above accessible-type ceilings.

Figure 410-3. Branch-circuit conductors terminating at each fixture (no feed-through).

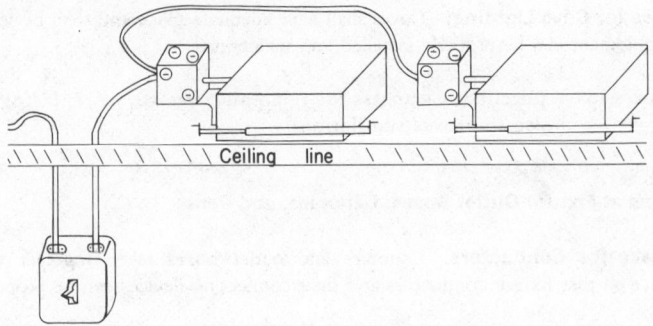

Figure 410-4. Lighting fixtures that are designed for "feed-through" branch-circuit conductors.

410-12. Outlet Boxes to Be Covered. In a completed installation, each outlet box shall be provided with a cover unless covered by means of a fixture canopy, lampholder, receptacle, rosette, or similar device.

Lighting fixtures are to be designed and installed not only to prevent overheating of conductors but also to prevent overheating of adjacent combustible wall or ceiling finishes. Hence, the requirement that any combustible finish between the edge of a fixture canopy and an outlet box be covered with a noncombustible material or fixture accessory. See Section 370-11 for requirements covering noncombustible finishes.

Where lighting fixtures are not directly mounted on outlet boxes, suitable outlet box covers are to be provided.

410-13. Covering of Combustible Material at Outlet Boxes. Any combustible wall or ceiling finish exposed between the edge of a fixture canopy or pan and an outlet box shall be covered with noncombustible material.

See commentary following Section 410-12.

410-14. Connection of Electric-Discharge Lighting Fixtures.

(a) Independently of the Outlet Box. Where electric-discharge lighting fixtures are supported independently of the outlet box, they shall be connected through metal raceways, metal-clad cables, or nonmetallic-sheathed cables.

Exception: Cord-connected fixtures shall be permitted as provided in Sections 410-30(b) and (c).

(b) Access to Boxes. Electric discharge lighting fixtures surface mounted over concealed outlet, pull, or junction boxes shall be installed with suitable openings in back of the fixture to provide access to the boxes.

D. Fixture Supports

410-15. Supports — General. Fixtures, lampholders, rosettes, and receptacles shall be securely supported. A fixture that weighs more than 6 pounds (2.72 kg) or exceeds 16 inches (406 mm) in any dimension shall not be supported by the screw shell of a lampholder.

410-16. Means of Support.

(a) Outlet Boxes. Where the outlet box or fitting will provide adequate support, a fixture shall be attached thereto or be supported as required by Section 370-13 for boxes. A fixture that weighs more than 50 pounds (22.7 kg) shall be supported independently of the outlet box.

(b) Inspection. Fixtures shall be so installed that the connections between the fixture conductors and the circuit conductors can be inspected without requiring the disconnection of any part of the wiring.

Exception: Fixtures connected by attachment plugs and receptacles.

(c) Suspended Ceilings. Framing members of suspended ceiling systems used to support fixtures shall be securely fastened to each other and shall be securely attached to the building structure at appropriate intervals. Fixtures so supported shall be securely fastened to the ceiling framing member by mechanical means, such as bolts, screws, or rivets. Clips identified for use with the type of ceiling framing member(s) and fixture(s) shall also be permitted.

(d) Fixture Studs. Fixture studs that are not a part of outlet boxes, hickeys, tripods, and crowfeet shall be made of steel, malleable iron, or other material suitable for the application.

(e) Insulating Joints. Insulating joints that are not designed to be mounted with screws or bolts shall have an exterior metal casing, insulated from both screw connections.

(f) Raceway Fittings. Raceway fittings used to support lighting fixture(s) shall be capable of supporting the weight of the complete fixture assembly and lamp(s).

Whether a lighting fixture is attached to an outlet box or supported independently of the outlet box, care should be taken to securely and rigidly fasten the outlet box or support the independent rod or pipe hanger (as shown in Figure 370-4).

So-called drop-in fixtures or surface mounted fixtures are to be securely fastened to the framing members of "hung" or suspended ceilings by mechanical means, such as bolts, screws, or rivets, or clips identified for use with the type of ceiling framing member(s) and fixture(s), and no other support of the fixture is necessary. However, the suspended ceiling framing members must be securely attached to each other and to the building structure and, also, additional supporting wires, rods, etc., may be necessary to provide ample support of the ceiling in areas where fixtures are installed.

(g) Busways. Fixtures shall be permitted to be connected to busways in accordance with Section 364-12.

E. Grounding

410-17. General. Fixtures and lighting equipment shall be grounded as provided in Part E of this article.

410-18. Exposed Fixture Parts.

(a) With Exposed Conductive Parts. The exposed conductive parts of lighting fixtures and equipment directly wired or attached to outlets supplied by a wiring method which provides an equipment ground shall be grounded.

(b) Made of Insulating Material. Fixtures directly wired or attached to outlets supplied by a wiring method which does not provide a ready means for grounding shall be made of insulating material and shall have no exposed conductive parts.

410-19. Equipment Over 150 Volts to Ground.

(a) Metal Fixtures, Transformers, and Transformer Enclosures. Metal fixtures, transformers, and transformer enclosures on circuits operating at over 150 volts to ground shall be grounded.

(b) Other Exposed Metal Parts. Other exposed metal parts shall be grounded or insulated from ground and other conducting surfaces and inaccessible to unqualified persons.

Exception: Lamp tie wires, mounting screws, clips, and decorative bands on glass lamps spaced not less than 1½ inches (38 mm) from lamp terminals shall not be required to be grounded.

410-20. Equipment Grounding Conductor Attachment. Fixtures with exposed metal parts shall be provided with a means for connecting an equipment grounding conductor for such fixtures.

410-21. Methods of Grounding. Equipment shall be considered grounded where mechanically connected in a permanent and effective manner to metal raceway, the armor of armored cable, mineral-insulated, metal-sheathed cable, and the continuous sheath of Type MC cable, the grounding conductor in nonmetallic-sheathed cable, or to a separate grounding conductor sized in accordance with Table 250-95, provided that the raceway, armor, or grounding conductor is grounded in a manner specified in Article 250.

F. Wiring of Fixtures

410-22. Fixture Wiring — General. Wiring on or within fixtures shall be neatly arranged and shall not be exposed to physical damage. Excess wiring shall be avoided. Conductors shall be so arranged that they shall not be subjected to temperatures above those for which they are rated.

410-23. Polarization of Fixtures. Fixtures shall be so wired that the screw shells of lampholders will be connected to the same fixture or circuit conductor or terminal. The grounded conductor, where connected to a screw-shell lampholder, shall be connected to the screw shell.

410-24. Conductors.

(a) Insulation. Fixtures shall be wired with conductors having insulation suitable for the environmental conditions, current, voltage, and temperature to which the conductors will be subjected.

(b) Conductor Size. Fixture conductors shall not be smaller than No. 18.

(FPN): For ampacity of fixture wire, see Table 402-5.

(FPN): For maximum operating temperature and voltage limitation of fixture wires, see Section 402-3.

410-25. Conductors for Certain Conditions.

(a) Mogul-Base Lampholders. Fixtures provided with mogul-base, screw-shell lampholders and operating at not over 300 volts between conductors shall be wired with Type AF, SF-1, SF-2, SFF-1, SFF-2, PF, PGF, PFF, PGFF, PTF, PTFF, PAF, PAFF, XF, XFF, ZF or ZFF fixture wire.

(b) Other than Mogul-Base, Screw-Shell Lampholders. Fixtures provided with other than mogul-base, screw-shell lampholders and operating at not over 300 volts between conductors shall be wired with Type AF, SF-1, SF-2, PF, PGF, PFF, PGFF, PTF, PTFF, PAF, PAFF, XF, XFF, ZF or ZFF fixture wire or Type AFC or AFPD flexible cord.

Exception No. 1: Where temperatures do not exceed 90°C (194°F), Types CF, TFN and TFFN fixture wire or Type CFPD flexible cord shall be permitted.

Exception No. 2: Where temperatures exceed 60°C (140°F) but are not higher than 75°C (167°F), Types RH and RHW rubber-covered wire and Types RFH-1, RFH-2, FFH-1, and FFH-2 fixture wires shall be permitted.

Exception No. 3: Where temperatures do not exceed 60°C (140°F), Type T thermoplastic wire, Types TF and TFF fixture wires shall be permitted, including fixtures of decorative types on which lamps of not over 60-watt rating are used in connection with imitation candles.

(FPN): See Table 402-3 and Section 402-3 for fixture wires and conductors; and Table 400-5 for flexible cords.

410-27. Pendant Conductors for Incandescent Filament Lamps.

(a) Support. Pendant lampholders with permanently attached leads, where used for other than festoon wiring, shall be hung from separate stranded rubber-covered conductors that are soldered directly to the circuit conductors but supported independently thereof.

(b) Size. Such pendant conductors shall not be smaller than No. 14 for mogul-base or medium-base screw-shell lampholders, nor smaller than No. 18 for intermediate or candelabra-base lampholders.

Exception: Approved Christmas tree and decorative lighting outfits shall be permitted to be smaller than No. 18.

(c) Twisted or Cabled. Pendant conductors longer than 3 feet (914 mm) shall be twisted together where not cabled in a listed assembly.

410-28. Protection of Conductors and Insulation.

(a) Properly Secured. Conductors shall be secured in a manner that will not tend to cut or abrade the insulation.

(b) Protection Through Metal. Conductor insulation shall be protected from abrasion where it passes through metal.

(c) Fixture Stems. Splices and taps shall not be located within fixture arms or stems.

(d) Splices and Taps. No unnecessary splices or taps shall be made within or on a fixture.

(FPN): For approved means of making connections, see Section 110-14.

(e) Stranding. Stranded conductors shall be used for wiring on fixture chains and on other movable or flexible parts.

(f) Tension. Conductors shall be so arranged that the weight of the fixture or movable parts will not put a tension on the conductors.

410-29. Cord-Connected Showcases.
Individual showcases, other than fixed, shall be permitted to be connected by flexible cord to permanently installed receptacles, and groups of not more than six such showcases shall be permitted to be coupled together by flexible cord and separable locking-type connectors with one of the group connected by flexible cord to a permanently installed receptacle.

The installation shall comply with the following requirements:

(a) Cord Requirements. Flexible cord shall be hard-service type, having conductors not smaller than the branch-circuit conductors, having ampacity at least equal to the branch-circuit overcurrent device, and having an equipment grounding conductor.

(FPN): See Table 250-95 for size of grounding conductor.

(b) Receptacles, Connectors, and Attachment Plugs. Receptacles, connectors, and attachment plugs shall be of a listed grounding type rated 15- or 20-amperes.

(c) Support. Flexible cords shall be secured to the undersides of showcases so that: (1) wiring will not be exposed to mechanical damage; (2) a separation between cases not in excess of 2 inches (50.8 mm), nor more than 12 inches (305 mm) between the first case and the supply receptacle will be assured; and (3) the free lead at the end of a group of showcases will have a female fitting not extending beyond the case.

(d) No Other Equipment. Equipment other than showcases shall not be electrically connected to showcases.

(e) Secondary Circuit(s). Where showcases are cord connected, the secondary circuit(s) of electric discharge lighting shall be limited to one showcase.

410-30. Cord-Connected Lampholders and Fixtures.

(a) Lampholders. Where a metal lampholder is attached to a flexible cord, the inlet shall be equipped with an insulating bushing which, if threaded, shall not be smaller than nominal ⅜-inch pipe size. The cord hole shall be of a size appropriate for the cord, and all burrs and fins shall be removed in order to provide a smooth bearing surface for the cord.

Metal (brass-shell and aluminum-shell type) lampholders used with flexible cord pendants should be equipped with smooth and permanently secured insulating bushings. Nonmetallic-type lampholders do not require a bushing because the material and design afford equivalent protection.

Bushing having holes ⁹⁄₃₂ inch (7.14 mm) in diameter shall be permitted for use with plain pendant cord and holes ¹³⁄₃₂ inch (10.3 mm) in diameter with reinforced cord.

(b) Adjustable Fixtures. Fixtures which require adjusting or aiming after installation shall not be required to be equipped with an attachment plug or cord connector provided the exposed cord is of the hard usage or extra-hard usage type and is not longer than that required for maximum adjustment. The cord shall not be subject to strain or physical damage.

(c) Electric-Discharge Fixtures. It shall be permissible to locate cord-equipped fixtures directly below the outlet box, if the cord is continuously visible for its entire length outside the fixture and is not subject to strain or physical damage. Such cord-equipped fixtures shall terminate at the outer end of the cord in a grounding-type attachment plug (cap) or busway plug.
Electric-discharge lighting fixtures provided with mogul-base, screw-shell lampholders shall be permitted to be connected to branch circuits of 50 amperes or less by cords complying with Section 240-4. Receptacles and attachment plugs shall be permitted to be of lower ampere rating than the branch circuit but not less than 125 percent of the fixture full-load current.
Electric-discharge lighting fixtures equipped with a flanged surface inlet shall be permitted to be supplied by cord pendants equipped with cord connectors. Inlets and connectors shall be permitted to be of lower ampere rating than the branch circuit but not less than 125 percent of the fixture load current.

This section permits electric-discharge lighting fixtures to be connected by means of a continuously visible cord only where such cords are not used as a supporting means and the fixture is suspended directly below the outlet boxes supplying such fixtures. Electric-discharge lighting fixtures are not permitted to be supplied by cord where installed in lift-out-type ceilings. Electric-discharge fixtures are permitted to be connected to busways by cords plugged directly into the busway or suspended from the busway as permitted in Section 364-12.

410-31. Fixtures as Raceways. Fixtures shall not be used as a raceway for circuit conductors.

Exception No. 1: Fixtures listed for use as a raceway.

Fixtures approved for use as raceways are labeled by Underwriters Laboratories Inc. as "fixtures suitable for use as raceways."

Exception No. 2: Fixtures designed for end-to-end assembly to form a continuous raceway or fixtures connected together by recognized wiring methods shall be permitted to carry through conductors of a two-wire or multiwire branch circuit supplying the fixtures.

Exception No. 3: One additional two-wire branch circuit separately supplying one or more of the connected fixtures described in Exception No. 2 shall be permitted to be carried through the fixtures.

Exception No. 3 permits an additional 2-wire circuit to be carried through the fixtures to supply switched night lighting commonly used to conserve energy.

(FPN): See Article 100 for definition of multiwire branch circuit.

Branch-circuit conductors within 3 inches (76 mm) of a ballast within the ballast compartment shall be recognized for use at temperatures not lower than 90°C (194°F), such as Types RHH, THW, THHN, FEP, FEPB, SA, XHHW, and AVA.

G. Construction of Fixtures

410-34. Combustible Shades and Enclosures.   Adequate air space shall be provided between lamps and shades or other enclosures of combustible material.

410-35. Fixture Rating.

(a) Marking.   All fixtures requiring ballasts or transformers shall be plainly marked with their electrical rating and the manufacturer's name, trademark, or other suitable means of identification. A fixture requiring supply wire rated higher than 90°C shall be so marked, in letters ¼ inch (6.35 mm) high prominently displayed on the fixture and shipping carton or equivalent.

(b) Electrical Rating.   The electrical rating shall include the voltage and frequency and shall indicate the current rating of the unit, including the ballast, transformer, or autotransformer.

410-36. Design and Material.   Fixtures shall be constructed of metal, wood, or other material suitable for the application and shall be so designed and assembled as to secure requisite mechanical strength and rigidity. Wireways, including their entrances, shall be such that conductors may be drawn in and withdrawn without injury.

410-37. Nonmetallic Fixtures.   In all fixtures not made entirely of metal or noncombustible material, wireways shall be lined with metal.

Exception: Where armored or lead-covered conductors with suitable fittings are used.

410-38. Mechanical Strength.

(a) Tubing for Arms.   Tubing used for arms and stems where provided with cut threads shall not be less than 0.040 inch (0.1 mm) in thickness and where provided with rolled (pressed) threads shall not be less than 0.025 inch (0.635 mm) in thickness. Arms and other parts shall be fastened to prevent turning.

(b) Metal Canopies. Metal canopies supporting lampholders, shades, etc., exceeding 8 pounds (3.63 kg), or incorporating attachment-plug receptacles, shall not be less than 0.020 inch (508 micrometers) in thickness. Other canopies shall not be less than 0.016 inch (406 micrometers) if made of steel and not less than 0.020 inch (508 micrometers) if of other metals.

(c) Canopy Switches. Pull-type canopy switches shall not be inserted in the rims of metal canopies that are less than 0.025 inch (635 micrometers) in thickness unless the rims are reinforced by the turning of a bead or the equivalent. Pull-type canopy switches, whether mounted in the rims or elsewhere in sheet metal canopies, shall not be located more than 3½ inches (89 mm) from the center of the canopy. Double set-screws, double canopy rings, a screw ring, or equal method shall be used where the canopy supports a pull-type switch or pendant receptacle.

The above thickness requirements shall apply to measurements made on finished (formed) canopies.

410-39. Wiring Space. Bodies of fixtures, including portable lamps, shall provide ample space for splices and taps and for the installation of devices, if any. Splice compartments shall be of nonabsorbent, noncombustible material.

410-42. Portable Lamps.

(a) General. Portable lamps shall be wired with flexible cord, recognized by Section 400-4 and an attachment plug of the polarized or grounding type. When used with Edison-based lampholders, the grounded conductor shall be identified and attached to the screw shell and the identified blade of the attachment plug.

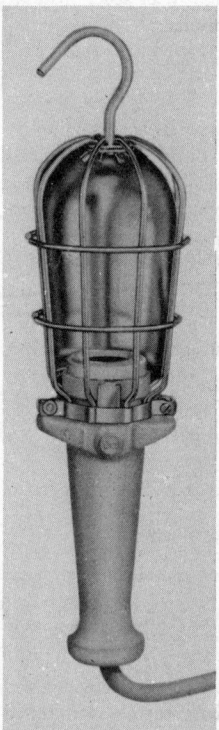

Figure 410-5. A portable handlamp with a grounded metallic guard and reflector, and a swivel-type hook that permits positioning the lamp in any location. (*Daniel Woodhead Co.*)

(b) Portable Handlamps. In addition to the provisions of Section 410-42(a), portable handlamps shall comply with the following: (1) metal shell, paperlined lampholders shall not be used; (2) handlamps shall be equipped with a handle of molded composition or other insulating material; (3) handlamps shall be equipped with a substantial guard attached to the lampholder or handle; (4) metallic guards shall be grounded by the means of an equipment grounding conductor run with circuit conductors within the power supply cord.

410-44. Cord Bushings. A bushing or the equivalent shall be provided where flexible cord enters the base or stem of a portable lamp. The bushing shall be of insulating material unless a jacketed type of cord is used.

410-45. Tests. All wiring shall be free from short circuits and grounds and shall be tested for these defects prior to being connected to the circuit.

410-46. Live Parts. Exposed live parts within porcelain fixtures shall be suitably recessed and so located as to make it improbable that wires will come in contact with them. There shall be a spacing of at least ½ inch (12.7 mm) between live parts and the mounting plane of the fixture.

H. Installation of Lampholders

410-47. Screw-Shell Type. Lampholders of the screw-shell type shall be installed for use as lampholders only. Where supplied by a circuit having a grounded conductor, the grounded conductor shall be connected to the screw shell.

In past years it was common practice to install screw-shell lampholders with screw-shell adapters in baseboards and walls for connecting cord-connected appliances and lighting equipment. This now prohibited practice permitted exposed live parts to be contacted by persons when the adapters were removed.

See Section 410-56(a) for permitted uses of receptacles.

410-48. Double-Pole Switched Lampholders. Where used on unidentified two-wire circuits tapped from the ungrounded conductors of multiwire circuits, the switching device of lampholders of the switched type shall simultaneously disconnect both conductors of the circuit in accordance with Section 210-10.

Single-pole switching may be used to interrupt the ungrounded conductor of a 2-wire circuit having one conductor grounded. The grounded conductor is required to be connected to the screw shell of the socket.

Where a 2-wire circuit is tapped from two ungrounded conductors of a multiwire circuit (3- or 4-wire system) and used with switched lampholders, the switching device is required to be double-pole and simultaneously disconnect both ungrounded conductors of the circuit. See Section 410-52.

410-49. Lampholders in Wet or Damp Locations. Lampholders installed in wet or damp locations shall be of the weatherproof type.

J. Construction of Lampholders

410-50. Insulation. The outer metal shell and the cap shall be lined with insulating material which shall prevent the shell and cap from becoming a part of the circuit. The lining shall not extend beyond the metal shell more than ⅛ inch (3.17 mm), but shall prevent any current-carrying part of the lamp base from being exposed when a lamp is in the lampholding device.

410-51. Lead Wires. Lead wires, furnished as a part of weatherproof lampholders and intended to be exposed after installation, shall be of approved stranded, rubber-covered conductors not less than No. 14 and shall be sealed in place or otherwise made raintight.

Exception: No. 18 rubber-covered conductors shall be permitted for candelabra sockets.

410-52. Switched Lampholders. Switched lampholders shall be of such construction that the switching mechanism interrupts the electrical connection to the center contact. The switching mechanism shall also be permitted to interrupt the electrical connection to the screw shell if the connection to the center contact is simultaneously interrupted.

K. Lamps and Auxiliary Equipment

410-53. Bases, Incandescent Lamps. An incandescent lamp for general use on lighting branch circuits shall not be equipped with a medium base if rated over 300 watts, nor with a mogul base if rated over 1500 watts. Special bases or other devices shall be used for over 1500 watts.

410-54. Enclosures for Electric-Discharge Lamp Auxiliary Equipment. Auxiliary equipment for electric-discharge lamps shall be enclosed in noncombustible cases and treated as sources of heat.

Underwriters Laboratories Inc. provides the following information under Electric-Discharge Lamp Control Equipment, Ballasts, in the UL Electrical Construction Materials Directory.

OPEN TYPE:

Open core and coil constructions (i.e. ballasts without complete metal enclosures) are intended for use within suitable enclosures.

INDOOR BALLAST:

An indoor ballast is suitable for use in an indoor location only.

OUTDOOR BALLAST:

Outdoor Ballast, Type 1—Outdoor ballast, Type 1, is suitable for use in outdoor fixtures and outdoor signs or other outdoor equipment if the ballast is provided with a complete metal enclosure in addition to its own enclosure. Ballasts of this type are marked "Type 1 Outdoor" or "Type 1."

Outdoor Ballast, Type 2—Outdoor ballast, Type 2, is suitable for use in outdoor fixtures, outdoor signs, or other outdoor equipment if the ballast is provided with an enclosure (not necessarily metal) in addition to its own enclosure. Ballasts of this type are marked "Type 2 Outdoor" or "Type 2."

WEATHERPROOF BALLAST:

A weatherproof ballast is suitable for use where completely exposed to the weather without an additional enclosure and is marked "Weatherproof" or "WP."

410-55. Arc Lamps. Arc lamps used in theaters shall comply with Section 520-61, and arc lamps used in projection machines shall comply with Section 540-20. Arc lamps used on constant-current systems shall comply with the general requirements of Article 710.

L. Receptacles, Cord Connectors, and Attachment Plugs (Caps)

410-56. Rating and Type.

(a) Receptacles. Receptacles installed for the attachment of portable cords shall be rated at not less than 15 amperes, 125 volts, or 15 amperes, 250 volts, and shall be of a type not suitable for use as lampholders.

Exception: The use of receptacles of 10-ampere, 250-volt rating used in nonresidential occupancies for the supply of equipment other than portable hand tools, portable handlamps, and extension cords shall be permitted.

(b) CO/ALR Receptacles. Receptacles rated 20 amperes or less directly connected to aluminum conductors shall be marked CO/ALR.

This requires that 15- and 20-A receptacles directly connected to aluminum conductors be suitable for such use. If the receptacle is not of the CO/ALR type, it can be connected with a copper pigtail to an aluminum branch-circuit conductor if a wire connector suitable for such a connection, and marked with the letters "AL" and "CU," is used.

(c) Faceplates. Metal faceplates shall be of ferrous metal not less than 0.030 inch (762 micrometers) in thickness or of nonferrous metal not less than 0.040 inch (1 mm) in thickness. Metal faceplates shall be grounded. Faceplates of insulating material shall be noncombustible and not less than 0.10 inch (2.54 mm) in thickness but shall be permitted to be less than 0.10 inch (2.54 mm) in thickness if formed or reinforced to provide adequate mechanical strength.

(d) Position of Receptacle Faces. After installation, receptacle faces shall be flush with or project from faceplates of insulating material and shall project a minimum of 0.015 inch (381 micrometers) from metal faceplates. Faceplates shall be installed so as to completely cover the opening and seat against the mounting surface. Boxes shall be installed in accordance with Section 370-10.

(e) Attachment Plugs. All 15- and 20-ampere attachment plugs and connectors shall be so constructed that there are no exposed current-carrying parts except the prongs, blades, or pins. The cover for wire terminations shall be a part, which is essential for the operation of an attachment plug or connector (dead-front construction).

Paragraph (d) requires boxes to be properly and securely mounted to provide a solid backing for receptacles so that attachment plugs can be inserted or removed without difficulty.

The reason for requiring receptacles to project from metal faceplates is to prevent faults caused by attachment plugs with exposed bare terminal screws. The design requirements of paragraph (e) for attachment plugs (dead-front construction) should prevent such faults at metal plates with new devices; however, existing attachment plugs with terminal screws exposed on the face are still in use.

Mounting boxes properly (Sections 370-10 and 370-13) requires the cooperation of other crafts (plasterers, dry-wall applicators, carpenters, building designers, etc.), and the proper installation of receptacles and faceplates assures that attachment plugs can be fully inserted, thus providing a better contact.

(f) Attachment Plug Ejector Mechanisms. Attachment plug ejector mechanisms shall not adversely affect engagement of the blades of the attachment plug with the contacts of the receptacle.

Section 410-56(f) permits a device designed for use by the aged, infirm, and the blind to reduce the likelihood of damage to the cord when pulling on the cord to remove the plug.

(g) Noninterchangeability. Receptacles, cord connectors, and attachment plugs shall be constructed so that the receptacle or cord connectors will not accept an attachment plug with a different voltage or current rating than that for which the device is intended. Nongrounding-type receptacles and connectors shall not accept grounding-type attachment plugs.

See Figures 210-6 and 210-7 for ANSI C73 configuration chart.

Exception: A 20-ampere T-slot receptacle or cord connector shall be permitted to accept a 15-ampere attachment plug of the same voltage rating.

410-57. Receptacles in Damp or Wet Locations.

(a) Damp Locations. A receptacle installed outdoors in a location protected from the weather or in other damp locations shall have an enclosure for the receptacle that is weatherproof when the receptacle is covered (attachment plug cap not inserted and receptacle covers closed).

An installation suitable for wet locations shall also be considered suitable for damp locations.

A receptacle shall be considered to be in a location protected from the weather where located under roofed open porches, canopies, marquees, and the like, and will not be subjected to a beating rain or water run-off.

(b) Wet Locations. A receptacle installed outdoors where exposed to weather or in other wet locations shall be in a weatherproof enclosure, the integrity of which is not affected when the receptacle is in use (attachment plug cap inserted).

Exception: An enclosure that is weatherproof only when a self-closing receptacle cover is closed shall be permitted to be used for a receptacle installed outdoors where the receptacle is not to be used with other than portable tools or other portable equipment not left connected to the outlet indefinitely.

(c) Protection for Floor Receptacles. Standpipes of floor receptacles shall allow floor-cleaning equipment to be operated without damage to receptacles.

(d) Flush Mounting with Faceplate. The enclosure for a receptacle installed in an outlet box flush-mounted on a wall surface shall be made weatherproof by means of a weatherproof faceplate assembly that provides a watertight connection between the plate and the wall surface.

(e) Installation. A receptacle outlet installed outdoors shall be located so that water accumulation is not likely to touch the outlet cover or plate.

Outdoor receptacle outlets are required for one-family and two-family dwellings and for swimming pool areas and are very common at other locations, such as shopping centers for children's rides and decorative lighting, truck terminals for refrigeration units and motor warmers, marinas, mobile home and recreational vehicle sites, and various other outdoor locations.

In "wet" locations the receptacle outlet must remain weatherproof with the cover open and the attachment plug inserted, except for temporary uses of portable equipment.

The enclosure for an outdoor receptacle may be flush or surface mounted or supported by conduits and used with a variety of receptacles and covers; however, it is the installer's responsibility to provide a watertight seal.

410-58. Grounding-type Receptacles, Adapters, Cord Connectors, and Attachment Plugs.

(a) Grounding Poles. Grounding-type receptacles, cord connectors, and attachment plugs shall be provided with one fixed grounding pole in addition to the circuit poles.

Exception: The grounding contacting pole of grounding-type attachment plugs on the power supply cords of portable hand-held, hand-guided, or hand-supported tools or appliances shall be permitted to be of the movable self-restoring type on circuits operating at not over 150 volts between any two conductors nor over 150 volts between any conductor and ground.

(b) Grounding-Pole Identification. Grounding-type receptacles, adapters, cord connections and attachment plugs shall have a means for connection of a grounding conductor to the grounding pole. A terminal for connection to the grounding pole shall be designated by:

(1) A green-colored hexagonal headed or shaped terminal screw or nut, not readily removable; or

(2) A green-colored pressure wire connector body (a wire barrel); or

(3) A similar green-colored connection device in the case of adapters. The grounding terminal of a grounding adapter shall be a green-colored rigid ear, lug, or similar device. The grounding connection shall be so designed that it cannot make contact with current-carrying parts of the receptacle, adapter, or attachment plug. The adapter shall be polarized.

Subparagraph (b)(3) requires the grounding terminal of an adapter to be a green-colored ear, lug, or similar device, thereby prohibiting the recognition of an adapter with an attached pigtail grounding wire.

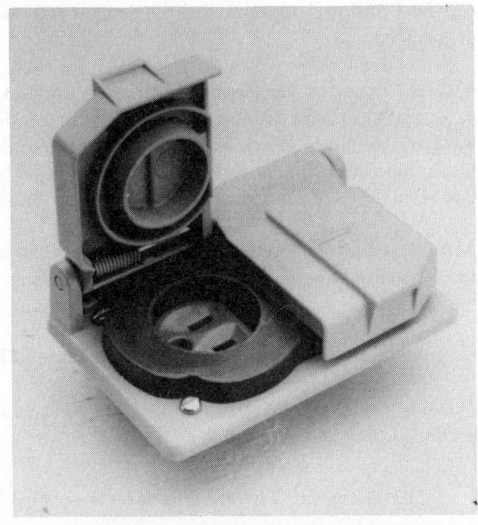

Figure 410-6. Weatherproof receptacle cover suitable for wet locations. (*Crouse-Hinds*)

(4) If the terminal for the equipment grounding conductor is not visible, the conductor entrance hole shall be marked with the word "Green" or otherwise identified by a distinctive green color.

(c) Grounding Terminal Use. A grounding terminal or grounding-type device shall not be used for purposes other than grounding.

(d) Grounding-Pole Requirements. Grounding-type attachment plugs and mating cord connectors and receptacles shall be so designed that the grounding connection is made before the current-carrying connections. Grounding-type devices shall be designed so grounding poles of attachment plugs cannot be brought into contact with current-carrying parts of receptacles or cord connectors.

The grounding member of the attachment plug is longer to ensure a "make-first break-last" grounding connection.

(e) Use. Grounding-type attachment plugs shall be used only where an equipment ground is to be provided.

M. Rosettes

The most common use for rosettes is to permit connection of a pendant fixture to open wiring on insulators or nonmetallic-sheathed cable without use of a box. See Section 300-15(b), Exception No. 2.

410-59. Unapproved Types.

(a) Fusible Rosettes. Fusible rosettes shall not be installed.

(b) Separable Rosettes. Separable rosettes that may change polarity shall not be used.

410-60. Rosettes in Damp or Wet Locations. Rosettes installed in damp or wet locations shall be of the weatherproof type.

410-61. Rating. Rosettes shall be rated at 660 watts, 250 volts, with a maximum current rating of 6 amperes.

410-62. Rosettes for Exposed Wiring. Rosettes for exposed wiring shall be provided with bases that shall have at least two holes for supporting screws, shall be high enough to keep the wires and terminals at least ½ inch (12.7 mm) from the surface wired over, and shall have a lug of insulating material under each terminal to prevent the rosette from being placed over projections that would reduce the separation to less than ½ inch (12.7 mm).

410-63. Rosettes for Use with Boxes or Raceways. Rosettes for use with conduit boxes or raceways shall have bases high enough to keep wires and terminals at least ⅜ inch (9.52 mm) from the surface wired over.

N. Special Provisions for Flush and Recessed Fixtures

410-64. General. Fixtures installed in recessed cavities in walls or ceilings shall comply with Sections 410-65 through 410-72.

The following Formal Interpretation No. FI 81-6 was issued in October, 1982 for the 1981 NEC:

Question: Is it intended that fixtures installed in suspended ceilings be subject to the requirements of Part N of Article 410?

Answer: Yes.

410-65. Temperature.

(a) Combustible Material. Fixtures shall be so installed that adjacent combustible material will not be subjected to temperatures in excess of 90°C (194°F).

(b) Fire-Resistant Construction. Where a fixture is recessed in fire-resistant material in a building of fire-resistant construction, a temperature higher than 90°C (194°F), but not higher than 150°C (302°F), shall be considered acceptable if the fixture is plainly marked that it is approved for that service.

(c) Recessed Incandescent Fixtures. Incandescent fixtures shall have thermal protection and shall so be identified as thermally protected.

Because many recessed incandescent fixtures are suitable for a wide variety of lamp sizes and types, and finish trims, the temperature close to the lamp can vary widely. Therefore, many manufacturers have chosen to locate their thermal protectors some distance from the source of heat, such as in the outlet box, and to design the protector so that it will detect a change in temperature resulting from the addition of thermal insulation around the fixture. This prevents "nuisance tripping" of the protector as a result of changing lamp wattage, for example, but still provides protection against gross overheating as a result of thermal insulation around a fixture not designed for such use.

Exception No. 1: Recessed incandescent fixtures identified for use and installed in poured concrete.

Exception No. 2: Recessed incandescent fixtures identified as suitable for installation in cavities where the thermal insulation will be in direct contact with the fixture.

Such fixtures are known as "Type IC" fixtures because of the marking required by UL on recessed-type incandescent (and HID) fixtures listed for use in insulated ceilings. Energy conservation measures have led to the installation of additional thermal insulation in attics. Many fires have been reported on recessed fixtures where thermal insulation, particularly blown-in insulation, is installed directly around the fixtures. The possibility of fire exists if the insulation is installed so as to entrap the heat of the fixture and prevent the free circulation of air.

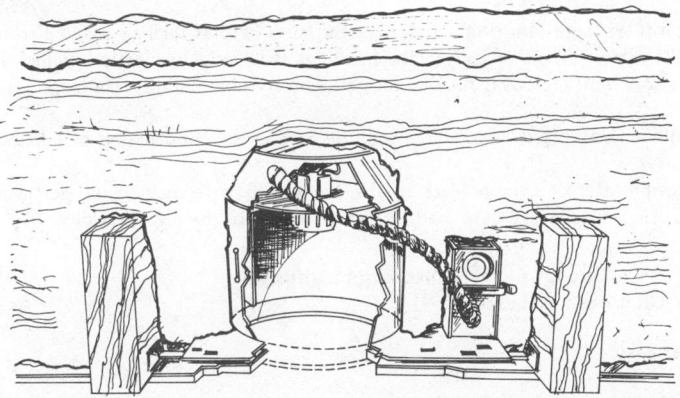

Figure 410-7. A listed recessed fixture suitable for use in insulated ceilings in direct contact with thermal insulation. (*Thomas Industries Inc.*)

410-66. Clearance and Installation.

(a) Clearance. Recessed portions of incandescent lighting fixture enclosures, other than at the points of support, shall be spaced at least ½ inch (12.7 mm) from combustible materials.

Exception: Recessed fixtures identified as suitable for insulation to be in direct contact with the fixture.

(b) Installation. Thermal insulation shall not be installed within 3 inches (76 mm) of the recessed fixture enclosure, wiring compartment, or ballast, and shall not be so installed above the fixture so as to entrap heat and prevent the free circulation of air.

ARTICLE 410—LIGHTING FIXTURES, ETC.

Exception: Recessed fixtures identified as suitable for insulation to be in direct contact with the fixture.

410-67. Wiring.

(a) **General.** Conductors having insulation suitable for the temperature encountered shall be used.

(b) **Circuit Conductors.** Branch-circuit conductors having an insulation suitable for the temperature encountered shall be permitted to terminate in the fixture.

(c) **Tap Conductors.** Tap conductors of a type suitable for the temperature encountered shall be permitted to run from the fixture terminal connection to an outlet box placed at least 1 foot (305 mm) from the fixture. Such tap conductors shall be in a suitable metal raceway of at least 4 feet (1.22 m) but not more than 6 feet (1.83 m) in length.

P. Construction of Flush and Recessed Fixtures

410-68. Temperature. Fixtures shall be so constructed that adjacent combustible material will not be subject to temperatures in excess of 90°C (194°F).

410-69. Enclosure. Sheet metal enclosures shall be protected against corrosion and shall not be less than No. 22 MSG.

Exception: Where a wireway cover is within the No. 22 MSG enclosure, it shall be permitted to be of No. 24 MSG metal.

410-70. Lamp Wattage Marking. Incandescent lamp fixtures shall be marked to indicate the maximum allowable wattage of lamps. The markings shall be permanently installed, in letters at least ¼ inch (6.35 mm) high, and shall be located where visible during relamping.

410-71. Solder Prohibited. No solder shall be used in the construction of a fixture box.

410-72. Lampholders. Lampholders of the screw-shell type shall be of porcelain or other suitable insulating materials. Where used, cements shall be of the high-heat type.

Q. Special Provisions for Electric-Discharge Lighting Systems of 1000 Volts or Less

410-73. General.

(a) **Open-Circuit Voltage of 1000 Volts or Less.** Equipment for use with electric-discharge lighting systems and designed for an open-circuit voltage of 1000 volts or less shall be of a type intended for such service.

(b) **Considered as Alive.** The terminals of an electric-discharge lamp shall be considered as alive where any lamp terminal is connected to a circuit of over 300 volts.

(c) **Transformers of the Oil-Filled Type.** Transformers of the oil-filled type shall not be used.

(d) **Additional Requirements.** In addition to complying with the general requirements for lighting fixtures, such equipment shall comply with Part Q of this article.

(e) **Thermal Protection.** Where fluorescent fixtures are installed indoors, the ballasts shall have thermal protection integral within the ballast. Replacement ballasts for all fluorescent fixtures installed indoors shall also have thermal protection integral within the ballast.

Thermal protection integral with the ballast is to be provided for fluorescent fixtures installed indoors. Ballasts not provided with integral thermal protection are not to be used as replacements for such fixtures. This paragraph was revised in the 1984 NEC to make it clear that thermally protected ballasts are required as replacements for nonthermally protected ballasts in older fixtures not originally provided with thermally protected ballasts.

As different "Class P" ballasts have different heating characteristics, the heating characteristics should be considered when selecting replacements for nonthermally protected ballasts.

This type of ballast is listed and marked by Underwriters Laboratories Inc. as "Class P" and is set at a predetermined temperature to prevent abnormal ballast heat buildup caused by a fault in one or more of the ballast components, or by some lampholder or wiring faults.

Exception to (e) above: Fluorescent fixtures with simple reactance ballasts.

Figure 410-8 illustrates a reactance-type ballast used in series with a 30-W or less preheat-type fluorescent lamp. This type ballast does not require thermal protection and the fixture may be equipped with automatic-type starters (such as used with medicine cabinet fixtures) or a manual momentary contact starter (such as used with desk lamps and some small under-cabinet fixtures).

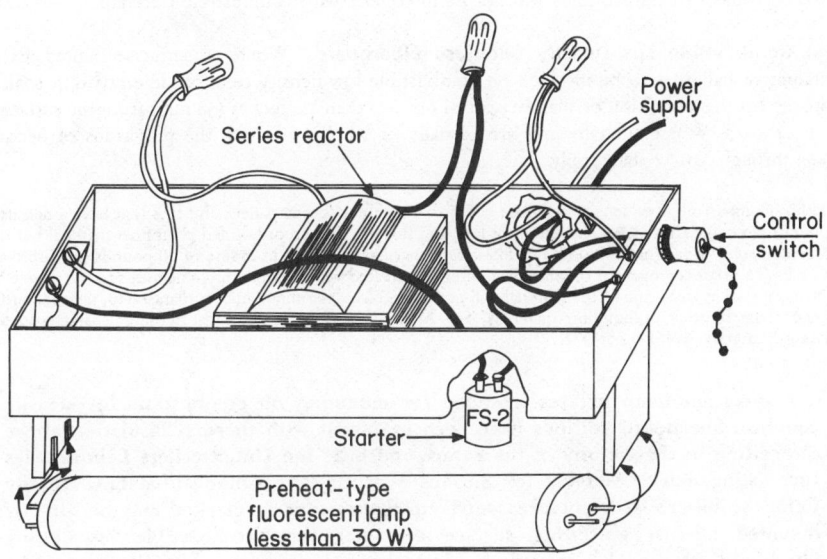

Figure 410-8. The circuitry for a simple reactance-type ballast for fluorescent lighting.

(f) Recessed High-Intensity Discharge Fixtures. Where recessed high-intensity discharge fixtures with integral ballast are installed indoors, the ballast shall have thermal protection integral within the ballast. Replacement ballasts for fixtures with integral ballasts shall also have thermal protection integral within the ballast.

The requirement in the last sentence is applicable only to recessed-type HID fixtures with integral ballasts.

410-74. Direct-Current Equipment. Fixtures installed on direct-current circuits shall be equipped with auxiliary equipment and resistors especially designed and for direct-current operation, and the fixtures shall be so marked.

410-75. Voltages — Dwelling Occupancies.

(a) Open-Circuit Voltage Exceeding 1000 Volts. Equipment having an open-circuit voltage exceeding 1000 volts shall not be installed in dwelling occupancies.

(b) Open-Circuit Voltage Exceeding 300 Volts. Equipment having an open-circuit voltage exceeding 300 volts shall not be installed in dwelling occupancies unless such equipment is so designed that there will be no exposed live parts when lamps are being inserted, are in place, or are being removed.

Fixtures intended for use in other than dwelling occupancies are so marked. This usually indicates that the fixture has maintenance features that are considered to be beyond the capabilities of the ordinary householder or involve voltages in excess of those permitted by this *Code* for dwelling occupancies. See Sections 210-6(c)(1) and (c)(2).

410-76. Fixture Mounting.

(a) Exposed Ballasts. Fixtures having exposed ballasts or transformers shall be so installed that such ballasts or transformers will not be in contact with combustible material.

(b) Combustible Low-Density Cellulose Fiberboard. Where a surface-mounted fixture containing a ballast is to be installed on combustible low-density cellulose fiberboard, it shall be approved for this condition or shall be spaced not less than 1½ inches (38 mm) from the surface of the fiberboard. Where such fixtures are partially or wholly recessed, the provisions of Sections 410-64 through 410-72 shall apply.

(FPN): Combustible low-density cellulose fiberboard includes sheets, panels, and tiles that have a density of 20 pounds per cubic foot (320.36 kg/cu m) or less, and that are formed of bonded plant fiber material but does not include solid or laminated wood, nor fiberboard that has a density in excess of 20 pounds per cubic foot (320.36 kg/cu m) or is a material that has been integrally treated with fire-retarding chemicals to the degree that the flame spread in any plane of the material will not exceed 25, determined in accordance with tests for surface burning characteristics of building materials. See Method of Test for Surface Burning Characteristics of Building Materials, ANSI A2.5-1977.

Fluorescent lamp fixtures intended for mounting on combustible low-density cellulose fiberboard ceilings have been evaluated with thermal insulation above the ceiling in the vicinity of the fixture and bear the Underwriters Laboratories Inc. listing mark "Suitable for Surface Mounting on Combustible Low-Density Cellulose Fiberboard." Fluorescent lamp fixtures not so marked may be directly mounted against a ceiling surface of other than combustible low-density fiberboard or may be spaced not less than 1½ in. from the surface of the low-density fiberboard.

Further information may be obtained from the Underwriters Laboratories Inc. publication, "Building Materials Directory," and also from the American National Standards Institute publication, "Method of Test for Surface Burning Characteristics of Building Materials."

410-77. Equipment Not Integral with Fixture.

(a) Metal Cabinets. Auxiliary equipment, including reactors, capacitors, resistors, and similar equipment, where not installed as part of a lighting fixture assembly, shall be enclosed in accessible, permanently installed metal cabinets.

(b) Separate Mounting. Separately mounted ballasts that are intended for direct connection to a wiring system shall not be required to be separately enclosed.

410-78. Autotransformers. An autotransformer which is used to raise the voltage to more than 300 volts, as part of a ballast for supplying lighting units, shall be supplied only by a grounded system.

410-79. Switches. Snap switches shall comply with Section 380-14.

R. Special Provisions for Electric-Discharge Lighting Systems of More than 1000 Volts

These sections apply to interior electric-discharge "neon-tube"-type lighting (containing neon, helium, or argon gas, with or without mercury, at low vapor pressure), long-length fluorescent tube lighting requiring more than 1,000 V, and cold-cathode fluorescent-lamp installations arranged to operate with several tubes in series.

410-80. General.

(a) Open-Circuit Voltage Exceeding 1000 Volts. Equipment for use with electric-discharge lighting systems and designed for an open-circuit voltage exceeding 1000 volts shall be of a type intended for such service.

(b) Considered as Alive. The terminal of an electric-discharge lamp shall be considered as alive when any lamp terminal is connected to a circuit of over 300 volts.

(c) Additional Requirements. In addition to complying with the general requirements for lighting fixtures, such equipment shall comply with Part R of this article.

(FPN): For signs and outline lighting, see Article 600.

410-81. Control.

(a) Disconnection. Fixtures or lamp installations shall be controlled either singly or in groups by an externally operable switch or circuit breaker that opens all ungrounded primary conductors.

(b) Within Sight or Locked Type. The switch or circuit breaker shall be located within sight from the fixtures or lamps, or it shall be permitted elsewhere if it is provided with a means for locking in the open position.

Providing that the switch or circuit breaker is within view or capable of being locked "off" assures the service person that the disconnecting means will not be closed while servicing the equipment.

410-82. Lamp Terminals and Lampholders. Parts that must be removed for lamp replacement shall be hinged or held captive. Lamps or lampholders will be so designed that there shall be no exposed live parts when lamps are being inserted or are being removed.

410-83. Transformer Ratings. Transformers and ballasts shall have a secondary open-circuit voltage of not over 15,000 volts with an allowance on test of 1000 volts additional. The secondary-current rating shall not be more than 120 milliamperes if the open-circuit voltage is over 7500 volts, and not more than 240 milliamperes if the open-circuit voltage is 7500 volts or less.

410-84. Transformer Type. Transformers shall be enclosed and listed.

410-85. Transformer Secondary Connections.

(a) High-Voltage Windings. The high-voltage windings of transformers shall not be connected in series or in parallel.

Exception: Two transformers, each having one end of its high-voltage winding grounded and connected to the enclosure, shall be permitted to have their high-voltage windings connected in series to form the equivalent of a midpoint grounded transformer.

(b) Grounded Ends of Paralleled Transformers. The grounded ends of paralleled transformers as permitted in (a) above shall be connected by an insulated conductor not smaller than No. 14.

410-86. Transformer Locations.

(a) Accessible. Transformers shall be accessible after installation.

(b) Secondary Conductors. Transformers shall be installed as near to the lamps as practicable to keep the secondary conductors as short as possible.

(c) Adjacent to Combustible Materials. Transformers shall be so located that adjacent combustible materials will not be subjected to temperatures in excess of 90°C (194°F).

410-87. Transformer Loading. The lamps connected to any transformer shall be of such length and characteristics as not to cause a condition of continuous overvoltage on the transformer.

Transformers are required to be enclosed and listed, and should be rated to supply the proper current and voltage for the lamp or tube. See Section 600-32.

410-88. Wiring Method — Secondary Conductors. Conductors shall be installed in accordance with Section 600-31.

Table 310-13, which lists various types of insulated conductors, does not include this type of cable. Underwriters Laboratories Inc., however, does have standards for this type of cable. The following information is an excerpt from the Underwriters Laboratories Inc. Electrical Construction Materials List:

Gas tube sign and ignition cable may be Type GTO-5 (5,000 volts), GTO-10 (10,000 volts), or GTO-15 (15,000 volts), and is listed in sizes Nos. 18-10 AWG copper and Nos. 12-10 AWG aluminum and copper-clad aluminum. This material is intended for use with gas tube signs, oil burners, and inside lighting.

L, used as a suffix in combination with any of the preceding type letter designations indicates that an outer covering of lead has been applied.

Underwriters Laboratories Inc.
®
LISTED
GAS TUBE SIGN
AND IGNITION CABLE

The UL symbol on the product and the listing mark of Underwriters Laboratories Inc. on the attached tag, coil, reel or smallest unit container in which the product is packaged is the only method provided by UL to identify these products manufactured under its listing and follow-up service. The listing mark for these products includes the name and/or symbol of Underwriters Laboratories Inc. together with the word "Listed," a control number, and one of the following product names as appropriate: A gas tube sign and ignition cable that contain copper or copper-clad aluminum conductor has the product name "Gas Tube Sign and Ignition Cable," a gas tube sign and ignition cable that contains aluminum conductor has the product name, "Gas Tube Sign and Ignition Aluminum Cable."

410-89. Lamp Supports. Lamps shall be adequately supported as required in Section 600-33.

410-90. Exposure to Damage. Lamps shall not be located where normally exposed to physical damage.

410-91. Marking. Each fixture or each secondary circuit of tubing having an open-circuit voltage of over 1000 volts shall have a clearly legible marking in letters not less than ¼ inch (6.35 mm) high reading "Caution....volts." The voltage indicated shall be the rated open-circuit voltage.

410-92. Switches. Snap switches shall comply with Section 380-14.

S. Lighting Track

Part S is new in the 1984 *NEC*

410-100. Definition. Lighting track is a manufactured assembly designed to support and energize lighting fixtures which are capable of being readily repositioned on the track. Its length may be altered by the addition or subtraction of sections of track.

410-101. Installation.

(a) Lighting Track. Lighting track shall be permanently installed and permanently connected to a branch circuit. Only lighting track fittings shall be installed on lighting track.

A lighting track fitting differs from a fitting as defined in Article 100 in that it usually performs both an electrical and a mechanical function. A lighting track fitting, for example, often includes a lampholder.

(b) Connected Load. The connected load on lighting track shall not exceed the rating of the track. Lighting track shall be supplied by a branch circuit having a rating not more than that of the track.

(c) Locations Not Permitted. Lighting track shall not be installed: (1) where subject to physical damage; (2) in wet or damp locations; (3) where subject to corrosive vapors; (4) in storage battery rooms; (5) in hazardous (classified) locations; (6) where concealed; (7) where extended through walls or partitions; (8) less than 5 feet (1.52 m) above the finished floor except where protected from physical damage.

(d) Support. Fittings identified for use on lighting track shall be designed specifically for the track on which they are to be installed. They shall be securely fastened to the track, maintain polarization and grounding, and shall be designed to be suspended directly from the track.

See commentary following Section 410-101(a).

410-102. Track Load. For branch-circuit calculations a maximum of 2 feet (609.6 mm) of lighting track or fraction thereof shall be considered 180 VA.

410-103. Heavy-Duty Track. Heavy-duty lighting track is lighting track identified for use exceeding 20 amperes. Each fitting attached to a heavy-duty lighting track shall have individual overcurrent protection.

See commentary following Section 410-101(a).

410-104. Fastening. Lighting track shall be securely mounted to the ceiling or the wall so that each fastening will be suitable for supporting the maximum weight of fixtures which can be installed. Unless specially approved for supports at greater intervals, a single section 4 feet (1.22 m) or shorter in length shall have two supports, and when installed in a continuous row each individual section of not more than 4 feet (1.22 m) in length shall have one additional support.

410-105. Construction Requirements.

(a) Construction. The housing for the lighting track system shall be of substantial construction to maintain rigidity. The conductors shall be installed within the track housing permitting insertion of a fixture, and designed to prevent tampering and accidental contact. Components of lighting track systems of different voltages shall not be interchangeable.

Exception: Fittings which incorporate an integral device to reduce the line voltage for a lower voltage lamp.

(b) Grounding. Lighting track shall be grounded in accordance with Article 250 and the track sections shall be securely coupled to maintain continuity of the circuitry, polarization and grounding throughout. The track conductors shall be a minimum No. 12 AWG or equal, and shall be copper. The track system ends shall be insulated and capped.

ARTICLE 422 — APPLIANCES

Contents

D. Control and Protection of Appliances

422-20. Disconnecting Means.

422-21. Disconnection of Permanently Connected Appliances.

(a) Rated at Not Over 300 Volt Amperes or ⅛ Horsepower.

(b) Permanently Connected Appliances of Greater Rating.

422-22. Disconnection of Cord- and Plug-Connected Appliances.

(a) Separable Connector or an Attachment Plug and Receptacle.

(b) Connection at the Rear Base of a Range.

(c) Rating.

(d) Requirements for Attachment Plugs and Connectors.

422-24. Unit Switch(es) as Disconnecting Means.

(a) Multifamily Dwellings.

(b) Two-Family Dwellings.

(c) One-Family Dwellings.

(d) Other Occupancies.

422-25. Switch and Circuit Breaker to Be Indicating.

422-26. Disconnecting Means for Motor-Driven Appliances.

422-27. Overcurrent Protection.

(a) Appliances.

(b) Household-type Appliance with Surface Heating Elements.

(c) Infrared Lamp Commercial and Industrial Heating Appliances.

(d) Open-Coil or Exposed Sheathed-Coil Types of Surface Heating Elements in Commercial-type Heating Appliances.

(e) Single Nonmotor-Operated Appliance.

(f) Electric Heating Appliances Employing Resistance-type Heating Elements Rated More than 48 Amperes.

E. Marking of Appliances

422-30. Nameplate.

(a) Nameplate Marking.

(b) To Be Visible.

422-31. Marking of Heating Elements.

422-32. Appliances Consisting of Motors and Other Loads.

(a) Marking.

(b) Alternate Marking Method.

A. General

422-1. Scope. This article covers electric appliances used in any occupancy.

This article covers electric appliances such as found in a dwelling unit, or commercial and industrial locations, and which may be fastened in place or cord- and plug-connected, such as air-conditioning units, dishwashers, heating appliances, water heaters, infrared heating lamps, etc. See Section 422-3 for requirements of other articles. Also see Article 100 for definition of "Appliance."

422-2. Live Parts. Appliances shall have no live parts normally exposed to contact.

Exception: Toasters, grills, or other appliances in which the current-carrying parts at high temperatures are necessarily exposed.

422-3. Other Articles. All requirements of this Code shall apply where applicable. Appliances for use in hazardous (classified) locations shall comply with Articles 500 through 517.

The requirements of Article 430 shall apply to the installation of motor-operated appliances and the requirements of Article 440 shall apply to the installation of appliances containing hermetic refrigerant motor-compressor(s), except as specifically amended in this article.

B. Branch-Circuit Requirements

422-5. Branch-Circuit Sizing. This section specifies sizes of conductors capable of carrying appliance current without overheating under the conditions specified. This section shall not apply to conductors that form an integral part of an appliance.

ARTICLE 422—APPLIANCES

(a) **Individual Circuits.** The rating of an individual branch circuit shall not be less than the marked rating of the appliance or the marked rating of an appliance having combined loads as provided in Section 422-32.

Exception No. 1: For motor-operated appliances not having a marked rating the branch-circuit size shall be in accordance with Part B of Article 430.

Exception No. 2: For an appliance, other than a motor-operated appliance, that is continuously loaded, the branch-circuit rating shall not be less than 125 percent of the marked rating; or not less than 100 percent if the branch-circuit device and its assembly is approved for continuous loading at 100 percent of its rating.

Exception No. 3: Branch circuits for household cooking appliances shall be permitted to be in accordance with Table 220-19.

(b) **Circuits Supplying Two or More Loads.** For branch circuits supplying appliance and other loads, the rating shall be determined in accordance with Section 210-23.

If a labeled or listed appliance is provided with installation instructions from the manufacturer, the branch-circuit size is not permitted to be less than the minimum size required by the installation instructions. See Section 110-3(b).

422-6. Branch-Circuit Overcurrent Protection. Branch circuits shall be protected in accordance with Section 240-3.

If a protective device rating is marked on an appliance, the branch-circuit overcurrent device rating shall not exceed the protective device rating marked on the appliance.

C. Installation of Appliances

422-7. General. All appliances shall be installed in an approved manner.

422-8. Flexible Cords.

(a) **Heater Cords.** All cord- and plug-connected smoothing irons and electrically heated appliances that are rated at more than 50 watts and produce temperatures in excess of 121°C (250°F) on surfaces with which the cord is likely to be in contact shall be provided with one of the types of approved heater cords listed in Table 400-4.

(b) **Other Heating Appliances.** All other cord- and plug-connected electrically heated appliances shall be connected with one of the approved types of cord listed in Table 400-4, selected in accordance with the usage specified in that table.

(c) **Other Appliances.** Flexible cord shall be permitted: (1) for connection of appliances to facilitate their frequent interchange or to prevent the transmission of noise or vibration, or (2) to facilitate the removal or disconnection of appliances, that are fastened in place, for maintenance or repair.

(d) **Specific Appliances.**

(1) Electrically operated kitchen waste disposers intended for dwelling unit use and provided with a Type S, SO, ST, STO, SJ, SJO, SJT, SJTO, SP-3, SPE-3, or SPT-3, three-conductor cord terminated with a grounding-type attachment plug shall be permitted where all of the following conditions are met:

a. The length of the cord shall not be less than 18 inches (457 mm) and not over 36 inches (914 mm).

b. Receptacles shall be located to avoid physical damage to the flexible cord.

c. The receptacle shall be accessible.

(2) Built-in dishwashers and trash compactors intended for dwelling unit use and provided with a Type S, SO, ST STO, SJ, SJO, SJT, SJTO, SP-3, SPE-3, or SPT-3, three-conductor cord terminated with a grounding-type attachment plug shall be permitted where all of the following conditions are met:

a. The length of the cord shall be 3 to 4 feet (0.914 to 1.22 m).

b. Receptacles shall be located to avoid physical damage to the flexible cord.

c. The receptacle shall be located in the space occupied by the appliance or adjacent thereto.

d. The receptacle shall be accessible.

Exception: Listed kitchen waste disposers, dishwashers and trash compactors protected by a system of double insulation, or its equivalent, shall not be required to be grounded. Where such a system is employed, the equipment shall be distinctively marked.

422-9. Cord- and Plug-Connected Immersion Heaters. Electric heaters of the cord- and plug-connected immersion type shall be so constructed and installed that current-carrying parts are effectively insulated from electrical contact with the substance in which they are immersed. The authority having jurisdiction may make exceptions for special applications of apparatus if suitable precautions are taken.

422-10. Protection of Combustible Material. Each electrically heated appliance that is intended by size, weight, and service to be located in a fixed position shall be so placed as to provide ample protection between the appliance and adjacent combustible material.

422-11. Stands for Cord- and Plug-Connected Appliances. Each smoothing iron and other cord- and plug-connected electrically heated appliance intended to be applied to combustible material shall be equipped with an approved stand, which shall be permitted to be a separate piece of equipment or a part of the appliance.

422-12. Signals for Heated Appliances. In other than dwelling-type occupancies, each electrically heated appliance or group of appliances intended to be applied to combustible material shall be provided with a signal.

Exception: If an appliance is provided with an integral temperature-limiting device.

A common way to provide a signal light for electrically heated appliances in commercial or industrial locations is to use a red light so connected to and within sight of the appliance as to indicate that the appliance is energized and operating.
No signal is required for an electrically heated appliance provided with a thermostat that limits it to a certain temperature.

422-13. Flatirons. Electrically heated smoothing irons intended for use in residences shall be equipped with approved temperature-limiting means.

422-14. Water Heaters.

(a) **Storage- and Instantaneous-type Water Heaters.** Each storage- or instantaneous-type water heater shall be equipped with a temperature-limiting means in addition to its control

ARTICLE 422—APPLIANCES

thermostat to disconnect all ungrounded conductors, and such means shall be: (1) installed to sense maximum water temperature and, (2) either a trip-free, manually reset type or a type having a replacement element. Such water heaters shall be marked to require the installation of a temperature and pressure relief valve.

(FPN): See Listing Requirements for Relief Valves and Automatic Gas Shutoff Devices for Hot Water Supply Systems (ANSI Z21.22-1972).

Exception: Water heaters with supply water temperature of 82°C (180°F) or above and a capacity of 60 kW or above and identified as being suitable for this use; and water heaters with a capacity of 1 gallon (3.785 L) or less and identified as being suitable for such use.

(b) Storage-type Water Heaters. All fixed storage-type water heaters having a capacity of 120 gallons (454.2 L) or less shall have a branch-circuit rating not less than 125 percent of the nameplate rating of the water heater.

(FPN): For branch-circuit sizing, see Section 422-5(a), Exception No. 2.

422-15. Infrared Lamp Industrial Heating Appliances.

(a) 300 Watts or Less. Infrared heating lamps rated at 300 watts or less shall be permitted with lampholders of the medium-base, unswitched porcelain type or other types identified as suitable for use with infrared heating lamps rated 300 watts or less.

(b) Over 300 Watts. Screw-shell lampholders shall not be used with infrared lamps over 300 watts rating.

Exception: Lampholders identified as suitable for use with infrared heating lamps rated more than 300 watts.

(c) Lampholders. Lampholders shall be permitted to be connected to any of the branch circuits of Article 210 and, in industrial occupancies, shall be permitted to be operated in series on circuits of over 150 volts to ground provided the voltage rating of the lampholders is not less than the circuit voltage.

Each section, panel, or strip carrying a number of infrared lampholders (including the internal wiring of such section, panel, or strip) shall be considered an appliance. The terminal connection block of each such assembly shall be considered an individual outlet.

Infrared (heat) radiation lamps are tungsten-filament incandescent lamps that are similar in appearance to lighting lamps; however, they are designed to operate at a lower temperature, thus transferring more heat radiation and less light intensity. Infrared lamps are used for a variety of heating and drying purposes in residential, commercial, and industrial locations.

422-16. Grounding.
Appliances required by Article 250 to be grounded shall have exposed noncurrent-carrying metal parts grounded in the manner specified in Article 250.

(FPN): See Sections 250-42, 250-43 and 250-45 for equipment grounding of refrigerators and freezers and Sections 250-57 and 250-60 for equipment grounding of electric ranges, wall-mounted ovens, counter-mounted cooking units, and clothes dryers.

422-17. Wall-Mounted Ovens and Counter-Mounted Cooking Units.

(a) Permitted to Be Cord- and Plug-Connected or Permanently Connected. Wall-mounted ovens and counter-mounted cooking units complete with provisions for mounting and for making electrical connections shall be permitted to be cord- and plug-connected or permanently connected.

(b) Separable Connector or a Plug and Receptacle Combination. A separable connector or a plug and receptacle combination in the supply line to an oven or cooking unit used only for ease in servicing or for installation shall:

(1) Not be installed as the disconnecting means required by Section 422-20.

(2) Be approved for the temperature of the space in which it is located.

422-18. Other Installation Methods. Appliances employing methods of installation other than covered by this article may be used only by special permission.

D. Control and Protection of Appliances

422-20. Disconnecting Means. A means shall be provided to disconnect each appliance from all ungrounded conductors as required by the following sections of Part D. If an appliance is supplied by more than one source, the disconnecting means shall be grouped and identified.

422-21. Disconnection of Permanently Connected Appliances.

(a) Rated at Not Over 300 Volt Amperes or ⅛ Horsepower. For permanently connected appliances rated at not over 300 volt amperes or ⅛ horsepower, the branch-circuit overcurrent device shall be permitted to serve as the disconnecting means.

(b) Permanently Connected Appliances of Greater Rating. For permanently connected appliances of greater rating the branch-circuit switch or circuit breaker shall be permitted to serve as the disconnecting means where readily accessible to the user of the appliance.

(FPN): For motor-driven appliances of more than ⅛ horsepower, see Section 422-26.

Exception: Appliances employing unit switches as permitted by Section 422-24.

422-22. Disconnection of Cord- and Plug-Connected Appliances.

(a) Separable Connector or an Attachment Plug and Receptacle. For cord- and plug-connected appliances, a separable connector or an attachment plug and receptacle shall be permitted to serve as the disconnecting means.

(b) Connection at the Rear Base of a Range. For cord- and plug-connected household electric ranges, an attachment plug and receptacle connection at the rear base of a range, if it is accessible from the front by removal of a drawer, shall be considered as meeting the intent of Section 422-22(a).

(c) Rating. The rating of a receptacle or of a separable connector shall not be less than the rating of any appliance connected thereto.

Exception: Demand factors authorized elsewhere in this Code shall be permitted to be applied.

(d) Requirements for Attachment Plugs and Connectors. Attachment plugs and connectors shall conform to the following:

(1) Live Parts. They shall be so constructed and installed as to guard against inadvertent contact with live parts.

(2) Interrupting Capacity. They shall be capable of interrupting their rated current without hazard to the operator.

(3) Interchangeability. They shall be so designed that they will not fit into receptacles of lesser rating.

422-24. Unit Switch(es) as Disconnecting Means. A unit switch(es) with a marked "off" position that is a part of an appliance and disconnects all ungrounded conductors shall be permitted as the disconnecting means required by this article where other means for disconnection are provided in the following types of occupancies:

(a) Multifamily Dwellings. In multifamily dwellings, the disconnecting means shall be within the dwelling unit, or on the same floor as the dwelling unit in which the appliance is installed, and shall be permitted to control lamps and other appliances.

(b) Two-Family Dwellings. In two-family dwellings, the disconnecting means shall be permitted to be outside the dwelling unit in which the appliance is installed. In this case an individual switch for the dwelling unit shall be permitted.

(c) One-Family Dwellings. In one-family dwellings, the service disconnecting means shall be permitted to be used.

(d) Other Occupancies. In other occupancies, the branch-circuit switch or circuit breaker, where readily accessible to the user of the appliance, shall be permitted for this purpose.

422-25. Switch and Circuit Breaker to Be Indicating. Switches and circuit breakers used as disconnecting means shall be of the indicating type.

422-26. Disconnecting Means for Motor-Driven Appliances. If a switch or circuit breaker serves as the disconnecting means for a permanently connected motor-driven appliance of more than ⅛ horsepower, it shall be located within sight from the motor controller and shall comply with Part H of Article 430.

Exception: A switch or circuit breaker that serves as the other disconnecting means as required in Section 422-24(a), (b), (c) or (d) shall be permitted to be out of sight from the motor controller of an appliance provided with a unit switch(es) with a marked "off" position and which disconnects all ungrounded conductors.

422-27. Overcurrent Protection.

(a) Appliances. Appliances shall be permitted to be protected against overcurrent if supplied by branch circuits as specified in (e) and (f) below and in Sections 422-5 and 422-6.

Exception: Motors of motor-operated appliances shall be provided with overload protection in accordance with Part C of Article 430. Hermetic refrigerant motor-compressors in air-conditioning or refrigerating equipment shall be provided with overload protection in accordance with Part F of Article 440. When appliance overcurrent protective devices separate from the appliance are required, data for selection of these devices shall be marked on the appliance. The minimum marking shall be that specified in Sections 430-7 and 440-3.

(b) Household-type Appliance with Surface Heating Elements. A household-type appliance with surface heating elements having a maximum demand of more than 60 amperes computed in accordance with Table 220-19 shall have its power supply subdivided into two or more circuits, each of which is provided with overcurrent protection rated at not over 50 amperes.

(c) Infrared Lamp Commercial and Industrial Heating Appliances. Infrared lamp commercial and industrial heating appliances shall have overcurrent protection not exceeding 50 amperes.

(d) Open-Coil or Exposed Sheathed-Coil Types of Surface Heating Elements in Commercial-type Heating Appliances. Open-coil or exposed sheathed-coil types of surface heating elements in commercial-type heating appliances shall be protected by overcurrent protective devices rated at not over 50 amperes.

(e) Single Nonmotor-Operated Appliance. If the branch circuit supplies a single nonmotor-operated appliance, rated at 16.7 amperes or more, the overcurrent device rating shall not exceed 150 percent of the appliance rating.

(f) Electric Heating Appliances Employing Resistance-type Heating Elements Rated More than 48 Amperes. Electric heating appliances employing resistance-type heating elements rated more than 48 amperes shall have the heating elements subdivided. Each subdivided load shall not exceed 48 amperes and shall be protected at not more than 60 amperes.

These supplementary overcurrent protective devices shall be: (1) factory installed within or on the heater enclosure or provided as a separate assembly by the heater manufacturer; (2) accessible, but need not be readily accessible; and (3) suitable for branch-circuit protection.

The main conductors supplying these overcurrent protective devices shall be considered branch-circuit conductors.

Exception No. 1: Household-type appliances with surface heating elements as covered in Section 422-27(b) and commercial-type heating appliances as covered in Section 422-27(d).

Exception No. 2: Commercial kitchen and cooking appliances using sheathed-type heating elements not covered in Section 422-27(d) shall be permitted to be subdivided into circuits not exceeding 120 amperes and protected at not more than 150 amperes where one of the following is met:

a. Elements are integral with and enclosed within a cooking surface;

b. Elements are completely contained within an enclosure identified as suitable for this use; or

c. Elements are contained within an ASME rated and stamped vessel.

Exception No. 3: Water heaters and steam boilers employing resistance-type immersion electric heating elements contained in an ASME rated and stamped vessel shall be permitted to be subdivided into circuits not exceeding 120 amperes and protected at not more than 150 amperes.

E. Marking of Appliances

422-30. Nameplate.

(a) Nameplate Marking. Each electric appliance shall be provided with a nameplate, giving the identifying name and the rating in volts and amperes, or in volts and watts. If the appliance is to be used on a specific frequency or frequencies, it shall be so marked.

When motor overload protection external to the appliance is required, the appliance shall be so marked.

(FPN): See Section 422-27(a), Exception for overcurrent protection requirements.

(b) To Be Visible. Marking shall be located so as to be visible or easily accessible after installation.

422-31. Marking of Heating Elements. All heating elements that are rated over one ampere, replaceable in the field, and a part of an appliance shall be legibly marked with the ratings in volts and amperes, or in volts and watts, or with the manufacturer's part number.

422-32. Appliances Consisting of Motors and Other Loads. Appliances shall be marked in accordance with (a) or (b) below.

(a) Marking. In addition to the marking required in Section 422-30, the marking on an appliance consisting of a motor with other load(s) or motors with or without other load(s) shall specify the minimum circuit size and the maximum rating of the circuit overcurrent protective device.

Exception No. 1: Appliances factory-equipped with cords and attachment plugs, complying with Section 422-30.

Exception No. 2: An appliance where both the minimum circuit size and maximum rating of the circuit overcurrent protective device are not more than 15 amperes and complies with Section 422-30.

(b) Alternate Marking Method. An alternate marking method shall be permitted to specify the rating of the largest motor in volts and amperes, and the additional load(s) in volts and amperes, or volts and watts in addition to the marking required in Section 422-30.

Exception No. 1: Appliances factory-equipped with cords and attachment plugs. complying with Section 422-30.

Exception No. 2: The ampere rating of a motor ⅛ horsepower or less or a nonmotor load 1 ampere or less shall be permitted to be omitted unless such loads constitute the principal load.

ARTICLE 424 — FIXED ELECTRIC SPACE
HEATING EQUIPMENT

Contents

424-95. Clearances of Branch-Circuit Wiring in Walls.
  (a) Exterior Walls.
  (b) Interior Walls.
424-96. Connection to Branch-Circuit Conductors.
  (a) General.
  (b) Heating Panels.
  (c) Heating Panel Sets.
424-97. Nonheating Leads.

424-98. Installation in Concrete or Poured Masonry.
  (a) Maximum Heated Area.
  (b) Secured in Place and Identified as Suitable.
  (c) Expansion Joints.
  (d) Spacings.
  (e) Protection of Leads.
  (f) Bushings or Fittings Required.

A. General

424-1. Scope. This article covers fixed electric equipment used for space heating. For the purpose of this article, heating equipment shall include heating cable, unit heaters, boilers, central systems, or other approved fixed electric space heating equipment. This article shall not apply to process heating and room air conditioning.

424-2. Other Articles. All requirements of this Code shall apply where applicable. Fixed electric space heating equipment for use in hazardous (classified) locations shall comply with Articles 500 through 517. Fixed electric space heating equipment incorporating a hermetic refrigerant motor-compressor shall also comply with Article 440.

424-3. Branch Circuits.

(a) Branch-Circuit Requirements. Individual branch circuits shall be permitted to supply any size fixed electric space heating equipment.

Branch circuits supplying two or more outlets for fixed electric space heating equipment shall be rated 15, 20, or 30 amperes.

Exception: In other than residential occupancies, fixed infrared heating equipment shall be permitted to be supplied from branch circuits rated not over 50 amperes.

(b) Branch-Circuit Sizing. The ampacity of the branch-circuit conductors and the rating or setting of overcurrent protective devices supplying fixed electric space heating equipment consisting of resistance elements with or without a motor shall not be less than 125 percent of the total load of the motors and the heaters. The rating or setting of overcurrent protective devices shall be permitted in accordance with Section 240-3, Exception No. 1. A contactor, thermostat, relay, or similar device, approved for continuous operation at 100 percent of its rating, shall be permitted to supply its full-rated load as provided in Section 210-22(c), Exception No. 2.

The size of the branch-circuit conductors and overcurrent protective devices supplying fixed electric space heating equipment consisting of mechanical refrigeration with or without resistance units shall be computed in accordance with Sections 440-34 and 440-35.

The provisions of this section shall not apply to conductors which form an integral part of approved fixed electric space heating equipment.

The sizing of branch-circuit conductors supplying fixed electric space heating equipment at 125 percent of the total load of the heaters (and motors) is predicated on the need to protect the insulation of the conductors from overheating during periods of prolonged operation.

B. Installation

424-9. General. All fixed electric space heating equipment shall be installed in an approved manner.

Heating equipment and systems often have special instructions for installation regarding spacings, types of supply wires, or special control equipment which must be considered in determining the suitability of the installation. See Section 110-3(b).

424-10. Special Permission. Fixed electric space heating equipment and systems installed by methods other than covered by this article may be used only by special permission.

424-11. Supply Conductors. Fixed electric space heating equipment requiring supply conductors with over 60°C insulation shall be clearly and permanently marked. This marking shall be plainly visible after installation and shall be permitted to be adjacent to the field-connection box.

Fixed electric space heating equipment often requires high temperature supply conductors.

424-12. Locations.

(a) Exposed to Severe Physical Damage. Fixed electric space heating equipment shall not be used where exposed to severe physical damage unless adequately protected.

(b) Damp or Wet Locations. Heaters and related equipment installed in damp or wet locations shall be approved for such locations and shall be constructed and installed so that water cannot enter or accumulate in or on wired sections, electrical components, or duct work.

(FPN): See Section 110-11 for equipment exposed to deteriorating agents.

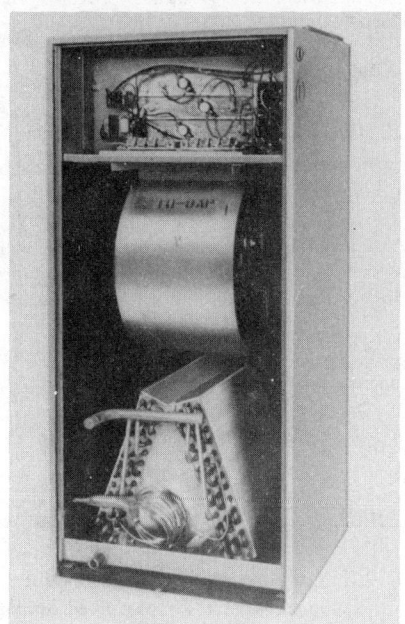

Figure 424-1. An electric furnace with cooling coils for air conditioning. (*Square D Co.*)

424-13. Spacing from Combustible Materials. Fixed electric space heating equipment shall be installed to provide the required spacing between the equipment and adjacent combustible material, unless it has been found to be acceptable where installed in direct contact with combustible material.

424-14. Grounding. All exposed noncurrent-carrying metal parts of fixed electric space heating equipment likely to become energized shall be grounded as required in Article 250.

C. Control and Protection of Fixed Electric Space Heating Equipment

424-19. Disconnecting Means. Means shall be provided to disconnect the heater, motor controller(s), and supplementary overcurrent protective device(s) of all fixed electric space heating equipment from all ungrounded conductors. Where heating equipment is supplied by more than one source, the disconnecting means shall be grouped and identified.

(a) Heating Equipment with Supplementary Overcurrent Protection. The disconnecting means for fixed electric space heating equipment with supplementary overcurrent protection shall be within sight from and on the supply side of the supplementary overcurrent protective device(s), and in addition shall comply with either (1) or (2) below.

(1) Heater Containing No Motor Rated Over ⅛ Horsepower. The above disconnecting means or unit switches complying with Section 424-19(b) (3) shall be permitted to serve as the required disconnecting means for both the motor controller(s) and heater under either (a) or (b) below.

a. The disconnecting means provided is also within sight from the motor controller(s) and the heater; or

b. The disconnecting means provided shall be capable of being locked in the open position.

(2) Heater Containing a Motor(s) Rated Over ⅛ Horsepower.

a. The above disconnecting means shall be permitted to serve as the required disconnecting means for both the motor controller(s) and heater if this disconnecting means is also in sight from the motor controller(s) and the heater.

b. Where the disconnecting means is not within sight from the heater a separate disconnecting means shall be installed, or the disconnecting means shall be capable of being locked in the open position, or unit switches complying with Section 424-19(b) (3) shall be permitted.

c. Where the disconnecting means is not within sight from the motor controller location a disconnecting means complying with Section 430-102 shall be provided.

d. Where the motor is not in sight from the motor controller location, Section 430-86 shall apply.

(b) Heating Equipment Without Supplementary Overcurrent Protection.

(1) Without Motor or with Motor Not Over ⅛ Horsepower. For fixed electric space heating equipment without a motor rated over ⅛ horsepower, the branch-circuit switch or circuit breaker shall be permitted to serve as the disconnecting means, where readily accessible for servicing.

(2) Over ⅛ Horsepower. For motor-driven electric space heating equipment with a motor rated over ⅛ horsepower, a disconnecting means shall be located within sight from the motor controller.

Exception: As permitted by Section 424-19(a)(2).

(3) Unit Switches as Disconnecting Means. Unit switches with a marked "off" position that are part of a fixed heater and disconnect all ungrounded conductors shall be permitted as the disconnecting means required by this article where other means for disconnection are provided in the following types of occupancies.

a. Multifamily Dwellings. In multifamily dwellings, the other disconnecting means shall be within the dwelling unit or on the same floor as the dwelling units in which the fixed heater is installed, and shall also be permitted to control lamps and appliances.

b. Two-Family Dwellings. In two-family dwellings, the other disconnecting means shall be permitted either inside or outside of the dwelling unit in which the fixed heater is installed.

c. One-Family Dwellings. In one-family dwelling units the service disconnecting means shall be permitted to be the other disconnecting means.

d. Other Occupancies. In other occupancies, the branch-circuit switch or circuit breaker, where readily accessible for servicing of the fixed heater, shall be permitted as the other disconnecting means.

424-20. Thermostatically Controlled Switching Devices.

(a) Serving as Both Controllers and Disconnecting Means. Thermostatically controlled switching devices and combination thermostats and manually controlled switches shall be permitted to serve as both controllers and disconnecting means provided all of the following conditions are met:

(1) Provided with a marked "off" position.

(2) Directly open all ungrounded conductors when manually placed in the "off" position.

(3) Designed so that the circuit cannot be energized automatically after the device has been manually placed in the "off" position.

(4) Located as specified in Section 424-19.

(b) Thermostats that Do Not Directly Interrupt All Ungrounded Conductors. Thermostats that do not directly interrupt all ungrounded conductors and operate remote control circuits shall not be required to meet the requirements of (a) above. These devices shall not be permitted as the disconnecting means.

424-21. Switch and Circuit Breaker to Be Indicating. Switches and circuit breakers used as disconnecting means shall be of the indicating type.

424-22. Overcurrent Protection.

(a) Branch-Circuit Devices. Electric space heating equipment, other than such motor-operated equipment as required by Articles 430 and 440 to have additional overcurrent protection, shall be permitted to be protected against overcurrent where supplied by one of the branch circuits in Article 210.

(b) Resistance Elements. Resistance-type heating elements in electric space heating equipment shall be protected at not more than 60 amperes. Equipment rated more than 48 amperes and employing such elements shall have the heating elements subdivided, and each subdivided load shall not exceed 48 amperes. Where a subdivided load is less than 48 amperes the rating of the supplementary overcurrent protective device shall comply with Section 424-3(b).

Exception: As provided in Section 424-72(a).

(c) Overcurrent Protective Devices. The supplementary overcurrent protective devices for the subdivided loads specified in (b) above shall be: (1) factory installed within or on the heater enclosure or supplied for use with the heater as a separate assembly by the heater manufacturer; (2) accessible, but shall not be required to be readily accessible; and (3) suitable for branch-circuit protection.

(FPN): See Section 240-10.

Where cartridge fuses are used to provide this overcurrent protection, a single disconnecting means shall be permitted to be used for the several subdivided loads.

(FPN): See Section 240-40.

Where subdivided loads are required, the heating equipment manufacturer is required to furnish the necessary overcurrent protective devices.

The main branch-circuit conductors supplying the overcurrent protective devices for subdivided loads are considered as branch circuits to make it clear that the 125 percent requirement in Section 424-3(b) is for the branch circuit only.

(d) Branch-Circuit Conductors. The conductors supplying the supplementary overcurrent protective devices shall be considered branch-circuit conductors.

Exception: For heaters rated 50 kW or more, the conductors supplying the supplementary overcurrent protective devices specified in (c) above shall be permitted to be sized at not less than 100 percent of the nameplate rating of the heater provided all of the following conditions are met:

a. The heater is marked with a minimum conductor size; and

b. The conductors are not smaller than the marked minimum size; and

c. A temperature-actuated device controls the cyclic operation of the equipment.

(e) Conductors for Subdivided Loads. Field-wired conductors between the heater and the supplementary overcurrent protective devices shall be sized at not less than 125 percent of the load served. The supplementary overcurrent protective devices specified in (c) shall protect these conductors in accordance with Section 240-3.

Exception: For heaters rated 50 kW or more, the ampacity of field-wired conductors between the heater and the supplementary overcurrent protective devices shall be permitted to be not less than 100 percent of the load of their respective subdivided circuits provided all of the following conditions are met:

a. The heater is marked with a minimum conductor size; and

b. The conductors are not smaller than the marked minimum size; and

c. A temperature-activated device controls the cyclic operation of the equipment.

D. Marking of Heating Equipment

424-28. Nameplate.

(a) Marking Required. Each unit of fixed electric space heating equipment shall be provided with a nameplate giving the identifying name and the normal rating in volts and watts, or in volts and amperes.

Electric space heating equipment intended for use on alternating current only or direct current only shall be marked to so indicate. The marking of equipment consisting of motors over ⅛ horsepower and other loads shall specify the rating of the motor in volts, amperes, and frequency, and the heating load in volts and watts, or in volts and amperes.

(b) Location. This nameplate shall be located so as to be visible or easily accessible after installation.

424-29. Marking of Heating Elements. All heating elements that are replaceable in the field and are a part of an electric heater shall be legibly marked with the ratings in volts and watts, or in volts and amperes.

E. Electric Space Heating Cables

424-34. Heating Cable Construction. Heating cables shall be furnished complete with factory-assembled nonheating leads at least 7 feet (2.13 m) in length.

424-35. Marking of Heating Cables. Each unit shall be marked with the identifying name or identification symbol, catalog number, ratings in volts and watts, or in volts and amperes.
Each unit length of heating cable shall have a permanent legible marking on each nonheating lead located within 3 inches (76 mm) of the terminal end. The lead wire shall have the following color identification to indicate the circuit voltage on which it is to be used: 120-volt nominal, yellow; 208-volt nominal, blue; 240-volt nominal, red; and 277-volt nominal, brown.

424-36. Clearances of Wiring in Ceilings. Wiring located above heated ceilings shall be spaced not less than 2 inches (50.8 mm) above the heated ceiling and shall be considered as operating at an ambient of 50°C. The ampacity of conductors shall be computed on the basis of the correction factors given in Tables 310-16 through 310-19.

Exception: Wiring above heated ceilings and located above thermal insulation having a minimum thickness of 2 inches (50.8 mm) shall not require correction for temperature.

424-37. Location of Branch-Circuit Wiring in Exterior Walls. Where located in exterior walls, wiring shall be located outside the thermal insulation.

424-38. Area Restrictions.

(a) Shall Not Extend Beyond the Room or Area. Heating cables shall not extend beyond the room or area in which they originate.

(b) Uses Prohibited. Cables shall not be installed in closets, over walls or partitions that extend to the ceiling, or over cabinets whose clearance from the ceiling is less than the minimum horizontal dimension of the cabinet to the nearest cabinet edge that is open to the room or area.

Exception: Isolated single runs of cable shall be permitted to pass over partitions where they are embedded.

(c) In Closet Ceilings as Low Temperature Heat Sources to Control Relative Humidity. This provision shall not prevent the use of cable in closet ceilings as low temperature heat sources to control relative humidity, provided they are used only in those portions of the ceiling that are unobstructed to the floor by shelves or other permanent fixtures.

424-39. Clearance from Other Objects and Openings. Heating elements of cables shall be separated at least 8 inches (203 mm) from the edge of outlet boxes and junction boxes that are to be used for mounting surface lighting fixtures. A clearance of not less than 2 inches (50.8 mm) shall be provided from recessed fixtures and their trims, ventilating openings, and other such openings in room surfaces. Sufficient area shall be provided to assure that no heating cable will be covered by any surface-mounted units.

424-40. Splices. Embedded cables shall be spliced only where necessary and only by approved means, and in no case shall the length of the heating cable be altered.

424-41. Installation of Heating Cables on Dry Board, in Plaster and on Concrete Ceilings.

(a) **Shall Not Be Installed in Walls.** Cables shall not be installed in walls.

Exception: Isolated single runs of cable shall be permitted to run down a vertical surface to reach a dropped ceiling.

(b) **Adjacent Runs.** Adjacent runs of cable not exceeding 2¾ watts per foot shall be installed not less than 1½ inches (38 mm) on centers.

(c) **Surfaces to Be Applied.** Heating cables shall be applied only to gypsum board, plaster lath or other fire-resistant material. With metal lath or other electrically conductive surfaces, a coat of plaster shall be applied to completely separate the metal lath or conductive surface from the cable.

(FPN): See also (f) below.

(d) **Splices.** All heating cables, the splice between the heating cable and nonheating leads, and 3-inch (76-mm) minimum of the nonheating lead at the splice shall be embedded in plaster or dry board in the same manner as the heating cable.

(e) **Ceiling Surface.** The entire ceiling surface shall have a finish of thermally noninsulating sand plaster having a nominal thickness of ½ inch (12.7 mm), or other noninsulating material identified as suitable for this use and applied according to specified thickness and directions.

(f) **Secured.** Cables shall be secured at intervals not exceeding 16 inches (406 mm) by means of approved stapling, tape, plaster, nonmetallic spreaders, or other approved means. Staples or metal fasteners that straddle the cable shall not be used with metal lath or other electrically conductive surfaces.

Exception: Cables identified to be secured at intervals not to exceed 6 feet (1.83 m).

(g) **Dry Board Installations.** In dry board installations, the entire ceiling below the heating cable shall be covered with gypsum board not exceeding ½ inch (12.7 mm) thickness. The void between the upper layer of gypsum board, plaster lath, or other fire-resistant material and the surface layer of gypsum board shall be completely filled with thermally conductive nonshrinking plaster or other approved material or equivalent thermal conductivity.

(h) **Free from Contact with Conductive Surfaces.** Cables shall be kept free from contact with metal or other electrical conductive surfaces.

(i) **Joists.** In dry board applications, cable shall be installed parallel to the joist, leaving a clear space centered under the joist of 2½ inches (64 mm) (width) between centers of adjacent runs of cable. Crossing of joist by cable shall be kept to a minimum. Surface layer of gypsum board shall be mounted so that the nails or other fasteners do not pierce the heating cable.

(FPN): Where practicable, cables shall cross joists only at the ends of a room.

424-42. Finished Ceilings. Finished ceilings shall not be covered with decorative panels or beams constructed of materials which have thermal insulating properties, such as wood, fiber, or plastic. Finished ceilings shall be permitted to be covered with paint, wallpaper, or other approved surface finishes.

424-43. Installation of Nonheating Leads of Cables.

(a) Free Nonheating Leads. Free nonheating leads of cables shall be installed in accordance with approved wiring methods from the junction box to a location within the ceiling. Such installations shall be permitted to be single conductors in approved raceways, single or multiconductor Type UF, Type NMC, Type MI, or other approved conductors.

(b) Leads in Junction Box. Not less than 6 inches (152 mm) of free nonheating lead shall be within the junction box. The marking of the leads shall be visible in the junction box.

(c) Excess Leads. Excess leads of heating cables shall not be cut but shall be secured to the underside of the ceiling and embedded in plaster or other approved material, leaving only a length sufficient to reach the junction box with not less than 6 inches (152 mm) of free lead within the box.

424-44. Installation of Cables in Concrete or Poured Masonry Floors.

(a) Watts per Linear Foot. Heating cables shall not exceed 16½ watts per lineal foot (305 mm) of cable.

(b) Spacing Between Adjacent Runs. The spacing between adjacent runs of cable shall not be less than 1 inch (25.4 mm) on centers.

(c) Secured in Place. Cables shall be secured in place by nonmetallic frames or spreaders or other approved means while the concrete or other finish is applied.
Cables shall not be installed where they bridge expansion joints unless protected from expansion and contraction.

(d) Spacings Between Heating Cable and Metal Embedded in the Floor. Spacings shall be maintained between the heating cable and metal embedded in the floor.

Exception: Grounded metal-clad cable shall be permitted to be in contact with metal embedded in the floor.

(e) Leads Protected. Leads shall be protected where they leave the floor by rigid metal conduit, intermediate metal conduit, rigid nonmetallic conduit, electrical metallic tubing, or by other approved means.

(f) Bushings or Approved Fittings. Bushings or approved fittings shall be used where the leads emerge within the floor slab.

424-45. Inspection and Tests. Cable installations shall be made with due care to prevent damage to the cable assembly and shall be inspected and approved before cables are covered or concealed.

F. Duct Heaters

424-57. General. Part F shall apply to any heater mounted in the air stream of a forced-air system where the air moving unit is not provided as an integral part of the equipment.

Figure 424-2. An insert-type electric duct heater. (*Square D Co.*)

424-58. Identification. Heaters installed in an air duct shall be identified as suitable for the installation.

424-59. Air Flow. Means shall be provided to assure uniform and adequate air flow over the face of the heater in accordance with the manufacturer's instructions.

(FPN): Heaters installed within 4 feet (1.22 m) of the outlet of an air-moving device, heat pump, air conditioner, elbows, baffle plates, or other obstructions in duct work may require turning vanes, pressure plates, or other devices on the inlet side of the duct heater to assure an even distribution of air over the face of the heater.

424-60. Elevated Inlet Temperature. Duct heaters intended for use with elevated inlet air temperature shall be identified as suitable for use at the elevated temperatures.

424-61. Installation of Duct Heaters with Heat Pumps and Air Conditioners. Heat pumps and air conditioners having duct heaters closer than 4 feet (1.22 m) to the heat pump or air conditioner shall have both the duct heater and heat pump or air conditioner identified as suitable for such installation and so marked.

424-62. Condensation. Duct heaters used with air conditioners or other air-cooling equipment that may result in condensation of moisture shall be identified as suitable for use with air conditioners.

424-63. Fan Circuit Interlock. Means shall be provided to ensure that the fan circuit is energized when any heater circuit is energized. However, time- or temperature-controlled delay in energizing the fan motor shall be permitted.

424-64. Limit Controls. Each duct heater shall be provided with an approved, integral, automatic-reset temperature-limiting control or controllers to de-energize the circuit or circuits.

In addition, an integral independent supplementary control or controllers shall be provided in each duct heater that will disconnect a sufficient number of conductors to interrupt current flow. This device shall be manually resettable or replaceable.

424-65. Location of Disconnecting Means. Duct heater controller equipment shall be accessible with the disconnecting means installed at or within sight from the controller.

Exception: As permitted by Section 424-19(a).

424-66. Installation. Duct heaters shall be installed in accordance with the manufacturer's instructions in a manner so that operation will not create a hazard to persons or property. Furthermore, duct heaters shall be located with respect to building construction and other equipment so as to permit access to the heater. Sufficient clearance shall be maintained to permit replacement of controls and heating elements and for adjusting and cleaning of controls and other parts requiring such attention. See Section 110-16.

For additional installation information, see Air Conditioning and Ventilating Systems, NFPA 90A-1981 (ANSI) and Warm Air Heating and Air Conditioning Systems, NFPA 90B-1980 (ANSI).

G. Resistance-type Boilers

424-70. Scope. The provisions in Part G of this article shall apply to boilers employing resistance-type heating elements. Electrode-type boilers shall not be considered as employing resistance-type heating elements. See Part H of this article.

424-71. Identification. Resistance-type boilers shall be identified as suitable for the installation.

424-72. Overcurrent Protection.

(a) Boiler Employing Resistance-type Immersion Heating Elements in an ASME Rated and Stamped Vessel. A boiler employing resistance-type immersion heating elements contained in an ASME rated and stamped vessel shall have the heating elements protected at not more than 150 amperes. Such a boiler rated more than 120 amperes shall have the heating elements subdivided into loads not exceeding 120 amperes.

Where a subdivided load is less than 120 amperes, the rating of the overcurrent protective device shall comply with Section 424-3(b).

(b) Boiler Employing Resistance-type Heating Elements Rated More than 48 Amperes and Not Contained in an ASME Rated and Stamped Vessel. A boiler employing resistance-type heating elements not contained in an ASME rated and stamped vessel shall have the heating elements protected at not more than 60 amperes. Such a boiler rated more than 48 amperes shall have the heating elements subdivided into loads not exceeding 48 amperes.

Where a subdivided load is less than 48 amperes, the rating of the overcurrent protective device shall comply with Section 424-3(b).

(c) Supplementary Overcurrent Protective Devices. The supplementary overcurrent protective devices for the subdivided loads as required by Section 424-72(a) and (b) shall be: (1) factory installed within or on the boiler enclosure or provided as a separate assembly by the boiler manufacturer; and (2) accessible, but need not be readily accessible; and (3) suitable for branch-circuit protection.

Where cartridge fuses are used to provide this overcurrent protection, a single disconnecting means shall be permitted for the several subdivided circuits. See Section 240-40.

(d) Conductors Supplying Supplementary Overcurrent Protective Devices. The conductors supplying these supplementary overcurrent protective devices shall be considered branch-circuit conductors.

Exception: Where the heaters are rated 50 kW or more, the conductors supplying the overcurrent protective device specified in (c) above shall be permitted to be sized at not less than 100 percent of the nameplate rating of the heater provided all of the following conditions are met:

a. The heater is marked with a minimum conductor size; and

b. The conductors are not smaller than the marked minimum size; and

c. A temperature or pressure-actuated device controls the cyclic operation of the equipment.

(e) Conductors for Subdivided Loads. Field-wired conductors between the heater and the supplementary overcurrent protective devices shall be sized at not less than 125 percent of the load served. The supplementary overcurrent protective devices specified in (c) shall protect these conductors in accordance with Section 240-3.

Exception: For heaters rated 50 kW or more, the ampacity of field-wired conductors between the heater and the supplementary overcurrent protective devices shall be permitted to be not less than 100 percent of the load of their respective subdivided circuits provided all of the following conditions are met:

a. The heater is marked with a minimum conductor size; and

b. The conductors are not smaller than the marked minimum size; and

c. A temperature-activated device controls the cyclic operation of the equipment.

424-73. Over-Temperature Limit Control. Each boiler designed, so that in normal operation there is no change in state of the heat transfer medium, shall be equipped with a temperature sensitive limiting means. It shall be installed to limit maximum liquid temperature and shall directly or indirectly disconnect all ungrounded conductors to the heating elements. Such means shall be in addition to a temperature regulating system and other devices protecting the tank against excessive pressure.

424-74. Over-Pressure Limit Control. Each boiler designed, so that in normal operation there is a change in state of the heat transfer medium from liquid to vapor, shall be equipped with a pressure sensitive limiting means. It shall be installed to limit maximum pressure and shall directly or indirectly disconnect all ungrounded conductors to the heating elements. Such means shall be in addition to a pressure regulating system and other devices protecting the tank against excessive pressure.

424-75. Grounding. All noncurrent-carrying metal parts shall be grounded in accordance with Article 250. Means for connection of equipment grounding conductor(s) sized in accordance with Table 250-95 shall be provided.

H. Electrode-type Boilers

424-80. Scope. The provisions in Part H of this article shall apply to boilers for operation at 600 volts, nominal, or less, in which heat is generated by the passage of current between electrodes through the liquid being heated.

424-81. Identification. Electrode-type boilers shall be identified as suitable for the installation.

424-82. Branch-Circuit Requirements. The size of branch-circuit conductors and overcurrent protective devices shall be calculated on the basis of 125 percent of the total load (motors not included). A contactor, relay or other device, approved for continuous operation at 100 percent of its rating, shall be permitted to supply its full-rated load. See Section 210-22(c), Exception No. 2. The provisions of this section shall not apply to conductors that form an integral part of an approved boiler.

Exception: For an electrode boiler rated 50 kW or more, the conductors supplying the boiler electrode(s) shall be permitted to be sized at not less than 100 percent of the nameplate rating of the electrode boiler provided all the following conditions are met:

    a. The electrode boiler is marked with a minimum conductor size; and

    b. The conductors are not smaller than the marked minimum size; and

    c. A temperature or pressure-actuated device controls the cyclic operation of the equipment.

424-83. Over-Temperature Limit Control. Each boiler designed, so that in normal operation there is no change in state of the heat transfer medium, shall be equipped with a temperature sensitive limiting means. It shall be installed to limit maximum liquid temperature and shall directly or indirectly interrupt all current flow through the electrodes. Such means shall be in addition to the temperature regulating system and other devices protecting the tank against excessive pressure.

424-84. Over-Pressure Limit Control. Each boiler designed, so that in normal operation there is a change in state of the heat transfer medium from liquid to vapor, shall be equipped with a pressure sensitive limiting means. It shall be installed to limit maximum pressure and shall directly or indirectly interrupt all current flow through the electrodes. Such means shall be in addition to a pressure regulating system and other devices protecting the tank against excessive pressure.

424-85. Grounding. For those boilers designed such that fault currents do not pass through the pressure vessel and the pressure vessel is electrically isolated from the electrodes, all exposed noncurrent-carrying metal parts including the pressure vessel, supply, and return connecting piping shall be grounded in accordance with Article 250.

For all other designs the pressure vessel containing the electrodes shall be isolated and electrically insulated from ground.

424-86. Markings. All electrode-type boilers shall be marked to show: (1) the manufacturer's name; (2) the normal rating in volts, amperes, and kilowatts; (3) the electrical supply required specifying frequency, number of phases, and number of wires; (4) the marking: "Electrode-type Boiler"; (5) a warning marking — "ALL POWER SUPPLIES SHALL BE DISCONNECTED BEFORE SERVICING INCLUDING SERVICING THE PRESSURE VESSEL."

The nameplate shall be located so as to be visible after installation.

I. Electric Radiant Heating Panels and Heating Panel Sets

    Part I is new in the 1984 *NEC.* It includes the requirements for heating panels and heating panel sets originally provided in Part E.

424-90. Scope. The provisions of Part I of this article shall apply to radiant heating panels and heating panel sets.

424-91. Definitions.

    (a) Heating Panel. A heating panel is a complete assembly provided with a junction box or a length of flexible conduit for connection to a branch circuit.

    (b) Heating Panel Set. A heating panel set is a rigid or nonrigid assembly provided with nonheating leads or a terminal junction assembly identified as being suitable for connection to a wiring system.

424-92. Markings.

    (1) Markings shall be permanent and in a location that is visible prior to application of panel finish.

(2) Each unit shall be identified as suitable for the installation.

(3) Each unit shall be marked with the identifying name or identification symbol, catalog number, rating in volts and watts, or in volts and amperes.

(4) The manufacturer of heating panels or heating panel sets shall provide marking labels indicating that space heating installations incorporate heating elements and instructions that the labels shall be affixed to the panelboards to identify which branch circuits supply the circuits to those space heating installations.

424-93. Installation.

(a) General.

(1) Heating panels and heating panel sets shall be installed in accordance with the manufacturer's instructions.

(2) The heating portion shall not:

a. Be installed in or behind surfaces where subject to physical damage.

b. Be run through or above walls, partitions, cupboards or similar portions of structures that extend to the ceiling.

c. Be run in or through thermal insulation, but shall be permitted to be in contact with the surface of thermal insulation.

(3) Edges of panels and panel sets shall be separated by not less than 8 inches (203 mm) from the edges of any outlet boxes and junction boxes that are to be used for mounting surface lighting fixtures. A clearance of not less than 2 inches (50.8 mm) shall be provided from recessed fixtures and their trims, ventilating openings and other such openings in room surfaces. Sufficient area shall be provided to assure that no heating panel or heating panel set is to be covered by any surface-mounted units.

Exception: Heating panels and panel sets listed and marked for lesser clearances shall be permitted to be installed at the marked clearances.

(4) After the heating panels or heating panel sets are installed and inspected, it shall be permitted to install a surface which has been identified by the manufacturer's instructions as being suitable for the installation. The surface shall be secured so that the nails or other fastenings do not pierce the heating panels or heating panel sets.

(5) Surfaces permitted by Section 424-93(a)(4) shall be permitted to be covered with paint, wallpaper or other approved surfaces identified in the manufacturer's instructions as being suitable.

(b) Heating Panel Sets.

(1) Heating panel sets shall be permitted to be secured to the lower face of joists or mounted in between joists, headers or nailing strips.

(2) Heating panel sets shall be installed parallel to joists or nailing strips.

(3) Nailing or stapling of heating panel sets shall be done only through the unheated portions provided for this purpose. Heating panel sets shall not be cut through or nailed through any point closer than ¼ inch (6.35 mm) to the element. Nails, staples or other fasteners shall not be used where they penetrate current-carrying parts.

(4) Heating panel sets shall be installed as complete units unless identified as suitable for field cutting in an approved manner.

424-94. Clearances of Wiring in Ceilings. Wiring located above heated ceilings shall be spaced not less than 2 inches (50.3 mm) above the heated ceiling and shall be considered as operating at an ambient of 50°C (122°F). The ampacity shall be computed on the basis of the correction factors given in Tables 310-16 through 310-19.

Exception: Wiring above heated ceilings and located above thermal insulations having a minimum thickness of 2 inches (50.8 mm) shall not require correction for temperature.

424-95. Clearances of Branch-Circuit Wiring in Walls.

(a) Exterior Walls. Where located in exterior walls, wiring shall be located outside the thermal insulation.

(b) Interior Walls. Any wiring behind heating panels or heating panel sets located in interior walls or partitions shall be considered as operating at an ambient of 40°C (104°F) and the ampacity shall be computed on the basis of the correction factors given in Tables 310-16 and 310-18.

424-96. Connection to Branch-Circuit Conductors.

(a) General. Heating panels or heating panel sets assembled together in the field to form a heating installation in one room or area shall be connected in accordance with the manufacturer's instructions.

(b) Heating Panels. Heating panels shall be connected to branch-circuit wiring by an approved wiring method.

(c) Heating Panel Sets.

(1) Heating panel sets shall be connected to branch-circuit wiring by a method identified as being suitable for the purpose.

(2) A heating panel set provided with terminal junction assembly shall be permitted to have the nonheating leads attached at the time of installation in accordance with the manufacturer's instructions.

424-97. Nonheating Leads. Excess nonheating leads of heating panels or heating panel sets shall be permitted to be cut to the required length. They shall meet the installation requirements of the wiring method employed in accordance with Section 424-96. Nonheating leads shall be an integral part of a heating panel and a heating panel set and shall not be subjected to the ampacity requirements of Section 424-3(b) for branch circuits.

424-98. Installation in Concrete or Poured Masonry.

(a) Maximum Heated Area. Heating panels or heating panel sets shall not exceed 33 watts per square foot (0.093 sq m) of heated area.

(b) Secured in Place and Identified as Suitable. Heating panels or heating panel sets shall be secured in place by means specified in the manufacturer's instructions and identified as suitable for the installation.

(c) Expansion Joints. Heating panels or heating panel sets shall not be installed where they bridge expansion joints unless protected from expansion and contraction.

(d) Spacings. Spacings shall be maintained between heating panels or heating panel sets and metal embedded in the floor.

Exception: Grounded metal-clad heating panels shall be permitted to be in contact with metal embedded in the floor.

(e) Protection of Leads. Leads shall be protected where they leave the floor by rigid metal conduit, intermediate metal conduit, rigid nonmetallic conduit, electrical metallic tubing or by other approved means.

(f) Bushings or Fittings Required. Bushings or approved fittings shall be used where the leads emerge within the floor slabs.

ARTICLE 426 — FIXED OUTDOOR ELECTRIC DE-ICING AND SNOW-MELTING EQUIPMENT

Contents

(b) Temperature Controller without "Off" Position.

(c) Remote Temperature Controller.

(d) Combined Switching Devices.

426-52. Overcurrent Protection.

A. General

426-1. Scope. The requirements of this article shall apply to electrically energized heating systems and the installation of these systems.

(a) Embedded. Embedded in driveways, walks, steps, and other areas.

(b) Exposed. Exposed on drainage systems, bridge structures, roofs, and other structures.

Article 426 includes requirements for resistance heating elements, impedance heating systems, or skin effect heating systems. These systems are defined in Section 426-2. In addition, specific requirements are provided for exposed resistance heating elements of the type commonly used on residences for gutter and roof de-icing and snow melting. See Sections 426-21 and 426-23. See commentary following Section 426-11.

426-2. Definitions. For the purpose of this article:

Heating System. A complete system consisting of components such as heating elements, fastening devices, nonheating circuit wiring, leads, temperature controllers, safety signs, junction boxes, raceways, and fittings.

Resistance Heating Element. A specific separate element to generate heat which is embedded in or fastened to the surface to be heated.

(FPN): Tubular heaters, strip heaters, heating cable, heating tape, and heating panels are examples of resistance heaters.

Impedance Heating System. A system in which heat is generated in a pipe or rod, or combination of pipes and rods, by causing current to flow through the pipe or rod by direct connection to an ac voltage source from a dual-winding transformer. The pipe or rod shall be permitted to be embedded in the surface to be heated, or constitute the exposed components to be heated.

Skin Effect Heating System. A system in which heat is generated on the inner surface of a ferromagnetic envelope embedded in or fastened to the surface to be heated.

(FPN): Typically, an electrically insulated conductor is routed through and connected to the envelope at the other end. The envelope and the electrically insulated conductor are connected to an ac voltage source from a dual-winding transformer.

426-3. Application of Other Articles. All requirements of this Code shall apply except as specifically amended in this article. Cord- and plug-connected fixed outdoor electric de-icing and snow-melting equipment intended for specific use and identified as suitable for this use shall be installed according to Article 422. Fixed outdoor electric de-icing and snow-melting equipment for use in hazardous (classified) locations shall comply with Articles 500 through 516.

This section was revised for the 1984 *Code* to include a new second sentence based on Tentative Interim Amendment No. 70-81-6 issued for the 1981 edition of the *Code*. See Sections 422-7 and 422-8.

ARTICLE 426—ELECTRIC DE-ICING, SNOW-MELTING EQUIPMENT

426-4. Branch-Circuit Sizing. The ampacity of branch-circuit conductors and the rating or setting of overcurrent protective devices supplying fixed outdoor electric de-icing and snow-melting equipment shall be not less than 125 percent of the total load of the heaters. The rating or setting of overcurrent protective devices shall be permitted in accordance with Section 240-3, Exception No. 1.

B. Installation

426-10. General. Equipment for outdoor electric de-icing and snow melting shall be identified as being suitable for:

(1) The chemical, thermal, and physical environment, and

(2) Installation in accordance with the manufacturer's drawings and instructions.

426-11. Use. Electrical heating equipment shall be installed in such a manner as to be afforded protection from physical damage.

The instructions required by UL for UL listed mat or cable de-icing and snow-melting equipment intended for burial in concrete specifically indicate that the slab is required to be a double pour (poured in two parts) if that is the only acceptable means of installation. If such a limitation is not specifically mentioned, either a single or double pour may be used. See Section 110-3(b).

426-12. Thermal Protection. External surfaces of outdoor electric de-icing and snow-melting equipment which operate at temperatures exceeding 60°C (140°F) shall be physically guarded, isolated, or thermally insulated to protect against contact by personnel in the area.

See Section 110-17.

426-13. Identification. The presence of outdoor electric de-icing and snow-melting equipment shall be evident by the posting of appropriate caution signs or markings where clearly visible.

426-14. Special Permission. Fixed outdoor de-icing and snow-melting equipment employing methods of construction or installation other than covered by this article shall be permitted only by special permission.

See definition of "Special Permission" in Article 100.

C. Resistance Heating Elements

426-20. Embedded De-Icing and Snow-Melting Equipment.

(a) Watt Density. Panels or units shall not exceed 120 watts per square foot (0.093 sq m) of heated area.

(b) Spacing. The spacing between adjacent cable runs is dependent upon the rating of the cable, and shall be not less than 1 inch (25.4 mm) on centers.

(c) Cover. Units, panels, or cables shall be installed:

(1) On a substantial asphalt or masonry base at least 2 inches (50.8 mm) thick and have at least 1½ inches (38 mm) of asphalt or masonry applied over the units, panels, or cables; or

(2) They shall be permitted to be installed over other approved bases and embedded within 3½ inches (89 mm) of masonry or asphalt but not less than 1½ inches (38 mm) from the top surface; or

(3) Equipment that has been specially investigated for other forms of installation shall be installed only in the manner for which it has been investigated.

(d) Secured. Cables, units, and panels shall be secured in place by frames or spreaders or other approved means while the masonry or asphalt finish is applied.

(e) Expansion and Contraction. Cables, units, and panels shall not be installed where they bridge expansion joints unless adequately protected from expansion and contraction.

426-21. Exposed De-Icing and Snow-Melting Equipment.

(a) Secured. Heating element assemblies shall be secured to the surface being heated by approved means.

(b) Overtemperature. Where the heating element is not in direct contact with the surface being heated, the design of the heater assembly shall be such that its temperature limitations shall not be exceeded.

(c) Expansion and Contraction. Heating elements and assemblies shall not be installed where they bridge expansion joints unless provision is made for expansion and contraction.

(d) Flexural Capability. Where installed on flexible structures, the heating elements and assemblies shall have a flexural capability compatible with the structure.

426-22. Installation of Nonheating Leads for Embedded Equipment.

(a) Grounding Sheath or Braid. Nonheating leads having a grounding sheath or braid shall be permitted to be embedded in the masonry or asphalt in the same manner as the heating cable without additional physical protection.

(b) Raceways. All but 1 to 6 inches (25.4 to 152 mm) of nonheating leads of Type TW and other approved types not having a grounding sheath shall be enclosed in a rigid conduit, electrical metallic tubing, intermediate metal conduit, or other raceways within asphalt or masonry; and the distance from the factory splice to raceway shall be not less than 1 inch (25.4 mm) or more than 6 inches (152 mm).

(c) Bushings. Insulating bushings shall be used in the asphalt or masonry where leads enter conduit or tubing.

See commentary following Section 373-6(c).

(d) Expansion and Contraction. Leads shall be protected in expansion joints and where they emerge from masonry or asphalt by rigid conduit, electrical metallic tubing, intermediate metal conduit, other raceways, or other approved means.

(e) Leads in Junction Boxes. Not less than 6 inches (152 mm) of free nonheating lead shall be within the junction box.

426-23. Installation of Nonheating Leads for Exposed Equipment.

(a) Nonheating Leads. Power supply nonheating leads (cold leads) for resistance elements shall be suitable for the temperature encountered. Preassembled nonheating leads on approved heaters shall be permitted to be shortened if the markings specified in Section 426-25 are retained. Not less than 6 inches (152 mm) of nonheating leads shall be provided within the junction box.

(b) Protection. Nonheating power supply leads shall be enclosed in a rigid conduit, intermediate metal conduit, electrical metallic tubing, or other approved means.

426-24. Electrical Connection.

(a) Heating Element Connections. Electrical connections, other than factory connections of heating elements to nonheating elements embedded in masonry or asphalt or on exposed surfaces, shall be made with insulated connectors identified for the use.

(b) Circuit Connections. Splices and terminations at the end of the nonheating leads, other than the heating element end, shall be installed in a box or fitting in accordance with Sections 110-14 and 300-15.

426-25. Marking.
Each factory-assembled heating unit shall be legibly marked within 3 inches (76 mm) of each end of the nonheating leads with the permanent identification symbol, catalog number, and ratings in volts and watts, or in volts and amperes.

426-26. Corrosion Protection.
Ferrous and nonferrous metal raceways, cable armor, cable sheaths, boxes, fittings, supports, and support hardware shall be permitted to be installed in concrete or in direct contact with the earth, or in areas subject to severe corrosive influences, when made of material suitable for the condition, or when provided with corrosion protection identified as suitable for the condition.

426-27. Grounding.

(a) Metal Parts. Exposed noncurrent-carrying metal parts of equipment likely to become energized shall be grounded as required in Article 250.

(b) Grounding Braid or Sheath. Grounding means, such as copper braid, metal sheath, or other approved means, shall be provided as part of the heated section of the cable, panel, or unit.

(c) Bonding and Grounding. All noncurrent-carrying metal parts that are likely to become energized shall be bonded together and connected to an equipment grounding conductor sized in accordance with Table 250-95, extending to the distribution panelboard.

D. Impedance Heating

426-30. Personnel Protection.
Exposed elements of impedance heating systems shall be physically guarded, isolated, or thermally insulated with weatherproof jacket to protect against contact by personnel in the area.

426-31. Voltage Limitations.
The impedance heating elements shall not operate at a voltage greater than 30 volts ac.

Exception: The voltage shall be permitted to be greater than 30 volts, but not more than 80 volts, if a ground-fault circuit-interrupter for personnel protection is provided.

426-32. Isolation Transformer.
A dual-winding transformer with a grounded shield between the primary and secondary windings shall be used to isolate the distribution system from the heating system.

426-33. Induced Currents.
All current-carrying components shall be installed in accordance with Section 300-20.

426-34. Grounding. An impedance heating system that is operating at a voltage greater than 30, but not more than 80, shall be grounded at designated point(s).

E. Skin Effect Heating

426-40. Conductor Ampacity. The ampacity of the electrically insulated conductor inside the ferromagnetic envelope shall be permitted to exceed the values shown in Article 310, provided it is identified as suitable for this use.

426-41. Pull Boxes. Where pull boxes are used they shall be accessible without excavation by location in suitable vaults or above grade. Outdoor pull boxes shall be of watertight construction.

426-42. Single Conductor in Enclosure. The provisions of Section 300-20 shall not apply to the installation of a single conductor in a ferromagnetic envelope (metal enclosure).

426-43. Corrosion Protection. Ferromagnetic envelopes, ferrous or nonferrous metal race-ways, boxes, fittings, supports, and support hardware shall be permitted to be installed in concrete or in direct contact with the earth, or in areas subjected to severe corrosive influences, where made of material suitable for the condition, or where provided with corrosion protection identified as suitable for the condition. Corrosion protection shall maintain the original wall thickness of the ferromagnetic envelope.

426-44. Grounding. The ferromagnetic envelope shall be grounded at both ends; and, in addition, it shall be permitted to be grounded at intermediate points as required by its design.

The provisions of Section 250-26 shall not apply to the installation of skin effect heating systems.

(FPN): See Section 250-26(d).

F. Control and Protection

426-50. Disconnecting Means.

(a) **Disconnection.** All fixed outdoor de-icing and snow-melting equipment shall be provided with a means for disconnection from all ungrounded conductors. Where readily accessible to the user of the equipment, the branch-circuit switch or circuit breaker shall be permitted to serve as the disconnecting means. Switches used as the disconnecting means shall be of the indicating type.

(b) **Cord- and Plug-Connected Equipment.** The factory-installed attachment plug of cord- and plug-connected equipment rated 20 amperes or less and 150 volts or less shall be permitted to be the disconnecting means.

426-51. Controllers.

(a) **Temperature Controller with "Off" Position.** Temperature controlled switching devices which indicate an "off" position and which interrupt line current shall open all ungrounded conductors when the control device is in the "off" position. These devices shall not be permitted to serve as the disconnecting means unless provided with a positive lockout in the "off" position.

(b) **Temperature Controller Without "Off" Position.** Temperature controlled switching devices which do not have an "off" position shall not be required to open all ungrounded conductors and shall not be permitted to serve as the disconnecting means.

(c) Remote Temperature Controller. Remote controlled temperature actuated devices shall not be required to meet the requirements of Section 426-51(a). These devices shall not be permitted to serve as the disconnecting means.

(d) Combined Switching Devices. Switching devices consisting of combined temperature actuated devices and manually controlled switches which serve both as the controller and the disconnecting means shall comply with all of the following conditions:

(1) Open all ungrounded conductors when manually placed in the "off" position; and

(2) Be so designed that the circuit cannot be energized automatically if the device has been manually placed in the "off" position; and

(3) Be provided with a positive lockout in the "off" position.

426-52. Overcurrent Protection. Fixed outdoor electric de-icing and snow-melting equipment shall be permitted to be protected against overcurrent where supplied by a branch circuit as specified in Section 426-4.

ARTICLE 427 — FIXED ELECTRIC HEATING EQUIPMENT FOR PIPELINES AND VESSELS

Contents

A. General

427-1. Scope. The requirements of this article shall apply to electrically energized heating systems and the installation of these systems used with pipelines and/or vessels.

Article 427 includes requirements for impedance heating, induction heating, and skin effect heating, in addition to resistance heating elements. Definitions of the various systems are provided in Section 427-2.

427-2. Definitions. For the purpose of this article:

Pipeline. A length of pipe including pumps, valves, flanges, control devices, strainers and/or similar equipment for conveying fluids.

Vessels. A container such as a barrel, drum, or tank for holding fluids or other material.

Integrated Heating System. A complete system consisting of components such as pipelines, vessels, heating elements, heat transfer medium, thermal insulation, moisture barrier, nonheating leads, temperature controllers, safety signs, junction boxes, raceways, and fittings.

Resistance Heating Element. A specific separate element to generate heat which is applied to the pipeline or vessel externally or internally.

(FPN): Tubular heaters, strip heaters, heating cable, heating tape, heating blankets, and immersion heaters are examples of resistance heaters.

Impedance Heating System. A system in which heat is generated in a pipeline or vessel wall by causing current to flow through the pipeline or vessel wall by direct connection to an ac voltage source from a dual-winding transformer.

Induction Heating System. A system in which heat is generated in a pipeline or vessel wall by inducing current and hysteresis effect in the pipeline or vessel wall from an external isolated ac field source.

Skin Effect Heating System. A system in which heat is generated on the inner surface of a ferromagnetic envelope attached to a pipeline and/or vessel.

(FPN): Typically, an electrically insulated conductor is routed through and connected to the envelope at the other end. The envelope and the electrically insulated conductor are connected to an ac voltage source from a dual-winding transformer.

427-3. Application of Other Articles. All requirements of this Code shall apply except as specifically amended in this article. Cord-connected pipe heating assemblies intended for specific use and identified as suitable for this use shall be installed according to Article 422. Fixed electric pipeline and vessel heating equipment for use in hazardous (classified) locations shall comply with Articles 500 through 516.

See Sections 422-7 and 422-8.

427-4. Branch-Circuit Sizing. The ampacity of branch-circuit conductors and the rating or setting of overcurrent protective devices supplying fixed electric heating equipment for pipelines and vessels shall be not less than 125 percent of the total load of the heaters. The rating or setting of overcurrent protective devices shall be permitted in accordance with Section 240-3, Exception No. 1.

ARTICLE 427—ELECTRIC HEATING FOR PIPELINES, VESSELS

B. Installation

427-10. General. Equipment for pipeline and vessel electrical heating shall be identified as being suitable for: (1) the chemical, thermal and physical environment; and (2) installation in accordance with the manufacturer's drawings and instructions.

427-11. Use. Electrical heating equipment shall be installed in such a manner as to be afforded protection from physical damage.

427-12. Thermal Protection. External surfaces of pipeline and vessel heating equipment which operate at temperatures exceeding 60°C (140°F) shall be physically guarded, isolated, or thermally insulated to protect against contact by personnel in the area.

427-13. Identification. The presence of electrically heated pipelines and/or vessels shall be evident by the posting of appropriate caution signs or markings at frequent intervals along the pipeline or vessel.

C. Resistance Heating Elements

427-14. Secured. Heating element assemblies shall be secured to the surface being heated by means other than the thermal insulation.

427-15. Not in Direct Contact. Where the heating element is not in direct contact with the pipeline or vessel being heated, means shall be provided to prevent overtemperature of the heating element unless the design of the heater assembly is such that its temperature limitations will not be exceeded.

427-16. Expansion and Contraction. Heating elements and assemblies shall not be installed where they bridge expansion joints unless provisions are made for expansion and contraction.

427-17. Flexural Capability. Where installed on flexible pipelines, the heating elements and assemblies shall have a flexural capability compatible with the pipeline.

427-18. Power Supply Leads.

   (a) Nonheating Leads. Power supply nonheating leads (cold leads) for resistance elements shall be suitable for the temperature encountered. Preassembled nonheating leads on approved heaters may be shortened if the markings specified in Section 427-20 are retained. Not less than 6 inches (152 mm) of nonheating leads shall be provided within the junction box.

   (b) Power Supply Leads Protection. Nonheating power supply leads shall be protected where they emerge from electrically heated pipeline or vessel heating units by rigid metal conduit, intermediate metal conduit, electrical metallic tubing, or other raceways identified as suitable for the application.

   (c) Interconnecting Leads. Interconnecting nonheating leads connecting portions of the heating system shall be permitted to be covered by thermal insulation in the same manner as the heaters.

427-19. Electrical Connections.

   (a) Nonheating Interconnections. Nonheating interconnections, where required under thermal insulation, shall be made with insulated connectors identified as suitable for this use.

   (b) Circuit Connections. Splices and terminations outside the thermal insulation shall be installed in a box or fitting in accordance with Sections 110-14 and 300-15.

427-20. Marking. Each factory-assembled heating unit shall be legibly marked within 3 inches (76 mm) of each end of the nonheating leads with the permanent identification symbol, catalog number, and ratings in volts and watts, or in volts and amperes.

427-21. Grounding. Exposed noncurrent-carrying metal parts of electric heating equipment which are likely to become energized shall be grounded as required in Article 250.

D. Impedance Heating

427-25. Personnel Protection. All accessible external surfaces of the pipeline and/or vessel being heated shall be physically guarded, isolated, or thermally insulated (with weatherproof jacket for outside installations) to protect against contact by personnel in the area.

427-26. Voltage Limitations. The pipeline or vessel being heated shall not operate at a voltage greater than 30 volts ac.

Exception: The voltage shall be permitted to be greater than 30 volts but not more than 80 volts if a ground-fault circuit-interrupter for personnel protection is provided.

427-27. Isolation Transformer. A dual-winding transformer with a grounded shield between the primary and secondary windings shall be used to isolate the distribution system from the heating system.

427-28. Induced Currents. All current-carrying components shall be installed in accordance with Section 300-20.

427-29. Grounding. The pipeline and/or vessel being heated which is operating at a voltage greater than 30 but not more than 80 shall be grounded at designated points.

427-30. Secondary Conductor Sizing. The ampacity of the conductors connected to the secondary of the transformer shall be rated at least 100 percent of the total load of the heater.

E. Induction Heating

427-35. Scope. This part covers the installation of line frequency induction heating equipment and accessories for pipelines and vessels.

(FPN): See Article 665 for other applications.

427-36. Personnel Protection. Induction coils that operate or may operate at a voltage greater than 30 volts ac shall be enclosed in a nonmetallic or split metallic enclosure, isolated or made inaccessible by location to protect personnel in the area.

427-37. Induced Current. Induction coils shall be prevented from inducing circulating currents in surrounding metallic equipment, supports, or structures by shielding, isolation, or insulation of the current paths. Stray current paths shall be bonded to prevent arcing.

F. Skin Effect Heating

427-45. Conductor Ampacity. The ampacity of the electrically insulated conductor inside the ferromagnetic envelope shall be permitted to exceed the values given in Article 310 provided it is identified as suitable for this use.

427-46. Pull Boxes. Pull boxes for pulling the electrically insulated conductor in the ferromagnetic envelope shall be permitted to be buried under the thermal insulation providing their locations are indicated by permanent markings on the insulation jacket surface and on drawings. For outdoor installations, pull boxes are to be of watertight construction.

427-47. Single Conductor in Enclosure. The provisions of Section 300-20 shall not apply to the installation of a single conductor in a ferromagnetic envelope (metal enclosure).

427-48. Grounding. The ferromagnetic envelope shall be grounded at both ends and, in addition, it shall be permitted to be grounded at intermediate points as required by its design. The ferromagnetic envelope shall be bonded at all joints to assure electrical continuity.

The provisions of Section 250-26 shall not apply to the installation of skin effect heating systems.

(FPN): See Section 250-26(d).

G. Control and Protection

427-55. Disconnecting Means.

(a) Switch or Circuit Breaker. Means shall be provided to disconnect all fixed electric pipeline or vessel heating equipment from all ungrounded conductors. The branch-circuit switch or circuit breaker, where readily accessible to the user of the equipment, shall be permitted to serve as the disconnecting means. Switches used as disconnecting means shall be of the indicating type, and shall be provided with a positive lockout in the "off" position.

(b) Cord- and Plug-Connected Equipment. The factory-installed attachment plug of cord- and plug-connected equipment rated 20 amperes or less and 150 volts or less to ground shall be permitted to be the disconnecting means.

427-56. Controls.

(a) Temperature Control with "Off" Position. Temperature controlled switching devices which indicate an "off" position and which interrupt line current shall open all ungrounded conductors when the control device is in this "off" position. These devices shall not be permitted to serve as the disconnecting means unless provided with a positive lockout in the "off" position.

(b) Temperature Control Without "Off" Position. Temperature controlled switching devices which do not have an "off" position shall not be required to open all ungrounded conductors and shall not be permitted to serve as the disconnecting means.

(c) Remote Temperature Controller. Remote controlled temperature actuated devices shall not be required to meet the requirements of Section 427-56(a) and (b). These devices shall not be permitted to serve as the disconnecting means.

(d) Combined Switching Devices. Switching devices consisting of combined temperature actuated devices and manually controlled switches which serve both as the controllers and the disconnecting means shall comply with all the following conditions:

(1) Open all ungrounded conductors when manually placed in the "off" position; and

(2) Be so designed that the circuit cannot be energized automatically if the device has been manually placed in the "off" position; and

(3) Be provided with a positive lockout in the "off" position.

427-57. Overcurrent Protection. Heating equipment shall be considered as protected against overcurrent where supplied by a branch circuit as specified in Section 427-4.

ARTICLE 430 — MOTORS, MOTOR CIRCUITS, AND CONTROLLERS

Contents

A. General

430-1. Motor Feeder and Branch Circuits. The following general requirements cover provisions for motors, motor circuits, and controllers that do not properly fall into the other parts of this article.

(FPN): See Article 440 for air-conditioning and refrigerating equipment.

(FPN): See Diagram 430-1.

Diagram 430-1 is intended to assist the user in following the provisions of Article 430. It is not a *Code* requirement.

430-2. Adjustable Speed Drive Systems. The incoming branch circuit or feeder to power conversion equipment included as a part of an adjustable speed drive system shall be based on the rated input to the power conversion equipment. If the power conversion equipment provides overload protection for the motor, additional overload protection is not required.

The disconnecting means shall be permitted to be in the incoming line to the conversion equipment and shall have a rating not less than 115 percent of the rated input current of the conversion unit.

430-3. Part-Winding Motors. A part-winding-start induction or synchronous motor is one arranged for starting by first energizing part of its primary (armature) winding and, subsequently, energizing the remainder of this winding in one or more steps. The purpose is to reduce the initial values of the starting current drawn or the starting torque developed by the motor. A standard part-winding-start induction motor is arranged so that one-half of its primary winding can be energized initially and, subsequently, the remaining half can be energized, both halves then carrying equal current. A hermetic refrigerant compressor motor shall not be considered a standard part-winding-start induction motor.

Where separate overload devices are used with a standard part-winding-start induction motor, each half of the motor winding shall be individually protected in accordance with Sections 430-32 and 430-37 with a trip current one-half that specified.

Each motor-winding connection shall have branch-circuit short-circuit and ground-fault protection rated at not more than one-half that specified by Section 430-52.

ARTICLE 430—MOTORS, CIRCUITS, CONTROLLERS

Exception: A single device having this half rating shall be permitted for both windings if it will allow the motor to start. Where a time-delay (dual-element) fuse is used as a single device for both windings, it shall be permitted to have a rating not exceeding 150 percent of motor full-load current.

Diagram 430-1

General	Part A
Requirements for over 600 volts, nominal	Part J
Protection of live parts all voltages	Part K
Grounding	Part L
Tables	Part M

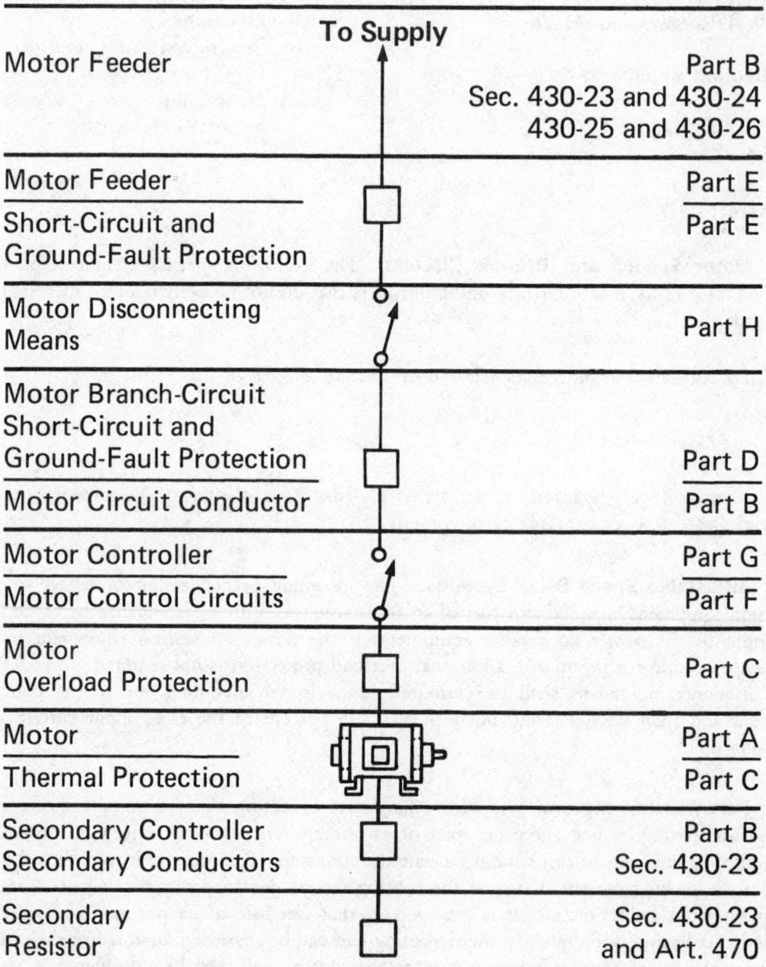

To Supply

Motor Feeder	Part B Sec. 430-23 and 430-24 430-25 and 430-26
Motor Feeder	Part E
Short-Circuit and Ground-Fault Protection	Part E
Motor Disconnecting Means	Part H
Motor Branch-Circuit Short-Circuit and Ground-Fault Protection	Part D
Motor Circuit Conductor	Part B
Motor Controller	Part G
Motor Control Circuits	Part F
Motor Overload Protection	Part C
Motor	Part A
Thermal Protection	Part C
Secondary Controller Secondary Conductors	Part B Sec. 430-23
Secondary Resistor	Sec. 430-23 and Art. 470

430-5. Other Articles. Motors and controllers shall also comply with the applicable provisions of the following:

430-6. Ampacity and Motor Rating Determination. Conductor ampacity and motor ratings shall be determined as specified in (a) and (b) below.

(a) General Motor Applications. Other than as specified for torque motors in (b) below, where the current rating of a motor is used to determine the ampacity of conductors or ampere ratings of switches, branch-circuit short-circuit and ground-fault protection, etc., the values given in Tables 430-147, 430-148, 430-149, and 430-150, including notes, shall be used instead of the actual current rating marked on the motor nameplate. Separate motor overload protection shall be based on the motor nameplate current rating. Where a motor is marked in amperes, but not horsepower, the horsepower rating shall be assumed to be that corresponding to the value given in Tables 430-147, 430-148, 430-149, and 430-150, interpolated if necessary.

Exception No. 1: Multispeed motors shall be in accordance with Sections 430-22(a) and 430-52.

Exception No. 2: For equipment employing a shaded-pole or permanent-split-capacitor-type fan or blower motor that is marked with the motor type, the full-load current for such motor marked on the nameplate of the equipment in which the fan or blower motor is employed shall be used instead of the horsepower rating to determine the ampacity or rating of the disconnecting means, the branch-circuit conductors, the controller, the branch-circuit short-circuit and ground-fault protection, and the separate overload protection. This marking on the equipment nameplate shall not be less than the current marked on the fan or blower motor nameplate.

(b) Torque Motors. For torque motors the rated current shall be locked-rotor current, and this nameplate current shall be used to determine the ampacity of the branch-circuit conductors covered in Sections 430-22 and 430-24 and the ampere rating of the motor overload protection.

(FPN): For motor controllers and disconnecting means, see Section 430-83, Exception No. 3 and Section 430-110.

(c) AC Adjustable Voltage Motors. For motors used in alternating-current, adjustable voltage, variable torque drive systems, the ampacity of conductors, or ampere ratings of switches, branch-circuit short-circuit and ground-fault protection, etc., shall be based on the maximum operating current marked on the motor and/or control nameplate. If the maximum operating current does not appear on the nameplate, the ampacity determination shall be based on 150 percent of the values given in Tables 430-149 and 430-150.

430-7. Marking on Motors and Multimotor Equipment.

(a) Usual Motor Applications. A motor shall be marked with the following information:

(1) Maker's name.

(2) Rated volts and full-load amperes. For a multispeed motor full-load amperes for each speed, except shaded-pole and permanent-split capacitor motors where amperes are required only for maximum speed.

(3) Rated frequency and number of phases, if an alternating-current motor.

(4) Rated full-load speed.

(5) Rated temperature rise or the insulation system class and rated ambient temperature.

(6) Time rating. The time rating shall be 5, 15, 30, or 60 minutes, or continuous.

(7) Rated horsepower if ⅛ horsepower or more. For a multispeed motor ⅛ horsepower or more, rated horsepower for each speed, except shaded-pole and permanent-split capacitor motors ⅛ horsepower or more where rated horsepower is required only for maximum speed. Motors of arc welders are not required to be marked with the horsepower rating.

(8) Code letter if an alternating-current motor rated ½ horsepower or more. On polyphase wound-rotor motors the code letter shall be omitted.

(FPN): See (b) below.

(9) Secondary volts and full-load amperes if a wound-rotor induction motor.

(10) Field current and voltage for direct-current excited synchronous motors.

(11) Winding: straight shunt, stabilized shunt, compound, or series, if a direct-current motor. Fractional horsepower dc motors 7 inches (178 mm) or less in diameter shall not be required to be marked.

(12) A motor provided with a thermal protector complying with Section 430-32(a) (2) or (c) (2) shall be marked "Thermally Protected." Thermally protected motors rated 100 watts or less and complying with Section 430-32(c) (2) shall be permitted to use the abbreviated marking, "T.P."

(13) A motor complying with Section 430-32(c) (4) shall be marked "Impedance Protected." Impedance protected motors rated 100 watts or less and complying with Section 430-32(c) (4) shall be permitted to use the abbreviated marking "Z.P."

(b) Locked-Rotor Indicating Code Letters. Code letters marked on motor nameplates to show motor input with locked rotor shall be in accordance with Table 430-7(b).

The code letter indicating motor input with locked rotor shall be in an individual block on the nameplate, properly designated. This code letter shall be used for determining branch-circuit short-circuit and ground-fault protection by reference to Table 430-152, as provided in Section 430-52.

(1) Multispeed motors shall be marked with the code letter designating the locked-rotor kVA per horsepower for the highest speed at which the motor can be started.

Exception: Constant-horsepower multispeed motors shall be marked with the code letter giving the highest locked-rotor kVA per horsepower.

(2) Single-speed motors starting on Y connection and running on delta connections shall be marked with a code letter corresponding to the locked-rotor kVA per horsepower for the Y connection.

(3) Dual-voltage motors that have a different locked-rotor kVA per horsepower on the two voltages shall be marked with the code letter for the voltage giving the highest locked-rotor kVA per horsepower.

(4) Motors with 60- and 50-hertz ratings shall be marked with a code letter designating the locked-rotor kVA per horsepower on 60 hertz.

(5) Part-winding-start motors shall be marked with a code letter designating the locked-rotor kVA per horsepower that is based upon the locked-rotor current for the full winding of the motor.

Table 430-7(b). Locked-Rotor Indicating Code Letters

Code Letter		Kilovolt-Amperes per Horsepower with Locked Rotor
A		0 — 3.14
B		3.15 — 3.54
C		3.55 — 3.99
D		4.0 — 4.49
E		4.5 — 4.99
F		5.0 — 5.59
G		5.6 — 6.29
H		6.3 — 7.09
J		7.1 — 7.99
K		8.0 — 8.99
L		9.0 — 9.99
M		10.0 — 11.19
N		11.2 — 12.49
P		12.5 — 13.99
R		14.0 — 15.99
S		16.0 — 17.99
T		18.0 — 19.99
U		20.0 — 22.39
V		22.4 — and up

(c) Torque Motors. Torque motors are rated for operation at standstill and shall be marked in accordance with (a) above.

Exception: Locked-rotor torque shall replace horsepower.

(d) Multimotor and Combination-Load Equipment. Multimotor and combination-load equipment shall be provided with a visible nameplate marked with the maker's name, the rating in volts, frequency, number of phases, minimum supply circuit conductor ampacity, and the maximum ampere rating of the circuit short-circuit and ground-fault protective device. The conductor ampacity shall be computed in accordance with Section 430-25 and counting all of the motors and other loads that will be operated at the same time. The short-circuit and ground-fault protective device rating shall not exceed the value computed in accordance with Section 430-53. Multimotor equipment for use on two or more circuits shall be marked with the above information for each circuit.

Where the equipment is not factory-wired and the individual nameplates of motors and other loads are visible after assembly of the equipment, the individual nameplates shall be permitted to serve as the required marking.

The nameplate marking of the maximum ampere rating of the branch-circuit short-circuit and ground-fault protective device may limit the type of protective device to a fuse by stipulating "fuse" without reference to a circuit breaker. This means that the circuit to the equipment is required to be protected by fuses, such as in a fused disconnect switch. The fused switch could be supplied from a circuit breaker in a panelboard.

ARTICLE 430—MOTORS, CIRCUITS, CONTROLLERS

430-8. Marking on Controllers. A controller shall be marked with the maker's name or identification, the voltage, the current or horsepower rating, and such other necessary data to properly indicate the motors for which it is suitable. A controller that includes motor overload protection suitable for group motor application shall be marked with the motor overload protection and the maximum branch-circuit short-circuit and ground-fault protection for such applications.

Combination controllers employing adjustable instantaneous trip circuit breakers shall be clearly marked to indicate the ampere settings of the adjustable trip element.

Where a controller is built in as an integral part of a motor or of a motor-generator set, individual marking of the controller shall not be required if the necessary data are on the nameplate. For controllers that are an integral part of equipment approved as a unit, the above marking shall be permitted on the equipment nameplate.

430-9. Marking at Terminals. Terminals of motors and controllers shall be suitably marked or colored where necessary to indicate the proper connections.

430-10. Wiring Space in Enclosures.

(a) General. Enclosures for motor controllers and disconnecting means shall not be used as junction boxes, auxiliary gutters, or raceways for conductors feeding through or tapping off to the other apparatus unless designs are employed which provide adequate space for this purpose.

(FPN): See Section 373-8 for switch and overcurrent-device enclosures.

During the planning stages of a motor(s) installation, consideration should be given to location and adequate work space for motor controllers and disconnects, including provisions for the use of auxiliary gutters or junction boxes to assure adequate space for conductors "feeding through" or "tapping off" to other apparatus.

For switch and overcurrent device enclosures, see Section 373-8.

(b) Wire Bending Space in Enclosures. Minimum wire bending space within the enclosures for motor controllers shall be in accordance with Table 430-10(b) when measured in a straight line from the end of the lug or wire connector (in the direction the wire leaves the terminal) to the wall or barrier. Where alternate wire termination means is substituted for that supplied by the manufacturer of the controller, it shall be of a type identified by the manufacturer for use with the controller and shall not reduce the minimum wire bending space.

Where the enclosure is a motor control center, the minimum wire bending space shall be in accordance with requirements of Article 373.

See Figure 430-1 for illustration of measurement in accordance with Section 430-10(b).

430-11. Protection Against Liquids. Suitable guards or enclosures shall be provided to protect exposed current-carrying parts of motors and the insulation of motor leads where installed directly under equipment, or in other locations where dripping or spraying oil, water, or other injurious liquid may occur, unless the motor is designed for the existing conditions.

Exposed current-carrying parts and insulated leads of motors should be suitably protected from injurious liquids (dripping oil, water, or excessive moisture) whose presence may cause an unnecessary breakdown or, in many cases, a fire.

430-12. Motor Terminal Housings.

(a) Material. Where motors are provided with terminal housings, the housings shall be of metal and of substantial construction.

Exception: In other than hazardous (classified) locations, substantial nonmetallic, nonburning housings shall be permitted on motors larger than 34 inches (864 mm) in diameter provided internal grounding means between the machine frame and the conduit connection is incorporated within the housing.

(FPN): See Method of Test for Flammability of Self-Supporting Plastics (ANSI K65.21-1975) for over 0.127 CM (0.050 inch) in thickness, for nonburning test.

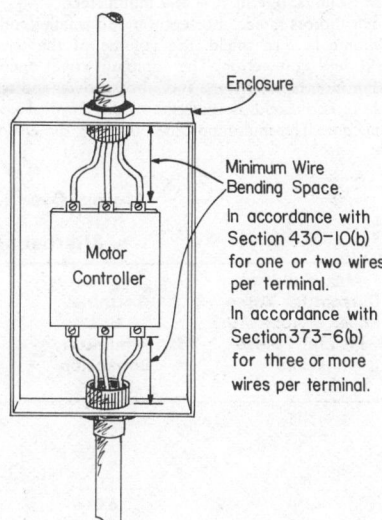

Figure 430-1. Wire bending space in enclosures for motor controllers.

Table 430-10(b). Minimum Wire Bending Space at the Terminals of Enclosed Motor Controllers (in Inches)

AWG or Circular-Mil Size of Wire	*Wires per Terminal	
	1	2
14-10	Not specified	—
8-6	1½	—
4-3	2	—
2	2½	—
1	3	—
1/0	5	5
2/0	6	6
3/0-4/0	7	7
250	8	8
300	10	10
350-500	12	12
600-700	14	16
750-900	18	19

* Where provision for 3 or more wires per terminal exists the minimum wire bending space shall be in accordance with the requirements of Article 373.

(b) Dimensions and Space — Wire-to-Wire Connections. When these terminal housings enclose wire-to-wire connections, they shall have minimum dimensions and usable volumes in accordance with Table 430-12(b).

Table 430-12(b).   Terminal Housings — Wire-to-Wire Connections
Motors 11 Inches in Diameter or Less

HP	Cover Opening, Minimum Dimension, Inches	Usable Volume, Minimum, Cubic Inches
1 and smaller*	1⅜	7½
1½, 2 and 3†	1¾	12
5 and 7½	2	16
10 and 15	2½	26

For SI units: one inch = 25.4 millimeters.

* For motors rated 1 horsepower and smaller and with the terminal housing partially or wholly integral with the frame or end shield, the volume of the terminal housing shall be not less than 0.8 cubic inch per wire-to-wire connection. The minimum cover opening dimension is not specified.

† For motors rated 1½, 2 and 3 horsepower and with the terminal housing partially or wholly integral with the frame or end shield, the volume of the terminal housing shall not be less than 1.0 cubic inch per wire-to-wire connection. The minimum cover opening dimension is not specified.

Motors Over 11 Inches in Diameter

Alternating-Current Motors

Max. Full-load Current for Three-phase Motors with Max. of Twelve Leads Amperes	Terminal Box Minimum Dimension Inches	Usable Volume Minimum Cubic Inches	Typical Maximum Horsepower Three Phase	
			230 Volt	460 Volt
45	2.5	26	15	30
70	3.3	55	25	50
110	4.0	100	40	75
160	5.0	180	60	125
250	6.0	330	100	200
400	7.0	600	150	300
600	8.0	1100	250	500

For SI units: one inch = 25.4 millimeters.

Direct-Current Motors

Maximum Full-Load Current for Motors with Maximum of Six Leads Amperes	Terminal Box Minimum Dimensions Inches	Usable Volume, Minimum Cubic Inches
68	2.5	26
105	3.3	55
165	4.0	100
240	5.0	180
375	6.0	330
600	7.0	600
900	8.0	1100

For SI units: one inch = 25.4 millimeters.

Auxiliary leads for such items as brakes, thermostats, space heater, exciting fields, etc., may be neglected if their current-carrying area does not exceed 25 percent of the current-carrying area of the machine power leads.

(c) Dimensions and Space — Fixed Terminal Connections. Where these terminal housings enclose rigidly mounted motor terminals, the terminal housing shall be of sufficient size to provide minimum terminal spacings and usable volumes in accordance with Tables 430-12(c)(1) and (c)(2).

Table 430-12(c) (1).   Terminal Spacings — Fixed Terminals

	Minimum Spacing, Inches	
Nominal Volts	Between Line Terminals	Between Line Terminals and Other Uninsulated Metal Parts
240 or less	¼	¼
Over 250 through 600	⅜	⅜

For SI units: one inch = 25.4 millimeters.

Table 430-12(c) (2).   Usable Volumes — Fixed Terminals

Power-Supply Conductor Size, AWG	Minimum Usable Volume per Power-Supply Conductor, Cubic Inches
14	1.0
12 and 10	1¼
8 and 6	2¼

For SI units: one inch = 25.4 millimeters.

(d) Large Wire or Factory Connections. For motors with larger ratings, greater number of leads, or larger wire sizes, or where motors are installed as a part of factory-wired equipment, without additional connection being required at the motor terminal housing during equipment installation, the terminal housing shall be of ample size to make connections, but the foregoing provisions for the volumes of terminal housings shall not be considered applicable.

(e) Equipment Grounding Connections. A means for attachment of an equipment grounding conductor termination in accordance with Section 250-113 shall be provided at motor terminal housings for wire-to-wire connections or fixed terminal connections. The means for such connections shall be permitted to be located either inside or outside the motor terminal housing.

Exception: Where a motor is installed as a part of factory-wired equipment, which is required to be grounded and without additional connection being required at the motor terminal housing during equipment installation, a separate means for motor grounding at the motor terminal housing shall not be required.

430-13. Bushing. Where wires pass through an opening in an enclosure, conduit box, or barrier, a bushing shall be used to protect the conductors from the edges of openings having sharp edges. The bushing shall have smooth well-rounded surfaces where it may be in contact with the conductors. If used where oils, greases, or other contaminants may be present, the bushing shall be made of material not deleteriously affected.

(FPN): For conductors exposed to deteriorating agents, see Section 310-9.

430-14. Location of Motors.

(a) Ventilation and Maintenance. Motors shall be located so that adequate ventilation is provided and so that maintenance, such as lubrication of bearings and replacing of brushes, can be readily accomplished.

(b) Open Motors. Open motors having commutators or collector rings shall be located or protected so that sparks cannot reach adjacent combustible material, but this shall not prohibit the installation of these motors on wooden floors or supports.

ARTICLE 430—MOTORS, CIRCUITS, CONTROLLERS

430-16. Exposure to Dust Accumulations. In locations where dust or flying material will collect on or in motors in such quantities as to seriously interfere with the ventilation or cooling of motors and thereby cause dangerous temperatures, suitable types of enclosed motors that will not overheat under the prevailing conditions shall be used.

(FPN): Especially severe conditions may require the use of enclosed pipe-ventilated motors, or enclosure in separate dusttight rooms, properly ventilated from a source of clean air.

For motors exposed to combustible dust or readily ignitible flying material, see the requirements of Sections 502-8 and 502-9 (Class II, Divisions 1 and 2) and Sections 503-6 and 503-7 (Class III, Divisions 1 and 2). For classification of locations, see Sections 500-5 (Class II locations) and 500-6 (Class III locations).

430-17. Highest Rated (Largest) Motor. In determining compliance with Sections 430-24, 430-53(b), and 430-53(c), the highest rated (largest) motor shall be considered to be that motor having the highest rated full-load current. The full-load current used to determine the highest rated motor shall be the equivalent value corresponding to the motor horsepower rating selected from Tables 430-147, 430-148, 430-149, and 430-150.

430-18. Nominal Voltage of Rectifier Systems. The nominal value of the ac voltage being rectified shall be used to determine the voltage of a rectifier derived system.

Exception: The nominal dc voltage of the rectifier shall be used if it exceeds the peak value of the ac voltage being rectified.

B. Motor Circuit Conductors

430-21. General. Part B specifies sizes of conductors capable of carrying the motor current without overheating under the conditions specified.

Exception: The provisions of Section 430-124 shall apply over 600 volts, nominal.

The provisions of Articles 250, 300, and 310 shall not apply to conductors that form an integral part of approved equipment, or to integral conductors of motors, motor controllers, and the like.

(FPN): See Sections 300-1(b) and 310-1.

430-22. Single Motor.

(a) General. Branch-circuit conductors supplying a single motor shall have an ampacity not less than 125 percent of the motor full-load current rating.

In case of a multispeed motor, the selection of branch-circuit conductors on the line side of the controller shall be based on the highest of the full-load current ratings shown on the motor nameplate; selection of branch-circuit conductors between the controller and the motor, which are energized for that particular speed, shall be based on the current rating for that speed.

Exception No. 1: Conductors for a motor used for short-time, intermittent, periodic, or varying duty shall have an ampacity not less than the percentage of the motor nameplate current rating shown in Table 430-22(a) Exception unless the authority having jurisdiction grants special permission for conductors of smaller size.

Exception No. 2: For direct-current motors operating from a rectified single-phase power supply, the conductors between the controller and the motor shall have an ampacity of not less than the following percent of the motor full-load current rating:

a. Where a rectifier bridge of the single-phase half-wave type is used, 190 percent.

b. Where a rectifier bridge of the single-phase full-wave type is used, 150 percent.

Table 430-22(a) Exception.   Duty-Cycle Service

Classification of Service	Percentages of Nameplate Current Rating			
	5-Minute Rated Motor	15-Minute Rated Motor	30 & 60 Minute Rated Motor	Con-tinuous Rated Motor
Short-Time Duty				
Operating valves, raising or lowering rolls, etc.........	110	120	150	. . .
Intermittent Duty				
Freight and passenger elevators, tool heads, pumps, drawbridges, turntables, etc.				
For arc welders, see Section 630-21	85	85	90	140
Periodic Duty				
Rolls, ore- and coal-handling machines, etc.............	85	90	95	140
Varying Duty	110	120	150	200

Any motor application shall be considered as continuous duty unless the nature of the apparatus it drives is such that the motor will not operate continuously with load under any condition of use.
See Example No. 8, Chapter 9 and Diagram 430-1.

The provision for a conductor with an ampacity of at least 125 percent of the motor full-load current rating is not a conductor derating. It is based on the need to provide for a sustained running current greater than the rated full-load current and for protection of the conductors by the motor overload protective device set above the motor full-load current rating.

The ampacity of the motor branch-circuit conductors is based on the full-load current rating values provided in Tables 430-147 through 430-150.

(b) Separate Terminal Enclosure. The conductors between a stationary motor rated 1 horsepower or less and the separate terminal enclosure permitted in Section 430-145(b) shall be permitted to be smaller than No. 14 but not smaller than No. 18, provided they have an ampacity as specified in (a) above.

Section 240-40 requires a disconnecting means on the supply side of cartridge fuses to disconnect the fuses from the source of electrical energy.

Figure 430-2 illustrates each motor on an individual branch circuit with branch-circuit short-circuit and ground-fault protective devices located at a distribution panel and disconnecting means, controllers, and overload protection at the motor locations.

Figure 430-3 also illustrates each motor on an individual branch circuit, but, unlike Figure 430-2, the branch circuits are tapped from a subfeeder at a convenient location such as a junction box, wireway, or from open wiring. The tap conductors are required to terminate in a branch-circuit protective device located not more than 25 ft from where the taps are connected to the subfeeder in accordance with Section 430-28. Also see Section 430-28, Exception which permits a 100-ft tap under some conditions.

Where motors or motor-operated appliances are connected to a 15- or 20-A branch circuit that also supplies lighting, or other appliance loads, as illustrated in Figure 430-4, the provisions of Articles 210 and 430 apply. Motors rated less than 1 hp may be connected to these circuits and are required to be provided with overload protective devices unless the motors are not permanently installed, are started manually, and are within sight from the controller location. For additional information for the installation of motors (1 hp or less), see Sections 430-32(b) and (c), and 430-53(a).

Figure 430-5 illustrates the essential parts of a motor branch circuit: (1) the branch-circuit conductors, (2) the disconnecting means, (3) the branch-circuit short-circuit and ground-fault protective devices, and (4) the motor overload protective devices. The branch-circuit short-circuit and ground-fault protective device may be fuses or a circuit breaker and must be capable of carrying the starting current of the motor without opening the circuit. See Table 430-152.

In general, it is required that every motor be provided with overload protective devices intended to protect motors, motor-control apparatus and motor branch-circuit conductors against excessive heating due to motor overloads and failure to start. Overload in equipment is considered to be operation in excess of normal, full-load rating, which, when it persists for a sufficient length of time, will cause damage or dangerous overheating. Overload in a motor includes stalled rotor, but does not include fault currents due to short circuits or grounds. See Section 430-44 for conditions where providing automatic opening of a motor circuit due to overload may be objectionable.

A motor is considered to be for continuous duty unless the nature of the apparatus it drives is such that the motor cannot operate continuously with load under any condition of use. Conductors for a motor used for short-time, intermittent, periodic, or varying duty are required to have an ampacity in accordance with Table 430-22(a), Exception. Branch-circuit conductors for a motor with a rated horsepower used for 5-minute short-time duty service are permitted to be sized smaller than for the same motor with a 60-minute rating, due to the cooling intervals between operating periods.

When selecting the smallest permissible size branch-circuit conductors for

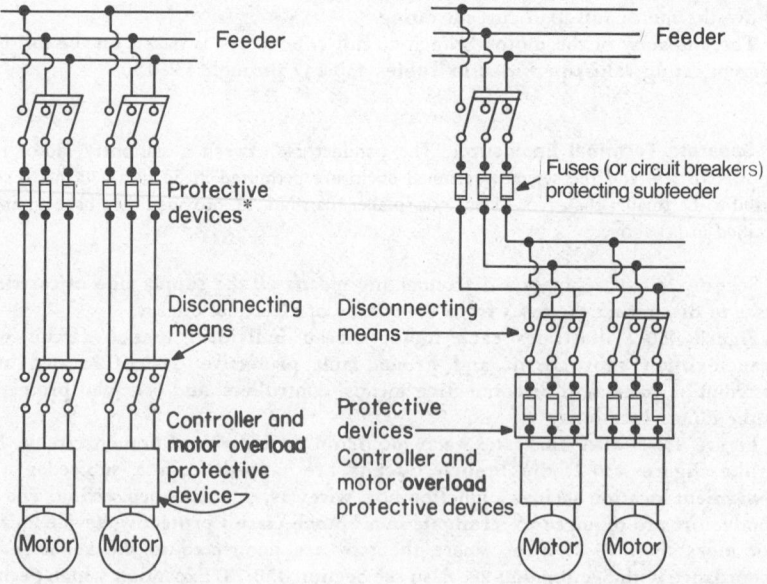

Figure 430-2. Layout showing each motor supplied by an individual branch circuit from a distribution center. (*branch-circuit, short-circuit, and ground-fault protective devices)

Figure 430-3. Layout showing a subfeeder supplying individual branch circuits to each motor.

elevator motors, which are generally considered intermittent duty motors, it is safest to be guided by the recommendations of the manufacturer of the equipment. This also applies to feeders of two or more elevator motors or other types of similar equipment.

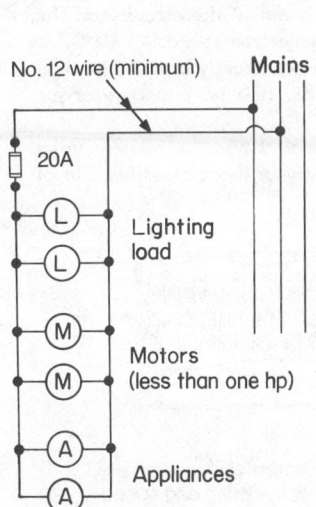

Figure 430-4. Layout showing a 20-A branch circuit supplying small motors, lamps, and appliances.

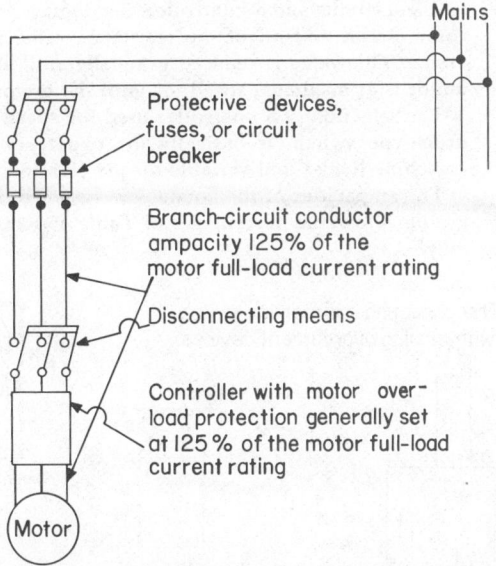

Figure 430-5. A motor branch circuit showing the three essential parts, that is, the branch-circuit conductors, branch-circuit overcurrent protection, and motor overload protection.

430-23. Wound-Rotor Secondary.

(a) Continuous Duty. For continuous duty, the conductors connecting the secondary of a wound-rotor alternating-current motor to its controller shall have an ampacity not less than 125 percent of the full-load secondary current of the motor.

(b) Other than Continuous Duty. For other than continuous duty, these conductors shall have an ampacity, in percent of full-load secondary current, not less than that specified in Table 430-22(a) Exception.

(c) Resistor Separate from Controller. Where the secondary resistor is separate from the controller, the ampacity of the conductors between controller and resistor shall not be less than that given in Table 430-23(c).

Table 430-23(c).   Secondary Conductor

Resistor Duty Classification	Ampacity of Conductor in Percent of Full-Load Secondary Current
Light starting duty	35
Heavy starting duty	45
Extra-heavy starting duty	55
Light intermittent duty	65
Medium intermittent duty	75
Heavy intermittent duty	85
Continuous duty	110

Wound-rotor ac motors are generally used where speed control is desired, where high starting torque for a rapid smooth acceleration to full load is required, for frequent starting, and for low starting current. These motors are also known as slip-ring motors because three slip rings are mounted on the shaft, and brushes, which are in contact with the slip rings, are connected to field-installed external resistance units and a controller. See Figure 430-6. The resistors are a part of the rotor circuit and all of the resistance value is in the circuit when starting the motor. This value is reduced gradually until all of it is out of the circuit and the motor is at maximum speed, or until the motor is at a desired speed.

The selection of a controller used for speed regulation, usually a dial-type or a drum-type switch, is basically for two types of loads, that is, constant-torque (machine loads) and variable-torque (fan loads).

The ampacities of the conductors between the controller and the resistor units are the allowable percentages of Table 430-23(c) for the resistor classification of duty.

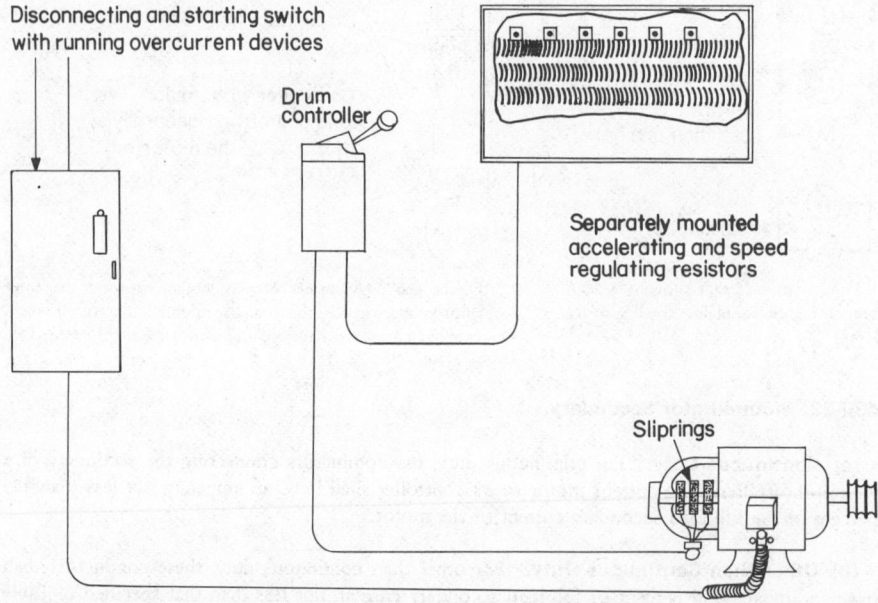

Disconnecting and starting switch
with running overcurrent devices

Drum
controller

Separately mounted
accelerating and speed
regulating resistors

Sliprings

Figure 430-6. A branch circuit to a wound-rotor induction motor showing a drum controller and separate bank of resistors for motor starting and speed regulation.

430-24. Conductors Supplying Several Motors. Conductors supplying two or more motors shall have an ampacity equal to the sum of the full-load current rating of all the motors plus 25 percent of the highest rated motor in the group.

Where one or more motors of the group are used on short-time, intermittent, periodic, or varying duty, the ampacity of the conductors shall be computed as follows:

(1) Determine the needed ampere rating for each motor used for other than continuous duty from Table 430-22(a) Exception.

(2) Determine the needed ampere rating for each continuous-duty motor based on 100 percent motor full-load current rating.

(3) Multiply the largest single motor ampere rating determined from (1) or (2) above by 1.25. Add all other motor ampere ratings from (1) and (2) above and select the conductor ampacity for this total ampere rating.

Exception: Where the circuitry is so interlocked as to prevent the starting and running of a second motor or group of motors, the conductor size shall be determined from the larger motor or group of motors that is to be operated at a given time.

(FPN): See Example No. 8, Chapter 9.

Where the conductors are feeders, the highest rating or setting of the feeder short-circuit and ground-fault protective devices for the minimum size feeder conductor permitted by this section is specified in Section 430-62.

The size of the feeder conductors is required to be increased accordingly where the selection of a feeder protective device of higher rating or setting is based on the simultaneous starting of two or more motors.

These requirements, and those of Section 430-62 for the short-circuit and ground-fault protection of power feeders, are based upon the principle that a power feeder should be of such size that it will have an ampacity equal to 125 percent of the running current of the largest motor, plus the full-load running currents of all other motors supplied by the feeder. Except when two or more motors may be started simultaneously, the heaviest load that a power feeder will ever be required to carry occurs when the largest motor is started at a time when all the other motors supplied by the same feeder are running and delivering their full-rated horsepower.

Where the conductors are branch-circuit conductors to multimotor equipment, Section 430-53 specifies the maximum rating of the branch-circuit short-circuit and ground-fault protective device. Section 430-7(d) requires the maximum ampere rating of the short-circuit and ground-fault protective device to be marked on the equipment.

430-25. Conductors Supplying Motors and Other Loads.

(a) Combination Load. Conductors supplying a motor load and in addition a lighting or appliance load shall have an ampacity sufficient for the lighting or appliance load computed in accordance with Article 220 and other applicable sections plus the motor load determined in accordance with Section 430-24 or, for a single motor, in accordance with Section 430-22.

Exception: The ampacity of conductors supplying motor-operated fixed electric space heating equipment shall conform with Section 424-3(b).

(b) Multimotor and Combination-Load Equipment. The ampacity of the conductors supplying multimotor and combination-load equipment shall not be less than the minimum circuit ampacity marked on the equipment in accordance with Section 430-7(d).

To compute the load for the minimum allowable conductor size for a combination lighting (or lighting and appliance) load and motor load, the capacity for the lighting load is determined in accordance with Article 220 (and other applicable sections, Article 424, etc.) plus the sum of the motor load, determined in accordance with Section 430-22 (single motor), or Section 430-24 (two or more motors).

430-26. Feeder Demand Factor.

Where reduced heating of the conductors results from motors operating on duty-cycle, intermittently, or from all motors not operating at one time, the authority having jurisdiction may grant permission for feeder conductors to have an ampacity less than specified in Sections 430-24 and 430-25, provided the conductors have sufficient ampacity for the maximum load determined in accordance with the sizes and number of motors supplied and the character of their loads and duties.

ARTICLE 430—MOTORS, CIRCUITS, CONTROLLERS

The authority having jurisdiction may grant permission to allow a demand factor of less than 100 percent for industrial plants where operational procedures, production demands, or the nature of the work is such that all the motors are not running at one time.

430-27. Capacitors with Motors. Where capacitors are installed in motor circuits, conductors shall comply with Sections 460-8 and 460-9.

430-28. Feeder Taps. Feeder tap conductors shall have an ampacity not less than that required by Part B, shall terminate in a branch-circuit protective device and, in addition, shall meet one of the following requirements: (1) be enclosed by either an enclosed controller or by a raceway and be not more than 10 feet (3.05 m) in length; or (2) have an ampacity of at least one-third that of the feeder conductors, be protected from physical damage and be not more than 25 feet (7.62 m) in length; or (3) have the same ampacity as the feeder conductors.

No short-circuit and ground-fault protection is required at a point where a tap conductor, equal in size to the feeder conductor from which it is supplied, is used. The tap conductors are required to be protected by the same short-circuit and ground-fault protection (fuses or circuit breakers) protecting the feeder conductors.

In addition to the above, short-circuit and ground-fault protection may be omitted at the point of connection to a feeder where a tap conductor, which may be less than ⅓ of the feeder size, is limited to 10 ft or less in length and enclosed within a controller or raceway, and where a tap conductor, which is at least ⅓ the ampacity of the feeder, is limited to 25 ft or less in length and suitably protected from physical damage. In high bay manufacturing buildings, feeder taps up to 100 ft long are permitted under Section 430-28, Exception.

Tap conductors are required to terminate in a branch-circuit short-circuit and ground-fault protective device. Conductors from this point to the motor-running protective device and to the motor are required to have an ampacity that is 125 percent of the full-load motor current, as specified in Section 430-22.

Example: A 15-hp 230-V 3-phase motor with autotransformer starter is to be supplied by a tap made to a 250,000 CM feeder. Assuming three conductors in an individual raceway, all to be Type THW copper, and no ambient correction factor, the feeder has an ampacity of 255 A (see Table 310-16). Where the tap conductors are not over 25 ft long (see Figure 430-7), No. 4 AWG conductors with an ampacity of 85 A are permitted (⅓ × 255 A = 85 A).

The full-load current of the motor is 42 A and, according to Part D of Article 430, assuming that the motor is not marked with a code letter, the branch-circuit fuses or circuit breakers are permitted to be rated at 90 A (nontime-delay fuse) or less in accordance with Table 430-152 and Section 430-52, Exception No. 1. With the motor overload protection set at 50 A the tap conductors are well protected from overload.

Tap conductors connected to feeders are not permitted to be sized smaller than the ampacity of branch-circuit conductors required by Section 430-22.

Exception: Feeder Taps Over 25 Feet (7.62 m) Long. In high-bay manufacturing buildings (over 35 feet (10.67 m) high at walls) conductors tapped to a feeder shall be permitted to be not over 25 feet (7.62 m) long horizontally and not over 100 feet (30.5) total length where all of the following conditions are met:

a. The ampacity of the tap conductors is not less than one-third that of the feeder conductors.

b. The tap conductors terminate with a single circuit breaker or a single set of fuses conforming with (1) Part D if the tap is a branch circuit or (2) Part E if the tap is a feeder.

c. The tap conductors are suitably protected from physical damage and are installed in raceways.

d. The tap conductors are continuous from end-to-end and contain no splices.

e. The tap conductors shall be No. 6 AWG copper or No. 4 AWG aluminum or larger.

f. The tap conductors shall not penetrate walls, floors, or ceilings.

430-29. Constant Voltage DC Motors — Power Resistors. Conductors connecting the motor controller to separately mounted power accelerating and dynamic braking resistors in the armature circuit shall have an ampacity not less than the value calculated from Table 430-29 using motor full-load current. If an armature shunt resistor is used, the power accelerating resistor conductor ampacity shall be calculated using the total of motor full-load current and armature shunt resistor current.

Armature shunt resistor conductors shall have an ampacity of not less than that calculated from Table 430-29 using rated shunt resistor current as full-load current.

Table 430-29. Conductor Rating Factors for Power Resistors

Time in Seconds		Ampacity of Conductor in Percent of Full-Load Current
On	Off	
5	75	35
10	70	45
15	75	55
15	45	65
15	30	75
15	15	85
Continuous Duty		110

C. Motor and Branch-Circuit Overload Protection

430-31. General. Part C specifies overload devices intended to protect motors, motor-control apparatus, and motor branch-circuit conductors against excessive heating due to motor overloads and failure to start.

Overload in electrical apparatus is an operating overcurrent which, when it persists for a sufficient length of time, would cause damage or dangerous overheating of the apparatus. It does not include short circuits or ground faults.

These provisions shall not be interpreted as requiring overload protection where it might introduce additional or increased hazards, as in the case of fire pumps.

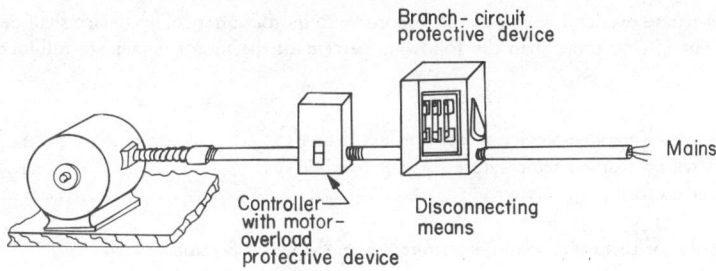

Figure 430-7. Protective devices (branch-circuit, short-circuit, and ground-fault) for a branch circuit located not more than 25 ft from the point where the conductors are tapped to the main feeder.

ARTICLE 430—MOTORS, CIRCUITS, CONTROLLERS

(FPN): See Installation of Centrifugal Fire Pumps, NFPA 20-1983 (ANSI).

See Section 230-90(a), Exception No. 5 for the commentary on centrifugal fire pumps.

The provisions of Part C shall not apply to motor circuits rated over 600 volts, nominal. See Part J.

(FPN): See Example No. 8, Chapter 9.

NFPA 20-1983 contains, in general, the minimum requirements for the selection and installation of centrifugal fire pumps.

Table 430-152 gives the allowable percentages of full-load current for the selection of the maximum rating or setting of motor branch-circuit short-circuit and ground-fault protective devices. The motor branch-circuit, short-circuit and ground-fault protective device is required to be capable of carrying the starting current of the motor without opening the circuit; therefore, the protective device is required to have a rating that is too high to provide overload protection for the motor.

Fire pump motors require circuit breakers and are allowed much larger short-circuit and ground-fault protection than other motors recognizing that the pump should be allowed to operate to failure rather than being removed from the line, under adverse fire conditions. A manually operated fuseless isolating switch is required to be connected ahead (supply side) of the circuit breaker.

For squirrel-cage induction motors, which are generally used, the circuit breaker is required to be of the time-delay type and have a time delay of not over 20 seconds at locked-rotor current (approximately 600 percent of the rated full-load motor current) and is required to be calibrated up to and set at 300 percent of the motor full-load current.

Combined overload protection (special-type fuses), as described in Section 430-55, is permitted as a single protective device. In most cases where motor overload protection is provided, however, the motor controller consists of a switch or contactor to control the circuit to the motor, and the motor-overload protective device is an overload relay with a heater coil selected to match the motor.

430-32. Continuous-Duty Motors.

(a) More than 1 Horsepower. Each continuous-duty motor rated more than 1 horsepower shall be protected against overload by one of the following means:

(1) A separate overload device that is responsive to motor current. This device shall be selected to trip or rated at no more than the following percent of the motor nameplate full-load current rating.

Motors with a marked service factor not less than 1.15 .... 125%
Motors with a marked temperature rise not over 40°C 125%
All other motors 115%

Modification of this value shall be permitted as provided in Section 430-34.

For a multispeed motor, each winding connection shall be considered separately.

Where a separate motor overload device is so connected that it does not carry the total current designated on the motor nameplate, such as for wye-delta starting, the proper percentage of nameplate current applying to the selection or setting of the overload device shall be clearly designated on the equipment, or the manufacturer's selection table shall take this into account.

(2) A thermal protector integral with the motor, approved for use with the motor it protects on the basis that it will prevent dangerous overheating of the motor due to overload and failure to start. The ultimate trip current of a thermally protected motor shall not exceed the following percentage of motor full-load current given in Tables 430-148, 430-149, and 430-150.

Motor full-load current not exceeding 9 amperes 170%
Motor full-load current 9.1 to and including 20 amperes 156%
Motor full-load current greater than 20 amperes 140%

If the motor current-interrupting device is separate from the motor and its control circuit is operated by a protective device integral with the motor, it shall be so arranged that the opening of the control circuit will result in interruption of current to the motor.

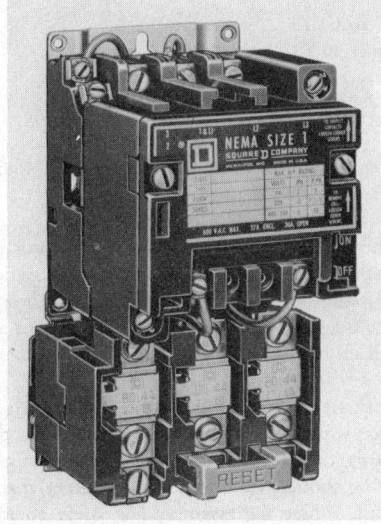

Figure 430-8. Line-voltage magnetic starter. (*Square D Co.*)

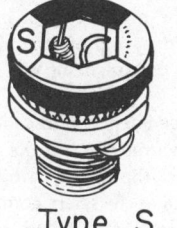

Type S

Figure 430-9. A Type S nonrenewable plug.

(3) A protective device integral with a motor that will protect the motor against damage due to failure to start shall be permitted if the motor is part of an approved assembly that does not normally subject the motor to overloads.

(4) For motors larger than 1500 horsepower, a protective device having embedded temperature detectors that cause current to the motor to be interrupted when the motor attains a temperature rise greater than marked on the nameplate in an ambient of 40°C.

(b) One Horsepower or Less, Nonautomatically Started.

(1) Each continuous-duty motor rated at 1 horsepower or less that is not permanently installed, is nonautomatically started, and is within sight from the controller location shall be permitted to be protected against overload by the branch-circuit short-circuit and ground-fault protective device. This branch-circuit protective device shall not be larger than that specified in Part D of Article 430.

ARTICLE 430—MOTORS, CIRCUITS, CONTROLLERS

Exception: Any such motor shall be permitted on a nominal 120-volt branch circuit protected at not over 20 amperes.

(2) Any such motor that is not in sight from the controller location shall be protected as specified in Section 430-32(c). Any motor rated at 1 horsepower or less that is permanently installed shall be protected in accordance with Section 430-32(c).

(c) One Horsepower or Less, Automatically Started. Any motor of 1 horsepower or less that is started automatically shall be protected against overload by one of the following means:

(1) A separate overload device that is responsive to motor current. This device shall be selected to trip or rated at no more than the following percentage of the motor nameplate full-load current rating.

Motors with a marked service factor not less than 1.15 .... 125%
Motors with a marked temperature rise not over 40°C 125%
All other motors 115%

For a multispeed motor, each winding connection shall be considered separately. Modification of this value shall be permitted as provided in Section 430-34.

(2) A thermal protector integral with the motor, approved for use with the motor which it protects on the basis that it will prevent dangerous overheating of the motor due to overload and failure to start. Where the motor current interrupting device is separate from the motor and its control circuit is operated by a protective device integral with the motor, it shall be so arranged that the opening of the control circuit will result in interruption of current to the motor.

(3) A protective device integral with a motor that will protect the motor against damage due to failure to start shall be permitted (1) if the motor is part of an approved assembly that does not normally normally subject the motor to overloads, or (2) if the assembly is also equipped with other safety controls (such as the safety combustion controls on a domestic oil burner) that protect the motor against damage due to failure to start. Where the assembly has safety controls that protect the motor, it shall be so indicated on the nameplate of the assembly where it will be visible after installation.

(4) In case the impedance of the motor windings is sufficient to prevent overheating due to failure to start, the motor shall be permitted to be protected as specified in Section 430-32(b)(1) for manually started motors if the motor is part of an approved assembly in which the motor will limit itself so that it will not be dangerously overheated.

(FPN): Many alternating-current motors of less than $\frac{1}{20}$ horsepower, such as clock motors, series motors, etc., and also some larger motors such as torque motors, come within this classification. It does not include split-phase motors having automatic switches that disconnect the starting windings.

(d) Wound-Rotor Secondaries. The secondary circuits of wound-rotor alternating-current motors, including conductors, controllers, resistors, etc., shall be permitted to be protected against overload by the motor-overload device.

Operation of a motor in excess of its normal full-load rating for a prolonged period of time would cause damage or dangerous overheating. Overload protection is intended to protect the motor and the system components from damaging overload currents.

A continuous-duty motor with a marked service factor not less than 1.15 or with a marked temperature rise not over 40°C can carry a 25 percent overload for an extended period of time without damage to the motor. Other types of motors, that is those with a service factor less than 1.15 or with a marked temperature rise greater than 40°C, are not capable of withstanding a prolonged overload and the motor-overload protective device should open the circuit should the motor continue to draw 115 percent of its rated full-load current.

A thermal protector located inside the motor housing is connected in series with the motor winding. This protective device commonly consists of two contacts attached to a bimetallic disk through which the circuit is normally "closed." The thermal protector heating coil (in series with the motor winding) causes the disk to heat rapidly and the heat-actuated disk snaps "open" to protect the motor against failure to start, a sudden heavy overload, or dangerous overheating due to a prolonged overload.

After opening the circuit and after the motor has cooled to a normal temperature, the contacts will automatically close and restart the motor. In some cases this may not be desirable. For such applications the protective device is so designed that it must be returned to the closed position by a manually controlled reset button as required by Section 430-43. See Figures 430-10 and 430-11. For

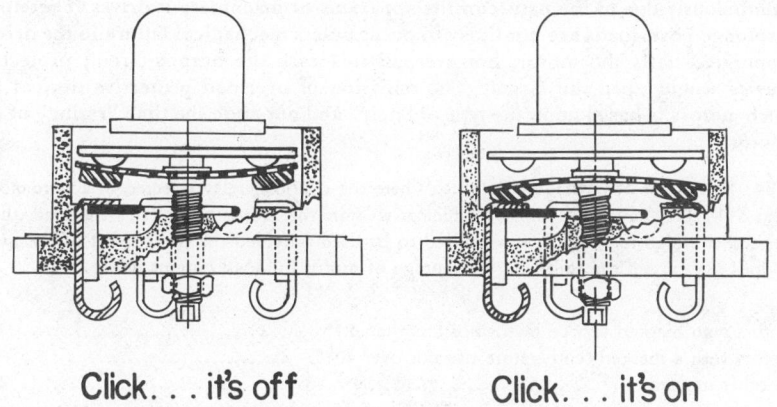

Click... it's off   Click... it's on

Figure 430-10. A thermal protector for a motor. A heat-sensitive, snap-action disk opens contacts and protects the motor against dangerous overheating. (*Texas Instruments, Inc.*)

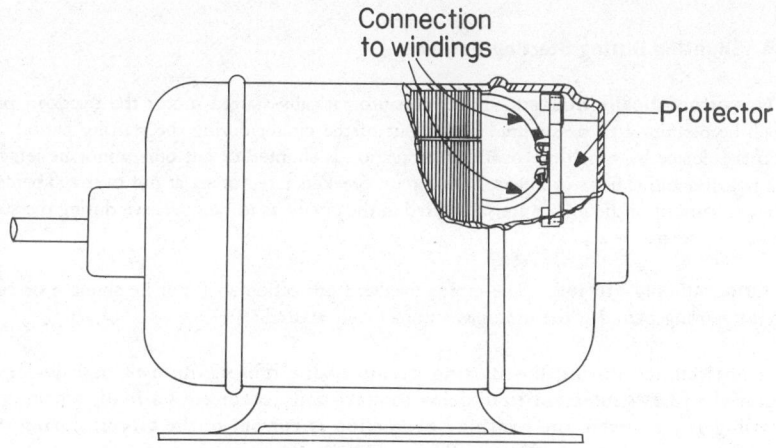

Figure 430-11. Integral mounting of the thermal protective device (Figure 430-10) in a motor housing.

larger motors (usually over 1 hp) a similar device is used. This device, upon abnormal overload, acts as a control circuit switch and operates the control circuit of a motor current-interrupting device located separately from the motor, usually a motor contactor or starter. A thermal protector and circuit-interrupting device should be approved for use with the motor it protects and is required to open the circuit on an overcurrent as specified in Section 430-32(a)(2).

430-33. Intermittent and Similar Duty. A motor used for a condition of service that is inherently short-time, intermittent, periodic, or varying duty, as illustrated by Table 430-22(a) Exception, shall be permitted to be protected against overload by the branch-circuit short-circuit and ground-fault protective device, provided the protective device rating or setting does not exceed that specified in Table 430-152.

Any motor application shall be considered to be for continuous duty unless the nature of the apparatus it drives is such that the motor cannot operate continuously with load under any condition of use.

Where a motor is selected for duty-cycle service (intermittent, short-time, periodic, or varying), it can be assumed that the motor will not operate continuously due to the nature of the apparatus or machinery it drives. Therefore, prolonged overloads are not likely to occur unless mechanical failure in the driven apparatus stalls the motor; however, in this case the branch-circuit protective device would open the circuit. The omission of overload protective devices for such motors is based upon the type of "duty" and not upon the time "rating" of the motor.

430-34. Selection of Overload Relay. Where the overload relay selected in accordance with Section 430-32(a)(1) and (c)(1) is not sufficient to start the motor or to carry the load, the next higher size overload relay shall be permitted to be used provided the trip current of the overload relay does not exceed the following percentage of motor full-load current rating.

Motors with marked service factor not less than 1.15 .... 140%
Motors with a marked temperature rise not over 40°C 140%
All other motors 130%

If not shunted during the starting period of the motor as provided in Section 430-35, the overload device shall have sufficient time delay to permit the motor to start and accelerate its load.

430-35. Shunting During Starting Period.

(a) Nonautomatically Started. For a nonautomatically started motor the overload protection shall be permitted to be shunted or cut out of the circuit during the starting period of the motor if the device by which the overload protection is shunted or cut out cannot be left in the starting position and if fuses or inverse time circuit breakers rated or set at not over 400 percent of the full-load current of the motor are so located in the circuit as to be operative during the starting period of the motor.

(b) Automatically Started. The motor overload protection shall not be shunted or cut out during the starting period if the motor is automatically started.

If not shunted during the starting period of the motor, the overload device is required to have sufficient time delay to start and accelerate its load; whereas if shunting is employed, the overload protection is cut out of the circuit during the starting period of the motor. See Figure 430-12.

Where fuses are used as overload protection, they may be shunted or cut out of the circuit during the starting period by a device (in this case a double-throw switch designed so that it cannot be left in the starting position). Therefore, during the starting period, the motor is protected only by the branch-circuit fuses that are always rated within the limits of this section. If there are no branch-circuit fuses, as permitted by Section 430-53, then a starter (shunting) device is not allowed during the starting period unless the feeder protection is within the limits of this section (not over 400 percent of the full-load motor current).

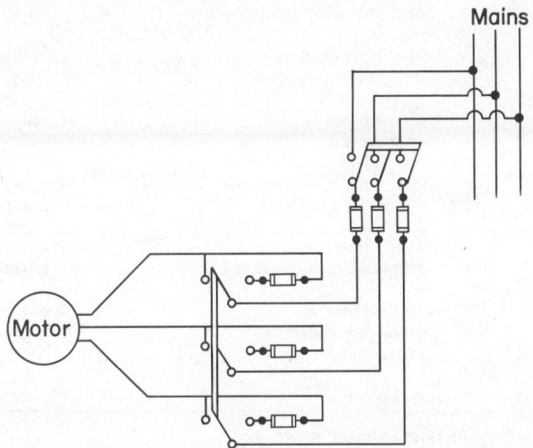

Figure 430-12. Arrangement for across-the-line starting of a motor. When the switch is thrown momentarily to the left to start the motor, the running fuses are shunted or cut out of the circuit. The switch is then thrown to the right (running position) and must be so designed that it cannot be left in the starting position.

Exception: The motor overload protection shall be permitted to be shunted or cut out during the starting period on an automatically started motor where:

(1) The motor starting period exceeds the time delay of available motor overload protective devices, and

(2) Listed means are provided to:

a. Sense motor rotation and to automatically prevent the shunting or cutout in the event that the motor fails to start, and

b. Limit the time of overload protection shunting or cutout to less than the locked rotor time rating of the protected motor, and

c. Provide for shutdown and manual restart if motor running condition is not reached.

430-36. Fuses — In Which Conductor. Where fuses are used for motor overload protection, a fuse shall be inserted in each ungrounded conductor.

A fuse shall also be inserted in the grounded conductor if the supply system is 3-wire, 3-phase ac with one conductor grounded.

430-37. Devices Other than Fuses — In Which Conductor. Where devices other than fuses are used for motor overload protection, Table 430-37 shall govern the minimum allowable number and location of overload units such as trip coils, relays, or thermal cutouts.

Table 430-37. Overload Units

Kind of Motor	Supply System	Number and location of overload units, such as trip coils, relays, or thermal cutouts
1-phase ac or dc	2-wire, 1-phase ac or dc ungrounded	1 in either conductor
1-phase ac or dc	2-wire, 1-phase ac or dc, one conductor grounded	1 in ungrounded conductor
1-phase ac or dc	3-wire, 1-phase ac or dc, grounded-neutral	1 in either ungrounded conductor
2-phase ac	3-wire, 2-phase ac, ungrounded	2, one in each phase
2-phase ac	3-wire, 2-phase ac, one conductor grounded	2 in ungrounded conductors
2-phase ac	4-wire, 2-phase ac, grounded or ungrounded	2, one per phase in ungrounded conductors
2-phase ac	5-wire, 2-phase ac, grounded neutral or ungrounded	2, one per phase in any ungrounded phase wire
3-phase ac	Any 3-phase	*3, one in each phase

Exception: Where protected by other approved means.

All 3-phase motors should be provided with three-unit protection (one in each phase). The exceptions are those protected by other approved means. Specially designed or integral-type detectors with or without supplementary external protective devices are some exceptions.

430-38. Number of Conductors Opened by Overload Device. Motor overload devices other than fuses, thermal cutouts, or thermal protectors shall simultaneously open a sufficient number of ungrounded conductors to interrupt current flow to the motor.

430-39. Motor Controller as Overload Protection. A motor controller shall also be permitted to serve as an overload device if the number of overload units complies with Table 430-37 and if these units are operative in both the starting and running position in the case of a direct-current motor, and in the running position in the case of an alternating-current motor.

For the purpose of this article, a controller may be a switch, a circuit breaker, a contactor, or other device to start and stop a motor by making and breaking the motor circuit current and is required to be capable of interrupting the stalled-rotor current of the motor and have a hp rating not lower than the hp rating of the motor.

Dual-element fuses can be sized to provide motor overload protection. See Section 430-36. Automatically operated contactors or circuit breakers (with trip units) are governed by the requirements of Sections 430-37 and 430-38.

430-40. Thermal Cutouts and Overload Relays. Thermal cutouts, overload relays, and other devices for motor overload protection that are not capable of opening short circuits shall be protected by fuses or circuit breakers with ratings or settings in accordance with Section 430-52 or by a motor short-circuit protector in accordance with Section 430-52.

Exception No. 1: Where approved for group installation and marked to indicate the maximum size of fuse or inverse time circuit breaker by which they must be protected.

Exception No. 2: The fuse or circuit breaker ampere rating shall be permitted to be marked on the nameplate of approved equipment in which the thermal cutout or overload relay is used.

(FPN): For instantaneous trip circuit breakers or motor short-circuit protectors, see Section 430-52.

430-42. Motors on General-Purpose Branch Circuits. Overload protection for motors used on general-purpose branch circuits as permitted in Article 210 shall be provided as specified in (a), (b), (c), or (d) below.

(a) Not Over 1 Horsepower. One or more motors without individual overload protection shall be permitted to be connected to a general-purpose branch circuit only where the installation complies with the limiting conditions specified in Section 430-53(a)(1) and (a)(2).

(b) Over 1 Horsepower. Motors of larger ratings than specified in Section 430-53(a) shall be permitted to be connected to general-purpose branch circuits only where each motor is protected by overload protection selected to protect the motor as specified in Section 430-32. Both the controller and the motor overload device shall be approved for group installation with the short-circuit and ground-fault protective device selected in accordance with Section 430-53.

(c) Cord- and Plug-Connected. Where a motor is connected to a branch circuit by means of an attachment plug and receptacle and individual overload protection is omitted as provided in (a) above, the rating of the attachment plug and receptacle shall not exceed 15 amperes at 125 volts or 10 amperes at 250 volts. Where individual overload protection is required as provided in (b) above for a motor or motor-operated appliance that is attached to the branch circuit through an attachment plug and receptacle, the overload device shall be an integral part of the motor or of the appliance. The rating of the attachment plug and receptacle shall determine the rating of the circuit to which the motor may be connected, as provided in Article 210.

(d) Time Delay. The branch-circuit short-circuit and ground-fault protective device protecting a circuit to which a motor or motor-operated appliance is connected shall have sufficient time delay to permit the motor to start and accelerate its load.

Two or more motors, or one or more motors and other loads, may be connected to the same 120-V, 15- or 20-A single-phase lighting circuit. The provision is that each motor is to be rated not more than 1 hp, the full-load rating of each motor is not to exceed 6 A, and the rating of the branch-circuit protective device is not to be exceeded.

Motors with ratings larger than 1 hp or 6 A may be connected to general-purpose branch circuits only if the motor is protected against overload as required by Section 430-32.

It is to be noted that the requirements for overload protection as provided in Section 430-32 are required to be applied in all cases regardless of the number (one or more) of motors or the type of branch circuit.

430-43. Automatic Restarting. A motor overload device that can restart a motor automatically after overload tripping shall not be installed unless approved for use with the motor it protects. A motor that can restart automatically after shutdown shall not be installed if its automatic restarting can result in injury to persons.

An integral motor overload protective device may be of the type that, after tripping and sufficiently cooling, will automatically restart the motor, or it may be of the type that, after tripping, returns to a closed position by use of a manually operated reset button. See commentary following Section 430-32.

ARTICLE 430—MOTORS, CIRCUITS, CONTROLLERS

430-44. Orderly Shutdown. If immediate automatic shutdown of a motor by a motor overload protective device(s) would introduce additional or increased hazard(s) to a person(s) and continued motor operation is necessary for safe shutdown of equipment or process, a motor overload sensing device(s) conforming with the provisions of Part C of this article shall be permitted to be connected to a supervised alarm instead of causing immediate interruption of the motor circuit, so that corrective action or an orderly shutdown can be initiated.

D. Motor Branch-Circuit Short-Circuit and Ground-Fault Protection

430-51. General. Part D specifies devices intended to protect the motor branch-circuit conductors, the motor control apparatus, and the motors against overcurrent due to short circuits or grounds. They add to or amend the provisions of Article 240. The devices specified in Part D do not include the types of devices required by Sections 210-8, 230-95, and 305-4.

The provisions of Part D do not apply to motor circuits rated over 600 volts, nominal. See Part J.

(FPN): See Example No. 8, Chapter 9.

430-52. Rating or Setting for Individual Motor Circuit. The motor branch-circuit short-circuit and ground-fault protective device shall be capable of carrying the starting current of the motor. A protective device having a rating or setting not exceeding the value calculated according to the values given in Table 430-152 shall be permitted.

Exception No. 1: Where the values for branch-circuit short- circuit and ground-fault protective devices determined by Table 430-152 do not correspond to the standard sizes or ratings of fuses, nonadjustable circuit breakers, or thermal protective devices, or possible settings of adjustable circuit breakers adequate to carry the load, the next higher size, rating, or setting shall be permitted.

Exception No. 2: Where the rating specified in Table 430-152 is not sufficient for the starting current of the motor:

a. The rating of a nontime-delay fuse not exceeding 600 amperes shall be permitted to be increased but shall in no case exceed 400 percent of the full-load current.

b. The rating of a time-delay (dual element) fuse shall be permitted to be increased but shall in no case exceed 225 percent of the full-load current.

c. The rating of an inverse time circuit breaker shall be permitted to be increased but shall in no case exceed (1) 400 percent for full-load currents of 100 amperes or less, or (2) 300 percent for full-load currents greater than 100 amperes.

d. The rating of a fuse of 601-6000 ampere classification shall be permitted to be increased but shall in no case exceed 300 percent of the full-load current.

Exception No. 3: Torque motor branch circuits shall be protected at the motor nameplate current rating in accordance with Section 240-3, Exception No. 1.

(FPN): See Section 240-6 for standard ratings of fuses and circuit breakers.

An instantaneous trip circuit breaker shall be used only if adjustable, and if part of a combination controller having motor overload and also short-circuit and ground-fault protection in each conductor. A motor short-circuit protector shall be permitted in lieu of devices listed in

Table 430-152 if the motor short-circuit protector is part of a combination controller having both motor overload protection and short-circuit and ground-fault protection in each conductor and if it will operate at not more than 1300 percent of full-load motor current. An instantaneous trip circuit breaker or motor short-circuit protector shall be used only as part of a combination motor controller which provides coordinated motor branch-circuit overload and short-circuit and ground-fault protection.

Exception: Where the setting specified in Table 430-152 is not sufficient for the starting current of the motor, the setting of an instantaneous trip circuit breaker shall be permitted to be increased but shall in no case exceed 1300 percent of the motor full-load current.

For a multispeed motor, a single short-circuit and ground-fault protective device shall be permitted for two or more windings of the motor, provided the rating of the protective device does not exceed the above applicable percentage of the nameplate rating of the smallest winding protected.

Where maximum branch-circuit short-circuit and ground-fault protective device ratings are shown in the manufacturer's overload relay table for use with a motor controller or are otherwise marked on the equipment, they shall not be exceeded even if higher values are allowed as shown above.

(FPN): See Example No. 8 in Chapter 9 and Diagram 430-1.

Suitable fuses shall be permitted in lieu of devices listed in Table 430-152 for an adjustable speed drive system provided that the marking for replacement fuses is provided adjacent to the fuses.

This section defines the maximum allowable ratings or settings of devices acceptable (fuses or circuit breakers) for motor branch-circuit short-circuit and ground-fault protection and states that these devices are expected to carry the starting currents of the motor and to provide short-circuit and ground-fault protection.

For certain exceptions to the maximum rating or setting of these motor branch-circuit protective devices as specified in Table 430-152, see Sections 430-52, 430-53, and 430-54. See Figure 430-2.

Section 430-6 provides that where the current rating of a motor is used to determine the ampacity of conductors or ampere ratings of switches, branch-circuit overcurrent devices, etc., the values given in Tables 430-147 through 430-150 (including notes) are to be used instead of the actual motor nameplate current rating. Separate motor overload protection is to be based on the motor nameplate current rating.

Figure 430-5 illustrates a typical motor circuit where the branch-circuit short-circuit and ground-fault protective fuses or circuit breaker rating must carry the starting current and may be sized 150 to 300 percent of the motor full-load current (depending on the type of motor). It should be noted 'that it is not necessary to size the branch-circuit conductors to the percentages (150 to 300) permitted for the branch-circuit short-circuit and ground-fault protective devices.

The rules for short-circuit and ground-fault protection are specific for particular situations. A short circuit is a fault between two conductors or between phases. A ground fault is a fault to ground. During a short-circuit or fault-to-ground condition, the extreme excess current would cause the protective fuses or circuit breakers to open the circuit. Excess current flow caused by an overload condition must pass through the overload protective device at the motor controller thereby causing this device to open the circuit. Branch-circuit conductors with an ampacity of 125 percent (Note: not 150 to 300 percent) of the motor full-load current are reasonably protected by motor-protective devices set to operate at nearly the same current as the ampacity of the conductors. Branch-circuit short-circuit and ground-fault protective devices will open the circuit under short-circuit conditions and thereby provide short-circuit and ground-fault protection for both the motor and overload protective device; however, the overload protective device is not intended to open short circuits or ground faults.

Section 430-7 provides for information that is to be marked on motor nameplates. AC motors, rated ½ hp or more, are required to be marked with code letters in accordance with Table 430-7(b) which are used to determine the correct rating of the branch-circuit protective devices. For motors smaller than ½ hp, or for the many motors still in use without code letters, the provisions of Table 430-152 apply.

The rating or setting of the branch-circuit short-circuit and ground-fault protective device should be selected as low as possible for maximum protection; however, where the rating or setting specified in Table 430-152 is not sufficient for the starting current of the motor, such as in the case of severe starting conditions where the motor and its driven machinery requires an extended period of time to reach its desired speed, it is allowable to use a higher rating or setting as permitted in the exception to Section 430-52.

Two or more small motors, each not over 1 hp and not over 6 A, may be connected to 120-V, 20-A, or 208 through 600-V, 15-A branch circuits if each motor has overload protection and the rating of the branch-circuit protective device does not exceed the rating specified on the motor controller (for the overhead relay heater coil). See Section 430-53(a). Also, if the branch-circuit short-circuit and ground-fault protective device can be selected for the smallest motor in the group, two or more motors may be connected to the same branch circuit. This may be feasible where two motors are very nearly the same size and cannot start simultaneously. See Section 430-53(b).

For other than the conditions specified in Sections 430-53(a) and (b) as described above, the equipment or controllers and protective devices are required to be listed (see Article 100). Where listed multimotor equipment is installed, it is required to be marked with the maximum rating of the branch-circuit short-circuit and ground-fault protective device in accordance with Section 430-7(d), and the protective device is not permitted to exceed this marked rating. Where the short-circuit and ground-fault protective device, the controller and the overload protective device are field installed, they are required to be listed for such use and provided with instructions for use with each other. See Section 450-53(c).

430-53. Several Motors or Loads on One Branch Circuit. Two or more motors or one or more motors and other loads shall be permitted to be connected to the same branch circuit under the conditions specified in (a), (b), or (c) below.

(a) Not Over 1 Horsepower. Several motors each not exceeding 1 horsepower in rating shall be permitted on a nominal 120 volt branch circuit protected at not over 20 amperes or a branch circuit of 600 volts, nominal, or less, protected at not over 15 amperes, if all of the following conditions are met:

(1) The full-load rating of each motor does not exceed 6 amperes.

(2) The rating of the branch-circuit short-circuit and ground-fault protective device marked on any of the controllers is not exceeded.

(3) Individual overload protection conforms to Section 430-32.

(b) If Smallest Motor Protected. If the branch-circuit short-circuit and ground-fault protective device is selected not to exceed that allowed by Section 430-52 for the motor of the smallest rating, two or more motors or one or more motors and other load(s), with each motor having individual overload protection, shall be permitted to be connected to a branch circuit where it can be determined that the branch-circuit short-circuit and ground-fault protective device will not open under the most severe normal conditions of service that might be encountered.

(c) Other Group Installations. Two or more motors of any rating or one or more motors and other load(s), with each motor having individual overload protection, shall be permitted to be connected to one branch circuit where the motor controller(s) and overload device(s) are (1) installed as a listed factory assembly and the motor branch-circuit short-circuit and ground-fault protective device is either provided as part of the assembly or is specified by a marking on the assembly, or (2) the motor branch-circuit short-circuit and ground-fault protective device, the motor controller(s) and overload device(s) are field-installed as separate assemblies listed for such use and provided with manufacturers' instructions for use with each other, and (3) all of the following conditions are complied with:

(1) Each motor overload device is listed for group installation with a specified maximum rating of fuse and/or inverse time circuit breaker.

(2) Each motor controller is listed for group installation with a specified maximum rating of fuse and/or circuit breaker.

(3) Each circuit breaker is one of the inverse time type and listed for group installation.

(4) The branch circuit shall be protected by fuses or inverse time circuit breakers having a rating not exceeding that specified in Section 430-52 for the largest motor connected to the branch circuit plus an amount equal to the sum of the full-load current ratings of all other motors and the ratings of other loads connected to the circuit. Where this calculation results in a rating less than the ampacity of the supply conductors, it shall be permitted to increase the maximum rating of the fuses or circuit breaker to a value not exceeding that permitted by Section 240-3, Exception No. 1.

(5) The branch-circuit fuses or inverse time circuit breakers are not larger than allowed by Section 430-40 for the thermal cutout or overload relay protecting the smallest motor of the group.

(d) Single Motor Taps. For group installations described above, the conductors of any tap supplying a single motor shall not be required to have an individual branch-circuit short-circuit and ground-fault protective device, provided they comply with either of the following: (1) no conductor to the motor shall have an ampacity less than that of the branch-circuit conductors, or (2) no conductor to the motor shall have an ampacity less than one-third that of the branch-circuit conductors, with a minimum in accordance with Section 430-22; the conductors to the motor overload device being not more than 25 feet (7.62 m) long and being protected from physical damage.

The following two examples describe installations permitting the omission of individual motor branch-circuit short-circuit and ground-fault protective devices. See Figures 430-13 and 430-14.

Figure 430-13 illustrates main branch-circuit conductors supplying a motor that is part of a group installation. The tap conductors have an ampacity equal to the ampacity of the main branch-circuit conductors; therefore, branch-circuit short-circuit and ground-fault protective devices, fuses or circuit breakers for the conductors in the tap are not required at the point of connection of the tap conductors to the main conductors, provided that the motor controller and motor overload protective device are listed for group installation with the size of main branch-circuit short-circuit and ground-fault protective device used.

Figure 430-14 illustrates main branch-circuit conductors supplying a motor that is part of a group installation. The tap conductors have an ampacity at least one-third the ampacity of the main branch-circuit conductors, are no more than 25 ft in length, and are suitably protected from physical damage, as shown in Figure 430-13. The motor controller and motor overload protective device are required to be listed for group installation with the size of main branch-circuit short-circuit and ground-fault protective device used.

In both examples, the main branch-circuit fuses or circuit breakers would operate in the event of a short circuit and the overload protective device would operate to protect the motor and the tap conductors under overload conditions.

It should be noted that the tap conductors should never be of a smaller size and ampacity than the branch-circuit conductors required by Section 430-22; that is, a tap conductor (25 ft or less) may be ⅓ the ampacity of the main branch-circuit conductor to which it is connected. However, this ampacity is required to be equal to or larger than 125 percent of the motor full-load current rating (see Section 430-22). For example, a feeder sized at No. 2/0 copper THW typically has an ampacity of 175 A and a tap conductor (25 ft or less) would normally be permitted to be sized at No. 6 copper THW (65 A). However, if a 25-hp, 230-V, 3-phase, squirrel-cage motor is to be supplied from this feeder, a No. 6 tap conductor would not meet the requirements of Section 430-22; that is, 125 percent of the full-load current of the motor is 85 A [1.25 × 68 A (Table 430-150) = 85 A]. Therefore, the branch-circuit tap conductors are not permitted to be smaller than a No. 4 copper THW with a normal ampacity of 85 A (see Table 310-16). Note that the ampacities in Table 310-16 are reduced for ambient temperatures above 30 o C and for more than 3 conductors in the raceway or cable.

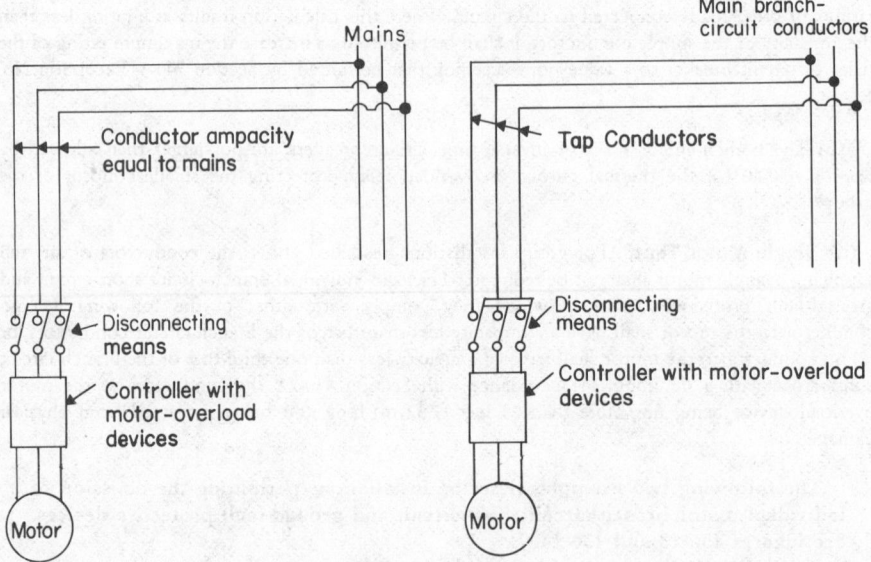

Figure 430-13. Motor branch-circuit protective devices can be omitted for tap conductors that have the same ampacity as the main branch-circuit conductors.

Figure 430-14. Motor branch-circuit protective devices can be omitted when the tap conductors have at least ⅓ the ampacity of the main conductors, are not over 25 ft long, and are protected from physical damage.

430-54. Multimotor and Combination-Load Equipment. The rating of the branch-circuit short-circuit and ground-fault protective device for multimotor and combination-load equipment shall not exceed the rating marked on the equipment in accordance with Section 430-7(d).

430-55. Combined Overcurrent Protection. Motor branch-circuit short-circuit and ground-fault protection and motor overload protection shall be permitted to be combined in a single protective device where the rating or setting of the device provides the overload protection specified in Section 430-32.

Either a circuit breaker with inverse time characteristics or a dual-element (time-delay) fuse may serve as both motor overload protection and also as the branch-circuit short-circuit and ground-fault protection. Figures 430-9, 430-15, and 430-16 are examples of dual-element fuses that are able to withstand the normal motor starting current when sized at or near the motor full-load rating, but open on a prolonged overload or "blow" rapidly on a short circuit or ground fault.

Figure 430-9 illustrates a dual-element Type S fuse that is available up to a 30-A rating and is designed to prevent oversize fusing. See Sections 240-51 through 240-54.

Figures 430-15 and 430-16 illustrate time-delay cartridge-type dual-element fuses. The dual-element characteristics, similar to those of the Type S fuse shown in Figure 430-9, are the "thermal cutout element," which permits harmless high inrush currents to flow for short periods (but would open the circuit during a prolonged period), and the "fuse link element," which has current limiting ability for short-circuit currents (and would "blow" rapidly). Dual-element fuses may be used in larger sizes to provide only short-circuit and ground-fault protection.

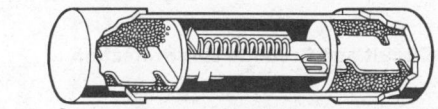

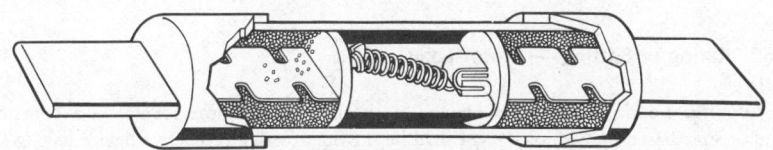

Figure 430-15. A Fusetron cartridge-type fuse. (*Bussmann Mfg. Co.*)

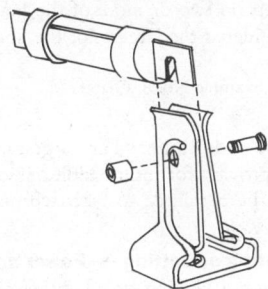

Figure 430-16. Class R dual-element fuse with physical rejection feature to prevent interchangeability. (*International Association of Electrical Inspectors*)

430-56. Branch-Circuit Protective Devices — In Which Conductor. Branch-circuit protective devices shall comply with the provisions of Section 240-20.

ARTICLE 430—MOTORS, CIRCUITS, CONTROLLERS

430-57. Size of Fuseholder. Where fuses are used for motor branch-circuit short-circuit and ground-fault protection, the fuseholders shall not be of a smaller size than required to accommodate the fuses specified by Table 430-152.

Exception: Where fuses having time delay appropriate for the starting characteristics of the motor are used, fuseholders of smaller size than specified in Table 430-152 shall be permitted.

Dual-element (time-delay) fuses make possible the use of sizes much smaller than with ordinary fuses and thus provide better protection because of the lower rating. This also permits a considerable saving in installation cost by using smaller size switches and panels and allows for easier arrangement of equipment where space is at a premium at motor control centers.

430-58. Rating of Circuit Breaker. A circuit breaker for motor branch-circuit short-circuit and ground-fault protection shall have a current rating in accordance with Sections 430-52 and 430-110.

An instantaneous trip circuit breaker has no intentional time-delay and opens only in response to currents in excess of its trip setting. Combination motor controller assemblies (see Section 430-52) are available with either interchangeable or noninterchangeable instantaneous trip units. In such a combination controller, the motor overload protective device in each conductor is relied upon to protect against excessive heating due to motor overloads and failure to start.

E. Motor Feeder Short-Circuit and Ground-Fault Protection

430-61. General. Part E specifies protective devices intended to protect feeder conductors supplying motors against overcurrents due to short circuits or grounds.

(FPN): See Example No. 8, Chapter 9.

430-62. Rating or Setting — Motor Load.

(a) Specific Load. A feeder supplying a specific fixed motor load(s) and consisting of conductor sizes based on Section 430-24 shall be provided with a protective device having a rating or setting not greater than the largest rating or setting of the branch-circuit short-circuit and ground-fault protective device for any motor of the group (based on Table 430-152), plus the sum of the full-load currents of the other motors of the group.

Where the same rating or setting of the branch-circuit short-circuit and ground-fault protective device is used on two or more of the branch circuits of the group, one of the protective devices shall be considered the largest for the above calculations.

(FPN): See Example No. 8, Chapter 9.

(b) Future Additions. For large-capacity installations, where heavy-capacity feeders are installed to provide for future additions or changes, the rating or setting of the feeder protective devices shall be permitted to be based on the ampacity of the feeder conductors.

430-63. Rating or Setting — Power and Light Loads. Where a feeder supplies a motor load, and in addition a lighting or a lighting and appliance load, the feeder protective device shall be permitted to have a rating or setting sufficient to carry the lighting or the lighting and appliance load as determined in accordance with Articles 210 and 220, plus for a single motor, the rating permitted by Section 430-52, and for two or more motors, the rating permitted by Section 430-62.

F. Motor Control Circuits

430-71. General. Part F contains modifications of the general requirements and applies to the particular conditions of motor control circuits.

Definition of Motor Control Circuit: The circuit of a control apparatus or system that carries the electric signals directing the performance of the controller, but does not carry the main power current.

430-72. Overcurrent Protection.

(a) General. A motor control circuit tapped from the load side of a motor branch-circuit short-circuit and ground-fault protective device(s) and functioning to control the motor(s) connected to that branch circuit shall be protected against overcurrent in accordance with Section 430-72. Such a tapped control circuit shall not be considered to be a branch circuit and shall be permitted to be protected by either a supplementary or branch-circuit overcurrent protective device(s). A motor control circuit other than such a tapped control circuit shall be protected against overcurrent in accordance with Section 725-12 or 725-35, as applicable.

(b) Conductor Protection. The overcurrent protection for conductors shall not exceed the values specified in Column A of Table 430-72(b).

Exception No. 1: Conductors which do not extend beyond the motor control equipment enclosure shall require only short-circuit and ground-fault protection and shall be permitted to be protected by the motor branch-circuit short-circuit and ground-fault protective device(s) where the rating of the protective device(s) is not more than the value specified in Column B of Table 430-72(b).

Exception No. 2: Conductors which extend beyond the motor control equipment enclosure shall require only short-circuit and ground-fault protection and shall be permitted to be protected by the motor branch-circuit short-circuit and ground-fault protective device(s) where the rating of the protective device(s) is not more than the value specified in Column C of Table 430-72(b).

Exception No. 3: Conductors supplied by the secondary side of a single-phase transformer having only a two-wire (single-voltage) secondary shall be permitted to be protected by overcurrent protection provided on the primary (supply) side of the transformer, provided this protection is in accordance with Section 450-3 and does not exceed the value determined by multiplying the appropriate maximum rating of the overcurrent device for the secondary conductor from Table 430-72(b) by the secondary-to-primary voltage ratio. Transformer secondary conductors (other than two-wire) are not considered to be protected by the primary overcurrent protection.

Table 430-72(b). Maximum Rating of Overcurrent
Protective Device-Amperes

Control Circuit Conductor Size, AWG	Column A Basic Rule		Column B Exception No. 1		Column C Exception No. 2	
	Copper	Alum. or Copper-Clad Alum.	Copper	Alum. or Copper-Clad Alum.	Copper	Alum. or Copper-Clad Alum.
18	7	—	25	—	7	—
16	10	—	40	—	10	—
14	Note 1	—	100	—	45	—
12	Note 1	Note 1	120	100	60	45
10	Note 1	Note 1	160	140	90	75
larger than 10	Note 1	Note 1	Note 2	Note 2	Note 3	Note 3

Note 1: Value specified in Tables 310-16 through 310-19, as applicable.
Note 2: 400 percent of value specified in Table 310-17 for 60°C conductors.
Note 3: 300 percent of value specified in Table 310-16 for 60°C conductors.

Exception No. 4: Conductors of control circuits shall require only short-circuit and ground-fault protection and shall be permitted to be protected by the motor branch-circuit short-circuit and ground-fault protective device(s) where the opening of the control circuit would create a hazard as, for example, the control circuit of a fire pump motor, and the like.

(c) Control Circuit Transformer. Where a motor control circuit transformer is provided, the transformer shall be protected in accordance with Article 450.

Exception No. 1: Control circuit transformers rated less than 50 VA and an integral part of the motor controller and located within the motor controller enclosure.

Exception No. 2: Where the control circuit transformer rated primary current is less than 2 amperes, an overcurrent device rated or set at not more than 500 percent of the rated primary current shall be permitted in the primary circuit.

Exception No. 3: Where the transformer supplies a Class 1 power-limited, circuit [see Section 725-11(a)] Class 2, or Class 3 remote control circuit conforming with the requirements of Article 725 (see Article 725 Part C).

Exception No. 4: Where protection is provided by other approved means.

Exception No. 5: Overcurrent protection shall be omitted where the opening of the control circuit would create a hazard, as, for example, the control circuit of a fire pump motor and the like.

430-73. Mechanical Protection of Conductor. Where damage to a motor control circuit would constitute a hazard, all conductors of such a remote motor control circuit that are outside the control device itself shall be installed in a raceway or be otherwise suitably protected from physical damage.

Where one side of the motor control circuit is grounded, the motor control circuit shall be so arranged that an accidental ground in the remote-control devices will not start the motor.

Where damage to the motor control circuit conductors would constitute a fire or accident hazard, physical protection of the motor control circuit conductors is necessary. Conductors are required to be installed in raceways where damage to the control circuit conductors could result in an accidental ground causing the device to operate or breakage of conductors could render the device inoperative. Either condition could constitute a hazard to persons or property. Where boilers or furnaces are equipped with an automatic safety control device, damage to the conductors of the low-voltage (Article 725, Class 2) control circuit (thermostat, etc.) does not constitute a hazard.

The second paragraph of Section 430-73 requires that if one side of the motor control circuit is grounded, the circuit be arranged so that an accidental ground in the remote control devices will not start the motor. For example, if the control circuit is a 227-V single-phase circuit derived from a 480-V wye, 3-phase system supplying the motor, one side of the control circuit will be the grounded neutral. If the "start" button of the motor control circuit is in the grounded neutral, a ground fault on the coil side of the "start" button can short-circuit the "start" circuit and start the motor. The same condition will exist if the ground fault is in the wiring rather than the control device itself. By locating the "start" button in the ungrounded side of the control circuit, this hazardous condition is avoided. See Figure 430-17.

Combinations of ground faults in motor and motor-control circuits can produce the same problem. If the circuit is ungrounded, the first fault may go undetected. One solution is to use double-pole control devices, one pole in each of the two control lines.

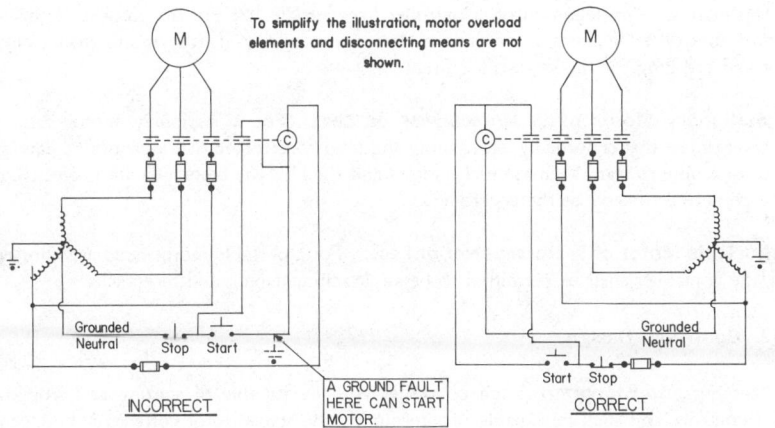

Figure 430-17. Control wiring in violation of Paragraph 2, Section 430-73(left) and in compliance with Paragraph 2, Section 430-73 (right).

430-74. Disconnection.

(a) **General.** Motor control circuits shall be so arranged that they will be disconnected from all sources of supply when the disconnecting means is in the open position. The disconnecting means shall be permitted to consist of two or more separate devices, one of which disconnects the motor and the controller from the source(s) of power supply for the motor, and the other(s), the motor control circuit(s) from its power supply. Where separate devices are used, they shall be located immediately adjacent one to each other.

Exception No. 1: Where more than twelve motor control circuit conductors are required to be disconnected, the disconnecting means shall be permitted to be located other than immediately adjacent one to each other where all of the following conditions are complied with:

a. Access to live parts is limited to qualified persons in accordance with Part K of this article.

b. A warning sign is permanently located on the outside of each equipment enclosure door or cover permitting access to the live parts in the motor control circuit(s), warning that motor control circuit disconnecting means are remotely located and specifying the location and identification of each disconnect. Where live parts are not in an equipment enclosure as permitted by Sections 430-132 and 430-133, an additional warning sign(s) shall be located where visible to persons who may be working in the area of the live parts.

Exception No. 2: Where the opening of one or more motor control circuit disconnect means may result in potentially unsafe conditions for personnel or property and the conditions a. and b. of Exception No. 1 above are complied with.

(b) **Control Transformer in Controller.** Where a transformer or other device is used to obtain a reduced voltage for the motor control circuit and is located in the controller, such transformer or other device shall be connected to the load side of the disconnecting means for the motor control circuit.

G. Motor Controllers

430-81. General. Part G is intended to require suitable controllers for all motors.

ARTICLE 430—MOTORS, CIRCUITS, CONTROLLERS

(a) Definition. For definition of "Controller," see Article 100. For the purpose of this article, the term "Controller" includes any switch or device normally used to start and stop a motor by making and breaking the motor circuit current.

(b) Stationary Motor of ⅛ Horsepower or Less. For a stationary motor rated at ⅛ horsepower or less that is normally left running and is so constructed that it cannot be damaged by overload or failure to start, such as clock motors and the like, the branch-circuit protective device shall be permitted to serve as the controller.

(c) Portable Motor of ⅓ Horsepower or Less. For a portable motor rated at ⅓ horsepower or less, the controller shall be permitted to be an attachment plug and receptacle.

430-82. Controller Design.

(a) Starting and Stopping. Each controller shall be capable of starting and stopping the motor it controls, and shall be capable of interrupting the stalled-rotor current of the motor.

(b) Autotransformer. An autotransformer starter shall provide an "off" position, a running position, and at least one starting position. It shall be so designed that it cannot rest in the starting position or in any position that will render the overload device in the circuit inoperative.

(c) Rheostats. Rheostats shall be in compliance with the following:

(1) Motor-starting rheostats shall be so designed that the contact arm cannot be left on intermediate segments. The point or plate on which the arm rests when in the starting position shall have no electrical connection with the resistor.

(2) Motor-starting rheostats for direct-current motors operated from a constant voltage supply shall be equipped with automatic devices that will interrupt the supply before the speed of the motor has fallen to less than one-third its normal value.

430-83. Rating. The controller shall have a horsepower rating not lower than the horsepower rating of the motor.

Exception No. 1: For a stationary motor rated at 2 horsepower or less, and 300 volts or less, the controller shall be permitted to be a general-use switch having an ampere rating not less than twice the full-load current rating of the motor.
On ac circuits, general-use snap switches suitable only for use on ac (not general-use ac-dc snap switches) shall be permitted to control a motor rated at 2 horsepower or less and 300 volts or less having a full-load current rating not more than 80 percent of the ampere rating of the switch.

Exception No. 2: A branch-circuit inverse time circuit breaker rated in amperes only shall be permitted as a controller. Where this circuit breaker is also used for overload protection, it shall conform to the appropriate provisions of this article governing overload protection.

Exception No. 3: The motor controller for a torque motor shall have a continuous-duty, full-load current rating not less than the nameplate current rating of the motor. For a motor controller rated in horsepower but not marked with the foregoing current rating, the equivalent current rating shall be determined from the horsepower rating by using Tables 430-147, 430-148, 430-149, or 430-150.

A controller, as defined in Section 430-81(a), includes any switch or device normally used to start and stop a motor by making and breaking the motor circuit current. Circuit breakers are suitable for this use; however, circuit breakers used for branch-circuit short-circuit and ground-fault protection are not well adapted for motor overload protective devices.

556

430-84. Need Not Open All Conductors. The controller shall not be required to open all conductors to the motor.

Exception: Where the controller serves also as a disconnecting means, it shall open all ungrounded conductors to the motor as provided in Section 430-111.

A controller that does not also serve as a disconnecting means is required to open only as many motor-circuit conductors as may be necessary to stop the motor. That is, one conductor for a dc or single-phase motor circuit; two conductors for a 3-phase motor circuit; and three conductors for a 2-phase motor circuit.

430-85. In Grounded Conductors. One pole of the controller shall be permitted to be placed in a permanently grounded conductor, provided the controller is so designed that the pole in the grounded conductor cannot be opened without simultaneously opening all conductors of the circuit.

Generally, one conductor of a 120-V circuit is grounded and a single-pole device is required to be connected in the ungrounded conductor to serve as a controller. A 2-pole controller is permitted for such a circuit, where both conductors (grounded and ungrounded) are opened simultaneously. The same requirement can be applied to other circuits, such as 240-V, 3-wire circuits with one conductor grounded.

430-86. Motor Not in Sight from Controller. Where a motor and the driven machinery are not in sight from the controller location, the installation shall comply with one of the following conditions:

(a) Capable of Being Locked in the Open Position. The controller disconnecting means shall be capable of being locked in the open position.

(b) Within Sight from the Motor Location. A manually operable switch that will disconnect the motor from its source of supply shall be placed within sight from the motor location.

(FPN): See Section 430-108 for type and rating.

The basic rule is that a motor and its driven machinery should be within sight from the controller location. However, when several motors are controlled from one location, such as a motor-control center, it may be impossible to locate the control center within sight from all of the motors. Article 100 defines "in sight from" as one equipment visible and not more than 50 ft from the other equipment. Where a motor is not in sight, or more than 50 ft from its controller, the controller disconnecting means is required to be capable of being locked in the "off" position or a manually operable switch in the motor circuit (not control circuit) is required to be placed within sight from the motor location. Figures 430-18 through 430-20 illustrate installations of motors that are not in sight from the controller location.

It should be noted that a control center enclosing several controllers should not be locked because controllers of other circuits would also be inaccessible. Also, this rule does not permit the removal of "pull-out"-type fuse blocks in lieu of locking because a spare could be inserted into the opening.

Figure 430-20 illustrates a pushbutton station located adjacent to a motor. In this case the controller is a magnetic contactor located out of sight from the motor and is a separate part of a combination fused-switch unit within a control center which has individual lock-open provisions. A pushbutton station is not a controller. Its function is to operate the holding coil of the contactor. Should the control wires or the pushbutton station malfunction, the "stop" button would not release the holding coil. In this case the fused switch would disconnect the supply to the controller and de-energize the motor, hence the requirement that a disconnecting means be placed within sight from the controller. See also Section 430-102.

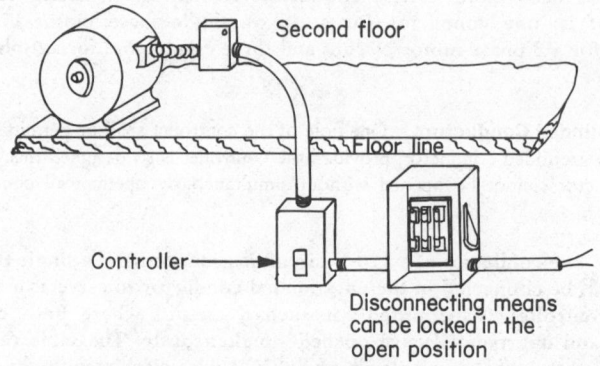

Figure 430-18. A controller disconnecting means that is not in sight of the motor installation must be designed to be locked in the "off" postion.

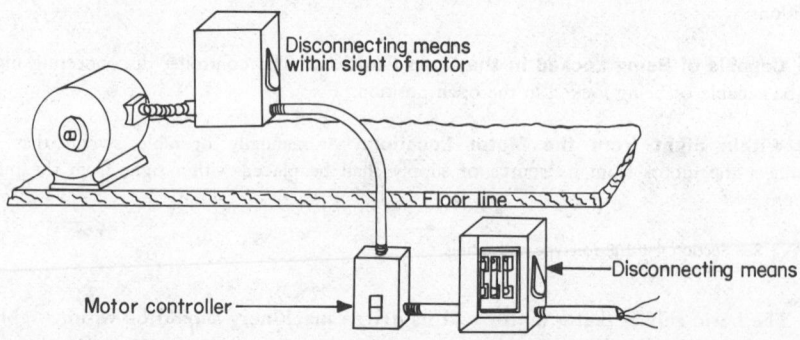

Figure 430-19. A motor installation where a disconnecting means is located within sight of the controller and another disconnecting means within sight of the motor.

430-87. Number of Motors Served by Each Controller. Each motor shall be provided with an individual controller.

Exception: For motors rated 600 volts or less, a single controller rated at not less than the sum of the horsepower ratings of all of the motors of the group shall be permitted to serve the group of motors under any one of the following conditions:

a. Where a number of motors drive several parts of a single machine or piece of apparatus, such as metal and woodworking machines, cranes, hoists, and similar apparatus.

b. Where a group of motors is under the protection of one overcurrent device as permitted in Section 430-53(a).

c. Where a group of motors is located in a single room within sight from the controller location.

These requirements for an individual controller are the same as those specified in Section 430-112 permitting the use of a single disconnecting means for a group of motors.

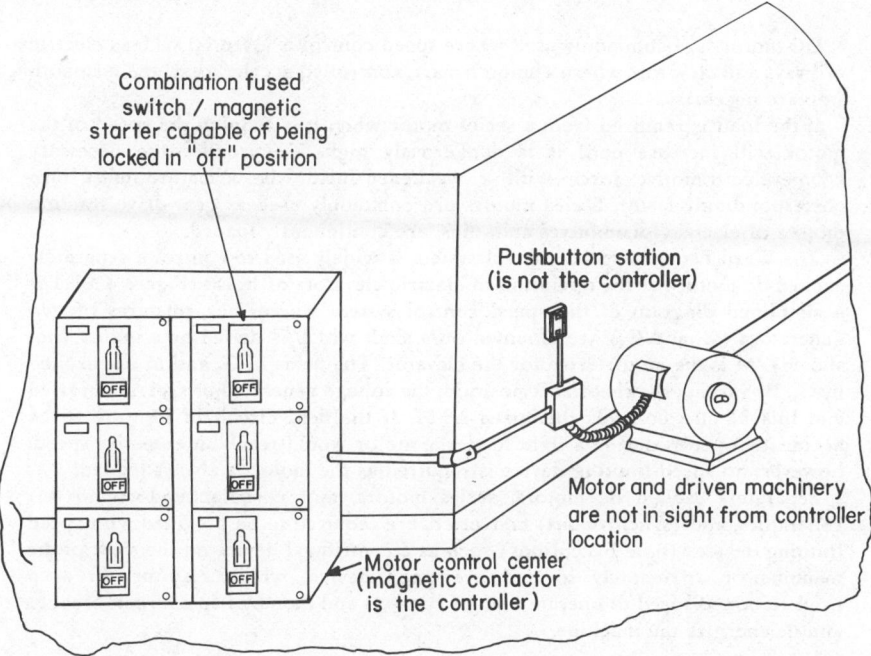

Combination fused switch / magnetic starter capable of being locked in "off" position

Pushbutton station (is not the controller)

Motor and driven machinery are not in sight from controller location

Motor control center (magnetic contactor is the controller)

Figure 430-20. A fused switch within the motor control center has lock-open provisions. The pushbutton station at the motor location is not a controller.

430-88. Adjustable-Speed Motors. Adjustable-speed motors that are controlled by means of field regulation shall be so equipped and connected that they cannot be started under weakened field.

Exception: Where the motor is designed for such starting.

The speed of a motor will increase or decrease with variations in the amount of magnetic flux passing through the armature. Since the speed of the armature increases until the necessary counterelectromotive force is produced, it is evident that weakening the field by decreasing the current flow through the field magnets will increase the motor speed; and increasing the current flow through the field magnets will decrease the motor speed. Because of excessive starting currents, this type motor is not permitted to be started under a weakened field condition unless the motor is designed for such starting.

430-89. Speed Limitation. Machines of the following types shall be provided with speed limiting devices or other speed limiting means:

(a) Separately Excited DC Motors. Separately excited direct-current motors.

(b) Series Motors. Series motors.

(c) Motor-Generators and Converters. Motor-generators and converters that can be driven at excessive speed from the direct-current end, as by a reversal of current or decrease in load.

Exception No. 1: When the inherent characteristics of the machines, the system, or the load and the mechanical connection thereto are such as to safely limit the speed.

Exception No. 2: When the machine is always under the manual control of a qualified operator.

DC motors are commonly used where speed control is essential such as electric railways and elevators where a smooth start, controlled acceleration, and a smooth stop are necessary.

If the load is removed from a series motor when it is running the speed of the motor will increase until it is dangerously high. To produce the necessary counterelectromotive force with a weakened field, the armature must turn correspondingly faster. Series motors are commonly used as gear-drive traction motors of electric locomotives and, thus, are continuously loaded.

The Ward Leonard speed control system is widely used to control a separately excited dc motor for the operation of electric elevators or hoists. Figure 430-21 is a simplified diagram of the speed control system where the armatures of two generators (G_1 and G_2) are mounted on a shaft which is driven by a motor (not shown). M is the motor-drive for the elevator. The fields of G_1 and M are excited by G_1. By varying the rheostat R position, the voltage generated by G_2 is also varied and this in turn controls the speed of M. If the field circuit of M were to be accidently opened during a light load, the motor would reach an excessive speed; however, no speed-limiting device is required as the motor is always loaded.

Separately excited dc motors, series motors, motor (compound-wound dc) generators, and (synchronous) converters are required to be provided with speed limiting devices (note Exceptions) such as a centrifugal device on the shaft of the machine or a remotely located overspeed device, which may be set at a predetermined speed to operate a set of contacts and thereby trip a circuit breaker and de-energize the machine.

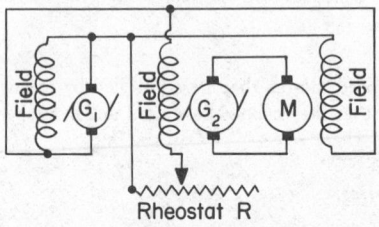

Rheostat R

Figure 430-21. A schematic diagram of the Ward Leonard speed control system.

430-90. Combination Fuseholder and Switch as Controller. The rating of a combination fuseholder and switch used as a motor controller shall be such that the fuseholder will accommodate the size of the fuse specified in Part C of this article for motor-running overload protection.

Exception: Where fuses having time delay appropriate for the starting characteristics of the motor are used, fuseholders of smaller size than specified in Part C of this article shall be permitted.

Time-delay (dual element) fuses can commonly be used for both motor overload and branch-circuit short-circuit and ground-fault protection and can be sized in accordance with Section 430-32. See also Sections 430-36, 430-55, and 430-57.

430-91. Motor Controller Enclosure Types. Table 430-91 provides the basis for selecting enclosures for use in specific nonhazardous locations. The enclosures are not intended to protect against conditions such as condensation, icing, corrosion or contamination which may occur within the enclosure or enter via the conduit or unsealed openings. These internal conditions require special consideration by the installer and/or user.

Table 430-91. Motor Controller Enclosure Selection Table

Provides a Degree of Protection Against the Following Environmental Conditions	For Outdoor Use						
	Enclosure Type Number†						
	3	3R	3S	4	4X	6	6P
Incidental contact with the enclosed equipment	X	X	X	X	X	X	X
Rain, snow and sleet	X	X	X	X	X	X	X
Sleet	—	—	X	—	—	—	—
Windblown dust	X	—	X	X	X	X	X
Hosedown	—	—	—	X	X	X	X
Corrosive agents	—	—	—	—	X	—	X
Occasional temporary submersion	— .	—	—	—	—	X	X
Occasional prolonged submersion	—	—	—	—	—	—	X

Provides a Degree of Protection Against the Following Environmental Conditions	For Indoor Use										
	Enclosure Type Number†										
	1	2	4	4X	5	6	6P	11	12	12K	13
Incidental contact with the enclosed equipment	X	X	X	X	X	X	X	X	X	X	X
Falling dirt	X	X	X	X	X	X	X	X	X	X	X
Falling liquids and light splashing	—	X	X	X	—	X	X	X	X	X	X
Dust, lint, fibers and flyings	—	—	X	X	X	X	X	—	X	X	X
Hosedown and splashing water	—	—	X	X	—	X	X	—	—	—	—
Oil and coolant seepage	—	—	—	—	—	—	—	—	X	X	X
Oil or coolant spraying and splashing	—	—	—	—	—	—	—	—	—	—	X
Corrosive agents	—	—	—	X	—	—	X	X	—	—	—
Occasional temporary submersion	—	—	—	—	—	X	X	—	—	—	—
Occasional prolonged submersion	—	—	—	—	—	—	X	—	—	—	—

† Enclosure type number, except type number 1, shall be marked on the motor controller enclosure.

Enclosure-type numbers are described in more detail in industry standards such as ANSI/NEMA IC6-1978, NEMA Pub. 250-179, UL 508, and controller manufacturers' literature. For other than general-use Type No. 1 enclosures, the type number is required to be marked on the motor controller enclosure.

H. Disconnecting Means

430-101. General. Part H is intended to require disconnecting means capable of disconnecting motors and controllers from the circuit.

(FPN): See Diagram 430-1.

(FPN): See Section 110-22 for identification of disconnecting means.

430-102. In Sight from Controller Location. A disconnecting means shall be located in sight from the controller location.

Exception No. 1: For motor circuits over 600 volts, nominal, the controller disconnecting means shall be permitted to be out of sight of the controller, provided the controller is marked with a warning label giving the location and identification of the disconnecting means to be locked in the open position.

Exception No. 2: A single disconnecting means shall be permitted to be located adjacent to a group of coordinated controllers mounted adjacent one to each other on a multimotor continuous process machine.

For motors located remote from the controller location, see the commentary following Section 430-86.

430-103. To Disconnect Both Motor and Controller. The disconnecting means shall disconnect the motor and the controller from all ungrounded supply conductors and shall be so designed that no pole can be operated independently. The disconnecting means shall be permitted in the same enclosure with the controller.

(FPN): See Section 430-113 for equipment receiving energy from more than one source.

The *Code* requires that a switch, circuit breaker, or other device serve as a disconnecting means for both the controller and the motor, thereby providing safety during maintenance and inspection shutdown periods. The disconnecting means also disconnects the controller; therefore, it cannot be a part of the controller. However, separate disconnects and controllers may be mounted on the same panel or contained in the same enclosure, such as combination fused-switch, magnetic-starter units.

Depending upon the size of the motor and other conditions, the type of disconnecting means required may be a motor-circuit switch, a circuit breaker, a general-use switch, an isolating switch, an attachment plug and receptacle, or a branch-circuit short-circuit and ground-fault protective device. See Section 430-109.

If a motor is stalled, or under heavy overload, and the motor controller fails to properly open the circuit, the disconnecting means, which is required to be rated to interrupt locked-rotor current, can be used to open the circuit. Switches rated up to 100 hp are readily obtainable, but for motors larger than 100 hp ac or 40 hp dc, the disconnecting means are to be permitted to be a general-use or isolating switch when plainly marked "Do not operate under load." See Section 430-109, Exception No. 4.

Figure 430-22. Heavy duty safety switches UL listed for use on systems up to 200,000 A fault current rms symmetrical with Class J or Class R fuses installed. (*Square D Co.*)

430-104. To Be Indicating. The disconnecting means shall plainly indicate whether it is in the open (off) or closed (on) position.

430-105. Grounded Conductors. One pole of the disconnecting means shall be permitted to disconnect a permanently grounded conductor, provided the disconnecting means is so designed that the pole in the grounded conductor cannot be opened without simultaneously disconnecting all conductors of the circuit.

430-106. Service Switch as Disconnecting Means. Where an installation consists of a single motor, the service switch may serve as the disconnecting means if it complies with this article and is within sight from the controller location.

430-107. Readily Accessible. One of the disconnecting means shall be readily accessible.

430-108. Every Switch. Every disconnecting means in the motor circuit between the point of attachment to the feeder and the point of connection to the motor shall comply with the requirements of Sections 430-109 and 430-110.

430-109. Type. The disconnecting means shall be a motor-circuit switch rated in horsepower, a circuit breaker, or a molded case switch (nonautomatic circuit interrupter).

Exception No. 1: For stationary motors of ⅛ horsepower or less, the branch-circuit overcurrent device shall be permitted to serve as the disconnecting means.

Exception No. 2: For stationary motors rated at 2 horsepower or less and 300 volts or less, the disconnecting means shall be permitted to be a general-use switch having an ampere rating not less than twice the full-load current rating of the motor.
On ac circuits, general-use snap switches suitable only for use on ac (not general-use ac-dc snap switches) shall be permitted to disconnect a motor rated 2 horsepower or less and 300 volts or less having a full-load current rating not more than 80 percent of the ampere rating of the switch.

Exception No. 3: For motors of over 2 horsepower to and including 100 horsepower, the separate disconnecting means required for a motor with an autotransformer-type controller shall be permitted to be a general-use switch where all of the following provisions are met:

a. The motor drives a generator that is provided with overload protection.

b. The controller (1) is capable of interrupting the locked-rotor current of the motor; (2) is provided with a no-voltage release; and (3) is provided with running overload protection not exceeding 125 percent of the motor full-load current rating.

c. Separate fuses or an inverse time circuit breaker rated or set at not more than 150 percent of the motor full-load current are provided in the motor branch circuit.

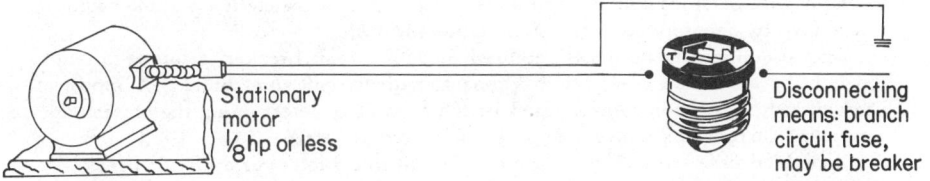

Figure 430-23. Exception No. 1: The branch-circuit overcurrent device may serve as the disconnecting means for stationary motors of ⅛ hp or less.

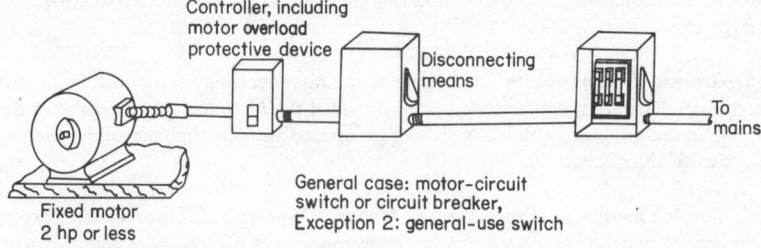

Figure 430-24. Exception No. 2: A general-use switch having an ampere rating not less than twice the motor full-load rating may serve as the disconnecting means for motors rated 2 hp or less and operating at 300 V or less.

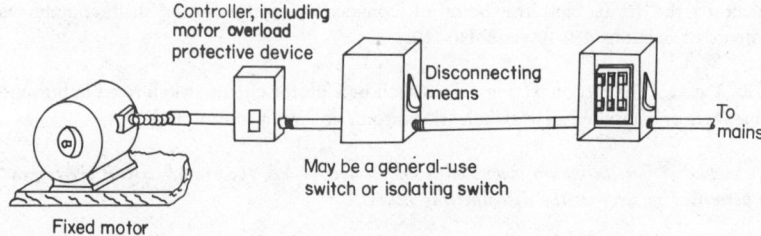

Figure 430-25. Exception No. 4: A general-use switch or isolation switch may serve as the disconnecting means for stationary motors rated more than 40 hp or 100 hp ac, if marked "Do ·not operate under load."

Exception No. 4: For stationary motors rated at more than 40 horsepower direct-current or 100 horsepower alternating-current, the disconnecting means shall be permitted to be a general-use or isolating switch when plainly marked "Do not operate under load."

Exception No. 5: For a cord- and plug-connected motor, an attachment plug and receptacle having ratings no less than the motor ratings shall be permitted to serve as the disconnecting means. A horsepower rated attachment plug and receptacle shall not be required for a cord- and plug-connected appliance in accordance with Section 422-22 or a room air conditioner in accordance with Section 440-63.

Exception No. 6: For torque motors the disconnecting means shall be permitted to be a general-use switch.

Section 430-108 requires every disconnecting means in the motor circuit to comply with Sections 430-109 and 430-110, including a manually operable switch permitted by Section 430-86(b). See Figure 430-19.

The disconnecting means is required to be a circuit breaker, a motor-circuit switch, or a molded case switch (nonautomatic circuit interrupter). A motor-circuit switch is a horsepower-rated switch capable of interrupting the maximum overload current of a motor (see Definitions, Article 100).

A molded case switch (nonautomatic circuit interrupter) is a circuit breaker-like device without the overcurrent element and automatic trip mechanism. It is rated in amperes and is suitable for use as a motor circuit disconnect based on its ampere rating, like a circuit breaker.

Figures 430-23 through 430-26 illustrate the exceptions to this general requirement.

When horsepower-rated fused switches are required, it is to be noted that marking within the enclosure usually permits a dual horsepower rating. The "standard" horsepower rating is based on the largest nontime-delay (nondual-element) fuse rating which can be used in the switch and which will permit the motor to start. The "maximum" horsepower rating is based on the largest rated time-delay (dual-element) fuse which can be used in the switch and which will permit the motor to start. Thus, when time-delay fuses are used, smaller sized switches and fuseholders can be used. See Section 430-57, Exception.

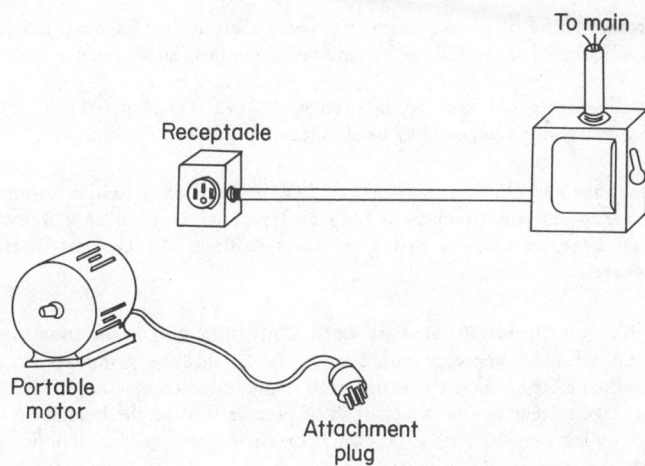

Figure 430-26. Exception No. 5: An attachment plug and receptacle of the proper rating may serve as the disconnecting means for cord-and-plug connected motors.

430-110. Ampere Rating and Interrupting Capacity.

(a) General. The disconnecting means for motor circuits rated 600 volts, nominal, or less, shall have an ampere rating of at least 115 percent of the full-load current rating of the motor.

(b) For Torque Motors. Disconnecting means for a torque motor shall have an ampere rating of at least 115 percent of the motor nameplate current.

(c) For Combination Loads. Where two or more motors are used together or where one or more motors are used in combination with other loads, such as resistance heaters, and where the combined load may be simultaneous on a single disconnecting means, the ampere and horsepower ratings of the combined load shall be determined as follows:

(1) The rating of the disconnecting means shall be determined from the summation of all currents, including resistance loads, at the full-load condition and also at the locked-rotor condition. The combined full-load current and the combined locked-rotor current so obtained shall be considered as a single motor for the purpose of this requirement as follows:

The full-load current equivalent to the horsepower rating of each motor shall be selected from Table 430-148, 430-149, or 430-150. These full-load currents shall be added to the rating in amperes of other loads to obtain an equivalent full-load current for the combined load.

ARTICLE 430—MOTORS, CIRCUITS, CONTROLLERS

The locked-rotor current equivalent to the horsepower rating of each motor shall be selected from Table 430-151. The locked-rotor currents shall be added to the rating in amperes of other loads to obtain an equivalent locked-rotor current for the combined load. Where two or more motors and/or other loads cannot be started simultaneously, appropriate combinations of locked-rotor and full-load current shall be permitted to be used to determine the equivalent locked-rotor current for the simultaneous combined loads.

Exception: Where part of the concurrent load is resistance load, and where the disconnecting means is a switch rated in horsepower and amperes, the switch used shall be permitted to have a horsepower rating not less than the combined load of the motor(s), if the ampere rating of the switch is not less than the locked-rotor current of the motor(s) plus the resistance load.

(2) The ampere rating of the disconnecting means shall not be less than 115 percent of the summation of all currents at the full-load condition determined in accordance with (c)(1) above.

(3) For small motors not covered by Tables 430-147, 430-148, 430-149, or 430-150, the locked-rotor current shall be assumed to be six times the full-load current.

A general-use switch, fuse, circuit breaker, molded case switch (nonautomatic circuit interrupter), or attachment plug and receptacle used as a disconnecting means must have an ampere rating of not less than 115 percent of the motor full-load current.

430-111. Switch or Circuit Breaker as Both Controller and Disconnecting Means. A switch or circuit breaker complying with Section 430-83 shall be permitted to serve as both controller and disconnecting means if it opens all ungrounded conductors to the motor, if it is protected by an overcurrent device (which shall be permitted to be the branch-circuit fuses) that opens all ungrounded conductors to the switch or circuit breaker, and if it is of one of the following types:

(a) Air-Break Switch. An air-break switch, operable directly by applying the hand to a lever or handle.

(b) Inverse Time Circuit Breaker. An inverse time circuit breaker operable directly by applying the hand to a lever or handle.

(c) Oil Switch. An oil switch used on a circuit whose rating does not exceed 600 volts or 100 amperes, or by special permission on a circuit exceeding this capacity where under expert supervision.
The oil switch or circuit breaker specified above shall be permitted to be both power and manually operable.
The overcurrent device protecting the controller shall be permitted to be part of the controller assembly or shall be permitted to be separate.
An autotransformer-type controller shall be provided with a separate disconnecting means.

Where the controller consists of a manually operable air-break switch, an inverse time circuit breaker, or a 100-A maximum oil switch (higher rating by special permission), the controller is considered to be a satisfactory disconnecting means. It is the intent of this section to permit omission of an additional device to serve as a disconnecting means. See Figure 430-27.
It should be noted that a separate disconnecting means is required to be provided if the controller is of the autotransformer or "compensator" type (this switch may be combined in the same enclosure with a motor overload protective device).

Where used as a controller, the switch or circuit breaker is required to meet all of the requirements for controllers and be protected by branch-circuit short-circuit and ground-fault protective devices (fuses or a circuit breaker), which ensure that all ungrounded conductors will be opened.

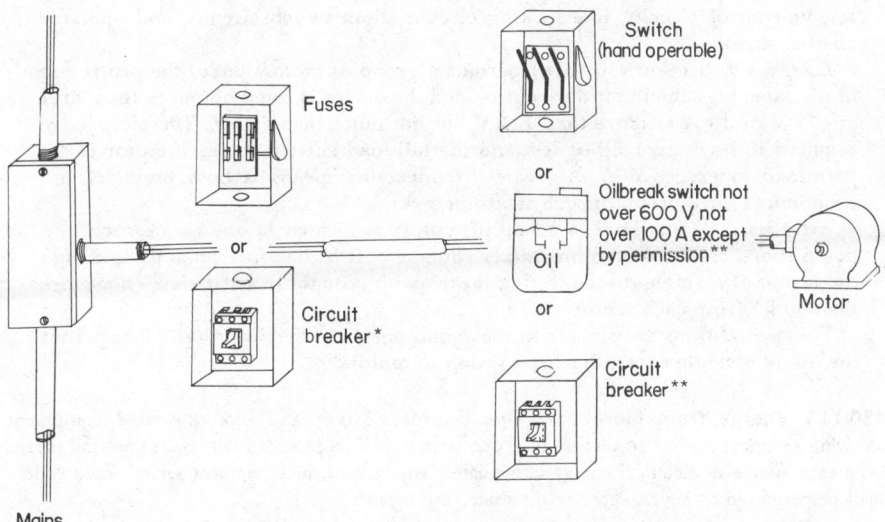

Figure 430-27. Three alternative arrangements where a switch, or circuit breaker, or oilbreak switch can serve satisfactorily as both the controller and disconnecting means. (* and ** oilbreak switch or circuit breaker may be hand operated or power operated.)

430-112. Motors Served by Single Disconnecting Means. Each motor shall be provided with an individual disconnecting means.

Exception: A single disconnecting means shall be permitted to serve a group of motors under any one of the following conditions:

a. Where a number of motors drive several parts of a single machine or piece of apparatus, such as metal and woodworking machines, cranes, and hoists.

b. Where a group of motors is under the protection of one set of branch-circuit protective devices as permitted by Section 430-53(a).

c. Where a group of motors is in a single room within sight from the location of the disconnecting means.

The single disconnecting means shall have a rating not less than is required by Section 430-110 for a single motor, the rating of which equals the sum of the horsepowers or currents of all the motors of the group.

The exception permits a single disconnecting means to serve a group of motors. The disconnecting means is required to have a rating equal to the sum of the horsepowers or currents of all the motors of the group. If the total horsepower is over 2 hp, a motor-circuit switch (horsepower-rated) is required to be used. Thus, for five 2-hp motors the disconnecting means should be a motor-circuit switch rated at not less than 10 hp.

Exception a. A single disconnecting means may be used where a number of motors drive several parts of a single machine such as cranes (see Sections 610-31 and 610-32), metal or woodworking machines, steel rolling mill machinery, etc. The single disconnecting means for multimotor machinery provides a positive means of simultaneously de-energizing all motor branch circuits, including remote-control circuits, interlocking circuits, limit-switch circuits, and operator control stations.

Exception b. Section 430-53(a) permits a group of motors under the protection of the same branch-circuit device provided the device is rated not more than 20 A at 125 V or 15 A at more than 125 V but not more than 600 V. The motors are required to be rated 1 hp or less and the full-load current for each motor is not permitted to exceed 6 A. A single disconnecting means is both practical and economical for a group of such small motors.

Exception c. Many times, a group of motors is located in one room, such as a pump room, compressor room, mixer room, etc. It is therefore possible to design the layout of a single disconnecting means with an unobstructed view (not more than 50 ft) from each motor.

These conditions are similar to the requirements in Section 430-87 that permit the use of a single controller for a group of motors.

430-113. Energy from More than One Source. Motor and motor-operated equipment receiving electrical energy from more than one source shall be provided with disconnecting means from each source of electrical energy immediately adjacent to the equipment served. Each source shall be permitted to have a separate disconnecting means.

Exception No. 1: Where a motor receives electrical energy from more than one source, the disconnecting means for the main power supply to the motor shall not be required to be immediately adjacent to the motor provided the controller disconnecting means is capable of being locked in the open position.

Exception No. 2: A separate disconnecting means shall not be required for a Class 2 remote-control circuit conforming with Article 725, rated not more than 30 volts, and which is isolated and ungrounded.

Exception No. 1 applies to large synchronous motors that receive electrical energy from more than one source. Exception No. 2 applies to low voltage control circuits, such as thermostat circuits used with heating and air-conditioning equipment.

J. Over 600 Volts, Nominal

430-121. General. Part J recognizes the additional hazard due to the use of high voltage. It adds to or amends the other provisions of this article. Other requirements for circuits and equipment operating at over 600 volts, nominal, are in Article 710.

430-122. Marking on Controllers. In addition to the marking required by Section 430-8, a controller shall be marked with the control voltage.

430-123. Conductor Enclosures Adjacent to Motors. Flexible metal conduit or liquidtight flexible metal conduit not exceeding 6 feet (1.83 m) in length shall be permitted to be employed for raceway connection to a motor terminal enclosure.

430-124. Size of Conductors. Conductors supplying motors shall have an ampacity not less than the current at which the motor overload protective device(s) is selected to trip.

430-125. Motor Circuit Overcurrent Protection.

(a) General. The high-voltage circuit for each motor shall include coordinated protection to automatically interrupt overload and fault currents in the motor, the motor circuit conductors, and the motor control apparatus.

Exception: Where a motor is vital to operation of the plant and the motor should operate to failure if necessary to prevent a greater hazard to persons, the sensing device(s) is permitted to be connected to a supervised annunciator or alarm instead of interrupting the motor circuit.

(b) Overload Protection.

(1) Each motor shall be protected against dangerous heating due to motor overloads and failure to start by a thermal protector integral with the motor or external current sensing devices, or both.

(2) The secondary circuits of wound-rotor alternating-current motors including conductors, controllers, and resistors rated for the application shall be considered as protected against overcurrent by the motor overload protection means.

(3) Operation of the overload interrupting device shall simultaneously disconnect all ungrounded conductors.

(4) Overload sensing devices shall not automatically reset after trip unless resetting of the overload sensing device does not cause automatic restarting of the motor or there is no hazard to persons created by automatic restarting of the motor and its connected machinery.

(c) Fault-Current Protection.

(1) Fault-current protection shall be provided in each motor circuit by one of the following means:

a. A circuit breaker of suitable type and rating so arranged that it can be serviced without hazard. The circuit breaker shall simultaneously disconnect all ungrounded conductors. The circuit breaker shall be permitted to sense the fault current by means of integral or external sensing elements.

b. Fuses of a suitable type and rating placed in each ungrounded conductor. Fuses shall be used with suitable disconnecting means or they shall be of a type that can also serve as the disconnecting means. They shall be so arranged that they cannot be serviced while they are energized.

(2) Fault-current interrupting devices shall not reclose the circuit automatically.

Exception: Where circuits are exposed to transient faults and where automatic reclosing of the circuit does not create a hazard to persons.

(3) Overload protection and fault-current protection shall be permitted to be provided by the same device.

430-126. Rating of Motor Control Apparatus. Motor controllers and motor branch-circuit disconnecting means shall have a continuous ampere rating not less than the current at which the overload protective device(s) is selected to trip.

430-127. Disconnecting Means. The controller disconnecting means shall be capable of being locked in the open position.

ARTICLE 430—MOTORS, CIRCUITS, CONTROLLERS

K. Protection of Live Parts — All Voltages

430-131. General. Part K specifies that live parts shall be protected in a manner judged adequate to the hazard involved.

430-132. Where Required. Exposed live parts of motors and controllers operating at 50 volts or more between terminals shall be guarded against accidental contact by enclosure or by location as follows:

(a) **In a Room or Enclosure.** By installation in a room or enclosure that is accessible only to qualified persons.

(b) **On a Suitable Balcony.** By installation on a suitable balcony, gallery, or platform, so elevated and arranged as to exclude unqualified persons.

(c) **Elevation.** By elevation 8 feet (2.44 m) or more above the floor.

Exception: Stationary motors having commutators, collectors, and brush rigging located inside of motor-end brackets and not conductively connected to supply circuits operating at more than 150 volts to ground.

430-133. Guards for Attendants. Where live parts of motors or controllers operating at over 150 volts to ground are guarded against accidental contact only by location as specified in Section 430-132, and where adjustment or other attendance may be necessary during the operation of the apparatus, suitable insulating mats or platforms shall be provided so that the attendant cannot readily touch live parts unless standing on the mats or platforms.

(FPN): For working space, see Sections 110-16 and 110-34.

L. Grounding

430-141. General. Part L specifies the grounding of motor and controller frames to prevent a potential above ground in the event of accidental contact between live parts and frames. Insulation, isolation, or guarding are suitable alternatives to grounding of motors under certain conditions.

430-142. Stationary Motors. The frames of stationary motors shall be grounded under any of the following conditions: (1) where supplied by metal-enclosed wiring; (2) where in a wet location and not isolated or guarded; (3) if in a hazardous (classified) location as covered in Articles 500 through 517; (4) if the motor operates with any terminal at over 150 volts to ground.

Where the frame of the motor is not grounded, it shall be permanently and effectively insulated from the ground.

Any motor in a wet location and subject to contact by personnel constitutes a serious hazard and, unless it is isolated, elevated or guarded from reach, should be grounded.

Stationary motors are usually supplied by wiring enclosed in metal raceways (rigid metal conduit, EMT, flexible metal conduit, etc.) or by cables with metallic sheaths (Types AC, MC). Upon being effectively attached to the motor junction box or frame, the metal raceway or cable armor serves as the equipment grounding conductor. See Section 250-91(b).

430-143. Portable Motors. The frames of portable motors that operate at over 150 volts to ground shall be guarded or grounded.

(FPN): See Section 250-45(d) for grounding of portable appliances in other than residential occupancies.

(FPN): See Section 250-59(b) for color of grounding conductor.

430-144. Controllers. Controller enclosures shall be grounded regardless of voltage.

Exception No. 1: Enclosures attached to ungrounded portable equipment.

Exception No. 2: Lined covers of snap switches.

430-145. Method of Grounding. Where required, grounding shall be done in the manner specified in Article 250.

(a) Grounding Through Terminal Housings. Where the wiring to fixed motors is metal-enclosed cable or in metal raceways, junction boxes to house motor terminals shall be provided, and the armor of the cable or the metal raceways shall be connected to them in the manner specified in Article 250.

(FPN): See Section 430-12(e) for grounding connection means required at motor terminal housings.

(b) Separation of Junction Box from Motor. The junction box required by (a) above shall be permitted to be separated from the motor not more than 6 feet (1.83 m), provided the leads to the motor are Type AC cable or armored cord or are stranded leads enclosed in liquidtight flexible metal conduit, flexible metal conduit, intermediate metal conduit, rigid metal conduit or electrical metallic tubing not smaller than ⅜-inch electrical trade size, the armor or raceway being connected both to the motor and to the box. Where stranded leads are used, protected as specified above, they shall not be larger than No. 10, and shall comply with other requirements of this Code for conductors to be used in raceways.

(c) Grounding of Controller Mounted Devices. Instrument transformer secondaries and exposed noncurrent-carrying metal or other conductive parts or cases of instrument transformers, meters, instruments, and relays shall be grounded as specified in Sections 250-121 through 250-125.

Most motors are subject to vibration and good practice requires that, in nearly all cases, the wiring to motors that are fixed be installed with a short section of liquidtight flexible metal conduit, or flexible metal conduit, to the motor terminal housing.

Table 430-147. Full-Load Current in Amperes, Direct-Current Motors

The following values of full-load currents* are for motors running at base speed.

HP	Armature Voltage Rating*					
	90V	120V	180V	240V	500V	550V
¼	4.0	3.1	2.0	1.6		
⅓	5.2	4.1	2.6	2.0		
½	6.8	5.4	3.4	2.7		
¾	9.6	7.6	4.8	3.8		
1	12.2	9.5	6.1	4.7		
1½		13.2	8.3	6.6		
2		17	10.8	8.5		
3		25	16	12.2		
5		40	27	20		
7½		58		29	13.6	12.2
10		76		38	18	16
15				55	27	24
20				72	34	31
25				89	43	38
30				106	51	46
40				140	67	61
50				173	83	75
60				206	99	90
75				255	123	111
100				341	164	148
125				425	205	185
150				506	246	222
200				675	330	294

* These are average direct-current quantities.

Table 430-148. Full-Load Currents in Amperes Single-Phase Alternating-Current Motors

The following values of full-load currents are for motors running at usual speeds and motors with normal torque characteristics. Motors built for especially low speeds or high torques may have higher full-load currents, and multispeed motors will have full-load current varying with speed, in which case the nameplate current ratings shall be used.

To obtain full-load currents of 208- and 200-volt motors, increase corresponding 230-volt motor full-load currents by 10 and 15 percent, respectively.

The voltages listed are rated motor voltages. The currents listed shall be permitted for system voltage ranges of 110 to 120 and 220 to 240.

HP	115V	230V
⅙	4.4	2.2
¼	5.8	2.9
⅓	7.2	3.6
½	9.8	4.9
¾	13.8	6.9
1	16	8
1½	20	10
2	24	12
3	34	17
5	56	28
7½	80	40
10	100	50

Table 430-149. Full-Load Current
Two-Phase Alternating-Current Motors (4-Wire)

The following values of full-load current are for motors running at speeds usual for belted motors and motors with normal torque characteristics. Motors built for especially low speeds or high torques may require more running current, and multispeed motors will have full-load current varying with speed, in which case the nameplate current rating shall be used. Current in the common conductor of a 2-phase, 3-wire system will be 1.41 times the value given.

The voltages listed are rated motor voltages. The currents listed shall be permitted for system voltage ranges of 110 to 120, 220 to 240, 440 to 480, and 550 to 600 volts.

HP	Induction Type Squirrel-Cage and Wound-Rotor Amperes				
	115V	230V	460V	575V	2300V
½	4	2	1	.8	
¾	4.8	2.4	1.2	1.0	
1	6.4	3.2	1.6	1.3	
1½	9	4.5	2.3	1.8	
2	11.8	5.9	3	2.4	
3		8.3	4.2	3.3	
5		13.2	6.6	5.3	
7½		19	9	8	
10		24	12	10	
15		36	18	14	
20		47	23	19	
25		59	29	24	
30		69	35	28	
40		90	45	36	
50		113	56	45	
60		133	67	53	14
75		166	83	66	18
100		218	109	87	23
125		270	135	108	28
150		312	156	125	32
200		416	208	167	43

Table 430-150.   Full-Load Current*
Three-Phase Alternating-Current Motors

HP	Induction Type Squirrel-Cage and Wound-Rotor Amperes					Synchronous Type †Unity Power Factor Amperes			
	115V	230V	460V	575V	2300V	230V	460V	575V	2300V
½	4	2	1	.8					
¾	5.6	2.8	1.4	1.1					
1	7.2	3.6	1.8	1.4					
1½	10.4	5.2	2.6	2.1					
2	13.6	6.8	3.4	2.7					
3		9.6	4.8	3.9					
5		15.2	7.6	6.1					
7½		22	11	9					
10		28	14	11					
15		42	21	17					
20		54	27	22					
25		68	34	27		53	26	21	
30		80	40	32		63	32	26	
40		104	52	41		83	41	33	
50		130	65	52		104	52	42	
60		154	77	62	16	123	61	49	12
75		192	96	77	20	155	78	62	15
100		248	124	99	26	202	101	81	20
125		312	156	125	31	253	126	101	25
150		360	180	144	37	302	151	121	30
200		480	240	192	49	400	201	161	40

For full-load currents of 208- and 200-volt motors, increase the corresponding 230-volt motor full-load current by 10 and 15 percent, respectively.

* These values of full-load current are for motors running at speeds usual for belted motors and motors with normal torque characteristics. Motors built for especially low speeds or high torques may require more running current, and multispeed motors will have full-load current varying with speed, in which case the nameplate current rating shall be used.

† For 90 and 80 percent power factor the above figures shall be multipled by 1.1 and 1.25 respectively.

The voltages listed are rated motor voltages. The currents listed shall be permitted for system voltage ranges of 110 to 120, 220 to 240, 440 to 480, and 550 to 600 volts.

**Table 430-151.   Conversion Table of Locked-Rotor Currents
for Selection of Disconnecting Means and Controllers
as Determined from Horsepower and Voltage Rating**

For use only with Sections 430-110, 440-12 and 440-41.

| Motor Locked-Rotor Current Amperes* | | | | | | | Max. HP Rating |
| Single Phase | | Two or Three Phase | | | | | |
115V	230V	115V	200V	230V	460V	575V	
58.8	29.4	24	18.8	12	6	4.8	½
82.8	41.4	33.6	19.3	16.8	8.4	6.6	¾
96	48	43.2	24.8	21.6	10.8	8.4	1
120	60	62	35.9	31.2	15.6	12.6	1½
144	72	81	46.9	40.8	20.4	16.2	2
204	102	—	66	58	26.8	23.4	3
336	168	—	105	91	45.6	36.6	5
480	240	—	152	132	66	54	7½
600	300	—	193	168	84	66	10
—	—	—	290	252	126	102	15
—	—	—	373	324	162	132	20
—	—	—	469	408	204	162	25
—	—	—	552	480	240	192	30
—	—	—	718	624	312	246	40
—	—	—	897	780	390	312	50
—	—	—	1063	924	462	372	60
—	—	—	1325	1152	576	462	75
—	—	—	1711	1488	744	594	100
—	—	—	2153	1872	936	750	125
—	—	—	2484	2160	1080	864	150
—	—	—	3312	2880	1440	1152	200

* These values of motor locked-rotor current are approximately six times the full-load current values given in Tables 430-148 and 430-150.

Table 430-152. Maximum Rating or Setting of Motor Branch-Circuit Short-Circuit and Ground-Fault Protective Devices

Type of Motor	Percent of Full-Load Current			
	Nontime Delay Fuse	Dual Element (Time-Delay) Fuse	Instan-taneous Trip Breaker	* Inverse Time Breaker
Single-phase, all types				
No code letter.........................	300	175	700	250
All ac single-phase and polyphase squirrel-cage and synchronous motors† with full-voltage, resistor or reactor starting:				
No code letter.........................	300	175	700	250
Code letter F to V	300	175	700	250
Code letter B to E	250	175	700	200
Code letter A	150	150	700	150
All ac squirrel-cage and synchronous motors† with autotransformer starting:				
Not more than 30 amps				
No code letter.........................	250	175	700	200
More than 30 amps				
No code letter.........................	200	175	700	200
Code letter F to V	250	175	700	200
Code letter B to E	200	175	700	200
Code letter A	150	150	700	150
High-reactance squirrel-cage				
Not more than 30 amps				
No code letter.........................	250	175	700	250
More than 30 amps				
No code letter.........................	200	175	700	200
Wound-rotor —				
No code letter.........................	150	150	700	150
Direct-current (constant voltage)				
No more than 50 hp				
No code letter.........................	150	150	250	150
More than 50 hp				
No code letter.........................	150	150	175	150

For explanation of Code Letter Marking, see Table 430-7(b).

For certain exceptions to the values specified, see Sections 430-52 through 430-54.

* The values given in the last column also cover the ratings of nonadjustable inverse time types of circuit breakers that may be modified as in Section 430-52.

† Synchronous motors of the low-torque, low-speed type (usually 450 rpm or lower), such as are used to drive reciprocating compressors, pumps, etc. that start unloaded, do not require a fuse rating or circuit-breaker setting in excess of 200 percent of full-load current.

ARTICLE 440 — AIR-CONDITIONING AND REFRIGERATING EQUIPMENT

Contents

(c) Where Lighting Units or Other Appliances Are Also Supplied.

440-63. Disconnecting Means.

440-64. Supply Cords.

A. General

440-1. Scope. The provisions of this article apply to electric motor-driven air-conditioning and refrigerating equipment, and to the branch circuits and controllers for such equipment. It provides for the special considerations necessary for circuits supplying hermetic refrigerant motor-compressors and for any air-conditioning and/or refrigerating equipment which is supplied from an individual branch circuit which supplies a hermetic refrigerant motor-compressor.

Hermetic Refrigerant Motor-Compressor: A combination consisting of a compressor and motor, both of which are enclosed in the same housing, with no external shaft or shaft seals, the motor operating in the refrigerant.

440-2. Other Articles.

(a) **Article 430.** These provisions are in addition to, or amendatory of, the provisions of Article 430 and other articles in this Code, which apply except as modified in this article.

(b) **Article 422, 424, or 430.** The rules of Article 422, 424, or 430, as applicable, shall apply to air-conditioning and refrigerating equipment which does not incorporate a hermetic refrigerant motor-compressor.Examples of such equipment are devices which employ refrigeration compressors driven by conventional motors, furnaces with air-conditioning evaporator coils installed, fan-coil units, remote forced air-cooled condensers, remote commercial refrigerators, etc.

(c) **Article 422.** Devices such as room air conditioners, household refrigerators and freezers, drinking water coolers, and beverage dispensers shall be considered appliances and the provisions of Article 422 shall also apply.

(d) **Other Applicable Articles.** Hermetic refrigerant motor-compressors, circuits, controllers, and equipment shall also comply with the applicable provisions of the following:

Capacitors .... Section 460-9
Garages, Aircraft Hangars, Gasoline Dispensing and
  Service Stations, Bulk Storage Plants, Spray Application,
  Dipping and Coating Processes, Inhalation Anesthetizing
  Locations .... Articles 511, 513, 514, 515, 516, and 517-G
Hazardous (Classified) Locations .... Articles 500 through 503
Motion-Picture and Television Studios .... Article 530
Resistors and Reactors .... Article 470

Article 440 provides for special considerations necessary for circuits supplying hermetic refrigerant motor-compressors and is in addition to, or amendatory of, the provisions of Article 430 and other applicable articles. However, many requirements, such as disconnecting means, controllers, single or group installations, and sizing of conductors, are the same as, or very similar to, those applied in Article 430.

Article 440 does not apply unless a hermetic refrigerant motor-compressor is supplied. Article 440 must be applied in conjunction with Article 430.

Note the term "rated load current," defined in the Fine Print Note following Section 440-3(a), and the term "branch-circuit selection current," defined in the Fine Print Note following Section 440-3(c).

When a "branch-circuit selection current" is marked on a nameplate, it is required to be used instead of the "rated-load current" in order to determine the size of the disconnecting means, the controller, the motor branch-circuit conductors, and the overcurrent protective devices for the branch-circuit conductors and the motor. The value of "branch-circuit selection current" will always be greater than the marked "rated-load current."

440-3. Marking on Hermetic Refrigerant Motor-Compressors and Equipment.

(a) Hermetic Refrigerant Motor-Compressor Nameplate. A hermetic refrigerant motor-compressor shall be provided with a nameplate which shall give the manufacturer's name, trademark or symbol; identifying designation; phase; voltage; and frequency. The rated load current in amperes of the motor-compressor shall be marked by the equipment manufacturer on either or both the motor-compressor nameplate and the nameplate of the equipment in which the motor-compressor is used. The locked-rotor current of each single-phase motor-compressor having a rated-load current of more than 9 amperes at 115 volts or more than 4.5 amperes at 230 volts and each polyphase motor-compressor shall be marked on the motor-compressor nameplate. Where a thermal protector complying with Section 440-52(a)(2) and (b)(2) is used, the motor-compressor nameplate or the equipment nameplate shall be marked with the words "Thermally Protected." Where a protective system, complying with Section 440-52(a)(4) and (b)(4), is used and is furnished with the equipment, the equipment nameplate shall be marked with the words, "Thermally Protected System." Where a protective system complying with Section 440-52(a)(4) and (b)(4) is specified, the equipment nameplate shall be appropriately marked.

(FPN): Definition: The rated-load current for a hermetic refrigerant motor-compressor is the current resulting when the motor-compressor is operated at the rated load, rated voltage and rated frequency of the equipment it serves.

(b) Multimotor and Combination-Load Equipment. Multimotor and combination-load equipment shall be provided with a visible nameplate marked with the maker's name, the rating in volts, frequency and number of phases, minimum supply circuit conductor ampacity, and the maximum rating of the branch-circuit short-circuit and ground-fault protective device. The ampacity shall be calculated by using Part D and counting all the motors and other loads which will be operated at the same time. The branch-circuit short-circuit and ground-fault protective device rating shall not exceed the value calculated by using Part C. Multimotor or combination-load equipment for use on two or more circuits shall be marked with the above information for each circuit.

Exception No. 1: Multimotor and combination-load equipment which is suitable under the provisions of this article for connection to a single 15- or 20-ampere, 120-volt, or a 15-ampere, 208- or 240-volt single-phase branch circuit shall be permitted to be marked as a single load.

Exception No. 2: Room air conditioners as provided in Part G of Article 440.

(c) Branch-Circuit Selection Current. Hermetic refrigerant motor-compressors or equipment containing such compressor(s) in which the protection system, approved for use with the motor-compressor which it protects, permits continuous current in excess of the specified percentage of nameplate rated-load current given in Section 440-52(b)(2) or (b)(4) shall also be marked with a branch-circuit selection current that complies with Section 440-52(b)(2) or (b)(4). This marking shall be provided by the equipment manufacturer and shall be on the nameplate(s) where the rated-load current(s) appears.

(FPN): Definition: Branch-circuit selection current is the value in amperes to be used instead of the rated-load current in determining the ratings of motor branch-circuit conductors, disconnecting means, controllers and branch-circuit short-circuit and ground-fault protective devices wherever the running overload protective device permits a sustained current greater than the specified percentage of the rated-load current. The value of branch-circuit selection current will always be greater than the marked rated-load current.

ARTICLE 440—AIR-CONDITIONING AND REFRIGERATING EQUIPMENT

440-4. Marking on Controllers. A controller shall be marked with the maker's name, trademark, or symbol; identifying designation; the voltage; phase; full-load and locked-rotor current (or horsepower) rating; and such other data as may be needed to properly indicate the motor-compressor for which it is suitable.

440-5. Ampacity and Rating. Ampacity of conductors and rating of equipment shall be determined as follows:

(a) Hermetic Refrigerant Motor-Compressor. For a hermetic refrigerant motor-compressor, the rated-load current marked on the nameplate of the equipment in which the motor-compressor is employed shall be used in determining the rating or ampacity of the disconnecting means, the branch-circuit conductors, the controller, the branch-circuit short-circuit and ground-fault protection, and the separate motor overload protection. Where no rated-load current is shown on the equipment nameplate, the rated-load current shown on the compressor nameplate shall be used. For disconnecting means and controllers, see also Sections 440-12 and 440-41.

Exception No. 1: When so marked, the branch-circuit selection current shall be used instead of the rated-load current to determine the rating or ampacity of the disconnecting means, the branch-circuit conductors, the controller, and the branch-circuit short-circuit and ground-fault protection.

Exception No. 2: As permitted in Section 440-22(b) for branch-circuit short-circuit and ground-fault protection of cord- and plug-connected equipment.

(b) Multimotor Equipment. For multimotor equipment employing a shaded-pole or permanent split-capacitor-type fan or blower motor, the full-load current for such motor marked on the nameplate of the equipment in which the fan or blower motor is employed shall be used instead of the horsepower rating to determine the ampacity or rating of the disconnecting means, the branch-circuit conductors, the controller, the branch-circuit short-circuit and ground-fault protection, and the separate overload protection. This marking on the equipment nameplate shall not be less than the current marked on the fan or blower motor nameplate.

440-6. Highest Rated (Largest) Motor. In determining compliance with this article and with Sections 430-24, 430-53(b) and (c), and 430-62(a), the highest rated (largest) motor shall be considered to be that motor which has the highest rated-load current. Where two or more motors have the same rated-load current, only one of them shall be considered as the highest rated (largest) motor. For other than hermetic refrigerant motor-compressors, and fan or blower motors as covered in Section 440-5(b), the full-load current used to determine the highest rated motor shall be the equivalent value corresponding to the motor horsepower rating selected from Tables 430-148, 430-149, or 430-150.

Exception: When so marked, the branch-circuit selection current shall be used instead of the rated-load current in determining the highest rated (largest) motor-compressor.

440-7. Single Machine. An air-conditioning or refrigerating system shall be considered to be a single machine under the provisions of Section 430-87, Exception and Section 430-112, Exception. The motors shall be permitted to be located remotely from each other.

B. Disconnecting Means

440-11. General. The provisions of Part B are intended to require disconnecting means capable of disconnecting air-conditioning and refrigerating equipment including motor-compressors, and controllers, from the circuit feeder. See Diagram 430-1.

440-12. Rating and Interrupting Capacity.

(a) Hermetic Refrigerant Motor-Compressor. A disconnecting means serving a hermetic refrigerant motor-compressor shall be selected on the basis of the nameplate rated-load current or branch-circuit selection current, whichever is greater, and locked-rotor current, respectively, of the motor-compressor as follows:

(1) The ampere rating shall be at least 115 percent of the nameplate rated-load current or branch-circuit selection current, whichever is greater.

(2) To determine the equivalent horsepower in complying with the requirements of Section 430-109, the horsepower rating shall be selected from Tables 430-148, 430-149, or 430-150 corresponding to the rated-load current or branch-circuit selection current, whichever is greater, and also the horsepower rating from Table 430-151 corresponding to the locked-rotor current. In case the nameplate rated-load current or branch-circuit selection current and locked-rotor current do not correspond to the currents shown in Tables 430-148, 430-149, 430-150, or 430-151, the horsepower rating corresponding to the next higher value shall be selected. In case different horsepower ratings are obtained when applying these tables, a horsepower rating at least equal to the larger of the values obtained shall be selected.

(b) Combination Loads. Where one or more hermetic refrigerant motor-compressors are used together or are used in combination with other motors and/or loads such as resistance heaters and where the combined load may be simultaneous on a single disconnecting means, the rating for the combined load shall be determined as follows:

(1) The horsepower rating of the disconnecting means shall be determined from the summation of all currents, including resistance loads, at the rated-load condition and also at the locked-rotor condition. The combined rated-load current and the combined locked-rotor current so obtained shall be considered as a single motor for the purpose of this requirement as follows:

a. The full-load current equivalent to the horsepower rating of each motor, other than a hermetic refrigerant motor-compressor, and fan or blower motors as covered in Section 440-5(b) shall be selected from Tables 430-148, 430-149, or 430-150. These full-load currents shall be added to the motor-compressor rated-load current(s) or branch-circuit selection current(s), whichever is greater, and to the rating in amperes of other loads to obtain an equivalent full-load current for the combined load.

b. The locked-rotor current equivalent to the horsepower rating of each motor, other than a hermetic refrigerant motor-compressor, shall be selected from Table 430-151, and for fan and blower motors of the shaded-pole or permanent split-capacitor type marked with the locked-rotor current, the marked value shall be used. The locked-rotor currents shall be added to the motor-compressor locked-rotor current(s) and to the rating in amperes of other loads to obtain an equivalent locked-rotor current for the combined load. Where two or more motors and/or other loads cannot be started simultaneously, appropriate combinations of locked-rotor and rated-load current or branch-circuit selection current, whichever is greater, shall be an acceptable means of determining the equivalent locked-rotor current for the simultaneous combined load.

Exception: Where part of the concurrent load is a resistance load and the disconnecting means is a switch rated in horsepower and amperes, the switch used shall be permitted to have a horsepower rating not less than the combined load to the motor-compressor(s) and other motor(s) at the locked-rotor condition, if the ampere rating of the switch is not less than this locked-rotor load plus the resistance load.

(2) The ampere rating of the disconnecting means shall be at least 115 percent of the summation of all currents at the rated-load condition determined in accordance with Section 440-12(b)(1).

(c) Small Motor-Compressors. For small motor-compressors not having the locked-rotor current marked on the nameplate, or for small motors not covered by Tables 430-147, 430-148, 430-149, or 430-150, the locked-rotor current shall be assumed to be six times the rated-load current. See Section 440-3(a).

(d) Every Switch. Every disconnecting means in the refrigerant motor-compressor circuit between the point of attachment to the feeder and the point of connection to the refrigerant motor-compressor shall comply with the requirements of Section 440-12.

(e) Disconnecting Means Rated in Excess of 100 Horsepower. Where the rated-load or locked-rotor current as determined above would indicate a disconnecting means rated in excess of 100 horsepower, the provisions of Section 430-109, Exception No. 4 shall apply.

440-13. Cord-Connected Equipment. For cord-connected equipment such as room air conditioners, household refrigerators and freezers, drinking water coolers, and beverage dispensers, a separable connector or an attachment plug and receptacle shall be permitted to serve as the disconnecting means. See also Section 440-63.

440-14. Location. A disconnecting means shall be located within sight from and readily accessible from the air-conditioning or refrigerating equipment.

Exception: Cord- and plug-connected appliances.

(FPN): See Parts G and H of Article 430 for additional requirements.

The reference to Parts G and H of Article 440 in the Fine Print Note is intended to call attention to the additional disconnect location requirements in Sections 430-86, 430-102, 430-107 and 430-113. Since Section 440-7(a) makes the requirements in Article 440 in addition to or amendatory of the provisions of Article 430, the requirement of Section 440-14 mandates equipment disconnecting means within sight from and readily accessible from the equipment, even if there is also a remote disconnect capable of being locked in the open position under the provision of Section 430-86(a). This special requirement for air-conditioning and refrigeration equipment covered by Article 440 is more stringent than the provisions in Article 430 in order to provide protection for service personnel working on equipment located in an attic, on the roof, or outside in a remote location where it is difficult to gain access to a remote lockable disconnect.

C. Branch-Circuit Short-Circuit and Ground-Fault Protection

440-21. General. The provisions of Part C specify devices intended to protect the branch-circuit conductors, control apparatus and motors in circuits supplying hermetic refrigerant motor-compressors against overcurrent due to short circuits and grounds. They are in addition to or amendatory of the provisions of Article 240.

Where an air conditioner is listed by a qualified electrical testing laboratory with the nameplate stating "maximum fuse size," the listing restricts the use of this unit to fuse protection only and does not cover its use with circuit breakers. If the air conditioner has been evaluated for both fuses and ordinary circuit breakers, or both fuses and "HACR Type" circuit breakers it may be so marked. UL listed circuit breakers which have been found suitable for use with heating, air conditioning, and refrigeration equipment comprising multimotor or combination loads are marked as "Listed HACR Type." It is the intent of Section 110-3(b) to have any restriction of listing applied to the installation of the equipment in order to comply with the *Code*.

The UL Electrical Appliance and Utilization Equipment Directory states the following under "Air-Conditioners, Central Cooling": "This marked protective device rating is the maximum for which the equipment has been investigated and found acceptable. Where the marking specifies fuses, or "HACR" type circuit breakers, the equipment is intended to be protected only by the type of protective device specified." (See Figure 440-1.)

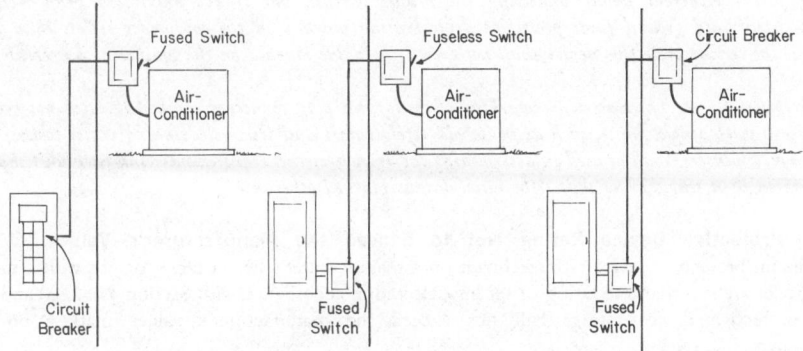

Figure 440-1. Illustrated are three correct wiring methods indicating, where the nameplate specifies fuses, that the equipment is intended to be protected by fuses only.

440-22. Application and Selection.

(a) Rating or Setting for Individual Motor-Compressor. The motor-compressor branch-circuit short-circuit and ground-fault protective device shall be capable of carrying the starting current of the motor. A protective device having a rating or setting not exceeding 175 percent of the motor-compressor rated-load current or branch-circuit selection current, whichever is greater, shall be permitted, provided that where the protection specified is not sufficient for the starting current of the motor, the rating or setting shall be permitted to be increased, but shall not exceed 225 percent of the motor rated-load current or branch-circuit selection current, whichever is greater.

Exception: The rating of the branch-circuit short-circuit and ground-fault protective device shall not be required to be less than 15 amperes.

(b) Rating or Setting for Equipment. The equipment branch-circuit short-circuit and ground-fault protective device shall be capable of carrying the starting current of the equipment. Where the hermetic refrigerant motor-compressor is the only load on the circuit, the protection shall conform with Section 440-22(a). Where the equipment incorporates more than one hermetic refrigerant motor-compressor or a hermetic refrigerant motor-compressor and other motors or other loads, the equipment short-circuit and ground-fault protection shall conform with Section 430-53 and the following:

(1) Where a hermetic refrigerant motor-compressor is the largest load connected to the circuit, the rating or setting of the branch-circuit short-circuit and ground-fault protective device shall not exceed the value specified in Section 440-22(a) for the largest motor-compressor plus the sum of the rated-load current or branch-circuit selection current, whichever is greater, of the other motor-compressor(s) and the ratings of the other loads supplied.

(2) Where a hermetic refrigerant motor-compressor is not the largest load connected to the circuit, the rating or setting of the branch-circuit short-circuit and ground-fault protective device shall not exceed a value equal to the sum of the rated-load current or branch-circuit selection

ARTICLE 440—AIR-CONDITIONING AND REFRIGERATING EQUIPMENT

current, whichever is greater, rating(s) for the motor-compressor(s) plus the value specified in Section 430-53(c)(4) where other motor loads are supplied, or the value specified in Section 240-3 where only nonmotor loads are supplied in addition to the motor-compressor(s).

Exception No. 1: Equipment which will start and operate on a 15- or 20-ampere 120-volt, or 15-ampere 208- or 240-volt single-phase branch circuit shall be permitted to be protected by the 15- or 20-ampere overcurrent device protecting the branch circuit, but if the maximum branch-circuit short-circuit and ground-fault protective device rating marked on the equipment is less than these values, the circuit protective device shall not exceed the value marked on the equipment nameplate.

Exception No. 2: The nameplate marking of cord- and plug-connected equipment rated not greater than 250 volts, single-phase, such as household refrigerators and freezers, drinking water coolers, and beverage dispensers, shall be used in determining the branch-circuit requirements, and each unit shall be considered as a single motor unless the nameplate is marked otherwise.

(c) Protective Device Rating Not to Exceed the Manufacturer's Values. Where maximum protective device ratings shown on a manufacturer's heater table for use with a motor controller are less than the rating or setting selected in accordance with Section 440-22(a) and (b), the protective device rating shall not exceed the manufacturer's values marked on the equipment.

D. Branch-Circuit Conductors

440-31. General. The provisions of Part D and Articles 300 and 310 specify sizes of conductors required to carry the motor current without overheating under the conditions specified, except as modified in Section 440-5(a), Exception No. 1.

The provisions of these articles shall not apply to integral conductors of motors, motor controllers and the like, or to conductors which form an integral part of approved equipment.

(FPN): See Sections 300-1(b) and 310-1 for similar requirements.

440-32. Single Motor-Compressor. Branch-circuit conductors supplying a single motor-compressor shall have an ampacity not less than 125 percent of either the motor-compressor rated-load current or the branch-circuit selection current, whichever is greater.

440-33. Motor-Compressor(s) With or Without Additional Motor Loads. Conductors supplying one or more motor-compressor(s) with or without additional load(s) shall have an ampacity not less than the sum of the rated-load or branch-circuit selection current ratings, whichever is larger, of all the motor-compressor(s) plus the full-load currents of the other motor(s), plus 25 percent of the highest motor or motor-compressor rating in the group.

Exception No. 1: When the circuitry is so interlocked as to prevent the starting and running of a second motor-compressor or group of motor-compressors, the conductor size shall be determined from the largest motor-compressor or group of motor-compressors that is to be operated at a given time.

Exception No. 2: Room air conditioners as provided in Part G of Article 440.

440-34. Combination Load. Conductors supplying a motor-compressor load in addition to a lighting or appliance load as computed from Article 220 and other applicable articles shall have an ampacity sufficient for the lighting or appliance load plus the required ampacity for the motor-compressor load determined in accordance with Section 440-33, or, for a single motor-compressor, in accordance with Section 440-32.

Exception: When the circuitry is so interlocked as to prevent simultaneous operation of the motor-compressor(s) and all other loads connected, the conductor size shall be determined from the largest size required for the motor-compressor(s) and other loads to be operated at a given time.

440-35. Multimotor and Combination-Load Equipment. The ampacity of the conductors supplying multimotor and combination-load equipment shall not be less than the minimum circuit ampacity marked on the equipment in accordance with Section 440-3(b).

E. Controllers for Motor-Compressors

440-41. Rating.

(a) **Motor-Compressor Controller.** A motor-compressor controller shall have both a continuous-duty full-load current rating, and a locked-rotor current rating, not less than the nameplate rated-load current or branch-circuit selection current, whichever is greater, and locked-rotor current, respectively (see Sections 440-5 and 440-6) of the compressor. In case the motor controller is rated in horsepower, but is without one or both of the foregoing current ratings, equivalent currents shall be determined from the ratings as follows: use Tables 430-148, 430-149, or 430-150 to determine the equivalent full-load current rating. Use Table 430-151 to determine the equivalent locked-rotor current ratings.

(b) **Controller Serving More than One Load.** A controller, serving more than one motor-compressor or a motor-compressor and other loads, shall have a continuous-duty full-load current rating, and a locked-rotor current rating not less than the combined load as determined in accordance with Section 440-12(b).

F. Motor-Compressor and Branch-Circuit Overload Protection

440-51. General.
The provisions of Part F specify devices intended to protect the motor-compressor, the motor-control apparatus, and the branch-circuit conductors against excessive heating due to motor overload and failure to start. See Section 240-3, Exception No. 3.

(FPN): Note: Overload in electrically driven apparatus is an operating overcurrent which, when it persists for a sufficient length of time, would cause damage or dangerous overheating. It does not include short circuits or ground faults.

440-52. Application and Selection.

(a) **Protection of Motor-Compressor.** Each motor-compressor shall be protected against overload and failure to start by one of the following means:

(1) A separate overload relay which is responsive to motor-compressor current. This device shall be selected to trip at not more than 140 percent of the motor-compressor rated-load current.

(2) A thermal protector integral with the motor-compressor, approved for use with the motor-compressor which it protects on the basis that it will prevent dangerous overheating of the motor-compressor due to overload and failure to start. If the current-interrupting device is separate from the motor-compressor and its control circuit is operated by a protective device integral with the motor-compressor, it shall be so arranged that the opening of the control circuit will result in interruption of current to the motor-compressor.

(3) A fuse or inverse time circuit breaker responsive to motor current, which shall also be permitted to serve as the branch-circuit short-circuit and ground-fault protective device. This device shall be rated at not more than 125 percent of the motor-compressor rated-load current. It shall have sufficient time delay to permit the motor-compressor to start and accelerate its load. The equipment or the motor-compressor shall be marked with this maximum branch-circuit fuse or inverse time circuit breaker rating.

(4) A protective system, furnished or specified and approved for use with the motor-compressor which it protects on the basis that it will prevent dangerous overheating of the motor-compressor due to overload and failure to start. If the current interrupting device is separate from the motor-compressor and its control circuit is operated by a protective device which is not integral with the current-interrupting device, it shall be so arranged that the opening of the control circuit will result in interruption of current to the motor-compressor.

(b) Protection of Motor-Compressor Control Apparatus and Branch-Circuit Conductors. The motor-compressor controller(s), the disconnecting means and branch-circuit conductors shall be protected against overcurrent due to motor overload and failure to start by one of the following means which shall be permitted to be the same device or system protecting the motor-compressor in accordance with Section 440-52(a).

Exception: For motor-compressors and equipment on 15- or 20-ampere single-phase branch circuits as provided in Sections 440-54 and 440-55.

(1) An overload relay selected in accordance with Section 440-52(a)(1).

(2) A thermal protector applied in accordance with Section 440-52(a)(2) and which will not permit a continuous current in excess of 156 percent of the marked rated-load current or branch-circuit selection current.

(3) A fuse or inverse time circuit breaker selected in accordance with Section 440-52(a)(3).

(4) A protective system in accordance with Section 440-52(a)(4) and which will not permit a continuous current in excess of 156 percent of the marked rated-load current or branch-circuit selection current.

440-53. Overload Relays. Overload relays and other devices for motor overload protection, which are not capable of opening short circuits, shall be protected by fuses or inverse time circuit breakers with ratings or settings in accordance with Part C unless approved for group installation or for part-winding motors and marked to indicate the maximum size of fuse or inverse time circuit breaker by which they shall be protected.

Exception: The fuse or inverse time circuit breaker size marking shall be permitted on the nameplate of approved equipment in which the overload relay or other overload device is used.

440-54. Motor-Compressors and Equipment on 15- or 20-Ampere Branch Circuits — Not Cord-and-Attachment Plug-Connected. Overload protection for motor-compressors and equipment used on 15- or 20-ampere 120-volt, or 15-ampere 208- or 240-volt single-phase branch circuits as permitted in Article 210 shall be permitted as indicated in (a) and (b) below.

(a) Overload Protection. The motor-compressor shall be provided with overload protection selected as specified in Section 440-52(a). Both the controller and motor overload protective device shall be approved for installation with the short-circuit and ground-fault protective device for the branch circuit to which the equipment is connected.

(b) Time Delay. The short-circuit and ground-fault protective device protecting the branch circuit shall have sufficient time delay to permit the motor-compressor and other motors to start and accelerate their loads.

440-55. Cord-and-Attachment Plug-Connected Motor-Compressors and Equipment on 15- or 20-Ampere Branch Circuits. Overload protection for motor-compressors and equipment that are cord-and-attachment plug-connected and used on 15- or 20-ampere 120-volt, or 15-ampere 208- or 240-volt single-phase branch circuits as permitted in Article 210 shall be permitted as indicated in (a), (b), and (c) below.

(a) Overload Protection. The motor-compressor shall be provided with overload protection as specified in Section 440-52(a). Both the controller and the motor overload protective device shall be approved for installation with the short-circuit and ground-fault protective device for the branch circuit to which the equipment is connected.

(b) Attachment Plug and Receptacle Rating. The rating of the attachment plug and receptacle shall not exceed 20 amperes at 125 volts or 15 amperes at 250 volts.

(c) Time Delay. The short-circuit and ground-fault protective device protecting the branch circuit shall have sufficient time delay to permit the motor-compressor and other motors to start and accelerate their loads.

G. Provisions for Room Air Conditioners

440-60. General. The provisions of Part G shall apply to electrically energized room air conditioners that control temperature and humidity. For the purpose of Part G, a room air conditioner (with or without provisions for heating) shall be considered as an alternating-current appliance of the air-cooled window, console, or in-wall type that is installed in the conditioned room and which incorporates a hermetic refrigerant motor-compressor(s). The provisions of Part G cover equipment rated not over 250 volts, single phase, and such equipment shall be permitted to be cord-and-attachment plug-connected.

A room air conditioner that is rated three phase or rated over 250 volts shall be directly connected to a wiring method recognized in Chapter 3, and provisions of Part G shall not apply.

440-61. Grounding. Room air conditioners shall be grounded in accordance with Sections 250-42, 250-43, and 250-45.

440-62. Branch-Circuit Requirements.

(a) Room Air Conditioner as a Single Motor Unit. A room air conditioner shall be considered as a single motor unit in determining its branch-circuit requirements when all the following conditions are met:

(1) It is cord-and-attachment plug-connected.

(2) Its rating is not more than 40 amperes and 250 volts, single phase.

(3) Total rated-load current is shown on the room air-conditioner nameplate rather than individual motor currents, and

(4) The rating of the branch-circuit short-circuit and ground-fault protective device does not exceed the ampacity of the branch-circuit conductors or the rating of the receptacle, whichever is less.

(b) Where No Other Loads Are Supplied. The total marked rating of a cord-and-attachment plug-connected room air conditioner shall not exceed 80 percent of the rating of a branch circuit where no other loads are supplied.

(c) Where Lighting Units or Other Appliances Are also Supplied. The total marked rating of a cord-and-attachment plug-connected room air conditioner shall not exceed 50 percent of the rating of a branch circuit where lighting units or other appliances are also supplied.

440-63. Disconnecting Means. An attachment plug and receptacle shall be permitted to serve as the disconnecting means for a single-phase room air conditioner rated 250 volts or less if: (1) the manual controls on the room air conditioner are readily accessible and located within 6 feet (1.83 m) of the floor, or (2) an approved manually operable switch is installed in a readily accessible location within sight from the room air conditioner.

440-64. Supply Cords. Where a flexible cord is used to supply a room air conditioner, the length of such cord shall not exceed: (1) 10 feet (3.05 m) for a nominal, 120-volt rating, or (2) 6 feet (1.83 m) for a nominal 208- or 240-volt rating.

ARTICLE 445 — GENERATORS

Contents

445-1. General. Generators and their associated wiring and equipment shall comply with the applicable provisions of Articles 230, 250, 700, 701, and 702.

445-2. Location. Generators shall be of a type suitable for the locations in which they are installed. They shall also meet the requirements for motors in Section 430-14. Generators installed in hazardous (classified) locations as described in Articles 500 through 503, or in other locations as described in Articles 510 through 517, and in Articles 520, 530, and 665 shall also comply with the applicable provisions of those articles.

445-3. Marking. Each generator shall be provided with a nameplate giving the maker's name, the rated frequency, power factor, number of phases if of alternating current, the rating in kilowatts or kilovolt amperes, the normal volts and amperes corresponding to the rating, rated revolutions per minute, insulation system class and rated ambient temperature or rated temperature rise, and time rating.

445-4. Overcurrent Protection.

(a) Constant-Voltage Generators. Constant-voltage generators, except alternating-current generator exciters, shall be protected from overloads by inherent design, circuit breakers, fuses, or other acceptable current-limiting means, suitable for the conditions of use.

(b) Two-Wire Generators. Two-wire, direct-current generators shall be permitted to have overcurrent protection in one conductor only if the overcurrent device is actuated by the entire current generated other than the current in the shunt field. The overcurrent device shall not open the shunt field.

(c) 65 Volts or Less. Generators operating at 65 volts or less and driven by individual motors shall be considered as protected by the overcurrent device protecting the motor if these devices will operate when the generators are delivering not more than 150 percent of their full-load rated current.

(d) Balancer Sets. Two-wire, direct-current generators used in conjunction with balancer sets to obtain neutrals for 3-wire systems shall be equipped with overcurrent devices that will disconnect the 3-wire system in case of excessive unbalancing of voltages or currents.

(e) 3-Wire, Direct-Current Generators. Three-wire, direct-current generators, whether compound or shunt wound, shall be equipped with overcurrent devices, one in each armature lead, and so connected as to be actuated by the entire current from the armature. Such overcurrent devices shall consist either of a double-pole, double-coil circuit breaker, or of a 4-pole circuit breaker connected in the main and equalizer leads and tripped by two overcurrent devices, one in each armature lead. Such protective devices shall be so interlocked that no one pole can be opened without simultaneously disconnecting both leads of the armature from the system.

Exception to (a) through (e): Where deemed by the authority having jurisdiction, a generator is vital to the operation of an electrical system and the generator should operate to failure to prevent a greater hazard to persons, the overload sensing device(s) is permitted to be connected to an annunciator or alarm supervised by authorized personnel instead of interrupting the generator circuit.

Alternating-current generators can be designed so that, during short periods of time when the generator may carry an excessive overload, the voltage will fall off sufficiently to limit the current and power output to values that will not damage the generator.

The connection of a 2-wire generator, protected by a single-pole circuit breaker, is illustrated in Figure 445-1. Where two or more dc generators are operated in parallel or multiple, an equalizer conductor lead is connected to the positive terminal of each generator or, in effect, is the connecting of the series fields in parallel to maintain equal output voltage for each generator. The current could divide at the positive terminal, some flowing through the series field and positive lead and some flowing through the equalizer lead. The entire current generated flows through the negative lead; therefore, the fuse or circuit breaker (or at least the operating coil of a circuit breaker) must be placed in the negative lead. Overcurrent devices are required to be connected so as to be actuated by the entire armature output current.

An overcurrent device should not be placed in the shunt-field circuit because, if this circuit were to open when the field is at full strength, an extremely high voltage would be induced which could damage the field-winding insulation and injure the generator.

Section 445-4(c) indicates that generators operating at 65 V or less are to be thought of as protected by the overcurrent devices that also protect the drive-motor, providing these devices will operate when the generator delivers 150 percent of its rated full-load current.

Figure 445-2 illustrates a double-pole circuit breaker with one pole connected in each lead of the main generator and with the operating coil properly designed to be connected in the neutral lead from the balancer, and so arranged as to be operated by either one of the "A" coils or by the "B" coil. Each of the two generators used as a balancer set carries approximately one-half of the unbalanced load and, thus, is always smaller than the main generator. During an excessive imbalance of the load, the balancer set would be overloaded with no overload on the main generator; hence, a double-pole circuit breaker is connected (as noted) to guard against this condition.

It should be noted that the authority having jurisdiction may judge that the generator should operate to failure rather than providing automatic means to shut it down, which, in many cases, could present a greater hazard to personnel. An overload sensing device(s) would be permitted to be connected to an annunciator or an alarm (instead of interrupting the generator) and allow operating personnel to shut down load-side equipment in a safe and orderly fashion.

445-5. Ampacity of Conductors. The ampacity of the phase conductors from the generator terminals to the first overcurrent device shall not be less than 115 percent of the nameplate current rating of the generator. It shall be permitted to size the neutral conductors in accordance with Section 220-22. Conductors which must carry ground-fault currents shall not be smaller than required by Section 250-23(b).

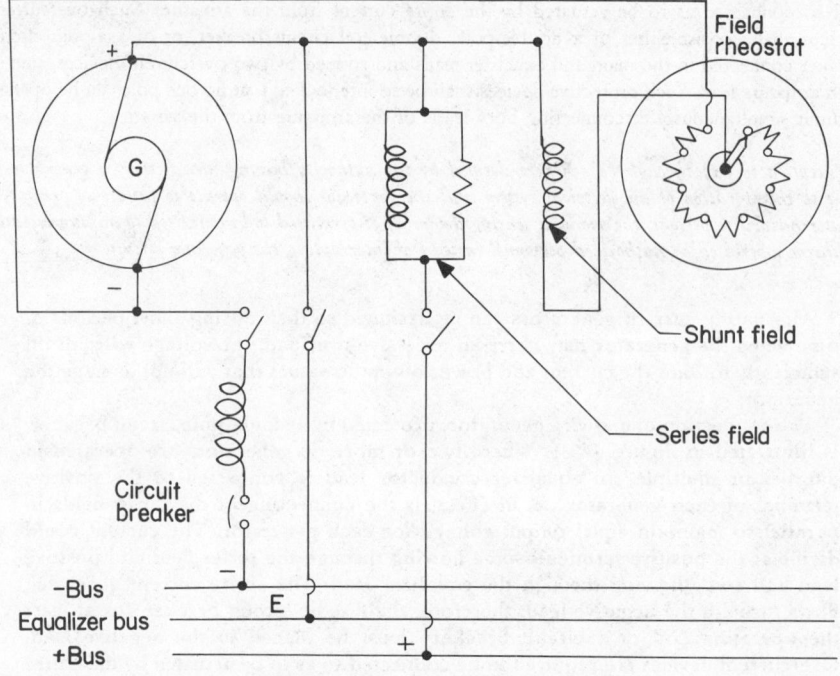

Figure 445-1. A schematic diagram of a 2-wire dc generator protected by a single-pole circuit breaker.

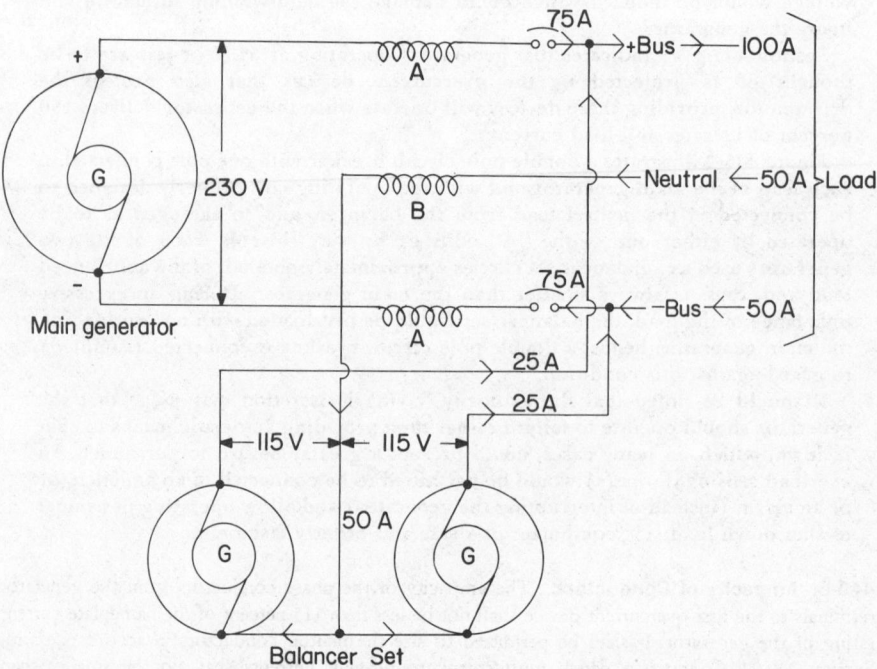

Figure 445-2. A schematic diagram of a double-pole circuit breaker (one pole connected in each lead of the main generator) with the opening coil arranged to be connected in the neutral of the balancer set.

Exception No. 1: Where the design and operation of the generator prevent overloading, the ampacity of the conductors shall not be less than 100 percent of the nameplate current rating of the generator.

Exception No. 2: Where the generator manufacturer's leads are connected directly to an overcurrent device that is an integral part of the generator set assembly.

445-6. Protection of Live Parts. Live parts of generators operated at more than 50 volts to ground shall not be exposed to accidental contact where accessible to unqualified persons.

445-7. Guards for Attendants. Where necessary for the safety of attendants, the requirements of Section 430-133 shall apply.

445-8. Bushings. Where wires pass through an opening in an enclosure, conduit box, or barrier, a bushing shall be used to protect the conductors from the edges of an opening having sharp edges. The bushing shall have smooth, well-rounded surfaces where it may be in contact with the conductors. If used where oils, grease, or other contaminants may be present, the bushing shall be made of a material not deleteriously affected.

ARTICLE 450 — TRANSFORMERS AND TRANSFORMER VAULTS

(Including Secondary Ties)

Contents

ARTICLE 450—TRANSFORMERS AND TRANSFORMER VAULTS

C. Transformer Vaults
450-41. Location.
450-42. Walls, Roof and Floor.
450-43. Doorways.
  (a) Type of Door.
  (b) Sills.
  (c) Locks.
450-45. Ventilation Openings.
  (a) Location.

  (b) Arrangement.
  (c) Size.
  (d) Covering.
  (e) Dampers.
  (f) Ducts.
450-46. Drainage.
450-47. Water Pipes and Accessories.
450-48. Storage in Vaults.

450-1. Scope. This article covers the installation of all transformers.

Exception No. 1: Current transformers.

Exception No. 2: Dry-type transformers that constitute a component part of other apparatus and comply with the requirements for such apparatus.

Exception No. 3: Transformers which are an integral part of an X-ray, high-frequency, or electrostatic-coating apparatus.

Exception No. 4: Transformers used with Class 2 and Class 3 circuits that comply with Article 725.

Exception No. 5: Transformers for sign and outline lighting that comply with Article 600.

Exception No. 6: Transformers for electric-discharge lighting that comply with Article 410.

Exception No. 7: Transformers used for power-limited fire protective signaling circuits that comply with Part C of Article 760.

Exception No. 8: Liquid-filled or dry-type transformers used for research, development, or testing, where effective arrangements are provided to safeguard unqualified persons from contacting high-voltage terminals or energized conductors.

> Exception No. 8 permits an exemption for liquid-filled or dry-type transformers because they are usually energized only when tests are being made, are under constant supervision by qualified personnel, and high-voltage circuits are guarded and interlocked to protect against accidental contact by unqualified persons.

This article also covers the installation of transformers in hazardous (classified) locations as modified by Articles 501 through 503.

A. General Provisions

450-2. Location. Transformers and transformer vaults shall be readily accessible to qualified personnel for inspection and maintenance.

Exception No. 1: Dry-type transformers 600 volts, nominal, or less, located in the open on walls, columns, or structures, shall not be required to be readily accessible.

Exception No. 2: Dry-type transformers not exceeding 600 volts, nominal, and 50 kVA shall be permitted in fire-resistant hollow spaces of buildings not permanently closed in by structure and provided they meet the ventilation requirements of Section 450-8.

Unless specified otherwise in this article, the term fire resistant means a construction having a minimum fire rating of 1 hour.

(FPN): See ASTM Standard E119-75; Fire Tests of Building Construction and Materials, NFPA 251-1979; and Methods of Fire Tests of Building Construction and Materials, ANSI A2.1-1972.

(FPN): The location of oil-insulated transformers and transformer vaults is covered in Sections 450-26, 450-27, and 450-41; dry-type transformers in Section 450-21; and askarel-insulated transformers in Section 450-25.

450-3. Overcurrent Protection. Overcurrent protection shall comply with (a) through (c) below. As used in this section, the word "transformer" shall mean a transformer or polyphase bank of two or three single-phase transformers operating as a unit.

(a) Transformers Over 600 Volts, Nominal.

(1) Primary. Each transformer over 600 volts, nominal, shall be protected by an individual overcurrent device on the primary side. Where fuses are used, their continuous current rating shall not exceed 250 percent of the rated primary current of the transformer. Where circuit breakers are used, they shall be set at not more than 300 percent of the rated primary current of the transformer.

Exception No. 1: Where 250 percent of the rated primary current of the transformer does not correspond to a standard rating of a fuse, the next higher standard rating shall be permitted.

Exception No. 2: An individual overcurrent device shall not be required where the primary circuit overcurrent device provides the protection specified in this section.

Exception No. 3: As provided in (a)(2) below.

(2) Primary and Secondary. A transformer over 600 volts, nominal, having an overcurrent device on the secondary side rated or set to open at not more than the values noted in Table 450-3(a)(2),. or a transformer equipped with a coordinated thermal overload protection by the manufacturer, shall not be required to have an individual overcurrent device in the primary connection provided the primary feeder overcurrent device is rated or set to open at not more than the values noted in Table 450-3(a)(2).

Table 450-3(a)(2)
Transformers Over 600 Volts
Having Overcurrent Protection on the Primary and Secondary Sides

	Maximum Overcurrent Device				
	Primary		Secondary		
	Over 600 Volts		Over 600 Volts		600 Volts or Below
Transformer Rated Impedance	Circuit Breaker Setting	Fuse Rating	Circuit Breaker Setting	Fuse Rating	Circuit Breaker Setting or Fuse Rating
Not more than 6%	600%	300%	300%	250%	250%
More than 6% and not more than 10%	400%	300%	250%	225%	250%

(b) Transformers 600 Volts, Nominal, or Less.

(1) Primary. Each transformer 600 volts, nominal, or less, shall be protected by an individual overcurrent device on the primary side, rated or set at not more than 125 percent of the rated primary current of the transformer.

Exception No. 1: Where the rated primary current of a transformer is 9 amperes or more and 125 percent of this current does not correspond to a standard rating of a fuse or nonadjustable circuit breaker, the next higher standard rating described in Section 240-6 shall be permitted. Where the rated primary current is less than 9 amperes, an overcurrent device rated or set at not more than 167 percent of the primary current shall be permitted.

Where the rated primary current is less than 2 amperes, an overcurrent device rated or set at not more than 300 percent shall be permitted.

Exception No. 2: An individual overcurrent device shall not be required where the primary circuit overcurrent device provides the protection specified in this section.

Exception No. 3: As provided in (b)(2) below.

(2) Primary and Secondary. A transformer 600 volts, nominal, or less, having an overcurrent device on the secondary side rated or set at not more than 125 percent of the rated secondary current of the transformer shall not be required to have an individual overcurrent device on the primary side if the primary feeder overcurrent device is rated or set at a current value not more than 250 percent of the rated primary current of the transformer.

A transformer 600 volts, nominal, or less, equipped with coordinated thermal overload protection by the manufacturer and arranged to interrupt the primary current, shall not be required to have an individual overcurrent device on the primary side if the primary feeder overcurrent device is rated or set at a current value not more than six times the rated current of the transformer for transformers having not more than 6 percent impedance, and not more than four times the rated current of the transformer for transformers having more than 6 but not more than 10 percent impedance.

Exception: Where the rated secondary current of a transformer is 9 amperes or more and 125 percent of this current does not correspond to a standard rating of a fuse or nonadjustable circuit breaker, the next higher standard rating described in Section 240-6 shall be permitted.

Where the rated secondary current is less than 9 amperes, an overcurrent device rated or set at not more than 167 percent of the rated secondary current shall be permitted.

(c) Potential (Voltage) Transformers. Potential transformers installed indoors or enclosed shall be protected with primary fuses.

(FPN): See also Section 384-22.

Questions frequently arise as to whether the overcurrent protection required for transformers, as specified in Section 450-3, will provide satisfactory protection for the primary and secondary conductors. Where polyphase transformers are involved, primary and secondary conductors will usually not be properly protected. The rules are intended to protect the transformer alone. The primary overcurrent device provides short-circuit protection for the transformer, and the secondary overcurrent device prevents the transformer from being overloaded. The transformer is considered the point of supply, and the conductors that it supplies are required to be protected in accordance with their ampacity.

Exceptions to this rule are permitted under special conditions outlined in Section 230-207, and Exception No. 8 of Section 240-21. See Figures 230-22 and 240-4.

Single-phase transformers having a 2-wire (single voltage) secondary may also omit the secondary overcurrent device if the primary overcurrent protection is provided in accordance with this section, and its rating does not exceed the value determined by multiplying the secondary conductor ampacity by the secondary to primary voltage ratio. See commentary following Section 240-3, Exception No. 5.

Single-phase transformers with a 3-wire secondary are not included in this exception because of the possibility of a severe unbalanced load which the primary protection would not recognize.

In those cases in which the primary feeder to the transformer incorporates overcurrent protective devices that are rated (or set) at a level not to exceed those prescribed herein, it is not necessary to duplicate them at the transformer.

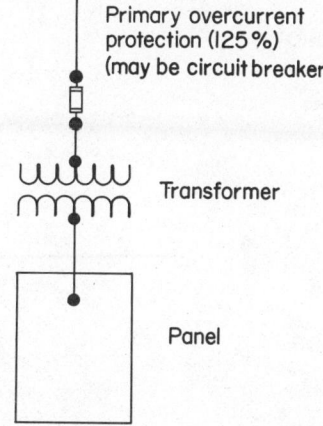

Figure 450-1. Transformers of 600 V or less must be protected by an individual overcurrent device on the primary side. Exceptions to the basic rule are given in Section 450-3(b)(1).

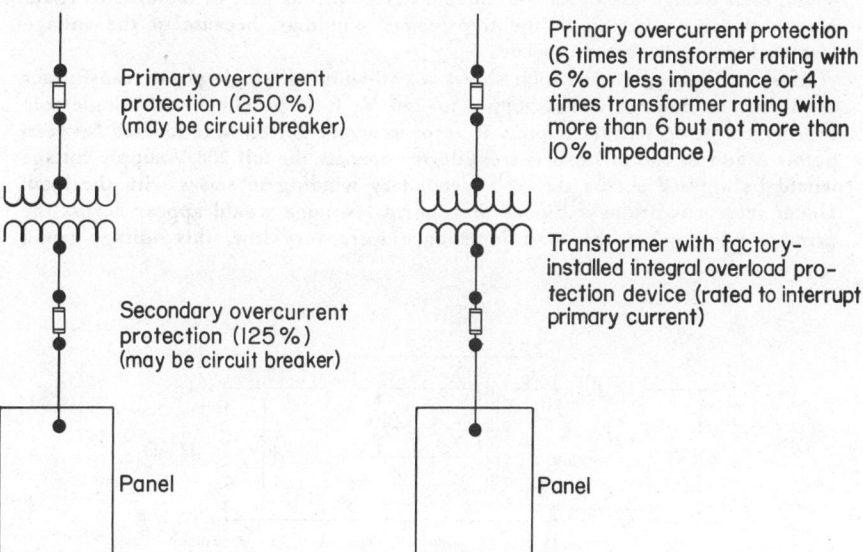

Figure 450-2. Overcurrent protection on the primary and secondary sides of transformers rated 600 V or less. Exceptions to the basic rule are given in Section 450-3(b)(2).

450-4. Autotransformers 600 Volts, Nominal, or Less.

(a) Overcurrent Protection. Each autotransformer 600 volts, nominal, or less shall be protected by an individual overcurrent device installed in series with each ungrounded input conductor. Such overcurrent device shall be rated or set at not more than 125 percent of the rated full-load input current of the autotransformer. An overcurrent device shall not be installed in series with the shunt winding (the winding common to both the input and the output circuits) of the autotransformer between Points A and B as shown in Diagram 450-4.

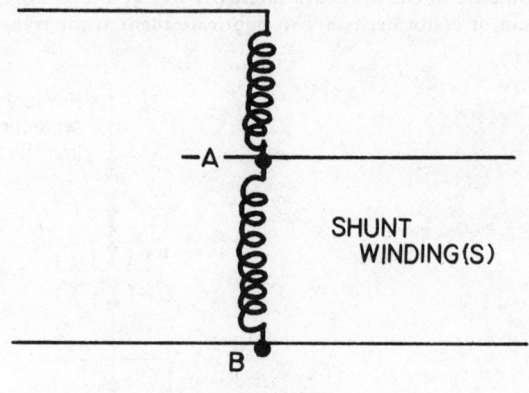

Diagram 450-4

An overcurrent device is not permitted between **Points A and B in Diagram 450-4,** even though use of an overcurrent device in this part of the circuit would permit closer protection of the transformer windings, because of the voltage feed-back problem that can occur.

Refer to Figure 450-3, which shows a two-winding, single-phase transformer connected to boost a 208-V supply to 240 V. It is provided with single-pole overcurrent devices in the supply. If an overcurrent device were located between points A and B, and this overcurrent device opened, the full 208-V supply voltage would be applied across the 32-V secondary winding in series with the load. Under these conditions a higher than normal voltage would appear across the primary winding. If the load impedance were very low, this voltage could approach $^{208}\!/_{32} \times 208 = 1352$ V.

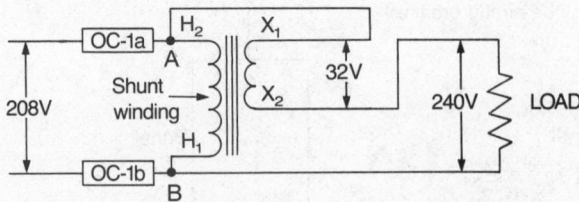

Figure 450-3. Overcurrent device in series with shunt winding of autotransformer is not permitted by Section 450-4(a).

Exception: Where the rated input current of an autotransformer is 9 amperes or more and 125 percent of this current does not correspond to a standard rating of a fuse or nonadjustable circuit breaker, the next higher standard rating described in Section 240-6 shall be permitted. Where the rated input current is less than 9 amperes, an overcurrent device rated or set at not more than 167 percent of the input current shall be permitted.

(b) Transformer Field-Connected as an Autotransformer. A transformer field-connected as an autotransformer shall be identified for use at elevated voltage.

This requirement is necessary because of the dielectric voltage withstand test requirements applied to transformers. The test is conducted at 2,500 volts for windings rated 250 V or less, and 4,000 V for higher rated windings. A transformer intended for buck or boost operation would require that the test for the low voltage winding be based on the sum of the primary and secondary voltage ratings.

450-5. Grounding Autotransformers. Grounding autotransformers covered in this section are zig-zag or T-connected transformers connected to 3-phase, 3-wire ungrounded systems for the purpose of creating a 3-phase, 4-wire distribution system or to provide a neutral reference for grounding purposes. Such transformers shall have a continuous per phase current rating and a continuous neutral current rating.

(FPN): The phase current in a grounding autotransformer is one-third the neutral current.

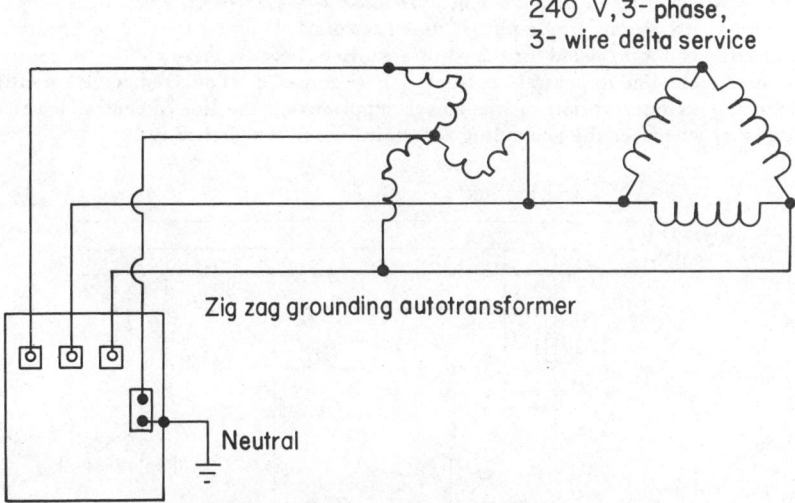

240 V, 3- phase,
3- wire delta service

Zig zag grounding autotransformer

Neutral

Figure 450-4. A zig-zag autotransformer used to create a 3-phase, 4-wire distribution system or to provide a neutral reference for grounding purposes.

(a) Three-Phase, 4-Wire System. A grounding autotransformer used to create a 3-phase, 4-wire distribution system from a 3-phase, 3-wire ungrounded system shall conform to the following:

(1) Connections. The transformer shall be directly connected to the ungrounded phase conductors and shall not be switched or provided with overcurrent protection which is independent of the main switch and common-trip overcurrent protection for the 3-phase, 4-wire system.

(2) Overcurrent Protection. An overcurrent sensing device shall be provided that will cause the main switch or common-trip overcurrent protection referred to in (a)(1) above to open if the load on the autotransformer reaches or exceeds 125 percent of its continuous current per phase or neutral rating. Delayed tripping for temporary overcurrents sensed at the autotransformer overcurrent device shall be permitted for the purpose of allowing proper operation of branch or feeder protective devices on the 4-wire system.

(3) Transformer Fault Sensing. A fault sensing system that will cause the opening of a main switch or common-trip overcurrent device for the 3-phase, 4-wire system shall be provided to guard against single-phasing or internal faults.

(FPN): This can be accomplished by the use of two subtractive-connected donut-type current transformers installed to sense and signal when an unbalance occurs in the line current to the autotransformer of 50 percent or more of rated current.

(4) Rating. The autotransformer shall have a continuous neutral current rating sufficient to handle the maximum possible neutral unbalanced load current of the 4-wire system.

The donut-type current transformers shown as CT-1, CT-2, and CT-3 in Figure 450-5 are intended to trip the main breaker if the current in any phase or the neutral conductor exceeds 125 percent of the rated current [see Section 450-4(a)(2)]. The current transformers CT-2 and CT-3 are also differentially connected to protect against an internal failure of the autotransformer [see Section 450-5(a)(3)].

Figure 450-5 shows the proper method of protecting a grounding autotransformer where used to provide a neutral for a 3-phase system when necessary to supply a group of single-phase, line-to-neutral loads. Separate overcurrent protection is not provided for the autotransformer because there will be no control of the system line-to-neutral voltages if it becomes disconnected; consequently, simultaneous interruption of the power supply to all the line-to-neutral loads is necessary whenever the grounding autotransformer is switched off.

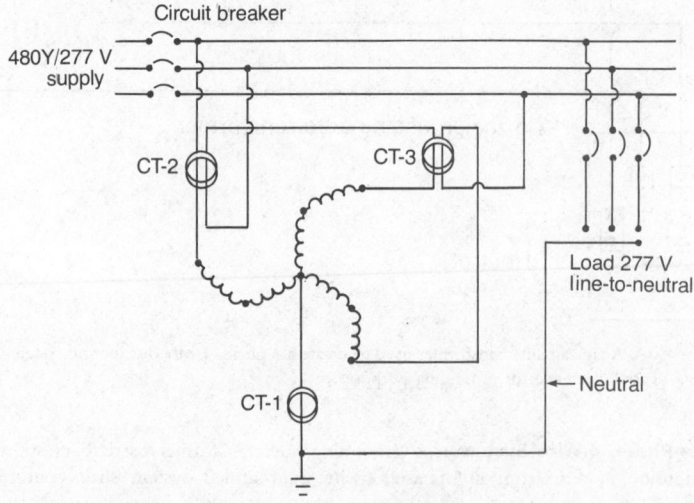

Figure 450-5. Zig-zag autotransformer for establishing a neutral connection for a 480Y/277-V, 3-phase ungrounded system to supply single-phase line-to-neutral loads. See Section 450-5(a).

CT-1 is connected to an overload relay responsive to excess neutral current being supplied. See Section 450-5(a)(2).

CT-2 and CT-3 are connected to differential-type fault-current sensing relays responsive to an unbalance of neutral current among the three phases of the grounding autotransformer (indicating an internal fault). See Section 450-5(a)(3).

All three relays are to be arranged to trip the circuit breaker located upstream of both the autotransformer and the line-to-neutral connected loads to satisfy the requirements of Section 450-5(a)(1).

(b) Ground Reference for Fault Protection Devices. A grounding autotransformer used to make available a specified magnitude of ground-fault current for operation of a ground responsive protective device on a 3-phase, 3-wire ungrounded system shall conform to the following requirements:

(1) Rating. The autotransformer shall have a continuous neutral current rating sufficient for the specified ground-fault current.

(2) Overcurrent Protection. An overcurrent protective device of adequate short-circuit rating that will open simultaneously all ungrounded conductors when it operates shall be applied in the grounding autotransformer branch circuit and rated or set at a current not exceeding 125 percent of the autotransformer continuous per phase current rating or 42 percent of the continuous current rating of any series connected devices in the autotransformer neutral connection. Delayed tripping for temporary overcurrents to permit the proper operation of ground responsive tripping devices on the main system shall be permitted, but shall not exceed values which would be more than the short-time current rating of the grounding autotransformer or any series connected devices in the neutral connection thereto.

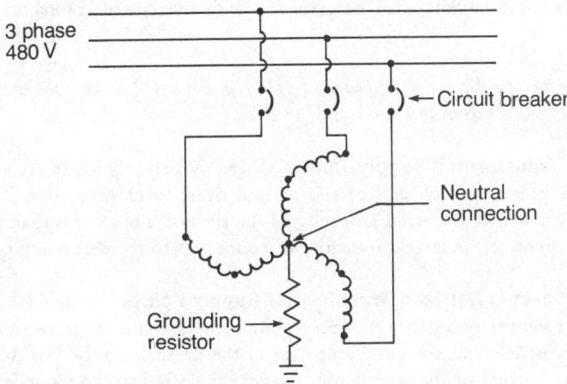

Figure 450-6. Zig-zag autotransformer for establishing a reference ground-fault current for fault-protective device operation or for damping transitory overvoltage surges. See Section 450-5(b) and (c).

The OC protective device is to have a rating (or setting) not in excess of 125 percent of the rated phase current of the autotransformer (42 percent of the neutral current rating) and not more than 42 percent of the continuous current rating of the neutral grounding resistor or other current-carrying device in the neutral connection. See Section 450-5(b)(2).

(c) Ground Reference for Damping Transitory Overvoltages. A grounding autotransformer used to limit transitory overvoltages shall be of suitable rating and connected in accordance with (a)(1) above.

For this case involving a high-resistance grounding package, the *NEC* text seems to suggest that the connections and overcurrent protection should conform with Section 450-5(a)(1), but this is not the case. The functional performance parallels that involved in Section 450-5(b), differing only in that the magnitude of available ground-fault current would likely be a lower value. It would be appropriate to employ the connections displayed on Figure 450-6, and conform with the overcurrent protection requirements prescribed in Section 450-5(b)(2).

With any of the grounding autotransformer applications covered by Sections 450-5(a), (b), or (c), it is important to emphasize the use of a ganged 3-pole switching interrupter for connecting and disconnecting the autotransformer in order to accomplish simultaneous connection (and disconnection) of the three line terminals. If at any time one or two of the line connections to the autotransformer should become "open," which could occur if the protective devices were single-pole, the grounding autotransformer ceases to function in the desired fashion and acts as a high-inductive-reactance connection between the electrical system and "ground." The latter connection is prone to create high-value transitory overvoltages, line-to-ground — a most unwanted result.

450-6. Secondary Ties. A secondary tie is a circuit operating at 600 volts, nominal, or less, between phases that connects two power sources or power supply points, such as the secondaries of two transformers. The tie may consist of one or more conductors per phase.

(FPN): As used in this section, the word "transformer" means a transformer or a bank of transformers operating as a unit.

(a) Tie Circuits. Tie circuits shall be provided with overcurrent protection at each end as required in Article 240.

Exception: Under the conditions described in (a)(1) and (a)(2) below, the overcurrent protection shall be permitted to be in accordance with (a)(3) below.

(1) Loads at Transformer Supply Points Only. Where all loads are connected at the transformer supply points at each end of the tie and overcurrent protection is not provided in accordance with Article 240, the rated ampacity of the tie shall not be less than 67 percent of the rated secondary current of the largest transformer connected to the secondary tie system.

(2) Loads Connected Between Transformer Supply Points. Where load is connected to the tie at any point between transformer supply points and overcurrent protection is not provided in accordance with Article 240, the rated ampacity of the tie shall not be less than 100 percent of the rated secondary current of the largest transformer connected to the secondary tie system.

Exception: As otherwise provided in (a)(4) below.

(3) Tie Circuit Protection. Under the conditions described in (a)(1) and (a)(2) above, both ends of each tie conductor shall be equipped with a protective device that will open at a predetermined temperature of the tie conductor under short-circuit conditions. This protection shall consist of one of the following: (1) a fusible link cable connector, terminal, or lug, commonly known as a limiter, each being of a size corresponding with that of the conductor and of construction and characteristics according to the operating voltage and the type of insulation on the tie conductors, or (2) automatic circuit breakers actuated by devices having comparable current-time characteristics.

(4) Interconnection of Phase Conductors Between Transformer Supply Points. Where the tie consists of more than one conductor per phase, the conductors of each phase shall be interconnected in order to establish a load supply point, and the protection specified in (a)(3) above shall be provided in each tie conductor at this point.

Exception: Loads shall be permitted to be connected to the individual conductors of a paralleled conductor tie without interconnecting the conductors of each phase and without the protection specified in (a)(3) above at load connection points provided the tie conductors of each phase have a combined capacity of not less than 133 percent of the rated secondary current of the largest transformer connected to the secondary tie system; the total load of such taps does not exceed the rated secondary current of the largest transformer; and the loads are equally divided on each phase and on the individual conductors of each phase as far as practicable.

(5) Tie Circuit Control. Where the operating voltage exceeds 150 volts to ground, secondary ties provided with limiters shall have a switch at each end that, when open, will de-energize the associated tie conductors and limiters. The current rating of the switch shall not be less than the rated current of the conductors connected to the switch. It shall be capable of opening its rated current, and it shall be constructed so that it will not open under the magnetic forces resulting from short-circuit current.

(b) Overcurrent Protection for Secondary Connections. Where secondary ties are used, an overcurrent device rated or set at not more than 250 percent of the rated secondary current of the transformers shall be provided in the secondary connections of each transformer. In addition, an automatic circuit breaker actuated by a reverse-current relay set to open the circuit at not more than the rated secondary current of the transformer shall be provided in the secondary connection of each transformer.

The rules of Section 450-6 apply specifically to network systems for power distribution that are commonly employed where the load density is high and reliability of service is important. Such a system is illustrated in Figure 450-9. This type of distribution system introduces a variety of problems not encountered in the more common radial-type distribution system and must be designed by experienced electrical engineers. The sketch shows a typical 3-phase network system for an industrial plant fed by two primary feeders, preferably from separate substations, which are energized at any standard voltage up to 34,500 V. Each of the transformers is supplied by the two primary feeders which are arranged by means of a double-throw switch at the transformer so that either feeder may supply it.

Each of the network transformers is rated in the range of 300 kVA to 1,000 kVA and is required to be protected as illustrated in Figure 450-7. The primary and secondary protection is in accordance with Section 450-3, but an additional protective device is also required to be provided on the secondary side known as a network protector consisting of a circuit breaker and a reverse-power relay. This operates on reverse current to prevent power being fed back into the transformer through the secondary ties should a fault occur in the transformer or in a primary feeder. The reverse-power relay is set to trip the circuit breaker at a current value not more than the rated secondary current of the transformer. The relay is not designed to trip the circuit breaker in the event of an overload on the secondary of the transformer.

The secondary ties shown in Figure 450-9 are required to be protected at each end with an overcurrent device in accordance with Section 450-6(a)(3). The overcurrent device most commonly provided for this purpose is a special type of fuse known as a current limiter (see Figure 450-8). This is a high interrupting capacity device designed to provide short-circuit protection only for the secondary ties and will open safely before temperatures damaging to the cable insulation are reached. See Section 240-11 for definition of current-limiting overcurrent protective device. See also commentary following Section 240-11. The secondary ties form a closed loop that is equipped with switching devices so that any part of the loop may be isolated when repairs are needed or a current limiter must be replaced.

450-7. Parallel Operation. Transformers shall be permitted to be operated in parallel and switched as a unit provided that the overcurrent protection for each transformer meets the requirements of Section 450-3 (a)(2) or (b)(2).

450-8. Guarding. Transformers shall be guarded as specified in (a) through (d) below.

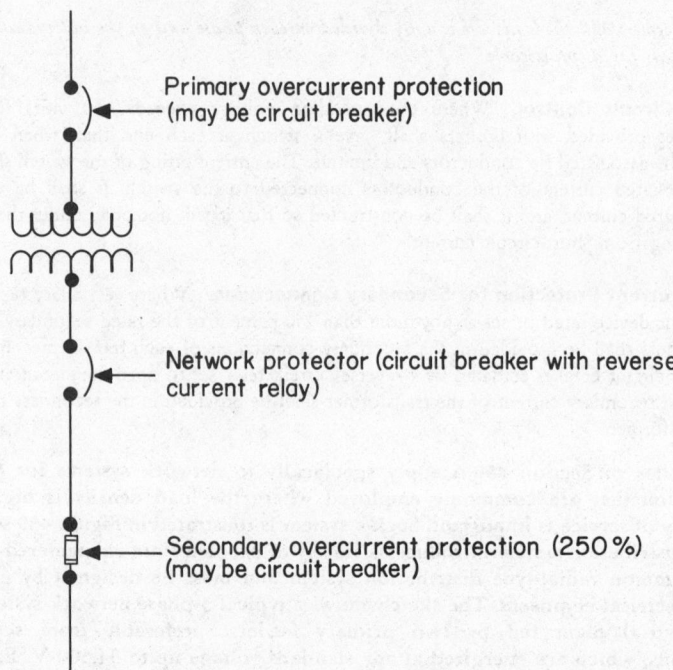

Figure 450-7. Primary and secondary overcurrent protection for a transformer in a network system showing a network protector (an automatic circuit breaker actuated by a reverse-current relay).

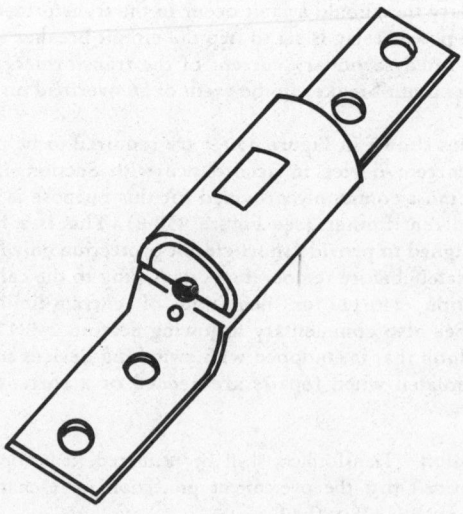

Figure 450-8. A current-limiter is a special type of high-interrupting capacity fuse.

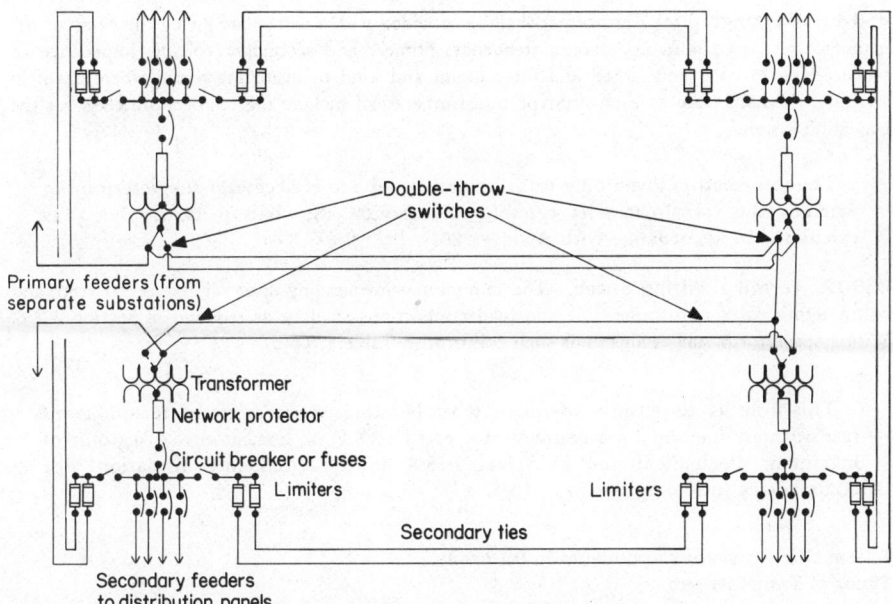

Figure 450-9. A typical 3-phase network system for an industrial plant fed by two primary feeders.

(a) Mechanical Protection. Appropriate provisions shall be made to minimize the possibility of damage to transformers from external causes where the transformers are exposed to physical damage.

One example of mechanical protection would be in the form of 3-in. to 4-in. inside diameter vertical steel pipes embedded in the ground and filled with concrete. This method can be used where transformers may otherwise be subjected to damage by vehicles.

(b) Case or Enclosure. Dry-type transformers shall be provided with a noncombustible moisture-resistant case or enclosure that will provide reasonable protection against the accidental insertion of foreign objects.

(c) Exposed Live Parts. Transformers shall be so installed that live parts are guarded in accordance with Section 110-17.

(d) Voltage Warning. The operating voltage of exposed live parts of transformer installations shall be indicated by signs or visible markings on the equipment or structures.

450-9. Ventilation. The ventilation shall be adequate to dispose of the transformer full-load losses without creating temperature rise which is in excess of the transformer rating.

(FPN): See ANSI/IEEE C57.12.00-1980, General Requirements for Liquid-Immersed Distribution, Power, and Regulating Transformers and ANSI/IEEE C57.12.01-1979, General Requirements for Dry-Type Distribution and Power Transformers.

450-10. Grounding. Exposed noncurrent-carrying metal parts of transformer installations, including fences, guards, etc., shall be grounded where required under the conditions and in the manner specified for electric equipment and other exposed metal parts in Article 250.

ARTICLE 450—TRANSFORMERS AND TRANSFORMER VAULTS

450-11. Marking. Each transformer shall be provided with a nameplate giving the name of the manufacturer; rated kilovolt-amperes; frequency; primary and secondary voltage; impedance of transformers 25 kVA and larger; and the amount and kind of insulating liquid where used. In addition, the nameplate of each dry-type transformer shall include the temperature class for the insulation system.

The information given on a transformer nameplate is necessary for determining whether the transformer is capable of carrying the load it is supplying as calculated in accordance with Article 220.

450-12. Terminal Wiring Space. The minimum wire bending space at fixed, 600 volts and below terminals of transformer line and load connections shall be as required in Section 373-6. Wiring space for pigtail connections shall conform to Table 370-6(b).

This rule is to ensure adequate wire bending space at fixed terminals of transformer line and load connections, rated 600 V or less, as this is a point of maximum mechanical and electrical stress on the conductor insulation. See commentary following Section 370-6.

B. Specific Provisions Applicable to Different Types of Transformers

450-21. Dry-type Transformers Installed Indoors.

(a) Not Over 112½ kVA. Transformers installed indoors and rated 112½ kVA or less shall have a separation of at least 12 inches (305 mm) from combustible material unless separated therefrom by a fire-resistant, heat-insulating barrier, or unless of a rating not over 600 volts and completely enclosed except for ventilating openings.

(b) Over 112½ kVA. Individual transformers of more than 112½ kVA rating shall be installed in a transformer room of fire-resistant construction.

Exception No. 1 to (b): Transformers constructed with Class 80°C rise or higher insulation and separated from combustible material by a fire-resistant, heat-insulating barrier or by not less than 6 feet (1.83 m) horizontally and 12 feet (3.66 m) vertically.

Exception No. 2 to (b): Transformers constructed with Class 80°C rise or higher insulation and of completely enclosed and ventilated-type construction.

(c) Over 35,000 Volts. Transformers rated over 35,000 volts shall be installed in a vault complying with Part C of this article.

Dry-type transformers depend on the surrounding air for adequate ventilation and where rated less than 112½ kVA are not required to be installed in a fire-resistive transformer room.

Transformers of the dry type, gas-filled, or less flammable liquid-insulated transformers (see Section 450-23) installed indoors with a primary voltage of not more than 35,000 volts are commonly used because a transformer vault is not required.

For the same reason, askarel-filled transformers have been extensively used indoors in the past. However, askarel, which contains a polychlorinated biphenyl (PCB), is no longer being manufactured, but acceptable substitutes that comply with Section 450-23 are now available. See Figure 450-10.

Figure 450-10 shows a 1,500 kVA gas-filled dry-type transformer available in ratings through 5,000 kVA, 34½ kV for use indoors or outdoors. These units are built using the conventional ventilated dry-type core and coils, but sealed in a heavy welded steel tank and filled with fluorocarbon gas for dielectric strength as well as cooling. Since the transformers are completely hermetically sealed in a heavy gage steel tank, they are considered safe indoors and outdoors, and there is little likelihood of flames or gases escaping in the event of a short circuit or transformer failure. These units can be used for any explosive, highly combustible, or dangerous area and offer high resistance to fire or explosion. See Sections 501-2, 502-2, and 503-2.

Figure 450-11 shows a dry-type transformer with the outside casing in place and with the latest core and coil design for a typical dry-type power transformer rated at 1,000 kVA, 13,800-V to 480-V, 3-phase, 60 Hz. This transformer has a high-voltage and low-voltage flange for connection to switchgear and a high-voltage, 2-position (double-throw), 3-pole load break air switch which may be attached to the case and arranged as a selector switch for the connection of the transformer primary to either of two feeder sources.

Dry-type transformers rated less than 112½ kVA are required to be separated from combustible material or rated less than 600 V and completely enclosed, except for ventilating openings. Noncombustible insulations used in transformers, such as mica, porcelain, and glass, which can withstand high temperatures, have permitted the application of larger dry-type transformers. However, combustible materials, such as varnish, are used with those insulations, and under short-circuit conditions, flames can escape from the transformer enclosure. Hence, transformers rated 112½ kVA or less are required to be spaced 12 in. or separated by fire-resistive barriers from combustibles or be completely enclosed. Those rated over 112½ kVA are required to be located in fire-resistive transformer rooms or vaults.

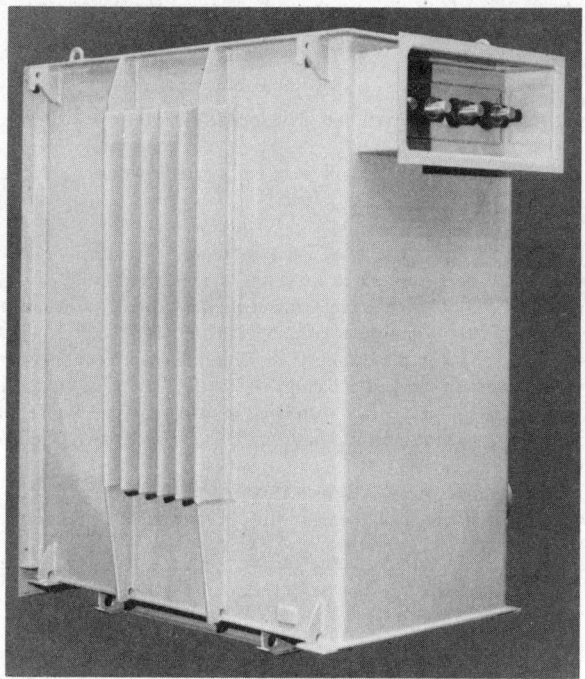

Figure 450-10. 1,500-kVA gas-filled dry-type transformer aviailable in ratings through 5,000 kVA, 34½ kV for use indoors or outdoors. (*Westinghouse Electric Corp.*)

Figure 450-11. A dry-type transformer with a core and coil design rated at 1,000 kVA, 13,800 V to 480 V, 3-phase, 60 Hz. (*Westinghouse Electric Corp.*)

450-22. Dry-type Transformers Installed Outdoors. Dry-type transformers installed outdoors shall have a weatherproof enclosure.

Transformers exceeding 112½ kVA shall not be located within 12 inches (305 mm) of combustible materials of buildings.

450-23. Less-Flammable Liquid-Insulated Transformers. Transformers insulated with listed less-flammable liquids shall be permitted to be installed without a vault in Type I and Type II buildings in areas in which no combustible materials are stored, provided there is a liquid confinement area, the liquid has a fire point of not less than 300°C, and the installation complies with all restrictions provided for in the listing of the liquid. Such indoor transformer installations not meeting the restrictions of the liquid listing, or installed in other than Type I or Type II buildings, or in areas where combustible materials are stored, shall (1) be provided with an automatic fire extinguishing system and a liquid confinement area, or (2) be installed in a vault complying with Part C of this article.

Transformers installed indoors and rated over 35,000 volts shall be installed in a vault.

Transformers installed outdoors shall comply with the safeguards of Section 450-27.

(FPN): As used in this section, "Noncombustible" refers to Type I and Type II building construction and noncombustible materials as defined in Types of Building Construction, NFPA 220-1979.

NFPA 220 defines Type I building construction as that type in which the structural members, including walls, columns, beams, floors, and roofs, are of approved noncombustible or limited-combustible materials and have fire resistance ratings not less than those set forth in Table 3 of NFPA 220.

Type II building construction is defined as that type not qualifying as Type I construction in which the structural members including walls, columns, beams, floors, and roofs are of approved noncombustible or limited-combustible materials and have fire resistance ratings not less than those set forth in Table 3 of NFPA 220.

(FPN): See definition of "Listed" in Article 100.

Figure 450-12 shows a liquid-insulated transformer filled with a listed, less flammable liquid with a fire point of at least 300°C. This type of transformer may be installed indoors without a vault in Types I and II buildings in areas where no combustible materials are stored provided they are not rated over 35,000 V, there is a liquid confinement area, and the installation complies with all restrictions provided for in the listing of the liquid. Factory Mutual Research Corp. has listings of the "less flammable" liquids covered in this section. See also commentary following Section 450-27.

Figure 450-12. A liquid-insulated transformer filled with a listed, less flammable liquid with a fire point of at least 300°C. (*Square D Co.*)

450-24. Nonflammable Fluid-Insulated Transformers. Transformers insulated with a dielectric fluid identified as nonflammable shall be permitted to be installed indoors or outdoors. Such transformers installed indoors and rated over 35,000 volts shall be installed in a vault.

For the purposes of this section, a nonflammable dielectric fluid is one which does not have a flash point or fire point, and is not flammable in air.

450-25. Askarel-Insulated Transformers Installed Indoors. Askarel-insulated transformers installed indoors and rated over 25 kVA shall be furnished with a pressure-relief vent. Where installed in a poorly ventilated place, they shall be furnished with a means for absorbing any gases generated by arcing inside the case, or the pressure-relief vent shall be connected to a chimney or flue that will carry such gases outside the building. Askarel-insulated transformers rated over 35,000 volts shall be installed in a vault.

450-26. Oil-Insulated Transformers Installed Indoors. Oil-insulated transformers installed indoors shall be installed in a vault constructed as specified in Part C of this article.

Exception No. 1: Where the total capacity does not exceed 112½ kVA, the vault specified in Part C of this article shall be permitted to be constructed of reinforced concrete not less than 4 inches (102 mm) thick.

Exception No. 2: Where the nominal voltage does not exceed 600, a vault shall not be required if suitable arrangements are made to prevent a transformer oil fire from igniting other materials, and the total capacity in one location does not exceed 10 kVA in a section of the building classified as combustible, or 75 kVA where the surrounding structure is classified as fire-resistant construction.

Exception No. 3: Electric furnace transformers having a total rating not exceeding 75 kVA shall be permitted to be installed without a vault in a building or room of fire-resistant construction, provided suitable arrangements are made to prevent a transformer oil fire from spreading to other combustible material.

Exception No. 4: Transformers shall be permitted to be installed in a detached building that does not comply with Part C of this article if neither the building nor its contents presents a fire hazard to any other building or property, and if the building is used only in supplying electric service and the interior is accessible only to qualified persons.

Exception No. 5: Oil-insulated transformers shall be permitted to be used without a vault in portable and mobile surface mining equipment (such as electric excavators) if each of the following conditions is met:

a. Provision is made for draining leaking fluid to the ground.

b. Safe egress is provided for personnel.

c. A minimum ¼ -inch (6.35-mm) steel barrier is provided for personnel protection.

450-27. Oil-Insulated Transformers Installed Outdoors. Combustible material, combustible buildings, and parts of buildings, fire escapes, and door and window openings shall be safeguarded from fires originating in oil-insulated transformers installed on roofs, attached to, or adjacent to a building or combustible material.

Space separations, fire-resistant barriers, automatic water spray systems, and enclosures that confine the oil of a ruptured transformer tank are recognized safeguards. One or more of these safeguards shall be applied according to the degree of hazard involved in cases where the transformer installation presents a fire hazard.

Oil enclosures shall be permitted to consist of fire-resistant dikes, curbed areas or basins, or trenches filled with coarse crushed stone. Oil enclosures shall be provided with trapped drains where the exposure and the quantity of oil involved are such that removal of oil is important. Transformers installed on poles or structures or underground shall conform to the National Electrical Safety Code, ANSI C2-1981.

The following Formal Interpretation No. 81-2 was issued in June, 1981. The words "high fire point liquid" in Section 450-23 of the 1981 *NEC* were changed to "less-flammable liquid" in the 1984 *NEC*.

Question 1: Is it the intent of the 1981 *National Electrical Code* to consider a high fire point liquid as described in Section 450-23 a substitute for any of the fire safeguards described in Section 450-27?

Answer: No.

Question 2: Is it the intent of the 1981 *National Electrical Code* that a high fire point liquid-insulated transformer have one or more of the fire safeguards described in Section 450-27 if the installation (e.g. location) of the transformer presents a fire hazard?

Answer: Yes.

450-28. Modification of Transformers. When modifications are made to a transformer in an existing installation which changes the type of the transformer with respect to Part B of this article, such transformer shall be marked to show the type of insulating liquid installed and the modified transformer installation shall comply with the applicable requirements for that type of transformer.

This section is new in the 1984 *Code*. Many askarel-insulated transformers are being modified by replacing the askarel with either oil or a less-flammable liquid. When such a modification takes place the completed installation is required to have the same degree of safety as a new installation. For example, replacement of askarel with oil in an indoor installation without a vault may not be acceptable. See Section 450-26 and exceptions. If the replacement liquid is a less-flammable liquid, see Section 450-23.

C. Transformer Vaults

450-41. Location. Vaults shall be located where they can be ventilated to the outside air without using flues or ducts wherever such an arrangement is practicable.

450-42. Walls, Roof and Floor. The walls and roofs of vaults shall be constructed of materials which have adequate structural strength for the conditions with a minimum fire resistance of 3 hours according to ASTM Standard E119-75; Fire Tests of Building Construction and Materials, NFPA 251-1972; and Methods of Fire Tests of Building Construction and Materials, ANSI A2.1-1972. The floors of vaults in contact with the earth shall be of concrete not less than 4 inches (102 mm) thick, but when the vault is constructed with a vacant space or other stories below it, the floor shall have adequate structural strength for the load imposed thereon and a minimum fire resistance of 3 hours.

(FPN): Six-inch (152-mm) thick reinforced concrete is a typical 3-hour construction.

Exception: Where transformers are protected with automatic sprinkler, water spray, carbon dioxide, or halon, construction of 1-hour rating shall be permitted.

450-43. Doorways. Vault doorways shall be protected as follows:

(a) Type of Door. Each doorway leading into a vault from the building interior shall be provided with a tight-fitting door having a minimum fire rating of 3 hours as defined in the Standard for the Installation of Fire Doors and Windows, NFPA 80-1979 (ANSI). The authority having jurisdiction shall be permitted to require such a door for an exterior wall opening where conditions warrant.

Exception: Where transformers are protected with automatic sprinkler, water spray, carbon dioxide, or halon, construction of 1-hour rating shall be permitted.

(b) Sills. A door sill or curb of sufficient height to confine within the vault the oil from the largest transformer shall be provided, and in no case shall the height be less than 4 inches (102 mm).

(c) Locks. Entrance doors shall be equipped with locks, and doors shall be kept locked, access being allowed only to qualified persons. Locks and latches shall be so arranged that the door can be readily and quickly opened from the inside.

450-45. Ventilation Openings. Where required by Section 450-9, openings for ventilation shall be provided in accordance with (a) through (f) below.

(a) Location. Ventilation openings shall be located as far away as possible from doors, windows, fire escapes, and combustible material.

(b) Arrangement. A vault ventilated by natural circulation of air shall be permitted to have roughly half of the total area of openings required for ventilation in one or more openings near the floor and the remainder in one or more openings in the roof or in the sidewalls near the roof, or all of the area required for ventilation shall be permitted in one or more openings in or near the roof.

(c) Size. For a vault ventilated by natural circulation of air to an outdoor area, the combined net area of all ventilating openings, after deducting the area occupied by screens, gratings, or louvers, shall not be less than 3 square inches (1936 sq mm) per kVA of transformer capacity in service, and in no case shall the net area be less than 1 square foot (0.093 sq m) for any capacity under 50 kVA.

(d) Covering. Ventilation openings shall be covered with durable gratings, screens, or louvers, according to the treatment required in order to avoid unsafe conditions.

(e) Dampers. All ventilation openings to the indoors shall be provided with automatic closing fire dampers that operate in response to a vault fire. Such dampers shall possess a standard fire rating of not less than 1½ hours.

(FPN): See Standard for Fire Dampers, ANSI/UL 555-1972.

(f) Ducts. Ventilating ducts shall be constructed of fire-resistant material.

450-46. Drainage. Where practicable, vaults containing more than 100 kVA transformer capacity shall be provided with a drain or other means that will carry off any accumulation of oil or water in the vault unless local conditions make this impracticable. The floor shall be pitched to the drain where provided.

450-47. Water Pipes and Accessories. Any pipe or duct system foreign to the electrical installation shall not enter or pass through a transformer vault. Piping or other facilities provided for vault fire protection, or for transformer cooling, shall not be considered foreign to the electrical installation.

450-48. Storage in Vaults. Materials shall not be stored in transformer vaults.

ARTICLE 460 — CAPACITORS

Contents

460-10. Grounding.
460-12. Marking.

B. Over 600 Volts, Nominal

460-24. Switching.
  (a) Load Current.
  (b) Isolation.
  (c) Additional Requirements for Series Capacitors.
460-25. Overcurrent Protection.
  (a) Provided to Detect and Interrupt Fault-Current.

  (b) Single-Phase or Multiphase Devices.
  (c) Protected Individually or in Groups.
  (d) Protective Devices Rated or Adjusted.
460-26. Identification.
460-27. Grounding.
460-28. Means for Discharge.
  (a) Means to Reduce the Residual Voltage.
  (b) Connection to Terminals.

460-1. Scope. This article covers the installation of capacitors on electric circuits.

Surge capacitors or capacitors included as a component part of other apparatus and conforming with the requirements of such apparatus are excluded from these requirements.

This article also covers the installation of capacitors in hazardous (classified) locations as modified by Articles 501 through 503.

460-2. Enclosing and Guarding.

(a) Containing More than 3 Gallons (11.36 L) of Flammable Liquid. Capacitors containing more than 3 gallons (11.36 L) of flammable liquid shall be enclosed in vaults or outdoor fenced enclosures complying with Article 710.

(b) Accidental Contact. Capacitors shall be enclosed, located, or guarded so that persons cannot come into accidental contact or bring conducting materials into accidental contact with exposed energized parts, terminals, or buses associated with them.

Exception: No additional guarding is required for enclosures accessible only to authorized and qualified persons.

A. 600 Volts, Nominal, and Under

460-6. Drainage of Stored Charge. Capacitors shall be provided with a means of draining the stored charge.

(a) Time of Discharge. The residual voltage of a capacitor shall be reduced to 50 volts, nominal, or less, within 1 minute after the capacitor is disconnected from the source of supply.

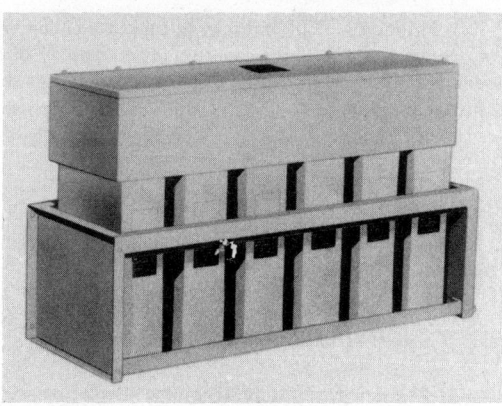

Figure 460-1. Single-tier, six capacitor rack with prewired connections. (*Sprague Electric Co.*)

ARTICLE 460—CAPACITORS

(b) Means of Discharge. The discharge circuit shall be either permanently connected to the terminals of the capacitor or capacitor bank, or provided with automatic means of connecting it to the terminals of the capacitor bank on removal of voltage from the line. Manual means of switching or connecting the discharge circuit shall not be used.

Means are required to be provided to drain off the stored charge in a capacitor after the supply circuit has been opened. Otherwise, a person servicing the equipment could receive a severe shock or damage may occur to the equipment.

Figures 460-2(a) and (b) show the method in which capacitors are connected in a motor circuit so that they may be switched with the motor. In either arrangement the stored charge will drain off through the windings when the circuit is opened. Figure 460-2(c) shows a third arrangement where the capacitor is permanently connected to the system. This arrangement eliminates the need for a separate switch to disconnect the capacitors.

Capacitors may be equipped with built-in resistors to drain off the stored charge, although this type is not needed when connected as shown in Figures 460-2(a) and (b).

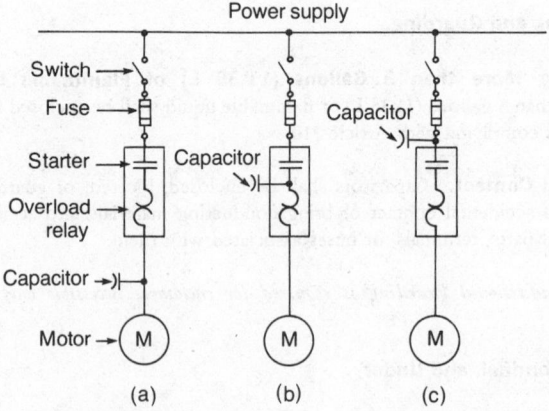

Figure 460-2. Methods of connecting capacitors in induction motor circuit for power factor correction.

460-8. Conductors.

(a) Ampacity. The ampacity of capacitor circuit conductors shall not be less than 135 percent of the rated current of the capacitor. The ampacity of conductors that connect a capacitor to the terminals of a motor or to motor circuit conductors shall not be less than one third the ampacity of the motor circuit conductors and in no case less than 135 percent of the rated current of the capacitor.

(b) Overcurrent Protection.

(1) An overcurrent device shall be provided in each ungrounded conductor for each capacitor bank.

Exception: A separate overcurrent device shall not be required for a capacitor connected on the load side of a motor overload protective device.

(2) The rating or setting of the overcurrent device shall be as low as practicable.

(c) Disconnecting Means.

(1) A disconnecting means shall be provided in each ungrounded conductor for each capacitor bank.

Exception: Where a capacitor is connected on the load side of a motor overload protective device.

(2) The disconnecting means shall open all ungrounded conductors simultaneously.

(3) The disconnecting means shall be permitted to disconnect the capacitor from the line as a regular operating procedure.

(4) The rating of the disconnecting means shall not be less than 135 percent of the rated current of the capacitor.

Capacitors are rated in kilovars, which is abbreviated kVAr and means reactive kilovolt-amperes. The kVAr rating shows how many reactive kilovolt-amperes the capacitor will supply in order to cancel out the reactive kilovolt-amperes caused by inductance. For example, a 20-kVAr capacitor will cancel out 20 kVA of inductive reactive kilovolt-amperes.

The basic unit is 3-phase and delta-connected internally but single-phase and 2-phase units are also available. They are constructed with built-in fuses for short-circuit protection and discharge resistors that reduce the voltage to 50-V crest or less when disconnected from the power supply. This will occur within one minute on 600-V units and within 5 minutes for 2,400- and 4,160-V units.

The capacitor circuit conductors and disconnecting means are required to have an ampacity not less than 135 percent of the rated current of the capacitor. This is because all capacitors are manufactured with a tolerance of -0 percent to +15 percent, so that a 100-kVAr capacitor may actually draw a current equivalent to a 115-kVAr capacitor. In addition, the current drawn by a capacitor varies directly with the line voltage, and any variation in the line voltage from a pure sine wave form causes the capacitor to draw an increased current. Considering these several factors, the increased current can amount to 135 percent of the rated current of the capacitor.

The current corresponding to the kVAr rating of a 3-phase capacitor is computed from the formula

$$Ic = \frac{kVAr \times 1,000}{1.73 \times volts}.$$

The ampacity of the conductors and the switching device is then determined by multiplying $Ic \times 1.35$. The most effective power factor correction is obtained when the individual capacitors are connected directly to the terminals of the motors, transformers, and other inductive machinery.

When connected together and operated as a unit, no complicated calculations are needed to determine the proper size capacitor to use. Capacitor manufacturers publish tables in which the required capacitor value is indicated by referring to the speed and hp of the motor. These values will improve the motor power factor to approximately 95 percent. To improve a plant power factor, capacitor manufacturers also publish tables to assist in calculating the total kVAr rating of capacitors required to improve the power factor to any desired value.

ARTICLE 460—CAPACITORS

460-9. Rating or Setting of Motor Overload Device. Where a motor installation includes a capacitor connected on the load side of the motor overload device, the rating or setting of the motor overload device shall be determined in accordance with Section 430-32.

Exception: Instead of using the full-load rated current of the motor as provided in Section 430-32, a lower value corresponding with the improved power factor of the motor circuit shall be used. Section 430-22 applies with respect to the rating of the motor circuit conductors.

Where a capacitor is connected on the load side of the overload relays, as shown in Figure 460-2(a), consideration is required to be given to the reduction in line current due to the improved power factor when selecting the rating or setting of the motor running overcurrent device. A value lower than indicated in Section 430-32 should be used for proper protection of the motor.

460-10. Grounding. Capacitor cases shall be grounded in accordance with Article 250.

Exception: Where the capacitor units are supported on a structure which is designed to operate at other than ground potential.

460-12. Marking. Each capacitor shall be provided with a nameplate giving the name of the manufacturer, rated voltage, frequency, kilovar or amperes, number of phases, and, if filled with a combustible liquid, the amount of liquid in gallons. When filled with a nonflammable liquid, the nameplate shall so state. The nameplate shall also indicate if a capacitor has a discharge device inside the case.

B. Over 600 Volts, Nominal

460-24. Switching.

(a) Load Current. Group-operated switches shall be used for capacitor switching and shall be capable of (1) carrying continuously not less than 135 percent of the rated current of the capacitor installation; (2) interrupting the maximum continuous load current of each capacitor, capacitor bank, or capacitor installation that will be switched as a unit; (3) withstanding the maximum inrush current, including contributions from adjacent capacitor installations; (4) carrying currents due to faults on capacitor side of switch.

(b) Isolation.

(1) A means shall be installed to isolate from all sources of potential each capacitor, capacitor bank, or capacitor installation that will be removed from service as a unit.

(2) The isolating means shall provide a visible gap in the electrical circuit adequate for the operating voltage.

(3) Isolating or disconnecting switches (with no interrupting rating) shall be interlocked with the load interrupting device or shall be provided with prominently displayed caution signs in accordance with Section 710-22 to prevent switching load current.

(c) Additional Requirements for Series Capacitors. The proper switching sequence shall be assured by use of one of the following: (1) mechanically sequenced isolating and bypass switches; (2) interlocks; or (3) switching procedure prominently displayed at the switching location.

460-25. Overcurrent Protection.

(a) Provided to Detect and Interrupt Fault-Current. A means shall be provided to detect and interrupt fault current likely to cause dangerous pressure within an individual capacitor.

(b) Single-Phase or Multiphase Devices. Single-phase or multiphase devices shall be permitted for this purpose.

(c) Protected Individually or in Groups. Capacitors may be protected individually or in groups.

(d) Protective Devices Rated or Adjusted. Protective devices for capacitors or capacitor equipment shall be rated or adjusted to operate within the limits of the Safe Zone for individual capacitors as defined by ANSI Standard for Shunt Power Capacitors, C55.1-1968.

Exception: If the protective devices are rated or adjusted to operate within the limits of the ANSI Standard for Zone 1 or Zone 2, the capacitors shall be enclosed or isolated.

In no event shall the rating or adjustment of the protective devices exceed the maximum limit of the ANSI Standard, Zone 2.

The reference to Zones 1 and 2 of ANSI Standard C55.1-1968 pertains to the performance of the capacitors under fault conditions. If a fault current exceeds the limit established for Zone 2, the capacitor tank may burst.

460-26. Identification. Each capacitor shall be provided with a permanent nameplate giving the maker's name, rated voltage, frequency, kilovar or amperes, number of phases, and the amount of liquid in gallons identified as flammable, if such is the case.

460-27. Grounding. Capacitor neutrals and cases, if grounded, shall be grounded in accordance with Article 250.

Exception: Where the capacitor units are supported on a structure which is designed to operate at other than ground potential.

460-28. Means for Discharge.

(a) Means to Reduce the Residual Voltage. A means shall be provided to reduce the residual voltage of a capacitor to 50 volts or less within 5 minutes after the capacitor is disconnected from the source of supply.

(b) Connection to Terminals. A discharge circuit shall be either permanently connected to the terminals of the capacitor or provided with automatic means of connecting it to the terminals of the capacitor bank after disconnection of the capacitor from the source of supply. The windings of motors, or transformers, or of other equipment directly connected to capacitors without a switch or overcurrent device interposed must meet the requirements of (a) above.

ARTICLE 470 — RESISTORS AND REACTORS

For Rheostats, see Section 430-82.

Contents

ARTICLE 470—RESISTORS AND REACTORS

A. 600 Volts, Nominal, and Under

470-1. Scope. This article covers the installation of separate resistors and reactors on electric circuits.

Exception: Resistors and reactors that are component parts of other apparatus.

This article also covers the installation of resistors and reactors in hazardous (classified) locations as modified by Articles 501 through 503.

470-2. Location. Resistors and reactors shall not be placed where exposed to physical damage.

470-3. Space Separation. A thermal barrier shall be required if the space between the resistors and reactors and any combustible material is less than 12 inches (305 mm).

470-4. Conductor Insulation. Insulated conductors used for connections between resistance elements and controllers shall be suitable for an operating temperature of not less than 90°C (194°F).

Exception: Other conductor insulations shall be permitted for motor starting service.

Resistors are made in many different sizes and shapes and for different purposes. They may be wire or ribbon wound, form wound, edgewise wound, cast grid, punched steel grid, or box resistors. They may be mounted in the open or in ventilated metal boxes or cabinets depending upon their use and location. Since they give off heat, they are required to be guarded and located at safe distances from combustible materials. When mounted on switchboards or installed in control panels, they are not required to have additional guards.

Reactors are installed in a circuit to introduce inductance for motor starting, controlling the current, and paralleling of transformers. Current-limiting reactors are installed to limit the amount of current that can flow in a circuit when a short circuit occurs. Reactors can be divided into two classes, those with iron cores and those that use no magnetic materials in the windings. Both types may be air cooled or oil immersed.

Mechanical stresses due to their external fields exist between air core reactors, and the manufacturer's recommendations should be followed in spacing and bracing between units and fastening of supporting insulators.

Saturable reactors are used for theater dimming. These have, in addition to the ac winding, an auxiliary winding connected line-to-line or line-to-ground in order to neutralize charging current and prevent a voltage rise. Those used on high voltage systems are usually oil immersed.

B. Over 600 Volts, Nominal

470-18. General.

(a) Protected Against Physical Damage. Resistors and reactors shall be protected against physical damage.

(b) Isolated by Enclosure or Elevation. Resistors and reactors shall be isolated by enclosure or elevation to protect personnel from accidental contact with energized parts.

(c) Combustible Materials. Resistors and reactors shall not be installed in close enough proximity to combustible materials to constitute a fire hazard and in no case closer than within 1 foot (305 mm) of combustible materials.

(d) Clearances. Clearances from resistors and reactors to grounded surfaces shall be adequate for the voltage involved.

(FPN): See Article 710.

(e) Temperature Rise from Induced Circulating Currents. Metallic enclosures of reactors and adjacent metal parts shall be installed so that the temperature rise from induced circulating currents will not be hazardous to personnel or constitute a fire hazard.

470-19. Grounding. Resistor and reactor cases or enclosures shall be grounded in accordance with Article 250.

470-20. Oil-Filled Reactors. Installation of oil-filled reactors, in addition to the above requirements, shall comply with applicable requirements of Article 450.

ARTICLE 480 — STORAGE BATTERIES

Contents

480-1. Scope. The provisions of this article shall apply to all stationary installations of storage batteries.

There are two general types of storage cells, the lead-acid type and the alkali type.

Basically, a lead-acid cell consists of a positive plate, usually lead peroxide (a semisolid compound) mounted on a framework or grid for support, and a negative plate made of sponge lead mounted on a grid. Grids are generally made of a lead-antimony alloy and the electrolyte is usually sulfuric acid and distilled water.

In the alkali-type cell (or Edison cell), the positive plate material is nickel oxide and the negative plate material is iron oxide. The electrolyte is a solution consisting mostly of potassium hydroxide (an alkaline).

480-2. Definitions.

Storage Battery: A battery comprised of one or more rechargeable cells of the lead-acid, nickel-cadmium, or other rechargeable electrochemical types.

Sealed Cell or Battery: A sealed cell or battery is one which has no provision for the addition of water or electrolyte or for external measurement of electrolyte specific gravity. The individual cells shall be permitted to contain a venting arrangement as described in Section 480-9(b).

ARTICLE 480—STORAGE BATTERIES

Nominal Battery Voltage: The voltage computed on the basis of 2.0 volts per cell for the lead-acid type and 1.2 volts per cell for the alkali type.

480-3. Wiring and Equipment Supplied from Batteries. Wiring and equipment supplied from storage batteries shall be subject to the requirements of this Code applying to wiring and equipment operating at the same voltage.

Exception: As otherwise provided for communication systems in Article 800.

480-4. Grounding. The requirements of Article 250 shall apply.

480-5. Insulation of Batteries of Not Over 250 Volts. This section shall apply to storage batteries having cells so connected as to operate at a nominal battery voltage of not over 250 volts.

(a) Vented Lead-Acid Batteries. Cells and multicompartment batteries with covers sealed to containers of nonconductive, heat-resistant material shall not require additional insulating support.

(b) Vented Alkaline-type Batteries. Cells with covers sealed to jars of nonconductive, heat-resistant material shall require no additional insulation support. Cells in jars of conductive material shall be installed in trays of nonconductive material with not more than 20 cells (24 volts, nominal) in the series circuit in any one tray.

(c) Rubber Jars. Cells in rubber or composition containers shall require no additional insulating support where the total nominal voltage of all cells in series does not exceed 150. Where the total voltage exceeds 150, batteries shall be sectionalized into groups of 150 volts or less and each group shall have the individual cells installed in trays or on racks.

(d) Sealed Cells or Batteries. Sealed cells and multicompartment sealed batteries constructed of nonconductive, heat-resistant material shall not require additional insulating support. Batteries constructed of a conducting container shall have insulating support if a voltage is present between the container and ground.

480-6. Insulation of Batteries of Over 250 Volts. The provisions of Section 480-5 shall apply to storage batteries having the cells so connected as to operate at a nominal voltage exceeding 250 volts, and, in addition, the provisions of this section shall also apply to such batteries. Cells shall be installed in groups having a total nominal voltage of not over 250 volts on any one rack. Insulation, which can be air, shall be provided between racks and shall have a minimum separation between live battery parts of opposite polarity of 2 inches (50.8 mm) for battery voltages not exceeding 600 volts. Maximum protection can be secured by sectionalizing high-voltage batteries into groups.

480-7. Racks and Trays. Racks and trays shall comply with (a) and (b) below.

(a) Racks. Racks, as required in this article, are rigid frames designed to support cells or trays. They shall be substantial and made of:

(1) Metal, so treated as to be resistant to deteriorating action by the electrolyte and provided with nonconducting members directly supporting the cells or with continuous insulating material other than paint or conducting members; or

(2) Other construction such as fiberglass or other suitable nonmetallic materials.

(b) Trays. Trays are frames, such as crates or shallow boxes usually of wood or other nonconductive material, so constructed or treated as to be resistant to deteriorating action by the electrolyte.

480-8. Battery Locations. Battery locations shall conform to (a) and (b) below.

(a) Ventilation. Provisions shall be made for sufficient diffusion and ventilation of the gases from the battery to prevent the accumulation of an explosive mixture.

Compliance with this section is necessary to prevent classification of a battery location as a hazardous (classified) location in accordance with Article 500.

It is not the intent of Section 480-8(a) to mandate mechanical ventilation. Hydrogen disperses rapidly and requires very little air movement to prevent accumulation. Unrestricted natural air movement in the vicinity of the battery together with normal air changes for occupied spaces or heat removal will normally be sufficient. If the space is confined, mechanical ventilation may be required in the vicinity of the battery.

Ventilation can be a fan, roof ridge vent, or louvered areas.

(b) Live Parts. Guarding of live parts shall comply with Section 110-17.

Batteries are required to be located in a clean, dry room and arranged to provide sufficient work space for inspection and maintenance. Provision is required to be made for adequate ventilation to prevent an accumulation of an explosive mixture of the gases from the batteries.

The fumes given off by storage batteries are very corrosive; therefore, wiring and its insulation must be of a type that will withstand corrosive action. See Section 310-9. Special precautions are necessary to ensure that all metalwork (metal raceways, metal racks, etc.) is designed or treated so as to be corrosion resistant. Manufacturers suggest that aluminum conduit be used to withstand the corrosive battery fumes, or, if steel conduits are used, it is recommended that they be zinc-coated and corrosion protected with a coating of an asphaltum-type paint. See Section 300-6.

Overcharging heats a battery and causes gassing and loss of water. A battery should not be allowed to reach temperatures over 110°F because heat causes a shedding of active materials from the plates that will eventually form a sediment buildup in the bottom of the case and short-circuit the plates and the cell. Because mixtures of oxygen and hydrogen are highly explosive, flame or sparks should never be allowed near a cell, especially if the filler cap is removed.

480-9. Vents.

(a) Vented Cells. Each vented cell shall be equipped with a flame arrestor designed to prevent destruction of the cell due to ignition of gases within the cell by an external spark or flame under normal operating conditions.

(b) Sealed Cells. Sealed battery/cells shall be equipped with a pressure-release vent to prevent excessive accumulation of gas pressure or the battery/cell shall be designed to prevent scatter of cell parts in event of a cell explosion.

5 SPECIAL OCCUPANCIES

ARTICLE 500 — HAZARDOUS (CLASSIFIED) LOCATIONS

Contents

500-1. Scope — Articles 500 Through 503. Articles 500 through 503 cover the requirements for electrical equipment and wiring for all voltages in locations where fire or explosion hazards may exist due to flammable gases or vapors, flammable liquids, combustible dust, or ignitible fibers or flyings.

Locations are classified depending on the properties of the flammable vapors, liquids or gases, or combustible dusts or fibers which may be present and the likelihood that a flammable or combustible concentration or quantity is present.

Each room, section, or area shall be considered individually in determining its classification.

Exception: Except as modified in Articles 500 through 503, all other applicable rules contained in this Code shall apply to electric equipment and wiring installed in hazardous (classified) locations.

(FPN): For definitions of "approved" and "explosionproof" as used in these articles, see Article 100; "dust-ignition-proof" is defined in Section 502-1.

Equipment and associated wiring approved as intrinsically safe shall be permitted in any hazardous (classified) location for which it is approved, and the provisions of Articles 500 through 517 shall not be considered applicable to such installations. Means shall be provided to prevent the passage of gases and vapors. Intrinsically safe equipment and wiring shall not be capable of releasing sufficient electrical or thermal energy under normal or abnormal conditions to cause ignition of a specific flammable or combustible atmospheric mixture in its most easily ignitible concentration.

Abnormal conditions shall include accidental damage to any field-installed wiring, failure of electrical components, application of overvoltage, adjustment and maintenance operations, and other similar conditions.

(FPN): For further information, see Intrinsically Safe Apparatus and Associated Apparatus for Use in Class I, II, and III, Division 1 Hazardous Locations, NFPA 493-1978 (ANSI) and Installation of Intrinsically Safe Instrument Systems in Class I Hazardous Locations (ANSI/ISA RP 12.6-1976).

The purpose of NFPA 493, Intrinsically Safe Apparatus and Associated Apparatus for Use in Class I, II, and III, Division 1 Hazardous Locations, is to provide requirements for the construction and testing of electrical apparatus, or parts of such apparatus, in which the circuits themselves are incapable of causing ignition in Class I, II, or III, Division 1 locations, in accordance with Articles 500, 501, 502, and 503 of the *NEC*.

This standard applies not only to apparatus or parts of apparatus in the hazardous (classified) location, but also to any parts, such as power supplies and recorders, located outside of the hazardous (classified) location, where the intrinsic safety of the electrical circuits in the hazardous (classified) location may be influenced by the design and construction of such parts. The detailed requirements apply only to apparatus for use in, or associated with, a location made hazardous by the presence of flammable gas or vapor, combustible dust, or easily ignitible fibers or flyings in air under normal atmospheric conditions. If other than normal atmospheric conditions exist, equipment approved as intrinsically safe may not be intrinsically safe. This is especially true if the atmosphere is oxygen-enriched.

In evaluating safety, all interconnected apparatus and circuits are to be considered, even though located in a Division 2 hazardous (classified) location, a nonhazardous location, or protected by other means, such as an explosionproof or purged and pressurized enclosure. They are to be examined to be sure that, under normal or fault conditions, they cannot provide a source of ignition-capable energy to the apparatus in the Divison 1 hazardous (classified) location. Associated apparatus and circuits are to conform to the requirements of the location in which the apparatus and circuits are installed.

An intrinsically safe circuit is one in which any spark or a thermal effect produced either normally or in specified fault conditions is, in the test conditions prescribed in NFPA 493, incapable of causing ignition of a specified mixture of gas or vapor in air in its most easily ignited concentration. Intrinsically safe circuits are required to be identified as intrinsically safe.

Although the scope of ANSI/RP 12.6, Installation of Intrinsically Safe Instrument Systems in Class I Hazardous Locations, is limited to instrument systems, the principles are applicable to other types of intrinsically safe systems. Precautions must be taken to ensure against intrusion of unsafe energy from nonintrinsically safe circuits, particularly in nonhazardous locations where there are fewer restrictions on the wiring methods used. Separation of intrinsically safe and nonintrinsically safe circuits is usually necessary to ensure that the circuits in the hazardous (classified) locations remain intrinsically safe.

The requirement that means be provided to prevent the passage of gases and vapors will necessitate, in Class I locations, some type of sealing or ventilation for raceways and cables capable of transmitting gases or vapors, if these cables or raceways provide communication between a Division 1 and Division 2 or nonhazardous location, or between a Division 2 and a nonhazardous location. Raceways and some cables can act to transmit gases. This requirement is intended to provide the same degree of safety for intrinsically safe wiring as provided for in Section 501-5(a)(4), for example. However, for intrinsically safe wiring, an explosionproof seal is not required. The seal can be similiar to that required in Section 300-7(a).

(FPN): Through the exercise of ingenuity in the layout of electrical installations for hazardous (classified) locations, it is frequently possible to locate much of the equipment in less hazardous or in nonhazardous locations and thus to reduce the amount of special equipment required. In some cases, hazards may be reduced or hazardous (classified) locations limited or eliminated by adequate positive-pressure ventilation from a source of clean air in conjunction with effective safeguards against ventilation failure. For further information, see Purged and Pressurized Enclosures for Electrical Equipment in Hazardous Locations, NFPA 496-1982 (ANSI).

NFPA 496, Purged and Pressurized Enclosures for Electrical Equipment in Hazardous Locations, covers purged enclosures for electrical equipment in Class I hazardous (classified) locations, and pressurized enclosures for electrical equipment in Class II hazardous (classified) locations.

Class I Hazardous (Classified) Locations: The object of NFPA 496 for Class I hazardous (classified) locations is to provide information for the design of purged and pressurized enclosures to eliminate or reduce within the enclosure a Class I hazardous (classified) location classification, as defined in Article 500 of the *Code*. By this means, equipment that is not otherwise acceptable for hazardous (classified) locations may be utilized in accordance with the *Code*.

Purging is defined as the process of supplying an enclosure with clean air or an inert gas, at sufficient flow and positive pressure to reduce to an acceptably safe level the concentration of any flammable gases or vapors initially present, and to maintain this safe level by positive pressure with or without continuous flow.

Type X purging reduces the classification within an enclosure from Division 1 to nonhazardous.

Type Y purging reduces the classification within an enclosure from Division 1 to Division 2.

Type Z purging reduces the classification within an enclosure from Division 2 to nonhazardous.

Class II Hazardous (Classified) Locations: The object of NFPA 496 for Class II locations is to provide information for the design of pressurized enclosures to eliminate within the enclosure a Class II hazardous (classified) location classification, as defined in Article 500 of the *Code*. By this means, equipment that is not otherwise acceptable for hazardous (classified) locations may be utilized in accordance with the *Code*. Pressurization, for the purposes of NFPA 496, may be defined as the process of supplying an enclosure with clean air or an inert gas, with or without continuous flow, at sufficient pressure to prevent the entrance of combustible dust.

It should be noted that an atmosphere made hazardous by combustible dust inside an enclosure cannot be reduced to a safe level by supplying a flow of clean air in the same manner as gases or vapors. The enclosure must be opened and the dust removed. Visual inspection can determine if the dust has been removed. Positive pressure will prevent entrance of a dust into a clean enclosure.

(FPN): It is important that the authority having jurisdiction be familiar with such recorded industrial experience as well as with such standards of the National Fire Protection Association as may be of use in the classification of various areas with respect to hazard.

(FPN): For further information, see Flammable and Combustible Liquids Code, NFPA 30-1981; Drycleaning Plants, NFPA 32-1979; Manufacture of Organic Coatings, NFPA 35-1982 (ANSI); Solvent Extraction Plants, NFPA 36-1983 (ANSI); Storage and Handling of Liquefied Petroleum Gases, NFPA 58-1983; Storage and Handling of Liquefied Petroleum Gases at Utility Gas Plants, NFPA 59-1979; and Classification of Class I Hazardous Locations for Electrical Installations in Chemical Plants, NFPA 497-1975 (ANSI).

(FPN): For protection against static electricity hazards, see Recommended Practice on Static Electricity, NFPA 77-1977 (ANSI).

(FPN): For electrical classification of laboratory areas, see Standard for Fire Protection of Laboratories Using Chemicals, NFPA 45-1982.

All conduit referred to herein shall be threaded with a NPT standard conduit cutting die that provides ¾-inch taper per foot. Such conduit shall be made up wrenchtight to minimize sparking when fault current flows through the conduit system. Where it is impractical to make a threaded joint tight, a bonding jumper shall be utilized.

Care should be exercised if intermediate metal conduit is used, since other than National Pipe Threads may be used on the intermediate metal conduit.

500-2. Special Precaution. Articles 500 through 503 require equipment construction and installation that will ensure safe performance under conditions of proper use and maintenance.

(FPN): It is important that inspection authorities and users exercise more than ordinary care with regard to installation and maintenance.

ARTICLE 500—HAZARDOUS (CLASSIFIED) LOCATIONS

(FPN): The explosion characteristics of air mixtures of gases, vapors, or dusts vary with the specific material involved. For Class I locations, Groups A, B, C, and D, the classification involves determinations of maximum explosion pressure, maximum safe clearance between parts of a clamped joint in an enclosure, and the minimum ignition temperature of the atmospheric mixture. For Class II locations, Groups E and G, the classification involves the tightness of the joints of assembly and shaft openings, to prevent entrance of dust in the dust-ignition-proof enclosure, the blanketing effect of layers of dust on the equipment that may cause overheating, electrical conductivity of the dust, and the ignition temperature of the dust. It is necessary, therefore, that equipment be approved not only for the class, but also for the specific group of the gas, vapor, or dust that will be present.

(FPN): Low ambient conditions require special consideration. Explosionproof or dust-ignition-proof equipment may not be suitable for use at temperatures lower than -25°C (-13°F) unless they are approved for low-temperature service. However at low ambient temperatures flammable concentrations of vapors may not exist in a location classified Class I, Division 1 at normal ambient temperature.

At low ambient temperatures, such as those encountered in the arctic, the strengths of materials change. This is particularly true for some sealing materials. In addition, explosion pressures increase at very low temperatures. However, the extent of the hazardous (classified) location may also change at low ambient conditions, depending on the flash point of the material involved.

(FPN): For purposes of testing, approval, and area classification, various air mixtures (not oxygen-enriched) have been grouped on the basis of their characteristics and facilities have been made available for testing and approving equipment for use in the following atmospheric groups:

Determining the proper group classification for flammable gases and vapors involves a determination of explosion pressures and maximum safe clearance between parts of a clamped joint under several conditions, and comparison of the values obtained with those obtained for presently classified materials under the same test conditions. Although some work has been done on the classification of flammable materials on the basis of chemical structure, the method is not sufficiently refined or accurate to ensure proper classification of all flammable materials.

For additional information on the rationale for classification, reference may be made to the following: "Rationale for Classification of Combustible Gases, Vapors, and Dusts with Reference to the National Electrical Code," Publication NMAB 353-6, 1982, a report of the Committee on Evaluation of Industrial Hazards, The National Materials Advisory Board, Commission on Engineering and Technical Systems, National Research Council. This publication is available from the National Technical Information Service (NTIS), Springfield, VA 22151. "An Investigation of Fifteen Flammable Gases or Vapors with Respect to Explosion-Proof Electrical Equipment," Bulletin of Research No. 58 by Underwriters Laboratories Inc., August 1969 (also Bulletin of Research Nos. 58A and 58B, which supplement No. 58). These are available from Underwriters Laboratories Inc., Publications Stock, 333 Pfingsten Rd., Northbrook, IL 60062.

(FPN): Group A: Atmospheres containing acetylene.

(FPN): Group B: Atmospheres such as butadiene*, ethylene oxide**, propylene oxide**, acrolein**, or hydrogen (or gases or vapors equivalent in hazard to hydrogen, such as manufactured gas).

(FPN): Group C: Atmospheres such as cyclopropane, ethyl ether, ethylene, or gases or vapors of equivalent hazard.

(FPN): Group D: Atmospheres such as acetone, alcohol, ammonia***, benzene, benzol, butane, gasoline, hexane, lacquer solvent vapors, naphtha, natural gas, propane, or gases or vapors of equivalent hazard.

(FPN): *Group D equipment may be used for this atmosphere if such equipment is isolated in accordance with Section 501-5(a) by sealing all conduit ½-inch size or larger.

(FPN): **Group C equipment may be used for this atmosphere if such equipment is isolated in accordance with Section 501-5(a) by sealing all conduit ½-inch size or larger.

(FPN): ***For classification of areas involving ammonia atmosphere, see Safety Code for Mechanical Refrigeration (ANSI/ASHRAE 15-1978) and Safety Requirements for the Storage and Handling of Anhydrous Ammonia (ANSI/CGA G2.1-1972).

(FPN): For a complete list noting properties of flammable liquids, gases, and solids, see Classification of Gases, Vapors and Dusts for Electrical Equipment in Hazardous (Classified) Locations, NFPA 497M-1983.

The following table is reprinted from NFPA 497M-1983. Additional tables in NFPA 497M cover materials with flash points 100°F (37.8°C) and higher.

Group Classification and Autoignition Temperature (AIT) of Selected Flammable Gases and Vapors of Liquids having Flash Points below 100°F (37.8°C).

Material	Group	AIT °F	AIT °C
Acetaldehyde	C*	347	175
Acetone	D*	869	465
Acetonitrile	D	975	524
Acetylene	A*	581	305
Acrolein (inhibited)	B(C)*¹	455	235
Acrylonitrile	D*	898	481
Allyl Alcohol	C*	713	378
Allyl Chloride	D	905	485
Ammonia	D*²	928	498
n-Amyl Acetate	D	680	360
sec-Amyl Acetate	D	—	—
Benzene	D*	1040	560
1,3-Butadiene	B(D)*¹	788	420
Butane	D*	550	288
1-Butanol	D*	650	343
2-Butanol	D*	761	405
n-Butyl Acetate	D*	790	421
iso-Butyl Acetate	D*	790	421
sec-Butyl Acetate	D	—	—
Butylamine	D	594	312
Butylene	D	725	385
Butyl Mercaptan	C	—	—
n-Butyraldehyde	C*	425	218
Carbon Disulfide	-*³	194	90
Carbon Monoxide	C*	1128	609
Chlorobenzene	D	1099	593
Chloroprene	D	—	—
Crotonaldehyde	C*	450	232
Cyclohexane	D	473	245
Cyclohexene	D	471	244
Cyclopropane	D*	938	503
1,1-Dichloroethane	D	820	438
1,2-Dichloroethylene	D	860	460
1,3-Dichloropropene	D	—	—
Dicyclopentadiene	C	937	503
Diethyl Ether	C*	320	160
Diethylamine	C*	594	312
Di-isobutylene	D*	736	391
Di-isopropylamine	C	600	316
Dimethylamine	C	752	400
1,4-Dioxane	C	356	180
Di-n-propylamine	C	570	299
Epichlorohydrin	C*	772	411
Ethane	D*	882	472
Ethanol	D*	685	363

Group Classification and Autoignition Temperature (AIT) (Continued)

Material	Group	AIT °F	AIT °C
Ethyl Acetate	D*	800	427
Ethyl Acrylate (inhibited)	D*	702	372
Ethylamine	D*	725	385
Ethyl Benzene	D	810	432
Ethyl Chloride	D	966	519
Ethylene	C*	842	450
Ethylenediamine	D*	725	385
Ethylene Dichloride	D*	775	413
Ethylenimine	C*	608	320
Ethylene Oxide	B(C)*[1]	804	429
Ethyl Formate	D	851	455
Ethyl Mercaptan	C*	572	300
n-Ethyl Morpholine	C	—	—
Formaldehyde (Gas)	B	795	429
Gasoline	D*	536-880	280-471
Heptane	D*	399	204
Heptene	D	500	260
Hexane	D*	437	225
2-Hexanone	D	795	424
Hexenes	D	473	245
Hydrogen	B*	752	400
Hydrogen Cyanide	C*	1000	538
Hydrogen Selenide	C	—	—
Hydrogen Sulfide	C*	500	260
Isoamyl Acetate	D	680	360
Isoamyl Alcohol	D	662	350
Isobutyl Acrylate	D	800	427
Isobutyraldehyde	C	385	196
Isoprene	D*	743	395
Isopropyl Acetate	D	860	460
Isopropylamine	D	756	402
Isopropyl Ether	D*	830	443
Isopropyl Glycidyl Ether	C	—	—
Liquefied Petroleum Gas	D	761-842	405-450
Manufactured Gas (containing more than 30% H_2 by volume)	B*	—	—
Mesityl Oxide	D*	652	344
Methane	D*	999	537
Methanol	D*	725	385
Methyl Acetate	D	850	454
Methylacetylene	C*	—	—
Methylacetylene-Propadiene (stabilized)	C	—	—
Methyl Acrylate	D	875	468
Methylamine	D	806	430
Methylcyclohexane	D	482	250
Methyl Ether	C*	662	350
Methyl Ethyl Ketone	D*	759	404
Methyl Formal	C*	460	238
Methyl Formate	D	840	449
Methyl Isobutyl Ketone	D*	840	440
Methyl Isocyanate	D	994	534
Methyl Mercaptan	C	—	—
Methyl Methacrylate	D	792	422
2-Methyl-l-Propanol	D*	780	416
2-Methyl-2-Propanol	D*	892	478
Monomethyl Hydrazine	C	382	194
Naphtha (Petroleum)	D*[4]	550	288
Nitroethane	C	778	414
Nitromethane	C	785	418
Nonane	D	401	205
Nonene	D	—	—
Octane	D*	403	206
Octene	D	446	230
Pentane	D*	470	243

Group Classification and Autoignition Temperature (AIT) (Continued)

Material	Group	AIT °F	AIT °C
1-Pentanol	D*	572	300
2-Pentanone	D	846	452
1-Pentene	D	527	275
Propane	D*	842	450
1-Propanol	D*	775	413
2-Propanol	D*	750	399
Propionaldehyde	C	405	207
n-Propyl Acetate	D	842	450
Propylene	D*	851	455
Propylene Dichloride	D	1035	557
Propylene Oxide	B(C)*[1]	840	449
n-Propyl Ether	C*	419	215
Propyl Nitrate	B*	347	175
Pyridine	D*	900	482
Styrene	D*	914	490
Tetrahydrofuran	C*	610	321
Toluene	D*	896	480
Triethylamine	C*	—	—
Tripropylamine	D	—	—
Turpentine	D	488	253
Unsymmetrical Dimethyl Hydrazine (UDMH)	C*	480	249
Valeraldehyde	C	432	222
Vinyl Acetate	D*	756	402
Vinyl Chloride	D*	882	472
Vinylidene Chloride	D	1058	570
Xylenes	D*	867-984	464-529

Notes To Table

*Material has been classified by test.

[1]If equipment is isolated by sealing all conduit ½ in. or larger, in accordance with Section 501-5(a) of NFPA 70, *National Electrical Code,* equipment for the group classification shown in parentheses is permitted.

[2]For classification of areas involving Ammonia, see *Safety Code for Mechanical Refrigeration,* ANSI/ASHRAE 15, and *Safety Requirements for the Storage and Handling of Anhydrous Ammonia,* ANSI/CGA G2.1

[3]Certain chemicals may have characteristics that require safeguards beyond those required for any of the above groups. Carbon disulfide is one of these chemicals because of its low autoignition temperature and the small joint clearance to arrest its flame propagation.

[4]Petroleum Naphtha is a saturated hydrocarbon mixture whose boiling range is 20° to 135°C. It is also known as benzine, ligroin, petroleum ether, and naphtha.

References: Autoignition temperatures listed above are the lowest value for each material as listed in NFPA 325M, *Fire Hazard Properties of Flammable Liquids, Gases, and Volatile Solids,* or as reported in an article by Hilado, C.J. and Clark, S.W., in *Chemical Engineering,* September 4, 1972.

(FPN): Group E: Atmospheres containing combustible metal dusts regardless of resistivity, or other combustible dusts of similarly hazardous characteristics having resistivity of less than 10^5 ohm-centimeter.

(FPN): Group G: Atmospheres containing combustible dusts having resistivity of 10^5 ohm-centimeter or greater.

(FPN): Equipment approved for Group F, but not for Group E, in accordance with earlier editions of this Code, is not suitable for use in Group E locations where the hazard is caused by the presence of metal dusts. Such equipment is suitable for use in Group E locations where the hazard is caused by the presence of carbonaceous dusts.

(FPN): For materials which were previously classified in Group F, see Classification of Gases, Vapors, and Dusts for Electrical Equipment in Hazardous (Classified) Locations, NFPA 497M-1983. Atmospheres containing carbon black, charcoal, coal or coke dusts which have more than 8 percent total volatile material (carbon black per ASTM D1620, charcoal, coal and coke dusts per ASTM D271) or atmospheres containing these dusts sensitized by other materials so that they present an explosion hazard may be Groups E or G depending on their resistivity.

The following table is part of Table 3-5 in NFPA 497M-1983. For the complete table and information on Group E dusts, see NFPA 497M.

Selected Nonconductive Dusts Classified as Group G—Ignition Sensitivity Equal to or Greater than 0.2; Explosion Severity Equal to or Greater than 0.5.

Material	°F	Minimum Cloud or Layer Ignition Temp.[1]	°C
AGRICULTURAL DUSTS			
Alfalfa Meal	392		200
Cellulose	500		260
Cinnamon	446		230
Cocoa, natural, 19% fat	464		240
Corn	482		250
Corncob Grit	464		240
Corn Dextrine	698		370
Cornstarch, commercial	626		330
Cork	410		210
Cottonseed Meal	392		200
Garlic, dehydrated	680	NL	360
Malt Barley	482		250
Milk, Skimmed	392		200
Potato Starch, Dextrinated	824	NL	440
Rice	428		220
Rice Bran	914	NL	490
Rice Hull	428		220
Safflower Meal	410		210
Soy Flour	374		190
Soy Protein	500		260
Sucrose	662	Cl	350
Sugar, Powdered	698	Cl	370
Wheat	428		220
Wheat Flour	680		360
Wheat Starch	716	NL	380
Wheat Straw	428		220
Woodbark, Ground	482		250
Wood Flour	500		260
Yeast, Torula	500		260
CARBONACEOUS DUSTS			
Charcoal[2]	356		180
Coal, Kentucky Bituminous[2]	356		180
Coal, Pittsburgh Experimental[2]	338		170
Lignite, California[2]	356		180
Pitch, Coal Tar	1310	NL	710
Pitch, Petroleum	1166	NL	630
CHEMICALS			
Acetoacetanilide	824	M	440
Adipic Acid	1022	M	550
Anthranilic Acid	1076	M	580
Azelaic Acid	1130	M	610
2,2-Azo-bis-butyronitrile	662		350
Benzoic Acid	824	M	440
Benzotriazole	824	M	440
Bisphenol-A	1058	M	570
Chloroacetoacetanilide	1184	M	640
Diallyl Phthalate	896	M	480
Dihydroacetic Acid	806	NL	430
Dimethyl Isophthalate	1076	M	580
Dimethyl Terephthalate	1058	M	570
3,5-Dinitrobenzoic Acid	860	NL	460
Diphenyl	1166	M	630
Ethyl Hydroxyethyl Cellulose	734	NL	390

Selected Nonconductive Dusts Classified as Group G (Continued)

Material	°F	Minimum Cloud or Layer Ignition Temp.[1]	°C
Fumaric Acid	968	M	520
Hexamethylene Tetramine	770	S	410
Hydroxyethyl Cellulose	770	NL	410
Isotoic Anhydride	1292	NL	700
Paraphenylene Diamine	1148	M	620
Paratertiary Butyl Benzoic Acid	1040	M	560
Pentaerythritol	752	M	400
Phthalic Anhydride	1202	M	650
Salicylanilide	1130	M	610
Sorbic Acid	860		460
Stearic Acid, Aluminum Salt	572		300
Stearic Acid, Zinc Salt	950	M	510
Sulfur	428		220
Terephthalic Acid	1256	NL	680
DRUGS			
Aspirin	1220	M	660
Gulasonic Acid, Diacetone	788	NL	420
Mannitol	860	M	460
l-Sorbose	698	M	370
Vitamin B1, mononitrate	680	NL	360
Vitamin C (Ascorbic Acid)	536		280
DYES, PIGMENTS, INTERMEDIATES			
Green Base Harmon Dye	347		175
Red Dye Intermediate	347		175
Violet 200 Dye	347		175
PESTICIDES			
Crag No. 974	590	Cl	310
Dieldrin (20%)	1022	NL	550
Dithane	356		180
Ferbam	302		150
Manganese Vancide	248		120
Sevin	284		140
THERMOPLASTIC RESINS AND MOLDING COMPOUNDS			
Acetal Resins			
Acetal, Linear (Polyformaldehyde)	824	NL	440
Acrylic Resins			
Acrylamide Polymer	464		240
Acrylonitrile Polymer	860		460
Acrylonitrile-Vinyl Chloride-Vinylidene Chloride Copolymer (70-20-10)	410		210
Methyl Methacrylate Polymer	824	NL	440
Methyl Methacrylate-Ethyl Acrylate Copolymer	896	NL	480
Methyl Methacrylate-Ethyl Acrylate-Styrene Copolymer	824	NL	440
Methyl Methacrylate-Styrene-Butadiene-Acrylonitrile Copolymer	896	NL	480
Methacrylic Acid Polymer	554		290
Cellulosic Resins			
Cellulose Acetate	644		340
Cellulose Triacetate	806	NL	430
Cellulose Acetate Butyrate	698	NL	370
Nylon (Polyamide) Resins			
Nylon Polymer (Polyhexa-methylene Adipamide)	806		430
Polycarbonate Resins			
Polycarbonate	1310	NL	710
Polyethylene Resins			
Polyethylene, High Pressure Process	716		380
Polyethylene, Low Pressure Process	788	NL	420
Polyethylene Wax	752	NL	400
Polymethylene Resins			
Carboxypolymethylene	968	NL	520

Selected Nonconductive Dusts Classified as Group G (Continued)

Material	Minimum Cloud or Layer Ignition Temp.[1]		
	°F		°C
Polypropylene Resins			
Polypropylene (No Antioxidant)	788	NL	420
Rayon Resins			
Rayon (Viscose) Flock	482		250
Styrene Resins			
Polystyrene Molding Cmpd.	1040	NL	560
Polystyrene Latex	932		500
Styrene-Acrylonitrile (70-30)	932	NL	500
Styrene-Butadiene Latex (> 75% Styrene; Alum Coagulated)	824	NL	440
Vinyl Resins			
Polyvinyl Acetate	1022	NL	550
Polyvinyl Acetate/Alcohol	824		440
Vinyl Chloride-Acrylonitrile Copolymer	878		470
Vinyl Toluene-Acrylonitrile Butadiene Copolymer	936	NL	530
THERMOSETTING RESINS AND MOLDING COMPOUNDS			
Allyl Resins			
Allyl Alcohol Derivative (CR-39)	932	NL	500
Amino Resins			
Urea Formaldehyde Molding Compound	860	NL	460
Urea Formaldehyde-Phenol Formaldehyde Molding Compound (Wood Flour Filler)	464		240
Epoxy Resins			
Epoxy	1004	NL	540
Epoxy-Bisphenol A	950	NL	510
Phenolic Resins			
Phenol Formaldehyde	1076	NL	580
Phenol Formaldehyde Molding Cmpd. (Wood Flour Filler)	932	NL	500
Polyester Resins			
Polyethylene Terephthalate	932	NL	500
Styrene Modified Polyester-Glass Fiber Mixture	680		360
Polyurethane Resins			
Polyurethane Foam, No Fire Retardant	824		440
SPECIAL RESINS AND MOLDING COMPOUNDS			
Ethylene Oxide Polymer	662	NL	350
Ethylene-Maleic Anhydride Copolymer	1004	NL	540
Petroleum Resin (Blown Asphalt)	932		500
Rubber, Crude, Hard	662	NL	350
Rubber, Synthetic, Hard (33% S)	608	NL	320

Notes to Table

[1]Normally, the minimum ignition temperature of a layer of a specific dust is lower than the minimum ignition temperature of a cloud of that dust. Since this is not universally true, the lower of the two minimum ignition temperatures is listed. If no symbol appears between the two temperature columns, then the layer ignition temperature is shown. "Cl" means the cloud ignition temperature is shown. "NL" means that no layer ignition temperature is available and the cloud ignition temperature is shown. "M" signifies that the dust layer melts before it ignites; the cloud ignition temperature is shown. "S" signifies that the dust layer sublimes before it ignites; the cloud ignition temperature is shown.

[2]These materials may be classified in Group E, depending on their resistivity.

(FPN): 1. Certain chemical atmospheres may have characteristics that require safeguards beyond those required for any of the above groups. Carbon disulfide is one of these chemicals because of its low ignition temperature, 100°C (212°F), and the small joint clearance to arrest its flame.

(FPN): 2. Certain metal dusts may have characteristics that require safeguards beyond those required for atmospheres containing the dusts of aluminum, magnesium, and their commercial alloys. For example, zirconium, thorium and uranium dusts have extremely low ignition temperatures [as low as 20°C (68°F)], and minimum ignition energies lower than any material classified in any of the Class I or Class II Groups.

(FPN): 3. Certain dusts may require additional precautions due to chemical phenomena that can result in the generation of ignitible gases. See National Electrical Safety Code (ANSI C2-1981), Section 127A-Coal Handling Areas.

(FPN): For a complete list noting properties of flammable liquids, gases and solids, see Fire Hazard Properties of Flammable Liquids, Gases, and Volatile Solids, NFPA 325M-1977.

Publication NMAB 353-4, "Classifications of Dusts Relative to Electrical Equipment in Class II Hazardous Locations," published in 1982 by the Committee on Evaluation of Industrial Hazards, National Materials Advisory Board, Commission on Engineering and Technical Systems, National Research Council, National Academy of Sciences, includes a description of test methods to determine the ignition temperatures and electrical resistivity of combustible dusts. The publication is available from the National Technical Information Service (NTIS), Springfield, VA 22151.

(a) Approval for Class and Properties. Equipment shall be approved not only for the class of location but also for the explosive, combustible, or ignitible properties of the specific gas, vapor, dust, fiber, or flyings that will be present. In addition, Class I equipment shall not have any exposed surface that operates at a temperature in excess of the ignition temperature of the specific gas or vapor. Class II equipment shall not have an external temperature higher than that specified in Section 500-2(d). Class III equipment shall not exceed the maximum surface temperatures specified in Section 503-1.

Equipment that has been approved for a Division 1 location shall be permitted in a Division 2 location of the same class and group.

Where specifically permitted in Articles 501 through 503, general-purpose equipment or equipment in general-purpose enclosures shall be permitted to be installed in Division 2 locations if the equipment does not constitute a source of ignition under normal operating conditions.

Unless otherwise specified, normal operating conditions for motors shall be assumed to be rated full-load steady conditions.

It is not intended that locked-rotor or other motor overload conditions be considered when evaluating motor operating temperatures in Class I, Division 2 locations. However, abnormal load conditions are considered when evaluating explosionproof motors for Class I, Division 1 locations and motors for Class II locations, such as dust-ignition-proof motors.

Where flammable gases or combustible dusts are or may be present at the same time, the simultaneous presence of both shall be considered when determining the safe operating temperature of the electrical equipment.

For example, coal-handling facilities where methane gas and coal dust may be present at the same time.

(FPN): The characteristics of various atmospheric mixtures of gases, vapors, and dusts depend on the specific material involved.

(b) Marking. Approved equipment shall be marked to show the Class, Group, and operating temperature or temperature range referenced to a 40°C ambient.

It should be noted that the marked operating temperature or temperature range is referenced to a 40°C (104°F) ambient. Unless the equipment is provided with thermally actuated sensors which limit the temperature to that marked on the equipment, operation in ambient temperatures higher than 40°C (104°F) will probably increase the operating temperature of the equipment. Many explosion-proof and dust-ignition-proof motors are equipped with thermal protectors. In a like manner, operation in ambient temperatures lower than 40°C (104°F) will usually reduce the operating temperature.

The temperature range, if provided, shall be indicated in identification numbers, as shown in Table 500-2(b).

Identification numbers marked on equipment nameplates shall be in accordance with Table 500-2(b).

Equipment which is approved for Class I and Class II shall be marked with the maximum safe operating temperature, as determined by simultaneous exposure to the combinations of Class I and Class II conditions.

Exception No. 1: Equipment of the nonheat-producing type, such as junction boxes, conduit, and fittings and equipment of the heat-producing type having a maximum temperature not more than 100°C (212°F), shall not be required to have a marked operating temperature or temperature range.

Exception No. 2: Fixed lighting fixtures marked for use in Class I, Division 2 or Class II, Division 2 locations only need not be marked to indicate the group.

Exception No. 3: Fixed general-purpose equipment in Class I locations, other than fixed lighting fixtures, which is acceptable for use in Class I, Division 2 locations shall not be required to be marked with the Class, Group, Division or operating temperature.

An example of such equipment is a squirrel-cage induction motor without brushes, switching mechanisms, or similar arc-producing devices. See the second paragraph of Section 501-8(b).

Exception No. 4: Fixed dusttight equipment other than fixed lighting fixtures which are acceptable for use in Class II, Division 2 and Class III locations shall not be required to be marked with the Class, Group, Division or operating temperature.

(FPN): For purposes of testing and approval, various atmospheric mixtures (not oxygen-enriched) have been grouped on the basis of their characteristics, and facilities have been made available for testing and approving equipment for use in the atmospheric groups listed in Classification of Gases, Vapors, and Dusts for Electrical Equipment in Hazardous (Classified) Locations, NFPA 497M-1983. Since there is no consistent relationship between explosion properties and ignition temperature, the two are independent requirements.

Table 500-2(b). Identification Numbers

Maximum Temperature		Identification
Degrees C	Degrees F	Number
450	842	T1
300	572	T2
280	536	T2A
260	500	T2B
230	446	T2C
215	419	T2D
200	392	T3
180	356	T3A
165	329	T3B
160	320	T3C
135	275	T4
120	248	T4A
100	212	T5
85	185	T6

(c) **Class I Temperature.** The temperature marking specified in (b) above shall not exceed the ignition temperature of the specific gas or vapor to be encountered.

The ignition temperature of a solid, liquid, or gaseous substance is the minimum temperature required to initiate or cause self-sustained combustion independent of the heating or heated element.

(FPN): For information regarding ignition temperatures of gases and vapors, see Classification of Gases, Vapors, and Dusts for Electrical Equipment in Hazardous (Classified) Locations, NFPA 497M-1983, and Fire Hazard Properties of Flammable Liquids, Gases, and Volatile Solids, NFPA 325M-1977.

Formerly the temperature limit of each Group was assumed to be the lowest ignition temperature of any material in the Group, i.e., 280°C for Group D, 180°C for Group C.

(FPN): To avoid revising this limit as new gases are added (see hexane in Group D and acetaldehyde in Group C), temperature will be specified in future markings.

The ignition temperature for which equipment was approved prior to this requirement shall be assumed to be as follows:

Group A — 280°C (536°F)   Group C — 180°C (356°F)
Group B — 280°C (536°F)   Group D — 280°C (536°F)

Maximum surface temperatures for equipment in Class II locations are covered in Section 502-1.

The preceding information on ignition temperatures for Class I materials was added as a Tentative Interim Amendment to the 1968 edition of the *NEC* and has been part of the *Code* since the 1971 edition. Listed or labeled heat-producing equipment, such as lighting fixtures and motors, manufactured before circa 1975 may not be marked with the operating temperature or temperature range. Unless the actual operating temperatures are marked on the equipment or are otherwise known, the intent is that the operating temperatures noted above be assumed. For multiple rated equipment (e.g., Class I, Groups C and D), the lowest operating temperature [180°C (356°F)] may be assumed.

Flammable gases or vapors are separated into four different atmospheric groups: Groups A, B, C, and D. It is to be noted that *Code* requirements for Class I locations do not vary for different kinds of gas or vapor contained in the atmosphere except in those cases where seals may be used in all conduits to change the group classification. See the Fine Print Notes to Section 500-2 on materials such as butadiene and ethylene oxide. It is necessary to select equipment that is designed for use in the particular group involved; however, equipment may be listed for use in Class I, Group D or use in Class I, Group C, etc. The reason for designating the groups in this way is that explosive mixtures have different explosion pressures and maximum safe clearances between parts of a joint in an enclosure.

Underwriters Laboratories Inc. and Factory Mutual Research Corp. list or "approve" electrical equipment suitable for use in all groups of Class I locations and further information is available from the UL Hazardous Locations Equipment Directory and FM Approval Guide. It is to be noted (from the UL Directory) that "only those products bearing the appropriate Listing Mark and the company's name, trade name, trademark, or other recognized identification should be considered as covered by UL's Listing and Follow-Up Service."

(d) Class II Temperature. The surface temperature marking specified in (b) above shall be less than the ignition temperature of the specific dust and in no case shall it be greater than the temperature given below for Groups E and G. (See Classification of Gases, Vapors, and Dusts for Electrical Equipment in Hazardous (Classified) Locations, NFPA 497M-1983 for minimum ignition temperatures of specific dusts.)

The maximum surface temperature for which equipment was approved prior to this requirement shall be assumed to be as follows:

Class II Group	Equipment that Is Not Subject to Overloading		Equipment (such as Motors or Power Transformers) that May Be Overloaded			
			Normal Operation		Abnormal Operation	
	Degrees C	Degrees F	Degrees C	Degrees F	Degrees C	Degrees F
E	200	392	200	392	200	392
F	200	392	150	302	200	392
G	165	329	120	248	165	329

Class II locations are hazardous because of the presence of combustible dust. Prior to the 1984 *NEC*, combustible dusts were separated into three different groups: Groups E, F, and G. Combustible dusts are now separated into two different groups based on the electrical resistivity of the dust: Groups E and G (see Fine Print Notes following Section 500-2). Group E includes aluminum and magnesium metal dusts, which are electrically conductive. It may include some carbonaceous dusts, depending on their resistivity. Group G includes nonconductive carbonacous dusts and dusts from flour, starch, grain, or combustible plastics or chemicals. See commentary and tables following Sections 500-2 and 502-1.

As in Class I locations, equipment must be approved not only for the "class" but also for the specific "group." It is important that in addition to the proper selection of equipment, high standards of installation be maintained for subsequent additions or alterations.

The NFPA and ANSI standards referenced in Articles 500 through 517 should be obtained for more information on specific hazardous (classified) locations.

The following NFPA standards include information on the extent of hazardous (classified) locations in specific occupancies or industries.

NFPA No.	Title of Standard	NFPA No.	Title of Standard
30	Flammable and Combustible Liquids Code	56A	Inhalation Anesthetics
32	Dry Cleaning Plants	56C	Laboratories in Health-Related Facilities
33	Spray Application Using Flammable and Combustible Materials	56D	Hyperbaric Facilities
		56E	Hypobaric Facilities
34	Dip Tanks	56F	Nonflammable Medical Gas Systems
35	Manufacture of Organic Coatings	58	Liquefied Petroleum Gases, Storage and Handling of
36	Solvent Extraction		
40	Cellulose Nitrate Motion Picture Film, Storage and Handling of	59	Liquefied Petroleum Gases at Utility Gas Plants
44A	Fireworks Code, Manufacture, Transportation and Storage of	59A	Liquefied Natural Gas, Storage and Handling
48	Magnesium Storage, Handling	61A	Manufacturing and Handling Starch
50A	Gaseous Hydrogen Systems	61B	Grain Elevators, Bulk Handling Facilities
50B	Liquefied Hydrogen Systems at Consumer Sites	61C	Feed Mills, Dust Explosion Prevention
51	Welding and Cutting, Oxygen-Fuel Gas System for	61D	Agricultural Commodities for Human Consumption
51A	Acetylene Cylinder Charging Plants	65	Aluminum Processing and Finishing
		81	Fur Storage, Cleaning

NFPA No.	Title of Standard	NFPA No.	Title of Standard
85D	Fuel Oil-Fired Multiple Burner Boiler-Furnaces		Enclosures for Electrical Equipment
88A	Parking Structures	497	Class I Hazardous Locations for Electrical Installations in Chemical Plants
88B	Repair Garages		
407	Aircraft Fueling Servicing		
409	Aircraft Hangars		
481	Titanium Storage, Handling	651	Aluminum or Magnesium Powder, for the Manufacture of
493	Intrinsically Safe Process Control Equipment		
495	Explosive Materials, Manufacturer, Transportation, Storage and Use of	653	Coal Preparation Plants, Dust Hazards
		654	Plastics Industry, Dust Hazards
		655	Sulfur Fires, Explosions, Prevention
496	Purged and Pressurized		

500-3. Specific Occupancies. Articles 510 through 517 cover garages, aircraft hangars, gasoline dispensing and service stations, bulk storage plants, finishing processes, and health care facilities.

500-4. Class I Locations. Class I locations are those in which flammable gases or vapors are or may be present in the air in quantities sufficient to produce explosive or ignitible mixtures. Class I locations shall include those specified in (a) and (b) below.

(a) Class I, Division 1. A Class I, Division 1 location is a location: (1) in which ignitible concentrations of flammable gases or vapors can exist under normal operating conditions; or (2) in which ignitible concentrations of such gases or vapors may exist frequently because of repair or maintenance operations or because of leakage; or (3) in which breakdown or faulty operation of equipment or processes might release ignitible concentrations of flammable gases or vapors, and might also cause simultaneous failure of electric equipment.

(FPN): This classification usually includes locations where volatile flammable liquids or liquefied flammable gases are transferred from one container to another; interiors of spray booths and areas in the vicinity of spraying and painting operations where volatile flammable solvents are used; locations containing open tanks or vats of volatile flammable liquids; drying rooms or compartments for the evaporation of flammable solvents; locations containing fat and oil extraction equipment using volatile flammable solvents; portions of cleaning and dyeing plants where flammable liquids are used; gas generator rooms and other portions of gas manufacturing plants where flammable gas may escape; inadequately ventilated pump rooms for flammable gas or for volatile flammable liquids; the interiors of refrigerators and freezers in which volatile flammable materials are stored in open, lightly stoppered, or easily ruptured containers; and all other locations where ignitible concentrations of flammable vapors or gases are likely to occur in the course of normal operations.

(b) Class I, Division 2. A Class I, Division 2 location is a location: (1) in which volatile flammable liquids or flammable gases are handled, processed, or used, but in which the liquids, vapors, or gases will normally be confined within closed containers or closed systems from which they can escape only in case of accidental rupture or breakdown of such containers or systems, or in case of abnormal operation of equipment; or (2) in which ignitible concentrations of gases or vapors are normally prevented by positive mechanical ventilation, and which might become hazardous through failure or abnormal operation of the ventilating equipment; or (3) that is adjacent to a Class I, Division 1 location, and to which ignitible concentrations of gases or vapors might occasionally be communicated unless such communication is prevented by adequate positive-pressure ventilation from a source of clean air, and effective safeguards against ventilation failure are provided.

ARTICLE 500—HAZARDOUS (CLASSIFIED) LOCATIONS

(FPN): This classification usually includes locations where volatile flammable liquids or flammable gases or vapors are used, but which, in the judgment of the authority having jurisdiction, would become hazardous only in case of an accident or of some unusual operating condition. The quantity of flammable material that might escape in case of accident, the adequacy of ventilating equipment, the total area involved, and the record of the industry or business with respect to explosions or fires are all factors that merit consideration in determining the classification and extent of each location.

(FPN): Piping without valves, checks, meters, and similar devices would not ordinarily introduce a hazardous condition even though used for flammable liquids or gases. Locations used for the storage of flammable liquids or of liquefied or compressed gases in sealed containers would not normally be considered hazardous unless subject to other hazardous conditions also.

Electrical conduits and their associated enclosures separated from process fluids by a single seal or barrier shall be classed as a Division 2 location if the outside of the conduit and enclosures is a nonhazardous location.

500-5. Class II Locations. Class II locations are those that are hazardous because of the presence of combustible dust. Class II locations shall include those specified in (a) and (b) below.

(a) Class II, Division 1. A Class II, Division 1 location is a location: (1) in which combustible dust is in the air under normal operating conditions in quantities sufficient to produce explosive or ignitible mixtures; or (2) where mechanical failure or abnormal operation of machinery or equipment might cause such explosive or ignitible mixtures to be produced, and might also provide a source of ignition through simultaneous failure of electric equipment, operation of protection devices, or from other causes; or (3) in which combustible dusts of an electrically conductive nature may be present in hazardous quantities.

(FPN): Combustible dusts which are electrically nonconductive include dusts produced in the handling and processing of grain and grain products, pulverized sugar and cocoa, dried egg and milk powders, pulverized spices, starch and pastes, potato and woodflour, oil meal from beans and seed, dried hay, and other organic materials which may produce combustible dusts when processed or handled. Electrically conductive dusts are dusts with a resistivity less than 10^5 ohm-centimeter. Dusts containing magnesium or aluminum are particularly hazardous and the use of extreme precaution will be necessary to avoid ignition and explosion.

(b) Class II, Division 2. A Class II Division 2 location is a location where combustible dust is not normally in the air in quantities sufficient to produce explosive or ignitible mixtures, and dust accumulations are normally insufficient to interfere with the normal operation of electrical equipment or other apparatus, but combustible dust may be in suspension in the air as a result of infrequent malfunctioning of handling or processing equipment and where combustible dust accumulations on, in, or in the vicinity of the electrical equipment may be sufficient to interfere with the safe dissipation of heat from electrical equipment or may be ignitible by abnormal operation or failure of electrical equipment.

(FPN): The quantity of combustible dust that may be present and the adequacy of dust removal systems are factors that merit consideration in determining the classification and may result in an unclassified area.

(FPN): Where products such as seed are handled in a manner which produces low quantities of dust, the amount of dust deposited may not warrant classification.

500-6. Class III Locations. Class III locations are those that are hazardous because of the presence of easily ignitible fibers or flyings, but in which such fibers or flyings are not likely to be in suspension in the air in quantities sufficient to produce ignitible mixtures. Class III locations shall include those specified in (a) and (b) below.

(a) Class III, Division 1. A Class III, Division 1 location is a location in which easily ignitible fibers or materials producing combustible flyings are handled, manufactured, or used.

(FPN): Such locations usually include some parts of rayon, cotton, and other textile mills; combustible fiber manufacturing and processing plants; cotton gins and cotton-seed mills; flax-processing plants; clothing manufacturing plants; woodworking plants; and establishments and industries involving similar hazardous processes or conditions.

(FPN): Easily ignitible fibers and flyings include rayon, cotton (including cotton linters and cotton waste), sisal or henequen, istle, jute, hemp, tow, cocoa fiber, oakum, baled waste kapok, Spanish moss, excelsior, and other materials of similar nature.

(b) Class III, Division 2. A Class III, Division 2 location is a location in which easily ignitible fibers are stored or handled.

Exception: In process of manufacture.

Sections 500-4, 500-5, and 500-6 recognize three classes of hazardous (classified) locations with varying degrees of hazards, and each class is then subdivided into two divisions. The requirements for Division 1 of each class are more stringent than those for Division 2.

Briefly, the hazards of the three classes are defined as follows: Class I, flammable gases or vapors; Class II, combustible dust; and Class III, combustible fibers or flyings.

When a given location is classified as hazardous, it should not be difficult to determine in which of the three classes it belongs; however, when it is unknown whether a location is definitely hazardous, it would be difficult to apply rules to an area that may, because of a change in process or material, become hazardous. In this case common sense and good judgment must prevail in classifying an area that is likely to become hazardous and in determining those portions of the premises to be classed Division 1 or Division 2.

ARTICLE 501 — CLASS I LOCATIONS

Contents

ARTICLE 501—CLASS I LOCATIONS

501-14. Signaling, Alarm, Remote-Control, and Communication Systems.
  (a) Class I, Division 1.
  (b) Class I, Division 2.
501-15. Live Parts, Class I, Divisions 1 and 2.

501-16. Grounding, Class I, Divisions 1 and 2.
  (a) Bonding.
  (b) Types of Equipment Grounding Conductors.
501-17. Surge Protection, Class I, Divisions 1 and 2.

501-1. General. The general rules of this Code shall apply to the electric wiring and equipment in locations classified as Class I in Section 500-4.

Exception: As modified by this article.

The more common Class I locations are those areas involved in the handling or processing of volatile flammable liquids such as gasoline, naphtha, benzene, diethyl ether, and acetone, or flammable gases such as hydrogen, methane, and propane.

Where ignitible concentrations (concentrations within the flammable or explosive limits) of flammable gases or vapors are present, atmospheres that are explosive when ignited by an arc, a spark, or high temperature exist. NFPA 325M includes information on the explosive limits of flammable liquids, gases, and volatile solids. All electrical equipment that may cause ignition-capable arcs or sparks should be kept out of Class I locations where practicable. If this is not practicable, such apparatus must be approved for the purpose and installed properly. The arc produced at the contacts of listed or labeled intrinsically safe equipment is not ignition-capable because the energy available is insufficient to cause ignition.

Hermetic sealing of all electric equipment is impractical because equipment such as motors, switches, and circuit breakers have movable parts that must be operated through the enclosing case, that is, the lever of a switch or the shaft of a motor must have sufficient clearance to operate freely. In addition, in many cases it is necessary to have access to the inside of enclosures for installation, servicing, or alterations.

It is practically impossible to make threaded conduit joints gastight. The conduit system and apparatus enclosure "breathe" due to temperature changes, and any flammable gases or vapors in the room may slowly enter the conduit or enclosure creating an explosive mixture. Should an arc occur, an explosion could take place.

When an explosion occurs within the enclosure or conduit system, the burning mixture, or hot gases, must be sufficiently confined within the system to prevent ignition of any explosive mixture that might be present in the room. An apparatus enclosure must be designed with sufficient strength to withstand the maximum pressure that can be generated by an internal explosion in order to prevent rupture and the release of burning or hot gases. Enclosures can and have been designed to withstand such internal explosions. Such enclosures are "explosionproof."

It has been found that during an explosion within an enclosure gases will escape through any paths or openings that exist, but that the gases will be sufficiently cooled where carried out through an opening that is long in proportion to its width; that is, the spiral path of at least five fully engaged threads of a screwed-on junction box cover, as illustrated in Figure 501-1. This principle is also applied in the design of explosionproof enclosures for apparatus by providing a wide machined flange on the body of the enclosure and a similar machined flange on the cover. These machined flanges are so ground that, when the cover is seated in place, the clearance between the two surfaces will at no point exceed, for example, 0.0015 in. If an explosion occurs within the enclosure, escaping gas travels a considerable distance through a very small opening. It is, therefore, sufficiently cooled when it enters and mixes with the surrounding atmosphere that ignition of the external explosive mixture cannot occur.

The clearance between flat surfaces may increase somewhat under explosion conditions because the internal pressures created by the explosion tend to force the surfaces apart. The amount of increase in the joint clearance depends on the "stiffness" of the enclosure parts, the size, strength, and spacing of the bolts, and the explosion pressure. See Figure 501-2. Simply measuring the joint width and clearance when there are no internal pressures will not indicate what the clearances will be under the dynamic conditions of an explosion. Actual explosion tests are usually needed to demonstrate the acceptability of the design.

Figure 501-1. An explosionproof junction box with a screw-type cover.

Figure 501-2. Effect of internal explosion on cover-to-body joint clearance in explosionproof enclosure. (*Underwriters Laboratories Inc.*)

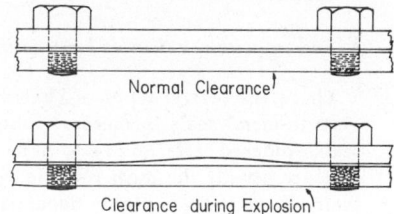

501-2. Transformers and Capacitors.

(a) Class I, Division 1. In Class I, Division 1 locations, transformers and capacitors shall comply with the following:

(1) Containing Liquid that Will Burn. Transformers and capacitors containing a liquid that will burn shall be installed only in approved vaults that comply with Sections 450-41 through 450-48, and in addition: (1) there shall be no door or other communicating opening between the vault and the Division 1 location; and (2) ample ventilation shall be provided for the continuous removal of flammable gases or vapors; and (3) vent openings or ducts shall lead to a safe location outside of buildings; and (4) vent ducts and openings shall be of sufficient area to relieve explosion pressures within the vault, and all portions of vent ducts within the buildings shall be of reinforced concrete construction.

(2) Not Containing Liquid that Will Burn. Transformers and capacitors that do not contain a liquid that will burn shall: (1) be installed in vaults complying with (a)(1) above, or (2) be approved for Class I locations.

(b) Class I, Division 2. In Class I, Division 2 locations, transformers and capacitors shall comply with Sections 450-21 through 450-27.

501-3. Meters, Instruments, and Relays.

(a) Class I, Division 1. In Class I, Division 1 locations, meters, instruments, and relays, including kilowatt-hour meters, instrument transformers, resistors, rectifiers, and thermionic tubes, shall be provided with enclosures approved for Class I, Division 1 locations.

> See the comments on purged and pressurized enclosures for electrical equipment in hazardous (classified) locations following the Fine Print Notes in Section 500-1 and the comments on explosionproof enclosures following the exception to Section 501-1.

Enclosures approved for Class I, Division 1 locations include: (1) explosionproof enclosures, and (2) purged and pressurized enclosures. See NFPA 496-1982 (ANSI), Purged and Pressurized Enclosures for Electrical Equipment in Hazardous Locations.

(b) Class I, Division 2. In Class I, Division 2 locations, meters, instruments, and relays shall comply with the following:

(1) Contacts. Switches, circuit breakers, and make-and-break contacts of pushbuttons, relays, alarm bells, and horns shall have enclosures approved for Class I, Division 1 locations in accordance with (a) above.

Exception: General-purpose enclosures shall be permitted, if current-interrupting contacts are:

a. Immersed in oil; or,

b. Enclosed within a chamber hermetically sealed against the entrance of gases or vapors; or,

> There are several types of "hermetic" seals, including fusion seals such as the glass-to-metal seals in mercury tube switches and some "reed" switches, welded seals, soldered seals, and seals made with gaskets. Seals of the glass-to-metal fusion type are usually the most reliable. Soft solder seals can be relatively porous, and their effectiveness is highly dependent on workmanship. Although gasketed seals can be very effective, depending on the gasket material used, gasket materials are easily damaged and can deteriorate rapidly when exposed to atmospheres containing solvent vapors.

c. In circuits that under normal conditions do not release sufficient energy to ignite a specific ignitible atmospheric mixture; i.e., are nonincendive.

> The word "nonincendive" as used here originated in publications of the Instrument Society of America (ISA), such as ISA Monogram No. 1110. It first appeared in this section and Section 501-14(b)(1) in the 1975 edition of the *Code*. It means that under the conditions specified, there is insufficient energy available

to cause ignition. "Nonincendive" is similar to "intrinsically safe" as defined in Section 500-1 and NFPA 493, but does not include consideration of fault and all of the abnormal conditions inherent in the definition of "intrinsically safe." A circuit may be "nonincendive" in a Group D atmosphere, but not in a Group C atmosphere, as the minimum ignition energies for the various flammable materials differ.

(2) Resistors and Similar Equipment. Resistors, resistance devices, thermionic tubes, rectifiers, and similar equipment that is used in or in connection with meters, instruments, and relays shall comply with (a) above.

Exception: General-purpose-type enclosures shall be permitted if such equipment is without make-and-break or sliding contacts [other than as provided in (b)(1) above] and if the maximum operating temperature of any exposed surface will not exceed 80 percent of the ignition temperature in degrees Celsius of the gas or vapor involved or has been tested and found incapable of igniting the gas or vapor.

The intent of "or has been tested and found incapable of igniting the gas or vapor" is to permit approved equipment with operating temperatures higher than 80 percent of the ignition temperature. If the equipment has been tested, the "safety factor" inherent in this "80 percent rule" is not needed. The system of temperature measurement must be specified, as 80 percent of a temperature in degrees Celsius is not the same temperature as 80 percent of that temperature in degrees Fahrenheit.

(3) Without Make-or-Break Contacts. Transformer windings, impedance coils, solenoids, and other windings that do not incorporate sliding or make-or-break contacts shall be provided with enclosures that may be of the general-purpose type.

(4) General-Purpose Assemblies. Where an assembly is made up of components for which general-purpose enclosures are acceptable as provided in (b)(1), (b)(2), and (b)(3) above, a single general-purpose enclosure shall be acceptable for the assembly. Where such an assembly includes any of the equipment described in (b)(2) above, the maximum obtainable surface temperature of any component of the assembly shall be clearly and permanently indicated on the outside of the enclosure. Alternatively, approved equipment shall be permitted to be marked to indicate the temperature range for which it is suitable, using the identification numbers of Table 500-2(b).

(5) Fuses. Where general-purpose enclosures are permitted in (b)(1), (b)(2), (b)(3) and (b)(4) above, fuses for overcurrent protection of instrument circuits not subject to overloading in normal use shall be permitted to be mounted in general-purpose enclosures if each such fuse is preceded by a switch complying with (b)(1) above.

(6) Connections. To facilitate replacements, process control instruments shall be permitted to be connected through flexible cord, attachment plug, and receptacle, provided: (1) a switch complying with (b)(1) above is provided so that the attachment plug is not depended on to interrupt current; and (2) the current does not exceed 3 amperes at 120 volts, nominal; and (3) the power-supply cord does not exceed 3 feet (914 mm), is of a type approved for extra-hard usage or for hard usage if protected by location, and is supplied through an attachment plug and receptacle of the locking and grounding type; and (4) only necessary receptacles are provided; and (5) the receptacle carries a label warning against unplugging under load.

501-4. Wiring Methods. Wiring methods shall comply with (a) and (b) below.

(a) Class I, Division 1. In Class I, Division 1 locations, threaded rigid metal conduit, threaded steel intermediate metal conduit, or Type MI cable with termination fittings approved for the location shall be the wiring method employed. All boxes, fittings, and joints shall be threaded for connection to conduit or cable terminations, and shall be explosionproof. Threaded joints shall be made up with at least five threads fully engaged. Type MI cable shall be installed and supported in a manner to avoid tensile stress at the termination fittings. Where necessary to employ flexible connections, as at motor terminals, flexible fittings approved for Class I locations shall be used.

This section indicates that termination fittings used with Type MI cable are to be approved for the specific purpose. It is intended that Type MI cable fittings approved and marked [see Section 500-2(b)] for the hazardous (classified) location class and group be used. Type MI cable fittings have a clamp-type joint, which must be investigated to determine that it is explosionproof. Type MI cable fittings suitable for nonhazardous locations may not be suitable for Class I, Division 1 hazardous (classified) locations. Rigid metal conduit and intermediate metal conduit are to be threaded with a (NPT) standard conduit cutting die that provides ¾-in. taper per ft, and five full threads must be engaged. Each joint is to be made up tight at couplings, unions, and threaded hubs of junction boxes, device boxes, conduit bodies, etc.

Figure 501-1 shows an explosionproof junction box having three hubs and a threaded opening for the screw-type cover. Unused openings must be effectively closed by inserting threaded metal plugs engaging at least five full threads and affording protection equivalent to that of the wall of the box. Figure 501-3 shows a larger type explosionproof junction box with a bolted flanged cover.

Figure 501-4 shows a flexible fitting, which is available in lengths up to 3 ft, for use in Class I, Division 1 locations. The design of the flexible fitting consists of a deeply corrugated bronze tube with an internal fibrous tubular protective liner and an outer cover of braided fine bronze wires. A threaded fitting is securely attached to each end of the flexible tube. The flexible fitting is commonly used at motor connections, can withstand continuous vibration for long periods of time, is explosionproof, and affords maximum protection to any enclosed conductors.

Figure 501-3. Cutaway view of explosionproof junction box and bolted flanged cover. (*Appleton Electric Co.*)

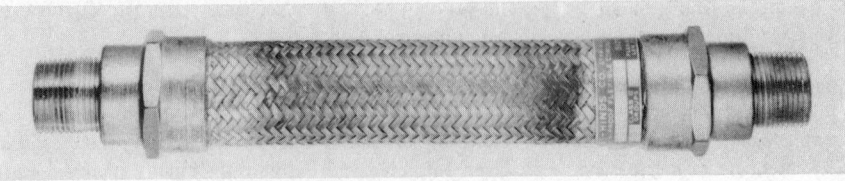

Figure 501-4. A flexible explosionproof fitting. (*Crouse-Hinds*)

(b) Class I, Division 2. In Class I, Division 2 locations, threaded rigid metal conduit, threaded steel intermediate metal conduit, enclosed gasketed busways, enclosed gasketed wireways, or Type PLTC cable in accordance with the provisions of Article 725, Type MI, MC, MV, TC, or SNM cable with approved termination fittings shall be the wiring method employed. Type PLTC, MI, MC, MV, TC, or SNM cable shall be permitted to be installed in cable tray systems and shall be installed in a manner to avoid tensile stress at the termination fittings. Boxes, fittings, and joints shall not be required to be explosionproof except as required by Sections 501-3(b)(1), 501-6(b)(1), and 501-14(b)(1). Where provision must be made for limited flexibility, as at motor terminals, flexible metal fittings, flexible metal conduit with approved fittings, liquidtight flexible metal conduit with approved fittings, or flexible cord approved for extra-hard usage and provided with approved bushed fittings shall be used. An additional conductor for grounding shall be included in the flexible cord unless other acceptable means of grounding are provided.

In Class I, Division 2 locations, boxes, fittings, and joints are not required to be explosionproof at lighting outlets or at enclosures containing no arcing devices. Where general-purpose enclosures are permitted by this section, rigid or intermediate metal conduit may be used with locknuts and bushings, but a bonding jumper with proper fittings is to be used between the enclosure and the raceway to assure adequate bonding from the hazardous area to the point of grounding for the service equipment. See Section 501-16(a).

Where limited flexibility is necessary and approved "fittings" are required for use with flexible metal conduit, liquidtight flexible metal conduit, and extra-hard usage flexible cord, it should be noted that such approved "fittings" are not required to be specifically approved for Class I locations. Also, where flexible conduit is used, internal or external bonding jumpers with proper fittings are to be provided as required in Section 501-16(b).

This section also permits a variety of cables, cable tray systems in accordance with Section 318-2(d), enclosed gasketed wireways, and enclosed gasketed busways. The cable and cable fittings, cable trays, wireways, and busways are not required to be specifically listed or labeled for Class I locations. For example, if Type MC cable is used, neither the cable nor the fittings need to be listed for use in hazardous (classified) locations.

Exception: Wiring, which under normal conditions cannot release sufficient energy to ignite a specific ignitible atmospheric mixture by opening, shorting or grounding, shall be permitted using any of the methods suitable for wiring in ordinary locations.

This exception is intended to permit what have been termed "nonincendive field circuits" [see comments on "nonincendive" following Item c of the exception to Section 501-3(b)(1)]. Many low-voltage, low-energy circuits are of this type. However, a Class 2 circuit as defined in Article 725 is not necessarily "nonincendive." There is considerable equipment listed by such testing laboratories as Factory Mutual Research Corp. and Underwriters Laboratories Inc. that have "nonincendive" circuits intended for field wiring in the various groups in Class I, Division 2 locations. Some common telephone circuits and thermocouple circuits are also "nonincendive."

501-5. Sealing and Drainage. Seals in conduit and cable systems shall comply with (a) through (f) below. Sealing compound shall be of a type approved for the conditions and use. Sealing compound shall be used in Type MI cable termination fittings to exclude moisture and other fluids from the cable insulation.

(FPN): Seals are provided in conduit and cable systems to minimize the passage of gases and vapors and prevent the passage of flames from one portion of the electrical installation to another through the conduit. Such communication through Type MI cable is inherently prevented by construction of the cable. Unless specifically designed and tested for the purpose, conduit and cable seals are not intended to prevent the passage of liquids, gases or vapors at a continuous pressure differential across the seal. Even at differences in pressure across the seal equivalent to a few inches of water, there may be a slow passage of gas or vapor through a seal, and through conductors passing through the seal. See Section 501-5(e)(2). Temperature extremes and highly corrosive liquids and vapors can affect the ability of seals to perform their intended function. See Section 501-5(c)(2).

The sealing material used in conduit fittings for sealing is somewhat porous, so that gases, particularly those under slight pressure and gases with small molecules, such as hydrogen, can pass slowly through the sealing compound. Also, the seal is around the insulation on the conductor, and gases can be transmitted slowly through the air spaces (the interstices) between strands of stranded conductors. See the second Fine Print Note to Section 501-5(e)(2). However, experience has shown that under normal conditions, and with only normal atmospheric pressure differentials across the seal, the passage of gas through a seal is not sufficient to result in a hazard.

(a) Conduit Seals, Class I, Division 1. In Class I, Division 1 locations, conduit seals shall be located as follows:

(1) In each conduit run entering an enclosure for switches, circuit breakers, fuses, relays, resistors, or other apparatus which may produce arcs, sparks, or high temperatures. Seals shall be placed as close as practicable and in no case more than 18 inches (457 mm) from such enclosures. Explosionproof unions, couplings, elbows, capped elbows and conduit bodies similar to "L," "T," and "Cross" type shall be the only enclosures or fittings permitted between the sealing fitting and the enclosure. The conduit bodies shall not be larger than the largest trade size of the conduits.

Exception: Conduit 1½ inches and smaller entering an explosionproof enclosure for switches, circuit breakers, fuses, relays, or other apparatus which may produce arcs or sparks need not be sealed if the current-interrupting contacts are:

a. Enclosed within a chamber hermetically sealed against the entrance of gases or vapors; or,

b. Immersed in oil in accordance with Section 501-6(b)(1)(2).

(2) In each conduit of 2-inch size or larger entering the enclosure or fitting housing terminals, splices, or taps and within 18 inches (457 mm) of such enclosure or fitting.

(FPN): See notes under Group B in sixth Fine Print Note to Section 500-2.

(3) Where two or more enclosures for which seals are required under (a)(1) and (a)(2) above are connected by nipples or by runs of conduit not more than 36 inches (914 mm) long, a single seal in each such nipple connection or run of conduit shall be considered sufficient if located not more than 18 inches (457 mm) from either enclosure.

(4) In each conduit run leaving the Class I, Division 1 location. The sealing fitting shall be permitted on either side of the boundary of such location but shall be so designed and installed to minimize the amount of gas or vapor which may have entered the conduit system within the Division 1 location from being communicated to the conduit beyond the seal. There shall be no union, coupling, box, or fitting in the conduit between the sealing fitting and the point at which the conduit leaves the Division 1 location.

Exception: Metal conduit containing no unions, couplings, boxes, or fittings that passes completely through a Class I, Division 1 location with no fittings less than 12 inches (305 mm) beyond each boundary shall not be required to be sealed if the termination points of the unbroken conduit are in nonhazardous locations.

(b) Conduit Seals, Class I, Division 2. In Class I, Division 2 locations, conduit seals shall be located as follows:

(1) For connections to explosionproof enclosures that are required to be approved for Class I locations, seals shall be provided in accordance with (a)(1), (a)(2) and (a)(3) above. All portions of the conduit run or nipple between the seal and such enclosure shall comply with Section 501-4(a).

(2) In each conduit run passing from a Class I, Division 2 location into a nonhazardous location. The sealing fitting shall be permitted on either side of the boundary of such location but shall be so designed and installed to minimize the amount of gas or vapor which may have entered the conduit system within the Division 2 location from being communicated to the conduit beyond the seal. Rigid metal conduit or threaded steel intermediate metal conduit shall be used between the sealing fitting and the point at which the conduit leaves the Division 2 location, and a threaded connection shall be used at the sealing fitting. There shall be no union, coupling, box, or fitting in the conduit between the sealing fitting and the point at which the conduit leaves the Division 2 location.

Exception: Metal conduit containing no unions, couplings, boxes or fittings that passes completely through a Class I, Division 2 location with no fittings less than 12 inches (305 mm) beyond each boundary shall not be required to be sealed if the termination points of the unbroken conduit are in nonhazardous locations.

(c) Class I, Divisions 1 and 2. Where required, seals in Class I, Division 1 and 2 locations shall comply with the following:

(1) Fittings. Enclosures for connections or equipment shall be provided with an approved integral means for sealing, or sealing fittings approved for Class I locations shall be used. Sealing fittings shall be accessible.

(2) Compound. Sealing compound shall be approved and shall provide a seal against passage of gas or vapors through the seal fitting, shall not be affected by the surrounding atmosphere or liquids, and shall not have a melting point of less than 93°C (200°F).

(3) Thickness of Compounds. In a completed seal, the minimum thickness of the sealing compound shall not be less than the trade size of the conduit, and in no case less than ⅝ inch (16 mm).

(4) Splices and Taps. Splices and taps shall not be made in fittings intended only for sealing with compound, nor shall other fittings in which splices or taps are made be filled with compound.

(5) Assemblies. In an assembly where equipment that may produce arcs, sparks, or high temperatures is located in a compartment separate from the compartment containing splices or taps, and an integral seal is provided where conductors pass from one compartment to the other, the entire assembly shall be approved for Class I locations. Seals in conduit connections to the compartment containing splices or taps shall be provided in Class I, Division 1 locations where required by (a)(2) above.

(d) Cable Seals, Class I, Division 1. In Class I, Division 1 locations each multiconductor cable in conduit shall be considered as a single conductor if the cable is incapable of transmitting gases or vapors through the cable core. These cables shall be sealed in accordance with (a) above.

Cables with a gas/vapor-tight continuous sheath capable of transmitting gases or vapors through the cable core shall be sealed in the Division 1 location after removing the jacket and any other coverings so that the sealing compound will surround each individual insulated conductor and the outer jacket.

(e) Cable Seals, Class I, Division 2. In Class I, Division 2 locations, cable seals shall be located as follows:

(1) Cables entering enclosures which are required to be approved for Class I locations shall be sealed at the point of entrance. The sealing fitting shall comply with (b)(1) above. Multiconductor cables with a gas/vapor-tight continuous sheath capable of transmitting gases or vapors through the cable core shall be sealed in an approved fitting in the Division 2 location after removing the jacket and any other coverings so that the sealing compound will surround each individual insulated conductor in such a manner as to prevent the passage of gases or vapors. Multiconductor cables in conduit shall be sealed as described in (d) above.

(2) Cables with a gas/vapor-tight continuous sheath and which will not transmit gases or vapors through the cable core in excess of the quantity permitted for seal fittings shall not be required to be sealed except as required in (e)(1) above. The minimum length of such cable run shall not be less than that length which limits gas or vapor flow through the cable core to the rate permitted for seal fittings [0.007 cubic feet per hour (198 cubic centimeters per hour) of air at a pressure of 6 inches of water (1493 pascals)].

The ability of a cable to transmit gases or vapors through the core (primarily between insulated conductors) depends not only on how tightly packed the conductors are within the outer sheaths, and the location and composition of "fillers," but also on how the cable has been handled and the geometry of the cable run. If there is any question as to whether or not the cable run is capable of transmitting gases or vapors through the core, sealing is suggested.

(FPN): See Outlet Boxes and Fittings for Use in Hazardous Locations, ANSI C33.27-1974.

(FPN): The cable core does not include the interstices of the conductor strands.

The intent is that the conductors themselves be individually sealed, such as by dipping the ends in wax, before measuring the rate of flow. However, if this is done, the wax should be removed before making electrical connections or putting the system into service.

(3) Cables with a gas/vapor-tight continuous sheath capable of transmitting gases or vapors through the cable core shall not be required to be sealed except as required in (e)(1) above, unless the cable is attached to process equipment or devices that may cause a pressure in excess of 6 inches (1493 pascals) of water to be exerted at a cable end, in which case a seal, barrier or other means shall be provided to prevent migration of flammables into an unclassified area.

Exception: Cables with an unbroken gas/vapor-tight continuous sheath shall be permitted to pass through a Class I, Division 2 location without seals.

(4) Cables which do not have gas/vapor-tight continuous sheath shall be sealed at the boundary of the Division 2 and nonhazardous location in such a manner as to prevent passage of gases or vapors into a nonhazardous location.

(FPN): The sheath mentioned in (d) and (e) above may be either metal or a nonmetallic material.

(f) Drainage.

(1) Control Equipment. Where there is a probability that liquid or other condensed vapor may be trapped within enclosures for control equipment or at any point in the raceway system, approved means shall be provided to prevent accumulation or to permit periodic draining of such liquid or condensed vapor.

(2) Motors and Generators. Where the authority having jurisdiction judges that there is a probability that liquid or condensed vapor may accumulate within motors or generators, joints and conduit systems shall be arranged to minimize entrance of liquid. If means to prevent accumulation or to permit periodic draining are judged necessary, such means shall be provided at the time of manufacture and shall be considered an integral part of the machine.

(3) Canned Pumps, Process Connections, Etc. For canned pumps, process connections for flow, pressure, or analysis measurement, etc., that depend upon a single seal diaphragm or tube to prevent process fluids from entering the electrical conduit system, an additional approved seal, barrier or other means shall be provided to prevent the process fluid from entering the conduit system beyond the additional devices or means, if the primary seal fails.

The additional approved seal or barrier and the interconnecting enclosure shall meet the temperature and pressure conditions to which they will be subjected upon failure of the primary seal unless other approved means are provided to accomplish the purpose above.

Other means which are used in the liquefied natural gas industry consist of a vented enclosure containing busbars. The conduit from the canned pump terminates at the enclosure, and the conductors are connected to one end of the (solid) busbars. The circuit continues through the short busbar section to another set of conductors and a sealed conduit.

Drains, vents or other devices shall be provided so that primary seal leakage will be obvious.

(FPN): See also the last paragraph of Section 500-4(b) and Fine Print Note to Section 501-5.

Seals in conduits are used to prevent an explosion from traveling through the conduit to another enclosure, and to minimize the passage of gases or vapors from a hazardous (classified) location to a nonhazardous location. Sealing compound must be used as soon as possible on Type MI cable terminations to exclude moisture from cable insulation.

Where the conduit enters an enclosure containing arcing or high-temperature equipment, a sealing fitting is required to be placed within 18 in. of the enclosure it isolates; conduit bodies ("L," "T," etc.), couplings, unions, and elbows are the only enclosures or fittings permitted between the seal and the enclosure. See Figure 501-9 for an approved type of union. If two enclosures are spaced not more than 36 in. apart, a single seal may be placed between two connecting nipples if the seal is located not more than 18 in. from either enclosure.

In each 2-in. or larger conduit, a sealing fitting is required to be placed within 18 in. of the entrance to an explosionproof enclosure that houses terminals, splices, or taps.

A sealing fitting is required where the conduit leaves a Division 1 location or passes from a Division 2 location to a nonhazardous location. The sealing fitting is permitted on either side of the boundary, and there is to be no union, coupling, box, etc., between the seal and the boundary. It is preferable to locate the fitting on the nonhazardous location side. This sealing fitting serves two purposes. It completes the explosionproof wiring and enclosure system. Note that a ½-in. conduit connected to an explosionproof box containing only splices, even in a Division 1 location, is not required to be sealed within 18 in. of the box. The seal at the boundary of the Division 1 location serves to complete the explosionproof system. The sealing fitting at the boundary also prevents the conduit system from serving as a pipe to transmit flammable mixtures from a Division 1 or Division 2 location to a less hazardous (classified) location.

In Class I, Division 2 locations, a seal is required in each conduit entering an enclosure that is required to be explosionproof. This is to complete the explosionproof enclosure.

Figure 501-5 illustrates the sealing of a fitting. A dam must be provided to prevent the sealing material from running out of the fitting while it is still in the liquid state. All conductors must be separated to permit the sealing material to run between them. The sealing compound is required to have a minimum thickness of not less than the trade size of the conduit and in no case less than ⅝ in. Conduit fittings for sealing are for use only with sealing compound supplied with the fitting and specified by the manufacturer in instructions furnished with the fitting.

Unless the additional seal or barrier, described in Section 501-5(f)(3), and interconnecting enclosures meet the performance requirements of the primary seal, the application of pressure or exposure to extreme temperatures must be prevented at the additional seal or barrier, so that the process fluid will not enter the conduit system if the primary seal fails. If the process fluid is a gas or can become a gas under ordinary atmospheric conditions (liquefied natural gas, for example), the "drain" mentioned in Section 501-5(f)(3) should be a vent. See commentary following Section 501-5(f)(3).

The necessary sealing may be accomplished by a sealing fitting and compound. To eliminate the time-consuming task of field-poured seals, a factory-sealed device with the seal designed into the device is permissible. A wide selection of factory-sealed devices is available for a variety of installations in hazardous (classified) locations. Factory-sealed devices are usually marked as such. Explosionproof motors are normally factory sealed, and no other seal is required. Where a conduit terminates in a motor, however, and if the conduit is 2 in. or larger, a seal is required to be placed within 18 in. of the motor terminal housing.

Figure 501-7 shows a sealing fitting designed for use in a vertical run of conduit to provide drainage for any condensation of moisture trapped by the seal above an enclosure. Any accumulation of water runs over the surface of the sealing compound down to an explosionproof drain, through which it automatically drains. Figure 501-6 shows a sealing fitting designed for either a horizontal or vertical conduit run. Figure 501-8 shows a combination drain and breather fitting. These fittings are specially designed to serve as a water drain and an air vent while providing positive explosionproof protection. The fitting permits the escape of accumulated water through the passage of its drain, and the breather allows the continuous circulation of air, preventing condensation of any moisture that may be present. Individual drain or breather fittings are also available. It is good practice to consider the installation of drain, breather, or combination fittings in order to guard against water accumulation with subsequent insulation failures, even though prevalent conditions may not indicate a need.

Figure 501-10 illustrates a Class I, Division 1 location using threaded rigid metal conduit or threaded intermediate metal conduit and explosionproof fittings and equipment including motors, motor controllers, pushbutton stations, lighting outlets, and junction boxes. The enclosures for the disconnecting means and motor controller for the motor (right part of the drawing) are placed in a nonhazardous location and are thus not required to be explosionproof.

Each of the three conduits is sealed on the nonhazardous side before passing into the hazardous (classified) location. The pigtail leads of both motors are factory sealed at the motor-terminal housing, and, unless the size of the flexible fitting entering the motor-terminal housing is 2 in. or larger, no other seals are needed at this point. Because the pushbutton control station and the motor controller and disconnect (left part of the drawing) are considered arc-producing devices, conduits are sealed within 18 in. of the entrance to these enclosures. It should be noted that seals are required even though the contacts may be immersed in oil.

A seal is provided within 18 in. of the lighting switch. The design of the lighting fixture, as required by Underwriters Laboratories Inc. (UL), is such that the explosionproof chamber for the wiring must be separated or sealed from the lamp compartment, hence a separate seal is not required adjacent to UL listed lighting fixtures. The lighting fixture is suspended on a conduit stem threaded into the cover of an explosionproof ceiling box. See Section 501-9.

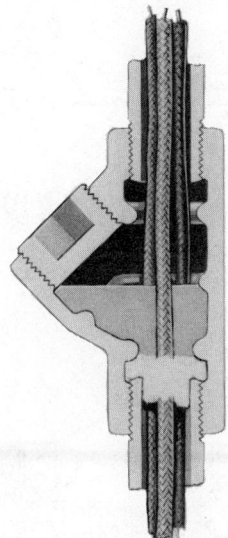

Figure 501-5. A seal fitting placed in a run of conduit to minimize the passage of gases from one portion of the electrical installation to another. (*Crouse-Hinds*)

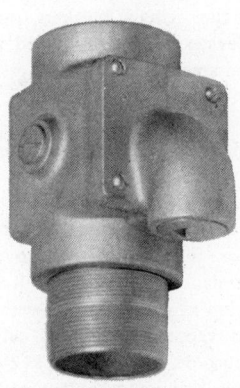

Figure 501-6. A sealing fitting for a horizontal or vertical conduit run with a removable screw-type fitting for draining purposes. (*Appleton Electric Co.*)

Figure 501-7. A sealing fitting with an automatic drain plug. (*Appleton Electric Co.*)

Figure 501-8. A combination breather-drainage fitting. (*Appleton Electric Co.*)

Figure 501-9. An explosionproof union. (*Appleton Electric Co.*)

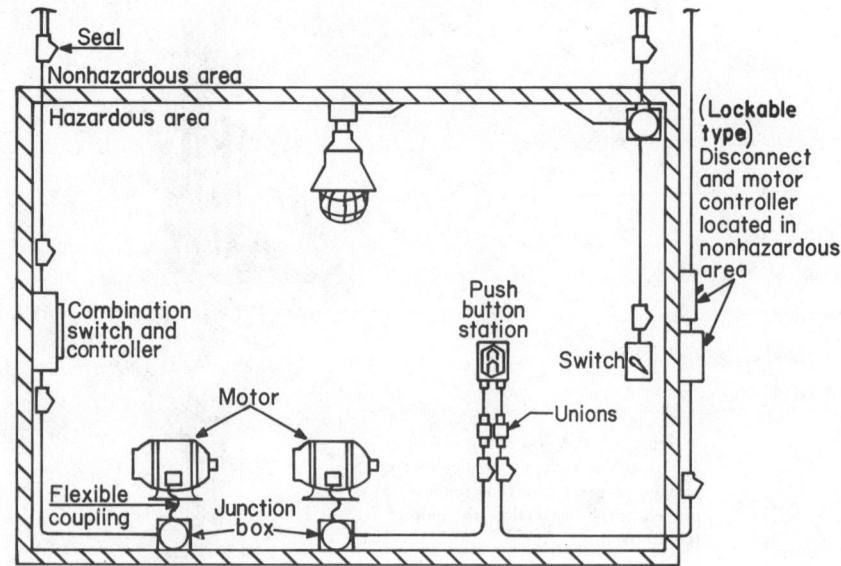

Figure 501-10. A Class I, Division 1 location where threaded metal conduits, sealing fittings, explosionproof fittings, and equipment for power and lights are used.

501-6. Switches, Circuit Breakers, Motor Controllers, and Fuses.

(a) **Class I, Division 1.** In Class I, Division 1 locations, switches, circuit breakers, motor controllers, and fuses, including pushbuttons, relays, and similar devices, shall be provided with enclosures and the enclosure in each case, together with the enclosed apparatus, shall be approved as a complete assembly for use in Class I locations.

(b) **Class I, Division 2.** Switches, circuit breakers, motor controllers, and fuses in Class I, Division 2 locations shall comply with the following:

(1) **Type Required.** Circuit breakers, motor controllers, and switches intended to interrupt current in the normal performance of the function for which they are installed shall be provided with enclosures approved for Class I, Division 1 locations in accordance with Section 501-3(a), unless general-purpose enclosures are provided and (1) the interruption of current occurs within a chamber hermetically sealed against the entrance of gases and vapors, or (2) the current make-and-break contacts are oil-immersed, and of the general-purpose type having a 2-inch (50.8-mm) minimum immersion for power and a 1-inch (25.4-mm) minimum immersion for control.

(2) **Isolating Switches.** Fused or unfused disconnect and isolating switches for transformers or capacitor banks that are not intended to interrupt current in the normal performance of the function for which they are installed, shall be permitted to be installed in general-purpose enclosures.

(3) **Fuses.** For the protection of motors, appliances, and lamps, other than as provided in (b)(4) below, standard plug or cartridge fuses shall be permitted, provided they are placed within enclosures approved for the location; or fuses shall be permitted if they are within general-purpose enclosures, and if they are of a type in which the operating element is immersed in oil or other approved liquid or the operating element is enclosed within a chamber hermetically sealed against the entrance of gases and vapors.

(4) Fuses or Circuit Breakers for Overcurrent Protection. Where not more than ten sets of approved enclosed fuses or not more than ten circuit breakers that are not intended to be used as switches for the interruption of current are installed for branch-circuit or feeder protection in any one room, area, or section of the Class I, Division 2 location, general-purpose-type enclosures for such fuses or circuit breakers shall be permitted if the fuses or circuit breakers are for the protection of circuits or feeders supplying lamps in fixed positions only.

(FPN): A set of fuses is all the fuses required to protect all the ungrounded conductors of a circuit. For example, a group of three fuses protecting an ungrounded 3-phase circuit and a single fuse protecting the ungrounded conductor of an identified 2-wire single-phase circuit is a set of fuses in each instance.

Fuses complying with (b)(3) above shall not be required to be included in counting the ten sets of fuses permitted in general-purpose enclosures.

(5) Fuses Internal to Lighting Fixtures. Approved cartridge fuses shall be permitted within lighting fixtures.

Figure 501-11 shows an explosionproof panelboard consisting of an assembly of branch-circuit devices enclosed in a cast-metal explosionproof housing. These panelboards are provided with bolted access covers and threaded conduit-entry hubs designed to withstand the force of any internal explosion.

Figure 501-12 shows an open and closed view of a cylindrical-type ("spin-top") combination motor controller, a motor control starter and circuit breaker in an explosionproof enclosure. The top and bottom covers are threaded on for quick removal for installation and servicing. Figure 501-13 shows the same type of equipment in a rectangular enclosure with a hinged, bolted-on cover. These types of housings are designed to accomodate a wide variety of either manually or magnetically operated across-the-line types of motor starters in a variety of ratings.

Figure 501-14 illustrates a standard toggle switch in an explosionproof enclosure.

In Class I, Division 2 locations, it is assumed that fuses or circuit breakers will seldom open the circuit when used to protect feeders or branch circuits supplying lamps in fixed positions only. Division 2 locations are not normally hazardous but

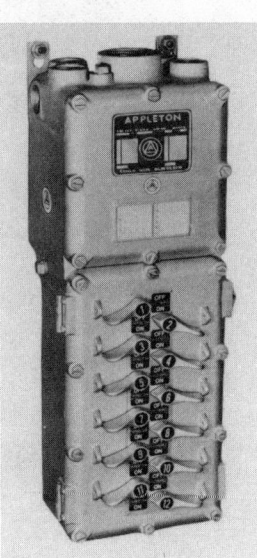

Figure 501-11. An explosionproof panelboard with provisions for twelve circuits. (*Appleton Electric Co.*)

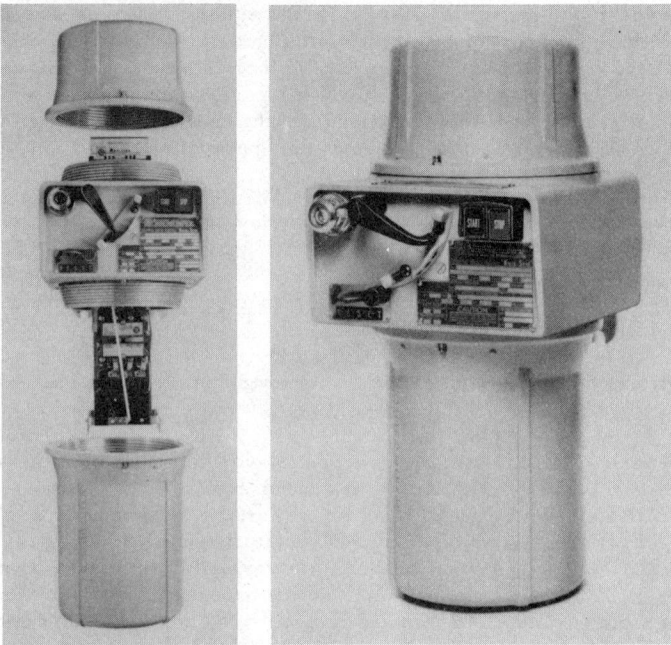

Figure 501-12. An explosionproof enclosure for a motor control starter and circuit breaker (open and closed views). (*Appleton Electric Co.*)

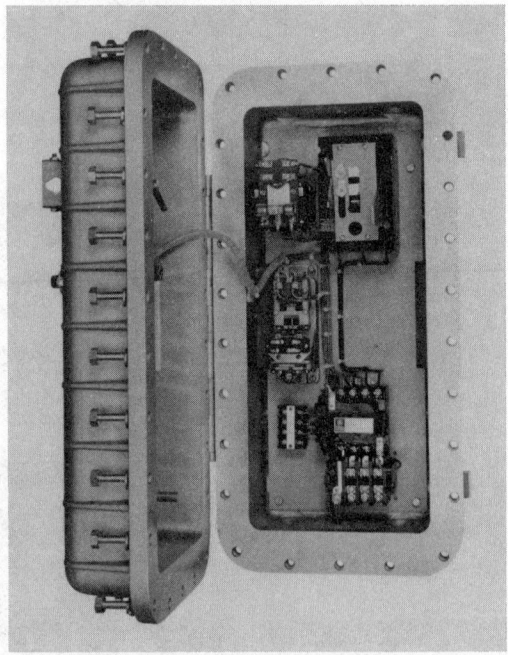

Figure 501-13. A magnetic motor starter for use in a Class I, Group D location. Note the number of securing bolts and the width of the flange. (*General Electric Co.*)

may become so [see Section 500-4(b)], and since it is unlikely that the fuse or circuit breaker in such a circuit will operate simultaneously with the occurrence of an explosive mixture inside the enclosure, general-purpose enclosures are permitted for such overcurrent devices.

Section 501-6(b)(5) permits fuses, often used for ballast protection in high-intensity-discharge and outdoor fluorescent fixtures.

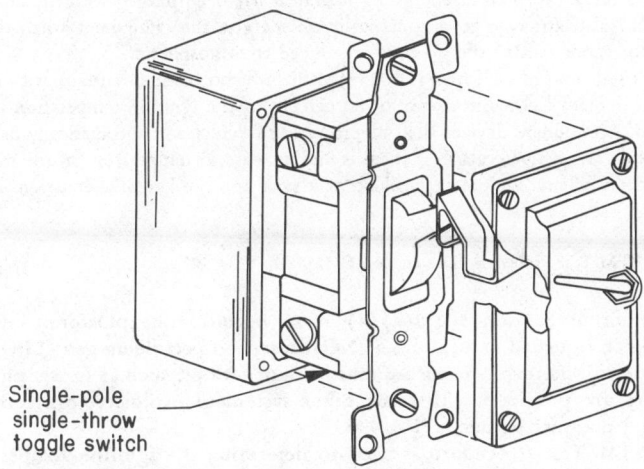

Single-pole
single-throw
toggle switch

Figure 501-14. A standard toggle switch in an explosionproof enclosure.

501-7. Control Transformers and Resistors. Transformers, impedance coils, and resistors used as, or in conjunction with, control equipment for motors, generators, and appliances shall comply with (a) and (b) below.

(a) Class I, Division 1. In Class I, Division 1 locations, transformers, impedance coils, and resistors, together with any switching mechanism associated with them, shall be provided with enclosures approved for Class I, Division 1 locations in accordance with Section 501-3(a).

(b) Class I, Division 2. In Class I, Division 2 locations, control transformers and resistors shall comply with the following:

(1) Switching Mechanisms. Switching mechanisms used in conjunction with transformers, impedance coils, and resistors shall comply with Section 501-6(b).

(2) Coils and Windings. Enclosures for windings of transformers, solenoids, or impedance coils shall be permitted to be of the general-purpose type.

(3) Resistors. Resistors shall be provided with enclosures; and the assembly shall be approved for Class I locations, unless resistance is nonvariable and maximum operating temperature, in degrees Celsius, will not exceed 80 percent of the ignition temperature of the gas or vapor involved, or has been tested and found incapable of igniting the gas or vapor.

501-8. Motors and Generators.

(a) Class I, Division 1. In Class I, Division 1 locations, motors, generators, and other rotating electric machinery shall be: (1) approved for Class I, Division 1 locations; or (2) of the totally enclosed type supplied with positive-pressure ventilation from a source of clean air with discharge to a safe area, so arranged to prevent energizing of the machine until ventilation has been established and the enclosure has been purged with at least 10 volumes of air, and also arranged to automatically de-energize the equipment when the air supply fails; or (3) of the totally enclosed inert gas-filled type supplied with a suitable reliable source of inert gas for pressuring the enclosure, with devices provided to ensure a positive pressure in the enclosure and arranged to automatically de-energize the equipment when the gas supply fails; or (4) of a type designed to be submerged in a liquid which is flammable only when vaporized and mixed with air, or in a gas or vapor at a pressure greater than atmospheric and which is flammable only when mixed with air; and the machine is so arranged to prevent energizing it until it has been purged with the liquid or gas to exclude air, and also arranged to automatically de-energize the equipment when the supply of liquid, or gas or vapor fails or the pressure is reduced to atmospheric.

Totally enclosed motors of Types (2) or (3) shall have no external surface with an operating temperature in degrees Celsius in excess of 80 percent of the ignition temperature of the gas or vapor involved. Appropriate devices shall be provided to detect and automatically de-energize the motor or provide an adequate alarm if there is any increase in temperature of the motor beyond designed limits. Auxiliary equipment shall be of a type approved for the location in which it is installed.

(FPN): See ASTM Test Procedure (Designation D 2155-69).

The intent of Section 501-8(a)(4) is to permit nonexplosionproof motors submerged in liquefied natural gas (LNG), liquefied petroleum gas (LPG), etc. It does not permit nonexplosionproof motors under water, such as in wet pits, unless the motors are provided with some other system of explosion protection, e.g., purged and pressurized per NFPA 496.

The ASTM Test Procedure is used to determine the ignition temperature of some flammable and combustible liquids.

(b) Class I, Division 2. In Class I, Division 2 locations, motors, generators, and other rotating electric machinery in which are employed sliding contacts, centrifugal or other types of switching mechanism (including motor overcurrent, overloading and overtemperature devices), or integral resistance devices, either while starting or while running, shall be approved for Class I, Division 1 locations, unless such sliding contacts, switching mechanisms, and resistance devices are provided with enclosures approved for Class I, Division 2 locations in accordance with Section 501-3(b). When operated at rated voltage, the exposed surface of space heaters used to prevent condensation of moisture during shut-down periods shall not exceed 80 percent of the ignition temperature in degrees Celsius of the gas or vapor involved.

The last sentence is new in the 1984 *NEC*. Many motor heaters are deenergized automatically when the motor is running. However, the heater ratings are usually low when compared to the normal heat generated during motor operation. Unless otherwise indicated on the motor wiring diagram or in instructions provided with the motor, there is no need to deenergize the heater except to save energy.

In Class I, Division 2 locations, the installation of open or nonexplosionproof enclosed motors, such as squirrel-cage induction motors without brushes, switching mechanisms, or similar arc-producing devices shall be permitted.

(FPN): It is important to consider the temperature of internal and external surfaces which may be exposed to the flammable atmosphere.

It is intended that the phrase "other rotating electric machinery" include electric brakes. Listed and labeled electric brakes are available for Class I, Division 1, Group C and D locations.

Figures 501-15 and 501-16 show closed and opened views of a totally enclosed fan-cooled motor approved for use in explosive atmospheres. The main frame and

Figure 501-15. Terminal housing of a motor approved for use in specific hazardous locations. Note integral sealing of the motor. (*General Electric Co.*)

Figure 501-16. View showing internal fan of motor in Figure 501-15.

end-bells are designed with sufficient strength to withstand an internal explosion, and flames or hot gases are cooled while escaping because of the wide metal-to-metal joints between the frame and the end-bells and the long, close-tolerance clearance provided for the free-turn of the shaft. Air circulation outside the motor is maintained by nonsparking (aluminum, bronze, or a nonstatic-generating-type plastic) fan on the end opposite the shaft end of the motor. A sheet metal housing surrounds this fan to reduce the likelihood of a person or object contacting the moving blades and to direct the flow of air. Internal fans on the shaft circulate air around the windings.

Motors that have arcing or sparking devices, such as commutators, internal switches, or other control devices, must be explosionproof. General-purpose squirrel-cage induction motors may be used in Division 2 locations.

The Fine Print Note is new in the 1984 *NEC*. Since some open-type motors are permitted in Class I, Division 2 locations, care should be exercised in selecting the motor types when flammable gases or vapors with very low ignition temperatures may be present. Modern motors with high temperature insulation systems, such as Class H (180°C), may operate close to or above the ignition temperature of the flammable mixture.

501-9. Lighting Fixtures. Lighting fixtures shall comply with (a) or (b) below.

(a) Class I, Division 1. In Class I, Division 1 locations, lighting fixtures shall comply with the following:

(1) Approved Fixtures. Each fixture shall be approved as a complete assembly for the Class I, Division 1 location and shall be clearly marked to indicate the maximum wattage of lamps for which it is approved. Fixtures intended for portable use shall be specifically approved as a complete assembly for that use.

(2) Physical Damage. Each fixture shall be protected against physical damage by a suitable guard or by location.

(3) Pendant Fixtures. Pendant fixtures shall be suspended by and supplied through threaded rigid metal conduit stems or threaded steel intermediate conduit stems, and threaded joints shall be provided with set-screws or other effective means to prevent loosening. For stems longer than 12 inches (305 mm), permanent and effective bracing against lateral displacement shall be provided at a level not more than 12 inches (305 mm) above the lower end of the stem, or flexibility in the form of a fitting or flexible connector approved for the Class I, Division 1 location shall be provided not more than 12 inches (305 mm) from the point of attachment to the supporting box or fitting.

(4) Supports. Boxes, box assemblies, or fittings used for the support of lighting fixtures shall be approved for Class I locations.

(b) Class I, Division 2. In Class I, Division 2 locations, lighting fixtures shall comply with the following:

(1) Portable Lighting Equipment. Portable lighting equipment shall comply with (a)(1) above.

Exception: Where portable lighting equipment are mounted on movable stands and are connected by flexible cords, as covered in Section 501-11, they shall be permitted, when mounted in any position, provided that they conform to Section 501-9(b)(2) below.

(2) Fixed Lighting. Lighting fixtures for fixed lighting shall be protected from physical damage by suitable guards or by location. Where there is danger that falling sparks or hot metal from lamps or fixtures might ignite localized concentrations of flammable vapors or gases, suitable enclosures or other effective protective means shall be provided. Where lamps are of a size or type that may, under normal operating conditions, reach surface temperatures exceeding 80 percent of the ignition temperature in degrees Celsius of the gas or vapor involved, fixtures shall comply with (a)(1) above or shall be of a type which has been tested and found incapable of igniting the gas or vapor if the ignition temperature is not exceeded.

(3) **Pendant Fixtures.** Pendant fixtures shall be suspended by threaded rigid metal conduit stems, threaded steel intermediate metal conduit stems or by other approved means. For rigid stems longer than 12 inches (305 mm), permanent and effective bracing against lateral displacement shall be provided at a level not more than 12 inches (305 mm) above the lower end of the stem, or flexibility in the form of an approved fitting or flexible connector shall be provided not more than 12 inches (305 mm) from the point of attachment to the supporting box or fitting.

(4) **Switches.** Switches that are a part of an assembled fixture or of an individual lampholder shall comply with Section 501-6(b)(1).

(5) **Starting Equipment.** Starting and control equipment for electric-discharge lamps shall comply with Section 501-7(b).

Exception: A thermal protector potted into a thermally protected fluorescent lamp ballast if the lighting fixture is approved for locations of this Class and Division.

Figures 501-17 and 501-18 show typical lighting fixtures for Class I, Group C and D locations and a variety of parts of a complete lighting fixture assembly. The outlet boxes have an internally threaded opening designed to receive the cover. A pendant fixture is attached to the cover by threaded rigid metal conduit or threaded intermediate metal conduit. To prevent loosening from vibration or lamp changing, threaded joints are to be provided with set-screws. The set-screws should not interrupt the explosionproof joint. Rigid metal conduit or intermediate metal conduit stems longer than 12 in. require effective bracing or a flexible fitting approved for the purpose and placed not more than 12 in. from the point of attachment to the supporting box, cover, or fitting.

A globeholder is threaded onto the body of the fixture housing and supports a heavy glass globe, guard, and reflector. It is available in sizes suitable for lamps from 40 W through 500 W. In designing any hazardous (classified) location

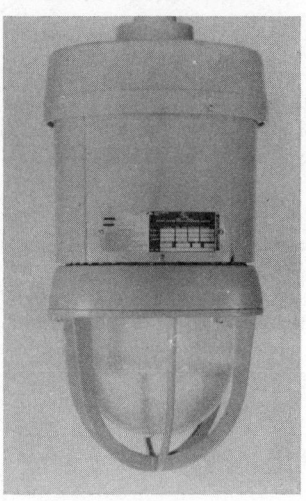

Figure 501-17. A typical lighting fixture for use in Class I, Group C and D locations. (*Crouse-Hinds*)

lighting system, operating temperatures must be considered. Therefore, if the area is Class I, Division 1, fixtures approved for this location, and properly marked, must be used. Generally, enclosed and gasketed fixtures (previously called vaportight fixtures) without guards, if breakage is unlikely, or fixtures approved for Class I, Division 2 locations, are required in Division 2 locations. Fixtures listed by Underwriters Laboratories Inc. (UL) for use in any of the groups under Class I, either Division 1 or 2 locations, or both, are designed to operate without causing ignition of surrounding flammable gas or vapor atmospheres, and are marked with the operating temperature or temperature range code [see Table 500-2(b)].

Figure 501-19 shows an explosionproof handlamp. It is required that lamp compartments be sealed from the terminal compartment. Provisions are to be made for the connection of 3-conductor (one, a grounding conductor), flexible, extra-hard usage cord. See Section 501-11.

501-10. Utilization Equipment.

(a) Class I, Division 1. In Class I, Division 1 locations, all utilization equipment shall be approved for Class I, Division 1 locations.

(b) Class I, Division 2. In Class I, Division 2 locations, all utilization equipment shall comply with the following:

(1) Heaters. Electrically heated utilization equipment shall conform with either (a) or (b) below.

a. The heater shall not exceed 80 percent of the ignition temperature in degrees Celsius of the gas or vapor involved on any surface which is exposed to the gas or vapor when continuously energized at the maximum rated ambient temperature. If a temperature controller is not provided, these conditions shall apply when the heater is operated at 120 percent of rated voltage.

b. The heater shall be approved for Class I, Division 1 locations.

(2) Motors. Motors of motor-driven utilization equipment shall comply with Section 501-8(b).

(3) Switches, Circuit Breakers, and Fuses. Switches, circuit breakers, and fuses shall comply with Section 501-6(b).

The requirements for utilization equipment in Class I locations are virtually identical for Division 1 and 2 locations, except for heaters. Electric pipe tracing systems listed for Class I, Division 2 locations and complying with Section 501-10(b)(1)a are available.

501-11. Flexible Cords, Class I, Divisions 1 and 2. A flexible cord shall be permitted only for connection between portable lighting equipment or other portable utilization equipment and the fixed portion of its supply circuit; and where used shall: (1) be of a type approved for extra-hard usage; (2) contain, in addition to the conductors of the circuit, a grounding conductor complying with Section 400-23; (3) be connected to terminals or to supply conductors in an approved manner; (4) be supported by clamps or by other suitable means in such a manner that there will be no tension on the terminal connections; and (5) be provided with suitable seals where the flexible cord enters boxes, fittings, or enclosures of the explosionproof type.

Exception: As provided in Sections 501-3(b)(6) and 501-4(b).

Electric submersible pumps with means for removal without entering the wet-pit shall be considered portable utilization equipment.

(FPN): See Section 501-13 for flexible cords exposed to liquids having a deleterious effect on the conductor insulation.

The second paragraph recognizes a wet-pit type of installation that is finding increasing acceptance for waste-water systems. Listed equipment for this use is available. See commentary following Section 501-8(a)(4).

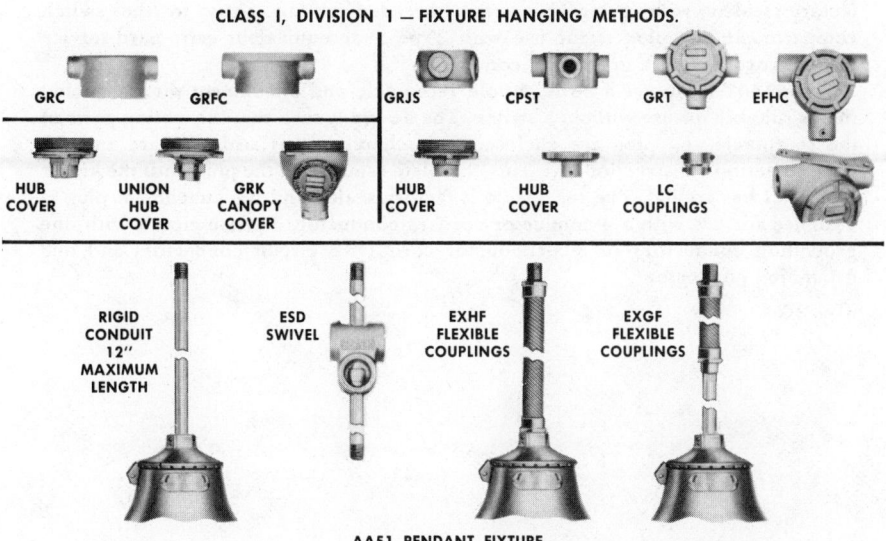

Figure 501-18. Various components used in an explosionproof lighting fixture installation. (*Appleton Electric Co.*)

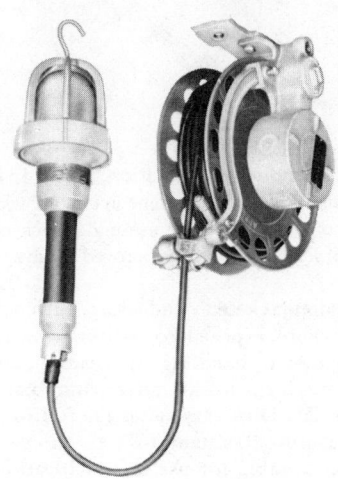

Figure 501-19. An explosionproof handlamp for use in Class I locations. (*Appleton Electric Co.*)

501-12. Receptacles and Attachment Plugs, Class I, Divisions 1 and 2. Receptacles and attachment plugs shall be of the type providing for connection to the grounding conductor of a flexible cord and shall be approved for Class I locations.

Exception: As provided in Section 501-3(b)(6).

Figure 501-20 shows an explosionproof receptacle and attachment plug with an interlocking switch. The design of this device is such that when the switch is in the "on" position, the plug cannot be removed, and also the switch cannot be placed in the "on" position when the plug has been removed; that is, the plug cannot be inserted or removed unless the switch is in the "off" position. The receptacle is factory sealed with a provision for threaded-conduit entry to the switch compartment; the plug is for use with Type S or equivalent extra-hard-service flexible cord having a grounding conductor.

Figure 501-21 shows a 30-A, 4-pole receptacle and attachment plug assembly that is suitable for use without a switch. The design is such that the mating parts of the receptacle and plug are enclosed in a chamber that seals the arc and, by delayed-action construction, prevents complete removal of the plug until the arc or hot metal has cooled. The receptacle is factory sealed and the attachment plug is designed for use with a 4-conductor cord (3-conductor, 3-phase circuit with one grounding conductor) or a 3-conductor cord (two circuit conductors and one grounding conductor).

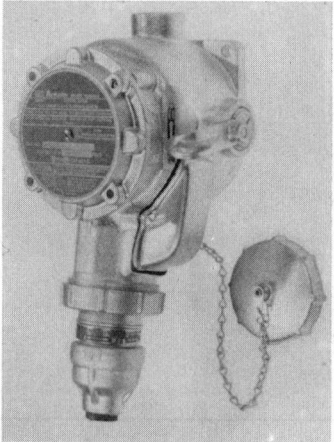

Figure 501-20. A receptacle and attachment plug of the explosionproof type with an interlocking switch. The switch must be in the off position to remove the attachment plug. (*Appleton Electric Co.*)

501-13. Conductor Insulation, Class I, Divisions 1 and 2. Where condensed vapors or liquids may collect on, or come in contact with, the insulation on conductors, such insulation shall be of a type approved for use under such conditions; or the insulation shall be protected by a sheath of lead or by other approved means.

Nylon-jacketed conductors, such as Types THWN and TW that are suitable for use where exposed to gasoline, have gained widespread acceptance because of their ease of handling, application, and economics.

An excerpt from Underwriters Laboratories Inc. (UL) Electrical Construction Materials Directory states the following: Wires, Thermoplastic

Gasoline Resistant TW — Indicates a TW conductor with a jacket of extruded nylon suitable for use in wet locations, and for exposure to mineral oil, and to liquid gasoline and gasoline vapors at ordinary ambient temperature. It is

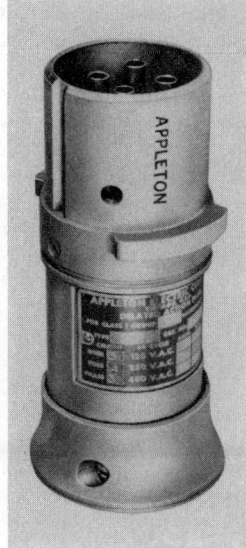

Figure 501-21. A four-pole (delayed action) explosionproof receptacle and attachment plug suitable for use without a switch. (*Appleton Electric Co.*)

identified by tag marking and by printing on the insulation or nylon jacket with the designation "Type TW Gasoline and Oil Resistant I."

Also listed for the above use is "Gasoline Resistant THWN" with the designation "Type THWN Gasoline and Oil Resistant II."

It should be noted that other thermoplastic wires may be suitable for exposure to mineral oil; but with the exception of those marked "Gasoline and Oil Resistant," reference to mineral oil does not include gasoline or similar light-petroleum solvents.

The conductor itself must bear the marking legend designating its use as suitable for gasoline exposure; such designation on the tag alone is not sufficient.

501-14. Signaling, Alarm, Remote-Control, and Communication Systems.

(a) Class I, Division 1. In Class I, Division 1 locations, all apparatus and equipment of signaling, alarm, remote-control, and communication systems, regardless of voltage, shall be approved for Class I, Division 1 locations, and all wiring shall comply with Sections 501-4(a) and 501-5(a) and (c).

(b) Class I, Division 2. In Class I, Division 2 locations, signaling, alarm, remote-control, and communication systems shall comply with the following:

(1) Contacts. Switches, circuit breakers, and make-and-break contacts of pushbuttons, relays, alarm bells, and horns shall have enclosures approved for Class I, Division 1 locations in accordance with Section 501-3(a).

Exception: General-purpose enclosures shall be permitted if current interrupting contacts are:

a. Immersed in oil; or

b. Enclosed within a chamber hermetically sealed against the entrance of gases or vapors; or

661

c. In circuits that under normal conditions do not release sufficient energy to ignite a specific ignitible atmospheric mixture, i.e., are nonincendive.

See commentary following Item c of Section 501-3(b)(1), Exception.

(2) Resistors and Similar Equipment. Resistors, resistance devices, thermionic tubes, rectifiers, and similar equipment shall comply with Section 501-3(b)(2).

(3) Protectors. Enclosures shall be provided for lightning protective devices and for fuses. Such enclosures shall be permitted to be of the general-purpose type.

(4) Wiring and Sealing. All wiring shall comply with Sections 501-4(b) and 501-5(b) and (c).

Audible-signaling devices, such as bells, sirens, and horns, other than the newer electronic types, usually involve make-and-break contacts that are capable of producing a spark of sufficient energy to cause ignition of a hazardous atmospheric mixture. Therefore, when used in Class I locations, this type of equipment is to be contained in explosionproof enclosures and wiring methods are to comply with Section 501-4 and sealing fittings are to be provided in accordance with Section 501-5. Figure 501-22 shows a signal siren for use in Class I locations.

Explosionproof devices or explosionproof enclosures may prove more practical than oil-immersed contacts because maintaining the condition and level of the oil can be a problem. Hermetically sealed enclosures, such as float-operated mercury-tube switches, are available for some applications. Electronic signal devices without make-and-break contacts will usually not require explosionproof enclosures in Division 2 locations.

Figure 501-22. A signal siren mounted on an explosionproof enclosure for use in hazardous areas. (*Crouse-Hinds*)

501-15. Live Parts, Class I, Divisions 1 and 2. There shall be no exposed live parts.

Contact with the circuit could produce sparks that could cause an explosion in a hazardous (classified) location.

501-16. Grounding, Class I, Divisions 1 and 2. Wiring and equipment in Class I, Division 1 and 2 locations shall be grounded as specified in Article 250 and with the following additional requirements:

(a) Bonding. The locknut-bushing and double-locknut types of contacts shall not be depended upon for bonding purposes but bonding jumpers with proper fittings or other approved means of bonding shall be used.

(b) Types of Equipment Grounding Conductors. Where flexible conduit is used as permitted in Section 501-4(b), it shall be installed with internal or external bonding jumpers in parallel with each conduit and complying with Section 250-79.

Special consideration is necessary in the grounding and bonding of exposed noncurrent-carrying metal parts of equipment, such as the frames or metal exteriors of motors, fixed or portable lamps, lighting fixtures, enclosures, and conduits to ensure permanent and effective mechanical and electrical connections to prevent the possibility of arcs or sparks caused by ineffective or poor grounding methods. To be effective, proper grounding and bonding applies to all interconnected raceways, fittings, enclosures, etc., between hazardous (classified) locations and the point of grounding for service equipment. Where conduit is used in hazardous (classified) locations, it is preferable that threaded connections also be employed in the nonhazardous location.

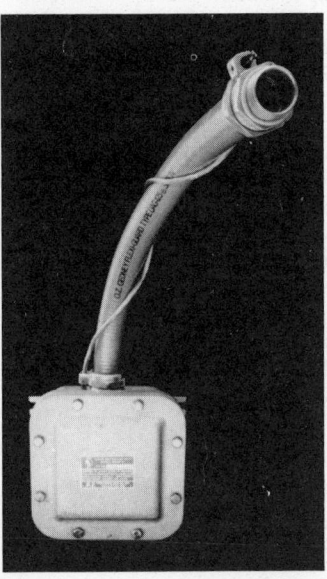

Figure 501-23. A fitting for the connection of an external bonding jumper used with liquidtight flexible metal conduit.

501-17. Surge Protection, Class I, Divisions 1 and 2. Surge arresters, including their installation and connection, shall comply with Article 280. In addition, surge arresters if installed in a Class I, Division 1 location shall be in suitable enclosures.

Some surge arresters, such as the older style lightning arresters, are spark-producing devices. Others, such as solid-state types, are not. Surge arresters should be connected to the service conductors outside the building and be bonded to the service-entrance raceway system. For services less than 1,000 V, the arrester grounding conductor is connected as provided in Section 280-21.

Where the service voltage is less than 600 V, the supply system is a secondary system; thus the grounded service conductor should always be bonded to the equipment grounding conductor as required by the provisions of Article 250.

In Class I, Division 1 locations, all surge arresters are required to be installed in explosionproof or purged and pressurized enclosures. In Class I, Division 2 locations, only the spark-producing types of surge arresters need such protection. They can also be installed in oil-filled enclosures or have the arcing or sparking contacts in hermetically sealed chambers. The nonsparking type of surge arrester needs no special enclosure in a Class I, Division 2 location.

ARTICLE 502 — CLASS II LOCATIONS

Contents

502-1. General. The general rules of this Code shall apply to the electric wiring and equipment in locations classified as Class II locations in Section 500-5

Exception: As modified by this article.

"Dust-ignition-proof," as used in this article, shall mean enclosed in a manner that will exclude ignitible amounts of dusts or amounts that might affect performance or rating and that, where installed and protected in accordance with this Code, will not permit arcs, sparks, or heat otherwise generated or liberated inside of the enclosure to cause ignition of exterior accumulations or atmospheric suspensions of a specified dust on or in the vicinity of the enclosure.

Equipment installed in Class II locations shall be able to function at full rating without developing surface temperatures high enough to cause excessive dehydration or gradual carbonization of any organic dust deposits that may occur.

(FPN): Dust that is carbonized or excessively dry is highly susceptible to spontaneous ignition.

Equipment and wiring of the type defined in Article 100 as explosionproof shall not be required and shall not be acceptable in Class II locations unless approved for such locations.

See Figure 502-3.

Where Class II, Group E dusts having a resistivity less than 10^5 ohm-centimeter are present in hazardous quantities, there are only Division 1 locations.

Class II, Division 1 and 2 locations are defined in Section 500-5 as hazardous due to the presence of combustible dust. These locations are separated into two groups:

Group E, atmospheres containing metal dusts, regardless of resistivity, such as aluminum and magnesium, and dusts of similarly hazardous characteristics having a resistivity of less than 10,000 ohm-centimeter;

Group G, atmospheres containing nonconductive carbonaceous dusts, such as most coal dusts, and flour, starch, grain, or combustible plastics or chemical dusts having a resistivity of 10,000 ohm-centimeter or greater.

Group F locations, in which coal, coke, charcoal, and coke dusts were formerly classified, has been deleted in the 1984 *NEC*.

Most of the Group F dusts are now classified in Group G. There may be a few, however, that should be classified in Group E: those with resistivities of less than 10,000 ohm-centimeter.

Since it is likely that considerable Group F equipment will be available for a number of years, new Section 500-2(d) is included to provide guidance on use of such equipment.

Note that the last paragraph specifically indicates that there are no Division 2 locations (only Division 1) if electrically conductive Group E dusts are present (i.e., dusts with a resistivity less than 100,000 ohm-centimeter). The Instrument Society of America Standard ISA-S12.10-1973, Area Classification in Hazardous Dust Locations, provides some measurements of electrical resistivity of dusts.

It should be noted that equipment suitable for one class and group is not necessarily suitable for any other class and group. To protect against explosion in hazardous (classified) locations, all electrical equipment exposed to the hazardous atmospheres is required to be suitable for such locations. Look for the Underwriters Laboratories (UL) Listing Mark or Factory Mutual (FM) approval. Do not take for granted that equipment suitable for Class I use is also suitable for Class II use. Grain dust, for example, will ignite at a temperature lower than that of many flammable vapors.

Any one, or more, of the following four hazards may be present in a Class II location:

1. An explosive mixture of air and dust;
2. Accumulations of dust that interfere with the safe dissipation of heat from electrical equipment;
3. Accumulation of electrically conductive dust lodging on live parts; and
4. Deposits of dust that could be ignited by arcs or sparks.

In the layout of electrical installations for hazardous (classified) locations, it is preferable to locate service equipment, switchboards, panelboards, and much of the electrical equipment in less hazardous areas, usually in a separate room.

502-2. Transformers and Capacitors.

(a) Class II, Division 1. In Class II, Division 1 locations, transformers and capacitors shall comply with the following:

(1) Containing Liquid that Will Burn. Transformers and capacitors containing a liquid that will burn shall be installed only in approved vaults complying with Sections 450-41 through 450-48, and in addition: (1) doors or other openings communicating with the Division 1 location shall have self-closing fire doors on both sides of the wall, and the doors shall be carefully fitted and provided with suitable seals (such as weather stripping) to minimize the entrance of dust into the vault; (2) vent openings and ducts shall communicate only with the outside air; and (3) suitable pressure-relief openings communicating with the outside air shall be provided.

(2) Not Containing Liquid that Will Burn. Transformers and capacitors that do not contain a liquid that will burn shall: (1) be installed in vaults complying with Sections 450-41 through 450-48, or (2) be approved as a complete assembly, including terminal connections for Class II locations.

(3) Metal Dusts. No transformer or capacitor shall be installed in a location where dust from magnesium, aluminum, aluminum bronze powders, or other metals of similarly hazardous characteristics may be present.

(b) Class II, Division 2. In Class II, Division 2 locations, transformers and capacitors shall comply with the following:

(1) Containing Liquid that Will Burn. Transformers and capacitors containing a liquid that will burn shall be installed in vaults complying with Sections 450-41 through 450-48.

(2) Containing Askarel. Transformers containing askarel and rated in excess of 25 kVA shall: (1) be provided with pressure-relief vents; (2) be provided with a means for absorbing any gases generated by arcing inside the case, or the pressure-relief vents shall be connected to a chimney or flue that will carry such gases outside the building; and (3) have an air space of not less than 6 inches (152 mm) between the transformer cases and any adjacent combustible material.

(3) Dry-type Transformers. Dry-type transformers shall be installed in vaults or shall: (1) have their windings and terminal connections enclosed in tight metal housings without ventilating or other openings, and (2) operate at not over 600 volts, nominal.

At this time no UL listed dry-type or high fire point liquid-insulated transformers that are dusttight and suitable for use in a Class II location are available. It may be possible to construct a small, low-voltage, dusttight (without ventilating openings) dry-type transformer, but transformers having a primary voltage rating of over 600 V are required to be either high fire point liquid-insulated or installed in a vault. In almost all cases, transformers can be located remote from dust atmospheres.

Capacitors used for power-factor correction of individual motors are of sealed construction but, if installed in Class II locations, are also required to be provided with dusttight terminal enclosures. The only special requirement for capacitors in Division 2 locations is that they are not permitted to contain oil or any other liquid that will burn; otherwise they are to be installed in vaults.

Capacitor and transformer oils (such as askarel) that do not burn have, in the past, contained PCBs, and production of such oil has been stopped.

Figure 502-1 illustrates suitable protection for wiring systems in Class II locations supplied from overhead transmission lines. This protection includes surge (lightning) arresters on the primary side of the transformers (within 1,000 ft of the service entrance), surge-protective capacitors connected to the supply side of the main service disconnecting means, and interconnection of all grounds. Arresters should be of the proper voltage rating for the system to which they are connected and where protecting the primary supply should be located within 300 ft of the transformers. Surge capacitors are to protect against abrupt increases in voltage and should be provided with automatic means for dissipating any stored charge.

Detailed information for the application of lightning arresters and surge protectors may be obtained from Mill Mutual Fire Prevention Bureau, 2 North Riverside Plaza, Chicago, IL 60606.

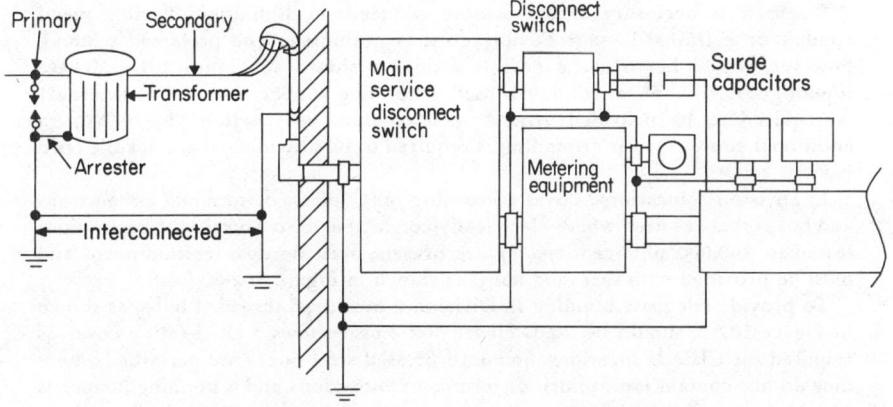

Figure 502-1. Lightning protection: arrester, interconnected grounding, and surge capacitors.

502-4. Wiring Methods. Wiring methods shall comply with (a) and (b) below.

(a) Class II, Division 1. In Class II, Division 1 locations, threaded rigid metal conduit, threaded steel intermediate metal conduit or Type MI cable with termination fittings approved for the location shall be the wiring method employed. Type MI cable shall be installed and supported in a manner to avoid tensile stress at the termination fittings.

(1) Fittings and Boxes. Fittings and boxes shall be provided with threaded bosses for connection to conduit or cable terminations, shall have close-fitting covers, and shall have no openings (such as holes for attachment screws) through which dust might enter or through which sparks or burning material might escape. Fittings and boxes in which taps, joints, or terminal connections are made, or that are used in locations where dusts are of a combustible electrically conductive nature, shall be approved for Class II locations.

(2) Flexible Connections. Where necessary to employ flexible connections, dusttight flexible connectors, liquidtight flexible metal conduit with approved fittings, or flexible cord approved for extra-hard usage and provided with bushed fittings shall be used. Where flexible cords are used and electrically conducting dusts are encountered, they shall be provided with dusttight seals at both ends. An additional conductor for grounding shall be provided in the flexible cord unless other acceptable means of grounding is provided. Where flexible connections are subject to oil or other corrosive conditions, the insulation of the conductors shall be of a type approved for the condition or shall be protected by means of a suitable sheath.

(b) Class II, Division 2. In Class II, Division 2 locations, rigid metal conduit, intermediate metal conduit, electrical metallic tubing, dusttight wireways, or Type MI, MC, or SNM cable with approved termination fittings shall be the wiring method employed.

(1) Wireways, Fittings, and Boxes. Wireways, fittings, and boxes in which taps, joints, or terminal connections are made shall be designed to minimize the entrance of dust, and: (1) shall be provided with telescoping or close-fitting covers or other effective means to prevent the escape of sparks or burning material, and (2) shall have no openings (such as holes for attachment screws) through which, after installation, sparks or burning material might escape or through which adjacent combustible material might be ignited.

(2) Flexible Connections. Where flexible connections are necessary, (a)(2) above shall apply.

Where it is necessary to use flexible connections, liquidtight flexible metal conduit or extra-hard usage flexible cord is permitted. The preferred method, however, would be to use a flexible fitting as shown in Figure 501-4. Where liquidtight flexible metal conduit is used, a bonding jumper (internal or external) is required to be provided around such conduit. See Section 502-16(b). An additional conductor for grounding is required to be provided where flexible cord is used.

In Division 1 locations, boxes containing taps, joints, or terminal connections and boxes that are used where electrically-conductive dusts (dusts with resistivities less than 100,000 ohm-centimeter) are present must be dust-ignition-proof and must be provided with threaded hubs, as shown in Figure 502-2.

To provide adequate bonding in Division 2 locations, threaded hubs, as shown in Figure 502-2, should be used. Figure 502-2 also shows a close-fitting cover as required for Class II locations. Standard pressed steel boxes are permitted where they do not contain taps, joints, or terminal connections and a bonding jumper is provided around the box.

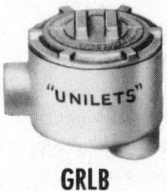

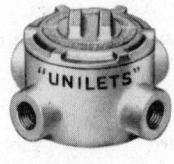

GRLB　　　　　　**GRX**

Figure 502-2. Junction boxes with threaded hubs suitable for use in Class II, Group E hazardous atmospheres. (*Appleton Electric Co.*)

502-5. Sealing, Class II, Divisions 1 and 2. Where a raceway provides communication between an enclosure that is required to be dust-ignition-proof and one that is not, suitable means shall be provided to prevent the entrance of dust into the dust-ignition-proof enclosure through the raceway. One of the following means shall be permitted: (1) a permanent and effective seal; (2) a horizontal raceway not less than 10 feet (3.05 m) long; or (3) a vertical raceway not less than 5 feet (1.52 m) long and extending downward from the dust-ignition-proof enclosure.

Where a raceway provides communication between an enclosure that is required to be dust-ignition-proof and an enclosure in an unclassified location, seals will not be required.

Sealing fittings shall be accessible.

This section provides three suitable ways to prevent dust from entering the dust-ignition-proof enclosure through the raceway where a raceway connects an enclosure that is required to be dust-ignition-proof to one that is not. If sealing fittings are used, any of the fittings designed for use in Class I locations can be used. No sealing method is needed in the special, but not unusual, situation in which no dust can enter the raceway in the hazardous (classified) location. See Figure 502-4.

502-6. Switches, Circuit Breakers, Motor Controllers, and Fuses.

(a) Class II, Division 1. In Class II, Division 1 locations, switches, circuit breakers, motor controllers, and fuses shall comply with the following:

(1) Type Required. Switches, circuit breakers, motor controllers, and fuses, including pushbuttons, relays, and similar devices that are intended to interrupt current during normal operation or that are installed where combustible dusts of an electrically conductive nature may be present, shall be provided with dust-ignition-proof enclosures, which, together with the enclosed equipment in each case, shall be approved as a complete assembly for Class II locations.

(2) Isolating Switches. Disconnecting and isolating switches containing no fuses and not intended to interrupt current and not installed where dusts may be of an electrically conductive nature shall be provided with tight metal enclosures that shall be designed to minimize the entrance of dust, and that shall: (1) be equipped with telescoping or close-fitting covers or with other effective means to prevent the escape of sparks or burning material, and (2) have no openings (such as holes for attachment screws) through which, after installation, sparks or burning material might escape or through which exterior accumulations of dust or adjacent combustible material might be ignited.

(3) Metal Dusts. In locations where dust from magnesium, aluminum, aluminum bronze powders, or other metals of similarly hazardous characteristics may be present, fuses, switches, motor controllers, and circuit breakers shall have enclosures specifically approved for such locations.

(b) Class II, Division 2. In Class II, Division 2 locations, enclosures for fuses, switches, circuit breakers, and motor controllers, including pushbuttons, relays, and similar devices, shall be dusttight.

Figure 502-3 shows a push-button station with pilot light suitable for both Class I and Class II hazardous (classified) locations. Figure 502-5 shows a panelboard suitable for use in Class II locations only. Most, but not necessarily all, of the switches or circuit breakers approved for Class I, Division 1 locations are also approved for Class II locations, but always look for the listing and identification of the hazardous (classified) locations for which the listing has been given.

Figure 502-3. An explosionproof and dusttight pushbutton control station that is suitable for use in Class I, Group C and D and Class II, Group E and G locations. (*Appleton Electric Co.*)

502-7. Control Transformers and Resistors.

(a) Class II, Division 1. In Class II, Division 1 locations, control transformers, solenoids, impedance coils, resistors, and any overcurrent devices or switching mechanisms associated with them shall have dust-ignition-proof enclosures approved for Class II locations. No control transformer, impedance coil, or resistor shall be installed in a location where dust from magnesium, aluminum, aluminum bronze powders, or other metals of similarly hazardous characteristics may be present unless provided with an enclosure approved for the specific location.

(b) Class II, Division 2. In Class II, Division 2 locations, transformers and resistors shall comply with the following:

(1) Switching Mechanisms. Switching mechanisms (including overcurrent devices) associated with control transformers, solenoids, impedance coils, and resistors shall be provided with dusttight enclosures.

(2) Coils and Windings. Where not located in the same enclosure with switching mechanisms, control transformers, solenoids, and impedance coils shall be provided with tight metal housings without ventilating openings.

(3) Resistors. Resistors and resistance devices shall have dust-ignition-proof enclosures approved for Class II locations.

Exception: Where the maximum normal operating temperature of the resistor will not exceed 120°C (248°F), nonadjustable resistors or resistors that are part of an automatically timed starting sequence shall be permitted to have enclosures complying with (b)(2) above.

502-8. Motors and Generators.

(a) Class II, Division 1. In Class II, Division 1 locations, motors, generators, and other rotating electrical machinery shall be:

(1) Approved for Class II, Division 1 locations, or

(2) Totally enclosed pipe-ventilated, meeting temperature limitations in Section 502-1.

It is intended that the phrase "other rotating electrical machinery" include electric brakes. Listed and labeled electric brakes are available for Class I, Group E and G locations.

Although some explosionproof (Class I, Division 1) motors are also dust-ignition-proof, and approved for both Class I and II locations, this is by no means true of all motors. Always look for the marking to be sure the motor is designed and tested for the Class II location involved. If control wiring to the motor is necessary (see motor installation instruction), be sure the control circuit is properly installed and connected. Most motors for Class II locations require internal thermal protection to comply with the temperature limitations in Section 500-2(d), and integral horsepower Class II motors may require both power and control circuit wiring from the motor controller to the motor.

(b) Class II, Division 2. In Class II, Division 2 locations, motors, generators, and other rotating electrical equipment shall be totally enclosed nonventilated, totally enclosed pipe ventilated, totally enclosed fan cooled or dust-ignition-proof for which maximum full-load external temperature shall not exceed 120°C (248°F) when operating in free air (not dust blanketed) and shall have no external openings.

Exception: If the authority having jurisdiction believes accumulations of nonconductive nonabrasive dust will be moderate, and if machines can be easily reached for routine cleaning and maintenance, the following may be installed:

a. Standard open-type machines without sliding contacts, centrifugal or other types of switching mechanism (including motor overcurrent, overloading and overtemperature devices), or integral resistance devices.

b. Standard open-type machines with such contacts, switching mechanisms, or resistance devices enclosed within dusttight housings without ventilating or other openings.

c. Self-cleaning textile motors of the squirrel-cage type.

Section 502-8(b) permits all types of totally enclosed motors in Class II, Division 2 locations if the external surface temperatures without a dust blanket do not exceed 120°C (248°F). Totally enclosed fan-cooled (TEFC) motors are specifically mentioned. The motor should be examined carefully to be sure there are no external openings, even though the motor may be marked "TEFC."

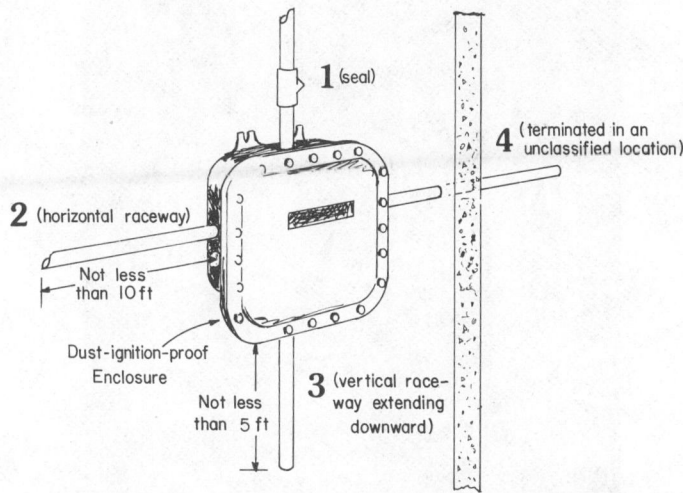

Figure 502-4. Illustrated are four methods permitted for preventing the entrance of dust into the dust-ignition-proof enclosure through the raceway.

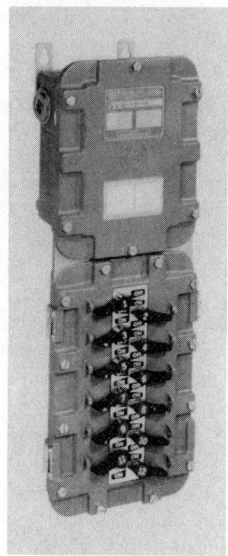

Figure 502-5. A dust-ignition-proof panelboard for use in Class II, Group E and G locations. (*Appleton Electric Co.*)

Figure 502-6 shows a totally enclosed pipe-ventilated motor showing intake piping through which cool, clean air is delivered to the motor from a fan or blower. The exhaust opening is connected to a pipe discharging to the outside of the building in order to prevent dust accumulation inside the motor.

Totally enclosed motors that have no special provision for cooling may be used in Class II, Division 2 locations, but to deliver the same horsepower, they must be considerably larger than an open-type, fan-cooled, or pipe-ventilated motor.

Figure 502-6. A pipe-ventilated motor that meets temperature limitations of Section 502-1. (*General Electric Co.*)

502-9. Ventilating Piping. Ventilating pipes for motors, generators, or other rotating electric machinery, or for enclosures for electric equipment, shall be of metal not lighter than No. 24 MSG, or of equally substantial noncombustible material, and shall comply with the following: (1) lead directly to a source of clean air outside of buildings; (2) be screened at the outer ends to prevent the entrance of small animals or birds; and (3) be protected against physical damage and against rusting or other corrosive influences.

Ventilating pipes shall also comply with (a) and (b) below.

(a) Class II, Division 1. In Class II, Division 1 locations, ventilating pipes, including their connections to motors or to the dust-ignition-proof enclosures for other equipment, shall be dusttight throughout their length. For metal pipes, seams and joints shall comply with one of the following: (1) be riveted and soldered; (2) be bolted and soldered; (3) be welded; or (4) be rendered dusttight by some other equally effective means.

(b) Class II, Division 2. In Class II, Division 2 locations, ventilating pipes and their connections shall be sufficiently tight to prevent the entrance of appreciable quantities of dust into the ventilated equipment or enclosure, and to prevent the escape of sparks, flame, or burning material that might ignite dust accumulations or combustible material in the vicinity. For metal pipes, lock seams and riveted or welded joints shall be permitted; and tight-fitting slip joints shall be permitted where some flexibility is necessary, as at connections to motors.

502-10. Utilization Equipment.

(a) Class II, Division 1. In Class II, Division 1 locations, all utilization equipment shall be approved for Class II locations. Where dust from magnesium, aluminum, aluminum bronze powders, or other metals of similarly hazardous characteristics may be present, such equipment shall be approved for the specific location.

(b) Class II, Division 2. In Class II, Division 2 locations, all utilization equipment shall comply with the following:

(1) Heaters. Electrically heated utilization equipment shall be approved for Class II locations.

(2) Motors. Motors of motor-driven utilization equipment shall comply with Section 502-8(b).

(3) Switches, Circuit Breakers, and Fuses. Enclosures for switches, circuit breakers, and fuses shall be dusttight.

(4) Transformers, Impedance Coils, and Resistors. Transformers, solenoids, impedance coils, and resistors shall comply with Section 502-7(b).

502-11. Lighting Fixtures. Lighting fixtures shall comply with (a) and (b) below.

(a) Class II, Division 1. In Class II, Division 1 locations, lighting fixtures for fixed and portable lighting shall comply with the following:

(1) Approved Fixtures. Each fixture shall be approved for Class II locations and shall be clearly marked to indicate the maximum wattage of the lamp for which it is approved. In locations where dust from magnesium, aluminum, aluminum bronze powders, or other metals of similarly hazardous characteristics may be present, fixtures for fixed or portable lighting and all auxiliary equipment shall be approved for the specific location.

(2) Physical Damage. Each fixture shall be protected against physical damage by a suitable guard or by location.

(3) Pendant Fixtures. Pendant fixtures shall be suspended by threaded rigid metal conduit stems, threaded steel intermediate metal conduit stems, by chains with approved fittings, or by other approved means. For rigid stems longer than 12 inches (305 mm), permanent and effective bracing against lateral displacement shall be provided at a level not more than 12 inches (305 mm) above the lower end of the stem, or flexibility in the form of a fitting or a flexible connector approved for the location shall be provided not more than 12 inches (305 mm) from the point of attachment to the supporting box or fitting. Threaded joints shall be provided with set-screws or other effective means to prevent loosening. Where wiring between an outlet box or fitting and a pendant fixture is not enclosed in conduit, flexible cord approved for hard usage shall be used, and suitable seals shall be provided where the cord enters the fixture and the outlet box or fitting. Flexible cord shall not serve as the supporting means for a fixture.

(4) Supports. Boxes, box assemblies, or fittings used for the support of lighting fixtures shall be approved for Class II locations.

(b) Class II, Division 2. In Class II, Division 2 locations, lighting fixtures shall comply with the following:

ARTICLE 502—CLASS II LOCATIONS

(1) Portable Lighting Equipment. Portable lighting equipment shall be approved for Class II locations. They shall be clearly marked to indicate the maximum wattage of lamps for which they are approved.

(2) Fixed Lighting. Lighting fixtures for fixed lighting, where not of a type approved for Class II locations, shall provide enclosures for lamps and lampholders that shall be designed to minimize the deposit of dust on lamps and to prevent the escape of sparks, burning material, or hot metal. Each fixture shall be clearly marked to indicate the maximum wattage of the lamp that shall be permitted without exceeding an exposed surface temperature of 165°C (329°F) under normal conditions of use.

(3) Physical Damage. Lighting fixtures for fixed lighting shall be protected from physical damage by suitable guards or by location.

(4) Pendant Fixtures. Pendant fixtures shall be suspended by threaded rigid metal conduit stems, threaded steel intermediate metal conduit stems, by chains with approved fittings, or by other approved means. For rigid stems longer than 12 inches (305 mm), permanent and effective bracing against lateral displacement shall be provided at a level not more than 12 inches (305 mm) above the lower end of the stem, or flexibility in the form of an approved fitting or a flexible connector shall be provided not more than 12 inches (305 mm) from the point of attachment to the supporting box or fitting. Where wiring between an outlet box or fitting and a pendant fixture is not enclosed in conduit, flexible cord approved for hard usage shall be used. Flexible cord shall not serve as the supporting means for a fixture.

(5) Electric-Discharge Lamps. Starting and control equipment for electric-discharge lamps shall comply with the requirements of Section 502-7(b).

Figure 502-7 shows a fixture listed by Underwriters Laboratories Inc. as suitable for use in Groups E and G of Class II locations. Lighting fixtures are required to be approved for use in Group E atmospheres where metal dusts are present.

Other than the requirement that the fixture is to be marked to indicate maximum lamp wattage, the only requirements for fixtures in Division 2 locations are that the lamps be enclosed in suitable glass globes to minimize dust deposits on the lamps and to prevent the escape of sparks or burning material. Guards are required to be provided unless, of course, globe breakage is unlikely.

Flexible cord of the hard-usage type is permitted with approved sealed connections for the wiring of chain-suspended or hook-and-eye suspended fixtures. Flexible cords are not intended to be used as a cord pendant or drop cord.

The portable handlamp shown in Figure 501-18 is approved as a complete assembly for use in Class I locations and also in any Class II, Group G location.

502-12. Flexible Cords, Class II, Divisions 1 and 2. Flexible cords used in Class II locations shall comply with the following: (1) be of a type approved for extra-hard usage; (2) contain, in addition to the conductors of the circuit, a grounding conductor complying with Section 400-23; (3) be connected to terminals or to supply conductors in an approved manner; (4) be supported by clamps or by other suitable means in such a manner that there will be no tension on the terminal connections; and (5) be provided with suitable seals to prevent the entrance of dust where the flexible cord enters boxes or fittings that are required to be dust-ignition-proof.

502-13. Receptacles and Attachment Plugs.

(a) Class II, Division 1. In Class II, Division 1 locations, receptacles and attachment plugs shall be of the type providing for connection to the grounding conductor of the flexible cord and shall be approved for Class II locations.

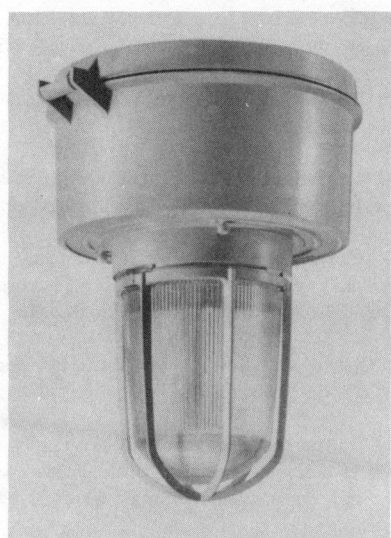

Figure 502-7. A typical lighting fixture for use in Class II, Division 1 locations. Where breakage is unlikely, a metal guard is not required.

(b) Class II, Division 2. In Class II, Division 2 locations, receptacles and attachment plugs shall be of the type providing for connection to the grounding conductor of the flexible cord and shall be so designed that connection to the supply circuit cannot be made or broken while live parts are exposed.

502-14. Signaling, Alarm, Remote-Control, and Communication Systems, Meters, Instruments, and Relays.

(FPN): See Article 800 for rules governing the installation of communication circuits.

(a) Class II, Division 1. In Class II, Division 1 locations, signaling, alarm, remote-control, and communication systems; and meters, instruments, and relays shall comply with the following:

(1) Wiring Methods. Where accidental damage or breakdown of insulation might cause arcs, sparks, or high temperatures, the wiring method shall be rigid metal conduit, intermediate metal conduit, electrical metallic tubing, or Type MI cable with approved termination fittings. For rigid conduit, intermediate metal conduit, or electrical metallic tubing, the number of conductors shall be limited only by the requirement that the cross-sectional area of all conductors shall not exceed 40 percent of the area of the raceway. Where limited flexibility is desirable or where exposure to physical damage is not severe, flexible cord approved for extra-hard usage shall be permitted.

(2) Contacts. Switches, circuit breakers, relays, contactors, fuses and current-breaking contacts for bells, horns, howlers, sirens, and other devices in which sparks or arcs may be produced shall be provided with enclosures approved for a Class II location.

Exception: Where current-breaking contacts are immersed in oil, or where the interruption of current occurs within a chamber sealed against the entrance of dust, enclosures shall be permitted to be of the general-purpose type.

(3) Resistors and Similar Equipment. Resistors, transformers, choke coils, rectifiers, thermionic tubes, and other heat-generating equipment shall be provided with enclosures approved for Class II locations.

Exception: Where resistors or similar equipment are immersed in oil, or enclosed in a chamber sealed against the entrance of dust, enclosures shall be permitted to be of the general-purpose type.

(4) Rotating Machinery. Motors, generators, and other rotating electric machinery shall comply with Section 502-8(a).

(5) Combustible Electrically Conductive Dusts. Where dusts are of a combustible electrically conductive nature, all wiring and equipment shall be approved for Class II locations.

(6) Metal Dusts. Where dust from magnesium, aluminum, aluminum bronze powders, or other metals of similarly hazardous characteristics may be present, all apparatus and equipment shall be approved for the specific conditions.

(b) Class II, Division 2. In Class II, Division 2 locations, signaling, alarm, remote-control, and communication systems; and meters, instruments, and relays shall comply with the following:

(1) Contacts. Enclosures shall comply with (a)(2) above; or contacts shall have tight metal enclosures designed to minimize the entrance of dust, and shall have telescoping or tight-fitting covers and no openings through which, after installation, sparks or burning material might escape.

Exception: In circuits that under normal conditions do not release sufficient energy to ignite a dust layer, enclosures shall be permitted to be of the general-purpose type.

(2) Transformers and Similar Equipment. The windings and terminal connections of transformers, choke coils, and similar equipment shall be provided with tight metal enclosures without ventilating openings.

(3) Resistors and Similar Equipment. Resistors, resistance devices, thermionic tubes, rectifiers, and similar equipment shall comply with (a)(3) above.

Exception: Enclosures for thermionic tubes, nonadjustable resistors, or rectifiers for which maximum operating temperature will not exceed 120°C (248°F) shall be permitted to be of the general-purpose type.

(4) Rotating Machinery. Motors, generators, and other rotating electric machinery shall comply with Section 502-8(b).

502-15. Live Parts, Class II, Divisions 1 and 2. Live parts shall not be exposed.

502-16. Grounding, Class II, Divisions 1 and 2. Wiring and equipment in Class II, Division 1 and 2 locations shall be grounded as specified in Article 250 and with the following additional requirements:

(a) Bonding. The locknut-bushing and double-locknut types of contact shall not be depended upon for bonding purposes but bonding jumpers with proper fittings or other approved means of bonding shall be used.

(b) Types of Equipment Grounding Conductors. Where flexible conduit is used as permitted in Section 502-4 it shall be installed with internal or external bonding jumpers in parallel with each conduit and complying with Section 250-79.

Single locknuts or double locknuts and bushings are not to be depended upon for bonding purposes. Bonding jumpers or other approved means with proper fittings are required for the interconnection of all raceways, junction boxes, fittings, enclosures, etc., between the hazardous area and all the way to the

grounding electrode conductor connection point at the service equipment. Where installed outside the raceway or enclosure, the grounding conductor is not to exceed 6 ft and is to be routed with the raceway or enclosure. See Section 250-79.

502-17. Surge Protection, Class II, Divisions 1 and 2. Surge arresters, including their installation and connection shall comply with Article 280. In addition, surge arresters if installed in a Class II, Division 1 location shall be in suitable enclosures.

Surge-protective capacitors shall be of a type designed for specific duty.

ARTICLE 503 — CLASS III LOCATIONS

Contents

503-1. General. The general rules of this Code shall apply to electric wiring and equipment in locations classified as Class III locations in Section 500-6.

Exception: As modified by this article.

Equipment installed in Class III locations shall be able to function at full rating without developing surface temperatures high enough to cause excessive dehydration or gradual carbonization of accumulated fibers or flyings.Organic material that is carbonized or excessively dry is highly susceptible to spontaneous ignition. The maximum surface temperatures under operating conditions shall not exceed 165°C (329°F) for equipment that is not subject to overloading, and 120°C (248°F) for equipment (such as motors or power transformers) that may be overloaded.

ARTICLE 503—CLASS III LOCATIONS

(FPN): For electric trucks, see Powered Industrial Trucks Including Type Designations, Areas of Use, Maintenance and Operation, NFPA 505-1982 (ANSI).

Class III locations usually include textile mills (cotton, rayon, etc.) where easily ignitible fibers or combustible flyings are present in the manufacturing process. Sawmills and other woodworking plants, where sawdust, wood shavings, and combustible fibers or flyings are present, may also become hazardous. If wood flour (dust) is present, the location is a Class II, Group G location, not a Class III location.

Fibers or flyings are hazardous not only because they are easily ignited, but also because flames spread through them quickly. Such fires travel with a rapidity approaching an explosion and are commonly called "flash fires."

Division 1 of Class III applies to locations where material is handled, manufactured, or used. Division 2 applies to locations where material is stored or handled, but where no manufacturing processes are performed. There are no group designations in Class III locations.

503-2. Transformers and Capacitors, Class III, Divisions 1 and 2. Transformers and capacitors shall comply with Section 502-2(b).

503-3. Wiring Methods. Wiring methods shall comply with (a) and (b) below.

(a) Class III, Division 1. In Class III, Division 1 locations, the wiring method shall be rigid metal conduit, rigid nonmetallic conduit, intermediate metal conduit, electrical metallic tubing, dusttight wireways, or Type MI, MC, or SNM cable with approved termination fittings.

(1) Boxes and Fittings. Fittings and boxes in which taps, joints, or terminal connections are made shall: (1) be provided with telescoping or close-fitting covers or other effective means to prevent the escape of sparks or burning material, and (2) shall have no openings (such as holes for attachment screws) through which, after installation, sparks or burning material might escape, or through which adjacent combustible material might be ignited.

(2) Flexible Connections. Where flexible connections are necessary, Section 502-4(a)(2) shall apply.

(b) Class III, Division 2. In Class III, Division 2 locations, the wiring method shall comply with (a) above.

Exception: In sections, compartments, or areas used solely for storage and containing no machinery, open wiring on insulators shall be permitted where installed in accordance with Article 320, but only on condition that protection as required by Section 320-14 be provided where conductors are not run in roof spaces and are well out of reach of sources of physical damage.

503-4. Switches, Circuit Breakers, Motor Controllers, and Fuses, Class III, Divisions 1 and 2. Switches, circuit breakers, motor controllers, and fuses, including pushbuttons, relays, and similar devices, shall be provided with tight metal enclosures designed to minimize entrance of fibers and flyings, and which shall: (1) be equipped with telescoping or close-fitting covers or with other effective means to prevent escape of sparks or burning material, and (2) have no openings (such as holes for attachment screws) through which, after installation, sparks or burning material might escape, or through which exterior accumulations of fibers or flyings or adjacent combustible material might be ignited.

503-5. Control Transformers and Resistors, Class III, Divisions 1 and 2. Transformers, impedance coils, and resistors used as or in conjunction with control equipment for motors, generators, and appliances shall comply with Section 502-7(b).

Exception: In Class III, Division 1 locations where these devices are in the same enclosure with switching devices of such control equipment and are used only for starting or short-time duty, the enclosure shall comply with Section 503-4.

503-6. Motors and Generators, Class III, Divisions 1 and 2. In Class III, Division 1 and 2 locations, motors, generators, and other rotating machinery shall be totally enclosed nonventilated, totally enclosed pipe-ventilated, or totally enclosed fan-cooled.

Exception: In locations where, in the judgment of the authority having jurisdiction, only moderate accumulations of lint or flyings will be likely to collect on, in, or in the vicinity of a rotating electric machine, and where such machine is readily accessible for routine cleaning and maintenance, one of the following shall be permitted:

a. Self-cleaning textile motors of the squirrel-cage types;

b. Standard open-type machines without sliding contacts, centrifugal or other types of switching mechanism, including motor overload devices; or

c. Standard open-type machines having such contacts, switching mechanisms, or resistance devices enclosed within tight housings without ventilating or other openings.

It is intended that the phrase "other rotating electric machinery" include electric brakes. Listed and labeled electric brakes are available for Class II, Group G locations, and according to Underwriters Laboratories Inc. (UL) Hazardous Location Equipment Directory, such brakes are suitable for Class III locations.

503-7. Ventilating Piping, Class III, Divisions 1 and 2. Ventilating pipes for motors, generators, or other rotating electric machinery, or for enclosures for electric equipment shall be of metal not lighter than No. 24 MSG, or of equally substantial noncombustible material, and shall comply with the following: (1) lead directly to a source of clean air outside of buildings; (2) be screened at the outer ends to prevent the entrance of small animals or birds; and (3) be protected against physical damage and against rusting or other corrosive influences.

Ventilating pipes shall be sufficiently tight, including their connections, to prevent the entrance of appreciable quantities of fibers or flyings into the ventilated equipment or enclosure and to prevent the escape of sparks, flame, or burning material that might ignite accumulations of fibers or flyings or combustible material in the vicinity. For metal pipes, lock seams and riveted or welded joints shall be permitted; and tight-fitting slip joints shall be permitted where some flexibility is necessary, as at connections to motors.

503-8. Utilization Equipment, Class III, Divisions 1 and 2.

(a) Heaters. Electrically heated utilization equipment shall be approved for Class III locations.

(b) Motors. Motors of motor-driven utilization equipment shall comply with Section 503-6.

(c) Switches, Circuit Breakers, Motor Controllers, and Fuses. Switches, circuit breakers, motor controllers, and fuses shall comply with Section 503-4.

503-9. Lighting Fixtures, Class III, Divisions 1 and 2.

(a) Fixed Lighting. Lighting fixtures for fixed lighting shall provide enclosures for lamps and lampholders that are designed to minimize entrance of fibers and flyings and to prevent the escape of sparks, burning material, or hot metal. Each fixture shall be clearly marked to show the maximum wattage of the lamps that shall be permitted without exceeding an exposed surface temperature of 165°C (329°F) under normal conditions of use.

(b) Physical Damage. A fixture that may be exposed to physical damage shall be protected by a suitable guard.

(c) Pendant Fixtures. Pendant fixtures shall be suspended by stems of threaded rigid metal conduit, threaded intermediate metal conduit, threaded metal tubing of equivalent thickness, or by chains with approved fittings. For stems longer than 12 inches (305 mm), permanent and effective bracing against lateral displacement shall be provided at a level not more than 12 inches (305 mm) above the lower end of the stem, or flexibility in the form of an approved fitting or a flexible connector shall be provided not more than 12 inches (305 mm) from the point of attachment to the supporting box or fitting.

(d) Portable Lighting Equipment. Portable lighting equipment shall be equipped with handles and protected with substantial guards. Lampholders shall be of the unswitched type with no provision for receiving attachment plugs. There shall be no exposed current-carrying metal parts and all exposed noncurrent-carrying metal parts shall be grounded. In all other respects, portable lighting equipment shall comply with (a) above.

503-10. Flexible Cords, Class III, Divisions 1 and 2. Flexible cords shall comply with the following: (1) be of a type approved for extra-hard usage; (2) contain, in addition to the conductors of the circuit, a grounding conductor complying with Section 400-23; (3) be connected to terminals or to supply conductors in an approved manner; (4) be supported by clamps or other suitable means in such a manner that there will be no' tension on the terminal connections; and (5) be provided with suitable means to prevent the entrance of fibers or flyings where the cord enters boxes or fittings.

503-11. Receptacles and Attachment Plugs, Class III, Divisions 1 and 2. Receptacles and attachment plugs shall be of the grounding type and shall be so designed to minimize the accumulation or the entry of fibers or flyings, and shall prevent the escape of sparks or molten particles.

Exception: In locations where, in the judgment of the authority having jurisdiction, only moderate accumulations of lint or flyings will be likely to collect in the vicinity of a receptacle, and where such receptacle is readily accessible for routine cleaning, general-purpose grounding-type receptacles mounted so as to minimize the entry of fibers or flyings shall be permitted.

503-12. Signaling, Alarm, Remote-Control, and Local Loudspeaker Intercommunication Systems, Class III, Divisions 1 and 2. Signaling, alarm, remote-control, and local loudspeaker intercommunication systems shall comply with the requirements of Article 503 regarding wiring methods, switches, transformers, resistors, motors, lights, and related components.

503-13. Electric Cranes, Hoists, and Similar Equipment, Class III, Divisions 1 and 2. Where installed for operation over combustible fibers or accumulations of flyings, traveling cranes and hoists for material handling, traveling cleaners for textile machinery, and similar equipment shall comply with (a) through (d) below.

(a) Power Supply. Power supply to contact conductors shall be isolated from all other systems and shall be equipped with an acceptable ground detector that will give an alarm and automatically de-energize the contact conductors in case of a fault to ground or will give a visual and audible alarm as long as power is supplied to the contact conductors or the ground fault remains.

(b) Contact Conductors. Contact conductors shall be so located or guarded as to be inaccessible to other than authorized persons and shall be protected against accidental contact with foreign objects.

(c) Current Collectors. Current collectors shall be so arranged or guarded as to confine normal sparking and prevent escape of sparks or hot particles. To reduce sparking, two or more separate surfaces of contact shall be provided for each contact conductor. Reliable means shall be provided to keep contact conductors and current collectors free of accumulations of lint or flyings.

(d) Control Equipment. Control equipment shall comply with Sections 503-4 and 503-5.

In a Class III location, cranes installed over accumulations of fibers or flyings and equipped with rolling or sliding collectors making contact with bare conductors introduce two hazards:

1. Any arcing between a conductor and a collector rail may ignite combustible fibers or "lint" accumulated on or near the bare conductor. This hazard may be prevented by maintaining the proper alignment of the bare conductor, by using a collector designed so that proper contact is always maintained, and by using guards or shields to confine hot metal particles that may be caused by arcing.

2. If enough moisture is present, fibers and flyings accumulating on the insulating supports of the bare conductors may form a conductive path between the conductors, or from one conductor to ground, thereby permitting enough current to flow to ignite the fibers. Where the system is ungrounded, a current flow to ground is unlikely to start a fire. A suitable recording ground detector will give an alarm and automatically deenergize contact conductors when the insulation resistance is being lowered by an accumulation of fibers on the insulators or in case of a fault to ground. A ground-fault indicator is permitted that will maintain an alarm until the system is deenergized or the ground fault is cleared.

503-14. Storage-Battery Charging Equipment, Class III, Divisions 1 and 2. Storage-battery charging equipment shall be located in separate rooms built or lined with substantial noncombustible materials so constructed as to adequately exclude flyings or lint and shall be well ventilated.

503-15. Live Parts, Class III, Divisions 1 and 2. Live parts shall not be exposed.

Exception: As provided in Section 503-13.

503-16. Grounding, Class III, Divisions 1 and 2. Wiring and equipment in Class III, Divisions 1 and 2 shall be grounded as specified in Article 250 and with the following additional requirements:

(a) Bonding. The locknut-bushing and double-locknut types of contacts shall not be depended upon for bonding purposes but bonding jumpers with proper fittings or other approved means of bonding shall be used.

(b) Types of Equipment Grounding Conductors. Where flexible conduit is used as permitted in Section 503-3, it shall be installed with internal or external bonding jumpers in parallel with each conduit and complying with Section 250-79.

ARTICLE 510 — HAZARDOUS (CLASSIFIED)
LOCATIONS — SPECIFIC

Contents

510-1. Scope. Articles 511 through 517 cover occupancies or parts of occupancies that are or may be hazardous because of atmospheric concentrations of flammable liquids, gases, or vapors, or because of deposits or accumulations of materials that may be readily ignitible.

510-2. General. The general rules of this Code shall apply to electric wiring and equipment in occupancies within the scope of Articles 511 through 517, except as such rules are modified in those articles. Where unusual conditions exist in a specific occupancy, the authority having jurisdiction shall judge with respect to the application of specific rules.

Information and copies of standards may be obtained from the National Fire Protection Association (NFPA), Batterymarch Park, Quincy, MA 02269.

ARTICLE 511 — COMMERCIAL GARAGES, REPAIR
AND STORAGE

Contents

511-1. Scope. These occupancies shall include locations used for service and repair operations in connection with self-propelled vehicles (including passenger automobiles, buses, trucks, tractors, etc.) in which volatile flammable liquids are used for fuel or power. Areas in which flammable fuel is transferred to vehicle fuel tanks shall conform to Article 514. Parking garages used for parking or storage and where no repair work is done except exchange of parts and routine maintenance requiring no use of electrical equipment, open flame, welding, or the use of volatile flammable liquids are not classified, but they shall be adequately ventilated to carry off the exhaust fumes of the engines.

(FPN): For further information, see Parking Structures, NFPA 88A-1979, and Repair Garages, NFPA 88B-1979.

Article 100 defines "Garage" as a building or portion of a building in which one or more self-propelled vehicles carrying volatile flammable liquid for fuel or power are kept for use, sale, storage, rental, repair, exhibition, or demonstrating purposes, and all that portion of a building which is on or below the floor or floors in which such vehicles are kept and which is not separated therefrom by suitable cutoffs.

A mechanical ventilating system capable of continuously providing at least six air changes per hour is required for all enclosed, basement, and underground parking garages.

Operations involving open flame or electric arcs, including fusion gas and electric welding, are to be restricted to areas specifically provided for such purposes.

Approved suspended unit heaters may be used provided they are located not less than 8 ft above the floor and are installed in accordance with the conditions of their approval.

511-2. Class I Locations. Classification under Article 500.

(a) Up to a Level of 18 Inches (457 mm) Above the Floor. For each floor the entire area up to a level of 18 inches (457 mm) above the floor shall be considered to be a Class I, Division 2 location except where the enforcing agency determines that there is mechanical ventilation providing a minimum of four air changes per hour.

(b) Any Pit or Depression Below Floor Level. Any pit or depression below floor level shall be considered to be a Class I, Division 1 location which shall extend up to said floor level, except that any pit or depression in which six air changes per hour are exhausted at the floor level of the pit shall be permitted to be judged by the enforcing agency to be a Class I, Division 2 location.

(c) Areas Adjacent to Defined Locations with Positive Pressure Ventilation. Areas adjacent to defined locations in which flammable vapors are not likely to be released such as stock rooms, switchboard rooms, and other similar locations shall not be classified when mechanically ventilated at a rate of four or more air changes per hour or when effectively cut off by walls or partitions.

(d) Adjacent Areas by Special Permission. Adjacent areas which by reason of ventilation, air pressure differentials, or physical spacing are such that, in the opinion of the authority enforcing this Code, no ignition hazard exists shall be classified as nonhazardous.

(e) Fuel Dispensing Units. When fuel dispensing units (other than liquid petroleum gas which is prohibited) are located within buildings, the requirements of Article 514 shall govern.

When mechanical ventilation is provided in the dispensing area, the controls shall be interlocked so that the dispenser cannot operate without ventilation as prescribed in Section 500-4(b).

(f) Portable Lighting Equipment. Portable lighting equipment shall be equipped with handle, lampholder, hook and substantial guard attached to the lampholder or handle. All exterior surfaces which might come in contact with battery terminals, wiring terminals, or other objects shall be of nonconducting material or shall be effectively protected with insulation. Lampholders

Figure 511-1. This cord, which is part of a portable lamp assembly, is to be arranged so that the lamp cannot be used in a Class I location; otherwise, the lamp must be of a type approved for Class I, Division 1 hazardous locations (explosionproof). (*Appleton Electric Co.*)

shall be of unswitched type and shall not provide means for plug-in of attachment plugs. Outer shell shall be of molded composition or other suitable material. Unless the lamp and its cord are supported or arranged in such a manner that they cannot be used in the locations classified in Section 511-2 they shall be of a type approved for Class I, Division 1 locations.

Sections 511-2(a) and (b) classify Class I, Divisions 1 and 2 locations of commercial garages. Fuel dispensing units located within the garage are to be governed by the requirements of Article 514.

The Class I, Division 2 location above grade within a commercial garage extends 18 in. above the floor level unless the authority having jurisdiction determines otherwise because there is mechanical ventilation providing at least four air changes per hour.

The Class I, Division 1 location below grade extends from the floor of the pit or depression to floor level, unless the authority having jurisdiction permits the pit or depression to be classified Class I, Division 2 because ventilation providing at least six air changes per hour exhausts air at the floor level of the pit or depression.

511-3. Wiring and Equipment in Class I Locations. Within Class I locations as defined in Section 511-2, wiring and equipment shall conform to applicable provisions of Article 501. Raceways embedded in a masonry wall or buried beneath a floor shall be considered to be within the Class I location above the floor if any connections or extensions lead into or through such areas.

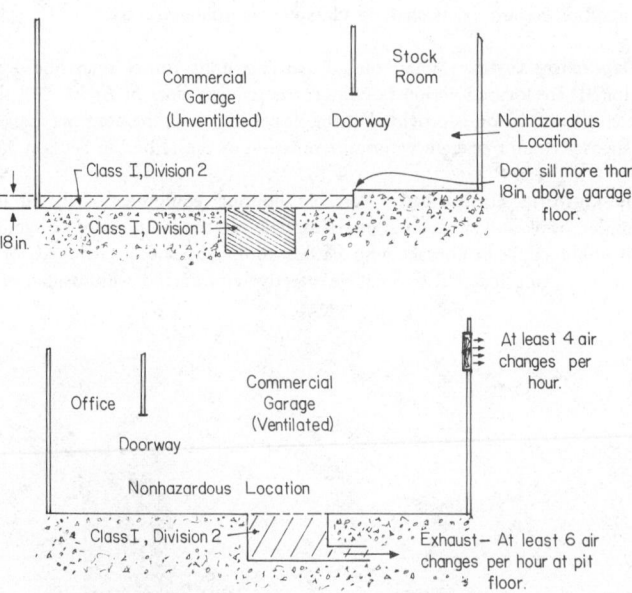

Figure 511-2. Classification of locations in commercial garages.

This section applies to raceways in walls and below floors of Class I locations in commercial garages. A raceway that is in a masonry wall or buried beneath a floor may not have any connections or extensions leading into or through a Class I, Division 1 or 2 location if it is to be considered in a nonhazardous location and not subject to the provisions of Article 501. However, any extension into a hazardous (classified) location sealed off in accordance with Section 501-5 isolates the sealed part from the unsealed part.

Article 501 applies to the raceway if any part of it is not imbedded in the wall or the wall is not masonry. Article 501 applies to the raceway if any part of it is not buried beneath the floor. The floor material is not specified.

511-4. Sealing. Approved seals conforming to the requirements of Section 501-5 shall be provided, and Section 501-5(b)(2) shall apply to horizontal as well as vertical boundaries of the defined Class I locations.

Seals are required if any part of the raceway is in, or passes through, a Class I, Division 2 location. See commentary on seals with Section 501-5.

511-5. Wiring in Spaces Above Class I Locations.

(a) Fixed Wiring Above Class I Locations. All fixed wiring above Class I locations shall be in metallic raceways, rigid nonmetallic conduit, or shall be Type MI, TC, SNM, or Type MC cable. Cellular metal floor raceways or cellular concrete floor raceways shall be permitted to be used only for supplying ceiling outlets or extensions to the area below the floor, but such raceways shall have no connections leading into or through any Class I location above the floor. No electrical conductor shall be installed in any cell, header, or duct which contains a pipe for any service except electrical or compressed air.

(b) Pendants. For pendants, flexible cord suitable for the type of service and approved for hard usage shall be used.

(c) Grounded Conductor. When a circuit which supplies portables or pendants includes a grounded conductor as provided in Article 200, receptacles, attachment plugs, connectors, and similar devices shall be of polarized type, and the grounded conductor of the flexible cord shall be connected to the screw shell of any lampholder or to the grounded terminal of any utilization equipment supplied.

(d) Attachment Plug Receptacles. Attachment plug receptacles in fixed position shall be located above the level of any defined Class I location, or be approved for the location.

511-6. Equipment Above Class I Locations.

(a) Arcing Equipment. Equipment that is less than 12 feet (3.66 m) above the floor level and that may produce arcs, sparks, or particles of hot metal, such as cutouts, switches, charging panels, generators, motors, or other equipment (excluding receptacles, lamps and lampholders) having make-and-break or sliding contacts, shall be of the totally enclosed type or so constructed as to prevent escape of sparks or hot metal particles.

(b) Fixed Lighting. Lamps and lampholders for fixed lighting that is located over lanes through which vehicles are commonly driven or that may otherwise be exposed to physical damage shall be located not less than 12 feet (3.66 m) above floor level, unless of the totally enclosed type or so constructed as to prevent escape of sparks or hot metal particles.

511-7. Battery Charging Equipment. Battery chargers and their control equipment, and batteries being charged shall not be located within locations classified in Section 511-2.

511-8. Electric Vehicle Charging.

(a) Connections. Flexible cords and connectors used for charging shall be suitable for the type of service and approved for extra-hard usage. Their ampacity shall be adequate for the charging current.

(b) Connector Design and Location. Connectors shall be so designed and installed that they will disconnect readily at any position of the charging cable, and live parts shall be guarded from accidental contact. No connector shall be located within a Class I location as defined in Section 511-2.

(c) Plug Connections to Vehicles. Where plugs are provided for direct connection to vehicles, the point of connection shall not be within a Class I location as defined in Section 511-2, and where the cord is suspended from overhead, it shall be so arranged that the lowest point of sag is at least 6 inches (152 mm) above the floor. Where the vehicle is equipped with an approved plug that will disconnect readily, and where an automatic arrangement is provided to pull both cord and plug beyond the range of physical damage, no additional connector shall be required in the cable or at the outlet.

ARTICLE 513 — AIRCRAFT HANGARS

Contents

513-1. Definition. An aircraft hangar is a location used for storage or servicing of aircraft in which gasoline, jet fuels, or other volatile flammable liquids or flammable gases are used. It shall not include locations used exclusively for aircraft that have never contained such liquids or gases, or that have been drained and properly purged.

513-2. Classification of Locations.

(a) Below Floor Level. Any pit or depression below the level of the hangar floor shall be classified as a Class I, Division 1 location that shall extend up to said floor level.

(b) Areas Not Cut Off or Ventilated. The entire area of the hangar, including any adjacent and communicating areas not suitably cut off from the hangar, shall be classified as a Class I, Division 2 location up to a level 18 inches (457 mm) above the floor.

(c) Vicinity of Aircraft. The area within 5 feet (1.52 m) horizontally from aircraft power plants or aircraft fuel tanks shall be classified as a Class I, Division 2 location that shall extend upward from the floor to a level 5 feet (1.52 m) above the upper surface of wings and of engine enclosures.

In order to properly classify the area in accordance with this section, it is necessary to obtain information on the aircraft parking patterns, the types of aircraft, and the operations to be performed in the hangar. See Figure 513-1.

Consideration of future changes in aircraft types and locations is appropriate to avoid the need for costly wiring and equipment changes as a result of changes in the area classification.

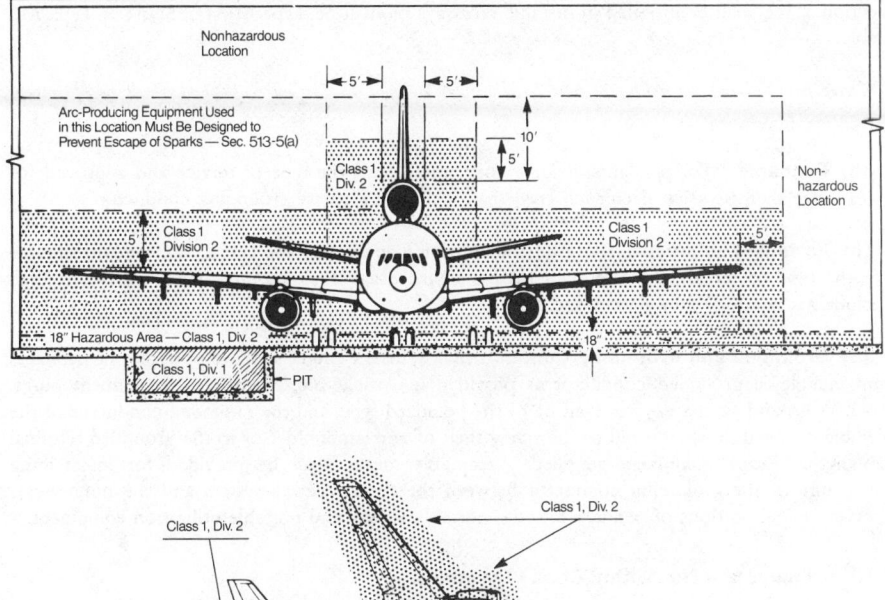

Figure 513-1. Area classification in aircraft hangars.

(d) Areas Suitably Cut Off and Ventilated. Adjacent areas in which flammable liquids or vapors are not likely to be released, such as stock rooms, electrical control rooms, and other similar locations, shall not be classified where adequately ventilated and where effectively cut off from the hangar itself by walls or partitions.

ARTICLE 513—AIRCRAFT HANGARS

513-3. Wiring and Equipment in Class I Locations. All wiring and equipment that is or may be installed or operated within any of the Class I locations defined in Section 513-2 shall comply with the applicable provisions of Article 501. All wiring installed in or under the hangar floor shall comply with the requirements for Class I, Division 1 locations. Where such wiring is located in vaults, pits, or ducts, adequate drainage shall be provided; and the wiring shall not be placed within the same compartment with any service other than piped compressed air.

Attachment plugs and receptacles in Class I locations shall be approved for Class I locations or shall be so designed that they cannot be energized while the connections are being made or broken.

513-4. Wiring Not Within Class I Locations.

(a) **Fixed Wiring.** All fixed wiring in a hangar, but not within a Class I location as defined in Section 513-2, shall be installed in metallic raceways or shall be Type MI, TC, SNM or Type MC cable.

Exception: Wiring in nonhazardous locations as defined in Section 513-2(d) shall be of a type recognized in Chapter 3.

(b) **Pendants.** For pendants, flexible cord suitable for the type of service and approved for hard usage shall be used. Each such cord shall include a separate grounding conductor.

(c) **Portable Equipment.** For portable utilization equipment and lamps, flexible cord suitable for the type of service and approved for extra-hard usage shall be used. Each such cord shall include a separate grounding conductor.

(d) **Grounded and Grounding Conductors.** Where a circuit supplies portables or pendants and includes a grounded conductor as provided in Article 200, receptacles, attachment plugs, connectors, and similar devices shall be of the polarized type, and the grounded conductor of the flexible cord will be connected to the screw shell of any lampholder or to the grounded terminal of any utilization equipment supplied. Acceptable means shall be provided for maintaining continuity of the grounding conductor between the fixed raceway system and the noncurrent-carrying metal portions of pendant fixtures, portable lamps, and portable utilization equipment.

513-5. Equipment Not Within Class I Locations.

(a) **Arcing Equipment.** In locations other than those described in Section 513-2, equipment that is less than 10 feet (3.05 m) above wings and engine enclosures of aircraft and that may produce arcs, sparks, or particles of hot metal, such as lamps and lampholders for fixed lighting, cutouts, switches, receptacles, charging panels, generators, motors, or other equipment having make-and-break or sliding contacts, shall be of the totally enclosed type or so constructed as to prevent escape of sparks or hot metal particles.

Exception: Equipment in areas described in Section 513-2(d) shall be permitted to be of the general-purpose type.

(b) **Lampholders.** Lampholders of metal-shell, fiber-lined types shall not be used for fixed incandescent lighting.

(c) **Portable Lighting Equipment.** Portable lighting equipment that are used within a hangar shall be approved for the location in which they are used.

(d) **Portable Equipment.** Portable utilization equipment that is or may be used within a hangar shall be of a type suitable for use in Class I, Division 2 locations.

513-6. Stanchions, Rostrums, and Docks.

(a) In Class I Location. Electric wiring, outlets, and equipment (including lamps) on or attached to stanchions, rostrums, or docks that are located or likely to be located in a Class I location as defined in Section 513-2(c) shall comply with the requirements for Class I, Division 2 locations.

(b) Not in Class I Location. Where stanchions, rostrums, or docks are not located or likely to be located in a Class I location as defined in Section 513-2(c), wiring and equipment shall comply with Sections 513-4 and 513-5, except that such wiring and equipment not more than 18 inches (457 mm) above the floor in any position shall comply with (a) above. Receptacles and attachment plugs shall be of a locking type that will not readily disconnect.

(c) Mobile Type. Mobile stanchions with electric equipment complying with (b) above shall carry at least one permanently affixed warning sign to read: "WARNING — KEEP 5 FEET CLEAR OF AIRCRAFT ENGINES AND FUEL TANK AREAS."

513-7. Sealing. Approved seals shall be provided in accordance with Section 501-5. Sealing requirements specified in Section 501-5(a)(4) and (b)(2) shall apply to horizontal as well as to vertical boundaries of the defined Class I locations. Raceways embedded in a masonry floor or buried beneath a floor shall be considered to be within the Class I location above the floor where any connections or extensions lead into or through such location.

513-8. Aircraft Electrical Systems. Aircraft electrical systems shall be de-energized when the aircraft is stored in a hangar, and, whenever possible, while the aircraft is undergoing maintenance.

513-9. Aircraft Battery — Charging and Equipment. Aircraft batteries shall not be charged when installed in an aircraft located inside or partially inside a hangar.

Battery chargers and their control equipment shall not be located or operated within any of the Class I locations defined in Section 513-2, and shall preferably be located in a separate building or in an area such as defined in Section 513-2(d). Mobile chargers shall carry at least one permanently affixed warning sign to read: "WARNING — KEEP 5 FEET CLEAR OF AIRCRAFT ENGINES AND FUEL TANK AREAS." Tables, racks, trays, and wiring shall not be located within a Class I location, and, in addition, shall comply with Article 480.

513-10. External Power Sources for Energizing Aircraft.

(a) Not Less than 18 Inches (457 mm) Above Floor. Aircraft energizers shall be so designed and mounted that all electric equipment and fixed wiring will be at least 18 inches (457 mm) above floor level and shall not be operated in a Class I location as defined in Section 513-2(c).

(b) Marking for Mobile Units. Mobile energizers shall carry at least one permanently affixed warning sign to read: "WARNING — KEEP 5 FEET CLEAR OF AIRCRAFT ENGINES AND FUEL TANK AREAS."

(c) Cords. Flexible cords for aircraft energizers and ground support equipment shall be approved for the type of service and extra-hard usage and shall include an equipment grounding conductor.

513-11. Mobile Servicing Equipment with Electric Components.

(a) General. Mobile servicing equipment (such as vacuum cleaners, air compressors, air movers, etc.) having electric wiring and equipment not suitable for Class I, Division 2 locations shall be so designed and mounted that all such fixed wiring and equipment will be at least 18 inches (457 mm) above the floor. Such mobile equipment shall not be operated within the Class I location defined in Section 513-2(c) and shall carry at least one permanently affixed warning sign to read: "WARNING — KEEP 5 FEET CLEAR OF AIRCRAFT ENGINES AND FUEL TANK AREAS."

(b) Cords and Connectors. Flexible cords for mobile equipment shall be suitable for the type of service and approved for extra-hard usage, and shall include an equipment grounding conductor. Attachment plugs and receptacles shall be approved for the location in which they are installed, and shall provide for connection of the grounding conductor to the raceway system.

(c) Restricted Use. Equipment not suitable for Class I, Division 2 locations shall not be operated in locations where maintenance operations likely to release flammable liquids or vapors are in progress.

513-12. Grounding. All metal raceways and all noncurrent-carrying metal portions of fixed or portable equipment, regardless of voltage, shall be grounded as provided in Article 250.

ARTICLE 514 — GASOLINE DISPENSING
AND SERVICE STATIONS

Contents

514-1. Definition. A gasoline dispensing and service station is a location where gasoline or other volatile flammable liquids or liquefied flammable gases are transferred to the fuel tanks (including auxiliary fuel tanks) of self-propelled vehicles.

Other areas used as lubritoriums, service rooms, repair rooms, offices, salesrooms, compressor rooms, and similar locations shall comply with Articles 510 and 511 with respect to electric wiring and equipment.

Where the authority having jurisdiction can satisfactorily determine that flammable liquids having a flash point below 38°C (100°F), such as gasoline, will not be handled, such authority may classify that location as nonhazardous.

(FPN): For further information regarding safeguards for gasoline dispensing and service stations, see Flammable and Combustible Liquids Code, NFPA 30-1981 (ANSI).

514-2. Class I Locations. Table 514-2 shall be applied where Class I liquids are stored, handled, or dispensed and shall be used to delineate and classify service stations. A Class I location shall not extend beyond an unpierced wall, roof, or other solid partition.

Table 514-2 is essentially the same as Table 7-1 in NFPA 30.

514-3. Wiring and Equipment Within Class I Locations. All electric equipment and wiring within Class I locations defined in Section 514-2 shall comply with the applicable provisions of Article 501.

Exception: As permitted in Section 514-8.

(FPN): For special requirements for conductor insulation, see Section 501-13.

For "gasoline and oil-resistant" insulated conductors, see the commentary following Section 501-13.

Table 514-2. Class I Locations — Service Stations

Location	Class I, Group D Division	Extent of Class I Location
Underground Tank		
Fill Opening	1	Any pit, box, or space below grade level, any part of which is within the Division 1 or 2 location.
	2	Up to 18 inches above grade level within a horizontal radius of 10 feet from a loose fill connection and within a horizontal radius of 5 feet from a tight fill connection.
Vent — Discharging Upward	1	Within 3 feet of open end of vent, extending in all directions.
	2	Space between 3 feet and 5 feet of open end of vent, extending in all directions.
Dispensing Units (except overhead type)		
Pits	1	Any pit, box, or space below grade level, any part of which is within the Division 1 or 2 location.
Dispenser	1	The space within a dispenser enclosure up to 4 feet vertically above the base except that space defined as Division 2. Any space within a nozzle boot.
	2	Spaces within a dispenser enclosure above the Division 1 location. Spaces within a dispenser enclosure isolated from Division 1 by a solid partition or a solid nozzle boot but not completely surrounded by Division 1 location. Within 18 inches horizontally in all directions from the Division 1 location located within the dispenser enclosure. Within 18 inches horizontally in all directions from the opening of a nozzle boot not isolated by a vaportight partition, except that the classified location need not be extended around a 90 degree or greater corner.
Outdoor	2	Up to 18 inches above grade level within 20 feet horizontally of any edge of enclosure.
Indoor with Mechanical Ventilation	2	Up to 18 inches above grade or floor level within 20 feet horizontally of any edge of enclosure.
with Gravity Ventilation	2	Up to 18 inches above grade or floor level within 25 feet horizontally of any edge of enclosure.

Table 514-2 (Continued)

Location	Class I, Group D Division	Extent of Class I Location
Dispensing Units, Overhead Type	1	Within the dispenser enclosure and 18 inches in all directions from the enclosure where not suitably cut off by ceiling or wall. All electrical equipment integral with the dispensing hose or nozzle.
	2	A space extending 2 feet horizontally in all directions beyond the Division 1 location and extending to grade below this classified location.
	2	Up to 18 inches above grade level within 20 feet horizontally measured from a point vertically below the edge of any dispenser enclosure.
Remote Pump — Outdoor	1	Any pit, box, or space below grade level if any part is within a horizontal distance of 10 feet from any edge of pump.
	2	Within 3 feet of any edge of pump, extending in all directions. Also up to 18 inches above grade level within 10 feet horizontally from any edge of pump.
Remote Pump — Indoor	1	Entire space within any pit.
	2	Within 5 feet of any edge of pump, extending in all directions. Also up to 3 feet above floor or grade level within 25 feet horizontally from any edge of pump.
Lubrication or Service Room — with Dispensing	1	Any pit within any unventilated area.
	2	Any pit with ventilation.
	2	Space up to 18 inches above floor or grade level and 3 feet horizontally from a lubrication pit.
Dispenser for Class I Liquids	2	Within 3 feet of any fill or dispensing point, extending in all directions.
Lubrication or Service Room — without Dispensing	2	Entire space within any pit used for lubrication or similar services where Class I liquids may be released.
	2	Space up to 18 inches above any such pit, and extending a distance of 3 feet horizontally from any edge of the pit.

Table 514-2 (Continued)

Location	Class I, Group D Division	Extent of Class I Location
Special Enclosure Inside Building (See NFPA 30, Flammable and Combustible Liquids Code, paragraph 7-2.2.)	1	Entire enclosure.
Sales, Storage and Rest Rooms	Ordinary	If there is any opening to these rooms within the extent of a Division 1 location, the entire room shall be classified as Division 1.
Vapor Processing Systems Pits	1	Any pit, box, or space below grade level, any part of which is within a Division 1 or 2 location or which houses any equipment used to transport or process vapors.
Vapor Processing Equipment Located Within Protective Enclosures	2	Within any protective enclosure housing vapor processing equipment.
Vapor Processing Equipment Not Within Protective Enclosures (excluding piping and combustion devices)	2	The space within 18 inches in all directions of equipment containing flammable vapor or liquid extending to grade level. Up to 18 inches above grade level within 10 feet horizontally of the vapor processing equipment.
Equipment Enclosures	1	Any space within the enclosure where vapor or liquid is present under normal operating conditions.
	2	The entire space within the enclosure other than Division 1.
Vacuum Assist Blowers	2	The space within 18 inches in all directions extending to grade level. Up to 18 inches above grade level within 10 feet horizontally.

For SI units: one inch = 25.4 millimeters; one foot = 0.3048 meter.

514-4. Wiring and Equipment Above Class I Locations. Wiring and equipment above the Class I locations defined in Section 514-2 shall comply with Sections 511-5 and 511-6.

514-5. Circuit Disconnects. Each circuit leading to or through a dispensing pump shall be provided with a switch or other acceptable means to disconnect simultaneously from the source of supply all conductors of the circuit, including the grounded neutral, if any.

It is important to note that all conductors of a circuit, including the grounded conductor, that may be present within a dispensing device are to be provided with a switch or special-type circuit breaker to simultaneously disconnect all conductors. The intent is that no "hot" wires be in the dispenser vicinity during maintenance or alteration. Considering possible accidental reversal of the polarities of conductors at panelboards, the grounded conductor must be able to be switched to the "open" or "off" position. Grounded conductors may be present in old-style pump motors, or they may pass through a dispenser as part of a circuit for the island lighting.

ARTICLE 514—GASOLINE DISPENSING AND SERVICE STATIONS

Since a fire or large gasoline spill at the dispensing island may make it impossible to operate the switches on the dispensing island that shut off the flow of gasoline, Subsection 7-4.1.2 of NFPA 30, the Flammable and Combustible Liquids Code, requires a clearly identified emergency power cutoff to be provided at a location remote from the dispensing device. The term "clearly identified" means that a sign is to be posted indicating where the cutoff switch is located. This emergency power cutoff should be readily accessible and not blocked by the storage of such things as tires or cases of lubricating oil. All service station operators as well as responding fire fighters should know the location of the emergency power cutoff.

514-6. Sealing.

(a) At Dispenser. An approved seal shall be provided in each conduit run entering or leaving a dispenser or any cavities or enclosures in direct communication therewith. The sealing fitting shall be the first fitting after the conduit emerges from the earth or concrete.

(b) At Boundary. Additional seals shall be provided in accordance with Section 501-5. Section 501-5(a)(4) and (b)(2) shall apply to horizontal as well as to vertical boundaries of the defined Class I locations.

It should be noted that sealing fittings are required in all conduits leaving a Class I location. All conduits passing under the boundaries of the hazardous (classified) locations (20-ft radius from dispenser) or the tank fill-pipe (10-ft radius from a loose fill connection and 5-ft radius from a tight-fill connection) are considered as being in a Class I, Division 1 location (see Section 514-8), and the seal is to be the first fitting at the point of emergence. A seal is required to be provided in each conduit run entering or leaving a dispenser, so even though a conduit runs from dispenser to dispenser and does not leave the hazardous (classified) location, a seal is necessary when leaving and again when entering the dispenser. Panelboards are generally located in a room classified as a nonhazardous location; however, any conduit coming from the dispenser, or passing under the hazardous (classified) location boundaries from the dispenser or tank fill-pipe, would require a seal at the panelboard location. Where the panelboard is located in the lube or repair room, all conduits emerging into the 18-in. hazardous (classified) location would require seals. See Figures 514-1 and 514-2.

514-7. Grounding.
Metal portions of dispensing pumps, metal raceways, and all noncurrent-carrying metal parts of electric equipment, regardless of voltage, shall be grounded as provided in Article 250.

514-8. Underground Wiring.
Underground wiring shall be installed in rigid metal conduit or threaded steel intermediate metal conduit. Any portion of electrical wiring or equipment which is below the surface of a Class I, Division 1 or Division 2 location (as defined in Table 514-2) shall be considered to be in a Class I, Division 1 location. Refer to Exception No. 3 of Section 300-5(a).

Experience has shown that the fuel spilled in the vicinity of gasoline pumps tends to accumulate underground where it can enter electrical conduits and accumulate in voids. This section therefore classifies the space below surface areas subject to fuel spills as Class I, Division 1 locations.

Exception No. 1: Type MI cable shall be permitted where it is installed in accordance with Article 330.

Exception No. 2: Rigid nonmetallic conduit complying with Article 347 shall be permitted when buried under not less than 2 feet (610 mm) of earth. Where rigid nonmetallic conduit is used, threaded rigid metal conduit or threaded steel intermediate metal conduit shall be used for the last 2 feet (610 mm) of the underground run to emergence or to the point of connection to the aboveground raceway; an equipment grounding conductor shall be included to provide electrical continuity of the raceway system and for grounding of noncurrent-carrying metal parts.

Exception No. 2 to Section 514-8 makes it clear that, if rigid nonmetallic conduit is used for underground wiring, threaded rigid metal conduit or threaded steel intermediate metal conduit must be used for the last 2 ft of the underground

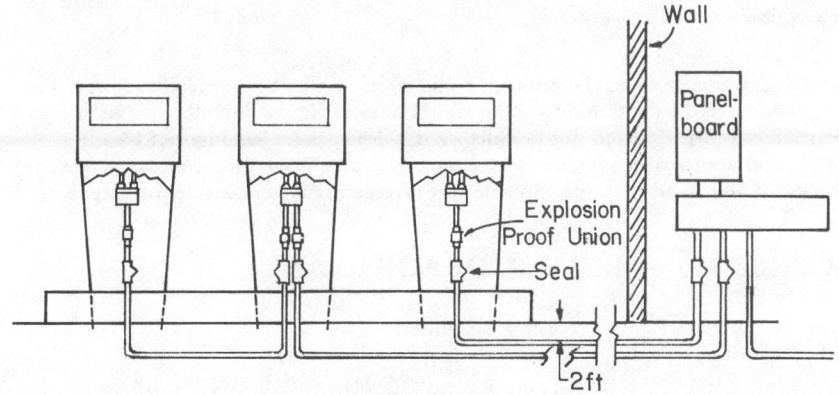

Figure 514-1. A gasoline dispensing installation indicating locations for sealing fittings.

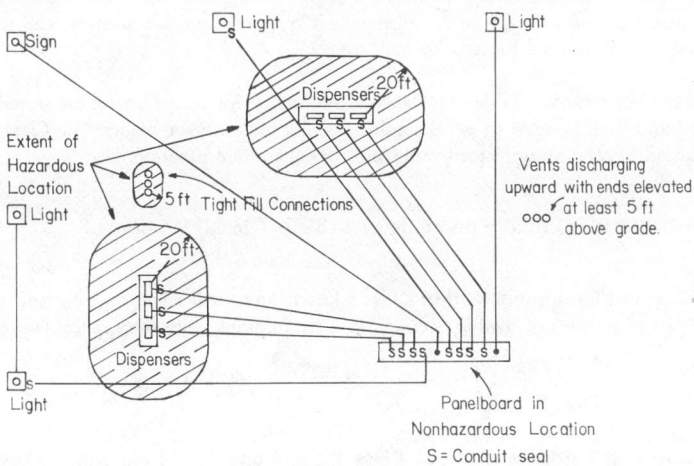

Figure 514-2. Seals are required at points marked "S." Seals are not required at the sign and two lights because conduit runs do not pass through a hazardous location.

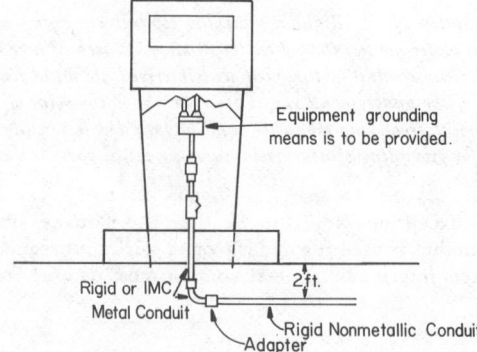

Figure 514-3. Location and permitted use of rigid nonmetallic conduit.

Equipment grounding means is to be provided.

Rigid or IMC Metal Conduit

Rigid Nonmetallic Conduit Adapter

2 ft.

run to emergence or to the point of connection to the aboveground raceway. The rigid nonmetallic conduit, including rigid nonmetallic conduit elbows and fittings, is required to be located not less than 2 ft below grade. See Figure 514-3.

If rigid nonmetallic conduit is used, an equipment grounding conductor must be included and bonded to the explosionproof raceway system inside the dispenser.

ARTICLE 515 — BULK STORAGE PLANTS

Contents

515-1. Definition.
515-2. Class I Locations.
515-3. Wiring and Equipment Within Class I Locations.
515-4. Wiring and Equipment Above Class I Locations.
515-5. Underground Wiring.

(a) Wiring Method.
(b) Insulation.
(c) Nonmetallic Wiring.
515-6. Sealing.
515-7. Gasoline Dispensing.
515-8. Grounding.

515-1. Definition. A bulk storage plant is a location where gasoline or other volatile flammable liquids are stored in tanks having an aggregate capacity of one carload or more, and from which such products are distributed (usually by tank truck).

515-2. Class I Locations. Table 515-2 shall be applied where Class I liquids are stored, handled, or dispensed and shall be used to delineate and classify bulk storage plants. The Class I location shall not extend beyond an unpierced wall, roof, or other solid partition.

Table 515-2 is essentially the same as Table 6-1 in NFPA 30.

515-3. Wiring and Equipment Within Class I Locations. All electric wiring and equipment within the Class I locations defined in Section 515-2 shall comply with the applicable provisions of Article 501.

Exception: As permitted in Section 515-5.

515-4. Wiring and Equipment Above Class I Locations. All fixed wiring above Class I locations shall be in metallic raceways or be Type MI, TC, SNM, or Type MC cable. Fixed equipment that may produce arcs, sparks, or particles of hot metal, such as lamps and lampholders for fixed lighting, cutouts, switches, receptacles, motors, or other equipment having make-

Table 515-2.   Class I Locations — Bulk Plants

Location	Class I, Group D Division	Extent of Class I Location
Tank Vehicle and Tank Car		
Loading Through Open Dome When classifying extent of space, consideration shall be given to fact that tank cars or tank vehicles may be spotted at varying points. Therefore, the extremities of the loading or unloading positions shall be used.	1	Within 3 feet of edge of dome, extending in all directions.
	2	Space between 3 feet and 15 feet from edge of dome, extending in all directions.
Loading Through Bottom Connections with Atmospheric Venting	1	Within 3 feet of point of venting to atmosphere, extending in all directions.
	2	Space between 3 feet and 15 feet from point of venting to atmosphere, extending in all directions. Also up to 18 inches above grade within a horizontal radius of 10 feet from point of loading connection.
Loading Through Closed Dome with Atmospheric Venting	1	Within 3 feet of open end of vent, extending in all directions.
	2	Space between 3 feet and 15 feet from open end of vent, extending in all directions. Also within 3 feet of edge of dome, extending in all directions.
Loading Through Closed Dome with Vapor Recovery	2	Within 3 feet of point of connection of both fill and vapor lines, extending in all directions.
Bottom Loading with Vapor Recovery or Any Bottom Unloading	2	Within 3 feet of point of connections, extending in all directions. Also up to 18 inches above grade within a horizontal radius of 10 feet from point of connection.
Pumps, Bleeders, Withdrawal Fittings, Meters and Similar Devices		
Indoors	2	Within 5 feet of any edge of such devices, extending in all directions. Also up to 3 feet above floor or grade level within 25 feet horizontally from any edge of such devices.
Outdoors	2	Within 3 feet of any edge of such devices, extending in all directions. Also up to 18 inches above grade level within 10 feet horizontally from any edge of such devices.
Storage and Repair Garage for Tank Vehicles	1	All pits or spaces below floor level.
	2	Space up to 18 inches above floor or grade level for entire storage or repair garage.
Drainage Ditches, Separators, Impounding Basins	2	Space up to 18 inches above ditch, separator, or basin. Also up to 18 inches above grade within 15 feet horizontally from any edge.

Table 515-2 (Continued)

Location	Class I, Group D Division	Extent of Class I Location
Garages for Other than Tank Vehicles	Ordinary	If there is any opening to these rooms within the extent of an outdoor Division 1 or 2 location, the entire room shall be classified the same as the area classification at the point of the opening.
Outdoor Drum Storage	Ordinary	
Indoor Warehousing Where There Is No Flammable Liquid Transfer	Ordinary	If there is any opening to these rooms within the extent of an indoor Division 1 or 2 location, the room shall be classified the same as if the wall, curb or partition did not exist.
Office and Rest Rooms	Ordinary	
Drum and Container Filling Outdoors, or Indoors with Adequate Ventilation	1	Within 3 feet of vent and fill opening, extending in all directions.
	2	Space between 3 feet and 5 feet from vent or fill opening, extending in all directions. Also up to 18 inches above floor or grade level within a horizontal radius of 10 feet from vent or fill opening.
Tank — Aboveground* Shell, Ends, or Roof and Dike Area	2	Within 10 feet from shell, ends, or roof of tank. Space inside dikes to level of top of dike.
Vent	1	Within 5 feet of open end of vent, extending in all directions.
	2	Space between 5 feet and 10 feet from open end of vent, extending in all directions.
Floating Roof	1	Space above the roof and within the shell.
Pits Without Mechanical Ventilation	1	Entire space within pit if any part is within a Division 1 or 2 location.
With Mechanical Ventilation	2	Entire space within pit if any part is within a Division 1 or 2 location.
Containing Valves, Fittings or Piping, and Not Within a Division 1 or 2 Location	2	Entire pit.

For SI units: one inch = 25.4 millimeters; one foot = 0.3048 meter.
* For Tanks — Underground, see Section 514-2.

and-break or sliding contacts, shall be of the totally enclosed type or be so constructed as to prevent escape of sparks or hot metal particles. Portable lamps or other utilization equipment and their flexible cords shall comply with the provisions of Article 501 for the class of location above which they are connected or used.

515-5. Underground Wiring.

(a) Wiring Method. Underground wiring shall be installed in rigid metal conduit, threaded steel intermediate metal conduit, or where buried under not less than 2 feet (610 mm) of earth shall be permitted in rigid nonmetallic conduit or an approved cable. Where rigid nonmetallic conduit is used, threaded rigid metal conduit or threaded steel intermediate metal conduit shall be used for the last 2 feet (610 mm) of the conduit run to emergence or to the point of connection to the aboveground raceway. Where cable is used, it shall be enclosed in rigid or threaded steel intermediate metal conduit from the point of lowest buried cable level to the point of connection to the aboveground raceway.

See commentary following Section 514-8.

(b) Insulation. Conductor insulation shall comply with Section 501-13.

(c) Nonmetallic Wiring. Where rigid nonmetallic conduit or cable with a nonmetallic sheath is used, an equipment grounding conductor shall be included to provide for electrical continuity of the raceway system and for grounding of noncurrent-carrying metal parts.

515-6. Sealing. Approved seals shall be provided in accordance with Section 501-5. Sealing requirements in Section 501-5(a)(4) and (b)(2) shall apply to horizontal as well as to vertical boundaries of the defined Class I locations. Buried raceways under defined Class I locations shall be considered to be within such locations.

515-7. Gasoline Dispensing. Where gasoline dispensing is carried on in conjunction with bulk station operations, the applicable provisions of Article 514 shall apply.

515-8. Grounding. All metal raceways and all noncurrent-carrying metal parts of electric equipment shall be grounded as provided in Article 250.

ARTICLE 516 — SPRAY APPLICATION, DIPPING AND COATING PROCESSES

Contents

ARTICLE 516—SPRAY APPLICATIONS, DIPPING AND COATING PROCESSES

516-1. Definition. This article covers the regular or frequent application of flammable liquids, combustible liquids and combustible powders by spray operations and the application of flammable liquids, or combustible liquids at temperatures above their flashpoint, by dipping, coating, or other means.

(FPN): For further information regarding safeguards for these processes, such as fire protection, posting of warning signs, and maintenance, see Standard for Spray Application Using Flammable and Combustible Materials, NFPA 33-1982 (ANSI), and Standard for Dipping and Coating Processes Using Flammable or Combustible Liquids, NFPA 34-1981. For additional information regarding ventilation, see Blower and Exhaust Systems, Dust, Stock and Vapor Removal or Conveying, NFPA 91-1973.

516-2. Classification of Locations. Classification is based on dangerous quantities of flammable vapors, combustible mists, residues, dusts or deposits.

(a) Class I or Class II, Division 1 Locations. The following spaces shall be considered Class I or Class II, Division 1 locations as applicable.

(1) The interiors of spray booths and rooms except as specifically provided in Section 516-3(d).

(2) The interior of exhaust ducts.

(3) Any area in the direct path of spray operations.

(4) For dipping and coating operations, all space within 5 feet (1.52 m) in any direction from the vapor sources extending from these surfaces to the floor. The vapor source shall be the liquid surface in the dip tank, the wetted surface of the drain board and the surface of the dipped object over either the liquid surface or the wetted surface of the drain board and extending from these surfaces to the floor.

(5) Pits within 25 feet (7.62 m) horizontally of the vapor source. If pits are in the classified area and extend beyond 25 feet (7.62 m) the Class I, Division 1 area shall include the entire pit unless a vapor stop is provided.

(b) Class I or Class II, Division 2 Locations. The following spaces shall be considered Class I or Class II, Division 2 as applicable.

(1) For open spraying, all space outside of but within 20 feet (6.10 m) horizontally and 10 feet (3.05 m) vertically of the Class I, Division 1 location as defined in Section 516-2(a), and not separated from it by partitions. See Figure 1.

(2) For spraying operations conducted within a closed top, open face, or front spray booth, the space shown in Figure 2, and the space within 3 feet (914 mm) in all directions from openings other than the open face or front.

The Class I or Class II, Division 2 location shown in Figure 2 shall extend from the open face or front of the spray booth in accordance with the following:

a. If the ventilation system is interlocked with the spraying equipment so as to make the spraying equipment inoperable when the ventilation system is not in operation, the space shall extend 5 feet (1.52 m) from the open face or front of the spray booth, and as otherwise shown in Figure 2A.

b. If the ventilation system is not interlocked with the spraying equipment so as to make the spraying equipment inoperable when the ventilation system is not in operation, the space shall extend 10 feet (3.05 m) from the open face or front of the spray booth, and as otherwise shown in Figure 2B.

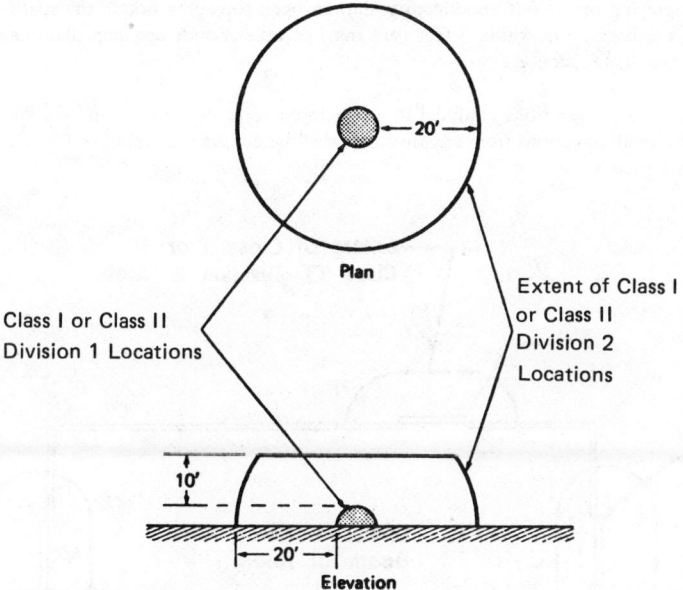

For SI units: one inch = 25.4 millimeters; one foot = 0.3048 meter.

Figure 1.   Class I or Class II, Division 2 Locations Adjacent to an Unenclosed Spray Operation.

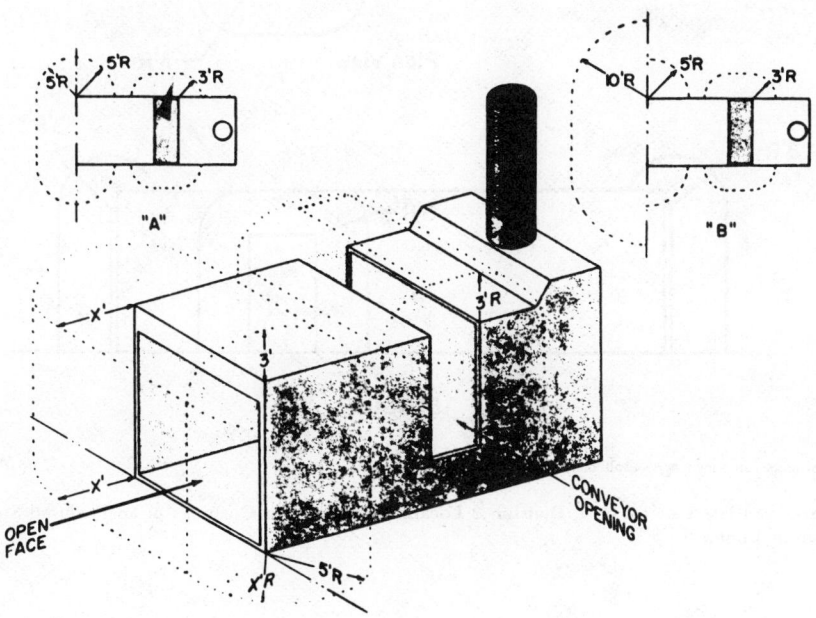

For SI units: one inch = 25.4 millimeters; one foot = 0.3048 meter.

Figure 2.   Class I or Class II, Division 2 Locations Adjacent to a Closed Top, Open Faced or Open Front Spray Booth.

A.   When ventilation system is interlocked with spray equipment.

B.   When ventilation system is not interlocked with spray equipment.

(3) For spraying operations conducted within an open top spray booth, the space 3 feet (914 mm) above the booth and within 3 feet (914 mm) of other booth openings shall be considered Class I or Class II, Division 2.

(4) For spraying operations confined to an enclosed spray booth or room, the space within 3 feet (914 mm) in all directions from any openings shall be considered Class I or Class II, Division 2 as shown in Figure 3.

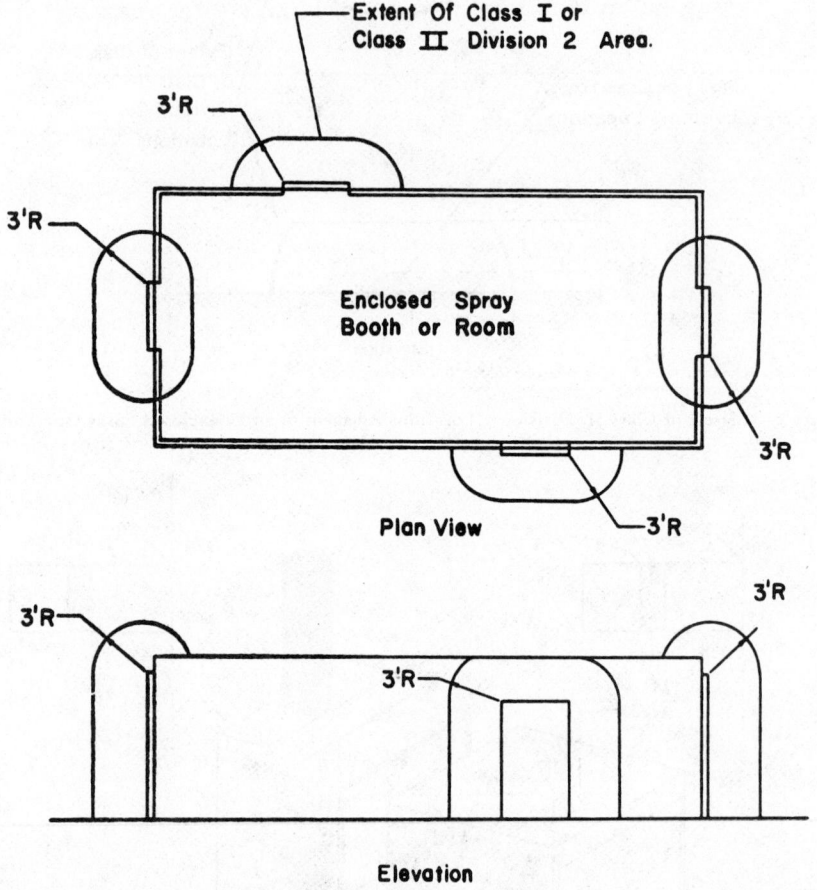

For SI units: one inch = 25.4 millimeters; one foot = 0.3048 meter.

Figure 3. Class I or Class II, Division 2 Locations Adjacent to Openings in an Enclosed Spray Booth or Room.

(5) For dip tanks and drain boards, and for other hazardous operations, all space beyond the limits for Class I, Division 1 and within 8 feet (2.44 m) of the vapor source as defined in (a)(4). In addition, all space from the floor to 3 feet (914 mm) above the floor, and extending 25 feet (7.62 m) horizontally from the vapor source as defined in (a)(4) as shown in Figure 4.

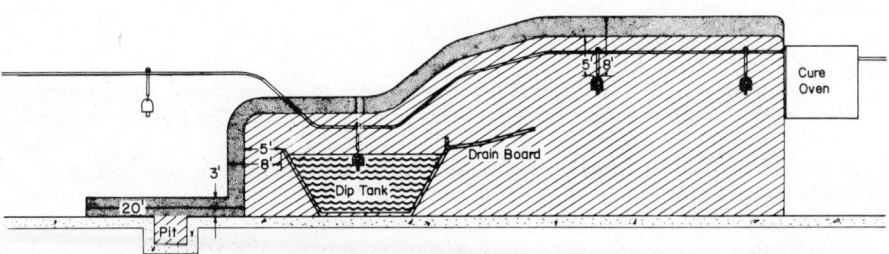

For SI units: one inch = 25.4 millimeters; one foot = 0.3048 meter.

Figure 4. The Extent of Class I, Division 1 and Class I, Division 2 Hazardous (Classified) Locations for a Point Dipping Operation.

(c) **Adjacent Locations.** Adjacent locations that are cut off from the defined Class I or Class II locations by tight partitions without communicating openings, and within which hazardous vapors or combustible powders are not likely to be released, shall be classified as nonhazardous.

(d) **Nonhazardous Locations.** Locations utilizing drying, curing, or fusion apparatus and provided with positive mechanical ventilation adequate to prevent accumulation of flammable concentrations of vapors, and provided with effective interlocks to de-energize all electric equipment (other than equipment approved for Class I locations) in case the ventilating equipment is inoperative, may be classified as nonhazardous where the authority having jurisdiction so judges.

(FPN): For further information regarding safeguards, see Ovens and Furnaces, Design, Location and Equipment, NFPA 86A-1977 (ANSI).

516-3. Wiring and Equipment in Class I Locations.

(a) **Wiring and Equipment — Vapors.** All electric wiring and equipment within the Class I location (containing vapor only—not residues) defined in Section 516-2 shall comply with the applicable provisions of Article 501.

(b) **Wiring and Equipment — Vapors and Residues.** Unless approved for both readily ignitible deposits and the flammable vapor location, no electric equipment shall be installed or used where it may be subject to hazardous accumulations of readily ignitible deposits or residues, as the susceptibility to spontaneous heating and ignition of some residues may be greatly increased with rise in temperature. Type MI cable and wiring in threaded rigid metal conduit or threaded steel intermediate metal conduit may be installed in such locations.

Where readily ignitible vapors and residues are present, the "only" wiring methods permitted are threaded rigid metal conduit, threaded steel intermediate metal conduit, and Type MI cable.

Electric equipment and lighting fixtures approved for Class I, Division 1 locations may be installed where not subjected to readily ignitible deposits or residues.

(c) Illumination. Illumination of readily ignitible areas through panels of glass or other transparent or translucent material shall be permitted only if it complies with the following: (1) fixed lighting units are used as the source of illumination; (2) the panel effectively isolates the Class I location from the area in which the lighting unit is located; (3) the lighting unit is approved for its specific location; (4) the panel is of a material or is so protected that breakage will be unlikely; and (5) the arrangement is such that normal accumulations of hazardous residue on the surface of the panel will not be raised to a dangerous temperature by radiation or conduction from the source of illumination.

The following Formal Interpretation of NFPA 33, Spray Application Using Flammable and Combustible Materials, was issued by NFPA. (See Fire News, July 1979).

"Question: Can an illumination fixture with self-contained or attached glass panel comply with Paragraph 3-9?

"Answer: Yes, provided that the glass panel accomplishes what is specified in Paragraph 3-9.

"Question: Can an illumination fixture with self-contained or attached glass panel be installed in the field or be used to replace an existing fixture?

"Answer: Yes, provided that the fixture meets the following requirements: (a) the glass panel meets the requirements of Paragraph 3-9, (b) the fixture meets the requirements of Paragraph 4-7 if applicable, and (c) the installation is done is a safe manner."

Underwriters Laboratories Inc. Hazardous Locations Equipment Directory indicates that UL listed fixtures suitable for use in hazardous (classified) locations having deposits of readily combustible paint residue are so marked.

(d) Portable Equipment. Portable electric lamps or other utilization equipment shall not be used in a spray area during spray operations.

Exception No. 1: Where portable electric lamps are required for operations in spaces not readily illuminated by fixed lighting within the spraying area, they shall be of the type approved for Class I, Division 1 locations where readily ignitible residues may be present.

Exception No. 2: Where portable electric drying apparatus are used in automobile refinishing spray booths and the following requirements are met: (1) the apparatus and its electrical connections are not located within the spray enclosure during spray operations; (2) electrical equipment within 18 inches (45.7 cm) of the floor is approved for Class I, Division 2 locations; (3) all metallic parts of the drying apparatus are electrically bonded and grounded; and (4) interlocks are provided to prevent the operation of spray equipment while drying apparatus is within the spray enclosure, to allow for a 3-minute purge of the enclosure before energizing the drying apparatus and to shut off drying apparatus on failure of ventilation system.

(e) Electrostatic Equipment. Electrostatic spraying or detearing equipment shall be installed and used only as provided in Section 516-4.

(FPN): For further information, see Standard for Spray Application Using Flammable and Combustible Materials, NFPA 33-1982 (ANSI).

516-4. Fixed Electrostatic Equipment. This section shall apply to any equipment using electrostatically charged elements for the atomization, charging, and/or precipitation of hazardous materials for coatings on articles or for other similar purposes in which the charging or atomizing device is attached to a mechanical support and is not hand held or manipulated. Where fixed electrostatic spraying and detearing equipment is installed, such equipment shall be of an approved type and shall comply with (a) through (h) below.

(a) Power and Control Equipment. Transformers, power packs, control apparatus, and all other electric portions of the equipment shall be installed outside of the Class I location as defined in Section 516-2 or be of a type approved for the location.

Exception: High-voltage grids, electrodes, electrostatic atomizing heads, and their connections shall be permitted within the Class I location.

(b) Electrostatic Equipment. Electrodes and electrostatic atomizing heads shall be: (1) located in suitable areas provided with adequate mechanical ventilation; (2) adequately supported in permanent locations; and (3) effectively insulated from ground. Electrodes and electrostatic atomizing heads that are permanently attached to their bases, supports, or reciprocators shall be considered as complying with this section. Insulators shall be nonporous.

(FPN): Fine-wire elements, where used, shall be under tension at all times and be of unkinked hardened steel or material of comparable strength.

(c) High-Voltage Leads. High-voltage leads shall be properly insulated and protected from mechanical injury or exposure to destructive chemicals. Any exposed element at high voltage shall be effectively and permanently supported on suitable insulators and shall be effectively guarded against accidental contact or grounding. An automatic means shall be provided for grounding the electrode system when the primary of its high-voltage supply is electrically de-energized for any reason.

(d) Separation of Goods from Electrostatic Equipment. A safe distance of at least twice the sparking distance shall be maintained between goods being painted and electrodes or electrostatic atomizing heads or conductors. A suitable sign indicating this safe distance shall be conspicuously posted near the assembly.

(e) Support of Goods. Goods being coated or deteared shall be supported on conveyors or hangers. The conveyors or hangers shall be so arranged as to assure that the parts being coated or deteared are electrically connected to ground with a resistance of 1 megohm or less, and to maintain safe distances between goods and the electrodes or electrostatic atomizing heads at all times. Goods shall be supported to prevent such swinging or movement which would reduce the clearance to less than that specified in (d) above.

(f) Automatic Controls. Electrostatic apparatus shall be equipped with automatic means which will rapidly de-energize the high-voltage elements under any of the following conditions: (1) stoppage of ventilating fans or failure of ventilating equipment from any cause; (2) stoppage of the conveyor carrying goods through the high-voltage field; (3) occurrence of a ground or excessive current leakage at any point in the high-voltage system; (4) de-energizing of the high voltage supply; (5) reduction of clearances below that specified in (d) above.

(g) Grounding. All electrically conductive objects within the charging influence of the electrodes except those required by the process to be at high voltage shall be adequately grounded. This requirement shall apply to paint containers, wash cans, guards, and any other electrically conductive objects or devices in the area. The equipment shall carry a prominent permanently installed warning regarding the necessity for grounding these objects.

(h) Isolation. Safeguards such as adequate booths, fencing, railings or other means shall be placed about the equipment so that they, either by their location or character, or both, assure that a safe isolation of the process is maintained from plant storage or personnel.

516-5. Electrostatic Hand-Spraying Equipment. This section shall apply to any equipment using electrostatically charged elements for the atomization, charging, and/or precipitation of materials for coatings on articles, or for other similar purposes in which the atomizing device is hand held or manipulated during the spraying operation. Electrostatic hand-spraying equipment and devices used in connection with paint-spraying operations shall be of approved types and shall comply with (a) through (e) below.

(a) General. The high-voltage circuits shall be designed so as not to produce a spark of sufficient intensity to ignite the most readily ignitible of those vapor-air mixtures likely to be encountered, nor result in appreciable shock hazard upon coming in contact with a grounded object under all normal operating conditions. The electrostatically charged exposed elements of the hand gun shall be capable of being energized only by an actuator which also controls the coating material supply.

(b) Power Equipment. Transformers, power packs, control apparatus, and all other electric portions of the equipment shall be located outside of the Class I location or be approved for the location.

Exception: The hand gun itself and its connections to the power supply shall be permitted within the Class I location.

(c) Handle. The handle of the spraying gun shall be electrically connected to ground by a metallic connection and be so constructed that the operator in normal operating position is in intimate electrical contact with the grounded handle to prevent buildup of a static charge on the operator's body. Signs indicating the necessity for grounding other persons entering the spray area shall be conspicuously posted.

(d) Electrostatic Equipment. All electrically conductive objects in the spraying area shall be adequately grounded. This requirement shall apply to paint containers, wash cans, and any other electrically conductive objects or devices in the area. The equipment shall carry a prominent, permanently installed warning regarding the necessity for this grounding feature.

(e) Support of Objects. Objects being painted shall be maintained in metallic contact with the conveyor or other grounded support. Hooks shall be regularly cleaned to ensure adequate grounding of 1 megohm or less. Areas of contact shall be sharp points or knife edges where possible. Points of support of the object shall be concealed from random spray where feasible; and where the objects being sprayed are supported from a conveyor, the point of attachment to the conveyor shall be so located as to not collect spray material during normal operation.

516-6. Powder Coating. This section shall apply to processes in which combustible dry powders are applied. The hazards associated with combustible dusts are present in such a process to a degree, depending upon the chemical composition of the material, particle size, shape, and distribution.

(FPN): The hazards associated with combustible dusts are inherent in this process. Generally speaking, the hazard rating of the powders employed is dependent upon the chemical composition of the material, particle size, shape, and distribution.

(a) Electric Equipment and Sources of Ignition. Electric equipment and other sources of ignition shall comply with the requirements of Article 502. Portable electric lamps and other utilization equipment shall not be used within a Class II location during operation of the finishing processes. When such lamps or utilization equipment are used during cleaning or repairing operations, they shall be of a type approved for Class II, Division 1 locations, and all exposed metal parts shall be effectively grounded.

Exception: Where portable electric lamps are required for operations in spaces not readily illuminated by fixed lighting within the spraying area, they shall be of the type approved for Class II, Division 1 locations where readily ignitible residues may be present.

(b) Fixed Electrostatic Spraying Equipment. The provisions of Sections 516-4 and (a) above shall apply to fixed electrostatic spraying equipment.

(c) Electrostatic Hand-Spraying Equipment. The provisions of Sections 516-5 and (a) above shall apply to electrostatic hand-spraying equipment.

(d) Electrostatic Fluidized Beds. Electrostatic fluidized beds and associated equipment shall be of approved types. The high-voltage circuits shall be so designed that any discharge produced when the charging electrodes of the bed are approached or contacted by a grounded object shall not be of sufficient intensity to ignite any powder-air mixture likely to be encountered nor to result in an appreciable shock hazard.

(1) Transformers, power packs, control apparatus, and all other electric portions of the equipment shall be located outside the powder-coating area or shall otherwise comply with the requirements of (a) above.

Exception: The charging electrodes and their connections to the power supply shall be permitted within the powder-coating area.

(2) All electrically conductive objects within the powder-coating area shall be adequately grounded. The powder-coating equipment shall carry a prominent, permanently installed warning regarding the necessity for grounding these objects.

(3) Objects being coated shall be maintained in electrical contact (less than 1 megohm) with the conveyor or other support in order to ensure proper grounding. Hangers shall be regularly cleaned to ensure effective electrical contact. Areas of electrical contact shall be sharp points or knife edges where possible.

(4) The electric equipment and compressed-air supplies shall be interlocked with a ventilation system so that the equipment cannot be operated unless the ventilating fans are in operation.

516-7. Wiring and Equipment Above Class I and II Locations.

(a) Wiring. All fixed wiring above the Class I and II locations shall be in metal raceways, rigid nonmetallic conduit, or shall be Type MI, TC, SNM, or Type MC cable. Cellular metal floor raceways shall be permitted only for supplying ceiling outlets or extensions to the area below the floor of a Class I or II location, but such raceways shall have no connections leading into or through the Class I or II location above the floor unless suitable seals are provided. No electric conductor shall be installed in any cell or header that contains a pipe for steam, water, air, gas, drainage, or for other than the electrical service.

(b) Equipment. Equipment that may produce arcs, sparks, or particles of hot metal, such as lamps and lampholders for fixed lighting, cutouts, switches, receptacles, motors, or other equipment having make-and-break or sliding contacts, where installed above a Class I or II location or above a location where freshly finished goods are handled, shall be of the totally enclosed type or be so constructed as to prevent escape of sparks or hot metal particles.

516-8. Grounding. All metal raceways and all noncurrent-carrying metal parts of fixed or portable equipment, regardless of voltage, shall be grounded as provided in Article 250.

NFPA 33, Spray Application Using Flammable and Combustible Materials, covers the application of flammable or combustible materials as a spray by compressed air, "airless" or "hydraulic atomization," or by steam, electrostatic methods, or any other means in continuous or intermittent processes. It also covers the application of combustible powders when applied by powder spray guns, electrostatic powder spray guns, and fluidized beds or electrostatic fluidized beds.

NFPA 33 outlines the requirements for the maintenance of safe conditions.

The proper maintenance and operation of processes and process areas where flammable and combustible materials are handled and applied are critical with respect to the protection of life and property from fire or explosion.

It has been shown that the largest fire losses and frequency of fires have occurred where the proper application of codes and standards has not been used.

Spray Area: Any area in which dangerous quantities of flammable or combustible vapors, mists, residues, dusts, or deposits are present due to the operation of spray processes.

A spray area shall include:

(a) The interior of spray booths and rooms (with certain exceptions).

(b) The interior of ducts exhausting from spraying processes.

(c) Any area in the direct path of spraying operations.

The authority having jurisdiction may, for the purpose of NFPA 33, define the limits of the spray area in any specific case. The "spray area" in the vicinity of spraying operations will necessarily vary with the design and arrangement of equipment and method of operation. When spraying operations are strictly confined to predetermined spaces provided with adequate and reliable ventilation, such as a properly constructed spray booth, the "spray area" will ordinarily not extend beyond the booth enclosure. When spraying operations are not confined to adequately ventilated spaces, the "spray area" may extend throughout the entire room containing spraying operations.

Spray Booth: A power-ventilated structure provided to enclose or accommodate a spraying operation, to confine and limit the escape of spray, vapor, and residue, and to conduct or direct them safely to an exhaust system. Spray booths are manufactured in a variety of forms, including automotive refinishing, downdraft, open-face, traveling, tunnel, and updraft booths.

Spray Room: A power-ventilated, fully enclosed room used exclusively for open spraying of flammable or combustible materials. The entire spray room is a spray area. A spray booth is not a spray room.

Waterwash Spray Booth: A spray booth equipped with a water washing system designed to minimize dusts or residues entering exhaust ducts and to permit the recovery of overspray finishing material.

Dry Spray Booth: A spray booth not equipped with a water washing system. A dry spray booth may be equipped with (1) distribution or baffle plates to promote an even flow of air through the booth or cause deposit of overspray before it enters exhaust duct; (2) overspray dry filters to minimize dusts or residues entering exhaust ducts; (3) overspray dry filter rolls designed to minimize dusts or residues entering exhaust ducts; or (4) powder collection systems so arranged in the exhaust to capture oversprayed material (when dry powders are sprayed).

Notes on Electrical Installations:

The safety of life and property from fire or explosion as a result of spray applications of flammable and combustible paints and finishes varies depending upon the arrangement and operation of a particular installation.

The principal hazards of spray application operations originate from flammable or combustible liquids or powders and their vapors or mists as well as from highly combustible residues or powders.

Properly constructed spray booths, with adequate mechanical ventilation, may be used to discharge vapors or powder to a safe location and reduce the possibility of an explosion. In like manner, the accumulation of overspray residues, many of which are not only highly combustible but also subject to spontaneous ignition, can be controlled.

The elimination of all sources of ignition in areas where flammable or combustible liquids, vapors, mists, or combustible residues are present, together with constant supervision and maintenance, is essential to the safe operation of spraying.

The human element necessitates careful consideration of the location of the operation and the installation of extinguishing equipment in order to reduce the possibility of fire spreading to other property and minimize the probability of damage to other property.

It is obvious that there should be no open flames or spark-producing equipment in any area where, because of inadequate ventilation, explosive vapor-air mixtures or mists are present. It is equally obvious that no open flames or spark-producing equipment should be located where highly combustible spray residues will be deposited on them. Because some residues may be ignited at very low temperatures, additional consideration must be given to operating temperatures of equipment subject to residue deposits. Many deposits may be ignited at temperatures produced by low-pressure steam pipes or by incandescent light globes, even those of explosionproof types.

It will be noted that electrical equipment is generally not permitted inside any spray booth, in the exhaust duct from a spray booth, in the entrained air of an exhaust system from a spraying operation, or in the direct path of spray, unless such equipment is specifically listed for both readily ignitible deposits and flammable vapor.

The determination of the extent of hazardous areas involved in spray application requires an understanding of the dual hazards of flammable vapors, mists, or powders, and highly combustible deposits applied to each individual installation.

When electrical equipment is installed in locations not subject to deposits of combustible residues but, due to inadequate ventilation, is subject to explosive concentrations of flammable vapors or mists, only approved explosionproof or other types of equipment approved for Class I, Division 1 locations (for example, purged and pressurized or intrinsically safe equipment or systems) are permitted.

When spraying areas containing dangerous quantities of flammable or combustible vapors, mists, residues, dusts, or deposits under normal operation have been determined, the adjacent unpartitioned areas, which are safe under normal operating conditions, but which may become dangerous due to accident or careless operation, should be given consideration. Equipment known to produce sparks or flames under normal operating conditions should not be installed in these adjacent unpartitioned areas.

When spraying operations are confined to adequately ventilated spray booths or rooms, there should be no deposits of combustible residues or dangerous concentrations of flammable vapors, mists, or dusts outside the spray booth under normal operating conditions.

In the interest of safety, however, it will be noted that, unless separated by partitions, an area within a certain distance [see Section 516-2(b)] of the Class I (or II), Division 1 spraying area, depending upon the arrangement, is classified as Division 2; that is, it should contain no equipment that produces ignition-capable sparks under normal operation. Furthermore, within this distance, electric lamps are required to be enclosed to prevent hot particles from falling on freshly painted stock or other readily ignitible material and, if subject to mechanical injury, are required to be properly guarded. See Section 516-7(b).

Even though it is contemplated that areas adjacent to spray booths (particularly where coating material stocks are located) will be provided with ventilation sufficient to prevent the presence of flammable vapors or deposits, it is nevertheless advisable that electric lamps be totally enclosed to prevent the falling of hot particles in any area where there may be freshly painted stock, accidentally spilled flammable or combustible materials, readily ignitible refuse, or flammable or combustible liquid containers accidentally left open. See Section 516-7(b).

Where electric lamps are in areas subject to atmospheres of flammable vapor, lamps should be replaced when electricity is off; otherwise there may be a spark from this source.

Sufficient lighting for coating operations, booth cleaning, and booth repair work should be provided at the time the equipment is installed in order to avoid the use of "temporary" or "emergency" lamps connected to ordinary extension cords in this area. See Section 516-3(d). A satisfactory and practical method of lighting is the use of ¼-in. thick wired or tempered glass panels in the top or sides of the spray booth with electrical light fixtures outside the booth, hence not in the direct path of the spray. See Section 516-3(c).

In order to prevent sparks from the accumulation of static electricity, all electrically conductive objects, including metal parts of spray booths, exhaust ducts, piping systems conveying flammable or combustible liquids or paint, solvent tanks, and canisters should be properly grounded. See Section 4-9.1 of NFPA 33.

Automobile undercoating operations in garages, conducted in areas having adequate natural or mechanical ventilation, are exempt from the requirements pertaining to spray-coating operations when (1) undercoating materials not more hazardous than kerosene (as classified by Underwriters Laboratories Inc. with respect to fire hazard rating 30-40) are used, or (2) undercoating materials using only solvents having a flash point in excess of 38°C (100°F) are used, and (3) no open flames are within 20 ft while such operations are conducted.

ARTICLE 517 — HEALTH CARE FACILITIES

Contents

ARTICLE 517—HEALTH CARE FACILITIES

K. X-ray Installations
517-140. Definitions.
517-141. Connection to Supply Circuit.
  (a) Fixed and Stationary Equipment.
  (b) Portable, Mobile, and Transportable Equipment.
  (c) Over 600-Volt Supply.
517-142. Disconnecting Means.
  (a) Capacity.
  (b) Location.
  (c) Portable Equipment.
517-143. Rating of Supply Conductors and Overcurrent Protection.

  (a) Diagnostic Equipment.
  (b) Therapeutic Equipment.
517-145. Control Circuit Conductors.
  (a) Number of Conductors in a Raceway.
  (b) Minimum Size of Conductors.
517-146. Equipment Installations.
517-148. Transformers and Capacitors.
517-151. Guarding and Grounding.
  (a) High-Voltage Parts.
  (b) Low-Voltage Cables.
  (c) Noncurrent-Carrying Metal Parts.

A. General

517-1. Scope.

The provisions of this article shall apply to electrical construction and installation criteria in health care facilities.

(FPN): The primary responsibility for developing performance, maintenance and testing criteria for installations in health care facilities rests with the Technical Committees which are directed by the Health Care Facilities Correlating Committee. For information concerning performance, maintenance and testing criteria refer to the appropriate health care facilities documents.

(FPN): NOTICE: Sections identified by an asterisk (*) include text extracted from Standard for Essential Electrical Systems for Health Care Facilities, NFPA 76A-1977, and Tentative Interim Amendments to that standard. Requests for interpretations or proposed revisions of the extracted text will be referred to the Committee on Essential Electrical Systems in Health Care Facilities. Sections identified by a double asterisk (**) include text extracted from Standard for the Use of Inhalation Anesthetics, NFPA 56A-1978, and Tentative Interim Amendments to that standard. Requests for interpretations or proposed revisions of the extracted text will be referred to the Committee on Anesthetizing Agents.

The requirements in Parts C, D, and E apply not only to single-function buildings, but are also intended to be individually applied to their respective forms of occupancy within a multifunction building (i.e., a doctor's examining room located within a residential custodial care facility would be required to meet the provisions of Part C).

The requirements of this article are intended to apply to all types of health care facilities. The requirements for each type of health care facility are nevertheless intended to be applied in a very specific manner. An example of the application of this article could be a suite of doctors' offices within a hospital. The doctor's business office would be treated as an ordinary occupancy and would be required to meet the applicable portion of the balance of this *Code*. The examining rooms attached to the doctor's business office would be required to meet the provisions of Part C of Article 517, and a nearby X-ray unit, whether operated by a group of doctors or the hospital itself, would be required to meet the provisions of Part K of Article 517.

The scope also includes health care facilities that may be mobile or supply very limited outpatient services.

Other standards referenced in this article are Essential Electrical Systems for Health Care Facilities, NFPA 76A-1977; Standard on Safe Use of Electricity in Patient Care Areas of Hospitals, NFPA 76B-1980; *Life Safety Code*®, NFPA 101®-1981; Inhalation Anesthetics, NFPA 56A-1978; Installation of Centrifugal Fire Pumps, NFPA 20-1983; and Standard for Nonflammable Medical Gas Systems, NFPA 56F-1983.

517-2. Definitions.

Alternate Power Source. One or more generator sets, or battery systems where permitted, intended to provide power during the interruption of the normal electrical services or the public utility electrical service intended to provide power during interruption of service normally provided by the generating facilities on the premises.

Anesthetizing Location. Any area of a health care facility which has been designated to be used for the administration of any flammable or nonflammable inhalation anesthetic agent in the course of examination or treatment.

This definition recognizes that in an emergency it may be necessary to administer an anesthetic almost anywhere in a health care facility; however, only those areas in a health care facility set aside by intent for the induction of anesthetics are required to meet the provisions of Part G of Article 517. This definition, as well as the provisions of Part G, is not intended to apply to the administration of analgesic anesthetics such as might be employed in a dental office.

Critical Branch. A subsystem of the emergency system consisting of feeders and branch circuits supplying energy to task illumination, special power circuits, and selected receptacles serving areas and functions related to patient care, and which are connected to alternate power sources by one or more transfer switches during interruption of the normal power source.

Emergency System. A system of feeders and branch circuits meeting the requirements of Article 700, and intended to supply alternate power to a limited number of prescribed functions vital to the protection of life and patient safety, with automatic restoration of electrical power within 10 seconds of power interruption.

Equipment System. A system of feeders and branch circuits arranged for delayed, automatic or manual connection to the alternate power source and which serves primarily 3-phase power equipment.

Essential Electrical System. A system comprised of alternate sources of power and all connected distribution systems and ancillary equipment, designed to assure continuity of electrical power to designated areas and functions of a health care facility during disruption of normal power sources, and also designed to minimize disruption within the internal wiring system.

Exposed Conductive Surfaces. Those surfaces which are capable of carrying electric current and which are unprotected, unenclosed, or unguarded, permitting personal contact. Paint, anodizing, and similar coatings are not considered suitable insulation, unless they are listed for the use.

This definition is intended to clarify the requirements of Section 517-81. Specifically, it points out that the mere application of paint or similar coatings does not necessarily render a metallic surface nonconductive. Under the terms of this definition, the coating material must be listed as an electrical insulating medium. See definition of "Listed" in Article 100.

Flammable Anesthetics. Gases or vapors such as fluroxene, cyclopropane, divinyl ether, ethyl chloride, ethyl ether, and ethylene, which may form flammable or explosive mixtures with air, oxygen, or reducing gases such as nitrous oxide.

Flammable Anesthetizing Location. Any inhalation anesthetizing location designated for the use of flammable anesthetizing agents.

713

Hazard Current. For a given set of connections in an isolated power system, the total current that would flow through a low impedance if it were connected between either isolated conductor and ground.

FAULT HAZARD CURRENT: The hazard current of a given isolated system with all devices connected except the line isolation monitor.

MONITOR HAZARD CURRENT: The hazard current of the line isolation monitor alone.

TOTAL HAZARD CURRENT: The hazard current of a given isolated system with all devices, including the line isolation monitor, connected.

Health Care Facilities. Buildings or parts of buildings that contain but are not limited to hospitals, nursing homes, residential custodial care facilities, clinics, and medical and dental offices, whether fixed or mobile.

Hospital. A building or part thereof used for the medical, psychiatric, obstetrical or surgical care, on a 24-hour basis, of four or more inpatients. Hospital, wherever used in this Code, shall include general hospitals, mental hospitals, tuberculosis hospitals, children's hospitals, and any such facilities providing inpatient care.

Isolated Power System. A system comprising an isolating transformer or its equivalent, a line isolation monitor, and its ungrounded circuit conductors.

Isolation Transformer. A transformer of the multiple-winding type, with the primary and secondary windings physically separated, which inductively couples its secondary winding to the grounded feeder systems that energize its primary winding.

Life Safety Branch. A subsystem of the emergency system consisting of feeders and branch circuits, meeting the requirements of Article 700 and intended to provide adequate power needs to ensure safety to patients and personnel, and which are connected to alternate power sources by one or more transfer switches.

Line Isolation Monitor. A test instrument designed to continually check the balanced and unbalanced impedance from each line of an isolated circuit to ground and equipped with a built-in test circuit to exercise the alarm without adding to the leakage current hazard.

(FPN): "Line isolation monitor" was formerly known as "ground contact indicator."

Nursing Home. A building or part thereof used for the lodging, boarding and nursing care, on a 24-hour basis, of four or more persons who, because of mental or physical incapacity, may be unable to provide for their own needs and safety without the assistance of another person. Nursing home, wherever used in this Code, shall include nursing and convalescent homes, skilled nursing facilities, intermediate care facilities, and infirmaries of homes for the aged.

Nurses' Stations. Areas intended to provide a center of nursing activity for a group of nurses serving bed patients, where the patient calls are received, nurses are dispatched, nurses' notes written, inpatient charts prepared, and medications prepared for distribution to patients. Where such activities are carried on in more than one location within a nursing unit, all such separate areas are considered a part of the nurses' station.

Patient Equipment Grounding Point. A jack or terminal bus which serves as the collection point for redundant grounding of electric appliances serving a patient vicinity.

Patient Vicinity. In an area in which patients are normally cared for, the patient vicinity is the space with surfaces likely to be contacted by the patient or an attendant who can touch the patient. This encloses a space within the room not less than 6 feet (1.83 m) beyond the perimeter of the bed in its nominal location, and extending vertically not less than 7½ feet (2.29 m) above the floor.

This area is limited to patients in bed. It is also limited to the bed in its nominal position, that is, the position of the bed as called for in the architect's plans, rather than the position of the bed as it may be found in daily use subject to movement by housekeeping staff or the convenience of the medical staff. It is not intended that a "halo" of electrical hazard follow the bed as it is moved about the room or the health care facility.

Definitions for hospital, nursing home, and residential custodial care facility are all identical to the same definitions as employed in NFPA *101, Life Safety Code.*

Psychiatric Hospital. A building used exclusively for the psychiatric care, on a 24-hour basis, of four or more inpatients.

Reference Grounding Point. A terminal bus which is the equipment grounding bus or an extension of the equipment grounding bus and is a convenient collection point for grounding all electric appliances, equipment, and, when necessary and appropriate, exposed conductive surfaces in a patient vicinity.

Residential Custodial Care Facility. A building, or part thereof, used for the lodging or boarding of four or more persons who may be incapable of self-preservation because of age, or physical or mental limitation. This includes facilities such as homes for the aged, nurseries (custodial care for children under 6 years of age), and mentally retarded care institutions. Day care facilities that do not provide lodging or boarding for institutional occupants are not classified as residential custodial care facilities.

Room Bonding Point. A grounding terminal or group of terminals which serves as a collection point for grounding exposed metal or conductive building surfaces in a room.

Selected Receptacles. Minimal electrical receptacles to accommodate appliances ordinarily required for local tasks or likely to be used in patient care emergencies.

Task Illumination. Provision for the minimum lighting required to carry out necessary tasks in the described areas, including safe access to supplies and equipment, and access to exits.

Therapeutic High-Frequency Diathermy Equipment. Therapeutic high-frequency diathermy equipment is therapeutic induction and dielectric heating equipment.

Wet Location, Health Care Facility. A patient care area that is normally subject to wet conditions, including standing water on the floor, or routine dousing or drenching of the work area. Routine housekeeping procedures and incidental spillage of liquids do not define a wet location.

This definition excludes such areas as laundry rooms, boiler rooms, and utility areas which, although routinely wet, are not patient care areas. The governing body of the health care facility may elect to include under this definition such areas as hydrotherapy areas, dialysis laboratories, and certain wet laboratories. No lavatories or bathrooms within a health care facility are intended to be classified as a wet location.

B. Wiring Systems — General

517-6. Applicability. Part B shall apply to all health care facilities. Installations in facilities which provide patient care, equipment or services identified in other parts of this article shall also comply with the requirements of that part.

517-10. Wiring Methods. Except as modified in this article, wiring methods shall comply with the applicable requirements of Chapters 1 through 4 of this Code.

ARTICLE 517—HEALTH CARE FACILITIES

517-11. Grounding of Receptacles and Fixed Electrical Equipment. In areas used for patient care, all receptacles and all noncurrent-carrying conductive surfaces of fixed electrical equipment likely to become energized that are subject to personal contact, operating at over 100 volts, shall be grounded by an insulated copper conductor sized in accordance with Table 250-95 and installed with the branch-circuit conductors supplying these receptacles or fixed equipment.

Exception No. 1: Metal faceplates shall be permitted to be grounded by means of a metal mounting screw(s) securing the faceplate to a grounded outlet box or grounded wiring device.

Exception No. 2: An equipment grounding conductor enclosed in the sheath of a nonmetallic-sheathed cable assembly installed in accordance with the limitations of Sections 336-3 and 336-4 shall be permitted to be used in accordance with Parts C and D of this article.

This rule applies to any area used for patient care and is not limited to patient rooms. Additional areas, such as therapy areas, recreational areas, solaria, and certain patient corridors, would also be included. It should be clearly understood that this section requires grounding by means of a copper conductor, usually insulated, installed with the branch-circuit conductors. The conductor can be either solid or stranded. A separate insulated equipment grounding conductor is not required to be run upstream from the branch-circuit panelboard with the feeder conductors in a metal raceway.

Exception No. 1 permits metallic plates to be grounded by means of the metal mounting screws rather than having a separate equipment grounding conductor run to the metal plate.

Exception No. 2 recognizes that the equipment grounding conductor (covered or bare) enclosed in the sheath of Type NM or NMC cable in accordance with the provisions of this exception is permitted in lieu of a separate insulated grounding conductor.

This rule differs from the general grounding rule for such equipment under Section 250-45 in that not just specific items, but all cord- and plug-connected equipment (over 100 V) is covered.

517-13. Receptacles with Insulated Grounds. Receptacles with insulated grounds as permitted in Section 250-74, Exception No. 4, shall be identified; such identification shall be visible after installation.

(FPN): Care is important in specifying such a system with receptacle insulated grounds since the grounding impedance is controlled only by the grounding wires and does not benefit functionally from any parallel grounding paths.

This section prevents the indiscriminate use of such devices, and the compromising of the potential difference requirements within critical care areas.

Proper identification may be by color-coding the receptacle "orange" or by other approved means.

517-14. Ground-Fault Protection.

(a) Feeders. When ground-fault protection is provided for operation of the service disconnecting means, an additional step of ground-fault protection shall be provided in the next level of feeder downstream toward the load. Such protection shall consist of overcurrent devices and current transformers or other equivalent protective equipment which shall cause the feeder disconnecting devices to open.

(b) Selectivity. Ground-fault protection for operation of the service and feeder disconnecting means shall be fully selective such that the feeder device and not the service device shall open on ground faults on the load side of the feeder device. A six-cycle minimum separation between the service and feeder ground-fault tripping bands shall be provided. Operating time of the disconnecting devices shall be considered in selecting the time spread between these two bands to achieve 100 percent selectivity.

(FPN): See Section 230-95, Fine Print Note, for transfer of alternate source where ground-fault protection is applied.

Whenever ground-fault protective equipment is applied to the service providing power to a health care facility, whether by design or by reason of the requirements of Section 230-95, an additional level of ground-fault protection is required downstream. Under this rule, ground-fault protection is required to be applied to every feeder, and additional ground-fault protective devices may be applied farther downstream at the option of the governing body of the health care facility. With proper coordination, this additional ground-fault protection is intended to limit a ground fault to a single feeder and thereby prevent a total outage of the entire health care system.

However, when a health care installation, such as a doctor's office, is a part of a larger general-use facility (for example, a business office building) that has service ground-fault protection in accordance with Section 230-95, it is not intended that ground-fault protection be required on the health care facility (doctor's office) feeder since no additional protection will be achieved insofar as the doctor's office is concerned.

A Fine Print Note to Section 230-95 calls attention to problems that may arise when ground-fault protected systems are transferred to another supply system.

(c) Testing. When equipment ground-fault protection is first installed, each level shall be performance tested to ensure compliance with (b) above.

Section 517-14(c) is new in the 1984 *NEC.* See also Section 230-95(c) and its commentary.

C. Clinics, Medical and Dental Offices, Outpatient Facilities and Other Health Care Facilities Not Covered in Parts D and E

These forms of occupancy are required to comply with grounding requirements in accordance with Sections 517-10 and 517-11. Note Exception No. 2 to Section 517-11 which permits Types NM and NMC for health care areas covered in Part C.

(FPN): For performance, maintenance and testing requirements of essential electrical systems in clinics, medical and dental offices and outpatient facilities, see Standard for Essential Electrical Systems for Health Care Facilities, NFPA 76A-1977.

517-30. General. Part C applies to those portions of clinics, medical and dental offices, and outpatient facilities wherein patients are intended to be examined or treated. It does not apply to business offices, corridors, waiting rooms, and the like.

D. Nursing Homes and Residential Custodial Care Facilities

(FPN): For performance, maintenance and testing requirements of essential electrical systems in nursing homes and residential custodial care facilities, see Standard for Essential Electrical Systems for Health Care Facilities, NFPA 76A-1977.

517-40.* Applicability. The requirements of Part D, Sections 517-42 through 517-47, shall apply to nursing homes and residential custodial care facilities.

ARTICLE 517—HEALTH CARE FACILITIES

Exception: Any free-standing building used for health care other than those described in Parts C and E of this article shall be exempted from the requirements of Sections 517-44 through 517-47 provided:

a. It maintains admitting and discharge policies that preclude the provision of care for any patient or resident who may need to be sustained by electrically operated or mechanical life support devices, and

b. Offers no surgical treatment requiring general anesthesia, and

c. Provides an automatic battery-operated system(s) or equipment that shall be effective for 4 or more hours and is otherwise in accordance with Section 700-12, and that shall be capable of supplying lighting for exit lights, exit corridors, stairways, nursing stations, medical preparation areas, boiler rooms and communication areas. This system shall also supply battery power to operate all alarm systems.

(FPN): See *Life Safety Code,* NFPA *101*-1981 (ANSI).

NFPA 76A recognizes two classes of nursing homes or residential custodial care facilities. For the smaller, less complex facility only a minimum alternate service need be furnished.

Where treatment of patients is of a more complex nature, the requirements of Sections 517-44 through 517-47 are required to be applied. The branches of the emergency system for this class of occupancy bear identical titles to their counterparts for hospital-type occupancies.

517-41. Inpatient Hospital Care Facilities. Nursing homes and residential custodial care facilities which provide inpatient hospital care shall comply with the requirements of Part E, Hospitals.

Regardless of the name applied to the facility, the type of electrical system is dependent upon the type of patient care provided. Where such care is clearly inpatient hospital care, a hospital-type electrical system is required to be installed.

517-42. Facilities Contiguous with Hospitals. Nursing homes and residential custodial care facilities which are contiguous with a hospital shall be permitted to have their essential electrical systems supplied by that of the hospital.

When a hospital, nursing home, or residential custodial care facility share what is essentially the same building, the nursing home need not have its own essential electrical system but may derive its supply from the hospital. It should be noted, however, that this rule applies only to the electrical supply and does not permit the sharing of transfer devices and the like.

517-44. Essential Electrical Systems.

(a) General. Essential electrical systems for nursing homes and residential custodial care facilities shall be comprised of two separate branches capable of supplying a limited amount of lighting and power service which is considered essential for the protection of life safety and effective operation of the institution during the time normal electrical service is interrupted for any reason. These two separate branches shall be the life safety branch and the critical branch. The essential electrical systems shall be installed and connected to the alternate power source so that all functions specified herein shall be restored to operation after interruption of the normal source.

(b) Transfer Switches.* The number of transfer switches to be used shall be based upon reliability, design, and load considerations. Each branch of the essential electrical system shall be served by one or more transfer switches as shown in Diagrams 517-44(1) and 517-44(2). One transfer switch shall be permitted to serve one or more branches or systems in a small facility as shown in Diagram 517-44(3).

(FPN): See Standard for Essential Electrical Systems for Health Care Facilities, NFPA 76A-1977: Section 5-6.2, Description of Transfer Switch Operation; Section 3-2.4, Automatic Transfer Switch Features; and Section 3-2.6, Nonautomatic Transfer Device Features.

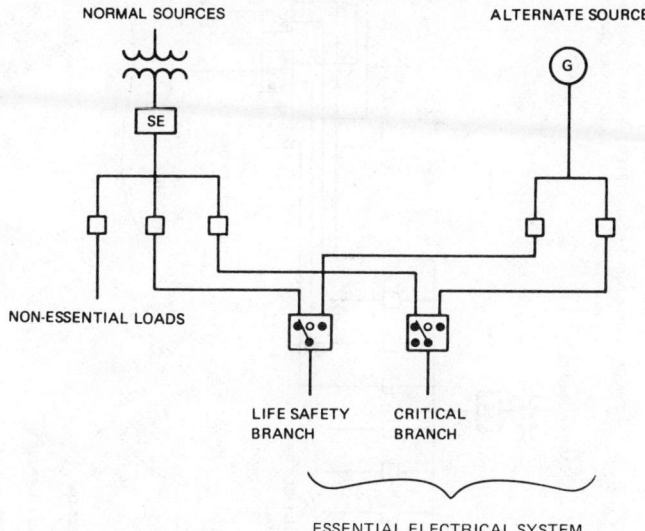

MINIMUM ELECTRICAL SYSTEM – TYPICAL SMALL NURSING HOMES
AND RESIDENTIAL CUSTODIAL
CARE FACILITIES

SE	SERVICE ENTRANCE
	OVERCURRENT PROTECTION
	AUTOMATIC SWITCHING EQUIPMENT
	DELAYED AUTOMATIC SWITCHING EQUIPMENT
	TRANSFORMER
G	GENERATOR

Diagram 517-44(1)

719

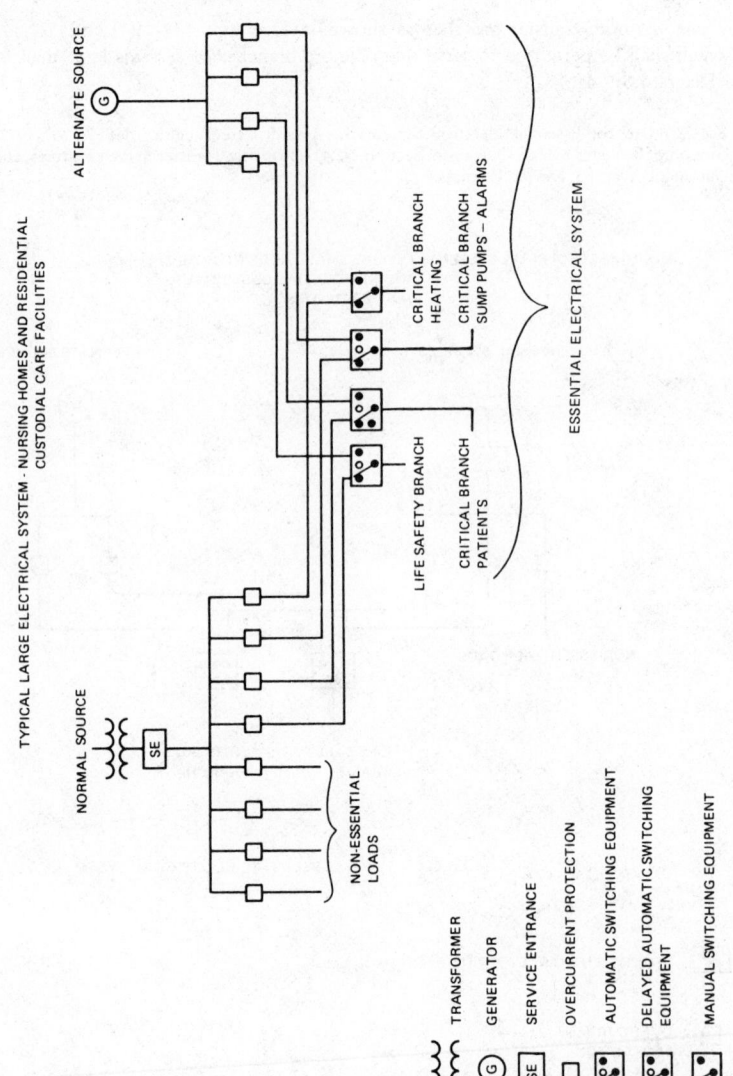

Diagram 517-44(2)

MINIMUM ELECTRICAL SYSTEM---TYPICAL SMALL NURSING HOMES
AND RESIDENTIAL CUSTODIAL
CARE FACILITIES
(SINGLE TRANSFER SWITCH)

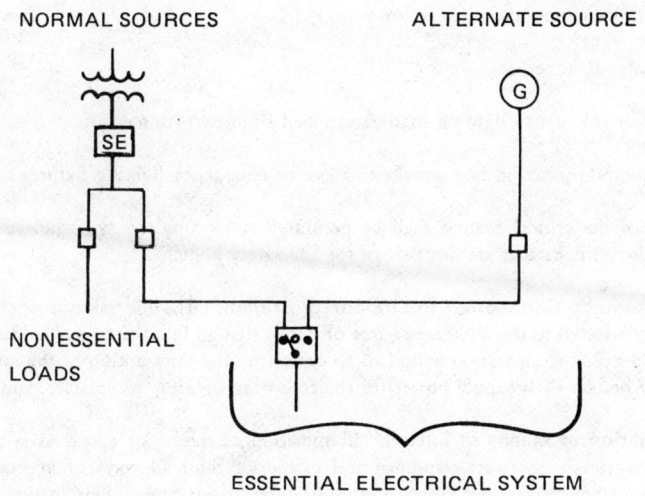

SE   SERVICE ENTRANCE

☐   OVERCURRENT
    PROTECTION

    AUTOMATIC SWITCHING
    EQUIPMENT

    TRANSFORMER

G   GENERATOR

Diagram 517-44(3)

(c) Capacity of System. The essential electrical system shall have adequate capacity to meet the demand for the operation of all functions and equipment to be served by each branch at one time.

(d) Separation from Other Circuits. The life safety branch shall be kept entirely independent of all other wiring and equipment and shall not enter the same raceways, boxes or cabinets with other wiring except as follows:

(1) In transfer switches,

(2) In exit or emergency lighting fixtures supplied from two sources, or

(3) In a common junction box attached to exit or emergency lighting fixtures supplied from two sources.

The wiring of the critical branch shall be permitted to occupy the same raceways, boxes or cabinets of other circuits that are not part of the life safety branch.

517-45.* Automatic Connection to Life Safety Branch. The life safety branch shall be so installed and connected to the alternate source of power that all functions specified herein shall be automatically restored to operation within 10 seconds after the interruption of the normal source. The life safety branch shall supply power for the following lighting, receptacles, and equipment:

(a) Illumination of Means of Egress. Illumination of means of egress as is necessary for corridors, passageways, stairways, landings and exit doors and all ways of approach to exits. Switching arrangement to transfer patient corridor lighting from general illumination circuits shall be permitted providing only one of two circuits can be selected, and both circuits cannot be extinguished at the same time.

(FPN): See *Life Safety Code*, NFPA *101*-1981 (ANSI), Section 5-10.

(b) Exit Signs. Exit signs and exit directional signs.

(FPN): See *Life Safety Code*, NFPA *101*-1981 (ANSI), Section 5-11.

(c) Alarm and Alerting Systems. Alarm and alerting systems, including:

(1) Fire alarms activated at manual stations, electric water flow alarm devices in connection with sprinkler systems, and automatic fire or smoke or products of combustion detection devices.

(FPN): See *Life Safety Code*, NFPA *101*-1981 (ANSI), Sections 7-6, 12-3.4, and 12-3.5.

(2) Alarms required for systems used for the piping of nonflammable medical gases.

(FPN): See Standard for Nonflammable Medical Gas Systems, NFPA 56F-1983 (ANSI).

(d) Communication Systems. Communication systems, where used for issuing instructions during emergency conditions.

(e) Dining and Recreation Areas. Sufficient lighting in dining and recreation areas to provide illumination to exit ways.

(f) Generator Set Location. Task illumination and selected receptacles in the generator set location.

...ian those listed above in (a) through (f) shall be connected to the life safety

...on to Critical Branch. The critical branch shall be so installed and ...ternate power source that the equipment listed in Section 517-46(a) shall be ...red to operation at appropriate time-lag intervals following the restoration of the lite ....ch to operation. Its arrangement shall also provide for the additional connection of equipment listed in Section 517-46(b) by either delayed automatic or manual operation.

(a) Delayed Automatic Connection. The following equipment shall be connected to the critical branch and shall be arranged for delayed automatic connection to the alternate power source:

(1) Patient care areas — task illumination and selected receptacles in:

a. Medication preparation areas.

b. Pharmacy dispensing areas.

c. Nurses' stations (unless adequately lighted by corridor luminaires).

(2) Sump pumps and other equipment required to operate for the safety of major apparatus and associated control systems and alarms.

(3) Elevator cab lighting and communication system.

(b) Delayed Automatic or Manual Connection. The following equipment shall be connected to the critical branch and shall be arranged for either delayed automatic or manual connection to the alternate power source:

(1) Heating equipment to provide heating for patient rooms.

Exception: Heating of general patient rooms during disruption of the normal source shall not be required under any of the following conditions:

a. The outside design temperature is higher than + 20°F (-6.7°C), or

b. The outside design temperature is lower than + 20°F (-6.7°C) and where a selected room(s) is provided for the needs of all confined patients, then only such room(s) need be heated, or

It has become common practice in some areas of the country to install individual room heating/air conditioners rather than have a central heating/air conditioning plant. When these individual units are electrically powered, it may not be practical to apply this high demand load to the generator. When the governing body of the nursing home has full-time skilled attendants who can move people to one room(s) which will be heated when this smaller load is picked up by the generator, then the intent of the *Code* is satisfied. The provisions for limited heating during emergency conditions are based on consideration of "outside" design temperature.

c. The facility is served by a dual source of normal power as described in Section 517-47(c), Fine Print Note.

(FPN): The outside design temperature is based on the 97½ percent design values as shown in Chapter 33 of the ASHRAE Handbook of Fundamentals (1972).

(2) Elevator Service. In instances where disruption of power would result in elevat stopping between floors, throw-over facilities shall be provided to allow the temporary operation of any elevator for the release of passengers.

(3) Additional illumination, receptacles, and equipment shall be permitted to be connected only to the critical branch.

517-47. Sources of Power.

(a) Two Independent Sources of Power. Essential electrical systems shall have a minimum of two independent sources of power: a normal source generally supplying the entire electrical system, and one or more alternate sources for use when the normal source is interrupted.

(b)* Alternate Source of Power. The alternate source of power shall be a generator(s) driven by some form of prime mover(s), and located on the premises.

(FPN): For information as to facilities where battery sources are permitted, see Standard for Essential Electrical Systems for Health Care Facilities, NFPA 76A-1977.

Exception No. 1: Where the normal source consists of generating units on the premises, the alternate source shall be either another generator set, or an external utility service.

Exception No. 2: Nursing homes or residential custodial care facilities meeting the requirements of the Exception to Section 517-40 shall be permitted to use a battery system or self-contained battery integral with the equipment.

(c) Location of Essential Electrical System Components. Careful consideration shall be given to the location of the spaces housing the components of the essential electrical system to minimize interruptions caused by natural forces common to the area (e.g., storms, floods, earthquakes, or hazards created by adjoining structures or activities). Consideration shall also be given to the possible interruption of normal electrical services resulting from similar causes as well as possible disruption of normal electrical service due to internal wiring and equipment failures.

(FPN): Facilities whose normal source of power is supplied by two or more separate central station-fed services experience greater than normal electrical service reliability than those with only a single feed. Such a dual source of normal power consists of two or more electrical services fed from separate generator sets or a utility distribution network having multiple power input sources and arranged to provide mechanical and electrical separation so that a fault between the facility and the generating sources will not likely cause an interruption of more than one of the facility service feeders.

E. Hospitals

(FPN): For performance, maintenance and testing requirements of essential electrical systems in hospitals, see Standard for Essential Electrical Systems for Health Care Facilities, NFPA 76A-1977. For installation of centrifugal fire pumps, see Standard for the Installation of Centrifugal Fire Pumps, NFPA 20-1983 (ANSI).

(FPN): For additional information, see Standard on Safe Use of Electricity in Patient Care Areas of Hospitals, NFPA 76B-1980.

517-58. Applicability. The requirements of Part E, Sections 517-60 through 517-65, shall apply to hospitals where an essential electrical system is required.

Exception: Those facilities covered by Parts C and D.

(FPN): For information as to the need for an essential electrical system, see Standard for Essential Electrical Systems for Health Care Facilities, NFPA 76A-1977.

517-60. Essential Electrical Systems.

(a) **General.**

(1) Essential electrical systems for hospitals shall be comprised of two separate systems capable of supplying a limited amount of lighting and power service which is considered essential for life safety and effective hospital operation during the time the normal electrical service is interrupted for any reason. These two systems shall be the emergency system and the equipment system.

(2)* The emergency system shall be limited to circuits essential to life safety and critical patient care. These are designated the life safety branch and the critical branch.

(3)* The equipment system shall supply major electrical equipment necessary for patient care and basic hospital operation.

(4)* The number of transfer switches to be used shall be based upon reliability, design, and load considerations. Each branch of the essential electrical system shall be served by one or more transfer switches as shown in Diagrams 517-60(1) and 517-60(2). One transfer switch shall be permitted to serve one or more branches or systems in a small facility as shown in Diagram 517-60(3).

(FPN): See Standard for Essential Electrical Systems for Health Care Facilities, NFPA 76A-1977: Section 3-2.4, Automatic Transfer Switch Features; Section 5-6.2, Description of Transfer Switch Operation; and Section 3-2.6, Nonautomatic Transfer Device Features.

Diagrams 517-60(1), 517-60(2), and 517-60(3) indicate possible electrical system connections for small and large hospitals. Diagram 517-60(2) illustrates a common situation where the expansion of the facility necessitates the addition of a normal source to that already in place. As shown in the diagram, this would not necessarily require the addition of another alternate source. Provided the alternate source has a capacity for all of the intended load, it may serve multiple services.

For a small hospital, see Diagram 517-60(3). A small hospital can be served by a single transfer switch that would handle the loads associated with both the emergency system and the equipment system. This, of course, is on the assumption that the transfer switch has sufficient capacity to handle the combined loads and the alternate source of power is sufficiently large to withstand the impact of the simultaneous transfer of both systems in the event of a normal power loss.

(b) **Wiring Requirements.**

(1) **Separation from Other Circuits.** The life safety branch and critical branch of the emergency system shall be kept entirely independent of all other wiring and equipment and shall not enter the same raceways, boxes or cabinets with each other or other wiring, except as follows:

a. In transfer switches,

b. In exit or emergency lighting fixtures supplied from two sources, or

c. In a common junction box attached to exit or emergency lighting fixtures supplied from two sources.

The wiring of the equipment system shall be permitted to occupy the same raceways, boxes or cabinets of other circuits that are not part of the emergency system.

ARTICLE 517—HEALTH CARE FACILITIES

MINIMUM ELECTRICAL SYSTEM - TYPICAL SMALL HOSPITALS

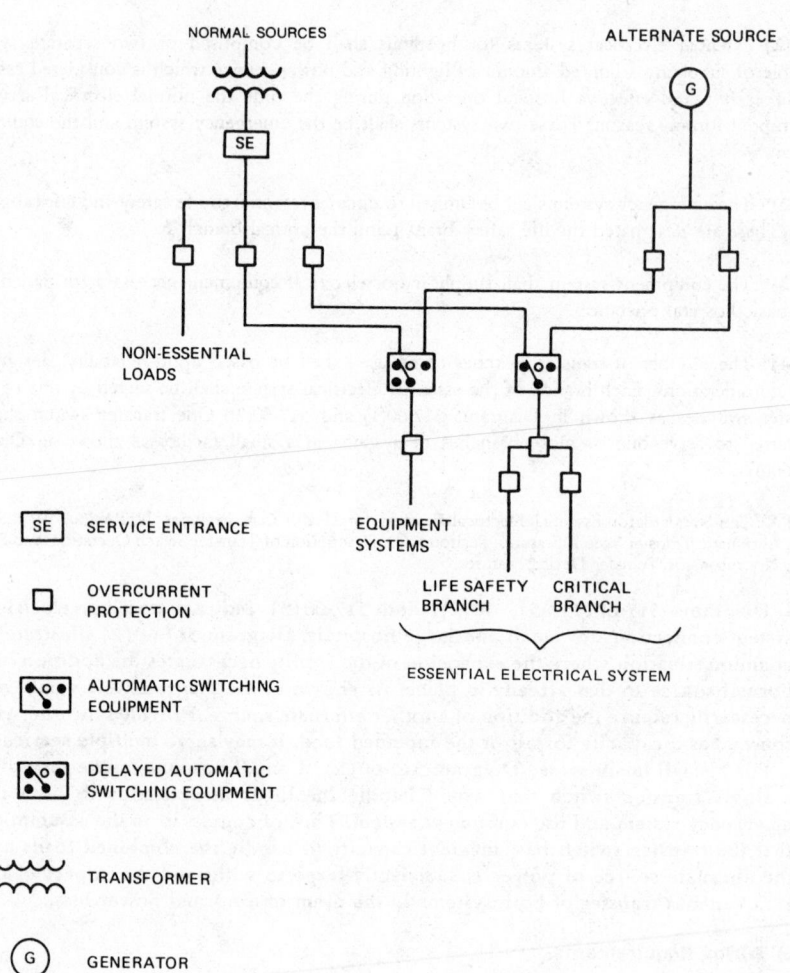

Diagram 517-60(1)

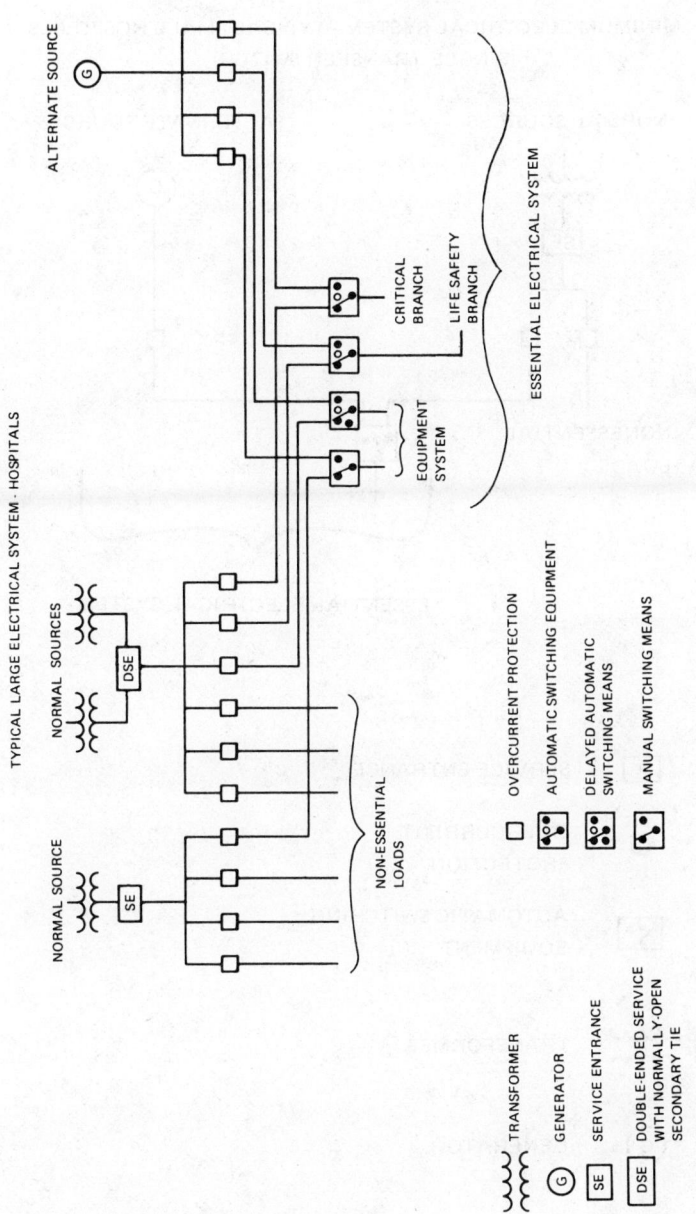

Diagram 517-60(2)

ARTICLE 517—HEALTH CARE FACILITIES

MINIMUM ELECTRICAL SYSTEM---TYPICAL SMALL HOSPITALS
(SINGLE TRANSFER SWITCH)

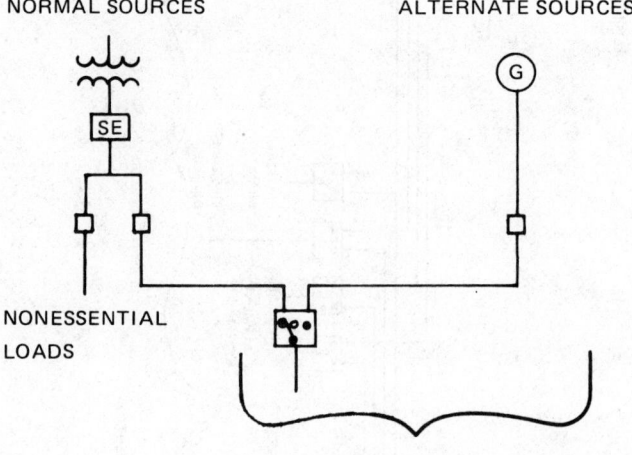

SE   SERVICE ENTRANCE

☐   OVERCURRENT
PROTECTION

AUTOMATIC SWITCHING
EQUIPMENT

TRANSFORMER

Ⓖ   GENERATOR

Diagram 517-60(3)

(2) Isolated Power Systems. Where isolated power systems are installed in any of the areas in Section 517-63(a)(1) and (a)(2), each system shall be supplied by an individual circuit serving no other load.

(3) Mechanical Protection of the Emergency System. The wiring of the emergency system of a hospital shall be mechanically protected by installation in metallic raceways.

Exception No. 1: Flexible power cords of appliances, or other utilization equipment, connected to the emergency system shall not be required to be enclosed in raceways.

Exception No. 2: Secondary circuits of transformer-powered communication or signaling systems shall not be required to be enclosed in raceways unless otherwise specified by Chapter 7 or 8.

This exception exempts nurse call, telephone, and alarm circuits from being run in metal raceways, provided they comply with their applicable articles elsewhere in the *Code*. Although this provides substantial latitude in the wiring method, it should be noted that the restrictions of Section 300-22 (ducts and plenums) still apply unless conductors listed as having adequate fire-resistant and low smoke-producing characteristics are used as required by the exceptions under Sections 725-2(b), 760-4(d), and 800-3(d).

(c) Capacity of Systems. The essential electrical system shall have adequate capacity to meet the demand for the operation of all functions and equipment to be served by each system and branch.

517-61.* Emergency System. Those functions of patient care depending on lighting or appliances that are connected to the emergency system shall be divided into two mandatory branches: the life safety branch and the critical branch, described in Sections 517-62 and 517-63.

The branches of the emergency system shall be installed and connected to the alternate power source so that all functions specified herein for the emergency system shall be automatically restored to operation within 10 seconds after interruption of the normal source.

517-62.* Life Safety Branch. The life safety branch of the emergency system shall supply power for the following lighting, receptacles, and equipment:

(a) Illumination of Means of Egress. Illumination of means of egress, such as lighting required for corridors, passageways, stairways and landings at exit doors, and all necessary ways of approach to exits. Switching arrangements to transfer patient corridor lighting in hospitals from general illumination circuits to night illumination circuits shall be permitted provided only one of two circuits can be selected, and both circuits cannot be extinguished at the same time.

(FPN): See *Life Safety Code*, NFPA *101*-1981 (ANSI), Section 5-10.

(b) Exit Signs. Exit signs and exit directional signs.

(FPN): See *Life Safety Code*, NFPA *101*-1981 (ANSI), Section 5-11.

(c) Alarm and Alerting Systems. Alarm and alerting systems including:

(1) Fire alarms, actuated at manual stations.

(2) Electric water-flow alarm devices in connection with sprinkler systems.

(3) Automatic fire or smoke or products of combustion detection devices.

(FPN): See *Life Safety Code*, NFPA *101*-1981 (ANSI), Sections 12-1 and 12-2.

(4) Alarms required for systems used for the piping of nonflammable medical gases.

(FPN): See Nonflammable Medical Gas Systems, NFPA 56F-1983 (ANSI).

(d) Communication Systems. Hospital communication systems, where used for issuing instructions during emergency conditions.

(e) Generator Set Location. Task illumination and selected receptacles at the generator set location.

No function other than those listed above in (a) through (e) shall be connected to the life safety branch.

517-63.* Critical Branch.

(a) Task Illumination and Selected Receptacles. The critical branch of the emergency system shall supply power for task illumination and selected receptacles serving the following areas and functions related to patient care.

The critical branch is intended to serve a limited number of receptacles and locations to reduce the load and to minimize the chances of a fault condition. Receptacles in general patient care area corridors are permitted on the critical branch, but they are required to be identified in some manner (color coded or labeled) as part of the critical branch.

(1) Anesthetizing locations — task illumination only.

(2) The isolated power systems required in anesthetizing locations and in special environments.

(3) Patient care areas — task illumination and selected receptacles in:

a. Infant nurseries,

b. Medication preparation areas,

c. Pharmacy dispensing areas,

d. Selected acute nursing areas,

e. Psychiatric bed areas (omit receptacles),

f. Ward treatment rooms, and

g. Nurses' stations (unless adequately lighted by corridor luminaires).

(4) Additional specialized patient care task illumination and receptacles, where needed.

(5) Nurse call systems.

(6) Blood, bone and tissue banks.

(7) Telephone equipment room and closets.

(8) Task illumination, receptacles, and special power circuits for:

a. Acute care beds (selected),

b. Angiographic labs,

c. Cardiac catheterization labs,

d. Coronary care units,

e. Hemodialysis rooms or areas,

f. Emergency room treatment areas (selected),

g. Human physiology labs,

h. Intensive care units, and

i. Postoperative recovery rooms (selected).

(9) Additional task illumination, receptacles and special power circuits needed for effective hospital operation.

(b) Subdivision of the Critical Branch. It shall be permitted to subdivide the critical branch into two or more branches.

517-64.* Equipment System Connection to Alternate Power Source. The equipment system shall be installed and connected to the alternate source, such that the equipment described in Section 517-64(a) is automatically restored to operation at appropriate time-lag intervals following the energizing of the emergency system. Its arrangement shall also provide for the subsequent connection of equipment described in Section 517-64(b).

(a) Equipment for Delayed Automatic Connection. The following equipment shall be arranged for delayed automatic connection to the alternate power source:

(1) Central suction systems serving medical and surgical functions, including controls.

(2) Sump pumps and other equipment required to operate for the safety of major apparatus, including associated control systems and alarms.

(3) Compressed air systems serving medical and surgical functions, including controls.

(FPN): The above equipment may be arranged for sequential delayed automatic action to the alternate power source to prevent overloading the generator where engineering studies indicate it is necessary.

(b) Equipment for Delayed Automatic or Manual Connection. The following equipment shall be arranged for either delayed automatic or manual connection to the alternate power source:

(1) Heating equipment to provide heating for operating, delivery, labor, recovery, intensive care, coronary care, nurseries and general patient rooms.

Exception: Heating of general patient rooms during disruption of the normal source shall not be required under any of the following conditions:

a. The outside design temperature is higher than + 20°F (-6.7°C), or

b. The outside design temperature is lower than + 20°F (-6.7°C) and where a selected room(s) is provided for the needs of all confined patients then only such room(s) need be heated, or

See commentary following Section 517-46(b)(1) Exception b.

c. The facility is served by a dual source of normal power as described in Section 517-65(c), Fine Print Note.

(FPN): The design temperature is based on the 97½ percent design value as shown in Chapter 33 of the ASHRAE Handbook of Fundamentals (1972).

(2) Elevator(s) selected to provide service to patient, surgical, obstetrical and ground floors during interruption of normal power. This shall include connection for cab lighting, control and signal systems.

In instances where interruption of normal power would result in other elevators stopping between floors, throw-over facilities shall be provided to allow the temporary operation of any elevator for the release of patients or other persons who may be confined between floors.

(3) Supply and exhaust ventilating systems for surgical and obstetrical delivery suites, infant nurseries, infection isolation rooms, emergency treatment spaces, and laboratory fume hoods.

(4) Hyperbaric facilities.

(5) Hypobaric facilities.

(6) Automatically operated doors.

(7) Such other loads as may be deemed necessary by the hospital, subject to the approval of the authority having jurisdiction.

Careful consideration should be given to the effect of placing fire pumps on the equipment system. In spite of the fact that manual connection of fire pumps is permitted, future additions of other equipment to the equipment system may eventually compromise its ability to handle the fire pump load. For this reason a separate alternate source may provide the best assurance of continued capacity for the fire pump load.

(8) Minimal electrically heated autoclaving equipment shall be permitted to be arranged for either automatic or manual connection to the alternate source.

(9) Other selected equipment shall be permitted to be served by the equipment system.

517-65. Sources of Power.

(a) Two Independent Sources of Power. Essential electrical systems shall have a minimum of two independent sources of power: a normal source generally supplying the entire electrical system, and one or more alternate sources for use when the normal source is interrupted.

(b) Alternate Source of Power. The alternate source of power shall be a generator(s) driven by some form of prime mover(s), and located on the premises.

Exception: Where the normal source consists of generating units on the premises, the alternate source shall be either another generating set, or an external utility service.

(c) Location of Essential Electrical System Components. Careful consideration shall be given to the location of the spaces housing the components of the essential electrical system to minimize interruptions caused by natural forces common to the area (e.g., storms, floods, earthquakes, or hazards created by adjoining structures or activities). Consideration shall also be given to the possible interruption of normal electrical services resulting from similar causes as well as possible disruption of normal electrical service due to internal wiring and equipment failures.

(FPN): Facilities whose normal source of power is supplied by two or more separate central station-fed services experience greater than normal electrical service reliability than those with only a single feed. Such a dual source of normal power consists of two or more electrical services fed from separate generator sets or a utility distribution network having multiple power input sources and arranged to provide mechanical and electrical separation so that a fault between the facility and the generating sources will not likely cause an interruption of more than one of the facility service feeders.

F. Patient Care Areas

The provisions of Part F apply to hospitals, nursing homes, and residential custodial care facilities that are not limited to specific services. Nursing homes and residential custodial care facilities that provide limited service may not be required to be provided with an essential electrical system, and are not covered by this part. See the following.

The following is extracted from the NFPA 76A-1977:

Chapter 5   Essential Electrical Systems for Nursing Homes
and Residential Custodial Care Facilities

5-1 Applicability.   The requirements of this chapter shall apply to nursing homes and residential custodial care facilities.

Exception: Any free-standing building used for health care other than those described in Chapters 4 and 6 shall be exempted from the requirements of this standard and the remainder of this chapter provided:

(1) It maintains admitting and discharge policies that preclude the provision of care for any patient or resident who may need to be sustained by electro-mechanical means such as respirators, suction apparatus, etc., and

(2) Offers no surgical treatment requiring general anesthesia, and

(3) Provides an automatic battery operated system(s) or equipment that will be effective for 4 or more hours and is otherwise in accordance with NFPA 101-1976, Life Safety Code, and NFPA 70-1978, National Electrical Code, that will be capable of supplying lighting of at least 1 foot candle to exit lights, exit corridors, stairways, nursing stations, medication preparation areas, boiler rooms, and communication areas. This system must also supply battery power to operate all alarm systems.

(FPN): See the Standard for the Safe Use of Electricity in Patient Care Areas of Hospitals, NFPA 76B-1980.

517-80. General.

(a) **Installation/Construction Criteria.** It is the purpose of Part F to specify the installation criteria and/or wiring methods which will minimize electrical hazards by the maintenance of adequately low-potential differences only between exposed conductive surfaces which are likely to become energized and could be contacted by a patient.

(FPN): In a health care facility, it is difficult to prevent the occurrence of a conductive or capacitive path from the patient's body to some grounded object, because that path may be established accidentally or through instrumentation directly connected to the patient. Other electrically conductive surfaces which may make an additional contact with the patient, or instruments which may be connected to the patient, then become possible sources of electric currents which can traverse the patient's body. The hazard is increased as more apparatus is associated with the patient, and therefore more intensive precautions must be taken. Control of electric shock hazard requires the limitation of electric current that might flow in an electric circuit involving the patient's body, by raising the resistance of the conductive circuit which includes the patient, or by insulating exposed surfaces which might become energized, in addition to reducing the potential difference which can appear between exposed conductive surfaces in the patient vicinity, or by combinations of these methods. A special problem is presented by the patient with an externalized direct conductive path to the heart muscle. The patient may be electrocuted at current levels so low that additional protection in the design of appliances, insulation of the catheter, and control of medical practice are required.

The Fine Print Note recognizes the possibility of increased sensitivity to electric shock by patients whose body resistance may be compromised either accidentally or by a necessary medical procedure. Such diverse situations as incontinence or the insertion of a catheter may render a patient much more vulnerable to the effects of an electric current. For these reasons it is essential that those responsible for the design, installation, and maintenance of the electrical system in patient care areas be well acquainted with at least the rudiments of the hazard as explained in this note.

Since the original recognition of this hazard in the 1971 *Code*, continued clinical evaluation of the problem has provided a better understanding of the limits of the hazard, bringing about the changes in both value and wiring methods in the *Code*.

The *Code* clearly assigns designation of the types of patient care areas to the governing body of the health care facility. Both the design and inspection of a patient care area must therefore be based on the governing body's designation rather than the superficial appearance of the area.

(b) Patient Care Areas. Patient care areas, classified as follows, shall be those areas designated by the governing body of the health care facility in accordance with the type of patient care anticipated.

(1) General care areas are patient bedrooms, examining rooms, treatment rooms, clinics, and similar areas in which it is intended that the patient shall come in contact with ordinary appliances such as a nurse call system, electrical beds, examining lamps, telephone, and entertainment devices. In such areas, it may also be intended that patients be connected to electromedical devices (such as heating pads, electrocardiographs, drainage pumps, monitors, otoscopes, ophthalmoscopes, peripheral intravenous lines).

(2) Critical care areas are those special care units, intensive care units, coronary care units, angiography laboratories, cardiac catheterization laboratories, delivery rooms, operating rooms, and similar areas in which patients are intended to be subjected to invasive procedures and connected to line-operated, electro-medical devices.

(3) A wet location is a patient care area that is normally subject to wet conditions including standing water on the floor or routine dousing or drenching of the work area. Routine housekeeping procedures and incidental spillage of liquids do not define a wet location.

517-81. Grounding Performance. Any two exposed conductive surfaces in the patient vicinity shall not exceed the following potential differences at frequencies of 1000 hertz or less measured across a 1000-ohm resistance.

(a) General Care Areas. 500 mV under normal operation.

(b) Critical Care Areas. 40 mV under normal operation.

Only exposed conductive surfaces (defined in Section 517-2) within the patient vicinity are required to meet the limitations of this section. The patient vicinity does not apply to ambulatory patients, only to the nominal location of the patient bed. The 1000-ohm resistance is intended to represent the patient in his or her nominal worst case condition.

Figure 517-1. A portable field probe used to detect leakage currents, static electricity, and improper grounds in patient care areas. (*Daniel Woodhead Co.*)

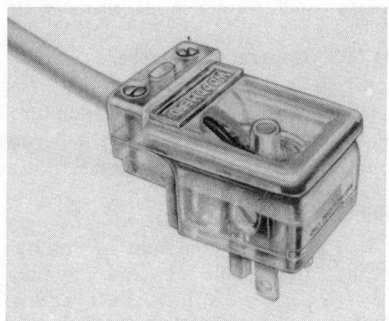

Figure 517-2. A "hospital grade" attachment plug that is designed for maximum performance in hospital environments. The plastic construction contributes to visible check of connections and toward preventing accidental energization of exposed conductive parts. (*Daniel Woodhead Co.*)

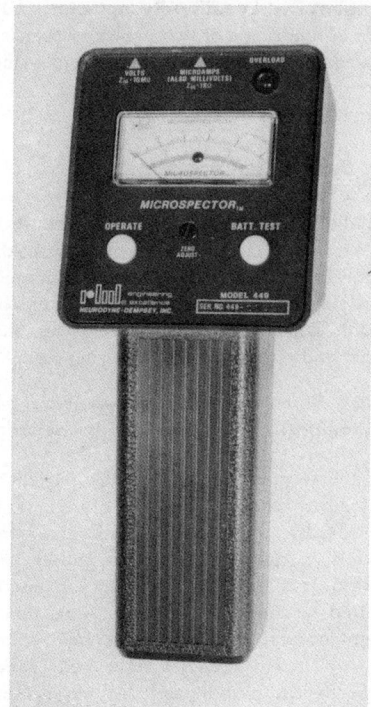

Figure 517-3. A battery-operated precision instrument for use on all hospital electrical equipment. This instrument measures and detects line voltage and leakage current between the grounding pole of a receptacle and the exposed conductive surfaces of nonelectrical equipment, and/or between the grounding pole and conductive surfaces of fixed or portable electrical equipment. (*Neurodyne-Dempsey, Inc.*)

Voltage limitations for general care areas will ordinarily be met by a reasonable level of electrical installation and maintenance. The voltage levels required for critical care areas may necessitate an additional degree of inspection and maintenance, but much of the problem can be eliminated by the use of electrical insulating or insulation-coated surfaces utilizing approved materials within the patient vicinity.

517-82. Panelboard Bonding. The equipment grounding terminal bars of the normal and essential electrical system panelboards shall be bonded together with an insulated continuous copper conductor not smaller than No. 10.

517-83. General Care Areas.

(a) Patient Bed Location Branch Circuits. Each patient bed location where inpatient care is provided shall be supplied by at least two branch circuits, at least one of which originated in a normal system panelboard; all branch circuits from the normal system shall originate in the same panelboard.

Patient bed locations in this type of area are prohibited from deriving all of their branch circuits from the emergency system. At least one branch circuit for each patient bed location is required to originate in a normal system panelboard. This is a reflection of the requirements stated in Section 517-63.

Exception No. 1: Branch circuits serving only special-purpose outlets or receptacles, such as portable X-ray outlets, need not be served from the same distribution panel or panels.

Exception No. 2: Clinics, medical and dental offices, outpatient facilities; nursing homes and residential custodial care facilities meeting the requirements of the Exception to Section 517-40.

(b) Patient Bed Location Receptacles. Each patient bed location shall be provided with a minimum of four single or two duplex receptacles; each receptacle shall be grounded by means of an insulated copper conductor sized in accordance with Table 250-95.

Exception: Psychiatric security rooms.

517-84. Critical Care Areas.

(a) Patient Bed Location Branch Circuits. Each patient bed location shall be supplied by at least two branch circuits, one or more from the emergency system. At least one branch circuit shall supply an outlet(s) only at that bed location. All branch circuits from the normal system shall be from a single panelboard; all branch circuits from the emergency system shall be from a single panelboard. Emergency system receptacles shall be identified, and shall also indicate the panelboard and circuit number supplying them.

Exception: Branch circuits serving only special-purpose receptacles or equipment in critical care areas shall be permitted to be served by other panelboards.

Conversely to Section 517-83, patient bed locations in critical care areas are required to have at least one branch circuit derived from the emergency system. Additionally, at least one individual branch circuit is required at each bed location; it may not have any other receptacle outlets serving any other bed location. It is left up to the designer whether this individual branch circuit is to be supplied by the normal or the emergency system. Furthermore, each emergency system receptacle is required to bear some form of identification indicating that it is part of the emergency system, and a label or other appropriate means is required to specify the panelboard and circuit number from which it is derived. These requirements are intended to ensure that critical care patients will not be without electrical power regardless of whether the equipment, the branch circuits, or the normal system itself is at fault.

(b) Patient Bed Location Receptacles. Each patient bed location shall be provided with a minimum of six single or three duplex receptacles, and grounded to the reference grounding point by means of an insulated copper equipment grounding conductor.

(c) Grounding and Bonding, Patient Vicinity.

(1) A patient bed location shall be permitted to have a patient equipment grounding point, grounded to the reference grounding point by means of an insulated continuous copper conductor, not smaller than No. 10, running directly to the reference grounding point or by means of a conductor permanently connected to the grounding conductor of a nearby power receptacle. The patient equipment grounding point, where supplied, shall be permitted to contain one or more jacks listed for the purpose.

(2) Fixed exposed conductive surfaces in the patient vicinity likely to become energized shall be connected to the room bonding point(s) or the reference grounding point by continuous copper conductors, or conductive building structural members having conductance at least equal to AWG No. 10 copper wire. The bonding conductors, if installed, may be arranged centrically or looped as convenient.

Exception: Small wall-mounted conductive surfaces not likely to become energized, such as surface-mounted towel and soap dispensers, mirrors, and so forth, need not be connected to the room bonding point. Similarly, large metal surfaces not likely to become energized (such as window and door frames) need not be intentionally grounded by connection to the room bonding point.

(3) The requirements in Section 517-84(c)(2) shall not apply to bedside stands, over-bed tables, chairs, portable IV poles, and small portable nonelectrical devices such as trays, pitchers, bedpans and the like. The requirements in Section 517-84(c)(2) shall not apply to portable appliances or furniture.

(4) Any of the grounding and bonding points in Section 517-84(c)(1) and (c)(2) shall be permitted to be combined into a single point.

(d) Panelboard Grounding. When a grounded electrical distribution system is used, and metallic feeder raceway or Type MC or MI cables are installed, grounding of a panelboard or switchboard shall be assured by one of the following means at each termination or junction point of the raceway or Type MC or MI cable:

(1) A grounding bushing and a continuous copper bonding jumper, sized in accordance with Section 250-95, where a locknut-bushing connection is provided.

(2) Connection of feeder raceways or Type MC or MI cables to threaded hubs or bosses on terminating enclosures.

(3) Other approved devices, such as bonding-type locknuts or bushings.

(e) Isolated Power System Grounding. Where an isolated ungrounded power source is used and limits the first-fault current to a low magnitude, the grounding conductor associated with the secondary circuit shall be permitted to be run outside of the enclosure of the power conductors in the same circuit.

(f) Special Purpose Receptacle Grounding. The equipment grounding conductor for special purpose receptacles such as the operation of mobile X-ray equipment shall be extended to the reference grounding points for all locations likely to be served from such receptacles. When such a circuit is served from an isolated ungrounded system, the grounding conductor need not be run with the power conductors; however, the equipment grounding terminal of the special purpose receptacle shall be connected to the reference grounding point.

517-90. Additional Protective Techniques.

(a) Critical Care Areas.

(1) Isolated power systems shall be permitted to be used for critical care areas.

(2) Isolated power system equipment shall be listed for the purpose and the system so designed and installed that it meets the provisions and is in accordance with Section 517-104.

Exception: The audible and visual indicators of the line isolation monitor shall be permitted to be located at the nursing station for the area being served.

(b) Pediatric and Psychiatric Locations. Fifteen- and 20-ampere, 125-volt receptacles intended to supply areas designated by the governing body of the health care facilities as pediatric or psychiatric wards, rooms and/or areas shall be tamperproof. For the purpose of this section, a tamperproof receptacle is a receptacle which by its construction limits improper access to its energized contacts.

(c) Wet Locations. Fifteen- and 20-ampere, 125-volt, single-phase receptacles supplying wet locations shall be provided with ground-fault circuit-interrupters if interruption of power under fault conditions can be tolerated, or an isolated power system if such interruption cannot be tolerated.

In areas that the governing body of the facility designates a wet location, ground-fault circuit-interrupters are required to be provided for the protection of receptacles, provided a circuit interruption can be tolerated. This rule applies only to receptacles and not to fixed, permanently wired equipment.

(FPN): For requirements for installation of therapeutic pools and tubs, see Part F of Article 680.

G. Inhalation Anesthetizing Locations

(FPN): For further information regarding safeguards for anesthetizing locations, see Standard for the Use of Inhalation Anesthetics, NFPA 56A-1978.

517-100. Anesthetizing Location Classifications.

(a) Hazardous (Classified) Location.

(1)** In a location where flammable anesthetics are employed, the entire area shall be considered to be a Class I, Division 1 location which shall extend upward to a level 5 feet (1.52 m) above the floor. The remaining volume up to the structural ceiling is considered to be above a hazardous (classified) location.

(2) Any room or location in which flammable anesthetics or volatile flammable disinfecting agents are stored shall be considered to be a Class I, Division 1 location from floor to ceiling.

(b) Other-than-Hazardous (Classified) Location. Any inhalation anesthetizing location designated for the exclusive use of nonflammable anesthetizing agents shall be considered to be an other-than-hazardous (classified) location. In such cases, the locations are excluded from the requirements of Section 517-101(a) and (b) as applied to X-ray systems only.

This section divides anesthetizing locations into either a hazardous (classified) location, where flammable or nonflammable anesthetics may be interchangeably employed, or an other-than-hazardous location, where only nonflammable anesthetics may be employed. In the case of the flammable anesthetizing location, the entire volume of the room extending upward from a level 5 ft above the floor to the surface of the structural ceiling of the room, and including the space between a drop ceiling and the structural ceiling, is considered to be above a "hazardous (classified) location."

517-101. Wiring and Equipment.

(a) Within Hazardous Anesthetizing Locations.

(1) In hazardous (classified) location(s) referred to in Section 517-100, all fixed wiring and equipment, and all portable equipment, including lamps and other utilization equipment, operating at more than 8 volts between conductors shall comply with the requirements of Sections 501-1 through 501-15 and Section 501-16(a) and (b) for Class I, Division 1 locations. All such equipment shall be specifically approved for the hazardous atmospheres involved.

(2) Where a box, fitting, or enclosure is partially, but not entirely, within a hazardous (classified) location(s), the hazardous (classified) location(s) shall be considered to be extended to include the entire box, fitting, or enclosure.

(3) Receptacles and attachment plugs in hazardous (classified) location(s) shall be listed for use in Class I, Group C hazardous (classified) locations, and shall have provision for the connection of a grounding conductor.

(4) Flexible cords used in hazardous areas for connection to portable utilization equipment, including lamps operating at more than 8 volts between conductors, shall be of a type approved for extra-hard usage in accordance with Table 400-4, and shall include an additional conductor for grounding.

(5) A storage device for the flexible cord shall be provided, and shall not subject the cord to bending at a radius of less than 3 inches (76 mm).

(b) Above Hazardous Anesthetizing Locations.

(1) Wiring above a hazardous area referred to in Section 517-100 shall be installed in rigid metal conduit, electrical metallic tubing, intermediate metal conduit, Type MI cable, or Type MC cable which employs a continuous, gas/vapor-tight metallic sheath.

(2) Installed equipment which may produce arcs, sparks, or particles of hot metal, such as lamps and lampholders for fixed lighting, cutouts, switches, generators, motors, or other equipment having make-and-break or sliding contacts, shall be of the totally enclosed type or so constructed as to prevent escape of sparks or hot metal particles.

Exception: Wall-mounted receptacles installed above the hazardous area in flammable anesthetizing locations shall not be required to be totally enclosed or have openings guarded or screened to prevent dispersion of particles.

(3) Surgical and other lighting fixtures shall conform to Section 501-9(b).

Exception No. 1: The surface temperature limitations set forth in Section 501-9(b)(2) shall not apply.

Exception No. 2: Integral or pendant switches which are located above and cannot be lowered into the hazardous (classified) location(s) shall not be required to be explosionproof.

(4) Approved seals shall be provided in conformance with Section 501-5, and Section 501-5(a)(4) shall apply to horizontal as well as to vertical boundaries of the defined hazardous (classified) locations.

Exception: Seals shall be permitted within 18 inches (457 mm) of the point at which a conduit emerges from a wall forming the boundary of an anesthetizing location if all of the following conditions are met:

a. The junction box, switch or receptacle contains a seal-off device between the arcing contacts and the conduit.

b. The conduit is continuous (without coupling or fitting) between the junction box and the sealing fitting within 18 inches (457 mm) of the point where the conduit emerges from the wall.

(5) Receptacles and attachment plugs located above hazardous anesthetizing locations shall be listed for hospital use for services of prescribed voltage, frequency, rating, and number of conductors with provision for the connection of the grounding conductor. This requirement shall apply to attachment plugs and receptacles of the 2-pole, 3-wire grounding type for single-phase 120-volt, nominal, ac service.

See Figure 517-2 for a "hospital grade" attachment plug. "Hospital grade" receptacles are identified by the marking "Hospital Only" or by the marking "Hospital Grade" and a green dot on the receptacle. The green dot is on the face of the receptacle where visible after installation.

"Hospital grade" receptacles and plugs are subject to special tests and requirements intended to provide a greater degree of reliability, particularly of grounding, than other plugs and receptacles.

(6) Plugs and receptacles for connection of 250-volt, 50-ampere and 60-ampere ac medical equipment for use above hazardous (classified) locations shall be so arranged that the 60-ampere receptacle will accept either the 50-ampere or the 60-ampere plug. Fifty-ampere receptacles shall be designed so as not to accept the 60-ampere attachment plug. The plugs shall be of the 2-pole, 3-wire design with a third contact connecting to the insulated (green or green with yellow stripe) equipment grounding conductor of the electrical system.

(c) Other-than-Hazardous Anesthetizing Locations.

(1) Wiring serving other than hazardous (classified) locations as defined in Section 517-100 shall be installed in rigid metal conduit, intermediate metal conduit, or electrical metallic tubing or shall be in Type MI or Type MC cable.

Exception: Pendant receptacle constructions employing at least SJO or equivalent flexible cords suspended not less than 6 feet (1.83 m) from the floor.

(2) Receptacles and attachment plugs installed and used in other-than-hazardous (classified) locations shall be listed for hospital use for services of prescribed voltage, frequency, rating, and number of conductors with provision for connection of the grounding conductor. This requirement shall apply to attachment plugs and receptacles of the 2-pole, 3-wire grounding type for single-phase 120-, 208-, or 240-volt, nominal, ac service.

See commentary following Section 517-101(b)(5).

(3) Plugs and receptacles for connection of 250-volt, 50-ampere, and 60-ampere ac medical equipment for use in other-than-hazardous (classified) locations shall be so arranged that the 60-ampere receptacle will accept either the 50-ampere or the 60-ampere plug. The 50-ampere receptacle shall be designed so as not to accept the 60-ampere attachment plug. The plug shall be of the 2-pole, 3-wire design with a third contact connecting to the insulated (green or green with yellow stripe) equipment grounding conductor of the electrical system.

517-103. Grounding. In any anesthetizing area, all metallic raceways, and all noncurrent-carrying conductive portions of fixed or portable electric equipment shall be grounded.

Exception: Equipment operating at not more than 8 volts between conductors shall not be required to be grounded.

It should be noted that the grounding requirements for anesthetizing locations apply only to metallic raceways and electrical equipment. Carts, tables, and other nonelectrical items need not be grounded. However, in flammable anesthetizing locations, portable carts and tables usually have a resistance to ground of not over 1,000,000 ohms, through use of conductive tires and wheels and conductive flooring, to avoid the build-up of static electrical charges. Such requirements will be found in NFPA 56A.

517-104. Circuits in Anesthetizing Locations.

(a) Isolated Power Systems.

(1)** Except as permitted in Section 517-104(c), each power circuit within, or partially within, an anesthetizing location as referred to in Section 517-100 shall be isolated from any distribution system supplying other-than-anesthetizing locations. Each isolated power circuit shall be controlled by a switch having a disconnecting pole in each isolated circuit conductor. Such isolation shall be accomplished by means of one or more transformers having no electrical connection between primary and secondary windings, by means of motor generator sets, or by means of suitably isolated batteries.

(2) Circuits supplying primaries of isolating transformers shall operate at not more than 600 volts between conductors and shall be provided with proper overcurrent protection. The secondary voltage of such transformers shall not exceed 600 volts between conductors of each circuit. All circuits supplied from such secondaries shall be ungrounded, and shall have an approved overcurrent device of proper ratings in each conductor. Circuits supplied directly from batteries or from motor generator sets shall be ungrounded, and shall be protected against overcurrent in the same manner as transformer-fed secondary circuits. If an electrostatic shield is present, it shall be connected to the reference grounding point.

(3) The isolating transformers, motor generator sets, or batteries and battery chargers, together with their primary and/or secondary overcurrent devices, shall not be installed in hazardous (classified) locations. The isolated secondary circuit wiring extending into a hazardous anesthetizing location shall be installed in accordance with Section 501-4.

(4) An isolated branch circuit supplying an anesthetizing location shall supply no other location. The insulation of the branch-circuit conductors on the secondary side of the isolated power supply shall have a dielectric constant of 3.5 or less. Wire pulling compounds that increase the dielectric constant shall not be used on the secondary conductors of the isolated power supply.

(5) The isolated circuit conductors shall be identified as follows:

Isolated Conductor No. 1 — Orange
Isolated Conductor No. 2 — Brown

For three-phase systems, the third conductor shall be identified as yellow.

ARTICLE 517—HEALTH CARE FACILITIES

(b)** Line Isolation Monitor.

(1) In addition to the usual control and overcurrent protective devices, each isolated power system shall be provided with a continually operating line isolation monitor that indicates possible leakage or fault currents from either isolated conductor to ground. The monitor shall be designed so that a green signal lamp, conspicuously visible to persons in the anesthetizing location, remains lighted when the system is adequately isolated from ground; an adjacent red signal lamp and an audible warning signal (remote if desired) shall be energized when the total hazard current (consisting of possible resistive and capacitive leakage currents) from either isolated conductor to ground reaches a threshold value of 5 milliamperes under nominal line voltage conditions. The line isolation monitor is not to alarm for a fault hazard current of less than 0.7 milliamperes. The line isolation monitor is not to alarm for a total hazard current of less than 1.7 milliamperes.

Exception: A system may be designed to operate at a lower threshold value of total hazard current. A line isolation monitor for such a system may be approved with the provision that the fault hazard current may be reduced but not to less than 35 percent of the corresponding threshold value of the total hazard current, and the monitor hazard current is to be correspondingly reduced to no more than 50 percent of the alarm threshold value of the total hazard current.

(FPN): Such systems contribute little additional electrical safety and are used for special applications.

(2) The line isolation monitor shall be designed to have sufficient internal impedance such that when properly connected to the isolated system the maximum internal current that can flow through the line isolation monitor, when any point of the isolated system is grounded, shall be 1 milliampere.

The following Tentative Interim Amendment No. 70-81-10 was issued on July 8, 1981 for the 1981 *NEC*:

Add the following Exception immediately following the wording of Section 517-104(b)(2), but prior to the Fine Print Note:

Exception: The line isolation monitor may be of the low impedance type such that the current through the line isolation monitor, when any point of the isolated system is grounded, will not exceed twice the alarm threshold value for a period not exceeding 5 milliseconds.

(FPN): Reduction of the monitor hazard current, provided this reduction results in an increased "not alarm" threshold value for the fault hazard current, will increase circuit capacity.

(3) An ammeter calibrated in the total hazard current of the system (contribution of the fault hazard current plus monitor hazard current) shall be mounted in a plainly visible place on the line isolation monitor with the "alarm on" zone at approximately the center of the scale. It is desirable to locate the ammeter so that it is conspicuously visible to persons in the anesthetizing location.

Exception: The line isolation monitor may be a composite unit, with a sensing section cabled to a separate display panel section on which the alarm and/or test functions are located.

See Figure 517-4.

(c) Grounded Power Systems.

(1) ** The general-purpose lighting circuit connected to the normal grounded service shall be installed in each operating room.

Exception: Where connected to any alternate source permitted in Section 700-12 which is separate from the source serving the emergency system.

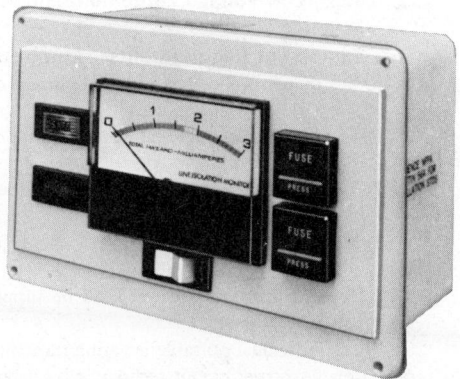

Figure 517-4. Line isolation monitor (right) for use with isolated power systems, remote indicator alarm (top left), and multiple annunciator panel (bottom left), which can monitor several operating rooms from a central location such as a nurses' station. (*Square D Co.*)

The failure of the emergency circuit feeder that supplies the operating room will ordinarily plunge the room into darkness. By requiring a general-purpose lighting circuit supplied by a normal source feeder, the effect of this kind of failure is minimized.

(2) Branch circuits supplying only listed, fixed, therapeutic and diagnostic equipment, permanently installed above the hazardous (classified) location and in other-than-hazardous (classified) locations, shall be permitted to be supplied from a normal grounded service, single- or three-phase system, provided:

a. Wiring for grounded and isolated circuits does not occupy the same raceway,

b. All conductive surfaces of equipment are grounded,

c. Equipment (except enclosed X-ray tubes and the leads to the tubes) are located at least 8 feet (2.44 m) above the floor or outside the anesthetizing location, and

d. Switches for the grounded branch circuit are located outside the hazardous (classified) location.

(3) Branch circuits supplying only fixed lighting shall be permitted to be supplied by a normal grounded service provided.

a. Such fixtures are located at least 8 feet (2.44 m) above the floor,

b. All conductive surfaces of fixtures are grounded,

c. Wiring for circuits supplying power to fixtures does not occupy the same raceway for circuits supplying isolated power, and

d. Switches are wall-mounted and located above hazardous (classified) locations.

(4) Wall-mounted remote control stations for remote control switches operating at 24 volts or less shall be permitted to be installed in any anesthetizing location.

(5) An isolated power center listed for the purpose and its grounded primary feeder shall be permitted to be located in an anesthetizing location provided it is installed above a hazardous (classified) location, or in an other-than-hazardous (classified) location.

517-105.** Low-Voltage Equipment and Instruments.

(a) Equipment Requirements. Low-voltage equipment which is frequently in contact with the bodies of persons or has exposed current-carrying elements shall:

(1) Operate on an electrical potential of 8 volts or less, or

(2) Be approved as intrinsically safe or double-insulated equipment.

(3) Be moisture-resistant.

(b) Power Supplies. Power shall be supplied to low-voltage equipment from:

(1) An individual portable isolating transformer (autotransformers shall not be used) connected to an isolated power circuit receptacle by means of an appropriate cord and attachment plug, or

(2) A common low-voltage isolating transformer installed in a nonhazardous location, or

(3) Individual dry-cell batteries, or

(4) Common batteries made up of storage cells located in a nonhazardous location.

(c) Isolated Circuits. Isolating-type transformers for supplying low-voltage circuits shall:

(1) Have approved means for insulating the secondary circuit from the primary circuit, and

(2) Have the core and case grounded.

(d) Controls. Resistance or impedance devices shall be permitted to control low-voltage equipment but shall not be used to limit the maximum available voltage to the equipment.

(e) Battery-Powered Appliances. Battery-powered appliances shall not be capable of being charged while in operation unless their charging circuitry incorporates an integral isolating-type transformer.

(f) Receptacles or Attachment Plugs. Any receptacle or attachment plug used on low-voltage circuits shall be of a type which does not permit interchangeable connection with circuits of higher voltage.

(FPN): Any interruption of the circuit, even circuits as low as 8 volts, either by any switch, or loose or defective connections anywhere in the circuit, may produce a spark sufficient to ignite flammable anesthetic agents. [See Section 3-5.2 of Standard for the Use of Inhalation Anesthetics (Flammable and Nonflammable), NFPA 56A-1978.]

H. Communications, Signaling Systems, Data Systems, Fire Protective Signaling Systems, and Low-Voltage Systems

Part H calls attention to the fact that certain wiring methods, although appropriate to a nonhealth care facility installation, could be inappropriate in a patient care area. This part recognizes a common necessity for connecting appliances within the patient vicinity to other appliances that may be located some distance away.

517-120. Patient Care Areas. Equivalent insulation, isolation, and grounding to that required for the electrical distribution systems in patient care areas shall be provided for communications, signaling systems, data system circuits, fire protective signaling systems, and low-voltage systems.

(FPN): An acceptable alternate means of providing isolation for patient/nurse call systems is by the use of nonelectrified signaling, communication or control devices held by the patient, or within reach of the patient.

(FPN): For grounding requirements, see Section 250-95.

517-121. Other-than-Patient-Care Areas. See Articles 725, 760, and 800.

517-122. Signal Transmission Between Appliances.

(a) General. Permanently installed signal cabling from an appliance in a patient location to remote appliances shall employ a signal transmission system which prevents hazardous grounding interconnection of the appliances. See Section 517-81.

(b) Common Signal Grounding Wire. Common signal grounding wires (i.e., the chassis ground for single-ended transmission) shall be permitted to be used between appliances all located within the patient vicinity, provided the appliances are served from the same reference grounding point.

K. X-ray Installations

Nothing in this part shall be construed as specifying safeguards against the useful beam or stray X-ray radiation.

(FPN): Radiation safety and performance requirements of several classes of X-ray equipment are regulated under Public Law 90-602 and are enforced by the Department of Health and Human Services.

(FPN): In addition, information on radiation protection by the National Council on Radiation Protection and Measurements is published as Reports of the National Council on Radiation Protection and Measurement. These reports are obtainable from NCRP Publications, P. O. Box 30175, Washington, D.C. 20014.

517-140. Definitions.

Long-Time Rating. A rating based on an operating interval of 5 minutes or longer.

Mobile. X-ray equipment mounted on a permanent base with wheels and/or casters for moving while completely assembled.

Momentary Rating. A rating based on an operating interval that does not exceed 5 seconds.

Portable. X-ray equipment designed to be hand carried.

Transportable. X-ray equipment to be installed in a vehicle or that may be readily disassembled for transport in a vehicle.

517-141. Connection to Supply Circuit.

(a) Fixed and Stationary Equipment. Fixed and stationary X-ray equipment shall be connected to the power supply by means of a wiring method meeting the general requirements of this Code.

Exception: Equipment properly supplied by a branch circuit rated at not over 30 amperes shall be permitted to be supplied through a suitable attachment plug and hard-service cable or cord.

ARTICLE 517—HEALTH CARE FACILITIES

(b) **Portable, Mobile, and Transportable Equipment.** Individual branch circuits shall not be required for portable, mobile, and transportable medical X-ray equipment requiring a capacity of not over 60 amperes.

(c) **Over 600-Volt Supply.** Circuits and equipment operated on a supply circuit of over 600 volts shall comply with Article 710.

517-142. Disconnecting Means.

(a) **Capacity.** A disconnecting means of adequate capacity for at least 50 percent of the input required for the momentary rating or 100 percent of the input required for the long-time rating of the X-ray equipment, whichever is greater, shall be provided in the supply circuit.

(b) **Location.** The disconnecting means shall be operable from a location readily accessible from the X-ray control.

(c) **Portable Equipment.** For equipment connected to a 120-volt branch circuit of 30 amperes or less, a grounding-type attachment plug and receptacle of proper rating shall be permitted to serve as a disconnecting means.

517-143. Rating of Supply Conductors and Overcurrent Protection.

(a) **Diagnostic Equipment.**

(1) The ampacity of supply branch-circuit conductors and the current rating of overcurrent protective devices shall not be less than 50 percent of the momentary rating or 100 percent of the long-time rating whichever is greater.

(2) The ampacity of supply feeder and the current rating of overcurrent protective devices supplying two or more branch circuits supplying X-ray units shall not be less than 50 percent of the momentary demand rating of each of the two largest diagnostic X-ray units plus 20 percent of the momentary ratings of each of the additional diagnostic X-ray units. Where simultaneous byplane examinations are undertaken with the X-ray units the supply conductors and overcurrent protective devices shall be 100 percent of the momentary rating of each X-ray unit.

(FPN): The minimum conductor size for branch and feeder circuits is also governed by voltage regulation requirements. For a specific installation, the manufacturer usually specifies: minimum distribution transformer and conductor sizes, rating of disconnect means, and overcurrent protection.

(b) **Therapeutic Equipment.** The ampacity of conductors and rating of overcurrent protective devices shall not be less than 100 percent of the current rating of medical X-ray therapy equipment.

(FPN): The ampacity of the branch-circuit conductors and the ratings of disconnecting means and overcurrent protection for X-ray equipment are usually designated by the manufacturer for the specific installation.

517-145. Control Circuit Conductors.

(a) **Number of Conductors in Raceway.** The number of control circuit conductors installed in a raceway shall be determined in accordance with Section 300-17.

(b) Minimum Size of Conductors. Sizes No. 18 or No. 16 fixture wires as specified in Section 725-16 and flexible cords shall be permitted for the control and operating circuits of X-ray and auxiliary equipment where protected by not larger than 20-ampere overcurrent devices.

517-146. Equipment Installations. All equipment for new X-ray installations and all used or reconditioned X-ray equipment moved to and reinstalled at a new location shall be of an approved type.

517-148. Transformers and Capacitors. Transformers and capacitors that are part of an X-ray equipment shall not be required to comply with Articles 450 and 460.

Capacitors shall be mounted within enclosures of insulating material or grounded metal.

517-151. Guarding and Grounding.

(a) High-Voltage Parts. All high-voltage parts, including X-ray tubes, shall be mounted within grounded enclosures. Air, oil, gas, or other suitable insulating media shall be used to insulate the high voltage from the grounded enclosure. The connection from the high-voltage equipment to X-ray tubes and other high-voltage components shall be made with high-voltage shielded cables.

(b) Low-Voltage Cables. Low-voltage cables connecting to oil-filled units that are not completely sealed, such as transformers, condensers, oil coolers, and high-voltage switches, shall have insulation of the oil-resistant type.

(c) Noncurrent-Carrying Metal Parts. Noncurrent-carrying metal parts of X-ray and associated equipment (controls, tables, X-ray tube supports, transformer tanks, shielded cables, X-ray tube heads, etc.) shall be grounded in the manner specified in Article 250, as modified by Section 517-11(a) and (b) under the criteria set forth in Section 517-81 for critical care areas.

Exception: Battery-operated equipment.

ARTICLE 518 — PLACES OF ASSEMBLY

Contents

518-1. Scope. This article covers all buildings or portions of buildings or structures designed or intended for the assembly of 100 or more persons.

Places of Assembly shall include, but are not limited to:

Assembly Halls	Museums
Exhibition Halls	Skating Rinks
Armories	Gymnasiums
Dining Facilities	Multipurpose Rooms
Restaurants	Bowling Lanes
Church Chapels	Pool Rooms
Dance Halls	Club Rooms
Mortuary Chapels	

ARTICLE 518—PLACES OF ASSEMBLY

Places of Awaiting
Transportation
Court Rooms
Conference Rooms
Auditoriums

Auditoriums within:
Schools
Mercantile Establishments
Business Establishments
Other Occupancies.

Occupancy of any room or space for assembly purposes by less than 100 persons in a building of other occupancy, and incidental to such other occupancy, shall be classed as part of the other occupancy and subject to the provisions applicable thereto.

When any such building structures or portion thereof contain a projection booth or stage platform or area for the presentation of theatrical or musical production, either fixed or portable, the wiring for that area shall comply with all applicable provisions of Article 520.

(FPN): For methods of determining population capacity, see local building code or in its absence *Life Safety Code*, NFPA *101*-1981 (ANSI).

This article applies to places of assembly designed or intended for the assembly of 100 or more persons. It would apply, for example, to a church chapel for occupancy by 100 or more persons, determined by the methods for occupancy population capacity appearing in NFPA *101*—1981, *Life Safety Code*. But the article does not apply to a supermarket, even though it may contain 100 or more persons, because a supermarket is not specifically designed or intended for the assembly of persons; nor is it an auditorium.

The following information for determining occupancy capacity is contained in NFPA *101*—1981, *Life Safety Code*.

8-1.7 Occupant Load

8-1.7.1 The occupant load permitted in any assembly building, structure, or portion thereof shall be determined by dividing the net floor area or space assigned to that use by the square foot (square meter) per occupant as follows:

(a) An assembly area of concentrated use without fixed seats such as an auditorium, church, chapel, dance floor, or lodge room — 7 sq ft (.65 sq m) per person.

(b) An assembly area of less concentrated use such as a conference room, dining room, drinking establishment, exhibit room, gymnasium, or lounge — 15 sq ft (1.39 sq m) per person.

(c) Standing room or waiting space — 3 sq ft (.28 sq m) per person.

(d) Bleachers, pews, and similar bench-type seating — 18 linear in. (45.72 linear cm) per person.

(e) Fixed seating. The occupant load of an area having fixed seats shall be determined by the number of fixed seats installed. Required aisle space serving the fixed seats shall not be used to increase the occupant load.

(f) Libraries. In stack areas — 100 sq ft (9.3 sq m) per person; in reading rooms — 50 sq ft (4.7 sq m) per person.

8-1.7.2 The occupant load permitted in a building or portion thereof may be increased above that specified in 8-1.7.1 if the necessary aisles and exits are provided. To increase the occupant load, a diagram indicating placement of equipment, aisles, exits, and seating shall be provided to and approved by the authority having jurisdiction prior to any increase in occupant load.

518-2. Other Articles.

(a) Hazardous (Classified) Areas. Hazardous (classified) areas located in any assemblage occupancy shall be installed in accordance with Article 500 — Hazardous (Classified) Locations.

(b) Temporary Wiring. In exhibition halls used for display booths, as in trade shows, the temporary wiring shall be installed in accordance with Article 305 — Temporary Wiring, except that approved flexible cables and cords shall be permitted to be laid on floors where protected from contact by the general public.

See Figure 518-1.

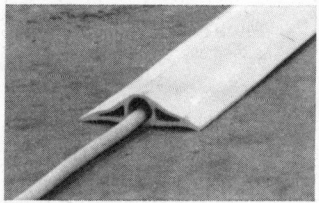

Figure 518-1. A treadle, such as this one, can be used to protect cords from abuse where they are laid across pedestrian ways, for instance, as part of a temporary wiring scheme such as may be used in exhibition halls. (*Daniel Woodhead Co.*)

(c) Emergency Systems. Control of emergency systems shall comply with Article 700 — Emergency Systems.

518-3. Wiring Methods. The fixed wiring methods shall be metal raceways, nonmetallic raceways encased in not less than 2 inches (50.8 mm) of concrete, Type MI cable, or Type MC cable.

Exception No. 1: Nonmetallic-sheathed cable, Type AC cable, and rigid nonmetallic conduit shall be permitted to be installed in those buildings or portions thereof that are not required to be fire-rated construction by the applicable building code.

Exception No. 2: As provided in Article 640 — Sound Reproduction and Similar Equipment, in Article 800 — Communication Circuits, and in Article 725 for Class 2 and Class 3 remote-control and signaling circuits, and in Article 760 for fire protective signaling circuits.

(FPN): Fire-rated construction is the fire-resistive classification used in building codes.

Refer to Figure 518-2. The washrooms and office area of this single-story facility are not places of assembly as defined in Section 518-1, and therefore require no special wiring methods. On the inside surface of the storage area walls, and on or in the partitions between storage areas, ordinary wiring methods can be used as these, too, are not places of assembly. However, inside any hollow spaces of the fire-rated storage area walls, the main requirement of Section 518-3 and Exception No. 2 are applicable as the serving corridors are part of the places of assembly as a result of this particular building design.

In a like manner, wiring in ceilings or floors required to be of fire-rated construction in a place of assembly as defined in Section 518-1 are required to comply with the main rule of Section 518-1, except as noted in Exception No. 2.

Although the partitions between the places of assembly and the central serving corridors, the partitions between the reception area and adjacent place of assembly, and the partitions between the food preparation area and the adjacent places of assembly are not required to be fire-rated by the local building code (in

749

this case) they are part of the place of assembly. The wiring in or on these partitions still comes under the main rule of Section 518-3 and Exception No. 1 is not applicable.

The intent is that within a place of assembly as defined in Section 518-1, the main rule of Section 518-3 and Exception No. 2 apply to any wall, floor, or ceiling. Exception No. 1 applies to those portions of the building and those places of assembly not required to be fire-rated.

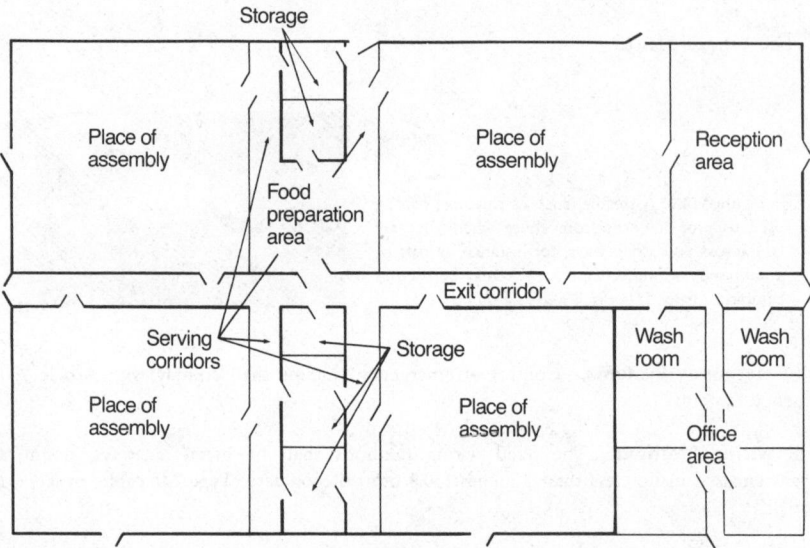

Figure 518-2. The heavy lines represent walls required by the local building code to be of fire-rated construction. See the commentary text for discussion. The light lines represent walls not required by the local building code to be of fire-rated construction.

ARTICLE 520 — THEATERS AND SIMILAR LOCATIONS

Contents

A. General

520-1. Scope. This article covers all buildings or that part of a building or structure designed or intended to be used for dramatic, musical, motion picture projection, or similar purposes and to areas of motion picture and television studios which incorporate assembly areas.

These special requirements apply only to that part of a building used as a theater or for a similar purpose and do not necessarily apply to the entire building. For example, they would apply to an auditorium in a school building used for dramatic or other performances. The special requirements of this chapter would be applicable to the stage, auditorium, dressing rooms, and main corridors leading to the auditorium, but not to other parts of the building that are not involved in the use of the auditorium for performances or entertainment.

520-2. Motion Picture Projectors. Motion picture equipment and its installation and use shall comply with Article 540.

520-3. Sound Reproduction. Sound-reproducing equipment and its installation shall comply with Article 640.

ARTICLE 520—THEATERS AND SIMILAR LOCATIONS

520-4. Wiring Methods. The fixed wiring method shall be metal raceways, nonmetallic raceways encased in at least 2 inches (50.8 mm) of concrete, mineral-insulated, metal-sheathed cable, or Type MC cable.

Exception No. 1: As provided in Article 640 for sound reproduction, in Article 800 for communication circuits, in Article 725 for Class 2 and Class 3 remote-control and signaling circuits, and in Article 760 for fire protective signaling circuits.

Exception No. 2: The wiring for stage set lighting and stage effects and other wiring that is not fixed as to location shall be permitted with approved flexible cords and cables.

Theaters and similar buildings are usually required to be of fire-rated construction by applicable building codes; therefore, the fixed wiring methods are limited to metal raceways such as rigid metal conduit, intermediate metal conduit, electrical metallic tubing, nonmetallic conduit encased in 2 in. of concrete, or Type MI or MC cable.

Exceptions to the rules requiring raceways are permitted for the installation of communication circuits, Class 2 and 3 remote-control and signaling circuits, and fire-protective signaling circuits. Where portability, flexibility, and adjustments are necessary for stage lighting and special effects, approved cords and cables are permitted.

520-5. Number of Conductors in Raceway. The number of conductors permitted in any metal conduit, rigid nonmetallic conduit as permitted in this article, or electrical metallic tubing for border or stage pocket circuits or for remote-control conductors shall not exceed the percentage fill shown in Table 1 of Chapter 9. Where contained within an auxiliary gutter or a wireway, the sum of the cross-sectional areas of all contained conductors at any cross section shall not exceed 20 percent of the interior cross-sectional area of the auxiliary gutter or wireway. The thirty-conductor limitation of Sections 362-5 and 374-5 shall not apply.

520-6. Enclosing and Guarding Live Parts. Live parts shall be enclosed or guarded to prevent accidental contact by persons and objects. All switches shall be of the externally operable type. Dimmers, including rheostats, shall be placed in cases or cabinets that enclose all live parts.

Figure 520-1. An electronic dimmer board for stage lighting. (*Packaged Lighting Systems, Inc.*)

520-7. Emergency Systems. Control of emergency systems shall comply with Article 700 — Emergency Systems.

B. Fixed Stage Switchboard

520-21. Dead Front. Stage switchboards shall be of the dead-front type and shall comply with Part C of Article 384 unless approved based on suitability as a stage switchboard as determined by a qualified testing laboratory and recognized test standards and principles.

520-22. Guarding Back of Switchboard. Stage switchboards having exposed live parts on the back of such boards shall be enclosed by the building walls, wire mesh grills, or by other approved methods. The entrance to this enclosure shall be by means of a self-closing door.

520-23. Control and Overcurrent Protection of Receptacle Circuits. Means shall be provided at a stage lighting switchboard to which load circuits are connected for individual overcurrent protection of stage lighting branch circuits and stage and gallery receptacles used for cord- and plug-connected stage equipment. Where the stage switchboard contains dimmers to control nonstage lighting, the locating of the overcurrent protective devices for these branch circuits at the stage switchboard shall be permitted.

> Any receptacles intended for the connection of stage lighting equipment, no matter where located, are covered by the term "gallery receptacles." The circuits supplying such receptacles are required to be controlled from the same location as the other stage lighting circuits.

520-24. Metal Hood. A stage switchboard that is not completely enclosed dead-front and dead-rear or recessed into a wall shall be provided with a metal hood extending the full length of the board to protect all equipment on the board from falling objects.

> Because stages are usually crowded and a great deal of flammable material is often present, a stage switchboard is not permitted to have exposed live parts on its front. Moreover, the space at the rear of a stage switchboard is required to be guarded in order to prevent entrance or contact by unqualified and unauthorized persons. One accepted method of accomplishing this is by enclosing the space between the rear of the switchboard and the wall in a sheet steel housing with a door at one end.
>
> Major stage switchboards are usually of the remote control type. Pilot switches on the stage switchboard control the operation of remotely installed contactors in a conveniently located available space, such as below the stage. In turn, these contactors control the lighting circuits.
>
> The front view of a small stage switchboard of the partial remote control type is shown in Figure 520-2. Dimmers for individual circuits are operated by the egg-shaped handles. The usual location of a stage switchboard is in a recess in the proscenium wall. After passing through switches and dimmers, many of the main circuits are required to be subdivided into branch circuits so that no branch circuit will be loaded to more than 20 A (see Section 520-41). In a switchboard of the remote control type, the branch-circuit fuses are located on the same panel as the contactors. In a direct control-type switchboard, and sometimes in a remote control-type switchboard, branch-circuit fuses are located on special panelboards, called "magazine panels," placed in the space behind the switchboard, usually in the location of the junction box.

520-25. Dimmers. Dimmers shall comply with (a) through (d) below.

(a) Disconnection and Overcurrent Protection. Where dimmers are installed in ungrounded conductors, each dimmer shall have overcurrent protection not greater than 125 percent of the dimmer rating, and shall be disconnected from all ungrounded conductors when the master or individual switch or circuit breaker supplying such dimmer is in the open position.

(b) Resistance- or Reactor-type Dimmers. Resistance- or series reactor-type dimmers may be placed in either the grounded or the ungrounded conductor of the circuit. Where designed to open either the supply circuit to the dimmer or the circuit controlled by it, the dimmer shall then comply with Section 380-1. Resistance- or reactor-type dimmers placed in the grounded neutral conductor of the circuit shall not open the circuit.

(c) Autotransformer-type Dimmers. The circuit supplying an autotransformer-type dimmer shall not exceed 150 volts between conductors. The grounded conductor shall be common to the input and output circuits.

(d) Solid-State-type Dimmers. The circuit supplying a solid-state dimmer shall not exceed 150 volts between conductors unless the dimmer is specifically approved for higher voltage operation. When a grounded conductor supplies a dimmer, it shall be common to the input and output circuits. Dimmer chassis shall be connected to the equipment ground conductor.

(FPN): See Section 210-9 for circuits derived from autotransformers.

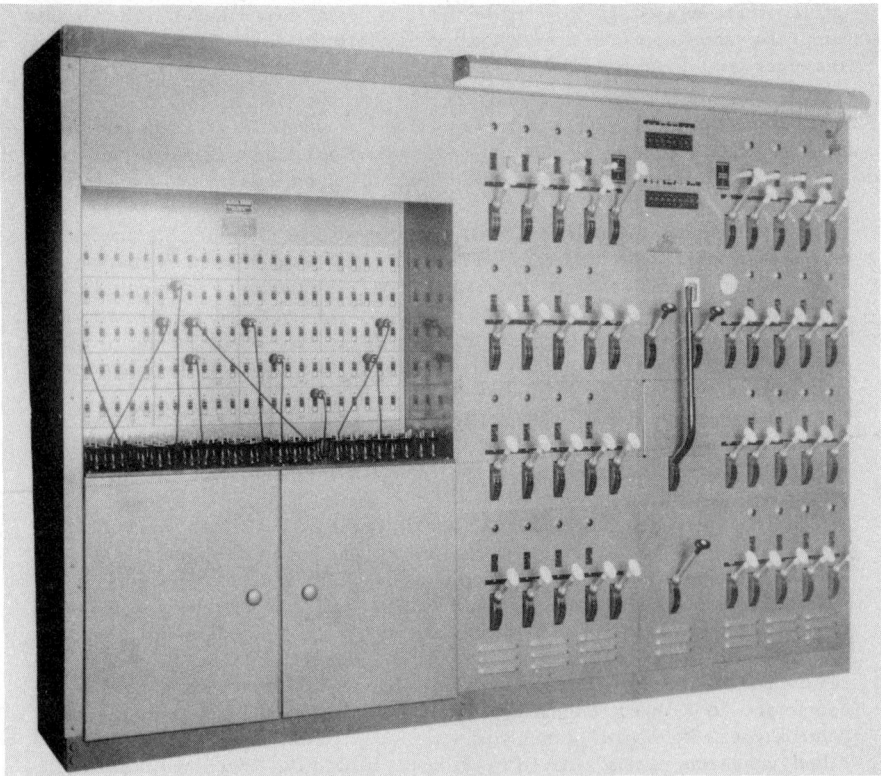

Figure 520-2. An autotransformer-type dimmer switchboard. (*Kliegl Bros.*)

Figure 520-3 illustrates three branch circuits arranged to be controlled by a single switch and a single dimmer plate. A single-pole switch on the stage switchboard feeds a short bus on the magazine panel. The magazine panel is like an ordinary panelboard but branch circuits are directly connected to the bus (without switches), and the circuits are divided into several sections which contain separate feeder buses. One side of the variable resistor or dimmer plate is connected to the neutral bus at the switchboard, and the other side is connected to the neutral bus in the magazine panel. In order to avoid shunting of the dimmer, causing it to lose its control of the brightness of the lamps, the neutral bus in the magazine is required to be effectively insulated from ground and separate from other neutral buses in the panel.

The dimmer is permanently connected to the neutral of the wiring system, which is required to be effectively grounded; hence, the dimmer is essentially at ground potential.

Circuits supplying autotransformer-type dimmers are not permitted to exceed 150 V between conductors and, by means of a movable contact, any desired voltage may be applied to the lamps from full line voltage to such a low voltage that the lamps provide no illumination. See Figure 520-4. This type of dimmer produces very little heat, operates at a high efficiency, and, within its maximum rating, its dimming effect is independent of the wattage of the load.

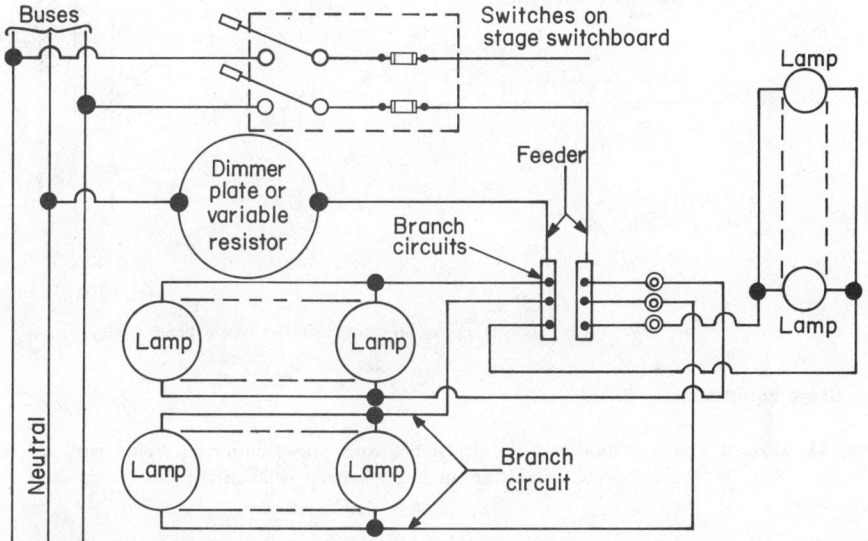

Figure 520-3. A schematic diagram of a typical stage switchboard showing connections for control switches, dimmer plate, and one section of a magazine panel showing feeder and branch-circuit connections for control of three lighting circuits.

520-26. Type of Switchboard. Stage switchboard shall be either one or a combination of the following types:

(a) Manual. Dimmers and switches are operated by handles mechanically linked to the control devices.

(b) Remotely Controlled. Devices are operated electrically from a pilot-type control console or panel. Pilot control panels shall either be part of the switchboard or shall be permitted to be at another location.

520-27. Stage Switchboard Feeders. Feeders supplying stage switchboards shall be one of the following:

(a) **Single Feeder.** A single feeder disconnected by a single disconnect device.

(b) **Multiple Feeders.** Multiple feeders disconnected and/or protected by separate devices in an intermediate stage switchboard, provided that all feeders are part of a single system. Where multiple feeders are used, all conductors are to be of the same length. Neutral conductors of multiple feeders shall be combined; however, neutral conductors shall be arranged so that the sum of the neutral conductors in a given wireway is of adequate ampacity to carry the maximum unbalanced phase current which shall be permitted to be supplied by other feeder conductors in the same wireway.

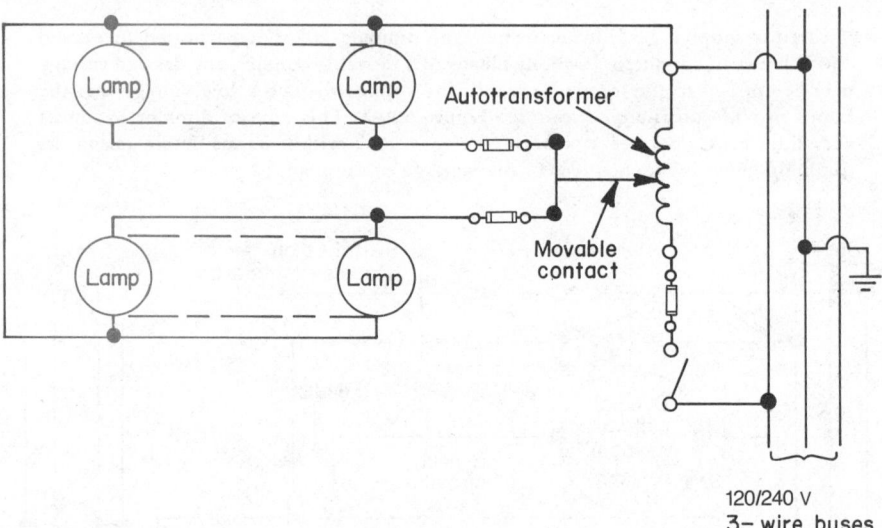

Figure 520-4. Typical connections for an autotransformer-type dimmer.

C. Stage Equipment — Fixed

520-41. Circuit Loads. Footlights, border lights, and proscenium side lights shall be so arranged that no branch circuit supplying such equipment will carry a load exceeding 20 amperes.

Exception: Where heavy-duty lampholders only are used, such circuits shall be permitted to comply with Article 210 for circuits supplying heavy-duty lampholders.

Sections 210-23(b) and (c) permit 30-A, 40-A, or 50-A branch circuits if heavy-duty lampholders, such as admedium or mogul-base Edison screw shell types, are used for fixed lighting.

520-42. Conductor Insulation. Foot, border, proscenium, or portable strip light fixtures and connector strips shall be wired with conductors having insulation suitable for the temperatures at which the conductors will be operated and not less than 125°C (257°F).

(FPN): See Table 310-13 for conductor types.

520-43. Footlights.

(a) **Metal Trough Construction.** Where metal trough construction is employed for footlights, the trough containing the circuit conductors shall be made of sheet metal not lighter than No. 20 MSG treated to prevent oxidation. Lampholder terminals shall be kept at least ½ inch (12.7 mm) from the metal of the trough. The circuit conductors shall be soldered to the lampholder terminals.

(b) Other-than-Metal-Trough Construction. Where the metal trough construction specified in Section 520-43(a) is not used, footlights shall consist of individual outlets with lampholders, wired with rigid metal conduit, intermediate metal conduit, or flexible metal conduit, Type MC cable, or mineral-insulated, metal-sheathed cable. The circuit conductors shall be soldered to the lampholder terminals. Disappearing footlights shall be so arranged that the current supply will be automatically disconnected when the footlights are replaced in the recess designed for them.

Metal troughs are commonly employed for footlights because the installation costs are less than individual outlets. Figure 520-5 illustrates a view of footlights in a typical installation.

Disappearing footlights are arranged so as to automatically disconnect the current supply when the footlights are in the closed position, thereby preventing heat-entrapment that could cause a fire.

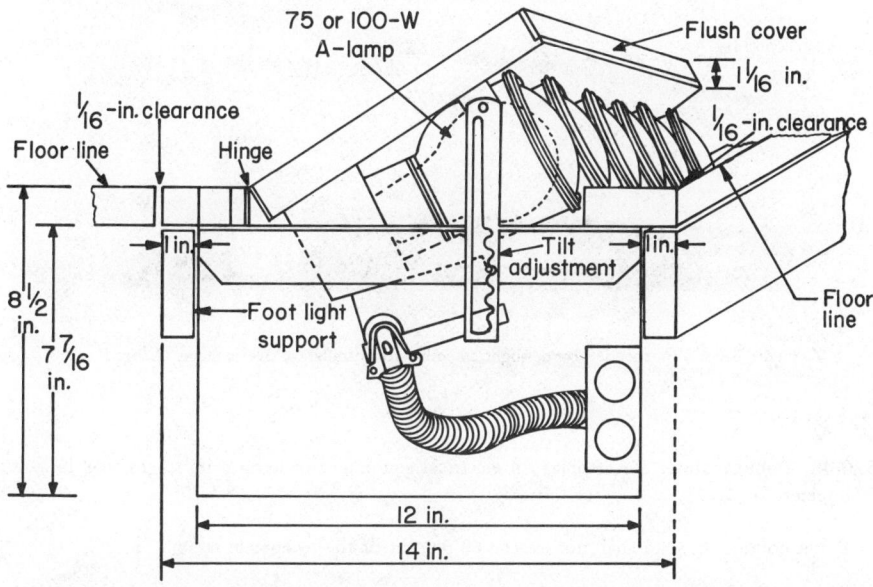

Figure 520-5. Disappearing footlights arranged to automatically disconnect the current supply when in the closed position to prevent heat-entrapment.

520-44. Borders and Proscenium Sidelights.

(a) General. Borders and proscenium sidelights shall be: (1) constructed as specified in Section 520-43; (2) suitably stayed and supported; and (3) so designed that the flanges of the reflectors or other adequate guards will protect the lamps from mechanical injury and from accidental contact with scenery or other combustible material.

(b) Cables for Border Lights. Cables for supply to border lights shall be Type S, SO, ST, or STO flexible cable as provided in Table 400-4. The cables shall be suitably supported. Such cables shall be employed only where flexible conductors are necessary.

Figure 520-6 shows a modern border light installed over a stage. Figure 520-7 is a cross-sectional view giving construction details. This particular border light is designed for 200-W lamps. Each lamp is provided with its own reflector to obtain the highest illumination efficiency. Fitted to each reflector is a glass roundel available in any color. Commonly red, white, and blue are used for three-color equipment, and red, white, blue, and amber for four-color equipment. A splice box is provided on top of the housing for enclosing connections between the cable supplying the border light and the border light's internal wiring which consists of wiring from the splice box to the lamp sockets in a trough extending the length of the border.

To facilitate height adjustment for cleaning and lamp replacement, border lights are usually supported by steel cables. Therefore, the circuit conductors supplying the border lights are required to be carried to the border in a flexible cable. The size of the individual conductor of the cable may be No. 14, though No. 12 is more commonly used.

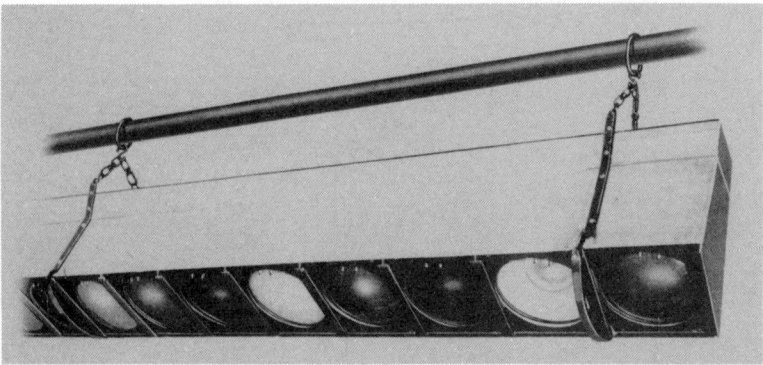

Figure 520-6. A suspended border-light assembly for installation over a stage. (*Kliegl Bros*).

520-45. Receptacles. Receptacles for electrical equipment or fixtures on stages shall be rated in amperes.

(1) A continuous load shall not exceed 80 percent of the receptacle rating.

(2) A noncontinuous load shall not exceed 100 percent of the receptacle rating. Conductors supplying receptacles shall be in accordance with Article 310.

This section was revised for the 1984 *Code* to clarify receptacle ratings for continuous and noncontinuous loads. A continuous load is one where the maximum current is expected to continue for three hours or more.

520-46. Stage Pockets. Receptacles intended for the connection of portable stage lighting equipment shall be mounted in suitable pockets or enclosures and shall comply with Section 520-45.

Figure 520-8 shows a single-receptacle stage floor pocket designed for flush mounting, and Figure 520-9 shows a three-gang floor pocket designed for flush mounting. The standard-type plug which is used with either floor pockets or wall pockets of these types is also shown.

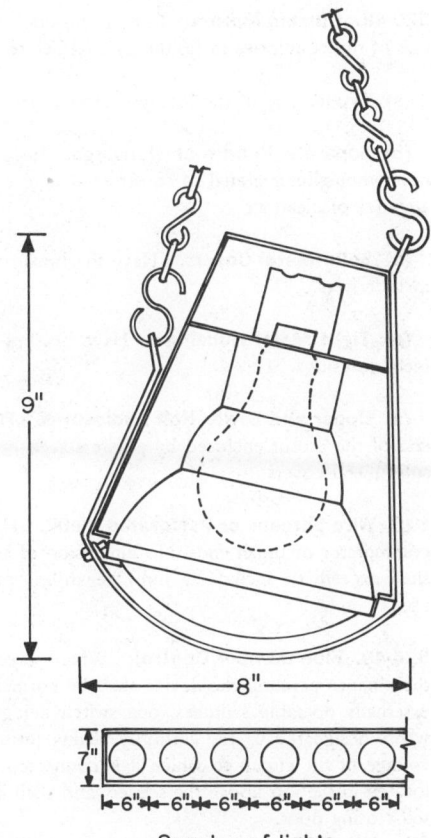

9"

8"

7"

|←6"→|←6"→|←6"→|←6"→|←6"→|←6"→|

Figure 520-7. A cross-sectional view of a typical light in the border assembly shown in Figure 520-6. (*Kliegl Bros.*)

Spacing of lights

Figure 520-8. A single receptacle in a stage floor pocket. (*Kliegl Bros.*)

Figure 520-9. A three-gang, three-receptacle stage floor pocket designed for flush mounting. (*Kliegl Bros.*)

520-47. Lamps in Scene Docks. Lamps installed in scene docks shall be so located and guarded as to be free from physical damage and shall provide an air space of not less than 2 inches (50.8 mm) between such lamps and any combustible material.

759

520-48. Curtain Motors. Curtain motors having brushes or sliding contacts shall comply with one of the conditions in (a) through (f) below.

(a) Types. Be of the totally enclosed, enclosed-fan-cooled, or enclosed-pipe-ventilated type.

(b) Separate Rooms or Housings. Be enclosed in separate rooms or housings built of noncombustible material so constructed as to exclude flyings or lint, and properly ventilated from a source of clean air.

(c) Solid Metal Covers. Have the brush or sliding-contact end of motor enclosed by solid metal covers.

(d) Tight Metal Housings. Have brushes or sliding contacts enclosed in substantial, tight metal housings.

(e) Upper and Lower Half Enclosures. Have the upper half of the brush or sliding-contact end of the motor enclosed by a wire screen or perforated metal and the lower half enclosed by solid metal covers.

(f) Wire Screens or Perforated Metal. Have wire screens or perforated metal placed at the commutator of brush ends. No dimension of any opening in the wire screen or perforated metal shall exceed .05 inch (1.27 mm), regardless of the shape of the opening and of the material used.

520-49. Flue Damper Control. Where stage flue dampers are released by an electrical device, the circuit operating the device shall be normally closed and shall be controlled by at least two externally operable switches, one switch being placed at the electrician's station and the other where designated by the authority having jurisdiction. The device shall be designed for the full voltage of the circuit to which it is connected, no resistance being inserted. The device shall be located in the loft above the scenery and shall be enclosed in a suitable metal box having a tight, self-closing door.

In addition to the flue dampers being controlled from two externally operable switches at different locations, the design of a normally closed circuit ensures that the flue dampers will operate when the circuit opens for any reason, such as a circuit breaker tripping or a fuse blowing.

D. Portable Switchboards on Stage

520-51. Supply. Portable switchboards shall be supplied only from outlets of sufficient voltage and ampere rating. Such outlets shall include only externally operable, enclosed fused switches or circuit breakers mounted on stage or at the permanent switchboard in locations readily accessible from the stage floor. Provisions for connection of an equipment grounding conductor shall be provided.

520-52. Overcurrent Protection. Circuits from portable switchboards directly supplying equipment containing incandescent lamps of not over 300 watts shall be protected by overcurrent devices having a rating or setting of not over 20 amperes. Circuits for lampholders over 300 watts shall be permitted where overcurrent protection complies with Article 210. Other circuits shall be provided with overcurrent devices with a rating or setting not higher than the current required for the connected load.

520-53. Construction. Portable switchboards for use on stages shall comply with (a) through (n) below.

(a) Enclosure. Portable switchboards shall be placed within an enclosure of substantial construction, which shall be permitted to be so arranged that the enclosure is open during operation. Enclosures of wood shall be completely lined with sheet metal of not less than No. 24 MSG and shall be well galvanized, enameled, or otherwise properly coated to prevent corrosion or be of a corrosion-resistant material.

(b) Live Parts. There shall be no exposed live parts within the enclosure.

Exception: For dimmer faceplates as provided in (e) below.

(c) Switches and Circuit Breakers. All switches and circuit breakers shall be of the externally operable, enclosed type.

(d) Circuit Protection. Overcurrent devices shall be provided in each ungrounded conductor of every circuit supplied through the switchboard. Enclosures shall be provided for all overcurrent devices in addition to the switchboard enclosure.

(e) Dimmers. The terminals of dimmers shall be provided with enclosures, and dimmer faceplates shall be so arranged that accidental contact cannot be readily made with the faceplate contacts.

(f) Interior Conductors. All conductors other than busbars within the switchboard enclosure shall be stranded. Conductors shall be approved for an operating temperature at least equal to the approved operating temperature of the dimming devices used in the switchboard and in no case less than the following: (1) resistance-type dimmers: 200°C (392°F); or (2) reactor-type, autotransformer, and solid-state dimmers: 125°C (257°F). All control wiring shall comply with Article 725.

Each conductor shall have an ampacity at least equal to the rating of the circuit breaker, switch, or fuse which it supplies. Circuit interrupting and bus bracing shall be in accordance with Sections 110-9 and 110-10. Switchboards with inadequate short-circuit withstand rating shall be protected on the line side by current-limiting devices. The short-circuit withstand rating shall be marked on the switchboard.

Exception: Conductors for pilot light circuits having overcurrent protection of not over 20 amperes.

Conductors shall be enclosed in metal wireways or be securely fastened in position and shall be bushed where they pass through metal.

(g) Pilot Light. A pilot light shall be provided within the enclosure and shall be so connected to the circuit supplying the board that the opening of the master switch will not cut off the supply to the lamp. This lamp shall be on an independent circuit having overcurrent protection rated or set at not over 15 amperes.

(h) Supply Connections. The supply to a portable switchboard shall be by means of Type S, SO, ST, or STO flexible cord terminating within the switchboard enclosure or in an externally operable fused master switch or circuit breaker. The supply cable shall have sufficient ampacity to carry the total load connected to the switchboard and shall be protected by overcurrent devices.

Exception No. 1: Supply Conductors Not Over 10 Feet (3.05 m) Long. In cases where supply conductors do not exceed 10 feet (3.05 m) in length between supply and switchboard or supply and a subsequent overcurrent device, the ampacity of the supply conductors shall be at least one-quarter of the ampacity of the supply overcurrent protection device where all of the following conditions are met:

a. The supply conductors shall terminate in a single overcurrent protection device that will limit the load to the ampacity of the supply conductors. This single overcurrent device shall be permitted to supply additional overcurrent devices on its load side.

b. The supply conductors shall not penetrate walls, floors, or ceilings, or be run through doors or traffic areas. The supply conductors shall be adequately protected from physical damage.

c. The supply conductors shall be suitably terminated in an approved manner.

d. Conductors shall be continuous without splices or connectors.

e. Conductors shall not be bundled.

f. Conductors shall be supported above the floor in an approved manner.

Exception No. 2: Supply Conductors Not Over 20 Feet (6.1 m) Long. In cases where supply conductors do not exceed 20 feet (6.1 m) in length between supply and switchboard or supply and a subsequent overcurrent protection device, the ampacity of the supply conductors shall be at least one-half the rating of the supply overcurrent protection device where all of the following conditions are met:

a. The supply conductors shall terminate in a single overcurrent protection device that will limit the load to the ampacity of the supply conductors. This single overcurrent device shall be permitted to supply additional overcurrent devices on its load side.

b. The supply conductors shall not penetrate walls, floors, or ceilings, or be run through doors or traffic areas. The supply conductors shall be adequately protected from physical damage.

c. The supply conductors shall be suitably terminated in an approved manner.

d. The supply conductors shall be supported in an approved manner at least 7 feet (2.13 m) above the floor except at terminations.

e. The supply conductors shall not be bundled.

f. Tap conductors shall be in unbroken lengths.

Exception Nos. 1 and 2 are new in the 1984 *Code.* Loads of 144 kVA and greater are not uncommon, even on portable switchboard equipment. Installations in the field include lighting for theatrical-type productions with large numbers of lighting fixtures. However, only a fraction of the many fixtures installed are used at any one time. The intent is that the supply conductors are required to be sized according to their overcurrent protection, and not by the total connected load. These exceptions are similar to those found in Section 240-21 for taps.

(i) Cable Arrangement. Cables shall be protected by bushings where they pass through enclosures and shall be so arranged that tension on the cable will not be transmitted to the connections.

(j) Number of Supply Interconnections. Where connectors are used in a supply conductor, there shall be a maximum number of three interconnections (mated connector pairs) when the total length from supply to switchboard does not exceed 100 feet (30.5 m). In cases where the total length from supply to switchboard exceeds 100 feet (30.5 m), one additional interconnection shall be permitted for each additional 100 feet (30.5 m) of supply conductor.

Subparagraph (j) was added to the 1984 *Code* because excessive numbers of interconnects could jeopardize the mechanical and electrical integrity of the supply conductors.

(k) Protection of Supply Conductors and Connectors. All supply conductors and connectors shall be adequately protected against physical and mechanical abuse. Supply conductors and connectors need not be in raceways.

(l) Flanged Surface Inlets. Flanged surface inlets (recessed plugs) that are used to accept the power shall be rated in amperes.

(m) Terminals. Terminals to which stage cables are connected shall be so located as to permit convenient access to the terminals.

(n) Supply Neutral Terminal. In portable switchboard equipment designed for use with 3-phase, 4-wire with ground supply, the supply neutral terminal and its associated busbar and/or equivalent wiring shall have an ampacity equal to twice the ampacity of the largest ungrounded supply terminal.

Exception: Portable solid-state switchboard equipment specifically constructed to be internally converted in the field, in an approved manner, from use with 3-phase, 4-wire with ground supply to use with single-phase, three-wire with ground supply. In such equipment, the supply neutral terminal and its associated busbar and/or equivalent wiring shall have a minimum ampacity equal to that of 200 percent of the largest ungrounded single phase supply terminal. The power supply lines to said solid-state dimmer board, if going through raceways or if a multiconductor cable, shall be sized considering the neutral as a conductor. If being supplied by single conductors in air, the neutral conductor shall be sized with an ampacity of 100 percent larger than the required size of the ungrounded conductors.

Subparagraph (n) and its exception are new in the 1984 *Code*. Portable switchboards designed for 3-phase, 4-wire with ground supply are often used in locations where only single-phase, 3-wire with ground supply is available. Since most stage lighting loads are single-phase, 2-wire, 120-V lamps are not necessarily operated simultaneously. Further, all grounded conductor (neutral) connections within the switchboard are common. Larger than normal neutral currents will result when two phases of a 3-phase, 4-wire with ground switchboard are tied together and supplied from a single-phase, 3-wire with ground supply. The neutral can also be caused to carry excessive current when connected to a 3-phase, 4-wire system and supplying an electronic dimmer board because of the sine wave clipping action of the SCRs in such boards. Therefore, the requirements for oversizing of the neutral are considered necessary in order to safely carry additional neutral currents. The exception covers equipment which has been designed for internal conversion from 3-phase, 4-wire with ground supply to single-phase, 3-wire with ground supply, thus preventing abnormal neutral currents.

E. Stage Equipment — Portable

520-61. Arc Lamps. Arc lamps shall be listed.

520-62. Portable Plugging Boxes. Portable plugging boxes shall comply with (a) through (d) below.

(a) Enclosure. The construction shall be such that no current-carrying part will be exposed.

(b) Receptacles and Overcurrent Protection. Each receptacle shall have a rating of not less than 30 amperes, and shall have overcurrent protection installed in an enclosure equipped with self-closing doors.

(c) Busbars and Terminals. Busbars shall have an ampacity equal to the sum of the ampere ratings of all the receptacles. Lugs shall be provided for the connection of the master cable.

(d) Flanged Surface Inlets. Flanged surface inlets (recessed plugs) that are used to accept the power shall be rated in amperes.

520-63. Bracket Fixture Wiring.

(a) Bracket Wiring. Brackets for use on scenery shall be wired internally, and the fixture stem shall be carried through to the back of the scenery where a bushing shall be placed on the end of the stem.

Exception: Externally wired brackets or other fixtures shall be permitted where wired with cords designed for hard usage that extend through scenery and without joint or splice in canopy of fixture back and terminate in an approved-type stage connector located, where practical, within 18 inches (457 mm) of the fixture.

(b) Mounting. Fixtures shall be securely fastened in place.

520-64. Portable Strips. Portable strips shall be constructed in accordance with the requirements for border lights and proscenium side lights in Section 520-44(a). The supply cable shall be protected by bushings where it passes through metal and shall be so arranged that tension on the cable will not be transmitted to the connections.

(FPN): See Section 520-42 for wiring of portable strips.

520-65. Festoons. Joints in festoon wiring shall be staggered. Lamps enclosed in lanterns or similar devices of combustible material shall be equipped with guards.

Festoon wiring is a string of lights which is suspended between two points more than 15 ft apart. Joints in festoon wiring are required to be staggered and properly insulated. This ensures that connections will not be opposite one another, which could cause sparking due to improper insulation or unraveling of insulation which, in turn, could ignite lanterns or other combustible material enclosing lamps. It should also be noted that when lampholders have terminals of a type that puncture the conductor insulation and make contact with the conductors, stranded-type conductors should be used.

520-66. Special Effects. Electrical devices used for simulating lightning, waterfalls, and the like shall be so constructed and located that flames, sparks, or hot particles cannot come in contact with combustible material.

520-67. Cable Connectors. Cable connectors, male and female, for flexible conductors shall be constructed so that tension on the cord or cable will not be transmitted to the connections. The female half shall be attached to the load end of the power supply cord or cable. The connector shall be rated in amperes and designed so that differently rated devices cannot be connected together.

(FPN): See Section 400-10 for pull at terminals.

520-68. Conductors for Portables. Flexible conductors used to supply portable stage equipment shall be Type S, SO, ST, or STO.

Exception: Reinforced cord shall be permitted to supply stand lamps where the cord is not subject to severe physical damage and is protected by an overcurrent device rated at not over 20 amperes.

F. Dressing Rooms

520-71. Pendant Lampholders. Pendant lampholders shall not be installed in dressing rooms.

520-72. Lamp Guards. All incandescent lamps in dressing rooms, where less than 8 feet (2.44 m) from the floor, shall be equipped with open-end guards riveted to the outlet box cover or otherwise sealed or locked in place.

Because of the varied types of flammable materials, such as costumes, wigs, etc., present in dressing rooms, pendant lampholders are not permitted. Lamps are required to be provided with suitable guards that are not easily removed. This makes it difficult to circumvent their intended purpose of preventing contact between the lamps and flammable material.

520-73. Switches Required. All lights and receptacles in dressing rooms shall be controlled by wall switches installed in the dressing rooms. Each switch controlling receptacles shall be provided with a pilot light to indicate when the receptacles are energized.

G. Grounding

520-81. Grounding. All metal raceways shall be grounded. The metal frames and enclosures of all equipment, including border lights and portable lighting fixtures, shall be grounded. Grounding, where employed, shall be in accordance with Article 250.

ARTICLE 530 — MOTION PICTURE AND TELEVISION STUDIOS AND SIMILAR LOCATIONS

Contents

ARTICLE 530—MOTION PICTURE AND TELEVISION STUDIOS

A. General

530-1. Scope. The requirements of this article shall apply to television studios and motion picture studios using either film or electronic cameras, except as provided in Section 520-1, and exchanges, factories, laboratories, stages, or a portion of the building in which film or tape more than ⅞ inch (22 mm) in width is exposed, developed, printed, cut, edited, rewound, repaired, or stored.

(FPN): For methods of protecting against cellulose nitrate film hazards, see Standard for the Storage and Handling of Cellulose Nitrate Motion Picture Film, NFPA 40-1982.

The requirements for motion picture studios and television studios are virtually the same, and are intended to apply "only" to those locations presenting special hazards. Otherwise, the conditions are similar to theater stages; therefore, the applicable provisions of Article 520 should be observed, such as for stages, dressing rooms, etc.

The special hazards are temporary structures constructed of wood or other flammable material.

B. Stage or Set

530-11. Permanent Wiring. The permanent wiring shall be Type MC cable, Type MI cable, or in approved raceways.

Exception: Communication circuits, and sound recording and reproducing equipment shall be permitted to be wired as permitted by Articles 640 and 800.

530-12. Portable Wiring. The wiring for stage set lighting, stage effects, electric equipment used as stage properties, and other wiring not fixed as to location shall be done with approved flexible cords and cables. Splices or taps shall be permitted in flexible cords used to supply stage properties when such are made with approved devices and the circuit is protected at not more than 20 amperes. Such cables and cords shall not be fastened by staples or nailing.

530-13. Stage Lighting and Effects Control. Switches used for studio stage set lighting and effects (on the stages and lots and on location) shall be of the externally operable type. Where contactors are used as the disconnecting means for fuses, an individual externally operable switch, such as a tumbler switch, for the control of each contactor shall be located at a distance of not more than 6 feet (1.83 m) from the contactor, in addition to remote-control switches.

Exception: A single externally operable switch shall be permitted to simultaneously disconnect all the contactors on any one location board, where located at a distance of not more than 6 feet (1.83 m) from the location board.

530-14. Plugging Boxes. Each receptacle of plugging boxes shall be rated at not less than 30 amperes.

530-15. Enclosing and Guarding Live Parts.

(a) Live Parts. Live parts shall be enclosed or guarded to prevent accidental contact by persons and objects.

(b) Switches. All switches shall be of the externally operable type.

(c) Rheostats. Rheostats shall be placed in approved cases or cabinets that enclose all live parts, having only the operating handles exposed.

(d) Current-Carrying Parts. Current-carrying parts of bull-switches, location boards, spiders, and plugging boxes shall be so enclosed, guarded, or located that persons cannot accidentally come into contact with them or bring conductive material into contact with them.

530-16. Portable Lamps. Portable lamps and work lights shall be equipped with flexible cords, composition or metal-sheathed porcelain sockets, and substantial guards.

Exception: Portable lamps used as properties in a motion picture set or television stage set, on a studio stage or lot, or on location.

530-17. Portable Arc Lamps. Portable arc lamps shall be substantially constructed. The arc shall be provided with an enclosure designed to retain sparks and carbons and to prevent persons or materials from coming into contact with the arc or bare live parts. The enclosures shall be ventilated. All switches shall be of the externally operable type.

530-18. Overcurrent Protection — Short-Time Rating.*

General. Automatic overcurrent protective devices (circuit breakers or fuses) for motion picture studio stage set lighting and the stage cables for such stage set lighting shall be as given in (a) through (e) below.

(FPN): Note: *Special consideration is given to motion picture studios and similar locations because filming periods are of short duration.

(a) Stage Cables. Stage cables for stage set lighting shall be protected by means of overcurrent devices set at not more than 400 percent of the ampacity given in Tables 310-16 through 310-19 and Table 400-5.

(b) Feeders. In buildings used primarily for motion picture production, the feeders from the substations to the stages shall be protected by means of overcurrent devices (generally located in the substation) having suitable ampere rating. The overcurrent devices shall be permitted to be multipole or single-pole gang-operated. No pole or overcurrent device shall be required in the neutral conductor. The overcurrent device setting for each feeder shall not exceed 400 percent of the ampacity of the feeder, as given in Tables 310-16 and 310-18 for the kind of insulation used.

(c) Location Boards. Overcurrent protection (fuses or circuit breakers) shall be provided at the "location boards." Fuses in the "location boards" shall have an ampere rating of not over 400 percent of the ampacity of the cables between the "location boards" and the plugging boxes.

(d) Plugging Boxes. Cables and cords supplied through plugging boxes shall be of copper. Cables and cords smaller than No. 8 shall be attached to the plugging box by means of a plug containing two cartridge fuses or a 2-pole circuit breaker. The rating of the fuses or the setting of the circuit breaker shall not be over 400 percent of the safe ampacity of the cables or cords as given in Tables 310-16 through 310-19, and 400-5 for the kind of insulation used.

(e) Lighting. Work lights, stand lamps, and fixtures shall be connected to plugging boxes by means of plugs containing two cartridge fuses not larger than 20 amperes, or they shall be permitted to be connected to special outlets on circuits protected by fuses or circuit breakers rated at not over 20 amperes. Plug fuses shall not be used unless they are on the load side of the fuse or circuit breakers on the "location boards."

530-19. Sizing of Feeder Conductors for Television Studio Sets.

(a) General. It shall be permissible to apply the demand factors listed in Table 530-19(a) to that portion of the maximum possible connected load for studio or stage set lighting for all permanently installed feeders between substations and stages and to all permanently installed subfeeders between the main stage switchboard and stage distribution centers or location boards.

Table 530-19(a). Demand Factors for Stage Set Lighting

Total Stage Set Lighting Load (Wattage)	Feeder Demand Factor
First 50,000 or less at	100%
Next 50,001 to 100,000 at	75%
Next 100,001 to 200,000 at	60%
All over 200,000	50%

(b) Portable Feeders. A demand factor of 50 percent of maximum possible connected load shall be permitted for all portable feeders.

530-20. Grounding. Metal-clad cable, metal raceways, and all noncurrent-carrying metal parts of appliances, devices, and equipment shall be grounded as specified in Article 250. This shall not apply to pendant and portable lamps, to stage lighting and stage sound equipment, nor to other portable and special stage equipment operating at not over 150 volts to ground.

530-21. Plugs and Receptacles. Plugs and receptacles shall be rated in amperes.

C. Dressing Rooms

530-31. Dressing Rooms. Fixed wiring in dressing rooms shall be installed in accordance with wiring methods covered in Chapter 3. Wiring for portable dressing rooms shall be approved.

D. Viewing, Cutting, and Patching Tables

530-41. Lamps at Tables. Only composition or metal-sheathed, porcelain, keyless lampholders equipped with suitable means to guard lamps from physical damage and from film and film scrap shall be used at patching, viewing, and cutting tables.

E. Film Storage Vaults

530-51. Lamps in Cellulose Nitrate Film Storage Vaults. Lamps in cellulose nitrate film storage vaults shall be rigid fixtures of the glass enclosed and gasketed type. Lamps shall be controlled by a switch having a pole in each ungrounded conductor. This switch shall be located outside of the vault and provided with a pilot light to indicate whether the switch is on or off. This switch shall disconnect from all sources of supply all ungrounded conductors terminating in any outlet in the vault.

530-52. Motors and Other Equipment in Cellulose Nitrate Film Storage Vaults. No receptacles, outlets, electric motors, heaters, portable lights, or other portable electric equipment shall be located in film storage vaults.

F. Substations

530-61. Substations. Wiring and equipment of over 600 volts, nominal, shall comply with Article 710.

530-62. Low-Voltage Switchboards. On 600 volts, nominal, or less, switchboards shall comply with Article 384.

530-63. Overcurrent Protection of DC Generators. Three-wire dc generators shall have protection consisting of overcurrent devices having an ampere rating or setting in accordance with the generator ampere rating. Single-pole or double-pole overcurrent devices shall be permitted, and no pole or overcurrent coil shall be required in the neutral lead (whether it is grounded or ungrounded).

530-64. Working Space and Guarding. Working space and guarding in permanent fixed substations shall comply with Sections 110-16 and 110-17.

(FPN): For guarding of live parts on motors and generators, see Sections 430-11 and 430-14.

Exception: Switchboards of not over 250 volts dc between conductors, when located in substations or switchboard rooms accessible to qualified persons only, shall not be required to be dead-front.

530-65. Portable Substations. Wiring and equipment in portable substations shall conform to the sections applying to installations in permanently fixed substations, but, due to the limited space available, the working spaces shall be permitted to be reduced, provided that the equipment shall be so arranged that the operator can do his work safely, and so that other persons in the vicinity cannot accidentally come into contact with current-carrying parts or bring conducting objects into contact with them while they are energized.

530-66. Grounding at Substations. Noncurrent-carrying metal parts shall be grounded.

Exception: Frames of dc circuit breakers installed on switchboards.

ARTICLE 540 — MOTION PICTURE PROJECTORS

Contents

A. General

540-1. Scope. The provisions of this article apply to motion picture projection rooms, motion picture projectors, and associated equipment of the professional and nonprofessional types using incandescent, carbon arc, Xenon, or other light source equipment which develops hazardous gases, dust, or radiation.

(FPN): For further information, see Storage and Handling of Cellulose Nitrate Motion Picture Film, NFPA 40-1982.

The definitions of hazardous (classified) locations in Article 500 do not classify a motion picture projection room as a hazardous (classified) location, even though some of the older types of film, such as cellulose nitrate film, rarely used now, are highly flammable. In comparison, cellulose acetate film, called "safety film," a much safer film, is in wide use today. Since film is not volatile at ordinary temperatures and no flammable gases are present, the wiring installation need not be suitable for hazardous (classified) locations as defined in Article 500, but should be done with special care to protect against the hazards of fire.

B. Definitions

540-2. Professional Projector. The professional projector is a type using 35- or 70-millimeter film which has a minimum width of 1⅜ inches (35 mm) and has on each edge 5.4 perforations per inch, or a type using carbon arc, Xenon, or other light source equipment which develops hazardous gases, dust, or radiation.

540-3. Nonprofessional Projector. Nonprofessional projectors are those types other than described in Section 540-2.

C. Equipment and Projectors of the Professional Type

540-10. Motion Picture Projection Room Required. Every professional-type projector shall be located within a projection room. Every projection room shall be of permanent construction, approved for the type of building in which the projection room is located. All projection ports, spotlight ports, viewing ports, and similar openings shall be provided with glass or other approved material so as to completely close the opening. Such rooms shall not be considered as hazardous (classified) locations as defined in Article 500.

(FPN): For further information on protecting openings in projection rooms handling cellulose nitrate motion picture film, see *Life Safety Code*, NFPA *101*-1981 (ANSI).

540-11. Location of Associated Electrical Equipment.

(a) Motor Generator Sets, Transformers, Rectifiers, Rheostats, and Similar Equipment. Motor generator sets, transformers, rectifiers, rheostats, and similar equipment for the supply or control of current to projection or spotlight equipment shall, if practicable, be located in a separate room. Where placed in the projection room, they shall be so located or guarded that arcs or sparks cannot come in contact with film, and motor generator sets shall have the commutator end or ends protected as provided in Section 520-48.

(b) Switches, Overcurrent Devices, or Other Equipment. Switches, overcurrent devices, or other equipment not normally required or used for projectors, sound reproduction, flood or other special effect lamps, or other equipment shall not be installed in projection rooms.

Exception No. 1: Remote control switches for the control of auditorium lights or switches for the control of motors operating curtains and masking of the motion picture screen.

Exception No. 2: In projection rooms approved for use only with cellulose acetate (safety) film, the installation of appurtenant electrical equipment used in conjunction with the operation of the projection equipment and the control of lights, curtains, and audio equipment, etc., shall be permitted. In such projection rooms, a sign reading "Safety Film Only Permitted in This Room" shall be posted on the outside of each projection room door and within the projection room itself in a conspicuous location.

(c) Emergency Systems. Control of emergency systems shall comply with Article 700 — Emergency Systems.

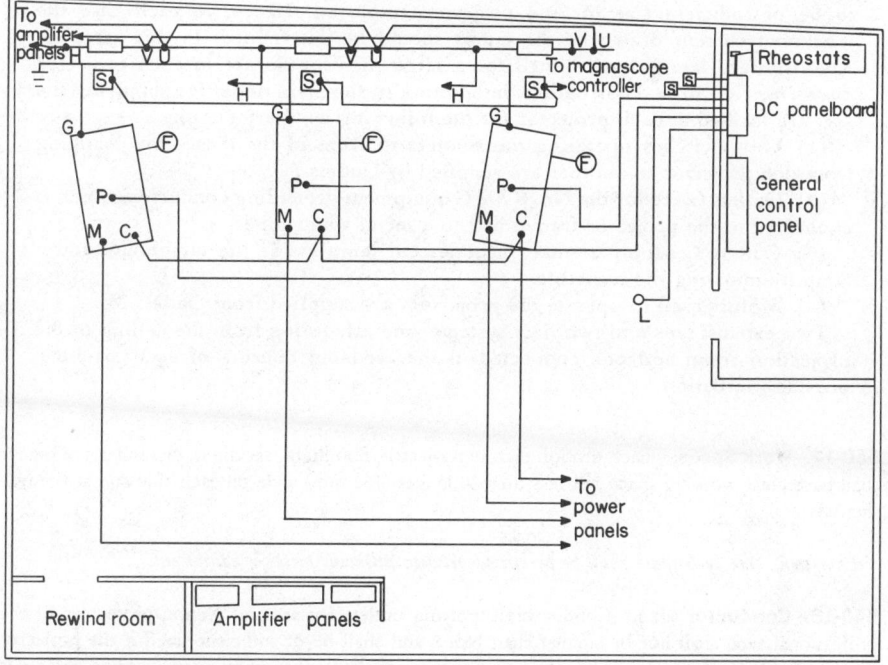

Figure 540-1. A typical layout of a projection room including associated generator equipment. Modern projectors contain rectifiers as an integral part of their equipment, thereby eliminating generators and other associated equipment.

The plan of a projection room of a motion picture theater is illustrated in Figure 540-1. This plan shows one stereopticon or "effect machine" (L), two spot machines (S), and three motion picture projectors (P).

A dc arc lamp is the light source in each of the six machines. The dc supply is furnished by two motor generator sets that are usually installed in soundproof areas so as not to interfere with the sound-reproducing equipment and are controlled from the generator panel in the projection room or booth. Two 500 MCM feeder cables are run from each generator to the dc panelboard.

A branch circuit consisting of two No. 2/0 cables runs from the dc panelboard to each projector (P) and to each spot machine (S). One of the two branch-circuit conductors runs directly to projector (P); the other passes through an auxiliary gutter to the bank of resistors in the rheostat room and then to the projector. The resistors are equipped with short-circuiting switches so that the total resistance in series with each arc may be preset to a desired value.

Since the stereopticon or effect machine (L) contains two arc lamps, two circuits with No. 1 AWG conductors are routed to this machine.

Section 540-13 requires that the conductors supplying outlets for arc and Xenon projectors of the professional type are not to be smaller than No. 8 AWG and are to be of sufficient size for the projector employed. Hence, in each case the maximum current drawn by the lamps should be determined. In this example, when the arc lamps are adjusted for a large picture, the arc in each projector draws nearly 150 A. Four outlets, in addition to the main outlet for supplying the arc, are located at each projector for the following auxiliary circuits:

(1) Foot switches operating the shutters in front of the lenses for changing from one projector to another are supplied by Outlets F.

(2) Outlets G are for the No. 8 AWG equipment grounding conductor, which is connected to the projector frames and to a metal water pipe.

(3) Outlets C supply a small incandescent lamp inside the lamphouse and a lamp illuminating the turntable.

(4) Motors used to operate the projectors are supplied from Outlets M.

Two exhaust fans and two duct systems, one exhausting from the ceiling of the projection room and one connected to the arc-lamp housing of each machine, provide ventilation.

540-12. Work Space. Each motion picture projector, floodlight, spotlight, or similar equipment shall have clear working space not less than 30 inches (762 mm) wide on each side and at the rear thereof.

Exception: One such space shall be permitted between adjacent pieces of equipment.

540-13. Conductor Size. Conductors supplying outlets for arc and Xenon projectors of the professional type shall not be smaller than No. 8 and shall be of sufficient size for the projector employed. Conductors for incandescent-type projectors shall conform to normal wiring standards as provided in Section 210-24.

540-14. Conductors on Lamps and Hot Equipment. Asbestos-covered conductors Type AA or other types of insulated conductors having a maximum operating temperature of 200°C (392°F) shall be used on all lamps or other equipment where the ambient temperature at the conductors as installed will exceed 50°C (122°F).

540-15. Flexible Cords. Cords approved for hard usage as provided in Table 400-4 shall be used on portable equipment.

540-20. Approval. Projectors and enclosures for arc, Xenon and incandescent lamps and rectifiers, transformers, rheostats and similar equipment shall be approved.

540-21. Marking. Projectors and other equipment shall be marked with the maker's name or trademark and with the voltage and current for which they are designed in accordance with Section 110-21.

D. Nonprofessional Projectors

540-31. Motion Picture Projection Room Not Required. Projectors of the nonprofessional or miniature type, when employing cellulose acetate (safety) film, shall be permitted to be operated without a projection room.

540-32. Approval. Projection equipment shall be listed.

E. Sound Recording and Reproduction

540-50. Sound Recording and Reproduction. Sound recording and reproduction equipment shall be installed as provided in Article 640.

ARTICLE 545 — MANUFACTURED BUILDING

Contents

A. General

545-1. Scope. This article covers requirements for a manufactured building and/or building components as herein defined.

545-2. Other Articles. Wherever the requirements of other articles of this Code and Article 545 differ, the requirements of Article 545 shall apply.

545-3. Definitions.

Manufactured Building. "Manufactured Building" means any building which is of closed construction and which is made or assembled in manufacturing facilities on or off the building site for installation, or assembly and installation on the building site, other than mobile homes or recreational vehicles.

Building Component. "Building Component" means any subsystem, subassembly, or other system designed for use in or integral with or as part of a structure, which can include structural, electrical, mechanical, plumbing, and fire protection systems, and other systems affecting health and safety.

Building System. "Building System" means plans, specifications, and documentation for a system of manufactured building or for a type or a system of building components, which can include structural, electrical, mechanical, plumbing, and fire protection systems, and other systems affecting health and safety, and including such variations thereof as are specifically permitted by regulation, and which variations are submitted as part of the building system or amendment thereto.

Closed Construction. "Closed Construction" means any building, building component, assembly, or system manufactured in such a manner that all concealed parts of processes of manufacture cannot be inspected before installation at the building site without disassembly, damage, or destruction.

545-4. Wiring Methods.

(a) Methods Permitted. All raceway and cable wiring methods included in this Code and such other wiring systems specifically intended and approved for use in manufactured building shall be permitted with approved fittings and with fittings approved for manufactured building. Where wiring devices with integral enclosures are used, sufficient length of conductor shall be provided to facilitate replacement.

(b) Securing Cables. In closed construction, cables shall be permitted to be secured only at cabinets, boxes, or fittings where No. 10 AWG or smaller conductors are used and protection against physical damage is provided as required by Section 300-4.

545-5. Service-Entrance Conductors. Service-entrance conductors shall meet the requirements of Article 230. Provisions shall be made to route the service-entrance conductors from the service equipment to the point of attachment of the service.

545-6. Installation of Service-Entrance Conductors. Service-entrance conductors shall be installed after erection at the building site.

Exception: Where point of attachment is known prior to manufacture.

545-7. Service Equipment Location. The service equipment shall be located at a readily accessible point nearest to the entrance of the conductors either inside or outside the building.

545-8. Protection of Conductors and Equipment. Protection shall be provided for exposed conductors and equipment during processes of manufacturing, packaging, in transit, and erection at the building site.

545-9. Outlet Boxes.

(a) Other Dimensions. Outlet boxes of dimensions other than those required in Table 370-6(a) shall be permitted to be installed when tested and approved to applicable standards.

(b) Not Over 100 Cubic Inches. Any outlet box not over 100 cubic inches in size, intended for mounting in closed construction, shall be affixed with approved anchors or clamps so as to provide a rigid and secure installation.

545-10. Receptacle or Switch with Integral Enclosure. A receptacle or switch with integral enclosure and mounting means, when tested and approved to applicable standards, shall be permitted to be installed.

See Figure 545-1 and the commentary following Section 300-15, Exception No. 5.

545-11. Bonding and Grounding. Prewired panels and/or building components shall provide for the bonding and/or grounding of all exposed metals likely to become energized, in accordance with Article 250, Parts E, F, and G.

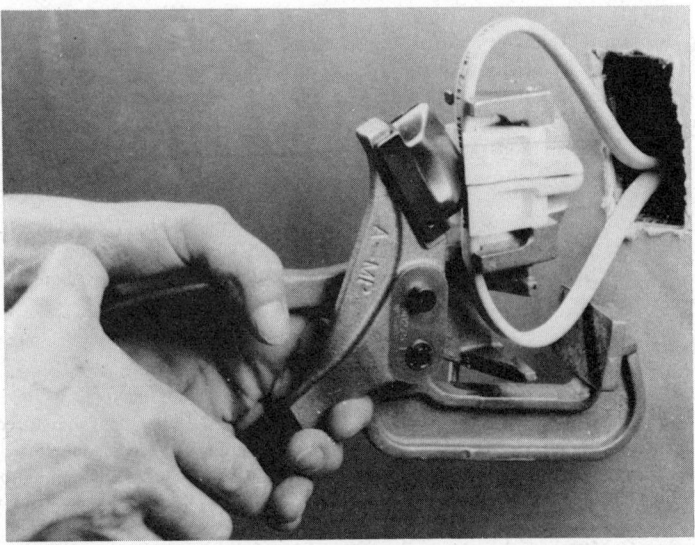

Figure 545-1. A special type of tool that is used to connect nonmetallic-sheathed cable to an approved boxless switch or receptacle. (*Amp Inc.*)

545-12. Grounding Electrode Conductor. The grounding electrode conductor shall meet the requirements of Article 250, Part J. Provisions shall be made to route the grounding electrode conductor from the service equipment to the point of attachment to the grounding electrode.

545-13. Component Interconnections. Fittings and connectors which are intended to be concealed at the time of on-site assembly, when tested and approved to applicable standards, shall be permitted for on-site interconnection of modules or other building components. Such fittings and connectors shall be equal to the wiring method employed in insulation, temperature rise, fault-current withstand and shall be capable of enduring the vibration and minor relative motions occurring in the components of manufactured building.

Structural components or modules are usually constructed in manufacturing facilities and then transported over the road to a building site for complete assembly of, for instance, a dwelling unit, a motel, an office building, etc. At the on-site location, approved wiring methods are employed to interconnect two or more modules. Figures 545-2 and 545-3 show types of nonmetallic-sheathed cable connectors permitted for such interconnections.

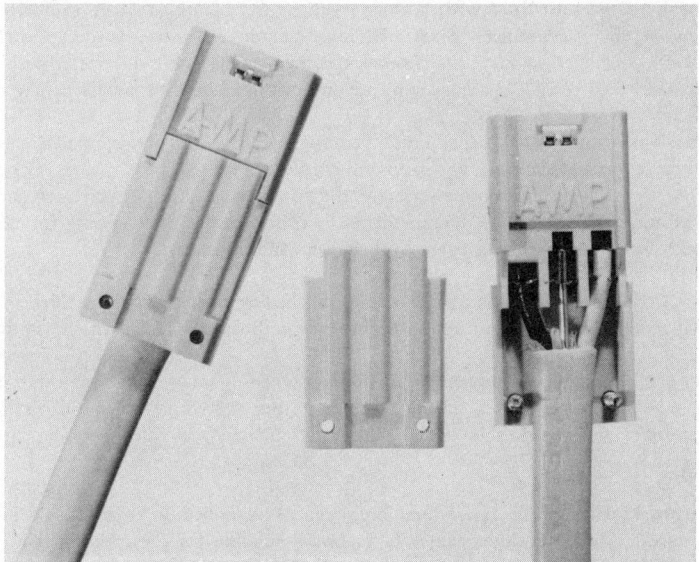

Figure 545-2. A type of nonmetallic-sheathed cable connector used for interconnecting modules in a manufacturing building. The parts are shown before mating together. (*Amp Inc.*)

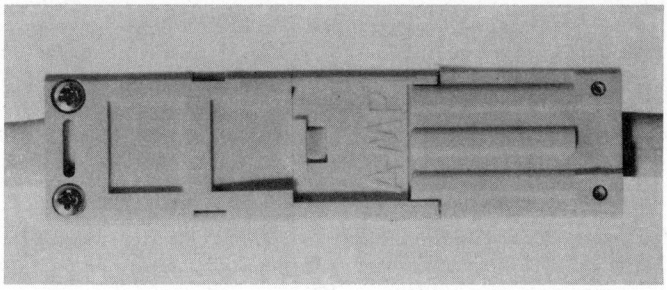

Figure 545-3. The nonmetallic-sheathed cable connector shown in Figure 545-2 after being joined together (*Amp Inc.*)

ARTICLE 547 — AGRICULTURAL BUILDINGS

Contents

547-1. Scope. The provisions of this article shall apply to the following agricultural buildings or that part of a building as specified in (a), (b), or (c) below.

(a) Excessive Dust and Dust with Water. Agricultural buildings where excessive dust and dust with water may accumulate. Such buildings include all areas of totally enclosed and environmentally controlled poultry and livestock confinement systems, where litter dust, feed dust, including mineral feed particles, may accumulate and enclosed areas of similar or like nature.

(b) Corrosive Atmosphere. Agricultural buildings where a corrosive atmosphere exists. Such buildings include totally enclosed and environmentally controlled areas where (1) poultry and animal excrement may cause corrosive vapors in the confinement area; (2) corrosive particles may combine with water; (3) the area is damp and wet by reason of periodic washing for cleaning and sanitizing with water and cleansing agents; (4) similar conditions exist.

(c) Other Articles. For agricultural buildings not having conditions as specified in (a) or (b), the electrical installations shall be made in accordance with the applicable articles in this Code.

547-2. General. Electrical equipment or devices installed in accordance with the provisions of this article shall be installed in a manner such that they will function at full rating without developing surface temperatures in excess of the specified normal safe operating range of the equipment or device.

547-3. Wiring Methods. In agricultural buildings as described in Section 547-1(a) and (b), Types UF, NMC, SNM, or other cables or raceways suitable for the location, with approved termination fittings, shall be the wiring methods employed. Article 320 wiring methods shall be permitted for Section 547-1(a). Buildings wired in accordance with the provisions of Article 502 shall be permitted. All cables shall be secured within 8 inches (203 mm) of each cabinet, box, or fitting.

> When cables are installed in agricultural buildings, cables are required to be secured within 8 in. of cabinets, boxes, or fittings. This distance is less than that required for cables in other types of occupancies.

(a) Boxes, Fittings, and Wiring Devices. All boxes in which devices are installed, where taps, joints, or terminal connections are made shall be dust- and water-tight and shall be made of corrosion-resistant material.

(b) Flexible Connections. Where necessary to employ flexible connections, dusttight flexible connectors, liquidtight flexible metal conduit, or flexible cord approved for hard usage shall be used. All shall be used with approved fittings.

547-4. Switches, Circuit Breakers, Motor Controllers, and Fuses. Switches, circuit breakers, motor controllers, and fuses, including pushbuttons, relays and similar devices, used in buildings described in Section 547-1(a) and (b), shall be provided with a weatherproof, corrosion-resistant enclosure designed to minimize the entrance of dust, water, and corrosive elements, and shall be equipped with a telescoping or close-fitting cover.

547-5. Motors. Motors and other rotating electrical machinery shall be totally enclosed or so designed as to minimize the entrance of dust, moisture, or corrosive particles.

547-6. Lighting Fixtures. Lighting fixtures installed in agricultural buildings described in Section 547-1 shall comply with the following:

(a) Minimize the Entrance of Dust. Lighting fixtures shall be installed to minimize the entrance of dust, foreign matter, moisture, and corrosive material.

(b) Exposed to Physical Damage. Any lighting fixture that may be exposed to physical damage shall be protected by a suitable guard.

(c) Exposed to Water. A fixture that may be exposed to water from condensation and/or building cleansing water or solution shall be watertight.

547-7. Grounding. Grounding shall comply with Article 250.

(FPN): Bonding together of all separate grounding electrode systems will limit potential differences between them and between their associated wiring systems.

ARTICLE 550 — MOBILE HOMES
AND MOBILE HOME PARKS

Contents

550-1. Scope.

(a) Mobile Homes and Mobile Home Parks. The provisions of this article cover the electrical conductors and equipment installed within or on mobile homes, the conductors that connect mobile homes to a supply of electricity, and the installation of electrical wiring, fixtures, equipment, and appurtenances related to electrical installations within a mobile home park up to the mobile home service-entrance conductors or, if none, the mobile home service equipment.

Wherever the requirements of other articles of this Code and Article 550 differ, the requirements of Article 550 shall apply.

(b) Mobile Home Not Intended as a Dwelling Unit. A mobile home not intended as a dwelling unit, as for example equipped for sleeping purposes only, contractor's on-site offices, construction job dormitories, mobile studio dressing rooms, banks, clinics, mobile stores, or intended for the display or demonstration of merchandise or machinery, shall not be required to meet the provisions of this article pertaining to the number or capacity of circuits required. It shall, however, meet all other applicable requirements of this article if provided with an electrical installation intended to be energized from a 115-volt or 115/230-volt ac power supply system. Where different voltage is required by either design or available power supply system, adjustment shall be made in accordance with other articles and sections for the voltage used.

(c) In Other than Mobile Home Parks. Mobile homes installed in other than mobile home parks shall comply with the provisions of this article.

(d) Connection to Wiring System. The provisions of this article apply to mobile homes intended for connection to a wiring system rated 115/230-volts, nominal, 3-wire ac, with grounded neutral.

(e) Listed or Labeled. All electrical materials, devices, appliances, fittings, and other equipment shall be listed or labeled by a qualified testing agency and shall be connected in an approved manner when installed.

The Federal Mobile Home Construction and Safety Standard, issued by the Federal Housing and Urban Development Administration (HUD), has incorporated most of the provisions of Article 550 of the *NEC*. The federal standard contains the requirements for electrical systems, conductors, and equipment installed within or on mobile homes and the conductors that connect mobile homes to a supply of electricity.

The regulations pertaining to electrical systems are located in the Code of Federal Regulations, Title 24, Sections 3280.801 through 3280.816. It is required that new mobile homes comply with the federal standard. In some cases HUD has delegated the enforcement of this standard to state and private inspection agencies and to qualified testing laboratories.

550-2. Definitions.

Appliance, Fixed. An appliance which is fastened or otherwise secured at a specific location.

Appliance, Portable. An appliance which is actually moved or can easily be moved from one place to another in normal use.

(FPN): For the purpose of this article, the following major appliances other than built-in are considered portable if cord-connected: refrigerators, gas range equipment, clothes washers, dishwashers without booster heaters, or other similar appliances.

Appliance, Stationary. An appliance which is not easily moved from one place to another in normal use.

Distribution Panelboard. See definition of panelboard in Article 100.

Feeder Assembly. The overhead or under-chassis feeder conductors, including the grounding conductor, together with the necessary fittings and equipment or a power-supply cord approved for mobile home use, designed for the purpose of delivering energy from the source of electrical supply to the distribution panelboard within the mobile home.

Laundry Area. An area containing or designed to contain either a laundry tray, clothes washer, and/or a clothes dryer.

Mobile Home. A factory-assembled structure or structures equipped with the necessary service connections and made so as to be readily movable as a unit or units on its own running gear and designed to be used as a dwelling unit(s) without a permanent foundation.

(FPN): The phrase "without a permanent foundation" indicates that the support system is constructed with the intent that the mobile home placed thereon will be moved from time to time at the convenience of the owner.

ARTICLE 550—MOBILE HOMES AND MOBILE HOME PARKS

Mobile Home Accessory Building or Structure. Any awning, cabana, ramada, storage cabinet, carport, fence, windbreak, or porch established for the use of the occupant of the mobile home upon a mobile home lot.

Mobile Home Lot. A designated portion of a mobile home park designed for the accommodation of one mobile home and its accessory buildings or structures for the exclusive use of its occupants.

Mobile Home Park. A contiguous parcel of land which is used for the accommodation of occupied mobile homes.

Mobile Home Service Equipment. The equipment containing the disconnecting means, overcurrent protective devices, and receptacles or other means for connecting a mobile home feeder assembly.

Park Electrical Wiring Systems. All of the electrical wiring, fixtures, equipment, and appurtenances related to electrical installations within a mobile home park, including the mobile home service equipment.

A. Mobile Homes

550-3. Power Supply.

(a) Service Equipment. The mobile home service equipment shall be located adjacent to the mobile home and not mounted in or on the mobile home. The power supply to the mobile home shall be a feeder assembly consisting of not more than one approved 50-ampere mobile home power-supply cord with integral molded cap, or a permanently installed circuit.

Exception: A mobile home that is factory-equipped with gas or oil-fired central heating equipment and cooking appliances shall be permitted to be provided with an approved mobile home power-supply cord rated 40 amperes.

(b) Power-Supply Cord. If the mobile home has a power-supply cord, it shall be permanently attached to the distribution panelboard or to a junction box permanently connected to the distribution panelboard, with the free end terminating in an attachment plug cap.

(c) Cords. Cords with adapters and pigtail ends, extension cords, and similar items shall not be attached to, or shipped with, a mobile home.

(d) Suitable Clamp. A suitable clamp or the equivalent shall be provided at the distribution panelboard knockout to afford strain relief for the cord to prevent strain from being transmitted to the terminals when the power-supply cord is handled in its intended manner.

(e) Approved-type Cord. The cord used shall be of an approved type with four conductors, one of which shall be identified by a continuous green color or a continuous green color with one or more yellow stripes for use as the grounding conductor.

(f) Attachment Plug Cap. The attachment plug cap shall be a 3-pole, 4-wire, grounding type, rated 50 amperes, 125/250 volts with a configuration as shown in Figure 550-3(f) and intended for use with the 50-ampere, 125/250 receptacle configuration shown in Figure 550-3(f). It shall be molded of butyl rubber, neoprene, or other materials which have been found suitable for the purpose, and shall be molded to the flexible cord so that it adheres tightly to the cord at the point where the cord enters the attachment plug cap. If a right-angle cap is used, the configuration shall be so oriented that the grounding member is farthest from the cord.

(FPN): Complete details of the 50-ampere plug and receptacle shown in Figure 550-3(f) can be found in ANSI Standard Dimensions of Caps, Plugs and Receptacles, C73.17-1972.

Figure 550-3(f). 50-ampere, 125/250 volt receptacle and attachment-plug-cap configurations, 3-pole, 4-wire, grounding types, used for mobile home supply cords and mobile home parks.

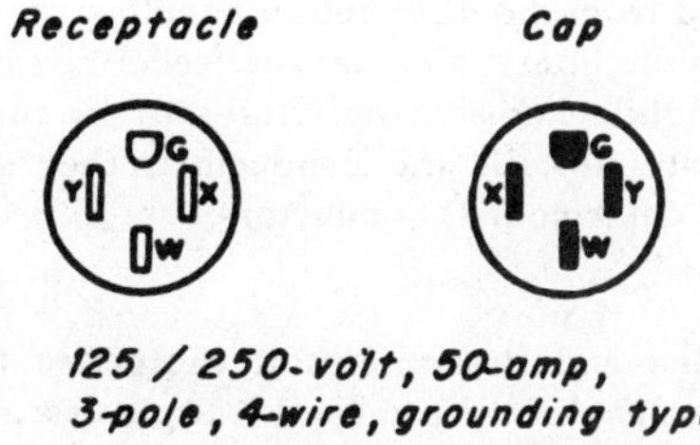

Receptacle   *Cap*

125 / 250-volt, 50-amp,
3-pole, 4-wire, grounding type

(g) Overall Length of a Power-Supply Cord. The overall length of a power-supply cord, measured from the end of the cord, including bared leads, to the face of the attachment plug cap shall not be less than 21 feet (6.4 m) and shall not exceed 36½ feet (11.13 m). The length of the cord from the face of the attachment plug cap to the point where the cord enters the mobile home shall not be less than 20 feet (6.1 m).

(h) Marking. The power-supply cord shall bear the following marking: "For use with mobile homes — 40 amperes" or "For use with mobile homes — 50 amperes."

(i) Point of Entrance. The point of entrance of the feeder assembly to the mobile home shall be in the exterior wall, floor, or roof.

> **This section permits the point of entrance of the power supply to the mobile home to be in locations other than the rear third of the mobile home. This allows greater flexibility in selecting the location of the power supply entry at the manufacturing level to fit the needs of the installation site, thus minimizing field modifications.**

(FPN): For location of distribution panelboard, see Section 550-4(a).

(FPN): For location of attachment of feeder assembly, see Section 550-23(d).

(j) Protected. Where the cord passes through walls or floors, it shall be protected by means of conduits and bushings or equivalent. The cord shall be permitted to be installed within the mobile home walls, provided a continuous raceway having a maximum size of 1¼ inches (31.8 mm) is installed from the branch-circuit panelboard to the underside of the mobile home floor.

(k) Protection Against Corrosion and Mechanical Damage. Permanent provisions shall be made for the protection of the attachment plug cap of the power-supply cord and any connector cord assembly or receptacle against corrosion and mechanical damage if such devices are in an exterior location while the mobile home is in transit.

(l) Mast Weatherhead or Metal Raceway. Where the calculated load exceeds 50 amperes or where a permanent feeder is used, the supply shall be by means of:

(1) One mast weatherhead installation installed in accordance with Article 230 containing four continuous, insulated, color-coded, feeder conductors, one of which shall be an equipment grounding conductor; or,

(2) A metal raceway from the disconnecting means in the mobile home to the underside of the mobile home with provisions for the attachment to a suitable junction box or fitting to the raceway on the underside of the mobile home [with or without conductors as in Section 550-3(l)(1)].

ARTICLE 550—MOBILE HOMES AND MOBILE HOME PARKS

In some localities mobile homes are permanently connected, as permitted in Section 550-3(1). In this regard local requirements must be checked for the approved method of installing overhead and underground feeder assemblies.

A raceway is required from the distribution panelboard in the mobile home to the underside of the mobile home. Whether the feeder conductors in this raceway are pulled in by the mobile home manufacturer or by installers in the field is optional. No matter who installs the conductors, they should comprise four continuous, insulated, color-coded conductors, as indicated in Section 550-3(1)(1).

550-4. Disconnecting Means and Branch-Circuit Protective Equipment. The branch-circuit equipment shall be permitted to be combined with the disconnecting means as a single assembly. Such a combination shall be permitted to be designated as a distribution panelboard. If a fused distribution panelboard is used, the maximum fuse size for the mains shall be plainly marked, with lettering at least ¼ inch (6.4 mm) high and visible when fuses are changed.

When plug fuses and fuseholders are used, they shall be tamper-resistant, Type S enclosed in dead-front fuse panelboards. Electrical distribution panelboards containing circuit breakers shall also be dead-front type.

(FPN): See Section 110-22 concerning identification of each disconnecting means and each service, feeder, or branch circuit at the point where it originated and the type marking needed.

(a) Disconnecting Means. A single disconnecting means shall be provided in each mobile home consisting of a circuit breaker, or a switch and fuses and its accessories installed in a readily accessible location near the point of entrance of the supply cord or conductors into the mobile home. The main circuit breakers or fuses shall be plainly marked "Main." This equipment shall contain a solderless type of grounding connector or bar for the purposes of grounding with sufficient terminals for all grounding conductors. The neutral bar termination of the grounded circuit conductors shall be insulated. The disconnecting equipment shall have a rating suitable for the connected load. The distribution equipment, either circuit breaker or fused type, shall be located a minimum of 24 inches (610 mm) from the bottom of such equipment to the floor level of the mobile home.

(FPN): See Section 550-13(b) for information on disconnecting means for branch circuits designed to energize heating and/or air-conditioning equipment located outside the mobile home, other than room air conditioners.

A distribution panelboard main circuit breaker shall be rated 50 amperes and employ a 2-pole circuit breaker rated 40 amperes for a 40-ampere supply cord, or 50 amperes for a 50-ampere supply cord. A distribution panelboard employing a disconnect switch and fuses shall be rated 60 amperes and shall employ a single 2-pole, 60-ampere fuseholder with 40- or 50-ampere main fuses for 40- or 50-ampere supply cords, respectively. The outside of the distribution panelboard shall be plainly marked with the fuse size.

The distribution panelboard shall be located in an accessible location, shall not be located in a bathroom, and shall be permitted to be located just inside a closet entry if the location is such that a clear space of 6 inches (152 mm) to easily ignitible materials is maintained in front of the distribution panelboard, and the distribution panelboard door can be extended to its full open position (at least 90 degrees). A clear working space at least 30 inches (762 mm) wide and 30 inches (762 mm) in front of the distribution panelboard shall be provided. This space shall extend from floor to the top of the distribution panelboard.

(b) Branch-Circuit Protective Equipment. Branch-circuit distribution equipment shall be installed in each mobile home and shall include overcurrent protection for each branch circuit consisting of either circuit breakers or fuses.

The branch-circuit overcurrent devices shall be rated: (1) not more than the circuit conductors; and (2) not more than 150 percent of the rating of a single appliance rated 13.3 amperes or more which is supplied by an individual branch circuit; but (3) not more than the fuse size marked on the air conditioner or other motor-operated appliance.

A 15-ampere multiple receptacle shall be acceptable when connected to a 20-ampere laundry circuit.

(c) Two-Pole Circuit Breakers. When circuit breakers are provided for branch-circuit protection, 230-volt circuits shall be protected by a 2-pole common or companion trip, or handle-tied paired circuit breakers.

(d) Electrical Nameplates. A metal nameplate on the outside adjacent to the feeder assembly entrance shall read: "This Connection for 120/240-Volt, 3-Pole, 4-Wire, 60 Hertz, . . . Ampere Supply." The correct ampere rating shall be marked in the blank space.

550-5. Branch Circuits. The number of branch circuits required shall be determined in accordance with (a) through (c) below.

(a) Lighting. Based on 3 watts per square foot (0.093 sq m) times outside dimensions of the mobile home (coupler excluded) divided by 115 volts to determine the number of 15- or 20-ampere lighting area circuits, e.g.,

$$\frac{3 \times \text{Length} \times \text{Width}}{115 \times 15 \text{ (or 20)}} = \text{No. of 15- (or 20-) ampere circuits.}$$

The lighting circuits shall be permitted to serve built-in gas ovens with electric service only for lights, clocks or timers, or listed cord-connected garbage disposal units.

(b) Small Appliances. For the small appliance load in kitchen, pantry, family room, dining room, and breakfast rooms of mobile homes, two or more 20-ampere appliance branch circuits in addition to the branch circuits specified in Section 550-5(a) shall be provided for all receptacle outlets in these rooms, and such circuits shall have no other outlets. Receptacle outlets supplied by at least two appliance receptacle branch circuits shall be installed in the kitchen.

(c) General Appliances. (Including furnace, water heater, range, and central or room air conditioner, etc.) There shall be one or more circuits of adequate rating in accordance with the following:

(1) Ampere rating of fixed appliances not over 50 percent of circuit rating if lighting outlets (receptacles, other than kitchen, dining area, and laundry, considered as lighting outlets) are on the same circuit;

(2) For fixed appliances on a circuit without lighting outlets, the sum of rated amperes shall not exceed the branch-circuit rating. Motor loads or other continuous duty loads shall not exceed 80 percent of the branch-circuit rating;

(3) The rating of a single cord- and plug-connected appliance on a circuit having no other outlets shall not exceed 80 percent of the circuit rating;

(4) The rating of a range branch circuit shall be based on the range demand as specified for ranges in Section 550-11(b)(5).

(FPN): For the laundry branch circuit, see Section 220-3(c).

(FPN): For central air conditioning, see Article 440.

550-6. Receptacle Outlets.

(a) **Grounding-type Receptacle Outlets.** All receptacle outlets: (1) shall be of grounding type; (2) shall be installed according to Section 210-7; and (3) except when supplying specific appliances, receptacles shall be parallel-blade, 15-ampere, 125-volt, either single or duplex.

(b) **Ground-Fault Circuit-Interrupters.** All 120-volt, single-phase, 15- and 20-ampere receptacle outlets installed outdoors and in bathrooms, including receptacles in light fixtures, shall have ground-fault circuit protection for personnel. Ground-fault circuit protection for personnel shall be provided for receptacle outlets located adjacent to any lavatory. Feeders supplying branch circuits shall be permitted to be protected by a ground-fault circuit-interrupter in lieu of the provision for such interrupters specified herein.

No receptacle shall be required in the area occupied by a toilet, toilet and/or shower, or toilet and tub/shower enclosure area. If a receptacle is installed in such an area, it shall have ground-fault circuit protection for personnel.

(c) **Cord-Connected Fixed Appliance.** There shall be an individual outlet of the grounding type for each cord-connected fixed appliance installed.

(d) **Required Receptacle Outlets.** Receptacle outlets required in all rooms other than the bath, closet, and hall areas shall be installed so that no point along the floor line is more than 6 feet (1.83 m) measured horizontally from an outlet in that space. Countertops shall have receptacles located every 6 feet (1.83 m). The contiguous measurement of countertop and floor line shall be permitted when measured from the required receptacle in rooms requiring small appliance circuits. Receptacle outlets on small appliance circuits shall not be included in determining the spacing for receptacle outlets of other circuits.

Exception No. 1: Where the measured distance is interrupted by an interior doorway, sink, refrigerator, range, oven, or cooktop, an additional receptacle outlet shall be provided when the interrupted space is at least 2 feet (610 mm) wide at the floor line and at least 12 inches (305 mm) wide at the countertop.

Exception No. 2: Receptacles concealed by stationary appliances shall not be considered as the required outlets.

Exception No. 3: The distance along a floor line occupied by a door opened fully against that space need not be included in establishing the horizontal measurement if the door swing is limited to 90 degrees nominal by that wall space.

Exception No. 4: Receptacle requirements for bar-type counters and for fixed room dividers no more than 8 feet (2.44 m) in length shall be permitted to be provided by a receptacle outlet in the wall at the nearest point where the counter or room divider attaches to the wall.

(FPN): To qualify as a "fixed room divider" the divider cannot be more than 8 feet (2.44 m) in length nor more than 4 feet (1.22 m) in height and may be attached to a wall at one end only.

(e) **Outdoor Receptacle Outlets.** At least one receptacle outlet shall be installed outdoors. A receptacle outlet located in a compartment accessible from the outside of the mobile home shall be considered an outdoor receptacle. Outdoor receptacle outlets shall be protected as required in Section 550-6(b).

(f) **Receptacle Outlets Not Permitted.** Receptacle outlets shall not be installed in or within reach [30 inches (762 mm)] of a shower or bathtub space.

(g) Heat Tape Outlet. A heat tape outlet, if installed, and if located on the underside of the mobile home at least 3 feet (914 mm) from the outside edge, shall not be considered an outdoor receptacle outlet. A heat tape outlet, if installed, shall be located within 2 feet (610 mm) of the cold water inlet.

550-7. Fixtures and Appliances.

(a) Fasten Appliances in Transit. Facilities shall be provided to securely fasten appliances when the mobile home is in transit. (See Section 550-9 for provisions on grounding.)

(1) Specifically approved pendant-type fixtures or pendant cords shall be permitted in mobile homes.

(2) Where a lighting fixture is installed over a bathtub or in a shower stall, it shall be of the enclosed and gasketed type approved for wet locations.

(3) The switch for shower lighting fixtures and exhaust fans located over a tub or in a shower stall shall be located outside the tub or shower space.

(b) Accessibility. Every appliance shall be accessible for inspection, service, repair, or replacement without removal of permanent construction.

550-8. Wiring Methods and Materials.
Except as specifically limited in this section, the wiring methods and materials included in this Code shall be used in mobile homes.

(a) Nonmetallic Outlet Boxes. Nonmetallic outlet boxes shall be acceptable only with nonmetallic cable.

(b) Nonmetallic Cable Protection. Nonmetallic cable located 15 inches (381 mm) or less above the floor, if exposed, shall be protected from physical damage by covering boards, guard strips, or conduit. Cable likely to be damaged by stowage shall be so protected in all cases.

(c) Metal-Clad and Nonmetallic Cable Protection. Metal-clad and nonmetallic cables shall be permitted to pass through the centers of the wide side of 2-inch by 4-inch studs. However, they shall be protected where they pass through 2-inch by 2-inch studs or at other studs or frames where the cable or armor would be less than 1½ inches (38 mm) from the inside or outside surface of the studs where the wall covering materials are in contact with the studs. Steel plates on each side of the cable, or a tube, with not less than No. 16 MSG wall thickness shall be required to protect the cable. These plates or tubes shall be securely held in place.

(d) Metallic Faceplates. Where metallic faceplates are used, they shall be effectively grounded.

(e) Installation Requirements. If a range, clothes dryer, or similar appliance is connected by metal-clad cable or flexible metal conduit, a length of free cable or conduit shall be provided to permit moving the appliance. The cable or flexible metal conduit shall be adequately secured to the wall. A length of not less than 3 feet (914 mm) of free cable or conduit shall be provided to permit moving the appliance. Type NM or Type SE cable shall not be used to connect a range or dryer. This shall not prohibit the use of Type NM or Type SE cable between the branch-circuit overcurrent protective device and a junction box or range or dryer receptacle.

(f) Metal Conduit. Threaded rigid metal conduit and intermediate metal conduit shall be provided with a locknut inside and outside the box, and a conduit bushing shall be used on the inside. Rigid nonmetallic conduit shall be permitted. Inside ends of the conduit shall be reamed.

(g) Switches. Switches shall be rated as follows:

(1) For lighting circuits, switches shall have a 10-ampere, 120- 125-volt rating, or higher, if needed for the connected load.

(2) For motors or other loads, switches shall have ampere or horsepower ratings, or both, adequate for loads controlled. (An "ac general-use" snap switch shall be permitted to control a motor 2 horsepower or less with full-load current not over 80 percent of the switch ampere rating.)

(h) Free Conductor at Each Outlet Box. At least 4 inches (102 mm) of free conductor shall be left at each outlet box except where conductors are intended to loop without joints.

(i) Under-Chassis Wiring. (Exposed to weather.)

(1) Where outdoor or under-chassis line-voltage wiring is exposed to moisture or physical damage, it shall be protected by rigid metal conduit or intermediate metal conduit. The conductors shall be suitable for wet locations.

Exception: Electrical metallic tubing shall be permitted where closely routed against frames and equipment enclosures.

(2) The cables or conductors shall be Type NMC, TW, or equivalent.

(j) Boxes, Fittings, and Cabinets. Boxes, fittings, and cabinets shall be securely fastened in place and shall be supported from a structural member of the home, either directly or by using a substantial brace.

Exception: Snap-in type boxes. Boxes provided with special wall or ceiling brackets and wiring devices with integral enclosures, which securely fasten to walls or ceilings and are identified for the use, shall be permitted without support from a structural member or brace. The testing and approval shall include the wall and ceiling construction systems for which the boxes and devices are intended to be used.

(k) Appliance Terminal Connections. Appliances having branch-circuit terminal connections which operate at temperatures higher than 60°C (140°F) shall have circuit conductors as described in (1) or (2) below.

(1) Branch-circuit conductors having an insulation suitable for the temperature encountered shall be permitted to be run directly to the appliance.

(2) Conductors having an insulation suitable for the temperature encountered shall be run from the appliance terminal connection to a readily accessible outlet box placed at least 1 foot (305 mm) from the appliance. These conductors shall be in a suitable raceway which shall extend for at least 4 feet (1.22 m).

(l) Component Interconnections. Fittings and connectors which are intended to be concealed at the time of assembly, when tested and approved to applicable standards, shall be permitted for the interconnection of building components. Such fittings and connectors shall be equal to the wiring method employed in insulation, temperature rise, fault-current withstanding, and shall be capable of enduring the vibration and shock occurring in mobile home transportation.

550-9. Grounding. Grounding of both electrical and nonelectrical metal parts in a mobile home shall be through connection to a grounding bus in the mobile home distribution panelboard. The grounding bus shall be grounded through the green-colored insulated conductor in the supply cord or the feeder wiring to the service ground in the service-entrance equipment located adjacent to the mobile home location. Neither the frame of the mobile home nor the frame of any appliance shall be connected to the neutral conductor in the mobile home.

(a) Insulated Neutral.

(1) The grounded circuit conductor (neutral) shall be insulated from the grounding conductors and from equipment enclosures and other grounded parts. The grounded (neutral) circuit terminals in the distribution panelboard and in ranges, clothes dryers, counter-mounted cooking units, and wall-mounted ovens shall be insulated from the equipment enclosure. Bonding screws, straps, or buses in the distribution panelboard or in appliances shall be removed and discarded.

(2) Connections of ranges and clothes dryers with 115/230-volt, 3-wire ratings shall be made with 4-conductor cord and 3-pole, 4-wire, grounding-type plugs, or by Type AC cable or conductors enclosed in flexible metal conduit.

For 115-volt rated devices, a 3-conductor cord and a 2-pole, 3-wire, grounding-type plug shall be permitted.

(b) Equipment Grounding Means.

(1) The green-colored insulated grounding wire in the supply cord or permanent feeder wiring shall be connected to the grounding bus in the distribution panelboard or disconnecting means.

(2) In the electrical system, all exposed metal parts, enclosures, frames, lamp fixture canopies, etc., shall be effectively bonded to the grounding terminal or enclosure of the distribution panelboard.

(3) Cord-connected appliances, such as washing machines, clothes dryers, refrigerators, and the electrical system of gas ranges, etc., shall be grounded by means of a cord with grounding conductor and grounding-type attachment plug.

(c) Bonding of Noncurrent-Carrying Metal Parts.

(1) All exposed noncurrent-carrying metal parts that may become energized shall be effectively bonded to the grounding terminal or enclosure of the distribution panelboard. A bonding conductor shall be connected between the distribution panelboard and accessible terminal on the chassis.

(2) Grounding terminals shall be of the solderless type and approved as pressure-terminal connectors recognized for the wire size used. The bonding conductor shall be solid or stranded, insulated or bare, and shall be No. 8 copper minimum, or equal. The bonding conductor shall be routed so as not to be exposed to physical damage.

(3) Metallic gas, water, and waste pipes and metallic air-circulating ducts shall be considered bonded if they are connected to the terminal on the chassis [see Section 550-9(c)(1)] by clamps, solderless connectors, or by suitable grounding-type straps.

(4) Any metallic roof and exterior covering shall be considered bonded if (a) the metal panels overlap one another and are securely attached to the wood or metal frame parts by metallic fasteners, and (b) if the lower panel of the metallic exterior covering is secured by metallic fasteners at a cross member of the chassis by two metal straps per mobile home unit or section at opposite ends.

The bonding strap material shall be a minimum of 4 inches (102 mm) in width of material equivalent to the skin or a material of equal or better electrical conductivity. The straps shall be fastened with paint-penetrating fittings, such as screws and starwashers or equivalent.

ARTICLE 550—MOBILE HOMES AND MOBILE HOME PARKS

The provisions of Section 550-3 require that the feeder assembly for a mobile home consist of four color-coded insulated conductors, one of which is the grounded conductor (white) and one of which is used for grounding purposes (green). Thus, the "grounded" and "grounding" conductors are kept independent of each other and are connected only at the service equipment (at the point of connection of the grounding electrode conductor). Grounding of both electrical and nonelectrical metal parts, including the frame of the mobile home or the frame of any appliance, is accomplished by connection to the equipment grounding bus [never to the grounded conductor (neutral bus)].

Bonding screws, straps, or buses which bond the grounded (neutral) circuit conductors to the noncurrent-carrying metal parts in the mobile home panelboard or in appliances (ranges, clothes dryers, etc.) are to be removed and discarded.

550-10. Testing.

(a) Dielectric Strength Test. The wiring of each mobile home shall be subjected to a 1-minute, 900-volt, dielectric strength test (with all switches closed) between live parts (including neutral) and the mobile home ground. Alternatively, the test shall be permitted to be performed at 1,080 volts for 1 second. This test shall be performed after branch circuits are complete and after fixtures or appliances are installed.

Exception: Fixtures or appliances which are approved shall not be required to withstand the dielectric strength test.

(b) Continuity and Operational Tests and Polarity Checks. Each mobile home shall be subjected to:

(1) An electrical continuity test to assure that all exposed electrically conductive parts are properly bonded;

(2) An electrical operational test to demonstrate that all equipment, except water heaters and electric furnaces, is connected and in working order; and

(3) Electrical polarity checks of permanently wired equipment and receptacle outlets to determine that connections have been properly made.

550-11. Calculations.
The following method shall be employed in computing the supply-cord and distribution-panelboard load for each feeder assembly for each mobile home in lieu of the procedure shown in Article 220 and shall be based on a 3-wire, 115/230-volt supply with 115-volt loads balanced between the two legs of the 3-wire system.

(a) Lighting and Small Appliance Load:
Lighting Volt-Amperes: Length times width of mobile home floor (outside dimensions) times 3 volt-amperes per square foot; e.g.,
Length × width × 3 =..................lighting volt-amperes.
Small Appliance Volt-Amperes: Number of circuits times 1,500 volt-amperes for each 20-ampere appliance receptacle circuit (see definition of Appliance, Portable with note) including 1,500 volt-amperes for laundry circuit; e.g.,
Number of circuits × 1,500 =..............small appliance volt-amperes.
Total: Lighting volt-amperes plus small appliance =...................total volt-amperes.
First 3,000 total volt-amperes at 100 percent plus remainder at 35 percent =...................volt-amperes to be divided by 230 volts to obtain current (amperes) per leg.

(b) Total Load for Determining Power Supply. Total load for determining power supply is the summation of:

(1) Lighting and small appliance load as calculated in Section 550-11(a).

(2) Nameplate amperes for motors and heater loads (exhaust fans, air conditioners, electric, gas, or oil heating).

Omit smaller of the heating and cooling loads, except include blower motor if used as air-conditioner evaporator motor. Where an air conditioner is not installed and a 40-ampere power supply cord is provided, allow 15 amperes per leg for air conditioning.

(3) 25 percent of current of largest motor in (2).

(4) Total of nameplate amperes for: disposal, dishwasher, water heater, clothes dryer, wall-mounted oven, cooking units.

Where number of these appliances exceeds three, use 75 percent of total.

(5) Derive amperes for free-standing range (as distinguished from separate ovens and cooking units) by dividing values below by 230 volts.

Nameplate Rating	Use
10,000 watts or less	80 percent of rating
10,001-12,500 watts	8,000 volt-amperes
12,501-13,500 watts	8,400 volt-amperes
13,501-14,500 watts	8,800 volt-amperes
14,501-15,500 watts	9,200 volt-amperes
15,501-16,500 watts	9,600 volt-amperes
16,501-17,500 watts	10,000 volt-amperes

(6) If outlets or circuits are provided for other than factory-installed appliances, include the anticipated load.

See following Example for illustration of application of this calculation.

Example

A mobile home floor is 70 feet × 10 feet and has two portable appliance circuits, a 1000 watt 230 volt heater, a 200 watt 115 volt exhaust fan, a 400 watt 115 volt dishwasher, and a 7000 watt electric range.

Lighting and small appliance load

Lighting 70 × 10 × 3 VA/sq ft =	2100 volt-amperes
Small appliance 1500 × 2 =	3000 volt-amperes
Laundry 1500 × 1 =	1500 volt-amperes
	6600 volt-amperes

1st 3000 volt-amperes at 100 percent	3000
Remainder (6600 − 3000 = 3600) at 35 percent	1260
	4260

$\frac{4260}{230} = 18.5$ amperes per leg

			Amperes per leg	
			A	B
		Lighting and appliances	18.5	18.5
1000 watt heater ÷ 230 =	4.4 amp	Heater (230 volt)	4	4
200 watt (fan) ÷ 115 =	1.7 amp	Fan (115 volt)	2	—
400 watt (dishwasher) ÷ 115 =	3.5 amp	Dishwasher (115 volt)	—	4
7000 watt (range) × .8 ÷ 230 =	24. amp	Range	24	24
		Totals	48.5	50.5

Based on the higher current calculated for either leg, use one 50-ampere supply cord.

(c) Optional Method of Calculation for Lighting and Appliance Load. For mobile homes, the optional method for calculating lighting and appliance load shown in Section 220-30 and Table 220-30 shall be permitted.

550-12. Interconnection of Multiple Section Mobile Home Units.

(a) Fixed-type Wiring. Approved and listed fixed-type wiring methods shall be used to join portions of a circuit which must be electrically joined which are located in adjacent sections of mobile homes after the home is installed on its support foundation. The circuit's junction shall be accessible for disassembly when the home is prepared for relocation.

(b) Disconnecting Means. Multiple section mobile homes not having permanently installed feeders, and which are to be moved from one location to another, shall be permitted to have disconnecting means with branch-circuit protective equipment in each unit when so located that after assembly or joining together of units, they shall not be interconnected on either the line side or the load side, except that the grounding means shall be electrically interconnected.

(FPN): Subsection (b) above applies to connection of previously constructed mobile homes where multiple feeder assemblies were allowed. The present Code does not permit more than one cord or feeder to a mobile home.

550-13. Outdoor Outlets, Fixtures, Air-Cooling Equipment, Etc.

(a) Approved for Outdoor Use. Outdoor fixtures and equipment shall be approved for outdoor use. Outdoor receptacle or convenience outlets shall be of a gasketed-cover type for use in wet locations.

(b) Outside Heating and/or Air-Conditioning Equipment. A mobile home provided with a branch circuit designed to energize heating and/or air-conditioning equipment located outside the mobile home, other than room air conditioners, shall have such branch-circuit conductors terminate in a listed outlet box, or disconnecting means, located on the outside of the mobile home. A label shall be permanently affixed adjacent to the outlet box and contain the following information:

> This connection is for heating and/or air-conditioning equipment. The branch circuit is rated at not more than _____ amperes, at _____ volts, 60-Hertz, _____ conductor ampacity. A disconnecting means shall be located within sight of the equipment.

The correct voltage and ampere rating shall be given. The tag shall be not less than 0.020 inch (508 micrometers), etched brass, stainless steel, anodized or alclad aluminum or equivalent. The tag shall not be less than 3 inches (76 mm) by 1¾ inches (44.5 mm) minimum size.

B. Mobile Home Parks

550-21. Distribution System.
The mobile home park secondary electrical distribution system to mobile home lots shall be single-phase, 120/240 volts, nominal. For the purpose of Part B, where the park service exceeds 240 volts, nominal, transformers and secondary distribution panelboards shall be treated as services.

(FPN): See Table 550-22 for calculation of load.

Section 550-1(d) applies to mobile homes intended for connection to a wiring system nominally rated 115/230 V, 3 wire ac, with a grounded neutral; therefore, distribution systems at mobile home parks must supply 115/230 V to the mobile home lot. Because appliances and other equipment are usually installed during the manufacturing process of mobile homes and are rated 115/230 V, a 120/208-V supply derived from a 4-wire, 120/208-V wye system is unsuitable.

Section 550-22(a) requires park electrical wiring systems to be calculated on the basis of not less than 16,000 VA (at 115/230 V) for each mobile home service; however, the ampacity of the feeder circuit conductors to each mobile home lot is not to be less than 100 A (at 115/230 V) according to Section 550-22(c).

550-22. Calculated Load.

(a) Minimum Allowable Demand Factors. Park electrical wiring systems shall be calculated on the basis of not less than 16,000 volt-amperes (at 115/230 volts) per each mobile home service. The demand factors which are set forth in Table 550-22 shall be considered the minimum allowable demand factors which shall be permitted in calculating load on feeders and service. No demand factor shall be allowed for any other load, except as provided in this Code.

Table 550-22
Demand Factors and Volt-Amperes per Mobile Home Site (Minimum) for Feeders and Service-Entrance Conductors

Number of Mobile Homes	Demand Factor (Percent)	Volt-Amperes per Mobile Home Site (Min.)
1	100	16,000
2	55	8,800
3	44	7,040
4	39	6,240
5	33	5,280
6	29	4,640
7-9	28	4,480
10-12	27	4,320
13-15	26	4,160
16-21	25	4,000
22-40	24	3,840
41-60	23	3,680
61 and over	22	3,520

(b) Demand Factor Shall Apply to All Lots. The demand factor for a given number of lots shall apply to all lots indicated.

Example: 20 lots calculated at 25 percent of 16,000 volt-amperes result in a permissible demand of 4,000 volt-amperes per lot or a total of 80,000 volt-amperes for 20 lots.

(c) Adequate Feeder Capacity. Mobile home lot feeder circuit conductors shall have adequate capacity for the loads supplied, and shall be rated at not less than 100 amperes at 115/230 volts.

See commentary following Section 550-21.

550-23. Mobile Home Service Equipment.

(a) Rating. Mobile home service equipment shall be rated at not less than 100 amperes, and provision shall be made for connecting a mobile home feeder assembly by a permanent wiring method. Power outlets used as mobile home service equipment shall also be permitted to contain receptacles rated up to 50 amperes with appropriate overcurrent protection. Fifty-ampere receptacles shall conform to the configuration shown in Figure 550-3(f).

(FPN): Complete details on the 50-ampere attachment plug cap configuration can be found in American National Standard Dimensions of Caps, Plugs and Receptacles, ANSI C73.17-1972.

(b) Additional Outside Electrical Equipment. Mobile home service equipment shall also contain a means for connecting a mobile home accessory building or structure or additional electrical equipment located outside a mobile home by a fixed wiring method.

(c) Additional Receptacles. Additional receptacles shall be permitted for connection of electrical equipment located outside the mobile home, and all such 125-volt, single-phase, 15- and 20-ampere receptacles shall be protected by approved ground-fault circuit protection for personnel.

(d) Location. Mobile home service equipment shall be readily accessible and shall be located in sight from and not more than 30 feet (9.14 m) from the exterior wall of the mobile home it serves.

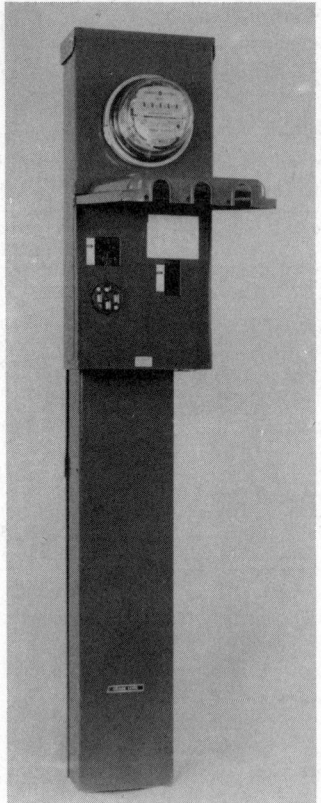

Figure 550-1. Mobile home service equipment and power outlet assembly showing metering, disconnecting means, overcurrent protective devices, and receptacle. (*Midwest*)

This section was revised for the 1984 *Code*. It now requires that the mobile home service equipment be located in sight from the mobile home, but permits the equipment to be not more than 30 ft from any point on the exterior wall of the mobile home. This recognizes use of feeder raceways external to the mobile home.

(e) Grounded. Each mobile home service equipment shall be grounded in accordance with Article 250 for service equipment.

550-24. Feeder. Mobile home feeder equipment shall consist of an approved type cord factory-installed in accordance with Section 550-3(e), or a permanently installed feeder containing four continuous, insulated, color-coded conductors, one of which shall be identified by a continuous solid green color of insulation or by factory coloring or painting the insulation green.

ARTICLE 551 — RECREATIONAL VEHICLES
AND RECREATIONAL VEHICLE PARKS

Contents

A. Recreational Vehicles

551-1. Scope.

(a) Covered. The provisions of Part A cover the electrical conductors and equipment installed within or on recreational vehicles and also the conductors that connect them to a supply of electricity. Wherever the requirements of other articles of this Code and Article 551 differ, the requirements of Article 551 shall apply.

(FPN): For requirements on the installation of plumbing and heating systems in recreational vehicles, refer to Standard for Recreational Vehicles, NFPA 501C-1982 (ANSI).

(b) Not Covered. A recreational vehicle not used for the purposes as defined in Section 551-2 shall not be required to meet the provisions of Part A pertaining to the number or capacity of circuits required. It shall, however, meet all other applicable requirements of this article if the recreational vehicle is provided with an electrical installation intended to be energized from a 115- or 115/230-volt, nominal, ac power-supply system.

(c) Systems. Part A covers battery and direct-current power (12-volt or less) systems, combination electrical systems, generator installations, and 115- or 115/230-volt, nominal, systems.

Laws in some states require factory inspection by state inspectors. The requirements of such laws follow closely the requirements of NFPA 501C, Standard for Recreational Vehicles. Section 1-5 in NFPA 501C specifies that electrical installations in recreational vehicles shall comply with Part A of Article 551 of the *Code*.

551-2. Definitions. (See Article 100 for other definitions.)

Air-Conditioning or Comfort-Cooling Equipment. All of that equipment intended or installed for the purpose of processing the treatment of air so as to control simultaneously its temperature, humidity, cleanliness, and distribution to meet the requirements of the conditioned space.

Appliance, Fixed. An appliance which is fastened or otherwise secured at a specific location.

Appliance, Portable. An appliance which is actually moved or can easily be moved from one place to another in normal use.

(FPN): For the purpose of this article, the following major appliances other than built-in are considered portable if cord-connected: refrigerators, gas range equipment, clothes washers, dishwashers without booster heaters, or other similar appliances.

Appliance, Stationary. An appliance which is not easily moved from one place to another in normal use.

Camping Trailer. A vehicular portable unit mounted on wheels and constructed with collapsible partial side walls which fold for towing by another vehicle and unfold at the campsite to provide temporary living quarters for recreational, camping, or travel use. (See "Recreational Vehicle.")

Converter. A device which changes electrical energy from one form to another, as from alternating current to direct current.

Dead Front. (As applied to switches, circuit breakers, switchboards, and distribution panelboards.) So designed, constructed, and installed that no current-carrying parts are normally exposed on the front.

Disconnecting Means. The necessary equipment usually consisting of a circuit breaker or switch and fuses, and their accessories, located near the point of entrance of supply conductors in a recreational vehicle and intended to constitute the means of cutoff for the supply to that recreational vehicle.

Receptacles used as disconnecting means shall be accessible (as applied to wiring methods) and capable of interrupting their rated current without hazard to the operator.

Distribution Panelboard. A single panel or group of panel units designed for assembly in the form of a single panel; including buses, and with or without switches and/or automatic overcurrent protective devices for the control of light, heat, or power circuits of small individual as well as aggregate capacity; designed to be placed in a cabinet or cutout box placed in or against a wall or partition and accessible only from the front.

ARTICLE 551—RECREATIONAL VEHICLES, PARKS

Low-Voltage. An electromotive force rated nominal 24 volts, nominal, or less, supplied from a transformer, converter, or battery.

Motor Home. A vehicular unit designed to provide temporary living quarters for recreational, camping, or travel use built on or permanently attached to a self-propelled motor vehicle chassis or on a chassis cab or van which is an integral part of the completed vehicle. (See "Recreational Vehicle.")

Power-Supply Assembly. The conductors, including the grounding conductors, insulated from one another, the connectors, attachment plug caps, and all other fittings, grommets, or devices installed for the purpose of delivering energy from the source of electrical supply to the distribution panel within the recreational vehicle.

Recreational Vehicle. A vehicular-type unit primarily designed as temporary living quarters for recreational, camping, or travel use, which either has its own motive power or is mounted on or drawn by another vehicle. The basic entities are: travel trailer, camping trailer, truck camper, and motor home.

Transformer. A device, which when used, will raise or lower the voltage of alternating current of the original source.

Travel Trailer. A vehicular unit mounted on wheels, designed to provide temporary living quarters for recreational, camping, or travel use, of such size or weight as not to require special highway movement permits when drawn by a motorized vehicle, and with a living area of less than 220 square feet (20.44 sq m), excluding built-in equipment (such as wardrobes, closets, cabinets, kitchen units or fixtures) and bath and toilet rooms. (See "Recreational Vehicle.")

Truck Camper. A portable unit constructed to provide temporary living quarters for recreational, travel, or camping use, consisting of a roof, floor, and sides, designed to be loaded onto and unloaded from the bed of a pick-up truck. (See "Recreational Vehicle.")

551-3. Low-Voltage Systems.

(a) Low-Voltage Circuits. Low-voltage circuits furnished and installed by the recreational vehicle manufacturer, other than those related to braking, are subject to this Code. Circuits supplying lights subject to federal or state regulations shall be in accordance with applicable government regulations, but shall not be lower than provided by this Code.

(b) Low-Voltage Wiring.

(1) Copper conductors shall be used for low-voltage circuits.

Exception: Metal chassis or frame shall be permitted as the return path for exterior lighting. Terminals for connection to the chassis or frame shall be of the solderless type and approved for the size and type wire used. Mechanical connections to the frame or chassis shall be made secure.

(2) Conductors shall conform to the requirements for Type HDT, SGT, or SGR, or Type SXL, or shall have insulation rated at least 60°C and a minimum wall thickness of 30 mils of thermoplastic insulation or equal.

(FPN): See SAE Standard J1128 for Types HDT and SXL, and SAE Standard J1127 for Types SGT and SGR in the 1977 SAE Handbook.

(3) Single-wire, low-voltage conductors shall be of the stranded type.

(4) All insulated low-voltage conductors shall be surface marked at intervals no greater than 4 feet (1.22 m) as follows:

a. Listed conductors shall be marked as required by the listing agency.

b. SAE conductors shall be marked with the name or logo of the manufacturer, specification designation, and wire gage.

c. Other conductors shall be marked with the name or logo of the manufacturer, temperature rating, wire gage, conductor material, and insulation thickness.

(c) Low-Voltage Wiring Methods.

(1) Conductors shall be protected against physical damage and shall be secured. Where insulated conductors are clamped to the structure, the conductor insulation shall be supplemented by an additional wrap or layer of equivalent material, except that jacketed cables need not be so protected. Wiring shall be routed away from sharp edges, moving parts, or heat sources.

(2) Conductors shall be spliced or joined with approved splicing devices or by brazing, welding, or soldering with a fusible metal or alloy. Soldered splices shall first be so spliced or joined as to be mechanically and electrically secure without solder and then soldered. All splices, joints, and free ends of conductors shall be covered with an insulation equivalent to that on the conductors.

(3) Battery and direct-current circuits shall be physically separated by at least a ½-inch (12.7-mm) gap or other approved means from circuits of a different power source. Acceptable methods shall be by clamping, routing, or equivalent means which ensure permanent total separation. Where circuits of different power sources cross, the external jacket of the nonmetallic-sheathed cables shall be deemed adequate separation.

(4) Ground terminals shall be accessible for service. The surface on which ground terminals make contact shall be cleaned and free from oxide or paint, or shall be electrically connected through use of a cadmium, tin, or zinc plated external toothed lockwasher or lockring terminals. Ground terminal attaching screws, rivets or bolts, nuts and lockwashers shall be cadmium, tin or zinc plated, except rivets shall be permitted to be unanodized aluminum when attaching to aluminum structures.

(5) The chassis-grounding terminal of the battery shall be bonded to the vehicle chassis with a No. 8 AWG copper conductor minimum or equivalent.

Section 551-3(c)(5) requires that the chassis-grounding terminal of the battery is to be bonded to the vehicle chassis with a No. 8 AWG copper conductor minimum or equivalent. This minimizes the possibility of low-voltage circuit-fault current paths through the ac panelboard bonding conductor and the grounding conductor of the combination ac/dc appliance and then through the negative dc conductor feeding the appliance which may be also bonded to the external metal cover of the appliance. The ac grounding conductor of the appliance may not have sufficient ampacity to safely conduct the dc fault current. This will necessitate installation of the battery bonding conductor. Some recreational vehicles have one side of the battery circuit already bonded to the frame by a No. 8 AWG copper or larger conductor.

(d) Battery Installations. Storage batteries subject to the provisions of this Code shall be securely attached to the vehicle and installed in an area vaportight to the interior and ventilated directly to the exterior of the vehicle. When batteries are installed in a compartment, the compartment shall be ventilated with openings having a minimum area of 1.7 square inches (1100 sq mm) at both the top and at the bottom. When compartment doors are equipped for ventilation the openings shall be within 1 inch (25.4 mm) of the top and bottom. Batteries shall not be installed in a compartment containing spark or flame producing equipment except that they shall be permitted to be installed in the engine generator compartment if the only charging source is from the engine generator.

(e) Overcurrent Protection.

(1) Low-voltage circuit wiring shall be protected by overcurrent protective devices rated not in excess of the ampacity of copper conductors, as follows:

Wire Size	Ampacity	Wire Type
18	6	Stranded only
16	8	Stranded only
14	15	Stranded or Solid
12	20	Stranded or Solid
10	30	Stranded or Solid

(2) Circuit breakers or fuses shall be of an approved type, including automotive types. Fuseholders shall be clearly marked with maximum fuse size and shall be protected against shorting and physical damage by a cover or equivalent means.

The requirement for protection of fuseholders by a cover or equivalent means is intended to reduce the possibility of the low-voltage system shorting to ground.

(FPN): For further information, see Society of Automotive Engineers (SAE) Standard J554-1973, and Standard for Electric Fuses, ANSI C118.1-1973, and Underwriters Laboratories Inc. Standard for Automotive Glass Tube Fuses, UL 275b-1973.

(3) Higher current-consuming, direct-current appliances such as pumps, compressors, heater blowers, and similar motor-driven appliances shall be installed in accordance with the manufacturer's instructions.

Motors which are controlled by automatic switching or by latching-type manual switches shall be protected in accordance with Section 430-32(c).

(4) The overcurrent protective device shall be installed in an accessible location on the vehicle within 18 inches (457 mm) of the point where the power supply connects to the vehicle circuits. If located outside the recreational vehicle, the device shall be protected against weather and physical damage.

Exception: External low-voltage supply shall be permitted to be fused within 18 inches (457 mm) after entering the vehicle or after leaving a metal raceway.

(f) Switches. Switches shall have a direct-current rating not less than the connected load.

(g) Lighting Fixtures. All low-voltage interior lighting fixtures shall be approved.

(h) Cigarette Lighter Receptacles. Twelve-volt receptacles that will accept and energize cigarette lighters shall be installed in a noncombustible outlet box.

Twelve-V systems for running and signal lights, similar to those in a conventional automobile, are covered in Sections 551-3, 551-4, and 551-5. In many recreational vehicles, 12-V systems are also used for interior lighting and other

small loads. The 12-V system is often supplied from an onboard battery or through a transfer switch from a 120/12-V transformer in conjunction with a full-wave rectifier.

551-4. Combination Electrical Systems.

(a) General. Vehicle wiring suitable for connection to a battery or direct-current supply source shall be permitted to be connected to a 115-volt source provided that the entire wiring system and equipment are rated and installed in full conformity with Part A requirements covering 115-volt electrical systems. Circuits fed from alternating-current transformers shall not supply direct-current appliances.

(b) Voltage Converters (115-Volt Alternating Current to Low-Voltage Direct Current). The 115-volt alternating current side of the voltage converter shall be wired in full conformity with Part A requirements for 115-volt electrical systems.

Exception: Converters supplied as an integral part of an approved appliance shall not be subject to the above.

All converters and transformers shall be listed for use in recreation vehicles and designed or equipped to provide over-temperature protection. To determine the converter rating the following formula shall be applied to the total connected load, including average battery charging rate, of all 12-volt equipment:
The first 20 amperes of load at 100 percent; plus
The second 20 amperes of load at 50 percent; plus
All load above 40 amperes at 25 percent.

Exception: A low-voltage appliance which is controlled by a momentary switch (normally "open") which has no means for holding in the "closed" position shall not be considered as a "connected load" when determining the required converter rating. Momentarily energized appliances shall be limited to those used to prepare the vehicle for occupancy or travel.

(c) Bonding Voltage Converter Enclosures. The noncurrent-carrying metal enclosure of the voltage converter shall be bonded to the frame of the vehicle with a No. 8 AWG copper conductor minimum or equivalent. The grounding conductor for the battery and the metal enclosure may be the same conductor.

The intent of this section is to reduce the possibility of damage to the power supply cord by large dc fault currents which may find their way back to the vehicle frame or the battery through the ac grounding conductor of the converter. Metal enclosures of UL listed converters are provided with an external pressure terminal connector for this purpose. See commentary following Section 551-3(c)(5).

(d) Dual-Voltage Fixtures or Appliances. Fixtures or appliances having both 115-volt and low-voltage connections shall be approved for dual voltage.

In such fixtures, barriers are used to separate the 115-V and the 12-V wiring connections.

(e) Autotransformers. Autotransformers shall not be used.

(f) Receptacles and Plug Caps. Where a recreational vehicle is equipped with a 120-volt or 120/240-volt alternating-current system and/or a low-voltage system, receptacles and plug caps of the low-voltage system shall differ in configuration from those of the 120- or 120/240-volt system. When a vehicle equipped with a battery or direct-current system has an external connection for low-voltage power, the receptacle shall have a configuration that will not accept 120-volt power.

551-5. Generator Installations.

(a) Mounting. Generators shall be mounted in such a manner as to be effectively bonded to the recreational vehicle chassis.

(b) Generator Protection. Approved equipment shall be installed to ensure that the current-carrying conductors from the engine generator and from an outside source are not connected to a vehicle circuit at the same time. If required the generator field shall be protected by appropriately rated, approved equipment.

(c) Installation of Storage Batteries and Generators. Storage batteries and internal-combustion-driven generator units (subject to the provisions of this Code) shall be secured in place to avoid displacement from vibration and road shock.

(d) Ventilation of Generator Compartments. Compartments accommodating internal-combustion-driven generator units shall be provided with approved ventilation in accordance with instructions provided by the manufacturer of the generator unit.

(e) Supply Conductors. The supply conductors from the engine generator shall terminate in (1) a junction box with a blank cover, or (2) a panelboard mounted on the outside of the generator compartment wall.

Supply conductors from the generator(s) to their first termination shall be of the stranded type installed in flexible metal conduit.

(f) Compartment Construction. Generator compartments shall be lined with galvanized steel, not less than 26 MSG thick. Seams and joints shall be lapped, mechanically secured and made vaportight to the interior of the vehicle. Alternate materials and methods of construction may be used if they provide equivalent quality, strength, effectiveness, fire resistance, durability and safety. Fuel lines and exhaust systems shall not penetrate into the living area. Holes for electrical conduit, conductors or cables into the living area shall be sealed vaportight.

This section was added to the 1984 *NEC* in order to provide increased protection from fire or carbon monoxide which could enter the vehicle.

551-6. 115- or 115/230-Volt, Nominal, Systems.

(a) General Requirements. The electrical equipment and material of recreational vehicles indicated for connection to a wiring system rated 115 volts, nominal, 2-wire with ground, or a wiring system rated 115/230 volts, nominal, 3-wire with ground, shall be approved and installed in accordance with the requirements of Part A.

(b) Materials and Equipment. Electrical materials, devices, appliances, fittings, and other equipment installed, intended for use in, or attached to the recreational vehicle shall be listed. All products shall be used only in the manner in which they have been tested and found suitable for the intended use.

551-7. Receptacle Outlets Required.

(a) Spacing. Receptacle outlets shall be installed at wall spaces 2 feet (610 mm) wide or more so that no point along the floor line is more than 6 feet (1.83 m), measured horizontally, from an outlet in that space.

Exception No. 1: Bath and hall areas.

Exception No. 2: Wall spaces occupied by kitchen cabinets, wardrobe cabinets, built-in furniture, behind doors which may open fully against a wall surface, or similar facilities.

(b) Location. Receptacle outlets shall be installed:

(1) Adjacent to counter tops in the kitchen [at least one on each side of the sink if counter tops are on each side and are 12 inches (305 mm) or over in width].

(2) Adjacent to the refrigerator and gas range space, except when a gas-fired refrigerator or cooking appliance, requiring no external electrical connection, is factory-installed.

(3) Adjacent to counter top spaces of 12 inches (305 mm) or more in width which cannot be reached from a receptacle required in Section 551-7(b)(1) by a cord of 6 feet (1.83 m) without crossing a traffic area, cooking appliance, or sink.

(c) Ground-Fault Circuit Protection. Where provided, each 120-volt, single-phase, 15- or 20-ampere receptacle outlet shall have ground-fault circuit protection for personnel in the following locations:

(1) Adjacent to a bathroom lavatory. [The receptacle outlet shall be a minimum of 24 inches (610 mm) from the compartment floor.]

This section permits mounting of a bathroom receptacle in the side of a lavatory cabinet when installation of a receptacle is not possible in a thin wall.

(2) Adjacent to any lavatory.

(3) In the area occupied by a toilet, toilet and/or shower, or toilet and tub-shower enclosure.

(4) On the exterior of the vehicle.

The receptacle outlet shall be permitted in a listed lighting fixture. A receptacle outlet shall not be installed in a tub or combination tub-shower compartment.

(d) Face-Up Position. A receptacle shall not be installed in a face-up position in any counter top or similar horizontal surfaces within the living area.

551-8. Branch Circuits Required. Each recreational vehicle containing a 120-volt electrical system shall contain one of the following:

(a) One 15-Ampere Circuit. One 15-ampere circuit to supply lights, receptacles outlets and fixed appliances. Such recreational vehicles shall be equipped with one 15-ampere switch and fuse, or 15-ampere circuit breaker.

(b) One 20-Ampere Circuit. One 20-ampere circuit to supply lights, receptacle outlets and fixed appliances. Such recreational vehicles shall be equipped with one 20-ampere switch and fuse, or 20-ampere circuit breaker.

(c) Two or More 15- or 20-Ampere Circuits. Two or more 15- or 20-ampere circuits to supply lights, receptacle outlets and fixed appliances. Such recreational vehicles shall be equipped with a 30-ampere rated main power supply assembly.

(FPN): See Section 210-23(a) for permissible loads. See Section 551-11(c) for main disconnect and overcurrent protection requirements.

(d) Power Supply Assembly. A 40- or 50-ampere power supply assembly which shall be calculated in accordance with the following method:

ARTICLE 551—RECREATIONAL VEHICLES, PARKS

A. Lighting. If electric lighting is provided either directly or indirectly (through a voltage converter) by the 115-volt or 115/230-volt system, calculate lighting wattage at 3 volt-amperes per square foot using exterior dimensions (exclusive of hitch and cab) as follows:

Length (feet) × width (feet) × 3 = _____ lighting volt-amperes.

B. Small Appliance. Number of circuits times 1,500 volt-amperes for each 20-ampere appliance receptacle circuit, e.g.,

Number of Circuits × 1,500 = _____ small appliance volt-amperes.

C. Total. Lighting volt-amperes plus small appliance volt-amperes = _____ total volt-amperes.

D. First 3,000 total volt-amperes at 100 percent plus remainder at 35 percent = _____ volt-amperes to be divided by voltage to obtain current (amperes) per leg.

	Amperes per Leg	
	A	*B*
Lighting and small appliance current (amperes) per leg (from D above) =		_____

E. Add nameplate amperes for motors and heater loads (exhaust fans, air conditioners*, electric, gas, or oil heating*). Also include anticipated loads in above categories when prewired outlets or circuits are installed for other than factory-installed major appliances.
*Omit smaller of heating or air conditioning load, except include any motor common to both functions.

F. Add 25 percent of amperes of largest motor in E = _____

G. Add nameplate amperes of the following appliances. Include anticipated loads when prewired outlets or circuits are installed for other than factory-installed major appliances. When number of appliances is four or more, use 75 percent of total.

Disposal	____	____
Water Heater	____	____
Wall-Mounted Ovens	____	____
Cooking Units	____	____
TOTAL	____	____ = _____

H. Add amperes for free-standing range as distinguished from separate ovens and cooking units. Derive from following table by dividing volt-amperes by 230 volts.

Range	Nameplate Rating (watts)	Use (volt-amperes)
(Freestanding range as	10,000 or less	80 percent of rating
distinguished from separate	10,001-12,500	8,000
oven and cooking units)	12,501-13,500	8,400
	13,501-14,500	8,800
	14,501-15,500	9,200
	15,501-16,500	9,600
	16,501-17,500	10,000

551-9. Branch-Circuit Protection.

(a) Rating. The branch-circuit overcurrent devices shall be rated:

(1) Not more than the circuit conductors; and

(2) Not more than 150 percent of the rating of a single appliance rated 13.3 amperes or more and supplied by an individual branch circuit; but

(3) Not more than the fuse size marked on an air conditioner or other motor-operated appliances.

(b) Protection for Smaller Conductors. A 20-ampere fuse or circuit breaker shall be permitted for protection for fixture leads, cords, or small appliances, and No. 14 tap conductors, not over 6 feet (1.83 m) long for recessed lighting fixtures.

(c) 15-Ampere Receptacle Considered Protected by 20 Amperes. If more than one outlet or load is on a branch circuit, a 15-ampere receptacle shall be permitted to be protected by a 20-ampere fuse or circuit breaker.

551-10. Power-Supply Assembly.

(a) 15-Ampere Main Power-Supply Assembly. Recreational vehicles wired in accordance with Section 551-8(a) shall use an approved 15-ampere, or larger, main power-supply assembly.

(b) 20-Ampere Main Power-Supply Assembly. Recreational vehicles wired in accordance with Section 551-8(b) shall use an approved 20-ampere, or larger, main power-supply assembly.

(c) 30-Ampere Main Power-Supply Assembly. Recreational vehicles wired in accordance with Section 551-8(c) shall use an approved 30-ampere, or larger, main power-supply assembly.

(d) 40- or 50-Ampere Power-Supply Assembly. In accordance with Section 551-8(d), any recreational vehicle with a rating in excess of 30 amperes, 115 volts, shall use an approved 40-ampere or 50-ampere, 115/230-volt power-supply assembly.

Exception No. 1: When the calculated load of the recreational vehicle exceeds 30 amperes, 115 volts, a second power-supply cord shall be permitted. Where a two-cord supply system is installed, they shall not be interconnected on either the line side or the load side. The grounding circuits and grounding means shall be electrically interconnected.

Exception No. 2: For a dual-supply source consisting of a generator and a power-supply cord, see Section 551-12.

551-11. Distribution Panelboard.

(a) Listed and Appropriately Rated. A listed and appropriately rated distribution panelboard or other equipment specifically listed for the purpose shall be used. The distribution panelboard shall be of the insulated neutral type, with the grounding bar attached to the metal frame of the panelboard or other approved grounding means.

(b) Location. The distribution panelboard shall be installed in a readily accessible location. Working clearance for the panelboard shall be no less than 24 inches (610 mm) wide and 30 inches (762 mm) deep.

Exception: Where the panelboard cover is exposed to the inside aisle space, then one of the working clearance dimensions shall be permitted to be reduced to a minimum of 22 inches (559 mm). A panelboard is considered exposed where the panelboard cover is within 2 inches (50.8 mm) of the aisle's finished surface.

(c) Dead-Front Type. The distribution panelboard shall be of the dead-front type and shall consist of one or more circuit breakers or Type S fuseholders. A main disconnecting means shall be provided where fuses are used or where more than two circuit breakers are employed. A main overcurrent protective device not exceeding the power-supply assembly rating shall be provided where more than two branch circuits are employed.

551-12. Dual-Supply Source.

(a) Dual-Supply System. Where a dual-supply system, consisting of a generator and a power-supply cord is installed, the feeder from the generator shall be protected by an overcurrent protective device. Installation shall be in accordance with Section 551-5(a) and (b).

(b) Calculation of Loads. Calculation of loads shall be in accordance with Section 551-8.

(c) Two Supply Sources Capacity. The two supply sources shall not be required to be of the same capacity.

(d) AC Generator Exceeding 30 Amperes. If the ac generator source exceeds 30 amperes, 115 volts, nominal, it shall be permissible to wire either as a 115-volt, nominal, system or a 115/230-volt, nominal, system, providing an overcurrent protective device of the proper rating is installed in the feeder.

(e) Power-Supply Assembly Not Less than 30 Amperes. The external power-supply assembly shall be permitted to be less than the calculated load but not less than 30 amperes and shall have overcurrent protection not greater than the capacity of the external power-supply assembly.

551-13. Means for Connecting to Power Supply.

(a) Assembly. The power-supply assembly or assemblies shall be factory-supplied or factory-installed when of the permanently connected type as specified herein:

(1) Separable. Where a separable power-supply assembly consisting of a cord with a female connector and molded attachment plug cap is provided, the vehicle shall be equipped with a permanently mounted, approved flanged surface inlet (male-recessed-type motor-base receptacle) wired directly to the distribution panelboard by an approved wiring method. The attachment plug cap shall be of an approved type.

(2) Permanently Connected. Each power-supply assembly shall be connected directly to the terminals of the distribution panelboard or conductors within an approved junction box and provided with means to prevent strain from being transmitted to the terminals. The ampacity of the conductors between each junction box and the terminals of each distribution panelboard shall be at least equal to the ampacity of the power-supply cord. The supply end of the assembly shall be equipped with an attachment plug of the type described in Section 551-13(c). Where the cord passes through the walls or floors, it shall be protected by means of conduit and bushings or equivalent.

(b) Cord. The cord exposed usable length shall be measured from the point of entrance to the recreational vehicle or the face of the flanged surface inlet (motor-base attachment plug) to the face of the attachment plug at the supply end.

The cord exposed usable length, measured to the point of entry on the vehicle exterior, shall be a minimum of 23 feet (7.0 m) when the point of entrance is at the side of the vehicle, or shall be a minimum 28 feet (8.5 m) when the point of entrance is at the rear of the vehicle.

When the cord entrance into the vehicle is more than 3 feet (0.9 m) above the ground, the minimum cord lengths above shall be increased by the vertical distance of the cord entrance heights above 3 feet (0.9 m).

(FPN): See Section 551-13(e).

(c) Attachment Plugs.

(1) Recreational vehicles having only one 15-ampere branch circuit as permitted by Section

551-8(a) shall have an attachment plug which shall be 2-pole, 3-wire, grounding type, rated 15 amperes, 125 volts, conforming to the configuration shown in Figure 551-13(c).

(FPN): Complete details of this configuration can be found in American National Standard ANSI C73.11-1972.

(2) Recreational vehicles having only one 20-ampere branch circuit as permitted in Section 551-8(b) shall have an attachment plug which shall be 2-pole, 3-wire, grounding type, rated 20 amperes, 125 volts, conforming to the configuration shown in Figure 551-13(c).

(FPN): Complete details of this configuration can be found in American National Standard ANSI C73.12-1972.

(3) Recreational vehicles wired in accordance with Section 551-8(c) shall have an attachment plug which shall be 2-pole, 3-wire, grounding type, rated 30 amperes, 125 volts, conforming to the configuration shown in Figure 551-13(c) intended for use with units rated at 30 amperes, 125 volts.

(FPN): Complete details of this configuration can be found in American National Standard Dimensions of Caps, Plugs and Receptacles, ANSI C73.13-1972.

(4) Recreational vehicles having a power-supply assembly rated 40 amperes or 50 amperes as permitted by Section 551-8(d) shall have a 3-pole, 4-wire, grounding-type attachment plug rated 50 amperes, 125/250 volts, conforming to the configuration shown in Figure 551-13(c).

(FPN): Complete details of this configuration can be found in American National Standard Dimensions of Caps, Plugs and Receptacles, ANSI C73.17-1972.

Figure 551-13(c). Configurations for grounding-type receptacles and attachment plug caps used for recreational vehicle supply cords and recreational vehicle lots.

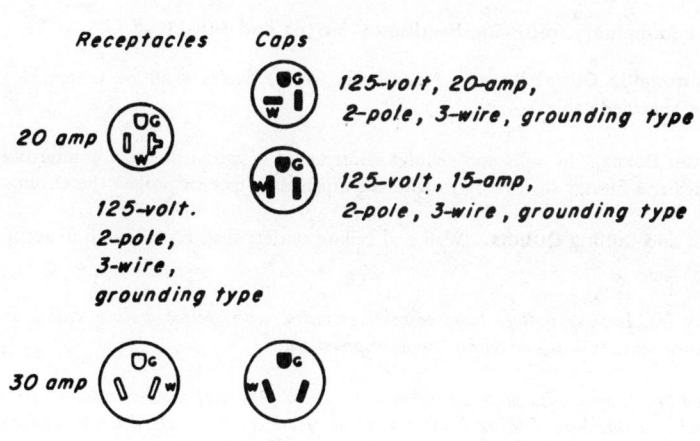

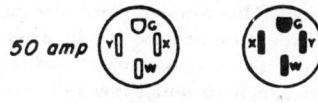

(d) Labeling at Electrical Entrance. Each recreational vehicle shall have permanently affixed to the exterior skin at or near the point of entrance of the power-supply cord(s) a label 3 inches (76 mm) by 1¾ inches (44.5 mm) minimum size, made of etched, metal-stamped or embossed brass, stainless steel, anodized or alclad aluminum not less than 0.020 inch (508 micrometers) thick, or other approved material [e.g., 0.005-inch (127-micrometers) plastic laminates], which reads, as appropriate, either:

"This connection is for 110-125 volt ac, 60 Hz ＿ ampere supply," or
"This connection is for 120/240 volt ac, 3-pole, 4-wire 60 Hz ＿ ampere supply."
The correct ampere rating shall be marked in the blank space.

(e) Location. The point of entrance of a power-supply assembly shall be located within 15 feet (4.57 m) of the rear, on the left (road) side or at the rear, left of the longitudinal center of the vehicle, within 18 inches (457 mm) of the outside wall.

Exception: A recreational vehicle equipped with only a listed flexible drain system or a side-vent drain system shall be permitted to have the electrical point of entrance located on either side provided the drain(s) for the plumbing system is (are) located on the same side.

551-14. Wiring Methods.

(a) Permitted. Electrical metallic tubing, flexible metal conduit, metal-clad cable, and nonmetallic-sheathed cable with a grounding conductor shall terminate by means of listed fittings, clamps, or connectors. Flexible metal conduit shall be permitted as a grounding means where installed in accordance with the requirements of Section 350-5.

See commentary following Section 350-5.

(b) Double Locknuts and Bushings. Rigid metal conduit and intermediate metal conduit shall be provided with a locknut inside and outside the box, and a conduit bushing shall be used on the inside. Inside ends of the conduit shall be reamed.

See commentary following Sections 373-6(c) and 348-11.

(c) Nonmetallic Outlet Boxes. Nonmetallic outlet boxes shall be acceptable only with nonmetallic-sheathed cable.

(d) Outlet Boxes. In walls and ceilings constructed of wood or other combustible material, outlet boxes and fittings shall be flush with the finished surface or project therefrom.

(e) Wall and Ceiling Outlets. Wall and ceiling outlets shall be mounted in accordance with Article 370.

Exception No. 1: Snap-in type boxes or boxes provided with special wall or ceiling brackets that securely fasten boxes in walls or ceilings shall be permitted.

Exception No. 2: A wooden plate providing a 1½-inch (38-mm) minimum width backing around the box and of a thickness of ½-inch (12.7 mm) or greater (actual) glued to the wall panel shall be considered as approved means for mounting outlet boxes.

This exception permits mounting of outlet boxes by screws to a wooden plate secured by adhesive to the back of the wall panel. This wooden plate is required to be not less than ½ in. thick, and is required to extend at least 1½ in. around the box. This recognizes the special construction of recreational vehicle walls which often makes it quite difficult or impossible to attach an outlet box to a structural member as required by Section 370-13(d).

(f) Sheath or Armor. The sheath of nonmetallic cable or the armor of metal-clad cable shall be continuous between outlet boxes and other enclosures.

(g) Protected. Metal-clad and nonmetallic cables shall be permitted to pass through the centers of the wide side of 2-inch by 4-inch studs. However, they shall be protected where they pass through 2-inch by 2-inch studs or at other studs or frames where the cable would be less than 1½ inches (38 mm) from the inside or outside surface. Steel plates on each side of the cable, or a steel tube, with not less than No. 16 MSG wall thickness, shall be installed to protect the cable. These plates or tubes shall be securely held in place.

(h) Bends. No bend shall have a radius of less than five times the cable diameter.

(i) Cable Supports. When connected with cable connectors or clamps, cables shall be supported within 12 inches (305 mm) of outlet boxes, distribution panelboards, and splice boxes on appliances. Supports shall be provided every 4½ feet (1.37 m) at other places.

(j) Nonmetallic Box Without Cable Clamps. Nonmetallic-sheathed cables shall be supported within 8 inches (203 mm) of a nonmetallic outlet box without cable clamps.

Exception: Where approved devices of insulating material are employed with a loop of extra cable to permit future replacement of the device, the cable loop shall be considered as an integral portion of the device.

(k) Physical Damage. Where subject to physical damage, exposed nonmetallic cable shall be protected by covering boards, guard strips, or conduit.

(l) Metallic Faceplates. Metallic faceplates shall be of ferrous metal not less than 0.030 inch (762 micrometers) in thickness or of nonferrous metal not less than 0.040 inch (1.02 mm) in thickness. Nonmetallic faceplates shall be of an approved type.

(m) Metallic Faceplates Effectively Grounded. Where metallic faceplates are used, they shall be effectively grounded.

(n) Moisture or Physical Damage. Where outdoor or underchassis wiring is 115 volts, nominal, or over and is exposed to moisture or physical damage, the wiring shall be protected by rigid metal conduit, intermediate metal conduit, or by electrical metallic tubing that is closely routed against frames and equipment enclosures.

(o) Component Interconnections. Fittings and connectors which are intended to be concealed at the time of assembly, when tested and approved to applicable standards, shall be permitted for the interconnection of components. Such fittings and connectors shall be equal to the wiring method employed in insulation, temperature rise, fault-current withstanding, and shall be capable of enduring the vibration and shock occurring in recreational vehicles.

(p) Method of Connecting Expandable Units.

(1) That portion of a branch circuit that is installed in an expandable unit shall be permitted to be connected to the portion of the branch circuit in the main body of the vehicle by means of an attachment plug and cord listed for hard usage. The cord and its connections shall conform to all provisions of Article 400 and shall be considered as a permitted use under Section 400-7.

(2) If the receptacle provided for connection of the cord to the main circuit is located on the outside of the vehicle it shall be protected with a ground-fault circuit-interrupter for personnel and be listed for wet locations. A cord located on the outside of a vehicle shall be identified for outdoor use.

(3) Unless removable or stored within the vehicle interior, the cord assembly shall have permanent provisions for protection against corrosion and mechanical damage while the vehicle is in transit.

(4) The cord shall be installed so as not to permit exposed live attachment plug pins.

(q) Prewiring for Air Conditioning Installation. Prewiring installed for the purpose of facilitating future air-conditioning installation shall conform to the following and other applicable portions of this article. The circuit shall serve no other purpose.

(1) An overcurrent protective device with a rating compatible with the circuit conductors shall be installed in the distribution panelboard and wiring connections completed.

(2) The load end of the circuit shall terminate in a junction box with a blank cover. The free ends of the conductors shall be adequately capped or taped.

(3) A label conforming to Section 551-13(d) shall be placed on or adjacent to the junction box and shall read:

AIR-CONDITIONING CIRCUIT. THIS

CONNECTION IS FOR AIR CONDITIONERS

RATED 110-125 VOLT AC, 60 HZ _____

AMPERES MAXIMUM. DO NOT EXCEED

CIRCUIT RATING.

An ampere rating, not to exceed 80 percent of the circuit rating, shall be legibly marked in the blank space.

(r) Prewiring for Generator Installation. Prewiring installed for the purpose of facilitating future generator installation shall conform to the following and other applicable portions of this article.

(1) Circuit conductors shall be appropriately sized in relation to the anticipated load and shall be protected by an overcurrent device in accordance with their ampacities.

(2) Where junction boxes are utilized at the circuit originating and/or terminus points, free ends of the conductors shall be adequately capped or taped.

(3) When devices such as receptacle outlet, transfer switch, etc., are installed, the installation shall be complete including circuit conductor connections. All devices shall be listed and appropriately rated.

(4) A label conforming to Section 551-13(d) shall be placed on the cover of each junction box containing incomplete circuitry and shall read, as appropriate, either:

GENERATOR CIRCUIT. THIS CONNECTION

IS FOR GENERATORS RATED 110-125 VOLT

AC, 60 HZ _____AMPERES MAXIMUM.

OR

GENERATOR CIRCUIT. THIS CONNECTION

IS FOR GENERATORS RATED 115/230 VOLT

AC, 60 HZ _____AMPERES MAXIMUM.

The correct ampere rating shall be legibly marked in the blank space.

551-15. Conductors and Outlet Boxes.

(a) Maximum Number of Conductors. The maximum number of conductors permitted in outlet and junction boxes shall be in accordance with Section 370-6.

(b) Free Conductor at Each Outlet Box. At least 4 inches (102 mm) of free conductor shall be left at each outlet box except where conductors are intended to loop without joints.

551-16. Grounded Conductors. The identification of grounded conductors shall be in accordance with Section 200-6.

551-17. Connection of Terminals and Splices. Conductor splices and connections at terminals shall be in accordance with Section 110-14. If splices of the grounding wire in nonmetallic-sheathed cable are made in outlet boxes, the splices shall be insulated.

551-18. Switches. Switches shall be rated as follows:

(a) Lighting Circuits. For lighting circuits, switches shall be rated not less than 10 amperes, 120-125 volts and in no case less than the connected load.

(b) Motors or Other Loads. For motors or other loads, switches shall have ampere or horsepower ratings, or both, adequate for loads controlled. (An ac general-use snap switch shall be permitted to control a motor 2 horsepower or less with full-load current not over 80 percent of the switch ampere rating.)

551-19. Receptacles. All receptacle outlets shall be: (1) of the grounding type, and (2) installed in accordance with Sections 210-7 and 210-21.

551-20. Lighting Fixtures.

(a) General. Any combustible wall or ceiling finish exposed between the edge of a fixture canopy, or pan and the outlet box, shall be covered with noncombustible material or a material identified for the purpose.

(b) Shower Fixtures. If a lighting fixture is provided over a bathtub or in a shower stall, it shall be of the enclosed and gasketed type and approved for the type of installation.
The switch for shower lighting fixtures and exhaust fans, located over a tub or in a shower stall, shall be located outside the tub or shower space.

(c) Outdoor Outlets, Fixtures, Air-Cooling Equipment, Etc. Outdoor fixtures and other equipment shall be approved for outdoor use.

551-21. Grounding. (See also Section 551-23 on bonding of noncurrent-carrying metal parts.)

(a) Power-Supply Grounding. The grounding conductor in the supply cord or feeder shall be connected to the grounding bus or other approved grounding means in the distribution panelboard.

(b) Distribution Panelboard. The distribution panelboard shall have a grounding bus with sufficient terminals for all grounding conductors or other approved grounding means.

(c) Insulated Neutral.

(1) The grounded circuit conductor (neutral) shall be insulated from the equipment grounding conductors and from equipment enclosures and other grounded parts. The grounded (neutral) circuit terminals in the distribution panelboard and in ranges, clothes dryers, counter-mounted cooking units, and wall-mounted ovens shall be insulated from the equipment enclosure. Bonding screws, straps, or buses in the distribution panel board or in appliances shall be removed and discarded.

(2) Connection of electric ranges and electric clothes dryers utilizing a grounded (neutral) conductor, if cord-connected, shall be made with 4-conductor cord and 3-pole, 4-wire, grounding-type plug caps and receptacles.

551-22. Interior Equipment Grounding.

(a) Exposed Metal Parts. In the electrical system, all exposed metal parts, enclosures, frames, lighting fixture canopies, etc., shall be effectively bonded to the grounding terminals or enclosure of the distribution panelboard.

(b) Equipment Grounding Conductors. Bare wires, green-colored wires, or green wires with yellow stripe(s) shall be used for equipment grounding conductors only.

(c) Grounding of Electrical Equipment. Where grounding of electrical equipment is specified, it shall be permitted as follows:

(1) Connection by metallic raceway (conduit or electrical metallic tubing) or the sheath of metal-clad cable to metallic outlet boxes.

(2) A connection between the one or more grounding conductors and a metallic box by means of a grounding screw, which shall be used for no other purpose, or an approved grounding device.

(3) The grounding wire in nonmetallic-sheathed cable shall be permitted to be secured under a screw threaded into the fixture canopy other than a mounting screw or cover screw, or attached to an approved grounding means (plate) in a nonmetallic outlet box for fixture mounting (grounding means shall also be permitted for fixture attachment screws).

(d) Grounding Connection in Nonmetallic Box. A connection between the one or more grounding conductors brought into a nonmetallic outlet box shall be so arranged that a connection can be made to any fitting or device in that box that requires grounding.

(e) Grounding Continuity. Where more than one equipment grounding conductor of a branch circuit enters a box, all such conductors shall be in good electrical contact with each other, and the arrangement shall be such that the disconnection or removal of a receptacle, fixture, or other device fed from the box will not interfere with or interrupt the grounding continuity.

(f) Cord-Connected Appliances. Cord-connected appliances, such as washing machines, clothes dryers, refrigerators, and the electrical system of gas ranges, etc., shall be grounded by means of an approved cord with grounding conductor and grounding-type attachment plug.

551-23. Bonding of Noncurrent-Carrying Metal Parts.

(a) Required Bonding. All exposed noncurrent-carrying metal parts that may become energized shall be effectively bonded to the grounding terminal or enclosure of the distribution panelboard.

(b) Bonding Chassis. A bonding conductor shall be connected between any distribution panelboard and an accessible terminal on the chassis. Aluminum or copper-clad aluminum conductors shall not be used for bonding if such conductors or their terminals are exposed to corrosive elements.

Exception: Any recreational vehicle which employs a unitized metal chassis-frame construction to which the distribution panelboard is securely fastened with a bolt(s) and nut(s) or by welding or riveting shall be considered to be bonded.

(c) Bonding Conductor Requirements. Grounding terminals shall be of the solderless type and approved as pressure terminal connectors recognized for the wire size used. The bonding conductor shall be solid or stranded, insulated or bare, and shall be No. 8 copper minimum, or equal

(d) Metallic Roof and Exterior Bonding. The metallic roof and exterior covering shall be considered bonded where:

(1) The metal panels overlap one another and are securely attached to the wood or metal frame parts by metallic fasteners, and

(2) The lower panel of the metallic exterior covering is secured by metallic fasteners at each cross member of the chassis, or the lower panel is bonded to the chassis by a metal strap.

(e) Gas, Water, and Waste Pipe Bonding. The gas, water, and waste pipes shall be considered grounded if they are bonded to the chassis.

(FPN): See Section 551-23(b) for chassis bonding.

(f) Furnace and Metallic Air Duct Bonding. Furnace and metallic circulating air ducts shall be bonded.

551-24. Appliance Accessibility and Fastening. Every appliance shall be accessible for inspection, service, repair, and replacement without removal of permanent construction. Means shall be provided to securely fasten appliances in place when the recreational vehicle is in transit.

551-25. Factory Tests (Electrical). Each recreational vehicle shall be subjected to the following tests:

(a) Circuits of 115 Volts or 115/230 Volts. Each recreational vehicle designed with a 115-volt or a 115/230-volt electrical system shall withstand the applied potential without electrical breakdown of a 1-minute, 900-volt dielectric strength test, or a 1-second, 1080-volt dielectric strength test, with all switches closed, between current-carrying conductors, including neutral, and the recreational vehicle ground. During the test, all switches and other controls shall be in the "on" position. Fixtures and permanently installed appliances shall not be required to withstand this test.

Each recreational vehicle shall be subjected to: (1) a continuity test to assure that all metallic parts are properly bonded; (2) operational tests to demonstrate that all equipment is properly connected and in working order; and (3) polarity checks to determine that connections have been properly made.

(b) Low-Voltage Circuits. Low-voltage circuit conductors in each recreational vehicle shall withstand the applied potential without electrical breakdown of a 1-minute, 500-volt or a 1-second, 600-volt dielectric strength test. The potential shall be applied between live and grounded conductors.

The test shall be permitted on running light circuits before the lights are installed provided the vehicle's outer covering and interior cabinetry has been secured. The braking circuit shall be permitted to be tested before being connected to the brakes, provided the wiring has been completely secured.

ARTICLE 551—RECREATIONAL VEHICLES, PARKS

B. Recreational Vehicle Parks

551-40. Application and Scope. Part B covers electrical systems on recreational vehicle parks. It does not apply to the electrical systems of recreational vehicles or the conductors that connect them to the park electrical supply facilities. Wherever the requirements of other articles of this Code and Article 551 differ, the requirements of Article 551 shall apply.

551-41. Definitions.

Power-Supply Assembly. The conductors, including the grounding conductors, insulated from one another, the connectors, attachment plug caps, and all other fittings, grommets, or devices installed for the purpose of delivering energy from the source of electrical supply to the distribution panelboard within the recreational vehicle.

Recreational Vehicle Park. A plot of land upon which two or more recreational vehicle sites are located, established, or maintained for occupancy by recreational vehicles of the general public as temporary living quarters for recreation or vacation purposes.

Recreational Vehicle Site. A plot of ground within a recreational vehicle park intended for the accommodation of either a recreational vehicle, tent, or other individual camping unit on a temporary basis.

Recreational Vehicle Site Feeder Circuit Conductors. The conductors from the park service equipment to the recreational vehicle site supply equipment.

Recreational Vehicle Site Supply Equipment. The necessary equipment, usually a power outlet, consisting of a circuit breaker or switch and fuse and their accessories, located near the point of entrance of supply conductors to a recreational vehicle site and intended to constitute the disconnecting means for the supply to that site.

Recreational Vehicle Stand. That area of a recreational vehicle site intended for the placement of a recreational vehicle.

551-42. Type Receptacles Provided. A minimum of 75 percent of all recreational vehicle sites with electrical supply shall each be equipped with a 30-ampere, 125-volt receptacle conforming to Figure 551-13(c). This supply shall be permitted to include additional receptacle configurations conforming to Section 551-52. The remainder of all recreational vehicle sites with electrical supply shall be equipped with one or more of the receptacle configurations conforming to Section 551-52.

All 15- and 20-ampere, 125-volt receptacles shall have approved ground-fault circuit-interrupter protection for personnel. Additional receptacles shall be permitted, for the connection of electrical equipment outside the recreational vehicle within the recreational vehicle park, and all such 125-volt, single-phase, 15- and 20-ampere receptacles shall have ground-fault circuit-interrupter protection for personnel.

551-43. Distribution System. The recreational vehicle park secondary electrical distribution system to recreational vehicle sites shall be derived from a single-phase 120/240-volt, 3-wire system.

551-44. Calculated Load.

(a) **Basis of Calculations.** Electrical service and feeders shall be calculated on the basis of not less than 3,600 volt-amperes per site equipped with both 20-ampere and 30-ampere supply facilities and 2,400 volt-amperes per site equipped with only 20-ampere supply facilities. The demand factors set forth in Table 551-44 shall be the minimum allowable demand factors that shall be permitted in calculating load for service and feeders.

Table 551-44
Demand Factors for Feeders and Service-Entrance Conductors for Park Sites

Number of Recreational Vehicle Sites	Demand Factor (percent)	Number of Recreational Vehicle Sites	Demand Factor (percent)
1	100	10-12	47
2	100	13-15	45
3	100	16-18	44
4	89	19-21	42
5	71	22-40	40
6	63	41-100	39
7-9	53	101 plus	37

(b) Transformers and Secondary Distribution Panelboards. For the purpose of this Code, where the park service exceeds 240 volts, transformers and secondary distribution panelboards shall be treated as services.

(c) Demand Factors. The demand factor for a given number of sites shall apply to all sites indicated. For example: twenty sites calculated at 42 percent of 3,600 volt-amperes result in a permissible demand of 1512 volt-amperes per site or a total of 30,240 volt-amperes for twenty sites.

(FPN): These demand factors may be inadequate in areas of extreme hot or cold temperature with loaded circuits for heating or air conditioning.

(d) Feeder Circuit Capacity. Recreational vehicle site feeder circuit conductors shall have adequate ampacity for the loads supplied, and shall be rated at not less than 30 amperes.

551-45. Overcurrent Protection. Overcurrent protection shall be provided in accordance with Article 240.

551-46. Grounding. All electrical equipment and installations in recreational vehicle parks shall be grounded as required by Article 250.

551-47. Recreational Vehicle Site Supply Equipment.

(a) Location. Where provided, the recreational vehicle site electrical supply equipment shall be located on the left (road) side of the parked vehicle, on a line which is 9 feet (2.74 m), ± 1 foot (0.3 m), from the longitudinal centerline of the stand and shall be located at any point on this line from the rear of the stand to 15 feet (4.57 m) forward of the rear of the stand.

(b) Disconnecting Means. A disconnecting switch or circuit breaker shall be provided in the site supply equipment for disconnecting the power supply to the recreational vehicle.

(c) Access. All site supply equipment shall be accessible by an unobstructed entrance or passageway not less than 2 feet (610 mm) wide and 6½ feet (1.98 m) high.

(d) Mounting Height. Site supply equipment shall be located not less than 2 feet (610 mm) nor more than 6½ feet (1.98 m) above the ground.

(e) Working Space. Sufficient space shall be provided and maintained about all electric equipment to permit ready and safe operation, in accordance with Section 110-16.

551-48. Grounding, Recreational Vehicle Site Supply Equipment.

(a) Exposed Noncurrent-Carrying Metal Parts. Exposed noncurrent-carrying metal parts of fixed equipment, metal boxes, cabinets, and fittings, which are not electrically connected to

813

grounded equipment, shall be grounded by a continuous grounding conductor run with the circuit conductors from the service equipments or from the transformer of a secondary distribution system. Equipment grounding conductors shall be sized in accordance with Section 250-95.

(b) Secondary Distribution System. Each secondary distribution system shall be grounded at the transformer.

(c) Neutral Conductor Not to Be Used as an Equipment Ground. The neutral conductor shall not be used as an equipment ground for recreational vehicles or equipment within the recreational vehicle park.

(d) No Connection on the Load Side. No connection to a grounding electrode shall be made to the neutral conductor on the load side of the service disconnecting means or transformer distribution panelboard.

551-49. Protection of Outdoor Equipment.

(a) Wet Locations. All switches, circuit breakers, receptacles, control equipment, and metering devices located in wet places or outside of a building shall be rainproof equipment.

(b) Meters. If secondary meters are installed, meter sockets without meters installed shall be blanked-off with an approved blanking plate.

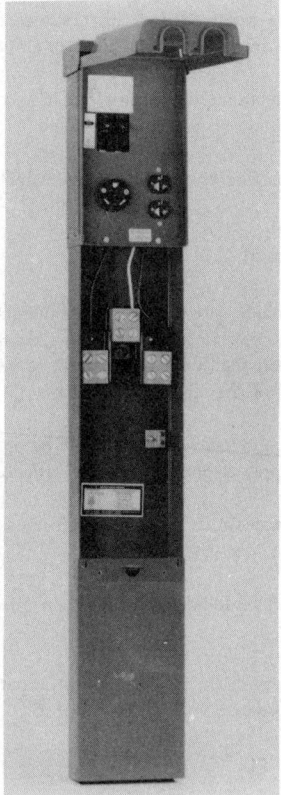

Figure 551-1. Recreational vehicle site supply equipment in accordance with Section 551-42. (*Midwest*)

551-50. Overhead Conductors.

(a) Vertical Clearance. Open conductors of not over 600 volts, nominal, shall have a vertical clearance of not less than 18 feet (5.49 m) in all areas subject to recreational vehicle movement. In all other areas, vertical clearances shall conform to Section 225-18.

(FPN): For clearance of conductors of over 600 volts, nominal, see National Electrical Safety Code, ANSI C2-1981.

(b) Horizontal Clearance. The horizontal clearance from structures and recreational vehicles for overhead conductors shall be not less than 3 feet (914 mm) for 600 volts, nominal, or less.

551-51. Underground Service, Feeder, Branch-Circuit and Recreational Vehicle Site Feeder Circuit Conductors.

(a) General. All direct-burial conductors, including the equipment grounding conductor if of aluminum, shall be insulated and identified for the use. All conductors shall be continuous from fitting to fitting. All splices shall be made in approved junction boxes.

(b) Mechanical Protection. Where underground conductors enter or leave a building or trench, they shall have mechanical protection in the form of rigid metal conduit, intermediate metal conduit, rigid nonmetallic conduit Schedule 80, electrical metallic tubing, or other approved mechanical means, extending a minimum of 18 inches (457 mm) into the trench from the finished grade.

(FPN): See Section 300-5 and Article 339 for conductors or Type UF cable used underground or in direct burial in earth.

551-52. Receptacles. A receptacle to supply electric power to a recreational vehicle shall be one of the configurations shown in Figure 551-13(c) in the following ratings:

(a) 50 Ampere. 125/250 volts, 50-ampere, 3-pole, 4-wire, grounding type for 115/230-volt systems.

(b) 30 Ampere. 125-volt, 30-ampere, 2-pole, 3-wire, grounding type for 115-volt systems.

(c) 20 Ampere. 125-volt, 20-ampere, 2-pole, 3-wire, grounding type for 115-volt systems.

(FPN): Complete details of these configurations can be found in American National Standard Dimensions of Caps, Plugs and Receptacles, ANSI C73.17-1972; ANSI C73.13-1972; and C73.12-1972.

ARTICLE 555 — MARINAS AND BOATYARDS

Contents

ARTICLE 555—MARINAS AND BOATYARDS

555-8. Wiring Over and Under Navigable Water.
555-9. Gasoline Dispensing Stations —
Hazardous (Classified) Locations.
  (a) Class I, Division 1 Location.
  (b) Class I, Division 2 Location.
555-11. Sealing.
  (a) At Dispenser.

  (b) At Boundary.

B. Floating Dwelling Units (FDU)
555-20. General.
555-21. Application of Other Articles.
555-22. Services.
555-23. Connection of Service and Feeders.
555-24. Grounding.

555-1. Scope. This article covers the installation of wiring and equipment in the areas comprising fixed or floating piers, wharfs, docks, and other areas in marinas, boatyards, boat basins, and similar establishments that are used, or intended for use, for the purpose of repair, berthing, launching, storage, or fueling of small craft and the moorage of floating dwelling units.

(FPN): See Part B for Floating Dwelling Units.

A. Marinas and Boatyards

555-2. Application of Other Articles. Wiring and equipment for marinas and boatyards shall comply with this article and also with the applicable provisions of other articles of this Code.

See notes following Sections 210-19(a) and 215-2(c) for voltage drop on branch circuits and feeders respectively.

(FPN): For disconnection of auxiliary power from boats, see Motor Craft, NFPA 302-1980 (ANSI).

555-3. Receptacles. Receptacles that provide shore power for boats shall be rated not less than 20 amperes and shall be single and of the locking and grounding types.

Fifteen- and 20-ampere, single-phase, 125-volt receptacles other than those supplying shore power to boats located at piers, wharfs, and other locations shall be protected by ground-fault circuit-interrupters.

(FPN): For various configurations and ratings of locking- and grounding-type receptacles and caps, see Dimensions of Caps, Plugs, and Receptacles, ANSI C73-1972.

(FPN): In locating receptacles consideration should be given to the maximum tide level and wave action.

    Receptacles that provide shore power for boats are required to be single and of the locking and grounding types. See Figure 555-1 and also Figure 210-7 for a complete chart of grounding-type locking plug and receptacle configurations. See Figure 555-2 for a power outlet assembly used at marinas and boatyards.

    Each single receptacle that supplies shore power to boats is required to be supplied from an individual branch circuit. Locking- and grounding-type receptacles and attachment caps are required to ensure proper connections to prevent unintentional disconnection of onboard equipment such as bilge pumps, refrigerators, etc. Fifteen- and 20-A, single-phase, 125-V receptacles, other than those supplying shore power to boats, that are used for maintenance or other purposes at piers, wharves, etc., may be of the general-purpose, nonlocking and nongrounding types and are required to be protected by ground-fault circuit-interrupters. See Figure 210-11.

    The second Fine Print Note is new in the 1984 *Code*. It was added to bring attention to the possibility of high waves (4 to 5 ft) which are often created by large cruisers and freighter traffic. This condition causes outlets and boxes to become filled with water which results in loss of power and corrosion of the receptacle and attachment plugs.

555-4. Branch Circuits. Each single receptacle that supplies shore power to boats shall be supplied from a power outlet or panelboard by an individual or multiwire branch circuit of the voltage class and rating corresponding to the rating of the receptacle.

This section was revised for the 1984 *Code* to clarify that either an individual or a multiwire branch circuit may be used with a common neutral. See commentary following Section 300-13.

555-5. Feeders and Services. The load for each ungrounded feeder and service conductor supplying receptacles that supply shore power for boats shall be calculated as follows:

For 1 to 4 receptacles	100% of the sum of the rating of the receptacles						
For 5 to 8	90%	"	"	"	"	"	"
For 9 to 13	80%	"	"	"	"	"	"
For 14 to 30	70%	"	"	"	"	"	"
For 31 to 50	50%	"	"	"	"	"	"
For 50 to 100	40%	"	"	"	"	"	"
For over 100	30%	"	"	"	"	"	"

555-6. Wiring Methods. The wiring method shall be one or more of the following identified as suitable for use where exposed to the weather or water: (1) rigid nonmetallic conduit; (2) mineral-insulated, metal-sheathed cable; (3) nonmetallic cable; (4) corrosion-resistant rigid metal conduit; (5) corrosion-resistant intermediate metal conduit; (6) underground wiring that complies with the requirements of this Code; (7) Type MC cable.

Exception No. 1: Where flexibility is required, other types identified for the purpose.

Exception No. 2: Open wiring shall be permitted by special permission.

(FPN): In granting special permission, major factors include possible contact of open wires with masts, cranes, or similar structures or equipment.

(FPN): For further information on wiring methods for various locations, see Fire Protection Standard for Marinas and Boatyards, NFPA 303-1975.

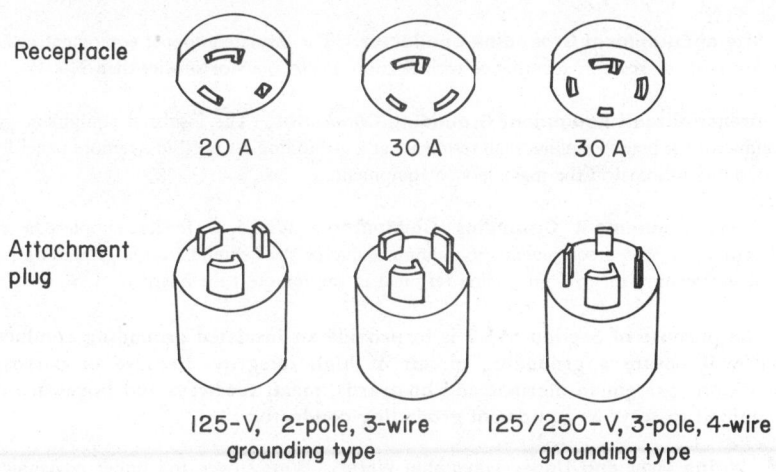

Figure 555-1. Typical configurations for single, locking- and grounding-type receptacles and attachment plug caps used to provide shore power for boats in marinas and boatyards.

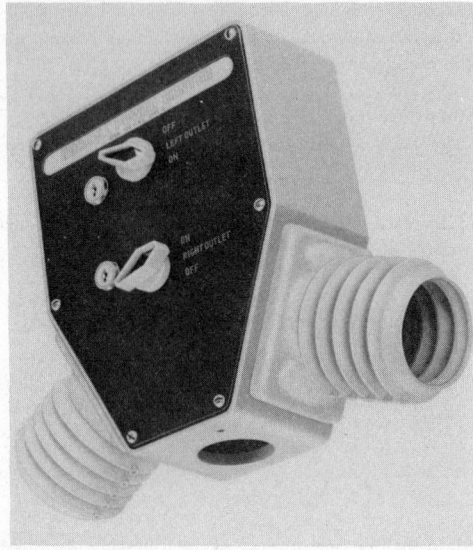

Figure 555-2. Power outlet assembly suitable for use at docks, wharves, piers, and other locations that provide shore power to boats. (*Hubbell*)

555-7. Grounding.

(a) **Equipment to Be Grounded.** The following items shall be connected to an equipment grounding conductor run with the circuit conductors in a raceway or cable:

(1) Boxes, cabinets, and all other metal enclosures.

(2) Metal frames of utilization equipment.

(3) Grounding terminals of grounding-type receptacles.

(b) **Type of Equipment Grounding Conductor.** The equipment grounding conductor shall be an insulated copper conductor with a continuous outer finish that is either green or green with one or more yellow stripes.

(c) **Size of Equipment Grounding Conductor.** The insulated copper equipment grounding conductor shall be sized in accordance with Section 250-95 but not smaller than No. 12.

(d) **Branch-Circuit Equipment Grounding Conductor.** The insulated equipment grounding conductor for branch circuits shall terminate at a grounding terminal in a remote panelboard or the grounding terminal in the main service equipment.

(e) **Feeder Equipment Grounding Conductors.** Where a feeder supplies a remote panelboard, an insulated equipment grounding conductor shall extend from a grounding terminal in the service equipment to a grounding terminal in the remote panelboard.

The purpose of Section 555-7 is to provide an insulated grounding conductor that will ensure a grounding circuit of high integrity. Because of corrosive conditions present in marinas and boatyards, metal raceways and boxes are not permitted to serve as equipment grounding conductors.

555-8. Wiring Over and Under Navigable Water. Wiring over and under navigable water shall be subject to approval by the authority having jurisdiction.

Some federal and local agencies have specific authority over navigable waterways; therefore, their approval of any proposed installation over or under such a waterway should be obtained.

555-9. Gasoline Dispensing Stations — Hazardous (Classified) Locations.

(a) **Class I, Division 1 Location.** The following spaces shall be considered a Class I, Division 1 location:

(1) The space within the dispenser from its base to a level measured 4 feet (1.22 m) vertically from its base.

(2) The space outside the dispenser for a distance measured 4 feet (1.22 m) horizontally from all points of the dispenser and measured vertically upwards for a distance of 18 inches (457 mm) from the base of the dispenser.

(3) The entire space between the base of the dispenser and the lowest water surface for a distance of 4 feet (1.22 m) measured horizontally from any point on the outside of the dispenser.

(b) **Class I, Division 2 Location.** In an outside location, the following space shall be considered a Class I, Division 2 location (spaces which are Class I, Division 1 as defined above are excluded. Buildings within the following space which are not suitably cut off shall be included.) This space shall include the entire volume enveloped within the following limits:

(1) A horizontal limit of 20 feet (6.1 m) from all points on the exterior enclosure of a dispenser.

(2) An upper limit of 18 inches (457 mm) measured vertically from the base of the dispenser.

(3) A lower limit which shall be the lowest water surface.

(FPN): For further information, see Marinas and Boatyards, NFPA 303-1975.

Section 4-3 in NFPA 303 and Chapter 4 in NFPA 30 include requirements pertaining to gasoline dispensing stations. See also Chapter 5 of NPFA 303 for electrical wiring and equipment requirements for marinas and boatyards.

555-11. Sealing.

(a) **At Dispenser.** An approved seal shall be provided in each conduit run entering or leaving a dispenser or any cavities or enclosures in direct communication therewith.

(b) **At Boundary.** Additional seals shall be provided in accordance with Section 501-5. Section 501-5(a)(4) and (b)(2) shall apply to horizontal as well as to vertical boundaries of the defined hazardous (classified) locations.

B. Floating Dwelling Units (FDU)

555-20. General. This part covers floating dwelling units and services and feeders to the associated pier, dock, or wharf to which they are moored.

555-21. Application of Other Articles. Wiring and equipment for floating dwelling units shall comply with this article, and also with the applicable provisions of other articles of this Code.

ARTICLE 555—MARINAS AND BOATYARDS

555-22. Services. Overhead service wiring shall be installed so that changes in water level will not result in unsafe clearances. The floating dwelling unit service equipment shall be located adjacent to the floating dwelling unit and not mounted in or on the unit.

The second sentence of this section is new in the 1984 *Code*. The intent here is to ensure that supply conductors to a floating dwelling unit can be disconnected in an emergency, such as during a storm, where the floating dwelling unit has to be moved quickly.

Overcurrent protection for supply conductors is also provided where these conductors may develop excessive leakage when underwater or where a short circuit or fault may occur.

555-23. Connection of Service and Feeders. Flexibility of the wiring system shall be maintained between the floating dwelling units and the supply conductors.

555-24. Grounding. Ground continuity shall be assured between an earth ground on the shore, the floating dwelling unit and the incoming electric distribution system.

6 SPECIAL EQUIPMENT

ARTICLE 600 — ELECTRIC SIGNS AND
OUTLINE LIGHTING

Contents

A. General

600-1. Scope. This article covers the installation of conductors and equipment for electric signs and outline lighting as defined in Article 100.

600-2. Disconnect Required. Each outline lighting installation, and each sign of other than the portable type, shall be controlled by an externally operable switch or breaker which will open all ungrounded conductors.

(a) In Sight of Sign. The disconnecting means shall be within sight of the sign or outline lighting which it controls.

Exception: Signs operated by electronic or electromechanical controllers located external to the sign shall have a disconnecting means located within sight from the controller location. The disconnecting means shall disconnect the sign and the controller from all ungrounded supply conductors and shall be so designed that no pole can be operated independently. The disconnecting means shall be permitted to be in the same enclosure with the controller. The disconnecting means shall be capable of being locked in the open position.

Disconnect means are required to be located in a direct line of sight from the sign or outline lighting which it controls. This requirement is for the protection of a worker who can keep the disconnecting means within view while working on the sign. The exception permits disconnecting means capable of being locked in the "open" position to be located elsewhere.

See Figure 600-1.

(b) Control Switch Rating. Switches, flashers, and similar devices controlling transformers shall be either rated for controlling inductive load(s) or have an ampere rating not less than twice the ampere rating of the transformer.

Exception: For other than motors, ac general-use snap switches shall be permitted to be used on alternating-current circuits to control inductive loads not exceeding the ampere rating of the switch.

(FPN): See Section 380-14 for rating of snap switches.

A switching device that controls the primary circuit of a transformer supplying a luminous gas tube encounters unusually severe arcing of its contacts. Therefore, the switch or flasher is required to be a general-use ac snap switch or have a current rating of at least twice the rating of the transformer it controls.

600-3. Enclosures as Pull Boxes. The wiring method used to supply signs and outline lighting shall terminate in the sign or transformer enclosures.

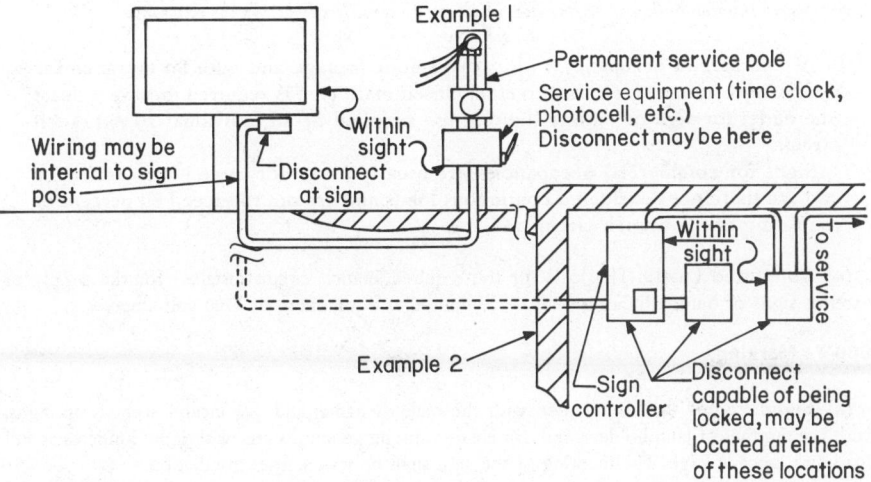

Figure 600-1. Example 1 depicts the disconnecting means placement which satisfies the requirements of Section 600-2(a). Example 2 illustrates the location of a disconnecting means as permitted by the Exception to Section 600-2(a).

Exception: Such signs and transformer boxes shall be permitted to be used as pull or junction boxes for conductors supplying other adjacent signs, outline lighting systems and floodlights that are part of signs provided the conductors extending from the equipment are protected by an overcurrent device rated 20 amperes or less.

600-4. Listing Required. Every electric sign of any type, fixed or portable, shall be listed and installed in conformance with that listing, unless otherwise permitted by special permission.

Section 600-4 requires every electric sign of any type to be listed, unless otherwise permitted by special permission. Many times signs of large dimensions are transported, in several parts, from the manufacturer to a location site where they are assembled. It is at this time that an inspection authority should be present to ensure that the components are assembled in conformance with their listing.

600-5. Grounding. Signs, troughs, tube terminal boxes, and other metal frames shall be grounded in the manner specified in Article 250.

Exception No. 1: Insulated and Inaccessible. Where they are insulated from ground and from other conducting surfaces and are inaccessible to unauthorized persons, they need not be grounded.

Exception No. 2: Isolated Parts. Isolated noncurrent-carrying metal parts of outline lighting may be bonded by No. 14 conductors, protected from physical damage, and grounded in accordance with Article 250.

600-6. Branch Circuits.

(a) Rating. Circuits which supply lamps, ballasts, and transformers, or combinations, shall be rated not to exceed 20 amperes. Circuits containing electric-discharge lighting transformers exclusively shall not be rated in excess of 30 amperes.

(b) Required Branch Circuit. Each commercial building and each commercial occupancy with ground floor footage accessible to pedestrians shall be provided at an accessible location outside the occupancy, with at least one outlet for sign or outline lighting use. This outlet shall be supplied by an individual 20-ampere branch circuit.

Exception: Interior hallways or corridors shall not be considered outside the occupancy.

A commercial occupancy with ground floor footage and with an entrance for pedestrians from a sidewalk, street, enclosed mall, etc., is required to have at least one outlet for sign or outline lighting use supplied by an individual 20-A branch circuit.

Signs for commercial occupancies are usually in use for three hours or longer and are therefore considered continuous loads and are not to exceed 80 percent of the rating of the branch circuit (16 A).

(c) Computed Load. The load for the required branch circuit installed for the supply of exterior signs or outline lighting shall be computed at a minimum of 1200 volt-amperes.

600-7. Marking.

(a) Signs. Signs shall be marked with the maker's name; and, for incandescent lamp signs, with the number of lampholders; and, for electric-discharge-lamp signs, with input amperes at full load and input voltage. The marking of the sign shall be visible after installation.

(b) Transformers. Transformers shall be marked with the maker's name; and transformers for electric-discharge-lamp signs shall be marked with the input rating in amperes or volt-amperes, the input voltage, and the open-circuit output voltage.

600-8. Enclosures.

(a) Conductors and Terminals. Conductors and terminals in sign boxes, cabinets, and outline troughs shall be enclosed in metal or other noncombustible material.

Exception: The supply leads shall not be required to be enclosed.

(b) Cutouts, Flashers, etc. Cutouts, flashers, and similar devices shall be enclosed in metal boxes, the doors of which shall be arranged so they can be opened without removing obstructions or finished parts of the enclosure.

(c) Strength. Enclosures shall have ample strength and rigidity.

(d) Material. Signs and outline lighting shall be constructed of metal or other noncombustible material. Wood shall be permitted for external decoration if placed not less than 2 inches (50.8 mm) from the nearest lampholder or current-carrying part.

Exception: Portable signs of the indoor type shall not be required to meet this requirement.

(e) Minimum Thickness — Enclosure Metal. Sheet copper shall be at least 20 ounce [0.028 inch (711 micrometers)]. Sheet steel shall be of No. 28 MSG.

Exception: For outline lighting and for electric-discharge signs, sheet steel shall be of No. 24 MSG if not ribbed, corrugated, or embossed over its entire surface and of No. 26 MSG if it is so ribbed, corrugated, or embossed.

(f) Protection of Metal. All steel parts of enclosures shall be galvanized or otherwise protected from corrosion.

(g) Enclosures Exposed to Weather. Enclosures for outdoor use shall be weatherproof and shall have at least two drain holes, each not larger than ½ inch (12.7 mm) or smaller than ¼ inch (6.35 mm). Wiring connections shall not be made through the bottoms of nonraintight enclosures exposed to the weather.

600-9. Portable Signs. Portable signs, letters, fixtures, symbols, and similar displays used in conjunction with fixed outdoor signs shall only be used when in compliance with all applicable provisions of this Code and, in addition, shall meet all of the following requirements:

(a) Weatherproof Receptacle and Attachment Plug. A weatherproof receptacle and attachment plug having one pole for grounding shall be provided for each individual letter, fixture, or sign.

(b) Cords. All cords shall be Type S, SJ, SJO, SJT, SJTO, SO, or ST, 3-conductor, with one conductor grounded as provided in the foregoing.

(c) Cord from Ground Level. No cord shall be less than 10 feet (3.05 m) from the ground level directly underneath.

Section 600-9 is not intended to apply to portable outdoor electric signs, such as those mounted on trailers. It is intended to apply only to portable parts used in conjunction with fixed outdoor signs.

600-10. Clearances.

(a) Vertical and Horizontal. Signs and outline system enclosures shall have not less than the vertical and horizontal clearances from open conductors specified in Article 225.

(b) Elevation. The bottom of sign and outline lighting enclosures shall not be less than 16 feet (4.88 m) above areas accessible to vehicles.

Exception: The bottom of such enclosures may be less than 16 feet (4.88 m) above areas accessible to vehicles where such enclosures are protected from physical damage.

600-11. Outdoor Portable Signs. The internal wiring of an outdoor sign that is portable or mobile and is readily accessible shall be supplied from, and protected by, ground-fault circuit-interrupters identified for use with portable electric signs, thereby providing protection for personnel. The required ground-fault circuit-interrupter shall be permitted on or within the sign or as an integral part of the attachment plug of the supply cord connected to the sign. Conductive supports of a sign covered by this section shall be considered part of the sign.

A GFCI in or on the sign will not provide protection for faults on the line (supply) side of the GFCI, so inspection of the cord used for supplying portable outdoor signs protected in this manner is desirable. See Figure 600-2 for a GFCI designed to serve as an attachment plug, and therefore capable of protecting both the sign and the supply cord.

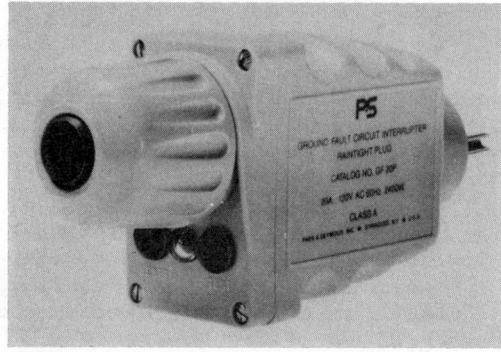

Figure 600-2. Raintight ground-fault circuit-interrupter with open neutral protection. This unit is designed for use on the line end of a flexible cord. (*Pass & Seymour, Inc.*)

ARTICLE 600—ELECTRIC SIGNS AND OUTLINE LIGHTING

It is the intent that a ground-fault circuit-interrupter identified for use with portable electric signs be provided with open neutral protection, so that the GFCI will provide protection even if the neutral conductor supplying the sign and GFCI opens.

B. 600 Volts, Nominal, or Less

600-21. Installation of Conductors.

(a) **Wiring Method.** Conductors shall be installed in rigid metal conduit, intermediate metal conduit, rigid nonmetallic conduit subject to the installation provisions of Chapter 3, flexible metal conduit, liquidtight flexible metal conduit, electrical metallic tubing, metal-clad cable, metal troughing, and mineral-insulated, metal-sheathed cable.

(b) **Insulation and Size.** Conductors shall be of a type listed for general use and shall not be smaller than No. 14.

Exception No. 1: Conductors not smaller than No. 18 of a type listed in Table 402-3 shall be permitted:

a. In portable signs.

b. As short leads permanently attached to lampholders or electric-discharge ballasts.

c. As leads not more than 8 feet (2.44 m) long permanently attached to electric-discharge lampholders or electric-discharge ballasts if the leads are enclosed in wiring channels.

d. For signs with multiple incandescent lamps requiring one conductor from a control to one or more lamps whose total load does not exceed 250 watts, if in an approved cable assembly of two or more conductors.

Exception No. 2: Conductors not smaller than No. 20 shall be permitted as short leads permanently attached to synchronous motors.

(c) **Exposed to Weather.** Conductors in raceways, metal-clad cable, or enclosures exposed to the weather shall be of the lead-covered type or other type specially approved for the conditions.

Exception: This shall not apply when rigid metal conduit, intermediate metal conduit, electrical metallic tubing, or enclosures are made raintight and arranged to drain.

(d) **Number of Conductors in Raceway.** The number of conductors in a raceway for sign fixtures shall be in accordance with Table 1 of Chapter 9.

(e) **Conductors Soldered to Terminals.** Where the conductors are fastened to lampholders other than of the pin type, they shall be soldered to the terminals or made with wire connectors, and the exposed parts of conductors and terminals shall be treated to prevent corrosion. Where the conductors are fastened to pin-type lampholders that protect the terminals from the entrance of water, and that have been found acceptable for sign use, the conductors shall be of the stranded type but shall not be required to be soldered to the terminals.

Conductors are required to be sized No. 14 or larger (note exceptions) and installed in the specified raceways or metal-clad cables. Unless raceways or enclosures exposed to the weather are made raintight and arranged to drain, conductors are required to be lead-covered or approved for wet locations. See Table 310-13.

600-22. Lampholders. Lampholders shall be of the unswitched type having bodies of suitable insulating material and shall be so constructed and installed as to prevent turning. Miniature lampholders shall not be employed for outdoor signs and outline lighting. The screw-shell contact of all sign lampholders in grounded circuits shall be connected to the grounded conductor of the circuit.

600-23. Conductors Within Signs and Troughs. Wires within the sign and outline lighting troughs shall be installed as to be mechanically secure.

600-24. Protection of Leads. Bushings shall be employed to protect wires feeding through enclosures.

C. Over 600 Volts, Nominal

600-31. Installation of Conductors.

(a) Wiring Method. Conductors shall be installed as concealed conductors on insulators, in rigid metal conduit, in intermediate metal conduit, in rigid nonmetallic conduit, in flexible metal conduit, in liquidtight flexible metal conduit, or in electrical metallic tubing, or as Type MC cable.

(b) Insulation and Size. Conductors shall be of a type identified for voltage not less than the voltage of the circuit and shall not be smaller than No. 14.

Exception: Conductors not smaller than No. 18 shall be permitted:

a. As leads not more than 8 feet (2.44 m) long permanently attached to electric-discharge lampholders or electric-discharge ballasts if the leads are enclosed in wiring channels.

b. In show window displays or small portable signs, as leads not more than 8 feet (2.44 m) long that run from the line ends of the tubing to the secondary windings of transformers if the leads are permanently attached within the transformer enclosure.

(c) Bends in Conductors. Sharp bends in the conductors shall be avoided.

(d) Concealed Conductors on Insulators — Indoors. Concealed conductors on insulators shall be separated from each other and from all objects other than the insulators on which they are mounted by a spacing of not less than 1½ inches (38 mm) for voltages above 10,000 and not less than 1 inch (25.4 mm) for voltages of 10,000 or less. They shall be installed in channels lined with noncombustible material and used for no other purpose, except that the primary circuit conductors shall be permitted to be in the same channel. The insulators shall be of noncombustible, nonabsorbent material. Concealed conductors on insulators shall not be allowed outside the sign enclosure.

(e) Conductors in Raceways. Where the conductors are covered with lead or other metal sheathing, the covering shall extend beyond the end of the raceway, and the surface of the cable shall not be injured where the covering terminates.

(1) In damp or wet locations, the insulation on all conductors shall extend beyond the metal covering or raceway not less than 4 inches (102 mm) for voltages over 10,000, 3 inches (76 mm) for voltages over 5000 but not exceeding 10,000, and 2 inches (50.8 mm) for voltages of 5000 or less.

(2) In dry locations the insulation shall extend beyond the end of the metal covering or raceways not less than 2½ inches (64 mm) for voltages over 10,000, 2 inches (50.8 mm) for voltages over 5000 but not exceeding 10,000, and 1½ inches (38 mm) for voltages of 5000 or less.

(3) For conductors at grounded midpoint terminals, no spacing shall be required.

(4) A metal raceway containing a single conductor from one secondary terminal of a transformer shall not exceed 20 feet (6.1 m) in length.

(f) Show Windows and Similar Locations. Conductors that hang freely in the air, away from combustible material, and where not subject to physical damage, as in some show window displays, shall not be required to be otherwise protected.

(g) Between Tubing and Grounded Midpoint. Conductors shall be permitted to be run from the ends of tubing to the grounded midpoint of transformers specifically designed for the purpose and provided with terminals at the midpoint. Where such connections are made to the transformer grounded midpoint, the connections between the high-voltage terminals of the transformer and the line ends of the tubing shall be as short as possible.

600-32. Transformers.

(a) Voltage. The transformer secondary open-circuit voltage shall not exceed 15,000 volts with an allowance on test of 1000 volts additional. For end-grounded transformers, the secondary open-circuit voltage shall not exceed 7500 volts with an allowance on test of 500 volts additional.

(b) Type. Transformers shall be of a type identified for use with electrical-discharge tubing and shall be limited in rating to a maximum of 4500 volt-amperes.

Open core-and-coil-type transformers shall be limited to 5000 volts with an allowance on test of 500 volts and to indoor applications in small portable signs.

Transformers for outline lighting installations shall have secondary current ratings not more than 30 milliamperes.

Exception: Where the transformers and all wiring connected to them are installed in accordance with Article 410 for electric-discharge lighting of the same voltage.

(c) Exposed to Weather. Transformers used outdoors shall be of the weatherproof type or shall be protected from the weather by enclosure in the sign body or in a separate metal box.

(d) Transformer Secondary Connections. The high-voltage windings of transformers shall not be connected in parallel or in series.

Exception No. 1: Two transformers each having one end of its high-voltage winding connected to the metal enclosure shall be permitted to have their high-voltage windings connected in series to form the equivalent of a midpoint-grounded transformer. The grounded ends shall be connected by insulated conductors not smaller than No. 14.

Exception No. 2: Transformers for small portable signs, show windows, and similar locations that are equipped with leads permanently attached to the secondary winding within the transformer enclosure and that do not extend more than 8 feet (2.44 m) beyond the enclosure for attaching to the line ends of the tubing shall not be smaller than No. 18.

(e) Accessibility. Transformers shall be located where accessible and shall be securely fastened in place.

(f) Working Space. A work space at least 3 feet (914 mm) high and measuring at least 3 feet (914 mm) by 3 feet (914 mm) horizontally shall be provided about each transformer or its enclosure where not installed in a sign.

(g) Attic Locations. Transformers may be located in attics provided there is a passageway at least 3 feet (914 mm) in height and at least 2 feet (610 mm) in width, provided with a suitable permanent fixed walkway or catwalk at least 12 inches (305 mm) in width extending from the point of entry into the attic to each transformer.

It is intended that Article 600 provide the necessary safeguards for personnel who are required to perform maintenance on signs and outline lighting by requiring a disconnecting means, by requiring that the use of open wiring be permitted "only" as concealed wiring on insulators within a sign enclosure, and by further requiring that transformers be located in a safe, accessible location.

600-33. Electric-Discharge Tubing.

(a) Design. The tubing shall be of such length and design as not to cause a continuous overvoltage on the transformer.

(b) Support. Tubing shall be adequately supported on noncombustible, nonabsorbent supports. Tubing supports shall, where practicable, be adjustable.

(c) Contact with Flammable Material and Other Surfaces. The tubing shall be free from contact with flammable material and shall be located where not normally exposed to physical damage. Where operating at over 7500 volts, the tubing shall be supported on noncombustible, nonabsorbent insulating supports that maintain a spacing of not less than ¼ inch (6.35 mm) between the tubing and the nearest surface.

600-34. Terminals and Electrode Receptacles for Electric-Discharge Tubing.

(a) Terminals. Terminals of the tubing shall be inaccessible to unqualified persons and isolated from combustible material and grounded metal or shall be enclosed. Where enclosed, they shall be separated from grounded metal and combustible material by noncombustible, nonabsorbent insulating material or by not less than 1½ inches (38 mm) of air. Terminals shall be relieved from stress by the independent support of the tubing.

(b) Tube Connections Other than with Receptacles. Where tubes do not terminate in receptacles designed for the purpose, all live parts of tube terminals and conductors shall be supported so as to maintain a separation of not less than 1½ inches (38 mm) between conductors or between conductors and any grounded metal.

(c) Receptacles. Electrode receptacles for the tubing shall be of noncombustible, nonabsorbent insulating material.

(d) Bushings. Where electrodes enter the enclosure of outdoor signs or of an indoor sign operating at a voltage in excess of 7500 volts, bushings shall be used unless receptacles are provided. Electrode terminal assemblies shall be supported not more than 6 inches (152 mm) from the electrode terminals.

(e) Show Windows. In the exposed type of show-window signs, terminals shall be enclosed by receptacles.

(f) Receptacles and Bushing Seals. A flexible, nonconducting seal shall be permitted to close the opening between the tubing and the receptacle or bushing against the entrance of dust or moisture. This seal shall not be in contact with grounded conductive material and shall not be depended upon for the insulation of the tubing.

(g) Enclosures of Metal. Enclosures of metal for electrodes shall not be less than No. 24 MSG sheet metal.

(h) Enclosures of Insulating Material. Enclosures of insulating material shall be noncombustible, nonabsorbent, and suitable for the voltage of the circuit.

(i) Live Parts. Live parts shall be enclosed or suitably guarded to prevent contact.

Electric-discharge tubing is required to be of such length and design as not to cause a continuous overload on the transformer. A tube too long and/or too small in diameter increases the impedance of the load and, thus, would burden the transformer. Generally, primary voltages of transformers are 120 V, and proper installation and maintenance of transformers and high-voltage secondary conductors will minimize the possibility of injury or fire. Precautions should be taken to ensure that secondary conductors are properly terminated to the tube electrodes, and that these connections are protected from contact by unauthorized persons or by any flammable or combustible material. Broken tubes should be replaced or de-energized.

600-35. Switches on Doors. Doors or covers giving access to uninsulated parts of indoor signs or outline lighting exceeding 600 volts, nominal, and accessible to the general public shall either be provided with interlock switches that on the opening of the doors or covers disconnect the primary circuit, or shall be so fastened that the use of other than ordinary tools will be necessary to open them.

600-36. Fixed Outline Lighting and Skeleton-type Signs for Interior Use.

(a) Tube Support. Gas tubing shall be supported independently of the conductors by means of insulators of noncombustible, nonabsorptive materials such as glass or porcelain or by suspension from suitable wires or chains.

(b) Transformers. Transformers shall be installed in metal enclosures and as near as practicable to the gas tubing system.

(c) Supply Conductors. The supply conductors for the transformers shall be enclosed in grounded metallic raceway or rigid nonmetallic conduit where installed in accordance with the requirements of Article 347.

(d) High-Tension Conductors. High-tension conductors shall be insulated for the voltage of the circuit and shall be enclosed in grounded metallic raceway.

Exception: Conductors not exceeding 4 feet (1.22 m) in length between gas tubing and adjacent metallic enclosures shall be permitted to be enclosed in continuous glass or other insulating sleeves.

600-37. Portable Gas Tube Signs for Show Windows and Interior Use. This section shall apply to the installation and use of portable gas tube signs.

(a) Location. Portable gas tube signs shall be for indoor use only.

(b) Transformer. The transformer shall be of the window type or shall be within a metal enclosure.

(c) Supply Conductors. Supply conductors shall consist of hard or extra-hard usage-type cord containing a grounding conductor. The cord shall not exceed more than 10 feet (3.05 m) in length.

(d) High-Voltage Conductors. High-voltage conductors shall not be more than 6 feet (1.83 m) long and shall be located where not subject to mechanical injury, and shall be insulated for the voltage of the circuit and be protected by continuous glass or other insulating sleeves or tubing.

(e) Grounding. Transformers and attached noncurrent-carrying metal parts shall be grounded in accordance with Article 250.

(f) Support. Portable indoor signs shall be held in place by not more than two open hooks attached to the transformer case.

ARTICLE 604 — MANUFACTURED WIRING SYSTEMS

Contents

604-1. Scope. The provisions of this article apply to field-installed wiring using off-site manufactured subassemblies for branch circuits, remote-control circuits, signaling circuits, and communication circuits in accessible areas.

604-2. Definition.

Manufactured Wiring System. A system containing component parts that are assembled in the process of manufacture and cannot be inspected at the building site without damage or destruction to the assembly.

604-3. Uses Permitted. The manufactured wiring systems shall be permitted in accessible and dry locations and in plenums and spaces used for environmental air, when listed for this application, and installed in accordance with Section 300-22.

Exception: In concealed spaces, one end of tapped cable shall be permitted to extend into hollow walls for direct termination at switch and outlet points in an approved manner.

604-4. Uses Not Permitted. Where conductors or cables are limited by the provisions in Articles 333 and 334.

604-5. Other Articles. Installations shall conform with, but not be limited only to, applicable sections of the following articles: 110, 200, 210, 220, 250, 300, 310, 333, 334, 350, 410, 545, 640, 700, 725 and 800.

604-6. Construction.

(a) Cable Types. Cable shall be listed Type AC or MC nominal 600 volt No. 12 AWG copper insulated conductors with a bare No. 12 AWG copper bonding conductor or listed flexible metal conduit with 600 volt No. 12 AWG copper insulated conductors with an insulated No. 12 AWG copper grounding conductor. Each section shall be marked to identify the type cable.

(b) Receptacles and Connectors. Receptacles and connectors shall be locking type, uniquely polarized and identified for the purpose and shall be part of a listed assembly for the appropriate system.

See Figure 604-1.

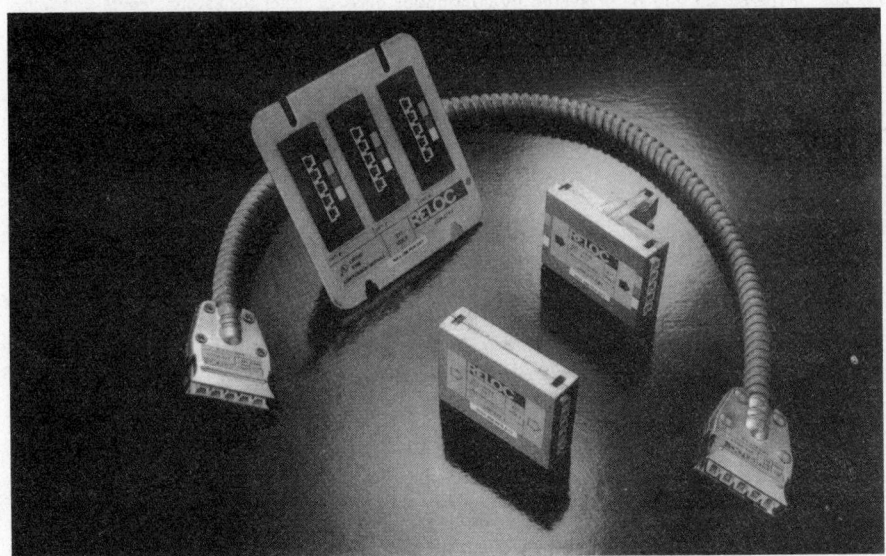

Figure 604-1. Components of a manufactured wiring system. (*RELOC a Div. of Lithonia Lighting*)

(c) Other Component Parts. Other component parts shall be listed for the appropriate system.

604-7. Unused Outlets. All unused outlets shall be capped to effectively close the connector openings.

ARTICLE 605 — OFFICE FURNISHINGS

(Consisting of Lighting Accessories and Wired Partitions)

Contents

605-1. Scope. This article covers electrical equipment, lighting accessories and wiring systems used to connect, or contained within, or installed on relocatable wired partitions.

This article is new in the 1984 *NEC*.

605-2. General. Wiring systems shall be identified as suitable for providing power for lighting accessories and appliances in wired partitions. These partitions shall not extend from floor to ceiling.

(a) Use. These assemblies shall be installed and used only as provided for by this article.

(b) Other Articles. Except as modified by the requirements of this article, all other articles of this Code shall apply.

(c) Hazardous (Classified) Locations. Where used in hazardous (classified) locations, manufactured wiring systems shall conform with Articles 500 through 517 in addition to this article.

605-3. Wireways. All conductors and connections shall be contained within wiring channels of metal or other material identified as suitable for the conditions of use. Wiring channels shall be free of projections or other conditions that may damage conductor insulation.

(FPN): Conductors as used in this section do not include flexible cord.

605-4. Partition Interconnections. The electrical connection between partitions shall be a flexible assembly identified for use with wired partitions.

Exception: Flexible cord shall be permitted for the connection between partitions provided all of the following conditions are met:

a. The cord is extra-hard usage type.

b. The partitions are mechanically contiguous.

c. The cord is not longer than necessary for maximum positioning of the partitions but in no case to exceed 2 feet (610 mm).

d. The cord is terminated at an attachment plug and cord-connector with strain relief.

605-5. Lighting Accessories. Lighting equipment identified for use with wired partitions shall comply with all of the following:

(a) Support. A means for secure attachment or support shall be provided.

(b) Connection. Where cord- and plug-connection is provided, the cord length shall be suitable for the intended application, but shall not exceed 8 feet (2.44 m) in length. Connection by other means shall be identified as suitable for the condition of use.

(c) Receptacle Outlet. Convenience receptacles shall not be permitted in lighting accessories.

605-6. Fixed-type Partitions. Wired partitions that are fixed (secured to building surfaces) shall be permanently connected to the building electrical system by one of the wiring methods of Chapter 3.

605-7. Free-Standing Type Partitions. Partitions of the free-standing type (not fixed) shall be permitted to be permanently connected to the building electrical system by one of the wiring methods of Chapter 3.

605-8. Free-Standing Type Partitions, Cord- and Plug-Connected. Individual partitions of the free-standing type, or groups of individual partitions which are electrically connected, mechanically contiguous and do not exceed 30 feet (9.14 m) when assembled shall be permitted to be connected to the building electrical system by a single flexible cord and plug provided all of the following conditions are met:

(a) Flexible Power Supply Cord. The flexible power-supply cord shall be extra-hard usage type with No. 12 AWG or larger conductors with an insulated grounding conductor and not exceeding 2 feet (610 mm) in length.

(b) Receptacle Supplying Power. The receptacle(s) supplying power shall be on a separate circuit serving only panels and no other loads and shall be located not more than 12 inches (305 mm) from the partition which is connected to it.

(c) Receptacle Outlets, Maximum. Individual partitions or groups of interconnected individual partitions shall not contain more than thirteen 15-ampere, 125-volt receptacle outlets.

(d) Multiwire Circuits, Not Permitted. Individual partitions or groups of interconnected individual partitions shall not contain multiwire circuits.

ARTICLE 610 — CRANES AND HOISTS

Contents

A. General

610-1. Scope. This article covers the installation of electric equipment and wiring used in connection with cranes, monorail hoists, hoists, and all runways.

(FPN): For further information, see Safety Code for Cranes, Derricks, Hoists, Jacks, and Slings (ANSI B-30).

610-2. Special Requirements for Particular Locations.

(a) Hazardous (Classified) Locations. All equipment which operates in a hazardous (classified) location shall conform to Article 500.

(1) Equipment used in locations which are hazardous because of the presence of flammable gases or vapors shall conform to Article 501.

(2) Equipment used in locations which are hazardous because of combustible dust shall conform to Article 502.

(3) Equipment used in locations which are hazardous because of the presence of easily ignitible fibers or flyings shall conform to Article 503.

(b) Combustible Materials. Where a crane, hoist, or monorail hoist operates over readily combustible material, the resistors shall be placed in a well-ventilated cabinet composed of noncombustible material so constructed that it will not emit flames or molten metal.

Exception: Resistors shall be permitted to be located in a cage or cab constructed of noncombustible material which encloses the sides of the cage or cab from the floor to a point at least 6 inches (152 mm) above the top of the resistors.

(c) Electrolytic Cell Lines. See Section 668-32.

Special precautions are necessary on electrolytic cell lines to prevent introduction of exposed grounded parts, as described in Section 668-32.

B. Wiring

610-11. Wiring Method. Conductors shall be enclosed in raceways or be Type MC cable, or Type MI cable.

Exception No. 1: Contact conductors.

Exception No. 2: Short lengths of open conductors at resistors, collectors, and other equipment.

Exception No. 3: Where flexible connections are necessary to motors and similar equipment, flexible stranded conductors shall be installed in flexible metal conduit, liquidtight flexible metal conduit, multiconductor cable, or an approved nonmetallic enclosure.

Exception No. 4: Where multiconductor cable is used with a suspended pushbutton station, the station shall be supported in some satisfactory manner that protects the electric conductors against strain.

Use of short lengths of "open" wiring is a permitted wiring method on cranes and hoists where a separately bushed hole from a box or fitting is provided for each conductor and the method is used for the connection of resistors, collectors, or similar equipment. In addition to other types of raceways, flexible metal conduit and liquidtight flexible metal conduit are permissible where flexibility is necessary.

ARTICLE 610—CRANES AND HOISTS

Figure 610-1. A suitable grip for strain relief with a suspended pushbutton station. (*Hubbell, Kellems Div.*)

610-12. Raceway Terminal Fittings. Conductors leaving raceways shall comply with one of the following:

(a) Separately Bushed Hole. A box or terminal fitting having a separately bushed hole for each conductor shall be used wherever a change is made from rigid metal conduit, intermediate metal conduit, electrical metallic tubing, nonmetallic-sheathed cable, metal-clad cable, or mineral-insulated cable or surface raceway wiring to open wiring. A fitting used for this purpose shall contain no taps or splices and shall not be used at fixture outlets.

(b) Bushing in Lieu of a Box. A bushing shall be permitted to be used in lieu of a box at the end of a rigid metal conduit, intermediate metal conduit or electrical metallic tubing where the raceway terminates at unenclosed controls or similar equipment including contact conductors, collectors, resistors, brakes, power circuit limit switches, and dc split frame motors.

610-13. Types of Conductors. Conductors shall comply with Table 310-13.

Exception No. 1: Conductor(s) exposed to external heat or connected to resistors shall have a flame-resistant outer covering or be covered with flame-resistant tape individually or as a group.

Exception No. 2: Contact conductors along runways, crane bridges, and monorails shall be permitted to be bare, and shall be copper, aluminum, steel, or other alloys or combinations thereof in the form of hard drawn wire, tees, angles, tee rails, or other stiff shapes.

Exception No. 3: Flexible conductors shall be permitted to be used to convey current and, where practicable, cable reels or take-up devices shall be employed.

610-14. Rating and Size of Conductors.

(a) Ampacity. The allowable ampacities of conductors shall be as shown in Table 610-14(a).

(FPN): For the ampacities of conductors between controllers and resistors, see Section 430-23.

Table 610-14(a).   Ampacities of Insulated Conductors up to Four Conductors in Raceway or Cable Used with Short-Time Rated Crane and Hoist Motors**

Max. Operating Temp. Size AWG MCM	75°C Type MTW, RH, RHW, THW, THWN, XHHW		90°C Type AVB, FEP, FEPB, PFA, PFAH, RHH, SA, TA, THHN, XHHW*, Z		110°C Type AVA	
	60 min	30 min	60 min	30 min	60 min	30 min
16	10	12	..	..	..	..
14	25	26	31	32	38	40
12	30	33	36	40	45	50
10	40	43	49	52	60	65
8	55	60	63	69	73	80
6	76	86	83	94	93	105
5	85	95	95	106	109	121
4	100	117	111	130	126	147
3	120	141	131	153	145	168
2	137	160	148	173	163	190
1	143	175	158	192	177	215
0	190	233	211	259	239	294
00	222	267	245	294	275	331
000	280	341	305	372	339	413
0000	300	369	319	399	352	440
250	364	420	400	461	447	516
300	455	582	497	636	554	707
350	486	646	542	716	616	809
400	538	688	593	760	666	856
450	600	765	660	836	740	930
500	660	847	726	914	815	1004

Other insulations shown in Table 310-13 and approved for the temperatures and location shall be permitted to be substituted for those shown in Table 610-14(a). The allowable ampacities of conductors used with 15-minute motors shall be the 30-minute ratings increased by 12 percent.   * For dry locations only. See Table 310-13.   ** For 5 or more simultaneously energized power conductors in raceway or cable, the ampacity of each power conductor shall be reduced to a value of 80 percent of that shown in the table.

(b) Secondary Resistor Conductors. Where the secondary resistor is separate from the controller, the minimum size of the conductors between controller and resistor shall be calculated by multiplying the motor secondary current by the appropriate factor from Table 610-14(b) and selecting a wire from Table 610-14(a).

Table 610-14(b). Secondary Conductor Rating Factors

Time in Seconds		Ampacity of Wire in Percent of Full-Load Secondary Current
On	Off	
5	75	35
10	70	45
15	75	55
15	45	65
15	30	75
15	15	85
Continuous Duty		110

(c) Minimum Size. Conductors external to motors and controls shall not be smaller than No. 16.

Exception No. 1: No. 18 wire in multiple conductor cord shall be permitted for control circuits at not over 7 amperes.

Exception No. 2: Wires not smaller than No. 20 shall be permitted for electronic circuits.

(d) Contact Conductors. Contact wires shall have an ampacity not less than that required by Table 610-14(a) for 75°C wire, and in no case shall they be smaller than the following:

Distance Between End Strain Insulators or Clamp-type Intermediate Supports	Size of Wire
0-30 feet	No. 6
30-60 feet	No. 4
Over 60 feet	No. 2

For SI units: one foot = 0.3048 meter.

(e) Calculation of Motor Load.

(1) For one motor, use 100 percent of motor nameplate full-load ampere rating.

(2) For multiple motors on a single crane or hoist, the minimum circuit ampacity of the power supply conductors on a crane or hoist shall be the nameplate full-load ampere rating of the largest motor or group of motors for any single crane motion, plus 50 percent of the nameplate full-load ampere rating of the next largest motor or group of motors, using that column of Table 610-14(a) which applies to the longest time-rated motor.

(3) For multiple cranes and/or hoists supplied by a common conductor system, compute the motor minimum ampacity for each crane as defined in Section 610-14(e), add them together, and multiply the sum by the appropriate demand factor from Table 610-14(e).

Table 610-14(e). Demand Factors

Number of Cranes or Hoists	Demand Factor
2	0.95
3	0.91
4	0.87
5	0.84
6	0.81
7	0.78

(f) Other Loads. Additional loads, such as heating, lighting, and air conditioning, shall be provided for by application of the appropriate sections of this Code.

(g) Nameplate. Each crane, monorail, or hoist shall be provided with a visible nameplate marked with the maker's name, the rating in volts, frequency, number of phases, and circuit amperes as calculated in Section 610-14(e) and (f).

610-15. Common Return. Where a crane or hoist is operated by more than one motor, a common-return conductor of proper ampacity shall be permitted.

C. Contact Conductors

610-21. Installation of Contact Conductors. Contact conductors shall comply with (a) through (h) below.

(a) Locating or Guarding Contact Conductors. Runway contact conductors shall be guarded and bridge contact conductors shall be located or guarded in a manner that persons cannot inadvertently touch energized current-carrying parts.

(b) Contact Wires. Wires that are used as contact conductors shall be secured at the ends by means of approved strain insulators and shall be so mounted on approved insulators that the extreme limit of displacement of the wire will not bring the latter within less than 1½ inches (38 mm) from the surface wired over.

(c) Supports Along Runways. Main contact conductors carried along runways shall be supported on insulating supports placed at intervals not exceeding 20 feet (6.1 m).

Exception: Supports for grounded rail conductors as provided in (f) below shall not be required to be of the insulating type.

Such conductors shall be separated not less than 6 inches (152 mm) other than for monorail hoists where a spacing of not less than 3 inches (76 mm) shall be permitted. Where necessary, intervals between insulating supports shall be permitted to be increased up to 40 feet (12.2 m), the separation between conductors being increased proportionately.

(d) Supports on Bridges. Bridge wire contact conductors shall be kept at least 2½ inches (64 mm) apart, and where the span exceeds 80 feet (24.4 m), insulating saddles shall be placed at intervals not exceeding 50 feet (15.2 m).

(e) Supports for Rigid Conductors. Conductors along runways and crane bridges, which are of the rigid type specified in Section 610-13, Exception No. 2, and not contained within an approved enclosed assembly, shall be carried on insulating supports spaced at intervals of not more than eighty times the vertical dimension of the conductor, but in no case greater than 15 feet (4.57 m), and spaced apart sufficiently to give a clear electrical separation of conductors or adjacent collectors of not less than 1 inch (25.4 mm).

(f) Track as Circuit Conductor. Monorail, tramrail, or crane-runway tracks shall be permitted as a conductor of current for one phase of a 3-phase, alternating-current system furnishing power to the carrier, crane, or trolley, provided all of the following conditions are met:

(1) The conductors supplying the other two phases of the power supply are insulated.

(2) The power for all phases is obtained from an insulating transformer.

(3) The voltage does not exceed 300 volts.

839

(4) The rail serving as a conductor is effectively grounded at the transformer and also shall be permitted to be grounded by the fittings used for the suspension or attachment of the rail to a building or structure.

Crane-runway tracks are permitted as a current-carrying conductor where part of a 3-phase system is furnishing power to the crane. Figure 610-2 illustrates a 3-phase isolated-delta secondary with one phase grounded at the transformer. It is also permitted to be grounded through the metal supporting means attached to the metal frame of a building.

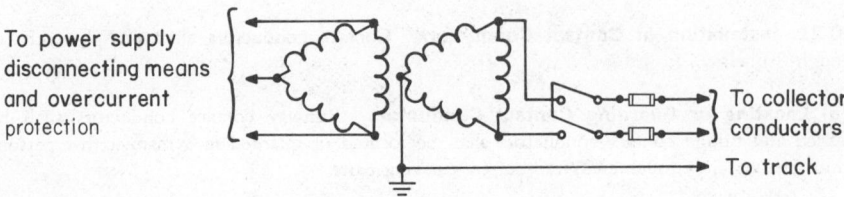

To power supply disconnecting means and overcurrent protection

To collector conductors

To track

Figure 610-2. Three-phase delta isolating transformer.

(g) Electrical Continuity of Contact Conductors. All sections of contact conductors shall be mechanically joined to provide a continuous electrical connection.

(h) Not to Supply Other Equipment. Contact conductors shall not be used as feeders for any equipment other than the crane or cranes which they are primarily designed to serve.

610-22. Collectors. Collectors shall be so designed as to reduce to a minimum sparking between them and the contact conductor; and where operated in rooms used for the storage of easily ignitible combustible fibers and materials, they shall comply with Section 503-13.

D. Disconnecting Means

610-31. Runway Conductor Disconnecting Means. A disconnecting means having a continuous ampere rating not less than that computed in Section 610-14(e) and (f) shall be provided between the runway contact conductors and the power supply. Such disconnecting means shall consist of a motor circuit switch or circuit breaker. This disconnecting means shall be readily accessible and operable from the ground or floor level, shall be arranged to be locked in the open position, shall open all ungrounded conductors simultaneously, and shall be placed within view of the crane or hoist and the runway contact conductors.

610-32. Disconnecting Means for Cranes and Monorail Hoists. A motor circuit switch or circuit breaker arranged to be locked in the open position shall be provided in the leads from the runway contact conductors or other power supply on all cranes and monorail hoists.

Exception: Where a monorail hoist or hand-propelled crane bridge installation meets all of the following, the disconnect shall be permitted to be omitted.

a. The unit is floor controlled.

b. The unit is within view of the power supply disconnecting means.

c. No fixed work platform has been provided for servicing the unit.

Where the disconnecting means is not readily accessible from the crane or monorail hoist operating station, means shall be provided at the operating station to open the power circuit to all motors of the crane or monorail hoist.

Many crane installations are not arranged so that the unit is within view of the power supply disconnecting means, hence the requirement that a disconnecting means (lock-open type) be provided in the contact conductors. However, personnel should be aware that, while servicing one crane, another unit on the same system could remain energized and could be run into the person performing maintenance on the locked-out unit.

610-33. Rating of Disconnecting Means. The continuous ampere rating of the switch or circuit breaker required by Section 610-32 shall not be less than 50 percent of the combined short-time ampere rating of the motors, nor less than 75 percent of the sum of the short-time ampere rating of the motors required for any single motion.

E. Overcurrent Protection

610-41. Feeders, Runway Conductors. The runway supply conductors and main contact conductors of a crane or monorail shall be protected by an overcurrent device(s) which shall not be greater than the largest rating or setting of any branch-circuit protective device, plus the sum of the nameplate ratings of all the other loads with application of the demand factors from Table 610-14(e).

610-42. Branch-Circuit Short-Circuit and Ground-Fault Protection. Branch circuits shall be protected as follows:

(a) Fuse or Circuit Breaker Rating. Crane, hoist, and monorail hoist motor branch circuits shall be protected by fuses or inverse-time circuit breakers having a rating in accordance with Table 430-152. Taps to control circuits shall be permitted to be taken from the load side of a branch-circuit protective device, provided each tap and piece of equipment is properly protected.

Exception No. 1: When two or more motors operate a single motion, the sum of their nameplate current ratings shall be considered as a single motor current in the above calculations.

Exception No. 2: Two or more motors shall be permitted to be connected to the same branch circuit if no tap to an individual motor has an ampacity less than one-third that of the branch circuit and if each motor is protected for overload according to Section 610-43.

(b) Taps to Brake Coils. Taps to brake coils do not require separate overcurrent protection.

610-43. Motor and Branch-Circuit Overload Protection. Each motor, motor control, and branch-circuit conductor shall be protected from overload by one of the following means:

(1) A single motor shall be considered as protected when the branch-circuit overcurrent device meets the rating requirements of Section 610-42.

(2) Overload relay elements in each ungrounded circuit conductor, with all relay elements protected from short circuit by the branch-circuit protection.

(3) Thermal sensing device(s), sensitive to motor temperature or to temperature and current which are thermally in contact with the motor winding(s). A hoist or trolley is considered to be protected if the sensing device is connected in the hoist's upper limit switch circuit so as to prevent further hoisting during an overload condition of either motor.

Exception No. 1: If the motor is manually controlled, with spring return controls, the overload protective device need not protect the motor against stalled rotor conditions.

Exception No. 2: Where two or more motors drive a single trolley, truck, or bridge and are controlled as a unit by a single set of overload devices with a rating equal to the sum of their rated full-load currents. A hoist or trolley is considered to be protected if the sensing device is connected in the hoist's upper limit switch circuit so as to prevent further hoisting during an overtemperature condition of either motor.

Exception No. 3: Hoists and monorail hoists and their trolleys which are not used as part of an overhead traveling crane do not require individual motor overload protection provided the largest motor does not exceed 7 ½ horsepower and all motors are under manual control of the operator.

F. Control

610-51. Separate Controllers. Each motor shall be provided with an individual controller.

Exception No. 1: Where two or more motors drive a single hoist, carriage, truck, or bridge, they shall be permitted to be controlled by a single controller.

Exception No. 2: One controller shall be permitted to be switched between motors provided,

a. The controller shall have a horsepower rating which shall not be lower than the horsepower rating of the largest motor.

b. Only one motor is operated at one time.

610-53. Overcurrent Protection. Conductors of control circuits shall be protected against overcurrent. Control circuits shall be considered as protected by overcurrent devices that are rated or set at not more than 300 percent of the ampacity of the control conductors.

Exception No. 1: Taps to control transformers shall be considered as protected when the secondary circuit is protected by a device rated or set at not more than 200 percent of the rated secondary current of the transformer and not more than 200 percent of the ampacity of the control circuit conductors.

Exception No. 2: Such conductors shall be considered as being properly protected by the branch-circuit overcurrent devices where the opening of the control circuit would create a hazard, as for example, the control circuit of a hot metal crane.

610-55. Limit Switch. A limit switch or other device shall be provided to prevent the load block from passing the safe upper limit of travel of all hoisting mechanisms.

610-57. Clearance. The dimension of the working space in the direction of access to live parts which are likely to require examination, adjustment, servicing, or maintenance while alive shall be a minimum of 2½ feet (762 mm). Where controls are enclosed in cabinets, the door(s) shall either open at least 90 degrees or be removable.

G. Grounding

610-61. Grounding. All exposed metal parts of cranes, monorail hoists, hoists and accessories including pendant controls shall be metallically joined together into a continuous electrical conductor so that the entire crane or hoist will be grounded in accordance with Article 250. Moving parts, other than removable accessories or attachments having metal-to-metal bearing surfaces, shall be considered to be electrically connected to each other through the bearing surfaces for grounding purposes. The trolley frame and bridge frame shall be considered as electrically grounded through the bridge and trolley wheels and its respective tracks unless local conditions, such as paint or other insulating material, prevent reliable metal-to-metal contact. In this case a separate bonding conductor shall be provided.

It is not the intent that the trolley frame or bridge frame serve as the equipment grounding conductor for electric equipment (such as motors, motor controllers, etc.) on a crane. Electric equipment is required to be grounded in accordance with Article 250. See Section 250-91(b) for acceptable types of equipment grounding conductors. However, it is intended that the trolley frame and bridge frame be bonded together and grounded. The bonding and grounding of these nonelectrical structural parts can be through the bridge and trolley wheels and the respective tracks unless local conditions prevent reliable metal-to-metal contact.

ARTICLE 620 — ELEVATORS, DUMBWAITERS, ESCALATORS, AND MOVING WALKS

Contents

ARTICLE 620—ELEVATORS, DUMBWAITERS

A. General

620-1. Scope. This article covers the installation of electric equipment and wiring used in connection with elevators, dumbwaiters, escalators, and moving walks.

(FPN): For further information, see Safety Code for Elevators and Escalators (ANSI/ASME A17.1-1981).

    This article is also applicable to similar equipment, such as moving theater stages. The Fine Print Note is necessary to provide for lighting requirements for and about the equipment, including workspace areas.

620-2. Voltage Limitations. The nominal voltage used for elevator, dumbwaiter, escalator, and moving-walk operating control and signaling circuits, operating equipment, driving machine motors, machine brakes, and motor-generator sets shall not exceed the following:

(a) 300 Volts. For operating control and signaling circuits and related equipment, including door operator motors.

Exception: Higher potentials shall be permitted for frequencies of 25- through 60-hertz alternating current or for direct current provided the current in the system cannot, under any conditions, exceed 8 milliamperes for alternating current or 30 milliamperes for direct current.

(b) 600 Volts. Driving machine motors, machine brakes, and motor-generator sets.

Exception: Higher potentials shall be permitted for driving motors of motor-generator sets.

620-3. Live Parts Enclosed. All live parts of electric apparatus in the hoistways, at the landings, or in or on the cars of elevators and dumbwaiters or in the wellways or the landings of escalators or moving walks shall be enclosed to protect against accidental contact.

B. Conductors

620-11. Insulation of Conductors. The insulation of conductors installed in connection with elevators, dumbwaiters, escalators, and moving walks shall comply with (a) through (e) below.

(a) Control Panel Wiring. Conductors from panels to main circuit resistors shall be flame-retardant and suitable for a temperature of not less than 90°C (194°F). All other wiring on control panels shall be flame-retardant and moisture-resistant.

(b) Hoistway Door Interlock Wiring. The conductors to the hoistway door interlocks from the hoistway riser shall be flame-retardant, moisture-resistant, and suitable for a temperature of not less than 200°C (392°F).

(c) Traveling Cables. Traveling cables used as flexible connections between the elevator or dumbwaiter car and the raceway shall be of the types of elevator cable listed in Table 400-4 or other approved types.

(d) Other Wiring. All conductors in raceways; in or on the cars of elevators and dumbwaiters; in the wellways of escalators and moving walks; and in the machine room of elevators, dumbwaiters, escalators, and moving walks shall have flame-retardant and moisture-resistant insulation.

(e) Thickness of Insulation. The thickness of the insulation of all conductors shall be suitable for the voltage to which the conductors are subjected.

Conductors from control panels to main circuit resistors are required to be suitable for temperatures of not less than 90°C (194°F). All other control panel wiring and all other wiring on control panels is required to be flame-retardant and moisture-resistant. Hoistway door interlock wiring is required to be suitable for 200°C (392°F). See Table 310-13 for conductor application and insulation. See also Table 310-16.

See Table 400-4 for approved types of elevator cables to be used in hazardous (classified) and nonhazardous locations. See also Notes 4 and 6 to Table 400-4. A characteristic equally important with respect to safety is the prevention of twisting of cables during their rise and fall with the elevator or dumbwaiter.

620-12. Minimum Size of Conductors. The minimum size of conductors used for elevator, dumbwaiter, escalator, and moving-walk wiring, other than conductors that form an integral part of control equipment, shall be as follows:

(a) Traveling Cables.

(1) For lighting circuits: No. 14.

Exception: No. 20 or larger conductors shall be permitted in parallel provided the ampacity is equivalent to at least that of No. 14 wire.

(2) Operating control and signaling circuits: No. 20.

(b) Other Wiring. All operating control and signaling circuits: No. 24.

Extensive use of electronics with the correspondingly lower currents permits the use of smaller wire sizes; hence, conductors of elevator cables may be sized as small as No. 20 AWG conforming to the description in Table 400-4. Operating control and signal circuits in other than traveling cables may be as small as No. 24 AWG. They should, of course, have the necessary strength and durability for the purpose.

620-13. Motor Circuit Conductors. Conductors supplying elevator, dumbwaiter, escalator or moving-walk motors shall have an ampacity in accordance with (a), (b), and (c) below based on the nameplate current rating of the motors. With generator field control, the ampacity shall be based on the nameplate current rating of the driving motor of the motor-generator set which supplies power to the elevator motor.

ARTICLE 620—ELEVATORS, DUMBWAITERS

(FPN): The heating of conductors depends on root-mean-square current values which, with generator field control, are reflected by the nameplate current rating of the motor-generator set driving motor rather than by the rating of the elevator motor, which represents actual but short-time and intermittent full-load current values.

(a) Conductors Supplying Single Motor. Conductors supplying a single motor shall have an ampacity in conformance with Section 430-22, and Table 430-22(a) Exception.

(b) Conductors Supplying Several Motors. Conductors supplying two or more motors shall have an ampacity of not less than 125 percent of the nameplate current rating of the highest rated motor in the group plus the sum of the nameplate current ratings of the remainder of the motors in the group.

(c) Feeder Demand Factor. Feeder conductors of less ampacity than required by (b) above shall be permitted subject to the requirements of Section 430-26.

C. Wiring

620-21. Wiring Methods. Conductors located in hoistways, in escalator and moving-walk wellways, in or on cars, and in machine and control rooms, not including the traveling cables connecting the car and hoistway wiring, shall be installed in rigid metal conduit, intermediate metal conduit, electrical metallic tubing, wireways, or be Type MC cable or Type MI cable.

Exception No. 1: Flexible metal conduit or Type AC cable shall be permitted in hoistways and in escalator and moving-walk wellways between risers and limit switches, interlocks, operating buttons, and similar devices. Low-voltage cables (24 volts or less) shall be permitted to be installed between risers and signal fixtures.

Exception No. 2: Short runs of flexible metal conduit or Type AC cable shall be permitted on cars where so located as to be free from oil and if securely fastened in place.

Exception No. 3: Type S, SO, ST, STO, SJ, or SJO shall be permitted as flexible connections between the fixed wiring on the car and devices on the car doors or gates. Type S, SO, ST or STO shall be permitted as flexible connections for the top-of-car operating device or the car-top work light. These devices or fixtures shall be grounded by means of a grounding conductor run with the circuit conductors.

Exception No. 4: Conductors between control panels and machine motors, machine brakes, and motor-generator sets, not exceeding 6 feet (1.83 m) in length, shall be permitted to be grouped together and taped or corded without being installed in a raceway provided the taping or cording is painted with an insulating paint. Such cable groups shall be supported at intervals of not more than 3 feet (914 mm) and so located as to be free from physical damage.

Exception No. 5: Flexible metal conduit of ⅜ inch nominal trade size shall be permitted in lengths not in excess of 6 feet (1.83 m).

Where motor-generators and machine motors are located adjacent to or underneath control equipment and are provided with extra length terminal leads not exceeding 6 feet (1.83 m) in length, such leads shall be permitted to be extended to connect directly to controller terminal studs without regard to the carrying-capacity requirements of Articles 430 and 445. Auxiliary gutters shall be permitted in machine and control rooms between controllers, starters, and similar apparatus.

620-22. Car Light Source. On multicar installations, a separate branch circuit shall supply the car lights for each elevator.

D. Installation of Conductors

620-31. Raceway Terminal Fittings. Conductors shall comply with Section 300-16(b). In locations where conduits project from the floor and terminate in other than a wiring enclosure, they shall extend at least 6 inches (152 mm) above the floor.

620-32. Wireways. Section 362-5 shall not apply to wireways. The sum of the cross-sectional area of the individual conductors in a wireway shall not be more than 50 percent of the interior cross-sectional area of the wireway.

Vertical runs of wireways shall be securely supported at intervals not exceeding 15 feet (4.57 m) and shall have not more than one joint between supports. Adjoining wireway sections shall be securely fastened together to provide a rigid joint.

620-33. Number of Conductors in Raceways. The sum of the cross-sectional area of the operating and control circuit conductors in raceways shall not exceed 40 percent of the interior cross-sectional area of the raceway.

Exception: In wireways as permitted in Section 620-32.

620-34. Supports. Supports for cables or raceways in a hoistway or in an escalator or moving-walk wellway shall be securely fastened to the guide rail or to the hoistway or wellway construction.

620-35. Auxiliary Gutters (Wiring Troughs). Auxiliary gutters shall not be subject to the restrictions of Section 374-2 as to length or of Section 374-5 as to number of conductors.

620-36. Different Systems in One Raceway or Traveling Cable. Conductors for operating, control, power, signaling, and lighting circuits of 600 volts or less shall be permitted to be run in the same traveling cable or raceway system if all conductors are insulated for the maximum voltage found in the cables or raceway system and if all live parts of the equipment are insulated from ground for this maximum voltage. Such a traveling cable or raceway shall also be permitted to include a pair of telephone conductors for the car telephone, provided such conductors are insulated for the maximum voltage found in the cable or raceway system.

With the use of greater numbers of individual cables and the use of much longer cables in tall buildings, there is a possibility of intertwisting cable loops. In order to eliminate the practice of tying a cable to the traveling cable, one elevator cable or raceway is permitted to enclose all the conductors of power, control, lighting, video, and communication circuits where all conductors are insulated for the maximum voltage of any conductor within the cable or raceway.

620-37. Wiring in Hoistways. Main feeders for supplying power to elevators and dumbwaiters shall be installed outside the hoistway. Only such electric wiring, conduit, and cable used directly in connection with the elevator or dumbwaiter, including wiring for signals, for communication with the car, for lighting and ventilating the car, and wiring for fire-detecting systems for the hoistways, shall be permitted inside the hoistway.

Exception: In existing structures, feeders for elevators or other purposes shall be permitted within a hoistway by special permission provided no conductors are spliced within the hoistway.

620-38. Electric Equipment in Garages and Similar Occupancies. Electric equipment and wiring used for elevators, dumbwaiters, escalators, and moving walks in garages shall comply with the requirements of Article 511. Wiring and equipment located on the underside of the car platform shall be considered as being located in the hazardous area.

ARTICLE 620—ELEVATORS, DUMBWAITERS

620-39. Sidewalk Elevators. Sidewalk elevators with sidewalk doors located exterior to the building shall have all electric wiring in rigid metal conduit, intermediate metal conduit, liquidtight flexible metal conduit or electrical metallic tubing and all electrical outlets, switches, junction boxes, and fittings shall be weatherproof.

E. Traveling Cables

620-41. Suspension of Traveling Cables. Traveling cables shall be so suspended at the car and hoistways' ends as to reduce the strain on the individual copper conductors to a minimum.

Traveling cables shall be supported by one of the following means: (1) by its steel supporting fillers; (2) by looping the cables around supports for unsupported lengths less than 100 feet (30.5 m); (3) by suspending from the supports by a means that automatically tightens around the cable when tension is increased for unsupported lengths up to 200 feet (61 m).

620-42. Hazardous (Classified) Locations. In hazardous (classified) locations, traveling cables shall be of a type approved for hazardous (classified) locations and shall be secured to explosionproof cabinets as provided in Section 501-11.

620-43. Location of and Protection for Cables. Traveling cable supports shall be so located as to reduce to a minimum the possibility of damage due to the cables coming in contact with the hoistway construction or equipment in the hoistway. Where necessary, suitable guards shall be provided to protect the cables against damage.

620-44. Installation of Traveling Cables. Traveling cable shall be permitted to be run without the use of raceway or conduit for a distance not exceeding 6 feet (1.83 m) in length as measured from the first point of support on the elevator car or hoistway wall, providing the conductors are grouped together and taped or corded, or in the original sheath.

Traveling cables may be continued to elevator control panels and to elevator car and machine room connections, as fixed wiring, providing it is suitably supported and protected from damage.

F. Control

620-51. Disconnecting Means. Elevators, dumbwaiters, escalators, and moving walks shall have a single means for disconnecting all ungrounded main power supply conductors for each unit. Where multiple driving machines are connected to a single elevator, escalator, moving walk, or pumping unit, there shall be one disconnecting means to disconnect the motor(s) and control valve operating magnets.

Where there is more than one driving machine in a machine room, disconnecting means shall be numbered to correspond to the number of the driving machine which they control.

(a) Type. The disconnecting means shall be an enclosed externally operable fused motor circuit switch or circuit breaker arranged to be locked in the open position. No provision shall be made to close this disconnecting means from any other part of the premises, nor shall circuit breakers be opened automatically by a fire alarm system.

(b) Location. The disconnecting means shall be located where it is readily accessible to qualified persons.

(1) On ac control and rheostatic controlled elevators, the disconnecting means shall be located in the vicinity of the controller. When the machine is not in the vicinity of the controller, an additional manually operated switch shall be provided at the machine, connected in the control circuit to prevent starting.

(2) On elevators with generator field control, the disconnecting means shall be located within sight of the motor starter for the driver motor of the motor-generator set. When the disconnecting means is not within sight of the hoist machine, the control panel, or the motor-generator set, an additional manually operated switch shall be installed adjacent to the remote equipment, connected in the control circuit to prevent starting.

(3) On escalators and moving walks, the disconnecting means shall be installed in the space where the controller is located.

620-52. Power from More than One Source.

(a) Single- and Multi-Car Installations. On single- and multi-car installations, equipment receiving electrical power from more than one source shall be provided with a disconnecting means from each source of electrical power within sight of the equipment served.

(b) Warning Sign for Multiple Disconnecting Means. Where multiple disconnecting means are used and parts of the control panel remain energized from a source other than the one disconnected, a warning sign shall be mounted on or adjacent to the disconnecting means. The sign shall be clearly legible and shall read "Warning — Parts of the control panel are not de-energized by this switch."

(c) Interconnection Multicar Control Panels. Where interconnections between control panels are necessary for the operation of the system on multicar installations that remain energized from a source other than the one disconnected, a warning sign in accordance with Section 620-52(b) shall be mounted on or adjacent to the disconnecting means.

620-53. Phase Protection.

(a) Electric Elevators. Electric elevators driven by polyphase alternating-current motors shall be provided with a means to prevent starting of the elevator motor when: (1) the phase rotation is in the wrong direction, or (2) there is a failure in any phase.

If the motor rotation were in the wrong direction, the elevator car would also travel in the wrong direction, hence the use of a reverse-phase relay which would prevent the controller from energizing the motor. This condition is possible when a worker unintentionally crosses two conductor leads of the motor circuit during maintenance or replacement.

(b) Hydraulic Elevators. Hydraulic elevators powered by a polyphase alternating-current motor shall be provided with the means to prevent overheating of the drive system (pump and motor) due to phase rotation reversals or failure.

Although phase reversal will not result in the car traveling in the wrong direction if the elevator is hydraulically operated, phase reversal can cause overheating of the drive system because the pump will run backwards.

G. Overcurrent Protection

620-61. Overcurrent Protection. Overcurrent protection shall be provided as follows:

(a) Control and Operating Circuits. Control and operating circuits and signaling circuits shall be protected against overcurrent in accordance with the requirements of Section 725-12.

(b) Motors.

(1) Duty on elevator and dumbwaiter driving machine motors and driving motors of motor-generators used with generator field control shall be classed as intermittent. Such motors shall be protected against overcurrent in accordance with Section 430-33.

(2) Duty on escalator and moving-walk driving machine motors shall be classed as continuous. Such motors shall be protected against overcurrent in accordance with Section 430-32.

(3) Escalator and moving-walk driving machine motors and driving motors of motor-generator sets shall be protected against running overcurrent as provided in Table 430-37.

H. Machine Room

620-71. Guarding Equipment. Elevator, dumbwaiter, escalator, and moving-walk driving machines, motor-generator sets, motor controllers, and disconnecting means shall be installed in a room or enclosure set aside for that purpose. The room or enclosure shall be secured against unauthorized access.

Exception: Dumbwaiter, escalator, or moving-walk motor controllers shall be permitted outside the spaces herein specified, provided they are enclosed in cabinets with doors or removable panels capable of being locked in the closed position and the disconnecting means is located adjacent to the motor controller. Such cabinets shall be permitted in the balustrading on the side away from the moving steps or moving treadway.

620-72. Clearance Around Control Panels and Disconnecting Means. Sufficient clear working space shall be provided around control panels and disconnecting means to provide safe and convenient access to all live parts of the equipment necessary for maintenance and adjustment. The minimum clear working space about live parts on control panels and disconnecting means shall not be less than specified in Section 110-16.

Exception: Where an escalator or moving walk control panel and disconnecting means are mounted in the same space as the escalator or moving walk drive machine and the clearances specified cannot be provided, the clearance requirements of Section 110-16 shall be permitted to be waived where the entire panel and disconnecting means are arranged so that they can be readily removed from the machine space and are provided with flexible leads to all external connections.

Where control panels are not located in the same space as the drive machine, they shall be located in cabinets with doors or removable panels capable of being locked in the closed position. Such cabinets shall be permitted in the balustrading on the side away from the moving steps or moving treadway.

J. Grounding

620-81. Metal Raceways Attached to Cars. Conduit, Type MC cable, or Type AC cable attached to elevator cars shall be bonded to grounded metal parts of the car with which they come in contact.

620-82. Electric Elevators. For electric elevators, the frames of all motors, elevator machines, controllers, and the metal enclosures for all electric devices in or on the car or in the hoistway shall be grounded.

620-83. Nonelectric Elevators. For elevators other than electric having any electric conductors attached to the car, the metal frame of the car, where normally accessible to persons, shall be grounded.

620-85. Inherent Ground. Equipment mounted on members of the structural metal frame of a building shall be considered to be grounded. Metal car frames supported by metal hoisting cables attached to or running over sheaves or drums of elevator machines shall be considered to be grounded where the machine is grounded in accordance with Article 250.

K. Overspeed

620-91. Overspeed Protection for Elevators. Under overhauling load conditions a means shall be provided on the load side of each elevator power disconnecting means to prevent the elevator from attaining a speed equal to the governor tripping speed or a speed in excess of 125 percent of the elevator rated speed, whichever is the lesser.

Overhauling load conditions shall include all loads up to rated elevator loads for freight elevators and all loads up to 125 percent of rated elevator loads for passenger elevators.

620-92. Motor-Generator Overspeed Device. Motor-generators driven by direct-current motors and used to supply direct current for the operation of elevator machine motors shall be provided with speed-limiting devices as required by Section 430-89(c) that will prevent the elevator from attaining at any time a speed of more than 125 percent of its rated speed.

620-101. Emergency Power. An elevator can be powered by an emergency power system provided that when operating on such emergency power there is conformance with Section 620-91.

Exception: Where the emergency power system is designed to operate only one elevator at a time, the energy absorption means, if required, shall be permitted on the power side of the disconnecting means, provided all other requirements of Section 620-91 are conformed to when operating any of the elevators the system might serve.

(a) Other Building Loads. Other building loads, such as power and light that can be supplied by the emergency power system, shall not be considered as means of absorbing the regenerated energy for the purpose of conforming to Section 620-91 unless such loads are using their normal power from the emergency power system when it is activated.

(b) Disconnecting Means. The disconnecting means required by Section 620-51 shall disconnect the emergency power service and the normal power service.

ARTICLE 630 — ELECTRIC WELDERS

Contents

A. General

630-1. Scope. This article covers electric arc welding, resistance welding apparatus, and other similar welding equipment that is connected to an electric supply system.

ARTICLE 630—ELECTRIC WELDERS

The two general types of electric welding are resistance welding and arc welding. Resistance welding or "spot" welding is the process of joining or fusing together electrically two or more metal sheets or parts without any preparation of stock. The metal parts are placed between two electrodes, or welding points, and a heavy current at a low voltage is passed through the electrodes. The metal parts offer a great resistance to the flow of current so that they heat to a molten state and a weld is made.

Arc welding is the "butting" of two metal parts to be welded and striking an arc at this joint with a metal electrode (a flux coated wire rod). The electrode, itself, is melted and supplies the extra metal necessary for joining the metal parts.

A transformer supplies current for one ac arc welder and a generator supplies current for one or more dc arc welders.

B. AC Transformer and DC Rectifier Arc Welders

630-11. Ampacity of Supply Conductors. The ampacity of conductors for ac transformer and dc rectifier arc welders shall be as follows:

(a) Individual Welders. The rated ampacity of the supply conductors shall not be less than the current values determined by multiplying the rated primary current in amperes given on the welder nameplate and the following factor based upon the duty cycle or time rating of the welder.

Duty Cycle (percent)	100	90	80	70	60	50	40	30	20 or less
Multiplier	1.00	.95	.89	.84	.78	.71	.63	.55	.45

For a welder having a time rating of 1 hour, the multiplying factor shall be 0.75.

(b) Group of Welders. The rated ampacity of conductors that supply a group of welders shall be permitted to be less than the sum of the currents, as determined in accordance with (a) above, of the welders supplied. The conductor rating shall be determined in each case according to the welder loading based on the use to be made of each welder and the allowance permissible in the event that all the welders supplied by the conductors will not be in use at the same time. The load value used for each welder shall take into account both the magnitude and the duration of the load while the welder is in use.

(FPN): Conductor ratings based on 100 percent of the current, as determined in accordance with (a) above, of the two largest welders, 85 percent for the third largest welder, 70 percent for the fourth largest welder, and 60 percent for all the remaining welders, can be assumed to provide an ample margin of safety under high-production conditions with respect to the maximum permissible temperature of the conductors. Percentage values lower than those given are permissible in cases where the work is such that a high-operating duty cycle for individual welders is impossible.

Even under high-production conditions the loads on transformer arc welders are considered intermittent; therefore, it is permissible to reduce the ampacity of feeder conductors supplying several transformers (three or more) to the allowable percentages described in the Fine Print Note. It is obvious that intermittent transformer arc welder loads would be considerably less than a continuous load equal to the sum of the full-load current ratings of all the transformers. See also Section 630-31(b).

630-12. Overcurrent Protection. Overcurrent protection for ac transformer and dc rectifier arc welders shall be as provided in (a) and (b) below. Where the nearest standard rating of the overcurrent device used is under the value specified in this section, or where the rating or setting specified results in unnecessary opening of the overcurrent device, the next higher rating or setting shall be permitted.

(a) For Welders. Each welder shall have overcurrent protection rated or set at not more than 200 percent of the rated primary current of the welder.

Exception: An overcurrent device shall not be required for a welder having supply conductors protected by an overcurrent device rated or set at not more than 200 percent of the rated primary current of the welder.

(b) For Conductors. Conductors that supply one or more welders shall be protected by an overcurrent device rated or set at not more than 200 percent of the conductor rating.

Some arc-welding machines have a welding-range involving an excess second-ary-current output capacity beyond that indicated by the marked secondary rating on the machines. This excess capacity (generally not more than 150 percent of the marked output capacity) is usually supplied by means of one or more secondary taps in addition to the tap, or taps, intended for normal output current; and the higher currents thus available are intended to provide for heavier welding work, including the use of larger size electrodes. This excess capacity is somewhat analogous to the inherent overload capacity of motors and transformers, and it is not covered at present by any definite requirements and is not investigated by Underwriters Laboratories Inc. However, the abuse of this excess current capacity, and overloading of a welding machine, except for relatively short periods of time, may be hazardous and should receive careful consideration by all those concerned.

630-13. Disconnecting Means. A disconnecting means shall be provided in the supply for each ac transformer and dc rectifier arc welder which is not equipped with a disconnect mounted as an integral part of the welder.

The disconnecting means shall be a switch or circuit breaker, and its rating shall not be less than that necessary to accommodate overcurrent protection as specified under Section 630-12.

630-14. Marking. A nameplate shall be provided for ac transformer and dc rectifier arc welders giving the following information: name of manufacturer; frequency; number of phases; primary voltage; rated primary current; maximum open-circuit voltage; rated secondary current; basis of rating, such as the duty cycle or time rating.

C. Motor-Generator Arc Welders

630-21. Ampacity of Supply Conductors. The ampacity of conductors for motor-generator arc welders shall be as follows:

(a) Individual Welders. The rated ampacity of the supply conductors shall not be less than the current values determined by multiplying the rated primary current in amperes given on the welder nameplate and the following factor based upon the duty cycle or time rating of the welder.

Duty Cycle (percent)	100	90	80	70	60	50	40	30	20 or less
Multiplier	1.00	.96	.91	.86	.81	.75	.69	.62	.55

For a welder having a time rating of 1 hour, the multiplying factor shall be 0.80.

(b) Group of Welders. The rated ampacity of conductors that supply a group of welders shall be permitted to be less than the sum of the currents, as determined in accordance with (a) above, of the welders supplied. The conductor rating shall be determined in each case according to the welder loading based on the use to be made of each welder and the allowance permissible in the event that all the welders supplied by the conductors will not be in use at the same time. The load value used for each welder shall take into account both the magnitude and the duration of the load while the welder is in use.

(FPN): Conductor ratings based on 100 percent of the current, as determined in accordance with (a) above, of the two largest welders, 85 percent for the third largest welder, 70 percent for the fourth largest welder, and 60 percent for all the remaining welders, can be assumed to provide an ample margin of safety under high-production conditions with respect to the maximum permissible temperature of the conductors. Percentage values lower than those given are permissible in cases where the work is such that a high-operating duty cycle for individual welders is impossible.

The ampacity of supply conductors for a welder that is not wired for a specific function, that is, one operated at varying intervals for different applications such as dissimilar metals or thicknesses, is permitted to be 70 percent of the rated primary current for automatically fed welders and 50 percent of the rated primary current for manually operated welders.

Rated primary current = kVA × 1,000 ÷ rated primary voltage (using values given on nameplate).

Where the "actual" primary current and duty cycle are known, such as for a welder wired for a specific operation, the ampacity of the supply conductors is not permitted to be less than the product of the actual primary current (current drawn during weld operation) and the multiplier [as given in (a)(2)] for the duty cycle at which the welder will be operated. For example, a spot welder is specifically set to perform 300 welds per hour on a 60-Hz system. Each weld draws current for 16 cycles. During the one-hour period, the welder draws current for 4,800 cycles (300 × 16). There are 216,000 cycles per hour (60 × 60 × 60).

$$\frac{4,800}{216,000} \times 100 \text{ percent} = 2.2 \text{ percent (duty cycle)}$$

Or, a seam welder draws current for 3 cycles and is off for 4 cycles during every 7-cycle period.

$$\frac{3}{7} \times 100 \text{ percent} = 42.9 \text{ percent (duty cycle)}$$

An ammeter capable of measuring current impulses for 3 cycles (1/20th of a second), as per the example, is required to measure the actual primary current. The duty cycle is set for a specific operation by adjusting the controller for the welder. When sizing supply conductors, voltage drop should be limited to a value permissible for the satisfactory performance of the welder.

630-22. Overcurrent Protection. Overcurrent protection for motor-generator arc welders shall be as provided in (a) and (b) below. Where the nearest standard rating of the overcurrent device used is under the value specified in this section, or where the rating or setting specified results in unnecessary opening of the overcurrent device, the next higher rating or setting shall be permitted.

(a) For Welders. Each welder shall have overcurrent protection rated or set at not more than 200 percent of the rated primary current of the welder.

Exception: An overcurrent device shall not be required for a welder having supply conductors protected by an overcurrent device rated or set at not more than 200 percent of the rated primary current of the welder.

(b) For Conductors. Conductors that supply one or more welders shall be protected by an overcurrent device rated or set at not more than 200 percent of the conductor rating.

630-23. Disconnecting Means. A disconnecting means shall be provided in the supply connection of each motor-generator arc welder.

The disconnecting means shall be a circuit breaker or motor-circuit switch, and its rating shall not be less than that necessary to accommodate overcurrent protection as specified under Section 630-22.

630-24. Marking. A nameplate shall be provided for each motor-generator arc welder giving the following information: name of manufacturer; rated frequency; number of phases; input voltage; input current; maximum open-circuit voltage; rated output current; basis of rating, such as duty cycle or time rating.

D. Resistance Welders

630-31. Ampacity of Supply Conductors. The ampacity of the supply conductors for resistance welders necessary to limit the voltage drop to a value permissible for the satisfactory performance of the welder is usually greater than that required to prevent overheating as prescribed in (a) and (b) below.

(a) Individual Welders. The rated ampacity for conductors for individual welders shall comply with the following:

(1) The rated ampacity of the supply conductors for a welder that may be operated at different times at different values of primary current or duty cycle shall not be less than 70 percent of the rated primary current for seam and automatically fed welders, and 50 percent of the rated primary current for manually operated nonautomatic welders.

(2) The rated ampacity of the supply conductors for a welder wired for a specific operation for which the actual primary current and duty cycle are known and remain unchanged shall not be less than the product of the actual primary current and the multiplier given below for the duty cycle at which the welder will be operated.

Duty Cycle (percent)	50	40	30	25	20	15	10	7.5	5.0 or less
Multiplier	.71	.63	.55	.50	.45	.39	.32	.27	.22

(b) Groups of Welders. The rated ampacity of conductors that supply two or more welders shall not be less than the sum of the value obtained in accordance with (a) above for the largest welder supplied, and 60 percent of the values obtained for all the other welders supplied.

(FPN): Explanation of Terms. (1) The rated primary current is the rated kVA multiplied by 1000 and divided by the rated primary voltage, using values given on the nameplate. (2) The actual primary current is the current drawn from the supply circuit during each welder operation at the particular heat tap and control setting used. (3) The duty cycle is the percentage of the time during which the welder is loaded. For instance, a spot welder supplied by a 60-hertz system (216,000 cycles per hour) making four hundred 15-cycle welds per hour would have a duty cycle of 2.8 percent (400 multiplied by 15, divided by 216,000, multiplied by 100). A seam welder operating 2 cycles "on" and 2 cycles "off" would have a duty cycle of 50 percent.

630-32. Overcurrent Protection. Overcurrent protection for resistance welders shall be as provided in (a) and (b) below. Where the nearest standard rating of the overcurrent device used is under the value specified in this section, or where the rating or setting specified results in unnecessary opening of the overcurrent device, the next higher rating or setting shall be permitted.

(a) For Welders. Each welder shall have an overcurrent device rated or set at not more than 300 percent of the rated primary current of the welder.

Exception: An overcurrent device shall not be required for a welder having a supply circuit protected by an overcurrent device rated or set at not more than 300 percent of the rated primary current of the welder.

(b) For Conductors. Conductors that supply one or more welders shall be protected by an overcurrent device rated or set at not more than 300 percent of the conductor rating.

Conductors of resistance welders and arc welders are provided with overcurrent protection against short circuits. Proper application and operation of the welder will safeguard against overload conditions. See commentary following Section 630-12(b).

630-33. Disconnecting Means. A switch or circuit breaker shall be provided by which each resistance welder and its control equipment can be isolated from the supply circuit. The ampere rating of this disconnecting means shall not be less than the supply conductor ampacity determined in accordance with Section 630-31. The supply circuit switch shall be permitted as the welder disconnecting means where the circuit supplies only one welder.

630-34. Marking. A nameplate shall be provided for each resistance welder giving the following information: name of manufacturer; frequency; primary voltage rated kVA at 50 percent duty cycle; maximum and minimum open-circuit secondary voltage; short-circuit secondary current at maximum secondary voltage; and specified throat and gap setting.

ARTICLE 640 — SOUND-RECORDING AND
SIMILAR EQUIPMENT

Contents

640-1. Scope. This article covers equipment and wiring for sound-recording and reproduction, centralized distribution of sound, public address, speech-input systems, and electronic organs.

Equipment covered by this article includes amplifiers, public address (PA) and centralized sound systems such as those utilized in schools, factories and similar locations, intercommunication devices and systems, and devices used for recording and reproducing voice or music.

640-2. Application of Other Articles.

(a) Wiring to and Between Devices. Wiring and equipment from source of power to and between devices connected to the interior wiring systems shall comply with the requirements of Chapters 1 through 4, except as modified by this article.

(b) Wiring and Equipment. Wiring and equipment for public-address, speech-input, radio-frequency and audio-frequency systems, and amplifying equipment associated with radio receiving stations in centralized distribution systems shall comply with Article 725.

> Chapters 1 through 4 apply generally to branch-circuit wiring that supplies power to sound systems and to wiring that supplies power between components of the system, unless modified by this article (see Sections 640-3 and 640-4, Exceptions).
>
> Wiring and equipment with electrical power limitations that differentiate them from light and power circuits are required to comply with Article 725 (see Section 640-5).
>
> Radio equipment is required to comply with Article 810 unless specifically referenced therein, such as in Section 810-2.

640-3. Number of Conductors in Raceway.
The number of conductors in a conduit or other raceway shall comply with Tables 1 through 7 of Chapter 9.

Exception No. 1: Special permission may be granted for the installation of two 2-conductor lead-covered cables in ¾-inch conduit, provided the cross-sectional area of each cable does not exceed .11 square inch.

Exception No. 2: Special permission may be granted for the installation of two 2-conductor No. 19 lead-covered cables in ½-inch conduit, provided the sum of the cross-sectional areas of the cables does not exceed 32 percent of the internal cross-sectional area of the conduit.

640-4. Wireways and Auxiliary Gutters.
Wireways shall comply with the requirements of Article 362, and auxiliary gutters shall comply with the requirements of Article 374.

Exception: Where used for sound-recording and reproduction, the following shall be complied with:

a. Conductors in wireways or gutters shall not fill the raceway to more than 75 percent of its depth.

b. Where the cover of auxiliary gutters is flush with the flooring and is subject to the moving of heavy objects, it shall be of steel at least ¼ inch (6.35 mm) in thickness; where not subject to moving of heavy objects, as in the rear of patch or other equipment panels, the cover shall be at least No. 10 MSG.

c. Wireways shall be permitted in concealed places provided they are run in a straight line between outlets or junction boxes. Covers of boxes shall be accessible. Edges of metal shall be rounded at outlet or junction boxes and all rough projections smoothed to prevent abrasion of insulation or conductors. Wireways made of sections shall be bonded and grounded as specified in Section 250-76.

d. Wireways and auxiliary gutters shall be grounded in accordance with the requirements of Article 250. Where the wireway or auxiliary gutter does not contain power-supply wires, the grounding conductor shall not be required to be larger than No. 14 copper or its equivalent. Where the wireway or auxiliary gutter contains power-supply wires, the grounding conductor shall not be smaller than specified in Section 250-95.

ARTICLE 640—SOUND-RECORDING AND SIMILAR EQUIPMENT

640-5. Conductors. Amplifier output circuits carrying audio-program signals of 70 volts or less and whose open-circuit voltage will not exceed 100 volts shall be permitted to employ Class 2 or Class 3 wiring as covered in Article 725.

(FPN): The above is based on amplifiers whose open-circuit voltage will not exceed 100 volts when driven with a signal at any frequency from 60 to 100 hertz sufficient to produce rated output (70.7 volts) into its rated load. This also accepts the known fact that the average program material is 12 db below the amplifier rating — thus the average rms voltage for an open-circuit 70-volt output would be only 25 volts.

640-6. Grouping of Conductors. Conductors of different systems grouped in the same conduit or other metal enclosure or in portable cords or cables shall comply with (a) through (c) below.

(a) Power-Supply Conductors. Power-supply conductors shall be properly identified and shall be used solely for supplying power to the equipment to which the other conductors are connected.

(b) Leads to Motor-Generator or Rotary Converter. Input leads to a motor-generator or rotary converter shall be run separately from the output leads.

(c) Conductor Insulation. The conductors shall be insulated individually, or collectively in groups, by insulation at least equivalent to that on the power supply and other conductors.

Exception: Where the power supply and other conductors are separated by a lead sheath or other continuous metallic covering.

640-7. Flexible Cords. Flexible cords and cables shall be of Type S, SJ, ST, SJO, or SJT or other approved types. The conductors of flexible cords, other than power-supply conductors, shall be permitted to be of a size not smaller than No. 26, provided such conductors are not in direct electrical connection with the power-supply conductors and are equipped with a current-limiting means so that the maximum power under any condition will not exceed 150 watts.

640-8. Terminals. Terminals shall be marked to show their proper connections. Terminals for conductors other than power-supply conductors shall be separated from the terminals of the power-supply conductors by a spacing at least as great as the spacing between power-supply terminals of opposite polarity.

Branch-circuit wiring that supplies power to sound systems and their components is usually a 120-V or 240-V power circuit and is not considered to be a part of the sound system and therefore is kept separate from sound system cables or conductors. It is permitted in the same enclosure, however, where terminals are spaced according to this section.

640-9. Storage Batteries. Storage batteries shall comply with (a) and (b) below.

(a) Installation. Storage batteries shall be installed in accordance with Article 480.

(b) Conductor Insulation. Storage-battery leads shall be rubber-covered or thermoplastic-covered.

640-10. Circuit Overcurrent Protection. Overcurrent protection shall be provided as follows:

(a) Heater or Filament (Cathode). Circuits to the heater or filament (cathode) of an electronic tube shall have overcurrent protection not exceeding 15 amperes where supplied by lighting branch circuits, or by storage batteries exceeding 20 ampere-hour capacity.

(b) Plate (Anode-Positive). Circuits to the plate (anode-positive) and to the screen grid of an electronic tube shall have overcurrent protection not exceeding 1.0 ampere.

(c) Control Grid. Circuits to the control grid of an electronic tube shall have overcurrent protection not exceeding 1.0 ampere where supplied by lighting branch circuits or by storage batteries exceeding 20 ampere-hour capacity.

(d) Location. Overcurrent devices shall be located as near as practicable to the source of power supply.

> Overcurrent protection is required to be located at the point where the conductor to be protected receives its supply from a battery or other power source. The three circuits in subparagraphs (a), (b), and (c) are defined for clarity to assure proper application and value of overcurrent devices.

640-11. Amplifiers and Rectifiers — Type.

(a) Approved Type. Amplifiers and rectifiers shall be of an approved type and shall be suitably housed.

(b) Readily Accessible. Amplifiers and rectifiers shall be so located as to be readily accessible.

(c) Ventilation. Amplifiers and rectifiers shall be so located as to provide sufficient ventilation to prevent undue temperature rise within the housing.

640-12. Hazardous (Classified) Locations. Equipment used in hazardous (classified) locations shall comply with Article 500.

640-13. Protection Against Physical Damage. Amplifiers, rectifiers, loudspeakers, and other equipment shall be so located or protected as to guard against physical damage, such as might result in fire or personal hazard.

ARTICLE 645 — DATA PROCESSING SYSTEMS

Contents

645-1. Scope. This article covers equipment, power-supply wiring, equipment interconnecting wiring, and grounding of data processing systems, including data communications equipment used as a terminal unit in a data processing room.

(FPN): For further information, see Standard for the Protection of Electronic Computer/Data Processing Equipment, NFPA 75-1981 (ANSI).

> Article 645 includes only equipment and wiring *in the data processing room.* A data processing room is usually an enclosed area, with one or more means of entry, that contains data processing equipment. Small terminals, such as remote telephone terminal units and cash registers in supermarkets, are not covered by Article 645.

ARTICLE 645—DATA PROCESSING SYSTEMS

A data processing room is a room designed to comply with the special construction and fire protection provisions of NFPA 75. Because of these special provisions, not all of the usual *Code* rules are applicable; for example, the wiring under the raised floor. The requirements in Article 645 are based on the assumption that the room will comply with NFPA 75.

645-2. Supply Circuits and Interconnecting Cables.

(a) Branch-Circuit Conductors. The branch-circuit conductors to which one or more units of a data processing system are connected to a source of supply shall have an ampacity not less than 125 percent of the total connected load.

(b) Connecting Cables. The data processing system shall be permitted to be connected by means of computer or data processing cable or flexible cord and an attachment plug cap or cord-set assembly specifically approved as a part of the data processing system. Separate units shall be permitted to be interconnected by means of flexible cords and cables specifically approved as part of the data processing system. When run on the surface of the floor, they shall be protected against physical damage.

(c) Under Raised Floors. Power cables, communications cables and interconnecting cables associated with the data processing equipment shall be permitted under a raised floor provided:

(1) The raised floor is of suitable construction.

(FPN): See Standard for Electronic Computer/Data Processing Equipment, NFPA 75-1981 (ANSI).

(2) The branch-circuit supply conductors to receptacles are in rigid metal conduit, intermediate metal conduit, electrical metallic tubing, metal wireway, metal surface raceway with metal cover, flexible metal conduit, liquidtight flexible metal conduit, mineral-insulated, metal-sheathed cable, metal-clad cable, or Type AC cable.

(3) Ventilation in the underfloor area is used for the data processing equipment and data processing area only.

645-3. Disconnecting Means.
A disconnecting means shall be provided to disconnect the power to all electronic equipment in the data processing room. This disconnecting means shall be controlled from locations readily accessible to the operator at the principal exit doors. There shall also be a similar disconnecting means to disconnect the air-conditioning system serving this area.

This section requires two separate disconnecting means. The disconnecting means is required to disconnect the conductors of each circuit from its source of supply. See definition of "Disconnecting Means" in Article 100. The disconnecting means could be remotely controlled switching devices, such as relays, with separate pushbutton stations at the principal exit doors.

645-4. Grounding.
All exposed noncurrent-carrying metal parts of a data processing system shall be grounded in accordance with Article 250.

645-5. Marking.
Each unit of a data processing system that is intended to be supplied by a branch circuit shall be provided with a manufacturer's nameplate, which shall also include the rating in volts, the operating frequency, and the total load in amperes.

ARTICLE 650 — ORGANS

Contents

650-1. Scope.
650-2. Source of Energy.
650-3. Insulation — Grounding.
650-4. Conductors.
  (a) Size.

(b) Insulation.
(c) Conductors to Be Cabled.
(d) Cable Covering.
650-5. Installation of Conductors.
650-6. Overcurrent Protection.

650-1. Scope. This article covers those electric circuits and parts of electrically operated organs which are employed for the control of the sounding apparatus and keyboards. Electronic organs shall comply with the appropriate provisions of Article 640.

650-2. Source of Energy. The source of energy shall have a potential of not over 15 volts and shall be a self-excited generator, a two-coil transformer-type rectifier, or a battery.

650-3. Insulation — Grounding. The generator shall be effectively insulated from ground and from the motor driving it, or both the generator and the motor frames shall be grounded in the manner specified in Article 250.

> The energy source required to power electrically operated organs has a potential of less than 15 V and is generally supplied by a motor-driven generator, although a rectifier or a battery may be used.
>
> Usually the motor and generator are mounted on the same metal frame and are effectively grounded. However, if this is not the case, the generator is required to be effectively insulated from the motor and from ground. If the motor and generator were not grounded and the generator not effectively insulated, then a motor-winding fault could energize the motor housing and also the generator housing to a potential of 120 V or 240 V (depending on the motor branch-circuit) and damage to the generator windings or the organ circuit conductors could result.

650-4. Conductors. Conductors shall comply with (a) through (d) below.

(a) Size. No conductor shall be smaller than No. 26, and the common-return conductor shall not be smaller than No. 14.

(b) Insulation. Conductors shall have rubber, thermoplastic, asbestos, cotton, or silk insulation.

Exception: The common-return conductors shall be rubber-covered, thermoplastic, or asbestos-covered (Type AA, AI, or AIA).

The cotton or silk shall be permitted to be saturated with paraffin if desired.

(c) Conductors to Be Cabled. Except the common-return conductor and conductors inside the organ proper, the organ sections and the organ console conductors shall be cabled. The common-return conductor shall be permitted under an additional covering enclosing both cable and return conductor, or shall be permitted as a separate conductor and shall be permitted to be in contact with the cable.

(d) Cable Covering. The cable shall be provided with one or more braided outer coverings, or a tape shall be permitted in place of an inner braid. Where not installed in metal raceways, the outer braid shall be flame-retardant or shall be covered with a closely wound fireproof tape.

ARTICLE 660—X-RAY EQUIPMENT

The common-return conductor carries the full voltage (usually about 10 V) of the control system and must be sized No. 14 AWG or larger. The other wires of the control system may be as small as No. 26 AWG and, being of the same polarity and potential, are not required to be overly protected from each other because they are required to be effectively insulated from the common-return conductor.

650-5. Installation of Conductors. Cables shall be securely fastened in place and shall be permitted to be attached directly to the organ structure without insulating supports. Cables shall not be placed in contact with other conductors.

Insulating supports are not required for such a low-voltage system; however, conductors that are required to be cabled are required to have a flame-retardant outer covering or are required to be run in metal raceways. Measures should be taken to prevent contact between cables and conductors of other systems.

650-6. Overcurrent Protection. Circuits shall be so arranged that all conductors shall be protected from overcurrent by an overcurrent device rated at not over 15 amperes.

Exception: The main supply conductors and the common-return conductor.

The two conductors that are run from the generator to the point of connection to the common-return conductor and to the many circuit conductors necessary for the system are the "main supply conductors" and do not require overcurrent protection. The common-return conductor also does not require overcurrent protection; however, the circuit conductors are required to be arranged to be protected by a 15-A overcurrent device at their connection point to the main supply conductor.

ARTICLE 660 — X-RAY EQUIPMENT

Contents

A. General

660-1. Scope. This article covers all X-ray equipment operating at any frequency or voltage for industrial or other nonmedical or nondental use.

(FPN): See Article 517 for medical and dental X-ray.

Nothing in this article shall be construed as specifying safeguards against the useful beam or stray X-ray radiation.

(FPN): Radiation safety and performance requirements of several classes of X-ray equipment are regulated under Public Law 90-602 and are enforced by the Department of Health and Human Services.

(FPN): In addition, information on radiation protection by the National Council on Radiation Protection and Measurements is published as Reports of the National Council on Radiation Protection and Measurement. These reports are obtainable from NCRP Publications, P.O. Box 30175, Washington, D.C. 20014.

660-2. Definitions.

Long-Time Rating. A rating based on an operating interval of 5 minutes or longer.

Mobile. X-ray equipment mounted on a permanent base with wheels and/or casters for moving while completely assembled.

Momentary Rating. A rating based on an operating interval that does not exceed 5 seconds.

Portable. X-ray equipment designed to be hand carried.

Transportable. X-ray equipment to be installed in a vehicle or that may be readily disassembled for transport in a vehicle.

660-3. Hazardous (Classified) Locations. Unless approved for the location, X-ray and related equipment shall not be installed or operated in hazardous (classified) locations.

(FPN): See Article 517, Part G.

X-ray equipment used in industrial establishments or similar locations is usually for the purpose of inspection of a process or product. This method permits testing without dismantling or applying stress to detect cracks, flaws, or structural defects. Welded joints are frequently inspected with X-ray equipment to detect hidden defects that may cause failure under stress.

Among the industrial applications of X-rays, the most common is radiography where shadow pictures of the subject matter are produced on photographic film. The type and thickness of the material involved governs the voltage to be employed and may range from a few thousand volts (kilovolts) to millions of volts (megavolts). It is possible to X-ray metal objects that are 20 in. thick.

Fluoroscopy is another X-ray technique that is used for industrial or commercial applications. This method is similar to radiography, but operates at a much lower voltage range (less than 250 kilovolts) and, instead of producing a film, a shadow picture is projected upon a screen such as is used for security checks of luggage at airport terminals. Fluoroscopy is capable of detecting extremely minute flaws or defects.

660-4. Connection to Supply Circuit.

(a) Fixed and Stationary Equipment. Fixed and stationary X-ray equipment shall be connected to the power supply by means of a wiring method meeting the general requirements of this Code.

ARTICLE 660—X-RAY EQUIPMENT

Exception: Equipment properly supplied by a branch circuit rated at not over 30 amperes shall be permitted to be supplied through a suitable attachment plug cap and hard-service cable or cord.

(b) Portable, Mobile, and Transportable Equipment. Individual branch circuits shall not be required for portable, mobile, and transportable medical X-ray equipment requiring a capacity of not over 60 amperes. Portable and mobile types of X-ray equipment of any capacity shall be supplied through a suitable hard-service cable or cord. Transportable X-ray equipment of any capacity shall be permitted to be connected to its power supply by suitable connections and hard-service cable or cord.

(c) Over 600 Volts, Nominal. Circuits and equipment operated at more than 600 volts, nominal, shall comply with Article 710.

660-5. Disconnecting Means. A disconnecting means of adequate capacity for at least 50 percent of the input required for the momentary rating or 100 percent of the input required for the long-time rating of the X-ray equipment, whichever is greater, shall be provided in the supply circuit. The disconnecting means shall be operable from a location readily accessible from the X-ray control. For equipment connected to a 120-volt, nominal, branch circuit of 30 amperes or less, a grounding-type attachment plug cap and receptacle of proper rating shall be permitted to serve as a disconnecting means.

660-6. Rating of Supply Conductors and Overcurrent Protection.

(a) Branch-Circuit Conductors. The ampacity of supply branch-circuit conductors and the overcurrent protective devices shall not be less than 50 percent of the momentary rating or 100 percent of the long-time rating, whichever is the greater.

(b) Feeder Conductors. The rated ampacity of conductors and overcurrent devices of a feeder for two or more branch circuits supplying X-ray units shall not be less than 100 percent of the momentary demand rating [as determined by (a)] of the two largest X-ray apparatus plus 20 percent of the momentary ratings of other X-ray apparatus.

(FPN): The minimum conductor size for branch and feeder circuits is also governed by voltage regulation requirements. For a specific installation, the manufacturer usually specifies: minimum distribution transformer and conductor sizes, rating of disconnect means, and overcurrent protection.

660-7. Wiring Terminals. X-ray equipment shall be provided with suitable wiring terminals or leads for the connection of power supply conductors of the size required by the rating of the branch circuit for the equipment.

Exception: Where provided with a permanently attached cord or a cord set.

660-8. Number of Conductors in Raceway. The number of control circuit conductors installed in a raceway shall be determined in accordance with Section 300-17.

660-9. Minimum Size of Conductors. Sizes No. 18 or 16 fixture wires as specified in Section 725-16 and flexible cords shall be permitted for the control and operating circuits of X-ray and auxiliary equipment where protected by not larger than 20-ampere overcurrent devices.

660-10. Equipment Installations. All equipment for new X-ray installations and all used or reconditioned X-ray equipment moved to and reinstalled at a new location shall be of an approved type.

B. Control

660-20. Fixed and Stationary Equipment.

(a) Separate Control Device. A separate control device, in addition to the disconnecting means, shall be incorporated in the X-ray control supply or in the primary circuit to the high-voltage transformer. This device shall be a part of the X-ray equipment, but shall be permitted in a separate enclosure immediately adjacent to the X-ray control unit.

(b) Protective Device. A protective device, which shall be permitted to be incorporated into the separate control device, shall be provided to control the load resulting from failures in the high-voltage circuit.

660-21. Portable and Mobile Equipment. Portable and mobile equipment shall comply with Section 660-20, but the manually controlled device shall be located in or on the equipment.

660-23. Industrial and Commercial Laboratory Equipment.

(a) Radiographic and Fluoroscopic Types. All radiographic- and fluoroscopic-type equipment shall be effectively enclosed or shall have interlocks that de-energize the equipment automatically to prevent ready access to live current-carrying parts.

(b) Diffraction and Irradiation Types. Diffraction- and irradiation-type equipment shall be provided with a positive means to indicate when it is energized. The indicator shall be a pilot light, readable meter deflection, or equivalent means.

Exception: Equipment or installations effectively enclosed or provided with interlocks to prevent access to live current-carrying parts during operation.

660-24. Independent Control. Where more than one piece of equipment is operated from the same high-voltage circuit, each piece or each group of equipment as a unit shall be provided with a high-voltage switch or equivalent disconnecting means. This disconnecting means shall be constructed, enclosed, or located so as to avoid contact by persons with its live parts.

A control device provides means for initiating and terminating X-ray exposures and automatically times their duration.

C. Transformers and Capacitors

660-35. General. Transformers and capacitors that are part of an X-ray equipment shall not be required to comply with Articles 450 and 460.

High-ratio step-up transformers that are an integral part of an X-ray are not required to comply with Article 450 and are generally used to provide the high voltage necessary for X-ray tubes. There is a lesser degree of fire hazard due to the low primary voltage; therefore, X-ray transformers are not required to be installed in fire-resistant vaults.

660-36. Capacitors. Capacitors shall be mounted within enclosures of insulating material or grounded metal.

D. Guarding and Grounding

660-47. General.

(a) High-Voltage Parts. All high-voltage parts, including X-ray tubes, shall be mounted within grounded enclosures. Air, oil, gas, or other suitable insulating media shall be used to insulate the high voltage from the grounded enclosure. The connection from the high-voltage equipment to X-ray tubes and other high-voltage components shall be made with high-voltage shielded cables.

(b) Low-Voltage Cables. Low-voltage cables connecting to oil-filled units that are not completely sealed, such as transformers, condensers, oil coolers, and high-voltage switches, shall have insulation of the oil-resistant type.

Grounded enclosures are required to be provided for all high-voltage X-ray equipment, including X-ray tubes. High-voltage shielded cables are required to be used to connect high-voltage equipment to X-ray tubes and the shield is required to be grounded as specified in Section 660-48.

660-48. Grounding. Noncurrent-carrying metal parts of X-ray and associated equipment (controls, tables, X-ray tube supports, transformer tanks, shielded cables, X-ray tube heads, etc.) shall be grounded in the manner specified in Article 250. Portable and mobile equipment shall be provided with an approved grounding-type attachment plug cap.

Exception: Battery-operated equipment.

ARTICLE 665 — INDUCTION AND DIELECTRIC HEATING EQUIPMENT

Contents

A. General

665-1. Scope. This article covers the construction and installation of induction and dielectric heating equipment and accessories for industrial and scientific applications, but not for medical or dental applications, appliances, or line frequency pipelines and vessels heating.

(FPN): See Article 517 for medical and dental therapeutic equipment.

(FPN): See Article 422 for appliances.

(FPN): See Article 427, Part E for line frequency pipelines and vessels heating.

To prevent spurious radiation caused by induction and dielectric heating equipment and to ensure that the frequency spectrum is utilized equitably, the Federal Communications Commission (FCC) has established rules (Code of Federal Regulations, Title 47, Part 18) that govern the use of industrial heating equipment of this type operating above 10 kHz.

665-2. Definitions.

Dielectric Heating.   Dielectric heating is the heating of a nominally insulating material due to its own dielectric losses when the material is placed in a varying electric field.

Heating Equipment.   The term "heating equipment" as used in this article includes any equipment used for heating purposes whose heat is generated by induction or dielectric methods.

Induction Heating.   Induction heating is the heating of a nominally conductive material due to its own I^2R losses when the material is placed in a varying electromagnetic field.

Induction and dielectric heating are used for ovens, furnaces, and industrial equipment where pieces of material are heated by a rapidly alternating magnetic or electric field. For further information on electric heating systems using an induction heater or a dielectric heater on ovens and furnaces, see NFPA 86A, Ovens and Furnaces, Design, Location and Equipment; and NFPA 86D, Industrial Furnaces Using Vacuum as an Atmosphere.

Theory of Operation — Solid State Converter Power Circuit
The circuit consists of three sections: the rectifier section, the inverter section, and the tank circuit which includes the load coil located on the outside. The rectifier section input power is 480 V ac nominal, 3-phase, 60 Hz. See Figure 665-1. The output of the rectifier section is most generally a fixed 600-V dc

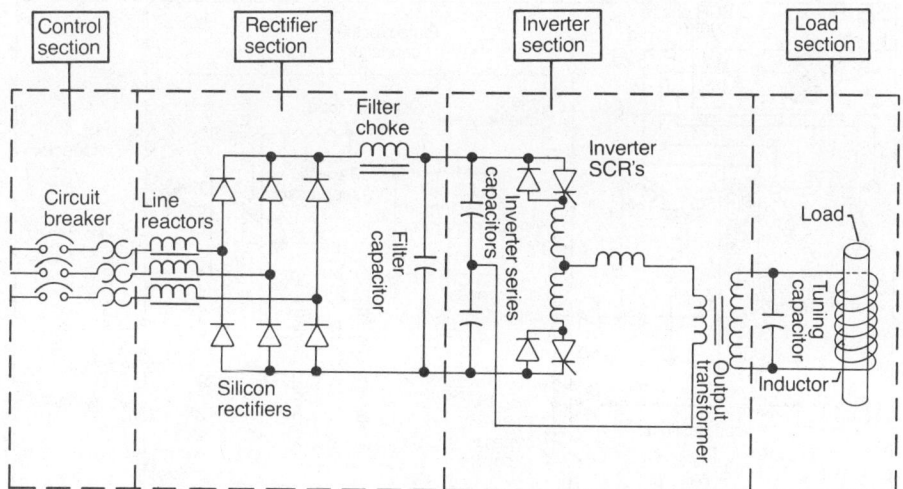

Figure 665-1. Simplified diagram of the components of a solid-state converter used for induction heating. (*Tocco Div. Park Ohio Industries*)

nominal. This feeds the inverter section which is a tuned variable frequency switching network that converts the dc power to single-phase nominal, 180 Hz, 1 kHz, 3 kHz, or 10 kHz square wave or sinusoidal power. The operating frequency is determined by the control section. The single-phase output drives the tank circuit which consists of a load coil and tuning capacitors.

Variable output power is achieved by frequency variation of the inverter section. Since the tank circuit is a tuned load, as the output approaches the frequency of the tank circuit, the power into the load approaches the maximum output. At minimum frequency the output power is very low. As the frequency increases, the power increases until a maximum is reached. This is the resonant frequency of the tank circuit.

Most induction heating loads exhibit a dynamic change as the work piece passes through the Curie temperature point (where the work load changes from the magnetic to the nonmagnetic state). The converter automatically adjusts to maintain a constant output power during this dynamic load change. If this maximum power is below the operator power setting, the converter unit will automatically limit at this maximum power point.

Induction Heating

Induction heating is accomplished with the aid of a current-carrying conductor that induces the transfer of electrical energy to the work by an eddy current. Induction heating, in general, involves frequencies ranging from 3 to about 500 kHz, and power outputs from a few hundred watts to several thousand kilowatts.

When induction heating is employed, a nominally conductive material is placed in an inductor coil. The effective intensity of inductance is caused by a current flow in the coil at a high frequency which produces a rapidly alternating magnetic field, thereby inducing a voltage in the material to be heated and causing a current to flow through the resistance of the material (I^2R loss), producing induction heating. See Figure 665-2.

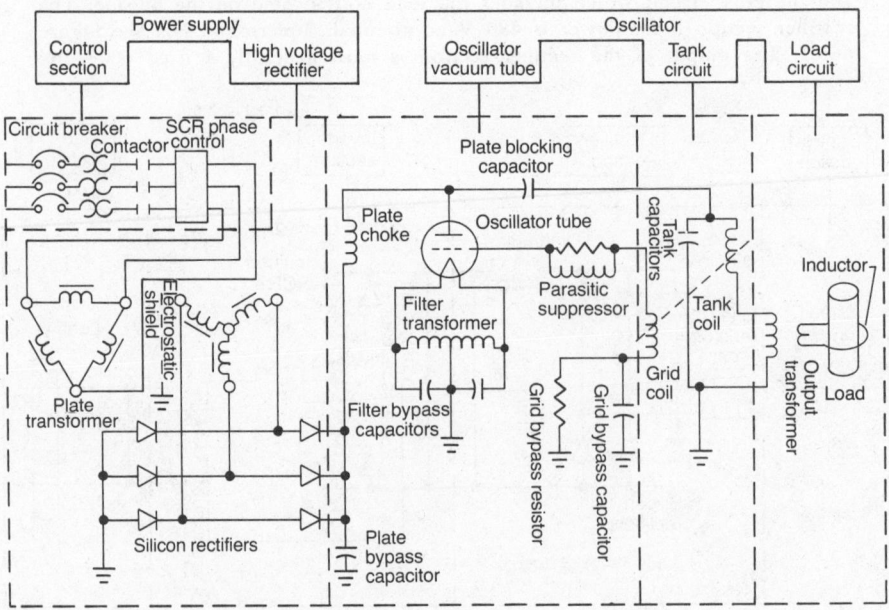

Figure 665-2. Simplified diagram of the components of a vacuum-tube generator used for induction heating. *(Tocco Div. Park Ohio Industries)*

Dielectric Heating

Dielectric heating equipment is similar to induction heating equipment; however, the frequencies are generally higher (in the order of 3 MHz or more) than those in induction heating. This type of heater is useful for heating materials that are commonly thought of as being nonconductive, for instance, heating plastic preforms before molding, curing glue and plywood, drying rayon cakes, and for many similar applications. Frequencies for this type of equipment range from 1 to 200 MHz, especially in the 1 to 50 MHz range. Vacuum tube generators are used exclusively to supply dielectric heating power, and outputs range from a few hundred watts to several hundred kilowatts.

A typical wiring diagram of a vacuum tube generator is shown in Figure 665-3. Whereas induction heating uses a varying magnetic field, dielectric heating employs a varying electric field. This is done by placing the material to be heated between a pair of metal plates, called electrodes, in the output circuit of the generator. When high-frequency voltage is applied to the electrodes, a rapidly alternating electric field is set up between them, passing through the material to be heated. Because of the electrical charges within the molecules of this material, the field causes the molecules to vibrate in proportion to its frequency. This internal molecular action generates the heat used for dielectric heating.

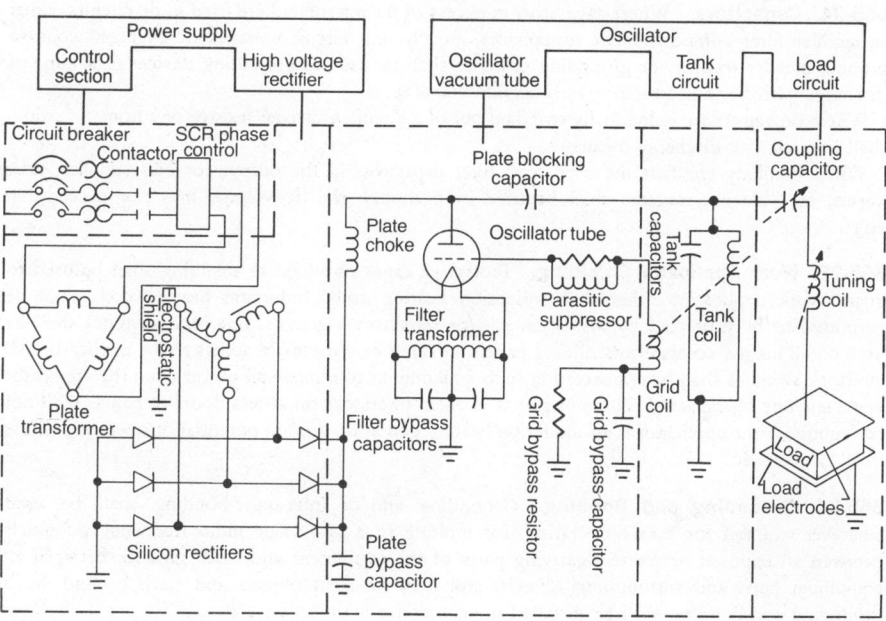

Figure 665-3. Simplified diagram of the components of a vacuum-tube generator used for dielectric heating. (*Tocco Div. Park Ohio Industries*)

665-3. Other Articles. Wiring from the source of power to the heating equipment shall comply with Chapters 1 through 4. Circuits and equipment operated at more than 600 volts, nominal, shall comply with Article 710.

665-4. Hazardous (Classified) Locations. Induction and dielectric heating equipment shall not be installed in hazardous (classified) locations as defined in Article 500.

Exception: Where the equipment and wiring are designed and approved for the hazardous (classified) locations.

ARTICLE 665—INDUCTION AND DIELECTRIC HEATING EQUIPMENT

B. Guarding, Grounding, and Labeling

665-20. Enclosures. The converting apparatus (including the dc line) and high-frequency electric circuits (excluding the output circuits and remote-control circuits) shall be completely contained within an enclosure or enclosures of noncombustible material.

665-21. Panel Controls. All panel controls shall be of dead-front construction.

665-22. Access to Internal Equipment. Doors or detachable panels shall be employed for internal access. Where doors are used giving access to voltages from 500 to 1000 volts ac or dc, either door locks shall be provided or interlocking shall be installed. Where doors are used giving access to voltages of over 1000 volts ac or dc, either mechanical lockouts with a disconnecting means to prevent access until voltage is removed from the cubicle, or both door interlocking and mechanical door locks shall be provided. Detachable panels not normally used for access to such parts shall be fastened in a manner that will make them inconvenient to remove.

665-23. Warning Labels. "Danger" labels shall be attached on the equipment, and shall be plainly visible even when doors are open or panels are removed from compartments containing voltages of over 250 volts ac or dc.

665-24. Capacitors. Where capacitors in excess of 0.1 microfarad are used in dc circuits, either as rectifier filter components or suppressors, etc., having circuit voltages of over 240 volts to ground, bleeder resistors or grounding switches shall be used as grounding devices. The time of discharge shall be in accordance with Section 460-6(a).

Where capacitors are individually switched out of a circuit, a bleeder resistor or automatic switch shall be used as a discharge means.

Where auxiliary rectifiers are used with filter capacitors in the output for bias supplies, tube keyers, etc., bleeder resistors shall be used even though the dc voltage may not exceed 240 volts.

665-25. Work Applicator Shielding. Protective cages or adequate shielding shall be used to guard work applicators other than induction heating coils. Induction heating coils shall be permitted to be protected by insulation and/or refractory materials. Interlock switches shall be used on all hinged access doors, sliding panels, or other easy means of access to the applicator. All interlock switches shall be connected in such a manner as to remove all power from the applicator when any one of the access doors or panels is open. Interlocks on access doors or panels shall not be required if the applicator is an induction heating coil at dc ground potential or operating at less than 150 volts ac.

665-26. Grounding and Bonding. Grounding and/or inter-unit bonding shall be used wherever required for circuit operation, for limiting to a safe value radio frequency potentials between all exposed noncurrent-carrying parts of the equipment and earth ground, between all equipment parts and surrounding objects, and between such objects and earth ground. Such grounding and bonding shall be installed in accordance with Article 250.

Bonding presents special problems at radio frequencies due to stray currents flowing between units of the equipment or to ground. These special bonding requirements are especially needed at dielectric heating frequencies (100 to 200 MHz) due to the differences in radio-frequency potential that can exist between the equipment and surrounding metal units or other units of the installation. Satisfactory bonding can be accomplished by placing all of the units of the equipment on a flooring or base consisting of a copper or aluminum sheet and thoroughly bonded where necessary by soldering, welding, or bolting.

By such special bonding, the radio-frequency resistance and reactance between units is held to a minimum and any stray circulating currents flowing through this bonding will not cause a dangerous voltage drop.

It is necessary to provide operator protection from high radio-frequency potentials by shielding at dielectric heating frequencies. Interference with radio communication systems at such high frequencies may be eliminated by totally enclosing all components of the circuiting in a shielding of copper or aluminum.

665-27. Marking. Each heating equipment shall be provided with a nameplate giving the manufacturer's name and model identification and the following input data: line volts, frequency, number of phases, maximum current, full-load kVA, and full-load power factor.

665-28. Control Enclosures. Direct current or low-frequency ac shall be permitted in the control portion of the heating equipment. This shall be limited to not over 150 volts. Solid or stranded wire No. 18 or larger shall be used. A step-down transformer with proper overcurrent protection shall be permitted in the control enclosure to obtain an ac voltage of less than 150 volts. The higher-voltage terminals shall be guarded to prevent accidental contact. 60-hertz components shall be permitted to control high frequency where properly rated by the induction heating equipment manufacturer. Electronic circuits utilizing solid-state devices and tubes shall be permitted printed circuits or wires smaller than No. 18.

C. Motor-Generator Equipment

665-40. General. Motor-generator equipment shall include all rotating equipment designed to operate from an ac or dc motor or by mechanical drive from a prime mover, producing an alternating current of any frequency for induction and/or dielectric heating.

665-41. Ampacity of Supply Conductors. The ampacity of supply conductors shall be determined in accordance with Article 430.

665-42. Overcurrent Protection. Overcurrent protection shall be provided as specified in Article 430 for the electric supply circuit.

665-43. Disconnecting Means. The disconnecting means shall be provided as specified in Article 430.
A readily accessible disconnecting means shall be provided by which each heating equipment can be isolated from its supply circuit. The ampere rating of this disconnecting means shall not be less than the nameplate current rating of the equipment. The supply circuit disconnecting means shall be permitted as a heating equipment disconnecting means where the circuit supplies only one equipment.

665-44. Output Circuit. The output circuit shall include all output components external to the generator, including contactors, transformers, busbars, and other conductors, and shall comply with (a) and (b) below.

(a) Generator Output. The output circuit shall be isolated from ground.

Exception No. 1: Where the capacitive coupling inherent in the generator causes the generator terminals to have voltages from terminal to ground that are equal.

Exception No. 2: Where a vacuum or controlled atmosphere is used with a coil in a tank or chamber, the center point of the coil shall be grounded to maintain an equal potential between each terminal and ground.

Where rated at over 500 volts, the output circuit shall incorporate a dc ground protector unit. The dc impressed on the output circuit shall not exceed 30 volts and shall not exceed a current capability of 5 milliamperes.
An isolating transformer for matching the load and the source shall be permitted in the output circuit if the output secondary is not at dc ground potential.

ARTICLE 665—INDUCTION AND DIELECTRIC HEATING EQUIPMENT

(b) Component Interconnections. The various components required for a complete induction heating equipment installation shall be connected by properly protected multiconductor cable, busbar, or coaxial cable. Cables shall be installed in nonferrous raceways. Busbars shall be protected, where required, by nonferrous enclosures.

665-47. Remote Control.

(a) Selector Switch. Where remote controls are used for applying power, a selector switch shall be provided and interlocked to provide power from only one control point at a time.

(b) Foot Switches. Switches operated by foot pressure shall be provided with a shield over the contact button to avoid accidental closing of a switch.

D. Equipment Other than Motor-Generator

665-60. General. Equipment other than motor-generators shall consist of all static multipliers and oscillator-type units utilizing vacuum tubes and/or solid-state devices. The equipment shall be capable of converting ac or dc to an ac frequency suitable for induction and/or dielectric heating.

665-61. Ampacity of Supply Conductors. The ampacity of supply conductors shall be determined in accordance with (a) and (b) below.

(a) Nameplate Rating. The ampacity of the circuit conductors shall not be less than the nameplate current rating of the equipment.

(b) Two or More. The ampacity of conductors supplying two or more equipments shall not be less than the sum of the nameplate current ratings on all equipments.

Figure 665-4. An 80-kW oscillator used to harden the exhaust valve seats of an automotive engine. (*Tocco Div. Park Ohio Industries*)

872

Exception: If simultaneous operation of two or more equipments supplied from the same feeder is not possible, the ampacity of the feeder shall not be less than the sum of the nameplate ratings for the largest group of machines capable of simultaneous operation, plus 100 percent of the stand-by currents of the remaining machines supplied.

665-62. Overcurrent Protection. Overcurrent protection shall be provided as specified in Article 240 for the equipment as a whole. This overcurrent protection shall be provided separately or as a part of the equipment.

665-63. Disconnecting Means. A readily accessible disconnecting means shall be provided by which each heating equipment can be isolated from its supply circuit. The rating of this disconnecting means shall not be less than the nameplate rating of the equipment. The supply circuit disconnecting means shall be permitted for disconnecting the heating equipment where the circuit supplies only one equipment.

665-64. Output Circuit. The output circuit shall include all output components external to the converting device, including contactors, transformers, busbars, and other conductors and shall comply with (a) and (b) below.

(a) Converter Output. The output circuit shall be isolated from ground.

Exception: Where a dc voltage can exist at the terminals because of an internal component failure, then the output circuit (direct or coupled) shall be at dc ground potential.

(b) Converter and Applicator Connection. Where the connections between the converter and the work applicator exceed 2 feet (610 mm) in length, the connections shall be enclosed or guarded with nonferrous, noncombustible material.

665-66. Line Frequency in Converter Equipment Output. Commercial frequencies of 25- to 60-hertz alternating-current output shall be permitted to be coupled for control purposes, but shall be limited to not over 150 volts during periods of circuit operation.

665-67. Keying. Where high-speed keying circuits dependent on the effect of "oscillator blocking" are employed, the peak radio-frequency output voltage during the blocked portion of the cycle shall not exceed 100 volts in units employing radio-frequency converters.

665-68. Remote Control.

(a) Selector Switch. Where remote controls are used for applying power, a selector switch shall be provided and interlocked to provide power from only one control point at a time.

(b) Foot Switches. Switches operated by foot pressure shall be provided with a shield over the contact button to avoid accidental closing of the switch.

ARTICLE 668 — ELECTROLYTIC CELLS

Contents

668-12. Cell Line Conductors.
(a) Insulation and Material.
(b) Size.
(c) Connections.
668-13. Disconnecting Means.
(a) More than One Process Power Supply.
(b) Removable Links or Conductors.
668-14. Shunting Means.
(a) Partial or Total Shunting.
(b) Shunting One or More Cells.
668-15. Grounding.
668-20. Portable Electrical Equipment.
(a) Portable Electrical Equipment Not to Be Grounded.
(b) Isolating Transformers.
(c) Marking.
668-21. Power Supply Circuits and Receptacles for Portable Electrical Equipment.

(a) Isolated Circuits.
(b) Noninterchangeability.
(c) Marking.
668-30. Fixed and Portable Electrical Equipment.
(a) Electrical Equipment Not Required to Be Grounded.
(b) Exposed Conductive Surfaces Not Required to Be Grounded.
(c) Wiring Methods.
(d) Circuit Protection.
(e) Bonding.
668-31. Auxiliary Nonelectric Connections.
668-32. Cranes and Hoists.
(a) Conductive Surfaces to be Insulated from Ground.
(b) Hazardous Electrical Conditions.
668-40. Enclosures.

668-1. Scope. The provisions of this article apply to the installation of the electrical components and accessory equipment of electrolytic cells, electrolytic cell lines and process power supply for the production of aluminum, cadmium, chlorine, copper, fluorine, hydrogen peroxide, magnesium, sodium, sodium chlorate and zinc.

Not covered by this article are cells used as a source of electric energy and for electroplating processes and cells used for the production of hydrogen.

(FPN): In general, any cell line or group of cell lines operated as a unit for the production of a particular metal, gas, or chemical compound may differ from any other cell line or group of cell lines producing the same product because of variations in the particular raw materials used, output capacity, use of proprietary methods or process practices, or other modifying factors to the extent that detailed Code requirements become overly restrictive and do not accomplish the stated purpose of this Code.

(FPN): For further information, see IEEE Standard for Electrical Safety Practices in Electrolytic Cell Line Working Zones: IEEE Std. 463-1977.

An electrolytic cell line and its dc process power supply circuit, both within a cell line working zone, constitute and are treated as an individual machine supplied from a single source, even though they may cover acres of space, have a load current in excess of 400,000 A dc, or a circuit voltage in excess of 1,000 V dc. The cell line process current passes through each cell in a series connection, and the load current cannot be subdivided, as it can, for example, in the heating circuit of a resistance-type electric furnace.

Because a cell line is supplied by its individual dc rectifier system, the rectifier or the entire cell line circuit is de-energized by removing its source of primary power.

In some electrolytic cell systems, the terminal voltage of the process supply can be appreciable. The voltage-to-ground of exposed live parts from one end of a cell line to the other is variable between the limits of the terminal voltage. Hence, operating and maintenance personnel and their tools are required to be insulated from ground.

Figure 668-1. A typical potroom in an aluminum reduction plant. (*Alcoa*)

668-2. Definitions.

Cell Line. An assembly of electrically interconnected electrolytic cells supplied by a source of direct-current power.

Cell Line Attachments and Auxiliary Equipment. As applied to Article 668, cell line attachments and auxiliary equipment include, but are not limited to: auxiliary tanks; process piping; duct work; structural supports; exposed cell line conductors; conduits and other raceways; pumps, positioning equipment and cell cutout or by-pass electrical devices. Auxiliary equipment includes tools, welding machines, crucibles, and other portable equipment used for operation and maintenance within the electrolytic cell line working zone.

In the cell line working zone, auxiliary equipment includes the exposed conductive surfaces of ungrounded cranes and crane-mounted cell-servicing equipment.

Electrolytic Cell. A receptacle or vessel in which electrochemical reactions are caused by applying electrical energy for the purpose of refining or producing usable materials.

Electrolytic Cell Line Working Zone. The cell line working zone is the space envelope wherein operation or maintenance is normally performed on or in the vicinity of exposed energized surfaces of electrolytic cell lines or their attachments.

668-3. Other Articles.

(a) Lighting, Ventilating, Material Handling. Chapters 1 through 4 shall apply to service feeders, branch circuits, and apparatus for supplying lighting, ventilating, material handling, and the like, which are outside the electrolytic cell line working zone.

ARTICLE 668—ELECTROLYTIC CELLS

(b) Systems Not Electrically Connected. Those elements of a cell line power-supply system that are not electrically connected to the cell supply system, such as the primary winding of a two-winding transformer, the motor of a motor-generator set, feeders, branch circuits, disconnecting means, motor controllers, and overload protective equipment shall be required to comply with all applicable provisions of this Code.

(FPN): For the purpose of this section, "electrically connected" shall mean connection capable of carrying current as distinguished from connection through electromagnetic induction.

(c) Electrolytic Cell Lines. Electrolytic cell lines shall comply with the provisions of Chapters 1, 2, 3, and 4.

Exception No. 1: The electrolytic cell line conductors shall not be required to comply with the provisions of Articles 110, 210, 215, 220, and 225. (See Section 668-11.)

Exception No. 2: Overcurrent protection of electrolytic cell dc process power circuits shall not be required to comply with the requirements of Article 240.

Exception No. 3: Equipment located or used within the electrolytic cell line working zone or associated with the cell line dc power circuits shall not be required to comply with the provisions of Article 250.

Exception No. 4: The electrolytic cells, cell line attachments and the wiring of auxiliary equipments and devices within the cell line working zone shall not be required to comply with the provisions of Articles 110, 210, 215, 220, and 225. (See Section 668-30.)

(FPN): See Section 668-15 on equipment, apparatus, and structural component grounding.

668-10. Cell Line Working Zone.

(a) Area Covered. The space envelope of the cell line working zone shall encompass any space:

(1) Within 96 inches (2.44 m) above energized surfaces of electrolytic cell lines or their energized attachments.

(2) Below energized surfaces of electrolytic cell lines or their energized attachments, provided the head room in the space beneath is less than 96 inches (2.44 m).

(3) Within 42 inches (1.07 m) horizontally from energized surfaces of electrolytic cell lines or their energized attachments or from the space envelope described in Section 668-10(a)(1) or (a)(2).

(b) Area Not Covered. The cell line working zone shall not be required to extend through or beyond walls, floors, roofs, partitions, barriers, or the like.

668-11. DC Cell Line Process Power Supply.

(a) Not Grounded. The dc cell line process power supply conductors shall not be required to be grounded.

(b) Metal Enclosures Grounded. All metal enclosures of dc cell line process power supply apparatus operating at a power supply potential between terminals of over 50 volts shall be grounded:

(1) Through protective relaying equipment, or

(2) By No. 2/0 AWG minimum copper grounding conductor or a conductor of equal ampacity.

(c) Grounding Requirements. The grounding connections required by Section 668-11(b) shall be installed in accordance with Sections 250-112, 250-113, 250-115, 250-117, and 250-118.

668-12. Cell Line Conductors.

(a) Insulation and Material. Cell line conductors shall be either bare, covered, or insulated and of copper, aluminum, copper-clad aluminum, steel, or other suitable material.

(b) Size. Cell line conductors shall be of such cross-sectional area that the temperature rise under maximum load conditions and at maximum ambient shall not exceed the safe operating temperature of the conductor insulation or the material of the conductor supports.

(c) Connections. Cell line conductors shall be joined by bolted, welded, clamped, or compression connectors.

668-13. Disconnecting Means.

(a) More than One Process Power Supply. Where more than one dc cell line process power supply serves the same cell line, a disconnecting means shall be provided on the cell line circuit side of each power supply to disconnect it from the cell line circuit.

(b) Removable Links or Conductors. Removable links or removable conductors shall be permitted to be used as the disconnecting means.

668-14. Shunting Means.

(a) Partial or Total Shunting. Partial or total shunting of cell line circuit current around one or more cells shall be permitted.

(b) Shunting One or More Cells. The conductors, switches, or combination of conductors and switches used for shunting one or more cells shall comply with the applicable requirements of Section 668-12.

668-15. Grounding.
For equipment, apparatus, and structural components which are required to be grounded by provisions of Article 668, the provisions of Article 250 shall apply.

Exception No. 1: A water pipe electrode shall not be required to be used.

Exception No. 2: Any electrode or combination of electrodes described in Sections 250-81 and 250-83 shall be permitted.

668-20. Portable Electrical Equipment.

(a) Portable Electrical Equipment Not to Be Grounded. The frames and enclosures of portable electrical equipment used within the cell line working zone shall not be grounded.

Exception No. 1: Where the cell line circuit voltage does not exceed 200 volts dc these frames and enclosures shall be permitted to be grounded.

Exception No. 2: These frames and enclosures shall be permitted to be grounded where guarded.

(b) Isolating Transformers. Electrically powered, hand-held, cord-connected portable equipment with ungrounded frames or enclosures used within the cell line working zone shall be connected to receptacle circuits having only ungrounded conductors such as a branch circuit supplied by an isolating transformer with an ungrounded secondary.

Exception: Where frames and enclosures of such equipments are grounded as permitted in Section 668-20(a), Exception No. 1.

(c) Marking. Ungrounded portable electrical equipment shall be distinctively marked and shall employ plugs and receptacles of a configuration which prevents connection of this equipment to grounding receptacles and which prevents inadvertent interchange of ungrounded and grounded portable electrical equipments.

668-21. Power Supply Circuits and Receptacles for Portable Electrical Equipment.

(a) Isolated Circuits. Circuits supplying power to ungrounded receptacles for hand-held, cord-connected equipments shall be electrically isolated from any distribution system supplying areas other than the cell line working zone and shall be ungrounded. Power for these circuits shall be supplied through isolating transformers. Primaries of such transformers shall operate at not more than 600 volts between conductors and shall be provided with proper overcurrent protection. The secondary voltage of such transformers shall not exceed 300 volts between conductors, and all circuits supplied from such secondaries shall be ungrounded and shall have an approved overcurrent device of proper rating in each conductor.

(b) Noninterchangeability. Receptacles and their mating plugs for ungrounded equipment shall not have provision for a grounding conductor and shall be of a configuration which prevents their use for equipment required to be grounded.

(c) Marking. Receptacles on circuits supplied by an isolating transformer with an ungrounded secondary shall be a distinctive configuration, distinctively marked, and shall not be used in any other location in the plant.

668-30. Fixed and Portable Electrical Equipment.

(a) Electrical Equipment Not Required to Be Grounded. AC systems supplying fixed and portable electrical equipments within the cell line working zone shall not be required to be grounded.

(b) Exposed Conductive Surfaces Not Required to Be Grounded. Exposed conductive surfaces, such as electrical equipment housings, cabinets, boxes, motors, raceways, and the like that are within the cell line working zone shall not be required to be grounded.

(c) Wiring Methods. Auxiliary electrical devices such as motors, transducers, sensors, control devices, and alarms, mounted on an electrolytic cell or other energized surface, shall be connected to premises wiring systems by any of the following means:

(1) Multiconductor hard-usage cord;

(2) Wire or cable in suitable raceways, metal or nonmetallic cable trays. If metal conduit, cable tray, armored cable, or similar metallic systems are used, they shall be installed with insulating breaks such that they will not cause a potentially hazardous electrical condition.

(d) Circuit Protection. Circuit protection shall not be required for control and instrumentation that are totally within the cell line working zone.

(e) Bonding. Bonding of fixed electrical equipment to the energized conductive surfaces of the cell line, its attachments or auxiliaries shall be permitted. Where fixed electrical equipment is mounted on an energized conductive surface it shall be bonded to that surface.

668-31. Auxiliary Nonelectric Connections. Auxiliary nonelectric connections, such as air hoses, water hoses, and the like, to an electrolytic cell, its attachments, or auxiliary equipments shall not have continuous conductive reinforcing wire, armor, braids and the like. Hoses shall be of a nonconductive material.

668-32. Cranes and Hoists.

(a) Conductive Surfaces to Be Insulated from Ground. The conductive surfaces of cranes and hoists that enter the cell line working zone shall not be required to be grounded. The portion of an overhead crane or hoist which contacts an energized electrolytic cell or energized attachments shall be insulated from ground.

(b) Hazardous Electrical Conditions. Remote crane or hoist controls which may introduce hazardous electrical conditions into the cell line working zone shall employ one or more of the following systems:

(1) Insulated and ungrounded control circuit in accordance with Section 668-21(a);

(2) Nonconductive rope operator;

(3) Pendant pushbutton with nonconductive supporting means and having nonconductive surfaces or ungrounded exposed conductive surfaces;

(4) Radio.

668-40. Enclosures. General-purpose electrical equipment enclosures shall be permitted where a natural draft ventilation system prevents the accumulation of gases.

ARTICLE 669 — ELECTROPLATING

Contents

669-1. Scope. The provisions of this article apply to the installation of the electrical components and accessory equipment that supply the power and controls for electroplating, anodizing, electropolishing, and electrostripping. For purposes of this article the term electroplating shall be used to identify any or all of these processes.

Because of the extremely high currents and low voltages normally involved, conventional wiring methods cannot be used in electroplating, anodizing, electropolishing, and electrostripping processes. Note the permission to use bare conductors even in systems exceeding 50 V dc. See Figures 669-1 and 669-2. Some systems in the aluminum anodizing process have potentials up to 240 V. Warning signs are required to be posted to indicate the presence of bare conductors.

669-2. Other Articles. Except as modified by this article, wiring and equipment used for electroplating processes shall comply with the applicable requirements of Chapters 1 through 4.

ARTICLE 669—ELECTROPLATING

669-3. General. Equipment for use in electroplating processes shall be identified for such service.

669-5. Branch-Circuit Conductors. Branch-circuit conductors supplying one or more units of equipment shall have an ampacity of not less than 125 percent of the total connected load. The ampacities for busbars shall be in accordance with Section 374-6.

669-6. Wiring Methods. Conductors connecting the electrolyte tank equipment to the conversion equipment shall be as follows:

(a) Systems Not Exceeding 50 Volts DC. Insulated conductors shall be permitted to be run without insulated support provided they are protected from physical damage. Bare copper or aluminum conductors shall be permitted where supported on insulators.

(b) Systems Exceeding 50 Volts DC. Insulated conductors shall be permitted to be run on insulated supports provided they are protected from physical damage. Bare copper or aluminum conductors shall be permitted where supported on insulators and guarded against accidental contact in accordance with Section 110-17.

Exception: Unguarded bare conductors shall be permitted at the terminals.

Figure 669-1. A typical electroplating line.

669-7. Warning Signs. Warning signs shall be posted to indicate the presence of bare conductors.

669-8. Disconnecting Means.

(a) More than One Power Supply. Where more than one power supply serves the same dc system a disconnecting means shall be provided on the dc side of each power supply.

Figure 669-2. Bare busbar to supply an electro-plating tank.

(b) Removable Links or Conductors. Removable links or removable conductors shall be permitted to be used as the disconnecting means.

669-9. Overcurrent Protection. DC conductors shall be protected from overcurrent by one or more of the following: (1) fuses or circuit breakers; (2) a current sensing device which operates a disconnecting means; or (3) other approved means.

ARTICLE 670 — METALWORKING MACHINE TOOLS AND PLASTICS MACHINERY

Contents

670-1. Scope. This article covers the definition of, the size and overcurrent protection of supply conductors to, and the nameplate data required on metalworking machine tools and plastics machinery.

(FPN): For further information, see Electrical Standard for Metalworking Machine Tools and Plastics Machinery, NFPA 79-1980, (ANSI).

670-2. Definition of Metalworking Machine Tools or Plastics Machinery. For the purposes of this article, a machine tool is defined as a power-driven machine not portable by hand, used to shape or form metal or plastic by cutting, impact, pressure, electrical techniques, or combination of these processes; plastics machinery is defined as a power-driven machine not portable by hand, used to shape or form plastic by application of thermal and/or mechanical energy, by cutting, impact, pressure, or a combination of these processes.

The requirements of this article do not apply to any motor-driven machine not covered by this definition. Thus, these provisions do not apply to woodworking machine tools or to a machine or tool that can be carried from place to place by hand and is not normally used in a fixed location.

670-3. Machine Nameplate Data.

(a) Permanent Nameplate. A permanent nameplate listing supply voltage, phase, frequency, full-load current, ampere rating of largest motor or load, short-circuit interrupting capacity of the machine overcurrent-protective device if furnished, and diagram number shall be attached to the control equipment enclosure or machine where plainly visible after installation.

The full-load current shown on the nameplate shall not be less than the sum of the full-load currents required for all motors and other equipment which may be in operation at the same time under normal conditions of use. Where unusual type loads, duty cycles, etc., require oversized conductors, the required capacity shall be included in the marked "full-load current."

Where more than one incoming supply circuit is to be provided, the nameplate shall state the above information for each circuit.

(b) Overcurrent Protection. Where overcurrent protection is provided in accordance with Section 670-4(b), the machine shall be marked "overcurrent protection provided at machine supply terminals."

670-4. Supply Conductors.

(a) Size. The size of the supply conductor shall be such as to have an ampacity not less than 125 percent of the full-load current rating of all resistance heating loads plus 25 percent of the full-load current rating of highest rated motor plus the sum of the full-load current ratings of all other connected motors and apparatus which may be in operation at the same time.

(FPN): For the protection of supply conductors to the machine, see Section 240-3.

(b) Overcurrent Protection. A machine covered by NFPA 79 (ANSI) shall be considered as an individual unit and therefore shall be provided with a disconnecting means. The disconnecting means shall be permitted to be supplied by branch circuits protected by either fuses or circuit breakers. The disconnecting means shall not be required to incorporate overcurrent protection. When furnished as part of the machine, overcurrent protection shall consist of a single circuit breaker or set of fuses, the machine shall bear the marking required in Section 670-3, and the supply conductors shall be considered either as feeders or taps as covered by Section 240-21.

Section 3-10 in NFPA 79 states: "The operating handle of the disconnecting means shall be readily accessible. The center of the grip of the operating handle of the disconnecting means, when in its highest position, shall not be more than 6½ ft (1.98 m) above the floor. A permanent operating platform, readily accessible by means of a permanent stair or ladder, shall be considered as the floor for the purpose of this requirement. The operating handle shall be capable of being locked only in the "off" position. When the control enclosure door is closed, the operating handle shall positively indicate whether the disconnecting means is in the open or closed position."

ARTICLE 675 — ELECTRICALLY DRIVEN OR
CONTROLLED IRRIGATION MACHINES

Contents

A. General

675-1. Scope. The provisions of this article apply to electrically driven or controlled irrigation machines, and to the branch circuits and controllers for such equipment.

Electric pump motors used to supply water to irrigation machines are governed by the general requirements of the *Code*, not by Article 675.

675-2. Definitions.

Center Pivot Irrigation Machines. A center pivot irrigation machine is a multimotored irrigation machine which revolves around a central pivot and employs alignment switches or similar devices to control individual motors.

Collector Rings. A collector ring is an assembly of slip rings for transferring electrical energy from a stationary to a rotating member.

Irrigation Machines. An irrigation machine is an electrically driven or controlled machine, with one or more motors, not hand portable, and used primarily to transport and distribute water for agricultural purposes.

675-3. Other Articles. These provisions are in addition to, or amendatory of, the provisions of Article 430 and other articles in this Code which apply except as modified in this article.

The requirements of this section apply to special equipment for a particular condition to supplement or modify the general rules. See Section 90-3, Code Arrangement.

675-4. Irrigation Cable.

(a) Construction. The cable used to interconnect enclosures on the structure of an irrigation machine shall be an assembly of stranded, insulated conductors with nonhygroscopic and nonwicking filler in a core of moisture- and flame-resistant, nonmetallic material overlaid with a metallic covering and jacketed with a moisture-, corrosion- and sunlight-resistant nonmetallic material.

ARTICLE 675—ELECTRICALLY DRIVEN IRRIGATION MACHINES

The conductor insulation shall be of a type listed in Table 310-13 for an operating temperature of 75°C and for use in wet locations. The core insulating material thickness shall not be less than 30 mils and the metallic overlay thickness shall not be less than 8 mils. The jacketing material thickness shall not be less than 50 mils.

A composite of power, control, and grounding conductors in the cable shall be permitted.

(b) Alternate Wiring Methods. Other cables listed for the purpose.

(c) Supports. Irrigation cable shall be secured by approved straps, hangers, or similar fittings so designed and installed as not to injure the cable. Cable shall be supported at intervals not exceeding 4 feet (1.22 m).

(d) Fittings. Fittings shall be used at all points where irrigation cable terminates. The fittings shall be designed for use with the cable and shall be suitable for the conditions of service.

675-5. More than Three Conductors in a Raceway or Cable. The signal and control conductors of a raceway or cable shall not be counted for the purpose of derating the conductors as required in Note 8 of Tables 310-16 through 310-19.

675-6. Marking on Main Control Panel. The main control panel shall be provided with a nameplate which shall give the following information: (1) the manufacturer's name, the rated voltage, the phase, and the frequency; (2) the current rating of the machine; and (3) the rating of the main disconnecting means and size of overcurrent protection required.

675-7. Equivalent Current Ratings. Where intermittent duty is not involved the provisions of Article 430 shall be used for determining ratings for controllers, disconnecting means, conductors, and the like. Where irrigation machines have inherent intermittent duty the following determinations of equivalent current ratings shall be used.

(a) Continuous-Current Rating. The equivalent continuous-current rating for the selection of branch-circuit conductors and branch-circuit devices shall be equal to 125 percent of the motor nameplate full-load current rating of the largest motor plus a quantity equal to the sum of each of the motor nameplate full-load current ratings of all remaining motors on the circuit multiplied by the maximum percent duty cycle at which they can continuously operate.

(b) Locked-Rotor Current. The equivalent locked-rotor current rating shall be equal to the numerical sum of the locked-rotor current of the two largest motors plus 100 percent of the sum of the motor nameplate full-load current ratings of all the remaining motors on the circuit.

675-8. Disconnecting Means.

(a) Main Controller. A controller which is used to start and stop the complete machine shall meet all of the following requirements:

(1) An equivalent continuous current rating not less than specified in Section 675-7(a) or 675-22(a).

(2) A horsepower rating not less than the value from Table 430-151 based on the equivalent locked-rotor current specified in Section 675-7(b) or 675-22(b).

(b) Main Disconnecting Means. The main disconnecting means for the machine shall be at the point of connection of electrical power to the machine or shall be visible and not more than 50 feet (15.2 m) from the machine and shall be readily accessible and capable of being locked in the open position. This disconnecting means shall have the same horsepower and current rating as required for the main controller.

This section permits the main disconnecting means to be up to 50 ft from the machine if readily accessible and capable of being locked in the open position. This eliminates one set of overcurrent protective devices and one disconnecting means when the circuit originates at the motor control panel for the irrigation pump and this panel is within 50 ft of the center pivot machine. It also alleviates some potential problems with machines designed to be towed to a second site.

(c) Disconnecting Means for Individual Motors and Controllers. A disconnecting means shall be provided for each motor and controller and shall be located as required by Article 430, Part H. The disconnecting means shall not be required to be readily accessible.

Article 430, Part H, provides for safety during maintenance and inspection shutdown periods. See commentary following Section 430-103.

675-9. Branch-Circuit Conductors. The branch-circuit conductors shall have an ampacity not less than specified in Section 675-7(a) or 675-22(a).

675-10. Several Motors on One Branch Circuit.

Section 430-53 provides for motor branch-circuit short-circuit and ground-fault protection for several motors on one branch circuit. A combination of these requirements, which are more or less stringent for this special equipment application, is found in Section 675-10.

(a) Protection Required. Several motors, each not exceeding 2-horsepower rating, shall be permitted to be used on an irrigation machine circuit protected at not more than 30 amperes at 600 volts, nominal, or less, provided all of the following conditions are met:

(1) The full-load rating of any motor in the circuit shall not exceed 6 amperes.

(2) Each motor in the circuit shall have individual running overcurrent protection in accordance with Section 430-32.

(3) Taps to individual motors shall not be smaller than No. 14 copper and not more than 25 feet (7.62 m) in length.

(b) Individual Protection Not Required. Individual branch-circuit short-circuit protection for motors and motor controllers shall not be required where the requirements of Section 675-10(a) are met.

675-11. Collector Rings.

(a) Transmitting Current for Power Purposes. Collector rings shall have an ampacity not less than 125 percent of the full-load current of the largest device served plus the full-load current of all other devices served, or as determined from Section 675-7(a) or 675-22(a).

(b) Control and Signal Purposes. Collector rings for control and signal purposes shall have an ampacity not less than 125 percent of the full-load current of the largest device served plus the full-load current of all other devices served.

(c) Grounding. The collector ring used for grounding shall be of the same ampacity as the largest collector ring in the assembly.

(d) Protection. Collector rings shall be protected from the expected environment and from accidental contact by means of a suitable enclosure.

ARTICLE 675—ELECTRICALLY DRIVEN IRRIGATION MACHINES

675-12. Grounding. The following equipment shall be grounded:

(1) All electrical equipment on the irrigation machine; (2) all electrical equipment associated with the irrigation machine; (3) metallic junction boxes and enclosures; and (4) control panels or control equipment that supply or control electrical equipment to the irrigation machine.

Exception: Grounding shall not be required on machines where all of the following provisions are met:

a. The machine is electrically controlled but not electrically driven.

b. The control voltage is 30 volts or less.

c. The control or signal circuits are current-limited as specified in Section 725-31.

675-13. Methods of Grounding. Machines which require grounding shall have a noncurrent-carrying equipment grounding conductor provided as an integral part of each cord, cable, or raceway. This grounding conductor shall be equal in size to the supply conductors in each cord cable or raceway, but not smaller than No. 14 copper. Feeder circuits supplying power to irrigation machines shall have an equipment grounding conductor sized according to Table 250-95.

675-14. Bonding. Where electrical grounding is required on an irrigation machine, the metallic structure of the machine, metallic conduit, or metallic sheath of cable shall be bonded to the grounding conductor. Metal-to-metal contact with a part which is bonded to the grounding conductor and the noncurrent-carrying parts of the machine shall be considered as an acceptable bonding path.

675-15. Lightning Protection. If an irrigation machine has a stationary point, a driven ground rod shall be connected to the machine at the stationary point for lightning protection.

Where the electrical power supply to irrigation machine equipment is a service, provisions in Sections 250-81 and 250-83 would require a made grounding electrode, specifically a driven ground rod. Consideration should be given to Section 250-86 and NFPA 78, Lightning Protection Code, in areas where lightning protection is critical.

675-16. Energy from More than One Source. Equipment within an enclosure receiving electrical energy from more than one source shall not be required to have a disconnecting means for the additional source, provided that its voltage is 30 volts or less and meets the requirements of Section 725-31.

675-17. Connectors. External plugs and connectors on the equipment shall be of the weatherproof type.
Unless provided solely for the connection of circuits meeting the requirements of Section 725-31, external plugs and connectors shall be constructed as specified in Section 250-99(a).

B. Center Pivot Irrigation Machines

675-21. General. The provisions of Part B are intended to cover additional special requirements which are peculiar to center pivot irrigation machines. See Section 675-2 for definition of Center Pivot Irrigation Machines.

675-22. Equivalent Current Ratings. In order to establish ratings of controllers, disconnecting means, conductors, and the like, for the inherent intermittent duty of center pivot irrigation machines, the following determination shall be used:

Figure 675-1. A center pivot irrigation machine. (*Lockwood Corp.*)

The ratings of electrical components of any circuit should be selected so as to avoid extensive damage to the equipment during a short-circuit or a ground-fault condition. Section 675-22 gives the requirements for establishing ratings of components of special equipment for inherent intermittent duty. Also see commentary following Sections 110-10 and 430-52.

(a) Continuous-Current Rating. The equivalent continuous-current rating for the selection of branch-circuit conductors and branch-circuit devices shall be equal to 125 percent of the motor nameplate full-load current rating of the largest motor plus 60 percent of the sum of the motor nameplate full-load current ratings of all remaining motors on the circuit.

(b) Locked-Rotor Current. The equivalent locked-rotor current rating shall be equal to the numerical sum of two times the locked-rotor current of the largest motor plus 80 percent of the sum of the motor nameplate full-load current ratings of all the remaining motors on the circuit.

ARTICLE 680 — SWIMMING POOLS, FOUNTAINS, AND SIMILAR INSTALLATIONS

Contents

(b) Other Enclosures.
(c) Protection.
(d) Grounding Terminals.
680-22. Bonding.
  (a) Bonded Parts.
  (b) Common Bonding Grid.
  (c) Pool Water Heaters.
680-23. Underwater Audio Equipment.
  (a) Speakers.
  (b) Wiring Methods.
  (c) Forming Shell and Metal Screen.
680-24. Grounding.
680-25. Methods of Grounding.
  (a) General.
  (b) Pool Lighting Fixtures and Related Equipment.
  (c) Motors.
  (d) Panelboards.
  (e) Cord-Connected Equipment.
  (f) Other Equipment.
680-26. Electrically Operated Pool Covers.
  (a) Motors and Controllers.
  (b) Wiring Methods.
680-27. Deck Area Heating.
  (a) Unit Heaters.
  (b) Permanently Wired Radiant Heaters.
  (c) Radiant Heat Cables Not Permitted.

C. Storable Pools

680-30. Pumps.
680-31. Ground-Fault Circuit-Interrupters Required.

D. Spas, Hot Tubs and Hydromassage Bathtubs

680-40. Outdoor Installations.
680-41. Indoor Installations.
  (a) Receptacles.
  (b) Lighting Fixtures and Lighting Outlets.
  (c) Wall Switches.
  (d) Bonding.
  (e) Methods of Bonding.
  (f) Grounding.

(g) Methods of Grounding.

E. Fountains

680-50. General.
680-51. Lighting Fixtures, Submersible Pumps and Other Submersible Equipment.
  (a) Ground-Fault Circuit-Interrupter.
  (b) Operating Voltage.
  (c) Lighting Fixture Lenses.
  (d) Overheating Protection.
  (e) Wiring.
  (f) Servicing.
  (g) Stability.
680-52. Junction Boxes and Other Enclosures.
  (a) General.
  (b) Underwater Junction Boxes and Other Underwater Enclosures.
680-53. Bonding.
680-54. Grounding.
680-55. Methods of Grounding.
  (a) Applied Provisions.
  (b) Supplied by a Flexible Cord.
680-56. Cord- and Plug-Connected Equipment.
  (a) Ground-Fault Circuit-Interrupter.
  (b) Cord Type.
  (c) Sealing.
  (d) Terminations.

F. Therapeutic Pools and Tubs in Health Care Facilities

680-60. General.
680-61. Permanently Installed Therapeutic Pools.
680-62. Therapeutic Tubs (Hydrotherapeutic Tanks).
  (a) Ground-Fault Circuit-Interrupter.
  (b) Bonding.
  (c) Methods of Bonding.
  (d) Grounding.
  (e) Methods of Grounding.
  (f) Receptacles.
680-63. Lighting Fixtures.

A. General

680-1. Scope. The provisions of this article apply to the construction and installation of electric wiring for and equipment in or adjacent to all swimming, wading, therapeutic, and decorative pools, fountains, hot tubs, and spas, whether permanently installed or storable, and to metallic auxiliary equipment, such as pumps, filters, and similar equipment.

(FPN): The term "pool" as used in the balance of this article shall include swimming, wading, and permanently installed therapeutic pools. The term "fountain" as used in the balance of this article shall include fountains, ornamental pools, display pools, and reflection pools.

This article applies to swimming pools and similar installations, indoors or outdoors, permanent or storable, and whether or not served by any electrical circuits of any nature. Studies conducted by Underwriters Laboratories, various manufacturers and others indicate that a person in a swimming pool can receive a severe electric shock by reaching over and touching the energized casing of a faulty appliance, such as a radio, hair dryer, etc., as the person's body establishes a conductive path through the water and pool to earth. Also, a person not in contact with a faulty appliance or any grounded object may receive an electric shock and be rendered immobile by a potential gradient in the water itself. Accordingly, requirements of this article covering effective bonding and grounding, installation of receptacles and lighting fixtures, use of ground-fault circuit-interrupters, modified wiring methods, etc., apply not only to the installation of the pool, but also to installations and equipment adjacent to, or associated with, the pool.

680-2. Approval of Equipment. All electric equipment installed in the water, walls, or decks of pools, fountains, and similar installations shall comply with the provisions of this article.

680-3. Other Articles. Except as modified by this article, wiring and equipment in or adjacent to pools and fountains shall comply with the applicable requirements of Chapters 1 through 4.

(FPN): See Section 370-13 for junction boxes, Section 347-3 for rigid nonmetallic conduit, and Article 720 for low-voltage lighting.

Note that Section 370-13(f) specifies the requirements for the support of empty threaded boxes and Section 347-3(b) does not permit equipment to be supported by rigid nonmetallic conduit. See Figure 680-1. See also commentary following Section 370-13(f).

680-4. Definitions.

Dry-Niche Lighting Fixture. A lighting fixture intended for installation in the wall of a pool or fountain in a niche that is sealed against the entry of pool water.

Forming Shell. A metal structure designed to support a wet-niche lighting fixture assembly and intended for mounting in a pool or fountain structure.

Hydromassage Bathtub. A bathtub equipped with a recirculating piping system, pump and associated equipment. It is designed so it can accept, circulate, and discharge water upon each use.

This definition is new in the 1984 *Code*. It was added to correlate with Section 680-41(a)(1), Exception.

Permanently Installed Decorative Fountains and Reflection Pools. Those that are constructed in the ground, on the ground, or in a building in such a manner that the fountain cannot be readily disassembled for storage and are served by electrical circuits of any nature. These units are primarily constructed for their aesthetic value and not intended for swimming or wading.

Permanently Installed Swimming, Wading, and Therapeutic Pools. Those that are constructed in the ground, on the ground, or in a building in such a manner that the pool cannot be readily disassembled for storage, whether or not served by electrical circuits of any nature.

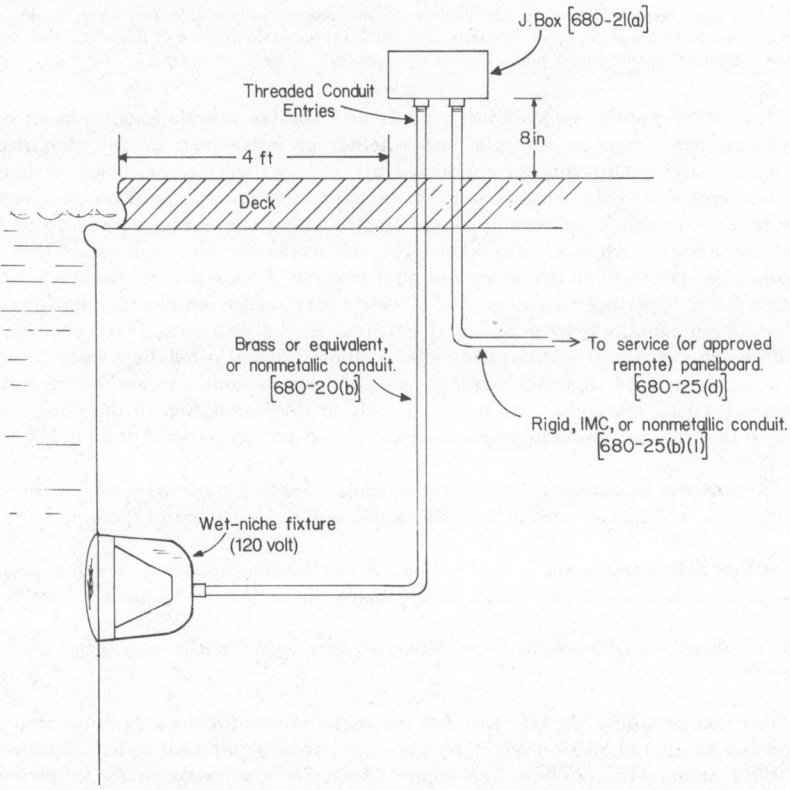

Figure 680-1. Where boxes are supported according to the provisions of Section 370-13(f), as above, additional supporting means may be required where nonmetallic conduit is used. See Section 347-3(b).

See commentary following Part F, heading.

Pool Cover, Electrically Operated.   Motor-driven equipment designed to cover and uncover the water surface of a pool by means of a flexible sheet or rigid frame.

This definition is new in the 1984 *Code*. See new Section 680-26.

Spa or Hot Tub.   A hydromassage pool designed for immersion of users and usually having a filter, heater, and motor-driven blower. It may be installed indoors or outdoors, on the ground or supporting structure, or in the ground or supporting structure.

See commentary following Part D, heading.

Storable Swimming or Wading Pool.   A pool with a maximum dimension of 18 feet (5.49 m) and a maximum wall height of 42 inches (1.07 m) and so constructed that it may be readily disassembled for storage and reassembled to its original integrity.

See commentary following Section 680-31 and Figure 680-9.

Wet-Niche Lighting Fixture.   A lighting fixture intended for installation in a metal forming shell mounted in a pool or fountain structure where the fixture will be completely surrounded by water.

See Figures 680-1 and 680-5.

680-5. Transformers and Ground-Fault Circuit-Interrupters.

(a) Transformers. Transformers used for the supply of fixtures, together with the transformer enclosure, shall be identified for the purpose. The transformer shall be a two-winding type having a grounded metal barrier between the primary and secondary windings.

> Unless marked otherwise, UL listed swimming pool and spa transformers are not suitable for connection to a conduit which extends directly to an underwater pool light forming shell. Swimming pool and spa transformers are not permitted to be used outdoors unless they are marked "For Outdoor Use" or equivalent, in which case they have been found to be acceptable for both outdoor and indoor use. See Section 110-3(b).

(b) Ground-Fault Circuit-Interrupters. Ground-fault circuit-interrupters shall be self-contained units, circuit-breaker types, receptacle types, or other approved types.

> See definition of "Ground-Fault Circuit-Interrupter" in Article 100.
> A ground-fault circuit-interrupter is intended to be used only in a circuit that has a solidly grounded conductor. A Class A GFCI trips when the current to ground has a value in the range of 4 through 6 milliamperes and is suitable for use in swimming pool circuits. It should be noted, however, that swimming pool circuits installed before local adoption of the 1965 *National Electrical Code* may include sufficient leakage current to cause a Class A GFCI to trip. A Class B GFCI trips when the current to ground exceeds 20 milliamperes and is suitable for use with underwater swimming pool lighting fixtures only.

(c) Wiring. Conductors on the load side of a ground-fault circuit-interrupter or of a transformer, used to comply with provisions of Section 680-20(a)(1), shall not occupy conduit, boxes, or enclosures containing other conductors.

Exception No. 1: Ground-fault circuit-interrupters shall be permitted in a panelboard that contains circuits protected by other than ground-fault circuit-interrupters.

Exception No. 2: Supply conductors to a feed-through, receptacle-type, ground-fault circuit-interrupter shall be permitted in the same enclosure.

680-6. Receptacles, Lighting Fixtures, Lighting Outlets and Switching Devices.

(a) Receptacles.

(1) Receptacles on the property shall be located at least 10 feet (3.05 m) from the inside walls of a pool.

Exception: A receptacle that provides power for a recirculating pump motor for a permanently installed pool, as permitted in Section 680-7, shall be permitted not less than 5 feet (1.52 m) from the inside walls of the pool and shall be single and of the locking and grounding types and all receptacles shall be protected by a ground-fault circuit-interrupter.

(2) Where a permanently installed pool is installed at a dwelling unit(s), at least one 125-volt convenience receptacle shall be located a minimum of 10 feet (3.05 m) from and not more than 20 feet (6.08 m) from the inside wall of the pool.

(3) All 125-volt receptacles located within 20 feet (6.08 m) of the inside walls of a pool shall be protected by a ground-fault circuit-interrupter. See Section 210-8(a)(3).

Section 680-6(a) makes it clear that a locking- and grounding-type receptacle used for a recirculating pump motor is permitted where it will be not less than 5 ft from the inside walls of the pool and is protected by a GFCI. This requirement also makes it clear that all receptacles located within 20 ft of a permanently installed pool (outdoors or indoors, for dwelling unit or commerical use) are required to be protected by GFCIs. This distance of 20 ft is intended to provide for location of receptacles beyond a pool deck. If located within the perimeter of a pool deck, the receptacle installation is likely to be a tripping hazard.

See Figure 680-2.

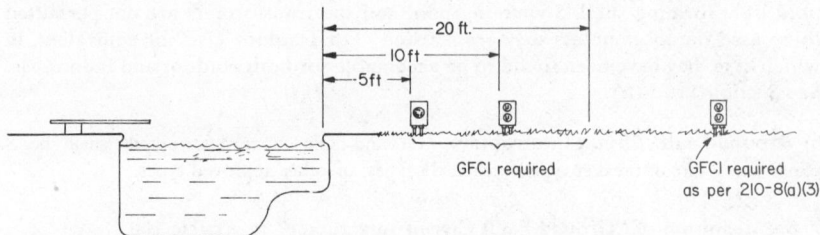

Figure 680-2. For permanently installed pools at dwelling unit(s), it is mandatory to install a 125-V receptacle between 10 and 20 ft from the inside wall of the pool.

(FPN): In determining the above dimensions, the distance to be measured is the shortest path the supply cord of an appliance connected to the receptacle would follow without piercing a floor, wall, or ceiling of a building or other effective permanent barrier.

See Figure 680-3.

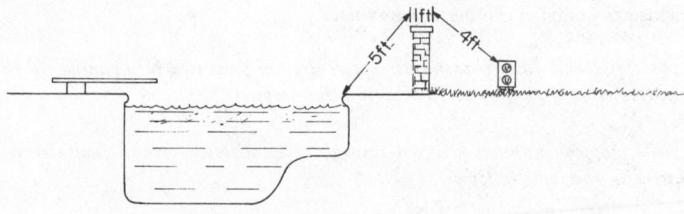

Figure 680-3. This figure illustrates the shortest path a supply cord of an appliance connected to the receptacle would follow without piercing the wall.

(b) Lighting Fixtures and Lighting Outlets.

(1) Lighting fixtures and lighting outlets shall not be installed over the pool or over the area extending 5 feet (1.52 m) horizontally from the inside walls of a pool unless 12 feet (3.66 m) above the maximum water level.

Exception No. 1: Existing lighting fixtures and lighting outlets located less than 5 feet (1.52 m) measured horizontally from the inside walls of a pool shall be at least 5 feet (1.52 m) above the surface of the maximum water level and shall be rigidly attached to the existing structure.

See Figure 680-4.

Exception No. 2: In indoor pool areas, the limitations of Section 680-6(b)(1) shall not apply if all of the following conditions are complied with: (1) fixtures are of totally enclosed type; (2) a ground-fault circuit-interrupter is installed in the branch circuit supplying the fixture(s); and (3) the distance from the bottom of the fixture to the maximum water level is not less than 7.5 feet (2.29 m).

(2) Lighting fixtures and lighting outlets installed in the area extending between 5 feet (1.52 m) and 10 feet (3.05 m) horizontally from the inside walls of a pool shall be protected by a ground-fault circuit-interrupter unless installed 5 feet (1.52 m) above the maximum water level and rigidly attached to the structure adjacent to or enclosing the pool.

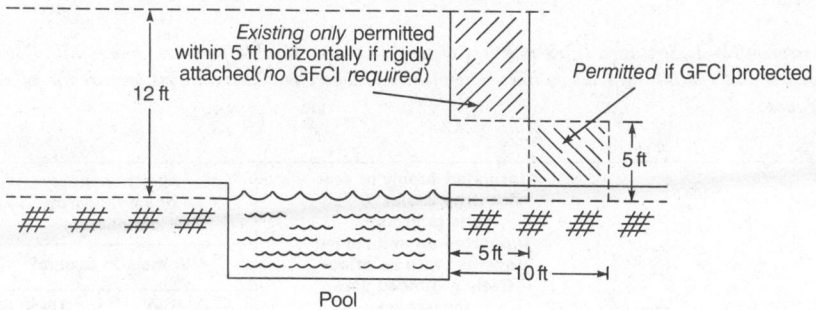

Figure 680-4. The requirements for ground-fault circuit-interrupter protection for lighting fixtures and lighting outlets over pools.

(3) Cord-connected lighting fixtures shall meet the same specifications as other cord- and plug-connected equipment as set forth in Section 680-7 when installed within 16 feet (4.88 m) of any point on the water surface, measured radially.

(c) Switching Devices. Switching devices on the property shall be located at least 5 feet (1.52 m) from the inside walls of a pool unless separated from the pool by a solid fence, wall, or other permanent barrier.

This subsection is new in the 1984 *Code*. Panelboards, time clocks and pool light switches, etc., where located not less than 5 ft from the inside walls of a pool, without a solid fence, wall or other permanent barrier, will be out of reach of persons who are in a pool, thereby preventing contact and possible shock hazards.

680-7. Cord- and Plug-Connected Equipment. Fixed or stationary equipment rated 20 amperes or less, other than an underwater lighting fixture for a permanently installed pool, shall be permitted to be connected with a flexible cord to facilitate the removal or disconnection for maintenance or repair. For other than storable pools, the flexible cord shall not exceed 3 feet (914 mm) in length and shall have a copper equipment grounding conductor not smaller than No. 12 with a grounding-type attachment plug.

(FPN): See Section 680-25(e) for connection with flexible cords.

In some geographic areas, it is preferable to disconnect the filter pump for a permanent pool during the cold weather months, and a 3-ft cord is permitted to facilitate the removal of fixed or stationary equipment for maintenance and storage.

The 3-ft cord limitation does not apply to cord- and plug-connected filter pumps used with storable-type pools, covered in Part C of this article, since these pumps are neither fixed nor stationary. Listed filter pumps for use with storable pools are considered portable and are permitted to be equipped with cords longer than 3 ft.

680-8. Overhead Conductor Clearances. The following parts of pools shall not be placed under existing service-drop conductors or any other open overhead wiring; nor shall such wiring be installed above the following: (1) pools and the area extending 10 feet (3.05 m) horizontally from the inside of the walls of the pool; (2) diving structure; or (3) observation stands, towers, or platforms.

Exception No. 1: Structures listed in (1), (2), and (3) above shall be permitted under utility-owned, -operated and -maintained supply lines or service drops where such installations provide the following clearances:

	Insulated supply or service drop cables, 0-750 volts to ground, supported on and cabled together with an effectively grounded bare messenger	All other supply or service drop conductors	
		Voltage to Ground	
		0-15 kV	15-50 kV
A. Clearance in any direction to the water level, edge of water surface, base of diving platform or permanently-anchored raft	18 feet (5.49m)	25 feet (7.62m)	27 feet (8.23m)
B. Clearance in any direction to the diving platform or tower	14 feet (4.27m)	16 feet (4.88m)	18 feet (5.49m)
C. Horizontal limit of clearance measured from inside wall of the pool.	This limit shall extend to the outer edge of the structures listed in (1) and (2) above but not less than 10 feet (3.05m).		

Figure 680-8, Exception No. 1

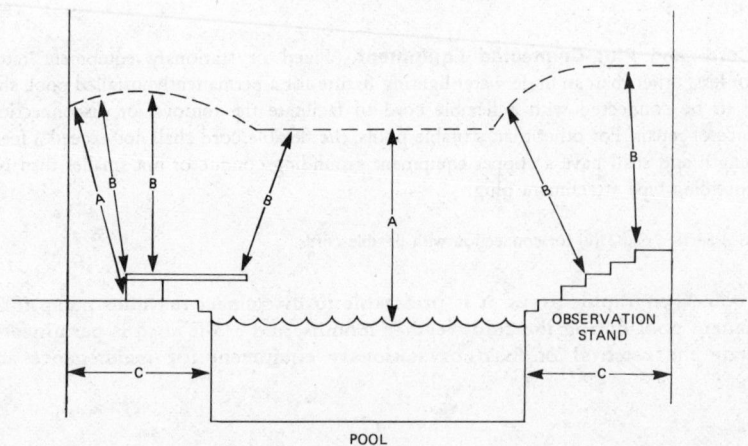

OBSERVATION STAND

POOL

Exception No. 2: Utility-owned, -operated, and -maintained communication conductors, community antenna system coaxial cables complying with Article 820, and the supporting messengers shall be permitted at a height of not less than 10 feet (3.05 m) above swimming and wading pools, diving structures and observation stands, towers or platforms.

(FPN): See Sections 225-18 and 225-19 for clearances for conductors not covered by this section.

680-9. Electric Pool Water Heaters. All electric pool water heaters shall have the heating elements subdivided into loads not exceeding 48 amperes and protected at not more than 60 amperes.

680-10. Underground Wiring Location. Underground wiring shall not be permitted under the pool or under the area extending 5 feet (1.52 m) horizontally from the inside wall of the pool.

Exception No. 1: Wiring necessary to supply pool equipment permitted by this article shall be allowed within this area.

Exception No. 2: When space limitations prevent wiring from being routed 5 feet (1.52 m) or more from the pool, such wiring shall be permitted when installed in rigid metal conduit, intermediate metal conduit, or a nonmetallic raceway system. All metallic conduit shall be corrosion-resistant and suitable for the location. The Exceptions to Section 300-5(a) shall not apply.

680-11. Equipment Rooms and Pits. Electric equipment shall not be installed in rooms or pits which do not have adequate drainage to prevent water accumulation during normal operation or filter maintenance.

The addition of the word "pits" in the 1984 *Code* is intended to recognize that pits for electrically operated pool covers will be provided with drainage.

B. Permanently Installed Pools

680-20. Underwater Lighting Fixtures.

(a) General. Paragraphs (a) through (c) of this section apply to all lighting fixtures installed below the normal water level of the pool. All lighting fixtures shall be installed for operation at 150 volts or less between conductors.

(1) The design of an underwater lighting fixture supplied from a branch circuit either directly or by way of a transformer meeting the requirements of Section 680-5(a) shall be such that, when the fixture is properly installed without a ground-fault circuit-interrupter, there is no shock hazard with any likely combination of fault conditions during normal use (not relamping).
In addition, a ground-fault circuit-interrupter shall be installed in the branch circuit supplying fixtures operating at more than 15 volts, so that there is no shock hazard during relamping. The installation of the ground-fault circuit-interrupter shall be such that there is no shock hazard with any likely fault-condition combination that involves a person in a conductive path from any ungrounded part of the branch circuit or the fixture to ground.
Compliance with this requirement shall be obtained by the use of an approved underwater lighting fixture and by installation of an approved ground-fault circuit-interrupter in the branch circuit.

(2) No lighting fixtures shall be installed for operation at over 150 volts between conductors.

(3) Lighting fixtures mounted in walls shall be installed with the top of the fixture lens at least 18 inches (457 mm) below the normal water level of the pool. A lighting fixture facing upward shall have the lens adequately guarded to prevent contact by any person.

ARTICLE 680—SWIMMING POOLS, FOUNTAINS

Exception: Lighting fixtures identified for use at a depth of not less than 4 inches (102 mm) below the normal water level of the pool shall be permitted.

(4) Fixtures that depend on submersion for safe operation shall be inherently protected against the hazards of overheating when not submerged.

> Fixtures that depend on submersion for safe operation are required to be inherently protected against the hazards of overheating when not submerged, for instance, during a relamping process. Protection against overheating is required to be built into or be a part of the fixture. A remotely located low-water cutoff switch would not provide the intended protection.

(b) Wet-Niche Fixtures.

(1) Approved metal forming shells shall be installed for the mounting of all wet-niche underwater fixtures and shall be equipped with provisions for threaded conduit entries. Rigid metal conduit or intermediate metal conduit of brass or other approved corrosion-resistant metal or rigid nonmetallic conduit shall extend from the forming shell to a suitable junction box or other enclosure located as provided in Section 680-21. Where rigid nonmetallic conduit is used, a No. 8 insulated copper conductor shall be installed in this conduit with provisions for terminating in the forming shell, junction box or transformer enclosure, or ground-fault circuit-interrupter enclosure. The termination of the No. 8 conductor in the forming shell shall be covered with, or encapsulated in, a listed potting compound to protect such connection from the possible deteriorating effect of pool water. Metal parts of the fixture and forming shell in contact with the pool water shall be of brass or other approved corrosion-resistant metal.

(2) The end of the flexible-cord jacket and the flexible-cord conductor terminations within a fixture shall be covered with, or encapsulated in, a suitable potting compound to prevent the entry of water into the fixture through the cord or its conductors. In addition, the grounding connection within a fixture shall be similarly treated to protect such connection from the deteriorating effect of pool water in the event of water entry into the fixture.

(3) The fixture shall be bonded to and secured to the forming shell by a positive locking device that assures a low-resistance contact and requires a tool to remove the fixture from the forming shell.

(c) Dry-Niche Fixtures.
A dry-niche lighting fixture shall be provided with: (1) provision for drainage of water, and (2) means for accommodating one equipment grounding conductor for each conduit entry.

Approved rigid metal conduit, intermediate metal conduit, or rigid nonmetallic conduit shall be installed from the fixture to the service equipment or panelboard. A junction box shall not be required, but if used shall not be required to be elevated or located as specified in Section 680-21(a)(4) if the fixture is specifically identified for the purpose.

> Underwater lighting fixtures of either dry-niche or wet-niche types operating at more than 15 V require ground-fault circuit-interrupter protection. See commentary following Section 680-5(b).
> Branch-circuit conductors for dry-niche fixtures are required to be installed in rigid metal conduit, intermediate metal conduit, or rigid nonmetallic conduit from the fixture to the source of supply. Branch-circuit conductors for wet-niche fixtures leaving the pool junction box are required to be enclosed in rigid metal conduit, intermediate metal conduit, or rigid nonmetallic conduit, except in or on buildings where the conductors may be protected by electrical metallic tubing as permitted by Section 680-25(b)(1), Exception No. 1. However, unlike wet-niche fixtures, a junction box is not required for dry-niche fixtures, but, if used, is not required to

be elevated or located as specified in Section 680-21 (a) (4). See Figures 680-1 and 680-5.

Where rigid nonmetallic conduit is used between a forming shell for a wet-niche fixture and a junction box or other enclosure, a No. 8 insulated, copper bonding conductor is required to be installed within this conduit to provide electrical continuity between the forming shell and the junction box or other enclosure. This rigid nonmetallic conduit should be sized large enough to enclose both the No. 8 insulated, copper bonding conductor and the approved flexible cord that supplies the wet-niche fixture to facilitate easy withdrawal and insertion of the bonding conductor and the cord.

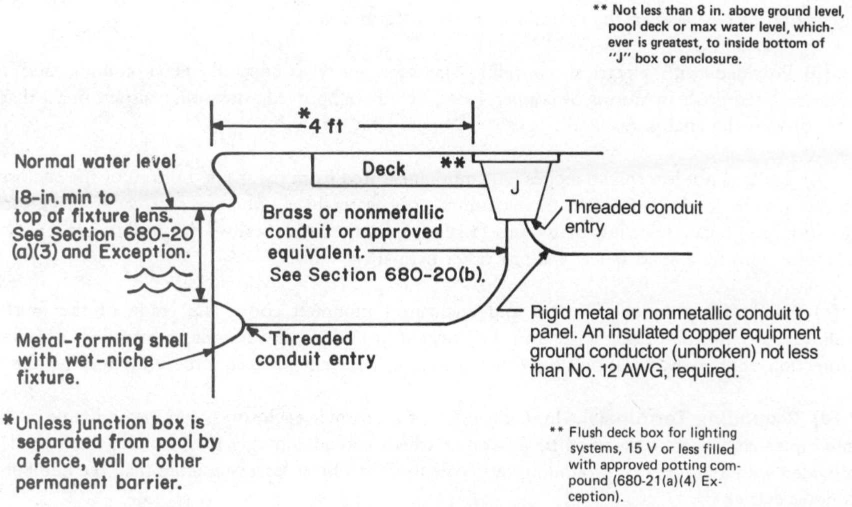

Figure 680-5. Installation requirements for wet-niche forming shell and deck box.

680-21. Junction Boxes and Enclosures for Transformers or Ground-Fault Circuit-Interrupters.

(a) Junction Boxes. A junction box connected to a conduit that extends directly to a forming shell shall be:

(1) Equipped with provisions for threaded conduit entries; and

(2) Of copper, brass, suitable plastic, or other approved corrosion-resistant material; and

(3) Provided with electrical continuity between every connected metal conduit and the grounding terminals by means of copper, brass, or other approved corrosion-resistant metal that is integral with the box; and

(4) Located not less than 8 inches (203 mm), measured from the inside of the bottom of the box, above the ground level, pool deck, or maximum pool water level, whichever provides the greatest elevation, and located not less than 4 feet (1.22 m) from the inside wall of the pool unless separated from the pool by a solid fence, wall, or other permanent barrier.

Exception: On lighting systems of 15 volts or less, a flush deck box shall be permitted provided:

a. An approved potting compound is used to fill the box to prevent the entrance of moisture; and

b. The flush deck box is located not less than 4 feet (1.22 m) from the inside wall of the pool.

Melted wax is often used to meet this requirement.

(b) Other Enclosures. An enclosure for a transformer, ground-fault circuit-interrupter, or a similar device connected to a conduit that extends directly to a forming shell shall be:

(1) Equipped with provisions for threaded conduit entries; and

(2) Provided with an approved seal, such as duct seal at the conduit connection, that prevents circulation of air between the conduit and the enclosures; and

(3) Provided with electrical continuity between every connected metal conduit and the grounding terminals by means of copper, brass, or other approved corrosion-resistant metal that is integral with the enclosures; and

(4) Located not less than 8 inches (203 mm), measured from the inside bottom of the enclosure to the ground level, pool deck, or maximum pool water level, whichever provides the greatest elevation, and located not less than 4 feet (1.22 m) from the inside wall of the pool unless separated from the pool by a solid fence, wall, or other permanent barrier.

(c) Protection. Junction boxes and enclosures mounted above the grade of the finished walkway around the pool shall not be located in the walkway unless afforded additional protection, such as by location under diving boards, adjacent to fixed structures, and the like.

(d) Grounding Terminals. Junction boxes, transformer enclosures, and ground-fault circuit-interrupter enclosures connected to a conduit which extends directly to a forming shell shall be provided with a number of grounding terminals that shall be at least one more than the number of conduit entries.

(e) Strain Relief. The termination of a flexible cord of an underwater lighting fixture within a junction box, transformer enclosure, ground-fault circuit-interrupter, or other enclosure shall be provided with a strain relief.

680-22. Bonding.

(FPN): It is not the intent of this subsection to require that the No. 8 or larger solid copper bonding conductor be extended or attached to any remote panelboard, service equipment or any electrode, but only that it be employed to eliminate voltage gradients in the pool area as prescribed.

This Fine Print Note was added to the 1984 *Code* to clear up previous misinterpretation.

(a) Bonded Parts. The following parts shall be bonded together:

(1) All metallic parts of the pool structure, including the reinforcing metal of the pool shell, coping stones, and deck.

(2) All forming shells.

(3) All metal fittings within or attached to the pool structure.

(4) Metal parts of electric equipment associated with the pool water circulating system, including pump motors.

(5) Metal parts of equipment associated with pool covers including electric motors.

(6) Metal conduit, metal piping, and all fixed metal parts that are within 5 feet (1.52 m) of the inside walls of the pool and that are not separated from the pool by a permanent barrier.

This subsection would also include, for example, a metal door frame or metal window frame.

Exception No. 1: The usual steel tie wires shall be considered suitable for bonding the reinforcing steel together, and welding or special clamping shall not be required.

Exception No. 2: Structural reinforcing steel or the walls of bolted or welded metal pool structures shall be permitted as a common bonding grid for nonelectrical parts where connections can be made in accordance with Section 250-113.

Exception No. 3: Isolated parts which are no more than 4 inches (102 mm) in any dimension and do not penetrate into the pool structure more than 1 inch (25.4 mm) shall not require bonding.

(b) Common Bonding Grid. These parts shall be connected to a common bonding grid with a solid, copper conductor, insulated, covered, or bare, not smaller than No. 8. Connection shall be made by pressure connectors or clamps of brass, copper, or copper alloy. The common bonding grid may be any of the following:

(1) The structural reinforcing steel of a concrete pool where the reinforcing rods are bonded together by the usual steel tie wires or the equivalent; or,

(2) The wall of a bolted or welded metal pool; or,

(3) A solid, copper conductor, insulated, covered, or bare, not smaller than No. 8.

(c) Pool Water Heaters. For pool water heaters rated at more than 50 amperes which have specific instructions regarding bonding and grounding, only those parts designated to be bonded shall be bonded, and only those parts designated to be grounded shall be grounded.

It is important to know the difference between the terms "bonding" and "grounding" as they apply to this article. As defined in Article 100, "Bonding" is the permanent joining of metallic parts to form an electrically conductive path that will assure electrical continuity and the capacity to conduct safely any current likely to be imposed. See comments following Section 680-26(b).

This section indicates the metal parts that are required to be "bonded" together, including all metal parts of electric equipment associated with the pool water circulating system, all metal parts of the pool structure, and all fixed metal parts, which include conduit and piping, metal door frames, and metal window frames, etc. within 5 ft of the inside walls of the pool and not separated by a permanent barrier. It should be understood that the "bonding together of these parts" does not mean that they are required to be connected to each other; it means that they are required to be connected to a common bonding grid with an insulated, covered, or bare solid copper conductor not smaller than No. 8. See Figures 680-6 and 680-7. Connections are required to be made by pressure connectors, clamps, or other approved means in accordance with Section 250-113. See Fine Print Note following Section 680-22.

The reason for connecting metal parts (ladders, hand-rails, water-circulating equipment, forming shells, diving boards, etc.) to a common bonding grid (pool reinforcing steel, pool metal wall, or a No. 8 solid conductor) is to ensure that all such metal parts will be at the same electrical potential. This will reduce any possible shock hazard created by stray currents in the ground or piping connected to the swimming pool. This includes plastic piping as water containing salt or chemicals can have a low resistivity, thereby permitting dangerous currents to flow.

Since corrosion is normally associated with the wet conditions of swimming pool areas, wiring and connections should be checked periodically, especially bonding connections between the No. 8 copper conductor and, for instance, an aluminum (or other dissimilar metal) ladder.

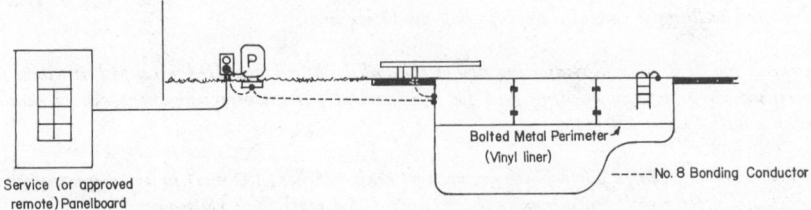

Figure 680-6. Illustrated is a metal (i.e., steel, aluminum) perimeter pool with bolted (may be welded) sections. The metal perimeter serves as the common bonding grid to which the metal ladder, the metal diving board, and pump motor are connected. Note that the pump motor is connected to a receptacle as per Sections 680-6 and 680-7.

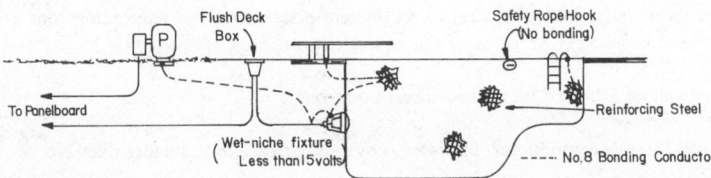

Figure 680-7. Illustrated is a poured concrete pool. The structural reinforcing steel serves as the common bonding grid to which all metal appurtenances associated with the pool are connected. Safety rope hooks are not required to be bonded as per Section 680-22(a), Exception No. 3. The flush deck box meets the provisions of Section 680-21(a), Exception.

680-23. Underwater Audio Equipment. All underwater audio equipment shall be identified for the purpose.

(a) Speakers. Each speaker shall be mounted in an approved metal forming shell, the front of which is enclosed by a captive metal screen, or equivalent, that is bonded to and secured to the forming shell by a positive locking device that assures a low resistance contact and requires a tool to open for installation or servicing of the speaker. The forming shell shall be installed in a recess in the wall or floor of the pool.

(b) Wiring Methods. Rigid metal conduit or intermediate metal conduit of brass or other identified corrosion-resistant metal or rigid nonmetallic conduit shall extend from the forming shell to a suitable junction box or other enclosure as provided in Section 680-21. Where rigid nonmetallic conduit is used, a No. 8 insulated, solid copper conductor shall be installed in this conduit with provisions for terminating in the forming shell and the junction box. The termination of the No. 8 conductor in the forming shell shall be covered with, or encapsulated in, a suitable potting compound to protect such connection from the possible deteriorating effect of pool water.

(c) Forming Shell and Metal Screen. The forming shell and metal screen shall be of brass or other approved corrosion-resistant metal.

680-24. Grounding. The following equipment shall be grounded: (1) wet-niche underwater lighting fixtures; (2) dry-niche underwater lighting fixtures; (3) all electric equipment located within 5 feet (1.52 m) of the inside wall of the pool; (4) all electric equipment associated with the recirculating system of the pool; (5) junction boxes; (6) transformer enclosures; (7) ground-fault circuit-interrupters; (8) panelboards that are not part of the service equipment and that supply any electric equipment associated with the pool.

680-25. Methods of Grounding.

(a) General. The following provisions shall apply to the grounding of underwater lighting fixtures, junction boxes, metal transformer enclosures, panelboards, motors and other electrical enclosures and equipment.

(b) Pool Lighting Fixtures and Related Equipment.

(1) Wet-niche lighting fixtures shall be connected to an equipment grounding conductor sized in accordance with Table 250-95 but not smaller than No. 12. It shall be an insulated copper conductor and shall be installed with the circuit conductors in rigid metal conduit, intermediate metal conduit, or rigid nonmetallic conduit.

Exception No. 1: Electrical metallic tubing shall be permitted to be used to protect conductors where installed on or within buildings.

Exception No. 2: The equipment grounding conductor between the wiring chamber of the secondary winding of a transformer and a junction box shall be sized in accordance with the overcurrent device in this circuit.

(2) The junction box, transformer enclosure, or other enclosure in the supply circuit to a wet-niche lighting fixture and the field-wiring chamber of a dry-niche lighting fixture shall be grounded to the equipment grounding terminal of the panelboard. This terminal shall be directly connected to the panelboard enclosure. The equipment grounding conductor shall be installed without joint or splice.

Exception No. 1: Where more than one underwater lighting fixture is supplied by the same branch circuit, the equipment grounding conductor, installed between the junction boxes, transformer enclosures, or other enclosures in the supply circuit to wet-niche fixtures or between the field-wiring compartments of dry-niche fixtures, shall be permitted to be terminated on grounding terminals.

Exception No. 2: Where the underwater lighting fixture is supplied from a transformer, ground-fault circuit-interrupter, or clock-operated switch which is located between the panelboard and a junction box connected to the conduit that extends directly to the underwater lighting fixture, the equipment grounding conductor shall be permitted to terminate on grounding terminals on the transformer, ground-fault circuit-interrupter, or clock-operated switch enclosure.

See commentary following Section 680-5(a).

(3) Wet-niche lighting fixtures that are supplied by a flexible cord or cable shall have all exposed noncurrent-carrying metal parts grounded by an insulated copper equipment grounding conductor that is an integral part of the cord or cable. This grounding conductor shall be connected to a grounding terminal in the supply junction box, transformer enclosure, or other enclosure. The grounding conductor shall not be smaller than the supply conductors and not smaller than No. 16.

(c) Motors. Pool-associated motors shall be connected to an equipment grounding conductor sized in accordance with Table 250-95 but not smaller than No. 12. It shall be an insulated copper conductor and shall be installed with the circuit conductors in rigid metal conduit, intermediate metal conduit or rigid nonmetallic conduit.

Exception No. 1: Electrical metallic tubing shall be permitted to be used to protect conductors where installed on or within buildings.

Exception No. 2: Where necessary to employ flexible connections at or adjacent to the motor, liquidtight flexible conduit with approved fittings shall be permitted.

See Section 351-8, Exception No. 1.

(d) Panelboards. A panelboard, not part of the service equipment, shall have an equipment grounding conductor installed between its grounding terminal and the grounding terminal of the service equipment. This conductor shall be sized in accordance with Table 250-95 but not smaller than No. 12. It shall be an insulated conductor and shall be installed with the feeder conductors in rigid metal conduit, intermediate metal conduit, or rigid nonmetallic conduit. The equipment grounding conductor shall be connected to an equipment grounding terminal of the panelboard.

The insulated equipment grounding conductor may be aluminum or copper and installed in a raceway. It should be understood that, for an "existing" remote panelboard, Exception No. 1 permits an approved cable assembly with an insulated "or covered" aluminum or copper equipment grounding conductor. See Figure 680-8.

Exception No. 1: The equipment grounding conductor between an existing remote panelboard and the service equipment shall not be required to be in one of the conduits listed in paragraph (c) if the interconnection is by means of a flexible metal conduit or an approved cable assembly with an insulated or covered equipment grounding conductor.

Exception No. 2: Electrical metallic tubing shall be permitted to be used to protect conductors where installed on or within the building.

(FPN): See Section 348-1.

(e) Cord-Connected Equipment. Where fixed or stationary equipment is connected with a flexible cord to facilitate removal or disconnection for maintenance, repair, or storage as provided in Section 680-7, the equipment grounding conductors shall be connected to a fixed metal part of the assembly. The removable part shall be mounted on or bonded to the fixed metal part.

(f) Other Equipment. Other electrical equipment shall be grounded in accordance with Article 250 and connected by wiring methods of Chapter 3.

Equipment, other than underwater lighting fixtures, are permitted to be connected by wiring methods of Chapter 3 and grounded in accordance with Article 250. For example, equipment such as a filter pump motor is permitted to be wired with Type UF cable containing an insulated or bare conductor for equipment grounding purposes. See Figure 680-8.

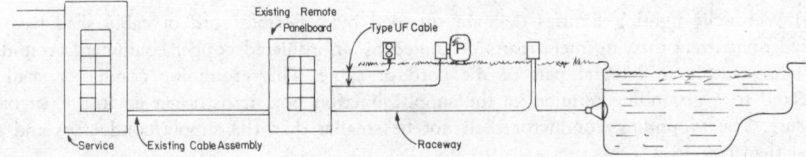

Figure 680-8. Circuits for pools may be derived from an existing remote panelboard that is supplied by an approved cable assembly as specified in Section 680-25(d), Exception No. 1. Section 680-25(f) permits Type UF cable to be used for the filter pump, the receptacle required by Section 680-6(a)(2), and other equipment; but circuit conductors for underwater lighting are required to be run in raceways.

When the provisions of Sections 680-24 and 680-25 are considered, the difference between "bonding" and "grounding" becomes apparent. As required in these sections, "grounding" is the connection of noncurrent-carrying metal parts of "electric" equipment associated with the pool (or located within 5 ft of the inside wall of the pool) to the grounding terminal bus of an approved panelboard [see Section 680-25(d)] or to the grounding terminal of the service equipment. This "equipment grounding conductor" provides a path of low impedance that limits the voltage to ground and facilitates the operation of the circuit overcurrent protective device(s). Furthermore, this "grounding" conductor is required to be an insulated copper conductor not smaller than No. 12, and for underwater lighting it is required to be run with the circuit conductors in rigid metal conduit, intermediate metal conduit, rigid nonmetallic conduit, or, where installed in or on buildings, it may be protected by electrical metallic tubing. Also, all equipment grounding conductors are required to terminate at an equipment grounding terminal located within lighting fixtures, junction boxes, transformer enclosures, panelboards, service equipment, etc.

Bonding conductors, however, may be insulated, covered, or bare, and are required to be No. 8 copper or larger. They may be direct buried, and, where connected to metal parts of the pool structure or metal parts of electric equipment, they may be externally clamped or attached and are not required to be accessible. All of these parts form a common bonding grid that establishes an equipotential grounding system, and they do not have to be run to the equipment grounding terminals of panelboards or service equipment.

680-26. Electrically Operated Pool Covers.

(a) Motors and Controllers. The electric motors, controllers and wiring shall be located at least 5 feet (1.52 m) from the inside wall of the pool unless separated from the pool by a wall, cover or other permanent barrier. Electric motors installed below grade level shall be of the totally enclosed type.

(FPN): See Sections 373-2, 380-4 and 430-11.

(b) Wiring Methods. The electric motor and controller shall be connected to a circuit protected by a ground-fault circuit-interrupter.

680-27. Deck Area Heating. The provisions of this section apply to all pool deck areas, including a covered pool, where electrically operated comfort heating units are installed within 20 feet (6.1 m) of the inside wall of the pool.

(a) Unit Heaters. Unit heaters shall be rigidly mounted to the structure and shall be of the totally enclosed or guarded types. Unit heaters shall not be mounted over the pool or over the area extending 5 feet (1.52 m) horizontally from the inside walls of a pool.

(b) Permanently Wired Radiant Heaters. Radiant electric heaters shall be suitably guarded and securely fastened to their mounting device(s). Heaters shall not be installed over a pool or over the area extending 5 feet (1.52 m) horizontally from the inside walls of the pool and shall be mounted at least 12 feet (3.66 m) vertically above the pool deck unless otherwise approved.

(c) Radiant Heat Cables Not Permitted. Radiant heating cables embedded in or below the deck shall not be permitted.

Only unit heaters and permanently connected radiant heaters are permitted in the area extending 5 to 20 ft horizontally from the inside walls of a pool. Radiant heat cables embedded in the deck are not permitted.

C. Storable Pools

680-30. Pumps. A cord-connected pool filter pump shall incorporate an approved system of double insulation or its equivalent, and shall be provided with means for grounding only the internal and nonaccessible noncurrent-carrying metal parts of the appliance.

The means for grounding shall be an equipment grounding conductor run with the power-supply conductors in the flexible cord that is properly terminated in a grounding-type attachment plug having a fixed grounding contact member.

680-31. Ground-Fault Circuit-Interrupters Required. All electric equipment, including power supply cords, used with storable pools shall be protected by ground-fault circuit-interrupters.

A storable pool may be readily disassembled and has a maximum dimension of 18 ft and a maximum wall height of 42 in. See definition, Section 680-4. This type of pool, and its associated equipment, does not require "bonding" conductors. However, the filter pump is required to be double insulated or equivalent, and "grounding" means consisting of an equipment grounding conductor that is an integral part of the flexible cord is required to be provided. There are portable filter pumps for use with storable pools listed by Underwriters Laboratories Inc.

Receptacles are required to be located at least 10 ft from pools [see Section 680-6(a)], and all electric equipment is required to have a ground-fault circuit-interrupter for personnel protection. See Figure 680-9.

(FPN): When flexible cords are used, see Section 400-4.

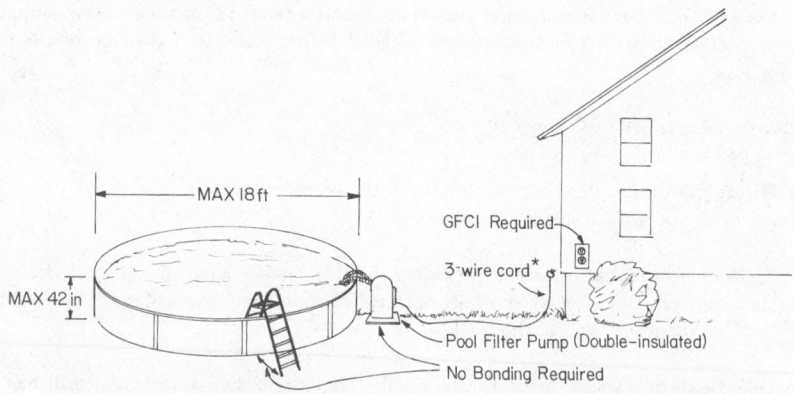

MAX 18 ft

MAX 42 in

GFCI Required

3-wire cord*

Pool Filter Pump (Double-insulated)

No Bonding Required

Figure 680-9. Illustrated are the requirements for a storable-type pool. Metal appurtenances are not required to be bonded. The 3-wire cord* may be longer than 3 ft. (Some listed filter pumps are equipped with cords 25 ft long.) The receptacle shown can be either a GFCI receptacle or one protected by a remote GFCI such as a GFCI circuit breaker.

D. Spas, Hot Tubs, and Hydromassage Bathtubs

The requirements of this part are divided into two categories: outdoor installations and indoor installations.

Outdoor installations fall under the requirements of both Parts A and B of Article 680 with three exceptions:

1. Metal bands or hoops used to secure wooden staves are not required to be bonded.

2. Listed packaged units may be cord connected and are required to be protected by a GFCI.

3. Bonding by metal-to-metal mounting on a common frame or base is permitted.

Indoor installations are subject to basically the same requirements, but take into consideration the more restricted confines of an indoor location.

Receptacles, wall switches, and electrical devices and controls not associated with a spa or hot tub are required to be located at least 5 ft away. A hydromassage bathtub installed in an existing bathroom, where located less than 5 ft from receptacles or wall switches, is permitted when receptacles and wall switches are protected by a GFCI. Receptacles within 20 ft and those providing power to a spa or hot tub are required to be protected by a GFCI.

Lighting fixtures located over a spa or hot tub or within 5 ft horizontally are required to be protected by a GFCI.

Bonding and grounding requirements are similar to those in Parts A and B of Article 680, except that metal-to-metal mounting on a common frame or base is an acceptable bonding method.

Listed packaged units may be cord connected.

680-40. Outdoor Installations. A spa or hot tub installed outdoors shall comply with the provisions of Parts A and B.

Exception No. 1: Metal bands or hoops used to secure wooden staves are exempt from Section 680-22.

Exception No. 2: Listed packaged units may be cord connected with a cord no longer than 15 feet (4.57 m) and shall be protected by a ground-fault circuit-interrupter.

Exception No. 3: Bonding by metal-to-metal mounting on a common frame or base shall be permitted.

680-41. Indoor Installations. A spa or hot tub installed indoors shall conform to the requirements of this part and shall be connected by wiring methods of Chapter 3.

Exception: Listed packaged units rated 20 amperes or less shall be permitted to be connected with a flexible cord to facilitate the removal or disconnection for maintenance and repair.

(a) Receptacles.

(1) Receptacles on the property shall be located at least 5 feet (1.52 m) from the inside walls of the spa or hot tub.

Exception: In an existing bathroom where a hydromassage bathtub is installed, an existing receptacle shall be permitted to be less than 5 feet (1.52 m) and shall be protected by a ground-fault circuit-interrupter.

(2) 125-volt receptacles located within 20 feet (6.1 m) of the inside walls of a spa or hot tub shall be protected by a ground-fault circuit-interrupter.

(FPN): In determining the above dimensions, the distance to be measured is the shortest path the supply cord of an appliance connected to the receptacle would follow without piercing a floor, wall, or ceiling of a building or other effective permanent barrier.

(3) Receptacles that provide power for a spa or hot tub shall be ground-fault circuit-interrupter protected.

(b) **Lighting Fixtures and Lighting Outlets.**

(1) Lighting fixtures and lighting outlets located over the spa or hot tub or within 5 feet (1.52 m) from the inside walls of the spa or hot tub shall be a minimum of 7 feet 6 inches (2.29 m) above the maximum water level and shall be protected by a ground-fault circuit-interrupter.

Exception: Lighting fixtures and lighting outlets located 12 feet (3.66 m) or more above the maximum water level shall not require protection by a ground-fault circuit-interrupter.

(2) Underwater lighting fixtures shall comply with the provisions of Part B of this article.

(c) **Wall Switches.** Switches shall be located at least 5 feet (1.52 m), measured horizontally, from the inside walls of the spa or hot tub.

Exception: In an existing bathroom where a hydromassage bathtub is installed, an existing wall switch shall be permitted to be less than 5 feet (1.52 m) and shall be protected by a ground-fault circuit-interrupter.

(d) **Bonding.** The following parts shall be bonded together:

(1) All metal fittings within or attached to the spa or hot tub structure.

(2) Metal parts of electric equipment associated with the spa or hot tub water circulating system, including pump motors.

(3) Metal conduit and metal piping within 5 feet (1.52 m) of the inside walls of the spa or hot tub and that are not separated from the spa or hot tub by a permanent barrier.

(4) All metal surfaces that are within 5 feet (1.52 m) of the inside walls of the spa or hot tub and not separated from the spa or hot tub area by a permanent barrier.

(5) Electrical devices and controls not associated with the spas or hot tubs shall be located a minimum of 5 feet (1.52 m) away from such units or be bonded to the spa or hot tub system.

(e) **Methods of Bonding.** All metallic parts associated with the spa or hot tub shall be bonded by any of the following methods: the interconnection of threaded metallic piping and fittings, metal-to-metal mounting on a common frame or base, or by the provisions of a copper bonding jumper, insulated, covered, or bare, not smaller than No. 8 solid.

(f) **Grounding.** The following equipment shall be grounded:

(1) All electric equipment located within 5 feet (1.52 m) of the inside wall of the spa or hot tub.

(2) All electric equipment associated with the circulating system of the spa or hot tub.

(g) **Methods of Grounding.**

(1) All electrical equipment shall be grounded in accordance with Article 250 and connected by the wiring methods of Chapter 3.

(2) Where equipment is connected with a flexible cord, the equipment grounding conductor shall be connected to a fixed metal part of the assembly.

E. Fountains

680-50. General. The provisions of Part E shall apply to all fountains as defined in Section 680-4. Fountains which have water common to a pool shall comply with the pool requirements of this article.

Exception: Self-contained, portable fountains no larger than 5 feet (1.52 m) in any dimension are not covered by Part E.

680-51. Lighting Fixtures, Submersible Pumps, and Other Submersible Equipment.

   (a) Ground-Fault Circuit-Interrupter. A ground-fault circuit-interrupter shall be installed in the branch circuit supplying fountain equipment.

Exception: Ground-fault circuit-interrupters shall not be required for equipment operating at 15 volts or less and supplied by a transformer complying with Section 680-5(a).

   (b) Operating Voltage. All lighting fixtures shall be installed for operation at 150 volts or less between conductors. Submersible pumps and other submersible equipment shall operate at 300 volts or less between conductors.

   (c) Lighting Fixture Lenses. Lighting fixtures shall be installed with the top of the fixture lens below the normal water level of the fountain unless approved for above water locations. A lighting fixture facing upward shall have the lens adequately guarded to prevent contact by any person.

   (d) Overheating Protection. Electric equipment which depends on submersion for safe operation shall be protected against overheating by a low-water cut-off or other approved means if the water level drops below normal.

   (e) Wiring. Equipment shall be equipped with provisions for threaded conduit entries or be provided with a suitable flexible cord. The maximum length of exposed cord in the fountain shall be limited to 10 feet (3.05 m). Cords extending beyond the fountain perimeter shall be enclosed in approved wiring enclosures. Metal parts of equipment in contact with water shall be of brass or other approved corrosion-resistant metal.

   (f) Servicing. All equipment shall be removable from the water for relamping or normal maintenance. Fixtures shall not be permanently imbedded into the fountain structure so that the water level must be reduced or the fountain drained for relamping, maintenance, or inspection.

   (g) Stability. Equipment shall be inherently stable or be securely fastened in place.

680-52. Junction Boxes and Other Enclosures.

   (a) General. Junction boxes and other enclosures used for other than underwater installation shall comply with Section 680-21(a) (1), (2), (3); and (b), (c), and (d).

   (b) Underwater Junction Boxes and Other Underwater Enclosures. Junction boxes and other underwater enclosures shall be watertight and (1) be equipped with provisions for threaded conduit entries or compression glands or seals for cord entry; (2) be of copper, brass, or other approved corrosion-resistant material; (3) be filled with an approved potting compound to prevent the entry of moisture; and (4) be firmly attached to the supports or directly to the fountain surface and bonded as required. When the junction box is supported only by the conduit the conduit shall be of copper, brass, or other approved corrosion-resistant metal. When the box is fed by nonmetallic conduit, it shall have additional supports and fasteners of copper, brass, or other approved corrosion-resistant material.

680-53. Bonding. All metallic piping systems associated with the fountain shall be bonded to the equipment grounding conductor of the branch circuit supplying the fountain.

(FPN): See Section 250-95 for sizing of these conductors.

680-54. Grounding. The following equipment shall be grounded: (1) all electric equipment located within 5 feet (1.52 m) of the inside wall of the fountain; (2) all electric equipment associated with the recirculating system of the fountain; (3) panelboards that are not part of the service equipment and that supply any electric equipment associated with the fountain.

680-55. Methods of Grounding.

(a) **Applied Provisions.** The provisions of Section 680-25 shall apply excluding paragraph (e).

(b) **Supplied by a Flexible Cord.** Electric equipment that is supplied by a flexible cord shall have all exposed noncurrent-carrying metal parts grounded by an insulated copper equipment grounding conductor that is an integral part of this cord. This grounding conductor shall be connected to a grounding terminal in the supply junction box, transformer enclosure, or other enclosure.

680-56. Cord- and Plug-Connected Equipment.

(a) **Ground-Fault Circuit-Interrupter.** All electric equipment, including power supply cords, shall be protected by ground-fault circuit-interrupters.

(b) **Cord Type.** Flexible cord immersed in or exposed to water shall be a water-resistant Type SO or ST.

(c) **Sealing.** The end of the flexible cord jacket and the flexible cord conductor termination within equipment shall be covered with or encapsulated in a suitable potting compound to prevent the entry of water into the equipment through the cord or its conductors. In addition, the ground connection within equipment shall be similarly treated to protect such connections from the deteriorating effect of water which may enter into the equipment.

(d) **Terminations.** Connections with flexible cord shall be permanent, except that grounding-type attachment plugs and receptacles shall be permitted to facilitate removal or disconnection for maintenance, repair, or storage of fixed or stationary equipment not located in any water-containing part of a fountain.

F. Therapeutic Pools and Tubs in Health Care Facilities

Portable therapeutic appliances are covered by the provisions of Article 422. They are required to be protected by a GFCI unless protected by an approved system of double insulation.

Permanently installed therapeutic pools that cannot be readily disassembled are required to comply with Parts A and B of Article 680. The limitations regarding lighting fixtures over and around a swimming pool do not apply to therapeutic pools and tubs if the lighting fixtures are totally enclosed.

Therapeutic tubs not easily moved are subject to basically the same requirements.

Bonding and grounding requirements are similar to those in Parts A and B of Article 680, except that metal-to-metal mounting on a common frame or base is acceptable. Where equipment is connected by a flexible cord, the equipment grounding conductor is required to be connected to a fixed metal part of the assembly.

680-60. General. The provisions of Part F include therapeutic pools and tubs in health care facilities. See Section 517-2 for definition of Health Care Facilities. Portable therapeutic appliances shall comply with Article 422.

680-61. Permanently Installed Therapeutic Pools. Therapeutic pools which are constructed in the ground, on the ground, or in a building in such a manner that the pool cannot be readily disassembled shall comply with Parts A and B of this article.

Exception: The limitations of Section 680-6(b)(1) and (2) shall not apply where all lighting fixtures are of the totally enclosed type.

680-62. Therapeutic Tubs (Hydrotherapeutic Tanks). Therapeutic tubs, used for the submersion and treatment of patients, which are not easily moved from one place to another in normal use or which are fastened or otherwise secured at a specific location including associated piping systems shall conform to this part.

(a) Ground-Fault Circuit-Interrupter. A ground-fault circuit-interrupter shall protect all therapeutic equipment.

Exception: Portable therapeutic appliances shall comply with Section 250-45.

(b) Bonding. The following parts shall be bonded together:

(1) All metal fittings within or attached to the tub structure.

(2) Metal parts of electric equipment associated with the tub water circulating system, including pump motors.

(3) Metal conduit and metal piping that are within 5 feet (1.52 m) of the inside walls of the tub and not separated from the tub by a permanent barrier.

(4) All metal surfaces that are within 5 feet (1.52 m) of the inside walls of the tub and not separated from the tub area by a permanent barrier.

(5) Electrical devices and controls not associated with the therapeutic tubs shall be located a minimum of 5 feet (1.52 m) away from such units or be bonded to the therapeutic tub system.

(c) Methods of Bonding. All metallic parts associated with the tub shall be bonded by any of the following methods: the interconnection of threaded metallic piping and fittings; metal-to-metal mounting on a common frame or base; connections by suitable metallic clamps; or by the provisions of a copper bonding jumper, insulated, covered, or bare, not smaller than No. 8 solid.

(d) Grounding. The following equipment shall be grounded:

(1) All electric equipment located within 5 feet (1.52 m) of the inside wall of the tub.

(2) All electric equipment associated with the circulating system of the tub.

(e) Methods of Grounding:

(1) All electric equipment shall be grounded in accordance with Article 250 and connected by wiring methods of Chapter 3.

(2) Where equipment is connected with a flexible cord, the equipment grounding conductor shall be connected to a fixed metal part of the assembly.

(f) Receptacles. All receptacles within 5 feet (1.52 m) of a therapeutic tub shall be protected by a ground-fault circuit-interrupter.

680-63. Lighting Fixtures. All lighting fixtures used in therapeutic pool areas shall be of the totally enclosed type.

ARTICLE 685 — INTEGRATED ELECTRICAL SYSTEMS

Contents

A. General

685-1. Scope. This article covers integrated electrical systems, other than unit equipment, in which orderly shutdown is necessary to ensure safe operation. An integrated electrical system as used in this article is a unitized segment of an industrial wiring system where all of the following conditions are met: (1) an orderly shutdown is required to minimize personnel hazard and equipment damage; (2) the conditions of maintenance and supervision assure that qualified persons will service the system; and (3) effective safeguards, acceptable to the authority having jurisdiction, are established and maintained.

Integrated electrical systems are commonly used in large industrial establishments where the electrical system and equipment are designed, installed, and operated by engineering workforces. The control equipment, including overcurrent devices, are located to be accessible to qualified personnel, but may not be "readily accessible" as defined in Article 100.

685-2. Application of Other Articles. In other articles applying to particular cases of installation of conductors and equipment, there are orderly shutdown requirements that are in addition to those of this article or are modifications of them:

	Section
Ground-Fault Protection of Equipment	230-95(a), Exception No. 1
Protection of Conductors	240-3, Exception No. 8
Electrical System Coordination	240-12
Grounding ac Systems of 50 to 1000 Volts	250-5(b), Exception No. 3
Orderly Shutdown	430-44
Disconnection	430-74, Exceptions No. 1 and 2
Disconnecting Means in Sight from Controller	430-102, Exception No. 2
Energy from More than One Source	430-113, Exceptions No. 1 and 2

B. Orderly Shutdown

685-10. Location of Overcurrent Devices In or On Premises. Location of overcurrent devices which are critical to integrated electrical systems shall be permitted to be accessible with mounting heights allowed to assure security from operation by nonqualified personnel.

685-12. Direct-Current System Grounding. Two-wire direct-current circuits shall be permitted to be ungrounded.

685-14. Ungrounded Control Circuits. Where operational continuity is required, control circuits of 150 volts or less from separately derived systems shall be permitted to be ungrounded.

ARTICLE 690 — SOLAR PHOTOVOLTAIC SYSTEMS

Contents

A. General

690-1. Scope. The provisions of this article apply to solar photovoltaic electrical energy systems including the array circuit(s), power conditioning unit(s) and controller(s) for such systems. Solar photovoltaic systems covered by this article may be interactive with other electric power production sources or stand alone, with or without electrical energy storage such as batteries. These systems may have alternating- or direct-current output for utilization.

ARTICLE 690—SOLAR PHOTOVOLTAIC SYSTEMS

690-2. Definitions.

Array. A mechanically integrated assembly of modules or panels with a support structure and foundation, tracking, thermal control, and other components, as required, to form a direct-current power-producing unit.

Blocking Diode. A diode used to block reverse flow of current into a photovoltaic source circuit.

Interactive System. A solar photovoltaic system that operates in parallel with and may be designed to deliver power to another electric power production source connected to the same load. For the purpose of this definition, an energy storage subsystem of a solar photovoltaic system, such as a battery, is not another electric power production source.

Module. The smallest complete, environmentally protected assembly of solar cells, optics and other components, exclusive of tracking, designed to generate direct-current power under sunlight.

Panel. A collection of modules mechanically fastened together, wired, and designed to provide a field-installable unit.

Photovoltaic Output Circuit. Circuit conductors between the photovoltaic source circuit(s) and the power conditioning unit or direct-current utilization equipment. See Diagram 690-1.

Photovoltaic Power Source. An array or aggregate of arrays which generates direct-current power at system voltage and current.

Photovoltaic Source Circuit. Conductors between modules and from modules to the common connection point(s) of the direct-current system. See Diagram 690-1.

Power Conditioning Unit. Equipment which is used to change voltage level or waveform or both of electrical energy. Commonly a power conditioning unit is an inverter which changes a direct-current input to an alternating-current output.

Power Conditioning Unit Output Circuit. Conductors between the power conditioning unit and the connection to the service equipment or another electric power production source such as a utility. See Diagram 690-1.

Solar Cell. The basic photovoltaic device which generates electricity when exposed to light.

Solar Photovoltaic System. The total components and subsystems which in combination convert solar energy into electrical energy suitable for connection to a utilization load.

Stand-Alone System. A solar photovoltaic system that supplies power independently but which may receive control power from another electric power production source.

690-3. Other Articles. Wherever the requirements of other articles of this Code and Article 690 differ, the requirements of Article 690 shall apply.

690-4. Installation.

(a) **Photovoltaic System.** A solar photovoltaic system shall be permitted to supply a building or other structure in addition to any service(s) of another electricity supply system(s).

(b) **Conductors of Different Systems.** Photovoltaic source circuits and photovoltaic output

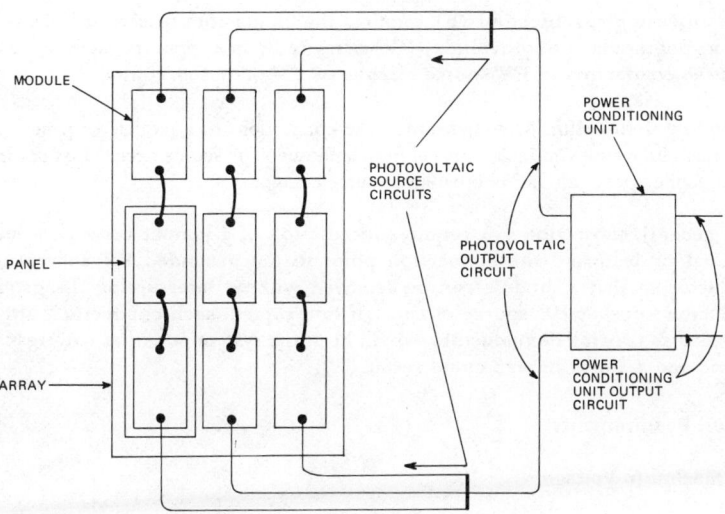

Diagram 690-1   Solar Photovoltaic Circuits

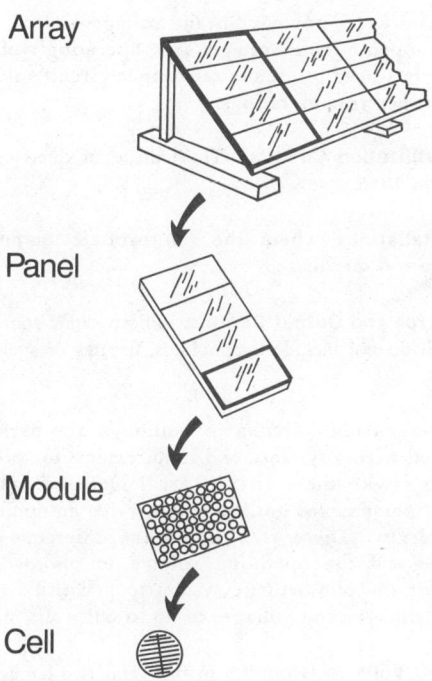

Array

Panel

Module

Cell

Figure 690-1. Array components.

circuits shall not be contained in the same raceway, cable tray, cable, outlet box, junction box or similar fitting as feeders or branch circuits of other systems.

Exception: Where the conductors of the different systems are separated by a partition or are connected together.

ARTICLE 690—SOLAR PHOTOVOLTAIC SYSTEMS

As an example, subsection (b) requires the conductors of a yard light located near a roof-mounted photovoltaic (PV) array to be in a separate raceway or cable from the conductors of PV source circuits or PV output circuit.

(c) Module Connection Arrangement. The connections to a module or panel shall be so arranged that removal of a module or panel from a photovoltaic source circuit does not interrupt a grounded conductor to another photovoltaic source circuit.

In general, subsection (c) requires installation of a jumper between a module terminal or lead and the connection point to the grounded PV source circuit conductor so that a module can be removed without interrupting the grounded conductor to other PV source circuits. If interrupted, such conductors, although identified as grounded conductors, would be at the system potential with respect to ground and a shock hazard could result.

B. Circuit Requirements

690-7. Maximum Voltage.

(a) Voltage Rating. In a photovoltaic power source and its direct-current circuits, the voltage considered shall be the rated open-circuit voltage.

A photovoltaic source is not a constant voltage source, and the difference between the rated open-circuit voltage and operating voltage is significant. Consequently, there is a need to use the rated open-circuit voltage to select circuit components with proper voltage ratings.

(b) Direct-Current Utilization Circuits. The voltage of direct-current utilization circuits shall conform with Section 210-6.

This covers installations where the photovoltaic output is connected to direct-current utilization circuits.

(c) Photovoltaic Source and Output Circuits. Photovoltaic source circuits and photovoltaic output circuits which do not include lampholders, fixtures or standard receptacles shall be permitted up to 600 volts.

Photovoltaic direct-current circuits in buildings are permanently connected using *Code* recognized wiring systems, and requirements for protecting unqualified persons from contact with these circuits are included in (b) and (d) of this section. Unqualified persons are not likely to service equipment in these circuits due to their complexity. There is a significant difference between the rated open-circuit voltage and the operating voltage in photovoltaic direct-current circuits. In order for the photovoltaic system to perform its intended function, rated direct-current open-circuit voltages of up to 600 volts may be present.

(d) Circuits Over 150 Volts to Ground. In one- and two-family dwellings, live parts in photovoltaic source circuits and photovoltaic output circuits over 150 volts to ground shall not be accessible while energized to other than qualified persons.

Where direct-current circuitry over 150 volts to ground is present in one- and two-family dwellings, additional protection for unqualified persons is needed. This may take the form of a locked cabinet or an enclosure that requires tools to open and in which entry is necessary only for servicing purposes. Section 110-17 applies in any case.

690-8. Circuit Sizing and Current.

(a) Ampacity and Overcurrent Devices. The ampacity of the conductors and the rating or setting of overcurrent devices in a circuit of a solar photovoltaic system shall not be less than 125 percent of the current computed in accordance with (b) below. The rating or setting of overcurrent devices shall be permitted in accordance with Section 240-3, Exception No. 1.

Exception: Circuits containing an assembly together with its overcurrent device(s) that is listed for continuous operation at 100 percent of its rating.

Sizing of the circuits for 125 percent of the rating is necessary because of continuous (3-hour or more) loads.

The exception permits use at the full rating of assemblies, such as panelboards, incorporating overcurrent devices which are listed for continuous operation at 100 percent of the rating.

(b) Computation of Circuit Current. The current for the individual type of circuit shall be computed as follows:

(1) Photovoltaic Source Circuits. The sum of parallel module operating current ratings.

(2) Photovoltaic Output Circuit. The photovoltaic power source current rating.

(3) Power Conditioning Unit Output Circuit. The power conditioning unit output current rating.

Exception: The current rating of a circuit without an overcurrent device, as permitted by the Exception to Section 690-9(a), shall be the short-circuit current, and it shall not exceed the ampacity of the circuit conductors.

Because photovoltaic arrays have a limited capacity, the power conditioning unit supplies to the load (or the utility system) whatever power is available from the arrays. Due to this characteristic, the sizing of photovoltaic circuits has to be based on the source rather than the load.

The exception specifies the use of the short-circuit current rating rather than the operating current rating to determine the current rating of a PV source circuit, PV output circuit or the power conditioning unit output circuit, if these circuits do not incorporate an overcurrent device. The short-circuit current rating is then used to determine the needed ampacity for the conductors in these circuits.

690-9. Overcurrent Protection.

(a) Circuits and Equipment. Photovoltaic source circuit, photovoltaic output circuit, power conditioning unit output circuit, and storage battery circuit conductors and equipment shall be protected in accordance with the requirements of Article 240. Circuits connected to more than one electrical source shall have overcurrent devices so located as to provide overcurrent protection from all sources.

Exception: A conductor in a photovoltaic source circuit, photovoltaic output circuit, or power conditioning unit output circuit having an ampacity not less than the maximum available current under short-circuit or ground-fault conditions with the condition of a shorted blocking diode shall be permitted without an overcurrent device.

(FPN): Possible backfeed of current from any source of supply, including a supply through a power conditioning unit into the photovoltaic output circuit and photovoltaic source circuits, must be considered in determining whether adequate overcurrent protection from all sources is provided for conductors and modules.

ARTICLE 690—SOLAR PHOTOVOLTAIC SYSTEMS

In the circuit illustrated in Figure 690-2 the PV source circuit overcurrent devices are required to be rated so that the source circuit conductors are protected in accordance with Article 240 and the overcurrent device ratings do not exceed the maximum overcurrent device rating marked on the modules. Possible backfeed from the other PV source circuits, from other supply sources through the power conditioning unit, and from storage battery circuits, if any, has to be considered.

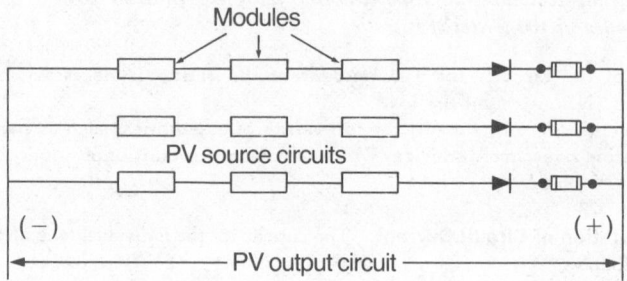

Figure 690-2. Application of blocking diodes and source circuit overcurrent devices.

Because the diodes may lose their blocking ability (due to over-temperature conditions or internal breakdown), overcurrent protection has to be considered with a condition of shorted blocking diodes, if used in the circuit.

If the rated short-circuit current of the PV power source does not exceed the ampacity of the PV output circuit conductors, overcurrent protective devices at the connections to the PV power source are not necessary. At the power conditioning unit end of the PV output circuit, the need for overcurrent protection has to be considered with respect to the maximum back feed fault current available from the power conditioning unit.

(b) Power Transformers. Overcurrent protection for a transformer with a source(s) on each side shall be provided in accordance with Section 450-3 by considering first one side of the transformer, then the other side of the transformer as the primary.

Exception: A power transformer with a current rating on the side connected toward the photovoltaic power source not less than the short-circuit output current rating of the power conditioning unit shall be permitted without overcurrent protection from that source.

(c) Photovoltaic Source Circuits. Branch-circuit or supplementary type overcurrent devices shall be permitted to provide overcurrent protection in photovoltaic source circuits. The overcurrent devices shall be accessible, but shall not be required to be readily accessible.

By considering the overcurrent protection of photovoltaic source circuits as supplementary overcurrent protection, use of overcurrent device types and ratings, other than those suitable for branch-circuit protection, can be permitted. Use of such devices permits module protection closer to the specified ratings. It is anticipated that replacement or resetting of overcurrent devices in photovoltaic source circuits will be accomplished by qualified service personnel. Consequently, ready access (such as by the user) need not be provided.

C. Disconnecting Means

690-13. All Conductors. Means shall be provided to disconnect all current-carrying conductors of a photovoltaic power source from all other conductors in a building or other structure.

690-14. Additional Provisions. The provisions of Article 230, Part H shall apply to the photovoltaic power source disconnecting means.

Exception No. 1: The disconnecting means shall not be required to be suitable as service equipment and shall be rated in accordance with Section 690-17.

Exception No. 1 permits use of disconnecting means rated in accordance with Section 690-17, but which need not be marked as suitable for use as service equipment.

Exception No. 2: Equipment such as photovoltaic source circuit isolating switches, overcurrent devices, and blocking diodes shall be permitted ahead of the photovoltaic power source disconnecting means.

690-15. Disconnection of Photovoltaic Equipment. Means shall be provided to disconnect equipment, such as a power conditioning unit, filter assembly and the like from all ungrounded conductors of all sources. If the equipment is energized (live) from more than one source, the disconnecting means shall be grouped and identified.

690-16. Fuses. Disconnecting means shall be provided to disconnect a fuse from all sources of supply if the fuse is energized from both directions and is accessible to other than qualified persons. Such a fuse in a photovoltaic source circuit shall be capable of being disconnected independently of fuses in other photovoltaic source circuits.

Switches, pullouts or similar devices having suitable ratings may serve as means to disconnect fuses from all sources of supply.

690-17. Switch or Circuit Breaker. The disconnecting means for ungrounded conductors shall consist of a manually operable switch(es) or circuit breaker(s): (1) located where readily accessible, (2) externally operable without exposing the operator to contact with live parts, (3) plainly indicating whether in the open or closed position, and (4) having ratings not less than the load to be carried. Where disconnect equipment may be energized from both sides, the disconnect equipment shall be provided with a marking to indicate that all contacts of the disconnect equipment may be live.

Exception: A disconnecting means located on the direct-current side shall be permitted to have an interrupting rating less than the current-carrying rating when the system is designed so that the direct-current switch cannot be opened under load.

690-18. Disablement of an Array. Means shall be provided to disable an array or portions of an array.

(FPN): Photovoltaic modules are energized while exposed to light. Installation, replacement, or servicing of array components while a module(s) is irradiated may expose persons to electric shock.

There are a number of methods which may accomplish disablement of an array or portions of an array for installation, servicing or other functions during which persons may come in contact with energized parts.

One method is to cover all or portions of an array with an opaque material. Care has to be taken so that all of the area to be covered is shielded from light.

Another method is to have provisions whereby the array may be segmented to nonhazardous portions. This may be accomplished by switches or connectors. Also see Section 690-33.

Short-circuiting all or portions of an array by means of switches or plug-in connectors in conjunction with by-pass diodes may also provide the necessary disablement. (By-pass diodes are incorporated in PV power sources for performance purposes.)

ARTICLE 690—SOLAR PHOTOVOLTAIC SYSTEMS

D. Wiring Methods

690-31. Methods Permitted.

(a) Wiring Systems. All raceway and cable wiring methods included in this Code and other wiring systems and fittings specifically intended and identified for use on photovoltaic arrays shall be permitted. Where wiring devices with integral enclosures are used, sufficient length of cable shall be provided to facilitate replacement.

(b) Single Conductor Cable. Type UF single conductor cable shall be permitted in photovoltaic source circuits where installed in the same manner as a Type UF multiconductor cable in accordance with Article 339. Where exposed to direct rays of the sun, cable identified as sunlight-resistant shall be used.

> Some photovoltaic modules are designed for a direct series connection by having terminations at both ends. To accommodate such a direct series connection without the waste of one or more conductors in a multi-conductor cable, use of a single-conductor, Type UF cable, is permitted in photovoltaic source circuits. The reference to installation as a multiconductor cable permits the single-conductor cable to be routed separately, not necessarily with the other conductors of a circuit. Since photovoltaic source circuits are direct-current circuits, increased impedance due to separated circuit conductors is not a problem.

690-32. Component Interconnections.
Fittings and connectors which are intended to be concealed at the time of on-site assembly, when listed for such use, shall be permitted for on-site interconnection of modules or other array components. Such fittings and connectors shall be equal to the wiring method employed in insulation, temperature rise and fault-current withstand, and shall be capable of resisting the effects of the environment in which they are used.

690-33. Connectors.
The connectors permitted by Section 690-32 shall comply with (a) through (e) below.

(a) Configuration. The connectors shall be polarized and shall have a configuration that is noninterchangeable with receptacles in other electrical systems on the premises.

(b) Guarding. The connectors shall be constructed and installed so as to guard against inadvertent contact with live parts by persons.

(c) Type. The connectors shall be of the latching or locking type.

(d) Grounding Member. The grounding member shall be the first to make and the last to break contact with the mating connector.

(e) Interruption of Circuit. The connectors shall be capable of interrupting the circuit current without hazard to the operator.

690-34. Access to Boxes.
Junction, pull and outlet boxes located behind modules or panels shall be installed so that the wiring contained in them can be rendered accessible directly or by displacement of a module(s) or panel(s) secured by removable fasteners and connected by a flexible wiring system.

E. Grounding

690-41. System Grounding.
For a photovoltaic power source, one conductor of a 2-wire system and a neutral conductor of a 3-wire system shall be solidly grounded.

Exception: Other methods which accomplish equivalent system protection and which utilize equipment listed and identified for the use shall be permitted.

(FPN): See Fine Print Note under Section 250-1.

With respect to the exception, other methods, using available equipment, may be used to achieve objectives contained in the Fine Print Note to Section 250-1, thereby providing protection equivalent to solid grounding for the photovoltaic power source circuits.

690-42. Point of System Grounding Connection. The direct-current circuit grounding connection shall be made at any single point on the photovoltaic output circuit.

(FPN): Locating the grounding connection point as close as practicable to the photovoltaic source will better protect the system from voltage surges due to lightning.

If other than solid grounding is utilized as permitted by Section 690-41, Exception, the connections should be made in accordance with the markings on the equipment or its installation instructions.

690-43. Size of Equipment Grounding Conductor. The equipment grounding conductor shall be no smaller than the required size of the circuit conductors in systems: (1) where the available photovoltaic power source short-circuit current is less than twice the current rating of the overcurrent device, or (2) where overcurrent devices are not employed as permitted in the Exception to Section 690-9(a). In other systems, the equipment grounding conductor shall be sized in accordance with Section 250-95.

690-44. Common Grounding Electrode. Exposed noncurrent-carrying metal parts of equipment and conductor enclosures of a photovoltaic system shall be grounded to the grounding electrode that is used to ground the direct-current system. Two or more electrodes that are effectively bonded together shall be considered as a single electrode in this sense.

This requirement ensures that direct-current circuits from the photovoltaic system do not enter enclosures that are grounded only by a grounding electrode of an alternating-current system without the grounding electrodes of both systems being effectively bonded together. For example, if the electrodes are not bonded together, it is possible that a small current flow through the alternating-current electrode, through the earth and back through the direct-current electrode, could result in raising the voltage on the array frame to close to line voltage.

F. Marking

690-51. Modules. Modules shall be marked with identification of terminals or leads as to polarity, maximum overcurrent device rating for module protection and with rated: (1) open-circuit voltage, (2) operating voltage, (3) maximum permissible system voltage, (4) operating current, (5) short-circuit current, and (6) maximum power.

690-52. Photovoltaic Power Source. A marking, specifying the photovoltaic power source rated: (1) operating current, (2) operating voltage, (3) open-circuit voltage, and (4) short-circuit current, shall be provided at an accessible location at the disconnecting means for the photovoltaic power source.

(FPN): Reflecting systems used for irradiance enhancement may result in increased levels of output current and power.

ARTICLE 690—SOLAR PHOTOVOLTAIC SYSTEMS

After installation of photovoltaic arrays, it may be difficult to determine the system rated voltage and current. These ratings, along with the open-circuit voltage and short-circuit current, are necessary to size the remainder of the system components as specified elsewhere in Article 690.

Generally, this marking is to be provided by the installer. The rated values for the PV power source can be calculated by adding voltage ratings of series-connected modules and adding current ratings of parallel-connected modules or PV source circuits.

With respect to the Fine Print Note, deliberate increase in the level or irradiance by reflectors or the like can cause the power source to operate at levels above those recommended by the manufacturer. See Section 110-3.

G. Connection to Other Sources

690-61. Loss of Utility Voltage. The power output from a utility interactive power conditioning unit shall be automatically disconnected from all ungrounded conductors of the utility system upon loss of voltage in the utility system and shall not reconnect until the utility voltage is restored.

This requirement prevents energizing of otherwise deenergized utility conductors and is intended to prevent electric shock. This feature is normally provided as part of the power conditioning unit.

690-62. Ampacity of Neutral Conductor. If a single-phase, 2-wire power conditioning unit output is connected to the neutral and one ungrounded conductor (only) of a 3-wire system or of a 3-phase, 4-wire wye-connected system, the maximum load connected between the neutral and any one ungrounded conductor plus the power conditioning unit output rating shall not exceed the ampacity of the neutral conductor.

690-63. Unbalanced Interconnections.

(a) Single-Phase. The output of a single-phase power conditioning unit shall not be connected to a 3-phase, 3- or 4-wire electrical service derived directly from a delta-connected transformer.

(b) Three-Phase. A 3-phase power conditioning unit shall be automatically disconnected from all ungrounded conductors of the interconnected system when one of the phases opens in either source.

Exception for (a) and (b): Where the interconnected system is designed so that significant unbalanced voltages will not result.

With respect to connections to other sources, the point of interconnection has not been specified. Section 230-82, Exception No. 6 permits connection of interconnected electric power production sources to the supply side of service disconnecting means of a premises. This could be a point of interconnection.

If the interconnections are made on the load side of the service disconnecting means, such as at a distribution panelboard, possible overloading of panelboard buses, suitability of equipment such as circuit breakers for back feeding, and a need for cautionary markings due to the presence of two sources need to be considered.

7 SPECIAL CONDITIONS

ARTICLE 700 — EMERGENCY SYSTEMS

Contents

A. General

700-1. Scope. The provisions of this article apply to the electrical safety of the design, installation, operation, and maintenance of emergency systems consisting of circuits and equipment intended to supply, distribute, and control electricity for illumination and/or power to required facilities when the normal electrical supply or system is interrupted.

The provisions of this article apply to the installation of emergency systems where such systems are legally required by municipal, state, federal, or other codes or a governmental agency having jurisdiction.

This article of the *Code* does not determine whether emergency systems are required or the location of emergency or exit lights. This function is covered in NFPA *101*-1981, *Life Safety Code.*

ARTICLE 700—EMERGENCY SYSTEMS

Emergency systems are those systems legally required and classed as emergency by municipal, state, federal, or other codes, or by any governmental agency having jurisdiction. These systems are intended to automatically supply illumination and/or power to designated areas and equipment in the event of failure of the normal supply or in the event of accident to elements of a system intended to supply, distribute, and control power and illumination essential for safety to human life.

(FPN): For further information regarding wiring and installation of emergency systems in health care facilities, see Article 517.

(FPN): For further information regarding performance and maintenance of emergency systems in health care facilities, see Standard for Essential Electric Systems for Health Care Facilities, NFPA 76A-1977.

(FPN): Emergency systems are generally installed in places of assembly where artificial illumination is required for safe exiting and for panic control in buildings subject to occupancy by large numbers of persons, such as hotels, theaters, sports arenas, health care facilities, and similar institutions. Emergency systems may also provide power for such functions as ventilation when essential to maintain life, fire detection and alarm systems, elevators, fire pumps, public safety communication systems, industrial processes where current interruption would produce serious life safety or health hazards, and similar functions.

(FPN): For specification of locations where emergency lighting is considered essential to life safety, see *Life Safety Code*, NFPA *101*-1981 (ANSI).

Emergency systems are designed to maintain a specific degree of illumination or provide power for essential equipment, such as fire pumps, operating room equipment, etc., in the event of failure of the normal power supply.

Where authorities determine that emergency lighting, including the proper placement of exit signs, is required for safe egress from various classes of buildings, or parts of buildings, sufficient illumination is to be provided for corridors, passageways, stairways, lobbies, etc.

700-2. Application of Other Articles.   Except as modified by this article, all applicable articles of this Code shall apply.

700-3. Equipment Approval.   All equipment shall be approved for use on emergency systems.

700-4. Tests and Maintenance.

   (a) Conduct or Witness Test.   The authority having jurisdiction shall conduct or witness a test on the complete system upon installation and periodically afterward.

   (b) Tested Periodically.   Systems shall be tested periodically on a schedule acceptable to the authority having jurisdiction to assure their maintenance in proper operating condition.

   (c) Battery Systems Maintenance.   Where battery systems or unit equipments are involved, including batteries used for starting or ignition in auxiliary engines, the authority having jurisdiction shall require periodic maintenance.

   (d) Written Record.   A written record shall be kept of such tests and maintenance.

   (e) Testing Under Load.   Means for testing all emergency lighting and power systems during maximum anticipated load conditions shall be provided.

700-5. Capacity.

   (a) Capacity and Rating.   An emergency system shall have adequate capacity and rating for all loads to be operated simultaneously.

It is essential that the emergency system be designed with adequate capacity and rating to carry safely the entire load connected to the emergency system at one time. The emergency operation of the equipment may be something less than the nameplate rating. Further, some equipment may be "spared," and with both normal and spare, it may be necessary for the emergency system to be sized for both to operate at the same time. The emergency system is required to be capable of restarting emergency loads that may have stopped.

Where such equipment is connected, in the event of a loss of normal power supply, emergency systems are required to be capable of supplying power to emergency lights for the illumination of specific areas, exit signs, and paths of egress, or for the operation of elevators, alarm systems, essential refrigeration, breathing apparatus or ventilation when essential to maintain life, fire pumps, public address systems, or other equipment.

The alternate power source in hospital facilities is required to be capable of supplying power to illuminate all exit signs and ways of approach to exits, alarm systems, communication systems, and task illumination, as well as for illumination of operating rooms and power for elevators, heating for specific areas, and special equipment such as inhalators, incubators, etc.

(b) Selective Load Pickup and Load Shedding. The alternate power source may supply emergency, legally required standby, and optional standby system loads where automatic selective load pickup and load shedding is provided as needed to assure adequate power to (1) the emergency circuits; (2) the legally required standby circuits; and (3) the optional standby circuits, in that order of priority.

This recognizes the use of a generator to serve more than one level of emergency, standby, and other loads. It also permits the use of a generator for load peak shaving, supplying backup power, and other uses. However, it is required that there be assurance that priority loads will be properly and reliably served. Such systems are required to be maintained and tested periodically to provide the necessary assurance.

A portable or temporary alternate source shall be available whenever the emergency generator is out of service for major maintenance or repair.

The added use that may result from serving other loads may necessitate major maintenance of emergency generator sets. The requirement for a portable or temporary alternate source is to provide emergency power when the generator set is out of service for a prolonged period of time. A major maintenance or repair procedure is one that keeps the generator set out of service for more than a few hours.

700-6. Transfer Equipment. Transfer equipment shall be automatic and identified for emergency use or approved by the authority having jurisdiction. Transfer equipment shall be designed and installed to prevent the inadvertent interconnection of normal and emergency sources of supply in any operation of the transfer equipment. See Section 230-83.

Means shall be permitted to isolate the transfer switch equipment. Where isolation switches are used, inadvertent parallel operation shall be avoided.

700-7. Signals. Audible and visual signal devices shall be provided, where practicable, for the following purposes:

(a) Derangement. To indicate derangement of the emergency source.

(b) Carrying Load. To indicate that the battery or generator set is carrying load.

(c) Not Functioning. To indicate that the battery charger is not functioning.

(d) Prime Mover. To indicate derangement of the prime mover starting equipment.

(e) Ground Fault. To indicate a ground fault in solidly grounded wye emergency systems of more than 150 volts to ground and circuit protective devices rated 1000 amperes or more. The sensor for the ground-fault signal devices shall be located at, or ahead of, the main system disconnecting means for the emergency source, and the maximum setting of the signal devices shall be for a ground-fault current of 1200 amperes. Instructions on the course of action to be taken in event of indicated ground fault shall be located at or near the sensor location.

Improper testing or lack of testing, inadequate maintenance, and negligence by attendants to observe visual signals indicating a malfunction of battery-charging equipment are the major causes of emergency equipment failures.

Signal devices should be located in an area where they will be readily visible to or heard by attendants or other personnel familiar with the operation of the emergency equipment.

In locations such as theaters or assembly halls, audible signal bells or horns should be located where they will not cause panic.

Battery-operated unit equipment generally have test switches to simulate a failure of the normal system and an indicating light that glows bright while charging and dim when ready. Transparent plastic cases are required to be provided for lead acid batteries for easy viewing of electrolyte levels.

A storage battery system is normally capable of delivering 12 V, 24 V, 32 V, or 120 V and consists of monitoring and distribution cabinets and console with battery and charger. It generally includes audio, visual, and remote signal devices, a test switch, and may provide a trouble bell and silence switch.

Although Section 700-26 indicates that ground-fault protection of equipment is not required on the alternate source for emergency systems, ground-faults can occur on such systems and they can result in equipment burn-down. Because of the emergency nature of such systems, automatic disconnect in the event of a ground fault is not appropriate. However, detection of such a fault is desirable. Section 700-7(e) is new in the 1984 *NEC*, and provides information for such ground-fault detection and signaling equipment.

700-8. Signs. A sign shall be placed at the service entrance equipment indicating type and location of on-site emergency power sources.

B. Circuit Wiring

700-9. Wiring, Emergency System. Wiring from emergency source or emergency source distribution overcurrent protection to emergency loads shall be kept entirely independent of all other wiring and equipment and shall not enter the same raceway, cable, box, or cabinet with other wiring.

Exception No. 1: In transfer equipment enclosures.

Exception No. 2: In exit or emergency lighting fixtures supplied from two sources.

Exception No. 3: In a common junction box attached to exit or emergency lighting fixtures supplied from two sources.

Exception No. 4: Wiring of two or more emergency circuits supplied from the same source shall be permitted in the same raceway.

Exception No. 5: In a common junction box attached to a unit equipment, and which contains only the branch circuit supplying the unit equipment and the emergency circuit supplied by the unit equipment.

Emergency circuit wiring is not permitted to enter the same raceway, cable, box, or cabinet with the regular or normal wiring of the building concerned. Wiring for the emergency circuits is required to be completely independent of all other wiring and equipment, thus ensuring that any fault on the normal wiring circuits will not affect the performance of the emergency wiring or equipment.

To effect an immediate throw-over from one system to the other, it is necessary for both the normal source and the emergency source to be present within a transfer switch enclosure as per Exception No. 1.

Exceptions No. 2 and 3 permit the use of two-lamp exit or two-lamp emergency fixtures where one lamp is connected to the normal supply and one lamp is connected to the alternate supply. It is to be noted that both lamps may be illuminated as part of the regular lighting operation.

C. Sources of Power

700-12. General Requirements. Current supply shall be such that in the event of failure of the normal supply to, or within, the building or group of buildings concerned, emergency lighting, emergency power, or both will be available within the time required for the application but not to exceed 10 seconds. The supply system for emergency purposes, in addition to the normal services to the building and meeting the general requirements of this section, shall be permitted to comprise one or more of the types of systems described in (a) through (e) below. Unit equipments in accordance with Section 700-12(f) shall satisfy the applicable requirements of this article.

In selecting an emergency source of power, consideration shall be given to the type of service to be rendered, whether of short-time duration, as for exit lights of a theater, or long duration, as for supplying emergency power and lighting due to a long period of current failure from trouble either inside or outside the building, as in the case of a hospital.

Consideration shall be given to the location and/or design of all equipment to minimize the hazards that might cause complete failure due to floods, fires, icing, and vandalism.

(FPN): Assignment of degree of reliability of the recognized emergency supply system depends upon the careful evaluation of the variables at each particular installation.

(a) Storage Battery. A storage battery of suitable rating and capacity to supply and maintain at not less than 87½ percent of system voltage the total load of the circuits supplying emergency lighting and emergency power for a period of at least 1½ hours.

Batteries, whether of the acid or alkali type, shall be designed and constructed to meet the requirements of emergency service and shall be compatible with the charger for that particular installation.

For a sealed battery, the container shall not be required to be transparent. However, for the lead acid battery which requires water additions, transparent or translucent jars shall be furnished. Automotive-type batteries shall not be used.

An automatic battery charging means shall be provided.

(b) Generator Set.

(1) A generator set driven by a prime mover acceptable to the authority having jurisdiction and sized in accordance with Section 700-5. Means shall be provided for automatically starting the prime mover on failure of the normal service and for automatic transfer and operation of all required electrical circuits. A time delay feature permitting a 15-minute setting shall be provided to avoid retransfer in case of short-time reestablishment of the normal source.

(2) Where internal combustion engines are used as the prime mover, an on-site fuel supply shall be provided with an on-premise fuel supply sufficient for not less than 2 hours full-demand operation of the system.

(3) Prime movers shall not be solely dependent upon a public utility gas system for their fuel supply or municipal water supply for their cooling systems. Means shall be provided for automatically transferring from one fuel supply to another where dual fuel supplies are used.

Exception: Where acceptable to the authority having jurisdiction, the use of other than on-site fuels shall be permitted when there is a low probability of a simultaneous failure of both the off-site fuel delivery system and power from the outside electrical utility company.

(4) Where the means of starting the prime mover is a storage battery, it shall be suitable for the purpose and shall be equipped with an automatic charging means.

(5) Generator sets which require more than 10 seconds to develop power are acceptable providing an auxiliary power supply will energize the emergency system until the generator can pick up the load.

(FPN): See Section 700-4 for test and maintenance requirements.

(c) Uninterruptible Power Supplies. Uninterruptible power supplies used to provide power for emergency systems shall comply with the applicable provision of Section 700-12(a) and (b).

(d) Separate Service. Where acceptable to the authority having jurisdiction, a second service shall be permitted. This service shall be in accordance with Article 230, with separate service drop or lateral, widely separated electrically and physically from the normal service to minimize the possibility of simultaneous interruption of supply.

(e) Connection Ahead of Service Disconnecting Means. Where acceptable to the authority having jurisdiction, connections ahead of, but not within, the main service disconnecting means shall be permitted. The emergency service shall be sufficiently separated from the normal main service disconnecting means to prevent simultaneous interruption of supply through an occurrence within the building or groups of buildings served.

When designing emergency systems, whether for lighting, power, or both, it is required that consideration be given to the type of service rendered.

Supply systems for emergency systems can be one or more of the following:

1. One, or a group of storage batteries, provided with an automatic battery-charging means. See also Article 480 and paragraph (a) of this section.

2. A generator set driven by a prime mover, acceptable to the authority having jurisdiction, and with adequate capacity to carry the maximum load connected at one time. Prime movers may be internal-combustion engines, steam turbines, or other approved types. A storage battery used to start the prime mover is required to be provided with an automatic battery-charging means. An on-site fuel supply sufficient to operate internal-combustion engines at full load for 2 hours is required to be available.

Off-site fuel supplies may be used where experience has demonstrated their reliability. Off-site fuel supplies may also be used where they will provide greater reliability for gasoline or diesel engines or in isolated areas where maintenance or refueling could be a problem.

Some types of drivers, particularly large ones, may take longer than 10 seconds to accelerate and develop voltage. Gas and steam turbines and large internal-combustion engines may have prolonged starting times. Depending on the specific loads, short-time supply could be provided by an uninterruptible power supply; a generator shared with other loads; or a generator with limited emergency supply, such as an expander, steam turbine, or waste heat system.

3. Two services, overhead or underground, widely separated electrically and physically, and preferred by some authorities to be completely independent of each

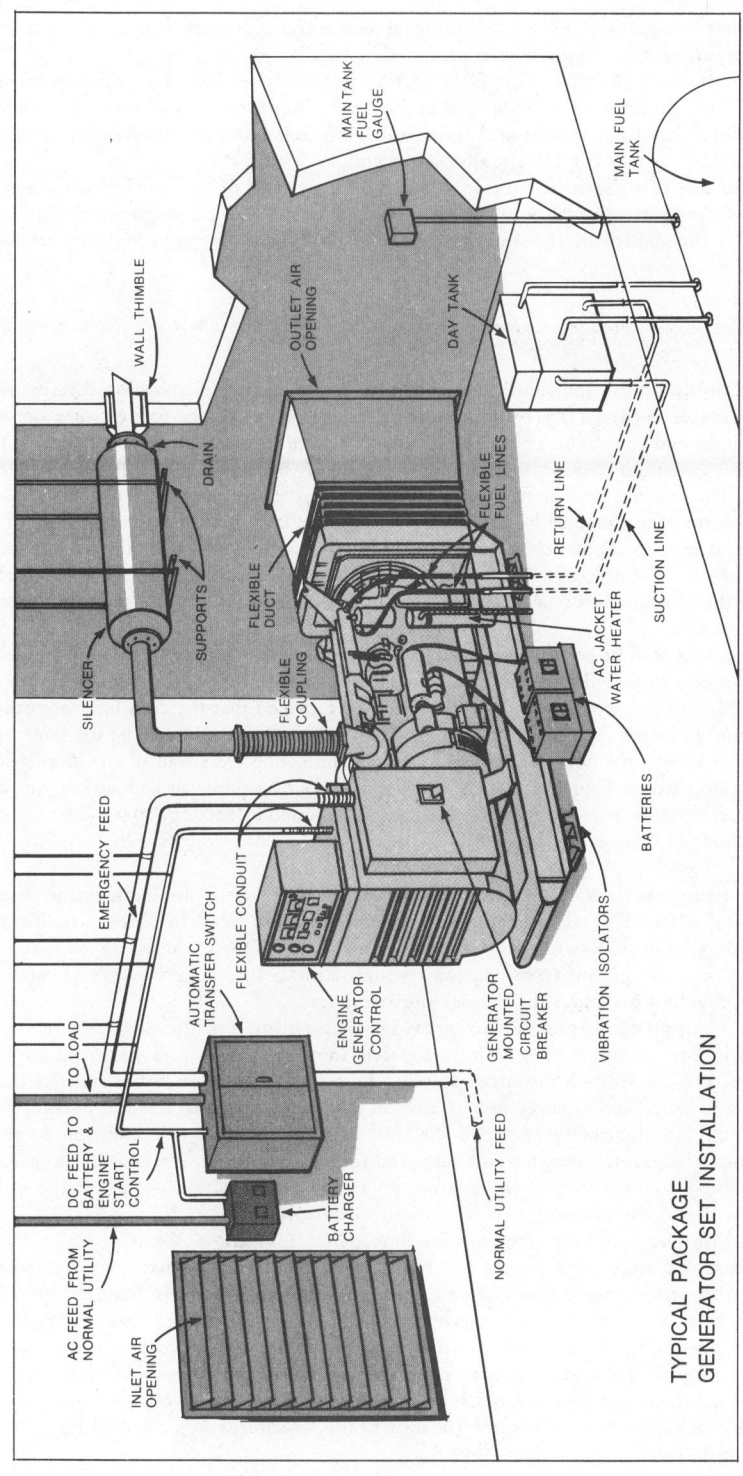

WALL THIMBLE

MAIN TANK FUEL GAUGE

OUTLET AIR OPENING

MAIN FUEL TANK

DRAIN

DAY TANK

SILENCER

SUPPORTS

FLEXIBLE DUCT

FLEXIBLE COUPLING

FLEXIBLE FUEL LINES

RETURN LINE

SUCTION LINE

AC JACKET WATER HEATER

BATTERIES

VIBRATION ISOLATORS

GENERATOR MOUNTED CIRCUIT BREAKER

ENGINE GENERATOR CONTROL

FLEXIBLE CONDUIT

AUTOMATIC TRANSFER SWITCH

EMERGENCY FEED

TO LOAD

DC FEED TO BATTERY & ENGINE START CONTROL

AC FEED FROM NORMAL UTILITY

INLET AIR OPENING

BATTERY CHARGER

NORMAL UTILITY FEED

TYPICAL PACKAGE GENERATOR SET INSTALLATION

Figure 700-1. A typical generator installation supplying standby power in ratings from 55 kW to 930 kW, 60 Hz. (*Caterpillar*)

other, that is, separate service locations, separate transformers, and supplied from separate utility substations where practical.

4. Uninterruptible power supplies (UPS) generally include a rectifier, storage battery, and inverter to ac. These may be very complex systems with redundant components and high-speed solid-state switching. It is common practice to include an automatic bypass for UPS malfunction and to permit maintenance.

5. The use of a separate service or connection ahead of the service disconnect requires a judgment by the authority having jurisdiction. Such judgment should be based on the nature of the emergency loads and the expected reliability of the other available sources.

(FPN): See Section 230-82 for equipment permitted on the supply side of a service disconnecting means.

(f) Unit Equipment. Individual unit equipment for emergency illumination shall consist of: (1) a rechargeable battery; (2) a battery charging means; (3) provisions for one or more lamps mounted on the equipment and/or shall be permitted to have terminals for remote lamps; and (4) a relaying device arranged to energize the lamps automatically upon failure of the supply to the unit equipment. The batteries shall be of suitable rating and capacity to supply and maintain at not less than 87½ percent of the nominal battery voltage for the total lamp load associated with the unit for a period of at least 1½ hours, or the unit equipment shall supply and maintain not less than 60 percent of the initial emergency illumination for a period of at least 1½ hours. Storage batteries, whether of the acid or alkali type, shall be designed and constructed to meet the requirements of emergency service.

Unit equipment shall be permanently fixed in place (i.e., not portable) and shall have all wiring to each unit installed in accordance with the requirements of any of the wiring methods in Chapter 3. Flexible cord- and plug-connection shall be permitted provided that the cord does not exceed 3 feet (914 mm) in length. The branch circuit feeding the unit equipment shall be the same branch circuit as that serving the normal lighting in the area and connected ahead of any local switches. Emergency illumination fixtures that obtain power from a unit equipment and are not part of the unit equipment shall be wired to the unit equipment as required by Section 700-9 and by one of the wiring methods of Chapter 3.

Unit equipment may be wired with a flexible cord- and plug-connection (not exceeding 3 ft). This equipment must be permanently fixed in place, usually by mounting screws accessible only from within the unit. One or more lamps may be mounted on, or remote from, the unit which should be located where it can be readily checked or tested for proper performance.

Unit equipment is intended to provide illumination for the area where it is installed. For instance, if a unit is located in a corridor it is required to be connected to the branch circuit supplying the normal corridor lights (on the line side of any switching arrangements) and, in the event of loss of normal power, the unit would automatically energize the unit lamps, restoring illumination to the corridor. A separate circuit is not required for unit equipment because, if applied to the above case, failure of the normal corridor circuit would not affect the unit equipment and the corridor would remain in darkness.

Notes on General Requirements for Emergency Lighting Systems

At least two sources of power are required to be provided, that is, one normal supply and one or more types of emergency systems described in Section 700-12. The sources may be (1) two services, one normal supply and one emergency supply (preferably from separate utility stations); (2) one normal service and a storage battery (or unit equipment) system; (3) one normal service and a generator set; or (4) one normal service and one emergency service connected to the line side of the normal service (usually at the weatherhead). See Figures 700-3, 700-4, and 700-5.

A transfer means (or throw-over switch) is to be provided to energize the emergency equipment from the alternate supply when the normal source of supply is interrupted.

Where two services are used both may operate normally, but equipment for emergency lighting and power is to be arranged to be energized from either service.

Where the alternate or emergency source of supply is a storage battery or a generator set, the single emergency system would usually be operated on the normal service, and the battery (or batteries) or generator would operate only if the normal service failed. See Figure 700-5.

Two or more separate and complete systems may be used to provide current for emergency lighting, but means are required to be provided for energizing either system upon the failure of the other.

It should be noted that provisions for disconnecting means and overcurrent protection (see Figures 700-3, 700-4, and 700-5) are to be provided for emergency systems as required by Article 230. See also Section 230-83.

Figure 700-2. Self-contained fully automatic unit equipment to operate emergency lighting located on the unit or for remotely located exit signs or lighting heads. (*Dual-Lite Inc.*)

D. Emergency System Circuits for Lighting and Power

700-15. Loads on Emergency Branch Circuits. No appliances and no lamps, other than those specified as required for emergency use, shall be supplied by emergency lighting circuits.

700-16. Emergency Illumination. Emergency illumination shall include all required exit lights, illuminated exit signs, and all other lights specified as necessary to provide required illumination.

Emergency lighting systems shall be so designed and installed that the failure of any individual lighting element, such as the burning out of a light bulb, cannot leave in total darkness any space which requires emergency illumination.

700-17. Circuits for Emergency Lighting. Branch circuits which supply emergency lighting shall be installed to provide service from a source complying with Section 700-12 when the normal supply for lighting is interrupted. Such installations shall provide either one of the following: (1) an emergency lighting supply, independent of the general lighting supply, with provisions for automatically transferring the emergency lights upon the event of failure of the general lighting system supply, or (2) two or more separate and complete systems with independent power supply, each system providing sufficient current for emergency lighting purposes. Unless both systems are used for regular lighting purposes and are both kept lighted, means shall be provided for automatically energizing either system upon failure of the other. Either or both systems shall be permitted to be a part of the general lighting system of the protected occupancy if circuits supplying lights for emergency illumination are installed in accordance with other sections of this article.

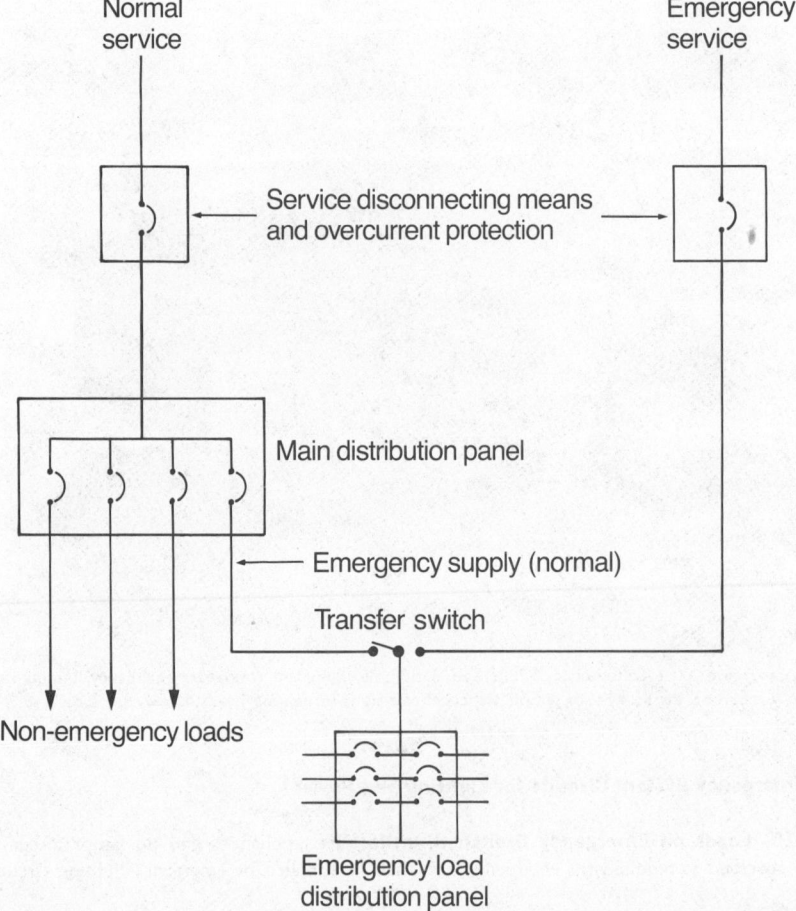

Figure 700-3. Emergency load arranged to be supplied from two widely separated services [Section 700-12(d)]. Upon failure of one service the emergency load will be transferred to the other service.

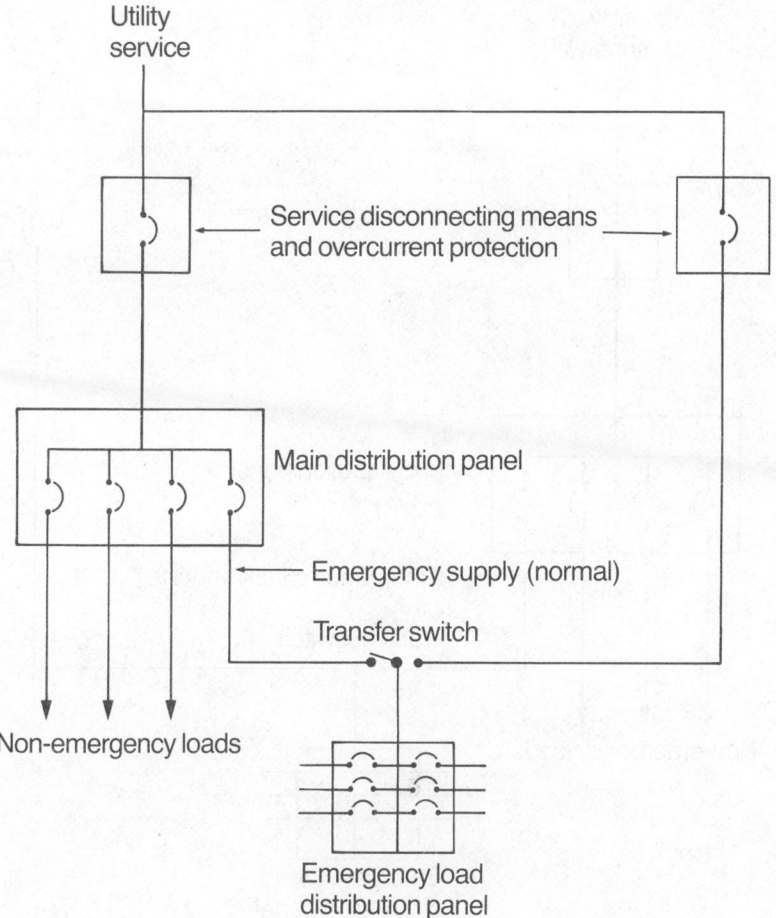

Utility service

Service disconnecting means and overcurrent protection

Main distribution panel

Emergency supply (normal)

Transfer switch

Non-emergency loads

Emergency load distribution panel

Figure 700-4. Emergency service arranged to be supplied by the tap ahead of the main [Section 700-12(e)].

1. General Considerations for Transfer Switches

Automatic transfer switches of double-throw construction are used primarily for emergency and standby power generation systems rated 600 V and less. These transfer switches do not normally incorporate overcurrent protection and are designed and applied in accordance with the *Code*, particularly Articles 700 and 701. They are available in ratings from 30 to 3,000 A. For reliability, most automatic transfer switches rated above 100 A are mechanically held and electrically operated from the power source to which the load is to be transferred.

An automatic transfer switch is usually located in the main or secondary distribution bus which feeds the branch circuits. Because of its location in the system, the abilities which must be designed into the transfer switch are unique and extensive as compared with the design requirements for other branch-circuit devices. For example, special consideration should be given to the following characteristics of an automatic transfer: (1) its ability to close against high in-rush currents, (2) its ability to carry full-rated current continuously from normal and emergency sources, (3) its ability to withstand fault currents, and (4)

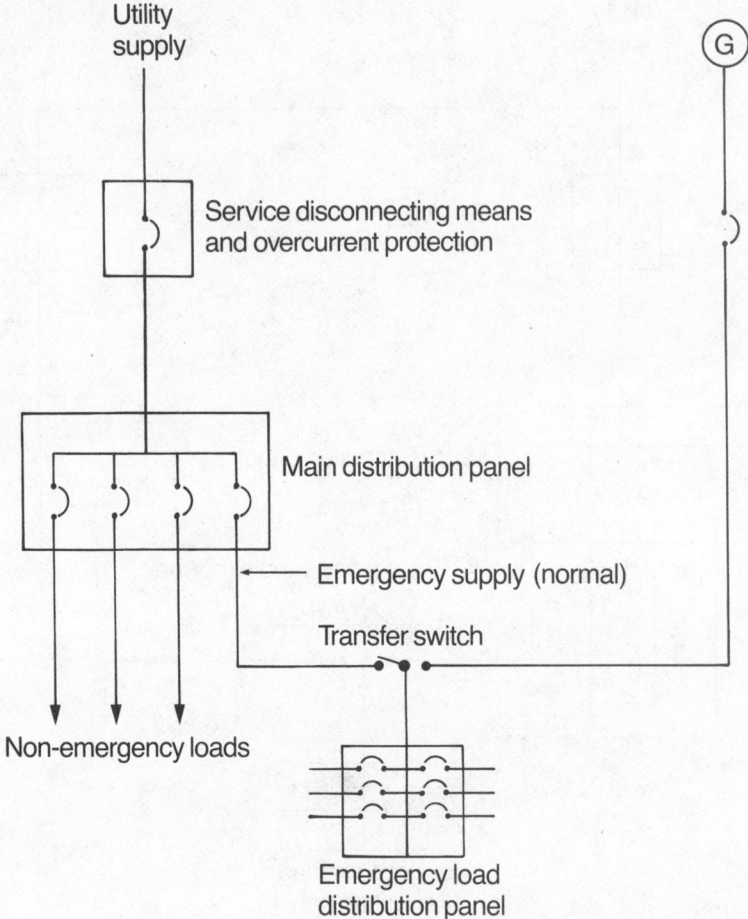

Figure 700-5. Emergency load arranged to be supplied from a generator [Section 700-12(b)] or storage battery [Section 700-12(a)].

its ability to interrupt six times the full-load currents. In addition to considering each of the above characteristics individually, it is also necessary to consider the effect each has upon the other.

In arrangements to provide protection against failure of the utility service, consideration should also be given to (1) an open circuit within the building area on the load side of the incoming service, (2) overload or fault condition, and (3) electrical or mechanical failure of the electric power distribution system within the building. It is therefore desirable to locate transfer switches close to the load and have the operation of the transfer switches independent of overcurrent protection. It is often desirable to use multiple transfer switches of lower current located near the load rating rather than one large transfer switch at the point of incoming service.

2. Location of Overcurrent Devices
The location of overcurrent devices for both normal and emergency power is covered by Section 240-21 and is not effected by the installation of an automatic transfer switch. Transfer switches should be rated for continuous duty and have low contact temperature rise.

3. Solid Neutral on AC and DC Systems

Solid neutrals can be used with the grounding connections made as required in Section 250-23 where automatic ac to ac transfer switches are used. Where multiple grounding creates objectionable ground current, corrective action specified in Section 250-21(b) is required to be made.

Section 230-95 requires ground-fault protection of equipment. Because the normal source and emergency source are typically grounded at their locations, the multiple neutral-to-ground connections usually require some additional means or devices to assure proper ground-fault sensing by the ground-fault protection device. Additional means or devices are generally required because the normal alterations to stop objectionable current per Section 250-21(b) do not apply when the objectionable current is a ground-fault current. See Section 250-21(c). Rather, solutions such as an overlapping neutral transfer pole or conventional fourth pole are often added to the transfer switch. Other solutions are isolation transformers and special ground-fault circuits, or using the service ground to also ground the generator neutral with 3-pole transfer switches.

On ac to dc automatic transfer switches, a solid neutral tie between the ac and dc neutrals is not permitted where both sources of supply are exterior distribution systems. Section 250-22 regarding location of grounds for dc exterior systems clearly specifies that the dc system can be grounded only at the supply station.

Where the dc system is an interior isolated system, such as a storage battery, solid neutral connection between the ac system neutral and the dc source is acceptable.

On an ac to dc automatic transfer switch where the neutral must be switched, the size of the neutral switching pole must be considered. A 4-pole, double-throw switch must be used where a 3-phase, 4-wire normal source and a 2-wire dc emergency source are transferred. Due to the neutral being switched, a 4-pole, double-throw transfer switch would be required. In this instance, one pole of the dc emergency source would carry three times the current of the other poles.

4. Close Differential Voltage Supervision of Normal Source

Most often the normal source is an electric utility company whose power is transmitted many miles to the point of utilization. The automatic transfer switch control panel continuously monitors the voltage of all phases. (Because utility frequency is, for all practical purposes, constant, only the voltage need be monitored.) For single-phase power systems, the line-to-line voltage is monitored. For 3-phase power systems, all three line-to-line voltages should be monitored to provide full-phase protection.

In addition, monitoring protects against operation at reduced voltage, such as brownouts, which can damage loads. Since the voltage sensitivity of loads vary, the pickup (acceptable) voltage setting, and dropout (unacceptable) voltage setting of the monitors should be adjustable. Typical range of adjustment for the pickup is 85 percent to 100 percent of nominal, while the dropout setting, which is a function of the pickup setting, is 75 percent to 98 percent of the pickup selected. Usual settings for most loads are 95 percent of nominal for pickup and 85 percent of nominal for dropout (90 percent of pickup).

Consideration must be given to voltage supervision at closer differential for many installations where the load circuits are critical to voltage.

Starter-type fluorescent lighting is extremely voltage sensitive and at voltages below 105 V it becomes uncertain as to whether the fluorescent lamp will burn. Therefore, a closer differential of transfer and retransfer is required for this type of lighting.

Electronic equipment load is frequently voltage critical. These installations include patient care equipment in health care facilities, X-ray equipment, television stations, microwave communications, telephone communications, computer centers, and similar applications.

Polyphase motors operating at low load have a tendency to single phase, despite the loss of voltage in one phase, leading to burnout of the motor. A close differential of voltage supervision should be applied to automatic transfer switches for motor installations of the polyphase type. Differential voltage relays with a close adjustment of 2 percent for transfer and retransfer values will aid in the detection of phase outages and provide protection from single phasing.

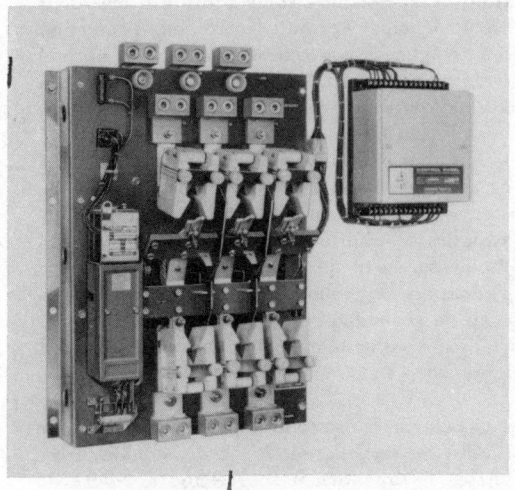

Figure 700-6. Automatic emergency transfer switch and control panel. (*Automatic Switch Co.*)

5. Automatic Transfer Switches with Emergency Source on Automatically Started Power Plant

In these installations the normal source is usually a utility power line, and the emergency source is an automatically started engine generator set which starts upon failure of the normal source. To ensure maximum reliability, a minimum installation should be arranged to:

1. Initiate engine starting of the power plant from a contact on the automatic transfer switch control panel (see Figure 700-7),

2. Sustain connection of load circuits to the normal source during the starting period to provide utilization of any existing service on the normal source,

3. Measure output voltage and frequency of emergency source through the use of voltage-frequency-sensitive monitor (see Figure 700-7) and effect transfer of the load circuits to the power plant only when both voltage and frequency of the power plant are approximately normal. Sensing of the emergency source need only be single phase since most applications involve an on-site engine generator with a relatively short line run to the ATS. In addition to monitoring voltage, the emergency source's frequency should also be monitored. Unlike the utility power, the engine generator frequency can vary during startup. Frequency monitoring will avoid overloading the engine generator while it is starting and can thus avoid stalling the engine. Combined frequency and voltage monitoring will protect against transferring loads to an engine generator set with an unacceptable output, and

4. Provide visual signal and auxiliary contact for remote indication when power plant is feeding the load per Section 700-7(b).

6. Time-Delay Devices on Automatic Transfer Switches

Time delays are provided to program operation of the automatic transfer switch. To avoid unnecessary starting and transfer to the alternate supply, a nominal 1-second time delay, adjustable up to 6 seconds, can override momentary

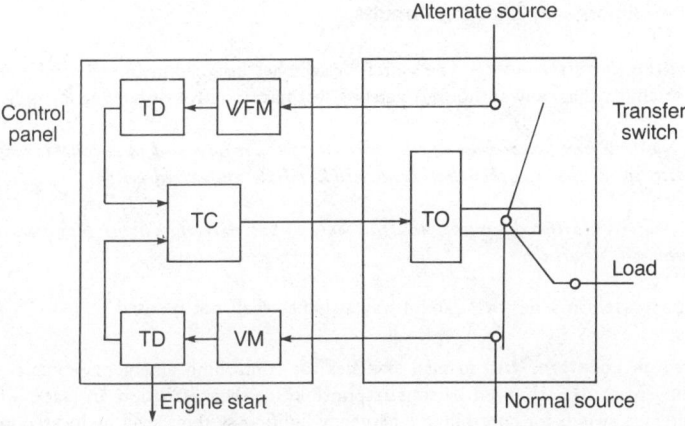

Figure 700-7. Diagram of connections of the automatic transfer switch shown in Figure 700-6. TD, Time Delay; TO, Transfer; TC, Transfer Controls; V/FM, Voltage Frequency Monitor; VM, Voltage Monitor. (*Automatic Switch Co.*)

interruptions and reductions in normal source voltage but allow starting and transfer if the reduction or outage is sustained. See Figure 700-7. The advantages of this feature are realized in all types of automatic transfer installations. In standby plant installations the reduced number of false starts is especially important to minimize wear on the starting gear, battery, and associated equipment. This delay is generally set at 1 second, but may be set higher if reclosers on the high lines take longer to operate or if momentary power dips exceed 1 second. If longer delay settings are used, care must be taken to ensure that sufficient time remains to meet 10-second power restoration requirements.

Once the load is transferred to the alternate source, another timer delays retransfer to the normal source until that source has time to stabilize. This timer is required by Section 700-12(b)(1) and is controlled by the preferred source voltage monitors. The timer is adjustable from 0 to 30 minutes and is normally set at 30 minutes. Another important function of this retransfer timer is to allow an engine generator to operate under load for a preselected minimum time to ensure continued good performance of the set and its starting system. This delay should be automatically nullified if the alternate source fails and the normal source is available as determined by the voltage monitors.

Engine generator manufacturers often recommend a cool-down period for their sets which allows them to run unloaded after the load is retransferred to the normal source. A third time delay, usually 5 minutes, is provided for this purpose. Running an unloaded engine for more than 5 minutes is neither necessary nor recommended since it can cause deterioration in engine performance.

It is sometimes prescribed to purposely sequence transfer of the loads to the alternate source where more than one automatic transfer switch is connected to the same engine generator. Utilization of such a sequencing scheme can reduce starting kVA capacity requirements of the generator. A fourth timer, adjustable from 0 to 5 minutes, will delay transfer to emergency for this and other similar requirements.

700-18. Circuits for Emergency Power.   For branch circuits that supply equipment classed as emergency, there shall be an emergency supply source to which the load will be transferred automatically upon the failure of the normal supply.

E. Control — Emergency Lighting Circuits

700-20. Switch Requirements. The switch or switches installed in emergency lighting circuits shall be so arranged that only authorized persons will have control of emergency lighting.

Exception No. 1: Where two or more single-throw switches are connected in parallel to control a single circuit, at least one of these switches shall be accessible only to authorized persons.

Exception No. 2: Additional switches that act only to put emergency lights into operation but not disconnect them are permissible.

Switches connected in series or 3- and 4-way switches shall not be used.

700-21. Switch Location. All manual switches for controlling emergency circuits shall be in locations convenient to authorized persons responsible for their actuation. In places of assembly, such as theaters, a switch for controlling emergency lighting systems shall be located in the lobby or at a place conveniently accessible thereto.

In no case shall a control switch for emergency lighting in a theater, or motion-picture theater or place of assembly be placed in a motion-picture projection booth or on a stage or platform.

Exception: Where multiple switches are provided, one such switch shall be permitted in such locations where so arranged that it can energize the circuit only, but it cannot de-energize the circuit.

700-22. Exterior Lights. Those lights on the exterior of a building that are not required for illumination when there is sufficient daylight shall be permitted to be controlled by an automatic light-actuated device.

F. Overcurrent Protection

700-25. Accessibility. The branch-circuit overcurrent devices in emergency circuits shall be accessible to authorized persons only.

700-26. Ground-Fault Protection of Equipment. The alternate source for emergency systems shall not be required to have ground-fault protection of equipment.

This is an exception to the general ground-fault protection requirement of Section 230-95 for protective devices set to, or rated at, 1,000 A or more. It permits the designer to exercise judgment in risking equipment damage in order to keep emergency circuits in operation as long as they will continue to function. See Section 700-7(e).

ARTICLE 701 — LEGALLY REQUIRED
STANDBY SYSTEMS

Contents

701-8. Signals.
(a) Derangement.
(b) Carrying Load.
(c) Not Functioning.
(d) Prime Mover.
701-9. Signs.

B. Circuit Wiring
701-9. Wiring Legally Required Standby Systems.

C. Sources of Power
701-10. Legally Required Standby Systems.

(a) Storage Battery.
(b) Generator Set.
(c) Uninterruptible Power Supplies.
(d) Separate Service.
(e) Connection Ahead of Service Disconnecting Means.
(f) Unit Equipment.

D. Overcurrent Protection
701-15. Accessibility.
701-17. Ground-Fault Protection of Equipment.

A. General

701-1. Scope. The provisions of this article apply to the electrical safety of the design, installation, operation, and maintenance of legally required standby systems consisting of circuits and equipment intended to supply, distribute, and control electricity to required facilities for illumination and/or power when the normal electrical supply or system is interrupted.

The systems covered by this article shall be permanently installed in their entirety including power source.

(FPN): For additional information, see Article 517 and NFPA 76A-1977, Standard for Essential Electrical Systems for Health Care Facilities.

In earlier editions of the *Code*, these requirements were included with the requirements for optional standby systems in Article 750. This tended to obscure an important level of standby systems.

Legally required standby systems are intended to provide electric power to aid in fire fighting, rescue operations, control of health hazards, and similar operations. In comparison, emergency systems (Article 700) are those which are essential for safety to human life. Optional standby systems are those whose failure could cause such effects as physical discomfort, serious interruption of an industrial process, damage to process equipment, or disruption of business.

Legally required standby systems have much the same needs as emergency systems; however, there are some differences in requirements. Upon loss of normal power, legally required systems are required to be able to supply standby power in 60 seconds or less instead of the 10 seconds or less required of emergency systems. Wiring for legally required standby systems may occupy the same raceways, cables, boxes, and cabinets as other general wiring. Wiring for emergency systems is required to be kept entirely independent of other wiring. Legally required standby systems take second order priority to emergency systems where they are involved in sharing an alternate supply and/or load shedding schemes.

701-2. Legally Required Standby Systems. Legally required standby systems are those systems required and so classed as legally required standby by municipal, state, federal, or other codes or by any governmental agency having jurisdiction. These systems are intended to automatically supply power to selected loads (other than those classed as emergency systems) in the event of failure of the normal source.

(FPN): Legally required standby systems are typically installed to serve loads, such as heating and refrigeration systems, communication systems, ventilation and smoke removal systems, sewerage disposal, lighting systems and industrial processes, that, when stopped during any interruption of the normal electrical supply, could create hazards or hamper rescue or fire fighting operations.

ARTICLE 701—LEGALLY REQUIRED STANDBY SYSTEMS

701-3. Application of Other Articles. Except as modified by this article, all applicable articles of this Code shall apply.

701-4. Equipment Approval. All equipment shall be approved for the intended use.

701-5. Tests and Maintenance for Legally Required Standby Systems.

(a) **Conduct or Witness Test.** The authority having jurisdiction shall conduct or witness a test on the complete system upon installation.

(b) **Tested Periodically.** Systems shall be tested periodically on a schedule and in a manner acceptable to the authority having jurisdiction to assure their maintenance in proper operating condition.

(c) **Battery Systems Maintenance.** Where batteries are used for starting or ignition of prime movers the authority having jurisdiction shall require periodic maintenance.

(d) **Written Record.** A written record shall be kept on such tests and maintenance.

(e) **Testing under Load.** Means for testing legally required standby systems under load shall be provided.

701-6. Capacity and Rating. A legally required standby system shall have adequate capacity and rating for the supply of all equipment intended to be operated at one time.

The alternate power source may supply legally required standby and optional standby system loads when automatic selective load pickup and load shedding is provided as needed to assure adequate power to the legally required standby circuits.

701-7. Transfer Equipment. Transfer equipment shall be automatic and identified for standby use or approved by the authority having jurisdiction. Transfer equipment shall be designed and installed to prevent the inadvertent interconnection of normal and alternate sources of supply in any operation of the transfer equipment.

Means to isolate the transfer switch equipment shall be permitted. Where isolation switches are used, inadvertent parallel operation shall be avoided.

701-8. Signals. Audible and visual signal devices shall be provided, where practicable, for the following purposes:

(a) **Derangement.** To indicate derangement of the standby source.

(b) **Carrying Load.** To indicate that the standby source is carrying load.

(c) **Not Functioning.** To indicate that the battery charger is not functioning.

(d) **Prime Mover.** To indicate derangement of the prime mover starting equipment.

701-9. Signs. A sign shall be placed at the service entrance indicating type and location of on-site legally required standby power sources.

B. Circuit Wiring

701-10. Wiring Legally Required Standby Systems. The legally required standby system wiring shall be permitted to occupy the same raceways, cables, boxes and cabinets with other general wiring.

C. Sources of Power

701-11. Legally Required Standby Systems. Current supply shall be such that in event of failure of the normal supply to, or within, the building or group of buildings concerned, legally required standby power will be available within the time required for the application but not to exceed 60 seconds. The supply system for legally required standby purposes, in addition to the normal services to the building, shall be permitted to comprise one or more of the types of systems described in (a) through (e) below. Unit equipment in accordance with Section 701-11(f) shall satisfy the applicable requirements of this article.

In selecting a legally required standby source of power, consideration shall be given to the type of service to be rendered whether of short-time duration or long duration.

Consideration shall be given to the location and/or design of all equipment to minimize the hazards that might cause complete failure due to floods, fires, icing, and vandalism.

(FPN): Assignment of degree of reliability of the recognized legally required standby supply system depends upon the careful evaluation of the variables at each particular installation.

(a) Storage Battery. A storage battery of suitable rating and capacity to supply and maintain at not less than 87½ percent of system voltage the total load of the circuits supplying legally required standby power for a period of at least 1½ hours.

Batteries, whether of the acid or alkali type, shall be designed and constructed to meet the service requirements of emergency service and shall be compatible with the charger for that particular installation.

For a sealed battery, the container shall not be required to be transparent. However, for the lead acid battery which requires water additions, transparent or translucent jars shall be furnished. Automotive-type batteries shall not be used.

An automatic battery charging means shall be provided.

(b) Generator Set.

(1) A generator set driven by a prime mover acceptable to the authority having jurisdiction and sized in accordance with Section 701-6. Means shall be provided for automatically starting the prime mover on failure of the normal service and for automatic transfer and operation of all required electrical circuits. A time delay feature permitting a 15-minute setting shall be provided to avoid retransfer in case of short-time reestablishment of the normal source.

(2) Where internal combustion engines are used as the prime mover, an on-site fuel supply shall be provided with an on-premise fuel supply sufficient for not less than 2 hours full-demand operation of the system.

(3) Prime movers shall not be solely dependent upon a public utility gas system for their fuel supply or municipal water supply for their cooling systems. Means shall be provided for automatically transferring one fuel supply to another where dual fuel supplies are used.

Exception: Where acceptable to the authority having jurisdiction, the use of other than on-site fuels shall be permitted when there is a low probability of a simultaneous failure of both the off-site fuel delivery system and power from the outside electrical utility company.

(4) Where the means of starting the prime mover is a storage battery, it shall be suitable for the purpose and shall be equipped with an automatic charging means.

(FPN): See Section 701-5 for test and maintenance requirements.

(c) Uninterruptible Power Supplies. Uninterruptible power supplies used to provide power for legally required standby systems shall comply with the applicable provision of Section 701-11(a) and (b).

(d) Separate Service. Where acceptable to the authority having jurisdiction, a second service shall be permitted. This service shall be in accordance with Article 230 with separate service drop or lateral widely separated electrically and physically from the normal service to minimize the possibility of simultaneous interruption of supply.

(e) Connection Ahead of Service Disconnecting Means. Where acceptable to the authority having jurisdiction, connections ahead of, but not within, the main service disconnecting means shall be permitted. The legally required standby service shall be sufficiently separated from the normal main service disconnecting means to prevent simultaneous interruption of supply through an occurrence within the building or groups of buildings served.

(FPN): See Section 230-82 for equipment permitted on the supply side of a service disconnecting means.

(f) Unit Equipment. Individual unit equipment for legally required standby illumination shall consist of (1) a rechargeable battery; (2) a battery charging means; (3) provisions for one or more lamps mounted on the equipment and/or shall be permitted to have terminals for remote lamps; and (4) a relaying device arranged to energize the lamps automatically upon failure of the supply to the unit equipment. The batteries shall be of suitable rating and capacity to supply and maintain at not less than 87½ percent of the nominal battery voltage for the total lamp load associated with the unit for a period of at least 1½ hours, or the unit equipment shall supply and maintain not less than 60 percent of the initial legally required standby illumination for a period of at least 1½ hours. Storage batteries, whether of the acid or alkali type, shall be designed and constructed to meet the requirements of emergency service.

Unit equipment shall be permanently fixed in place (i.e., not portable) and shall have all wiring to each unit installed in accordance with the requirements of any of the wiring methods in Chapter 3. Flexible cord-and plug-connection shall be permitted provided that the cord does not exceed 3 feet (914 mm) in length. The branch circuit feeding the unit equipment shall be the same branch circuit as that serving the normal lighting in the area and connected ahead of any local switches. Legally required standby illumination fixtures that obtain power from a unit equipment and are not part of the unit equipment shall be wired to the unit equipment by one of the wiring methods of Chapter 3.

D. Overcurrent Protection

701-15. Accessibility. The branch-circuit overcurrent devices in legally required standby circuits shall be accessible to authorized persons only.

701-17. Ground-Fault Protection of Equipment. The alternate source for legally required standby systems shall not be required to have ground-fault protection of equipment.

ARTICLE 702 — OPTIONAL STANDBY SYSTEMS

Contents

A. General

702-1. Scope. The provisions of this article apply to the installation and operation of optional standby systems.

The systems covered by this article consist only of those that are permanently installed in their entirety, including prime movers.

702-2. Optional Standby Systems. Optional standby systems are intended to protect private business or property where life safety does not depend on the performance of the system. Optional standby systems are intended to supply on-site generated power to selected loads either automatically or manually.

(FPN): Optional standby systems are typically installed to provide an alternate source of electric power for such facilities as industrial and commercial buildings, farms, and residences, and to serve loads such as heating and refrigeration systems, data processing and communications systems, and industrial processes that, when stopped during any power outage, could cause discomfort, serious interruption of the process, damage to the product or process, or the like.

702-3. Application of Other Articles. Except as modified by this article all applicable articles of this Code shall apply.

702-4. Equipment Approval. All equipment shall be approved for the intended use.

702-5. Capacity. An optional standby system shall have adequate capacity and rating for the supply of all equipment intended to be operated at one time.

(FPN): The optional standby system rating need only be sufficient to carry loads selected by the user.

702-6. Transfer Equipment. Transfer equipment shall be suitable for the intended use and so designed and installed as to prevent the inadvertent interconnection of normal and alternate sources of supply in any operation of the transfer equipment.

702-7. Signals. Audible and visual signal devices shall be provided, where practicable, for the following purposes:

(a) Derangement. To indicate derangement of the optional standby source.

(b) Carrying Load. To indicate that the optional standby source is carrying load.

702-8. Signs. A sign shall be placed at the service-entrance equipment indicating type and location of on-site optional standby power sources.

B. Circuit Wiring

702-9. Wiring Optional Standby Systems. The optional standby system wiring shall be permitted to occupy the same raceways, cables, boxes and cabinets with other general wiring.

ARTICLE 710 — OVER 600 VOLTS, NOMINAL
GENERAL

Contents

ARTICLE 710—OVER 600 VOLTS, NOMiNAL, GENERAL

A. General

710-1. Scope. This article covers the general requirements for all circuits and equipment operated at more than 600 volts, nominal. For specific installations, see the articles referred to in Section 710-2.

710-2. Other Articles. Provisions applicable to specific types of installations are included in Article 225, Outside Branch Circuits and Feeders; Article 230, Services; Article 240, Overcurrent Protection; Article 250, Grounding; Article 300, Wiring Methods; Article 318, Cable Trays; Article 326, Medium Voltage Cable; Article 345, Intermediate Metal Conduit; Article 346, Rigid Metal Conduit; Article 347, Rigid Nonmetallic Conduit; Article 364, Busways; Article 365, Cablebus; Article 370, Outlet, Device, Pull and Junction Boxes, Conduit Bodies and Fittings; Article 410, Lighting Fixtures, Lampholders, Lamps, Receptacles, and Rosettes; Article 427, Fixed Electric Heating Equipment for Pipelines and Vessels; Article 430, Motors, Motor Circuits, and Controllers; Article 450, Transformers and Transformer Vaults; Article 460, Capacitors; Article 600, Electric Signs and Outline Lighting; Article 660, X-Ray Equipment; Article 665, Induction and Dielectric Heating Equipment; and for construction and ampacities of high-voltage conductors, see Article 310.

710-3. Wiring Methods.

(a) Aboveground Conductors. Aboveground conductors shall be installed in rigid metal conduit, in intermediate metal conduit, in rigid nonmetallic conduit, in cable trays, as busways, as cablebus, in other suitable raceways, or as open runs of metal-clad cable suitable for the use and purpose.

In locations accessible to qualified persons only, open runs of nonmetallic-sheathed cable, bare conductors and bare busbars shall also be permitted.

(b) Underground Conductors. Underground conductors shall be suitable for the voltage and conditions under which they are installed.

Direct burial cables shall comply with the provisions of Section 310-7.

Underground cables shall be permitted to be direct buried or installed in raceways identified for the use and shall meet the depth requirements of Table 710-3(b).

Nonshielded cables shall be installed in rigid metal conduit, in intermediate metal conduit, or in rigid nonmetallic conduit encased in not less than 3 inches (76 mm) of concrete.

Exception No. 1: Type MC cable with nonshielded conductor where the metallic sheath is grounded through an effective grounding path meeting the requirements of Section 250-51.

Exception No. 2: Lead sheath cable with nonshielded conductor where the lead sheath is grounded through an effective grounding path meeting the requirements of Section 250-51.

Table 710-3(b)

Minimum Cover Requirements
(Cover Means the Distance in Inches Between the Top Surface of Cable or Raceway and the Grade)

Circuit Voltage	Direct Buried Cables	Rigid Nonmetallic Conduit Approved for Direct Burial*	Rigid Metal Conduit and Intermediate Metal Conduit
Over 600-22kV	30	18	6
Over 22kV-40kV	36	24	6
Over 40kV	42	30	6

For SI units: one inch = 25.4 millimeters.

* Listed by a qualified testing agency as suitable for direct burial without encasement. All other nonmetallic systems shall require 2 inches (50.8mm) of concrete or equivalent above conduit in addition to above depth.

Exception No. 1: The above minimum cover requirements shall be permitted to be reduced 6 inches (152 mm) for each 2 inches (50.8 mm) of concrete or equivalent above the conductors.

Exception No. 2: Areas subject to heavy vehicular traffic, such as thoroughfares or commercial parking areas, shall have a minimum cover of 24 inches (610 mm).

Exception No. 3: Lesser depths are permitted where cables and conductors rise for terminations or splices or where access is otherwise required.

Exception No. 4: In airport runways, including adjacent defined areas where trespass is prohibited, cable shall be permitted to be buried not less than 18 inches (457 mm) deep and without raceways, concrete enclosement, or equivalent.

Exception No. 5: Raceways installed in solid rock shall be permitted to be buried at lesser depth when covered by 2 inches (50.8 mm) of concrete which may extend to the rock surface.

(1) Protection from Damage. Conductors emerging from the ground shall be enclosed in approved raceway. Raceways installed on poles shall be of rigid metal conduit, intermediate metal conduit, PVC Schedule 80 or equivalent extending from the ground line up to a point 8 feet (2.44 m) above finished grade. Conductors entering a building shall be protected by an approved enclosure from the ground line to the point of entrance. Metallic enclosures shall be grounded.

(2) Splices. Direct burial cables shall be permitted to be spliced or tapped without the use of splice boxes provided they are installed using materials suitable for the application. The taps and splices shall be watertight and protected from mechanical injury. Where cables are shielded, the shielding shall be continuous across the splice or tap.

(3) Backfill. Backfill containing large rock, paving materials, cinders, large or sharply angular substance, or corrosive materials shall not be placed in an excavation where materials can damage raceways, cables, or other substructures or prevent adequate compaction of fill or contribute to corrosion of raceways, cables, or other substructures.

(4) Raceway Seal. Where a raceway enters from an underground system the end within the building shall be sealed with suitable compound so as to prevent the entrance of moisture or gases, or it shall be so arranged to prevent moisture from contacting live parts.

In switch rooms, transformer vaults, and similar areas that are restricted to qualified personnel, any suitable wiring method may be used. Open wiring using bare or insulated conductors on insulators is commonly employed, as is rigid metal conduit and rigid nonmetallic conduit.

(c) Busbars. Busbars shall be permitted to be either copper or aluminum.

710-4. Braid-Covered Insulated Conductors — Open Installation. Open runs of braid-covered insulated conductors shall have a flame-retardant braid. If the conductors used do not have this protection, a flame-retardant saturant shall be applied to the braid covering after installation. This treated braid covering shall be stripped back a safe distance at conductor terminals, according to the operating voltage. This distance shall not be less than 1 inch (25.4 mm) for each kilovolt of the conductor-to-ground voltage of the circuit, where practicable.

710-6. Insulation Shielding. Metallic and semiconducting insulation shielding components of shielded cables shall be removed for a distance dependent on the circuit voltage and insulation. Stress reduction means shall be provided at all terminations of factory applied shielding.

Metallic shielding components such as tapes, wires or braids, or combinations thereof and their associated conducting or semiconducting components shall be grounded.

Special kits are available from several manufacturers that permit a quick and easy means of providing the required stress reductions when terminating solid dielectric cables.

710-7. Grounding. Wiring and equipment installations shall be grounded in accordance with the applicable provisions of Article 250.

710-8. Moisture or Mechanical Protection for Metal-Sheathed Cables. Where cable conductors emerge from a metal sheath and where protection against moisture or physical damage is necessary, the insulation of the conductors shall be protected by a cable termination.

710-9. Protection of Service Equipment, Metal-Enclosed Power Switchgear, and Industrial Control Assemblies. Pipes or ducts foreign to the electrical installation which require periodic maintenance or whose malfunction would endanger the operation of the electrical system shall not be located in the vicinity of the service equipment, metal-enclosed power switchgear, or industrial control assemblies. Protection shall be provided where necessary to avoid damage from condensation leaks and breaks in such foreign systems. Piping and other facilities shall not be considered foreign if provided for fire protection of the electrical installation.

B. Equipment — General Provisions

710-11. Indoor Installations. See Section 110-31(a).

710-12. Outdoor Installations. See Section 110-31(b).

710-13. Metal-Enclosed Equipment. See Section 110-31(c).

710-14. Oil-Filled Equipment. Installation of electrical equipment, other than transformers, covered in Article 450, containing more than 10 gallons (37.85 L) of flammable oil per unit shall meet the requirements of Parts B and C of Article 450.

C. Equipment — Specific Provisions

(FPN): See also references to specific types of installations in Section 710-2.

710-20. Overcurrent Protection. Overcurrent protection shall be provided for each ungrounded conductor by one of the following:

(a) Overcurrent Relays and Current Transformers. Circuit breakers used for overcurrent protection of ac 3-phase circuits shall have a minimum of three overcurrent relays operated from three current transformers.

Exception No. 1: On 3-phase, 3-wire circuits, an overcurrent relay in the residual circuit of the current transformers shall be permitted to replace one of the phase relays.

Exception No. 2: An overcurrent relay, operated from a current transformer which links all phases of a 3-phase, 3-wire circuit, shall be permitted to replace the residual relay and one of the phase conductor current transformers.

(b) Fuses. A fuse shall be connected in series with each ungrounded conductor.

710-21. Circuit-Interrupting Devices.

(a) Circuit Breakers.

(1) Indoor installations shall consist of metal-enclosed units or fire-resistant cell-mounted units.

ARTICLE 710—OVER 600 VOLTS, NOMINAL, GENERAL

Exception: Open mounting of circuit breakers shall be permitted in locations accessible to qualified persons only.

(2) Circuit breakers used to control oil-filled transformers shall be either located outside the transformer vault or be capable of operation from outside the vault.

(3) Oil circuit breakers shall be so arranged or located that adjacent readily combustible structures or materials are safeguarded in an approved manner.

(4) Circuit breakers shall have the following equipment or operating characteristics:

a. An accessible mechanical or other approved means for manual tripping, independent of control power.

b. Be release free (trip free).

c. If capable of being opened or closed manually while energized, the main contacts shall operate independently of the speed of the manual operation.

d. A mechanical position indicator at the circuit breaker to show the open or closed position of the main contacts.

e. A means of indicating the open and closed position of the breaker at the point(s) from which they may be operated.

f. A permanent and legible nameplate showing manufacturer's name or trademark, manufacturer's type or identification number, continuous current rating, interrupting rating in MVA or amperes, and maximum voltage rating. Modification of a circuit breaker affecting its rating(s) shall be accompanied by an appropriate change of nameplate information.

For the control and protection of feeders leaving a substation, Figure 710-1 shows a typical example of modern, metal-enclosed switchgear. This industrial unit substation includes a high-voltage disconnect switch, transformer, and low-voltage switchgear with a full functioning ground-fault relay protection system.

Indicating instruments, such as voltmeters, ammeters, wattmeters, and protective relays, may be mounted on the panel doors as desired. This switchgear affords a high degree of safety because all live parts are metal enclosed, and interlocks are provided for safe operation. It is also available with air circuit breakers which eliminate the fire hazard associated with oil breakers.

(5) The continuous current rating of a circuit breaker shall be not less than the maximum continuous current through the circuit breaker.

(6) The interrupting rating of a circuit breaker shall not be less than the maximum fault current the circuit breaker will be required to interrupt, including contributions from all connected sources of energy.

(7) The closing rating of a circuit breaker shall not be less than the maximum asymmetrical fault current into which the circuit breaker can be closed.

(8) The momentary rating of a circuit breaker shall not be less than the maximum asymmetrical fault current at the point of installation.

(9) The rated maximum voltage of a circuit breaker shall not be less than the maximum circuit voltage.

Figure 710-1. An assembly of metal-enclosed switchgear. (*Federal Pacific Electric Co.*)

(b) Power Fuses and Fuseholders.

(1) Use. Where fuses are used to protect conductors and equipment a fuse shall be placed in each ungrounded conductor. Two power fuses shall be permitted to be used in parallel to protect the same load, if both fuses have identical ratings, and both fuses are installed in an identified common mounting with electrical connections that will divide the current equally. Power fuses of the vented type shall not be used indoors, underground or in metal enclosures unless identified for the use.

(2) Interrupting Rating. The interrupting rating of power fuses shall not be less than the maximum fault current the fuse will be required to interrupt, including contributions from all connected sources of energy.

(3) Voltage Rating. The maximum voltage rating of power fuses shall not be less than the maximum circuit voltage. Fuses having a minimum recommended operating voltage shall not be applied below this voltage.

(4) Identification of Fuse Mountings and Fuse Units. Fuse mountings and fuse units shall have permanent and legible nameplates showing the manufacturer's type or designation, continuous current rating, interrupting current rating, and maximum voltage rating.

(5) Fuses. Fuses that expel flame in opening the circuit shall be so designed or arranged that they will function properly without hazard to persons or property.

(6) Fuseholders. Fuseholders shall be designed or installed so that they will be de-energized while replacing a fuse.

Exception: Fuse and fuseholder designed to permit fuse replacement by qualified persons using equipment designed for the purpose without de-energizing the fuseholder.

(7) High-Voltage Fuses. Metal-enclosed switchgear and substations that utilize high-voltage fuses shall be provided with a gang-operated disconnecting switch. Isolation of the fuses from the circuit shall be provided by either connecting a switch between the source and the fuses or providing roll-out switch and fuse type of construction. The switch shall be of the load-interrupter type, unless mechanically or electrically interlocked with a load-interrupting device arranged to reduce the load to the interrupting capability of the switch.

(c) Distribution Cutouts and Fuse Links — Expulsion Type.

(1) Installation. Cutouts shall be so located that they may be readily and safely operated and re-fused, and so that the exhaust of the fuses will not endanger persons. Distribution cutouts shall not be used indoors, underground, or in metal enclosures.

(2) Operation. Where fused cutouts are not suitable to interrupt the circuit manually while carrying full load, an approved means shall be installed to interrupt the entire load. Unless the fused cutouts are interlocked with the switch to prevent opening of the cutouts under load, a conspicuous sign shall be placed at such cutouts reading, "WARNING — DO NOT OPEN UNDER LOAD."

(3) Interrupting Rating. The interrupting rating of distribution cutouts shall not be less than the maximum fault current the cutout will be required to interrupt, including contributions from all connected sources of energy.

(4) Voltage Rating. The maximum voltage rating of cutouts shall not be less than the maximum circuit voltage.

(5) Identification. Distribution cutouts shall have on their body, door, or fuse tube a permanent and legible nameplate or identification showing the manufacturer's type or designation, continuous current rating, maximum voltage rating, and interrupting rating.

(6) Fuse Links. Fuse links shall have a permanent and legible identification showing continuous current rating and type.

(7) Structure Mounted Outdoors. The height of cutouts mounted outdoors on structures shall provide safe clearance between lowest energized parts (open or closed position) and standing surfaces, in accordance with Section 110-34(e).

(d) Oil-Filled Cutouts.

(1) Continuous Current Rating. The continuous current rating of oil-filled cutouts shall not be less than the maximum continuous current through the cutout.

(2) Interrupting Rating. The interrupting rating of oil-filled cutouts shall not be less than the maximum fault current the oil-filled cutout will be required to interrupt, including contributions from all connected sources of energy.

(3) Voltage Rating. The maximum voltage rating of oil-filled cutouts shall not be less than the maximum circuit voltage.

(4) Fault Closing Rating. Oil-filled cutouts shall have a fault closing rating not less than the maximum asymmetrical fault current that can occur at the cutout location, unless suitable interlocks or operating procedures preclude the possibility of closing into a fault.

(5) Identification. Oil-filled cutouts shall have a permanent and legible nameplate showing the rated continuous current, rated maximum voltage, and rated interrupting current.

(6) Fuse Links. Fuse links shall have a permanent and legible identification showing the rated continuous current.

(7) Location. Cutouts shall be so located that they will be readily and safely accessible for re-fusing, with the top of the cutout not over 5 feet (1.52 m) above the floor or platform.

(8) Enclosure. Suitable barriers or enclosures shall be provided to prevent contact with nonshielded cables or energized parts of oil-filled cutouts.

(e) Load Interrupters. Load-interrupter switches shall be permitted if suitable fuses or circuit breakers are used in conjunction with these devices to interrupt fault currents. Where these devices are used in combination, they shall be so coordinated electrically that they will safely withstand the effects of closing, carrying, or interrupting all possible currents up to the assigned maximum short-circuit rating.

(1) Continuous Current Rating. The continous current rating of interrupter switches shall equal or exceed the maximum continuous current at the point of installation.

(2) Voltage Rating. The maximum voltage rating of interrupter switches shall equal or exceed the maximum circuit voltage.

(3) Identification. Interrupter switches shall have a permanent and legible nameplate including the following information: manufacturer's type or designation, continuous current rating, interrupting current rating, fault closing rating, maximum voltage rating.

(4) Switching of Conductors. The switching mechanism shall be arranged to be operated from a location where the operator is not exposed to energized parts and shall be arranged to open all ungrounded conductors of the circuit simultaneously with one operation. Switches shall be arranged to be locked in the open position. Metal-enclosed switches shall be operable from outside the enclosure.

(5) Stored Energy for Opening. The stored energy operator shall be permitted to be left in the uncharged position after the switch has been closed if a single movement of the operating handle charges the operator and opens the switch.

(6) Supply Terminals. Fused interrupter switches shall be so installed that all supply terminals shall be at the top of the switch enclosure.

Exception: Supply terminals are not required to be at the top of the switch enclosure if barriers are installed to prevent persons from accidentally contacting energized parts or dropping tools or fuses into energized parts.

710-22. Isolating Means. Means shall be provided to completely isolate an item of equipment. The use of isolating switches shall not be required where there are other ways of de-energizing the equipment for inspection and repairs, such as drawout-type metal-enclosed switchgear units and removable truck panels.

Isolating switches not interlocked with an approved circuit-interrupting device shall be provided with a sign warning against opening them under load.

A fuseholder and fuse, designed for the purpose, shall be permitted as an isolating switch.

710-23. Voltage Regulators. Proper switching sequence for regulators shall be assured by use of one of the following: (1) mechanically sequenced regulator bypass switch(es); (2) mechanical interlocks; or (3) switching procedure prominently displayed at the switching location.

710-24. Metal-Enclosed Power Switchgear and Industrial Control Assemblies.

(a) Scope. This section covers assemblies of metal-enclosed power switchgear and industrial control, including but not limited to switches, interrupting devices and their control, metering, protection and regulating equipment, where an integral part of the assembly, with associated interconnections and supporting structures. This section also includes metal-enclosed power switchgear assemblies that form a part of unit substations, power centers, or similar equipment.

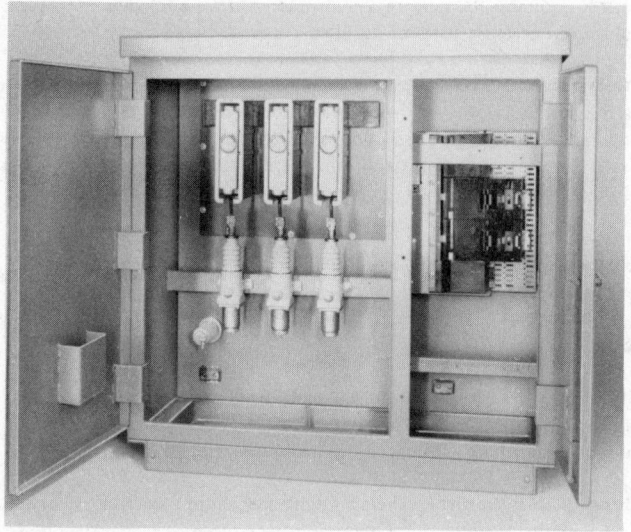

Figure 710-2. A 300-kVA, 15-kV pad-mounted transformer integral unit containing a primary hook-stick operated switch with a limited number of secondary breakers or switches. (*Square D Co.*)

(b) Arrangement of Devices in Assemblies. Arrangement of devices in assemblies shall be such that individual components can safely perform their intended function without adversely affecting the safe operation of other components in the assembly.

(c) Guarding of High-Voltage Energized Parts Within a Compartment. When access for other than visual inspection is required to a compartment that contains energized high-voltage parts, barriers shall be provided as follows:

(1) To prevent accidental contact with energized parts.

Exception No. 1: Fuse and fuseholder designed to permit fuse replacement by qualified persons using equipment designed for the purpose without de-energizing the fuseholder.

Exception No. 2: Exposed live parts shall be permitted within the compartment where accessible to qualified persons only.

(2) To prevent tools or other equipment from being dropped on energized parts.

(d) Guarding of Low-Voltage Energized Parts Within a Compartment. Energized bare parts mounted on doors shall be guarded where the door must be opened for maintenance of equipment or removal of drawout equipment.

(e) Clearance for Cable Conductors Entering Enclosure. The unobstructed space opposite terminals or opposite conduits or other raceways entering a switchgear or control assembly shall be adequate for the type of conductor and method of termination.

(f) Accessibility of Energized Parts.

(1) Doors which would provide nonqualified persons access to high-voltage energized parts shall be locked.

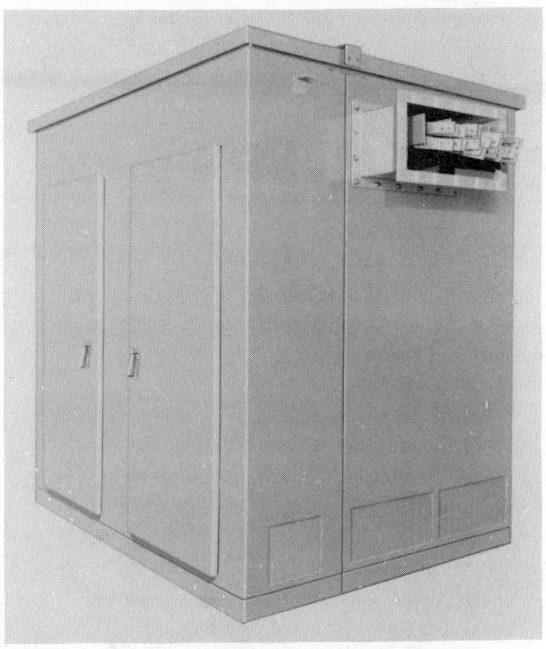

Figure 710-3. A 1,500-kVA, 15-kV unit substation transformer or power center type which is adaptable to a line-up of a high-voltage switch, transformer, and low-voltage secondary. (*Square D Co.*)

(2) Low-voltage control equipment, relays, motors, and the like shall not be installed in compartments with exposed high-voltage energized parts or high-voltage wiring unless the access door or cover is interlocked with the high-voltage switch or disconnecting means to prevent door or cover from being opened or removed unless the switch or disconnecting means is in its isolating position.

Exception No. 1: Instrument or control transformers connected to high voltage.

Exception No. 2: Space heaters.

(g) Grounding. Frames of switchgear and control assemblies shall be grounded.

(h) Grounding of Devices. Devices with metal cases and/or frames, such as instruments, relays, meters, and instrument and control transformers, located in or on switchgear or control, shall have the frame or case grounded.

(i) Door Stops and Cover Plates. External hinged doors or covers shall be provided with stops to hold them in the open position. Cover plates intended to be removed for inspection of energized parts or wiring shall be equipped with lifting handles and shall not exceed 12 square feet (1.11 sq m) in area or 60 pounds (27.22 kg) in weight, unless they are hinged and bolted or locked.

(j) Gas Discharge from Interrupting Devices. Gas discharged during operating of interrupting devices shall be so directed as not to endanger personnel.

(k) Inspection Windows. Windows intended for inspection of disconnecting switches or other devices shall be of suitable transparent material.

(l) Location of Devices. Control and instrument transfer switch handles or pushbuttons shall be in a readily accessible location at an elevation not over 78 inches (1.98 m).

Exception No. 1: Operating handles requiring more than 50 pounds (22.68 kg) of force shall not be higher than 66 inches (1.68 m) in either the open or closed position.

Exception No. 2: Operating handles for infrequently operated devices, such as drawout fuses, fused potential or control transformers and their primary disconnects, and bus transfer switches, shall not be required to be readily accessible, where they are otherwise safely operable and serviceable from a portable platform.

(m) Interlocks — Interrupter Switches. Interrupter switches equipped with stored energy mechanisms shall have mechanical interlocks to prevent access to the switch compartment unless the stored energy mechanism is in the discharged or blocked position.

(n) Stored Energy for Opening. The stored energy operator may be left in the uncharged position after the switch has been closed if a single movement of the operating handle charges the operator and opens the switch.

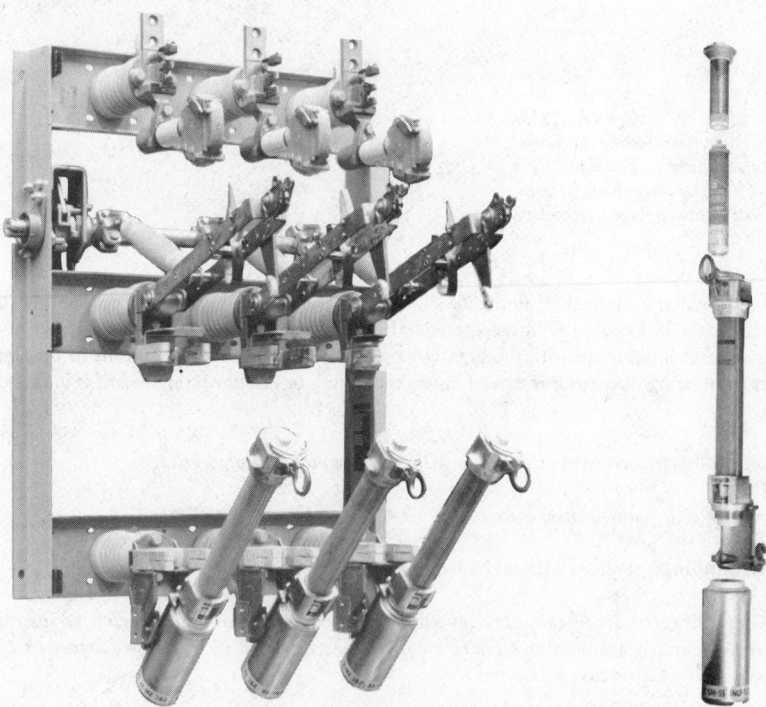

Figure 710-4 (left) Group-operated interrupter-switch and power-fuse combination rated at 13.8 kV, 600 A continuous and interrupting, 40,000 A momentary, 40,000 A fault closing. Figure 710-5 (right). Components of the indoor solid-material (SM) power fuseholder (boric-acid arc-extinguishing type) with a 14.4 kV, 400 E A max, 40,000 A RMS asym. interrupting rating. Shown here are the spring and cable assembly, refill unit, holder, and snuffler. (S & C Electric Co.)

(o) Fused Interrupter Switches.

(1) Fused interrupter switches shall be so installed that all supply terminals shall be at the top of the switch enclosure.

Exception: Supply terminals shall not be required to be at the top of the switch enclosure if barriers are installed to prevent persons from accidentally contacting energized parts or dropping tools or fuses into energized parts.

(2) Where fuses can be energized by backfeed, a sign shall be placed on the enclosure door reading, "WARNING — FUSES MAY BE ENERGIZED BY BACKFEED."

(p) Interlocks — Circuit Breakers.

(1) Circuit breakers equipped with stored energy mechanisms shall be designed to prevent the release of the stored energy unless the mechanism has been fully charged.

(2) Mechanical interlocks shall be provided in the housing to prevent the complete withdrawal of the circuit breaker from the housing when the stored energy mechanism is in the fully charged position.

Exception: Where a suitable device is provided that prevents the complete withdrawal of the circuit breaker unless the closing function is blocked.

D. Installations Accessible to Qualified Persons Only

710-31. Enclosure for Electrical Installations. See Section 110-31.

710-32. Circuit Conductors. Circuit conductors shall be permitted to be installed in raceways, in cable trays, as metal-clad cable, as bare wire, cable, and busbars, or as nonmetallic-sheathed cables, or conductors as provided in Sections 710-3 through 710-6. Bare live conductors shall conform with Sections 710-33 and 710-34.

Insulators, together with their mounting and conductor attachments, where used as supports for wires, single-conductor cables, or busbars, shall be capable of safely withstanding the maximum magnetic forces that would prevail when two or more conductors of a circuit were subjected to short-circuit current.

Open runs of insulated wires and cables having a bare lead sheath or a braided outer covering shall be supported in a manner designed to prevent physical damage to the braid or sheath. Supports for lead-covered cables shall be designed to prevent electrolysis of the sheath.

710-33. Minimum Space Separation. In field-fabricated installations, the minimum air separation between bare live conductors and between such conductors and adjacent grounded surfaces shall not be less than the values given in Table 710-33. These values shall not apply to interior portions or exterior terminals of equipment designed, manufactured, and tested in accordance with accepted national standards.

710-34. Work Space and Guarding. See Section 110-34.

E. Mobile and Portable Equipment

710-41. General.

(a) Covered. The provisions of this part shall apply to installations and use of high-voltage power distribution and utilization equipment which is portable and/or mobile, such as substations and switch houses mounted on skids, trailers, or cars, mobile shovels, draglines, cranes, hoists, drills, dredges, compressors, pumps, conveyors, underground excavators, and the like.

Table 710-33. Minimum Clearance of Live Parts*

Nominal Voltage Rating, kV	Impulse Withstand, B.I.L. kV		Minimum Clearance of Live Parts, in Inches			
			Phase-to-Phase		Phase-to-Ground	
	Indoors	Outdoors	Indoors	Outdoors	Indoors	Outdoors
2.4-4.16	60	95	4.5	7	3.0	6
7.2	75	95	5.5	7	4.0	6
13.8	95	110	7.5	12	5.0	7
14.4	110	110	9.0	12	6.5	7
23	125	150	10.5	15	7.5	10
34.5	150	150	12.5	15	9.5	10
	200	200	18.0	18	13.0	13
46		200		18		13
		250		21		17
69		250		21		17
		350		31		25
115		550		53		42
138		550		53		42
		650		63		50
161		650		63		50
		750		72		58
230		750		72		58
		900		89		71
		1050		105		83

For SI units: one inch = 25.4 millimeters.

* The values given are the minimum clearance for rigid parts and bare conductors under favorable service conditions. They shall be increased for conductor movement or under unfavorable service conditions, or wherever space limitations permit. The selection of the associated impulse withstand voltage for a particular system voltage is determined by the characteristics of the surge protective equipment.

(b) **Other Requirements.** The requirements of this part shall be additional to, or amendatory of, those prescribed in Articles 100 through 725 of this Code. Special attention shall be paid to Article 250.

(c) **Protection.** Adequate enclosures and/or guarding shall be provided to protect portable and mobile equipment from physical damage.

(d) **Disconnecting Means.** Disconnecting means shall be installed for mobile and portable high-voltage equipment according to the requirements of Part K of Article 230 and shall disconnect all ungrounded conductors.

710-42. Overcurrent Protection. Motors driving single or multiple dc generators supplying a system operating on a cyclic load basis do not require running overcurrent protection, provided that the thermal rating of the ac drive motor cannot be exceeded under any operating condition. However, the branch-circuit protective device(s), which may be external to the equipment, shall provide short-circuit and locked-rotor protection.

710-43. Enclosures. All energized switching and control parts shall be enclosed in effectively grounded metal cabinets or enclosures. These cabinets or enclosures shall be marked "WARNING — HIGH VOLTAGE" and shall be locked so that only authorized and qualified persons can enter. Circuit breakers and protective equipment shall have the operating means projecting through the metal cabinet or enclosure so these units can be reset without opening locked doors. With doors closed, reasonable safe access for normal operation of these units shall be provided.

710-44. Collector Rings. The collector ring assemblies on revolving-type machines (shovels, draglines, etc.) shall be guarded to prevent accidental contact with energized parts by personnel on or off the machine.

710-45. Power Cable Connections to Mobile Machines. A metallic enclosure shall be provided on the mobile machine for enclosing the terminals of the power cable. The enclosure shall include provisions for a solid connection for the ground wire(s) terminal to effectively ground the machine frame. Ungrounded conductors shall be attached to insulators or terminated in approved high-voltage cable couplers (which include ground wire connectors) of proper voltage and ampere rating. The method of cable termination used shall prevent any strain or pull on the cable from stressing the electrical connections. The enclosure shall have provision for locking so only authorized and qualified persons may open, and shall be marked "WARNING — HIGH VOLTAGE."

710-46. High-Voltage Portable Cable for Main Power Supply. Flexible high-voltage cable supplying power to portable or mobile equipment shall comply with Article 250 and Article 400, Part C.

710-47. Grounding. Mobile equipment shall be grounded in accordance with Article 250.

F. Tunnel Installations

710-51. General.

(a) **Covered.** The provisions of this part shall apply to installation and use of high-voltage power distribution and utilization equipment which is portable and/or mobile, such as substations, trailers, or cars, mobile shovels, draglines, hoists, drills, dredges, compressors, pumps, conveyors, underground excavators, and the like.

(b) **Other Articles.** The requirements of this part shall be additional to, or amendatory of, those prescribed in Articles 100 through 710 of this Code. Special attention shall be paid to Article 250.

(c) **Protection Against Physical Damage.** Conductors and cables in tunnels shall be located above the tunnel floor and so placed or guarded to protect them from physical damage.

710-52. Overcurrent Protection. Motor-operated equipment shall be protected from overcurrent in accordance with Article 430. Transformers shall be protected from overcurrent in accordance with Article 450.

710-53. Conductors. High-voltage conductors in tunnels shall be installed in (1) metal conduit or other metal raceway; (2) Type MC cable; or (3) other approved multiconductor cable. Multiconductor portable cable shall be permitted to supply mobile equipment.

710-54. Bonding and Equipment Grounding Conductor.

(a) **Grounded and Bonded.** All nonenergized metal parts of electric equipment and all metal raceways and cable sheaths shall be effectively grounded and bonded to all metal pipes and rails at the portal and at intervals not exceeding 1000 feet (305 m) throughout the tunnel.

(b) **Equipment Grounding Conductor.** An equipment grounding conductor shall be run with circuit conductors inside the metal raceway or inside the multiconductor cable jacket. The equipment grounding conductor shall be permitted to be insulated or bare.

710-55. Transformers, Switches, and Electric Equipment. All transformers, switches, motor controllers, motors, rectifiers, and other equipment installed below ground shall be protected from physical damage by location or guarding.

710-56. Energized Parts. Bare terminals of transformers, switches, motor controllers, and other equipment shall be enclosed to prevent accidental contact with energized parts.

710-57. Ventilation System Controls. Electrical controls for the ventilation system shall be so arranged that the air flow can be reversed.

710-58. Disconnecting Means. A switching device meeting the requirements of Article 430 or 450 shall be installed at each transformer or motor location for disconnecting the transformer or motor. The switching device shall open all ungrounded conductors of a circuit simultaneously.

710-59. Enclosures. Enclosures for use in tunnels shall be dripproof, weatherproof, or submersible as required by the environmental conditions. Switch or contactor enclosures shall not be used as junction boxes or raceways for conductors feeding through or tapping off to other switches, unless special designs are used to provide adequate space for this purpose.

710-60. Grounding. Tunnel equipment shall be grounded in accordance with Article 250.

G. Electrode-type Boilers

710-70. General. The provisions of this part shall apply to boilers operating over 600 volts, nominal, in which heat is generated by the passage of current between electrodes through the liquid being heated.

710-71. Electric Supply System. Electrode-type boilers shall be supplied only from a 3-phase, 4-wire solidly grounded wye system, or from isolating transformers arranged to provide such a system. Control circuit voltages shall not exceed 150 volts, shall be supplied from a grounded system, and shall have the controls in the ungrounded conductor.

710-72. Branch Circuit Requirements.

(a) **Rating.** Each boiler shall be supplied from an individual branch circuit rated not less than 100 percent of the total load.

(b) **Common-Trip Fault Interrupting Device.** The circuit shall be protected by a 3-phase common-trip fault interrupting device, which shall be permitted to automatically reclose the circuit upon removal of an overload condition but shall not reclose after a fault condition.

(c) **Phase Fault Protection.** Phase fault protection shall be provided in each phase, consisting of a separate phase overcurrent relay connected to a separate current transformer in the phase.

(d) **Ground Current Detection.** Means shall be provided for detection of the sum of the neutral and ground currents and shall trip the circuit interrupting device if the sum of those currents exceeds the greater of 5 amperes or 7½ percent of the boiler full-load current for 10 seconds or exceeds an instantaneous value of 25 percent of the boiler full-load current.

(e) **Grounded Neutral Conductor.** The grounded neutral conductor shall:

(1) Be connected to the pressure vessel containing the electrodes.

(2) Be insulated for not less than 600 volts.

(3) Have not less than the ampacity of the largest ungrounded branch-circuit conductor.

(4) Be installed in the same raceway or cable tray with the ungrounded conductors.

(5) Not be used for any other circuit.

710-73. Pressure and Temperature Limit Control. Each boiler shall be equipped with a means to limit the maximum temperature and/or pressure by directly or indirectly interrupting all current flow through the electrodes. Such means shall be in addition to the temperature and/or pressure regulating systems and pressure relief or safety valves.

710-74. Grounding. All exposed noncurrent-carrying metal parts of the boiler and associated exposed grounded structures or equipment shall be bonded to the pressure vessel or to the neutral conductor to which the vessel is connected, in accordance with Section 250-79, except the ampacity of the bonding jumper shall be not less than the ampacity of the neutral conductor.

ARTICLE 720 — CIRCUITS AND EQUIPMENT
OPERATING AT LESS THAN 50 VOLTS

Contents

720-1. Scope. This article covers installations operating at less than 50 volts, direct current or alternating current.

Exception: As covered in Articles 650, 725, and 760.

720-2. Hazardous (Classified) Locations. Installations coming within the scope of this article and installed in hazardous (classified) locations shall also comply with the appropriate provisions of Articles 500 through 517.

It should be noted that low voltage alone does not make a circuit incapable of igniting flammable atmospheres. Under some conditions, even ordinary flashlights using two 1½-V "D" cells can be a source of ignition in hazardous (classified) locations.

720-4. Conductors. Conductors shall not be smaller than No. 12 copper or equivalent. Conductors for appliance branch circuits supplying more than one appliance or appliance receptacle shall not be smaller than No. 10 copper or equivalent.

720-5. Lampholders. Standard lampholders having a rating of not less than 660 watts shall be used.

720-6. Receptacle Rating. Receptacles shall have a rating of not less than 15 amperes.

720-7. Receptacles Required. Receptacles of not less than 20-ampere rating shall be provided in kitchens, laundries, and other locations where portable appliances are likely to be used.

720-8. Overcurrent Protection. Overcurrent protection shall comply with Article 240.

720-9. Batteries. Installations of storage batteries shall comply with Article 480.

720-10. Grounding. Grounding shall comply with Sections 250-5(a) and 250-45.

ARTICLE 725 — CLASS 1, CLASS 2, AND CLASS 3 REMOTE-CONTROL, SIGNALING, AND POWER-LIMITED CIRCUITS

Contents

A. Scope and General

725-1. Scope. This article covers remote-control, signaling, and power-limited circuits that are not an integral part of a device or appliance.

(FPN): The circuits described herein are characterized by usage and electrical power limitations which differentiate them from electric light and power circuits and, therefore, special consideration is given with regard to minimum wire sizes, derating factors, overcurrent protection, and conductor insulation requirements.

Included within the scope of Article 725 are such systems as burglar alarm circuits (a signaling system) and the coaxial cable wiring often associated with interconnection of electronic data processing (EDP) and computer equipment not within a data processing room as covered in Article 645. See Article 760 for fire protective signaling systems, Article 800 for communication circuits, Article 810 for radio and television equipment other than cable TV, and Article 820 for cable TV systems.

725-2. Locations and Other Articles. Circuits and equipment shall comply with (a), (b), (c), (d), and (e) below.

(a) Prevention of Spread of Fire or Products of Combustion. Section 300-21.

(b) Ducts, Plenums and Other Air-Handling Spaces. Section 300-22 where installed in ducts or plenums or other space used for environmental air.

Exception to (b): Single- and multiconductor cables of Class 2 and Class 3 circuits listed as having adequate fire-resistant and low-smoke producing characteristics shall be permitted for ducts and plenums as described in Section 300-22(b) and other space used for environmental air as described in Section 300-22(c).

See commentary following Sections 300-22(b) and 300-22(c).

(FPN): One method of defining low-smoke producing materials is by establishing an acceptable value of the smoke produced per the UL 910 test to a maximum peak optical density of 0.5 and a maximum average optical density of 0.15.

(FPN): Similarly, fire-resistant cables may be defined as having a maximum allowable flame travel distance of 5.0 feet (1.52 m) in the UL 910 test.

Underwriters Laboratories Inc. (UL) classifies cables as having adequate fire-resistant and low-smoke producing characteristics in accordance with UL 910 and the exceptions to Sections 725-2(b), 760-4(d), 800-3(d), and 820-15. The cables are marked to indicate the *NEC* section for which they have been investigated.

The term "listed" as used in the *NEC* includes materials that have been "classified" by UL. See definition of "Listed" in Article 100.

(c) Hazardous (Classified) Locations. Articles 500 through 516, and Article 517, Part G where installed in hazardous (classified) locations.

(d) Cable Trays. Article 318 where installed in cable tray.

(e) Motor Control Circuits. Article 430, Part F where tapped from the load side of the motor branch-circuit protective device(s) as specified in Section 430-72(a).

725-3. Classifications. A remote-control, signaling, or power-limited circuit is the portion of the wiring system between the load side of the overcurrent device or the power-limited supply and all connected equipment, and shall be Class 1, Class 2, or Class 3 as defined in (a) and (b) below.

(a) Class 1 Circuits. Circuits that comply with Part B of this article and in which the voltage and power limitations are in accordance with Section 725-11.

(b) Class 2 and Class 3 Circuits. Circuits that comply with Part C of this article and in which the voltage and power limitations are in accordance with Section 725-31.

ARTICLE 725—REMOTE-CONTROL, SIGNALING CIRCUITS

(FPN): Due to their power limitations, both Class 2 and 3 circuits consider safety from a fire initiation standpoint. In addition, Class 2 circuits provide acceptable protection from electric shock. However, since Class 3 circuits permit higher allowable levels of voltage and current, additional safeguards are specified to provide protection against the electric shock hazard that could be encountered.

725-4. Safety-Control Equipment. Remote-control circuits to safety-control equipment shall be Class 1 if the failure of the equipment to operate introduces a direct fire or life hazard. Room thermostats, water temperature regulating devices, and similar controls used in conjunction with electrically controlled household heating and air conditioning shall not be considered safety-control equipment.

725-5. Communication Cables. Class 1 circuits shall not be run in the same cable with communication circuits. Class 2 and Class 3 circuit conductors shall be permitted in the same cable with communication circuits, in which case the Class 2 and Class 3 circuits shall be classified as communication circuits and shall meet the requirements of Article 800.

B. Class 1 Circuits

725-11. Power Limitations for Class 1 Circuits.

(a) Class 1 Power-Limited Circuits. These circuits shall be supplied from a source having a rated output of not more than 30 volts and 1000 volt-amperes. The source shall be protected by overcurrent devices rated at not more than 167 percent of the volt-ampere rating of the source divided by the rated voltage. The overcurrent devices shall not be interchangeable with overcurrent devices of higher ratings. The overcurrent device shall be permitted to be an integral part of the power supply.

(1) Transformers. Transformers used to supply power-limited Class 1 circuits shall comply with Article 450.

(2) Other Power Sources. To comply with the 1000 volt-ampere limitation of Section 725-11(a), the maximum output of power sources other than transformers shall be limited to 2500 volt-amperes and the product of the maximum current and maximum voltage shall not exceed 10,000 volt-amperes. These ratings shall be determined with any overcurrent protective device bypassed.

(FPN): For definitions of V_{max}, I_{max}, VA_{max}, see Note 1, Tables 725-31(a) and (b).

(b) Class 1 Remote-Control and Signaling Circuits. Class 1 remote-control and signaling circuits shall not exceed 600 volts; however, the power output of the source shall not be required to be limited.

725-12. Overcurrent Protection. Conductors No. 14 and larger shall be protected against overcurrent in accordance with their ampacities. The ampacities shall be those given in Tables 310-16 through 310-19, without derating factors. Overcurrent protection shall not exceed 7 amperes for No. 18 conductors and 10 amperes for No. 16.

Exception No. 1: Where other articles of this Code permit or require other overcurrent protection.

(FPN): For example, see Section 430-72 for motors and Section 610-53 for cranes and hoists.

See Section 240-4, Exception No. 2 for another example.

Exception No. 2: Transformer Secondary Conductors. Class 1 circuit conductors supplied by the secondary of a single-phase transformer having only a 2-wire (single-voltage) secondary shall be permitted to be protected by overcurrent protection provided on the primary (supply) side of the transformer, provided this protection is in accordance with Section 450-3 and does not exceed the value determined by multiplying the secondary conductor ampacity by the secondary-to-primary transformer voltage ratio. Transformer secondary conductors other than 2-wire shall not be considered to be protected by the primary overcurrent protection.

Exception No. 2 correlates with Section 240-3, Exception No. 5 and Section 430-72(b), Exception No. 3.

Exception No. 3: Class 1 circuit conductors No. 14 and larger which are tapped from the load side of the overcurrent protective device(s) of the controlled light and power circuit shall require only short-circuit and ground-fault protection and shall be permitted to be protected by the branch-circuit overcurrent protective device(s) where the rating of the protective device(s) is not more than 300 percent of the ampacity of the Class 1 circuit conductor.

Exception No. 3 correlates with Section 240-3, Exception No. 4.

725-13. Location of Overcurrent Devices. Overcurrent devices shall be located at the point where the conductor to be protected receives its supply.

Exception: Where the overcurrent device protecting the larger conductor also protects the smaller conductor.

725-14. Wiring Method. Installations of Class 1 circuits shall be in accordance with the appropriate articles in Chapter 3.

Exception No. 1: As provided in Sections 725-15 through 725-17.

Exception No. 2: Where other articles of this Code permit or require other methods.

725-15. Conductors of Different Circuits in Same Enclosure, Cable, or Raceway. Class 1 circuits shall be permitted to occupy the same enclosure, cable, or raceway without regard to whether the individual circuits are alternating current or direct current, provided all conductors are insulated for the maximum voltage of any conductor in the enclosure, cable, or raceway. Power supply and Class 1 circuit conductors shall be permitted in the same enclosure, cable, or raceway only where the equipment powered is functionally associated.

Exception: When installed in factory- or field-assembled control centers.

725-16. Conductors.

(a) Sizes and Use. Conductors of Nos. 18 and 16 shall be permitted to be used provided they supply loads that do not exceed the ampacities given in Section 402-5 and are installed in a raceway or a listed cable. Conductors larger than No. 16 shall not supply loads greater than the ampacities given in Tables 310-16 through 310-19. Flexible cords shall comply with Article 400.

(b) Insulation. Insulation on conductors shall be suitable for 600 volts. Conductors larger than No. 16 shall comply with Article 310. Conductors in sizes No. 18 and 16 shall be Type RFH-2, RFHH-2, RFHH-3, FFH-2, TF, TFF, TFN, TFFN, PF, PFF, PGF, PGFF, PTF, PTFF, SF-2, SFF-2, PAF, PAFF, ZF, ZFF, KF-2, or KFF-2. Conductors with other types and thicknesses of insulation shall be permitted if listed for Class 1 circuit use.

725-17. Number of Conductors in Raceways, Cable Trays, and Cables, and Derating.

(a) Class 1 Circuits. Where only Class 1 circuits are in a raceway, the number of conductors shall be determined in accordance with Section 300-17. The derating factors given in Note 8 to Tables 310-16 through 310-19 shall apply only if such conductors carry continuous loads.

(b) Power-Supply Conductors and Class 1 Circuit Conductors. Where power-supply conductors and Class 1 circuit conductors are permitted in a raceway in accordance with Section 725-15, the number of conductors shall be determined in accordance with Section 300-17. The derating factors given in Note 8 to Tables 310-16 through 310-19 shall apply as follows:

(1) To all conductors when the Class 1 circuit conductors carry continuous loads and where the total number of conductors is more than three.

(2) To the power-supply conductors only, when the Class 1 circuit conductors do not carry continuous loads and where the number of power-supply conductors is more than three.

(c) Class 1 Circuit Conductors in Cable Trays. Where Class 1 circuit conductors are installed in cable trays they shall comply with the provisions of Sections 318-8 through 318-10.

725-18. Physical Protection. Where damage to remote-control circuits of safety control equipment would introduce a hazard, as covered in Section 725-4, all conductors of such remote-control circuits shall be installed in rigid metal conduit, intermediate metal conduit, rigid nonmetallic conduit, electrical metallic tubing, Type MI cable, Type MC cable, or be otherwise suitably protected from physical damage.

725-19. Circuits Extending Beyond One Building. Class 1 circuits that extend aerially beyond one building shall also meet the requirements of Article 225.

725-20. Grounding. Class 1 circuits and equipment shall be grounded in accordance with Article 250.

C. Class 2 and Class 3 Circuits

725-31. Power Limitations of Class 2 and Class 3 Circuits. As specified in Table 725-31(a) for ac circuits and Table 725-31(b) for dc circuits, the power for Class 2 and Class 3 circuits shall be either inherently limited requiring no overcurrent protection or limited by a combination of a power source and overcurrent protection.

725-32. Interconnection of Power Supplies. Class 2 or Class 3 power supplies shall not be paralleled or otherwise interconnected unless listed for such interconnection.

725-34. Marking. A Class 2 or Class 3 power supply unit shall be durably marked where plainly visible to indicate the class of supply and its electrical rating.

725-35. Overcurrent Protection. Where overcurrent protection is required, the overcurrent protective devices shall not be interchangeable with devices of higher ratings. The overcurrent device shall be permitted as an integral part of the power supply.

725-36. Location of Overcurrent Devices. Overcurrent devices shall be located at the point where the conductor to be protected receives its supply.

725-37. Wiring Methods on Supply Side. Conductors and equipment on the supply side of overcurrent protection, transformers, or current-limiting devices shall be installed in accordance with the appropriate requirements of Chapter 3. Transformers or other devices supplied from electric light or power circuits shall be protected by an overcurrent device rated not over 20 amperes.

Exception: The input leads of a transformer or other power source supplying Class 2 and Class 3 circuits shall be permitted to be smaller than No. 14, but not smaller than No. 18 if they are not over 12 inches (305 mm) long and if they have insulation that complies with Section 725-16(b).

Table 725-31(a). Power Limitations for Alternating Current (Class 2 and Class 3 Circuits)

Circuit	Inherently Limited Power Source (Overcurrent protection not required)				Not Inherently Limited Power Source (Overcurrent protection required)			
	Class 2		Class 3		Class 2			Class 3
	0-20†	Over 20-30†	Over 30-150	Over 30-100	0-20†	Over 20-30†	Over 30-100	Over 100-150
Circuit Voltage V_{max} (Note 1)								
Power Limitation $(VA)_{max}$ (Note 1) (Volt-Amps)	—	—	—	—	250 (see Note 3)	250	250	N.A.
Current Limitation I_{max} (Note 1) (Amps)	8.0	8.0	0.005	$150/V_{max}$	$1000/V_{max}$	$1000/V_{max}$	$1000/V_{max}$	1.0
Maximum Overcurrent Protection (Amps)	—	—	—	—	5.0	$100/V_{max}$	$100/V_{max}$	1.0
Power Source Maximum Nameplate Ratings — VA (Volt-Amps)	$5.0 \times V_{max}$	100	$0.005 \times V_{max}$	100	$5.0 \times V_{max}$	100	100	100
Current (Amps)	5.0	$100/V_{max}$	0.005	$100/V_{max}$	5.0	$100/V_{max}$	$100/V_{max}$	$100/V_{max}$
Supply Conductors and Cables	See Section 725-37							
Circuit Conductors and Cables	See Section 725-40							

† Voltage ranges shown are for sinusoidal ac in indoor locations or where wet contact is not likely to occur. For nonsinusoidal or wet contact conditions, see Note 2.

Table 725-31(b). Power Limitations for Direct Current (Class 2 and Class 3 Circuits).

Circuit	Inherently Limited Power Source (Note 4) (Overcurrent protection not required)					Not Inherently Limited Power Source (Overcurrent protection required)			
	Class 2			Class 3		Class 2		Class 3	
Circuit Voltage V_{max} (Note 1)	0-20††	Over 20-30††	Over 30-60††	Over 60-150	Over 60-100	0-20††	Over 20-60††	Over 60-100	Over 100-150
Power Limitation $(VA)_{max}$ (Note 1) (Volt-Amps)	—	—	—	0.005	—	250 (see Note 3)	250	250	N.A.
Current Limitation I_{max} (Note 1) (Amps)	8.0	8.0	$150/V_{max}$	—	$150/V_{max}$	$1000/V_{max}$	$1000/V_{max}$	$1000/V_{max}$	1.0
Maximum Overcurrent Protection (Amps)	—	—	—	—	—	5.0	100	100	1.0
Power Source Maximum Nameplate Ratings — VA (Volt-Amps)	$5.0 \times V_{max}$	100	100	$0.005 \times V_{max}$	100	$5.0 \times V_{max}$	100	100	100
Power Source Maximum Nameplate Ratings — Current (Amps)	5.0	$100/V_{max}$	$100/V_{max}$	0.005	$100/V_{max}$	5.0	$100/V_{max}$	$100/V_{max}$	$100/V_{max}$
Supply Conductors and Cables	See Section 725-37					See Section 725-40			
Circuit Conductors and Cables	See Sections 725-31(a) and (b)								

†† Voltage ranges shown are for continuous dc in indoor locations or where wet contact is not likely to occur. For interrupted dc or wet contact conditions, see Note 5.

Notes for Tables 725-31(a) and (b)

Note 1. V_{max}: Maximum output voltage regardless of load with rated input applied. I_{max}: Maximum output current under any noncapacitive load, including short circuit, and with overcurrent protection bypassed if used. VA_{max}: Maximum volt-ampere output regardless of load and overcurrent protection bypassed if used. Note 2. For nonsinusoidal ac, V_{max} shall be not greater than 42.4 volts peak. Where wet contact (immersion not included) is likely to occur, Class 3 wiring methods shall be used or V_{max} shall be not greater than: 15 volts for sinusoidal ac: 21.2 volts peak for nonsinusoidal ac. Note 3. If the power source is a transformer, $(VA)_{max}$ is 350 or less when V_{max} is 15 or less. Note 4. A dry cell battery shall be considered an inherently limited power source provided the voltage is 30 volts or less and the capacity is equal to or less than that available from series connected No. 6 carbon zinc cells. Note 5. For dc interrupted at a rate of 10 to 200 Hz, V_{max} shall not be greater than 24.8 volts. Where wet contact (immersion not included) is likely to occur, Class 3 wiring methods shall be used or V_{max} shall not be greater than: 30 volts for continuous dc; 12.4 volts for dc that is interrupted at a rate of 10 to 200 Hz.

725-38. Wiring Methods on Load Side. Conductors on the load side of overcurrent protection, transformers, and current-limiting devices shall be insulated at not less than the requirements of Section 725-40 and shall comply with (a) and (b) below.

(a) Separation from Electric Light, Power, and Class 1 Conductors.

(1) Open Conductors. Conductors of Class 2 and Class 3 circuits shall be separated at least 2 inches (50.8 mm) from conductors of any electric light, power, or Class 1 circuits.

Exception No. 1: Where the electric light or power, and Class 1 circuit conductors are in a raceway or in metal-sheathed, metal-clad, nonmetallic-sheathed, or Type UF cables.

Exception No. 2: Where the conductors are permanently separated from the conductors of the other circuits by a continuous and firmly fixed nonconductor, such as porcelain tubes or flexible tubing in addition to the insulation on the wire.

(2) In Enclosures, Raceways, Cable Trays, and Cables. Conductors of Class 2 and Class 3 circuits shall not be placed in any enclosure, raceway, cable tray, cable, compartment, outlet box, or similar fitting with conductors of electric light, power, and Class 1 circuits.

Exception No. 1: Where the conductors of the different circuits are separated by a partition.

Exception No. 2: Conductors in outlet boxes, junction boxes, or similar fittings, or compartments where power-supply conductors are introduced solely for supplying power to the equipment connected to Class 2 or Class 3 circuits to which the other conductors in the enclosure are connected.

An example would be power circuit and Class 2 circuit conductors in the same motor starter enclosure where the Class 2 circuit source is the secondary of a control transformer in the same motor starter enclosure. In such an installation, the Class 2 conductor insulation is not required to have the same voltage rating as the insulation on the power conductors in the same enclosure.

(3) In Shafts. Class 2 or Class 3 conductors run in the same shaft with conductors for electric light, power, or Class 1 circuits shall be separated by not less than 2 inches (50.8 mm) from the light, power, and Class 1 conductors.

Exception No. 1: Where the conductors of either the electric light, power, or Class 1 circuits or the Class 2 or Class 3 circuits are encased in noncombustible tubing.

Exception No. 2: Where the electric light, power, or Class 1 circuit conductors are in a raceway, or are in metal-sheathed, metal-clad, nonmetallic-sheathed, or Type UF cables.

(4) In Hoistways. Class 2 or Class 3 conductors shall be installed in rigid conduit, intermediate metal conduit, or electrical metallic tubing in hoistways.

Exception: As provided for in Section 620-21, Exceptions No. 1 and 2 for elevators and similar equipment.

(b) Vertical Runs. Conductors in a vertical run in a shaft or partition shall have a fire-resistant covering capable of preventing the carrying of fire from floor to floor.

Exception: Where conductors are encased in noncombustible tubing or other outer covering of noncombustible materials or are located in a fireproof shaft having fire stops at each floor.

ARTICLE 725—REMOTE-CONTROL, SIGNALING CIRCUITS

725-39. Conductors of Different Class 2 and Class 3 Circuits in Same Cable, Enclosure, or Raceway.

(a) Two or More Class 2 Circuits. Conductors of two or more Class 2 circuits shall be permitted within the same cable, enclosure, or raceway provided all conductors in the cable, enclosure, or raceway are insulated for the maximum voltage of any conductor.

(b) Two or More Class 3 Circuits. Conductors of two or more Class 3 circuits shall be permitted within the same cable, enclosure, or raceway.

(c) Class 2 Circuits with Class 3 Circuits. Conductors of one or more Class 2 circuits shall be permitted within the same cable, enclosure, or raceway with conductors of Class 3 circuits provided that the insulation of the Class 2 circuit conductors in the cable, enclosure, or raceway is at least that required for Class 3 circuits.

725-40. Conductors.

(a) Class 2 Circuits. The conductor material size and insulation shall be suitable for the particular application.

(FPN): The conductor insulation is not specified in further detail as reliance is placed on Class 2 power supplies which limit voltage and current to safe values.

Exception: Where the conductors are installed in (1) cable tray, (2) in hazardous (classified) locations except as permitted by Section 501-4(b), Exception, or (3) both, the conductors shall comply with (b)(3) below except conductors used for thermocouple circuits shall be permitted to be any of the materials used for thermocouple extension wire.

(b) Class 3 Circuits. Conductors shall comply with (1), (2), (3), or (4) below.

Exception: Where installed in cable tray or in hazardous (classified) locations, or both, conductors shall comply with (3) below.

(1) Single conductors shall not be smaller than No. 18 and shall be insulated in accordance with Section 725-16(b).

(2) Conductors of a multiconductor cable shall be of solid or stranded copper not smaller than No. 22, and shall have thermoplastic insulation of not less than 12 mils nominal (10 mils minimum) thickness. The cable conductors shall have an overall thermoplastic jacket having a nominal thickness of not less than 35 mils (30 mils minimum). Where the number of conductors in a cable exceeds four, the thickness of the thermoplastic jacket shall be increased so as to provide equivalent performance characteristics. Similarly, where the size of conductors in a cable exceeds No. 16, the thickness of the conductor insulation shall be increased so as to provide equivalent performance characteristics.

Exception No. 1: Cables with smaller conductors and other types and thicknesses of insulations and jackets shall be permitted, if listed for this use.

Exception No. 2: Two conductors assembled in a flat parallel construction with a 30-mil nominal integral insulation-jacket and a 47-mil minimum web shall be permitted.

(3) Type PLTC nonmetallic-sheathed, power-limited tray cable shall be a factory assembly of two or more insulated conductors under a nonmetallic jacket. The insulated conductors shall be a No. 22 through 12. The conductor material shall be copper (solid or stranded). Insulation on conductors shall be suitable for 300 volts. The cable core shall be either (1) two or more parallel conductors; (2) one or more group assemblies of twisted or parallel conductors; or (3) a combination thereof. A metallic shield or a metallized foil shield with drain wire(s) shall be permitted to be applied either over the cable core, over groups of conductors, or both. The outer jacket shall be a flame-retardant, sunlight- and moisture-resistant nonmetallic material. The cable shall be marked in accordance with Section 310-11. Where the use of PLTC cable is permitted in Section 501-4(b), the cable shall be installed in cable trays, in raceways, supported by messenger wires, or directly buried where the cable is listed for this use.

Exception: Where a smooth metallic sheath, welded and corrugated metallic sheath, or interlocking tape armor is applied over the nonmetallic jacket, an overall nonmetallic jacket shall not be required. On metallic-sheathed cable without an overall nonmetallic jacket, the information required in Section 310-11 shall be located on the nonmetallic jacket under the sheath.

(4) Approved power-limited (low-energy) circuit cable, Class 3 circuit cable, or other equivalent cable.

General Discussion of Remote-Control, Signaling, and Power-Limited Circuits.

The wiring methods required by Chapters 1 through 4 of the *Code* apply to remote-control, signaling, and power-limiting circuits, except as amended by Article 725 for the particular conditions.

A remote-control, signaling, or power-limited circuit is the portion of the wiring system between the load side of the overcurrent device or the power-limited supply and all connected equipment, and is separated into Class 1, Class 2, and Class 3 circuits.

Class 1 circuits are not to exceed 600 V. A remote-control circuit to safety control equipment is a Class 1 circuit if the failure of the safety control introduces a hazard to life or property. Room thermostats and water-temperature regulating devices used in conjunction with household heating and air-conditioning systems are not considered safety-control equipment. In many cases, Class 1 circuits are extensions of power systems and are subject to the requirements of the power systems, except for the following: (1) conductors sized Nos. 16 and 18 may be used if properly protected against overcurrent (see Section 725-12); (2) where damage to the circuit would introduce a hazard, the circuit is to be mechanically protected by a suitable means (see Section 725-18); (3) the derating factors of Note 8 to Tables 310-16 through 310-19 are to apply only if such conductors carry a continuous load (see Section 725-17).

Class 1 remote-control circuits are commonly used to operate motor-controllers in conjunction with moving equipment or mechanical processes, elevators, conveyors, and such equipment where it is necessary to control the equipment from one or more locations to prevent a hazard to life. Class 1 wiring is required in this case even though a low-voltage, low-energy system is used. See Section 725-4.

Another example of such a Class 1 circuit is a hospital nurses call system where it is intended that the system be used for issuing instructions during emergency conditions.

Class 1 signaling circuits often operate at 120 V, though not limited to this value, and are often used for alarm and security systems.

Conductors and equipment on the supply side of overcurrent protection, a transformer, or current-limiting devices of Class 2 and Class 3 circuits are required to be installed according to the applicable requirements of Chapter 3. Load-side conductors and equipment are required to comply with Article 725. They are required to be separated from, and not occupy the same raceways, cable trays, cables, or enclosures as electric light, power, and Class 1 conductors (exceptions are noted in Section 725-38).

Primary batteries are satisfactory with respect to current limitations provided the voltage is 30 or less and the capacity is equal to or less than that available from series connected No. 6 carbon zinc cells.

Where dry cells are used, the requirements of Note 4 to Tables 725-31(a) and 725-31(b) are applicable for inherent power limitation.

Figure 725-1 illustrates a simplified diagram of an automatic domestic oil burner unit. A thermostat is supplied by a current-limiting transformer at 24 V and the opening and closing of the thermostat contacts controls a relay that operates the oil burner ignition and pump motor. Failure of the thermostat would not introduce a hazard. Assume that the thermostat failed in the closed-contact position thereby energizing the ignition and motor. The Class 1 circuit, in this case an extension of the power circuit, would operate and open the circuit, that is the high-limit control (forced warm air) or pressure switch control (circulating hot water or steam). Therefore, the safety controls and ignition circuit would be considered a Class 1 circuit and the thermostat circuit would be considered a Class 2 circuit.

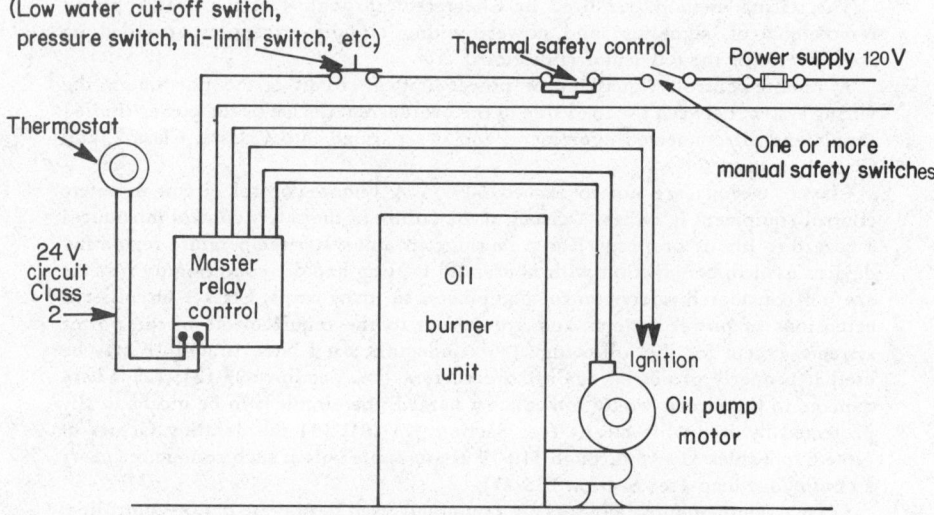

Figure 725-1. Typical installation of an automatic oil burner unit.

725-41. Circuits Extending Beyond One Building.
Class 2 or Class 3 circuits that extend beyond one building and are so run as to be subject to accidental contact with electric light or power conductors operating at over 300 volts to ground shall also meet the requirements of Sections 800-2, 800-11, and 800-12 for communication circuits.

725-42. Grounding.
Class 2 and Class 3 circuits and equipment shall be grounded in accordance with Article 250.

ARTICLE 760 — FIRE PROTECTIVE SIGNALING SYSTEMS

A. Scope and General

760-1. Scope. This article covers the installation of wiring and equipment of fire protective signaling systems operating at 600 volts, nominal, or less.

ARTICLE 760—FIRE PROTECTIVE SIGNALING SYSTEMS

(FPN): For further information for fire alarm, guard tour, sprinkler waterflow, and sprinkler supervisory systems, refer to the following:

NFPA 71-1982 — Central Station Signaling Systems.
NFPA 72A-1979 — Local Protective Signaling Systems.
NFPA 72B-1979 — Auxiliary Protective Signaling Systems.
NFPA 72C-1982 — Remote Station Protective Signaling Systems.
NFPA 72D-1979 — Proprietary Protective Signaling Systems.
NFPA 72E-1982 — Automatic Fire Detectors.
NFPA 74-1980 — Household Fire Warning Equipment.

(FPN): Class 1, 2 and 3 circuits are defined in Article 725.

NFPA 71, Central Station Signaling Systems. This standard covers the installation, maintenance, and use of central station signaling systems. These systems include the central station physical plant, exterior communication channels, satellite stations, and the signaling facilities located at the protected premises.

This standard is intended to apply primarily to supervisory and alarm service furnished by operators constantly in attendance at a central station, manually or automatically controlled, with the required maintenance, inspection, and testing force and runner service readily available. Central station companies customarily follow this standard for maintenance, testing, and inspection with respect to other classes of contract service that they furnish.

Such systems are controlled and operated by a person, firm, or corporation whose principal business is the furnishing and maintaining of supervised signaling service.

NFPA 72A, Local Protective Signaling Systems. The provisions of this standard contemplate supervised systems providing fire alarm or supervisory signals within the protected premises. These systems are primarily for the protection of life by indicating the necessity for building evacuation and secondarily for the protection of property.

NFPA 72B, Auxiliary Protective Signaling Systems. An auxiliary alarm system provides protection to an individual occupancy or building or to a group of buildings of a single occupancy and utilizes municipal fire alarm facilities in order to transmit an alarm to the fire department.

Alarms from an auxiliary system are received at municipal fire alarm headquarters on the same equipment and by the same methods as alarms transmitted from municipal fire alarm boxes located on streets.

An auxiliary alarm system is maintained and supervised by a responsible person or corporation. The auxiliary alarm system deals with equipment and circuits in the protected property which, of themselves, are insufficient for notifying the fire department in the event of fire, but which, in combination with a suitable municipal fire alarm system, are arranged to summon fire department response when operated.

NFPA 72C, Remote Station Protective Signaling Systems. This standard deals with the installation, maintenance, testing, and use of a remote station protective signaling system which serves properties under various ownership from a remote station where trained, competent personnel are in constant attendance. It covers the minimum requirements for operating personnel, the remote station, power supplies, signal initiation, signal notification, and recording of signals.

NFPA 72D, Proprietary Protective Signaling Systems. This standard deals with the installation, maintenance, testing, and use of a proprietary protective signaling system which serves contiguous or noncontiguous properties under one ownership from a central supervising station at the protected property, where trained, competent personnel are in constant attendance. It covers the minimum requirements for operating personnel, the central supervising station, power supplies, signal initiation, signal notification, and automatic permanent visual recording of signals.

NFPA 72E, Automatic Fire Detectors. The purpose of this standard is to provide basic minimum requirements for performance of automatic fire detectors to ensure timely warning for the purposes of life safety and property protection.

This standard is intended for use by persons knowledgeable in fire protection. It covers minimum performance, location, mounting, testing, and maintenance requirements of automatic fire detectors for the protection of the occupant, building, space, structure, area, or object in accordance with the stated purpose.

This standard is intended to be used with other NFPA standards that deal specifically with fire alarm, extinguishment, or control. Automatic fire detectors add to fire protection by initiating emergency action but only when used in conjunction with other equipment.

NFPA 74, Household Fire Warning Equipment. This standard is primarily concerned with life protection, not with the protection of property. It contemplates that the family has an exit plan and covers the requirements for the proper selection, installation, operation, and maintenance of fire warning equipment for use within family living units.

A control and associated equipment, single or multiple station alarm device(s), or any combination thereof, may be used to form a household fire warning system.

Detection and alarm systems covered by this standard are solely for the use of the protected household. If the alarm is extended to any other location, such as the fire department, the system is then considered to be one of the aforementioned systems (as applicable), except that the requirements of detector location and spacing, as they apply to home warning systems, would continue to be followed.

NFPA 1221, Public Fire Service Communications. This standard covers the installation, maintenance, and use of all public fire service communication facilities. These facilities include public reporting, dispatching, telephone, and both two-way and microwave radio systems, all of which fulfill two principal functions: that of receiving fire alarms or other emergency calls from the public and that of retransmitting these alarms and emergency calls to fire companies and other interested agencies.

760-2. Classifications. Fire protective signaling circuits shall be classified as nonpower limited or power limited. All fire protective signaling circuits shall comply with Part A and, in addition, nonpower-limited circuits shall comply with Part B and power-limited circuits shall comply with Part C. Circuits not marked according to Section 760-23 shall comply with Part B.

(FPN): Circuits which do not comply with all of the requirements of Part C are classified as nonpower-limited circuits and must comply with all of the requirements of Part B.

760-3. Identification. Fire protective signaling circuits shall be identified at terminal and junction locations, in a manner which will prevent unintentional interference with the signaling circuit during testing and servicing.

760-4. Location and Other Articles. Circuits and equipment shall comply with (a), (b), (c), and (d) below.

(a) Prevention of Spread of Fire or Products of Combustion. Section 300-21.

(b) Hazardous (Classified) Locations. Articles 500 through 516 and Article 517, Part G where installed in hazardous (classified) locations.

(c) Corrosive, Damp, or Wet Locations. Sections 110-11, 300-6 and 310-9 where installed in corrosive, damp, or wet locations.

(d) Ducts, Plenums and Other Air-Handling Spaces. Section 300-22 where installed in ducts or plenums or other space used for environmental air.

Exception to (d): Single- and multiconductor cables covered under Part C and listed as having adequate fire-resistant and low-smoke producing characteristics shall be permitted for ducts and plenums as described in Section 300-22(b) and other space used for environmental air as described in Section 300-22(c).

See commentary following Sections 300-22(b) and 300-22(c).

(FPN): One method of defining low-smoke producing materials is by establishing an acceptable value of the smoke produced per the UL 910 test to a maximum peak optical density of 0.5 and a maximum average optical density of 0.15. Similarly, fire-resistant cables may be defined as having a maximum allowable flame travel distance of 5.0 feet (1.52 m) in the UL 910 test.

See commentary following Section 725-2(b).

760-5. Signaling Line Circuits Extending Beyond One Building. Fire protective signaling line circuits that extend aerially beyond one building shall either meet the requirements of Article 800 and be classified as communications circuits, or shall meet the requirements of Article 225.

760-6. Grounding. Fire protective signaling circuits and equipment shall be grounded in accordance with Article 250.

Exception: DC power-limited fire protective signaling circuits having a maximum current of 0.030 amperes.

760-7. Supervision. The circuit shall be electrically supervised so that a trouble signal shall indicate the occurrence of a single open or a single ground fault on any installation wiring circuit that would prevent proper alarm operation.

Exception: Interconnecting circuits of household fire warning equipment wholly within a dwelling unit.

(FPN): For additional information, see NFPA 74-1980, Household Fire Warning Equipment.

(FPN): See articles on electrical supervision in NFPA 71, 72A, 72B, 72C, and 72D for more information about electrical supervision.

B. Nonpower-Limited Fire Protective Signaling Circuits

760-11. Power Limitations. The power supply of nonpower-limited fire protective signaling circuits shall comply with Chapters 1 through 4 and the output voltage shall not be more than 600 volts, nominal.

760-12. Overcurrent Protection. Conductors No. 14 and larger shall be protected against overcurrent in accordance with their ampacities. The ampacities shall be those given in Tables 310-16 through 310-19, without derating factors. Overcurrent protection shall not exceed 7 amperes for No. 18 conductors and 10 amperes for No. 16.

Exception: Where other articles of this Code require other overcurrent protection.

See Section 240-4, Exception No. 2 for example.

760-13. Location of Overcurrent Devices. Overcurrent devices shall be located at the point where the conductor to be protected receives its supply.

Exception: Where the overcurrent device protecting the larger conductor also protects the smaller conductor.

760-14. Wiring Method. Wiring installation shall be in accordance with the appropriate articles in Chapter 3.

Exception No. 1: As provided in Sections 760-15 through 760-18.

Exception No. 2: Where other articles of this Code require other methods.

760-15. Conductors of Different Circuits in Same Enclosure, Cable, or Raceway. Class 1 and nonpower-limited fire protective signaling circuits shall be permitted to occupy the same enclosure, cable, or raceway without regard to whether the individual circuits are alternating current or direct current, provided all conductors are insulated for the maximum voltage of any conductor in the enclosure or raceway. Power supply and fire protective signaling circuit conductors shall be permitted in the same enclosure, cable, or raceway only when connected to the same equipment.

760-16. Copper Conductors.

(a) Sizes and Use. Copper conductors of Nos. 18 and 16 shall be permitted to be used provided they supply loads that do not exceed the ampacities given in Table 402-5 and are installed in a raceway or a listed cable. Copper conductors larger than No. 16 shall not supply loads greater than the ampacities given in Tables 310-16 through 310-19.

(b) Insulation. Insulation on conductors shall be suitable for 600 volts. Conductors larger than No. 16 shall comply with Article 310. Conductors in sizes Nos. 18 and 16 shall be Type RFH-2, RFHH-2, RFHH-3, TF, TFN, PF, PGF, SF-2, ZF, or KF-2. Conductors with other type and thickness of insulation shall be permitted if listed for nonpower-limited fire protective signaling circuit use.

(FPN): For application provisions, see Table 402-3.

(c) Conductor Materials. Conductors shall be solid or bunch-tinned (bonded) stranded copper.

Exception No. 1: Stranded copper with a maximum of 7 strands for sizes 16 and 18 shall be permitted.

Exception No. 2: Stranded copper with a maximum 19 strands for sizes 14 and larger shall be permitted.

Control of the stranding is required to prevent a single fine strand of wire from completing a circuit, making it appear the circuit is operational. The fine strand could remain intact under the current used for the supervisory signal, but burn open when required to carry the higher current of an alarm signal.
Exception No. 2 is new in the 1984 *NEC*. It permits, for example, No. 14 AWG conductors which are dual rated THW/MTW.

Exception to (b) and (c): Wire Types PTF and PAF shall be permitted only for high-temperature applications between 90°C and 250°C.

760-17. Multiconductor Cable for Circuits Operating at 150 Volts or Less. A multiconductor cable of two or more No. 16 or 18 solid or stranded (maximum of 7 strands) copper conductors listed for this use shall be permitted to be used on fire protective signaling circuits operating at 150 volts or less. The multiconductor cable shall be installed in a raceway or exposed in accordance with the requirements of Chapter 3 except that surface-mounted cable shall not be permitted within 7 feet (2.13 m) of the floor.

760-18. Number of Conductors in Raceways, Cable Trays, and Cables, and Derating.

(a) Nonpower-Limited Fire Protective Signaling Circuits and Class 1 Circuits. Where only nonpower-limited fire protective signaling circuits and Class 1 circuits are in a raceway, the number of conductors shall be determined in accordance with Section 300-17. The derating factors given in Note 8 to Tables 310-16 through 310-19 shall apply if such conductors carry continuous loads.

(b) Power-Supply Conductors and Fire Protective Signaling Circuit Conductors. Where power-supply conductors and fire protective signaling circuit conductors are permitted in a raceway in accordance with Section 760-15, the number of conductors shall be determined in accordance with Section 300-17. The derating factors given in Note 8 to Tables 310-16 through 310-19 shall apply as follows:

(1) To all conductors when the fire protective signaling circuit conductors carry continuous loads and where the total number of conductors is more than three.

(2) To the power-supply conductors only, when the fire protective signaling circuit conductors do not carry continuous loads and where the number of power-supply conductors is more than three.

(c) Cable Trays. Where fire protective signaling circuit conductors are installed in cable trays, they shall comply with Sections 318-8 through 318-10.

C. Power-Limited Fire Protective Signaling Circuits

760-21. Power Limitations. As specified in Table 760-21(a) for ac circuits and Table 760-21(b) for dc circuits, the power for power-limited fire protective signaling circuits shall be either inherently limited requiring no overcurrent protection or limited by a combination of a power source and overcurrent protection.

760-22. Supervision. In addition to the requirements of Section 760-7, either a trouble or alarm signal shall indicate the occurrence of a multiple ground fault or any short-circuit fault on the fire alarm system primary (main) power supply, alarm initiating, signaling line, or required alarm indicating circuits that would prevent proper alarm operation.

Exception: Interconnecting circuits of household fire warning equipment wholly within a dwelling unit.

(FPN): For additional information see Household Fire Warning Equipment, NFPA 74-1980.

760-23. Marking. The circuit shall be durably marked where plainly visible at terminations to indicate that it is a power-limited fire protective signaling circuit.

760-25. Overcurrent Protection. Where overcurrent protection is required, the overcurrent protective devices shall not be interchangeable with devices of higher ratings. The overcurrent device shall be permitted as an integral part of the power supply.

760-26. Location of Overcurrent Device. Overcurrent devices shall be located at the point where the conductor to be protected receives its supply.

Table 760-21(a).   Power Limitations for Alternating-Current Fire Protective Signaling Circuits

	Inherently Limited Power Source (Overcurrent protection not required)			Not Inherently Limited Power Source (Overcurrent protection required)		
Circuit Voltage V_{max} (Note 1)	0–20	Over 20–30	Over 30–100	0–20	Over 20–100	Over 100–150
Power Limitation $(VA)_{max}$ (Note 1) (Volt-Amps)	—	—	—	250 (see Note 2)	250	N.A.
Current Limitation I_{max} (Note 1) (Amps)	8.0	8.0	$150/V_{max}$	$1000/V_{max}$	$1000/V_{max}$	1.0
Maximum Over-current Protection (Amps)	—	—	—	5.0	$100/V_{max}$	1.0
Power Source Maximum Name-plate Ratings — VA (Volt-Amps)	$5.0 \times V_{max}$	100	100	$5.0 \times V_{max}$	100	100
Power Source Maximum Name-plate Ratings — Current (Amps)	5.0	$100/V_{max}$	$100/V_{max}$	5.0	$100/V_{max}$	$100/V_{max}$
Supply Conductors and Cables	See Section 760-27					
Circuit Conductors and Cables	See Section 760-30					

975

Table 760-21(b).   Power Limitations for Direct-Current Fire Protective Signaling Circuits

	Inherently Limited Power Source (Note 4) (Overcurrent protection not required)				Not Inherently Limited Power Source (Overcurrent protection required)		
Circuit Voltage V_{max} (Note 1)	0-20	Over 20-30	Over 30-100	Over 100-250	0-20	Over 20-100	Over 100-150
Power Source Maximum Nameplate Ratings — Power Limitation $(VA)_{max}$ (Note 1) (Volt-Amps)	—	—	—	—	250 (see Note 2)	250	N.A.
Current Limitation I_{max} (Note 1) (Amps)	8.0	8.0	$150/V_{max}$	0.030	$1000/V_{max}$	$1000/V_{max}$	1.0
Maximum Overcurrent Protection (Amps)	—	—	—	—	5.0	$100/V_{max}$	1.0
VA (Volt-Amps)	$5.0 \times V_{max}$	100	100	$0.030 \times V_{max}$	$5.0 \times V_{max}$	100	100
Current (Amps)	5.0	$100/V_{max}$	$100/V_{max}$	0.030	5.0	$100/V_{max}$	$100/V_{max}$
Supply Conductors and Cables	See Section 760-27						
Circuit Conductors and Cables	See Section 760-30						

Notes for Tables 760-21(a) and (b)

Note 1. V_{max}: Maximum output voltage regardless of load with rated input applied.

I_{max}: Maximum output current after one minute of operation under any noncapacitive load, including short circuit, and with overcurrent protection bypassed if used.

VA_{max}: Maximum volt-ampere output regardless of load and overcurrent protection bypassed if used.

Note 2. If the power source is a transformer, $(VA)_{max}$ is 350 or less when V_{max} is 15 or less.

760-27. Wiring Methods on Supply Side. Conductors and equipment on the supply side of overcurrent protection, transformers, or current-limiting devices shall be installed in accordance with the appropriate requirements of Part B and Chapter 3. Transformers or other devices supplied from power-supply conductors shall be protected by an overcurrent device rated not over 20 amperes.

Exception: The input leads of a transformer or other power source supplying power-limited fire protective signaling circuits shall be permitted to be smaller than No. 14 but not smaller than No. 18, if they are not over 12 inches (305 mm) long and if they have insulation that complies with Section 760-16(b).

760-28. Wiring Methods and Materials on Load Side. Circuits on the load side of overcurrent protection, transformers, and current-limiting devices shall be permitted to use wiring methods and materials in accordance with (a) and (b) below.

(a) Nonpower-Limited Wiring Methods and Materials. The appropriate articles of Chapter 3 including Section 300-17 shall apply.

Exception No. 1: Conductors and multiconductor cables described in and installed in accordance with Sections 760-16 and 760-17 shall be permitted.

The intent of Section 760-28(a) and Exception No. 1 is to permit the same wiring methods for power-limited circuits as are permitted for electric power and light circuit wiring in Chapter 3, or for nonpower-limited circuits in Sections 760-16 and 760-17. The special wiring covered by Section 760-28(b) is not the only acceptable method for wiring power-limited fire protective signaling systems. However, Section 760-29 is still applicable. Even if a Chapter 3 wiring method is used for a power-limited circuit, the conductors are required to be separated as required by Section 760-29.

Exception No. 2: The derating factors given in Note 8 to Tables 310-16 through 310-19 shall not apply.

(b) Power-Limited Wiring Methods and Materials. Power-limited circuit conductors and cables described in Section 760-30 shall be installed as follows:

(1) In raceway or exposed on surface of ceiling and sidewalls or "fished" in concealed spaces. Cable shall be adequately supported and terminated in approved fittings and installed in such a way that maximum protection against physical injury is afforded by building construction such as baseboards, door frames, ledges, etc. When located within 7 feet (2.13 m) of the floor, cable shall be securely fastened in an approved manner, such as insulated stapling at intervals of not more than 18 inches (457 mm).

(2) In metal raceway or rigid nonmetallic conduit when passing through a floor or wall to a height of 7 feet (2.13 m) above the floor unless adequate protection can be afforded by building construction such as detailed in (1) above, or unless an equivalent solid guard is provided.

(3) In rigid conduit, intermediate metal conduit or electrical metallic tubing when installed in hoistways.

Exception: As provided for in Section 620-21, Exceptions No. 1 and 2 for elevators and similar equipment.

(4) Encased in noncombustible tubing or other outer covering of noncombustible materials or located in a fireproof shaft having fire stops at each floor when installed in a vertical run in a shaft or partition.

Exception: Power-limited circuit conductors and cables listed as having a fire-resistant covering capable of preventing the carrying of fire from floor to floor.

760-29. Separation of Conductors. Conductors and cables on the load side of overcurrent protection, transformers, and current-limiting devices shall comply with (a) and (b) below.

(a) Separation from Electric Light, Power, Class 1 and Nonpower-Limited Fire Protective Signaling Circuits.

(1) Power-limited circuits shall be separated at least 2 inches (50.8 mm) from open conductors of any electric light, power, Class 1, or nonpower-limited fire protective signaling circuits.

Exception No. 1: Where the electric light, power, Class 1, or nonpower-limited fire protective signaling circuit conductors are in raceway or in metal-sheathed, metal-clad, nonmetallic-sheathed, or Type UF cables.

Exception No. 2: Where the power-limited circuit conductors are permanently separated from the conductors of the other circuits by a continuous and firmly fixed nonconductor, such as porcelain tubes or flexible tubing in addition to the insulation on the wire.

(2) Power-limited circuits shall not be placed in any enclosure, raceway, cable, compartment, outlet box, or similar fitting containing conductors of electric light, power, Class 1, or nonpower-limited fire protective signaling circuits.

Exception No. 1: Where the conductors of the different systems are separated by a partition.

Exception No. 2: Conductors in outlet boxes, junction boxes, or similar fittings or compartments where power-supply conductors are introduced solely for supplying power to the power-limited fire protective signaling system to which the other conductors in the enclosure are connected.

(3) Power-limited circuits shall be separated by not less than 2 inches (50.8 mm) from electric light, power, Class 1, or nonpower-limited fire protective signaling circuit conductors run in the same shaft.

Exception No. 1: Where the conductors of either the electric light, power, Class 1, the nonpower-limited fire protective signaling circuits, or the power-limited fire protective signaling circuits are encased in noncombustible tubing.

Exception No. 2: Where the electric light, power, Class 1, or the nonpower-limited fire protective signaling circuit conductors are in a raceway or are in metal-sheathed, metal-clad, nonmetallic-sheathed, or Type UF cables.

The requirements for separation from electric light, power, Class 1, and nonpower-limited fire protective signaling circuits as noted in Section 760-29(a) apply even if the power-limited circuits are wired using nonpower-limited circuit wiring methods. See commentary following Section 760-28(a), Exception No. 1.

(b) Conductors of Different Power-Limited Fire Protective Signaling Circuits and Class 2 and Class 3 Circuits in Same Cable, Enclosure, or Raceway.

(1) Cables and conductors of two or more power-limited fire protective signaling circuits or Class 3 circuits shall be permitted in the same cable, enclosure, or raceway.

(2) Conductors of one or more Class 2 circuits shall be permitted within the same cable, enclosure, or raceway with conductors of power-limited fire protective signaling circuits provided that the insulation of the Class 2 circuit conductors in the cable, enclosure, or raceway is at least that required by the power-limited fire protective signaling circuits.

760-30. Conductors and Cables. Conductors and cables for use with power-limited fire protective signaling circuits installed in accordance with Section 760-28(b) shall be listed for this use and shall meet or exceed the requirements of (a) through (e) or where coaxial cable is used, the requirements of (f) below.

(a) Conductor Materials. Conductors shall be solid copper or bunch-tinned (bonded) stranded copper.

Exception No. 1: Stranded copper with a maximum of 7 strands for sizes 16 and 18 shall be permitted.

Exception No. 2: Stranded copper with a maximum of 19 strands for sizes 14 and larger shall be permitted.

(b) Sizes. Conductors shall be not smaller than No. 16 for single conductor, No. 19 for two or three conductor and No. 22 for four or more conductor multiconductor cables.

(c) Insulation — Multiconductor Cables. Conductors of multiconductor cables shall be covered by approved thermoplastic insulation of not less than 12 mils nominal (10 mils minimum) thickness. The cable conductor shall have an overall thermoplastic jacket having a nominal thickness of not less than 35 mils (30 mils minimum). Where the number of conductors in a cable exceeds four, the thickness of the thermoplastic jacket shall be increased so as to provide equivalent performance characteristics. Similarly, where the size of conductors in a cable exceeds No. 16, the thickness of the conductor insulation shall be increased so as to provide equivalent performance characteristics.

Exception No. 1: Two conductors assembled in a flat parallel construction with a 30 mils nominal integral insulation-jacket and a 47 mils minimum web shall be permitted.

Exception No. 2: Other types and thicknesses of insulation and jackets shall be permitted if listed for this use.

Exception No. 3: Where a smooth metallic sheath, welded and corrugated metallic sheath, or interlocking tape armor is applied over the nonmetallic jacket, an overall nonmetallic jacket shall not be required.

(d) Insulation — Single Conductors. Single conductors shall be covered by approved thermoplastic insulation of not less than 30 mils nominal (28 mils minimum) thickness.

Exception: Other types and thicknesses of insulation shall be permitted if listed for this use.

(e) Ratings. The cable shall have a voltage rating of not less than 300 volts and the jacket compound shall have a high degree of abrasion resistance.

(f) Coaxial Cables. Coaxial cables shall have a minimum No. 22 AWG copper or 30 percent minimum conductivity copper covered steel center conductor, an overall insulation rated at 300 volts, an overall metallic shield covered by a flame retardant nonmetallic jacket having a minimum thickness not less than 35 mils nominal (30 mils minimum), and they shall have a high degree of abrasion resistance.

760-31. Current-Carrying Continuous Line-type Fire Detectors.

(a) Application. Listed continuous line-type fire detectors, including insulated copper tubing of pneumatically operated detectors, employed for both detection and carrying signaling currents shall be permitted to be used in circuits having power-limiting characteristics in accordance with Section 760-21.

(b) Insulation. Continuous line-type fire detectors shall be insulated in accordance with Section 760-30(c) through (e), or with an equivalent type of insulation.

(c) Installation. Continuous line-type fire detectors shall be installed in accordance with Sections 760-22 through 760-29.

ARTICLE 770 — OPTICAL FIBER CABLES

Contents

770-1. Scope. The provisions of this article apply to the installation of optical fiber cables along with electrical conductors. This article does not cover the construction of optical fiber cables. It also does not cover the installation of optical fiber cables in circumstances other than those covered in this article.

> Article 770 is new in the 1984 *NEC*. It is included to permit the orderly development and usage of optical fiber technology when used in conjunction with electrical conductors for communication, signaling, and control circuits in lieu of metallic conductors.
>
> Article 770 is not applicable to optical fiber cables except when they are installed along with electrical conductors.
>
> Optical fiber cables may be desirable in some circumstances where electrical noise is a problem, as such systems are not affected by electrical noise.

770-2. Optical Fiber Cables. Optical fiber cables transmit light for control, signaling and communications through an optical fiber.

770-3. Types. Optical fiber cables can be grouped into three types.

(a) Nonconductive. These cables contain no metallic members and no other electrically conductive materials.

(b) Conductive. These cables contain noncurrent-carrying conductive members such as metallic strength members and metallic vapor barriers.

(c) Hybrid. These cables contain optical fibers and current-carrying electrical conductors and shall be classified as electrical cables in accordance with the type of electrical conductors.

770-4. Optical Fibers and Electrical Conductors.

(a) With Conductors for Electric Light, Power, or Class 1 Circuits. Optical fibers shall be permitted within the same hybrid cable for electric light, power, or Class 1 circuits operating at 600 volts or less only where the functions of the optical fibers and the electrical conductors are associated. Nonconductive optical fiber cables shall be permitted to occupy the same raceway or cable tray with conductors for electric light, power or Class 1 circuits operating at 600 volts or less.

Nonconductive optical fiber cables shall not be permitted to occupy the same cabinet, panel, outlet box or similar enclosure housing the electrical terminations of an electric light, power or Class 1 circuit.

Exception No. 1: Where nonconductive optical fiber cable is functionally associated with the electric light, power or Class 1 circuit.

Exception No. 2: Where nonconductive optical fiber cables are installed in factory- or field-assembled control centers.

Installations in raceway shall comply with Section 300-17.

(b) With Other Conductors. Optical fibers shall be permitted in the same cable, and conductive and nonconductive optical fiber cables shall be permitted in the same raceway, cable tray or enclosure with conductors of any of the following:

(1) Class 2 and Class 3 remote-control, signaling and power-limited circuits in compliance with Article 725.

(2) Power-limited fire protective signaling systems in compliance with Article 760.

(3) Communications circuits in compliance with Article 800.

(4) Radio and television circuits in compliance with Part B of Article 810.

(5) Community antenna television and radio distribution systems in compliance with Article 820.

(c) Grounding. Noncurrent-carrying conductive members of optical fiber cables shall be grounded in accordance with Article 250.

770-5. Spread of Fire or Products of Combustion. Installations in hollow spaces, vertical shafts, and ventilation or air-handling ducts shall be so made that the possible spread of fire or products of combustion will not be substantially increased. Openings around penetrations through fire-resistance rated walls, partitions, floors, or ceilings shall be firestopped using approved methods.

770-6. Vertical Runs. Optical fiber cables in a vertical run in a shaft shall be listed as having fire-resistance characteristics capable of preventing the carrying of fire from floor to floor.

Exception: Where the cables are encased in noncombustible tubing or are located in a fireproof shaft having fire stops at each floor.

770-7. Ducts and Plenums and Other Spaces Used for Environmental Air. Installations of optical fiber cables in ducts or plenums or other spaces used for environmental air shall comply with Section 300-22 as to installation methods.

Exception: Optical fiber cables listed as having adequate fire-resistant and low-smoke producing characteristics shall be permitted for ducts and plenums as described in Section 300-22(b) and other space used for environmental air as described in Section 300-22(c).

See commentary following Sections 300-22(b) and 300-22(c).

(FPN): One method of defining low-smoke producing materials is by establishing an acceptable value of the smoke produced per the UL 910 test to a maximum peak optical density of 0.5 and a maximum average optical density of 0.15.

(FPN): Similarly, fire-resistant cables may be defined as having a maximum allowable flame travel distance of 5.0 feet (1.52 m) in the UL 910 test.

See commentary following Section 725-2(b). Although UL has not, as of this writing, classified optical fiber cables in accordance with the exception to Section 770-7, testing and classification, along the same lines as for the exceptions to Sections 725-2(b), 760-4(d), 800-3(d), and 820-15, is expected following adoption of the 1984 *NEC* and new Article 770.

770-8. Grounding of Entrance Cables. Where exposed to contact with electric light or power conductors, the noncurrent-carrying metallic members of aerial optical fiber cables entering buildings shall be grounded or shall be interrupted close to the entrance of the building by an insulating joint or equivalent device.

8 COMMUNICATION SYSTEMS

ARTICLE 800 — COMMUNICATION CIRCUITS

Contents

A. General

800-1. Scope. This article covers telephone, telegraph (except radio), district messenger, outside wiring for fire alarm and burglar alarms, and similar central station systems; and telephone systems not connected to a central station system but using similar types of equipment, methods of installation, and maintenance. Where optical fiber cable is used Article 770 shall apply.

(FPN): For further information for fire alarm, sprinkler, supervisory, or watchman systems, see Article 760.

Section 90-3, "Code Arrangement," states that Chapter 8, which includes Articles 800, 810, and 820, covers communication systems and is independent of the other chapters except where they are specifically referenced therein. For instance, Section 800-2(b) references Article 500, Section 800-3(d) references Section 300-22, Section 800-11(a)(3) references Section 225-14(d), etc.

Although electronic data processing (EDP) systems are often used for or with communications systems, Article 800 does not cover EDP system wiring. It is covered by Article 725 (Article 760 if for a fire protective signaling system). In some cases, the telephone system wiring is also used for data transmission, and this use is covered by Article 800.

ARTICLE 800—COMMUNICATION CIRCUITS

B. Protection

800-2. Protective Devices. A listed protector shall be provided on each circuit run partly or entirely in aerial wire or aerial cable not confined within a block. Also, a listed protector shall be provided on each circuit, aerial or underground, so located within the block containing the building served as to be exposed to accidental contact with electric light or power conductors operating at over 300 volts to ground.

(FPN): The word "block" as used in this article means a square or portion of a city, town, or village enclosed by streets and including the alleys so enclosed but not any street.

(FPN): The word "exposed" as used in this article means that the circuit is in such a position that, in case of failure of supports or insulation, contact with another circuit may result.

(a) Location. The protector shall be located in, on, or immediately adjacent to the structure or building served and as close as practicable to the point at which the exposed conductors enter or attach.

(b) Hazardous (Classified) Locations. The protector shall not be located in any hazardous (classified) location as defined in Article 500, nor in the vicinity of easily ignitible material.

(c) Protector Requirements. The protector shall consist of an arrester connected between each line conductor and ground in an appropriate mounting. Protector terminals shall be marked to indicate line and ground as applicable.

(1) Fuseless-type protectors shall be permitted under any of the following conditions:

a. Where circuits enter a building through metallic-sheathed cable or through a nonmetallic-sheathed cable having a metallic grounding shield between the sheath and the conductor assembly, if the metallic sheath or shield of the cable is effectively grounded, and if the conductors in the cable safely fuse on all currents greater than the current-carrying capacity of the protector, and the ampacity of the protector grounding conductor.

b. Where insulated conductors in accordance with Section 800-11(c)(1) or (c)(2) are used to extend circuits to a building from a metallic-sheathed cable or from a nonmetallic-sheathed cable having a metallic grounding shield between the sheath and the conductor assembly, if the metallic sheath or shield is effectively grounded and if the conductors in the cable or cable stub, or the connections between the insulated conductors and the exposed plant safely fuse on all currents greater than the current-carrying capacity of the protector, and the ampacity of the associated insulated conductors and the protector grounding conductor.

c. Where insulated conductors in accordance with Section 800-11(c)(1) or (c)(2) are used to extend circuits to a building from other than a grounded metallic-sheathed or shielded cable, if (1) the protector is listed for this purpose, and (2) the connections of the insulated conductors to the exposed plant or the conductors of the exposed plant safely fuse on all currents greater than the current-carrying capacity of the protector, and the ampacity of the associated insulated conductors and the protector grounding conductor.

d. Where insulated conductors in accordance with Section 800-11(c)(1) or (c)(2) are used to extend circuits aerially to a building from an unexposed buried or underground circuit.

(FPN): Effectively grounded means intentionally connected to earth through a ground connection or connections of sufficiently low impedance and having sufficient current-carrying capacity to prevent the buildup of voltages which may result in undue hazard to connected equipment or to persons.

e. Where insulated conductors in accordance with Section 800-11(c)(1) or (c)(2) are used to extend circuits to a building from an effectively grounded metallic-sheathed or shielded cable, and if (1) the combination of the protector and insulated conductors is listed for this purpose, and (2) the insulated conductors safely fuse on all currents greater than the current-carrying capacity of the protector and the ampacity of the protector grounding conductor.

(2) Where the requirements listed under (c)(1)a, (1)b, (1)c, or (1)d above are not met, fused-type protectors shall be used. Fused-type protectors shall consist of an arrester connected between each line conductor and ground, a fuse in series with each line conductor, and an appropriate mounting arrangement. Protector terminals shall be marked to indicate line, instrument, and ground, as applicable.

800-3. Installation of Conductors. Conductors from the protector to the equipment or, where no protector is required, conductors attached to the outside or inside of the building shall comply with (a) through (d) below.

(a) Separation from Other Conductors.

(1) Open Conductors. Conductors shall be separated at least 2 inches (50.8 mm) from conductors of any electric light or power circuits or Class 1 circuits.

Exception No. 1: Where the electric light or power or Class 1 circuit conductors are in a raceway or in metal-sheathed, metal-clad, nonmetallic-sheathed, or Type UF cables.

Exception No. 2: Where the conductors are permanently separated from the conductors of the other circuit by a continuous and firmly fixed nonconductor, such as porcelain tubes or flexible tubing, in addition to the insulation on the wire.

(2) In Raceways and Boxes. Communication conductors shall not be placed in any raceway, compartment, outlet box, junction box, or similar fitting with conductors of electric light or power circuits or Class 1 circuits.

Exception No. 1: Where the conductors of the different systems are separated by a partition.

Exception No. 2: Conductors in outlet boxes, junction boxes, or similar fittings or compartments where such conductors are introduced solely for power supply to communication equipment or for connection to remote-control equipment.

(3) In Shafts. Conductors run in the same shaft with conductors of electric light or power shall be separated from light or power conductors by not less than 2 inches (50.8 mm).

Exception No. 1: Where the conductors of either system are encased in noncombustible tubing.

Exception No. 2: Where the electric light or power conductors are in a raceway, or in metal-sheathed, metal-clad, nonmetallic-sheathed, or Type UF cables.

(b) Vertical Runs. Communications wires and cables, both metallic conductor and optical fiber types, in a vertical run in a shaft shall be listed as having fire-resistant characteristics capable of preventing the carrying of fire from floor to floor.

Exception: Where the wires and cables are encased in noncombustible tubing or are located in a fireproof shaft having fire stops at each floor.

(c) Spread of Fire or Products of Combustion. Installations in hollow spaces, vertical shafts, and ventilation or air-handling ducts shall be so made that the possible spread of fire or products of combustion will not be substantially increased. Openings around penetrations through fire resistance rated walls, partitions, floors, or ceilings shall be firestopped using approved methods.

(FPN): The conductors referred to in this section would ordinarily be insulated, but the kind of insulation is not specified as reliance is placed on the protective device to limit excessive currents and voltages.

(d) Wiring in Ducts, Plenums and Other Air Handling Spaces. Communications wires and cables, both metallic conductor and optical fiber types, and equipment installed in ducts or plenums or other spaces used for environmental air shall also comply with Section 300-22 as to installation methods.

Exception to (d): Communications wires and cables, both metallic conductor and optical fiber types, listed as having adequate fire-resistant and low-smoke producing characteristics shall be permitted for ducts and plenums as described in Section 300-22(b) and other space used for environmental air as described in Section 300-22(c).

See commentary following Sections 300-22(b) and 300-22(c).

(FPN): One method of defining low-smoke producing materials is by establishing an acceptable value of the smoke produced per the UL 910 test to a maximum peak optical density of 0.5 and a maximum average optical density of 0.15. Similarly, fire-resistant cables may be defined as having a maximum allowable flame travel distance of 5 feet (1.52 m) in the UL 910 test.

See commentary following Section 725-2(b).

C. Outside Conductors

800-11. Overhead Conductors. Overhead conductors entering buildings shall comply with (a) through (c) below.

(a) On Poles and In-Span. Where communication conductors and electric light or power conductors are supported by the same pole or run in parallel in-span, the following conditions shall be met:

(1) Relative Location. Where practicable, the communications conductors shall be located below the electric light or power conductors.

(2) Attachment to Crossarms. Conductors shall not be attached to a crossarm that carries electric light or power conductors.

(3) Climbing Space. The climbing space through communication conductors shall comply with the requirements of Section 225-14(d).

(4) Clearance. Supply service drops of 0-750 volts running above and parallel to communication service drops shall be permitted to have a minimum separation of 12 inches (30.48 cm) at any point in the span including the point of and at their attachment to the building provided the nongrounded conductors are insulated and that a clearance of 40 inches (1.02 m) is maintained between the two services at the pole.

(b) On Roofs. Conductors passing over buildings shall be kept at least 8 feet (2.44 m) above any roof that may be readily walked upon.

Exception No. 1: Auxiliary buildings, such as garages and the like.

Exception No. 2: A reduction in clearance above only the overhanging portion of the roof to not less than 18 inches (457 mm) shall be permitted if (1) not more than 4 feet (1.22 mm) of communication service-drop conductors pass above the roof overhang, and (2) they are terminated at a through-the-roof raceway or support.

(c) Circuits Requiring Protectors. Circuits that require protectors as provided in Section 800-2 shall comply with the following:

(1) Insulation, Single or Paired Conductors. Each conductor from the last outdoor support to the protector shall have 30-mil (0.762-mm) rubber insulation, except that where such conductors are entirely within a block the insulation on the conductor may be less than 30 mils (0.762 mm), but not less than 25 mils (0.635 mm) in thickness. In addition, the conductor, either individually or over the pair, shall be covered with a substantial fibrous covering or equivalent protection. Listed conductors having rubber insulation of a thickness less than specified above, or having other kinds of insulation, shall be permitted.

(2) Insulation, Cables. Conductors within a cable of the metal-sheathed type or within a cable having a rubber sheath of at least 30-mil (0.762-mm) thickness and covered with a substantial fibrous covering shall be permitted to have paper or other suitable insulation. Where the metal or rubber sheath is omitted, each conductor shall be insulated as required in (c)(1) above, and the bunched conductors shall be covered with a substantial fibrous covering or equivalent covering.

(3) On Buildings. Open conductors shall be separated at least 4 inches (102 mm) from electric light or power conductors not in conduit or cable, or be permanently separated from conductors of the other system by a continuous and firmly fixed nonconductor in addition to the insulation on the wires, such as porcelain tubes or flexible tubing. Open conductors exposed to accidental contact with electric light and power conductors operating at over 300 volts to ground and attached to buildings shall be separated from woodwork by being supported on glass, porcelain, or other insulating material.

Exception: Separation from woodwork shall not be required where fuses are omitted as provided for in Section 800-2(c)(1), or where conductors are used to extend circuits to a building from a cable having a grounded metal sheath.

(4) Entering Buildings. Where a protector is installed inside the building, the conductors shall enter the building either through a noncombustible, nonabsorbent insulating bushing, or through a metal raceway. The insulating bushing shall not be required where the entering conductors (1) are in metal-sheathed cable; (2) pass through masonry; (3) meet the requirements of (c)(1) above and fuses are omitted as provided in Section 800-2(c)(1); or (4) meet the requirements of (c)(1) above and are used to extend circuits to a building from a cable having a grounded metal sheath. Raceways or bushings shall slope upward from the outside or, where this cannot be done, drip loops shall be formed in the conductors immediately before they enter the building. Raceways shall be equipped with an approved service head. More than one conductor shall be permitted to enter through a single raceway or bushing. Conduits or other metal raceways located ahead of the protector shall be grounded.

800-12. Lightning Conductors. Where practicable, a separation of at least 6 feet (1.83 m) shall be maintained between open conductors of communication systems on buildings and lightning conductors.

D. Underground Circuits

800-21. Underground Circuits Entering Buildings. Underground conductors of communication circuits entering buildings shall comply with (a) and (b) below.

(a) With Electric Light or Power Conductors. Underground conductors in a duct, handhole, or manhole containing electric light or power conductors shall be in a section separated from such conductors by means of brick, concrete, or tile partitions.

(b) Underground Block Distribution. Where the entire street circuit is run underground and the circuit within the block is so placed as to be free from likelihood of accidental contact with electric light or power circuits of over 300 volts to ground, the insulation requirements of Section 800-11(c)(1) and (c)(4) shall not apply, insulating supports shall not be required for the conductors, and bushings shall not be required where the conductors enter the building.

E. Grounding

800-31. Grounding. Equipment shall be grounded as specified in (a) and (b) below.

(a) Cable Sheath. Where exposed to contact with electric light or power conductors, the metal sheath of aerial cables entering buildings shall be grounded or shall be interrupted close to the entrance to the building by an insulating joint or equivalent device.

(b) Protector Ground. The protector ground shall comply with the following:

(1) Insulation. The grounding conductor shall have a 30-mil rubber insulation and shall be covered by a substantial fibrous covering. Conductors listed for this use having less than 30-mil rubber insulation or having other kinds of insulation shall be permitted.

(2) Size. The grounding conductor shall not be smaller than No. 14 AWG copper or equivalent.

(3) Run in Straight Line. The grounding conductor shall be run to the grounding electrode in as straight a line as practicable.

(4) Physical Damage. Where necessary, the grounding conductor shall be guarded from physical damage.

(5) Electrode. The grounding conductor shall be connected as follows:

a. To the nearest accessible location on (1) the building or structure grounding electrode system as covered in Section 250-81, (2) the grounded interior metal water piping system as covered in Section 250-80(a), (3) the power service accessible means external to enclosures as covered in Section 250-71(b), (4) the metallic power service raceway, (5) the service equipment enclosure, or (6) the grounding electrode conductor or the grounding electrode conductor metal enclosure; or

b. If the building or structure served has no grounding means as described in (5)a, to any one of the individual electrodes described in Section 250-81; or

c. If the building or structure served has no grounding means as described in (5)a or (5)b, to: (1) an effectively grounded metal structure, or (2) a continuous and extensive underground gas piping system where acceptable to both the gas supplier and to the authority having jurisdiction, or (3) to a ground rod or pipe driven into permanently damp earth and separated from lightning conductors as covered in Section 800-12 and at least 6 feet (1.83 m) from electrodes of other systems. Steam or hot water pipes or lightning-rod conductors shall not be employed as electrodes for protectors.

(6) Electrode Connection. The grounding conductor shall be attached to a pipe electrode by means of a bolted clamp to which the conductor is connected in an effective manner. Where a gas pipe electrode is used, connection shall be made between the gas meter and the street main. Connectors, clamps, fittings, or lugs used to attach grounding conductors and bonding jumpers to grounding electrodes or to each other which are to be concrete-encased or buried in the earth shall be suitable for its application.

(7) Bonding of Electrodes. A bonding jumper not smaller than No. 6 copper or equivalent shall be connected between the communication and the power grounding electrodes where the requirements of (5) above result in the use of separate electrodes. Bonding together of all separate electrodes shall be permitted.

(FPN): See Section 250-86 for use of lightning rods.

(FPN): Bonding together of all separate electrodes will limit potential differences between them and between their associated wiring systems.

ARTICLE 810 — RADIO AND TELEVISION EQUIPMENT

Contents

ARTICLE 810—RADIO AND TELEVISION EQUIPMENT

A. General

810-1. Scope. This article covers radio and television receiving equipment and amateur radio transmitting and receiving equipment, but not equipment and antennas used for coupling carrier current to power line conductors.

> The requirements for Article 810 are similar to the requirements for Article 800. See Section 800-11 for the provisions that cover outside conductor location, clearances, and insulation. It should be noted that 30-mil insulation is required except where such conductors are entirely within a block, that is, where conductors are run separately from light and power conductors, such as between buildings or from building to building, not less than 25-mil insulation is permitted.
>
> See Section 800-21 for underground circuits. Note, particularly, the provisions of paragraph (b) regarding minimum permitted insulation.

810-2. Other Articles. Wiring from the source of power to and between devices connected to the interior wiring system shall comply with Chapters 1 through 4 other than as modified by Sections 640-3, 640-4, and 640-5. Wiring for radio-frequency and audio-frequency equipment and loud speakers shall comply with Article 640. Where optical fiber is used Article 770 shall apply.

810-3. Community Television Antenna. The antenna shall comply with this article. The distribution system shall comply with Article 820.

810-4. Radio Noise Suppressors. Radio interference eliminators, interference capacitors, or noise suppressors connected to power-supply leads shall be of a listed type. They shall not be exposed to physical damage.

B. Receiving Equipment — Antenna Systems

810-11. Material. Antennas and lead-in conductors shall be of hard-drawn copper, bronze, aluminum alloy, copper-clad steel or other high-strength, corrosion-resistant material.

Exception: Soft-drawn or medium-drawn copper shall be permitted for lead-in conductors where the maximum span between points of support is less than 35 feet (10.67 m).

810-12. Supports. Outdoor antennas and lead-in conductors shall be securely supported. The antennas shall not be attached to the electric service mast. They shall not be attached to poles or similar structures carrying electric light or power wires or trolley wires of over 250 volts between conductors. Insulators supporting the antenna conductors shall have sufficient mechanical strength to safely support the conductors. Lead-in conductors shall be securely attached to the antennas.

810-13. Avoidance of Contacts with Conductors of Other Systems. Outdoor antennas and lead-in conductors from an antenna to a building shall not cross over electric light or power circuits and shall be kept well away from all such circuits so as to avoid the possibility of accidental contact. Where proximity to electric light or power service conductors of less than 250 volts between conductors cannot be avoided, the installation shall be such as to provide a clearance of at least 2 feet (610 mm).

Where practicable, antenna conductors shall be so installed as not to cross under electric light or power conductors.

> One of the leading causes of electrical shock and electrocution, according to statistical reports, is the accidental contact of radio and television receiving antennas and equipment, and amateur radio transmitting and receiving antennas and equipment, with light or power conductors. Extreme caution should therefore be exercised during this type of installation, and periodic visual inspections should be conducted thereafter.

810-14. Splices. Splices and joints in antenna spans shall be made mechanically secure with approved splicing devices or by such other means as will not appreciably weaken the conductors.

Conductor spans from antennas should be of sufficient size and strength to maintain clearances and avoid possible contact with light or power conductors. Splices and joints should be made with approved connectors or other means providing sufficient mechanical strength so as not to weaken appreciably the conductors.

810-15. Grounding. Masts and metal structures supporting antennas shall be grounded in accordance with Section 810-21.

810-16. Size of Wire-Strung Antenna — Receiving Station.

(a) **Size of Antenna Conductors.** Outdoor antenna conductors for receiving stations shall be of a size not less than given in Table 810-16(a).

Table 810-16(a)
Size of Receiving-Station Outdoor Antenna Conductors

Material	Minimum Size of Conductors		
	When Maximum Open Span Length Is		
	Less than 35 feet	35 feet to 150 feet	Over 150 feet
Aluminum alloy, hard-drawn copper	19	14	12
Copper-clad steel, bronze, or other high-strength material	20	17	14

For SI units: one foot = 0.3048 meter.

(b) **Self-Supporting Antennas.** Outdoor antennas, such as vertical rods or dipole structures, shall be of noncorrodible materials and of strength suitable to withstand ice and wind loading conditions, and shall be located well away from overhead conductors of electric light and power circuits of over 150 volts to ground, so as to avoid the possibility of the antenna or structure falling into or making accidental contact with such circuits.

810-17. Size of Lead-in — Receiving Station. Lead-in conductors from outside antennas for receiving stations shall, for various maximum open span lengths, be of such size as to have a tensile strength at least as great as that of the conductors for antennas as specified in Section 810-16. Where the lead-in consists of two or more conductors that are twisted together, are enclosed in the same covering, or are concentric, the conductor size shall, for various maximum open span lengths, be such that the tensile strength of the combination will be at least as great as that of the conductors for antennas as specified in Section 810-16.

810-18. Clearances — Receiving Stations.

(a) **On Outside of Buildings.** Lead-in conductors attached to buildings shall be so installed that they cannot swing closer than 2 feet (610 mm) to the conductors of circuits of 250 volts or less between conductors, or 10 feet (3.05 m) to the conductors of circuits of over 250 volts between conductors, except that in the case of circuits not over 150 volts between conductors, where all conductors involved are supported so as to ensure permanent separation, the clearance shall be permitted to be reduced but shall not be less than 4 inches (102 mm). The clearance between lead-in conductors and any conductor forming a part of a lightning rod system shall not be less than 6 feet (1.83 m) unless the bonding referred to in Section 250-86 is accomplished.

(b) Antennas and Lead-ins — Indoors. Indoor antennas and indoor lead-ins shall not be run nearer than 2 inches (50.8 mm) to conductors of other wiring systems in the premises.

Exception No. 1: Where such other conductors are in metal raceways or cable armor.

Exception No. 2: Where permanently separated from such other conductors by a continuous and firmly fixed nonconductor, such as porcelain tubes or flexible tubing.

810-19. Electric Supply Circuits Used in Lieu of Antenna — Receiving Stations. Where an electric supply circuit is used in lieu of an antenna, the device by which the radio receiving set is connected to the supply circuit shall be listed.

The approved device is usually a small fixed condenser connected between the antenna terminal of the receiving set and one wire of the lighting circuit. As is the case with most receiving sets, the condenser should be designed for operation at not less than 300 V and mica should be used as the dielectric. This ensures a high degree of safety and minimizes the possibility of a breakdown in the condenser thereby avoiding a short circuit to ground through the antenna coil of the set.

810-20. Antenna Discharge Units — Receiving Stations.

(a) Where Required. Each conductor of a lead-in from an outdoor antenna shall be provided with a listed antenna discharge unit.

Exception: Where the lead-in conductors are enclosed in a continuous metallic shield that is either permanently and effectively grounded, or is protected by an antenna discharge unit.

(b) Location. Antenna discharge units shall be located outside the building or inside the building between the point of entrance of the lead-in and the radio set or transformers, and as near as practicable to the entrance of the conductors to the building. The antenna discharge unit shall not be located near combustible material nor in a hazardous (classified) location as defined in Article 500.

A lightning arrester is not required where the lead-in conductors are enclosed in a continuous metal shield such as rigid or intermediate metal conduit, or electrical metallic tubing, or any metal raceway or metal-shielded cable that is effectively grounded. A lightning discharge will take the path of lower impedance and jump from the lead-in conductors to the metal raceway or shield rather than take the path through the antenna coil of the receiving set.

(c) Grounding. The antenna discharge unit shall be grounded in accordance with Section 810-21.

810-21. Grounding Conductors — Receiving Stations. Grounding conductors shall comply with (a) through (i) below.

(a) Material. The grounding conductor shall be of copper, aluminum, copper-clad steel, bronze, or similar corrosion-resistant material.

(b) Insulation. Insulation on grounding conductors shall not be required.

(c) Supports. The grounding conductors shall be securely fastened in place and shall be permitted to be directly attached to the surface wired over without the use of insulating supports.

Exception: Where proper support cannot be provided, the size of the grounding conductors shall be increased proportionately.

(d) Mechanical Protection. The grounding conductor shall be protected where exposed to physical damage, or the size of the grounding conductors shall be increased proportionately to compensate for the lack of protection.

(e) Run in Straight Line. The grounding conductor for an antenna mast or antenna discharge unit shall be run in as straight a line as practicable from the mast or discharge unit to the grounding electrode.

(f) Electrode. The grounding conductor shall be connected as follows:

(1) To the nearest accessible location on (1) the building or structure grounding electrode system as covered in Section 250-81, (2) the grounded interior metal water piping system as covered in Section 250-80(a), (3) the power service accessible means external to enclosures as covered in Section 250-71(b), (4) the metallic power service raceway, (5) the service equipment enclosure, or (6) the grounding electrode conductor or the grounding electrode conductor metal enclosures; or

(2) If the building or structure served has no grounding means as described in (f)(1), to any one of the individual electrodes described in Section 250-81; or

(3) If the building or structure served has no grounding means as described in (f)(1) or (f)(2), to: (1) an effectively grounded metal structure, or (2) a continuous and extensive underground gas piping system where acceptable to both the gas supplier and to the authority having jurisdiction and where a gas pipe electrode is used, connection shall be made between the gas meter and street main, or (3) to a ground rod or pipe driven into permanently damp earth and separated at least 6 feet (1.83 m) from lightning conductors and electrodes of other systems. Steam or hot water pipes or lightning-rod conductors shall not be employed as electrodes for protectors.

(g) Inside or Outside Building. The grounding conductor shall be permitted to be run either inside or outside the building.

(h) Size. The grounding conductor shall not be smaller than No. 10 copper or No. 8 aluminum or No. 17 copper-clad steel or bronze.

(i) Common Ground. A single grounding conductor shall be permitted for both protective and operating purposes.

The requirements for grounding are in accordance with the provisions of Article 250. It is required that antenna masts be grounded to the same grounding electrode used for the electrical system of the building. This is necessary to assure that all exposed dead metal parts are at the same potential. In many cases masts are (incorrectly) connected to conveniently located vent pipes, metal gutters, and down spouts. This could create potential differences between various metal parts located in or on buildings and lead-in conductors, resulting in potential shock and fire hazards.

(j) Bonding of Electrodes. A bonding jumper not smaller than No. 6 copper or equivalent shall be connected between the radio and television equipment ground and the power grounding electrodes where the requirements of (f) above result in the use of separate electrodes. Bonding together of all separate electrodes shall be permitted.

C. Amateur Transmitting and Receiving Stations — Antenna Systems

810-51. Other Sections. In addition to complying with Part C, antenna systems for amateur transmitting and receiving stations shall also comply with Sections 810-11 through 810-15.

810-52. Size of Antenna. Antenna conductors for transmitting and receiving stations shall be of a size not less than given in Table 810-52.

Table 810-52
Size of Amateur Station Outdoor Antenna Conductors

Material	Minimum Size of Conductors	
	Where Maximum Open Span Length is	
	Less Than 150 feet	Over 150 feet
Hard-drawn copper	14	10
Copper-clad steel, bronze or other high-strength material	14	12

For SI units: one foot = 0.3048 meter.

810-53. Size of Lead-in Conductors. Lead-in conductors for transmitting stations shall, for various maximum span lengths, be of a size at least as great as that of conductors for antennas as specified in Section 810-52.

810-54. Clearance on Building. Antenna conductors for transmitting stations, attached to buildings, shall be firmly mounted at least 3 inches (76 mm) clear of the surface of the building on nonabsorbent insulating supports, such as treated pins or brackets equipped with insulators having not less than 3-inch (76-mm) creepage and airgap distances. Lead-in conductors attached to buildings shall also comply with these requirements.

Exception: Where the lead-in conductors are enclosed in a continuous metallic shield that is permanently and effectively grounded, they shall not be required to comply with these requirements. Where grounded, the metallic shield shall also be permitted to be used as a conductor.

The creepage distance is measured from the conductor, across the face of the supporting insulator, to the building surface. The airgap distance is measured from the conductor (at its closest point) across the air space (not necessarily in a straight line) to the surface of the building. The exception covers coaxial cable with the shield permanently and effectively grounded.

810-55. Entrance to Building. Except where protected with a continuous metallic shield that is permanently and effectively grounded, lead-in conductors for transmitting stations shall enter buildings by one of the following methods: (1) through a rigid, noncombustible, nonabsorbent insulating tube or bushing; (2) through an opening provided for the purpose in which the entrance conductors are firmly secured so as to provide a clearance of at least 2 inches (50.8 mm); or (3) through a drilled window pane.

810-56. Protection Against Accidental Contact. Lead-in conductors to radio transmitters shall be so located or installed as to make accidental contact with them difficult.

810-57. Antenna Discharge Units — Transmitting Stations. Each conductor of a lead-in for outdoor antennas shall be provided with an antenna discharge unit or other suitable means that will drain static charges from the antenna system.

Exception No. 1: Where protected by a continuous metallic shield that is permanently and effectively grounded.

Exception No. 2: Where the antenna is permanently and effectively grounded.

Where a lightning arrester is not installed at a transmitting station, protection against lightning may be provided by a switch that connects the lead-in to ground during the time the station is not in operation.

810-58. Grounding Conductors — Amateur Transmitting and Receiving Stations. Grounding conductors shall comply with (a) through (c) below.

(a) Other Sections. All grounding conductors for amateur transmitting and receiving stations shall comply with Section 810-21(a) through (g).

(b) Size of Protective Grounding Conductor. The protective grounding conductor for transmitting stations shall be as large as the lead-in, but not smaller than No. 10 copper, bronze, or copper-clad steel.

(c) Size of Operating Grounding Conductor. The operating grounding conductor for transmitting stations shall not be less than No. 14 copper or its equivalent.

D. Interior Installation — Transmitting Stations

810-70. Clearance from Other Conductors. All conductors inside the building shall be separated at least 4 inches (102 mm) from the conductors of any lighting or signaling circuit.

Exception No. 1: As provided in Article 640.

Exception No. 2: Where separated from other conductors by conduit or some firmly fixed nonconductor, such as porcelain tubes or flexible tubing.

810-71. General. Transmitters shall comply with (a) through (d) below.

(a) Enclosing. The transmitter shall be enclosed in a metal frame or grille, or separated from the operating space by a barrier or other equivalent means, all metallic parts of which are effectively connected to ground.

(b) Grounding of Controls. All external metal handles and controls accessible to the operating personnel shall be effectively grounded.

(c) Interlocks on Doors. All access doors shall be provided with interlocks that will disconnect all voltages of over 350 volts between conductors when any access door is opened.

(d) Audio-Amplifiers. Audio-amplifiers that are located outside the transmitter housing shall be suitably housed and shall be so located as to be readily accessible and adequately ventilated.

ARTICLE 820 — COMMUNITY ANTENNA TELEVISION AND RADIO DISTRIBUTION SYSTEMS

Contents

ARTICLE 820—COMMUNITY ANTENNA TELEVISION

A. General

820-1. Scope. This article covers coaxial cable distribution of radio frequency signals typically employed in community antenna television (CATV) systems. Where the installation is other than coaxial, Articles 770 and 800 shall apply as applicable.

The coaxial cable shall be permitted to deliver low-energy power to equipment directly associated with this radio frequency distribution system if the voltage is not over 60 volts and if the current supply is from a transformer or other device having energy-limiting characteristics.

820-2. Material. Coaxial cable used for radio frequency distribution systems shall be suitable for the application.

B. Protection

820-7. Ground of Outer Conductive Shield of a Coaxial Cable. Where coaxial cable is exposed to lightning or to accidental contact with lightning arrester conductors or power conductors operating at a potential of over 300 volts to ground, the outer conductive shield of the coaxial cable shall be grounded at the building premises as close to the point of cable entry as practicable.

(a) Shield Grounding. Where the outer conductive shield of a coaxial cable is grounded, no other protective devices shall be required.

(b) Shield Protective Devices. Grounding of a coaxial drop cable shield by means of a protective device that does not interrupt the grounding system within the premises shall be permitted.

> This section permits the use of a shield protective device which does not interrupt the grounding system within the premises. This permits protection against overheating of the CATV service-drop cable. Overheating can occur due to neutral fault currents in the power and lighting system. Such a protective device would have to maintain the integrity of the coaxial system to prevent RF leakage. An ordinary fuse, for example, would not be suitable.

C. Installation of Cable

820-11. Outside Conductors. Coaxial cables, prior to the point of grounding, as defined in Section 820-7, shall comply with (a) through (e) below.

(a) On Poles. Where practicable, conductors on poles shall be located below the electric light or power conductors and shall not be attached to a cross-arm that carries electric light or power conductors.

(b) Lead-in Clearance. Lead-in or aerial-drop cables from a pole or other support, including the point of initial attachment to a building or structure, shall be kept away from electric light or power circuits so as to avoid the possibility of accidental contact.

Exception: Where proximity to electric light or power service conductors cannot be avoided, the installation shall be such as to provide clearances of not less than 12 inches (305 mm) from light or power service drops.

(c) Over Roofs. Cables passing over buildings shall be at least 8 feet (2.44 m) above any roof that may be readily walked upon.

Exception No. 1: Auxillary buildings such as garages and the like.

Exception No. 2: A reduction in clearance above only the overhanging portion of the roof to not less than 18 inches (457 mm) shall be permitted if (1) not more than 4 feet (1.22 m) of communication service drop conductors pass above the roof overhang, and (2) they are terminated at a through-the-roof raceway or support.

(d) Between Buildings. Cables extending between buildings and also the supports or attachment fixtures shall be acceptable for the purpose and shall have sufficient strength to withstand the loads to which they may be subjected.

Exception: Where a cable does not have sufficient strength to be self-supporting, it shall be attached to a supporting messenger cable that, together with the attachment fixtures or supports, shall be acceptable for the purpose and shall have sufficient strength to withstand the loads to which they may be subjected.

(e) On Buildings. Where attached to buildings, cables shall be securely fastened in such a manner that they will be separated from other conductors as follows:

(1) Electric Light or Power. The coaxial cable shall have a separation of at least 4 inches (102 mm) from electric light or power conductors not in conduit or cable, or be permanently separated from conductors of the other system by a continuous and firmly fixed nonconductor in addition to the insulation on the wires.

(2) Other Communication Systems. Coaxial cable shall be installed so that there will be no unnecessary interference in the maintenance of the separate systems. In no case shall the conductors, cables, messenger strand, or equipment of one system cause abrasion to the conductors, cable, messenger strand, or equipment of any other system.

(3) Lightning Conductors. Where practicable, a separation of at least 6 feet (1.83 m) shall be maintained between any coaxial cable and lightning conductors.

820-13. Conductors Inside Buildings. Beyond the point of grounding, as defined in Section 820-7, the cable installation shall comply with (a) through (d) below.

(a) Electric Light or Power. Coaxial cable shall be separated at least 2 inches (50.8 mm) from conductors of any electric light or power circuits or Class 1 circuits.

Exception No. 1: Where the electric light or power or Class 1 circuit conductors are in a raceway, or in metal-sheathed, metal-clad, nonmetallic-sheathed, or Type UF cables.

Exception No. 2: Where the conductors are permanently separated from the conductors of the other circuit by a continuous and firmly fixed nonconductor, such as porcelain tubes or flexible tubing, in addition to the insulation on the wire.

(b) In Raceways and Boxes. Coaxial cable shall not be placed in any raceway, compartment, outlet box, junction box, or other enclosures with conductors of electric light or power circuits or Class 1 circuits.

Exception No. 1: Where the conductors of the different systems are separated by a permanent partition.

Exception No. 2: Conductors in outlet boxes, junction boxes, or similar fittings or compartments where such conductors are introduced solely for power supply to the coaxial cable system distribution equipment or for power connection to remote-control equipment.

(c) In Shafts. Coaxial cable installed in the same shaft with conductors for electric light or power shall be separated from the electric light or power conductors by not less than 2 inches (50.8 mm).

Exception No. 1: Where the conductors of either system are encased in noncombustible tubing.

Exception No. 2: Where the electric light or power conductors are in a raceway, or in metal-sheathed, metal-clad, nonmetallic-sheathed, or Type UF cables.

(d) Vertical Runs. Coaxial cables bunched together in a vertical run in a shaft shall have a fire-resistant covering capable of preventing the carrying of flame from floor to floor.

Exception: Where cables are encased in noncombustible tubing or are located in a fireproof shaft having fire stops at each floor.

(FPN): There is no specific separation requirement between Class 2 or Class 3 circuits, wired distribution system cables, and communication cables or conductors, other than the clearance necessary to prevent conflict or abrasion.

820-14. Spread of Fire or Products of Combustion. Installations in hollow spaces, vertical shafts, and ventilation or air-handling ducts shall be so made that the possible spread of fire or products of combustion will not be substantially increased. Openings around penetrations through fire resistance rated walls, partitions, floors, or ceilings shall be firestopped using approved methods.

820-15. Wiring in Ducts, Plenums, and Other Air-Handling Spaces. Circuits and equipment installed in ducts or plenums or other space used for environmental air shall also comply with Section 300-22 as to installation methods.

Exception: Coaxial cables listed as having adequate fire-resistant and low-smoke producing characteristics shall be permitted for ducts and plenums as described in Section 300-22(b) and other space used for environmental air as described in Section 300-22(c).

See commentary following Sections 300-22(b) and 300-22(c).

(FPN): One method of defining low-smoke producing materials is by establishing an acceptable value of the smoke produced per the UL 910 test to a maximum peak optical density of 0.5 and a maximum average optical density of 0.15. Similarly, fire-resistant cables may be defined as having a maximum allowable flame travel distance of 5.0 feet (1.52 m) in the UL 910 test.

See commentary following Section 725-2(b).

D. Underground Circuits

820-18. Entering Buildings. Underground coaxial cables in a duct, pedestal, handhole, or manhole containing electric light or power conductors shall be in a section permanently separated from such conductors by means of a suitable barrier.

E. Grounding

820-22. Cable Grounding. Coaxial cable shall be grounded as specified in (a) through (h) below.

(a) Insulation. The grounding conductor shall have a rubber or other suitable kind of insulation.

(b) Material. The grounding conductor shall be copper or other corrosion-resistant conductive material, stranded or solid.

(c) Size. The grounding conductor shall not be smaller than No. 18; it shall have an ampacity approximately equal to that of the outer conductor of the coaxial cable.

(d) Run in Straight Line. The grounding conductor shall be run to the grounding electrode in as straight a line as practicable.

(e) Physical Protection. Where necessary, the grounding conductor shall be guarded from physical damage.

(f) Electrode. The grounding conductor shall be connected as follows:

(1) To the nearest accessible location on (1) the building or structure grounding electrode system as covered in Section 250-81, (2) the grounded interior metal water piping system as covered in Section 250-80(a), (3) the power service accessible means external to enclosures as covered in Section 250-71(b), (4) the metallic power service raceway, (5) the service equipment enclosure, or (6) the grounding electrode conductor or the grounding electrode conductor metal enclosure; or

(2) If the building or structure served has no grounding means as described in (f)(1), to any one of the individual electrodes described in Section 250-81; or

(3) If the building or structure served has no grounding means as described in (f)(1) or (f)(2), to: (1) an effectively grounded metal structure, or (2) a continuous and extensive underground gas piping system where acceptable to both the gas supplier and to the authority having jurisdiction, or (3) to a ground rod or pipe driven into permanently damp earth and separated from lightning conductors as covered in Section 820-11(e)(3), and at least 6 feet (1.83 m) from electrodes of other systems. Steam or hot water pipes or lightning rod conductors shall not be employed as electrodes for protectors.

(g) Electrode Connection. Connections to grounding electrodes shall comply with Section 250-115. Where a gas pipe electrode is used, connection shall be made between the gas meter and the street main.

(h) Bonding of Electrodes. A bonding jumper not smaller than No. 6 copper or equivalent shall be connected between the antenna systems and the power grounding electrodes where the requirements of (f) above result in the use of separate electrodes. Bonding together of all separate grounding electrodes shall be permitted.

(FPN): See Section 250-86 for use of lightning rods.

The most common error made in grounding CATV systems is to connect the coaxial cable sheath to a ground rod, often 4 ft long, driven by the CATV installer at a convenient location near the point of cable entry to the building. This is permitted by the *Code* only if the building or structure has none of the grounding means described in Sections 820-22(f)(1) or (f)(2), which is extremely unlikely. The *Code* does not say these grounding means must be readily available; if they exist they are required to be used.

Proper bonding of the CATV system coaxial cable sheath to the electrical power ground is needed to prevent potential fire and shock hazards. The earth cannot be used as an equipment grounding conductor or bonding conductor as it will not have the low impedance path needed. See Section 250-91(c).

Both CATV systems and power systems are subject to current surges as a result, for example, of induced voltages from lightning in the vicinity of the usually extensive outside distribution systems. Surges also result from switching operations on power systems. If the "grounded" conductors and parts of the two systems are not bonded by a low impedance path, such line surges can raise the potential difference between the two systems to many thousands of volts. This can result in arcing between the two systems, for example wherever the coaxial cable jacket contacts a grounded part inside the building, such as a metal water pipe or metal structural member.

If a person is the interface between the two systems, and the bonding has not been done in accordance with the *Code*, the high voltage surge could result in electric shock. More common, however, is burnout of the TV tuner, as this part is almost always an interface between the two systems. The tuner is connected to the power system ground through the grounded neutral of the power supply, even if the TV set itself is not provided with an equipment grounding conductor.

Also see commentary following Section 820-7.

820-23. Equipment Grounding. Unpowered equipment and enclosures or equipment powered by the coaxial cable shall be considered grounded where connected to the metallic cable shield.

9

Tables and Examples

Contents

A. Tables

Notes to Tables

1. Tables 3A, 3B and 3C apply only to complete conduit or tubing systems and are not intended to apply to short sections of conduit or tubing used to protect exposed wiring from physical damage.

2. Equipment grounding conductors, when installed, shall be included when calculating conduit or tubing fill. The actual dimensions of the equipment grounding conductor (insulated or bare) shall be used in the calculation.

TABLES AND EXAMPLES

3. When conduit nipples having a maximum length not to exceed 24 inches (610 mm) are installed between boxes, cabinets, and similar enclosures, the nipple shall be permitted to be filled to 60 percent of its total cross-sectional area, and Note 8 of Tables 310-16 through 310-19 does not apply to this condition.

4. For conductors not included in Chapter 9, such as compact or multiconductor cables, the actual dimensions shall be used.

5. See Table 1 for allowable percentage of conduit or tubing fill.

(FPN): Table 1 is based on common conditions of proper cabling and alignment of conductors where the length of the pull and the number of bends are within reasonable limits. It should be recognized that for certain conditions a larger size conduit or a lesser conduit fill should be considered.

Tables 3A, 3B, and 3C provide for the maximum allowable number of conductors (new work or rewiring) that may be enclosed in complete systems of conduit or tubing, based on the percentage fill of Table 1, and do not apply to short sections of conduit or tubing used for the physical protection of conductors and cables. Cables are commonly protected from physical damage by conduit or tubing sleeves sized to enable the cable to be passed through with relative ease without injuring or abrading the protective jacket of the cable.

Conduit nipples, not exceeding 24 in. in length, may be filled to 60 percent of their capacity and the derating factors of Note 8 to Tables 310-16 through 310-19 need not be applied.

All conductors occupy space in a raceway, and they must therefore all be counted, including equipment grounding conductors (insulated, bare or covered) and neutral or grounded conductors (insulated, bare or covered). The only exception to this rule is the addition of an uninsulated grounding conductor permitted within short lengths (not more than 72 in.) of ⅜-in. flexible metal conduit (see Fine Print Note to Table 350-3). The dimensions of bare conductors are given in Table 8.

For conductors not included in Chapter 9, such as high-voltage types, the cross-sectional area may be calculated in the following manner, using the actual dimensions of each conductor:

D = outside diameter of a conductor (including insulation)

CM = circular mils

1 in. = 1,000 mils (1 mil = 0.001 in.)

CM = [π (3.1416) ÷ 4] = 0.7854 of a square mil

Diameter in mils squared × 0.7854 = cross-sectional area

Table 1. Percent of Cross Section of Conduit and Tubing for Conductors

(See Table 2 for Fixture Wires)

Number of Conductors	1	2	3	4	Over 4
All conductor types except lead-covered (new or rewiring)	53	31	40	40	40
Lead-covered conductors	55	30	40	38	35

Note 1. See Tables 3A, 3B, and 3C for number of conductors all of the same size in trade sizes of conduit ½ inch through 6 inch.

Note 2. For conductors larger than 750 MCM or for combinations of conductors of different sizes, use Tables 4 through 8, Chapter 9, for dimensions of conductors, conduit and tubing.

Note 3. Where the calculated number of conductors, all of the same size, includes a decimal fraction, the next higher whole number shall be used where this decimal is 0.8 or larger.

Note 4. When bare conductors are permitted by other sections of this Code, the dimensions for bare conductors in Table 8 of Chapter 9 shall be permitted.

Note 5. A multiconductor cable of two or more conductors shall be treated as a single conductor cable for calculating percentage conduit fill area. For cables that have elliptical cross section, the cross-sectional area calculation shall be based on using the major diameter of the ellipse as a circle diameter.

Example: Three 15-kV single conductors are to be installed in conduit. The outside diameter of each conductor measures 1⅝ in. (1⅝ in. = 1.62 in.).

$$1.62 \times 1.62 \times .7854 \times 3 = 6.18 \text{ sq in.}$$

Table 1 allows 40 percent conduit fill for three or more conductors. Table 4 indicates that 40 percent of a 5-in. conduit is 8.00 sq in., thus accommodating three 15-kV single conductors.

The percentage fills of Table 1 for conduit and tubing are to be used where any conflict occurs in Tables 3A, 3B, or 3C and also when various conductor sizes are to be installed in the same conduit.

An example of computing the conduit size for various conductor sizes follows:

Number	Wire size and type	Table 5 cross-sectional area (ea.)	Subtotal cross-sectional area
4	12 THWN	0.0117	0.0468
3	8 TW	0.0471	0.1413
3	6 THW	0.0819	0.2457
		Total cross-sectional area	0.4338

The 40 percent column (three or more conductors) of Table 4 indicates that 40 percent of a 1¼-in. conduit is 0.60 sq in., the required conduit size for these ten conductors.

An example based on Note 3 (decimal fractions) would be to determine how many No. 12 THWN conductors are permitted in a ¾-in. conduit. Table 1 permits a 40 percent fill (three or more conductors), hence, from Table 4, 40 percent of a ¾-in. conduit is 0.21 sq in., and, from Table 5, the cross-sectional area of a No. 12 THWN conductor is 0.0117 sq in.

$$0.21 \div 0.0117 = 17.9$$

Eighteen such conductors are permitted in a ¾-in. conduit. [Since the decimal (0.9) is more than 0.8, it is increased to the next higher whole number. If the decimal had been less than 0.8, the decimal would have been dropped.]

Table 2. Maximum Number of Fixture Wires in Trade Sizes of Conduit or Tubing

(40 Percent Fill Based on Individual Diameters)

Conduit Trade Size (Inches)	½					¾					1					1¼					1½					2				
Wire Types	18	16	14	12	10	18	16	14	12	10	18	16	14	12	10	18	16	14	12	10	18	16	14	12	10	18	16	14	12	10
PTF, PTFF, PGFF, PGF, PFF, PF, PAF, PAFF, ZF, ZFF	23	18	14			40	31	24			65	50	39			115	90	70			157	122	95			257	200	156		
TFFN, TFN	19	15				34	26				55	43				97	76				132	104				216	169			
SF-1	16					29					47					83					114					186				
SFF-1, FFH-1	15					26					43					76					104					169				
CF	13	10	8	4	3	23	18	14	7	6	38	30	23	12	9	66	53	40	21	16	91	72	55	29	22	149	118	90	48	37
TF	11	10				20	18				32	30				57	53				79	72				129	118			
RFH-1	11					20					32					57					79					129				
TFF	11	10				20	17				32	27				56	49				77	66				126	109			
AF	11	9	7	4	3	19	16	12	7	5	31	26	20	11	8	55	46	36	19	15	75	63	49	27	20	123	104	81	44	34
SFF-2	9	7	6			16	12	10			27	20	17			47	36	30			65	49	42			106	81	68		
SF-2	9	8	6			16	14	11			27	23	18			47	40	32			65	55	43			106	90	71		
FFH-2	9	7				15	12				25	19				44	34				60	46				99	75			
RFH-2	7	5				12	10				20	16				36	28				49	38				80	62			
KF-1, KFF-1, KF-2, KFF-2	36	32	22	14	9	64	55	39	25	17	103	89	63	41	28	182	158	111	73	49	248	216	152	100	67	406	353	248	163	110

Table 3A. Maximum Number of Conductors in Trade Sizes of Conduit or Tubing

(Based on Table 1, Chapter 9)

Type Letters	Conductor Size AWG, MCM	½	¾	1	1¼	1½	2	2½	3	3½	4	5	6
TW, T, RUH, RUW, XHHW (14 thru 8)	14	9	15	25	44	60	99	142	171				
	12	7	12	19	35	47	78	111	131	176			
	10	5	9	15	26	36	60	85					
	8	2	4	7	12	17	28	40	62	84	108		
RHW and RHH (without outer covering), THW	14	6	10	16	29	40	65	93	143	192			
	12	4	8	13	24	32	53	76	117	157			
	10	4	6	11	19	26	43	61	95	127	163		
	8	1	3	5	10	13	22	32	49	66	85	133	
TW, T, THW, RUH (6 thru 2), RUW (6 thru 2)	6	1	2	4	7	10	16	23	36	48	62	97	141
	4	1	1	3	5	7	12	17	27	36	47	73	106
	3	1	1	2	4	6	10	15	23	31	40	63	91
	2	1	1	2	4	5	9	13	20	27	34	54	78
	1		1	1	3	4	6	9	14	19	25	39	57
FEPB (6 thru 2), RHW and RHH (without outer covering)	0		1	1	2	3	5	8	12	16	21	33	49
	00		1	1	1	3	5	7	10	14	18	29	41
	000		1	1	1	2	4	6	9	12	15	24	35
	0000			1	1	1	3	5	7	10	13	20	29
	250			1	1	1	2	4	6	8	10	16	23
	300			1	1	1	2	3	5	7	9	14	20
	350				1	1	1	3	4	6	8	12	18
	400				1	1	1	2	4	5	7	11	16
	500				1	1	1	1	3	4	6	9	14
	600					1	1	1	3	4	5	7	11
	700					1	1	1	2	3	4	7	10
	750					1	1	1	2	3	4	6	9

Conduit Trade Size (Inches)

Table 3B. Maximum Number of Conductors in Trade Sizes of Conduit or Tubing

(Based on Table 1, Chapter 9)

Type Letters	Conductor Size AWG, MCM	½	¾	1	1¼	1½	2	2½	3	3½	4	5	6
THWN,	14	13	24	39	69	94	154						
	12	10	18	29	51	70	114	164					
	10	6	11	18	32	44	73	104	160				
	8	3	5	9	16	22	36	51	79	106	136		
THHN, FEP (14 thru 2), FEPB (14 thru 8), PFA (14 thru 4/0), PFAH (14 thru 4/0), Z (14 thru 4/0)	6	1	4	6	11	15	26	37	57	76	98	154	
	4	1	2	4	7	9	16	22	35	47	60	94	137
	3	1	1	3	6	8	13	19	29	39	51	80	116
	2	1	1	3	5	7	11	16	25	33	43	67	97
	1		1	1	3	5	8	12	18	25	32	50	72
XHHW (4 thru 500MCM)	0		1	1	3	4	7	10	15	21	27	42	61
	00		1	1	2	3	6	8	13	17	22	35	51
	000		1	1	1	3	5	7	11	14	18	29	42
	0000			1	1	2	4	6	9	12	15	24	35
	250			1	1	1	3	4	7	10	12	20	28
	300			1	1	1	3	4	6	8	11	17	24
	350			1	1	1	2	3	5	7	9	15	21
	400						1	3	5	6	8	13	19
	500				1	1	1	2	4	5	7	11	16
	600				1	1	1	1	3	4	5	9	13
	700					1	1	1	3	4	5	8	11
	750					1	1	1	2	3	4	7	11
XHHW	6	1	3	5	9	13	21	30	47	63	81	128	185
	600				1	1	1	1	3	4	5	9	13
	700					1	1	1	3	4	5	7	11
	750					1	1	1	2	3	4	7	10

Table 3C.   Maximum Number of Conductors in Trade Sizes of Conduit or Tubing

(Based on Table 1, Chapter 9)

Conduit Trade Size (Inches) →	½	¾	1	1¼	1½	2	2½	3	3½	4	5	6
Type Letters / Conductor Size AWG, MCM												
RHW, — 14	3	6	10	18	25	41	58	90	121	155		
12	3	5	9	15	21	35	50	77	103	132		
10	2	4	7	13	18	29	41	64	86	110		
8	1	2	4	7	9	16	22	35	47	60	94	137
RHH (with outer covering) — 6	1	1	2	5	6	11	15	24	32	41	64	93
4	1	1	1	3	5	8	12	18	24	31	50	72
3	1	1	1	3	4	7	10	16	22	28	44	63
2		1	1	3	4	6	9	14	19	24	38	56
1		1	1	1	3	5	7	11	14	18	29	42
0		1	1	1	2	4	6	9	12	16	25	37
00			1	1	1	3	5	8	11	14	22	32
000			1	1	1	3	4	7	9	12	19	28
0000			1	1	1	2	4	6	8	10	16	24
250				1	1	1	3	5	6	8	13	19
300				1	1	1	3	4	5	7	11	17
350				1	1	1	2	4	5	6	10	15
400				1	1	1	1	3	4	6	9	14
500				1	1	1	1	3	4	5	8	11
600					1	1	1	2	3	4	6	9
700					1	1	1	1	3	3	6	8
750						1	1	1	3	3	5	8

Tables 4 through 8, Chapter 9. Tables 4 through 8 give the nominal size of conductors and conduit or tubing for use in computing size of conduit or tubing for various combinations of conductors. The dimensions represent average conditions only, and variations will be found in dimensions of conductors and conduits of different manufacture.

Table 4.   Dimensions and Percent Area of Conduit and of Tubing

Areas of Conduit or Tubing for the Combinations of Wires Permitted in Table 1, Chapter 9.

Area — Square Inches

Trade Size	Internal Diameter Inches	Total 100%	Not Lead Covered			Lead Covered				
			2 Cond. 31%	Over 2 Cond. 40%	1 Cond. 53%	1 Cond. 55%	2 Cond. 30%	3 Cond. 40%	4 Cond. 38%	Over 4 Cond. 35%
½	.622	.30	.09	.12	.16	.17	.09	.12	.11	.11
¾	.824	.53	.16	.21	.28	.29	.16	.21	.20	.19
1	1.049	.86	.27	.34	.46	.47	.26	.34	.33	.30
1¼	1.380	1.50	.47	.60	.80	.83	.45	.60	.57	.53
1½	1.610	2.04	.63	.82	1.08	1.12	.61	.82	.78	.71
2	2.067	3.36	1.04	1.34	1.78	1.85	1.01	1.34	1.28	1.18
2½	2.469	4.79	1.48	1.92	2.54	2.63	1.44	1.92	1.82	1.68
3	3.068	7.38	2.29	2.95	3.91	4.06	2.21	2.95	2.80	2.58
3½	3.548	9.90	3.07	3.96	5.25	5.44	2.97	3.96	3.76	3.47
4	4.026	12.72	3.94	5.09	6.74	7.00	3.82	5.09	4.83	4.45
5	5.047	20.00	6.20	8.00	10.60	11.00	6.00	8.00	7.60	7.00
6	6.065	28.89	8.96	11.56	15.31	15.89	8.67	11.56	10.98	10.11

Table 5.   Dimensions of Rubber-Covered and Thermoplastic-Covered Conductors

Size AWG MCM	Types RFH-2, RH, RHH,*** RHW,*** SF-2 — Approx. Diam. Inches	Approx. Area Sq. In.	Types TF, T, THW,† TW, RUH,** RUW** — Approx. Diam. Inches	Approx. Area Sq. In.	Types TFN, THHN, THWN — Approx. Diam. Inches	Approx. Area Sq. In.	Types**** FEP, FEPB, FEPW, TFE, PF, PFA, PFAH, PGF, PTF, Z, ZF, ZFF — Approx. Diam. Inches	Approx. Area Sq. Inches	Type XHHW, ZW†† — Approx. Diam. Inches	Approx. Area Sq. In.	Types KF-1, KF-2, KFF-1, KFF-2 — Approx. Diam. Sq. In.	Approx. Area Sq. In.
Col. 1	Col. 2	Col. 3	Col. 4	Col. 5	Col. 6	Col. 7	Col. 8	Col. 9	Col. 10	Col. 11	Col. 12	Col. 13
18	.146	.0167	.106	.0088	.089	.0062	.081	.0052	…	…	.065	.0033
16	.158	.0196	.118	.0109	.100	.0079	.092	.0066	…	…	.070	.0038
14	30 mils .171	.0230	.131	.0135	.105	.0087	.105 .105	.0087 .0087	.129	.0131	.083	.0054
14	45 mils .204*	.0327*	…	…	…	…	…	…	…	…	…	…
14	…	…	.162†	.0206†	…	…	…	…	…	…	…	…
12	30 mils .188	.0278	.148	.0172	.122	.0117	.121 .121	.0115 .0115	.146	.0167	.102	.0082
12	45 mils .221*	.0384*	…	…	…	…	…	…	…	…	…	…
12	…	…	.179†	.0252†	…	…	…	…	…	…	…	…
10	.242	.0460	.168	.0222	.153	.0184	.142 .142	.0158 .0158	.166	.0216	.124	.0121
10	…	…	.199†	.0311†	…	…	…	…	…	…	…	…
8	.328	.0845	.245	.0471	.218	.0373	.206 .186	.0333 .0272	.241	.0456	…	…
8	…	…	.276†	.0598†	…	…	…	…	…	…	…	…
6	.397	.1238	.323	.0819	.257	.0519	.244 .302	.0468 .0716	.282	.0625	…	…
4	.452	.1605	.372	.1087	.328	.0845	.292 .350	.0670 .0962	.328	.0845	…	…
3	.481	.1817	.401	.1263	.356	.0995	.320 .378	.0804 .1122	.356	.0995	…	…
2	.513	.2067	.433	.1473	.388	.1182	.352 .410	.0973 .1320	.388	.1182	…	…
1	.588	.2715	.508	.2027	.450	.1590	.420	.1385	.450	.1590	…	…
0	.629	.3107	.549	.2367	.491	.1893	.462	.1676	.491	.1893	…	…
00	.675	.3578	.595	.2781	.537	.2265	.498	.1948	.537	.2265	…	…
000	.727	.4151	.647	.3288	.588	.2715	.560	.2463	.588	.2715	…	…
0000	.785	.4840	.705	.3904	.646	.3278	.618	.3000	.646	.3278	…	…

Table 5 (Continued)

Size AWG MCM	Types RFH-2, RH, RHH,*** RHW,*** SF-2		Types TF, T, THW,† TW, RUH,** RUW***		Types TFN, THHN, THWN		Types***** FEP, FEPB, FEPW, TFE, PF, PFA, PFAH, PGF, PTF, Z, ZF, ZFF		Type XHHW, ZW††	
	Approx. Diam. Inches	Approx. Area Sq. In.	Approx. Diam. Inches	Approx. Area Sq. In.	Approx. Diam. Inches	Approx. Area Sq. In.	Approx. Diam. Inches	Approx. Area Sq. Inches	Approx. Diam. Inches	Approx. Area Sq. In.
Col. 1	Col. 2	Col. 3	Col. 4	Col. 5	Col. 6	Col. 7	Col. 8	Col. 9	Col. 10	Col. 11
250	.868	.5917	.788	.4877	.716	.4026	....	....	.716	.4026
300	.933	.6837	.843	.5581	.771	.4669	....	....	.771	.4669
350	.985	.7620	.855	.6291	.822	.5307	....	....	.822	.5307
400	1.032	.8365	.942	.6969	.869	.5931	....	....	.869	.5931
500	1.119	.9834	1.029	.8316	.955	.7163	....	....	.955	.7163
600	1.233	1.1940	1.143	1.0261	1.058	.8791	....	....	1.073	.9043
700	1.304	1.3355	1.214	1.1575	1.129	1.0011	....	....	1.145	1.0297
750	1.339	1.4082	1.249	1.2252	1.163	1.0623	....	....	1.180	1.0936
800	1.372	1.4784	1.282	1.2908	1.196	1.1234	....	....	1.210	1.1499
900	1.435	1.6173	1.345	1.4208	1.259	1.2449	....	....	1.270	1.2668
1000	1.494	1.7530	1.404	1.5482	1.317	1.3623	....	....	1.330	1.3893
1250	1.676	2.2062	1.577	1.9532	....	....	....	....	1.500	1.7671
1500	1.801	2.5475	1.702	2.2751	....	....	....	....	1.620	2.0612
1750	1.916	2.8832	1.817	2.5930	....	....	....	....	1.740	2.3779
2000	2.021	3.2079	1.922	2.9013	....	....	....	....	1.840	2.6590

* The dimensions of Types RHH and RHW.

** No. 14 to No. 2.

† Dimensions of THW in sizes No. 14 to No. 8. No. 6 THW and larger is the same dimension as T.

*** Dimensions of RHH and RHW without outer covering are the same as THW No. 18 to No. 10, solid; No. 8 and larger, stranded.

**** In Columns 8 and 9 the values shown for sizes No. 1 thru 0000 are for TFE and Z only. The right-hand values in Columns 8 and 9 are for FEPB, Z, ZF, and ZFF only.

†† No. 14 to No. 2.

Table 6.   Dimensions of Lead-Covered Conductors

Types RL, RHL, and RUL

Size AWG-MCM	Single Conductor		Two Conductor		Three Conductor	
	Diam. Inches	Area Sq. In.	Diam. Inches	Area Sq. In.	Diam. Inches	Area Sq. In.
14	.28	.062	.28 X .47	.115	.59	.273
12	.29	.066	.31 X .54	.146	.62	.301
10	.35	.096	.35 X .59	.180	.68	.363
8 sol.	.41	.132	.41 X .71	.255	.82	.528
8 str.	.43	.145	.43 X .75	.282	.86	.581
6	.49	.188	.49 X .86	.369	.97	.738
4	.55	.237	.54 X .96	.457	1.08	.916
2	.60	.283	.61 X 1.08	.578	1.21	1.146
1	.67	.352	.70 X 1.23	.756	1.38	1.49
0	.71	.396	.74 X 1.32	.859	1.47	1.70
00	.76	.454	.79 X 1.41	.980	1.57	1.94
000	.81	.515	.84 X 1.52	1.123	1.69	2.24
0000	.87	.593	.90 X 1.64	1.302	1.85	2.68
250	.98	.754	....	.....	2.02	3.20
300	1.04	.85	....	.....	2.15	3.62
350	1.10	.95	....	.....	2.26	4.02
400	1.14	1.02	....	.....	2.40	4.52
500	1.23	1.18	....	.....	2.59	5.28

The above cables are limited to straight runs or with nominal offsets equivalent to not more than two quarter bends.

Note — No. 14 to No. 10, solid conductors; No. 8, solid or stranded conductors; No. 6 and larger, stranded conductors.

Table 7. Dimensions of Asbestos-Varnished-Cambric Insulated Conductors

Types AVA, AVB, and AVL

Size AWG, MCM	Type AVA		Type AVB		Type AVL	
	Approx. Diam. Inches	Approx. Area Sq. In.	Approx. Diam. Inches	Approx. Area Sq. In.	Approx. Diam. Inches	Approx. Area Sq. In.
14	.245	.047	.205	.033	.320	.080
12	.265	.055	.225	.040	.340	.091
10	.285	.064	.245	.047	.360	.102
8 sol.	.310	.075	.270	.057	.390	.119
8 str.	.325	.083	.285	.064	.390	.119
6	.395	.122	.345	.094	.430	.145
4	.445	.155	.395	.123	.480	.181
2	.505	.200	.460	.166	.570	.255
1	.585	.268	.540	.229	.620	.300
0	.625	.307	.580	.264	.660	.341
00	.670	.353	.625	.307	.705	.390
000	.720	.406	.675	.358	.755	.447
0000	.780	.478	.735	.425	.815	.521
250	.885	.616	.855	.572	.955	.715
300	.940	.692	.910	.649	1.010	.800
350	.995	.778	.965	.731	1.060	.885
400	1.040	.850	1.010	.800	1.105	.960
500	1.125	.995	1.095	.945	1.190	1.118
550	1.165	1.065	1.135	1.01	1.265	1.26
600	1.205	1.140	1.175	1.09	1.305	1.34
650	1.240	1.21	1.210	1.15	1.340	1.41
700	1.275	1.28	1.245	1.22	1.375	1.49
750	1.310	1.35	1.280	1.29	1.410	1.57
800	1.345	1.42	1.315	1.36	1.440	1.63
850	1.375	1.49	1.345	1.43	1.470	1.70
900	1.405	1.55	1.375	1.49	1.505	1.78
950	1.435	1.62	1.405	1.55	1.535	1.85
1000	1.465	1.69	1.435	1.62	1.565	1.93

Note: No. 14 to No. 10, solid; No. 8, solid or stranded; No. 6 and larger, stranded; except AVL where all sizes are stranded.

Varnished-Cambric Insulated Conductors
Type V

The insulation thickness for varnished-cambric conductors, Type V, is the same as for rubber-covered conductors, Type RHH, except for No. 8 which has 45-mil insulation for varnished-cambric, and 60-mil insulation for rubber-covered conductors. See Table 310-13. Therefore, Table 3C shall be permitted to be used for the number of varnished-cambric insulated conductors in a conduit or tubing.

Table 8. Conductor Properties

Size AWG/ MCM	Area Cir. Mils	Stranding Quan-tity	Stranding Diam. In.	Overall Diam. In.	Overall Area In.²	Copper Uncoated ohm/MFT	Copper Coated ohm/MFT	Alumi-num ohm/ MFT
18	1620	1	—	0.040	0.001	7.77	8.08	12.8
18	1620	7	0.015	0.046	0.002	7.95	8.45	13.1
16	2580	1	—	0.051	0.002	4.89	5.08	8.05
16	2580	7	0.019	0.058	0.003	4.99	5.29	8.21
14	4110	1	—	0.064	0.003	3.07	3.19	5.06
14	4110	7	0.024	0.073	0.004	3.14	3.26	5.17
12	6530	1	—	0.081	0.005	1.93	2.01	3.18
12	6530	7	0.030	0.092	0.006	1.98	2.05	3.25
10	10380	1	—	0.102	0.008	1.21	1.26	2.00
10	10380	7	0.038	0.116	0.011	1.24	1.29	2.04
8	16510	1	—	0.128	0.013	0.764	0.786	1.26
8	16510	7	0.049	0.146	0.017	0.778	0.809	1.28
6	26240	7	0.061	0.184	0.027	0.491	0.510	0.808
4	41740	7	0.077	0.232	0.042	0.308	0.321	0.508
3	52620	7	0.087	0.260	0.053	0.245	0.254	0.403
2	66360	7	0.097	0.292	0.067	0.194	0.201	0.319
1	83690	19	0.066	0.332	0.087	0.154	0.160	0.253
1/0	105600	19	0.074	0.373	0.109	0.122	0.127	0.201
2/0	133100	19	0.084	0.419	0.138	0.967	0.101	0.159
3/0	167800	19	0.094	0.470	0.173	0.0766	0.0797	0.126
4/0	211600	19	0.106	0.528	0.219	0.0608	0.0626	0.100
250	—	37	0.082	0.575	0.260	0.0515	0.0535	0.0847
300	—	37	0.090	0.630	0.312	0.0429	0.0446	0.0707
350	—	37	0.097	0.681	0.364	0.0367	0.0382	0.0605
400	—	37	0.104	0.728	0.416	0.0321	0.0331	0.0529
500	—	37	0.116	0.813	0.519	0.0258	0.0265	0.0424
600	—	61	0.992	0.893	0.626	0.0214	0.0223	0.0353
700	—	61	0.107	0.964	0.730	0.0184	0.0189	0.0303
750	—	61	0.111	0.998	0.782	0.0171	0.0176	0.0282
800	—	61	0.114	1.03	0.834	0.0161	0.0166	0.0265
900	—	61	0.122	1.09	0.940	0.0143	0.0147	0.0235
1000	—	61	0.128	1.15	1.04	0.0129	0.0132	0.0212
1250	—	91	0.117	1.29	1.30	0.0103	0.0106	0.0169
1500	—	91	0.128	1.41	1.57	0.00858	0.00883	0.0141
1750	—	127	0.117	1.52	1.83	0.00735	0.00756	0.0121
2000	—	127	0.126	1.63	2.09	0.00643	0.00662	0.0106

These resistance values are valid ONLY for the parameters as given. Using conductors having coated strands, different stranding type, and especially, other temperatures, change the resistance.

Formula for temperature change: $R_{2 = R1} [1+\alpha(T_2\text{-}20)]$ where: $\alpha_{cu} = 0.00393$, $\alpha_{AL} = 0.00403$.

Class B stranding is listed as well as solid for some sizes. Its overall diameter and area is that of its circumscribing circle. The construction information is per NEMA WC8-1976 (Rev 5-1980). The resistance is calculated per National Bureau of Standards Handbook 100, dated 1966, and Handbook 109, dated 1972.

Conductors with compact and compressed stranding have about 9 percent and 3 percent, respectively, smaller bare conductor diameters than those shown.

The IACS conductivities used: bare copper = 100%, aluminum = 61%.

Table 9.   AC Resistance and Reactance
600 V cables, 3 phase, 60 Hz, 75°C—Three Single Conductors in Conduit

Size AWG, MCM	Uncoated Copper				Aluminum			
	Nonmagnetic		Magnetic		Nonmagnetic		Magnetic	
	Rac	X_L	Rac	X_L	Rac	X_L	Rac	X_L
14	3.1	0.054	3.1	0.068				
12	2.0	0.051	1.9	0.064	3.2	0.051	3.2	0.064
10	1.2	0.048	1.2	0.059	2.0	0.048	2.4	0.059
8	0.78	0.048	0.78	0.060	1.3	0.048	1.3	0.060
6	0.49	0.046	0.49	0.057	0.81	0.046	0.81	0.057
4	0.31	0.043	0.31	0.054	0.51	0.043	0.51	0.054
3	0.24	0.042	0.24	0.053	0.40	0.042	0.40	0.053
2	0.19	0.041	0.19	0.052	0.32	0.041	0.32	0.052
1	0.15	0.041	0.15	0.052	0.25	0.041	0.25	0.052
1/0	0.12	0.040	0.12	0.050	0.20	0.040	0.20	0.050
2/0	0.097	0.039	0.098	0.049	0.16	0.039	0.16	0.049
3/0	0.077	0.038	0.078	0.048	0.13	0.038	0.13	0.048
4/0	0.061	0.038	0.062	0.047	0.10	0.038	0.10	0.047
250	0.052	0.038	0.053	0.048	0.085	0.038	0.086	0.048
300	0.044	0.037	0.045	0.046	0.071	0.037	0.072	0.046
350	0.038	0.037	0.039	0.046	0.061	0.037	0.062	0.046
400	0.034	0.036	0.035	0.045	0.053	0.036	0.054	0.045
500	0.027	0.036	0.029	0.044	0.043	0.036	0.044	0.044
600	0.023	0.036	0.026	0.045	0.036	0.036	0.037	0.045
750	0.019	0.035	0.022	0.044	0.029	0.035	0.030	0.044
1000	0.016	0.034	0.019	0.043	0.022	0.034	0.024	0.043

Class B stranding was used; the computations are based upon 100 percent IACS copper, 61 percent IACS aluminum.

The values are valid ONLY for the parameters as given. Different operating temperatures and/or different installation configuration or environment will change the values.

At the stated parameters, capacitive reactance is negligible, so only inductive reactance is given.

B. Examples

Selection of Conductors. In the following examples, the results are generally expressed in amperes. To select conductor sizes, refer to Tables 310-16 through 310-19 and the Notes that pertain to such tables.

Voltage. For uniform application of Articles 210, 215 and 220, a nominal voltage of 120, 120/240, 240 and 208Y/120 volts shall be used in computing the ampere load on the conductor.

Fractions of an Ampere. Except where the computations result in a major fraction of an ampere (0.5 or larger), such fractions may be dropped.

Ranges. For the computation of the range loads in these examples, Column A of Table 220-19 has been used. For optional methods, see Columns B and C of Table 220-19.

SI Units: For SI units: one square foot = 0.093 square meter; one foot = 0.3048 meter.

In the following examples loads are assumed to be properly balanced on the system. Where loads are not properly balanced, additional feeder capacity may be required.

Example No. 1(a).   One-Family Dwelling

The dwelling has a floor area of 1500 sq. ft. exclusive of unoccupied cellar, unfinished attic, and open porches. Appliances are a 12-kW range and a 5.5 kW, 240-volt dryer. Assume range and dryer kW ratings equivalent to kVA ratings in accordance with Sections 220-18 and 220-19.

Computed Load [see Section 220-10(a)]:
General Lighting Load:
    1500 sq. ft. at 3 volt-amperes per sq. ft. = 4500 volt-amperes.

Minimum Number of Branch Circuits Required [see Section 220-2(b)]:
General Lighting Load:
    4500 volt-amperes ÷ 120 volts = 37.5 A: This requires three 15 A 2-wire or two 20 A 2-wire circuits
Small Appliance Load: Two 2-wire 20 A circuits [see Section 220-3(b)]
Laundry Load: One 2-wire 20 A circuit [see Section 220-3(c)]

Minimum Size Feeder Required [see Section 220-10(a)]:

General Lighting	4500 volt-amperes
Small Appliance Load	3000 volt-amperes
Laundry	1500 volt-amperes
Total General Light & Small Appliance	9000 volt-amperes
3000 volt-amperes at 100%	3000 volt-amperes
9000 − 3000 = 6000 volt-amperes at 35%	2100 volt-amperes
Net General Lighting & Small Appliance Load	5100 volt-amperes
Range Load (see Table 220-19)	8000 volt-amperes
Dryer Load (see Table 220-18)	5500 volt-amperes
Total Load	18,600 volt-amperes

For 120/240-volt 3-wire single-phase service or feeder,
18,600 volt-amperes ÷ 240 volts = 77.5 A.

Net computed load exceeds 10 kVA. Service conductors shall be 100 amperes [see Section 230-42(b)(2)].

Neutral for Feeder and Service

Lighting and Small Appliance Load	5100 volt-amperes
Range Load 8000 volt-amperes at 70%	5600 volt-amperes
Dryer Load 5500 volt-amperes at 70%	3850 volt-amperes
Total	14,550 volt-amperes

14,550 VA ÷ 240 V = 60.6 amperes

(Example 1(a) Continued Next Page.)

TABLES AND EXAMPLES

Example No. 1(a) (Continued)

The general lighting and general-use receptacle load is computed from the outside dimensions of the building, apartment, or other area involved. For a dwelling unit(s), the computed floor area is not to include open porches, garages, or unused or unfinished spaces unadaptable for future use. See Section 220-2(b).

Example: A two-story dwelling measures 30 ft × 30 ft for the first floor and 30 ft × 20 ft for the second floor.

$$30 \text{ ft} \times 30 \text{ ft} = \quad 900 \text{ sq ft (first floor)}$$
$$30 \text{ ft} \times 20 \text{ ft} = \quad \underline{600} \text{ sq ft (second floor)}$$
$$\text{Total area} = 1{,}500 \text{ sq ft}$$

The air-conditioning load in Example No. 2(b) is counted at 100 percent, and this load is calculated separately in order to comply with the requirements of Section 220-30 and Table 220-30.

Example No. 1(b). One-Family Dwelling

Same conditions as Example No. 1(a), plus addition of one 6-ampere 230-volt room air-conditioning unit and one 12-ampere 115-volt room air-conditioning unit*, one 8-ampere 115-volt rated disposal and one 10-ampere 120-volt rated dishwasher*. See Article 430 for general motors and Article 440, Part G for air-conditioning equipment. Motors have nameplate ratings of 115 V and 230 V for use on 120 V and 240 V nominal voltage systems.

From previous Example No. 1(a), feeder current is 78 amperes (3-wire 240 volts).

	Line A	Neutral	Line B
Amperes from Example No. 1(a)	78	61	78
One 230 V air conditioner	6	—	6
One 115 V air conditioner and 120 V dishwasher	12	12	10
One 115 V disposal	—	8	8
25% of largest motor (Section 430-24)	3	3	2
Amperes per line	99	84	104

* For feeder neutral, use largest of the two appliances for unbalance.

Example No. 2(a). Optional Calculation for One-Family Dwelling Heating Larger than Air-Conditioning
(See Section 220-30.)

Dwelling has a floor area of 1500 sq. ft. exclusive of unoccupied cellar, unfinished attic, and open porches. It has a 12-kW range, a 2.5-kW water heater, a 1.2-kW dishwasher, 9 kW of electric space heating installed in five rooms, a 5-kW clothes dryer, and a 6-ampere 230-volt room air-conditioning unit. Assume range, water heater, dishwasher, space heating, and clothes dryer kW ratings equivalent to kVA.

Air conditioner kVA is 6 × 230 ÷ 1000 = 1.38 kVA

1.38 kVA is less than the connected load of 9 kVA of space heating; therefore, the air conditioner load need not be included in the service calculation (see Section 220-21).

1500 sq. ft. at 3 volt-amperes	4.5 kVA
Two 20-amp. appliance outlet circuits at 1500 volt-amperes each	3.0 kVA
Laundry circuit	1.5 kVA
Range (at nameplate rating)..	12.0 kVA
Water heater	2.5 kVA
Dishwasher	1.2 kVA
Space heating..	9.0 kVA
Clothes dryer	5.0 kVA
	38.7 kVA

First 10 kVA at 100% = 10.00 kVA
Remainder at 40% (28.7 kVA × .4) = 11.48 kVA

Calculated load for service size 21.48 kVA = 21,480 volt-amperes
21,480 VA ÷ 240 volts = 89.5 amperes

Therefore, this dwelling may be served by a 100-ampere service.

(Example 2(a) Continued Next Page.)

Example No. 2(a) (Continued)

Feeder Neutral Load, per Section 220-22:

1500 sq. ft. at 3 volt-amperes	4500 volt-amperes
Three 20-amp. circuits at 1500 volt-amperes	4500 volt-amperes
Total	9000 volt-amperes
3000 volt-amperes at 100%.................................	3000 volt-amperes
9000 VA−3000 VA = 6000 volt-amperes at 35%	2100 volt-amperes
	5100 volt-amperes
Range—8 kVA at 70%	5600 volt-amperes
Clothes dryer—5 kVA at 70%	3500 volt-amperes
Dishwasher	1200 volt-amperes
Total..	15,400 volt-amperes

15,400 VA ÷ 240 volts = 64.2 amperes

Example No. 2(b). Optional Calculation for
One-Family Dwelling Air Conditioning Larger than Heating
(See Section 220-30.)

Dwelling has a floor area of 1500 sq. ft. exclusive of unoccupied cellar, unfinished attic, and open porches. It has two 20-ampere small appliance circuits, one 20-ampere laundry circuit, two 4-kW wall-mounted ovens, one 5.1-kW counter-mounted cooking unit, a 4.5-kW water heater, a 1.2-kW dishwasher, a 5-kW combination clothes washer and dryer, six 7-ampere 230-volt room air-conditioning units, and a 1.5-kW permanently installed bathroom-space heater. Assume wall-mounted ovens, counter-mounted cooking unit, water heater, dishwasher and combination clothes washer and dryer kW ratings equivalent to kVA.

Air Conditioning kVA Calculation:

Total amperes 6 × 7 = 42.00 amperes

42 × 240 ÷ 1000 = 10.08 kVA of air-conditioned load assume P.F. = 1.0

Load Included at 100%:

Air conditioning	10.08 kVA
Space heater (omit, see Section 220-21)	

Other Load:

	kVA
1500 sq. ft. at 3 volt-amperes	4.5
Two 20-amp. small appliance circuits	
at 1500 volt-amperes...	3.0
Laundry circuit	1.5
Two ovens	8.0
One cooking unit...	5.1
Water heater	4.5
Dishwasher	1.2
Washer/dryer	5.0
Total other load	32.8

1st 10 kVA at 100%	10.0	kVA
Remainder at 40% (22.8 kVA × .4).........................	9.12	kVA
Total calculated load	29.2	kVA = 29,200 volt-amperes

29,200 VA ÷ 240 V = 122 amperes (service rating)

Feeder Neutral Load, per Section 220-22:

(It is assumed that the two 4 kVA wall-mounted ovens are supplied by one branch circuit, the 5.1 kVA counter-mounted cooking unit by a separate circuit.)

1500 sq. ft. at 3 volt-amperes	4500 volt-amperes
Three 20-amp. circuits at 1500 volt-amperes	4500 volt-amperes
Total	9000 volt-amperes
3000 volt-amperes at 100%.............................	3000 volt-amperes
9000 VA−3000 VA = 6000 volt-amperes at 35%	2100 volt-amperes
	5100 volt-amperes

(Example 2(b) Continued Next Page.)

Example No. 2(b) (Continued)

Two 4 kVA ovens plus one 5.1 kVA cooking unit totals 13.1 kVA
    Table 220-19 permits 55% demand factor
    13.1 kVA × .55 = 7.2 kVA feeder capacity

7200 VA × 70% for neutral load	5040 volt-amperes
Clothes washer / dryer — 5 kVA	
× 70% for neutral load	3500 volt-amperes
Dishwasher	1200 volt-amperes
Total	14,840 volt-amperes

14,840 VA ÷ 240 V = 61.83, use 62 amperes

Example No. 3.   Store Building

A store 50 ft. by 60 ft., or 3000 sq. ft., has 30 ft. of show window. There are a total of 80 duplex receptacles. The service is 120/240-volt, single-phase (3-wire service).

Computed Load (Section 220-10):

* General Lighting Load:	
3000 sq. ft. at 3 volt-amperes per sq. ft. × 1.25	11,250 volt-amperes
Show Window Lighting Load:	
30 ft. at 200 volt-amperes per foot	6000 volt-amperes
Receptacle Load (Section 220-13)	
80 receptacles at 180 VA = 14,400 VA	
10,000 VA at 100%	10,000 volt-amperes
(14,400—10,000) VA at 50%	2200 volt-amperes
Outside sign circuit 1200 volt-amperes [Section 600-6(c)]	1,200 volt-amperes
Total...	30,650 volt-amperes

Minimum Number of Branch Circuits Required:

General Lighting Load:
   11,250 volt-amperes ÷ 240 volts = 47 amperes for 3-wire, 120/240.
The lighting load may be served by 2-wire or 3-wire 15- or 20-ampere circuits with combined capacity equal to 47 amperes or greater for 3-wire circuits or 94 amperes or greater for 2-wire circuits.

Show Window:

6000 volt-amperes ÷ 240 volts = 25 amperes for 3-wire, 120/240.
The show window lighting may be served by 2-wire or 3-wire circuits with a capacity equal to 25 amperes or greater for 3-wire circuits or 50 amperes or greater for 2-wire circuits.
Receptacles required by Section 210-62 are assumed to be included in the receptacle load above if these receptacles do not supply the show window lighting load.
Receptacle Load: 14,400 volt-amperes ÷ 240 volts = 60 amperes for 3-wire, 120/240.
The receptacle load may be served by 2-wire or 3-wire circuits with a capacity equal to 60 amperes or greater for 3-wire circuits or 120 amperes or greater for 2-wire circuits.

Minimum Size Feeders (or Service Conductors) Required (Section 215-3):

For 120/240-volt, 3-wire system:
   30,650 volt-amperes ÷ 240 volts = 128 amperes

* The above examples assume that the entire lighting load is continuous. The general lighting load is increased by 25 percent in accordance with Section 220-2. No branch circuit may serve a continous lighting load greater than 80 percent of its rating.

Example No. 4(a).   Multifamily Dwelling

Multifamily dwelling having 40 dwelling units.

Meters in two banks of 20 each and individual subfeeders to each dwelling unit.

One-half of the dwelling units are equipped with electric ranges not exceeding 12 kW each. Assume range kW rating equivalent to kVA rating in accordance with Section 220-19. Other half of ranges are gas ranges.

Area of each dwelling unit is 840 sq. ft.

Laundry facilities on premises available to all tenants. Add no circuit to individual dwelling unit. Add 1500 volt-amperes for each laundry circuit to house load and add to the example as a "house load."

(Example 4(a) Continued Next Page.)

Example No. 4(a) (Continued)

Computed Load for Each Dwelling Unit (Article 220):

General Lighting Load:
840 sq. ft. at 3 volt-amperes per sq. ft. .... 2520 volt-amperes
Special Appliance Load:
Electric Range (Section 220-19) .... 8000 volt-amperes

Minimum Number of Branch Circuits Required for Each Dwelling Unit (Section 220-3):

General Lighting Load: 2520 volt-amperes ÷ 120 volts = 21 amperes or two 15-ampere, 2-wire circuits; or two 20-ampere, 2-wire circuits.

Small Appliance Load: Two 2-wire circuits of No. 12 wire. [See Section 220-3(b).]

Range Circuit: 8000 volt-amperes ÷ 240 = 33 amperes or a circuit of two No. 8 and one No. 10 as permitted by Section 220-22. (See Section 210-19.)

Minimum Size Subfeeder Required for Each Dwelling Unit (Section 215-2):

Computed Load (Article 220):
General Lighting Load .... 2520 volt-amperes
Small Appliance Load, two 20-ampere circuits .... 3000 volt-amperes
Total Computed Load (without ranges) .... 5520 volt-amperes

Application of Demand Factor:
3000 volt-amperes at 100% .... 3000 volt-amperes
2520 volt-amperes at 35% .... 882 volt-amperes
Net Computed Load (without ranges).................................... 3882 volt-amperes
Range Load .... 8000 volt-amperes
Net Computed Load (with ranges)...................................... 11,882 volt-amperes

Size of Each Subfeeder (see Section 215-2).
For 120/240-volt, 3-wire system (without ranges):
Net Computed Load, 3882 volt-amperes ÷ 240 volts = 16.2 amperes.
For 120/240-volt, 3-wire system (with ranges):
Net Computed Load, 11,882 volt-amperes ÷ 240 volts = 49.5 amperes.

Subfeeder Neutral:
Lighting and Small Appliance Load .... 3882 volt-amperes
Range Load, 8000 volt-amperes at 70%
(see Section 220-22) .... 5600 volt-amperes
(Not included for apartments without electric range)
Net Computed Load (neutral) .... 9482 volt-amperes
9482 volt-amperes ÷ 240 volts = 39.5 amperes

Minimum Size Feeders Required from Service Equipment to Meter Bank (For 20 Dwelling Units — 10 with Ranges):

Total Computed Load:
Lighting and Small Appliance Load,
20 × 5520 volt-amperes.. 110,400 volt-amperes
Application of Demand Factor:
3000 volt-amperes at 100% .... 3000 volt-amperes
107,400 volt-amperes at 35% .... 37,950 volt-amperes
Net Computed Lighting and Small Appliance Load .... 40,590 volt-amperes
Range Load, 10 ranges (less than 12 kVA, Col. A,
Table 220-19) .... 25,000 volt-amperes
Net Computed Load (with ranges)...................................... 65,590 volt-amperes

For 120/240-volt, 3-wire system:
Net Computed Load, 65,590 volt-amperes ÷ 240 volt = 273 amperes.

Feeder Neutral:
Lighting and Small Appliance Load .... 40,590 volt-amperes
Range Load: 25,000 volt-amperes at 70%
(see Section 220-22) .... 17,500 volt-amperes
Computed Load (neutral)... 58,090 volt-amperes
58,090 volt-amperes ÷ 240 volts = 242 amperes.

Further Demand Factor (Section 220-22):
200 amperes at 100%   200 amperes
42 amperes at 70%   29 amperes
Net Computed Load (neutral) .... 229 amperes

(Example 4(a) Continued Next Page.)

TABLES AND EXAMPLES

Example No. 4(a) (Continued)

Minimum Size Main Feeder (or Service Conductors) Required (less house load). (For 40 Dwelling Units — 20 with Ranges):

Total Computed Load:
Lighting and Small Appliance Load, 40 × 5520
volt-amperes .... 220,800 volt-amperes

Application of Demand Factor:
3000 volt-amperes at 100% .... 3000 volt-amperes
117,000 volt-amperes at 35% .... 40,950 volt-amperes
100,800 volt-amperes at 25% .... <u>25,200 volt-amperes</u>
    Net Computed Lighting and Small Appliance Load .... 69,150 volt-amperes
Range Load, 20 ranges (less than 12 kVA, Col. A,
Table 220-19) .... <u>35,000 volt-amperes</u>
    Net Computed Load .... 104,150 volt-amperes

For 120/240-volt, 3-wire system:
    Net Computed Load, 104,150 volt-amperes ÷ 240 volts = 434 amperes.

Feeder Neutral:
Lighting and Small Appliance Load .... 69,150 volt-amperes
Range Load, 35,000 volt-amperes at 70%
(see Section 220-22) .... <u>24,500 volt-amperes</u>
Computed Load (neutral)... 93,650 volt-amperes
    93,650 volt-amperes ÷ 240 volts = 390 amperes.

Further Demand Factor (see Section 220-22):
200 amperes at 100% .... 200 amperes
190 amperes at 70% .... <u>133 amperes</u>
Net Computed Load (neutral) .... 333 amperes

See Tables 310-16 through 310-19, Notes 8 and 10.

Example No. 4(b).   Optional Calculation for Multifamily Dwelling

Multifamily dwelling equipped with electric cooking and space heating or air conditioning and having 40 dwelling units.

Meters in two banks of 20 each plus house metering and individual subfeeders to each dwelling unit.

Each dwelling unit is equipped with an electric range of 8-kW nameplate rating, four 1.5 kW separately controlled 240-volt electric space heaters, and a 2.5-kW 240-volt electric water heater. Assume range, space heater, and water heater kW ratings equivalent to kVA.

A common laundry facility is available to all tenants [Section 210-52(e), Exception No. 1].

Area of each dwelling unit is 840 square feet.

Computed Load for Each Dwelling Unit (Article 220):

General Lighting Load:
840 sq. ft. at 3 volt-amperes per sq. ft. .... 2520 volt-amperes
Electric Range .... 8000 volt-amperes
Electric Heat 6 kVA .... 6000 volt-amperes
(or air conditioning if larger)
Electric Water Heater.. 2500 volt-amperes

Minimum Number of Branch Circuits Required for Each Dwelling Unit:

General Lighting Load 2520 volt-amperes ÷ 120 volts = 21 amperes or two 15-ampere 2-wire circuits or two 20-ampere 2-wire circuits.

Small Appliance Loads: Two 2-wire circuits of No. 12 [see Section 220-3(b)].

Range circuit 8000 volt-amperes × 80% ÷ 240 volts = 27 amperes on a circuit of three No. 10 AWG as permitted in Column C of Table 220-19.

Space Heating 6000 volt-amperes ÷ 240 volts = 25 amperes

No. of circuits (see Section 220-3).

Minimum Size Subfeeder Required for Each Dwelling Unit (Section 215-2):

Computed Load (Article 220):
General Lighting Load .... 2520 volt-amperes
Small Appliance Load, two 20-ampere circuits .... <u>3000 volt-amperes</u>
Total Computed Load .... 5520 volt-amperes
(without range and space heating)

(Example 4(b) Continued Next Page.)

Example No. 4(b) (Continued)

Application of Demand Factor:

3000 volt-amperes at 100%	3000 volt-amperes
2520 volt-amperes at 35%	882 volt-amperes
Net Computed Load	3882 volt-amperes
(without range and space heating)	
Range Load	6400 volt-amperes
Space Heating (Section 220-15)	6000 volt-amperes
Water Heater	2500 volt-amperes
Net Computed Load for individual dwelling unit	18,782 volt-amperes

For 120/240-volt 3-wire system

Net Computed Load 18,782 volt-amperes ÷ 240 volts = 78 amperes

Subfeeder Neutral (Section 220-22)

Lighting and Small Appliance Load	3882 volt-amperes
Range Load 6400 volt-amperes at 70%	
(see Section 220-22)	4480 volt-amperes
Space and Water Heating (no neutral) 240 volt	0 volt-amperes
Net Computed Load (neutral)	8362 volt-amperes

8362 volt-amperes ÷ 240 volts = 35 amperes

Minimum Size Feeder Required from Service Equipment to Meter Bank for 20 Dwelling Units:

Total Computed Load:

Lighting and Small Appliance Load 20 × 5520	110,400 volt-amperes
Water and Space Heating Load 20 × 8500	170,000 volt-amperes
Range Load 20 × 8000 volt-amperes	160,000 volt-amperes
Net Computed Load (20 dwelling units)	440,400 volt-amperes

Net Computed Load Using Optional Calculation (Table 220-32)

440,400 volt-amperes × .38	167,352 volt-amperes

167,352 volt-amperes ÷ 240 volts = 697 amperes

Minimum Size Main Feeder Required (less house load) for 40 Dwelling Units:

Total Computed Load:

Lighting and Small Appliance Load 40 × 5520	220,800 volt-amperes
Water and Space Heating 40 × 8500	340,000 volt-amperes
Range Load 40 × 8000 volt-amperes	320,000 volt-amperes
Net Computed Load (40 dwelling units)	880,800 volt-amperes

Net Computed Load Using Optional Calculation (Table 220-32)

880,800 volt-amperes × .28	246,624 volt-amperes

246,624 volt-amperes ÷ 240 volts = 1028 amperes

Feeder Neutral Load for Feeder from Service Equipment to Meter Bank for 20 Dwelling Units:

Lighting and Small Appliance Load

20 × 5520 volt-amperes	110,400 volt-amperes
First 3000 volt-amperes at 100%	3000 volt-amperes
107,400 volt-amperes at 35%	37,500 volt-amperes
Subtotal	40,500 volt-amperes
20 Ranges = 35,000 volt-amperes at 70%	24,500 volt-amperes
(See Table 220-19 and Section 220-22.)	
Total	65,000 volt-amperes

65,000 volt-amperes ÷ 240 volts = 271 amperes

Further Demand Factor (Section 220-22)

First 200 amperes at 100%	200 amperes
Balance: 71 amperes at 70%	50 amperes
Total	250 amperes

Feeder Neutral Load of Main Feeder (less house load) for 40 Dwelling Units:

Lighting and Small Appliance Load

40 × 5520 volt-amperes	220,800 volt-amperes
First 3000 volt-amperes at 100%	3000 volt-amperes
120,000 volt-amperes—3000 volt-amperes =	
117,000 volt-amperes at 35%	40,950 volt-amperes
220,800 volt-amperes—120,000 volt-amperes =	
100,800 volt-amperes at 25%	25,200 volt-amperes

(Example 4(b) Continued Next Page.)

TABLES AND EXAMPLES

Example No. 4(b) (Continued)

Net Computed Lighting and Small Appliance Load	69,150 volt-amperes
40 Ranges = 55,000 volt-amperes at 70%	<u>38,500</u> volt-amperes
(See Table 220-19 and Section 220-22)	
Total	107,650 volt-amperes

107,650 volt-amperes ÷ 240 volts = 449 amperes

Further Demand Factor (Section 220-22)

First 200 amperes at 100%	200 amperes
Balance: 249 amperes at 70%	<u>174</u> amperes
Total	374 amperes

Example No. 5(a). Multifamily Dwelling Served at 208Y/120 Volts, Three Phase

All conditions and calculations the same as for Multifamily Dwelling [Example No. 4(a)] served at 120/240 volts, single phase except as follows:

Service to each dwelling unit shall be two phase legs and neutral.

Minimum Number of Branch Circuits Required for Each Dwelling Unit (Section 220-3):

Range Circuit: 8000 volt-amperes ÷ 208 volts = 38 amperes or a circuit of two No. 8 and one No. 10 as permitted by Section 220-22.

Minimum Size Subfeeder Required for Each Dwelling Unit (Section 215-2):

For 120/208-volt, 3-wire system (without ranges)
Net Computed Load: 3882 volt-amperes ÷ 208 volts = 18.7 amperes
For 120/208-volt, 3-wire system (with ranges)
Net Computed Load: 11,882 volt-amperes ÷ 208 volts = 57.1 amperes
Subfeeder neutral: 9482 volt-amperes ÷ 208 volts = 45.6 amperes

Minimum Size Feeders Required from Service Equipment to Meter Bank (For 20 Dwelling Units— 10 with Ranges):

For 208Y/120-volt, 3-phase, 4-wire system
Ranges: Maximum number between any two phase legs = 4
Twice 4 = 8. Table 220-19 Demand = 23,000 volt-amperes.
Per phase demand: 23,000 volt-amperes ÷ 2 = 11,500 volt-amperes
Equivalent 3-phase load = 34,500 volt-amperes
Net Computed Load (total): 40,590 volt-amperes + 34,500 volt-amperes = 75,090 volt-amperes
75,090 volt-amperes ÷ (208)(1.732) = 208.4 amperes

Feeder Neutral Size
40,590 volt-amperes + 34,500 volt-amperes at 70% = 64,700 volt-amperes
Net Computed Neutral Load:
64,700 volt-amperes ÷ (208)(1.732) = 179.6 amperes

Minimum Size Main Feeder (less house load) (For 40 Dwelling Units—20 with Ranges):

For 208Y/120-volt, 3-phase, 4-wire system
Ranges: Maximum number between any two phase legs = 7
Twice 7 = 14. Table 220-19 Demand = 29,000 volt-amperes.
Per phase demand: 29,000 ÷ 2 = 14,500 volt-amperes
Equivalent 3-phase load = 43,500 volt-amperes
Net Computed Load (total): 69,150 volt-amperes + 43,500 volt-amperes = 112,650 volt-amperes
112,650 volt-amperes ÷ (208)(1.732) = 312.7 amperes

Main Feeder Neutral Size
69,150 volt-amperes + 43,500 volt-amperes at 70% = 99,600 volt-amperes
99,600 volt-amperes ÷ (208)(1.732) = 276.5 amperes

Further Demand Factor (Section 220-22)

200 amperes at 100%	200.0 amperes
76.5 amperes at 70%	<u>53.6</u> amperes
Net Computed Load	253.6 amperes

Example No. 5(b). Optional Calculation for Multifamily Dwelling Served at 208Y/120 Volts, Three Phase

All conditions and calculations the same as for Optional Calculation for Multifamily Dwelling [Example No. 4(b)] served at 120/240 volt, single phase except as follows:
Service to each dwelling unit shall be two phase legs and neutral.

Minimum Number of Branch Circuits Required for Each Dwelling Unit (Section 220-3):

Range Circuit: 8000 volt-amperes at 80% ÷ 208 volts = 30.7 amperes or a circuit of two No. 8 and one No. 10 as permitted by Section 220-22.

Space Heating: 6000 volt-amperes ÷ 208 volts = 28.8 amperes. Two 20-ampere, 2-pole circuits required, No. 12.

Minimum Size Subfeeder Required for Each Dwelling Unit.

Computed Load (120/208-volt, 3-wire circuit)
Net Computed Load: 18,782 volt-amperes ÷ 208 volts = 90.3 amperes
Net Computed Load (neutral): 3882 volt-amperes + 6000 volt-amperes + 2500 volt-amperes + 6400 volt-amperes at 70% = 16,862 volt-amperes.
16,862 volt-amperes ÷ 208 volts = 81.1 amperes

Minimum Size Feeder Required for Service Equipment to Meter Bank (For 20 dwelling units):

Net Computed Load: 167,352 volt-amperes ÷ (208)(1.732) = 464.9 amperes
Feeder Neutral Load:
65,000 volt-amperes ÷ (208)(1.732) = 180.4 amperes

Minimum Size Main Feeder Required (less house load) (for 40 dwelling units):
Net Computed Load: 246,624 volt-amperes ÷ (208)(1.732) = 685.1 amperes
Main Feeder Neutral Load:
107,650 volt-amperes ÷ (208)(1.732) = 298.8 amperes

Further Demand Factor (Section 220-22)
200 amperes at 100%..200.0 amperes
98.8 amperes at 70% .... 69.2 amperes
Net Computed Load ....269.2 amperes

Example No. 6. Maximum Demand for Range Loads

Table 220-19, Column A applies to ranges not over 12 kW. The application of Note 1 to ranges over 12 kW (and not over 27 kW) is illustrated in the following examples:

A. Ranges all the same rating.

Assume 24 ranges each rated 16 kW.

From Column A the maximum demand for 24 ranges of 12 kW rating is 39 kW.
16 kW exceeds 12 kW by 4.
5% × 4 = 20% (5% increase for each kW in excess of 12).
39 kW × 20% = 7.8 kW increase.
39 + 7.8 = 46.8 kW: value to be used in selection of feeders.

B. Ranges of unequal rating.

Assume 5 ranges each rated 11 kW.
2 ranges each rated 12 kW.
20 ranges each rated 13.5 kW.
3 ranges each rated 18 kW

$$
\begin{array}{ll}
5 \times 12 & = \quad 60 \text{ Use 12 kW for range rated less than 12.} \\
2 \times 12 & = \quad 24 \\
20 \times 13.5 & = 270 \\
\underline{3 \times 18} & = \underline{\quad 54} \\
30 & \quad\ 408 \text{ kW}
\end{array}
$$

408 ÷ 30 = 13.6 kW (average to be used for computation)

From Column A the demand for 30 ranges of 12 kW rating is 15 + 30 = 45 kW.
13.6 exceeds 12 by 1.6 (use 2).
5% × 2 = 10% (5% increase for each kW in excess of 12).
45 kW × 10% = 4.5 kW increase.
45 + 4.5 = 49.5 kW: value to be used in selection of feeders.

TABLES AND EXAMPLES

Example No. 8.   Motors, Conductors, Overload, and Short-Circuit and Ground-Fault Protection

(See Sections 430-6, 430-7, 430-22, 430-24, 430-32, 430-34, 430-52, 430-62, and Tables 430-150 and 430-152.)

Determine the conductor size, the motor overload protection, the branch-circuit short-circuit and ground-fault protection, and the feeder protection, for one 25-horsepower squirrel-cage induction motor (full-voltage starting, service factor 1.15, Code letter F), and two 30-horsepower wound-rotor induction motors (40°C rise), on a 460-volt, 3-phase, 60-Hertz supply.

Conductor Loads

The full-load current of the 25-horsepower motor is 34 amperes (Table 430-150). A full-load current of 34 amperes × 1.25 = 42.5 amperes (Section 430-22). The full-load current of the 30-horsepower motor is 40 amperes (Table 430-150). A full-load current of 40 amperes × 1.25 = 50 amperes (Section 430-22).

The feeder ampacity will be 125 percent of 40 plus 40 plus 34, or 124 amperes (Section 430-24).

Overload and Short-Circuit and Ground-Fault Protection

Overload. Where protected by a separate overload device, the 25-horsepower motor, with full-load current of 34 amperes, must have overload protection of not over 42.5 amperes [Sections 430-6(a) and 430-32(a)(1)]. Where protected by a separate overload device, the 30-horsepower motor, with full-load current of 40 amperes, must have overload protection of not over 50 amperes [Sections 430-6(a) and 430-32 (a)(1)]. If the overload protection is not sufficient to start the motor or to carry the load, it may be increased according to Section 430-34. For a motor marked "thermally protected," overload protection is provided by the thermal protector [see Sections 430-7(a)(12) and 430-32(a)(2)].

Branch-Circuit Short-Circuit and Ground-Fault. The branch circuit of the 25-horsepower motor must have branch-circuit short-circuit and ground-fault protection of not over 300 percent for a nontime-delay fuse (Table 430-152) or 3.00 × 34 = 102 amperes. The next smaller standard size fuse is 100 amperes. The fuse size may be increased to 110 or 125 amperes (Section 430-52, Exception No. 1) if the 100-ampere fuse is not sufficient for the starting current of the motor.

For the 30-horsepower motor, the branch-circuit short-circuit and ground-fault protection is 150 percent (Table 430-152) or 1.50 × 40 = 60 amperes. Where the maximum value of branch-circuit short-circuit and ground-fault protection is not sufficient to start the motor, the value for a nontime-delay fuse may be increased to 400 percent (Section 430-52, Exception a.)

Feeder Circuit. The maximum rating of the feeder short-circuit and ground-fault protection device is based on the sum of the largest branch-circuit protective device (110-ampere fuse) plus the sum of the full-load currents of the other motors or 110 plus 40 plus 40 = 190 amperes. The nearest standard fuse which does not exceed this value is 175 amperes [Section 430-62(a)].

Appendix

The following rules on Tentative Interim Amendments and Formal Interpretations are excerpted from the NFPA Regulations Governing Committee Projects as adopted by the Board of Directors on December 3, 1983.

Section 15. Tentative Interim Amendments

15-1. Authorization. A Tentative Interim Amendment to any existing Document may be processed if the Tentative Interim Amendment is of an emergency nature requiring prompt action and has the endorsement of a Member of the involved Technical Committee.

15-2. Determination of Compliance. A proposed Tentative Interim Amendment shall be submitted to the Council Secretary who, after consultation with the appropriate Committee Chairman, shall determine compliance with 15-1.

15-3. Processing. If such compliance is determined, the proposed Tentative Interim Amendment shall be processed in the following manner:

(a) The text of a proposed Tentative Interim Amendment may be processed as submitted or may be changed, but only with the approval of the submitter.

(b) A proposed Tentative Interim Amendment which meets the provisions of 15-1 shall be published by the Association in appropriate media with a notice that the proposed Tentative Interim Amendment has been forwarded to the responsible Technical Committee for processing and that anyone interested may comment on the proposed Tentative Interim Amendment within the time period established and published.

(c) The proposed Tentative Interim Amendment shall be submitted for letter ballot and comment of the Technical Committee in accordance with Section 12. Such balloting shall be completed concurrently with the public review period. Any public comments inconsistent with the vote of any Committee Member shall be circulated to the Committee for supplemental letter ballot. A recommendation for approval shall be established if three-fourths of the voting Members calculated in accordance with Section 12 have voted in favor of the Tentative Interim Amendment.

(d) The proposed Tentative Interim Amendment shall be submitted for letter ballot and comment of the Correlating Committee, if any, which shall make a recommendation to the Council with respect to the disposition of the Tentative Interim Amendment.

(e) All public comments, Technical Committee and Correlating Committee ballots and comments on the proposed Tentative Interim Amendment shall be summarized in a staff report and forwarded to the Council for action in accordance with 15-4.

15-4. Action of the Council. The Council shall review the material submitted in accordance with 15-3(e) and shall take one of the following actions:

(a) issue the proposed Tentative Interim Amendment,

(b) issue the proposed Tentative Interim Amendment as amended by the Council,

(c) reject the proposed Tentative Interim Amendment,

(d) return the proposed Tentative Interim Amendment to the Technical Committee with appropriate instruction,

(e) direct a different action.

15-5. Publication of Tentative Interim Amendment. The Association shall publish in one of its publications sent to all members notice of the issuance of each Tentative Interim Amendment, shall issue a news release to applicable and interested technical journals, and shall also include in any subsequent distribution of the Document to which the Tentative Interim Amendment applies the text of the Tentative Interim Amendment in a manner judged most feasible to accomplish the desired objectives. The tentative character of the Tentative Interim Amendment shall be clearly indicated in the publication and release.

15-6. Subsequent Processing of Tentative Interim Amendments. The Technical Committee concerned shall process the subject matter of any Tentative Interim Amendment through normal Technical Committee procedures (see Sections 10, 11, and 12) at the next meeting of the Association to which the Technical Committee reports.

15-7. Exception. When the Board of Directors authorizes other procedures for the processing and/or issuance of Tentative Interim Amendments, the provisions of this Section shall not apply.

Section 16. Formal Interpretations Procedure

16-1. General. The following Formal Interpretation procedure is for the purpose of providing formal explanations of the meaning or intent of any specific provision or provisions of any Document.

A statement, written or oral, that is not processed in accordance with Section 16 of these Regulations shall not be considered the official position of NFPA or any of its Committees and shall not be considered to be, nor be relied upon as, a Formal Interpretation.

NOTE: This Formal Interpretation procedure does not prevent any Committee Chairman, Member of any Committee, or the Staff Liaison from expressing an opinion on the meaning or intent of any provision of any such Document, provided that:

(a) the person rendering the opinion orally or in writing clearly states that "the opinion is personal and does not represent the position of the Committee or the Association and may not be considered to be or relied upon as such"; and

(b) written opinions are rendered only in response to written requests and a copy of the request and the response is sent to the Staff Liaison.

16-2. Nature of Formal Interpretations. Two general forms of Formal Interpretations are recognized:

(a) those making an interpretation of the literal text, and

(b) those making an interpretation of the intent of the Technical Committee when the particular text was issued.

16-3. Editions to be Interpreted. Interpretations shall be rendered on the text of the latest adopted Document and any text of earlier editions which is identical to the text in the latest Document. Interpretations may be rendered to the requester on text of an outdated Document where such has been revised in or deleted from later editions. If possible, the requester should be informed why the text was revised or deleted.

16-4. Method of Requesting Formal Interpretations. A request for a Formal Interpretation shall be directed to the Council Secretary. The request shall include a statement in which shall appear specific references to a single problem and identifying the portion (article, section, paragraph, etc.) of the Document and edition of the Document on which an Interpretation is requested. Such a request shall be in writing and shall indicate the business interest of the requester. A request involving an actual field situation shall so state and all parties involved shall be named and notified.

16-5. Qualifications for Processing. A request for an Interpretation may be processed if it:

(a) complies with 16-2 and 16-4,

(b) does not involve a determination of compliance of a design, installation, or product or equivalency of protection,

(c) does not involve a review of plans or specifications, or require judgement or knowledge that can only be acquired as a result of on-site inspection,

(d) does not involve text that clearly and decisively provides the requested information.

16-6. Determination of Qualification. The Council Secretary, after consultation with the appropriate Staff Liaison, shall determine the qualification in accordance with 16-5.

16-7. Editing of Interpretation Request. A request for an Interpretation may be rephrased. The rephrased version and any pertinent background information shall be sent to the requester and all parties named in the request for agreement. A deadline for receipt of agreement shall be established.

16-8. Establishment of Interpretations Subcommittee. If accepted for consideration, each request shall then be submitted to letter ballot of an Interpretations Subcommittee made up of five or more Members of the Technical Committee(s) or Subcommittee having primary jurisdiction of the Document or portion thereof covering the subject under consideration. The Members shall be selected by the Committee Chairmen or the Council Secretary, if the Chairmen are not available. No Member shall be eligible for appointment to an Interpretations Subcommittee if he is directly involved in the particular case prompting the request for the Interpretation. The Interpretations Subcommittee should include Committee Members representing the same interest categories as the requester and the other parties involved, as well as representatives of other parties. The personnel of Interpretations Subcommittees may be varied for each request.

16-9. Voting on Interpretations. In any case where more than twenty percent of the Subcommittee Members disagree on the Interpretation, the request for Interpretation shall be referred to the entire Technical Committee(s). Under these conditions, a Formal Interpretation requires a two-thirds majority agreement of the Technical Committee(s) as tallied in accordance with 12-7. Where the necessary agreement is not received, the item shall be placed on the docket for regular processing by the Technical Committee(s) for subsequent possible action.

16-10. Publication of Interpretation. If the required agreement is secured from the Interpretations Subcommittee(s) or from the Technical Committee, the requester and all named parties shall be informed by the Staff Liaison and the Interpretation shall be published by the Association in one of its publications sent to all members and announced in an Association news release to other media.

Interpretations of text of an outdated Document which has been revised in or deleted from later editions shall not be published by the Association but shall be sent to the requester and all parties named in the request.

16-11. Action Following Issuance of Formal Interpretations. Any Technical Committee(s) whose Document has been the subject of a Formal Interpretation shall review the item on which the Interpretation has been issued to determine whether any change may be desired to the text of the Document on which the Interpretation has been rendered. If such a change is indicated, the Technical Committee(s) shall process such change in conformance with procedures set forth in Sections 10, 11, and 12.

16-12. Applicability of Formal Interpretations. Any Formal Interpretation issued shall apply to the edition of the Document for which the Interpretation is made and to any other edition of the Document if the text is identical to the text of the edition of which the Formal Interpretation was rendered.

Section 18. Operating Procedures

18-1. Authorization. A Committee may adopt internal operating procedures, provided that such procedures are consistent with the Bylaws of the Association and with these Regulations. Such procedures and amendments thereto shall be promptly transmitted to the Council Secretary who shall submit them to the Council for approval. Amendments to the Bylaws of the Association or to these Regulations shall automatically supersede any such procedures which may be in conflict therewith.

The following procedures on Tentative Interim Amendments and Formal and Informal Interpretations are excerpted from the "Operating Procedures for the National Electrical Code Committee" as adopted by the NFPA Standards Council on July 8, 1981 and amended October 7, 1982.

PART B—TENTATIVE INTERIM AMENDMENTS TO THE *NATIONAL ELECTRICAL CODE*

Section 110. Procedures for Processing Tentative Interim Amendments

111. A Proposal for a Tentative Interim Amendment shall include a specific statement of what new text or amendment of the existing text of the *National Electrical Code* is recommended, and a full explanation of the Proposal supported by all relevant data. The Proposal shall also include justification for qualification as being of an emergency nature requiring processing before the next scheduled edition of the *National Electrical Code*.

112. In order to determine compliance with Section 15-1 of the Regulations, the results of a ballot of a Special Subcommittee appointed by the Chairman of the Correlating Committee shall be submitted to the Standards Council Secretary. The Subcommittee shall consist of, in addition to the Correlating Committee Chairman, no less than two Members of the Correlating Committee and the Chairman or Chairmen of the Code-Making Panel(s) concerned with the proposed Tentative Interim Amendment. A majority vote by the Members of the Subcommittee to support the Proposal results in an affirmative recommendation.

PART C—FORMAL AND INFORMAL INTERPRETATIONS OF THE *NATIONAL ELECTRICAL CODE*

Section 200. General

201. Certain questions arise in the application of the requirements of the *National Electrical Code* which are not subject to Formal Interpretation under the established procedures. In addition to those outlined in the Regulations, these questions include the degree and extent of a hazardous (classified) location, interpretation of suitability of isolation or guarding, and interpretation of equivalent protection. However, such questions are suitable for "Informal" Interpretations and are covered in Section 220 of these Procedures.

Section 210. Procedures for Processing Formal Interpretations

211. The Secretary of the National Electrical Code Committee, after consultation with the Chairman of the Correlating Committee and any others as appropriate, shall advise the Standards Council Secretary of any request the Committee Secretary believes should be processed as a Formal Interpretation.

212. The National Electrical Code Committee Secretary with the assistance of the Correlating Committee Chairman shall, if necessary, rephrase the request so that it is suitable for balloting by an Interpretation Subcommittee. Any rewording shall be transmitted to the requester for concurrence.

213. The Interpretation Subcommittee shall consist of the following taking into account Section 16-8 of the Regulations

(a) The Chairman of the Correlating Committee, who shall be the Chairman of the Interpretation Subcommittee and a voting Member.

(b) The Chairman of that Code-Making Panel which is responsible for the affected Article of the Code for which an Interpretation is requested, and

(c) At least three other Members or Alternates of the National Electrical Code Committee selected by the Chairman of the Correlating Committee depending upon the availability, experience, knowledge, and interest of the Members or Alternates.

214. The appropriate Code-Making Panel shall review the text of any Section of the *National Electrical Code* for which a Formal Interpretation has been issued to the end that a suitable revision of the text may be recommended to eliminate the difficulty which prompted the request for a Formal Interpretation.

Section 220. Procedures for Processing Informal Interpretations

221. All requests for written Informal Interpretations shall be answered either by the Committee Member to which it is addressed or referred to the Secretary of the National Electrical Code Committee for reply.

As stated in Section 16-1 of the Regulations, a Committee Chairman, a Member of any Committee or the Secretary of the National Electrical Code Committee may express an opinion on the meaning or intent of any provision of the *National Electrical Code,* provided that the opinion is clearly identified as not being a Formal Interpretation of the National Electrical Code Committee or of the Association and shall not be relied upon as such.

A copy of the request, any necessary accompanying material, and the response shall be sent, as appropriate, to

a. The Chairman of the Correlating Committee

b. The Chairman of the appropriate Code-Making Panel(s)

c. The Secretary of the National Electrical Code Committee.

Time Schedule for the 1987 *National Electrical Code*

Nov. 23, 1984   Final date for receipt of proposals from the public for revision of the 1984 *National Electrical Code* preparatory to the issuance of the 1987 edition. Proposals should be forwarded to the Secretary of the Standards Council, National Fire Protection Association, Batterymarch Park, Quincy, MA 02269.

Jan. 7-26, 1985   Code-Making Panels Preliminary Meeting to consider proposals for *Code* changes.

May 6-10, 1985   Correlating Committee reviews the Preliminary Report submitted by the Code-Making Panels. Establishes that no conflicts exist, that satisfactory correlation is achieved among the recommendations of the Code-Making Panels, and that the Committee's activities have been conducted in accordance with the Regulations Governing Committee Projects and the NEC Operating Procedures.

June 17, 1985   *National Electrical Code Technical Committee Report* (NEC-TCR or "Preprint") for the 1987 *National Electrical Code* published for distribution to the National Electrical Code Committee and other interested parties.

June 17-
Oct. 28, 1985   Period of study by interested parties and submittal of recommendations for modifying report to the Secretary of the Standards Council, NFPA.

Oct. 28, 1985   Closing date for comments.

Dec. 2-14, 1985   Code-Making Panels meet to act on public comments.

March 10-14, 1986   Correlating Committee meeting to review the Code-Making Panel action on comments.

April 11, 1986   NFPA prints and distributes the *National Electrical Code Technical Committee Documentation* (NEC-TCD) and the Advanced Printing of the Proposed 1987 *National Electrical Code* to members of the National Electrical Code Committee and other interested parties.

May 19-22, 1986   Action by NFPA Annual Meeting.

July, 1986   Action by NFPA Standards Council.

September, 1986   Publication of the 1987 *National Electrical Code.*

NFPA Publications

The NFPA Electrical Codes and Standards which relate to electrical requirements are frequently revised. Booklet editions of those Codes and Standards available at the time of publication are listed below. Contact the NFPA Publications Sales Division, Batterymarch Park, Quincy, MA 02269 for current prices.

Pub. No.	Title
NFPA 20	Centrifugal Fire Pumps, 1983.
NFPA 70	*National Electrical Code®*, 1984.
NFPA 70A*	Electrical Code for One- and Two-Family Dwellings, 1984.
NFPA 70B	Electrical Equipment Maintenance, 1983.
NFPA 70L	Model State Electrical Law, Inspection of Electrical Installations, 1973.
NFPA 70E	Electrical Safety Requirements for Employee Workplaces, 1983.
NFPA 71	Central Station Signaling Systems, 1982.
NFPA 72A	Local Protective Signaling Systems, 1979.
NFPA 72B	Auxiliary Protective Signaling Systems, 1979.
NFPA 72C	Remote Station Protective Signaling Systems, 1982.
NFPA 72D	Proprietary Protective Signaling Systems, 1979.
NFPA 72E	Automatic Fire Detectors, 1982.
NFPA 74	Household Fire Warning Equipment, 1980.
NFPA 75	Protection of Electronic Computer/Data Processing Equipment, 1981.
NFPA 76A	Essential Electrical Systems for Health Care Facilities, 1977.
NFPA 76B	Safe Use of Electricity in Patient Care Areas of Hospitals, 1980.
NFPA 76C	Safe Use of High-Frequency Electricity in Health Care Facilities, 1980.
NFPA 77	Recommended Practice on Static Electricity, 1983.
NFPA 78	Lightning Protection Code, 1980.
NFPA 79	Electrical Standard for Metalworking Machine Tools and Plastics Machinery, 1980.
NFPA *101®*	*Life Safety Code®*, 1981.
NFPA 493	Intrinsically Safe Apparatus and Associated Apparatus for Use in Class I, II, and III, Division 1 Hazardous Locations, 1978.
NFPA 496	Purged and Pressurized Enclosures for Electrical Equipment in Hazardous (Classified) Locations, 1982.
NFPA 497	Classification of Class I Hazardous Locations for Electrical Installations in Chemical Plants, 1975.
NFPA 497M	Classification of Gases, Vapors and Dusts for Electrical Equipment in Hazardous (Classified) Locations, 1983.
NFPA 907M	Manual on the Investigation of Fires of Electrical Origin, 1983.
NFPA 1221	Public Fire Service Communications, 1980.

*Available January, 1984.

INDEX

AC and DC Conductors in Same Enclosures, 300-3(a), 725-15

AC-DC, General-Use Snap Switches
Definitions, Switches, Art. 100
Marking, 380-15
Motors, 430-83, Ex. 1
Panelboards, Use in, 384-16(b)
Ratings, Type Loads, 380-14
Signs, 600-2(b), Ex.

AC Resistance and Reactance Conversion,
Table 9, Chap. 9

AC Armored Cable, Art. 333

AC Systems
Conductor to be Grounded, 250-25
Grounding Connections for, 250-23
Grounding of, 250-5
In Same Metallic Enclosures, 215-4(b), 300-20

Access and Working Space, Electric Equipment
Machine Room Elevator, 520-72
Not Over 600 Volts, 110-16
Over 600 Volts, 110-B
Service Disconnecting Means, 230-73
Service Overcurrent Devices, 230-96
Substations, Motion Picture, TV Studios, 530-64
Switchboards, 384-8
Transformers, Electric Signs Over 600 Volts, 600-32(f)

Accessible, Definition, Art. 100

Accessible, Readily
Amplifiers and Rectifiers, 640-11(b)
Definitions, Art. 100

Accessible, Readily *(Continued)*
Grounding Electrode Connection, 250-112
Junction, Pull, and Outlet Boxes, 370-19
Sealing Fittings [See also Hazardous (Classified) Locations], 501-5(c)(1), 502-5
Splices and Taps in Auxiliary Gutters, 374-8(a)
Splices and Taps in Wireways, 362-6
Transformers and Vaults, 450-2
Transformers, Signs, Outline Lighting, 600-32(e)
Unfinished Attics, Roof Spaces, Knob-and-Tube Wiring, 324-11(a)

Aerial Cable, Art. 342 (see Nonmetallic Extensions)
Installation, 342-7(b)
Messenger Supported Wiring, Art. 321

Agricultural Buildings, Art. 547

Air-Conditioning and Refrigerating Equipment, Art. 440
Branch-Circuit
  Conductors, 440-D
    Ampacity, Determination of, 440-5
    Combination Loads for, 440-34
    General, 440-31
    Multimotor Equipment for, 440-35
    Several Motor-Compressors for, 440-33
    Single Motor-Compressor for, 440-32
  Ratings, 440-C
    Equipment for, 440-22(b)
    General, 440-21
    Individual Motor-Compressor for, 440-22(a)
  Selection Current
    Definition, 440-3(c) (FPN)
    Marking on Nameplate, 440-3(c)
Controllers for, 440-41(a-b)
  Marking, 440-4
Disconnecting Means, 440-B
  Cord-Connected as, 440-13

Community Antenna Systems *(Continued)*
   Equipment, 820-23
   Installation, 820-C
     Inside Buildings, 820-13
     Outside Buildings, 820-11
   Protection, 820-B
   Underground Circuits, 820-D
     Entering Buildings, 820-18

Compressors, Refrigeration, Art. 440

Concealed
   Definition, Art. 100
   Knob-and-Tube Wiring, Art. 324

Concentric Knockouts, Bonding Jumpers, Service, 250-72(d)

Concrete
   Encased Electrodes, 250-81(c)
   Metal Raceways and Equipment in, 300-6
   Service Conductors, 230-44

Conductor Fill
   Auxiliary Gutters, 374-5, 374-8
   Cable Trays, 318-8, 318-9, Tables 318-8 and 318-9
   Cellular Concrete Floor Raceways, 358-9
   Cellular Metal Floor Raceways, 356-5
   Electrical Metallic Tubing, 348-6
   Electrical Nonmetallic Tubing, 331-6
   Elevators, 620-33
   Entering Boxes, Conduit Bodies, or Fittings, 370-7
   Fixture Wire, 402-7
   Flexible Metal Conduit, 350-1, 350-3, Table 350-3
   Flexible Metallic Tubing, 349-12
   Intermediate Metal Conduit, 345-7
   Liquidtight Flexible Metal Conduit, 351-6
   Liquidtight Flexible Nonmetallic Conduit, 351-25
   Maximum Permitted, 300-17
   Rigid Metal Conduit, 346-6
   Rigid Nonmetallic Conduit, 347-11
   Signs, 600-21(d)
   Sound Recording, 640-3, 640-4
   Surface Metal Raceways, 352-4
   Surface Nonmetallic Raceways, 352-25
   Theaters, 520-5
   Wireways, 362-5, 362-6

Conductors (see also Cords, Flexible; and Fixture Wires)
   Aluminum and Copper-Clad Aluminum, Ampacities of, Tables 310-16 through 310-19 and 310-20(a) through 310-30
   Aluminum Conductor Material, 310-14
   Aluminum, Properties of, Table 8, Chap. 9
     Motors, 430-B
     Raceway (More than Three in), Note 8, Tables 310-16, 310-18
   Amplifier Circuits, 640-5
   Application, 310-12, 310-13
   Armored Cable, Type AC, Art. 333
   Bare, Definition, Art 100
   Boxes and Fittings, Junction, 370-6, 370-7
   Branch Circuits, Art. 210
   Buried, 310-7
   Busways, Art. 364
   Cabinets and Cutout Boxes, 373-5, 373-6, 373-7
   Cablebus, Art. 365

Conductors *(Continued)*
   Capacitor Circuits, 460-8
   Cellular Concrete Floor Raceways, Art. 358
   Cellular Metal Floor Raceways, Art. 356
   Circuit
     Less than 50 Volts, Art. 720
     Power, Signal, Remote-Control, Low-Energy, Art. 725
     Over 600 Volts, Art. 710
   Combinations, Table 1, Chap. 9
   Computations of, Examples, Chap. 9, Part B
   Concealed Knob-and-Tube, Art. 324
   Conduit or Tubing, Number in, 345-7, 346-6, 347-11, 348-6, Table 350-3, Tables 3A, 3B, 3C, Chap. 9
   Construction, General, Table 310-13
   Copper, Ampacities, Tables 310-16 through 310-19 and 310-20(a) through 310-30
   Copper-Clad Aluminum, Definition, Art. 100
   Copper, Properties, Table 8, Chap. 9
   Cords, Flexible, Art. 400
   Corrosive Conditions, 300-6, 310-9, 501-13
   Covered, Definition, Art. 100
   Cranes and Hoists, 610-B, 610-C, 610-31, 610-41
   Different Systems, 300-3, 318-25(f), 725-15, 725-38(a)(2)
   Dimension of
     Asbestos-Varnished-Cambric Insulated, Table 7, Chap. 9
     Lead-Covered, Table 6, Chap. 9
     Rubber-Covered and Thermoplastic-Covered, Table 5, Chap. 9
   Electrical Metallic Tubing, Art. 348
   Electrical Nonmetallic Tubing, Art. 331
   Elevators, Dumbwaiters, Escalators, and Moving Walks, 620-B, 620-C, 620-D
   Enclosure, Grounding, 250-1, 250-D
   Feeder, Art. 215
   Fixture Wires, Art. 402
   Flat Cable Assemblies, Type FC, Art. 363
   Flat Conductor Cable, Type FCC, Art. 328
   Flexible Metal Conduit, Art. 350
   Gages, (AWG) General Provisions, 110-6
   Generators, Size, 445-5
   Grounded
     Alternating Current Systems, 250-23, 250-25, Identification, 200-2, 210-5, 215-8
     Overcurrent Protection, 240-22
     Service, Disconnection, 230-75
       Overcurrent Protection, 230-90(b)
     Size, Change in, 240-23
     Switches, Disconnection, 380-2(b)
     Use and Identification, Art. 200
   Grounding, 250-J
     Connections, 250-K
   Indentification, 310-12
   Induction and Dielectric Heating Equipment
     Capacity of Supply, 665-41, 665-61
   In Free Air Tables 310-17, 317-19
   Insulating Materials, 310-12, 310-19
   Insulation, Art. 310
     Fixtures, Flush, Recessed, 410-67
     Hazardous Locations, Class I Installations, 501-13
     Motion Picture Projectors, 540-14
     Resistors and Reactors, 470-4
     Theaters, 520-42
   Insulation at Bushings, No. 4 and Larger, 373-6(c)
   Lighting Fixtures, 410-E
   Lightning Rods, Spacing from, 250-46

Disconnecting Means

Air-Conditioning and Refrigerating Equipment, 440-B
Appliances, 422-D
Capacitors, 460-8(c)
Cranes, 610-D
Definition, Art. 100
Electric Space Heating Equipment, 424-C
Elevators, 620-51
Fuses and Thermal Cutouts, 240-40
Induction and Dielectric Heating Equipment, 665-43
Mobile Homes, 550-4
Motor and Controllers, 430-H, 430-127
Recreational Vehicles, 551-11
Services, 230-H
  Connections, Ahead of, 230-82, 700-12(e)
  Over 600 Volts, 230-205, 230-206
Signs, 600-2(a)
Welders, Resistance, 630-33
X-ray Equipment, 517-142, 660-5, 660-24

Discontinued Outlets

Cellular Concrete Floor Raceways, 358-11
Cellular Metal Floor Raceways, 356-7
Underfloor Raceways, 354-7

Dissimilar Metals, 110-14, 250-115, 345-3(b), 346-1(b), 348-1(b)

Door(s), Transformer Vaults, 450-43

Double Insulated, Appliances and Tools, 250-45, 422-8(d) Exception

Dishwasher, Trash Compactor, Waste Disposers [see 422-8(d) Exception]

Double Locknuts, Where Required, 250-76(b), 373-6(c), 501-16(b), 550-8(f), 551-14(b)

Drainage

Capacitor Charge, 460-6
Equipment, 501-5(f)
Oil-Insulated Outdoor Transformers, 450-27
Raceways, 230-53, 225-22, 230-202(g)
Transformer Vaults for, 450-46

Dressing Rooms

Motion Picture Studios, 530-C
Theaters, 520-F

Drip Loops

Conductors Entering Buildings, 225-11, 230-52
Service Heads, 230-54

Driveways

Clearance of Conductors, 225-18
Clearance of Service Drop, 230-24(b)
Protection of Service-Entrance Cables, 230-50

Drop, Service, Definition, Art. 100

Drop, Voltage, 210-19(a) (FPN), 215-2 (FPN), 310-15(b)

Dry Location, Definition, Art. 100 (see also Damp or Wet Locations)

Dryers, Clothes

Demand Factors, 220-18, Table 220-18
Grounding, 250-60
Mobile Homes, 550-8(e)

Dry-Type Transformers, 450-2, 450-3(b), 450-21, 450-22

Dual-Voltage Motor, Locked-Rotor Rating, 430-7(b)(3)

Duct(s)

Lighting Fixtures in, 410-4(c)
Wiring in, 300-21, 300-22, 725-2(b), 760-4(d), 800-3(d), 820-15

Duct Heaters Installation of, 424-F

Dumbwaiters (see Elevators), Art. 620

Dust-Ignition-Proof, 502-1

Dustproof, Definition, Art. 100

Dusts [see Hazardous (Classified) Locations]

Dust-Tight, Definition, Art. 100

Duty, Type, Definition, Art. 100

Duty Cycle (Welding), 630-31

Dwellings [see also Appliance(s), Boxes, Branch Circuits, Fixtures, Grounding, and Similar General Categories]

Branch-Circuit Voltages, 210-6(c)
Clothes Dryers, Demand Factors, Table 220-18
Definition, Art. 100
  Multifamily, Art. 100
  One-family, Art. 100
  Two-family, Art. 100
  Unit, Art. 100
Farm, Services, 220-41
Feeder Load, Calculations for, 220-10(a), 220-30, 220-31, 220-32, Part B, Chap. 9
Lighting Loads for, Table 220-2(b)
Panelboards as Services, 384-3(c), 384-16(a)
Ranges, Demand Load, Table 220-19
Receptacle Circuits Required, 220-3(b)
Receptacle Outlets Required, 210-52, 680-6(a)(2)
  Protection by Ground-Fault Circuit-Interrupters,
Dwelling Units, 210-8(a), 680-6(a)(1) Exception
  Hotels and Motels, 210-8(b)

Eccentric Knockouts, Bonding Jumpers, Service, 250-72(d)

Elbows, Metallic, Protection from Corrosion, 300-6

Electric Discharge Lighting

Connection to Fixtures, 410-14, 410-30(c)
More than 1000 Volts, 410-R
1000 Volts or Less, 410-Q
Signs and Outline Lighting, Art. 600
Wiring, Equipment, 410-Q, 410-R

INDEX

Header(s)
Cellular Concrete Floor Raceways, 358-1, 358-2, 358-3, 358-6, 358-7
Cellular Metal Floor Raceways, 356-1, 356-2, 356-5, 356-6

Health Care Facilities, Art. 517
Clinics, Medical and Dental Offices, and Out-Patient Facilities, etc., 517-C
Communications, Signaling Systems, Data Systems, Fire Protective Signaling Systems, and Low-Voltage Systems, 517-H
General, 517-A
Definitions, 517-2
Hospitals, 517-E
Critical Branch, 517-63
Emergency System, 517-61
Equipment System, 517-64
Essential Electrical Systems, 517-60
Life Safety Branch, 517-62
Power Sources, 517-65
Inhalation Anesthetizing Locations, 517-G
Circuits in, 517-104
Classification of Locations, 517-100
Wiring and Equipment 517-101
Grounded Systems, 517-104(c)
Isolated, 517-104(a)
Line Isolation Monitor, 517-104(b)
Grounding, 517-103
Low-Voltage Equipment and Instruments, 517-105
Patient Care Areas, 517-120
Signal Transmission, 517-122
Nursing Homes and Residential Custodial Care Facilities, 517-D
Critical Branch, 517-46
Essential Electrical System, 517-44
Facilities, 517-41, 517-42
Life Safety Branch, 517-45
Power Sources, 517-47
Patient Care Areas, 517-F
Additional Protective Techniques, 517-90
Critical Care Areas, 517-84
General Care Areas, 517-83
Grounding, 517-81
Panelboard Bonding, 517-82
Wet Locations, 517-90(c)
Wiring, 517-B
Ground-Fault Protection, 517-14
Grounding, 517-11
Methods, 517-B, 517-10
Receptacles, Insulated Grounds, 517-13
X-ray Installation, 517-K
Connection, 517-141
Control Circuit Conductors, 517-145
Definitions, 517-140
Disconnecting Means, 517-142
Equipment Installations, 517-146
Rating, 517-143
Transformers and Capacitors, 517-148

Heat Generating Equipment, Art. 665

Heat Tape Outlet Mobile Homes, 550-6(g)

Heater Cords, Table 400-4, 422-8(a)

Heating Appliances, Art. 422

Heating Cables, Art. 424, 426

Heating Elements, Marking, 422-31

Heating, Fixed Electric Space, Art. 424

Heating Panels and Heating Panel Sets, Radiant, 424-I

Heavy-Duty Lampholders
Branch Circuits, 210-23, Table 210-24
Definition, 210-21(a)
Unit Loads, 220-2(c)

Hermetic Refrigerant Motor Compressors
(see Air-Conditioning and Refrigerating Equipment, Art. 440)

Hoists, Art. 610
Conductors, Contact, 610-C
Control, 610-F
Electric Cords, 400-7
Grounding, 250-7, 250-43, 610-G
Hazardous (Classified) Locations, 503-13
Motors, and Controllers, Disconnecting Means, 430-112, 610-D
Overcurrent Protection, 610-F
Wiring, 610-B

Hoistway
Definition, Art. 100
Wiring In, 620-37

Hood, Metal Theaters, 520-24

Hoods for Commercial Cooking, Lighting in, 410-4(c)

Hospitals (see Health Care Facilities, Art. 517)

Hot Tubs, 680-D

Houseboats (Floating Dwelling Units), 555-B

Hydromassage Bathtubs, 680-D

Identification
Disconnecting Means, 110-22
Flexible Cords
Grounded Conductor, 400-22
Grounding Conductor, 400-23
Grounded Conductors, Art. 200
High Leg, 215-8, 230-56, 384-3(e)
Service Disconnecting Means, 230-70

Identified, Definition, Art. 100

Immersion Heaters, Portable Types, 422-9

Incandescent Lamps [see also Hazardous (Classified) Locations]
Guards
Aircraft Hangars, 513-5(a)
Garages, 511-6(a), (b)
Theater Dressing Rooms, 520-72
Lamp Wattage, Marking on Fixture, 410-70

INDEX

INDEX

Metal-Clad Cable *(Continued)*
Bends, 334-11
Conductors, 334-20
Construction, 334-C
Definition, 334-1
Fittings for, 334-12
Grounding, 334-23
Marking, 310-11(b)(2) Ex. 3, 334-24
Supports, 334-10
Through Studs, Joists, and Rafters, 300-4
Uses Not Permitted, 334-3
Uses Permitted, 334-3
Voltages, 334-2

Metal-Enclosed Switchgear, 230-202(h), 230-208(b), 710-9, 710-24

Metal Frame of Building
Grounding Electrode, 250-81(b)
Not Permitted as Equipment Grounding Conductor, 250-58(a)
Permitted as Inherent Ground, 620-85

Metal Hood, Stage Switchboard, 520-24

Metal Working Machine Tools and Plastic Machinery, Art. 670

Metal Siding, Grounding of, 250-44 (FPN)

Metallic Outlet Boxes, 370-20

Metallic Raceways [see (FPN) to Definition of, Raceway, Art. 100]

Metals, Dissimilar, 110-14, 250-115, 345-3, 346-1, 348-1

Meter(s)
Cases, Grounding, 250-123, 250-124
Connection and Location at Services, 230-82 Ex. 3, 230-94 Ex. 5
Grounding to Circuit Conductor, 250-61(b) Ex. 3
Hazardous (Classified) Locations, Class I, 501-3, 502-14

Metric Units of Measurement, 90-8

Mineral-Insulated Metal-Sheathed Cable,
Type MI, Art. 330
Bends, 330-13
Construction Specifications, 330-C
Definition, 330-1
Fittings, 330-14
Supports, 330-12
Terminating Seals, 330-15
Through Studs, Joists, etc., 300-4, 330-11
Uses Not Permitted, 330-4
Uses Permitted, 330-3
Wet Locations, 300-6(c), 330-10

Mobile Home Parks, Art. 550
Definition of, 550-2
Distribution Systems, 550-21
Park Electrical Wiring System
Calculated Load, 550-22(a)

Mobile Home Parks *(Continued)*
Feeder and Service Demand Factors, Table 550-22
Per Mobile Home Service, 550-22(a)
Definition, 550-2
Mobile Home Lot, Definition, 550-2
Mobile Home Service Equipment, 550-23(a)
Definition, 550-2

Mobile Homes, Art. 550
Appliances, 550-7
Branch Circuits, 550-5
Branch-Circuit Protective Equipment, 550-4(b)
Calculations of Loads, 550-11
Definition, 550-2
Disconnecting Means, 550-4(a)
Expandable and Dual Units, Wiring, 550-12
Ground-Fault Circuit-Interrupter, 550-6(b)
Grounding, 550-9
Heat Tape Outlet, 550-6(g)
Insulated Neutral Required, 550-9(a)
Lighting Fixtures, 550-7(a)
Nameplates, 550-4(d)
Outdoor Outlet Fixtures, Air-Cooling Equipment, 550-13
Permanent Foundation on, Definition, 550-2
Power Supply, 550-3
Receptacle Outlets, Types, Where Required, 550-6
Testing, 550-10
Wiring Methods and Materials, 550-8

Mogul Base Lampholders, 210-6, 410-53

Monorails, 610-1

Motion Picture
Projectors, 520-2, Art. 540
Grounding, 250-43(h)
Studios, Art. 530
Theaters, Art. 520

Motor(s), Art. 430
Air Conditioning Units, Art. 440
Appliances, Motor Driven, 430-H
Branch Circuits, 430-B
Combination Loads, 430-25, 430-63
Continuous Duty, 430-22
Intermittent Duty, 430-22
Single Motor, 430-22
Taps, 430-28 Exception, 430-53
Two or More, 430-24
Wound Rotor Secondary, 430-23
Capacitor
Circuits, 460-8, 460-9
Rating, 460-9
Circuits, 430-B
Code Letters, Table 430-7(b)
Coded and Noncoded, Setting of Branch-Circuit Devices, Table 430-152
Combined Overcurrent Protection (Starting and Running), 430-55
Conductor(s), 430-B
Control Circuits, 430-F
Controllers, 430-G
Hazardous (Classified) Locations, 501-6, 502-6, 503-4
Current, Full Load
Alternating Current

1058

INDEX

INDEX

INDEX

Tamperability

Air Circuit Breakers, 240-82

Type S Fuses, 240-54(d), 550-4

Tamperproof Receptacles, 517-90(b)

Taps (see also Splices and Taps)

Branch-Circuit

Cooking Appliances, 210-19(c) Ex. 1

Individual Fixtures or Lampholders, 210-19(c) Ex. 2, 240-4

Busways, 364-12 Ex. 1

Feeders

10-ft. Rule, 240-21 Ex. 2

25-ft. Rule, 240-21 Exs. 3 and 8

100-ft. Rule, 240-21 Ex. 10

Motor, 430-28

100-ft. Rule, 430-28 Exception

Service-Entrance Conductors, 230-46

Telegraph Systems, Art. 800

Telephone Exchanges, Circuit Load, 220-2(c) Ex. 4

Telephone Systems, Art. 800

Television, Radio Equipment, Art. 810

Television Studios, Art. 520, 530

INDEX

Pursuant to Section 15 of the NFPA Regulations Governing Committee Projects, the National Fire Protection Association has issued the following Tentative Interim Amendments to the 1984 edition of the *National Electrical Code*, NFPA 70. These TIAs were processed by the National Electrical Code Committee, and were approved for release by the Standards Council on July 8, 1981.

A Tentative Interim Amendment is tentative because it has not been processed through the entire standards-making procedures. It is interim because it is effective only between editions of the standard. A TIA automatically becomes a Proposal of the proponent for the next edition of the standard; as such, it then is subject to all the procedures of the standards-making process.

(NOTE: This is TIA 70-81-10 reissued on the 1984 edition.)

Tentative Interim Amendment 70-84-1

to the

National Electrical Code

NFPA 70-1984

1. Add the following Exception immediately following the wording of Section 517-104(b)(2), but prior to the Fine Print Note:

Exception: The line isolation monitor may be of the low impedance type such that the current through the line isolation monitor, when any point of the isolated system is grounded, will not exceed twice the alarm threshold value for a period not exceeding 5 milliseconds.

(NOTE: This is TIA 70-81-11 reissued on the 1984 edition.)

Tentative Interim Amendment 70-84-2

to the

National Electrical Code

NFPA 70-1984

1. Revise Part C, Section 517-30, and add a new 517-31 and 517-32 to read as follows:

Part C. Clinics, Medical and Dental Offices, Outpatient Facilities, and Other Health Care Facilities Not Covered in Parts D and E

517-30. Applicability. Part C applies to those portions of clinics, medical and dental offices, and outpatient facilities wherein patients are intended to be examined or treated. It does not apply to business offices, corridors, waiting rooms, and the like.

517-31.* Wiring, Grounding and Receptacles. Wiring, grounding and receptacle installations shall be in accordance with Sections 517-10 and 517-11.

517-32.* Essential Electrical System.

(a) **General.** The requirements of this section shall apply to those health care facilities described in Section 517-30, in which

(1) Inhalation anesthetics are administered in any concentration to patients, or

(2) Patients require electrically operated or mechanical life support devices.

(b) **Scope.** The essential electrical system for these facilities shall comprise a system capable of supplying a limited amount of lighting and power service which is considered essential for life safety and orderly cessation of procedures during the time normal electrical service is interrupted for any reason.

(c) **Connections.** The essential electrical system shall supply power for

(1) Task illumination which is related to the safety of life and which is necessary for the safe cessation of procedures in progress.

(2) All anesthesia and resuscitative equipment used in areas where inhalation anesthetics are administered to patients including alarm and alerting devices.

(FPN): See Nonflammable Medical Gas Systems, NFPA 56F-1977, Chapters 3 and 6.

(3) All electrically operated and mechanical equipment in areas where procedures are performed that require such equipment for the support of the patient's life.

(d) **Alternate Source of Power.**

(1) **Power Source.** The alternate source of power for the system shall be specifically designed for this purpose and shall be either a generator, battery system or self-contained battery integral with the equipment.

(2) **System Capacity.** The alternate source of power shall be separate and independent from the normal source and shall have a capacity to sustain its connected loads for a minimum of 1½ hours after loss of the normal source.

(3) **System Operation.** The system shall be so arranged that, in the event of a failure of the normal power source, the alternate source of power shall be automatically connected to the load within 10 seconds.

(FPN): See Essential Electrical Systems for Health Care Facilities, NFPA 76A-1977, Section 6-6.2, Description of Transfer Switch Operation with Engine Generator Sets, and Section 6-6.3, Description of Transfer Switch Operation with Battery Systems.

The 1984 NEC®
The most up-to-date information available!

The new *1984 National Electrical Code®* approved at NFPA's Annual Meeting includes more than 1,000 additions, deletions and changes. Extensive revisions that are sure to affect your job if you are an electrician, inspector, contractor, electrical manufacturer, architect, builder or consulting engineer. Discover the changes by ordering your copy today!

YES! PLEASE SEND ME—

_____ Copies of the *1984 National Electrical Code®*
(6Q) NFPA 70-84 at $15.00 each; *NFPA Members: $13.50*

Tapping in to the NEC®
The informative companion to any edition of the NEC!

If you haven't yet ordered your copy of this unique NEC resource, now is the time to become more informed! You'll find answers to 75 of the most-asked questions, presented by a panel of six top NEC experts. *Tapping in to the NEC®* offers a variety of interesting, informal viewpoints on basic Code requirements that are often mis-understood . . . makes fine reading for anyone who regularly works with the NEC!

YES! PLEASE SEND ME—

_____ Copies of *Tapping in to the NEC®* (6Q-NEC-QUE) at $8.50 a copy; *NFPA Members $7.65*

BUSINESS REPLY MAIL
FIRST CLASS   PERMIT NO. 5347   QUINCY, MA

POSTAGE WILL BE PAID BY ADDRESSEE

National Fire Protection Association
Batterymarch Park
Quincy, Massachusetts 02269

BUSINESS REPLY MAIL
FIRST CLASS   PERMIT NO. 5347   QUINCY, MA

POSTAGE WILL BE PAID BY ADDRESSEE

National Fire Protection Association
Batterymarch Park
Quincy, Massachusetts 02269

Operational Amplifiers

G	Open loop gain	I_{io}	Input offset current
A	Closed loop gain	I_{Bias}	Input bias current
G_{cm}, A_{cm}	Common-mode gains		$(I_{Bias} = \dfrac{I_{B+} + I_{B-}}{2})$
V_+, v_+	Voltage at the noninverting input terminal	I_{B+}, I_{B-}	Input currents to noninverting and inverting terminals
V_-, v_-	Voltage at the inverting input terminal		
A_+	Ratio v_o/v_+	I_{os}	Offset current
A_-	Ratio v_o/v_-	CMRR	Common-mode rejection ratio
A_d	Differential gain	PSRR	Power-supply rejection ratio
V_{cm}	Common-mode voltage	SR	Slew rate
V_d, v_d	Differential input voltage	GBP	Voltage gain–bandwidth product
V_{os}	Output offset voltage		
V_{io}	Input offset voltage	R_{cm}	Common-mode resistance
V^+, V^-	Op-amp supply voltages	f_p	Power bandwidth

Transistor Amplifiers

A_i	Amplifier current gain	η	Amplifier efficiency	A_{im}	Midfrequency-range current gain
		α	Common-base current gain		
A_v	Amplifier voltage gain	β	Ratio i_C/i_B	ω_c	Corner frequency in rad/s
I_{CBO}	Leakage current in the collector-base junction	γ	Voltage feedback ratio (feedback attenuation factor)	f_H	High corner frequency in hertz
r_d	Dynamic transistor resistance	A_{vm}	Midfrequency-range voltage gain	f_L	Low corner frequency in hertz

Diodes

$V\gamma$	Turn-on voltage	R_f	Forward resistance of a diode
V_r	Ripple voltage		
I_D	Current in diode	R_r	Reverse resistance of a diode
I_o	Reverse saturation current		

FET Amplifiers

g_m	Transconductance
r_{DS}	FET dynamic resistance
V_p	Pinch-off voltage

ELECTRONIC CIRCUIT DESIGN

An Engineering Approach

C. J. Savant, Jr.
California State University, Los Angeles

Martin S. Roden
California State University, Los Angeles

Gordon L. Carpenter
California State University, Long Beach

The Benjamin/Cummings Publishing Company, Inc.

Menlo Park, California • Reading, Massachusetts
Don Mills, Ontario • Wokingham, U.K. • Amsterdam • Sydney
Singapore • Tokyo • Madrid • Bogota • Santiago • San Juan

To our loving wives,
Elnora Carpenter and Barbara Savant

Sponsoring Editor: Craig Bartholomew
Production Supervisors: George Calmenson, Betsy Dilernia
Consulting Designer and Art Coordinator: Wendy Calmenson
Copy Editor: Linda Thompson
Illustrators: Art by AYXA, Carl Brown, Becky and Al McCahon
Compositor: Graphic Typesetting Service
Cover Design: Wendy Calmenson
Cover Photograph: Courtesy of Aetna Life and Casualty;
photo by Al Ferreira

The basic text of this book was designed using the Modular Design System, as developed by Wendy Earl and Design Office Bruce Kortebein.

Library of Congress Cataloging-in-Publication Data

Savant, C. J.
   Electronic circuit design.

   Bibliography: p.
   Includes index.
   1. Electronic circuit design.   I. Roden, Martin S.
II. Carpenter, Gordon L. (Gordon Lee), 1928–
III. Title.
TK7867.S277   1987   621.3815′3   86-26365
ISBN 0-8053-7860-X

ABCDEFGHIJ-DO-8987

The Benjamin/Cummings Publishing Company, Inc.
2727 Sand Hill Road
Menlo Park, California 94025

PREFACE

Electronic Circuit Design: An Engineering Approach is written for use as a text in the core electronics courses in undergraduate programs in electrical engineering. The book provides coverage of three areas: discrete devices, linear integrated circuits, and digital integrated circuits. A practicing engineer looking for a current reference for self-study will also find this book valuable.

Why This Book?

With literally dozens of books to choose from in the field of analog and digital electronics, you may wonder why we have written yet another book on the subject. Our principal goal in writing this text was to relieve our frustrations. We had attempted to teach electronics to undergraduates using existing texts. These traditional texts look at the field from a theoretical point of view. They emphasize fundamentals, such as physics of semiconductors, but ignore the exciting applications. Fundamentals *do not* change with time, and are thus extremely important. However, dealing only with fundamentals detracts from the excitement of the subject and, indeed, the student may never develop the application skills required for a career in electronics. On the other hand, applications *do* change with time, so an approach that emphasizes these at the expense of presenting a superficial treatment of fundamentals is dangerous.

While this book covers the fundamentals in a thorough and direct fashion, it goes one step further toward a balanced approach to electronics. With both the accrediting agency (ABET) and industry demanding more design in engineering programs, we feel that it is time to balance the fundamentals with a strong but measured taste of design. It is our hope that this book will inspire the imaginations of tomorrow's engineers, who will be called upon to *design*, not just to analyze, electronic systems.

Uniqueness of the Design Approach

Contact with practicing engineers and engineering recruiters has led us to place significant emphasis upon *design* of electronic systems. The new engineer will be asked to design electronic systems and circuits using an ever-increasing inventory of new integrated circuits and discrete components. Thus, we have attempted to teach engineering students to *think* as designers, rather than to mimic just a few design approaches. Our goal is to "educate" rather than to "train."

Elementary design procedures are introduced early in the text to motivate the reader. It is our experience that analog and digital electronics is best comprehended through a "learn by doing" approach. Thus, topics such as small signal analysis have been presented immediately following dc analysis, to allow for presentation of some early meaningful and realistic design problems.

Wherever possible, a step-by-step design procedure is developed, which we feel will give the student confidence. Rather than replacing the theory, such procedures will reinforce and clarify it. This approach culminates in Chapter 17, which presents universal design procedures that can be applied to both analog and digital systems.

Drill Problems

The text contains a large number of drill problems that are evenly distributed throughout the book. Since drill problems are meant to offer immediate reinforcement for students, answers to these problems can be found right along with the problems.

SPICE Appendix

A comprehensive appendix on the SPICE circuit modeling program is included. This allows instructors the flexibility of introducing SPICE at any point in the course. Examples of SPICE program printouts are included as models for the student.

Other Appendices

The book includes appendices covering:

- Semiconductor Physics. This may be used as supplementary material to Chapter 1 if additional detail is desired.

- Noise in Electronic Systems
- Manufacturers' Data Sheets (for selected devices)
- Laplace Transforms
- Answers to Selected Problems

Accuracy of the Book

Every effort has been made to write and publish an *accurate* book. Since this text evolved out of the classroom environment, it has been extensively checked and class-tested with our students. Copies of the manuscript were used as the primary text in our classes, and students and colleagues were encouraged to freely criticize (a challenge they enthusiastically accepted). In addition, the manuscript was extensively reviewed and checked by Professor Mahmoud El Nokali of the University of Pittsburgh. Victor Valdivia of Stanford University provided additional "backup" fact-checking as the authors embarked on the proofreading phase of the project. We therefore feel confident in the accuracy and precision of this book.

Instructional Adjuncts

Overhead projector **Transparency Masters** of the important figures in the text are available for instructors. Also available for instructors is an **Instructor's Manual**, containing complete solutions to all the drill problems and end-of-chapter problems in the book. Many of the problems, particularly those in Chapter 17, have been drawn from actual industrial applications, where the resulting systems have been implemented.

The authors recommend that the latest manufacturers' data books be used in conjunction with this text. For example, the Texas Instruments *TTL Data Book, Volume II,* and the National Semiconductor *CMOS Data Book* would be suitable companions for the third portion of our book, on digital integrated circuits.

Guide for Classroom Use

The material in this book can be presented in a series of two or three one-semester courses or three one-quarter courses in the junior and/or senior years. The prerequisite for the book is a first course in circuit analysis.

Chapters 1 through 6 cover the analysis and design of diode circuits, bipolar junction and field effect transistors, and audio frequency power amplifiers. No s-plane concepts are needed for an understanding of this first portion of the text.

The second portion of the book (Chapters 7 through 13) is devoted to linear integrated circuits. This material includes thorough coverage of ideal and actual operational amplifiers, frequency response, feedback and stability, Bode plots, and transfer characteristic design. Chapter 13 covers the subject of active filters, including a design procedure for Butterworth and Chebyshev filters. Some background in the Laplace Transform method is helpful in covering this part of the text. With this in mind, an appendix is included for the review of Laplace Transforms.

The final four chapters in the book (Chapters 14 through 17) are devoted to a study of digital integrated circuits and systems. Steady state analysis of pulse driven circuits and relaxation oscillators is presented. Three logic families—TTL, CMOS, and ECL—are compared and analyzed. Numerous unclocked and clocked ICs are studied with many practical applications included.

Chapter 17 is a unique chapter, presenting a "universal" design methodology that can be used with either digital or analog circuits. Many of the examples of design in this chapter have been drawn from industry to illustrate real-life design problems.

Acknowledgments

We would like to express our appreciation to the students in the various electronic design classes the authors have taught while using the early versions of this text. Sincere thanks are extended to Professor Gene Hostetter, who provided much of the op-amp material, and to our colleagues Professors Hassan Babaie, Lou Balin, Roy Barnett, Ed Evans, Mike Hassul, and Ken James for their comments and assistance with various portions of the manuscript.

We would especially like to thank Paul Van Halen of Portland State University, who supplied the first draft of the appendix on Semiconductor Physics, and Mahmoud El Nokali of the University of Pittsburgh, who read every page of the final manuscript and made many valuable suggestions. Special thanks also go to Bernhard Schmidt of the University of Dayton, who checked every illustration and problem set in the text for clarity and comprehensiveness. Victor Valdivia of Stanford University deserves special mention for his superb job of error-checking the typeset proofs for the book.

Every book is the result of a number of iterations and revisions based on classroom experience and the expert advice of reviewers. We were fortunate to have twenty-eight readers review all or part of this volume. We would like to thank the following reviewers, and the many others who are not mentioned by name, for their efforts:

Jack Allison, Oklahoma State University
Kay D. Baker, Utah State University
W. L. Beasley, Texas A&M University
Robert L. Bernick, California Polytechnic State University, Pomona

Raymond Black, New Mexico State University
T. V. Blalock, University of Tennessee
Frank Brands, Washington State University
John Churchill, University of California, Davis
R. G. Deshmukh, Florida Institute of Technology
Mahmoud El Nokali, University of Pittsburgh
E. L. Gerber, Drexel University
Ward Helms, University of Washington
Alfred T. Johnson, Jr., Widener University
Jerrold Krenz, University of Colorado, Boulder
B. Lalevic, Rutgers University
John Lowell, Texas Tech University
Eugene Manus, Virginia Polytechnic Institute and State University
Richard Morris, University of Portland
David A. Navon, University of Massachusetts, Amherst
Harry Neinhaus, University of South Florida
Charles Nelson, California State University, Sacramento
David Pearlman, Rochester Institute of Technology
William Sayle, Georgia Institute of Technology
Bernhard Schmidt, University of Dayton
Paul Van Halen, Portland State University
Darrell L. Vines, Texas Tech University
J. L. Yeh, Rutgers University
Carl R. Zimmer, Arizona State University

In addition to our colleagues and reviewers, many students helped us out along the way. The following students deserve our appreciation for their special assistance: Gabriel Cocco, Ted Curmi, Jim Eckman, Kevin Kean, Lyle Mattes, Bob McBride, Mark Pendleton, Steve Phillips, Gloria Quinn, Bob Topper, Bob Tran, Phil Vrbancic, and Ann Weichbrod. Special thanks are due Julie Jarnagan, who made many fundamental and grammatical corrections.

On a project of this complexity, it is no simple task to create a finished book out of a manuscript. However, in the able hands of George and Wendy Calmenson of San Francisco, this critical task did indeed look simple. Their professionalism and attention to detail have contributed to a book of which we are proud.

We truly hope that each of the people who contributed to this book and had a hand in its development are as satisfied with the finished product as we are.

Gordon L. Carpenter
Martin S. Roden
C. J. Savant, Jr.

INTRODUCTION
TO THE STUDENT

Electronics is the backbone of electrical engineering. Whether you specialize in solid state electronic design, or in diverse areas such as power, computers, controls, or communications, you must first become familiar with the basics of the design and analysis of electronic circuits and systems.

This is not an easy task, since the field is changing at a rapid pace. You must be careful to concentrate upon *education*, rather than *training*, in the area of electronics. Those who were *trained* in vacuum tube electronic design during the 1950s found their training to be useless a decade later when transistors replaced vacuum tubes in all but a few high-power or high-frequency applications. Likewise, those who were *trained* in transistor design during the 1960s and early 1970s found that training to be obsolete with the advent of integrated circuits and op-amp systems. It is therefore important that you prepare yourself for the next revolution by both learning the fundamentals and "learning how to learn."

Many texts approach this challenge by overemphasizing the theory and completely avoiding applications. You will find this not to be the case in this text. A sterile theoretical presentation could leave you with some basic knowledge that you could someday apply. However, you would probably not experience the excitement of applying this knowledge to practical situations as you learn. Indeed, you would not even know if you are capable of it.

For that reason, this text is heavily *design oriented*. You will be led through many practical applications of the theory—and we do mean *practical*. We hope you will be motivated to construct some of the systems you will design on paper, for that will truly "close the loop" and make your education more meaningful.

Some of the problems at the back of the chapters might seem overwhelming at first glance. Learning design is gradual, so don't become discouraged. You will find you are capable of making progress on even the most complex design problems. Your professor should be able to provide guidance.

Most of all, enjoy the subject material. You have chosen an exciting career, but the same factors that make it exciting also make it challenging. You must sometimes strain to the limits of your mental abilities if you are to succeed, but the rewards of success will be fine compensation.

If you have any comments or suggestions about the text, please feel free to communicate them to any of the three authors. Professors Roden and Savant are at California State University, Los Angeles, and Professor Carpenter is at California State University, Long Beach. Because we take a genuine interest in engineering education, we welcome all your comments and suggestions.

CONTENTS

CHAPTER 8   IDEAL OPERATIONAL AMPLIFIERS   324

ELECTRONIC CIRCUIT DESIGN

An Engineering Approach

1

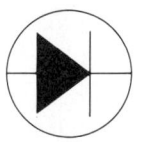

SEMICONDUCTOR DIODE CIRCUIT ANALYSIS

1.0 Introduction

The simplest nonlinear electronic device is known as a *diode*. A diode is composed of two different materials placed together so that charge flows easily in one direction but is impeded in the other direction. This device was developed by Henry Dunwoody in 1906 when he placed a piece of electric furnace carborundum between two brass holders. Later that year, Greenleaf Pickard developed a crystal radio detector in the form of a cat whisker in contact with a crystal. Various studies conducted between 1906 and 1940 indicated that silicon and germanium were excellent materials to use in the construction of these devices.

Many problems had to be overcome in the construction and fabrication of diodes. Engineers waited until the mid-1950s to solve the most critical of these problems. During the technological explosion of the late 1950s and early 1960s, solid-state technology received a great deal of attention. This was due to the need for lightweight, small, low-power-consuming electronic components for use in the development of intercontinental missiles and space vehicles. Emphasis was placed upon fabricating solid state devices that could achieve high reliability in applications where maintenance would be impossible. The result was the development of solid state components that are more economical and more reliable than vacuum tubes.

This chapter provides an introduction to the operation and applications of the solid-state diode. This two-terminal device, which is often smaller than a grain of rice, is *nonlinear*. In its simplest form, this means that applying the sum of two voltages produces a current that is not the sum of the two individual resulting currents. The diode behavior depends upon the polarity of the applied voltage. The diode's nonlinear characteristic is the reason it finds so many applications in electronics.

We first consider the basic physical concepts of semiconductors. The silicon junction diode is analyzed and an equivalent circuit is developed. Some important diode applications are then discussed, including rectification, demodulation, and detection. Appendix B expands greatly on the physics of semiconductors.

The *zener* diode is presented and its use for voltage regulation is investigated. A specific design technique is then developed.

A number of special-purpose diodes, such as *Schottky, varactor, tunnel, light-emitting* and *photo* are discussed. The chapter concludes with the design of a power supply using the MC7800 series integrated circuit regulator.

1.1   Theory of Semiconductors

We will be designing and analyzing systems using equivalent circuits to represent diodes. It is quite possible to use these circuits without understanding why they represent accurate models of the diodes. However, it is helpful to have an exposure to the physics of diodes in order to appreciate the origins of the equivalent circuits and to understand their shortcomings.

An *atom* consists of a nucleus, which has a positive charge. Electrons, with negative charges, move around the nucleus in elliptic paths. These electrons distribute themselves in *shells*. Electrons in the outermost shell are known as *valence electrons*.

When extremely pure elements, such as silicon and germanium, are cooled from the liquid state, their atoms arrange themselves in orderly patterns called *crystals,* as illustrated in Figure 1.1. The valence electrons determine the exact shape or lattice structure of the resulting crystal.

Silicon and germanium atoms each have four valence electrons. Hence, the atoms are bound in a lattice structure such that each atom "shares" its four valence electrons with neighboring atoms in the form of *covalent bonds*. The covalent bonds hold the lattice together.

Although the valence electrons are bound tightly in the crystalline structure, it is possible for these electrons to break their bonds and thus be capable of moving about in a conduction mode. This happens if sufficient external energy is supplied (e.g., from light or heat).

Figure 1.1
Crystal structure.

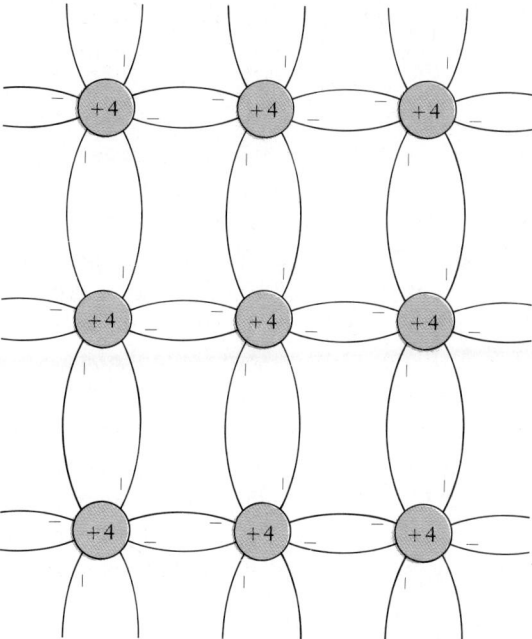

Because of interaction among the atoms in a crystal, it is possible for the valence electrons to possess energy levels within a range of values. The further an electron is away from atomic nucleii, the higher the energy level. Thus, as the crystal becomes "tighter," the levels decrease.

Just as there is a range, or band, of energies for the valence electrons, there is another range of energy values for free electrons—those that have broken loose and form a conduction channel. The two bands may or may not overlap.

1.1.1   Conduction in Materials

Figure 1.2 presents three energy-level diagrams. In Figure 1.2(a), the energy bands are widely separated. The unshaded region represents a *forbidden band* of energy levels in which no electrons are found. When this band is relatively large, as shown in the figure, the result is an *insulator*.

If the band is relatively small (on the order of 1 electron volt (eV), the amount of kinetic energy by which an electron increases when it falls through a potential of 1 V, or 1.6×10^{-19} J), the result is a *semiconductor*. This is illustrated in Figure 1.2(b).

The energy required to break a covalent bond is a function of the atomic spacing in the crystal. The smaller the atom, the closer the spacing and the greater the energy required to break the covalent bonds. It is more difficult to break a conductive electron from silicon than one from germanium because the silicon crystals have closer lattice spacing.

Figure 1.2
Energy levels.

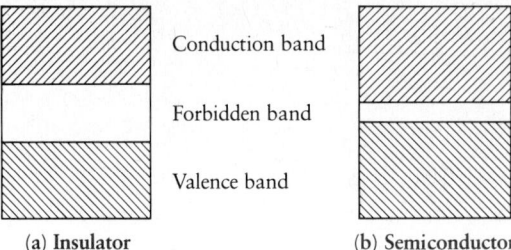
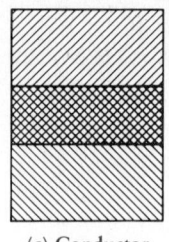

Conduction band

Forbidden band

Valence band

(a) **Insulator**　　　　(b) Semiconductor　　　　(c) Conductor

The *conductor,* or metal, results when the bands overlap, as shown in Figure 1.2(c). The conductor permits electric charges to move when a potential difference exists across the material.

There is no gap between the energy of a valence electron and that of a conduction electron in a conductor. This means that a particular valence electron is not strongly associated with its own nucleus. It is, therefore, free to move about throughout the structure. This movement of electrons, usually in response to an applied potential, is conduction.

Electrons in materials can be raised to higher energy bands by the application of heat, which causes vibration of the lattice. Materials that are insulators at room temperature can become conductors when the temperature is raised high enough. This causes some electrons to move to a higher energy band, where they become available for conduction. The energy band diagram of Figure 1.3 is used to illustrate the amount of energy required for electrons to reach the conduction band. The abscissa of this graph is the atomic spacing of the crystal. As the spacing increases, the nucleii exert a smaller force on the valence electrons. The axis is marked with the atomic spacing for four materials. Carbon (C) is an insulator in crystalline form (diamond). Silicon (Si) and Germanium (Ge) are semiconductors, and tin is a conductor. The energy gap shown on the figure represents the amount of external energy required to move the valence electrons into the conduction band.

1.1.2 *Conduction in Semiconductor Materials*

Electrons are tightly held together in silicon and germanium atoms. The inner electrons are buried deep within the atom, whereas the valence electrons are part of the covalent bonding—they cannot break away without receiving a considerable amount of energy. One way to supply such energy is by heating the material. At a temperature of absolute zero, there is no thermally induced vibration in the crystal. No covalent bonds can be broken, so there are no available electrons in the conduction band. Hence, current cannot exist and the semiconductor acts as an insulator.

Heat and other sources of energy cause valence band electrons to break their covalent bonds and become free electrons in the conduction band. As an

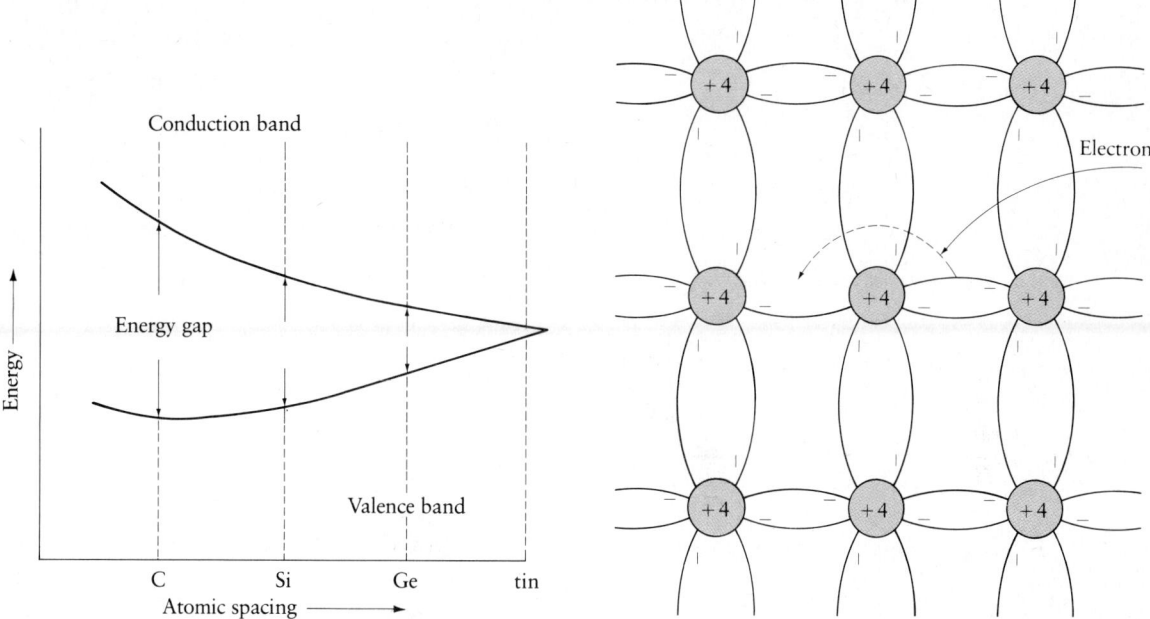

Figure 1.3 Energy band diagram.

Figure 1.4 Conduction from broken covalent bond.

electron leaves the valence band, it leaves a "hole." A nearby valence band electron can move in and fill the hole, thus creating another hole, with practically no exchange of energy. Figure 1.4 shows how the movement of electrons in covalent bonds contributes to conduction.

The conduction caused by the electrons in the conduction band is different from the conduction due to the holes left in the valence band. In pure semiconductors there are as many holes as there are free electrons.

Internal thermal energy increases the activity of electrons, thus moving valence electrons out of the influence of the covalent bond into the conduction band. In this way, there are a limited number of conduction band electrons under the influence of the applied electric field; these electrons move in one direction and establish a current, as shown in Figure 1.5.

Each time an electron is raised to a higher band, a hole is created in the valence band. The motion of holes is opposite in direction from that of electrons and is known as *hole current*. The holes act as if they are positive particles and contribute to the overall current.

As temperature is raised, a greater number of electrons is elevated to the conduction band, and current increases ([44], Volume I).

The two methods by which holes and electrons move through a silicon crystal are *diffusion* and *drift*. Thermal agitation causes random electron movement in a semiconductor. Although this phenomenon can be related to diffusion, it does not result in any net flow of charge. However if some other

Figure 1.5
Current.

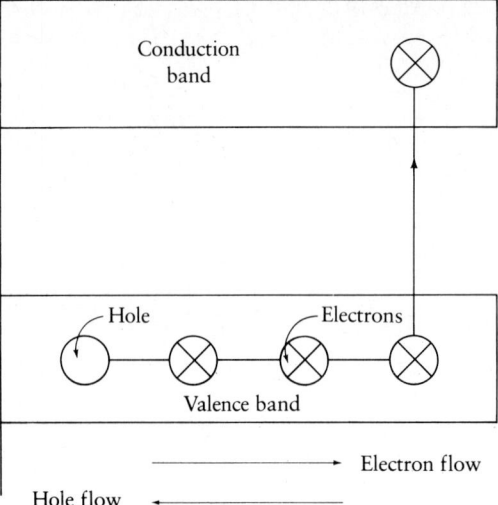

mechanism causes a concentration at one end of the semiconductor, the electrons will diffuse to the other end. This gives rise to a net charge flow, known as *diffusion current*. The other method of movement, drift, results when an electric field is applied to the semiconductor and the free holes and electrons are accelerated in the electric field. The velocity of this movement is called *drift velocity,* and the movement results in *drift currents*. The relationship between the applied electric field and the drift current is analogous to Ohm's law.

1.1.3 *Semiconductor Materials*

Silicon and germanium atoms are illustrated in Figure 1.6. The germanium atom has one more filled outer ring than does the silicon atom. This germanium outer ring is at a greater distance from the atom nucleus than is the silicon outer ring. Therefore, it takes less energy to raise electrons from the outer band into the conduction band for a germanium atom. This point is further illustrated by comparing the *energy gaps* of the two materials, as shown in Figure 1.7. Germanium has a smaller energy gap separating its valence and conduction bands, so less energy is required to cross the gap between bands.

1.1.4 *Doped Semiconductors*

Currents induced in pure semiconductors are too small (typically less than 10^{-9} A) for practical applications. In a pure semiconductor, the number of holes is the same as the number of electrons. The conductivity of a semicon-

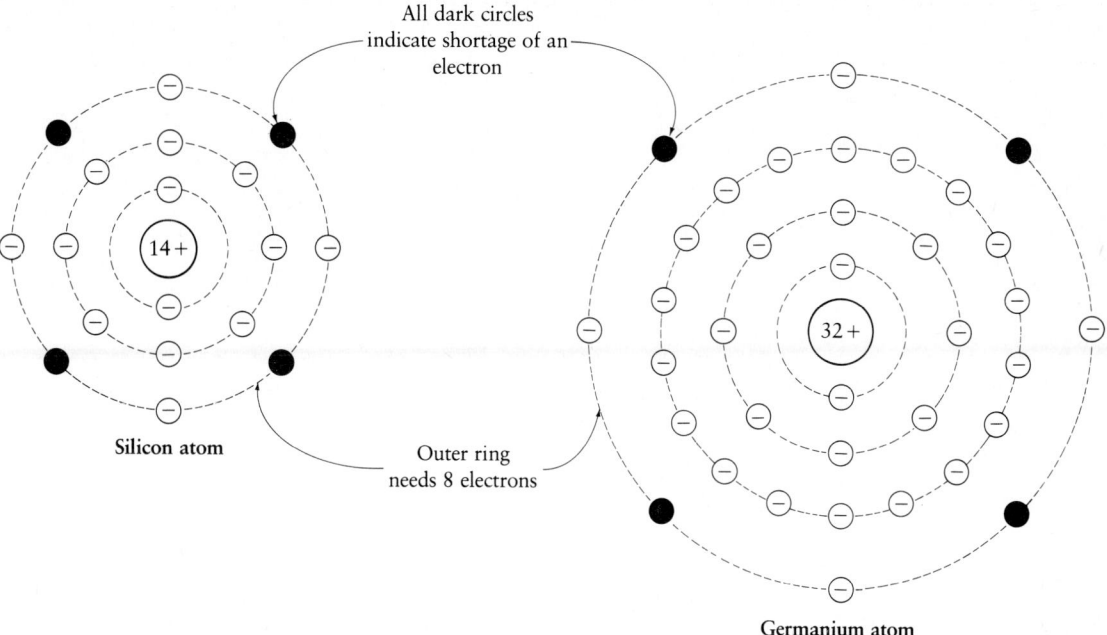

Figure 1.6   Atomic structure of silicon and germanium.

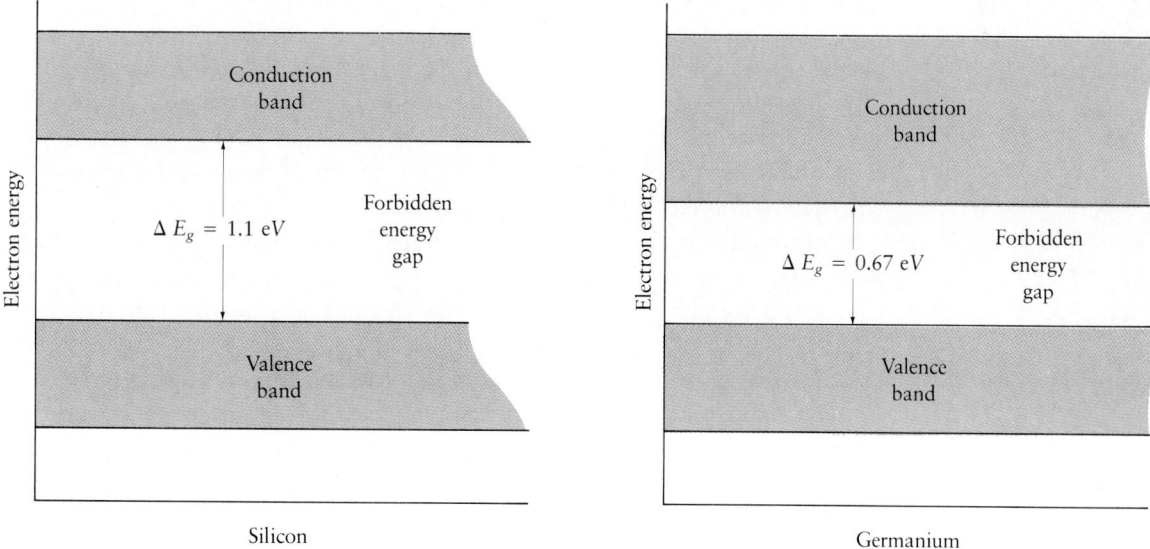

Figure 1.7   Energy gaps for germanium and silicon.

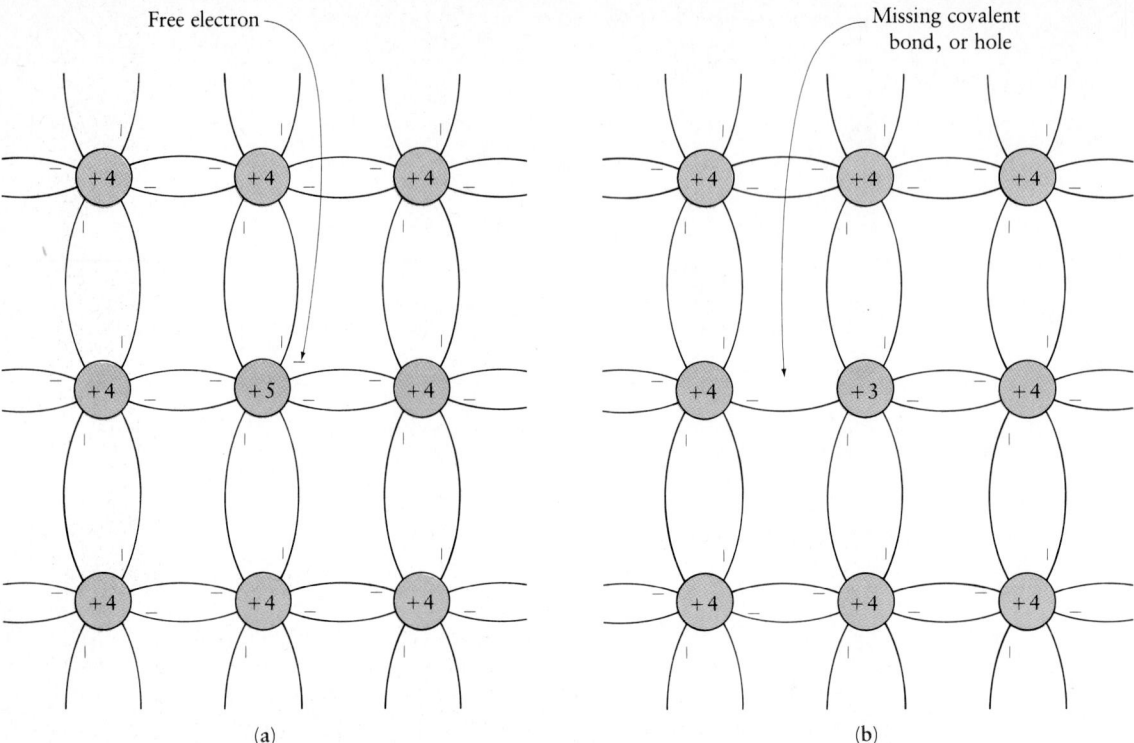

Figure 1.8   Crystal structure of doped semiconductors.

ductor can be greatly increased when small amounts of specific impurities are introduced into the crystal. This procedure is called *doping*. If the doping substance has extra free electrons, it is known as a *donor,* and the doped semiconductor is *n-type*. The *majority carriers* are electrons and the *minority carriers* are holes, since there are more electrons than holes.

If the doping substance has extra holes, it is known as an *acceptor,* and the doped semiconductor is *p-type*. The majority carriers are holes and the minority carriers are electrons. Figure 1.8 illustrates the crystal structure of *n*-type (Figure 1.8(a)) and *p*-type (Figure 1.8(b)) semiconductors. The doped materials are known as *extrinsic semiconductors,* whereas the pure substances are *intrinsic semiconductors*. The intrinsic semiconductor crystal has equal concentrations of free electrons and holes generated by thermal ionization. The density of electrons is denoted by *n*, and the density of holes is *p*. It can be shown that the product, *np*, is constant for a given material at a given temperature.

The intrinsic carrier density, denoted by n_i, is given by the square root of this product. Thus,

$$n_i^2 = np$$

Since these concentrations are caused by thermal ionization, n_i is dependent upon the temperature of the crystal. It then follows that n or p or both have to be a function of temperature. The minority hole concentration is a function of temperature in the n-type doped material and the majority electron density is independent of temperature. Similarly, the minority electron concentration is a function of temperature in p-type materials and the majority hole density is independent of temperature. Remember that the doped semiconductor is still electrically neutral, as the majority free carriers are neutralized by the bound charges associated with the impurity atoms.

The resistance of a semiconductor is known as *bulk resistance.* A lightly doped semiconductor has high bulk resistance.

1.2 Semiconductor Diodes

The simplest linear circuit element is the resistor. The voltage across this element is related to current through it by Ohm's law. This relationship is graphically depicted by a straight line, as shown in Figure 1.9(a). The slope of the line is the conductance of the resistor, i.e., the ratio of current to voltage. The reciprocal of this slope is the resistance in ohms. If the resistor is connected in any circuit, the operating point must fall somewhere on this curve.

The ideal diode is a nonlinear device with a current versus voltage characteristic, as shown in Figure 1.9(b). This characteristic is referred to as *piecewise linear,* since the curve is constructed from segments of straight lines. Note that as we attempt to impose a positive (or forward) voltage on the diode, we are not successful and the voltage is limited to zero. The slope of the curve is infinity. Therefore, under this condition the resistance is zero and the diode behaves as a short circuit. If we place a negative (or reverse) voltage across the diode, the current is zero and the slope of the curve is zero. Thus, the diode is now behaving as an infinite resistance, or open circuit.

Figure 1.9   Operating curves for resistor and ideal diode.

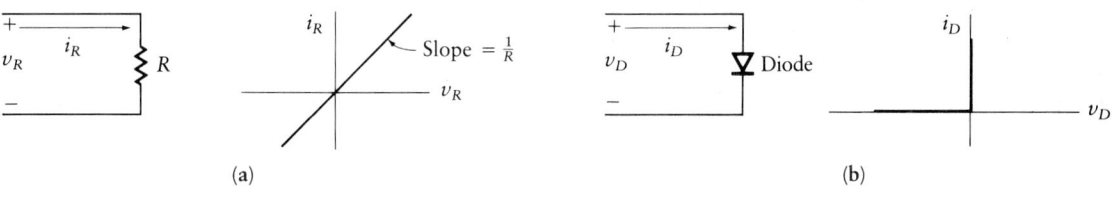

1.2.1   *Diode Construction*

Figure 1.10 shows a *p*-type material and an *n*-type material placed together to form a junction. This represents a simplified model of diode construction. The model ignores gradual changes in concentration of the impurities in the material. Practical diodes are constructed as a single piece of semiconductor material, where one side is doped with *p*-type material and the other side with *n*-type material.

Also shown in Figure 1.10 is the schematic symbol of the diode. Note that the "arrow" in this symbol points from the *p*- to the *n*-type material.

Three different materials are commonly used in the construction of diodes: germanium, silicon, and gallium arsenide. Silicon has generally replaced germanium for diodes because its larger energy gap allows higher temperature operation, and the material costs are much lower. Gallium arsenide is particularly useful in microwave and high-frequency applications. However, gallium arsenide is more expensive than silicon and the manufacture of gallium arsenide diodes is difficult.

The precise distance over which the change from *p*- to *n*-type material occurs within the crystal varies with the fabrication technique. The essential feature of the *pn* junction is that the change in impurity concentration must occur in a relatively short distance. Otherwise, the junction will not behave as a diode. There are cases where the *pn* junction cannot be treated as an abrupt change in material type, notably when the diode is formed by diffusion. This causes the doping near the junction to be *graded*—that is, the donor and acceptor concentrations are a function of distance across the junction [2, 14, 36, 37, 44, 53, 57, 61].

A *depletion region* will exist in the vicinity of the junction, as shown in Figure 1.11(a). This phenomenon is due to a combination of electrons and holes where the materials join. This depletion region will have few carriers. The minority carriers on each side of the depletion region (electrons in the *p*-region and holes in the *n*-region) will migrate to the other side and combine with ions in that material. Likewise, the majority carriers (electrons in the *n*-region and holes in the *p*-region) will migrate across the junction.

However, the two components of the current formed by the hole and electron movements across the junction add together to form the diffusion current, I_D. The direction of this current is from the *p*-side to the *n*-side. In addition to the diffusion current, a current exists due to the minority carrier drift across the junction, and this is referred to as I_S. Some of the thermally generated holes in the *n*-type material diffuse through the *n*-type material to the edge of the depletion region. There they experience the electric field and are swept across the depletion region into the *p*-type side. The electrons react in the same manner. The components of these actions combine to form the drift current, I_S.

Figure 1.10
Simplified diode
model.

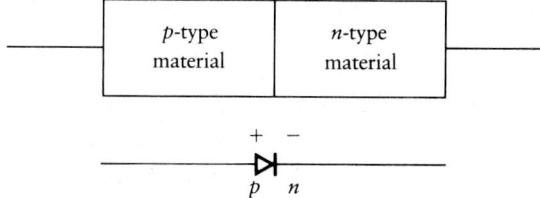

Figure 1.11
Depletion regions.

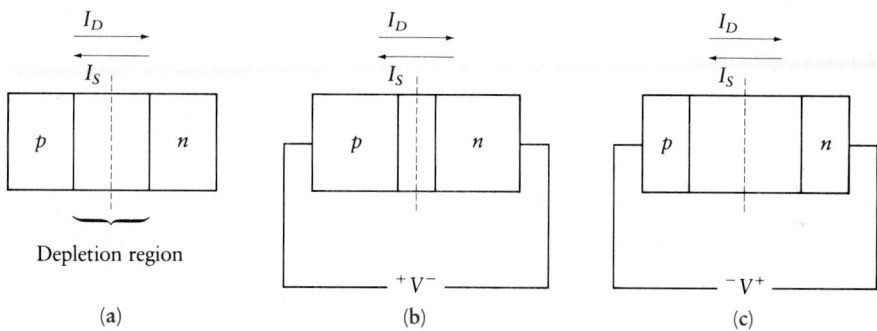

Depletion region

(a)   (b)   (c)

During open-circuit conditions, the diffusion current is equal to the drift current (at equilibrium).

If we now apply a positive potential to the p-material relative to the n-material, as shown in Figure 1.11(b), the diode is said to be *forward-biased*. The depletion region shrinks in size due to the attraction of majority carriers to the opposite side. That is, the negative potential at the right attracts holes in the p-region, and vice-versa. With a smaller depletion region, current can flow more readily. When forward-biased, $I_D - I_S = I$ after equilibrium is achieved, where I is the current through the junction.

Alternatively, if the applied voltage is as shown in Figure 1.11(c), the diode is *reverse-biased*. Free electrons are drawn from the n-material toward the right, and, similarly, holes are drawn to the left. The depletion region gets wider and the diode acts as an insulator. When reverse-biased, $I_S - I_D = I$ after equilibrium is achieved, where I is the current through the junction.

1.2.2   *Diode Operation*

Figure 1.12 illustrates the operating characteristics of a *practical* diode. This curve differs from the ideal characteristic of Figure 1.9(b) in the following ways: As the forward voltage increases beyond zero, current does not immediately start to flow. It takes a minimum voltage, denoted by $V\gamma$, to obtain any noticeable current. As the voltage tries to exceed $V\gamma$, the current increases

Figure 1.12
Diode operating
characteristics.

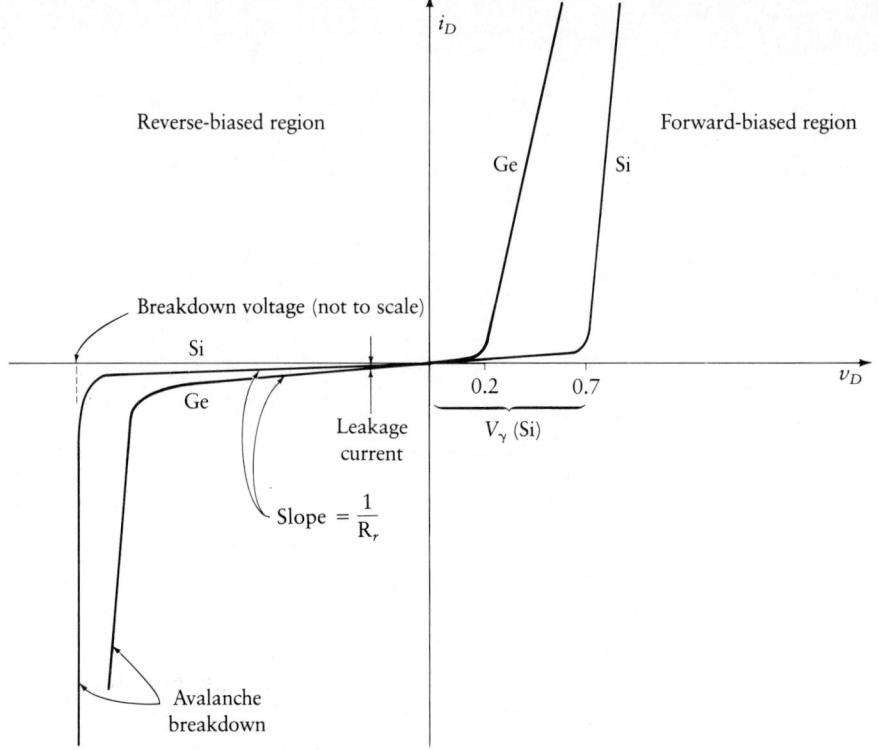

rapidly. The slope of the characteristic curve is large but not infinite, as is the case with the ideal diode. The minimum voltage required to obtain noticeable current, $V\gamma$, is approximately 0.7 V for silicon semiconductors (at room temperature) and 0.2 V for germanium semiconductors. The difference between the voltage for silicon and germanium stems from the atomic structure of the materials. For gallium arsenide diodes, $V\gamma$ is approximately 1.2 V.

When the diode is reverse-biased, there is some small leakage current. This current occurs provided that the reverse voltage is less than the voltage required to break down the junction. The leakage current is much greater for germanium diodes than it is for silicon or gallium arsenide diodes. If the negative voltage becomes large enough to be in the breakdown region, a normal diode may be destroyed. This breakdown voltage is defined as the *peak inverse voltage* (PIV) in manufacturers' specifications (Appendix D shows representative specification sheets. We refer to these often in this text, so you should take a minute to locate them at this time). The curve of Figure 1.12 is not to scale in the reverse region as the avalanche breakdown is usually at a large negative voltage (typically 50 V or more). The damage to the normal diode at breakdown is due to the avalanche of electrons, which flow across the junction with little increase in voltage. The large current can cause destruction of the diode if excessive

Figure 1.13
Diode models.

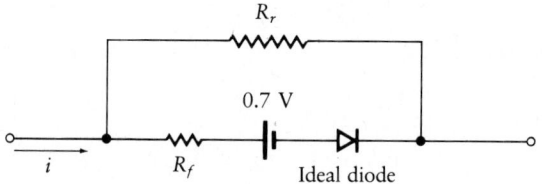

(a)   dc model (both forward and reverse)

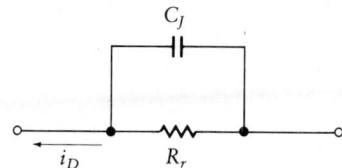

(b)   Simple ac model for reverse-biased diode

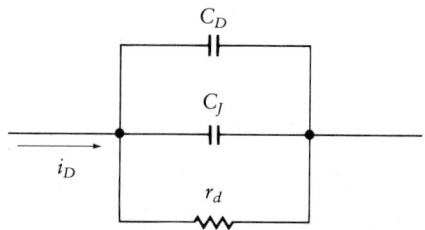

(c)   ac model for forward-biased diode

heat builds up. This breakdown is sometimes referred to as the diode voltage breakdown (V_{BR}).

Diodes can be constructed to utilize the breakdown voltage to simulate a voltage-control device. The result is a zener diode, which is discussed in Section 1.6.

1.2.3   *Diode Equivalent Circuit Models*

The circuit shown in Figure 1.13(a) represents a simplified model of the silicon diode under both forward and reverse *dc* operating conditions. The relationships for this model approximate the diode operating curve of Figure 1.12. The resistor R_r represents the reverse-bias resistance of the diode and is usually of the order of megohms. The resistor R_f represents the contact and bulk resistance of the diode and is usually less than 50 Ω. When forward-biased, the ideal diode is a short circuit, or zero resistance. The circuit resistance of the practical diode modeled in Figure 1.13(a) is

$$R_r \parallel R_f \approx R_f$$

Under reverse-bias conditions, the ideal diode has infinite resistance (open circuit), and the circuit resistance of the practical model is R_r. The ideal diode that is part of the model of Figure 1.13(a) is forward-biased when the terminal voltage exceeds 0.7 V.

The *ac* circuit models are more complex because the diode operation depends upon frequency. A simple ac model for a reverse-biased diode is shown in Figure 1.13(b). The capacitor, C_J, represents the junction capacitance. Figure 1.13(c) shows the ac equivalent circuit for a forward-biased diode. The model includes two capacitors, the *diffusion capacitor, C_D*, and the *junction capacitor, C_J*. The diffusion capacitance, C_D, approaches zero for reverse-biased diodes. The *dynamic resistance* is r_d and it is given by the slope of the voltage-current characteristic. At low frequencies, the capacitive effects are small and r_d is the only significant element.

1.3   Physics of Solid-State Diodes

Now that we have discussed diode construction and have had a brief introduction to practical diode models, we shall explore some of the more detailed aspects of the differences between practical and ideal diodes. Additional detail is presented in Appendix B.

1.3.1   *Charge Distribution*

Diodes can be visualized as a combination of an *n*-type semiconductor connected to a *p*-type semiconductor. However, in actual production, a single crystal of a semiconductor is formed with part of the crystal doped with *n*-type material and the other part doped with *p*-type material.

When the *p*- and *n*-type materials exist together in a crystal, a charge redistribution occurs. Some of the free electrons from the *n*-material migrate across the junction and combine with the free holes in the *p*-material. Similarly some of the free holes from the *p*-material migrate across the junction and combine with free electrons in the *n*-material. As a result of this charge redistribution, the *p*-material acquires a net negative charge and the *n*-material acquires a net positive charge. These charges create an electric field and a potential difference between the two types of material that will inhibit any further charge movement. The result is to reduce the number of current carriers near the junction. This happens in an area known as the *depletion region*. The resulting electric field provides a *potential barrier,* or *hill,* in a direction that inhibits the migration of carriers across the junction. This is shown in Figure

Figure 1.14
Barrier potentials.

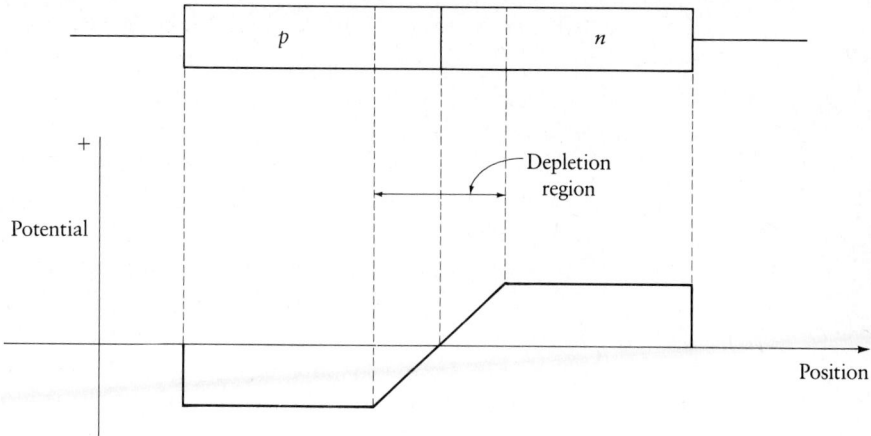

1.14. In order to produce a current across the junction, we must reduce the potential barrier, or hill, by applying a voltage of the proper polarity across the diode.

1.3.2 *Relationship Between Diode Current and Diode Voltage*

An exponential relationship exists between diode current and applied potential. It is possible to write a single expression for the current that applies for both the forward- and reverse-bias conditions. The expression applies as long as the voltage does not exceed the breakdown voltage. The relationship is described by equation (1.1).

$$i_D = I_o \left[\exp\left(\frac{qv_D}{nkT}\right) - 1 \right]$$ (1.1)

The terms in equation (1.1) are defined as follows:

i_D = current in the diode

v_D = potential difference across the diode

I_o = leakage current

q = electron charge: 1.6×10^{-19} coulombs (C)

k = Boltzmann's constant: 1.38×10^{-23} J/°K

T = absolute temperature in degrees Kelvin

n = empirical constant between 1 and 2, sometimes referred to as the *exponential ideality factor*

Equation (1.1) can be simplied by defining

$$V_T = \frac{kT}{q}$$

This yields

$$i_D = I_o \left[\exp\left(\frac{v_D}{nV_T}\right) - 1 \right] \tag{1.2}$$

If we operate at room temperature (25°C) and only in the forward-bias region $(v_D > 0)$, then the first term in parenthesis predominates and the current is approximately given by

$$i_D = I_o \exp\left(\frac{v_D}{nV_T}\right) \tag{1.3}$$

These equations are illustrated in Figure 1.15.

The reverse saturation current, I_o, is a function of the material purity, doping, and geometry of the diode. The empirical constant, n, is a number that is a property of the diode construction. It can vary in accordance with the voltage and current levels. However, some diodes may operate over a considerable voltage range with a fairly constant n. If $n = 1$, the value of nV_T is 26 mV at 25°C. When $n = 2$, nV_T becomes 52 mV. For germanium diodes, n is usually considered to be 1. For silicon diodes, the Sah-Noyce-Shockley (SNS) theory [47] predicts that n should equal 2. Although the value of 2 is predicted, most silicon diodes operate in the range $n = 1.3$ to 1.6. The value of n can vary somewhat even in a particular production run due to manufacturing tolerance, material purity, and doping levels ([36], Section 1.2).

We now have the necessary information to evaluate the relationship between current and voltage at an operating point Q. Although the curves for the forward region shown in Figure 1.15 resemble a straight line, we know the line is not straight, as it has to follow the exponential relationship. This means that the slope of the line is changing as i_D changes. We can differentiate the expression of equation (1.3) to find the slope at any fixed i_D:

$$\frac{di_D}{dv_D} = \frac{I_o \left[\exp\left(\frac{v_D}{nV_T}\right) \right]}{nV_T} \tag{1.4}$$

In order to eliminate the exponential function, we solve equation (1.2) to get

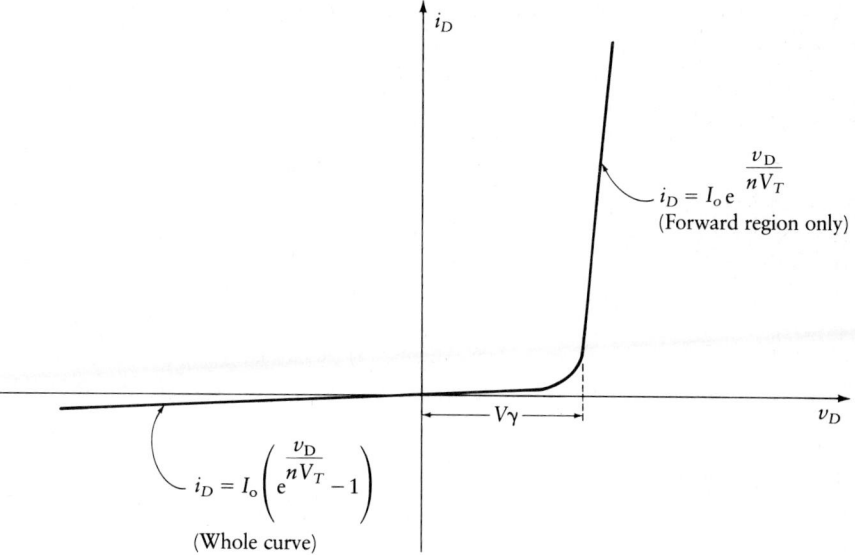

$$\exp\left(\frac{v_D}{nV_T}\right) = \frac{i_D}{I_o} + 1$$

Then, substituting this expression into equation (1.4) yields

$$\frac{di_D}{dv_D} = \frac{(i_D + I_o)}{nV_T}$$

The dynamic resistance, r_d, is the reciprocal of this expression, or

$$r_d = \frac{nV_T}{(i_D + I_o)} \approx \frac{nV_T}{i_D}$$

Although we know r_d changes when i_D changes, we can assume it is fixed for a specific operating range. We use the term R_f to denote diode forward resistance, which is composed of r_d and the contact resistance.

1.3.3 Temperature Effects

Temperature plays an important role in determining operational characteristics of diodes. Changes in the diode characteristics caused by changing temperature may require adjustments in the design and packaging of circuits.

Figure 1.16
Dependence of I_D
upon temperature.

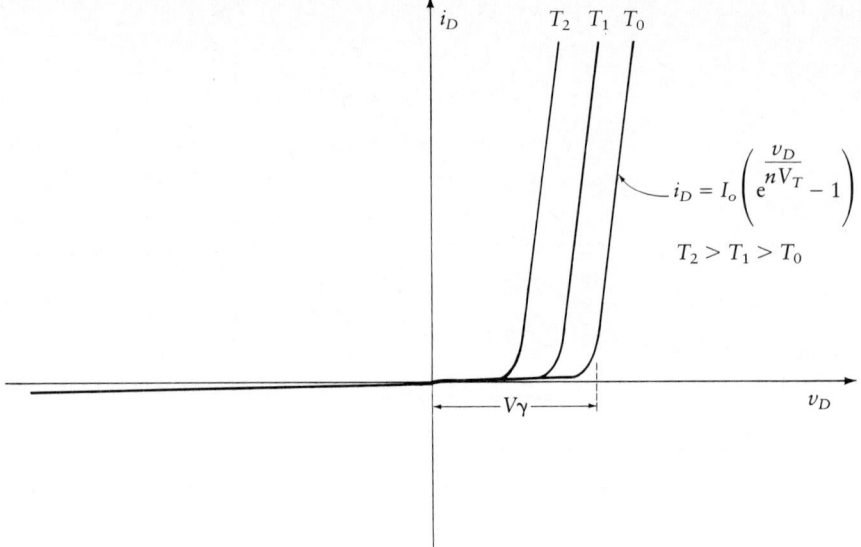

As temperature increases, the turn-on voltage, $V\gamma$, decreases. Alternatively, a decrease in temperature results in an increase in $V\gamma$. This is illustrated in Figure 1.16. Here $V\gamma$ varies linearly with temperature according to the following equation (we assume that the diode current, i_D, is held constant):

$$V\gamma(T_1) - V\gamma(T_o) = k(T_1 - T_o)$$

where

$$T_o = \text{room temperature, or } 25°C$$
$$T_1 = \text{new temperature of diode in } °C$$
$$V\gamma(T_o) = \text{diode voltage at room temperature (ambient)}$$
$$V\gamma(T_1) = \text{diode voltage at new temperature}$$
$$k = \text{temperature coefficient in V/}°C$$

Although k does in fact vary with changing operating parameters, standard engineering practice permits assuming that it is constant. Values of k for the various types of diodes are given as follows ([50], Section 1.11):

$$k = -2.5 \text{ mV/}°C \quad \text{for germanium diodes}$$
$$k = -2.0 \text{ mV/}°C \quad \text{for silicon diodes}$$
$$k = -1.5 \text{ mV/}°C \quad \text{for Schottky diodes}$$

$V\gamma(T_o)$ is equal to the value given below.

silicon diodes: 0.7 V

germanium diodes: 0.2 V

Schottky diodes: 0.3 V

gallium arsenide diodes: 1.2 V

The reverse saturation current, I_o, is another diode parameter that depends upon temperature. It increases approximately 7.2%/°C for both silicon and germanium diodes. In other words, I_o approximately doubles for every 10°C increase in temperature. The expression for the reverse saturation current as a function of temperature is

$$I_o(T_2) = I_o(T_1)\exp[k_i(T_2 - T_1)]$$

where

$$k_i = 0.072/°C$$

and T_1 and T_2 are two different temperatures. This expression can be simplified and rewritten as follows:

$$I_o(T_2) = I_o(T_1)2^{(T_2 - T_1)/10} \tag{1.5}$$

This simplification is possible because

$$e^{0.72} \approx 2$$

Drill Problems

D1.1   When a silicon diode is conducting at a temperature of 25°C, a 0.7 V drop exists across its terminals. What is the voltage, $V\gamma$, across the diode at 100°C?

   Ans: $V\gamma = 0.55$ V

D1.2   The diode described in Problem D1.1 is cooled to -100°C. What is the voltage required across the diode to establish a noticeable current at the new temperature?

   Ans: $V\gamma = 0.95$ V

1.3.4 *Diode Load Lines*

Since the diode is a nonlinear device, standard circuit-analysis techniques must be modified. We cannot simply write equations and solve for the variables, since the equations only hold within a particular operating region.

Figure 1.17
Circuit with diode.

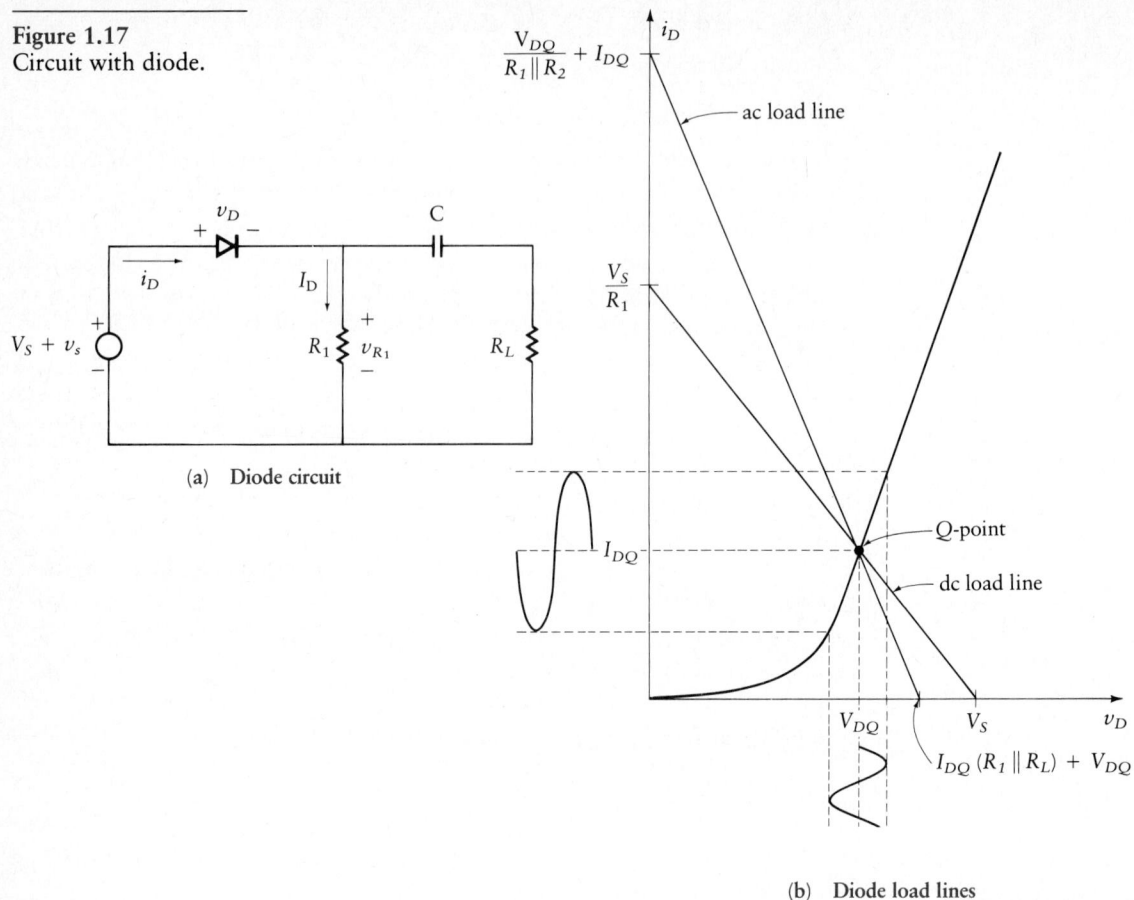

(a)   Diode circuit

(b)   Diode load lines

A circuit often contains both dc supply voltages and time-varying sources. If we set the time-varying sources equal to zero, the only energy supplied to the circuit comes from the dc supply voltages. With the time-varying sources out of the circuit, the diode voltage and current define what is known as the *quiescent operating point (Q-point)*.

Figure 1.17(a) illustrates a circuit with a diode, capacitor, source, and two resistors. If we designate the diode current and diode voltage as the two circuit unknowns, we need two independent equations involving these unknowns in order to find a unique solution for the operating point. One of the equations is the constraint provided by the circuitry connected to the diode. The second is the actual diode voltage-current relationship. These two equations must be simultaneously solved to yield the diode voltage and current. This simultaneous solution can be done graphically.

If we first look at the dc condition, the voltage source becomes simply V_S, and the capacitor is an open circuit (i.e., the impedance of the capacitor is infinity at a frequency of zero). Thus, the loop equation can be written as

$$V_S = V_D + V_{R1} = V_D + I_D R_1$$

or

$$V_D = -R_1 I_D + V_S \tag{1.6}$$

This is the first of two simultaneous equations involving the diode voltage and current. We need to combine this with the diode characteristic in order to solve for the operating point. The graph of this equation is shown in Figure 1.17(b) and is labeled "dc load line." The graph of the diode characteristic is also shown on this same set of axes. The intersection of the two plots yields the simultaneous solution of the two equations and is labeled "Q-point" on the figure. This is the point at which the circuit will operate with the time-varying inputs set to zero. The Q denotes the "quiescent," or rest, condition.

If a time-varying signal is now applied in addition to the dc input, one of the two simultaneous equations changes. If we assume that the time-varying input is of a high-enough frequency to allow approximation of the capacitor as a short circuit, the new equation is given by equation (1.7):

$$v_s = v_d + i_d(R_1 \parallel R_L)$$

or

$$v_d = -(R_1 \parallel R_L)i_d + v_s \tag{1.7}$$

We are considering only the time-varying components of the various parameters. (Note the use of lowercase letters for the variables. Refer to the labeling convention presented at the beginning of this text.) Thus, the total parameter values are given by

$$v_D = v_d + V_{DQ}$$

$$i_D = i_d + I_{DQ}$$

and equation (1.7) becomes

$$v_D - V_{DQ} = -(R_1 \parallel R_L)(i_D - I_{DQ}) + v_s$$

This last equation is labeled "ac load line" in Figure 1.17(b). The ac load line must pass through the Q-point, since at those times when the time-varying part of the input goes to zero, the two operating conditions (dc and ac) must coincide. Thus, the ac load line is uniquely determined.

Example 1.1

The source voltage,

$$v_S = 1.1 + 0.1 \sin 1000t$$

is placed across a series combination of a diode and a 100 Ω load resistance, as shown in Figure 1.18. Find the current, i_D, if

$$nV_T = 40 \text{ mV}$$

$$V\gamma = 0.7 \text{ V}$$

SOLUTION   We use KVL for the dc equation to yield

$$V_S = V\gamma + I_D R_L$$

$$I_D = \frac{V_S - V\gamma}{R_L} = \frac{1.1 - 0.7}{100} = 4 \text{ mA}$$

This sets the dc operating point of the diode. We need to determine the dynamic resistance (we use the symbol R_f instead of r_d, since it includes the contact resistance) so we can establish the resistance of the forward-biased junction for the ac signal.

Using equation (1.4a) and assuming that the contact resistance is negligible, we have

$$R_f = \frac{nV_T}{I_D} = \frac{40 \text{ mV}}{4 \text{ mA}} = 10 \text{ } \Omega$$

Now we can replace the diode with a 10 Ω resistor, provided it remains forward-biased during the entire period of the input ac signal. Again using KVL, we have

$$v_s = R_f i_d + R_L i_d$$

$$i_d = \frac{v_s}{R_f + R_L} = \frac{0.1 \sin 1000t}{110} = 0.91 \sin 1000t \text{ mA}$$

The diode current is then given by

$$i_D = 4 + 0.91 \sin 1000t \text{ mA}$$

Since i_D is always positive the diode is always forward-biased, and the solution is complete.

Figure 1.18
Diode series circuit.

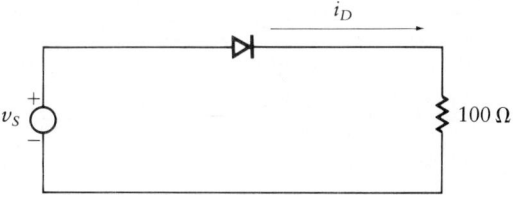

If the ac current amplitude becomes greater than the dc current value, the solution must be modified. In that case, when the ac current amplitude in the negative direction becomes larger than the dc value, the diode becomes reverse-biased and the current is cut off. This case is covered in Section 1.8. ✦

1.3.5 *Power-Handling Capability*

Diodes are rated according to their power-handling capability. The ratings are determined by the physical construction of the diode (e.g., size of junction, type of packaging, and size of diode). The manufacturer's specifications are used to determine the power capability of a diode for certain temperature ranges. Some diodes, such as power diodes, are rated by their current-carrying current-carrying capacity.

The instantaneous power dissipated by a diode is defined by the expression in equation (1.8):

$$p_D = v_D i_D \tag{1.8}$$

1.3.6 *Diode Capacitance*

The equivalent circuit of a diode includes a small capacitor. The size of this capacitor depends upon the magnitude and polarity of the voltage applied to the diode as well as upon the characteristics of the junction formed during manufacture.

In the simple model of a diode junction shown in Figure 1.19, the region at the junction is depleted of both electrons and holes. On the *p*-side of the junction, there is a high concentration of holes, and on the *n*-side of the junction, there is a high concentration of electrons. Diffusion of these electrons and holes occurs close to the junction, causing an initial *diffusion current*. When the holes diffuse across the junction into the *n*-region, they quickly combine with the majority electrons present in that area and disappear. Likewise, electrons also diffuse across the junction, recombine, and disappear. This causes a *depletion region* (sometimes called the *space charge region*) near the junction due to the recombination of electrons and holes. As a reverse voltage is applied across the junction, this region widens, causing the depletion region to increase in size.

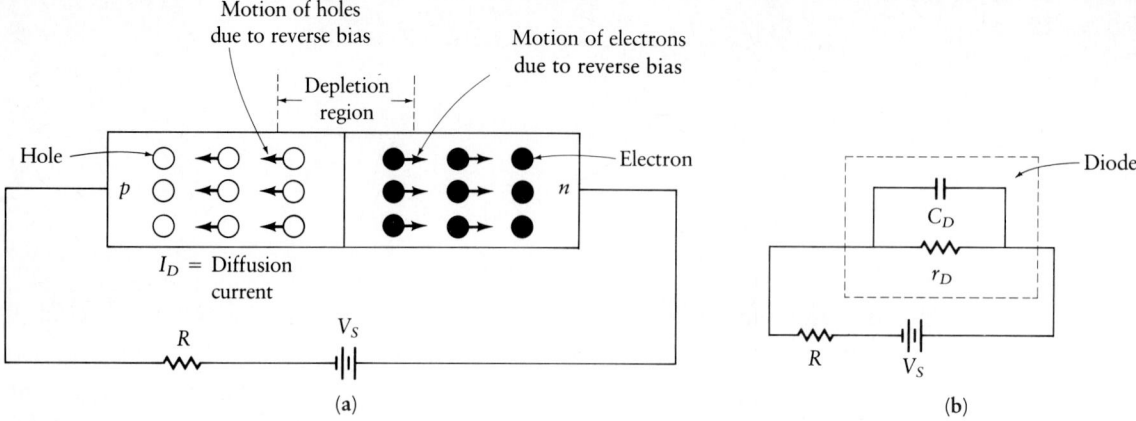

Figure 1.19   Diode model and equivalent circuit.

The depletion region acts like an insulator. Thus, a reverse-biased diode acts like a capacitor whose capacitance varies inversely with the square root of the voltage drop across the semiconductor material.

The equivalent capacitance for high-speed diodes is less than 5 pF. This capacitance can become as large as 500 pF in high-current (low-speed) diodes. The manufacturer's specifications should be consulted to determine the anticipated amount of capacitance for a given operating condition.

1.4   Rectification

We are now ready to see how the diode is configured to perform a useful function. The first major application we consider is that of *rectification*.

Rectification is the process of turning an alternating signal (ac) into one that is restricted to only one direction (dc). Rectification is classified as either *half-wave* or *full-wave*.

1.4.1   *Half-Wave Rectification*

Since an ideal diode can sustain current flow in only one direction, it can be used to change an ac signal into a dc signal.

Figure 1.20 illustrates a simple *half-wave rectifier* circuit. When the input voltage is positive, the diode is forward-biased and can be replaced (assume it is ideal) by a short circuit. When the input voltage is negative, the diode is reverse-biased and can be replaced by an open circuit (provided the voltage

Figure 1.20
Half-wave rectifier.

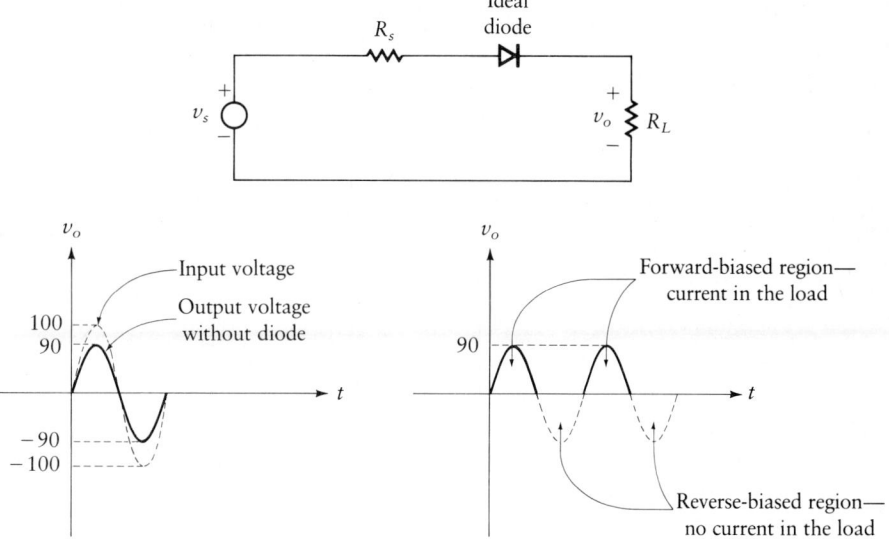

does not get sufficiently negative to break down the diode). Thus, when the diode is forward-biased, the output voltage across the load resistor can be found from the voltage divider relationship. Alternatively, in the reverse-biased condition, the current is zero, so the output voltage is also zero.

Figure 1.20 shows an example of the output waveform assuming a 100 V amplitude sinusoidal input, $R_s = 10 \ \Omega$, and $R_L = 90 \ \Omega$.

The half-wave rectifier can be used to create an almost-constant dc output if the resulting waveform of Figure 1.20 is filtered. The filtering operation is discussed in Section 1.4.3. We note that the half-wave rectifier is not very efficient. During one-half of each cycle, the input is completely blocked from the output. If we could transfer input energy to the output during this half-cycle, we would increase output power for a given input.

1.4.2 *Full-Wave Rectification*

A *full-wave rectifier* transfers input energy to the output during both halves of the cycle and provides increased average current per cycle over that obtained using the half-wave rectifier. A transformer is usually used in constructing a full-wave rectifier in order to obtain the positive and negative polarities. A representative circuit and the output voltage curve are shown in Figure 1.21.

The *average* of a periodic function is defined as the integral of the function over one period divided by the period. It is equal to the first term in a Fourier series expansion of the function. The full-wave rectifier produces *twice* the average current of that of the half-wave rectifier. (You should verify this statement.)

Figure 1.21
Full-wave rectifier.

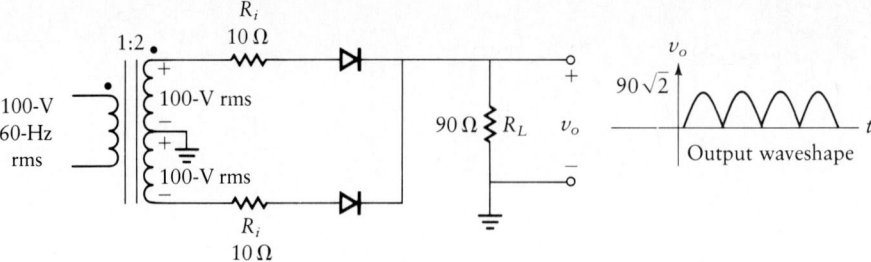

Figure 1.22
Full-wave bridge
rectifier.

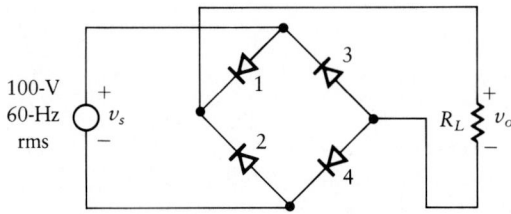

Figure 1.23
Bridge rectifier-diode
conduction times.

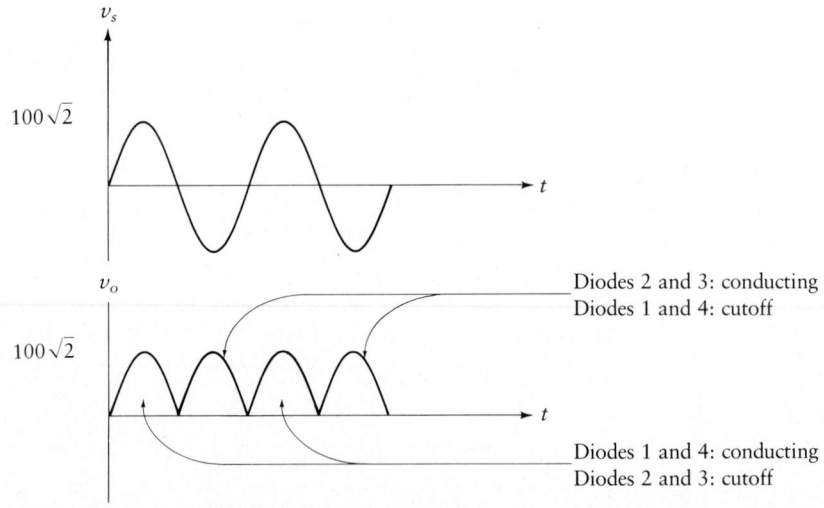

Full-wave rectification is possible without the use of a transformer. The *bridge rectifier* of Figure 1.22 accomplishes full-wave rectification. When the source voltage is positive, diodes 1 and 4 conduct and diodes 2 and 3 are open circuit. When the source voltage goes negative, the reverse situation occurs, and diodes 2 and 3 conduct. This is indicated in Figure 1.23. Study of Figure 1.22 indicates a possible practical shortcoming of the bridge rectifier circuit. If one terminal of the source is grounded, neither terminal of the load resistor can be grounded. To do so would cause a *ground loop,* which would effectively short out one of the diodes. Therefore, it may be necessary to add a transformer to this circuit in order to isolate the two grounds from each other.

Figure 1.24
Full-wave rectifier
with filter.

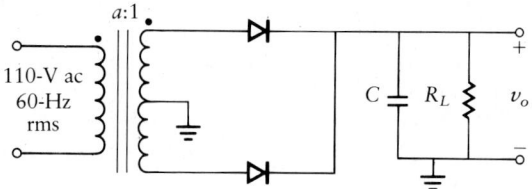

Figure 1.25
Filtered output
waveform.

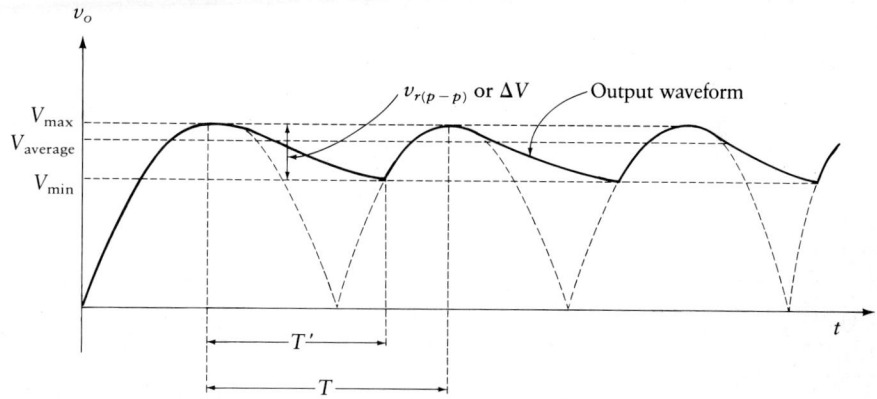

1.4.3 *Filtering*

The rectifier circuits of the previous section provide a *pulsating* dc voltage at the output. These pulsations (known as output *ripple*) can be reduced considerably by filtering the rectifier output. The most common type of filter employs a single capacitor.

Figure 1.24 shows the full-wave rectifier, where a capacitor has been added in parallel with the load resistor. The modified output voltage is shown in Figure 1.25.

The capacitor will charge to the highest voltage (V_{max}) when the input peaks at its most positive or negative value. When the input voltage falls below that value, the capacitor cannot discharge through either diode. Therefore, discharge takes place through R_L. This leads to an exponential decay given by the equation

$$v_o = V_{max}e^{-t/\tau} = V_{max}e^{-t/R_L C} \tag{1.9a}$$

As an example of a design situation, let us assume that the input is a sinusoid with amplitude 100 V and that the lowest output voltage we can accept in a given application is 95 V. Then

$$95 = 100e^{-T'/R_L C} \tag{1.9b}$$

where T' is the discharge time available, as indicated in the figure. We can solve for C in terms of T' and R_L by taking the natural logarithm of both sides of equation (1.9b):

$$\ln 1.053 = \frac{T'}{R_L C}$$

and, finally,

$$C = \frac{19.4 T'}{R_L}$$

This formula is difficult to use in filter design (i.e., choosing a value for C), since T' is dependent upon the $R_L C$ time constant and, therefore, upon the unknown C. Certainly it is known that

$$T' < T$$

For a 60-Hz input, the output fundamental frequency is doubled, or 120 Hz. Therefore,

$$T = \frac{1}{f} = \frac{1}{120} = 8.33 \text{ ms}$$

We can approximate the value of the filter capacitor needed for a particular load by using a straight-line approximation, as shown in Figure 1.26. The initial slope of the exponential of equation (1.9a) is

$$m_1 = \frac{-V_{max}}{R_L C}$$

which is the slope of line A in Figure 1.26.

The slope of line B of Figure 1.26 is

$$m_2 = \frac{V_{max}}{T/2}$$

Then

$$t_1 = \frac{-\Delta V}{m_1} = \frac{R_L C \, \Delta V}{V_{max}}$$

Using corresponding triangles, we find

Figure 1.26
Discharge time
approximation.

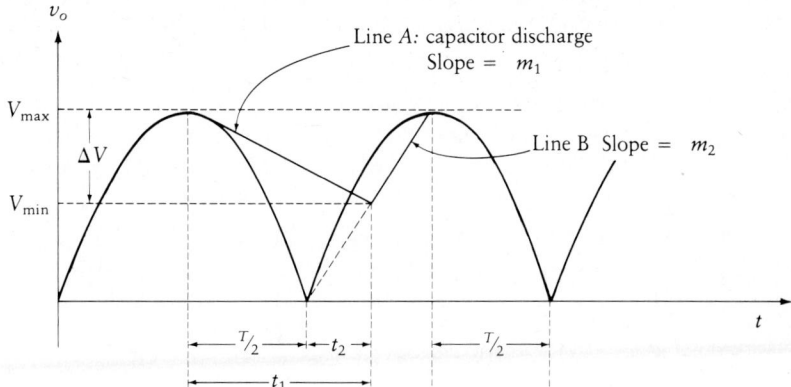

$$t_1 = \frac{T}{2} + t_2 = \frac{T}{2} + \frac{T V_{min}}{2 V_{max}}$$

and

$$t_1 = \frac{R_L C \Delta V}{V_{max}} = \frac{T(1 + V_{min}/V_{max})}{2}$$

$$= \frac{T}{2}\left(1 + \frac{V_{max} - \Delta V}{V_{max}}\right) = \frac{T(2 - \Delta V/V_{max})}{2}$$

Substituting $T = 1/f_p$, where f_p is the number of pulses per second (twice the original frequency), we have

$$R_L C \frac{\Delta V}{V_{max}} = \frac{1}{2f_p}\left[2 - \frac{\Delta V}{V_{max}}\right] = \frac{1}{f_p}\left[1 - \frac{\Delta V}{2 V_{max}}\right]$$

$$2\pi f_p R_L C = \frac{2\pi V_{max}}{\Delta V}\left[1 - \frac{\Delta V}{2 V_{max}}\right]$$

but since

$$\frac{\Delta V}{2 V_{max}} << 1$$

we neglect the second term and obtain

$$2\pi f_p R_L C = \frac{2\pi V_{max}}{\Delta V}$$

or

$$C = \frac{2\pi V_{max}}{\Delta V 2\pi f_p R_L}$$

This formula represents a conservative solution to the design problem: if the straight line never goes below V_{min}, the exponential curve certainly will stay above this value. A practical rule of thumb we suggest using in design is to choose

$$C = \frac{5 V_{max}}{\Delta V 2\pi f_p R_L} \qquad (1.10)$$

We now use equation (1.10) to solve for the capacitance in the example presented earlier. We assume that the input is a 60 Hz sinusoid of amplitude 100 V and that the lowest acceptable output voltage is 95 V. Thus, for this example, $V_{max} = 100$ V, $\Delta V = 5$ V, and the frequency after full-wave rectification is

$$f_p = 120 \text{ Hz}$$

Thus, from equation (1.10),

$$C = \frac{500}{5 \times 240\pi R_L} = \frac{0.133}{R_L}$$

This analysis shows that a filter can be designed to limit the output ripple from a rectifier. The amount of ripple is often an important design parameter. Since this ripple does not follow any standard shape (e.g., sinusoidal or sawtooth), we need some way to characterize its size. The ripple voltage, $V_r(rms)$ is given by

$$V_r(rms) = \frac{V_{max} - V_{min}}{2\sqrt{3}}$$

Note that we use $\sqrt{3}$ rather than $\sqrt{2}$ in the denominator. The latter figure would be used to find the rms value of a sinusoid, which is the amplitude divided by $\sqrt{2}$. For a sawtooth wave, the rms is the amplitude divided by $\sqrt{3}$. These figures are verified by taking the square root of the average of the square of the waveform over one period. The shape of the ripple is closer to that of a sawtooth waveform than it is to a sinusoid. The average value of the ripple voltage is assumed to be the midpoint of the waveform (this is an approximation). Defining the difference between the maximum and minimum as $V_r(p\text{-}p)$ for peak-to-peak ripple, the average or dc value is

$$V_{dc} = V_{max} - \frac{v_{r(p-p)}}{2}$$

The *ripple factor* is defined as

$$\text{ripple factor} = \frac{V_r(\text{rms})}{V_{dc}}$$

Drill Problems

D1.3 The circuit of Figure 1.24 is used to rectify a sinusoid of 100 V rms and 60 Hz. The minimum voltage output cannot drop below 70 V and the transformer has a turns ratio of 1:2. The load resistance is 2 kΩ. What size capacitor is needed across R_L?

Ans: 6.6 μF

D1.4 A half-wave rectifier output has 50 V amplitude at 60 Hz. Assuming no forward resistance in the diode, what minimum load could be added to the circuit when using a 50 μF capacitor to maintain the minimum voltage above 40 V?

Ans: 1.33 kΩ

D1.5 A full-wave rectifier similar to the one shown in Figure 1.24 has a transformer with a 5:1 turns ratio. What capacitance would be required to maintain a 10 V minimum voltage into a 100 Ω load if the input signal is 110-V rms at 60 Hz, as shown in the figure?

Ans: 185 μF

D1.6 If the voltage input in Problem D1.5 varies between 110 V and 120 V rms at 60 Hz, what capacitance is needed to keep a 10 V minimum into the load?

Ans: 161 μF

1.5 Demodulation

Amplitude modulation (AM) is a method of translating a low frequency signal to high frequency for transmission through a channel. The AM waveform is characterized by the following equation:

$$v(t) = V [1 + mf(t)] \sin \omega_c t$$

Figure 1.27
AM and the detection
process.

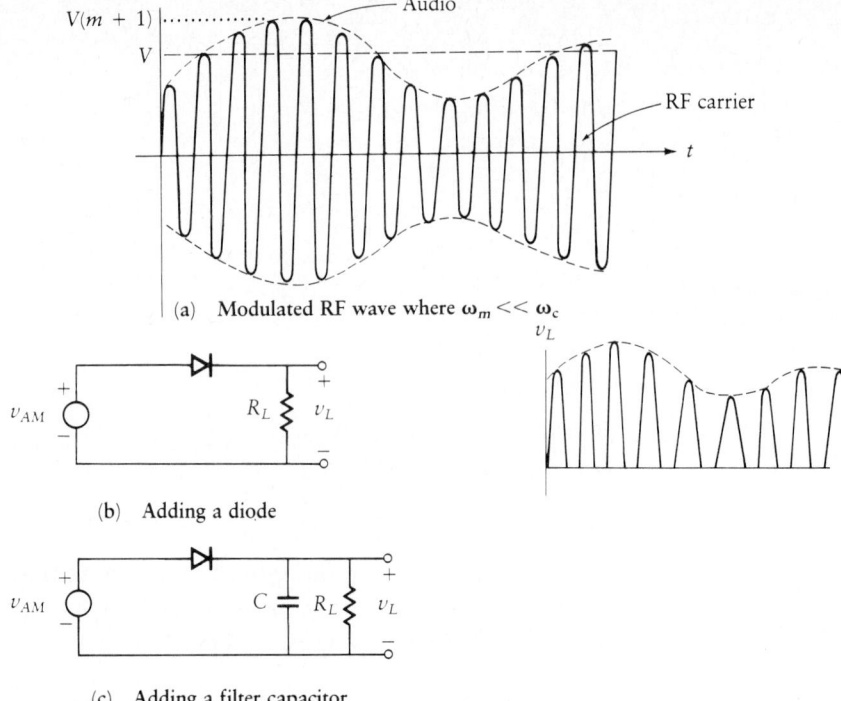

(a)   Modulated RF wave where $\omega_m \ll \omega_c$

(b)   Adding a diode

(c)   Adding a filter capacitor

where m is the *modulation index*, $f(t)$ is a normalized (amplitude limited to unity) low-frequency signal that we wish to transmit, and ω_c is the *carrier frequency*. Figure 1.27(a) is a sketch of a typical AM waveform. The dashed upper outline, labeled "audio," is given by

$$V\,[1 + mf(t)]$$

Demodulation, also known as *detection,* is the process of starting with the modulated waveform of Figure 1.27(a) and processing it in a manner to yield the audio signal, or upper outline of the sketch. This process is not significantly different from that of rectification, except that in the case of rectification the signal with which we start is a constant amplitude sinusoid. That is, rectification can be considered as a special case of demodulation, where $f(t)$ is a constant. If we build a rectifier but permit the output to vary as quickly as $f(t)$ varies, we have constructed a demodulator.

The circuit of Figure 1.27(b) performs half-wave rectification upon the input and yields the output signal, as shown. If a capacitor is now placed in parallel with the resistor, the effect is to provide for an exponential decay between pulses, much as is done in Figure 1.25, which showed the output of a filtered rectifier. Thus, with proper choice of parameters, the output of the circuit of Figure 1.27(c) is approximately equal to the audio signal.

The circuit time constant (the product of the resistance and capacitance) must be carefully selected in order not to distort the modulating signal (audio). If the time constant is selected properly, the output will track each peak of the pulsating rectified signal. If it is too large, the audio signal will be distorted, since the output will miss some of the peaks (i.e., it will not be able to change fast enough). If the time constant is too small, there will be too much ripple on the output waveform.

We can use our earlier straight-line approximations (see Figure 1.26) to yield the following design equation. For this equation, we assume that $f(t)$ is a sinusoid of frequency ω.

$$\frac{V}{R_L C} \geqslant m\omega V$$

The left side of this equation is the slope, m_1, from the analysis of the previous section. The right side is the maximum slope of the audio signal (i.e., the maximum value of the derivative of $Vm \sin \omega t$). Solving for the limiting value of capacitance, we find

$$C = \frac{1}{\omega R_L m} \tag{1.11}$$

This equation can be used to select the capacitor value once the load resistance is known.

Drill Problems

D1.7   A radio frequency carrier of 15 MHz is modulated by a 5 kHz signal at a modulation index of 0.5. If the detector load resistance is 5 kΩ, what value capacitor should be added across the detector load to filter out the radio frequency signal?

Ans: 0.013 µF

D1.8   If the detector capacitor in Problem D1.7 is changed to 0.01 µF, how high could the modulating frequency be raised to filter out the RF to the same degree as in Problem D1.7?

Ans: 6.37 kHz

1.6   Zener Diodes

A *zener diode* is a device where the doping is performed in such a way as to make the *avalanche* or *breakdown* voltage, V_Z, characteristic very steep. If the reverse voltage exceeds the breakdown voltage, the diode normally will not be destroyed. This is true as long as the current does not exceed a predetermined maximum and the device does not overheat.

When a thermally generated carrier (part of the reverse saturation current) falls down the junction barrier (see Figure 1.14) and acquires energy of the applied potential, the carrier collides with crystal ions and imparts sufficient energy to disrupt a covalent bond. In addition to the original carrier, a new electron-hole pair is generated, which may pick up sufficient energy from the applied field to collide with another crystal ion and create still another electron-hole pair. This action continues and thereby disrupts the covalent bonds; the process is referred to as *avalanche multiplication* or *avalanche breakdown*.

There is a second mechanism that disrupts the covalent bonds. The use of a sufficiently strong electric field at the junction can cause a direct rupture of the bond. If the electric field exerts a strong force on a bound electron, the electron can be torn from the covalent bond thus causing the electron-hole pair combination to multiply. This mechanism is called *zener breakdown*. The value of reverse voltage at which this phenomenon occurs is controlled by the amount of doping of the diode. A heavily doped diode has a low zener breakdown voltage, whereas a lightly doped diode has a high zener breakdown voltage.

Although we describe two distinctly different mechanisms to effect breakdown, they are commonly interchanged. At voltages above approximately 10 V, the mechanism most predominant is the avalanche breakdown ([35], Section 2.9). Since the zener effect (avalanche) occurs at a predictable point, the diode can be used as a voltage reference. The reverse voltage at which the avalanche occurs is called the *zener voltage*.

A typical zener diode characteristic is shown in Figure 1.28. The circuit symbol for the zener diode is different from that of a regular diode and is illustrated in Figure 1.28.

The maximum reverse current, $I_{Z\,max}$, that the zener diode can withstand is dependent upon the design and construction of the diode. The leakage current ($I_{Z\,min}$) below the knee of the characteristic curve is usually assumed to be $0.1I_{Z\,max}$. Use of $I_{Z\,min}$ assures that the avalanche curve remains parallel to the i_D axis between $I_{Z\,max}$ and $I_{Z\,min}$. The amount of power that the zener diode can withstand is $P_Z = I_{Z\,max}\,V_Z$.

1.6.1   *Zener Regulator*

A zener diode can be used as a voltage regulator in the configuration shown in Figure 1.29. The figure illustrates a load with resistance that can vary over a particular range. The circuit is designed so that the diode operates in the breakdown region, thereby approximating an ideal voltage source. The output voltage remains relatively constant even when the input source voltage varies over a relatively wide range ([49], Section 4.4).

Figure 1.28
Zener diode.

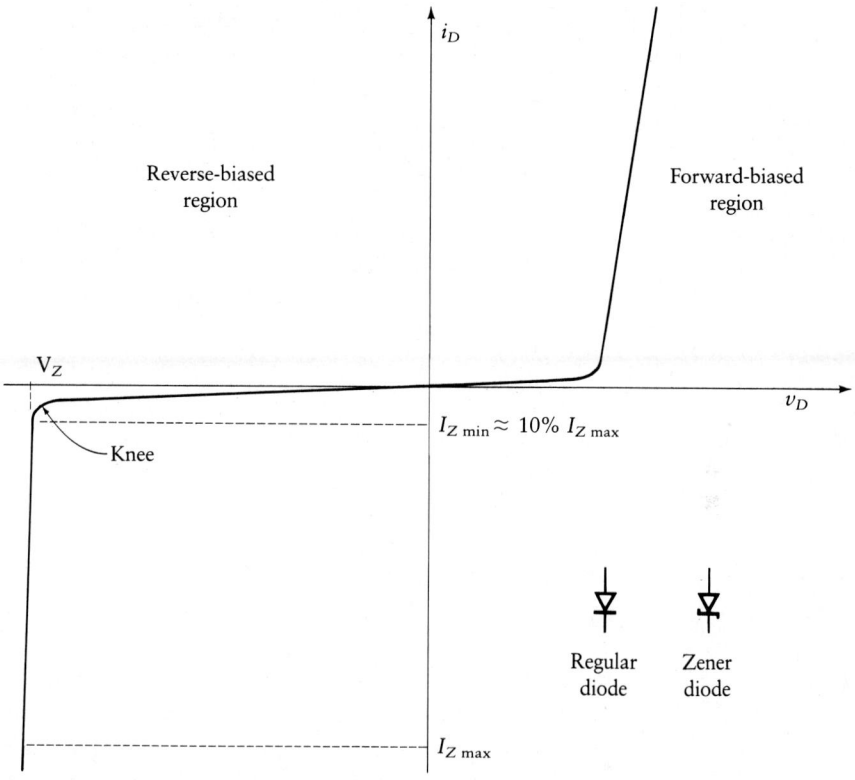

Figure 1.29
Zener regulator.

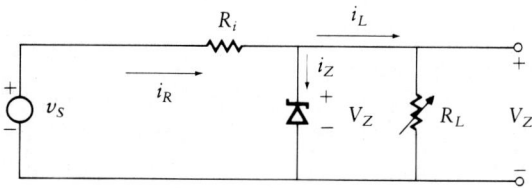

It is important to know the range of input voltage and load current in order to properly design this circuit. The resistance, R_i, must be such that the diode stays in the constant voltage mode over the entire range of variables.

The node equation for the circuit of Figure 1.29 yields

$$R_i = \frac{v_S - V_Z}{i_R} = \frac{v_S - V_Z}{i_Z + i_L} \tag{1.12}$$

In order to assure that the diode remains in the constant voltage (breakdown) region, we examine the two extremes of input/output conditions.

1. The current through the diode i_Z is a minimum when the load current i_L is maximum and the source voltage v_S is minimum.
2. The current through the diode i_Z is a maximum when the load current i_L is minimum and the source voltage v_S is maximum.

When these characteristics of the two extremes are inserted into equation (1.12), we find

$$\text{Condition 1:} \quad R_i = \frac{V_{S\,min} - V_Z}{I_{L\,max} + I_{Z\,min}} \tag{1.13a}$$

$$\text{Condition 2:} \quad R_i = \frac{V_{S\,max} - V_Z}{I_{L\,min} + I_{Z\,max}} \tag{1.13b}$$

We equate (1.13a) and (1.13b) to obtain

$$(V_{S\,min} - V_Z)(I_{L\,min} + I_{Z\,max}) = $$
$$(V_{S\,max} - V_Z)(I_{L\,max} + I_{Z\,min}) \tag{1.13c}$$

In a practical problem, it is reasonable to assume that we know the range of input voltages, the range of output load currents, and the desired zener voltage. Equation (1.13c) thus represents one equation in two unknowns, the maximum and minimum zener current. A second equation is found by examining Figure 1.28. In order to avoid the nonconstant portion of the characteristic curve, we use a rule of thumb that the maximum zener current should be 10 times the minimum ([46], Section 5.4); that is,

$$I_{Z\,min} = 0.1 I_{Z\,max}$$

This is an accepted design criterion.

We now rewrite equation (1.13c) as

$$(V_{S\,min} - V_Z)(I_{L\,min} + I_{Z\,max}) = (V_{S\,max} - V_Z)(I_{L\,max} + 0.1 I_{Z\,max})$$

Then solving for the maximum zener current, we obtain

$$I_{Z\,max} = \frac{I_{L\,min}(V_Z - V_{S\,min}) + I_{L\,max}(V_{S\,max} - V_Z)}{V_{S\,min} - 0.9 V_Z - 0.1 V_{S\,max}} \tag{1.14}$$

Now that we can solve for the maximum zener current, the value of R_i is calculated from either equation (1.13a) or equation (1.13b).

Example 1.2   **Zener Regulator Design**

Design a zener regulator (Figure 1.30) for each of the following conditions:

a. The load current ranges from 100 mA to 200 mA and the source voltage ranges from 14 V to 20 V.
b. The load current ranges from 20 mA to 200 mA and the source voltage ranges from 10.2 V to 14 V.

Use a 10-V zener diode in both cases.

SOLUTION

a. The design consists of choosing the proper value of resistance, R_i, and power rating for the zener. We use the equations from this section first to calculate the maximum current in the zener diode and then to find the input resistor value. From equation (1.14), we have

$$I_{Z\,max} = \frac{0.1(10 - 14) + 0.2(20 - 10)}{14 - 0.9(10) - 0.1(20)}$$

$$= \frac{1.6}{3} = 0.533 \text{ A}$$

Then, from equation (1.13b), we find R_i as follows:

$$R_i = \frac{V_{S\,max} - V_Z}{I_{Z\,max} + I_{L\,min}} = \frac{20 - 10}{0.533 + 0.1} = 15.8 \text{ }\Omega$$

It is not sufficient to specify only the resistance of R_i. We must also select the proper resistor power rating. The maximum power is given by the product of voltage and current, where we use the maximum for each value.

$$P_R = I_{R\,max}(V_{S\,max} - V_Z)$$

$$= (I_{Z\,max} + I_{L\,min})(V_{S\,max} - V_Z)$$

$$= 0.63 \times 10 = 6.3 \text{ W}$$

Figure 1.30
Zener diode regulator.

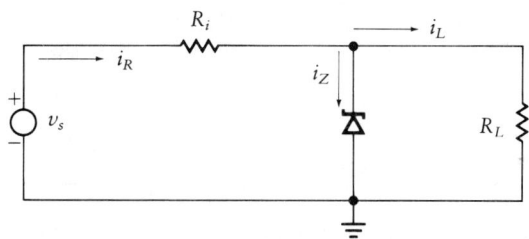

Finally, we must determine the power rating of the zener diode. The maximum power dissipated in the zener diode is given by the product of voltage and current.

$$P_Z = V_Z I_{Z\,max} = 10 \times 0.53 = 5.3 \text{ W}$$

b. Repeating these steps for the parameters of part (b) yields

$$I_{Z\,max} = \frac{0.02(10 - 10.2) + 0.2(14 - 10)}{10.2 - 0.9(10) - 0.1(14)} = -4 \text{ A}$$

The negative value of $I_{Z\,max}$ indicates that the margin between $V_{S\,min}$ and V_Z is not large enough to allow for the variation in load current. That is, under the worst case condition of a 10.2 V input and 200 mA load current, the zener cannot possibly sustain 10 V across its terminals. Therefore, the regulator will not operate correctly for any choice of resistance.   ▶┤

The zener regulator circuit of Figure 1.30 can be combined with the full-wave rectifier of Figure 1.24 to yield the full-wave zener regulator of Figure 1.31.

The component R_F is called a *bleeder resistor* and is used to provide a discharge path for the capacitor when the load is removed. Bleeder resistors are normally high resistances in order not to absorb significant power when the circuit is operating. Since R_F is much larger than R_i, we neglect it in the following analysis.

The value of C_F is found by adapting equation (1.10) to this situation. The resistance in the equation is the equivalent resistance across C_F. The zener diode is replaced by a voltage source, V_Z. The equivalent resistance is then the parallel combination of R_F with R_i. Since R_F is much larger than R_i, the resistance is approximately equal to R_i. Since the voltage across R_i does not go to zero, as is the case for the full-wave rectifier, V_{max} in equation (1.9) must be replaced by the total voltage swing. Thus, the capacitor is as specified in equation (1.15), where we are assuming a (the transformer ratio) is 1.

Figure 1.31   Full-wave zener regulator.

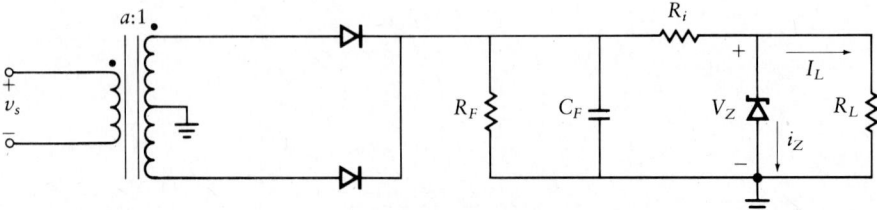

$$C_F = \frac{5(V_{S\,max} - V_Z)}{\Delta V 2\pi f_p R_i} \qquad (1.15)$$

The largest voltage imposed upon the regulator is $V_{S\,max}$. As before, ΔV is the peak-to-peak ripple and f_p is the fundamental frequency of the rectified waveform (i.e., twice the original frequency for full-wave rectification).

1.6.2 *Practical Zener Diodes and Percent Regulation*

In the previous section we assumed that the zener diode was ideal. That is, in the avalanche breakdown region, the diode behaves as a constant voltage source. This assumption means that the curve of Figure 1.28 is a vertical line in the breakdown region. In practice, this curve is not vertical, and the slope is caused by a series resistance. The breakdown voltage is then a function of current instead of being a constant. We model the practical zener diode as shown in Figure 1.32. This model replaces the practical zener diode with an ideal diode in series with a resistance, R_Z.

In order to show the effects of this series resistor, we once again solve Example 1.2. We assume that a practical zener diode is incorporated into the circuit, with the diode resistance $R_Z = 2\ \Omega$. In that example, the circuit of Figure 1.30 is used as a regulator where the maximum zener current is 0.53 A. We assume that $I_{Z\,min}$ is 10% of $I_{Z\,max}$, or 0.053 A. The output voltage (across the load) is no longer a constant 10 V because of R_Z. We find the minimum and maximum values of this voltage from Figure 1.32 using the minimum and maximum current values. The voltage across the ideal diode of Figure 1.32 is 10 V, so we can write

$$V_{o\,min} = 10 + (0.053 \times 2) = 10.1\ \text{V}$$

$$V_{o\,max} = 10 + (0.53 \times 2) = 11.1\ \text{V}$$

Figure 1.32 Zener equivalent circuit.

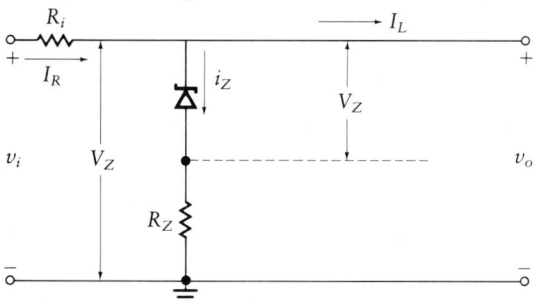

The *percent regulation* is defined as the total voltage swing divided by the nominal voltage. The smaller the percent regulation, the better the regulator. Therefore, for this example,

$$\text{percent reg.} = \frac{V_{o\,\text{max}} - V_{o\,\text{min}}}{V_{o\,\text{nominal}}} = \frac{11.1 - 10.1}{10}$$

$$= 0.1, \text{ or } 10\% \tag{1.16}$$

This value of regulation is poor and the regulation can be improved by limiting the zener current to a smaller value. This is accomplished by using an amplifier in series with the load. The effect of this amplifier is to limit the variations of current through the zener diode. We study such amplifiers in Chapter 6.

Drill Problems

D1.9   A zener diode regulator circuit (see Figure 1.30) has an input whose voltage varies between 10 and 15 V and a load whose current varies between 100 mA and 500 mA. Find the values of R_i and $I_{Z\,\text{max}}$ assuming that a 6 V zener is used.

   Ans: 6.33 Ω; 1.32 A

D1.10   In Problem D1.9, find the power ratings for the zener diode and for the input resistor.

   Ans: 7.94 W; 12.8 W

D1.11   In Problem D1.9, find the value of capacitor required if the source is a half-wave rectifier output with a 60 Hz input.

   Ans: 3800 μF

D1.12   If no resistor, R_F, were used in the circuit of Figure 1.31 and the transformer were a 4:1 center-tapped transformer with a 120 V rms 60 Hz input, what value of R_i would be needed to maintain 10 V across a load whose current varies from 50 mA to 200 mA? Assume that the minimum voltage allowed at the regulator input is 14 V.

   Ans: 14.8 Ω

D1.13   What value of capacitor is needed in the regulator of Problem D1.12 in order to maintain a minimum voltage of 14 V?

   Ans: 697 μF

D1.14   In the circuit of Problem D1.12, assume that the input voltage varies from 110 V to 120 V rms at 60 Hz. Select a value of capacitance that will accommodate both load current variation of 50 mA to 200 mA and the specified input voltage variation.

Ans: $C = 922 \ \mu F$

1.7 Power Supply Design Using Integrated Circuit Package

Regulators are packaged as integrated circuits (ICs); as an example, we focus our attention upon the MC78XX series. The appropriate specification sheets appear in Appendix D, and these should be referred to during the following discussion. There are a number of different voltages that can be obtained from the 7800 series IC; they are 5, 6, 8, 8.5, 10, 12, 15, 18, and 24 V. All that is required to design a regulator around one of these ICs is to select a transformer, diodes, and filter. A typical circuit is shown in Figure 1.33.

The specification sheet for this IC indicates that there must be a common ground between the input and output, and the minimum voltage at the IC input must be at least 2 to 4 V above the regulated output. In order to assure this last condition, it is necessary to filter the output from the rectifier. The C_F in Figure 1.33 performs this filtering when combined with the input resistance to the IC.

The smallest equivalent input resistance of the IC is given by $V_{S\,min}/I_{L\,max}$. Then

$$C_F = \frac{5(V_{S\,max} - V_L)}{\Delta V 2\pi f_p V_{S\,min}/I_{L\,max}} \tag{1.17}$$

where $V_{S\,max}$ is the largest voltage imposed on the IC, ΔV is the voltage decay of the capacitor (i.e., lowest peak voltage applied to the IC minus the IC output voltage plus 4 V) and f_p is the number of pulses per second.

The output capacitor, C_o, is added to aid in isolating the effects of the

Figure 1.33 Regulated voltage power supply.

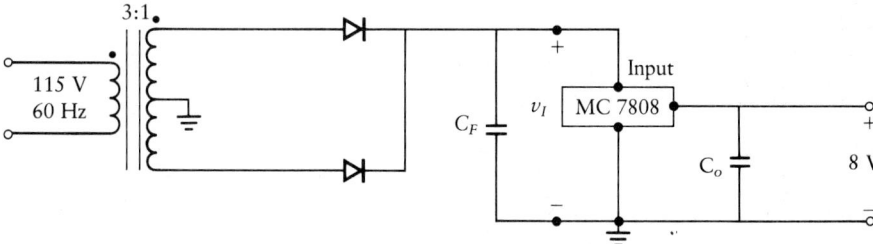

varying loads from each other. The capacitor will tend to short out high-frequency variations coming from the load circuitry.

The MC7900 series regulators are identical to the 7800 series except that they provide negative regulated voltages instead of positive.

Example 1.3

Suppose we wish to design an IC circuit regulator to generate a 12 V output into a load whose current varies from 5 to 800 mA.

SOLUTION We use the circuit of Figure 1.33 with a 7812 regulator. The output of the transformer is given by a full-wave rectified sine wave of amplitude, $115\sqrt{2}/6$, or 27.1 V (zero to peak) at 120 Hz.

The minimum voltage we desire at the IC input is

$$V_{S\,min} = 12 + 4 = 16 \text{ V}$$

where we use 4 V above the desired output.

The smallest equivalent load resistance is the ratio of the minimum voltage to the maximum current, or

$$R_L(\text{worst case}) = \frac{16}{0.8} = 20 \ \Omega$$

The voltage difference between maximum and minimum is

$$V = 27.1 - 16 = 11.1 \text{ V}$$

Then from equation (1.15), we solve for the filter capacitor:

$$C = \frac{5(27.1 - 12)}{11.1(4\pi60)20} = 451 \ \mu\text{F}$$

Using at least a 451-μF capacitor should ensure that the regulator provides a 12-V regulated output for any load drawing current up to 800 mA.   ➤─

Drill Problems

D1.15 An MC7812 IC is used as the regulator with a center-tapped transformer to full-wave rectify a 40 V peak-to-peak amplitude signal. What is the smallest capacitor required to provide an output of 12 V at 400 mA?

Ans: 332 μF

D1.16 In Problem D1.15, an MC7808 is used in place of the MC7812. What is the smallest-value capacitor needed to filter the full-wave rectified signal?

Ans: 332 μF

1.8 Clippers and Clampers

Diodes have other applications in addition to rectification and detection. Among these are clipping an input signal or limiting only parts of the signal. Diodes are also used in restoring a dc level to an input signal.

1.8.1 *Clippers*

Clipping circuits are used to eliminate a part of a waveform that lies above or below some reference level. Clipping circuits are sometimes referred to as *limiters, amplitude selectors,* or *slicers.* The rectification circuits of the previous section use clipping action at the zero level. If a battery is added in series with the diode, a rectification circuit will clip everything above or below the battery voltage, depending upon the orientation of the diode. This is illustrated in Figure 1.34.

The output waveforms indicated in Figure 1.34 assume that the diodes are ideal. We now relax this assumption for the circuit of Figure 1.34(a) by including two additional parameters in the diode model. First, we assume that a voltage of $V\gamma$ must be overcome before the diode will conduct. Second, when the diode is conducting, we include a forward resistance, R_f. The effect of $V\gamma$ is to make the clipping level $V\gamma + V_B$ instead of V_B. The effect of the resistance is to change the flat clipping action to one that proportionately follows the input voltage (i.e., a voltage-divider effect). The resulting output is calculated as follows, and it is illustrated in Figure 1.35 ([34], Section 10.2).

For

$$v_i < V_B + V\gamma, \qquad v_o = v_i$$

For

$$v_i > V_B + V\gamma, \qquad v_o = v_i \frac{R_f}{R + R_f} + (V_B + V\gamma) \frac{R}{R + R_f}$$

Positive and negative clipping can be performed simultaneously. The result is a *parallel-biased clipper,* which is designed by using two diodes and two

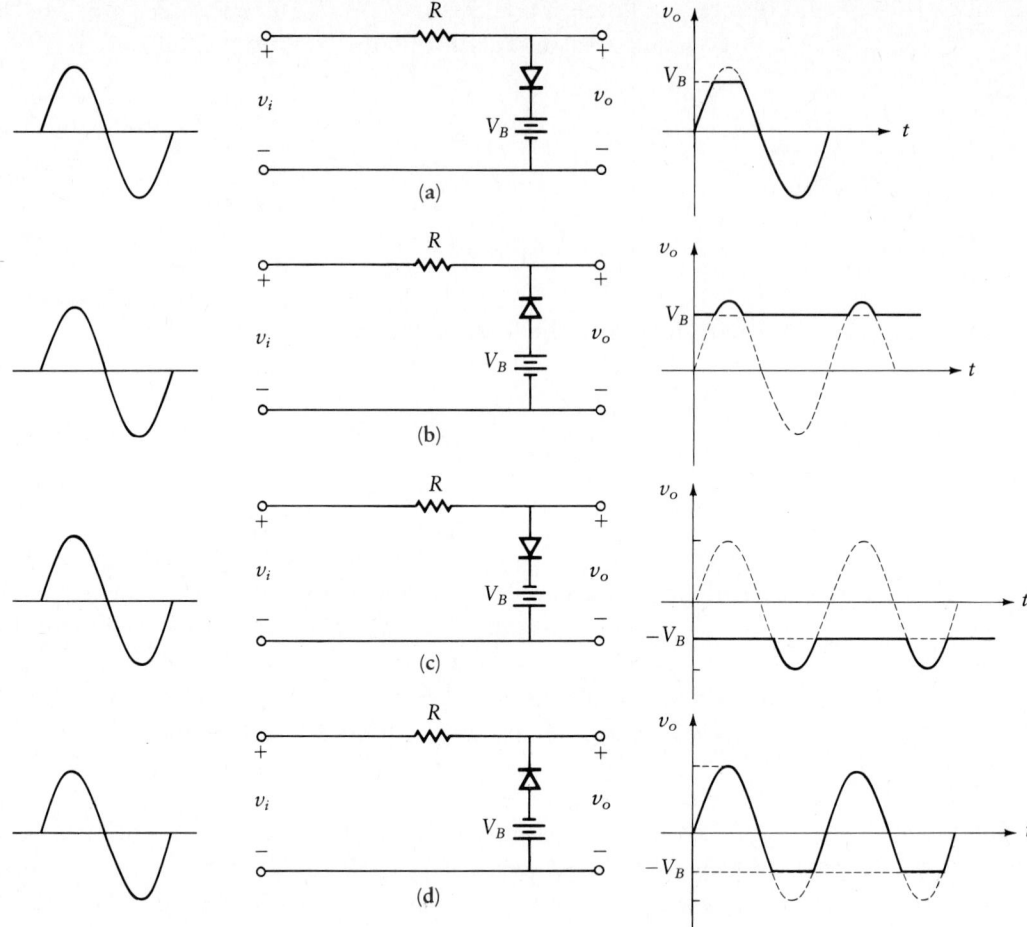

Figure 1.34   Ideal clipping circuits.

voltage sources oriented oppositely. The circuit produces the output waveshape as shown in Figure 1.36 when ideal diodes are assumed. The extension to practical diodes parallels the analysis leading to the results in Figure 1.35.

Another type of clipper is the *series-biased* clipper, which is shown in Figure 1.37. The 1-V battery in series with the input causes the input signal to be superimposed on a dc voltage of -1 V rather than being symmetrical about the zero axis. Assuming that this system uses an ideal diode, we find that the diode of Figure 1.37(a) will conduct only during the negative-going condi-tioned (i.e., shifted) input signal. When the diode is conducting, the output is zero. We have a nonzero output when the diode is not conducting. In Figure 1.37(b), the reverse is true. When the conditioned signal is positive, the diode conducts and an output signal exists, but when the diode is off, no output occurs. Although the operation of the two circuits is different, the two outputs

Figure 1.35
Output waveform for
circuit of Figure
1.34(a).

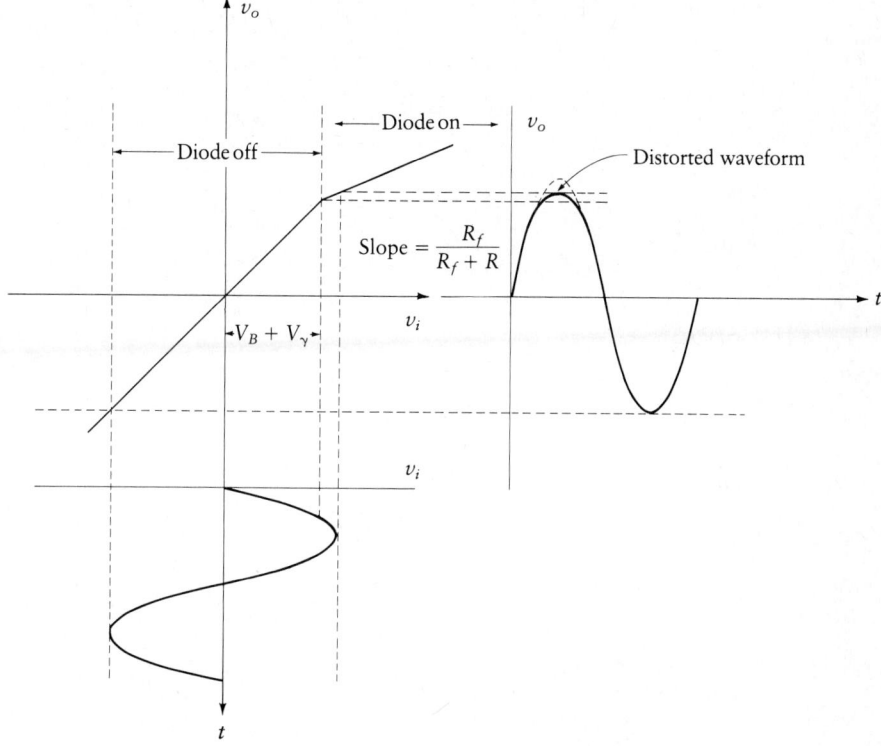

Figure 1.36
Parallel-biased clipper.

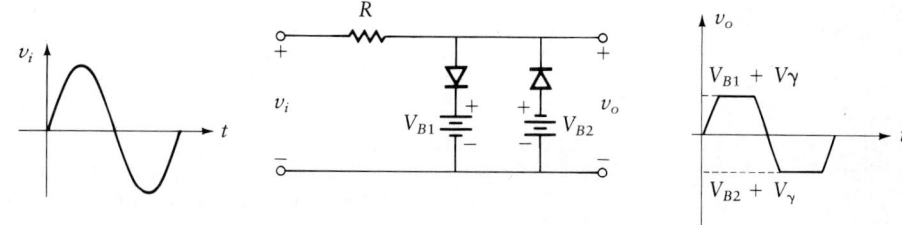

are identical. In Figure 1.37(c) and (d) we reverse the polarity of the battery
and obtain output waveforms as shown.

1.8.2 *Clampers*

A voltage waveform can be shifted by adding an independent voltage source,
either a constant or a time function, in series with the waveform. *Clamping* is
a shifting operation, but the amount of shift depends upon the actual waveform. Figure 1.38 shows an example of clamping. The input waveform is shifted
by an amount that makes the shifted waveform peak at a value of V_B. Thus,

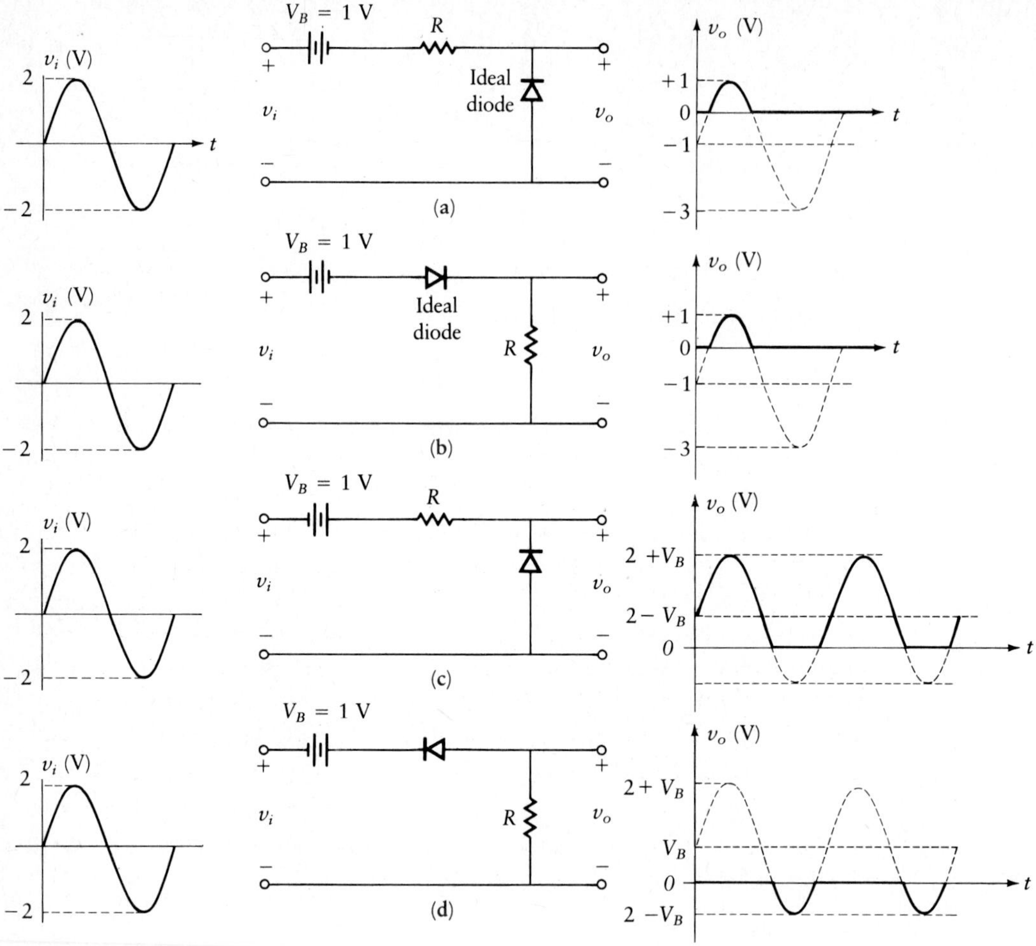

$V_B = 1$ V

v_i (V)

v_o (V)

Ideal diode

(a)

$V_B = 1$ V

v_i (V)

v_o (V)

Ideal diode

R

(b)

$V_B = 1$ V

v_i (V)

v_o (V)

R

$2 + V_B$

$2 - V_B$

(c)

$V_B = 1$ V

v_i (V)

v_o (V)

R

$2 + V_B$

V_B

$2 - V_B$

(d)

Figure 1.37 Series-biased clipper.

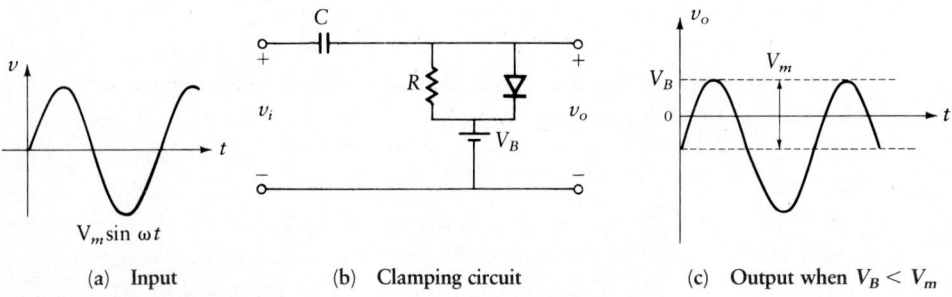

| (a) Input | (b) Clamping circuit | (c) Output when $V_B < V_m$ |

Figure 1.38 Clamping circuit.

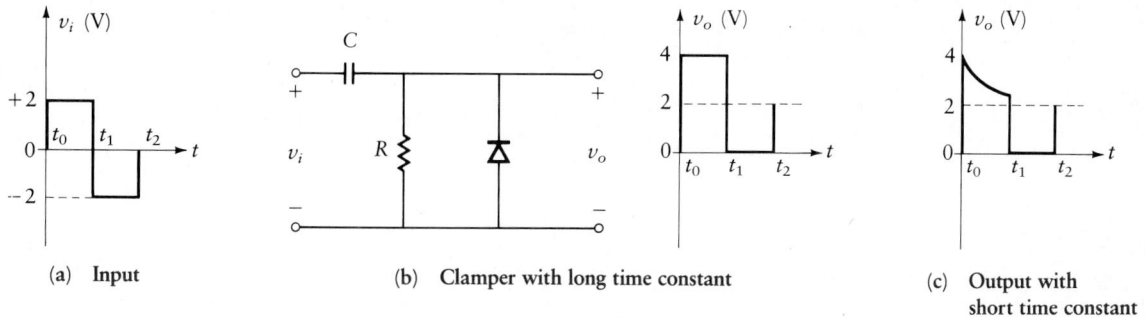

Figure 1.39 Clamping at zero.

the amount of shift is the exact amount necessary to change the original maximum, V_m, to a new maximum, V_B. The waveform is "clamped" to a value of V_B. If the input waveform changes, the amount of shift will change such that the output is always clamped to V_B. The clamping circuit thus provides a dc component in an amount necessary to achieve the desired clamping level.

A clamping circuit is composed of a battery (or dc supply), diode, capacitor, and resistor. The resistor and capacitor are chosen so that the time constant is large. It is desired that the capacitor charge to a constant value and remain at that value throughout the period of the input waveform. If this condition is met and the forward resistance of the diode is assumed to be zero, the output is a reproduction of the input with the appropriate shift. Whenever the output tries to exceed V_B, the diode forward-biases and the output is limited to V_B. During these times, the capacitor charges. When steady state is reached, the capacitor will be charged to a value of

$$V_C = V_m - V_B$$

Figure 1.39 illustrates a clamping circuit where the output is clamped to zero (i.e., there is no battery, so $V_B = 0$). Because the diode is in the reverse direction from that of the previous circuit, the *minimum* rather than *maximum* of the output is clamped. The circuit is shown with a square wave as input. It is important that the voltage across the capacitor remain approximately constant during the half-period of the input waveform. A design rule of thumb is to make the RC time constant at least five times the duration of the half-period (i.e., five times either $t_1 - t_0$ or $t_2 - t_1$). In this case, the RC circuit has less than 20% of a time constant to charge or discharge during the half-period. This places the final value within 18% of the starting value (i.e., $\exp(-0.2) = 0.82$). If the time constant is too small, the waveform will be distorted, as shown in Figure 1.39(c). ([6], Section 1.22). To reduce the error to less than 18%, the time constant can be increased (e.g., to 10 times the half-period duration).

1.9 **Alternate Types of Diodes**

This section briefly presents the following types of diodes:

- Schottky
- Varactor
- Tunnel
- Light-emitting
- Photo
- PIN

1.9.1 *Schottky Diodes*

A *Schottky diode* is formed by bonding a metal, such as aluminum or platinum, to an *n*-type silicon. It is often used in integrated circuits for high-speed switching applications. Its symbol and construction are shown in Figure 1.40. The Schottky diode has a voltage-current characteristic similar to that of the silicon *pn* junction diode, except that the forward voltage, $V\gamma$, is 0.3 V rather than 0.7 V. When the Schottky diode is operated in the forward mode, current is induced by the movement of electrons from the *n*-type silicon across the junction and through the metal. Since electrons move relatively unimpeded through metals, the recombination time is small, on the order of 10 ps. This is faster than an ordinary *pn* junction diode. Therefore, the Schottky diode is of great value in high-speed switching applications. The capacitance associated with this diode is small.

The metallic material in contact 1 and the lightly doped *n*-region form a rectifying junction, whereas the heavily doped *n*-region and contact 2 form an ohmic contact. The forward-direction electrons from the *n*-type silicon cross the junction into the metal, where there are numerous available electrons. This results in a *majority* carrier device. This is in contrast to a standard *pn* junction diode, where the *minority* carriers determine the diode characteristics.

The Schottky diode is sometimes called a *barrier diode,* since a barrier forms across the junction due to the movement of electrons from the semiconductor to the metal interface.

Schottky diodes are useful in IC technology because they are easy to fabricate and can be manufactured at the same time as the other components on the chip. Fabrication of a Schottky diode on a chip requires one less step than fabrication of a *pn* junction diode, since the *pn* junction diode requires the additional *p*-type diffusion. The low-noise characteristics of the Schottky diode make it ideal for application in power monitoring of low-level radio frequencies, detectors for high frequency, and Doppler radar mixers.

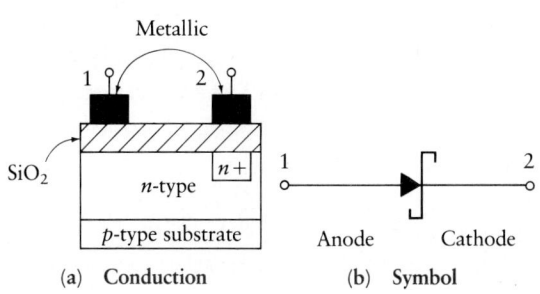

(a) Conduction   (b) Symbol

Figure 1.40 Schottky diode.

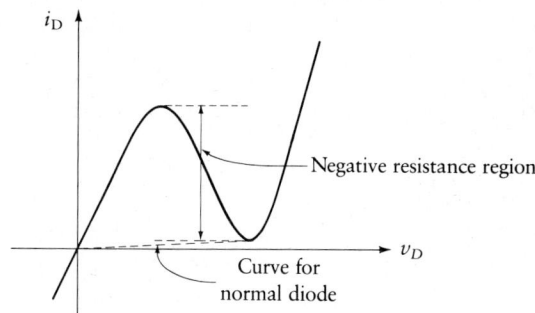

Figure 1.41 Tunnel diode characteristics.

1.9.2 *Varactor Diodes*

The normal *pn* junction exhibits capacitance when operated in the reverse-bias mode. The *varactor diode* is specifically manufactured to operate in this mode. The capacitance is a function of the reverse voltage. The diode therefore acts as a *variable capacitor,* where the value of capacitance is a function of the input voltage.

One common use of this diode is in the *voltage-controlled oscillator (VCO).* The VCO is a sinusoidal generator whose output frequency depends upon the input voltage.

1.9.3 *Tunnel Diodes (Esaki Diode)*

The *tunnel diode* is more heavily doped than a zener diode, causing the depletion region to be small. This increases speed of operation, so the tunnel diode is useful in high speed applications. As the forward bias is increased, the current rises rapidly until breakdown. The current then falls rapidly. This characteristic is shown in Figure 1.41. The negative-slope region of the characteristic can be modeled as a negative resistance in series with a dc source. The tunnel diode is useful because of this negative-resistance region. As an example, it may be used in conjunction with a tuned circuit to produce a high-frequency high-Q oscillator.

The negative-resistance region of a tunnel diode is typically developed over the range of 50 mV to 250 mV. This relatively low voltage limits its applications ([36], Section 3.4).

1.9.4 *Light-Emitting Diodes and Photo Diodes*

Certain types of diodes are capable of changing electric energy into light energy. The *light-emitting diode (LED)* transforms electric current into light. It is useful in various types of displays, and can sometimes be used as a light source for optical fiber communication applications.

An electron can fall from the conduction band into a hole and give up energy in the form of a photon of light. The momentum and energy relationships in silicon and germanium are such that the electron gives up its energy as heat when it returns from the conduction band to the valence band. However, the electron in a gallium arsenide crystal produces a photon when it returns from the conduction band to the valence band. Although there are not enough electrons in an intrinsic crystal to produce visible light, when a forward bias is applied, large numbers of electrons are injected from the *n*-material into the *p*-material. These electrons combine with holes in the *p*-material at the valence band energy level, and photons are released. The light intensity is proportional to the rate of recombination of electrons and, therefore, proportional to the diode current. The gallium arsenide diode emits light waves at a wavelength near the infrared band. To produce light in the visible range, gallium-phosphide must be mixed with the gallium arsenide.

A *photo diode* performs the inverse of an LED. That is, it transforms light energy into an electric current. Reverse bias is applied to the photo diode and the reverse saturation current is controlled by the light intensity that shines on the diode. The light generates electron hole pairs, which induce current. The result is a "photocurrent" in the external circuit, which is proportional to the effective light intensity on the device. The diode behaves as a constant current generator as long as the voltage does not exceed the avalanche voltage. The response times are less than 1 μs. The sensitivity of the diode can be increased if the junction area is made larger since more photons are collected, but this will also increase the response time since the junction capacitance gets larger.

Figure 1.42 shows a photo diode. The reverse current, $-I_p$, increases as the light intensity, H, increases. Equation (1.18) can be used to estimate photo diode current, I_p:

$$I_p = \eta q H \tag{1.18}$$

where

η = quantum efficiency

q = charge on an electron: 1.6×10^{-19} C

ϕ = photon flux density in photons/s-cm^2

A = junction area in cm^2

H = $\phi \times A$ = light intensity in photons/s

Most silicon light detectors consist of a photo diode junction and an amplifier, frequently on one chip. We defer discussion of this type of device until Chapter 3.

Figure 1.42
The photo diode.

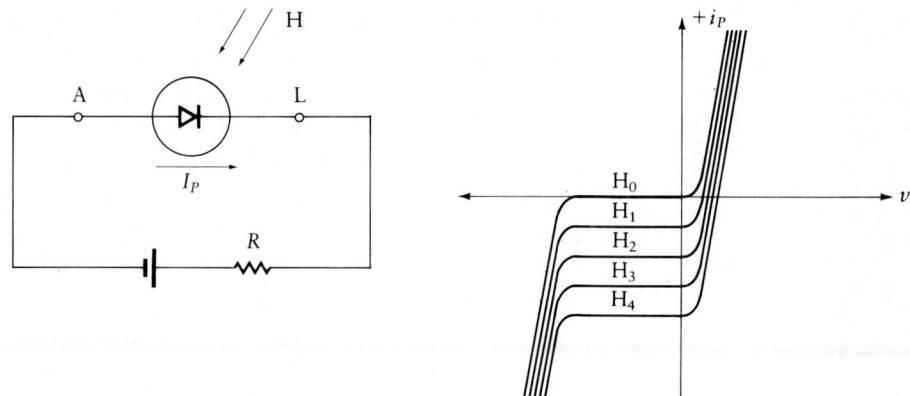

1.9.5 *PIN Diodes*

A diode that has a lightly doped, almost intrinsic region between the *p*- and *n*-regions is called a *PIN diode*. The name derives from the intrinsic material between the *p*- and *n*-layers. Due to its construction, the PIN diode has low capacitance and thus finds applications at high frequencies. When forward biased, minority carrier injection increases the conductivity of the intrinsic region. When reverse-biased, the *i*-region is fully depleted of carriers and the field strength across the region is constant. The maximum voltage rating of the diode is determined by the critical field strength for avalanche and the thickness of the *i*-region.

The PIN diodes are used in radio frequency switches, alternators, and radio frequency phase shifters. With the control current varying continuously, PIN diodes are used in amplitude modulation ([36], Section 3.4).

1.10 Manufacturers' Specifications

The construction of a diode determines the amount of current it is capable of handling, the amount of power it can dissipate, and the peak inverse voltage it will withstand without damage. Each manufacturer develops these criteria in specification sheets for the device. Examples of manufacturer specifications are given in Appendix D.

Listed next are the principal parameters that are found on a manufacturer's specification sheet for a rectifier diode:

1. Type of device with generic number or manufacturer's numbers.
2. Peak inverse voltage (PIV).
3. Maximum reverse current at PIV.

4. Maximum dc forward voltage.
5. Average half-wave rectified forward current.
6. Maximum junction temperature.
7. Current derating curves.
8. Characteristic curves for changes in temperature so that the device can be *derated* for higher temperatures.

In the case of zener diodes, the following parameters usually appear on the specification sheets:

1. Type of device with generic number or manufacturer's number.
2. Nominal zener voltage (avalanche breakdown voltage).
3. Voltage tolerance.
4. Maximum power dissipation (at 25°C).
5. Test current, I_{ZT}.
6. Dynamic impedance at I_{ZT}.
7. Knee current.
8. Maximum junction temperature.
9. Temperature coefficient.
10. Derating curves for higher temperatures.

Let us select an example specification and view the information given in the specification sheet. Using the 1N4001 rectifier diode shown in Appendix D, we find listings as follows:

1. PIV = 50 V.
2. Maximum reverse current (at rated dc voltage) at 25°C = 10 μA. At 100°C the maximum current is 5 μA.
3. Maximum instantaneous forward voltage drop at 25°C = 1.1 V.
4. Average rectified forward current at 25°C = 1 A.
5. Operating and storage junction temperature range (T_j) = −65° to +175°C.
6. A figure is presented for temperature versus printed circuit board mounting for various loads.
7. A figure is presented for effects of lead length for resistive loads versus temperature.

Figure 1.43 shows a typical *current derating curve*. This curve indicates the required adjustment in rated current as the temperature increases beyond ambient. A similar curve is often given for *power derating*.

Note that the manufacturer does not provide the standard current derating curves for the 1N4001. However, the information provided is more than adequate to assure that the diode junction is not overheated when operated in the various circuit modes. In practice, designers should assure that the diode will be subjected to current values that are at least 20 to 30% below the published

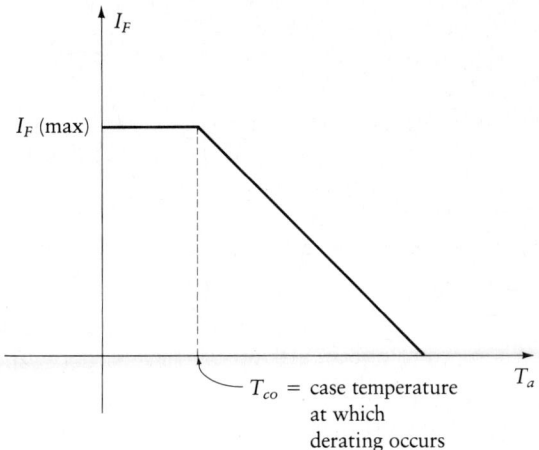

Figure 1.43
Current derating curve.

maximum ratings. In some applications (such as military or space) derating of up to 50% is required.

PROBLEMS

1.1 Sketch the output of the circuit shown in Figure P1.1 when the input, v_s, is a 100 V peak-to-peak square wave having a period of 2 s. Assume that the diode is ideal.

1.2 Sketch the output of the circuit shown in Figure P1.2 (the diode is ideal) when v_s is a:
  a. Square wave of 100 V peak-to-peak with a period of 2 s.
  b. Sine wave of 100 V peak-to-peak with a period of 2 s.
  c. Triangular wave of 40 V peak-to-peak with a period of 2 s.

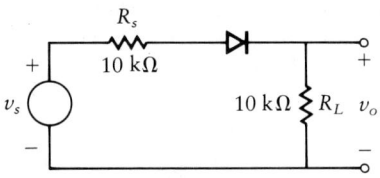

Figure P1.1

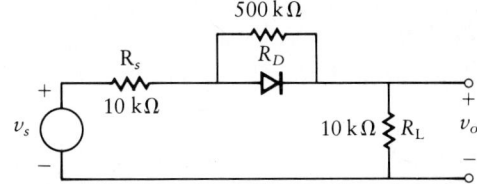

Figure P1.2

1.3 Sketch the output of the circuit shown in Figure P1.3 when v_s is a 100 V peak-to-peak sine wave with a period of 2 s. Assume that the diode is ideal.

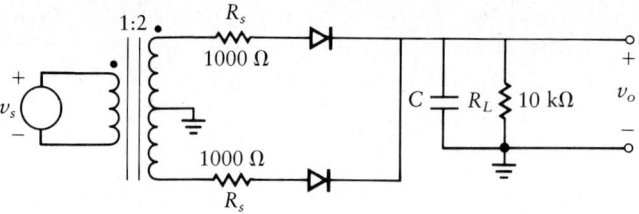

Figure P1.3

1.4 If the output load of a half-wave rectifier is 10 kΩ, what value of capacitor is required to obtain an output voltage that will not vary more than 5%? The input voltage is 100 V rms at 60 Hz. Refer to Figure P1.1. Draw the output waveform.

1.5 If the output load of a full-wave rectifier is 10 kΩ, what value of capacitor is required to maintain an output voltage that will not vary more than 10%? The input is 110 V rms at 60 Hz. Refer to Figure P1.3. Draw the output waveform.

1.6 A radio frequency (rf) signal of 2 MHz is modulated by a 15 kHz signal, with a modulation index of 0.5. What capacitance should be used across a 2 kΩ detector load to filter the rf yet not affect the modulating signal?

1.7 Plot I_D versus V_D for a silicon diode if the reverse saturation current, I_o = 0.1 μA using n = 1.5 for silicon. Also determine the turn-on voltage for the diode.

1.8 Plot I_D versus V_D for a germanium diode if the reverse saturation current, I_o = 0.01 mA. Also determine the turn-on voltage for the diode (this curve can be plotted on the same graph as that of Problem 1.7).

1.9 A particular diode has a reverse saturation current of 0.2 μA, n = 1.6, and V_T = 26 mV. Determine the diode current when the voltage across the diode is 0.4 V. Also determine the forward resistance of the diode at this operating point.

1.10 For the circuit shown in Figure P1.4, determine the current through the diode when the dc voltage across the diode is 0.6 V for this range of current and nV_T = 40 mV.

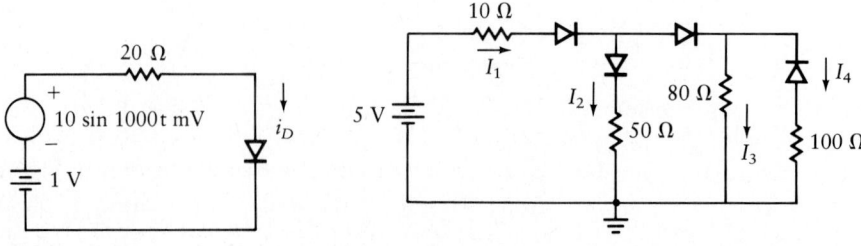

Figure P1.4   **Figure P1.5**

1.11 For the circuit shown in Figure P1.5, determine I_3 in each case.
a. When the diodes are considered ideal.
b. When the diodes are considered nonideal with $R_f = 10\ \Omega$ and $V_D = 0.7$ V.

Ignore the reverse saturation current.

1.12 A zener diode is connected in a circuit, as shown in Figure P1.6. What is the value of resistance R_i that will maintain the voltage at the load at 12 V (V_Z) if the load current is 1 A and the input voltage varies from 14 to 20 V? What is the power rating needed for the resistor and zener diode?

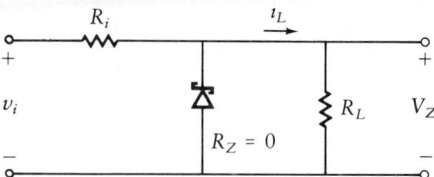

Figure P1.6

1.13 If a zener diode is connected in a circuit as shown in Figure P1.6, what is the value of resistor R_i that will maintain the load voltage at 12 V (V_Z) when the load varies from 50 mA to 500 mA and the input voltage varies from 15 to 20 V? Determine the power rating required for the resistor and zener diode.

1.14 The zener regulator shown in Figure P1.7 uses a 20-V zener diode to maintain a constant 20 V across the load resistor, R_L. If the input voltage varies from 32 to 43 V and the load current varies from 200 mA to 600 mA, select the value of R_i to maintain the constant voltage across the load. Determine the power rating required for the resistor and the zener diode. Assume $R_Z = 0$.

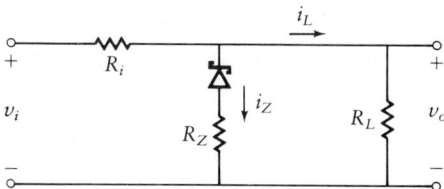

Figure P1.7

1.15 A zener regulator as shown in Figure P1.7 uses a 9-V zener diode to maintain a constant 9 V across the load, with the input varying from 16 to 25 V and the output varying from 100 mA to 800 mA. Assume $R_Z = 0$.
a. Select the value for R_i needed and determine its minimum power requirement.

b. Determine the power rating of the zener diode.

c. Calculate the peak-to-peak output variation if $R_Z = 1\ \Omega$.

1.16 Assuming no loss in the rectifier diodes of Figure P1.8, what is the value of R_i needed to maintain V_L at 16 V with a load current of 1 A using a 16-V zener? v_i varies between 110 and 120 V rms at 60 Hz. Assume $R_Z = 0$. The voltage to the regulator should not drop to more than 5 V above V_Z.

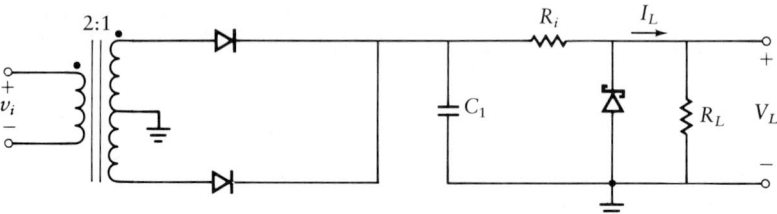

Figure P1.8

1.17 Assuming no voltage drop in the rectifier diode of Figure P1.8, what is the value of R_i necessary to maintain V_L at 16 V with a 1 A load? The input voltage to the transformer is 110 to 120 V rms at 60 Hz. The filtered output from the rectifier may not vary more than ± 5 V. Determine the power rating needed for the resistor and zener diode.

1.18 Using the values for the input voltage to R_i of Problem 1.17 but using a 12-V zener, what would the value of R_i be to maintain 12 V at the output if the load varied from 20 mA to 600 mA? What size capacitor is needed?

1.19 Using the circuit of Figure P1.8 and assuming no loss in the rectifier diodes, what is the value of R_i to maintain 12 V across the load using a 12-V zener when v_i is 110 to 120 V rms at 60 Hz? The output of the rectifier drops 20% due to the size of the capacitor, C_1, and the load varies from 20 mA to 500 mA. What is the size of the capacitor?

1.20 Repeat Problem 1.19 using an MC7812 to replace the discrete regulator shown. Determine the minimum-size capacitor needed.

1.21 With an input waveform of 10 sin ωt, what is the output waveform for the clipping circuits shown in Figure P1.9? Assume that all diodes are ideal.

1.22 Design a clamper which will provide a $+2$ V clamped level to a square wave input for the circuit shown in Figure P1.10. The square wave input magnitude is ± 4 V with a period of 100 μs.

1.23 In the diode clipping circuits of Figure P1.11, $v_i = 20$ sin ωt, $R = 2$ kΩ and $V_R = 10$ V. The reference voltage is obtained from a tap on a 10-kΩ divider connected to a 100-V source. Neglect all capacitances. The

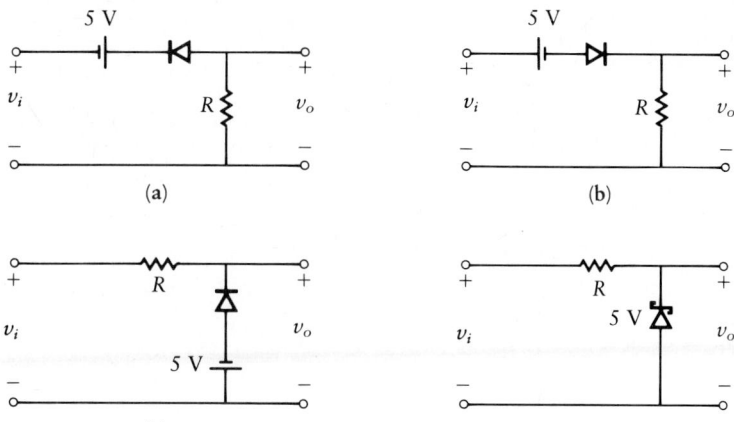

Figure P1.9

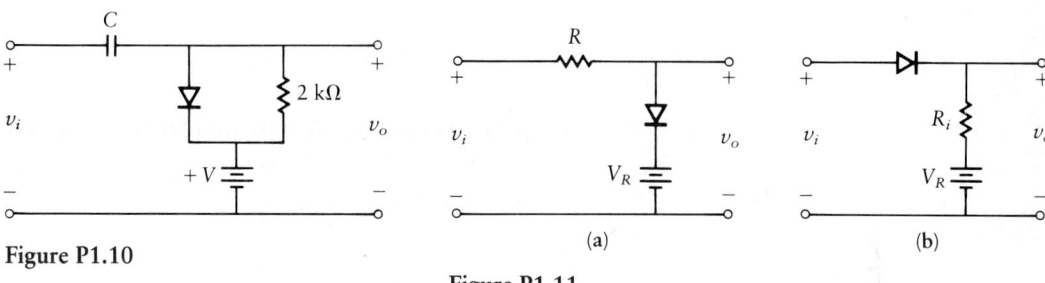

Figure P1.10

Figure P1.11

diode forward resistance is 100 Ω, $R_r = \infty$, and $V\gamma = 0$. Draw the input and output waveforms. Apply Thevenin's theorem to the reference voltage divider network.

1.24 a. The input voltage, v_i, to the clipper shown in Figure P1.12(a) varies linearly from 0 to 175 V. Sketch the output voltage v_o on the same time plot as the input. Assume ideal diodes.

b. Repeat part (a) for the circuit of Figure P1.12(b).

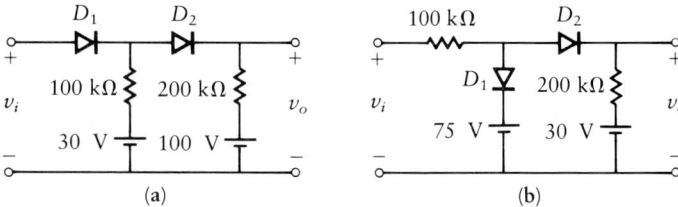

Figure P1.12

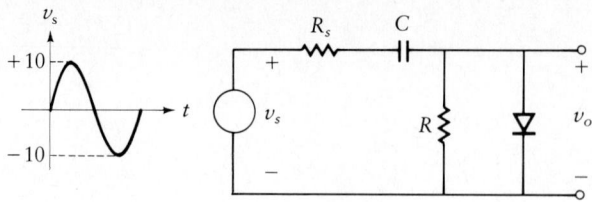

Figure P1.13

1.25 An ideal 10-kHz sinusoidal voltage source whose peak excursions are ± 10 V with respect to ground is applied to the diode clamping circuit of Figure P1.13. Assume $R = \infty$, $R_s = 0$, $C = 1$ μF, the diode has $R_r = \infty$, $R_f = 0$, and $V\gamma = 0$, and the source resistance is zero. Sketch the output waveform.

1.26 The signal shown in Figure P1.13 with a frequency of 10 kHz is applied to the circuit, with values $R_s = 0$, $R = 10$ kΩ, $C = 1$ μF, $R_f = 0$, $R_r = \infty$, and $V\gamma = 0$.
 a. Sketch the output waveform, v_o.
 b. Repeat part (a) if $R = 1$ kΩ and $C = 0.1$ μF.

1.27 What type of clipper is needed to obtain the waveforms illustrated for circuits shown in Figure P1.14? Assume the input is 10 sin t volts. Draw the circuits and label them.

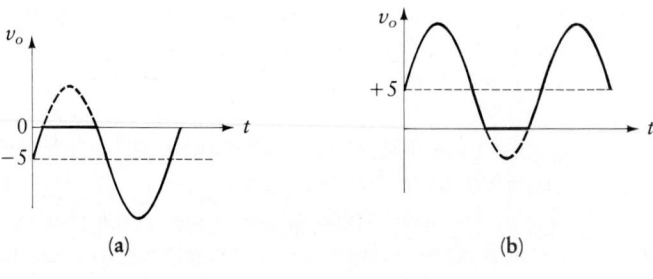

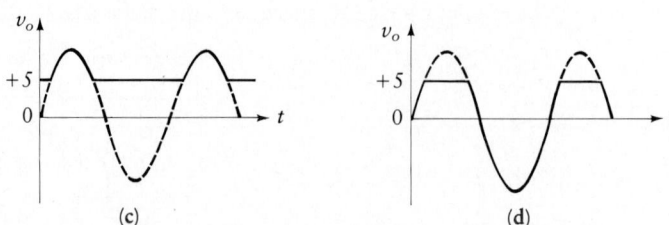

Figure P1.14

2

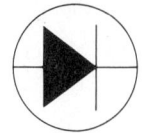

BIPOLAR JUNCTION
TRANSISTOR AMPLIFIERS

Introduction

Basic circuit analysis is the study of interconnections of passive devices and sources. *Passive linear devices* include resistors, capacitors, and inductors. These devices perform the linear operations of proportional multiplication, integration, and differentiation. *Independent sources* are either voltage or current, and their output values do not depend upon any other quantity in the circuit. *Dependent sources* are characterized by an output voltage or current that is a function of a parameter in some branch of the circuit separate from that of the source. Dependent sources usually arise from modeling of active devices such as bipolar junction transistors, field effect transistors, and operational amplifiers.

We begin our study of active devices with the bipolar junction transistor. In 1948, John Bardeen, Walter H. Brattain, and William Shockley of Bell Telephone Laboratories built and tested the first transistor. It was a crude device with low gain—really not of much use for purposes other than laboratory experiments. Meanwhile, in industry, the vacuum tube reigned supreme in applications ranging from consumer goods to military hardware. However, there were some roles that the tube could not fulfill without a great deal of expense. Even worse, certain applications were impossible to achieve using vacuum tubes. Soon after the invention of the transistor, engineers saw its advantages for small portable devices and set out to improve performance. A continuing evolution resulted, which has led to the transistor of today. During the 1960s, manufacturing processes and methods improved so that the transistor could be built reliably. This brought about a boom in the electronics industry, as many consumer products could be inexpensively constructed. Power-handling ability and maximum operating frequency improved steadily throughout this period. The transistor has now almost completely replaced the vacuum tube except in some high-power and high-frequency applications.

2.1   Dependent Voltage and Current Sources

Dependent sources produce a voltage or current whose value is determined by a voltage or current existing in some other location in the circuit (note that passive devices produce a voltage or current whose value is determined by a voltage or current existing at the *same* location in the circuit). Both independent and dependent voltage and current sources are *active* elements. That is, they are capable of delivering power to some external device. *Passive* elements are not capable of generating power, although they can store finite amounts of energy for delivery at a later time, as is the case with capacitors and inductors.

Figure 2.1 shows a circuit containing a dependent source. The source voltage is dependent upon the value of the voltage, V_{R2}. The amplification factor is 4. Kirchhoff's voltage law (KVL) is applied to the loop to obtain

$$10 = (5000)I + 4V_{R2} - V_{R2} = (5000)I + 3V_{R2}$$

Then, using Ohm's law, we have

$$V_{R2} = -(1000)I$$

Substituting this into the loop equation yields

$$10 = (5000)I + 3V_{R2} = (5000)I - (3000)I = (2000)I$$

Therefore,

$$I = 5 \text{ mA}$$
$$V_{R2} = -5 \text{ V}$$

and

$$4V_{R2} = -20 \text{ V}$$

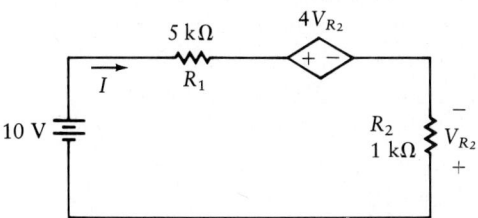

Figure 2.1 Circuit containing dependent voltage source.

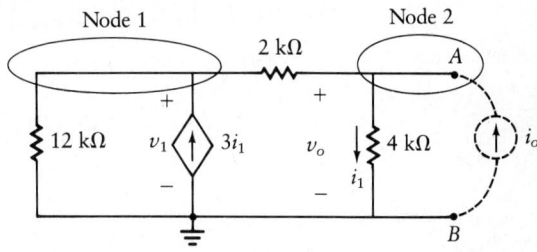

Figure 2.2 Circuit with dependent current source.

The voltage across the dependent source is twice as large as that of the independent source.

If the 10-V battery were replaced by an alternating voltage, the voltage across the dependent source would have twice the amplitude of the input voltage and be 180° out of phase.

We now analyze a simple circuit containing a dependent current source, as shown in Figure 2.2. Note that this circuit contains only a dependent source and resistors—there is no independent source of energy. Therefore, with no external connections, this circuit will remain with zero current and voltage for each branch (convince yourself that setting all parameters equal to zero satisfies Kirchhoff's current and voltage laws). This circuit is of interest only when additional circuitry is connected (in this case, to terminals A and B).

Let us find the Thevenin equivalent of the circuit when viewed across these two terminals. The open circuit voltage is zero, so the entire circuit is equivalent to a single resistance. The Thevenin resistance cannot be found using simple resistor combinations due to the presence of the dependent source. It also cannot be found using the technique of evaluating open-circuit voltage and short-circuit current and then taking the ratio. Both of these quantities are zero, so this approach leads to an indeterminate answer. The approach most often used in this type of problem is to assume that a current or voltage source is applied to the terminals, evaluate the resulting voltage or current, and then take the ratio to find the resistance.

Let us assume an applied current of i_o as shown by the dashed lines in the figure. Kirchhoff's current law (KCL) (nodal analysis) at node 1 yields

$$\frac{v_1}{12,000} - 3i_1 + \frac{v_1 - v_o}{2000} = 0$$

At node 2,

$$\frac{v_o - v_1}{2000} + \frac{v_o}{4000} = i_o$$

Substituting $i_1 = v_o/4000$ into the above equation yields

$$7v_1 - 15v_o = 0$$

$$-2v_1 + 3v_o = 4000i_o$$

Cramer's rule is used to solve these simultaneous equations to obtain

$$v_o = \frac{\begin{vmatrix} 7 & 0 \\ -2 & i_o \times 4000 \end{vmatrix}}{\begin{vmatrix} 7 & -15 \\ -2 & 3 \end{vmatrix}} = \frac{(28,000)i_o}{21 - 30} = (-3110)i_o \text{ V}$$

The equivalent resistance, R_{TH}, is then found by dividing v_o by i_o to get

$$R_{TH} = -3.11 \text{ k}\Omega$$

The fact that the resistance is negative suggests power gain or amplification. This circuit does not consume power. Instead, the circuit develops power, or produces a power gain.

Figure 2.3 illustrates a common configuration in solid-state circuit analysis. We will find the voltage and current gain of this system. *Voltage gain* is defined as the ratio of output to input voltage. Likewise, *current gain* is the ratio of output to input current. The input current is

$$i_{in} = \frac{v_i}{R_{in}} = \frac{20 \sin \omega t \text{ mV}}{1 \text{ k}\Omega} = 20 \sin \omega t \text{ }\mu A$$

A current-divider relationship can be used to find i_1.

$$i_1 = \frac{2000(20 \sin \omega t \text{ }\mu A)}{2000 + 2000} = 10 \sin \omega t \text{ }\mu A$$

The output voltage is then given by

$$v_o = -100i_1 \times (10 \text{ k}\Omega \parallel 10 \text{ k}\Omega)$$

where $\parallel$ indicates a parallel combination of resistors.

$$v_o = -(500,000)i_1 = -500,000(10 \times 10^{-6} \sin \omega t) = -5 \sin \omega t \text{ V}$$

Figure 2.3
Solid-state equivalent
circuit.

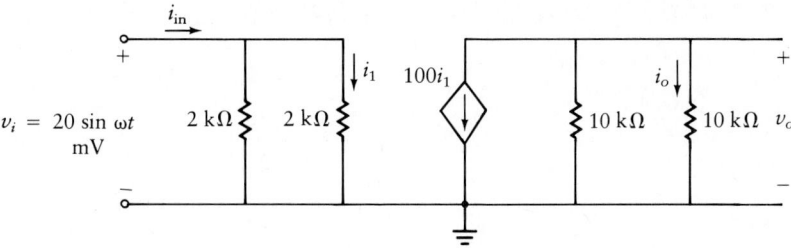

Then, using a current-divider relationship, the output current is found to be

$$i_o = \frac{10,000(-100i_1)}{10,000 + 10,000} = -50i_1$$

The voltage gain is

$$\frac{v_o}{v_i} = \frac{-5 \sin \omega t}{0.02 \sin \omega t} = -250$$

The current gain is

$$\frac{i_o}{i_{in}} = \frac{-50(10 \ \mu A)}{20 \ \mu A} = -25$$

2.2   **Bipolar Transistors**

The transistor is a three-terminal device, in contrast to the diode, which is a two-terminal device. The diode consists of a *p*-type material and an *n*-type material; the transistor consists of two *n*-type materials separated by a *p*-type material (*npn* transistor) or two *p*-type materials separated by an *n*-type material (*pnp* transistor). Figure 2.4(a) illustrates the schematic representation of a transistor [22].

The three different layers or sections are identified as emitter, base, and collector. The *emitter* is a heavily doped, medium-sized layer designed to emit or inject electrons. The *base* is a medium doped, small layer designed to pass electrons. The *collector* is a lightly doped, large layer design to collect electrons.

The transistor can be idealized as two *pn* junctions placed back to back; these are called *bipolar junction transistors (BJTs)*.

In order to provide an explanation for the operation of the transistor, we

Figure 2.4
The bipolar transistor.

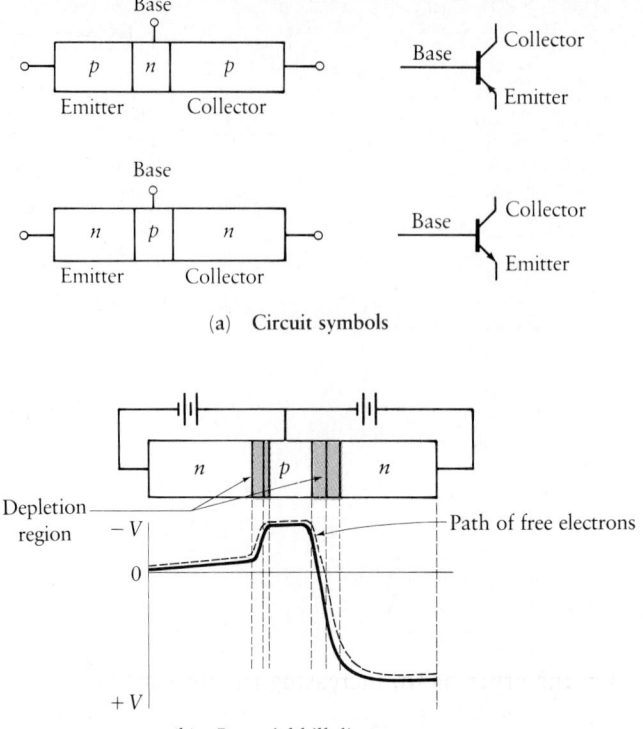

(a)   Circuit symbols

(b)   Potential-hill diagram

develop a simple mathematical model based upon the operational character-istics of the device for the region in which we are working. In order to keep the model simple, we confine our analysis to low frequencies. In Chapter 3 we modify our simple model to include input resistances. Then in Chapter 10, we expand the model to include additional components so that we can analyze transistor operation at high frequency.

The present model is sufficient to present concepts and to design for many useful low-frequency applications. It is intentionally kept uncomplicated so that a closed-form solution of the resulting equations is possible. If, however, more accurate results are required, computer analysis may be necessary. A computer-aided analysis program has been developed. It is known as *SPICE* (simulated program with integrated circuit emphasis; see Appendix A and [36], p. 254) and uses the *Gummel-Poon* model ([16], p. 286). Many U.S. companies use SPICE to develop multitransistor circuits and also for the purpose of doing "worst-case" analysis of circuits to determine the effects of component tolerance.

Models similar to the Gummel-Poon model as used in SPICE are discussed in Chapter 10, where high-frequency analysis and design are considered.

2.3 Transistor Operation

A simple but effective explanation of the *npn* transistor operation is developed using the potential-hill diagram technique of Figure 2.4(b). This approach illustrates a simplified visual picture of the basic operation of a bipolar transistor so that simple circuit applications can be understood. When the base-emitter junction is biased in the forward direction and the base-collector junction is biased in the reverse direction, electrons leaving the *n*-material of the emitter will see only a small potential hill at the *np* junction. Since the potential hill is small, most of the electrons have enough energy to progress to the top of the hill. Once on top of the potential hill, the electrons move easily through the *p*-material (base) to the *pn*- (base-collector) junction. When they approach that junction, the electrons are under the influence of the positive supply voltage and move forward rapidly as they move down the potential hill. If the forward bias on the base-emitter junction is reduced, the height of the potential hill is raised. Electrons leaving the emitter will have more difficulty in reaching the top. The electrons reaching the top are the ones with the highest amount of energy, and these will progress to the collector. The reduction of forward bias thus causes the current through the transistor to be considerably reduced. On the other hand, increasing the forward bias on the base-emitter junction will reduce the potential hill and allow more emitter electrons to flow through the transistor.

The current flow in a junction transistor can also be understood by examining charge-carrier behavior and the depletion regions. The depletion regions have been indicated on Figure 2.4(b). Note that since the base-emitter junction is forward-biased, the depletion region is relatively narrow. The reverse is true for the base-collector junction. A large number of majority carriers (electrons) will diffuse across the base-emitter junction, since this is forward-biased. These electrons then enter the base region and have two choices. They may either exit this region through the connection to the voltage sources, or they may continue flowing to the collector region across the wide depletion region of the reverse-biased junction. We would normally expect the major portion of this current to return to the source, except for the following observations. Since the base region is so thin, these electrons need to travel less distance to be attracted to the positive potential of the collector connection. In addition, the base material has a low conductivity, so the path to the source lead represents a high impedance path. In reality, a very small fraction of the electrons leave the base through the source connection—the major portion of current does flow into the collector.

The bipolar junction transistor exhibits a current gain, which can be used to amplify signals. A simplified *npn* transistor equivalent circuit is shown in

Figure 2.5
Simplified transistor
equivalent circuit.

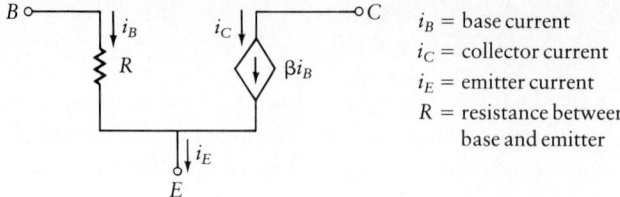

i_B = base current
i_C = collector current
i_E = emitter current
R = resistance between
       base and emitter

Figure 2.6
Simple transistor
circuit.

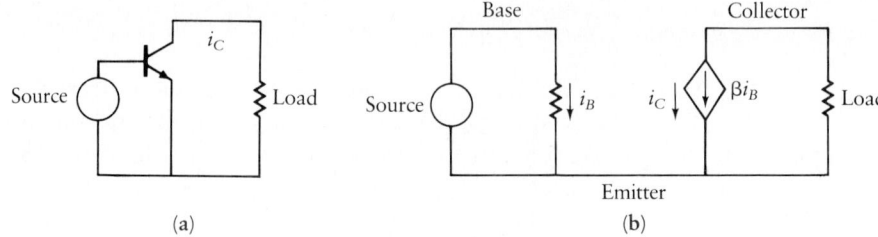

(a)   (b)

Figure 2.5. This model is usually adequate for design and analysis of most circuits.

Figure 2.6 shows a simple circuit for producing current gain. A source voltage is applied across the base-emitter, and a load resistance is connected between the collector and emitter. Figure 2.6(b) shows the same circuit, where the transistor is replaced by the model of Figure 2.5. Because of the presence of the dependent source, a current in the base lead controls the current from the collector to the emitter. The collector current source is dependent upon the base current, i_B. As i_B is increased, the collector current, i_C, increases proportionally. The proportionality constant is given the name *beta* (β).

Figure 2.7 shows a refined version of this model, known as the *Ebers-Moll model* [32]. The base-emitter junction acts as a forward-biased diode with a forward current of $i_B + i_C$. The base-collector junction is reverse-biased and exhibits a small leakage current. I_{CBO}, and a larger current, βi_B. This latter current is caused by the interaction of currents in the base. Clearly,

$$i_E = i_C + i_B \tag{2.1}$$

Note that the positive direction of base and collector currents are defined to be *into* the transistor, whereas the reverse is true for the emitter current. This is simply a convention, and we could have just as well reversed any of the directions. The Ebers-Moll model includes a current, I_{CBO}, which is independent of the base current.

Figure 2.7
Ebers-Moll model.

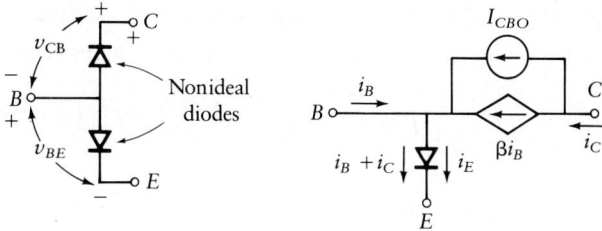

Figure 2.8
Internal currents in a transistor.

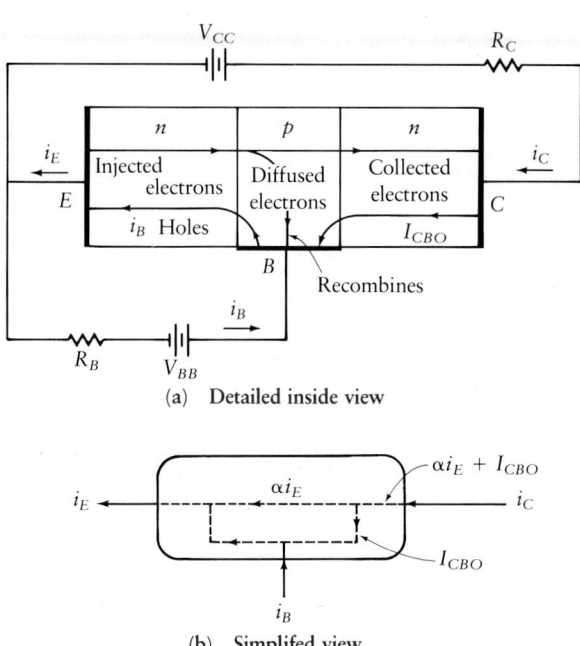

(a)   Detailed inside view

(b)   Simplifed view

The *common-base current gain,* α, is defined as the ratio of the change in collector current to the change in emitter current, assuming that the voltage between collector and base is a constant. Thus,

$$\alpha = \frac{\Delta i_C}{\Delta i_E}\bigg|_{v_{CB}=\text{constant}}$$

This is shown pictorially in Figure 2.8 where I_{CBO} is the leakage current between base and collector. We wish to find a relationship between the collector and base currents. The collector current is found by viewing Figure 2.8(b):

$$i_C = \alpha i_E + I_{CBO} \tag{2.2}$$

Combining equation (2.1) with equation (2.2) yields the emitter current,

$$i_E = \alpha i_E + I_{CBO} + i_B$$

and solving for the base current,

$$i_B = i_E(1 - \alpha) - I_{CBO} \qquad (2.3)$$

We can eliminate i_E from equation (2.3) by rewriting equation (2.2) as

$$i_E = \frac{i_C - I_{CBO}}{\alpha}$$

Finally, this is substituted in equation (2.3) to yield a relationship between i_B, i_C, and I_{CBO}:

$$
\begin{aligned}
i_B &= \frac{(i_C - I_{CBO})(1 - \alpha)}{\alpha} - I_{CBO} \\
&= \frac{(1 - \alpha)i_C}{\alpha} - \frac{I_{CBO}}{\alpha}
\end{aligned}
\qquad (2.4)
$$

The common-base current gain, α, usually lies in the range from 0.8 to 0.999. Therefore, the reciprocal can often be approximated as unity, thus yielding

$$i_B = \frac{(1 - \alpha)i_C}{\alpha} - I_{CBO}$$

Beta (β) was used earlier (see Figure 2.6) to define the ratio of changes in collector current to changes in base current. That is,

$$\beta = \frac{\Delta i_C}{\Delta i_B}$$

Therefore, we differentiate equation (2.4) and rearrange terms.

$$\beta = \frac{\alpha}{1 - \alpha}$$

Typical values of β range from 10 to 600. Making the substitution for β yields

$$i_B = \frac{i_C}{\beta} - I_{CBO}$$

We can usually neglect I_{CBO}, since it is small in magnitude. Thus,

$$i_C \approx \beta i_B \tag{2.5}$$

The term β is referred to as the *large-signal amplification factor,* or the *dc amplification factor.* Thus we are back to our original simplified model. In practice, the value of β varies with base current.

Design challenges exist because β varies with changes in the transistor current. Additionally, during the fabrication of the transistor, variation of the value of beta occurs within a single production run. Thus, two transistors fabricated at the same time will have different values of β, even at the same current levels. This leads us to develop a design procedure that makes the value of collector current relatively independent of changes in β. These methods are discussed in Section 2.5.

Another simplifying assumption often made is that the collector current is approximately equal to the emitter current. That is, since I_{CBO} is small compared to i_C and since α ranges from 0.9 to 0.999, we have

$$i_C \approx i_E \tag{2.6}$$

2.4 Transistor Circuits

2.4.1 *Common Circuit Configurations*

There are three general configurations utilized in transistor circuits. The most often used is the *common-emitter* (CE) *amplifier,* so called because the emitter is in both the input and output loops. The next most widely used circuit is the *common-collector* (CC) configuration, also known as the *emitter follower.* The third configuration is the *common-base* (CB) circuit. Examples of these amplifier configurations are shown in Figure 2.9, where we have illustrated the circuits using *npn* transistors.

In this chapter we consider the design of the bias, or dc circuit. This is characterized by the base resistor, R_B, the emitter resistor, R_E, the collector resistor, R_C, and the source voltage, V_{CC}. The bias technique for the CE amplifier is the same as that for the CB configuration, so these are considered together. The CC configuration is considered separately. When we use *pnp* transistors, the voltage polarities of V_{BB} and V_{CC} are reversed, but the ac equivalent circuits we have developed remain the same.

Figure 2.9
Amplifier circuits.

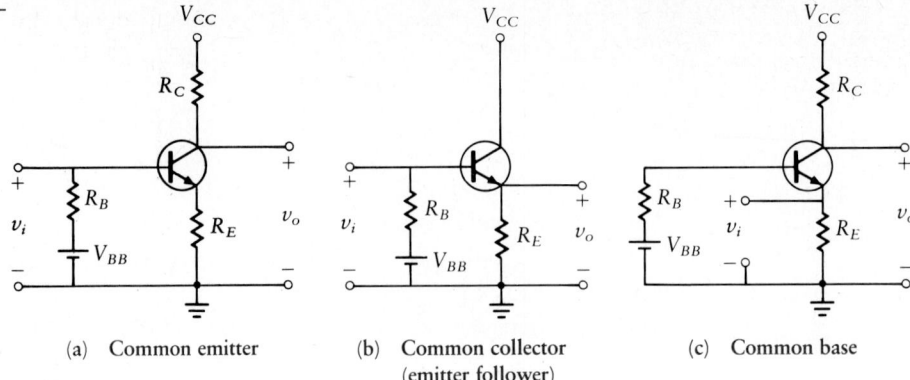

(a) Common emitter

(b) Common collector
(emitter follower)

(c) Common base

2.4.2 *Characteristic Curves*

Since the transistor is a nonlinear device, one way to define its operation is with a series of characteristic curves in a manner similar to that used for diodes in the previous chapter. There is a set of curves for each type of transistor. Since we are no longer dealing with two terminal devices, equations involve at least three variables. Therefore, *parametric curves* are usually used to describe transistor behavior. Figure 2.10 shows two typical plots. Figure 2.10(a) shows the emitter current as a function of the voltage between base and emitter when v_{CE} is held constant. Note that, as we might have expected, this curve is similar to the curve for a diode, since it is the characteristic of the current in the single junction. A load line is drawn using the two axis intercepts. When $i_E = 0$, $v_{BE} = V_{BB}$. The other intercept is found by setting $v_{BE} = 0$. The point where the load line crosses the i_E versus v_{BE} curve is called the *quiescent point*, or simply *Q-point*. The slope of the load line is $-1/(R_E + R_B)$. That is, the equivalent resistance seen by the base and emitter terminals is simply $R_E + R_B$. The slope of the characteristic curve is $1/r_d$, where r_d is the *dynamic resistance* of the transistor emitter-base junction. This slope can be calculated from equation (1.1) and the simplifications that follow that equation. Since this is a *pn* junction, $nV_T = 26$ mV (assuming a silicon junction at room temperature). Taking the derivative of equation (1.1) and performing appropriate simplifications, we find the dynamic resistance to approximately equal

$$r_d \approx \frac{0.026}{I_{EQ}}$$

where I_{EQ} is the emitter current at the Q-point.

Figure 2.10
Transistor characteris-
tic curves.

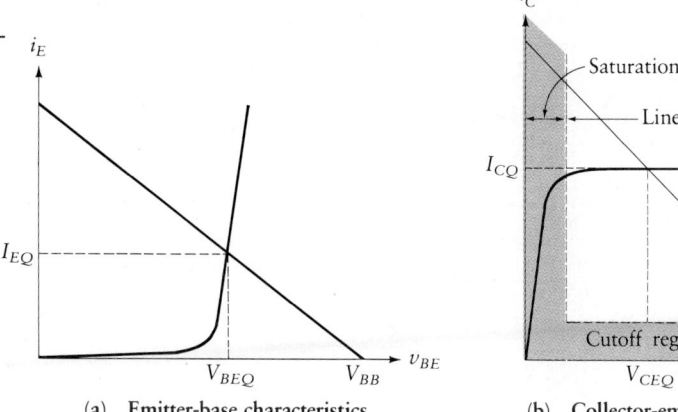

(a) **Emitter-base characteristics**

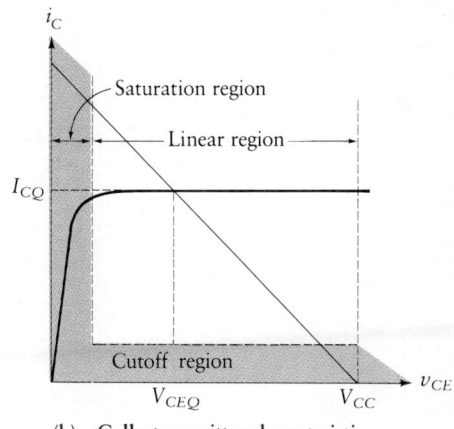

(b) **Collector-emitter characteristics**

Since $i_B = i_C/\beta$, the base-emitter junction is similar to that of a diode. Therefore, for the forward-biased junction,

$$i_B = \left(\frac{I_o}{\beta}\right) \exp\left(\frac{v_{BE}}{nV_T}\right)$$

For a silicon diode, n has a value of 1.3 to 1.6. However, in silicon transistors, the value of n has a value close to unity because of recombination effects caused by the collector and base currents combining in the emitter region. Diffused transistors exhibit an increase of 10 to 20% in the value of n for current levels above the normal operating range of the transistor. In this text, we use $n = 1$ and $nV_T = 26$ mV for silicon transistors.

A straight-line extension of the characteristic curve would intersect the v_{BE} axis at 0.7 V for silicon transistors, 0.2 V for germanium, and 1.2 V for gallium arsenide devices.

If we now hold i_B constant, the collector-emitter junction is defined by the curve of i_C versus v_{CE} shown in Figure 2.10(b). As can be seen from this typical curve, the collector current is almost independent of the voltage between the collector and the emitter, v_{CE}, throughout the "linear range" of operation. When i_B is close to zero, i_C approaches zero in a nonlinear manner. This is known as the *cutoff region* of operation. For the section of the characteristic curves where v_{CE} is near zero, i_C is maximum. This region, known as the *saturation region*, is also not usable for amplification because of nonlinear operation.

Transistor characteristic curves are parametric curves of i_C versus v_{CE}, where i_B is a parameter. Figure 2.11 shows an example of a family of such curves. Each transistor type has its own unique set of characteristic curves.

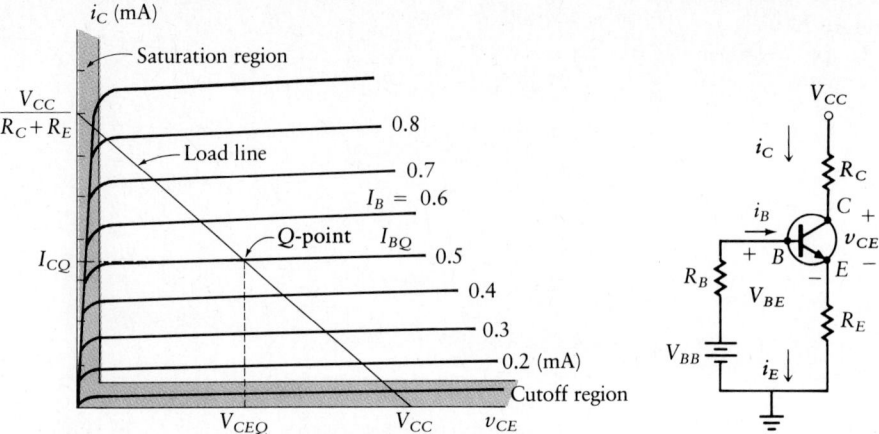

Figure 2.11   Family of transistor characteristic curves.   Figure 2.12   Simple transistor circuit.

As an example of the use of the characteristic curves, we shall analyze the circuit of Figure 2.12. Applying KVL around the collector to emitter loop, we obtain

$$V_{CC} = i_C R_C + v_{CE} + i_E R_E \qquad (2.7)$$

Since i_E is approximately equal to i_C, equation (2.7) can be simplified, as in equation (2.8).

$$V_{CC} = i_C(R_C + R_E) + v_{CE} \qquad (2.8)$$

Equation (2.8) defines a straight-line relationship between i_C and v_{CE}. That is,

$$i_C = \frac{V_{CC} - v_{CE}}{R_C + R_E} = -\frac{1}{R_C + R_E} v_{CE} + \frac{V_{CC}}{R_C + R_E} \qquad (2.9)$$

One way to plot this straight line is to solve for the two axis intercepts. If $i_C = 0$, $v_{CE} = V_{CC}$. If $v_{CE} = 0$, then

The dc load line is plotted on the characteristic curves of Figure 2.11. When we discuss design, we will see how properly to select the circuit parameters. For now, we assume that the operating point, the Q-point, can be selected anywhere on this load line. The point will have coordinates of V_{CEQ} and I_{CQ}, the quiescent values of v_{CE} and i_C, respectively. The quiescent point is the zero signal value of v_{CE} and i_C.

2.5 The CE Amplifier

The CE, or common emitter transistor amplifier, is so called because the base and collector current combine in the emitter. Figure 2.13 shows the configuration of the amplifier, where an *npn* transistor has been selected for illustration.

We first analyze the circuit of Figure 2.13 under dc conditions. The variable source, v_s, is set equal to zero. KVL around the base loop is written as follows:

$$I_B R_B + V_{BE} - V_{BB} = 0 \tag{2.10}$$

Recall that V_{BE} is equal to 0.6 to 0.7 V for silicon transistors, but in this text, we use 0.7 V unless otherwise specified.

We now write the KVL around the collector-emitter loop as follows:

$$V_{CC} = R_C I_C + V_{CE}$$

Then

$$I_C = \frac{V_{CC} - V_{CE}}{R_C} \tag{2.11}$$

Equation (2.11) defines the load line, which is drawn on the characteristic curves in Figure 2.14(a). A Q-point, or operating point, which is defined as the zero-signal point, can now be selected to lie on the load line. Now if we assume an ac input of

$$v_s = V \sin \omega t$$

Figure 2.13
Common emitter *npn*
transistor amplifier.

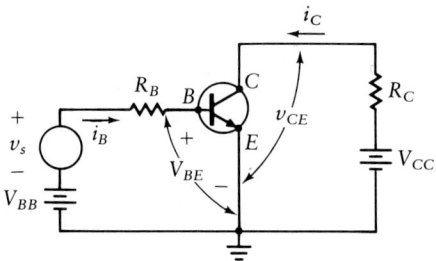

Figure 2.14
Characteristic curves
for CE amplifier.

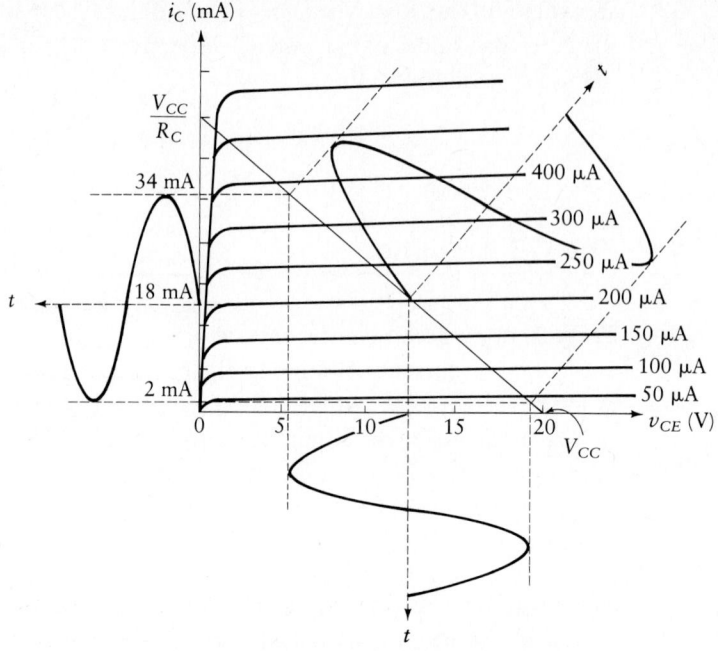

(a)   **Transistor characteristics curve**

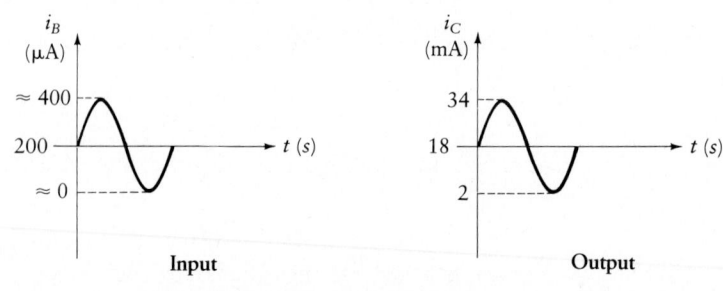

(b)   **Input-output current curves**

the output wave can be found graphically. By moving the operating point up and down along the load line as i_B varies, we can plot i_C, i_B, and v_{CE}, as shown in Figure 2.14.

Let us determine the change in collector current for a given change in base current. This ratio is the *current gain,* which is defined as

$$A_i = \frac{\Delta i_C}{\Delta i_B}$$

$$= \frac{32 \text{ mA}}{400 \text{ μA}} = 80$$

Figure 2.15
CE amplifier with
emitter resistor.

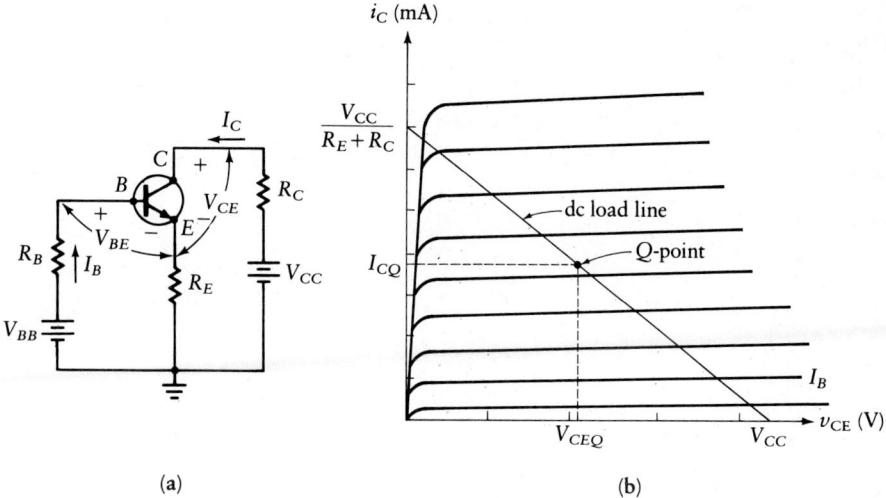

(a)

(b)

Δi_C and Δi_B are read from Figure 2.14 as the total swings in these parameter values. It is this gain that makes the device important for many engineering applications.

2.5.1 CE Amplifier with Emitter Resistor

Figure 2.15 illustrates a CE circuit to which an emitter resistor has been added. We write the Kirchhoff equations around the emitter-collector loop to determine the dc load line. Referring to Figure 2.15(a), we find

$$V_{CC} = R_C I_C + V_{CE} + R_E I_E$$

Since I_C is approximately equal to I_E, we have

$$I_C = \frac{V_{CC} - V_{CE}}{R_E + R_C} \qquad (2.12)$$

If $I_C = 0$, then

$$V_{CE} = V_{CC}$$

This operating point is in the cutoff region. If $V_{CE} = 0$, we have

$$I_C = \frac{V_{CC}}{R_E + R_C}$$

This operating point is in the saturation region. The resulting load line is as drawn in Figure 2.15(b).

In using the common emitter transistor, we avoid the nonlinear region of the characteristic curves occurring at low values of i_C (cutoff) and at low values of v_{CE} (saturation). In designing a transistor amplifier, we often desire maximum undistorted output swing. If the ac input signal is symmetrical about zero, we can achieve maximum swing by placing the Q-point in the center of the load line. Thus,

$$V_{CEQ} = \frac{V_{CC}}{2}$$

This equation establishes V_{CEQ} and I_{CQ}. Additionally, since the base-emitter junction acts as a diode,

$$V_{BE} = V_\gamma$$

Writing KVL equations around the base loop, we obtain

$$V_{BB} = R_B i_B + v_{BE} + i_C R_E$$

Note that we are using lowercase letters and uppercase subscripts for the variables. This indicates total (dc + ac) values. This would be an appropriate time to review the notation conventions presented at the beginning of this text. Because

$$i_C = \beta i_B$$

we have

$$V_{BB} = \frac{R_B i_C}{\beta} + V_{BE} + i_C R_E$$

and at the quiescent point,

$$I_{CQ} = \frac{V_{BB} - V_{BE}}{R_B/\beta + R_E} \tag{2.13}$$

The voltage, V_{BE}, is considered to be a constant at room temperature (25°C) and has a value of about 0.7 V for silicon transistors. In order to avoid using two separate dc sources, a voltage-divider network can be used to provide the dc source for the base circuit, as shown in Figure 2.16. The values for R_1 and

Figure 2.16
Transistor circuit using one source.

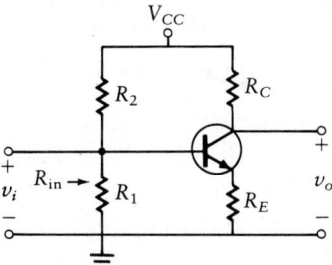

R_2 determine the location of the Q-point. If the resistor and source combination connected to the base in Figure 2.16 is replaced by a Thevenin equivalent, the new circuit is identical to that of Figure 2.15. Therefore, it is necessary only to properly choose R_1 and R_2.

The Thevenin equivalent voltage and resistance from base to ground are

$$V_{\text{TH}} = V_{BB} = \frac{R_1 V_{CC}}{(R_1 + R_2)} \tag{2.14}$$

$$R_{\text{TH}} = R_1 \| R_2 = R_B = \frac{R_1 R_2}{R_1 + R_2} \tag{2.15}$$

We can solve for R_1 and R_2 by substituting equation (2.14) into equation (2.15):

$$R_1 = \frac{R_B V_{CC}}{V_{CC} - V_{BB}} = \frac{R_B}{1 - V_{BB}/V_{CC}} \tag{2.16}$$

$$R_2 = \frac{V_{CC} R_B}{V_{BB}} \tag{2.17}$$

R_1 and R_2 need to be determined to establish the required bias point. The analysis of the previous section assumes that the collector current is equal to the emitter current. This is a good approximation, since β is usually greater than 100.

For the circuit under consideration, we wish to have about 10% of the input current going into the base and about 90% shunted through the equivalent external resistor, R_B. This provides bias stability and also permits the use of the simplified equations. Hence, the current in R_B should be about 10 times the base current. To achieve this, we set

$$R_B \leqslant 0.1 \ \beta R_E \tag{2.18}$$

or

$$\frac{R_B}{\beta} \leq 0.1R_E$$

This prevents variation in β from significantly affecting the dc operating point of the stage. We will have more to say about this later.

We can now use equation (2.13) to solve for the quiescent collector current. Letting R_B equal 0.1 βR_E, we have

$$I_{CQ} = \frac{V_{BB} - V_{BE}}{-0.1 \ \beta R_E/\beta + R_E} = \frac{V_{BB} - V_{BE}}{1.1R_E} \tag{2.19}$$

Equation (2.19) is used in the design process.

2.5.2   *Introduction to Analysis and Design*

In *analysis* problems, the circuit is completely specified. Therefore the Q-point is known, since both R_1 and R_2 are given. The bias point may not be optimally located, and, in fact, we may find that the transistor is in the saturation or cutoff region. Nonetheless, since the entire circuit is specified, we can only substitute values into equations and calculate the results.

In *design* problems, the circuit is *not* completely specified. The designer has the option of placing the quiescent point in the best possible location. If it is desired to have the maximum possible output voltage swing, the Q-point is placed in the center of the load line. If, on the other hand, the input signal is small, I_{CQ} can often be set at a smaller value to obtain a linear (nondistorted) output, while dissipating less power in the rest condition. Since specification of the Q-point does not yield a sufficient number of equations to solve for all components, additional constraints can be introduced to provide performance improvement. For example, we use the equation $R_B = 0.1 \ \beta R_E$ in order to find R_1 and R_2. Recall that choosing R_B according to this equation makes the Q-point location less sensitive to variations in β. Sometimes the circuit configuration will dictate other constraints upon the resistor values that will not permit satisfying this last relationship.

Example 2.1	**Analysis of CE Amplifier**

A CE amplifier is configured as shown in Figure 2.17 with $R_1 = 1$ kΩ, $R_2 = 9$ kΩ, $R_C = 1$ kΩ, $V_{CC} = 12$ V, $R_E = 100 \ \Omega$, $\beta = 100$, and $V_{BE} = 0.6$ V. Determine V_{BB}, R_B, and I_{CQ}.

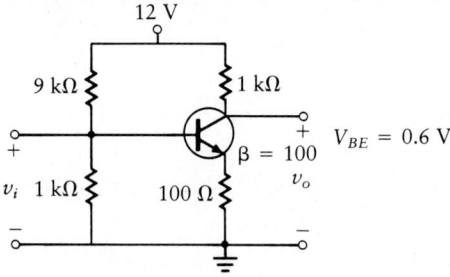

Figure 2.17
CE amplifier for
Example 2.1.

SOLUTION   We first find the Thevenin equivalent of the resistive network connected to the base.

$$V_{BB} = \frac{R_1 V_{CC}}{R_1 + R_2} = \frac{(1000)(12)}{(1000 + 9000)} = 1.2 \text{ V}$$

$$R_B = \frac{R_1 R_2}{R_1 + R_2} = \frac{(1000)(9000)}{(1000 + 9000)} = 900 \text{ }\Omega$$

We now use the KVL equation for the base loop, equation (2.13), to obtain

$$I_{CQ} = \frac{V_{BB} - V_{BE}}{R_B/\beta + R_E} = \frac{1.2 - 0.6}{900/100 + 100} = 5.5 \text{ mA}$$

Example 2.2   **Design of CE Amplifier**

In the circuit of Figure 2.17, we wish to place the Q-point in the middle of the load line. Here, $\beta = 100$, $V_{BE} = 0.6$ V, $R_E = 100$ Ω, $R_C = 1$ kΩ, and $V_{CC} = 12$ V. Find the required values of R_1 and R_2.

SOLUTION   The specification that the Q-point is in the middle of the load line requires that

$$V_{CEQ} = \frac{V_{CC}}{2}$$

We can then use KVL around the emitter-collector loop, equation (2.12), to find I_{CQ}:

$$I_{CQ} = \frac{V_{CC} - V_{CEQ}}{R_E + R_C} = \frac{V_{CC} - V_{CC}/2}{R_E + R_C} = \frac{12}{2(100 + 1000)} = 5.5 \text{ mA}$$

We need to know R_B and V_{BB} in order to find R_1 and R_2. R_B is found from the constraint

$$R_B = 0.1\, \beta R_E = 0.1(100)(100) = 1\ \text{k}\Omega$$

We now use the base loop KVL equation, equation (2.13), to find V_{BB} as follows:

$$V_{BB} = V_{BE} + I_{CQ}\left(\frac{R_B}{\beta} + R_E\right)$$

$$= 0.6 + (0.0055)\left(\frac{1000}{100} + 100\right) = 1.2\ \text{V}$$

With V_{BB} and R_B determined, equations (2.16) and (2.17) can be used to find R_1 and R_2.

$$R_2 = \frac{R_B V_{CC}}{V_{BB}} = \frac{1000 \times 12}{1.2} = 10\ \text{k}\Omega$$

$$R_1 = \frac{R_B}{1 - V_{BB}/V_{CC}} = \frac{1000}{1 - 1.2/12} = 1.11\ \text{k}\Omega$$

Drill Problems

D2.1   Given the circuit of Figure 2.16 with $V_{CC} = 16$ V, $R_1 = 2$ kΩ, $R_2 = 20$ kΩ, $R_C = 3$ kΩ, $R_E = 200$ Ω, $\beta = 200$, and $V_{BE} = 0.7$ V, determine the values of V_{BB}, R_B, and I_{CQ}.

   Ans.   1.46 V; 1.82 kΩ, 3.6 mA

D2.2   Given the circuit of Figure 2.16 with a *pnp* transistor, $V_{CC} = -6$ V, $R_1 = 2$ kΩ, $R_2 = 12$ kΩ, $R_C = 1$ kΩ, $R_E = 100$ Ω, $\beta = 100$, and $V_{BE} = -0.7$ V, determine the values of V_{BB}, I_{CQ}, and R_B.

   Ans. -0.86 V; -1.34 mA; 1.71 kΩ

D2.3   Given the circuit of Problem D2.1 but with R_1 and R_2 not specified, design a circuit for maximum output voltage swing. Determine the new values of R_1, R_2, and I_{CQ}.

   Ans: 4.34 kΩ; 51.2 kΩ; 2.5 mA

D2.4   Using the information given in Problem D2.2, design a circuit for maximum output voltage swing. Determine the new values of R_1, R_2, and I_{CQ}.

Ans: 1.2 kΩ; 6 kΩ; -2.73 mA

D2.5   In the amplifier of Problem D2.1, R_B is required to be 10 kΩ. What are the values of R_1, R_2, I_{CQ}, and R_E that make the amplifier operate with maximum output voltage swing and insensitivity to variations in β?

Ans: 11.4 kΩ; 81.8 kΩ; 2.29 mA; 500 Ω

2.6   Power Considerations

Power rating is an important consideration in selecting resistors. The resistors must be capable of withstanding the maximum anticipated power without overheating. Power considerations also affect transistor selection. Designers normally select components that have the lowest power-handling capability suitable for the design. Frequently, *derating* is used to improve the reliability of a device. This is similar to using safety factors in the design of mechanical systems where the system is designed to withstand values that exceed the maximum.

2.6.1   *Derivation of Power Equations*

Average power is calculated as follows:

$$\text{for dc:} \quad P = VI = I^2R = \frac{V^2}{R}$$

$$\text{for ac:} \quad P = \frac{1}{T}\int_0^T v(t)i(t)dt$$

In the ac equation, T is one period of the waveform. If the signal is not periodic, we let T approach infinity. The power supplied by the power source to the CE amplifier of Figure 2.16 can be written as follows:

$$
\begin{aligned}
P_{V_{CC}} &= P_{\text{(transistor circuit)}} + P_{\text{(bias current)}} \\
&= \frac{1}{T}\int_0^T V_{CC}\left[I_{CQ} + i_c(t)\right] dt + \frac{V^2_{CC}}{R_1 + R_2} + I^2_{BQ}R_2 \\
&= V_{CC}I_{CQ} + \frac{V^2_{CC}}{R_1 + R_2} + I^2_{BQ}R_2
\end{aligned}
$$

We have assumed that the average value of $i_c(t)$ is zero. For example, if the input ac signal is a sinusoid,

$$i_c(t) = A \sin \omega t$$

Then

$$\int_0^T A \sin \omega t \, dt = 0$$

where $T = 2\pi/\omega$. Since $I^2_{BQ}R_2$ is small, it usually can be ignored.

The average power dissipated by the transistor is

$$P_{\text{(transistor)}} = \frac{1}{T}\int_0^T v_{CE}(t)i_C(t) \, dt \tag{2.20}$$

For zero-signal input, this becomes

$$P_{\text{(transistor)}} = V_{CEQ}I_{CQ}$$

For an input signal with maximum possible swing,

$$v_{CE}(t) = V_{CEQ} - V_{CEQ} \sin \omega t = V_{CEQ}(1 - \sin \omega t)$$

$$i_C(t) = I_{CQ} + I_{CQ} \sin \omega t = I_{CQ} (1 + \sin \omega t)$$

$$P_{\text{(transistor)}} = \frac{1}{T}\int_0^T V_{CEQ}I_{CQ} (1 - \sin \omega t)(1 + \sin \omega t) \, dt$$

$$= \frac{V_{CEQ}I_{CQ}}{T}\int_0^T (1 - \sin^2 \omega t) \, dt$$

$$= \frac{V_{CEQ}I_{CQ}}{T}\int_0^T \cos^2 \omega t \, dt$$

$$= \frac{V_{CEQ}I_{CQ}}{2T}\int_0^T (1 + \cos 2\omega t) \, dt$$

$$= \frac{V_{CEQ}I_{CQ}}{2} \tag{2.21}$$

From the above derivation, we see that the transistor dissipates its maximum power when no ac signal input is applied. This is shown in Figure 2.18. Depending upon the amplitude of the input signal, the transistor will dissipate an average power between $V_{CEQ}I_{CQ}$ and one-half of this value. Therefore, the transistor is selected for zero input signal so it will handle the maximum power as follows:

Figure 2.18
Instantaneous transistor power.

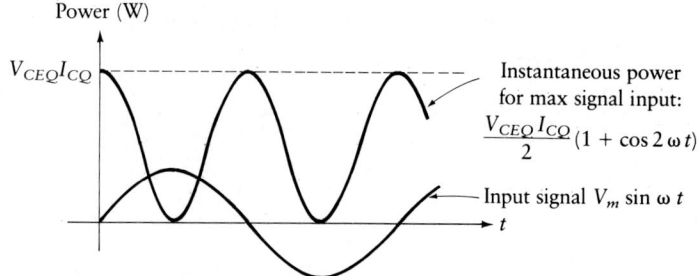

$$P_{(transistor\text{-}max\ average)} = V_{CEQ}\ I_{CQ} \qquad (2.22)$$

We need a measure of efficiency to determine how much of the power delivered by the source appears as signal power at the output. We define *conversion efficiency* as

$$\eta = \frac{P_o\ (\text{ac})}{P_{VCC}\ (\text{dc})} \times 100$$

Drill Problems

D2.6 What is the maximum power used from the power supply in Problem D2.1?

Ans: 69.2 mW

D2.7 What would the maximum undistorted ac power in R_C be in Problem D2.1 when an ac signal is injected into the amplifier to obtain a maximum symmetrical output swing?

Ans: 2.94 mW

D2.8 What is the actual conversion efficiency of the amplifier in Problem D2.3?

Ans: 21%

2.7 Bypass and Coupling Capacitors

Capacitors are approximated as short circuits for ac signals and open circuits for dc signals. *Bypass capacitors* are therefore used to effectively eliminate

Figure 2.19
Common emitter ac
amplifier stage.

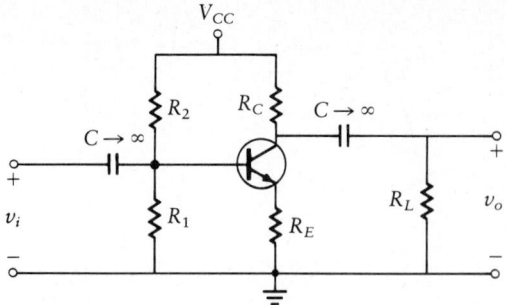

(short out) resistors during ac operation. *Coupling capacitors* are used to block the direct current yet allow the ac signal to pass.

2.7.1   *Bypass Capacitors*

Capacitors can be used to bypass the emitter resistor, thus increasing the voltage gain of an amplifier. To accomplish this, a capacitor is selected so that its impedance at operating frequencies is much less than the resistance of the emitter resistor. Since impedance increases with decreasing frequency, the capacitor impedance should be much less than the value of the equivalent resistance across the capacitance at the lowest operating frequency of the amplifier.

2.7.2   *Coupling Capacitors*

Each pair of stages of a multistage amplifier can be coupled together with a capacitor. The input impedance of the following stage is the load of the previous stage. A coupling capacitor is necessary to prevent interactions of dc currents between adjacent stages. A single-stage transistor amplifier has the form shown in Figure 2.19, where R_L is the equivalent input resistance of the next stage.

The capacitors are open circuits at dc, and they are short circuits for ac (at the midfrequency operating region that we are addressing). However, the capacitors assume a major role in determining the low-frequency portion of the response curve. That role is addressed in Chapter 10.

2.8   **ac Load Line for CE Configuration**

Before beginning discussion of load lines for the CE amplifier, we note that the bias methods for CE and CB configurations are identical. Thus, although we are presenting the theory for the CE, we use the same concepts for both CE and CB.

The resistance in the emitter-collector circuit for dc operation is $R_C + R_E$, which we define as R_{dc}. When a load is coupled to the transistor through a capacitor, the ac resistance is different. Under ac conditions, the resistance in the emitter-collector circuit is

$$R_{ac} = (R_L \parallel R_C) + R_E$$

Note that for ac operation, the V_{CC} terminal is grounded. If the emitter resistor is bypassed with a capacitor, then the ac resistance is only

$$R_{ac} = R_L \parallel R_C$$

The ac load line has a slope of $-1/R_{ac}$. Since a zero ac input places the operation at the Q-point, the ac load line intersects the dc load line at the Q-point. If the input signal is small, the Q-point should normally be located to minimize the quiescent collector current. In designing such circuits, we raise I_{CQ} above the zero point just enough to allow linear reproduction of the input signal (i.e., no distortion by entering the cutoff region). Under this condition, the transistor dissipates less power than if the Q-point is placed in the middle of the ac load line. We investigate this design procedure in Section 2.9.3.

2.8.1 ac Load Line Through Any Q-Point

We determined the dc load line from equation (2.12). This is then given by the equation

$$i_C = \frac{-v_{CE}}{R_E + R_C} + \frac{V_{CC}}{R_E + R_C}$$

Since the coupling capacitors are open circuits to dc, this load line applies to the circuit of Figure 2.19. The load line is plotted on the characteristic curves of Figure 2.20. The definitions of ac and dc resistance are repeated next.

R_{dc} = total resistance around the collector-emitter loop under dc conditions (capacitors considered open circuits)

R_{ac} = total resistance around the collector-emitter loop under ac conditions (dc sources set to zero and capacitors considered short circuits)

For the circuit in Figure 2.19, we have

$$R_{dc} = R_E + R_C \tag{2.23}$$
$$R_{ac} = R_L \parallel R_C + R_E \tag{2.24}$$

Figure 2.20
Characteristic curves.

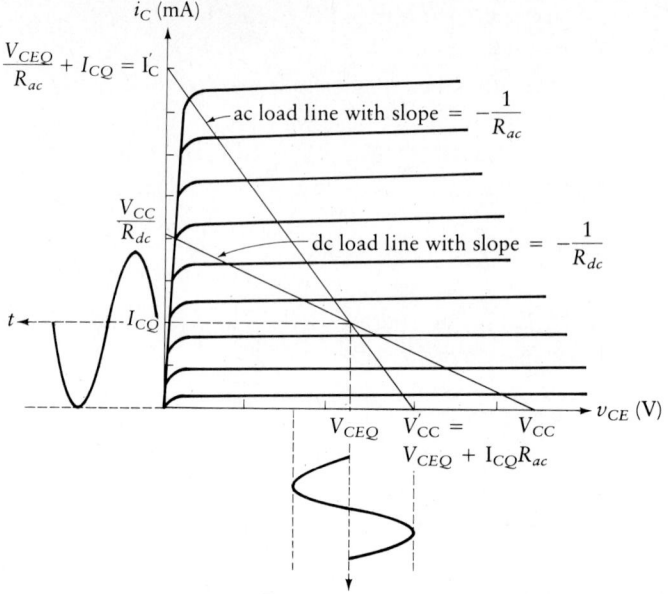

The equation for the dc load line is then

$$i_C = \frac{V_{CC}}{R_{dc}} - \frac{v_{CE}}{R_{dc}} = \frac{1}{R_{dc}}(V_{CC} - v_{CE})$$

The Q-point, which is specified for zero signal value, is on both the ac and dc load lines. The ac load line goes through the Q-point and has a slope of $-1/R_{ac}$. This slope is greater in magnitude than that of the dc load line. The ac load line is plotted in Figure 2.20. The intersections with the i_C-axis and the v_{CE}-axis can be obtained from the equation for a straight line through a given point (x_1, y_1) with known slope (m) as follows:

$$(y - y_1) = m(x - x_1)$$

$$(i_C - I_{CQ}) = \frac{-(v_{CE} - V_{CEQ})}{R_{ac}}$$

$$i_C = -\frac{v_{CE}}{R_{ac}} + \left(\frac{V_{CEQ}}{R_{ac}} + I_{CQ}\right)$$

The intersection of the ac load line with the i_C-axis is then

$$I'_C = \frac{V_{CEQ}}{R_{ac}} + I_{CQ}$$

Figure 2.21
Load lines for maximum ac swing.

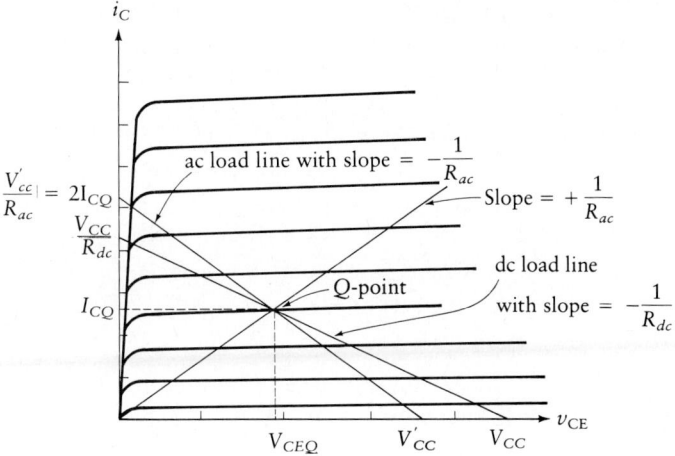

The intersection of the ac load line with the v_{CE}-axis is, with $i_C = 0$,

$$V'_{CC} = V_{CEQ} + I_{CQ}R_{ac}$$

2.8.2 *Choice of ac Load Line for Maximum Output Swing*

If we wish to design for the maximum output voltage swing from the amplifier, the Q-point must be placed in the center of the ac load line. Figure 2.21 shows the load lines for the circuit in Figure 2.19. It is a matter of geometry to set the Q-point for maximum swing. The dc load line is drawn as in Figure 2.20. That is,

$$V_{CC} = v_{CE} + i_C R_{dc} \qquad (2.25)$$

We write KVL equations for the ac case, where capacitors are replaced by short circuits and the dc sources are set to zero. We write the linear equation with the point-slope method, as follows:

$$(i_C - I_{CQ}) = -\frac{1}{R_{ac}}(v_{CE} - V_{CEQ}) \qquad (2.26)$$

The intersection of this line and the dc load line is the Q-point. Since i_C is maximum when $v_{CE} = 0$, the maximum collector current, I'_C, is given by

$$I'_C = \frac{V_{CEQ}}{R_{ac}} + I_{CQ}$$

However, I'_C is equal to $2I_{CQ}$ for maximum swing along the ac load line. Substituting this constraint in the previous equation, we obtain

$$2I_{CQ} - I_{CQ} = \frac{V_{CEQ}}{R_{ac}}$$

or

$$I_{CQ} = \frac{V_{CEQ}}{R_{ac}} \tag{2.27}$$

Equation (2.27) represents one equation in two unknowns for specifying the Q-point location for maximum output swing. The second equation is derived by using the dc load-line equation. Equation (2.27) is substituted into equation (2.25) as follows:

$$V_{CC} = V_{CEQ} + \frac{V_{CEQ}R_{dc}}{R_{ac}}$$

which reduces to

$$V_{CEQ} = \frac{V_{CC}}{1 + R_{dc}/R_{ac}} \tag{2.28}$$

This specifies v_{CE} at the Q-point. I_{CQ} is then found from equation (2.27) as follows:

$$I_{CQ} = \frac{V_{CC}}{R_{ac} + R_{dc}} \tag{2.29}$$

V'_{CC} is the intercept of the ac load line with the v_{CE}-axis, as shown in Figure 2.21. The slope of the ac load line is

$$\frac{-1}{R_{ac}} = \frac{-2I_{CQ}}{V'_{CC}}$$

so

$$V'_{CC} = 2I_{CQ}R_{ac} = \frac{2V_{CC}}{1 + R_{dc}/R_{ac}} \tag{2.30}$$

or

$$V'_{CC} = 2V_{CEQ}$$

2.9   **ac Analysis and Design**

We now have the necessary tools to permit analysis and design of amplifier circuits. It is necessary for us only to pull together the results derived in previous sections.

In *analyzing* an ac amplifier, the circuit components are specified. We begin the solution by determining the dc bias. The Thevenin equivalent circuit for the base-emitter loop is first derived. This provides the values needed to solve the bias equation for I_{CQ}. The dc and ac load lines are constructed next. If I_{CQ} is in the transistor operating region (i.e., not in the cutoff or saturation region), the maximum undistorted output ac voltage swing of the amplifier can be determined by examining the ac load line.

In *designing* an amplifier, the situation is reversed, since the designer must select the circuit components and has the option of selecting I_{CQ}. If a maximum output voltage swing is desired, I_{CQ} is placed in the center of the ac load line. On the other hand, if the input signal is small, I_{CQ} can be made just large enough so the ac signal output will not be clipped during the input signal maximum. In designing, the engineer starts calculations at the collector-emitter side of the amplifier rather than at the base-emitter side. After I_{CQ} has been determined, the bias equation is used to determine the values of R_1 and R_2 to cause the transistor to operate at the selected I_{CQ}.

2.9.1   *Analysis Procedure*

In analysis problems, the values of R_1, R_2, V_{CC}, V_{BE}, R_E, R_C, R_L, and β are given. We present an organized procedure for analysis. The equations used have been derived earlier in this chapter, and we cite references so the derivations can be consulted. We strongly recommend that you consult these derivations since it is important to be aware of the various assumptions. Our purposes in presenting this analysis procedure are not confined to teaching you the art of amplifier analysis. It is more important for you to appreciate the methodology of reducing theory to a step-by-step procedure. In this manner, you will be able to deal with new situations as they arise.

Step 1   Use R_1 and R_2 to determine V_{BB} and R_B from the following equations:

$$V_{BB} = \frac{R_1 V_{CC}}{R_1 + R_2}$$

$$R_B = R_1 \parallel R_2 = \frac{R_1 R_2}{R_1 + R_2}$$

(*Reference* equations (2.14) and (2.15))

Step 2   Use the bias equation to calculate I_{CQ}.

$$I_{CQ} = \frac{V_{BB} - V_{BE}}{R_B/\beta + R_E}$$

(*Reference* equation (2.13))

Step 3   The dc load line equation is used to determine V_{CEQ}.

$$V_{CEQ} = V_{CC} - (R_E + R_C)I_{CQ} = V_{CC} - R_{dc}I_{CQ}$$

(*Reference* equation (2.12))

Step 4   The dc load line is constructed on the characteristic curves. Since we know that the ac load line intersects the dc load line at the Q-point, the ac load line is constructed from the equation

$$V'_{CC} = V_{CEQ} + I_{CQ}(R_{ac})$$

where R_{ac} is the ac equivalent resistance in the collector-emitter loop.

(*Reference* last equation in Section 2.8.1)

Step 5   Determining the maximum possible symmetrical output voltage swing requires the use of the load-line construction on the characteristic curves. If the Q-point is on the upper half of the ac load line, I_{CQ} is subtracted from the maximum value of i_C (the point where the ac load line intersects the i_C axis). This provides the maximum amplitude ac output current of the transistor. Alternatively, if the Q-point is on the lower half of the ac load line, I_{CQ} is the maximum amplitude ac output current of the transistor. Then, the maximum peak-to-peak symmetrical output voltage swing is given by

$$2i_C(\text{maximum amplitude}) \times (R_C \parallel R_L)$$

2.9.2   *Design Procedure*

In design problems, we work first with the collector-emitter side of the transistor rather than with the base side. There are two conditions to satisfy. The first condition places the Q-point in the center of the ac load line for maximum output voltage swing. The second condition limits I_{CQ} to the value required to provide symmetrical output for a designated intput. V_{CC}, V_{BE}, β, and R_L are usually specified. R_C and R_E are determined by the other specified conditions of voltage gain, current gain, and input resistance. This is considered in Chapter 3. For now, the values of R_C and R_E are given.

Step 1   To place the Q-point in the center of the load line, use the following equation.

$$I_{CQ} = \frac{V_{CC}}{R_{ac} + R_{dc}}$$

(*Reference* equation (2.29))

Step 2   Use the ac load line equation to determine V_{CEQ}.

$$V_{CEQ} = \frac{V'_{CC}}{2}$$

where

$$V'_{CC} = 2I_{CQ}R_{ac}$$

(*Reference* equation (2.30))

Step 3   If no other restrictions exist, select R_B for bias stability.

$$R_B = 0.1\ \beta R_E$$

(*Reference* equation (2.18))

Step 4   Use the bias equation to determine V_{BB}.

$$V_{BB} = V_{BE} + I_{CQ}\left(\frac{R_B}{\beta} + R_E\right)$$

(*Reference* equation (2.13))

Step 5   Find R_1 and R_2 from R_B and V_{BB}.

$$R_1 = \frac{R_B}{1 - V_{BB}/V_{CC}}$$

$$R_2 = \frac{R_B V_{CC}}{V_{BB}}$$

(*Reference* equations (2.16) and (2.17))

Step 6   Determine $v_{o(p-p)}$ (maximum peak-to-peak symmetrical output) as in Step 5 of the analysis procedure.

$$V_o = 2i_C \text{ (maximum amplitude)} \times (R_C \parallel R_L)$$

Example 2.3   Analysis

Determine the Q-point for the circuit given in Figure 2.22 if $R_1 = 1.5$ kΩ and $R_2 = 6$ kΩ. A 2N3903 transistor (see Appendix D) is used with $\beta = 140$, $R_E = 100$ Ω, and $R_C = R_L = 1$ kΩ.

SOLUTION   Using the step-by-step procedure of this section, we obtain

$$V_{BB} = \frac{R_1 V_{CC}}{R_1 + R_2} = \frac{1500 \times 5}{1500 + 6000} = 1 \text{ V}$$

$$R_B = \frac{R_1 R_2}{R_1 + R_2} = 1200 \ \Omega$$

We determine if the amplifier maintains bias stability with changes in β by checking $R_B < 0.1 \beta R_E = 0.1(140)(100) = 1400 \ \Omega$. Since the inequality holds, bias stability is maintained. We find the Q-point as follows:

$$I_{CQ} = \frac{V_{BB} - V_{BE}}{R_B/\beta + R_E} = \frac{1 - 0.7}{1200/140 + 100} = 2.76 \text{ mA}$$

We find $R_{ac} = R_C \parallel R_L = 500 \ \Omega$ and $R_{dc} = R_C + R_E = 1.1$ kΩ. V_{CEQ} is found as in Step 3.

$$V_{CEQ} = V_{CC} - I_{CQ}R_{dc} = 5 - (2.76 \times 10^{-3})(1.1 \times 10^3) = 1.96 \text{ V}$$

Then

$$V'_{CC} = V_{CEQ} + I_{CQ}R_{ac} = 1.96 + (2.76 \times 10^{-3})(500) = 3.34 \text{ V}$$

Since the Q-point is on the lower half of the ac load line, the maximum possible symmetrical output voltage swing is then

$$2I_{CQ}(R_C \parallel R_L) = 2(2.76 \times 10^{-3})(500) = 2.76 \text{ V}$$

Figure 2.22
CE amplifier circuit.

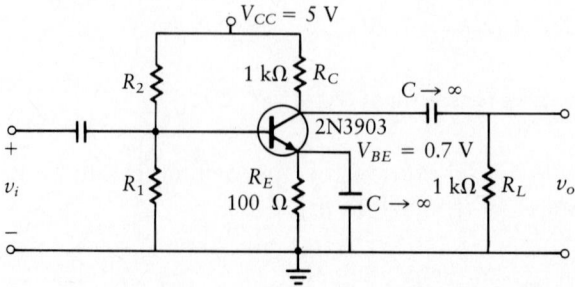

The Q-point in this example is not in the middle of the load line, so that output swing is not a maximum. However, if the input signal is small and maximum output is not required, a small I_{CQ} can be used to reduce the power dissipated in the circuit.   ◂┼

Example 2.4   **Design**

Select R_1 and R_2 for maximum output voltage swing in the circuit shown in Figure 2.22.

SOLUTION   Following the design steps of Section 2.9.2, we first determine I_{CQ} for the circuit:

$$I_{CQ} = \frac{V_{CC}}{R_{ac} + R_{dc}} = \frac{5}{500 + 1100} = 3.13 \text{ mA}$$

since

$$R_{ac} = R_C \parallel R_L = 500 \ \Omega$$

and

$$R_{dc} = R_E + R_C = 1100 \ \Omega$$

For maximum swing,

$$V'_{CC} = 2V_{CEQ}$$

V_{CEQ} is then given by

$$V_{CEQ} = (3.13 \text{ mA})(500 \ \Omega) = 1.56 \text{ V}$$

The intersection of the ac load line on the v_{CE}-axis is V'_{CC}. Since

$$V_{CEQ} = \frac{V'_{CC}}{2}$$

then

$$V'_{CC} = 3.12 \text{ V}$$

From the manufacturer's specification in Appendix D, β for the 2N3903 is approximately 140. R_B is set equal to 0.1 βR_E, so

$$R_B = 0.1(140)(100) = 1400\ \Omega$$

$$V_{BB} = (3.13 \times 10^{-3})\frac{1400}{140} + 100 + 0.7 = 1.044\ \text{V}$$

Since we know V_{BB} and R_B, we find R_1 and R_2:

$$R_1 = \frac{R_B}{1 - V_{BB}/V_{CC}} = \frac{1400}{1 - 1.044/5} = 1.77\ \text{k}\Omega$$

$$R_2 = \frac{R_B V_{CC}}{V_{BB}} = \frac{1400 \times 5}{1.044} = 6.7\ \text{k}\Omega$$

The maximum output voltage swing, ignoring the nonlinearities at saturation and cutoff, would then be

$$\text{maximum output swing} = 2I_{CQ}\,(R_C \parallel R_L)$$
$$= 2(3.13\ \text{mA})(500\ \Omega) = 3.13\ \text{V}$$

The load lines are shown on the characteristic curves of Figure 2.23.

We check the maximum power dissipated by the transistor to assure that it will not exceed the specifications. From equation (2.22), we have

$$P_{(\text{transistor})} = (1.56\ \text{V})(3.13\ \text{mA}) = 4.88\ \text{mW}$$

Figure 2.23   Load lines for Example 2.4.

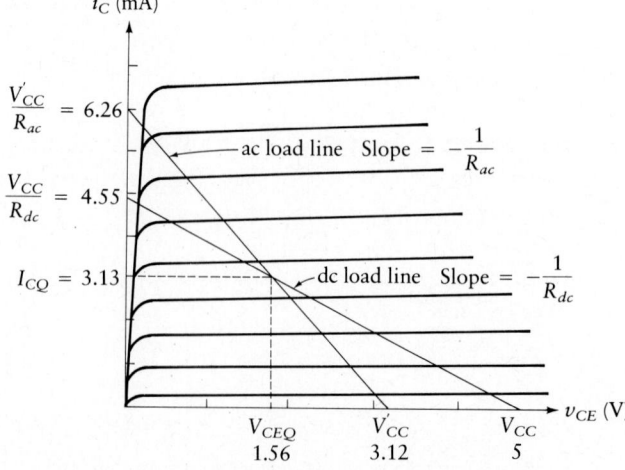

This is well within the 350 mW maximum given on the specification sheet. The maximum conversion efficiency is

$$\eta = \frac{P_o(\text{ac})}{P_{V_{CC}}(\text{dc})} \times 100 = \frac{(3.13 \times 10^{-3}/2)^2 1000/2 \times 100}{5 \times 3.13 \times 10^{-3} + 5^2/8470)} = 6.6\%$$ ⊁

Drill Problems

D2.9   Refer to Figure 2.19 and find the peak-to-peak output voltage swing when $R_1 = 2 \text{ k}\Omega$, $R_2 = 15 \text{ k}\Omega$, $R_E = 200 \ \Omega$, $R_C = 2 \text{ k}\Omega$, $R_L = 2 \text{ k}\Omega$, $\beta = 200$, $V_{BE} = 0.7 \text{ V}$, and $V_{CC} = 15 \text{ V}$.

Ans: 6.3 V peak-to-peak

D2.10   In Problem D2.9, design the amplifier for maximum symmetrical swing by finding the values of R_1 and R_2.

Ans: $R_1 = 4.5 \text{ k}\Omega$; $R_2 = 36 \text{ k}\Omega$

D2.11   What is the maximum symmetrical voltage swing for the configuration of Problem D2.10?

Ans.   8.8 V peak-to-peak

D2.12   What is the output power of the amplifier of Problem D2.10? What is the power supplied to the amplifier?

Ans: 4.9 mW; 71.7 mW

2.9.3   *Designing for Less than Maximum Swing*

As discussed earlier, it is not always desirable to design an amplifier for maximum possible swing. If the input signal is small, the operating point may move only a relatively small distance on either side of the Q-point and never get near saturation or cutoff. In that case, designing an amplifier with the Q-point in the middle of the load line wastes power. The power dissipated in the rest condition is greater than necessary for undistorted operation. In this section, we modify the previous design criteria to allow for placement of the Q-point below the center of the load line.

Suppose we wish to design for a quiescent current,

$$I_{CQ} = \delta I'_C \tag{2.31}$$

where I'_C is the intersection of the ac load line with the i_C axis and is seen to be (Figure 2.20)

$$I'_C = \frac{V'_{CC}}{R_{ac}} = I_{CQ} + \frac{V_{CEQ}}{R_{ac}} \qquad (2.32)$$

Here δ is a number between 0 and 1 and is equal to 0.5 for the maximum symmetrical swing case. Now since

$$I_{CQ} = \delta I'_C$$

we can solve equation (2.32) for V_{CEQ} to obtain

$$V_{CEQ} = \frac{(1 - \delta)I_{CQ}R_{ac}}{\delta} \qquad (2.33)$$

Since the Q-point must also lie on the dc load line, we have

$$V_{CEQ} = V_{CC} - I_{CQ}R_{dc} \qquad (2.34)$$

Equating equation (2.33) to equation (2.34) yields

$$\frac{(1 - \delta)I_{CQ}R_{ac}}{\delta} = V_{CC} - I_{CQ}R_{dc}$$

and solving for I_{CQ}, we obtain

$$I_{CQ} = \frac{V_{CC}}{(1 - \delta)R_{ac}/\delta + R_{dc}} \qquad (2.35)$$

Note that if $\delta = 0.5$, equation (2.35) reduces to

$$I_{CQ} = \frac{V_{CC}}{(R_{ac} + R_{dc})}$$

as found earlier.

2.10   Emitter-Follower (Common-Collector) Amplifier

The *emitter-follower (EF)*, or common-collector (CC), amplifier is illustrated in Figure 2.24. Its output is developed from the emitter to ground rather than from the collector to ground, as in the case of the CE. This type of amplifier configuration is used to obtain *current gain* and *power gain*.

The CE has a 180° phase shift between the base and collector voltages.

Figure 2.24
Emitter follower.

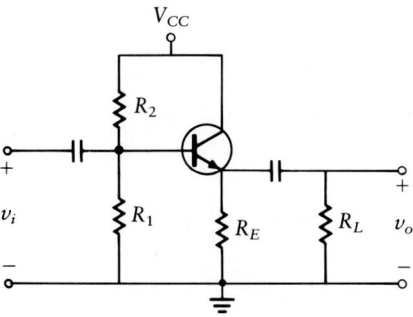

NOTE: *Throughout this text, when a capacitor in a circuit is unlabelled, assume its capacitance approaches infinity (i.e. it is a short circuit for all signal frequencies).*

That is, as the input signal increases in value, the output signal decreases. Alternatively, for an EF, the output signal is in phase with the input signal. The amplifier has a voltage gain of slightly less than unity. On the other hand, the current gain is significantly greater than 1. Note that the collector needs no resistor ($R_C = 0$), and no emitter bypass capacitor is required.

We analyze this circuit in the same manner as we did for the common emitter. The only differences are the values we use for R_{ac} and R_{dc}. For the emitter follower of Figure 2.24,

$$R_{ac} = R_E \parallel R_L$$

and

$$R_{dc} = R_E$$

and the dc load line is given by the equation

$$i_C = \frac{(V_{CC} - v_{CE})}{R_{dc}}$$

The ac load line, under conditions of maximum swing, is found in the same manner as for the common emitter circuit. For maximum swing, the Q-point is located at

$$I_{CQ} = \frac{V_{CC}}{R_{ac} + R_{dc}} = \frac{V_{CC}}{(R_E \parallel R_L) + R_E}$$

and

$$V_{CEQ} = I_{CQ}R_{ac} = I_{CQ}(R_E \parallel R_L)$$

2.10.1   *ac Analysis and Design of EF Amplifiers*

The procedures for both design and analysis of EF amplifier are the same as those for CE amplifiers. The only changes are in the equations for R_{ac}, R_{dc}, and the output voltage swing. The output swing for the EF is given by

$$V_{om} = 2i_C(\text{max amplitude}) \times (R_E \parallel R_L) \tag{2.36}$$

Example 2.5	**Design**

In the circuit of Figure 2.25(a), find the values of R_1 and R_2 that yield maximum symmetrical output swing as shown in Figure 2.25(b). Assume that a 2N2222 transistor is used (see Appendix D for data sheets) with an average β of 100.

SOLUTION

$$R_{dc} = R_E = 600\ \Omega$$

$$R_{ac} = R_E \parallel R_L = 300\ \Omega$$

$$I_{CQ} = \frac{V_{CC}}{R_{ac} + R_{dc}} = \frac{12}{600 + 300} = 13.3\ \text{mA}$$

Then

$$V_{CEQ} = I_{CQ}R_{ac} = (13.3 \times 10^{-3})(300) = 4\ \text{V}$$

Figure 2.25   EF amplifier for Example 2.5.

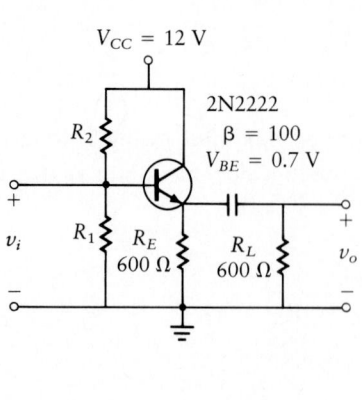

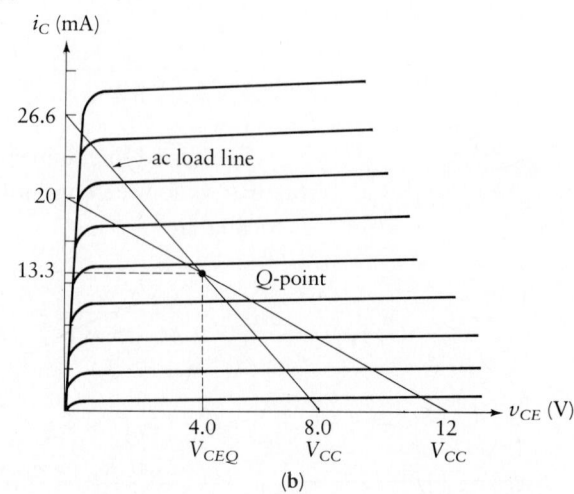

(a)   (b)

In order to reduce the effects of variations in β, we choose

$$R_B = 0.1\,\beta R_E = 0.1(100 \times 600) = 6\ \text{k}\Omega$$

$$V_{BB} = V_{BE} + I_{CQ}\left(\frac{R_B}{\beta} + R_E\right)$$

$$= 0.7 + 0.0133\left(\frac{6000}{1000} + 600\right) = 9.48\ \text{V}$$

From equations (2.16) and (2.17) we obtain

$$R_1 = \frac{R_B}{1 - V_{BB}/V_{CC}} = \frac{6000}{1 - 9.48/12} = 28.5\ \text{k}\Omega$$

$$R_2 = \frac{R_B V_{CC}}{V_{BB}} = \frac{6000 \times 12}{9.48} = 7.59\ \text{k}\Omega$$

From equation (2.36), we find

$$\text{maximum output swing} = 2I_{CQ}(R_E \parallel R_L)$$

$$= 2(0.0133)(300) = 7.98\ \text{V}$$

Example 2.6   **Analysis**

Find the Q-point and output voltage swing of the circuit of Figure 2.25(a) with $R_1 = 10\ \text{k}\Omega$ and $R_2 = 20\ \text{k}\Omega$.

SOLUTION Using equation (2.14) and equation (2.15), we have

$$R_B = R_1 \parallel R_2 = 6.67\ \text{k}\Omega$$

$$V_{BB} = \frac{R_1 V_{CC}}{R_1 + R_2} = \frac{12(10 \times 10^3)}{30 \times 10^3} = 4\ \text{V}$$

From equation (2.13), we have

$$I_{CQ} = \frac{V_{BB} - V_{BE}}{R_B/\beta + R_E} = \frac{4 - 0.7}{6670/100 + 600} = 4.9\ \text{mA}$$

The output swing is then given by

$$\text{output swing} = 2I_{CQ}(R_E \parallel R_L)$$

$$= 2(4.95 \times 10^{-3})(300) = 2.98\ \text{V}$$

Figure 2.26
Load lines for Example 2.6.

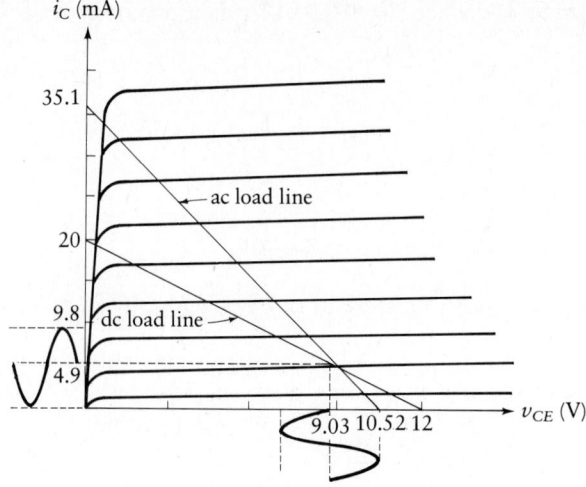

This is less than the maximum possible output swing. Continuing the analysis,

$$V_{CEQ} = V_{CC} - I_{CQ}R_E$$
$$= 12 - (4.95 \times 10^{-3})(600) = 9.03 \text{ V}$$
$$V'_{CC} = V_{CEQ} + I_{CQ}(R_E \parallel R_L)$$
$$= 9.03 + (4.95 \times 10^{-3})(300) = 10.52 \text{ V}$$
$$I'_C = \frac{10.52}{300} = 35.1 \text{ mA}$$

The load lines for this problem are shown in Figure 2.26   ▶┤

Drill Problems

D2.13   What is the maximum symmetrical voltage swing for the amplifier of Figure 2.24, where V_{CC} = 15 V, R_1 = 8 kΩ, R_2 = 2 kΩ, R_E = 1 kΩ, R_L = 1 kΩ, V_{BE} = 0.7 V, and β = 80?

Ans: 7.8 V peak-to-peak

D2.14   In Problem D2.13, redesign the amplifier for the maximum symmetrical voltage swing. What are the new values of R_1, R_2, and $V_{o(p-p)}$?

Ans: 36.4 kΩ; 10.3 kΩ; 10 V peak-to-peak

D2.15   What is the conversion efficiency of the amplifier design in Problem D2.14?

Ans: 8%

PROBLEMS

2.1 Find the location of the Q-point of the amplifier shown in Figure P2.1, where an *npn* transistor is used. Assume that V_{CC} = 10 V, V_{BB} = 1 V, R_B = 10 kΩ, R_C = 2 kΩ, R_E = 100 Ω, β = 100, I_{CBO} = 0, and V_{BE} = 0.7 V. What is the new location of the Q-point if R_B = 1 kΩ?

2.2 Find the Q-point of the amplifier shown in Figure P2.1 if a *pnp* transistor is used and V_{CC} = − 12 V, V_{BB} = − 1V, R_B = 10 kΩ, R_C = 1 kΩ, R_E = 100 Ω, β = 100, and V_{BE} = −0.7 V. What is the new Q-point location if the value of R_B is changed to 1 kΩ?

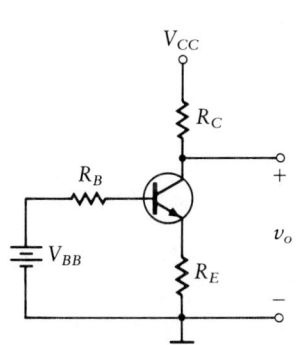

Figure P2.1

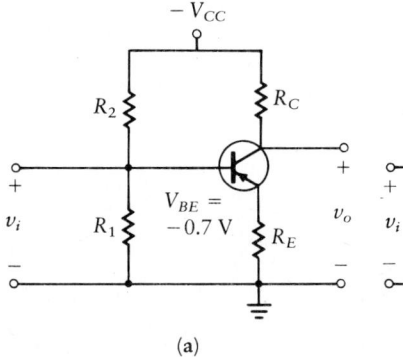

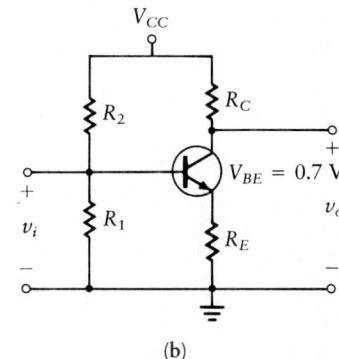

(a)　　　　　　　(b)

Figure P2.2

2.3 Find the values of R_1 and R_2 necessary to place the Q-point of the circuit of Figure P2.2(a) in the center of the dc load line. Assume that V_{CC} = − 25 V, R_C = 2 kΩ, and R_E = 1 kΩ, and β has the following value.
a. β = 150
b. β = 100
c. β = 50

2.4 Find the maximum peak-to-peak swing of i_C in the circuit of Figure P2.2(b). Assume that R_1 = 1 kΩ, R_2 = 7 kΩ, V_{CC} = 24 V, R_C = 2 kΩ, R_E = 400 Ω, and β = 100. Draw the dc load line.

2.5 Repeat Problem 2.4 if the value of R_2 changes to 10 kΩ and all other values remain the same.

2.6 With the circuit of Problem 2.5, find the values of R_1 and R_2 that yield the maximum possible peak-to-peak swing of i_C. Draw the dc load line.

2.7 For the amplifier of Problem 2.5, calculate the following:
a. Power supplied by the battery.
b. Power dissipated by R_1, R_2, R_E and R_C.
c. Power dissipated by the collector junction.

2.8   For the amplifier of Problem 2.6, calculate the following:
a. Power supplied by the battery.
b. Power dissipated by R_1, R_2, R_E and R_C.
c. Power dissipated by the collector junction.

Compare your answers with those of Problem 2.7.

2.9   For the amplifier of Figure P2.2(b) where $R_1 = 3$ kΩ, $R_2 = 20$ kΩ, $R_C = 1$ kΩ, $R_E = 200\ \Omega$, $\beta = 100$, and $V_{CC} = 20$ V, find the location of the Q-point. The transistor is replaced with another of different β. Find the minimum required value of β so that I_{CQ} does not change by more than 10%.

2.10 Use the amplifier of Figure P2.3.
a. Find the values of R_1 and R_2 to achieve $I_{CQ} = 10$ mA.
b. Find the output symmetrical swing for the resistors of part (a).
c. Draw the ac and dc load lines.
d. Sketch the waveforms for i_C and v_{CE}.

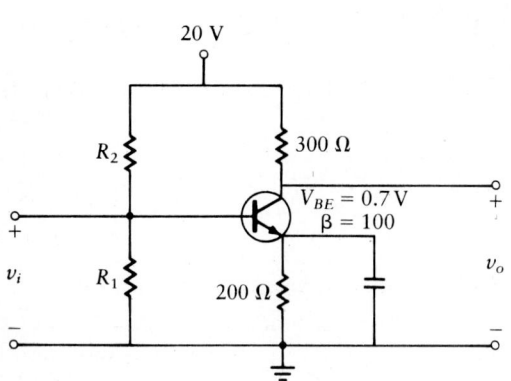

Figure P2.3   **Figure P2.4**

2.11 Use the amplifier of Figure P2.3.
a. Find the values of R_1 and R_2 for $I_{CQ} = 30$ mA.
b. Find the output symmetrical swing using the values of part (a).
c. Draw the ac and dc load lines.
d. Sketch the waveforms for i_C and v_{CE}.

2.12 Use the amplifier of Figure P2.3.
a. Find the values of R_1 and R_2 to achieve maximum symmetrical swing.
b. Determine the value of maximum symmetrical swing achieved in part (a).
c. Draw the ac and dc load lines.
d. Sketch waveforms for i_C and v_{CE}.

2.13 Use the amplifier of Figure P2.4.
  a. Find the values of R_1 and R_2 for $I_{CQ} = 8$ mA.
  b. Determine the symmetrical output voltage swing for the values of part (a).
  c. Draw the ac and dc load lines.
  d. Determine the power dissipated by the transistor and the power dissipated by R_L.

2.14 Use the amplifier shown in Figure P2.4.
  a. Find the values of R_1 and R_2 for $I_{CQ} = 4$ mA.
  b. Determine the symmetrical output voltage swing for the values of part (a).
  c. Draw the ac and dc load lines.
  d. Determine the power dissipated by the transistor and the power dissipated by R_L.

2.15 Use the amplifer of Figure P2.4.
  a. Find the values of R_1 and R_2 needed to achieve maximum symmetrical swing.
  b. Determine the symmetrical output voltage swing for the values of part (a).
  c. Draw the ac and dc load lines.
  d. Determine the power dissipated by the transistor and the power dissipated by R_L.

2.16 Determine the value of R_C for maximum symmetrical output swing for the circuit of Figure P2.5. Assume that a *pnp* transistor is used. Draw the dc and ac load lines. What is the peak-to-peak value of maximum symmetrical output voltage?

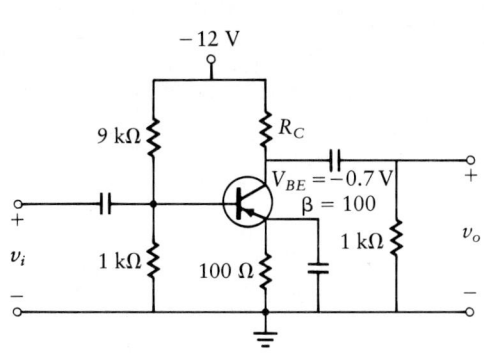

Figure P2.5

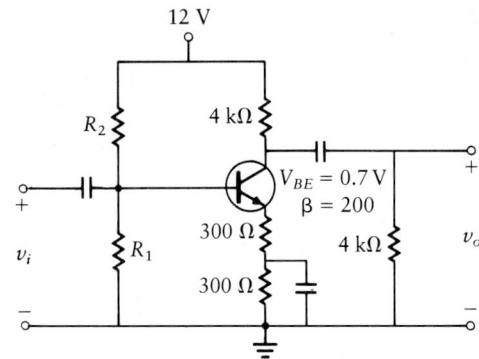

Figure P2.6

2.17 Select I_{CQ} and V_{CEQ} for maximum symmetrical output voltage swing for the circuit of Figure P2.6.

    a. Determine the values of R_1 and R_2 in order to achieve this operating point.

    b. Find the maximum symmetrical output voltage swing.

    c. Determine the power dissipated by the transistor and the power delivered to the load.

2.18 Use the circuit of Figure P2.7.

    a. Find I_{CQ} and V_{CEQ}.

    b. Determine if the amplifier is stable for large changes in β. You may assume that β is in the range $150 < \beta < 250$.

    c. Draw the load lines.

    d. Determine the symmetrical output voltage swing.

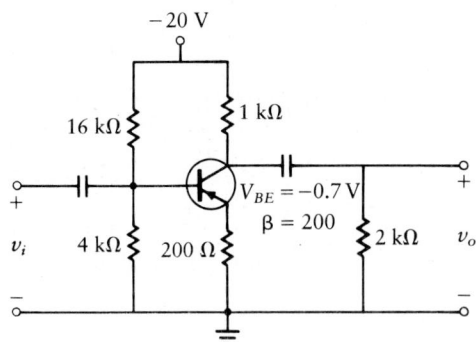

Figure P2.7

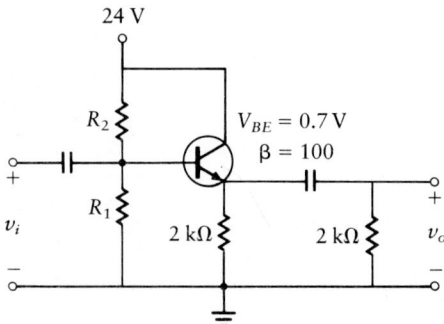

Figure P2.8

2.19 Use the circuit of Figure P2.8.

    a. Find the values of R_1 and R_2 if $I_{CQ} = 6$ mA.

    b. Draw the ac and dc load lines.

    c. Determine the symmetrical output voltage swing.

    d. Find the power dissipated by the transistor and the power delivered to the load.

2.20 Use the circuit shown in Figure P2.8.

    a. Find the values of R_1 and R_2 if $I_{CQ} = 10$ mA.

    b. Draw the ac and dc load lines.

    c. Determine the symmetrical output voltage swing.

    d. Find the power dissipated by the transistor and the power delivered to the load.

2.21 Use the circuit shown in Figure P2.8.

    a. Find the values of R_1 and R_2 needed to achieve maximum possible symmetrical swing.

b. Draw the ac and dc load lines.

c. Determine the maximum symmetrical output voltage swing.

d. Find the power dissipated by the transistor and the power delivered to the load.

2.22 Use the emitter follower amplifier of Figure P2.9.

a. Determine the values of V_{CEQ} and I_{CQ}.

b. Find the output voltage swing.

c. Find the power delivered to the load and the required power rating of the transistor.

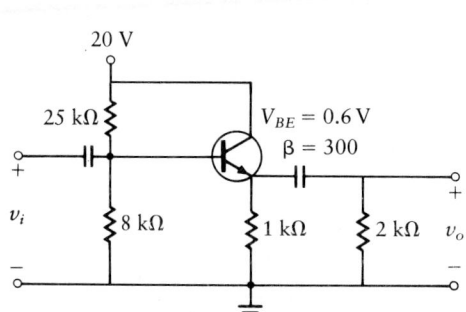

Figure P2.9

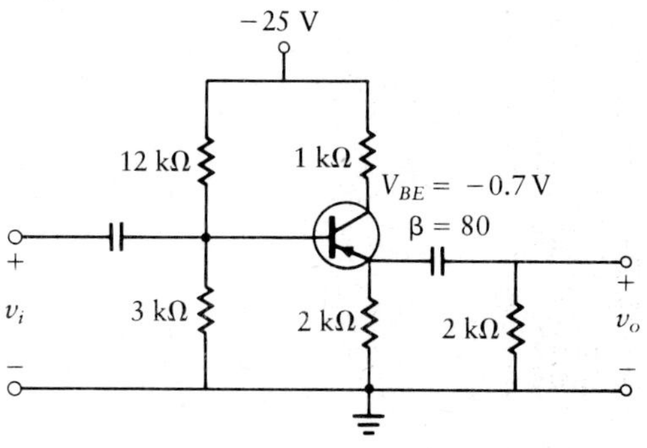

Figure P2.10

2.23 Use the emitter follower amplifier shown in Figure P2.10.

a. Determine the values of V_{CEQ} and I_{CQ}.

b. Draw the dc and ac load lines.

c. Determine the value of symmetrical output voltage swing.

d. The 1-kΩ resistor is now bypassed with a capacitor. Describe the changes that occur in the operation of the circuit.

2.24 Determine the maximum symmetrical output voltage swing for the circuit of Figure P2.10 by selecting new values of R_1 and R_2. What are the values of these resistors? Draw the new load lines.

2.25 The resistor, R_C, is bypassed by a capacitor in the circuit of Figure P2.10. Determine the maximum symmetrical output voltage swing by selecting new values of R_1 and R_2. What are the values of these resistors? Find the power delivered to the load and the necessary power rating of the transistor.

2.26 By selecting new values of R_1 and R_2, determine the maximum symmetrical output voltage swing for the circuit of Figure P2.8 if the load resistor is reduced to 500 Ω. Find the power delivered to the load and the required power rating of the transistor.

3

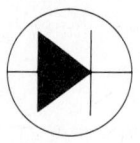

DESIGN OF BIPOLAR JUNCTION TRANSISTOR AMPLIFIERS

3.0 Introduction

In Chapter 2 we discuss the biasing, or dc operation, of BJT circuits. The transistor is biased to obtain the required peak-to-peak output voltage swing. In the current chapter we concentrate upon *small-signal analysis* through the use of equivalent circuit techniques. We describe the use of the equivalent circuit method using *hybrid parameters*. The transistor parameters required to accomplish this analysis can be obtained from manufacturer's data sheets. The data are provided by the manufacturers in a format as shown in the examples of Appendix D. The design method presented here reduces the dependence of the circuit upon the variations in the transistor parameters.

The chapter begins with an introduction to hybrid parameters that are used to develop a transistor mathematical model. We derive the equations for input resistance, voltage gain, current gain, and output resistance for the various amplifier configurations (i.e., CE, CC, and CB). In each case, both a precise and an approximate relationship are developed. Design examples are presented for each case. Multistage amplifier analysis is also discussed and example problems are given.

3.1 Analysis of Two-Port Networks

3.1.1 *Gain Impedance Formula*

We derive an important relationship between the ac quantities of voltage gain, A_v, and current gain, A_i. Figure 3.1 shows a block diagram of a four-terminal (two-port) network with input resistance R_{in} and load resistance, R_L, which are assumed to be resistors. In general, they can be complex impedances.

The relationships between the input variables, v_i and i_{in}, and the output variables, v_o and i_o, are derived directly from Ohm's law. That is,

$$v_o = i_o R_L$$

$$v_i = i_{in} R_{in}$$

Forming the ratio of these two equations yields

$$\frac{v_o}{v_i} = \frac{i_o}{i_{in}} \frac{R_L}{R_{in}}$$

Voltage gain is defined as

$$A_v = \frac{v_o}{v_i}$$

and current gain is defined as

$$A_i = \frac{i_o}{i_{in}}$$

Combining the various equations, we find

$$A_v = \frac{A_i R_L}{R_{in}} \tag{3.1}$$

Equation (3.1) is called the *gain impedance formula* and is used throughout this text.

Figure 3.1
Two-port network.

3.1.2 *Hybrid Parameters*

There are a number of ways to characterize four-terminal networks. In a four-terminal system, there are four circuit variables: the input voltage and current and the output voltage and current. These four variables can be related by various equations, depending upon which variables are considered to be independent and which are dependent.

The *hybrid parameter* (*h*-parameter) equation pair (and its equivalent circuit) is often used for BJT circuit analysis. The equation pair is specified as follows:

$$v_1 = h_{11}i_1 + h_{12}v_2 \tag{3.2}$$

$$i_2 = h_{21}i_1 + h_{22}v_2 \tag{3.3}$$

The first digit of the subscript on h denotes the dependent variable and the second digit denotes the independent variable associated with the particular h-parameter. Hence, for example, h_{12} relates v_2 to v_1. The values of h are assumed to be constants.

When h-parameters are used to describe a transistor network, the equation pair is written as follows:

$$v_1 = h_i i_1 + h_r v_2 \tag{3.4}$$

$$i_2 = h_f i_1 + h_o v_2 \tag{3.5}$$

where the h-parameters are defined as follows:

$h_i = h_{11} =$ input resistance of transistor

$h_r = h_{12} =$ reciprocal voltage gain of transistor

$h_f = h_{21} =$ forward current gain of transistor

$h_o = h_{22} =$ output conductance of transistor

When h-parameters are applied to transistor networks, the parameters take on a practical significance as related to the transistor performance. The circuit developed using the h-parameters is shown in Figure 3.2. A simple application of Kirchhoff's laws to the circuit of Figure 3.2 shows that it satisfies equation (3.4) and equation (3.5).

Figure 3.2
Equivalent circuit for
h-parameters.

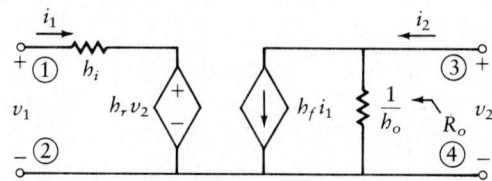

When the input and output parameters are individually set equal to zero, each hybrid parameter either represents a resistance, a conductance, a ratio of two voltages, or a ratio of two currents. The following equations are derived from equations (3.4) and (3.5). Following each equation are the units associated with the parameter and the name given to it.

$$R_{in} = h_i = \frac{v_1}{i_1}\bigg|_{v_2=0}$$

ohms: short-circuit input resistance with v_2 shorted

$$h_f = \frac{i_2}{i_1}\bigg|_{v_2=0}$$

dimensionless: forward current gain with v_2 shorted

$$h_r = \frac{v_1}{v_2}\bigg|_{i_1=0}$$

dimensionless: reverse voltage gain with i_1 open circuited

$$Y_{out} = h_o = \frac{i_2}{v_2}\bigg|_{i_1=0}$$

siemens (formerly mhos): output conductance with i_1 open-circuited

Although these parameters are ideally constant, the numerical values depend upon the transistor configuration. Thus, for example, if terminal 1 in Figure 3.2 is the base, 2 is the emitter and 3 is the collector, the circuit represents a CE configuration. Similarly, the transistor can be modeled as a CB configuration if terminals 1, 2, and 3 are the emitter, base, and collector, respectively.

It is helpful to have a way to distinguish among the three wiring configurations, i.e., CE, CC, and CB. A second subscript is added to each hybrid parameter to provide this bookeeping distinction. Thus, for example, a CE circuit normally has h_i in the base circuit, and it is renamed h_{ie}. Similarly for the CB, h_i is renamed h_{ib}, and for the CC, it is named h_{ic}. The three values of this short-circuit input impedance are related to each other as

$$h_{ie} = (1 + \beta)h_{ib} \approx \beta h_{ib} = h_{ic} \tag{3.6}$$

Figure 3.3 shows a CE amplifier with two different equivalent circuits. Although the h-parameter model defines the second subscript as associated with the type of amplifier configuration, h_{ib} and h_{ie} are values of resistance that are based upon the operating point of the amplifier and the location of these resistances within the equivalent circuit. In this case, the subscripts have nothing to do with the amplifier configuration. The same concept is also applied to h_{fe}, which refers to β regardless of how the transistor is placed within the amplifier configuration.

In each equivalent circuit, we have made the (usually reasonable) simplification that $h_r = h_o = 0$. Figure 3.3(b) uses the CE model, where the transistor has been replaced by the circuit of Figure 3.2 with terminal 1 as the base, 2 as the emitter, and 3 as the collector. In Figure 3.3(c), the transistor is replaced

Figure 3.3
CE and equivalent
circuits.

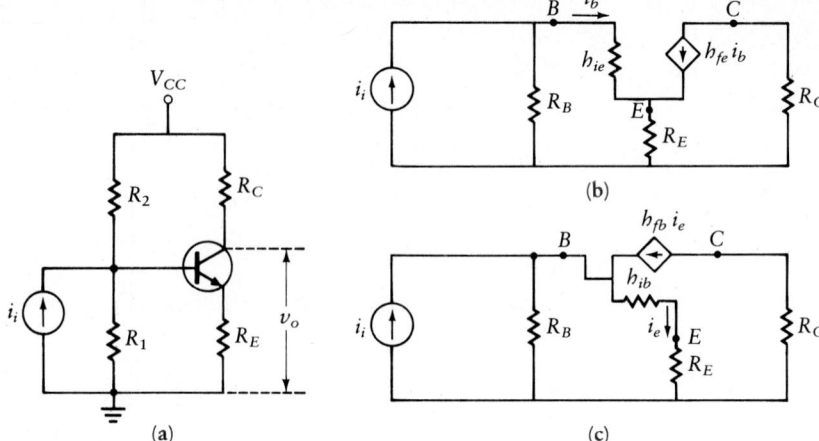

by the CB model. That is, using Figure 3.2, terminal 1 is the emitter, 2 is the base, and 3 is the collector.

For small-signal current, we see that h_{fe} is the ratio of the change in output current (Δi_C) to the change in input current (Δi_B). Recall that this relationship is also the defining expression for β. As a result,

$$h_{fe} = \beta = \frac{\Delta i_C}{\Delta i_B}\bigg|_{v_{CE} = \text{constant}}$$

The actual value of β is a function of the operating point (I_{CQ}) of the transistor. In the flat portion of the i_C versus v_{CE} curve with i_B constant, there is little change in β. As the transistor approaches saturation, β starts dropping. As the transistor approaches cutoff, β also approaches zero.

Manufacturer's specifications often present a graph of h_{fe} as a function of i_C. The output conductance, h_o, of the transistor is usually small. Therefore, the output resistance, r_o, is usually large. As an example, let us examine the manufacturer's specification sheet for the 2N3903 (see Appendix D). It can be seen that the output conductance varies from 4 μS to 65 μS as i_C varies from 0.1 mA to 10 mA. This means that the output resistance varies from 15 kΩ to 250 kΩ. As an example of a typical value, when I_{CQ} is equal to 1 mA, the transistor output resistance is approximately 115 kΩ. With a typical load of 4 kΩ, the parallel combination is approximately 4 kΩ (since 115 kΩ is much larger than 4 kΩ) and r_o can be assumed to be infinite. The reverse voltage gain of the network, h_r, is also small and is ignored in the transistor equivalent circuit used in this text.

Another two-port model that is used in the study of transistor circuits is

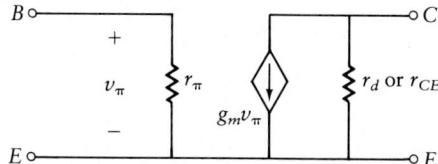

Figure 3.4
Hybrid-π model
equivalent circuit.

the *hybrid-π* model, which is important when the transistor is used at high frequency. It includes the effects of parameters that become significant at high frequency (this is discussed in Chapter 10).

A low-frequency small-signal hybrid-π transistor model is shown in Figure 3.4. The model for low frequency is similar to that of the *h*-parameter model for the CE. The major difference is that the current-controlled current source of Figure 3.2 has been replaced by a voltage-controlled current source. In fact, a comparison of the parameters is easily accomplished as follows:

$$g_m = \frac{1}{h_{ib}}$$

$$r_\pi = h_{ie}$$

$$r_{CE} = \frac{1}{h_o}$$

3.2 Short-Circuit Input Resistance

We explore the parameter values before discussing the actual use of equivalent circuits for design and analysis. We first develop equations for h_{ie} and h_{ib}, which display the dependence of these parameters upon the location of the operating point.

We begin with the equation for the operating characteristics of the base-emitter junction, which acts as a diode, as presented in Chapter 1.

$$i_B = I_o \left[\exp\left(\frac{v_{BE}}{V_T}\right) - 1 \right]$$

This equation is now differentiated with respect to v_{BE} to obtain

$$\frac{di_B}{dv_{BE}} = \frac{I_o}{V_T} \exp\left(\frac{v_{BE}}{V_T}\right)$$

In the forward-bias region, i_B is approximately given by

$$i_B = I_o \exp\left(\frac{v_{BE}}{V_T}\right)$$

Then

$$\frac{di_B}{dv_{BE}} = \frac{i_B}{V_T}$$

But from the definition of h_{ie}, we obtain (see Figure 3.2)

$$h_{ie} = \left.\frac{\Delta v_1}{\Delta i_1}\right|_{v_2=0} = \frac{dv_{BE}}{di_B} = \frac{V_T}{I_{BQ}}$$

Now recall that

$$h_{ib} = \frac{h_{ie}}{\beta}$$

Finally,

$$h_{ib} = \frac{V_T}{|\beta I_{BQ}|} = \frac{V_T}{|I_{CQ}|} \tag{3.7}$$

Equation (3.7) is known as the *Shockley equation*. Using the approximation $V_T = 26$ mV, which applies to the BJT, equation (3.7) becomes

$$h_{ib} = \frac{0.026 \text{ V}}{|I_{CQ}|} \tag{3.8}$$

Equation (3.8) is useful in estimating the value of h_{ib} to be used in the equivalent circuit of Figure 3.3(c) (or g_m in the equivalent circuit of Figure 3.4).

3.3 CE Parameters

The equations that define ac amplifier parameters are summarized in Table 3.1 and are derived in the following sections. Note that the table gives two defining equations for each parameter. These are designated as the *long form* and the *short form*. The short-form equation is a simplified version of the long-form equation and is derived by making assumptions about the relative sizes of some of the parameters. We point out the required assumptions as each equation is derived and the assumptions are in the table.

This double set of equations is used as the basis for our problem-solving technique. In general, we use the short-form equation because the parameters are not known more accurately. Then we verify that the assumptions necessary to make this short form valid do, in fact, hold. If short-form conditions apply, the component values are within the manufacturing tolerances. If short-form conditions do not apply, the calculations must be repeated using the long form equations.

Table 3.2 summarizes the equivalent circuits used in the derivations.

3.3.1　Input Resistance, R_{in}

The hybrid parameter circuit is used to derive the input resistance equation for each type of amplifier configuration. Figure 3.5 modifies the CE amplifier of Figure 3.3 by adding a capacitor-coupled load resistance. The basic circuit is shown in Figure 3.5(a), and two forms of equivalent circuit are shown in Figure 3.5(b) and (c). Note that we have omitted the reverse voltage gain, h_r, and the output admittance, h_o, from the model.

The equivalent circuit of Figure 3.5(b) is used to derive the input resistance, R_{in}. Usually β is large enough that we can approximate $1 + \beta$ as β. The current in R_E is therefore approximately equal to βi_b. If the circuit is now split as in Figure 3.5(c), the current through the resistor in series with h_{ie} in the input loop is i_b. Thus, to keep the voltage at the same value existing in the original circuit, we must change the resistor value to βR_E. The input resistance is then found by writing KVL and KCL equations for the input loop.

$$R_{in} = \frac{v_i}{i_{in}} = R_B \parallel (h_{ie} + \beta R_E) = \frac{R_B(h_{ie} + \beta R_E)}{R_B + h_{ie} + \beta R_E} \tag{3.9}$$

We substitute $h_{ie} = \beta h_{ib}$ to obtain

$$R_{in} = \frac{R_B(h_{ib} + R_E)}{R_B/\beta + h_{ib} + R_E} \tag{3.10}$$

If R_B is negligible compared to βR_E, equation (3.10) can be further simplified to the form given in equation (3.11).

$$R_{in} \approx \frac{R_B(h_{ib} + R_E)}{h_{ib} + R_E} = R_B \tag{3.11}$$

Table 3.1 Formula for Different Amplifier Configurations

Type	Voltage Gain (A_v)	Current Gain (A_i)	Input Resistance (R_{in})
Common emitter	Long forms: $$\dfrac{-(R_L\|R_C)}{h_{ib} + R_E}$$ Short forms, if $h_{ib} \ll R_E$ and $R_B \ll \beta R_E$: $$\dfrac{-R_L\|R_C}{R_E}$$	$$\dfrac{-R_B}{\dfrac{R_B}{\beta} + h_{ib} + R_E}\quad \dfrac{R_C}{R_L + R_C}$$ $$\dfrac{-R_B}{\dfrac{R_B}{\beta} + R_E}\ \dfrac{R_C}{R_C + R_L}$$	$$\dfrac{R_B\,(h_{ib} + R_E)}{\dfrac{R_B}{\beta} + h_{ib} + R_E}$$ R_B
Common collector (Emitter follower)	Long forms: $$\dfrac{R_E\|R_L}{h_{ib} + (R_E\|R_L)}$$ Short forms, if $h_{ib} \ll R_E\|R_L$ and $R_B \ll (R_E\|R_L)\beta$: 1	$$\dfrac{R_B}{\dfrac{R_B}{\beta} + h_{ib} + (R_E\|R_L)}\ \dfrac{R_E}{R_E + R_L}$$ $$\dfrac{R_B}{R_L}$$	$$\dfrac{R_B\,[h_{ib} + (R_E\|R_L)]}{\dfrac{R_B}{\beta} + h_{ib} + (R_E\|R_L)}$$ R_B
Common base	Long forms: $$\dfrac{R_C\|R_L}{h_{ib} + \dfrac{R_B}{\beta}}$$ Short forms, if $h_{ib} \ll R_E$ and $R_B \ll \beta R_E$: $$\dfrac{R_C\|R_L}{h_{ib} + \dfrac{R_B}{\beta}}$$	$$\dfrac{+R_C}{R_C + R_L}\ \dfrac{R_E}{R_E + h_{ib} + \dfrac{R_B}{\beta}}$$ $$\dfrac{R_C}{R_C + R_L}$$	$$R_E\|\left(h_{ib} + \dfrac{R_B}{\beta}\right)$$ $$h_{ib} + \dfrac{R_B}{\beta}$$

Table 3.2 Equivalent Circuits for Different Amplifier Configurations

Type	Circuit	Equivalent Circuit	Equivalent Circuit with R_E Bypassed
Common emitter			
Common collector			
Common base			With R_B bypassed

Figure 3.5
CE configuration.

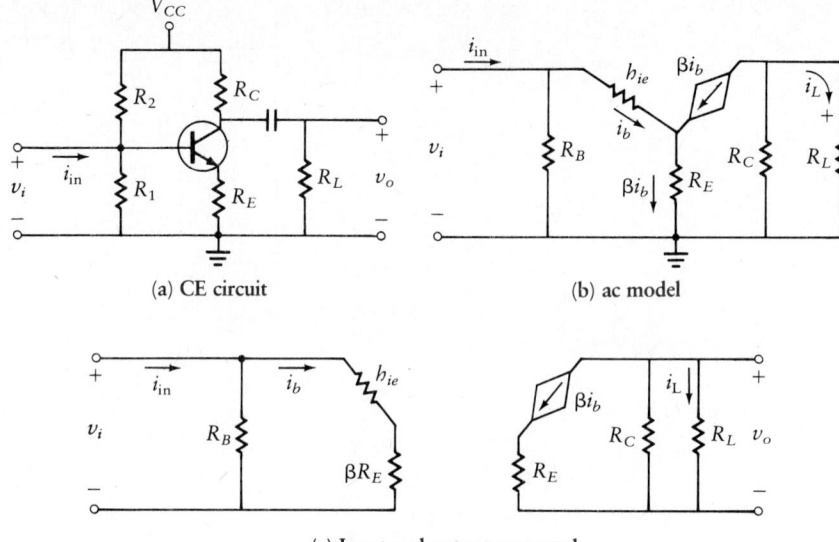

(a) CE circuit

(b) ac model

(c) **Input and output separated**

Equation (3.10) is the long-form equation and it requires only one approximation, that is, $\beta \gg 1$. Equation (3.11) is the short-form equation because it requires the additional approximation that $R_B \ll \beta R_E$, often expressed as $R_B \leq 0.1 \, \beta R_E$.

3.3.2   *Voltage Gain, A_v*

The voltage gain is found from the definition

$$A_v = \frac{v_o}{v_i} = \frac{i_L R_L}{v_i}$$

The current-division relationship applied at the output of Figure 3.5(b) yields

$$i_L = \frac{-R_C \beta i_b}{R_L + R_C}$$

The negative sign results from the opposite direction of βi_b with respect to i_L. Then

$$A_v = -\frac{\beta R_L i_b}{v_i} \frac{R_C}{R_L + R_C}$$

We wish to obtain an expression for A_v that does not contain other variables.

That is, we need to eliminate i_b and v_{in} from the above equation. Applying current division at the input yields the following expression for i_b:

$$i_b = \frac{R_B i_{in}}{R_B + h_{ie} + \beta R_E}$$

We then substitute this into the equation for A_v to obtain

$$A_v = \frac{-\beta R_L}{v_i} \frac{R_C}{R_L + R_C} \frac{R_B i_{in}}{R_B + h_{ie} + \beta R_E}$$

Since $v_i = i_{in} R_{in}$, we have

$$A_v = \frac{-\beta R_L}{i_{in} R_{in}} \frac{R_C}{R_L + R_C} \frac{R_B i_{in}}{R_B + h_{ie} + \beta R_E}$$

The i_{in} cancels from numerator and denominator. Since the parameter R_{in} is solved for in terms of transistor parameters and circuit elements, we can simplify this further. Substituting R_{in} from equation (3.9), we obtain

$$A_v = \frac{-\beta R_L R_C}{R_L + R_C} \frac{R_B}{R_B + h_{ie} + \beta R_E} \frac{R_B + h_{ie} + \beta R_E}{R_B(h_{ie} + \beta R_E)}$$

When like terms are canceled from the numerator and denominator and we recognize $h_{ie} = \beta h_{ib}$, this expression simplifies to the long form given in equation (3.12):

$$A_v = \frac{-\beta(R_L \parallel R_C)}{h_{ie} + \beta R_E} = \frac{-R_L \parallel R_C}{h_{ib} + R_E} \tag{3.12}$$

If $h_{ib} << R_E$, the equation further reduces to the short form given by equation (3.13):

$$A_v = \frac{-(R_L \parallel R_C)}{R_E} \tag{3.13}$$

If R_E is bypassed with a large capacitor so that the ac impedance is small, h_{ib} is no longer much less than R_E and the long form of equation (3.12) must be used. This becomes

$$A_v = \frac{-(R_L \parallel R_C)}{h_{ib}}$$

We can combine this with the h_{ib} approximation of equation (3.8) to obtain

$$A_v = \frac{-(R_L \parallel R_C)I_{CQ}}{0.026}$$

which shows that with R_E bypassed, the voltage gain of the amplifier is dependent upon the value of I_{CQ}.

3.3.3 *Current Gain, A_i*

The current gain is found from the gain impedance formula, equation (3.1).

$$A_i = \frac{R_{in}A_v}{R_L}$$

Substituting for A_v and R_{in} from equations (3.9) and (3.12), we obtain the long-form current gain of equation (3.14):

$$A_i = -\frac{R_B(h_{ie} + \beta R_E)}{(R_B + h_{ie} + \beta R_E)R_L}\frac{\beta(R_L \parallel R_C)}{h_{ie} + \beta R_E}$$

$$= -\frac{R_B R_C}{(R_B/\beta + h_{ib} + R_E)(R_C + R_L)} \tag{3.14}$$

If $R_B \ll \beta R_E$ and $h_{ib} \ll R_E$, the current gain simplifies to the short-form expression of equation (3.15):

$$A_i = -\frac{R_B R_C}{R_E(R_L + R_C)} \tag{3.15}$$

These equations for the CE amplifier are summarized in Table 3.1.

3.3.4 *Output Resistance, R_o*

In the equivalent circuit for the transistor, as shown in Figure 3.2, the output circuit contains an ideal current generator in parallel with a resistance of value $1/h_o$. The ideal current source exhibits an infinite impedance, since we measure output resistance with the input open circuited (i.e., $i_b = 0$). The output resistance for the CE transistor is then

$$r_o = \frac{v_2}{i_2} = \frac{1}{h_{oe}}$$

The parameter h_{oe} is usually small enough to be neglected in calculations, so the output resistance of the transistor becomes infinite in magnitude. The value of h_{oe} can be determined by consulting the transistor specifications. The output resistance, R_o, of a CE amplifier is the value of R_C when r_o is large. Most junction transistors typically have an r_o in excess of 50 kΩ.

Example 3.1   Capacitor-Coupled CE Amplifier (Design)

Design a CE amplifier (see Figure 3.6) with $A_v = -10$, $\beta = 200$ and $R_L = 1$ kΩ. A *pnp* transistor is used and maximum symmetrical output swing is required.

SOLUTION   Refer to Figure 3.7 during this derivation. In Section 2.9.2 we learn how to select R_1 and R_2 for maximum symmetrical output swing when the other circuit parameters are known. The only additional information provided here is the value of A_v, yet there are two additional unknowns, R_C and R_E. Thus, we need another equation. We shall choose the other equation to force $R_C = R_L = 1$ kΩ (see Problem 3.17 for justification). We first try using the short-form equation for A_v in order to solve for R_E:

$$A_v = \frac{-(R_L \parallel R_C)}{R_E}$$

When known values are substituted into this equation, we find $R_E = 50$ Ω. We need to find h_{ib} in order to see if use of the short-form equation is justified. We first find R_{ac} and R_{dc} and then calculate the Q-point as follows:

$$R_{ac} = R_E + R_C \parallel R_L = 550 \text{ Ω}$$

$$R_{dc} = R_E + R_C = 1050 \text{ Ω}$$

Figure 3.6
CE amplifier.

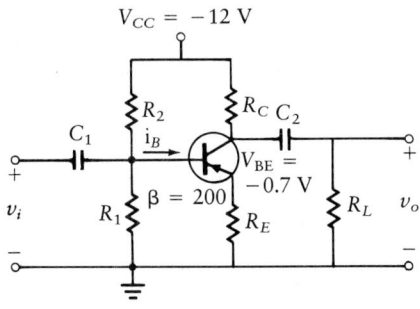

Figure 3.7
Load lines for
Example 3.1.

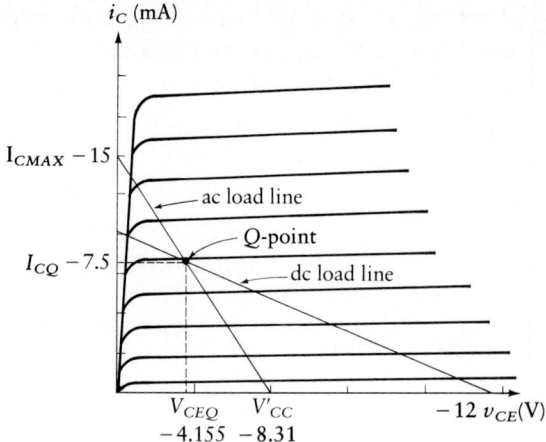

With R_{ac} and R_{dc} determined, the design of this circuit now parallels the step-by-step procedure for ac design given in Section 2.9.2. The first step is to calculate the quiescent collector current needed to place the Q-point in the center of the ac load line (i.e., maximum swing). The equation is

$$I_{CQ} = \frac{V_{CC}}{R_{ac} + R_{dc}} = -7.5 \text{ mA}$$

We now test the validity of the short-form equation for A_v. The quantity h_{ib} is found from equation (3.8) as follows:

$$h_{ib} = \frac{26 \text{ mV}}{|I_{CQ}|} = \frac{26 \text{ mV}}{7.5 \text{ mA}} = 3.47 \text{ }\Omega$$

Then

$$R_E = 50 \text{ }\Omega - h_{ib} = 46.5 \text{ }\Omega$$

Since h_{ib} is much less than R_E, the short-form equation is valid, and we continue with the design.

If there were a current gain or input resistance specification for this design, we would use it to solve for the value of R_B. Since there is no such specification, we use the expression

$$R_B = 0.1 \beta R_E = 0.1(200)(50) = 1 \text{ k}\Omega$$

Because we are, in effect, forcing R_B to be less than βR_E by a factor of 10, the short form expression for A_i is probably valid. Therefore,

$$A_i = \frac{-R_B R_C}{R_E(R_C + R_L)} = \frac{-1000 \times 1000}{50 \times 2000} = -10$$

We now check this result by recalculating the current gain using the long form. We have

$$R_B = 0.1 \, \beta R_E = 0.1(200)(46.5) = 930 \ \Omega$$

Then

$$A_i = \frac{-R_B}{R_B/\beta + h_{ib} + R_E} \frac{R_C}{R_C + R_L} = -8.5$$

This shows that using the short-form expression results in an error greater than 10%. We therefore abandon the short form and continue using the long form expressions as follows:

$$V_{CEQ} = V_{CC} - (R_C + R_E)I_{CQ}$$

$$= -12 - (1046)(-0.0075) = -4.155 \text{ V}$$

$$V_{BB} = I_{CQ}\left(R_E + \frac{R_B}{\beta}\right) + V_{BE}$$

$$= (-0.0075)\left(46.5 + \frac{930}{200}\right) + (-0.7) = -1.08 \text{ V}$$

$$R_1 = \frac{R_B}{1 - V_{BB}/V_{CC}} = \frac{930}{1 - 1.08/12} = 1.02 \text{ k}\Omega$$

$$R_2 = \frac{R_B V_{CC}}{V_{BB}} = \frac{(930)(-12)}{-1.08} = 10.3 \text{ k}\Omega$$

$$R_{\text{in}} = \frac{R_B(h_{ib} + R_E)}{R_B/\beta + h_{ib} + R_E} = \frac{930(50)}{930/200 + 50} = 851 \ \Omega$$

$$R_o = R_C = 1 \text{ k}\Omega \qquad \text{(assuming } r_o \text{ is large compared to } R_C\text{)}$$

The maximum peak-to-peak output swing is given by

$$2 \, |I_{CQ}| \, (R_C \parallel R_L) = 2(.0075)(500) = 7.5 \text{ V}$$

The power delivered into the load and the maximum power dissipated by the transistor are found using equations from Sections 2.9 and 2.11.

$$P_L = \frac{(I_{CQ})^2 R_L}{8} = 7 \text{ mW}$$

$$P_T = V_{CEQ} I_{CQ} = 30.9 \text{ mW}$$

The load lines for this circuit are shown in Figure 3.7. If R_{in} or A_i had been specified (instead of A_v), then the equation for R_{in} or A_i could be used to determine R_B. Next, the equation

$$R_B = 0.1 \, \beta R_E$$

could be used to solve for R_E. Thus,

$$R_E = \frac{R_B}{0.1\beta}$$ ▶+

3.4   Nonlinearities of BJTs

In Section 2.4.2, we learned that a transistor operates in a linear manner except in the saturation and cutoff regions. Operating in or near these regions causes distorted reproduction of an input signal. Therefore, the shaded regions shown in Figure 3.8 should be avoided. Designers frequently discard 5% of the characteristic curve in the vicinity of the saturation region and 5% of the curve near the cutoff region.

Using these guidelines and assuming the I_{CQ} has been placed in the center of the ac load line, the undistorted peak-to-peak output voltage is given by equation (3.16).

$$v_{o(p-p)} = 0.9 \times 2 \, |I_{CQ}| \, (R_L \parallel R_C)$$

$$= 1.8 \, |I_{CQ}| \, (R_L \parallel R_C) \tag{3.16}$$

Suppose now that I_{CQ} is not in the middle of the load line. The circuit will have a reduced output swing for a symmetrical input signal. Figures 3.9(a) and (b) show this reduced swing graphically. The maximum symmetrical output swing can be determined as follows. Let us assume that the input is a sinusoid so that

Figure 3.8
Nonlinear portions of
characteristic curve.

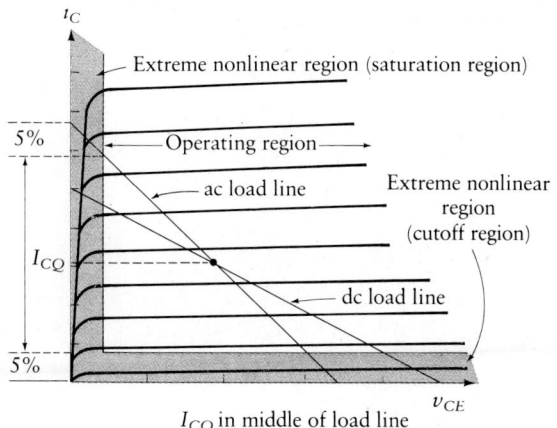

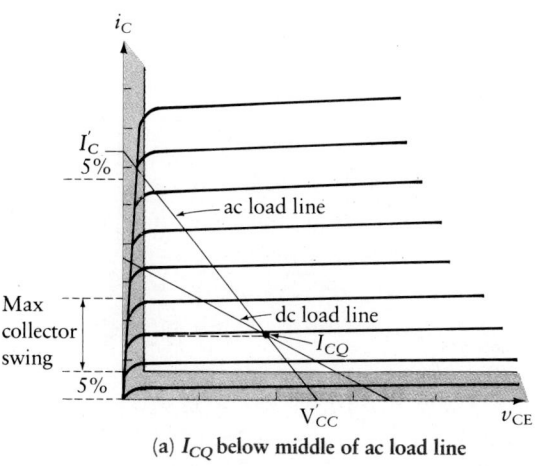

(a) I_{CQ} below middle of ac load line

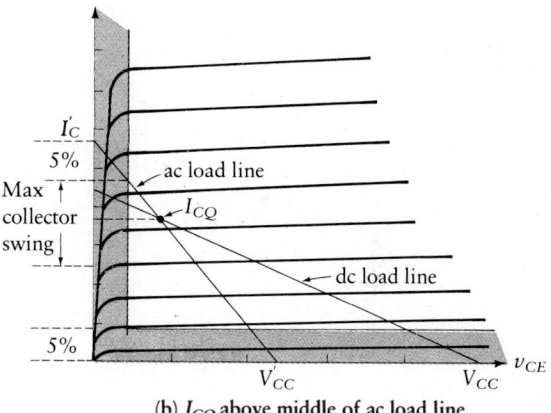

(b) I_{CQ} above middle of ac load line

Figure 3.9   Reduced swing on load line.

$$i_c(t) = I_{Cmax}\sin \omega t$$

Then

$$v_o(\text{max undistorted swing}) = 2I_{Cmax}(R_L \parallel R_C)$$

For the case where I_{CQ} is below the center of the ac load line as in Figure
3.9(a),

$$I_{Cmax} = I_{CQ} - 0.05 \times I_C'$$

where, from Figure 3.9(a),

$$I_C' = \frac{V_{CC}'}{R_{ac}}$$

Then

$$v_o(\text{max undistorted swing}) = 2(I_{CQ} - 0.05I_C')(R_L \parallel R_C) \qquad (3.17a)$$

For the case where I_{CQ} is above the center of the ac load line, as in Figure 3.9(b),

$$I_{C\,max} = 0.95I_C' - I_{CQ}$$

Then

$$v_o(\text{max undistorted swing}) = 2(0.95I_C' - I_{CQ})(R_L \parallel R_C) \qquad (3.17b)$$

Drill Problems

D3.1   The CE amplifier of Figure 3.5(a) has $V_{CC} = 15$ V, $R_L = \infty$, $V_{BE} = 0.7$ V, $R_C = 5$ kΩ, $R_E = 500$ Ω and $\beta = 200$. Determine R_1, R_2, A_v, A_i, and the maximum undistorted symmetrical output voltage when the Q-point is in the middle of the dc load line.

> **Ans.:** $R_1 = 11.1$ kΩ; $R_2 = 104$ kΩ; $A_v = -10$;
> $A_i = -20$; $v_{o(p-p)} = 12.2$ V

D3.2   In Problem D3.1, R_E is bypassed with a capacitor. What are the values of R_1, R_2, A_v, A_i, and R_o?

> **Ans:** $R_1 = 11.1$ kΩ; $R_2 = 101$ kΩ; $A_v = -275$;
> $A_i = -147$; $R_{in} = 2.67$ kΩ; $R_o = 5$ kΩ

D3.3   The *pnp* transistor amplifier shown in Figure 3.6 requires a voltage gain $A_v = v_o/v_i = -5$ and an input resistance, $R_{in} = 1$ kΩ. $R_L = 5$ kΩ, $V_{CC} = -12$V, $V_{BE} = -0.7$ V and $\beta = 200$. Determine the current gain, maximum output swing, and other resistor values.

> **Ans:** $A_i = -1$; $v_{o\,max} = 6.35$ V;
> $R_1 = 1.1$ kΩ; $R_2 = 8.5$ kΩ

D3.4   Design a CE amplifier (Figure 3.6) with a voltage gain of $A_v = -60$, $R_L = 5$ kΩ and $R_{in} = 5$ kΩ. Design for the maximum voltage output swing.

Ans: $R_E = 25.2\ \Omega;\ R_1 = 13.4\ k\Omega;\ R_2 = 179\ k\Omega;$
$A_i = -60;\ v_{o(p-p)} = 7.12\ V$
(Note that the amplifier is not bias stable.)

D3.5 Design a CE amplifier (Figure 3.6) for maximum output swing with $R_L = 6\ k\Omega,\ A_v = -60,$ and $A_i = -20$.

Ans: $R_E = 30\ \Omega;\ R_1 = 2.67\ k\Omega;\ R_2 = 40\ k\Omega;$
$R_{in} = 2\ k\Omega;\ v_o(\text{p-p}) = 7.12\ V$

3.5 Parameters for CC (EF) Amplifier

3.5.1 *Input Resistance, R_{in}*

The EF (emitter follower) circuit is shown in Figure 3.10. As before, C_1 and C_2 are considered to be short circuits for midrange frequencies.

If we write a KVL equation around the input loop and solve for the input resistance, we obtain (assuming $1 + \beta \approx \beta$)

$$R_{in} = R_B \parallel [h_{ie} + \beta(R_E \parallel R_L)]$$

$$= \frac{R_B\,[h_{ie} + \beta(R_E \parallel R_L)]}{R_B + h_{ie} + \beta(R_E \parallel R_L)} \tag{3.18}$$

This is the long-form equation for R_{in}. In comparing this to the entry in Table 3.1, recall that $h_{ie} = \beta h_{ib}$. If $R_B \ll \beta(R_E \parallel R_L)$, then R_B can be dropped from the denominator and the short form, equation (3.19), results:

$$R_{in} = R_B \tag{3.19}$$

Figure 3.10
CC amplifier.

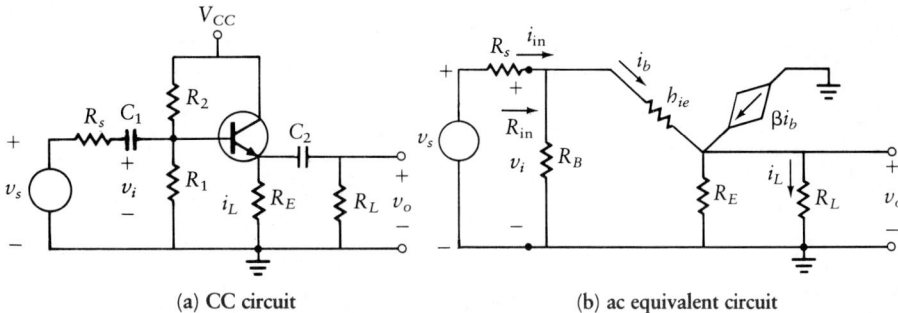

(a) CC circuit   (b) ac equivalent circuit

3.5.2   *Voltage Gain, A_v*

The voltage gain is given by

$$A_v = \frac{v_o}{v_i} = \frac{v_o}{i_{in}R_{in}}$$

Thus, the voltage gain is

$$A_v = \frac{\beta i_b(R_E \parallel R_L)}{i_{in}R_{in}}$$

We now apply current division in the input circuit to obtain

$$i_b = i_{in}\frac{R_B}{R_B + h_{ie} + \beta(R_E \parallel R_L)} \tag{3.20}$$

We next substitute the expression for i_b into the A_v equation to obtain

$$A_v = \frac{\beta i_{in}(R_E \parallel R_L)R_B}{[R_B + h_{ie} + \beta(R_E \parallel R_L)]i_{in}R_{in}}$$

Finally, substituting equation (3.18) for R_{in}, and cancelling i_{in} we obtain the long-form expression of equation (3.21).

$$A_v = \frac{\beta(R_E \parallel R_L)}{h_{ie} + \beta(R_E \parallel R_L)} = \frac{R_E \parallel R_L}{h_{ib} + (R_E \parallel R_L)} \tag{3.21}$$

If h_{ib} is small compared to $R_E \parallel R_L$, as is usually the case, we obtain the short-form expression

$$A_v = 1$$

Notice that the gain is positive since v_{in} is in phase with v_o.

3.5.3   *Current Gain, A_i*

Since

$$i_o = i_L = \frac{i_b\beta R_E}{R_E + R_L}$$

and by inverting equation (3.20), we obtain

$$i_{\text{in}} = \frac{i_b[R_B + h_{ie} + \beta(R_E \parallel R_L)]}{R_B}$$

then the long form for A_i is as shown in equation (3.22).

$$A_i = \frac{i_o}{i_{\text{in}}} = \frac{\beta i_b R_E R_B}{(R_E + R_L)i_b} \frac{1}{R_B + h_{ie} + \beta(R_E \parallel R_L)}$$

$$= \frac{R_B}{R_B/\beta + h_{ib} + (R_E \parallel R_L)} \frac{R_E}{R_E + R_L} \tag{3.22}$$

If h_{ib} and R_B/β are both much smaller than the parallel combination of R_E and R_L, then the following short-form equation results:

$$A_i = \frac{R_B}{R_L} \tag{3.23}$$

Note that current gain is positive for the EF amplifier.

3.5.4 Output Resistance, R_o

An alternative equivalent circuit for an EF amplifier is shown in Figure 3.11(a). Here we have used the CB model of the transistor instead of the CE employed in Figure 3.10. The resistance of the input voltage source is shown as R_s. The reduced equivalent of Figure 3.11(b) is found in a manner similar to that used in Figure 3.5(c). The current in h_{ib} is approximately β times the current in the circuitry to the left of h_{ib}. Therefore, when the controlled current source is removed, R_s and R_B have currents through them that are β times the actual currents. To maintain the same voltages, the resistor values must be divided by β. We obtain the output resistance of this circuit as follows:

$$R_o = \left(h_{ib} + \frac{R_s \parallel R_B}{\beta} \right) \parallel R_E \tag{3.24}$$

Figure 3.11
Output resistance of
EF configuration.

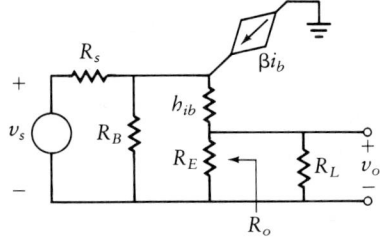

(a) Equivalent circuit—EF amplifier

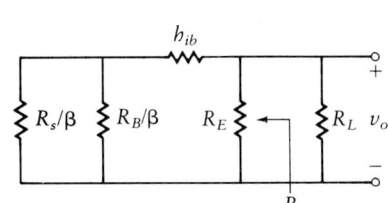

(b) Reduced equivalent circuit to find R_o

The output resistance is dependent upon the input parameters R_s and R_B. This is in contrast to the result for the CE amplifier, where R_o depends only upon R_C (see Section 3.3.4).

Example 3.2   Capacitor-Coupled CC Amplifier (Design)

Design a single-stage *npn* CC amplifier (Figure 3.10) with $\beta = 60$, $V_{BE} = 0.7$ V, $R_s = 1$ kΩ, and $V_{CC} = 12$ V. Determine the circuit element values for the stage to achieve $A_i = 10$ with a 100 Ω load resistor.

SOLUTION   We must select R_1, R_2, and R_E, but, again we have only two equations. These two equations are specified by the current gain and the placement of the Q-point. We shall, therefore, begin by constraining R_E to be equal to R_L. This yields a third equation. Therefore,

$$R_E = R_L = 100 \ \Omega$$

Now finding the load-line slopes,

$$R_{ac} = R_L \parallel R_E = 50 \ \Omega$$

$$R_{dc} = R_E = 100 \ \Omega$$

We now use the step-by-step design procedure introduced in Section 2.9.2. Since the amplitude of the input is not specified, we choose the quiescent current to place the Q-point in the center of the ac load line.

$$I_{CQ} = \frac{V_{CC}}{R_{ac} + R_{dc}} = 80 \text{ mA}$$

$$V_{CEQ} = I_{CQ} R_{ac} = 4 \text{ V}$$

We now check to see if the long- or short-form equation should be used to find R_B; h_{ib} is found from

$$h_{ib} = \frac{26 \text{ mV}}{|I_{CQ}|} = \frac{26 \text{ mV}}{80 \text{ mA}} = 0.33 \ \Omega$$

Since h_{ib} is insignificant compared to $R_E \parallel R_L$, it can be ignored. Because this is one of the conditions for use of the short-form equations, we first find R_B from the short-form current-gain equation.

$$A_i = \frac{R_B}{R_L} = \frac{R_B}{100} = 10$$

$$R_B = 1000 \ \Omega$$

A second condition for use of the short form is

$$R_B << \beta(R_E \parallel R_L)$$

Now that R_B has been found from the short-form equation, we can check this assumption.

$$0.1 \ \beta(R_E \parallel R_L) = (0.1)(60)(50) = 300 \ \Omega$$

Because 1000 Ω is larger than 300 Ω, we must go back and use the long-form equation. (Before continuing, you should convince yourself that you understand what we just did. It is similar to the guess-and-check technique often used in integral calculus.) The long-form equation yields

$$A_i = \frac{\beta R_E R_B}{(R_E + R_L)[R_B + (R_E \parallel R_L)\beta]}$$

where we have neglected h_{ib}. We solve for R_B from this equation, with the result

$$R_B = 1500 \ \Omega$$

V_{BB} is found as in Step 4 of the design procedure presented in Section 2.9.2:

$$V_{BB} = 0.7 + 0.08 \left(\frac{1.5 \times 10^3}{60} + 100 \right) = 10.7 \ \text{V}$$

Continuing with the design as presented earlier, we find

$$R_1 = 13.8 \ \text{k}\Omega$$

and

$$R_2 = 1.68 \ \text{k}\Omega$$

The voltage gain is approximately unity. The input resistance is found from equation (3.18).

$$R_{\text{in}} = R_B \parallel \beta(R_E \parallel R_L) = 1.5 \ \text{k}\Omega \parallel 3 \ \text{k}\Omega = 1 \ \text{k}\Omega$$

The output resistance is calculated from equation (3.24):

$$R_o = \left[0.33 + \frac{1000 \parallel 1500}{60} \right] \parallel 100 = 9.36 \ \Omega$$

The maximum peak-to-peak symmetrical output swing is given by equation (3.16), where we are interpreting maximum swing to mean the largest excursion without significant distortion (i.e., removing 5% of characteristic range on each end). Recall that distortion occurs when the circuit operation approaches cutoff or saturation.

$$v_{o(p-p)} = 1.8 \, |I_{CQ}|(R_E \parallel R_L) = 7.2 \ \text{V}$$

The power dissipated in the load, P_L, and the maximum power required of the transistor, P_T, are

$$P_L = \frac{(0.9 I_{CQ}/2)^2 R_L}{2} = 64.8 \ \text{mW}$$

$$P_T = I_{CQ} \, V_{CEQ} = 320 \ \text{mW} \qquad\qquad \blacktriangleright\!\!+$$

Drill Problems

D3.6   Design an EF amplifier (Figure 3.10) that has $A_i = 15$, $V_{CC} = 18$ V, $\beta = 100$, $R_s = 0$, $V_{BE} = 0.7$ V and $R_L = 200 \ \Omega$. Find the peak-to-peak undistorted output voltage.

   Ans: $R_1 = 28$ kΩ; $R_2 = 5.05$ kΩ; $R_E = 200 \ \Omega$;
   $v_{o(p-p)} = 10.8$ V

D3.7   Design an EF amplifier that has $R_{\text{in}} = 2$ kΩ, $R_C = 100 \ \Omega$, $V_{CC} = 18$ V, $\beta = 100$, $V_{BE} = 0.7$ V and $R_L = 200 \ \Omega$.

   Ans: $R_E = 200 \ \Omega$; $R_1 = 4.89$ kΩ ; $R_2 = 5.1$ kΩ;
   $A_i = 10$; $v_{o(p-p)} = 6.48$ V

3.6   Parameters for CB Amplifier

The CB amplifier is shown in Figure 3.12. The CB circuit is often drawn in the horizontal orientation, as shown in Figure 3.12(a). However, the circuit is more easily understood when drawn as in Figure 3.12(b). From this configuration, it is easily seen that the dc biasing is identical to that of the CE amplifier.

Figure 3.12
CB amplifier.

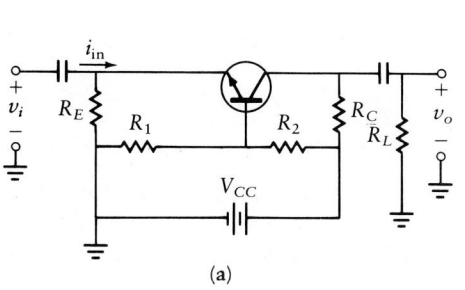 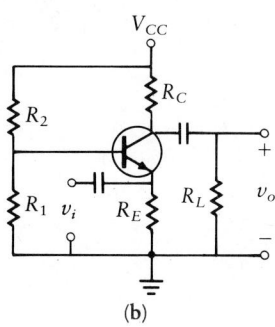

(a)   (b)

Figure 3.13
CB amplifier equivalent circuit.

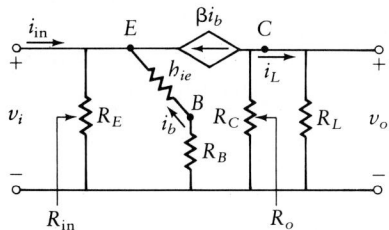

3.6.1   *Input Resistance, R_{in}*

The equivalent hybrid circuit for the CB is shown in Figure 3.13, where the CE hybrid model is used. R_B is the parallel combination of R_1 and R_2. The long-form equation for R_{in} is derived as follows. The current in R_E is $i_{in} + (1 + \beta)i_b$. In the following analysis, as throughout this text, we assume that β is large enough to permit substituting β for $1 + \beta$. Thus,

$$v_i = R_E(i_{in} + \beta i_b)$$

$$= -i_b(h_{ie} + R_B)$$

Substituting i_b from the second equation into the first yields

$$v_i = R_E\left[i_{in} - \frac{\beta v_i}{h_{ie} + R_B}\right]$$

Combining terms and solving for R_{in}, we have

$$R_{in} = \frac{R_E}{1 + R_E\beta/(h_{ie} + R_B)}$$

$$= \frac{R_E(h_{ie} + R_B)}{h_{ie} + R_B + \beta R_E}$$

$$= \frac{R_E(h_{ib} + R_B/\beta)}{h_{ib} + R_B/\beta + R_E} = R_E \parallel \left(h_{ib} + \frac{R_B}{\beta}\right) \tag{3.25}$$

The short-form equation is obtained by assuming that $h_{ib} \ll R_E$ and $R_B \ll \beta R_E$. Then

$$R_{in} = h_{ib} + \frac{R_B}{\beta} \tag{3.26}$$

Equation (3.26) indicates one of the most serious limitations of the CB configuration: Low input resistance. Both h_{ib} and R_B/β are usually only a few ohms, so R_{in} is quite small.

3.6.2   *Current Gain, A_i*

The current gain for the circuit of Figure 3.13 is found as follows:

$$A_i = \frac{i_L}{i_{in}} = -\frac{\beta i_b}{i_{in}} \frac{R_C}{R_C + R_L}$$

From the previous derivation for R_{in}, we have

$$i_b = \frac{-v_i}{h_{ie} + R_B} = \frac{-i_{in}R_{in}}{h_{ie} + R_B}$$

$$= \frac{-R_E i_{in}}{\beta R_E + h_{ie} + R_B}$$

We then substitute the i_b expression into the A_i equation and simplify to derive the long-form expression of equation (3.27).

$$A_i = \frac{R_E}{R_E + h_{ib} + R_B/\beta} \frac{R_C}{R_C + R_L} \tag{3.27}$$

Then, if $R_B \ll \beta R_E$ and $h_{ib} \ll R_E$, we obtain the short-form expression of equation (3.28).

$$A_i = \frac{R_C}{R_C + R_L} \tag{3.28}$$

3.6.3   *Voltage Gain, A_v*

The gain impedance formula of equation (3.1) is used to find A_v. We use A_i from equation (3.27) and R_{in} from equation (3.25) to obtain the long-form expression of equation (3.29):

$$A_v = A_i \frac{R_L}{R_{in}} = \frac{R_C \parallel R_L}{h_{ib} + R_B/\beta} \tag{3.29}$$

We cannot further simplify equation (3.29) since h_{ib} is approximately equal to R_B/β. If a bypass capacitor is added between base and ground, R_B/β is deleted from equation (3.29) and the expression simplifies to

$$A_v = \frac{R_L \parallel R_C}{h_{ib}}$$

Note that the voltage gain increases significantly with the addition of this bypass capacitor.

3.6.4   *Output Resistance, R_o*

As in the case of the CE amplifier, the dependent-current generator, βi_b, exhibits a high resistance. Therefore,

$$R_o = R_C.$$

Note that since R_E does not appear in the equations for R_{in}, A_i, A_v, or R_o, it may be chosen so that the inequalities, $R_B \ll \beta R_E$ and $h_{ib} \ll R_E$ are easily satisfied. In the examples and problems, we select a value for R_E.

Example 3.3   **Capacitor-Coupled CB Amplifier (Design)**

Design a CB amplifier using an *npn* transistor (Figure 3.12) with $\beta = 100$, $V_{CC} = 24$ V, $R_L = 2$ kΩ, $R_E = 400$ Ω and $V_{BE} = 0.7$ V. Design this amplifier for a voltage gain of 20.

SOLUTION   Again, we need an additional constraint, so we set

$$R_C = R_L = 2 \text{ k}\Omega$$

Then from equation (3.29)

$$h_{ib} + \frac{R_B}{\beta} = \frac{R_C \parallel R_L}{A_v} = 50 \ \Omega$$

$$R_{ac} = 1400 \ \Omega$$

$$R_{dc} = 2400 \ \Omega$$

$$I_{CQ} = \frac{V_{CC}}{R_{ac} + R_{dc}} = 6.32 \ \text{mA}$$

We check the conditions for the short-form equation.

$$h_{ib} = \frac{0.026}{I_{CQ}} = 4.12 \ \Omega$$

which is much less than R_E, so we may be able to use the short form.

$$R_B = \beta(50 - 4.13) = 4.59 \ \text{k}\Omega$$

which is much less than βR_E. Therefore, both conditions are met, and we can use the short-form expressions to calculate A_i and R_{in}.

$$A_i = \frac{R_C}{R_C + R_L} = \frac{2000}{(2000 + 2000)} = 0.5$$

$$R_{in} = h_{ib} + \frac{R_B}{\beta} = 4.12 + \frac{4590}{100} = 50 \ \Omega$$

We again use the bias equation of Section 2.9.2 to find the parameters of the input bias circuitry.

$$V_{BB} = V_{BE} + I_{CQ}\left(\frac{R_B}{\beta} + R_E\right)$$

$$= 0.7 + (6.32 \times 10^{-3})\left(\frac{4.59 \times 10^3}{100} + 400\right) = 3.52 \ \text{V}$$

The bias resistors are then given by

$$R_1 = \frac{R_B}{1 - V_{BB}/V_{CC}} = \frac{4.59 \times 10^3}{1 - 3.52/24} = 5.38 \ \text{k}\Omega$$

$$R_2 = \frac{R_B V_{CC}}{V_{BB}} = \frac{(4.59 \times 10^3)(24)}{3.52} = 31.3 \ \text{k}\Omega$$

The maximum peak-to-peak undistorted output voltage is

$$V_{o(p-p)} = 1.8 \ I_{CQ}(R_C \parallel R_L) = 11.38 \ \text{V}$$

Example 3.4 **Capacitor-Coupled CB Amplifier (Analysis)**

An *npn* transistor is connected in a CB configuration, as shown in Figure 3.12(b). The voltage source is $V_{CC} = 20$ V, $\beta = 200$, $V_{BE} = 0.7$ V, $R_E = 200$ Ω, $R_1 = 5$ kΩ, $R_2 = 80$ kΩ, and $R_C = R_L = 5$ kΩ. A large capacitor is placed between the base of the transistor and ground. Determine the voltage gain, current gain, input impedance, and maximum undistorted symmetrical output voltage swing.

SOLUTION We find the Thevenin equivalent of the base circuitry.

$$R_B = R_1 \parallel R_2 = 5 \text{ k}\Omega \parallel 80 \text{ k}\Omega = 4.7 \text{ k}\Omega$$

$$V_{BB} = 20 \times \frac{5 \text{ k}\Omega}{85 \text{ k}\Omega} = 1.18 \text{ V}$$

The Q-point location is found by writing a KVL equation around the base-emitter loop:

$$V_{BE} + I_{CQ} \left(R_E + \frac{R_B}{\beta} \right) = V_{BB}$$

where we assume that $I_C = I_E$. Substituting values and solving for I_{CQ} yields

$$I_{CQ} = \frac{1.18 - 0.7}{(4700/200 + 200)} = 2.13 \text{ mA}$$

Then

$$h_{ib} = \frac{26 \text{ mV}}{2.13 \text{ mA}} = 12.21 \ \Omega$$

We use equations (3.27) and (3.29) with $R_b = 0$ to find A_i and A_v as follows:

$$A_i = \frac{200}{2(200 + 12.21)} = 0.47$$

$$A_v = \frac{5000 \parallel 5000}{12.21} = 205$$

Note that we have not included R_B in the formula for A_v and A_i, since it is bypassed by a large capacitor.

Solving for R_{in} with $R_B = 0$ from equation (3.25), we obtain

$$R_{\text{in}} = 12.21 \parallel 200 = 11.5 \ \Omega$$

In order to determine the maximum output voltage swing, we evaluate the ac and dc load-line equations to determine whether I_{CQ} is above or below the center of the ac load line.

$$V_{CEQ} = V_{CC} - (R_C + R_E)I_{CQ}$$
$$= 20 - 5.2 \text{ k}\Omega \ (2.13 \text{ mA}) = 8.92 \text{ V}$$

The ac load line intersects the axis at

$$V'_{CC} = V_{CEQ} + I_{CQ}R_{ac}$$

where

$$R_{ac} = R_C \parallel R_L + R_E = 2.7 \text{ k}\Omega$$

Then

$$V'_{CC} = 8.92 + 2.13 \text{ mA}(2.7 \text{ k}\Omega) = 14.67 \text{ V}$$

$$I'_C = \frac{V'_{CC}}{R_{ac}} = \frac{14.67}{2.7 \text{ k}\Omega} = 5.4 \text{ mA}$$

Note that the Q-point is below the center of the load line since $I_{CQ} = 2.13$ mA and the center is at $5.4/2 = 2.7$mA. Therefore, using the appropriate equation from Section 3.4, we obtain the undistorted peak-to-peak output voltage swing,

$$v_{o(p\text{-}p)} = 2(I_{CQ} - 0.05I'_C)(R_L \parallel R_C)$$
$$= 2(2.13 - 0.05 \times 5.4)(2.5) = 9.3 \text{ V} \qquad \blacktriangleright\!\!-$$

Drill Problems

D3.8   Determine the voltage gain of a CB amplifier (Figure 3.12) with $R_L = 3$ kΩ, $R_E = 500 \ \Omega$, $V_{CC} = 15$ V, $V_{BE} = 0.7$ V, $R_B = 6$ kΩ, and $\beta = 200$. The circuit is designed for maximum voltage output swing.

   Ans: $A_v = 38$

D3.9   Rework Problem D3.8 assuming that a large capacitor is added from the base to ground.

   Ans: $A_v = 158$

D3.10   Design a CB amplifier (Figure 3.12) that has a voltage gain of 40.

Determine the component values when $V_{CC} = 20$ V, $R_L = 4$ kΩ, $R_E = 500$ Ω, $V_{BE} = 0.7$ V, and $\beta = 100$.

> **Ans:** $R_1 = 4.6$ kΩ; $R_2 = 36.4$ kΩ;
> $R_C = 4$ kΩ; $R_{in} = 45$ Ω

3.7 Transistor Amplifier Applications

In this section, we view the results of the previous section and suggest applications for the three types of amplifier configuration based upon their properties.

The CE amplifier is found to have significant current and voltage gain with high input and output impedance. The high input impedance is desirable, whereas the high output impedance poses some problems. Note that the higher the output impedance, the less current can be drawn from an amplifier without a significant drop in output voltage. The CE is used most often for voltage amplification. It can provide a large output voltage swing, which then becomes the input of the next stage of the system.

The EF (CC) amplifier provides a high current gain with a low output impedance. It has a high input impedance and a voltage gain near unity. Clearly, it is not used for voltage amplification. The low output impedance makes this circuit useful for driving high-current devices. It can be used as a type of *buffer* between a CE and a current drawing load. The CC is a power amplifier and also an impedance matching stage. This amplifier is normally found in the final output stage of a signal amplifier, as it not only drops the impedance to a low value but also provides the necessary power to drive the load.

The CB amplifier has a low input impedance and a relatively high output impedance. These properties are not desirable for signal amplification. If the base is bypassed to ground with a capacitor, the amplifier has high voltage gain, but the current gain is less than unity. Even without the bypass capacitor, the voltage gain is higher than that of the CE. Thus, if the source driving the amplifier has a low impedance and the load is drawing very little current, the CB can be used as a voltage amplifier. This amplifier is less frequency sensitive than the other amplifier types and is used quite often in integrated circuits to provide an output with a wide frequency range.

3.8 Amplifier Coupling

When a system is composed of more than one transistor stage, it is necessary to connect, or couple, the transistors to each other. There are several common

ways of accomplishing this interconnection between amplifiers. In the following sections, we discuss direct, capacitive, transformer, and optical coupling.

3.8.1   *Direct Coupling*

Two amplifiers are *direct-coupled* if the output of the first amplifier is directly
connected to the input of the second without the use of capacitors. An example
is shown in Figure 3.14(a). The ac output of the first stage is superimposed
upon the dc quiescent level of the second stage. The dc level of the output from
the previous stage has the effect of adding to the dc bias of the second stage.
In order to compensate for the changing of bias levels, the amplifier uses
different values of dc voltage sources instead of a single V_{CC} source.

Direct coupling can be used effectively when coupling a CE amplifier to
an EF amplifier, as shown in Figure 3.14(b), because the bias current in an EF
is usually high. Direct coupling eliminates the need for the coupling capacitor
and the resistors R_1 and R_2 of the second stage. The directly coupled amplifier
has good frequency response, since there are no series storage (i.e., frequency-
sensitive) elements to affect the output signal at low frequency.

Direct coupling is commonly used in the design of integrated circuits. The
resulting amplifier has excellent low-frequency response and can amplify dc
signals. It is also simpler to fabricate an integrated circuit, since there is no
need for capacitors.

3.8.2   *Capacitive Coupling*

Capacitive coupling is the type that is illustrated in the designs of this chapter.
It is the simplest and most effective way of decoupling the effects of the dc

Figure 3.14   Direct-coupled amplifier.

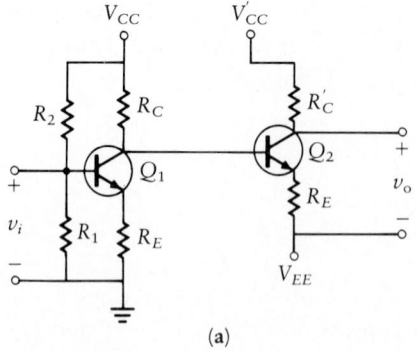

(a)

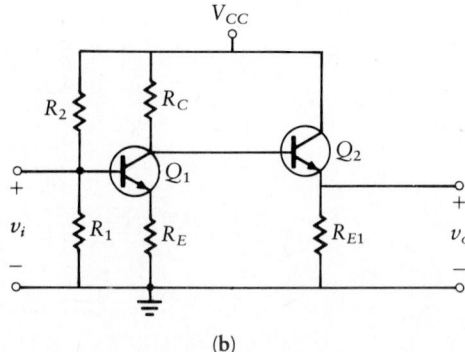

(b)

level of the first amplifier stage from those of the second stage. The capacitor removes the dc component from the ac signal. Thus, the biasing of the next stage is not affected by the previous stage. To ensure that the signal is not significantly changed by the addition of a capacitor, it is necessary for the capacitor to look like a short circuit to all frequencies being amplified. The specific criteria for choosing capacitor sizes are discussed in Chapter 10. For the present analysis, we assume that the capacitor is large, approaching infinity.

3.8.3 *Transformer Coupling*

A *transformer* can be used to couple two amplifier stages. This type of coupling is often used when high frequencies are being amplified. Although transformers are more costly than capacitors, their advantages can justify the additional cost. Through appropriate choice of turns ratio, a transformer can be used to increase either the voltage or current gain. For example, in the output stage of a power amplifier, the transformer is used to increase the current gain. There are other benefits associated with use of a transformer. For example, the transformer can be tuned to resonance so that it becomes a band-pass filter (a filter that passes desired frequencies while attenuating frequencies outside the desired band).

Tuned transformer coupling is used in television and radio receivers. In this manner, the transistor stages not only amplify the signal (video or audio) but also perform the function of separating the desired station from the others received by the antenna. In Figure 3.15, we illustrate the technique by which several stages are tuned to slightly different frequencies. The net effect is to produce a frequency characteristic that is approximately flat over the desired band of frequencies.

Figure 3.15
Transformer-coupled
tuned amplifier.

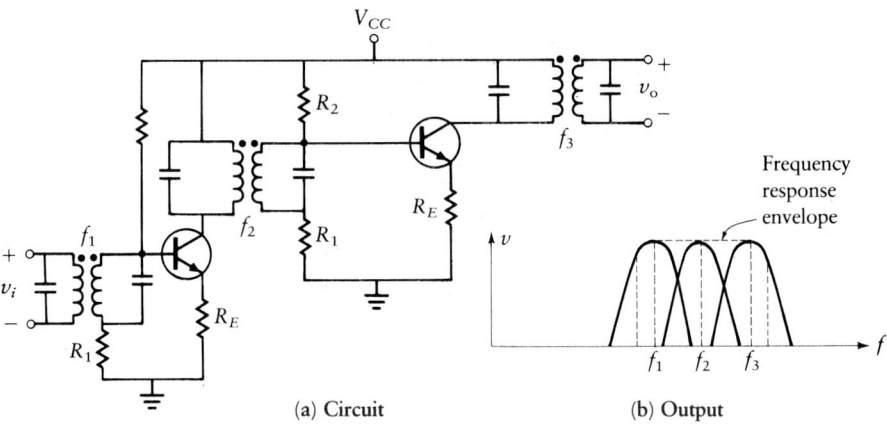

(a) Circuit

(b) Output

Figure 3.16
Transformer coupling
into a speaker.

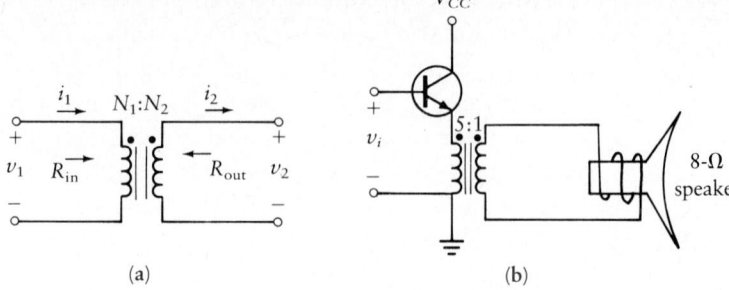

(a) (b)

Coupling the output stage to the load in an EF can be accomplished by using a transformer. Figure 3.16 illustrates this technique, where the amplifier is coupled into a speaker. We refer to Figure 3.16 in reviewing the operation of a transformer. The input and output voltages are proportional to the transformer turns ratio as follows:

$$v_2 = v_1 \left(\frac{N_2}{N_1} \right)$$

where N_1 is the number of turns in the primary coil and N_2 is the number of turns in the secondary coil. The input and output currents are related inversely to the voltage since power must be conserved. Thus,

$$i_2 = i_1 \left(\frac{N_1}{N_2} \right)$$

Taking the ratio of voltage to current yields the impedance relationship,

$$Z_1 = Z_2 \left(\frac{N_1}{N_2} \right)^2$$

Figure 3.16(b) illustrates an application of these results where the transformer is used to drive an 8-Ω speaker. If the transformer-turns ratio is 5:1, the equivalent resistance seen by the transistor emitter is $8 \times 5^2 = 200 \ \Omega$. If v_i is a sinusoid of amplitude 10 V, the emitter voltage is approximately the same value since the gain of an EF amplifier is unity. The voltage at the speaker is one-fifth of this amount, or a 2 V amplitude sinusoid. The current at the speaker is a 250 mA amplitude sinusoid (i.e., use Ohm's law at the speaker teminals), and the current in the transistor emitter is a 50 mA amplitude sinusoid.

Example 3.5

Transformer-Coupled Amplifier (Analysis)

Calculate the current gain, voltage gain, and input resistance for the trans-former coupled amplifier of Figure 3.17.

SOLUTION Note that the total amplification for the stage is obtained by taking the products of the gains of each section (the sections are separated by dashed lines in the figure).

The voltage gain of the transistor is found from the short form equation for the CE amplifier, where the collector resistance ($R_L \parallel R_C$ in the equation) is found by reflecting the 500 Ω load resistance back through the transformer. The overall voltage gain, A_v, includes the voltage-scaling effects of the two transformers. The results are shown directly on the figure.

The current gain, A_i, is found similarly using the short-form equation. Note that there is only one resistor in the collector circuit, that being the load reflected through the transformer.

The input resistance to the transistor is R_B, which is the parallel combi-nation of R_1 and R_2, or 2500 Ω. This is reflected through the transformer to obtain R_{in}.

Figure 3.17
Transformer-coupled amplifier of Example 3.5.

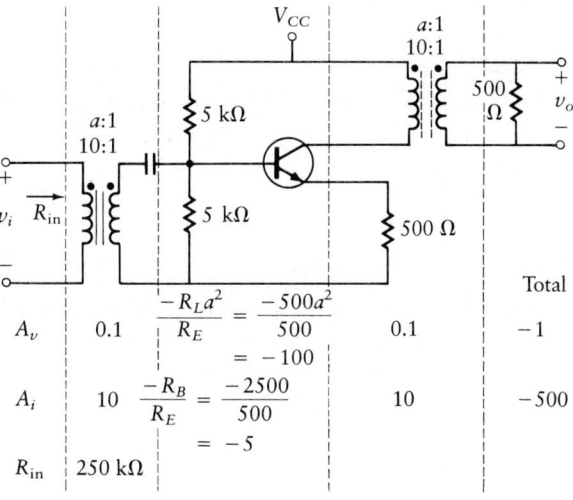

Drill Problems

D3.11 A CE amplifier (Figure 3.17) has a 1:5 input transformer and a 1:5 output transformer. Also, $R_L = 20$ kΩ, $R_E = 100$ Ω, $R_1 = 10$ kΩ and $R_2 = 100$ kΩ. Determine the overall A_i, A_v and R_{in}.

Ans: $A_v = -200$; $A_i = -3.64$; $R_{in} = 364 \ \Omega$

D3.12   An EF amplifier has a 10:1 input transformer and a 20:1 output transformer. Also, $R_L = 10 \ \Omega$, $R_1 = 100 \ k\Omega$, and $R_2 = 20 \ k\Omega$. Determine the overall A_i, A_v, and R_{in}.

Ans: $A_i = 417$; $A_v = 0.005$; $R_{in} = 1.67 \ M\Omega$

3.8.4   *Optical Coupling*

Numerous applications require *optical coupling* of electronic circuits. These applications can be categorized as follows:

- Light-sensitive and light-emitting devices.
- Discrete detectors and emitters for fiber-optic systems.
- Interrupter/reflector modules that detect objects modifying the light path.
- Isolators/couplers that transmit electrical signals without electrical connections.

As an example of this last application, suppose we desire to use the 60-Hz power line as the input signal to an electronic circuit. Because of the 15 to 25 A current available from the power line, we do not wish to make an electrical connection for our electronic needs but choose instead an optical connection. In the event of a component failure (e.g., a capacitor shorting) an optical coupler would prevent a dangerous, perhaps fatal, connection of the operator to the 110-V, 60-Hz power line. We discuss some of the major optical devices in the following paragraphs.

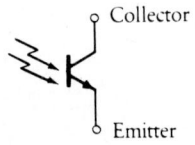

Collector

Emitter

Figure 3.18
Phototransistor.

Optoelectronic Detectors and Emitters   In Section 1.9.4 we consider the use of LEDs and light-sensitive diodes. The latter device operates, as shown in Figure 1.42, such that as the light intensity, H, increases, the current in the external circuit also increases. This, of course, is the same phenomenon that occurs as we increase the base current in a transistor. Such a device is a *phototransistor* and is illustrated in Figure 3.18. Note that there is no electrical connection to the base.

Optoelectronic components require packaging that both allows light to pass through the package to the chip and also protects the chip. The semiconductor package "window" can be modified to provide lens action, which gives improved response along the optical axis of the lens and greater directional sensitivity. A typical package configuration is shown in Figure 3.19. Communication systems (e.g., telephone lines) using optical fibers have replaced copper-wire systems. The light is emitted into and out of the optical fiber with devices such as the one shown in Figure 3.19.

Figure 3.19
Optoelectronic package configuration.
Courtesy of Power Electronics Semiconductor Department, General Electric Co.

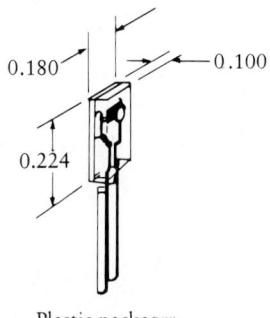

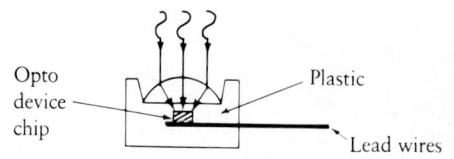

Plastic packages

Figure 3.20
Interrupter/reflector modules.
Courtesy of Power Electronics Semiconductor Department, General Electric Co.

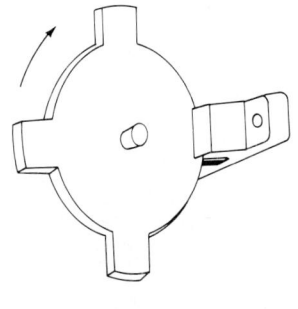

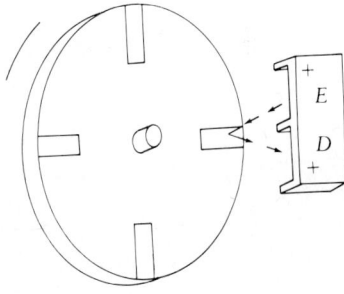

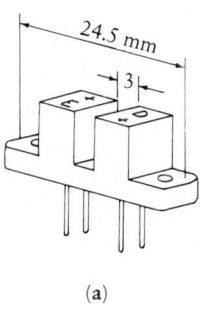

(a)

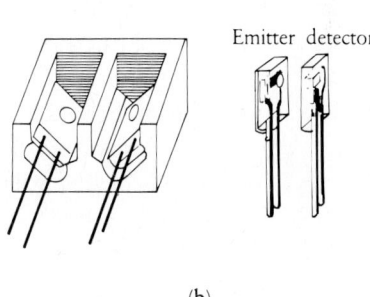

(b)

Interrupter/Reflector Modules   In many applications, it is necessary to determine the mechanical position or velocity of a shaft. Use of a light emitter and detector in either an interrupter mode, as shown in Figure 3.20(a), or in a reflector mode, as shown in Figure 3.20(b), allows the engineer to measure mechanical shaft motion.

Optocouplers   When we wish to couple two electrical circuits without making any electrical connections, we can use optocouplers (also called *optoisolators*), which are purely electronic components. The light path, emitter to detector, is

Figure 3.21
Optoisolator data
sheet.
Courtesy of Power
Electronics Semicon-
ductor Department,
General Electric Co.

Photon Coupled Isolator H11A1, H11A2

The H11A1 and H11A2 are gallium arsenide infrared
emitting diodes coupled with a silicon phototransistor
in a dual in-line package, with 6 terminals.

Absolute maximum ratings: (25°C)

Infrared Emitting Diode

Power Dissipation	*100	milliwatts
Forward Current (Continuous)	60	milliamps
Forward Current (Peak)	3	ampere
(Pulse width 1 μsec 300 P Ps)		
Reverse Voltage	3	volts

*Derate 1.33mW/°C above 25°C ambient

Phototransistor

Power Dissipation	150	milliwatts
V_{CEO}	30	volts
V_{CBO}	70	volts
V_{ECO}	7	volts
Collector Current (Continuous)	100	milliamps

totally enclosed in the component and cannot be modified externally. The
degree of electrical isolation between the two devices is controlled by the materials in the light path and by the physical distance between the emitter and
detector. The greater that distance, the better the isolation.

A portion of a data sheet for an optoisolator is shown in Figure 3.21. Notice
that this device isolates 1500 V peak and 1060 V rms input to output.

3.9   Phase Splitter

A *phase splitter,* shown in Figure 3.22, is an amplifier that is simultaneously
a CE and a CC. We choose $R_C = R_E = R_L$, so that the output voltage at the
collector is equal in magnitude to the output voltage at the emitter, but these
voltages are 180° out of phase. The two signal outputs from this circuit are
approximately equal to the input signal in amplitude: That is, the voltage-gain
ratios, v_1/v_i and v_2/v_i are approximately equal to unity in magnitude. The
two outputs resulting from a sinusoidal input are sketched on the figure. The
output at the emitter is in phase with the input signal, whereas the output of
the collector is 180° out of phase with the input signal.

Figure 3.22
Phase splitter.

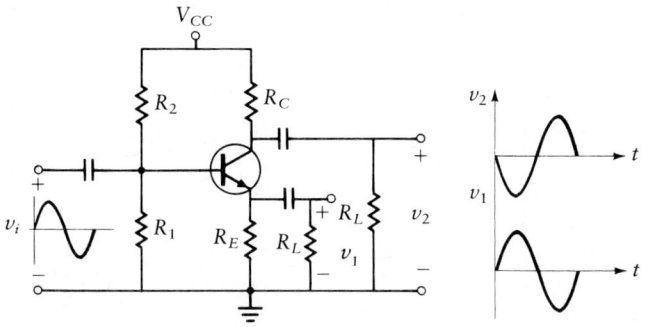

Figure 3.23
Multistage amplifier.

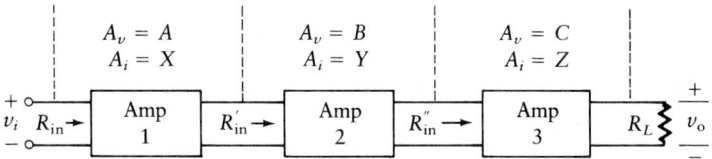

Drill Problem

D3.13 The outputs of Figure 3.22 are each connected to a 2 kΩ load. What would the output voltage swing of the phase splitter be when $V_{CC} = 20$ V? Also determine R_C, R_E, R_1, and R_2 for maximum output swing when $\beta = 200$ and $V_{BE} = 0.7$ V.

    Ans: $R_C = R_E = 2$ kΩ; $R_1 = 66.9$ kΩ; $R_2 = 99.6$ kΩ;
          $v_{o(p-p)} = 6$ V

3.10   ## Multistage Amplifier Analysis

Amplifiers are often connected in series (cascaded), as shown in Figure 3.23. The load on the first amplifier is the input resistance of the second amplifier. The various stages need not have the same voltage and current gain. In practice, the earlier stages are often voltage amplifiers and the last one or two stages are current amplifiers. The amount of gain in a stage is determined by the load on the amplifier stage, which is governed by the input resistance to the next stage. Therefore, in designing or analyzing multistage amplifiers, we start at the output and proceed toward the input.

Example 3.6   Multistage Amplifier (Analysis)

Determine the current and voltage gains for the two-stage capacitor coupled amplifier shown in Figure 3.24. Each capacitor is so large that it can be considered to be a short circuit to the ac signal.

SOLUTION   We develop the hybrid equivalent circuit for the multistage amplifier of Figure 3.24. This equivalent is shown in Figure 3.25. Primed variables denote output stage quantities and unprimed variables denote input stage quantities. Calculations for the output stage are

$$R_B' = \frac{10,000 \times 2000}{10,000 + 2000} = 1.67 \text{ k}\Omega$$

$$V_{BB}' = \frac{12 \times 2000}{10,000 + 2000} = 2 \text{ V}$$

$$I_{CQ}' = \frac{V_{BB}' - V_{BE}}{R_B'/\beta + R_E'} = \frac{2 - 0.7}{1670/200 + 50}$$

$$= 22 \text{ mA}$$

$$h_{ib}' = 26 \text{ mV}/|I_{CQ}'| = 1.17 \ \Omega$$

For the input stage,

$$R_B = \frac{7000 \times 1000}{7000 + 1000} = 875 \ \Omega$$

$$V_{BB} = \frac{12 \times 1000}{7000 + 1000} = 1.5 \text{ V}$$

$$I_{CQ} = \frac{1.5 - 0.7}{875/200 + 50} = 14.7 \text{ mA}$$

$$h_{ib} = \frac{26 \text{ mV}}{14.7 \text{ mA}} = 1.77 \ \Omega$$

We determine the input resistance using the long-form equation from Table 3.1 as follows:

$$R_{\text{in}} = R_B \parallel \beta(h_{ib} + R_E)$$

$$= \frac{875 \times 200 \times (1.77 + 50)}{875 + 10354} = 807 \ \Omega$$

Figure 3.24
Multistage amplifier
of Example 3.6.

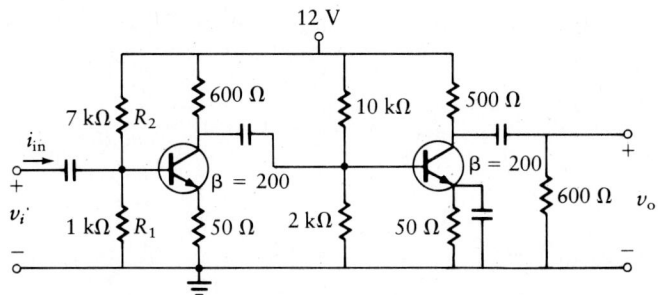

Figure 3.25
Equivalent circuit for
Example 3.6.

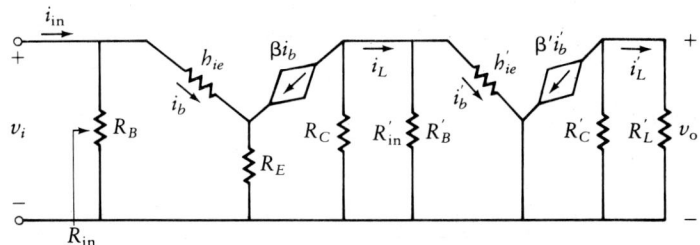

Figure 3.26
Current dividers for
circuit of Figure 3.25.

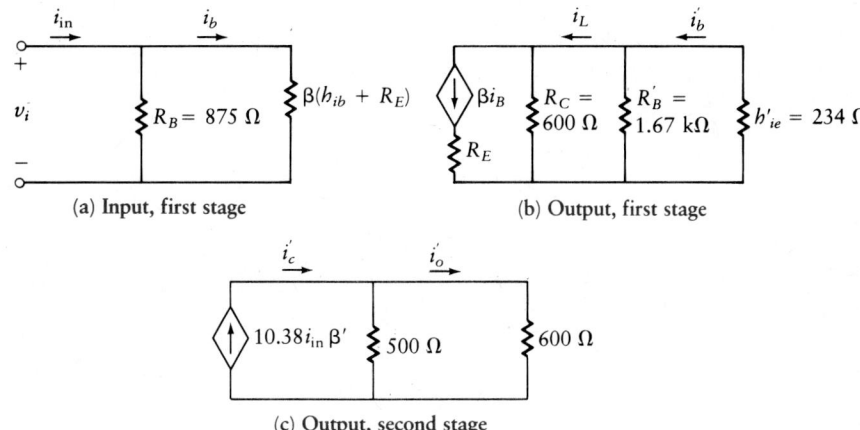

The current gain, A_i, is found by applying the equation from Table 3.1 twice, once for each stage. The first stage uses the value for R_L derived from the input to the second stage. We analyze Figure 3.25 by extracting three current dividers, as shown in Figure 3.26. The current division of the input stage is found from Figure 3.26(a).

$$i_b = \frac{R_B i_{\text{in}}}{R_B + \beta(h_{ib} + R_E)} = \frac{875 i_{\text{in}}}{875 + 200(1.77 + 50)} = 0.078\ i_{\text{in}}$$

The output of the first stage is coupled to the input of the second stage in Figure 3.26(b). The input resistance of the second stage is

$$R'_{in} = R'_B \parallel h'_{ie} = 205 \ \Omega$$

The current in R'_{in} is i_L and is given by

$$i_L = 15.6 \ i_{in} \times \frac{600}{805} = 11.63 \ i_{in}$$

Again, i_L is current divided at the input to the second stage. Thus

$$i'_b = \frac{-R'_B i_L}{R'_B + h'_{ie}} = \frac{-1670(11.63 i_{in})}{(1670 + 205)}$$

$$= -10.38 \ i_{in}$$

The output current is found from Figure 3.26(c):

$$i'_o = \frac{10.38 i_{in} \times 200 \times 500}{500 + 600} = 941 \ i_{in}$$

The current gain is

$$A_i = 941$$

Now, using equation (3.1), we find the voltage gain is

$$A_v = \frac{941 \times 600}{807} = 700$$

3.11 Four-Layer Devices

We have been discussing two-layer devices (diodes) and three-layer devices (transistors). The success of three-layer devices, such as the BJT and the field-effect transistor (FET), led researchers to the concept of the four-layer device. With improved manufacturing capability, four-layer devices do not present any major fabrication problems. In the following subsections, we mention a few of these devices and discuss their basic operation.

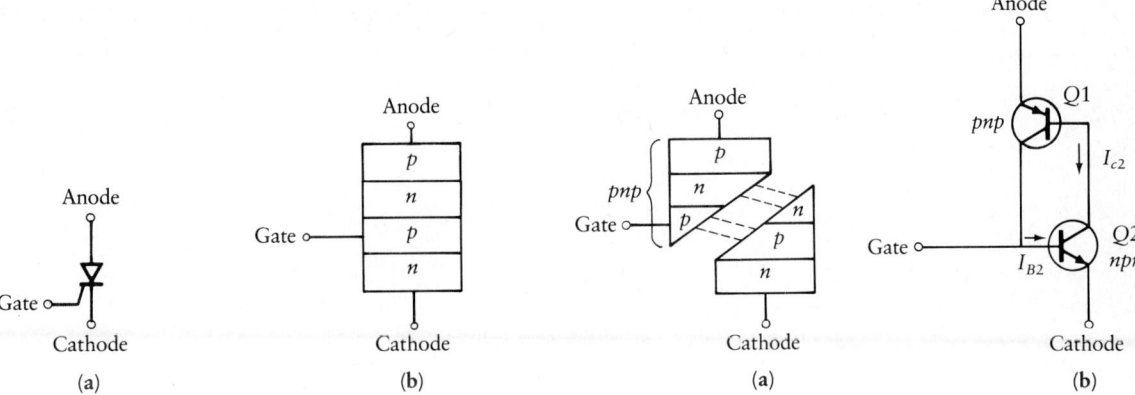

Figure 3.27   SCR symbol and construction.   **Figure 3.28**   SCR two-BJT equivalent circuit.

3.11.1   *Silicon-Controlled Rectifier (SCR)*

The *silicon-controlled rectifier (SCR)* is a four-layer device (*pnpn*) with useful switching characteristics ([6], Section 11.2–11.6). It is a member of the *thyristor* family and is used in relay controls, choppers, battery chargers, protective circuits, inverters, induction heating, ultrasonic cleaning, and control circuitry. SCRs can be built to control power in the megawatt region and to survive currents as high as 1500 A at 2000 V. The frequency ranges are somewhat limited, but some SCRs are able to perform at frequencies as high as 50 kHz.

Figure 3.27 illustrates the circuit symbol and construction of the SCR.

In Figure 3.28 the SCR is represented as a two-BJT equivalent circuit. We evaluate the performance of an SCR using the equivalent circuit. If a zero voltage appears at the gate, the gate is effectively grounded. Therefore, the base current, I_{B2}, is approximately equal to zero and I_{C2} is approximately equal to I_{CBO}. The base current of Q_1 is

$$I_{B1} = I_{C2} = I_{CBO}$$

which is too small to allow Q_1 to conduct. This results in almost no current between the anode and cathode, thereby presenting a high impedance between these elements. If a voltage that is impressed on the gate is sufficiently large to allow Q_1 to conduct, I_{C1} will increase, thus resulting in a corresponding increase in I_{B2}. Due to the interconnection, the effect is cumulative, and each transistor drives the other into saturation. Once in saturation, the junctions are forward-biased and the total voltage drop across the device is approximately 1 V. The SCR approximates a short circuit. To turn off the SCR, some type of interrup-

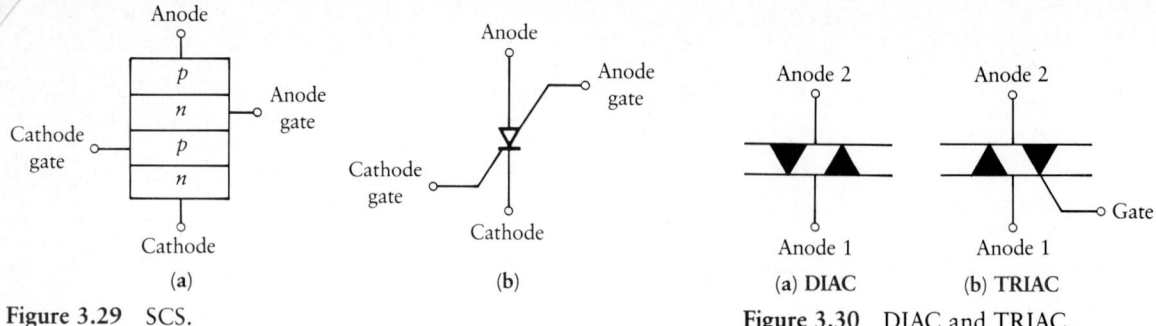

Figure 3.29 SCS.

Figure 3.30 DIAC and TRIAC.

tion must occur in the anode-voltage or cathode-voltage source. The regeneration action to turn on an SCR occurs in 0.1 μs to 1 μs, and the turn-off time ranges from 5 μs to 30 μs. This switching action is generally faster than that obtainable with a single transistor operating between saturation and cutoff at large currents.

3.11.2 Silicon-Controlled Switch (SCS)

The *silicon-controlled switch (SCS)* is constructed similarly to the SCR except that both center layers are connected to gates, one being called the anode gate and the other the cathode gate. This is shown in Figure 3.29.

The operation of the device is similar to that of the SCR. As the anode gate current becomes higher, the anode-to-cathode voltage required to turn on the device becomes lower. The anode gate can be used to either turn on or turn off the device. A negative pulse must be applied to the anode gate terminal to turn off the SCS, whereas a positive pulse is required to turn on the device.

3.11.3 DIAC and TRIAC

The *DIAC*, or trigger diode, is a two-terminal device that can be triggered in either direction. The device operates in the reverse region and breakdown occurs in either direction when the voltage increases to the necessary level. These devices are often used in the gate circuit of an SCR to initiate gate action. The DIAC symbol is illustrated in Figure 3.30(a).

The *TRIAC* is similar to the DIAC except that it has a gate terminal for controlling the turn on for either polarity of the voltage between the two anode terminals. The symbol is illustrated in Figure 3.30(b).

PROBLEMS

3.1 Derive equations for A_v, A_i, and R_{in} for the CE amplifier shown in Figure P3.1.

3.2 Calculate R_{in}, A_v, and A_i when $R_B = R_L = 5$ kΩ, $R_E = 1$ kΩ and $h_{ie} = 0$ for the CE amplifier shown in Figure P3.2. Let β be given by:
a. β = 200
b. β = 100
c. β = 10

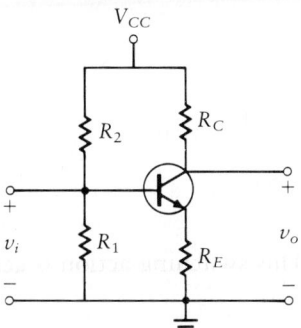

Figure P3.1

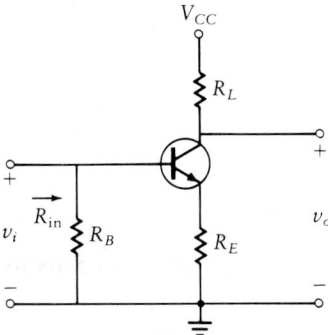

Figure P3.2

3.3 Determine A_v, A_i and R_{in} for the amplifier shown in Figure P3.2 when $R_L = R_B = 5$ kΩ, $h_{ib} = 40$ Ω, β = 300, and R_E is as follows:
a. $R_E = 1000$ Ω
b. $R_E = 500$ Ω
c. $R_E = 100$ Ω
d. $R_E = 0$

Discuss the effects of changing R_E.

3.4 For the CE amplifier shown in Figure P3.1, $V_{BE} = 0.6$ V, $V_{CC} = 12$ V, β = 300, P_L (max average) = 100 mW, and $A_v = -10$. Determine R_1, R_2, R_{in}, and A_i. How much power is dissipated in the transistor?

3.5 Find A_v for the amplifier shown in Figure P3.3, where $h_{ie} = 2$ kΩ, $h_{re} = 0$, $h_{fe} = 200$ and $1/h_{oc} = 8$ kΩ.

Figure P3.3

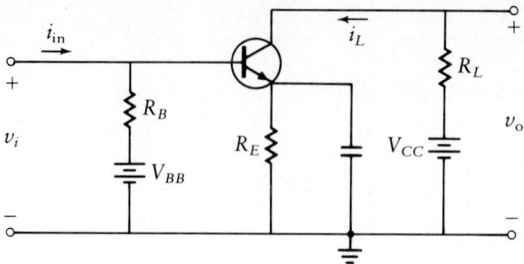

Figure P3.4

3.6   For the CE amplifier shown in Figure P3.4, where $h_{ie} = 1\ k\Omega$, $h_{oe} = 10\ \mu S$, $h_{fe} = 50$, plot each of the following.
a. $A_i = i_L/i_{in}$, assuming $R_B \ll h_{ie}$ as a function of the value of R_L. Let R_L vary from 0 to 500 kΩ.
b. A_i as a function of R_L but assume $h_{re} = 0 = h_{oe}$.

3.7   For the CE amplifier shown in Figure P3.5, determine the variation of A_i and R_{in} if h_{fe} varies from 50 to 150 for the silicon transistor.

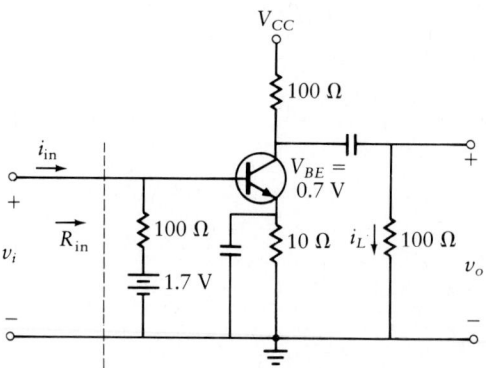

Figure P3.5

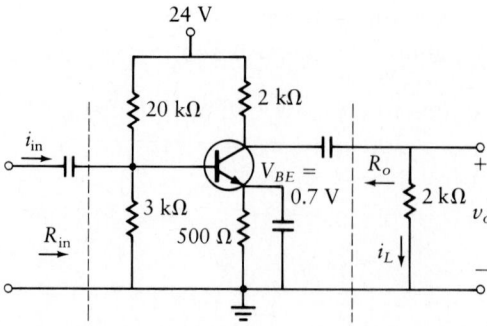

Figure P3.6

3.8 Determine h_{ie}, A_i, R_{in} and R_o for the CE amplifier shown in Figure P3.6 if $h_{fe} = 100$ and $h_{re} = h_{oe} = 0$.

3.9 Calculate h_{ib} for the silicon transistor circuits shown in Figure P3.7 and determine whether h_{ib} should be considered in the design equations.

3.10 Compare input resistances and voltage gains for the ac equivalent amplifier circuits shown in Figure P3.8.

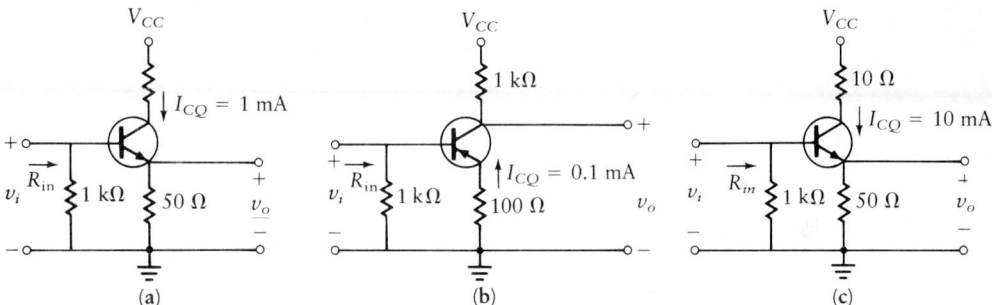

Figure P3.7

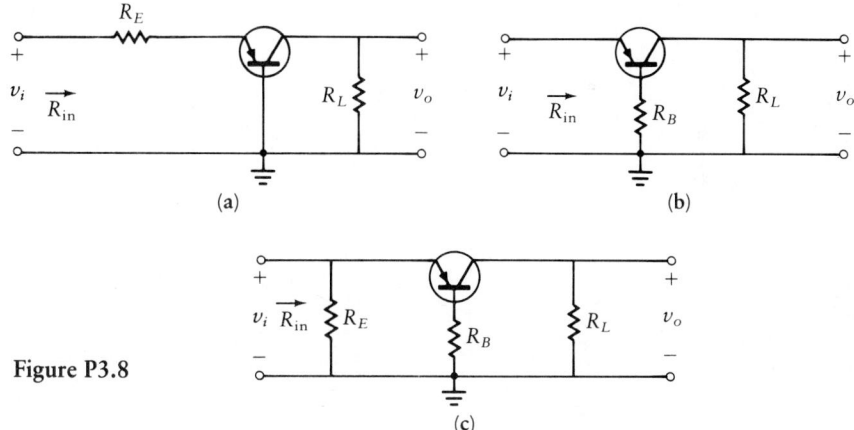

Figure P3.8

3.11 Calculate A_v, A_i and R_{in} when $\beta = 250$, $R_E = 100\ \Omega$, $R_C = R_L = 1100\ \Omega$, $R_1 = 10\ \text{k}\Omega$, $R_2 = 10\ \text{k}\Omega$ and $h_{ie} = 500\ \Omega$ for the CE amplifier shown in Figure P3.9.

3.12 Plot A_v versus R_L and A_i versus R_C for $100\ \Omega < R_L < 10\ \text{k}\Omega$ for the amplifier of Problem 3.11. Hold all other parameters constant.

3.13 Plot A_v versus R_E and A_i versus R_E for $10\ \Omega < R_E < 1000\ \Omega$ for the amplifier of Problem 3.11. Hold all other parameters constant.

3.14 Plot A_v versus β and A_i versus β for $50 < \beta < 300$ for the amplifier of Problem 3.11. Hold all other parameters constant.

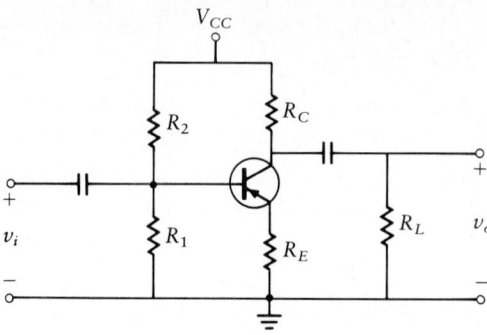

Figure P3.9

3.15 Plot R_{in} versus β for $50 < \beta < 300$ for the amplifier of Problem 3.11. Hold all other parameters constant.

3.16 Plot R_{in} versus R_E for $10\ \Omega < R_E < 1000\ \Omega$ for the amplifier of Problem 3.11. Hold all other parameters constant.

3.17 Design the CE amplifier in Figure P3.9 to drive a 2 kΩ load using a *pnp* silicon transistor. $V_{CC} = -24$ V, $\beta = 200$, $A_v = -10$, and $V_{BE} = -0.7$ V. Determine all element values and calculate A_i, R_{in}, and the undistorted symmetrical output voltage swing for each R_C given below:
  a. $R_C = R_L$
  b. $R_C = 0.1R_L$
  c. $R_C = 10R_L$

Compare your results.

3.18 Design a CE amplifier as shown in Figure P3.9 using a *pnp* transistor when $R_L = 3$ kΩ, $A_v = -10$, $V_{BE} = -0.7$ V, $\beta = 200$, and $V_{CC} = -12$ V. Determine all element values, A_i, R_{in} and the maximum voltage swing across R_L.

3.19 Design a CE amplifier as shown in Figure P3.9 using a *pnp* transistor when $R_L = 4$ kΩ, $A_v = -15$, $R_{in} = 20$ kΩ, $V_{CC} = -20$ V, $\beta = 300$, and $V_{BE} = -0.6$ V. Determine all element values and the maximum peak-to-peak output voltage swing.

3.20 Design a CE amplifier as shown in Figure 3.5(a) using an *npn* transistor when $R_L = 9$ kΩ, $A_v = -10$, $A_i = -10$, $V_{BE} = 0.7$ V, $\beta = 200$ and $V_{CC} = 15$ V. Determine all element values, R_{in}, and the maximum peak-to-peak output voltage swing.

3.21 Design a CE amplifier to obtain a voltage gain of -5 when $A_i = -2$, $R_L = 4$ kΩ, $V_{CC} = 15$ V, $V_{BE} = 0.6$ V, and $\beta = 200$. Determine all resistor values, input resistance and maximum output voltage swing. Use the circuit of Figure 3.5(a).

3.22 Design a CE amplifier to obtain a voltage gain of -25 when $R_{in} = 5$ kΩ, $R_L = 5$ kΩ, $V_{CC} = 12$ V, $\beta = 200$, and $V_{BE} = 0.7$ V. Determine all resistor values, current gain, and maximum output voltage swing. Use the circuit of Figure 3.5(a).

3.23 Design a CE amplifier to obtain a voltage gain of -10 when $R_{in} = 2$ kΩ, $R_L = 4$ kΩ, $V_{CC} = 15$ V, $V_{BE} = 0.6$ V and $\beta = 300$. This amplifier requires an output swing of only 2 V peak-to-peak, so the design should be made for minimum current drain from the dc power source. Determine all resistor values and current gain.

3.24 Calculate R_{in}, A_v, A_i, and $v_{o(p\text{-}p)}$ for symmetrical output swing for the EF amplifier shown in Figure P3.10. Let $R_L = 1$ kΩ, $R_B = 5$ kΩ, $h_{ib} = 40$ Ω, $\beta = 300$, $V_{CC} = 6$ V and $V_{BE} = 0.7$ V. Find the solution for each value of R_C given below:
a. $R_C = 1$ kΩ
b. $R_C = 0$

Discuss the effects on R_{in}, A_v, A_i, and $v_{o(p\text{-}p)}$ when R_C goes to zero.

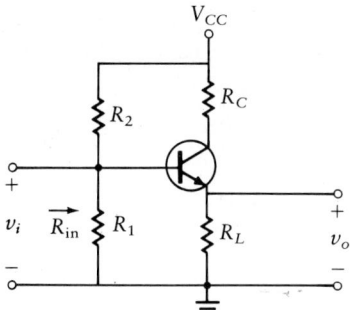

Figure P3.10

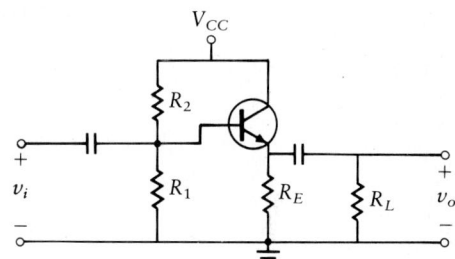

Figure P3.11

3.25 Design an EF amplifier as shown in Figure P3.11 using an *npn* transistor with $R_L = 500$ Ω, $V_{BE} = 0.7$ V, $A_i = 25$, $\beta = 200$, and $V_{CC} = 15$ V. Determine all element values, R_{in}, A_v, and the maximum output voltage swing.

3.26 Design an EF amplifier to drive an 8-Ω load when $\beta = 60$, $V_{CC} = 24$ V, $V_{BE} = 0.7$ V, $A_v = 1$, and $A_i = 10$. Use the circuit of Figure P3.11. Determine all element values, output voltage swing, and R_{in}.

3.27 Design an EF amplifier as shown in Figure P3.11 using a *pnp* transistor when $R_L = 500$ Ω, $V_{BE} = -0.7$ V, $\beta = 200$, $A_i = 10$, and $V_{CC} = -15$ V. Determine all element values, R_{in}, A_v, and the maximum output voltage swing.

3.28 Design an EF amplifier as shown in Figure P3.11 using an *npn* transistor when $R_L = 1500$ Ω, $V_{BE} = 0.7$ V, $R_{in} = 10$ kΩ, $\beta = 200$, and $V_{CC} = 16$ V. Determine all element values, A_i, A_v, and the maximum output voltage swing.

3.29 Design an EF amplifier as shown in Figure P3.11 to drive a 10-Ω load when V_{CC} = 24 V, V_{BE} = 0.6 V, A_v = 1, R_{in} = 100 Ω, and β = 200. Determine all element values, R_{in}, and maximum output voltage swing.

3.30 Design a CB amplifier (See Figure 3.12) that has a voltage gain of 10 and a 4-kΩ load. Use β = 100, V_{BE} = 0.7 V, V_{CC} = 18 V, and R_E = 500 Ω. Determine values of I_{CQ}, R_1, R_2, R_B, and the maximum voltage output swing. What is the voltage gain when R_1 is bypassed with a large capacitor?

3.31 Design a CB amplifier using the values given in Problem 3.30 except that the voltage gain is 100. Determine value of R_1, R_2, I_{CQ}, R_B, and the maximum output voltage swing.

3.32 Design a CB amplifier for maximum voltage swing and at least 100-Ω input impedance, R_L = 8 kΩ, V_{CC} = 12 V and R_E = 400 Ω. Use an *npn* transistor with a β = 200 and V_{BE} = 0.7 V. Determine the voltage gain and all resistor values.

3.33 Analyze a CB amplifier for R_{in}, A_v, and $V_{o(p-p)}$ that has the following values: V_{CC} = 16 V, R_1 = 2 kΩ, R_2 = 25 kΩ, R_E = 200 Ω, R_C = R_L = 4 kΩ, β = 200 and V_{BE} = 0.7 V. The base is ac grounded.

3.34 Determine A_v, A_i and R_{in} for the EF amplifier shown in Figure P3.12 when β = 200 and h_{ib} = 0.

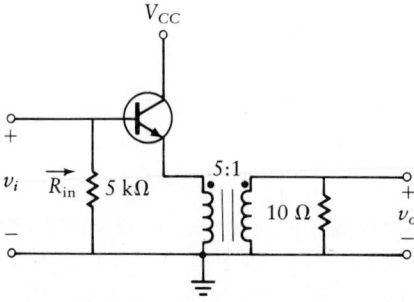

Figure P3.12

3.35 Determine the overall current and voltage gains and the input resistance for the transformer coupled amplifier shown in Figure P3.13. Use an *npn* transistor with a = 4, R_1 = 2 kΩ, R_2 = 4 kΩ, V_{CC} = 15 V, β = 200 and R_L = 500 Ω. Neglect h_{ie}.

3.36 Determine the overall current and voltage gains and the input resistance R_{in} for the transformer-coupled amplifier, as shown in Figure P3.13. Use a *pnp* transistor with a = 7, V_{CC} = −15 V, R_1 = 3 kΩ, R_2 = 4 kΩ, and R_L = 300 Ω. Neglect h_{ie}.

3.37 Directly couple a CE amplifier to an EF (see Figure 3.14(b)) for 4 V output swing with the following values: V_{CC} = 12 V, A_v = 10, Q_1 has

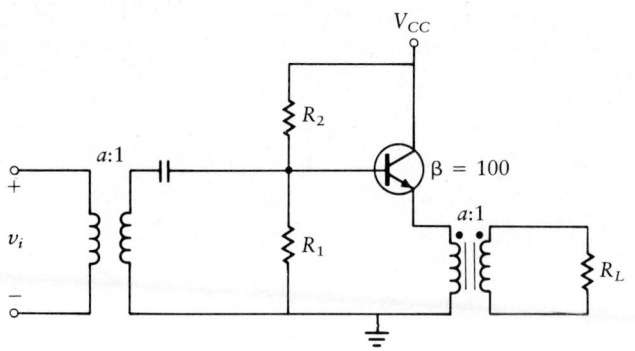

Figure P3.13

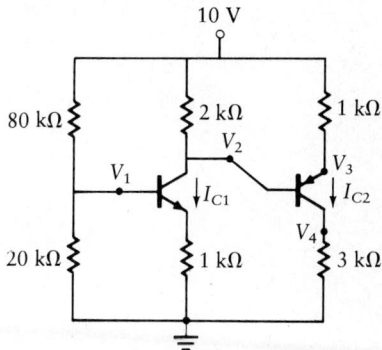

Figure P3.14

Figure P3.15

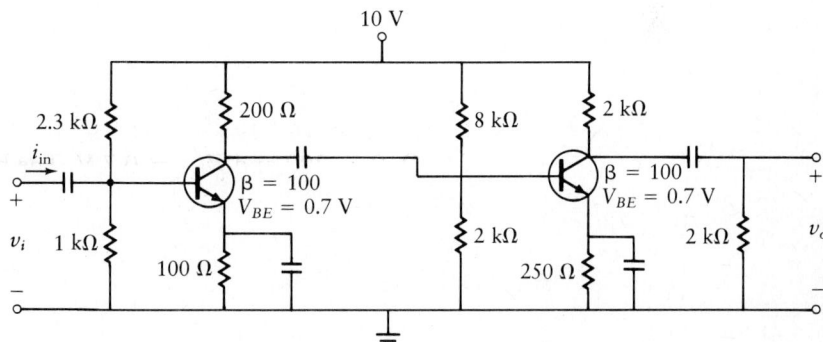

β = 200 and V_{BE} = 0.7 V, Q_2 has β = 100 and V_{BE} = 0.7 V, and R_{E1} = 100 Ω. Let R_C = 4 kΩ.

3.38 Determine the values of V_1, V_2, V_3, V_4, I_{C1}, and I_{C2} for the circuit shown in Figure P3.14. Assume that β is 300 or greater.

3.39 Determine A_i and A_v for the two-stage amplifier shown in Figure P3.15. The transistors are silicon.

3.40 Determine A_v and A_i for the two-stage amplifier shown in Figure P3.16. The transistors are silicon.

Figure P3.16

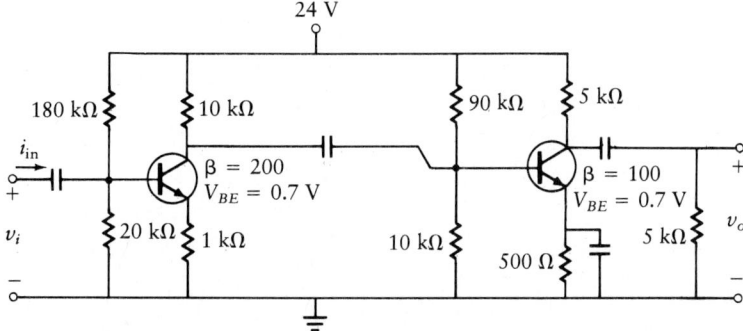

4

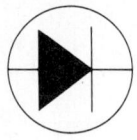

FIELD-EFFECT TRANSISTOR AMPLIFIERS

4.0 Introduction

The performance of the *field-effect transistor (FET)*, which was proposed by W. Shockley in 1952, is different from that of the BJT. The controlling parameter for an FET is *voltage* instead of *current*.

The FET is a *unipolar* device, since current exists *either* as electrons or holes. In an *n*-channel FET, electron current exists, and in a *p*-channel FET, hole current exists. Both types of FET are controlled by a voltage imposed between the *gate* and the *source*.

In comparing FETs to BJTs, we notice that the *drain* (*D*) is analogous to the collector and the *source* (*S*) is analogous to the emitter. A third contact, the *gate* (*G*), is analogous to the base. The source and drain of an FET can usually be interchanged without affecting transistor operation.

This chapter begins with a discussion of the FET characteristics and a comparison of these characteristics with the characteristics of the BJT. The construction and operation of both JFETs and MOSFETs are then described. We develop the biasing techniques for FETs followed by ac analysis using equivalent circuits. We then derive the gain equations for the common-source (CS) amplifier. This is followed by development of a step-by-step design procedure, which is applied to several design examples.

Analysis and design of common-drain (CD) (source follower (SF)) amplifiers are then presented. Step-by-step design procedures are developed followed by application of these procedures to examples.

The chapter concludes with a brief discussion of other speciality devices.

4.1   Advantages and Disadvantages of the FET

The advantages of FETs can be summarized as follows:

1. They are voltage-sensitive devices with high input impedance (on the order of 10^7 to 10^{12} Ω). Since this input impedance is considerably higher than that of BJTs, FETs are preferred over BJTs for use as the input stage to a multistage amplifier.
2. FETs generate a lower noise level than BJTs.
3. FETs are more temperature stable than BJTs.
4. FETs are generally easier to fabricate than BJTs, since they usually require fewer masking steps and fewer diffusions. Greater numbers of devices can be fabricated on a single chip (i.e., increased *packing density* is possible).
5. FETs react like voltage-controlled variable resistors for small values of drain source voltage.
6. The high input impedance of FETs permit them to store charge long enough to allow use as storage elements.
7. Power FETs can dissipate high power and can switch large currents.

There are several disadvantages that limit the use of FETs in some applications:

1. FETs usually exhibit poor frequency response because of high input capacitance.
2. Some types of FETs exhibit poor linearity.
3. FETs can be damaged in handling due to static electricity.

4.2   Types of FETs

We consider here three major types of FETs:

1. Junction FET (JFET)
2. Depletion-mode metal-oxide semiconductor FET (depletion MOSFET)

3. Enhancement-mode metal-oxide semiconductor FET (enchancement MOSFET)

The MOSFET is often called an insulated-gate FET (IGFET).

4.3   JFET Operation and Construction

Like the BJT, the FET is a three-terminal device, but it has only one *pn* juncton rather than two, as in the BJT. A schematic for the physical structure of the JFET is shown in Figure 4.1.

The *n*-channel JFET, shown in Figure 4.1(a), is constructed using a strip of *n*-type material with two *p*-type materials diffused into the strip, one on each side. The *p*-channel JFET has a strip of *p*-type material with two *n*-type materials diffused into the strip, as shown in Figure 4.1(b).

To understand the operation of the JFET, we connect the *n*-channel JFET of Figure 4.1(a) to an external circuit. A supply voltage, V_{DD}, is applied to the drain (this is analogous to the V_{CC} supply voltage for a BJT) and the source is brought to common. A gate supply voltage, V_{GG}, is applied to the gate (this is analogous to V_{BB} for the BJT). This circuit configuration is shown in Figure 4.2(a).

V_{DD} provides a drain-source voltage, v_{DS}, that causes a drain current, i_D, from drain to source. The drain current, i_D, which is identical to the source current, exists in the channel surrounded by the *p*-type gate. The gate-to-source voltage, v_{GS}, which is equal to $-V_{GG}$ (see Figure 4.2(a)), creates a *depletion region* in the channel, which reduces the channel width and hence increases the resistance between drain and source. Since the gate-source junction is reverse-biased, a zero gate current results.

We consider JFET operation with $v_{GS} = 0$, as shown in Figure 4.2(b). The drain current, i_D, through the *n*-channel from drain to source causes a voltage drop along the channel, with the higher potential at the drain-gate junction. This positive voltage at the drain-gate junction reverse-biases the *pn* junction and produces a depletion region, as shown by the shaded area in Figure 4.2(b).

Figure 4.1
Physical structure of JFET.

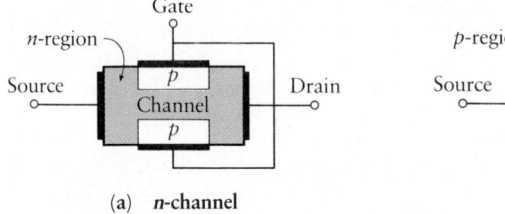
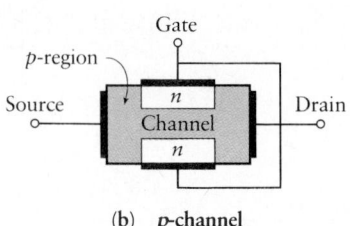

(a) *n*-channel   (b) *p*-channel

Figure 4.2
Operation of the JFET
in an external circuit.

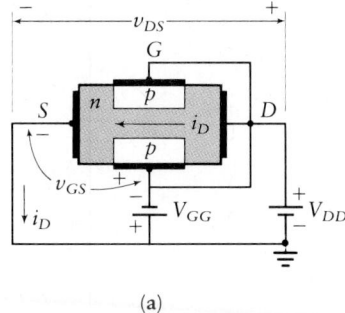

(a)

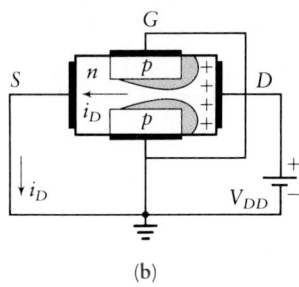

(b)

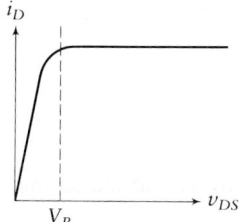

Figure 4.3
i_D-v_{DS} characteristic
for *n*-channel JFET.

When we increase v_{DS}, the drain current, i_D, also increases, as shown in Figure 4.3. This action results in a larger depletion region and an increased channel resistance between drain and source. As v_{DS} is further increased, a point is reached where the depletion region forms across the entire channel and the drain current reaches its saturation point. If we increase v_{DS} beyond this point, i_D remains constant. The value of the saturated drain current with $V_{GS} = 0$ is an important parameter and is denoted as the *drain-source saturation current*, I_{DSS}. As can be seen from Figure 4.3, increasing v_{DS} beyond this channel *pinch-off* point causes no further increase in i_D, and the i_D-v_{DS} characteristic curve becomes flat (i.e., i_D remains constant as v_{DS} is further increased).

4.3.1 *JFET Gate-to-Source Voltage Variation*

In the previous section, we developed the i_D-v_{DS} characteristic curve with $v_{GS} = 0$. In this section, we consider the complete i_D-v_{DS} characteristics for various values of the v_{GS} parameter. Note that in the case of the BJT, the characteristic curves (i_C-v_{CE}) have i_B as the parameter. The FET is a voltage-controlled device and is controlled by v_{GS}. Figure 4.4 shows the i_D-v_{DS} characteristic curves for both the *n*-channel and *p*-channel JFET. Before we discuss these curves, take note of the symbols for an *n*-channel and a *p*-channel JFET, which are also shown in Figure 4.4. These symbols are the same except for the direction of the arrow.

As v_{GS} is increased (more negative for an *n*-channel and more positive for a *p*-channel) the depletion region is formed and closes off for a lower value of i_D. Hence, for the *n*-channel JFET of Figure 4.4(a), the maximum i_D reduces from I_{DSS} as v_{GS} is made more negative. If v_{GS} is further decreased (more negative), a value of v_{GS} is reached, after which i_D will be zero regardless of the value of v_{DS}. This value of v_{GS} is called V_{GSOFF}, or *pinch-off voltage* (V_p). The value of V_p is negative for an *n*-channel JFET and positive for a *p*-channel JFET.

Figure 4.4
i_D-v_{DS} characteristic
curves for JFET.

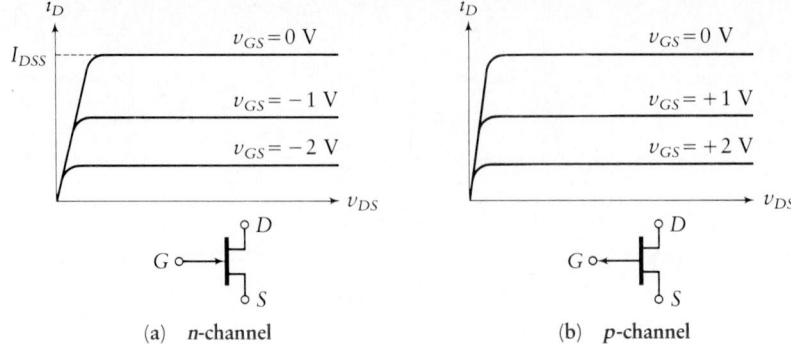

(a)   *n*-channel   (b)   *p*-channel

4.3.2   *JFET Transfer Characteristics*

Of great value in JFET design is the transfer characteristic, which is a plot of the drain current, i_D, as a function of gate-to-source voltage, v_{GS}, above pinch-off. Although this is plotted with v_{DS} equal to a constant, the transfer characteristic is essentially independent of v_{DS} since, after the FET reaches pinch-off, i_D remains constant for increasing values of v_{DS}. This can be seen from the i_D-v_{DS} curves of Figure 4.4, where each curve becomes flat for values of $v_{DS} > V_p$. Each curve has a different saturation point.

In Figure 4.5, we show the transfer characteristics and the i_D-v_{GS} characteristics for an *n*-channel JFET. We plot these with a common i_D axis. The transfer characteristics can be obtained from an extension of the i_D-v_{DS} curves. A useful method of determining the transfer characteristic is with the following relationship (the Shockley equation):

$$\frac{i_D}{I_{DSS}} \approx \left(1 - \frac{v_{GS}}{V_p}\right)^2 \tag{4.1}$$

Hence, we need to know only I_{DSS} and V_p, and the entire characteristic is then determined. Manufacturer's data sheets often give these two parameters, so the transfer characteristic can be constructed or equation (4.1) can be used directly. Note that i_D saturates (i.e., becomes constant) as v_{DS} exceeds the voltage necessary for the channel to pinch off. This can be expressed as an equation for $v_{DS(sat)}$ for each curve, as follows:

$$v_{DS(sat)} = v_{GS} + V_p$$

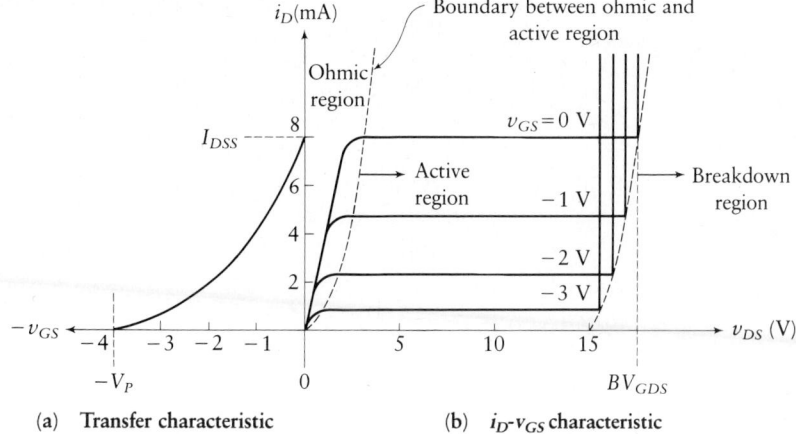

Figure 4.5
JFET characteristics.

(a)   **Transfer characteristic**   (b) i_D-v_{GS} characteristic

As v_{GS} becomes more negative, the pinch-off occurs at lower values of v_{DS} and the saturation current becomes smaller. The useful region for linear operation is above pinch-off and below the breakdown voltage. In this region, i_D is saturated and its value depends upon v_{GS}, according to equation (4.1) or the transfer characteristic.

The transfer and i_D-v_{GS} characteristic curves for the JFET, which are shown in Figure 4.5, are different from the similar curves for a BJT: The FET is a voltage-controlled device, whereas the BJT is a current-controlled device. The controlling parameter for the FET is gate-source voltage rather than base current, as in the BJT.

There are two other distinct differences between the FET and BJT. First, the vertical spacing between pairs of parametric curves for the FET is not linearly related to the value of the controlling parameter. Thus, for example, the distance between the $v_{GS} = 0$ V curve and $v_{GS} = -1$ V curve in Figure 4.5 is not the same as that between the $v_{GS} = -1$ V curve and $v_{GS} = -2$ V curve. This contrasts with the BJT curves, where a more linear relationship exists.

The second difference relates to the size and shape of the ohmic region of the characteristic curves. Recall that in using BJTs, we avoid nonlinear operation by not using the transistor at the lower 5% of values of v_{CE}, which is called the *saturation region*. We see that the width of the ohmic region for the JFET is a function of the gate-to-source voltage. As the magnitude of the gate-to-source voltage decreases, the width of the ohmic region increases. We also note from Figure 4.5 that the breakdown voltage is a function of the gate-to-source voltage. In fact, to obtain reasonably linear signal amplification, we must utilize only a relatively small segment of these curves—the area of linear operation is in the active region.

Note from Figure 4.5 that as v_{DS} increases from zero, a break point occurs on each curve, beyond which the drain current increases very little as v_{DS} continues to increase. At this drain-to-source voltage, pinch-off occurs. The pinch-off values in Figure 4.5 are connected with a dashed curve that separates the ohmic region from the active region. As v_{DS} continues to increase beyond the pinch-off point, a point is reached where the voltage between drain and source becomes so large that *avalanche breakdown* occurs. (This phenomenon also occurs in diodes and in BJTs.) At the breakdown point, i_D increases sharply with a negligible increase in v_{DS}. This breakdown occurs at the drain end of the gate-channel junction. Hence, when the drain-gate voltage, v_{DG}, exceeds the breakdown voltage, BV_{GDS} (for $v_{GS} = 0$ V), for the *pn* junction, avalanche occurs. At this point, the i_D-v_{DS} characteristic exhibits the peculiar shape shown on the right part of Figure 4.5.

The region between pinch-off and avalanche breakdown is called the *active region, amplifier operating region, saturation region,* or *pinch-off region,* as shown in Figure 4.5. The ohmic region (before pinch-off) is sometimes called the *voltage-controlled region.* The FET is operated in this region both when a variable resistor is desired and in switching applications.

The breakdown voltage is a function of v_{GS} as well as v_{DS}. As the magnitude of the voltage between gate and source is increased (more negative for *n*-channel and more positive for *p*-channel), the breakdown voltage decreases. With $v_{GS} = V_p$, the drain current is zero (except for a small leakage current), and with $v_{GS} = 0$, the drain current saturates at a value

$$i_D = I_{DSS}$$

where I_{DSS} is the *saturation drain-to-source current.*

Between pinch-off and breakdown, the drain current is saturated and does not change appreciably as a function of v_{DS}. After the FET passes the pinch-off operating point, the value of i_D can be obtained from the characteristic curves or from equation (4.1), which is repeated here for reference.

$$i_D \approx I_{DSS} \left(1 - \frac{v_{GS}}{V_p} \right)^2$$

The saturation drain-to-source current, I_{DSS}, is a function of temperature,

$$I_{DSS} = KT^{-3/2}$$

where K is a constant [51]. The pinch-off voltage is an approximately linear function of temperature (as is the case with the base-emitter current in the BJT); hence

$$\Delta V_p = -k_p \Delta T$$

where $k_p \approx 2$ mV/°C.

The currents and voltages in this section are presented for an *n*-channel JFET. The values for a *p*-channel JFET are the reverse of those just given for the *n*-channel.

4.3.3 *Equivalent Circuit, g_m and r_{DS}*

In order to obtain a measure of the amplification possible with a JFET, we introduce the parameter g_m, which is the *forward transconductance*. This parameter is similar to the current gain (or h_{fe}) for a BJT. The value of g_m, which is measured in siemens (S), is a measure of the change in drain current for a change in gate-source voltage. This can be expressed as

$$g_m = \frac{\partial i_D}{\partial v_{GS}} \approx \frac{\Delta i_D}{\Delta v_{GS}} \bigg|_{V_{DS} = \text{constant}} \tag{4.2}$$

The transconductance, g_m, does not remain constant as the Q-point is changed. This can be seen by geometrically determining g_m from the transfer characteristic curves. As i_D changes, the slope of the transfer characteristic curve of Figure 4.5 varies, thereby changing g_m.

We can find the transconductance by differentiating equation (4.1), with the result

$$g_m = \frac{\partial i_D}{\partial v_{GS}} = \frac{2I_{DSS}(1 - v_{GS}/V_p)}{-V_p} \tag{4.3}$$

We define

$$g_{mo} = \frac{2I_{DSS}}{-V_p}$$

which is the transconductance at $v_{GS} = 0$. Using this equation, the transconductance is given by

$$g_m = g_{mo}\left(1 - \frac{v_{GS}}{V_p}\right) \tag{4.4}$$

An alternate form of equation (4.4) can be found by defining

$$k_n = \frac{I_{DSS}}{V_p^2}$$

in equation (4.1), and rearranging terms, as follows:

$$i_D = I_{DSS}\left(1 - \frac{v_{GS}}{V_p}\right)^2 = \frac{I_{DSS}}{V_p^2}(V_p - v_{GS})^2 = k_n(V_p - v_{GS})^2$$

We select the Q-point so $i_D = I_{DQ}$ and $v_{GS} = V_{GSQ}$. Thus we obtain

$$V_p - V_{GSQ} = -\sqrt{\frac{I_{DQ}}{k_n}} \tag{4.5}$$

But from equation (4.3),

$$g_m = -\frac{2I_{DSS}}{V_p}\left(1 - \frac{V_{GSQ}}{V_p}\right) = -\frac{2I_{DSS}}{V_p^2}(V_p - V_{GSQ})$$

We use equation (4.5) and substitute for $V_p - V_{GSQ}$ to obtain

$$g_m = \frac{2I_{DSS}}{V_p^2}\sqrt{\frac{I_{DQ}}{k_n}} = 2k_n\sqrt{\frac{I_{DQ}}{k_n}} = 2\sqrt{k_n I_{DQ}} \tag{4.6}$$

The *inverse dynamic resistance*, r_{DS}, is defined as the inverse of the slope of the i_D-v_{DS} curve in the saturated region:

$$\frac{1}{r_{DS}} = \frac{\partial i_D}{\partial v_{DS}} \approx \frac{\Delta i_D}{\Delta v_{DS}}\bigg|_{\Delta v_{GS}=\text{constant}} \tag{4.7}$$

Because the slope of this curve is so small in the active region (see Figure 4.4), r_{DS} is large.

We develop the ac equivalent circuit for a JFET much as we did for the BJT, with the expression

$$\Delta i_D = \frac{\partial i_D}{\partial v_{GS}}\Delta v_{GS} + \frac{\partial i_D}{\partial v_{DS}}\Delta v_{DS} \tag{4.8}$$

Equation (4.8) can be rewritten using equations (4.2) and (4.7), as follows:

$$\Delta i_D = g_m\Delta v_{GS} + \frac{1}{r_{DS}}\Delta v_{DS} \tag{4.9}$$

Figure 4.6
FET equivalent circuit.

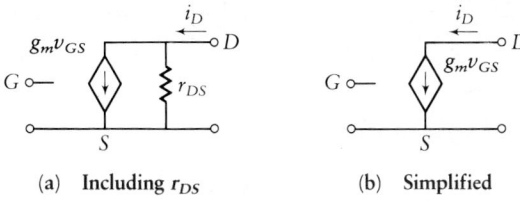

(a) Including r_{DS} (b) Simplified

Figure 4.7
i_D-v_{DS} JFET characteristic curves.

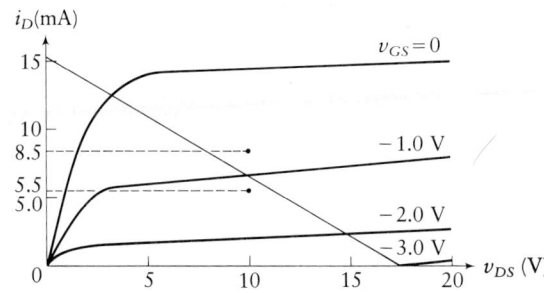

which leads to the equivalent circuit shown in Figure 4.6(a). Because r_{DS} is so large, we can usually use the simplified equivalent circuit of Figure 4.6(b) to determine the active region performance of a JFET. Equation (4.9) then reduces to

$$\Delta i_D = g_m \Delta v_{GS}$$

The performance of a JFET is specified by the values of g_m and r_{DS}. We now determine these parameters for an n-channel JFET using the characteristic curve shown in Figure 4.7. We select an operating region that is approximately in the middle of the curves, that is, between $v_{GS} = -0.8$ V and $v_{GS} = -1.2$ V and $i_D = 8.5$ mA and $i_D = 5.5$ mA. From equation (4.2), we find

$$g_m = \frac{\Delta i_D}{\Delta v_{GS}} \bigg|_{v_{DS} = \text{constant}} = \frac{(5.5 - 8.5) \text{ mA}}{-1.2 - (-0.8)} = 7.5 \text{ mS}$$

If the characteristic curves for a JFET are not available, g_m and v_{GS} can be obtained mathematically, provided I_{DSS} and V_p are known. These two parameters are usually given in the manufacturer's specifications. The quiescent drain current, I_{DQ}, can be selected to be between 0.3 and 0.7 times I_{DSS}, which locates the Q-point in the most linear region of the characteristic curves. Repeating equation (4.1), we have

$$i_D = I_{DSS}\left(1 - \frac{v_{GS}}{V_p}\right)^2$$

and at the quiescent point,

$$g_m = g_{mo}\left(1 - \frac{V_{GSQ}}{V_p}\right)$$

where

$$g_{mo} = \frac{-2I_{DSS}}{V_p}$$

The relationship between i_D and v_{GS} can be plotted on a dimensionless graph (i.e., a normalized curve), as shown in Figure 4.8. The vertical axis of this graph is $i_D/|I_{DSS}|$, and the horizontal axis is $v_{GS}/|V_p|$. The slope of the curve is g_m.

A reasonable procedure for locating the quiescent value near the center of the linear operating region is as follows:

1. Select $I_{DQ} = I_{DSS}/2$ and, from the curve, $V_{GSQ} = 0.3V_p$. Note from Figure 4.8 that this is near the midpoint of the curve.
2. Select $V_{DSQ} = V_{DD}/2$.

Figure 4.8
$i_D/|I_{DSS}|$ versus
$v_{GS}/|V_p|$.

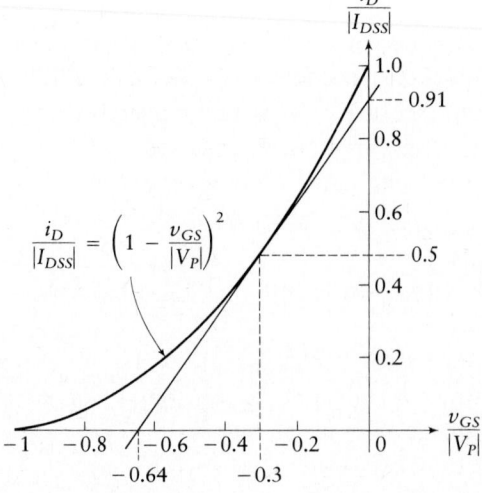

We find the transconductance at the Q-point from the slope of the curve of Figure 4.8. This is given by

$$g_m = \frac{0.91 I_{DSS}}{0.64 V_p} = \frac{1.42\ I_{DSS}}{V_p} = -0.71 g_{mo}$$

These values usually represent a good starting point for setting the quiescent values for the JFET.

Example 4.1

Determine g_m for a JFET where $I_{DSS} = 7$ mA, $V_p = -3.5$ V, and $V_{DD} = 15$ V. Choose a reasonable location for the Q-point.

SOLUTION We start by referring to Figure 4.8 and selecting the Q-point as follows:

$$I_{DQ} = \frac{I_{DSS}}{2} = 3.5\ \text{mA}$$

$$V_{DSQ} = \frac{V_{DD}}{2} = 7.5\ \text{V}$$

$$V_{GSQ} = 0.3 V_p = -1.05\ \text{V}$$

The transconductance, g_m, is found from the slope of the curve at the point $i_D/I_{DSS} = 0.5$ and $v_{GS}/V_p = 0.3$. Hence

$$g_m = \frac{1.42 I_{DSS}}{|V_p|} = \frac{1.42 \times 7\ \text{mA}}{3.5\ \text{V}} = 2840\ \mu\text{S}$$

4.4 MOSFET Operation and Construction

In this section, we consider the metal-oxide-semiconductor FET (MOSFET). This FET is constructed with the gate terminal insulated from the channel with a silicon dioxide (SiO_2) dielectric and is constructed in either a *depletion* or an *enhancement* mode. We define and consider these two types in the next sections.

Figure 4.9
The *n*-channel deple-
tion MOSFET.

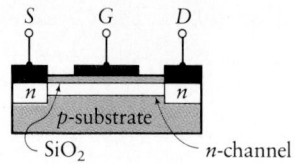

(a)   **Schematic of physical structure**

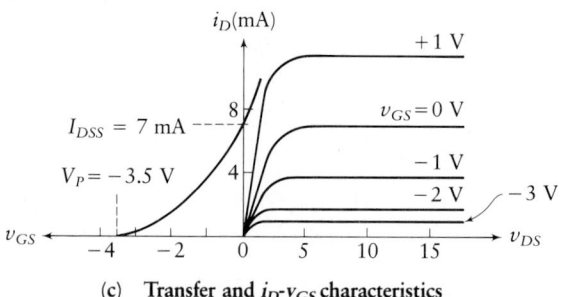

(b)   **Symbol**

(c)   **Transfer and i_D-v_{GS} characteristics**

4.4.1   *Depletion MOSFET*

The constructions of the *n*-channel and the *p*-channel depletion MOSFET are
shown in Figures 4.9 and 4.10, respectively. Each of these figures shows the
construction, the symbol, the transfer characteristic, and the i_D-v_{GS} characteristics. The depletion MOSFET is constructed (as shown in Figure 4.9(a) for
the *n*-channel and Figure 4.10(a) for the *p*-channel) with a physical channel
constructed between the drain and the source. As a result, i_D exists between
drain and source when a voltage, v_{DS}, is applied.

The *n*-channel depletion MOSFET of Figure 4.9 is established on a *p*-
substrate, which is a *p*-doped silicon. The *n*-doped source and drain wells form
low-resistance connections between the ends of the *n*-channel and the alumi-
nimum contacts of the source (S) and the drain (D). An SiO_2 layer, which is
an insulator, is grown on the top surface of the *n*-channel, as shown in Figure
4.9(a). An aluminum pad is deposited on the SiO_2 insulator to form the gate
(G) terminal. The performance of the depletion MOSFET, as can be seen from
Figures 4.9(c) and 4.10(c), is similar to that of the JFET. The JFET is controlled
by the *pn* junction between the gate and the drain end of the channel. No such
junction exists in the enhancement MOSFET, and the SiO_2 layer acts as the
insulator. For the *n*-channel MOSFET, shown in Figure 4.9, a negative v_{GS}
will push the electrons out of the channel region, hence depleting the channel.
When v_{GS} reaches V_p, the channel will be pinched off. Positive values of v_{GS}

Figure 4.10
The *p*-channel deple-
tion MOSFET.

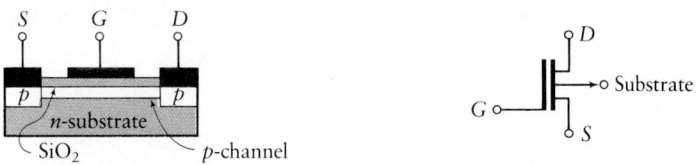

(a) Schematic of physical structure

(b) Symbol

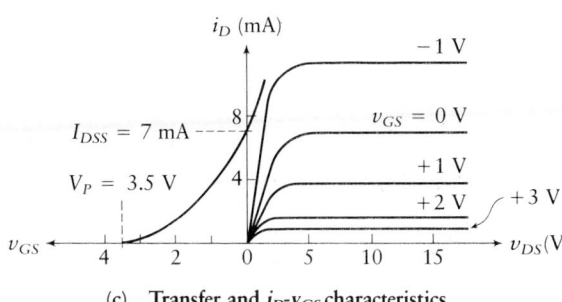

(c) Transfer and *i*$_D$-*v*$_{GS}$ characteristics

increase channel size, resulting in an increase of drain current. This is indicated
on the characteristic curves of Figure 4.9(c).

Notice that the depletion MOSFET can operate with either positive or
negative values of v_{GS}. We can use the same Shockley equation (equation (4.1))
to approximate the curves for negative v_{GS}. Notice, however, that the transfer
characteristic continues on for positive values of v_{GS}. Since the gate is insulated
from the channel, the gate current is negligibly small (10^{-12} A), and v_{GS} can
be of either polarity.

As we can see from Figures 4.9(b) and 4.10(b), the symbol for the MOSFET
has a fourth terminal, the *substrate*. The arrowhead points in for an *n*-channel
and out for a *p*-channel. The *p*-channel depletion MOSFET, which is shown
in Figure 4.10, is the same as Figure 4.9, except we reverse the *n*- and *p*-
materials and reverse the polarity of the voltages and currents.

Example 4.2

Calculate the drain current, i_D, for the depletion MOSFET of Figure 4.9 with
the following values of v_{GS}:

a. $v_{GS} = -1V$ c. $v_{GS} = -3$ V
b. $v_{GS} = -2$ V   d. $v_{GS} = +0.5$ V

SOLUTION   We use equation (4.1) for each case, where $I_{DSS} = 7$ mA and $V_p = -3.5$ V.

a. $i_D = I_{DSS}\left(1 - \dfrac{v_{GS}}{V_p}\right)^2 = 7\left(1 - \dfrac{-1}{-3.5}\right)^2 = 3.57$ mA

b. $i_D = I_{DSS}\left(1 - \dfrac{v_{GS}}{V_p}\right)^2 = 7\left(1 - \dfrac{-2}{-3.5}\right)^2 = 1.29$ mA

c. $i_D = I_{DSS}\left(1 - \dfrac{v_{GS}}{V_p}\right)^2 = 7\left(1 - \dfrac{-3}{-3.5}\right)^2 = 0.14$ mA

d. $i_D = I_{DSS}\left(1 - \dfrac{v_{GS}}{V_p}\right)^2 = 7\left(1 - \dfrac{0.5}{-3.5}\right)^2 = 9.14$ mA

It is interesting to note that i_D increases dramatically as v_{GS} becomes positive. The accuracy of the formula approximation deteriorates for positive values of v_{GS}. ◄►

4.4.2   *Enhancement MOSFET*

The enhancement MOSFET is shown in Figure 4.11. It differs from the depletion MOSFET in that it does not have the thin n-layer but requires a positive voltage between the gate and source to establish a channel. This channel is formed by the action of a positive gate-to-source voltage, v_{GS}, which attracts electrons from the substrate region between the n-doped drain and source. Positive v_{GS} causes electrons to accumulate at the surface beneath the oxide layer. When the voltage reaches a threshold value, V_T, enough electrons are attracted to this region to make it act like a conducting n-channel. No appreciable current i_D will exist until v_{GS} exceeds V_T.

No value of I_{DSS} exists for the enhancement MOSFET, since the drain current is zero until the channel has been formed. I_{DSS} is zero at $v_{GS} = 0$. For values of

$$v_{GS} > V_T$$

the drain current in saturation can be calculated from the equation

$$i_D = k(v_{GS} - V_T)^2 \tag{4.10}$$

The value of k depends upon the construction of the MOSFET and is primarily a function of the width and length of the channel. A typical value for k is 0.3 mA/V^2, and the threshold voltage, V_T, is specified by the manufacturer. We

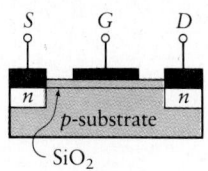

Figure 4.11
The *n*-channel
enhancement
MOSFET.

(a)   Schematic of physical structure

(b)   Symbol

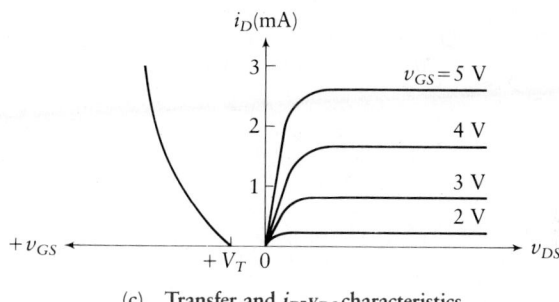

(c)   Transfer and i_D-v_{DS} characteristics

can find a value for g_m by differentiating equation (4.10), as we did with JFETs, with the result

$$g_m = \frac{\partial i_D}{\partial v_{GS}} = 2k(v_{GS} - V_T) \tag{4.11}$$

If

$$v_{GS} < V_T$$

then $i_D = 0$.

The *p*-channel enhancement MOSFET is shown in Figure 4.12 and, as can be seen, displays similar but opposite characteristics to those of the *n*-channel enhancement MOSFET.

Although it is more restricted in operating range than the depletion MOSFET, the enhancement MOSFET is useful in IC applications (see Chapter 15) because of its small size and simple construction. The gate for both *n*- and *p*-channel MOSFETs is a metal deposit on a silicon-oxide layer. The construction begins with a substrate material (*p*-type for *n*-channel; *n*-type for *p*-channel) on which the opposite type of material is diffused to form the source and drain. Notice that the symbol for an enhancement MOSFET, which is shown in Figures 4.11 and 4.12, shows a broken line between source and drain to indicate that no channel initially exists.

Figure 4.12
The *p*-channel
enhancement
MOSFET.

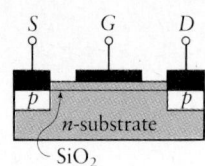

(a)   Schematic of physical structure

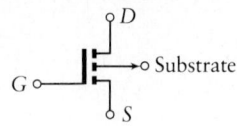

(b)   Symbol

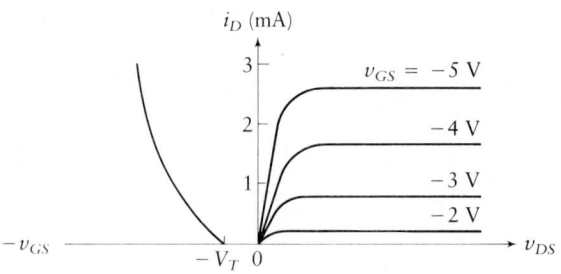

(c)   Transfer and i_D-v_{GS} characteristics

Example 4.3

Determine i_D for an *n*-channel enhancement MOSFET with $V_T = 3.0$ V when $k = 0.3$ mA/V^2 and v_{GS} is given by the following values:

a. 3.0 V
b. 4.0 V
c. 5.0 V

SOLUTION   From equation (4.10) we calculate the following values.

a. $i_D = 0.3(v_{GS} - V_T)^2 = 0.3(3 - 3)^2 = 0$ mA
b. $i_D = 0.3(4 - 3)^2 = 0.3$ mA
c. $i_D = 0.3(5 - 3)^2 = 1.2$ mA

4.5   Biasing of FETs

The same basic circuits of Figure 3.6 that are used for biasing BJTs can also be used for JFETs and depletion MOSFETS. However, for the active region of the JFET and the depletion-mode MOSFET, the polarity of v_{GS} can be opposite from that of the drain voltage source. In selecting the operating point, voltage

Figure 4.13
FET amplifier.

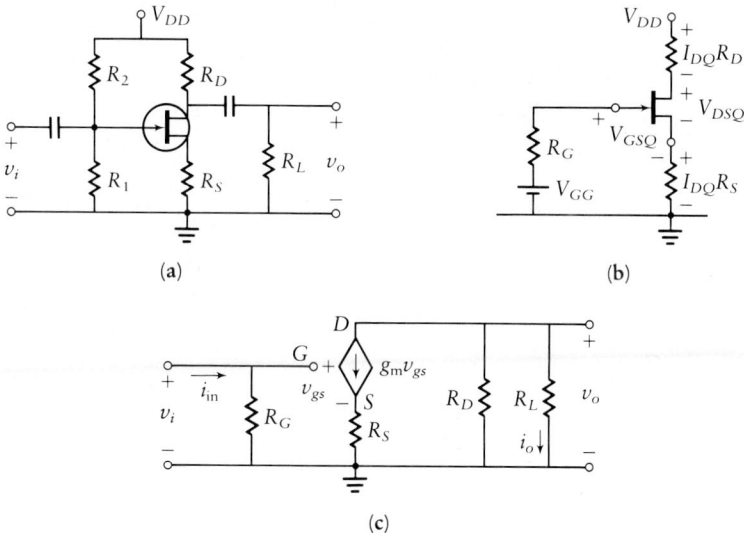

(a)

(b)

(c)

of the opposite polarity is not available from the source to meet the requirements of the circuit. It may be necessary to delete R_2 (see Figure 4.13) so only voltage of correct polarity is acquired. It is not always possible to find resistor values to achieve a particular Q-point. In such instances, selecting a new Q-point can sometimes provide a solution to the problem.

We consider here the bias equations for the CS amplifier, shown in Figure 4.13, where we use a JFET. The bias methods are similar for depletion MOSFETs.

Figure 4.13(a) illustrates a FET amplifier using one dc voltage source for biasing. We form the Thevenin equivalent of the bias circuit to obtain

$$R_G = R_1 \parallel R_2 = \frac{R_1 R_2}{R_1 + R_2} \tag{4.12a}$$

$$V_{GG} = \frac{V_{DD} R_1}{R_1 + R_2} \tag{4.12b}$$

Since we have three unknown variables, I_{DQ}, V_{GSQ}, and V_{DSQ}, we need three dc equations. First, the dc equation around the gate-source loop is formed from Figure 4.13(b), as follows:

$$V_{GG} = V_{GSQ} + I_{DQ} R_S \tag{4.13}$$

Notice that since the gate current is zero, a zero voltage drop exists across R_G.

A second dc equation is found from the Kirchhoff's law equation in the drain-source loop, as follows:

$$V_{DD} = V_{DSQ} + I_{DQ}(R_S + R_D) \tag{4.14}$$

The third dc equation necessary to establish the bias point is found from equation (4.1), which is repeated here with $i_D = I_{DQ}$ and $v_{GS} = V_{GSQ}$.

$$\frac{I_{DQ}}{I_{DSS}} = \left(1 - \frac{V_{GSQ}}{V_p}\right)^2 \tag{4.15}$$

These three equations are sufficient to establish the bias for the JFET and depletion MOSFET, which are used for linear amplifiers. The enhancement MOSFET is used for digital ICs.

Note that we do not need to put the Q-point in the center of the ac load line as we did for BJT biasing. This is because we normally use a FET amplifier at the input to the amplifier to take advantage of the high input resistance. At this point, the voltage levels are so small that we do not drive the amplifier with large excursions. Also, since the FET characteristic curves are nonlinear, we would produce distortion with large input excursions.

4.6   Analysis of a CS Amplifier

Figure 4.13(c) shows the ac equivalent circuit for the FET amplifier. We assume r_{DS} is large compared to $R_D \| R_L$, so it can be neglected. Writing a KVL equation around the gate circuit, we find

$$v_{gs} = v_i - R_S i_D = v_i - R_S g_m v_{gs}$$

Solving for v_{gs} yields

$$v_{gs} = \frac{v_i}{1 + R_S g_m}$$

The output voltage, v_o, is given by

$$v_o = -i_d(R_D \| R_L) = \frac{-(R_D \| R_L)g_m v_i}{1 + R_S g_m}$$

The voltage gain, A_v, is

$$A_v = \frac{v_o}{v_i} = \frac{-g_m(R_D \parallel R_L)}{1 + R_S g_m}$$

$$= \frac{-(R_D \parallel R_L)}{R_S + 1/g_m} \tag{4.16a}$$

The resistance, R_S, is sometimes bypassed by a capacitor, in which case the voltage gain increases to

$$A_v = -g_m(R_D \parallel R_L)$$

The input resistance and current gain are given by

$$R_{in} = R_G = R_1 \parallel R_2 \tag{4.16b}$$

$$A_i = \frac{i_o}{i_{in}} = \frac{A_v R_{in}}{R_L} = \frac{-R_D \parallel R_L}{R_S + 1/g_m} \frac{R_{in}}{R_L} = \frac{-R_G}{R_S + 1/g_m} \frac{R_D}{R_D + R_L} \tag{4.16c}$$

Example 4.4   ## CS Amplifier (Analysis)

Find A_v for the JFET amplifier of Figure 4.14(a). The Q-point is at $V_{DSQ} = 12$ V and $I_{DQ} = 7$ mA. The FET parameters are given by

$$g_m = 3.0 \text{ mS}$$

$$r_{DS} = 200 \text{ k}\Omega$$

SOLUTION   From the equivalent circuit of Figure 4.14(b), we obtain

$$A_v = \frac{v_o}{v_{gs}} = \frac{-i_D(R_D \parallel r_{DS})}{v_{gs}} = -g_m(R_D \parallel r_{DS}) = 52$$

Figure 4.14
JFET circuit for Example 4.4.

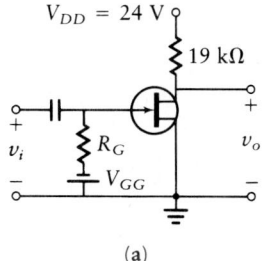

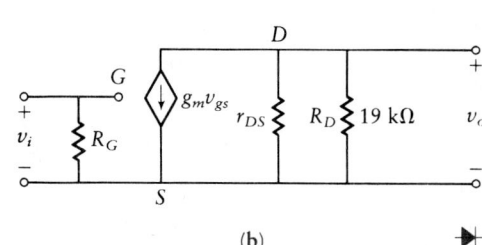

(a)   (b)

4.7 **Design of a CS Amplifier**

The design procedure of a CS amplifier is presented in this section. The JFET and the depletion MOSFET amplifier design is presented as a step-by-step procedure. You should convince yourself that you understand the origin of each step, since several variations may subsequently be required.

Amplifiers are designed to meet gain requirements if the desired specifications are within the range of the transistor. The supply voltage, load resistance, voltage gain and input resistance (or current gain) are usually specified. Our problem is to select the resistance values R_1, R_2, R_D, and R_S. Refer to Figure 4.15 as you follow the steps in the procedure. This procedure assumes that a device has been selected and that its characteristics are known—at least V_p and I_{DSS}.

Step 1 Select a Q-point in the most linear portion of the JFET characteristic curves. Refer to the curves of Figure 4.15(b) for an example. This identifies V_{DSQ}, V_{GSQ}, I_{DQ}, and g_m. If an i_D-v_{GS} characteristic curve is unavailable, use the dimensionless curve of Figure 4.8, with I_{DSS} and V_p given for the transistor type used.

Step 2 Write the dc KVL equation (equation (4.14)) around the drain-source loop,

$$V_{DD} = V_{DSQ} + (R_S + R_D)I_{DQ}$$

Solving for the sum of the two resistors yields

$$R_S + R_D = \frac{V_{DD} - V_{DSQ}}{I_{DQ}} = K_1 \tag{4.17}$$

Equation (4.17) represents one equation in two unknowns, R_S and R_D.

Step 3 Use the voltage-gain equations (equation (4.16a)) to yield a second equation in R_S and R_D. We can substitute equation (4.17) into equation (4.16a)

$$A_v = \frac{-R_L \parallel R_D}{R_S + 1/g_m} = \frac{-R_L \parallel R_D}{(K_1 - R_D) + 1/g_m} \tag{4.18}$$

The resistance, R_D, *is the only unknown in this equation.* Solving for R_D results in a quadratic equation with two solutions, one negative and one positive. If the positive solution results in $R_D > K_1$, thus implying a negative R_S, a new

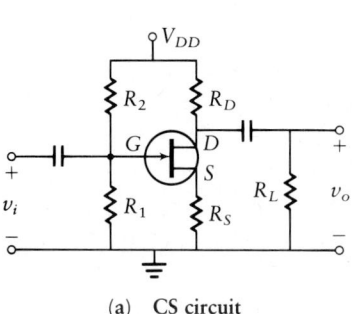

Figure 4.15
JFET CS amplifier.

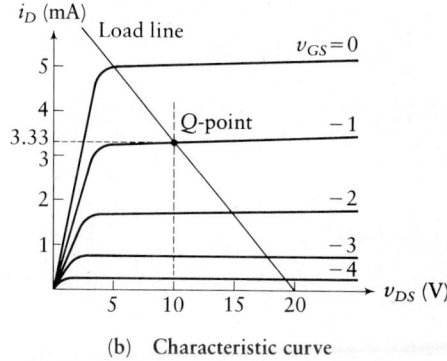

(a)   CS circuit

(b)   Characteristic curve

Q-point must be selected (i.e., restart the design at Step 1). If the positive solution yields $R_D < K_1$, we can proceed to Step 4.

Step 4   Solve for R_S using equation (4.17), the drain-to-source loop equation developed in Step 2.

$$R_S = \frac{V_{DD} - V_{DSQ}}{I_{DQ}} - R_D$$

With R_D and R_S known, we need find only R_1 and R_2.

Step 5   Write the KVL equation for the gate-source loop (equation (4.13)):

$$V_{GG} = V_{GSQ} + I_{DQ}R_S$$

The voltage V_{GSQ} is of opposite polarity from V_{DD}. Thus the term $I_{DQ}R_S$ must be greater than V_{GSQ} in magnitude. Otherwise, V_{GG} will have the opposite polarity from V_{DD}, which is not possible according to equation (4.12b).

Step 6   We now solve for R_1 and R_2 assuming that the V_{GG} found in Step 5 has the *same polarity* as V_{DD}. These resistor values are selected by finding the value of R_G from the current-gain equation or from the input resistance. We solve equation (4.12) to find R_1 and R_2:

$$R_1 = \frac{R_G}{1 - V_{GG}/V_{DD}}$$

$$R_2 = \frac{R_G V_{DD}}{V_{GG}}$$

Figure 4.16
JFET design with
bypassed source
resistor.

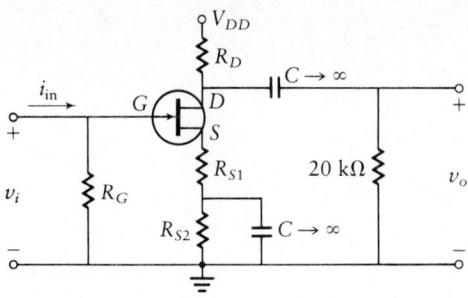

Step 7   If V_{GG} has the *opposite polarity* of V_{DD}, it is not possible to solve for R_1 and R_2. The practical way to proceed is to let $V_{GG} = 0$ V. Thus, $R_2 \to \infty$. Since V_{GG} is specified by equation (4.13), the previously calculated value of R_S now needs to be modified. In Figure 4.16, where a capacitor is used to bypass a part of R_S, we develop the new value of R_S as follows:

$$V_{GG} = 0 = V_{GSQ} + I_{DQ}R_{Sdc}$$

Therefore, solving for R_{Sdc} yields

$$R_{Sdc} = \frac{-V_{GSQ}}{I_{DQ}}$$

The value of R_{Sdc} is $R_{S1} + R_{S2}$ and the value of R_{Sac} is R_{S1}.

Now that we have a new R_{Sdc}, we must repeat several steps.

Step 8   Determine R_D using KVL for the drain-to-source loop (repeat Step 2):

$$R_D = K_1 - R_{Sdc}$$

The design problem now becomes one of calculating both R_{S1} and R_{S2} instead of finding only one source resistor.

With a new value for R_D of $K_1 - R_{Sdc}$, we go to the voltage-gain expression of equation (4.16a) with R_{Sac} used for this ac equation rather than R_S.

The following additional steps must be added to the design procedure.

Step 9   We find R_{Sac} (which is simply R_{S1}) from the voltage-gain equation, equation (4.16a):

$$A_v = \frac{-(R_L \| R_D)}{R_{Sac} + 1/g_m}$$

R_{Sac} is the only unknown in this equation. Therefore,

$$R_{Sac} = -\frac{R_L \| R_D}{A_v} - \frac{1}{g_m}$$

Suppose now that R_{Sac} is found to be positive but less than R_{Sdc}. This is the desirable condition since

$$R_{Sdc} = R_{Sac} + R_{S2}$$

Then our design is complete and

$$R_1 = R_{in} = R_G$$

Step 10   Suppose that R_{Sac} is found to be positive but *greater* than R_{Sdc}. The amplifier cannot be designed with the voltage gain and Q-point as selected. A new Q-point must be selected, and we return to Step 1. If the voltage gain is too high, it may not be possible to effect the design with any Q-point. A different transistor may be needed or the use of two separate stages may be required.

4.8   Selection of Components

A design is not yet complete when the various component values are specified. It is still necessary to select the actual components to be used (e.g., choose the manufacturer's part numbers from a catalog). Thus, when the design requires a resistor value, say 102.5 Ω, the designer will not be able to find this resistor in a standard parts catalog. Available nominal component values depend upon tolerances. As an example, a 100-Ω resistor with a 5% tolerance can have any value between 95 Ω and 105 Ω. It would not make much sense for the manufacturer to offer another off-the-shelf resistor with a nominal rating of 101 Ω, since that resistor could have a value between approximately 96 Ω and 106 Ω. The distance between adjacent nominal component values is therefore related to the tolerance, with such distance decreasing as the tolerance decreases (i.e., higher-precision components). Standard values of resistors and capacitors are included in Appendix E.

Since component values are not readily available to any degree of resolution, it would not make sense to carry out design calculations to an unreasonably large number of significant figures.

In our design examples, we specify values to at least three significant figures. This is important to ensure that we still maintain accuracy to two significant figures following arithmetic operations. For example, suppose we must add

$$0.274 + 0.474$$

If these two numbers are rounded to two significant figures, we obtain

$$0.27 + 0.47 = 0.74$$

If we first do the calculation, however, we obtain

$$0.274 + 0.474 = 0.748$$

which rounds to 0.75. Rounding the numbers prior to performing the addition results in an error in the second significant figure. Thus, to reduce accumulated errors and to increase the confidence that our answers are accurate to two significant figures, we maintain at least three figures throughout the calculations.

Example 4.5   JFET CS Amplifier (Design)

Design a CS JFET amplifier with a voltage gain of $A_v = -4$, $R_{in} = 100$ kΩ, $R_L = 20$ kΩ, $I_{DSS} = 6.67$ mA, $V_p = -3.33$ V and $V_{DD} = 20$ V. Since we do not know whether we will need an R_2, let us start with Figure 4.15(a) and the dimensionless curves of Figure 4.8.

SOLUTION

Step 1   The Q-point is selected from Figure 4.8 as follows:

$$I_{DQ} = \frac{I_{DSS}}{2} = 3.33 \text{ mA}$$

$$V_{GSQ} = 0.3V_p = -1 \text{ V}$$

$$V_{DSQ} = \frac{V_{DD}}{2} = 10 \text{ V}$$

Then

$$g_m = 1.42 \frac{I_{DSS}}{V_p} = 2.86 \times 10^{-3} \text{ S}$$

and

$$\frac{1}{g_m} = 350 \ \Omega$$

Step 2   From Step 2 in the design procedure, we have

$$R_D + R_{Sdc} = \frac{20 \text{ V} - 10 \text{ V}}{3.33 \text{ mA}} = 3 \text{ k}\Omega = K_1$$

Step 3   Using the ac gain equation, we obtain

$$A_v = \frac{-(20 \text{ k}\Omega \parallel R_D)}{3 \text{ k}\Omega - R_D + 350 \ \Omega)} = -4$$

$$R_D^2 + (21.65 \text{ k}\Omega)R_D - 67 \text{ M}\Omega^2 = 0$$

From the quadratic for R_D we select the positive root,

$$R_D = 2.747 \text{ k}\Omega$$

Step 4   This quantity is less than K_1, so we proceed to Step 4. We find R_S using equation (4.15):

$$R_S = 3 \text{ k}\Omega - R_D = 253 \ \Omega$$

Step 5   This step now yields

$$V_{GG} = -1 + 253(3.33 \times 10^{-3}) = -0.15 \text{ V}$$

Since this negative voltage cannot be obtained by dividing the source voltage using resistors, we skip to Step 7.

Step 7   Let

$$R_2 \to \infty$$

Then

$$V_{GG} = 0 = V_{GSQ} + I_{DQ}R_{Sdc}$$

$$= -1 + (3.33 \times 10^{-3})R_{Sdc}$$

Solving for R_{Sdc} we obtain

$$R_{Sdc} = 300 \ \Omega$$

Step 8   This step yields

$$R_D = 3 \text{ k}\Omega - R_{Sdc} = 2.7 \text{ k}\Omega$$

R_{Sac} is determined from Step 9.

Step 9

$$R_{Sac} = -\frac{R_L \| R_D}{A_v} - \frac{1}{g_m} = \frac{-(20 \text{ k}\Omega \| 2.7 \text{ k}\Omega)}{-4} - 350 \ \Omega = 245 \ \Omega$$

The final circuit is shown in Figure 4.16, where the component values are

$$R_D = 2.7 \text{ k}\Omega$$

$$R_{S1} = R_{Sac} = 245 \ \Omega$$

$$R_{S2} = R_{Sdc} - R_{Sac} = 300 \ \Omega - 245 \ \Omega = 55 \ \Omega$$

$$R_G = R_{\text{in}} = R_1 = 100 \text{ k}\Omega$$

Example 4.6   **JFET CS Amplifier (Design)**

Repeat Example 4.5 for Figure 4.17, but select a Q-point that is not in the center of the linear region.

SOLUTION   Let us arbitrarily select the new operating point as follows.

Step 1

$$I_{DQ} = 3.5 \text{ mA}$$

$$V_{GSQ} = -0.8 \text{ V}$$

$$V_{DSQ} = 6 \text{ V}$$

Then

$$g_m = 2.0 \times 10^{-3} \text{ S}$$

and

$$\frac{1}{g_m} = 500 \ \Omega$$

Step 2   This step in the design procedure yields

$$R_D + R_S = \frac{20 - 6}{3.5 \times 10^{-3}} = 4 \text{ k}\Omega = K_1$$

Step 3   Then we find

$$A_v = -4 = \frac{-R_D \parallel 20 \text{ k}\Omega}{4 \text{ k}\Omega - R_D + 500 \text{ }\Omega}$$

from which we obtain, after solving the quadratic equation,

$$R_D = 3.716 \text{ k}\Omega$$

This quantity is less than K_1, so we proceed to Step 4.

Step 4   From equation (4.17), we obtain

$$R_S = 4 \text{ k}\Omega - 3.716 \text{ k}\Omega = 284 \text{ }\Omega$$

Step 5   Using the bias equation of this step, we find

$$V_{GG} = -0.8 + 284(3.5 \times 10^{-3}) = 0.194 \text{ V}$$

Step 6   To determine R_1 and R_2 with $R_{in} = R_G$, we use Step 6, since V_{GG} is the same polarity as V_{DD}. (This contrasts with the situation in the previous example.) Thus,

$$R_1 = \frac{100 \text{ k}\Omega}{1 - 0.194/20} = 101 \text{ k}\Omega$$

$$R_2 = 100 \text{ k}\Omega \left(\frac{20}{0.194}\right) = 10.3 \text{ M}\Omega$$

The final circuit is shown in Figure 4.17.

Figure 4.17
CS amplifier for
Example 4.6.

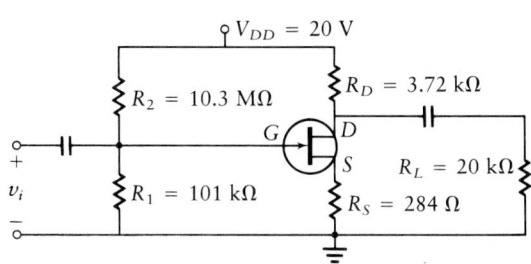

Example 4.7   **JFET CS Amplifier (Analysis)**

Analyze the single-stage JFET CS amplifier shown in Figure 4.18 and determine A_v, A_i, and R_{in}. Assume $I_{DSS} = 2$ mA and $V_p = 2$ V.

SOLUTION   We first calculate the Q-point, from which we determine g_m; both A_v and A_i depend upon this parameter. Remember that the value of g_m depends upon the Q-point location. We need two equations in order to find I_{DQ} and V_{GSQ}, as follows:

$$V_{GSQ} = -R_S I_{DQ} = -0.4 I_{DQ}$$

and from equation (4.1),

$$\frac{I_{DQ}}{I_{DSS}} = \left(1 - \frac{V_{GSQ}}{V_p}\right)^2$$

When we solve these two equations, we obtain a quadratic equation in I_{DQ}.

$$\frac{I_{DQ}}{2} = \left(1 - \frac{-0.4 I_{DQ}}{-2}\right)^2$$

where I_{DQ} is in milliamps.

This reduces to

$$I_{DQ}^2 - 22.5 I_{DQ} + 25 = 0$$

We solve this quadratic equation and obtain two values: 21.33 mA and 1.17 mA. Since I_{DSS} is only 2 mA, we discard the larger value and obtain

$$I_{DQ} = 1.17 \text{ mA}$$

Figure 4.18
CS amplifier for
Example 4.7.

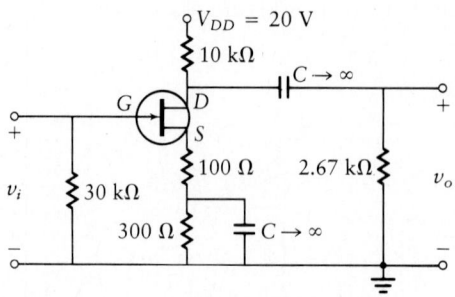

Hence

$$V_{GSQ} = (-0.4)(I_{DQ}) = -(0.4)(1.17) = -0.469 \text{ V}$$

We use equation (4.3) to find g_m as follows:

$$g_m = \frac{-2I_{DSS}}{V_p}\left(1 - \frac{V_{GSQ}}{V_p}\right) = \frac{(2)(2)}{-(-2)}\left(1 - \frac{-0.469}{-2}\right) = 1.53 \text{ mS}$$

and

$$\frac{1}{g_m} = 653 \ \Omega$$

We now find the voltage gain from equation (4.16a):

$$A_v = -\frac{R_D \| R_L}{R_{Sac} + 1/g_m} = \frac{10 \text{ k}\Omega \| 2.67 \text{ k}\Omega}{100 \ \Omega + 653 \ \Omega} = -2.8$$

and

$$R_{in} = 30 \text{ k}\Omega$$

$$A_i = \frac{A_v R_{in}}{R_L} = \frac{-2.8(30,000)}{2670} = -31.5$$

Drill Problems

D4.1   Design a CS JFET amplifier that has an R_L of 10 kΩ, $V_{DD} = 12$ V, R_{in} = 500 kΩ, and $A_v = -2$. Use the circuit of Figure 4.15(a). Select the Q-point as $V_{DSQ} = 6$ V, $V_{GSQ} = -1$ V, $I_{DQ} = 1$ mA, and $g_m = 2500$ μS.

> **Ans:** $R_S = 1.22$ kΩ; $R_D = 4.78$ kΩ;
> $R_1 = 509$ kΩ; $R_2 = 27$ MΩ;
> $A_i = -100$

D4.2   Redesign the amplifier of Problem D4.1 for a Q-point at $V_{DSQ} = 7$ V, $V_{GSQ} = -1.2$ V, $I_{DQ} = 0.5$ mA and $g_m = 3330$ μS.

> **Ans:** $R_1 = 500$ kΩ; $R_2 = \infty$;
> $R_D = 7.6$ kΩ; $R_{Sdc} = 2.4$ kΩ;
> $R_{Sac} = 1.86$ kΩ; $A_i = -100$

4.9 Analysis of CD (SF) Amplifiers

The CD (SF) JFET amplifier is illustrated in Figure 4.19(a) and the equivalent circuit is shown in Figure 4.19(b). Our approach to the analysis of this amplifier parallels that of Section 4.7. The input resistance is $R_{in} \approx R_G$. Note in the equivalent circuit that we ignore r_{DS}, since it is usually much larger than R_S. If r_{DS} is not much larger than R_S, we modify the following equations by replacing R_S with $r_{DS} \parallel R_S$.

Writing KVL equation around the gate-to-source loop, we have

$$v_{gs} = v_i - g_m(R_S \parallel R_L)v_{gs}$$

from which we obtain

$$v_i = v_{gs}\left[1 + g_m(R_S \parallel R_L)\right]$$

The output voltage is

$$v_o = g_m(R_S \parallel R_L)v_{gs}$$

and the voltage gain is the ratio

$$A_v = \frac{v_o}{v_i} = \frac{g_m(R_S \parallel R_L)}{1 + g_m(R_S \parallel R_L)} = \frac{R_S \parallel R_L}{(R_S \parallel R_L) + 1/g_m} \tag{4.19a}$$

Note that since $R_S \parallel R_L$ is of the same magnitude as $1/g_m$, the voltage gain of a SF amplifier is less than unity.

We find the current gain using the gain impedance formula as follows:

$$A_i = A_v \frac{R_{in}}{R_L} \tag{4.19b}$$

$$= \frac{R_S \parallel R_L}{(R_S \parallel R_L) + 1/g_m} \frac{R_{in}}{R_L} = \frac{R_S}{(R_S \parallel R_L) + 1/g_m} \frac{R_G}{R_S + R_L}$$

Figure 4.19   JFET SF amplifier.

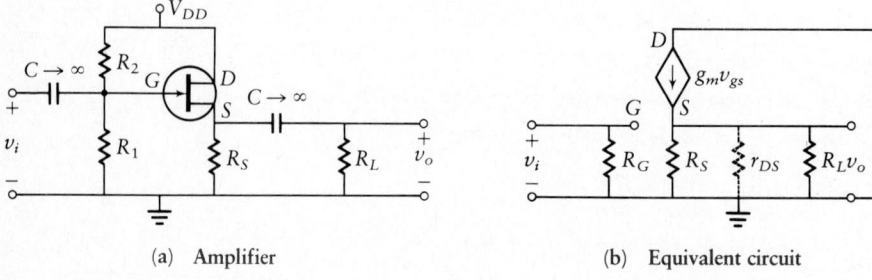

(a) Amplifier   (b) Equivalent circuit

4.10 CD Amplifier Design Procedure

In this section, we present the design procedure for the CD JFET amplifier. This procedure is the same as that used to design depletion MOSFET amplifiers. The following quantities are specified: current gain, load resistance, and V_{DD}. Input resistance may be specified instead of current gain. With A_i (or R_{in}) specified, we have three equations (two loop equations and the A_i equation) in three unknowns, R_1, R_2 and R_S. In this case, we refer to Figure 4.19(a).

If both A_i and R_{in} are specified, then we have four equations and only three unknowns. With one more equation than the number of unknowns, it usually will not be possible to find a solution without modifying the circuit. In such cases, we introduce a bypass capacitor across a portion of R_S, as shown in Figure 4.20. With that change, we now have four unknowns, R_1, R_2, R_{S1}, and R_{S2}, so the circuit can be solved.

Step 1 Select a Q-point in the center of the FET characteristic curves with the aid of Figure 4.8. This step determines V_{DSQ}, V_{GSQ}, I_{DQ}, and g_m.

Step 2 Write the dc KVL equation around the drain-to-source loop.

$$V_{DD} = V_{DSQ} + R_S I_{DQ}$$

from which we find the dc value of R_S,

$$R_{Sdc} = \frac{V_{DD} - V_{DSQ}}{I_{DQ}} \tag{4.20a}$$

Step 3 Find R_{Sac} from the rearranged current gain equation, equation (4.19b), as follows:

$$R_{Sac} = \frac{R_L}{(R_G/A_i - R_L)g_m - 1} \tag{4.20b}$$

Figure 4.20
CD amplifier.

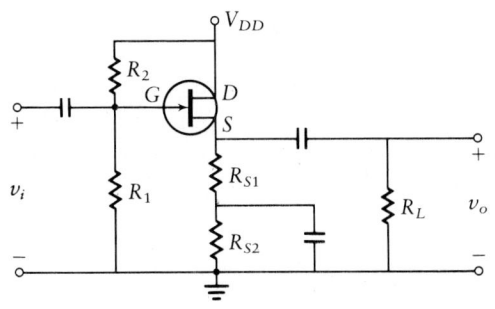

where

$$R_G = R_{in}$$

If the input resistance is not specified, let $R_{Sac} = R_{Sdc} = R_S$ and calculate the input resistance from equation (4.20b). If the input resistance is not high enough, it may be necessary to change the Q-point location.

If R_{in} is specified, it is necessary to calculate R_{Sdc} from equation (4.20a) and R_{Sac} from equation (4.20b). In such cases, R_{Sac} is different from R_{Sdc}, so we bypass part of R_S with a capacitor.

Step 4   Determine V_{GG} using the equation

$$V_{GG} = V_{GSQ} + I_{DQ}R_S$$

No phase inversion is produced in a source-follower FET amplifier, and V_{GG} is normally the same polarity as the supply voltage.

Step 5   Determine the values of R_1 and R_2 from equation (4.12):

$$R_1 = \frac{R_G}{1 - V_{GG}/V_{DD}}$$

$$R_2 = \frac{R_G V_{DD}}{V_{GG}}$$

There is usually enough drain current in an SF to develop the opposite polarity voltage needed to offset the negative voltages required by the JFET gate. Therefore, normal voltage division biasing can be used.

We now return to the problem of specifying the input resistance. We can assume that part of R_S is bypassed, as in Figure 4.20, which leads to different values of R_{Sac} and R_{Sdc}. Step 2 is used to solve for R_{Sdc}. In Step 3, we let R_G equal the specified value of R_{in} and use equation (4.20b) to solve for R_{Sac}.

If the R_{Sac} calculated above is smaller than R_{Sdc}, the design is accomplished by bypassing R_{S2} with a capacitor. Remember that $R_{Sac} = R_{S2}$ and $R_{Sdc} = R_{S1} + R_{S2}$. If, on the other hand, R_{Sac} is larger than R_{Sdc}, the Q-point must be moved to a different location. We select a smaller V_{DSQ}, thus causing increased voltage to be dropped across $R_{S1} + R_{S2}$, which makes R_{Sdc} larger. If V_{DSQ} cannot be reduced sufficiently to make R_{Sdc} larger than R_{Sac}, then the amplifier cannot be designed with the given current gain, R_{in}, and FET type. One of these three specifications must be changed, or a second amplifier stage must be used to provide the required gain.

Example 4.8   CD Amplifier (Design)

Design a CD JFET amplifier with the following specifications: $A_i = 12$, $R_L = 400\ \Omega$, $I_{DSS} = 20$ mA, $V_p = -6.67$ V, and $V_{DD} = 12$ V.

SOLUTION

Step 1   Select the Q-point as follows (see Figure 4.8):

$$I_{DQ} = \frac{I_{DSS}}{2} = 10 \text{ mA}$$

$$V_{DSQ} = \frac{V_{DD}}{2} = 6 \text{ V}$$

$$V_{GSQ} = (0.3)(-6.67) = -2 \text{ V}$$

$$g_m = \frac{1.42 I_{DSS}}{V_p} = 4.26 \text{ mS}$$

and

$$\frac{1}{g_m} = 235 \ \Omega$$

Step 2   Since no value of R_{in} is specified, $R_S = R_{Sac} = R_{Sdc}$ and we use Figure 4.19, with the result

$$R_S = \frac{V_{DD} - V_{DSQ}}{I_{DQ}} = \frac{12 - 6}{10 \times 10^{-3}} = 600 \ \Omega$$

Step 3   We use this step to find R_G by rearranging equation (4.19b):

$$R_G = A_i \left[R_L + \frac{1 + R_L/R_S}{g_m} \right] = 12 \left[400 + \frac{1 + 400/600}{4.26 \text{ mS}} \right] = 9.5 \text{ k}\Omega$$

Since R_G is greater than the minimum specified R_{in}, the design is acceptable and we can continue to Step 4.

Step 4

$$V_{GG} = -2 + (10 \times 10^{-3})(600) = 4 \text{ V}$$

Step 5   Finally, from this step we find

$$R_1 = \frac{9500}{1 - 4/12} = 14.25 \text{ k}\Omega$$

$$R_2 = \frac{9500 \times 12}{4} = 28.5 \text{ k}\Omega$$

$$A_v = A_i \frac{R_L}{R_{in}} = 12 \frac{400}{9500} = 0.51$$

Example 4.9   **CD Amplifier (Design)**

Design a CD amplifier (see Figure 4.19) to meet the following specifications: $A_i = 20$, $R_{in} = 50$ kΩ, $R_L = 1$ kΩ, $V_{DD} = 12$ V, $I_{DSS} = 20$ mA, and $V_p = -6.67$ V. Determine all component values for the circuit.

SOLUTION   The Q-point is selected as

$$V_{DSQ} = \frac{V_{DD}}{2} = 6 \text{ V}$$

$$I_{DQ} = \frac{I_{DSS}}{2} = 10 \text{ mA}$$

$$V_{GSQ} = 0.3(V_p) = -2 \text{ V}$$

We find g_m from the dimensionless curve of Figure 4.8 as follows:

$$g_m = 1.42 \frac{I_{DSS}}{|V_p|} = 4.26 \text{ mS}$$

and

$$\frac{1}{g_m} = 230 \text{ }\Omega$$

We use Step 2 to find R_{Sdc}. Note that since R_{in} is given, we will probably need values for R_{Sdc} and R_{Sac}.

$$R_{Sdc} = \frac{12 - 6}{10 \times 10^{-3}} = 600 \text{ }\Omega$$

Since R_{in} is specified, we use Step 3 to find R_{Sac}; from equation (4.20),

$$R_G = R_{in} = 50 \text{ k}\Omega$$

$$R_{Sac} = \frac{R_L}{(R_G/A_i - R_L)g_m - 1}$$

$$= \frac{1000}{(50,000/20 - 1000)4.26 \text{ mS} - 1} = 186 \ \Omega$$

Since R_{Sac} is less than R_{Sdc}, we find $R_{S1} = 186 \ \Omega$ and $R_{S2} = 414 \ \Omega$ in the configuration of Figure 4.20. We continue to Step 4.

$$V_{GG} = -2 + (10 \times 10^{-3})(600) = 4 \text{ V}$$

Finally, we use Step 5 to find R_1 and R_2:

$$R_1 = \frac{50,000}{1 - 4/12} = 75 \text{ k}\Omega$$

$$R_2 = \frac{50,000 \times 12}{4} = 150 \text{ k}\Omega$$

The design is complete.

Drill Problems

D4.3 Design a CD JFET amplifier as shown in Figure 4.19, with $R_L = 10$ kΩ, $R_{in} = 200$ kΩ, $V_{DD} = 12$ V and a Q-point selected to be at $V_{DSQ} = 6$ V, $V_{GSQ} = -1$ V, $I_{DQ} = 1$ mA, and $g_m = 4$ mS. Determine the value of resistors and the current gain of the amplifier.

Ans: $R_S = 6$ kΩ ; $R_1 = 342$ kΩ;
$R_2 = 480$ kΩ; $A_i = 18.8$

D4.4 Design a CD JFET amplifier as shown in Figure 4.21 to provide a current gain of 15 to a load of $R_L = 20$ kΩ using $V_{DD} = 12$ V and $R_{in} = 400$ kΩ. Select a Q-point at $V_{DSQ} = 6$ V, $I_{DQ} = 2$ mA, $V_{GSQ} = -0.5$ V, and $g_m = 3330$ μS.

Ans: $R_{Sdc} = 3$ kΩ; $R_{Sac} = 942$ Ω;
$R_1 = 873$ kΩ; $R_2 = 738$ kΩ

4.11   SF Bootstrap Amplifier

In this section we analyze an *SF (or CD) bootstrap FET amplifier*. This circuit is a special case of the SF called the *bootstrap circuit* and is illustrated in Figure 4.21. Here the bias is developed across only a part of the source resistor. This reduces the need for a capacitor bypass across part of the source resistor and thus reflects a much larger input resistance than normally can be attained. This design allows us to take advantage of the high impedance characteristics of the FET without using a high value of gate resistor, R_G.

The equivalent circuit of Figure 4.22 is used to evaluate the circuit operation. We assume that i_{in} is sufficiently small to approximate the current in R_{S2} as i_1. The output voltage is then found to be

$$v_o \approx g_m v_{gs}(R_S \| R_L) \tag{4.21}$$

where

$$R_S = R_{S1} + R_{S2}$$

If the assumption about i_{in} is not valid, R_S is replaced by the expression

$$R_{S1} + \frac{(i_{in} + i_1)R_{S2}}{i_1}$$

A KVL equation at the input yields v_i as follows:

$$v_i = v_{gs} + i_1 R_{S1} + (i_1 + i_{in})R_{S2} \tag{4.22}$$

The current, i_1, is found from a current-divider relationship,

$$i_1 = \frac{g_m v_{gs} R_L}{R_S + R_L}$$

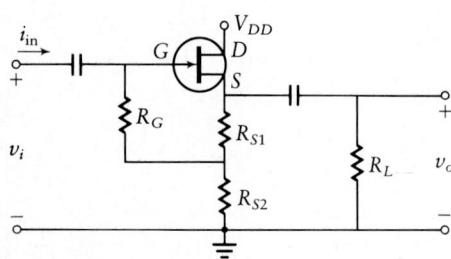

Figure 4.21   Bootstrap SF.

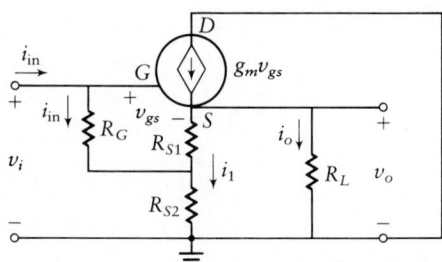

Figure 4.22   AC equivalent circuit for SF.

Using this in equation (4.22), we obtain

$$v_i = v_{gs} + \frac{g_m v_{gs} R_L R_S}{R_L + R_S} + i_{in} R_{S2} \tag{4.23}$$

A second equation for v_i is developed around the loop through R_G and R_{S2} as follows.

$$v_i = i_{in} R_G + \left(\frac{g_m v_{gs} R_L}{R_S + R_L} + i_{in} \right) R_{S2}$$

$$= i_{in}(R_G + R_{S2}) + \frac{g_m v_{gs} R_L R_{S2}}{R_S + R_L} \tag{4.24}$$

We eliminate v_i by setting equation (4.23) equal to equation (4.24) and solve for i_{in} to obtain

$$i_{in} = \frac{g_m v_{gs}}{R_G} \left[(R_L \parallel R_S) + \frac{1}{g_m} - \frac{R_L R_{S2}}{R_S + R_L} \right] \tag{4.25}$$

The input resistance, $R_{in} = v_i / i_{in}$, is found by dividing equation (4.24) by equation (4.25) with the result

$$R_{in} = \frac{R_G [1/g_m + (R_L \parallel R_S)]}{(R_L \parallel R_S) + 1/g_m - R_L R_{S2}/(R_S + R_L)} + R_{S2}$$

We solve for R_G as follows:

$$R_G = \frac{(R_{in} - R_{S2}) [R_{S1} R_L + (R_S + R_L)/g_m]}{R_L R_S + (R_S + R_L)/g_m} \tag{4.26}$$

The current gain is

$$A_i = \frac{i_o}{i_{in}} = \frac{v_o}{R_L i_{in}}$$

Using equation (4.21) and equation (4.25) and noting that $R_S - R_{S2} = R_{S1}$, we find

$$A_i = \frac{R_G R_S}{R_L R_{S1} + (R_L + R_S)/g_m} \tag{4.27}$$

The voltage gain is

$$A_v = \frac{A_i R_L}{R_{in}}$$

$$= \frac{R_G R_S R_L}{R_{in}[R_{S1}R_L + (R_S + R_L)/g_m]} \qquad (4.28)$$

Example 4.10   Bootstrap SF (Design)

Design a SF amplifier circuit for the following conditions: $R_{in} = 100 \text{ k}\Omega$, $R_L = 10 \text{ k}\Omega$, and $V_{DD} = 20 \text{ V}$. The circuit is connected as shown in Figure 4.21. The Q-point is selected at

$$V_{DSQ} = 10 \text{ V} \qquad I_{DQ} = 3.33 \text{ mA}$$

$$V_{GSQ} = -1 \text{ V} \qquad g_m = 2 \text{ mS}$$

SOLUTION   Designing this circuit consists of choosing values for R_{S1}, R_{S2}, and R_G. The relationship $V_{GSQ} = -1$ V is used to find R_{S1}. We sum voltages around the gate-to-source loop assuming that i_{in} is approximately equal to zero, as follows:

$$0 = V_{GSQ} + R_{S1}I_{DQ}$$

$$R_{S1} = \frac{1}{3.3 \times 10^{-3}} = 300 \text{ }\Omega$$

In order to find R_{S2}, we write a KVL equation around the source-to-drain loop:

$$V_{DD} = V_{DSQ} + (R_{S1} + R_{S2})I_{DQ}$$

$$20 = 10 + (300 + R_{S2})(3.33 \times 10^{-3})$$

Solving for R_{S2}, we obtain

$$R_{S2} = 2.7 \text{ k}\Omega$$

We find R_G using equation (4.26) as follows:

$$R_G = \frac{(R_{in} - R_{S2})[R_{S1}R_L + (R_S + R_L)/g_m]}{R_L R_S + (R_S + R_L)/g_m}$$

$$= \frac{(100,000 - 2700)[(300)(10,000) + (13,000)(500)]}{(10,000)(3000) + (13,000)(500)} = 25.3 \text{ k}\Omega$$

➤

Drill Problems

D4.5 Determine the value of the resistors and the current gain for a SF JFET bootstrap amplifier that requires $R_{in} = 200$ kΩ, $R_L = 20$ kΩ, and $V_{DD} = 10$ V. The Q-point is selected as

$$V_{DSQ} = 5 \text{ V} \qquad V_{GSQ} = -1.5 \text{ V}$$

$$I_{DQ} = 0.5 \text{ mA} \qquad g_m = 4 \text{ mS}$$

Use the configuration of Figure 4.21.

Ans: $R_G = 62.8$ kΩ; $R_{S1} = 3$ kΩ; $R_{S2} = 7$ kΩ; $A_i = 9.3$

4.12 Metal Semiconductor Barrier Junction Transistor

The *metal semiconductor barrier junction transistor* (MESFET) is similar to a FET, except that the junction is a metal semiconductor barrier, much as is the case with Schottky diodes (see Section 1.9.1). FETs made of silicon (Si) or gallium arsenide (GaAs) are constructed with diffused or ion-implanted gates. However, there are advantages to using a Schottky barrier metal gate when the channel is *n*-type and short channel widths are needed. It is difficult to work with GaAs, yet GaAs makes good Schottky barriers that are useful in high-frequency applications. Using GaAs in MESFETs results in a transistor that exhibits good performance in microwave applications. In comparison with the silicon bipolar transistor, GaAs MESFETs have better performance above input frequencies of 4 GHz. These MESFETs have high gains, lower noise, better efficiency, higher input impedance, and properties that prevent thermal runaway. They are used in microwave oscillators, amplifiers, mixers, and for high speed switching. GaAs MESFETs are used for high-frequency applications such as microwave oscillators, amplifiers, mixers, and high speed switching.

4.13 Other Devices

Other devices that are outgrowths of the normal two- and three-terminal devices are presented in this section.

Figure 4.23
The UJT.

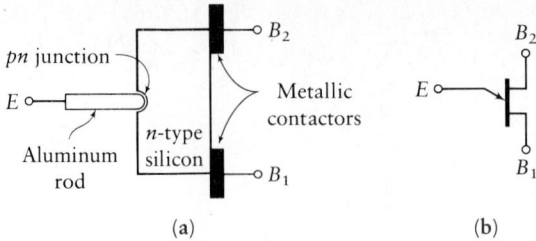

Figure 4.24
UJT characteristic curves.

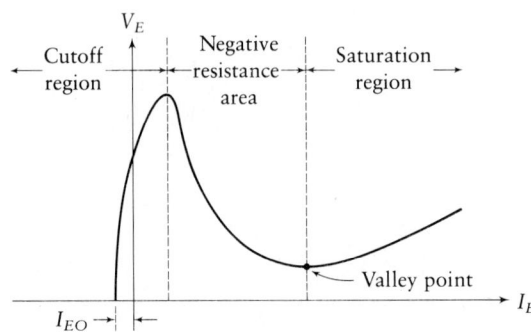

4.13.1   *Unijunction Transistor*

The *unijunction transistor (UJT)* ([47], Section 11.1) is a three-terminal device composed of a lightly doped slab of n-type silicon material with two base contacts. These are attached to both ends of one surface, and a small pellet of p-type material is alloyed to the opposite surface. The boundary of the p-type pellet forms the pn junction between it and the n-silicon. The single pn junction is where the unijunction acquires its name. One type of construction and its circuit symbol are shown in Figure 4.23.

The UJT provides a useful negative resistance portion of the characteristic curve, as shown in Figure 4.24.

If a voltage is applied to the terminal B_1, the potential at the junction results from a voltage division across the resistance from E to B_1 and from B_1 to B_2. If this value is greater than the voltage applied to terminal E, there is no injection of carriers across the E-B junction. However, if an external source raises V_E to a level higher than the voltage at the junction, injection of carriers will result.

Varying the voltage, V_E, has the effect of varying the resistance of the bar in the region of terminal E. As V_E is raised, the resistance between E and B_1

Figure 4.25
Relaxation oscillator.

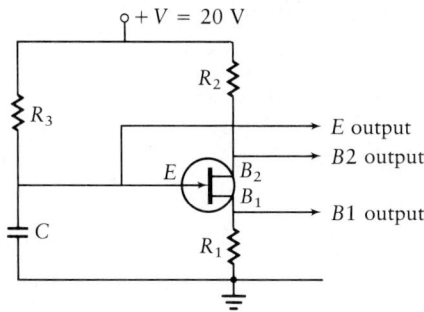

decreases, thus causing a decrease in the voltage at the junction. The net effect of these changes is to raise the current between B_1 and B_2.

The UJT is not used as a signal amplifier. Instead, it is used as a voltage-controlled switch. Unlike the SCR, which is triggered by a gate current (see Chapter 3), the UJT is triggered with a voltage. The UJT is used to trigger other types of devices and can also be used in oscillator circuits.

The area of negative resistance is stable and can be utilized in other circuit applications. Beyond the *valley point,* the transistor acts like a simple diode.

An example of the use of a UJT is the *relaxation oscillator* as shown in Figure 4.25. This circuit is the basic building block in most UJT timer and oscillator circuits. When power is applied, the capacitor charges through R_3 until the voltage is large enough at point E to trigger the UJT conduction. This causes the E-B_1 junction to become forward-biased, and the emitter characteristic goes into the negative resistance region. The capacitor discharges through the emitter and a positive-going pulse is available at the B_1 output. When conduction occurs, the voltage at B_2 decreases, thus causing a negative-going pulse at B_2. The frequency of the pulses is approximated by the equation

$$f_o \approx \frac{1.5}{R_3 C} \tag{4.29}$$

4.13.2   *VMOSFET (VMOS)*

Considerable research effort has been applied to increasing the power capability of solid-state devices. An area that has shown much promise is the MOSFET in which the conduction channel is modified to form a V rather than the conventional source-to-drain straight line. An additional semiconductor layer is added. The term *VMOS* is derived from the fact that the current between source and drain follows a vertical path due to the construction. The drain is

Figure 4.26
VMOS construction.

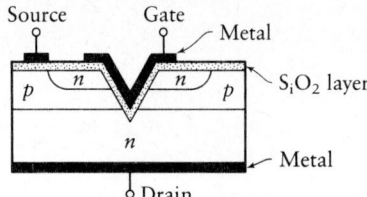

now located on a piece of added semiconductor material. Conventional FETs are limited to currents of the order of milliamperes, but VMOS FETs are available for operation in the 100-A current range. This provides a great improvement in power over the conventional FET. The construction of the VMOS is shown in Figure 4.26.

The VMOS device can provide a solution to high-frequency, high-power applications. Ten-watt devices have been developed at frequencies in the lower ultrahigh-frequency (UHF) band. Some other important advantages of VMOS FETs include the following: They have a negative temperature coefficient to prevent thermal runaway, they exhibit low leakage current and they are capable of achieving high switching speed. VMOS transistors can be made to have equal spacing of their characteristic curves for equal increments of gate voltage, so they can be used like BJTs for high-power linear amplifiers ([34], pp. 690–691).

4.13.3   *Other MOS Devices*

Another type of MOS device is a *double-diffused process fabricated FET*, sometimes called *DMOS*. This device has the advantage of decreasing the length of the channels, thus providing excellent low-power dissipation and high-speed capability.

Fabrication of a FET on small islands on a substrate of sapphire is sometimes referred to as *SOS*. The islands of silicon are formed by etching a thin layer of silicon grown on the sapphire substrate. This type of fabrication provides insulation between the islands of silicon, thus greatly reducing parasitic capacitance between devices.

MOS technology has the advantage that both capacitors and resistors are made at the same time as the FET, although large-value capacitors are not feasible. Using an enhancement MOSFET, a two-terminal resistance is made and the MOSFET gate connected to the drain causes the FET to operate at pinch-off. The MOSFET gate is connected to the drain through a power source, causing the FET to be biased where it will operate in the voltage-controlled resistance region of the characteristics. In this way, drain-load resistors are replaced by a MOSFET rather than a deposited resistor, hence saving chip area.

PROBLEMS

4.1 The characteristic curves for the operating region of a specific *n*-channel FET transistor can be approximated by the equation

$$i_D = 0.5(4 + v_{GS})^2 \text{ mA}$$

when the following conditions hold:

$$R_S = 500 \text{ }\Omega; \qquad R_D = 2 \text{ k}\Omega; \qquad R_{\text{in}} = 100 \text{ k}\Omega;$$

$$I_{DQ} = 5 \text{ mA}; \qquad V_{DD} = 20 \text{ V}$$

Determine the following parameters:
a. V_{GSQ}
b. V_D
c. V_{DSQ}
d. R_1 and R_2

Refer to Figure P4.1.

4.2 a. Design a CS amplifier (Figure P4.1) using a *p*-channel JFET when the specification calls for $A_v = -10$ and $R_{\text{in}} = 20$ kΩ. Assume the Q-point is chosen at $I_{DQ} = -1$ mA, $V_{DSQ} = -10$ V, $V_{GSQ} = 0.5$ V and $g_m = 1500$ μS.

b. Calculate A_i, R_1, R_2, R_S, and R_D. (Refer to the characteristic curve in Figure P4.2. Note that you may have to split R_S and bypass part of it.)

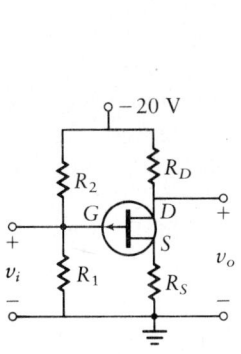

Figure P4.1

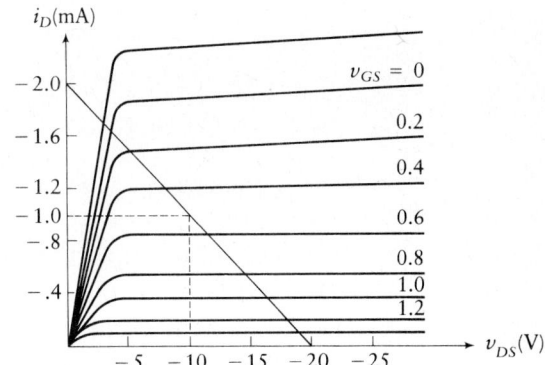

Figure P4.2

4.3 Repeat Problem 4.2 when an R_L of 20 kΩ is coupled to the drain with a capacitor. Note that you may need to choose a different Q-point.

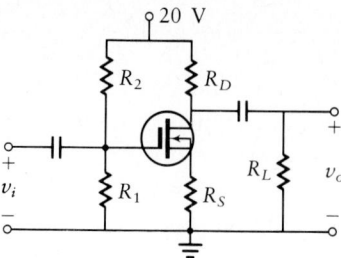

Figure P4.3

4.4 Design a CS amplifier using a MOSFET, as shown in Figure P4.3 Let R_L = 1 kΩ, A_v = -1, and R_{in} = 15 kΩ. The Q-point is chosen at V_{GSQ} = 3 V, I_{DQ} = 7 mA, V_{DSQ} = 10 V, where g_m = 2300 μS. Find values for all other elements.

4.5 Design a CS amplifier using an *n*-channel JFET for a circuit of the type shown in Figure 4.13(a) with A_v = -1, V_{DD} = 12 V, R_L = 1 kΩ, R_{in} = 15 kΩ, I_{DSS} = 10 mA, and V_p = -4 V. Use I_{DQ} = $I_{DSS}/2$.

4.6 Design a CS amplifier using an *n*-channel JFET when R_L = 4 kΩ, A_v = -3, and R_{in} = 50 kΩ. Assume a Q-point is chosen such that I_{DQ} = 3 mA, V_{DSQ} = 10 V, V_{GSQ} = -1 V, g_m = 2000 μS, and V_{DD} = 20 V. Use the circuit of Figure 4.15(a).

4.7 Design an *n*-channel JFET CS amplifier that has A_v = -5, A_i = -20, V_{DD} = 12 V, and R_L = 5 kΩ. Determine all component values and the power rating of the transistor. (The circuit may require changes to meet the design.) Select a Q-point of V_{DSQ} = 6 V, V_{GSQ} = -2 V, and I_{DQ} = 2 mA. The transistor has g_m = 4 mS.

4.8 Design a CS *p*-channel JFET amplifer with A_v = -5, A_i = -20, R_L = 8 kΩ, and V_{DD} = -16 V. The Q-point is at V_{DSQ} = -8 V, V_{GSQ} = 3 V, I_{DQ} = -2 mA, and g_m = 3.33 mS. Use the circuit of Figure P4.4. Determine the power rating of the transistor.

4.9 Design a CS *p*-channel JFET amplifier with a 5-kΩ load using the circuit shown in Figure P4.4. Let V_{DD} = -20 V, A_v = -2, A_i = -20, V_p = 6 V, and I_{DSS} = -5 mA. Determine the power rating of the transistor.

4.10 Design a CS *n*-channel MOSFET amplifier using a 3N128 transistor (see Appendix D) for a 10 kΩ load with a voltage gain of A_v = -10. Use the circuit of Figure P4.3. Select the Q-point using the characteristic curves shown in the specifications when R_{in} > 10 kΩ.

4.11 Design a CS *n*-channel MOSFET amplifier using a 3N128 transistor (see Appendix D) for a 2 kΩ load with A_v = -4 and R_{in} > 100 kΩ. Assume

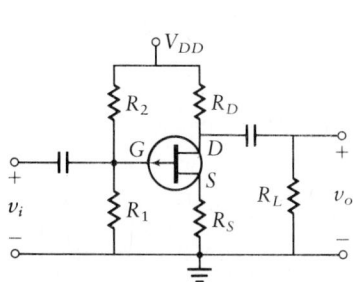

Figure P4.4

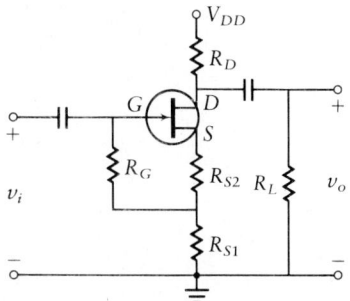

Figure P4.5

that the Q-point is chosen as $V_{GSQ} = -0.6$ V, $V_{DSQ} = 10$ V, $I_{DQ} = 10$ mA, and $V_{DD} = 20$ V.

4.12 Analyze a CS *n*-channel JFET amplifier as shown in Figure P4.5 when the load is 20 kΩ, $R_D = 8$ kΩ, $V_{DD} = 24$ V, and $R_{in} = 50$ kΩ. Select the Q-point as $V_{GSQ} = -1.5$ V, $V_{DSQ} = 12$ V, $I_{DQ} = 1$ mA, and $g_m = 2.83$ mS. Find all component values, A_i, and A_v.

4.13 If R_S in Figure 4.15(a) is bypassed with a capacitor, what is the voltage gain? Assume that the Q-point is selected so that $g_m = 1.5$ mS, $R_D = 3.2$ kΩ, and $R_L = 5$ kΩ. Determine the current gain when $R_S = 500$ Ω, $R_1 = 200$ kΩ, and $R_2 = 800$ kΩ.

4.14 What is the voltage gain, A_v, of the circuit shown in Figure 4.15(a) if a signal is fed into the amplifier, which has a source voltage resistance, R_i, of 10 kΩ? Assume $R_D = 4$ kΩ, $R_L = 10$ kΩ, $R_{Sac} = 500$ Ω, $g_m = 2$ mS, $R_1 = 25$ kΩ, and $R_2 = 120$ kΩ.

4.15 In the circuit shown in Figure P4.6, assume that R_S is bypassed entirely with a capacitor. $V_{DD} = 15$ V, $R_D = 2$ kΩ, $R_L = 3$ kΩ, $R_S = 200$ Ω, $R_1 = 500$ kΩ, $I_{DSS} = 8$ mA, and $V_P = -4$ V. Determine A_v, A_i, R_{in}, and the Q-point for the amplifier.

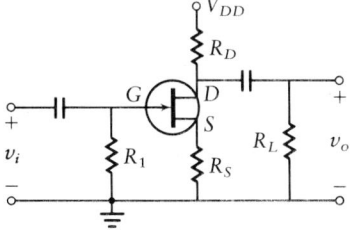

Figure P4.6

4.16 In the circuit shown in Figure P4.6, $V_{DD} = 20$ V, $R_D = 2$ kΩ, $R_L = 10$ kΩ, $R_S = 200$ Ω, $R_1 = 1$ MΩ, $I_{DSS} = 10$ mA, and $V_p = -5$ V. Determine the Q-point, A_v, A_i, and R_{in} for the amplifier.

4.17 For the amplifier shown in Figure P4.6, $V_{DD} = 20$ V, $R_D = 2$ kΩ, $R_L = 6$ kΩ, $R_S = 100$ Ω, $R_1 = 1$ MΩ, $I_{DSS} = 10$ mA, and $V_p = -5$ V. Determine the Q-point, A_v, A_i, and R_{in} for the amplifier.

4.18 A CS amplifier circuit as shown in Figure P4.1 uses a JFET for which $I_{DSS} = 2$ mA and $g_m = 2000$ μS. If the value of $R_D = 10$ kΩ and $R_S = 200$ Ω, what is the voltage gain, A_v, for each of the following values of V_{GSQ}?
a. -1 V
b. -0.5 V
c. 0 V

4.19 A CS amplifier circuit as shown in Figure P4.6 has a transistor with $V_p = -4$ V, $I_{DSS} = 4$ mA, and $r_{DS} = 500$ Ω. If $R_D = 2$ kΩ, $R_L = 4$ kΩ and $R_S = 200$ Ω, what is the voltage gain, A_v, of the circuit if $V_{GSQ} = -1$ V? What happens to A_v as r_{DS} approaches infinity?

4.20 Design a CS *n*-channel MOSFET amplifier when $V_{DD} = 20$ V, $R_L = 4$ kΩ, $A_v = -5$, and $A_i = -10$. The Q-point is selected as $V_{DSQ} = 10$ V, $V_{GSQ} = 4$ V, $I_{DQ} = 2$ mA, and $g_m = 4000$ μS.

4.21 Design an SF amplifier using a *p*-channel JFET as shown in Figure P4.7 with $R_{in} = 20$ kΩ. Try to obtain a voltage gain, A_v, as close to unity as possible. Calculate A_i, R_1, R_2, and R_S. Use the characteristic curves as shown in Figure P4.2.

4.22 Repeat Problem 4.21 when a 20 kΩ load is capacitively coupled to the amplifier.

4.23 Design a CD MOSFET amplifier when $R_L = 100$ Ω, $A_i = 100$, $I_{DQ} = 8$ mA, $V_{GSQ} = 1.5$ V, $V_{DSQ} = 6.3$ V, $R_{in} = 100$ kΩ, and $g_m = 2.9$ mS. Determine A_v and all resistor values. Use the circuit of Figure P4.8.

4.24 Design a CD amplifier using an *n*-channel MOSFET where $R_{in} = 12$ kΩ, $A_i = 10$, $R_L = 500$ Ω, $V_{DD} = 20$ V, and the Q-point is selected to be $V_{DSQ} = 10$ V, $V_{GSQ} = -3$ V, $I_{DQ} = 7$ mA, and $g_m = 2.3$ mS. Use the circuit of Figure P4.8 as a guide.

4.25 Design an SF amplifier using an *n*-channel JFET for a current gain of 100 and an input resistance of 500 kΩ. The load is 2 kΩ. Select the Q-point for the following parameters: $V_{DSQ} = 8$ V, $I_{DQ} = 5$ mA, V_{GSQ}

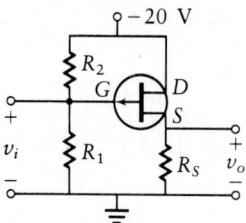

Figure P4.7

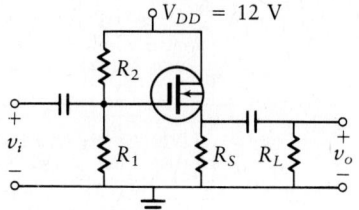

Figure P4.8

$= -1$ V, and $g_m = 4$ mS. Determine the resistances and the voltage gain and draw the circuit when $V_{DD} = 10$ V.

4.26 Repeat Problem 4.25 except with a different transistor having the following parameter values: $V_p = -3$ V, $I_{DSS} = 10$ mA.

4.27 Analyze the circuit shown in Figure 4.22 when $V_{DD} = 16$ V and $R_L = 8$ kΩ. Select a Q-point of $I_{DQ} = 5$ mA, $V_{GSQ} = -1$ V, $V_{DSQ} = 8$ V and $g_m = 5.5$ mS. Determine all component values, A_i, and A_v when $R_{in} = 12$ kΩ.

5

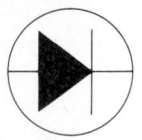

BIAS STABILITY OF TRANSISTOR AMPLIFIERS

5.0 Introduction

Parameter variations, such as those due to temperature changes, aging, and device substitutions, cause the operating-point location of a transistor circuit to vary from the nominal value. We often expend considerable effort to reduce the effects of these parameter changes, since such variations can adversely affect performance. For example, a change in the location of the Q-point can reduce the maximum symmetrical undistorted output swing. In extreme cases, such changes can saturate or cut off the transistor without any input signal being present.

Parameters vary because of changes in supply voltage, changes in temperature, and also because of tolerances in the transistor-manufacturing process. This chapter studies the effects of these changes. Once the effects are understood, we develop equations for several discrete amplifier configurations. Several design examples are given. We then analyze diode compensation as one method of reducing the effects of parameter variations upon circuit operation. The chapter concludes with a summary of the design steps needed to insure bias stability.

5.1   Types of Biasing

In this chapter, we illustrate the various biasing techniques using BJTs. The same biasing techniques can be applied to FETs, although the motivation is somewhat different. For example, temperature does not affect FET operation in the same manner as it does BJT operation.

The voltage-divider biasing system is commonly used and is discussed in Chapter 2. This method of biasing allows the amplifier to operate close to the intended design point regardless of variations that occur in the transistor.

Although we do discuss the concept of feedback with these two new biasing techniques, we are only showing that a part of the output signal is fed back to the input. The intent is to illustrate two other useful techniques of dc biasing of transistor circuits. We discuss feedback systems in more detail in Chapter 11 following the earlier treatment of frequency effects in amplifiers.

5.1.1   *Current Biasing*

Figure 5.1 illustrates one form of biasing with moderate stability known as *current feedback*, where collector current through R_E develops a negative feedback voltage. The base resistor, R_B, is connected to the supply, V_{CC}. The KVL equation for the bias current loop is given by

$$V_{CC} = I_{BQ}R_B + R_E I_{CQ} + V_{BE}$$

$$= V_{BE} + I_{CQ}\left(\frac{R_B}{\beta} + R_E\right)$$

We solve for I_{CQ} to obtain

$$I_{CQ} \doteq \frac{V_{CC} - V_{BE}}{R_B/\beta + R_E} \tag{5.1a}$$

Figure 5.1
Current feedback.

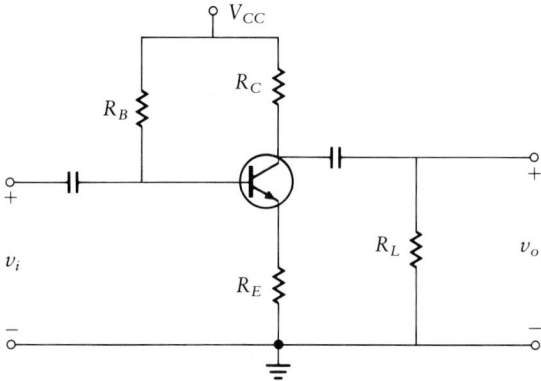

Dividing this by β yields

$$I_{BQ} = \frac{V_{CC} - V_{BE}}{R_B + \beta R_E} \tag{5.1b}$$

Note that the value of I_{BQ} is affected by R_B, R_E, V_{BE}, and β. The specific values of these parameters then determine the quiescent operating point of the transistor.

We examine the reason for calling this configuration "current feedback." *Feedback* occurs when a circuit is configured in such a manner that the input is affected by the output. The emitter resistor in the circuit of Figure 5.1 provides a form of feedback. As the collector current tends to increase, the voltage across the emitter resistor also increases. For a given input voltage, v_i, this increase in voltage across R_E reduces the base-emitter voltage and, therefore, also reduces the base current. This, in turn, decreases the collector current to reduce the effect of the original change. Because this effect is fighting against the increase in collector current, the situation is known as *negative current feedback*. The emitter resistor can be bypassed with a capacitor, thus removing the feedback for ac signals and preventing reduction of gain. The effect on dc stability is still present ([49], Chapter 12). In fact, we cannot achieve bias stability due to changes in β as the transistor will be driven into saturation for any reasonable value of voltage gain.

5.1.2   *Voltage and Current Biasing*

A second type of feedback, shown in Figure 5.2, is *voltage feedback*. Note that current shunt feedback is still present due to R_E. Better performance results when $R_E = 0$.

The feedback resistor, R_F, is connected between the collector and base. The base-to-ground voltage is then composed of two components, one arising from the input voltage and one from the collector voltage. We analyze this circuit by writing the dc equations between base and collector. In the following, we assume that the quiescent base current is much less than the quiescent collector current and therefore can be ignored in the equations.

$$V_{CC} = I_{CQ}R_C + I_{BQ}R_F + V_{BE} + I_{CQ}R_E$$

$$= I_{CQ}R_C + I_{CQ}R_F/\beta + V_{BE} + I_{CQ}R_E$$

Solving for I_{CQ} yields

$$I_{CQ} = \frac{V_{CC} - V_{BE}}{R_C + R_E + R_F/\beta} \tag{5.2a}$$

Figure 5.2
Voltage feedback.

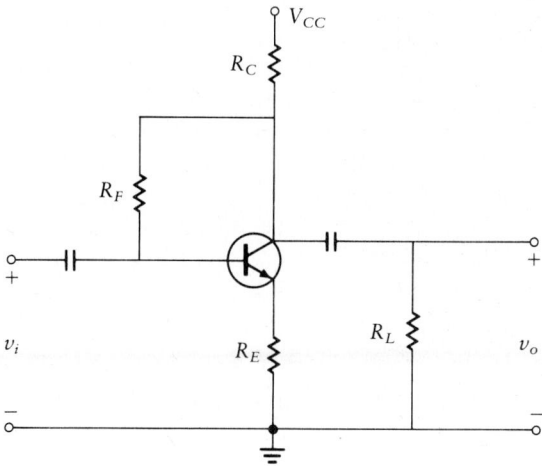

Dividing this by β, we get

$$I_{BQ} = \frac{V_{CC} - V_{BE}}{R_F + \beta(R_C + R_E)} \tag{5.2b}$$

Note that β appears in both equations (5.1) and (5.2). Variations in β therefore affect the Q-point location. We present techniques for reducing the effects of variations in β in later sections of this chapter. It proves desirable to make R_B equal to $0.1\beta R_E$ when using voltage-division biasing circuits, as studied in Chapter 2. However, in the circuit shown in Figure 5.1, using $R_B = 0.1\beta R_E$ causes the transistor to go into satuation. The equivalent expression for the biasing system of Figure 5.2 to reduce the effect of changes in β is as follows:

$$R_F = 0.1\beta(R_C + R_E)$$

Although this proves to be a good design criterion for reducing the effects of changes in β upon the Q-point location, it is not always possible to achieve this design value since to do so reduces the maximum output swing.

Drill Problems

D5.1 Design a CE amplifier for maximum output voltage swing with a voltage gain of -10 and an output resistance of 10 kΩ. Use the circuit shown in Figure 5.1 with $V_{CC} = 16$ V, $V_{BE} = 0.7$ V and $\beta = 100$.

Ans: $R_C = 10 \text{ k}\Omega; R_E = 474 \, \Omega;$
$R_B = 1.48 \text{ M}\Omega$

D5.2   Design a CE amplifier with $A_v = -10$. Use the circuit of Figure 5.2 with $R_L = 10 \text{ k}\Omega$, $V_{CC} = 16$ V, $V_{BE} = 0.7$ V and $\beta = 100$. Also determine the maximum undisorted voltage output swing.

Ans: $R_C = 10 \text{ k}\Omega; R_E = 474 \, \Omega;$
$R_F = 483 \text{ k}\Omega$
$v_{o(p\text{-}p)} = 9.0$ V

D5.3   Select a value of R_F in the amplifier of Problem D5.2 to provide bias stability against changes in β. What is the maximum undistorted symmetrical output voltage swing?

Ans: $R_F = 105 \text{ k}\Omega;$
$v_{o(p-p)} = 2.85$ V

5.2   Effects of Parameter Changes—Bias Stability

Temperature changes cause certain transistor parameters to change. In particular, the followng parameters are temperature-sensitive:

1. Collector leakage current between base and collector (I_{CBO})
2. Base-emitter voltage (V_{BE})

The supply voltage, V_{CC}, and the β of the transistor also vary, but these are usually not dependent upon temperature. In many cases, the supply is sufficiently well regulated that we can ignore changes in V_{CC}. However, for completeness in our derivation, such changes are included ([51], Chapter 4).

Variations in β can be significant, but the largest variations are not caused by changes in temperature. The more likely cause is random variations from device to device that occur during the manufacture process.

Viewing temperature changes first, we note that as the temperature increases, the changes in the parameters cause the Q-point to move up (i.e., an increase in I_{CQ}). If the temperature is reduced, the Q-point moves down (i.e., a decrease in I_{CQ}). Either condition causes the maximum possible peak-to-peak output voltage swing to be reduced, as shown in Figure 5.3.

We determine the amount of collector-current change using partial derivatives. The collector current is a function of four variables,

$$I_{CQ} = f(V_{BE}, I_{CBO}, \beta, V_{CC})$$

For small parameter changes, the variation in I_C is approximately given by

Figure 5.3
V_{CE} with changes in temperature.

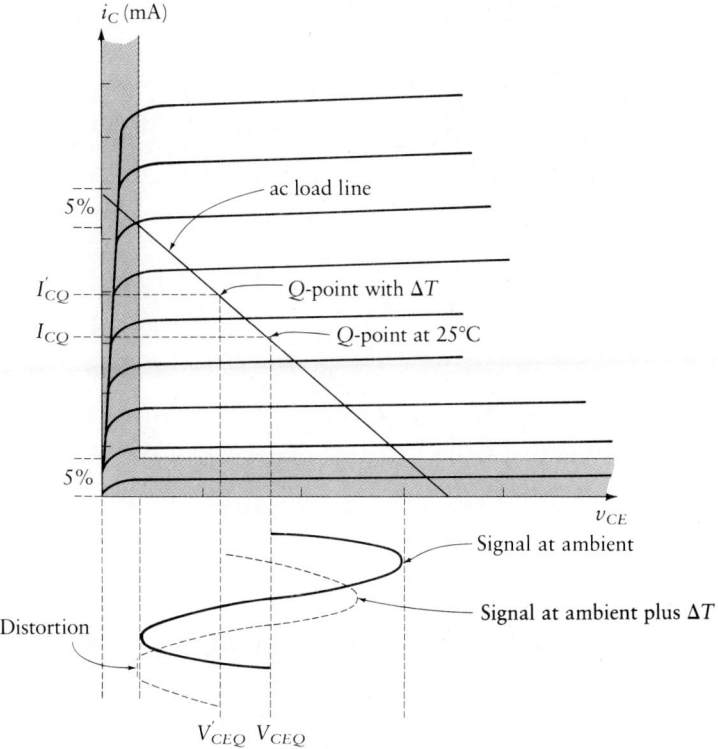

We define four *variation constants* as the partial derivatives of I_C with respect to the four variables. These constants are designated by δ_V, δ_I, δ_β, and δ_{VCC}. Then, in terms of these constants, we have

$$\Delta I_{CQ} = \frac{\partial I_{CQ}}{\partial V_{BE}} \Delta V_{BE} + \frac{\partial I_{CQ}}{\partial I_{CBO}} \Delta I_{CBO} + \frac{\partial I_{CQ}}{\partial \beta} \Delta\beta + \frac{\partial I_{CQ}}{\partial V_{CC}} \Delta V_{CC}$$

$$\Delta I_{CQ} = \delta_V \Delta V_{BE} + \delta_I \Delta I_{CBO} + \delta_\beta \Delta\beta + \delta_{VCC} \Delta V_{CC} \tag{5.3}$$

We now examine the four variables in equation (5.3).

The variation, ΔV_{BE}, is the change of the junction voltage between the base and emitter. This behaves in the same way as does the voltage across a diode. For silicon transistors, the voltage therefore varies linearly with temperature as

$$\Delta V_{BE} \approx -2(T_2 - T_1) \text{ mV} \tag{5.4}$$

where T_2 and T_1 are in degrees Celsius.

The leakage current between the collector and base (sometimes referred to as the *reverse saturation current*) is also a function of temperature. The collector-to-base leakage current, I_{CBO}, approximately doubles for every 10° temperature rise. This is given by the following formula where I_{CBO1} is the reverse leakage current at room temperature (25°C).

$$I_{CBO2} = I_{CBO1} \times 2^{(T_2 - 25°C)/10}$$

$$\Delta I_{CBO} = I_{CBO2} - I_{CBO1} = I_{CBO1} \left[2^{(T_2 - 25°C)/10} - 1 \right] \tag{5.5}$$

Since the primary variations of the other two parameters, V_{CC} and β, are due to factors other than temperature, information about the magnitude of these changes must be specified in the design statement.

In the following sections, we calculate values of the four variation constants for the CE and CC configurations.

5.2.1 CE Configuration

We find the variation constant for V_{BE}, δ_V, by first writing the KVL equation around the base-emitter loop. Refer to the circuit shown in Figure 5.4 where, as in Chapter 2, V_{BB} and R_B are the Thevenin equivalent parameters for the base bias circuit. That is,

$$V_{BB} = \frac{V_{CC}R_1}{R_1 + R_2}$$

and

$$R_B = R_1 \parallel R_2$$

Figure 5.4
CE amplifier.

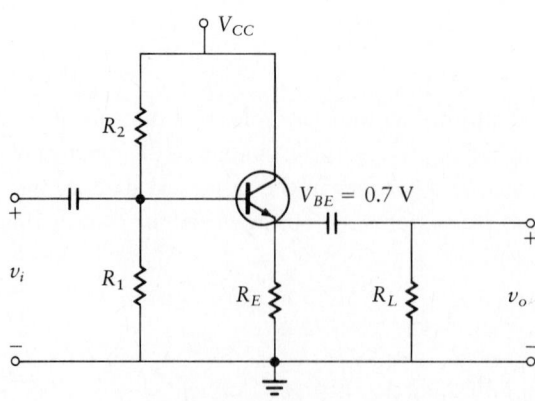

We then have

$$I_{CQ} = \frac{V_{BB} - V_{BE}}{R_E + R_B/\beta} \qquad (5.6)$$

and

$$\delta_V = \frac{\partial I_{CQ}}{\partial V_{BE}} = -\frac{1}{R_E + R_B/\beta} \qquad (5.7)$$

The variation constant for I_{CBO}, δ_I, is developed by referring to Figure 5.5:

$$I_{CQ} = I'_{CQ} + I_{CBO}$$

and

$$I'_{CQ} = \beta(I_{BQ} + I_{CBO})$$

Thus,

$$I_{CQ} = \beta(I_B + I_{CBO}) + I_{CBO} = \beta I_{BQ} + (\beta + 1)I_{CBO}$$

If we assume that $1 + \beta \approx \beta$, then

$$I_{CQ} = \beta I_{BQ} + \beta I_{CBO}$$

Figure 5.5
Current in the
transistor.

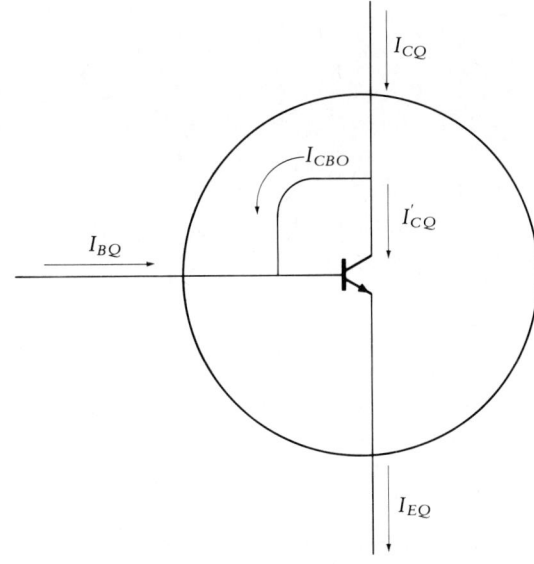

so

$$I_B = \frac{I_{CQ}}{\beta} - I_{CBO} \tag{5.8}$$

The base-emitter loop equation, equation (5.6), is rewritten as follows:

$$V_{BB} - V_{BE} = R_B I_{BQ} + R_E(I_{CQ} + I_{BQ})$$

In this case, we shall not assume that $1 + \beta = \beta$ as is done in the derivation of equation (5.6). If we assumed that $1 + \beta = \beta$, the I_B term would be absent from the parentheses. Substituting equation (5.8) for I_B yields,

$$V_{BB} - V_{BE} = (R_B + R_E)(I_{CQ}/\beta - I_{CBO}) + I_{CQ}R_E$$

Solving for I_{CQ}, we have

$$I_{CQ} = \frac{V_{BB} - V_{BE} + (R_B + R_E)I_{CBO}}{(R_B + R_E)/\beta + R_E} \tag{5.9}$$

and taking the partial derivative,

$$\delta_I = \frac{\partial I_{CQ}}{\partial I_{CBO}} = \frac{R_B + R_E}{(R_B + R_E)/\beta + R_E} = \frac{1}{1/\beta + R_E/(R_E + R_B)} \tag{5.10}$$

If $R_B = 0.1\beta R_E$ and β is large, we can assume $R_B >> R_E$. Under these conditions, δ_I is approximately given by

$$\delta_I = \frac{\beta}{1 + \beta R_E/R_B} \tag{5.11}$$

We now evaluate the variation constant for β. Although β varies with temperature, the predominant variation is due to external factors. The range of values is usually specified in the specification sheet. The value of β used in the following equations is normally the midvalue of the given range.

We start with the equation for collector current, equation (5.9), and differentiate this with respect to β. With a little algebra, we obtain

$$\frac{\partial I_{CQ}}{\partial \beta} = \frac{(R_B + R_E)[V_{BB} - V_{BE} + (R_B + R_E)I_{CBO}]}{(R_B + R_E + \beta R_E)^2}$$

If we can make the assumptions: $R_B >> R_E$, $\beta R_E >> R_B$ and $R_B I_{CBO} << (V_{BB} - V_{BE})$, the equation reduces to the following form:

$$\delta_\beta = \frac{\partial I_{CQ}}{\partial \beta} = \frac{R_B(V_{BB} - V_{BE})}{\beta^2 R_E^2} \tag{5.12}$$

Finally, the variation constant associated with changes in the voltage supply V_{CC} is found from the collector-to-emitter loop equation.

$$I_{CQ} = \frac{V_{CC} - V_{CE}}{R_E + R_C}$$

$$\delta_{VCC} = \frac{\partial I_{CQ}}{\partial V_{CC}} = \frac{1}{R_E + R_C} = \frac{1}{R_{dc}} \tag{5.13}$$

Putting all these relationships together, the total change in I_{CQ} is found from equation (5.3) to be

$$\Delta I_{CQ} = \left[\frac{-1}{R_E + R_B/\beta}\right]\Delta V_{BE} + \left[\frac{\beta}{1 + \beta R_E/R_B}\right]\Delta I_{CBO}$$

$$+ \frac{R_B(V_{BB} - V_{BE})}{\beta^2 R_E^2}\Delta\beta + \frac{\Delta V_{CC}}{R_{dc}} \tag{5.14}$$

We apply this equation to several examples in order to find the variation in I_{CQ} that occurs when the temperature rises or drops. Using this equation, we can determine which terms cause the largest changes in I_{CQ}. If the total variation is too large for the amplifier application, we concentrate upon the term that is causing the largest variation in I_{CQ}. Upon viewing this equation, we determine whether a parameter value should be raised or lowered. For example, if the second term is the largest, then it may be necessary to select a transistor that has a lower leakage current between collector and base (I_{CBO}) or change the design to reduce R_B. For temperatures lower than ambient, all terms in equation (5.14) become negative. Thus, they are causing I_{CQ} to become smaller.

5.2.2 EF Configuration

The EF amplifier is shown in Figure 5.6. The biasing technique for this amplifier is the same as that of the CE with the one exception that the collector resistor, R_C, is equal to zero. Thus, the derivation is based upon the same bias equation:

$$I_{CQ} = \frac{V_{BB} - V_{BE}}{R_B/\beta + R_E}$$

Figure 5.6
The EF amplifier.

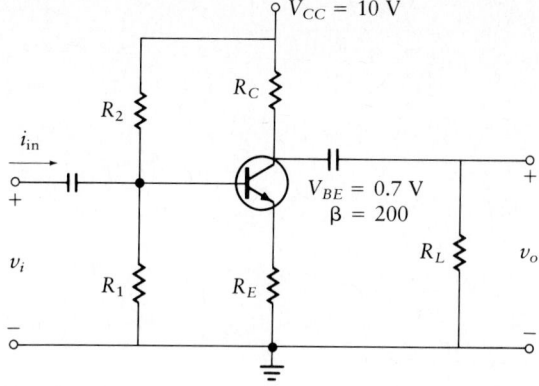

The variation constants are then the same as those of the common emitter except that R_{dc} is simply equal to R_E rather than $(R_E + R_C)$. Equation (5.14) is once again used to find the variation in quiescent collector current.

5.3 Examples of Parameter Variation

Example 5.1   CE Amplifier

Design a CE amplifier with $A_v = -8$ and $R_L = 2$ kΩ. Determine the maximum undistorted voltage output swing if the temperature changes from 25°C to 85°C and $V_{CC} = 10$ V.

The transistor has an $I_{CBO} = 1$ μA at 25°C and β varies between 150 and 250.

SOLUTION   Refer to Section 3.3 for the design procedure and let

$$R_C = R_L = 2 \text{ k}\Omega$$

The design equations can be reviewed in Table 3.1. Following the short form of these equations, we find

$$A_v = \frac{-(R_L \parallel R_C)}{R_E'} = -8$$

Then

$$R_E' = \frac{(R_L \parallel R_C)}{8} = 125 \ \Omega$$

$$R_L \parallel R_C = 1000 \ \Omega$$

$$R_{ac} = R_E' + R_L \parallel R_C = 1125 \ \Omega$$

$$R_{dc} = R_E' + R_C = 2125 \ \Omega$$

$$I_{CQ} = \frac{V_{CC}}{R_{ac} + R_{dc}} = \frac{10}{1125 + 2125} = 3.08 \text{ mA}$$

$$h_{ib} = \frac{26 \text{ mV}}{|I_{CQ}|} = \frac{26 \text{ mV}}{3.08 \text{ mA}} = 8.44 \ \Omega$$

We verify that $h_{ib} \leqslant 0.1 R_E$, so that we use the simplified equations.

$$R_B = 0.1 \beta R_E = 0.1(200)(125) = 2.5 \text{ k}\Omega$$

$$V_{BB} = I_{CQ} \left(\frac{R_B}{\beta} + R_E \right) + V_{BE}$$

$$= (3.08 \times 10^{-3}) \left(\frac{2500}{200} + 125 \right) + 0.7 = 1.12 \text{ V}$$

Now that the design is complete, we examine the variations in the various parameters. Using equation (5.4) we find

$$\Delta V_{BE} = -2\Delta T = -2(60) = -120 \text{ mV}$$

From equation (5.5), we have

$$\Delta I_{CBO} = I_{CBO1}(2^{60/10} - 1) = (1 \times 10^{-6})(63) = 63 \ \mu\text{A}$$

From the given information, we have (no variation in V_{CC} is mentioned)

$$\Delta \beta = 100$$

$$\Delta V_{CC} = 0$$

From equation (5.14) we obtain the variation in I_{CQ}:

$$\Delta I_{CQ} = \left[\frac{-1}{125 + 2500/200} \right] (-0.12)$$

$$+ \left[\frac{200}{1 + 200(125)/2500} \right] (63 \times 10^{-6}) + \left[\frac{2500(1.12 - 0.7)}{200^2 125^2} \right] 100$$

$$= 0.87 \text{ mA} + 1.15 \text{ mA} + 0.17 \text{ mA} = 2.19 \text{ mA}$$

Figure 5.7
Load line for Example
5.1.

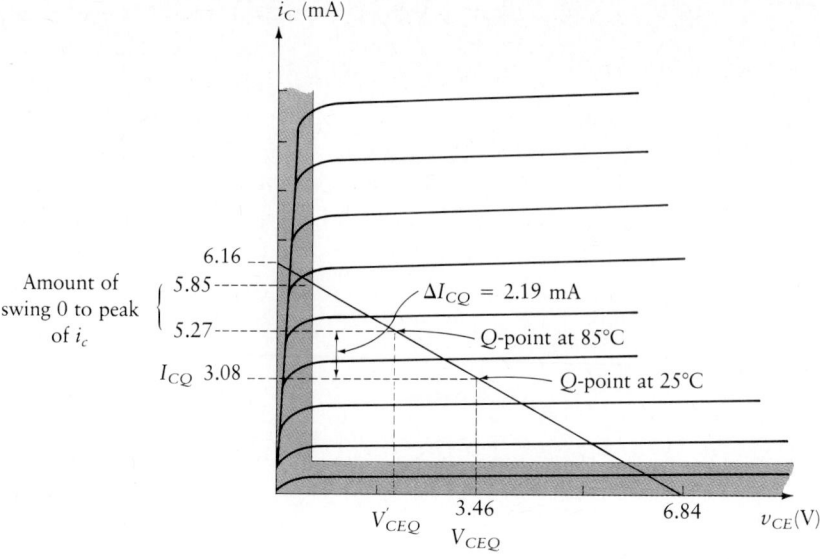

The new Q-point is then located at

$$I_{CQ} = 3.08 + 2.19 = 5.27 \text{ mA}$$

Figure 5.7, which illustrates the load line, can be used to determine how the increase in I_{CQ} reduces the distortion-free swing. We see that the maximum undistorted amplitude of i_C is

$$(95\%)(6.16) = 5.85 \text{ mA}$$

The total undistorted peak-to-peak current swing is then

$$2(5.85 - 5.27) \text{ mA} = 1.16 \text{ mA}$$

The total peak-to-peak voltage swing is

$$1.16 \text{ mA} \times 1000 = 1.16 \text{ V}$$

The parameter variations have reduced the peak-to-peak voltage output swing from 5.5 to 1.16 V. We discuss methods to decrease these changes later in this chapter. This is an extreme reduction and would probably be unacceptable in a practical design.

If we examine the equation for ΔI_{CQ}, we find the term that contributes the major change in I_{CQ} is the ΔI_{CBO} term. If the 2.19-mA change in I_{CQ} is more than can be tolerated, we should reduce the 1.15-mA term, as it is the major contributor to the change in I_{CQ}. There are several actions that can be taken to reduce this value. For example, we can select a different transistor with a lower I_{CBO}. Alternatively, we can reduce the total temperature change in the amplifier thereby reducing the ΔI_{CBO} term. We can also reduce R_B even further, or increase R_E. These actions change the current gain and input impedance, but since the design specification does not specify either the input impedance or the current gain, this must be viewed as a viable option. ▶︎╂

| **Example 5.2** | **EF Amplifier** |

Design an EF amplifier (see Figure 5.6) with $A_i = 10$, $I_{CBO1} = 10\ \mu A$ at 25°C, $V_{BE} = 0.7$ V at 25°C, and $R_L = 200\ \Omega$. The temperature varies between 25° and 85°C, and β varies between 80 and 120. The power supply voltage ranges between 17.5 V and 18.5 V.

SOLUTION Refer to Chapter 3 and Table 3.1 for the necessary design equations. We start by setting

$$R_E = R_L = 200\ \Omega.$$

Then

$$A_i = \frac{R_B}{R_L} = 10$$

which yields the following:

$$R_B = 2\ k\Omega$$

$$R_{ac} = R_E \parallel R_L = 100\ \Omega$$

$$R_{dc} = R_E = 200\ \Omega$$

$$I_{CQ} = \frac{V_{CC}}{R_{ac} + R_{dc}} = \frac{18}{100 + 200} = 60\ mA$$

$$h_{ib} = \frac{26\ mV}{|I_{CQ}|} = \frac{26\ mV}{60\ mA} = 0.43\ \Omega$$

In order to justify using the short-form A_i expression, we must check two conditions:

$$h_{ib} \leq 0.1 \, R_E$$

$$R_B \leq 0.1\beta(R_E \parallel R_L)$$

The first of these two conditions is met but the second is not. Therefore the short-form expression is *not* valid. We go back and use the long form. We are justified, however, in omitting h_{ib} from the expression.

$$A_i = 10 = \frac{R_B}{R_B/\beta + R_E \parallel R_L} \times \frac{R_E}{R_E + R_L}$$

so

$$R_B = 2.5 \text{ k}\Omega$$

$$V_{BB} = V_{BE} + I_{CQ}(R_B/\beta + R_E)$$

$$= 0.7 + (60 \times 10^{-3})\left(\frac{2500}{100} + 200\right) = 14.2 \text{ V}$$

Calculating the parameter variations based upon the given conditions, we have

$$\Delta V_{BE} = -2\Delta T = -2(60) = -120 \text{ mV}$$

$$\Delta I_{CBO} = I_{CBO1}\,(2^{(T_2 - 25°C)/10} - 1)$$

$$= (10 \times 10^{-6})(2^{60/10} - 1) = 0.63 \text{ mA}$$

$$\Delta\beta = 40$$

$$\Delta V_{CC} = 1$$

We find ΔI_{CQ} using equation (5.14), where we use the average β-value of 100.

$$\Delta I_{CQ} = \frac{-1}{200 + 2500/100}(-0.12) + \frac{100}{1 + 100(200)/2500}(0.63 \times 10^{-3})$$

$$+ \frac{2500(13.5)}{100^2 200^2}(40) + \frac{1}{200}(1)$$

$$= 0.53 \text{ mA} + 7 \text{ mA} + 3.38 \text{ mA} + 5 \text{ mA} = 1.59 \text{ mA}$$

This change in I_{CQ} is shown in Figure 5.8. We find the maximum current swing from zero to the peak is

$$i_{Cp} = 120 \times 0.95 - (60 + 15.9) = 38.1 \text{ mA}$$

Figure 5.8
Load line for Example 5.2.

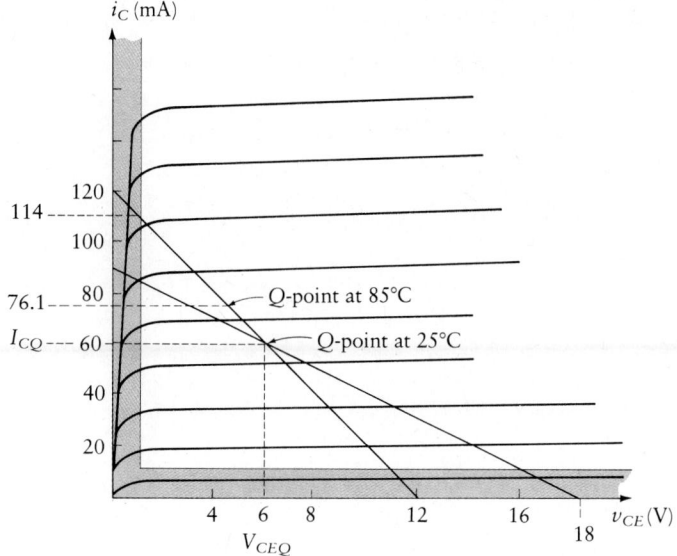

and the maximum undistorted voltage swing at the output load is

$$2(38.1)(100) = 7.62 \text{ V} \quad \text{peak-to-peak}$$

This represents a reduction in output voltage swing from 10.8 to 7.62 V.

Example 5.3   **CE Amplifier**

Design a CE amplifier (see Figure 5.4) with $A_v = -10$, $R_L = 1 \text{ k}\Omega$, and $V_{CC} = 12$ V. The temperature varies between $-50°C$ and $+65°C$. The selected transistor has $V_{BE} = 0.7$ V and $I_{CBO1} = 1.5 \text{ μA}$ at $25°C$ and a β that varies between 300 and 400. What is the maximum undistorted collector-current swing?

SOLUTION   Let us start the design by letting

$$R_C = R_L = 1 \text{ k}\Omega$$

We again use the short-form equations summarized in Table 3.1.

$$A_v = \frac{-(R_L \parallel R_C)}{R_E} = -10$$

so

$$R_E = 50 \ \Omega$$

$$R_{ac} = R_E + R_C \| R_L = 550 \ \Omega$$

$$R_{dc} = R_C + R_E = 1050 \ \Omega$$

$$I_{CQ} = \frac{V_{CC}}{R_{ac} + R_{dc}} = \frac{12}{550 + 1050} = 7.5 \text{ mA}$$

$$h_{ib} = \frac{26 \text{ mV}}{|I_{CQ}|} = \frac{26 \text{ mV}}{7.5 \text{ mA}} = 3.47 \ \Omega$$

Since $h_{ib} \leq 0.1 R_E$, we are justified in using the short-form equations, so we continue with the design by letting $R_E' = R_E = 50 \ \Omega$.

$$R_B = 0.1 \ \beta R_E = 0.1(350)(50) = 1.75 \text{ k}\Omega$$

$$V_{BB} = I_{CQ}(R_B/\beta + R_E) + V_{BE}$$

$$= (7.5 \times 10^{-3}) \left(\frac{1750}{350} + 50 \right) + 0.7 = 1.11 \text{ V}$$

Since the temperature ranges from below 25°C to above, we must separate the analysis into two parts. For the temperature change from 25° to 65°C, we first find the temperature dependent variations in I_{CBO} and V_{BE}.

$$\Delta T = 40°C$$

$$\Delta I_{CBO} = I_{CBO1}(2^{40/10} - 1) = (1.5 \times 10^{-6})(15) = 22.5 \ \mu A$$

$$\Delta V_{BE} = -2(40) = -80 \text{ mV}$$

The variation in β is

$$\Delta \beta = 100$$

Since the problem says nothing about variations in V_{CC}, we assume that

$$\Delta V_{CC} = 0$$

The change in I_{CQ} is now found from equation (5.14).

$$\Delta I_{CQ} = \frac{-1}{50 + 1750/350}(-0.08) + \frac{350}{1 + 350(50)/1750}(22.5 \times 10^{-6})$$

$$+ \frac{1750(1.11 - 0.7)}{350^2 50^2}(100)$$

$$\Delta I_{CQ} = 1.45 \text{ mA} + 0.72 \text{ mA} + 0.23 \text{ mA} = 2.4 \text{ mA}$$

For the temperature change from 25° to $-50°C$,

$$\Delta T = -75°C$$

$$\Delta I_{CBO} = I_{CBO1}(2^{-75/10} - 1)$$

$$= (1.5 \times 10^{-6})(-0.99) = -1.49 \text{ μA}$$

$$\Delta V_{BE} = -2(-50 - 25) = 150 \text{ mV}$$

The change in I_{CQ} is then

$$\Delta I_{CQ} = \frac{-1}{50 + 1750/350}(0.15) + \frac{350}{1 + 350(50)/1750}(-1.49 \times 10^{-6})$$

$$+ \frac{1750(1.11 - 0.7)}{350^2 50^2}(100)$$

$$= -2.73 \text{ mA} - 0.05 \text{ mA} + 0.23 \text{ mA} = -2.55 \text{ mA}$$

Now that the variations in both directions have been calculated, it is necessary to find the new maximum symmetrical collector current swing. The positive direction change in collector quiescent current is 2.4 mA, whereas the negative change is 2.55 mA. Thus, with the original Q-point in the center of the load line, the negative change will move the point closer to a nonlinear region than will the positive change. The negative excursion is therefore the limiting factor for the maximum symmetrical swing. After movement in the negative direction, the new Q-point is at

$$I_{CQ} = (7.5 - 2.55) \text{ mA} = 4.95 \text{ mA}$$

If we avoid the lower 5% of the load line because of nonlinearities, the maximum amplitude of the current swing is

$$(4.95 - 5\% \times 15) \text{ mA} = 4.2 \text{ mA}$$

The total swing therefore has a peak-to-peak of twice this amount, or 8.4 mA. This is the maximum peak-to-peak collector current for a distortion-free output and is illustrated in Figure 5.9. The maximum output voltage swing is reduced from 6.75 V to 4.2 V.

In this design, the first term in the ΔI_{CQ} equation is the largest. Thus, the temperature effect on V_{BE} causes the largest change in I_{CQ}. If the amount of reduction in symmetrical output swing were not acceptable, one approach

Figure 5.9
Load line for Example
5.3.

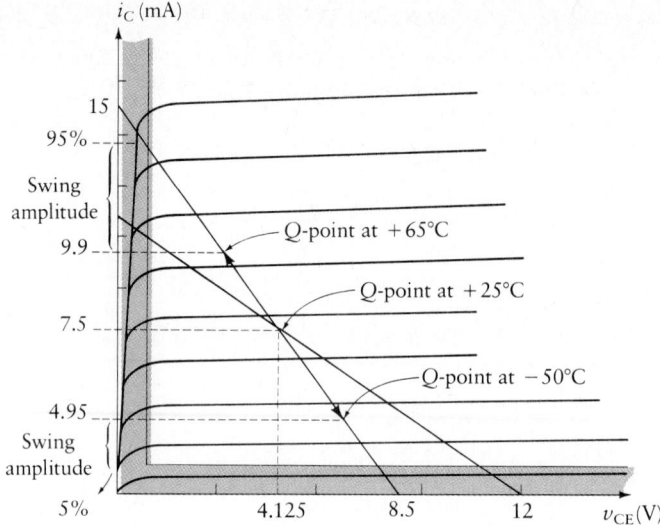

would be to try to reduce the first term in the expression. This could be accomplished by locating the amplifier in a cooler location or by providing for removal of heat from the transistor.   ➤━

Drill Problems

D5.4   Determine the variation of I_{CQ} for a CE amplifier that is designed using the following criteria: $A_v = -10$, $R_L = 4$ kΩ, $R_{in} = 5$ kΩ, and $I_{CBO} = 0.1$ μA at 25°C. The value of β varies from 100 to 300 and the temperature ranges from 25° to 85°C (see Figure 5.4).

Ans: I_{CQ} starts at 1.56 mA and increases to 2.58 mA at 85°C.

D5.5   What is the maximum undistorted symmetrical voltage output swing for the amplifier of Problem D5.4?

Ans: 1.54 V peak-to-peak

D5.6   If the amplifier in Problem D5.4 is designed to operate from −25°C to +25°C, what is the variation in I_{CQ}?

Ans: I_{CQ} decreases by 0.757 mA

D5.7   What is the maximum undistorted symmetrical voltage output swing for the amplifier of Problem D5.6?

Ans: 2.57 V peak-to-peak

D5.8 Design an EF amplifier for $R_L = 50\ \Omega$, $A_i = 15$, $V_{CC} = 15$ V, $V_{BE} = 0.7$ V, and $I_{CBO1}(25°C) = 2\ \mu A$. β ranges from 75 to 125 and the power supply voltage varies by ± 1 V. The amplifier is designed to operate at 100°C. What is I_{CQ} at 100°C and at 25°C?

    Ans: $I_{CQ}(25°C) = 200$ mA; $I_{CQ}(100°C) = 275$ mA

D5.9 What is the maximum undistorted symmetrical voltage swing for the amplifier of Problem D5.8 if the temperature is 100°C?

    Ans: 5.25 V peak-to-peak

5.4   Diode Compensation

The examples of the previous section show that changes in temperature can greatly affect the location of the Q-point. *Diode compensation* is a useful technique for reducing the effect of changes in temperature on I_{CQ}. A diode is selected that has temperature characteristics similar to those of the transistor. It may, in fact, be the junction of an identical transistor. This diode is connected in the circuit, as shown in Figure 5.10.

The addition of this diode in the base circuit compensates for changes arising from temperature variation, since V_γ varies in the same fashion as V_{BE}. R_f is the forward resistance of the diode. If the diode characteristic and the base-emitter junction characteristic are the same, then as the temperature changes both V_γ and V_{BE} change at the same rate. With proper diode selection, the effects of variations in V_{BE} are reduced. The new bias equation for the base-to-ground voltage is

$$V_B = V_\gamma + I_D R_f = V_{BE} + I_{CQ} R_E$$

Figure 5.10
Single diode
compensation.

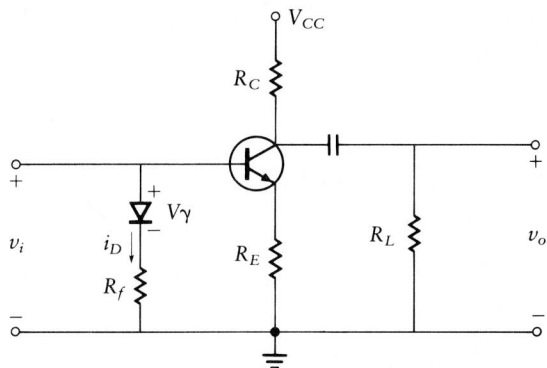

Solving for I_{CQ} yields

$$I_{CQ} = \frac{(V_\gamma - V_{BE} + I_D R_f)}{R_E}$$

Temperature affects both V_γ and V_{BE}. We neglect the term $I_D R_f$ since it is much smaller than $(V_\gamma - V_{BE})$ and the variation of I_D is small. The variation in I_{CQ} with temperature is found by taking the partial derivative as follows:

$$\frac{\partial I_{CO}}{\partial T} = \frac{\partial V_\gamma/\partial T - \partial V_{BE}/\partial T}{R_E} \qquad (5.15)$$

If

$$\frac{\partial V_\gamma}{\partial T} = \frac{\partial V_{BE}}{\partial T}$$

then

$$\frac{\partial I_{CQ}}{\partial T} = 0$$

Hence, I_{CQ} is essentially independent of changes in temperature.

Let us perform a similar analysis for the example shown in Figure 5.11(a). This circuit is biased in a different manner than that of the previous circuit. We begin the analysis by finding the Thevenin equivalent for the bias circuit. Figure 5.11(b) illustrates the circuit connected to the base of the transistor. In order to find the open-circuit voltage from the base to ground, we first find the diode current.

$$I_D = \frac{V_{CC} - V_\gamma}{R_1 + R_2 + R_f}$$

The Thevenin voltage, V_{TH}, is then given by

$$V_{\text{TH}} = I_D R_1 + V_\gamma + I_D R_f$$

$$= \frac{V_{CC}(R_1 + R_f) + V_\gamma R_2}{R_1 + R_2 + R_f}$$

and if $R_f << R_1$,

$$= \frac{V_{CC} R_1 + V_\gamma R_2}{R_1 + R_2}$$

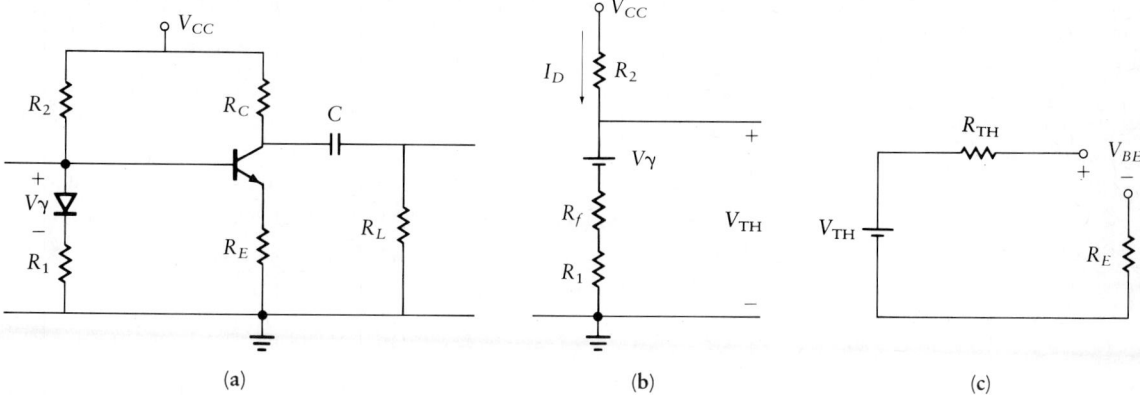

Figure 5.11   Diode compensation.

The Thevenin resistance is the parallel combination of R_2 with R_1.

$$R_{TH} = R_2 \parallel R_1$$

The equivalent of the bias circuit is shown in Figure 5.11(c). We find the quiescent base current as follows:

$$I_{BQ} = \frac{V_{TH} - V_{BE}}{R_{TH} + \beta R_E}$$

The quiescent collector current is found by multiplying the base current by β. Following substitution of the earlier expressions, we obtain

$$I_{CQ} = \frac{V_{TH} - V_{BE}}{R_{TH}/\beta - R_E}$$

$$= \frac{[V_{CC}R_1 + V_\gamma R_2]/(R_1 + R_2) - V_{BE}}{R_{TH}/\beta + R_E}$$

The sensitivity of this circuit to variations of temperature is found by forming the partial derivative, $\partial I_{CQ}/\partial T$ as follows:

$$\frac{\partial I_{CQ}}{\partial T} = \frac{[R_2/(R_1 + R_2)]\partial V_\gamma/\partial T - \partial V_{BE}/\partial T}{R_{TH}/\beta + R_E}$$

Now if $R_2 \gg R_1$, this is simplified to yield

$$\frac{\partial I_{CQ}}{\partial T} \approx \left(\frac{\partial V_\gamma}{\partial T} - \frac{\partial V_{BE}}{\partial T}\right)\left(\frac{1}{R_{TH}/\beta + R_E}\right) \tag{5.16}$$

This shows that if the diode temperature characteristic is matched to the base-emitter temperature characteristic, I_{CQ} is essentially independent of changes in temperature.

5.4.1   *Dual-Diode Compensation*

In the *single-diode compensator* of Figure 5.10, the current in the diode is not necessarily equal to the current in the transistor junction. Thus, although the characteristics of the diode might be matched to those of the base-emitter junction, there is no assurance that operating conditions are identical. If we use two diodes, as shown in Figure 5.12, this problem is eliminated and better compensation is achieved. We arrive at the equivalent circuit in two steps, as shown in Figure 5.12(b) and (c). The first simplification is made by finding the Thevenin equivalent of the bias circuitry. The second simplification involves the finding of a second Thevenin equivalent, where each diode is replaced by a dc voltage source of V_γ volts. In making this substitution, we assume that the two forward resistances of the diodes are included in an added resistor, R_D. We find the Thevenin voltage using superposition as follows:

$$V_{TH} = \frac{2V_\gamma R_B + R_D V_{BB}}{R_B + R_D}$$

The Thevenin resistance is R_B in parallel with R_D.

$$R_{TH} = R_B \parallel R_D$$

The base-emitter loop equation yields

$$I_{CQ} = \frac{V_{TH} - V_{BE}}{R_E + (R_B \parallel R_D)/\beta}$$

Figure 5.12   Dual-diode compensation.

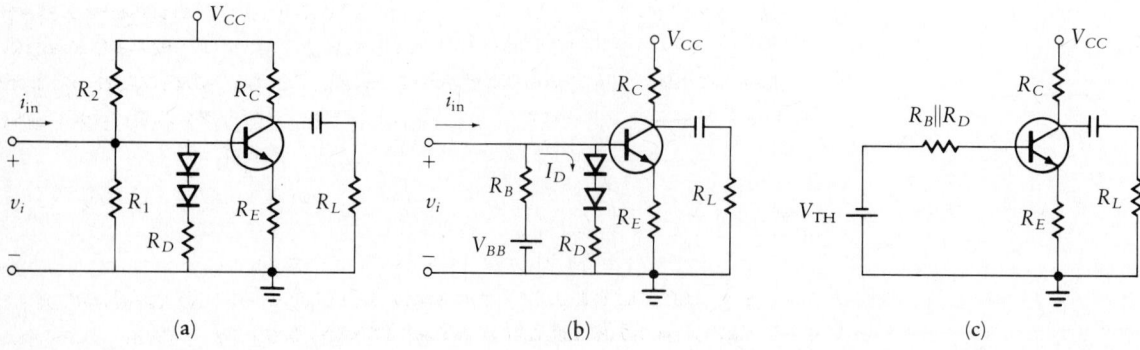

(a)   (b)   (c)

If $(R_B \parallel R_D)/\beta \ll R_E$, then I_{CQ} is given approximately by

$$I_{CQ} = \frac{V_{\text{TH}} - V_{BE}}{R_E}$$

Substituting the expression for V_{TH} yields

$$I_{CQ} = \frac{\dfrac{2V_\gamma R_B + R_D V_{BB}}{R_B + R_D} - V_{BE}}{R_E}$$

and the variation with temperature is given by

$$\frac{\partial I_{CQ}}{\partial T} = \frac{\partial V_\gamma}{\partial T} \frac{2R_B}{(R_B + R_D)R_E} - \frac{\partial V_{BE}}{\partial T} \frac{1}{R_E} \tag{5.17}$$

If we let $R_B = R_D$, then equation (5.17) becomes

$$\frac{\partial I_{CQ}}{\partial T} = \frac{1}{R_E}\left[\frac{\partial V_\gamma}{\partial T} - \frac{\partial V_{BE}}{\partial T}\right]$$

If the diode characteristic matches that of the base-emitter junction, this expression reduces to zero, and accurate temperature compensation is achieved. To ensure that the characteristics are matched, the diodes and the transistor can be fabricated on the same chip.

5.5 Reducing Temperature Variations

As the level of current increases in any semiconductor device, the junction temperature increases. This causes variations in the transistor parameters, which causes the I_{CQ} of the device to increase, thus reducing the maximum output voltage swing. To avoid this change in I_{CQ}, active or passive cooling techniques can be employed to keep the junction temperature fairly constant. Active cooling involves the use of fans or air conditioners. Such systems are expensive and bulky.

Passive cooling involves the use of heat sinks composed of a conductive material located so that the heat is conducted away from the transistor. The purpose of the heat sink is to provide a large surface area through which the heat can be removed from the device by conduction. The larger surface area permits the heat to be dissipated in the surrounding air by convection. When large amounts of heat must be removed from the device, cooling fins are added to the heat sink to increase the amount of surface area in contact with surrounding air. A metal chassis supporting the electronic components is sometimes used as an effective and economical heat sink.

If the problem is cold rather than heat, similar results can be achieved by using heaters.

5.6   Designing for BJT Amplifier Bias Stability

In order to reduce the effects of parameter changes on the Q-point location, we concentrate upon reducing each term in equation (5.14). The design approach toward accomplishing this goal is outlined by the following four steps.

1. Use diode compensation to subtract the changes that occur in V_{BE} from changes in temperature. The changes in V_{BE} are often significant and cause a large change in I_{CQ}. In using diode compensation, it is imperative that the characteristics of the diodes be the same as the characteristics of the transistor V_{BE}.
2. Select a transistor with low I_{CBO} so that the temperature change does not significantly affect I_{CQ}.
3. Ensure that the design reduces the effect of changes in β. For example, with voltage-division biasing, R_B should be less than $0.1\beta R_E$. This reduces the effect of changes in β, as can be seen from the third term in equation (5.14).
4. Use a well-regulated power supply to reduce the change in V_{CC}.

5.7   FET Temperature Effects

Temperature changes cause large variations in the bias point of BJTs. Fortunately, temperature instability is not as big a problem with FET amplifiers. However, the drain current is affected somewhat by temperature variations. Temperature increases cause the gate-to-source leakage current of a FET to increase, roughly doubling for every 10°C rise in temperature.

Increasing the temperature of a FET amplifier tends to decrease the mobility of charge carriers in the channel of the FET. The effect of the smaller number of charge carriers is to reduce the drain current. However, the increased temperature also narrows the depletion region, which tends to increase the drain current. These two effects are in opposition, thus giving the FET its relatively low temperature coefficient.

Figure 5.13
FET amplifier.

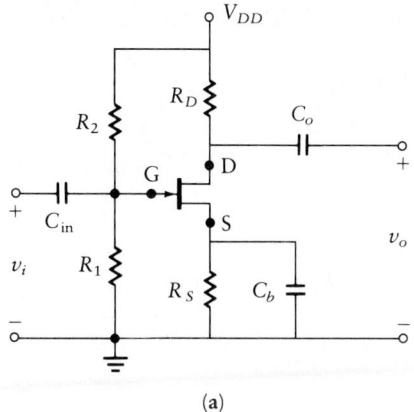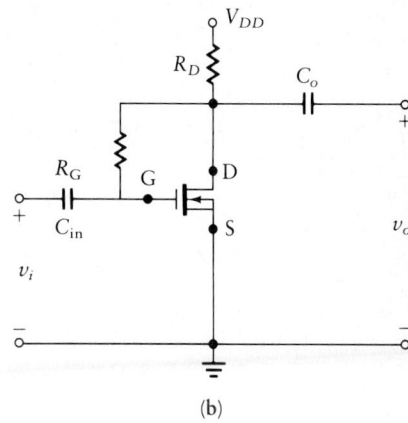

(a)   (b)

Figure 5.14
FET operating curves.

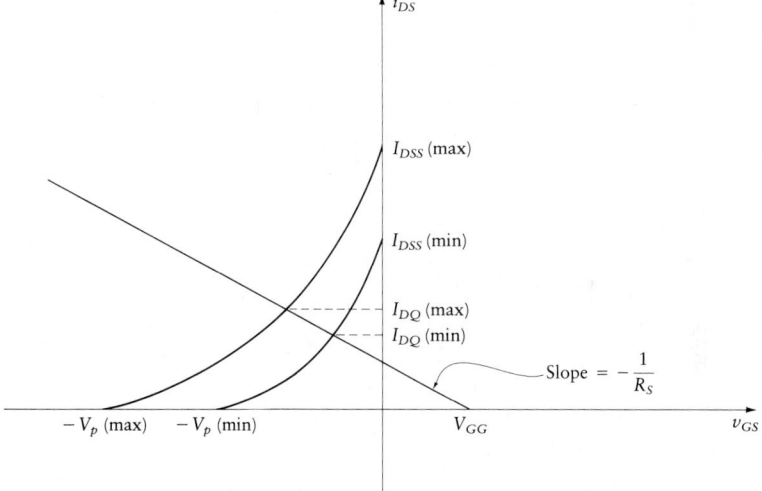

For some types of FET, the manufacturer specifies a quiescent drain current, which, when used, gives nearly a zero temperature coefficient. This results from the decreased conductivity of the channel.

Since the temperature coefficient is not zero, it is good practice to consider bias stability in all circuit design. One simple approach is to use a source resistor, which results in negative feedback. This is shown in Figure 5.13(a). When the drain current increases, v_S becomes more positive, causing v_{GS} to become more negative. Thus, as i_D increases, v_{GS} becomes more negative. This tends to decrease i_D. The result is that the amount of change in i_D is reduced. We illustrate this graphically in Figure 5.14. The manufacturer typically provides a range of V_p and I_{DSS}. The v_{GS}-i_D curve as shown in Figure 5.14 is used to account for the two extremes of these values. Note that as the value of the source resistor increases, the variation in i_D decreases. This allows us to design the amplifier to reduce the affects of changes in drain current. A typical value of R_S that provides a reasonable I_{DQ} deviation is 10% of the value of R_D ([34], Section 11.17).

Bias stability is provided for MOSFETs in the same manner. However, a simpler circuit can be used, as shown in Figure 5.13(b). An increase in i_D causes v_{DS} to decrease. Reducing v_{DS} reduces v_{GS}, thereby tending to decrease the original increase in i_D. This is a form of negative feedback ([51], Section 4.5).

Example 5.4

Determine the value of the source and drain resistors for a JFET amplifier (see Figure 4.15(a)) that will allow for only a 10% variation in I_{DQ} for the following specifications:

- V_p ranges from 5 V to 8V.
- I_{DSS} ranges from 7 mA to 10 mA.
- The nominal value of I_{DQ} is 5 mA.
- $V_{DD} = 12$ V.
- $V_{DSQ} = 4$ V.

SOLUTION   A 10% variation in I_{DQ} is a variation from a minimum of 4.5 mA to a maximum of 5.5 mA. The intercepts of these values on the curves of Figure 5.14 show that

v_{GS} varies from 0.7 V to 1.3 V

Then the source resistance is given by

$$R_S = \frac{\Delta v_{GS}}{I_{DQ\,max} - I_{DQ\,min}} = \frac{1.3 - 0.7}{5.5\ \text{mA} - 4.5\ \text{mA}} = 600\ \Omega$$

The line passing through these points intersects the v_{GS} axis, resulting in a value of V_{GG} of 2.1 V:

$$V_{GSQ} = V_{GG} - 5\ \text{mA}\ (600\ \Omega)$$

$$= -0.9\ \text{V}$$

$$V_{DD} = V_{DSQ} + (R_S + R_D)I_{DQ}$$

$$R_D + R_S = \frac{V_{DD} - V_{DSQ}}{I_{DQ}} = \frac{12 - 4}{5\ \text{mA}} = 1.6\ \text{k}\Omega$$

Then

$$R_D = 1.6 \text{ k}\Omega - R_S = 1 \text{ k}\Omega$$

By selecting

$$R_S = 600 \ \Omega$$

we can ensure that I_{DQ} will not vary more than 10% for any variation of the transistor parameters, V_p and I_{DSS}, within the specified range.   ➤

PROBLEMS

5.1 Prove that $V_{CC} = V_{BB}$ for the circuit shown in Figure 5.1. Use the equations derived in Chapter 2.

5.2 In the circuit of Figure 5.1, let $R_C = 1 \text{ k}\Omega$, $V_{CC} = 10$ V, and $A_v = -8$. Determine the values of R_B and R_E that would make the amplifier least susceptible to large changes in β. Assume $V_{BE} = 0.7$ V and $\beta = 150$.

5.3 For an amplifier of the type shown in Figure 5.2, determine the values of R_F and R_E that will make the amplifier operate consistently for large changes in β. Let $V_{CC} = 10$ V, $R_L = 1 \text{ k}\Omega$, $A_v = -10$, $V_{BE} = 0.7$ V and $\beta = 100$.

5.4 Design an EF amplifier to drive a 15-Ω load when $\beta = 60$, $V_{BE} = 0.7$ V, $I_{CBO}(25°\text{C}) = 1 \ \mu\text{A}$, $V_{CC} = 20$ V, and $A_i = 8$. If the temperature now changes from 25° to 85°C, determine the peak-to-peak output voltage swing at 85°C. Use the circuit of Figure 5.6.

5.5 Design a CE amplifier as shown in Figure P5.1 to obtain a voltage gain of -8. Do not exceed the power limit of the transistor, $P_{\text{max}} = 50$ mW. If the temperature changes from 25° to 85°C and $I_{CBO}(25°\text{C}) = 0.4 \ \mu\text{A}$, what is the peak-to-peak undistorted voltage output at 85°C when $V_{CC} = 12$ V?

5.6 Design an EF amplifier to drive an 8 Ω load, as shown in Figure P5.2. Set the current gain, $A_i = 10$. Determine the peak-to-peak output voltage swing if the temperature rises to 75°C. Assume $I_{CBO}(25°\text{C}) = 0.5 \ \mu\text{A}$, $V_{CC} = 24$ V, and that β varies over the range from 60 to 100.

5.7 For the design of Problem 5.5, determine the maximum peak-to-peak output voltage if β varies from 250 to 350 and the power supply varies from 11.5 to 12.5 V.

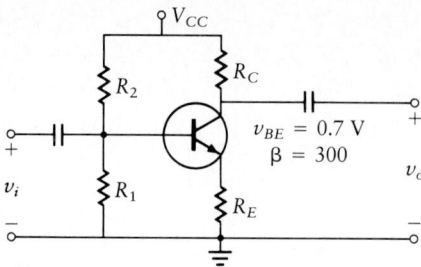

Figure P5.1

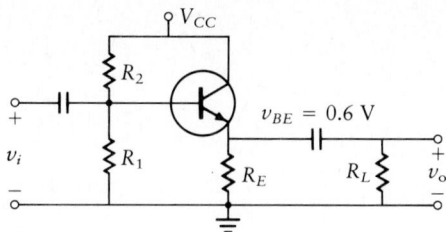

Figure P5.2

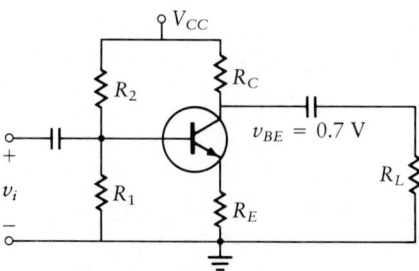

Figure P5.3

5.8 For the circuit of Figure P5.2, determine the maximum peak-to-peak output voltage swing if β varies from 40 to 80 and the voltage supply varies from 19 to 21 V with the temperature at 85°C. Assume $I_{CBO}(25°C) = 2$ μA, $R_L = 200$ Ω, and $A_i = 8.8$.

5.9 Design a CE amplifier to have a voltage gain of 8 and drive a 750-Ω load. Use the configuration of Figure P5.3 with a transistor that has $\beta = 300$ and $I_{CBO}(25°C) = 10$ μA. Determine the maximum peak-to-peak output voltage swing when the temperature rises to 85°C, β varies from 250 to 350, and $V_{CC} = 24$ V.

5.10 The amplifier shown in Figure P5.3 is designed for operation where the temperature is $-25°C$. Find the maximum peak-to-peak output voltage swing at $-25°C$ if all parameters are the same as in Problem 5.9 except that β varies from 200 to 350.

5.11 An amplifier similar to that shown in Figure P5.2 is being designed. It is required to have a current gain of 10 and to drive a 20-Ω load using a 24-V $\pm$ 2% regulated power supply. The transistor selected has a β variation of 60 to 100, $V_{BE} = 0.7$ V and $I_{CBO}(25°C) = 1$ μA. What is the maximum output voltage swing that can be obtained at $-30°C$ and at 80°C? Let $V_{CC} = 24$ V.

5.12 Using the stability factor, δ_β, find the value of R_E for an amplifier of the type shown in Figure P5.1. Use a silicon transistor designed such that the voltage across R_C will not vary more than ± 0.5 V. Assume the supply voltage is 20 V, $V_{BE} = 0.7$ V, $I_{CQ} = 10$ mA, and β varies from 50 to 100.

5.13 An amplifier similar to the one shown in Figure P5.3 is being designed for use where the temperature ranges from $80°$ to $-50°$C. The battery source is 24 V, the transistor selected has a β variation of 200 to 300, and $I_{CBO}(25°C) = 2$ μA. What is the maximum output voltage swing for a voltage gain of 10 if the load is 1 kΩ?

5.14 In the amplifier described in Problem 5.13, change the high temperature from 80°C to 50°C. What is the maximum output voltage swing for the amplifier after this modification?

5.15 For the amplifier described in Problem 5.13, the transistor originally planned for use went out of production and the only other transistor available that would meet the requirements had an $I_{CBO}(25°C)$ of 5 μA and a variation in β of 300 to 500. What is the maximum output voltage swing with the temperature changing from $-50°$ to $+50°$C?

5.16 An amplifier as in Figure P5.2 requires a current gain of 10 into a 50 Ω load. The specification requires the amplifier to operate from $-75°$ to 50°C. The transistor selected has an $I_{CBO}(25°C) = 5$ μA and a β variation of 200 to 300. Let $V_{CC} = 25$ V. Find the maximum output swing of the amplifier.

5.17 In Problem 5.16, change the high temperature to 100°C. With this change, what is the maximum output voltage swing?

6

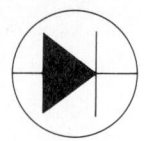

POWER AMPLIFIERS
AND POWER SUPPLIES

6.0 Introduction

In this chapter we consider the design of power amplifiers. The purpose of the power amplifier is to deliver a maximum undistorted symmetrical output voltage swing to a low resistance load. In practice, a system may consist of several stages of amplification, the last of which is usually a power amplifier. The load fed by this power amplifier may be a loudspeaker, an actuator, a solenoid, or some other analog device. The input to the system is a small signal, which is amplified through the voltage-gain stages. The output of the voltage-gain stages is of sufficient amplitude to drive the output power amplifier.

We begin the chapter with a discussion of the various biasing techniques leading to Class-A, Class-B, Class-AB, and Class-C operation. We then analyze the specific amplifier circuits and the effects of various coupling configurations. In particular, inductively coupled, capacitor-coupled, and transformer-coupled amplifiers are studied and several design examples are given.

The analysis of the zener-regulated supply of Chapter 1 is extended to include the use of power transistors. This allows regulation over a wider range of inputs and outputs. The IC regulator is also briefly discussed.

We conclude the chapter with a detailed analysis of Class-B power amplifier circuits.

6.1 Classes of Amplifiers

Power amplifiers are classified according to the percent of time that collector current is nonzero. There are four principal classifications: Class A, Class B, Class AB, and Class C. We discuss each of these in the following subsections.

6.1.1 *Class-A Operation*

Class-A is the type of operation considered in the amplifiers of Chapters 2, 3 and 4. In Class-A operation, the amplifier reproduces the input signal in its entirety. The collector current is nonzero all the time. This type of operation is inefficient, since, even with zero-input signal, I_{CQ} is nonzero and the transistor dissipates power. That is, the transistor dissipates power in the rest, or quiescent, condition.

Figure 6.1 illustrates typical characteristic curves for Class-A operation. The current, I_{CQ}, is usually set to be in the center of the ac load line. The figure shows an example of a sinusoidal input and the resulting collector current at the output. Note that we sketch the sinusoidal input with the ordinate aligned with the load line. We then vary v_{CE} as a function of time by moving up and down the load line. Variations in v_{CE} cause proportional variations in the collector current which is read by projecting the v_{CE} value to the load line and then horizontally to the i_C-axis. Note that if the nonlinear portions of the operating curves (the shaded regions of the diagram) are avoided, a sinusoidal input results in a sinusoidal output.

Figure 6.1
Class-A operation.

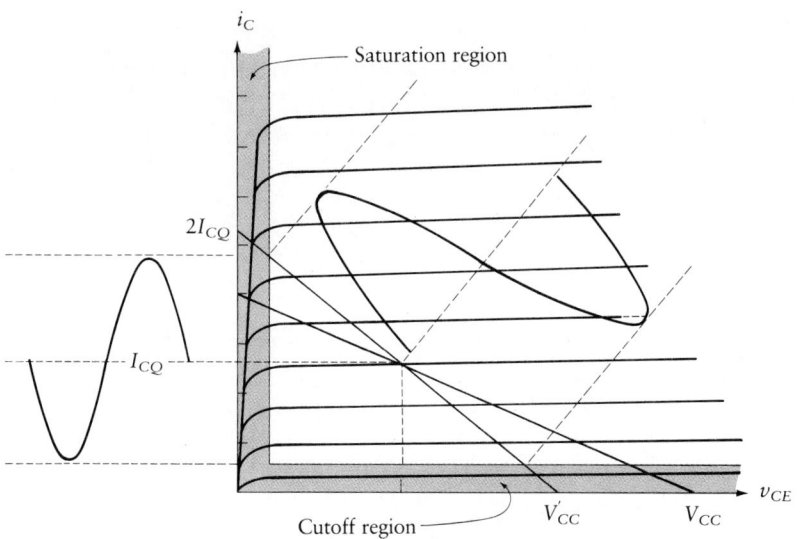

6.1.2   *Class-B Operation*

In *Class-B* operation, one amplifier is used to amplify the positive half-cycle of the input signal, and a second amplifier is used to amplify the negative half-cycle. This amplifier configuration is known as *push-pull,* or *complementary symmetry.* We present push-pull circuits in Section 6.3, but in the current section, we are interested only in the concept.

Since a single transistor can respond only to a half-cycle, two transistors are required to produce the complete waveform. Each of these transistors is biased at cutoff rather than in the middle of the operating range, as is the case for Class-A operation. Each transistor operates one-half of the time, so the collector current of each is nonzero 50% of the time.

The advantage of Class-B operation is that the collector current is zero when the signal input to the amplifier is zero. Therefore, the transistor dissipates no power in the quiescent condition.

Among the disadvantages of a Class-B amplifier is that the nonlinear cutoff region is included in the operating range. That is, unlike the Class-A situation, we are not able to eliminate the 5% of the operating region shaded at the bottom of Figure 6.1. Therefore, the distortion occurring near the Q-point is included in the output signal.

Figure 6.2 illustrates a typical characteristic curve for a pair of transistors in the push-pull configuration. This figure is intended for conceptual purposes only, since we discuss the amplifier in more detail later. Since two transistors are connected back to back, we have repeated the set of transistor curves for the second transistor, but the sign of the collector current and collector-to-emitter voltage have been reversed. That is, these two quantities increase in the downward and the left directions, respectively, for the second transistor characteristic. The upper left portion of the figure represents the first transistor, which conducts only during the positive half-cycle of the input. The lower right portion represents the second transistor, which is configured to conduct only during the negative half-cycle. A typical output waveform is shown in Figure 6.3. Note that the first transistor produces the positive part of the output and the second transistor produces the negative part. Also note that Figure 6.3(a) and (b) indicates some distortion near the point $i_C = 0$. When these two curves are added together, the output shown in Figure 6.3(c) results. This resembles the sinusoidal input, but the waveform is distorted near the zero axis.

It is important that the two transistors in a push-pull configuration be carefully matched. In this way, the positive and negative portions of the input are amplified by the same amount.

6.1.3   *Class-AB Operation*

Class-A operation has the advantage of little distortion, whereas Class-B has the advantage of higher efficiency. *Class-AB operation* is a compromise between

Figure 6.2
Class-B operation.

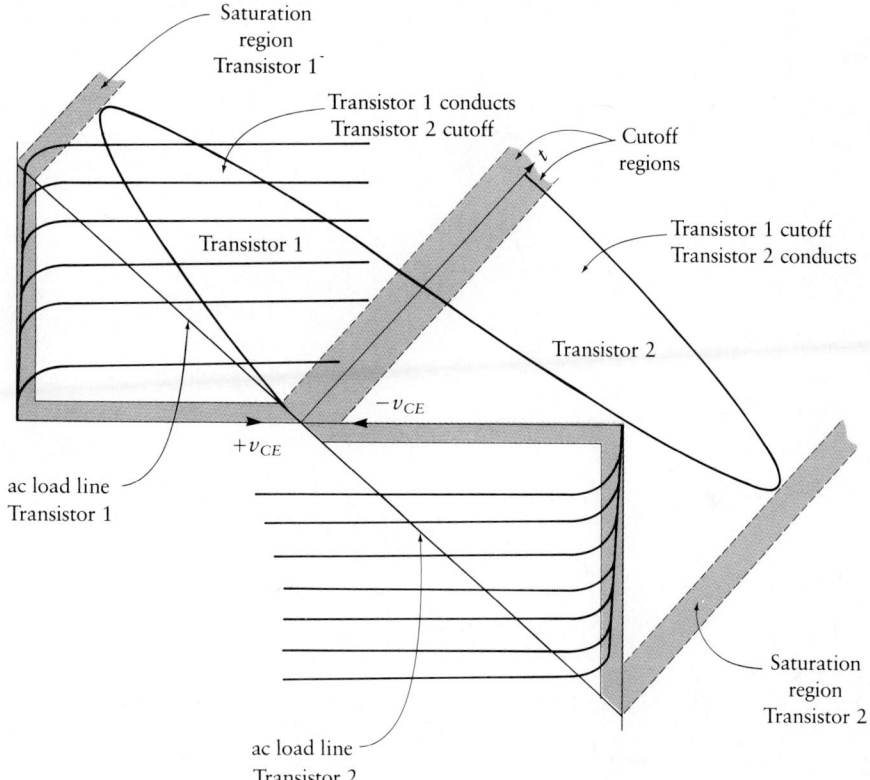

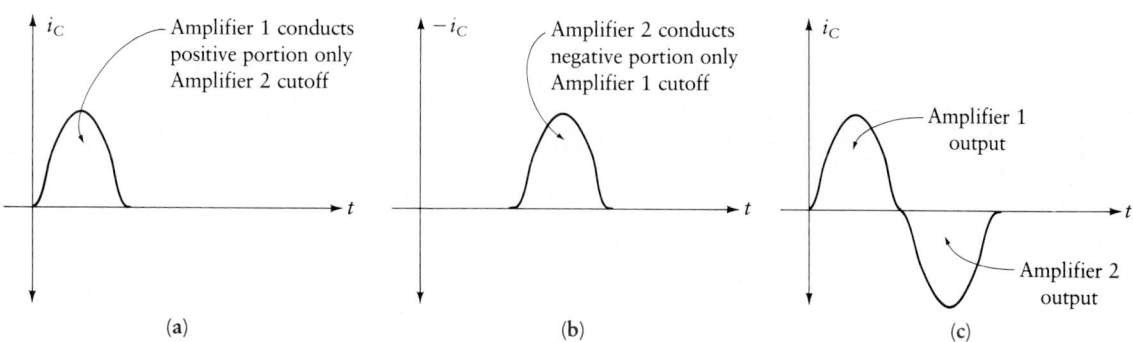

Figure 6.3   Push-pull output waveform.

these two extremes. The Q-point is set slightly above the cutoff value, so it is at the lower boundary of the linear (no distortion) portion of the operating curves. The transistor therefore supports a nonzero collector current over slightly more than 50% of the time.

Figure 6.4 illustrates the operating curve for a sinusoidal input and Class-AB operation. Note that with only one transistor, if the input is a sinusoid,

Figure 6.4
Class-AB operation.

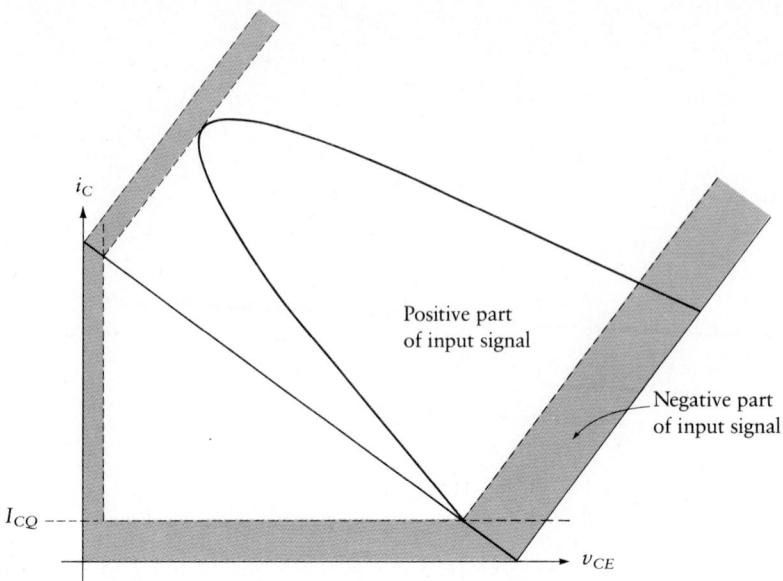

the negative portion of the waveform is severely distorted by the amplifier. The Class-AB amplifier is intended only for the positive portion of the input waveform. Either the input must be conditioned to never go negative or a push-pull type arrangement is necessary.

6.1.4   *Class-C Operation*

A *Class-C* amplifier load line is shown in Figure 6.5, where V_{BEQ} is set to a negative value. The transistor is biased with a negative V_{BB}. Thus it conducts only when the input signal is above a specified positive value. The output is less than one-half of a sinusoid and the collector current is nonzero less than 50% of the time.

If a sinusoid forms the input to a Class-C amplifier, the output consists of "blips" at the frequency of the input. This is shown to the left of Figure 6.5. Since this is a periodic signal, it contains a fundamental frequency component plus higher frequency harmonics. If this signal is passed through an inductor-capacitor (LC) circuit tuned to be resonant at the fundamental frequency, the output is a sinusoidal signal at the same frequency as the input. This approach is often used if the signal to be amplified is either a pure sinusoid or a more general signal with a limited range of frequencies.

Class-C amplifiers are capable of providing large amounts of power. They are often used for transmitter power stages, where a tuned circuit is included to eliminate the higher harmonics in the output signal.

Figure 6.5
Class-C operation.

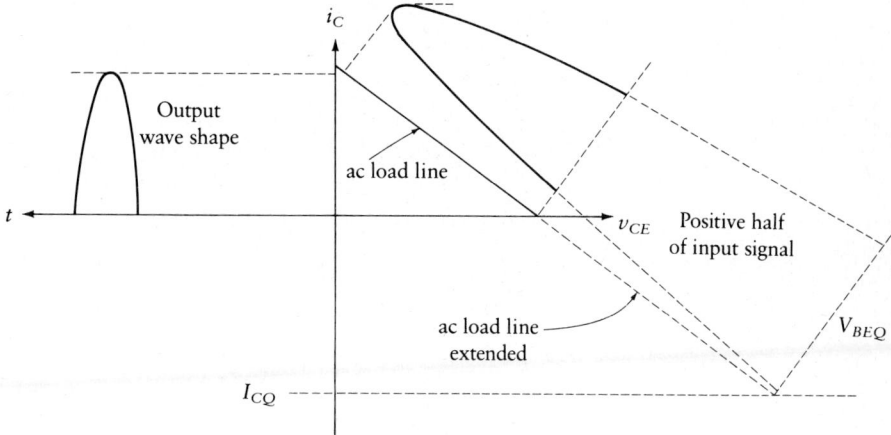

6.2 Power-Amplifier Circuits—Class-A Operation

Power-amplifier circuits usually contain transistors capable of handling high power. These normally operate at higher voltages than do low-power transistors, and they therefore often require a separate power supply. For example, voltages of power transistors can exceed 450 V. Current ratings are also high, often in excess of 10 A of continuous current. Since these transistors need to dissipate high power, they are designed differently than low-power transistors. They may include protective circuits to limit current. Additional effort is also expended to dissipate heat which builds up during operation.

In this section, we discuss the circuit configurations for power amplifiers. These are categorized according to the type of coupling.

6.2.1 *Inductively Coupled Amplifier*

High current gain is required to obtain power in the output load. The output voltage swing can be increased by using an inductor for the collector element instead of a resistor. We will see that this also increases the efficiency of the circuit. The inductor is selected so that it approximates an open circuit for the input frequency but a short circuit for dc. In other words,

$$\omega L \gg R_L$$

at the lowest frequency,

$$R_{\text{coil}} \ll R_L$$

and

$$R_{coil} << R_E.$$

Figure 6.6 illustrates the inductively coupled amplifier circuit and load lines.

We choose the Q-point for maximum output swing. The current, I_{CQ}, is then given by equation (2.29), which is developed in Chapter 2.

$$I_{CQ} = \frac{V_{CC}}{R_{ac} + R_{dc}}$$

The ac resistance is simply R_L, since the inductor is an approximate open circuit for ac and the capacitors are short circuits. The dc resistance is R_E, provided that we can neglect the resistance of the inductor. Therefore,

$$I_{CQ} = \frac{V_{CC}}{R_L + R_E}$$

Since both dc and ac load lines cross the Q-point, the ac load-line equation yields

$$I_{CQ} = \frac{V_{CEQ}}{R_L}$$

Equating these two expressions for I_{CQ}, we obtain equation (6.1):

$$V_{CEQ} = \frac{V_{CC}}{1 + R_E/R_L} \tag{6.1}$$

Suppose that $R_E << R_L$. Then from equation (6.1) we see that $V_{CEQ} \approx V_{CC}$ and the ac load line intersects the v_{CE} axis at approximately $2V_{CC}$. The use of the storage device (inductor) results in a voltage swing that is effectively equivalent to doubling the supply voltage. The inductor field stores energy during the conducting cycle, thus acting like a second V_{CC} source in series with the dc supply.

The inductively coupled amplifier has a higher efficiency than does the amplifier that contains a collector resistance. In order to prove this, we shall first calculate the efficiency of this amplifier. We do this assuming sinusoidal input signals.

The power supplied by the voltage source is

$$P_{supplied} = V_{CC}I_{CQ} = \frac{V^2_{CC}}{R_L}$$

where we assume that $R_E \ll R_L$; hence we ignore R_E in the equation. The power delivered to the load under the assumption that the input is sinusoidal with amplitude, $I_{L\,\text{max}}$, is

$$P_{\text{load}} = I^2_{L\,\text{max}} \frac{R_L}{2}$$

We observe from Figure 6.6 that the maximum swing in collector current has an amplitude of I_{CQ} (we ignore saturation and cutoff). Since the inductor is nearly an open circuit for ac, this is also the maximum swing in load current. Therefore, the maximum power to the load is

$$P_{\text{load}} = \frac{I^2_{CQ}R_L}{2} = \frac{V^2_{CC}}{2R_L}$$

We define *conversion efficiency* as the ratio of ac load power to the power delivered by the source. This efficiency measure therefore depends upon the power dissipated in the bias circuitry and in R_E. In order to derive a maximum value for efficiency, we assume that the power dissipated in the bias circuitry and in R_E and in R_{coil} is negligible. The maximum conversion efficiency (with output swing a maximum) is then given by

$$\eta = \frac{V^2_{CC}/2R_L}{V^2_{CC}/R_L} = 50\%$$

The circuit with a collector resistor is discussed in Section 2.6.1 where we derive the various power relationships. These can be used to show that the maximum efficiency of the amplifier with collector resistance is 25%, or one-half of the efficiency found for the inductively coupled amplifier. This is reasonable, since, in the circuit with a collector resistor, the load seen by the

Figure 6.6
Inductively coupled amplifier.

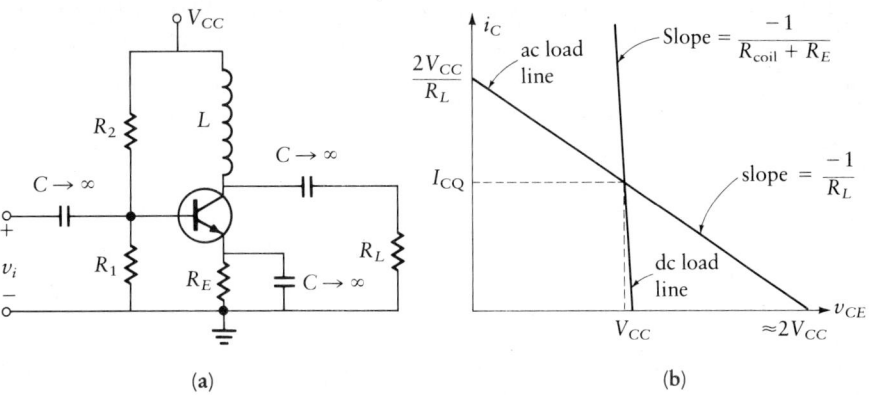

(a)

(b)

transistor is the parallel combination of the collector and load resistance. The maximum power delivered by the transistor is shared between these two resistors.

6.2.2   *Transformer-Coupled Power Amplifier*

The transformer-coupled amplifier is presented in Chapter 3 and basic relationships are developed ([51], Section 5.2). We examine this circuit in more detail in the present section, since it has useful application to power amplifiers. Figure 6.7 illustrates the CC (EF) transformer-coupled power amplifier. Also shown in the figure are the load lines. Note that the slope of the dc load line depends upon the resistance of the primary coil of the transformer. This resistance is usually very small. The slope of the ac load line depends upon the reflected load resistance.

If maximum output voltage swing is desired, we solve the design equation (equation (6.2)) in order to place the Q-point in the middle of the load line. Note that the load resistance reflected by the transformer is

$$R_{\text{trans}} = a^2 R_L$$
$$I_{CQ} = \frac{V_{CC}}{R_{ac} + R_{dc}} = \frac{V_{CC}}{a^2 R_L} \tag{6.2}$$

We have assumed that the transformer primary resistance is negligible and therefore that $R_{dc} = 0$.

In design of CE amplifiers, we select the base resistance, R_B, from the bias stability design equation,

$$R_B = 0.1\,\beta R_E$$

In the design of CC amplifiers, a different criterion is used. The base resistance is constrained by the desired current gain, A_i or by the specified input resistance, R_{in}. The voltage gain of this amplifier is near unity.

The remainder of the design follows equations derived in Chapter 3. We review these in the examples that follow.

We find the maximum conversion efficiency of the transformer-coupled power amplifier. The power supplied by the voltage source is

$$P_{\text{supplied}} = I_{CQ} V_{CC}$$

and from Figure 6.7(b), we see this is approximately equal to

$$P_{\text{supplied}} = \frac{V^2_{CC}}{a^2 R_L}$$

We have assumed that the power to the bias circuitry is negligible and that the slope of the ac load line is $-1/(a^2 R_L)$.

Figure 6.7
Transformer-coupled
power amplifier.

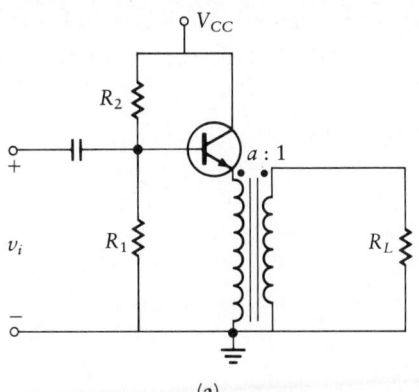
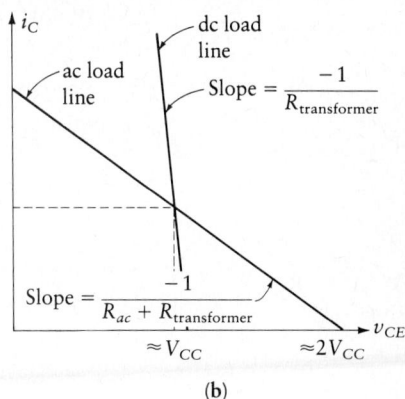

(a)   (b)

The maximum power transferred to the load, assuming a sinusoidal input at full drive and ignoring saturation effects, is

$$P_{\text{load}} = \frac{V^2_{L\,\text{max}}}{2R_L} = \frac{V^2_{CC}}{2a^2 R_L} \tag{6.3}$$

The maximum power-conversion efficiency is then given by

$$\eta = \frac{V^2_{CC}/2a^2 R_L}{V^2_{CC}/a^2 R_L} = 50\%$$

Thus the transformer-coupled amplifier has characteristics similar to those of the inductively coupled amplifier. The maximum conversion efficiency of both circuits is 50%, and although the EF has a voltage gain near unity, the turns ratio of the transformer determines the voltage gain to the load. The transformer-coupled amplifier possesses the additional advantage of providing for impedance matching, as is discussed in Chapter 3.

Example 6.1   **Inductively Coupled Amplifier**

Design an inductively coupled CE amplifier with the given specifications. Determine the power supplied to the load, the power required from the dc source, and the maximum undistorted symmetrical output-voltage swing.

$$A_v = \frac{v_o}{v_i} = -10 \qquad\qquad A_i = \frac{i_o}{i_{\text{in}}} = -30$$

$$R_L = 4\ \text{k}\Omega; \qquad V_{CC} = 16\text{V}; \qquad \beta = 200; \qquad V_{BE} = 0.7\ \text{V}$$

SOLUTION   The circuit of Figure 6.6 is used with the emitter resistor bypass capacitor removed. We use the short-form voltage-gain equation (refer to Table 3.1) for the CE amplifier with the observation that the impedance of the inductor is assumed to be infinite for ac operation. Then

$$R_E = -\frac{R_L}{A_v} = \frac{-4000}{-10} = 400 \ \Omega$$

We use the design equation for I_{CQ}, where

$$R_{ac} = R_L + R_E = 4.4 \text{ k}\Omega$$
$$R_{dc} = R_E = 400 \ \Omega$$

Then

$$I_{CQ} = \frac{V_{CC}}{R_{ac} + R_{dc}} = \frac{16}{4400 + 400} = 3.33 \text{ mA}$$

$$h_{ib} = \frac{26 \text{ mV}}{3.33 \text{ mA}} = 7.8 \ \Omega$$

Note that $h_{ib} < 0.1R_E$, so the short-form equation is justified. For this inductively coupled amplifier, using the short form for the current gain,

$$A_i = -\frac{R_B}{R_E}$$

We solve for the base resistance,

$$R_B = -A_iR_E = 30 \times 400 = 12 \text{ k}\Omega$$

The condition for allowing use of the short-form equation is that

$$R_B << \beta R_E$$

or, substituting values,

$$12 \text{ k}\Omega << 80 \text{ k}\Omega$$

Since 12 is not much less than 80, we recalculate R_B using the long-form equation:

$$A_i = \frac{-R_B}{R_B/\beta + R_E} = \frac{-R_B}{R_B/200 + 400} = -30$$

Solving for R_B yields $R_B = 14.1$ kΩ, which represents a change of 17.5% from the value found from the short-form equations. Since this is more than the tolerance of the average resistor used in such circuits, we are justified in rejecting the 12 kΩ value found from the short-form equations. Had the change been only 3 or 4%, the extra effort would not be justified, since most nonprecision resistors have a tolerance greater than this value (e.g., a 12 kΩ, ± 5% tolerance resistor could have an actual resistance between 11.4 kΩ and 12.6 kΩ).

We use the bias equations to find the bias resistor values:

$$V_{BB} = V_{BE} + I_{CQ}\left(\frac{R_B}{\beta} + R_E\right)$$

$$= 0.7 + (3.33 \times 10^{-3})\left[\frac{14.1 \times 10^3}{200} + 400\right] = 2.27 \text{ V}$$

Then solving for R_1 and R_2 yields

$$R_1 = \frac{R_B}{1 - V_{BB}/V_{CC}}$$

$$= \frac{14,100}{1 - 2.27/16} = 16.4 \text{ k}\Omega$$

$$R_2 = \frac{V_{CC}R_B}{V_{BB}}$$

$$= (14.1 \text{ k}\Omega)\frac{16}{2.27} = 99.4 \text{ k}\Omega$$

The circuit design is now complete, and we calculate power efficiency and maximum undistorted output swing. Because $I_{Cmax} = I_{CQ}$, the output power is given by

$$P_o = (0.95I_{CQ})^2\frac{R_L}{2} = (0.95)^2\frac{(3.33 \text{ mA})^2 \times 4 \text{ k}\Omega}{2} = 20.02 \text{ mW}$$

Note that we have restricted operation to the linear region by eliminating 5% of the maximum swing near cutoff and saturation. The power delivered by the dc source is

$$P_{VCC} = I_{CQ}V_{CC} + \frac{V^2_{CC}}{R_1 + R_2}$$

$$= 3.33 \text{ mA}(16 \text{ V}) + \frac{16^2}{16.4 \text{ k}\Omega + 99.4 \text{ k}\Omega} = 55.2 \text{ mW}$$

The efficiency of the amplifier is then given by the ratio

$$\eta = \frac{20.02}{55.2} = 0.36, \quad \text{or} \quad 36\%$$

The maximum undistorted symmetrical output swing is

$$v_o = 1.8(3.33 \text{ mA})(4 \text{ k}\Omega) = 24 \text{ V}$$

Note that this voltage swing is greater than the supply voltage. This is possible due to the energy-storing capability of the inductor.   ▶▌

Example 6.2   ## Transformer-Coupled Amplifier

Design a transformer-coupled amplifier (see Figure 6.8) for a current gain of $A_i = 80$. Find the power supplied to the load and the power required from the supply.

SOLUTION   We first use the design equation to find the location of the Q-point for maximum output swing:

$$I_{CQ} = \frac{V_{CC}}{R_{ac} + R_{dc}}$$

$$= \frac{12}{a^2 R_L} = \frac{12}{8^2 \times 8} = 23.4 \text{ mA}$$

Since the problem statement requires a current gain of 80, the amplifier must have a current gain of 10 because the transformer provides an additional gain of 8. We use the equations from Table 3.1 to find the base resistance, R_B:

$$A_i = \frac{R_B}{R_B/\beta + h_{ib} + R_E} = 10$$

where

$$R_E = a^2 R_L = 512 \ \Omega$$

We assume that h_{ib} is sufficiently small to be neglected. Then, solving for R_B yields

$$R_B = 5.69 \text{ k}\Omega$$

Figure 6.8
Transformer-coupled
amplifier for Example
6.2.

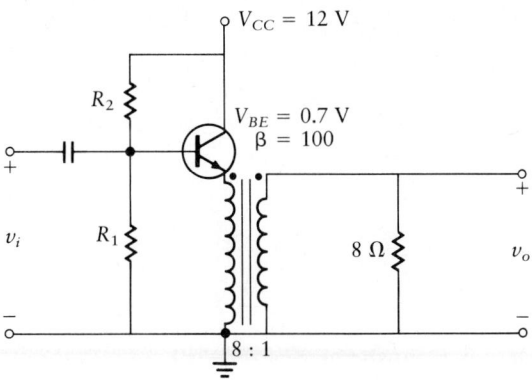

$$V_{BB} = \frac{I_{CQ}R_B}{\beta} + V_{BE}$$

$$= (23.4 \times 10^{-3})\left(\frac{5690}{100}\right) + 0.7 = 2.031 \text{ V}$$

Now solving for the bias resistors,

$$R_1 = \frac{R_B}{1 - V_{BB}/V_{CC}} = \frac{5690}{1 - 2.031/12} = 6.8 \text{ k}\Omega$$

$$R_2 = \frac{V_{CC}R_B}{V_{BB}} = \frac{12(5690)}{2.031} = 33.6 \text{ k}\Omega$$

The design is now complete. The power delivered by the source is given by

$$P_{VCC} = V_{CC}I_{CQ} + \frac{V^2_{CC}}{R_1 + R_2} = 284 \text{ mW}$$

The power dissipated in the load is

$$P_L = \frac{(0.95a\ I_{CQ})^2 R_L}{2} = 126.5 \text{ mW}$$

We have again restricted operation to the nonlinear region by eliminating 5% of the maximum swing near cutoff and saturation. The efficiency is the ratio of load power to source power.

$$\eta = \frac{126.5}{284} = 0.45, \quad \text{or} \quad 45\%$$

Drill Problems

D6.1   Design an inductively coupled CE amplifier for $A_v = -10$, $R_{in} = 4$ kΩ, $R_L = 2$ kΩ, $V_{CC} = 12$ V, $\beta = 200$ and $V_{BE} = 0.7$ V. Determine A_i, the power delivered to the load, and the maximum undistorted symmetrical voltage output swing.

> **Ans:** $R_E = 195$ Ω; $R_1 = 5.2$ kΩ;
> $R_2 = 29.8$ kΩ; $A_i = -20$;
> $P_o = 20.25$ mW; $v_{o\ (p\text{-}p)} = 18$ V

D6.2   Design a transformer-coupled EF amplifier to drive an 8 Ω load if $V_{CC} = 20$ V; $V_{BE} = 0.7$ V; $\beta = 100$; $R_{in} = 2$ kΩ and the transformer has a turns ratio of 10:1. Determine the current gain, A_i, power output, and maximum undistorted voltage output swing.

> **Ans:** $R_1 = 2.1$ kΩ; $R_2 = 33.8$ kΩ;
> $A_i = 250$; $P_o = 202.5$ mW;
> $v_{o\ (p\text{-}p)} = 3.6$ V

6.3 Power-Amplifier Circuits—Class-B Operation

A Class-B audio amplifier uses one transistor to amplify the positive portion of the input signal and another transistor to amplify the negative portion of the input signal.

6.3.1 *Push-Pull CE Circuits*

A *push-pull* CE circuit is shown in Figure 6.9. The input signals to the bases, which are equal and 180° out of phase with each other, are derived from a center-tapped transformer. Alternatively, they can be derived from a phase splitter, as shown in the figure.

The circuit operation is analyzed by viewing a single transistor, as shown in Figure 6.10. The load lines are shown in Figure 6.10(b). The current, I_{CQ}, is set at zero so that the transistor conducts only for a positive input signal. The ac load line is specified by the equation

$$V_{CC} = v_{CE} + i_C(a^2 R_L)$$

Note that when $v_{CE} = 0$,

$$i_C = \frac{V_{CC}}{a^2 R_L}$$

Figure 6.9
CE push-pull
amplifier.

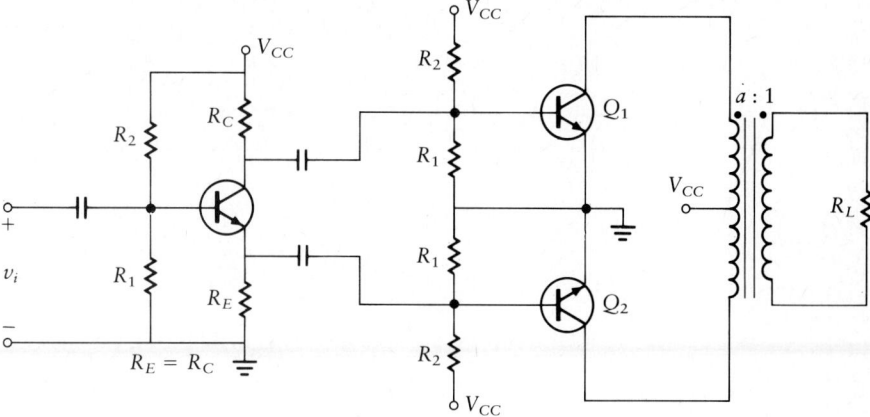

Figure 6.10
Single-transistor
amplifier from circuit
of Figure 6.9.

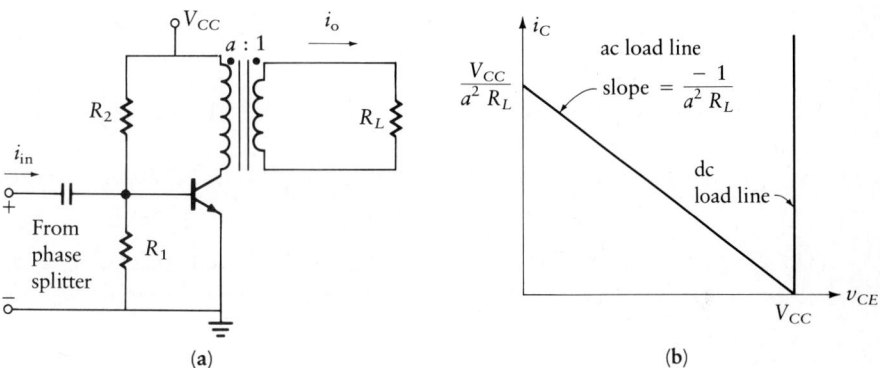

(a)   (b)

The current gain is given by

$$A_i = \frac{-i_{in}\beta a R_B/(R_B + h_{ie})}{i_{in}} = -a\beta$$

We have neglected h_{ie}, since it is much less than R_B.

The power dissipated in the push-pull circuit is

$$P_{VCC} = V_{CC}\frac{1}{T}\int_{-T/2}^{T/2}\left[i_{C1}(t) + i_{C2}(t)\right]dt \tag{6.4}$$

We have neglected the power dissipated in the bias resistors. The integrand of equation (6.4) is the sum of the two collector currents. If the input is sinusoidal, each of these currents is a half-wave rectified version of a sine wave. During the first half-cycle of the input wave, the upper transistor conducts and the lower transistor is cut off. During the second half-cycle, the reverse situation occurs. Thus, the sum of the two currents is a full-wave rectified sinusoid. Assuming that the full swing is used (i.e., we do not eliminate 5% on each end, as done earlier to avoid distortion), the maximum current is given by

$$I_{C\,max} = \frac{V_{CC}}{R_L a^2}$$

The power is then

$$P_{VCC} = \frac{V^2_{CC}}{R_L a^2} \frac{1}{T} \int_{-T/2}^{T/2} \left| \sin \frac{2\pi t}{T} \right| dt = \frac{2}{\pi} \frac{V^2_{CC}}{a^2 R_L}$$

6.3.2   *Complementary-Symmetry Class-B Power Amplifier*

A push-pull power amplifier can be designed without the use of transformers or phase splitters if one *pnp* and one *npn* transistor with symmetrical characteristics are used. The circuit is as shown in Figure 6.11. This circuit is commonly called a *complementary-symmetry power amplifier*. Because two power supplies of opposite polarity are used, the dc voltage at the junction between the two emitters is zero.

If the circuit is revised to isolate the load with a capacitor, a single power supply can be used. This circuit is shown in Figure 6.12. The capacitor blocks the dc ($V_{CC}/2$) from the load. The capacitor also provides the power supply voltage to Q_2 when Q_1 is not conducting. That is, the capacitor charges to a dc value of $V_{CC}/2$ at the connection of the two emitters.

The dc load line is still vertical, since the capacitor acts as an open circuit for dc. Since the amplifier is to operate as Class B, I_{CQ} is set to zero.

As is the case for the transformer-coupled power amplifier, R_B is determined from the current gain or input resistance equations. The input resistance, R_{in}, is determined as follows ($h_{ib} = 0$):

$$R_{in} = R_B \parallel (\beta R_L) = \frac{R_B R_L}{R_B/\beta + R_L}$$

The equivalent base resistance, R_B, is no longer equal to $R_1 \parallel R_2$. Instead, it is $R_2 \parallel R_2$ or $R_2/2$, since the two input capacitors effectively short both R_1 resistors for ac operation. With this value of R_B, we find R_{in} to be

$$R_{in} = \frac{R_L R_2/2}{R_2/2\beta + R_L} = \frac{R_2 R_L}{R_2/\beta + 2R_L} \tag{6.5}$$

Figure 6.11
Complementary symmetry using two power supplies.

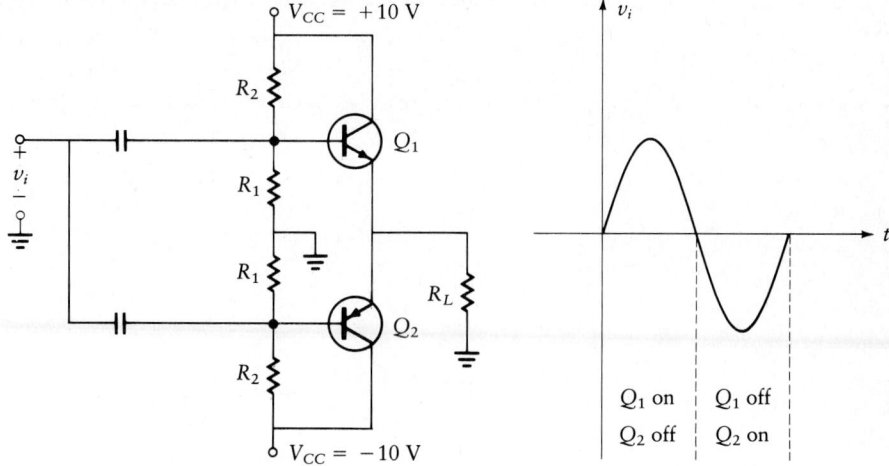

Figure 6.12
Complementary symmetry using one power supply.

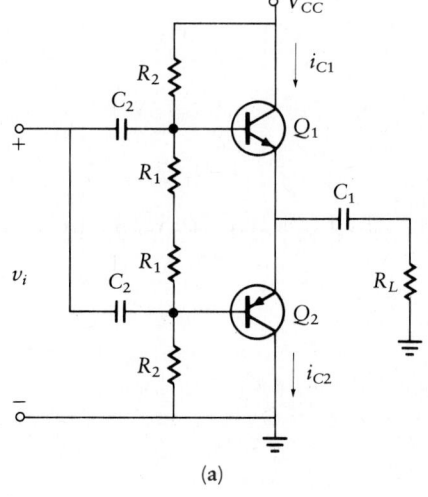

(a)

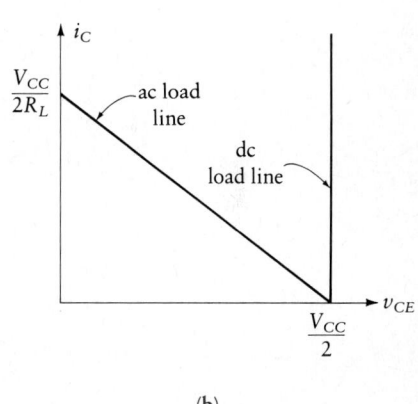

(b)

$$A_i = \frac{\beta R_B}{R_B + \beta R_L}$$

but

$$R_B = \frac{R_2}{2}$$

so

$$A_i = \frac{R_2}{R_2/\beta + 2R_L}$$

Since we now have the value of R_2, we determine the value of R_1 by using the dc equation:

$$V_{BB} = \frac{R_1}{R_1 + R_2} \frac{V_{CC}}{2} \quad \text{but} \quad V_{BB} = V_{BE}$$

so

$$R_1 = \frac{2R_2 V_{BE}}{V_{CC} - 2V_{BE}}$$

In order to avoid the nonlinear operating region near cutoff and thereby to obtain more symmetrical operation, the two R_1 resistors can be removed and replaced with a variable resistor, R_3, as shown in Figure 6.13. This resistor allows I_{CQ} to be raised above zero to compensate for the distortion that occurs when operating close to cutoff, as shown in Figure 6.3. This accomplishes Class-AB operation.

In the circuits of Figure 6.12 and Figure 6.13, a capacitor is used to isolate the load. The capacitor forms part of the current path for one transistor when the other is cut off. Thus, the capacitor charges during conduction of Q_1 and discharges during conduction of Q_2.

With capacitance present, the circuit becomes frequency-dependent. The low frequency response of the stage is determined by the RC network shown in Figure 6.14(a). As the signal frequency decreases, the voltage across the series capacitor increases and the voltage across R_L decreases. This effect reduces the signal developed across R_L and hence decreases the gain of the amplifier.

The *half-power*, or 3 *dB*, point specifies the lower frequency cutoff. This is the frequency which causes a 3 dB drop $(1/\sqrt{2})$ in the output amplitude. The point is specified by

$$R_L = \left| \frac{1}{j\omega C_1} \right|$$

or

$$\omega = \frac{1}{R_L C_1}$$

Figure 6.14(b) shows the amplitude response of the RC network. Note that at the half-power frequency, the amplitude drops by a factor of $1/\sqrt{2}$ from its peak value. This frequency is the lower radian cutoff frequency and normally represents the lowest frequency that can be effectively processed by the amplifier. That is, as frequency decreases, the output decreases. At some point, the

Figure 6.13
Complementary sym-
metry using one power
supply.

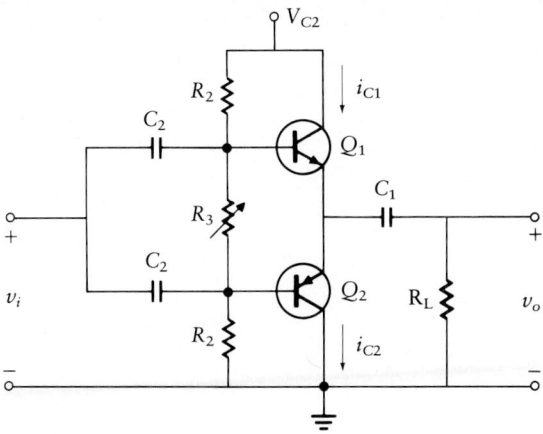

Figure 6.14
RC network.

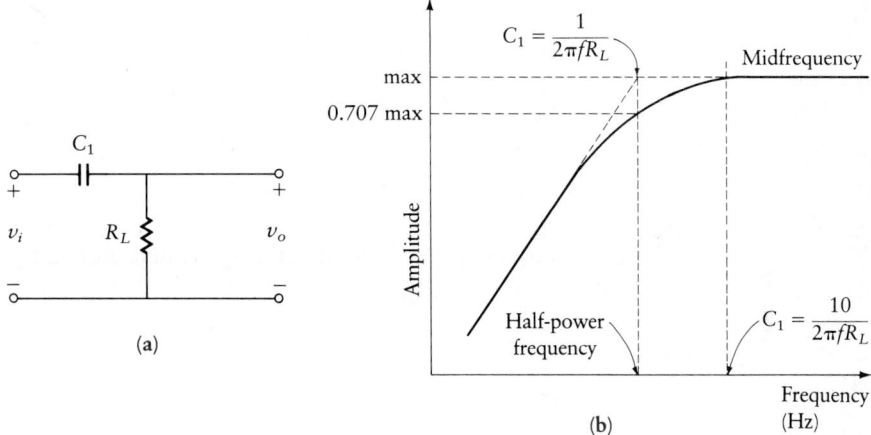

output amplitude is too small to be of use. For example, we might be able to
tolerate only a 1% drop in output amplitude. The half-power point represents
about a 30% drop in output voltage or current (i.e., $1/\sqrt{2} = 0.707$), and this
may be more than can be tolerated for the given application. Nonetheless, the
half-power point is generally accepted as the limiting frequency.

Referring to Figure 6.15, we see that if C_1 is large, the impedance is small
and v_L is almost equal to v'_L. The output power is therefore approximately at
its maximum value. Alternatively, if C_1 is relatively small, v_L is almost equal
to zero and the output power is small. The impedance of C_1 determines the
output amplitude, and this impedance depends upon frequency. The impedance of a fixed capacitor decreases with increasing frequency, so the worst case

Figure 6.15
Output voltage divider
at lowest frequency.

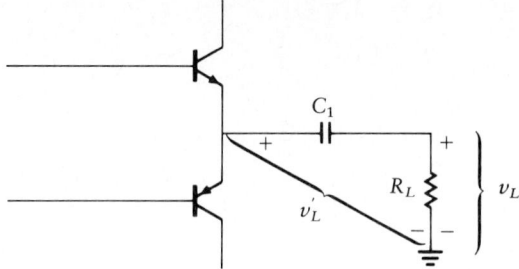

occurs at the lowest operating frequency. Let us assume that the lowest frequency (i.e., the cutoff frequency) is f_{low} hertz. Then the value of C_1 is found from the equation for the half-power point as follows:

$$C_1 = \frac{1}{2\pi f_{low} R_L}$$

For this value of C_1, the output voltage (in operator notation) is given by

$$V_L = \frac{R_L V'_L}{\sqrt{X^2_{C1} + R^2_L}} = \frac{V'_L}{\sqrt{2}} \tag{6.6}$$

Thus, as long as we operate above the cutoff frequency, V_L is greater than the value shown in equation (6.6).

Further improvement in circuit operation is possible. The fluctuations of V_{BE} with temperature can be reduced by replacing the two R_1 resistors with diodes. These diodes should have characteristics similar to those of the transistor and they should be mounted on the same heat sink. This form of compensation is discussed in Section 5.4 and is illustrated in Figure 6.16.

In the design of any complementary-symmetry amplifier, we must be aware of three areas of concern. One is the crossover distortion discussed in Section 6.1.2. This distortion can easily be reduced by placing small resistors in series with the diodes to cause I_{CQ} to be slightly above zero. This, in turn, causes both amplifiers to amplify the ac input signal simultaneously in the cutoff region, thus compensating for the lower individual amplification in that region. The second area of concern is the possibility of *thermal runaway,* which can be caused by the two complementary transistors not having the same characteristics or from an uncompensated V_{BE} being reduced by high temperatures. This would lead to higher collector current, resulting in additional power dissipation and heating. This process continues until the transistor overheats and fails. This problem is reduced by placing small resistors in series with the emitter to increase the bias level. With a 4 to 8 Ω load, the required resistances

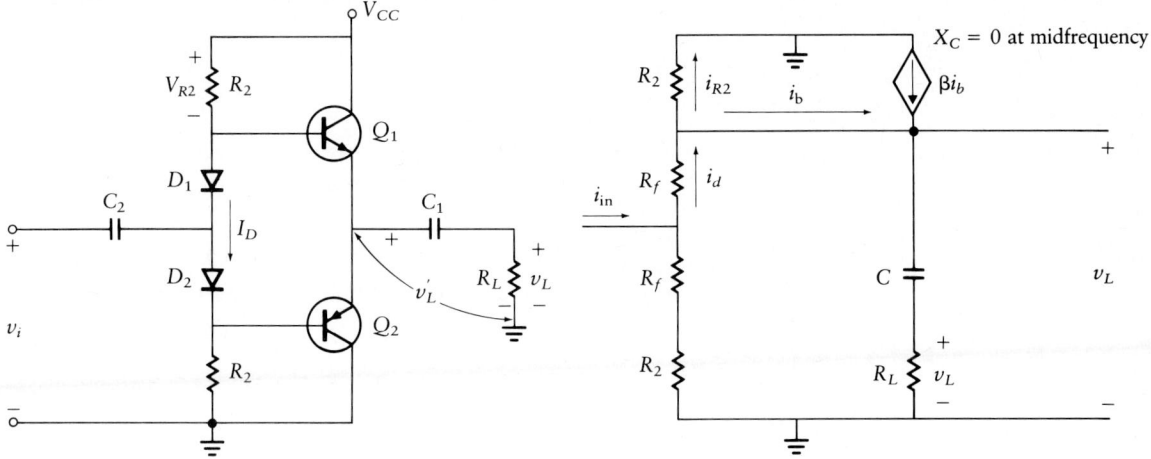

Figure 6.16 Complementary symmetry with diode compensation.

Figure 6.17 Base equivalent circuit.

are approximately 0.47 Ω. The third area of concern is to keep the bias diodes always turned on to avoid distortion.

The design of the power amplifier shown in Figure 6.16 requires knowledge of the diode forward resistance, which is typically less than 100 Ω. It is also important that the diode bias current be large enough to keep the diodes in the linear portion of their forward-biased region for all input voltages. The maximum negative peak current through the diode must be less than the direct current bias. That is, the dc component of current must be larger than the ac component, such that when it adds to the dc component, the resultant current does not go negative. If this were not true, the diode would be reverse-biased. This restriction is stated as

$$I_D > |i_{dp}| \tag{6.7}$$

where i_{dp} is the amplitude of the ac component of diode current.

The ac equivalent circuit is shown in Figure 6.17, where i_b is the transistor ac base current and v'_L is the ac voltage across the load, $R_L + jX_{CI}$, at the low frequency.

The following equation provides the direct current, I_D, through the diode.

$$I_D = \frac{V_{CC}/2 - 0.7}{R_2}$$

The *peak* signal current through the diode in the reverse direction, i_{dp}, is (refer to Figure 6.17)

$$i_{dp} = i_{bp} + i_{R_2p}$$

$$= i_{bp} + \frac{v'_{Lp}}{R_2} \tag{6.8}$$

Equation (6.8) is derived by noting that the voltage gain is unity for the EF amplifier. That is, the ac voltage across R_2 is the same as the voltage from the emitter to ground, v'_L.

By equating I_D with i_{dp}, we find the limiting condition for operating in the forward-biased diode condition (see equation (6.7)). From this, R_2 can be found as follows:

$$\frac{V_{CC}/2 - 0.7}{R_2} = i_{bp} + \frac{v'_{Lp}}{R_2}$$

so

$$R_2 = \frac{V_{CC}/2 - 0.7 - v'_{Lp}}{i_{bp}} \tag{6.9}$$

Since the amplifier is an EF, $v_i \approx v'_L$. At midfrequency, the voltage across C_1 is zero, so the entire voltage, v_L, appears across R_L. Therefore, $v'_L = v_L$. At the lower 3-dB cutoff frequency, the output power drops to $\frac{1}{2}$ of the power at midrange frequency, and the voltage across R_L is equal to the voltage across C_1. Each of these voltages is equal to $v_L/\sqrt{2}$. The peak magnitude of the voltage across the series combination of R_L and C_1 is

$$\left| v'_{Lp} \right| = \sqrt{\left(\frac{v_L}{\sqrt{2}} \right)^2 + \left(\frac{v_L}{\sqrt{2}} \right)^2} = v_L$$

Hence, the value of v'_{Lp} in equation (6.9) can be written as

$$v'_{Lp} = R_L \beta i_{bp} = R_L i_{Cp} \tag{6.10}$$

The input resistance is determined from the equivalent circuit shown in Figure 6.18 for the condition of $Z_L = R_L$ at the midfrequency of the amplifier where $X_{C1} = 0$.

The capacitor is assumed to be a short circuit for midfrequency operation. Note that R_L reflects back as βR_L. The diode has a forward resistance, R_f, and a reverse resistance, R_r.

The input resistance is found from Figure 6.18 as follows:

$$R_{in} = (R_f + R_2) \,\|\, [R_f + (R_2 \,\|\, \beta R_L)] \tag{6.11}$$

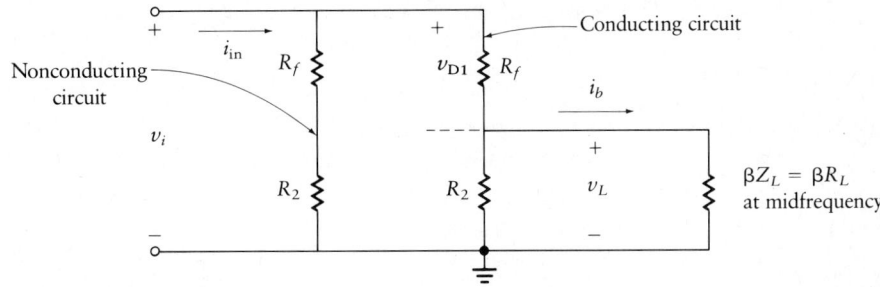

Figure 6.18
Input equivalent
circuit.

The current gain is found using current division. The voltage across D_1 with Q_1 conducting is

$$v_{D1} = R_f\left(i_{bp} + \frac{v_L}{R_2}\right)$$

$$i_{D2} = \frac{v_{D1} + v_L}{R_f + R_2}$$

$$i_{in} = \frac{v_{D1} + v_L}{R_f + R_2} + i_{bp} + \frac{v_L}{R_L} \qquad (6.12)$$

$$A_i = \beta\frac{i_b}{i_{in}} \qquad (6.13)$$

We add an additional subscript, p, to indicate that the peak value of the variable is being used (e.g. i_{bp}).

6.3.3 *Power Calculations for Class-B Push-Pull Amplifier*

The power delivered by the ac source is split between the transistor and the resistors in the bias circuitry. The ac signal source adds an insignificant additional amount of power, since base currents are small relative to collector currents. Part of the power to the transistor goes to the load, and the other part is dissipated by the transistor itself. The following equations specify the various power relationships in the circuit.

The input power is

$$P_{VCC} = V_{CC}I_{DC}$$

where I_{DC} is the average current drawn from the power supply for the transistor portion of the circuit. The current, I_{DC}, is determined by averaging across a full period. We use the equation

$$I_{DC} = \frac{1}{T}\int_0^{T/2} i_{C1}(t)dt = \frac{1}{\pi}I_{C\,max}$$

This result requires close examination. During the first half-cycle of the input, current flows through the upper transistor into the capacitor and load resistor. The second transistor is cut off. The power during this half-cycle goes to the upper transistor, the load, and toward storing energy in the capacitor. During the second half-cycle, the upper transistor is cut off. Thus, the V_{CC} source *does not supply any power* during this half-cycle. Instead, stored energy in the capacitor is returned to the load and to the lower transistor.

$$P_{VCC} \text{ (delivered to the transistor circuit)} = \frac{V_{CC} I_{C\,max}}{\pi} \tag{6.14}$$

The maximum value of collector current is

$$I_{C\,max} = \frac{V_{CC}}{2R_L}$$

The maximum power delivered to the transistor is

$$P_{VCC}(\text{max delivered to transistor}) = \frac{V^2_{CC}}{2\pi R_L}$$

The ac output power, assuming that the input is sinusoidal, is

$$P_{o(ac)} = \frac{I^2_{C\,max} R_L}{2} \tag{6.15}$$

and the maximum ac output power is found by substituting $I_{C\,max}$ to obtain

$$\max P_{o(ac)} = \frac{1}{2}\left(\frac{V_{CC}}{2R_L}\right)^2 R_L = \frac{V^2_{CC}}{8R_L}$$

The total dc power supplied to the stage is the sum of the power to the transistor and the power to the bias and compensation circuitry:

$$P_{VCC} = \frac{V_{CC} I_{C\,max}}{\pi} + \frac{V^2_{CC}}{2R_f + 2R_2} \tag{6.16}$$

If we subtract the power to the load from the power of equation (6.14), we find the power being dissipated in the transistors. Since this power is shared equally between the two transistors, the power dissipated by a single transistor is one-half of this value. Thus,

$$P_{transistor} = \frac{1}{2}\left[\frac{V_{CC} I_{C\,max}}{\pi} - \frac{I^2_{C\,max} R_L}{2}\right] \tag{6.17}$$

We are assuming that the base current is negligible. The maximum efficiency of the Class-B push-pull amplifier is the ratio of the output power to the power delivered to the transistor. Thus, when we neglect the power dissipated by the bias circuit ([34], Chapter 18):

$$\eta = \frac{V^2{}_{CC}/8R_L}{V^2{}_{CC}/2\pi R_L} = \frac{\pi}{4} = 0.785, \quad \text{or} \quad 78.5\%$$

This amplifier is more efficient than a Class-A amplifier.

The designer of this amplifier must specify the power rating of the transistor. That is, it is important to know the maximum power dissipated by a single transistor. This parameter is found by differentiating equation (6.17) with respect to $I_{C\,\max}$ in order to find the value that results in maximum dissipated power. Thus,

$$\frac{dP}{dI_{C\,\max}} = 0 = \frac{1}{2}\left[\frac{V_{CC}}{\pi} - I_{C\,\max}R_L\right] \tag{6.18}$$

and solving for $I_{C\,\max}$ yields

$$I_{C\,\max} = \frac{V_{CC}}{\pi R_L} \tag{6.19}$$

We now substitute this value back into equation (6.17) to find the maximum power:

$$\begin{aligned}
P_{\max} &= \frac{1}{2}\left[\frac{V_{CC}{}^2}{\pi^2 R_L} - \frac{V_{CC}{}^2}{2\pi^2 R_L}\right] \\
&= \frac{V^2{}_{CC}}{4\,\pi^2 R_L}
\end{aligned} \tag{6.20}$$

Since equation (6.20) represents the maximum power dissipated in each transistor, it is equivalent to the minimum transistor power rating. That is, in choosing a transistor, it is important that the power rating is equal to or exceeds this number.

Example 6.3   **Class-B Push-Pull Amplifier (Design)**

Design a diode compensated complementary symmetry circuit (Figure 6.16) for an audio amplifier with a frequency response of 60 Hz to 20 kHz and a power output of $\frac{1}{2}$ W into an 8-Ω speaker. Use silicon transistors with $\beta = 60$ and diode compensation. The diodes have forward resistance of 8 Ω. Use a

12 V power supply and determine the current gain, power delivered to the amplifier, and power ratings of the transistors.

SOLUTION   We first determine the value of $I_{C\,max}$ needed to achieve the specified load power:

$$P_L = \frac{I^2_{C\,max}R_L}{2} = \frac{1}{2}\,\text{W}$$

$$I_{C\,max} = \sqrt{\frac{1}{R_L}} = \sqrt{\frac{1}{8}} = 0.354\,\text{A}$$

The maximum base current is

$$I_{bp} = \frac{I_{C\,max}}{\beta} = \frac{0.354}{60} = 5.9\,\text{mA}$$

The lower frequency, 60 Hz, represents the half-power frequency used to find C_1. At this frequency,

$$R_L = \frac{1}{\omega C_1}$$

and

$$C_1 = \frac{1}{\omega R_L} = \frac{1}{60 \times 2\pi \times 8} = 331\,\mu\text{F}$$

At 60 Hz, the impedance of the RC circuit is $Z'_L = 8\sqrt{2} = 11.3\,\Omega$. Then Z_L, as seen from the base, is $Z_L = 60(11.0) = 678\,\Omega$. Using equation (6.10), we find, at midfrequency

$$v'_{Lp} = 0.354 \times 8 = 2.83\,\text{V}$$

We use equation (6.9) in order to find R_2.

$$R_2 = \frac{6 - 0.7 - 2.83}{5.9} = 419\,\Omega$$

R_{in} and A_i are determined at midfrequency as follows:

$$V_D = R_f\left(i_{bp} + \frac{V_L}{R_2}\right) = 8\left(5.9 \times 10^{-3} + \frac{2.83}{419}\right)$$

$$= 0.099 \text{ V}$$

Using equation (6.12) we find

$$i_{\text{in}} = \frac{0.1 + 2.83}{427} + 5.9 \times 10^{-3} + \frac{2.83}{419} = 19.8 \text{ mA}$$

Using equation (6.11), we find R_{in}:

$$R_{\text{in}} = (8 + 419) \,\|\, [8 + (419 \,\|\, 480)] = 150 \ \Omega$$

Equation (6.13) is then used to evaluate A_i:

$$A_i = \frac{60(5.9)}{19.8} = 17.9$$

The power to the amplifier, including the bias circuit, is given by equation (6.16):

$$P_{VCC} = \frac{12(0.354)}{\pi} + \frac{12^2}{2(8 + 419)} = 1.52 \text{ W}$$

The maximum power rating of each transistor is given by equation (6.20):

$$P_{\text{trans}} = \frac{V^2{}_{CC}}{4\pi^2 R_L} = 0.456 \text{ W}$$

Example 6.4	**Class-B Push-Pull Amplifier (Design)**

Design a complementary symmetry push-pull diode compensated Class-B amplifier (see Figure 6.19) to drive a 4-Ω load to ± 3 V for a frequency range of 50 to 20,000 Hz. Use *npn* and *pnp* transistors each having a β of 100 and $V_{BE} = \pm 0.7$ V. The diodes have forward resistance, $R_f = 10 \ \Omega$. Determine all quiescent voltages and currents for $V_{CC} = 16$ V. Calculate the maximum power that is delivered from the power supply, the power delivered to the load, and the power rating of the transistors to be used.

SOLUTION Choose C_1 so that the half-power frequency is 50 Hz. Thus, at this frequency we have

$$C_1 = \frac{1}{2\pi f_L R_L} = 796 \ \mu\text{F} \approx 800 \ \mu\text{F}$$

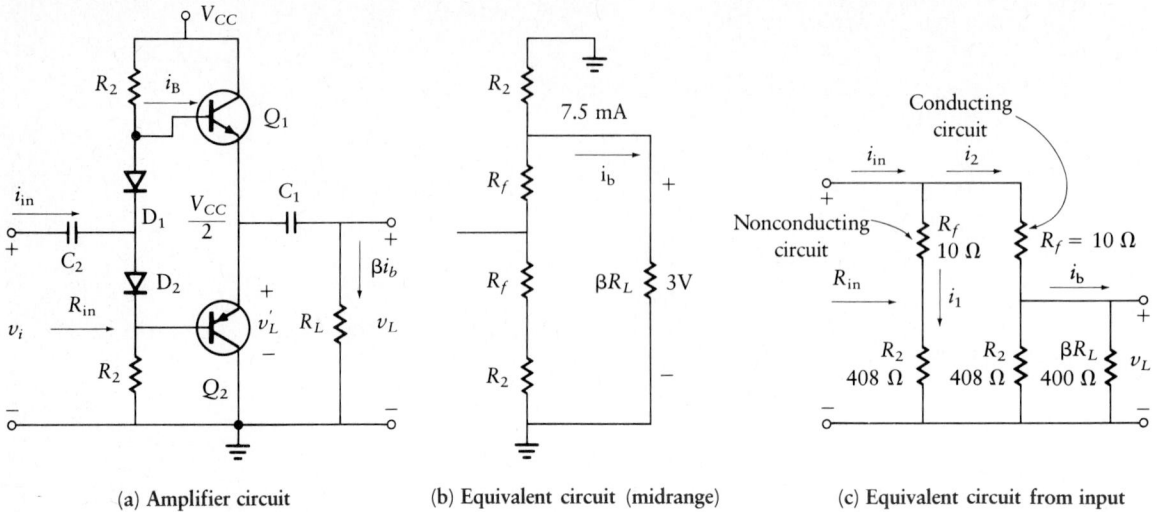

(a) Amplifier circuit   (b) Equivalent circuit (midrange)   (c) Equivalent circuit from input

Figure 6.19   Circuit for Example 6.4.

We discuss component selection in Section 4.8. Some points from that section bear repetition here. In most designs in this text, we specify component values to three significant digits. In the majority of practical designs, this is much more accuracy than is necessary. For example, in dealing with nonprecision (everyday) resistors, the tolerance is normally $\pm 5\%$. Thus, a resistor that is marked as 100 Ω can be expected to have an exact resistance anywhere between 95 and 105 Ω. Therefore, if a $\pm 5\%$ resistor is being used, it would not make much sense for the design engineer to specify a resistance value of 101.5936 Ω. The same is true of capacitors. The amount of rounding that is permitted in a design depends upon the precision of components being used and the confidence the designer has in device parameters (e.g., β). The more precision, the more expensive are the components. Since we have not specified any particular level of precision, we continue to carry most of our answers to three significant digits. Rounding numbers in intermediate computational steps can propagate errors.

In spite of all this, we feel justified in rounding the value of C_1 just found to 800 μF. This represents a change of only $\frac{1}{2}\%$.

The maximum collector and maximum base currents are related by β. Thus,

$$i_{bp} = \frac{i_{Cp}}{\beta}$$

but since $V_{L\,max}$ is given as 3, we find

$$i_{Cp} = \tfrac{3}{4} = 750 \text{ mA}$$

Therefore,

$$i_{bp} = 7.5 \text{ mA}$$

and from equation (6.9),

$$R_2 = \frac{8 - 0.7 - 3}{7.5 \text{ mA}} = 573 \ \Omega$$

At midfrequency, the input resistance is found from equation (6.11) to be

$$R_{in} = (10 + 573) \parallel (10 + 573 \parallel 400) = 173 \ \Omega$$

The supply power is given by equation (6.16).

$$P_{sup} = \frac{V_{CC} I_{C \, max}}{\pi} + \frac{V^2_{CC}}{2R_f + 2R_2}$$

$$= 3.82 + 0.22 = 4.04 \text{ W}$$

Equation (6.15) yields the output power.

$$P_o = \frac{i^2_{C \, max} R_L}{2} = 1.13 \text{ W}$$

Finally, equation (6.20) is used to find the required power rating of each transistor:

$$P_{trans} = \frac{V^2_{CC}}{4\pi^2 R_L} = \frac{16^2}{4\pi^2 4} = 1.62 \text{ W}$$

The current gain, A_i, is found by referring to Figure 6.19(c):

$$i_b = \frac{R_2 i_2}{R_2 + \beta R_L} = \frac{573 i_2}{973}$$

Therefore,

$$i_2 = \frac{973 i_b}{573} = 12.7 \text{ mA}$$

and i_2 and i_{in} are related by

$$i_2 = \frac{(R_f + R_2) i_{in}}{(R_f + R_2 + R_f + R_2 \parallel \beta R_L)} = \frac{583 i_{in}}{828}$$

Hence,

$$i_{\text{in}} = \frac{828(12.7 \text{ mA})}{583} = 18 \text{ mA}$$

Finally,

$$A_i = \frac{\beta i_b}{i_{\text{in}}} = \frac{7.5 \times 100}{18} = 41.7$$

◄

Drill Problems

D6.3   Design a complementary symmetry diode-compensated Class-B amplifier to drive a 4 Ω load with 1 W of power for a frequency range of 20 to 20,000 Hz. Use *npn* and *pnp* matched transistors each having β = 100 and V_{BE} = $\pm$ 0.7 V with equivalent characteristic diodes having R_f = 50 Ω. Let V_{CC} = 12 V. Determine R_2, R_{in}, C_1, P_{trans}, and $A_i = i_o/i_{\text{in}}$.

Ans: R_1 = 350 Ω; C_1 = 2000 μF;
P_{trans} = 0.91 W;
A_i = 29; R_{in} = 149 Ω

D6.4   Design a complementary symmetry diode-compensated Class-B power amplifier to deliver 2 W to a 10 Ω load over a range of 30 Hz and 30 kHz. Use a matched pair of *npn* and *pnp* transistors each having β = 100 and V_{BE} = $\pm$ 0.7 V with equivalent characteristic diodes having R_f = 5 Ω. Determine R_2, C_1, R_{in}, and A_i when V_{CC} = 16 V.

Ans: C_1 = 530 μF; R_2 = 154 Ω;
R_{in} = 74 Ω; A_i = 7.1

6.4   Darlington Circuit

Figure 6.20 illustrates a *Darlington circuit*. Such a circuit is a compound configuration composed of two cascaded transistors. This transistor combination possesses some desirable characteristics that make it more useful than a single transistor in certain applications. For example, the circuit has high input impedance, low output impedance, and high current gain. One disadvantage of the Darlington transistor pair is that the leakage current of the first transistor is amplified by the second transistor.

If the two transistors are connected in the manner shown in Figure 6.21,

Figure 6.20
Darlington transistor
pair.

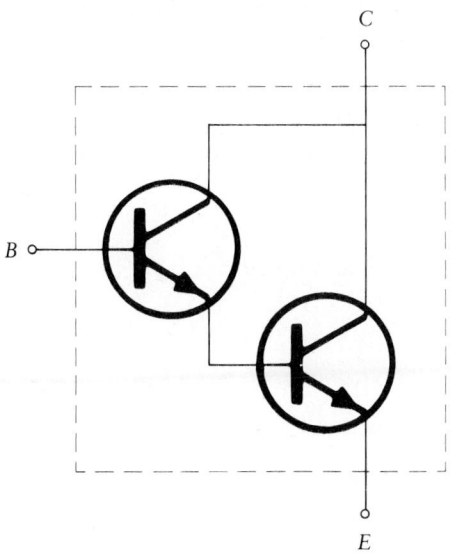

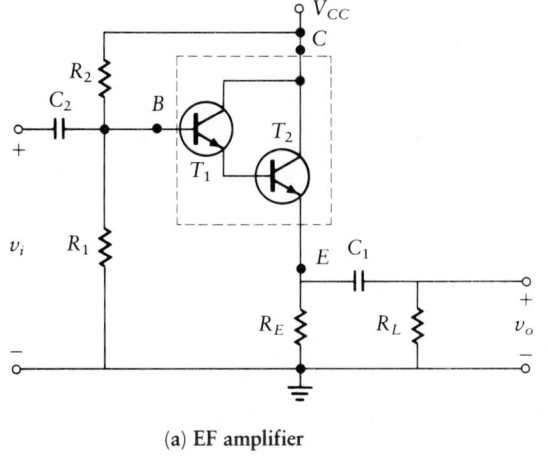

(a) EF amplifier

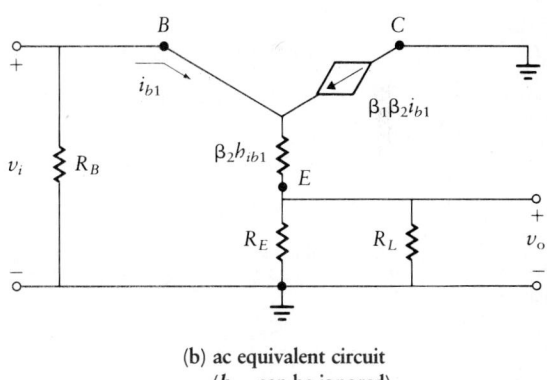

(b) ac equivalent circuit
(h_{ib2} can be ignored)

Figure 6.21 EF amplifier using Darlington pair.

the betas of the two transistors multiply together, forming a combination that looks like a single high-β transistor. The Darlington transistor pair can be used in either a CE or EF amplifier configuration. The h_{ie} of both transistors is not the same, since the quiescent point for the first transistor is different from that of the second. This is because the equivalent load on the first transistor is $\beta_2(R_L \parallel R_E)$, whereas the load on the second transistor is only $R_E \parallel R_L$. In practice, the first transistor can be of lower power rating than the second. The input resistance of the second transistor constitutes the emitter load for the first transistor.

To determine the ac parameters for a Darlington CE amplifier, we look at the equivalent circuit, which is shown in Figure 6.22(b). We write the equation for R_{in} as follows:

$$R_{in} = R_B \parallel (h_{ie1} + \beta_1 h_{ie2})$$

and

$$h_{ie1} = \beta_1 h_{ib1}$$
$$h_{ie2} = \beta_2 \, h_{ib2}$$

Then

$$R_{in} = R_B \parallel (\beta_1 h_{ib1} + \beta_1 \, \beta_2 h_{ib2})$$

but

$$h_{ib2} = \frac{V_T}{I_{CQ2}}$$

$$h_{ib1} = \frac{V_T}{I_{CQ1}} = \frac{V_T}{I_{BQ2}} = \frac{\beta_2 V_T}{I_{CQ2}} = \beta_2 h_{ib2}$$

and

$$R_{in} = R_B \parallel (\beta_1 \beta_2 h_{ib2} + \beta_1 \, \beta_2 h_{ib2})$$
$$= R_B \parallel 2\beta_1 \, \beta_2 h_{ib2}$$

Using current division, we obtain

$$i_{b1} = \frac{R_B}{R_B + h_{ie1} + \beta_1 h_{ie2}} \, i_{in} = \frac{R_B}{R_B + 2\beta_1 \, \beta_2 h_{ib2}} \, i_{in}$$

$$i_{in} = \frac{R_B + 2\beta_1 \, \beta_2 \, h_{ib2}}{R_B} \, i_{b1}$$

$$A_i = \frac{i_2}{i_{in}} = \frac{-\beta_1 \, \beta_2 i_{b1} R_C/(R_C + R_L)}{(R_B + 2\beta_1 \, \beta_2 h_{ib2}) i_{b1}/R_B}$$

$$= \frac{-\beta_1 \, \beta_2 R_B}{R_B + 2\beta_1 \, \beta_2 h_{ib2}} \frac{R_C}{R_C + R_L}$$

$$= \frac{-R_B}{R_B/\beta_1 \, \beta_2 + 2h_{ib2}} \frac{R_C}{R_C + R_L}$$

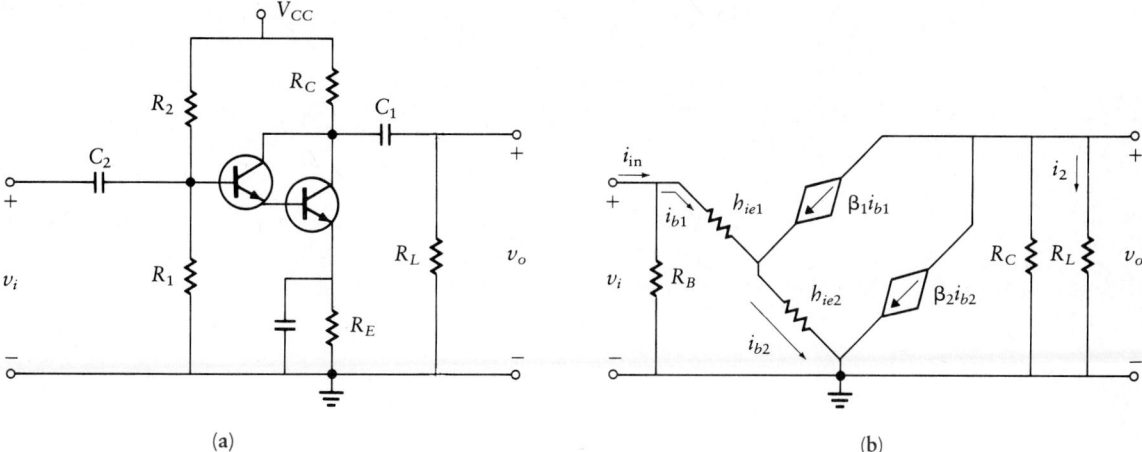

Figure 6.22 Darlington CE amplifier.

Using the gain-impedance formula, we have

$$A_v = A_i R_L/R_{in}$$

$$= \frac{-\beta_1 \beta_2 (R_C \parallel R_L)}{2\beta_1 \beta_2 h_{ib2}} = \frac{-R_C \parallel R_L}{2h_{ib2}}$$

Although this is normally considered a voltage-gain amplifier, it can provide high current gains due to extremely high input resistance. Most bypassed emitter-resistance configuration amplifiers have excellent voltage gains but have low input resistance, resulting in low current gain. However, this amplifier provides not only good voltage gain but excellent current gain.

Some manufacturers package the Darlington transistor pair into a single package with only three external leads. Darlington transistor pairs packaged into an integrated circuit are available with betas as high as 30,000 ([34], p. 395).

Although the Darlington circuit may be viewed as if it were a single transistor, there are some potentially important differences. One of these is speed of operation. Changing the voltage across a transistor junction requires a finite amount of time, since electrons must be moved. In fact, as capacitance increases, the time constant of any RC combination increases and the speed of operation decreases. Since the Darlington circuit has two base-emitter junctions in series with each other, the combination tends to operate more slowly than does a single transistor ([51], Section 7.6). To speed up the operation, a resistor is placed between the emitter of the first transistor and the base of the second transistor. These resistors have typical values of several hundred ohms for power transistors and several thousand ohms for signal transistors. In addition, since two base-emitter junctions exist, the overall $V_{BE} = 1.4$ V instead of 0.7 V.

The equivalent circuit of the Darlington pair used in EF amplifiers can be simplified as shown in Figure 6.22(b). The values of R_{in} and A_i are determined as follows:

$$R_{in} = R_B \parallel [\beta_1\beta_2(2h_{ib2} + R_E \parallel R_L)]$$

The current gain is given by

$$A_i = \frac{\beta_1\beta_2 i_{b1}}{i_{in}} \frac{R_E}{R_E + R_L}$$

where

$$i_{b1} = \frac{R_B}{R_B + (2h_{ib2} + R_E \parallel R_L)\beta_1\beta_2} i_{in}$$

and

$$i_{in} = \frac{R_B + (2h_{ib2} + R_E \parallel R_L)\beta_1\beta_2}{R_B} i_{b1}$$

so we obtain

$$A_i = \frac{R_B}{R_B/\beta_1\beta_2 + 2h_{ib2} + R_E \parallel R_L} \frac{R_E}{R_E + R_L}$$

We see from these equations that R_B can be made much larger than in the case of a single transistor. As a result, the input resistance and the current gain are both much larger for the Darlington pair.

Example 6.5   Darlington Pair in Class-A Amplifier (Design)

Design an EF amplifier using a Darlington transistor pair (Figure 6.21) that has a combined β of 10,000 and $V_{BE} = 1.4$ V. The amplifier must drive a load of 20 Ω with $R_{in} = 3$ kΩ. Use $V_{CC} = 12$ V, $f_L = 20$ Hz, and determine A_i and P_o.

SOLUTION   Set $R_E = R_L$, since there is one less equation than unknowns. We calculate R_B from knowledge of R_{in} as follows:

$$R_{\text{in}} = R_B \parallel [\beta_1\beta_2(R_E \parallel R_L)]$$

$$3\ k\Omega = \frac{R_B(100{,}000)}{R_B + 100{,}000}$$

We ignore h_{ib2} (since I_{CQ} is larger) and solve for R_B

$$R_B = 3.09\ k\Omega$$

The Q-point is at

$$I_{CQ} = \frac{V_{CC}}{R_{ac} + R_{dc}} = \frac{12}{10 + 20} = 400\ \text{mA}$$

We use the bias equation to find V_{BB}.

$$V_{BB} = V_{BE} + I_{CQ}\left(\frac{R_B}{\beta_1\beta_2} + R_E\right)$$

$$= 1.4 + (400 \times 10^{-3})\left(\frac{3090}{10{,}000} + 20\right) = 9.52\ \text{V}$$

The bias resistors are given by

$$R_1 = \frac{3090}{1 - 9.52/12} = 15.0\ k\Omega$$

$$R_2 = \frac{3090 \times 12}{9.52} = 3.87\ k\Omega$$

The current gain is given by

$$A_i = \frac{3.09\ k\Omega}{3090/10{,}000 + 10} \times \frac{1}{2} = 150$$

The output power is

$$P_o = \frac{1}{2}\left(\frac{I_{CQ}}{2}\right)^2 R_L = \frac{1}{2}\left(\frac{0.4}{2}\right)^2 20 = 0.4\ \text{W}$$

We calculate C_1 by noting that the total resistance in the discharge path of the capacitor is $(R_E + R_L)$, so

$$C_1 = \frac{1}{2\pi f_L (R_E + R_L)} = 199\ \mu\text{F}$$

The Darlington pair provides a large increase in current and power gain over the single transistor amplifier. It also provides a higher input resistance than what can be obtained by the single transistor amplifier.

Drill Problems

D6.5   Design an EF amplifier using a Darlington transistor pair (Figure 6.21) to drive an 8 Ω load with a combined β of 20,000, $V_{BE} = 1.4$ V, $V_{CC} = 20$ V and $A_i = 500$. Design the amplifier for a frequency range of 40 to 15,000 Hz. Find R_E, R_1, R_2, C_1, R_{in}, and P_o.

> **Ans:** $R_E = 8\ \Omega$; $R_1 = 17$ kΩ; $R_2 = 5.6$ kΩ;
> $C_1 = 250$ μF(3 dB down);
> $R_{in} = 4$ kΩ; $P_o = 2.79$ W

D6.6   Design an EF amplifier using a Darlington transistor pair (Figure 6.21) with a combined β of 5000, $V_{BE} = 1.4$ V, $V_{CC} = 20$ V, $R_{in} = 8$ kΩ and $R_L = 10\ \Omega$. The frequency range is 20 to 20,000 Hz. Find R_E, R_1, R_2, C_1, P_o, and A_i.

> **Ans:** $R_E = 10\ \Omega$; $R_1 = 108$ kΩ; $R_2 = 13.2$ kΩ;
> $C_1 = 398$ μF (3 dB down);
> $A_i = 800$; $P_o = 1.8$ W

6.5   Darlington Pair Quasi-Complementary Class-AB Amplifier

A high-current-gain amplifier can be designed using Darlington pair connected transistors ([6], Section 9.7). Such an amplifier is illustrated in Figure 6.23. This configuration is known as a *Darlington pair quasi-complementary class-AB amplifier*. It incorporates a Darlington pair with *npn* transistors and a feedback pair consisting of an *npn* and a *pnp* transistor.

Transistors Q_2 and Q_4 are matched *npn* transistors capable of handling high power. Transistors Q_1 and Q_3 are matched and need not handle high power. The effective load for Q_1 and Q_3 is βR_L (where β is the current gain of the output transistor), which is large compared to R_L. Therefore, the operating point for these transistors is much lower on the load line than are those of Q_2 and Q_4.

The positive input signal causes Q_1 to conduct, but Q_3 remains at cutoff since it is a *pnp* transistor. As the input signal goes negative, Q_1 cuts off and Q_3 conducts. Thus, the input circuit operates like the complementary-symmetry power amplifier discussed previously. Resistor R_1 can be adjusted

Figure 6.23
Quasi-complementary
push-pull amplifier.

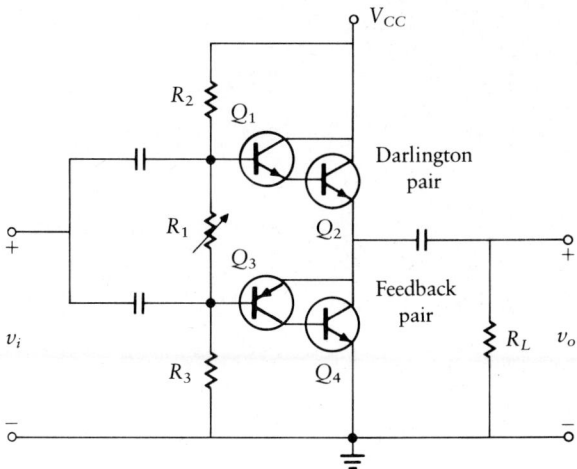

to minimize the crossover distortion by allowing both Q_1 and Q_2 to conduct when the input signal is near zero.

6.6   Power Supply Using Power Transistors

6.6.1   *Power Supply Using Discrete Components*

In Chapter 1 we analyzed the regulated power supply using a zener diode as the voltage-controlling device. As the zener diode regulates voltages, the current through the diode changes. That is, as the input voltage increases, the current in the zener also increases. Since the diode has a nonzero resistance, the voltage across the diode is a function of the current. This leads to poor regulation.

To obtain better regulation, the zener diode is connected to the base circuit of a power transistor, as is shown in Figure 6.24. This configuration reduces the current flow in the diode. The power transistor used in this configuration is known as a *pass* transistor. The purpose of C_L is to ensure that the variations in one of the regulated power-supply loads will not be fed to other loads. That is, the capacitor effectively shorts out any high-frequency variations.

Because of the current amplifying property of the transistor, the current in the zener diode is small. Hence there is little voltage drop across the diode resistance, and the zener acts like an ideal constant voltage source.

The current in the resistor, R_i, is the zener diode current plus the base current in the transistor. We set equations (1.13a) and (1.13b) equal to each other to obtain

Figure 6.24
Regulated power
supply.

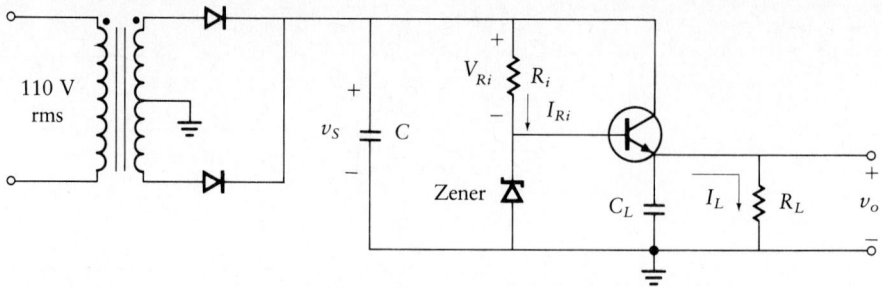

$$R_i = \frac{V_{S\,max} - V_Z}{I_{Z\,max} - I_{L\,min}/\beta} = \frac{V_{S\,min} - V_Z}{I_{Z\,min} + I_{L\,max}/\beta} \tag{6.21}$$

Then

$$(V_{S\,max} - V_Z)(0.1I_{Z\,max} + I_{L\,max}/\beta) = (V_{S\,min} - V_Z)(I_{Z\,max} + I_{L\,min}/\beta)$$
$$0.1I_{Z\,max}\,(V_{S\,max} - V_Z) + (I_{L\,max}/\beta)(V_{S\,max} - V_Z) =$$
$$I_{Z\,max}\,(V_{S\,min} - V_Z) + (I_{L\,min}/\beta)(V_{S\,min} - V_Z)$$

and finally,

$$I_{Z\,max} = \frac{I_{L\,min}\,(V_Z - V_{S\,min}) + I_{L\,max}\,(V_{S\,max} - V_Z)}{(V_{S\,min} - 0.1V_{S\,max} - 0.9V_Z)} \tag{6.22}$$

Equation (6.22) is the same as equation (1.14) except that the maximum of i_Z is reduced by the β of the transistor. The design is accomplished as in Section 1.6.1 with the exception that the value of $I_{Z\,max}$ is reduced. We solve for the equivalent load as seen from the capacitor, C_F,

$$R_L\,(\text{equivalent}) = R_i + R_z \parallel (h_{ie} + \beta\,R_L) \approx R_i \tag{6.23}$$

since $R_Z << R_i$.

We substitute equation (6.23) into equation (1.15) to estimate the capacitor size:

$$C_F = \frac{5(V_{S\,max} - V_Z)}{\omega_p(V_{S\,max} - V_{S\,min})(R_i)} \tag{6.24}$$

The value of ω_p is $2\pi f_p$ for a half-wave rectifier and $4\pi f_p$ for a full-wave rectifier.

Since the voltage gain of a CE amplifier is unity, the output voltage of the regulated power supply is

$$V_L = V_Z - V_{BE} \qquad (6.25)$$

The percent regulation of the power supply is given by

$$\% \text{ reg} = \frac{V_{Z\,max} - V_{Z\,min}}{V_Z} \times 100$$

$$= \frac{(V_Z + I_{Z\,max}R_Z) - (V_Z + I_{Z\,min}R_Z)}{V_Z} \times 100$$

$$= \frac{R_Z(I_{Z\,max} - I_{Z\,min})}{V_Z} \times 100 \qquad (6.26)$$

6.6.2 *Power Supply Using IC Regulator (Three-Terminal Regulator)*

For relatively low power requirements, an *IC regulator* is much less expensive than the discrete components required to make a regulated power supply and offers better regulation ($\pm 0.01\%$), overload protection, and reliability. For these reasons, it is often an attractive alternative to the zener diode regulator.

As examples, the 7800 and 7900 series IC regulator packages are readily available. The last two digits of the IC part number denote the output voltage of the device. Thus, for example, a 7808 IC package produces an 8-V regulated output. The 7800 series IC regulators provide only positive regulated voltages. The 7900 series is the complement of the 7800 series, as they provide the negative regulated voltages. This package, although internally complex, is inexpensive and easy to use.

Figure 6.25 illustrates the connections for a 7800 series IC regulator package. The external circuit is quite simple and is shown in Figure 6.25(b). Note that the IC regulator is a three-lead device. The external circuitry consists of two capacitors (C_L is optional) and a full-wave rectifier. If the currents in the regulator exceed about $\frac{3}{4}$ A, the IC package should be secured to a heat sink.

Figure 6.25 7800 series regulator.

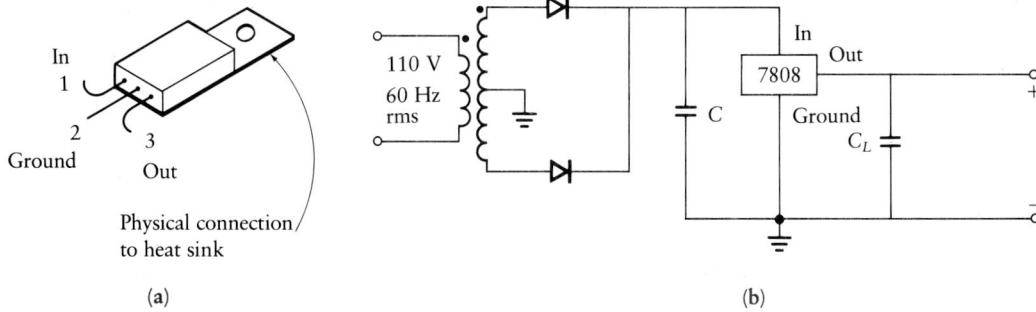

(a)

(b)

6.6.3   *Power Supply Using Three-Terminal Adjustable Regulator*

The *LM317* is an adjustable three-terminal positive-voltage regulator capable of supplying more than 1.5 A over a 1.2- to 37-V output range. It is easy to use and requires only two external resistors to set the output voltage. Both line and load regulation are better than in standard fixed-voltage regulators. The LM317 is packaged in a standard transistor package.

The LM317 offers full overload protection, including current-limiting and thermal-overload protection. Figure 6.26(a) shows a connection diagram for the LM317. The capacitor C_2 is optional and when it is included, the transient response improves. Output capacitors in the range of 1 to 100 μF (aluminum or tantalum electrolytic) are commonly used to provide improved output impedance and rejection of transients. The capacitor C_1 is needed if the device is physically located far from filter capacitors.

In operation, the LM317 has a precision internal voltage reference that develops a nominal 1.25-V voltage, V_{REF}, between the output and the adjustment terminal. The reference voltage is impressed across the *program resistor*, R_1. Since V_{REF} is constant, there is a constant current, I_1, through the program resistor. The output voltage is then given by

$$V_o = V_{REF} + (I_1 + I_{ADJ})R_2$$

$$= V_{REF} + \frac{V_{REF}R_2}{R_1} + I_{ADJ}R_2$$

$$= V_{REF}\left(1 + \frac{R_2}{R_1}\right) + I_{ADJ}R_2 \tag{6.27}$$

Note that if V_{REF}, R_1, R_2, and I_{ADJ} are all constants, then V_o is also a constant.

An input-bypass capacitor is usually used. A 0.1-μF disc or 1-μF solid tantalum capacitor is suitable for input bypassing for almost all applications. This capacitor shorts out high-frequency variations that occur in adjoining circuitry.

Figure 6.26
LM317 adjustable regulator.

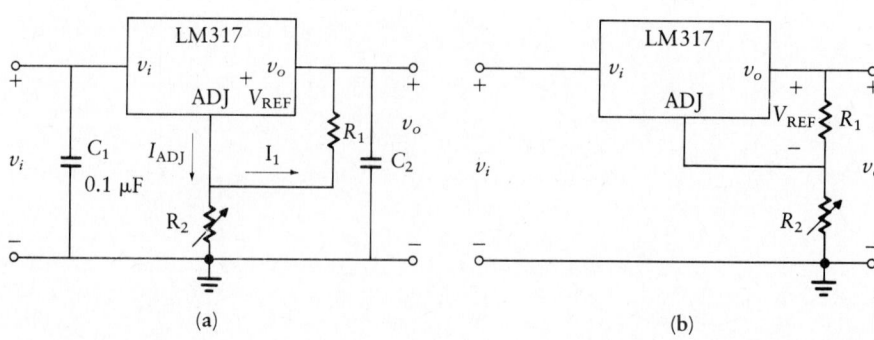

(a)   (b)

Although the LM317 is stable with no output capacitors, as in any feedback circuit, certain values of external capacitance can cause excessive oscillations known as *ringing*. Ringing occurs with capacitances between 500 and 5000 pF. A 1-μF solid tantalum (or 25-μF aluminum electrolytic) capacitor on the output reduces this effect and insures stability.

Example 6.6   **Regulated Power Supply Using Discrete Components (Design)**

Design an 11.3-V regulated power supply (see Figure 6.24) for a load current that varies from 400 to 500 mA. Assume an input of 120 V (rms) at 60 Hz into a 3:1 center-tapped transformer. Use a 12-V zener with $R_Z = 2\Omega$. The transistor has $V_{BE} = 0.7$ V and $\beta = 100$. Set C so $\Delta v_s = 10\%$.

SOLUTION   The design consists of choosing values for R_i and C_F. We first find $V_{S\,max}$ by multiplying by $\sqrt{2}$ to obtain 170 V. The transformer output on either side of the center tap is $\frac{1}{6}$ of the input, so $V_{S\,max}$ is 28.3 V. Since $\Delta v_S = 10\%$,

$$V_{S\,min} = (0.9)(V_{S\,max}) = 25.45 \text{ V}$$

$$I_{L\,max} = 500 \text{ mA}$$

$$I_{L\,min} = 400 \text{ mA}$$

and

$$V_Z = 0$$

Now using equation (6.22), we obtain,

$$I_{Z\,max} = \frac{0.4(12 - 25.45) + 0.5(28.3 - 12)}{100(25.45 - 2.83 - 10.8)}$$

$$= \frac{-5.38 + 8.15}{(100)11.82}$$

$$= 2.3 \text{ mA}$$

Notice that the transistor has kept the value of $I_{Z\,max}$ quite small since β appears in the denominator of equation (6.22). We calculate the value of R_i from equation (6.21).

$$R_i = \frac{V_{S\,max} - V_Z}{I_{Z\,max} + I_{L\,min}/\beta} = \frac{28.3 - 12}{2.3 + 400/100} = 2.59 \text{ k}\Omega$$

The capacitor size is estimated from equation (6.24):

$$C_F = \frac{5(28.3 - 12)}{(2.83)4\pi(60)(2590)} = 14.75 \ \mu F$$

Equation (6.26) can be used to evaluate the percent of regulation at the load.

$$\% \ reg = \frac{2(0.0023 - 0.00023)}{12} \times 100 = 0.0345\%$$

Example 6.7   Regulated Power Supply Using IC (Design)

Design a regulated power supply (see Figure 6.25(b)) using the 7808 IC regulator package to provide an 8 V output. The load current varies from 500 to 750 mA. The input voltage to the 20:1 transformer of the circuit is 120 V rms. Select C so $\Delta v_s = 10\%$.

SOLUTION   The maximum input voltage is found by multiplying by $\sqrt{2}$ which yields 17 V at the transformer output. We refer to Appendix D for the specifications of the 7808. The minimum voltage to the regulator must be at least 4 V above the regulated voltage to assure good regulation over the entire range or, in this case, $8 + 4$, or 12 V. In order to evaluate the size of the filter capacitor, C_F, we need the minimum value of R_L as seen from the capacitor. This equivalent resistance is found by dividing the minimum voltage by the current, where the current is the sum of the load current and the current drawn by the regulator. We can neglect the current drawn by the regulator and consider only load current.

To find R_L we use the output voltage of the voltage regulator, V_{oR}, divided by $I_{L \ max}$, or

$$R_L = \frac{V_{oR}}{I_{L \ max}} = \frac{8 \ V}{750 \ mA} = 10.7 \ \Omega$$

To estimate the capacitor value, we use a modification of equation (6.24), as follows:

$$C_F = \frac{5(V_{S \ max} - V_{oR} - 4)}{2\pi f_p(V_{S \ max} - V_{S \ min})R_L} = \frac{5(17 - 12)}{2\pi(120)(1.7)(10.7)}$$

$$= 1823 \ \mu F$$

The value of load capacitor, C_L, depends upon the variation that occurs in the load and the distance that load elements are from the power supply. Typically a 1-μF, high-quality electrolytic capacitor is used. The capacitor should be located physically close to the regulator in order to improve stability and transient response. ▶︎

Drill Problems

D6.7   Design a 7.3 V regulated power supply for an 800 ± 100 mA load. The input is 110 V rms at 60 Hz and a 4:1 center-tapped transformer is used. $V_Z = 8$ V and $\Delta v_s = 10\%$. The transistor has $V_{BE} = 0.7$ and $\beta = 100$. Assume a full wave rectifier $R_Z = 5$ Ω. Find R_i, C_F and the percentage of regulation.

Ans: $R_i = 2.88$ kΩ; $C_F = 18.3$ μF;
0.21% regulation

D6.8   Design a 12-V regulator power supply using a 7812 IC regulator for a 500-mA load. Use the transformer and power input given in Problem D6.7 and select C_F so $\Delta v_s = 10\%$.

Ans: $C = 1004$ μF

6.7   Switching Regulators

The series regulators, either discrete or IC type, were discussed in the previous sections. Although these series regulators are useful, they suffer from several serious limitations. The most serious difficulty lies in the area of the power generated within the regulator. These series regulators rely upon the variable voltage dropped across an internal series resistor, R_i, or across a power transistor. The input voltage must be greater than the regulated output voltage. The difference is dropped across an internal component. The greater the difference, the greater amount of power dissipated within the regulator. Because of the inefficiency of the series regulator, power supplies that generate high current output, in excess of 2 A, rely upon a switching regulator.

The block diagram of a switching regulator is shown in Figure 6.27. This feedback system compares a reference voltage, V_{REF}, with the regulated output voltage, V_{REG}. V_{REF} is obtained from a low-current-output series regulator as discussed in Section 6.6.2. Since little current, perhaps 20 mA, is required from this reference series regulator, it dissipates little internal power and provides an accurate reference voltage. The regulated output voltage, V_{REG}, is compared to a fraction, $R_A/(R_A + R_F)$, of V_{REF}. The error amplifier is an operational amplifier, which is discussed more completely in Chapters 8 and 9. For our immediate purposes, the output of the error amplifier, v_e, is applied to a pulse-

Figure 6.27
Switching regulator.

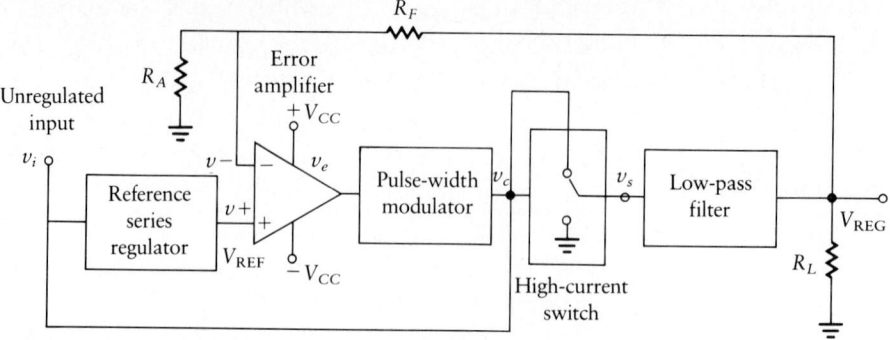

Figure 6.28
Low-pass filter for switching regulator.

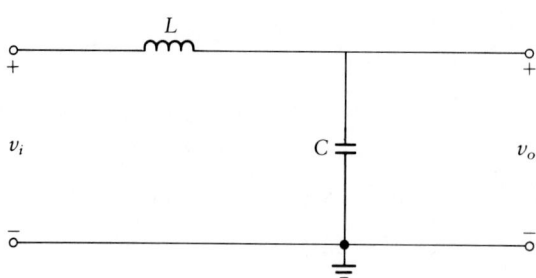

width modulator. The output of the pulse-width modulator, v_c, is used to control the high-current switch. This control voltage, v_c, is a square wave of period T whose duty cycle, σ, is given by

$$\sigma = kv_c \tag{6.28}$$

The high-current switch alternatively supplies either unregulated voltage or 0 V to the filter. Hence, the voltage at the filter input, v_s, is a square wave with a period T and duty cycle (just as the control voltage, v_c) but whose low value is zero and whose high value is v_i. The voltage, v_s, is passed through the low-pass filter to pass the fundamental frequency, $2\pi/T$, and reduce the higher harmonics in V_{REG}. The low-pass filter is shown in Figure 6.28, where $\sqrt{LC}$ must be chosen much larger than $T/2\pi$. As a result, the value of V_{REG} is a constant and is equal to the average value of v_s.

An analysis of this operational amplifier circuit yields the following equations:

$$v_- = \frac{V_{REG}R_A}{R_A + R_F}$$

and

$$v_+ = V_{\text{REF}}$$

Then since $v_+ = v_-$,

$$V_{\text{REG}} = V_{\text{REF}} \left(1 + \frac{R_F}{R_A} \right) \tag{6.29}$$

Hence, the regulated voltage output depends only upon the accuracy of V_{REF} and the resistor ratio, R_F/R_A. The output, V_{REG}, does not vary either as a function of input voltage, v_i, or load current.

Example 6.8   **Switching Regulator Supply**

Select values of R_F and R_A for the switching regulator of Figure 6.27. V_{REG} is to be 12 V and V_{REF} is 5 V.

SOLUTION   We use equation (6.29) and solve for the ratio R_F/R_A as follows:

$$\frac{R_F}{R_A} = \frac{V_{\text{REG}}}{V_{\text{REF}}} - 1 = \frac{12}{5} - 1 = 1.4$$

Now that the ratio is known, we can simply choose a value for R_A and solve for R_F. If, for example, R_A is 1 kΩ, then R_F would be equal to 1.4 kΩ.   ✦

We must be certain that $v_i > V_{\text{REG}}$ since V_{REG} is the average value of a chopped signal whose maximum value is v_i.

Some portions of the circuit of Figure 6.27 are consolidated onto one IC chip. These include the reference series regulator, the error amplifier, and the pulse-width modulator. As a result, the design of a switching regulator concentrates upon the output circuitry, especially the high-current switch and the low-pass filter.

6.7.1   *Efficiency of Switching Regulators*

The output current comes directly from the unregulated input voltage, v_i, through the high-current switch and the filter inductor, L, to the load. Thus, if we use a transistor switch with low "ON" voltage drop and a low loss inductor, the conversion efficiency can be high (greater than 90%). The significant saving in this regulator is based upon switching, or modulating, the input voltage with the high-current switch rather than dissipating power across a series resistor or a pass transistor.

PROBLEMS

6.1 Determine the output power of an inductively coupled amplifier as shown in Figure 6.6(a). Let $V_{CC} = 12$ V, $V_{BE} = 0.7$ V, $R_E = 100$ Ω, $R_L = 1$ kΩ, and $\beta = 60$. Also find R_1 and R_2, the power provided by the power supply, the power dissipated in the transistor, and the maximum output voltage swing.

6.2 An inductively coupled amplifier is designed for a current gain of $A_i = -15$. Determine the output power when $R_L = 2$ kΩ, $V_{CC} = 12$ V, $\beta = 200$, and $V_{BE} = 0.7$ V. Also determine the power supplied by the power supply, power rating required for the transistor, R_1, R_2, and R_E. Use the circuit of Figure 6.6(a) except delete the emitter-bypass capacitor.

6.3 Use the circuit of Figure 6.6(a) to obtain a current gain of -60. If the power supply is 15 V, $R_L = 1$ kΩ, $V_{BE} = 0.7$ V, and $\beta = 100$, can the circuit provide the required gain when $R_E = 100$ Ω? Find the values of the circuit elements, power required from the power source, power rating of the transistor, R_1, R_2, and maximum power dissipated in the load resistor.

6.4 Design a transformer-coupled EF power amplifier to drive a 10 Ω load with $A_i = 100$ if $V_{CC} = 12$ V, $V_{BE} = 0.7$ V, the step-down transformer turns ratio is 10:1, $\beta = 50$. Determine R_1, R_2, the power rating of the transistor, and the power dissipated in the load. Refer to the circuit of Figure 6.7(a).

6.5 What changes are required in the amplifier parameters of Problem 6.4 if the primary resistance of the transformer is 200 Ω?

6.6 A Class-A transformer-coupled EF power amplifier must deliver an output of $\frac{1}{2}$ W to an 8-Ω speaker. What transformer ratio is needed to provide this power if $V_{CC} = 18$ V? The transistor has $\beta = 100$ and $V_{BE} = 0.7$ V. Assume zero resistance in the transformer. What transistor power rating is needed?

6.7 Design a complementary symmetry Class B amplifier to drive a 12 Ω load. Refer to the circuit shown in Figure 6.12. Use $V_{CC} = 18$ V, $V_{BE} = 0.7$ V and $\beta = 60$. Calculate the total power dissipated in the load, the input resistance, and the power rating of the transistor. Select values of R_1 and R_2 and C_1 for a 20 Hz to 20 kHz frequency response and for a current gain of $A_i = 20$.

6.8 Design a complementary-symmetry Class-B amplifier to drive an 8 Ω load using $\beta = 60$, $V_{BE} = \pm 0.7$ V, $V_{CC} = 12$ V, and a frequency range of 100 Hz to 15 kHz. Use the circuit of Figure 6.12 with a required current gain of $A_i = 20$.

    a. Find the quiescent voltages and currents.

    b. Find the maximum power delivered to the load.

    c. Select values for R_1, R_2, and C_1.

    d. Determine R_{in}.

6.9 Design a complementary-symmetry Class-AB amplifier to drive an 8 Ω load using $\beta = 80$, $V_{BE} = \pm 0.7$ V, $V_{CC} = 16$ V and a frequency response of 20 Hz to 20 kHz. Use the circuit of Figure 6.13.

    a. Find all quiescent voltages and currents.

    b. Determine R_2, R_3, and C_1 for a current gain of $A_i = 40$.

    c. Find the maximum power delivered to the load.

    d. Determine R_{in} and the power rating of the transistors.

6.10 Design a complementary-symmetry Class-B diode-compensated amplifier to drive an 8-Ω load. Assume $\beta = 80$, peak-to-peak output voltage is 6 V, $R_f = 10$ Ω, $V_{CC} = 12$ V, and $V_{BE} = 0.7$ V. Let $C \rightarrow \infty$. Use the circuit of Figure 6.16.

    a. Find all quiescent voltages and currents at midfrequency.

    b. Find the maximum power delivered to the load.

    c. Determine the values of R_2 and R_{in}.

6.11 Design a $\frac{1}{2}$-W complementary-symmetry Class-B diode compensated amplifier to drive an 8 Ω load. Assume $\beta = 80$, $R_f = 4$ Ω, $V_{CC} = 12$ V, $V_{BE} = \pm 0.7$ V, and a frequency response of 50 Hz to 20 kHz. Use the circuit of Figure 6.16.

    a. Find all quiescent voltages and currents at midfrequency range.

    b. Find the maximum power delivered by the power supply.

    c. Determine R_2, C_1, A_i and R_{in}.

6.12 Design a 2-W complementary symmetry Class-B diode compensated amplifier to drive an 8 Ω load. Assume $\beta = 80$, $R_f = 20$ Ω, $V_{CC} = 16$ V and $V_{BE} = \pm 0.7$ V, and a frequency response of 20 Hz to 20 kHz. Use the circuit of Figure 6.16.

    a. Find all quiescent voltages and currents at midrange frequency.

    b. Find the maximum power delivered by the power supply.

    c. Find the power rating of the transistors.

    d. Determine R_2, R_{in}, A_i and C_1.

6.13 Design a $\frac{1}{2}$-W complementary-symmetry Class-B audio amplifier to drive an 8 Ω speaker. Use $\beta = 60$, $V_{BE} = \pm 0.7$ V, $V_{CC} = 12$ V, and a frequency response of 100 Hz to 20 kHz. Use the circuit of Figure 6.16. The diodes have forward resistance of 10 Ω and use a capacitor with the 3 dB point at 100 Hz.

    a. Determine the power rating of the transistors at low frequency.

    b. Determine R_2, R_{in}, and C_1.

    c. Determine the current gain.

6.14 Design an EF Class-A amplifier using a Darlington transistor pair that has a combined β of 8000 and $V_{BE} = 1.4$ V to an 8 Ω load with $R_{in} = 5$ kΩ. Determine all the component values for a frequency response of 20 Hz to 20 kHz, and find A_i, and P_o when $V_{CC} = 24$ V. Use the circuit of Figure 6.21.

6.15 Design an EF Class-A amplifier using a Darlington transistor pair that has a combined β of 6000 and $V_{BE} = 1.4$ V to drive a 10 Ω load. The system requires $A_i = 500$ for a frequency range of 500 Hz to 10 kHz. Use the circuit of Figure 6.21 with $V_{CC} = 12$ V. Determine all the component values for the amplifier and P_o.

6.16 Repeat Problem 6.13 but use a Darlington transistor pair with $\beta = 6000$ and $V_{BE} = 1.4$ V.

6.17 Design a Darlington pair CE amplifier as shown in Figure 6.22 to provide an A_i of -4000 to a 1 kΩ load. Design the amplifier for maximum output-voltage swing and determine the value of the required maximum-input voltage. $\beta_1 = 100$, $\beta_2 = 200$, V_{BE} for both transistors is 0.6 V, $V_{CC} = 12$ V.

6.18 A power supply is to provide an amplifier with 300 ± 50 mA of regulated power. Design a power source (see Figure 6.24) that will provide the power to the amplifier if the transformer has a turns ratio of 8:1 to each secondary and a 12-V zener diode is used. Assume the input voltage is 115 V at 60 Hz and that the forward resistance of the diodes is zero. Use $\beta = 50$ and $V_{BE} = 0.7$ V. Select C_F so $\Delta v_s = 10\%$. Determine C_1, R_i, and the power rating of the diodes.

6.19 A power supply is to provide an audio amplifier with a 500 ± 75 mA regulated current. Design a power source (see Figure 6.24) that uses a 20-V zener, and a 5:1 transformer ratio to each secondary. The input voltage is 110 V, 60 Hz, $\beta = 100$, $V_{BE} = 0.7$ V, and $\Delta v_s = 10\%$.

    a. Determine C_1 and R_i assuming zero diode forward resistance.

    b. Determine the power rating of the zener diode.

    c. Determine the voltage variation at the load if $R_Z = 2$ Ω.

7

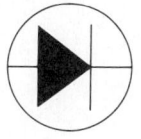

INTEGRATED CIRCUITS: OPERATIONAL AMPLIFIERS

7.0 ## Introduction

The rapid expansion of requirements for smaller, lighter, and more complex circuits resulted in the need to place not one but *hundreds* of transistors on a single silicon chip. Whenever more than one element is placed on a single chip, the resulting device is known as an *integrated circuit* (IC).

The unmodified term, IC, is used to describe those chips composed of less than 60 elements. If a chip contains more than 60 but less than 300 elements, the term *medium-scale integration* (MSI) is used. If the number of elements is over 300 but less than about 1000, the circuit is a *large-scale integration* (LSI). *Very large scale integration* (VLSI) refers to those chips with more than 1000 elements.

Integrated circuits can be linear or nonlinear, depending upon the relationship between output and input waveforms. *Linear integrated circuits* (LIC) are designed to replace standard circuits, and these LICs are then used as building blocks for more-complex systems. One of the most utilized analog circuits is the *operational amplifier* (op-amp). Ideally, this amplifier has infinite gain, infinite input impedance, and zero output impedance. Practical op-amps have performance characteristics that closely approach those of ideal op-amps.

We discuss the internal characteristics of the op-amp in this chapter. We begin with a discussion of techniques for fabricating transistors, resistors, and

285

capacitors on ICs. A summary of IC fabrication techniques is then presented. The basic building block, the difference, or differential, amplifier, is then analyzed. Several variations of the basic amplifier, including the constant-current source and single-ended input and output, are discussed. Various types of current sources are presented as examples of active sources used to simulate circuit elements on the chip.

The chapter concludes with information about the forms of packaging used for op-amps. A discussion of the 741 general-purpose operational amplifier is included.

7.1   IC Fabrication

A complex circuit may be fabricated on a single silicon chip. The circuit can be composed of transistors, resistors, and capacitors, all of which are small enough to be located on the chip. We discuss the fabrication of each of these elements in the following sections ([34], Chapter 4).

7.1.1   *Transistors and Diodes*

IC *transistors* and *diodes* are fabricated on a silicon substrate material. If the transistor is to be *npn*, a substrate *p*-type material is used. This insulates the *npn* transistor from the surrounding areas. A typical cross section is shown in Figure 7.1. The process begins on a small silicon wafer about 0.1 to 0.2 mm thick and 25 to 125 mm in diameter. The different layers are developed by either diffusion or epitaxial growth. *Diffusion* is the process where a heated slab of single-crystal *n*-type or *p*-type material is exposed to *p*-forming or *n*-forming impurities in vapor form. The impurity diffuses slowly into the surface of the material. However, the speed of the diffusion is greatly increased by elevating the temperature. The *epitaxial* process is accomplished by placing the silicon wafer in a furnace at a temperature of about 1200°C. A vapor of H_2 and $SiCl_4$ is passed over the wafer. During the ensuing chemical reaction, HCl is formed and silicon atoms are deposited on the wafer. These atoms arrange themselves along the axis of the crystalline structure of the wafer, thus causing new layers of single-crystal silicon to be grown. By introducing an impurity into the vapor, the impurity atoms are made to segregate and enter the crystal growth, thereby forming a layer with uniform impurity concentrations. The epitaxial process permits greater flexibility in controlling the impurity concentration than is provided by the diffusion process. The components on the chip are separated by either *p*-type or *n*-type material in order to assure isolation of elements from each other.

Figure 7.1
npn transistor on IC.

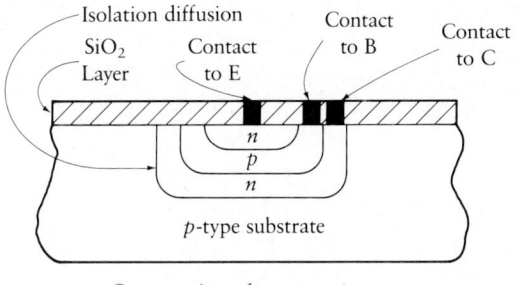
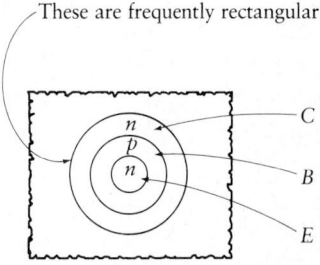

Cross section of *npn* transistor
fabricated on an IC

Top view with SiO₂ layer removed

Diodes are fabricated in a similar manner, but only single layers of *p*-material and *n*-material are needed.

7.1.2   Resistors

Resistors are produced on an IC at the same time as are the transistors. A *p*-type material is being used to produce the resistor in the illustration of Figure 7.1. This is isolated by use of a layer of *n*-type material. A thin channel of *p*-type material is used for the resistor, and it is diffused during the same step in production as the base of the transistor. The amount of resistance is controlled by varying the thickness and the impurity level of the material. The channel width and its length affect the value of the resistance. In fact, the resistance is directly proportional to the length of the channel (assuming a constant width). If this fabrication technique does not provide a sufficiently high resistance, the channel can be overlaid upon itself several times, thus increasing the effective length.

Because of physical size limitations, resistances above about 100 kΩ are usually avoided on ICs.

7.1.3   Capacitors

There are two types of capacitors used on an IC chip: a diffused capacitor and a MOS capacitor. The *diffused capacitor* takes advantage of the incremental junction capacitance of a reverse-biased *pn* junction.

The *MOS capacitor* is made in a manner similar to that of a conventional capacitor. The lower conductor is a highly doped *n*-material: The insulator is a film of silicon dioxide; the other plate is a metallized layer, which also forms one contact point. This type of capacitor provides about 400 to 600 pF/mm². Because of the relatively large amount of space needed for capacitors, the number used in a IC design is usually kept small.

7.1.4   *Lateral Transistors*

Lateral pnp transistors can be fabricated on ICs using simple planar technology ([34], Section 7.6). Small *p*-channels used as the emitter and collector are placed on a slab of *n*-material used as the base. A ring of *p*-channel material is used as the collector. The emitter *p*-channel material is placed within this ring, with separating *n*-material used as the base. Holes are injected from the emitter and flow parallel to the surface across the *n*-type base region and are collected by the *p*-type collector before reaching the base contact. The transistor action is lateral rather than vertical. Lateral *pnp* transistors have relatively low current gains because of the tendency of carriers to be injected toward the base and recombine instead of being collected at the laterally displaced collector. Because they are easy to fabricate on ICs, these transistors are used for active loads, current sources, and level shifters (these are discussed later in this chapter). These configurations are so easy to fabricate in IC design that parasitic lateral transistors may be unintentionally formed. This causes problems with IC performance. The IC design should be checked closely so that such inadvertent transistors do not appear on the chip.

7.1.5   *Schottky Barrier-Junction Technology*

In a *Schottky barrier semiconductor* junction, the forward current in the junction is caused by the flow of electrons over the barrier ([36], Chapter 2). The minority carrier flow does not play the important role that it does in a standard *pn* junction. Thus, the switching speed of the device is primarily limited by the RC time constant of the circuit. This is not true for standard BJTs. In fact, prior to the development of Schottky barrier-junction technology, a special type of doping was used to reduce the storage time in BJTs. The resulting doping effect was temperature-dependent. In ICs, the Schottky metallic semiconductor junction is used as a clamping diode between the base and collector to prevent excess minority-carrier storage. The need for extra doping of the transistor is then avoided. Clamping diodes are fabricated with the BJT on the IC, as shown in the schematic of Figure 7.2(a). A metallic layer cannot be used as the emitter of a transistor since the Schottky barrier junction is primarily a majority-carrier device. However, this is not true for the collector, since it can use a Schottky barrier junction. The symbol for a Schottky transistor is shown in the schematic of Figure 7.2(b). This transistor can have storage times of less than 1 ns (i.e., the time necessary to shift enough electrons to go from cutoff to saturation and vice versa). This makes the Schottky transistor ideal for high-speed switching circuits. Because of its ease of fabrication on IC chips, the Schottky junction is used extensively.

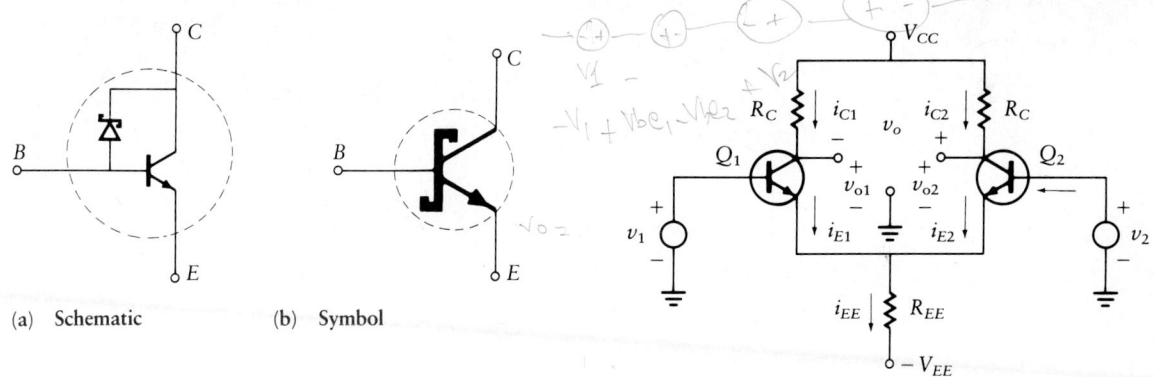

Figure 7.2 Schottky *npn* transistor.

Figure 7.3 Differential amplifier.

7.2 Difference Amplifiers

Most operational amplifiers are comprised of a series of transistors, resistors, and capacitors, which form a complete system on a single chip. The amplifiers available today are highly reliable, small in size, and consume a small amount of power.

The input stage of most op-amps is a *difference amplifier,* as shown in its simplest form in Figure 7.3. The *difference amplifier* (or differential amplifier) is composed of two emitter-coupled CE dc amplifiers with two inputs, v_1 and v_2, and three outputs, v_{o1}, v_{o2}, and v_o. The third output, v_o, is the difference between v_{o1} and v_{o2}. This can be verified by applying the superposition principle to the circuit.

7.2.1 dc Transfer Characteristics

The difference amplifier does not operate linearly with large signal inputs. In order to simplify the analysis, we assume that R_E is large, that the base resistance of the transistors is negligible, and that the output resistance of the transistors is large. The large R_E keeps the emitter resistor voltage drop constant.

We begin by writing a KVL equation around the base junction loop for the circuit of Figure 7.3 under ac conditions:

$$v_1 = v_{BE1} - v_{BE2} + v_2 \qquad (7.1)$$

We solve the circuit for the collector currents, i_{C1} and i_{C2}. The base-emitter voltage is given by the equation presented in Section 3.2.

$$v_{BE1} = V_T \ln\left(\frac{i_{C1}}{\beta I_{o1}}\right) \qquad (7.2)$$

$$v_{BE2} = V_T \ln\left(\frac{i_{C2}}{\beta I_{o2}}\right) \qquad (7.3)$$

Since the transistors are assumed to be identical, we have

$$I_{o1} = I_{o2}$$

Combining equations (7.1), (7.2), and (7.3) yields

$$v_1 - V_T \ln\left(\frac{i_{C1}}{\beta I_{o1}}\right) + V_T \ln\left(\frac{i_{C2}}{\beta I_{o2}}\right) - v_2 = 0$$

and

$$\frac{i_{C1}}{i_{C2}} = \exp\left[\frac{v_1 - v_2}{V_T}\right] \qquad (7.4)$$

We assume that i_C is approximately equal to i_E. Therefore,

$$i_{EE} = i_{C1} + i_{C2} \qquad (7.5)$$

Combining equation (7.4) and equation (7.5), we have

$$i_{C1} = \frac{i_{EE}}{1 + \exp\left[-(v_1 - v_2)/V_T\right]} \qquad (7.6)$$

$$i_{C2} = \frac{i_{EE}}{1 + \exp\left[(v_1 - v_2)/V_T\right]} \qquad (7.7)$$

Note that

$$v_o = (i_{C1} - i_{C2})R_C$$

An important observation can be made by viewing equations (7.6) and (7.7). If $v_1 - v_2$ becomes greater than several hundred millivolts, the collector current in transistor 2 becomes extremely small and the transistor is essentially cut off. The collector current in transistor 1 is approximately equal to i_{EE}, and this transistor is saturated. The collector currents, and therefore the output voltage v_o, become independent of the difference between the two input voltages. Linear amplification occurs only for input voltage differences less than approximately 100 mV.

In order to increase the linear range of the input voltage, small emitter resistors can be added. This causes a negative feedback condition, resulting in the reduction in the voltage amplification.

7.2.2 Common-Mode and Differential-Mode Gains

The difference amplifier is intended to respond only to the difference between the two input voltages, v_1 and v_2. However, in a practical op-amp, the output depends to some degree upon the sum of these inputs. Thus, for example, if both inputs are equal, the output voltage should be zero, but in a practical amplifier it is not. We label the case when the circuit responds to the difference as the *differential-mode* case. If the two inputs are made equal, we say the circuit is in its *common mode*. Ideally we would expect the circuit to produce an output only in the differential mode.

Any two input voltages can be resolved into a common and a differential part. That is, we define two new input voltages as follows:

$$v_{di} = v_1 - v_2$$

$$v_{ci} = \frac{v_1 + v_2}{2} \tag{7.8}$$

The voltage v_{di} is the differential-mode input voltage and it is simply the difference between the two input voltages. The voltage v_{ci} is the common-mode input voltage, and it is the average of the two input voltages. The original input voltages can be expressed in terms of these new quantities as follows:

$$v_1 = \frac{v_{di} + 2v_{ci}}{2}$$

$$v_2 = \frac{2v_{ci} - v_{di}}{2} \tag{7.9}$$

If we set the two input voltages equal, we have

$$v_1 = v_2 = v_{ci}$$

and

$$v_{di} = 0$$

Since the two inputs are equal and the transistors are identical, the emitter-base junction voltages will be equal. Thus, the collector currents must also be identical. Since the emitter currents will be equal, we analyze a half-circuit as shown in Figure 7.4(a). Note that the emitter resistance has been doubled, since

Figure 7.4
Differential-amplifier
analysis.

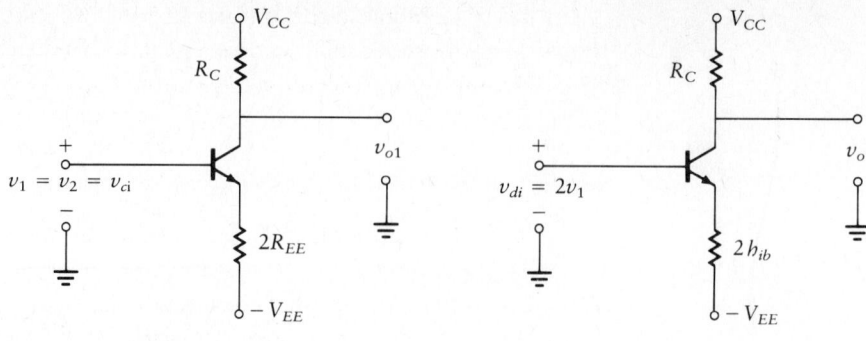

(a)   Common-mode circuit   (b)   Differential-mode circuit

the actual current in this resistor is twice that maintained by the illustrated half-circuit. The output of the half-circuit is v_{o1} or v_{o2}. We define a common-mode and differential-mode gain by resolving the output into two components,

$$v_{o1} = A_d v_{di} + A_c v_{ci}$$

The common-mode gain is found by setting the two inputs equal, since we have forced v_{di} to be zero. Thus, assuming the r_o of the BJT is large and $h_{ib} << R_{EE}$, then

$$A_c = \frac{v_{o1}}{v_{ci}} = \frac{-R_C}{2R_{EE}} \qquad (7.10a)$$

In order to find the differential-mode gain, we again use the technique of splitting the circuit in two parts and analyze the half-circuit of Figure 7.4(b). We let

$$v_1 = -v_2$$

so

$$v_{di} = 2v_1 = -2v_2$$

The ac current from one emitter flows directly into the other emitter, so the voltage across the emitter resistor remains constant. Since the ac signal voltage across the resistor is zero, it can therefore be replaced by a short circuit in the ac equivalent circuit. However, the resistance, h_{ib}, remains in the base-emitter loop of the transistor. The differential-mode gain is then given by

$$A_d = \frac{v_{o1}}{v_{di}} = \frac{-R_C}{2h_{ib}} \qquad (7.10b)$$

Note that the common-mode gain is defined in terms of only one of the two outputs. The differential output, v_o, should (ideally) cancel to zero. In the practical circuit, parameter variations occur. If the common-mode gain is high, these variations affect v_o as well as the two individual output voltages. For this reason, it is desirable for the differential-mode gain to be much larger than the common-mode gain. The *common-mode rejection ratio* (CMRR) is defined as the ratio of the differential-mode gain to the common-mode gain (usually expressed in decibels).

$$\text{CMRR} = 20 \log \frac{|-R_C/2h_{ib}|}{|-R_C/2R_{EE}|} \text{ dB} = 20 \log \left(\frac{R_{EE}}{h_{ib}}\right) \text{ dB} \tag{7.11}$$

It is desirable to make the CMRR as large as possible so that the amplifier will react only to the difference between the input voltages.

Before we evaluate the differential-mode and common-mode gain, let us look at the input resistance of the amplifier in both the differential mode and the common mode. For the differential mode, we look into the amplifier at the base of both transistors. This results in a complete circuit through the emitter of both transistors, and the input resistance is

$$R_i(\text{differential mode}) = 2h_{ie}$$

Now from the common-mode input, we look into the amplifier in Figure 7.4(a). Thus, the input resistance is

$$R_i(\text{common mode}) = 2\beta R_{EE}$$

These results indicate that the input resistance of the common mode is much higher than that of the differential mode.

Equation (7.11) shows that to make the CMRR large, we must make R_{EE} large. Since large resistances are hard to fabricate on IC chips, we seek an alternate approach. This is accomplished by replacing R_{EE} with a constant-current generator, as we discuss in the next section.

Our differential-amplifier analysis is based upon BJTs as the transistor building blocks. Junction field-effect transistors can also be used in differential amplifiers, with the resulting advantages of reduced input bias current and higher input impedance. However, the analysis of the differential amplifier using JFETs is accomplished in the same way as that of BJT analysis.

7.2.3 Differential Amplifier with Constant-Current Source

In the previous section, we saw that it is desirable to make R_{EE} as large as possible in order to reduce the common-mode output. An ideal constant-current source has infinite impedance, so we investigate the possibility of replacing

Figure 7.5
Differential amplifier
with constant-current
source.

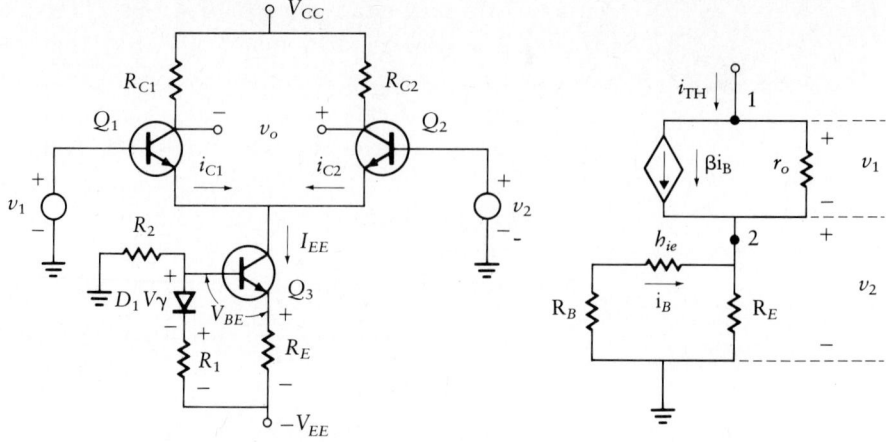

(a) Differential amplifier with
constant-current source

(b) Equivalent circuit of current source

R_{EE} with such a current source. Figure 7.5 illustrates a differential amplifier where the resistor, R_{EE}, is replaced with a constant-current source.

The closer the source is to the ideal constant current source, the higher the CMRR. We therefore show a diode-compensated current source. The compensation, as discussed in Section 5.4, makes the operation of the circuit less dependent upon temperature variations. Diode D_1 and transistor Q_3 are selected so that they have nearly identical characteristics over the range of operating temperatures.

In order to analyze the circuit of Figure 7.5(a) and find the CMRR, we need to determine the equivalent resistance, R_{TH}, the Thevenin equivalent of the constant current source circuit. Looking at the equivalent circuit of the current source as shown in Figure 7.5(b), we have

$$R_{TH} = \frac{v_1 + v_2}{i_{TH}}$$

Writing a KCL equation at node 1, we have

$$i_{TH} = \beta i_B + \frac{v_1}{r_o}$$

where r_o is the internal resistance of the transistor at the specified operating point (see Section 3.1.2).

A KCL equation at node 2 yields

$$\beta i_B + \frac{v_1}{r_o} + i_B - \frac{v_2}{R_E} = 0$$

but

$$v_1 = (i_{TH} - \beta i_B) r_o$$

and

$$v_2 = -i_B(h_{ie} + R_B)$$

Substituting v_1 and v_2 into the equation at node 2, we have

$$-i_{TH} = i_B + \frac{h_{ie} + R_B}{R_E} i_B = i_B \left(1 + \frac{h_{ie} + R_B}{R_E}\right)$$

The Thevenin resistance is given by

$$R_{TH} = \frac{h_{ie} + R_B + r_o[1 + (h_{ie} + R_B)/R_E] + \beta r_o}{1 + (h_{ie} + R_B)/R_E}$$

In order to maintain bias stability, we have used the guideline that

$$R_B = 0.1\beta R_E$$

Substituting this value of R_B in the equation for R_{TH} and dividing by β, we have

$$R_{TH} = \frac{h_{ib} + 0.1R_E + r_0[1/\beta + (h_{ib} + 0.1R_E)/R_E + 1]}{1/\beta + (h_{ib} + 0.1R_E)/R_E}$$

Since

$$1 >> \frac{1}{\beta}$$

and

$$\frac{h_{ib} + 0.1R_E}{R_E} >> \frac{1}{\beta}$$

we have

$$R_{TH} = \frac{h_{ib} + 0.1R_E + r_o[1 + (h_{ib} + 0.1R_E)/R_E]}{(h_{ib} + 0.1R_E)/R_E}$$

and

$$R_{\text{TH}} = R_E + r_o \left[1 + \frac{R_E}{h_{ib} + 0.1R_E} \right]$$

Since the second term in this equation is much greater than the first, we can ignore R_E to get

$$R_{\text{TH}} = r_o \left[1 + \frac{R_E}{h_{ib} + 0.1R_E} \right]$$

This equation can be further simplified if the following condition exists:

$$0.1R_E \gg h_{ib}$$

In that case, we have the simple result

$$R_{\text{TH}} \approx 11r_o \tag{7.12}$$

Hence, if all of the approximations are valid, R_{TH} is independent of β and its value is quite large.

7.2.4   *Differential Amplifier with Single-Ended Input and Output*

Figure 7.6 shows a differential amplifier where the second input, v_2, is set equal to zero and the output is taken as v_{o1}.

We use a constant-current source in place of R_E, as discussed in the previous section. This is known as a *single-ended input and output amplifier with phase reversal*. The amplifier is analyzed by setting $v_2 = 0$ in the earlier equations. The differential input is then simply

$$v_{di} = v_1 - v_2 = v_i$$

so the output is

$$v_o = v_{o1} = A_d v_{di} = \frac{-R_C v_i}{2h_{ib}}$$

The minus sign indicates that this amplifier exhibits a 180° phase shift between the output and input. A typical sinusoidal input and output are illustrated in the figure.

If an output signal is to be referenced to ground but a phase reversal is not desired, the output can be taken from transistor Q_2, as illustrated in Figure

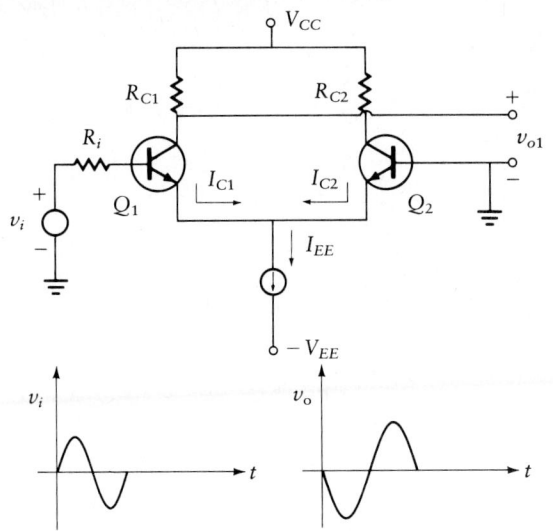

Figure 7.6   Single-ended input with phase reversal.

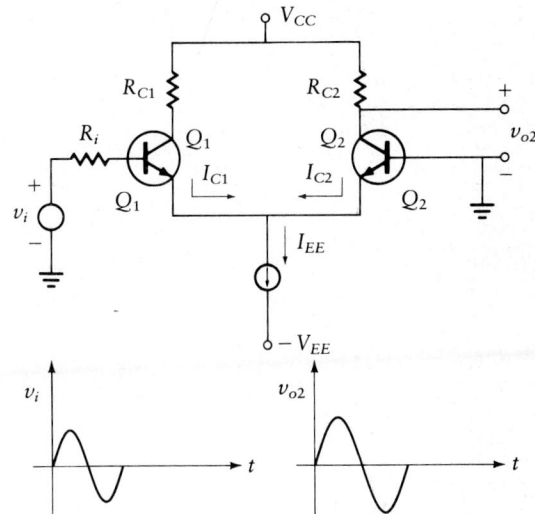

Figure 7.7   Single-ended input with in-phase output.

7.7. In order to show that the output of the circuit of Figure 7.7 is the inverse of that of Figure 7.6, take the mirror image of the first circuit. That is, suppose $v_1 = 0$ and $v_2 = v_i$ in the original differential amplifier of Figure 7.3. The differential-input voltage is then

$$v_{di} = v_1 - v_2 = -v_i$$

Thus, the output is the negative of that found earlier, and no phase reversal occurs.

Example 7.1   **Differential Amplifier (Analysis)**

Find the differential voltage gain, the common-mode voltage gain, and the CMRR for the circuit shown in Figure 7.3. Assume that $R_i = 0$, $R_C = 5$ kΩ, $V_{EE} = 15$ V, $V_{BE} = 0.7$ V, $V_T = 26$ mV, and $R_{EE} = 25$ kΩ. Let $v_2 = 0$ and take output from v_{o2}.

SOLUTION   The current in the current source is found at the quiescent conditions. Since the base of Q_2 is grounded, the emitter voltage is $-V_{BE} = -0.7$ V, and

$$I_{EE} = \frac{V_{EE} - V_{BE}}{R_{EE}} = \frac{15 - 0.7}{25,000} = 0.57 \text{ mA}$$

The quiescent current in each transistor is one-half of this amount

$$I_{C1} = I_{C2} = \frac{I_{EE}}{2} = 0.29 \text{ mA}$$

Since

$h_{eb} = \frac{1}{g_m}$

$$h_{ib} = \frac{V_T}{I_C} = \frac{26}{0.29} = 90 \ \Omega$$

the differential voltage gain in each transistor is

$$A_d = \frac{-R_C}{2h_{ib}} = \frac{5000}{2(90)} = -28$$

$-g_m R_C =$

The common-mode voltage gain is

$V_{be} - 15 V$

$$A_c = \frac{-R_C}{2R_{EE}} = \frac{-5000}{50,000} = -0.1$$

The common-mode rejection ratio is then given by

$$\text{CMRR} = 20 \log \left(\frac{|A_d|}{|A_c|} \right) = 49 \text{ dB}$$

Example 7.2

For the differential amplifier described in Example 7.1, design a current source to replace R_{EE} and determine the new CMRR for the differential amplifier, with $r_o = 105 \text{ k}\Omega$, $V_{BE} = 0.7 \text{ V}$, and $\beta = 100$.

SOLUTION   We place the transistor operating point in the middle of the dc load line.

$$V_{CEQ} = \frac{V_{EE} - V_{BE}}{2} = \frac{15 - 0.7}{2} = 7.15 \text{ V}$$

Then, referring to the current source of Figure 7.5a,

$$R_{EE} = \frac{7.15 \text{ V}}{0.57 \text{ mA}} = 12.54 \text{ k}\Omega$$

For bias stability,

$$R_B = 0.1 \, \beta R_{EE} = 0.1(100)(12,540) = 125.4 \text{ k}\Omega$$

Since $0.1R_E \gg h_{ib}$ (i.e., $1.25 \text{ k}\Omega \gg 90 \, \Omega$), then from equation (7.12), we have

$$R_{TH} \approx 11 r_o$$

so the equivalent resistance and CMRR are given by

$$R_{TH} \approx 11 \, (105 \text{ k}\Omega) = 1.155 \text{ M}\Omega$$

$$\text{CMRR} = 20 \log \left(\frac{R_{TH}}{h_{ib}} \right) = 20 \log \left(\frac{1.155 \times 10^6}{90} \right) = 82.2 \text{ dB} \qquad \blacktriangleright$$

Drill Problems

D7.1 What are the differential- and common-mode gains of the amplifiers of Figure 7.3 if $R_{C1} = R_{C2} = 5 \text{ k}\Omega$ and $R_{EE} = 20 \text{ k}\Omega$? Assume that $V_{CC} = 12$ V, $V_{BE} = 0.7$ V, $V_T = 26$ mV, and $V_{EE} = 12$ V.

Ans: $A_c = -0.125$; $A_d = -53.8$

D7.2 What are the differential- and common-mode gains of the amplifier of Figure 7.6 if $R_{C1} = R_{C2} = 5 \text{ k}\Omega$, $V_{CC} = 15$ V, $V_{EE} = 15$ V, $V_{BE} = 0.7$ V, and $V_T = 26$ mV? Assume that V_{EE}/R_{TH} is a constant-current source with $R_{TH} = 10 \text{ k}\Omega$.

Ans: $A_c = -0.25$; $A_d = -69$

D7.3 For the constant-current source shown in Figure 7.5, determine R_E, R_1, and R_2, where $V_{EE} = 10$ V, $I_{EE} = 2$ mA, and $V_{BE} = 0.7$ V. Also assume that $V_T = 26$ mV and $\beta = 200$.

Ans: $R_E = 2.33 \text{ k}\Omega$; $R_1 = 93 \text{ k}\Omega$; $R_2 = 93 \text{ k}\Omega$

7.3 Current Sources, Active Loads, and Level Shifters

In this section we explore alternate methods of simulating a constant-current source to replace the emitter resistor. One type of source was discussed in Section 7.2.3, where a compensated transistor current source was used.

7.3.1   *Widlar Current Source*

Due to the high gain of an operational amplifier, the bias currents must be small. Typical collector currents are in the range of 5 µA. Large resistors are often required to maintain small currents, and these large resistors occupy correspondingly large areas on the IC chip. It is therefore often desirable to replace these large resistors with current sources. One such device is the *Widlar current source* [63], as illustrated in Figure 7.8. The two transistors Q_1 and Q_2 are identical. We sum the voltages around the base loop of the two transistors to get

$$V_{BE1} - V_{BE2} - I_{C2}R_2 = 0 \tag{7.13}$$

We saw in Section 3.2 that

$$I_C = \beta I_o \exp\left(\frac{V_{BE}}{V_T}\right)$$

Solving this for V_{BE} yields

$$V_{BE} = V_T \ln\left(\frac{I_C}{\beta I_o}\right) \tag{7.14}$$

Substituting the expression of equation (7.14) into equation (7.13), we obtain

$$V_T \ln\left(\frac{I_{C1}}{\beta I_o}\right) - V_T \ln\left(\frac{I_{C2}}{\beta I_o}\right) - I_{C2}R_2 = 0$$

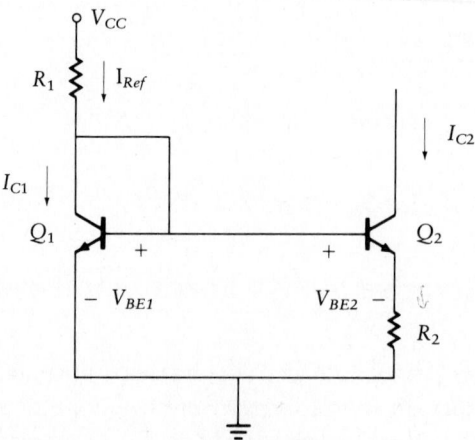

Figure 7.8   Widlar current source.

We assume that the two transistors are matched so that I_o, β, and V_T are the same for both transistors. Thus

$$V_T \ln\left(\frac{I_{C1}}{I_{C2}}\right) = I_{C2}R_2 \tag{7.15}$$

For design purposes, I_{C1} is usually known, since it is used as the reference, and I_{C2} is the desired output current. This allows us to solve equation (7.15) for the required value of R_2.

We use an example to illustrate how a current source can be designed to provide a small constant current while using resistors that are easily fabricated on an IC chip.

Example 7.3   **Widlar Current Source (Design)**

Design a Widlar current source to provide a constant current of 3 μA with $V_{CC} = 12$ V, $R_1 = 50$ kΩ, and $V_{BE} = 0.7$ V.

SOLUTION   Use the circuit of Figure 7.8. Apply KVL to the Q_1 transistor to obtain

$$I_{C1} \approx I_{Ref} = \frac{12 - 0.7}{50,000} = 0.226 \text{ mA}$$

From equation (7.15) we have

$$0.026 \ln\left(\frac{0.226 \times 10^{-3}}{3 \times 10^{-6}}\right) = 3 \times 10^{-6}R_2$$

and

$$R_2 = 37.5 \text{ k}\Omega$$

Since R_2 is less than 50 kΩ, it can be fabricated on an IC.

7.3.2   *Wilson Current Source*

The *Wilson current source* [65], as shown in Figure 7.9, uses three transistors, and its operation is almost independent of the internal transistor characteristics. Negative feedback from the collector to the base of Q_3 increases the output resistance of this current source.

Figure 7.9
Wilson current source.

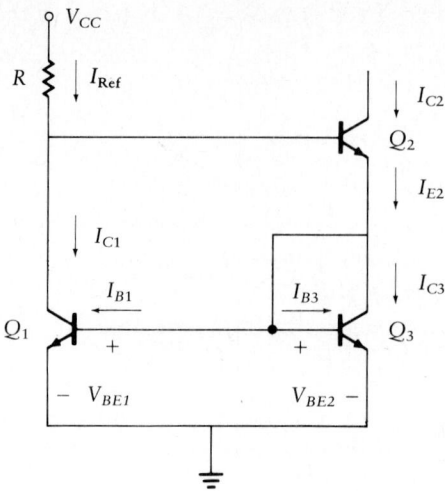

We solve for I_{C2} to illustrate the usefulness of this circuit. Applying KCL at the emitter of Q_2 yields

$$I_{E2} = I_{C3} + I_{B3} + I_{B1} \tag{7.16}$$

Using the relationship between collector and base current yields,

$$I_{E2} = I_{C3}\left(1 + \frac{1}{\beta}\right) + \frac{I_{C1}}{\beta} \tag{7.17}$$

Since all three transistors are assumed to be identical,

$$V_{BE1} = V_{BE3}$$

and

$$\beta_1 = \beta_2 = \beta_3$$

With identical transistors, current in the feedback path splits equally between the bases of Q_1 and Q_3, leading to the result that

$$I_{C1} = I_{C3}$$

Thus, equation (7.17) becomes

$$I_{E2} = I_{C3}\left(1 + \frac{2}{\beta}\right)$$

The collector current of Q_2 is

$$I_{C2} = \frac{I_{E2}\beta}{\beta + 1} = \frac{I_{C3}(1 + 2/\beta)\beta}{\beta + 1}$$

Solving for I_{C3} yields

$$I_{C3} = \frac{I_{C2}}{(1 + 2/\beta)\beta/(1 + \beta)} = I_{C2}\frac{\beta + 1}{\beta + 2} \tag{7.18}$$

Summing currents at the base of Q_2, we find

$$I_{C1} = I_{Ref} - \frac{I_{C2}}{\beta}$$

or

$$I_{C2} = \beta(I_{Ref} - I_{C1}) \tag{7.19}$$

Since $I_{C1} = I_{C3}$, we substitute I_{C3} from equation (7.18) for I_{C1} in equation (7.19) to get

$$I_{C2} = \beta I_{Ref} - \frac{\beta(\beta + 1)}{\beta + 2} I_{C2}$$

and solving for I_{C2},

$$I_{C2} = \frac{\beta^2 + 2\beta}{\beta^2 + 2\beta + 2} I_{Ref}$$

$$= \left(1 - \frac{2}{\beta^2 + 2\beta + 2}\right) I_{Ref} \tag{7.20}$$

Equation (7.20) shows that β has little effect upon I_{C2}, since, for reasonable values of β,

$$\frac{2}{\beta^2 + 2\beta + 2} << 1$$

7.3.3   Current Mirrors

The circuit shown in Figure 7.10 is known as a *current mirror*. It is used in op-amp circuit design to reproduce a current from one location to one or more other locations. In this circuit, Q_2 is in the linear mode, since the collector

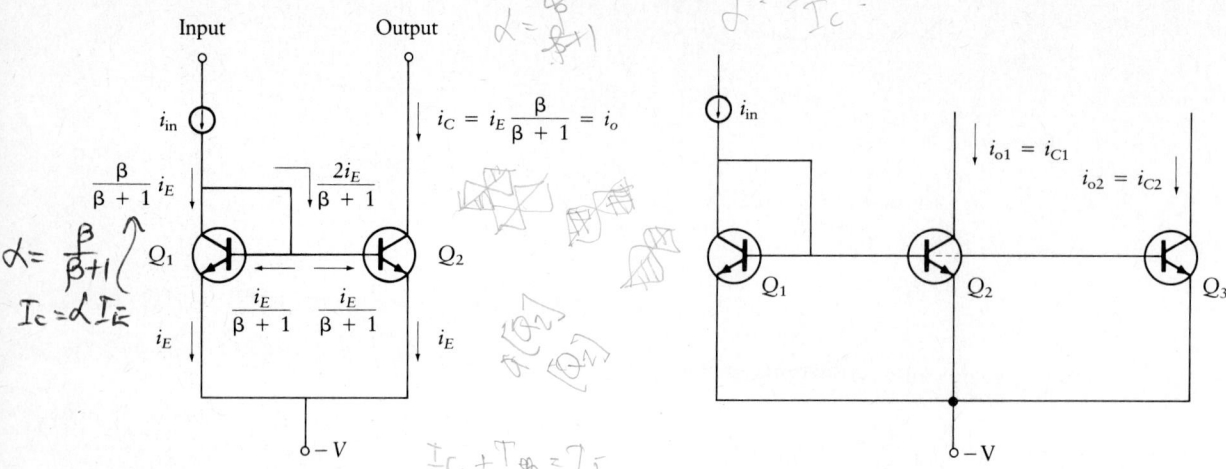

Figure 7.10   Current mirror.

Figure 7.11   Multiple-current mirrors.

voltage (output) is higher than the base voltage. The transistors Q_1 and Q_2 are identical devices fabricated on the same IC chip. The emitter currents are equal, since the emitters and bases are in parallel. If we sum the currents of Q_2, we obtain

$$i_B + i_C = i_E$$

so

$$i_o = i_C = i_E - \frac{i_E}{\beta + 1} = \frac{\beta i_E}{\beta + 1}$$

Summing currents at the collector of Q_1 yields

$$i_{in} = \left(\frac{\beta}{\beta + 1} + \frac{2}{\beta + 1} \right) i_E = \frac{\beta + 2}{\beta + 1} i_E$$

The current gain of the mirror is given by

$$A_i = \frac{i_o}{i_{in}} = \frac{\beta i_E}{\beta + 1} \frac{\beta + 1}{(\beta + 2)i_E} = \frac{1}{1 + 2/\beta} \approx 1$$

If β is much larger than 1, this current gain is approximately equal to unity, and the current mirror has reproduced the input current.

This concept is extended to several other circuits, as shown in Figure 7.11. The current input of Q_1 is mirrored into several other transistors, $Q_2, Q_3, \ldots$,

Figure 7.12
Widlar current-source
equivalent circuit.

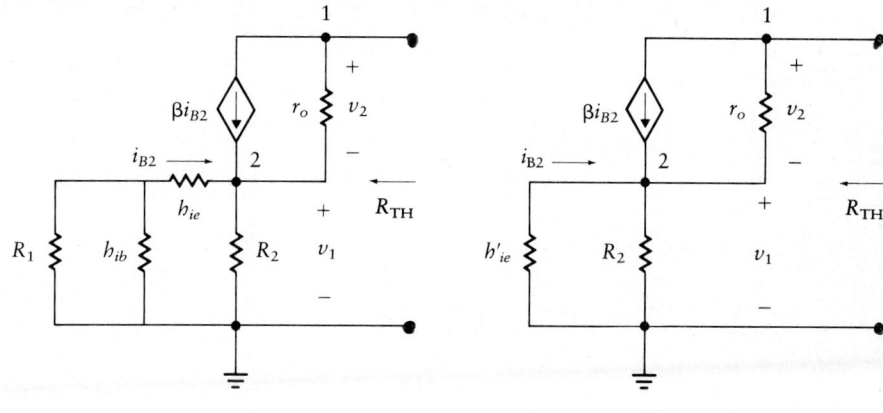

(a) Actual equivalent circuit   (b) Approximate equivalent circuit

Q_n. The errors in base current accumulate when multiple outputs are used, and the current gain tends to deviate from unity.

7.3.4 *Current Sources as Active Loads*

In the conventional differential amplifiers of Section 7.2, the collector loads consist of resistors. The differential gain is

$$A_v = \frac{v_o}{v_i} = \frac{-R_C}{h_{ib}} = \frac{-R_C I_{CQ}}{V_T}$$

In order to achieve a large voltage gain, the product $R_C I_{CQ}$ must be large. This requires large values of either resistance or power supply voltage. Since the power supply size is usually fixed, large resistors are required. The preceding sections illustrate several alternate forms of almost-ideal constant-current sources. We now show that these are equivalent to large resistors.

The Widlar circuit can be used to simulate a high resistance. The small-signal equivalent circuit is shown in Figure 7.12. Since this circuit has no independent sources, it is equivalent to a single Thevenin resistance. To find the value of this resistance, we assume a current, i_{TH}, find the resulting voltage, and take the ratio. We start by summing currents at node 1,

$$i_{TH} = \beta i_{B2} + \frac{v_2}{r_o} \tag{7.21}$$

and at node 2,

$$\beta i_{B2} + \frac{v_2}{r_o} - \frac{v_1}{R_2} + i_{B2} = 0 \tag{7.22}$$

From equation (7.21), we have

$$v_2 = (i_{TH} - \beta i_{B2})r_o \tag{7.23}$$

Also

$$v_1 = -i_{B2}h'_{ie} \tag{7.24}$$

where

$$h'_{ie} = h_{ie} + (h_{ib}\|R_1)$$

Substituting equations (7.23) and (7.24) into equation (7.22) yields

$$-i_{TH} = i_{B2}\left(1 + \frac{h'_{ie}}{R_2}\right) \tag{7.25}$$

Using the relationship

$$R_{TH} = \frac{v_{TH}}{i_{TH}}$$

yields

$$R_{TH} = \frac{r_o(1 + \beta + h'_{ie}/R_2) + h'_{ie}}{1 + h'_{ie}/R_2}$$

Since

$$r_o \gg h'_{ie}$$

we have

$$R_{TH} = r_o\left[\frac{1 + \beta + h'_{ie}/R_2}{1 + h'_{ie}/R_2}\right] = r_o\left[1 + \frac{\beta}{1 + h'_{ie}/R_2}\right]$$

In order to simplify this result, assume that

$$\frac{h'_{ie}}{R_2} \gg 1$$

and

$$h_{ie} = \frac{\beta V_T}{I_{CQ}}$$

Then

$$R_{TH} = r_o \left[1 + \frac{\beta}{h_{ie}/R_2} \right]$$

$$= r_o \left[1 + \frac{\beta R_2 I_{CQ}}{\beta V_T} \right]$$

Finally,

$$R_{TH} = r_o \left[1 + \frac{I_{CQ}R_2}{V_T} \right] \tag{7.26}$$

Equation (7.26) shows that R_{TH} depends upon $I_{CQ}R_2$, which is the dc voltage drop across R_2. The larger the voltage drop, the higher the output resistance. Generally, the output resistance of a simple current source is increased by the addition of resistances (R_2 in Figures 7.8 and 7.12) in the emitters of the current-source transistors.

We perform a similar analysis for the Wilson current source. This analysis is like that used for the Widlar source, so we simply state the result here. The equivalent resistance is given by

$$R_{TH} = \frac{\beta r_o}{2} \tag{7.27}$$

We now examine two applications of the constant-current circuits. Figure 7.13(a) illustrates a CE amplifier with an active load as the collector resistor. In Figure 7.13(b), a differential amplifier is shown using active loads, Widlar current sources, and current mirrors. Similar circuits of this type are found in many ICs, since large resistors are avoided in the fabrication process. Transistors Q_1 and Q_2 are the differential-amplifier transistors, Q_3 and Q_4 are the active loads for the amplifier, Q_3, Q_4, and Q_6 form the current source with current mirrors, and Q_5 and Q_7 form a Widlar current source.

7.3.5 Level Shifters

Amplifiers often produce dc voltages at the output. Even if the input has an average value of 0 V, the output usually has a nonzero average voltage due to

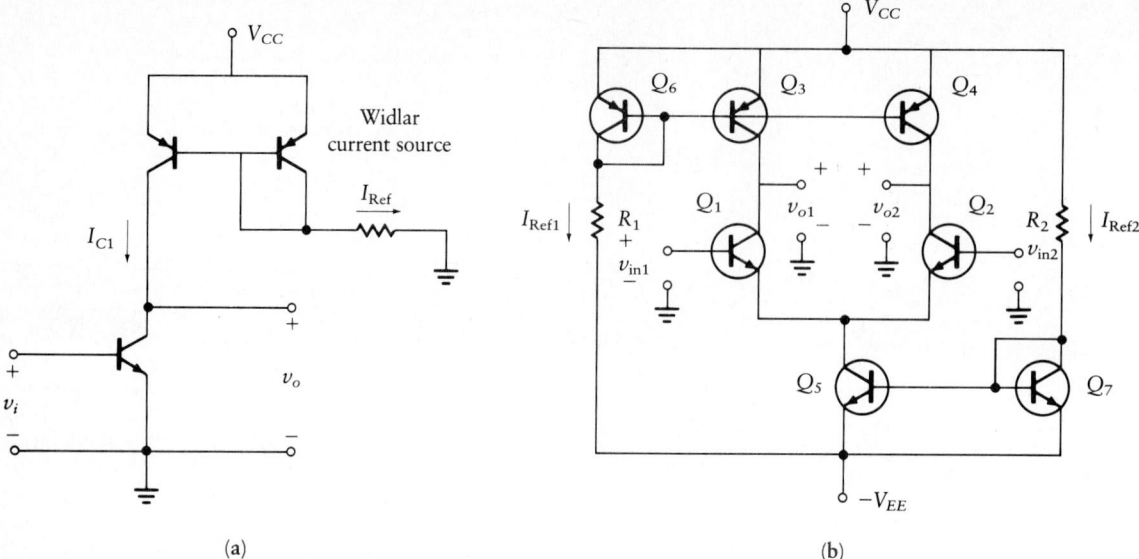

Figure 7.13   CE amplifier with active load.

biasing effects. These dc voltages can cause difficulties at the output, since they cause an undesired offset.

In Chapter 6 we study the Class B power amplifier, which provides a method of reducing the offset voltages in the output stage. However, we cannot always use Class-B amplifiers, so another technique is necessary. *Level shifters* are amplifiers that add or subtract a known voltage from the input in order to compensate for dc offset voltages.

Since the op-amp is a multistage dc amplifier with high gain, unwanted dc voltages are always a source of concern. That is, a small offset in an early stage can saturate a later stage. For this reason level shifters are included in the design of op-amps.

Figure 7.14 illustrates a simple level shifter. We show that this shifter acts as a unit-gain amplifier for ac while providing an adjustable dc output. We begin the analysis by using KVL in Figure 7.14(a) and letting $v_i = 0$ to get

$$V_{BB} = I_B R_B + V_{BE} + I_C R_E + V_o$$

Since

$$I_B = \frac{I_C}{\beta}$$

Figure 7.14
Level shifter.

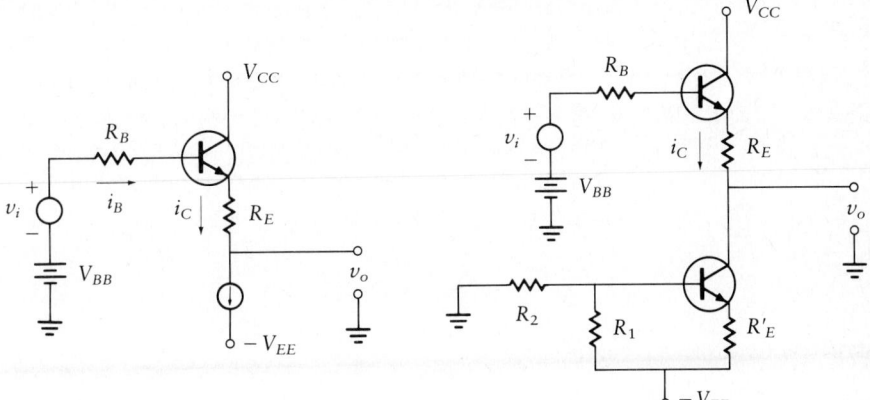

(a) Simple level shifter
     where $v_{in} = 0$

(b) Actual circuit

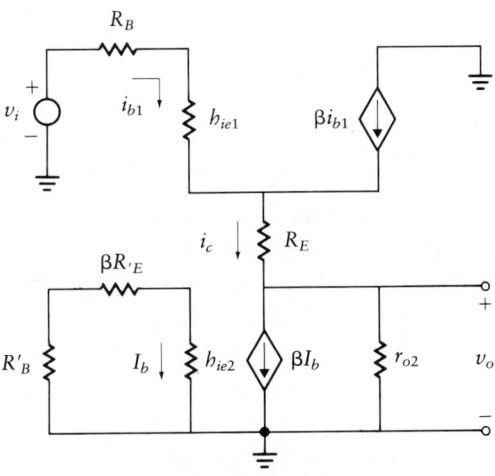

(c) Small-signal ac equivalent circuit

we solve for the dc value of output voltage, V_o:

$$V_o = V_{BB} - \frac{R_B I_C}{\beta} - I_C R_E - V_{BE} \qquad (7.28)$$

This equation shows that by selecting a value of R_E, V_o can be set to any desired dc level less than $V_{BB} - V_{BE}$. Since V_{BB} is the dc level acquired from the previous stage, this amplifier is used to shift the level *downward* (to a lower value). If *upward* shifting is required, a similar circuit is used, but *pnp* transistors are substituted for the *npn* transistors. A complete circuit with active current sources is shown in Figure 7.14(b).

We examine small-signal ac signals. Figure 7.14(c) illustrates the ac equivalent circuit. Note that βI_B is the collector current in the active current source, and we assume it to be a constant. Because the ac value of the current is zero, this current source is replaced by an open circuit in the following equations. We write the ac equations using KVL:

$$v_i = i_{b1}R_B + i_{b1}h_{ie1} + i_cR_E + v_o \tag{7.29}$$

and

$$v_o = i_c r_{o2}$$

$$i_c = \frac{v_o}{r_{o2}}$$

$$v_{\text{in}} = \frac{v_o R_B}{\beta r_{o2}} + \frac{v_o h_{ie1}}{\beta r_{o2}} + \frac{v_o R_E}{r_{o2}} + v_o$$

Finally, the ratio of ac output to ac input is

$$\frac{v_o}{v_i} = \frac{1}{1 + (R_B/\beta + h_{ie}/\beta + R_E)/r_{o2}} \tag{7.30}$$

Equation (7.30) shows that as r_{o2} becomes large, the ratio of output to input approaches unity, and the level shifter acts like an emitter follower to ac. This is the desired result.

Example 7.4

Two direct-coupled CE amplifiers are placed in series to achieve the desired voltage gain. Design a level shifter to be placed in between the two CE amplifiers to provide a dc voltage sufficiently low to prevent the second CE amplifier from saturating. Do this by providing a 1 V bias to the second stage. The collector voltage, V_C, of the first amplifier is 4 V, and the R_C of that amplifier is 1 kΩ. Design the level shifter to have an I_{CQ} of 1 mA using dc power of ± 10 V. Use a current source of the type shown in Figure 7.5 with transistors having $\beta = 100$, $V_{BE} = 0.7$ V, and $V\gamma = 0.7$ V.

SOLUTION   The level shifter is shown in Figure 7.14(b). We need to find the values of R_E, R_1, R_2, and R'_E. Since the first amplifier has a V_C of 4 V, the value of V_{BB} for equation (7.28) is 4 V, whereas the R_B of that formula is 1 kΩ. Note this is using Thevenin equivalent circuit of the previous amplifier. Equation (7.28) then yields

$$1 = 4 - 1000 \frac{10^{-3}}{100} - 10^{-3}R_E - 0.7$$

Solving for R_E, we find

$$R_E = 2.29 \text{ k}\Omega$$

Setting the current-source transistor operating point in the middle of the dc load line, we have

$$V_{CEQ} = \frac{10 + 1}{2} = 5.5 \text{ V}$$

$$R'_E = \frac{5.5 \text{ V}}{1 \text{ mA}} = 5.5 \text{ k}\Omega$$

and

$$R'_B = R_1 \| R_2 = 0.1 \, \beta R'_E = 55 \text{ k}\Omega$$

$$V_{R'E} = V_{R1} = 5.5 \text{ V}$$

Then

$$V_{R2} = 10 - 5.5 - 0.7 = 3.8 \text{ V}$$

We now know the voltages across R_1 and R_2 and the parallel resistance. This gives two equations as follows, where we assume that the base current in the lower transistor of Figure 7.14(b) is negligible.

$$R_B = \frac{(5.5/I)(3.8/I)}{(5.5/I) + (3.8/I)} = 55 \text{ k}\Omega$$

$$I = 0.041 \text{ mA}$$

and

$$R_1 = 134 \text{ k}\Omega$$

$$R_2 = 93 \text{ k}\Omega$$

The design is therefore complete. ▶+

7.4 Cascode Configuration

The *cascode* configuration, as shown in Figure 7.15, consists of a CE amplifier direct-coupled to a CB amplifier. It is used with the difference amplifier to provide the advantages of increased output resistance and wider-frequency bandwidth.

The CB amplifier possesses the advantage of favorable frequency-response characteristics (higher achievable frequency while maintaining high voltage gain). If the CE amplifier is replaced by a difference amplifier, the result is a two-stage difference amplifier with increased voltage gain and bandwidth. We prove this statement when we evaluate frequency response in Chapter 10. For

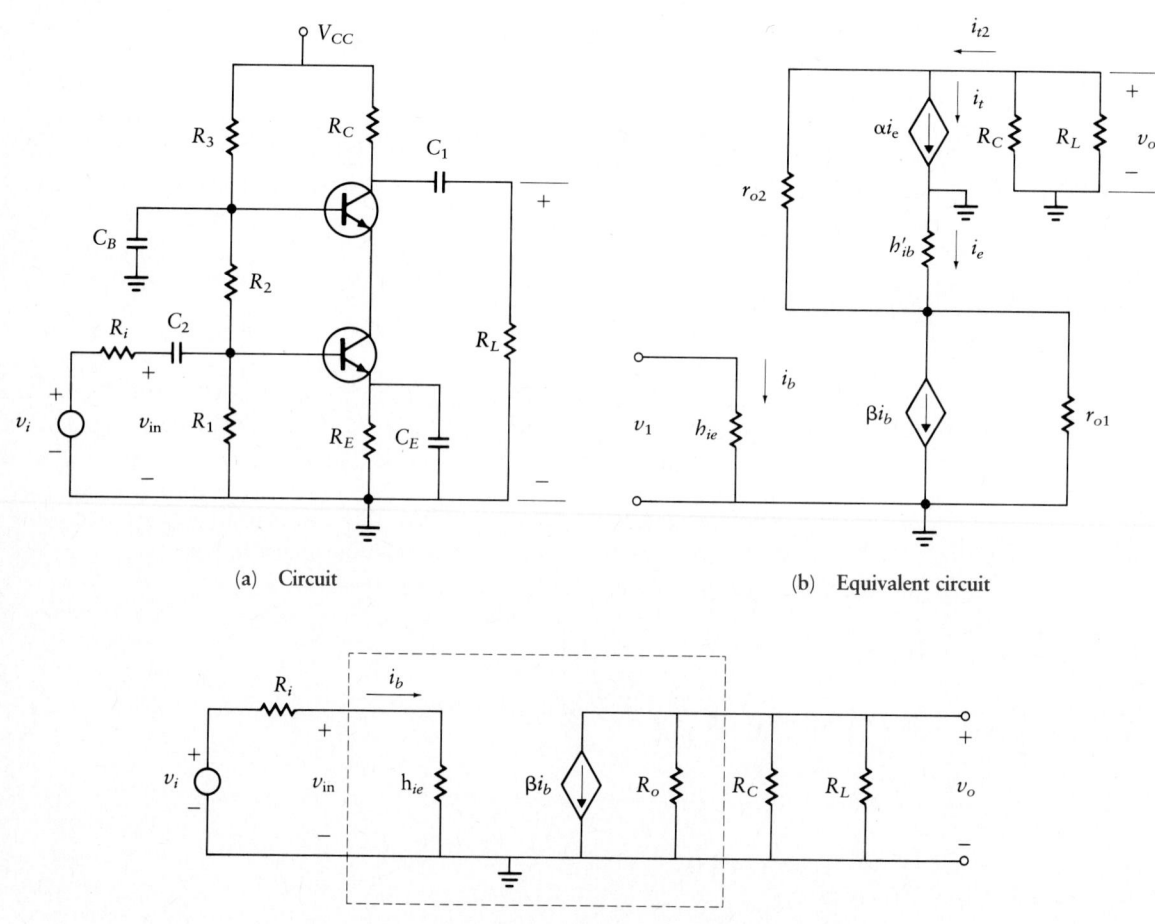

(a) Circuit

(b) Equivalent circuit

(c) Simplified equivalent circuit

Figure 7.15 Cascode amplifier.

now, the basic cascode configuration is analyzed to determine the change in output resistance of the amplifier. Although we illustrate the cascode amplifier with BJTs, the amplifier works equally well using FETs.

Figure 7.15(b) illustrates the equivalent circuit of the amplifier of Figure 7.15(a). The input resistance of the circuit is the input resistance of the first transistor, or h_{ie}. The current in r_{o2} is given by

$$i_{r_{o2}} = \frac{v_o}{r_{o2} + h'_{ib}} \approx \frac{v_o}{r_{o2}} = -i_e \tag{7.31}$$

In writing equation (7.31), we assume that r_{o1} and r_{o2} are each much larger than h'_{ib}. Then

$$i_t = \alpha i_e = -\frac{\alpha v_o}{r_{o2}}$$

and $\tag{7.32}$

$$i_{t2} = i_t + i_{r_{o2}} = \frac{v_o(1 - \alpha)}{r_{o2}} \approx \frac{v_o}{\beta r_{o2}}$$

The output resistance of the amplifier (as seen across v_o) is

$$R_o = \frac{v_o}{i_{t2}} = \beta r_{o2} \tag{7.33}$$

The amplifier combination displays an output resistance that is approximately a factor of beta larger than that of a single-transistor amplifier. A simplified equivalent circuit, including this output resistance, is shown in Figure 7.15(c).

If the CE amplifier in the cascode circuit is replaced with a single-ended output difference amplifier, the circuit of Figure 7.16 results. This circuit has

Figure 7.16
Cascode configuration using difference amplifier.

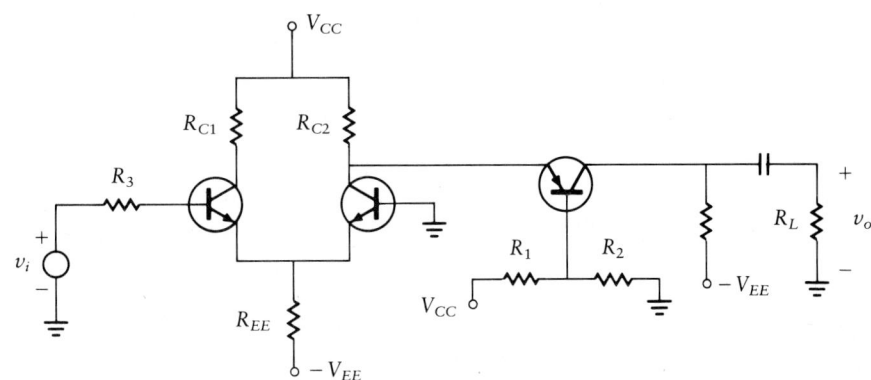

a high-output impedance and improved frequency characteristics. It is found in the input of many wideband operational amplifiers. We discuss the frequency characteristics of the cascode amplifier in Section 10.7.

Drill Problems

D7.4   Design a Widlar current source to obtain a constant current of 50 μA. The battery voltage is 20 V, and a 4 mA reference current is used. Determine the resistor value required and R_{TH} of the current source when r_o (transistor) = 50 kΩ, V_{BE} = 0.7 V, and V_T = 26 mV.

Ans: R_1 = 4.83 kΩ; R_2 = 2.28 kΩ; R_{TH} = 269 kΩ

D7.5   Design a Wilson current source to provide 100 μA when V_{CC} = 15 V. Use transistors with β = 100, V_{BE} = 0.7 V, and V_T = 26 mV. Determine R_{TH} when r_o of the transistor is 15 kΩ.

Ans: I_{REF} = 100 μA; R_1 = 143 kΩ; R_{TH} = 750 kΩ

D7.6   Design a level shifter to change V_C from 6 V to 2 V so the voltage is compatible with a following CE amplifier. Use a CE amplifier that has an R_C = 5 kΩ and a current source of 4 mA with V_{CC} = 15 V and V_{EE} = 15 V. The transistors have β = 200 and V_{BE} = 0.7 V.

Ans: R_E = 805Ω; R'_E = 2.13 kΩ;
R_1 = 110 kΩ; R_2 = 69 kΩ

7.5   Op-Amp Packaging

Op-amp circuits are packaged in standard IC packages, including cans, dual-in-line packages (DIP), and flat packs. Each of these packages has at least eight pins or connections. They are illustrated in Figures 7.17, 7.18, and 7.19. In a practical design, it is important to identify the various leads correctly (they are usually not numbered). The figures illustrate the manner in which pin 1 is identified from the physical configuration. In the *can package* of Figure 7.17, pin 1 is identified as the first pin to the left of the tab, and the pins are numbered consecutively counterclockwise looking from the top. In the *DIP* of Figure 7.18, the top of the package has an indentation to locate pin 1, and the pins are numbered down on the left and up on the right. Note that more than one op-amp (typically two or four) is packaged in one DIP.

In the *flat pack* of Figure 7.19, pin 1 is identified by a dot, and the pins are numbered as in the DIP.

Figure 7.17
Op-amp connection
for can package.

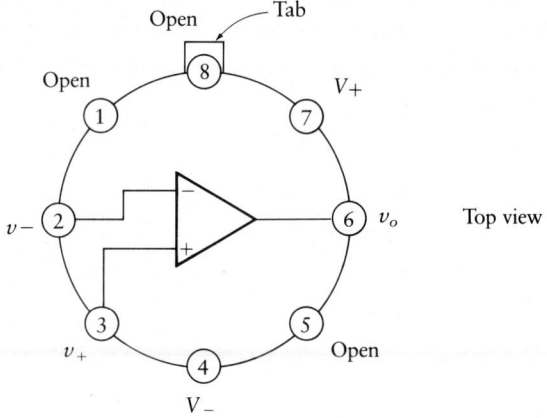

Figure 7.18
Op-amp connection
for 14-pin DIP.

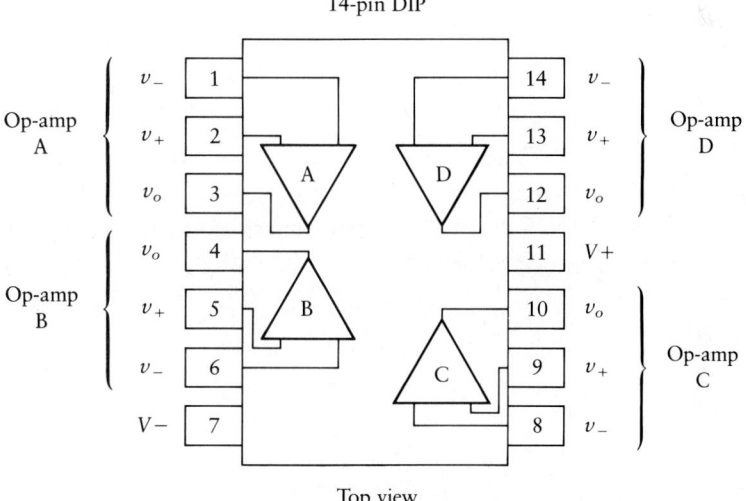

Figure 7.19
Op-amp connection
for 10-pin flat pack.

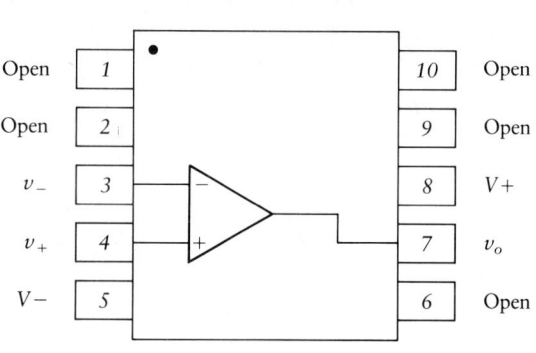

Figure 7.20
Power supply
connections.

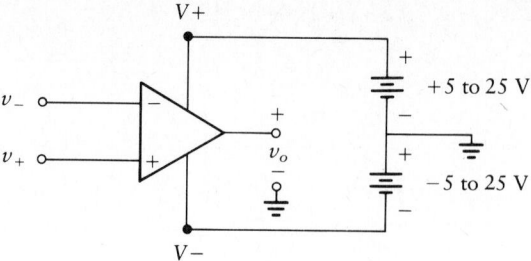

7.5.1   *Power Requirements*

Many op-amps require both a negative and a positive voltage source. Typical voltage sources range from ± 5 V to ± 25 V. Figure 7.20 shows typical power supply connections to the op-amp.

The maximum output voltage swing is limited by the dc voltage supplied to the op-amp. Some operational amplifiers can be operated from a single voltage source. The manufacturer's specifications define the limits of operation in those cases where the op-amp uses only one power supply.

7.6   **The 741 Op-Amp**

One of the most popular op-amps is the A741 illustrated in Figure 7.21. It has been produced since 1966 by most IC manufacturers, and although there have been many advances since its introduction, the 741 is still widely used.

We briefly describe this op-amp. The external behavior and specifications of this circuit are discussed later in this chapter. For now, we concentrate upon the internal construction.

The 741 op-amp has *internal compensation,* which refers to the RC network that causes the amplitude response to fall off at higher frequencies. Two cascoded difference amplifiers drive a complementary-symmetry power amplifier through another voltage amplifier.

The 741 op-amp consists of three major stages: an input differential amplifier, an intermediate single-ended high-gain amplifier, and an output-buffering amplifier. Other circuitry important to its operation include a level shifter to shift the dc level of the signal so that the output can swing both positive and negative, bias circuits to provide reference currents to the various amplifiers, and circuits that protect the op-amp from short circuits at the output. The 741 is internally frequency-compensated by means of an on-chip capacitor-resistor network.

The op-amp is further improved by adding more stages of amplification, isolating the input circuits, and adding more emitter followers at the output

Figure 7.21
The 741 op-amp.
Courtesy of Fairchild
Semiconductor Corp.

EQUIVALENT CIRCUIT

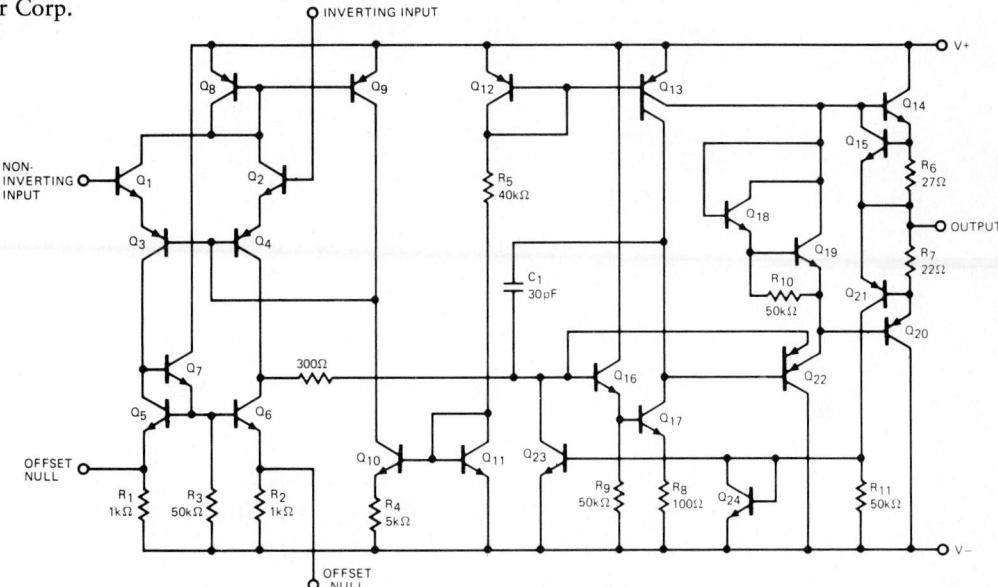

to decrease the output impedance. Other improvements result in increased CMRR, higher input impedance, wider frequency response, decreased output impedance, and increased power.

7.6.1 Bias Circuits

Several current sources can be seen in the 741 op-amp of Figure 7.21. Transistors Q_{11} and Q_{12}, which have their bases and collectors connected together, are being used as diodes. They provide a reference current in R_5 for the op-amp output stage. This bias current is used to provide a reference current to Q_{13}. Thus, Q_{12} and Q_{13} form a two-output current mirror. A Widlar current source, formed by Q_{10}, Q_{11}, and R_4, creates bias current for the first stage. Another current source that provides an active load for the first stage is composed of Q_8 and Q_9.

7.6.2 Short-Circuit Protection

The 741 circuit includes a number of transistors that are normally cut off and conduct only in the event that a large current exists at the output. The bias on the output transistors is then changed to reduce this current to an acceptable level. In the circuit of Figure 7.21, this short-circuit protection network consists of transistors Q_{15} and Q_{21} and resistors R_{11} and R_9.

7.6.3   *Input Stage*

The input stage of the 741 op-amp is relatively complicated in that it is required to provide voltage gain, level shifting, and a single-ended differential amplifier output. The complexity of the circuitry causes a large offset-voltage error. In contrast to this, the standard resistor-loaded differential amplifier causes less offset-voltage error. However, the standard amplifier has limited gain, which means that more stages would be required to achieve the desired amplification. The resistor-loaded differential amplifiers are used in op-amps having less voltage drift than the 741.

BJTs used in the input stage require large bias currents, introducing offset-current problems. To reduce the offset-current error, FETs are often used in the input stage.

The input stage of the 741 is a differential amplifier with an active load formed by transistors Q_5, Q_6, and Q_7 and resistors R_1, R_2, and R_3. This circuit provides a high resistance load and converts the signal from differential to single-ended with no loss in gain or common-mode rejection capability. The single-ended output is taken from the collector of Q_6. The input-stage level shifter consists of lateral *pnp* transistors, Q_3 and Q_4, which are connected in a CB configuration.

Use of the lateral transistors Q_3 and Q_4 results in an added advantage. They help protect the input transistors, Q_1 and Q_2, against emitter-base junction breakdown. The emitter-base junction of an *npn* transistor breaks down when the reverse bias exceeds about 7 V. Lateral transistor breakdown does not occur until the reverse bias exceeds about 50 V. Since the transistors are in series with Q_1 and Q_2, the breakdown voltage of the input circuit is increased.

7.6.4   *Intermediate Stage*

The intermediate stages in most op-amps provide high gain through several amplifiers. In the 741, the single-ended output of the first stage is connected to the base of Q_{16}, which is in an emitter-follower configuration. This provides a high input impedance to the input stage, which minimizes loading effects. The intermediate stage also consists of transistors Q_{17} and Q_{18} and resistors R_{11} and R_{12}. The output of the intermediate stage is taken from the collector of Q_{17} and provided to Q_{14} through a phase splitter. The capacitor in the 741 is used for frequency compensation.

7.6.5   *Output Stage*

The output stage of an op-amp is required to provide high current gain to a low output impedance. Most op-amps use a complementary-symmetry output stage to gain more efficiency without sacrificing current gain. In Chapter 6 we show that the maximum achievable efficiency for the CS amplifier is 78%. The single-ended output amplifier has a maximum efficiency of only 25%. Some op-amps use Darlington pair complementary symmetry to increase their output capability. The complementary-symmetry output stage in the 741 consists of Q14 and Q20.

7.7 Manufacturers' Specifications

Each op-amp has characteristics that are described in the manufacturer's specifications. These are combined into data books.

Each specification also provides the characteristics of the op-amp under various operational conditions. The major parameters are shown either in tabular or graphical form. There may also be manufacturer-recommended typical applications for the op-amp. Other items shown in the specification may include examples of the external circuits required to balance the op-amp. This would be an appropriate time to familiarize yourself with Appendix D, where we illustrate examples of specification sheets. The μA741 is included and should be viewed as a typical example.

Op-amps are versatile building blocks for use by the designer. As we explore the various applications of these building blocks (in the next five chapters), it would be most useful to obtain one of the latest copies of a manufacturer's *linear IC handbook*. This contains the various specification sheets and other valuable information.

PROBLEMS

7.1 What are the differential- and common-mode gains for the amplifier of Figure 7.3 if $R_{C1} = R_{C2} = 10$ kΩ, $R_E = 10$ kΩ and $V_{CC} = 15$ V? Assume that V_{EE}/R_E is a constant-current source and that $V_{BE} = 0.7$ V, $V_T = 26$ mV and $V_{EE} = 15$ V.

7.2 What are the differential- and common-mode gains of the amplifier of Figure 7.3 if $R_{EE} = 5$ kΩ, $R_{C1} = R_{C2} = 5$ kΩ, $V_{CC} = V_{EE} = 15$ V? Assume that $V_{BE} = 0.7$ V, $V_T = 26$ mV and $\beta = 100$.

7.3 Find the differential voltage for the circuit of Figure 7.3 if $v_1 = 0.6$ V and $v_2 = 0.55$ V. Let $R_C = 5$ kΩ, $R_{EE} = 5$ kΩ and $I_{EE} = 2.6$ mA.

7.4 A manufacturer lists the voltage gain of a differential amplifier as 200 and the CMRR as 80 dB. If a differential signal of 2 mV is applied to the input along with an unwanted common-mode signal of 10 mV, what is the amplitude of each signal at the output?

7.5 The differential amplifier of Figure 7.5 has $A_d = 200$, a differential voltage input of 3 mV, a common-mode voltage of 15 mV, and a CMRR of 95 dB. Calculate the differential voltage and the common-mode voltage at the output.

7.6 Calculate v_{o1}, v_{o2} and v_{o3} in terms of the input v_1 and v_2 for the circuit of Figure P7.1. Assume the differential voltage gain, A_d (double-ended output to double-ended input), is 100 and that the common-mode voltage gain, A_c, is -0.5 for each stage. All transistors can be assumed to be identical.

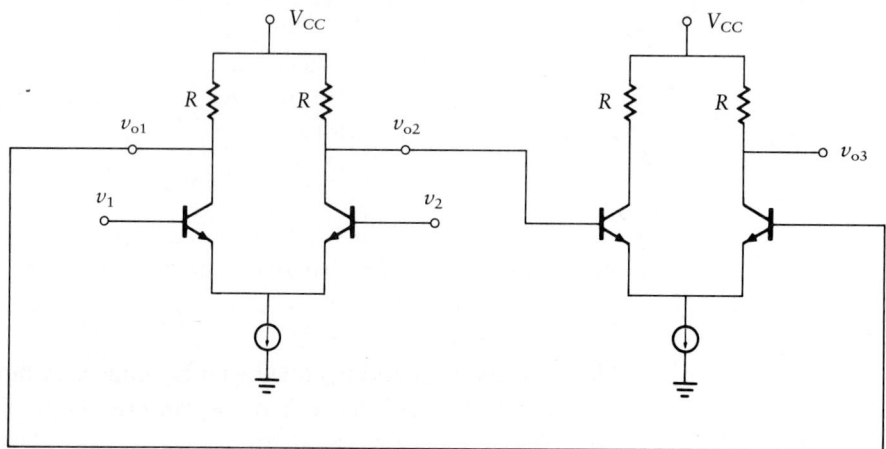

Figure P7.1

7.7 Calculate v_{o3} in terms of the inputs v_1 and v_2 for the circuit of Figure P7.2. The differential- and common-mode voltage gains for the first stage are the same as those in Problem 7.6. For transistor Q_3, $\beta = 100$, $R_C = 10\ \text{k}\Omega$, $h_{ib} = 50\ \Omega$ and $R_E = 200\ \Omega$.

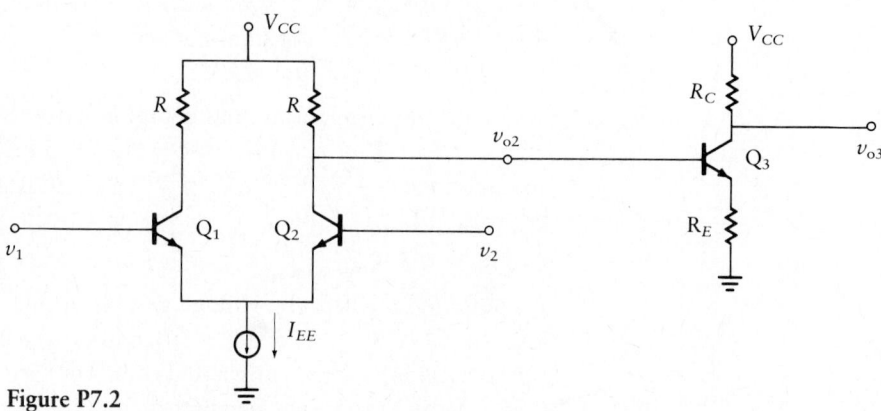

Figure P7.2

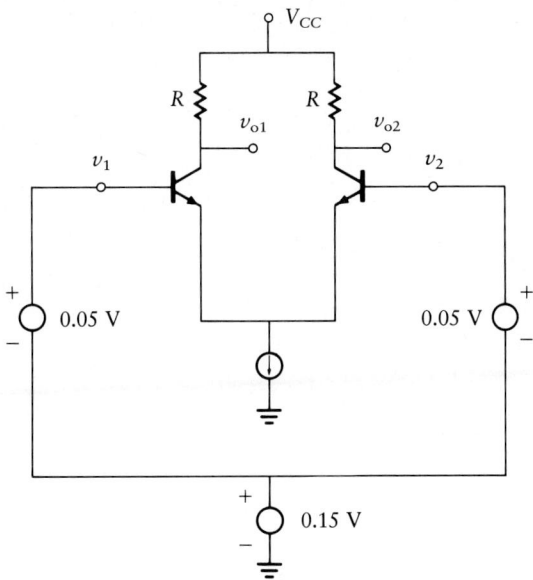

Figure P7.3

7.8 Calculate v_{o1} and v_{o2} for the input voltages as shown in Figure P7.3. A_d and A_c are the same as those in Problem 7.6.

7.9 Find A_c, A_d and the CMRR for the circuit of Figure 7.5 if $R_{C1} = R_{C2} = 3$ kΩ, $I_{EE} = 4$ mA, $R_E = 2$ kΩ, $r_o = 15$ kΩ, $V_{CC} = 12$ V and $V_{EE} = 12$ V.

7.10 Find A_c, A_d and the CMRR for v_{o2} of the circuit of Figure 7.3 if $R_C = 4$ kΩ, $I_{EE} = 3$ mA, $V_{CC} = V_{EE} = 12$ V, $v_1 = 0$, and $R_{EE} = 40$ kΩ.

7.11 Find A_c, A_d and the CMRR for the circuit of Figure P7.2 when R(current source) $= 50$ kΩ, $R = 6$ kΩ, V_2 is grounded, $I_{EE} = 2$ mA, $V_{CC} = 8$ V, $R_C = 2$ kΩ, $R_E = 500$ Ω, and $\beta = 200$.

7.12 In the current source shown in Figure 7.5, determine the values of R_1 and R_2 if $V_{EE} = 10$ V, $I_{EE} = 2$mA and $\beta = 200$. Make sure that V_γ can be used to balance out the temperature variations of V_{BE}.

7.13 If the current source shown in Figure 7.5 has $R_1 = 20$ kΩ, $R_2 = 18$ kΩ, $V_{EE} = 15$ V, $R_E = 10$ kΩ, and $\beta = 200$, what is the value of I_{EE} for the circuit? What are the values of I_{C1} and I_{C2} if the differential amplifier is balanced? Assume that $V_{BE} = V_\gamma$.

7.14 For the circuit shown in Figure P7.4, determine R_{C1}, R_{C2}, I_{EE}, A_c, A_d, v_o, and the CMRR. Assume $V_{BE} = 0.7$ V and $\beta = 200$.

7.15 If the CE bypass capacitor is removed from the circuit in Problem 7.14, would A_c, A_d, and CMRR change? If so, by how much?

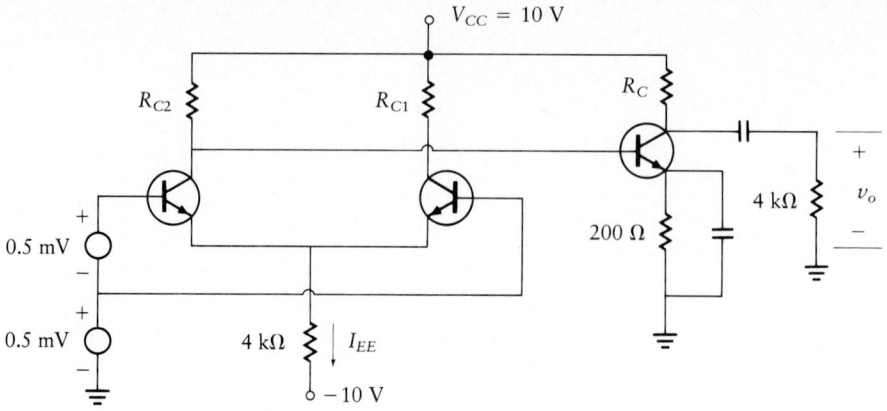

Figure P7.4

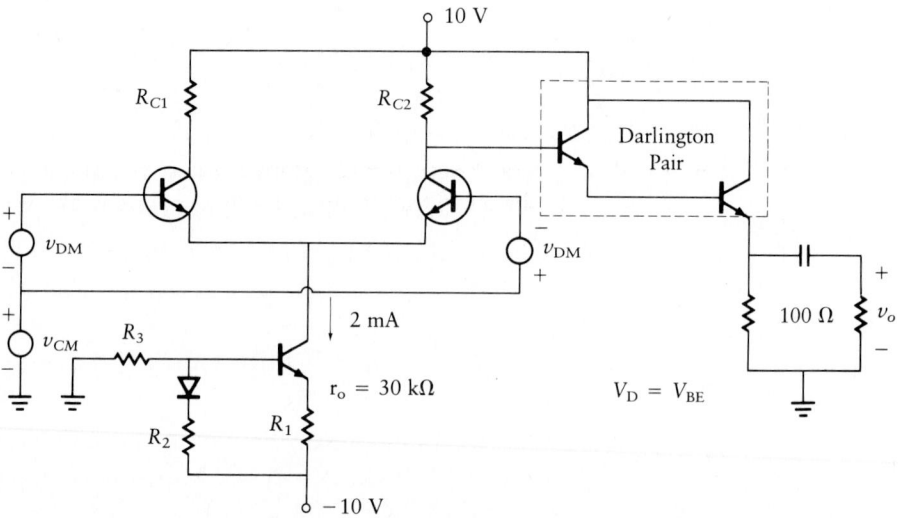

Figure P7.5

7.16 If R_{EE} in Problem 7.14 were replaced with a diode-compensated current source (where $r_o = 25$ kΩ and β $= 200$ for the transistor to be used), what is the new CMRR? Determine the values for R_1 and R_2.

7.17 For the amplifier shown in Figure P7.5, determine R_1, R_2, R_3, A_c, A_d, R_{C1}, R_{C2}, and CMRR when β $= 100$ and $V_{BE} = 0.7$ V for the single transistors and β $= 10,000$ and $V_{BE} = 1.4$ V for the Darlington pair.

7.18 Design a Widlar current source to provide $I_{C2} = 10$ μA. Assume $V_{CC} = 30$ V, $R_1 = 40$ kΩ, and $V_{BE} = 0.7$ V. Refer to Figure 7.8.

7.19 Design a Widlar current source to provide $I_{C2} = 100$ μA for a reference current of 1 mA. Assume that $V_{CC} = 20$ V and $V_{BE} = 0.7$ V. Refer to Figure 7.8.

7.20 The Widlar current source of Problem 7.19 is used as an active load. What is the equivalent resistance of the current source when used in this manner? Assume that 2N3903 transistors are employed (see Appendix D1).

7.21 For the Wilson current source of Figure 7.9, calculate the output resistance if $V_{CC} = 15$ V, $R = 12$ kΩ, $V_T = 26$ mV, $V_{BE} = 0.7$ V and $\beta = 100$. Assume that 2N3903 transistors are used in the 500-μA range (see Appendix D1).

7.22 In the circuit of Problem 7.21, what are the values of I_{REF} and I_{C2}?

7.23 What is the output of the level shifter of Figure 7.14 if $V_{BB} = 8$ V, $R_B = 5$ kΩ, $V_{CC} = 10$ V, the current source provides 4 mA, $R_E = 800$ Ω, $V_{BE} = 0.7$ V and $\beta = 100$?

7.24 Design a level shifter to attain a 4 V offset using the circuit of Figure 7.14(b). Assume that $R_B = 4$ kΩ, $V_{BB} = 8$ V, $V_{CC} = 12$ V, $V_{EE} = 12$ V, $\beta = 100$, and $V_{BE} = 0.7$ V. Use a current source that provides 6 mA.

7.25 A direct-coupled multistage amplifier has a CE amplifier for its last stage. The V_C for the CE amplifier is 6 V with an R_C of 5 kΩ. Design a level shifter to follow the CE amplifier and provide an ac output. The parameter values are $V_{CC} = 10$ V, $V_{EE} = 10$ V, $V_{BE} = 0.7$ V and $\beta = 100$. Design the current source to have a 5 mA output.

8

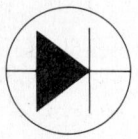

IDEAL OPERATIONAL AMPLIFIERS

8.0 Introduction

In Chapter 7, we introduced op-amps in the context of a study of the discrete circuits that make up an operational amplifier. The current chapter is the first of two devoted exclusively to a detailed study of the op-amps. We have discussed some overall aspects of op-amps, including packaging and specifications on data sheets. We now idealize this important IC and explore its use in design. The inverting amplifier and the noninverting amplifier are studied. A procedure is presented, which permits a general approach toward designing an amplifier that is configured to form a weighted sum of any number of input voltages. We then explore a variety of useful op-amp applications, including negative resistance circuits, integrators, and impedance converters.

In Chapter 9 we modify the ideal op-amp mathematical model of the current chapter by recognizing the changes required to the model to make it more closely coincide with the real op-amp.

8.1 Ideal Op-Amps

This section uses a *systems* approach to present the fundamentals of ideal op-amps [21]. As such, we consider the op-amp as a block with input and output

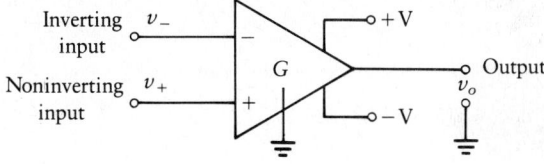

Figure 8.1   Symbol for ideal op-amp.

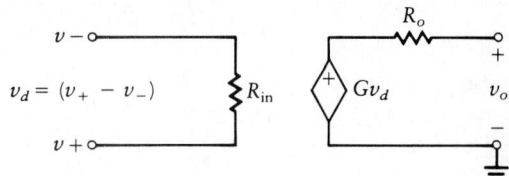

Figure 8.2   Equivalent circuit of op-amp.

terminals. We are not currently concerned with the electronic devices within the op-amp.

An op-amp is a high-gain direct-coupled amplifier, which is often powered by both a positive and a negative supply voltage. This allows the output voltage to swing both above and below ground. The op-amp finds wide application in many linear electronic systems.

The name *operational amplifier* is derived from one of the original uses of op-amp circuits; to perform mathematical operations in analog computers. Early op-amps used a single inverting input. A positive voltage change at the input caused a negative change at the output.

Figure 8.1 presents the symbol for the op-amp, and Figure 8.2 shows its equivalent circuit. The model contains a dependent voltage source, whose voltage depends upon the input voltage. The output impedance is represented in the figure as a resistance of value R_o. The amplifier is driven by two input voltages, v_+ and v_-. The two input terminals are known as the *noninverting* and *inverting* inputs, respectively. Ideally, the output of the amplifier depends not on the magnitudes of the two input voltages but upon the difference between them. We designate a new input voltage as this difference,

$$v_d = v_+ - v_-$$

where v_d is the *differential input voltage*. The input impedance of the op-amp is represented as a resistance in Figure 8.2. The output voltage is proportional to the input voltage, and we designate the ratio as the open loop gain, G. Thus, the output voltage is

$$v_o = G(v_+ - v_-) \tag{8.1}$$

As an example, an input of $E \sin \omega t$ (E is usually a small amplitude) applied to the inverting input with the noninverting terminal grounded, produces $-G(E \sin \omega t)$ at the output. When the same source signal is applied to the noninverting input, with the inverting terminal grounded, the output is $+G(E \sin \omega t)$.

The ideal operational amplifier is characterized as follows:

1. Input resistance, $R_{in} \to \infty$
2. Output resistance, $R_o = 0$
3. Open-loop voltage gain, $G \to \infty$
4. Bandwidth $\to \infty$
5. $v_o = 0$ when $v_+ = v_-$ (i.e., the common-mode gain is zero and the CMRR approaches infinity)

Let us explore the implication of the open-loop gain being infinite. If we rewrite equation (8.1) as

$$v_+ - v_- = \frac{v_o}{G}$$

and let G approach infinity, we see that

$$v_+ - v_- = 0$$

Hence, *the voltage between the two input terminals is zero,* or

$$v_+ = v_-$$

Since the input resistance, R_{in}, is infinite, *the current into each input, inverting and noninverting, is zero.*

Practical op-amps have high voltage gain (typically 10^5 at low frequency), but this gain varies with frequency. For this reason, an op-amp is not normally used in the form shown in Figure 8.1. This configuration is known as *open loop* because there is no feedback from output to input. We see later that the open-loop configuration is useful for *comparator* applications. The more common configuration for linear applications is the *closed-loop* circuit with *feedback*.

External elements are used to feed back a portion of the output signal to the input. If the feedback elements are placed between the output and the inverting input, the *closed-loop gain, or transfer ratio,* is decreased, since a portion of the output subtracts from the input. Feedback not only decreases the overall gain, but it also makes that gain less sensitive to the value of G. With feedback, the closed-loop gain depends upon the feedback circuit elements and not upon the basic op-amp voltage gain, G. Thus, the closed-loop gain is independent of the value of G and depends only upon values of the external circuit elements.

Figure 8.3 illustrates a single negative-feedback op-amp circuit. We analyze this circuit later. For now, note that a single resistor, R_F, is used to connect the output voltage, v_o, to the inverting input, v_-. Another resistor is connected from the inverting input, v_-, to the input voltage.

Figure 8.3
Op-amp circuit.

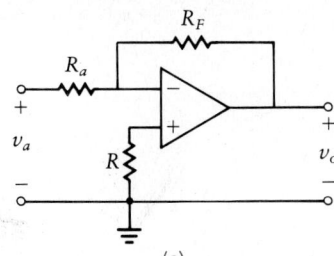

(a)

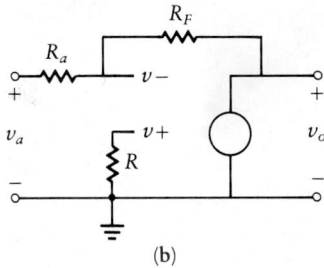

(b)

Circuits using op-amps, resistors, and capacitors can be configured to perform many useful operations, such as summing, subtracting, integrating, filtering, comparing, and amplifying.

8.1.1 Analysis Method

We use two important ideal op-amp properties:

1. The voltage between v_+ and v_- is zero, or $v_+ = v_-$.
2. The current into both the v_+ and v_- terminal is zero.

We develop a step-by-step procedure to analyze any ideal op-amp circuit as follows:

1. Write the Kirchhoff node equation at the noninverting terminal, v_+.
2. Write the Kirchhoff node equation at the inverting terminal, v_-.
3. Set $v_+ = v_-$ and solve for the desired closed-loop gains.

When performing the first two steps, remember that the current into both the v_+ and v_- terminal is zero.

8.2 The Inverting Amplifier

Figure 8.3(a) illustrates an inverting amplifier with feedback, and Figure 8.3(b) shows the equivalent-circuit form of this inverting amplifier. We wish to solve for the output voltage, v_o, in terms of the input voltage, v_a. Let us follow the step-by-step procedure of Section 8.1.1.

1. Kirchhoff's node equation at v_+ yields

$$v_+ = 0$$

2. Kirchhoff's node equation at v_- yields

$$\frac{v_a - v_-}{R_a} + \frac{v_o - v_-}{R_F} = 0$$

3. Setting $v_+ = v_-$ yields
$$v_+ = v_- = 0$$

We now solve for the closed-loop gain as

$$\frac{v_o}{v_a} = \frac{-R_F}{R_a}$$

Notice that the closed-loop gain, v_o/v_a, is dependent upon the ratio of two resistors, R_F/R_a, and is independent of the open-loop gain, G. This desirable result is caused by the use of feedback of a portion of the output voltage to subtract from the input voltage. The feedback from output to input through R_F serves to drive the differential voltage, $v_i = v_+ - v_-$, to zero. Since the noninverting input voltage, v_+, is zero, the feedback has the effect of driving v_- to zero. Hence, at the input of the op-amp,

$$v_+ = v_- = 0$$

and there is a *virtual ground* at v_-. The term *virtual* means that the voltage, v_-, is zero (ground potential), but no current actually flows into this short circuit since no current can flow into either the inverting or noninverting op-amp terminal.

No matter how complex the ideal op-amp circuit may be, by following this procedure the engineer can quickly begin to analyze (and soon design) op-amp systems.

We now expand this result to the case of multiple inputs. The amplifier shown in Figure 8.4(a) produces an output that is a negative summation of several input voltages. The node equation at v_+ yields $v_+ = 0$. The node equation at the inverting input is given by

$$\frac{v_- - v_o}{R_F} + \frac{v_- - v_a}{R_a} + \frac{v_- - v_b}{R_b} + \frac{v_- - v_c}{R_c} = 0$$

Since $v_+ = v_-$, then $v_+ = 0 = v_-$, and we solve for v_o in terms of the inputs as follows:

$$v_o = -R_F\left(\frac{v_a}{R_a} + \frac{v_b}{R_b} + \frac{v_c}{R_c}\right)$$

$$= -R_F \sum_{j=a}^{c} \left(\frac{v_j}{R_j}\right) \tag{8.2}$$

The extension to n inputs is obvious.

Figure 8.4
Op-amp circuit.

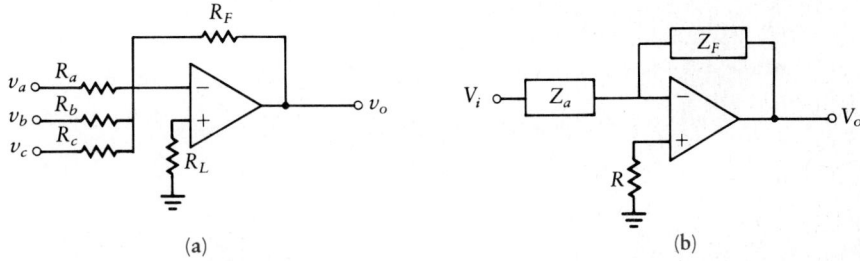

(a)   (b)

The relationship of equation (8.2) is easily extended to include nonresistive components if R_j is replaced by Z_j and R_F is replaced by Z_F. For a single input, as shown in Figure 8.4(b), the output reduces to

$$V_o = \frac{-Z_F V_i}{Z_A} \tag{8.3}$$

Since we are dealing in the ω-domain, we use uppercase letters for the voltages and currents, which represent the *complex amplitudes*.

One useful circuit based upon equation (8.3) is the *Miller integrator*. In this application, the feedback component is a capacitor, C, and the input component is a resistor, R, so

$$Z_F = \frac{1}{j\omega C}$$

and

$$Z_A = R$$

When we substitute these impedances into equation (8.3), we obtain

$$\frac{V_o}{V_i} = \frac{-1}{j\omega RC}$$

which has the form of an integral in the time domain:

$$v_o(t) = \left(\frac{-1}{RC}\right) \int_0^t v_i(\tau) \, d\tau$$

This is an *inverting integrator* because the expression contains a negative sign.

If the feedback element is a resistor and the input element is a capacitor, the input-output relationship becomes

$$\frac{V_o}{V_i} = -j\omega RC$$

and in the time domain, this becomes

$$v_o(t) = -RC\frac{dv_i}{dt}$$

The circuit is operating as an *inverting differentiator*.

Drill Problems

Using the step-by-step procedure of Section 8.1.1, determine v_o in terms of the input voltages for the following circuits. (The answers are shown on the figures.)

D8.1   Single inverting open loop

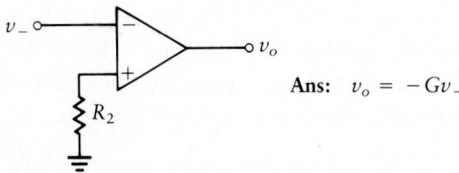

Ans: $v_o = -Gv_-$

Figure D8.1

D8.2   Open-loop voltage divider

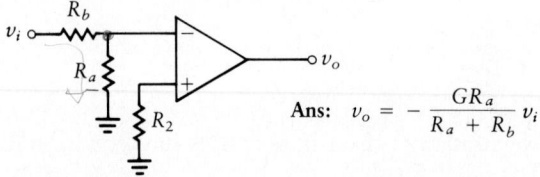

Ans: $v_o = -\dfrac{GR_a}{R_a + R_b}v_i$

Figure D8.2

D8.3   Inverter

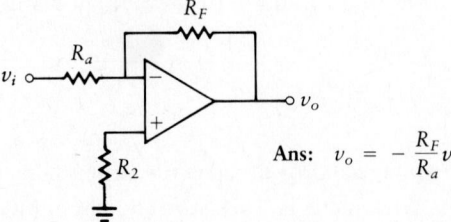

Ans: $v_o = -\dfrac{R_F}{R_a}v_i$

Figure D8.3

D8.4   Summing inverter

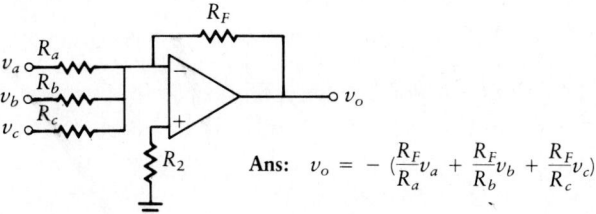

Ans: $v_o = -\left(\dfrac{R_F}{R_a}v_a + \dfrac{R_F}{R_b}v_b + \dfrac{R_F}{R_c}v_c\right)$

Figure D8.4

D8.5   Equal gain summing inverter

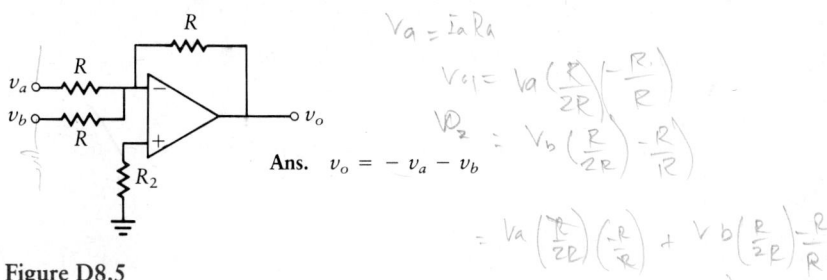

Ans. $v_o = -v_a - v_b$

$V_a = I_a R_a$

$V_{q1} = V_a\left(\dfrac{R}{2R}\right)\left(-\dfrac{R}{R}\right)$

$V_{q2} = V_b\left(\dfrac{R}{2R}\right) - \dfrac{R}{R}$

$= V_a\left(\dfrac{R}{2R}\right)\left(\dfrac{-R}{R}\right) + V_b\left(\dfrac{R}{2R}\right) - \dfrac{R}{R}$

$= \tfrac{1}{2} \times (-1) + \tfrac{1}{2}\left(-\dfrac{R}{R}\right)$

$= -\tfrac{1}{2} V_o + \tfrac{1}{2} V_{o1}$

Figure D8.5

D8.6   Dual inverted summer with gain

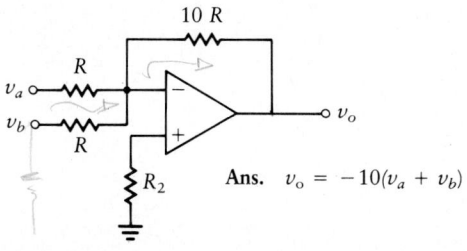

Ans. $v_o = -10(v_a + v_b)$

$V_+ = 0$

$\dfrac{V_a - 0}{R} = \dfrac{V_g}{R}$

$-10(V_a + 10)$

$=$

Figure D8.6

D8.7   Dual inverted weighted summer

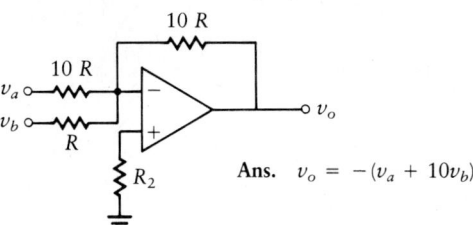

Ans. $v_o = -(v_a + 10v_b)$

Figure D8.7

8.3 The Noninverting Amplifier

The operational amplifier can be configured to produce either an inverted or noninverted output. In the previous section we analyzed the inverting amplifier, and in this section we repeat the analysis for the noninverting amplifier, which is shown in Figure 8.5. To analyze this circuit, we again follow the procedure of Section 8.1.1:

1. Write a node equation at the v_+ node to get

$$v_+ = v_i$$

2. Write a node equation at the v_- node to get

$$\frac{v_- - 0}{R_a} + \frac{v_- - v_o}{R_F} = 0$$

3. Set $v_+ = v_-$, and substitute for v_-, since

$$v_+ = v_i = v_-$$

Then

$$\frac{v_i}{R_a} + \frac{v_i - v_o}{R_F} = 0$$

Solving for the gain, we obtain

$$\frac{v_o}{v_i} = 1 + \frac{R_F}{R_a} \tag{8.4}$$

Figure 8.5 Noninverting amplifier.

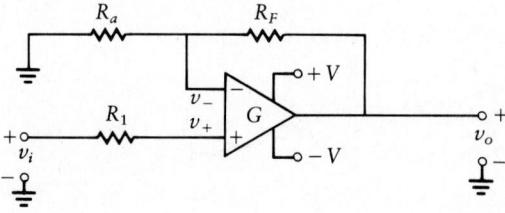

Drill Problems

Using the ideal op-amp approximations, determine v_o in terms of the input voltages for the following six circuits. (The answers are shown directly on the figures.)

D8.8   Noninverting amplifier

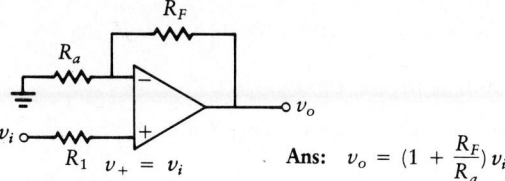

Ans: $v_o = (1 + \dfrac{R_F}{R_a}) v_i$

Figure D8.8

D8.9   Voltage follower

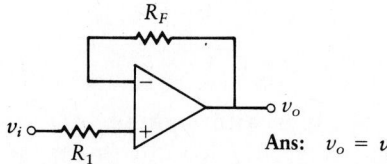

Ans: $v_o = v_i$

Figure D8.9

D8.10   Noninverting input with voltage divider

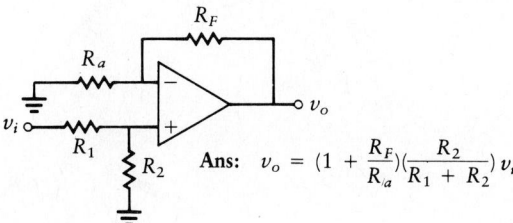

Ans: $v_o = (1 + \dfrac{R_F}{R_a})(\dfrac{R_2}{R_1 + R_2}) v_i$

Figure D8.10

D8.11   Less than unity gain

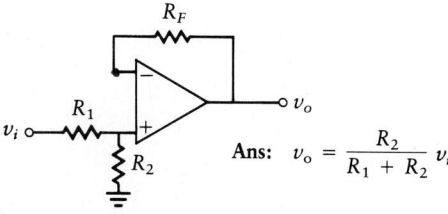

Ans: $v_o = \dfrac{R_2}{R_1 + R_2} v_i$

Figure D8.11

D8.12   Noninverting summer with gain

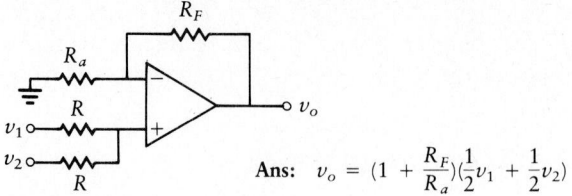

Ans: $v_o = (1 + \dfrac{R_F}{R_a})(\dfrac{1}{2}v_1 + \dfrac{1}{2}v_2)$

Figure D8.12

D8.13   Unity gain summer

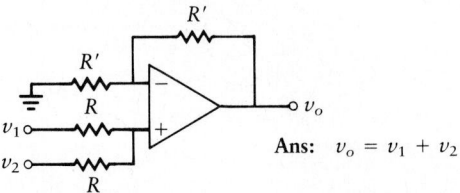

Ans: $v_o = v_1 + v_2$

Figure D8.13

We now analyze op-amps with multiple inputs. Figure 8.6 illustrates a circuit with two input voltages. These two inputs are applied to the noninverting input of the operational amplifier. The analysis of this circuit follows the procedure of Section 8.1.1. In order to find v_+, we apply KCL to the noninverting input terminal to yield (recall that the input current to the op-amp is zero)

$$\frac{v_1 - v_+}{R_1} + \frac{v_2 - v_+}{R_2} = 0$$

Solving for v_+, we obtain

$$v_+ = (R_1 \parallel R_2)\left(\frac{v_1}{R_1} + \frac{v_2}{R_2}\right)$$

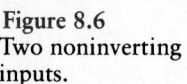

Figure 8.6
Two noninverting
inputs.

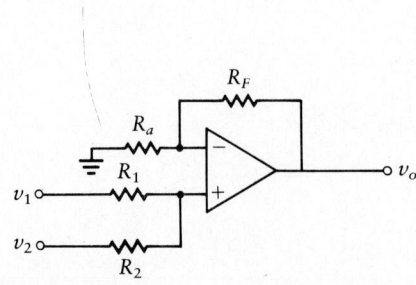

The inverting voltage, v_-, is found from the node equation at v_- with the result

$$v_- = \frac{R_a v_o}{R_a + R_F}$$

Setting v_+ equal to v_-, we obtain

$$v_o = (R_1 \parallel R_2)\left(\frac{v_1}{R_1} + \frac{v_2}{R_2}\right)\frac{R_a + R_F}{R_a} \tag{8.5}$$

Drill Problems

Determine v_o in terms of the input voltages for the following circuits. (The answers are shown directly on the figures.)

D8.14   Sum of two inputs

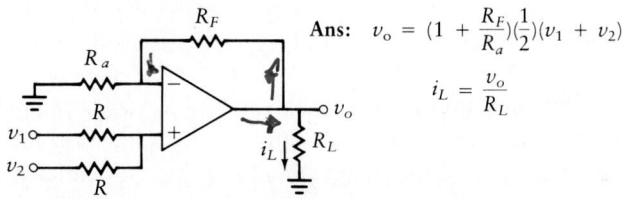

Ans: $v_o = (1 + \frac{R_F}{R_a})(\frac{1}{2})(v_1 + v_2);$

$$i_L = \frac{v_o}{R_L}$$

Figure D8.14

D8.15   Weighted sum of two inputs

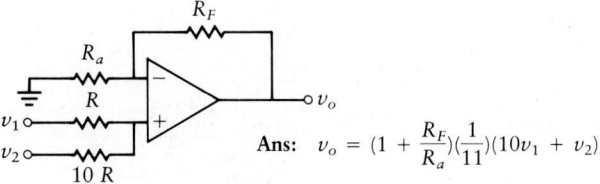

Ans: $v_o = (1 + \frac{R_F}{R_a})(\frac{1}{11})(10v_1 + v_2)$

Figure D8.15

D8.16   Sum of three inputs

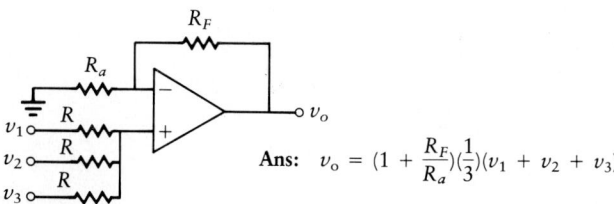

Ans: $v_o = (1 + \frac{R_F}{R_a})(\frac{1}{3})(v_1 + v_2 + v_3)$

Figure D8.16

D8.17   Voltage divider weighted sum of two inputs

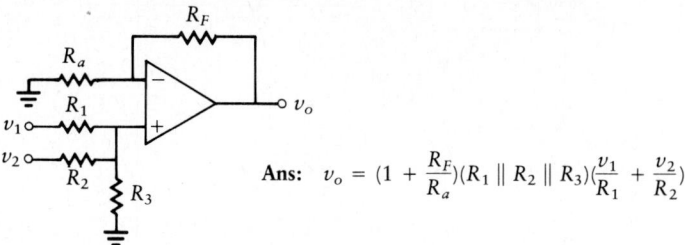

Ans: $v_o = (1 + \dfrac{R_F}{R_a})(R_1 \parallel R_2 \parallel R_3)(\dfrac{v_1}{R_1} + \dfrac{v_2}{R_2})$

Figure D8.17

8.4   Input Resistance of Op-Amp Circuit with Feedback

The input resistance of the ideal op-amp is infinite. The input resistance to a circuit composed of an ideal op-amp with external components is no longer infinite. We find the input resistance of the op-amp with feedback. The equivalent circuit for a noninverting op-amp is shown in Figure 8.7(a). Figure 8.7(b) shows the same circuit rearranged for simplicity of analysis. We have attached a voltage source to the input in order to calculate the equivalent resistance. Since the circuit contains a dependent-voltage source, we find the resistance by assuming a voltage and taking the ratio of that voltage to the resulting current. The loop equation is given by

$$R_F i = v - G v_i$$

but since

$$v_i = -v$$

then

$$R_F i = (1 + G)v$$

and

$$R_{in} = \frac{v}{i} = \frac{R_F}{1 + G} = 0 \tag{8.6}$$

The input resistance is zero, since the gain, G, approaches infinity.

If G is assumed to be large but finite, the input resistance is small and is proportional to R_F. Note that the input voltage is normally applied through a

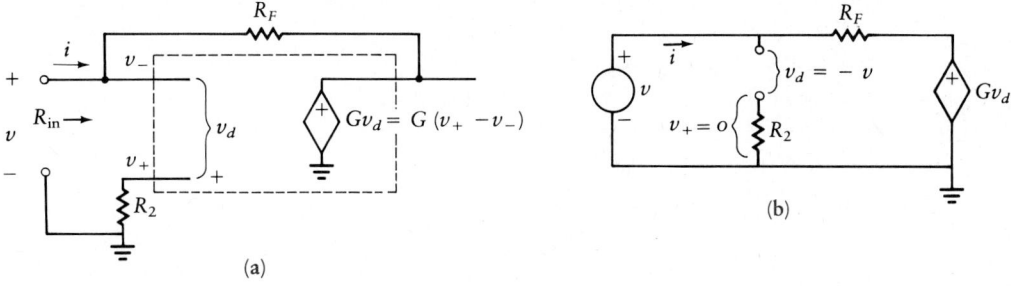

Figure 8.7 Input resistance, feedback amplifier.

Figure 8.8
Input resistance—summing inputs.

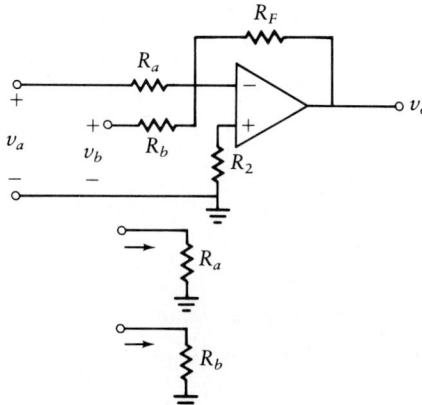

series resistor, which would be external to the circuit of Figure 8.7(a). Thus, the input resistance seen by the source is equal to the value of this external resistance.

Figure 8.8 shows an inverting amplifier with two inputs, each of which is applied through a corresponding input resistance. This is a special case of the circuit of Figure 8.4. Since the voltage at the inverting input to the op-amp is zero (virtual ground), the input resistance seen by v_a is R_a and that seen by v_b is R_b. The grounded inverting input also serves to isolate the two inputs from each other. That is, a variation in v_a does not affect the input v_b, and vice versa. The term *virtual ground* is used in this situation, since the v_- terminal is virtually grounded for ac signals.

8.5   Combined Inverting and Noninverting Inputs

The most general case of input configuration is a combination of the previous two sections. That is, we allow for both inverting and noninverting inputs. The general configuration is shown in Figure 8.9. The previous circuits can be

Figure 8.9
Inverting and noninverting inputs.

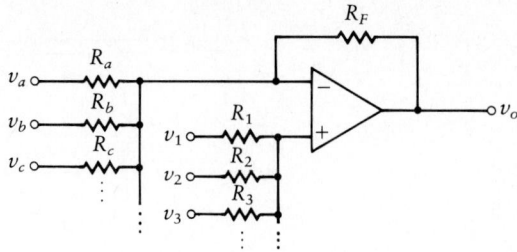

considered as special cases of this general problem. The output relationship is found by applying superposition as follows. (The following expression is derived by combining equation (8.2) with equation (8.3). The student should not just accept the result but should perform the simple derivation.)

$$v_o = \left[1 + \frac{R_F}{R_a \parallel R_b \parallel R_c \parallel \ldots} \right] (R_1 \parallel R_2 \parallel R_3 \parallel \ldots)$$

$$\times \left[\frac{v_1}{R_1} + \frac{v_2}{R_2} + \frac{v_3}{R_3} + \ldots \right] - \left[\frac{R_F}{R_a} v_a + \frac{R_F}{R_b} v_b + \frac{R_F}{R_c} v_c + \ldots \right] \quad (8.7)$$

Equation (8.7) represents a general result that will prove useful in analyzing a wide variety of circuits.

Drill Problems

Determine v_o in terms of all input voltages for the following configurations. The answers are shown directly on the figures.

D8.18   Positive and negative gain configuration

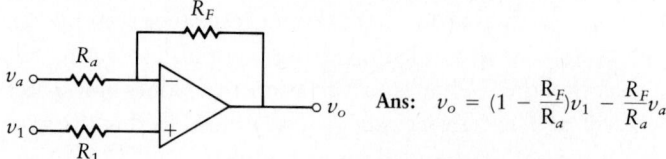

$\text{Ans:} \quad v_o = (1 - \frac{R_F}{R_a})v_1 - \frac{R_F}{R_a}v_a$

Figure D8.18

D8.19   Differencing amplifier

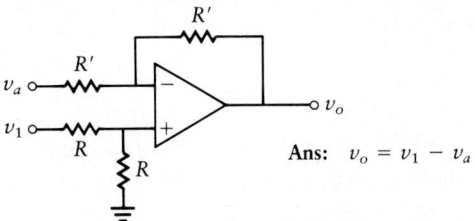

Figure D8.19

Ans: $v_o = v_1 - v_a$

D8.20 Weighted differencing amplifier

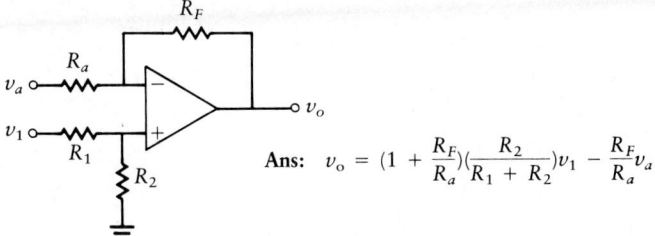

Ans: $v_o = (1 + \dfrac{R_F}{R_a})(\dfrac{R_2}{R_1 + R_2})v_1 - \dfrac{R_F}{R_a}v_a$

Figure D8.20

D8.21 Differencing amplifier with gain

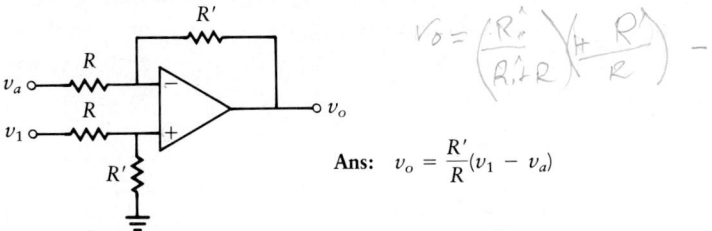

$V_0 = \left(\dfrac{R'}{R_1 + R}\right)\left(1 + \dfrac{R'}{R}\right) -$

Ans: $v_o = \dfrac{R'}{R}(v_1 - v_a)$

Figure D8.21

D8.22 Sign switcher

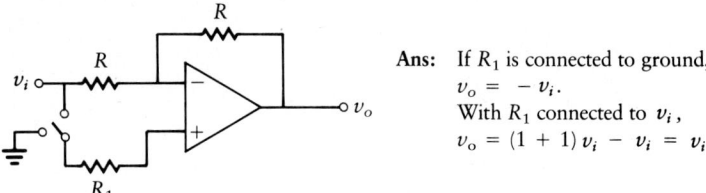

Ans: If R_1 is connected to ground,
$v_o = -v_i$.
With R_1 connected to v_i,
$v_o = (1 + 1)v_i - v_i = v_i$.

Figure D8.22

8.6   Design of Op-Amp Circuits

Given the configuration of an op-amp system, we *analyze* that system to determine the output in terms of the inputs using the procedure of Section 8.1.1.

If you wish to *design* a circuit that combines both inverting and noninverting inputs, the problem is more complex. We present a practical design technique in this section.* This technique allows us to design an op-amp summing circuit without elaborate solution of simultaneous equations.

In a design problem, a desired linear equation is given, and the op-amp circuit must be designed. The desired output of the op-amp summer can be expressed as a linear combination of inputs,

$$v_o = X_1 v_1 + \cdots + X_n v_n - Y_a v_a - \cdots - Y_m v_m \tag{8.8}$$

where $X_1, X_2, \ldots, X_n$ are the desired gains at the noninverting inputs and $Y_a, Y_b, \ldots, Y_m$ are the desired gains at the inverting inputs.

Equation (8.8) is easily implemented with the circuit of Figure 8.10. Equation (8.8) shows that the values of the resistors $R_a, R_b, \ldots, R_m$ and $R_1, R_2, \ldots, R_n$ are inversely proportional to the desired gains associated with the respective input voltages. In other words, if a large gain is desired at a particular input terminal, then the resistance at that terminal is small.

When the open-loop gain of the operational amplifier, G, is large, the output voltage may be written in terms of the resistors connected to the operational amplifier (see equation (8.7)).

$$v_o = \left[1 + \frac{R_F}{R_A} \right] (R_1 \parallel R_2 \parallel \cdots \parallel R_n \parallel R_x) \left[\frac{v_1}{R_1} + \frac{v_2}{R_2} + \cdots + \frac{v_n}{R_n} \right]$$
$$- R_F \left[\frac{v_a}{R_a} + \frac{v_b}{R_b} + \cdots + \frac{v_m}{R_m} \right] \tag{8.9}$$

where

$$R_A = R_a \parallel R_b \parallel \cdots \parallel R_m \parallel R_y \tag{8.10}$$

Let us define

$$R_{eq} = \left(1 + \frac{R_F}{R_A} \right) (R_1 \parallel R_2 \parallel \cdots \parallel R_n \parallel R_x) \tag{8.11}$$

---

*This technique was devised by Phil Vrbancic, a student at California State University, Long Beach, and was presented in a paper submitted to the *IEEE Region VI 1982 Prize Paper Contest*.

Figure 8.10
Multiple-input
summer.

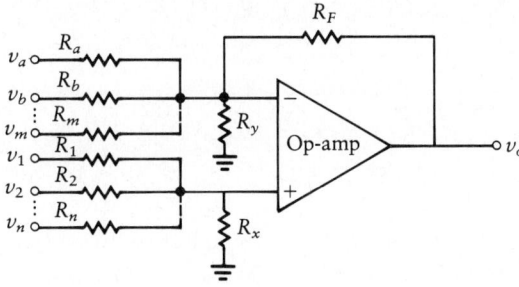

We see that the output voltage is a linear combination of inputs, where each input is divided by its associated resistance and multiplied by another resistance. The multiplying resistance is R_F for inverting inputs and R_{eq} for noninverting inputs.

The Thevenin resistance looking back from the inverting input is usually made equal to that looking back from the noninverting input. We find in Section 9.1 that this constraint minimizes the *dc bias current offset*. For the configuration shown in Figure 8.10, this constraint may be expressed as follows:

$$R_1 \parallel R_2 \parallel \cdots \parallel R_n \parallel R_x = R_a \parallel R_b \parallel \cdots \parallel R_m \parallel R_y \parallel R_F \qquad (8.12)$$

Substituting equations (8.10) and (8.11) into equation (8.12) yields

$$\frac{R_{eq}}{1 + R_F/R_A} = R_A \parallel R_F \qquad (8.13)$$

from which we obtain,

$$R_{eq} = R_F \qquad (8.14)$$

By comparing like terms in equations (8.8) and (8.9), we obtain the noninverting and inverting gains as follows:

$$X_i = \frac{R_{eq}}{R_i} = \frac{R_F}{R_i} \qquad (8.15)$$

and

$$Y_j = \frac{R_F}{R_j} \qquad (8.16)$$

The bias-offset relationship, equation (8.12), may be rewritten as follows:

$$\frac{1}{1/R_x + \sum_{i=1}^{n} 1/R_i} = \frac{1}{1/R_F + 1/R_y + \sum_{j=a}^{m} 1/R_j} \tag{8.17}$$

or

$$\frac{1}{R_x} + \sum_{i=1}^{n} \frac{1}{R_i} = \frac{1}{R_F} + \frac{1}{R_y} + \sum_{j=a}^{m} \frac{1}{R_j} \tag{8.18}$$

Substituting equations (8.15) and (8.16) into equation (8.18), we obtain

$$\frac{1}{R_x} + \sum_{i=1}^{n} \frac{X_i}{R_F} = \frac{1}{R_F} + \frac{1}{R_y} + \sum_{j=a}^{m} \frac{Y_j}{R_F}$$

$$\frac{1}{R_x} + \frac{1}{R_F} \sum_{i=1}^{n} X_i = \frac{1}{R_F} + \frac{1}{R_y} + \frac{1}{R_F} \sum_{j=a}^{m} Y_j \tag{8.19}$$

Recall that our goal is to solve for the Rs in terms of the X_i and Y_j. Let us define

$$X = \sum_{i=1}^{n} X_i \tag{8.20}$$

and

$$Y = \sum_{j=a}^{m} Y_j$$

We can then rewrite equation (8.19) as follows:

$$\frac{1}{R_x} + \frac{1}{R_F} X = \frac{1}{R_F} + \frac{1}{R_y} + \frac{1}{R_F} Y \tag{8.21}$$

This is a starting point for our step-by-step design procedure. Recall that R_x and R_y are the resistors between ground and the noninverting and inverting inputs, respectively. The feedback resistor is denoted by R_F.

We can eliminate either or both of the resistors R_x and R_y from the circuit of Figure 8.10. That is, either or both of these resistors can be set to infinity (i.e., open-circuited). This yields three design possibilities, which we denote by Case I, Case II, and Case III. Depending upon the desired multiplying factors relating output to input, one of these cases will yield the appropriate design. The following results are summarized in Table 8.1.

Case I   If $R_x \to \infty$, equation (8.21) becomes

$$\frac{X}{R_F} = \frac{1}{R_F} + \frac{1}{R_y} + \frac{Y}{R_F} \tag{8.22}$$

When we choose an R_F, R_y is the only unknown in this equation. Solving for this, we obtain

$$\frac{1}{R_y} = \frac{X}{R_F} - \frac{Y}{R_F} - \frac{1}{R_F}$$

$$= \frac{(X - Y - 1)}{R_F} \tag{8.23}$$

Let us now define

$$Z = X - Y - 1$$

Then equation (8.23) becomes

$$\frac{1}{R_y} = \frac{Z}{R_F}$$

Z must be positive in order for R_y to be physically realizable. If Z is negative, Case I does not apply.

Equations (8.15) and (8.16) yield the resistance values

$$R_i = \frac{R_F}{X_i}; \qquad R_j = \frac{R_F}{Y_j} \tag{8.24}$$

Case II   When $R_y \to \infty$, equation (8.21) becomes

$$\frac{1}{R_x} + \frac{X}{R_F} = \frac{1}{R_F} + \frac{Y}{R_F} \tag{8.25}$$

and

$$\frac{1}{R_x} = \frac{-(X - Y - 1)}{R_F} = \frac{-Z}{R_F} \tag{8.26}$$

Hence, Z must be negative.

Case III   When $R_x \to \infty$ and $R_y \to \infty$, equation (8.21) becomes

Table 8.1   Summary of Summing Amplifier Design

Z	R_y	R_x	R_i	R_j
>0	$\dfrac{R_F}{Z}$	∞		
<0	∞	$\dfrac{R_F}{-Z}$	$\dfrac{R_F}{X_i}$	$\dfrac{R_F}{Y_j}$
0	∞	∞		

$$\frac{X}{R_F} = \frac{1}{R_F} + \frac{Y}{R_F} \tag{8.27}$$

and

$$0 = \frac{X - Y - 1}{R_F} = \frac{Z}{R_F} \tag{8.28}$$

Therefore, $Z = 0$.

The results of all three cases are combined in Table 8.1. Note that $Z = X - Y - 1$, where

$$X = \sum_{i=1}^{n} X_i$$

$$Y = \sum_{j=a}^{m} Y_j$$

Example 8.1   **Op-Amp Summer (Design)**

Design an op-amp summer to yield the following input/output relationship:

$$v_o = 10v_1 + 6v_2 + 4v_3 - 5v_a - 2v_b$$

SOLUTION   The values of X, Y, and Z are calculated as follows:

$$X = \sum_{i=1}^{3} X_i = 10 + 6 + 4 = 20$$

Figure 8.11
Amplifier for Example 8.1.

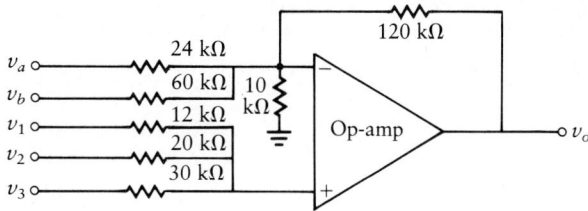

$$Y = \sum_{j=a}^{b} Y_j = 5 + 2 = 7$$

$$Z = X - Y - 1 = 20 - 7 - 1 = 12$$

In this example, Z is greater than zero, so we are dealing with Case I, where R_x is open-circuited. A suitable value of R_F must first be chosen. Once R_F is determined, all other resistor values are easily found. Suppose we want the minimum resistance, R_{min}, at any of the inputs to be 10 kΩ. Then the multiplying factor, K, would be the largest of any X_i, Y_j, or Z. Thus, $K = 12$ and $R_F = 10 \text{ k}\Omega \times 12 = 120 \text{ k}\Omega$. We do not want to choose too small a value, or the circuit will load previous circuitry. We also do not use an exceptionally large value for R_F, since this would increase the noise generated in that resistor. As a guide, all resistors used in the op-amp circuit should be between 1 kΩ and 1 MΩ. Having determined R_F, the resistors are found from equation (8.24) as follows:

$$R_1 = \frac{R_F}{X_1} = \frac{120 \text{ k}\Omega}{10} = 12 \text{ k}\Omega$$

$$R_2 = \frac{R_F}{X_2} = \frac{120 \text{ k}\Omega}{6} = 20 \text{ k}\Omega$$

$$R_3 = \frac{R_F}{X_3} = \frac{120 \text{ k}\Omega}{4} = 30 \text{ k}\Omega$$

$$R_a = \frac{R_F}{Y_a} = \frac{120 \text{ k}\Omega}{5} = 24 \text{ k}\Omega$$

$$R_b = \frac{R_F}{Y_b} = \frac{120 \text{ k}\Omega}{2} = 60 \text{ k}\Omega$$

$$R_y = \frac{R_F}{Z} = \frac{120 \text{ k}\Omega}{12} = 10 \text{ k}\Omega$$

The resulting amplifier is shown in Figure 8.11.

Example 8.2   Op-Amp Summer (Design)

Design an op-amp circuit to implement the following equation:

$$v_o = 4v_1 + v_2 - 8v_a - 6v_b$$

SOLUTION   We first calculate the values of X, Y, and Z.

$$X = 4 + 1 = 5$$
$$Y = 8 + 6 = 14$$
$$Z = 5 - 14 - 1 = -10$$

Since Z is less than zero, R_y is open circuit and we are dealing with an example of Case II. Suppose in this case, we want the equivalent resistance at the + and − terminal to be 10 kΩ. Then the multiplying factor would be the largest of X or $Y + 1$. This would make $K = 15$ and $R_F = 15 \times 10k = 150$ kΩ.

$$R_x = \frac{R_F}{Z} = \frac{150 \text{ k}\Omega}{10} = 15 \text{ k}\Omega$$

$$R_a = \frac{R_F}{Y_a} = \frac{150 \text{ k}\Omega}{8} = 18.75 \text{ k}\Omega$$

$$R_b = \frac{R_F}{Y_b} = \frac{150 \text{ k}\Omega}{6} = 25 \text{ k}\Omega$$

$$R_1 = \frac{R_F}{X_1} = \frac{150 \text{ k}\Omega}{4} = 37.5 \text{ k}\Omega$$

$$R_2 = \frac{R_F}{X_2} = \frac{150 \text{ k}\Omega}{1} = 150 \text{ k}\Omega$$

The complete circuit is shown in Figure 8.12. Note that at each input terminal, the equivalent resistance is 10 kΩ or calculated as follows:

$$37.5 \text{ k}\Omega \parallel 150 \text{ k}\Omega \parallel 15 \text{ k}\Omega = 25 \text{ k}\Omega \parallel 18.75 \text{ k}\Omega \parallel 150 \text{ k}\Omega = 10 \text{ k}\Omega$$

Figure 8.12
Amplifier for Example 8.2.

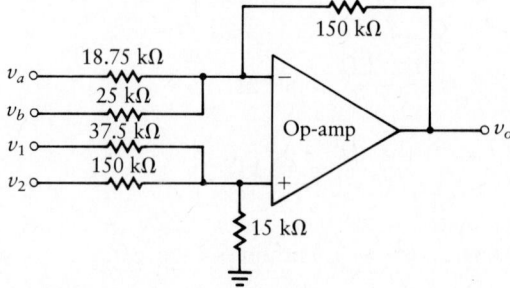

Recall that the derivation forced these to be equal to minimize the dc bias-current offset. Note also that if we are not happy with the resulting resistor values, they can all be multiplied by the same constant without changing the voltage relationships. ➤

8.7 Other Op-Amp Applications

We have seen that the op-amp can be used as an amplifier, differentiator, or integrator and to combine a number of inputs in a linear manner. In this section, we investigate some additional important applications of this versatile IC.

8.7.1 *Negative Impedance Circuit*

The circuit shown in Figure 8.13 produces a negative input resistance (impedance in the general case). This can be used to cancel an unwanted positive resistance and thus produce an oscillator. The input resistance, R_{in}, is defined as

$$R_{in} = \frac{v}{i}$$

The op-amp inputs are given by

$$v_+ = v_- = v$$

As before, a voltage-divider relationship is used to derive the following expression:

$$v_- = v = \frac{R_A v_o}{R_A + R_F}$$

Solving for v_o in terms of v yields

$$v_o = v\left(1 + \frac{R_F}{R_A}\right)$$

Since the input impedance to the v_+ terminal is infinite, the current in R is equal to i and can be found as follows:

$$i = \frac{v - v_o}{R} = \frac{v - v(1 + R_F/R_A)}{R} = \frac{-R_F v}{R_A R}$$

Figure 8.13
Negative impedance
circuit.

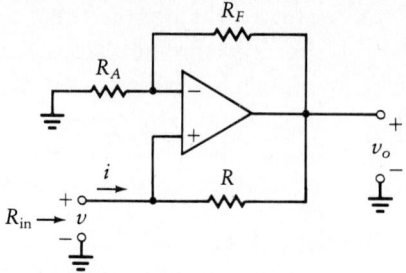

The input resistance, R_{in}, is given by

$$R_{\text{in}} = \frac{v}{i} = \frac{-R_A R}{R_F} \tag{8.29}$$

Equation (8.29) shows that the circuit of Figure 8.13 develops a negative resistance. If R is replaced by an impedance, Z, the circuit develops a negative impedance.

8.7.2   *Dependent-Current Generator*

With a slight modification of the negative impedance circuit, we can design a dependent-current generator, which produces a load current proportional to an applied voltage, v_i, and is independent of the load resistance. The circuit is shown in Figure 8.14(a). Suppose we let $R_1 = R_2$. Equation (8.29) then indicates that the input resistance to the op-amp circuit (enclosed in the dashed box) is $-R$. The input circuit can then be simplified as shown in Figure 8.14(b). We wish to calculate i_L, the current in R_L. Although the resistance is negative, the normal Kirchhoff's laws still apply, since nothing in their derivation assumed positive resistors. The input current, i_{in}, is then found by combining the resistances into a single resistor, R_{in}:

$$i_{in} = \frac{v_i}{R_{\text{in}}} = \frac{v_i}{R - RR_L/(R_L - R)} = \frac{v_i(R_L - R)}{R_L R - R^2 - RR_L} = \frac{v_i\,(R_L - R)}{-R^2}$$

We then apply a current-divider ratio to the current split between R_L and $-R$ to get

$$i_L = \frac{-iR}{R_L - R} = \frac{-v_i(R_L - R)}{R^2}\,\frac{-R}{R_L - R}$$

$$= \frac{v_i}{R} \tag{8.30}$$

Figure 8.14
Dependent-current
generator.

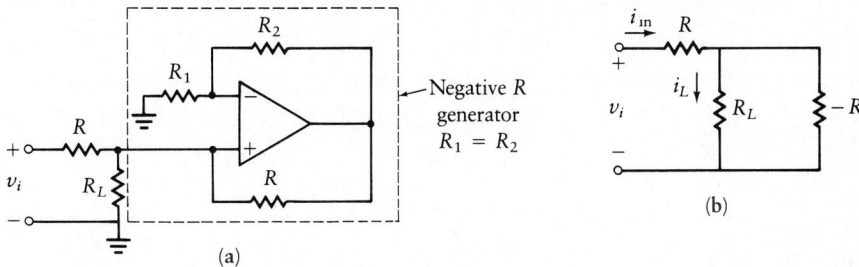

(a)

(b)

Thus the effect of the addition of the op-amp circuit is to make the current in the load proportional to the input voltage. It does not depend upon the value of the load resistance, R_L. The current is therefore independent of changes in the load resistance. The op-amp circuit effectively cancels out the load resistance. Since the current is independent of the load but depends only upon the input voltage, we call this a *current generator* (or voltage-to-current convertor).

8.7.3   *Noninverting Miller Integrator*

We use a modification of the dependent-current generator of the previous section to develop a noninverting integrator. The circuit is configured as shown in Figure 8.15. This is similar to the circuit of Figure 8.14, but the load resistance has been replaced by a capacitance. The current, I_L, is found from equation (8.30) as

$$I_L = \frac{V_i}{R}$$

The output voltage, V_o, is found from the voltage division between V_o and V_- as follows:

$$V_- = \frac{R_1 V_o}{R_1 + R_1} = \frac{V_o}{2}$$

Figure 8.15
Noninverting
integrator.

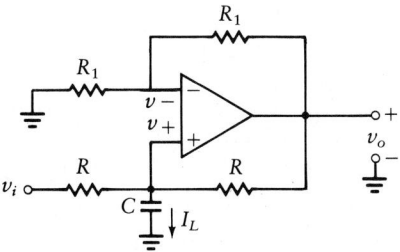

Since

$$V_+ = \frac{I_L}{j\omega C} = \frac{V_i}{j\omega RC} = V_-$$

then

$$\frac{V_o}{V_i} = \frac{2}{j\omega RC}$$

Thus, in the time domain we have

$$v_o(t) = \frac{2}{RC} \int_o^t v_i(\tau) \, d\tau$$

The circuit is therefore a noninverting integrator.

8.7.4   *Impedance Converter*

An extension of the negative resistance circuit of Figure 8.13 is shown in Figure 8.16, where the circuit uses impedances, Z_i, rather than resistances, R_i. We wish to calculate the input impedance, Z_{in}. The two op-amps are considered to be ideal, so that in each amplifier, $V_+ = V_-$. Because of this,

$$V_i = V_2 = V_4$$

The current through Z_4 and Z_5 is given by

$$I_5 = \frac{V_4}{Z_5} = \frac{V_i}{Z_5}$$

The voltage, V_3, is

$$V_3 = V_4 + I_5 Z_4 = V_i + \frac{Z_4 V_i}{Z_5} = V_i\left(1 + \frac{Z_4}{Z_5}\right)$$

The current in Z_3 is

$$I_3 = \frac{V_3 - V_2}{Z_3} = \frac{V_i(1 + Z_4/Z_5) - V_i}{Z_3} = \frac{V_i Z_4}{Z_3 Z_5}$$

The voltage, V_1, is given by

Figure 8.16
Impedance converter.

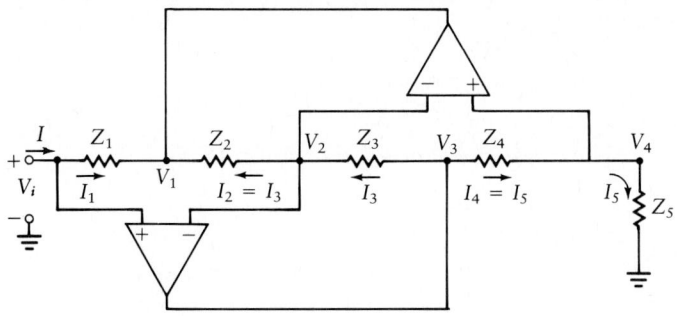

$$V_1 = V_2 - I_3 Z_2 = V_i - \frac{V_i Z_4 Z_2}{Z_3 Z_5}$$

The current is

$$I_1 = \frac{V_i - V_1}{Z_1} = \frac{V_i Z_2 Z_4}{Z_1 Z_3 Z_5}$$

Finally, the input impedance is given by

$$Z_{\text{in}} = \frac{V_i}{I_{\text{in}}} = \frac{V_i}{I_1} = \frac{Z_1 Z_3 Z_5}{Z_2 Z_4} \tag{8.31}$$

This is a valuable circuit, since, with proper selection of the five impedances, a wide variety of Z_{in} functions can be obtained.

Example 8.3   **Active Inductor (Design)**

Design an active circuit inductor without using any inductance elements.

SOLUTION   We use the circuit of Figure 8.16. Equation (8.31) is the key to designing the active inductor. We see that if either Z_2 or Z_4 is a capacitor and all other impedances are resistors, we have a total impedance function that represents an inductor. Thus, we let

$$Z_1 = R_1$$
$$Z_2 = R_2$$
$$Z_3 = R_3$$

$$Z_4 = \frac{1}{j\omega C}$$

$$Z_5 = R_5$$

The total impedance is then given by

$$Z_{\text{in}} = \frac{j\omega C R_1 R_3 R_5}{R_2} \tag{8.32}$$

Hence we have designed an active inductor using no inductive elements. The effective inductance is given by

$$L = \frac{R_1 R_3 R_5 C}{R_2} \qquad \blacktriangleright \text{(8.33)}$$

8.7.5   Op-Amps and Diodes

Numerous examples exist for using op-amps with diodes. We consider a wide range of these circuits in Chapter 12 and present several simple examples in this section.

Consider the ideal op-amp circuit shown in Figure 8.17 with

$$v_i = V \sin \omega t$$

The diode is conducting when v_+ attempts to go negative and nonconducting when v_+ is positive. When v_+ attempts to go negative, the diode short circuits and

$$v_+ = 0$$

The inverting input voltage is found using the following voltage divider relationship,

$$v_- = \frac{R_a v_o}{R_a + R_F}$$

Since $v_+ = v_- = 0$, we see that v_o must also equal zero.

When v_+ goes positive, the diode is open-circuited, and a voltage-divider relationship yields

$$v_+ = \frac{R_x v_i}{R_1 + R_x}$$

As before, the inverting voltage input is given by

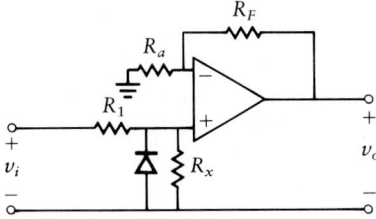

Figure 8.17 Half-wave rectifier circuit.

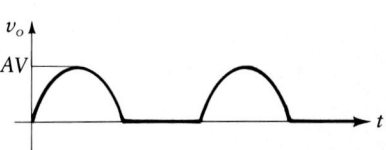

Figure 8.18 Output of half-wave rectifier.

$$v_- = \frac{R_a v_o}{R_a + R_F}$$

Since v_+ is equal to v_-, we can equate these two expressions to get

$$v_o = \frac{(1 + R_F/R_a)R_x v_i}{R_1 + R_x}$$

$$= v_i \frac{1 + R_F/R_a}{1 + R_1/R_x}$$

$$= A v_i$$

where

$$A = \frac{1 + R_F/R_a}{1 + R_1/R_x}$$

The output waveform is plotted as Figure 8.18 for $v_i = V \sin \omega t$. This shows that the circuit is operating as a half-wave rectifier.

As another example of the use of diodes with op-amps, consider the *electronic thermometer* shown in Figure 8.19. Recall from equation (1.2) that the voltage across a diode varies with temperature according to the expression

$$\Delta V_\gamma = -2(T_2 - T_1) \text{ mV}$$

At room temperature ($T_1 = 25°C$), the voltage across the diode is 700 mV. The diode voltage decreases as the temperature increases. For example, at $T_2 = 125°C$, the decrease in diode voltage is

$$\Delta V_\gamma = -2(125 - 25) \times 10^{-3} = -200 \text{ mV}$$

As a result, the diode voltage drops to 500 mV. This voltage variation can be used as the basis for an inexpensive thermometer. We choose the resistance R

Figure 8.19
Electronic
thermometer.

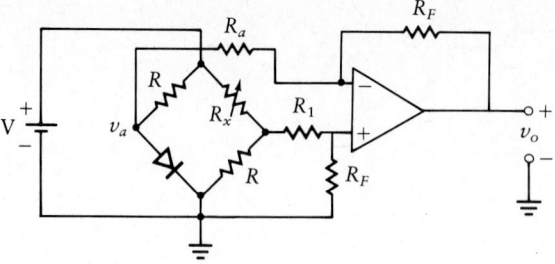

so the diode is conducting and the diode voltage, which is the v_a input to the op-amp, is

$$v_a = V_\gamma = 700 \text{ mV} - 2(T_2 - 25°C) \text{ mV}$$
$$= (750 - 2T_2) \text{ mV} \qquad (8.34)$$

The bias voltage, which is the v_1 input to the op-amp, is

$$v_1 = -10^4 \frac{R}{R + R_x} \text{ mV} \qquad (8.35)$$

If we let $V = 10$ V, the op-amp output voltage is

$$v_o = -\frac{R_F}{R_a} v_a - \frac{R_F}{R_b} v_b + \left[\frac{R_F}{R_1 + R_F} \frac{R_F}{R_a \| R_F} \right] v_1 \qquad (8.36)$$

If we let $R_a = R_1$ and substitute equations (8.34) and (8.35) into equation (8.36), we obtain

$$v_o = -\frac{R_F}{R_a} (750 - 2T_2) + \frac{R_F}{R_b} 10^4 \frac{R}{R + R_x}$$
$$= \frac{R_F}{R_1} \left[\frac{R}{R + R_x} - 750 + 2T_2 \right] \text{ mV}$$

We wish to cancel the dc components, so we let

$$750 = 10^4 \frac{R}{R + R_x} \qquad (8.37)$$

and we obtain

$$v_o = \frac{2R_F T_2}{R_1} \text{ mV} \qquad (8.38)$$

Proper selection of resistors yields the desired output voltages shown in equation (8.38). The design details are left for Problem 8.29.

PROBLEMS

In Problems **8.1–8.10**, find the output voltage, v_o, in terms of the input voltage for each of the circuits shown.

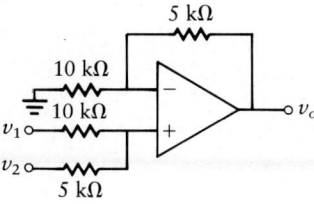

Figure P8.1

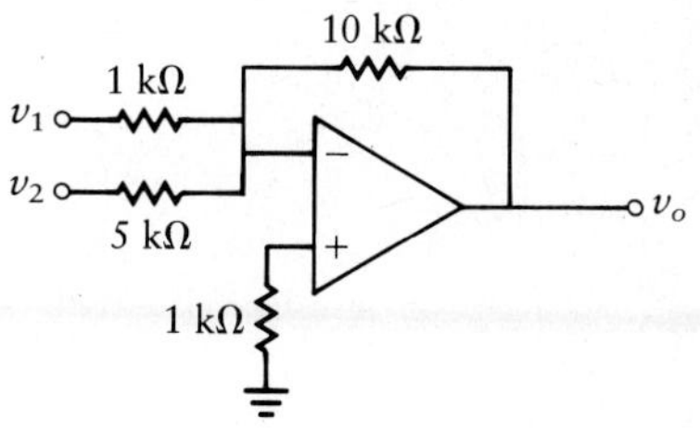

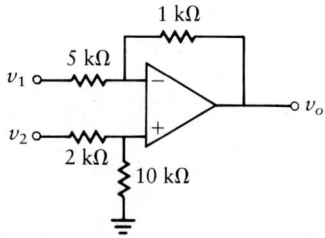

Figure P8.2

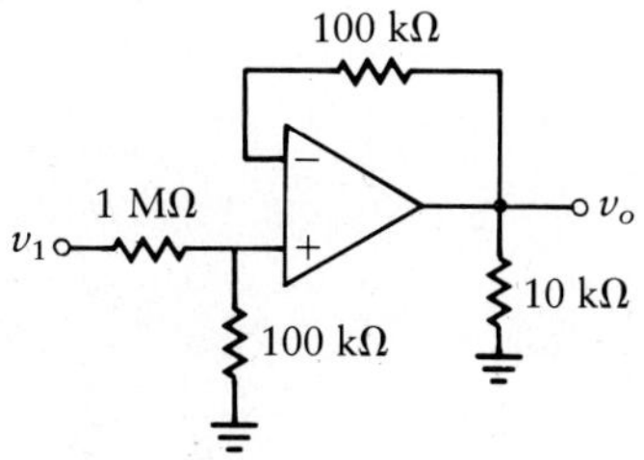

Figure P8.3

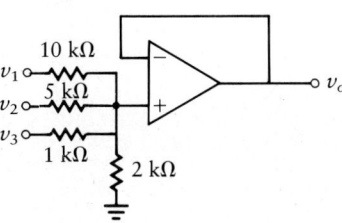

Figure P8.4

Figure P8.5

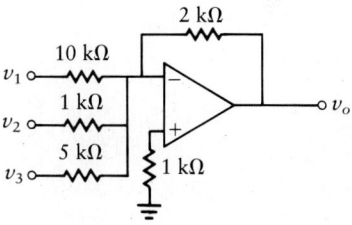

Figure P8.6

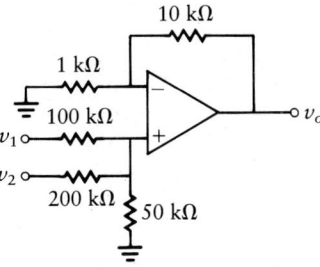

Figure P8.7

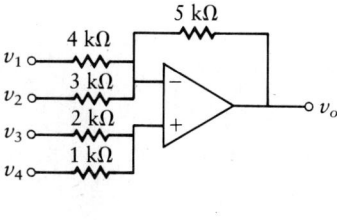

Figure P8.8

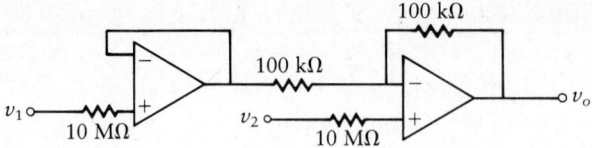

Figure P8.9

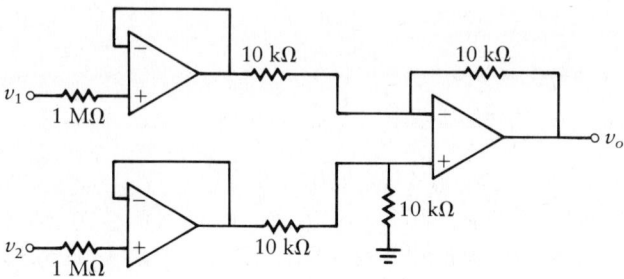

Figure P8.10

8.11 Construct an ideal op-amp mathematical model and solve for the gain ratio, v_o/v_i, for each of the configurations of Figure P8.11.

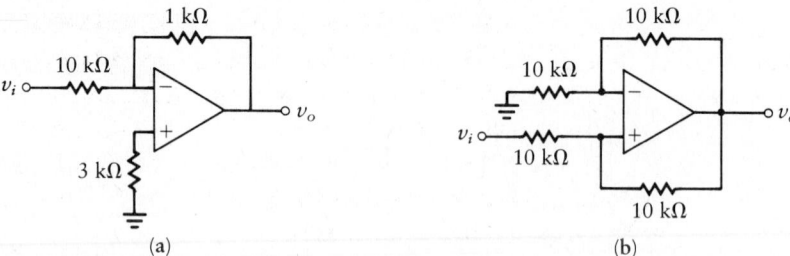

Figure P8.11

8.12 Find the output voltage, v_o, in terms of the input signals for the circuits of Figure P8.12. Use the ideal op-amp mathematical model.

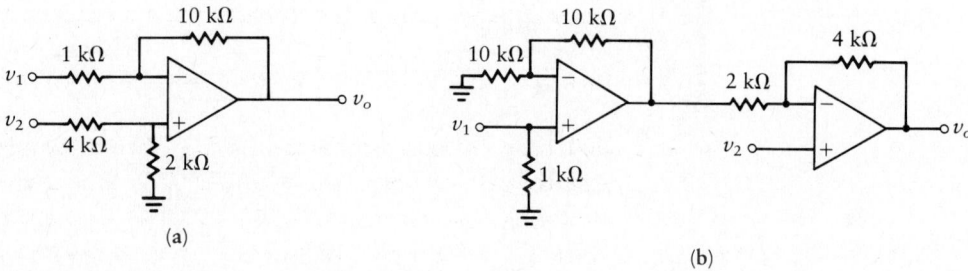

Figure P8.12

In Problems 8.13–8.16, design an op-amp circuit to yield the relationships shown in each equation. In each case, use the procedure of Examples 8.1 and 8.2 and compare the results.

8.13 $v_o = v_1 + 10v_2 - 30v_a - 100v_b$ $\qquad R_{min} = 5 \text{ k}\Omega.$

8.14 $v_o = 8v_1 + 8v_2 - 4v_a - 9v_b$ $\qquad R_{min} = 10 \text{ k}\Omega.$

8.15 $v_o = 6v_1 + 8v_2 - 3v_a - 12v_b$ $\qquad R_{min} = 8 \text{ k}\Omega.$

8.16 $v_o = 3v_1 + v_2 + 6v_3 - 4v_a - 5v_b$ $\quad R_{min} = 12 \text{ k}\Omega.$

8.17 A digital-to-analog (D/A) converter can be designed using an op-amp, as shown in Figure P8.13. Use the method of Section 8.6 to design a 6-bit D/A converter with $R_{min} = 10 \text{ k}\Omega$. What is a good choice for V_{CC} if logic 1 corresponds to 0.2 V?

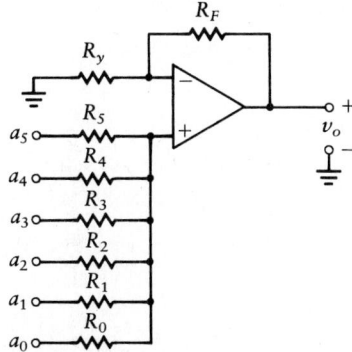

Figure P8.13

(*Hint*: The decimal equivalent of the binary number $a_5a_4a_3a_2a_1$, where a_i is either 0 or 1, is

$$N = a_5 2^5 + a_4 2^4 + a_3 2^3 + a_2 2^2 + a_1 2^1 + a_0 2^0$$
$$= 32a_5 + 16a_4 + 8a_3 + 4a_2 + 2a_1 + a_0)$$

8.18 Design an analog voltmeter using the circuit shown in Figure P8.14. The meter reads full scale with a current of 100 μA. Find R so that the full-scale reading is $v = +10$ V. Note that this design is independent of R_m, the meter resistance.

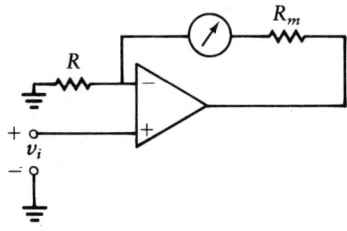

Figure P8.14

8.19 Design an op-amp circuit to produce a negative resistance of -10 kΩ.

8.20 Design a noninverting integrator to implement the equation

$$\frac{V_o}{V_i} = \frac{1}{j\omega}$$

8.21 Design an op-amp circuit to simulate a 0.5-H coil without using any inductors in the circuit.

8.22 Determine the gain v_o/v_i for the ideal op-amp circuit shown in Figure P8.15. Why does this circuit yield such a peculiar answer?

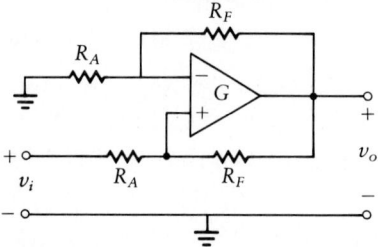

Figure P8.15

8.23 Determine the transfer ratio V_o/V_i for the circuit shown in Figure P8.16. The op-amp is ideal.

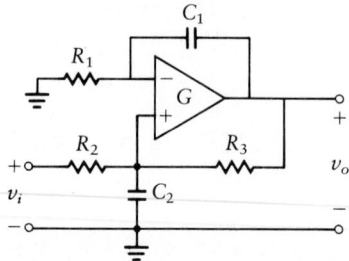

Figure P8.16

8.24 Calculate the transfer ratio V_o/V_i for the circuit shown in Figure P8.17. The op-amp is ideal.

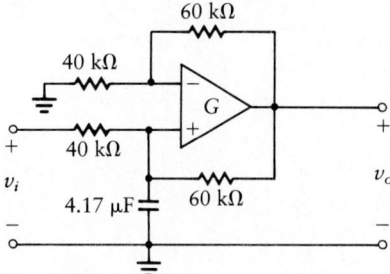

Figure P8.17

8.25 Find the gain v_o/v_i for the ideal op-amp circuit shown in Figure P8.18.

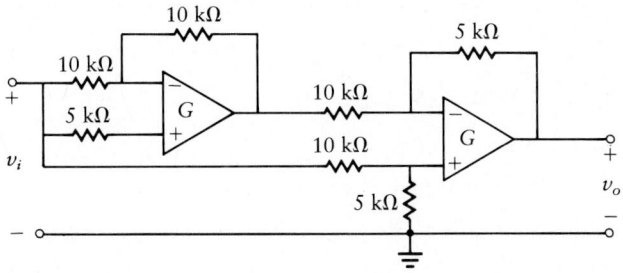

Figure P8.18

8.26 Determine the voltage gain v_o/v_i for the ideal op-amp circuit shown in Figure P8.19. This will be a function of the variable resistor. The maximum value of the resistor is R when $x = 1$, and x ranges from 1 to 0.

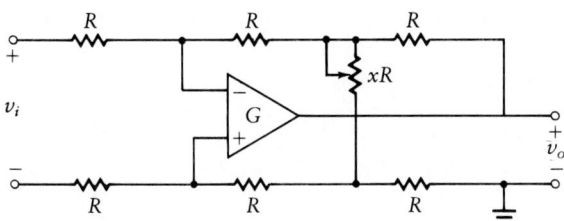

Figure P8.19

8.27 Plot the output voltage v_o as function of R/R_x for the ideal op-amp circuit of Figure P8.20. Assume that $V = 15$ V.

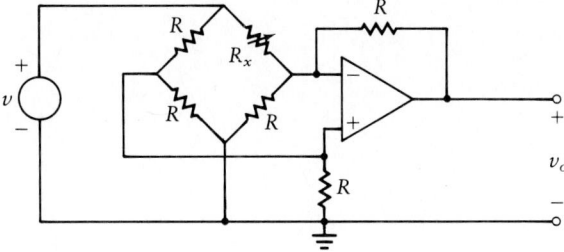

Figure P8.20

8.28 Plot the output voltage for the op-amp system shown in Figure P8.21 when the input voltage is given by

$$v_i = 10 \sin 20\, t$$

Assume that $v_\gamma = 0.7$ V and that $R_F = 0$.

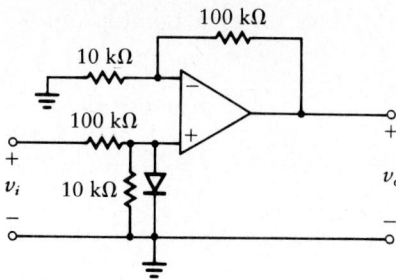

Figure P8.21

8.29 Figure 8.19 is an electronic thermometer. Plot the output voltage V_o as the temperature varies from room temperature (25°C) to 125°C. The change in voltage across the diode, ΔV_γ, varies according to the relationship

$$\Delta V_\gamma = -2(T_2 - 25°C) \text{ mV}$$

Select the resistor values so that the output v_o, given by equation (8.40), must be 5 V when the temperature is 125°C.

9

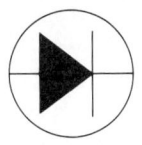

PRACTICAL OPERATIONAL AMPLIFIERS

9.0 Introduction

This chapter expands upon the results of the previous two chapters. We reexamine many of the same op-amp circuits, but in this chapter, the op-amps are no longer assumed to be ideal. We begin by identifying the variations of a practical op-amp from the ideal and then develop an improved equivalent circuit, which more accurately models the actual op-amp characteristics. The improved model is then applied to the analysis of noninverting and inverting amplifiers. Since the practical op-amp is frequency-dependent, we spend time analyzing the frequency characteristics of the various circuits.

The chapter continues with an exploration of the sensitivity of op-amp circuits to changes in supply voltage. We conclude with a discussion of audio amplifiers.

9.1 Practical Op-Amps

Practical op-amps approximate their *ideal* counterparts but differ in some important respects. It is important for the circuit designer to realize the differences between actual op-amps and ideal op-amps, since these differences can adversely affect circuit performance.

Table 9.1 Parameter Values for Op-Amps.

	Ideal	General-Purpose 741	High Speed 715	Low Noise 5534
Voltage gain, G	∞	$1 \times 10^{5*}$	3×10^4	10^5
Output impedance, Z_o	0	75 Ω	75 Ω	0.3 Ω
Input impedance, Z_{in} (open loop)	∞	2 MΩ	1 MΩ	100 kΩ
Offset current, I_{io}	0	20 nA	250 nA	300 nA
Offset voltage, V_{io}	0	2 mV	10 mV	5 mV
Bandwidth, BW	∞	1 MHz	65 MHz	10 MHz
Slew rate, SR	∞	0.7 V/ms	100 V/ms	13 V/ms

*The 741 op-amp has typical values of approximately 2 to 3 $\times$ 10^5; however in this text we use 10^5.

Our intent is to develop a detailed model of the practical op-amp—a model that takes into account the most significant characteristics of the nonideal device. We begin by defining the parameters used to describe practical op-amps. These parameters are specified in listings on data sheets supplied by the op-amp manufacturer.

Table 9.1 lists the parameter values for three particular op-amps, one of the three being the popular 741. As the various parameters are defined in the following sections, reference should be made to this table to find typical values.

The most significant difference between ideal and actual op-amps is in the voltage gain. The ideal op-amp has an infinite voltage gain. The actual op-amp has a finite voltage gain that decreases as the frequency increases. Most op-amps are frequency-compensated to provide a predictable voltage gain versus frequency characteristic. Some op-amps, like the 741, are internally compensated with a fixed capacitor. Other op-amps, like the 101, permit a capacitor to be added externally to the op-amp so the frequency characteristic can be changed.

9.1.1   Open-Loop Voltage Gain (G)

The *open-loop voltage gain* of an op-amp is the ratio of the change in output voltage to a change in the input voltage without feedback. Voltage gain is a dimensionless quantity. The symbol G is used to indicate the open-loop voltage gain. Op-amps have high voltage gain for inputs with frequencies in the range of dc to about 10 kHz. The op-amp specification lists the voltage gain in volts per millivolt or in decibels defined as $20 \log_{10}(v_o/v_i)$.

The open-loop voltage gain is frequency-dependent. Figure 9.1 illustrates this gain as a function of frequency for a typical op-amp. Note that the gain decreases with increasing frequency.

Figure 9.1
Voltage gain vs.
frequency.

Figure 9.1
Voltage gain vs.
frequency.

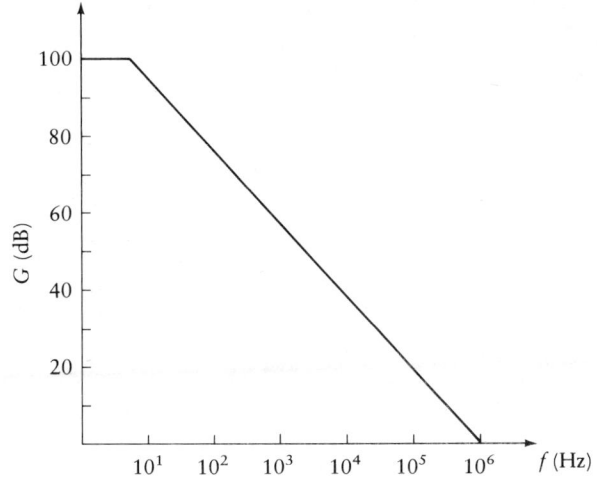

Figure 9.2
Technique for measur-
ing V_{io}.

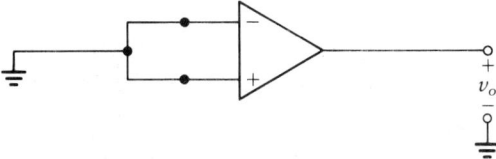

9.1.2 *Input Offset Voltage (V_{io})*

When the input voltage to an ideal op-amp is zero, the output voltage is also zero. This is not true for an actual op-amp. The *input offset voltage, V_{io}*, is defined as the input voltage required to make the output voltage equal to zero. V_{io} is zero for the ideal op-amp. A typical value of V_{io} for the 741 op-amp is 2 mV. A nonzero value of V_{io} is undesirable, since the op-amp will amplify any input offset, thus causing a larger output dc error.

The following technique may be used to measure the input offset voltage. Rather than vary the input voltage in order to force the output to zero, the input is set equal to zero, as shown in Figure 9.2, and the output voltage is measured. The output voltage resulting from a zero input voltage is known as the *output dc offset voltage*. If this quantity is divided by the open loop gain $\frac{V_{os}}{G} = V_{io}$ of the op-amp, the input offset-voltage is obtained.

The effects of input offset voltage can be incorporated into the op-amp model, as shown in Figure 9.3. Note that in addition to including input offset voltage, the ideal op-amp model has been further modified by the addition of four resistances. R_o is the output resistance. The input resistance of the op-amp, R_i, is measured between the inverting and noninverting terminals. The model also contains a resistor between each of the two inputs and ground. These are the *common-mode resistances* and are each equal to $2R_{cm}$. If the

Figure 9.3
Input offset voltage model.

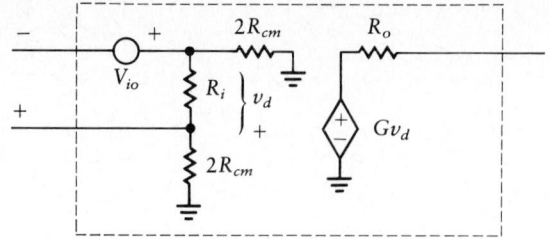

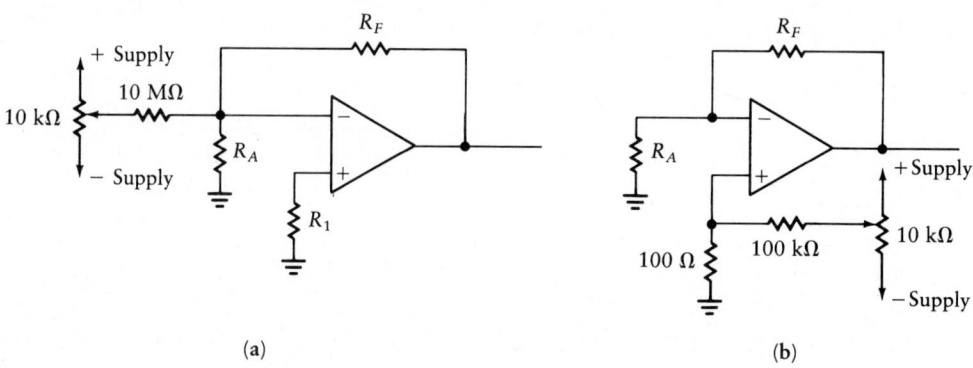

Figure 9.4   Offset voltage balancing.

inputs are connected together, as in Figure 9.2, these two resistors are in parallel, and the combined resistance to ground is R_{cm}. If the op-amp is ideal, R_i and R_{cm} are equal to infinity (i.e., open circuit) and R_o is zero (i.e., short circuit).

The external configuration shown in Figure 9.4(a) may be used to negate the effects of offset voltage. A variable voltage is applied to the inverting input terminal. Proper choice of this voltage can cancel the input offset. Similarly, Figure 9.4(b) illustrates this balancing circuit applied to the noninverting terminal.

9.1.3   *Input Bias Current (I_{Bias})*

Although ideal op-amp inputs draw no current, some bias current must enter each input terminal in the actual case. I_{Bias} is the base current of the input transistor, and a typical value is 2 μA. When the source impedance is low, I_{Bias} has little effect, since it causes a relatively small change in input voltage. However, in high-impedance circuits, a small current can lead to a large voltage.

The bias current can be modeled as two current sinks, as shown in Figure 9.5. The values of these sinks are independent of the source impedance. The bias current is defined as the average value of the two current sinks. Thus

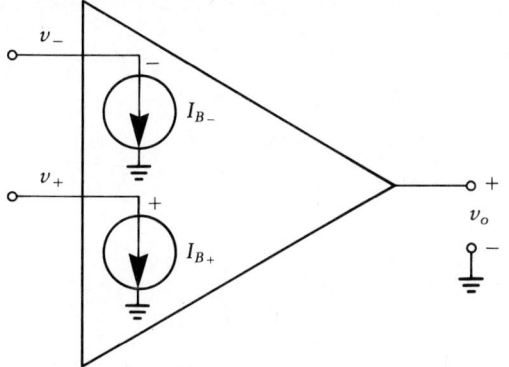

Figure 9.5   Input bias current.

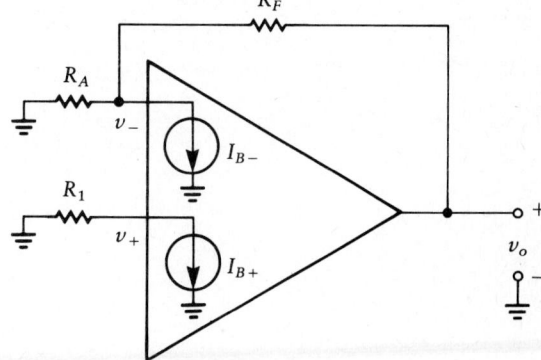

Figure 9.6   Reducing the effect of input bias current.

$$I_{\text{Bias}} = \frac{I_{B+} + I_{B-}}{2} \tag{9.1}$$

The difference between the two sink values is known as the *input offset current,* I_{io}, and is given by

$$I_{io} = I_{B+} - I_{B-} \tag{9.2}$$

Both the input bias current and the input offset current are temperature-dependent. The *input bias current temperature coefficient* is defined as the ratio of change in bias current to change in temperature. A typical value is 10 nA/°C. The *input offset current temperature coefficient* is defined as the ratio of the change in magnitude of the offset current to the change in temperature. A typical value is -2nA/°C.

It is possible to reduce the output dc voltage caused by the input bias current by connecting the op-amp as shown in Figure 9.6. This method consists of connecting a resistance in series with the noninverting terminal. The value of resistance is equal to the total equivalent resistance connected to the inverting terminal. If we assume that

$$I_{B+} = I_{B-} = I_B$$

the output voltage due to these currents is then given by

$$V_o = GI_B(R_1 - R_A \parallel R_F) \tag{9.3}$$

If the value of R_1 is selected to be equal to $R_A \parallel R_F$, then the output voltage is zero. We conclude from this analysis that the dc resistance from v_+ to ground

Figure 9.7
Input bias current
model.

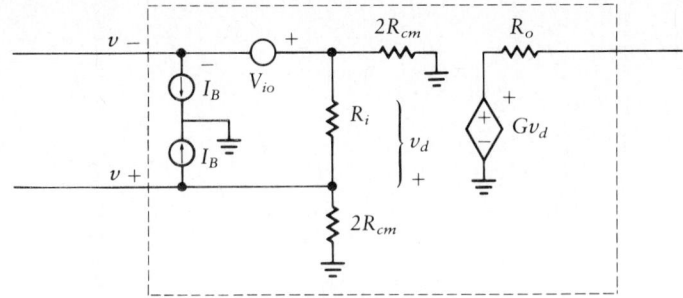

should equal the dc resistance from v_- to ground. We use this observation many times in our designs. It is important that both the inverting and non-inverting terminals have a dc path to ground to reduce the effects of input bias current.

The input bias currents are incorporated into the op-amp model of Figure 9.7.

We analyze this model in order to find the output voltage caused by the input bias currents. Figure 9.8(a) shows an op-amp circuit where the inverting and noninverting inputs are connected to ground through associated resistances. The circuit is replaced by its equivalent (see Figure 9.7) in Figure 9.8(b), where we have neglected V_{io}.

We further simplify the circuit in Figure 9.8(c) by neglecting R_o and R_L. That is, we assume

$$R_F \gg R_o$$

and

$$R_L \gg R_o$$

Output loading requirements usually assure that these inequalities are met.

The circuit is further simplified in Figure 9.8(d), where the series combination of the voltage source and resistor is replaced by a parallel combination of a current source and resistor.

Finally, we combine resistances and change the current source back to a voltage source to obtain the simplified equivalent of Figure 9.8(e). We use a loop equation to find

$$V_o = GV_d$$

$$= \frac{GR_i(R_A' \parallel R_F - R_1')I_B(R_A' + R_F)}{(R_A' + R_F)(R_i + R_A' \parallel R_F + R_1') + GR_iR_A'} \tag{9.4}$$

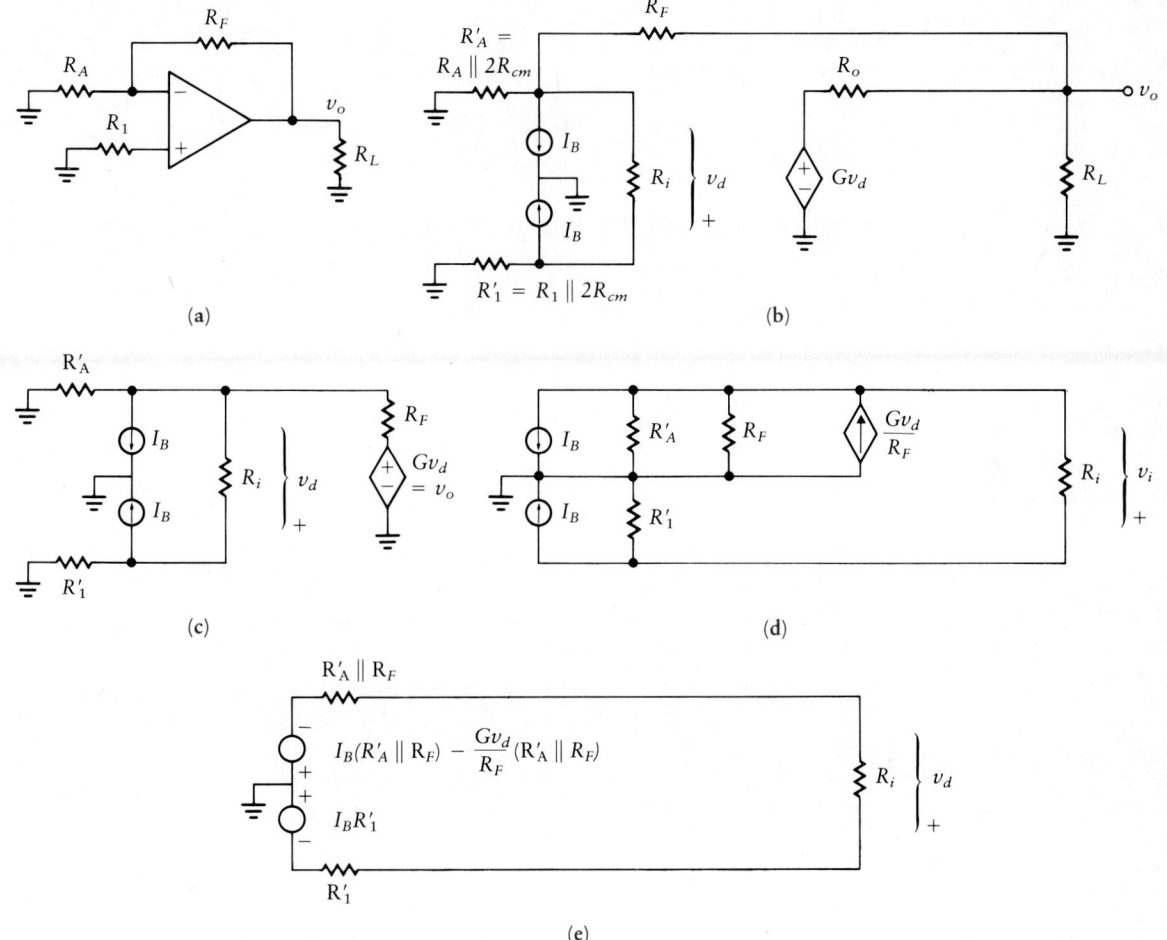

Figure 9.8 Input bias current effects.

where

$$R'_A = R_A \parallel 2R_{cm}$$

$$R'_1 = R_1 \parallel 2R_{cm}$$

$$R_F \gg R_o$$

$$R_L \gg R_o$$

The common-mode resistance, $2R_{cm}$, is in the range of several hundred megohms for most op-amps. Then

$$R'_A \approx R_A$$

and

$$R'_1 \approx R_1$$

We further assume that G is large, so equation (9.4) becomes equation (9.5):

$$V_o = \left(1 + \frac{R_F}{R_A}\right)I_B(R_A \parallel R_F - R_1) \qquad (9.5)$$

Example 9.1

Find the output voltage for the configurations of Figure 9.9, where

$$I_B = 80 \text{ nA} = 8 \times 10^{-8} \text{ A} \qquad V_0 = I_B R_2 = \qquad V_0 = -8mV.$$

SOLUTION   We use the simplified form of equation (9.5) to find the output voltages for the circuit of Figure 9.9(a).

$$V_o = \left(\frac{1 + 100,000}{10,000}\right)(8 \times 10^{-8})(9100 - 10,000) = -0.79 \text{ mV}$$

For the circuit of Figure 9.9(b), we obtain

$$V_o = \left(\frac{1 + 100,000}{10,000}\right)(8 \times 10^{-8})(9100) = 8 \text{ mV}$$

By selecting $R_1 = 10$ kΩ rather than 0Ω, we reduce the output voltage due to I_B by a factor of 10. We therefore balance the bias-current effect by equating the resistances connected between the positive terminal and ground with those connected between the negative terminal and ground.

9.1.4   *Common-Mode Rejection*

The op-amp is normally used to amplify the difference between two input voltages. It therefore operates in the *differential mode*. A constant voltage added to each of these two inputs should not affect the difference and should, therefore, not be transferred to the output. In the practical case, this constant, or average value of the inputs *does* affect the output voltage. If we consider

Figure 9.9
Configurations for
Example 9.1.

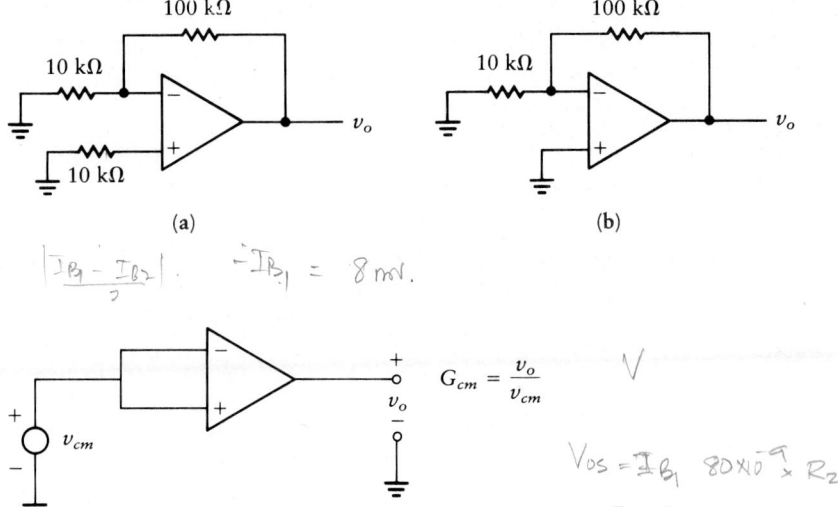

(a)　　　　　　　　　　　(b)

$\left|\dfrac{I_{B_1} - I_{B_2}}{2}\right|.$ $-I_{B_1} = 8\,mV.$

Figure 9.10
Common mode.

$G_{cm} = \dfrac{v_o}{v_{cm}}$ √

$V_{os} = I_{B_1}\ 80 \times 10^{-9} \times R_2$

$I_s = I_B$

$I_{os} =$

$V_2 \ne 0$

$V = V_2$

$V_1 - V_2 \ne 0$ —

only the equal parts of the two inputs, we have what is known as the *common mode*.

Let us assume that the two input terminals of a practical op-amp are connected together and then to a common source voltage. This is illustrated in Figure 9.10. The output voltage would be zero in the ideal case. In the practical case, this output is nonzero. The ratio of the nonzero output voltage to the applied input voltage is the *common-mode voltage gain*, G_{cm}. The common-mode rejection ratio (CMRR) is defined as the ratio of the open-loop gain, G, to the common mode gain. Thus,

$$\text{CMRR} = \frac{|G|}{|G_{cm}|} \tag{9.6a}$$

or in decibels,

$$\text{CMRR} = 20 \log_{10}\left(\frac{|G|}{|G_{cm}|}\right) \tag{9.6b}$$

Typical values of the CMRR range from 80 to 100 dB. It is desirable to have the CMRR as high as possible.

9.1.5 *Power Supply Rejection Ratio (PSRR)*

The *power supply rejection ratio* (PSRR) is a measure of the ability of the op-amp to ignore changes in the power supply voltage. If the output stage of a system draws a variable amount of current, the supply voltage could change. This load-induced change in supply voltage could then cause changes in the operation of other amplifiers sharing the same supply. This is known as *crosstalk,* and it can lead to instability.

The PSRR is the ratio of the change in v_o to the total change in power supply voltage. For example, if the positive and negative supplies vary from ± 5 V to ± 5.5 V, the total change is $11 - 10 = 1$ V. PSRR is usually specified in microvolts per volt or sometimes in decibels. Typical op-amps have a PSRR of about 30 μV/V.

To decrease changes in supply voltage, the power supply for each group of op-amps should be *decoupled* (i.e., isolated) from those of other groups. This confines the interaction to a single group of op-amps. In practice, each printed circuit card should have the supply lines bypassed to ground via a 0.1-μF ceramic or 1-μF tantalum capacitor. This assures that load variations will not feed significantly through the supply to other cards.

9.1.6   Phase Shift

If a sinusoidal signal forms the inverting input to an ideal op-amp, the output is 180° out of phase with this input. However, with practical op-amps, the phase shift between input and output signals decreases as the frequency of the input signal increases. At high frequencies, the phase difference approaches zero and a portion of the output signal is fed back in phase. This changes the feedback from negative to positive, and the amplifier can exhibit behavior characteristics of an oscillator.

Op-amp manufacturers prevent this situation by adding an internal filter. This is done in a manner such that the op-amp has a gain of less than unity as the phase difference between output and input approaches zero. Oscillation does not occur with positive feedback as long as the gain is less than unity. This modification of the op-amp is known as *internal frequency compensation.* If the manufacturer does not provide for this internal compensation, an external capacitor can be added to accomplish the same result.

9.1.7   Slew Rate (SR)

Because a practical op-amp has a frequency-dependent response, the output due to a step input is not an ideal step. The op-amp would need to respond uniformly to all frequencies if it were to accurately reproduce the instantaneous change in voltage that occurs with a step input.

If an attempt is made to drive the output from one extreme to the other by applying a step input, the output goes through a transition between the two extremes. The rate of change of the output voltage under these input conditions is known as the *slew rate* (SR). Slew rate is therefore a measure of the speed at which the output signal can change.

Figure 9.11
Example of slew rate.

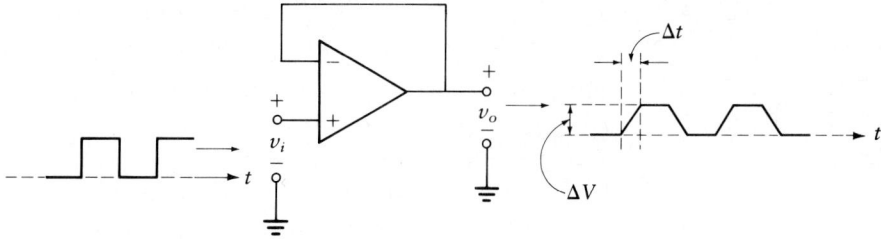

Slew rate limiting occurs because the amplifier is incapable of rapidly driving internal or external capacitive loads. These loads limit the frequencies to which the amplifier can respond.

If a square wave forms the input to the amplifier configuration of Figure 9.11, the output can be approximated as shown in the figure (this is an approximation since the actual curve cannot have any sharp corners). As the frequency of the pulse train input is increased, the ability to reproduce the square wave is impaired, since the widened pulses can overlap. The amplifier output is capable of changing at the maximum slew rate of

$$\text{SR} = \frac{\Delta V}{\Delta t} \tag{9.7}$$

Slew rate is related to the *power bandwidth*, f_p, which is defined as the frequency at which a sine wave output, at rated output voltage, starts to experience distortion. That is, it is the frequency above which the amplifier can no longer keep up with the maximum slope of a sinusoid. If the output signal is

$$v_o = V \sin 2\pi f_p t$$

then the maximum slope is

$$\text{SR} = \frac{dv}{dt}\bigg|_{\text{max}} = 2\pi f_p V$$

The power bandwidth is given by

$$f_p = \frac{\text{SR}}{2\pi V}$$

As an example, if SR = 1 V/μs for an op-amp where the maximum output is ±15 V, then

$$f_p = \frac{1 \text{ V/μs}}{2\pi \times 15 \text{ V}} = 10.6 \text{ kHz}$$

Example 9.2

Find the slew rate if a 741 op-amp supplies 16 μA to its compensating capacitor of value 30 pF.

SOLUTION   Since the amplifier is capable of supplying 16 μA, we can replace it with a 16 μA source, which feeds the 30-pF capacitor. When a constant-current source forms the input to a capacitor, the voltage across the capacitor follows a ramp. The slope of the ramp is the slew rate. Therefore,

$$SR = \frac{\Delta \text{ output voltage}}{\Delta \text{ time}} = \frac{I}{C} = \frac{16 \text{ μA}}{30 \text{ pF}} = 0.53 \text{ V/μs}$$

Drill Problems

D9.1   If the slew rate for a unity gain inverting 741 op-amp is 0.5 V/μs, how long will it take for the output to change by 5 V?

Ans: 10 μs

D9.2   For an op-amp with SR = 0.6 V/μs, find f_p for a peak undistorted input voltage of (a) 1 V and (b) 10 V.

Ans: (a) 95.5 kHz, (b) 9.6 kHz

D9.3   For a 741 op-amp with SR = 0.5 V/μs, find f_p with peak output voltage of 13 V.

Ans: 6.1 kHz

9.2   Improved Op-Amp Model

Figure 9.12 shows a modified version of the idealized op-amp model. We have altered the idealized model by adding input resistance, output resistance, and common mode resistance.

Typical values of these parameters (for the 741 op-amp) are

Input resistance:	$R_i = 2 \text{ M}\Omega$
Resistance to ground:	$2R_{cm} = 400 \text{ M}\Omega$
Output resistance:	$R_o = 75 \text{ }\Omega$
Open-loop gain at dc:	$G = 1 \times 10^5$

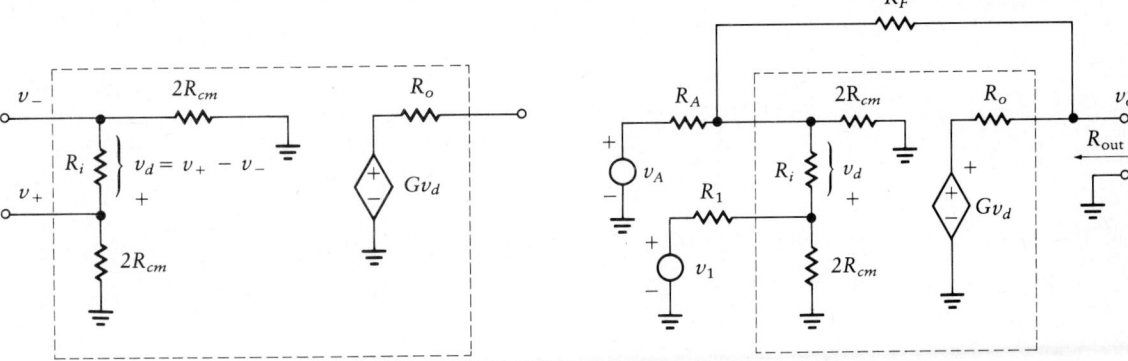

Figure 9.12 Improved op-amp model.

Figure 9.13 Op-amp circuit.

Figure 9.14
Thevenin equivalent
for output resistance.

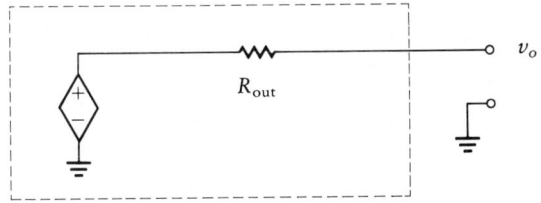

We consider the circuit of Figure 9.13. The inverting and noninverting inputs of the op-amp are driven by sources that have series resistance. The output of the op-amp is fed back to the input through a resistor, R_F.

The sources driving the two inputs are denoted by v_A and v_1, and the associated series resistances are R_A and R_1. If the input circuitry is more complex, these resistances can be considered as Thevenin equivalents of that circuitry.

As a first step in the analysis of this configuration, we find the Thevenin equivalent for the portion of the op-amp circuit shown in the box of Figure 9.13 enclosed by a dashed line, which is shown in Figure 9.14. Since the circuit contains no independent sources, the Thevenin equivalent voltage is zero, and the short-circuit current is zero, so the circuit is equivalent to a single resistor. The value of the resistor cannot be found using resistor combinations. To find the equivalent resistance, assume that a voltage source, v, is applied to the output leads. We then calculate the resulting current, i, and take the ratio, v/i. This yields the Thevenin resistance.

Figure 9.15(a) shows the applied voltage source. The circuit is simplified to that shown in Figure 9.15(b) and further reduced to the circuit shown in Figure 9.15(c) by defining new resistances as follows:

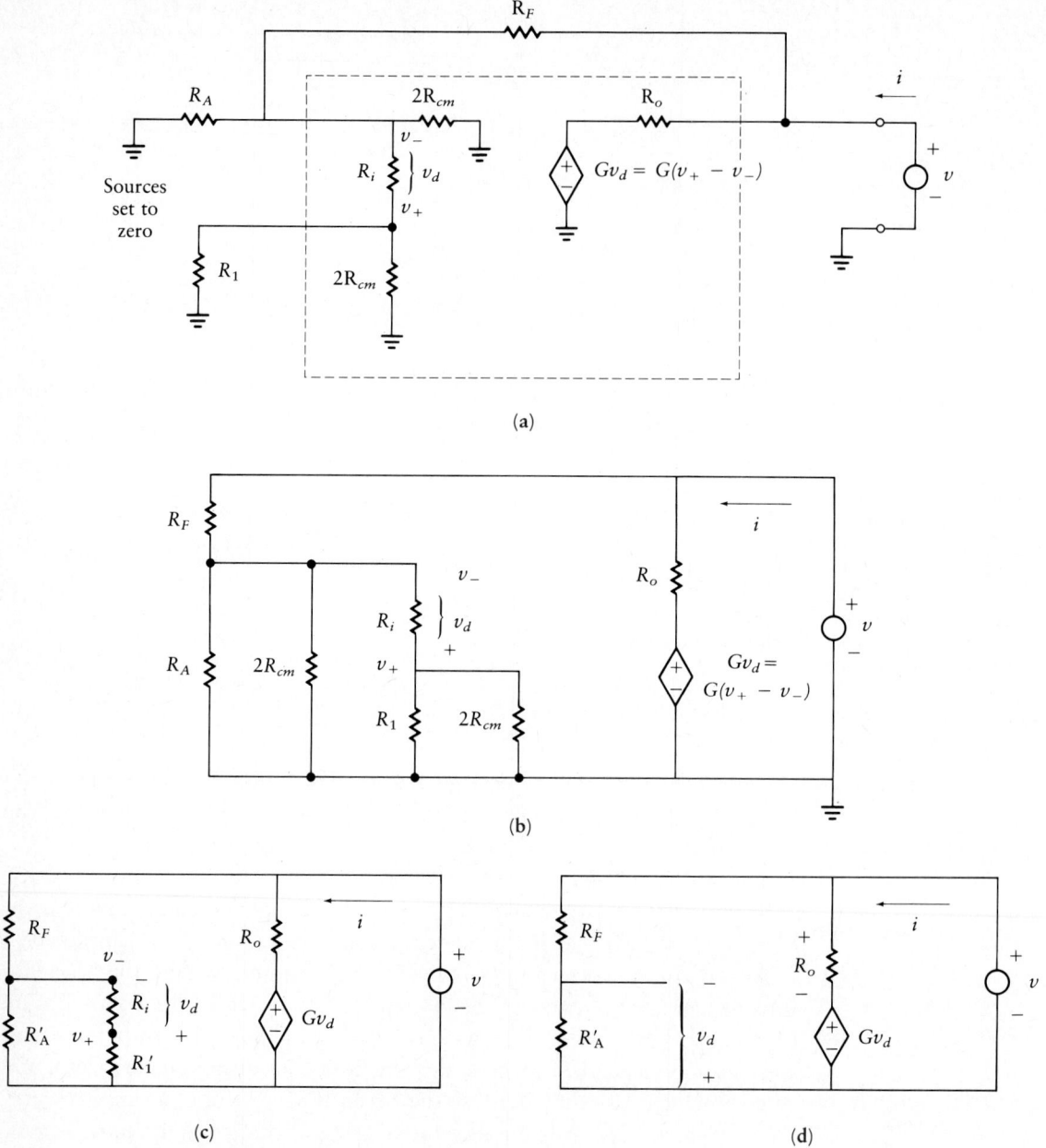

Figure 9.15   Reduced Thevenin equivalent circuits.

$$R'_A = R_A \parallel 2R_{cm}$$

$$R'_1 = R_1 \parallel 2R_{cm}$$

We make the assumption that

$$R'_A \ll (R'_1 + R_i)$$

and

$$R_o \ll R'_A \parallel (R'_1 + R_i)$$

The simplified circuit of Figure 9.15(d) results. The input voltage is found from this simplified circuit using a voltage-divider ratio, as follows:

$$v_d = \frac{-R'_A v}{R'_A + R_F}$$

The output-loop equation is

$$iR_o = v - Gv_d$$

$$= v \left(1 + \frac{GR'_A}{R'_A + R_F} \right)$$

Finally,

$$R_{\text{out}} = \frac{v}{i} = \frac{R_o}{1 + R'_A G/(R_F + R'_A)} \tag{9.8}$$

R_{out} is typically 1 Ω or less.

In most cases, R_{cm} is so large that

$$R'_A = R_A$$

and

$$R'_1 = R_1$$

Therefore, R_{out} can be reduced to

$$R_{\text{out}} = \frac{R_o}{1 + R_A G/(R_F + R_A)} = \frac{R_o}{G} \left(1 + \frac{R_F}{R_A} \right)$$

Example 9.3

Find the output impedance of a unity-gain buffer as shown in Figure 9.16.

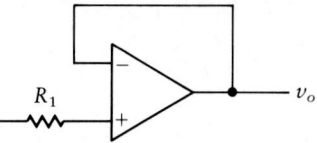

Figure 9.16   Unity-gain buffer.

SOLUTION   When the circuit of Figure 9.16 is compared to the feedback circuit of Figure 9.13, we find that

$$R_A \rightarrow \infty$$

Therefore,

$$R'_A = \infty \parallel 2R_{cm} = 2R_{cm}$$

Equation (9.8) cannot be used, since we are not sure that the inequalities leading to the simplification of Figure 9.15(c) apply in this case. That is, the necessary simplification is

$$2R_{cm} << R_1 \parallel (2R_{cm} + R_i)$$

Without this simplification, the circuit takes the form shown in Figure 9.17. This circuit is analyzed to find the following relations:

$$v_d = \frac{-R_i v}{R'_1 + R_i}$$

$$R_o i = v - G v_d = 1 + \frac{G R_i}{R_i + R'_1}$$

The output resistance is then given by

$$R_{out} = \frac{v}{i} = \frac{R_o}{1 + R_i G/(R'_1 + R_i)} \tag{9.9}$$

if we use the assumption

$$R_o << (R'_1 + R_i) << 2R_{cm}$$

Figure 9.17
Equivalent circuit—
unity-gain buffer.

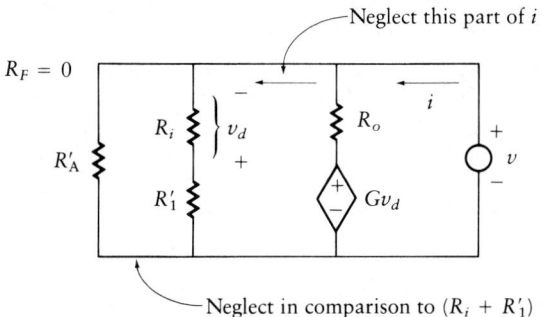

9.3 Noninverting Amplifier

Figure 9.18(a) illustrates the *noninverting amplifier,* and Figure 9.18(b) shows the equivalent circuit. The input voltage is applied between the noninverting terminal and ground.

9.3.1 *Noninverting Input and Output Resistance*

The input resistance of this amplifier is found by determining the Thevenin equivalent of the circuit surrounded by the dashed curve. The load resistance is normally such that

$$R_L \gg R_o$$

If this were not true, the effective gain would be reduced and the effective value of R_o would be the parallel combination of R_o with R_L. Let us again define

Figure 9.18
The noninverting
amplifier.

$R_L \gg R_o$

$R'_A = R_A \parallel 2R_{cm}$

$R'_F = R_F + R_o$

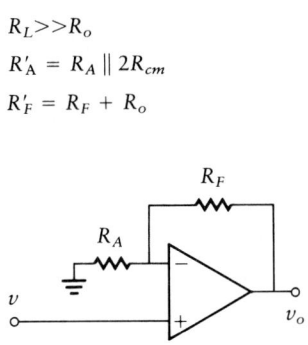

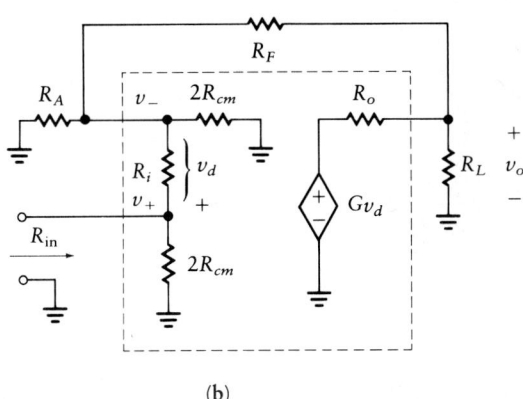

(a)   (b)

Figure 9.19
Reduced circuits for
input resistance.

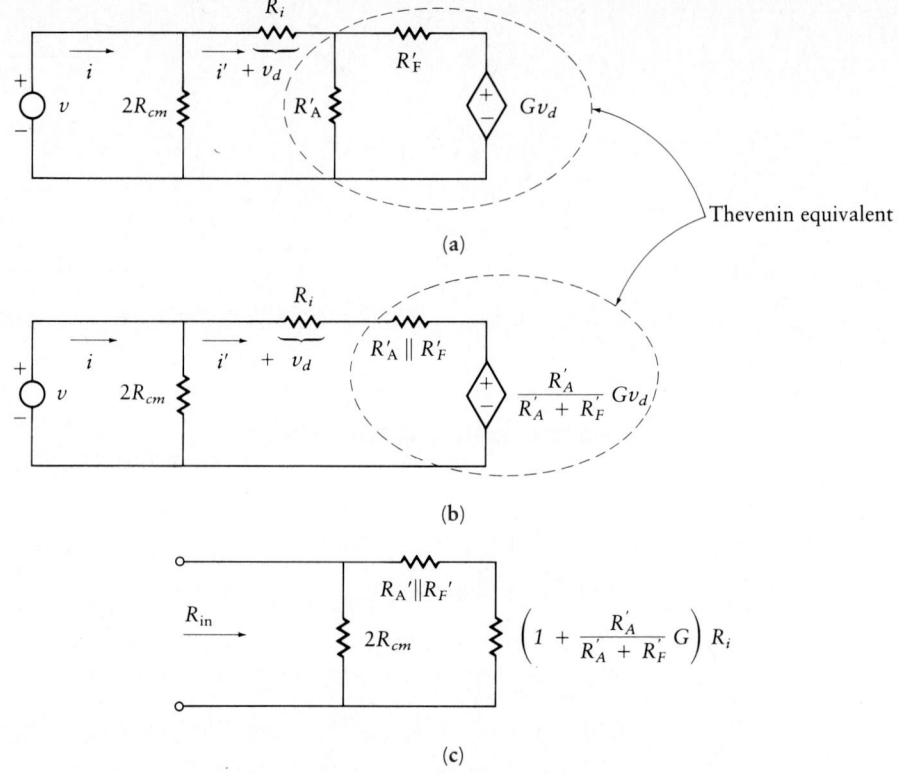

(a)

Thevenin equivalent

(b)

(c)

$$R'_A = R_A \parallel 2R_{cm}$$

and

$$R'_F = R_F + R_o$$

Now since $R_L \gg R_o$, we can reduce Figure 9.18(a) to the simplified form of
Figure 9.19(a). We find the Thevenin equivalent of the circuit surrounded by
the dashed curve, resulting in Figure 9.19(b). We write a loop equation to
obtain

$$(R_i + R'_A \parallel R'_F)i' = v - \frac{R'_A G v_d}{R'_A + R'_F}$$

$$= v - \frac{R'_A G R_i i'}{R'_A + R'_F}$$

since

$$v_d = R_i i'$$

The resistance to the right of $2R_{cm}$ is given by

$$\frac{v}{i'} = (R'_A \parallel R'_F) + \left(1 + \frac{R'_A G}{R'_A + R'_F}\right) R_i$$

This is used to yield the simplified circuit of Figure 9.19(c). Finally, the input resistance is calculated:

$$R_{in} = 2R_{cm} \middle\| \left[(R'_A \parallel R'_F) + \left(1 + \frac{R'_A G}{R'_A + R'_F}\right) R_i \right] \tag{9.10}$$

Recall that

$$R'_A = R_A \parallel 2R_{cm}$$

$$R'_F = R_F + R_o$$

$$R_L \gg R_o$$

If we retain only the most significant terms and assume R_{cm} is very large, equation (9.10) reduces to

$$R_{in} = 2R_{cm} \middle\| \frac{R'_A G R_i}{R'_A + R'_F}$$

$$= 2R_{cm} \middle\| \frac{G R_i}{1 + R'_F/R'_A} \tag{9.11}$$

If we use the parameter values for the 741 op-amp, equation (9.11) becomes

$$R_{in} = 400 \times 10^6 \middle\| \frac{(10^5)(2 \times 10^6)}{1 + R_F/R_A} \approx 400 \text{ M}\Omega \tag{9.12}$$

The *output resistance* is found from equation (9.8). We again use the assumption that R_{cm} is large, i.e.,

$$R'_F = R_F$$

and

$$R'_A = R_A$$

Then the output resistance is given by

$$R_{\text{out}} = \frac{R_o(1 + R_F/R_A)}{G}$$

$$= \frac{75(1 + R_F/R_A)}{10^5} \tag{9.13}$$

Example 9.4

Calculate the input resistance for the unity-gain amplifier shown in Figure 9.20(a).

SOLUTION   The equivalent circuit is shown in Figure 9.20(b). Since we assume the gain, G, and common-mode resistance, R_{cm}, are high, we can neglect the term $2R_{cm} \parallel R_F$ compared to $(1 + G)R_i$. Equation (9.10) cannot be used where we note that $R_F = 0$ and $R_A = 0$. The input resistance is then given by

$$R_{\text{in}} \approx 2R_{cm} \parallel (1 + G)R_i = 2R_{cm}$$

This is typically equal to 200 MΩ or more.

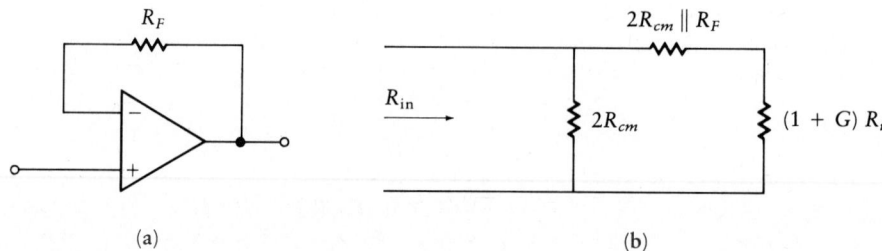

Figure 9.20   Unity-gain follower—Example 9.4.

9.3.2   *Noninverting Amplifier Voltage Gain*

We wish to determine the voltage gain, A_+, for the circuit shown in Figure 9.21. This gain is defined by

$$A_+ = \frac{v_o}{v_+}$$

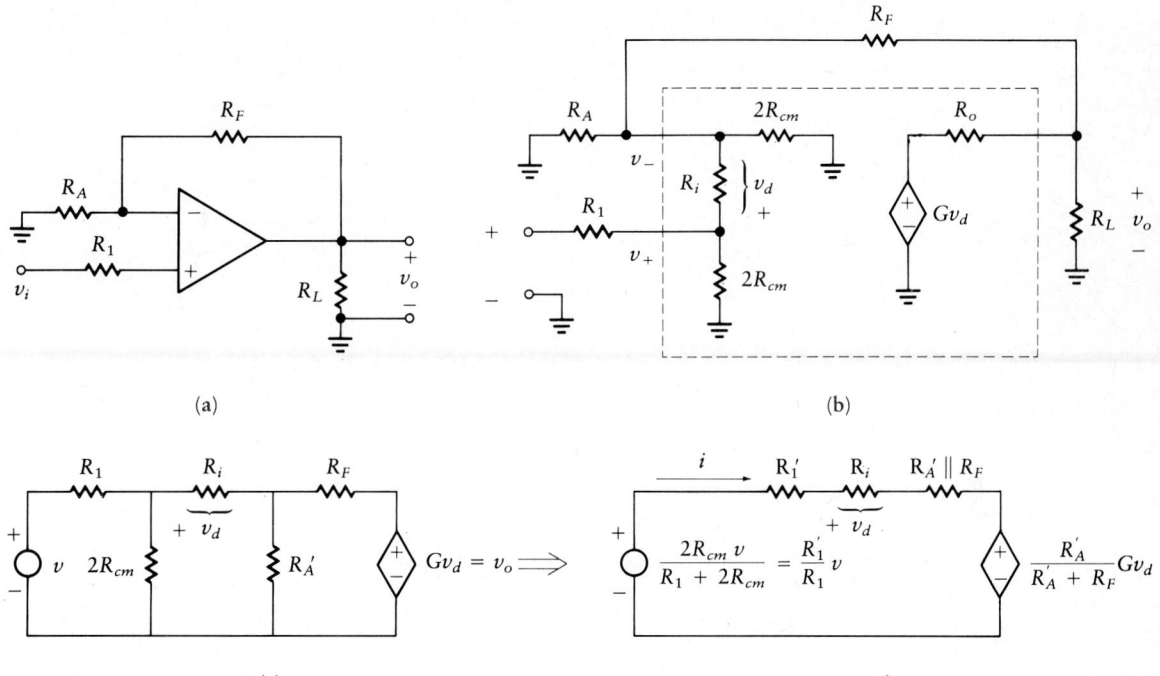

Figure 9.21 Noninverting amplifier.

The equivalent circuit is shown in Figure 9.21(b). We define

$$R'_A = R_A \| 2R_{cm}$$

The circuit then reduces to that shown in Figure 9.21(c). If we make the additional definition

$$R'_1 = R_1 \| 2R_{cm}$$

then the circuit can be further reduced to that shown in Figure 9.21(d). In this reduction, we make use of the following assumptions:

$$R_L \gg R_o$$

$$R_F \gg R_o$$

These conditions are desirable in order to prevent reduction of the effective gain. KVL is applied to the circuit of Figure 9.21(d) to obtain

$$(R_1' + R_i + R_A' \| R_F)i = \frac{R_1' v_i}{R_1} - \frac{R_A' G v_d}{R_A' + R_F}$$

where

$$v_d = R_i i$$

Solving for i yields

$$i = \frac{R_1' v_i / R_1}{(R_A' \| R_F) + R_1' + [1 + R_A' G/(R_A' + R_F)]R_i}$$

The output voltage is given by

$$v_o = G v_d = R_i i G$$

Finally, the voltage gain is given by the ratio

$$A_+ = \frac{v_o}{v_i} = \frac{R_1' G R_i / R_1}{R_A' \| R_F + R_1' + [1 + R_A' G/(R_A' + R_F)]R_i} \tag{9.14}$$

As a check of this result, we can reduce the model to that of the ideal op-amp by using the following information:

$$R_1 = R_1'$$

$$R_A = R_A'$$

$$R_i G \gg R_F$$

$$R_i G \gg R_1$$

$$R_i G \gg R_L$$

Equation (9.14) then becomes

$$A_+ = \frac{R_A + R_F}{R_A}.$$

which agrees with the result for the idealized model presented in Chapter 8.

Example 9.5

Find the gain of the unity-gain follower shown in Figure 9.22.

SOLUTION   In this circuit,

$$R_A = \infty$$

$$R_A' = 2R_{cm}$$

$$R_F << R_A'$$

In equation (9.14), we assume that G is large and that $R_1' \approx R_1$. Then equation (9.14) reduces to

$$A_+ = \frac{R_A' + R_F}{R_A'} = 1$$

so

$$v_o = v_i$$

as expected.

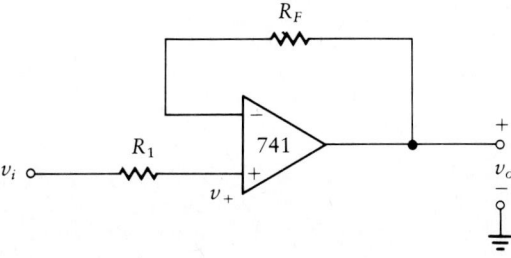

Figure 9.22   Unity-gain follower.

9.3.3   Bandwidth Considerations

A practical op-amp has neither infinite gain nor infinite bandwidth. The characteristic gain and bandwidth typically vary with operating frequency. However, the *gain-bandwidth product* (GBP) is frequently constant. The GBP is defined as

$$\text{GBP} = A_v \text{BW} \tag{9.15}$$

Table 9.2   Summary of Equations for Nonideal Op-Amp.

Variable	Noninverting Op-Amp		Inverting Op-Amp	
	Nonideal	741	Nonideal	741
R_{in}	$2\,R_{cm}\left\|\dfrac{GR_i}{1 + R_F/R_A}\right.$	$(4 \times 10^8)\left\|\dfrac{2 \times 10^4}{1 + R_F/R_A}\right.$	R_A	R_A
R_{out}	$\dfrac{R_o}{1 + \dfrac{R_A G}{R_F + R_A}}$	$75\left(1 + \dfrac{R_F}{R_A}\right)10^{-5}$	$\dfrac{R_o}{1 + \dfrac{R_A G}{R_F + R_A}}$	$75\left(1 + \dfrac{R_F}{R_A}\right)10^{-5}$
BW	$\dfrac{GBP}{1 + R_F/R_A}$	$\dfrac{10^6}{1 + R_F/R_A}$	$\dfrac{GBP}{1 + R_F/R_A}$	$\dfrac{10^6}{1 + R_F/R_A}$
Voltage gain	$A_+ = \left(1 + \dfrac{R_F}{R_A}\right)$		$A_- = -\dfrac{R_F}{R_A}$	

where A_v is the closed-loop voltage gain (i.e., with feedback) of the op-amp and BW is the bandwidth that corresponds to this gain. Since A_v is dimensionless, the units of GBP are those of the bandwidth, or Hertz. A typical value is 1 MHz. For the noninverting amplifier of Figure 9.18, the (ideal) closed-loop gain is given by

$$A_v = \frac{v_o}{v_i} = 1 + \frac{R_F}{R_A} \tag{9.16}$$

In order to approach this value in the practical case, we can choose

$$R_1 = R_A \,\|\, R_F$$

to achieve bias balance. Then the bandwidth is given by

$$\text{BW} = \frac{\text{GBP}}{A_v} = \frac{1\ \text{MHz}}{1 + R_F R_A} \tag{9.17}$$

since the gain bandwidth product is typically 1 MHz.

The variables for the noninverting op-amp are summarized in Table 9.2.

9.3.4   *Multiple Input Noninverting Amplifiers*

We extend the previous results to the case of the noninverting amplifier with multiple voltage inputs. If inputs $v_1, v_2, v_3, \ldots, v_n$ are applied through input resistances $R_1, R_2, R_3, \ldots, R_n$, we obtain a special case of the general result derived in Section 8.5, as follows:

$$v_o = \left(1 + \frac{R_F}{R_A}\right)(R_1 \| R_2 \| \cdots \| R_n) \sum_{k=1}^{n} \frac{v_k}{R_k} \tag{9.18}$$

We choose

$$R_A \| R_F = R_1 \| R_2 \| \cdots \| R_n$$

in order to achieve bias balance. The input resistance, output resistance, and bandwidth are found from equations (9.12), (9.13), and (9.17), respectively and these are summarized in Table 9.2.

Example 9.6

Find the output voltage of the two-input summer of Figure 9.23.

SOLUTION   The output voltage is found from equation (9.18) as follows:

$$v_o = \left(1 + \frac{R_F}{R_A}\right)\left(\frac{R_2 v_1}{R_1 + R_2} + \frac{R_1 v_2}{R_1 + R_2}\right) \tag{9.19}$$

We choose

$$R_A \| R_F = R_1 \| R_2$$

to achieve bias balance. If we assume

$$R_F = R_1 = R_2 = R_A$$

then equation (9.19) reduces to

$$v_o = v_1 + v_2$$

which is a unity-gain two-input summer.
  To construct a multiple-input noninverting summer, we simply extend the previous result.

Figure 9.23
Two-input summer—
Example 9.6.

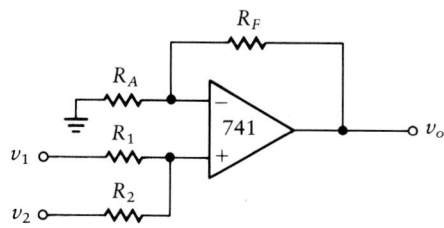

Drill Problems

D9.4   Find the input resistance and bandwidth of the 741 op-amp circuit of Figure D9.1. Let $R_A = R_F = R_L = 10 \text{ k}\Omega = 2 R_1$.

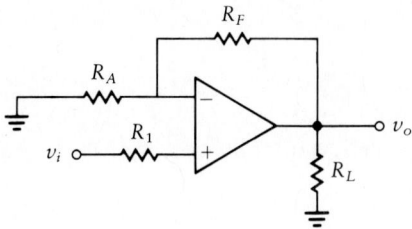

Figure D9.1

   Ans: $R_{in} = 400 \text{ M}\Omega$; BW = 0.5 MHz.

D9.5   Calculate the output resistance, R_{out}, for the amplifier of Figure D9.1. Use a 741 op-amp with $R_A = R_F = R_L = 10 \text{ k}\Omega = 2 R_1$.

   Ans: 1.5 mΩ

D9.6   Find the voltage gain and bandwidth of the 741 op-amp circuit of Figure D9.1. Let $R_F = R_L = 10 \text{ k}\Omega$ and $R_1 = R_A = 1 \text{ k}\Omega$.

   Ans: $A_V = 11$; BW = 91 kHz.

Example 9.7

Design and analyze a three-input summer using a 741 amplifier where

$$v_o = 3v_1 + 2v_2 + 5v_3$$

The minimum resistance to the $+$ and $-$ op-amp terminals is $R_{min} = 10 \text{ k}\Omega$.

SOLUTION   We use the design method of Section 8.6, as follows:

$$X = 10; \quad Y = 0; \quad Z = 10 - 0 - 1 = 9$$

$$R_F = 10(10 \text{ k}\Omega) = 100 \text{ k}\Omega$$

$$R_1 = \frac{100 \text{ k}\Omega}{3} \approx 33.3 \text{ k}\Omega$$

$$R_2 = \frac{100 \text{ k}\Omega}{2} = 50 \text{ k}\Omega$$

$$R_3 = \frac{100 \text{ k}\Omega}{5} = 20 \text{ k}\Omega$$

$$R_y = \frac{R_F}{Z} = 100 \text{ k}\Omega/9 = 11.1 \text{ k}\Omega$$

The gain of the amplifier is $(1 + R_F/R_A) = 10$. The bandwidth of the amplifier is 1 MHz/10 = 100 kHz. The output resistance is $75(10)/10^5 = 7.5$ mΩ. The design method of Section 8.6 assures us that

$$R_1 \parallel R_2 \parallel R_3 = R_F \parallel R_A = 10 \text{ k}\Omega$$

or

$$33.3 \text{ k}\Omega \parallel 50 \text{ k}\Omega \parallel 20 \text{ k}\Omega = 100 \text{ k}\Omega \parallel 11.1 \text{ k}\Omega = 10 \text{ k}\Omega$$

9.4 Inverting Amplifier

Figure 9.24 illustrates an inverting amplifier. Figure 9.25(a) shows the equivalent circuit using the op-amp model developed earlier in this chapter.

9.4.1 *Inverting Amplifier—Input and Output Resistance*

Figure 9.25(a) is reduced to Figure 9.25(b) if we let

$$R_1' = R_1 \parallel 2R_{cm}$$

$$R_F \gg R_o$$

$$R_L \gg R_o$$

Figure 9.24
Inverting amplifier.

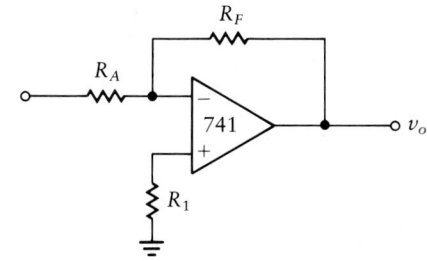

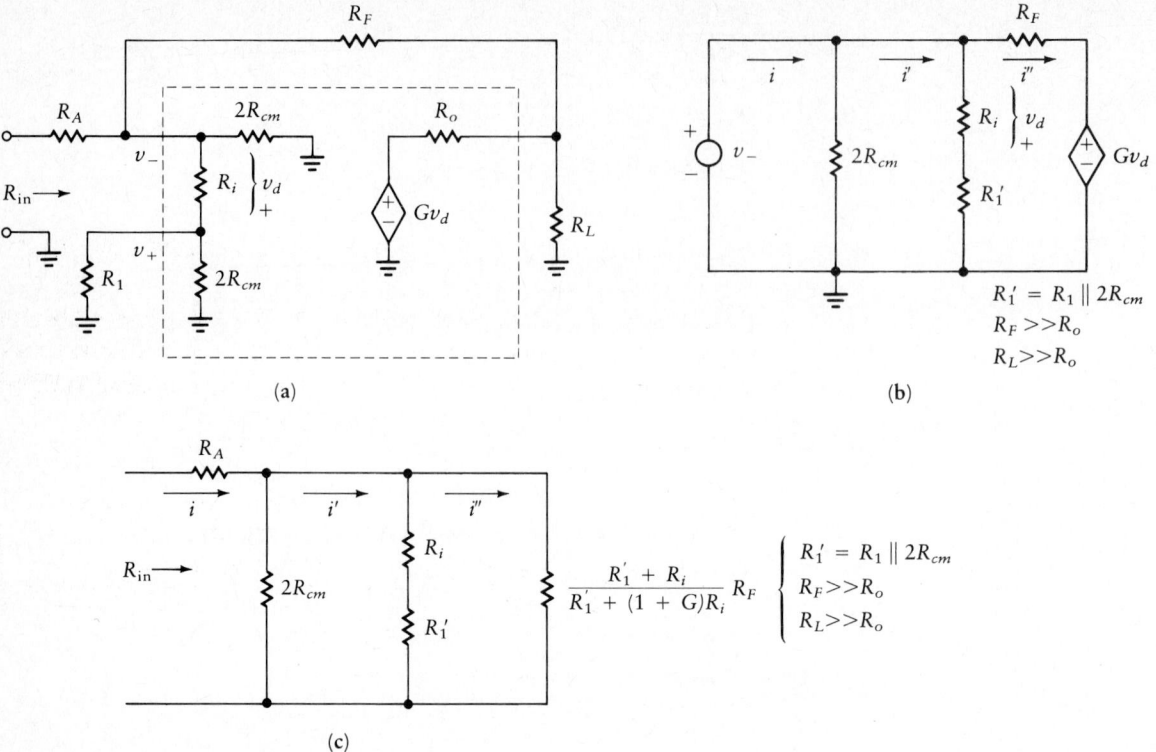

Figure 9.25   Inverting amplifier model.

It is reasonable to assume the above inequalities, since, were they not true, the output would load the input and the gain would be reduced.

A voltage-divider relationship can be used to yield

$$v_d = \frac{-R_i v_-}{R_i + R_1'}$$

and a loop equation yields

$$R_F i'' = v_- - G v_d$$

$$R_F i'' = \left(1 + \frac{G R_i}{R_i + R_1'} \right) v_-$$

$$= \frac{R_1' + (1 + G) R_i}{R_i + R_1'} v_-$$

The input resistance, R_{in}, is obtained from Figure 9.25(c), where we have replaced the dependent source with an equivalent resistance. The value of this resistor is v_-/i'', which is found from the previous equation. For large G, the rightmost resistance in Figure 9.25(c) is zero, and

$$R_{in} \approx R_A \tag{9.20}$$

The output resistance of the inverting amplifier is the same as that of the noninverting amplifier. Thus,

$$R_{out} = \frac{R_o(1 + R_F/R_A)}{G} \tag{9.21}$$

Using the typical values for the 741 op-amp, the output resistance becomes

$$R_{out} = \frac{75(1 + R_F/R_A)}{10^5} \tag{9.22}$$

9.4.2   *Inverting Input Voltage Gain*

The equivalent circuit of Figure 9.25(a) is repeated as Figure 9.26(a). The inverting input gain, A_-, is obtained from the circuit of Figure 9.26(a) by again making the assumptions that

$$R_1' = R_1 \| 2R_{cm}$$

$$R_A' = R_A \| 2R_{cm}$$

$$R_L \gg R_o$$

$$R_F \gg R_o$$

These assumptions reduce the circuit to that shown in Figure 9.26(b). The circuit is further reduced to that of Figure 9.26(c) by changing the voltage source in series with a resistance to a current source in parallel with a resistance. The resistors can then be combined to yield the circuit of Figure 9.26(d). Finally, the current source is converted back to the voltage source to yield the simplified circuit of Figure 9.26(e). The loop equation for this circuit is given by

$$v_d = \frac{-R_i}{R_i + R_1' + R_A'R_F/(R_A' + R_F)}\left[\frac{R_A'R_F}{R_A' + R_F}\frac{v_i}{R_A} + \frac{R_A'G}{R_A' + R_F}v_d\right]$$

Since $v_o = Gv_d$, the inverting voltage gain is

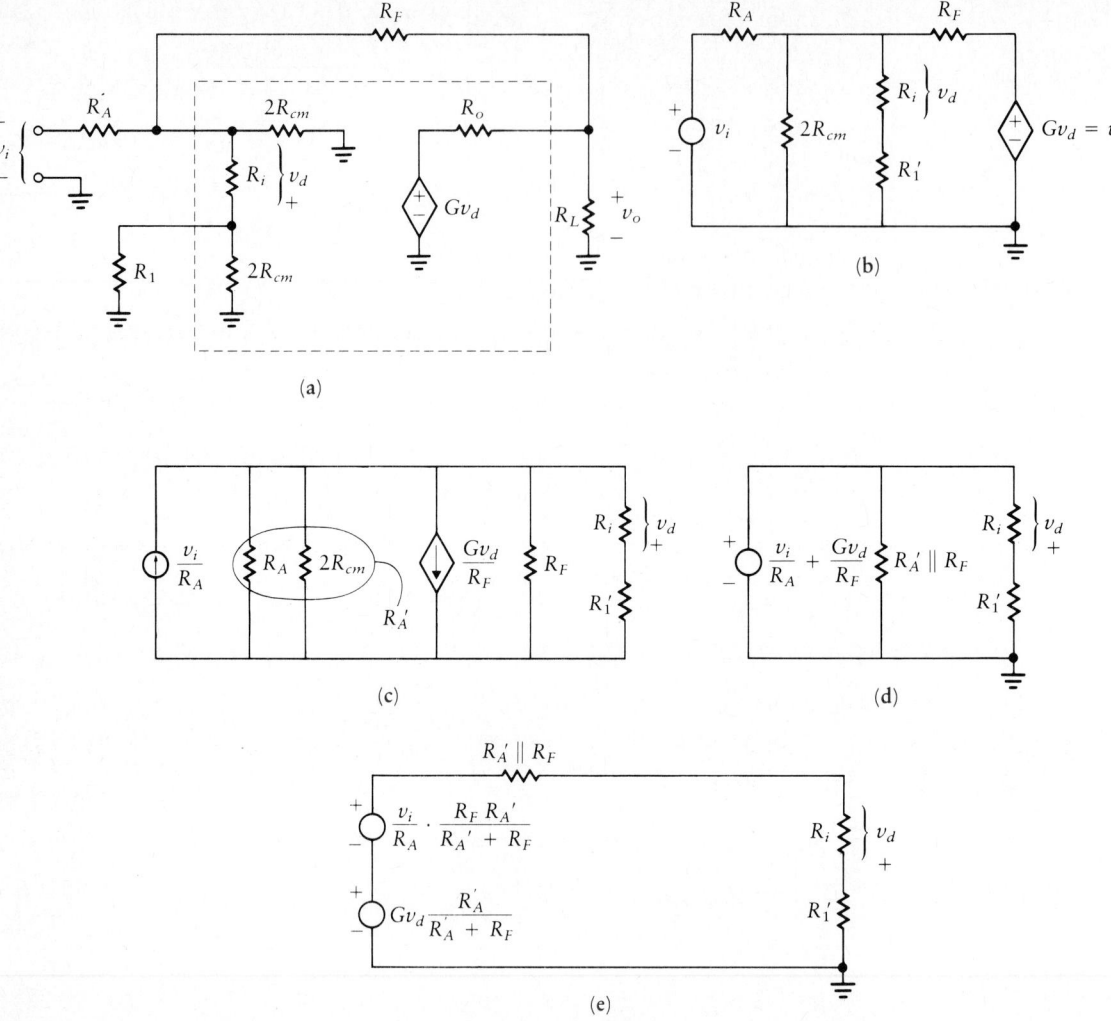

Figure 9.26   Inverting input gain.

$$A_- = v_o/v_i = -\frac{GR'_AR_iR_F/R_A}{(R_i + R'_1)(R'_A + R_F) + R'_AR_F + R_iR'_AG} \qquad (9.23)$$

We can compare this to the result for the ideal op-amp by making the following approximations.

$$R_A \ll 2R_{cm}$$

$$G \gg 1$$

Then

$$R_A' = R_A \parallel 2R_{cm} = R_A$$

and

$$A_- = \frac{-R_F}{R_A}$$

This is the same as the result found earlier for the simplified model. In design, we choose $R_1 = R_A \parallel R_F$ to achieve bias balance.

The variables for the inverting op-amp are summarized in Table 9.2.

9.4.3 *Multiple Input—Inverting Amplifier*

If the voltages $v_a, v_b, \ldots, v_m$ are applied to the summing junction (inverting input to op-amp) through resistors $R_a, R_b, \ldots, R_m$,

$$
\begin{aligned}
v_o &= -\frac{R_F v_a}{R_a} - \frac{R_F v_b}{R_b} - \cdots - \frac{R_F v_m}{R_m} \\
&= -R_F \sum_{j=a}^{m} \frac{v_j}{R_j}
\end{aligned}
\tag{9.24}
$$

To achieve bias balance, we choose

$$R_1 = R_F \parallel R_a \parallel R_b \parallel \cdots \parallel R_m \parallel R_L$$

Let us define

$$R_A = R_a \parallel R_b \parallel \cdots \parallel R_m$$

The output resistance is then given by

$$R_{\text{out}} = \frac{R_o(1 + R_F/R_A)}{G}$$

and the bandwidth is

$$\text{BW} = \frac{\text{GBP}}{1 + R_F/R_A}$$

If only two inputs are used, the output voltage is

$$v_o = \frac{-R_F v_a}{R_a} - \frac{R_F v_b}{R_b} \qquad (9.25)$$

The input resistance at v_a is approximately equal to R_a, and the input resistance at v_b is approximately R_b. We can obtain a unity-gain two-input summer with an output voltage of

$$v_o = -v_a - v_b \qquad (9.26)$$

by setting the following values of resistance:

$$R_F = R_a = R_b$$

The resistance from the noninverting input terminal to ground is chosen to achieve bias balance. Thus,

$$R_1 = \frac{R_F}{3}$$

We then have

$$1 + \frac{R_F}{R_A} = 1 + \frac{R_F}{R_a \parallel R_b} = 3$$

An equal-gain (i.e., not unity) two-input summer is obtained by setting

$$R_a = R_b = R$$

and

$$R_1 = \frac{R_F \parallel R}{2}$$

In this case, the output voltage is

$$v_o = -\left(\frac{R_F}{R}\right)(v_a + v_b) \qquad (9.27)$$

The input resistance is approximately R. Since

$$R_A = \frac{R}{2}$$

then

$$1 + \frac{R_F}{R_A} = 1 + \frac{2R_F}{R}$$

If m inputs are summed through equal resistors (R), the output voltage is

$$v_o = -\left(\frac{R_F}{R}\right) \sum_{j=1}^{m} v_j \tag{9.28}$$

For this equal-gain multiple-input inverting summer, the input resistance to each input is approximately R:

$$R_A = \frac{R}{m}$$

so

$$1 + \frac{R_F}{R_A} = 1 + \frac{mR_F}{R}$$

and

$$R_1 = \frac{R_F \parallel R}{m}$$

The output resistance is

$$R_{\text{out}} = \left(\frac{R_o}{G}\right) \left(1 + \frac{mR_F}{R}\right) \tag{9.29}$$

Example 9.8

Design and analyze a three-input inverting amplifier using a 741 op-amp, where

$$v_o = -4v_a - 2v_b - 3v_c$$

and the minimum input resistance between the + and − terminal is $R_{\text{min}} = 8\ \text{k}\Omega$.

SOLUTION We use the design method of Section 8.6 to find

$$X = 0; \quad Y = 9; \quad Z = -10$$

Then

$$R_F = 10 \times 8 \text{ k}\Omega = 80 \text{ k}\Omega$$

$$R_a = \frac{80 \text{ k}\Omega}{4} = 20 \text{ k}\Omega$$

$$R_b = \frac{80 \text{ k}\Omega}{2} = 40 \text{ k}\Omega$$

$$R_c = \frac{80 \text{ k}\Omega}{3} = 26.7 \text{ k}\Omega$$

$$R_x = \frac{80 \text{ k}\Omega}{10} = 8 \text{ k}\Omega$$

The gain of the amplifier is $1 + R_F/R_A = 10$ and the bandwidth of the amplifier is 1 MHz/10 = 100 kHz. We find the input resistance as follows:

$$R_{in}(v_a) = 20 \text{ k}\Omega$$

$$R_{in}(v_b) = 40 \text{ k}\Omega$$

$$R_{in}(v_c) = 26.7 \text{ k}\Omega$$

The output resistance is approximately $75(10)/10^5 = 7.5 \text{ m}\Omega$. To achieve bias balance, we see that

$$R_x = R_a \parallel R_b \parallel R_c \parallel R_F = 8 \text{ k}\Omega \qquad \blacktriangleright$$

9.5   Differential Summing

We have seen that an op-amp can be configured to produce an output that is a weighted sum of multiple inputs. If the sum includes both positive and negative signs, *differential summing* results. The op-amp configuration of Figure 9.27 produces an output voltage, v_o, given by

$$v_o = \left(1 + \frac{R_F}{R_A}\right)(R_1 \parallel R_2 \parallel R_3 \parallel \cdots \parallel R_n \parallel R_x) \sum_{i=1}^{n} \frac{v_i}{R_i} - R_F \sum_{j=a}^{m} \frac{v_j}{R_j}$$

$$(9.30)$$

Figure 9.27
Differential summing.

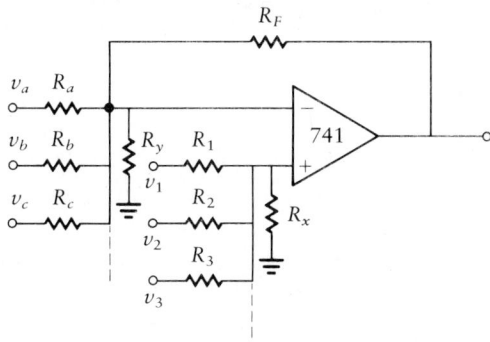

Figure 9.28
Differencing amplifier.

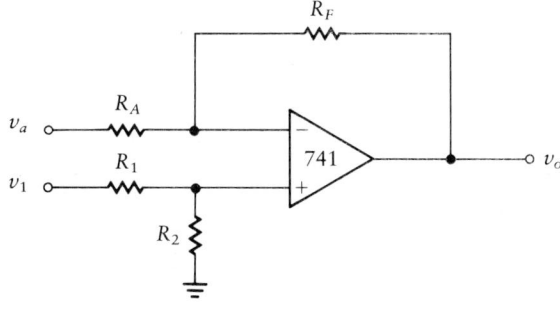

where

$$R_A = R_a \parallel R_b \parallel R_c \parallel \cdots \parallel R_m \parallel R_y$$

We would normally choose the resistors to achieve bias balance. That is,

$$R_1 \parallel R_2 \parallel R_3 \cdots \parallel R_x = R_F \parallel R_a \parallel R_b \parallel R_c \parallel \cdots \parallel R_y$$

The input resistance for each inverting input v_j is R_j.

If the inverting and noninverting terminals each have only one input, the result is a *differencing amplifier*. This is illustrated in Figure 9.28. The output voltage for this configuration is

$$v_o = \left(1 + \frac{R_F}{R_A}\right)\left(\frac{R_2}{R_1 + R_2}\right)v_1 - \frac{R_F v_a}{R_A} \tag{9.31}$$

In order to achieve bias balance, we normally choose

$$R_1 \parallel R_2 = R_A \parallel R_F$$

The input resistance for the v_a terminal is R_A. The input resistance for the v_1 terminal is $R_1 + (R_2 \parallel R_{in})$, where R_{in} is found from equation (9.11) to be

$$R_{in} = 2R_{cm} \left\| \left(\frac{GR_i}{1 + R_F/R_A} \right) \approx 2R_{cm} \right. \tag{9.32}$$

R_{out} is found in equation (9.13) and is equal to

$$R_{out} = \frac{R_o(1 + R_F/R_A)}{G} \tag{9.33}$$

The bandwidth was found in equation (9.17), and is given by

$$BW = \frac{GBP}{1 + R_F/R_A} \tag{9.34}$$

If we wish to achieve unit-gain differencing, the output is given by

$$v_o = v_1 - v_a$$

and we set

$$R_A = R_F = R_1 = R_2$$

If a 741 op-amp is used, a typical value for these four resistors is 10 kΩ. The bandwidth is approximately 500 kHz. The input resistance into v_a is then 10 kΩ, and into the v_1 terminal, the resistance is 20 kΩ.

Suppose that equal-gain differencing is desired, but that the gains need not be unity. We then set

$$R_1 = R_A$$

and

$$R_2 = R_F$$

The output voltage is then

$$v_o = \frac{R_F(v_1 - v_a)}{R_A} \tag{9.35}$$

The input resistance into the v_a terminal is R_A, and into the noninverting terminal, it is $R_A + (R_F \parallel R_{in})$, which is approximately $R_A + R_F$, since $R_{in} \gg R_F$. Values for input resistance, R_{out}, and the bandwidth are easily determined with the use of equations (9.32), (9.33), and (9.34).

Drill Problems

D9.7 Find the gain and bandwidth for the 741 op-amp of Figure 9.24 with $R_F = 10 \text{ k}\Omega$ and $R_A = 1 \text{ k}\Omega$.

Ans: $A_v = -10$; BW = 91 kHz

D9.8 Find the bandwidth and input resistance for the differencing amplifier of Figure 9.28 using the 741 op-amp. $R_F = R_2 = 10 \text{ k}\Omega$ and $R_A = R_1 = 1 \text{ k}\Omega$.

Ans: $R_{in}(v_1) = 11 \text{ k}\Omega$; BW = 91 kHz;
$R_{in}(v_a) = 1 \text{ k}\Omega$

A useful modification of the configuration of Figure 9.28 is the *sign switcher*, as shown in Figure 9.29. With the switch in the position shown in Figure 9.29(a),

$$v_o = -v_i$$

For the opposite switch position,

$$v_o = 2v_i - v_i = v_i$$

The input resistance is 10 kΩ for each position, and the bias is balanced in each position. Figure 9.29(a) uses a single-pole double-throw switch. The sign switcher can also be accomplished with the single-throw switch shown in Fig-

Figure 9.29
Sign switcher.

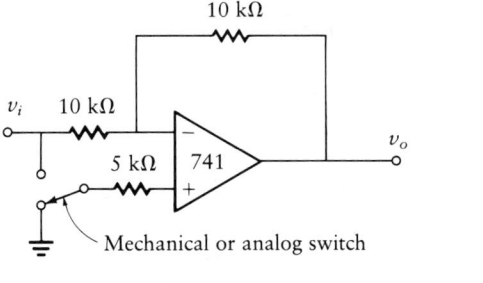

(a)

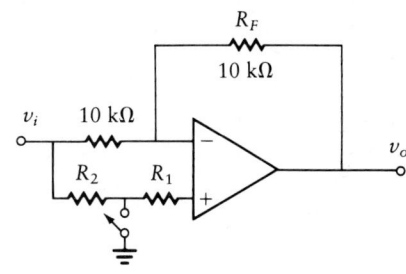

(b)

ure 9.29(b). However, for this implementation, the bias and input resistances are not equal in the two switch positions.

9.6   101 Amplifier

The 101 op-amp has similar characteristics to those of the 741. An additional feature is that the 101 amplifier provides capability for external compensation, which can be used to increase the bandwidth.

The principal characteristics for the 101 op-amp are

$$R_i = 2 \text{ M}\Omega$$

$$2R_{cm} = 400 \text{ M}\Omega$$

$$R_o = 100 \text{ }\Omega$$

$$G = 10^5 \quad \text{(externally compensated)}$$

Offset adjustment for the 101 op-amp is accomplished with either arrangement shown in Figure 9.30. Pin 1 of the op-amp is also used to *compensate* for offset adjustment.

Single-pole compensation is accomplished by placing a capacitor, C, between pins 1 and 8 of the op-amp package (see Figure 9.31(a)). If a value of $C = 30$ pF is used, the GBP is

$$GBP = 10^6 \text{ Hz}$$

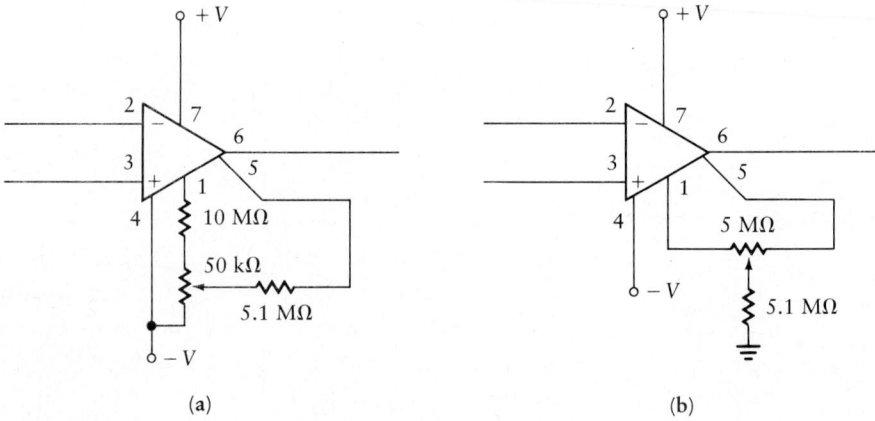

(a)   (b)

Figure 9.30 Input offset adjustment.

Figure 9.31
101 compensation.

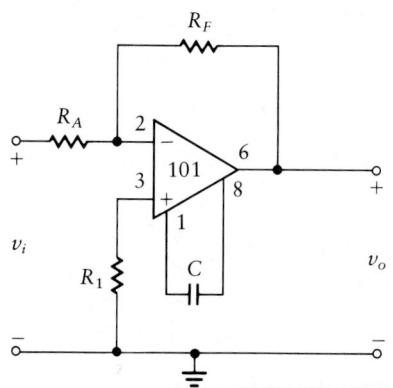

(a) Single-pole compensation

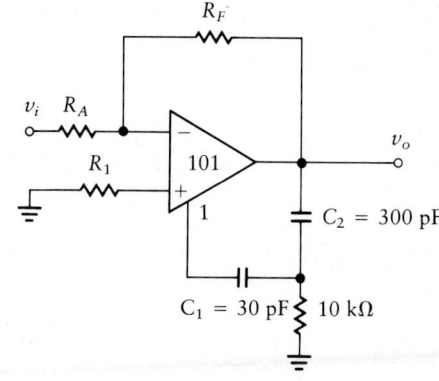

(b) Two-pole compensation

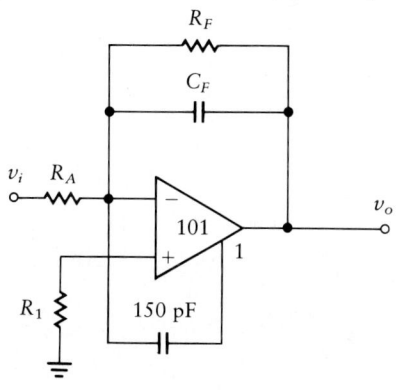

(c) Feedforward compensation

The amplitude response as a function of frequency is shown in Figure 9.32(a). If the capacitor value is changed to $C = 3$ pF, the GBP increases to

$$GBP = 10^7 \text{ Hz}$$

3 pF compensation should not be used for amplifiers having gains less than 20 dB. The resulting frequency response is shown in Figure 9.32(b). The figures illustrate straight line *Bode plot* approximations. These plots are discussed in Chapter 10.

   If the compensation is *two-pole* instead of one-pole, the circuit is as shown in Figure 9.31(b). The frequency response exhibits a drop with frequency at twice the slope (-40 dB per decade) of one-pole compensation.

   Figure 9.32(c) illustrates *feedforward compensation*. That is, instead of pin 1 being tied to the output through a capacitor, it is connected to the input. This system has a GBP of

$$GBP = 10^7 \text{ Hz}$$

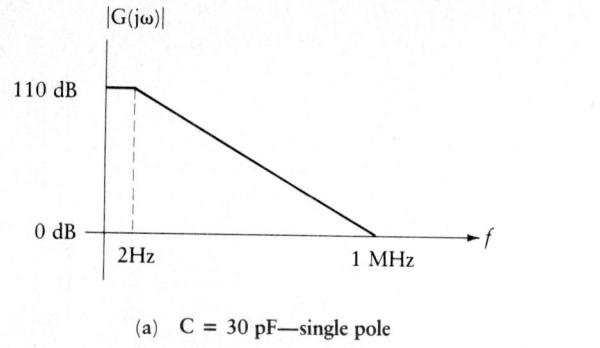 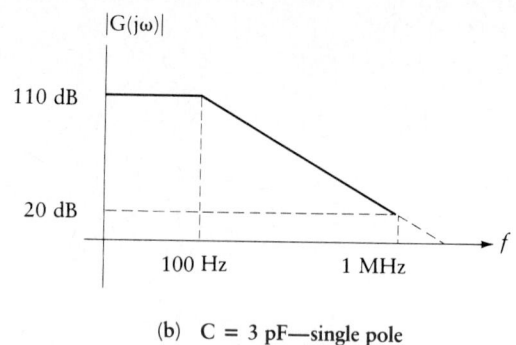

(a)   C = 30 pF—single pole   (b)   C = 3 pF—single pole

Figure 9.32   101 compensation.

The capacitance, C_F, is calculated from equation (9.36):

$$C_F = \frac{1}{2\pi \times 3 \times 10^6 \times R_F} \tag{9.36}$$

R_F is selected using gain considerations.

9.6.1   *Noninverting 101 Amplifiers*

If the configuration of Figure 9.33 is used, the voltage output is

$$v_o = \left(1 + \frac{R_F}{R_A}\right)v_i$$

The input resistance and output resistance of this amplifier are found by applying equations (9.11) and (9.13) as follows:

$$R_{\text{in}} = 2R_{cm}\left\|\left[\frac{R_A G R_i}{R_A + R_F}\right]\right.$$

$$= 400 \text{ M}\Omega\left\|\left[\frac{10^5(2 \text{ M}\Omega)}{1 + (R_F/R_A)}\right]\right. \approx 400 \text{ M}\Omega$$

$$R_{\text{out}} = \frac{R_o}{R_A G/(R_F + R_A)}$$

$$= \frac{100(1 + R_F/R_A)}{10^5}$$

The bandwidth is defined as the range of frequencies over which the gain is within 0.707 of its maximum value. This is derived in equation (9.17). If a 30-

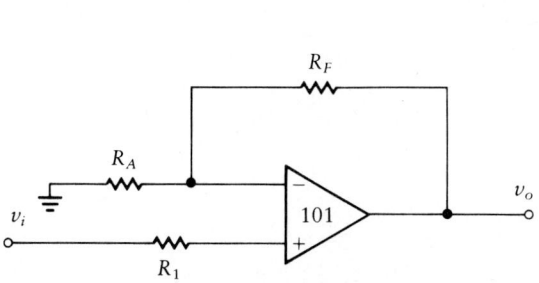

Figure 9.33   Noninverting 101 amplifier.

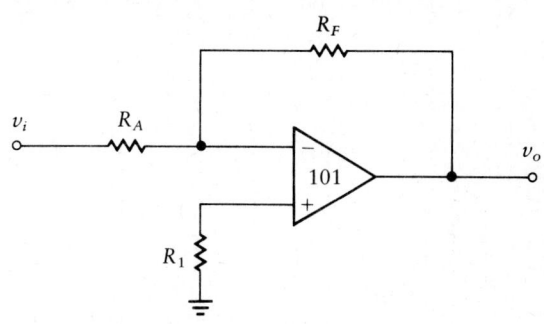

Figure 9.34   101 inverting amplifier.

pF capacitor is used in single-pole compensation, the bandwidth is given by

$$\mathrm{BW}_{30} = \frac{\mathrm{GBP}_{30}}{1 + R_F/R_A} = \frac{10^6}{1 + R_F/R_A} \tag{9.37}$$

If a 3-pF capacitor is used in single-pole compensation or with feedforward compensation, the bandwidth is

$$\mathrm{BW}_3 = \frac{\mathrm{GBP}_3}{1 + R_F/R_A} = \frac{10^7}{1 + R_F/R_A} \tag{9.38}$$

To achieve bias balance, we set

$$R_1 = R_A \parallel R_F$$

9.6.2   Inverting 101 Amplifiers

The output voltage for an inverting 101 amplifier, as shown in Figure 9.34, is

$$v_o = \frac{-R_F v_i}{R_A}$$

Once again, to achieve bias balance, we choose

$$R_1 = R_F \parallel R_A$$

R_{in} and R_{out} are found as in equations (9.12) and (9.13) and are given by

$$R_{\mathrm{in}} = R_A$$

$$R_{\mathrm{out}} = \frac{R_o(1 + R_F/R_A)}{G} = \frac{100(1 + R_F/R_A)}{10^5}$$

With 30 pF single-pole compensation, the bandwidth is found from the equation

$$BW_{30} = \frac{GBP_{30}}{1 + R_F/R_A} = \frac{10^6}{1 + R_F/R_A}$$

This is the same as for the noninverting amplifier of the previous section.

9.7   Designing Amplifiers Using Multiple Op-Amps

We now have knowledge of the external electrical characteristics of the op-amp and are able to use this knowledge as a building block in the design of amplifiers requiring more than one op-amp. The specified input resistance at each terminal is important to the designer, as are the characteristics of bandwidth and output resistance. Other characteristics that aid in selecting the correct op-amp type include CMRR, PSRR, and the slew rate.

The first step in designing multiple op-amp circuits is to determine the amount of gain per stage. This is accomplished by dividing the gain-bandwidth product of the selected op-amp by the required frequency response (bandwidth).

The next step is to determine which inputs are negative and which are positive. This determines whether connections should be made to the negative or positive terminal of the op-amp.

If the required input resistance is above 1 MΩ, the input voltage must be fed to the noninverting teminal of the op-amp. This is true, since the input resistance to the inverting terminal is the value of the coupling resistance used, and this is considerably less than 1 MΩ. There are other considerations in the design, such as isolation of various sources from each other and phase relationships. We tie these concepts together through the following two design examples.

Example 9.9   Multiple Op-Amp (Design)

Design an amplifier that is composed of 741 op-amps in order to obtain a gain of 800 with an input impedance of at least 20 MΩ. The amplifier must respond to a frequency of 40 kHz. Determine all resistor values, the output resistance, the input resistance, and the bandwidth.

SOLUTION   The maximum gain per stage is determined by the gain-bandwidth product for the 741 op-amp and the specified bandwidth. Thus,

$$\frac{\text{maximum gain}}{\text{stage}} = \frac{1 \text{ MHz}}{40 \text{ kHz}} = 25$$

In order to achieve an overall gain of 800, we therefore need at least three stages of amplification. To achieve the high input impedance, the input to the first op-amp must be connected to the noninverting input. The overall gain must be split among the three stages, so one possible choice is to design two of the stages with gains of 10 each and the third with a gain of 8. All stages are noninverting.

In designing single op-amp stages in earlier sections of this text, we found that there is usually not enough given information to specify all the design values. We must choose the value of one or more resistors before proceeding with the design. The same is true in this case, and if the procedures are followed, one possible set of resistor values for the op-amps with gains of 10 is

$$R_F = 90 \text{ k}\Omega; \quad R_A = 10 \text{ k}\Omega; \quad R_1 = 9 \text{ k}\Omega$$

For the op-amp requiring a gain of 8, we can use

$$R_F = 70 \text{ k}\Omega; \quad R_A = 10 \text{ k}\Omega; \quad R_1 = 8.75 \text{ k}\Omega$$

The resulting design is shown in Figure 9.35. The bandwidth of the amplifier is the smallest of the three individual bandwidths of the various stages. Using the stage with gain of 10 yields

$$1 + \frac{R_F}{R_A} = 1 + \frac{90 \text{ k}\Omega}{10 \text{ k}\Omega} = 10$$

The bandwidth is then given by

$$\text{BW} = \frac{1 \text{ MHz}}{10} = 100 \text{ kHz}$$

which exceeds the requirement. The input resistance is approximately 400 MΩ (see equation (9.12)), which also exceeds the requirement. The output resistance is found from equation (9.8) to be

$$R_{\text{out}} = \frac{75(1 + R_F/R_A)}{10^5} = 7.5 \text{ m}\Omega$$

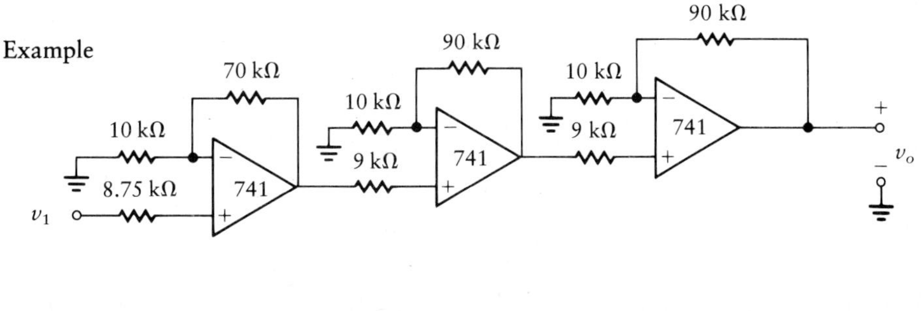

Figure 9.35
Solution for Example 9.9.

Example 9.10   Multiple Op-Amp (Design)

Design an amplifier that is composed of 741 op-amps to obtain an output of

$$v_o = 20v_1 - 40v_2 - 45v_3$$

The amplifier must respond to frequencies up to 50 kHz. Determine all resistor values, the output resistance, the input resistance, and the bandwidth of the amplifier.

SOLUTION   The design procedure of Section 8.6 is used. We can reduce the number of resistors in the design by forcing the parameter, Z, to be zero. This would be correct if the input-output relationship were

$$v_o = 20v_1 - 10v_2 - 9v_3$$

At this point, the maximum gain in any one stage is checked using the bandwidth requirements, as follows:

$$\frac{\text{maximum gain}}{\text{stage}} = \frac{\text{GBP}}{\text{BW}} = \frac{1 \text{ MHz}}{50 \text{ kHz}} = 20$$

Thus, we can achieve the required gain of the v_1 channel. If the gain of any channel is greater than 20, we obtain the gain with two series amplifiers.

Since this input-output equation is not the same as the given relationship, it is necessary to have additional amplifier stages that multiply v_2 by 4 and v_3 by 5. The main amplifier stage is designed using the following resistor values (we choose R_F and then solve for the other values).

$$R_F = 180 \text{ k}\Omega$$

$$R_1 = \frac{180 \text{ k}\Omega}{20} = 9 \text{ k}\Omega$$

$$R_2 = \frac{180 \text{ k}\Omega}{10} = 18 \text{ k}\Omega$$

$$R_3 = \frac{180 \text{ k}\Omega}{9} = 20 \text{ k}\Omega$$

The first voltage, v_1, is connected directly to the noninverting terminal, yielding an input resistance of approximately 400 MΩ. The amplification of v_2 by 4 is achieved with a stage using

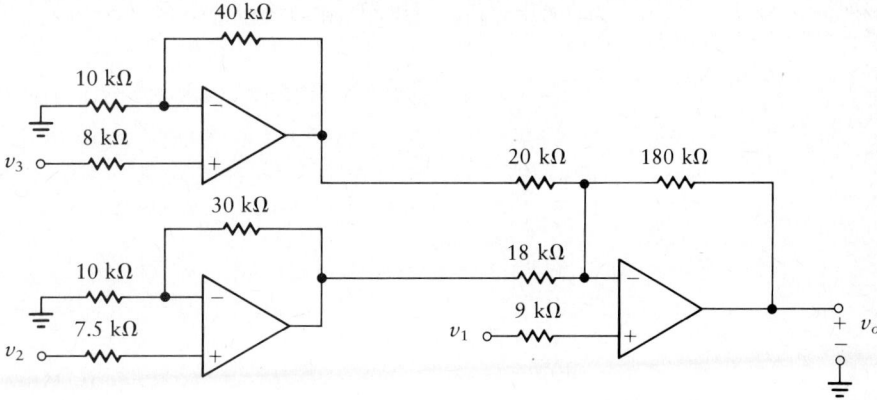

Figure 9.36   Solution for Example 9.10.

$$R_A = 10 \text{ k}\Omega$$

$$R_F = 30 \text{ k}\Omega$$

$$R_1 = 7.5 \text{ k}\Omega$$

The amplification of v_3 by 5 is achieved with a stage using

$$R_A = 10 \text{ k}\Omega$$

$$R_F = 40 \text{ k}\Omega$$

$$R_1 = 8 \text{ k}\Omega$$

The output resistance is given by

$$R_{\text{out}} = \frac{75[1 + R_F/(R_2 \parallel R_3)]}{10^5} = 15 \text{ m}\Omega$$

The bandwidth for the design is determined by the amplifier with the largest gain ($20v_1$),

$$BW = \frac{1 \text{ MHz}}{1 + R_F/(R_2 \parallel R_3)} = 50 \text{ kHz}$$

The resulting amplifier is shown in Figure 9.36.

9.8   Amplifiers with Balanced Inputs and Outputs

The effects of offsets can be eliminated or balanced in several ways. One direct method is to apply a small voltage at the input to cancel the effects of offset. This voltage is often developed across a potentiometer so that it can be adjusted. A second method is to cascade two op-amps in such a manner that the offsets cancel each other.

Various configurations of balanced inputs and outputs are illustrated in Figure 9.37. These use the second method of balancing, that of cascading two op-amps.

In the configuration shown, for example, in Figure 9.37(b), if v_i is supplied from a high-impedance source, the 5 kΩ resistors are no longer useful. Bias current may not be balanced in each amplifier. However, the effects of equal offsets due to unbalanced bias currents in the two input amplifiers should cancel one another. The alternate arrangement shown in the figure avoids this problem.

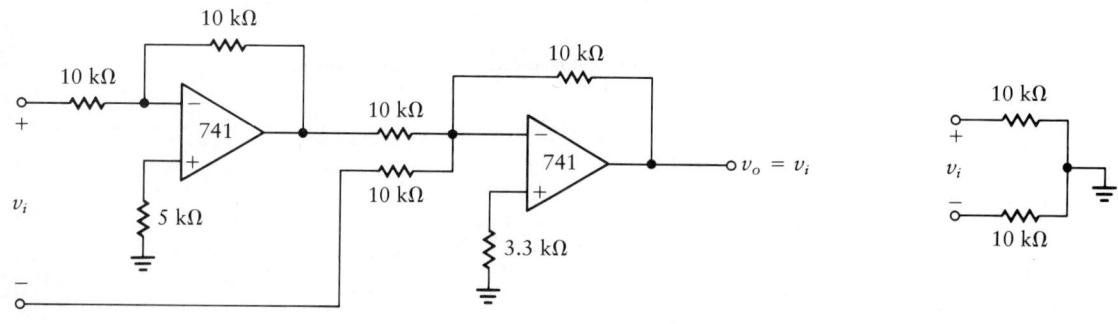

(a)   Balanced input, unbalanced output

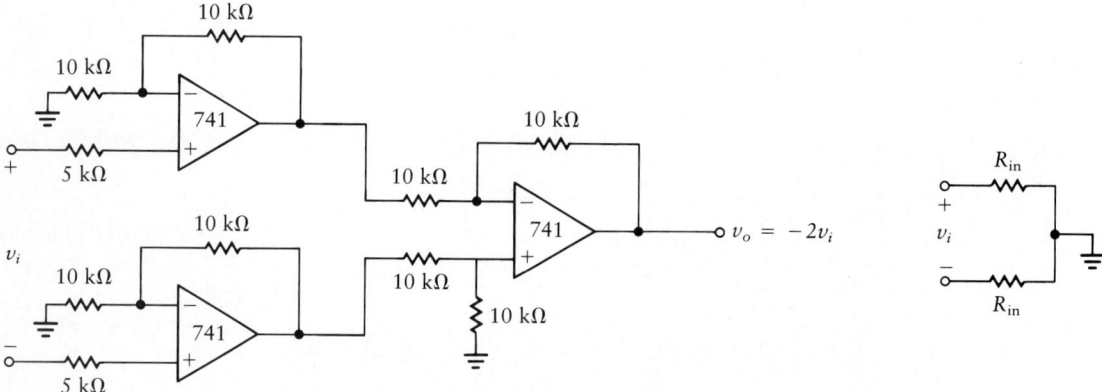

(b)   Balanced high-impedance input, unbalanced output

Figure 9.37   Balanced inputs and outputs.

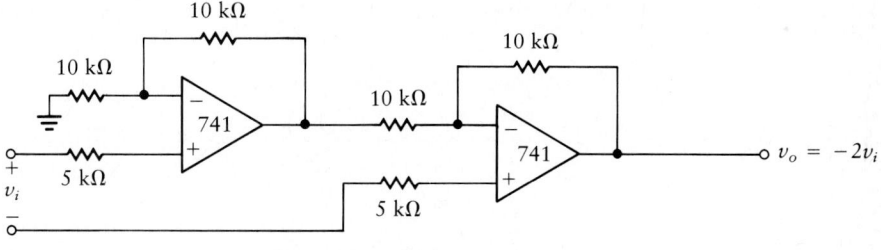

Alternate arrangement for (b)

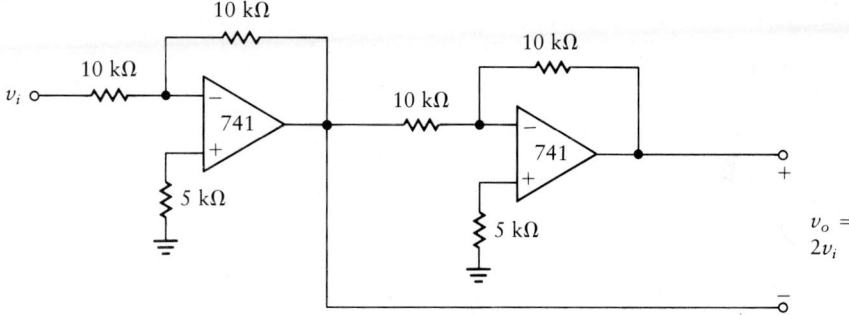

(c)   Unbalanced input, balanced output

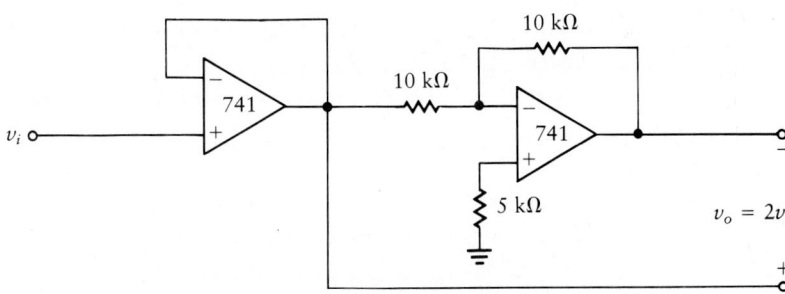

(d)   Unbalanced high-impedance input, balanced output

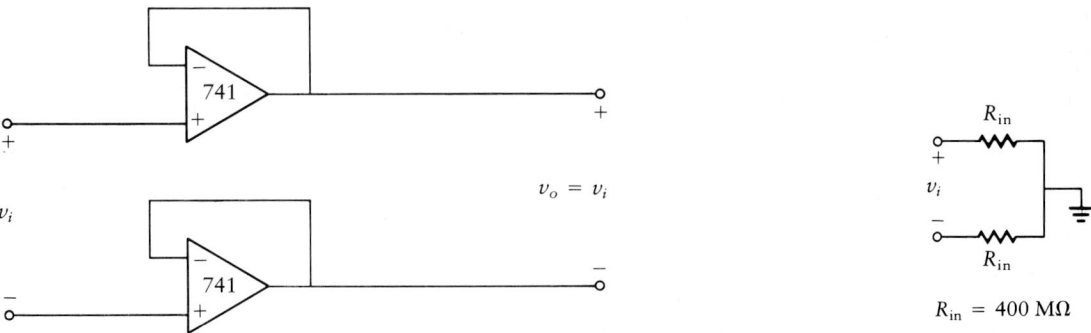

(e)   Differential high-impedance input, balanced output

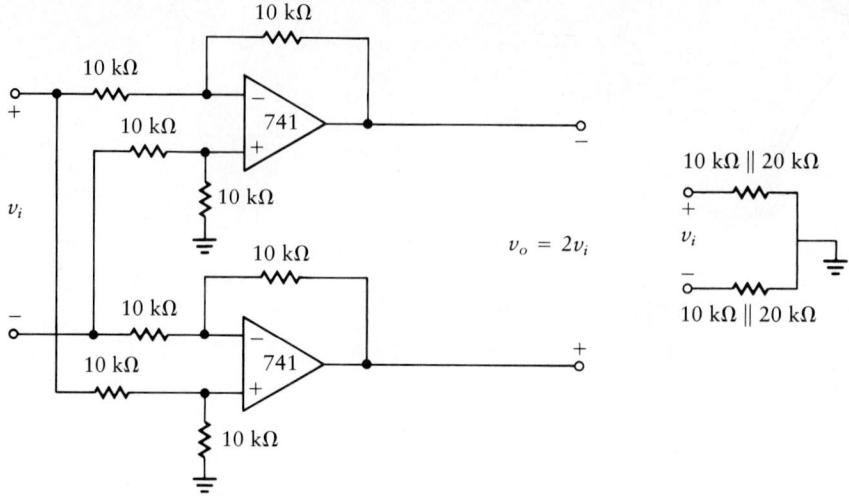

(f)   Balanced input, balanced output

Figure 9.37   (continued)

9.9 **Coupling Between Multiple Inputs**

When more than one input signal is connected either to the inverting or to the noninverting input to the op-amp, coupling between the inputs can result. This is frequently a disturbing problem, since a variation in one channel can produce an input into an adjoining channel. Consider the dual-input, noninverting op-amp of Figure 9.38(a), where each channel is driven with a voltage source in series with a source resistance. Here, v_1 and v_2 are ideal source voltages with series resistances r_1 and r_2, respectively. Let us write the equations for the effective voltages v_1' and v_2' into the summing amplifier. With v_2 set equal to zero, as shown in Figure 9.38(b), the voltage into the op-amp, v_2', is

$$v_2' = v_1 \frac{r_2}{r_1 + r_2 + R_1 + R_2}$$

When $v_1 = 0$, the v_1' voltage is (see Figure 9.38(c)),

$$v_1' = v_2 \frac{r_1}{r_1 + r_2 + R_1 + R_2}$$

Notice that the v_2' voltage comes from v_1 and the v_1' voltage comes from v_2. This coupling effect produces an undesirable crosstalk between the two inputs. The effect can be eliminated by designing a system with $r_1 = 0$ and $r_2 = 0$.

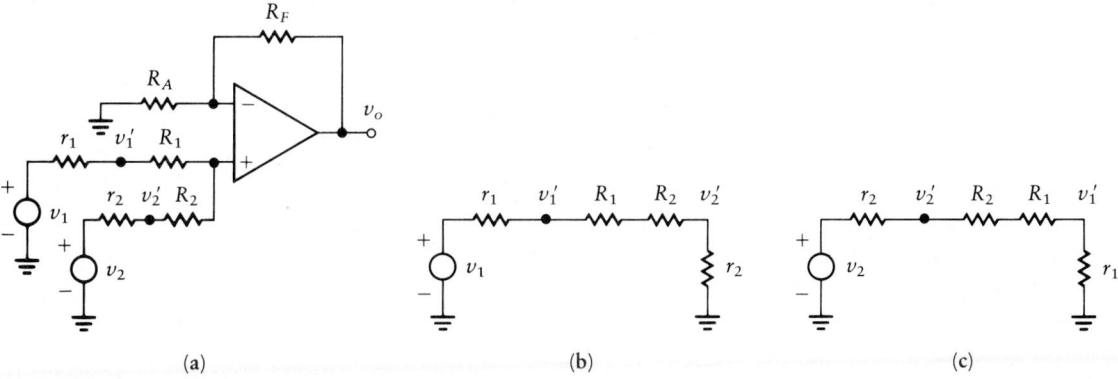

Figure 9.38 Coupling between multiple inputs.

Hence, to eliminate coupling, each noninverting multiple input should be driven with an op-amp that has zero (or very low) output impedance.

9.10 Audio Amplifiers

A common use for linear amplifiers is to provide gain for audio systems. An *audio amplifier* receives an input signal from a microphone, phonograph cartridge, tape deck, or an AM/FM tuner. The output of the amplifier drives a speaker system, headphones, or a tape recorder. These input devices usually have low output voltage and high output impedance. Therefore, the input impedance of the amplifier must be very high so it is much greater than the output impedance of the input device. If this is not true, the amplifier significantly loads the input device, and the gain decreases accordingly.

The devices that are driven by the amplifier usually have low impedance. For example, the impedance of a single speaker is normally 8 Ω. These devices may require powers on the order of 1 to 10 W.

Example 9.11 Audio Amplifier

Find the maximum output resistance for an audio amplifier that must develop 1 W of output power into an 8-Ω speaker. Also find the current that the op-amp must be capable of supplying. Assume that a 16 V peak-to-peak output voltage is available from the amplifier with no load.

SOLUTION   The peak-load current is given by

$$i_{\text{peak}} = \frac{v_{\text{peak}}}{R_s + R_L} = \frac{8}{R_s + 8}$$

where R_s is the output resistance of the amplifier. If we assume that the output is sinusoidal, the power delivered to the load is

$$P_L = \frac{i_{\text{peak}}^2 R_L}{2}$$

$$= 4i_{\text{peak}}^2 = 4\left[\frac{8}{R_s + 8}\right]^2 = 1$$

Since the load power was given to be 1 W, we set this expression equal to 1. We then solve for the equation for the output resistance, R_s:

$$R_s = 8\ \Omega$$

This is the maximum output resistance for the amplifier.

We now find the required output current. In order to develop 1 W of power in an 8 Ω load, the required rms current is 0.353 A. That is, if this quantity is squared and multiplied by 8 Ω (the load resistance), the result is unity. The op-amp must therefore be capable of supplying this amount of current. Typically, op-amps do not provide enough power to drive speakers to the desired level. The 741 op-amp, for example, is limited to approximately 20 mA. One alternative is for the designer to use the op-amp to drive a Darlington, or CSDC, amplifier, as discussed in Section 6.4.   ✦

PROBLEMS

9.1   Consider the improved op-amp model with

$$G = 10^5$$
$$R_i = 1\ \text{M}\Omega$$
$$R_{cm} = 200\ \text{M}\Omega$$

Solve the network of Figure P9.1 for the resistance, R_o.

9.2   In each of the op-amp circuits of Figure P9.2, $V_{io} = 10$ mV, the input offset voltage temperature coefficient is 10 μV/°C, the temperature is 50°C, and $R_i = 1$ MΩ. Find the largest possible offset in v_o due to V_{io}.

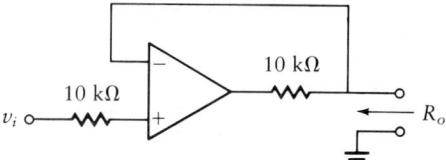

Figure P9.1

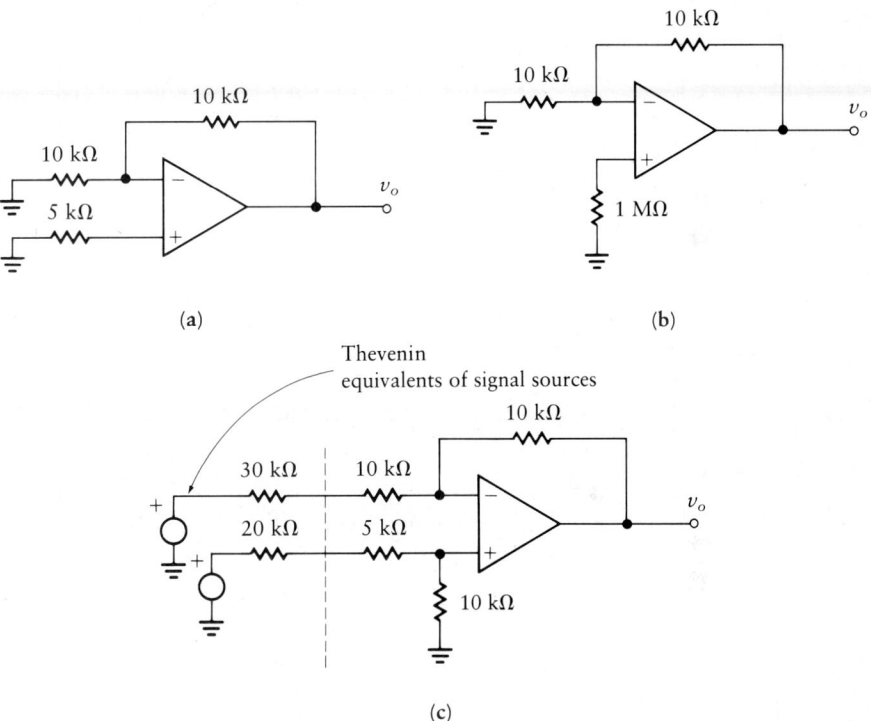

(a)

(b)

Thevenin
equivalents of signal sources

(c)

Figure P9.2

9.3 For each of the circuits of Figure P9.2, the op-amp input bias current is 800 nA, the bias offset is 20 nA, the input bias current-temperature coefficient is -10 nA/°C, and the input offset bias current-temperature coefficient is -2 nA/°C. Find each of the following.

   a. The largest possible offset in v_o due to average bias current effects.

   b. The largest possible offset in v_o due to bias offset effects.

   c. The largest possible offset in v_o due to voltage offset bias current and bias offset combined.

9.4 Design a single 741 op-amp amplifier that will yield an output given by the equation

$$v_o = 10v_1 + 6v_2 + 4v_3$$

The equivalent resistance at the negative and positive terminals is 10 kΩ. Determine each resistor value, the bandwidth, the input resistance of each amplifier input, and the output resistance.

9.5   Design a single 741 op-amp amplifier that will yield an output given by the equation

$$v_o = -10v_1 - 5v_2 - 4v_3$$

The equivalent resistance at the negative and positive terminals is 10 kΩ. Determine each resistor value, the bandwidth, input resistance at each amplifier input, and the output resistance.

9.6   Design a single 741 op-amp amplifier that will yield an output given by the equation

$$v_o = 10v_1 + 6v_2 - 3v_3 - 4v_4$$

The equivalent resistance at the negative and positive terminals is 10 kΩ. Determine each resistor value, the bandwidth, the input resistance at each amplifier input, and the output resistance.

In Problems 9.7–9.16, design 741 op-amp circuits that will generate the indicated output voltage, v_o, from the input voltages v_1, v_2, and v_3. Be sure to balance the bias currents in each design. For each design, find the input resistance for each input, the output resistance, and the bandwidth. The input resistance must be at least 100 MΩ and the bandwidth must be greater than 20 kHz. It may be necessary to use more than one op-amp in some of these designs.

9.7 $v_o = 700\, v_1$

9.8 $v_o = \dfrac{v_1}{700}$

9.9 $v_o = -700v_1$

9.10 $v_o = \dfrac{-v_1}{700}$

9.11 $v_o = v_1 - v_2$

9.12 $v_o = 10v_1 - v_2$

9.13 $v_o = v_1 - 10v_2$

9.14 $v_o = v_1 + 700v_2$

9.15 $v_o = -(v_1 + 700v_2)$

9.16 $v_o = v_1 - 2v_2 + 3v_3$

In Problems 9.17–9.22, design multiple 741 op-amp circuits to develop the indicated output voltage, v_o, from the input voltages v_1, v_2, and v_3. The input resistance to each input must be 100 MΩ or greater, and the inputs should not be directly coupled to one another. For each design, find R_{in}, R_{out}, and the bandwidth. A minimum bandwidth of 50 kHz must be achieved.

9.17 $v_o = 3(v_1 + v_2)$

9.18 $v_o = 3(v_1 - v_2)$

9.19 $v_o = 1000v_1 - 300v_2$

9.20 $v_o = v_1 + v_2 - v_3$

9.21 $v_o = 0.63v_1 + 0.3v_2 + 0.42v_3$

9.22 $v_o = 100v_1 + 50v_2$

In Problems 9.23–9.26, design single-amplifier 101 circuits that will generate the indicated output voltage, v_o, from the input voltages v_1 and v_2. Use a 3-pF compensating capacitor wherever possible. Be sure to balance the bias currents in each input. Calculate R_{in}, R_{out}, and the bandwidth.

9.23 $v_o = 700v_1$

9.24 $v_o = 10v_1 - v_2$

9.25 $v_o = 20v_1 + 30v_2$

9.26 $v_o = v_1 - 15v_2$

In Problems 9.27–9.29, design multiple 101 operational amplifier circuits to develop the voltage v_o from the input voltages v_1 and v_2. The input resistance into each input must be at least 100 MΩ and the inputs should not be directly coupled to one another. The bandwidth should be as great as possible using 30 pF or 3 pF 101 compensation. Find the bandwidth in each case.

9.27 $v_o = 10(v_1 + v_2)$

9.28 $v_o = 10v_1 - v_2$

9.29 $v_o = 1000v_1 - 300v_2$

9.30 Design a circuit using 741 op-amps, which, from the *differential* voltages, v_1 and v_2, develops an output voltage

$$v_o = 100v_1 + 50v_2$$

Input resistances should be balanced to ground and should be in excess of 100 MΩ. The minimum bandwidth must be 50 kHz.

9.31 Design a circuit using 741 op-amps, which, from voltages v_1 and v_2, develops a *balanced* output voltage

$$v_o = 100v_1 - 50v_2$$

The output resistances should be less than 1 Ω.

9.32 Design a circuit using 741 op-amps that has a balanced input, a balanced output, a gain of 100, input impedance greater than 100 MΩ, and output impedance less than 1 Ω.

9.33 Two differential voltages v_A and v_B, each of which are balanced with respect to ground, are available as inputs. The v_A source has a Thevenin resistance between 10 kΩ and 210 kΩ, whereas the v_B source has a Thevenin resistance between 50 kΩ and 150 kΩ. Design a multiple 741 circuit to generate the voltage

$$v_o = 10(v_A - v_B)$$

with respect to ground without coupling between the two input sources. The bias current balance should be as good as is possible.

9.34 Design a single-supply audio amplifier using a 741 op-amp and having a gain of 100. Find the input impedance, output impedance, and frequency response of your design. (Use specification sheets for the 741 op-amp as given in Appendix D.)

10

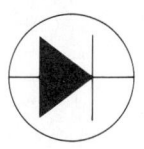

FREQUENCY-RESPONSE CHARACTERISTICS

10.0 Introduction

Upon receiving your electrical engineering degree, you were employed by the XYZ Audio Corporation, a company that designs and manufactures stereo equipment. Since your supervisor knew you had a solid background in electronic design, you were assigned the task of designing an amplifier as part of a compact disc player system. You mustered all your knowledge of electronics, made a number of trade-off decisions, and chose a CE amplifier. The amplifier was designed using the techniques of the earlier chapters, and in order to achieve the necessary gain using only one stage, you bypassed the emitter resistor with a capacitor.

A prototype of the system was constructed, and a disc was played as a test. The result was a disaster! The sound was far less than full, and, in fact, you determined that the amplifier was not responding well to the low frequencies in the audio signal. The output was distorted! What went wrong?

You completely forgot that capacitors (and inductors) are frequency-dependent elements. As soon as they are present in a circuit, the response becomes a function of frequency. You failed to perform a frequency analysis of your amplifier! The current chapter teaches you how to correct this design error.

Our earlier work treated amplifiers as though their behavior was independent of the frequency of the input signal. This is not true in the practical case.

415

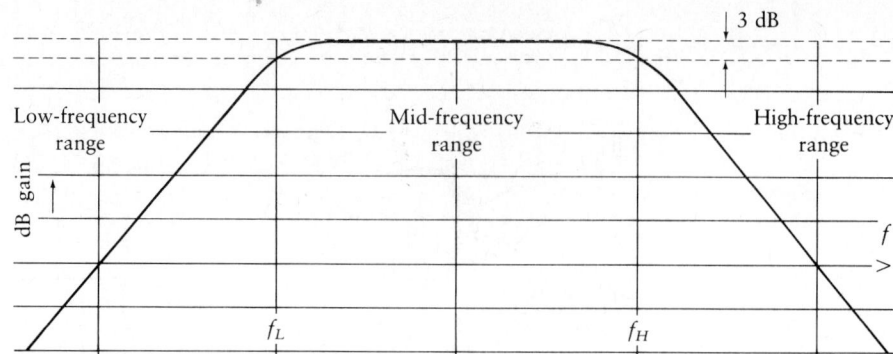

The current chapter concentrates upon the frequency-dependent aspects of various amplifiers.

Capacitance within an amplifier, which causes the response to be frequency-dependent, may be present by design or it may be present unintentionally. *Coupling* and *bypass* capacitors are often designed into the system, with the desired condition being a short circuit for all signal frequencies. That is, these capacitors are intended to provide an open circuit for the dc bias voltages but allow all signal components to pass through them without attenuation. Capacitors do not suddenly change from a short-circuit to an open-circuit condition when the frequency reaches zero. Instead they approach an open circuit as the frequency gets smaller, so the performance is degraded as the input frequencies decrease.

The second type of capacitance found in an amplifier is present unintentionally. Any time that two conductors are separated by any nonconducting material, capacitance exists. There is thus internal capacitance within every semiconductor, capacitance between contacts, and wiring capacitances due to the circuit configuration. As frequencies increase, these capacitances tend to short out the signal and thereby decrease the gain.

Figure 10.1 illustrates a typical amplitude-frequency response for an RC-coupled amplifier. Note that the maximum gain occurs for a *midrange* of frequencies and that the gain decreases at both low and high frequencies. The low and high limits of the midrange, f_L and f_H, are known as the *corner frequencies*. They are defined as the points at which the gain drops to 0.707 of its midrange value. This figure is the square root of 0.5 and therefore represents the frequency at which the output power reduces to one-half of its midrange value. It is known as the *half-power point*.

Amplifiers can be analyzed as linear systems—the frequency response can be described by a complex function yielding the magnitude and phase-shift response for each input frequency. We spend the first portion of this chapter learning how to draw these two response curves from the transfer function equation of the system. In particular, we concentrate upon a simple method, known as the *Bode plot*, which permits drawing of the graphs almost by inspection.

The concept of Bode plots is then applied to analysis of the frequency response of operational amplifiers. This is followed by a parallel treatment of BJT amplifiers and FET amplifiers. Attention is given to both the low-frequency and high-frequency response of these amplifiers.

10.1 Bode Plots

When a system contains capacitance and/or inductance, the response of that system is a function of the frequency of the input signal. Frequency plots of amplitude and phase are important measures of system behavior. Analysis of frequency-dependent systems can be performed using the impedance method, also known as *sinusoidal steady-state analysis*. These analyses result in formulas relating output to input. We will see how these formulas can be translated into frequency-response curves, which clearly demonstrate how the amplifier behaves for varying input signal frequencies.

We begin with a simple example. Consider the series circuit of Figure 10.2. The complex (phasor) output voltage of the circuit is given by

$$V_o(j\omega) = \frac{j\omega RC \; V_i(j\omega)}{1 + j\omega RC}$$

where $V_i(j\omega)$ is the phasor of the input voltage. It thus represents the magnitude and phase of that sinusoid. As a specific example, let us assume that the resistor and capacitor are chosen such that

$$RC = \frac{1}{4}$$

Then the ratio of output to input phasor, known as the *transfer function*, is given by

$$G(j\omega) = \frac{V_o(j\omega)}{V_i(j\omega)} = \frac{j\omega}{j\omega + 4}$$

Figure 10.2
A series circuit.

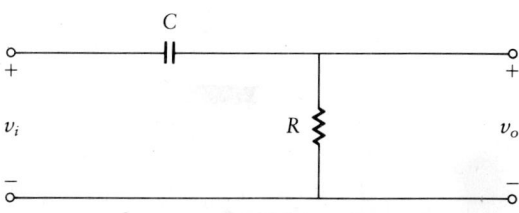

This is a complex function of the radian frequency, ω. In dealing with complex numbers (or functions), we are actually dealing with two sets of numbers (or functions). These are commonly selected as either real and imaginary parts or magnitudes and phases. The magnitude and phase representation is more common in sinusoidal steady-state analysis since it has physical significance in terms of the amplitudes and phase shifts of the sinusoidal signals.

We denote the amplitude and phase of the transfer function as $A(\omega)$ and $\phi(\omega)$, respectively. For this example, they are given by

$$A(\omega) = |G(j\omega)| = \left| \frac{j\omega}{j\omega + 4} \right|$$

$$= \frac{\omega}{\sqrt{\omega^2 + 16}}$$

$$\phi(\omega) = \angle G(j\omega) = 90° - \tan^{-1}\left(\frac{\omega}{4}\right)$$

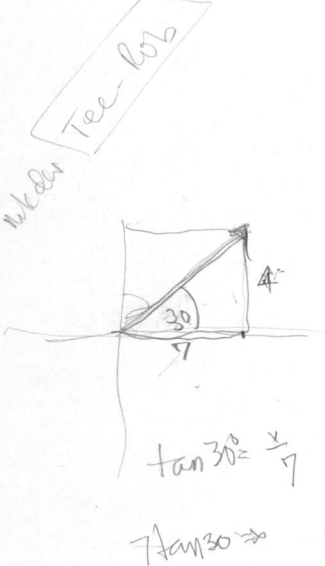

As an example of the application of these results, suppose that the input to the system is given by

$$v_i(t) = 3\cos(7t + 30°)$$

The steady-state output of the system is a sinuoid with the same frequency, 7 rad/s, but with altered amplitude and phase. In order to find the new amplitude and phase, we need only evaluate $A(\omega)$ and $\phi(\omega)$ at the given frequency. Thus,

$$A(\omega)|_{\omega=7} = \frac{7}{\sqrt{7^2 + 16}} = \frac{7}{\sqrt{65}} = 0.87$$

$$\phi(\omega)|_{\omega=7} = 90° - \tan^{-1}\left(\frac{7}{4}\right) = 90° - 60° = 30°$$

The output amplitude is equal to the input amplitude multiplied by $A(\omega)$, and the output phase is the input phase shifted by $\phi(\omega)$. Therefore, the output time signal is given by

$$v_o(t) = 2.6 \cos(7t + 60°)$$

Suppose you were asked to measure the frequency response of a system in the laboratory. You could take advantage of the amplitude and phase relationships by simply applying a sinusoidal input and observing the output amplitude and phase shift. Since you will be taking the ratio of output amplitude to input amplitude, the actual value of input amplitude is not critical. It need only be large enough so that the signal is not masked by noise, yet not so large that it saturates the system. In practice, the transfer function is evaluated at a particular frequency (the frequency of the input). Then the input frequency is changed to find the transfer function at other values of frequency.

The Laplace transform is closely related to the sinusoidal steady state transfer function, and we use it for part of the following analysis. The variable in the Laplace transform is s instead of $j\omega$. The variable s is complex, whereas the radian frequency, ω, is a real variable. We can change an expression from sinusoidal steady state to Laplace transform by making the following substitution:

$$s = j\omega$$

Although this may seem like a minor modification, it simplifies the mathematics considerably, since we will be factoring polynomials in s. If $j\omega$ is used instead of s, it is necessary to deal with complex polynomials. We note that sinusoidal steady-state analysis is a special case of Laplace transform analysis, where the complex variable s is restricted to lie on the imaginary axis. We are avoiding arguments relative to existence of the transform, since it is true that if the sinusoidal steady-state expression exists, the Laplace transform must converge along the imaginary axis. There is no need for us to deal with functions for which the transform does not exist along the imaginary axis, since they could not result from real circuits.

Many electronic systems contain feedback paths. This is particularly true in the case of control systems. Although the results of this chapter apply to systems with or without feedback, we relate the initial discussion to the feedback case.

It is useful to define some new terms. We define $G(s)$ as the product of all forward-path input-output ratios. This transfer function, $G(s)$, thus represents the transfer function of the system if all feedback paths are open-circuited (i.e., cut). We also defined $H(s)$ as the product of all feedback input-output ratios. The product of these two is known as the *loop-transfer function*, and it is an important characteristic of the overall system. This product function, $G(s)H(s)$, may be characterized by a ratio of polynomials for any linear system and is given in equation (10.1):

$$G(s)H(s) = \frac{b_m s^m + b_{m-1} s^{m-1} + \cdots + b_1 s + b_0}{a_n s^n + a_{n-1} s^{n-1} + \cdots + a_1 s + a_0} \tag{10.1}$$

A *zero* of $G(s)H(s)$ is defined as any numerical value of s that causes the numerator polynomial in equation (10.1) to have a value of zero. Therefore, at this value of s,

$$G(s)H(s) = 0$$

A *pole* of $G(s)H(s)$ is defined as any numerical value of s that causes the denominator polynomial in equation (10.1) to have zero value. Therefore, at this value of s,

$$G(s)H(s) \rightarrow \infty$$

We obtain the sinusoidal response by letting $s = j\omega$ in equation (10.1).

Our current objective is to plot the frequency response represented by $G(s)H(s)$. We start with the limiting values of frequency, since these will prove critical in devising the inspection method for plotting the response. As the frequency, ω, approaches infinity, all but the highest powers of s in the numerator and denominator may be ignored. That is, if ω is very large, ω^n is much larger than ω^{n-1}. Thus, letting $s = j\omega$ and retaining only the highest powers, we have

$$G(j\omega)H(j\omega) \approx \frac{b_m(j\omega)^m}{a_n(j\omega)^n} = \left(\frac{b_m}{a_n}\right)j^{m-n}\omega^{m-n}$$

This shows that as the frequency approaches infinity, the amplitude curve is proportional to ω^{m-n}. The phase curve approaches $(m - n)$ times $90°$, since this is the angle of the j^{m-n} term.

We now examine the other extreme, as ω approaches zero. For this case, all but the lowest power of ω are negligible. That is, if ω is very small, ω^{n-1} is much larger than ω^n. Thus, as frequency approaches zero, the response function approaches

$$G(j\omega)H(j\omega) = \frac{b_0}{a_0}$$

This is true provided both a_0 and b_0 are nonzero. If either or both of these constants are equal to zero, it is necessary to include the lowest power of ω that is present.

As an example, consider the loop-transfer function,

$$G(s)H(s) = \frac{6s^3 + 2s^2 + 3s}{s^5 + 4s^4 + 2s^3 + s^2 + 10}$$

At high frequencies, this is approximately equal to

$$G(j\omega)H(j\omega) = \frac{6(j\omega)^3}{(j\omega)^5}$$

and the amplitude and phase are given by

$$A(\omega) = |G(j\omega)H(j\omega)| \approx \frac{6}{\omega^2} = 6\omega^{-2}$$

$$\phi(\omega) = \angle\, G(j\omega)H(j\omega) \approx -180°$$

At low frequencies, we maintain the lowest powers of the numerator and denominator to get

$$G(j\omega)H(j\omega) \approx \frac{3j\omega}{10}$$

and the amplitude and phase are given by

$$A(\omega) = |G(j\omega)H(j\omega)| = \frac{3\omega}{10}$$

$$\phi(\omega) = \angle\, G(j\omega)H(j\omega) \approx 90°$$

Once the behavior of the curve is found for extreme values of ω, a few more measurements should suffice to plot the entire curve. It is useful to make more measurements at frequencies where the largest changes in amplitude or phase occur and fewer measurements over ranges where the function is almost constant.

Now that we have determined the behavior of the curve for limiting values, we examine the other critical parameters in the frequency-response curves.

10.1.1 G(s)H(s) *Function Terms*

Since polynomials in s can be factored, the $G(s)H(s)$ functions with which we deal can be viewed as products of simple terms. When complex terms are multiplied together, the resulting amplitude is the product of the individual amplitudes, and the resulting phase is the algebraic sum of the individual phases. We thus find it useful first to learn to deal with the simplest terms that will result from factoring of the $G(s)H(s)$ polynomials.

Instead of dealing with the amplitude curves directly, their logarithms are usually used. In this manner, multiplication of the various amplitudes is equivalent to addition of the logarithms. The *decibel* (dB) is used to describe amplitude-response curves as a function of frequency. The decibel is defined as in equation (10.2):

$$dB = 20\log_{10}A(\omega) = 20\log_{10}|G(j\omega)H(j\omega)| \tag{10.2}$$

We use the observations of the previous section to aid in the plotting of the various components of $G(s)H(s)$. That is, we first concentrate upon the behavior of these curves for very small and for very large values of frequency. We see that the decibel gain is usually proportional to the log of the frequency.

Therefore, if we use a logarithmic scale for the frequency axis, these curves will be straight lines and, therefore, will be much easier to plot by inspection. For this reason, semilog paper is usually used to plot the components of $G(s)H(s)$. The frequency is plotted on the horizontal logarithmic scale and the decibel amplitude and the phase are plotted along the linear vertical scale. The number of cycles of the semilog paper determines how many orders of magnitude of frequency variation can be plotted. Three- or four-cycle semilog paper is commonly used for general-purpose applications.

10.1.2   *The Asymptotic Approximation*

The numerator and denominator of $G(s)H(s)$, as given by equation (10.1), can be factored into a product of functions. The individual factors are of one of the following forms:

1. Frequency-invariant factors (constants), K.
2. Terms corresponding to simple (order 1) zeros or poles at the origin, s or $1/s$.
3. Linear terms corresponding to simple zeros (not at the origin), $s\tau_1 + 1$.
4. Linear terms corresponding to simple poles, $(s\tau_2 + 1)^{-1}$.
5. Quadratic terms corresponding to simple zeros and poles,

$$\left(\frac{s}{\omega_n}\right)^2 + \frac{2\zeta s}{\omega_n} + 1$$

or

$$\frac{1}{(s/\omega_n)^2 + 2\zeta s/\omega_n + 1}$$

We shall now see how to plot each of these factors. These could, of course, be plotted point by point by evaluating the function for various values of frequency. We shall find that by using the limiting values of frequency (i.e., the asymptotes of the curve), we can draw fairly accurate curves almost by inspection.

1. *Frequency invariant factors.* The gain constant K, which is independent of frequency, is plotted from the decibel representation of equation (10.3):

$$K_{\text{dB}} = 20 \log_{10} K \tag{10.3}$$

The constant K represents the product of all frequency-invariant terms in the $G(s)H(s)$ function. Equation (10.3) is plotted as Figure 10.3. Note that the phase of this real constant is zero for all frequencies.

Figure 10.3
Gain and phase for a
constant factor.

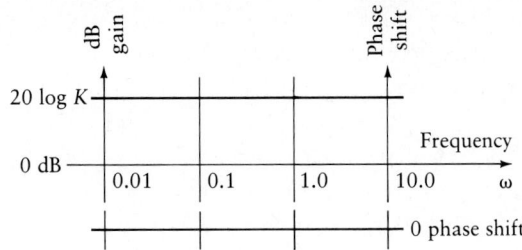

2. *Zeros or poles at the origin.* The factors are of the form

$$s \tag{10.4a}$$

or

$$\frac{1}{s} \tag{10.4b}$$

We set $s = j\omega$ and find the amplitude and phase for the zero as follows:

$$A(\omega)_{dB} = 20 \log(|j\omega|) = 20 \log \omega \tag{10.5a}$$

$$\phi(\omega) = \angle j\omega = 90° \tag{10.5b}$$

For the pole,

$$A(\omega)_{dB} = -20 \log \omega \tag{10.5c}$$

and

$$\phi(\omega) = \angle 1/j\omega = -90° \tag{10.5d}$$

We shall divert our attention for a moment to explore multiple zeros or poles at the origin. If the factors s or $1/s$ are raised to the power n, we have multiple zeros or poles. Since these factors multiply together in the expression for $G(s)H(s)$, the decibel amplitudes add, as do the phases. Thus, the amplitude for a multiple zero is

$$20n \log \omega \text{ dB} \tag{10.6}$$

and for a multiple pole, it is

$$-20n \log \omega \text{ dB}$$

The phase for the multiple zero is

$$n90° \qquad\qquad (10.7)$$

and for the pole, it is

$$-n90°$$

Figure 10.4 illustrates the amplitude and phase plots for multiple zeros and poles. If $n = 1$, we are dealing with simple zeros and poles. Note that the amplitude curve goes through 0 dB when $\omega = 1$. This is true because log 1 = 0. A *decade* is defined as a change in frequency by a factor of 10. When the frequency increases 10-fold, the log of the frequency increases by 1. Thus, the slope of the curves in Figure 10.4 is $\pm 20n$ db/decade. An *octave* is defined as a change in frequency by a factor of 2. Since the log of 2 is approximately 0.3, a slope of $20n$ dB per decade is nearly the same as a slope of $6n$ dB per octave.

We have not yet found it necessary to make any approximations. The curves of Figure 10.4 are exact representations of the amplitude and phase of the factors s^n and s^{-n}.

If a transfer function polynomial contains both a constant (frequency invariant term) and poles and zeros at the origin, the combined plot is formed by adding together the results of (1) and (2). For ease in plotting, the constant portion of the transfer function, K, can be combined with the s^n terms. As an example, consider a single pole at the origin, as given by equation (10.8).

$$\frac{K}{j\omega} = \frac{1}{j\omega/K} \qquad\qquad (10.8)$$

We can view the frequency variable as being ω/K instead of simply ω. Multiplication of the frequency by 10 results in multiplication of ω/K by 10. Thus, the amplitude response for this term has the same slope as that corresponding to the single pole at the origin, $1/s$. The only difference is that the amplitude curve intersects the 0 dB line at a frequency of $\omega = K$ instead of $\omega = 1$. The phase remains constant at $-90°$, as is the case without the constant K. It should be clear that these results are not any different from those that would occur if the two individual components of the amplitude curve were added together.

3. *Zeros.* Let us now consider zeros that are not at the origin. If these are simple (not multiple), the factor is of the form

$$(j\omega\tau + 1) \qquad\qquad (10.9)$$

The resulting amplitude plot is no longer a straight line, so we shall resort to asymptotic approximations. If the frequency is very small, such that $\omega\tau << 1$, we can approximate the decible (dB) amplitude by

Figure 10.4
Phase and gain for
multiple zeros and
poles at origin.

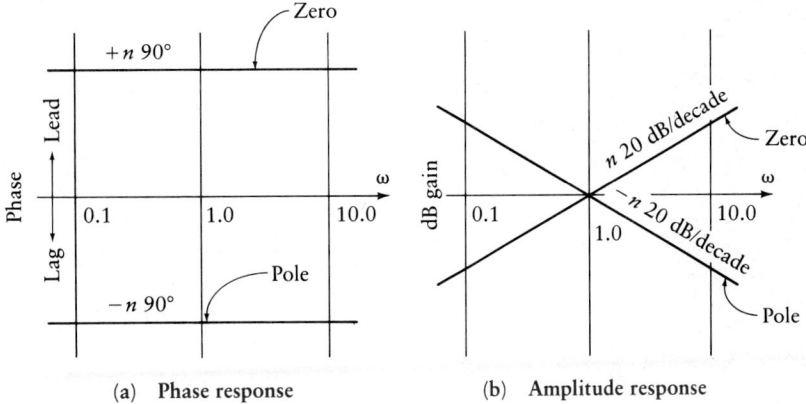

(a) Phase response   (b) Amplitude response

$$20 \log_{10} |j\omega\tau + 1| \approx 20 \log_{10} 1 = 0 \text{ dB} \qquad (10.10)$$

Thus, for small values of frequency, the magnitude remains close to 0 dB. Now when the frequency becomes very large, $\omega\tau \gg 1$, we can neglect the constant term to get

$$20 \log_{10} |j\omega\tau + 1| \approx 20 \log_{10} \omega\tau \qquad (10.11)$$

This is similar to the result for a zero at the origin, so the amplitude and phase plot resembles that of a plot for the term $j\omega\tau$. The slope (for large ω) is thus 20 dB/decade, and this straight-line asymptote intersects the 0-dB line at $\omega\tau = 1$, or $\omega = 1/\tau$. This point of intersection is known as the *corner frequency*. The two straight-line plots, one for small frequency and one for large frequency, intersect at the corner frequency and represent the asymptotic approximation to the curves. These are illustrated in Figure 10.5(a).

We have shown that once the corner frequency is known, the approximate curve for the amplitude of a simple zero is easily drawn by inspection. Suppose the approximation is not good enough and that additional accuracy is required. The first steps in approaching the exact curve can also be accomplished by inspection. In fact, the actual amplitude curve deviates only slightly from the straight-line asymptotes. Figure 10.5(a) shows both the asymptotic approximation and the exact curve. At the corner frequency, the actual curve is 3 dB above the approximation. One octave away from the corner frequency, the actual curve deviates from the approximation by about 1 dB. These variations can be seen from the equation. At the corner frequency, $\omega = 1/\tau$, the value of the function is

$$20 \log(|j1 + 1|) = 20 \log\sqrt{2} = 3 \text{ dB}$$

Figure 10.5
Response curves for
zeros and poles.

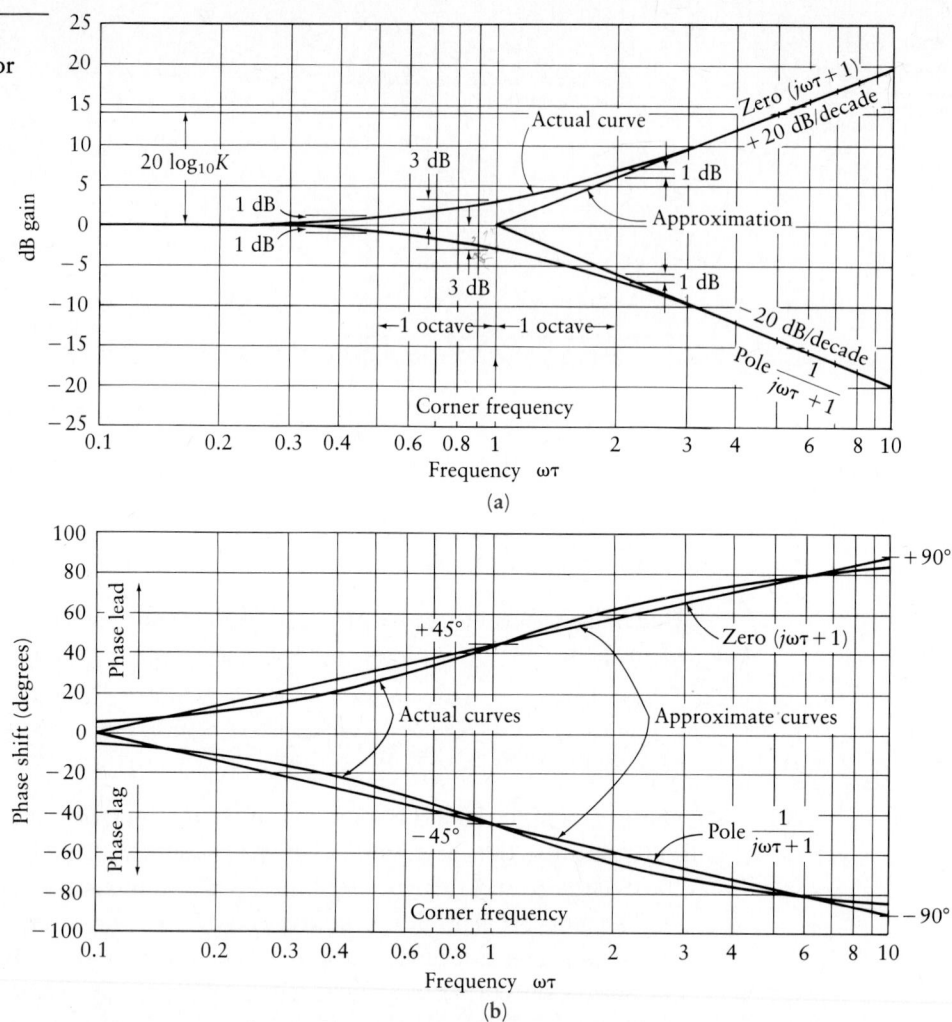

Since the approximate curve is at 0 dB at the corner frequency, the deviation is 3 dB as stated above.

One octave above the corner frequency, $\omega = 2/\tau$, and the value of the function is

$$20 \log(|\,j2 + 1|) = 20 \log\sqrt{5} = 6.99 \text{ dB}$$

The approximate curve is at about 6 dB, 1 octave above the corner frequency, so the deviation is about 1 dB, as just stated.

One octave below the corner frequency, at $\omega = 1/2\tau$, the value of the function is

Figure 10.6
Phase curve.

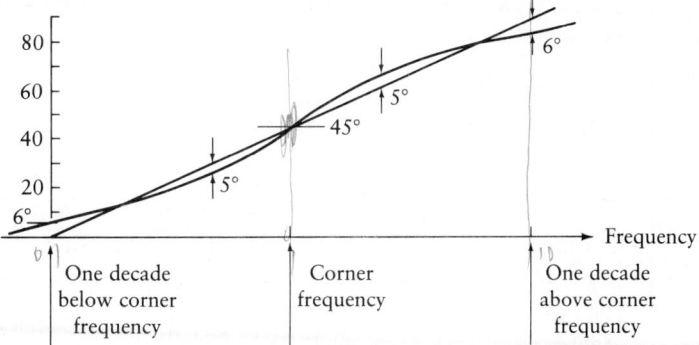

$$20 \log\left(\left|\frac{j}{2} + 1\right|\right) = 20 \log\sqrt{\frac{5}{4}} = 0.97 \text{ dB}$$

The approximate curve is at 0 dB, 1 octave below the corner frequency, so the deviation is once again about 1 dB.

The phase of the expression in equation (10.9) is simply the angle whose tangent is the ratio of the imaginary to the real part of the function. Thus,

$$\phi(\omega) = \angle 1 + j\omega\tau$$

$$= \tan^{-1}\omega\tau \tag{10.12}$$

In the plot of Figure 10.5(b), the frequency variable, $\omega\tau$, is on the horizontal logarithmic scale. The arctangent curve has a value of 45° when $\omega\tau = 1$, which is at the corner frequency. The phase curve starts at 0°, increases to a maximum of 90°, and is symmetric about the 45° point. The complete frequency-response curve for the zero comprises the amplitude curve shown in Figure 10.5(a) and the phase curve shown in Figure 10.5(b).

In sketching a first approximation to the phase curve, three straight lines can be used. The curve is horizontal from low frequency to one-tenth of the corner frequency. A straight line, with a slope of 45°/decade, goes from $0.1\omega_c$ to $10\ \omega_c$ passing through 45° at the corner frequency. For frequencies above $10\omega_c$, the line is again horizontal through 90° at 10 times the corner frequency. The slope of this approximate curve is 45°/decade. The maximum amount that the straight-line approximation deviates from the actual curve is 6°. The approximation and the actual curve are shown in Figure 10.6.

4. *Poles.* Simple pole factors of the form $1/(j\omega\tau + 1)$ can be treated in a fashion similar to that of simple zero factors. Since the logarithm of a reciprocal

quantity is equal to the negative of the logarithm of the quantity, we simply have

$$20 \log\left(\frac{1}{j\omega\tau + 1}\right) = -20 \log(j\omega\tau + 1) \tag{10.13}$$

The curve for a simple pole factor is similar to that for a simple zero factor, except that it is reflected about the 0 dB line. For small frequencies, the amplitude remains at 0 dB. For large frequencies, the asymptote is a straight line of slope -20 dB/decade. This asymptotic approximation is shown in Figure 10.5(a). Note that it intersects the 0 dB axis at $\omega = 1/\tau$, which is the corner frequency. As was the case with the zero, the actual amplitude curve deviates from the straight-line approximation by -3dB at the corner frequency and by about -1 dB at both one-half and double the corner frequency.

The phase curve of a pole is similar to that of a zero, but it is reflected about the $\phi = 0$ line. Since the pole is in the denominator of $G(s)H(s)$, the sign is changed when the angle is brought into the numerator. Thus,

$$\phi(\omega) = -\tan^{-1}\omega\tau \tag{10.14}$$

Equation (10.14) represents an arctangent curve, which starts from zero at a frequency of zero and approaches a value of $-90°$ for large frequencies. The $-45°$ phase point occurs at the corner frequency. The actual phase curve and its straight-line approximation is the negative of that included in Figure 10.6.

If the transfer function has multiple zeros or poles, the various amplitude and phase curves must simply be added to themselves a number of times equal to the order of the root. Thus, for example, for two repeated poles or zeros, the slope changes from ± 20 dB/decade to ± 40 dB/decade, and the phase angle is $\pm 90°$ at the corner frequency. The phase angle varies from $0°$ to $\pm 180°$ rather than from $0°$ to $\pm 90°$, and the slope is $\pm 90°$/decade rather than $\pm 45°$/decade. The corresponding functions are shown in Figure 10.7.

5. *Quadratic poles.* Quadratic pole factors are of the form

$$G(s)H(s) = \frac{\omega_n^2}{s^2 + 2s\zeta\omega_n + \omega_n^2}$$

$$= \frac{1}{(s/\omega_n)^2 + 2s\zeta/\omega_n + 1} \tag{10.15}$$

We normalize this by making a change of variables, letting

$$u = \frac{\omega}{\omega_n}$$

Figure 10.7
Double poles and zeros.

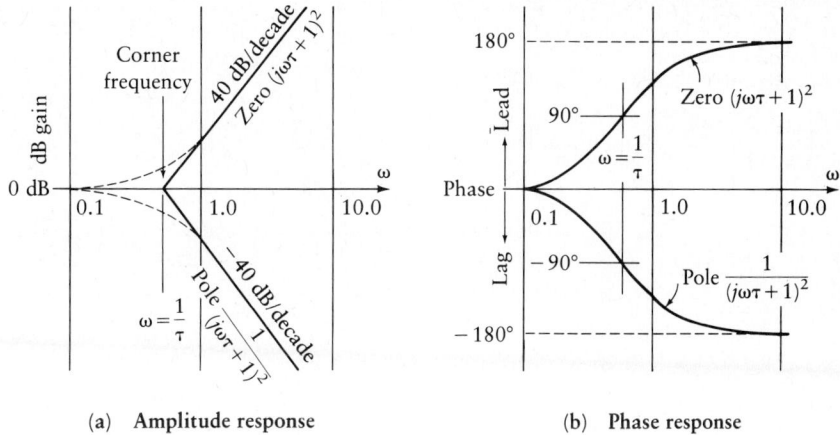

(a) Amplitude response

(b) Phase response

This is done after substituting $s = j\omega$. The equation then becomes

$$G(u)H(u) = \frac{1}{1 - u^2 + j2\zeta u} \tag{10.16}$$

The amplitude and phase of the expression in equation (10.16) are plotted in Figure 10.8.

Because the amplitude and phase response for quadratic pole factors depend not only upon the corner frequency but also upon the *damping ratio,* ζ, a parametric chart of the form shown in Figure 10.8 is used to make the plot. The amplitude and phase response are plotted by locating the corner frequency and damping ratio for the particular quadratic factor, as found by comparison of the given expression with equation (10.15).

The results of Figure 10.8 can be compared with those of a double pole with corner frequency of unity. The amplitude for the double pole is a line of slope -40 dB/decade starting at the corner frequency. The phase is a line of slope $-90°$/decade starting at $\frac{1}{10}$ and ending at 10 times the corner frequency. The difference between the double pole plot and the quadratic pole can be viewed as a correction factor. These differences (correction factors) are plotted as Figure 10.9 for various values of the damping ratio, ζ. Thus, in solving a problem with a quadratic pole, we can first treat it as a double pole and then apply the corrections of Figure 10.9.

10.1.3   *Examples of Bode Plots*

The concepts presented in the previous section are now applied to a number of examples.

Figure 10.8
Amplitude and phase
of quadratic pole.

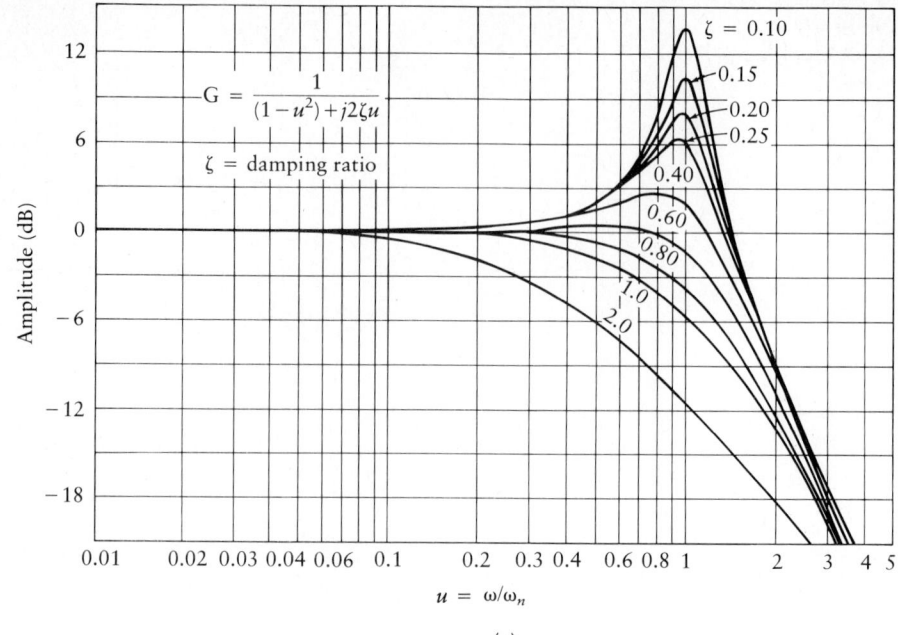

$$G = \frac{1}{(1 - u^2) + j2\zeta u}$$

ζ = damping ratio

(a)

$$G = \frac{1}{(1 - u^2) + j2\zeta u}$$

ζ = damping ratio

$$-\tan \Phi = \frac{2\zeta u}{1 - u^2}$$

(b)

Figure 10.9
Correction factors for quadratic pole.

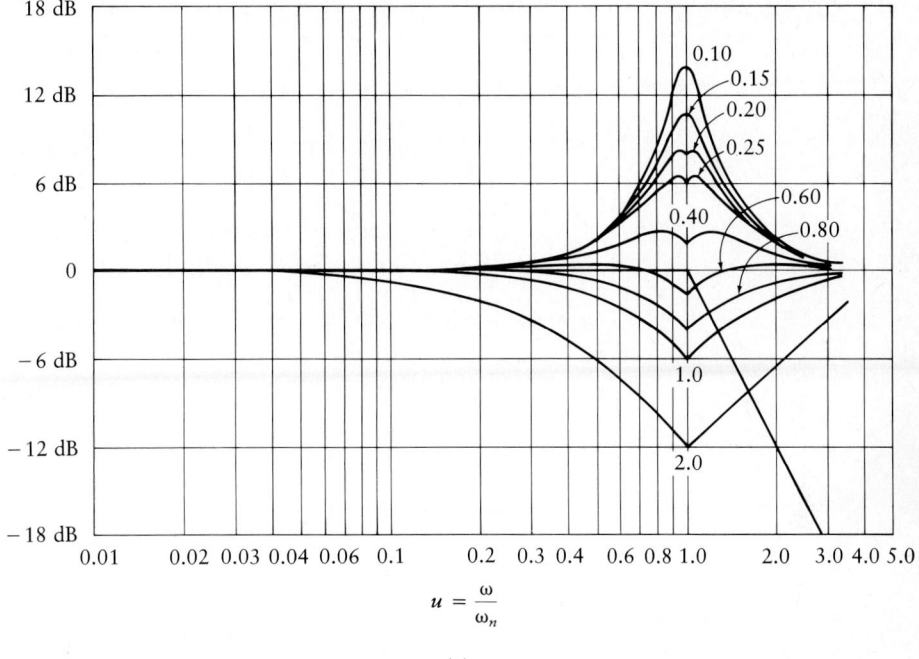

(a)

(b)

Example 10.1

Draw the Bode plot for the loop-transfer function

$$G(s)H(s) = 100$$

SOLUTION This is a simple case of a frequency-invariant factor, and

$$K_{dB} = 20 \log(100) = 20(2) = 40 \text{ dB} \qquad \text{for all } \omega$$

The phase is zero for all frequencies, since the loop-transfer function is real. The plot is shown in Figure 10.10.   ▶⊢

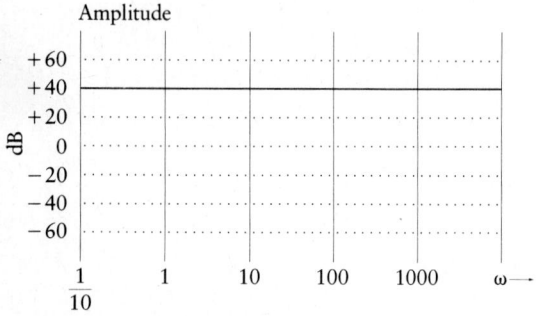

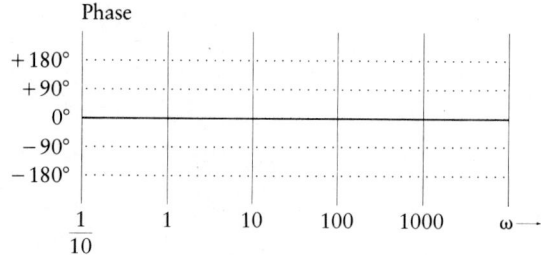

Figure 10.10 Frequency response for Example 10.1.

Example 10.2

Draw the Bode plot for the loop-transfer function

$$G(s)H(s) = s$$

SOLUTION This is a case of a simple zero at the origin. The resulting amplitude plot is a straight line of slope 20 dB/decade. The line passes through the 0-dB axis at $\omega = 1$. The phase is a constant at 90° for all frequencies since the transfer function for $s = j\omega$ is pure imaginary. The result is shown in Figure 10.11.   ▶⊢

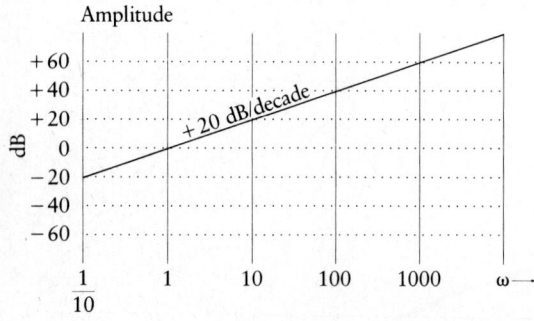

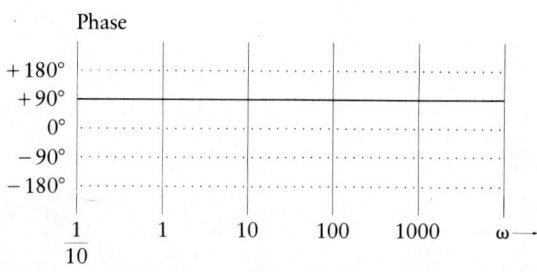

Figure 10.11 Frequency response for Example 10.2.

Example 10.3

Draw the Bode plot for the loop-transfer function

$$G(s)H(s) = \frac{10}{s + 10} = \frac{1}{s/10 + 1}$$

SOLUTION This expression contains a simple pole. The corner frequency is $\omega = 10$. As the frequency approaches zero, the amplitude approaches 1, which corresponds to 0 dB. To the right of the corner frequency, the slope of the amplitude curve is -20 dB/decade. The phase curve starts at 0° and goes through $-45°$ at the corner frequency. The center portion of the phase approximation has a slope of $-45°$/decade, so the approximation starts decreasing from 0° at a frequency of 1. It reaches the maximum negative phase of $-90°$ at a frequency of 100. The resulting curves are shown in Figure 10.12

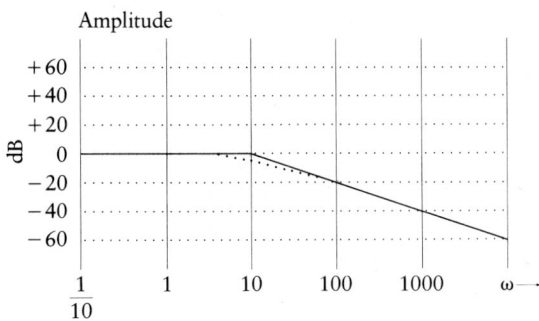
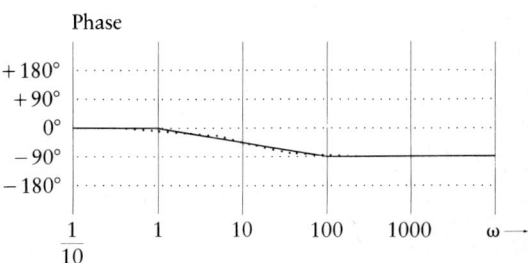

Figure 10.12 Frequency response for Example 10.3.

Example 10.4

Draw the Bode plot for the transfer function

$$G(s)H(s) = \frac{s}{s + 10} = \frac{0.1s}{0.1s + 1}$$

SOLUTION This transfer function is the product of two factors. One of these is a simple zero at the origin, as in Example 10.2, and the other is a simple pole, as in Example 10.3. We can either plot each of these separately and add the results, or we can plot them simultaneously. We choose the latter approach.

The zero is at the origin, and the pole has a corner frequency of 10. Therefore, if we begin the amplitude plot at small values of frequency, the zero is the dominating term. The plot begins as a straight line with a slope of 20 dB/decade. For small values of frequency, the transfer function is approximated by $s/10$, so the plot intersects the 0-dB axis at $\omega = 10$. As the frequency increases, the next effect occurs at the corner frequency of $\omega = 10$. At this

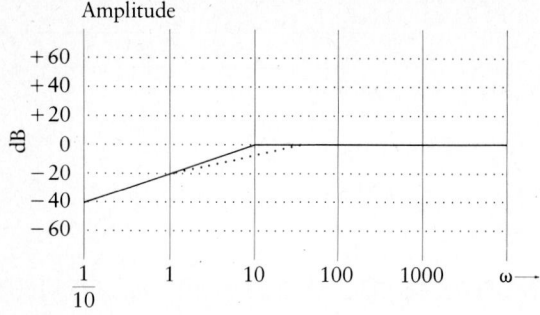

Figure 10.13   Frequency response for Example 10.4.

point, we add a straight line of slope -20 dB/decade. The result is to change the slope of the curve from $+20$ dB/decade to 0 (i.e., horizontal). The resulting curve is shown in Figure 10.13. Note that we illustrate both the approximation and the corrected curve, where the corrected curve is shown as a dotted line. At the corner frequency, the correction is -3 dB.

The phase plot is developed in a similar manner. We again start with small frequency, where the zero predominates. The phase is then 90° until the effects of the pole come into play. Recall that the phase plot for the pole is a straight line with a slope of $-45°$/decade starting at $\frac{1}{10}$ of the corner frequency and ending at 10 times the corner frequency. The result is shown in Figure 10.13.

Example 10.5

Draw the Bode plot for the transfer function

$$G(s)H(s) = \frac{1}{s^2 + 3s + 10} = \frac{0.1}{0.1s^2 + 0.3s + 1}$$

SOLUTION   This is an example of a quadratic pole. We begin by putting this into the form of equation (10.15) as follows:

$$G(s)H(s) = \frac{0.1}{(s/\omega_n)^2 + 2\zeta s/\omega_n + 1} \tag{10.17}$$

where

$$\omega_n = \sqrt{10} = 3.16 \text{ rad/s} \tag{10.18}$$

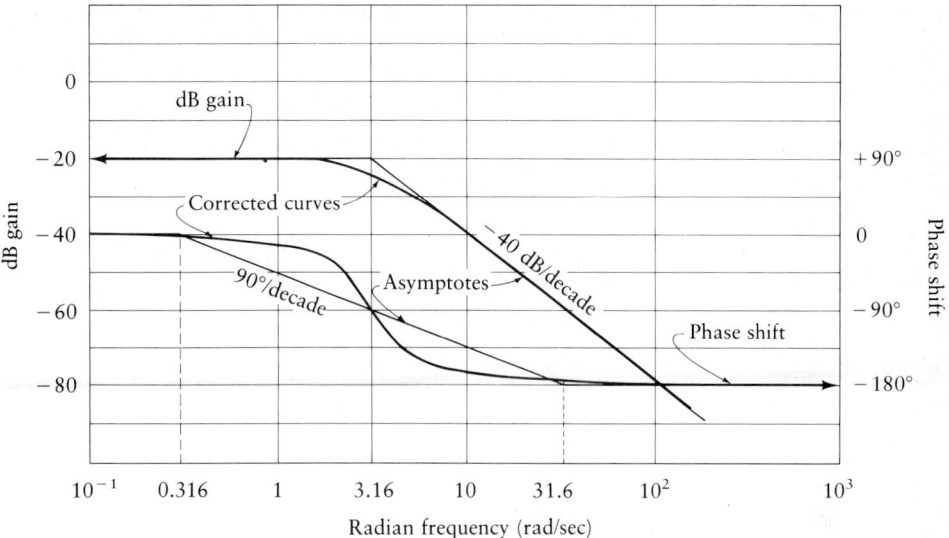

Figure 10.14 Bode plots for Example 10.5.

and

$$\zeta = \frac{0.3\omega_n}{2} = 0.474 \tag{10.19}$$

The corner frequency is first located on the Bode plot. The first approximation is drawn in the same manner as for a double pole located at the corner frequency. That is, for the amplitude plot, we start from this frequency and draw a -40-dB/decade line extending to the right. The phase plot is an approximation to the arctangent curve extending from 0 to $-180°$. These asymptotic approximations are shown in Figure 10.14. Because the correction from the asymptotes depends upon the damping ratio, it is necessary to refer to Figure 10.8 or Figure 10.9. The actual shape of the amplitude plot is as shown in Figure 10.8(a) for a damping ratio of 0.475 and for a corner frequency of $\sqrt{10}$. It is necessary to interpolate between the two curves shown for damping ratios of 0.4 and 0.6. To make the plot, start with the approximations of Figure 10.14 and apply the corrections of Figure 10.9(a). We interpolate since no curve is shown for a damping ratio of 0.475. The phase curve is also drawn by starting with the approximation of Figure 10.14 and applying the deviations given in Figure 10.9(b). The resulting amplitude and phase curves are also shown in Figure 10.14. Notice that the correction for the phase shift curve is more severe than that for the amplitude curve. ➤+

Drill Problems

D10.1   Draw a Bode plot for the loop-transfer function

$$G(s)H(s) = -0.1$$

Ans: See Figure D10.1.

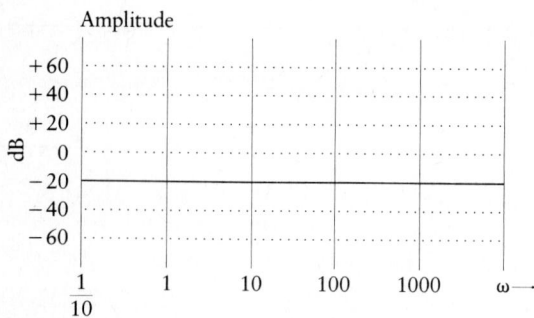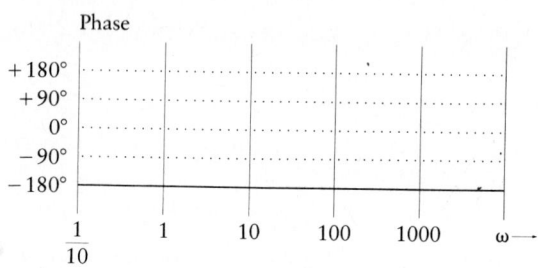

Figure D10.1

D10.2   Draw a Bode plot for the loop-transfer function

$$G(s)H(s) = \frac{K}{s}$$

Ans: See Figure D10.2.

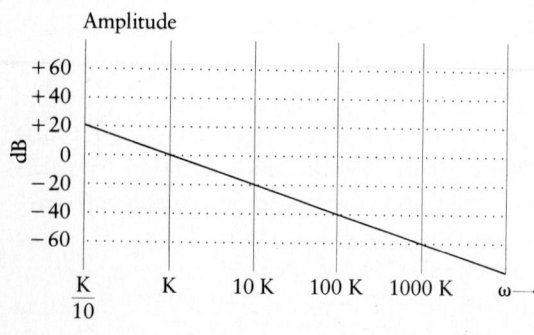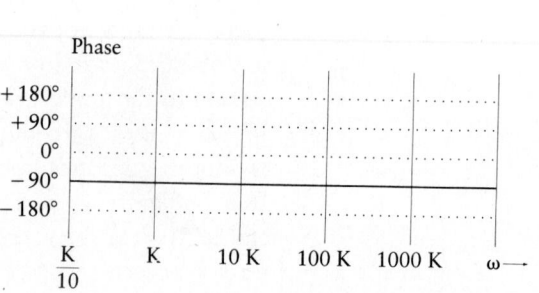

Figure D10.2

D10.3   Draw a Bode plot for the loop-transfer function

$$G(s)H(s) = 0.1s + 1$$

Ans: See Figure D10.3.

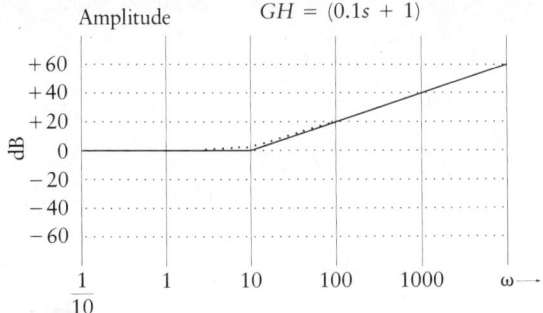

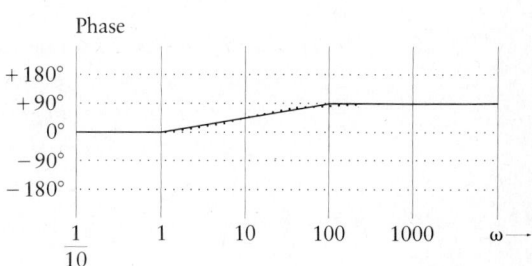

Figure D10.3

D10.4   Draw the Bode plot for the system with loop-transfer function

$$G(s)H(s) = \frac{0.03}{s(0.5s + 1)(0.06s^2 + 0.1s + 1)}$$

Ans: Note that for the quadratic term, $\omega_n = 4.08$ and $\zeta = 0.204$. The resulting plots are shown in Figure D10.4.

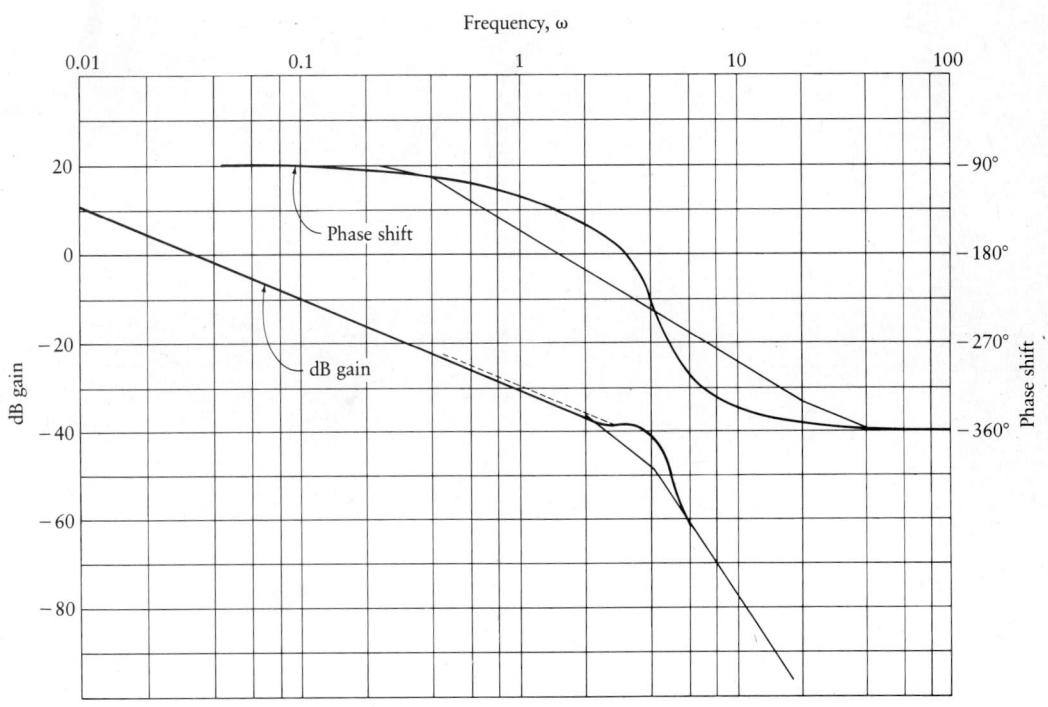

Figure D10.4

10.2   **Op-Amp Frequency Response**

Having gained some skill in making Bode plots, we are ready to apply these concepts to the frequency analysis of op-amp circuits.

Typical open loop op-amp amplitude characteristics as a function of frequency are shown in Figure 10.15. The numbers are typical of a general-purpose μA741 op-amp. We can approximate this plot with the expression in equation (10.20).

$$G(s) = \frac{G_o}{1 + s/\omega_c} \tag{10.20}$$

The constant G_o is the dc open-loop gain of the op-amp, and ω_c is the corner frequency. This amplitude-frequency characteristic results from the internal compensation built into the op-amp. The curve shown is for single-pole internal compensation. The manufacturer's specification sheets usually show both amplitude and phase response of the op-amp. This information is shown in Appendix D.

Figure 10.15
Op-amp open-loop
gain characteristics.

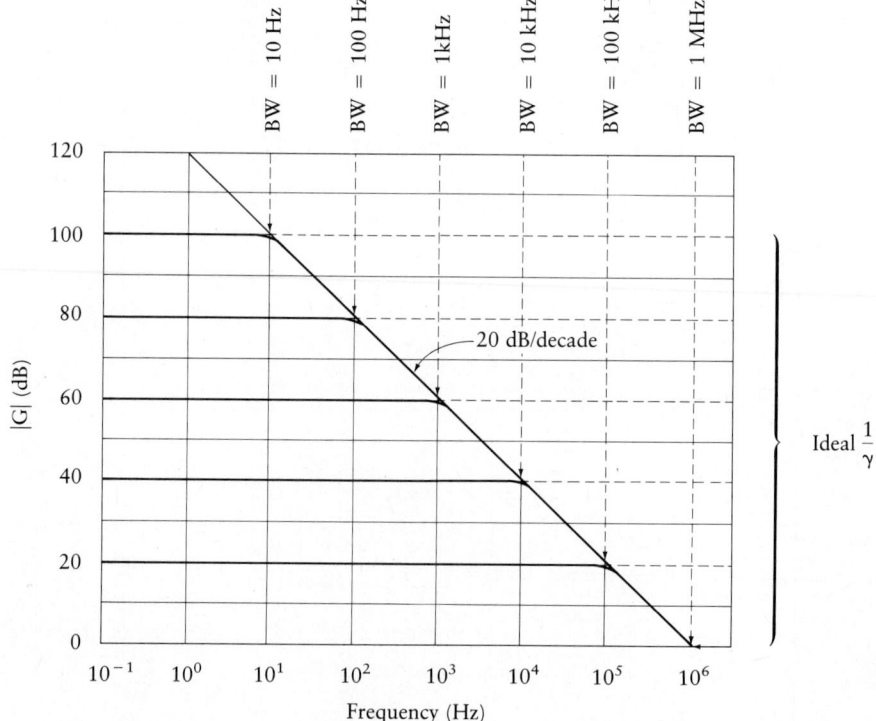

Examination of the curve in Figure 10.15 shows that the gain is 100 dB at low frequency, and then the gain falls off at a slope of -20 dB/decade to 0 dB at a frequency of 10^6 Hz. The GBP is a constant and is equal to 10^6 Hz.

We now find the closed-loop gain for this op-amp in a typical inverting amplifier application, as illustrated in Figure 10.16. The closed-loop gain is found by writing the nodal equations at v_+ and v_- as follows:

$$v_+ = 0$$

$$\frac{v_- - v_i}{R_A} = \frac{v_o - v_-}{R_F}$$

Solving for the inverting voltage input yields

$$v_- = \frac{v_i R_F + v_o R_A}{R_F + R_A}$$

We now use the open-loop gain relationship to solve for the output voltage:

$$v_o = -G v_-$$

$$= \frac{-G v_i R_F}{R_A + R_F} - \frac{G v_o R_A}{R_A + R_F}$$

This expression can be simplified by defining a new parameter as the voltage-divider ratio between R_A and R_F:

$$\gamma = \frac{R_A}{R_A + R_F}$$

Figure 10.16
Inverting op-amp.

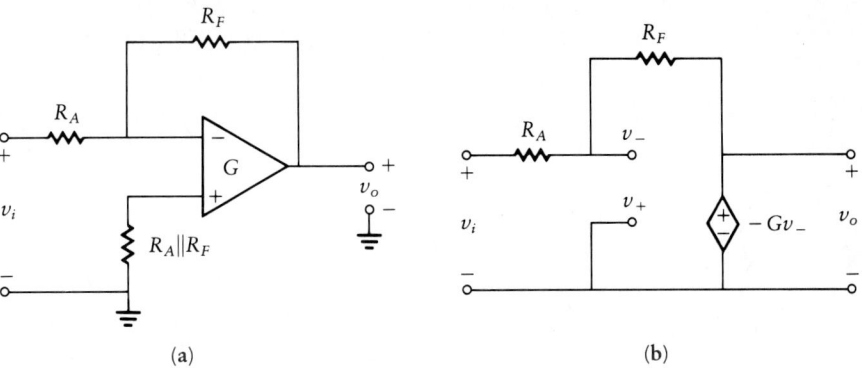

(a)   (b)

Then the output voltage is given by

$$v_o = \frac{-Gv_iR_F\gamma}{R_A} - Gv_o\gamma$$

and voltage gain is the ratio of output to input voltage,

$$A_v = \frac{v_o}{v_i} = \frac{-G\gamma R_F/R_A}{1 + G\gamma} \qquad (10.21)$$

As the gain, G, approaches infinity, the voltage gain, A_v approaches

$$A_v = \frac{-R_F}{R_A}$$

Recall that G is a function of frequency as given by equation (10.20). Substituting this for G in equation (10.21), we obtain

$$A_v = \frac{-R_F}{R_A}\frac{G_o\gamma}{1 + G_o\gamma + s/\omega_c}$$

$$= \frac{-R_F}{R_A}\frac{G_o\gamma/(1 + G_o\gamma)}{1 + \dfrac{s}{\omega_c(1 + G_o\gamma)}} \qquad (10.22)$$

If the dc gain is large, we can assume that $\gamma G_o \gg 1$. Equation (10.22) then reduces to

$$A_v = \frac{-R_F}{R_A}\frac{1}{1 + s/\gamma G_o\omega_c}$$

This gain equation contains a single pole. Therefore, the Bode plot starts at $20 \log(R_F/R_A)$ and has a corner frequency at

$$\omega = \frac{G_o\omega_c}{1 + R_F/R_A}$$

Note that the product $G_o\omega_c$ appears in these equations. Thus, if the closed-loop gain is to remain at a fixed value, there is an inverse relationship between G_o and ω_c. As the gain increases, the corner frequency (i.e., bandwidth) must decrease so that their product remains constant. This inverse relationship between gain and bandwidth is an important trade-off design consideration.

10.3 **Low-Frequency Response—BJT**

The BJT amplifier normally contains capacitors in order to couple the output to the load and to bypass the emitter resistor. These capacitors are intended to be open circuits for dc bias conditions but short circuits for the signal frequencies of interest. In practice, the capacitor deviates from the short-circuit condition as the frequency decreases. This causes a degradation in response—the amplifier is now frequency-dependent. In this section, we study the low-frequency response of the amplifier. We shall examine the effects of the coupling and bypass capacitors separately.

10.3.1 *Coupling Capacitance*

Figure 10.17 shows a CE amplifier with coupling capacitors C_1 and C_2. The equivalent circuit is shown in Figure 10.18. As the frequency reduces toward zero, both of the coupling capacitors approach open-circuit conditions, and the input signal is attenuated. The input impedance is given by

$$Z_{\text{in}} = R_{\text{in}} + \frac{1}{sC_2}$$

$$= [R_B \parallel (h_{ie} + \beta R_E)] + \frac{1}{sC_2}$$

where

$$R_B = R_1 \parallel R_2$$

Figure 10.17   CE amplifier.

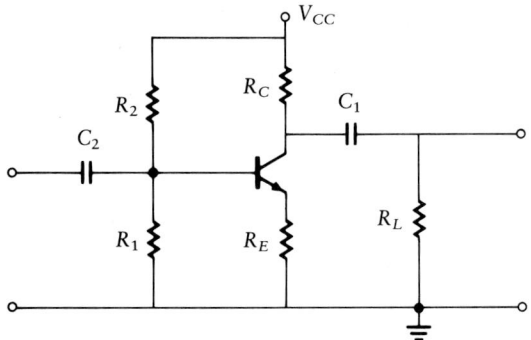

Figure 10.18   Equivalent circuit—CE amplifier.

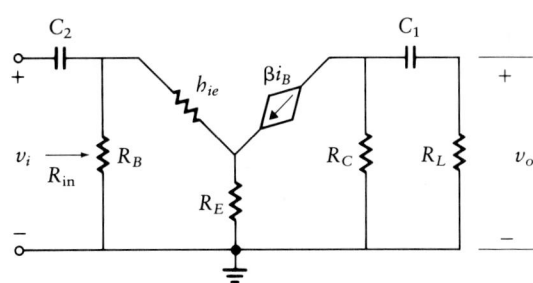

If we now assume that the source resistance is much less than the input resistance, then the input current is given by

$$I_{in} = \frac{V_i}{R_{in} + 1/sC_2}$$

and the base current is

$$I_B = \frac{V_i}{R_{in} + 1/sC_2} \frac{R_B}{R_B + h_{ie} + \beta R_E}$$

$$= \frac{V_i R_B}{R_B + h_{ie} + \beta R_E} \frac{sC_2}{sC_2 R_{in} + 1}$$

$$= \frac{V_i R_B}{R_B + h_{ie} + \beta R_E} \frac{sC_2 R_{in}}{sC_2 R_{in} + 1} \frac{1}{R_{in}}$$

but

$$R_{in} = R_B \parallel (h_{ie} + \beta R_E)$$

so we simplify this expression to get

$$I_B = \frac{V_i}{h_{ie} + \beta R_E} \frac{\tau_2 s}{\tau_2 s + 1}$$

where τ_2 is the time constant of the base resistor-capacitor combination. That is,

$$\tau_2 = R_{in} C_2$$

If the source resistance, R_i, is not much less than R_{in}, we must add R_i to R_{in} when calculating τ_2.

The output voltage is given by

$$V_o = \frac{-\beta I_B R_C R_L}{R_C + R_L + 1/sC_1} = \frac{-\beta I_B R_C R_L s C_1}{sC_1(R_C + R_L) + 1}$$

$$= -\beta I_B (R_C \parallel R_L) \frac{\tau_1 s}{\tau_1 s + 1}$$

where τ_1 is the time constant associated with the output RC loop. That is,

$$\tau_1 = C_1(R_C + R_L)$$

The voltage gain is now given by

$$A_v = \frac{V_o}{V_i} = \frac{-R_C \parallel R_L}{h_{ib} + R_E} \frac{\tau_1 \tau_2 s^2}{(s\tau_1 + 1)(s\tau_2 + 1)}$$

$$= \frac{-R_C \parallel R_L}{h_{ib} + R_E} \frac{s^2}{(s + 1/\tau_1)(s + 1/\tau_2)} \tag{10.23}$$

The current gain is given by

$$A_i = A_v \frac{Z_{in}}{Z_L}$$

$$= \frac{-R_C \parallel R_L}{h_{ib} + R_E} \frac{\tau_1 \tau_2 \, s^2}{(\tau_1 s + 1)(\tau_2 s + 1)} \frac{R_{in} + 1/sC_2}{R_L}$$

$$= \frac{-R_B^2 R_C C_1 C_2}{R_E} \frac{s^2(1 + 1/sR_BC_2)}{(s\tau_1 + 1)(s\tau_2 + 1)}$$

$$= \frac{-R_C \parallel R_L}{h_{ib} + R_E} \frac{\tau_1 \tau_2 \, s^2}{(\tau_1 s + 1)(\tau_2 s + 1)} \frac{R_B(h_{ie} + \beta R_E)}{R_B + h_{ie} + \beta R_E} \frac{\tau_2 s + 1}{\tau_2 s R_L}$$

$$= - \frac{R_B}{R_B/\beta + h_{ib} + R_E} \frac{s}{s + 1/\tau_1} \frac{R_C}{R_C + R_L} \tag{10.24}$$

Suppose we wish to draw the Bode plot of the current gain in equation (10.24). First note that the expression has a first-order zero at the origin and one pole. The corner frequency occurs at a frequency of $1/\tau_1$. For frequencies below the corner frequency, the zero causes the plot to rise at 20 dB/decade. At the corner frequency, $1/\tau_1$, a negative-going line of slope -20 dB/decade is added. The resultant therefore stays constant. We plot these results for a particular example following discussion of one simplification. Equations (10.23) and (10.24) can be simplified by defining a midrange gain as the value of the gain at frequencies to the right of the corner frequency. This is equivalent to taking the limit of the expressions in the two equations as s approaches infinity. Doing this and substituting for τ_1 and τ_2, we find, from equation (10.23),

$$A_{vm} = A_v|_{s\to\infty} = \frac{-R_C \parallel R_L}{R_E + h_{ib}} \tag{10.25}$$

Similarly, equation (10.24) yields

$$A_{im} = A_i|_{s\to\infty} = \frac{-R_B}{R_B/\beta + h_{ib} + R_E} \frac{R_C}{R_C + R_L} \tag{10.26}$$

We can now use these midrange gains to normalize the expressions of equations (10.23) and (10.24). That is, we divide by the midrange values to get

$$\frac{A_v}{A_{vm}} = \frac{s^2}{(s + 1/\tau_1)(s + 1/\tau_2)} \tag{10.27}$$

$$\frac{A_i}{A_{im}} = \frac{s}{s + 1/\tau_1} \tag{10.28}$$

Example 10.6

Plot the low-frequency response for the amplifier shown in Figure 10.19. Assume zero source resistance.

SOLUTION We need simply calculate the midrange gains and the corner frequencies. In order to find the corner frequencies, we need the two time constants τ_1 and τ_2.

$$V_{BB} = \frac{2200(10)}{22,200} = 0.991 \text{ V}$$

$$R_B = 2.2 \text{ k}\Omega \parallel 20 \text{ k}\Omega = 1.98 \text{ k}\Omega$$

$$I_{CQ} = \frac{0.991 - 0.7}{1980/200 + 100} = 2.65 \text{ mA}$$

$$h_{ib} = \frac{26 \text{ mV}}{2.65 \text{ mA}} = 9.8 \text{ }\Omega$$

$$R_{in} = 1.98 \text{ k}\Omega \parallel [(9.8 + 100)200] \text{ }\Omega = 1.82 \text{ k}\Omega$$

$$\tau_1 = C_1(R_C + R_L)$$

$$= (5 \times 10^{-6})(2 \text{ k}\Omega) = 0.01 \text{ s}$$

so

$$\omega_1 = 100 \text{ rad/s}$$

$$\tau_2 = C_2 R_{in} = (50 \times 10^{-6})(1.82 \text{ k}\Omega) = 0.091 \text{ s}$$

and

$$\omega_2 = 11 \text{ rad/s}$$

The midrange gains are given by equations (10.25) and (10.26).

Figure 10.19
CE amplifier for
Example 10.6.

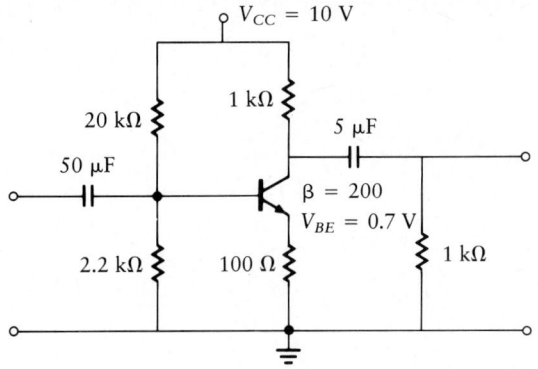

$$A_{vm} = \frac{-R_C \parallel R_L}{R_E + h_{ib}} = \frac{500}{100 + 9.8} = -4.55$$

$$A_{im} = \frac{-R_B}{R_B/\beta + h_{ib} + R_E} \frac{R_C}{R_C + R_L}$$

$$= \frac{-2000}{9.9 + 9.8 + 100} \frac{1000}{2000} = -8.28$$

The normalized gains are plotted on the Bode plot from the equations

$$\frac{A_v}{A_{vm}} = \frac{s^2}{(s + 1/\tau_1)(s + 1/\tau_2)} = \tau_1\tau_2 \frac{s^2}{(\tau_1 s + 1)(\tau_2 s + 1)}$$

$$= 0.91 \times 10^{-3} \frac{s^2}{(0.01s + 1)(0.091s + 1)} \tag{10.29a}$$

$$\frac{A_i}{A_{vm}} = \frac{s}{s + 1/\tau_1} = 10^{-2} \frac{s}{0.01s + 1} \tag{10.29b}$$

The voltage-amplitude plot starts at a slope of 40 dB/decade. At the first corner frequency, $\omega = 11$, the slope changes to 20 dB/decade. The actual curve deviates from the straight-line asymptotic approximation by 3 dB at the corner frequency and by 1 dB at one-half and at double this corner frequency. At the second corner frequency, $\omega = 100$, the slope changes to 0 dB/decade. To the right of this point, the amplitude remains at 0 dB. This is shown as Figure 10.20.

The phase curve starts at 180°. The corner frequencies are located at $\omega = 11$ and $\omega = 100$ rad/s. Starting at $\frac{1}{10}$ of the first corner frequency, or 1.1 rad/s, the curve follows a $-45°$/decade asymptote until $\frac{1}{10}$ of the second corner frequency, or 10 rad/s. At $\omega = 100$ rad/s, the effect of the first pole disappears and the asymptotic curve has a slope of $-45°$/decade until a frequency of 1000. Thereafter, the slope of the phase curve is 0°/decade.

Figure 10.20
Bode plot for Example
10.6.

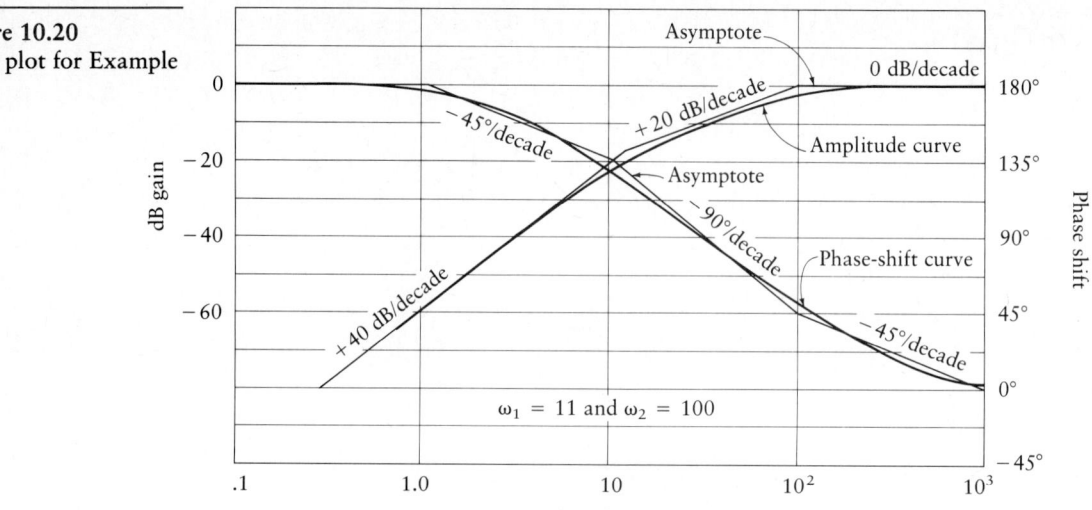

The corrections to the asymptotic curves for both phase and gain are shown in Figure 10.20.

The current amplitude plot starts at a slope of 20 dB/decade. It continues at this slope until the corner frequency at 100 rad/s. At this point the slope decreases to 0 dB/decade and the amplitude remains constant at 0 dB. The phase shift starts at $-90°$ at low frequency. At 10 rad/s, the slope becomes $-45°$/decade until 100 rad/s, at which point the phase shift becomes zero. ➤+

10.3.2   *Design for a Given Frequency Characteristic*

Suppose we wish to design an amplifier with a specific low-frequency cutoff. That is, the gain falls off at low frequency, and the point is specified at which the response falls by 3 dB below the midrange value. If there were only one corner frequency, the design task would be trivial. We would simply set the corner frequency equal to the given frequency.

In fact, we usually have two corner frequencies that interact with each other, so the design is more complex. We present three design approaches. The specific approach that is used in a particular design depends upon the degree of separation of the two corner frequencies. The first approach requires sufficient separation such that there is virtually no interaction and therefore reduces to the single-corner frequency-design problem. The other two approaches allow for partial and total interaction of the two effects. We discuss the three approaches and then apply them to an example.

Approach 1   We let one pole reflect the total 3-dB drop and set the other pole one decade lower in frequency. Thus, as frequency is reduced toward zero, the 3-dB design requirement is achieved before the second pole takes effect.

Approach 2   We set the two pole-corner frequencies equal and allow each of the two poles to decrease the magnitude by 1.5 dB at the specified frequency. The total decrease is therefore 3 dB, as required by the design. The actual pole-corner frequencies are below the specified design (3-dB) frequency. If we set both poles at the design-corner frequency, the drop at that frequency is 6 dB instead of the required 3 dB. We use equation (10.27), where

$$\frac{1}{\tau_1} = \frac{1}{\tau_2} = \omega_c$$

Therefore, the normalized voltage gain is

$$\frac{A_v}{A_{vm}} = \frac{s^2}{(s + \omega_c)^2}$$

The 3-dB point occurs when this normalized magnitude drops to 0.707. Thus, we let $s = j\omega_o$, where ω_o is the specified 3-dB frequency:

$$\frac{\omega_o^2}{\omega_o^2 + \omega_c^2} = \frac{1}{\sqrt{2}}$$

Solving for ω_o yields

$$\omega_o = 1.55\omega_c \qquad\qquad (10.30)$$

Approach 3   The first approach separates the corner frequencies sufficiently so that the lower frequency can be ignored. The second approach sets the two frequencies equal. The third approach chooses equal capacitor values, which lead to corner frequencies that interact but are not equal. This allows for interchanging of components and often represents an efficient design approach. We begin the analysis with equation (10.27), where we set

$$\omega_1 = \frac{1}{\tau_1}$$

and

$$\omega_2 = \frac{1}{\tau_2}$$

Thus, setting the normalized gain equal to 0.707 at a frequency of ω_o, we have

$$\frac{A_v}{A_{vm}} = \frac{(j\omega)^2}{(j\omega + \omega_1)(j\omega + \omega_2)}\bigg|_{\omega = \omega_o}$$

$$= \frac{\omega_o^2}{\sqrt{\omega_o^2 + \omega_1^2}\ \sqrt{\omega_o^2 + \omega_2^2}}$$

$$= \frac{1}{\sqrt{2}}$$

Solving for ω_o yields

$$2\omega_o^4 = (\omega_o^2 + \omega_1^2)(\omega_o^2 + \omega_2^2)$$

$$= \omega_o^4 + \omega_o^2(\omega_1^2 + \omega_2^2) + \omega_1^2\omega_2^2$$

In many cases, both ω_1 and ω_2 are less than ω_o. We can then approximate

$$\omega_o^4 = \omega_o^2(\omega_1^2 + \omega_2^2)$$

Finally

$$\omega_o = \sqrt{\omega_1^2 + \omega_2^2}$$

and, substituting for ω_1 and ω_2, we have

$$\omega_o = \sqrt{\frac{1}{C_1^2(R_C + R_L)^2} + \frac{1}{R_{in}^2 C_2^2}}$$

If we let $C_1 = C_2 = C$ and solve for C, this yields

$$C = \frac{1}{\omega_o R_{in}(R_C + R_L)}\ \sqrt{R_{in}^2 + (R_C + R_L)^2} \tag{10.31}$$

Again, if the source resistance, R_i, is significant in comparison with R_{in}, we will have to include the resistance R_i in with the value of R_{in} in these expressions. That is, we replace R_{in} with $R_i + R_{in}$.

Example 10.7

A CE amplifier is designed with

$$R_C = R_L = 2\ \text{k}\Omega$$

$$R_{in} \approx R_B = 5\ \text{k}\Omega$$

Determine the capacitor sizes that will yield a low-frequency cutoff at 20 Hz.

SOLUTION   We illustrate each of the three approaches.

Approach 1   We place one pole at the given frequency and the second pole one decade below this point. Thus,

$$C_1 = \frac{1}{2\pi f(R_L + R_C)} = 2 \ \mu F$$

$$C_2 = \frac{1}{2\pi (f/10)R_{in}} = 15.9 \ \mu F$$

Approach 2   We set both corner frequencies to the same value. From equation (10.30) we have

$$f_o = 1.55 f_c$$

or

$$f_c = \frac{20}{1.55} = 12.9 \ Hz$$

Then the capacitors are calculated to be

$$C_1 = \frac{1}{2\pi f(R_L + R_C)} = 3.08 \ \mu F$$

$$C_2 = \frac{1}{2\pi f R_{in}} = 2.46 \ \mu F$$

Approach 3   We set both capacitors equal in value. Then, from equation (10.31),

$$C = \frac{1}{2\pi f R_{in}(R_C + R_L)} \sqrt{R_{in}^2 + (R_C + R_L)^2} = 2.55 \ \mu F$$

Then the corner frequencies are given by

$$f_1 = \frac{1}{2\pi \tau_1} = \frac{1}{2\pi C(R_C + R_L)} = 15.6 \ Hz$$

$$f_2 = \frac{1}{2\pi \tau_2} = \frac{1}{2\pi C R_{in}} = 12.5 \ Hz$$

Drill Problem

D10.5 Determine the low-frequency response for the amplifier of Figure 10.17 when $C_2 = 2 \ \mu F$, $R_1 = 10 \ k\Omega$, $R_2 = 90 \ k\Omega$, $R_C = 1 \ k\Omega$, $R_E = 200 \ \Omega$, $C_1 = 4 \ \mu F$, $R_L = 2 \ k\Omega$, $\beta = 100$, $V_{BE} = 0.7$ V, and $V_{CC} = 20$ V.

Ans: $\tau_1 = C_1(R_L + R_C) = 0.012$;

$\tau_2 = C_2 R_{\text{in}} = 0.0125$;

$f_1 = \dfrac{1}{2\pi\tau_1} = 13.3$ Hz;

$f_2 = \dfrac{1}{2\pi\tau_2} = 12.7$ Hz.

The low-frequency decibel gain curve starts at a slope of 40 dB/decade until f_1 is reached, then the slope changes to 20 dB/decade until f_2 is reached. Finally, the curve becomes horizontal to the right of f_2.

10.3.3 Emitter-Resistor Bypass Capacitor

The effects of the coupling capacitors upon the frequency response of amplifiers has been presented. This section explores the addition of a bypass capacitor in parallel with the emitter resistor.

The single-stage CE amplifier with bypass capacitor is shown in Figure 10.21(a). Figure 10.21(b) shows the equivalent circuit of this amplifier. The following equations are derived from the equivalent circuit:

$$Z_{\text{in}} = R_B \parallel \beta\left(h_{ib} + R_E \parallel \frac{1}{sC}\right)$$

Figure 10.21 CE amplifier with bypass capacitor.

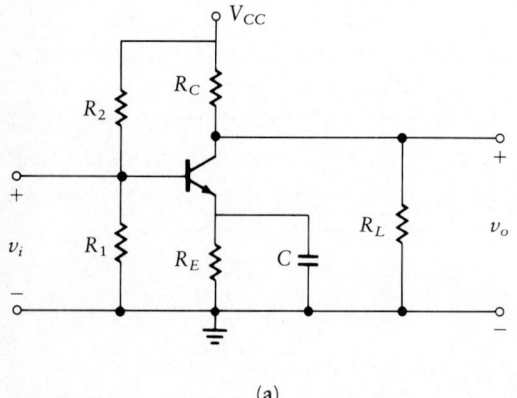

(a)

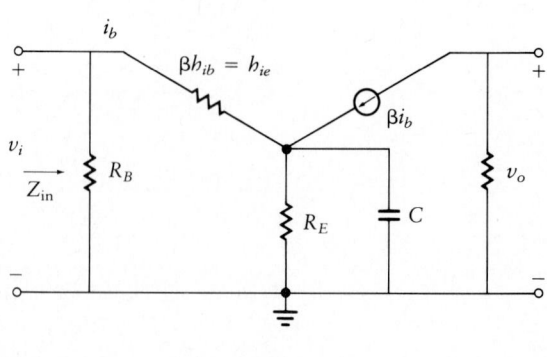

(b)

$$I_b = \frac{V_i}{\beta[h_{ib} + R_E \parallel 1/sC]}$$

$$V_o = -\beta I_b R_L' = \frac{-V_i R_L'}{h_{ib} + R_E \parallel 1/sC}$$

where

$$R_L' = R_L \parallel R_C$$

We now find the voltage gain.

$$A_v = \frac{V_o}{V_i} = \frac{-R_L'}{h_{ib} + \dfrac{R_E/sC}{R_E + 1/sC}}$$

$$= \frac{-R_L'(1 + 1/sCR_E)}{h_{ib}(1 + 1/sCR_E) + R_E/sCR_E} \qquad (10.32)$$

To normalize this gain, we divide by the midrange gain, A_{vm}, to obtain

$$\frac{A_v}{A_{vm}} = \frac{s + 1/R_E C}{s + (1 + R_E/h_{ib})/R_E C} = \frac{s + 1/\tau_a}{s + 1/\tau_b} \qquad (10.33)$$

where

$$A_{vm} = -R_L'/h_{ib}$$

$$\tau_a = R_E C$$

$$\tau_b = \frac{R_E C}{1 + R_E/h_{ib}} = C(R_E \parallel h_{ib})$$

Note that τ_a is greater than τ_b. The Bode plot of the normalized gain of equation (10.33) contains two corner frequencies. The lower of these two is due to the zero. We therefore start at low frequency with a horizontal line. At the corner frequency of the zero, $1/\tau_a$, the curve turns upward at a slope of $+20$ dB/decade. When the second corner frequency, that of the pole, is reached, the curve once again turns horizontal. This is illustrated in Figure 10.22.

10.3.4 *Combined Effect of Coupling Capacitor and Bypass Capacitor*

In many circuits of interest, both coupling and bypass capacitors are present. The bypass capacitors are often selected to have corner frequencies below

Figure 10.22
Amplitude plot for CE
amplifier of Figure
10.21.

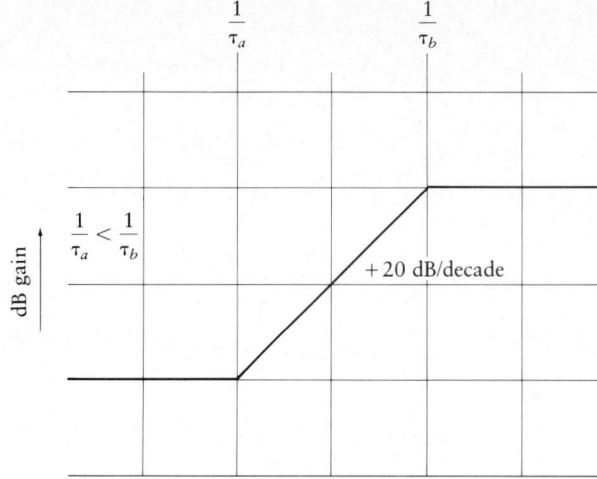

those of the coupling capacitors. Since the resistance in parallel with the bypass capacitors is usually smaller than the resistance in parallel with the coupling capacitors, the bypass capacitors must be considerably larger than the coupling capacitors to meet the corner-frequency requirement. That is, for the corner frequency to be smaller, the RC time constant must be larger. If we are able to meet this condition, the effects of the bypass capacitors can be ignored in the frequency analysis and design of amplifiers.

Let us examine the equations derived in Sections 10.3.1 and 10.3.3. We can solve for the three capacitors in terms of the time constants

$$C_1 = \frac{\tau_1}{R_C + R_L} \tag{10.34a}$$

$$C_2 = \frac{\tau_2}{R_{\text{in}}} \tag{10.34b}$$

$$C_b = \frac{\tau_b}{R_E \parallel h_{ib}} \tag{10.34c}$$

We ignore the effects of the zero in equation (10.33), since we assume that the coupling capacitors reduce the gain considerably over the range affected by this zero. That is, we once again assume that the corner frequencies due to the bypass capacitors are much lower than those of the coupling capacitors. The zero of the bypass response therefore does not affect the output until the frequency is very small.

10.3.5 *Low-Frequency Response—EF Amplifier*

The low-frequency characteristic of the EF amplifier is similar to that of the CE amplifier, and the response function is given by the following equation

$$\frac{A_v}{A_{vm}} = \frac{s^2}{(s + 1/\tau_1)(s + 1/\tau_2)}$$

Since the time constants are functions of the RC combination, we can write them as follows:

$$\tau_1(\text{output}) = C_1[R_L + R_E \parallel (R_B/\beta + h_{ib})]$$

$$\tau_2(\text{input}) = C_2(R_{\text{in}} + R_i)$$

R_{in} for an EF amplifier is much larger than the output resistance. Thus the input time constant is much less than the output time constant, and we usually allow the 3-dB loss to occur at the output circuit. This results in capacitor sizes that are as low as possible. Thus, we design the input capacitor-resistor combination to reflect no loss at the corner frequency. We do this by setting the input corner frequency one decade lower than the output circuit corner frequency.

10.3.6 *Low-Frequency Response—CB Amplifier*

The design of the CB amplifier is almost identical to that of the EF amplifier except the predominant pole shifts from the output circuit to the input circuit. Therefore, to keep the capacitor sizes reasonable, we allow the 3-dB loss to occur at the input circuit while setting the corner frequency of the output circuit to 1 decade below the required lower frequency limit. The time constant for these circuits are as follows:

$$\tau_1(\text{output}) = C_1(R_C + R_L)$$

$$\tau_2(\text{input}) = C_2[R_E \parallel (h_{ib} + R_B/\beta) + R_i]$$

$$= C_2(R_{\text{in}} + R_i)$$

If the base resistor is bypassed with a capacitor, C_B, we set the time constant for this circuit to also be 1 decade away from the required lower frequency limit. This base time constant is given by

$$\tau_b = C_B[R_B \parallel (h_{ie} + \beta R_E)]$$

With the base capacitor present, τ_2 changes to

$$\tau_2(\text{input}) = C_2[(R_E \parallel h_{ib}) + R_i]$$

This change is caused by setting C_b to a lower frequency, thus causing C_B to look like a short circuit at the corner frequency at which the design is being accomplished.

10.4   Low-Frequency Response—FET Amplifiers

10.4.1   *Low-Frequency Response for a CS Amplifier*

Figure 10.23(a) illustrates a single-stage FET amplifier with coupling and bypass capacitors. The equivalent circuit is shown in Figure 10.23(b).

Since the input impedance of an FET amplifier is generally high, the input time constant is also high. This results in a very low corner frequency. We can usually ignore the effects of the input coupling capacitor upon the low-frequency response of the amplifier.

The low-frequency performance is thus determined by the source resistor bypass capacitor, C_2, and the output coupling capacitor, C_1.

We first calculate the midrange voltage gain by assuming that the capacitors are short circuits. We write a loop equation around the gate-to-source loop, with the result

$$A_{vm} = \frac{-g_m(R_D \parallel R_L)}{(1 + g_m R_{S1})} \tag{10.35}$$

Figure 10.23   Single-stage FET amplifier.

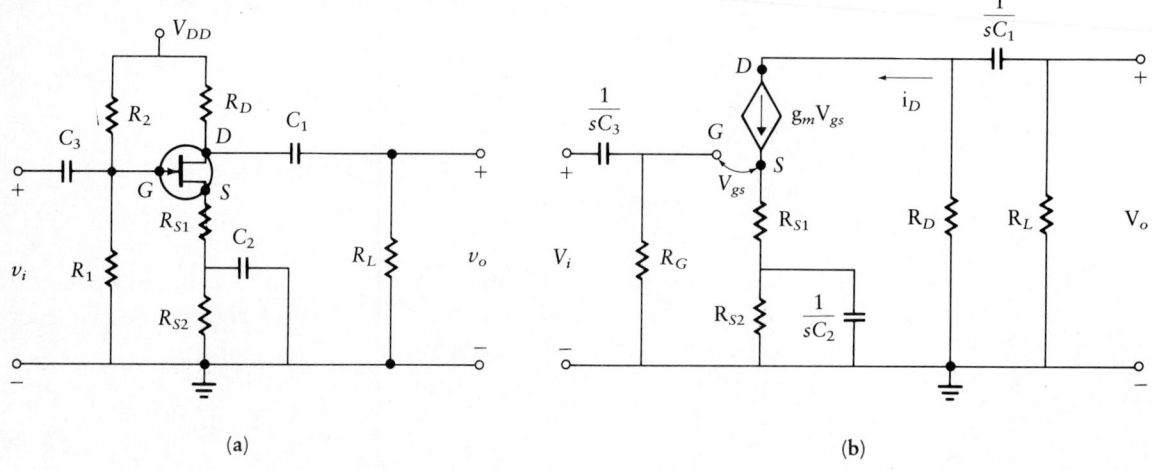

(a)   (b)

When the capacitors are not short circuits, the output voltage is found from a current-divider relationship as follows:

$$A_v = \frac{V_o}{V_i} = \frac{R_L R_D}{R_L + R_D + 1/sC_1} \frac{-V_{gs} g_m}{V_i} \tag{10.36}$$

Writing a loop equation around the gate-to-source loop yields

$$V_{gs} = V_i - g_m V_{gs}(R_{S1} + Z_{S2})$$

$$= \frac{V_i}{1 + g_m(R_{S1} + Z_{S2})}$$

where Z_{S2} is the parallel combination of R_{S2} and C_2, i.e.,

$$Z_{S2} = \frac{R_{S2}/sC_2}{R_{S2} + (1/sC_2)} = \frac{R_{S2}}{sC_2 R_{S2} + 1}$$

Substituting the expressions for V_{gs} and Z_{S2} into equation (10.36) yields the final form for the voltage gain,

$$A_v = \frac{-R_L R_D g_m}{(R_L + R_D + 1/sC_1)[1 + g_m(R_{S1} + Z_{S2})]}$$

$$= \frac{-R_L R_D s C_1}{sC_1(R_L + R_D) + 1} \frac{g_m}{1 + g_m R_{S1} + \dfrac{g_m R_{S2}}{sC_2 R_{S2} + 1}}$$

This is simplified by defining three time constants,

$$\tau_1 = C_1(R_L + R_D) \tag{10.37a}$$

$$\tau_2 = R_{S2} C_2 \tag{10.37b}$$

$$\tau_3 = \frac{C_2 R_{S2}}{1 + g_m R_{S2}/(1 + g_m R_{S1})} \tag{10.37c}$$

Using these time constants, the voltage gain reduces to

$$A_v = \frac{-g_m R_L R_D C_1}{(1 + g_m R_{S1})[1 + g_m R_{S2}/(1 + g_m R_{S1})]} \frac{s(\tau_2 s + 1)}{(\tau_1 s + 1)(\tau_3 s + 1)}$$

$$\tag{10.38}$$

The normalized voltage gain is found by dividing equation (10.38) by the midrange gain of equation (10.35)

$$\frac{A_v}{A_{vm}} = \frac{\tau_1 \tau_3}{\tau_2} \frac{s}{\tau_1 s + 1} \frac{\tau_2 s + 1}{\tau_3 s + 1} \tag{10.39}$$

Example 10.8

Derive the Bode plot for an FET amplifier with the following parameters.

$$R_{S2} = 200 \ \Omega \qquad g_m = 2000 \ \mu S$$
$$C_1 = 0.1 \ \mu F \qquad R_L = R_D = 5 \ k\Omega$$
$$C_2 = 1.0 \ \mu F \qquad R_{S1} = 500 \ \Omega$$

SOLUTION   We calculate the time constants using equation (10.37):

$$\tau_1 = 1 \times 10^{-3} \ s$$

$$\tau_2 = (200)(10^{-6}) = 2 \times 10^{-4} \ s$$

$$\tau_3 = \frac{\tau_2}{1 + (0.002 \times 200)/[1 + (0.002 \times 500)]}$$

$$= \frac{\tau_2}{1.2} = 1.67 \times 10^{-4} \ s$$

The normalized voltage gain is obtained from equation (10.39):

$$\frac{A_v}{A_{vm}} = \frac{\tau_1 \tau_3}{\tau_2} \frac{s}{\tau_1 s + 1} \frac{\tau_2 s + 1}{\tau_3 s + 1}$$

$$= (0.84 \times 10^{-3}) \frac{s}{10^{-3} s + 1} \frac{(2 \times 10^{-4} s + 1)}{(1.67 \times 10^{-4} s + 1)}$$

The Bode plot is shown in Figure 10.24.

Note that there are two zeros and two poles, where one of the zeros is at the origin. The amplitude curve therefore starts at a slope of 20 dB/decade until the first corner frequency is reached. The corner frequency of the second zero is 5000 rad/s, and the corner frequency of the two poles are 1000 rad/s and 6000 rad/s. Thus, the first corner frequency is due to the pole at 1000 rad/s, and, at that point, the curve slope reduces to 0 dB/decade. At 5000 rad/s, the effect of the zero is to increase the slope to 20 dB/decade. Finally, at the corner frequency of the pole at 6000 rad/s, the slope once again reduces to zero. The midrange gain (normalized) is 0 dB, so to the right of the corner frequency of 6000 rad/s, the curve follows the 0 dB axis.   ►+

Figure 10.24
Bode plot for Example 10.8.

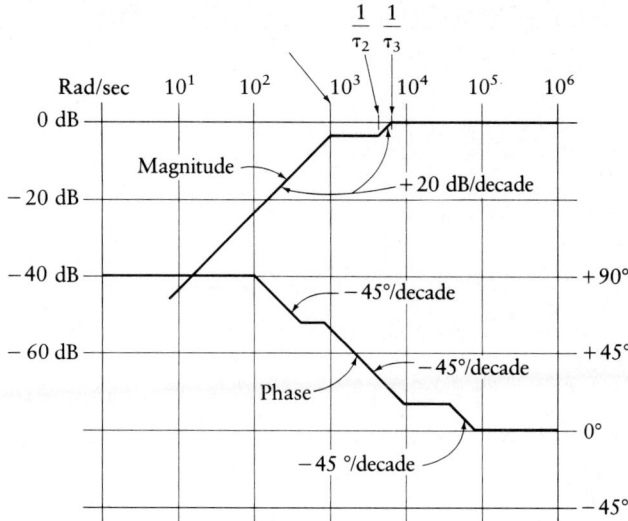

Example 10.9

Design an *n*-channel CS amplifier with $A_v = -2$, $V_{DD} = 18$ V, $R_L = 2$ kΩ and $R_{in} = 100$ kΩ. Determine all the resistance and capacitance values so that the 3-dB point is at 20 Hz. Select the Q-point for the amplifier as $I_{DQ} = 2$ mA, $V_{GSQ} = -1$ V, $V_{DSQ} = 9$ V, and $g_m = 2 \times 10^{-3}$ S.

SOLUTION   We use the design procedure of Section 4.9 and the circuit of Figure 10.23. We first solve for the resistance in the drain-source loop.

$$(R_S + R_D)I_{DQ} + V_{DSQ} = V_{DD}$$

$$(R_S + R_D)(2 \times 10^{-3}) + 9 = 18$$

where

$$R_S = R_{S1} + R_{S2}$$

and

$$R_S + R_D = 4.5 \text{ k}\Omega \tag{10.40}$$

Now from the given gain and equation (10.36), we have

$$A_v = -2 = \frac{-R_D \| R_L}{R_S + 1/g_m} = \frac{-R_D \| 2 \text{ k}\Omega}{R_S + 1/g_m}$$

$$= \frac{-R_D \| 2 \text{ k}\Omega}{4.5 \text{ k}\Omega - R_D + 500 \text{ }\Omega} \tag{10.41}$$

Solving equation (10.40) and equation (10.41) for R_D and R_S, we have

$$R_D = 4.32 \text{ k}\Omega$$

$$R_S = 180 \ \Omega$$

The gate voltage, V_{GG}, is given by

$$V_{GG} = R_S(I_{DQ}) + V_{GSQ}$$

$$= 180(2 \times 10^{-3}) - 1 = -640 \text{ mV}$$

Now since V_{GG} is negative, we let $R_2 \to \infty$, $V_{GG} = 0$, and $R_1 = 100$ kΩ. We cannot achieve the design with a single source resistor, so we split R_S into R_{S1} and R_{S2}, as shown in the figure. Then

$$R_{Sdc} = \frac{-V_{GSQ}}{I_{DQ}} = \frac{1}{2 \times 10^{-3}}$$

and

$$R_{Sdc} = 500 \ \Omega = R_{S1} + R_{S2}$$

$$R_D = 4.5 \text{ k}\Omega - R_{Sdc} = 4 \text{ k}\Omega$$

The midband gain is

$$A_v = -2 = \frac{4 \text{ k}\Omega \parallel 2 \text{ k}\Omega}{R_{S2} + 500}$$

$$R_{S1} = 167 \ \Omega$$

$$R_{S2} = 500 \ \Omega - R_{S1} = 333 \ \Omega$$

The time constants are calculated as follows:

$$\tau_1 = C_1(R_L + R_D) = C_1(2 \text{ k}\Omega + 4 \text{ k}\Omega) = (6 \text{ k}\Omega)C_1$$

$$\tau_2 = R_{S2}C_2 = 333 \ C_2$$

$$\tau_3 = \frac{\tau_2}{1 + \dfrac{g_m R_{S2}}{1 + g_m R_{S1}}} = \frac{333 \ C_2}{1 + \dfrac{(2 \times 10^{-3})(333)}{1 + (2 \times 10^{-3})(0.167)}}$$

$$= (0.24 \text{ k}\Omega)C_2$$

We place the corner frequency, $1/\tau_3$, at 20 Hz as specified in the problem statement. We place the other two corner frequencies 1 decade lower, at 2 Hz. Thus,

$$\frac{1}{\tau_3} = 2\pi(20) = 40\pi = \frac{1}{240C_2}$$

and

$$C_2 = 33.2 \ \mu\text{F}$$

$$\frac{1}{\tau_1} = 2\pi(2) = 4\pi = \frac{1}{6000C_1}$$

Therefore,

$$C_1 = 13.3 \ \mu\text{F}$$

C_3 is selected so that

$$\frac{1}{\tau_4} = 2\pi(2)$$

But

$$\tau_4 = R_{\text{in}}C_3 = R_1C_3$$

so

$$\frac{1}{\tau_4} = 4\pi = \frac{1}{10^5C_3}$$

and

$$C_3 = 0.8 \ \mu\text{F}$$

Example 10.10

Given the FET amplifier of Figure 10.23 with the following parameter values: $R_{S2} = 200 \ \Omega$, $R_{S1} = 100 \ \Omega$, $R_D = 3\text{k}\Omega$, $R_L = 40 \ \text{k}\Omega$, $R_2 = \infty$, $R_1 = 10^6 \ \Omega$, $I_{DQ} = 3.33 \ \text{mA}$, $V_{GSQ} = -1 \ \text{V}$, $V_{DSQ} = 10 \ \text{V}$, and $g_m = 2 \times 10^{-3} \ \text{S}$, select values of C_1, C_2, and C_3 so that the low-frequency 3 dB point is at 20 Hz.

SOLUTION   Equation (10.37) yields the following time constants:

$$\tau_1 = C_1(R_L + R_D) = C_1(43\ k\Omega)$$

$$\tau_2 = R_{S1}C_2 = C_2(200\ \Omega)$$

$$\tau_3 = \frac{R_{S2}C_2}{1 + g_m R_{S2}/(1 + g_m R_{S1})} = C_2(150\ \Omega)$$

We use a different approach from that of the previous example. Recall that there are two zeros and two poles in the response characteristic for this amplifier. We let one of the zeros cancel one of the poles. That is, we let

$$\tau_1 = \tau_2$$

The normalized voltage gain now reduces to

$$\frac{A_v}{A_{vm}} = \frac{\tau_3 s}{\tau_3 s + 1}$$

By setting $\tau_1 = \tau_2$, we force

$$C_2(200\ \Omega) = C_1(43\ k\Omega)$$

This is one equation in the two unknown capacitors. The second equation comes from setting the remaining corner frequency to 20 Hz. Thus, we let

$$\frac{1}{\tau_3} = 2\pi \times 20$$

and

$$C_2 = \frac{1}{(150)(2\pi)(20)} = 53\ \mu F$$

From the first equation, we then have

$$C_1 = \frac{C_2 \times 200\ \Omega}{43\ k\Omega} = 0.25\ \mu F$$

Looking now at the input coupling capacitor, we have

$$R_G = R_1 = 10^6\ \Omega$$

$$C_3 R_G = C_3 10^6$$

We set this corner frequency at 1 decade below 20 Hz so it does not interact with the corner frequency of the pole. Thus,

$$10^6 C_3 = \frac{1}{4\pi}$$

$$C_3 = \frac{10^{-6}}{4\pi} = 0.08 \ \mu F$$

10.4.2 Low-Frequency Response—CD Amplifier

In the case of the CD amplifier, the input frequency characteristic has an effect upon the output of the amplifier. In this section, we develop the normalized gain equation for all frequencies in a manner similar to that used for the CS amplifier in Section 10.4.1.

Figure 10.25 shows the CD amplifier and its equivalent circuit.

We specify the midrange voltage gain (see Chapter 4) as follows:

$$A_{vm} = \frac{g_m(R_S \parallel R_L)}{1 + g_m(R_S \parallel R_L)}$$

When the capacitors are not short circuits, the voltage gain is found from the current-divider relationship as follows:

$$A_v = \frac{V_o}{V_i} = \frac{g_m V_{gs}}{V_i} \frac{R_S}{R_S + Z_1} R_L$$

where

$$Z_1 = \frac{1}{sC_1} + R_L$$

Figure 10.25
CD amplifier.

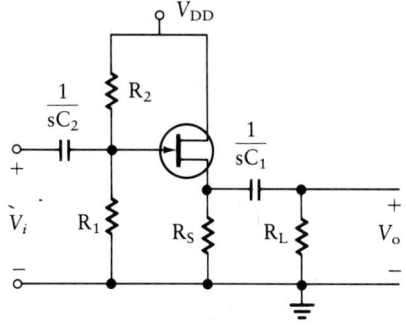

(a) Common drain amplifier

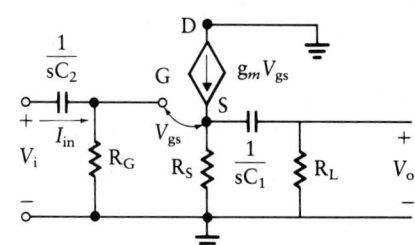

(b) Equivalent circuit

Writing a loop equation around the gate-to-source loop yields

$$V_i = \frac{1}{sC_2} I_{in} + V_{gs} + g_m V_{gs}(R_S \parallel Z_1)$$

but

$$I_{in} = \frac{V_i s C_2}{R_G C_2 s + 1}$$

Then

$$V_i = \frac{R_G C_2 s + 1}{R_G C_2 s} \left[V_{gs} + g_m V_{gs} \frac{R_S R_L C_1 s + R_S}{sC_1(R_L + R_S) + 1} \right]$$

Substituting back into the A_v equation, we have

$$A_v = \frac{g_m V_{gs} R_S R_L s C_1}{sC_1(R_L + R_S) + 1} \frac{R_G C_2 s}{R_G C_2 s + 1} \frac{1}{V_{gs} + g_m V_{gs} \left[\dfrac{R_S R_L C_1 s + R_S}{sC_1(R_L + R_S) + 1} \right]}$$

If we let

$$\tau_2 = R_G C_2$$

then the gain equation becomes

$$A_v = \frac{\tau_2 s}{\tau_2 s + 1} \frac{g_m V_{gs} R_S R_L C_1 s}{sC_1(R_L + R_S) + 1} \cdot$$

$$\frac{sC_1(R_L + R_S) + 1}{[sC_1(R_L + R_S) + 1]V_{gs} + g_m V_{gs}[R_S R_L C_1 s + R_S]}$$

Reducing this equation further yields

$$A_v = \frac{\tau_2 s}{\tau_2 s + 1} \frac{g_m(R_S \parallel R_L)C_1 s(R_S + R_L)}{sC_1(R_L + R_S + g_m R_S R_L) + 1 + g_m R_S}$$

If we now let

$$\tau_1 = C_1 \left[\frac{1 + g_m(R_S \parallel R_L)}{1 + g_m R_S} \right] (R_S + R_L)$$

and normalize the gain, we have

$$\frac{A_v}{A_{vm}} = \frac{\tau_1 s}{\tau_1 s + 1} \frac{\tau_2 s}{\tau_2 s + 1} = \frac{s^2}{(s + 1/\tau_1)(s + 1/\tau_2)}$$

In this case, we place the corner frequency for the input circuit 1 decade below the desired corner frequency and allow the output circuit to cause a drop of 3 dB in magnitude at the desired corner frequency (i.e. we use Approach 1 of Section 10.3.2).

Example 10.11

A CD amplifier, as shown in Figure 10.25, has the following specifications: $R_L = 1 \text{ k}\Omega$, $R_S = 800 \, \Omega$, $g_m = 2 \text{ mS}$, and $R_G = 500 \text{ k}\Omega$. Determine the size of the coupling capacitors for a low-frequency cutoff of 300 Hz.

SOLUTION   The normalized voltage gain is given by

$$\frac{A_v}{A_{vm}} = \frac{s^2}{(s + 1/\tau_1)(s + 1/\tau_2)}$$

The input circuit is designed to provide no loss to the signal at the low-frequency cutoff. Thus,

$$f_L = 30 \text{ Hz}$$

$$\frac{1}{\tau_2} = 2\pi 30 = \frac{1}{R_G C_2} = \frac{1}{500{,}000 C_2}$$

and solving for the capacitance,

$$C_2 = \frac{1}{500{,}000(2\pi 30)} = 0.011 \ \mu F$$

Then

$$\frac{1}{\tau_1} = 2\pi 300 = \frac{1}{C_1(R_S + R_L)[1 + g_m(R_S \parallel R_L)]/(1 + g_m R_S)}$$

$$= \frac{1}{C_1(1800)[1 + 0.002(444)]/[1 + 0.002(800)]}$$

Solving for the capacitor value yields

$$C_1 = \frac{1}{2\pi 300(1800)(0.726)} = 0.406 \ \mu F$$

10.5   High-Frequency Response—BJT Amplifier

The low-frequency response of transistor circuits depends upon the external capacitors used for coupling and for bypass. The high-frequency response depends upon the *internal* capacitance of the transistor. The simplified equivalent circuit is expanded to include the effects of these internal capacitors.

These capacitors, which affect the high-frequency response, exist between the terminals of the device. We can view each of the capacitors as being in series with the equivalent (Thevenin) resistance of the associated circuitry. We thus begin by examining the simple RC circuit of Figure 10.26. As the frequency of the input increases, the output signal decreases in amplitude at 20 dB/decade according to the expression

$$\frac{V_o}{V_i} = \frac{1}{j\omega RC + 1} = \frac{1}{j\omega \tau + 1} \tag{10.42}$$

We set the time constant $\tau = RC$. We can usually ignore the wiring and stray capacitances and consider only the *parasitic* terminal capacitance.

The high-frequency performance is evaluated in this section. The coupling and bypass capacitors are not considered in the discussion, since they are assumed to be short circuits at these high frequencies.

10.5.1   *CE Response at High Frequency*

We use the *hybrid-π* model to estimate the high-frequency response of BJT amplifiers. The hybrid-π is similar to the *h*-parameter model studied in Section 3.1. The parameters of the two different models are related to each other. Figure 10.27(a) shows the hybrid-π model at low frequencies. The symbol B' represents the base junction and B represents the base terminal. These are not identical, since leads are connected to the base junction, and the base terminal is separated from the junction by these leads.

We define the resistances in the model and relate them to the *h*-parameters.

Base-Spreading Resistance   The base-spreading resistance, $r_{bb'}$, is related to the *h*-parameter, h_{ie}, which is the input resistance with the output shorted.

Figure 10.26
RC equivalent circuit.

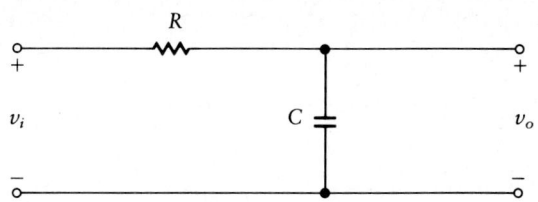

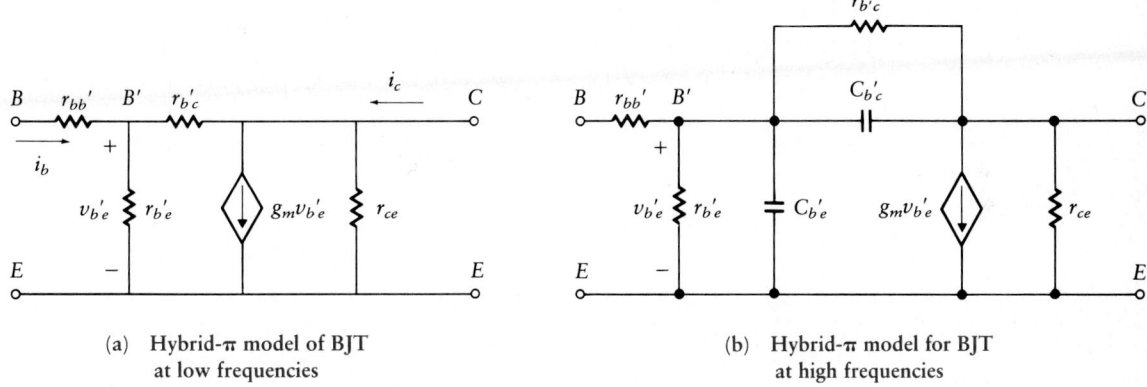

(a) Hybrid-π model of BJT
at low frequencies

(b) Hybrid-π model for BJT
at high frequencies

Figure 10.27 Hybrid-π transistor model.

We apply a short circuit at the output of the circuit of Figure 10.27(a) in order to find h_{ie}. This yields

$$h_{ie} = r_{bb'} + r_{b'e} \parallel r_{b'c} \tag{10.43}$$

$$\approx r_{bb'} + r_{b'e}$$

The last approximation is made since $r_{b'c} \gg r_{b'e}$. A typical value of $r_{bb'}$ is 100 Ω at room temperature with $I_c \approx 1$ mA.

Input Resistance   The input resistance, $r_{b'e}$, is approximated by the ratio

$$r_{b'e} \approx \frac{v_{b'e}}{i_b}$$

since $r_{b'c} \gg r_{b'e}$. The short-circuit collector current, i_c, is found from Figure 10.27(a) by short-circuiting the output.

$$i_c = g_m v_{b'e} \approx g_m r_{b'e} i_b$$

But this quantity is related to the base current according to the h-parameter, h_{fe}; i.e.,

$$i_c = h_{fe} i_b$$

We therefore obtain

$$r_{b'e} = \frac{i_c}{g_m i_b} = \frac{h_{fe}}{g_m}$$

[handwritten: $h_{fe} = \beta$.]

[handwritten: $r_\pi = \frac{I_c}{g_m I_B}$]

[handwritten: $r_\pi = \frac{\beta}{g_m}$]

[handwritten: $r_\pi = $]

We can estimate the value of g_m from the equation,

$$g_m \approx \frac{|I_{CQ}|}{26} = \frac{1}{h_{ib}} \qquad\qquad g_m \approx \frac{I_c}{2 v_T} = \qquad\qquad\qquad\qquad \text{(10.44)}$$

where I_{CQ} is in milliamps. Thus

$$r_{b'e} = \frac{h_{fe} \times 26}{|I_{CQ}|}$$

Recall from Chapter 3 that

$$h_{ib} = \frac{26}{|I_{CQ}|}$$

Therefore,

$$r_{b'e} = h_{fe} h_{ib} = h_{ie}$$

A typical value for $r_{b'e}$ is 2 kΩ.

Feedback Resistance   The feedback resistance, $r_{b'c}$, is related to h_{re}, the reverse voltage gain, as follows:

$$h_{re} = \frac{v_{b'e}}{v_{ce}}$$

We now use a voltage-divider relationship to find

$$h_{re} = \frac{r_{b'e}}{r_{b'e} + r_{b'c}} \approx \frac{r_{b'e}}{r_{b'c}} \qquad\qquad\qquad\qquad \text{(10.45)}$$

The last approximation results since $r_{b'c} \gg r_{b'e}$. Finally,

$$r_{b'e} = h_{re}r_{b'c}$$

$r_{b'c}$ is typically in the megohm range.

Output Resistance The output conductance is given by h_{oe} in h-parameters, and it is determined with the input open-circuited. We see from the circuit of Figure 10.27(a) that

$$h_{oe} = \frac{i_c}{v_{ce}}$$

An output-node equation yields

$$i_c = \frac{v_{ce}}{r_{ce}} + \frac{v_{ce}}{r_{b'c} + r_{b'e}} + g_m v_{b'e}$$

Therefore,

$$h_{oe} = \frac{1}{r_{ce}} + \frac{1}{r_{b'c}} + g_m h_{re} \tag{10.46}$$

We have again used the fact that $r_{b'c} \gg r_{b'e}$. Also note that

$$v_{b'e} = h_{re}v_{ce}$$

The hybrid-π model can be used to evaluate the high-frequency performance of BJTs if two capacitances are added, as shown in Figure 10.27(b). The *collector-junction capacitor*, $C_{b'c}$, is small (typically 30 pF for a low frequency transistor and 1 pF for a high-frequency transistor). The collector-junction capacitance is the capacitance of the collector-base junction. This junction behaves like a graded junction for small bias voltages, since it is formed by diffusion. The doping density is a function of distance near the junction. For larger reverse-bias voltages, the junction depletion region spreads into the collector region (which is more uniformly doped) and the junction behaves as an "abrupt junction" with uniform doping. The collector-junction capacitance thus follows similar variations. In practice, although this is a varying capacitance, we consider it as constant for the particular transistor operating region. The value of this capacitance appears in the manufacturer's data sheets as C_{oB}, which is the output capacitance of the CB configuration.

The capacitance, $C_{b'e}$, is the sum of the emitter diffusion capacitance and the emitter-junction capacitance. Because the former capacitor is the larger of the two, $C_{b'e}$ is approximately equal to the diffusion capacitance (also known as the base-charging capacitance).

The change in base-emitter voltage, Δv_{BE}, causes a change in the minority carrier charge in the base, Δq. Thus

$$C_{b'e} = \frac{\Delta q}{\Delta v_{BE}}$$

We can define a new term, τ_F, which has the dimensions of time and is called the *base transit time* of a carrier crossing the base region. Thus,

$$\tau_F = \frac{\Delta q}{\Delta i_C}$$

or

$$\Delta q = \tau_F \Delta i_C$$

We then have

$$C_{b'e} \approx \tau_F \frac{\Delta i_C}{\Delta v_{BE}} = \frac{g_m}{\omega_T} = \frac{1}{\omega_T h_{ib}}$$

$$= \frac{I_{CQ}}{2\pi f_T (26 \text{ mV})} = \frac{I_{CQ}}{52\pi f_T \times 10^{-3}} \tag{10.47}$$

In this equation, f_T is the frequency at which the CE short-circuit current gain is 0 dB. The frequency, f_T, is also the current gain-bandwidth product and is found in the manufacturer's specification sheets (see Appendix D).

We now show that the equivalent capacitance of a circuit can be considerably higher than the actual capacitor values present in the circuit. This is called the *Miller effect,* and in order to derive it, we start with a simple circuit transformation. Consider the circuits shown in Figure 10.28.

By appropriately selecting the values of the impedances, Z_1 and Z_2, in the circuit of Figure 10.28(b), the two circuits can be made identical. This is Miller's theorem and it is most useful in high-frequency amplifier analysis.

In order to derive this important result, let us first write the equation for I_1 in the circuit of Figure 10.27(a):

$$I_1 = \frac{V_1 - V_2}{Z} = \left(\frac{V_1}{Z}\right)\left(1 - \frac{V_2}{V_1}\right)$$

Now let V_2/V_1 be the voltage gain of the stage, A_v. Then

$$I_1 = \frac{V_1(1 - A_v)}{Z}$$

Figure 10.28
Miller's theorem.

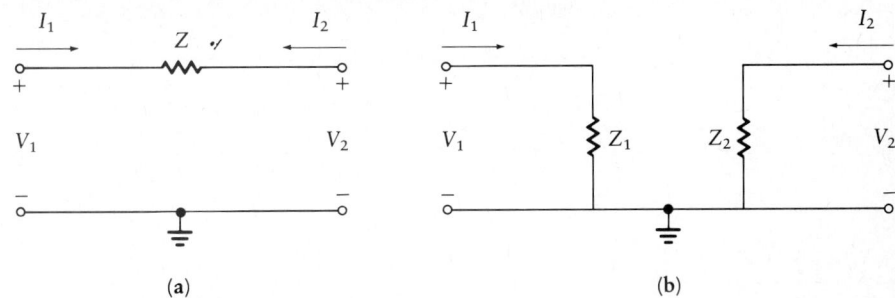

(a)　　　　　　　　　　　　(b)

For the circuit of Figure 10.28(b) to be identical to that of Figure 10.28(a), we must set the currents equal. Thus,

$$I_1 = \frac{V_1}{Z_1} = \frac{V_1(1 - A_v)}{Z}$$

and

$$Z_1 = \frac{Z}{1 - A_v} \tag{10.48}$$

In a similar manner, for the first circuit,

$$I_2 = \frac{V_2 - V_1}{Z} = \left(\frac{V_2}{Z}\right)\left(1 - \frac{V_1}{V_2}\right) = \left(\frac{V_2}{Z}\right)\left(1 - \frac{1}{A_v}\right)$$

where, again, $A_v = \dfrac{V_2}{V_1}$. We set the currents in the two circuits equal and solve for Z_2, with the result

$$Z_2 = \frac{Z}{1 - 1/A_v} \tag{10.49}$$

Let us now apply this result to the CE amplifier stage of Figure 10.29(a). If the hybrid-π model of Figure 10.27(b) is substituted for the transistor, the result is as shown in Figure 10.29(b). We make several simplifications as follows:

$r_{ce} \gg R_L \parallel R_C$, so r_{ce} is deleted.

$r_{b'c} \gg$ other resistors, so $r_{b'c}$ is deleted.

$r_{bb'} \ll r_{b'e}$, so $r_{bb'}$ is deleted.

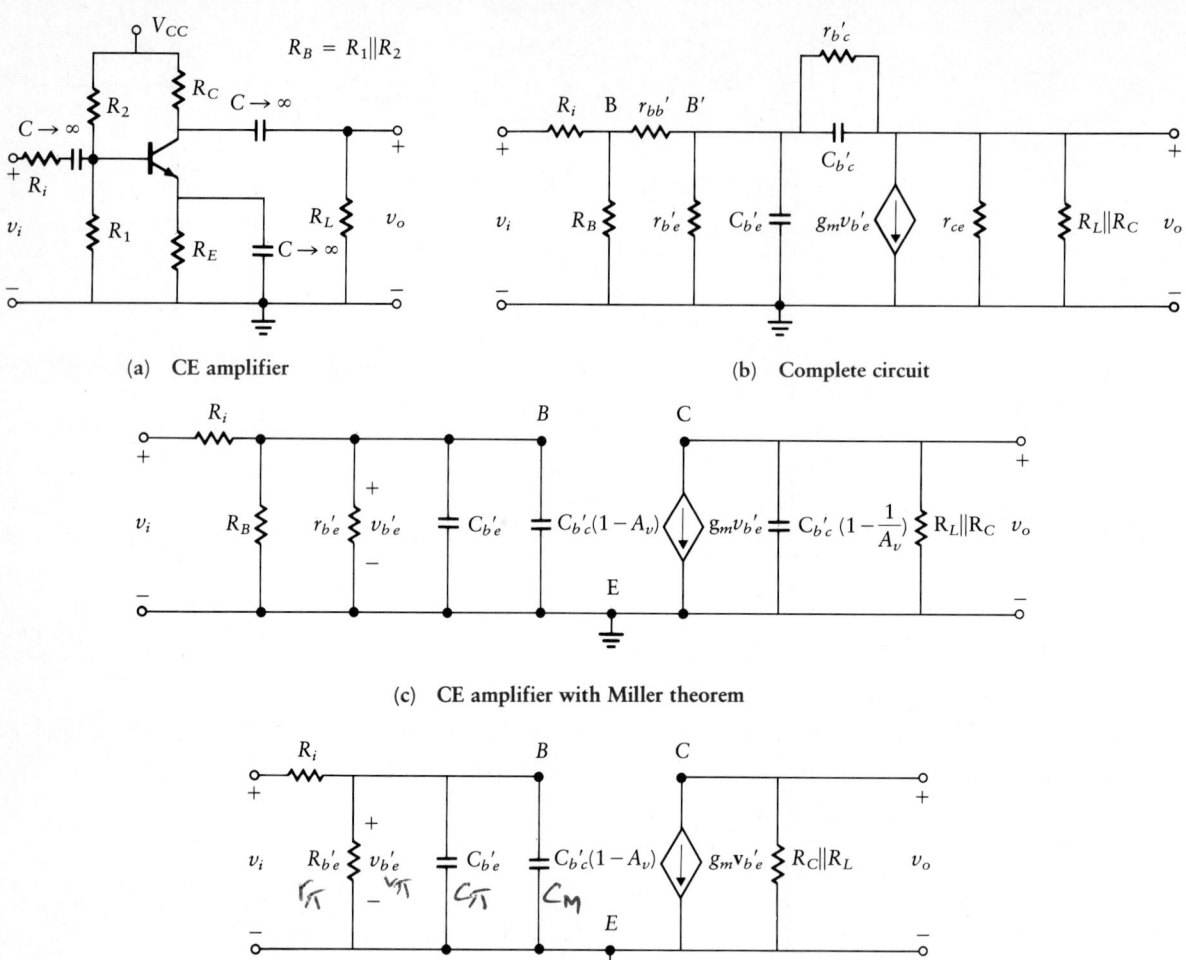

Figure 10.29   CE amplifier.

We now use Miller's theorem to reflect $C_{b'c}$ to the input and output. This yields the result shown in Figure 10.29(c), which is further simplified by combining R_B and $r_{b'e}$ into a single resistance, as follows:

$$R_{b'e} = R_B \parallel r_{b'e}$$

In Figure 10.29(c), we find that there are two poles in the transfer function, one in the base circuit and the other in the collector circuit. This becomes the dominant pole, since the input capacitance is so large (because it is multiplied by A_v). This results from the fact that A_v is usually much greater than 1 and the output capacitance is approximately equal to $C_{b'c}$, which is ignored to develop Figure 10.29(d).

We combine the two capacitors into a total capacitance, C_t, as follows:

$$C_t = C_{b'e} + C_{b'c}(1 - A_v) \tag{10.50}$$

The voltage gain for the CE amplifier at midrange frequency is then given by

$$A_v = \frac{V_{ce}}{V_{be}} = \frac{-R_L \parallel R_C}{h_{ib}} \approx -g_m (R_L \parallel R_C)$$

This expression for gain is used in equation (10.50) to find the total capacitance, C_t, as follows:

$$C_t = C_{b'e} + C_{b'c}[1 + g_m(R_L \parallel R_C)] \tag{10.51}$$

The Miller capacitance is defined as

$$C_M = C_{b'c}[1 + g_m(R_L \parallel R_C)] \tag{10.52}$$

The high-frequency cutoff, f_H, is determined from the input resistance and capacitance, where the resistance is $R_i \parallel R_{b'e}$ and the capacitance is

$$C_t = C_{b'e} + C_M$$

The high-frequency cutoff is then given by the reciprocal of the RC time constant:

$$f_H = \frac{1}{2\pi[R_i \parallel R_{b'e}]\{C_{b'e} + C_{oB}[1 + g_m(R_L \parallel R_C)]\}} \tag{10.53}$$

This equation is only valid for emitter-bypassed CE amplifiers. For non-emitter-bypassed CE amplifiers, we replace the factor $[1 + g_m(R_L \parallel R_C)]$ in equation (10.53) with $(1 - A_v)$. This results in an amplifier with higher bandwidth and greatly reduced gain. We have used C_{oB} in place of $C_{b'c}$, since the former notation is usually found on the data sheets. However, when R_i approaches zero, the dominant pole changes from the input circuit to the output circuit (see equation (10.53)). This then raises the frequency of the dominant pole, resulting in a higher-frequency capability of the amplifier. The dominant pole is then

$$f_H = \frac{1}{2\pi(r_{ce} \parallel R_L \parallel R_C) C_{b'c}}$$

For transistors that are fabricated on ICs, another capacitance might become large enough to be added to $C_{b'c}$ in the formula just given. This capacitance is the collector-to-substrate capacitance, which is normally insignificant in discrete devices and IC devices where the dominant pole is a function of the input circuit.

Example 10.12

Calculate the high-frequency cutoff, f_H, for the 2N3904 transistor. Assume that a CE amplifier is used and that $\beta = 200$, $I_{CQ} = 10$ mA, $R_B = 5$ kΩ, $R_i = 1$ kΩ and $R_L = R_C = 1$ kΩ. Further assume that you have checked the data sheets (see Appendix D) and found that $f_T = 0.25 \times 10^9$ Hz and that $C_{oB} = 4.5$ pF.

SOLUTION   In order to use equation (10.53), we need to find $R_{b'e}$, $C_{b'e}$, and C_m. These are found from the equations derived in this section:

$$r_{b'e} = \frac{26\beta}{I_{CQ}} = \frac{26(200)}{10} = 520 \ \Omega$$

$$g_m = \frac{I_{CQ}}{26 \text{ mA}} = \frac{10}{26} = 0.385 \text{ S}$$

$$C_{b'e} = \frac{g_m}{2\pi f_T} = \frac{0.385}{2\pi \times 0.25 \times 10^9} = 245 \text{ pF}$$

$$C_M = C_{oB}[1 + g_m(R_L \parallel R_C)] = 4.5(1 + 0.385 \times 500) = 870 \text{ pF}$$

$$R_{b'e} = 5 \text{ k}\Omega \parallel 520 \ \Omega = 471 \ \Omega$$

$$R_i \parallel R_{b'e} = 1 \text{ k}\Omega \parallel 471 \ \Omega = 320 \ \Omega$$

Finally,

$$f_H = \frac{10^{12}}{(2\pi)(320)(245 + 870)} = 446 \text{ kHz}$$

Equation (10.53) indicates that the high-frequency cutoff can be increased by lowering R_i and R_b, by lowering the voltage gain of the stage, or by selecting a high-frequency transistor with lower capacitance values. As an example, suppose we recalculate f_H for Example 10.12, where the source impedance, R_i, is now reduced from 1 kΩ to 250 Ω. We calculate

$$R_i \parallel R_{b'e} = 250 \ \Omega \parallel 471 \ \Omega = 163 \ \Omega$$

and

$$f_H = \frac{10^{12}}{(2\pi)(163)(245 + 870)} = 874 \text{ kHz}$$

↦

Drill Problem

D10.6 Determine the high-frequency cutoff for the CE amplifier of Figure 10.17. The transistor parameters are $f_T = 0.4 \times 10^9$ Hz, $C_{oB} = 2$ pF, $\beta = 200$, $r_{b'e} = 400$ Ω, $g_m = 0.5$ S, $R_B = 10$ kΩ, and $R_C \parallel R_L = 670$ Ω.

Ans: $R_{b'e} = 385$ Ω; $C_{b'e} = 200$ pF; $C_M = 672$ pF; $f_H = 474$ kHz

10.5.2 *EF Amplifier Response at High Frequency*

The EF amplifier has a voltage gain approximately equal to unity. The load for most EF amplifiers is capacitive, so we include the load capacitor in our models. Figure 10.30 shows an EF amplifier, its equivalent circuit, and a modified equivalent circuit illustrating the Miller effect. Since the amplifier gain is close to unity, $C_{b'e}$ is close to zero and h_{ie}, which is in the input circuit, becomes infinite. In the output circuit, $C_{b'e}$ also becomes zero. Then the system reduces to a two-pole amplifier with normalized gain as follows:

$$\frac{A_v}{A_{vm}} = \frac{1}{[(R_i \parallel R_B)(C_{b'c} s + 1)](C_L R_L s + 1)}$$

This approximation does not contain the effects of $C_{b'e}$. In an attempt to provide a better approximation, we derive the gain for the amplifier in terms of its components:

$$V_o = \beta I_b \left[R_L \parallel \left(\frac{1}{sC_L} \right) \right] = \beta I_b \frac{R_L}{R_L C_L s + 1}$$

The base-to-ground voltage, V_i', is given by

$$V_i' = I_b h_{ie} = \beta I_b h_{ib}$$

Then,

$$\frac{V_o}{V_i} = \frac{\beta I_b R_L / (R_L C_L s + 1)}{\beta I_b h_{ib}} = \frac{R_L}{R_L C_L s + 1} \frac{1}{h_{ib}}$$

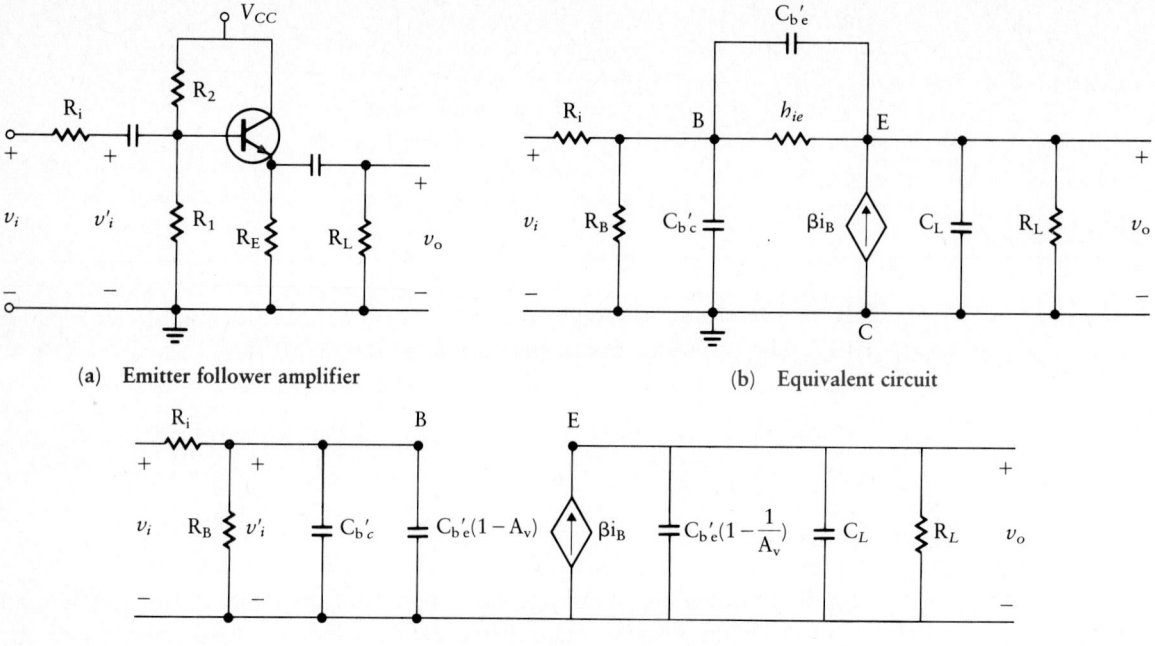

(a)   Emitter follower amplifier

(b)   Equivalent circuit

(c)   Equivalent circuit using Miller theorem

Figure 10.30   EF amplifier.

Since we know that V_o/V_i is approximately unity, then

$$\frac{R_L}{R_L C_L s + 1} \frac{I_{CQ}}{V_T} \approx 1$$

where we have used the relationship

$$h_{ib} = \frac{V_T}{I_{CQ}}$$

Putting this in terms of frequency, we let $s = j\omega_H$ to get

$$1 = \left| \frac{R_L}{j\omega_H R_L C_L + 1} \right| \frac{I_{CQ}}{V_T} \approx \frac{R_L}{2\pi f_H R_L C_L} \frac{I_{CQ}}{V_T}$$

and

$$\frac{1}{2\pi f_H C_L} = \frac{V_T}{I_{CQ}}$$

Now since

$$C_{b'e} = \frac{I_{CQ}}{V_T 2\pi f_T}$$

then

$$\frac{V_T}{I_{CQ}} = \frac{1}{C_{b'e} 2\pi f_T}$$

Thus

$$\frac{1}{2\pi f_H C_L} = \frac{1}{C_{b'e}(2\pi f_T)}$$

and

$$f_H \approx \frac{f_T C_{b'e}}{C_L}$$

This last equation is valid only if

$$C_L R_L \gg (R_i \parallel R_B) C_{b'c}$$

10.5.3 *CB Amplifier Response at High Frequency*

In Section 10.5.2, we stated that the CB amplifier has a higher frequency response than that of the CE amplifier. In Section 10.5.1 we explained the Miller effect, which causes the input capacitance to increase by the factor of $(1 - A_v)C_{b'c}$. When the gain is large, the input capacitance becomes so large that the amplifier is essentially a one-pole amplifier with the input circuit providing the dominant pole. In the case of the CB amplifier, this effect does not exist, and there is no multiplying factor for $C_{b'c}$. This is shown in Figure 10.31, where the CB amplifier and its equivalent circuit are illustrated.

The CB amplifier has two poles, as with the CE amplifier. In the CB configuration, the input circuit will usually not provide the dominant pole. The normalized gain is given by

$$\frac{A_v}{A_{vm}} = \frac{1}{(\tau_1 s + 1)(\tau_2 s + 1)}$$

where

$$\tau_1 = (R_L \parallel R_C)C_{b'c}$$

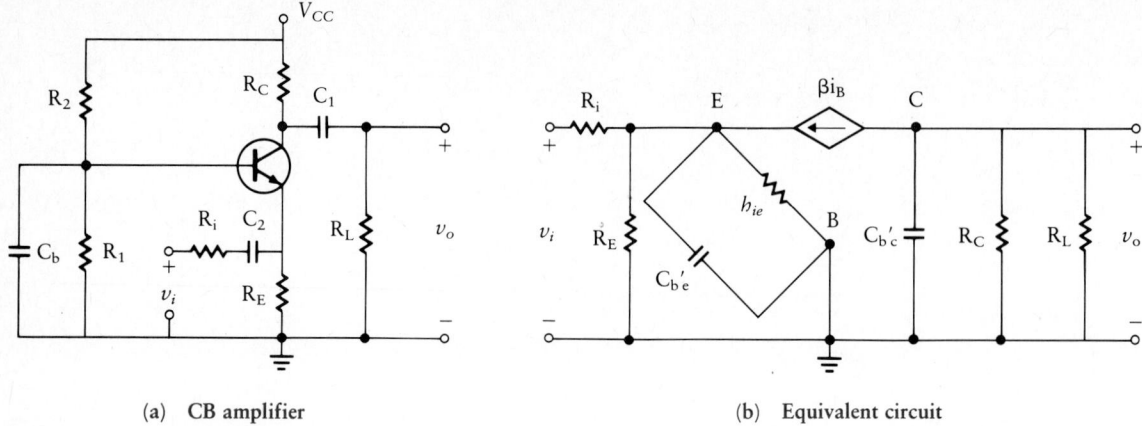

(a) CB amplifier   (b) Equivalent circuit

Figure 10.31   CB amplifier.

and

$$\tau_2 = (R_E \parallel h_{ib} \parallel R_i)C_{b'e}$$

A comparison of time constants indicates that the frequency response for CB amplifiers is much greater than that for CE amplifiers providing the same voltage gain.

Example 10.13

Determine the frequency response of the CB amplifer shown in Figure 10.31, with the following specifications: $V_{CC} = 12$ V, $V_{BE} = 0.7$ V, $\beta = 100$, $R_i = 600\ \Omega$, $R_E = 200\ \Omega$, $R_L = 2$ kΩ, $C_{oB} = 2$ pF, and $f_T = 10^8$ Hz. Then compare this with the response of a CE amplifier having the same gain.

SOLUTION   First determine the Q-point for maximum output swing.

$$I_{CQ} = \frac{12}{2200 + 1200} = 3.53 \text{ mA}$$

Then,

$$h_{ib} = \frac{26}{3.53} = 7.37\ \Omega$$

The voltage gain is given by

$$A_v = \frac{2 \text{ k}\Omega \parallel 2 \text{ k}\Omega}{7.37} = 136$$

Since $C_{b'c} = C_{oB} = 2$ pF, we have

$$\tau_1 = (R_L \parallel R_C)(2 \text{ pF}) = 2 \text{ ns}$$

$$\tau_2 = (R_E \parallel h_{ib} \parallel R_i)C_{b'e}$$

where

$$C_{b'e} = \frac{I_{CQ}}{52 \times 10^{-3}\pi f_T} = 216 \text{ pF}$$

Then

$$\tau_2 = (200 \parallel 7.37 \parallel 600)(216 \text{ pF}) = 1.52 \text{ ns}$$

$$f_1 = 80 \text{ MHz}$$

$$f_2 = 105 \text{ MHz}$$

The high-frequency response is then

$$f_H = 105 \text{ MHz}$$

The comparable CE amplifier has

$$R_{b'e} = R_B \parallel r_{b'e} = [0.1(100)(200)] \parallel (7.37 \times 100) = 538 \ \Omega$$

and

$$f_H = \frac{1}{2\pi(600 \parallel 538)[216 \text{ pF} + (2 \text{ pF})(1 + 136)]} = 1.14 \text{ MHz}$$

Notice that the CB amplifier has a frequency response 80 times higher than that of the CE amplifier. ►►

10.6   High-Frequency Response—FETs

10.6.1   *CS Amplifier*

The high-frequency equivalent circuit for a FET is obtained by adding three capacitors to the model developed in Chapter 4, as shown in Figure 10.32. The capacitors are defined as follows:

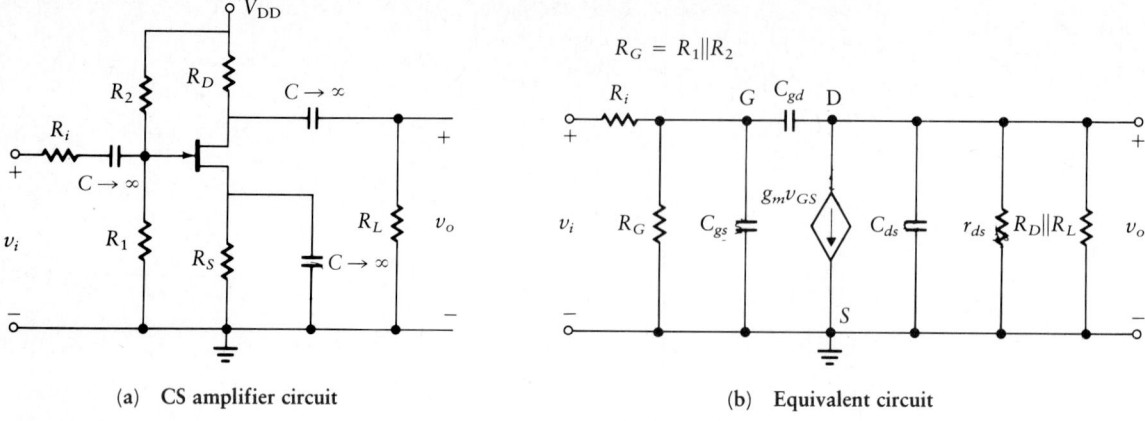

(a) CS amplifier circuit   (b) Equivalent circuit

Figure 10.32   CS amplifier, high-frequency model.

C_{gs} is the capacitance between gate and source.

C_{gd} is the capacitance between gate and drain.

C_{ds} is the capacitance between drain and source.

Manufacturer's data sheets show these capacitances in terms of the two-port model, which we discussed in Chapter 3.

We refer to Figure 10.32(b) for the following equations. The input admittance, Y_{is}, is found by shorting the output (D to S) and finding the ratio of input current to input voltage. Thus,

$$Y_{is} = \frac{I_g}{V_{gs}} = j\omega(C_{gs} + C_{gd}) \tag{10.54}$$

The equivalent input capacitance, as shown in data sheets, is

$$C_{is} = C_{gs} + C_{gd} \tag{10.55}$$

We look at the forward transfer admittance, Y_{fs}, which is the ratio of *output* current to input voltage with the output short-circuited. Thus,

$$Y_{fs} = \frac{I_o}{V_{gs}} = g_m - j\omega C_{gd} \tag{10.56}$$

The equivalent forward transfer capacitance, as shown in the data sheets, is

$$C_{fs} = C_{gd} \tag{10.57}$$

The reverse transfer admittance, Y_{rs}, is the ratio of input current to output voltage with the input short-circuited:

$$Y_{rs} = \frac{I_G}{V_{ds}} = -j\omega C_{gd} \tag{10.58}$$

Thus, the reverse transfer capacitance is

$$C_{rs} = C_{gd} \tag{10.59}$$

Finally, the output admittance, Y_{os}, is the ratio of output current to output voltage with the input short-circuited.

$$Y_{os} = \frac{I_o}{V_{ds}} = 1/r_{ds} + j\omega(C_{gd} + C_{ds}) \tag{10.60}$$

The output capacitance is then

$$C_{os} = C_{gd} + C_{ds} \tag{10.61}$$

The input and reverse transfer capacitors, C_{is} and C_{rs}, are usually shown in the manufacturer's specification sheets as C_{iss} and C_{rss}. The second s is used to designate that one of the ports is short-circuited.

The capacitors of Figure 10.32(a) can be approximately related to C_{rss} and C_{iss} by

$$C_{gd} = C_{rss}$$

and

$$C_{gs} = C_{iss} - C_{rss}$$

C_{ds} is so small that it can be neglected.

The CS amplifier of Figure 10.32(a) is then modeled at high frequencies, with the small-signal equivalent circuit of Figure 10.32(b).

Note that at mid-range frequencies the capacitors are neglected, and the voltage gain is

$$\frac{v_o}{v_i} = -g_m[r_{ds} \parallel (R_L \parallel R_D)] \approx -g_m(R_L \parallel R_D)$$

The final approximation is true, since r_{ds} is usually much larger than the parallel combination of R_L and R_D.

Now we apply the Miller theorem to the circuit of Figure 10.32(b) in a manner similar to that used for the BJT analysis. The input capacitance is

$$C_{gs} + C_{gd}[1 + g_m(R_L \parallel R_D)] \tag{10.62}$$

and the output capacitance is

$$C_{ds} + C_{gd}\left[1 + \frac{1}{g_m(R_L \parallel R_D)}\right] \approx C_{ds} + C_{gd}$$

The simplified circuit is shown in Figure 10.33, where C_{ds} is neglected because of its small size. The largest capacitor is the Miller capacitor because of the amplification of the stage. The dominant pole is normally formed by the input characteristics of the circuit.

As in the case of BJT amplifiers, the high-frequency cutoff, f_H, is determined by the RC combination made up of the resistance

$$R_G \parallel R_i$$

and the capacitance

$$C_{gs} + C_{gd}[1 + g_m(R_L \parallel R_D)]$$

The high-frequency cutoff is then given by the reciprocal of the RC time constant:

$$f_H = \frac{1}{2\pi(R_G \parallel R_i)\{C_{gs} + C_{gd}[1 + g_m(R_L \parallel R_D)]\}} \tag{10.63}$$

Again, as in the BJT high-frequency case, the equation is valid only when R_S is totally bypassed. If R_S is not bypassed, we must replace the term $[1 + g_m(R_L \parallel R_D)]$ with $(1 - A_v)$.

As in the case of the BJT, when R_i approaches zero, the dominant pole

Figure 10.33
Simplified high-frequency equivalent circuit.

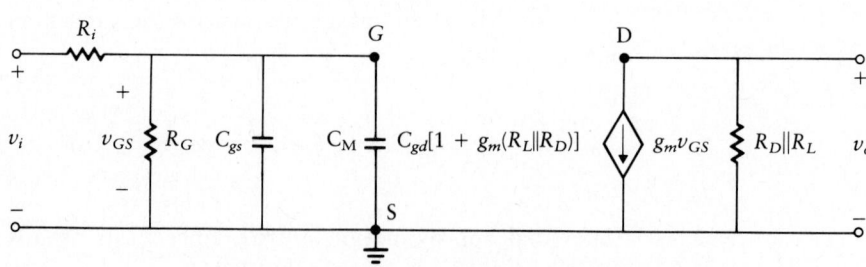

Assuming $C_{GD} + C_{DS} < C_M$ and $r_{DS} \gg R_L$ or R_D

shifts from the effect of the input circuit to the output circuit. Then, the high-frequency cutoff is

$$f'_H = \frac{1}{2\pi(r_{DS} \| R_D \| R_L)(C_{gd} + C_{ds})}$$

In this case, any existing load capacitance must be added to C_{gd} and C_{ds}. This has the effect of reducing the frequency response of the amplifier.

Example 10.14

Determine the high-frequency cutoff for the CS amplifier of Figure 10.32(a). Let $R_L = 20$ kΩ, $R_D = 4$ kΩ, $R_G = 100$ kΩ, $R_i = 100$ kΩ, $g_m = 2000$ μS, $C_{gs} = C_{gd} = 16$ pF, and $C_{ds} = 0$.

SOLUTION   We use equation (10.63) to find f_H as follows:

$$f_H = \frac{1}{(2\pi)(100 \text{ k}\Omega \| 100 \text{ k}\Omega)\{10 \times 10^{-12} + 16 \times 10^{-12} [1 + (0.002)(20 \text{ k}\Omega \| 4 \text{ k}\Omega)]\}}$$

$$= \frac{1}{(2\pi)(50 \times 10^3)(139 \times 10^{-12})} = 22.9 \text{ kHz}$$

This is a relatively low cutoff frequency because of the large values of the capacitors, C_{gs} and C_{gd}. We can increase this frequency by lowering C_{gs} and C_{gd} and by lowering the input and source resistors or by reducing the voltage gain of the stage. ➤+

Drill Problem

D10.7   Determine the high-frequency cutoff, f_H, for the FET amplifier of Figure 10.32(a) with

$$C_{gs} = C_{gd} = 3 \text{ pF}$$

$$C_{ds} = 0$$

$$R_L = 20 \text{ k}\Omega, \qquad R_D = 4 \text{ k}\Omega, \qquad R_G = R_i = 10 \text{ k}\Omega$$

$$g_m = 2000 \text{ }\mu\text{S}$$

Ans: $f_H = 1.22$ MHz

Note the great improvement in high-frequency cutoff from that obtained in Example 10.14.

Example 10.15

Given an FET transistor with the following parameters: $g_m = 0.8$ mS, $r_{ds} = 50$ kΩ, $C_{gs} = 2.5$ pF, $C_{ds} = 5$ pF, and $C_{gd} = 0.1$ pF. Determine the admittance parameters at a frequency of 20 kHz.

SOLUTION   We need simply apply equations (10.54) through (10.61).

$$Y_{is} = j(2\pi \times 2 \times 10^4)(2.5 + 0.1) \times 10^{-12}$$

$$= j3.27 \times 10^{-7} \text{ S}$$

$$Y_{fs} = 0.8 \times 10^{-3} - j(2\pi \times 2 \times 10^4 \times 0.1 \times 10^{-12})$$

$$= 0.8 \times 10^{-3} - j1.26 \times 10^{-8}$$

$$Y_{os} = \frac{1}{50 \text{ k}\Omega} + j2\pi \times 2 \times 10^4(2.5 + 0.1) \times 10^{-12}$$

$$= 2 \times 10^{-5} + j3.27 \times 10^{-7}$$

$$Y_{rs} = j(2\pi \times 2 \times 10^4 \times 0.1 \times 10^{-12}) = -j1.26 \times 10^{-8} \text{ S}$$

10.6.2   *CD Amplifier*

Figure 10.34 shows a CD amplifier, its high-frequency equivalent circuit, and a modification of the equivalent circuit that illustrates the Miller effect. The high-frequency cutoff of CD amplifiers is much higher than that of CS amplifiers using the same transistor. This phenomenon is attributed to the Miller effect, as shown in Figure 10.34(c). Remember that the CD amplifier has a gain that is positive and less than unity. This allows the Miller effect to *reduce* the capacitance rather than increase it, as was the case with the CS amplifier. The gate-to-source resistance, r_{GS}, is reduced considerably by the Miller effect, but since JFETs already have large gate-to-source resistances (on the order of megohms), it is still ignored in the model. MOSFETs have even higher values of gate-to-source resistance in the order of hundreds of megohms. The reduction of the gate-to-source capacitance by the Miller effects reduces the effect of the pole at the output so the dominant pole is usually found at the input circuit, even though JFETs sometimes have small drain-to-source resistances. The amplifier then can be reduced to a single-pole amplifier as follows:

$$\frac{A_v}{A_{vm}} = \frac{1}{\tau_2 s + 1}$$

where

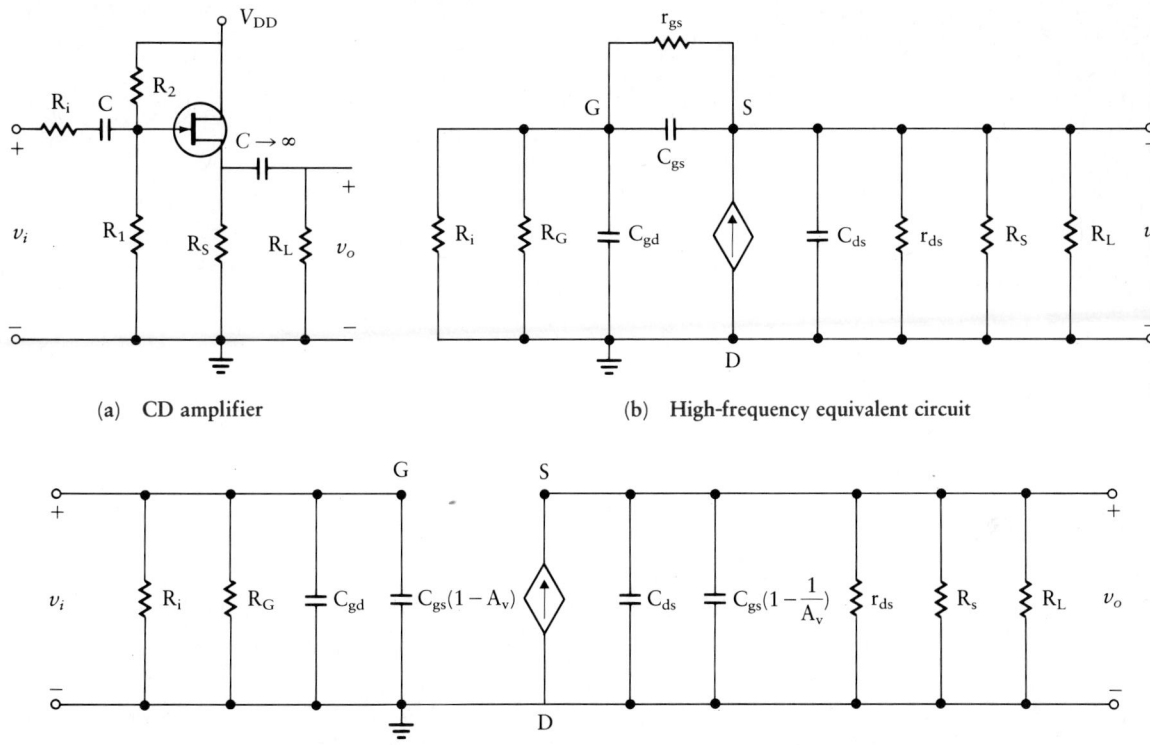

(a) CD amplifier

(b) High-frequency equivalent circuit

(c) High-frequency equivalent curcuit with Miller effect

Figure 10.34 CD amplifier.

$$\tau_2 = (R_G \parallel R_i)[C_{gd} + C_{gs}(1 - A_v)]$$

Since R_G is usually very large, we can approximate $R_G \parallel R_i$ by R_i. The cutoff frequency is then given by

$$f_H = \frac{1}{2\pi R_i[C_{gd} + C_{gs}(1 - A_v)]}$$

10.7 Cascode Amplifiers

We now revisit the cascode amplifier, first presented in Section 7.4. The circuit is repeated in Figure 10.35.

The cascode configuration exhibits a higher cutoff frequency than is experienced with cascaded CE amplifiers using the same type of transistor. Since

Figure 10.35
Cascode amplifier.

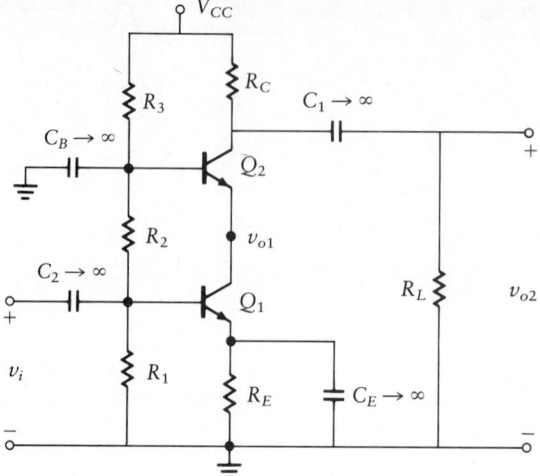

the CE amplifier (Q_1) in the cascode configuration sees the low-input impedance of the common base amplifier, the gain of the CE amplifier (Q_1) is approximately equal to -1. This reduces the effect of the capacitance between the base and collector. Since the capacitance of this junction is the source of the dominant high-frequency pole, the Miller effect, $(1 - A_v)C_{bc}$, is greatly diminished and the pole occurs at a higher frequency. The CB amplifier (with Q_2), however, is not affected by the Miller effect of the capacitance of the BC junction and already has a wide bandwidth. It also has a high voltage gain and compensates for the low voltage gain of the CE amplifier (Q_1).

Since we assume the transistors to have the same current gain,

$$i_{C1} = i_{C2}$$

and

$$i_{B1} = i_{B2}$$

Since the base currents are both small, we can calculate V_{B1} by applying a voltage-divider relationship as follows:

$$V_{B1} = \frac{R_1 V_{CC}}{R_1 + R_2 + R_3}$$

I_{C1} is found from the expression

$$I_{C1} = I_{C2} = \frac{V_{B1} - V_{BE}}{R_E}$$

and

$$h_{ib1} = h_{ib2} = \frac{26 \text{ mV}}{I_{C1}}$$

The gain of the first stage is

$$A_{v1} = \frac{-h_{ib2}}{h_{ib1}} = -1$$

The gain to the output is

$$A_{v2} = \frac{R_L \parallel R_C}{h_{ib2}}$$

Example 10.16

Given the circuit of Figure 10.35 with

$$R_1 = R_2 = R_3 = 5 \text{ k}\Omega$$

$$V_{CC} = 24 \text{ v}$$

$$R_E = 1 \text{ k}\Omega$$

$$r_o = 11 \text{ k}\Omega$$

$$\beta = 100$$

$$R_L = R_C = 5 \text{ k}\Omega$$

Find the voltage gains A_{v1} and A_{v2} and the output resistance R_o.

SOLUTION   The following equations follow from the results in this section.

$$V_{B1} = \frac{5 \text{ k}\Omega \times 24}{5 \text{ k}\Omega + 5 \text{ k}\Omega + 5 \text{ k}\Omega} = 8 \text{ V}$$

$$I_{C1} = I_{C2} = \frac{8 - 0.7}{1 \text{ k}\Omega} = 7.3 \text{ mA}$$

$$h_{ib1} = h_{ib2} = \frac{26 \text{ mV}}{7.3 \text{ mA}} = 3.56 \ \Omega$$

$$A_{v1} = -1$$

$$A_{v2} = \frac{5 \text{ k}\Omega \parallel 5 \text{ k}\Omega}{3.56} = 702$$

The total gain is then given by

$$A_{v1}A_{v2} = -702$$

From Chapter 7,

$$R_o = \beta r_o$$
$$R_o = 100 \times 11 \text{ k}\Omega = 1.1 \text{ M}\Omega$$

10.8   High-Frequency Amplifier Design

In the previous section, we learned to analyze amplifiers to determine the high-frequency cutoff point. We now consider the design changes to the amplifier to attain a specific high-frequency cutoff. It is difficult to set the cutoff frequency using a particular transistor, circuit parameters, and configuration. When the amplifier is constructed, it will attain a high-frequency cutoff point based upon these parameters. The designer has the following options to attain a high cutoff frequency:

1. Reduce the gain per stage to reduce the Miller effect.
2. Reduce the source impedance of the input signal, R_i.
3. Select a higher frequency transistor.
4. Use a configuration that is not as frequency-sensitive, such as the CB or cascode configuration.

For high-frequency design, changing the above parameters requires a new analysis with each change. This is time-consuming. A computer program called SPICE (Simulated Program with Integrated Circuit Emphasis) can be of great help since parameters can be changed and the computer will readily provide an analysis of the circuit with the complete frequency response characteristics. Although SPICE was developed more for internal IC analysis, it can be of great assistance to the circuit designer. In Appendix A, we provide a simplified explanation of how circuit elements can be modeled to be entered into the computer for a SPICE analysis. We also present some sample runs for simple circuits.

10.9 **Concluding Remarks**

Let us return to the XYZ Audio Corporation discussion given in the introduction to this chapter. Recall that as a fresh graduate engineer, you designed an audio amplifier to be used in a compact disc player, but, alas, that amplifier was found to have poor low frequency response. Since the problem was identified as being at low frequencies rather than high frequencies, it can be traced to the presence of coupling and bypass capacitors. The techniques of Section 10.3 are used to analyze your design. It is, of course, preferable to use the bandwidth criteria as part of the design process, but we assume that in this case, the design was completed and we are now in the troubleshooting phase. The corner frequencies are found and compared to the design specifications. Since the amplifier must handle audio signals, it is reasonable to desire response down to 15 or 20 Hz. When the corner frequencies are calculated, they will probably be undesirably high. To lower these frequencies, we must raise the time constants. This requires either raising the resistances or the capacitances. Raising the resistances requires complete redesign in order to maintain the same gain. Therefore, if your original design is close to specification, you would probably want to work with the capacitances.

It is not our intent to minimize the practical problems associated with a real-life design. While our study of electronics attempts to *model* the real world closely, realize that we are simply working with models. There is a difference between real-world behavior and mathematical-model performance.

PROBLEMS

Draw the amplitude and phase curves as a function of frequency for the loop transfer functions given in Problems 10.1–10.12.

10.1 $G(s)H(s) = \dfrac{100}{s^2}$

10.2 $G(s)H(s) = \dfrac{s}{s + 10}$

10.3 $G(s)H(s) = \dfrac{10(s + 10)}{s + 1}$

10.4 $G(s)H(s) = \dfrac{0.1s + 1}{s + 1}$

10.5 $G(s)H(s) = \dfrac{10s}{0.1s + 1}$

10.6 $G(s)H(s) = \dfrac{s + 1}{s(0.1s + 1)}$

10.7 $G(s)H(s) = \dfrac{2}{s}$

10.8 $G(s)H(s) = \dfrac{1}{s(s + 8)}$

10.9 $G(s)H(s) = \dfrac{1}{(s + 5)(s + 10)}$

10.10 $G(s)H(s) = \dfrac{1}{s^2 + 2s + 30}$

10.11 $G(s)H(s) = \dfrac{1}{s(s^2 + 2s + 30)}$

10.12 $G(s)H(s) = \dfrac{1}{s(s^2 + 3s + 2)}$

10.13 Construct Bode plots for V_o/V_i for the circuits of Figure P10.1 and determine the lower and upper 3-dB frequencies.

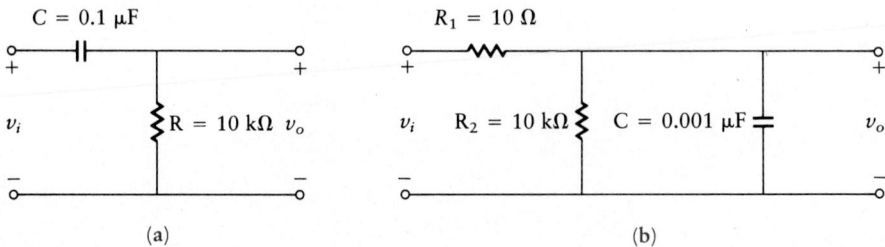

(a)   (b)

Figure P10.1

10.14 A 2N3903 transistor is incorporated in the circuit of Figure 10.17. Calculate the lower-corner 3-dB frequency and draw the Bode plot for this amplifier. Let $R_L = R_C = 1$ kΩ, $C_1 = 0.1$ μF, $R_E = 100$ Ω, $R_1 = 1.5$ kΩ, $R_2 = 10$ kΩ, $C_2 = 0.01$ μF, and $V_{CC} = 12$ V.

10.15 Given the circuit of Figure 10.17 with $V_{CC} = 12$ V, $\beta = 250$, $R_L = 1$ kΩ and $A_v = -5$, select C_1 and C_2 so that the amplifier has a lower 3-dB frequency of 20 Hz.

10.16 Use a 2N3903 transistor in the circuit of Figure 10.17. Draw the Bode plot for this amplifier when $R_1 = 1$ kΩ, $R_2 = 9$ kΩ, $\beta = 200$, $R_L = R_C = 1$ kΩ, $R_E = 100$ Ω, $C_2 = 0.01$ μF and $C_1 = 0.1$ μF.

10.17 Design a CE amplifier with $R_{in} = 15$ kΩ, $A_v = -10$, $R_L = 10$ kΩ, and a low-frequency cutoff of 40 Hz. Use a transistor with $\beta = 200$, $V_{BE} = 0.7$ V and $V_{CC} = 12$ V. What are the values of C_1 and C_2 in each case?

a. If the poles are one decade apart.

b. If both poles are identically located.

c. If C_1 and C_2 are equal. Determine the new corner frequencies.

Compare the results of parts (a), (b), and (c).

10.18 The emitter resistor is bypassed in the amplifier of Problem 10.17. What value is required for the bypass capacitor if the cutoff frequency is 40 Hz?

10.19 An EF amplifier has $R_1 = 20$ kΩ, $R_2 = 2$ kΩ, $R_L = 100$ Ω, $R_E = 50$ Ω, C(output) $= 100$ μF, and C(input) $= 3.3$ μF. Draw the Bode plots for this amplifier if $V_{CC} = 10$ V, $\beta = 200$, and $V_{BE} = 0.7$ V.

10.20 Design an EF amplifier with $A_i = 10$, $R_L = 20$ Ω and a low-frequency cutoff of 20 Hz. Use $V_{CC} = 10$ V and a transistor with $\beta = 80$ and $V_{BE} = 0.7$ V. What are the values of C_1 and C_2 in each case?

a. If the poles are one decade apart.

b. If both poles are identically located.

c. If C_1 and C_2 are equal. Determine the new corner frequencies.

10.21 Given the FET amplifier of Figure 10.23 with a 3N128 MOSFET and $V_{DD} = 12$ V, $R_{in} = 50$ kΩ.

a. Design the amplifier to have a midrange voltage gain of -2 when $R_L = 3$ kΩ. Use $g_m = 5000$ μS, $V_{DSQ} = 7.5$ V and $I_{DQ} = 2$ mA.

b. Select C_1 and C_2 so that the lower 3-dB frequency is 10 Hz.

10.22 Design a JFET amplifier for $A_v = -10$, $R_{in} = 50$ kΩ, and $R_L = 20$ kΩ using $V_{CC} = 20$ V. The Q-point is selected at $V_{DSQ} = 7$ V, $V_{GSQ} = -0.35$ V, $I_{DQ} = 1.3$ mA, and $g_m = 1600$ μS. Select C_1, C_2, and C_3 for a lower 3 dB frequency of 20 Hz.

10.23 In the amplifier of Problem 10.22, the transistor is replaced by a MOSFET, which has $g_m = 3333$ μS at a Q-point of $V_{DSQ} = 6$ V, $I_{DQ} = 1$ mA and $V_{GSQ} = 2$ V.

a. Design the amplifier.

b. Select C_1, C_2, and C_3.

10.24 Design a JFET CS amplifier for a 3-dB lower frequency cutoff of 40 Hz for $A_v = -2$ and $R_{in} = 100$ kΩ. The Q-point is selected at $V_{DSQ} = 6$ V, $V_{GSQ} = -1$ V, $I_{DQ} = 0.5$ mA, and $g_m = 2000$ μS. Determine each of the following.

    a. All resistor values when $V_{CC} = 12$ V and $R_L = 10$ kΩ.

    b. τ values.

    c. Values of C_1, C_2, and C_b.

10.25 Draw the amplitude and phase Bode plots for the operational amplifier of Figure 10.16. Let $G_o = 120$ dB and $\omega_c = 2\pi$ rad/s in the equations

$$G = \frac{G_o}{1 + s/\omega_c}$$

Use the following resistor values:

    a. $\dfrac{R_F}{R_A} = 10^3$

    b. $\dfrac{R_F}{R_A} = 10$

    c. $\dfrac{R_F}{R_A} = 1$

10.26 Using a 2N3904 transistor with the circuit of Figure 10.17, determine the upper and lower 3 dB frequency and construct the Bode plot. Let $R_L = R_C = 10$ kΩ, $C_1 = 0.1$ μF, $R_E = 100$ Ω, $R_1 = 1.5$ kΩ, $R_2 = 21$ kΩ, $R_i = 500$ Ω, $C_2 = 0.01$ μF, $V_{CC} = 12$ V, $V_{BE} = 0.7$ V, $C_{oB} = 4.5$ pF, $f_T = 200$ MHz, and $\beta = 100$.

10.27 Calculate the f_H for a junction transistor with the following values: $f_T = 500$ MHz, $h_{fe} = 400$, $C_{oB} = 0.5$ pF, $R_L = 2$ kΩ, $I_{CQ} = 5$ mA, $R_L = R_C = 7$ kΩ, $R_B = 20$ kΩ, and $R_i = 2$ kΩ.

10.28 The specifications for a particular FET show that at 200 MHz, $C_{oss} = 2$ pF, $C_{iss} = 6$ pF, $C_{rss} = 0.5$ pF, $RE(Y_{os}) = 20$ μS, $RE(Y_{is}) = 0.8$ mS, and $RE(Y_{fs}) = 2000$ μS. Develop the model shown in Figure 10.32(b).

10.29 Determine the parameters of the model of Figure 10.32(b) from the information for the 3N128 given in the appendix. Use a frequency of 200 MHz at $V_{DS} = 15$ V and $I_D = 5$ mA. Assume the capacitor values are the same for 1 MHz as for 200 MHz and ignore the series resistors in the gate and source.

10.30 According to the manufacturer's specification for a particular FET, the Y-parameter values at 100 MHz are: $Y_{iss} = 0.2 + j2.5$ mS, $Y_{rss} = -0.01 - j0.7$ mS, $Y_{fss} = 3 - j0.7$ mS and $Y_{os} = 0.05 + j0.8$ mS. Determine the values of C_{gd}, C_{gs}, C_{ds}, g_m, and r_{ds}.

10.31 For the circuit of Figure 10.32(a), develop the high-frequency portion of the Bode plot for an amplifier when $R_i = 2$ kΩ, $R_L = 4$ kΩ, $R_D = 3$ kΩ, $R_G = 20$ kΩ, $r_{ds} = 10$ kΩ, $C_{gs} = 5$ pF, and $C_{ds} = 1.1$ pF. Assume that $C_{gd} = 2$ pF and $g_m = 0.002$ S.

10.32 Construct a Bode plot for the amplifier given in Problem 10.31 when R_i approaches zero.

10.33 Determine the frequency response for the FET amplifier shown in Figure P10.2 where $r_{ds} = 100$ kΩ, $g_m = 2.5$ mS, $C_{dg} = 2$ pF, $C_{gs} = 10$ pF, and $C_{ds} = 2$ pF.

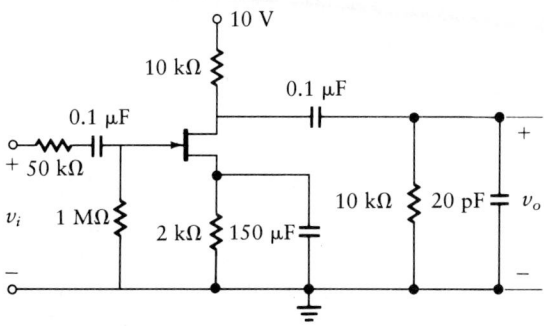

Figure P10.2

11

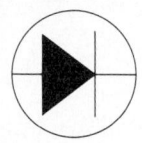

FEEDBACK AND STABILITY

Introduction

You have studied hard, learned well, and can now design amplifiers using BJTs, FETs, and ICs. You have designed many such amplifiers for the XYZ Audio Company and have been promoted to group leader. A new engineer has just joined your group, and you gave that person the assignment of designing a simple audio amplifier. The new engineer was knowledgeable regarding frequency response, and the resulting amplifiers produced distortionless sound. However, one day during a demonstration for a prospective customer, a loud whistling sound came from the speaker. Instead of simply amplifying the audio signal, the system had become an oscillator! Pity! Both you and your young charge had failed to perform a stability analysis of the amplifier system. Heed well what follows in this chapter, and you can avoid such embarrassing situations!

Feedback exists when the output of a system is connected to the input in such a way that voltages appearing at the output affect the input signal.

We have already seen several forms of feedback. The transistor amplifiers of Chapter 2 often include an emitter resistor. If that emitter resistor is left unbypassed, a form of feedback occurs, since the output voltage is subtracted from the input voltage and thereby affects the base to emitter voltage.

We study op-amp circuits in Chapters 7 through 9. Most of these amplifiers include a feedback connection between output and input. This feedback has the desirable effect of reducing the sensitivity of the overall amplifier to changes in the op-amp parameters. Most notably, the gain of the open loop (without feedback) op-amp varies significantly with changes in frequency, whereas the overall gain of the feedback amplifier is much less sensitive to frequency changes.

The advantages of feedback are summarized as follows:

1. Gain is relatively independent of the variation of device parameters.
2. Input and output resistances of the closed-loop system are controlled.
3. Amplifier bandwidth is increased.
4. Nonlinearities and distortion are reduced.
5. Unwanted noise signals are reduced. (See Appendix F for a discussion of noise and noise generators.)

The potential disadvantage of feedback is that the gain is reduced. In the last discussion, we confined our attention to *negative feedback,* which occurs when the portion of the output fed back to the input subtracts from that input.

Positive feedback, where the signal fed back from the output is *added* rather than *subtracted* from the input, is frequently used in electronic circuits. Such feedback is intentionally introduced when we wish to design an *oscillator.* This makes the amplifier unstable, and it begins to oscillate, producing a sinusoidal output signal when there is no input signal.

This chapter develops the mathematical analysis tools for studying feedback systems. Attention is given to the problem of stability.

11.1   Feedback Amplifier Considerations

Figure 11.1 shows a mathematical system model of a feedback system. This model can be used to represent an amplifier or any other feedback system. The circle denotes a summing operation, and with the polarity markings as shown, it has the meaning that the signal leaving the circle, ϵ, is equal to the difference between the two signals entering. Thus,

$$\epsilon = R + (-Y) = R - Y$$

Each of the parameters in this equation can represent time functions, Laplace transforms, or complex phasors, as used in the case of sinusoidal inputs. For the present analysis, we use Laplace transform notation. (A review of the Laplace transform method is presented in Appendix C.)

Figure 11.1
Feedback model.

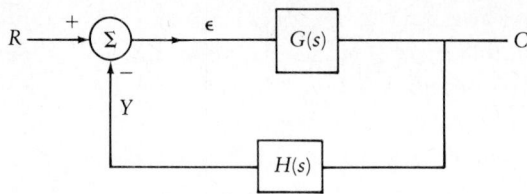

The system of Figure 11.1 is a *negative-feedback* system, since the signal driving the forward loop block, $G(s)$, is equal to the input signal, $R(s)$, *minus* some function of the output signal, $C(s)$. In this case,

$$Y(s) = H(s)C(s)$$

and

$$C(s) = G(s)\epsilon(s)$$

where $H(s)$ and $G(s)$ are transfer functions. The *closed-loop* transfer function, $C(s)/R(s)$, is derived as follows:

$$\epsilon(s) = R(s) - H(s)C(s)$$

and

$$\begin{aligned} C(s) &= G(s)\epsilon(s) \\ &= G(s)R(s) - G(s)H(s)C(s) \end{aligned}$$

Therefore,

$$\frac{C(s)}{R(s)} = \frac{G(s)}{1 + G(s)H(s)} \tag{11.1}$$

11.2 Types of Feedback

Feedback exists when a portion of the output is connected through a circuit to the input. Since both the output and input can be characterized by either a voltage or a current, there are four possible forms of feedback. For example, the output voltage can be fed back to the input in the form of a voltage signal that then subtracts from the input voltage signal. Similarly, either or both of

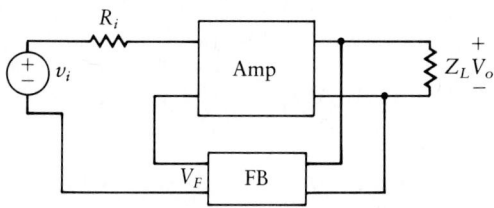

(a) Voltage feedback—voltage subtraction

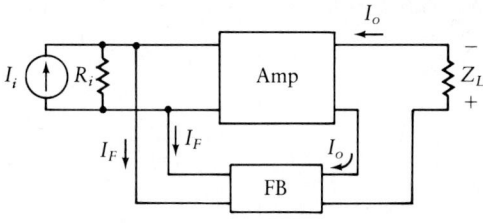

(b) Current feedback—current subtraction

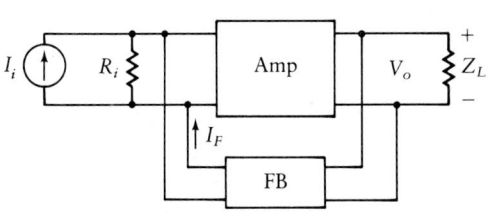

(c) Voltage feedback—current subtraction

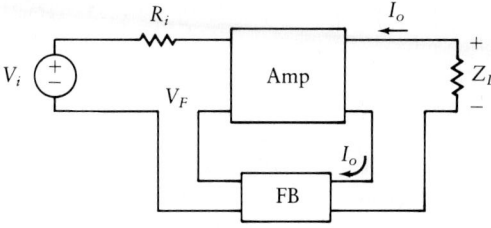

(d) Current feedback—voltage subtraction

Figure 11.2 Four types of feedback.

these voltage parameters can be replaced with current parameters. This gives rise to the following four forms of feedback. We summarize the important impedance characteristics, which are discussed in the following sections.

1. *Voltage feedback–voltage subtraction:*
   Input is a voltage.
   Output is a voltage.
   Input impedance is high.
   Output impedance is low.
   Voltage is fed back as in Figure 11.2(a).
2. *Current feedback–current subtraction:*
   Input is a current.
   Output is a current.
   Input impedance is low.
   Output impedance is high.
   Current is fed back as in Figure 11.2(b).
3. *Voltage feedback–current subtraction:*
   Input is a current.
   Output is a voltage.
   Input impedance is low.
   Output impedance is low.
   Voltage is fed back as in Figure 11.2(c).

4. *Current feedback–voltage subtraction:*
   Input is a voltage.
   Output is a current.
   Input impedance is high.
   Output impedance is high.
   Current is fed back as in Figure 11.2(d).

11.3   Feedback Amplifiers

In this section, we discuss examples of both voltage and current feedback. In most cases, such as shown in Figure 11.2, the amplifier networks consist of active elements, whereas the feedback networks consist of passive networks. The feedback networks can be either resistive or frequency-sensitive. In the frequency-sensitive feedback networks, the amount of feedback is determined by the frequency of the input signals. In other words, as the frequency changes, the amount of feedback changes.

As indicated in the previous summary, negative feedback either increases or decreases the input impedance of an amplifier, depending upon whether the feedback network is in series or in parallel with the input signal path.

11.3.1   *Current Feedback—Voltage Subtraction for Discrete Amplifiers*

Consider a CE BJT amplifier with an emitter resistor that is not bypassed. Therefore, a voltage proportional to the output current is subtracted from, or fed back, to the input signal voltage. This form of feedback is illustrated in Figure 11.2(d).

Figure 11.3(a) shows the CE circuit with a bypass capacitor. We can use this circuit to consider both feedback and no feedback simply by varying the value of the bypass capacitance. That is, as the capacitor value approaches zero, the capacitor approaches an open circuit and we have the feedback situation. As the capacitance approaches infinity, the capacitor becomes a short circuit, and the amplifier has no feedback. Figure 11.3(b) shows the equivalent circuit of the amplifier.

The voltage gain for the CE amplifier is calculated from this equivalent circuit as follows:

$$V_o = -\beta I_b (R_C \| R_L)$$

where

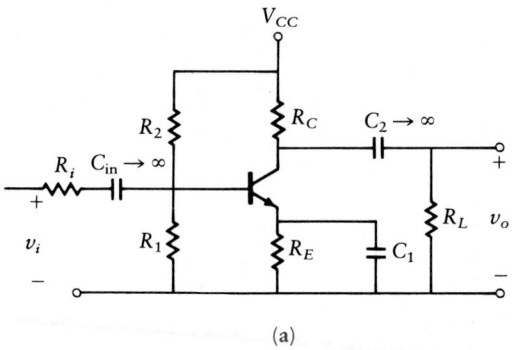

(a)   (b)

Figure 11.3   CE stage.

$$I_b = I_{\text{in}} \frac{R_B}{R_B + h_{ie} + \beta(R_E \parallel 1/sC)}$$

Now since

$$I_{\text{in}} = \frac{V_i}{R_{\text{in}}} = \frac{V_i}{R_B \parallel [h_{ie} + \beta(R_E \parallel 1/sC)]}$$

the voltage gain, A_v, is given by

$$A_v = \frac{V_o}{V_i} = \frac{-\beta(R_C \parallel R_L)}{h_{ie} + \beta(R_E \parallel 1/sC)} = \frac{-(R_C \parallel R_L)}{h_{ib} + (R_E \parallel 1/sC)} \tag{11.2}$$

The voltage gain with feedback is known as the *closed-loop gain* and is found by letting C approach zero in equation (11.2). Also assume that

$$R_E \gg h_{ib}$$

Equation (11.2) for the closed-loop gain reduces to

$$A_v = \frac{-(R_C \parallel R_L)}{R_E}$$

The voltage gain without feedback is known as the *open-loop gain* and is found by letting C approach infinity in equation (11.2), as follows:

$$A_{vo} = \frac{-(R_C \parallel R_L)}{h_{ib}} = \frac{-\beta(R_C \parallel R_L)}{h_{ie}}$$

Example 11.1

Given a CE amplifier with the following component values: $R_C = R_L = 1$ kΩ, $R_E = 100$ Ω, $h_{ie} = 600$ Ω, and β = 300, determine both the open- and closed-loop voltage gains.

SOLUTION The gain with no feedback (open-loop) is given by

$$A_{vo} = \frac{-\beta(R_C \parallel R_L)}{h_{ie}} = \frac{-(300)(500)}{600} = -250$$

The gain with feedback (closed-loop) is

$$A_v = \frac{-(R_C \parallel R_L)}{R_E} = \frac{-500}{100} = -5$$

As can be seen from this example, A_{vo} is much larger than A_v, since the feedback considerably reduces the gain.

The equation for gain with feedback does not, however, include any transistor parameter values. Thus, the gain with feedback depends only upon the ratio of resistance values. This is the desired case. The higher gain, obtained when the capacitance approaches infinity, is dependent upon the transistor parameters. Recall, from Chapter 5, that these parameters can vary considerably.

The use of feedback improves the performance of the single-stage amplifier. We analyze this in a slightly different manner by observing Figure 11.4. We have isolated the unbypassed emitter resistor for the feedback case. When we write the base-emitter loop equation for the circuit of Figure 11.4, the effect of the negative feedback becomes evident. The voltage, V_{BE}, is given by

$$V_{BE} = V_i - I_C R_E \tag{11.3}$$

Equation (11.3) shows that the voltage driving the transistor, V_{BE}, is reduced by a signal proportional to the output current, I_C. We now return to equation (11.2) and rewrite it in a form that emphasizes the feedback, i.e.,

$$A_v = \frac{-R_C \parallel R_L}{h_{ib}} \frac{1}{1 + (R_E \parallel 1/sC)/h_{ib}} \tag{11.4}$$

We define γ as the ratio of feedback voltage, V_f, to output voltage V_o, where V_f is defined in Figure 11.3(b) as the voltage across $(R_E \parallel 1/sC)$. This *feedback attenuation factor* corresponds to $H(s)$ in Figure 11.1. In this case, $H(s)$ is a constant, since the feedback circuit is purely resistive. (Note that the symbol β

Figure 11.4
Unbypassed R_E.

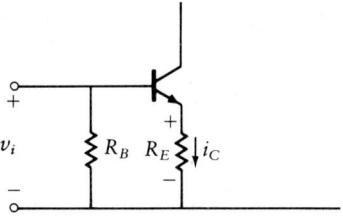

is often used for the feedback factor. We have chosen γ in order not to confuse this with the current gain in a transistor.) Therefore,

$$\gamma = \frac{V_f}{V_o} = \frac{R_E \parallel (1/sC)}{R_C \parallel R_L}$$

Recall that the gain without feedback, or the open-loop gain, is

$$A_{vo} = \frac{-(R_C \parallel R_L)}{h_{ib}}$$

Using the equations for A_{vo} and for γ, we rewrite equation (11.4) in the simplified form,

$$A_v = \frac{A_{vo}}{1 - \gamma A_{vo}} \tag{11.5}$$

This equation is now in the same form as the general feedback equation, equation (11.1). Keep in mind that A_{vo} is negative, so the denominator in equation (11.5) is really of the form $1 + |\gamma A_{vo}|$.   ➤

Drill Problem

D11.1   Calculate γ for the amplifier stage of Example 11.1.

    Ans: $\gamma = 0.2$

Example 11.2

In a given feedback amplifier, $A_{vo} = -80$ and the ratio of feedback voltage to output voltage is $\gamma = 0.1$. What is the closed-loop voltage gain of the amplifier? Now suppose that the gain without feedback increases by 25%. Find the new overall gain.

SOLUTION   The closed loop gain is given by equation (11.5).

$$A_v = \frac{-80}{1 + 0.1 \times 80} = -8.89$$

We now let A_{vo} change from -80 to -100. The new closed-loop gain is

$$A_v = \frac{-100}{1 + 0.1 \times 100} = -9.09$$

Thus, a 25% change in the open loop gain results in only a 1.1% change in the closed-loop gain.

Example 11.2 considers a specific example of the *sensitivity* of an amplifier to changes in gain. This sensitivity is determined in general by differentiating equation (11.5) with respect to the open-loop gain. Thus,

$$A_v = \frac{1}{1/A_{vo} - \gamma}$$

and

$$\frac{dA_v}{dA_{vo}} = \frac{1}{(1 - \gamma A_{vo})^2}$$

If we now divide this derivative by A_v as in equation (11.5), we have

$$\frac{dA_v}{A_v} = \frac{1}{1 - \gamma A_{vo}} \frac{dA_{vo}}{A_{vo}} \approx -\frac{1}{\gamma A_{vo}} \frac{dA_{vo}}{A_{vo}} \qquad (11.6)$$

The approximation of equation (11.6) holds if

$$\gamma A_{vo} \gg 1$$

The expression on the left side of equation (11.6) is the variation in closed-loop gain as a ratio of the gain value. The variation in closed-loop gain is therefore approximately equal to the variation in open loop gain divided by γA_{vo}. Of course, since γA_{vo} is usually a large number, the variation in closed-loop gain is greatly reduced for a given variation of open-loop gain.   ⟶

11.3.2   *Voltage Feedback–Current Subtraction for a Discrete Amplifier*

Figure 11.5(a) illustrates an amplifier where the output voltage is fed back to the input through a resistor, R_F. The equivalent circuit is shown in Figure

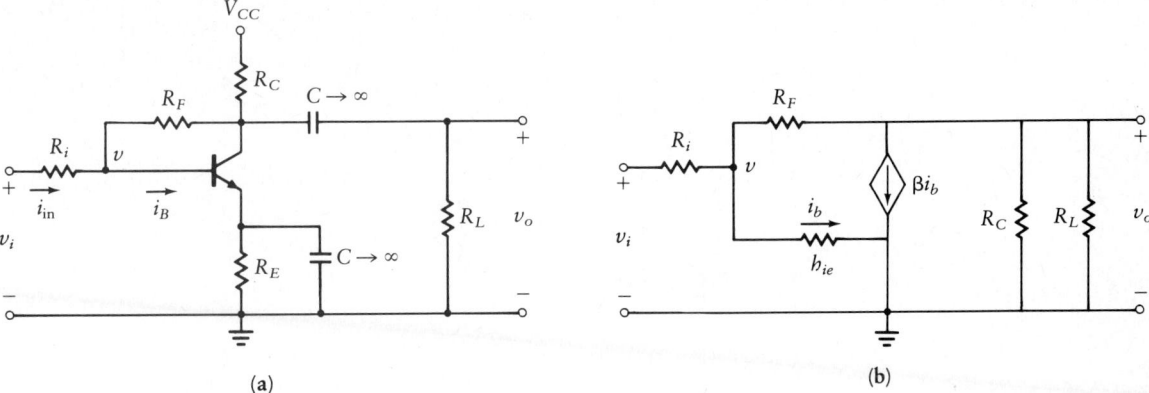

Figure 11.5 Voltage feedback—current subtraction.

11.5(b). Here we bypass R_E with a large capacitor to eliminate the type of feedback presented in Section 11.3.

We develop equations for the gain of this circuit by using equation (11.5). We find the output voltage by assuming that the current through R_F is negligible with respect to βi_b. Thus,

$$v_o = -(R_C \parallel R_L)\beta i_b \tag{11.7a}$$

The current, i_b, is found by writing a nodal equation at the node labeled v in Figure 11.5(b).

$$i_b = \frac{v_i - v}{R_i} + \frac{v_o - v}{R_F} = \frac{v_i}{R_i} + \frac{v_o}{R_F} - \frac{v}{R_i \parallel R_F}$$

Now since

$$i_b = \frac{v}{h_{ie}}$$

we can multiply through by h_{ie} and solve for v as follows:

$$v\left(1 + \frac{h_{ie}}{R_i \parallel R_F}\right) = \left[\frac{v_i}{R_i} + \frac{v_o}{R_F}\right]h_{ie}$$

This simplifies to

$$\frac{v}{h_{ie}} = i_b = \frac{v_i/R_i + v_o/R_F}{\alpha} \tag{11.7b}$$

where we define

$$\alpha = 1 + \frac{h_{ie}}{R_i \parallel R_F}$$

We now substitute equation (11.7b) into equation (11.7a) to obtain the output voltage,

$$v_o = \frac{-\beta(R_C \parallel R_L)}{\alpha}\left[\frac{v_i}{R_i} + \frac{v_o}{R_F}\right] \tag{11.8}$$

The voltage gain is found by dividing v_o in equation (11.8) by v_i to obtain

$$A_v = \frac{v_o}{v_i} = \frac{-\beta(R_C \parallel R_L)/\alpha R_i}{1 + \beta(R_C \parallel R_L)/R_F\alpha} \tag{11.9}$$

If R_F approaches infinity, we have the situation with no feedback, and A_v of equation (11.9) becomes

$$A_{vo} = \frac{-\beta(R_C \parallel R_L)}{\alpha_\infty R_i} \tag{11.10}$$

The value of α_∞ in equation (11.10) is the value that applies when R_F approaches infinity. That is,

$$\alpha_\infty = 1 + \frac{h_{ie}}{R_i} \tag{11.11}$$

Suppose now that R_F does not approach infinity, so we have feedback, but as is often the case, we can assume

$$R_i \ll R_F$$

Under this assumption, α is still approximated by the expression just given, and the gain of equation (11.9) reduces to

$$A_v = \frac{A_{vo}}{1 - R_i A_{vo}/R_F} \tag{11.12}$$

Once again, we have reduced the result to the form of equation (11.2), the general feedback relationship.

Example 11.3

In the single-stage amplifier of Figure 11.5(a), let $R_C = R_L = 1\ k\Omega$, $R_E = 100\ \Omega$, $h_{ie} = 800\ \Omega$, $\beta = 300$, $R_i = 1\ k\Omega$, and $R_F = 100\ k\Omega$. Determine the open- and closed-loop voltage gain of this amplifier.

SOLUTION   We first solve for α.

$$\alpha = 1 + \frac{h_{ie}}{R_i} = 1 + \frac{800}{1000} = 1.8$$

From equation (11.10), we have

$$A_{vo} = \frac{-300 \times 500}{1.8 \times 1000} = -83.3$$

This is the voltage gain for no feedback (open loop). The gain with feedback (closed-loop) is given by equation (11.12):

$$A_v = \frac{-83.3}{1 - (1\ k\Omega/100\ k\Omega)(-83.3)} = -45.4$$

11.4   Multistage Feedback Amplifiers

The performance of an amplifier can be altered by the use of feedback whether the amplifier consists of one stage or many stages. Since we desire negative feedback, the number of amplifier stages must be odd, so there are an odd number of polarity changes. The analysis of single or multistage amplifiers with an odd number of polarity reversals is the same since we can portray any number of stages as a single amplifier.

Examples of multistage feedback amplifiers are shown in Figure 11.6. In Figure 11.6(a), we have illustrated voltage feedback. In this circuit, R_{E1} is small to allow the first stage to have reasonable gain, and R_F is large in order not to load the amplifier. Most of the current from the feedback flows through R_{E1} and provides a voltage that is out of phase with the input signal. The ratio of the feedback voltage to the output voltage is then

$$\gamma_v = \frac{R_{E1}}{R_{E1} + R_F}$$

Figure 11.6
Multistage feedback
amplifiers.

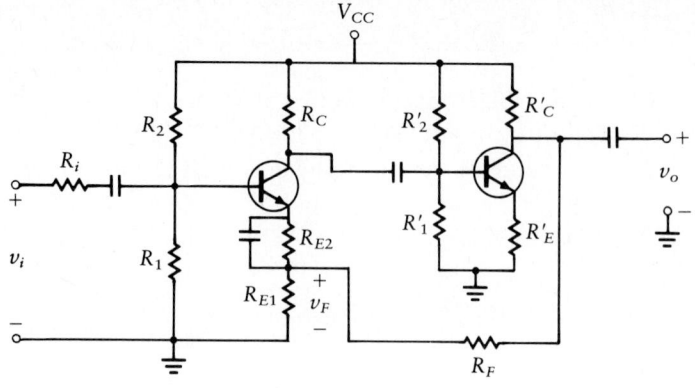

(a)   Voltage feedback

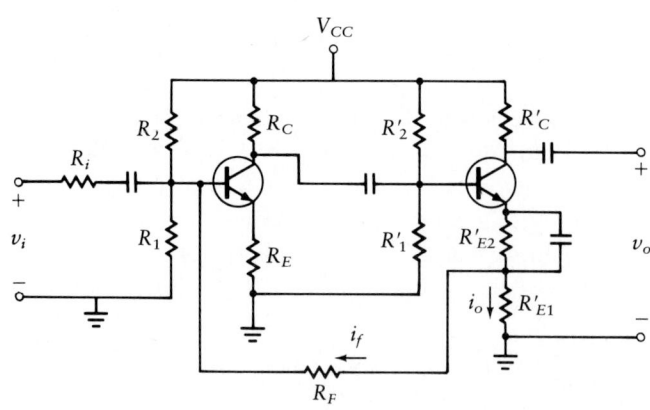

(b)   Current feedback

A multistage amplifier with a current-feedback system is shown in Figure 11.6(b). In this circuit, the output current exists in the resistor, R'_{E1}, and the voltage across the resistor is proportional to the output current. The ratio of the feedback current to the output current is then

$$\gamma_i = \frac{R'_{E1}}{R_F}$$

An example of a feedback amplifier with an odd number of polarity changes is shown in Figure 11.7. Increasing the number of stages before feedback does not pose a major problem, since we can represent the amplifier of many stages as a single amplifier as long as we carefully monitor the number of phase reversals in the amplifier. In many system designs, you will encounter voltage or current feedback to the input to improve the amplified signal over a variety of conditions.

Figure 11.7
Multistage feedback
amplifier.

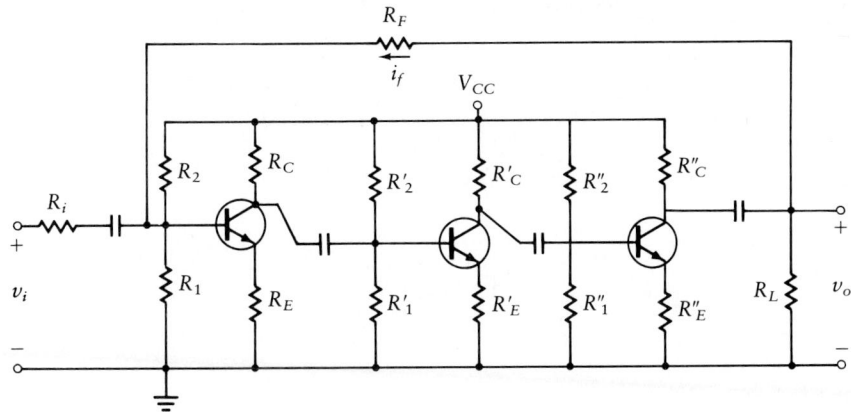

Example 11.4

A three-stage amplifier is shown in Figure 11.8(a). Each identical stage has a gain, $-K$, and an input RC network, as shown in the figure. Plot the Bode diagram when $RC = 10^{-5}$ s and determine the gain, K, that will produce *marginal stability* (this is the point where the phase shift is $-180°$ and the gain is 0 dB).

Figure 11.8
Three-stage amplifier.

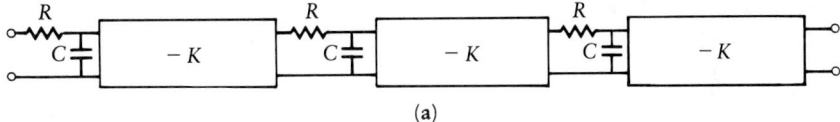

(a)

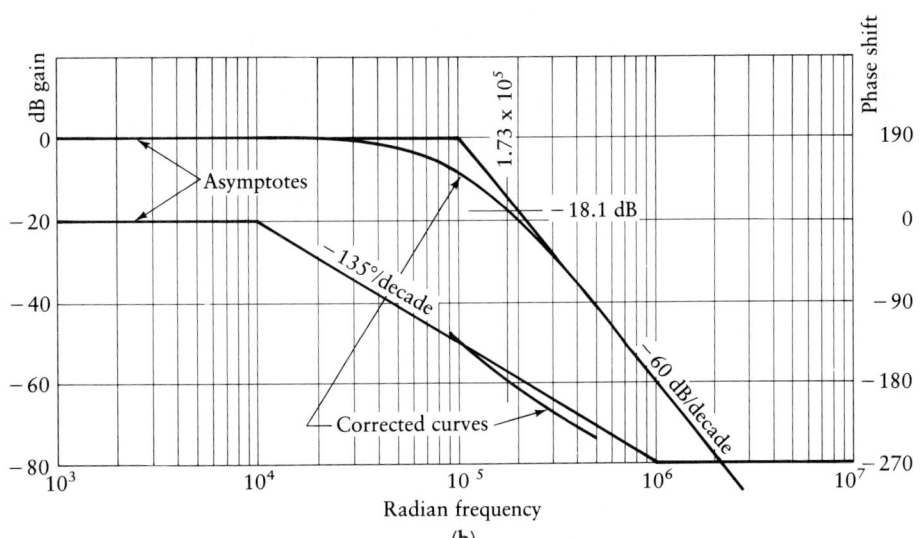

(b)

SOLUTION The Bode diagram is plotted in Figure 11.8(b). The frequency at which the phase shift crosses $-180°$ is 1.73×10^5 rad/s, or 27.53 kHz. At this frequency, the gain is -18.1 dB, which indicates that we can raise the combined gain, K^3, by 18.1 dB or

$$K^3 = 8.04$$

so

$$K = 2$$

11.5 Feedback in Operational Amplifiers

In the previous chapter, we saw that the gain of the practical op-amp is high at dc but decreases as frequency increases. This frequency-dependence is built into the op-amp by the manufacturer. Numerous op-amps permit the engineer to select external compensation networks. Figure 11.9 shows a curve of the open-loop gain for a μA741 op-amp (see Appendix D for a complete data sheet for this op-amp) as a function of frequency.

We find that, just as for discrete amplifiers, op-amps exhibit less sensitivity when feedback is employed. To calculate the error due to gain variations, we assume that all characteristics of the op-amp are ideal except for the gain variation with frequency.

We use the inverting amplifier circuit of Figure 11.10(a) for the analysis and begin by finding the effect of the output voltage upon the op-amp input. This effect is characterized by the ratio v_i/v_o. We assume that $v_i = 0$, since we are finding only that portion of v_i due to v_o. Once again, γ is defined as the feedback attenuation factor. We thus have

Figure 11.9
μA 741 op-amp open-loop gain response.

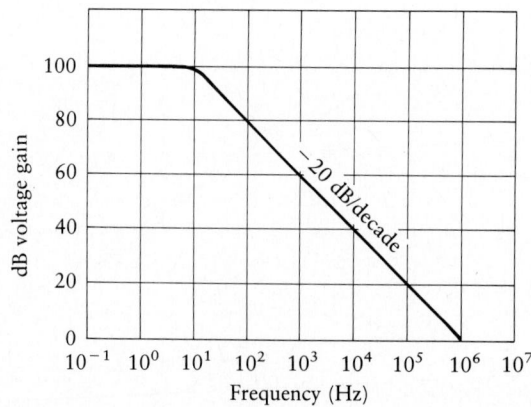

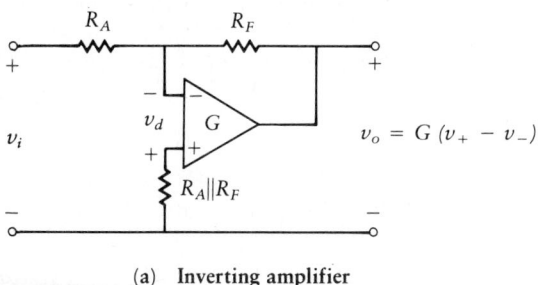

(a) Inverting amplifier

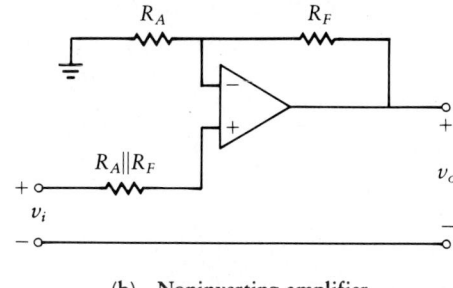

(b) Noninverting amplifier

Figure 11.10   Inverting and noninverting amplifier.

$$\gamma = \frac{v_i}{v_o} = \frac{R_A}{R_A + R_F} = \frac{1}{1 + R_F/R_A} \qquad (11.13)$$

The signal v_i is amplified by $+G$ to produce an output voltage, v_o (note the polarity of v_i).

We write a nodal equation at the inverting terminal of the amplifier of Figure 11.10(a) as follows:

$$\frac{v_o - v_-}{R_F} + \frac{v_i - v_-}{R_A} = 0$$

Now since $v_+ = 0$,

$$v_- = \frac{-v_o}{G}$$

then

$$v_o \left[1 + \frac{R_F}{G(R_F \parallel R_A)} \right] = -v_i \frac{R_F}{R_A}$$

and the closed-loop gain is

$$A_v = \frac{v_o}{v_i} = \frac{-R_F}{R_A} \frac{1}{1 + (1 + R_F/R_A)/G} \qquad (11.14)$$

We again use the feedback attenuation factor of equation (11.13) to obtain the expression in standard feedback form,

$$\frac{v_o}{v_i} = -\frac{R_F}{R_A} \frac{G\gamma}{1 + G\gamma} \qquad (11.15)$$

As the op-amp gain, G, approaches infinity, equation (11.14) becomes

$$A_{v_\infty} = \frac{-R_F}{R_A}$$

Note that as the op-amp gain approaches infinity, A_v becomes independent of the specific value of G and is a function only of the two resistor values R_F and R_A.

We next consider a noninverting op-amp shown in Figure 11.10(b). We assume that the op-amp is ideal except that the gain, G, depends upon frequency, as in Figure 11.9. We find the closed-loop gain in a manner similar to that just determined. Thus, we write the node voltages for the inverting and the noninverting inputs as follows:

$$v_- = v_o \frac{R_A}{R_A + R_F}$$

and

$$v_+ = v_i$$

The output voltage is

$$v_o = G(v_+ - v_-) = G\left[v_i - v_o \frac{R_A}{R_A + R_F}\right]$$

We solve for v_o using equation (11.13) for γ as follows:

$$v_o \left[1 + G\frac{1}{1 + R_F/R_A}\right] = Gv_i$$

and the closed-loop voltage gain is

$$A_v = \frac{v_o}{v_i} = \frac{G}{1 + \gamma G} = \left(1 + \frac{R_F}{R_A}\right)\frac{G\gamma}{1 + \gamma G} \qquad (11.16)$$

For very large G, equation (11.16) reduces to

$$A_{v\infty} = \frac{1}{\gamma} = 1 + \frac{R_F}{R_A}$$

The two gain expressions, equations (11.15) and (11.16), can be *normalized* by dividing by $A_{v\infty}$, the gain for infinite G. The same expression results for both the inverting and noninverting amplifier, as follows:

$$\frac{A_v}{A_{v_\infty}} = \frac{G\gamma}{1 + G\gamma} \tag{11.17}$$

The expression $G\gamma$ is the *loop gain*. This is the gain obtained by tracing a loop through the amplifier and feedback path back to the starting point. Note that the loop gain of both amplifiers is identical.

The variation of the overall gain from the value that we would obtain with infinite G is sometimes expressed as an error. We define the *percent error* as the difference between the gain for infinite G and the actual gain expressed as a percentage of the gain for infinite G. Thus,

$$\% \text{ error} = \frac{-R_F/R_A - [-R_F/R_A G\gamma/(1 + G\gamma)]}{-R_F/R_A} \times 100$$

$$= \left[1 - \frac{G\gamma}{1 + G\gamma} \right] \times 100 \tag{11.18}$$

The same expression applies to both the inverting and noninverting amplifier.

As an example, if the loop gain, $G\gamma$, is 100 (40 dB), the error is approximately 1%. As the gain decreases, as it will for increasing frequency, the error becomes larger.

Drill Problem

D.11.2 Find the voltage gain for the op-amp circuit of Figure D11.1.

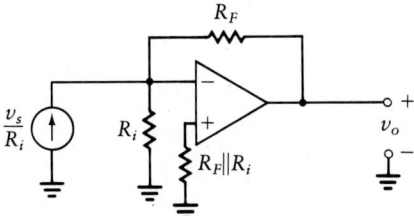

Figure D11.1

Ans: $A_v = \dfrac{v_o}{v_i} = \dfrac{-R_F}{R_i}$

11.6 Stability of Feedback Amplifiers

Negative feedback is advantageous since the operation of the amplifier becomes less sensitive to parameter variations. Negative feedback requires that a portion of the output signal be subtracted from the input signal. Although we might design a system to provide such perfect subtraction, as soon as frequencies vary out of the midrange, phase shifts may make the subtraction less than perfect. In particular, at certain frequencies a phase shift of 180° could occur. This would change the subtraction to an addition and change negative feedback into positive feedback. In order to illustrate this problem, suppose that $A_{vo} = +100$ and $\gamma = 0.01$. The positive sign on A_{vo} represents a 180° phase shift. That is,

$$A_{vo} = -100 \exp(j180°) = +100$$

Under this set of assumptions, we substitute into equation (11.5) with the result

$$
\begin{aligned}
A_v &= \frac{A_{vo}}{1 - \gamma A_{vo}} \\
&= \frac{100}{1 - 0.01 \times 100} = \frac{100}{0} \rightarrow \infty
\end{aligned}
\tag{11.19}
$$

The fact that the gain goes to infinity indicates that the system is not stable. This would indicate that an infinitesimal input (even simply random noise) would cause an infinite output. Of course, in a practical system the output could never reach infinity. In many cases, such a circuit will oscillate. At the very least, the output will no longer depend upon the input value. It is therefore important in amplifier design that the circuit be stable for all operating frequencies.

We previously considered stability primarily by looking at the Bode plot and checking whether the gain is greater than or equal to unity at the frequency where the phase shift is 180°. An equivalent test for stability is to look at the roots of the overall transfer function, $T(s)$, and observe where they are located in the s-plane. If all the roots are in the left half of the s-plane, the system is stable.

Suppose that a feedback system has a transfer function that can be put into the following form:

$$T(s) = \frac{*}{1 + KG(s)} \tag{11.20}$$

The * in equation (11.20) stands for any polynomial expression, and we look for the roots of $1 + KG(s)$.

In order to place the op-amp relationships in the form of equation (11.20), we begin by repeating the equations developed in Chapter 8 for the inverting and noninverting amplifiers.

The noninverting gain, A_+, is

$$A_+ = \frac{G(s)R_i(R_1'/R_1)}{R_A' \parallel R_F + R_1' + [1 + (R_A'G(s))/(R_A' + R_F)]R_i}$$

This is a repeat of equation (9.14). The various terms are defined as

$$A_+ = \frac{v_o}{v_+}$$

$$R_A' = R_A \parallel 2R_{cm}$$

$$R_1' = R_1 \parallel 2R_{cm}$$

$$R_L \gg R_o$$

$$R_F \gg R_o$$

This expression for A_+ is reduced to

$$
\begin{aligned}
A_+ &= \frac{G(s)R_i}{R_A'R_F/(R_A' + R_F) + R_i + R_1' + R_A'R_iG(s)/(R_A' + R_F)} \\
&= \frac{G(s)R_i(R_A' + R_F)/[(R_i + R_1')(R_A' + R_F) + R_A'R_F]}{1 + R_A'R_iG(s)/[(R_i + R_1')(R_A' + R_F) + R_A'R_F]}
\end{aligned}
\tag{11.21}
$$

If we now assume that R_i is large, the second term in the denominator can be replaced by $R'_A/(R'_A + R_F)$. Large R_i represents a desirable condition, since the gain reduces with smaller R_i. With this substitution, the denominator of equation (11.21) becomes

$$1 + \frac{R_A'G(s)}{R_A' + R_F}$$

In a similar manner, we find the inverting gain

$$
\begin{aligned}
A_- &= \frac{-G(s)R_A'R_iR_F/R_A}{(R_i + R_1')(R_A' + R_F) + R_A'R_F + R_iR_A'G(s)} \\
&= \frac{G(s)(R_A'/R_A)R_iR_F/[(R_i + R_1')(R_A' + R_F) + (R_A'R_F)]}{1 + R_iR_A'G(s)/[(R_i + R_1')(R_A' + R_F) + R_A'R_F]}
\end{aligned}
\tag{11.22}
$$

Once again we approximate the second term in the denominator of equation (11.22) by

$$\frac{R_A'G(s)}{R_A' + R_F}$$

We thus obtain the same denominator as in the equation for the noninverting gain. This result could have been predicted immediately, since, in general, all transfer functions in a given system have the same denominator polynomial. This is determined by the source-free system behavior (i.e., the characteristic equation of the system). Given the stable open-loop system with gain function, $G(s)$, the closed-loop system is specified by

$$T(s) = \frac{*}{1 + R_A' G(s)/(R_A' + R_F)} \tag{11.23}$$

Once again, * is used to denote any numerator polynomial. This system is stable if the phase shift of the denominator $G(s)H(s)$ function crosses 180° at a point where

$$G(s)H(s) = \frac{R_A' G(s)}{R_A' + R_F}$$

is less than unity (0 dB). The steady-state operation of the circuit is characterized from the s-plane by moving an operating point along the imaginary (vertical) axis. Thus, if all the roots of $T(s)$ are in the left half-plane, the system is stable. Hence, the 180° condition and the left half-plane condition are equivalent.

Example 11.5

Investigate the stability of a typical uncompensated 101 op-amp with three dominant poles. The frequency response is as shown in Figure 11.11.

SOLUTION   We see from equation (11.23) that the closed-loop system is stable only for noninverting gains in excess of the value $1/K$, where

Figure 11.11
Op-amp frequency response.

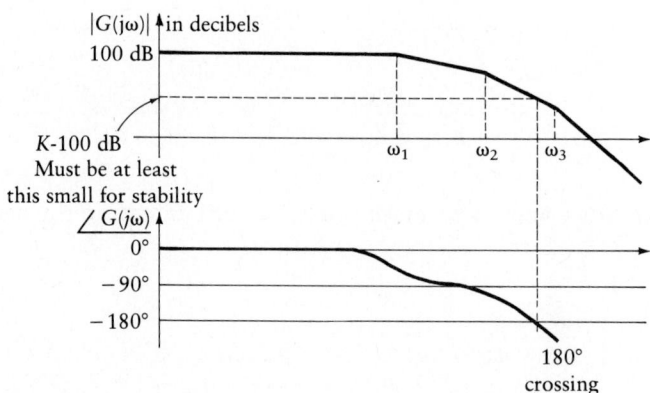

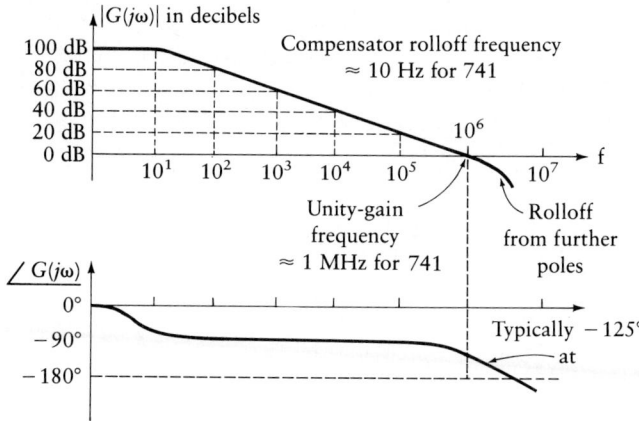

Figure 11.12 Single-pole compensation frequency response.

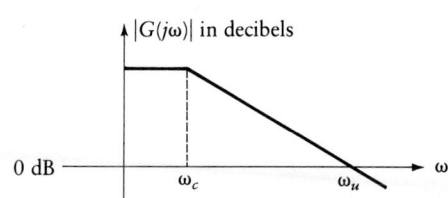

Figure 11.13 Closed-loop frequency response.

$$K = \frac{R'_A}{R'_A + R_F}$$

That is, if the gain is equal to this value and the phase is 180°, $T(s)$ approaches infinity.

A compensated op-amp has one predominant pole provided by a compensation network. A typical open-loop frequency response is illustrated in Figure 11.12. We now calculate the corner frequency for the closed loop system. This corner frequency is also the *bandwidth* of the system. Although we assume that $G(s)$ has three dominant poles, if two of these are much higher in frequency than the third, we can use a single-pole model to achieve accurate results up to the frequencies at which the other poles begin to affect $G(s)$. We therefore approximate $G(s)$ with a single-pole model as follows,

$$G(s) = \frac{\sqrt{\omega_c^2 + \omega_u^2}}{s + \omega_c}$$

where ω_c is the compensated corner frequency and ω_u is the unity-gain frequency, as shown in Figure 11.13. The numerator of this expression for $G(s)$ is chosen so that at a frequency of ω_u, the magnitude of the function is unity. The overall transfer function is then given by

$$T(s) = \frac{\text{numerator term}}{1 + \dfrac{R'_A}{R'_A + R_F}G(s)} = \frac{(\text{numerator term})(s + \omega_c)}{s + \omega_c + \dfrac{R'_A \sqrt{\omega_c^2 + \omega_u^2}}{R'_A + R_F}}$$

The corner frequency (or bandwidth) for the closed-loop system is seen from this expression to be

$$\text{BW} = \omega_c + \frac{R_A'}{R_A' + R_F} \sqrt{\omega_c^2 + \omega_u^2}$$

$$= \omega_c \left[1 + \frac{R_A'}{R_A' + R_F} \sqrt{1 + \left(\frac{\omega_u}{\omega_c}\right)^2} \right]$$

If we assume that $\omega_c \ll \omega_u$, as is normally the case, this reduces to

$$\text{BW} \approx \frac{R_A' \omega_u}{R_A' + R_F} \qquad\qquad (11.24)$$

11.6.1   *Gain-Bandwidth Product*

Equation (11.21), the noninverting gain of the closed-loop op-amp system, reduces to the following expression for large values of gain and large R_i.

$$A_+ = 1 + \frac{R_F}{R_A'}$$

If we now multiply this by the bandwidth found in equation (11.24), we obtain the *gain-bandwidth product* (GBP):

$$A_+\text{BW} = \frac{R_A' + R_F}{R_A'} \frac{R_A'}{R_A' + R_F} \omega_u = \text{GBP} = \omega_u$$

Thus, the gain-bandwidth product is equal to the unity-gain frequency. Hence, for a single-pole amplifier, this gain-bandwidth product is constant.

11.7   Frequency Response—Feedback Amplifier

The stability of a negative feedback system is dependent upon the loop phase being less than 180° when the gain is 0 dB (unit amplitude). If the system has 180° of phase shift when the gain is 0 dB, the system is unstable and can oscillate. That is, an output exists when no input signal is applied.

11.7.1   *Single-Pole Amplifier*

Let us return to the basic feedback system of Figure 11.1 and assume that $G(s)$ is a polynomial with one pole and that $H(s)$ is a constant. That is,

$$G(s) = \frac{-G_o}{1 + s/\omega_c}$$

and

$$H(s) = -\gamma$$

Since we are interested in the stability of the amplifier, we wish to examine the phase of the loop-gain expression to assure that the stability condition is met. Figure 11.14 illustrates the Bode plot of the normalized amplitude and phase. For purposes of illustration, the break frequency is selected to be $\omega_c = 4$. Since the maximum phase shift for any frequency is $-90°$, this amplifier can never be unstable. A necessary condition for instability is that the phase shift reach 180°.

The *single-pole amplifier* has a closed-loop gain, $T(s)$, given by

$$T(s) = \frac{G(s)}{1 + G(s)H(s)}$$

$$= \frac{-G_o}{1 + s/\omega_c + G_o\gamma}$$

$$= \frac{-G_o}{1 + G_o\gamma} \frac{1}{1 + \dfrac{s}{(1 + G_o\gamma)\omega_c}} \tag{11.25}$$

Figure 11.14
Response for single-pole amplifier.

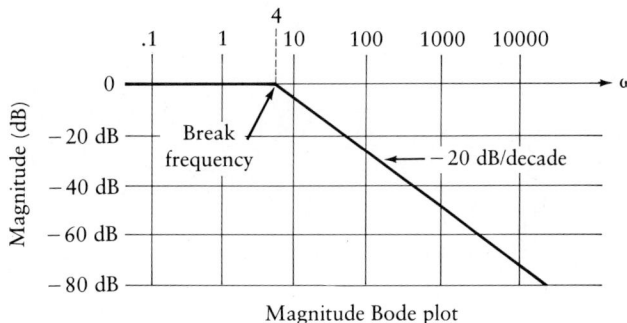

Magnitude Bode plot

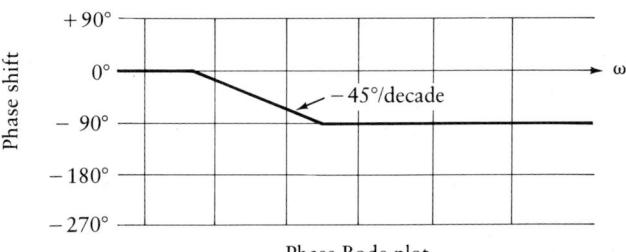

Phase Bode plot

The 3-dB point for the closed-loop gain characteristic is at a frequency of

$$\omega = (1 + \gamma G_o)\omega_c$$

Since $\gamma G_o \gg 1$, the 3-dB frequency is approximately $\gamma G_o \omega_c$.

11.7.2   *Two-Pole Amplifier*

Let us now assume that $G(s)$ has two poles at the same location. Thus,

$$G(s) = \frac{-G_o}{(1 + s/\omega_c)^2} \tag{11.26}$$

We again assume that $H(s)$ is a constant,

$$H(s) = -\gamma$$

The closed-loop gain function, $T(s)$, is given by

$$
\begin{aligned}
T(s) &= \frac{-G_o/[(1 + s/\omega_c)^2]}{1 + G_o\gamma/[(1 + s/\omega_c)^2]} \\
&= \frac{-G_o}{1 + \gamma G_o} \; \frac{1}{s^2/[\omega_c^2(1 + \gamma G_o)] + 2s/[\omega_c(1 + \gamma G_o)] + 1}
\end{aligned} \tag{11.27}
$$

This can be written in a more useful form using the following two definitions:

$$\omega_n = \omega_c \sqrt{1 + \gamma G_o} \tag{11.28}$$

and

$$\xi = \frac{1}{\sqrt{1 + \gamma G_o}} \tag{11.29}$$

We defined ω_n as the undamped natural radian frequency and ξ as the damping ratio. When these new terms are used in equation (11.27), the gain function can be written as

$$T(s) = \frac{-G_o}{1 + \gamma G_o} \; \frac{1}{s^2/\omega_n^2 + 2\xi s/\omega_n + 1} \tag{11.30}$$

If we are interested in the stability of this amplifier, we need first to examine the roots of the $T(s)$ expression. For $\gamma = 0$, the roots lie on the negative real axis. When we substitute $\gamma = 0$ into equations (11.28) and (11.29), the denominator polynomial of equation (11.30) becomes

$$\left(\frac{s}{\omega_c} + 1\right)^2$$

so there exist two equal real roots at $s = -\omega_c$. For any nonzero gain, γ, the roots are complex conjugates with value

$$s_{1,2} = -\omega_n(\xi \pm \sqrt{\xi^2 + 1}) \tag{11.31}$$

We can draw the Bode plot for the gain expression in order to evaluate the stability of the system. Since this represents an example of a quadratic denominator function, the plots resemble those of Figure 10.8. Observe that the phase-shift plot of Figure 10.8 never touches the $-180°$ line. Each of these curves becomes asymptotic to $-180°$ but never actually crosses the $-180°$ line. Since there is no frequency for which the phase shift is equal to $-180°$, this amplifier is stable.

Example 11.6

Determine the stability for the op-amp circuit shown in Figure 11.15 by plotting the Bode diagram for the $G(s)H(s)$ function. The 741 op-amp has a gain function given by

$$G(s) = \frac{G_o}{1 + s/\omega_c}$$

where $G_o = 10^5$ and $\omega_c = 20\pi$.

SOLUTION The node equation at V_- yields

$$\frac{V_-}{R} + \frac{V_- - V_o}{1/sC} = 0$$

so

$$V_- = \frac{RsCV_o}{1 + RsC}$$

At V_+, we obtain

$$V_+ = V_i$$

Figure 11.15
Amplifier for Example
11.6.

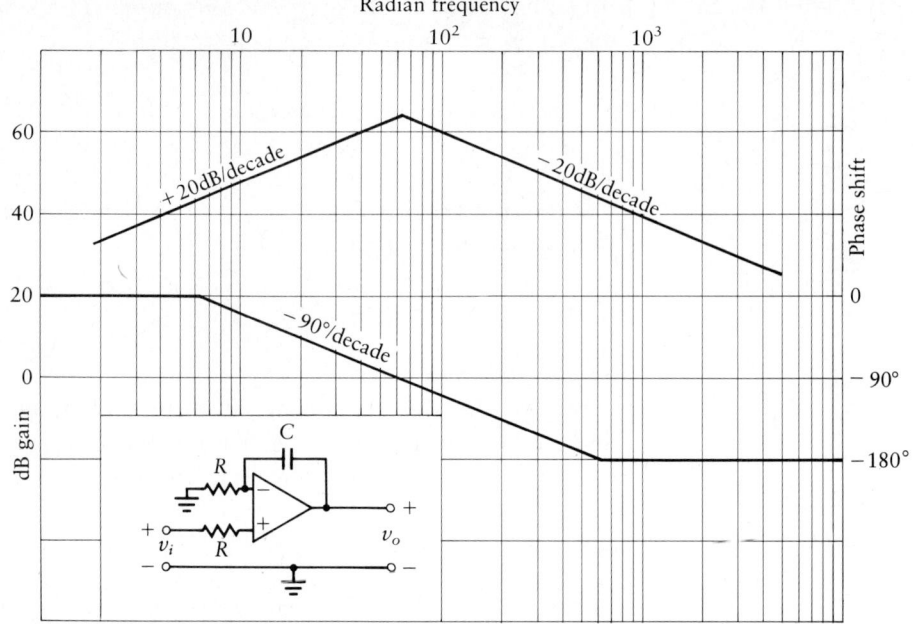

But since

$$V_o = G(V_+ - V_-) = G\left[V_i - \frac{RsCV_o}{1 + RsC}\right]$$

we solve for the gain,

$$\frac{V_o}{V_i} = \frac{G}{1 + GRsC/(1 + RsC)} = \frac{G_o/(1 + s/\omega_c)}{1 + G_oRsC/[(1 + s/\omega_c)(1 + sRC)]}$$

This is now in the form of

$$\frac{G(s)}{1 + G(s)H(s)}$$

so we can plot the $G(s)H(s)$ function from the following:

$$G(s)H(s) = \frac{G_o sRC}{(1 + s/\omega_c)(1 + sRC)}$$

where $G_o = 10^5$, $RC = 0.016$ s, and $\omega_c = 62.83$. Hence, we obtain

$$G(s)H(s) = \frac{1.6 \times 10^3 \, s}{(1 + s/62.83)^2}$$

where $1/RC \approx \omega_c$. We therefore have two identical poles. This is plotted in the Bode diagram of Figure 11.15. Only the straight-line asymptotes are shown. We see that the phase shift never reaches $-180°$, so the system is always stable, which is the reason that the straight-line approximation proves sufficient. This is not true in the following example. ➤⊢

Example 11.7

Determine the stability for the op-amp system of Figure 11.16 using Bode plots. Note that the op-amp gain function is given by

$$G(s) = \frac{G_o}{(1 + s/20\pi)^2}$$

SOLUTION We again write the node equation at V_- and V_+ as follows:

$$V_- = V_o \frac{1/sC}{1/sC + R}$$

Figure 11.16
Amplifier for Example 11.7.

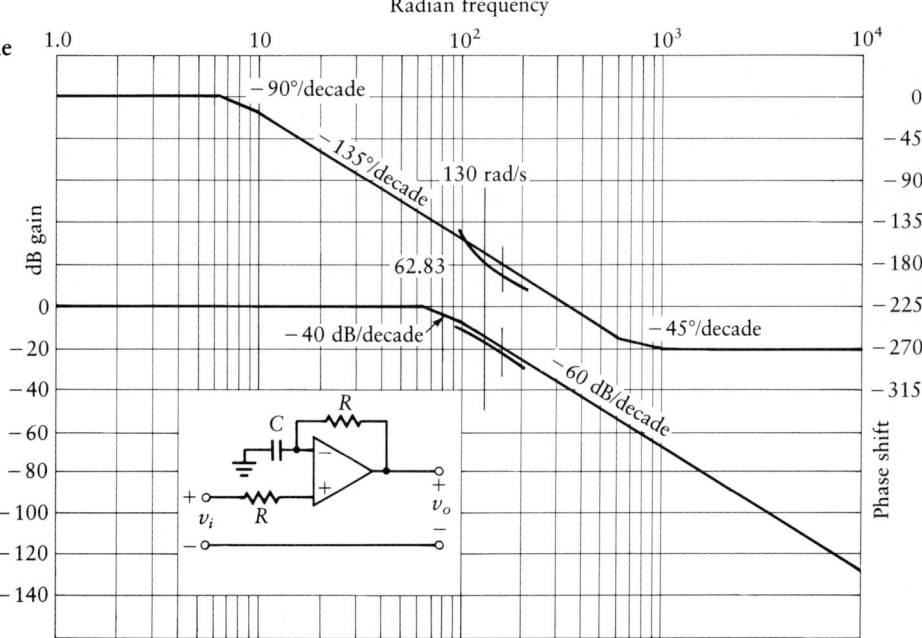

and

$$V_+ = V_i$$

The output voltage is

$$V_o = G(V_+ - V_-)$$

so combining terms, we obtain

$$V_o = G\left(V_i - \frac{V_o}{1 + sRC}\right)$$

The closed-loop gain is

$$\frac{V_o}{V_i} = \frac{G(s)}{1 + G(s)/(1 + sRC)} = \frac{G(s)}{1 + G(s)H(s)}$$

and the $G(s)H(s)$ function is given by

$$G(s)H(s) = \frac{G_o}{(1 + sRC)(1 + s/20\pi)^2}$$

with C = 0.1 μF, R = 100 kΩ, and $RC = 10^{-2}$. Let us set $G_o = 1$ and plot the resulting function:

$$G(s)H(s) = \frac{1}{(1 + s/10^2)(1 + s/62.8)^2}$$

This result is shown plotted in Figure 11.16. The straight-line asymptotes are first plotted, and the curves are corrected in the vicinity of the frequency where the phase shift is $-180°$. From this corrected plot, we can see that the phase-shift curve intersects the $-180°$ line at a frequency of 130 rad/s, and the gain at this frequency is -18.7 dB (or 8.61). Thus, 18.7 dB is the gain for marginal stability.   ➤❘

11.8   Design of a Three-Pole Amplifier with a Lead Equalizer

Consider an amplifier with three poles located at the same point, i.e.,

$$G(s) = \frac{-G_o}{(1 + s/\omega_c)^3}$$

Again, let $H(s)$ be a constant,

$$H(s) = -\gamma$$

and the loop function is

$$G(s)H(s) = \frac{\gamma G_o}{(1 + s/\omega_c)^3}$$

Figure 11.17 illustrates the Bode plot for the loop-transfer function, $G(s)H(s)$, where we have let γG_o be normalized to 1. For purposes of illustration, we have selected a corner frequency of $\omega_c = 10$ rad/s.

We determine stability of the amplifier system with the loop-transfer function rather than with the closed-loop gain of the amplifier system. We check for instability by seeing whether the $G(s)H(s)$ function has an amplitude of unity when its phase shift is $-180°$. We note that the phase does reach $-180°$ at a frequency of 18 rad/s. The amplitude at this point is -18 dB, but recall that we have normalized the function by dividing it by γG_o. Thus, if the loop gain, γG_o, reaches $+18$ dB, the overall gain will reach 0 dB and the system will become unstable. This gain, $+18$ dB, is relatively low, so this particular amplifier would probably be unstable in a practical application.

This leaves us with two options. We must either abandon this amplifier, since it is inherently unstable, or change it so the instability does not occur. Fortunately, it is not difficult to alter the amplifier to reduce the chances of instability. *Compensation networks* (or *equalizers*) are used to alter the gain-phase characteristics in order to prevent instabilities. One way to view these

Figure 11.17
Bode plot for three-pole amplifier.

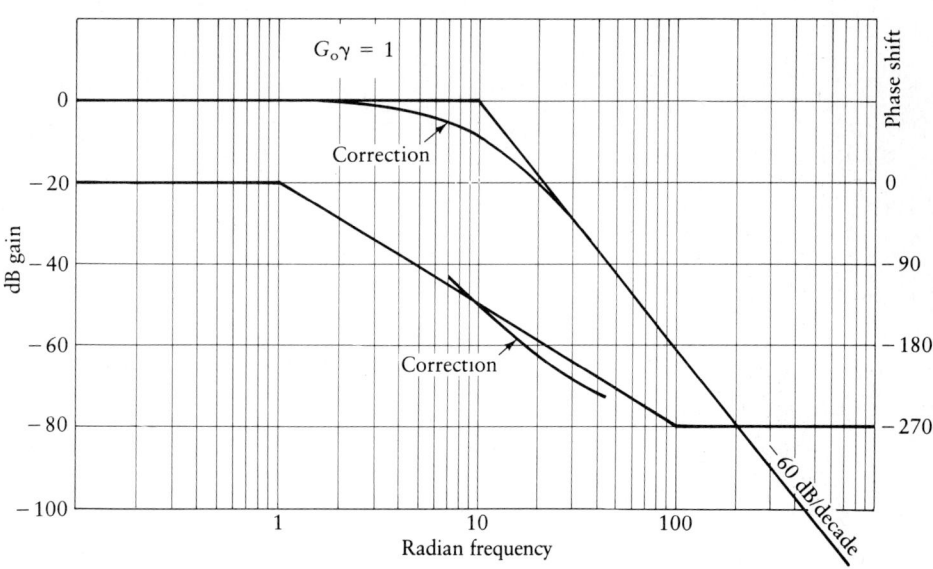

Figure 11.18
Passive-circuit lead
network.

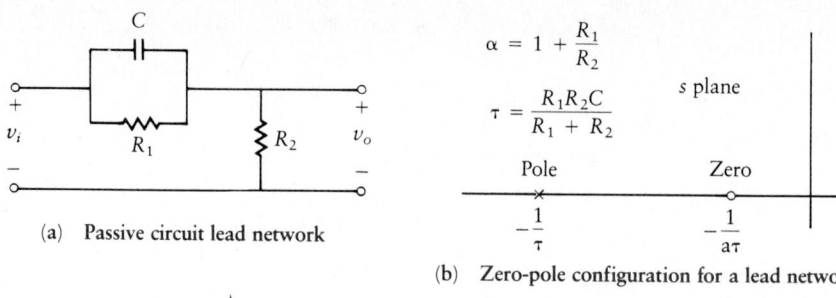

(a)   Passive circuit lead network

(b)   Zero-pole configuration for a lead network

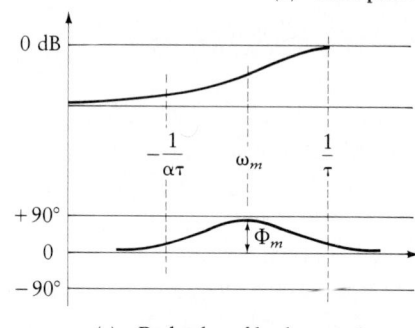

(c)   Bode plot of lead network

networks is that they change the phase characteristic so that the shift is no longer 180° at frequencies where the gain exceeds 0 dB.

In the following analysis, we consider a *lead network*. The word *lead* refers to the relationship between input and output phase. The circuit for a passive-lead network, sometimes referred to as a *passive-circuit differentiator*, is shown in Figure 11.18.

We can solve for the output voltage as follows:

$$V_o = \frac{R_2}{R_2 + (R_1 \parallel 1/sC)} \, V_i$$

Dividing output by input yields the transfer function for this circuit:

$$G(s) = \frac{V_o}{V_i} = \frac{R_2}{R_2 + R_1/(sCR_1 + 1)}$$

$$= \frac{R_2(1 + R_1 sC)}{(R_1 + R_2)[1 + sCR_1 R_2/(R_1 + R_2)]}$$

$$= \frac{R_2}{R_1 + R_2} \frac{1 + sR_1 C}{1 + s(R_1 \parallel R_2)C} \tag{11.32}$$

The phase shift of this expression is found by setting $s = j\omega$ and subtracting the denominator phase shift from that of the numerator. Note that the phase shift of the numerator is larger than the phase of the denominator, since

$$R_1 C \geqslant (R_1 \parallel R_2) C$$

Therefore, the overall phase shift of this expression is positive, and the output phase shift leads the input phase.

Equation (11.32) is written in a different form by defining

$$\alpha = 1 + \frac{R_1}{R_2} \tag{11.33}$$

and

$$\tau = \frac{R_1 R_2 C}{R_1 + R_2} \tag{11.34}$$

With these two definitions, the transfer function becomes

$$G(s) = \frac{V_o}{V_i} = \frac{s + 1/\alpha\tau}{s + 1/\tau} = \frac{\alpha\tau s + 1}{\alpha(\tau s + 1)} \tag{11.35}$$

Figure 11.18(b) shows the representation of this function in the s-plane. There is a pole at $s = 1/\tau$ and a zero at $s = -1/\alpha\tau$. The Bode plot for this network is shown in Figure 11.18(c). Note that the maximum phase lead is a function of α. It approaches 90° as α approaches infinity.

The peak phase shift, ϕ_m, and the frequency at which it occurs, ω_m, can be related to the parameters α and τ by setting the derivative of the phase expression to zero. We obtain

$$\omega_m = \frac{1}{\sqrt{\alpha\tau}}$$

$$\phi_m = \sin^{-1}\left(\frac{\alpha - 1}{\alpha + 1}\right)$$

Example 11.8

Select a lead network with

$$\tau = \frac{1}{40}$$

$$\alpha = 4$$

to compensate a 3-pole op-amp circuit adequately.

SOLUTION   The transfer function for the lead network is

$$G(s) = \frac{0.1s + 1}{4(s/40 + 1)}$$

Figure 11.19 illustrates the gain and phase curves for the function that results when this is multiplied by the transfer function of the three-pole system. Shown in Figure 11.19 is a repeat of the three-pole amplitude and phase curves from Figure 11.17. When the compensation network is placed in cascade with this system, we add the Bode plots (both decibel gain and phase) for the uncompensated amplifier and the compensation network. Thus note that the amplitude curve has a slope that increases by 20 dB/decade between a frequency of 10 and 40 and then decreases by 20 dB/decade to return to a slope of −60 dB/decade. These two changes are due to the zero and pole of the compensation network function at frequencies of 10 and 40, respectively. The phase curve is similarly altered at the break frequencies of $\frac{1}{10}$ and 10 times the two corner frequencies (10 and 40). We now view the point at which the compensated phase curve crosses a phase shift of −180°. At this frequency (approximately 35 rad/s), the compensated gain is −34 dB. The system can therefore have any gain below 34 dB and still be stable. This is the overall gain, including the

Figure 11.19   Bode plots for Example 11.8.

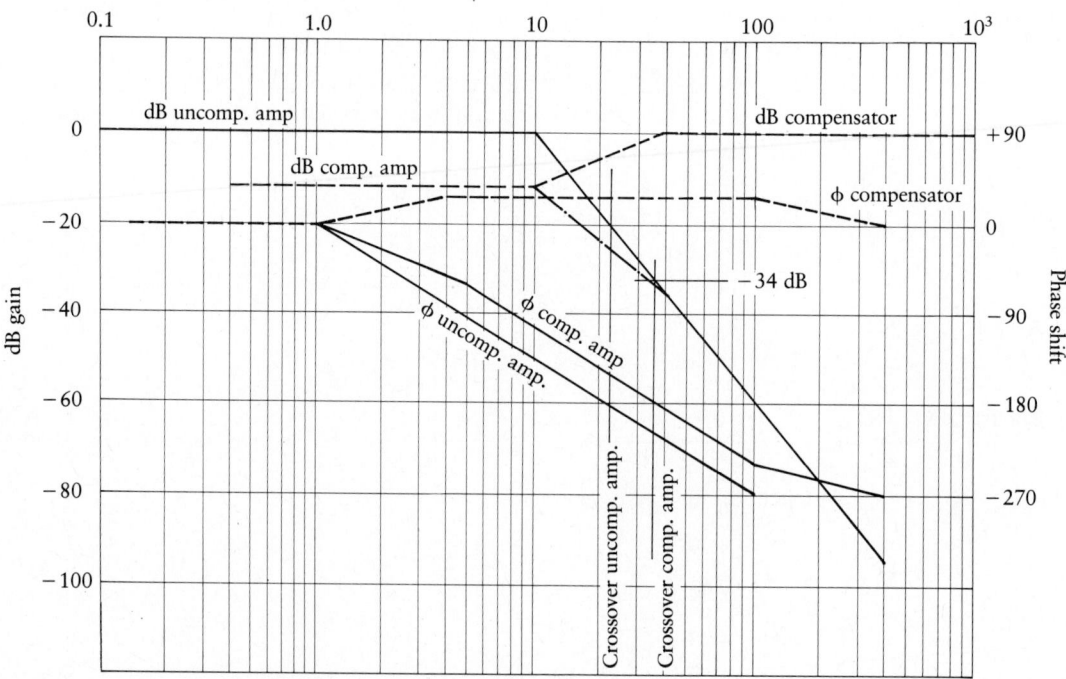

compensation network. Since the compensation network has a gain (attenuation) of $\frac{1}{4}$ (-6 dB), the gain of the op-amp can be as high as

$$G_o = 34 \text{ dB} + 6 \text{ dB} = 40 \text{ dB}$$

Without compensation, the allowable gain is about 20 dB. Thus, an improvement of approximately 20 dB is realized. The system can be further improved if we vary the location of the zero and pole. ▶️

Example 11.9

Consider the negative gain op-amp system of Figure 11.20(a). Investigate the stability of this 3-pole amplifier.

SOLUTION The equivalent circuit of the amplifier is shown in Figure 20(b). The closed loop gain, V_o/V_i, is found in the usual way, with equation (11.15), which is repeated here for convenience.

Figure 11.20
Amplifier for Example 11.9.

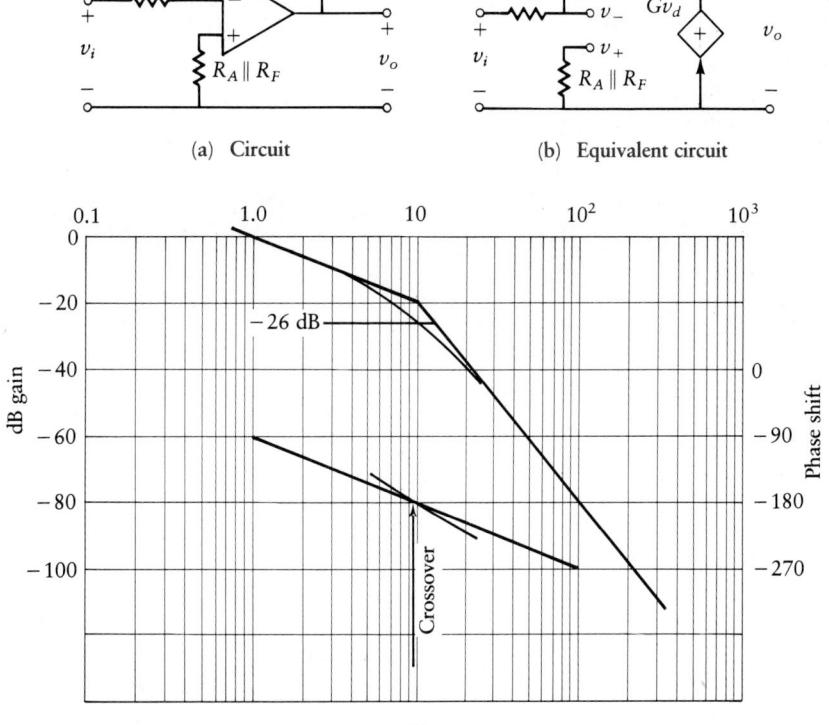

(a) Circuit

(b) Equivalent circuit

(c)

$$\frac{V_o}{V_i} = \frac{-G\gamma R_F/R_A}{1 + G\gamma}$$

where

$$\gamma = \frac{1}{1 + R_F/R_A}$$

The amplifier has the following third-order transfer function:

$$G = \frac{G_o}{s(1 + s/\omega_c)^2}$$

where

$$\omega_c = 10$$

We solve the system with the Bode plot shown in Figure 11.20(c). Notice that we are making a Bode plot for the loop gain, $G\gamma$, where we set $\gamma G_0 = 1$. The phase shift reaches $-180°$ at a frequency of 10 rad/s, and the associated gain is -26 dB. Thus, the design allows for a gain of 26 dB before instability is experienced. The -6 dB is due to the correction to the straight-line asymptote.

▶︎

11.9   Phase-Lag Equalizer

A *passive phase-lag network,* often termed an *integrator,* is shown in Figure 11.21(a), with the zero-pole configuration shown in Figure 11.21(b). We obtain the input-output relationships,

$$V_o = \frac{R_2 + 1/sC}{R_1 + R_2 + 1/sC} V_i$$

$$\frac{V_o}{V_i} = \frac{CR_2 s + 1}{C(R_1 + R_2)s + 1} \tag{11.36}$$

Since

$$C(R_1 + R_2) > CR_2$$

the phase shift of the output lags the phase shift of the input. That is, the phase shift of the denominator in equation (11.36) is larger than the phase shift of the numerator, so the overall phase shift is negative.

Figure 11.21
Passive circuit-lag
network.

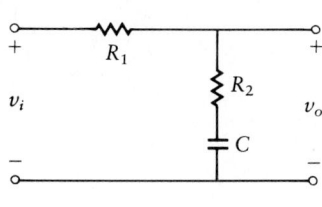

(a) Passive circuit lag network

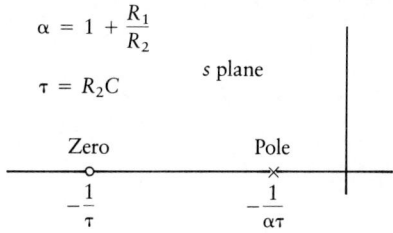

(b) Zero-pole configuration for a lag network

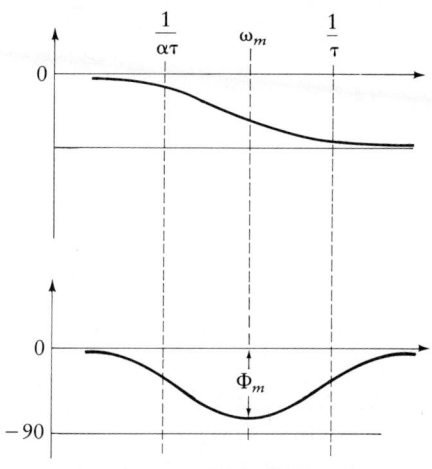

(c) Polar plot of phase-lag network

The transfer function is simplified by again defining two constants

$$\alpha = 1 + \frac{R_1}{R_2}$$

$$\tau = R_2 C$$

The transfer function then becomes

$$\frac{V_o}{V_i} = G(s) = \frac{1}{\alpha}\left[\frac{s + 1/\tau}{s + 1/\alpha\tau}\right] \tag{11.37}$$

The Bode plot for this expression is shown in Figure 11.21(c). Note that the maximum phase lag increases as α increases, and it approaches 90° as α approaches infinity. The frequency, ω_m, at which the maximum occurs decreases with increasing α.

Lag networks possess certain disadvantages when contrasted with other forms of compensation. If the time constant of the lag network is too large, a large root occurs in the system function, which can lead to undesirable transients. The effect of this root can be minimized by keeping the zero close to the pole.

Figure 11.22
Capacitive loading.

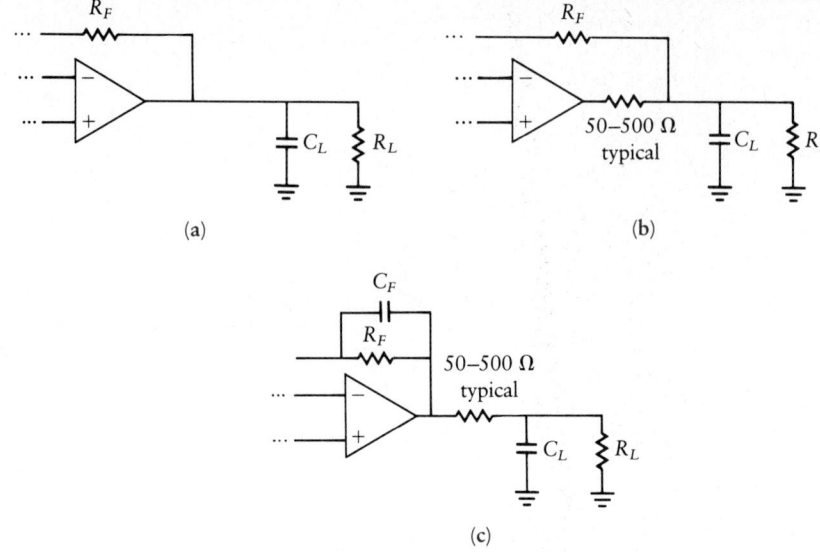

(a)   (b)

(c)

11.10   Effects of Capacitive Loading

The op-amp transfer function includes the output capacitance and the effects of chip capacitance. A capacitive load lowers the corner frequency (i.e., a longer time constant leads to lower frequency) and is troublesome for capacitor values (C_L) of more than about 100 pF in a typical circuit configuration (Figure 11.22(a)). The effect can be reduced by addition of a series resistance, as shown in Figure 11.22(b). This adds attenuation and modifies the gain-phase characteristic.

Input impedance is frequently modeled as a capacitor, C_i, in parallel with a resistor, R_i. This $R_i C_i$ network accounts for another of the poles of $G(s)$ and leads to a phase shift at high frequencies. Additional external capacitance across the input is troublesome when R_F is large because the corner frequency is lowered. Additional compensation comprising a capacitor, C_F, in parallel with R_F can be used as a cure (Figure 11.22(c)). This is known as *Miller-effect compensation,* and it places a zero coincident with the pole to effect cancellation. Typical values for C_F are 3 to 10 pF.

11.11   Oscillators

Sinusoidal driving sources are the building blocks of many systems. They are extensively used in communication systems, as well as in virtually every other application of electronics. A feedback system will oscillate if the loop-transfer

Figure 11.23
Oscillator circuit.

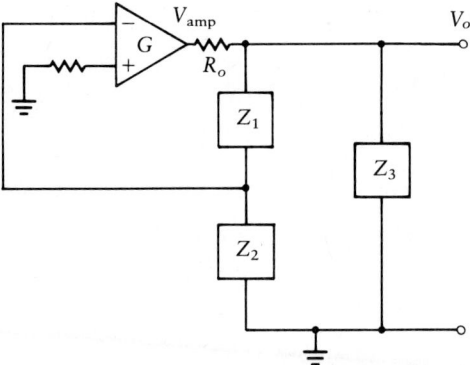

function reaches unity (0 dB) when the phase shift is $-180°$. Such a system produces an output with no input. In a sense, it "chases its tail," with the signal constantly recirculating and regenerating itself.

Two equivalent techniques exist for determining whether a feedback circuit will oscillate. One is to look at the loop gain of a negative-feedback system. If a phase shift of 180° occurs where the loop gain is 0 dB, the circuit is unstable and will oscillate. The second technique is to look for poles of the overall transfer function that lie on the imaginary axis.

While the basic concept of instability and positive feedback is common to all oscillators, there are a number of variations of the basic design. Common oscillators include the *Wien bridge,* the *phase shift, Colpitts,* and *Hartley* oscillators. We examine a number of these in this section.

The feedback model shown in Figure 11.1 is a good starting point for oscillator analysis. Instead of the negative feedback as shown, the feedback is positive. This occurs if the phase shift of the feedback network is 180°. The input signal can be removed without changing the output, since the output is fed back in phase with the input. If the circuit is to sustain oscillations, the loop gain must be unity at $-180°$ phase shift.

We begin by analyzing the circuit shown in Figure 11.23. Several of the standard oscillators can be modeled in this manner. If Z_1 and Z_2 are capacitors and Z_3 is an inductor, the circuit is known as a *Colpitts oscillator.* Alternatively, if Z_1 and Z_2 are inductors and Z_3 is a capacitor, the circuit is a *Hartley oscillator.*

The circuit of Figure 11.23 is redrawn in a different manner as Figure 11.24. This new configuration clearly shows the presence of feedback. R_o is the op-amp output resistance and Z_L is the total load seen by the op-amp. The feedback is as follows:

$$H = \frac{Z_2}{Z_1 + Z_2} \tag{11.38}$$

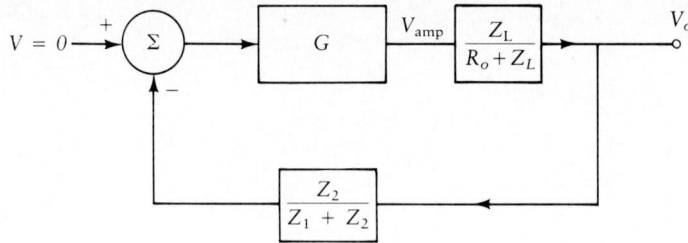

Figure 11.24
Feedback model for
oscillator circuit.

The output is then given by

$$V_o = \frac{Z_L V_{\text{amp}}}{R_o + Z_L} \tag{11.39}$$

where V_{amp} is the op-amp output voltage.

For the Colpitts oscillator, for example,

$$Z_1 = \frac{1}{sC_1}$$

$$Z_2 = \frac{1}{sC_2}$$

$$Z_3 = sL$$

$$Z_L = sL \,\|\, \left[\frac{1}{sC_1} \,\|\, \frac{1}{sC_2} \right]$$

If we define an equivalent capacitance to be

$$C_{\text{eq}} = C_1 + C_2$$

We have

$$Z_L = \frac{sL}{LC_{\text{eq}}s^2 + 1} \tag{11.40}$$

If equation (11.40) is substituted into equation (11.39), we have the output voltage,

$$V_o = \frac{sL/(LC_{\text{eq}}s^2 + 1)}{sL/(LC_{\text{eq}}s^2 + 1) + R_o} V_{\text{amp}}$$

$$= \frac{Ls/R_o}{LC_{\text{eq}}s^2 + Ls/R_o + 1} V_{\text{amp}} \tag{11.41}$$

Equation (11.41) indicates that there is damping in the circuit due to the negative real part of the poles of the expression. If L/R_o is made very small, equation (11.41) reduces to

$$V_o = \frac{Ls/R_o}{LC_{eq}s^2 + 1}\, V_{amp} \tag{11.42}$$

The loop gain is

$$A_L = \frac{C_1}{C_1 + C_2}\, \frac{GLs/R_o}{LC_{eq}s^2 + 1} \tag{11.43}$$

Because the poles of A_L are on the imaginary axis, this system oscillates.

If the op-amp has only a small output resistance, it may be necessary to add a resistor in series with the op-amp output to increase R_o so that the ratio of L/R_o becomes small and the damping becomes negligible. The frequency of oscillation is given by the location of the pole of A_L. That is,

$$f_o = \frac{1}{2\pi\sqrt{LC_{eq}}} \tag{11.44}$$

The Hartley oscillator configuration, where Z_1 and Z_2 of Figure 11.23 are inductors, has two disadvantages when compared to the Colpitts oscillator. When two inductors are in proximity, a mutual coupling occurs, and one inductor has an effect upon the other. This causes the output frequency to be different from the calculated frequency. Another shortcoming is that inductors cannot be varied easily over a wide range of values. This is not the case with capacitors, so the Colpitts oscillator frequency can be varied over a wide range with relative ease. In most applications, the Colpitts oscillator is used, and the capacitor values are varied to change the frequency. One exception to this is in the traditional (nonelectronic) TV tuner, where a Colpitts oscillator is used with a varying inductor. The capacitors are fixed, and the inductor is connected to the tuner, which is changed for each station frequency. Tuning slugs are used in the inductor to fine-tune the frequency to the station carrier.

Low resistance inductors are required in oscillators. This increases the cost of using LC-type oscillators such as the Hartley and Colpitts. Other oscillators that do not employ inductors are frequently used in op-amp circuits. We briefly present several of these alternatives.

Figures 11.25 and 11.26 illustrate the *Wien bridge oscillator*. The impedances, Z_3 and Z_4, are resistive, whereas Z_1 and Z_2 are each series-parallel combinations of resistors and capacitors. The conditions for oscillation to exist in the circuit are those of bridge balance. That is,

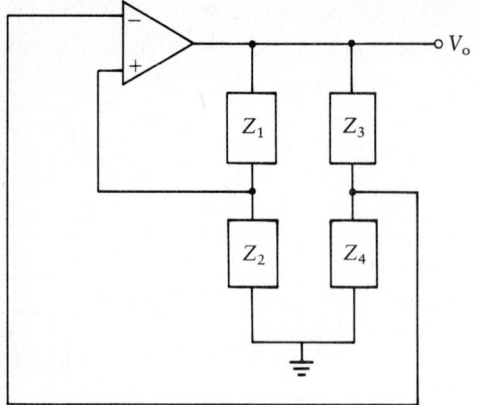

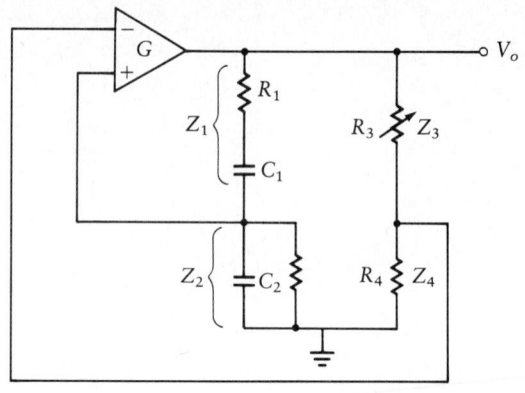

Figure 11.25   Wien bridge oscillator block diagram.

Figure 11.26   Wien bridge oscillator.

$$\frac{Z_1}{Z_2} = \frac{Z_3}{Z_4} \qquad\qquad (11.45)$$

Note that since Z_3 and Z_4 are resistive, this ratio is real.

The *phase-shift oscillator* is shown in Figure 11.27. It consists of three identical RC networks, which each provide a $-60°$ phase shift, resulting in the required $-180°$ total phase shift. This oscillator is a simple form of an op-amp oscillator and is relatively low in cost.

If we now write the transfer function of the feedback network, we find that its angle is $-180°$ when the frequency is

$$f_o = \frac{1}{2\sqrt{6}\,\pi RC} \qquad\qquad (11.46)$$

which therefore represents the oscillator frequency. In practice, more than three RC networks are required due to each section loading the previous section and thereby changing its characteristics. An alternative to using more than three networks is to add a buffer stage between each pair of RC networks in order to reduce the loading effects.

A very simple oscillator, shown in Figure 11.28(a), can be constructed using a *piezo-electric crystal,* commonly known as a *quartz crystal,* and an amplifier. Since the crystal is electrically a resonant circuit, it is used in conjunction with discrete or integrated circuits. Crystal oscillators can be made to achieve accurate frequency control. Stabilities in the range of several parts per million frequency variation over normal temperature ranges can be achieved. Quartz crystals are readily available with frequencies from 10 kHz to 10 MHz. Crystals with other frequency ranges can be obtained, but they are generally not off-the-shelf items. A simple crystal oscillator circuit is shown in Figure 11.28(b).

Figure 11.27
The phase-shift
oscillator.

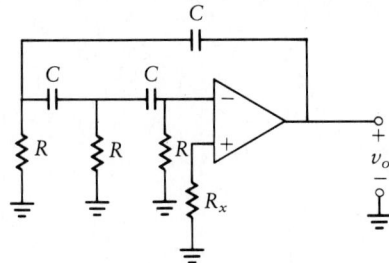

Figure 11.28
Crystal oscillator.

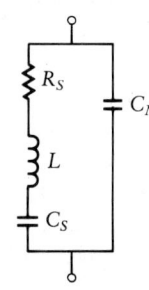

(a) Crystal electrical
equivalent circuit

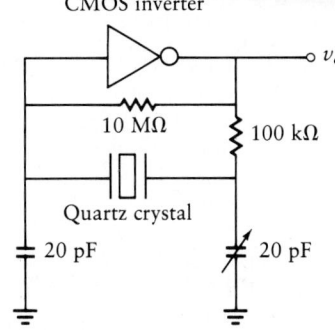

(b) Crystal oscillator circuit

Example 11.10

Design a Colpitts oscillator to resonate at 712 kHz, and determine the transfer function, $G(s)$.

SOLUTION The transistor version of the Colpitts oscillator is shown in Figure 11.29. The capacitor C_1 corresponds to Z_1 in Figure 11.23, C_2 corresponds to Z_2, and L corresponds to Z_3. The frequency of oscillation is given by

$$f_o = \frac{1}{2\pi\sqrt{LC_1C_2/(C_1 + C_2)}}$$

Only the frequency of oscillation has been specified in this design problem. We therefore have one equation in three unknowns. We must select two of the values using other considerations. Suppose we choose standard values for the capacitors, say 0.001 μF. We then use the equation to find L, and if a reasonable value is obtained, the design is complete. In fact, solving for L yields a value of 100 μH, which is a readily obtainable inductor. The loop gain from V'_b around to V_b is given by

Figure 11.29
Colpitts oscillator.

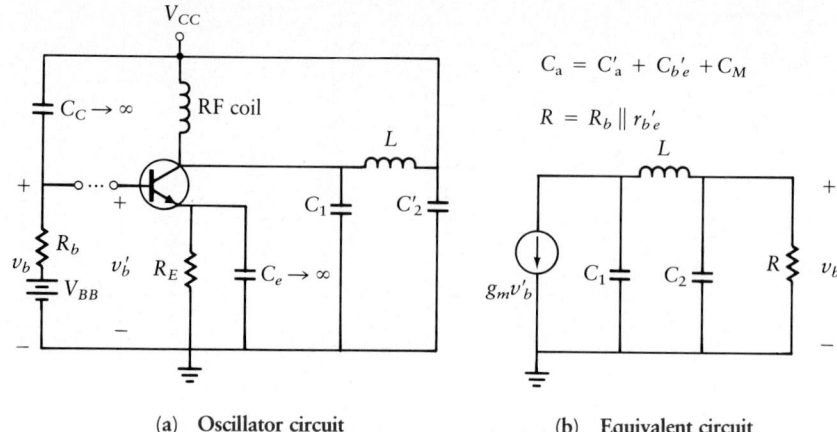

(a) Oscillator circuit   (b) Equivalent circuit

$$G(s) = \frac{V_b}{V'_b} = \frac{-g_m}{s^3 LRC_1 C_2 + s^2 LC_1 + s(RC_1 + RC_2) + 1} \tag{11.47}$$

The resistor values would be selected for proper biasing. As an example, suppose that the parallel combination,

$$R = r_{b'e} \,\|\, R_b = 1 \text{ k}\Omega$$

Note that $r_{b'e}$ is typically about 1 kΩ, so we assume that R_b is considerably larger than this value. If we further assume that $g_m = 0.4$ mS, equation (11.47) can be factored to yield

$$G(s) = \frac{-0.4}{(1.98 \times 10^{-6}s + 1)(5.06 \times 10^{-14}s^2 + 2.5s + 1)} \tag{11.48}$$

The quadratic in the denominator of equation (11.48) can be factored to obtain the roots

$$s = -2.5 \times 10^5 \pm j4.4 \times 10^6$$

Note that the imaginary part of the roots is an order of magnitude higher than the real part. The frequency of oscillation is approximately given by 4.4×10^6 rad/s, which is 700 kHz, as specified in the problem statement. ◄┼

PROBLEMS

11.1   For the circuit of Figure P11.1, determine the voltage gain, input resistance, and current gain when $C_E \to \infty$.

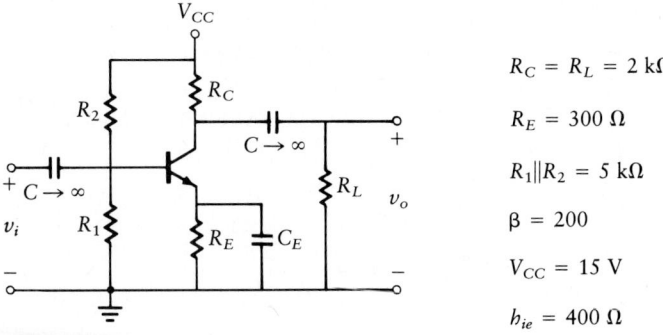

$R_C = R_L = 2 \text{ k}\Omega$

$R_E = 300 \ \Omega$

$R_1 \| R_2 = 5 \text{ k}\Omega$

$\beta = 200$

$V_{CC} = 15 \text{ V}$

$h_{ie} = 400 \ \Omega$

Figure P11.1

11.2 Repeat Problem 11.1 when $C_E = 0$. Compare the values of A_v, R_{in} and A_i found in each of these problems, and explain any differences.

11.3 For the amplifier of Figure P11.1, determine A_v, R_{in}, and A_i when $R_1 \rightarrow \infty$ and $R_2 = 200 \text{ k}\Omega$.

11.4 For the amplifier shown in Figure P11.1, determine the feedback attenuation factor.

11.5 A feedback amplifier of the type shown in Figure 11.3(a) with $C_1 = 0$ has a gain of -200 with no feedback and the ratio of the feedback voltage to the output voltage is 0.2. What is the voltage gain of the amplifier? If the gain with no feedback increases to -300, what is the new voltage gain?

11.6 For the amplifier of Figure P11.2, determine A_v, R_{in}, and A_i when $R_F = 14 \text{ k}\Omega$.

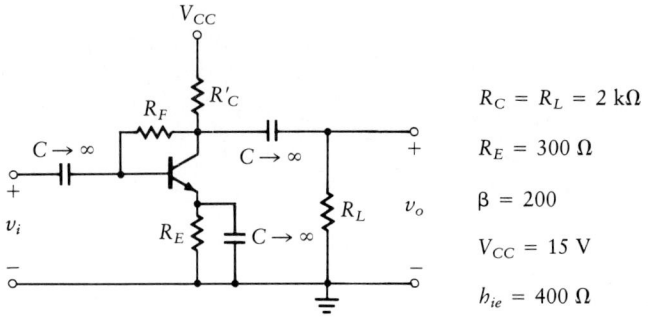

$R_C = R_L = 2 \text{ k}\Omega$

$R_E = 300 \ \Omega$

$\beta = 200$

$V_{CC} = 15 \text{ V}$

$h_{ie} = 400 \ \Omega$

Figure P11.2

11.7 A single-stage amplifier using voltage feedback, as shown in Figure P11.2, has a source voltage resistance of 2 kΩ and an R_F of 20 kΩ. Determine the open-loop and closed-loop gain of the amplifier.

11.8 Using the same amplifier as in Problem 11.7, select the value of R_F to make the amplifier bias stable and determine the closed loop gain.

11.9 For the circuit shown in Figure 11.6(a), determine the closed-loop gain and the value of R_F of the amplifier. Assume $\beta = 200$, $R_{E1} = 100\ \Omega$, $h_{ib} = 4\ \Omega$, $R_{C1} = 2\ k\Omega$, $R_{C2} = 1\ k\Omega$, $R_i = 2\ k\Omega$, all $C \to \infty$, $R_1 \parallel R_2 = 2\ k\Omega$, $R'_1 \parallel R'_2 = 5\ k\Omega$, and the ratio of the feedback voltage to the output voltage is 0.005.

11.10 Use the data sheets in Appendix D to determine the worst-case values for the following quantities for each of the three op-amps and given conditions.

  a. 741E op-amp at 25°C, ± 15 V supplies, and a load resistance of 10 kΩ.

  b. 741E op-amp at 50°C, ± 20 V supplies, and a load resistance of 2 kΩ.

  c. 101A op-amp at 50°C, ± 15 V supplies, and a load resistance of 5 kΩ.

   i. Gain (smallest is worst case).
   ii. Input resistance (smallest is worst case).
   iii. Input offset voltage (largest is worst case).
   iv. Input bias current (largest is worst case).
   v. Input offset current (largest is worst case).
   vi. Output resistance (largest is worst case).
   vii. Output voltage swing (smallest is worst case).
   viii. Gain-bandwidth product (smallest is worst case).
   ix. Power supply current (largest is worst case).

11.11 For the op-amp inverting amplifier shown in Figure 11.10(a), what is the percent error if the open loop gain is only 50,000? Use $R_F = 200$ kΩ and $R_A = 10$ kΩ.

In Problems 11.12–11.17, sketch decibel gain and phase curves for each function, and discuss the stability of each amplifier as a function of K.

11.12 $\dfrac{K}{s(s + 10)}$

11.13 $\dfrac{K}{s^2(s + 10)}$

11.14 $\dfrac{K(s + 1)}{s^2(s + 10)}$

11.15 $\dfrac{K}{s(s + 1)(s + 100)}$

11.16 $\dfrac{K(s + 1)}{s^3(s + 100)}$

11.17 $\dfrac{K}{s(s^2 + 20s + 100)}$

11.18 The op-amp system of Figure 11.16(a) has a gain function that is

$$G(s) = \frac{G_o}{1 + s/2\pi}$$

R = 100 kΩ and C = 0.1 μF. Determine the open- and closed-loop functions.

11.19 For the op-amp system of Problem 11.18, plot a Bode diagram with $G_o = 1$. Determine the stability for this system.

11.20 For the op-amp system of Figure 11.15(a), use

$$G(s) = \frac{G_o}{(1 + s/20\pi)^2}$$

R = 159 kΩ and C = 0.1 μF. Note the square in the op-amp gain function. Determine the open- and closed-loop functions.

11.21 For the op-amp system of Problem 11.20, plot a Bode diagram with $G_o = 1$. Determine the stability of the system.

For the expressions in Problems 11.22–11.25, sketch Bode plots and discuss stability of each amplifier. Let $K = 1$ in each function.

11.22 $\dfrac{K}{s(s^2 + s + 25)}$

11.23 $\dfrac{K}{s^2(s^2 + s + 25)}$

11.24 $\dfrac{Ks}{s^2 + s + 25}$

11.25 $\dfrac{K(s + 1)}{s^2(s^2 + s + 100)}$

11.26 Find a function G(s) that has the approximate frequency response shown in Figure P11.3

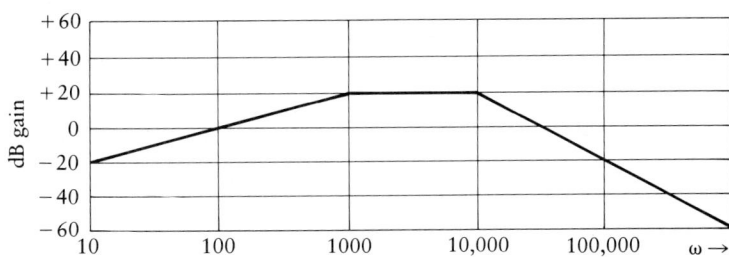

Figure P11.3

11.27 Determine the ratio of R_F to R_A to meet the condition for oscillations of the Wien bridge oscillator shown in Figure P11.4 and determine the formula for frequency of oscillation.

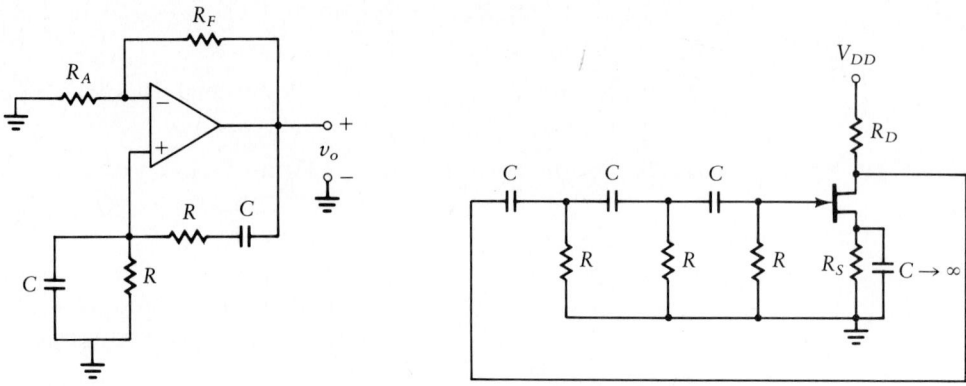

Figure P11.4　　　　　　　　　　　**Figure P11.5**

11.28 Design a phase-shift oscillator using a FET transistor, as shown in Figure P11.5. Let $g_m = 5000$ μS, $r_d = 50$ kΩ, and the feedback resistors $R = 20$ kΩ. Select the value of C for the oscillator to operate at 10 kHz. Make sure the gain of the amplifier is at least -50 to compensate for loading.

11.29 Determine the value of the capacitor needed in the Colpitts oscillator of Figure P11.6 if a 0.001-mH inductor is the only value inductor available. The frequency of oscillation is specified to be 500 kHz.

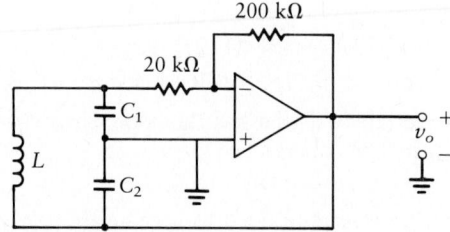

Figure P11.6

11.30 In Problem 11.27, design the Wien bridge oscillator to oscillate at 100 MHz using resistor values (R) of 10 kΩ, 20 kΩ, . . . , 100 kΩ.

11.31 Prove equation (11.46) by developing the transfer function of the feedback network of a phase-shift oscillator.

12

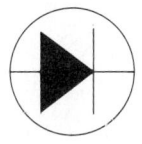

NONLINEAR CIRCUITS

12.0 Introduction

Several nonlinear diode circuits were considered in Chapter 1. One of the examples was the power supply circuit, which converts an ac signal into dc. We also analyzed various clipping and clamping configurations that were used either to chop off a portion of a time varying signal or to change its dc level. In the current chapter, we combine diodes with op-amps in various circuit configurations. The advantage of this approach is that the diodes are able to operate more closely to their ideal characteristics. We consider rectifiers, limiters, comparators, and Schmitt triggers. Our objective is to design a system that achieves a specified instantaneous nonlinear output-to-input voltage-transfer characteristic. The characteristics are *instantaneous* since the circuit contains no energy storage devices (e.g., inductors or capacitors). The output at any particular time depends only upon the present value of the input.

12.1 Rectifiers

One of the most basic and useful nonlinear circuits is the *rectifier*. Rectifiers operate upon an input signal in a manner that depends upon the sign of the instantaneous input voltage. They can be designed either to chop off the neg-

Figure 12.1
Inverting half-wave
rectifier.

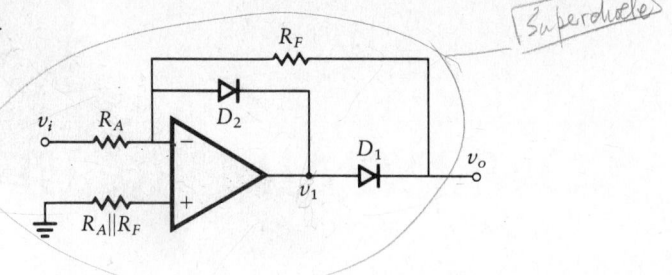

ative (or positive) part of the signal or to yield an output that is the mathematical absolute value of the input.

The circuit shown in Figure 12.1 is known as an *inverting half-wave rectifier*. Since a diode can operate in either of two states, we analyze the rectifier as two separate circuits. Which of the two separate circuits applies depends upon the sign of v_1.

We assume the op-amp to be ideal. Then

$$v_- = v_+ = 0$$

For positive v_i, the amplifier output voltage, v_1, is less than 0. Diode D_2 *conducts* and it can therefore be replaced by a small resistor, R_f. The diode forward resistance represents a small feedback resistor, thus leading to lowered amplifier gain. Diode D_1 acts as an open circuit under this condition, so

$$v_o = v_- = 0$$

Alternatively, when v_1 is positive, D_2 is nonconducting (off) and D_1 is *conducting* (on). Figure 12.2(a) repeats the circuit of Figure 12.1 where the diodes are replaced by their equivalents for the situation when v_1 is positive. That is, D_1 is replaced by a forward resistance and D_2 is open-circuited. Figure 12.2(b) shows the same circuit where the op-amp is replaced by its simplified equivalent.

We see from Figure 12.2(b) that

$$v_+ = 0$$
$$v_- = v_i - iR_A \tag{12.1}$$

Since $v_- = v_+ = 0$, we set the right side of equation (12.1) to zero and solve for i to obtain,

$$i = \frac{v_i}{R_A}$$

The output voltage is given by

Figure 12.2
Inverting half-wave
rectifier.

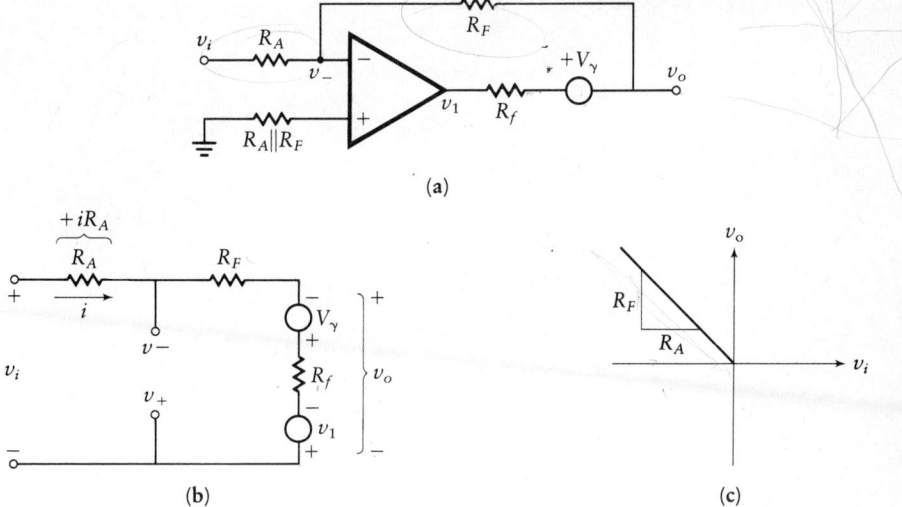

(a)

(b)

(c)

$$v_o = -R_F i$$

$$= -R_F \frac{v_i}{R_A} \tag{12.2}$$

The expression in equation (12.2) does not depend upon the diode forward voltage, V_γ. Thus, the feedback acts to cancel the diode turn on (forward) voltage. This leads to improved performance since the diode more closely approximates the ideal device. The transfer characteristic is shown in Figure 12.2(c).

The half-wave rectifier is one of the simplest nonlinear circuits. There are a number of variations of the basic circuit. Some of these alternate forms are illustrated in Table 12.1. We strongly recommend that you not proceed beyond this point until you review the operation of each circuit in the table.

A *full-wave rectifier,* or *magnitude operator,* produces an output that is the absolute value, or magnitude, of the input signal waveform. One method of accomplishing full-wave rectification is to use two half-wave rectifiers. One of these effectively operates upon the positive portion of the input and the second operates upon the negative portion. The outputs are summed with the proper polarities. Figure 12.3 illustrates one such configuration. This method of full-wave rectification requires three separate amplifiers, and there are simpler methods.

One of these simpler methods of full-wave rectification follows from an arithmetic observation. First note that the mathematical operation of taking the absolute value is the same as that of reversing the sign of the negative part of the signal. If the original signal is subtracted from twice the half-wave

Table 12.1   Half-Wave Rectifier Configurations.

1. Basic positive output, inverting

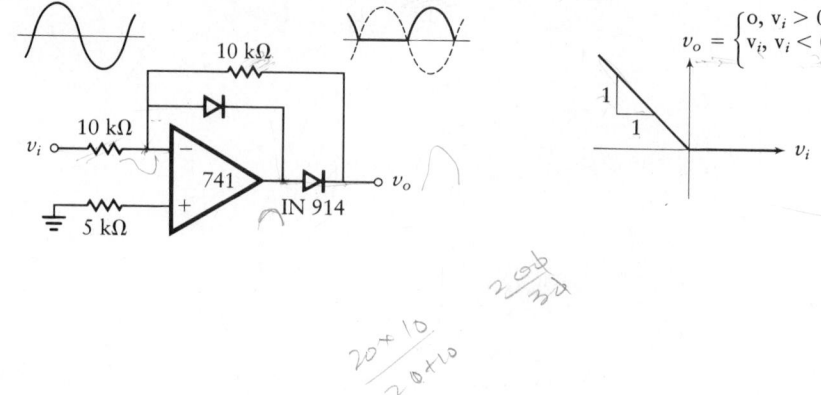

$$v_o = \begin{cases} 0, & v_i > 0 \\ v_i, & v_i < 0 \end{cases}$$

2. Positive output, inverting with gain

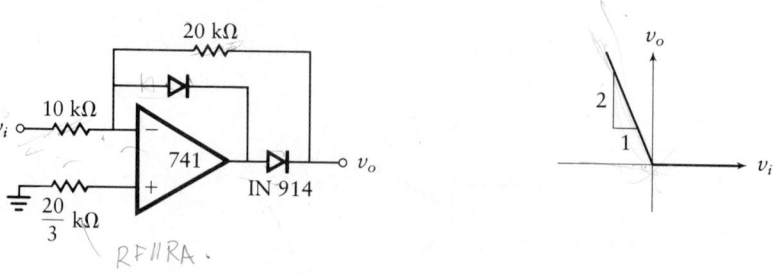

3. Positive output, inverting and summing

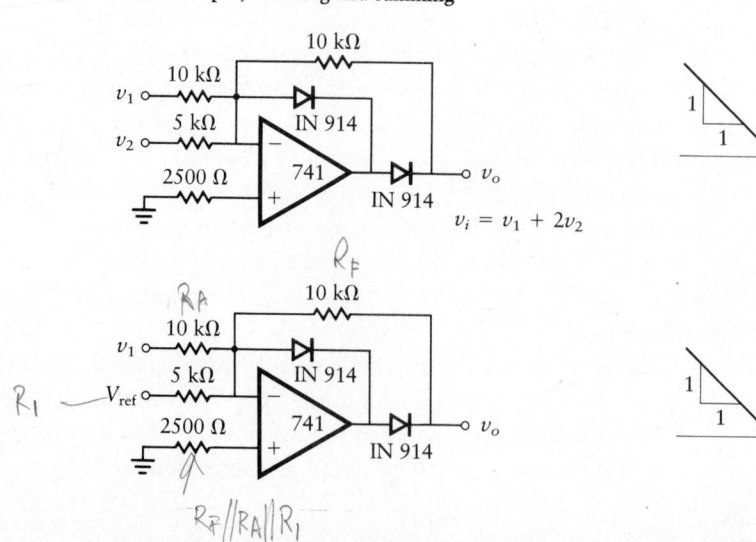

$v_i = v_1 + 2v_2$

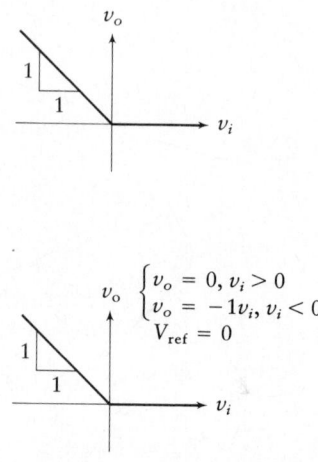

$$v_o \begin{cases} v_o = 0, \; v_i > 0 \\ v_o = -1v_i, \; v_i < 0 \\ V_{ref} = 0 \end{cases}$$

Table 12.1 Half-Wave Rectifier Configurations. (*Continued*)

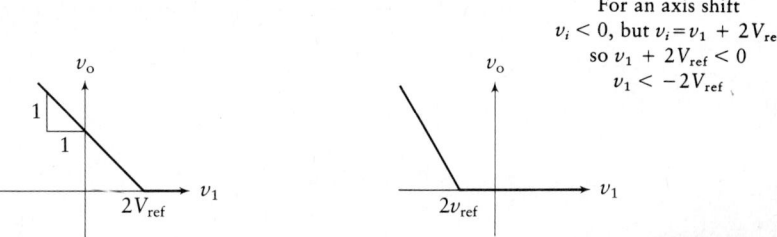

For an axis shift
$v_i < 0$, but $v_i = v_1 + 2V_{ref}$
so $v_1 + 2V_{ref} < 0$
$v_1 < -2V_{ref}$

For a positive V_{ref}, the output voltage (v_{o2}) is shifted to the left, and for a negative V_{ref}, the output (v_{o1}) is shifted to the right.

4. Basic negative output, inverting

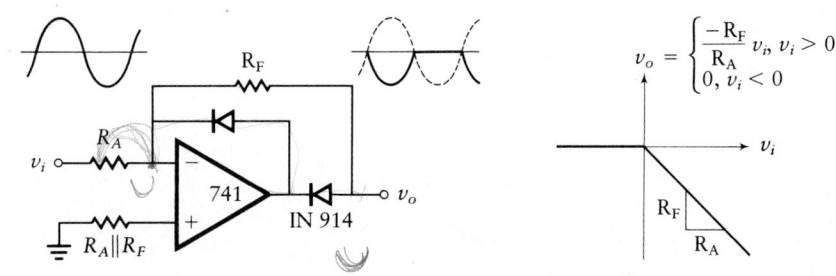

$$v_o = \begin{cases} \dfrac{-R_F}{R_A} v_i, & v_i > 0 \\ 0, & v_i < 0 \end{cases}$$

Figure 12.3
Full-wave rectifier.

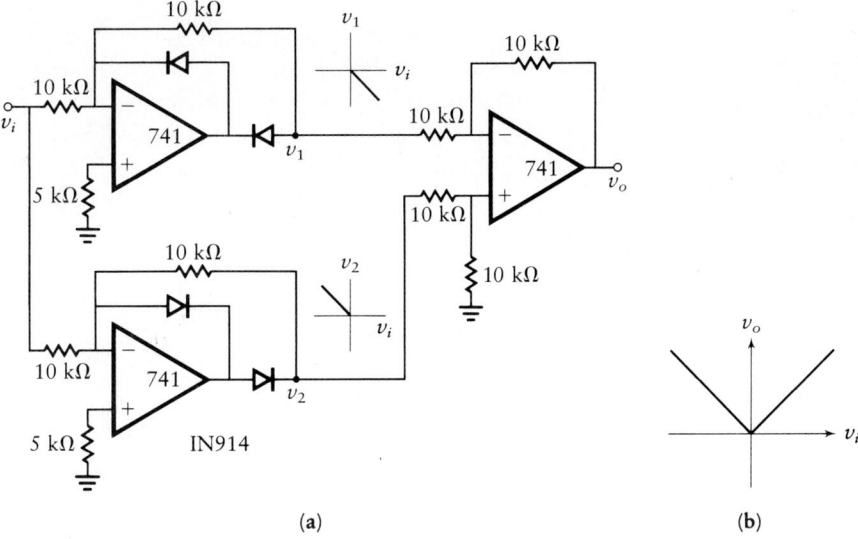

(a) (b)

output, the result is the full-wave rectified waveform. This is easily proven by considering the two operating conditions separately. First, suppose that the input is positive. Then the half-wave output is equal to the input, and the difference described above becomes

$$2v_i(t) - v_i(t) = v_i(t)$$

Thus, the output is equal to the input. If the input is now negative, the half-wave output is zero, and the difference becomes

$$2 \times 0 - v_i(t) = -v_i(t)$$

Thus, the output is equal to the negative of the input. The composite output is then the absolute value of the input. This form of the full-wave rectifier is shown as the first entry in Table 12.2. The remaining entries in this table illustrate alternate methods of forming the full-wave rectified output. Some careful study should easily verify the operation of each system.

Example 12.1

Start with the inverting half-wave rectifier of Figure 12.1 but reverse the diodes and place a reference voltage, $V_{ref} = 5$ V, at the negative terminal of the op-amp fed through a 20 kΩ resistor. Let $R_A = 10$ kΩ and $R_F = 20$ kΩ. The resulting circuit is shown in Figure 12.4(a). Assume that the op-amp is DC bias balanced. Find the input-output voltage characteristic.

SOLUTION   If the reference voltage were zero, the output would be nonzero only in the fourth quadrant of the v_o versus v_i characteristic. This differs from the situation of Figure 12.2(c) by 180°, since the diodes are reversed. In that quadrant, the slope is $-R_F/R_A$ or -2, and the curve intercepts the origin. With a reference voltage of $+5$ V and an associated gain of unity (based upon the given resistor values), the axis of the line is moved to where $v_i = -5$ when $v_o = 0$. That is, v_i is -5 V for the summed input to equal zero. The 5-V reference causes the diode to conduct when the v_i voltage is -5 V or less. A gain of -2 will be realized for all input voltages less than -5 V. The v_o versus v_i characteristic is shown in Figure 12.4(b).   ▸┤

Figure 12.4
Circuit for Example 12.1.

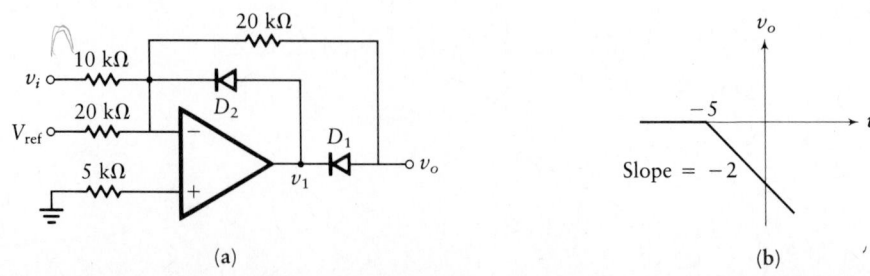

(a)   (b)

12.2 Feedback Limiters

A *limiter,* in its ideal basic form, constrains a signal to be below (or above) a particular specified value (breakpoint). The output signal is proportional to the input below (or above) this breakpoint and stays constant for inputs above (or below) this value.

There are a wide variety of variations of the basic limiter circuit. In fact, any characteristic composed of two straight lines intersecting at a point can be considered as a form of limiter and can be realized by using a diode in the feedback path of an op-amp.

As an example, consider the system of Figure 12.5. Because of the presence of the diode, this circuit is analyzed by considering the two cases separately. That is, the diode is first assumed to be an open circuit, and the circuit is solved. The solution is repeated for the case when the diode is a short circuit. It is then simply necessary to find the location of the breakpoint between the two regions.

When the diode of Figure 12.5 is not conducting, the circuit operates as an inverting amplifier with the output given by

$$v_o = -v_i \left(\frac{R_F}{R_A} \right)$$

and the gain is $-R_F/R_A$.

To find the breakpoint, we solve for v_1 as follows:

$$v_1 = \frac{V_{ref} - v_o}{R_1 + R_2} R_2 + v_o = \frac{R_2 V_{ref} + R_1 v_o}{R_1 + R_2}$$

$$= (R_1 \| R_2) \left[\frac{V_{ref}}{R_1} + \frac{v_o}{R_2} \right]$$

Figure 12.5 Feedback limiter.

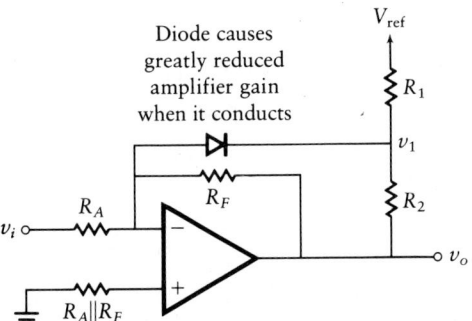

Table 12.2   Full-Wave Rectifiers.

1. General case

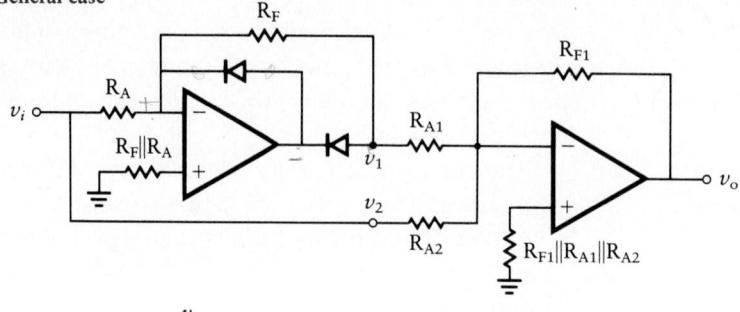

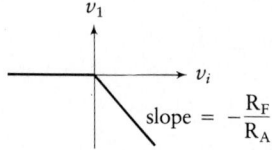

① v_1 due to v_i:

$$v_1\big|_{v_2\,=\,0} = -\frac{R_F}{R_A}v_i$$

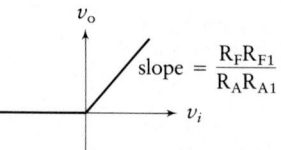

② v_o due to v_1:

$$v_o\big|_{v_2\,=\,0} = -\frac{R_{F1}}{R_{A1}}v_1 = \frac{R_F R_{F1}}{R_A R_{A1}}v_i$$

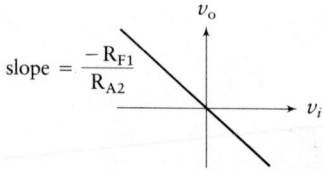

③ v_o due to v_2:

$$v_o\big|_{v_1\,=\,0} = -\frac{R_{F1}}{R_{A2}}v_2 = \frac{R_{F1}}{R_{A2}}v_i$$

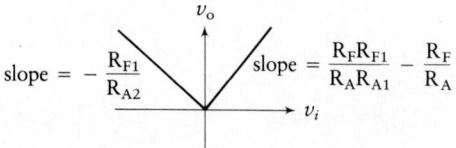

④ v_o due to v_1 and v_2

Table 12.2   Full-Wave Rectifiers. (*Continued*)

2. Numerical examples

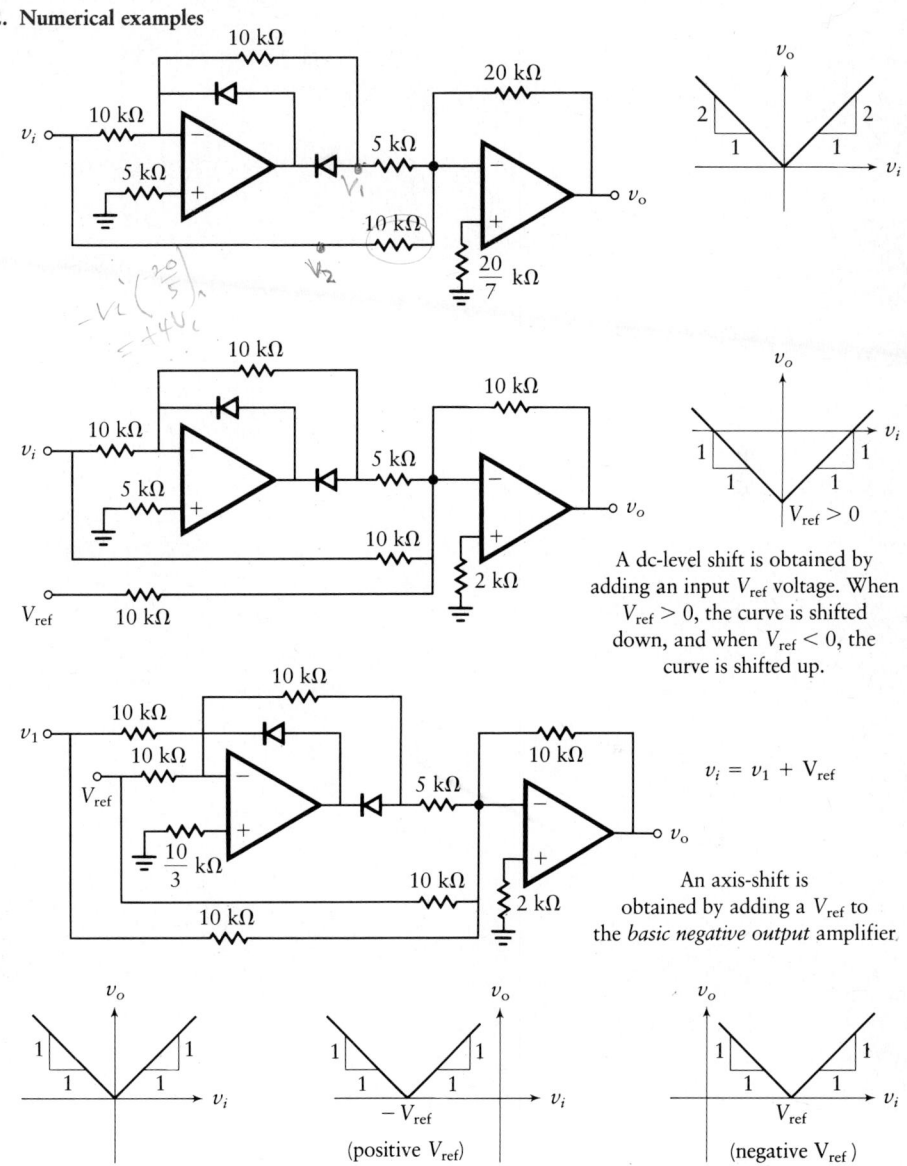

A dc-level shift is obtained by adding an input V_{ref} voltage. When $V_{ref} > 0$, the curve is shifted down, and when $V_{ref} < 0$, the curve is shifted up.

$$v_i = v_1 + V_{ref}$$

An axis-shift is obtained by adding a V_{ref} to the *basic negative output* amplifier.

(positive V_{ref})   (negative V_{ref})

The diode conducts when v_1 tries to go below $V\gamma$. (Note that $v_- = v_+ = 0$). That is,

$$v_1 = \frac{R_2 V_{ref} + R_1 v_o}{R_1 + R_2} < V\gamma$$

We solve for v_o by setting $v_1 = -V\gamma$ as follows:

$$v_o = \frac{-(R_1 + R_2)}{R_1} V\gamma - \frac{R_2}{R_1} V_{ref}$$

If we assume that $V\gamma$ is zero, this becomes

$$v_o = \frac{-R_2 V_{ref}}{R_1} \qquad (12.3)$$

This represents the breakpoint between the two circuit conditions.

To analyze the other condition, we find the Thevenin equivalent of the resistor divider network to the right of the diode, as shown in Figure 12.6. When the diode is on, it is replaced by a "turn-on" voltage generator, $V\gamma$, and a forward resistance, R_f. The circuit of Figure 12.5 then takes the form shown in Figure 12.7. The voltage v_o is determined from the circuit as follows:

$$v_o = -\frac{R_F}{R_A} v_i - \frac{R_F}{R_1 \| R_2 + R_f} \left[\frac{R_2 V_{ref} + R_1 v_o}{R_1 + R_2} + V\gamma \right]$$

$$\text{and} \left[1 + \frac{R_F}{R_1 \| R_2 + R_f} \frac{R_1}{R_1 + R_2} \right] v_o$$

$$= -\frac{R_F}{R_A} v_i - \frac{R_F}{R_1 \| R_2 + R_f} \left[\frac{R_2}{R_1 + R_2} V_{ref} + V\gamma \right]$$

We now assume that

$$\frac{R_F}{R_1 \| R_2 + R_f} \gg 1$$

as is normally the case. The equation then reduces to

$$v_o = \frac{-R_F v_i / R_A}{[R_F/(R_1 \| R_2 + R_f)][R_1/(R_1 + R_2)]} - \frac{R_2}{R_1} V_{ref} - \frac{R_1 + R_2}{R_1} V\gamma$$

$$= -\left(\frac{1}{R_A} \right)\left(1 + \frac{R_2}{R_1} \right)(R_1 \| R_2 + R_f) v_i - \frac{R_2}{R_1} V_{ref} - \left(1 + \frac{R_2}{R_1} \right) V\gamma \qquad (12.4)$$

Figure 12.6
Thevenin equivalent for feedback limiter.

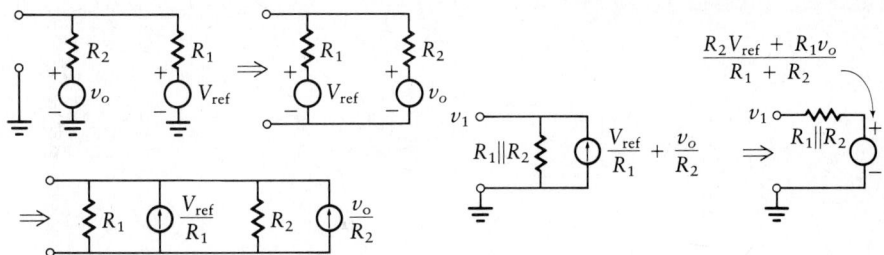

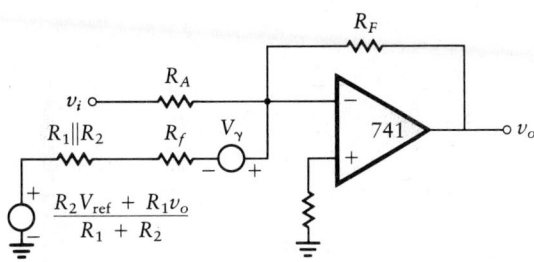

Figure 12.7
Reduced circuit—feedback limiter.

The gain is given by

$$-\left(\frac{1}{R_A}\right)\left(1 + \frac{R_2}{R_1}\right)(R_1 \| R_2 + R_f)$$ (12.5)

If $R_2 \ll R_1$ or if $R_f \ll (R_1 \| R_2)$, the expression for the gain in equation (12.5) reduces to

$$\frac{-R_2}{R_A}$$

The resulting characteristic curve is shown in Figure 12.8. The slope changes from $-R_F/R_A$ to approximately $-R_2/R_A$ as v_i increases beyond the breakpoint. If V_{ref} is negative, the break in the characteristic curve occurs at a positive value of v_o.

Notice that R_2 must be much smaller than R_A if good limiting is to be achieved. That is, if the limiter is to have near-zero slope beyond the breakpoint, $R_2/R_A \ll 1$.

The values of v_o and v_i when the slope changes (we define these as V_{oc} and V_{ic}, respectively) are given by the following equations:

$$V_{oc} = \frac{-R_2 V_{ref}}{R_1} - \left(1 + \frac{R_2}{R_1}\right)V\gamma$$ (12.6)

Figure 12.8
Limiter characteristics.

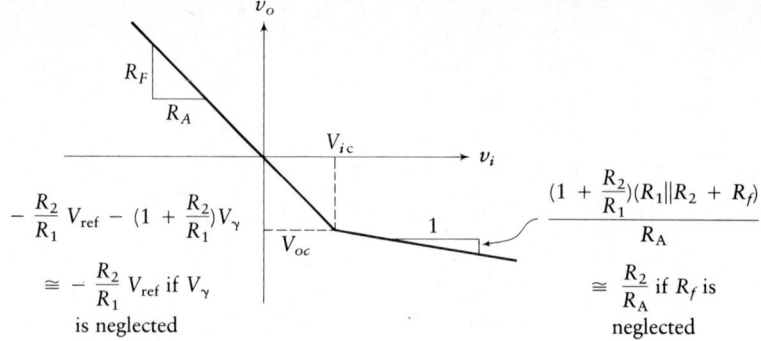

$$V_{ic} = \frac{R_A}{R_F}\left[\frac{R_2 V_{ref}}{R_1} + \left(1 + \frac{R_2}{R_1}\right)V\gamma\right] \tag{12.7}$$

It is important to realize that the value of the output voltage when the slope changes, V_{oc}, must be less than the saturation voltage, $-E$, for the op-amp. This is true since the amplifier cannot produce a voltage greater than the saturation voltage, so if the break is beyond this value, it will never be achieved. If $E = V_{ref}$, as is frequently the case, R_2 must be less than R_1.

Table 12.3 presents a variety of limiter configurations. These should be carefully studied before proceeding.

Table 12.3   Limiter Configurations.

1. Basic lower limit

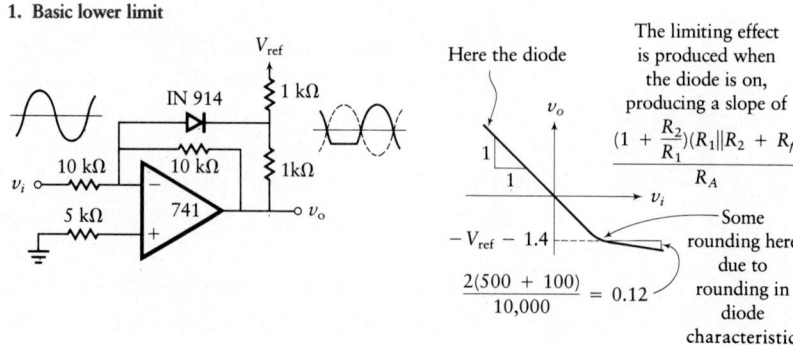

Table 12.3 Limiter Configurations. (*Continued*)

2. Negative reference voltage

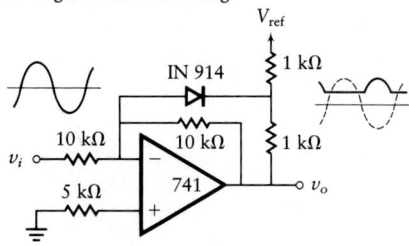

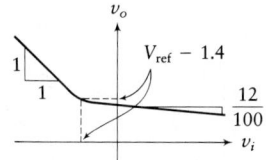

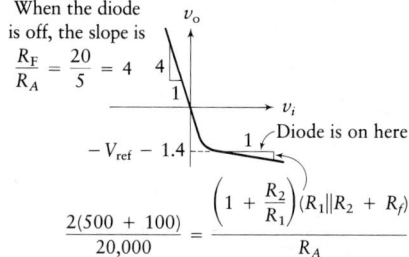

We have a negative reference voltage with the slopes the same as before, except now the output voltage is limited above zero.

3. Lower limit with gain

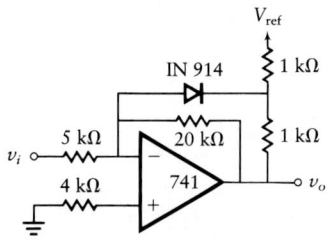

When the diode is off, the slope is

$$\frac{R_F}{R_A} = \frac{20}{5} = 4$$

$$\frac{2(500 + 100)}{20,000} = \frac{\left(1 + \dfrac{R_2}{R_1}\right)(R_1\|R_2 + R_f)}{R_A}$$

4. Summation and lower limit

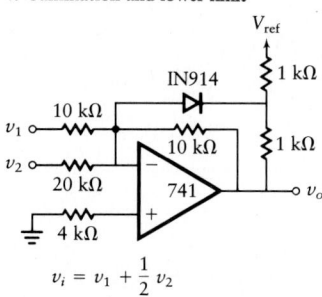

$$v_i = v_1 + \frac{1}{2}v_2$$

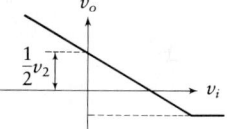

Instead of just one input, we have two. Purpose is to get dc bias of $\frac{1}{2}v_2$ while varying v_1 or vice-versa.

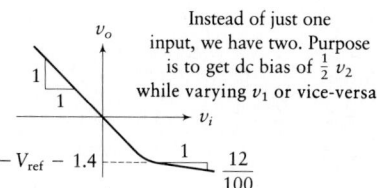

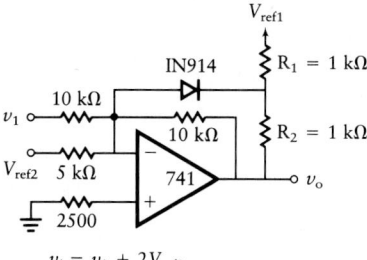

$$v_i = v_1 + 2V_{ref2}$$

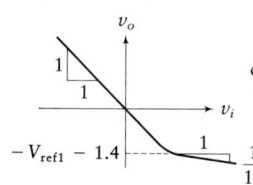

Same as above, except different coefficient for V_{ref}, which produces a larger bias.

Table 12.3 Limiter Configurations. (*Continued*)

5. **Unequal divider resistances**

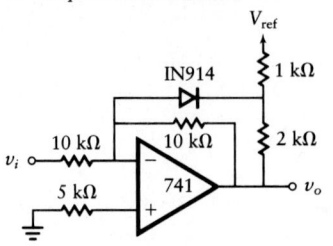

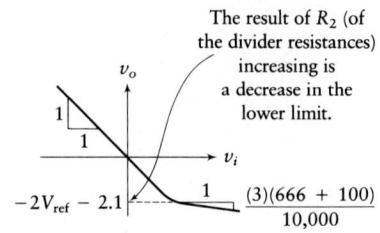

The result of R_2 (of the divider resistances) increasing is a decrease in the lower limit.

6. **Basic upper limit**

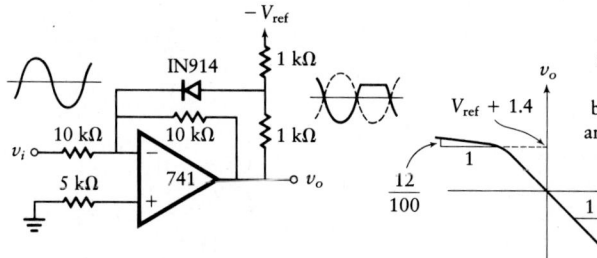

Instead of limiting the output voltage when v_i is positive, we can limit v_o when v_i is negative by having a negative V_{ref} and by changing the diode polarity.

7. **Positive reference voltage**

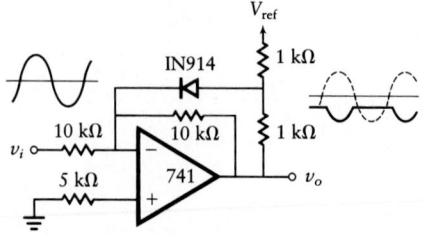

Comparing with the negative reference voltage circuit, the output voltage here is limited below zero because the diode polarity is reversed.

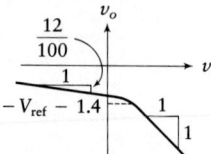

8. **Upper and lower limiting**

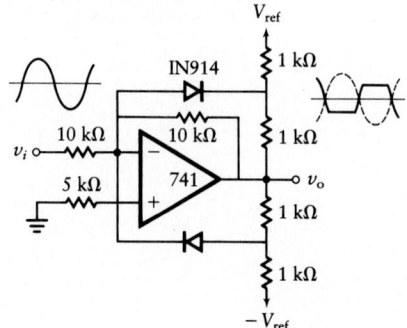

The basic lower limit and basic upper limit circuits are combined.

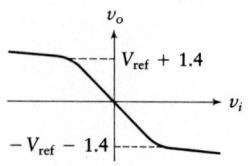

Table 12.3   Limiter Configurations. (*Continued*)

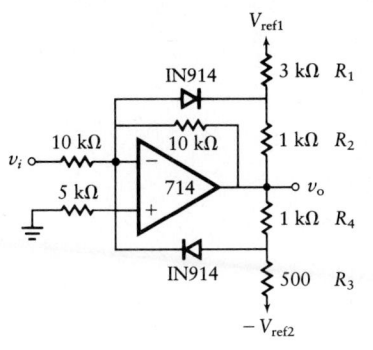

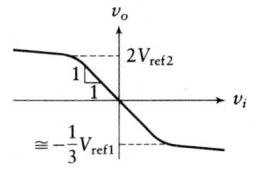

This is an example
of the effects of changing
R_1 values. The saturation points differ.

9. Adjustable limiting

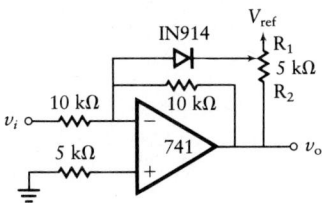

From the characteristic
plot, we can see that by using
a potentiometer for R_1 and R_2,
the lower limit decreases as
R_2 gets larger.

"break" level
set by
potentiometer

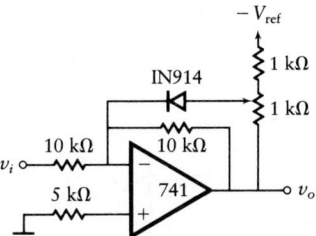

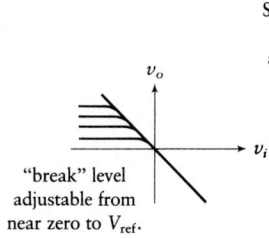

Some as above, except
with a negative V_{ref}
and reversed polarity
of the diode, the
saturation curves
are above zero.

"break" level
adjustable from
near zero to V_{ref}.

Table 12.3   Limiter Configurations. (*Continued*)

10. Here are shown the combined effects of the two previous circuits

11. Voltage-controlled limiting

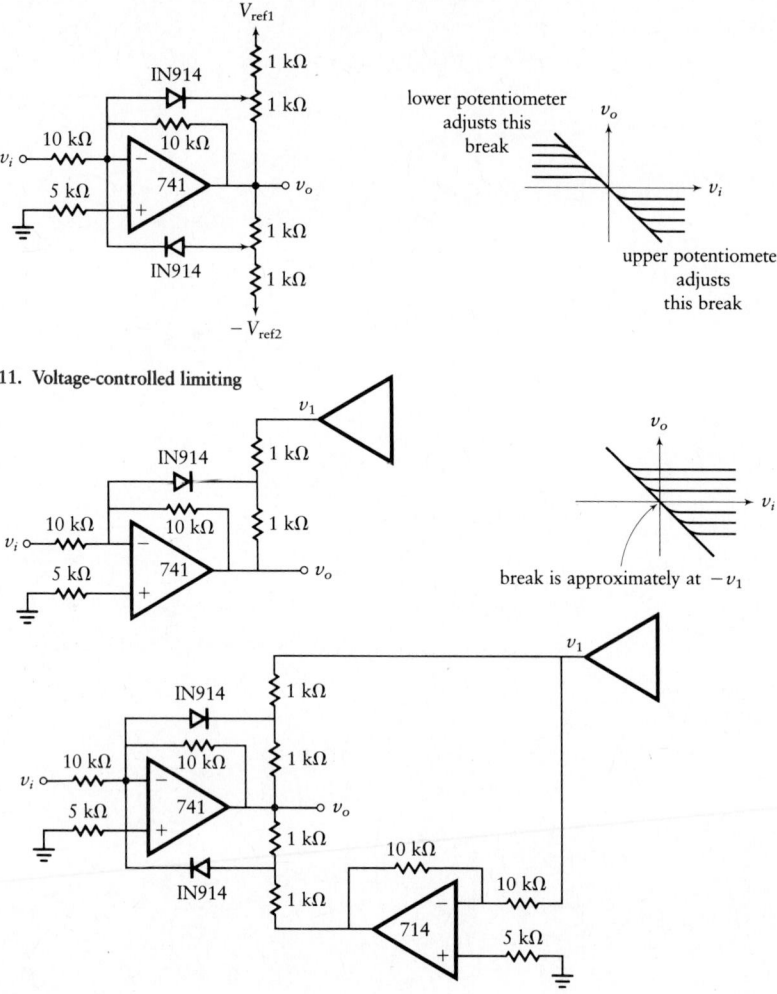

Drill Problems

Design 741 circuits with transfer characteristics, as shown in the figures. Assume that the reference supply available is ± 10 V and that $V\gamma = 0.7$ V and $R_f = 100 \ \Omega$. The answers are shown in Figures D12.1 and D12.2.

D12.1

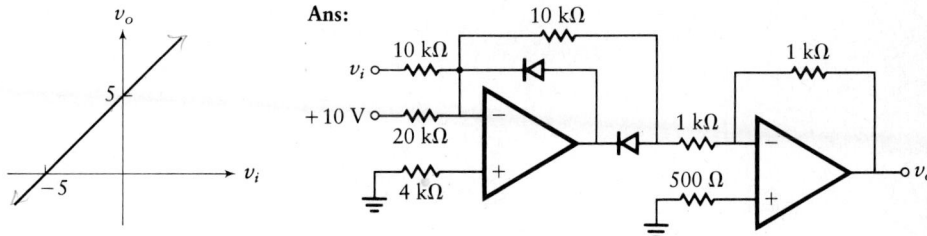

Figure D12.1

D12.2

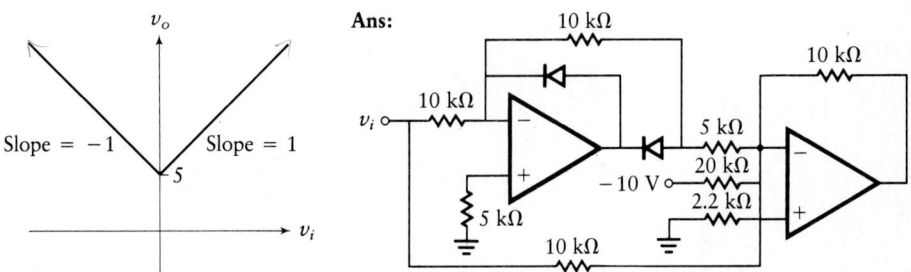

Figure D12.2

Find approximate relationships between the input voltages, v_1 and v_2, and the output voltage, v_o, for each of the circuits shown. Assume that $V\gamma = 0.7$ V and that $R_f = 100 \ \Omega$. The answers are shown in Figures D12.3 and D12.4.

D12.3

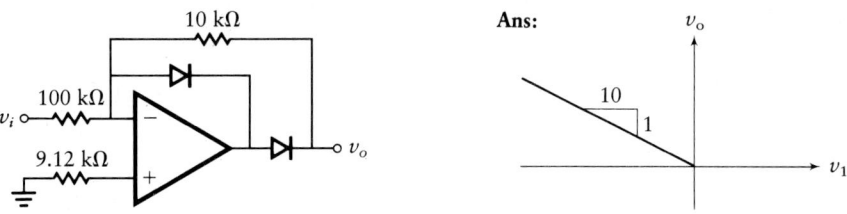

Figure D12.3

D12.4

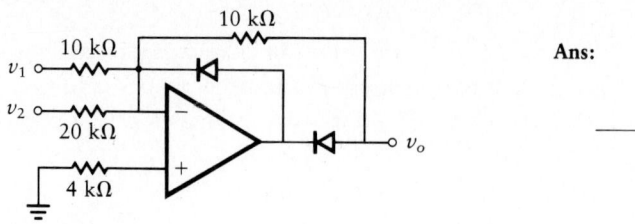

Figure D12.4

Ans: $v_i = v_1 + \frac{1}{2} v_2$

Example 12.2

A feedback limiter, as shown in Figure 12.5, has $R_A = 10\ k\Omega$, $R_F = 20\ k\Omega$, $R_1 = 4\ k\Omega$, $R_2 = 2\ k\Omega$, $V_{ref} = 10\ V$, $V\gamma = 0.7\ V$, and $R_f = 50\ \Omega$. Determine where the characteristic of v_o versus v_i changes slope and also find the slope in the saturation region (diode on).

SOLUTION   From the equations for the breakpoint, equations (12.6) and (12.7), we find

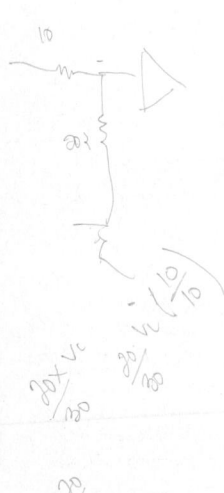

$$V_{oc} = \frac{-R_2 V_{ref}}{R_1} - \left[1 + \frac{R_2}{R_1}\right] V\gamma$$

$$= \frac{-2\ k\Omega \times 10}{4\ k\Omega} - \left[1 + \frac{2\ k\Omega}{4\ k\Omega}\right](0.7)$$

$$= -6.05$$

$$V_{ic} = \frac{R_A}{R_F}\left[\frac{R_2 V_{ref}}{R_1} + \left(1 + \frac{R_2}{R_1}\right)V\gamma\right]$$

$$= \left(\frac{10\ k\Omega}{20\ k\Omega}\right)\left[\frac{2\ k\Omega \times 10}{4\ k\Omega} + \left(1 + \frac{2\ k\Omega}{4\ k\Omega}\right)0.7\right]$$

$$= 3.02$$

The slope is given by equation (12.5) as follows:

$$\text{slope} = -\left(\frac{1}{R_A}\right)\left(1 + \frac{R_2}{R_1}\right)(R_1 \| R_2 + R_f)$$

$$= -\frac{1}{10\ k\Omega}\left(1 + \frac{2\ k\Omega}{4\ k\Omega}\right)(4\ k\Omega \| 2\ k\Omega + 50\ \Omega)$$

$$= -0.21$$

The v_o versus v_i characteristics are shown in Table 12.3 as the "Basic Lower Limit" limiter. Several additional limiter applications are included in Table 12.4.

Table 12.4 Limiter Applications.

1. TTL interface

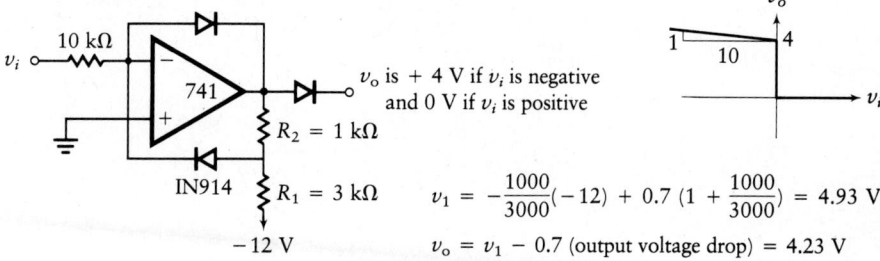

v_o is $+ 4$ V if v_i is negative
and 0 V if v_i is positive

$v_1 = -\dfrac{1000}{3000}(-12) + 0.7 \left(1 + \dfrac{1000}{3000}\right) = 4.93$ V

$v_o = v_1 - 0.7$ (output voltage drop) $= 4.23$ V

Other values of R_1 and R_2 will accommodate other reference voltages.

2. Inverting summation

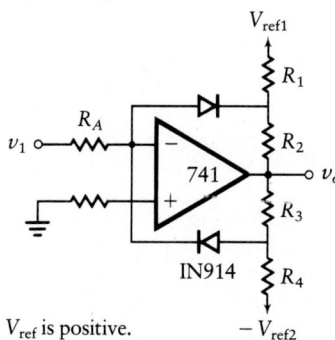

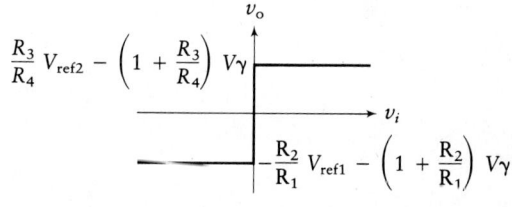

$\dfrac{R_3}{R_4} V_{ref2} - \left(1 + \dfrac{R_3}{R_4}\right) V\gamma$

$-\dfrac{R_2}{R_1} V_{ref1} - \left(1 + \dfrac{R_2}{R_1}\right) V\gamma$

V_{ref} is positive.

3. Adjustable saturation levels

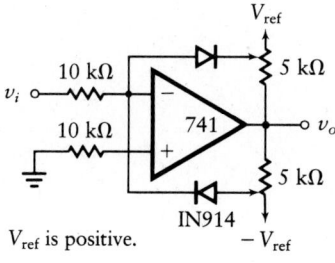

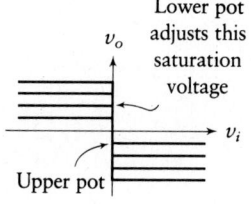

V_{ref} is positive.

Lower pot adjusts this saturation voltage

Upper pot

Similar to above, except the 5-kΩ potentiometer varies the ratio of the resistors. The effect is to adjust the upper and lower saturation voltages.

Table 12.4　Limiter Applications. (*Continued*)

4. Voltage-controlled saturation levels

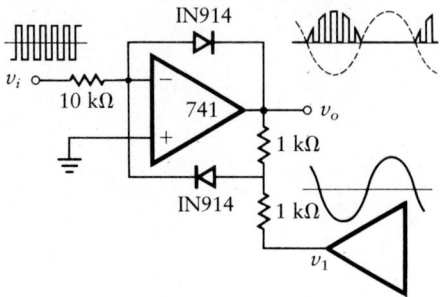

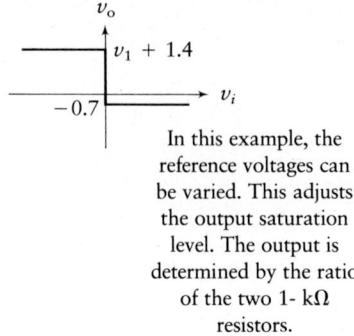

In this example, the reference voltages can be varied. This adjusts the output saturation level. The output is determined by the ratio of the two 1- kΩ resistors.

5. Input-axis shifting

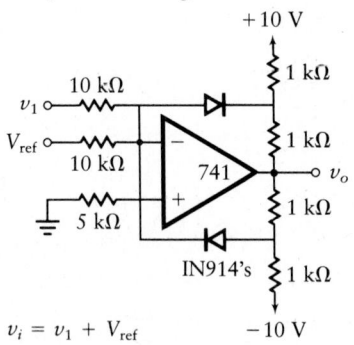

$v_i = v_1 + V_{ref}$

In this case, V_{ref} is added to v_1. This changes the value of v_1 that is required to swing from one saturation voltage to another.

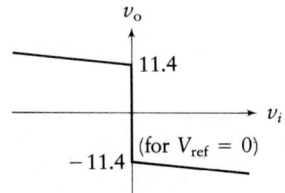

(for $V_{ref} = 0$)

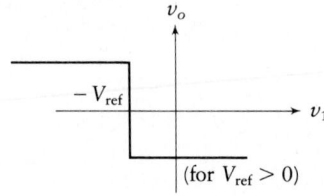

(for $V_{ref} > 0$)

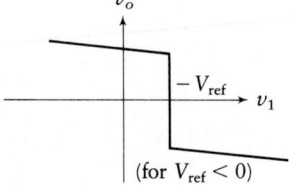

(for $V_{ref} < 0$)

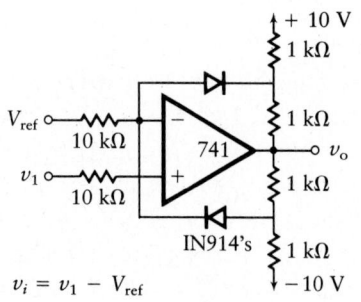

$v_i = v_1 - V_{ref}$

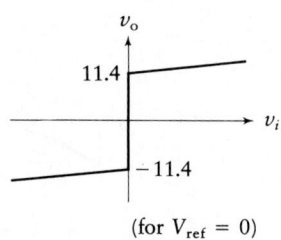

(for $V_{ref} = 0$)

Table 12.4 Limiter Applications. (*Continued*)

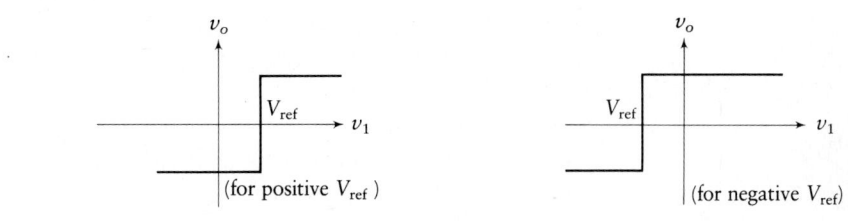

6. Voltage-controlled saturation levels

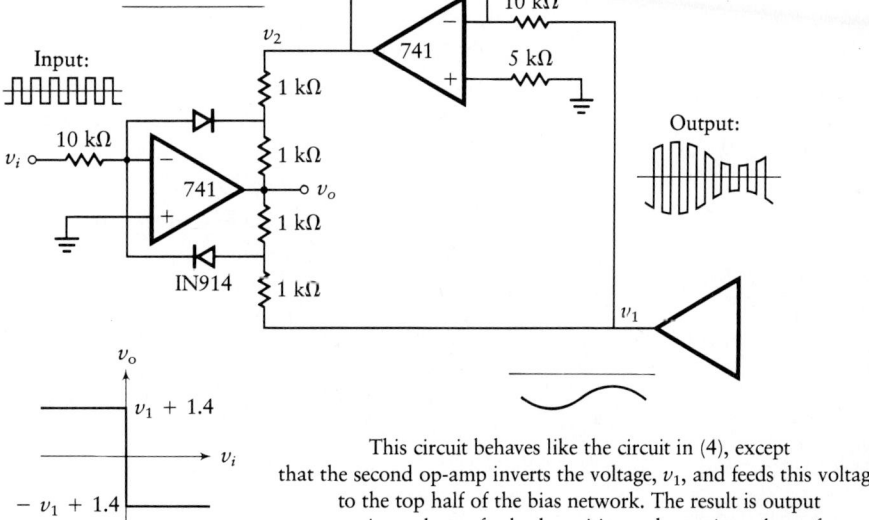

This circuit behaves like the circuit in (4), except that the second op-amp inverts the voltage, v_1, and feeds this voltage to the top half of the bias network. The result is output saturation voltages for both positive and negative values of v_1.

12.3 Comparators

It is frequently important to compare two voltages to determine which is the larger. As a simple application, consider an electronic thermostat where the temperature is converted to a voltage. When the voltage corresponding to the room temperature is less than that corresponding to the desired temperature (setting of thermostat), the system should produce a signal that turns on the heater. As a more complex application, one form of digital communication (delta modulation) requires that a continuous time signal be replaced by a staircase approximation. At each sampling point, the decision of whether the approximation should step up or step down is based upon a comparison of the staircase approximation with the original continuous function.

Since feedback control systems usually operate upon the difference between two signals (inverting and noninverting), comparators are ideally suited to these applications.

The output of one type of *comparator* is positive when the circuit voltage, v_i, is less than the reference voltage, V_{ref}. The output becomes negative when v_i is greater than V_{ref}. If the gain of the circuit is large, the output will saturate. That is, as soon as v_i becomes slightly below V_{ref}, the output rapidly changes to the positive supply voltage. Likewise, the voltage saturates at the negative supply voltage for any value of v_i greater than V_{ref}. Thus, the output takes on only one of two possible values: positive or negative.

When the input is varying around V_{ref}, there are transitions in the output whenever v_i crosses the V_{ref} axis. That is, at one instant, v_i is less than V_{ref}, and at the next instant, the reverse is true. Ideally, the output should instantaneously jump from its positive saturation value to its negative value. In practice, a small amount of response time is required due to capacitive effects in the circuit. A typical value of this response time is a few microseconds. For example, the 741 switches in about 40 μs.

The *accuracy* of a practical comparator is the voltage difference required between the input and reference to cause the output to change its state from one saturation value to the other.

Saturation comparators, which operate the op-amp in the open-loop mode, depend upon high open-loop gain to drive the op-amp into saturation. Figure 12.9 shows a 741 op-amp used in two saturating comparator configurations. Figures 12.10 and 12.11 show other comparator configurations that can be used to vary the *crossover* voltage.

A *limiting comparator* is formed with a diode as the feedback element, as shown in Figure 12.12(a). When the diode is open-circuited, the lack of feedback causes the op-amp to operate in the open-loop mode and to saturate for negative input voltages, and

$$v_o = \text{op-amp saturation voltage}$$

As v_i increases, the diode forward biases (turns on). This happens when v_i exceeds $(V_{ref} + V\gamma)$. The equivalent circuit for this condition is shown in Figure 12.12(b), where we neglect the diode forward resistance. That is, we assume

$$R_f << (R_1 \parallel R_2)$$

We also neglect the diode forward voltage, $V\gamma$.

We simplify the resulting circuit. The Thevenin equivalent voltage source yields a series resistance of $R_1 \parallel R_2$ and a Thevenin voltage of

$$v_{TH} = \left(\frac{V_{ref}}{R_1} + \frac{v_o}{R_2}\right)(R_1 \parallel R_2) \tag{12.8}$$

Figure 12.9
Saturation
comparator.

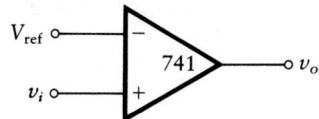

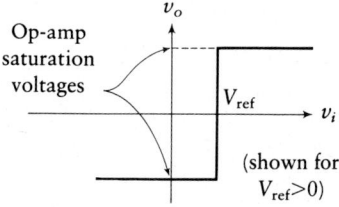

v_o high when $v_i > V_{ref}$
V_{ref} may be positive or negative

(a)

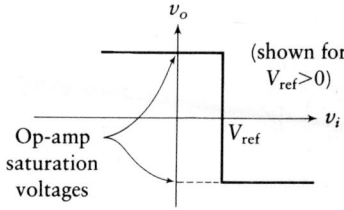

v_o high when $v_i < V_{ref}$
V_{ref} may be positive or negative

(b)

Figure 12.10
Variable crossover
comparator.

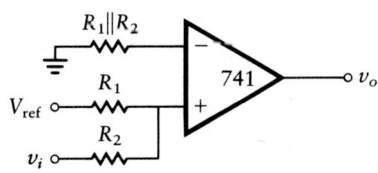

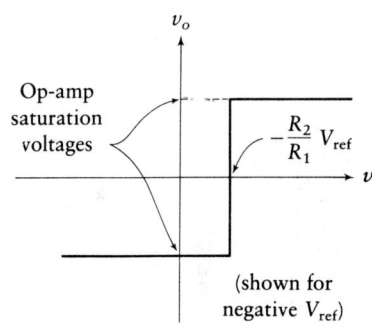

v_o high when $\dfrac{V_{ref}}{R_1} + \dfrac{v_i}{R_2} > 0$ or

$$v_i > -\frac{R_2}{R_1} V_{ref}$$

Either polarity of V_{ref} may be used

Figure 12.11
Variable crossover
comparator.

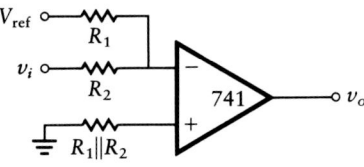

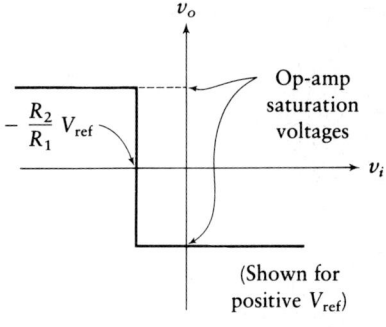

v_o high when $\dfrac{V_{ref}}{R_1} + \dfrac{v_i}{R_2} < 0$ or

$$v_i < -\frac{R_2}{R_1} V_{ref}$$

Either polarity of V_{ref} may be used

Figure 12.12
Limiting comparator.

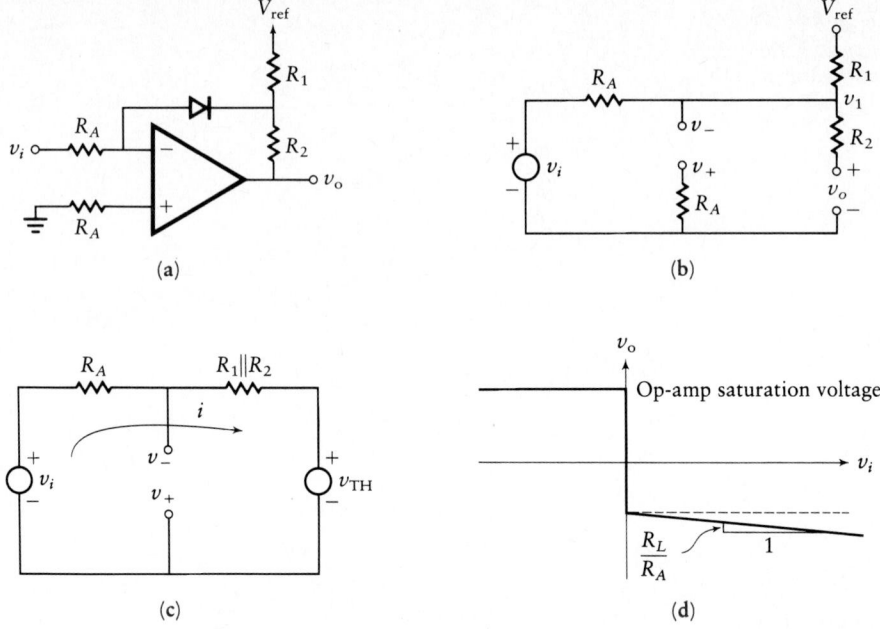

(a)

(b)

(c)

(d)

This is shown in the equivalent circuit of Figure 12.12(c). To determine the equations relating v_o to v_i, we use the equations

$$v_- = v_i - iR_A$$

$$= v_i - \frac{(v_i - v_{TH})R_A}{R_A + R_1 \| R_2} \tag{12.9}$$

and since

$$v_+ = v_-$$

we set the expression in equation (12.9) to zero and obtain

$$(R_1 \| R_2)v_i + v_{TH}R_A = 0$$

Replacing v_{TH} by the expression in equation (12.8) yields

$$0 = (R_1 \| R_2)v_i + V_{ref}\frac{R_2R_A}{R_1 + R_2} + v_o\frac{R_1R_A}{R_1 + R_2}$$

or

$$(R_1 \| R_2)v_i + V_{ref}\frac{R_2R_A}{R_1 + R_2} = \frac{-v_oR_1R_A}{R_1 + R_2}$$

Figure 12.13
Balanced limiting
comparator.

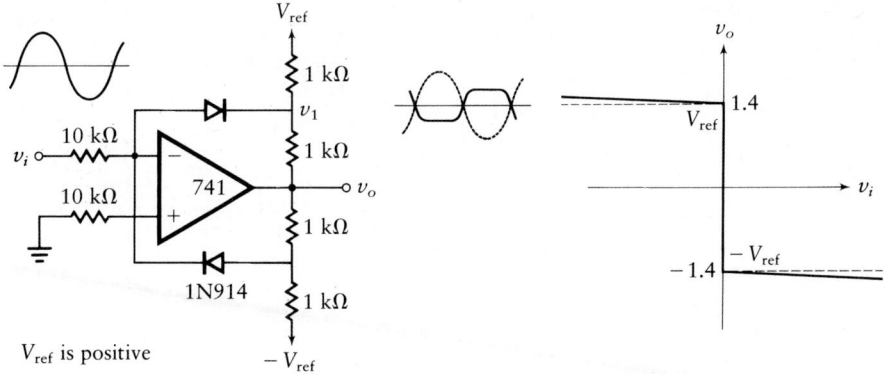

Solving for the output voltage yields

$$v_o = \frac{-R_2}{R_A} v_i - V_{ref} \frac{R_2}{R_1} \tag{12.10}$$

The slope of the curve, for positive input voltage, is given by

$$\frac{v_o}{v_i} = -\frac{R_2}{R_A}$$

The transfer characteristics for equation (12.10) are shown in Figure 12.12(d).
Note that the output voltage for an input of $v_i = V_{ref}$ is given by

$$-R_2 V_{ref} \left(\frac{1}{R_A} + \frac{1}{R_1} \right)$$

The limiter described here is not *balanced*, since the switching transfer characteristics are not symmetrical. We can modify the circuit to provide for balanced operation. The transfer characteristic for the resulting balanced positive and negative limiter is shown in Figure 12.13. The analysis is performed in a manner similar to that used for the unbalanced limiter.

Drill Problems

Design 741 circuits with the following approximate transfer characteristics. Available reference supply voltages are ± 10 V. Op-amp supply voltages are ±15 V. Assume that $V\gamma = 0.7$ V. The answers are shown in Figures D12.5 and D12.6.

D12.5

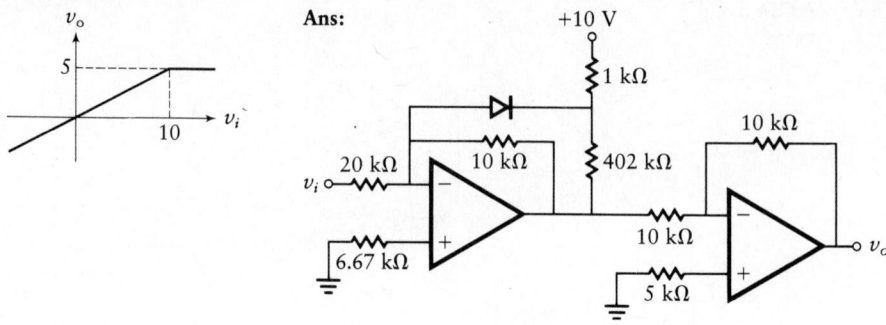

Figure D12.5

D12.6

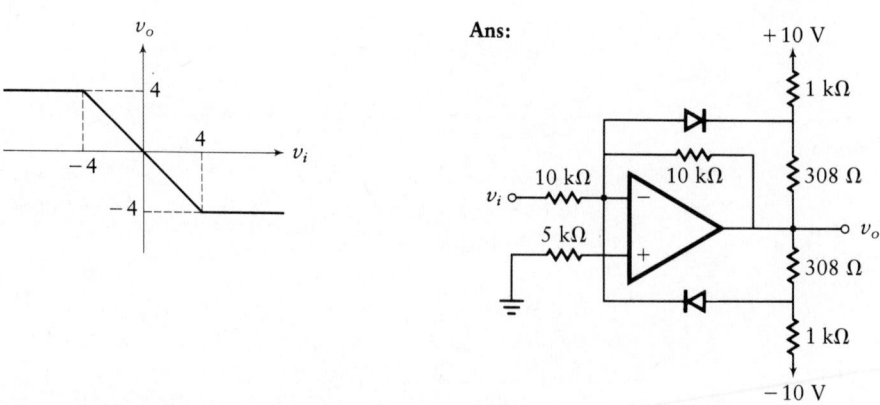

Figure D12.6

Find approximate relationships between the input voltage, v_i, and the output voltage, v_o, for the circuits shown. Assume that $V\gamma = 0.7$ V. The answers are shown in Figures D12.7 and D12.8.

D12.7

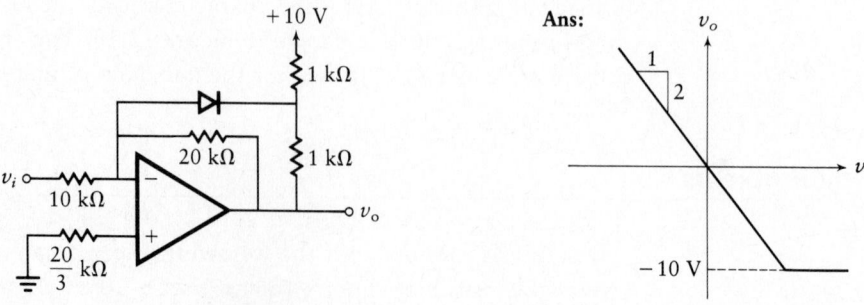

Figure D12.7

D12.8

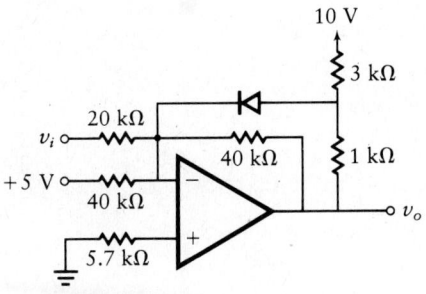

Ans:

Figure D12.8

Example 12.3

Design a limiter that will provide limiting at $v_o = \pm 6$ V with a gain of -4 and a slope in the saturation region of $-\frac{1}{25}$. Assume that $V_{ref} = \pm 10$ V, $V\gamma = 0.7$ V and $R_f = 100$ Ω.

SOLUTION The number of constraints is one less than the number of unknown component values. Let us select $R_A = 10$ kΩ. If this leads to unreasonable values of other components, we will return and revise our selection. Solving for the other parameters,

$$R_F = 40 \text{ k}\Omega$$

$$V_{oc} = 6 = \frac{R_2 V_{ref}}{R_1} + \left(1 + \frac{R_2}{R_1}\right) V\gamma$$

$$6 = \frac{R_2 \times 10}{R_1} + \left(1 + \frac{R_2}{R_1}\right) 0.7$$

Finally,

$$\frac{R_2}{R_1} = 0.495$$

which represents one equation in R_1 and R_2. The slope is $-\frac{1}{25}$, which yields

$$-\frac{1}{25} = -\left(1 + \frac{R_2}{R_1}\right) \frac{(R_1 \| R_2 + R_f)}{R_A}$$

This is a second equation in R_1 and R_2, which we solve for the resistor values as follows:

$$R_2 = 250 \ \Omega$$

$$R_1 = 505 \ \Omega$$

The final circuit is of the type shown in Table 12.3 for "Upper and Lower Limiting."

Example 12.4

Design a balanced limiting comparator of the type shown in Figure 12.13 with limiting required at ± 8 V and the slope of the limited part of the characteristic to be $-\frac{1}{20}$. Assume that $V_{ref} = \pm 10$ V, $R_A = 10$ kΩ, $V\gamma = 0.7$ V and $R_f = 100 \ \Omega$.

SOLUTION We use the equations of this section to find

$$V_{oc} = 8 = V\gamma\left(1 + \frac{R_2}{R_1}\right) + \frac{V_{ref}R_2}{R_1}$$

$$8 = 0.7\left(1 + \frac{R_2}{R_1}\right) + \frac{10R_2}{R_1}$$

Then

$$\frac{R_2}{R_1} = 0.682$$

which represents one equation in two unknowns. The second equation comes from the given slope. That is,

$$-\frac{1}{20} = -\frac{(1 + R_2/R_1)(R_f + R_1 \parallel R_2)}{R_A}$$

Finally, solving for the two resistor values yields

$$R_2 = 332 \ \Omega$$

$$R_1 = 486 \ \Omega$$

The design is complete.

12.4 Schmitt Triggers

One class of comparator, known as the *Schmitt trigger,* uses positive feedback to speed up the switching cycle. This increases the gain and therefore steepens the transition between the two output levels. Positive feedback holds a comparator in one of the two saturation states unless a sufficiently large input is applied to overcome the feedback.

Figure 12.14(a) illustrates one form of Schmitt trigger, where a reference voltage of 0 is implied, since $v_- = 0$. We use Figure 12.14(a) to develop the characteristic curves. We start with v_i as a large positive voltage. This causes the output voltage, v_o, to be at $+E$, the op-amp saturation voltage. The non-inverting voltage, v_+, is calculated by writing a node equation at the v_+ node as follows:

$$\frac{v_+ - v_i}{R_1} + \frac{v_+ - v_o}{R_2} = 0 \qquad = \frac{V_+}{R_1} - \frac{V_i}{R_1}$$

so

$$v_+ \left(\frac{1}{R_1} + \frac{1}{R_2} \right) = \frac{v_i}{R_1} + \frac{v_o}{R_2} \tag{12.11}$$

We start reducing the magnitude of v_i to find the switching point. Since $v_- = 0$ and $v_+ = v_-$ (once the op-amp comes out of saturation), we set the above equation to zero to obtain

$$v_i = \frac{-R_1 v_o}{R_2} = \frac{-R_1 E}{R_2} \tag{12.12}$$

As v_i is reduced from a large positive voltage, the output voltage, v_o, is switched from $+E$ to $-E$ at the point where v_+ goes to 0. This happens at the point when v_i reaches $-R_1 E/R_2$. As the input voltage, v_i, is reduced further, v_o remains at $-E$.

If we now increase the input voltage from a large negative value, the output voltage will switch to $+E$ when $v_+ = 0 = v_-$. Hence, the switching takes place at

$$v_i = \frac{-R_1 v_o}{R_2} = \frac{-R_1(-E)}{R_2} = \frac{+R_1 E}{R_2} \tag{12.13}$$

v_o will remain at $+E$ as v_i is further increased past $+R_1 E/R_2$.

Figure 12.14
Schmitt trigger.

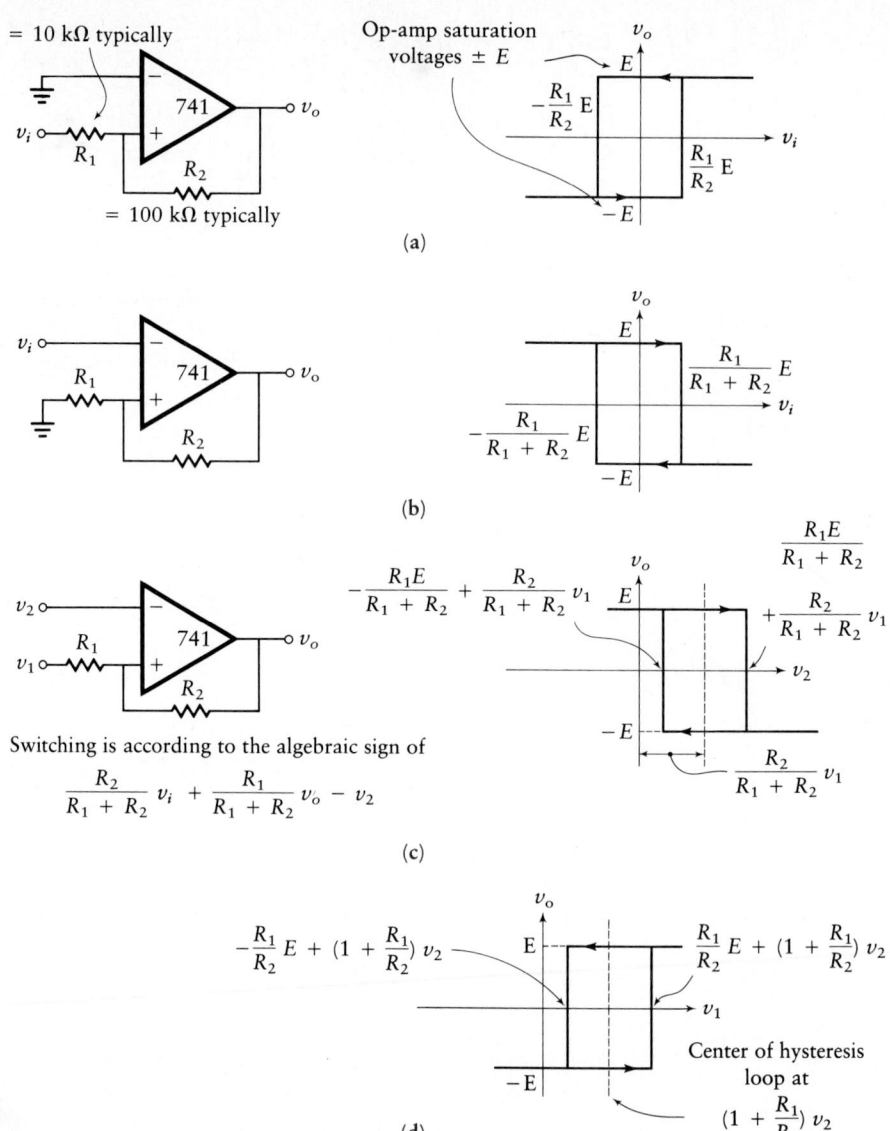

(a)

(b)

Switching is according to the algebraic sign of

$$\frac{R_2}{R_1 + R_2} \, v_i + \frac{R_1}{R_1 + R_2} \, v_o - v_2$$

(c)

(d)

The loop shown in the characteristic curve of Figure 12.14(a) is a form of *hysteresis*. This word is used to describe a situation where the system has *memory*. That is, the output at any particular time does not depend only upon the present value of the input but also upon past values. For example, for an input voltage of $v_i = 0$, there are two possible values of v_o, depending on the direction in which we approach $v_i = 0$.

This observation about hysteresis indicates one important application of the Schmitt trigger. This circuit can be used as a *binary memory device*. That is, since the output depends upon past values of the input, we can apply a voltage to the input and then remove that voltage. The trigger circuit remembers whether the voltage was above or below the reference level. We can therefore write one of two possible values into this memory.

A second important application of the Schmitt trigger is as a square-wave generator. A slow-moving continuous signal at the input (e.g., a sine wave) produces an output that rapidly jumps between two levels. The jump occurs as the input moves across the reference level. In this manner, a pulse-type waveform can be generated from a continuous input.

The inverting Schmitt trigger of Figure 12.14(b) interchanges the ground and the input voltages at the op-amp input. It is analyzed in a manner similar to that applied above. The switching point is found from the equations

$$v_- = v_i$$

$$v_+ = \frac{R_1 v_o}{R_1 + R_2}$$

The states switch when the two voltages are equal, so

$$v_i = \frac{R_1 v_o}{R_1 + R_2}$$

When $v_o = +E$ and v_i is increasing from a large negative voltage toward a positive voltage, the switching point occurs at

$$v_i = \frac{R_1 v_o}{R_1 + R_2} = \frac{R_1 E}{R_1 + R_2}$$

If $v_o = -E$ and v_i is decreasing from a large positive voltage toward a negative voltage, the switching point occurs at

$$v_i = \frac{-R_1 E}{R_1 + R_2}$$

The circuit of Figure 12.14(c) replaces the ground of the v_+ input of Figure 12.14(b) with a reference voltage v_1. The second voltage, v_2, is the input voltage. The equations are derived in the same manner as those just derived and are included along with the hysteresis curve on the figure. Note that the entire characteristic is shifted to the right, so it is no longer symmetrical about the origin. You should verify these results before continuing.

The same circuit can be viewed in a different manner when v_2 is the reference and v_1 is the input (assume a series input resistor is present). This then represents a variation of the circuit of Figure 12.14(a), where the ground input to v_- is replaced by the v_2 reference. The curve of Figure 12.14(d) results.

Example 12.5

Determine the output voltage from the Schmitt trigger of Figure 12.14(a). The input voltage is

$$v_i = 20 \sin 200\pi t$$

$E = 5$ V, $R_1 = 20$ kΩ, and $R_2 = 100$ kΩ.

SOLUTION   The hysteresis curve for these values is plotted in Figure 12.15(a). When an input sinusoid, $v_i = 20 \sin 200\pi t$, is applied to the Schmitt trigger of Figure 12.15(a), a square wave results. Figure 12.15(b) shows the input sinusoid (shown as a solid line) and the output pulse train (shown as a dashed line). The peak-to-peak voltage is 10 V and the zero crossing is offset by ±1 V because of the hysteresis loop of Figure 12.15(a).

Figure 12.15
Schmitt trigger output for Example 12.5.

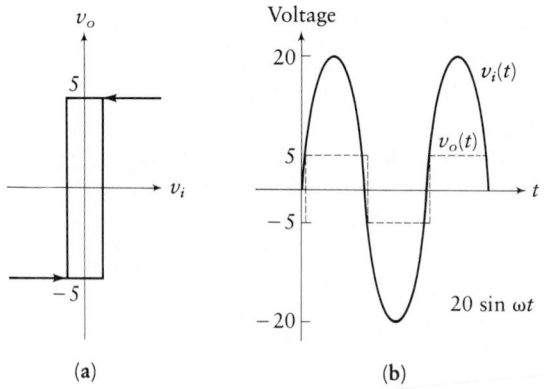

(a)   (b)

12.4.1 *Schmitt Triggers with Limiters*

The limiting comparator, which is studied in Section 12.3, can be used in conjunction with any of the Schmitt triggers of Figure 12.14. In so doing, the op-amp saturation voltage, E, which is not very accurate, is replaced with an accurate voltage, V_{ref}. Figure 12.16(a) illustrates an unbalanced limiting comparator. The diode D_1 controls the lower saturation point, and D_2 controls the upper saturation point. The resulting characteristic curve is shown in Figure 12.16(b).

Using this configuration, the saturation voltages, $\pm E$, are replaced with the limiting voltages shown on the figure.

As an example of the use of a limiter with a Schmitt trigger, consider the

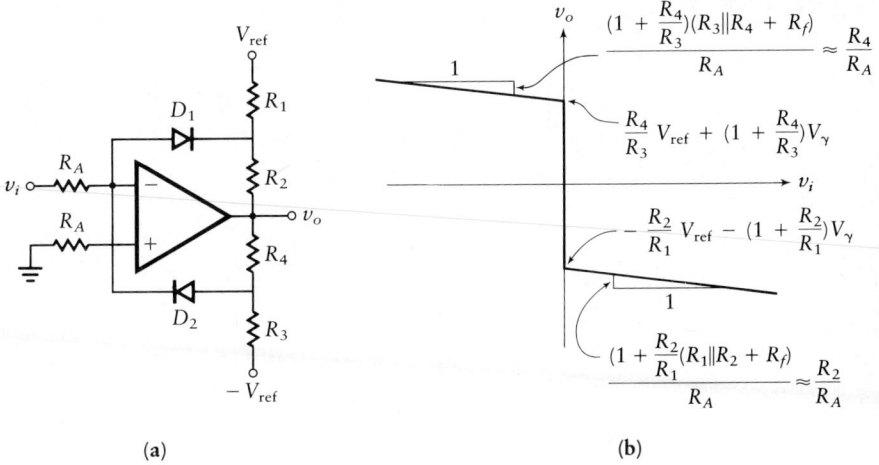

Figure 12.16
Unbalanced limiting
comparator.

(a)   (b)

circuit of Figure 12.17. These circuits use positive feedback to achieve the faster switching action required for a Schmitt trigger but with the limits of the voltage output curve determined by V_{ref}.

When a dc voltage is placed at one input of a Schmitt trigger, it causes the hysteresis loop to move along the v_i-axis. This is shown by using Figure 12.14(c) with v_1 as a dc reference voltage and v_2 as v_i. KCL is used to derive

$$\frac{v_1 - v_+}{R_1} + \frac{v_o - v_+}{R_2} = 0$$

so

$$v_+\left(\frac{1}{R_1} + \frac{1}{R_2}\right) = \frac{v_1}{R_1} + \frac{v_o}{R_2}$$

Since the op-amp is operating in its linear region until v_o reaches *rail* voltage (the rail voltage is the $\pm V_{CC}$ applied to the op-amp),

$$v_+ = v_- = v_2$$

Thus,

$$v_2 = \frac{R_2 v_1}{R_1 + R_2} + \frac{R_1 v_o}{R_1 + R_2}$$

$$v_1 = V_{ref}$$

$$v_2 = v_i$$

Figure 12.17
Schmitt trigger with limited values.

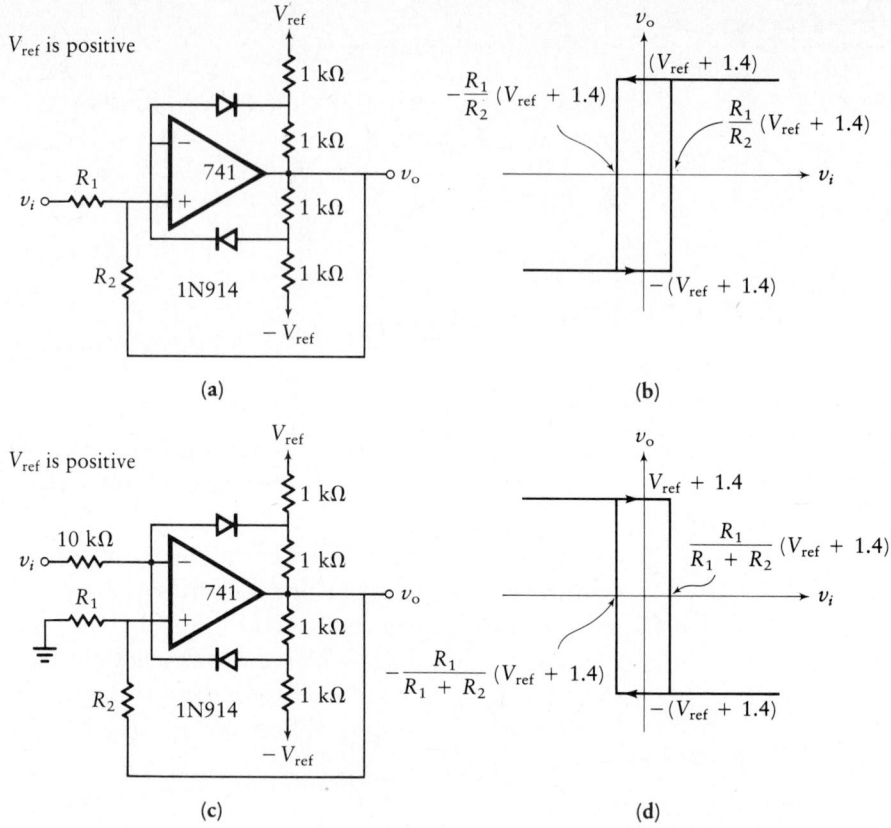

Since positive feedback has caused the amplifier to drive to the rail voltage, E, then $v_o = E$ and

$$v_i = \frac{R_2 V_{ref}}{R_1 + R_2} + \frac{R_1 E}{R_1 + R_2}$$

When switched to the negative rail, $v_o = -E$ and

$$v_2 = \frac{R_2 V_{dc}}{R_1 + R_2} - \frac{R_1 E}{R_1 + R_2}$$

In this manner, the hysteresis loop is moved along the v_i axis as shown in Figure 12.14(c). To move the hysteresis loop up and down the v_o axis, a dc voltage is added at the output of the Schmitt trigger.

Drill Problems

Design op-amp circuits with the following approximate transfer characteristics. Reference supplies available are ± 10 V. Op-amp supply voltages are ± 15 V. The answers are shown in Figures D12.9 and D12.10. Assume $V\gamma = 0.7$ V and $R_f = 100\ \Omega$.

D12.9

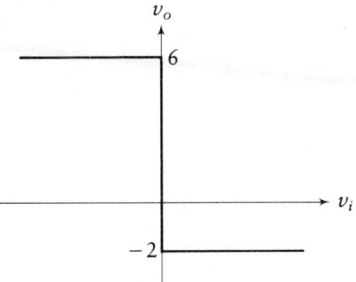

Figure D12.9

Ans:

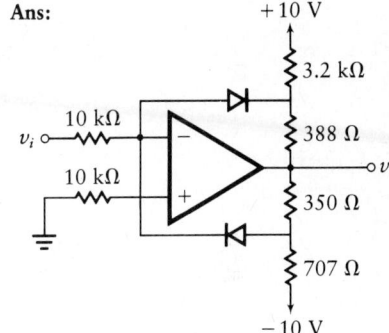

D12.10

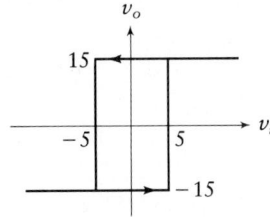

Figure D12.10

Ans:

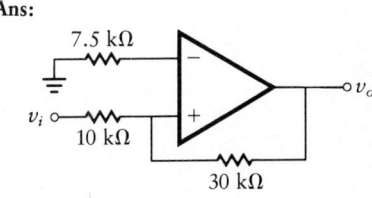

Find approximate relationships between the input voltage v_i and the output voltage v_o in each circuit shown. The answers are shown in Figures D12.11 and D12.12.

D12.11

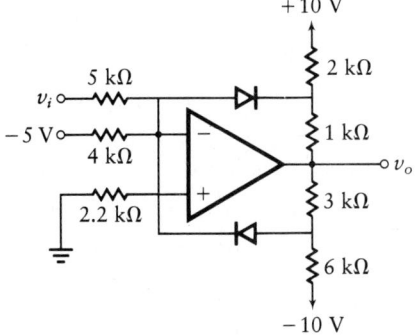

Figure D12.11

Ans:

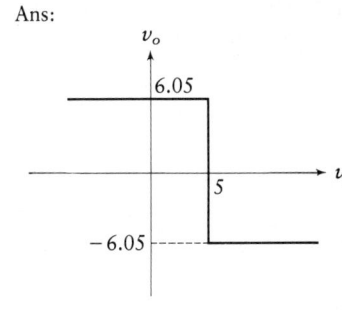

D12.12

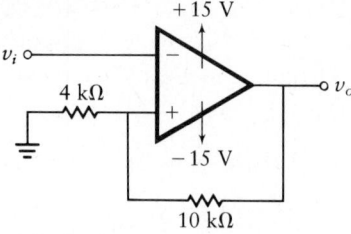

Ans:

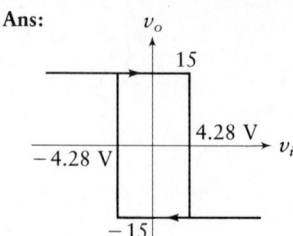

Figure D12.12

Example 12.6

Design an unbalanced limiter comparator of the type shown in Figure 12.16. Limiting should occur at $+6$ V and -4 V, with the slope of the limiting characteristic as $-\frac{1}{25}$. Assume $V_{\text{ref}} = 10$ V, $R_A = 10$ kΩ, $V\gamma = 0.7$ V, and $R_f = 100$ Ω.

SOLUTION   Using equations from this chapter, we find

$$V_{oc} = +6 = V\gamma\left(1 + \frac{R_2}{R_1}\right) + \frac{V_{\text{ref}}R_2}{R_1}$$

$$= 0.7\left(1 + \frac{R_2}{R_1}\right) + \frac{10R_2}{R_1}$$

Solving for R_2/R_1 yields

$$\frac{R_2}{R_1} = 0.495$$

The slope requirement provides us with the second equation in R_1 and R_2.

$$-\frac{1}{25} = \frac{-(1 + R_2/R_1)(100 + R_1 \| R_2)}{10 \text{ k}\Omega}$$

Solving for R_1 and R_2, we obtain:

$$R_2 = 250 \ \Omega$$

$$R_1 = 505 \ \Omega$$

Note that this first part of the design parallels that of Example 12.3. We now solve for the remaining two resistors.

$$V_{oc} = -4 = -V\gamma \left(1 + \frac{R_4}{R_3}\right) - \frac{V_{ref}R_4}{R_3}$$

$$\frac{R_4}{R_3} = 0.308$$

The second equation in R_3 and R_4 comes from the slope requirement,

$$-\frac{1}{25} = \frac{-(1 + R_4/R_3)(100 + R_3 \| R_4)}{10 \text{ k}\Omega}$$

Solving for the resistances, we obtain:

$$R_4 = 269 \ \Omega$$
$$R_3 = 873 \ \Omega$$

PROBLEMS

Find approximate relationships between the input voltages v_1 and v_2 and the output voltage v_o in each of the circuits of Problems 12.1–12.4. Assume $V\gamma = 0.7$ V and $R_f = 100 \ \Omega$.

12.1

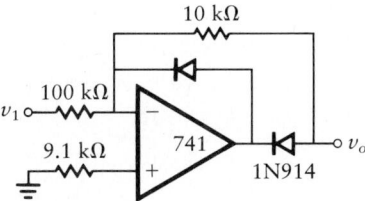

Figure P12.1

12.2

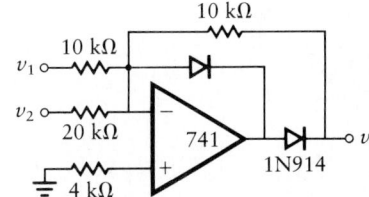

Figure P12.2

12.3

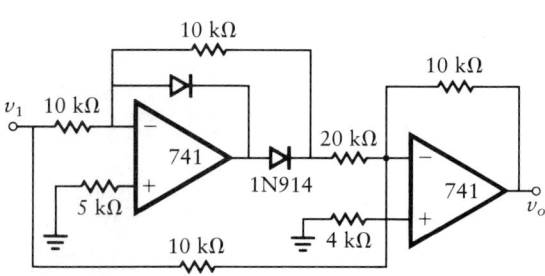

Figure P12.3

12.4

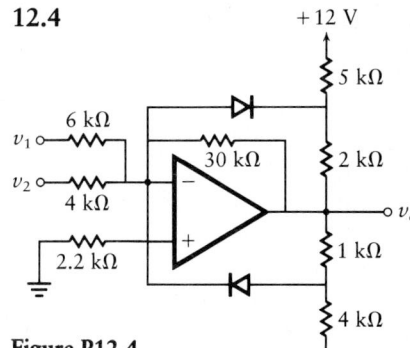

Figure P12.4

Design circuits with the approximate transfer characteristics shown in Problems 12.5–12.11. Reference supplies of $+10$ V and -10 V are available. Assume that $V_\gamma = 0.7$ V and $R_f = 100$ Ω.

12.5

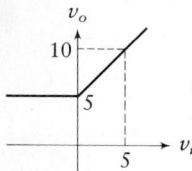

Figure P12.5

12.6

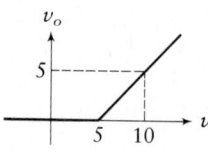

Figure P12.6

12.7

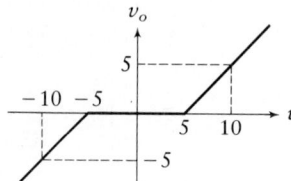

Figure P12.7

12.8

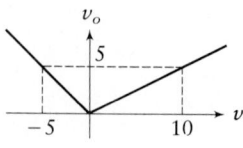

Figure P12.8

12.9

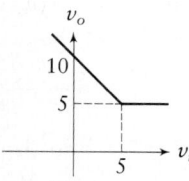

Figure P12.9

12.10

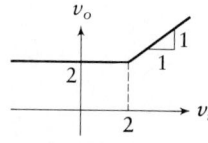

Figure P12.10

12.11

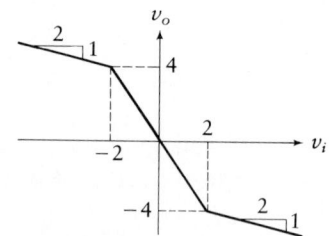

Figure P12.11

Find approximate relationships between the input voltages v_1 and v_2 and the output voltage v_o in each of the circuits shown in Problems 12.12–12.15. Assume that $V_\gamma = 0.7$ V and $R_f = 100$ Ω.

12.12

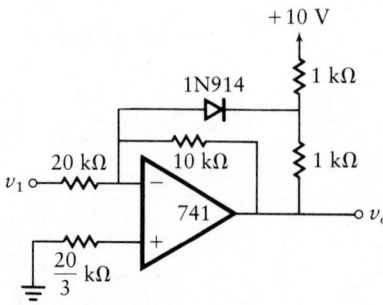

Figure P12.12

12.13

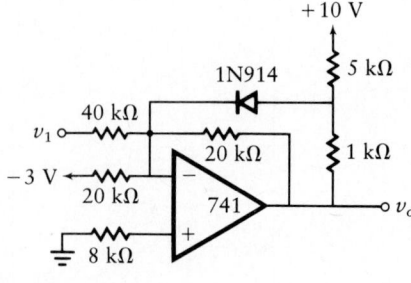

Figure P12.13

12.14

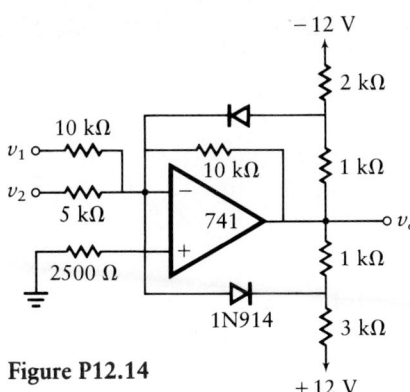

Figure P12.14

12.15

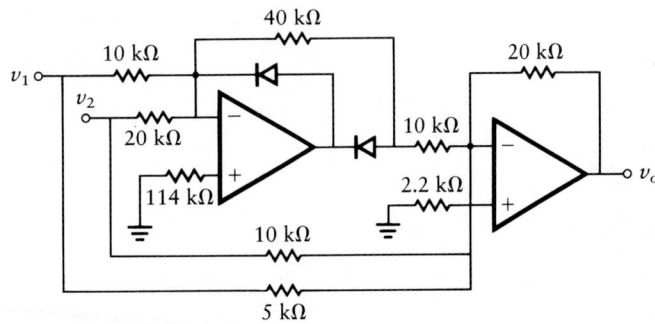

Figure P12.15

Design 741 circuits with the approximate transfer characteristics shown in Problems 12.16–12.22. Reference supplies of ± 10 V are available. Op-amp supply voltages are ± 15 V. Assume that $V\gamma = 0.7$ V and $R_f = 100$ Ω.

12.16

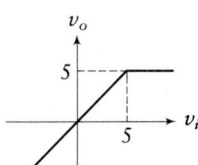

Figure P12.16

12.17

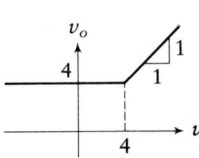

Figure P12.17

12.18

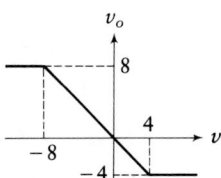

Figure P12.18

12.19

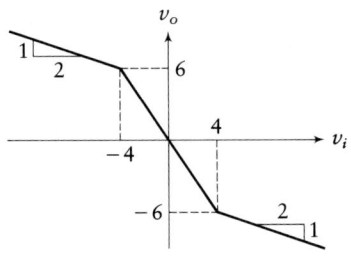

Figure P12.19

12.20

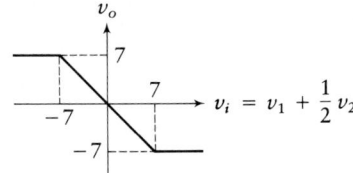

Figure P12.20

12.21

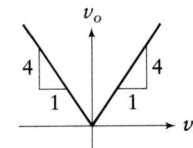

Figure P12.21

12.22

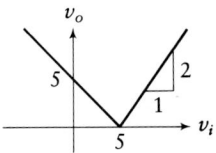

Figure P12.22

Find approximate relationships between the input voltages v_1 and v_2 and the output voltage v_o in each of the circuits shown in Problems 12.23–12.26. Assume that $V\gamma = 0.7$ V and $R_f = 100$ Ω.

12.23

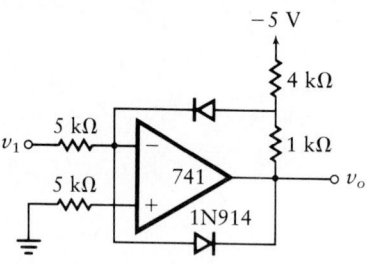

Figure P12.23

12.24

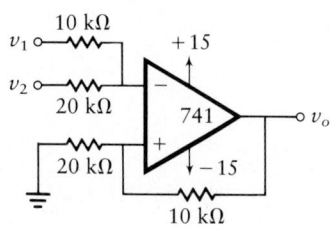

Figure P12.24

12.25

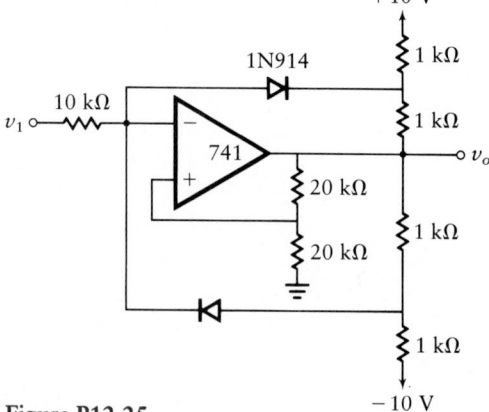

Figure P12.25

12.26

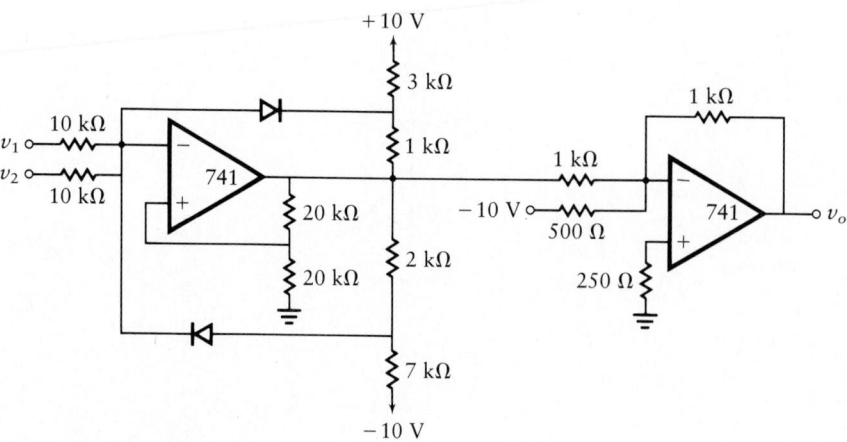

Figure P12.26

Design 741 circuits with the approximate transfer characteristics shown in Problems 12.27–12.33. Reference supplies of ±10 V are available. Op-amp supply voltages are ±15 V. Assume $V\gamma = 0.7$ V and $R_f = 100$ Ω.

12.27

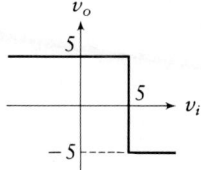

Figure P12.27

12.28

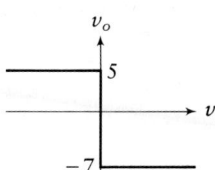

Figure P12.28

12.29

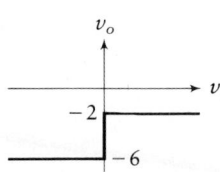

Figure P12.29

12.30

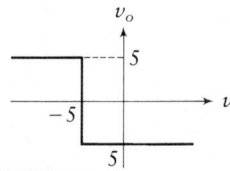

Figure P12.30

12.31

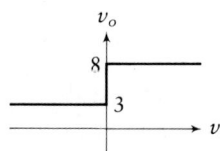

Figure P12.31

12.32

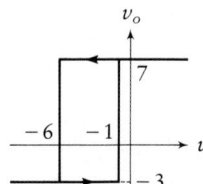

Figure P12.32

12.33

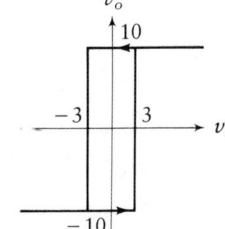

Figure P12.33

13

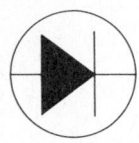

ACTIVE FILTERS

Introduction

You are employed by a company that designs and manufactures video games. The company has just embarked upon manufacturing a new generation of games coupling compact-disc technology with traditional microprocessor-controlled video games. The pioneer entry into this market is a game that has been named "The Colonization of Mars." This couples actual footage of film taken on the surface of Mars with superimposed images of the actual player of the game. The Federal Communications Commission (FCC) must license the game since video signals of the player are transmitted from a small remote camera to the game module. Unfortunately, the FCC refused approval due to spurious signals. They claimed your transmitter was interfering with signals in adjacent frequency bands. Your company has given you a small budget to eliminate the problem as quickly as possible since firm orders for the game (at fixed price) must be filled within 30 days.

Having taken undergraduate courses in network synthesis, you muster your knowledge and design a filter that meets the FCC specifications for reducing out-of-band transmissions. However, the specifications are so stiff that your filter requires a large number of components. Since components are inexpensive, this did not bother you until you became aware of the "real estate" problem. That is, the expense of the components is not so much the problem as is the space to house them. Alas, after searching your storehouse of experience and knowledge, you cannot come up with a solution. Another engineer working for the same company asks you if you considered active filters. Indeed, you have not. The current chapter will help you correct this deficiency in your background and will give you the tools to solve the problem just described.

A *filter* is a system designed to achieve a desired transfer characteristic. That is, it operates upon an input signal (or signals) in a predetermined manner. *Passive linear filters* are normally considered as part of a study of circuits, networks, or linear systems. They are composed of combinations of resistors, inductors, and capacitors. Although it is possible to achieve a wide variety of transfer characteristics using these elements, a large number of components is often required. This leads us to explore alternatives to passive filters.

Active filters contain amplifiers, which permit the design of a wide range of transfer functions (within some broad restrictions relating to the properties of the transfer function).

The practical details of active filters are presented in this chapter. Integrators and differentiators are first considered, followed by first- and second-order active filters. The important concepts of transfer function, impulse response, frequency response, and filter classification are developed.

The low-pass, high-pass, band-pass, and band-stop filters are then discussed. Transfer functions are analyzed prior to presentation of actual filter circuits. A general configuration is presented and then adapted to the various types of filters.

Section 13.6 explores classical analog filters. In particular, the Butterworth and Chebyshev filters are analyzed. Practical design techniques are presented throughout the chapter.

13.1   Integrators and Differentiators

A simple two-element passive circuit can approximate an integrator or differentiator. For example, a series RC circuit can perform this function. Figure 13.1 illustrates an RC circuit with a voltage source applied.

Figure 13.1
RC circuit.

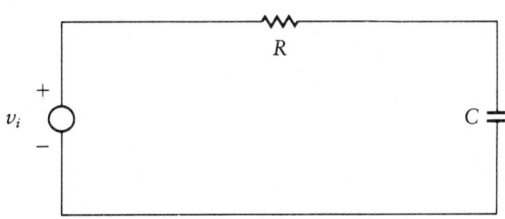

The current in a capacitor is proportional to the derivative of the voltage across the capacitor. The circuit acts as a differentiator if the resistance, R, is made small compared to the capacitive impedance, $1/\omega C$, at the frequencies of interest. The input voltage is then almost equal to the capacitor voltage, since the voltage across R is small. The current is therefore approximately equal to the derivative of the input voltage. The output is taken across the resistor, so it is approximately proportional to the derivative of the input voltage.

In order to approximate an integrator, the opposite approach is used. That is, we want the current in the circuit to be proportional to the input voltage. This is achieved by making the resistance predominate over the capacitive impedance. Since the voltage across a capacitor is proportional to the integral of the current through it, the output is taken across the capacitor.

This passive circuit approximates the operations of differentiation and integration, and the approximation gets better as the impedance of one of the elements is made much smaller than that of the other. Unfortunately, as this impedance gets smaller, the magnitude of the output voltage also gets smaller.

Considerable improvement of performance is possible if we switch from passive to active circuits. Let us begin our study with the basic op-amp of Figure 13.2(a). The gain of this op-amp is given by equation (13.1), where Z_F is the impedance in the feedback path and Z_A is the impedance between the source and the inverting input terminal.

$$\frac{V_o}{V_i} = -\frac{Z_F}{Z_A} \qquad (13.1)$$

The Laplace transform operator notation for an integrator is $1/s$. Therefore, if we choose impedances that make the right side of equation (13.1) proportional to $1/s$, we have accomplished integration. For example, if Z_F is the impedance of a capacitor and Z_A is that of a resistor, the gain takes the desired form.

Figure 13.2   Op-amp circuits.

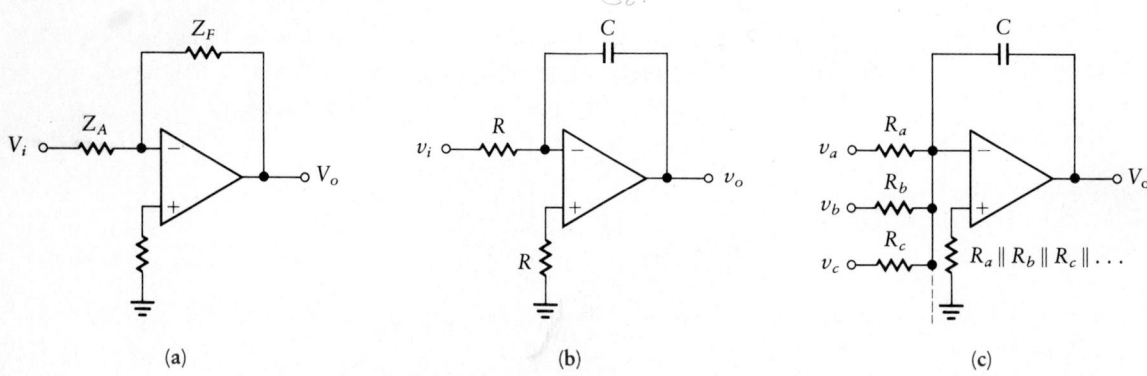

(a)   (b)   (c)

Figure 13.2(b) shows one form of the integrator. The behavior of this circuit is described by the following equation:

$$V_o(s) = -\left(\frac{1}{sCR}\right) V_i(s)$$

When this operator notation equation is converted to the time domain, we obtain

$$v_o(t) = -\left(\frac{1}{RC}\right) \int_0^t v_i(\tau) \, d\tau \tag{13.2}$$

The above analysis makes this active filter appear to be a perfect integrator. Of course, we are using the ideal model for the op-amp, so this is still an approximation. However, this active circuit yields a much better approximation to an integrator than can be achieved with passive circuits. Another advantage of using op-amps is due to their ability to easily sum inputs.

A *summing inverting integrator* is illustrated in Figure 13.2(c). This configuration yields the following equations:

$$V_o(s) = -\frac{1}{s}\left[\frac{V_a(s)}{R_a C} + \frac{V_b(s)}{R_b C} + \cdots\right] \tag{13.3}$$

In the time domain, this becomes

$$v_o(t) = -\int_0^t \left[\frac{v_a(\tau)}{R_a C} + \frac{v_b(\tau)}{R_b C} + \cdots\right] d\tau$$

It is easy to form differences between input signals when op-amps are used in the circuits. A *differencing integrator* is shown in Figure 13.3. The equations are obtained by finding V_- and V_+ and then equating them, as follows:

$$V_- = \frac{(V_o - V_1)R}{R + 1/sC} + V_1$$

$$= \frac{RCsV_o + V_1}{RCs + 1}$$

$$V_+ = \frac{1/Cs}{R + 1/Cs} V_2 = \frac{RCsV_o + V_1}{RCs + 1}$$

Note that we are using uppercase notation, since the voltages are functions of s. Since $G \to \infty$, $V_+ = V_-$,

Figure 13.3
Differencing
integrator.

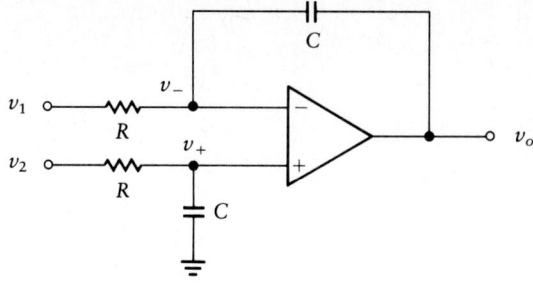

$$V_o = \frac{V_2 - V_1}{RCs} \tag{13.4}$$

and in the time domain,

$$v_o(t) = \left(\frac{1}{RC}\right) \int_0^t [v_2(t) - v_1(t)] \, dt$$

The components R and C are chosen to achieve the required dc gain.

If the capacitor and resistor of the previous circuit are interchanged, the result is the *basic differentiator*, as shown in Figure 13.4(a). Since $V_+ = V_- = 0$, we write a node equation at the inverting terminal of the op-amp, yielding

$$\frac{V_i}{1/Cs} = \frac{-V_o}{R}$$

and

$$V_o = \frac{-RV_i}{1/sC} = -RCsV_i \tag{13.5}$$

In the time domain, equation (13.5) becomes

$$v_o(t) = -RC \frac{dv_i(t)}{dt}$$

Differentiation circuits are not often used. One of the reasons for this is the effect the circuit has upon random noise. Integration is a smoothing process, whereas differentiation has the opposite effect. For example, if noise spikes are present, differentiation leads to higher spikes because of the presence of large slopes in the noise voltage waveform.

As with integrators, we can sum or take the difference between inputs. A *differencing differentiator* is shown in Figure 13.4(b). The equations describing

Figure 13.4
Differentiator.

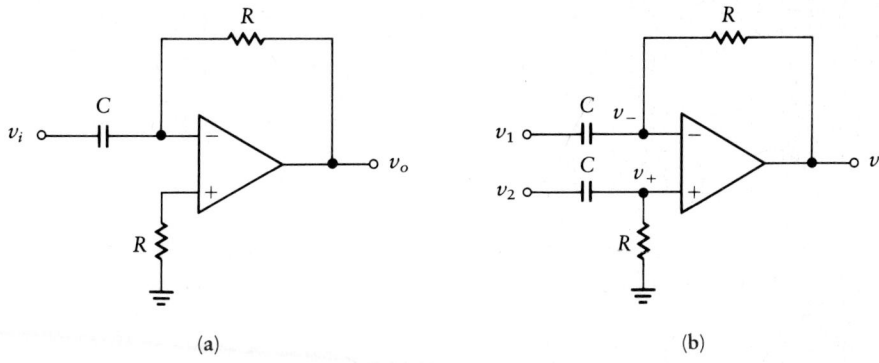

(a)   (b)

its operation are derived from the basic op-amp relationships, as follows:

$$V_+ = \frac{V_2 R}{R + 1/Cs} = \frac{V_2 RCs}{RCs + 1}$$

$$V_- = (V_o - V_1)\frac{1/Cs}{1/Cs + R} + V_1$$

$$= \frac{V_o + RCsV_1}{RCs + 1}$$

Since $G \to \infty$, $V_+ = V_-$, and we obtain

$$V_o = (V_2 - V_1)RCs \tag{13.6}$$

In the time domain, this becomes

$$v_o(t) = RC\frac{d[v_2(t) - v_1(t)]}{dt}$$

The process of differentiation accentuates high-frequency components. That is, taking the derivative of a sinusoid multiplies the amplitude by the frequency of the waveform. For this reason, if differentiators are used, they are often combined with filters whose transfer function attenuates high frequencies. In reality, the op-amp frequency limitations often provide this attenuation without the need for additional circuitry. Thus, at low frequency, the transfer function approaches a multiple of s, whereas at high frequencies, the function approaches either a constant or zero. Examples of typical composite transfer functions are

$$T_1(s) = \frac{100s}{s + 100}$$

$$T_2(s) = \frac{100s}{s^2 + 20s + 100}$$

Both of these functions approximate $T(s) = s$ at low frequencies.

13.2   Active-Network Design

Network synthesis is the study of techniques for going from a desired transfer function to a practical circuit implementation. The addition of an amplifier to the passive circuit results in a transfer function that has the form of a ratio of two polynomials. The constant multiplier (overall gain) may be changed, but the form of the transfer function remains the same.

The general form of the active network is repeated as Figure 13.5.

There are a number of advantages associated with using active networks as compared to passive networks. We list a few of these next:

- *Low cost*   In low-frequency applications, inductors can become quite large and expensive. Active filters that use op-amps can be designed without inductors.

- *Cascadability*   Because of good isolation, complex filters can be broken down into a series of simple sections. Cascadability allows each filter section to be designed separately and then cascaded so that the total transfer function becomes the product of the individual section functions.

- *Gain*   Active filters can produce gain as needed to suit system or filter requirements.

Figure 13.5
Operational amplifier used for active-network synthesis.

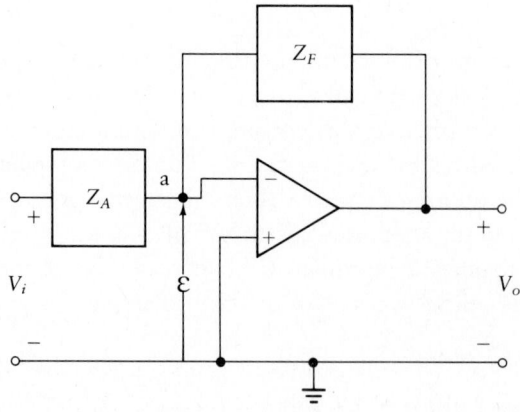

Along with these advantages are some limitations.

- *Supply power*   A power supply is needed for all active filters, whereas passive filters do not require any supply.
- *Signal limits*   The op-amp inherently has definite signal limits beyond which nonlinear operation occurs.
- *Frequency limits*   The op-amp does not respond at high frequencies, since it may have a cutoff frequency too low to allow it to be used in a particular application.

One of the most direct methods of active network design is based upon equation (13.1). The impedances Z_F and Z_A need not represent single elements. In fact, they can be any achievable two-terminal functions resulting from combinations of elements. Table 13.1 illustrates some common two-terminal configurations and their associated impedance functions.

Example 13.1

Use Table 13.1 and the circuit of Figure 13.5 to synthesize the following transfer function:

$$\frac{V_o}{V_i} = \frac{-(s + 30)^2}{(s + 5)(s + 100)} = \frac{-(s + 30)}{s + 5} \frac{(s + 30)}{s + 100} \tag{13.7}$$

SOLUTION   Comparing equation (13.7) with equation (13.1) and solving for the two-terminal impedance functions, we find one possible implementation, as follows:

$$Z_F = \frac{s + 30}{s + 5}$$

and

$$Z_A = \frac{s + 100}{s + 30} \tag{13.8}$$

Reference to Table 13.1 indicates several two-terminal networks that satisfy equation (13.8). In particular, entries (b) or (e) can be used.

Table 13.1   Two-Terminal Functions.

	Circuit	Transfer Function
(a)	C R C_1	$\dfrac{s + \dfrac{1}{RC}}{C_1 s \left(s + \dfrac{1}{R}\dfrac{C_1 + C}{C_1 C} \right)}$
(b)	R C R_1	$\dfrac{RR_1 \left(s + \dfrac{1}{RC} \right)}{(R + R_1) \left[s + \dfrac{1}{C(R + R_1)} \right]}$
(c)	R C	$\dfrac{RCs + 1}{Cs}$
(d)	R C_1 C	$\dfrac{(C + C_1) \left[s + \dfrac{1}{R\,(C + C_1)} \right]}{CC_1 s \left[s + \dfrac{1}{RC} \right]}$
(e)	C R_1 R	$\dfrac{R_1 \left(s + \dfrac{1}{C}\dfrac{R + R_1}{R_1 R} \right)}{s + \dfrac{1}{RC}}$
(f)	C R	$\dfrac{1}{C \left(s + \dfrac{1}{RC} \right)}$

Drill Problem

D13.1   Design an active network to generate the following transfer function.

$$\frac{V_o}{V_i} = -\frac{(s + 4)^2}{s(s + 20)^2}$$

Use no inductors and one op-amp.

Ans: Use circuit (b) from Table 13.1 for Z_A and circuit (d) for Z_F. The result is shown in Figure D13.1.

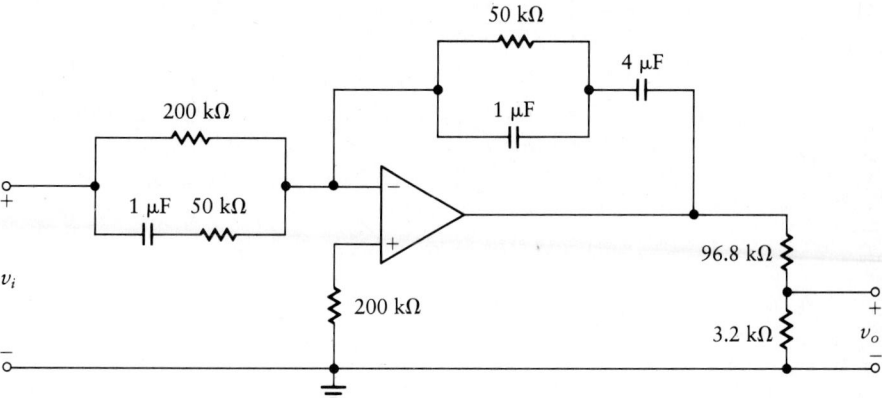

Figure D13.1

13.3 Active Filters

The word *filter* refers to the removal of the undesired portions of the frequency spectrum. It was originally applied to systems that eliminate undesired frequency components from a time waveform. The word has been used in a much more general way to include systems that simply weight the various frequency components of a function in a desired manner. Four of the most commonly encountered classes of filters are low-pass, high-pass, band-pass and band-stop.

Ideal *low-pass* filters allow frequencies up to a given limit to pass and attenuate frequencies above that limit. Ideal *high-pass* filters are just the reverse of low-pass filters in that they pass frequencies above the limit and attenuate those below. Ideal *band-pass* filters allow only a particular band of frequencies to pass and attenuate the remaining frequencies. Ideal *band-stop* filters are just the reverse of band-pass filters in that they pass frequencies outside of the particular band and reject those frequencies within the band.

Active filters produce gain and usually consist only of resistors and capacitors along with integrated circuits. The op-amp, when combined with resistors and capacitors, can simulate the performance of passive inductive-capacitive filters. For high-order filters, the active configurations are much simpler than the passive ones.

When designing a circuit or system, constraints are usually imposed. Meeting the desired specifications is the heart of the design. Specifications can include the *roll-off* (the rate of attenuation of a signal with frequency outside of the pass band), the *corner* (or *cutoff*) frequency, and the *peaking* (amount of gain produced at the resonant frequency of the circuit). These are frequency-domain requirements. Time-domain requirements are usually also important, since they determine the transient response. These are commonly expressed in terms of *rise time, overshoot,* and *settling time* for prescribed inputs (usually step functions).

Often one constraint can be met only at the expense of another. In these situations, the engineer is forced to make a trade-off between the desired parameter and its unwanted counterpart.

13.3.1   *Filter Properties and Classification*

The transfer function, $T(s)$, for a single-input, single-output linear time-invariant system is the ratio of the Laplace transformed output, $Y(s)$, to the Laplace transformed input, $R(s)$, with all initial conditions set equal to zero. Note that since we are talking about general systems rather than specific circuits, we have used the more general notation of $r(t)$ for the input and $y(t)$ for the output. For specific circuits, these become the voltages $v_i(t)$ and $v_o(t)$.

Figure 13.6(a) illustrates a general system and introduces the notation just described. The transfer function is the same as the ratio of output to input as a function of s when each varies as e^{st}. This is shown in Figure 13.6(b).

The output and input for a linear time-invariant system are related by a differential equation as follows:

$$\frac{d_n y}{dt^n} + a_{n-1}\frac{d_{n-1}y}{dt^{n-1}} + \cdots + a_1\frac{dy}{dt} + a_o y = \frac{d_m r}{dt^m} + \cdots + b_o r$$

The transfer function is then given by

$$T(s) = \frac{b_m s^m + b_{m-1}s^{m-1} + \cdots + b_1 s + b_o}{s^n + a_{n-1}s^{n-1} + \cdots + a_1 s + a_o} \tag{13.9}$$

Figure 13.6
Definition of transfer function.

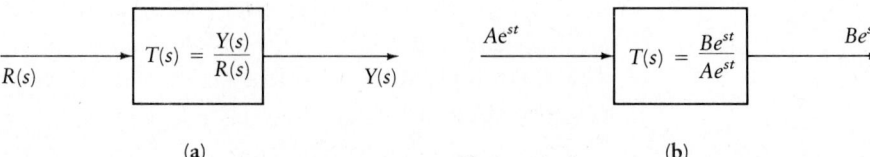

(a)   (b)

Example 13.2

Determine the transfer function of a system described by the following differential equation:

$$\frac{d^2y}{dt^2} + 3\frac{dy}{dt} + 2y = -4\frac{dr}{dt} + 5r$$

Assume zero initial conditions.

SOLUTION We can either write the transfer function directly from the differential equation or derive it by substituting

$$r(t) = Ae^{st}$$

$$y(t) = Be^{st}$$

to obtain

$$(s^2 + 3s + 2)Be^{st} = (-4s + 5)Ae^{st}$$

and

$$T(s) = \frac{-4s + 5}{s^2 + 3s + 2}$$

Example 13.3

Determine the transfer function of the system described by the following differential equation with zero initial conditions.

$$\frac{d^2y}{dt^2} + 2\frac{dy}{dt} + 10y = 6\frac{d^2r}{dt^2}$$

$$s^2 + 2s + 10 = 6s^2 \qquad \frac{6s^2}{s^2 + 2s + 10}$$

SOLUTION We take the Laplace transform of each term in the equation with zero initial conditions to obtain

$$T(s) = \frac{Y(s)}{R(s)} = \frac{6s^2}{s^2 + 2s + 10}$$

The transfer function is obtained from the impulse response, as indicated in Figure 13.7(a). If an impulse function is applied as the system input, the system

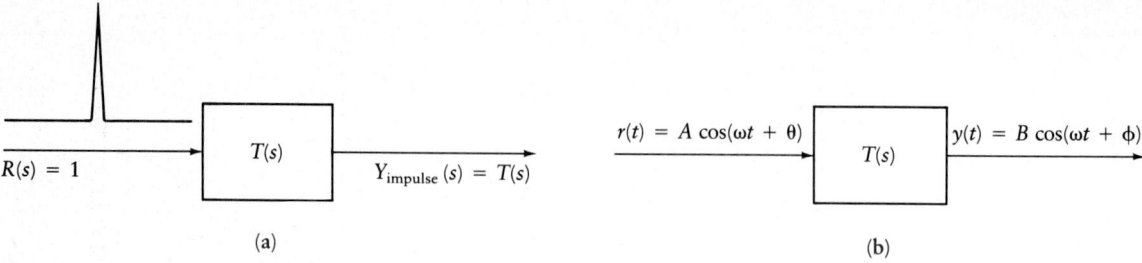

(a)   (b)

Figure 13.7   Impulse and frequency response.

output has a Laplace transform equal to the transfer function of the system. The impulse response of the system is thus the inverse Laplace transform of the transfer function.

$$Y_{impulse}(s) = T(s)$$

$$y_{impulse}(t) = L^{-1}[T(s)]$$

The transfer function can also be determined from the sinusoidal steady-state response. If a sinusoidal signal is the input to a system, the ratio of output magnitude to input magnitude is the magnitude of the transfer function evaluated at $s = j\omega$. The difference in phase between output and input is the phase shift of the transfer function at this frequency.   ➤┼

Example 13.4

A system has transfer function given by

$$T(s) = \frac{10}{s + 4}$$

Determine the response of the system to a function

$$r(t) = 3 \cos 4t$$

by the frequency-response method.

SOLUTION   The frequency of the input is 4 rad/s. For $s = j4$, we have

$$T(j4) = \frac{10}{4 + j4} = \frac{10}{4\sqrt{2}} \angle -45°$$

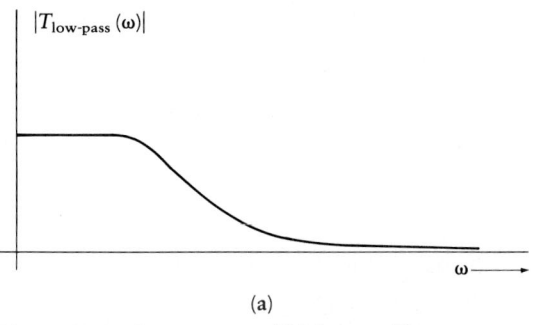

$|T_{\text{low-pass}}(\omega)|$

(a)

$|T_{\text{high-pass}}(\omega)|$

(b)

Figure 13.8   Low-pass and high-pass filter.

Then

$$y(t) = \left(\frac{15}{2\sqrt{2}}\right)\cos(4t - 45°)$$

The overall frequency response of this system is given by

$$|T(s = j\omega)| = \frac{10}{\sqrt{16 + \omega^2}}$$

$$\underline{/T(s = j\omega)} = -\tan^{-1}\left(\frac{\omega}{4}\right)$$

We now examine the frequency response of the general classification of filters. A *low-pass* filter has a frequency response that is nonzero for $\omega = 0$ and zero as $\omega \to \infty$, as shown in Figure 13.8(a). Note we are considering amplitude only and ignoring phase.

Example 13.5

Describe the frequency response of a system with transfer function

$$T(s) = \frac{10}{s + 2}$$

SOLUTION   The gain at $\omega = 0$ is 5 and declines at -20 dB/decade for frequencies larger than the corner frequency of $\omega = 2$ rad/s. This is a low-pass filter.

Example 13.6

Describe the frequency response of a system with transfer function

$$T(s) = \frac{3s - 8}{s^2 + s + 100}$$

SOLUTION   The constant term, $\frac{-8}{100}$, determines the behavior for $\omega = 0$. Since $T(s)$ has a denominator one order higher than the numerator, the magnitude declines with increasing frequency at a rate of -20 dB/decade and approaches zero for large values of ω. This is a low-pass filter.   ◄

A *high-pass* filter has a magnitude characteristic that is zero for $\omega = 0$ and nonzero, approaching a constant, as $\omega \to \infty$. This characteristic is shown in Figure 13.8(b).

Example 13.7

Describe the frequency response of a system with transfer function

$$T(s) = \frac{s}{s + 2}$$

SOLUTION   The zero at the origin yields a zero magnitude for $\omega \to 0$. The magnitude approaches a constant, 1, for $\omega \to \infty$. This is a high-pass filter.

◄

Example 13.8

Describe the frequency response of a system with transfer function

$$T(s) = \frac{s^3 - 10s^2 + 20s}{3s^3 + s + 70}$$

SOLUTION   The unit power term, s, is a factor of the numerator but not of the denominator. This makes the magnitude zero for $\omega = 0$. Since the numerator and denominator are of equal order, the magnitude approaches a constant for $\omega \to \infty$. This is a high-pass filter.   ◄

A *band-pass* filter has a magnitude characteristic that is zero for $\omega = 0$ *and* for $\omega \to \infty$, as shown in Figure 13.9(a).

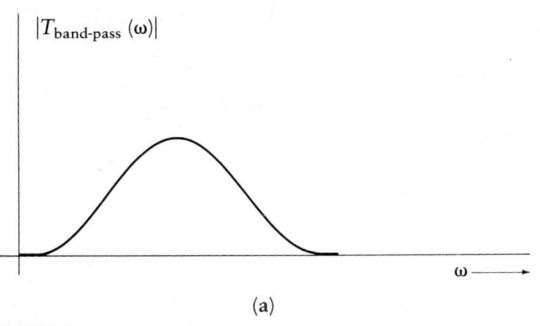
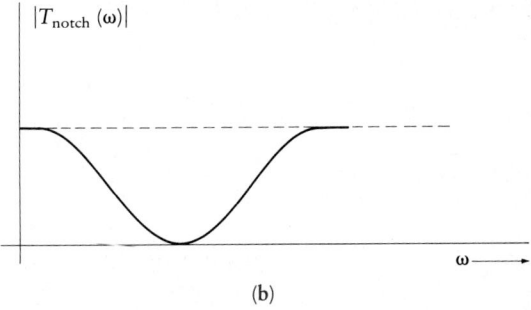

(a)   (b)

Figure 13.9   Amplitude response of band-pass and band-stop filter.

Example 13.9

Describe the frequency response of a system with transfer function

$$T(s) = \frac{s}{s^2 - s + 20}$$

SOLUTION   The zero at the origin leads to a magnitude of zero for $\omega = 0$. The higher-order denominator causes the magnitude to be zero for $\omega \to \infty$. This is a band-pass filter.   ▶┤

A *band-stop* or *notch* filter has a magnitude characteristic that is nonzero for $\omega = 0$ and has the same nonzero value for $\omega \to \infty$. The amplitude is zero (or nearly zero) over some range of values of frequency. This is shown in Figure 13.9(b).

Example 13.10

Describe the frequency response of a system with transfer function

$$T(s) = \frac{3s^2 + 60}{s^2 + s + 20}$$

SOLUTION   The numerator of this transfer function is zero for $\omega = \sqrt{20}$ (i.e., $s = j\sqrt{20}$) and the constant term and the highest-power terms have the same ratio, in this case 3:1. This is a notch filter.   ▶┤

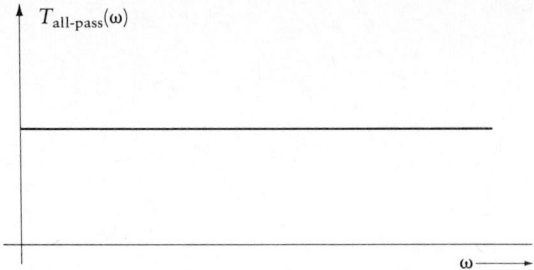

Figure 13.10 All-pass network.

A nontrivial filter for which the magnitude is constant (or near constant) is termed an *all-pass* filter or *delay equalizer*. A magnitude characteristic plot for such a filter is shown in Figure 13.10. Only the magnitude is shown in the figure, since the phase may vary depending upon the application.

The following two examples show typical forms of the transfer functions for an all-pass filter.

$$T(s) = \frac{s - 10}{s + 10}$$

$$T(s) = \frac{s^2 - 3s + 20}{s^2 + 3s + 20}$$

It is not possible to achieve a phase that is identically zero, $\phi(\omega) = 0°$. In fact, if the phase were zero, the filter would be "trivial." That is, the resulting circuit would not produce any change in a signal. The closest approximation for many applications is to let the phase shift be proportional to frequency, as follows:

$$\phi(\omega) = -\tau\omega$$

where τ is a constant corresponding to a constant *time delay* of signals passing through the filter. The delay is τ seconds if ϕ is expressed in radians.

Drill Problems

Find the transfer function, $T(s)$, for the circuits shown in Problems D13.2 to D13.5. Let all resistors, R_1, R_2, R_3, R_4, and R_5, be 100 kΩ. Also let $C_1 = C_3 = 10$ μF; $C_2 = C_4 = 0.01$ μF.

D13.2

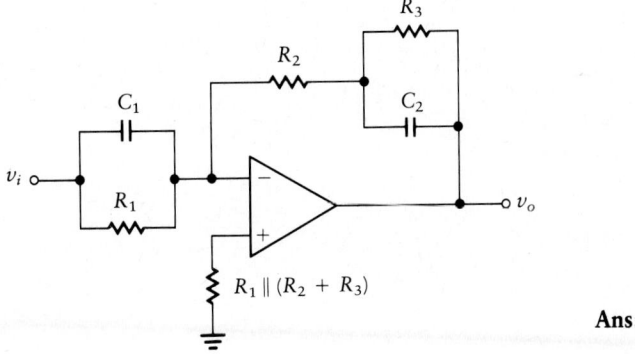

Ans: $-\dfrac{(s + 2000)}{(s + 1000)}(s + 1)$

Figure D13.2

D13.3

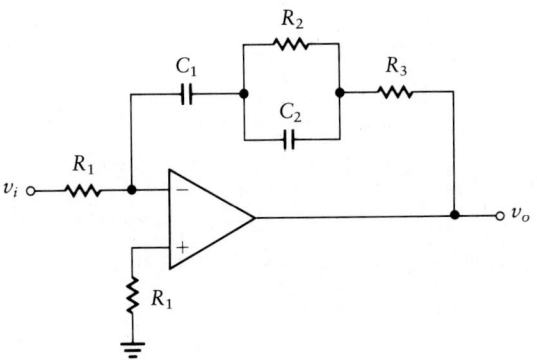

Ans: $-\dfrac{s^2 + 2000s + 1000}{s(s + 1000)}$

Figure D13.3

D13.4

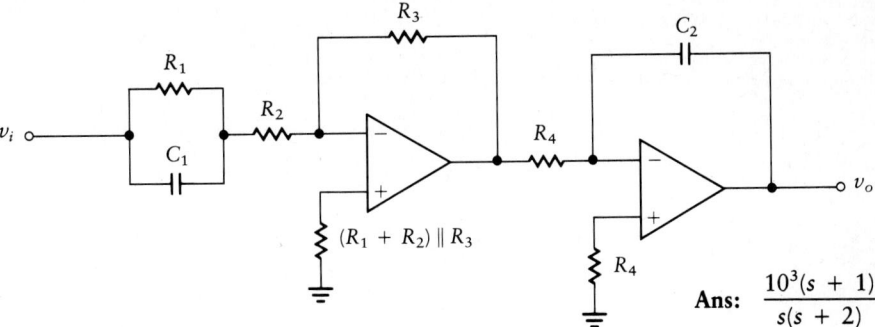

Ans: $\dfrac{10^3(s + 1)}{s(s + 2)}$

Figure D13.4

D13.5

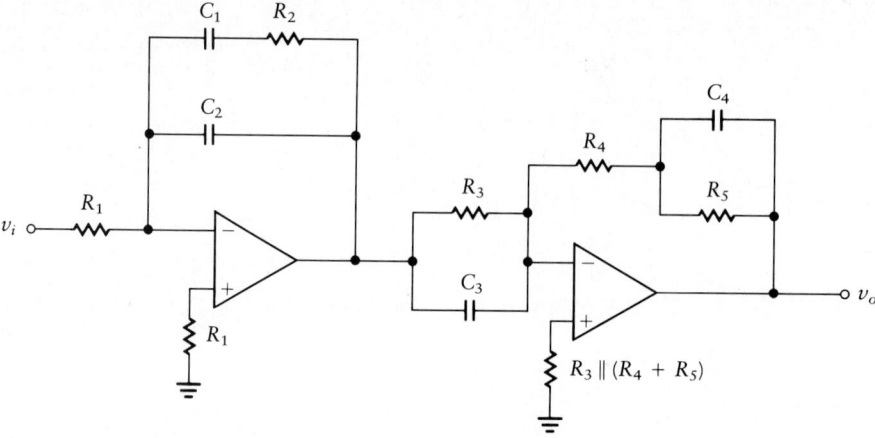

Figure D13.5

Ans: $\dfrac{10^3(s + 1)^2(s + 2000)}{s(s + 1000)^2}$

D13.6 Determine the Laplace transform of the following differential equation.

$$\frac{d^2y}{dt^2} + 5\frac{dy}{dt} + 20y = 10\frac{d^2r}{dt^2}$$

Assume zero initial conditions.

Ans: $(s^2 + 5s + 20)Y(s) = 10s^2R(s)$

D13.7 What type of filter does the following transfer function describe?

$$T(s) = \frac{5s - 10}{s^2 + s + 200}$$

Ans: Low-pass filter

13.3.2   First-Order Active Filters

An active RC low-pass filter is shown in Figure 13.11(a). The equations are found by letting $V_+ = V_-$ as follows:

$$V_+ = \frac{(1/sC)V_i}{R + 1/sC} = \frac{V_i}{RsC + 1}$$

$$V_- = \frac{R_A V_o}{R_A + R_F}$$

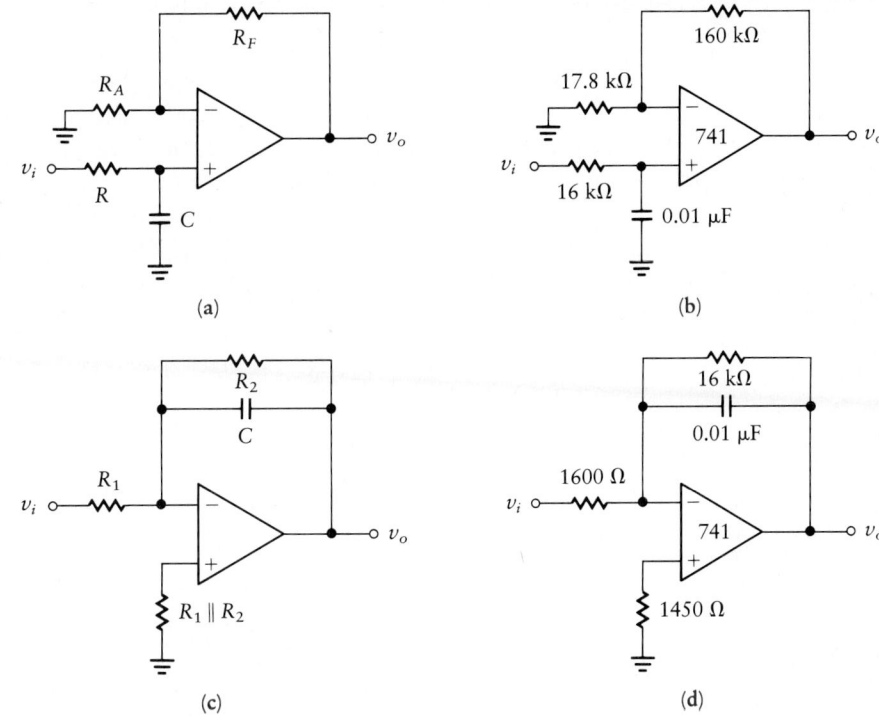

Figure 13.11
The low-pass filter.

(a)

(b)

(c)

(d)

Setting these two expressions equal and solving for the transfer function yields

$$T(s) = \frac{V_o}{V_i} = \frac{(1 + R_F/R_A)/RC}{s + 1/RC} \tag{13.10}$$

This is of the same form as the expression in Example 13.5.

Notice that the first-order active filter has one pole (a first-order denominator polynomial). The corner frequency is at $1/RC$ and the dc gain (found by setting $s = 0$) is $1 + R_F/R_A$.

Example 13.11

Design a first-order active low-pass filter with a dc gain of 10 and a corner frequency of 1 kHz.

SOLUTION There are four unknown variables (R, R_A, R_F, and C) and only three equations: the dc gain, the corner frequency, and the equation for bias current balance. (Note that if we had specified the input impedance, we would have had four equations in four unknowns.) We therefore are free to choose one element value at will. In practice, we choose this to put all component values into reasonable ranges. (For example, it would be senseless to solve the equations and find that a 100 F capacitor is needed! A large baked potato with two spikes might serve this purpose, but it is preferable to keep component values in a range that permits use of off-the-shelf components.) Let us choose C as the specified component and use a 0.01 μF capacitor. We use the equation for corner frequency in order to solve for R—that is

$$\omega = 2\pi f = 6280 = \frac{1}{RC}$$

and

$$R = \frac{10^8}{6280} = 16 \text{ k}\Omega$$

If bias-current balance is to be achieved,

$$R_A \parallel R_F = R = 16 \text{ k}\Omega$$

Thus,

$$R_A \parallel R_F = \frac{R_A R_F}{R_A + R_F} = 16 \text{ k}\Omega$$

The dc gain gives a second equation in R_A and R_F.

$$T(0) = 1 + \frac{R_F}{R_A} = 10$$

Solving these two equations yields

$$R_F = 160 \text{ k}\Omega$$

$$R_A = 17.8 \text{ k}\Omega$$

The complete circuit is shown in Figure 13.11(b).

An alternate form of low-pass filter is shown in Figure 13.11(c). The transfer function is derived in the same manner as was done in the previous circuit. That is, we set $V_- = V_+$ to get

$$T(s) = \frac{-R_2}{R_1} \frac{1}{R_2 C s + 1} \tag{13.11}$$

The dc gain is R_2/R_1 and the corner frequency is at $1/R_2 C$.

If desired, we can couple the input to the noninverting terminal of the op-amp instead of to the inverting terminal. This will achieve a high-impedance input and the output will no longer be inverted. ➤┼

Example 13.12

Design a first-order active filter with a dc gain of 10 and a corner frequency of 1 kHz. Use the circuit of Figure 13.11(c).

SOLUTION Using the equation for corner frequency, we find

$$\omega = 2\pi f = 6280 = \frac{1}{R_2 C}$$

The dc gain equation yields

$$T(0) = \frac{-R_2}{R_1} = -10$$

There is one more unknown than the number of constraints. Suppose we choose $C = 0.01 \ \mu F$. Then

$$R_2 = \frac{10^8}{6280} = 16 \ k\Omega$$

$$R_1 = \frac{R_2}{10} = 1.6 \ k\Omega$$

The complete filter is shown in Figure 13.11(d). ➤┼

One advantage of active filters is that it is often quite simple to vary parameter values. As an example, a first-order low-pass filter with adjustable corner frequency is shown in Figure 13.12. The voltage at v_- is

$$v_- = \frac{v_1 R_A}{R_A + R_F}$$

Figure 13.12
Low-pass filter with
adjustable corner
frequency.

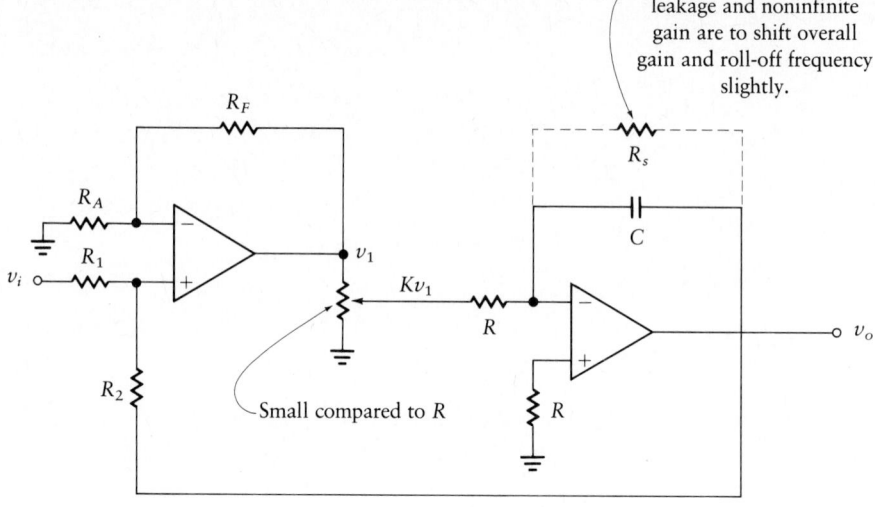

Where $K = \dfrac{\text{resistance from slider to ground}}{\text{total resistance}}$

The voltage at the noninverting input is found by writing the node equation at v_+ and solving for v_+.

$$v_+ = \frac{R_2 v_i}{R_1 + R_2} + \frac{R_1 v_o}{R_1 + R_2}$$

Setting $v_+ = v_-$ we obtain the voltage, v_1, as follows:

$$v_1 = \left(1 + \frac{R_F}{R_A}\right)\left[\left(\frac{R_2}{R_1 + R_2}\right)v_i + \frac{R_1}{R_1 + R_2}v_o\right]$$

$$= A_1 v_i + A_2 v_o$$

where

$$A_1 = \frac{(1 + R_F/R_A)R_2}{R_1 + R_2}$$

$$A_2 = \frac{(1 + R_F/R_A)R_1}{R_1 + R_2}$$

The second op-amp acts as an inverting integrator, and

$$V_o = \frac{-KV_1}{RCs}$$

Note that we use uppercase letters for voltages since these are functions of s. K is the fraction of V_1 sent to the integrator. That is, it is the potentiometer ratio, which is a number between 0 and 1.

$$V_o = \frac{-K(A_1 V_i + A_2 V_o)}{RCs}$$

The transfer function is given by

$$T(s) = \frac{V_o}{V_i} = \frac{-KA_1}{RCs + KA_2} \tag{13.12}$$

The dc gain is given by

$$\frac{-A_1}{A_2} = \frac{-R_2}{R_1}$$

The corner frequency is at KA_2/RC. Thus, the frequency is proportional to K. Without use of the op-amp, we would normally have a corner frequency that is inversely proportional to the resistor value. With a frequency proportional to K, we can use a *linear taper* potentiometer. The frequency is then linearly proportional to the setting of the potentiometer.

Example 13.13

Design a first-order adjustable low-pass filter with a dc gain of 10 and a corner frequency adjustable from near 0 to 1 kHz.

SOLUTION   There are six unknowns in this problem (R_A, R_F, R_1, R_2, R, and C) and only three equations (gain, frequency and bias balance). This leaves three parameters open to choice. Suppose we choose the following values:

$$C = 0.1 \ \mu F$$
$$R = 10 \ k\Omega$$
$$R_1 = 10 \ k\Omega$$

The ratio of R_2 to R_1 is the dc gain, so with a given value of $R_1 = 10 \ k\Omega$, R_2 must be 100 kΩ. We solve for A_1 and A_2 in order to find the ratio R_F/R_A.

The maximum corner frequency occurs at $K = 1$, so this frequency is set to $2\pi \times 1000 = 6280$.

$$\frac{A_2}{RC} = \frac{A_2}{10^4 \times 10^{-7}} = 6280$$

and solving for A_2,

$$A_2 = 6.28$$

A_2 and A_1 are related by the dc gain, so

$$\frac{A_1}{A_2} = 10$$

Therefore,

$$A_1 = 62.8$$

Now substituting the expression for A_2, we find

$$\frac{(1 + R_F/R_A)(R_1)}{R_1 + R_2} = A_2 = 6.28$$

But

$$\frac{R_1}{R_1 + R_2} = \frac{1}{11}$$

so

$$1 + \frac{R_F}{R_A} = 11(6.28) = 69$$

$$\frac{R_F}{R_A} = 68$$

R_A is chosen to achieve bias balance. The impedance attached to the noninverting input is

$$10 \text{ k}\Omega \parallel 100 \text{ k}\Omega \approx 10 \text{ k}\Omega$$

If we assume that R_F is large compared with R_A (we can check this after solving for these resistors), the parallel combination will be close to the value of R_A.

Figure 13.13
First-order filter for
Example 13.13.

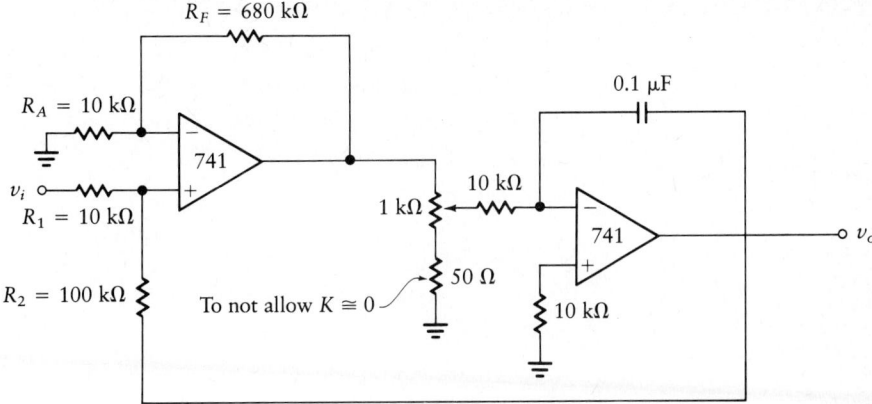

Figure 13.14
RC high-pass filter.

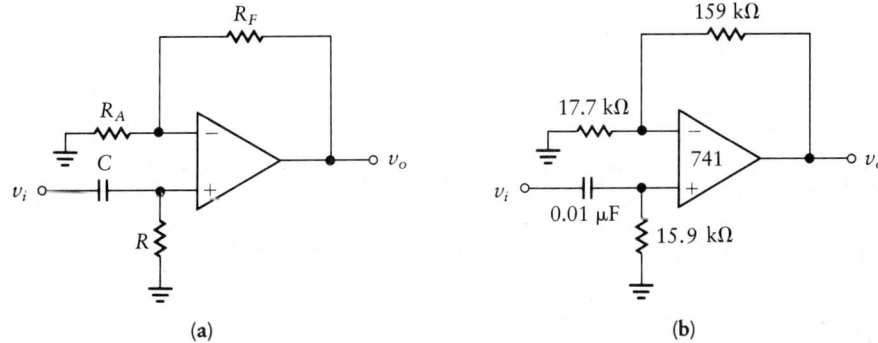

(a)   (b)

Therefore, we can choose $R_A = 10$ kΩ. With this choice of R_A, R_F is found to be 680 kΩ and bias balance is achieved.

The complete filter is shown in Figure 13.13.

An RC *high-pass filter* is shown in Figure 13.14(a). Once again, we solve for V_+ and V_-, and then set these equal to find the transfer function.

$$T(s) = \frac{R}{R + 1/Cs}\left(1 + \frac{R_F}{R_A}\right) = \left(1 + \frac{R_F}{R_A}\right)\frac{s}{s + 1/RC}$$

The high-frequency gain is $1 + R_F/R_A$ and the corner frequency is at $1/RC$.

Example 13.14

Design an RC high-pass filter with a high-frequency gain of 10 and a corner frequency of 1 kHz.

SOLUTION In this problem we have three equations (high-frequency gain, corner frequency, and bias balance) and four unknowns (R, C, R_A, and R_F). Therefore, one parameter is arbitrary. Let us choose $C = 0.01 \ \mu F$. We find R from the equation for corner frequency.

$$\omega = 2\pi f = 6280 = \frac{1}{RC}$$

and

$$R = 15.9 \ k\Omega$$

The high-frequency gain equation yields

$$1 + \frac{R_F}{R_A} = 10$$

This represents one equation in two unknowns, R_F and R_A. We derive a second equation from the bias balance relationship,

$$R_A \parallel R_F = R = 15.9 \ k\Omega$$

Solving these two equations yields

$$R_F = 159 \ k\Omega$$

$$R_A = 17.7 \ k\Omega$$

The complete circuit is shown in Figure 13.14(b).   ►

Drill Problem

D13.8 What is the dc gain and corner frequency of the circuit shown in Figure D13.6? What type of circuit is this?

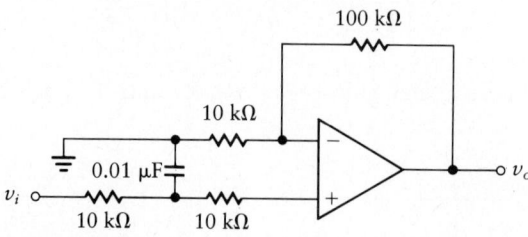

Figure D13.6

Ans: dc gain = 11; corner frequency is 10^4 rad/s; low-pass filter

We now analyze the circuit for an adjustable high-pass filter. The circuit of Figure 13.15 combines an amplifier for signal summing with a second amplifier for low-pass summing. Analysis yields the following equations:

$$V_o = \frac{(1 + R_F/R_A)(R_1)V_1}{R_1 + R_2} - \frac{R_F V_i}{R_A}$$

$$= A_1 V_1 - A_2 V_i$$

where

$$A_1 = \frac{(1 + R_F/R_A)(R_1)}{R_1 + R_2}$$

$$A_2 = \frac{R_F}{R_A}$$

If K is the potentiometer attenuation, then

$$V_1 = \frac{-KV_o}{RCs}$$

Figure 13.15
Adjustable high-pass filter.

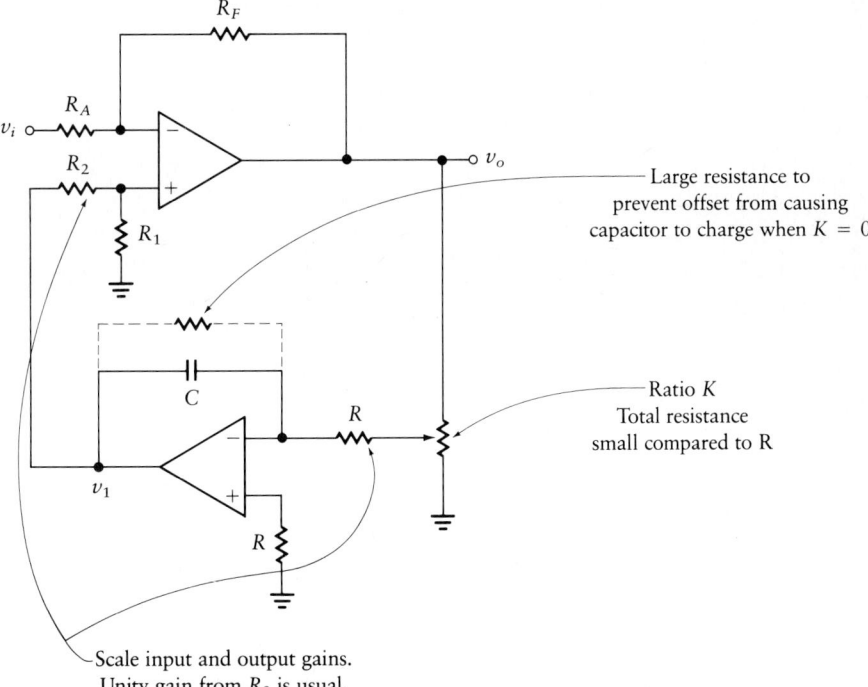

Large resistance to prevent offset from causing capacitor to charge when $K = 0$

Ratio K
Total resistance small compared to R

Scale input and output gains.
Unity gain from R_2 is usual.

and

$$V_o = \frac{-KA_1 V_o}{RCs} - A_2 V_i$$

The transfer function is given by

$$T(s) = \frac{V_o}{V_i} = \frac{-A_2 RCs}{RCs + KA_1}$$

$$= -A_2 \frac{s}{s + KA_1/RC}$$

The result is a high-pass filter with adjustable corner frequency.

Example 13.15

Design a high-pass filter with a high-frequency gain of 10 and a corner frequency adjustable from 100 Hz to 400 Hz.

SOLUTION   We have three equations and six unknowns, so we choose values for three variables: R_A, A_1, and C. We start with the high-frequency gain equation,

$$A_2 = \frac{R_F}{R_A} = 10$$

If we now choose $R_A = 10$ kΩ, we find $R_F = 100$ kΩ. We select $A_1 = 1$ to achieve unity gain for the noninverting input. Then

$$A_1 = \frac{(1 + R_F/R_A)(R_1)}{R_1 + R_2}$$

$$= \frac{11R_1}{R_1 + R_2} = 1$$

The bias balance equation yields

$$R_1 \parallel R_2 = R_A \parallel R_F = 10 \text{ k}\Omega \parallel 100 \text{ k}\Omega$$

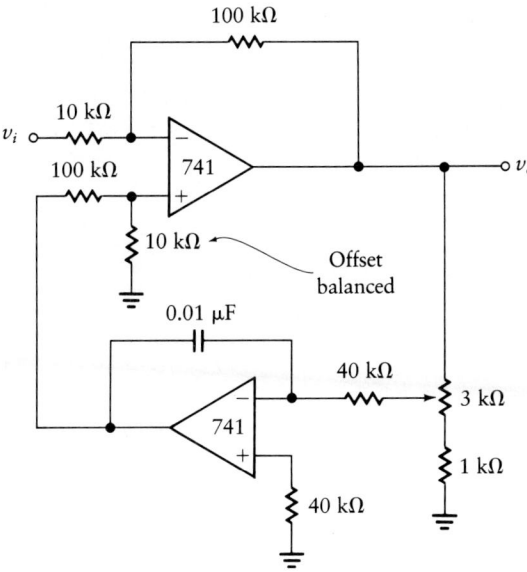

Figure 13.16 Circuit for Example 13.15.

We thus have two equations in R_1 and R_2. Solving these yields

$$R_1 = 10 \text{ k}\Omega$$

$$R_2 = 100 \text{ k}\Omega$$

Since K cannot exceed unity, we design for the maximum corner frequency at $K = 1$ to yield

$$\frac{A_1}{RC} = \frac{1}{RC} = \omega = 2\pi f = 2513 \text{ rad/s}$$

If we now choose $C = 0.01 \text{ μF}$, we find

$$R = \frac{10^8}{2513} = 40 \text{ k}\Omega$$

Adjustment of K from 0.25 to 1 yields the desired frequency range of 100 Hz to 400 Hz. This is accomplished using a 4-kΩ potentiometer with a limiting tab or by placing a 1-kΩ fixed resistor between ground and the 3-kΩ potentiometer. This latter approach is shown in the input of the feedback op-amp in the circuit of Figure 13.16. ◀▌

Drill Problem

D13.9   Given the circuit shown in Figure D13.7, what is the gain and the adjustable frequency range?

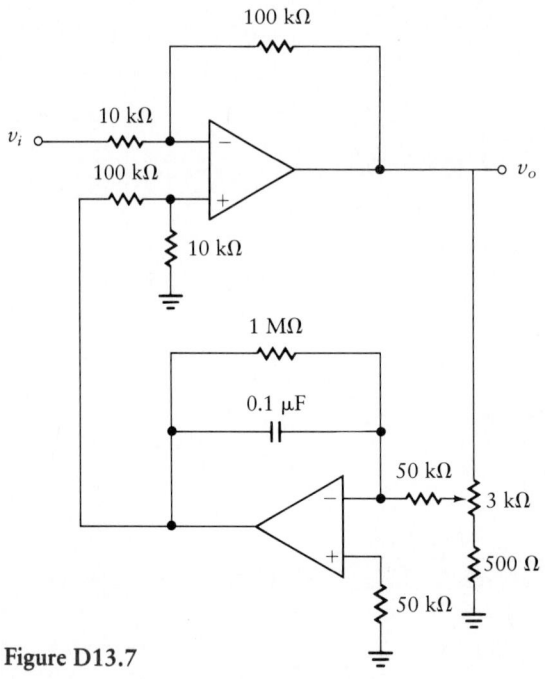

Figure D13.7

Ans: $A_1 = 1$; range of frequencies is 28.6 rad/s to 200 rad/s

13.3.3   *General First-Order Filters*

We considered the low-pass and high-pass filters in the previous sections. These are specific examples of first-order filters. We now examine the more general case. The circuit diagram for a general first-order filter is shown in Figure 13.17. Cascading two stages allows this filter to achieve any first order transfer function (i.e., both numerator and denominator of the transfer function can be any first-order polynomials in s). The second stage sums a portion of the input with a low-pass-filtered version of this input. The gains of the input and output stages are set by R_1 and R_3, respectively. The zero frequency gain of the input stage (the low-pass filter) is usually selected to be unity. This permits v_1 and v_i to be comparable in amplitude when forming the input to the second stage.

The transfer function of the filter is found by superposition as follows:

Figure 13.17
General first-order
filter.

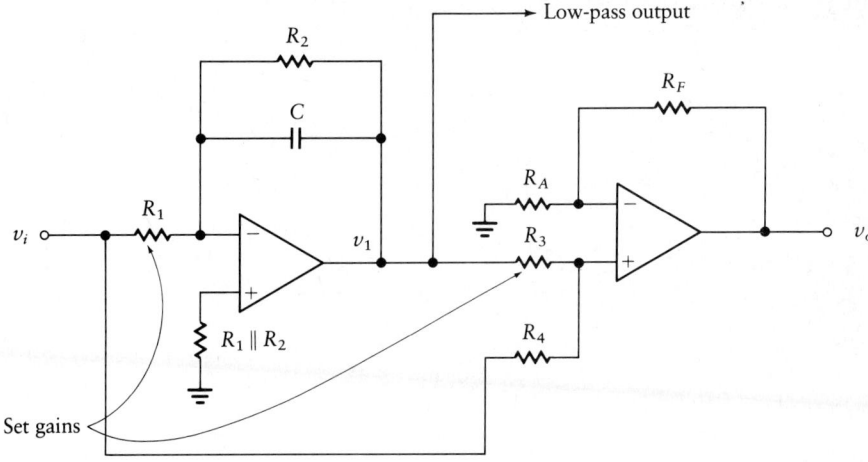

$$V_o = \left(1 + \frac{R_F}{R_A}\right) \frac{R_3 V_i + R_4 V_1}{R_3 + R_4} \tag{13.13}$$

but

$$V_1 = \frac{-(R_2/R_1)V_i}{1 + sCR_2}$$

which is the equation of a single-order low-pass filter (see Figure 13.11(c) and equation (13.11)). We substitute this into equation (13.13) to yield

$$\frac{V_o}{V_i} = T(s) = \left(1 + \frac{R_F}{R_A}\right) \frac{R_3}{R_3 + R_4} \left[1 - \frac{R_4}{R_3} \frac{1/R_1C}{s + 1/R_2C}\right]$$

$$T(s) = \left(1 + \frac{R_F}{R_A}\right) \frac{R_3}{R_3 + R_4} \frac{s + (1/R_2 - R_4/R_1R_3)/C}{s + 1/R_2C} \tag{13.14a}$$

With proper choice of the capacitor and the six resistors, this can simulate any first-order system.

As an example, to make this into a high-pass filter, we need to make the numerator equal to a constant multiple of s. If we let

$$R_1 R_3 = R_2 R_4$$

then

$$T(s) = \left(1 + \frac{R_F}{R_A}\right) \frac{R_3}{R_3 + R_4} \frac{s}{s + 1/R_2C} \tag{13.14b}$$

The high-frequency gain is

$$\frac{(1 + R_F/R_A)(R_3)}{R_3 + R_4}$$

and the corner frequency is at $1/R_2C$.

Example 13.16

Design a high-pass filter with a high-frequency gain of 10 and a corner frequency of 400 Hz.

SOLUTION The filter contains seven unknowns, but we have only five equations (gain, corner frequency, high-pass filter resistor constraint, bias balance, and forcing the gain of the first stage to be unity). We therefore choose two parameter values at will. Let us select C and R_3 as follows:

$$C = 0.01 \ \mu F$$

$$R_3 = 10 \ k\Omega$$

We then solve for R_2 from the corner-frequency equation,

$$\frac{1}{R_2C} = \frac{10^8}{R_2} = \omega = 2\pi f = 2513 \ \text{rad/s}$$

$$R_2 = 40 \ k\Omega$$

The low-pass filter section is designed for unity dc gain, so R_1 must equal R_2, or 40 kΩ. We know R_1, R_2, and R_3, so we can solve for R_4 from the high-pass constraint

$$R_1R_3 = R_2R_4$$

which yields

$$R_4 = R_3 = 10 \ k\Omega$$

The high-frequency gain is used to specify the ratio of R_F to R_A.

$$T(s \to \infty) = \frac{(1 + R_F/R_A)(R_3)}{R_3 + R_4}$$

$$= \left(1 + \frac{R_F}{R_A}\right)\left(\frac{1}{2}\right) = 10$$

Therefore,

$$\frac{R_F}{R_A} = 19$$

To achieve bias balance, we choose

$$R_A \parallel R_F = R_3 \parallel R_4$$

From these two conditions we find $R_A = 5.26 \text{ k}\Omega$ and $R_F = 100 \text{ k}\Omega$. The complete high-pass circuit is shown in Figure 13.18.   ▸┼

As another example of the utility of this general design for various filters, we can change equation (13.14a) to represent an all-pass filter. The pole and zero should be symmetrically located around the imaginary *s*-axis. Thus,

$$\frac{-1}{R_2} + \frac{R_4}{R_1 R_3} = \frac{1}{R_2}$$

or

$$R_1 R_3 = \frac{R_2 R_4}{2}$$

Substituting these values into equation (13.14a) yields

$$T(s) = \left(1 + \frac{R_F}{R_A}\right) \frac{R_3}{R_3 + R_4} \frac{s - 1/R_2 C}{s + 1/R_2 C} \tag{13.15}$$

Figure 13.18
High-pass filter for
Example 13.16.

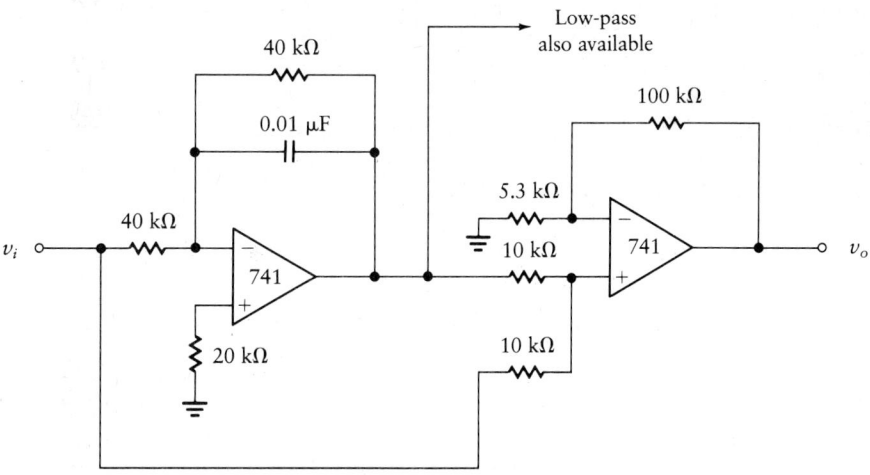

The dc gain is given by

$$-\frac{R_3(1 + R_F/R_A)}{R_3 + R_4}$$

and the corner frequency is at $1/R_2C$. For an all-pass filter, the corner frequency can be considered to be the frequency where the phase of both the numerator and of the denominator is $-45°$. Thus, the overall phase is $-90°$, and we no longer think of this as the break frequency, where the amplitude characteristic starts decreasing.

Example 13.17

Design an all-pass filter with a dc gain of 10 and a corner frequency of 400 Hz.

SOLUTION   There are seven unknowns (R_F, R_A, R_1, R_2, R_3, R_4, and C) and only five equations (the gain, corner frequency, all-pass constraint, bias balance, and unity gain for the first stage). We therefore can select two parameters, so we choose

$$C = 0.01 \ \mu F$$

$$R_3 = 10 \ k\Omega$$

Then, from the corner-frequency relationship, we have

$$\frac{1}{R_2C} = \frac{10^8}{R_2} = \omega = 2\pi f = 2513 \ \text{rad/s}$$

and

$$R_2 = 40 \ k\Omega$$

We use the unity-gain relationship of the first stage to find R_1. Thus,

$$R_1 = R_2 = 40 \ k\Omega$$

We use the all-pass constraint to find R_4. Thus,

$$R_1R_3 = \frac{R_2R_4}{2}$$

and substituting previously found values,

$$40 \text{ k}\Omega \times 10 \text{ k}\Omega = 40 \text{ k}\Omega \times \frac{R_4}{2}$$

and

$$R_4 = 20 \text{ k}\Omega$$

The bias-balance relationship yields

$$R_A = R_3 \parallel R_4 = 10 \text{ k}\Omega \parallel 20 \text{ k}\Omega = 6.67 \text{ k}\Omega$$

Again, since

$$R_A \ll R_F$$

then

$$R_A \parallel R_F \approx R_A$$

The gain relationship yields

$$\frac{(1 + R_F/R_A)(R_3)}{R_3 + R_4} = 10$$

Solving for R_F, we have

$$R_F = 193 \text{ k}\Omega$$

The complete circuit is shown in Figure 13.19.

Figure 13.19
All-pass filter for
Example 13.17.

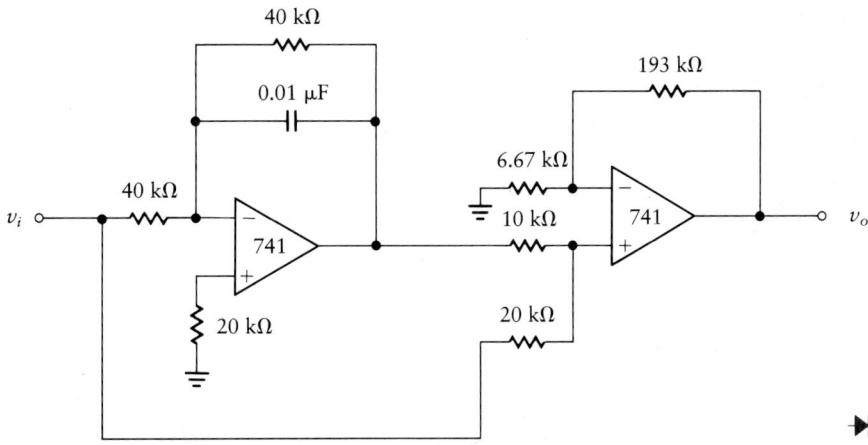

Drill Problem

D13.10　Find the transfer function for the first-order filter shown in Figure D13.8. Find the dc gain and corner frequency.

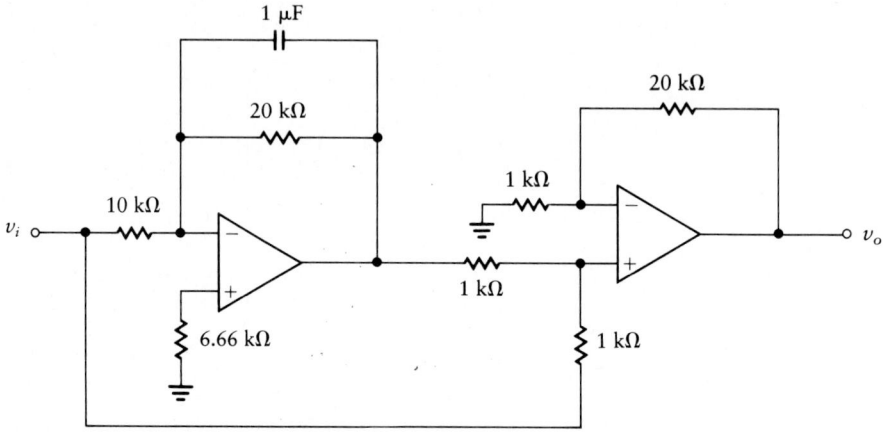

Figure D13.8

Ans:　$10.5\dfrac{0.02s - 1}{0.02s + 1}$; gain = 10.5 and corner frequency = 50 rad/s

---

13.4　Single Amplifier—General Type

In Section 13.3.3 we considered a general first-order filter using two op-amps. In this section, we achieve a comparable result using only one op-amp. Figure 13.20 shows the circuit for the general single amplifier. The transfer function is developed as follows:

$$
\begin{aligned}
T(s) &= \left[1 + \frac{R_2/R_1}{R_2Cs + 1}\right]\frac{R_4}{R_3 + R_4} - \frac{R_2/R_1}{R_2Cs + 1} \\
&= \frac{(R_2sC + 1 + R_2/R_1)[R_4/(R_3 + R_4)]}{R_2Cs + 1} - \frac{R_2/R_1}{R_2Cs + 1}
\end{aligned}
\tag{13.16}
$$

Finally,

$$
T(s) = \frac{R_4}{R_3 + R_4}\frac{s + (1/R_1C)(R_1/R_2 - R_3/R_4)}{s + 1/R_2C}
\tag{13.17}
$$

Figure 13.20
Single amplifier—general type.

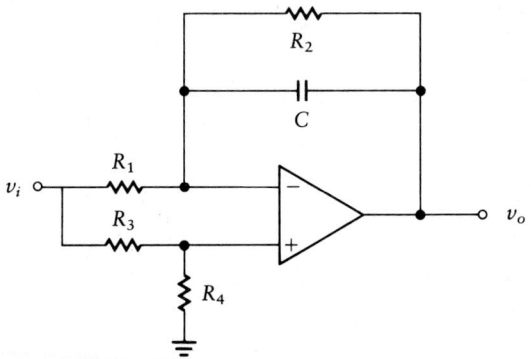

In order to make this a *high-pass filter,* we want the zero of the numerator to be at the origin. We therefore let

$$R_1 R_4 = R_2 R_3$$

Then

$$T(s) = \frac{R_4}{R_3 + R_4} \frac{s}{s + 1/R_2 C} \tag{13.18}$$

The gain at zero frequency is zero, and as the frequency approaches infinity, the gain is

$$\frac{V_o}{V_i} = \frac{R_4}{R_3 + R_4} \tag{13.19}$$

If we wish to make this circuit into an *all-pass filter,* we set

$$R_2 R_3 = 2 R_1 R_4$$

in equation (13.17). Then

$$T(s) = \frac{R_4}{R_3 + R_4} \frac{s - 1/R_2 C}{s + 1/R_2 C} \tag{13.20}$$

Finally, if we wish to construct a *low-pass filter,* we let R_3 approach infinity in equation (13.17). This yields

$$T(s) = \frac{-(1/R_1 C)}{s + 1/R_2 C}$$

Example 13.18

Design a high-pass filter with a high-frequency gain of $\frac{1}{2}$ and a corner frequency of 4 kHz.

SOLUTION   The unknowns are R_1, R_2, R_3, R_4, and C. We have equations for gain, corner frequency, bias balance, and the high-pass constraint. This leaves one unknown, which we can select. Let us choose $C = 0.01$ μF. Then from the corner frequency, we have

$$\frac{10^8}{R_2} = 2\pi f = 25,130 \text{ rad/s}$$

Therefore,

$$R_2 = 4 \text{ k}\Omega$$

For a high-frequency gain of $\frac{1}{2}$, we obtain, from equation (13.19), that

$$R_3 = R_4$$

Therefore, the high-pass resistor constraint yields

$$R_1 R_4 = R_2 R_3$$

and

$$R_1 = R_2 = 4 \text{ k}\Omega$$

To achieve bias balance, we choose

$$R_3 = R_4 = 4 \text{ k}\Omega$$

Example 13.19

Design an all-pass filter with a gain of $\frac{1}{2}$ and a corner frequency of 4 kHz.

SOLUTION   Let us choose $C = 0.01$ μF. From the corner frequency equations, we have

$$\frac{1}{R_2 C} = \frac{10^8}{R_2} = 2\pi f = 25,130 \text{ rad/s}$$

and

$$R_2 = 4 \text{ k}\Omega$$

To achieve a gain of $\frac{1}{2}$,

$$R_3 = R_4$$

and the all-pass constraint yields

$$R_2 R_3 = 2R_1 R_4$$

but since $R_3 = R_4$, we have

$$R_1 = \frac{R_2}{2} = 2 \text{ k}\Omega$$

The parallel combination of R_1 and R_2 has a resistance of 1.33 kΩ, so to achieve bias balance, we require

$$R_3 = R_4 = 2.67 \text{ k}\Omega$$

▶┤

13.5 Second-Order Single Amplifier Filters

Second-order filters can more closely model ideal characteristics than can first-order filters. A second-order low-pass filter is shown in Figure 13.21(a). The resistors are chosen to provide for bias balance. The equivalent circuit is shown in Figure 13.21(b). The loop equations are given by

$$\left(R_1 + \frac{1}{sC_1}\right)I_1 - \left(\frac{1}{sC_1}\right)I_2 = V_i - V_+$$

$$\left(-\frac{1}{sC_1}\right)I_1 + \left(R_2 + \frac{1}{sC_1} + \frac{1}{sC_2}\right)I_2 = V_+$$

$$V_+ = V_o = \left(\frac{1}{sC_2}\right)I_2$$

We multiply the first equation by sC_1 and the second by $sC_1 C_2$. Substituting V_o for V_+ yields

Figure 13.21
Second-order low-pass
filter.

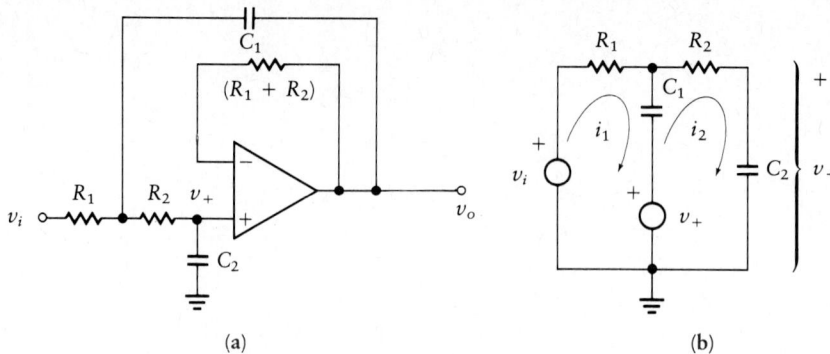

(a)   (b)

$$(R_1C_1s + 1)I_1 - I_2 = sC_1V_i - sC_1V_o$$

$$-C_2I_1 + (R_2C_1C_2s + C_2 + C_1)I_2 = C_1C_2sV_o$$

$$I_2 = sC_2V_o$$

Finally, solving for V_o and eliminating I_1 and I_2 yields the transfer function, V_o/V_i:

$$T(s) = \frac{1}{(R_1R_2C_1C_2)s^2 + (R_1 + R_2)C_2s + 1} \qquad (13.21)$$

Example 13.20

Design a second-order low-pass filter to achieve the transfer function

$$T(s) = \frac{1000}{s^2 + 10s + 1000} = \frac{1}{s^2/1000 + s/100 + 1}$$

SOLUTION   We have four unknowns (R_1, R_2, C_1, and C_2) and two equations (the coefficients of s^2 and s). We therefore can choose two parameters.
    If we choose $C_2 = 0.1 \ \mu\text{F}$, then

$$(R_1 + R_2)C_2 = \frac{1}{100}$$

and

$$R_1 + R_2 = 100 \ \text{k}\Omega$$

If we choose $R_1 = 50 \ \text{k}\Omega$, we find

$$R_2 = 50 \ \text{k}\Omega$$

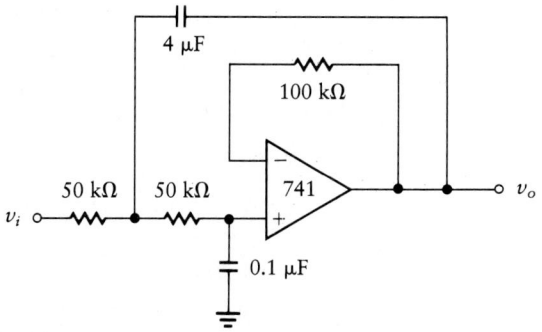

Figure 13.22 Circuit for Example 13.20.

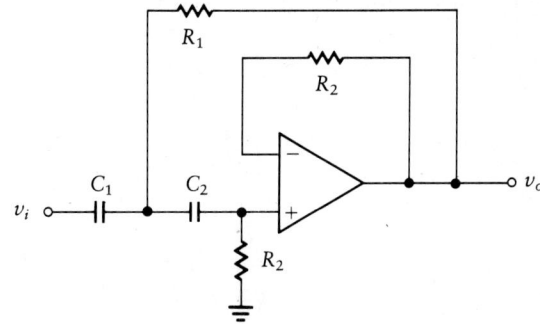

Figure 13.23 Second-order high-pass filter.

Now since

$$R_1 R_2 C_1 C_2 = (5 \times 10^4)(5 \times 10^4)(10^{-7})C_1 = 10^{-3}$$

we find C_1 to be

$$C_1 = 4 \ \mu F$$

The final circuit is shown in Figure 13.22.

A second-order high-pass filter is shown in Figure 13.23. Comparing this to the low-pass filter of Figure 13.21, we see that the resistors and capacitors are interchanged. Note that the resistor values are constrained to provide for bias balance. We repeat equation (13.21) for the low-pass filter:

$$T_{LP}(s) = \frac{1}{(R_1 R_2 C_1 C_2)s^2 + (R_1 + R_2)C_2 s + 1}$$

$$= \frac{1}{R_1 R_2 (C_1 s)(C_2 s) + (R_1 + R_2)C_2 s + 1}$$

There is no need to rederive the results for the new circuit. We simply interchange components to obtain the high-pass filter-transfer function. We interchange R_1 and $1/sC_1$ and also interchange R_2 and $1/sC_2$ to obtain

$$T_{HP}(s) = \frac{1}{(1/sC_1)(1/sC_2)(1/R_2)(1/R_1) + (1/sC_1 + 1/sC_2)(1/R_2) + 1}$$

$$= \frac{s^2}{s^2 + (1/R_2 C_1 + 1/R_2 C_2)s + 1/R_1 R_2 C_1 C_2} \tag{13.22}$$

Example 13.21

Design a high-pass filter to achieve the following transfer function:

$$T(s) = \frac{s^2}{s^2 + 10s + 1000}$$

SOLUTION   Two component values are selected since there are more unknowns than equations. If we choose $C_1 = C_2 = 10\ \mu F$, then equating coefficients of s yields

$$\frac{1}{R_2 C_1} + \frac{1}{R_2 C_2} = \left(\frac{1}{R_2}\right)(2 \times 10^5) = 10$$

and

$$R_2 = 20\ k\Omega$$

Equating the constant terms yields

$$R_1 R_2 C_1 C_2 = R_1(2 \times 10^4)(10^{-5})(10^{-5}) = 10^{-3}$$

and

$$R_1 = 500\ \Omega$$

The complete circuit is shown in Figure 13.24.

A second-order band-pass filter is shown in Figure 13.25(a), and the equivalent circuit is in Figure 13.25(b). We derive the transfer function as follows:

$$\left(\frac{1}{R_1} + C_1 s + C_2 s + \frac{1}{R_2}\right)V_1 = \frac{V_i}{R_1} + C_1 s V_o$$

$$V_1 = \frac{-V_o}{R_3 C_2 s}$$

$$\left(\frac{1}{R_1} + C_1 s + C_2 s + \frac{1}{R_2}\right)\left(\frac{-V_o}{R_3 C_2 s}\right) = \frac{V_i}{R_1} + C_1 s V_o$$

$$[R_2 + R_1 R_2 C_1 s + R_1 R_2 C_2 s + R_1 + C_1 s(R_1 R_2 R_3 C_2 s)]V_o$$

$$= -R_2 R_3 C_2 s V_i$$

Finally,

$$T(s) = \frac{-(1/R_1C_1)s}{s^2 + (1/R_3)(1/C_1 + 1/C_2)s + (R_1 + R_2)/(C_1C_2R_3R_1R_2)}$$ (13.23)

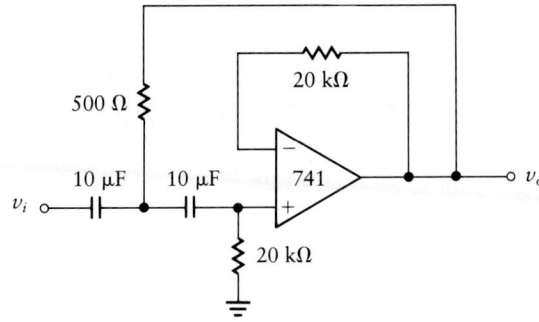

Figure 13.24
High-pass filter for
Example 13.21.

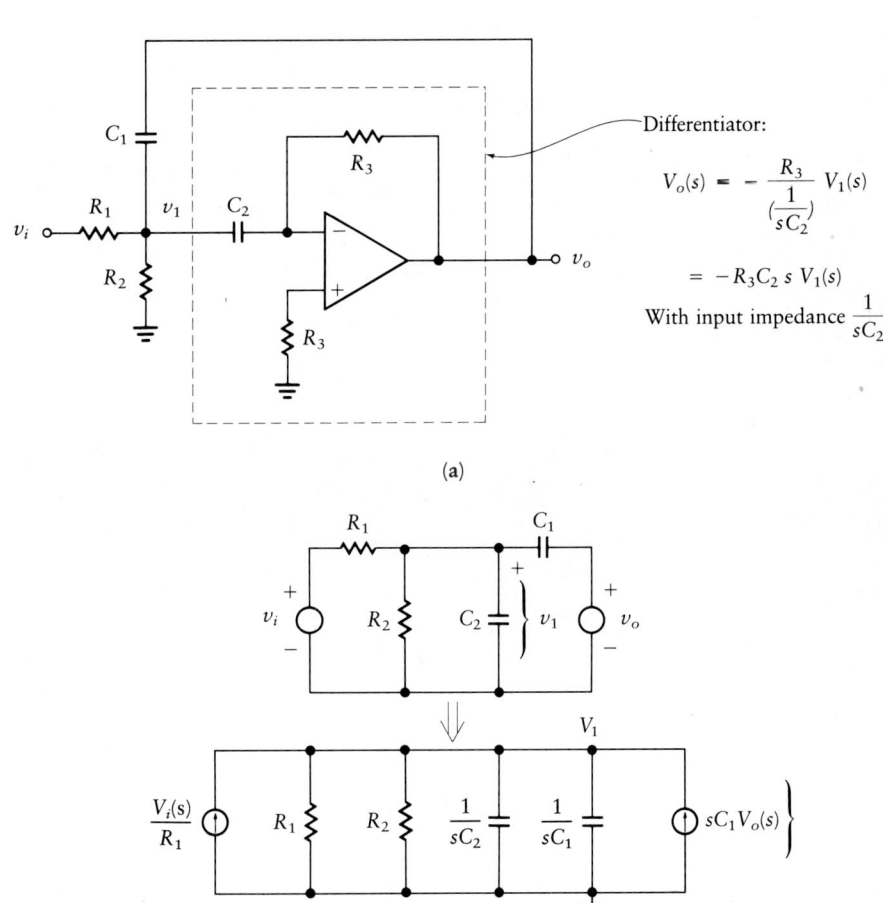

Figure 13.25
Band-pass filter.

(a)

(b)

Example 13.22

Design a band-pass filter to achieve the following transfer function:

$$T(s) = \frac{-s}{s^2 + 10s + 1000}$$

SOLUTION   There are five unknowns in the circuit (R_1, R_2, R_3, C_1, and C_2) and only three equations. Suppose we first choose $C_1 = 1.0\ \mu\text{F}$. Then equating the coefficients of s in the numerator yields

$$\frac{1}{R_1 C_1} = \frac{10^6}{R_1} = 1$$

and

$$R_1 = 1\ \text{M}\Omega$$

If we now choose $C_2 = 1\ \mu\text{F}$, then equating the coefficients of s in the denominator yields

$$\left(\frac{1}{R_3}\right)\left(\frac{1}{C_1} + \frac{1}{C_2}\right) = \left(\frac{1}{R_3}\right)(2 \times 10^6) = 10$$

so

$$R_3 = 200\ \text{k}\Omega$$

Finally, we equate the constants in the denominator to find

$$\frac{1/R_1 + 1/R_2}{C_1 C_2 R_3} = \frac{10^{-6} + 1/R_2}{10^{-6}(10^{-6})(2 \times 10^5)} = \frac{10^{-6} + 1/R_2}{2 \times 10^{-7}} = 1000$$

Therefore, $R_2 = 5\ \text{k}\Omega$ and the design is complete, with the final circuit shown in Figure 13.26.

Figure 13.26
Circuit for Example 13.22.

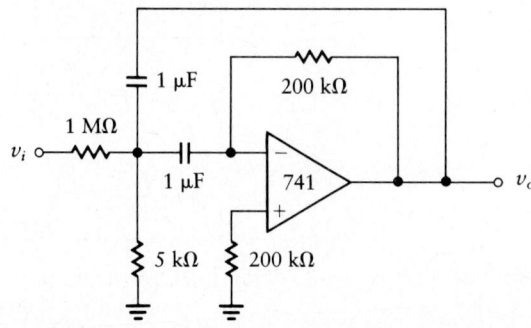

Drill Problem

D13.11 Find the transfer function for the circuit shown in Figure D13.9. What type of filter is this?

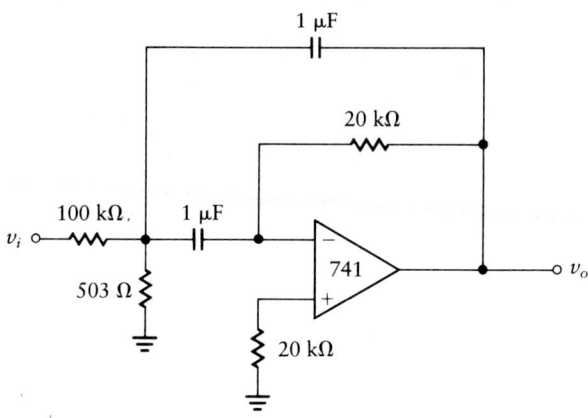

Figure D13.9

Ans: $T(s) = \dfrac{-10s}{s^2 + 10^2 s + 10^5}$; band-pass filter

---

13.6 Classical Analog Filters

Before we can design more-complex active filters, we first become familiar with some results in passive-filter theory.

There are many types of filters, each of which exhibits special characteristics. *Butterworth filters* produce no ripple in the pass-band and attenuate unwanted frequencies outside of this band. *Chebyshev filters* attenuate unwanted frequencies more effectively than Butterworth filters, but they exhibit ripple in the pass-band. Other important classical filters include the elliptic, parabolic, Bessel, Papoulis, and Gaussian. The current discussion is limited to Butterworth and Chebyshev filters, although similar design approaches can be used for the other types.

Specifications of filters are often presented by use of a modified amplitude versus frequency characteristic diagram. For example, Figure 13.27 is a diagram of the characteristics of a low-pass filter. The pass-band of the filter extends from zero frequency to a maximum frequency of f_{pass}. The range of frequencies between f_{pass} and f_{stop} is known as the *transition band,* and the range above f_{stop} is the *stop band.* The magnitudes shown on the diagram are in decibels. Within the pass band, the unshaded region indicates that the magnitude must be above A_p, the amplitude in the pass-band, throughout that

Figure 13.27
Low-pass filter
characteristic.

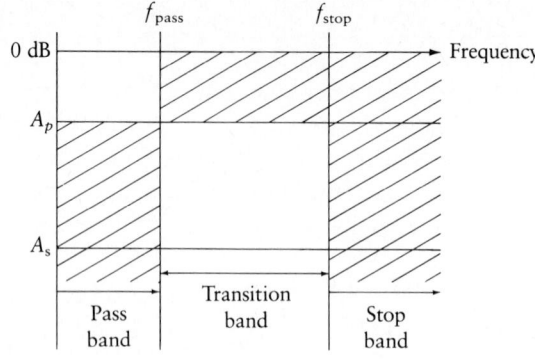

band. Some filters, such as the Chebyshev, have a *ripple* in the pass band. Nonetheless, the minimum magnitude is greater than A_p. Within the transition band, attenuation occurs as the frequency increases, with the magnitude at f_{stop} (the upper frequency) equal to A_s, the amplitude in the stop band.

The standard form of the transfer function of a filter is often given in the following form:

$$|T(j\omega)|^2 = \frac{1}{1 + e^2 s_n{}^2(\omega)} \qquad (13.24)$$

In this equation, $s_n(\omega)$ is a classical nth-order polynomial and e is related to the ripple in the pass band. We explore several specific examples in the following sections.

13.6.1   *Butterworth Filters*

Butterworth filters are also known as *maximally flat magnitude (MFM)* filters, since the transfer function is chosen so that the magnitude response curve is as flat as possible within the pass band of the filter. This is accomplished by setting as many derivatives of the function as possible equal to zero at the center of the pass band.

Suppose we set $s_n = \omega^n$ and $e = 1$ in equation (13.24). This yields the Butterworth filter. The magnitude-squared transfer function of the nth-order Butterworth filter is given as follows:

$$|T(j\omega)|^2 = \frac{1}{1 + \omega^{2n}} \qquad (13.25)$$

For example, the transfer function for a second order Butterworth filter is given by

$$T(s) = \frac{1}{s^2 + \sqrt{2}s + 1} \tag{13.26}$$

If $s = j\omega$ is substituted into equation (13.26), the magnitude of the resulting complex function is that given in equation (13.25) with $n = 2$. The magnitude of the transfer function is unity within the pass band, and the break frequency (i.e., the frequency where $|T(j\omega)| = 1/\sqrt{2}$) is also unity. We refer to this as a *normalized filter*.

Equation (13.25) is the general expression for the magnitude squared of the transfer function of the Butterworth filter. As the order of the filter, n, increases, the roll-off in the transition region becomes steeper.

Suppose a roll-off is specified in decibels per decade. The order of the filter is given by this quantity divided by 20. The roll-off is $20n$ dB/decade, where n is the filter order.

Suppose that the specifications give the magnitude of the characteristic at two points, that is, the magnitude is $|T_1|$ at a frequency of ω_1 and $|T_2|$ at a frequency of ω_2. We find the required order of the filter from equation (13.25). Substituting the two values into this equation, we find

$$n \geq \frac{\log(|T_2|^{-2} - 1)^{0.5}/(|T_1|^{-2} - 1)^{0.5}}{\log(\omega_2/\omega_1)} \tag{13.27}$$

The transfer function of the Butterworth filter is expressed as the reciprocal of a polynomial in s. If $T(s)$ is the transfer function and $B_n(s)$ is the polynomial for the nth-order filter, we obtain

$$T(s) = \frac{1}{B_n(s)}$$

The transfer function for the normalized filter has a corner frequency at $\omega = 1$. The magnitude at this corner frequency is 0.707.

The normalized polynomials for Butterworth filters are as follows:

$$B_1(s) = s + 1$$

$$B_2(s) = s^2 + 1.414s + 1$$

$$B_3(s) = s^3 + 2s^2 + 2s + 1$$

$$B_4(s) = s^4 + 2.61s^3 + 3.41s^2 + 2.61s + 1$$

$$B_5(s) = s^5 + 3.24s^4 + 5.24s^3 + 5.24s^2 + 3.24s + 1$$

$$B_6(s) = s^6 + 3.86s^5 + 7.46s^4 + 9.14s^3 + 7.46s^2 + 3.86s + 1 \tag{13.28}$$

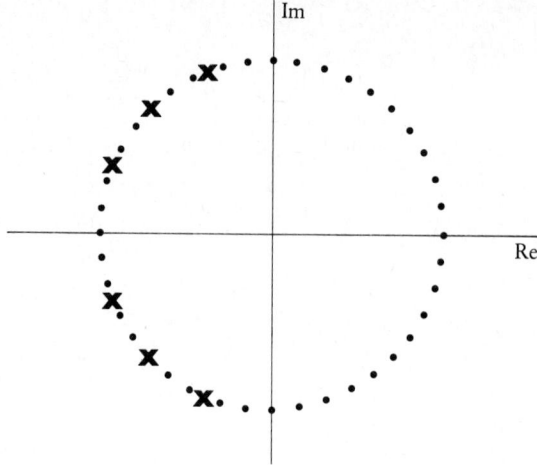

Figure 13.28
Poles for Butterworth
filter.

In equation (13.26) we use the polynomial of order 2, $B_2(s)$.

For each value of n, the poles of $T(s)$ are on the unit circle in the left half s-plane. The poles are symmetrically spaced, as shown in Figure 13.28.

Example 13.23

Determine the transfer function for a third-order Butterworth low-pass filter that has normalized transfer function given by

$$T(s) = \frac{1}{s^3 + 2s^2 + 2s + 1}$$

and Bode plot as shown in Figure 13.29.

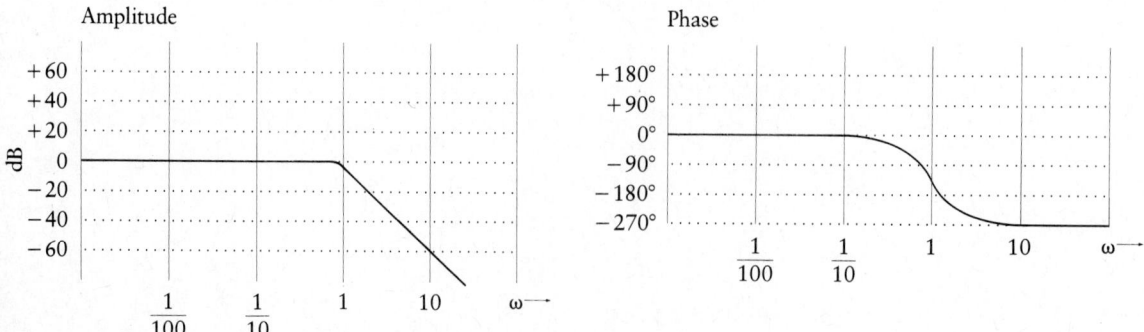

Figure 13.29   Bode plot for Example 13.23.

SOLUTION   A third-order Butterworth low-pass filter with a dc gain of 10 and a cutoff frequency of 1000 Hz is defined by the transfer function

$$T(s) = \frac{10}{\left(\dfrac{s}{2\pi \times 1000}\right)^3 + 2\left(\dfrac{s}{2\pi \times 1000}\right)^2 + 2\left(\dfrac{s}{2\pi \times 1000}\right) + 1}$$

◀▶

13.6.2   *Chebyshev Filters*

The Chebyshev low-pass filter has a transfer function built around a Chebyshev polynomial. The polynomials are sketched in Figure 13.30 and are given by the following equations:

$$C_0 = 1$$

$$C_1(x) = x$$

$$C_2(x) = 2x^2 - 1$$

$$C_3(x) = 4x^3 - 3x$$

$$C_4(x) = 8x^4 - 8x^2 - 1$$

$$C_5(x) = 16x^5 - 20x^3 + 5x$$

$$C_6(x) = 32x^6 - 48x^4 + 18x^2 + 1$$

and, in general,

$$C_{n+1}(x) = 2xC_n(x) - C_{n-1}(x)$$

Figure 13.30   Chebyshev polynomials.

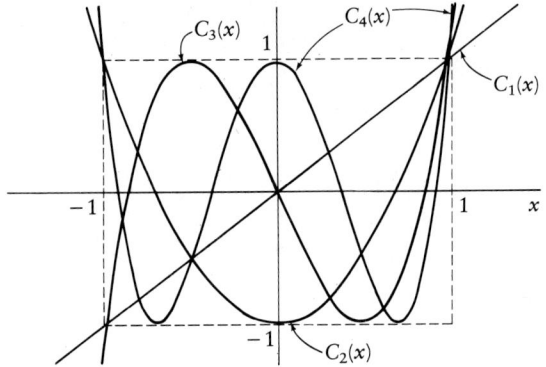

Chebyshev filters exhibit ripple in the pass band, and they have a steeper roll-off than Butterworth filters. For a given order, both filter characteristics have the same asymptotic slope. The magnitude of the transfer function is

$$|T^2(\omega)| = \frac{1}{1 + \epsilon^2 C_n{}^2(\omega)}$$

where C_n is the nth-order polynomial and ϵ determines the ripple magnitude. The constant ϵ is less than 1.

The normalized second-order Chebyshev low-pass filter with $\epsilon = 0.5$ has a ripple bounded by

$$\text{ripple} = \frac{1}{1 + \epsilon^2} = 0.8$$

The transfer function is found by substituting the value of ϵ and the Chebyshev polynomial into the general expression to find

$$|T^2(\omega)| = \frac{1}{1 + (0.5)^2 C_2{}^2(\omega)}$$

$$= \frac{1}{1 + 0.25(2\omega^2 - 1)^2}$$

$$= \frac{1}{\omega^4 - \omega^2 + 0.75}$$

Letting $s = j\omega$ yields

$$T^2(s) = \frac{1}{s^4 + s^2 + 0.75}$$

This is rewritten by factoring out the square, with the result

$$T^2(s) = \frac{1}{(s^2 + 0.5)^2 + 0.5}$$

If the filter order is odd, the response curve starts at $T(j\omega) = 1$ or, in decibels, at 0 dB. If the filter order is even, the curve starts at the magnitude of the ripple. Excluding the point where the curve crosses at $\omega_p = 1$, the order of the filter equals the sum of the response maxima and minima in the pass band. The curve of Figure 13.31 therefore represents an even order filter of order 4.

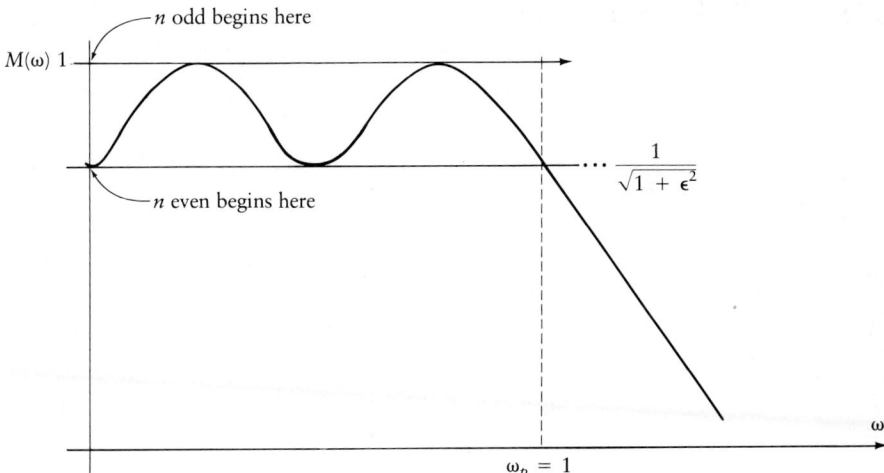

Figure 13.31 Example of a Chebyshev filter.

When designing higher-order filters, the most convenient approach is to break the function up into second- and third-order stages. These successive stages then combine to yield the desired response. This cascading is possible using op-amps because of the isolation, which yields good cascadability. If one stage were to load another stage, cascading would not be possible.

13.7 Transformations

There is a close relationship among the various classifications of filters. Once a design is completed for one type, it is often possible to modify the design to change the filter into one of a different classification. In this manner, lengthy redesigns may be avoided. We examine two particular transformations between one filter format and another.

13.7.1 *Low-Pass to High-Pass Transformation*

Substituting s for $1/s$ converts a normalized low-pass transfer function to a high-pass transfer function. This transformation has the effect of interchanging the resistors with all the capacitors, as we saw in an example in Section 13.5.

Example 13.24

Transform a third-order Butterworth low-pass filter into a high-pass filter.

SOLUTION The low-pass transfer function is given by

$$T_{LP}(s) = \frac{1}{s^3 + 2s^2 + 2s + 1}$$

We now replace s by $1/s$ to yield

$$T_{HP}(s) = \frac{1}{(1/s)^3 + 2(1/s)^2 + 2(1/s) + 1}$$

$$= \frac{s^3}{s^3 + 2s^2 + 2s + 1}$$

The amplitude and phase for this transformed Butterworth network are shown in Figure 13.32.

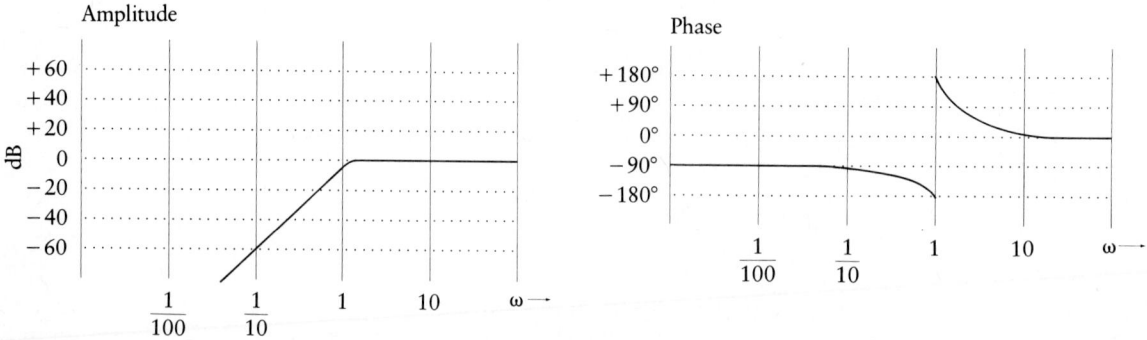

Figure 13.32 Bode plot of transformed Butterworth filter.

Example 13.25

Transform the following second-order Chebyshev low-pass filter into a high-pass filter:

$$T_{LP}(s) = \frac{1}{(s + 0.84)^2 + 0.87^2}$$

SOLUTION Starting with the low-pass transfer function,

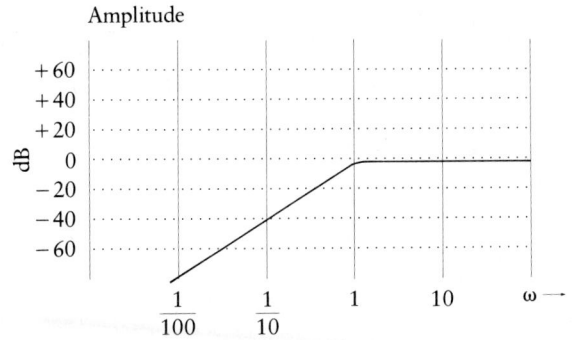

Figure 13.33 Bode plot of transformed Chebyshev filter.

$$T_{LP}(s) = \frac{1}{s^2 + 1.7s + 1.47}$$

We now replace s by $1/s$ to yield

$$T_{HP}(s) = \frac{1}{(1/s)^2 + 1.7(1/s) + 1.47}$$

$$= \frac{s^2}{1.47s^2 + 1.7s + 1}$$

The Bode plot for this transformed Chebyshev network is shown in Figure 13.33.

13.7.2 *Band-Pass Transformation*

We can convert a normalized low-pass transfer function into a normalized band-pass transfer function by making the substitution

$$\frac{s^2 + 1}{s}$$

in place of s. The order of the band-pass filter is twice that of the original low-pass filter.

Example 13.26

Transform a third-order Butterworth low-pass filter into a band-pass filter.

SOLUTION We start with the low-pass transfer function,

$$T_{LP}(s) = \frac{1}{s^3 + 2s^2 + 2s + 1}$$

Replacing s with $(s^2 + 1)/s$ yields

$$T_{BP}(s) = \frac{1}{[(s^2 + 1)/s]^3 + 2[(s^2 + 1)/s]^2 + 2[(s^2 + 1)/s] + 1}$$

$$= \frac{s^3}{s^6 + 2s^5 + 5s^4 + 5s^3 + 5s^2 + 2s + 1} \qquad \blacktriangleright\!\!+$$

13.8   Design Procedure for Butterworth and Chebyshev Filters

In this section, we examine a constant-resistance or constant-capacitance approach toward designing Butterworth and Chebyshev filters. The design approach set forth assumes 1 Ω values for the resistors in the low-pass filter shown in Figure 13.34. In this section we develop filters up to tenth order. Each order is formed by combining second- and third-order filters.

To design a high-pass Butterworth or Chebyshev filter, we interchange the capacitors and resistors from that of the low-pass design. In a high-pass filter, the capacitors are of equal value (instead of the resistors, as is the case in low-pass filters). The two-pole and three-pole high-pass filters are shown in Figure 13.35.

The circuit configuration for the Chebyshev filter is identical to that of the Butterworth filter. Only the component values are different.

13.8.1   *Low-Pass Filter Design*

Four parameters must be specified to enable us to design a Butterworth or Chebyshev filter. These four parameters can be stated in various ways. One set of choices is shown in Figure 13.36, and the parameters are as follows:

A_p = decibel attenuation in the pass band

A_s = decibel attenuation in the stop band

f_p = frequency at which A_p occurs

f_s = frequency at which A_s occurs

In the case of the Chebyshev filter, one additional parameter is specified. This parameter is the maximum ripple permitted in the pass band, given in decibels.

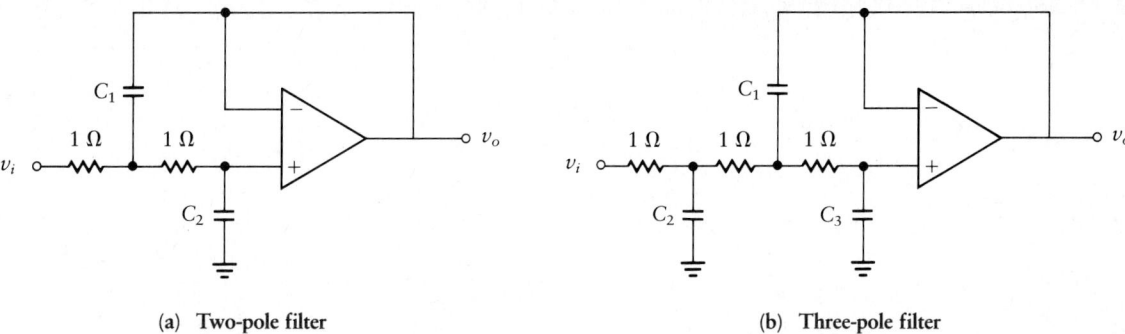

(a) Two-pole filter   (b) Three-pole filter

Figure 13.34   Unity-R active low-pass filter.

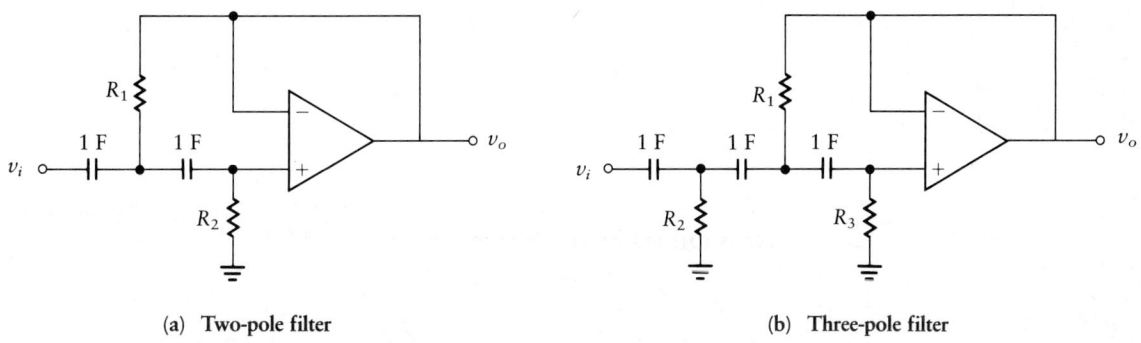

(a) Two-pole filter   (b) Three-pole filter

Figure 13.35   Unity-C active high-pass filters.

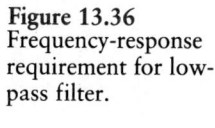

Figure 13.36
Frequency-response
requirement for low-
pass filter.

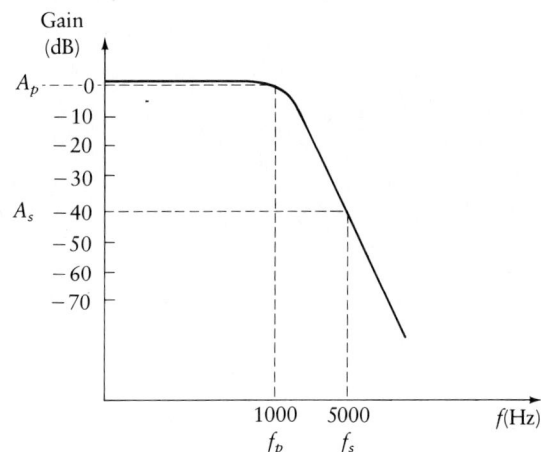

The design procedure is divided into two parts. It is first necessary to find the required *order* of the filter and then to find the *scale factor* that must be applied to the normalized parameter values.

13.8.2 *Filter Order*

We first determine what order filter is needed to satisfy the specification for A_p at f_p and A_s at f_s. Notice that A_p and A_s are magnitudes, so we need not be concerned with the minus sign that appears in the expressions.

The first step is to use the pass-band and stop-band amplitude information to find the required filter order. We denote this order as n_B for the Butterworth filter and n_C in the Chebyshev case. We use equation (13.27), where T_1 is A_p, ω_1 is ω_p, T_2 is A_s, and ω_2 is ω_s. Since A_p is the number of decibels *below* 0 dB, the value of T_1 is $10^{-A_p/20}$. Other quantities are similarly transformed. Therefore, the equation for the Butterworth order, n_B, is

$$n_B = \frac{\log(\epsilon_2/\epsilon_1)}{\log(f_s/f_p)} \tag{13.29a}$$

and the equation for the Chebyshev order, n_C, is

$$n_C = \frac{\ln(2\epsilon_2/\epsilon_1)}{\sqrt{2(f_s/f_p - 1)}} \tag{13.29b}$$

where

$$\epsilon_1 = \sqrt{10^{0.1A_p} - 1}$$

$$\epsilon_2 = \sqrt{10^{0.1A_s} - 1} \tag{13.30}$$

Example 13.27

Select the order for a low-pass filter that has the following specifications:

$$A_p = 3 \text{ dB} \quad \text{at} \quad f_p = 1 \text{ kHz}$$
$$A_s = 40 \text{ dB} \quad \text{at} \quad f_s = 5 \text{ kHz}$$

This filter characteristic is shown as Figure 13.36.

SOLUTION   Using equation (13.30), we obtain

$$\epsilon_1 = \sqrt{10^{(0.1)(3)} - 1} = \sqrt{10^{0.3} - 1} = \sqrt{2 - 1} = 1$$

$$\epsilon_2 = \sqrt{10^{(0.1)(40)} - 1} = \sqrt{10^4 - 1} = 100$$

We calculate n_B and n_C as follows:

$$n_B = \frac{\log(\epsilon_2/\epsilon_1)}{\log(f_s/f_p)} = \frac{\log(100)}{\log(5000/1000)} = 2.86 \qquad \text{so we use } n = 3.$$

$$n_C = \frac{\ln(2\epsilon_2/\epsilon_1)}{\sqrt{2(f_s/f_p - 1)}} = \frac{\ln(200)}{\sqrt{8}} = 1.87 \qquad \text{so we use } n = 2.$$

The order must be an integer, so we choose the next integer value above the calculated value.   ➤+

13.8.3   *Parameter Scale Factor*

Now that we know the required order for the filter, we need to choose the component values.

Various synthesis methods are available to design these filters. The constant-resistance or constant-capacitance technique presented here provides a direct and suitable method to design these filters easily ([64] provides additional information regarding the design process). Once we know the order of the filter, we can use Table 13.2 to select the capacitor coefficients for the Butterworth filter or Table 13.3, (a) through (e), for design of the Chebyshev filter.

Table 13.2 lists capacitor ratios for normalized Butterworth low-pass filters and resistor ratios for high-pass filters. For the low-pass filter, the resistors are assumed to be 1 Ω in value. Thus, as an example, viewing the first row of the table yields a second-order Butterworth filter design. We use one second-order stage with $C_1/C = 1.41$ and $C_2/C = 0.707$. For orders greater than 3, the table contains more than one row. The reason is that we build these filters using second- and third-order stages, so for order greater than 3, more than one stage is required. The table is configured for unit corner frequency, that is, $\omega_p = 1$.

To design a practical Butterworth filter, we obtain the capacitor or resistor ratios from the table and scale the values to practical sizes. That is, if the corner frequency is anything other than 1 rps, and/or the resistors are any value other than 1 Ω, the capacitor values from the table must be appropriately scaled. Since the product RC is inversely proportional to the frequency, then for a given frequency, R and C are themselves inversely related. If, for example, we double R, we halve C. Thus, if resistors of other than 1 Ω are used, the capacitor

Table 13.2   Butterworth Active Low-Pass Values.*

Order n	C_1/C or R/R_1	C_2/C or R/R_2	C_3/C or R/R_3
2	1.414	0.7071	
3	3.546	1.392	0.2024
4	1.082	0.9241	
	2.613	0.3825	
5	1.753	1.354	0.4214
	3.235	0.3090	
6	1.035	0.9660	
	1.414	0.7071	
	3.863	0.2588	
7	1.531	1.336	0.4885
	1.604	0.6235	
	4.493	0.2225	
8	1.020	0.9809	
	1.202	0.8313	
	1.800	0.5557	
	5.125	0.1950	
9	1.455	1.327	0.5170
	1.305	0.7661	
	2.000	0.5000	
	5.758	0.1736	
10	1.012	0.9874	
	1.122	0.8908	
	1.414	0.7071	
	2.202	0.4540	
	6.390	0.1563	

*See [64].

ratios from the table are scaled. Likewise, if a corner frequency other than 1 rps is used, the capacitor values are again scaled.

The resistor values, which are shown as 1 Ω in Fig. 13.34, are raised to a more practical value. The capacitor values are also adjusted to a practical value. We first select a value for all resistors, that is, $R_1 = R_2 = R_3 = R$. The actual capacitor values are found by using the scaling equation,

$$C_n = \frac{C_i}{2\pi f_p R} \tag{13.31}$$

where R is the chosen resistor value and C_i are read from the table.

Table 13.3a　0.01 dB Chebyshev Active Values.*

Order n	C_1/C or R/R_1	C_2/C or R/R_2
2	1.4826	0.7042
4	1.4874	1.1228
	3.5920	0.2985
6	1.8900	1.5249
	2.5820	0.5953
	7.0522	0.1486
8	2.3652	1.9493
	2.7894	0.8196
	4.1754	0.3197
	11.8920	0.08672

*See [64].

Table 13.3b　0.1 dB Chebyshev Active Values.*

Order n	C_1/C or R/R_1	C_2/C or R/R_2	C_3/C or R/R_3
2	1.638	0.6955	
3	6.653	1.825	0.1345
4	1.900	1.241	
	4.592	0.2410	
5	4.446	2.520	0.3804
	6.810	0.1580	
6	2.553	1.776	
	3.487	0.4917	
	9.531	0.1110	
7	5.175	3.322	0.5693
	4.546	0.3331	
	12.73	0.08194	
8	3.270	2.323	
	3.857	0.6890	
	5.773	0.2398	
	16.44	0.06292	
9	6.194	4.161	0.7483
	4.678	0.4655	
	7.170	0.1812	
	20.64	0.04980	
10	4.011	2.877	
	4.447	0.8756	
	5.603	0.3353	
	8.727	0.1419	
	25.32	0.04037	

*See [64].

Table 13.3c   0.25 dB Chebyshev Active Values.*

Order n	C_1/C or R/R_1	C_2/C or R/R_2	C_3/C or R/R_3
2	1.778	0.6789	
3	8.551	2.018	0.1109
4	2.221	1.285	
	5.363	0.2084	
5	5.543	2.898	0.3425
	8.061	0.1341	
6	3.044	1.875	
	4.159	0.4296	
	11.36	0.09323	
7	6.471	3.876	0.5223
	5.448	0.2839	
	15.26	0.06844	
8	3.932	2.474	
	4.638	0.6062	
	6.942	0.2019	
	19.76	0.05234	
9	7.766	4.891	0.6919
	5.637	0.3983	
	8.639	0.1514	
	24.87	0.04131	
10	4.843	3.075	
	5.368	0.7725	
	6.766	0.2830	
	10.53	0.1181	
	30.57	0.03344	

*See [64].

Table 13.3d   0.5 dB Chebyshev Active Values.*

Order n	C_1/C or R/R_1	C_2/C or R/R_2	C_3/C or R/R_3
2	1.950	0.6533	
3	11.23	2.250	0.0895
4	2.582	1.300	
	6.233	0.1802	
5	6.842	3.317	0.3033
	9.462	0.1144	

Table 13.3d 0.5 dB Chebyshev Active Values. (*Continued*)

Order n	C_1/C or R/R_1	C_2/C or R/R_2	C_3/C or R/R_3
6	3.592	1.921	
	4.907	0.3743	
	13.40	0.07902	
7	7.973	4.483	0.4700
	6.446	0.2429	
	18.07	0.05778	
8	4.665	2.547	
	5.502	0.5303	
	8.237	0.1714	
	23.45	0.04409	
9	9.563	5.680	0.6260
	6.697	0.3419	
	10.26	0.1279	
	29.54	0.03475	
10	5.760	3.175	
	6.383	0.6773	
	8.048	0.2406	
	12.53	0.09952	
	36.36	0.02810	

*See [64].

Table 13.3e 1 dB Chebyshev Active Values.*

Order n	C_1/C or R/R_1	C_2/C or R/R_2	C_3/C or R/R_3
2	2.218	0.6061	
3	16.18	2.567	0.06428
4	3.125	1.269	
	7.546	0.1489	
5	8.884	3.935	0.2540
	11.55	0.09355	
6	4.410	1.904	
	6.024	0.3117	
	16.46	0.06425	
7	10.29	5.382	0.4012
	7.941	0.1993	
	22.25	0.04684	

Table 13.3e   1 dB Chebyshev Active Values. (*Continued*)

Order n	C_1/C or R/R_1	C_2/C or R/R_2	C_3/C or R/R_3
8	5.756	2.538	
	6.792	0.4435	
	10.15	0.1395	
	28.94	0.03568	
9	12.33	6.853	0.5382
	8.281	0.2813	
	12.68	0.1038	
	36.51	0.02808	
10	7.125	3.170	
	7.897	0.5630	
	9.952	0.1962	
	15.50	0.08054	
	44.98	0.02269	

*See [64].

Example 13.28

Find component values for the design of Example 13.27. In that example, we specify

$$A_p = -3 \text{ dB} \quad \text{at} \quad f_p = 1 \text{ kHz}$$

$$A_s = -40 \text{ dB} \quad \text{at} \quad f_s = 5 \text{ kHz}$$

SOLUTION   Refer to Table 13.2 for the Butterworth filter of order $n_B = 3$. For order 3, the capacitor ratios are read as follows:

$$\frac{C_1}{C} = 3.546; \qquad \frac{C_2}{C} = 1.392; \qquad \frac{C_3}{C} = 0.2024$$

These values must be scaled inversely with the frequency and the selected resistor value. Suppose we choose resistors of value 1 kΩ. The scaling factor is then

$$\frac{1}{2\pi f_p R} = \frac{1}{2\pi \times 10^3 \times 10^3} = 0.16 \times 10^{-6}$$

This yields capacitors of value

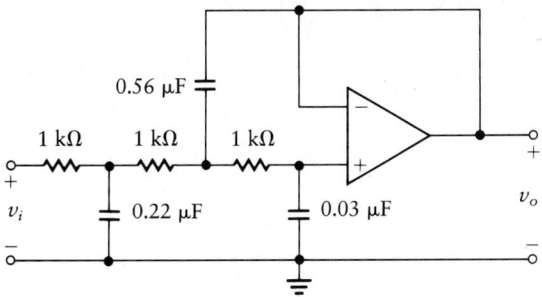

Figure 13.37
Three-pole Butterworth filter for Example 13.28.

$$C_1 = (0.16)(3.546) \ \mu F = 0.56 \ \mu F$$

$$C_2 = (0.16)(1.392) \ \mu F = 0.22 \ \mu F$$

$$C_3 = (0.16)(0.2024) \ \mu F = 0.03 \ \mu F$$

The complete filter is shown in Figure 13.37. All resistor values are equal to 1 kΩ. If the derived capacitor values were not practical because of size or availability, we could select a new value for R and recalculate the capacitor values.

Example 13.29

Derive the 0.1-dB Chebyshev filter for the specifications of Example 13.28.

SOLUTION   Let us again select $R = 1 \ \text{k}\Omega$ and use the capacitor coefficients for a Chebyshev low-pass filter of order 2 (recall that $n_C = 2$ from Example 13.27). These coefficients are taken from Table 13.3(b), since the maximum ripple is specified as 0.1 dB. Therefore,

$$\frac{C_1}{C} = 1.638$$

$$\frac{C_2}{C} = 0.6955$$

Using the scaling technique described above, we find the scale value to be

$$\frac{1}{2\pi f_p R} = 0.16 \times 10^{-6}$$

We thus obtain

Figure 13.38
Chebyshev filter for
Example 13.29.

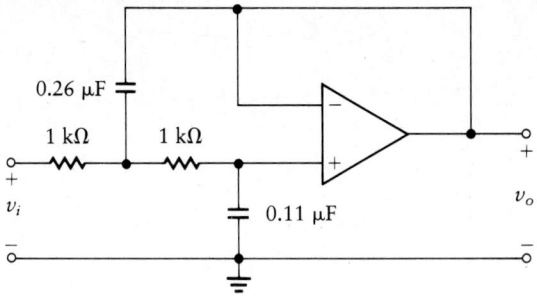

$$C_1 = (0.16)(1.638) \ \mu F = 0.26 \ \mu F$$

$$C_2 = (0.16)(0.6955) \ \mu F = 0.11 \ \mu F$$

The filter is shown in Figure 13.38.

13.8.4   *High-Pass Filter*

The circuits for a high-pass filter are shown in Figure 13.35(a) for a two-pole filter and Figure 13.35(b) for a three-pole filter. When calculating the order for a high-pass filter, f_p and f_s are interchanged, and all the capacitors are of the same value. We use the ratio of R/R_i rather than C_i/C in the tables.

Example 13.30

Design an active high-pass filter to meet the following requirements:

$$A_p = \ \ 3 \ dB \ \ at \ \ f_p = 100 \ Hz$$

$$A_s = 75 \ dB \ \ at \ \ f_s = 25 \ Hz$$

SOLUTION   We first calculate the filter order using equation (13.30):

$$\epsilon_1 = \sqrt{10^{(0.1)(3)} - 1} = 1$$

$$\epsilon_2 = \sqrt{10^{7.5} - 1} = 5623$$

The required order for the Butterworth and Chebyshev filters are then obtained from equation (13.29):

$$n_B = \frac{\log 5623}{\log(100/25)} = \frac{3.75}{0.6} = 6.25 \quad \text{so use 7}$$

$$n_C = \frac{\ln(2 \times 5623)}{\sqrt{2(100/25 - 1)}} = \frac{9.33}{2.45} = 3.81 \quad \text{so use 4}$$

We again go to the next-highest integer value for order.

Since the Chebyshev filter has a lower order than the Butterworth, we select the Chebyshev filter. We use the data for a 0.5-dB Chebyshev filter from Table 13.3(d). Note that the ratios in this table are *resistor* ratios, R/R_i, for a high-pass filter. They are *capacitor* ratios for the low-pass filter. Hence, for this fourth-order filter, we obtain the following information.

First Stage

$$\frac{R}{R_1} = 2.582 \qquad \frac{R}{R_2} = 1.3$$

Second Stage

$$\frac{R}{R_1'} = 6.233 \qquad \frac{R}{R_2'} = 0.1802$$

Let us choose $C = 0.015 \ \mu\text{F}$. The scaling factor is then given by

$$R = \frac{1}{2\pi f_p C} = \frac{1}{2\pi(15 \times 10^{-9})(100)} = 1.06 \times 10^5$$

We obtain the following resistor values:

$$R_1 = \frac{R}{2.582} = \frac{1.06 \times 10^5}{2.582} = 41.1 \ \text{k}\Omega$$

$$R_2 = \frac{1.06 \times 10^5}{1.3} = 81.6 \ \text{k}\Omega$$

$$R_1' = \frac{1.06 \times 10^5}{6.233} = 17 \ \text{k}\Omega$$

$$R_2' = \frac{1.06 \times 10^5}{0.1802} = 589 \ \text{k}\Omega$$

The circuit is shown in Figure 13.39. Note that it makes no difference which second-order filter is first and which is last.

Figure 13.39
High-pass Chebyshev
filter for Example
13.30.

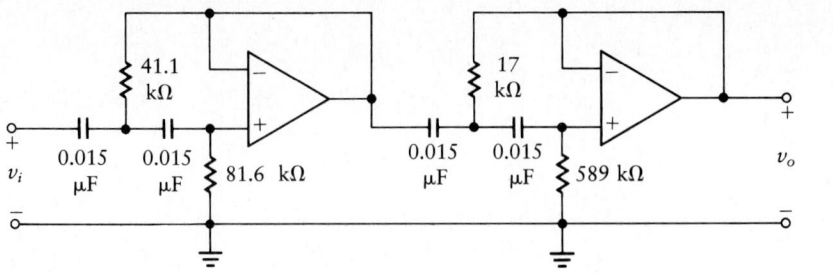

13.8.5 *Band-Pass and Band-Stop Filter Design*

The band-pass and band-stop filters are each formed from low-pass and high-pass filters. The frequency response for the band-pass filter is shown in Figure 13.40(a). We form this type of filter by placing a low-pass filter in series with a high-pass filter, as shown in Figure 13.40(b). The frequency response for the band-stop filter is shown in Figure 13.41(a). We form this filter by placing a low-pass filter in parallel with a high-pass filter, as shown in Figure 13.41(b).

Figure 13.40
Band-pass filter.

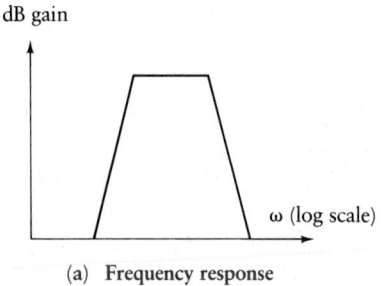

(a) Frequency response

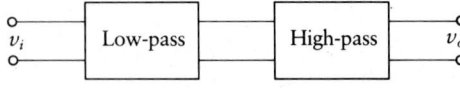

(b) Low-pass and high-pass filters in series

Figure 13.41
Band-stop filter.

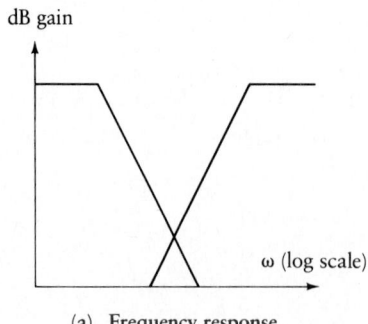

(a) Frequency response

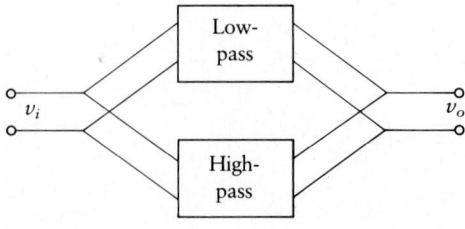

(b) Low-pass and high-pass filters in parallel

Example 13.31

Design a band-pass Butterworth filter that has the frequency response shown in Figure 13.42.

SOLUTION   This filter is designed using a low-pass filter in series with a high-pass filter, as shown in Figure 13.40(b). We start the design of the low-pass filter by using equation (13.29a) and equation (13.30) as follows:

$$\epsilon_1 = \sqrt{10^{(0.1)(3)} - 1} = 1$$

$$\epsilon_2 = \sqrt{10^{(0.1)(30)} - 1} = 31.6$$

$$n_B = \frac{\log(\epsilon_2/\epsilon_1)}{\log(f_s/f_p)} = \frac{\log(31.6)}{\log(8000/4000)} = 4.98 \qquad \text{so use 5}$$

We obtain the C_i/C coefficients from Table 13.2 as follows:

1.753	1.354	0.4214
3.235	0.309	

The scaling factor, C, is found, for a choice of $R = 10$ kΩ, to be

$$C = \text{scaling factor} = \frac{1}{2\pi f_p R} = \frac{1}{2\pi(4 \times 10^3)(10^4)} = 3.98 \times 10^{-9} \text{ F}$$

The scale factor is multiplied by each of the C_i/C coefficients to yield the capacitor values. The final circuit for the low-pass section is shown in Figure

---

Figure 13.42
Band-pass filter response for Example 13.31.

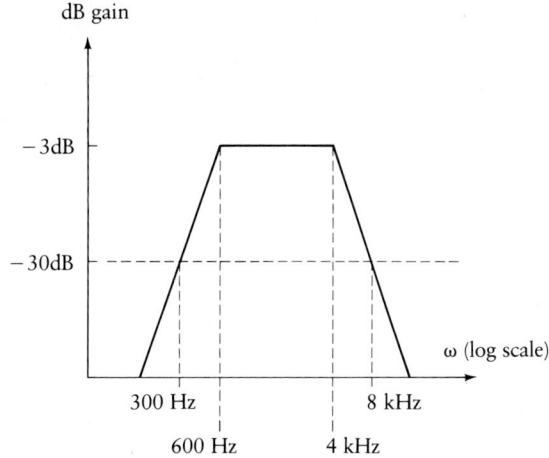

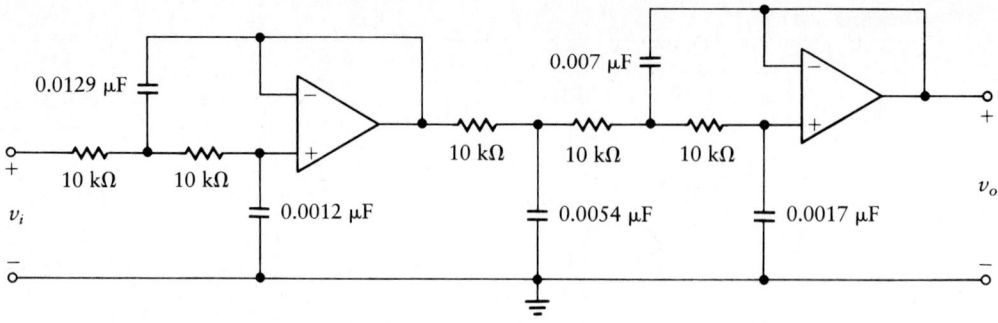

Figure 13.43 Low-pass filter for Example 13.31.

13.43. It makes no difference whether the third-order filter is before or after the second-order filter.

The second part of the filter comprises the design of the high-pass section. Equations (13.29a) and (13.30) are used as follows:

$$\epsilon_1 = \sqrt{10^{(0.1)(3)} - 1} = 1$$

$$\epsilon_2 = \sqrt{10^{(0.1)(30)} - 1} = 31.6$$

and $n_B = 5$ just as for the low-pass filter. The coeffients for the high-pass filter are the ratio of R/R_i but have the same numerical values as for the C_i/C ratios. Thus, they are given as follows:

1.753   1.354   0.4214

3.235   0.309

Let us choose $C = 0.05$ μF, yielding the scaling factor, R, to be

$$R = \text{scaling factor} = \frac{1}{2\pi(600)(0.5 \times 10^{-7})} = 5.305 \text{ k}\Omega$$

The resistor values, R_i, are found by dividing the coefficients into the scaling factor, R, as follows:

$$R_1 = \frac{5305}{1.753} = 3.03 \text{ k}\Omega$$

$$R_2 = \frac{5305}{1.354} = 3.92 \text{ k}\Omega$$

$$R_3 = \frac{5305}{0.4214} = 12.59 \text{ k}\Omega$$

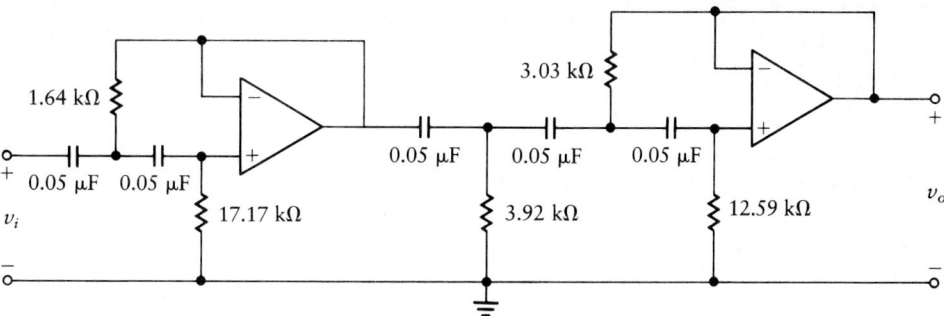

Figure 13.44 High-pass filter for Example 13.31.

$$R_4 = \frac{5305}{3.235} = 1.64 \text{ k}\Omega$$

$$R_5 = \frac{5305}{0.309} = 17.17 \text{ k}\Omega$$

The final circuit for the high-pass section is shown in Figure 13.44. The complete circuit is formed by placing the low-pass section of Figure 13.43 in series with the high-pass section of Figure 13.44.

13.9 Concluding Remarks

In the introduction to this chapter, we posed the problem of designing a filter to reduce out-of-band power output to the level required by the FCC. This design was to be accomplished quickly in order to bring the video game to market in a timely manner.

Because the filter has to be designed and manufactured quickly, it is probably not wise to attempt a custom design. The requirement for significant reduction outside of the pass band leads us to consider the Butterworth or Chebyshev design. Since the selling price of our game was calculated without considering the filter, it is important that cost be held to an absolute minimum. Example 13.27 illustrates that the same level of out-of-band attenuation can be accomplished with fewer stages using a Chebyshev as compared to a Butterworth filter. For this reason, we would probably select the Chebyshev bandpass filter of the order necessary to meet the FCC specification. One precaution is necessary here. The ripple within the pass band of the Chebyshev filter normally would not cause great difficulty. In particular, if audio signals are involved, the listener would probably not hear any distortion. However, with video signals, this ripple could lead to ghost images on the television screen. Given the tight time schedule, it would probably be best to build a prototype Chebyshev filter and test it in the game. If objectionable results occur, you could switch to a higher-order Butterworth filter.

PROBLEMS

In Problems 13.1–13.6, design active networks to provide the given V_o/V_i transfer function.

13.1 $T(s) = \dfrac{-10}{s}$

13.2 $T(s) = \dfrac{10}{s^2}$

13.3 $T(s) = \dfrac{-s}{s + 10}$

13.4 $T(s) = \dfrac{-10(s + 10)}{s + 1}$

13.5 $T(s) = \dfrac{10}{s(s + 1)}$

13.6 $T(s) = \dfrac{-(s + 1)^2}{s(s + 10)}$

In Problems 13.7–13.8, design a single-amplifier summing integrator to achieve the output voltage V_o related to input voltages, V_1, V_2, and V_3 as indicated.

13.7 $V_o = \dfrac{-(V_1 + 10V_2 + 0.53V_3)}{s}$

13.8 $V_o = \dfrac{V_1 - V_2 - 2V_3}{s}$

13.9 Design a multiple-amplifier integrator using a single capacitor that achieves the input-output relationships of Problems 13.7 and 13.8.

13.10 Design a single-input integrator circuit, which has a switch that will reset the integrator output voltage to $+10$ V when thrown. When integrating, the output voltage should be the negative of the integral of the input voltage. A ganged switch may be used if necessary.

13.11 Design a single amplifier summing differentiator with the following relationship between output voltage, V_o, and input voltages, V_1, V_2, and V_3.

$$V_o = -s(V_1 + 10V_2 + 0.5V_3)$$

13.12 Design a 741 low-pass filter with a dc gain of $\frac{1}{2}$ and a roll-off frequency of 10 kHz.

13.13 Design a 741 low-pass filter with a dc gain of 1000 and a roll-off frequency of 0.4 Hz.

13.14 Design a 741 low-pass filter that is adjustable between 10 Hz and 100 Hz roll-off frequency. The frequency adjustment should be made with a potentiometer.

13.15 Design a 741 low-pass filter that has independently adjustable dc gain and roll-off frequency. Gain should be adjustable between 0 and 10 and the frequency from near 0 Hz to 100 Hz. In addition, this system should have an input impedance greater than 50 MΩ.

13.16 Design a 741 high-pass filter with a high frequency gain of $\frac{1}{2}$ and a roll-off frequency of 20 Hz.

13.17 Design a 741 filter that has both a low-pass and a high-pass output. Gain of the low-pass (at dc) and of the high-pass (at high frequency) should each be 10. Roll-off frequency for each is to be at 200 Hz.

13.18 Repeat the design of Problem 13.14, making the roll-off frequency adjustable in the range between 500 Hz and 1500 Hz.

13.19 Design a 741 filter with transfer function

$$T(s) = \frac{3s - 10}{s + 100}$$

13.20 Design a 741 filter with transfer function

$$T(s) = \frac{-10s + 5}{3s + 40}$$

13.21 Derive equation (13.20) from Figure 13.17.

13.22 Design an unbuffered RC low-pass filter with a dc gain of 10 and a corner frequency of 2 kHz.

13.23 Design a buffered first-order low-pass filter with a dc gain of 20 and a corner frequency of 1 kHz.

13.24 Design a low-pass filter with adjustable roll-off frequency between 500 Hz and 1 kHz and a dc gain of 5.

13.25 Design a high-pass filter with a high frequency gain of 20 and a corner frequency of 500 Hz.

13.26 Design an all-pass filter with a dc gain of 5 and the corner frequency at 100 Hz.

13.27 Design an adjustable high-pass filter with a high-frequency gain of 20 and a corner frequency adjustable from 200 Hz to 600 Hz.

13.28 Design an adjustable high-pass filter with a high-frequency gain of 10 and a corner frequency adjustable from 100 Hz to 200 Hz.

13.29 Design an all-pass filter with a gain of 10 and a corner frequency of 100 Hz.

13.30 Using the single amplifier of the general type, design a filter with a high-frequency gain of 1 and a corner frequency of 3 kHz.

13.31 Design a second-order low-pass filter to obtain the transfer function

$$T(s) = \frac{5000}{5s^2 + 50s + 5000}$$

13.32 Design a high-pass filter to achieve the following transfer function:

$$T(s) = \frac{s^2}{s^2 + 25s + 2500}$$

13.33 Design a band-pass filter to achieve the following transfer function:

$$T(s) = \frac{-s}{s^2 + 25s + 2500}$$

13.34 Design a Butterworth low-pass filter with the following specifications:

$$f_p = 500 \text{ Hz} \qquad A_p = 3 \text{ dB}$$
$$f_s = 3 \text{ kHz} \qquad A_s = 50 \text{ dB}$$

13.35 Repeat Problem 13.34 using a Chebyshev filter with a 0.5-dB ripple.

13.36 Repeat Problem 13.35 but use a 1.0-dB ripple.

13.37 Design a Butterworth high-pass filter with the following specifications:

$$-3 \text{ dB at } 1 \text{ kHz}$$
$$-45 \text{ dB at } 300 \text{ Hz}$$

13.38 Repeat Problem 13.37 using a Chebyshev filter with a 0.25-dB ripple.

13.39 Design a "crossover" network to distribute the high frequencies of an audio signal into a high-frequency speaker and the low frequencies into a low-frequency speaker. This is shown in Figure P13.1. Choose either a Butterworth or Chebyshev filter, whichever requires fewer components. If you choose a Chebyshev filter, choose a maximum ripple of 0.25 dB. Draw the filter diagrams.

13.40 Determine the transfer function V_o/V_i for the ideal op-amp circuit shown in Figure P13.2. Since the op-amp is ideal, $V_+ = V_-$. The parameter values are

$$C_1 = 3.546C; \qquad C_2 = 1.392C; \qquad C_3 = 0.2024C$$
$$RC = 1.0$$

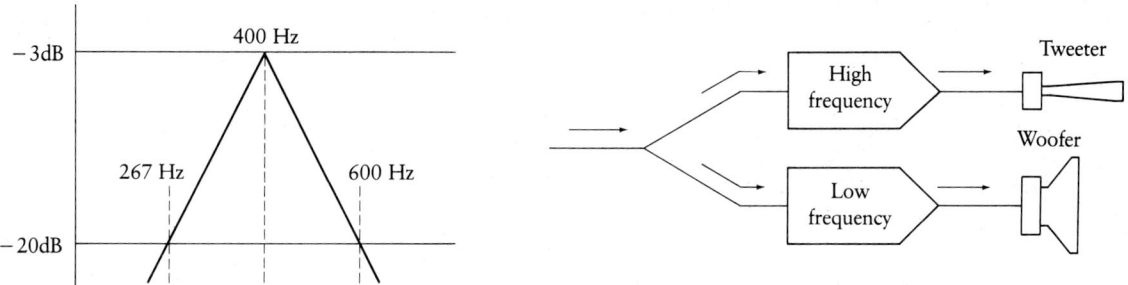

Figure P13.1

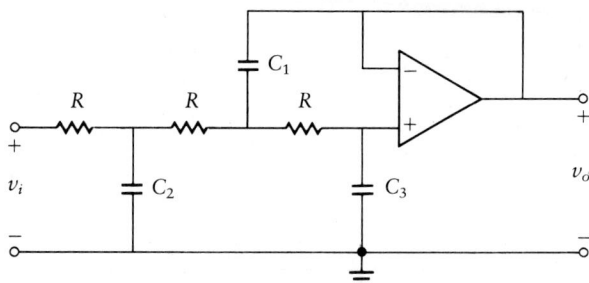

Figure P13.2

Solve this problem in two steps. First find the equations; then solve them using determinants. Construct a Bode plot for this network.

13.41 Design a Butterworth band-pass filter that has the amplitude characteristics shown in Figure P13.3.

13.42 Design a Chebyshev band-stop filter that has the amplitude characteristics shown in Figure P13.4. Set the maximum ripple at 1 dB.

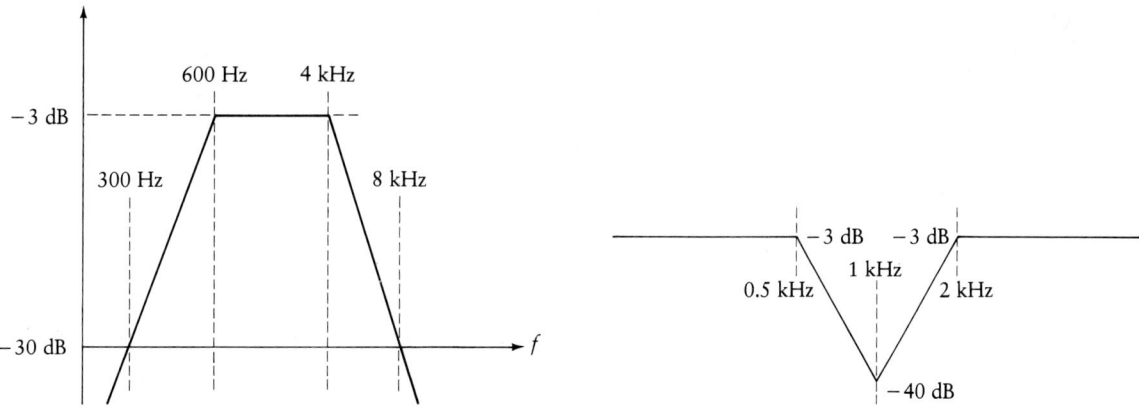

Figure P13.3   **Figure P13.4**

14

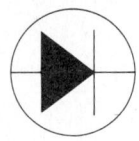

PULSED WAVEFORMS

14.0 Introduction

The topics covered throughout the first 13 chapters of this text emphasize *analog* electronics. In such circuits, we are interested in voltage and current gain, maximum undistorted amplitude swings, and input and output resistance. Typical applications include the amplification of music or speech.

The balance of this text is devoted to *digital* electronics. It has often been said that the world is going digital. Indeed, there are some good reasons for the continuing movement away from analog and toward digital systems.

Digital electronics deals with signals that are one of two values, high or low, on or off, 1 or 0. (We are describing *binary* digital electronics. Digital systems can be nonbinary, and many of the circuits we discuss can be generalized to be nonbinary.) Transistors are either in the *cutoff* or *saturated* condition. We are no longer interested in the linear operating region of electronic devices. Instead, we are concerned only with whether the device is operating in the saturation or cutoff region—that is, whether the output voltage is near zero or near the supply-voltage value. By reducing operations to one of two values, the circuitry often becomes simpler and the chance of making errors is greatly reduced. This last point deserves more emphasis. In an analog system, the output can take on any value within a continuum of values. Therefore, any disturbance, whether in the form of additive noise or distortion, results in an error. In a binary digital system, we are dealing with two possible signal values. Any disturbance must be large enough to make one value look like the other. If the disturbance is not that large, the error is zero.

Before getting to the actual digital electronic system, some preliminary circuit-analysis results are discussed. In particular, we analyze system behavior in the presence of pulse trains. The timing for many of the systems is provided by RC networks. We therefore begin our study of digital electronics by analyzing RC networks with a pulse train as the input. Many of these networks include diodes. In particular, we are interested in the *steady-state* output waveforms of such networks.

14.1   High-Pass RC Network

A series capacitor and a shunt resistor form a simple high-pass network. The input voltage is applied across the combination and the output voltage is taken across the resistor, as shown in Figure 14.1. We analyze the first-order high-pass filter in Chapter 13, and the transfer function is of the form

$$\frac{V_o}{V_i} = \frac{\tau s}{\tau s + 1}$$

where the time constant

$$\tau = RC$$

The sinusoidal steady-state amplitude plot of this response is shown in Figure 14.2. Notice that the corner frequency on this figure is f_c, which is equal to $1/2\pi RC$. Suppose the input to this system is a step function of amplitude V. That is,

$$v_i(t) = Vu(t)$$

where $u(t)$ is the unit-step function. We can use Laplace transform analysis to find the output. (See Appendix C for a review of the Laplace transform method.)

Figure 14.1
High-pass RC network.

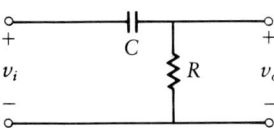

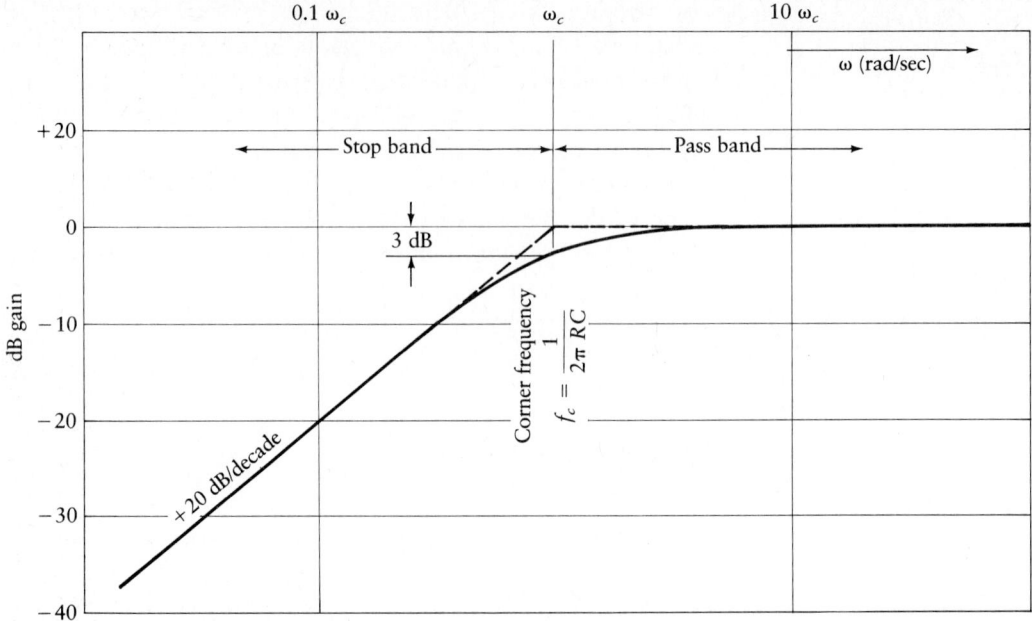

Figure 14.2   Amplitude response of high-pass network.

The Laplace transform of the output is found by multiplying the transfer function by V/s, the Laplace transform of the step input, with the result

$$V_o = \frac{\tau V}{\tau s + 1}$$

The corresponding time function is

$$v_o(t) = Ve^{-t/\tau}u(t) \qquad (14.1)$$

The input step function and the output exponential response are shown in Figure 14.3. Since the circuit equations for an RC network are given by first-order differential equations, the form of the response due to any constant input must be exponential. Thus, for example, the voltage functions must be of the form

$$v(t) = A + Be^{-t/\tau} \qquad (14.2)$$

The time constant, τ, is again equal to RC, and the constants A and B are chosen to match the initial and final values. If the initial and final values of $v(t)$ are given by V_i and V_f, respectively, we solve for A and B as follows:

Figure 14.3
Step response of high-pass network.

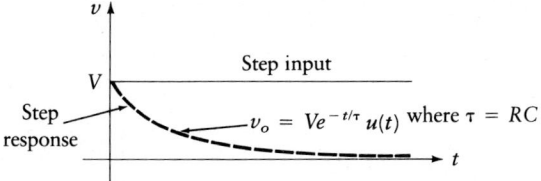

$$v_o(0) = V_i = A + Be^0 = A + B$$

$$v_o(\infty) = V_f = A + Be^{-\infty} = A$$

with the result

$$A = V_f$$

$$B = V_i - V_f$$

The equation for the curve is then

$$v(t) = V_f + (V_i - V_f)e^{-t/\tau} \tag{14.3}$$

As an example of the use of equation (14.3), let us once again find the network response to the step function shown in Figure 14.3.

The initial value of the output voltage is V, since the capacitor voltage cannot change instantaneously when the input jumps from 0 to V volts. The final value is zero, since the capacitor looks like an open circuit for a dc input. Therefore, we have

$$V_i = V$$

$$V_f = 0$$

Substituting these values into equation (14.3) yields

$$v_o(t) = Ve^{-t/\tau}$$

as we found earlier.

We now complicate the system by forming the input from a composite of two steps. Consider the input to be a pulse of amplitude V and duration T. This is formed by adding a step of amplitude V at the origin to a step of amplitude $-V$, which is delayed by T seconds. This is shown in Figure 14.4(a). We solve for the output waveform in two steps. We find the output for times

Figure 14.4
Single pulse formed
from two step
functions.

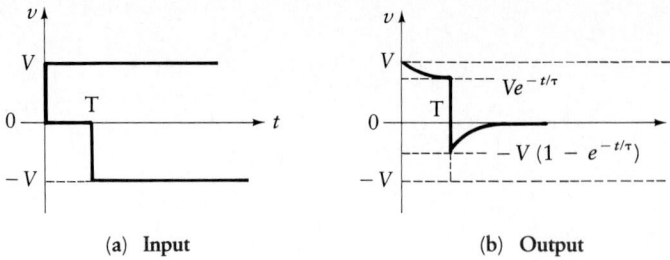

(a) Input   (b) Output

prior to $t = T$ as done previously. That is, since the system cannot see into the future (it is *causal*), it does not know that another step occurs at $t = T$ until the input reaches that point. Therefore, the output prior to time T is given by

$$v_o(t) = Ve^{-t/\tau}$$

We use this equation to find the output just prior to time T, the time at which the second step is applied:

$$v_o(T^-) = Ve^{-T/\tau}$$

The output voltage of the high-pass network of Figure 14.1 *can* jump instantaneously, so we use the notation T^- to indicate the time just prior to the transition time. At time $t = T$, the input voltage jumps negatively by V volts. Since the capacitor voltage cannot change instantaneously and the sum of voltages around the loop is zero, the output must jump down by V volts to equal

$$v_o(T^+) = v_o(T^-) - V = V(e^{-T/\tau} - 1)$$

This forms the initial value for the second portion of the output. The final value is zero. Therefore, we use equation (14.3) in a shifted version, as follows:

$$v_o(t) = V_f + (V_i - V_f)e^{-(t-T)/\tau}$$

You should verify that this equation reduces to V_i at $t = T$ and to V_f as t approaches infinity. We now find initial and final values for this segment:

$$V_i = V(e^{-T/\tau} - 1)$$

$$V_f = 0$$

The equation for the second portion of the output is then given by

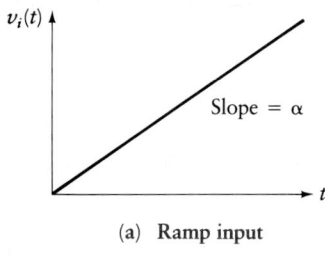

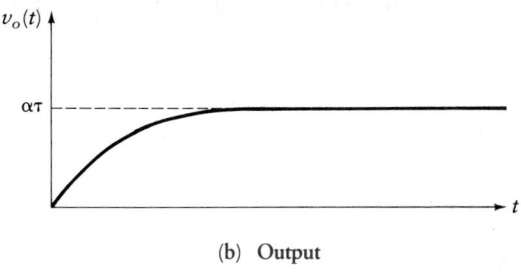

(a) Ramp input

(b) Output

Figure 14.5   Ramp response of high-pass RC network.

$$v_o(t) = -V(1 - e^{-T/\tau})e^{-(t-T)/\tau} \tag{14.4}$$

The composite output is plotted as Figure 14.4(b).

This same result could have been found by applying the principle of *superposition* to the system. The input is a sum of two step functions, so the output is the sum of the two individual step responses.

Before extending this single step result to apply to a pulse train input, we briefly consider the ramp input with slope α, as shown in Figure 14.5(a). We find the response of the RC network using Laplace transforms. The transform of the ramp is α/s^2. Therefore,

$$V_o(s) = \frac{\alpha}{s^2} \frac{s\tau}{s\tau + 1} = \alpha \frac{1}{s(s + 1/\tau)}$$

The inverse Laplace transform of this function is given by

$$v_o(t) = \alpha\tau(1 - e^{-t/\tau})u(t) \tag{14.5}$$

This is shown in Figure 14.5(b).

Example 14.1

The ramp of Figure 14.5(a) forms the input to a high-pass RC filter with a lower 3 dB frequency of 10^4 rad/s. The slope of the input ramp is 10 V/s.

   a. Find the steady-state output voltage.
   b. How long does it take the output to reach 90% of its steady-state value?
   c. Sketch the output-voltage waveform.

SOLUTION

   a. In Chapter 13, we learned that the 3 dB frequency is the reciprocal of the time constant. Therefore,

Figure 14.6
Output voltage for
Example 14.1.

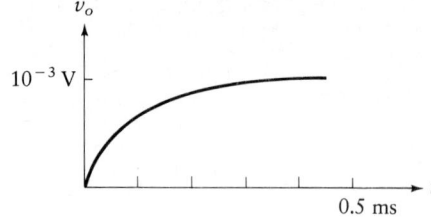

$$\tau = 10^{-4}$$

The steady-state output is found from equation (14.5) or Figure 14.5 to be $\alpha\tau$. Therefore,

$$v_o\Big|_{t\to\infty} = \alpha\tau = (10\ \text{V/s})(10^{-4}\ \text{s}) = 10^{-3}\ \text{V}$$

b. The output voltage will reach 90% of its steady-state value when

$$\alpha\tau(1 - e^{-t/\tau}) = 0.9\alpha\tau$$

$$t = -\tau\ln(0.1) = 0.23\ \text{ms}$$

Note that this result is independent of α.

c. The output voltage waveform is shown in Figure 14.6.   ▶┤

14.1.1 *Steady-State Response—High-Pass Network*

We now have the necessary background and tools to consider the periodic pulse input, as shown in Figure 14.7(a). We apply this square waveform to the high-pass network of Figure 14.1. Without making some logical assumptions, the solution of this circuit-analysis problem is quite tedious. Without such assumptions, we would start with the first pulse and repeat the analysis of Figure 14.4. But then when the second pulse comes along, we have a new initial value for the voltage, and we would have to repeat the analysis for this second pulse. This analysis would be repeated for each input pulse. We would know that steady state is reached only if the initial value no longer changes from that at the start of the previous cycle. That is, we would continue solving for the pulse response until the transient dies out. Of course, the transient is exponential, so it takes infinite time to die out. We present here a better way to evaluate the steady-state response.

We assume that the output resembles the waveform shown in Figure 14.7(b). (We will soon see the reason that three curves are shown, but for now, concentrate upon the center curve, labeled $\tau \approx T$.) We can make this assumption,

Figure 14.7
High-pass RC filter
response to periodic
waveform.

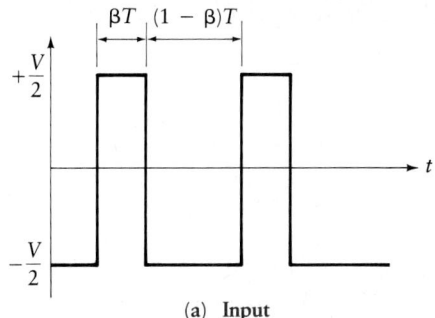

(a) Input

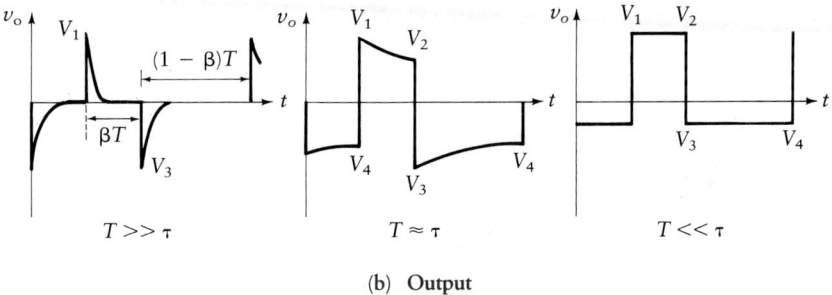

(b) Output

since the input remains constant over portions of the time axis, and during these periods, the output must exponentially approach zero. We next find the key starting values, V_1 and V_3. To do so, divide the problem into three scenarios, depending upon the relationship between the time constant and the period of the input.

If the time constant is much less than the period of the input, the exponential has time to decay almost to zero between transitions, and the output resembles the first sketch in Figure 14.7(b). We next use the fact that the output must have an average value of zero, since the series capacitor cannot pass dc— it acts as an open circuit to zero frequency. The areas of the positive output portions must therefore equal the areas of the negative portions. Since the positive and negative portions of the first sketch in Figure 14.7(b) are symmetrical, we draw the conclusion that

$$V_1 = -V_3 \tag{14.6a}$$

Since the input voltage jumps by V volts at each transition and the capacitor voltage cannot change instantaneously, we conclude that

$$V_1 = -V_3 = V \tag{14.6b}$$

Finally, the waveform is given by

$$v_o(t) = \pm V \exp\left[\frac{-(t - t_0)}{\tau}\right]$$

within each region. The plus sign applies for the positive pulses and the negative sign, for the negative pulses. The time t_0 is the time at which each transition begins.

Note that this result does not apply to the other two sketches of Figure 14.7(b) since we are assuming that the input square wave is asymmetrical—it does not spend equal time at positive and negative values.

Let us examine the case where the time constant and the period of the input are of the same order of magnitude. This is represented by the second sketch in Figure 14.7(b), where the output decays by a noticeable amount but does not reach zero between transitions. We still know that the size of each transition is V volts, so we can write,

$$V_1 = V_4 + V \tag{14.7a}$$

and

$$V_3 = V_2 - V \tag{14.7b}$$

This represents two equations in four unknowns. The remaining two equations in these four unknowns are found by taking the exponential decay into account. The voltage, V_2, results from an exponential relationship starting at V_1 and decaying toward zero for βT seconds. Likewise, V_4 results from an exponential that starts at V_3 and decays toward zero for $(1 - \beta)T$ seconds. Therefore,

$$V_2 = V_1 e^{-\beta T/\tau} \tag{14.7c}$$

and

$$V_4 = V_3 e^{-(1 - \beta)T/\tau} \tag{14.7d}$$

These equations are easily solved for the four voltage values. For example, we solve for V_1 to obtain

$$V_1 = \frac{V(1 - e^{-(1-\beta)T/\tau})}{1 - e^{-T/\tau}}$$

Solutions for the other three voltages follow directly from the equations, which we solve in Example 14.2.

Suppose that $\beta = \frac{1}{2}$. Then

$$V_1 = \frac{V}{1 + e^{-T/2\tau}}$$

and

$$V_3 = -V_1$$

$$V_4 = -V_2$$

$$V_2 = V - V_1$$

When the time constant is much larger than the input period, the output hardly has any time to decay between input transitions, and the output resembles the third sketch in Figure 14.7(b). Since $V_2 = V_1$ and $V_4 = V_3$ and since the height of the transitions must be V, we have

$$V_3 + V = V_1 \tag{14.8a}$$

Since the average value of the output is zero, we match negative and positive arcas to find

$$\beta T(V_1) = -(1 - \beta)TV_3$$

Finally,

$$V_1 = V_2 = V(1 - \beta) \tag{14.8b}$$

$$V_3 = V_4 = -V(\beta) \tag{14.8c}$$

Note that for this case, the output waveform is similar to that of the input but with a voltage shift.

In designing a system, the choice of time constant is often critical. If narrow pulses are required for a triggering operation, we want the output to look similar to the first sketch in Figure 14.7(b). We therefore design with a time constant much less than the period of the input. On the other hand, if we wish to reproduce the input at the output, we should choose a time constant much larger than the period of the input.

Example 14.2

A symmetrical square wave with a peak-to-peak voltage of 10 V is applied to a high-pass RC filter with $R = 1\ k\Omega$ and $C = 1\ \mu F$. Sketch the output waveform and identify key voltages. Assume each of the given frequencies of the square wave.

    a. 50 Hz
    b. 500 Hz
    c. 5 kHz

SOLUTION   Note that since the input waveform is symmetrical, it spends an equal portion of the period at positive and at negative values. Therefore, $\beta = \frac{1}{2}$ and the previous equations are considerably simplified.

    We first find the time constant,

$$\tau = RC = (1 \text{ k}\Omega)(1 \text{ }\mu\text{F}) = 1 \text{ ms}$$

and then compare this time constant to the period of the square wave for each condition given in the problem.

    a. $T = 1/f = 20$ ms, which is much larger than the time constant,

$$T \gg \tau$$

Therefore,

$$V_1 = V = 10 \text{ V}$$
$$V_3 = -V = -10 \text{ V}$$

The result is shown in Figure 14.8(a).

    b. For the second input condition,

$$T = \frac{1}{f} = \frac{1}{500} = 2 \text{ ms}$$

For this case, the input period and the time constant are of the same order of magnitude. We solve for the four voltages as follows:

$$V_1 = V_4 + V = -V_2 + V = -V_3$$
$$V_2 = V_1 e^{-T/2\tau} = -V_4$$

$$V_1 = \frac{V}{1 + e^{-T/2\tau}} = \frac{10}{1 + \exp(-2 \times 10^{-3}/2 \times 10^{-3})}$$
$$= 7.31 = -V_3$$

and

$$V_2 = V - V_1 = 10 - 7.31 = 2.69 \text{ V}$$

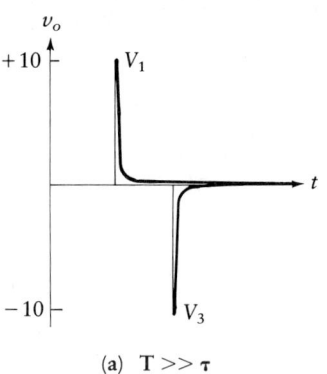

(a) T ≫ τ

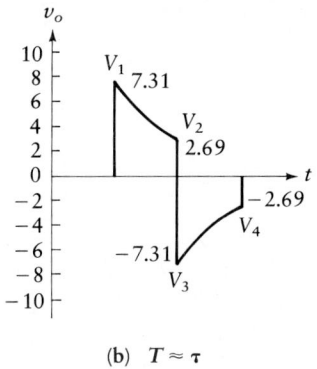

(b) T ≈ τ

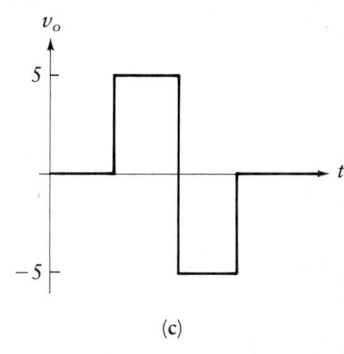

(c)

Figure 14.8   Output waveforms for Example 14.2.

This waveform is shown in Figure 14.8(b). Note that $V_1 = -V_3$ and $V_2 = -V_4$ due to symmetry.

c. For the third input condition,

$$T = \frac{1}{f} = \frac{1}{5000} = 0.2 \text{ ms}$$

This represents a case where the time constant is much larger than the period of the input. Therefore,

$$V_1 = V_2 = \frac{V}{2} = 5 \text{ V}$$

$$V_3 = V_4 = \frac{V}{2} = -5 \text{ V}$$

This waveform is plotted on Figure 14.8(c). Note that it resembles the input waveform.   ►┤

Drill Problems

The asymmetrical input signal of Figure 14.7(a) with $\beta = \frac{1}{3}$, $T = 10$ ms, and $V = 10$ V forms the input to the high-pass network of Figure 14.1. Calculate the four important voltages and sketch the output waveform for the conditions given in Problems D14.1–D14.3.

D14.1   Let $T/\tau = 100$.

   Ans: $V_1 = 10$ V; $V_2 = 0$ V; $V_3 = -10$ V; $V_4 = 0$ V

D14.2   Let $T/\tau = 1$.

   Ans: $V_1 = 7.7$ V; $V_2 = 5.52$ V; $V_3 = -4.48$ V; $V_4 = -2.3$ V

D14.3   Let $T/\tau = 0.01$.

   Ans: $V_1 = 6.678$ V; $V_2 = 6.655$ V; $V_3 = -3.345$ V; $V_4 = -3.322$ V

14.2   Low-Pass RC Network

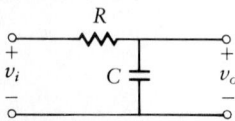

Figure 14.9
Low-pass RC
network.

We now reverse the situation of the previous section by taking the output across the capacitor instead of the resistor. The result is the low-pass RC network shown in Figure 14.9. This network passes low frequencies and attenuates high frequencies. The sinusoidal steady-state amplitude response is shown in Figure 14.10, where the solid line is the actual curve and the dashed line is the Bode plot asymptotic approximation. The transfer function is given by

$$\frac{V_o}{V_i} = \frac{1}{1 + s\tau}$$

Figure 14.10   Amplitude response of low-pass network.

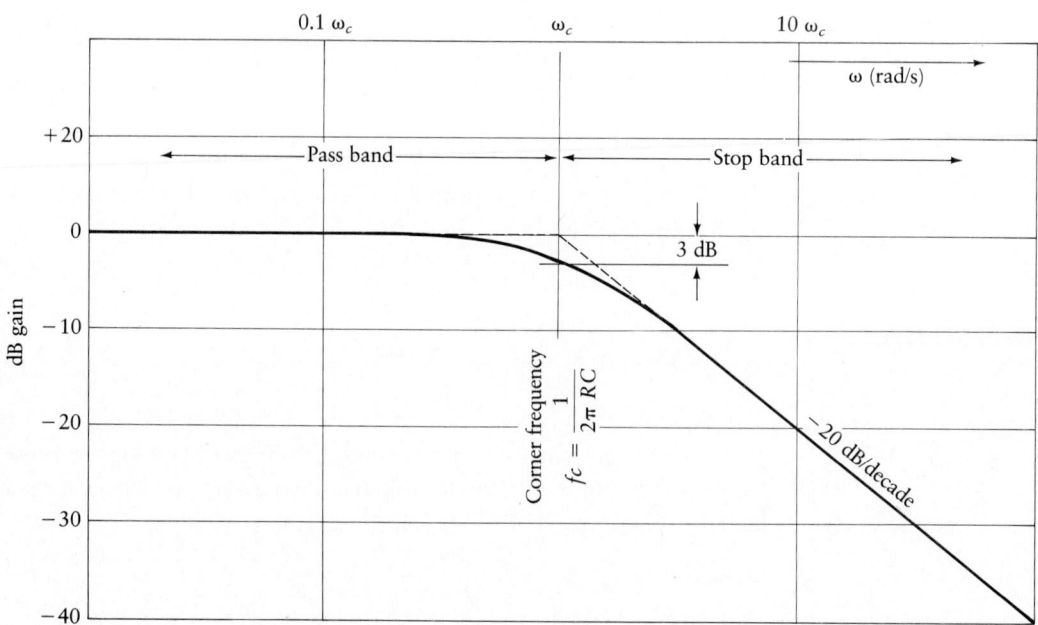

The time constant is

$$\tau = RC$$

Let us turn our attention to the pulse-train input shown in Figure 14.11(a). Both the square-wave input and the output are shown on the same set of axes. Note that the input square wave is no longer assumed to be symmetrical around the zero axis. The positive amplitude is shown as αV and the negative, as $-(1 - \alpha)V$. The total swing is, therefore, V volts.

The output is taken across the capacitor, and therefore it cannot change instantaneously. This "continuity" constraint on the output simplifies the solution, since there are only two unknown voltages, V_1 and V_2, as shown in the figure. We first examine the region between $t = 0$ and $t = \beta T$. The initial value of this exponential waveform is

$$V_i = V_1$$

The final value is the value the voltage would attain if given infinite time. This is seen to be the value of the input, or

$$V_f = \alpha V$$

These two values are used in the general expression of equation (14.3) to find the waveform in the first interval:

$$v_o(t) = \alpha V + (V_1 - \alpha V)e^{-t/\tau}$$

Evaluating this expression at $t = \beta T$ yields an expression for V_2 as follows:

$$v_o(\beta T) = V_2 = \alpha V + (V_1 - \alpha V)e^{-\beta T/\tau} \tag{14.9}$$

Figure 14.11   Input and output of low-pass filter.

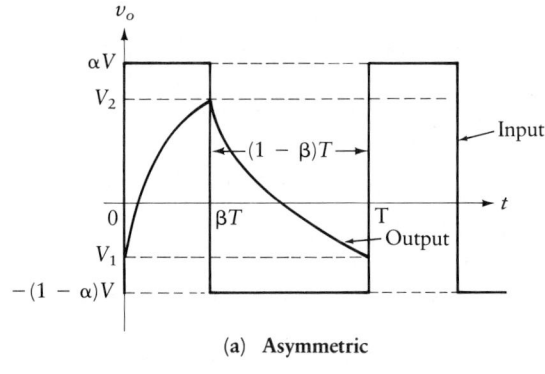

(a) **Asymmetric**

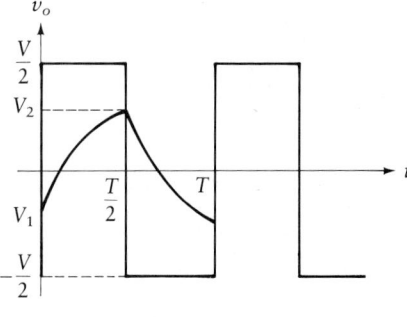

(b) **Symmetric**

For the next region, where $\beta T < t < T$, we have

$$V_f = -(1 - \alpha)V$$

$$V_i = V_2$$

so

$$v_o(t) = -(1 - \alpha)V + (V_2 + V - \alpha V)e^{-(t - \beta T)/\tau}$$

Evaluating this expression at $t = T$ yields the second equation in the two unknowns.

$$v_o(T) = V_1 = -(1 - \alpha)V + (V_2 + V - \alpha V)e^{-(1 - \beta)T/\tau} \qquad (14.10)$$

We next solve equations (14.9) and (14.10) to obtain expressions for V_1 and V_2.

If the input waveform is symmetrical, several simplifications result. That is,

$$\alpha = \beta = \tfrac{1}{2}$$

and

$$V_1 = -V_2$$

Under these conditions, we find

$$-V_1 = V_2 = \frac{V(1 - e^{-T/2\tau})}{2(1 + e^{-T/2\tau})} \qquad (14.11)$$

When a symmetrical square waveform is applied to the low-pass RC network of Figure 14.9, the output is as shown in Figure 14.12. Note the dependence of the output upon the relationship between the time constant, τ, and the period of the input, T. The critical voltages in the output waveforms of Figure 14.12 are as follows:

1. For a time constant much less than the input period,

$$-V_1 = +V_2 = \frac{V}{2} \qquad (14.12)$$

2. For a time constant of the same order as the input period,

$$-V_1 = +V_2 = \frac{V(1 - e^{-T/2\tau})}{2(1 + e^{-T/2\tau})} \qquad (14.13)$$

Figure 14.12
Output a low-pass RC filter with symmetrical square wave input.

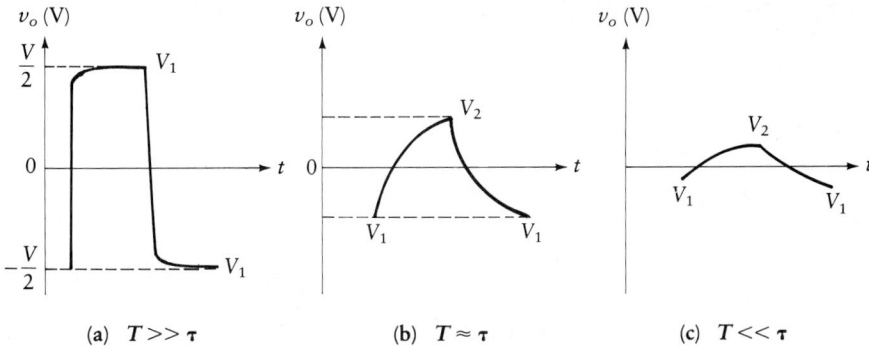

(a) $T \gg \tau$ (b) $T \approx \tau$ (c) $T \ll \tau$

3. For a time constant much greater than the input period, the same result is obtained as in case 2. It should, however, be realized that V_1 and V_2 will be small values.

If the input waveform is no longer symmetrical about the zero axis, α is no longer equal to $\frac{1}{2}$. It is not necessary to rederive all the expressions. The results of Figure 14.12 are simply shifted in the vertical direction by the average value of $v_i(t)$.

Example 14.3

A symmetrical square wave, with a peak-to-peak voltage of 5 V, is applied to the low-pass RC filter of Figure 14.9 with $R = 10$ kΩ and $C = 0.1$ μF. Sketch the output-voltage waveform and identify key voltages for the following three values of the square-wave frequency:

a. 50 Hz
b. 500 Hz
c. 5 kHz

SOLUTION   The time constant of the circuit is

$$\tau = RC = (10 \text{ k}\Omega)(0.1 \text{ }\mu\text{F}) = 1 \text{ ms}$$

a. The period of the input is

$$T = \frac{1}{f} = 20 \text{ ms}$$

In this case, the time constant is much less than the period, so

$$-V_1 = +V_2 = \frac{V}{2} = 2.5 \text{ V}$$

The output is as shown in Figure 14.12(a).

b. The period of the input is

$$T = \frac{1}{f} = 2 \text{ ms}$$

In this case, the time constant is of the same order of magnitude of the input, so we solve for the two key voltages:

$$V_2 = \frac{V}{2} \cdot \frac{1 - e^{-T/2\tau}}{1 + e^{-T/2\tau}} = 2.5 \frac{1 - e^{-1}}{1 + e^{-1}} = 1.155 \text{ V}$$

$$V_1 = -V_2 = -1.155 \text{ V}$$

The resulting waveform is shown in Figure 14.12(b).

c. The period is given by

$$T = \frac{1}{f} = 0.2 \text{ ms}$$

In this case, the time constant is much greater than the period and the output is close to zero, as shown in Figure 14.12(c). The actual values of the key voltages are found as in part (b) of this example:

$$V_2 = \frac{V}{2} \frac{1 - e^{-T/2\tau}}{1 + e^{-T/2\tau}} = 2.5 \frac{1 - e^{-0.1}}{1 + e^{-0.1}} = 0.125 \text{ V}$$

$$V_1 = -V_2 = -0.125 \text{ V}$$

Let us briefly examine the response of the low-pass filter to the ramp input shown in Figure 14.13(a). The output is found in the same manner as with the high-pass filter and is given by

$$v_o(t) = (-\alpha\tau + \alpha t + \alpha\tau e^{-t/\tau})u(t) \tag{14.14}$$

This is shown in Figure 14.13(b). Once again α is the slope of the input ramp in volts per second.

Figure 14.13
Low-pass RC filter-ramp response.

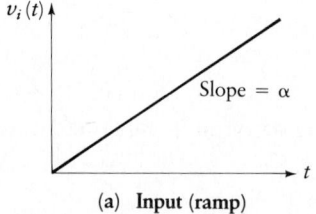

(a) Input (ramp)

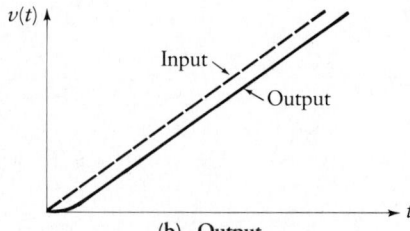

(b) Output

Example 14.4

The ramp input of Figure 14.13(a) is applied to a low-pass RC filter with a corner frequency of 5000 rad/s. The slope of the input ramp is 10 V/s. Calculate and sketch the output-voltage waveform.

SOLUTION   The time constant is the inverse of the 3-dB frequency, so

$$\tau = \frac{1}{5000} \text{ s}$$

The output waveform is written directly from equation (14.14):

$$v_o(t) = (-\alpha\tau + \alpha t + \alpha\tau e^{-t/\tau})u(t)$$
$$= (-0.002 + 10t + 0.002e^{-5000t})u(t) \text{ V}$$

This is plotted in Figure 14.14.

Figure 14.14
Response for Example 14.4.

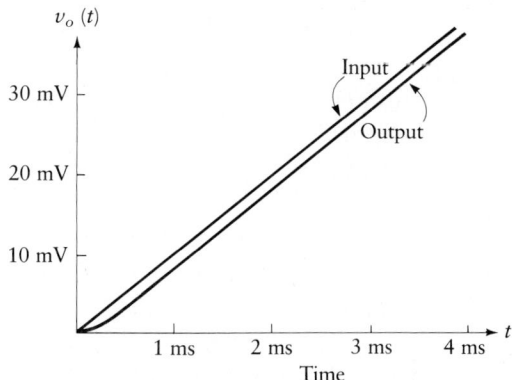

14.3   Diodes

Diodes are often coupled with RC networks in order to achieve desirable results. In analyzing such circuits, we use the piecewise-linear diode model shown in Figure 14.15. When the diode is forward-biased and therefore conducting, it is represented by a small forward resistance, R_f. (We are neglecting the forward voltage, V_γ). When the diode is reverse-biased, it is represented by a large reverse resistance, R_r.

Figure 14.15
Diode model.

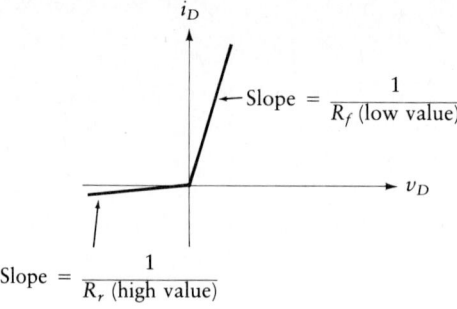

14.3.1   *Steady-State Response of Diode Circuit to Pulse Train*

Circuits used in digital applications often combine resistors, capacitors, and diodes. One such configuration is shown in Figure 14.16(a).

If the diode is ideal, the circuit acts as a *clamper*. The capacitor can never discharge, so it charges to the peak value of the input. The output is therefore "clamped" to a zero-voltage level.

We continue the analysis assuming that the diode is not ideal. The pulse train, as shown in Figure 14.17(a), forms the input to this circuit. The circuit behaves in a manner similar to that of the RC circuit analyzed earlier in this chapter. The only difference is that two different time constants apply, depending upon the state of the diode.

The steady-state output is shown in Figure 14.17(b). This sketch is exaggerated to illustrate the concept. That is, it is drawn as if the time constants are of the same order of magnitude as the period of the input. Since there are two time constants for this circuit, this assumption may not always be valid, since the two time constants are usually quite different. Additionally, V_1 and V_2 are less than V_3 or V_4. However, the derivation of the numerical results does not depend upon this assumption.

Figure 14.16(b) shows the equivalent circuit under the condition that the diode is forward-biased. This situation occurs whenever the output is positive. Figure 14.16(c) shows the comparable situation for negative outputs, when the diode is reverse-biased. The two time constants, for the forward- and reverse-biased condition, are therefore given by

$$\tau_f = (R_f + R_i)C$$

$$\tau_r = (R_r + R_i)C$$

Note that since $R_r \gg R_f$, then $\tau_r \gg \tau_f$.

We need four equations in order to find V_1, V_2, V_3, and V_4. As in the earlier

Figure 14.16
Steady-state response
to pulse train.

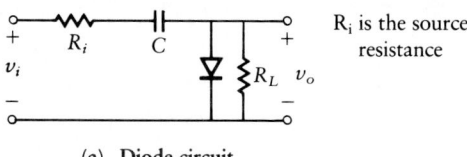

R$_i$ is the source
resistance

(a) Diode circuit

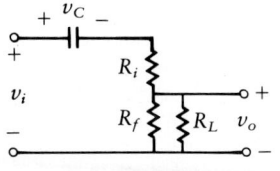

(b) Diode conducting

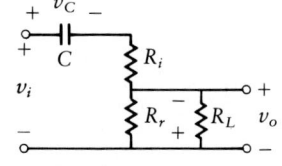

(c) Diode not conducting

Figure 14.17
Steady-state response
of diode circuit.

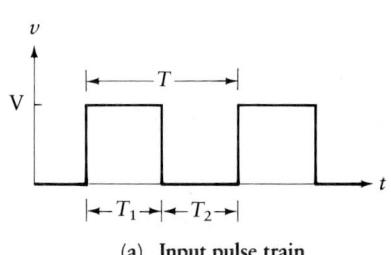

(a) Input pulse train

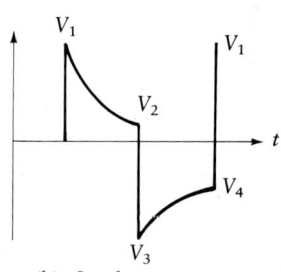

(b) Steady-state output waveform

circuit without the diode, two of these equations come from the exponential-decay relationship and the other two come from the size of the voltage transitions. The exponential-decay relationships yield

$$V_2 = V_1 \exp\left(\frac{-T_1}{\tau_f}\right) \tag{14.15a}$$

$$V_4 = V_3 \exp\left(\frac{-T_2}{\tau_r}\right) \tag{14.15b}$$

At the instant before the input voltage drops by V volts, the output is at V_2. When the input drops, the capacitor voltage cannot change instantaneously. Therefore, the voltage across the series combination of R_i and R_f must drop by V volts. If the resistor value did not change from R_f to R_r during this transition, we could simply use a voltage-divider formula to find the relationship between V_3 and V_2. Since the diode does indeed change state during this transition, we must find the new output by examining the capacitor voltage. The capacitor voltage just prior to this transition is found by writing a loop equation for the circuit of Figure 14.16 and realizing that

$$v_i = V$$

$$v_o = V_2$$

The capacitor voltage is

$$V_C = V - \frac{V_2(R_f + R_i)}{R_f}$$

At the instant after the input voltage drops to zero, the capacitor voltage is still at this value. The new value of the output is found by writing a loop equation for the circuit in Figure 14.16(c). This equivalent is used since the diode is now reverse-biased. The result is

$$V_3 = \frac{-R_r}{R_r + R_i} \left[V - V_2 \left(\frac{R_f + R_i}{R_f} \right) \right] \tag{14.15c}$$

We use a similar approach to find the relationship between V_1 and V_4. The result is (you should verify this expression before continuing):

$$V_1 = \frac{R_f V + V_4 R_f (R_r + R_i)/R_r}{R_f + R_i} \tag{14.15d}$$

The four equations (14.15a), (14.15b), (14.15c), and (14.15d) are sufficient to solve for the unknown reference points. They are rewritten as equations (14.16) for easy reference:

$$V = \frac{R_f + R_i}{R_f} V_1 - \frac{R_r + R_i}{R_r} V_4 \tag{14.16a}$$

$$V = \frac{R_f + R_i}{R_f} V_2 - \frac{R_r + R_i}{R_r} V_3 \tag{14.16b}$$

$$V_2 = V_1 \exp\left(\frac{-T_1}{\tau_f} \right) \tag{14.16c}$$

$$V_4 = V_3 \exp\left(\frac{-T_2}{\tau_r} \right) \tag{14.16d}$$

Example 14.5

Given the circuit of Figure 14.16(a) with

$$R_i = 100\ \Omega; \quad R_f = 100\ \Omega; \quad R_r = 1\ \text{M}\Omega; \quad R_L = 10\ \text{k}\Omega; \quad C = 1\ \mu\text{F}$$

Find the critical voltages of the output waveform if the input is as shown in Figure 14.18.

Figure 14.18
Input waveform for
Example 14.5.

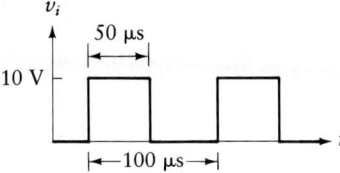

SOLUTION Since $R_L \gg R_f$ and $R_r \gg R_L$,

$$R_L \parallel R_f \approx R_f$$
$$R_r \parallel R_L \approx R_L$$

We now find the two time constants.

$$\tau_f = (R_f + R_i)C = 200\ \mu\text{s}$$
$$\tau_r = (R_L + R_i)C = 10\ \text{ms}$$

Equation (14.16) yields

$$10 = 2V_1 - 1.01V_4 \tag{14.17a}$$
$$10 = 2V_2 - 1.01V_3 \tag{14.17b}$$
$$V_2 = V_1\exp(-50\ \mu\text{s}/200\ \mu\text{s}) = V_1 e^{-1/4} = 0.78V_1 \tag{14.17c}$$
$$V_4 = V_3\exp(-50\ \mu\text{s}/10\ \text{ms}) = V_3 e^{-0.005} = 0.995V_3 \tag{14.17d}$$

Solving these four equations for the four unknown voltages yields

$$V_1 = 0.11\ \text{V} \qquad V_2 = 0.09\ \text{V}$$
$$V_3 = -9.73\ \text{V} \qquad V_4 = -9.68\ \text{V}$$

The resulting waveform is plotted in Figure 14.19. Note that both time constants are large compared to the period of the input, so the exponentials do

Figure 14.19
Solution to Example
14.5.

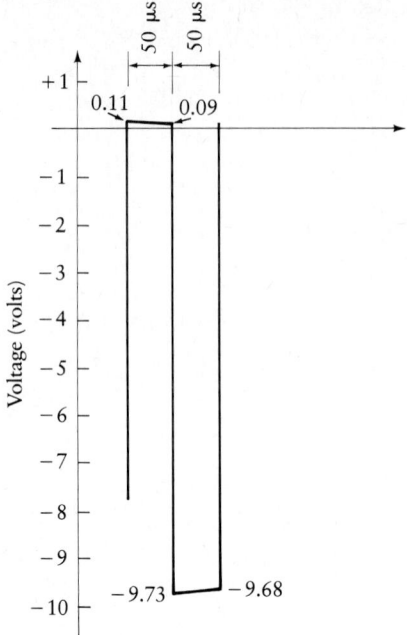

not decay appreciably between transitions. Further note that the derivation of this section neglected the diode forward voltage, V_γ. Since V_1 and V_2 turned out to be of the same order of magnitude as V_γ, the model used in this section is not accurate for this example. The values of V_1 and V_2 obtained should be considered to be approximations.   ▸

14.4 Trigger Circuits

Binary digital systems operate with discrete time signals. That is, since the information is contained in sequences of binary digits, each of these bits occurs at a specific time. *Timing* is therefore extremely important, and transitions must occur at carefully controlled points in time. Many digital circuits require a trigger pulse to be generated, and this trigger pulse is used to control the timing.

Trigger pulses are usually generated at either the leading or trailing edge of a pulse train. As one example, consider the *positive-edge trigger* of Figure 14.20(a). The input to the circuit is a pulse that has a transition between 0 and 5 V. This step function is applied to the high-pass RC network. Equation (14.1) can be used to find the output for $t > 0$:

$$v_o(t) = Ve^{-t/\tau}\, u(t)$$

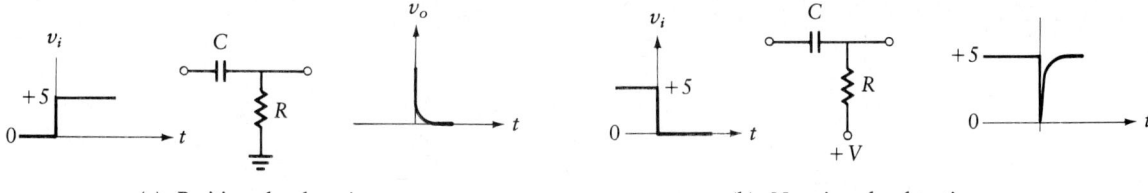

(a) Positive-edge detection   (b) Negative-edge detection

Figure 14.20 Trigger circuits.

where $\tau = RC$ and $V = 5$ V. This is a positive-going trigger. The trigger pulse is narrow, with the width dependent upon the RC time constant. It can be used for accurate timing purposes.

The *negative-edge trigger* is shown in Figure 14.20(b). The output is also shown in the diagram, and for $t > 0$, it is given by

$$v_o(t) = V(1 - e^{-t/\tau})$$

The exponential decay of both of these outputs can be shortened by reducing the time constant. We shall explore methods of making the output pulse even sharper. This is possible using inverters or buffers, both of which are discussed in the next chapter.

14.4.1 *Pulse-Train Response*

The networks of the previous section detect both a positive and negative edge of a single-step function. We now combine a series of steps to create a pulse train as the input to an RC circuit, as studied in Section 14.1. The input and corresponding output are shown in Figure 14.21(a). The output is comprised of a series of positive- and negative-going pulses of amplitude $\pm V$ volts. Recall from the discussion of Figure 14.7(b) that pulses of this type occur if the time constant is much smaller than the period of the input. Therefore, the RC product must be

$$\tau = RC << T$$

We often require only a negative-going pulse to act as a trigger, so a diode can be used to remove the positive-going pulses. This is shown in Figure 14.21(b). If the diode is reversed, the negative-going pulses are removed and the positive-going pulses remain. The circuit of Figure 14.21(c) will accomplish the same trigger as Figure 14.21(b), except that no V_{REF} is required.

Figure 14.21
Response to a pulse
train.

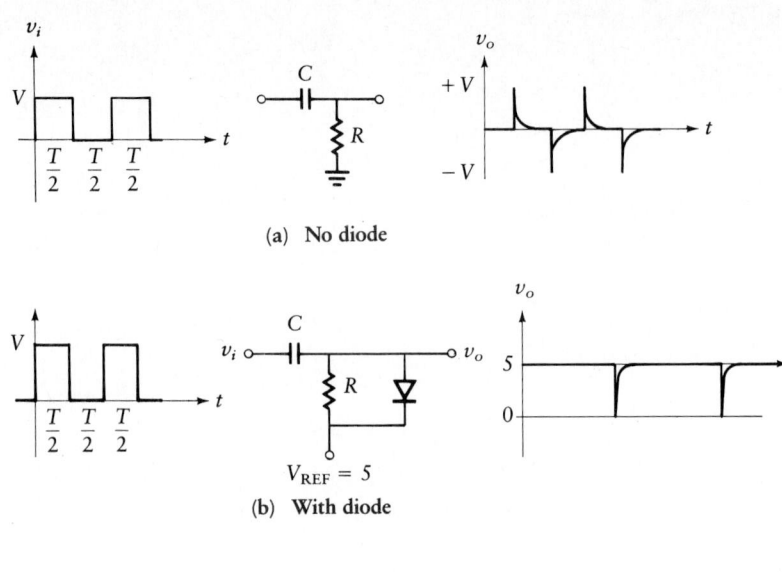

(a) No diode

(b) With diode

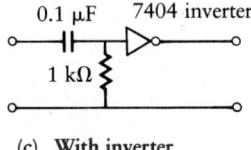

(c) With inverter

Example 14.6

A symmetrical 60-Hz rectangular-pulse train forms the input to the system shown in Figure 14.22(a). Design a circuit to develop a trigger pulse that must be less than 2 ms wide and exists only on the negative-going edges of the input-clock pulse train.

SOLUTION   The period of the input is 16.7 ms, so we want the RC time constant to be much less than this. The time constant must be sufficiently small so that the output pulse has decayed almost to zero within 2 ms, as specified in the problem statement. Suppose we choose a time constant of 0.5 ms. We choose a capacitor value of $C = 0.1$ μF and a resistance of 5 kΩ resulting in an RC time constant of 0.5 ms. The resulting circuit is shown in Figure 14.22(b).

A *buffer*, which can be formed from two inverters in series, can be used at the output of the circuit of Figure 14.22(b). The buffer changes this exponential signal to a rectangular pulse and provides a low output impedance.

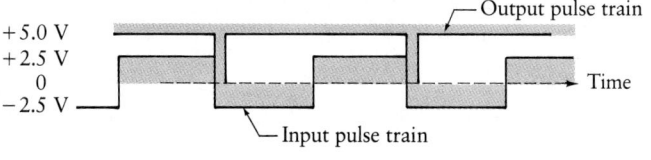

Figure 14.22
Circuit for Example
14.6.

(a) **Input and output signals**

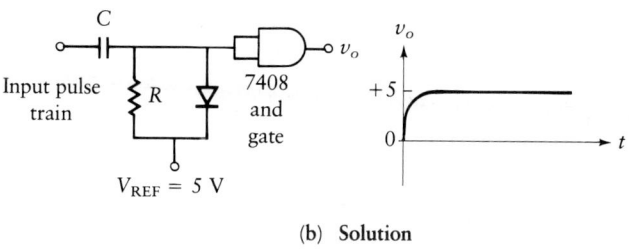

(b) **Solution**

14.5 The 555 Pulse Generator

Although this chapter is intended as an introduction to *digital* electronics, the circuits and signals we have been discussing are really analog. They operate upon and produce waveforms that take on a continuum of values rather than simply responding to one of two levels.

In between analog and digital circuits there exists a class of devices that possess the characteristics of both types. Within this class are timers and waveform-generator circuits that find wide use in both analog and digital circuitry. The major characteristic of these circuits is that the time (period) may be set either by an external voltage or by a resistor-capacitor combination. These devices often have external control lines so that the frequency or pulse width may be easily controlled by an external source. When these circuits are implemented as IC chips, the internal construction uses both analog and digital circuits to generate the timing and control signals required for operation.

14.5.1   *The Relaxation Oscillator*

We shall lead our way into timing circuits by first analyzing the *relaxation oscillator* made from an operational amplifier with positive feedback, as shown in Figure 14.23(a). The voltage at the noninverting input of the op-amp results from putting the output voltage through a resistor divider composed of R_1 and R_2. The voltage at the inverting input is developed across the capacitor as part

Figure 14.23
Relaxation oscillator.

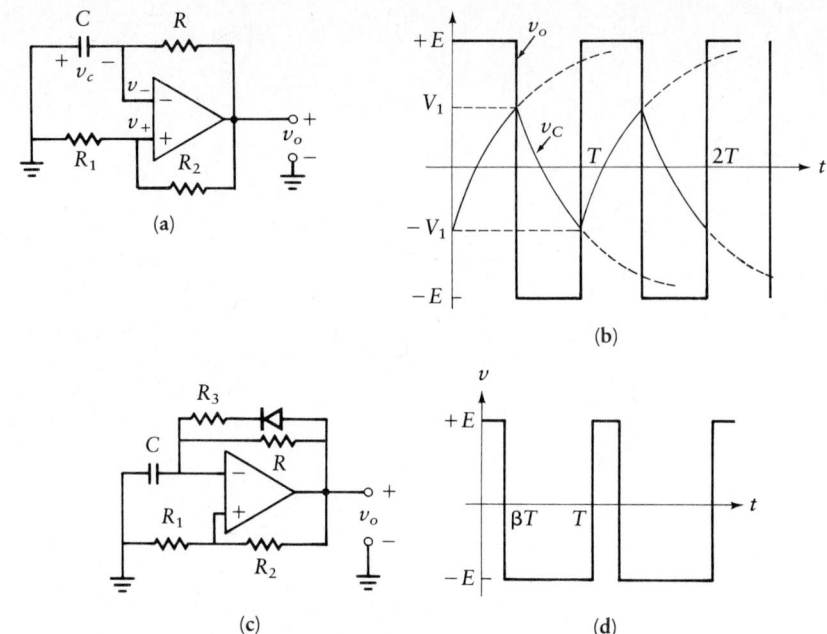

(a)

(b)

(c)

(d)

of an RC combination. If the differential input is positive, the op-amp output saturates near the positive supply voltage. If the differential input is negative, the output saturates near the negative of the supply voltage.

When the output is at the positive value, the capacitor charges toward this value exponentially with time constant RC. At some point, this increasing inverting input voltage causes the op-amp to switch to the other state, where the output voltage is negative. The capacitor then starts discharging toward this negative value until the differential input once again becomes positive.

The output is therefore a square wave, as shown in Figure 14.23(b). The exponential waveform in this figure represents the capacitor voltage. We find the equation for the exponential curve by using the initial and final values and the time constant, as described earlier in this chapter. For the first segment of the curve between times 0 and $T/2$, the initial value is $-V_1$, the final value is the supply voltage, $+E$, and the time constant is $\tau = RC$. The equation is, therefore,

$$v_-(t) = E + (-V_1 - E)e^{-t/\tau} \tag{14.18a}$$

For the next period, between $T/2$ and T, the starting value is V_1 and the final value is $-E$. Note that we are assuming that, in the steady state, the waveform is symmetrical around the zero axis:

$$v_-(t) = -E + (V_1 + E)e^{-(t - T/2)/\tau} \tag{14.18b}$$

Either equation (14.18a) or equation (14.18b) is evaluated at the transition time to obtain

$$v_-(T/2) = V_1 = E + (-V_1 - E)e^{-T/2\tau}$$

Therefore,

$$e^{-T/2\tau} = (E - V_1)/(E + V_1) \tag{14.19}$$

The unknowns in this equation are T and V_1. We need a second equation to find the period of oscillation. This equation comes from the noninverting input since the transitions occur when the *differential* input goes through zero (i.e., $v_- = v_+$). To simplify this, let us make the assumption that the resistors are equal. That is,

$$R_1 = R_2$$

The noninverting input during the first half-cycle is then given by

$$v_+ = \frac{R_1 E}{R_1 + R_2} = \frac{E}{2}$$

The change in state occurs when the inverting input reaches this value. Thus, from equation (14.17), we have

$$e^{-T/2\tau} = \frac{E - \dfrac{E}{2}}{E + \dfrac{E}{2}} = \frac{1}{3}$$

Taking natural logs of both sides yields

$$\frac{-T}{2\tau} = \ln\left(\frac{1}{3}\right) = -1.1$$

and

$$T = 2.2RC$$

The frequency of oscillation is the reciprocal of the period:

$$f = \frac{1}{T} = \frac{0.455}{RC} \text{ Hz}$$

This equation is based on ideal op-amp theory ($v_+ = v_-$). If the frequency is too high, the actual op-amp gain may reduce with increasing frequency, thus causing this equation to be in error.

Suppose now that we desire an *asymmetrical* pulse train at the output of the oscillator. The circuit of Figure 14.23(c) is used to produce the waveform of Figure 14.23(d). Note that a diode is added in order to permit two different time constants to occur.

When the diode is *on*, the charging path for the capacitor is through a resistance made up of R in parallel with R_3 (we are neglecting the forward resistance of the diode). When the diode is *off*, the discharge path is through a resistor of value R.

Example 14.7

Find the output of the circuit of Figure 14.23(c) if

$$C = 0.1 \ \mu\text{F}$$

$$R = 20 \ \text{k}\Omega$$

$$R_1 = R_2$$

$$R_3 = 1 \ \text{k}\Omega$$

SOLUTION　We first find the two time constants for charging and discharging the capacitor.

$$\tau_c = C(R \parallel R_3) = (0.1 \ \mu\text{F})(0.95 \ \text{k}\Omega) = 0.095 \ \text{ms}$$

$$\tau_d = RC = (0.1 \ \mu\text{F})(20 \ \text{k}\Omega) = 2 \ \text{ms}$$

The equation for the first portion of the waveform is

$$v_- = E + (-V_1 - E)e^{-t/0.095\text{ms}}$$

The transition occurs when this voltage reaches $E/2$, since $R_1 = R_2$. Thus,

$$v_-(\beta T) = E + (-V_1 - E)e^{-\beta T/0.095\text{ms}} = \frac{E}{2}$$

but setting $V_1 = E/2$ yields

$$\exp\left(\frac{-\beta T}{\tau_c}\right) = \frac{1}{3}$$

and

$$\beta T = 1.1 \times 0.095 \text{ ms} = 0.1 \text{ ms}$$

For the discharge region,

$$v_-(t) = -E + (V_1 + E)\exp\left[\frac{-(t - \beta T)}{\tau_d}\right]$$

Setting $t = T$ for the second transition yields

$$v_-(T) = \frac{-E}{2} = -E + \left(\frac{E}{2} + E\right)\exp\left[\frac{-(T - \beta T)}{\tau_d}\right]$$

with the result that

$$(1 - \beta)T = 2.2 \text{ ms}$$

The period is then

$$T = \beta T + (1 - \beta)T = (0.1 + 2.2) \text{ ms} = 2.3 \text{ ms}$$

14.5.2   *The 555 as an Oscillator*

We now examine the very useful *555 timer*. It consists of a mixture of digital and analog circuitry. A brief description of the internal operation of the 555 is presented in this section. Figure 14.24 shows a block diagram of the 555. The circuit contains comparators, amplifiers, and a flip-flop. Comparators are

Figure 14.24
Block diagram of the
555.

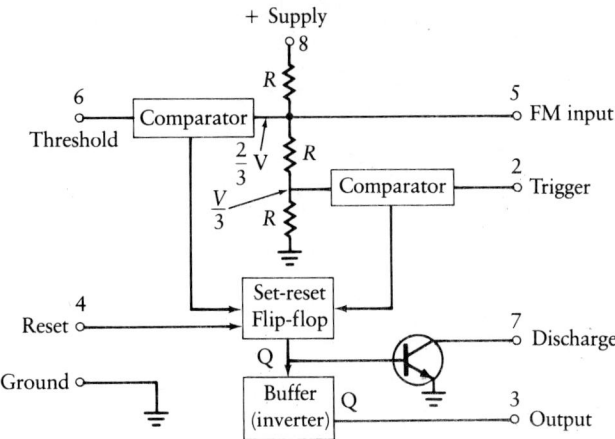

discussed in Section 12.3. Flip-flops are considered in Chapter 16. For now, it is sufficient to think of the *set-reset flip-flop* as an electrically operated switch. Setting the switch causes the output, Q, to go *high* (approximately to the supply voltage), and resetting the flip-flop causes the output to go low (almost to zero). The three resistors, R, are used as a voltage divider to provide $\frac{2}{3}$ of the supply- and $\frac{1}{3}$ of the supply-voltage levels to the comparators.

Pins 2 (trigger) and 6 (threshold) control the output of the 555 circuit. When the voltage at pin 6 goes above the $\frac{2}{3}$ supply level, the output of the comparator *sets* the flip-flop, causing its output to go *high*. The output of the flip-flop will then bias the discharge transistor on, causing its output (pin 7) to go low. A voltage at pin 2 of less than the $\frac{1}{3}$ supply level *resets* the flip-flop causing the output to go *low* and turns off the discharge transistor, allowing its output to float. Pin 4 is used to reset the flip-flop. By connecting pin 4 to common, the flip-flop is reset to *low*. When not in use, this pin is connected to the positive supply.

The 555 can be used as a pulse generator in an astable mode if configured as shown in Figure 14.25. In operation, the capacitor starts to charge through R_1 and R_2. The flip-flop is reset (turned off) since pin 2 starts at a low voltage. With the flip-flop reset, the input to the inverter is low and the circuit output is high. When the capacitor voltage gets high enough for the voltage on pin 6 to reach $\frac{2}{3}$ of the supply, the flip-flop *sets* and pin 7 goes low. The capacitor then starts to discharge through R_2. When it has discharged to a value of $\frac{1}{3}$ of the supply, the second comparator, pin 2, causes the flip-flop to *reset*, and the cycle repeats.

The capacitor voltage therefore goes exponentially between $\frac{1}{3}$ and $\frac{2}{3}$ of the supply voltage. During charging, the time constant is given by

$$\tau_c = (R_1 + R_2)C$$

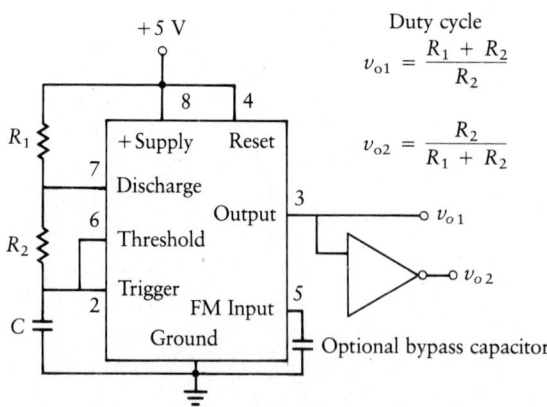

Figure 14.25
The 555 as a pulse generator.

Duty cycle

$$\nu_{o1} = \frac{R_1 + R_2}{R_2}$$

$$\nu_{o2} = \frac{R_2}{R_1 + R_2}$$

During discharge, the time constant is

$$\tau_d = R_2 C$$

The switching occurs when the exponential has gone one-half of the way between initial and final value. For example, during charging, the capacitor voltage starts at $\frac{1}{3}$ of the supply voltage and is exponentially charging toward the supply voltage. Switching takes place when the voltage reaches $\frac{2}{3}$ of the supply. The reverse is true during discharge. An exponential reaches $\frac{1}{2}$ of its total value after 0.693 of a time constant. That is, when

$$t = 0.693\tau$$

in the equation $e^{-t/\tau}$, we have

$$e^{-0.693} = 0.5$$

Therefore, the charging time is given by

$$T_c = 0.693(R_1 + R_2)C$$

The discharge time is

$$T_d = 0.693 R_2 C$$

The output is high during charge and low during discharge. The total period of the square-wave output is given by the sum of the two times.

$$T = 0.693(R_1 + 2R_2)C$$

The frequency is the reciprocal of this.

$$f = \frac{1}{T} = \frac{1.44}{(R_1 + 2R_2)C}$$

Example 14.8

Design an astable 555 square-wave generator to deliver a 10 kHz output signal.

SOLUTION We take this opportunity to give some practical limitations of the 555 timer. The capacitance should be kept larger than 500 pF (5×10^{-10} F) to swamp out stray capacitance. Each of the resistors R_1 and R_2 should be larger than 1 kΩ to limit the current. The sum $R_1 + R_2$ should be no larger than 3.3 MΩ. These limitations come from a detailed analysis of the operation of this circuit. It should be noted that with these constraints, we cannot achieve a frequency of greater than about 1 MHz using the circuit of Figure 14.25.

Let us select $C = 0.001$ μF. The problem did not specify whether the square wave had to be symmetrical or not. That is, although the period is specified at 0.1 ms, we have not been given information about the duty cycle.

The *duty cycle* is defined here to be the time high divided by the time low. For the 555, the equation is

$$\text{duty cycle} = \frac{\text{time high}}{\text{time low}} = \frac{R_1 + R_2}{R_2} \tag{14.20}$$

Suppose we desire the waveform to spend about as much time at the positive value as at the zero value. The discharge time should then be the same as the charging time. Equation (14.20) indicates that these times cannot be exactly equal. If we choose R_2 to be much greater than R_1, the times are close to being equal. Let us assume that this is the case. The frequency is then approximately given by

$$f = 10 \text{ kHz} \approx \frac{1.44}{2R_2C}$$

Using the assumed value of C, this yields

$$R_2 = 72 \text{ k}\Omega$$

We can choose R_1 to be about 1 kΩ and still be within the design guidelines given above. The design is then complete.

Since the duty cycle, given by equation (14.20), has $R_1 + R_2$ in the numerator and R_2 in the denominator, we are limited to duty-cycle values greater than 1. If we desire a duty cycle less than unity, we can use an inverter (the 7404 inverter is discussed in the next chapter) to invert equation (14.20). Hence, if we include an inverter as shown in Figure 14.25, the duty cycle for the output, v_{o2}, is given by

$$\text{duty cycle} = \frac{R_2}{R_1 + R_2} \tag{14.21}$$

14.5.3 *The 555 as a Monostable Circuit*

The 555 can be used in a *monostable mode* by eliminating R_2 and connecting C between pins 6 and 7 and ground, as shown in Figure 14.26. In the monostable mode, the circuit output consists of a single pulse with a specified duration each time a trigger pulse is delivered to pin 2 that drives the comparator below $\frac{1}{3}$ of the supply voltage. When pin 2 goes low, the flip-flop *resets* and the output (pin 3) goes high. Since the discharge transistor is turned off, pin 7 is allowed to float, and the capacitor starts to charge from its initial value of 0 V. When it has charged to $\frac{2}{3}$ of the supply voltage, the flip-flop *sets* and the output goes low. The trigger pulse must start at $+5$, drop to 0, and then return to $+5$, as shown in Figure 14.26. The trigger pulse must be of shorter duration than the desired output pulse. The *on-time* is the amount of time the output pulse is high. This is the time it takes the exponential charging voltage to go from 0 to $\frac{2}{3}$ of its final value. This will be 1.1 time constants, since

$$(1 - e^{-1.1}) = \frac{2}{3}$$

The on-time is therefore

$$T = 1.1RC \tag{14.22}$$

Figure 14.26
The 555 in a monostable mode.

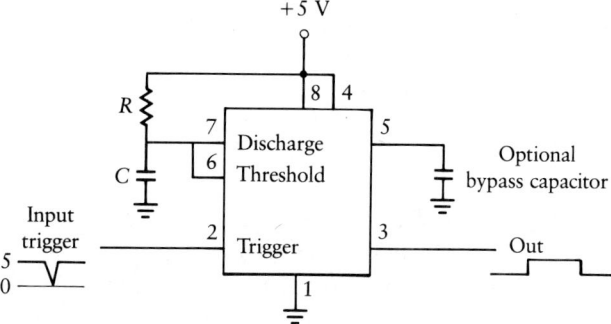

Example 14.9

Design a 555 in the monostable mode to provide a 100 ms pulse each time an input trigger is applied.

SOLUTION Let us use a capacitor of 1 μF. Equation (14.22) then yields the value of R:

$$R = \frac{T}{1.1C} = \frac{100 \times 10^{-3}}{1.1 \times 10^{-6}} = 91 \text{ k}\Omega$$

The circuit is as shown in Figure 14.26, with the parameter values as calculated above.

The form of the trigger pulse necessary to initiate the 555 monostable is most important. As shown on Figure 14.26, the trigger pulse, applied to pin 2, is at + 5 V. This voltage is briefly dropped to zero to initiate the timing sequence. At the instant that the trigger is brought to zero, an output pulse of duration 1.1RC is generated. In contrast to the astable mode of operation, the cycle does not repeat. Another trigger pulse is required to initiate another output pulse.

The method of obtaining these trigger pulses for the 555 in the monostable mode is shown in Figure 14.20(a) and (b). If a leading edge trigger is desired, use the circuit shown in Figure 14.20(a). The inverter (the inverter is covered in Chapter 15) is used to invert the pulse into the form necessary to trigger the 555.

A trailing-edge trigger is obtained with the circuit of Figure 14.20(b). Note that to obtain the proper trigger, the resistor is connected to +5 V rather than to ground. It may be desirable to use a noninverting buffer at the output of the circuit of Figure 14.20(b) to "square up" the trigger pulse and also to reduce the loading effect on the v_i source.

The reset pin (pin 4) can be used to disable or stop the timing cycle after it begins. When the reset pin is brought to ground, the operation is inhibited. When not required, pin 4 should be tied to the positive supply, as shown in Figure 14.26.   ➤

PROBLEMS

14.1   A 10 Hz symmetrical square wave has a peak-to-peak voltage of 5 V. It forms the input to a high-pass circuit with lower corner frequency of 5 Hz $\left(f_c = \dfrac{1}{2\pi RC} \right)$. Sketch the output waveform. What is the peak-to-peak output amplitude?

14.2   A 10 Hz square wave forms the input to an amplifier, which acts as a high-pass circuit. The peak-to-peak voltage is V. Plot the output waveform for each lower-corner frequency given.
a. 0.3 Hz
b. 3 Hz
c. 30 Hz

14.3 A square wave extends ± 2 V with respect to ground. The duration of the positive section is 0.1 s and that of the negative section is 0.2 s. The waveform is applied to a high-pass network with time constant $RC = 0.2$ s. Plot the steady-state output waveform and calculate the important maximum and minimum voltages.

14.4 The limited ramp of Figure P14.1 is applied to a high-pass network. Let $V_m = 1$ V. Draw the output waveform for each value of T.
  a. $T = 0.2(RC)$
  b. $T = RC$
  c. $T = 5(RC)$

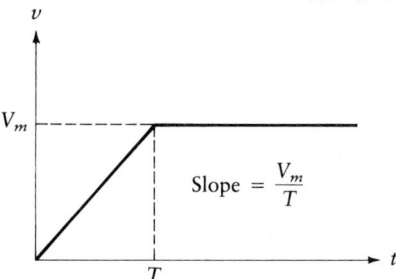

Figure P14.1

14.5 A symmetrical square wave with an average value of zero has a peak-to-peak voltage of 10 V and a period of 2 μs. This waveform is the input to a low-pass circuit with corner frequency of 0.16 MHz. Calculate and sketch the steady-state output waveform. What is the peak-to-peak output voltage?

14.6 The pulse train shown in Figure P14.2 is applied to the input of a diode-capacitor network. Plot the steady-state output voltage, $v_o(t)$, and calculate the four important voltages in the output. Assume that the diode voltage is zero when forward biased (i.e., $V_\gamma = 0$), $R_f = 100$ Ω, $R_r = 100$ kΩ, and $R_S = 1$ kΩ.

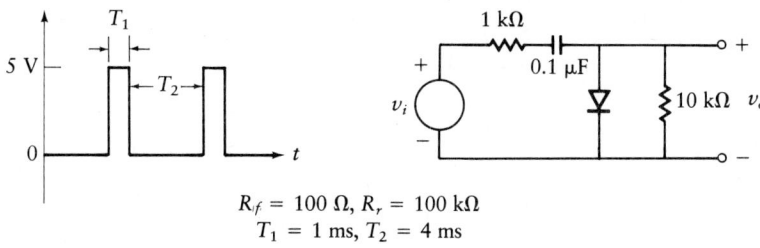

Figure P14.2

14.7   A 10 kHz pulse train with peak value $V_{peak} = 10$ V is applied to the diode-clamping circuit of Figure P14.3(b). The parameter values are $R = 10$ kΩ, and $C = 1$ μF. The diode has $R_r = \infty$, $R_f = 0$, and $V_\gamma = 0$, and the source impedance is zero.
   a. Sketch the output waveform.
   b. If the diode forward resistance is 1 kΩ, sketch the output waveform. Calculate the maximum and minimum voltage with respect to ground.
   c. Repeat part (b) if the source impedance is 1 kΩ.

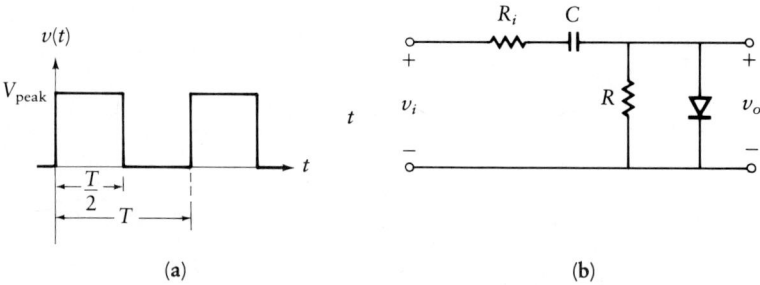

(a)   (b)

Figure P14.3

14.8   The pulse train shown in Figure P14.3(a) with $T = 50$ μs is applied to the circuit of Figure P14.3(b). The circuit has $R_i = 1$ kΩ, $R = 10$ kΩ, $C = 0.1$ μF, $R_f = 100$ Ω, $R_r = 100$ kΩ and $V_\gamma = 0$. Find the steady-state output waveform, $v_o(t)$.

14.9   The limited ramp of Figure P14.1 is applied to a low-pass network with $V_m = 1$ V. Draw the output waveform for each value of T.
   a. $T = 0.2(RC)$
   b. $T = RC$
   c. $T = 5(RC)$

14.10 Design a signal generator using a 555 circuit in the astable mode to provide pulse rates of 100 kHz, 10 kHz, and 1 kHz. Keep the duty cycle constant.

14.11 Design a trigger circuit and a monostable 555 to produce a train of 100 ms pulses. Use a 0 V to 5 V, 1 Hz, pulse train input to this circuit.

14.12 Use a 555 in the astable mode and an inverter (needed to obtain a duty cycle less than 1) to produce a pulse generator for the following continuously variable frequency ranges.

a. 10 Hz to 100 Hz
b. 100 Hz to 1 kHz
c. 1 kHz to 10 kHz

The duty cycle can be no greater than 0.2. Select all resistor and capacitor values and select the chip number for the inverter. Assume that you have available any power you need. Draw the circuit diagram for the design.

14.13 Develop a 60 Hz pulse train using the 60 Hz, 110 V power-line voltage with the system shown in Figure P14.4. The output is a pulse train with a 100% duty cycle. Select all resistor and capacitor values. Draw the circuit diagram for your complete design.

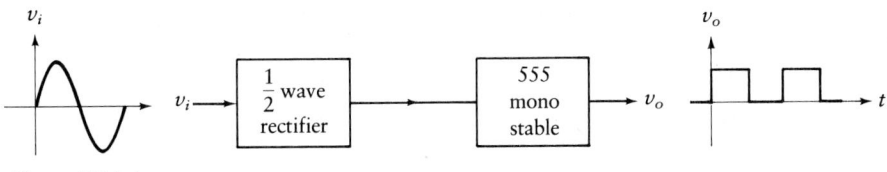

Figure P14.4

14.14 Design a pulse generator that will have the following continuously variable ranges.
a. 0.1 kHz to 1 kHz
b. 1 kHz to 10 kHz
c. 10 kHz to 100 kHz

A duty cycle of 1.0 is required. Assume you have available any power needed in the design.

14.15 Design a traffic-light-control system using digital circuitry. The traffic light is to be used at a four-way intersection, and each direction must have three lights: red, yellow, and green. To turn on a lamp, the circuit must provide an output of +5 V. If the output to a certain lamp circuit is zero volts, that lamp will be off. The required on times and a map of the intersection are shown in Figure P14.5

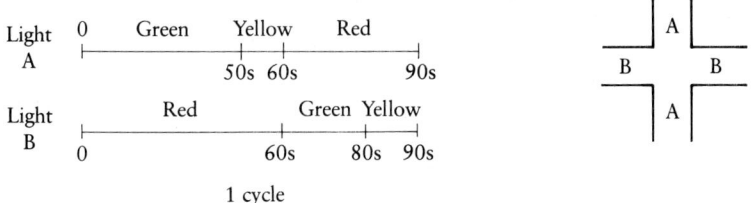

Figure P14.5

14.16 Design a pulse delay network to provide a 15 μs delay for a pulse input whose duration is 1 μs, as shown in Figure P14.6.

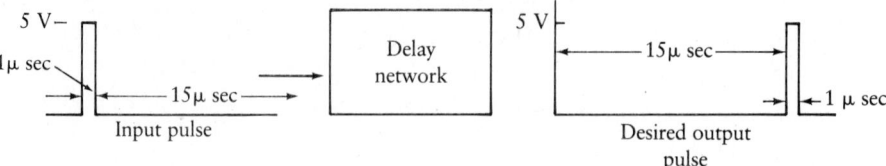

Figure P14.6

14.17 Design a pulse generator to provide the clock pulse for an electronic system. Use the 110 V 60 Hz power line as the basic drive for the pulse generator. The duty cycle of the clock pulse output is 0.5. Calculate all resistor and capacitor values and specify the type number of the ICs used.

14.18 Analyze the circuit shown in Figure P14.7. Sketch the output signal as a function of time. Calculate all important frequencies and pulse widths. Switch SW is normally closed. You are to plot the output signal after the time that the switch is open.

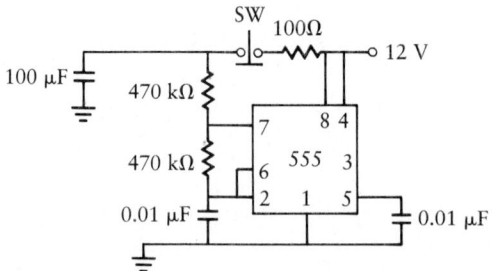

Figure P14.7

14.19 Design a 1 kHz pulse generator with a 0 V to 5 V output, using an astable 555 timer to provide the 1 kHz pulse train. The duty cycle of the output clock pulses must be variable from 0.2 to 10. Use one potentiometer and one monostable 555 to generate the duty cycle. Calculate all resistor and capacitor values and specify the type numbers of the ICs used in the design.

14.20 Use op-amps and a 555 monostable timer to design a signal-conditioning system. The input to the system is obtained from the ignition system for an engine. One hundred turns of wire are wrapped around the supply line to one of the spark plugs. This produces one voltage pulse for two revolutions of the engine. The signal has the form shown in Figure P14.8(a). The transients are large and do not die out for 10 ms.

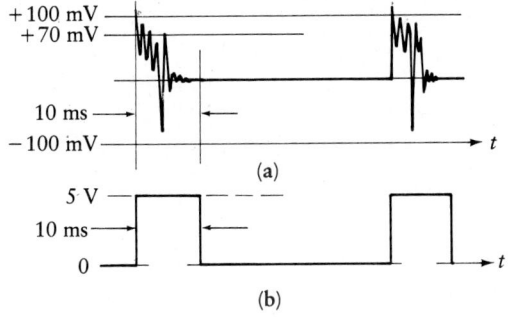

Figure P14.8

Design an electronic system to condition this input signal so it will be suitable to drive a TTL system. The signal will have only one output pulse for each firing of the spark plug. That is, the signal conditioning system should ignore the transients and only produce *one* pulse for each burst of energy. The pulse train should look like that shown in Figure P14.8(b). Each pulse of the output signal corresponds to two revolutions of the engine and the maximum engine speed is 6000 rpm.

15

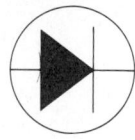

DIGITAL LOGIC FAMILIES

15.0 Introduction

You have secured an excellent engineering position working for a major auto corporation in their advanced design section. You have been assigned the task of designing an electronic control module for the safety features for next year's automobiles. The device specifications have been developed by the systems department of your corporation. They include requirements for a warning system that accomplishes the following: The system warns the driver if the headlights are off after dark. It also flashes a warning if the lights are left on after the car is parked and the passengers exit. Low fuel level, low tire pressure, low brake fluid, low oil pressure, and excessive engine temperature must also lead to warnings, as must driver intoxication, failure to turn on windshield wipers in the rain, and excessive speed. Finally, the device must also work as a sophisticated burglar alarm. Each of these functions has override switches.

You carefully review all of the specifications and assemble the necessary handbooks to choose the appropriate circuitry. You use amplifiers, filters, comparators, and oscillators (to generate warning tones) and design what you think is a sophisticated system. Unfortunately, you significantly exceed the budget for this device. Even more serious, you install a prototype and find that false alarms frequently occur. You trace this to ignition noise generating unwanted signals, which trigger the comparators and sound a false alarm. If you had not already run beyond your budget, you would consider reducing the noise by providing shielding and by using resistive ignition wires. Alas, you have run out of options, and you turn to your colleagues for help. One of them suggests that this is an ideal situation to use digital electronics rather than analog. You are told that this will not only reduce the probability of a false alarm, but that it will also lead to more compact, simpler and less expensive circuitry. You turn to this and the following chapters to review what you learned in school.

This and the next chapters deal specifically with *digital electronics*. Digital electronics forms a subset of the broader field of digital engineering. A typical study of digital engineering includes procedures for reducing digital functions to their simplest form. That is, a particular function is specified and then, prior to considering implementation, the function is reduced to its simplest form. It is only following that reduction that we consider filling in the blocks on the diagram with electronic circuitry. In this text, we concentrate upon the circuitry. We present a brief summary of some digital engineering results in Section 15.1. It is assumed that you either have had a course in digital engineering or will accept the specifications as being the result of logic operations.

We deal with *digital* ICs in this chapter. The previous ICs considered were analog; that is, they were able to accept inputs and produce outputs that range over a continuum of amplitudes. The op-amp is an example of an analog IC. Binary digital integrated circuits accept inputs consisting of either of two logic levels, usually denoted by a 0 or a 1. That is, the signals can only take on one of a set of specific amplitudes, with that set consisting of two entries in the case of binary circuits. Since each component of a (binary) digital IC produces a logic 0 or 1 at the output depending upon the value of the input(s), the components can be thought of as logic gates. A *gate* will let either a 1 or a 0 through to the output.

The first section of this chapter briefly discusses function tables for the most important logic gates. The basics of Boolean algebra are then summarized. This is needed for circuit simplification operations.

Three IC families are discussed: TTL, ECL, and CMOS. A comparison of these families is made to permit an optimum choice of the appropriate family for a given application.

15.1 Basic Concepts of Digital Logic

Logic has been a field of study since the days of the Greek philosophers. Many of the concepts that are used in digital logic were derived from earlier sources. Several of the basic functions were used by philosophers to prove statements and solve puzzles.

Two of these operations, known as AND and OR, form the basic building blocks of a logic system. These can be considered as analogous to addition and multiplication in the basic algebra system. We start with these two and then expand to more-complex functions.

Prior to defining the functions, we need to explore ways to express a digital relationship. In algebra, a function is usually expressed in one of three ways. First, we can give an equation for the function, where that equation contains basic operations such as addition and multiplication. Alternatively, we can present a graph of the function in two dimensions, with one variable (independent) on the abscissa and the other (dependent) on the ordinate of the graph. A third technique for specifying the function is to give the value of the function for every possible value of the independent variable. In the analog continuous case, this would involve a table with an infinite number of entries.

Two of these functional representation techniques lend themselves nicely to describing digital functions. An equation can be written once we define some notation for the basic logic operations. Alternatively, a table can be presented that specifies the value of the function for every possible input. In contrast with the analog case, this table will only have a finite number of entries. It is known as a *function table,* or *truth table,* and we use it to define the various functions.

Since binary digital signals can only take on one of two possible values, the inputs to the system can also only be one of these values. Although they are manifested as voltages in a circuit, they are usually referred to as 0 and 1. The two voltages developed by a widely used family of circuits consist of one near zero and the other near 5 V. Refer to these as LOW (or 0) and HIGH (or 1), respectively. In order to convey digital information, two distinct signals are needed. There is nothing magic about 0 and 1. For example, the digital number 10110, when appearing in this text, could just as well be represented by *XYXXY.* As long as two distinct signals are used, the information is conveyed. We therefore have two choices in assigning the binary numbers 0 and 1 to the two voltages present in a circuit. If we associate the higher voltage with 1 and the lower with 0, we are using what is known as *positive logic.* Conversely, a 0 can be represented by the higher voltage and a 1 by the lower. This latter situation is known as *negative logic.* Throughout this text, we use positive logic unless specifically stated to the contrary.

15.1.1   *Time-Independent, or Unclocked, Logic*

A *time-independent logic function* is one that has no memory. This form of logic responds only to the *present* inputs that are applied, and previous inputs have no effect upon the present output. In essence, the circuit forgets any previous logic conditions. Function tables for such circuits are easy to construct, since there are no clock signals or previous conditions to be considered. The elementary logic functions considered in this chapter are all time-independent. Time-independent logic is also known as *unclocked*, or *asynchronous*, *logic*.

15.1.2 *Time-Dependent, or Clocked, Logic*

A *time-dependent logic function* is one that has a *memory*. This form of logic responds not only to the present inputs that are applied to it but also depends upon previous input and/or output conditions. A dependency on the previous output state represents a form of feedback in digital circuits. Time-dependent logic functions often have inputs with labels such as *clock, strobe, enable, set,* or *reset*. We shall encounter these terms in the following chapters. The output may change state at the rising edge or at the falling edge (called "edge triggered") of an input, or it may be a function of a high or low logic level of a critical input or combination of inputs (called "level triggered"). Time-dependent logic is also known as *clocked*, or *synchronous*, *logic*.

15.1.3 *Elementary Logic Functions*

The first digital ICs produced were simple gates and inverters containing one to six devices in a package. The variety of gates has increased dramatically.

The various levels of integrated circuit complexity and size are as follows. *Small-scale integration (SSI)* includes simple devices such as gates and flip-flops. Devices within this classification contain between one and ten equivalent gates. *Medium-scale integration (MSI)* consists of more-complex devices such as counters, shift registers, encoders, decoders, and small memories. MSI devices contain from 10 to 100 equivalent gates. *Large-scale integration (LSI)* includes larger memories and microprocessors. LSI devices consists of between 100 and 1000 equivalent gates. *Very large scale integration (VLSI)* includes the largest memories and microprocessors. VLSI devices have more than 1000 equivalent gates.

We now briefly define eight of the most basic and common logic gates. Even with the continuing development of MSI and LSI logic functions and microprocessors, these basic functions still play a major role in digital electronic design.

Eight functions are presented in Figure 15.1. Each is described, but first we pick two for more detailed discussion. We do this to clarify the concept of the truth table.

Begin with the *inverter,* which is a device for which the output is the opposite of the input. If the input is 0, the output is 1, and vice versa. The output is always the *complement* of the input. The truth table for the function is exceedingly simple, since there are only two possible inputs. We therefore enter each possible input value (designated as *A*) and write the corresponding output (designated as *Y*) next to this value. The truth table is shown in Figure 15.1(b).

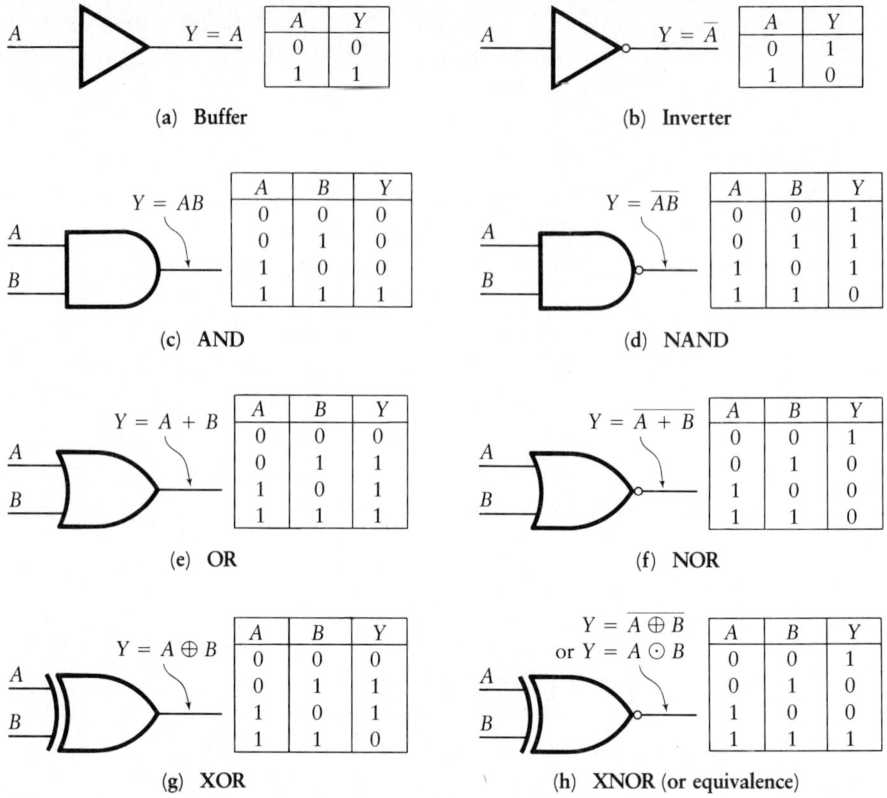

Figure 15.1
Elementary gate summary.

A	Y
0	0
1	1

$Y = A$

(a) Buffer

A	Y
0	1
1	0

$Y = \overline{A}$

(b) Inverter

A	B	Y
0	0	0
0	1	0
1	0	0
1	1	1

$Y = AB$

(c) AND

A	B	Y
0	0	1
0	1	1
1	0	1
1	1	0

$Y = \overline{AB}$

(d) NAND

A	B	Y
0	0	0
0	1	1
1	0	1
1	1	1

$Y = A + B$

(e) OR

A	B	Y
0	0	1
0	1	0
1	0	0
1	1	0

$Y = \overline{A + B}$

(f) NOR

A	B	Y
0	0	0
0	1	1
1	0	1
1	1	0

$Y = A \oplus B$

(g) XOR

A	B	Y
0	0	1
0	1	0
1	0	0
1	1	1

$Y = \overline{A \oplus B}$
or $Y = A \odot B$

(h) XNOR (or equivalence)

	BUFFER	INVERTER	AND	NAND
TTL ——	7417	7404	7408	7400
ECL ——	MC10188	MC10189	MC10104	MC10121
CMOS ——	MM74HC125	MM74HC04	MM74HC08	MM74HC00

	OR	NOR	XOR	XNOR
TTL ——	7432	7402	7486	74266
ECL ——	MC10103	MC10102	MC10113	MC10107
CMOS ——	MM74HC32	MM74HC02	MM74HC86	MM74HC266

The equation is given in the form

$$Y = \overline{A}$$

We have introduced the notation of a bar over the variable to indicate the logic operation of inversion. An alternate notation is to use a prime for the inversion operation, so in equation form this becomes

$$Y = A'$$

The notation used in the block diagram to denote inversion is a small circle at the output of the logic symbol. The inversion operation is sometimes referred to as a *NOT* gate. Thus, the output of the inverter with A as input is sometimes known as NOT A.

The second operation we discuss is that of the *OR* gate. The OR gate has more than one input, and a two-input gate is illustrated in Figure 15.1(e). The gate provides a logic 1 at the output when *any one or more* of the inputs is in the logic 1 state. That is, the output, Y, is 1 if A and/or B are equal to 1.

Since this gate has two inputs (A and B), the truth table has three columns, one for each input and one for the output (Y). Since there are two inputs and each of these can take on either of two values, there are four possible input combinations. These form the four rows of the table. In general, the truth table has 2^n rows, where n is the number of inputs.

Although it is a simple matter to develop a truth table with only four rows, the process can become quite complex if the number of input variables increases. For example, with 6 inputs, the number of possible combinations is 2^6, or 64. In cataloging the 64 possible input combinations, it is usually helpful to arrange them in binary counting order. Thus, for two inputs, the rows are ordered by input combination as follows: 00, 01, 10, 11. This is helpful to avoid omitting any possible combination in more complex situations.

The formula notation for the operation of OR is the plus sign. The circuit symbol contains a curved line at the left edge, as shown in Figure 15.1(e).

We now briefly define the remaining six functions in the figure.

A *buffer,* shown in Figure 15.1(a), has a single input and a single output. The output is always in the same logic state as the input. The purpose of a buffer is to provide additional power to drive other logic inputs. A buffer can be built by cascading two inverters together. That is, taking an inverse twice returns us to the original value.

An *AND* gate has two (or more) inputs and one output. The output is at logic level 1 only when *all* the inputs are in the logic 1 state. The AND gate is shown in Figure 15.1(c). Note that the notation of the AND operation used in the formula is to write the two variables next to each other as if we were talking about algebraic multiplication. We also sometimes use a dot between the variables. Thus,

$$AB$$

and

$$A \cdot B$$

are both read, "A and B." Also note that the circuit symbol has a straight line on the input edge and a semicircle on the output edge, as distinguished from the OR gate symbol, which uses a curved line on the input edge and two curved lines on the output edge.

The *NAND* gate provides a logic 0 at the output only when *all* the inputs are in the logic 1 state. The NAND gate can be viewed as an AND gate followed by an inverter. This is illustrated in Figure 15.1(d). Note that the equation and the circuit diagram are both developed by combining the notation for the AND with that of the inversion operation. Note that any 0 at the input produces a 1 at the output.

A *NOR* gate provides a logic 0 output when *any one or more* of the inputs is in the logic 1 state. This is shown in Figure 15.1(f). Note that the NOR gate can be viewed as an OR gate followed by an inverter. Both the equation and the circuit diagram are developed by combining the two individual representations.

The *XOR* gate, or *exclusive OR,* provides a logic 1 output when *any one, but only one,* of its inputs is in the logic 1 state. This is shown in Figure 15.1(g). Note that the formula notation is a plus sign (as used for the OR) with a circle around it. The circuit notation starts with the symbol for an OR gate and adds a second curved line at the input.

The final logic operation shown is the *exclusive NOR,* or *XNOR,* gate. The XNOR gate provides a logic 0 output when *any one, but only one,* of its inputs is in the logic 1 state. This gate is also called *equivalence,* since the output is logic 1 when the two inputs are equal. Note that the XNOR can be viewed as an exclusive OR gate followed by an inverter. This is shown in Figure 15.1(h), where two formula notations are shown.

Also included in Figure 15.1 are some IC part numbers for each of these gates in three different families.

15.1.4   *Boolean Algebra*

Whenever binary variables are manipulated, equations result. We need rules for working with these equations. Boolean algebra gives us the necessary set of rules. In Boolean algebra, the two elementary algebraic operations of addition and multiplication are replaced by the elementary logic operations of OR and AND. Functions are defined either through an equation or by giving the value of the function for every possible input. This latter approach gives rise to the truth (or function) table, as discussed in the previous section.

The Boolean equation is a shorthand way of writing the truth table. *Boolean identities* can be proven by referring to the function tables for the gates as shown in Figure 15.1.

The following drill problems present an overview of several important Boolean identities.

Drill Problems

Prove each of the relationships given in Problems D15.1–D15.16.

D15.1 $A + (B + C) = (A + B) + C$ (associative law)

D15.2 $A(BC) = (AB)C$ (associative law)

D15.3 $\overline{A + B} = \overline{A}\,\overline{B}$ (DeMorgan's theorem)

D15.4 $\overline{ABC} = \overline{A} + \overline{B} + \overline{C}$ (DeMorgan's theorem)

D15.5 $A + 0 = A$

D15.6 $A + A = A$

D15.7 $A + \overline{A} = 1$

D15.8 $A \cdot 0 = 0$

D15.9 $A \cdot 1 = A$

D15.10 $A \cdot A = A$

D15.11 $A \cdot \overline{A} = 0$

D15.12 $A + AB = A$

D15.13 $AB + A\overline{B} = A$

D15.14 $\overline{(\overline{A})} = A$

D15.15 $\overline{(A + B)}\,\overline{(\overline{A} + \overline{B})} = 0$

D15.16 $B + A\overline{B} = A + B$

DeMorgan's theorem (see Drill Problems D15.3 and D15.4) can be used to develop alternate forms for implementing the NOR and NAND operation. These alternate forms are sometimes preferable for reasons related to practical considerations, as we see later.

Starting with the NOR operation, we can use the theorem to show

$$\overline{A + B} = \overline{A}\overline{B} \tag{15.1}$$

For the case of three variables,

$$\overline{A + B + C} = \overline{A}\overline{B}\overline{C} \tag{15.2}$$

Alternatively, for the NAND operation, we have

$$\overline{AB} = \overline{A} + \overline{B} \tag{15.3}$$

Figure 15.2
Alternate forms for
NOR and NAND
gates.

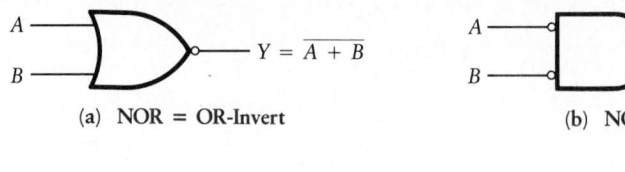

(a) NOR = OR-Invert   (b) NOR = Invert-AND

(c) NAND = AND-Invert   (d) NAND = Invert-OR

In the three-variable case,

$$\overline{ABC} = \overline{A} + \overline{B} + \overline{C} \qquad (15.4)$$

The resulting alternate forms of the basic gates are shown in Figure 15.2.

15.2 IC Construction and Packaging

ICs are fabricated using a sequence of processing steps, which include growing, slicing, and etching silicon wafers, masking and doping them with n- and p-type impurities, and depositing conductor patterns. This complex processing sequence produces complete functional circuits containing patterns of resistors, capacitors, diodes, and transistors.

A functional circuit pattern is repeated numerous times to fill the usable area of a silicon wafer. After the processing steps, the wafer is sliced into small rectangles, or "chips," each containing one or more functional circuits. Each chip is tested and mounted in a package. A typical package is the 14-pin *dual in-line package* (known as a *DIP*). Several of the popular packages are illustrated in Figure 15.3.

The package provides structural support, an arrangement of pins for external connections, and a sealed cover to keep out moisture and contamination. The complexity of VLSI chips with their large numbers of inputs and outputs has caused some decline in the use of the DIP. Newer package configurations provide for additional external connections and faster (and less expensive) manufacturing techniques. This is particularly true when these chips are incorporated into larger system modules.

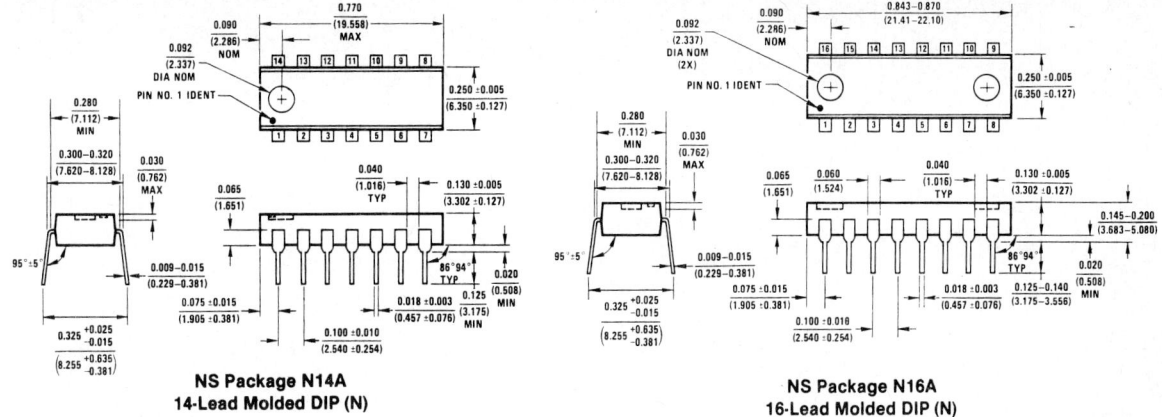

NS Package N14A
14-Lead Molded DIP (N)

NS Package N16A
16-Lead Molded DIP (N)

Figure 15.3
IC package
configurations.
Courtesy of National
Semiconductor Corp.

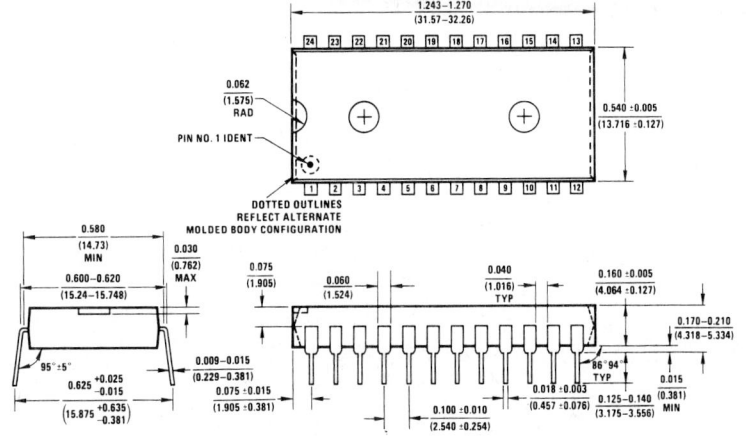

NS Package N24A
24-Lead Molded DIP (N)

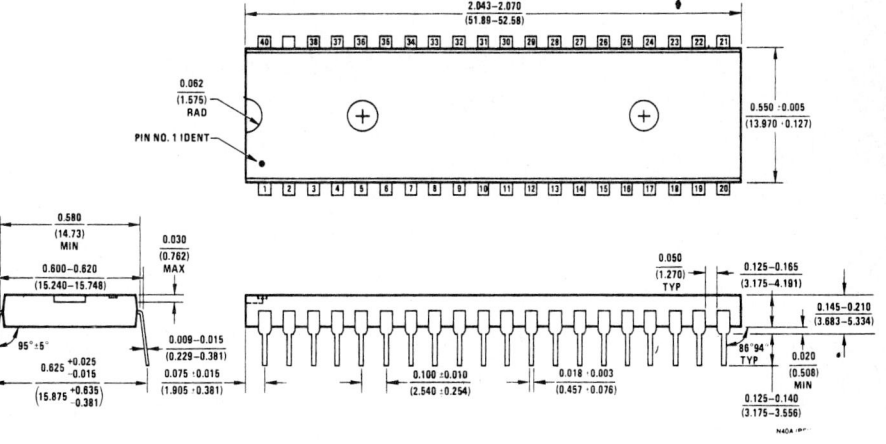

NS Package N40A
40-Lead Molded DIP (N)

15.3   **Practical Considerations in Digital Design**

A number of limitations or constraints must be taken into account when approaching a practical digital electronic design problem. We must be concerned with such factors as the number of inputs per device, the number of devices contained in each IC package, the number of packages required to implement a complete logic system, noise immunity, power consumptions, speed, time delay, and loading of logic outputs.

One of the first considerations is that gates come packaged in arrays with a fixed number in each package. Each gate in the array has the same number of inputs. A typical package contains either six inverters or buffers, four two-input gates, three three-input gates, two four-input gates, or a single eight-input gate. These numbers are chosen to match the number of input and output leads available on a DIP. For example, one standard DIP has 14 pins. Two of these must be used for supplying voltage and ground, which leaves 12 for the gates. A two-input, one-output gate requires three leads, so 4 of these gates can be packaged on a single chip.

Suppose, for example, a particular design required seven inverters. Since a typical package contains six inverters, you would need two packages, and this would leave five devices unused. On the other hand, consider the fact that a spare NAND or NOR gate may be used as an inverter. This can be seen from Figure 15.1. For example, suppose the first input to a NAND gate is set equal to 1 (tied to the HIGH of the supply). Then the relationship between the second input and the output is that of the inverter. We could also tie inputs *A* and *B* together and, in this manner, develop an inverter.

As another example, if you needed a five-input gate and only had an eight-input gate available, you can set the three unused inputs to the appropriate value and use the remaining five inputs to produce the desired function. In this manner, you may save purchase of additional chips and reduce the associated power and space requirements.

Unused input pins should never be left open. They should be connected to a suitable logic-low or logic-high level, or input pins may be connected together in groups. The function table is used to determine the proper logic level to be applied to unused inputs. For OR and NOR gates, the unused inputs should be connected to a logic 0, or LOW voltage. For AND and NAND gates, the unused inputs should be connected to a logic 1, or HIGH voltage.

Noise immunity, power consumption, and *speed* are important considerations in the design of a logic circuit. The location or environment in which the logic circuit must function should be carefully considered. Locations in which electrical noise is prevalent, such as in factories with large electric motors and tools or near radio, television, or radar transmitters, may require a logic family that has *high noise immunity*. High noise immunity means that the logic family is insensitive to noise voltages that are radiated or conducted into the electronic system. If this is not practical, then it may be necessary to use shielded enclosures, filtered power and shielded logic wiring.

Power consumption is usually of no consequence for equipment that is powered by a 110 V ac outlet. On the other hand, portable battery-powered equipment requires a logic family that consumes low power. High-operating-speed requirements also narrow the choice of logic families. Manufacturer's data books should be studied carefully to make the best selection of device or logic family for the specific application.

Output loading should also be carefully checked to make sure that each logic output is not being asked to drive an excessive number of logic inputs. This consideration also applies to any other type of load that exceeds the manufacturer's rating for the device. The number of logic inputs that an IC can drive is defined as *fan out*.

Another performance characteristic of logic circuits is *time delay,* often called *propagation delay*. This is the time between the application of a logic input and the appearance of the corresponding logic output. This delay can sometimes cause serious problems such as undesired transients, or *glitches*.

Consider the example shown in Figure 15.4, which demonstrates how a small delay of one logic input can cause a glitch. Below the circuit diagram is a series of five sketches, which comprise what is known as a *timing diagram*. We start by drawing an assumed shape for inputs *A* and *B*. In this case, we let *A* start HIGH, then go LOW, and, finally, go back to HIGH. The second input, *B,* starts LOW. It goes from LOW to HIGH at the same time that input *A* is changing from HIGH to LOW. Then *B* returns to LOW following the second transition in *A*.

The circuit performs an exclusive OR operation between *B* and the inverse of *A*. Thus the output, *Y,* should be HIGH if either *A* is low or *B* is high but

Figure 15.4
Generation of undesired glitch.

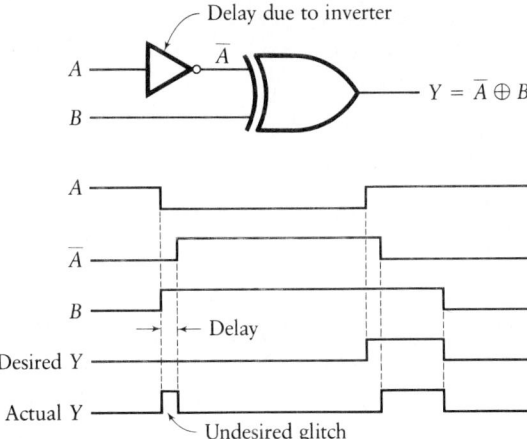

Figure 15.5
Example of useful
glitches.

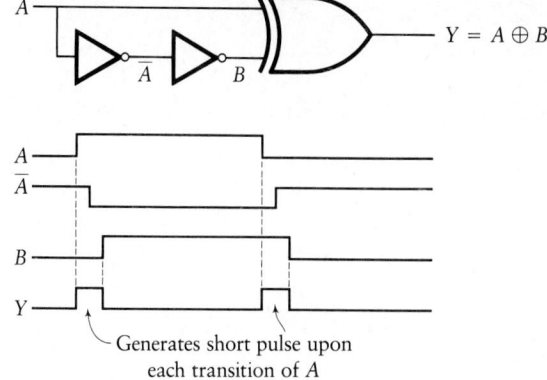

Generates short pulse upon
each transition of A

not both. Thus, the expected output is shown as "desired Y." However, now
suppose that the inverter introduces a delay so that the actual output, $\overline{A}$, is as
shown on the second line. The result of the exclusive OR operation is as labeled
"actual Y." Note that a narrow pulse has been generated at the first transition
time, and this undesired pulse is known as a glitch.

Sometimes glitches can be useful, as shown in the example of Figure 15.5.
This demonstrates how two inverters (or any even number) may be used with
an exclusive OR to generate a narrow pulse whenever a logic input changes
from one logic state to the other (i.e., at both the rising transition and the
falling transition).

Drill Problems

In Problems D15.17–D15.20, form a five-input AND gate using only the specified gates.

D15.17   Use two-input AND gates.

   Ans: See Figure D15.1.

Using 2-Input AND gates:

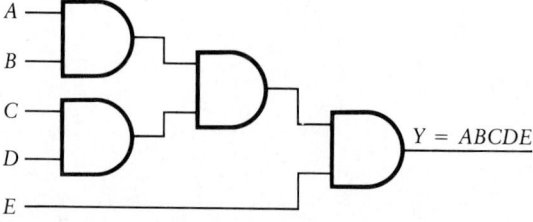

$Y = ABCDE$

Note: A, B, C, and D are delayed more than E.

Figure D15.1

D15.18   Use three-input AND gates.

   Ans: See Figure D15.2.

Using 3-Input AND gate:

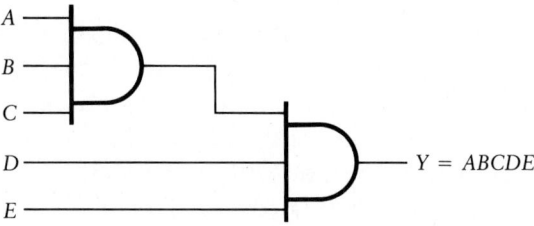

Note: A, B, and C are delayed more than D and E.

Figure D15.2

D15.19   Use four-input AND gates.

   Ans: See Figure D15.3.

Using 4-Input AND gate:

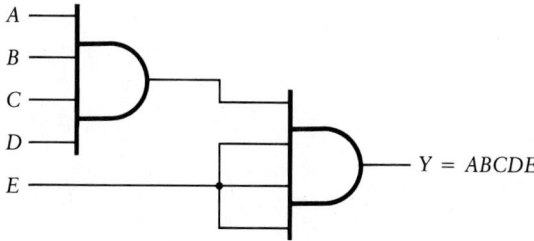

Note: A, B, C, and D are delayed more than E.

Figure D15.3

D15.20   Use eight-input AND gates.

   Ans: See Figure D15.4.

Using an 8-input AND gate:

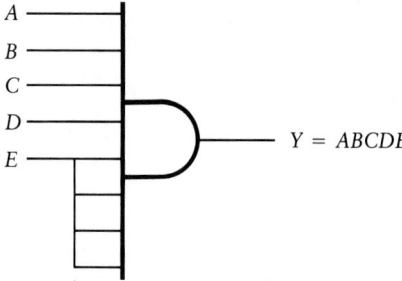

Note: All inputs are delayed the same amount.

Figure D15.4

15.4   Digital Circuit Characteristics of BJTs

The operation of junction transistors is considered in Chapters 2 and 3. The design techniques presented in those chapters concentrate upon assuring operation in the linear or active region of the characteristic curves. In the case of digital circuits, we require that the transistor be either ON (in the saturated condition) or OFF (in the cut-off condition). In effect, we operate at either of the two extremes of the transistor characteristic curves, as shown in Figure 15.6(a). The voltage from the collector to emitter, v_{CE}, is approximately 0.2 V when the transistor is saturated. That is,

$$V_{CEsat} = 0.2 \text{ V}$$

When the transistor is cut off, it acts like an open circuit between collector and emitter.

The i_B-versus-v_{BE} characteristic curve is shown in Figure 15.6(b). When v_{BE} is less than about 0.6 V, the transistor is cut off and

$$i_B = i_C = 0$$

When v_{BE} increases, i_B and i_C increase rapidly. The saturation voltage between base and emitter, V_{BEsat}, is approximately 0.7 to 0.8 V.

The first step in the analysis of the BJT family of ICs is to prepare a function table that shows the status of each transistor (either ON or OFF) for all possible combinations of high and low levels of each of the inputs. Next determine the numerical value of v_{BE} for each transistor. If v_{BE} is less than 0.6 V, the transistor is cut off, and

$$i_B = i_C = 0$$

Figure 15.6
npn silicon transistor characteristic.

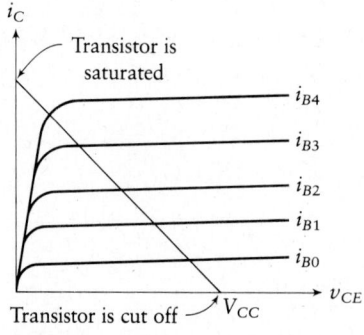

(a) Typical i_C vs v_{CE} characteristics

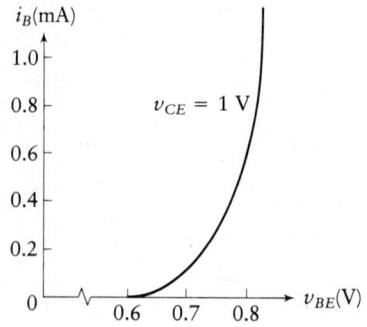

(b) Typical i_B vs v_{BE} characteristics

If v_{BE} is greater than 0.6 V, the transistor could be in the active region or it could be saturated. With digital ICs, transistors in this condition are saturated so the transistor is considered to be ON.

15.5 BJT Logic Families

There are six important families of bipolar logic. These are known as TTL, ECL, RTL, DTL, HTL, and HNIL. The first two of these are extremely important and are discussed in detail in Sections 15.6 and 15.7. The last four are of less current importance, and are included in this section only to provide historical perspective.

Resistor-transistor logic (RTL) was the earliest IC family. It utilizes only transistors and resistors and provides logic gating by placing transistor collectors in parallel.

Diode-transistor logic (DTL) was a popular logic family for several years. It provided improvements in noise immunity and fan-out capabilities as compared to RTL. The gating of DTL is performed by diode OR gates at the input to each logic circuit.

Several manufacturers developed digital logic families that were functionally similar to DTL but replaced some of the diodes with zener diodes so that the transistors would not conduct until the input voltages reached a level of about 6 V. This increased the noise immunity, making this logic family well suited for use in industrial environments such as factories and refineries, where heavy electrical equipment produces spikes, transients, and other variations in the power line voltage.

These logic families are known as *high-threshold logic* (HTL) and *high-noise immunity logic* (HNIL). They are currently available only in limited SSI and MSI functions.

15.6 Transistor-Transistor Logic (TTL)

Transistor-transistor logic (TTL) started as a single, unique logic family. As it grew, various requirements for higher speed, lower power, or higher output drive led to the development of several subgroups, as discussed shortly.

The original logic family is still in use, although most new logic functions are being manufactured in newer subgroups of the family. TTL utilizes BJTs and provides moderate speed and power consumption.

High-power TTL (H-TTL) was developed for driver circuits and other applications requiring a high fan-out (number of circuits which the output must drive) and high speed. The H-TTL family consumes more power than other TTL subgroups. It is not widely used and is available only in a few logic functions. It utilizes and attains higher speed by using lower resistor values than those used in TTL.

Low-power TTL (LP-TTL) was developed for applications requiring lower power consumption and where reduced operating speed can be tolerated. It utilizes saturating transistors and attains lower power consumption by using higher resistor values than those used in TTL. It has essentially been replaced by LS-TTL.

Schottky TTL (S-TTL) was developed for high-speed applications. It attains high-speed operation with lower power dissipation than H-TTL by using a nonsaturating type of transistor, called a *Schottky transistor*. It contains a built-in forward-voltage diode connected between the base and collector. Figure 15.7 shows a comparison between Schottky transistors and the standard BJT. The base-to-emitter voltage is typically 0.7 V, and the diode forward-voltage drop is typically 0.3 V. Thus, when the collector voltage drops to 0.4 V, the excess base current is shunted through the diode to the collector, and the transistor is prevented from saturating. Since the transistor is not saturated, it does not suffer from the delay required to remove the excess base charge and turn the transistor off.

Low-power Schottky TTL (LS-TTL) is a subgroup that provides the speed

Figure 15.7
Schottky transistor.

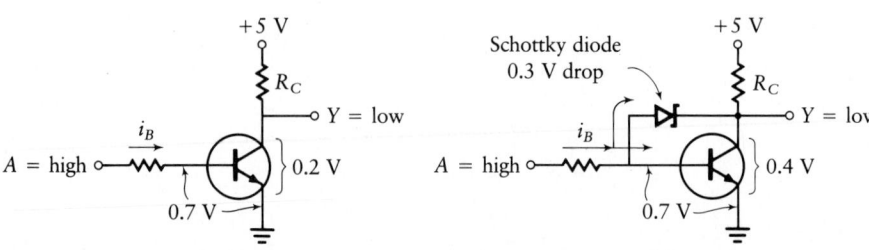

(a) Saturated transistor

(b) Schottky diode with normal transistor; excess base current shunted through diode

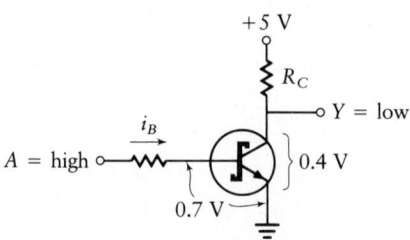

(c) Schottky transistor

of the original TTL family but with substantially reduced power consumption. It can be described as low-power TTL using Schottky transistors instead of saturating transistors. It has been one of the most popular subgroups for many years, and most logic functions are available in LS-TTL.

Advanced Schottky TTL (AS-TTL) is a TTL subgroup that provides somewhat higher speed and lower power than S-TTL.

Advanced low-power Schottky TTL (ALS-TTL) provides an excellent combination of desirable speed and power consumption properties. It utilizes Schottky transistors but incorporates material developments and smaller circuit layouts with reduced capacitance.

15.6.1 Open Collector

We are now ready to examine the internal circuitry of a TTL chip. Figure 15.8 shows the schematic diagram and function table for a two-input TTL NAND gate with open collector. The operation of this basic TTL gate depends upon the dual-emitter transistor, Q_1. The two inputs A and B are connected to the emitters. The diodes between the emitters and ground prevent damage to Q_1 if the signal at A or B should be negative. A TTL-compatible signal should be 0.2 V for the LOW level and between 2.4 and 5 V for the HIGH level. Since we are using positive logic in this text, 0.2 V to 0.7 V corresponds to a binary 0. When the output is logic 0, the TTL gate is capable of sinking 16 mA of current. A voltage between 2.4 V and 5 V (3.3 V is typical) corresponds to a binary 1.

The output of this open collector gate is taken from the collector of Q_3. A "pull-up" resistor is inserted externally from the IC output pin to a voltage of level V, frequently 5 V. This pull-up resistor causes the output of the IC to "pull up" to V when Q_3 is OFF. Since the logic block is a NAND gate, the output should be 1 when either or both of the inputs is 0. Notice that when either or both of the emitters of Q_1 is low, Q_1 will conduct. The base voltage of Q_1 is 0.2 V plus the $V_{BE}(Q_1)$ of 0.7 V, for a total of about 0.9 V. With Q_1 conducting, the current is flowing away from the base of Q_2, causing Q_2 to cut off. With Q_2 OFF, the base voltage on Q_3 is less than 0.6 V, so Q_3 is also

Figure 15.8
Two-input TTL NAND gate (open collector).

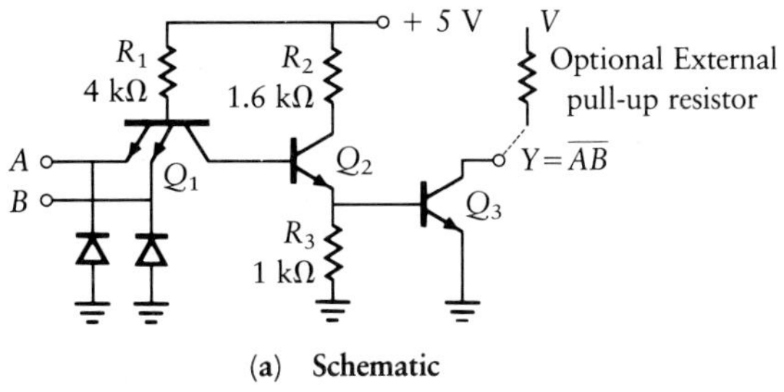

(a) **Schematic**

A	B	Q_1	Q_2	Q_3	Y
0	0	ON	OFF	OFF	1
0	1	ON	OFF	OFF	1
1	0	ON	OFF	OFF	1
1	1	OFF	ON	ON	0

(b) **Function table**

cut off. Since Q_3 is OFF, the output goes to HIGH, or logic level 1. This is summarized in the first three rows of the table in Figure 15.8(b). If both inputs are HIGH (logic level 1), Q_1 is OFF, which causes Q_2 to saturate. With Q_2 ON, the voltage on the base of Q_3 is greater than 0.7 V, and hence Q_3 is ON. This, in turn, causes the output to drop to 0.2 V, the saturated value of V_{CE}. This analysis is summarized in the last row of the table in Figure 15.8(b).

Let us now examine some of the major applications for the open collector gate. The gate can be used as a means of going from the TTL logic family to another logic family. For example, in a system that includes both TTL and CMOS ICs (discussed in Section 15.8), the HIGH and LOW voltage levels may be different. In particular, the high level for TTL is 5 V, whereas it can be 10 V for CMOS. If the pull-up resistor of Figure 15.8 is connected to 10 V, then the open collector gate acts as an interface between the TTL portion of the system and the CMOS portion.

A second application of the open collector gate occurs when several gates are attached to a common *bus*. In the operation of this common bus, each gate can control the logic level of the bus only by bringing it low but not high. With the collector left open, each gate that has Q_3 OFF exerts no control upon the bus. Only when the output transistor is ON does the gate bring the bus to logic level 0.

Another application for the open collector occurs when a lamp or relay is driven from the output of a gate. The lamp or relay is placed between the output terminal of the open collector IC and the voltage source through an appropriate limiting resistor. When Q_3 is saturated, a path to ground exists and the lamp or relay is ON. When Q_3 is OFF, there is no path to ground so the device is OFF.

15.6.2   *Active Pull-Up*

Figure 15.9(a) shows a two-input TTL NAND gate with active pull-up on the output. This circuit configuration is known as a *totem-pole* output. The circuit is the same as that of Figure 15.8(a) except for the addition of D_3, Q_4, and R_4. The same function table is generated as with the open collector NAND gate with a pull-up resistor. This type of gate is used when increased operating speed is required. The *propagation delay* (the time required for the gate to go from on to off) for an open collector gate is approximately 35 ns. The propagation delay for the active pull-up gate is about 8 ns, so the clear advantage is in increasing the speed of this totem-pole output compared to that of the open collector output gate.

The voltage at the base of Q_4 with both Q_2 and Q_3 ON is given by

$$V_B(Q_4) = V_{CE}(Q_2) + V_{BE}(Q_3)$$
$$= 0.2 + 0.7 = 0.9 \text{ V}$$

Figure 15.9
Two-input TTL
NAND gate (active
pull-up).

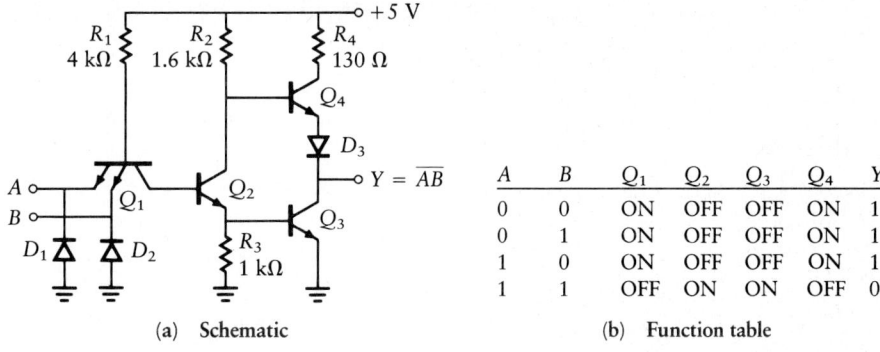

A	B	Q_1	Q_2	Q_3	Q_4	Y
0	0	ON	OFF	OFF	ON	1
0	1	ON	OFF	OFF	ON	1
1	0	ON	OFF	OFF	ON	1
1	1	OFF	ON	ON	OFF	0

(a) Schematic   (b) Function table

The voltage necessary to turn Q_4 ON must be greater than 1.4 V. That is,

$$V_{BE}(Q_4) + V(D_3) + V_{CE}(Q_3) = 0.6 + 0.6 + 0.2 = 1.4 \text{ V}$$

Since the base voltage of Q_4 is only 0.9 V, Q_4 is OFF. When the output goes to logic 1, Q_2 and Q_3 are OFF and Q_4 saturates. Since the load capacitance can now discharge through a smaller resistor (130 Ω plus the resistances of Q_4 and D_3, or about 150 Ω) the time to change from 1 to 0 is faster than for the open collector gate, which must discharge through a larger pull-up resistor.

The totem-pole output gate cannot be used for the applications cited in the previous section. For example, suppose we tried to connect two totem-pole outputs to a common bus. If the output of one gate is HIGH and the output of the other is LOW, an excessive amount of current results, and this could damage the ICs.

15.6.3 *H-TTL and LP-TTL Gates*

The two input NAND gates for the H-TTL and LP-TTL circuits are shown in Figures 15.10(a) and 15.11(a), respectively, and the function tables are presented as Figures 15.10(b) and 15.11(b).

Let us first examine the table for the H-TTL in Figure 15.10(b). The differences between this table and that of the TTL NAND gate of Figure 15.9 occur since there is an additional transistor in the H-TTL gate. The tables are identical through the column for Q_2. Starting with the next column, the state of Q_3 for the H-TTL gate is opposite that of Q_2. In the H-TTL gate, transistors Q_4 and Q_5 are fed by the collector and emitter of Q_3. In the TTL NAND gate of Figure 15.9, transistors Q_4 and Q_3 are fed by the collector and emitter of Q_2. Note that the resistors are smaller and the fan-out capability is greater.

The table for the LP-TTL gate (Figure 15.11(b)) is identical to that of the H-TTL gate (Figure 15.10(b)); however, the resistance values are increased.

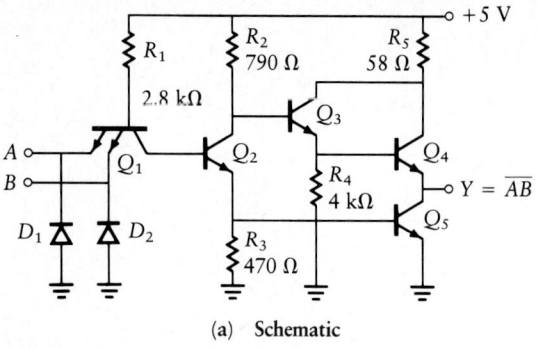

(a) Schematic

A	B	Q_1	Q_2	Q_3	Q_4	Q_5	Y
0	0	ON	OFF	ON	ON	OFF	1
0	1	ON	OFF	ON	ON	OFF	1
1	0	ON	OFF	ON	ON	OFF	1
1	1	OFF	ON	OFF	OFF	ON	0

(b)   Function table

Figure 15.10 Two-input H-TTL NAND gate.

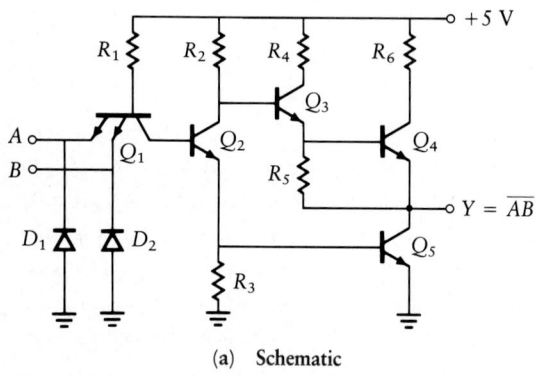

(a)   Schematic

A	B	Q_1	Q_2	Q_3	Q_4	Q_5	Y
0	0	ON	OFF	ON	ON	OFF	1
0	1	ON	OFF	ON	ON	OFF	1
1	0	ON	OFF	ON	ON	OFF	1
1	1	OFF	ON	OFF	OFF	ON	0

(b)   Function table

Figure 15.11 Two-input LP-TTL NAND gate.

This reduces the power but also decreases the speed of the IC, since the *RC* time constants are increased.

15.6.4   *Schottky TTL Gates*

The Schottky subgroup of the TTL family is designed to reduce the propagation-delay time of the standard TTL gates. The time needed for a transistor to switch from ON to OFF can be greatly reduced if the transistor does not go into saturation. Refer to Figure 15.7(b), where, by placing a Schottky diode between base and collector, we shunt the excess base current through the diode and hence prevent the transistor from going into saturation. A Schottky diode differs from a conventional diode in that the Schottky diode is formed with a

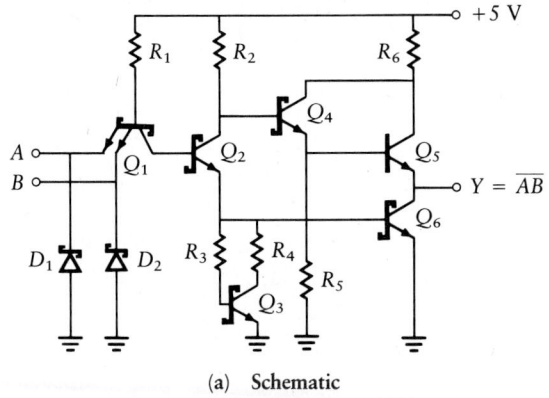

+5 V

(a)   Schematic

A	B	Q_1	Q_2	Q_4	Q_5	Q_6	Y
0	0	ON	OFF	ON	ON	OFF	1
0	1	ON	OFF	ON	ON	OFF	1
1	0	ON	OFF	ON	ON	OFF	1
1	1	OFF	ON	OFF	OFF	ON	0

(b)   **Function table** (Q_3 is used for base drive control of Q_4 and is not ON or OFF in a logic sense)

Figure 15.12   Two-input S-TTL NAND gate.

junction of a *metal* and a semiconductor rather than a junction of *p*- and *n*-type semiconductor material. The voltage across a conducting Schottky diode is 0.3 V rather than 0.7 V for a standard diode. The Schottky diode and the transistor are combined to form a Schottky transistor as in Figure 15.7(c).

The circuit schematic and the function diagram for the two-input NAND gate is shown in Figure 15.12. The transistors in the gate are of the Schottky type except for Q_5, which is of the standard type, since it does not saturate. In this circuit, Q_5 and Q_4 form a *Darlington pair*, providing a high current gain with low resistance (see Chapter 6 for a discussion of Darlington-pair transistor configurations).

The function table for the S-TTL gate (Figure 15.12(b)) is similar to that of the LP-TTL gate, except for the addition of a sixth transistor. The state of this sixth transistor, Q_3, is not carried in the table, since it only increases the speed of the IC and has no direct effect upon the states of the other transistors. The remaining five transistors follow the same table as for the LP-TTL. The verification of the entries in these tables is left to the student, with the procedure paralleling that of the previous sections.

A complete analysis of this circuit shows that the propagation delay is about 30% lower than that of the standard TTL circuit.

15.6.5   *Tri-State Gates*

The *tri-state* family of gates combines the high-speed advantage of the totem-pole output with the advantages of an open collector output. The tri-state gate has a totem-pole output. However, it has another terminal, which permits the

Figure 15.13
Tri-state bus driver.

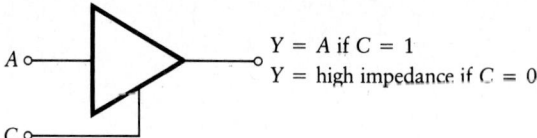

$Y = A$ if $C = 1$
$Y = $ high impedance if $C = 0$

gate to operate normally if the third terminal is HIGH. The gate exhibits a high impedance when the third terminal is LOW. The tri-state bus driver, shown in the schematic of Figure 15.13, produces an output of $Y = A$ when C is HIGH. A high input impedance occurs when C is LOW. This permits several of these gates to be attached to a common bus, as with the open collector gate.

Drill Problems

Determine the state of each transistor and the output in the circuits shown in Problems D15.21–D15.24.

D15.21

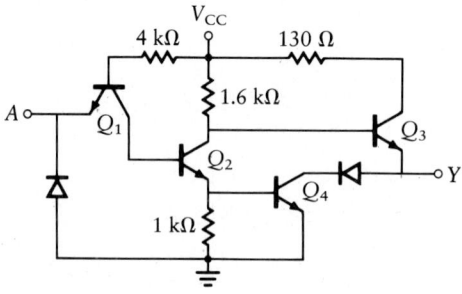

Figure D15.5

Ans:

A	Q_1	Q_2	Q_3	Q_4	Y
0	N	F	N	F	1
1	F	N	F	N	0

N = ON
F = OFF

D15.22

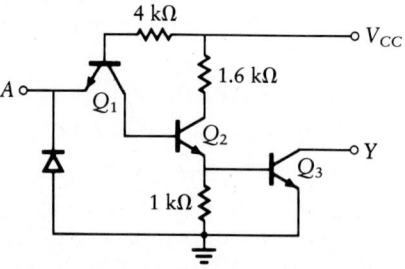

Figure D15.6

Ans:

A	Q_1	Q_2	Q_3	Y
0	N	F	F	U
1	F	N	N	0

U = undetermined
N = ON
F = OFF

D15.23

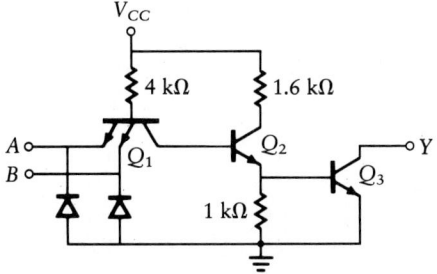

Ans:

A	B	Q_1	Q_2	Q_3	Y
0	0	N	F	F	U
0	1	N	F	F	U
1	0	N	F	F	U
1	1	F	N	N	0

U = undetermined
N = ON
F = OFF

Figure D15.7

D15.24

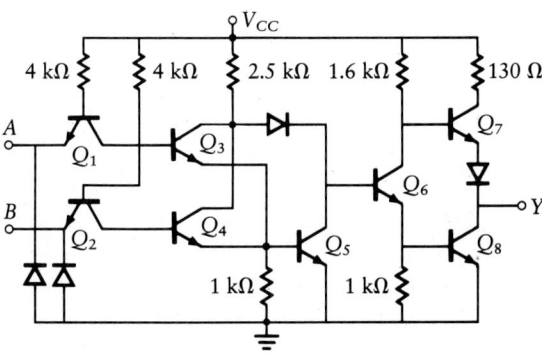

Ans:

A	B	Q_1	Q_2	Q_3	Q_4	Q_5	Q_6	Q_7	Q_8	Y
0	0	N	N	F	F	F	N	F	N	0
0	1	N	F	F	N	N	F	N	F	1
1	0	F	N	N	F	N	F	N	F	1
1	1	F	F	N	N	N	F	N	F	1

Figure D15.8

15.6.6 *Device Listings*

Table 15.1 shows a partial listing for the devices of the TTL family. At this point, we strongly suggest that the student obtain one or more of the *data books* supplied by the various IC manufacturers. These are listed in the references at the end of this text. It is virtually impossible to successfully complete digital electronic designs without access to these data books.

Table 15.1 Partial TTL Device Listing.

Type Number	Description
7400	Quad 2-input NAND
7401	Quad 2-input NAND, open collector
7402	Quad 2-input NOR
7403	Quad 2-input NOR, open collector
7404	Hex Inverter
7405	Hex Inverter, open collector
7406	Hex Inverter, open collector to 30 volts
7407	Hex Buffer/Driver, open collector to 30 volts
7408	Quad 2-input AND
7409	Quad 2-input AND, open collector
7410	Triple 3-input NAND
7411	Triple 3-input AND
7414	Hex Schmitt-trigger inverters
7420	Dual 4-input NAND
7421	Dual 4-input AND
7427	Triple 3-input OR
7430	8-input NAND
7432	Quad 2-input OR
7486	Quad 2-input XOR

TTL Data Book, Vol. 2, Texas Instruments, Inc., Dallas, Texas.

15.7 Emitter-Coupled Logic

Emitter-coupled logic (ECL) is used in specialized devices such as radar-signal processors and high-speed computers. This family utilizes a differential amplifier circuit, which performs a *current-steering* function. This causes current to flow in only one of the pair of transistors at a time. The transistor voltages and currents are controlled to prevent transistor saturation without requiring special Schottky transistors. ECL uses a negative supply voltage and consumes a large amount of power. Output voltage levels are -0.8 V for logic 1 and -1.8 V for logic 0. The devices are more susceptible to noise than most other logic families. The fast rise and fall times of the output waveform often require use of special wiring techniques to prevent overshoot, ringing, or reflections of the wave returning from the other end of a cable.

Figure 15.14 shows an example of an ECL gate that provides both an OR and a NOR function. One side of the differential pair is connected to an internal reference voltage, whereas the other side is composed of two or more transistors connected in parallel. If the base voltage of one or more of these

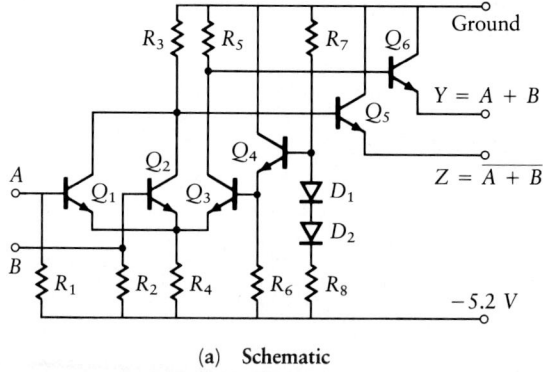

(a) Schematic

A	B	Q_1	Q_2	Q_3	Y	Z
0	0	OFF	OFF	ON	0	1
0	1	OFF	ON	OFF	1	0
1	0	ON	OFF	OFF	1	0
1	1	ON	ON	OFF	1	0

(b) Function table

Figure 15.14 Two-input ECL OR/NOR gate.

transistors is driven to a level higher than the internal reference voltage, the current is steered through the transistor with the highest input voltage. The collector voltages of the differential pair change only by about 0.8 V. The collector voltages are level-shifted by means of the emitter-follower transistor such that the HIGH and LOW logic-output voltages are suitable for driving other ECL inputs. Since the transistors do not saturate, propagation times of the order of 1 to 2 ns are achievable.

15.7.1 *Device Listings*

Table 15.2 presents a partial listing for devices of the ECL family. Once again, we suggest that you obtain a data book for additional details.

15.8 **Digital-Circuit Characteristics of FETs**

The characteristics of the *n*-channel and *p*-channel enhancement MOSFET for linear operation are presented in Section 4.4.2. In the current section, we consider the characteristic of the *n*- and *p*-channel enhancement MOSFET for use in digital applications.

15.8.1 n-*Channel Enhancement MOSFET*

Refer to Figure 4.11, where we present the schematic of the physical structure, the symbol, and the characteristics for an *n*-channel enhancement MOSFET.

Table 15.2 Partial ECL Device Listing.

Type Number	Description
10100/10500	Quad 2-input NOR with strobe
10101/10501	Quad OR/NOR
10102/10502	Quad 2-input NOR
10103/10503	Quad 2-input OR
10104/10504	Quad 2-input AND
10105/10505	Triple 2-3-2-input OR/NOR
10106/10506	Triple 4-3-3-input NOR
10107/10507	Triple 2-input exclusive OR/exclusive NOR
10109/10509	Dual 4-5-input OR/NOR
10110	Dual 3-input 3-output OR
10111	Dual 3-input 3-output NOR
10113/10513	Quad exclusive OR
10117/10517	Dual 2-wide 2-3-input OR-AND/OR-AND-invert
10118/10518	Dual 2-wide 3-input OR-AND
10119/10519	4-wide 4-3-3-input OR-AND
10121/10521	4-wide OR-AND/OR-AND-invert
10123	Triple 4-3-3-i bus driver

MECL Data Book, Motorola Semiconductor Products, Inc., Mesa, Arizona.

Note that this transistor has no channel between source and drain. However, as the gate-to-source voltage, v_{GS}, becomes more positive, it forms an n-channel region that extends from source to drain. This region provides an extremely low resistance between source and drain. In order to turn the transistor ON, we apply a v_{GS} that is greater than the threshold voltage, V_T, as shown in Figure 4.11(c). This voltage, V_T, can vary from 1 V to voltages above 1 V, depending upon the device. To turn the transistor OFF, we simply let $v_{GS} = 0$ V, so no channel is formed. With the gate grounded, the resistance between source and ground is extremely high, and the transistor is OFF. The enhancement MOSFET is normally OFF, because no channel exists between source and drain. The gate-to-source voltage, v_{GS}, must be greater than V_T to form the channel and hence turn the transistor ON.

It is important to note that the input gate is an open circuit that resembles a small capacitor. No input current is required, except for the brief period when we charge or discharge this small-input gate capacitor. When $v_{GS} = 0$, the resistance between source and drain is high and resembles an open switch. When v_{GS} is greater than V_T, the transistor turns on and the channel between source and drain becomes equivalent to a low-value resistor. The only voltage drop is a small drop from source to drain across this resistance.

15.8.2 *The p-Channel Enhancement MOSFET*

The *p*-channel enhancement MOSFET is shown in Figure 4.12, where we present the schematic of the physical structure, the symbol, and the characteristics. This device is the mirror image of the *n*-channel enhancement MOSFET. With a negative voltage applied to v_{GS} (i.e., when $v_{GS} < V_T$), the channel is formed and the transistor turns ON. When v_{GS} is zero, the transistor is an open circuit.

15.9 FET Transistor Families

In this section we consider the *n*-channel and the *p*-channel MOS integrated circuit.

15.9.1 *n-Channel MOS*

The *n-channel MOS* (NMOS) ICs are constructed with *n*-channel MOS transistors. The development of NMOS logic lagged several years behind PMOS, but once volume production was achieved, the superior performance characteristics of NMOS led to rapid expansion of MOS logic applications. One of the superior characteristics of NMOS is high carrier mobility, which enables each transistor to be small. Improvements in material processing and reduction in physical dimensions allow modern NMOS circuits to operate at lower supply voltages and higher speeds. Another improvement utilizes one MOSFET as a constant current supply for the switching transistor, replacing a pull-up resistor. This provides a linear rise time rather than an exponential one (resulting from an RC time constant) and reduces the power dissipated when the switching transistor is in its LOW (conducting) state. This family of circuits is widely used in memories and in microprocessors. An example of an NMOS inverter and its function table is shown in Figure 15.15.

We analyze the *n*-channel FET by noting that if the gate voltage and the substrate voltage are the same, the transistor is OFF. When the gate voltage is greater than the substrate voltage, the transistor is ON. With Q_n ON, the output voltage is zero, and with Q_n OFF, the output is raised to $+V$ volts.

Figure 15.15
NMOS inverter.

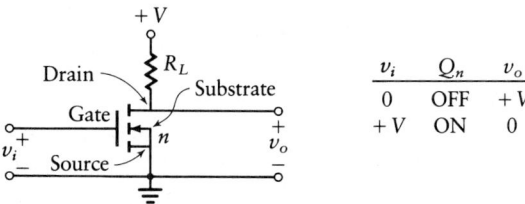

v_i	Q_n	v_o
0	OFF	$+V$
$+V$	ON	0

Figure 15.16
PMOS inverter.

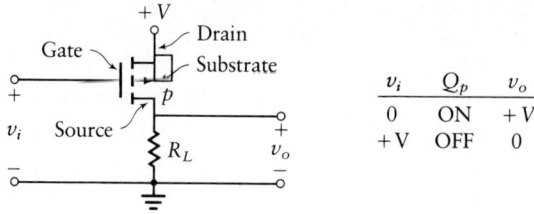

v_i	Q_p	v_o
0	ON	$+V$
$+V$	OFF	0

15.9.2   p-*Channel MOS*

The *p-channel MOS* (PMOS) ICs are constructed with *p*-channel MOS transistors and were the first types of memory circuits to be developed. Their speed and performance are poor and high supply voltages (typically 12 V) are required. This family of circuits has essentially been superceded by the NMOS and CMOS logic families.

An example of a PMOS inverter and its function table is shown in Figure 15.16. We analyze this circuit by noting that if the voltage on the gate (the input voltage) is the same as the voltage on the substrate, then the transistor is OFF. If the voltage on the gate is less than the substrate voltage, the transistor is ON. With Q_p ON, the output voltage is raised to $+V$, and with Q_p OFF, the output voltage is zero.

15.10   **Complementary MOS**

Complementary MOS (CMOS) ICs are constructed with complementary pairs, or sets, of *p*-channel and *n*-channel MOS transistors. This logic family has some very important advantages, which include low cost, extremely low and noncritical power requirements, good noise performance, infinite input impedance, high fan-out capability, and availability of new devices that do not exist in the other families (such as an analog switch, which we consider later).

A CMOS inverter is formed from one *p*- and one *n*-channel FET, as shown in Figure 15.17. The function table is constructed by reference to Figures 15.15 and 15.16. When v_i is zero, Q_p is ON and Q_n is OFF, so v_o is $+V$ volts. When v_i is $+V$ volts, Q_p is OFF and Q_n is ON, so v_o is zero. The function table of Figure 15.17 summarizes these results.

Figure 15.18 shows a CMOS two-input NAND gate. The circuit behaves like four switches, as shown in Figure 15.18(b). Two of the switches are connected in parallel to $+V$ and two are connected in series to ground. One switch in each pair is controlled by A and the other by B. When A is LOW, Q_1 is ON and Q_3 is OFF. When A is HIGH, Q_1 is OFF and Q_3 is ON. Likewise, when B is LOW, Q_2 is ON and Q_4 is OFF. When B is HIGH, Q_2 is OFF and Q_4 is

Figure 15.17
CMOS inverter.

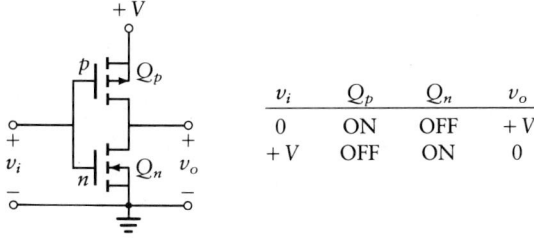

v_i	Q_p	Q_n	v_o
0	ON	OFF	$+V$
$+V$	OFF	ON	0

Q_1, Q_2 = p-channel

Q_3, Q_4 = n-channel

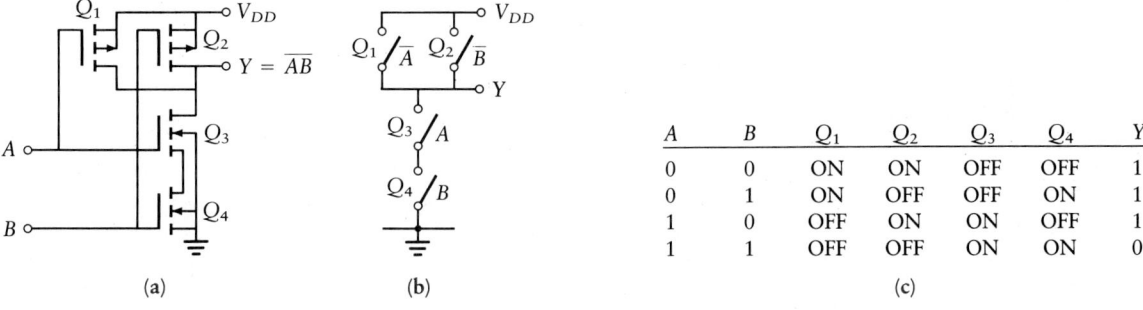

A	B	Q_1	Q_2	Q_3	Q_4	Y
0	0	ON	ON	OFF	OFF	1
0	1	ON	OFF	OFF	ON	1
1	0	OFF	ON	ON	OFF	1
1	1	OFF	OFF	ON	ON	0

(a)   (b)   (c)

Figure 15.18   Two-input CMOS NAND gate.

ON. The function table, shown in Figure 15.18(c), is developed column by column.

CMOS logic can operate over a wide range of supply voltages (3 V to 18 V) with moderate speed. The primary power consumption for CMOS logic involves the charging and discharging of input and load capacitance as logic levels switch between ground and the supply voltage. This results in a power consumption, which increases linearly as a function of clock rate or frequency. At maximum operating frequencies, CMOS circuits may consume as much power as some bipolar logic circuits. When used at low frequencies, CMOS provides excellent performance and is particularly well suited to use in battery-powered equipment. In general, CMOS is slower than most of the bipolar logic families and has a higher output impedance, so it is not capable of driving as much power into output devices. Since the input impedance of CMOS is composed primarily of a capacitance of a few picofarads, a large number of CMOS inputs can be driven by one CMOS output. The CMOS family also exhibits excellent noise immunity. Figure 15.19 shows a CMOS input/output transfer curve. The output voltage changes state at an input voltage of $V/2$. Thus, noise must be of sufficient magnitude to break this threshold voltage in order for an error to

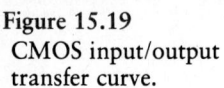

Figure 15.19
CMOS input/output
transfer curve.

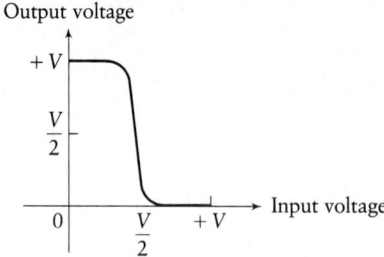

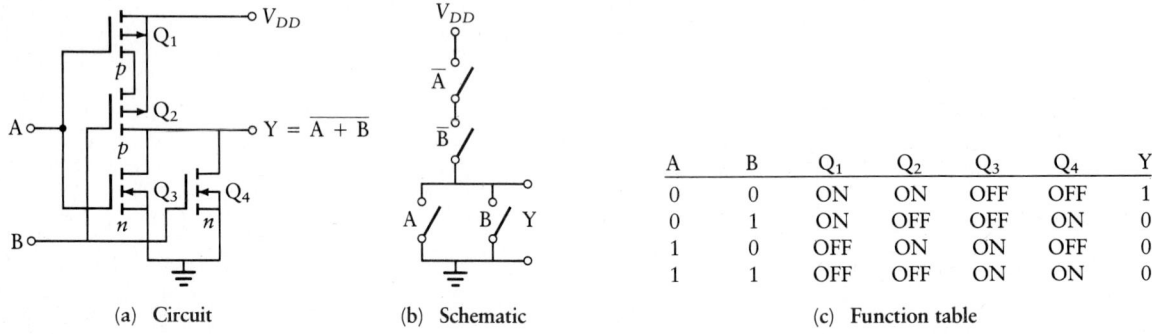

A	B	Q_1	Q_2	Q_3	Q_4	Y
0	0	ON	ON	OFF	OFF	1
0	1	ON	OFF	OFF	ON	0
1	0	OFF	ON	ON	OFF	0
1	1	OFF	OFF	ON	ON	0

(a) Circuit   (b) Schematic   (c) Function table

Figure 15.20   CMOS two-input NOR gate.

occur. In addition, the CMOS family allows for large swings in voltage from the high to low logic states.

We summarize the advantages and characteristics of the CMOS logic family as follows:

The input to all circuits is an open circuit.

Power-supply input current is low.

Good noise immunity exists, since the logic changes from LOW to HIGH at $V/2$.

CMOS power supply voltages vary from 5 V to 15 V.

CMOS creates little noise of its own.

We consider here another CMOS circuit; the CMOS two-input NOR gate, as shown in Figure 15.20. This circuit can be represented by two switches in series with V_{DD} and two switches in parallel to ground. The two switches in series are controlled by $\overline{A}$ and $\overline{B}$. The two switches in parallel are driven by A and B. We use the rule that if the voltage on the gate and on the substrate are the same, the transistor is OFF. If the gate voltage is different from the substrate voltage, the transistor is ON. We obtain the function table of Figure 15.20(c) by applying these conditions.

Drill Problems

Determine the status of each transistor and the output in the circuits shown in Problems D15.25–D15.28.

D15.25

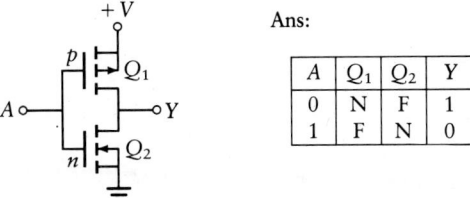

Ans:

A	Q_1	Q_2	Y
0	N	F	1
1	F	N	0

Figure D15.9

D15.26

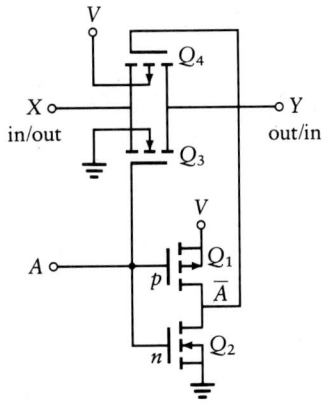

Figure D15.10

Ans:

A	$\overline{A}$	Q_1	Q_2	Q_3	Q_4	Condition
0	1	N	F	F	F	Open
1	0	F	N	N	N	X = Y

CD4016 digital switch
(bilateral switch)

D15.27

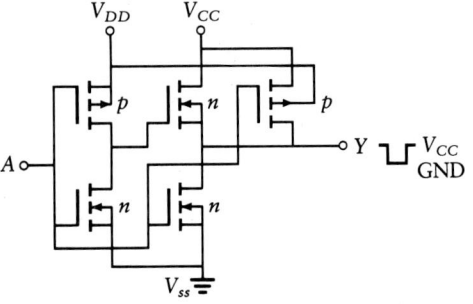

Ans:

A	Q_1	Q_2	Q_3	Q_4	Q_5	Y
0	N	F	N	F	N	1
1	F	N	F	N	F	0

Figure D15.11

D15.28

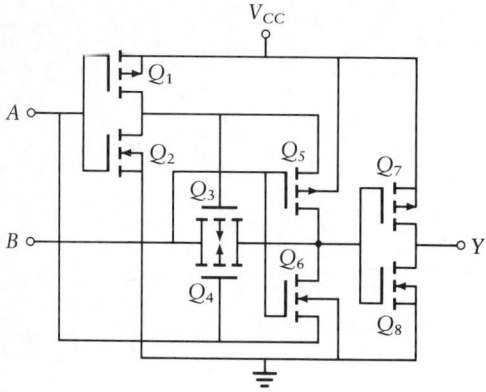

Ans:

A	B	Q_1	Q_2	Q_3	Q_4	Q_5	Q_6	Q_7	Q_8	Y
0	0	N	F	F	F	N	F	F	N	0
0	1	N	F	F	F	F	N	N	F	1
1	0	F	N	N	N	N	F	N	F	1
1	1	F	N	N	N	F	N	F	N	0

Figure D15.12

15.10.1   *CMOS Device Listings and Usage Rules*

Table 15.3 shows a partial listing of devices of the CMOS family. We once again refer you to the appropriate data books for more details and an expanded listing. We also include some rules that are important when using the CMOS family, as follows:

1. Attach every terminal to $+V$, ground, or to an input signal.
2. Avoid exceeding the limits of the IC, thereby preventing the input diodes from conducting.
3. Avoid static electricity by storing CMOS devices on conductive foam or foil.
4. Debounce all mechanical switches or contacts.

15.11   **Comparison of Logic Families**

Figure 15.21 summarizes the parameters of the various logic families. It is presented to provide comparisons among the various groups, which makes it useful as an aid in selecting the proper family of circuit for a particular application. The most important families are TTL, CMOS, and ECL.

15.12   **Concluding Remarks**

We have introduced the topic of digital electronics and gained some facility with the basic time-independent logic circuits. You are now in a position to

Table 15.3   Partial CMOS Device Listing.

Type Number	Description
MM54HC00/MM74HC00	Quad 2-input NAND gate
MM54HC02/MM74HC02	Quad 2-input NOR gate
MM54HC03/MM74HC03	Quad 2-input open drain NAND gate
MM54HC04/MM74HC04	Hex inverter
MM54HC08/MM74HC08	Quad 2-input AND gate
MM54HC10/MM74HC10	Triple 3-input NAND gate
MM54HC11/MM74HC11	Triple 3-input AND gate
MM54HC14/MM74HC14	Hex inverting Schmitt trigger
MM54HC20/MM74HC20	Dual 4-input NAND gate
MM54HC27/MM74HC27	Triple 3-input NOR gate
MM54HC30/MM74HC30	8-input NAND gate
MM54HC32/MM74HC32	Quad 2-input OR gate
MM54HC51/MM74HC51	Dual AND-OR-invert gate
MM54HC58/MM74HC58	Dual AND-OR gate
MM54HC86/MM74HC86	Quad 2-input exclusive OR gate
MM54HC132/MM74HC132	Quad 2-input NAND Schmitt trigger
MM54HC133/MM74HC133	13-input NAND gate
MM54HC266/MM74HC266	Quad 2-input exclusive NOR gate
MM54HC4002/MM74HC4002	Dual 4-input NOR gate
MM54HC4049/MM74HC4049	Hex inverting logic level down converter
MM54HC4050/MM74HC4050	Hex logic level down converter
MM54HC4075/MM74HC4075	Triple 3-input OR gate
MM54HC4078/MM74HC4078	8-Input NOR/OR gate
MM54HCT00/MM74HCT00	Quad 2-Input NAND Gate
MM54HCT04/MM74HCT04	Hex inverter
MM54HCT05/MM74HCT05	Hex inverter (open drain)
MM54HCT34/MM74HCT34	Noninverter gate (TTL input)
MM54HCU04/MM74HCU04	Hex inverter

CMOS Databook, National Semiconductor, Inc., Santa Clara, California.

execute the first level of digital electronic design and to formulate some useful circuits.

If we return to the auto safety-control box described in the introduction to this chapter, we find that this device can be effectively designed using the basic circuits presented in Chapters 14 and 15.

Observe that the change from analog to digital electronics goes a long way toward reducing the effects of ignition noise upon the control circuitry. You would probably choose the CMOS family for your design, since it provides excellent noise immunity and the operating frequencies in your system are low. Therefore, although power is not of critical concern (an automotive battery looks like a virtually unlimited source of power when compared to the power

Logic Family	Supply Voltage	Power per Gate	Propagation Delay per Gate	Maximum Clock Frequency	Maximum Logic Zero Input	Minimum Logic One Input	Maximum Logic Zero Ouput	Minimum Logic One Output
RTL	3.6 V	20 mW	10 nS		.50 V	.88 V	0.3 V	
DTL	5 V	8 mW	30 nS	5 MHz				
HTL	15 V	40 mW	110 nS	0.5 MHz	6.5 V	8.5 V	1.0 V	14.4 V
TTL	5 V	10 mW	10 nS	35 MHz	0.8 V	2.0 V	0.4 V	2.4 V
HTTL	5 V	22 mW	6 nS	50 MHz	0.8 V	2.0 V	0.4 V	2.4 V
LPTTL	5 V	1 mW	33 nS	3 MHz	0.8 V	2.0 V	0.4 V	2.4 V
STTL	5 V	16 mW	4 nS	75 MHz	0.8 V	2.0 V	0.5 V	2.7 V
LSTTL	5 V	2 mW	10 nS	40 MHz	0.8 V	2.0 V	0.5 V	2.7 V
ALSTTL	5 V	1 mW	4 nS	50 MHz	0.8 V	2.0 V	0.5 V	2.5 V
ASTTL	5 V	8 mW	2.5 nS	100 MHz	0.8 V	2.0 V	0.5 V	3.0 V
ECL	− 5.2 V	25 mW	2 nS		−1.48 V	−1.13 V	−1.6 V	−0.98 V
CMOS	3–15 V	0.5 mW*	100 nS	3 MHz**	1.5 V	3.5 V	0.5 V	4.5 V
HCMOS	5 V	0.5 mW*	10 nS	30 MHz	1.0 V	3.5 V	0.05 V	4.95 V
PMOS	− 9 V − 5 V	≈ 1 mW	4 µS	100 kHz	−4.0 V	−1.2 V	−8.5 V	−1.0 V
NMOS	+ 5 V +12 V	≈ .1 mW	≈100 nS	3 MHz	0.8 V	2.4 V	0.4 V	2.4 V

*at 1 MHz
**at 5 V
(Some parameters vary with device type or manufacturer)

Figure 15.21 Comparison of logic families.

required by ICs!), CMOS uses relatively little power. This could be a consideration if monitoring takes place during long periods when the automobile is not driven.

The actual design requires a series of basic gates such as AND and OR gates. Since several of the problems at the end of this chapter deal specifically with automotive systems, we shall not solve this problem for you and thereby compromise the excitement that your successful solution of these problems will yield.

PROBLEMS

Construct logic diagrams and function tables for the Boolean algebraic expressions of Problems 15.1–15.7.

15.1 $Y = \overline{A} \cdot B \cdot \overline{C} \cdot D$

15.2 $Y = \overline{A} \cdot B \cdot \overline{C} + A \cdot B \cdot \overline{C}$

15.3 $Y = AB + A\overline{B}$

15.4 $Y = A\overline{B} + B$

15.5 $Y = A + B$

15.6 $Y = \overline{A + B + C}$

15.7 $Y = \overline{A \cdot B \cdot C}$

15.8 Develop a logic circuit such that the output is HIGH if inputs *A*, *B*, and *C* are all HIGH or if inputs *D*, *E*, and *F* are all HIGH.

15.9 Develop a logic circuit such that the output is HIGH if inputs *A* and *B* are HIGH or if inputs *C* and *B* are HIGH.

Develop logic networks to satisfy the functions given in Problems 15.10–15.19.

15.10 To win a prize, you must send in a receipt and also have the correct answer to at least one of the questions.

15.11 Today's luncheon special consists of a hamburger with either soup or salad but not both.

15.12 The walls may be painted either blue or green, but not both colors. However, whether or not the walls are painted, the ceiling must be painted white.

15.13 A pair of kings or a pair of aces will win the hand.

15.14 They will rent the house to a couple or to a single person but not to both.

15.15 On this television set, you can get the sound and picture separately or together on Channel 2, but only the sound is available on Channel 4.

15.16 To get in, you must have either $3 and a discount card or you must pay an additional $1.

15.17 You must attend at least one night session or one afternoon session of either day of the 2-day conference.

15.18 If you take a course in law or history or both, you must also take one in either English or speech, but not in both.

15.19 You can play doubles at tennis, but if a player on either team fails to show up, the game is called off.

15.20 Design a four-passenger auto seat belt—warning system that will sound an alarm if the ignition is on and there is a passenger with an unfastened seat belt. Normally open switches with one contact grounded are available to sense the presence of passengers and to sense the connection of each seat belt. This is shown in Figure P15.1(a). A normally open switch with one contact grounded senses whether the engine ignition is on. This circuit is shown in Figure P15.1(b). An LED should light for an unsafe condition.

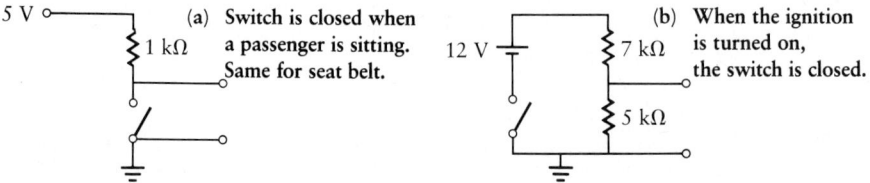

Figure P15.1

15.21 Design a safety reminder system for your automobile to alert the driver when the headlights are accidentally left on and the key is in the ignition switch. This system uses the following normally-open switches:
  a. Headlight switch is closed when lights are on and open when the lights are off.
  b. Ignition key switch is closed when key is in the lock and open when the key is removed from lock.
  c. The door switch is closed when the door is open, and open when the door is closed.
     The alarm sounds only when the door is open and the headlights are on and/or the key is in the ignition switch.

15.22 Design a burglar alarm system that will sound a 500 Hz, 5 W alarm signal in a speaker. An alarm switch is built into the left front fender. It is a normally open switch. When the key is turned to the "armed" position, the switch is closed, as shown in Figure P15.2(a). A motion switch is mounted in the automobile such that when any motion occurs, a momentary contact is made. This is shown in Figure P15.2(b). When

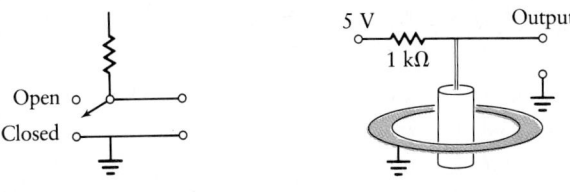

Figure P15.2(a)   Figure P15.2(b)

the automobile is disturbed, the output signal momentarily drops to 0 V (ground). The burglar alarm should then sound the 500 Hz signal *only* if the fender switch was previously armed.

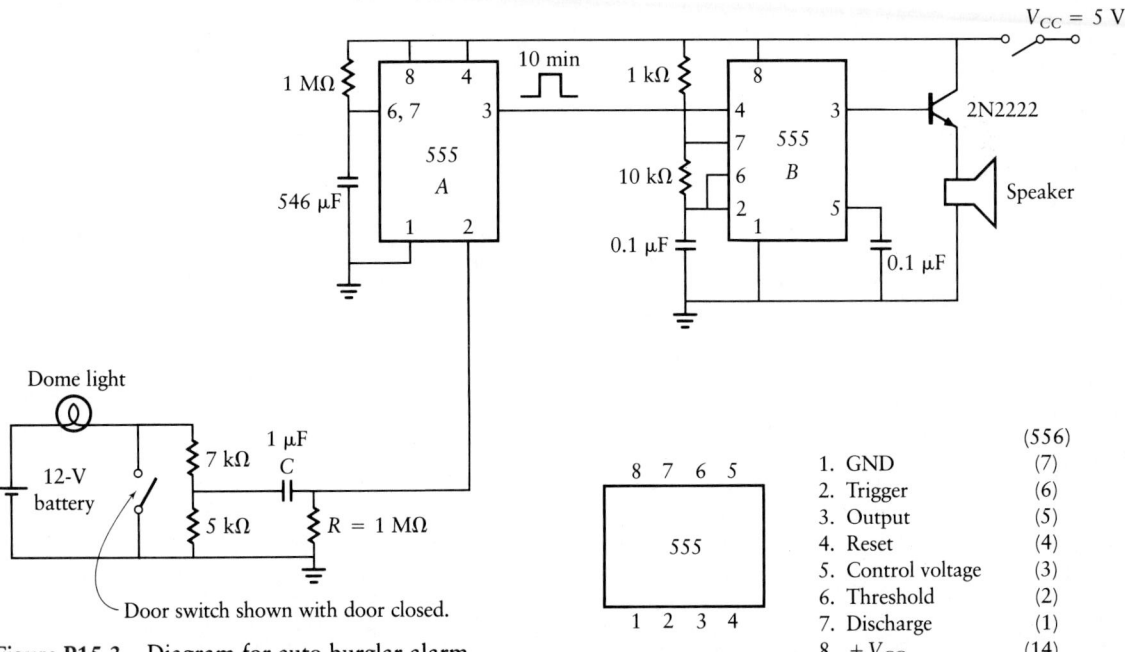

Figure P15.3   Diagram for auto burglar alarm.

(556)
1. GND   (7)
2. Trigger   (6)
3. Output   (5)
4. Reset   (4)
5. Control voltage (3)
6. Threshold (2)
7. Discharge (1)
8. $+V_{CC}$ (14)

15.23 Analyze the auto burglar-alarm system illustrated in Figure P15.3. Describe the operation of this electronic system.

15.24 Design the electronic circuitry to accomplish the following operation. A 3 ms-wide input pulse must reproduce and send a 3 ms wide input pulse to another circuit. After a 10 ms delay, an 3 ms echo pulse must follow, as shown in Figure P15.4.

Figure P15.4

15.25 Design a digital lock that operates in two steps. First, the code is set by activating three of the six two-position push-button switches. For this example, set the code to be: b d e. Second, the toggle switch connected to the output is thrown. If the correct code is selected, the output will go LOW and the lock will be released with a solenoid (a solenoid is an electromechanical device that produces a mechanical motion when a signal is applied to the solenoid coil). If the incorrect code is selected, a 1 kHz tone will sound for 1 min. See Figure P15.5 for details.

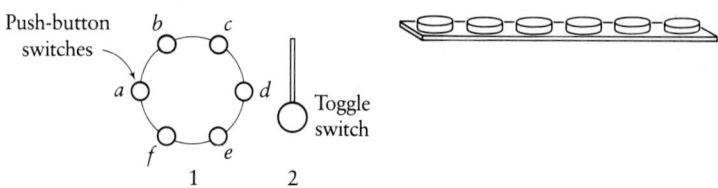

Figure P15.5

15.26 Sketch the output of Figure 15.5 if an odd number of inverters is used in the circuit. Assume the delay time for one inverter is 35 ns.

Determine the status of each transistor and prepare a function table for each of the TTL circuits given in Problems 15.27–15.30.

15.27 Figure P15.6: a 7486 quad two-input XOR, active collector output.

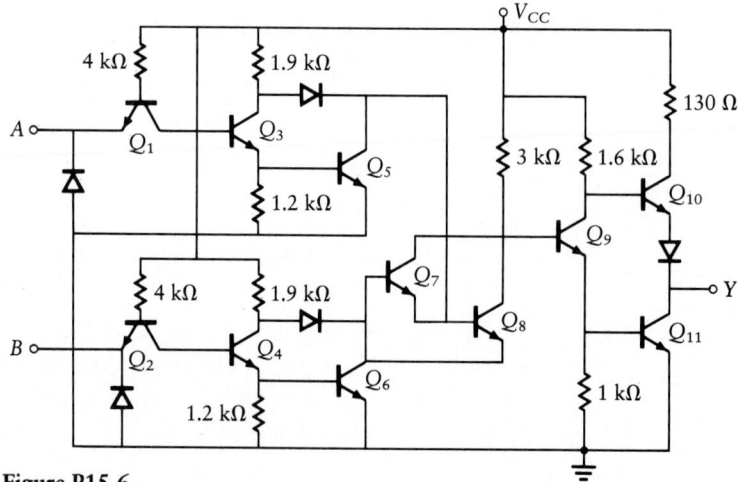

Figure P15.6

15.28 Figure P15.7: a 7407/17 hex driver, noninverting, open collector output.

15.29 Figure P15.8: a 7408 quad two-input AND, active collector output.

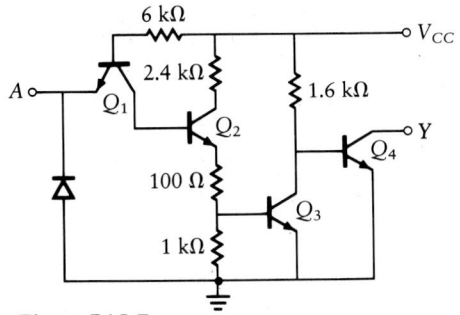

Figure P15.7

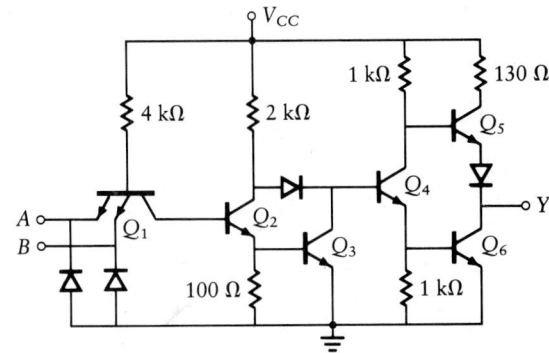

Figure P15.8

15.30 Figure P15.9: a 7400 quad two-input NAND, active collector output.

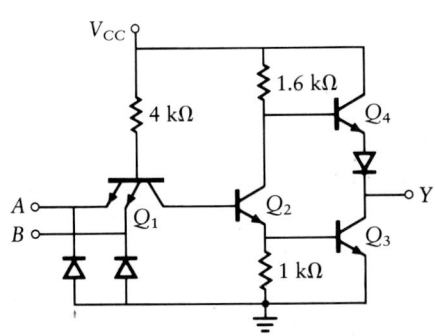

Figure P15.9

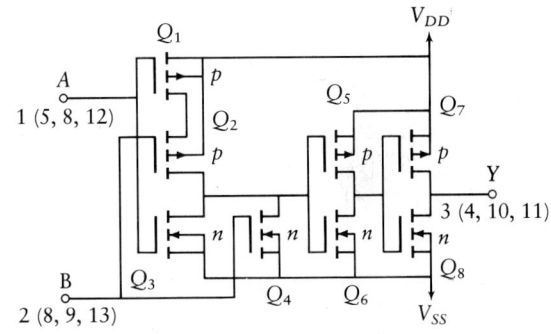

Figure P15.10

Determine the status of each FET and prepare a function table for the CMOS circuits of Problems 15.31–15.33.

15.31 Figure P15.10: a CD4001 quad two-input NOR.

15.32 Figure P15.11: a CD4-81 quad two-input AND.

15.33 Figure P15.12: a CD4001 quad two-input NAND.

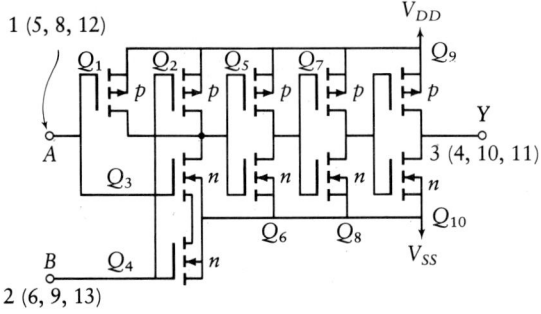

Figure P15.11

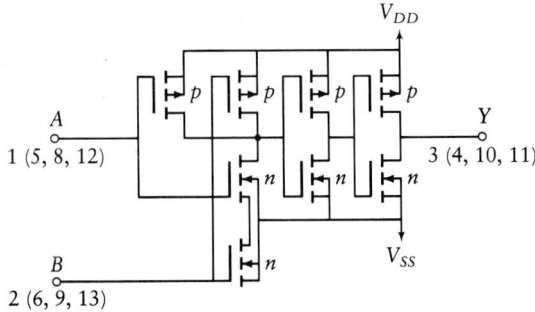

Figure P15.12

15.34 Complete the function table for the TTL-CMOS circuit shown in Figure P15.13.

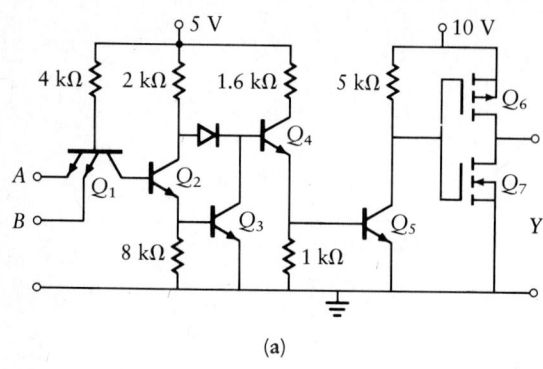

(a)

A	B	Q_1	Q_2	Q_3	Q_4	Q_5	Q_6	Q_7	Y
0	0								
0	1								
1	0								
1	1								

(b)

Figure P15.13

15.35 Design a seven-segment display driver to vary the brightness of the seven-segment LED from almost off to maximum brightness. Provide a single potentiometer control to produce a uniform intensity for all segments.

15.36 Design a circuit to sample a function of time every 100 ms. The sampling time must be no greater than 5 ms. Draw the circuit diagram showing the complete pin-out of each IC used. The function of time, $f(t)$, and the sampled output are shown in Figure P15.14.

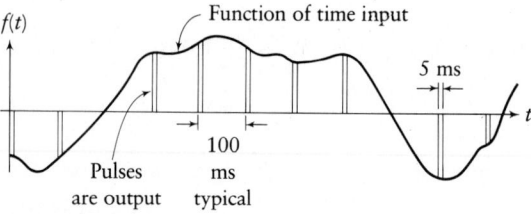

Figure P15.14

16

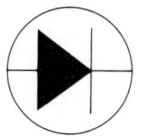

DIGITAL INTEGRATED CIRCUITS

16.0 **Introduction**

In Chapter 15 we introduce the major families of digital integrated circuits. Included in that chapter is a discussion of the various basic SSI circuits.

The intent of the present chapter is to expand this catalog of ICs so that the engineer has the necessary tools to perform a wide variety of designs. There are a large number of different circuits on the market. These can be divided into several major categories, which form the major sections of this chapter. Application examples are presented throughout.

The figures in the text often contain excerpts from data books. As in the previous chapter, we strongly urge you to obtain several of these books. Although they are listed in the references in Appendix D, we repeat the major listings here:

1. *The TTL Data Book for Design Engineers,* Vol. II, Texas Instruments Corp., Dallas, Texas.
2. *CMOS Data Book,* National Semiconductor Corp., Santa Clara, California.
3. *Linear and Data Acquisition Products,* Harris Semiconductor Products Division, Melbourne, Florida.
4. *CMOS Data Book,* Fairchild Camera and Instrument Corp., Mountain View, California.

735

5. *Master Selection Guide,* Motorola Semiconductor Products Inc., Phoenix, Arizona.

6. *Schottky and Low Power Schottky Data Book,* Advanced Micro Devices Inc., Sunnyvale, California.

We begin our study in Section 16.1 with decoders and encoders. The examples include binary to 7-segment displays, parity checkers, multiplexers, and arithmetic units.

Circuits with memory are examined in the later part of the chapter, beginning with Section 16.3. These include flip-flops, latches, shift registers, and counters. Since circuits with memory often require timing, we explore methods of accomplishing this. Particular attention is given to clocks, oscillators, phase-locked loops, and voltage controlled oscillators (VCOs).

Section 16.7 considers the important topic of memories with attention given to RAMs, ROMs, PROMs, and EPROMs.

The chapter concludes with a discussion of more complex devices, including arithmetic logic units, A/D and D/A converters, and the programmable array logic chip.

16.1 Decoders and Encoders

A wide variety of multiple-input-multiple-output ICs can be combined under the term *decoder.* Devices that fit into this category are given more specific names that accurately describe their function. Examples of these include *multiplexers* and *demultiplexers.* Whatever the specific name, decoders share a common trait with the elementary gates: These ICs have *no memory.* Regardless of the values of previous inputs and outputs, the device's present output depends only upon its present input.

The first example we present is a 3- to 8-line decoder/demultiplexer as shown in Figure 16.1. We have selected a 74LS138 TTL circuit for purposes of illustration. Note that the pin-out diagram and function table applies to several chip numbers. These chips differ in speed of operation and in power requirements. These properties are shown elsewhere in the manufacturer's data sheets. The 3- to 8-line decoder/demultiplexer is used to enable (turn on) 1 among 8 possible outputs. It is comprised of a series of gates, as shown in Figure 16.1(b). The 3- to 8-line decoder accepts 3-bit binary inputs representing a binary number between 000 and 111. These correspond to the decimal numbers 0 through 7. Of the 8 output lines, only 1 is LOW at any one time, as shown in the function table of Figure 16.1(c). The output that is LOW is the one numbered to match the binary input (SELECT). For example, if the binary

Figure 16.1
74LS138 3- to 8-line decoder.
Courtesy of Texas Instruments Incorporated.

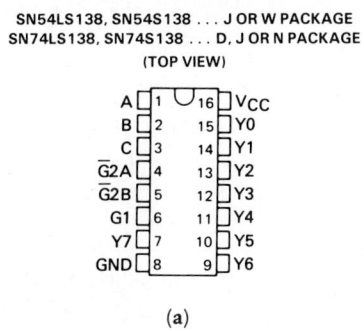

SN54LS138, SN54S138 . . . J OR W PACKAGE
SN74LS138, SN74S138 . . . D, J OR N PACKAGE
(TOP VIEW)

(a)

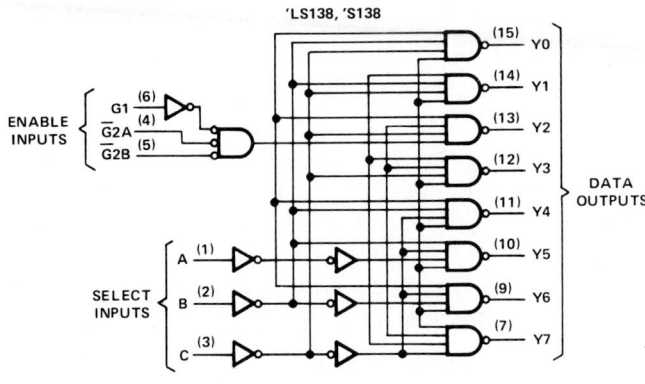

Pin numbers shown on logic notation are for D, J or N packages.

(b)

'LS138, 'S138
FUNCTION TABLE

INPUTS					OUTPUTS							
ENABLE		SELECT										
G1	Ḡ2*	C	B	A	Y0	Y1	Y2	Y3	Y4	Y5	Y6	Y7
X	H	X	X	X	H	H	H	H	H	H	H	H
L	X	X	X	X	H	H	H	H	H	H	H	H
H	L	L	L	L	L	H	H	H	H	H	H	H
H	L	L	L	H	H	L	H	H	H	H	H	H
H	L	L	H	L	H	H	L	H	H	H	H	H
H	L	L	H	H	H	H	H	L	H	H	H	H
H	L	H	L	L	H	H	H	H	L	H	H	H
H	L	H	L	H	H	H	H	H	H	L	H	H
H	L	H	H	L	H	H	H	H	H	H	L	H
H	L	H	H	H	H	H	H	H	H	H	H	L

*Ḡ2 = Ḡ2A + Ḡ2B
H = high level, L = low level, X = irrelevant

(c)

number 010 forms the input, output 2 (Y2) is LOW and all the others are HIGH. If we desire the selected output to be HIGH instead of LOW, we can feed the various outputs into an inverter.

The circuit diagram and the function table contain several *enable* lines. In order to operate the system as a decoder, enable input G1 must be HIGH and input G2 must be LOW. Note that G2 is formed as an OR operation on G2A and G2B. If enable input G1 is LOW, all the outputs are high regardless of the condition of the other enable or of the select lines. This is also true if G2 is HIGH.

Another way to view a decoder is that the input is a binary number and the output is another binary number. The two binary numbers are not of the same bit length. The decoder circuit can thus be thought of as a *translator* that accepts one language and changes it into another.

The 3- to 8-line decoder illustrates the concept that 3 bits of input data can control 2^3 lines of output. In more general terms, an *n*- to *m*-line decoder converts *n* input lines into a maximum of $m = 2^n$ output lines.

Before going on to the next topic, you should take the time to verify some of the entries in the function table. Do this by applying the appropriate logic HIGH and LOW inputs and tracing these through the logic-block diagram.

In its most general form, the decoder chip accepts one binary word as input and produces a second binary word as output. This leads to a large number of possible decoder configurations. Six of these configurations are used in many applications, and we discuss these next:

1. *Binary-to-single-output*   An n-bit binary word selects a single output from one of 2^n possible outputs. The circuit of Figure 16.1 is an example of this configuration with $n = 3$.

2. *Binary-to-7-segment-display*   This decoder accepts a binary input and produces a 7-bit binary code as the output. The input is a 4-bit binary number between 0000 and 1001, representing the decimal digit between 0 and 9. This is known as the *binary-coded decimal* (BCD) code. The output is matched to a 7-segment display. Seven straight-line segments (3 horizontal and 4 vertical) are used to display any digit between 0 and 9. The decoder yields the appropriate output to light the necessary segments thereby producing the decimal digit. We examine this decoder in more detail in Section 16.2.

3. *Multiple-input-to-multiple-output*   There are many devices used to convert numbers from one form to another. These devices are often used to perform simple mathematical operations or to multiplex several signals together.

   An important example of a multiple-input-to-multiple-output chip is the *BCD-to-binary converter*. The BCD code represents each decimal digit between 0 and 9 by a 4-bit binary number. Thus, for example, the decimal number 64 becomes 01100100 in BCD since each decimal digit is handled independently. Note that this differs from a simple conversion of 64 to binary. Such a conversion would result in the binary number, 1000000, which is only 7 bits in length instead of 8 bits as in the BCD code.

   The 74HC42 chip is an example of a *BCD-to-decimal* decoder and is illustrated in Figure 16.2. The input to this device is a 4-bit BCD code of a single decimal digit. There are 10 separate outputs, and only one of these is LOW for any valid input combination. The one that is LOW represents the decimal equivalent of the input BCD number. Note that the BCD code uses only 10 of the 16 possible 4-bit combinations. Therefore, six input combinations are invalid and should not exist in the BCD code. If the input matches any of these invalid combinations, an error must have occurred prior to that point in the circuitry. The 74HC42 chip is designed to respond to these invalid inputs by not allowing any of the 10 outputs to go LOW.

4. *Testers*   This group of devices performs tests upon coded information

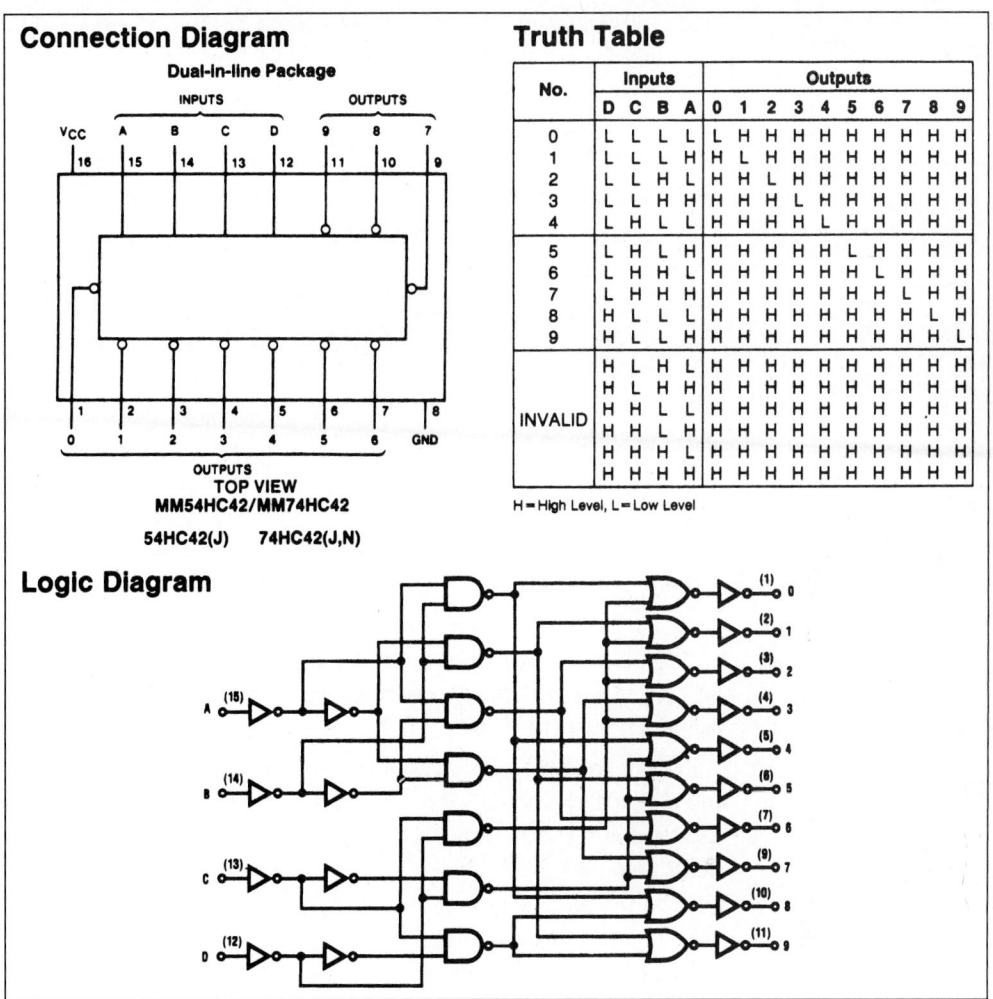

Connection Diagram

Dual-in-line Package

TOP VIEW
MM54HC42/MM74HC42

54HC42(J)   74HC42(J,N)

Truth Table

No.	Inputs				Outputs									
	D	C	B	A	0	1	2	3	4	5	6	7	8	9
0	L	L	L	L	L	H	H	H	H	H	H	H	H	H
1	L	L	L	H	H	L	H	H	H	H	H	H	H	H
2	L	L	H	L	H	H	L	H	H	H	H	H	H	H
3	L	L	H	H	H	H	H	L	H	H	H	H	H	H
4	L	H	L	L	H	H	H	H	L	H	H	H	H	H
5	L	H	L	H	H	H	H	H	H	L	H	H	H	H
6	L	H	H	L	H	H	H	H	H	H	L	H	H	H
7	L	H	H	H	H	H	H	H	H	H	H	L	H	H
8	H	L	L	L	H	H	H	H	H	H	H	H	L	H
9	H	L	L	H	H	H	H	H	H	H	H	H	H	L
INVALID	H	L	H	L	H	H	H	H	H	H	H	H	H	H
	H	L	H	H	H	H	H	H	H	H	H	H	H	H
	H	H	L	L	H	H	H	H	H	H	H	H	H	H
	H	H	L	H	H	H	H	H	H	H	H	H	H	H
	H	H	H	L	H	H	H	H	H	H	H	H	H	H
	H	H	H	H	H	H	H	H	H	H	H	H	H	H

H = High Level, L = Low Level

Logic Diagram

Figure 16.2   The 74HC42 BCD-to-decimal decoder. Courtesy of National Semiconductor Corp.

and produces an output containing information regarding the outcome of the test. The *comparator* is an example of a tester. It accepts two binary codes as the input, and the output indicates which of the two inputs is larger. *Parity checkers* represent another important application of testing chips. These are discussed in Section 16.1.2.

5. *Arithmetic*   Arithmetic chips perform simple mathematical operations such as addition and subtraction. A *full adder* is one example of such a chip. This adder accepts three input bits. Two of these are the bits to be added together, and the third is a *carry* bit from a previous, or lower-weight, addition. Thus, the full adder is suited to applications where

multiple-bit binary numbers must be added together. There are two outputs from a full adder. One of these is the sum, and the second is the carry bit. For example, the binary sum of $1 + 0 + 0$ is 1 with a carry of 0. The sum of $1 + 1 + 1$ is 1 with a carry of 1. We discuss full adders in more detail in Section 16.8.2.

6. *Multiplexers*   The multiplexer selects one of many inputs to be transferred to one output. This is the reverse of the *demultiplexer,* which routes one input to one of many outputs.

   Multiplexers are used to interleave data from several sources. For example, if only one transmission line were available to send four different signals, the bits would have to be interleaved (commutated) to form a *time-division-multiplexed* signal. The first bit of the first signal is followed by the first bit of the second, and so on. Finally, the first bit of the fourth signal is followed by the second bit of the first signal, and the cycle continues until the four signals are sent in their entirety.

   At the receiving end, a demultiplexer (decommutator) is used to separate the various signals and sort them out onto different transmission paths.

We now examine the *data selector/multiplexer* in more detail. This circuit selects one input from many possibilities and transfers this input to the output. Figure 16.3 shows the SN74150 data-selector/multiplexer chip.

There are four data-*select* inputs, labeled A, B, C, and D (pins 15, 14, 13, and 11, respectively). Depending upon the value of these select inputs, the corresponding data input is transferred to the output. This particular chip yields an output (W) on pin 10, which is the inverse of the selected input. Thus, for example, if the data select inputs are LHHL, representing the binary number 0110 (the decimal number 6), the output is the inverse of the signal connected to input pin 2, the sixth input bit (E6). This particular chip is *clocked,* and the appropriate input is transferred to the output only when a LOW signal is placed on the *strobe,* pin 9. If the strobe is HIGH, the output is HIGH, independent of the input levels.

It is important to supply proper timing to this chip to avoid transients in the output. This is true since the data select, which is a 4-bit binary number, changes whenever it is desired to transfer a different input to the output (pin 10). If, for example, the select is changing from 1010 to 0101, we desire that the input on pin 22 be transferred to the output prior to the change and that the input on pin 3 be transferred after the change. However, the four binary-select inputs may not change at the exact same moment, so there may be intermediate select configurations prior to arrival at 0101. Without clocking, the output will reflect each of these intermediate input values. The clock is

Figure 16.3
SN74150 data-selec-tor/multiplexer.
Courtesy of Texas
Instruments
Incorporated.

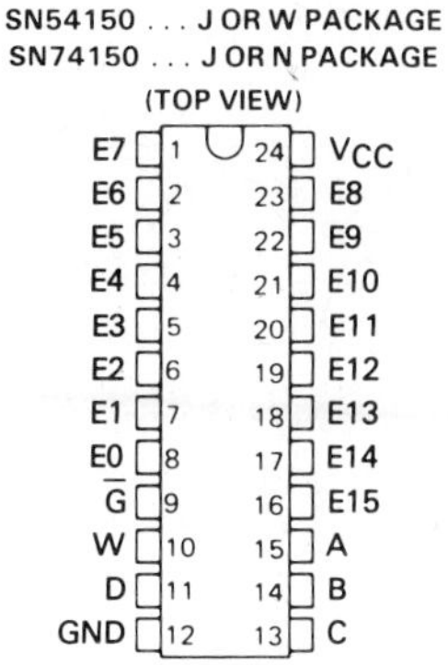

SN54150 . . . J OR W PACKAGE
SN74150 . . . J OR N PACKAGE
(TOP VIEW)

```
     E7 [ 1    24 ] VCC
     E6 [ 2    23 ] E8
     E5 [ 3    22 ] E9
     E4 [ 4    21 ] E10
     E3 [ 5    20 ] E11
     E2 [ 6    19 ] E12
     E1 [ 7    18 ] E13
     E0 [ 8    17 ] E14
     Ḡ  [ 9    16 ] E15
     W  [ 10   15 ] A
     D  [ 11   14 ] B
    GND [ 12   13 ] C
```

(a) **Connection diagram**

'150
FUNCTION TABLE

INPUTS					OUTPUT
SELECT				STROBE	W
D	C	B	A	$\bar{G}$	
X	X	X	X	H	H
L	L	L	L	L	$\overline{E0}$
L	L	L	H	L	$\overline{E1}$
L	L	H	L	L	$\overline{E2}$
L	L	H	H	L	$\overline{E3}$
L	H	L	L	L	$\overline{E4}$
L	H	L	H	L	$\overline{E5}$
L	H	H	L	L	$\overline{E6}$
L	H	H	H	L	$\overline{E7}$
H	L	L	L	L	$\overline{E8}$
H	L	L	H	L	$\overline{E9}$
H	L	H	L	L	$\overline{E10}$
H	L	H	H	L	$\overline{E11}$
H	H	L	L	L	$\overline{E12}$
H	H	L	H	L	$\overline{E13}$
H	H	H	L	L	$\overline{E14}$
H	H	H	H	L	$\overline{E15}$

(b) **Function table**

used to assure that the output changes only *after* the select has arrived at its final configuration.

Note that the chip has 24 pins in a DIP configuration. Two of these are for power (pin 24 for V_{CC} and pin 12 for ground), 1 is for strobe (pin 9), 1 for the output (pin 10), 4 for select, and the remaining 16 for the data inputs.

16.1.1 *Keyboard Encoders and Decoders*

A keyboard consists of a series of switches activated by keys. The keyboard can be in any of a wide variety of configurations, including that of a typewriter or of a numeric keypad. Prior to the development of digital electronics, each key was connected to the appropriate printing mechanism, often through a series of mechanical linkages. With the advent of digital electronics, it became preferable to code the input into an appropriate binary code, thus eliminating the necessity of connecting each key switch to the final output device.

The purpose of the encoder is to produce a binary output that contains information regarding which of the keys is being depressed.

As a specific example, we consider the HD0165 keyboard encoder, as illustrated in Figure 16.4. This is a 16-line-to-4-bit encoder intended for use with manual data-entry devices such as calculators or typewriter keyboards. Any 4-bit output code can be implemented.

Figure 16.4
The HD0165 keyboard encoder.
Courtesy of Harris Semiconductor.

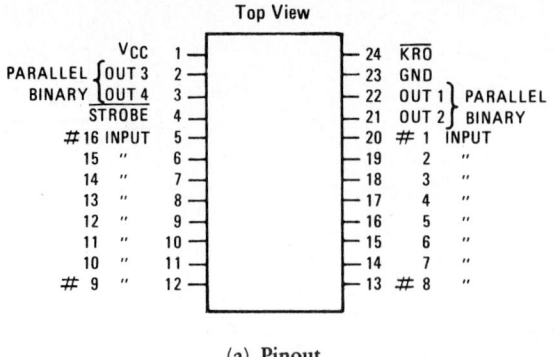

(a) **Pinout**

INPUTS																OUTPUTS					
1	2	3	4	5	6	7	8	9	10	11	12	13	14	15	16	1	2	3	4	St.	$\overline{K}_{RO}$
L	L	L	L	L	L	L	L	L	L	L	L	L	L	L	L	H	H	H	H	H	H
H	L	L	L	L	L	L	L	L	L	L	L	L	L	L	L	H	H	H	H	L	H
L	H	L	L	L	L	L	L	L	L	L	L	L	L	L	L	L	H	H	H	L	H
L	L	H	L	L	L	L	L	L	L	L	L	L	L	L	L	H	L	H	H	L	H
L	L	L	H	L	L	L	L	L	L	L	L	L	L	L	L	L	L	H	H	L	H
L	L	L	L	H	L	L	L	L	L	L	L	L	L	L	L	H	H	L	H	L	H
L	L	L	L	L	H	L	L	L	L	L	L	L	L	L	L	L	H	L	H	L	H
L	L	L	L	L	L	H	L	L	L	L	L	L	L	L	L	H	L	L	H	L	H
L	L	L	L	L	L	L	H	L	L	L	L	L	L	L	L	L	L	L	H	L	H
L	L	L	L	L	L	L	L	H	L	L	L	L	L	L	L	H	H	H	L	L	H
L	L	L	L	L	L	L	L	L	H	L	L	L	L	L	L	L	H	H	L	L	H
L	L	L	L	L	L	L	L	L	L	H	L	L	L	L	L	H	L	H	L	L	H
L	L	L	L	L	L	L	L	L	L	L	H	L	L	L	L	L	L	H	L	L	H
L	L	L	L	L	L	L	L	L	L	L	L	H	L	L	L	H	H	L	L	L	H
L	L	L	L	L	L	L	L	L	L	L	L	L	H	L	L	L	H	L	L	L	H
L	L	L	L	L	L	L	L	L	L	L	L	L	L	H	L	H	L	L	L	L	H
L	L	L	L	L	L	L	L	L	L	L	L	L	L	L	H	L	L	L	L	L	H
ANY TWO OR MORE HIGH																X	X	X	X	L	L

INPUTS:　L = Open Circuit or < +1.0V　　H = > +4.5V Current Source
OUTPUTS:　L = < +0.4V　　H = > +2.4V　　X = Erroneous Data

(b) **Function table**

Inputs are normally wired through the keyboard switches to the +5-V power supply. The 16 possible outputs represent all possible combinations of 4 bits. The outputs can be configured to yield the binary equivalent of the particular input that is HIGH. Thus, for example, if input 9 is HIGH (i.e., switch 9 is depressed), the output is LHHH, where, on Figure 16.4(b), we start with output 4 and work our way to the left to output 1. If L corresponds to 1 and H to 0, this is the binary number 1000, or in decimal equivalent, 8. That is correct since the input switches are labeled 1 through 16, whereas the output binary numbers range from 0 to 15. Thus, if we depress the input switches in order from number 1 to number 16, the output will count in binary numbers from 0 to 15. This one-to-one association between the ordered input switches and the output binary numbers is not the only way we could configure the output. That is, as input switches are depressed in order, we may wish the output to follow a sequence other than the standard counting sequence. Some thought will show that there are 16!, or about 2.1×10^{13}, ways to order the 16 output words. Particular configurations have been developed to yield desirable properties. The more common among these are the *Gray code* and the *1-2-4-2 BCD code*. You are referred to the references for details.

As the mechanical switch is depressed, a *bounce* effect sometimes occurs. The switch makes momentary contact, then momentarily breaks contact, and finally makes a solid connection. The STROBE can be used to *debounce* the switch, thus eliminating this effect. Note from the function table that when any key is depressed, thus causing the associated encoder input to go HIGH, the STROBE output goes LOW. Debouncing can be accomplished by using the STROBE output to trigger a monostable (such as a 555) with an on-time longer than the anticipated bounce time. Thus, the first contact of the switch causes the monostable output to go HIGH, and this output stays HIGH until the switch stops bouncing. When the monostable returns to the OFF state, a second strobe is activated, and it is this strobe that transfers the keyboard input to the switch. The debounce operation is a time-delay process where the keyboard input is transferred to the chip some time after the time of the first switch closure.

Examination of the function table of Figure 16.4 reveals an additional output, labeled *key rollover (KRO)*. This output goes LOW when more than one key is depressed at the same time. It informs the circuit that the encoded output word is not valid and should be ignored. A more sophisticated approach involves using this output to set up a delayed strobe, much as is done to debounce the keyboard. We assume that depression of two keys is normally a temporary condition, so the delay may be sufficient to return to a single depressed key situation.

16.1.2 *Parity Generators and Checkers*

The *parity* of a binary number indicates whether the total number of 1s is odd or even. Thus, for example, the binary number 101 has *even parity,* whereas the number 100 has *odd parity*. By adding one additional bit to a number, it is possible to force the enlarged number to have either even or odd parity. To create even parity, the added bit is a 1 if the original number had odd parity, whereas it is a 0 if the original number had even parity.

If a single bit in a word is changed, the parity of the word changes. Therefore, addition of a parity bit allows detection of single bit errors.

Suppose, for example, that a parity bit is added to each word to force the parity of the enlarged word to always be even. The system could then check parity at critical test points and if odd parity is detected, it knows a bit error occurred. In actuality, any odd number of bit errors causes a parity change, whereas any even number of errors causes no change. For example, if 2 bit errors occur, the word still has even parity and the errors go undetected.

The problem associated with detecting multiple bit errors can prove serious in applications where errors frequently occur, such as in a high-noise environment. In such cases, undetected multiple errors can be expected. Some improvement is possible by using additional parity bits.

16.2   Drivers and Associated Systems

Driver chips are used to power displays and other special-purpose devices. The driver circuits in this family of chips are designed to operate over a wide range of voltages and currents, since the display devices often use nonstandard voltages and currents. Figure 16.5 illustrates a 7447 BCD-to-7-segment decoder/driver. The function table for this device is shown in Figure 16.5(b). The chip accepts six inputs. Four of these represent a 4-bit binary number between 0 and 15. As can be seen from the "numerical designations and resultant displays" in Figure 16.5, the 4-bit binary numbers between 0 and 9 generate a display that is the decimal digit corresponding to the number. The remaining six input combinations generate symbols that may be used to convey various types of information (e.g., overload). Suppose, for example, the 4-bit input is HLLH, representing the binary number 1001 and the decimal digit 9. Reference to the 7-segment LED display shows that we wish to light segments a, b, c, f, and g of the display to show the integer 9. The function table verifies that it is these specific five outputs that will be ON. The outputs are designed to drive either LEDs or incandescent lamps. The driver portion of the circuit provides an open collector output, which is discussed in Chapter 15.

In addition to the 4-bit binary word, three additional binary inputs are provided. These are designated by *lamp test* (LT), *ripple blanking input* (RBI), and *blanking input/ripple blanking output* (BI/RBO). The last line of the table shows that a LOW input on the lamp test pin causes every display segment to light. This is used to test the circuit and the display.

The display is turned completely off if the binary number 1111 forms the input or if the blanking input is LOW. Ripple blanking is used to blank out leading zeroes in the display that exist before the most significant digit. This is used both to turn off the display and to *modulate* it. By modulating the display or turning it on and off periodically, the perceived brightness can be adjusted.

The 7447 chip is easily combined with a common-anode LED display, as shown in Figure 16.6. The typical forward voltage of the LED is in the range

Figure 16.5
7447 BCD-to-7-segment decoder/driver. Courtesy of Texas Instruments Incorporated.

SN54L46, SN54L47 . . . J PACKAGE
SN5446A, SN5447A, SN54LS47, SN5448,
SN54LS48 . . . J OR W PACKAGE
SN7446A, SN7447A,
SN7448 . . . J OR N PACKAGE
SN74LS47, SN74LS48 . . . D, J OR N PACKAGE
(TOP VIEW)

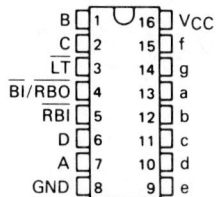

(a) **Connection diagram**

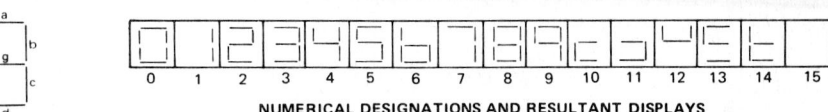

SEGMENT IDENTIFICATION

0 1 2 3 4 5 6 7 8 9 10 11 12 13 14 15

NUMERICAL DESIGNATIONS AND RESULTANT DISPLAYS

'46A, '47A, 'L46, 'L47, 'LS47 FUNCTION TABLE

DECIMAL OR FUNCTION	INPUTS						BI/RBO†	OUTPUTS						
	LT	RBI	D	C	B	A		a	b	c	d	e	f	g
0	H	H	L	L	L	L	H	ON	ON	ON	ON	ON	ON	OFF
1	H	X	L	L	L	H	H	OFF	ON	ON	OFF	OFF	OFF	OFF
2	H	X	L	L	H	L	H	ON	ON	OFF	ON	ON	OFF	ON
3	H	X	L	L	H	H	H	ON	ON	ON	ON	OFF	OFF	ON
4	H	X	L	H	L	L	H	OFF	ON	ON	OFF	OFF	ON	ON
5	H	X	L	H	L	H	H	ON	OFF	ON	ON	OFF	ON	ON
6	H	X	L	H	H	L	H	OFF	OFF	ON	ON	ON	ON	ON
7	H	X	L	H	H	H	H	ON	ON	ON	OFF	OFF	OFF	OFF
8	H	X	H	L	L	L	H	ON	ON	ON	ON	ON	ON	ON
9	H	X	H	L	L	H	H	ON	ON	ON	OFF	OFF	ON	ON
10	H	X	H	L	H	L	H	OFF	OFF	OFF	ON	ON	OFF	ON
11	H	X	H	L	H	H	H	OFF	OFF	ON	ON	OFF	OFF	ON
12	H	X	H	H	L	L	H	OFF	ON	OFF	OFF	OFF	ON	ON
13	H	X	H	H	L	H	H	ON	OFF	OFF	ON	OFF	ON	ON
14	H	X	H	H	H	L	H	OFF	OFF	OFF	ON	ON	ON	ON
15	H	X	H	H	H	H	H	OFF	OFF	OFF	OFF	OFF	OFF	OFF
BI	X	X	X	X	X	X	L	OFF	OFF	OFF	OFF	OFF	OFF	OFF
RBI	H	L	L	L	L	L	L	OFF	OFF	OFF	OFF	OFF	OFF	OFF
LT	L	X	X	X	X	X	H	ON	ON	ON	ON	ON	ON	ON

(b) **Function table**

of 1.6 V to 2.2 V with a current of 50 mA. We have used 330-Ω resistors to connect the open collector outputs of the 7447 to the $V_{CC} = +5$ V source through each segment of the LED. These resistors are necessary to limit the current through each LED segment.

Figure 16.6
LED display.

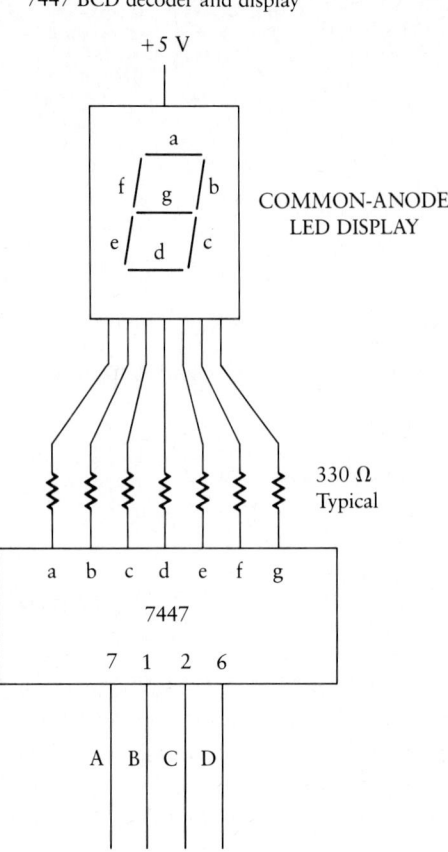

7447 BCD decoder and display

COMMON-ANODE
LED DISPLAY

330 Ω
Typical

Example 16.1

Design a circuit using a 555 oscillator to control the brightness of the 7-segment display.

SOLUTION   With the BCD-to-7-segment decoder (see Section 16.2), it is necessary to place a LOW input on the blanking in order to turn the display OFF. We use a 555 timer to construct a pulse generator to drive the decoder-blanking input. The 555 pulse generator modulates the blanking input so the brightness of the 7-segment display is adjustable. Variation of the duty cycle of the 555 changes the display brightness. The design is shown in Figure 16.7. The duty cycle is varied by adjusting the setting of the 50 kΩ potentiometer.

Figure 16.7
Variable brightness control for 7-segment display.

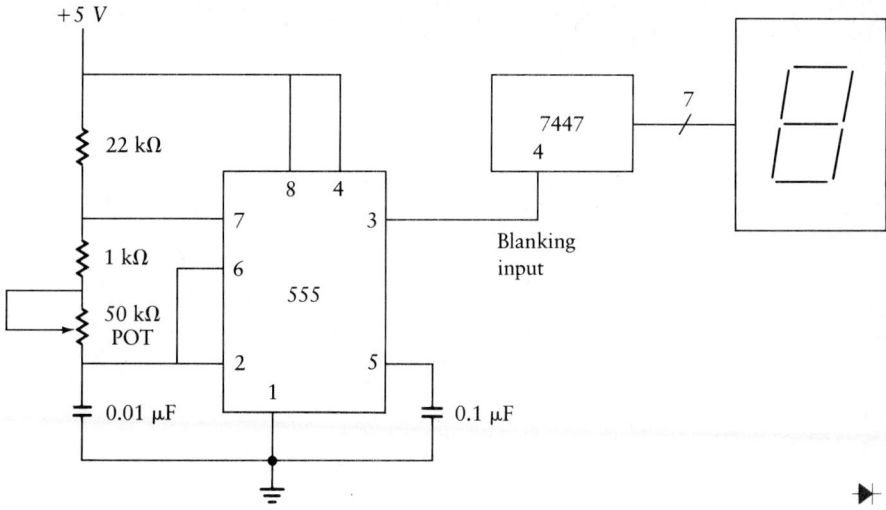

16.3 Flip-Flops, Latches, and Shift Registers

We now begin our study of circuits with memory. The outputs not only depend upon the current value of the inputs but also upon the past values. This is known as *clocked logic, synchronous logic,* or *time-dependent logic.*

The function tables considered so far contain only two symbols, 0 and 1 or L and H. We now expand our vocabulary of function-table symbols by introducing some new symbols in Figure 16.8. The first three entries in the figure represent symbols with which you are already familiar. The first entry is the data HIGH, or 1. The second is the data LOW, or 0. The third symbol, X, is used in function tables to represent values that do not matter—that is, they have no effect upon the output. These are sometimes referred to as *don't care* conditions.

In some cases, the transitions are important in determining system output. In Chapter 14, we briefly discuss edge triggering. A particular effect could occur on the leading (or trailing) edge of a clock input. In such a case, the

Figure 16.8
List of equivalent symbols.

Symbols	Common function table
1, H	Logical one or high
0, L	Logical zero or low
X	Don't care input; input can be any level or waveform
⬆ or ⌐	Low-to-high transition
⬇ or ⌐	High-to-low transition
NC	No change in output
Q_{n+1}	Output after a given event

Figure 16.9
Always gate.

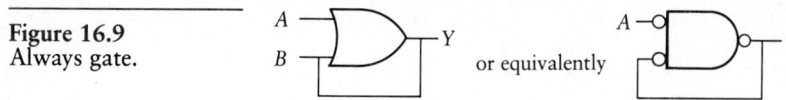

or equivalently

transitions are important, and we use the fourth and fifth entries in Figure 16.8 to specify the direction of transition. The symbol *NC* is used to designate no change in an output.

More than one function table is often used to indicate the values of outputs and inputs before and after a clock pulse or transition. It is possible to combine these tables and to apply a name to variables before and after the change. In such cases, a variable Q is rewritten as Q_n and Q_{n+1} to represent the values before and after a given event, respectively. Some authors and data books have adopted variations of this terminology; however, the particular choice of symbols is usually self-explanatory.

We start with circuits that have no memory and then change these to circuits with memory by feeding the output back to the input. A simple example is shown in Figure 16.9. The output of an OR gate is fed back to the input. An equivalent form uses a NAND gate with feedback. This configuration is known as an *always gate* for reasons that will shortly become clear.

Suppose we start with input and output equal to 0 (LOW). If we now apply a HIGH to input A, the output will go HIGH. If input A is now made LOW again, the output remains HIGH because the B input is now HIGH. Once A goes HIGH, the output will *always* be HIGH regardless of subsequent changes in A.

The always gate is an exceedingly simple circuit with limited applications. Nonetheless, it illustrates the fact that feedback can be used to create a circuit with memory capability from one that previously had none.

16.3.1   *Flip-Flops*

We can combine two NAND gates in the manner shown in Figure 16.10 to arrive at an extremely useful configuration. This is known as the *set-reset, or RS, flip-flop*. The flip-flop has two stable states and two complementary outputs, Q and $\overline{Q}$. The output will remain in either of these two stable states until the SET or RESET lines are changed. The function table is shown in Figure 16.10(b). $Q(t)$ is the logic value of Q before the application of the clock pulse, and $Q(t + 1)$ is the value of Q after the application of the clock pulse. The device acts like a memory since the outputs will remain the same until a momentary change occurs at the input.

If the flip-flop is told to SET and RESET at the same time ($\overline{S} = 0$ and $\overline{R} = 0$), we obtain a disallowed state, as shown in the last entry of the function

Figure 16.10
Set-reset flip-flop.

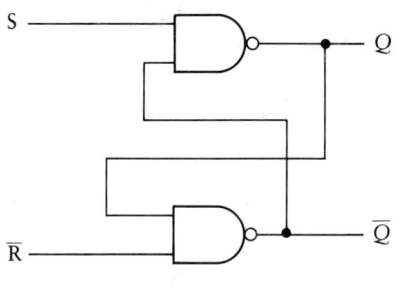

$\overline{S}$	$\overline{R}$	Q(t + 1)	
0	0	1	Disallowed
0	1	1	Set
1	0	0	Reset
1	1	Q(t)	No change

(a) Circuit

(b) Function table

Figure 16.11
Function table for *JK*
flip-flop.

J	K	Q (t + 1)
0	0	Q(t)
0	1	0
1	0	1
1	1	$\overline{Q(t)}$

table. The two outputs, Q and $\overline{Q}$, no longer form a complementary set. A second shortcoming of this simple circuit is that transitions can occur at any time, depending upon the state changes of the inputs. The circuit contains no clock. Careful control of the SET and RESET inputs is therefore required. For example, suppose we are making a transition from the RESET instruction ($\overline{S} = 1$ and $\overline{R} = 0$) to the SET instruction ($\overline{S} = 0$ and $\overline{R} = 1$). If, during this transition, both $\overline{S}$ and $\overline{R}$ are momentarily 0, then the disallowed-output state occurs. The presence of the disallowed state and the lack of a clock represent severe shortcomings of the basic *RS* flip-flop. Because of these shortcomings, we concentrate upon an improved circuit known as the *JK flip-flop*.

The *JK* flip-flop does not suffer from the problems of the *RS* flip-flop. It features both time-dependent and time-independent signals and uses a mixture of the two signals to control the output signals, Q and $\overline{Q}$. Figure 16.11 presents the function table for a *JK* flip-flop. The clock is omitted to simplify the table.

The table of Figure 16.11 should be carefully compared with that of Figure 16.10 to see the differences between the *RS* and *JK* flip-flops. Note that if the

J is considered as the SET input and the *K* as the RESET, two of the entries in the tables match. Thus a 0 on the *J* and a 1 on the *K* input RESETS the flip-flop, regardless of what state it was in before the application of these signals. The opposite conditions, *J* = 1 and *K* = 0, SETS the flip-flop. If both inputs are 1, then the *RS* flip-flop does not change output, whereas the *JK* flip-flop changes state. That is, the output of the *JK* flip-flop under the condition of *J* = 1 and *K* = 1 is given as

$$Q(t + 1) = \overline{Q(t)}$$

which means that the new output is the inverse of the old. We say that the flip-flop *toggles*.

If both inputs are 0, the *RS* flip-flop goes into a disallowed state with both outputs at 1. The *JK* flip-flop, with 0 as both inputs, remains in its current state. That is,

$$Q(t + 1) = Q(t)$$

Clocked flip-flops can change state only when the clock signal appears at the input. No matter how many changes occur in *J* or *K* between clock signals, the state of the circuit will not change. This form of logic can hold an output constant while some of the inputs are changing. A clocked logic device can therefore be used as a memory device to store an output so that it can be referred to again and again. Another advantage of clocked logic is that all changes in a complex circuit can be forced to occur at exactly the same time. This restriction is used to prevent potentially severe problems.

There are two basic types of clocking—level and edge. With *level clocking*, the input data cannot be changed except immediately after a clock pulse arrives. It is important that the input change only once during the period that the clock pulse is present. The state of the clock (either 0 or 1) determines whether changes in the output can occur. Alternatively, with *edge clocking*, the input data can change at any time. Changes in the output occur only during *transitions* of the clock signal, so it is the value of the inputs at these times that matter.

Figure 16.12 illustrates the 74108 dual *JK* flip-flop function table and connection diagram. Note that this chip contains both a PRESET and a CLEAR input. If the PRESET input is LOW and the CLEAR input is HIGH, the flip-flop SETS independent of the values of *J*, *K*, and the CLOCK. Thus, the output, *Q*, goes HIGH. If the CLEAR input is LOW and the PRESET input is HIGH, the flip-flop RESETS independent of the other inputs. Setting both PRESET and CLEAR to LOW is an illegal instruction, and both *Q* and $\overline{Q}$ temporarily go HIGH until the input signal is removed.

If both the PRESET and CLEAR are kept HIGH, the *J* and *K* inputs control

Figure 16.12
74108 dual *JK* flip-flop.
Courtesy of Texas Instruments Incorporated.

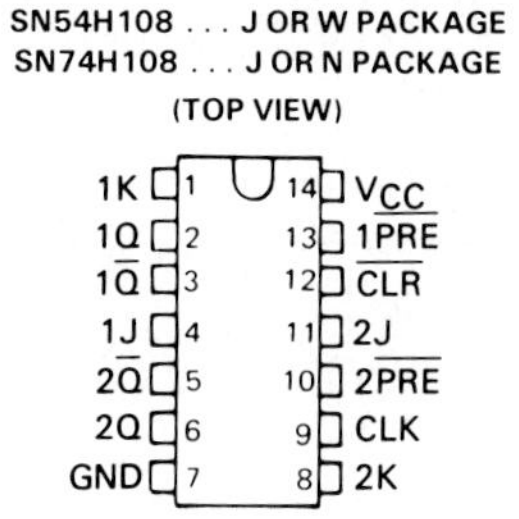

SN54H108 . . . J OR W PACKAGE
SN74H108 . . . J OR N PACKAGE
(TOP VIEW)

```
       ┌──┬─┬──┐
1K  ☐ 1 │  U  │ 14 ☐ V_CC
1Q  ☐ 2 │     │ 13 ☐ 1PRE
1Q̄  ☐ 3 │     │ 12 ☐ CLR
1J  ☐ 4 │     │ 11 ☐ 2J
2Q̄  ☐ 5 │     │ 10 ☐ 2PRE
2Q  ☐ 6 │     │ 9  ☐ CLK
GND ☐ 7 │     │ 8  ☐ 2K
       └─────┘
```

(a) Connection diagram

INPUTS					OUTPUTS	
PRE	CLR	CLK	J	K	Q	Q̄
L	H	X	X	X	H	L
H	L	X	X	X	L	H
L	L	X	X	X	H↑	H↑
H	H	↓	L	L	Q_0	Q̄_0
H	H	↓	H	L	H	L
H	H	↓	L	H	L	H
H	H	↓	H	H	TOGGLE	
H	H	H	X	X	Q_0	Q̄_0

(b) Function table

Figure 16.13
Function table for *D* flip-flop.

D	$Q (t + 1)$
0	0
1	1

the flip-flop whenever a CLOCK signal is present. The arrow notation in the CLOCK column of the table is used by this manufacturer to indicate that changes in state take place on the negative clock transition (that is, the pulse input goes from HIGH to LOW). The *J* input acts as a positive logic SET instruction, whereas the *K* acts as a RESET (or CLEAR). If both *J* and *K* are LOW, the flip-flop remains in its previous state, noted as Q_0. If both *J* and *K* are HIGH, the flip-flop changes state, or toggles.

There are two other major categories of flip-flops in addition to the *JK* flip-flop, these being the *D* and the *T* flip-flop. The *D*, or *data*, flip-flop has only one input instead of two (as is the case with the *RS* and *JK* flip-flops). Regardless of the input level, the *D* input is transferred to the output. Figure 16.13 illustrates the function table for this type of flip-flop. Notice that the next state of the output is given by the current value of the input. A 1 at the input SETS the flip-flop, whereas a 0 at the input RESETS the flip-flop.

The *D* flip-flop can be constructed from a *JK* flip-flop by setting *J* equal to the *D* input and *K* equal to the complement of the *D* input. Thus, if *D* = 1 for the *D* flip-flop, this is the same as *J* = 1 and *K* = 0 for the *JK* flip-flop, and this SETS the device. The reverse is true for an input of *D* = 0. By forcing *K* to be the complement of *J*, we have eliminated two rows from the *JK* function table.

The *T,* or *toggle,* flip-flop also has only one input. If the input, *T,* is equal to 1, then the flip-flop changes state. If the input is 0, the flip-flop remains in

Figure 16.14
Function table for T
flip-flop.

T	$Q(t + 1)$
0	$Q(t)$
1	$\overline{Q(t)}$

its current state. This is shown in the function table of Figure 16.14. A *JK* flip-flop can be turned into a T flip-flop by setting both J and K equal to T. That is, the inputs to the J and K are tied together to form a single input, T. Thus, if $T = 1$, this is the same as $J = 1$ and $K = 1$, which toggles the *JK* flip-flop. If $T = 0$, then $J = 0$ and $K = 0$, so the *JK* flip-flop does not change state.

16.3.2   *Latches and Memories*

The *latch memory* is a form of flip-flop that has the ability to remember a previous input and store it until the device is either cleared or the data are called up to be read by another chip. Latch ICs come in sizes ranging from chips with one latch to memory chips that store thousands of bits of information.

Figure 16.15 illustrates the pin diagram and function table for the 74C373 tri-state octal *D*-type latch, which is an 8-bit storage element.

There are 8 data-input lines, labeled $1D$ through $8D$, and 8 output lines, labeled $1Q$ through $8Q$. The device is assembled in a 20-pin DIP. Eight of the pins are used for data input, eight for data output, and two for power; there are two additional inputs, as described next. The outputs are specially designed to drive high-capacitive loads such as are found in a system bus. An additional input is labeled LATCH ENABLE. When this is HIGH, the Q outputs follow the D inputs just as in the case of the *D*-type flip-flop. In this state the latch is said to be *transparent* since the outputs follow the input. When the LATCH ENABLE input is LOW, the outputs do not change. This is indicated in the manufacturer's function table by showing Q to equal Q.

An additional input is labeled OUTPUT DISABLE. When this input is HIGH, all the outputs go to a high-impedance state regardless of the status of the other inputs.

A *memory chip* stores information until it is either cleared, set or written over by another bit of information. The write operation can be triggered either by a rising or falling clock transition or by a steady logic state. Some devices will write the true value of the input data and others will invert it before storage. Likewise, the output may be either true or inverted. The output normally has its own triggering mechanism and can therefore be read by means of an enabling signal.

Figure 16.15
74C373 tri-state octal
D-type latch.
Courtesy of Texas
Instruments
Incorporated.

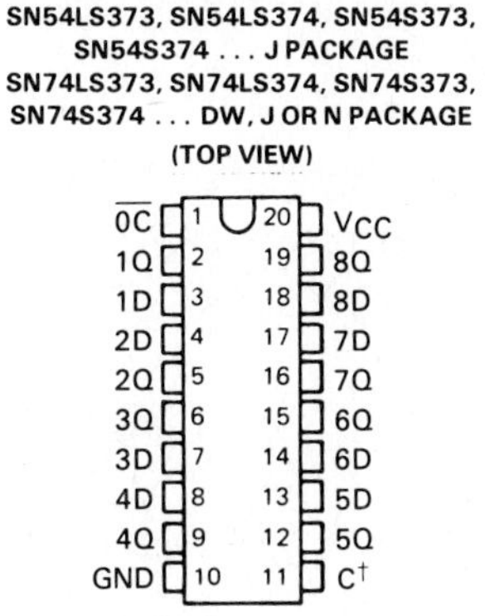

SN54LS373, SN54S374, SN54S373,
SN54S374 . . . J PACKAGE
SN74LS373, SN74LS374, SN74S373,
SN74S374 . . . DW, J OR N PACKAGE
(TOP VIEW)

$\overline{OC}$	1 ⌴ 20	Vcc
1Q	2 19	8Q
1D	3 18	8D
2D	4 17	7D
2Q	5 16	7Q
3Q	6 15	6Q
3D	7 14	6D
4D	8 13	5D
4Q	9 12	5Q
GND	10 11	C†

(a) **Connection diagram**

**'LS373, 'S373
FUNCTION TABLE**

OUTPUT ENABLE	ENABLE LATCH	D	OUTPUT
L	H	H	H
L	H	L	L
L	L	X	Q_0
H	X	X	Z

(b) **Function table**

Many memory elements *multiplex* the inputs and outputs. That is, a single line is used to read or write more than one bit. It is therefore necessary to have a read- and write-signaling system that controls the read and write process. This contrasts with most flip-flops and simple latches, since for these circuits, outputs are always available for reading.

Example 16.2

Design a drive for one 7-segment LED display that will hold the output fixed while the input is changing. This is often required when we are measuring quantities such as velocity.

SOLUTION One possible solution for this design problem is shown in Figure 16.16. Since only four data lines are required, we have chosen a 74175 latch to hold the data on the display while the inputs are changing. Information on the four input lines (pins 4, 5, 12, and 13) is transferred to the output lines (pins 2, 7, 10, and 15) on the positive-going edge of the clock pulse on pin 9. When the clock input is at either the HIGH or LOW level, the data input has no effect upon the output. The latch output feeds the 7447 BCD-to-7-segment decoder/driver, which in turn feeds the 7 inputs of the LED display through 330 Ω resistors. We have introduced the notation of a connection with a slash through it. This is shown in the figure as a slash with a 7 next to it. The slash-7 is a shorthand notation that avoids drawing 7 separate lines and represents 7 wires with seven 330 Ω resistors connecting the SN7447 to the common-anode LED display.

Figure 16.16
LED display with
latch.

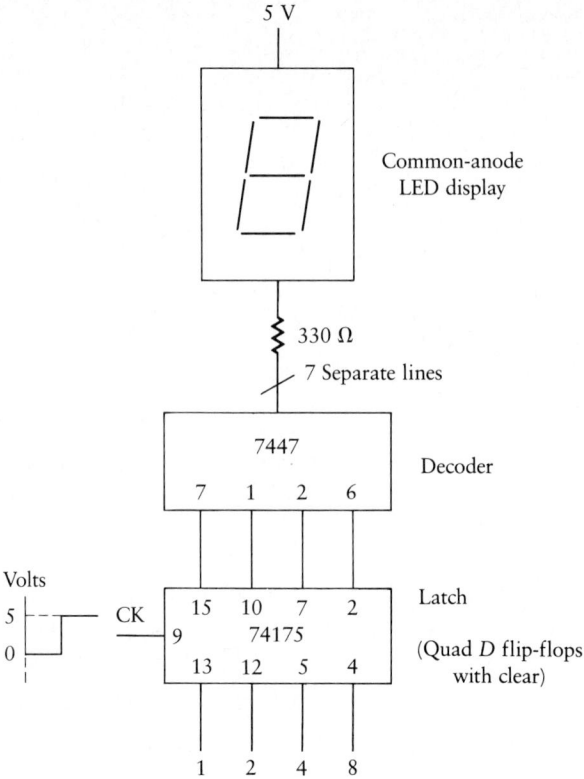

16.3.3 *Shift Registers*

A *shift register* is comprised of a number of *JK* or *D* flip-flops cascaded in a string so that, upon clocking, the contents contained in each stage are moved, or shifted, either one stage to the left or to the right. A simple shift register is shown in Figure 16.17. We illustrate eight stages, Q_A through Q_H. The bits of data, either 0 or 1, are passed on in order so the first bit in is the first bit out. The shifting takes place upon the rising edge of the clock signal. As a result, the eight-stage register of Figure 16.17 delays the input data for eight clock pulses.

A shift register can be thought of as a memory device that consists of N memory elements connected together in a chain. Each cell in the chain is capable of remembering one bit of information. That bit can be transferred to the adjacent cell, left or right, upon a proper control instruction.

Figure 16.18 illustrates one particular class of 4-bit shift registers, the 74194. This is known as a *universal* shift register since it can be configured in a variety of ways. The circuit contains 46 equivalent gates. The shift register can be loaded in a parallel fashion by setting both MODE controls, *S*1 and *S*0, HIGH.

Figure 16.17
Shift register.

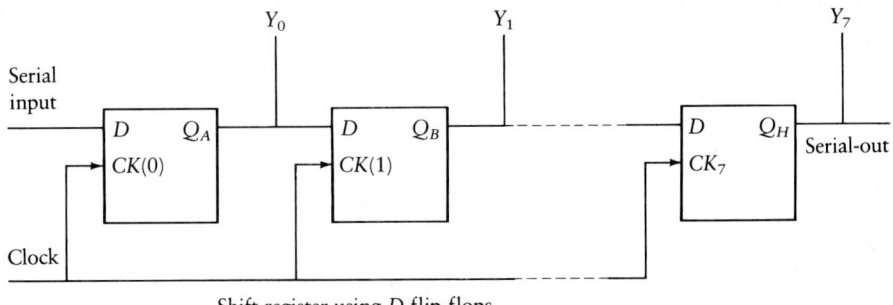

Shift register using *D* flip-flops

Figure 16.18
74194 4-bidirec-
tional universal shift
register.
Courtesy of Texas
Instruments
Incorported.

SN54194, SN54LS194A, SN54S194 . . . J OR W PACKAGE
SN74194 . . . J OR N PACKAGE
SN74LS194A, SN74S194 . . . D, J OR N PACKAGE
(TOP VIEW)

$\overline{CLR}$	1	16	V_{CC}
SR SER	2	15	Q_A
A	3	14	Q_B
B	4	13	Q_C
C	5	12	Q_D
D	6	11	CLK
SL SER	7	10	S1
GND	8	9	S0

(a) **Connection diagram**

INPUTS									**OUTPUTS**			
CLEAR	**MODE**		CLOCK	**SERIAL**		**PARALLEL**				Q_A	Q_B	Q_C	Q_D
	S1	S0		LEFT	RIGHT	A	B	C	D				
L	X	X	X	X	X	X	X	X	X	L	L	L	L
H	X	X	L	X	X	X	X	X	X	Q_{A0}	Q_{B0}	Q_{C0}	Q_{D0}
H	H	H	↑	X	X	a	b	c	d	a	b	c	d
H	L	H	↑	X	H	X	X	X	X	H	Q_{An}	Q_{Bn}	Q_{Cn}
H	L	H	↑	X	L	X	X	X	X	L	Q_{An}	Q_{Bn}	Q_{Cn}
H	H	L	↑	H	X	X	X	X	X	Q_{Bn}	Q_{Cn}	Q_{Dn}	H
H	H	L	↑	L	X	X	X	X	X	Q_{Bn}	Q_{Cn}	Q_{Dn}	L
H	L	L	X	X	X	X	X	X	X	Q_{A0}	Q_{B0}	Q_{C0}	Q_{D0}

H = high level (steady state)
L = low level (steady state)
X = irrelevant (any input, including transitions)
↑ = transition from low to high level
a, b, c, d = the level of steady-state input at
inputs A, B, C, or D, respectively.
Q_{A0}, Q_{B0}, Q_{C0}, Q_{D0} = the level of Q_A,
Q_B, Q_C, or Q_D, respectively, before the
indicated steady-state input conditions
were established.
Q_{An}, Q_{Bn}, Q_{Cn}, Q_{Dn} = the level of Q_A,
Q_B, Q_C, respectively, before the most-
recent ↑ transition of the clock.

(b) **Function table**

Then the 4 bits of data are loaded into the associated flip-flops by using inputs
A, B, C, and *D.* The output is read in parallel as Q_A through Q_D. The X in
the SERIAL columns of the table indicate that, during the parallel loading
mode, serial data flow is inhibited. If we now set the mode controls to $S0$ = HIGH
and $S1$ = LOW, the data shift to the right upon the rising edge of the clock
pulse (study the function table to convince yourself that the fourth and fifth
rows confirm this observation). Alternatively, a LOW input to mode control
$S0$ and a HIGH to $S1$ causes a shift to the left upon the rising edge of the clock

pulse. The sixth and seventh rows of the table confirm this. If both mode controls are LOW, the state of the register does not change, so clocking is inhibited. A CLEAR input is provided, which sets all registers to LOW independent of the values of the other inputs or of the clock. The mode inputs must change only while the clock input is not changing.

Although there exist numerous shift-register configurations, they can be divided into the following four broad categories, depending upon whether inputs and outputs are handled serially (one after another) or in parallel:

1. *Serial-in serial-out (SISO)*   Input data enter the shift register serially and the data are taken from the output lead in a serial fashion delayed by a number of clock pulses equal to the number of storage cells. Figure 16.17 is an example of a SISO shift register.
2. *Serial-in parallel-out (SIPO)*   Input data enter the shift register serially but the data are taken from the output leads in a parallel fashion. This requires more than one output lead, since the bits are read in groups of multiple bits. For example, if the bits represent a BCD code, the output bits are read in groupings of four to represent one BCD word.
3. *Parallel-in serial-out (PISO)*   This type of shift register has the capability of loading the data in parallel and shifting the data out serially. This register uses NAND gates and inverters with the flip-flops to sequence the input data properly.
4. *Parallel-in parallel-out (PIPO)*   This type of parallel-access shift register is considerably more complex because of the additional gates that must be added. It can be thought of as a parallel combination of SISO shift registers.

16.4   Counters

Counters can be either asynchronous (ripple) or synchronous. Figure 16.19 illustrates an *asynchronous counter*. Each of the blocks in this diagram is a *JK* flip-flop configured as a *T* flip-flop, since the *J* and *K* inputs are tied together. Note that the data input is used for the CLOCK. A *T* flip-flop toggles only when its input goes HIGH.

Suppose we feed a pulse train into the first flip-flop. The first time the input goes HIGH, the flip-flop SETs. The second time the input goes HIGH, the flip-flop CLEARs, and so on. Thus, the output of the first flip-flop, labeled 1, is a pulse waveform at one-half of the frequency of the input. The process repeats itself at the second flip-flop, and each device toggles once for every two toggles of the circuit to its left. The outputs are labeled according to the

Figure 16.19
Asynchronous
counter.

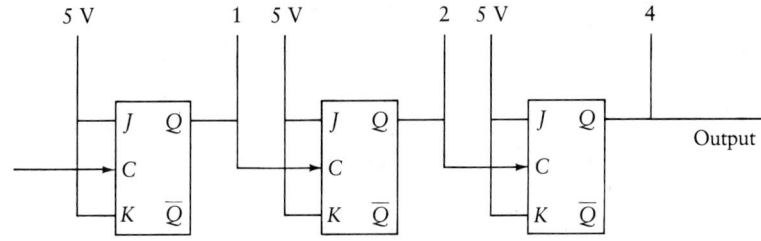

weight in a binary number. Thus, the third output corresponds to 2^2, or 4. The counter generates a 3-bit number, which cycles as follows:

000, 001, 010, 011, 100, 101, 110, 111, 000, . . .

Note that the frequency of each bit changing from 0 to 1 is one-half of that of the bit to its right. Thus, the circuit counts between 000 through 111 and back to 000 as the input is pulsed eight times. The counter is asynchronous, since counts occur in the right flip-flop only after the clock pulse "ripples" from the left to the right flip-flop.

The circuit of Figure 16.20 is a *synchronous counter,* since the clock input feeds into all three flip-flops simultaneously. The second flip-flop toggles upon a clock pulse only if the output of the first flip-flop is a 1. This represents a *carry* condition in the operation of adding 1 to the previous output. The third flip-flop toggles upon a clock pulse only if both the first and second outputs are 1.

Since the output of each flip-flop is at a frequency that is one-half that of its input, the flip-flop is often known as a *divide-by-2* circuit. The counter is therefore often called a *divide-by-n counter,* where *n* is the number of input cycles required to produce one output cycle.

Figure 16.20
Synchronous counter.

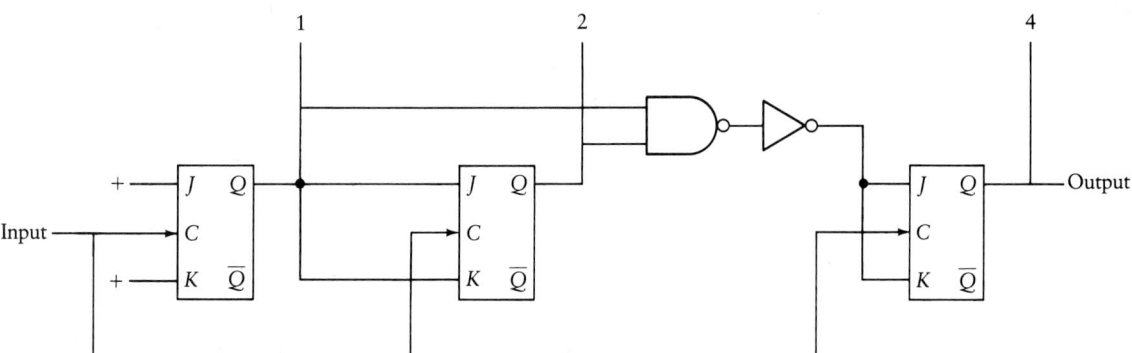

Figure 16.21
Connection diagram
to count from 8 to 14.

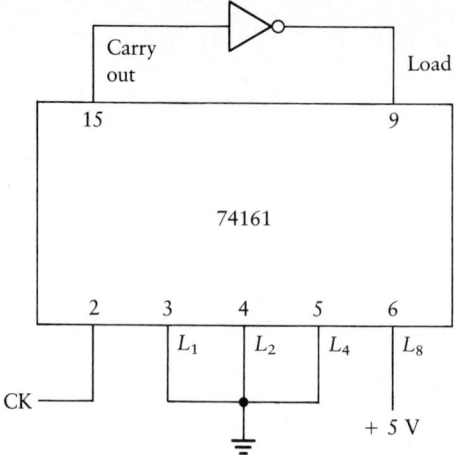

The majority of TTL and CMOS counters are *up-only* counters, that is, they count only in a direction of increasing binary numbers. Inverters can be used on the outputs in order to change an up-counter into a down-counter. This will work only if the counter counts to a binary length that is a power of two. That is, if a 3-bit counter counts from 000 to 111 (2^3 counts), the inversion operation will change from up-counting to down-counting. However, if the counter is used to count only between 000 and 101, then inversion will not have the desired effect.

An *up-down counter* either adds to, ignores, or subtracts from the current count at any time. Examples are the TTL 74190 and 74192 and the CMOS 74C192, 74HC160, 161, and 162. Although these are the most flexible and versatile of counters, they are usually also more expensive and consume more power than the up-only counters.

Counters can be connected in sequence with the output of the first forming the input to the second, and in this manner, the count is lengthened. It is possible to shorten the count sequence of a particular counter by presetting it to a nonzero number. An example is shown in Figure 16.21. This circuit uses a 74161 binary synchronous presettable counter to count from 8 to 14. The load inputs, L1, L2, L4, and L8, are used to preset the counter to any desired value. In this example, the connections preset the counter to 1000 or, in decimal, 8. These bits are loaded into the counter whenever the LOAD pin, 9, goes LOW. The CARRY-OUT lead (also known as carry lookahead), pin 15, goes HIGH when the count reaches 15 (1111). This is fed through the inverter so that the LOAD input goes LOW, thus resetting the counter to 1000.

Figure 16.22 shows another example of a truncated count sequence. In this case, we set the load input to 0000, so the counter will start counting at 0000. When the count output reaches 0111, or 7, all three inputs to the NAND gate

Figure 16.22
Connection diagram to cause counter to clear on 7.

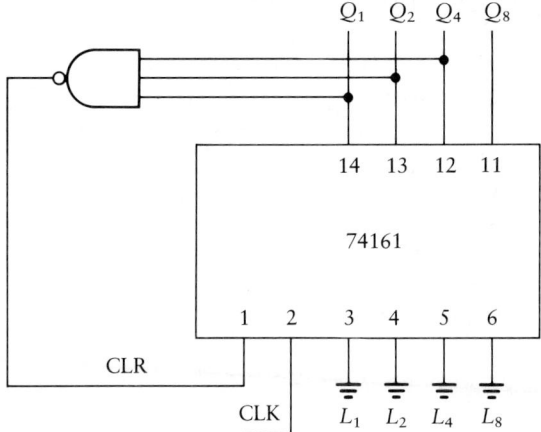

are HIGH, and the NAND output goes LOW. This clears the counter to 0000.

It should now be clear that the counter can be configured to start at any value and to end at any other value.

The 74161 chip is used in the previous two examples, and we now take a more detailed look at this group of ICs. Figure 16.23 presents some information regarding the 74160 through 74163 series of synchronous 4-bit counters. This figure is abstracted from the data sheets and represents only one piece of information available to the design engineer. The chips are composed of flip-flops that are all clocked from the same signal. This class of counters is *programmable*, that is, the output can be preset to any desired combination. When signals are placed into the load inputs and the LOAD is enabled, the counter presets, regardless of the values of the other inputs.

We examine the timing diagram in the figure. Moving from left to right (increasing time), the first action is that the CLEAR input goes LOW. Some of the chips in this grouping have *asynchronous clear* and others have *synchronous clear*. Note that in the asynchronous clear case, the outputs Q_A through Q_D clear as soon as the CLEAR input goes LOW. In the synchronous clear case, clearing occurs at the first positive clock transition following the CLEAR input.

The next action shown in the diagram is the LOAD input going LOW. This causes the data input to be loaded at the next clock transition. Note that the example shows 1100, or 12, as the load sequence (D is the most significant bit and A is the least significant). The count is then enabled with the enable inputs going HIGH. The counter is shown incrementing through 1100, 1101, 1110, 1111, 0000, 0001, 0010. At that point, the ENABLE P goes LOW and the counter holds the last value.

Figure 16.24 illustrates an MSI/TTL counter that includes, on the same

Figure 16.23
74160 through 74163
series, synchronous
4-bit counter.
Courtesy of Texas
Instruments
Incorporated.

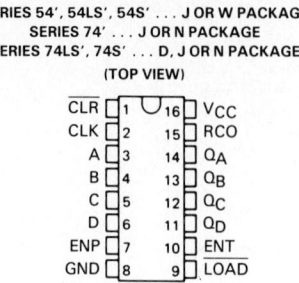

SERIES 54', 54LS', 54S' . . . J OR W PACKAGE
SERIES 74' . . . J OR N PACKAGE
SERIES 74LS', 74S' . . . D, J OR N PACKAGE
(TOP VIEW)

$\overline{CLR}$	1	16	V_{CC}
CLK	2	15	RCO
A	3	14	Q_A
B	4	13	Q_B
C	5	12	Q_C
D	6	11	Q_D
ENP	7	10	$\overline{ENT}$
GND	8	9	$\overline{LOAD}$

typical clear, preset, count, and inhibit sequences

Illustrated below is the following sequence:

1. Clear outputs to zero ('160 and 'LS160A are asynchronous; '162, 'LS162A, and 'S162 are synchronous)
2. Preset to BCD seven
3. Count to eight, nine, zero, one, two, and three
4. Inhibit

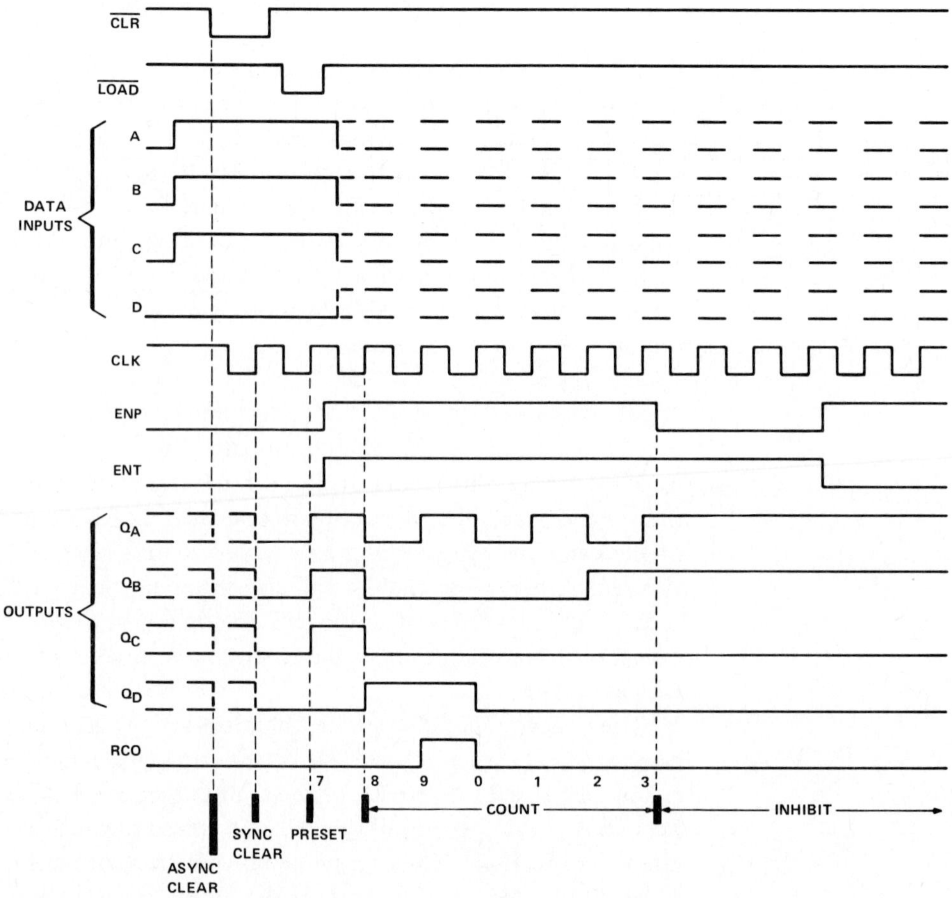

CLR

LOAD

DATA INPUTS

A

B

C

D

CLK

ENP

ENT

OUTPUTS

Q_A

Q_B

Q_C

Q_D

RCO

7   8   9   0   1   2   3

ASYNC CLEAR   SYNC CLEAR   PRESET   ←——— COUNT ———→   ←— INHIBIT —→

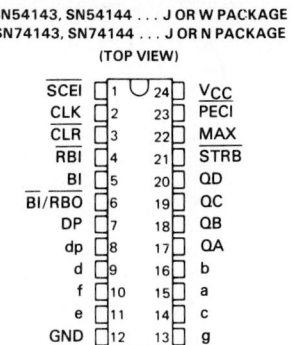

SN54143, SN54144 . . . J OR W PACKAGE
SN74143, SN74144 . . . J OR N PACKAGE
(TOP VIEW)

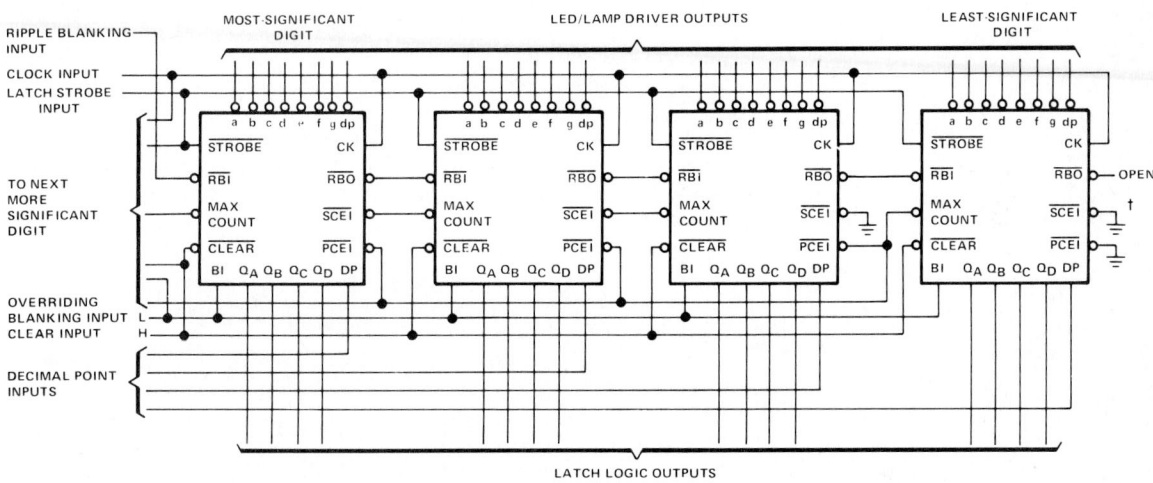

Figure 16.24   SN74143 and SN74144 series 4-bit counter/latch, 7-segment LED/lamp drivers. Courtesy of Texas Instruments Incorporated.

chip, the counter, latch, decoder, and the display drivers. This is a useful chip, since it combines the wide range of functions needed for LED/LAMP drivers. Also shown in the figure is an example of cascading these chips to lengthen the count.

The 74143 and 74144 series TTL MSI circuits contain the equivalent of 86 gates on a single chip. They include relatively large resistors in series with the bases of the input transistors, which lowers the drive current requirements.

The *SN74143 driver* has outputs designed to maintain a constant current of approximately 15 mA into the loads for the 7-segment outputs *a* through *g*. The *decimal point* output (dp) can sustain a 7 mA current, which applies for voltages ranging from 1 V to 5 V. It is important to note this IC latches and clears on the LEVEL of the applied signal rather than on the transition from HIGH to LOW. Reference to the data book is essential for understanding this complex IC.

The *SN74144 driver* has high-sink current-saturated outputs for driving indicators having voltage ratings up to 15 V or requiring up to 25 mA drive. The maximum clock frequency is typically 18 MHz, and power dissipation is typically 280 mW.

Drill Problems

D16.1   Design a drive circuit for a single 7-segment LED display that will hold the output fixed while the input is changing. Use a 74162 decade counter driven from a 555 asynchronous pulse generator.

Ans: Refer to Figure D16.1 for a solution to this problem. The 555 clock (CK1) drives the 74162 synchronous 4-bit counter providing a signal to the 74175 latch. Whenever the second clock signal (CK2) goes from LOW to HIGH, the data at the input of the latch are transferred to the output and then to the 7-segment display which does not change until the next CK2 transition.

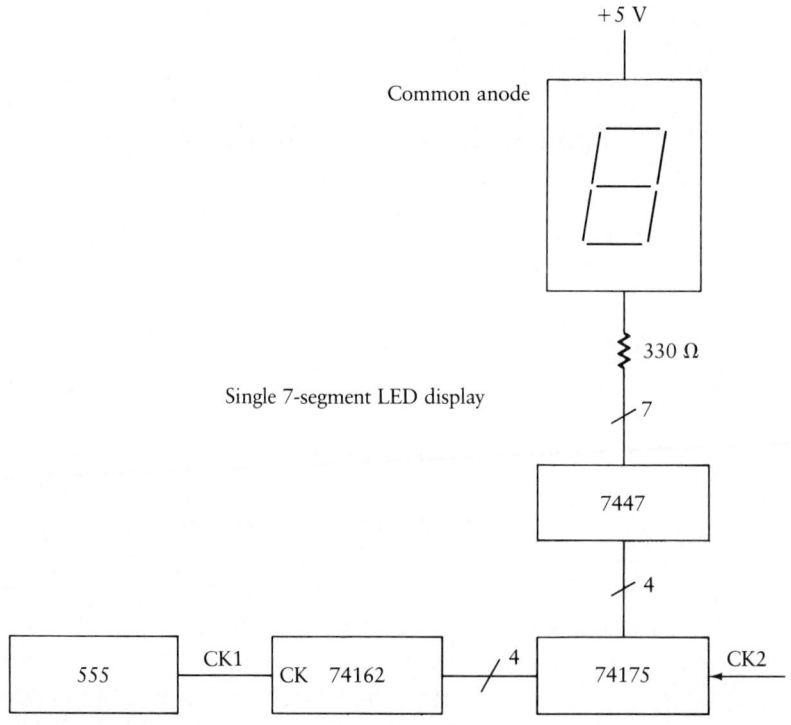

Figure D16.1

D16.2   Repeat Problem D16.1 using a 74143 4-bit counter/latch, 7-segment LED driver.

Ans: As can be seen from the block diagram of Figure D16.2, the single IC will solve the complete design, since contained within the IC are a BCD counter, 4-bit

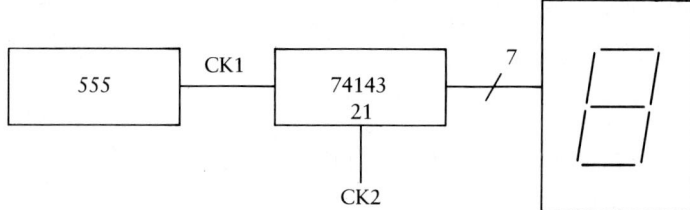

Figure D16.2

latch, and decoder/driver. An important difference in using the 74143 is that we latch the count into the display with a LEVEL latch strobe voltage. We must hold pin 21 high to latch the data into the display. This is shown in Figure D16.2 as CK2.

An important application of counters is in frequency or velocity measurement. A counter can be combined with a pulse generator to form a frequency counter. This is shown in Figure 16.25. The counter counts the number of pulses (or cycles) that occur during the time that the "window" pulse is HIGH. Since the width of the window pulse is known, the frequency of the input can be calculated. For example, if the window is exactly 1 s long, the counter will yield an output in hertz.

Figure 16.25 Frequency counter.

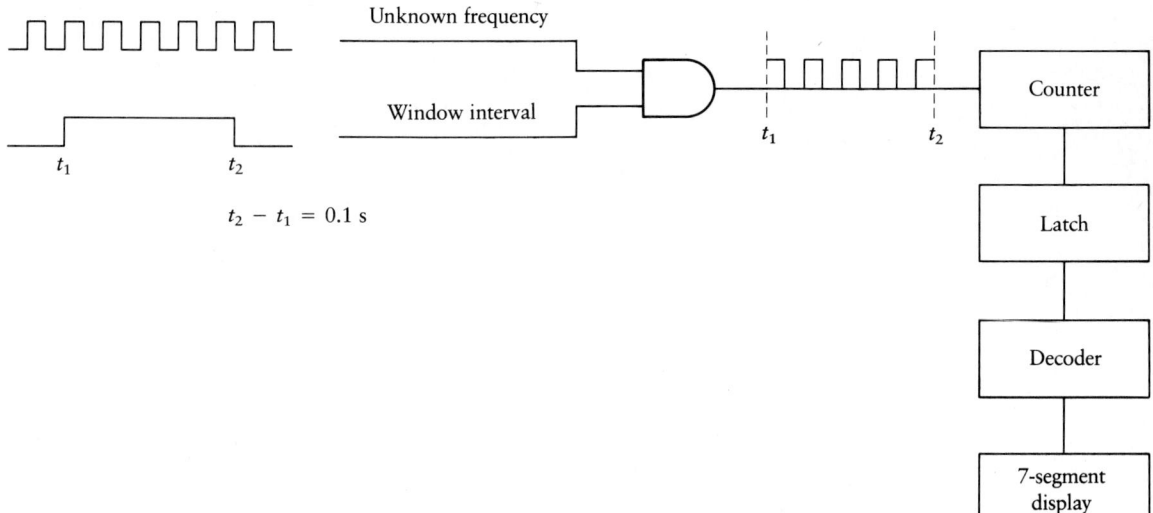

Example 16.3

Design a frequency counter to measure the frequency of a sinusoidal signal in the range between 5 kHz and 15 kHz. The amplitude of the input signal is 10 V rms. Display the output on three 7-segment LEDs with three significant digits (i.e., *XX.X* kHz).

SOLUTION We refer to the system block diagram shown in Figure 16.25, where we let the window period be 0.1 s long. At 5 kHz, we obtain 500 pulses and at 15 kHz, we obtain 1500 pulses within the window period. This meets the requirements of three significant figures. The sinusoidal signal is first conditioned to create pulses, as shown in Figure 16.26(a). We use a half-wave rectifier and then feed a 7414 Schmitt trigger inverter to yield the clean pulse train.

The window is developed with an astable 555 operating with a duty cycle of 10. We want the time low to be short, so that we waste little time to update the display. We will select the low time to be 10% of the high time. This circuit is shown in Figure 16.26(b). We select a period, *T* = 0.11 s, for the astable

Figure 16.26
Frequency measure-
ment for Example
16.3.

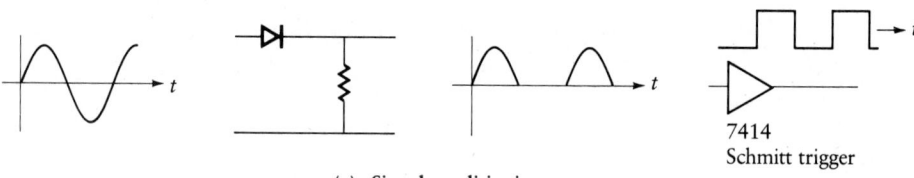

7414
Schmitt trigger

(a) **Signal conditioning**

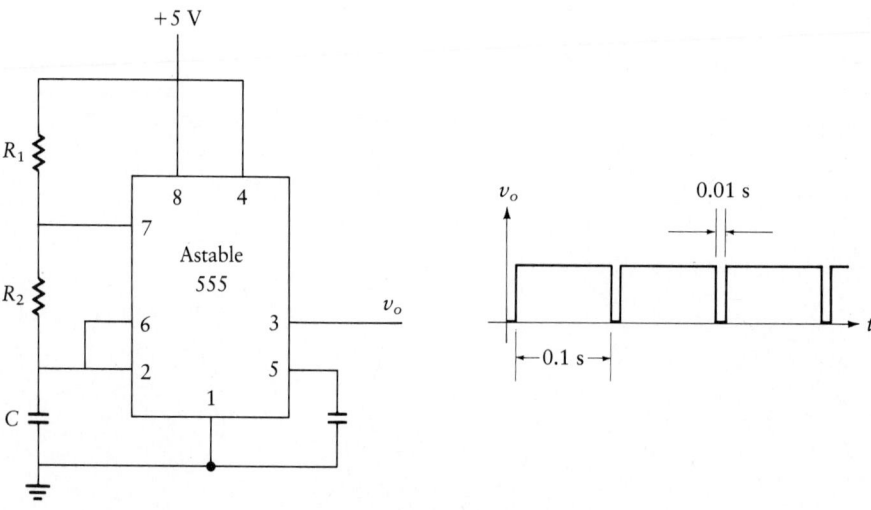

(b) **Creating the window**

555, so the frequency is $f = 1/T = 9.09$ Hz. We use the techniques of Chapter 14 to design the timer, as follows: Select $C = 1$ μF and obtain

$$9.09 = \frac{1.44}{C(R_1 + 2R_2)}$$

from which we obtain

$$(R_1 + 2R_2) = \frac{1.44}{9.09C} = 158.4 \text{ k}\Omega$$

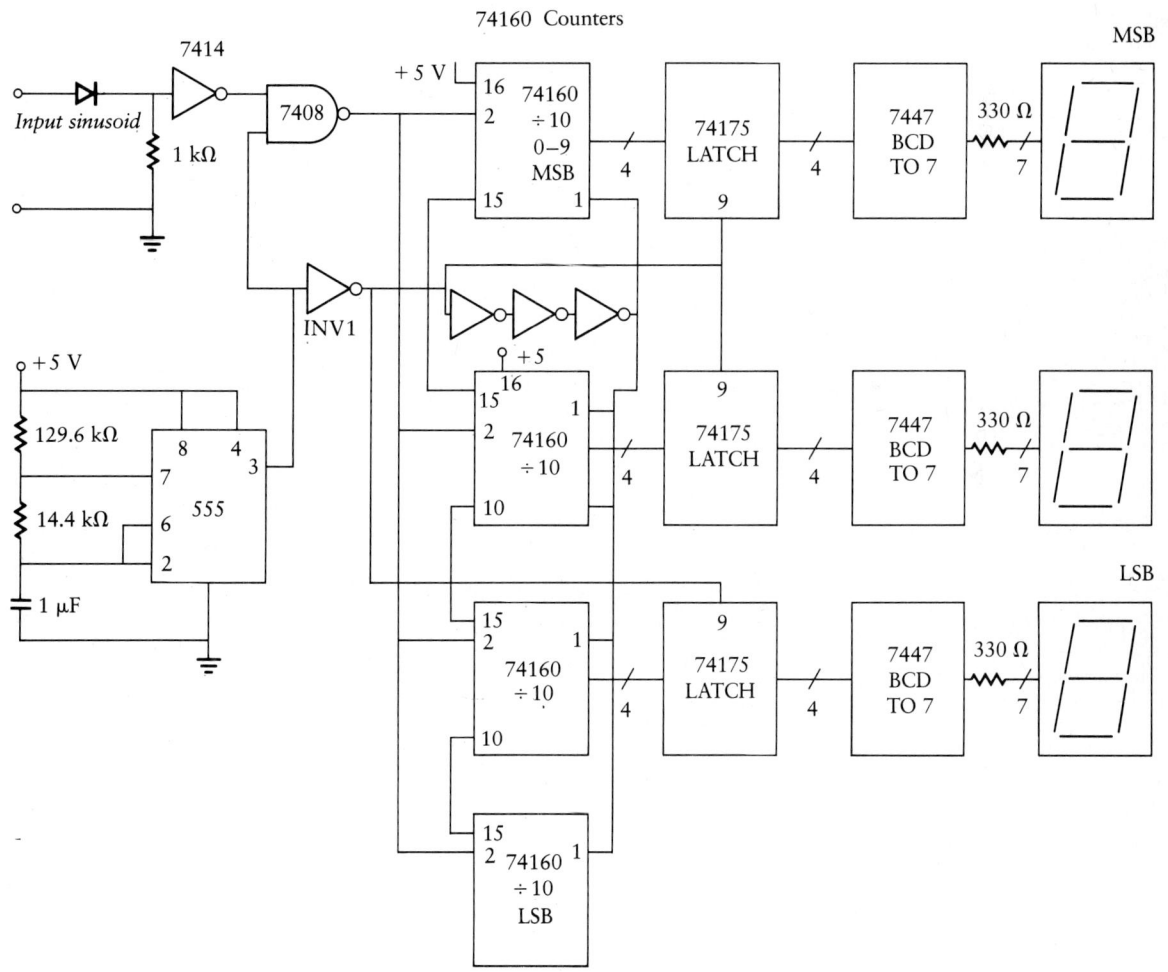

(c) **System block diagram**

Since the duty cycle is 10, we have

$$\text{Duty cycle} = \frac{\text{time high}}{\text{time low}} = \frac{R_1}{R_2} + 1 = 10$$

Hence,

$$\frac{R_1}{R_2} = 9$$

and

$$R_1 + 2R_2 = 9R_2 + 2R_2 = 158.4 \text{ k}\Omega$$

We solve for R_2 and R_1, with the result

$$R_2 = 14.4 \text{ k}\Omega$$
$$R_1 = 129.6 \text{ k}\Omega$$

We now AND the output of the pulse train from Figure 16.26(a) with the window of Figure 16.26(b) to yield the number of pulses in 0.1 s. The complete system block diagram is shown in Figure 16.26(c), where the pulses from the output of the 7408 AND gate are counted with four 74160 decade synchronous counters. Since we need only three 7-segment LED displays, we need only three 74175 latches and three 7447 BCD to 7-segment decoder drivers.

The trailing edge of the counter is used for two purposes:

1. To latch the ultimate count into the LED display and then later,
2. To clear the counter back to 0000.

To assure that the counter is cleared *after* the ultimate count is latched into the LED displays, the three extra inverters are included between the latch signal, after INV1, and the counter CLEAR signal. This is important, since if we do not delay the CLEAR signal, the display will show all zeroes for any input count.   ▶+

16.5   Clocks

Clocks are used to control the times at which changes occur in a digital circuit. One of the most popular clocks is formed using the 555 timer/oscillator, which is discussed in Chapter 14. A wide variety of other devices can be used for clocks, such as multivibrators, timers, and oscillator/dividers.

Figure 16.27
VCO using a 555.

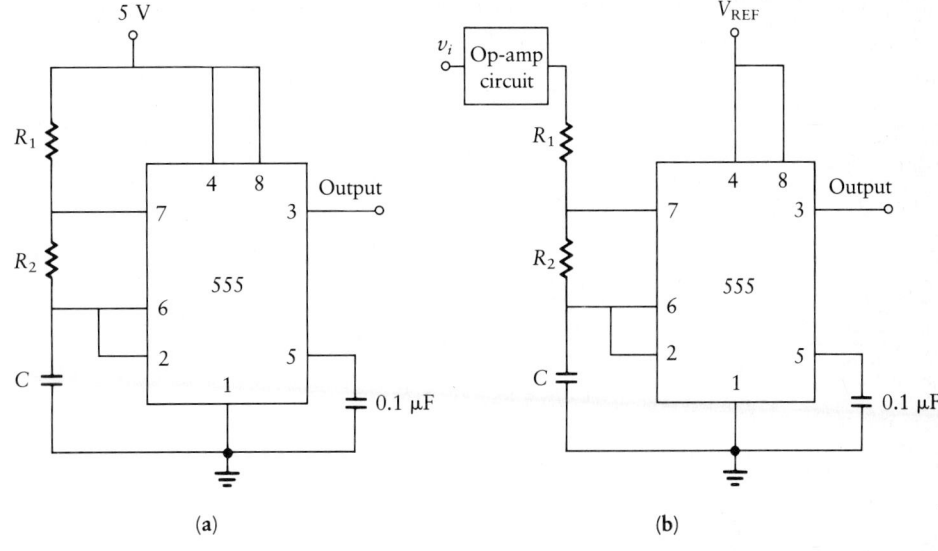

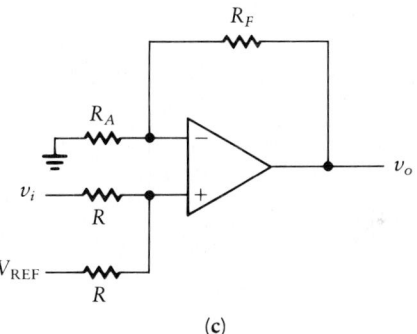

16.5.1 *Voltage-Controlled Oscillator (VCO)*

The output frequency of most oscillators depends upon the setting of an *RC* time constant. We sometimes require a frequency that varies with an input *voltage*. Examples of such situations include frequency modulators (FM), tone generators, A/D converters, and digital voltmeters. Oscillators of this type are called *voltage-controlled oscillators (VCOs)*.

The frequency of oscillation of a relaxation oscillator, such as the 555 in the astable mode, depends upon both the *RC* time constant and upon the voltage to which the capacitor charges. In the applications of the 555 discussed in Chapter 14, we drive the external charging circuit and the internal voltage dividers with the same voltage. We repeat the circuit diagram for a 555 in the astable mode, as in Figure 16.27(a). We use the same voltage drivers to assure that the output frequency is independent of the supply voltage variations.

Figure 16.28
74LS124 dual voltage-controlled oscillator. Courtesy of Texas Instruments Incorporated.

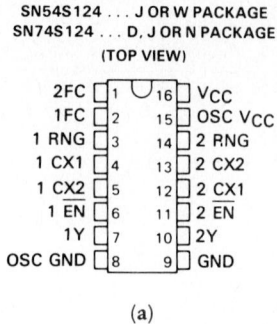

SN54S124 . . . J OR W PACKAGE
SN74S124 . . . D, J OR N PACKAGE
(TOP VIEW)

(a)

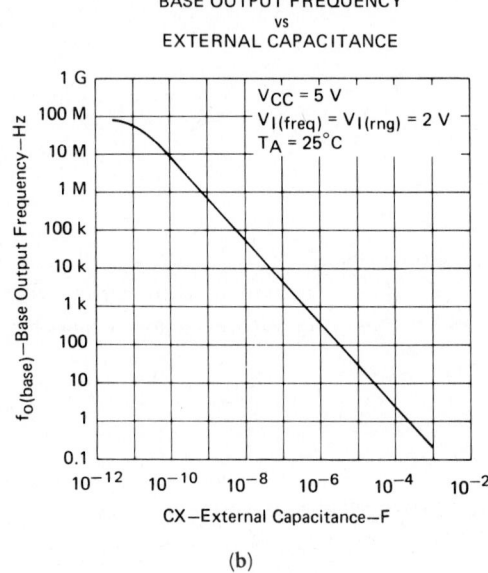

BASE OUTPUT FREQUENCY
vs
EXTERNAL CAPACITANCE

$V_{CC} = 5$ V
$V_{I(freq)} = V_{I(rng)} = 2$ V
$T_A = 25°C$

(b)

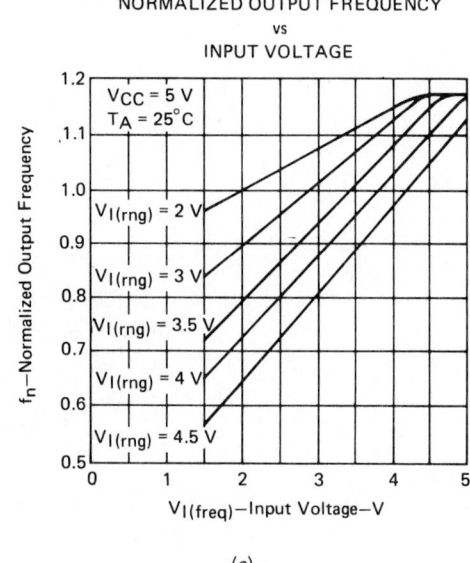

NORMALIZED OUTPUT FREQUENCY
vs
INPUT VOLTAGE

$V_{CC} = 5$ V
$T_A = 25°C$

(c)

We now configure the 555 as shown in Figure 16.27(b), with the external charging circuit driven by an input voltage, V_i, through an op-amp circuit, such as shown in Figure 16.27(c). The internal voltage dividers are driven by a fixed-reference voltage, V_{REF}. If we vary the voltage over a small region, the output frequency will change as a function of this voltage. The result is a simplified VCO with limitations of linearity and frequency range. These limitations cause us to consider a more sophisticated circuit.

Figure 16.28 shows the pin-out diagram and the typical characteristic curves for the 74LS124 dual voltage-controlled oscillator. This IC features two independent voltage-controlled oscillators in a single package. The output frequency of each VCO is established by a single external component, either a capacitor or a crystal, in combination with two voltage-sensitive inputs. One of the inputs controls the frequency range and the other controls the actual frequency. The relationship of these inputs to output frequency is shown in the curves of Figure 16.28. The curve of Figure 16.28(b) shows the center frequency as a function of the capacitance. The curves of Figure 16.28(c) show the range of output frequency, expressed as a multiple of the center frequency, as the input voltage varies. There are a number of parametric curves on this graph. Each represents a different voltage on the range input. These stable oscillators can be set to operate at any frequency between about 0.12 Hz and 85 MHz. They can operate from a single 5 V supply. However, one set of supply voltage and ground pins (V_{CC} and GND) is provided for the enable, synchronization-gating, and + output sections, and a separate set (OSC V_{CC} and OSC GND) is provided for the oscillator and associated frequency-control circuits. This is done so that effective isolation can be accomplished in the system.

Example 16.4

Use the 74S124 VCO to convert the voltage output of a temperature-sensitive bridge circuit to a frequency that is proportional to temperature. The center frequency should be 5 kHz. The temperature sensor provides the following outputs:

With 110° F, the output is 4 V.

With 90° F, the output is 2 V.

SOLUTION   The design consists of the 74S124 chip with appropriate voltage inputs. We first set the center frequency using the frequency curves of Figure 16.28(b). To achieve a frequency of 5 kHz, the capacitance is approximately 10^{-7} F, or 0.1 μF.

We must next decide what voltage value to use for the RANGE input. The second set of curves in Figure 16.28(b) gives the necessary information. The input voltage ranges from 2 V to 4 V, and this is read on the abscissa. We wish to choose a $V_{1(rng)}$ that will allow this voltage variation to cause a symmetrical swing around a normalized output frequency of unity, which corresponds to the center frequency, f_o. For example, if we choose a RANGE voltage of 4 V, the input of 2 V would create an output frequency of $0.72f_o$, where f_o is the center frequency. A voltage of 4 V would create an output frequency of $1.03f_o$. These values are read from the $V_{1(rng)} = 4$ V curve in Figure 16.28(c). For an input of 4 V, the curve yields a normalized frequency of 1.13, so the output frequency is 1.13 × 5 kHz, or 5.65 kHz. For an input of 2 V, the curve yields a normalized frequency of 0.9, so the output frequency would be 0.9 × 5 kHz, or 4.5 kHz. To achieve a more symmetrical frequency swing, we choose a range voltage that is slightly greater than 3 V.

This is a poor choice of range voltage for this particular input voltage variation since the frequencies are not symmetrical around f_o. Perhaps a better choice would be a range input of approximately 3 V. The output frequency range is then found from the figure.   ▸┤

We present here a step-by-step procedure to scale the SN74S124 voltage-controlled oscillator. We convert a specific voltage to a frequency that can then be measured using a window, as shown in Figure 16.25. We illustrate the procedure for the specifications of Example 16.4. That is, we wish to display the number 90 when the VCO reads 2 V and display the number 110 when the VCO reads 4 V. It does not matter what the 90 and 110 represent. Breaking the problem solution into steps, we have the following:

1. Decide what the frequency output of the VCO, f_{o1}, is going to be when the input voltage to the VCO is 2 V.

$$f_{o1} = \frac{90}{t_2 - t_1}$$

$t_2 - t_1$ is the window time used later to read the number 90 from counter outputs. The frequency output when the input voltage to the VCO is 4 V, f_{o2}, is given by

$$f_{o2} = \frac{110}{t_2 - t_1}$$

Hence the frequency range of the VCO output is from f_{o1} to f_{o2}. Note that for greater accuracy we might count 900 and 1100 pulses per window instead of 90 and 110 as indicated earlier.

2. Select the base frequency as the average:

$$f_{\text{base}} = \frac{f_{o1} + f_{o2}}{2}$$
$$= \frac{1}{2}\left(\frac{110}{T} + \frac{90}{T}\right)$$

where we define

$$T = t_2 - t_1$$

The effect is to allow a full frequency swing in the range of frequencies to be measured.

3. The external capacitor value is now calculated (or use specifications as in Figure 16.28(b)).

$$C_{\text{ext}} = \frac{5 \times 10^{-4}}{f_{\text{base}}}$$

4. Now that f_{base} and f_o are known, we calculate the normalized frequencies

$$f_{n1} = \frac{f_{o1}}{f_{\text{base}}}$$

$$f_{n2} = \frac{f_{o2}}{f_{\text{base}}}$$

5. With this information, we look at the characteristic curves for the 74S124 and find the input voltages needed to provide the f_n just calculated. Pick a voltage range $(V_{1(\text{rng})})$ that provides the greatest slope for the frequency range.

6. If the voltages corresponding to f_{n1} and f_{n2} are not equal to 2 V and 4 V, we need to use an operational amplifier to perform the necessary conversion. Let us denote the voltages corresponding to f_{n1} and f_{n2} as V_{11} and V_{12}, respectively. The op-amp must accept an input with voltages ranging between 2 V and 4 V and convert this to an output with voltage ranges between V_{11} and V_{12}. The output versus input characteristic is a straight line with slope

$$m = \frac{V_{12} - V_{11}}{4\text{ V} - 2\text{ V}} \tag{16.1}$$

and intercept

$$v_o = 2V_{11} - V_{12} \tag{16.2}$$

7. The op-amp configuration of Figure 16.27(c) can be used to develop an output voltage of

$$v_o = \left(\frac{1}{2} + \frac{R_F}{2R_A}\right)v_i + \left(\frac{1}{2} + \frac{R_F}{2R_A}\right)V_{\text{REF}} \tag{16.3}$$

The first expression in parentheses represents the op-amp gain, or the slope m. We equate terms and let

$$m = \frac{V_{12} - V_{11}}{2\text{ V}} = \frac{1}{2} + \frac{R_F}{2R_A} \tag{16.4}$$

The second term of equation (16.3) is the offset and can be found by equating terms, with the result:

$$2V_{11} - V_{12} = \left(\frac{1}{2} + \frac{R_F}{2R_A}\right)V_{REF} \qquad (16.5)$$

8. Select a value of R_F and solve for V_{REF} and R_A from equations (16.4) and (16.5).
9. Finally, connect the output of the op-amp to the voltage input of the VCO and the design is complete.

16.6   Conversion Between Analog and Digital

In Example 16.4, the VCO is used to develop a digital signal corresponding to a given analog signal. This electronic system is called an *analog-to-digital* (A/D) *converter*. A/D converters (and digital-to-analog converters) are not truly digital devices but rather are a combination of both analog and digital circuits. We include them in this chapter, since they often are important in applying digital circuitry to analog situations.

16.6.1   *Digital-to-Analog (D/A) Converter*

Digital-to-analog (D/A) *converters* change a digital word into an analog voltage or current. Numerous techniques are used to accomplish this. Two methods are presented here.

The magnitude of the D/A output is generally proportional to the current flowing through weighted resistors or inversely proportional to the resistor values. An example of an 8-bit binary D/A converter with a current-to-voltage converter operational amplifier is shown in Figure 16.29. Each of the inputs is weighted according to the input summing resistors so that the proper power of 2 is developed. An 8-bit signal at the input yields an analog output.

Another method is based upon using a CMOS switch to change the resistors in a resistance ladder, as shown in Figure 16.30(a). This method is called a current-switching R-2R ladder and uses a series of deposited silicon chromium resistors. These resistors, of value R or $2R$, are arranged in the ladder of Figure 16.30(a). The digital input code applied to the input of the D/A converter controls the position of the current switches. In this manner, the available ladder current is steered to either i_{OUT1} or i_{OUT2}, as determined by the logic level (either 0 or 1, respectively). The CMOS switches are bilateral so can switch currents of either polarity with only a small voltage drop.

Figure 16.29
D/A converter.

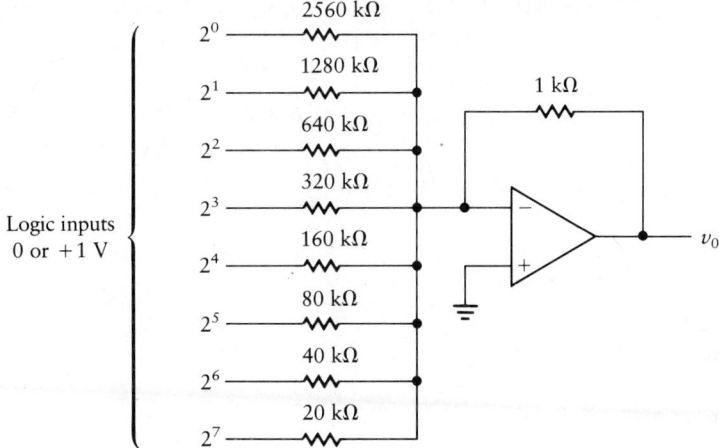

Figure 16.30
DAC0830: 8-bit D/A
converter.
Courtesy of National
Semiconductor Corp.

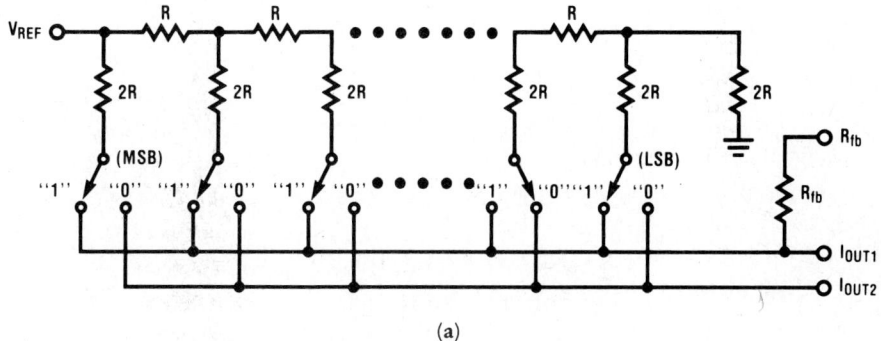

(a)

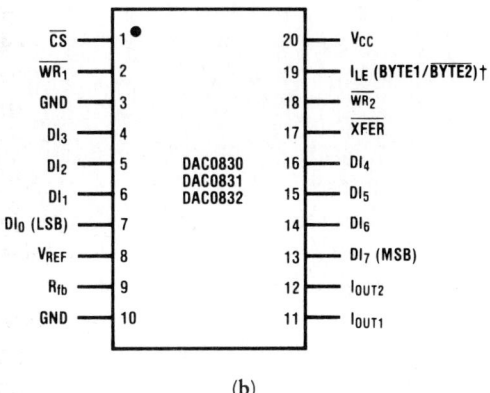

(b)

A pin diagram for the 8-bit D/A converter, the DAC0830, is shown in Figure 16.30(b). With the use of the *R-2R* ladder network, this D/A converter can produce 0.05% of full-scale maximum linearity error. Typical conversion time is 1 μs, and with an 8-bit input, this circuit is capable of generating 256 distinguishable output current levels. The resolution is 8-bit. Additional technical details are given in the manufacturer's data sheets.

16.6.2   *A/D Converter*

A/D converters change an analog voltage level into a corresponding digital word. There are numerous methods of producing an A/D converter. We discuss several in this section. One way of producing such a converter is to increment a counter, which feeds a D/A converter, and to stop the counter when the D/A converter's output exceeds the analog voltage in question. This method is illustrated in Figure 16.31. The D/A converter output is a staircase function. It can be thought of as a series of discrete ramp functions. The number of counts it takes before the ramp crosses the analog value is proportional to that value. The digital output word is the counter output. An 8-bit counter resets and starts from zero for each measurement.

A second method of generating a digital word from an analog voltage is to use successive approximations. If we assign binary numbers to various voltage levels starting with the lowest voltage (all 0s) and counting toward the highest (all 1s), we can use the basic properties of binary sequences to simplify the conversion. The most significant bit in the binary number indicates whether the voltage is in the upper or lower half of the range. The next bit subdivides this range in half, and so on. This is equivalent to the observation that in a binary counter, each bit is oscillating at half the frequency of the previous bit. The conversion is then accomplished by a series of comparisons with the regional dividing points.

A specific example of this type of A/D converter is the ADC0801 IC, which contains a high-input impedance comparator, 256 series resistors and analog switches, control logic, and output latches. Conversion is performed using a successive-approximation technique, where the unknown analog voltage is compared to the voltage at the resistor tie points using analog switches. When the appropriate tie-point voltage matches the unknown voltage, conversion is complete. The digital outputs contain an 8-bit complementary binary word corresponding to the unknown voltage.

16.6.3   *The $3\frac{1}{2}$-digit A/D Converter*

The $3\frac{1}{2}$-*digit A/D converter* is used in digital voltmeters. Incorporated into the design of this digital voltmeter IC is the *dual-slope* method of A/D conversion. We present the ICL7106/7107 CMOS A/D converter as an example. The pin-

Figure 16.31
A/D converter.

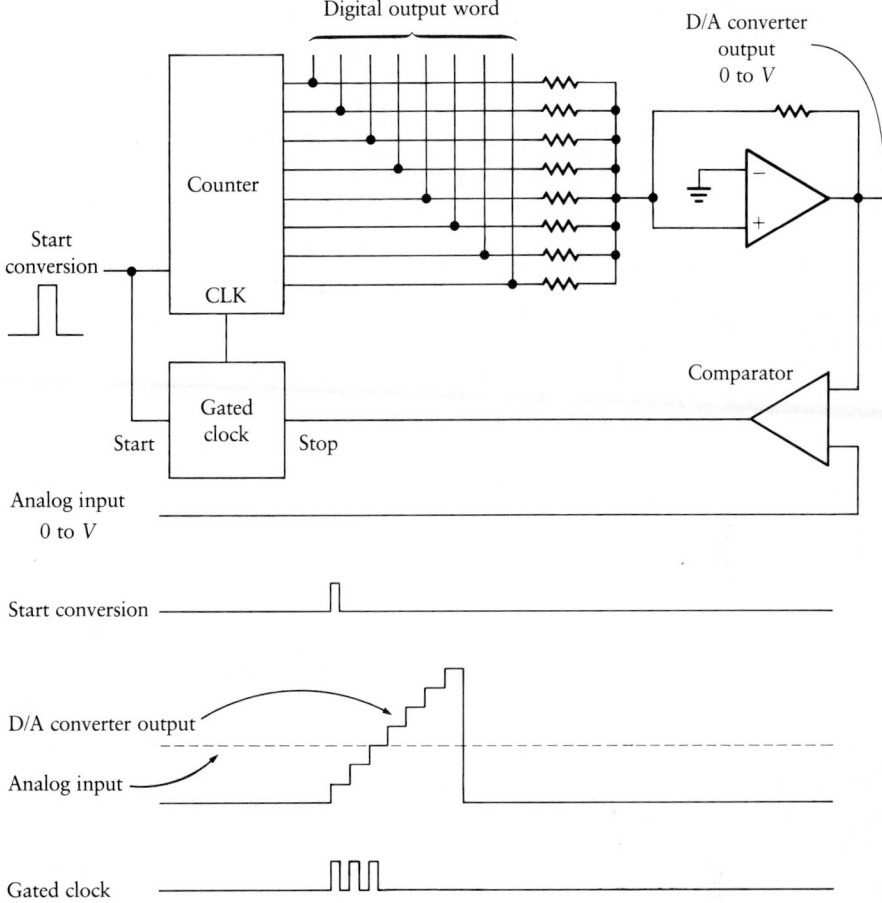

out diagram for this IC is shown in Figure 16.32. The ICL7106 drives a liquid crystal display (LCD) and the ICL7107 drives light emitting diode (LED) display. Included are 7-segment decoders, display drivers, references, and a clock. The IC operates in three phases: (1) auto-zero, (2) signal integrate, and (3) reference integrate. In Phase 1 of the dual-slope conversion, the cycle is zeroed for a new start. This process is known as the auto-zero phase. The block diagram is shown in Figure 16.33(a). In Phase 2 of the dual-slope method, the signal is integrated for a fixed period of time with the slope depending upon the RC combination of the integrating op-amp. In Phase 3, the integrator input is switched from v_i to V_{REF}. The polarity is determined during Phase 2 so that the integrator discharges back toward zero. The number of clock pulses counted between the beginning of this cycle (Phase 3) and the time when the integrator output passes through zero is a digital measure of the magnitude of

Figure 16.32
ICL7106/7107 digital
voltmeter IC.
Courtesy of Intersil Inc.

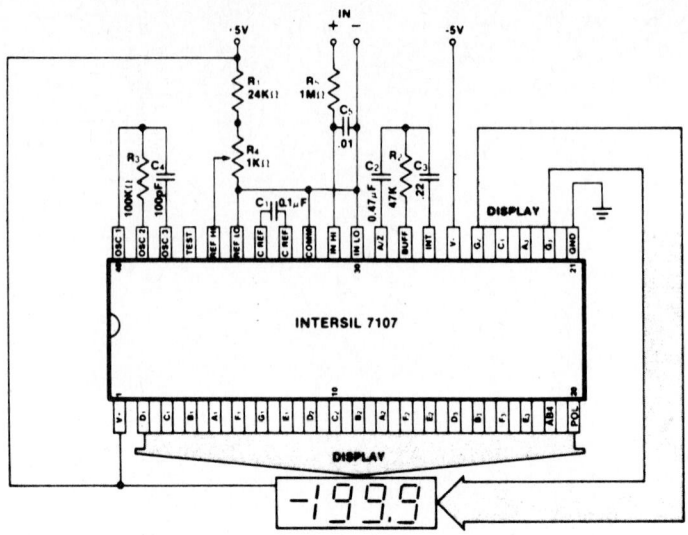

ICL7107 with LED Display

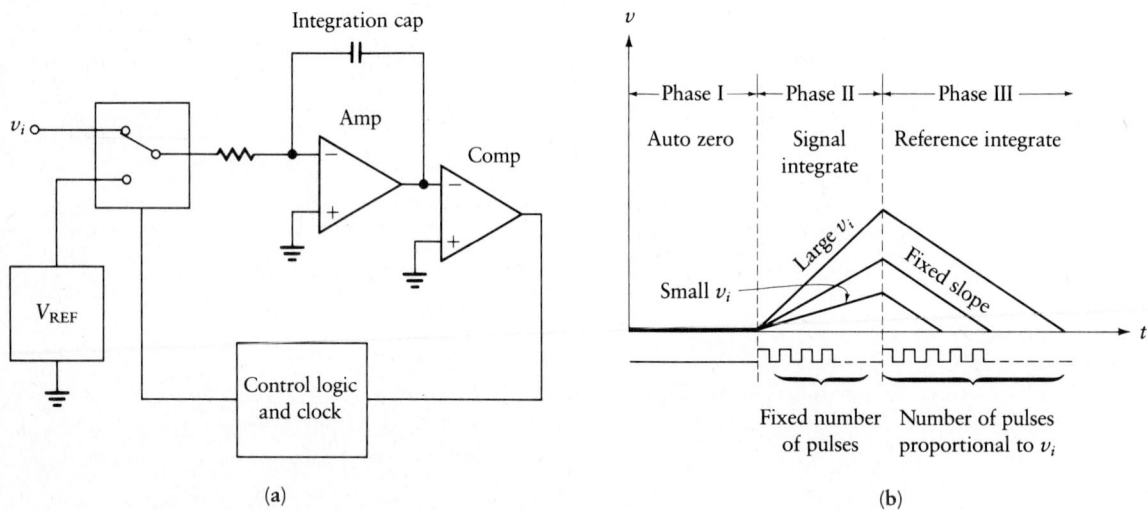

(a)

(b)

Figure 16.33   Phases in dual-slope conversion.

v_i. The conversion technique corresponds to creating a window whose length is proportional to the magnitude of the input voltage. We hence produce a pulse train proportional to the input voltage. This digital measurement is then fed to digital counters, which provide the digital output. The digital control logic synchronizes the display output for each cycle and begins the A/D conversion cycle again. When the analog input voltage is lower, the descending ramp is shorter. A fixed clock signal is generated internally from an external RC combination. The analog voltage is thus converted into a digital number. In the dual-slope comparison method, the accuracy of the system is limited by the number of bits of the counter and by the accuracy of the reference voltages. This A/D converter depends only upon the ratio of v_i to V_{REF}, a constant.

16.6.4 Liquid Crystal Display (LCD)

The *liquid crystal display* (LCD) requires very low power and is ideally suited for battery operated devices, such as digital watches. LCDs are driven by applying a symmetrical square wave to the back plane (BP). To turn on a segment, a waveform 180° out of phase with BP (and of equal amplitude) is applied to that segment. Excessive dc voltages (greater than 50 mV) will permanently damage the display if applied for more than a few minutes.

A schematic diagram for a liquid crystal cell is shown in Figure 16.34. As can be seen in Figure 16.34(b), when the cell is activated, the light is scattered so the display shows black. When the cell is unactivated, the cell shows white.

The segments of the 7-segment LCD display are driven to form the numbers from 0 to 9, as is done for the 7-segment LED display.

Figure 16.34
LCD.

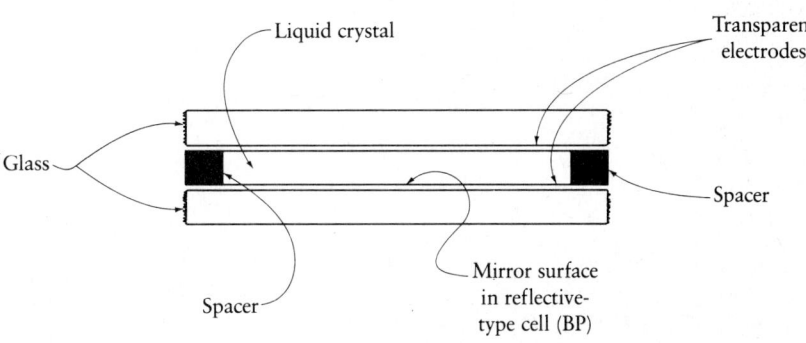

(a)   Construction of LC cell

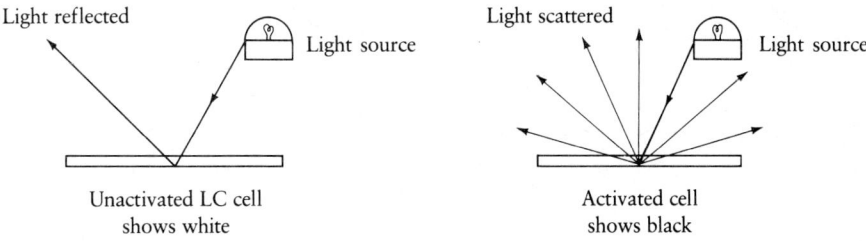

(b)   Operation of LC cell

16.7   Memories

We consider various types of memory devices, which are summarized in the block diagram of Figure 16.35.

16.7.1   *Serial Memories*

Data entered into the storage of serial memory devices are not immediately available for reading. Typically, each stored bit is transferred sequentially through 64 or more storage locations between the time it is written into memory and the time it first becomes available for reading. A shift register is a form of memory, where the data are transferred from cell to cell.

Moving-surface memories are the slowest form of serial memory. The moving magnetic tape player is an example of this type. This form of memory is cheaper than electronic memories because there is no need to define individual physical patterns or structures for each individual storage cell. However, precision mechanical components may be needed to transport the magnetic storage medium, leading to a high initial cost.

Figure 16.35   Memory overview.

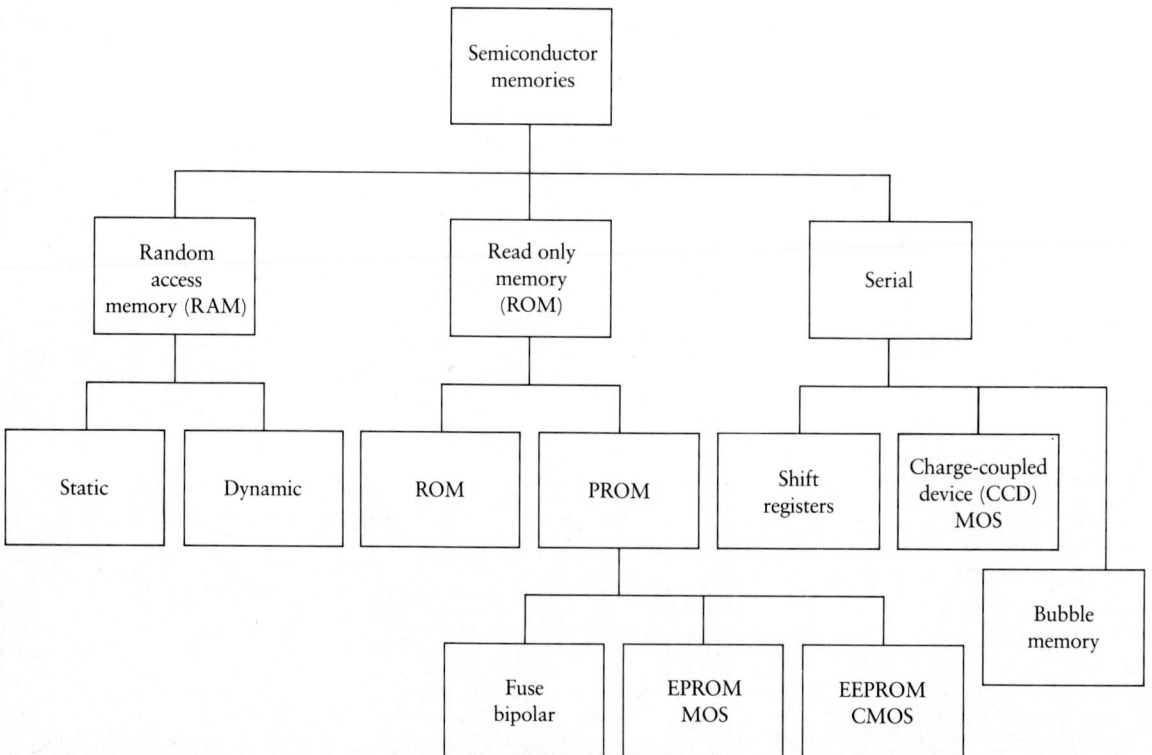

Bubble memories are serial in organization, so access time depends upon the number of storage locations in a serial path and upon the maximum shifting rate. Serial paths range in length from about 10 locations to over 1000 locations. Shifting rates range from a fraction of a microsecond to several microseconds. The most attractive potential application of bubble memories is the replacement of tape and disk memories with a capacity of between 1 million and 10 million bits. A key feature of bubble memories is that stored information is retained even when external power is interrupted.

When selecting a particular memory, it is important to consider the price per bit of storage capacity. Bubble memories are potentially cheaper than semiconductor memories.

Price depends strongly upon access time. In currently available systems, the access time ranges from about 10 ns for bipolar transistor memories to about 10 s or more for magnetic tape memories. The cost per bit varies over a very wide range. For bipolar memories, it is of the order of 1¢ per bit, while for tape, it is only about 10^{-5}¢ per bit. The relationship between price per bit and access time is approximately logarithmic over a wide range of prices per bit. This relationship is shown in Figure 16.36.

Figure 16.36 Access time versus price.

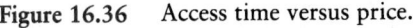

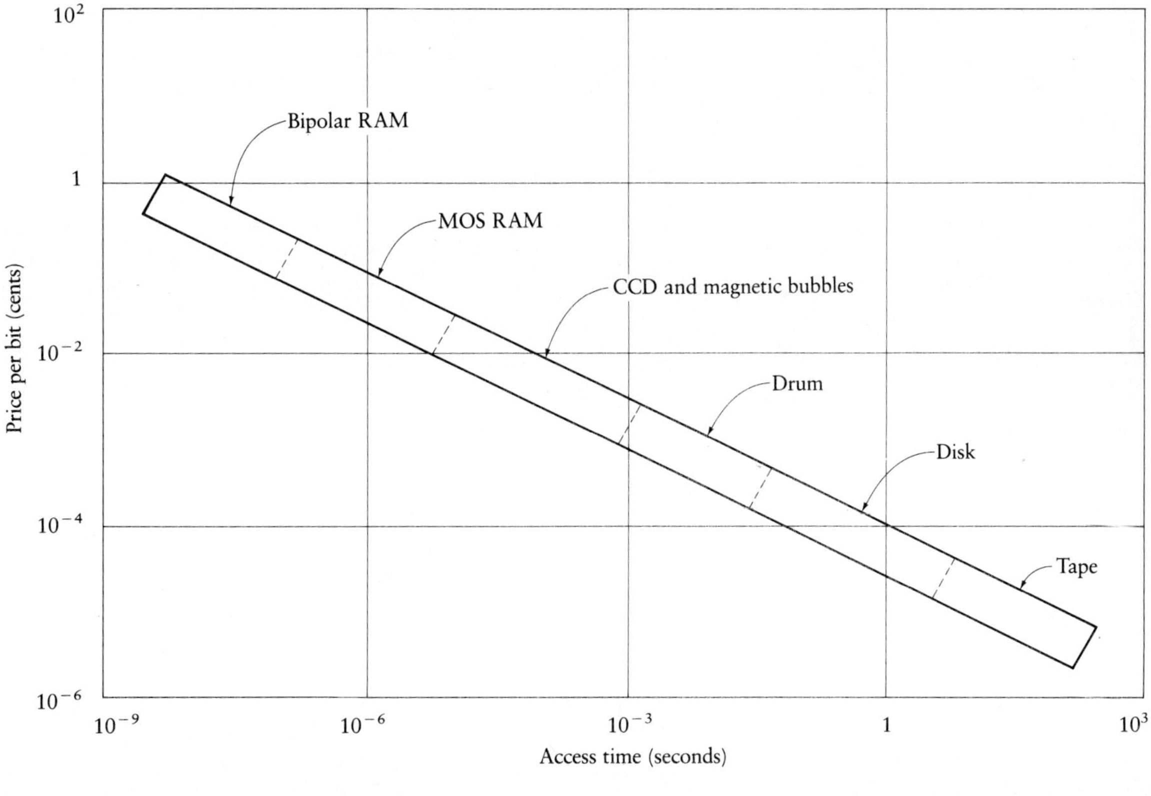

16.7.2   *Random-Access Memory (RAM)*

Dynamic memories store their data in the form of a charge on a small capacitor. A dynamic memory cell cannot store data indefinitely. The capacitor storage cell can lose stored information in two ways. First the capacitor itself has an associated leakage current. Second, when the cell is selected for a read operation, the charge stored is shared between the cell capacitor and the large capacitance of the data line.

For the dynamic memory to retain valid data, the capacitor charge must be periodically restored. This restoration must occur at least once every 2 ms. Rewriting is accomplished internally without the need to reapply the original external data. This rewriting operation is called *refresh*.

Memories that do not require refresh operations are called *static memories*. In spite of their higher cost per bit of storage, they are favored for small memory systems because they require a minimum of external support circuitry. At a further premium in cost, the power consumption of static memories can be significantly reduced. These memories are found in pocket calculators, where small batteries must provide sufficient power for operating over days and weeks.

A static RAM is an array of latches with a common addressing structure for both reading and writing. In the WRITE mode, the information at the data input is written into the latch selected by the ADDRESS. In the READ mode, the content of the selected latch is fed to the data output.

Semiconductor memories have *nondestructive readout*. That is, the memory can be read without destroying the data stored therein. Semiconductor read/write memories are *volatile*. That is, data can be stored only as long as the power is uninterrupted.

Memories are generally identified by specifying the number of words, number of bits per word, and function. For example, a 1024 × 16 RAM is a random-access read/write memory containing 1024 words of 16 bits each.

High density RAM memories are usually organized into arrays of *n* words of 1 bit each. Only one input/output lead is needed in addition to the address leads, thus optimizing lead usage.

Addressing (word selection) in a semiconductor memory consists of two operations. First, a given device or group of devices must be selected; second, a given location in a device or group of devices must be specified. The selection of the device can be done by supplying an input to the CHIP SELECT function of each device. The input is LOW for all but the desired device. The input can be derived from a binary-to-*n* decoder. The binary address of the device is fed in, and only the select output for that device is HIGH.

Figure 16.37 shows the block and connection diagrams for the NMC6164 8192 × 8-bit static RAM. This is a 8192-word by 8-bit random-access read/write memory that uses CMOS technology. The address is specified by a row and a column. Nine of the address bits specify one of 512 possible rows, while 4 address bits are used to specify one of 16 possible columns.

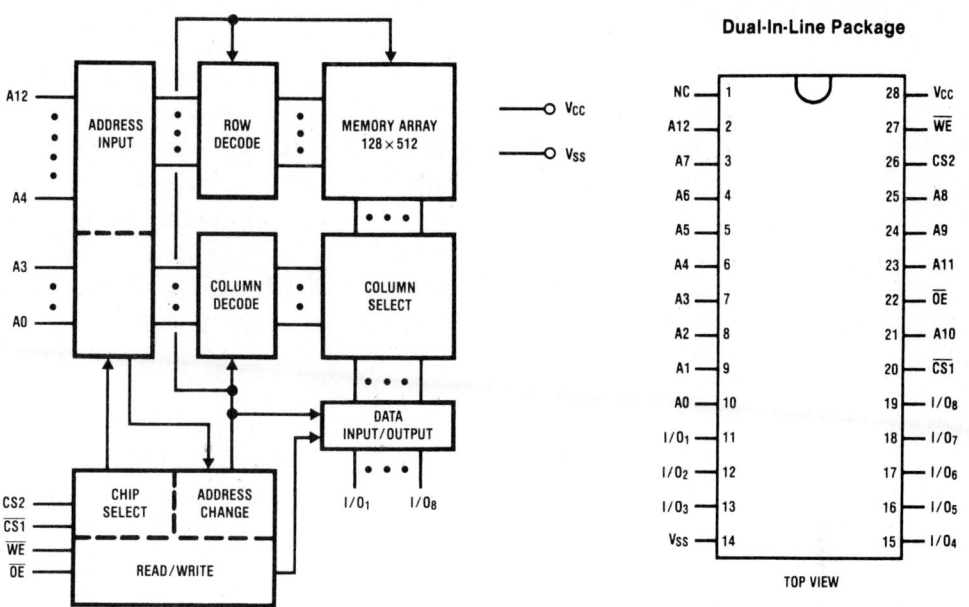

Figure 16.37   74C920 1024-bit static RAM.

The actual 8-bit word is fed into, or read out of pins 11-13 and 15-19. Data can be read when the write enable (WE) and chip select 2 (CS2) inputs are HIGH and $\overline{CS1}$ and $\overline{OE}$ are LOW. Writing into memory occurs with the write enable LOW. This chip has an access time on the order of 100 ns.

16.7.3   *ROMs and PROMs*

A *read-only memory* (ROM) is a random-access memory in which the stored information is fixed and nonvolatile. A semiconductor ROM is a circuit whose stored information is fixed during manufacture, whereas a *programmable ROM* (PROM) is a memory that can be programmed after manufacture. A ROM is best suited for systems produced in large volume. Here the tooling charge for a unique *mask* is relatively small on a per-unit basis and is often counterbalanced by the economies of batch processing. PROMs are the best choice in low-volume production or in systems having limited useful life, in short procurement cycle situations for applications where some degree of system tailoring is required for each installation, and where there is a high probability that the stored information will be changed at some future date.

16.7.4 *EPROMs*

PROMs can be programmed with any desired array of binary numbers. The process of programming is sometimes known as *burning* the PROM, since the programming can be thought of as *burning out* appropriate fuses. Once this process is performed, the PROM can never be reprogrammed, although it is possible to make additional outputs high by burning additional fuses. That is, none of the output 1s can be changed to 0s, but the reverse is possible.

A class of PROMs exists where the programmed data can be cleared and the PROM reprogrammed with new data. *Erasable PROMs* (EPROM) are available with MOS technology. An EPROM allows the programmed information to be erased by exposure to ultraviolet light of the correct intensity and wavelength. Figure 16.38 presents information for a 2048 × 8 EPROM. This 16K PROM is erased by applying an ultraviolet light to the window in the IC. The memory is reprogrammed electrically. The memory is packaged in a 24-pin DIP with a transparent window. This window permits the user to expose the chip to ultraviolet light for the purpose of erasing the bit pattern. The IC uses a single +5-V power supply. The EPROM operates in 5 modes, which are shown in Figure 16.41(b) and are summarized as follows:

1. *READ mode*   Two control functions: chip enable ($\overline{CE}$) and output enable ($\overline{OE}$) are required to gate the addressed data to the output.
2. *STANDBY mode*   When in this mode, the outputs are in a high-impedance state, independent of $\overline{OE}$. In this standby mode, the power dissipation is reduced by 98%.
3. *PROGRAM mode*   After erasure, all bits in the memory are in the logic 1 state. Data are introduced by selectively programming logic 0 into the desired bit locations. To change a 0 to a 1, however, we must use ultraviolet light erasure. The memory is in a programming mode when the V_{PP} power supply is at 25 V and $\overline{OE}$ is at a high input voltage (V_{IH}).
4. *PROGRAM VERIFY mode*   To be certain that the bit pattern is correctly programmed, we can use this mode. We verify the program with $V_{PP} = 25$ V and $\overline{CE}$/PGM and $\overline{OE}$ both at V_{IL}.
5. *PROGRAM INHIBIT mode*   When programming multiple memories in parallel, it is necessary to inhibit the memories that are not being programmed. A low level $\overline{CE}$/PGM input inhibits the other parallel memories from being programmed.

An *electrically erasable PROM* (EEPROM) is useful when we wish to alter stored data. Erasing and programming are accomplished by applying electrical signals to the appropriate inputs of the IC.

Figure 16.38
NMC27C16
(2048 × 8) UV
EPROM.
Courtesy of National
Semiconductor Corp.

Pin Names

A0–A14	Addresses
$\overline{CE}$	Chip Enable
$\overline{OE}$	Output Enable
O_0–O_7	Outputs
$\overline{PGM}$	Program
NC	No Connect

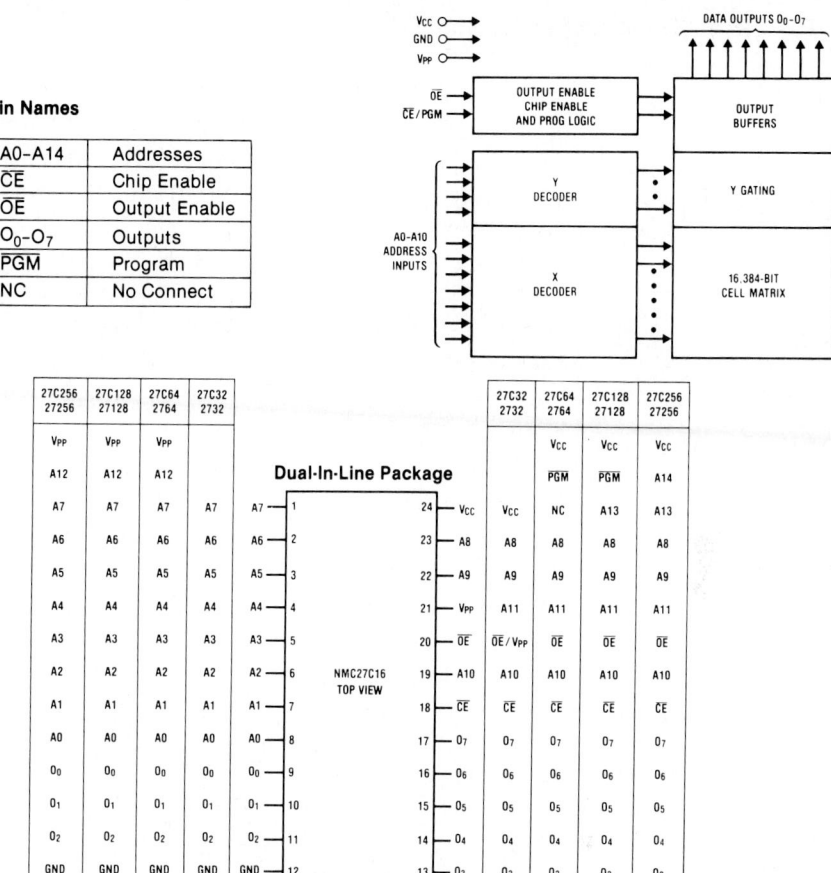

(a) Block and connection diagrams

Pins Mode	$\overline{CE}$/PGM (18)	$\overline{OE}$ (20)	V_{PP} (21)	V_{CC} (24)	Outputs (9–11, 13–17)
Read	V_{IL}	V_{IL}	V_{CC}	5	D_{OUT}
Standby	V_{IH}	Don't Care	V_{CC}	5	Hi-Z
Program	Pulsed V_{IL} to V_{IH}	V_{IH}	25	5	D_{IN}
Program Verify	V_{IL}	V_{IL}	25	5	D_{OUT}
Program Inhibit	V_{IL}	V_{IH}	25	5	Hi-Z

(b) Mode selection

16.8   **More Complex Circuits**

We now study some of the more complex digital ICs. We concentrate upon those that are used to perform mathematical operations.

16.8.1   *Arithmetic Logic Unit (ALU)*

The *arithmetic logic unit (ALU)* performs logic or arithmetic operations. We examine the SN74181 series as a typical example. The pin diagram and function table for these chips are shown in Figure 16.39. The ALU has a complexity of 75 equivalent gates. These circuits perform 16 binary arithmetic operations on two 4-bit words, as shown in the table of Figure 16.39(b). These operations are selected by the four function-select lines (S0, S1, S2, and S3). The 32 possible configurations of the select lines each lead to a form of *addition, subtraction, decrement by one,* and *straight transfer*. These functions are provided in various combinations, with and without carry bits.

In addition to its use as an arithmetic processor, the ALU can also be utilized as a *comparator* by placing it in the subtract mode so one input is subtracted from the other. The IC is then configured to test whether this difference is positive, negative, or zero.

This circuit has been designed to incorporate most of the requirements that a design engineer may desire for arithmetic operations and also to provide 16 possible functions of two Boolean variables without the need for external circuitry. These Boolean functions are shown in Figure 16.39(b). The Boolean logic functions are selected by use of the four function-select inputs, and with the mode-control input (M) at high to disable the internal carry operation. The 16 logic functions include AND, OR, NAND, NOR, and exclusive-OR.

16.8.2   *Full Adders*

A *full adder* is a circuit that forms the arithmetic sum of 3 input bits, as shown in the circuit of Figure 16.40. This circuit has three inputs and two outputs. Two of the input variables, denoted by A_i and B_i, represent the two significant bits to be added. The third input, C_i, represents the carry from the previous lower significant-position addition operation. Two outputs are necessary because the arithmetic sum of three binary digits ranges in value from 0 to 3, thus requiring 2 bits. The two outputs are designated by S (for sum) and C (for carry).

16.8.3   *Look-Ahead Carry Generators*

When two numbers are added together, we assume that the numbers are immediately available for computation at the same time. However, with digital

Figure 16.39
ALU/function
generators.
Courtesy of Texas
Instruments
Incorporated.

SN54181, SN54LS181, SN54S181 . . . J OR W PACKAGE
SN74181 . . . J OR N PACKAGE
SN74LS181, SN74S181 . . . DW, J OR N PACKAGE
(TOP VIEW)

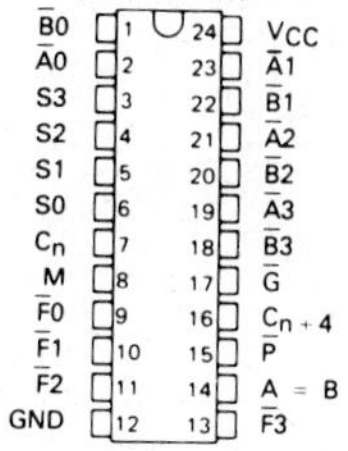

```
        B0  [ 1   24 ]  VCC
        A0  [ 2   23 ]  A1
        S3  [ 3   22 ]  B1
        S2  [ 4   21 ]  A2
        S1  [ 5   20 ]  B2
        S0  [ 6   19 ]  A3
        Cn  [ 7   18 ]  B3
         M  [ 8   17 ]  G
        F0  [ 9   16 ]  Cn+4
        F1  [10   15 ]  P
        F2  [11   14 ]  A = B
       GND  [12   13 ]  F3
```

(a)

| SELECTION | | | | ACTIVE-LOW DATA | | |
| | | | | M = H | M = L; ARITHMETIC OPERATIONS | |
S3	S2	S1	S0	LOGIC FUNCTIONS	C_n = L (no carry)	C_n = H (with carry)
L	L	L	L	F = $\overline{A}$	F = A MINUS 1	F = A
L	L	L	H	F = $\overline{AB}$	F = AB MINUS 1	F = AB
L	L	H	L	F = $\overline{A}$ + B	F = A$\overline{B}$ MINUS 1	F = A$\overline{B}$
L	L	H	H	F = 1	F = MINUS 1 (2's COMP)	F = ZERO
L	H	L	L	F = $\overline{A + B}$	F = A PLUS (A + $\overline{B}$)	F = A PLUS (A + $\overline{B}$) PLUS 1
L	H	L	H	F = $\overline{B}$	F = AB PLUS (A + $\overline{B}$)	F = AB PLUS (A + $\overline{B}$) PLUS 1
L	H	H	L	F = A $\oplus$ B	F = A MINUS B MINUS 1	F = A MINUS B
L	H	H	H	F = A + $\overline{B}$	F = A + $\overline{B}$	F = (A + $\overline{B}$) PLUS 1
H	L	L	L	F = $\overline{A}$B	F = A PLUS (A + B)	F = A PLUS (A + B) PLUS 1
H	L	L	H	F = A $\oplus$ B	F = A PLUS B	F = A PLUS B PLUS 1
H	L	H	L	F = B	F = A$\overline{B}$ PLUS (A + B)	F = A$\overline{B}$ PLUS (A + B) PLUS 1
H	L	H	H	F = A + B	F = (A + B)	F = (A + B) PLUS 1
H	H	L	L	F = 0	F = A	F = A PLUS A PLUS 1
H	H	L	H	F = A$\overline{B}$	F = AB PLUS A	F = AB PLUS A PLUS 1
H	H	H	L	F = AB	F = A$\overline{B}$ PLUS A	F = A$\overline{B}$ PLUS A PLUS 1
H	H	H	H	F = A	F = A	F = A PLUS 1

| SELECTION | | | | ACTIVE-HIGH DATA | | |
| | | | | M = H | M = L; ARITHMETIC OPERATIONS | |
S3	S2	S1	S0	LOGIC FUNCTIONS	$\overline{C}_n$ = H (no carry)	$\overline{C}_n$ = L (with carry)
L	L	L	L	F = $\overline{A}$	F = A	F = A PLUS 1
L	L	L	H	F = $\overline{A + B}$	F = A + B	F = (A + B) PLUS 1
L	L	H	L	F = $\overline{A}$B	F = A + $\overline{B}$	F = (A + $\overline{B}$) PLUS 1
L	L	H	H	F = 0	F = MINUS 1 (2's COMPL)	F = ZERO
L	H	L	L	F = $\overline{AB}$	F = A PLUS A$\overline{B}$	F = A PLUS A$\overline{B}$ PLUS 1
L	H	L	H	F = $\overline{B}$	F = (A + B) PLUS A$\overline{B}$	F = (A + B) PLUS A$\overline{B}$ PLUS 1
L	H	H	L	F = A $\oplus$ B	F = A MINUS B MINUS 1	F = A MINUS B
L	H	H	H	F = A$\overline{B}$	F = A$\overline{B}$ MINUS 1	F = A$\overline{B}$
H	L	L	L	F = $\overline{A}$ + B	F = A PLUS AB	F = A PLUS AB PLUS 1
H	L	L	H	F = A $\oplus$ B	F = A PLUS B	F = A PLUS B PLUS 1
H	L	H	L	F = B	F = (A + $\overline{B}$) PLUS AB	F = (A + $\overline{B}$) PLUS AB PLUS 1
H	L	H	H	F = AB	F = AB MINUS 1	F = AB
H	H	L	L	F = 1	F = A	F = A PLUS A PLUS 1
H	H	L	H	F = A + $\overline{B}$	F = (A + B) PLUS A	F = (A + B) PLUS A PLUS 1
H	H	H	L	F = A + B	F = (A + $\overline{B}$) PLUS A	F = (A + $\overline{B}$) PLUS A PLUS 1
H	H	H	H	F = A	F = A MINUS 1	F = A

(b)

Figure 16.40
Full adder.

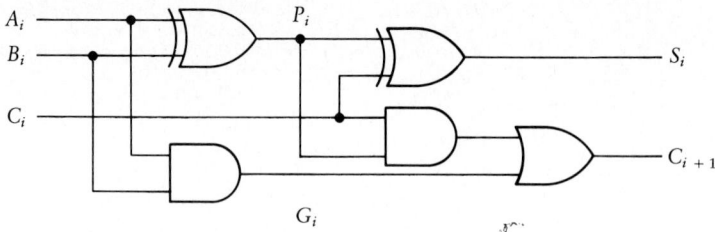

circuits the signals must propagate through gates before the correct level is available at the output terminals. Rather than wait for the signals to propagate through a group of adders, we consider two new variables defined as follows: The *carry generate*, G_i, is defined by

$$G_i = A_i B_i$$

The *carry propagate*, P_i, is defined by

$$P_i = A_i \oplus B_i$$

The sum, S_i, and the carry, C_{i+1}, can be written as

$$S_i = A_i \oplus B_i \oplus C_i = P_i \oplus C_i$$
$$C_{i+1} = G_i + P_i C_i$$

Look-ahead carry generator circuits are used to speed up the operation of a group of adders. The 74S182 look-ahead carry generator IC is illustrated in Figure 16.41. This is a high-speed look-ahead carry generator capable of anticipating a carry across four binary adders or a group of adders. The IC looks across all four individual binary summation operations and generates an overall carry generate, G, and carry propagate, P. That is, rather than wait for the four individual binary operations to be completed before passing information on to the next IC in an arithmetic operation, the IC examines the four individual operations and develops the resulting carry information before the arithmetic is completed.

16.8.4   *Magnitude Comparator*

The comparison of two numbers is an operation that determines if one number is greater than, less than, or equal to the other number. A *magnitude comparator* is a circuit that compares two numbers, A and B, to determine their relative

PIN DESIGNATIONS

ALTERNATIVE	DESIGNATIONS†	PIN NOS.	FUNCTION
$\overline{G}0, \overline{G}1, \overline{G}2, \overline{G}3$	G0, G1, G2, G3	3, 1, 14, 5	CARRY GENERATE INPUTS
$\overline{P}0, \overline{P}1, \overline{P}2, \overline{P}3$	P0, P1, P2, P3	4, 2, 15, 6	CARRY PROPAGATE INPUTS
C_n	$\overline{C}_n$	13	CARRY INPUT
$C_{n+x}, C_{n+y},$ C_{n+z}	$\overline{C}_{n+x}, \overline{C}_{n+y},$ $\overline{C}_{n+z}$	12, 11, 9	CARRY OUTPUTS
$\overline{G}$	Y	10	CARRY GENERATE OUTPUT
$\overline{P}$	X	7	CARRY PROPAGATE OUTPUT
V_{CC}		16	SUPPLY VOLTAGE
GND		8	GROUND

SN54182, SN54S182 . . . J OR W PACKAGE
SN74182 . . . J OR N PACKAGE
SN74S182 . . . D, J OR N PACKAGE
(TOP VIEW)

$\overline{G}1$	1	16	V_{CC}
$\overline{P}1$	2	15	$\overline{P}2$
$\overline{G}0$	3	14	$\overline{G}2$
$\overline{P}0$	4	13	C_n
$\overline{G}3$	5	12	C_{n+x}
$\overline{P}3$	6	11	C_{n+y}
$\overline{P}$	7	10	$\overline{G}$
GND	8	9	C_{n+z}

FUNCTION TABLE FOR $\overline{G}$ OUTPUT

INPUTS							OUTPUT
$\overline{G}3$	$\overline{G}2$	$\overline{G}1$	$\overline{G}0$	$\overline{P}3$	$\overline{P}2$	$\overline{P}1$	$\overline{G}$
L	X	X	X	X	X	X	L
X	L	X	X	L	X	X	L
X	X	L	X	L	L	X	L
X	X	X	L	L	L	L	L
All other combinations							H

FUNCTION TABLE
FOR $\overline{P}$ OUTPUT

INPUTS				OUTPUT
$\overline{P}3$	$\overline{P}2$	$\overline{P}1$	$\overline{P}0$	$\overline{P}$
L	L	L	L	L
All other combinations				H

FUNCTION TABLE
FOR C_{n+x} OUTPUT

INPUTS			OUTPUT
$\overline{G}0$	$\overline{P}0$	C_n	C_{n+x}
L	X	X	H
X	L	H	H
All other combinations			L

FUNCTION TABLE
FOR C_{n+y} OUTPUT

INPUTS					OUTPUT
$\overline{G}1$	$\overline{G}0$	$\overline{P}1$	$\overline{P}0$	C_n	C_{n+y}
L	X	X	X	X	H
X	L	L	X	X	H
X	X	L	L	H	H
All other combinations					L

FUNCTION TABLE FOR C_{n+z} OUTPUT

INPUTS							OUTPUT
$\overline{G}2$	$\overline{G}1$	$\overline{G}0$	$\overline{P}2$	$\overline{P}1$	$\overline{P}0$	C_n	C_{n+z}
L	X	X	X	X	X	X	H
X	L	X	L	X	X	X	H
X	X	L	L	L	X	X	H
X	X	X	L	L	L	H	H
All other combinations							L

Figure 16.41 The 74182 look-ahead carry generator.
Courtesy of Texas Instruments Incorporated.

magnitudes. The outcome of the comparison is specified by three binary variables that indicate whether $A > B$, $A = B$, or $A < B$.

The reduced circuit diagram for the comparator follows a bit-by-bit procedure to compare the two numbers. Suppose we are dealing with two 4-bit numbers, designated $A_3A_2A_1A_0$ and $B_3B_2B_1B_0$. The two numbers are equal if $A_i = B_i$ for all i between 0 and 3. To see if $A > B$, we first examine the most significant bits, A_3 and B_3. If these are unequal (one is 1 and the other is 0), the comparator need look no further. If they are equal, the comparator must look at the next set of bits. The 74LS85 is an example of a magnitude comparator and is illustrated in Figure 16.42. The function table in the figure expands upon this discussion. For example, the first row in the table indicates that

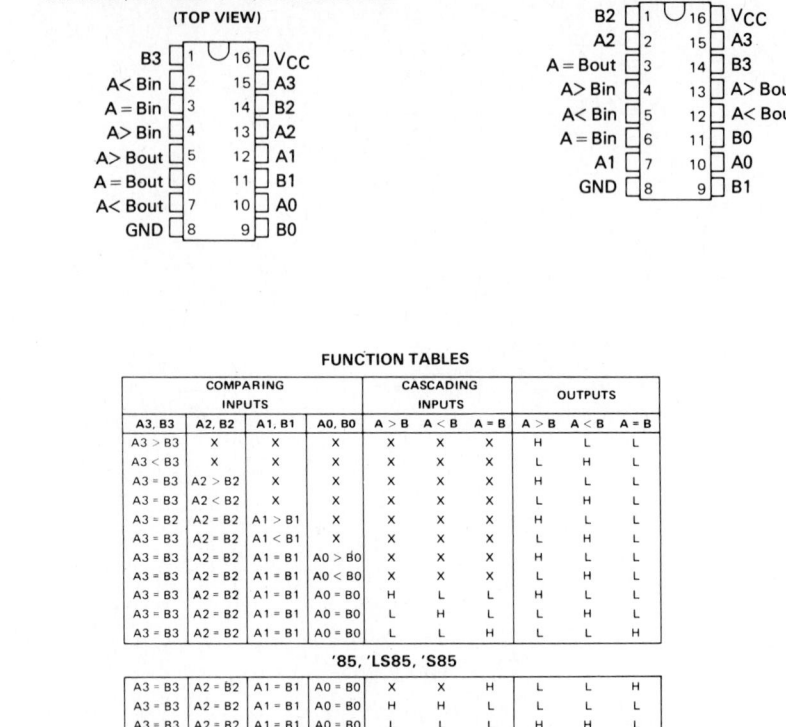

SN5485, SN54LS85, SN54S85 . . . J OR W PACKAGE
SN7485 . . . J OR N PACKAGE
SN74LS85, SN74S85 . . . D, J OR N PACKAGE
(TOP VIEW)

SN54L85 . . . J PACKAGE
(TOP VIEW)

FUNCTION TABLES

COMPARING INPUTS				CASCADING INPUTS			OUTPUTS		
A3, B3	A2, B2	A1, B1	A0, B0	A > B	A < B	A = B	A > B	A < B	A = B
A3 > B3	X	X	X	X	X	X	H	L	L
A3 < B3	X	X	X	X	X	X	L	H	L
A3 = B3	A2 > B2	X	X	X	X	X	H	L	L
A3 = B3	A2 < B2	X	X	X	X	X	L	H	L
A3 = B2	A2 = B2	A1 > B1	X	X	X	X	H	L	L
A3 = B3	A2 = B2	A1 < B1	X	X	X	X	L	H	L
A3 = B3	A2 = B2	A1 = B1	A0 > B0	X	X	X	H	L	L
A3 = B3	A2 = B2	A1 = B1	A0 < B0	X	X	X	L	H	L
A3 = B3	A2 = B2	A1 = B1	A0 = B0	H	L	L	H	L	L
A3 = B3	A2 = B2	A1 = B1	A0 = B0	L	H	L	L	H	L
A3 = B3	A2 = B2	A1 = B1	A0 = B0	L	L	H	L	L	H

'85, 'LS85, 'S85

A3 = B3	A2 = B2	A1 = B1	A0 = B0	X	X	H	L	L	H
A3 = B3	A2 = B2	A1 = B1	A0 = B0	H	H	L	L	L	L
A3 = B3	A2 = B2	A1 = B1	A0 = B0	L	L	L	H	H	L

'L85

A3 = B3	A2 = B2	A1 = B1	A0 = B0	L	H	H	L	H	H
A3 = B3	A2 = B2	A1 = B1	A0 = B0	H	L	H	H	L	H
A3 = B3	A2 = B2	A1 = B1	A0 = B0	H	H	H	H	H	H
A3 = B3	A2 = B2	A1 = B1	A0 = B0	H	H	L	H	H	L
A3 = B3	A2 = B2	A1 = B1	A0 = B0	L	L	L	L	L	L

H = high level, L = low level, X = irrelevant

Figure 16.42   74LS85 4-bit magnitude comparator.
Courtesy of Texas Instruments Incorporated.

that if $A_3 > B_3$, we need look no further. The $A > B$ output goes high, and the other two go low.

If we wish to compare words of length greater than 4 bits, we can cascade these ICs together. For example, for 8-bit comparisons, we cascade two ICs together. The inputs to the second (most significant) IC include the two 4-bit numbers plus the three outputs from the first IC. This is included in the function table. Note that as long as the 4 most significant bits are not the same (the first 8 rows in the table), there is no need even to look at the outputs from the previous IC. Therefore, the cascading inputs are marked as X for don't care, or irrelevant, inputs.

16.9 Programmable Array Logic (PAL)

A basic knowledge of digital engineering combined with the practical material presented so far in this chapter should be sufficient to design digital systems using the basic logic packages. It is not unusual for a design to require several hundred TTL logic circuits. For example, the early video games required about 150 ICs to control a simple simulated sport such as tennis. Although the cost of individual ICs is quite low, these systems become expensive both due to manufacturing costs associated with wiring all the ICs together and also because the large number of circuits requires an unreasonably large amount of space.

As IC technology developed, circuits became smaller and versatility increased until the ultimate goal of full programmability was reached. The microprocessor represents a major breakthrough in versatility and reduction of manufacturing complexity.

There exists a user-programmable array of logic gates that can be used to replace a number of separate packages with a single IC. The array is known as *programmable array logic (PAL)*. It uses Schottky components, so it operates at high speed. With this IC, we can implement registers, flip-flops, and basic logic. The PAL typically is packaged in a single 20-pin DIP and it can be used to replace between 4 and 12 SSI and MSI packages.

The basic logic structure of a PAL includes a programmable AND array that feeds a fixed OR array. The ICs are available in sizes ranging from 10×8 (10 input, 8 output) to 16×2. The wide variety of input/output formats allows the PAL to replace many different-sized blocks of combinational logic with a single package. Additional information can be obtained from manufacturer's data books.

PROBLEMS

16.1 Compare the 4028 and the 7442 decoders.

16.2 Contrast the 74150 TTL and 74C150 CMOS Data Selector/Multiplexer.

16.3 Draw a diagram showing the connection of a CD4511 to drive a 7-segment LED display.

16.4 Design a system to drive four 7-segment LED displays with 74143 drivers.

16.5 Use the circuit of Figure 16.25 to measure the frequency of the ac power line to one decimal point accuracy. Select $(t_2 - t_1)$ to be 10 s and use the 74160 decade counters and three LED displays.

16.6 Use a CD4047 as an astable multivibrator to operate at 50 kHz.

16.7   Design a VCO to operate at a base output frequency of 10 kHz. Use a 74LS124 and calculate the maximum obtainable output frequency variation.

16.8   Design a digital voltmeter using the ICL7106 IC (see Figure 16.32 and the manufacturer's data book) to measure voltages in the following ranges:

10 mV to 100 mV

100 mV to 1 V

1 V to 10 V

Use a voltage-divider network, since the maximum input to a $3\frac{1}{2}$ DVM is 199.9 mV.

16.9   Convert the 7493 binary counter into a decade counter.

16.10 Analyze the circuit of Figure P16.1, where the input voltage, v_i, varies linearly from 2 V to 3 V. Determine the frequency of the output voltage as a function of v_i. Do this by calculating the frequency of the output for the following values of v_i: 2 V, 2.5 V, and 3 V. This circuit exhibits an output frequency that varies with input voltage.

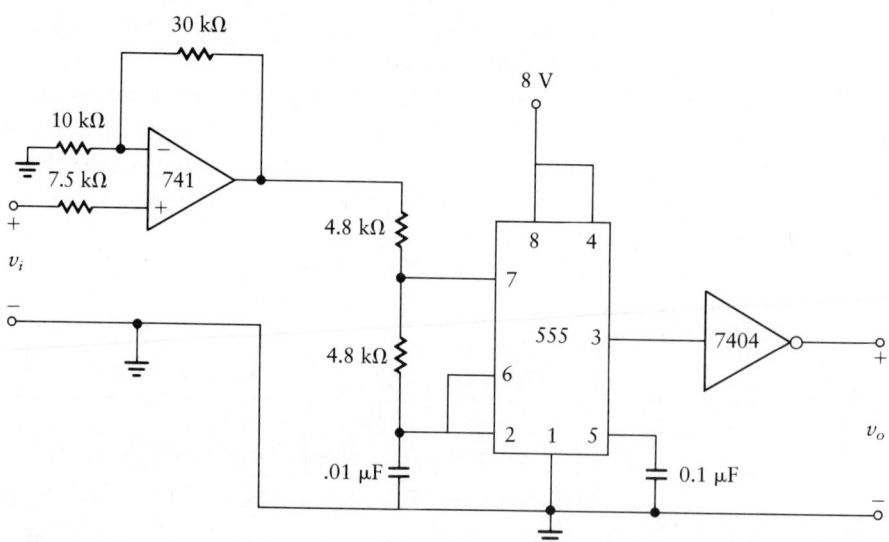

Figure P16.1

16.11 Design an instrument to measure the frequency of a sinusoidal signal over the range of 1.0 kHz to 9.0 kHz. The voltage level of the input signal is 10 V rms. Display the output on two 7-segment LED displays, as shown in Figure P16.2.

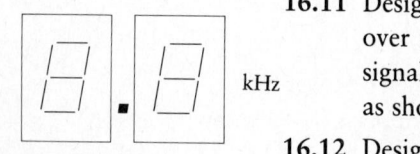
kHz

Figure P16.2

16.12 Design a 0–5 V pulse-train generator to develop the following continuously variable frequency ranges:

100 Hz to 1 kHz

1 kHz to 10 kHz

10 kHz to 100 kHz

Use a *JK* flip-flop to produce an output that is symmetrical—that is, the time high is the same as the time low.

16.13 Design a 1 kHz clock that has a variable duty cycle. One potentiometer should be used to vary the duty cycle from 0.2 to 10. The frequency must not change from 1 kHz. (Note that duty cycle is defined as time high divided by time low.)

16.14 Design a key chain that is equipped with an electronic system to help you locate your keys if they are lost. The device is to emit a 1 kHz tone for 30 s whenever you loudly clap your hands together. Use a duty cycle of 0.5 for the 1 kHz oscillator, and provide 0.25 W into the speaker. The crystal microphone outputs a 300 mV peak-to-peak signal when you clap your hands together within 20 ft of the key chain. Calculate all resistor and capacitor values and specify the type numbers for the ICs used in the design.

16.15 Design an electronic system to measure the total number of revolutions of an engine. This electronic system uses the conditioned pulse train from Problem 14.20 as the input, which is shown in Figure P14.8(b). The output of this electronic system is displayed on four 7-segment LED displays. This display is illustrated in Figure P16.3 and shows total revolutions in 10^6 revolutions. Remember that each pulse corresponds to two revolutions of the engine. Be sure to provide battery power to the critical parts of this system so that the total number of revolutions displayed is not lost during a power failure.

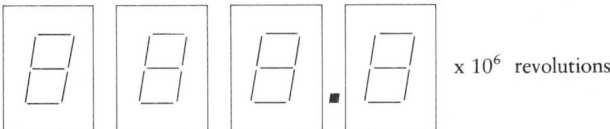

$\times\ 10^6$ revolutions

Figure P16.3

16.16 Design a pair of digital dice that uses the LED pattern shown in Figure P16.4. Each time the dice are electronically rolled, a button is pressed, and the digital dice box displays a random number between 1 and 6, as shown in the figure.

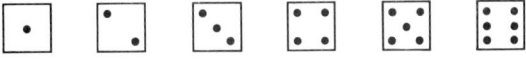

Figure P16.4

16.17 Design an rpm meter to display engine rpm, which ranges in value from 0 to 6000 rpm. The input to this system is the pulse train from Problem 14.20, which is shown in Figure P14.8(b). This conditioned pulse train is TTL compatible and each pulse corresponds to 2 revolutions of the engine. The output is shown on three 7-segment LED displays as shown in Figure P16.5.

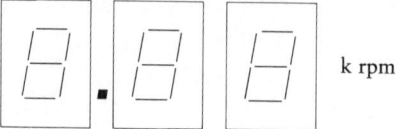
k rpm

Figure P16.5

16.18 Design a system to measure the audience viewing interest in the various TV channels. To sample which channels the audience is viewing, the TV channel selector is instrumented. Eight families are selected to have their TV receivers fitted with potentiometers. The signals from each of the 8 instrumented TV receivers are sent to a central station. The voltage on the lines, in volts, is identical to the channel being viewed. Thus, for example, if channel 4 is being viewed, the voltage is 4 V. If the set is off, the voltage is 0 V.

Each of the 8 TV receivers is continuously sampled for 8 seconds each, and while the receiver is being sampled, one display, which comprises three 7-segment LED displays, reads the TV family, from 0 to 7. The other two LED displays read the channel being viewed.

TV number   Channel viewed

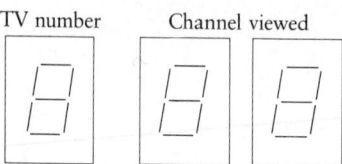

Figure P16.6

17

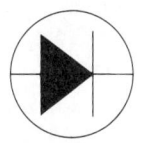

DIGITAL ELECTRONIC DESIGN

17.0 Introduction

In the previous three chapters, we studied the building blocks that make up digital electronic systems. We are now ready to put the pieces together in an orderly and rational fashion to design electronic systems. Problems facing the electronics engineer can involve material from every chapter in this text, including discrete components, linear ICs, and digital ICs. This chapter sets forth the necessary techniques to perform electronic system design. A number of examples are presented throughout the chapter. These require knowledge of the principles of discrete, linear integrated, and digital integrated circuits. Electronic system design, therefore, draws from a good portion of your past knowledge. This makes design extremely challenging—indeed, it has the potential to be discouraging. It is important to keep in mind that good design skills are acquired over a long period of time. You should not expect to be an expert electronic circuit designer having just taken your first course covering this material.

17.1 Principles of Design

The orderly approach to problem solving consists of five major steps. We briefly state the steps here and expand upon the discussion in the following sections.

1. *Define the problem*   State what your product is supposed to accomplish, including any special requirements and specifications.

2. *Subdivide the problem*   To simplify and speed the design process, break the main problem up into several smaller problems. It is difficult for even the most experienced engineer to solve a large, complex problem in one operation.

3. *Create documentation*   The essence of engineering is to generate drawings or plans so that the system can be manufactured and people can make use of it. The best piece of engineering design work is useless unless others are aware of it. It would not be satisfying or profitable if all your work had to be repeated each time the desired result is the same.

4. *Build a prototype*   We like to think that our theory and equations represent good models of real-life behavior. In practice, this is not always the case. Until a prototype is built and tested, you cannot be sure that all contingencies have been considered and that the design specifications have been met.

   Since the prototype is not built until you have some confidence that the "paper" design is complete, a section entitled "Design Checklist" is included. It is suggested that such a checklist be developed just prior to prototype construction.

5. *Finalize the design*   Once the prototype is working to your satisfaction, test it under the conditions in which it will be used. Then, complete any documentation that may be required in addition to the drawings that have already been generated.

This concludes the design cycle. A flowchart of the process is shown in Figure 17.1. Once the design process is complete, the finished documents are sent to the appropriate departments and construction of the product begins. If your job has been done properly, you have generated a clear set of plans, instructions, and additional information needed to build, service, and update the design.

Figure 17.1
Design-process
flowchart.

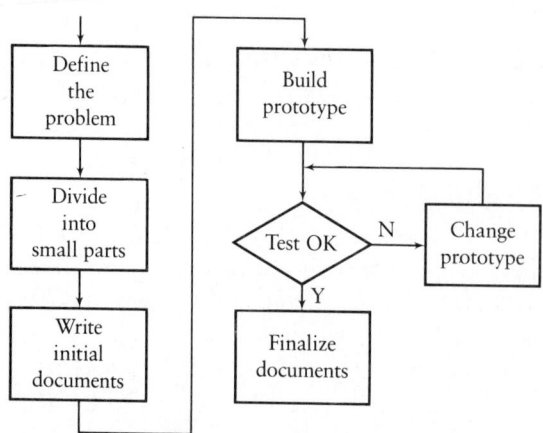

17.2 Problem Definition

The first step in the design process is to *define the problem*. In this stage of the design, the engineer faces one of two possibilities. A fully specified design may be available or the design may be a vague idea in the mind of a customer. The engineer will often be faced with a combination of these two, where part of the design must perform certain precise functions and the other part of the design is in the form of a hazy sketch.

In the case of the fully specified design, the engineer's job is to analyze and understand the specifications given by the customer. After reviewing the requirements, the engineer will often meet with the customer to make sure that they both understand and agree on what the product is supposed to do. It is now the engineer's task to design a product that will meet the specifications. If a product does not measure up to these requirements, the manufacturer will be forced to modify the design in order to make the product meet the standards or face loss of money, reputation, and time. The consequences of this course of action upon the design engineer are open to speculation. It is, at best, an unpleasant situation.

In cases where the design is not fully specified, the customer may have only a general idea of what the product should accomplish. It is then the job of the engineer to define the product for the customer. This will usually require that the engineer and customer work together until both sides have agreed upon the product definition. Once again, the engineer must exercise care in determining special customer requirements. If the product fails to perform to expectations, the customer may decide to take the business elsewhere.

17.3 Subdividing the Problem

Once the product has been defined and specified, the problem is usually broken up into a series of smaller designs. The number of smaller designs depends upon the complexity of the product.

As an example, consider the design of an electronically controlled toaster. One design group could be working on the toaster mechanism while another group works on the electronic control portion. In this case, the product design is broken into two parts. Even with such a simple example, there are many other ways to divide the problem. It is the project engineer's job to divide the problem into the best subsets so that the design can be rapidly and inexpensively implemented. Frequently, an engineering department is divided into groups that specialize in the various disciplines—for example, power supply, electronic circuits, and control electronics.

17.4   Documentation

A primary responsibility of an engineer is to tell someone else how to build, service, use, and update the product that has been designed. This information *must be written* so it will not be lost. We use many terms and symbols in specifying electronic hardware design. In order to put these words and symbols on paper, engineers were forced to create their own language. Like any living language, the language of electronics has certain standard symbols that everyone understands and other symbols that have come to mean something else for a certain group of users.

The language of electronics can be subdivided into three parts. The first is the set of universally recognized symbols and words—those that are used and accepted by a majority of the industry. Some of these words include the symbols for resistors and capacitors used in drawing schematics. Also included are universal measurements such as the ohm, volt, and henry. The engineer can use these symbols to communicate with others about electronics even if the readers do not speak the same conversational language.

The second part of the language consists of the symbol and word set that is recognized by most but is not standardized. For example, there are several different symbols used for the field-effect transistor (FET), all of which mean the same thing but look different from each other. This subset will be recognized and the meaning understood, but the people involved will continue to use their own symbols and words until the symbol becomes obsolete or nonstandard. Many "jargon" words such as *bus* and *interface* can be used in several ways and mean various things to different people.

The final portion of this language is composed of the special forms that each separate business uses to communicate internally. Many of these forms are specialized for use only by the company in question. Others are semistandard forms that are variants on industry standards. Every time a designer moves to a new company, a new dialect must be learned so that documents can be generated in acceptable form. Examples of these forms include schedules, requisitions, and product-change requests—information that the company must know but outsiders need not know.

17.4.1   *The Schematic Diagram*

The *schematic,* or *circuit, diagram* is a plan of an electronic device that is drawn using standard and nonstandard symbols. This diagram shows the interconnections and components used to build the circuit. A schematic usually shows only the electrical connections needed to build a circuit and not the physical layout and construction of the circuit.

The schematic is one of the most important documents that an engineer must draw. Most of the other documents needed for production and servicing are derived from the schematic drawing.

In order to draw a clear and understandable schematic, it is usually desirable first to draw individual schematics for each of the blocks in a subdivided system. The complete schematic is then drawn by using the smaller ones and combining them in appropriate ways.

The master schematic is arranged to put related modules next to each other so that the interconnecting signal lines traverse the shortest path. The master schematic is drawn so that each of the modules occupies a separate part of the plan. As a rule of good design, modules should be shown as a whole and not scattered over the drawing. Related stages that have inputs and outputs in common should be drawn next to each other.

17.4.2 *The Parts List*

Anyone who has ever used a list for grocery shopping understands the concept behind the parts list. This is a compendium of all of the parts needed to construct the product. This list is often subdivided into modules so that it is easier to read. Components of the same type are listed together for ease of reference. Parts lists are used by both engineers and management for purposes of cost evaluation and as a checklist for building the prototype. There is no standard way in which to make a parts list, since each manufacturer has its own ideas on what should be included. A sample list with some of the possibilities is shown in Figure 17.2.

17.4.3 *Running Lists and Other Documentation*

In addition to the schematic and the parts list, other lists are used at the prototype-production stages. These lists are assigned various names and can be arranged in several different ways. The purposes of these lists are to keep track of wiring, maintain a list of signals, and to ease the construction of the prototype. Typical lists, including running, wrapping, signal and wiring lists, are illustrated in Figure 17.3. These lists, in combination with the parts lists and the assembly drawings, are used by engineers to build and test the prototype and generate the paperwork that the production department needs in order to build the unit.

17.4.4 *Using Documents*

There are different types of documents and paperwork used throughout the engineering profession. Many of these documents are for company use in accounting, advertising, or management. We have covered a few types of doc-

Figure 17.2
Sample parts list.

Schematic symbol	Value in appropriate units	Additional descriptive information	Manufacturer's or in house part number	Quantity required
R_1, R_2	10 k 1/4 w	carbon film 5%	R10353	2
R_3	12 k 1/4 w	carbon composition 10%	R123102	1
C_1	0.01 μF	50 V disc ceramic	C18201	1

In addition, the following may also be listed:

1. Alternate parts
2. Parts manufacturer
3. Serial numbers if applicable
4. Other information deemed necessary by the engineering, marketing, and production departments.

Each parts list should also be identified as follows:

	Product name and number	Date issued	Which changes
XYZ	motor gauge parts list	Issued 6/5/86	Revision 4
			Page 1 of 4

Quantity	Part	Description	Number
2	R_1, R_2	10 k 1/4 w carbon film 5%	R10353
1	C_1	0.01 μF disc ceramic 50 V	C18201
2	C_2, C_3	0.1 μF disc ceramic 50 V	C17201
1	C_4	10 μF 25 wVdc electrolytic	C15803
1	Q_1	100 μF 15 wVdc electrolytic	C14803

uments used for building and planning a unit. To keep track of what changes have been made to a unit, schematics and lists must be constantly updated and changed. Whenever changes are made to the unit, all the appropriate documents should be changed as soon as possible. Trusting to memory is a sure way to create errors in the documents and to waste time for everyone who must use them in order to test and build the unit.

17.5   Design Checklist

We are almost ready to build and test the prototype. However, since the transition from "paper design" to hardware represents a major step in the design process, we recommend a pause at this point to double-check the previous work.

Signal	Location
CE	10C12, 5B6, 3D2, 2D3, 1D12
D1	10C11, 9C11, 8C11
D2	10C9, 9C9, 8C9
D3	10C8, 9C8, 8C8

OR

Signal	Location	X	Y
CE	10C12	1119	110
CE	5B6	509	90
CE	3D2	330	130
CE	2D3	220	120

Signal name — Location of signal — Chip identifier — Pin number

Grid system used to specify exact pin location

Wire number	Location	X	Y	Location	X	Y	Length	Signal
1	10C12	1119	110	5B6	509	90	Y3	CE
2	3D2	330	130	2D3	220	120	Y3	CE
3	5B6	509	90	3D2	330	130	Y3	CE
4	2D3	220	120	1D12	100	96	Y4	CE

Order in which wires get wrapped

Location for both ends of wire

Wire color and length code

Location	X	Y	Signal	Wire number
10C9	1117	110	X	34 36
10C10	1118	110	Y	58
10C11	1119	110	CE	1

Chip number and pin

Location

Figure 17.3   Running lists.

Some of the problems that may occur include the following: outputs that are inadvertently tied together, which then assume different states, floating IC terminals, ground-loop problems, intercoupling between circuits, and false triggering.

Most engineers who design digital circuitry have a checklist that they run through in their minds while they are designing the circuits. Unfortunately, these lists are usually developed as a result of making design errors. They represent attempts to avoid repeating the same mistake twice.

A short version of a typical checklist might contain the following four steps:

1. *Inputs and outputs*   Make sure that all unused inputs are tied to either an output, a ground, or a power supply. Inputs that are left floating

can assume incorrect levels and "fool" the circuit into thinking that another logic level has been applied. Another input-related item is to check that the number of inputs connected to any one output does not exceed the specifications for the device. If the number is too large, additional buffers must be added so that the circuit can properly feed the load.

2. *Timing problems*   Many troubles occur in circuits when events are expected to happen simultaneously but do not. These problems can be traced back to propagation delays. This causes a chip with several outputs to change state at different times, even though the design calls for the events to happen at the same time. Another problem that can occur is when several inputs require data at the same time and the inputs are delayed by first going through other circuitry. Although compensating time delays can be added, often the only sure way to cure time related problems is to redesign the circuit.

3. *Special requirements*   This category includes any special quirks of the circuit that must be taken into account. For example, certain memory ICs cause spikes to appear on their power inputs. In order that these pulses do not interfere with other devices, the power input pins must be bypassed with a capacitor. In addition, some TTL chips must have their outputs tied to the supply voltage through a resistor for proper operation.

4. *Power requirements*   The designer must make sure that the power supply can deliver the required current and voltage. Additionally, the supply must be adequately filtered and there must be sufficient bypass capacitors on the supply leads. Provision must be made for allowing excessive heat to escape. Some logic families such as TTL and ECL get quite warm when operated at maximum fan-out.

17.6   Prototyping Digital Circuits

While this text is not intended as a guide to circuit construction, a few words on the subject are in order. Engineers, experimenters, and hobbyists require fast, economical means of constructing digital circuits. None of these people need large numbers of their designs constructed. Production methods of building circuits are not usually warranted because of cost and complexity. Mass-produced digital circuits are built using printed circuit boards (often double-sided). These boards are plated and processed at a facility for making printed circuit boards. It is difficult to rectify mistakes on such a board or to make changes if required. When these changes are required, traces are cut and lifted from the board and/or jumper wires are added. To avoid this problem, several methods have been developed that permit easy alteration of circuits.

Figure 17.4
Prototype board.
Courtesy of A P
Products.

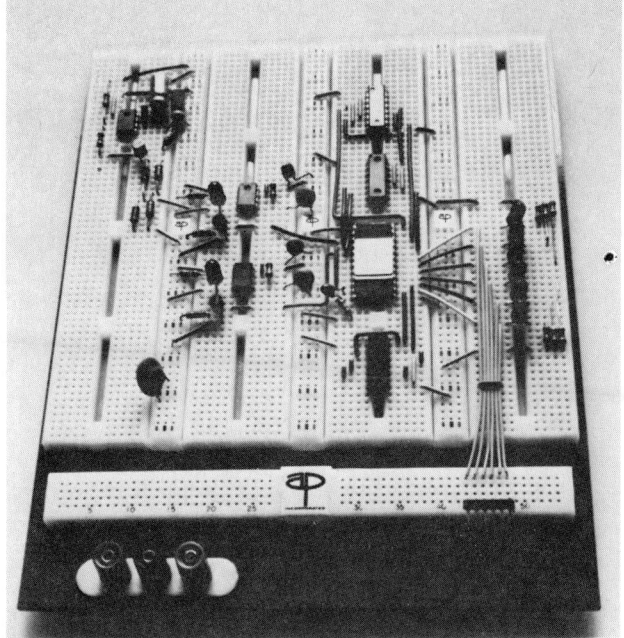

One device that is commonly used for simply circuits goes under a variety of trade names including *Proto-Board* and *Circuit Board*. A representative board is shown in Figure 17.4. It consists of a plastic base with a grid of interconnected holes that can be used to connect components together. These boards are designed to accept standard integrated circuits and component leads so that any element may be used. They are fast to use, and components may be reused. There are some disadvantages associated with using these boards. Because of their layout, they suffer from high interlead capacitance and, after much use, develop intermittent lead contacts.

Another popular method for prototyping and small production runs is *wirewrap*, as illustrated in Figure 17.5. Connections are made using a special tool-and-socket combination that permits fast and reliable circuit interconnections. The special socket consists of a top portion that allows the insertion of an IC, and the bottom portion consists of square posts around which the wire is wrapped. The tool is designed to wrap neat, compact coils around the posts. These wires are run by the assembler from post to post for interconnections within the circuit. Wirewrap boards have several advantages: The connections are secure, circuits are easy to change, and the boards are inexpensive for small production runs. Among their disadvantages are that they are susceptible to noise from other circuits and crosstalk. They can be miswired and they are bulkier than a printed circuit board.

Figure 17.5
Wirewrap.

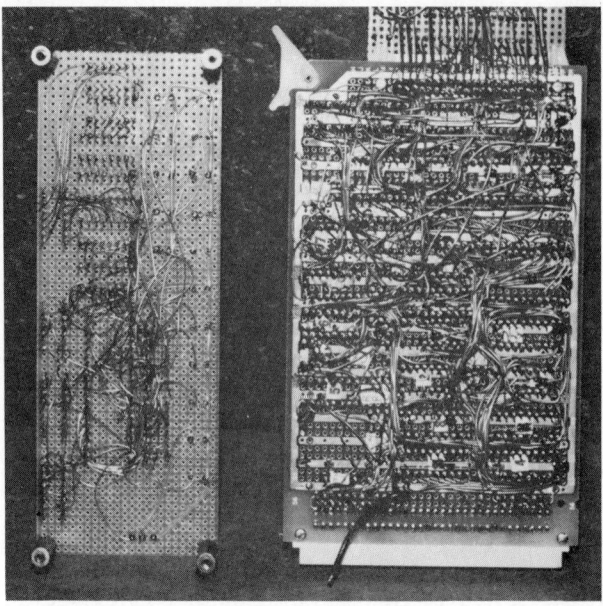

17.7 Design Examples

Although the design process follows a logical progression of specific steps, it is far from being simple. Decades ago, when design engineers were called upon to design power supplies and other well-developed systems, they used various handbooks that contained examples and all the necessary equations. Many of these people were affectionately referred to as "handbook engineers."

The diversity of applications of electronics and the myriad continuing developments in the field have made design much more difficult. Although you now have the necessary skills to perform many designs, you will have to work hard to polish these skills and become a good designer. You should continually study to keep abreast of new developments in electronics.

Since design skills are enhanced by practice, we present five design examples for your study in this section. Additionally, the problems at the back of this chapter contain many challenging situations to help you further develop your skills.

Example 17.1 | **Digital Tachometer**

The assignment: The XYZ Motor Company has determined that the mechanical tachometers used on their engine test stands have become too expensive. In hopes of finding a cheaper electronic alternative, they contact ABC Engineering Company and tell a salesperson what they want. You are the ABC engineer assigned to this project. Trace the steps in this design process.

SOLUTION You contact the customer to refine the problem accurately and define the desired product. The customer and you then discuss and work out the requirements of the new digital tachometer. You then make a list of specifications for the new digital tachometer. Let us assume the following is a list of functions and specifications.

1. Read out revolutions per minute.
2. Have a range from 200 to 8000 rev/min.
3. Have an accuracy of 1% and read out in tens of revolutions per minute.
4. Use the 60 Hz, 110–120 V power line for power supply and timing.
5. Use a timing transducer that produces one pulse for each revolution.

The problem has been defined and you now understand what the customer wants. This completes the first step in the design cycle.

You now move to subdividing the problem. You study this problem and define a block diagram much like the one shown in Figure 17.6. The problem is broken into five parts. One part consists of the input to the tachometer and the necessary processing required to make this input compatible with the remainder of the circuitry. Since the purpose of this circuit is to count the number of revolutions of an engine, the circuit will need a counting device. The count must last for a specified period of time because the specifications called out by the customer ask for revolutions per minute. Therefore, the circuit will need a clock to keep track of time. The revolutions-per-minute count must be displayed, so a display system is required. From past experience, you know that the displays will not "understand" the raw information output from the counter. A decoder circuit is needed between the displays and the counters.

You have now defined the five portions of the problem and draw a block diagram of the system, showing the interconnections of the separate modules.

Figure 17.6
Block diagram for
Example 17.1.

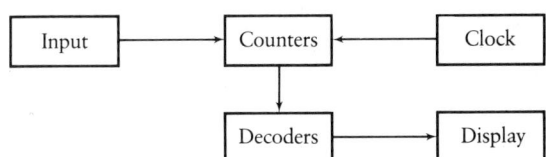

Figure 17.9
Decoder and latch
module.

Latch
enable

three ICs provide 1000 as the most sig
significant digit (LSD).
The decoder module, which is sh
of changing the format of the data
The data that come from the cou
The data lines are constantly
a short period of time during w
data, you place a latch in the d
input data are changing. A 7
The signal must be trans
display can understand. A
the 74LS47, which is des
driver output provides u
no more than 24 mA f
gain.
Before proceeding
single IC that comb
data book shows t
counter, latch, an
15 mA constant-c
16.) The schema
is shown in Fig
You now
d for the
signa
p

Figure 17.7
Input signal.

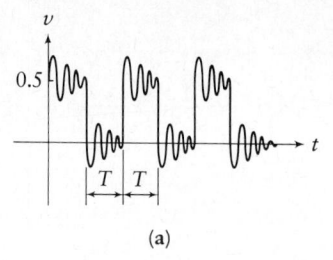

(a)

Figure 17.8
Counter circuit.

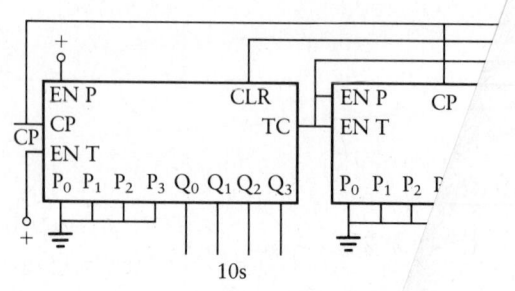

EN P   CLR   EN P   CP
CP   TC   EN T
$\overline{CP}$
EN T
$P_0\ P_1\ P_2\ P_3\ Q_0\ Q_1\ Q_2\ Q_3$ $P_0\ P_1\ P_2$

10s

This completes the second ph...
can now be designed.

The input module is cons...
the engine can generate for ...
from a small transducer m...
Figure 17.7(a), is contami...
must be cleaned up bef...
this "signal conditionin...
circuit exhibits a high...
0s. The output of th...
usable by the rest of...
use the inexpensive...
conditioning, as s...

The next sta...
required to cou...
output this nu...
and reset by ...
input. The d...
a decimal c...
divide-by-...
You selec...

Input   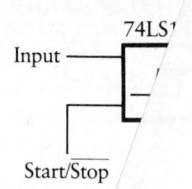   74LS1

Start/Stop

Figure 17.10
Counter/latch, 7-segment LED driver.

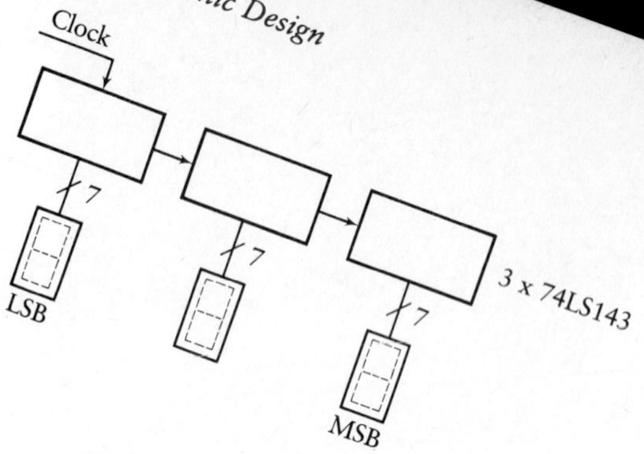

Clock

LSB

7   7   7

3 x 74LS143

MSB

Figure 17.11
Clock circuit.

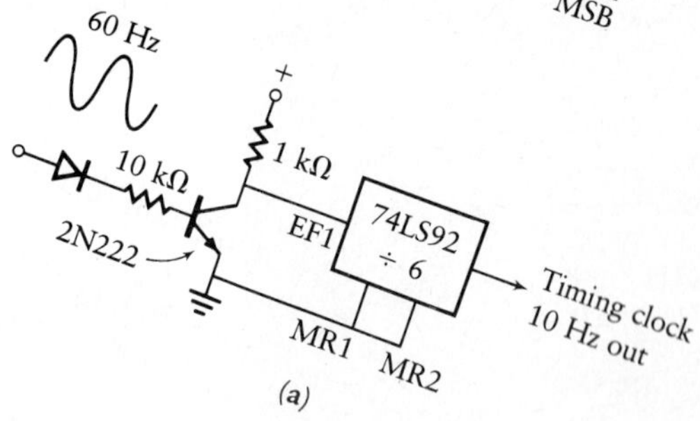

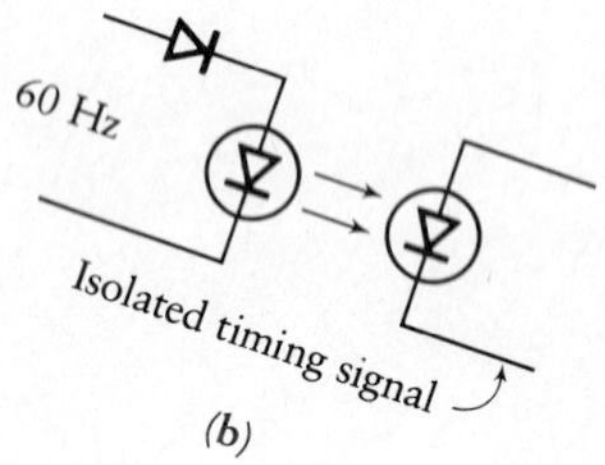

60 Hz

10 kΩ   1 kΩ

2N222   EF1   74LS92   ÷ 6   Timing clock 10 Hz out

MR1   MR2

(a)

60 Hz

Isolated timing signal

(b)

power from the same line. It would be well to provide electrical isolation from the power line. Such a circuit is called an optoisolator and is discussed in Chapters 1 and 3. This circuit combines a light-activated diode (LAD) with an LED to transmit only the 60 Hz signal. These devices commonly operate in the infrared region to eliminate the effects due to room lighting. The circuit is shown in Figure 17.11(b).

Several outputs are required from your timer circuit: a start/stop signal, a timing signal, a reset signal, and a data-ready signal. Since the output must only read tens of revolutions per minute, you decide to make the window pulse last for 0.1 min. During this time, the counting circuit will count the number of pulses entering the system. Since this also corresponds with the time that the timing pulse is on, it can be used as a start/stop signal. Once the counter has stopped, the data must be sent to the decoder circuits. A reversed or invert... start/stop signal is used to control the data latches in the three 74LS143 ... Remember that the 74143 is level-triggered.

You now are ready to turn your attention to the display. It is imp... because the customer will be viewing this part of your design more th... rest of the circuitry. The display must be bright enough to be seen ... variety of lighting conditions, and the numbers must be large enou... read without strain. You decide to use $\frac{3}{4}$-in. 7-segment LED displ... output. This is shown in Figure 17.12.

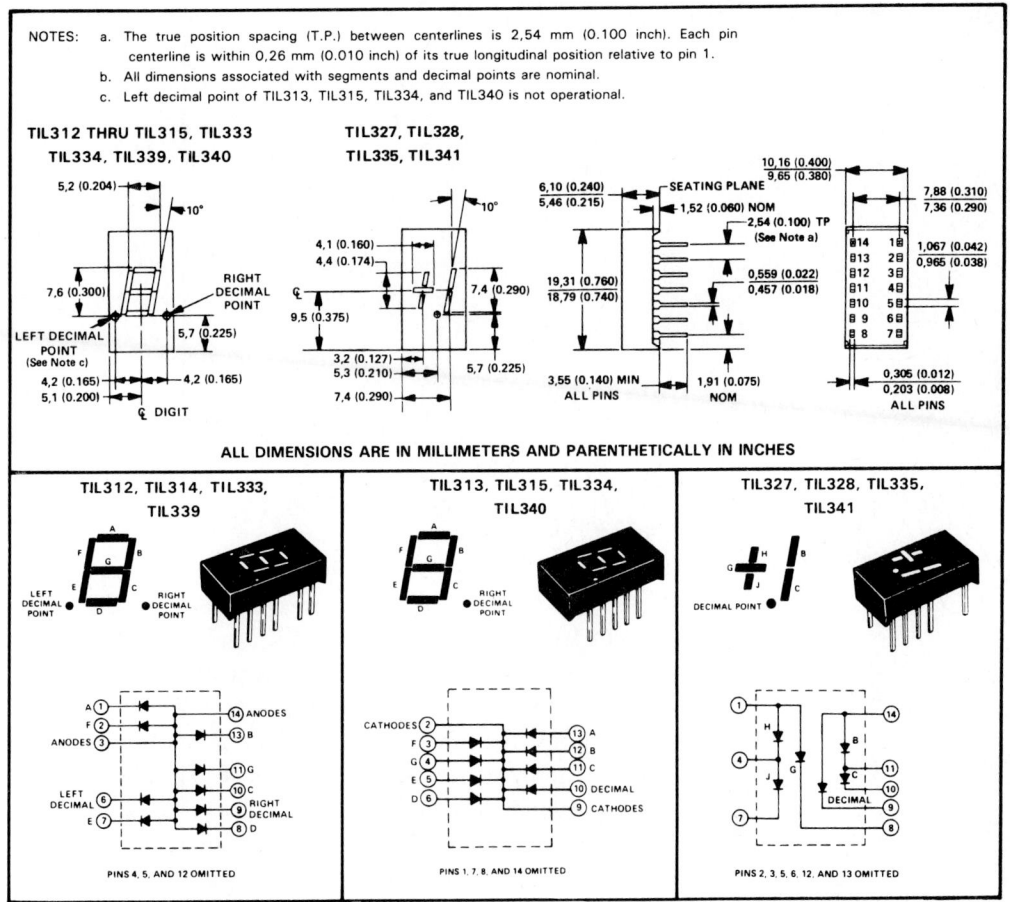

Figure 17.12 Display.
Courtesy of Texas Instruments, Inc.

Now that the system has been defined, you must determine the power requirements. Both the total power and the voltages necessary should be set forth.

With preliminary design of the system finished, the prototype stage is entered. Assuming that the prototype works in the lab and in the field, you would then complete all of the documentation and schematics and send them to other departments in the ABC Engineering Company. You have apparently done a good job!

Example 17.2   Faulty-Lamp Indicator

The assignment: Design a faulty-lamp indicator that monitors 64 lamps at the end of an airport runway. When a lamp is operating, the voltage at that lamp's terminal is 5 V. When the lamp is faulty, the voltage is 0. The output of the indicator must have two 7-segment LEDs, which indicate the number of the lamp being tested (0 to 63). If a fault is detected, a single LED must light to indicate that the lamp at this number position is faulty. Set the timing so that each lamp is tested once for 1 min during each 64-minute cycle. Derive power from the 60 Hz, 110 V line.

SOLUTION   Start with the block diagram shown in Figure 17.13. A 5-V power supply converts 110 V, 60 Hz to 5 V dc, with a maximum current of 750 mA. The unit also provides a 60 Hz clock pulse to a string of counters, which in turn produces a one-pulse-per-minute output. This is done by dividing by 6, 10, 6, and 10, successively.

A divide-by-64 binary counter generates addressing for a 64 input multiplexer (this is four 16-input multiplexers). A pair of BCD decade counters is used to count from 0 to 63 and drive BCD-to-7-segment decoders and LED displays. These indicate the number of the particular runway lamp being tested.

The 64-input multiplexer is comprised of four 16-input multiplexers (addressed simultaneously), whose outputs are combined by being fed to the inputs of a 4-input multiplexer. If the selected input (1 of 64) is low, the multiplexer output is low. This energizes an LED, which signifies that the runway lamp being tested is faulty. The complete schematic diagram is shown in Figure 17.14. The 7805 in the power supply must be able to handle the total current, so this is now checked. The current required by the various ICs is summarized in the accompanying table. These data are obtained from the TTL Data Book.

IC Number	Quantity	Current Required (mA)	Total Current (mA)
7492	2	31	62
7490	2	32	64
74161	2	34	68
74160	2	34	68
7447	2	43	86
74150	4	40	160
74151	1	29	29

Total IC current requirement =   537 mA

Figure 17.13
Block diagram for
Example 17.2.

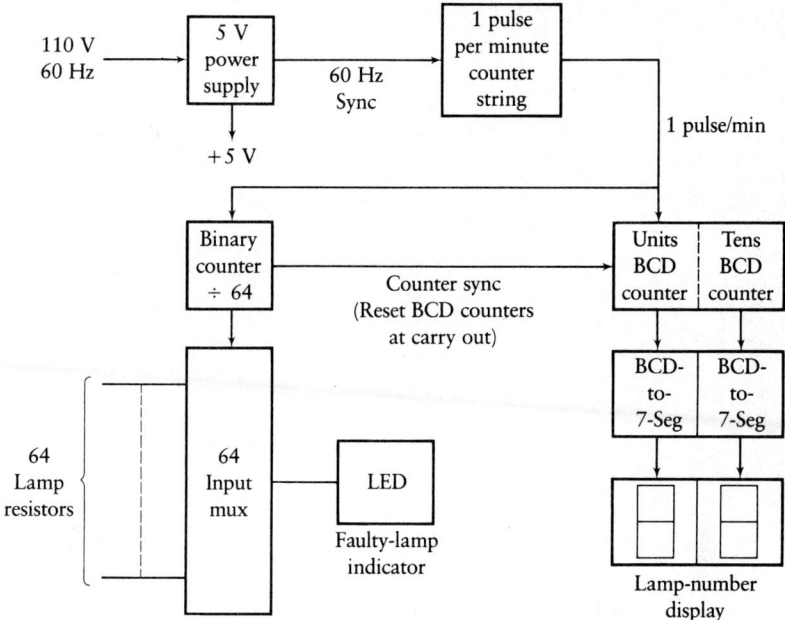

Each segment of the LED requires 10 mA, and a maximum of 12 segments must be lighted (e.g., to display 28, 38, or 58).

The maximum display current is	120
The faulty lamp LED requires	10
The 2N2222 transistor requires	10
The RC differentiator in the BCD reset line requires	2
The total current is then	679 mA

This is within the 750 mA rating of the 7805. The initial design is therefore complete, and the other steps of Section 17.1 must now be followed.

Figure 17.14
Schematic diagram for
Example 17.2.

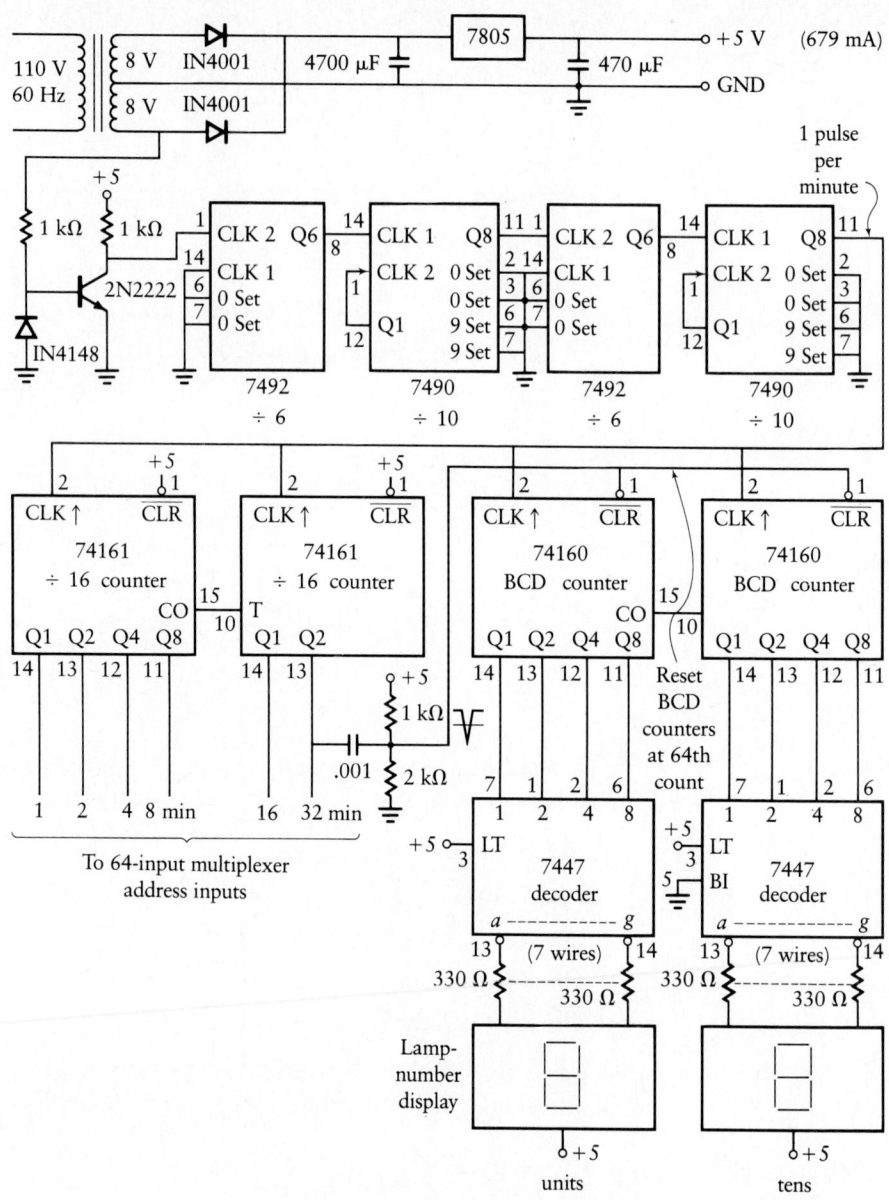

(a)   **Power supply clock, counters and lamp-number display**

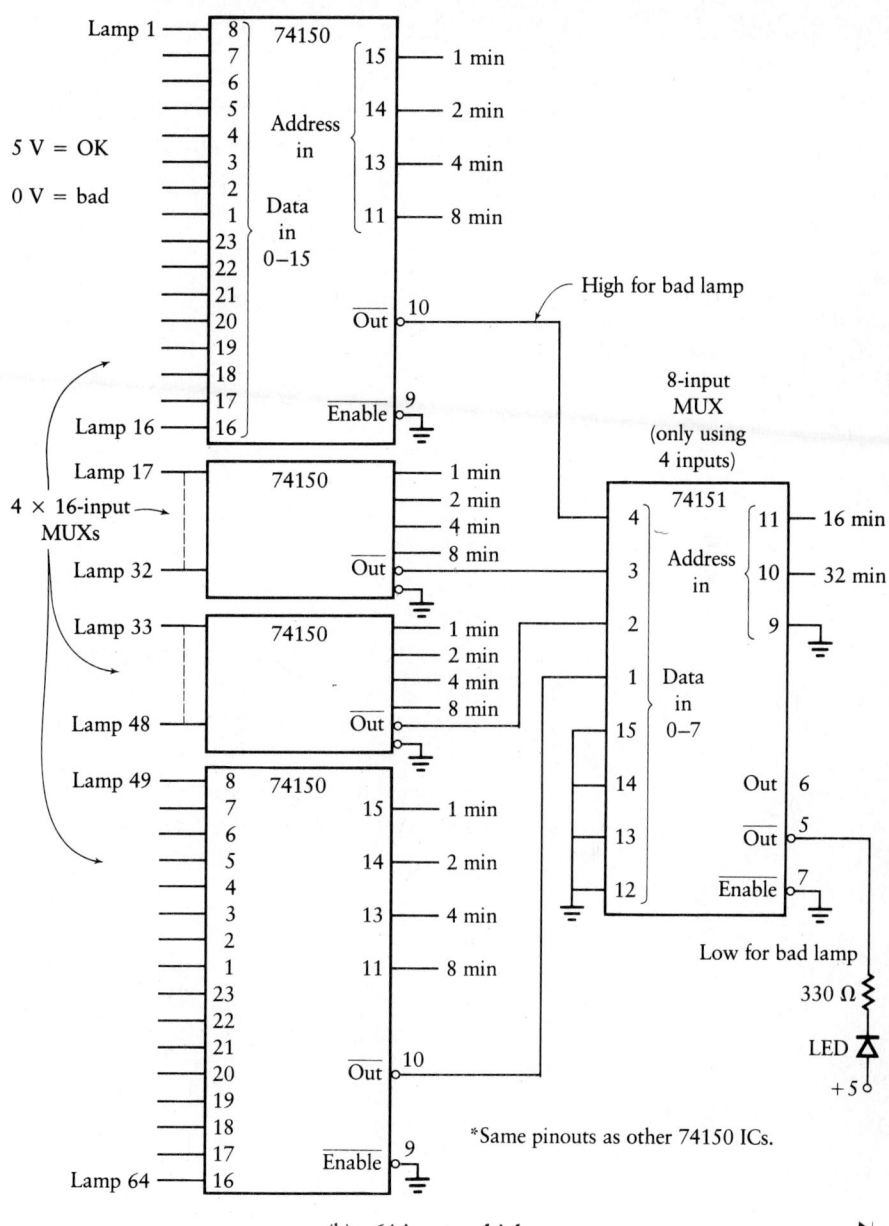

(b) **64-input multiplexer**

Example 17.3   Reactor-Chamber Pressure Detector

The assignment: Design a system to display reactor-chamber pressure. The pressure transducer outputs a 400 Hz signal with peak-to-peak voltage amplitude proportional to gauge pressure according to the equation:

$$\text{amplitude} = \frac{100 \; mV_{p-p}}{100 \; \text{psig}}$$

The pressure transducer has a range of 0 to 1000 psig. The system output is to be displayed on three 7-segment LEDs, which read psig from 0 to 999 psig. Derive power from the 60 Hz, 110 V line.

SOLUTION   The amplitude of the input signal is proportional to pressure, but this signal is amplitude-modulated on a 400 Hz carrier, so it must first be demodulated. We now have a dc voltage that is proportional to pressure. At this point, there are several approaches, including simply feeding this signal into a digital voltmeter ($3\frac{1}{2}$ DVM). After investigating several techniques and comparing costs, we have chosen to feed the voltage into a VCO and then use a counter to measure the output frequency. Since VCOs do not operate well at 0 V input for zero frequency, we decide to shift a 0-mV input to 2 V and a 1000 mV input to 3.4 V.

The block diagram is shown in Figure 17.15. The VCO is set to generate a frequency between 1000 and 1999 Hz. This frequency is counted during a 1-s window, and the count is displayed on the LEDs through a latch. The 1-s period is provided by a 555 timer operating in the astable mode. Only the last three digits are displayed (0–999, omitting the thousands digit). It is necessary to latch the data in the display before clearing the counters. The latch is therefore set approximately 30 ns before the counters are reset by feeding the reset signal through a series of inverters. The schematic diagram is shown in Figure 17.16.

Figure 17.15
Block diagram for Example 17.3.

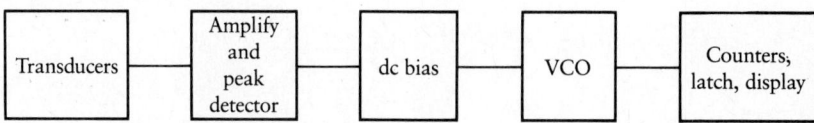

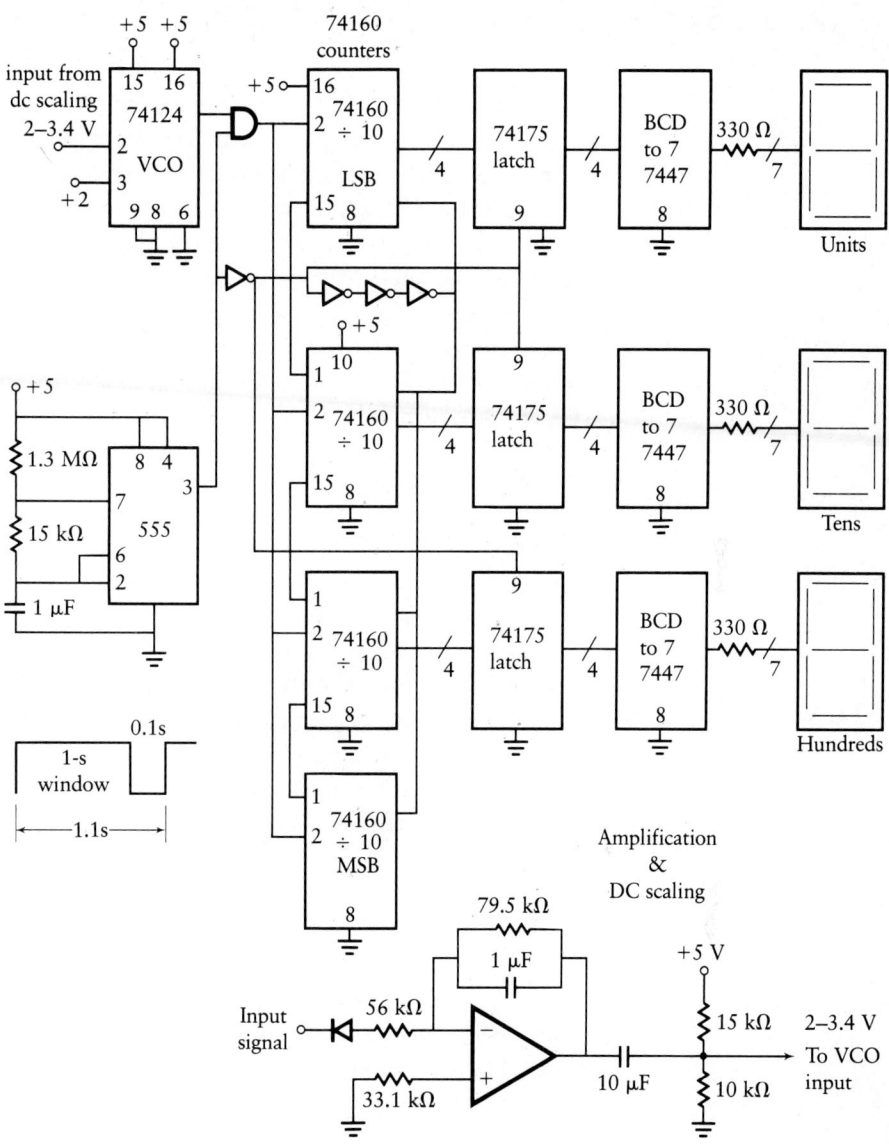

Figure 17.16 Schematic diagram for Example 17.3.

Example 17.4   Warning Speedometer

The assignment: Design a warning speedometer to measure the speed of an automobile. The input to the system is taken from one spark plug. Each pulse from the plug is of $\frac{1}{2}$ V magnitude, and occurs once for each 2 revolutions of the engine. An engine speed of 2500 rev/min results at a speed of 60 mi/h (in high gear). The speed is proportional to the revolutions per minute of the engine assuming that no slippage occurs and that the transmission stays in high gear.

Two outputs are required from the tachometer. These are in the form of a visual display of the speed and an audible tone warning of high speeds.

Three 7-segment LED readouts are to display the speed of the automobile to one decimal point accuracy. An audible tone increases in frequency as the velocity increases above 60 mi/h. The tone is interrupted at a 10 Hz rate. The frequency of the tone is 500 Hz between 60.0 and 69.9 mi/h, 2 kHz between 70.0 and 79.9 mi/h, and 5 kHz for speeds above 80.0 mi/h. We must drive an 8 Ω speaker with ½ W of power.

SOLUTION   A block diagram of one solution is shown in Figure 17.17. The input signal from the spark plug is conditioned to TTL compatibility with an op-amp and Schmitt trigger. Because we have so few input pulses, we must multiply and scale the input pulses. (See Section 17.8 for more information on this technique.) Output pulses are generated at a rate of 288 pulses for each input pulse. At this rate, 6000 pulses per second corresponds to 60 mi/h. Therefore, we need simply divide the number of output pulses per second by 10 to get the speed in mi/h to one decimal point accuracy.

The next step is to count the pulse rate. This is done by producing a window 0.1 s long and counting the number of pulses occurring during the window time. While the window is open, we count the pulses with three decade counters. As soon as the window closes, the count is latched into three 4-bit latches to produce an output to the decoder drivers. Once the count is latched, the counters are cleared and the window can be opened again. In the meantime the latched count is displayed on 3 LED displays. The MSD is sent to three 4-bit magnitude comparators. These comparators compare the MSD to 6, 7, and 8. The outputs of the comparators are used to enable the appropriate warning signal. The schematic diagram is shown in Figure 17.18. A partial parts list is shown in Table 17.1.

Figure 17.17
Block diagram for system of Example 17.4.

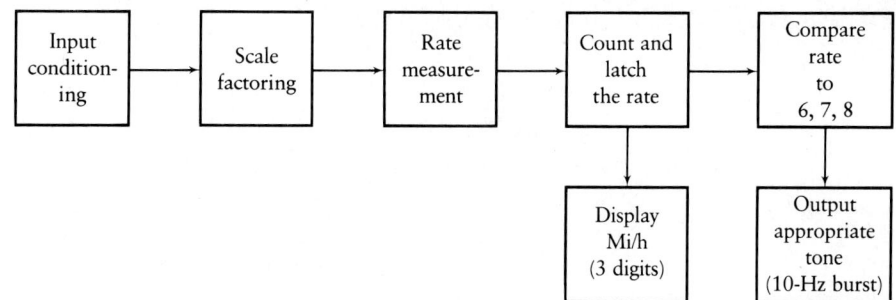

Table 17.1   Partial Parts List for Example 17.4.

Part Number	Description	Quantity
555	Timer	7
7447	BCD-to-7-segment decoder/driver	3
74175	Quad D flip-flop	3
74160	Presettable decade counter	3
7485	4-bit magnitude comparator	3
7492	Divide-by-12 counter	2
7493	4-bit binary counter	1
74132	Quad Schmitt trigger	1
7474	Dual D flip-flop	1
7402	Quad 2-input NOR gate	1
7404	Hex inverter	1
7408	Quad 2-input AND gate	1
7417	Hex driver, noninverting	1
741C	Op-amp	1
40-262	$2\frac{3}{4}$-in. 8-Ω speaker	1
LRT 173	Red LED digital display	3
	Assorted resistors	44
	Assorted capacitors	12

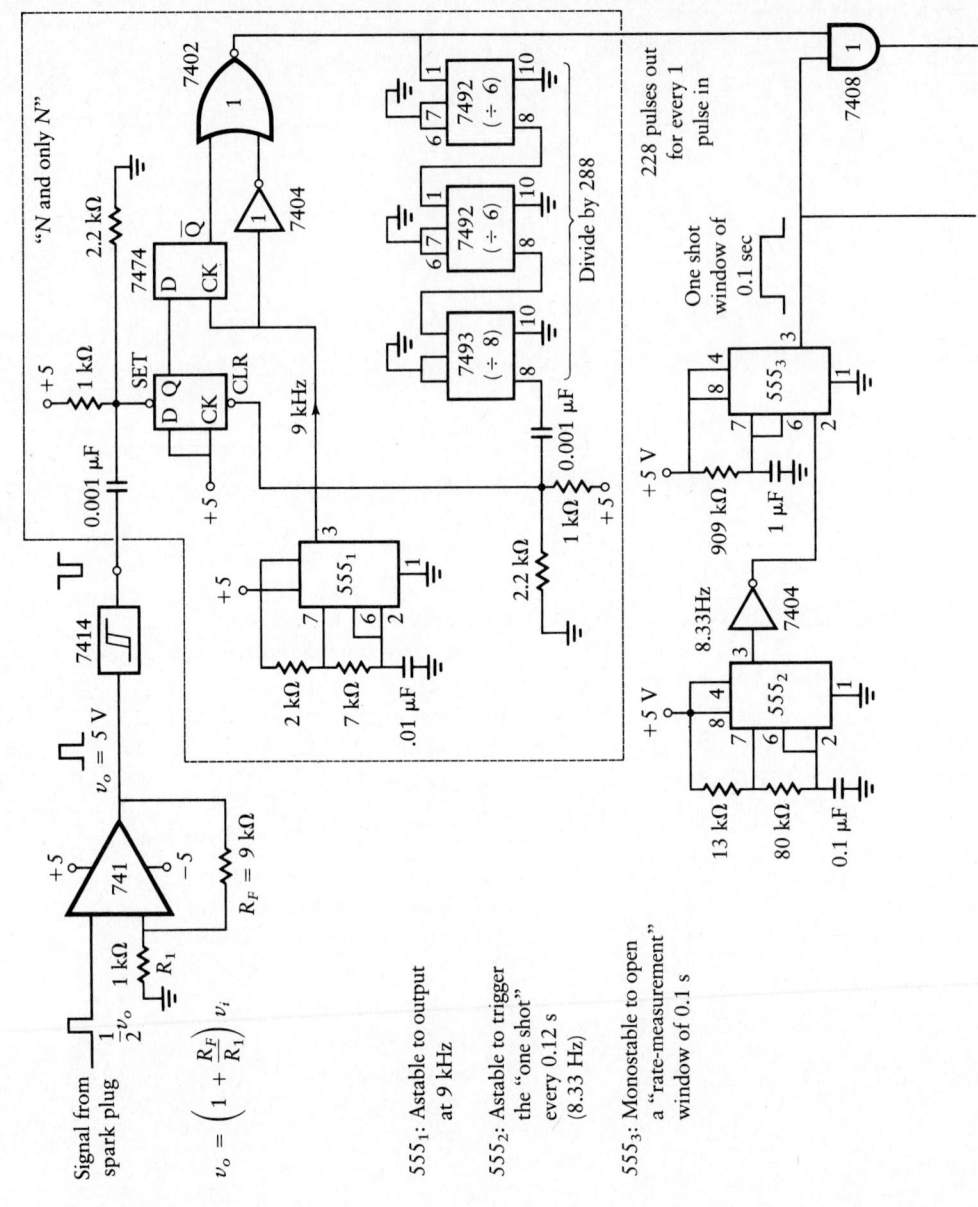

Figure 17.18 Schematic for Example 17.4.

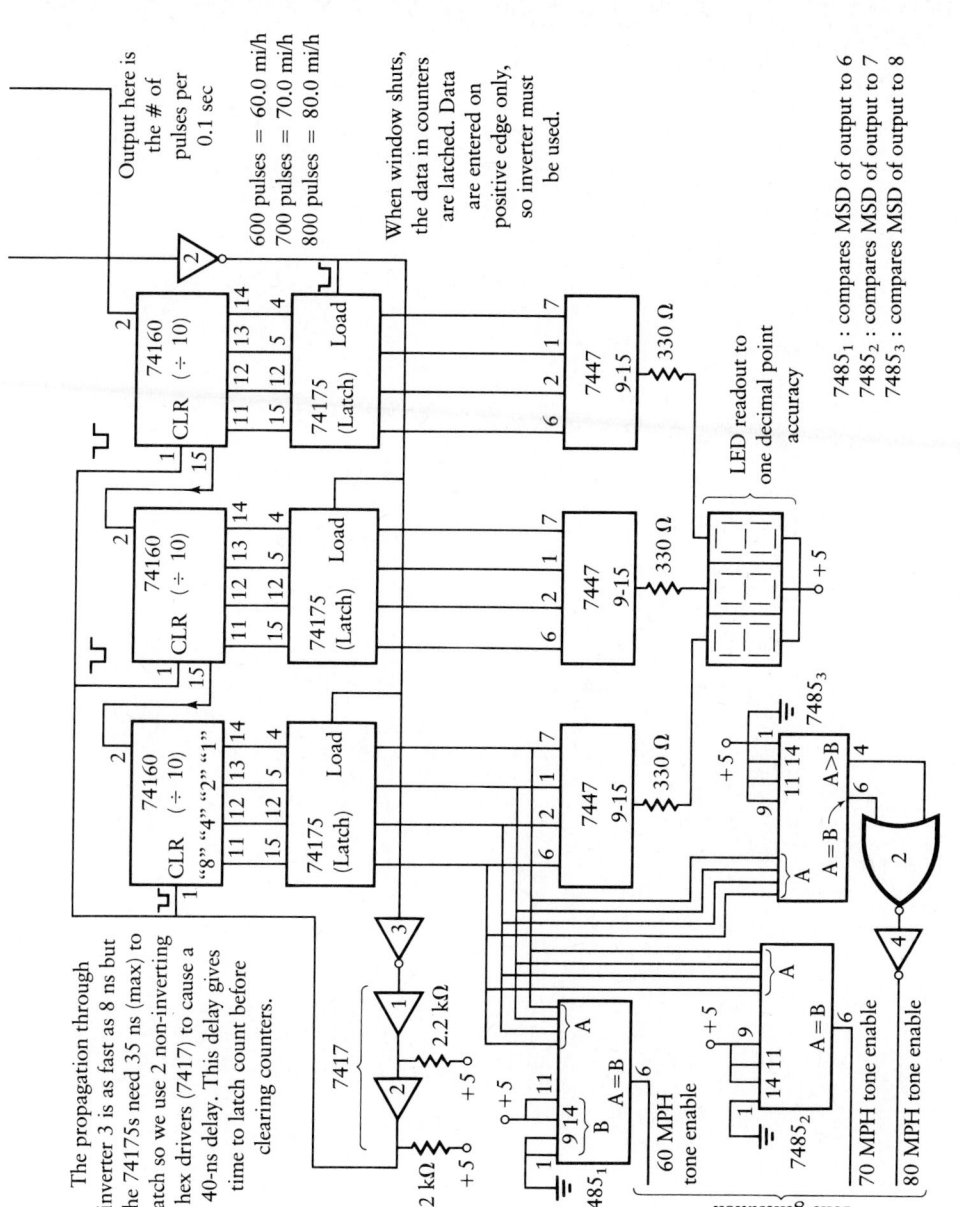

(a) **Schematic diagram for warning tachometer**

Figure 17.18
(continued)

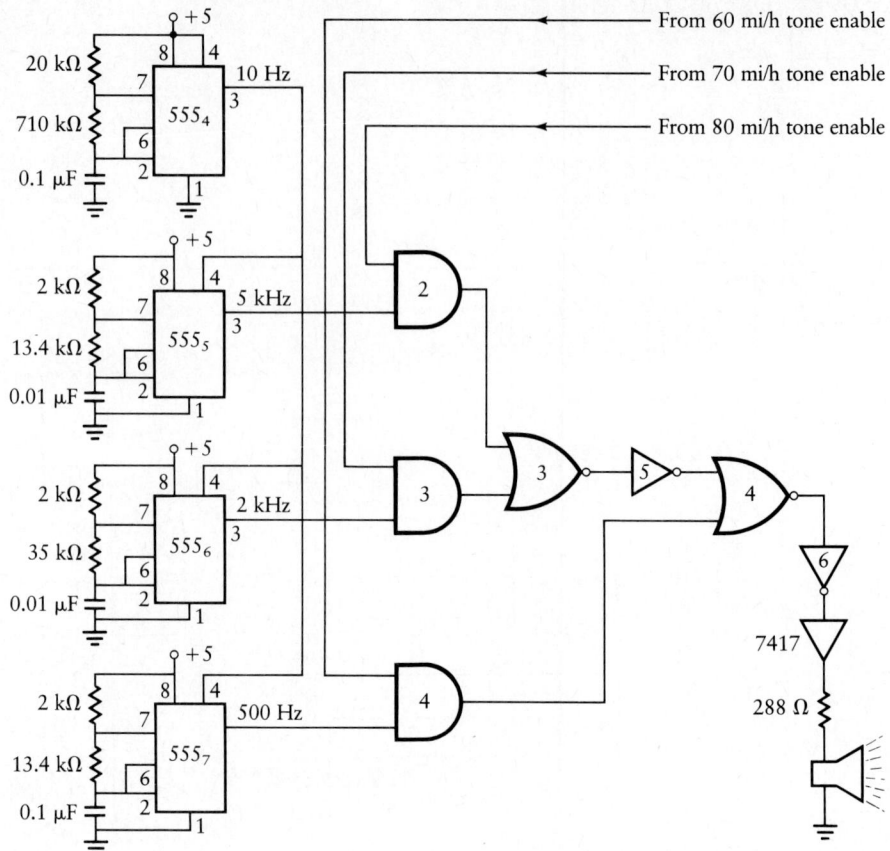

555_4 : A 10 Hz output to create a
tone burst. The output of
555_4 will reset the other
three so that the outputs
of the other three will
be in 10 Hz bursts.

555_5 : Creates the 5 kHz warning
tone for speeds greater than
80 mi/h

555_6 : Creates the 2 kHz warning
tone for speeds between 70.0 and 79.9 mi/h

555_7 : Creates the 500 Hz warning
tone for speeds between 60.0 and 69.9 mi/h

(b) Tone generation module for Example 17.4

Example 17.5   **Tape Controller**

The assignment: Design a digital tape-recorder controller that must have outputs and inputs as specified in Figure 17.19. There are no limits on the size, power supply, or type of integrated circuits that may be used in this problem, but the circuit must supply 12 V signals for the motor controllers.

Figure 17.19
Recorder-control
specifications.

Present state	Button pushed			
	Stop	Play	Fast forward	Rewind
Stop	NC	Wait 0 s. Start M1, M2. Turn audio on.	Wait 0 s. Start M1.	Wait 0 s. Start M3.
Play	Wait 0 s. Stop M1, M2. Turn audio off.	NC	Wait 0 s. Stop M2. Turn off audio.	Stop M1, M2. Turn off audio. Wait 1 s. Start M3.
Fast forward	Wait 0 s. Stop M1.	Wait 0 s. Start M2. Turn audio on.	NC	Stop M1. Wait 1 s. Start M3.
Rewind	Wait 0 s. Stop M3.	Stop M3. Wait 0 s. Start M1, M2. Turn audio on.	Stop M3. Wait 1 s. Start M1.	NC

SOLUTION   We first subdivide the problem into three parts: motor-control, audio-control, and switch-processing sections. Since the outputs require a voltage level of 12 V, we decide to use CMOS ICs. A block diagram is drawn with indications of what outputs and inputs each module expects. This is shown in Figure 17.20. After the problem has been subdivided, the individual blocks are designed.

Figure 17.20
Block diagram for
Example 17.5.

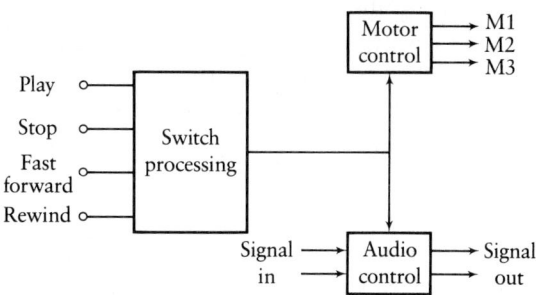

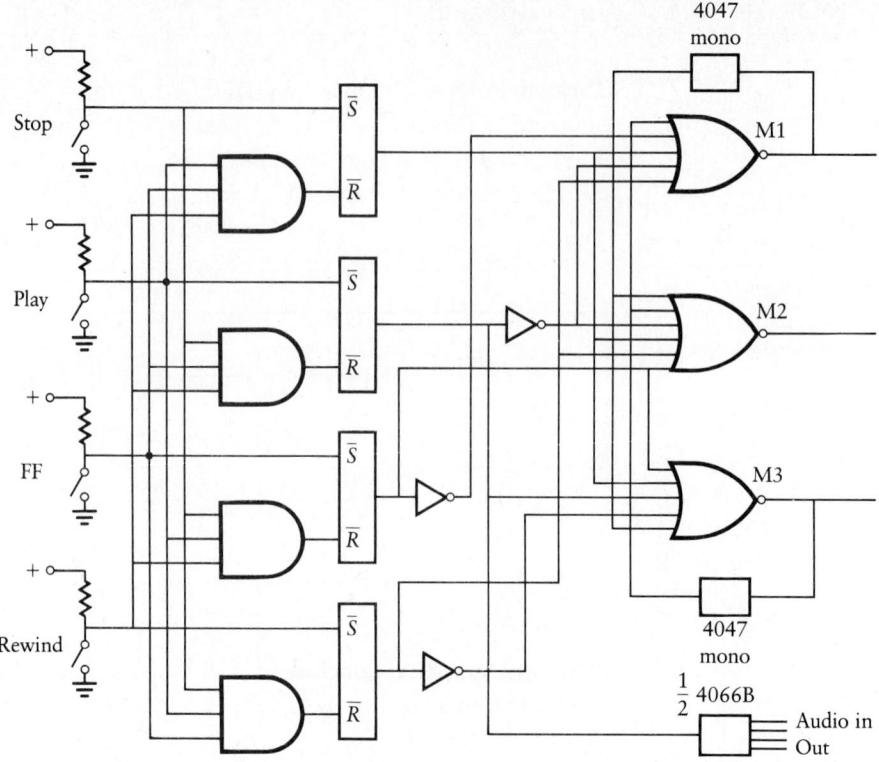

Figure 17.21   Schematic for Example 17.5.

The motor-control circuitry is required to generate delays depending upon the order of switch operation. Since the amount of delay time is not critical (i.e., 1.05 s is as good as 1.00 s), a monostable multivibrator circuit is used. We find, by referring to the CMOS data book, that the 4047B has the necessary inputs and outputs for generating the delays.

The audio portion of the system needs a special circuit to switch low-level (2 V or less) audio signals. The CMOS family includes the 74HC4066 Quad Bilateral Switch, which can be switched using digital signals. For the switch-processing portion of the unit, a memory device such as a *D*-type flip-flop can be used to debounce and remember which switch was last pressed. The rest of the logic is then designed to generate the waveforms needed to interface the signals. A schematic is drawn, as shown in Figure 17.21. Next, a prototype is built and tested. If the unit were to be put into production, a parts list would be developed, printed circuit boards designed, and other documents needed by production would be written.

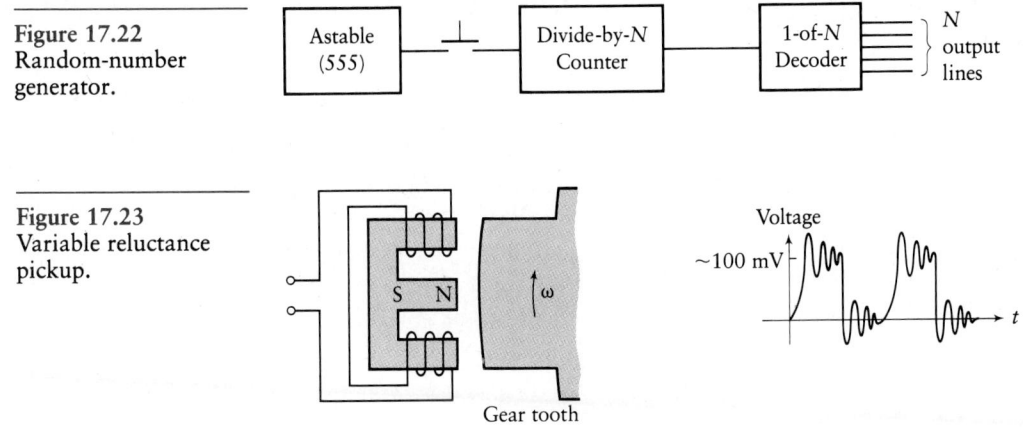

Figure 17.22
Random-number generator.

Figure 17.23
Variable reluctance pickup.

17.8   Introduction to Problems

The problems that conclude this chapter are generally quite challenging, and there are no single correct solutions. In fact, as time goes on and new and better devices are developed, the possible solutions to these problems will improve.

In formulating these problems, we have tried to pick situations for which you now have the necessary tools at least to make an attempt at the solution. There are, however, just a few loose ends we would like to tie up now to enlarge your repertoire of available tools.

In game-related situations, you will find it necessary to be able to generate *random numbers*. Fortunately, this is a simple process with a number of possible approaches. One of the simplest ways to generate a random number is as shown in Figure 17.22. A 555 timer is run at a high frequency. The output of the 555 is used to select one output line of a decoder. When the signal from the 555 to the decoder is interrupted, the decoder stops and one output line is high. All output lines of the decoder have an equal probability of going high. Since the frequency of the 555 is high compared to the other frequencies in the system (e.g., your reaction time if you are pushing a button), the instant at which the timer stops is random.

In a number of physical situations, you will need ways of providing input to digital systems from mechanical devices. A *variable reluctance pickup* is a common device for providing such a signal to a digital system. Figure 17.23 illustrates one example of the use of this pickup device in conjunction with a rotating gear. As the gear tooth, which is made of magnetic material, moves

Figure 17.24
Signal conditioning.

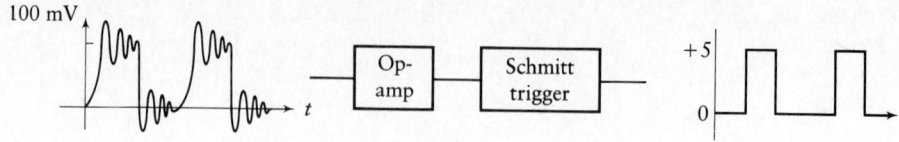

past the magnet, a voltage is generated at the output of the coils, which are wrapped about the magnetic circuit. The resulting output pulse train is noisy and the voltage level is generally incompatible with digital circuits because it is so small. The signal must therefore be conditioned.

The conditioning of the signal consists of amplifying it to a level compatible with the particular digital logic being used and then applying it to a Schmitt trigger, as shown in Figure 17.24. The output is then a 0 V to +5 V (in the case of TTL) signal that is compatible with the digital circuitry.

We often deal with magnets in the process of position sensing, thickness determination, weight measurement, speed control and pressure monitoring. We must be able to sense a magnetic field. This can be done with a *silicon Hall-effect switch*. The TL170C, as shown in Figure 17.25, is one example of such a switch. This is a low-cost magnetically operated switch, which is composed of a Hall-effect sensor, signal conditioning and hysteresis functions, and an output transistor. The outputs of these circuits are usually compatible with the digital ICs, so little, if any, signal conditioning is required.

We have used a *window* in the solution of several design problems. Before arriving at the design problems at the end of this chapter, we present three uses of a window for various electronic system applications.

Figure 17.25   Hall-effect generator.

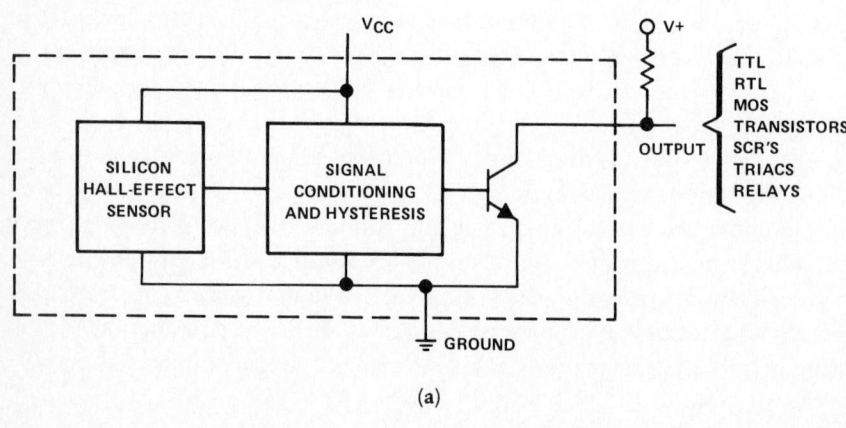

(a)

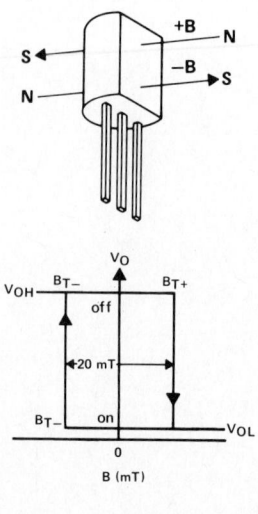

(b)

Figure 17.26
Use of windows.

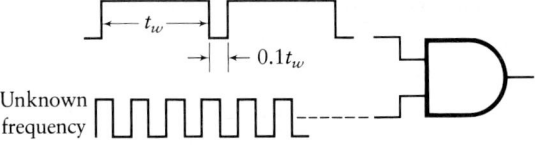

(a)   Use of a window to measure frequency

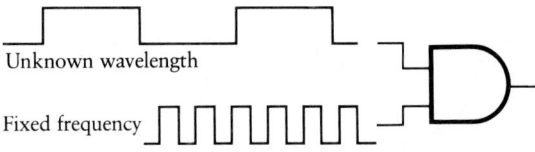

(b)   Use of a window to measure wavelength

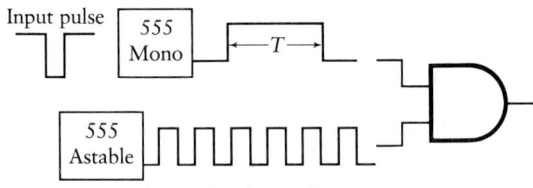

(c)   Frequency multiplication

1. Use of a window to measure frequency or velocity. If we hold a window high for a fixed time, t_w, we will count the number of pulses in a signal with unknown frequency. We accomplish this by ANDing the window with the pulse train of unknown frequency. This is shown in Figure 16.25, and repeated in Figure 17.26(a). The output of the AND circuit yields the number of pulses (of the signal with unknown frequency) that occur in the time period, t_w. As shown in Figure 17.26(a), the ideal window is high for the time t_w and low for a short time, $0.1t_w$. The trailing edge of the window is used to set the latch and then clear the counter in anticipation of the next time the window goes high. We desire a low time of $0.1t_w$ so we waste a minimum amount of time before we again update the display.

2. Use of a window to measure wavelength or $1/f$. This mode, which is shown in Figure 17.26(b), uses the signal with unknown wavelength as the window and a higher fixed-frequency signal as the input. These are ANDed, with the result that the number of pulses of fixed frequency is proportional to the length of time that the window is held open. Hence, the number of output pulses is proportional to the wavelength.

3. Use of a window to produce a multiplication of input pulses. In applications where the number of pulses coming from the sensor is insuffi-

cient to drive the counter, we must multiply the number of pulses by a constant. Suppose, for example, that we require 10 pulses each time we receive one pulse from the instrumentation. We set up a window so that with one pulse as input to the system, 10 pulses will be generated at the output. This is accomplished by letting the input pulses trigger the 555 monostable of Figure 17.26(c) to provide a window of duration T. We design a 555 astable in such a manner that during the time T, precisely 10 pulses are produced at the output. The window of period T is ANDed with the pulse train of the 555 astable to produce the 10 desired pulses for each input pulse.

17.9 Concluding Remarks

The design process probably appears overwhelming if this is your first exposure to it. It is important to realize that this is an area where practice is extremely important. You should also know that help is available in the form of data books, other engineers who may be working in the same company with you, your professors, application notes, books, magazines, and technical publications. Although your skill is an important asset in effective design, it is also critical that you be knowledgeable regarding new developments in the field. This requires extensive reading and attendance at meetings of professional societies. By being organized in methods, and willing to research information and by writing down the steps followed to produce a working prototype, you can solve many difficult problems.

With this assortment of tools combined with what you have learned in this book, you are now ready to approach the wide array of challenging electronic system design problems. After solving some of these problems, we hope you will be motivated to invent your own problems. You need only examine your daily environment to formulate a virtually unlimited list of projects.

Good luck in this exciting undertaking!

PROBLEMS

Use TTL or CMOS ICs and/or discrete elements in each of the following problems. Your final design should include a written explanation of how the system operates and a schematic diagram. Include the component values used and the type numbers of the ICs and discrete elements. Assume that any power-supply voltages you need are available, so do not design the power supply for these problems. Use as few components as possible.

17.1 Design an oil well monitoring system to measure the output of a field of 16 oil wells. The output of *each* well is measured with a flow meter that outputs a binary digital number corresponding to one of the following four flow conditions.

00   no flow

01   33.3% flow

10   66.6% flow

11   100% flow

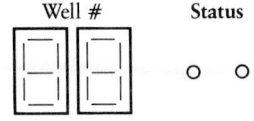

Well #   Status

Figure P17.1

The information from all 16 wells is transmitted to a control center, where two LEDs and two 7-segment LED displays are used in the format shown in Figure P17.1. The two 7-segment LED displays identify the oil well number (0 to 15) being measured. The two single LEDs indicate the flow information (status). Each oil well is to be sampled and read for 0.1 min, once every 1.6 min. In addition, when the flow is 00 for any oil well, a 1 kHz tone is sounded when that oil well number is displayed.

17.2 Design a lamp test indicator for a commercial aircraft to test 16 important running and landing lights about the aircraft. Each lamp has a small resistor between the light and ground, as shown in Figure P17.2. When the lamp is operational, the voltage across the resistor is 5 V. When the lamp is not operational, the voltage across the resistor drops to zero. Test each of the lamps for a period of 5 s and display the lamp number (0 to 15) on two 7-segment LED displays. Each time a lamp is faulty, sound a 1 kHz tone for the 5 s that the faulty lamp is being tested. Power of $\frac{1}{4}$ W is sufficient to drive the 8-Ω speaker.

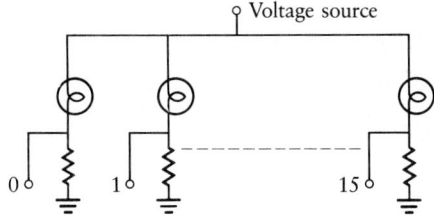

Figure P17.2

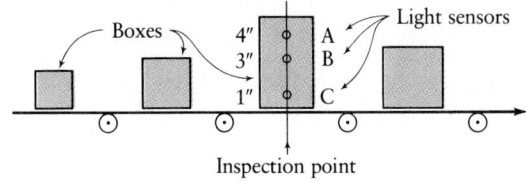

Figure P17.3

17.3 Design an assembly-line inspection system to sort boxes based upon the height of each box. The boxes pass down the assembly line, as shown in Figure P17.3. Light sensors A and B are used to determine the box height. Light sensor C is used to determine that a box is present. We wish to accept all boxes that are between 3 in. and 4 in. in height.

Other boxes are to be rejected by this inspection system. When a box passes the height sensor, check its height and if the height is *not* between 3 in. and 4 in., provide a $+5$ V pulse to energize a solenoid to push the box off the line (reject it).

The height sensors provide input to the system with the function table shown in Figure P17.4. Sensor C is high when a box is present and low when no box is present. The high level (logic 1) is 5 V and the low level (logic 0) is 0 V.

	Height		
	A	B	C
Box height $< 3''$	0	0	1
$3'' <$ box height $< 4''$	0	1	1
$4'' <$ box height	1	1	1
No box present	0	0	0

Figure P17.4

17.4 Use two 7-segment displays in the design of a frequency measuring circuit that shows the MSD on one 7-segment display and the "$\times 10^n$" range on another 7-segment display. The frequency of the input (0 to 5 V) pulse is between 1 Hz and 9999 Hz. The reading on this "*n*-display" would be as follows:

If frequency is 1 to 9, display 0, since the frequency is $\times 10^0$.

If frequency is 10 to 99, display 1, since the frequency is $\times 10^1$.

If frequency is 100 to 999, display 2, since the frequency is $\times 10^2$.

If frequency is 1000 to 9999, display 3, since the frequency is $\times 10^3$.

For example, if the frequency is 857, the MSD display would indicate 8 and the $\times 10^n$ display would show 2.

17.5 Design an electronic circuit that displays the amount of liquid in a large storage tank on one 7-segment display. The display shows the amount of liquid in the tank in percent full from 10% to 90% in 10% increments. Sound a 1 kHz alarm if the liquid level falls below 10% full or exceeds 90% full. The level is measured with a sonar device that provides pulses, as shown in Figure P17.5.

Figure P17.5

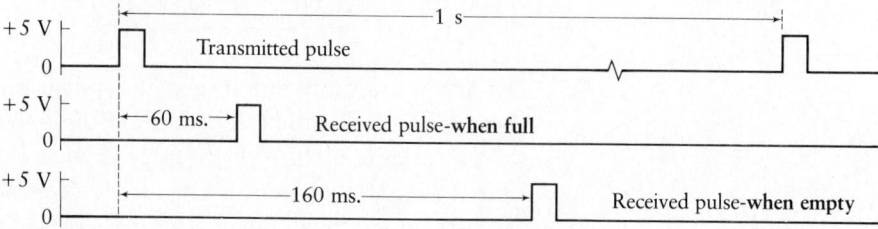

17.6 Design a countdown sequencer to time the firing of a sounding rocket. It is desired to countdown from 10 minutes before firing and then per the following schedule:

10.0 minutes	Start countdown
7.0 minutes	Transfer to rocket power
6.0 minutes	Activate the on-board cooling
4.0 minutes	Transfer to on-board computer
3.0 minutes	Fuse firing sequencer
2.0 minutes	Remove external cable
0.0 minutes	Fire

After firing, the same counter will keep track of the time after the launch of the rocket and will count up for at least 20 min. Use three 7-segment LED displays to show the time before and after firing to tenths of minutes, and use a digital CMOS switch (such as the CD4016) to activate each of the important times in the countdown. The three LED displays are to be arranged as shown in Figure P17.6. Preload a 74190 UP/DOWN decade counter with 10.0, and in the DOWN mode, go through the prefire events. When the count reaches 00.0, change the counter to count UP to record time. As a suggestion, use three 74190 decade up/down counters. (A zero on pin 5 makes the counter count up and a 1 makes it count down). An astable 555 operating at 100 Hz can be used for the clock.

Figure P17.6

17.7 Design a 24.0 hour clock and a system to control the turn-on and turn-off functions needed in an apartment complex.

If the clock reads 14.3, this means 2:18 P.M. since $\frac{3}{10}$ h is $\frac{3}{10}$ of 60 min, which is 18 min. For clock timing accuracy, use the 60 Hz line frequency. Design the system to activate the following:

1. Turn garden lights on at 18.0 h and off at 1.0 h by providing a 5 V signal to a relay.
2. Use a data distributor (74154) to turn on 10 possible sets of water sprinklers (one at a time). Turn on the first set of sprinklers by providing a +5 V signal to the voltage-controlled valve at 4.0 h. Provide a watering sequence by allowing the first set to flow for 0.1 h (6 min). Then turn the first set off and turn on the second set, also for 6 min. Continue this sequence until all 10 sets have been turned on and off.
3. Turn the music system on (by providing a 5 V signal to a relay) at 09.0 h and off at 21.0 h.

17.8 Design a controller to activate a large incandescent advertising sign, as shown in Figure P17.7. There are 64 lights around the circumference of the sign, and they are lighted four at a time in a sequence rotating as follows:

	Lights on
1st second	0, 16, 32, 48
2nd second	1, 17, 33, 49
3rd second	2, 18, 34, 50

.
.
.

There are 64 lights around sign

Figure P17.7

Each light is to remain on for 1 s. The letters are formed by an array of lights and are lighted in sequence as follows:

	Letter On
1st interval	C
2nd interval	CA
3rd interval	CAS
4th interval	CASI
5th interval	CASIN
6th interval	CASINO
7th interval	———
1st interval	Repeat sequence

Each interval is to be 4 s long. In this design, do not concern yourself with the output power requirements but only with the electronic design. The output of the electronic design is sufficient to drive one LED for each of the peripheral lights and only one LED to drive each letter *C, A, S, I, N,* and *O* (i.e. use backlighted templates for the letters).

17.9 Design a pressure-altitude-hold system for a small commercial aircraft. The system is to operate over the range of 0 to 50,000 ft with a 200-ft resolution. The actual pressure altitude, *A,* which is measured in feet, is obtained from a digital pressure transducer which outputs an 8-bit binary signal with each binary number equivalent to 200 ft. So if the pressure transducer outputs 01101101, the pressure altitude is 109 × 200 ft = 21,800 ft.

The pilot sets the desired altitude, B, in feet, with a 3-position switch on the control stick, as shown in Figure P17.8. This 3-position switch allows the pilot to increase, by pushing the switch forward, or decrease, by pushing the switch back, the set altitude. The set altitude will remain the same if the pilot's finger is removed from the switch.

Desired altitude switch

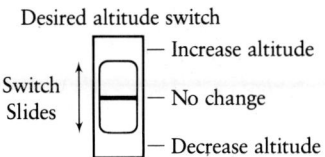

Switch Slides

— Increase altitude

— No change

— Decrease altitude

Figure P17.8

Three 7-segment LED displays indicate the set altitude (desired altitude) where the least significant digit corresponds to 200 ft. Compare the actual altitude with the set altitude, and provide a 5 V signal according to the following schedule:

Terminal	$A > B$	$A = B$	$A < B$
Altitude decreases	1	0	0
No change	0	1	0
Altitude increases	0	0	1

17.10 Design a temperature-monitoring system for an aircraft engine. It is necessary to monitor eight points throughout the engine with the circuit shown in Figure P17.9. The voltage V_γ across the diode is 0.7 V at 25°C = T_1, and this voltage reduces as the temperature increases, as follows:

$$\Delta V_\gamma = -2(T_2 - T_1) \text{ mV}$$

with T_1 and T_2 in degrees Celsius. The temperature varies from 25°C to 200°C. The output is displayed on three 7-segment LEDs, as shown in Figure P17.10. A single LED identifies the diode being read and the three 7-segment LEDs read the temperature at the point in question. Each temperature is to be sampled sequentially and read for 6 seconds.

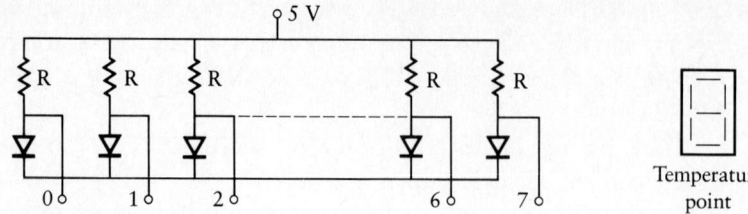

Figure P17.9

Temperature
point

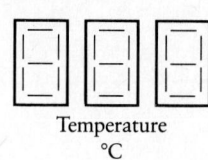

Temperature
°C

Figure P17.10

Figure P17.11

An analog multiplexer (74HC4051) is used to sample each of the eight values of voltage. The analog signal from the diode must be conditioned with the op-amp circuit of Figure P17.11.

The voltage V_γ is

$$V_\gamma = 700 - 2(T - 25) = 750 - 2T \text{ mV}$$

where T is expressed in degrees Celsius. The voltage V_c is

$$V_c = \frac{50}{r + 10} \text{ V}$$

where r is in kΩ. The output voltage, V_o, from the op-amp is

$$V_o = \frac{R}{175 \text{ k}\Omega} \left[V_c - V_\gamma \right]$$

and substituting, we obtain

$$V_o = \frac{-R}{175} \left[750 - 2T - \frac{50 \times 10^3}{r + 10} \right] \text{mV}$$

We choose r by letting

$$\frac{50 \times 10^3}{r + 10} - 750 = 0$$

We set the gain by selecting R from the equation

$$V_o = \frac{2R}{100\ \text{k}\Omega}\ T\ \text{mV}$$

Use a $3\frac{1}{2}$-digit DVM to process the signal.

17.11 Design a temperature-monitoring system that will display seven different temperatures on three 7-segment displays. Seven diodes are used to measure the seven temperatures. The output voltage of each diode, which varies linearly with temperature, is fed into an op-amp. When the op-amp output is properly calibrated and amplified, a dc signal is obtained, which ranges from 0.25 V for 25°C to 1.25 V for 125°C. Your design should monitor each of these outputs, in sequence, and display the temperature for a period of 1 minute. Seven single LEDs indicate which temperature point is being displayed, as shown in Figure P17.12.

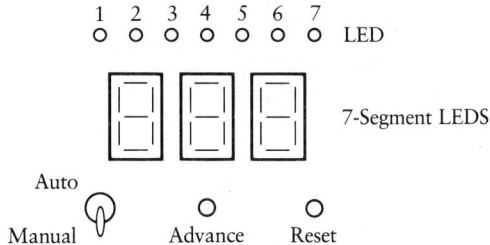

Figure P17.12

Two modes of operation are required, as follows:
a. Automatic mode: Each temperature is displayed for 1 minute.
b. Manual mode: The temperature displayed remains the same until the user presses the advance button to see the next temperature.

17.12 Energy is to be saved in a large museum by automatically turning the lights on and off in an infrequently visited exhibition room, as shown in Figure P17.13. Design an electronic circuit that will turn the lights on when the first person enters and turn the lights off when the last person leaves the room. The electronic system should be able to accommodate up to 99 people in the room at any time. The entrance sensor

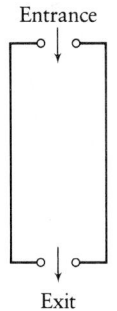

Figure P17.13

and the exit sensor each consists of a parallel light beam as shown in the figure. Assume these sensors normally provide a 0 V output, which changes to 5 V when the beam is broken. Provide a reset switch to set the count to 0. Assume that the entrance is narrow enough to allow only one person to enter at a time and that the light beams break only once per person.

17.13 Design a television monitor for a hotel with 14 rooms on each floor. Design the electronic system (for one floor only) to detect when any television receiver is ON. When the television is ON, a 5 V signal is delivered to the office from a switch installed on each television. When the television is OFF, the signal delivered to the office is 0 V. Each television is monitored for 1 min before the monitor passes to the next television on the floor, and the process continues with each television being monitored once every 14 min.

The readout comprises two 7-segment LED displays, which indicate the room numbers from 0 to 13, and a single LED, which is ON when the television in that room is ON and OFF when the television is OFF.

17.14 Design an electronic voting system to be used for Parliament, which consists of 256 members. Each member has two switches, as shown in Figure P17.14(a). The first switch is used to indicate that the member is present at the session. Each member in attendance turns this switch ON, thus sending a 5 V signal to the podium. When the member is absent, the signal at the podium is 0 V. A YES vote, as recorded by throwing the second switch, sends 5 V on the line to the podium, and a NO vote puts 0 V on the line at the podium.

The output is composed of three single LEDs, which indicate the result of the vote: either YES, TIE, or NO. In addition, three 7-segment LED displays indicate the number of members voting. This display is shown in Figure P17.14(b).

The head of Parliament, who stays at the podium, has one switch, which is used to disable the circuit. When all members have voted either YES or NO, the head of Parliament throws the podium switch to ON, which latches the results into the display. Once the switch is thrown ON, no votes can be changed.

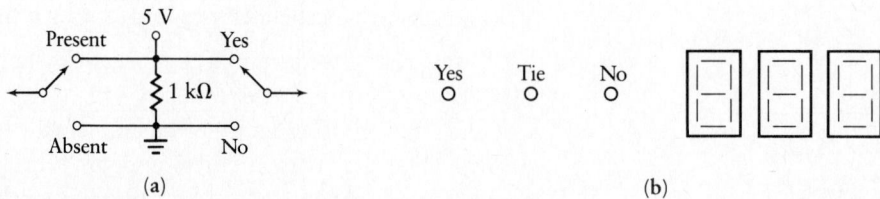

Figure P17.14

17.15 Design a digital control system to control the angular velocity of the main rotor of a helicopter. The system is shown in Figure P17.15. The actual rotor speed is displayed on two 7-segment LED displays. The desired rotor speed, which is displayed on two other 7-segment LEDs, is set on the control panel for the range of 50×10 to 70×10 rev/min. A three position switch allows the pilot to increase rev/min (pressing the switch forward) or decrease rev/min (pressing the switch backward). When the switch is in the center position, no change occurs.

The rotor, which rotates at a speed between 500 and 700 rev/min, is connected through a gear train to the turbine engine, which rotates at 5000 to 7000 rev/min. The difference between desired velocity, f_D, and the actual velocity, f_a, (in revolutions per minute) is used to change the setting of the throttle. Increasing the throttle will increase the speed of the turbine, which increases the speed of the rotor. Each pulse into the stepper motor advances (or retards) the throttle setting and hence increases (or decreases) the angular velocity of the rotor.

The actual velocity, f_a, is generated with a 500-tooth iron gear attached to the turbine shaft. This gear is used with a variable reluctance pickup, which produces a 100 mV peak-to-peak pulse train. Each time the rotor rotates one revolution, 500 pulses are generated at the output.

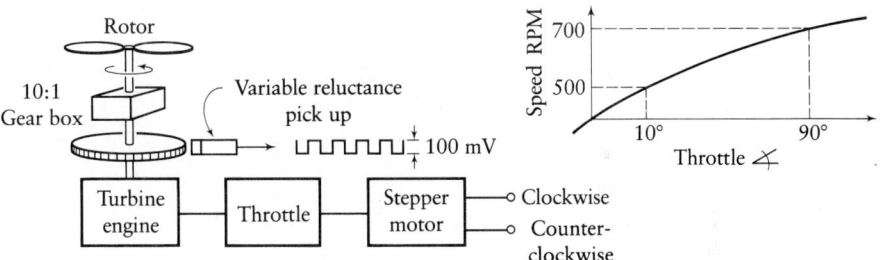

Figure P17.15

17.16 An experimental windmill must have the number of revolutions per minute of its blade monitored and displayed. The expected operating range is 60 to 240 rev/min. A 100-tooth iron gear is attached to the blade shaft and is sensed by a magnetic pickup, which provides a $+100$ mV pulse as each tooth passes the sensor.

    a. The circuit should process the signal from the magnetic sensor and display the speed of the windmill in revolutions per minute using three 7-segment LED displays.

    b. The circuit should energize a 400 Hz alarm if the speed exceeds 240 rev/min. Assume that the IC output can directly drive a small speaker.

17.17 Design a digital control system to measure precisely the error in angular velocity of a large centrifuge. This large centrifuge rotates at a precise angular velocity and is used to apply acceleration to large objects. This is an *A-V-E* (angular-velocity-error) indicator. The output comprises five 7-segment LED displays to yield the error velocity ω_E (in revolutions per minute) to three decimal places. The *A-V-E* indicator is used to detect the error in angular velocity of the centrifuge. The large arm is to rotate at 60 rev/min, and the motor rotates at 6000 rev/min. An accurate reference velocity, ω_R, is obtained from a crystal oscillator (temperature controlled) that produces a 1 MHz pulse train. The actual velocity, ω_a, is generated with a 500-tooth iron gear that is attached to the motor shaft and is sensed with a variable reluctance pick-up. This produces a noisy 100 mV pulse train with a frequency of ω_a. Use an UP-DOWN counter and two identical windows. First, up-count ω_R during a window period; then down-count ω_a during an identical window period. Assuming that $\omega_R > \omega_a$, the count left after the end of the second window is the error in revolutions per minute.

17.18 Use a comparator in the design of a speed-control system for your automobile. The throttle is positioned with a stepper motor that operates as shown in Figure P17.16. The desired speed is set by depressing a switch on the dashboard. This switch causes two 7-segment LED displays to advance and to indicate the set speed. When the switch is released, a latch holds this speed as the desired speed of your automobile. When the display reaches 80 mi/h, it resets to zero.

The actual speed is taken from the engine distributor, which outputs 8 pulses for each 2 revolutions of the engine. In drive gear, the ratio of engine speed to forward velocity is given by the following equation:

$$\text{Ratio} = \frac{1000 \text{ rev/min}}{25 \text{ mi/h}} = 40 \text{ (rev/min)/(mi/h)}$$

In the design, include a disable capability when the brake pedal is depressed, and provide an ON/OFF switch.

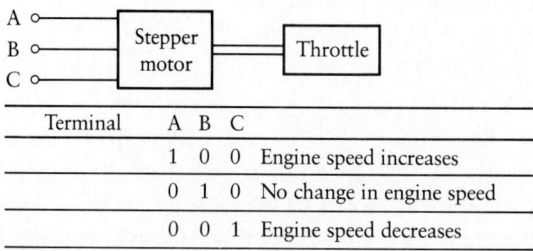

Terminal	A	B	C	
	1	0	0	Engine speed increases
	0	1	0	No change in engine speed
	0	0	1	Engine speed decreases

Figure P17.16

17.19 Design an electronic system to measure the rate at which your heart beats. The system is mounted on a stationary bicycle, so you are able to use the 60 Hz power line for power purposes. The device must read the heart rate from 150 to 250 beats per minute.

The heart rate is measured with an infrared sensor that produces a 100-mV pulse each time that the heart beats. This sensor is attached to the index finger of your hand. These pulses are not clean pulses, so they must be signal-conditioned.

The readout comprises three 7-segment LED displays, which read the heart rate in beats per minute.

17.20 Design a miles-per-gallon indicator to be used on an automobile. Two inputs are available as follows:
a. Odometer signal: This signal produces a 5 V pulse for every tenth of a mile traveled.
b. Fuel tank signal: The fuel tank is instrumented so that a 5 V pulse is produced each time the fuel reduces by 0.1 gal.

The output is composed of two 7-segment LED displays, which display miles per gallon to the nearest mile per gallon.

17.21 Design a wind-velocity meter. A propeller is mounted on a ball-bearing shaft so it will turn freely, and a 100-tooth iron gear is attached to the same shaft. A variable-reluctance sensor is used to sense the teeth on the gear, and it produces a 100 mV signal each time a gear tooth passes the sensor. Hence 100 pulses are produced for each revolution of the propeller. When the wind velocity, V_w, is 20 mi/h, the propeller velocity, f_p, is 90 rev/min. The relation is linear as follows:

$$f_p = 4.5\, V_w \text{ rev/min}$$

where V_w is the wind velocity in miles per hour. The output display is composed of two 7-segment LED displays to read the wind velocity to the nearest digit.

17.22 Design a warning tachometer for a gas turbine engine that operates in the range of 8000 to 9000 rev/min. A 100-tooth iron gear is mounted on the engine shaft. A variable-reluctance pickup is mounted near the gear, and it produces 100 pulses for each revolution of the engine. The pulses are only 100 mV in magnitude, so they must be conditioned. The display is comprised of two 7-segment LED displays, which display the word LO when the speed is 8000 rev/min or less and the word HI when the speed is 9000 rev/min or more. In the range between 8000 and 9000 rev/min, the LED displays are blank. When LO is displayed, a 500 Hz tone is sounded and when HI is displayed, a 1 kHz tone is sounded. One-quarter watt of power is needed for each tone.

17.23 Design an electronic display to read the wavelength of a low frequency transmitter signal. The wavelength, λ, is given by

$$\lambda = \frac{3 \times 10^5}{f} \text{ km}$$

The frequency varies from 54 kHz to 160 kHz, and the corresponding wavelength ranges from

5.56 km   at   54 kHz

to

1.87 km   at   160 kHz

Display the wavelength on three 7-segment LED displays to one-decimal-point accuracy. Form a window as described in Section 17.8 to find λ.

17.24 Design an electronic system to determine the number of cars in a parking garage containing 300 spaces. Each time a car enters the garage, the entrance gate lifts and a pulse of variable width is generated. The pulse is of variable width because of the difference in time required for the gate to drop after each car of different length and different speed passes through. Each time a car leaves the garage, the exit gate, at another location, lifts, and another pulse of variable width is generated. These pulses are shown in Figure P17.17. Provide a *CLEAR* for the system so that the counter can be reset to zero. The visual display is composed of the following:
1. Three 7-segment LED displays, which show the number of cars in the garage at any time.
2. Four 7-segment LED displays, which show the word FULL when the garage contains 300 cars.

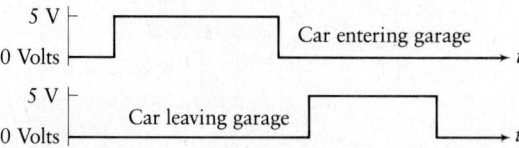

Figure P17.17

17.25 Design a digital thermometer using a thermistor bridge as the temperature sensor and a voltage-controlled oscillator (VCO). You may wish to use a 74124 VCO. The output of the thermistor bridge is as follows:

With 110°F, the output is 50 mV

With 90°F, the output is 34.4 mV.

The readout is to be three 7-segment LED displays yielding the temperature in degrees Fahrenheit to the nearest whole number. Compute the scale factor showing that your system will yield accurate temperature readings in the 90°–110° range.

17.26 Repeat Problem 17.25 using a $3\frac{1}{2}$ digit A/D converter (ICL7106).

17.27 Design a digital bathroom scale using a strain gauge load cell as the weight sensor. The load cell produces an output voltage that is proportional to weight. The system is shown in Figure P17.18, where we write the equation for V_1 and V_2 as follows:

$$V_1 = \frac{(R - \Delta R)V}{R - \Delta R + R + \Delta R} = \frac{V(R - \Delta R)}{2R}$$

and

$$V_2 = \frac{R}{2R}V = \frac{V}{2}$$

The equation for the output of the op-amp is

$$V_o = \frac{R_F}{R_A}\left(V_2 - V_1\right) = \frac{R_F}{R_A}\left[\frac{V}{2} - \frac{V(R - \Delta R)}{2R}\right] = \frac{R_F V}{2R_A R}\Delta R$$

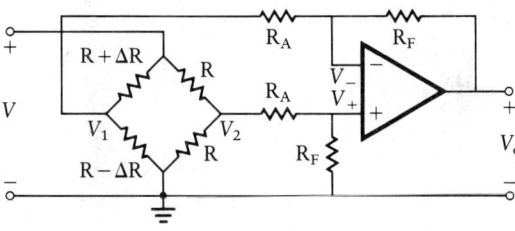

Figure P17.18

Select $R = 1\ \text{k}\Omega$ and $V = 9\ \text{V}$. The change in resistance, ΔR, is proportional to the weight. Figure P17.19(a) shows a schematic of the mechanical system. Strain gauges are attached on the top and bottom of the beam. The beam bends down because of the application of the weight on the scale. As a result, the resistance of the upper strain gauge increases $(R + \Delta R)$ and the resistance of the lower gauge decreases $(R - \Delta R)$. This provides the input to the bridge system of Figure P17.18.

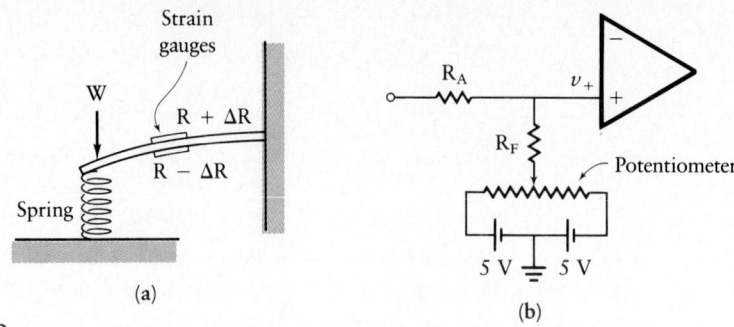

Strain gauges

W

R + ΔR

R − ΔR

Spring

(a)

R_A

v_+

R_F

Potentiometer

5 V   5 V

(b)

Figure P17.19

Two additional strain gauges, not shown on the diagram of Figure P17.19(a), are attached to the beam in a direction that causes no change in resistance, R, as the weight is applied. These two gauges form the other two legs of the bridge and are shown as R in Figure P17.18. Since resistance is a function of temperature, the bridge will remain balanced as the temperature changes and will yield a voltage output only for a change in weight.

The scale is to respond to changes in weight from 0 to 399 lb. The load cell is linear, and when the weight is 399 lb,

$$V_o = \frac{R_F}{R_A} (34 \text{ mV})$$

Hence, over the range of 0 to 399 lb, the output voltage of the system of Figure P17.18 varies from 0 to

$$\frac{R_F}{R_A}(34 \text{ mV})$$

When someone steps on the scale, a normally open switch closes and hence applies power to the device. Three 7-segment LED displays read the weight in pounds. Calculate the scale factor, R_F/R_A, and provide a zero adjustment, which can be accomplished with the circuit shown in Figure P17.19(b). The resistance of the potentiometer should be approximately 10% of the value of R_F.

17.28 Design an odometer to be used on a bicycle. A Hall-effect generator is mounted near the rear wheel. A magnet is mounted on one of the spokes of the rear wheel. As the magnet passes the generator, a 5 V pulse is generated. Hence, each time the wheel revolves once, the Hall-effect device generates a 5 V pulse. With a nominal 26-in. wheel (including the effect of the tire), the bicycle travels 7 ft each time the wheel turns through one revolution. Thus, each pulse corresponds to 7 ft of travel by the bicycle. Since there are so few pulses generated by the Hall-effect generator, use pulse multiplication as discussed in Section 17.8.

The readout is to be three 7-segment LED displays connected so that the least significant digit reads 100 ft increments, and the most significant digit reads 10,000 ft increments.

Consider the changes to the design required for the following improvements:

a. Change the output to read from 00.0 to 99.9 mi rather than feet.

b. Change the odometer to operate with variable bicycle-wheel diameters.

17.29 Design a run-in-place odometer to exercise by running in one place inside your home. A normally open switch closes each time either of your feet strikes the pad. The switch within the pad is a mechanical device, so it must be debounced. The controls comprise a reset button to activate the device and a potentiometer to set the length of each individual's stride in feet. The output is shown on three 7-segment LED displays with the MSD equal to 10^4 ft and the LSD equal to 10^2 ft. Use a monostable 555 to debounce the switch, and use the pulse multiplication technique as discussed in Section 17.8 to increase the number of pulses. The number of pulses we generate for each pulse from the mechanical switch should be related to the stride. The stride potentiometer sets the frequency of the astable 555.

For example, if a person, when running, travels 2.8 ft every time either foot hits the ground, the stride is 2.8 ft. In this case, the frequency of the astable 555, in the pulse-multiplication circuit, should be set for 28. Hence each time either foot strikes the pad, 28 pulses are generated for the counter.

A   SPICE

A.0   Introduction

SPICE is the acronym for a Simulation Program with Integrated Circuit Emphasis developed by the Electronics Research Laboratory of the University of California and released to the public in July 1975. The simulation program is written in various computer languages. Through continuing research and suggestions from SPICE users, the program has been modified and updated to expand its simulation capability. The SPICE program reads input data, processes the data in batch mode on a mainframe computer, and produces the output in tabular or graphic form on an ordinary line printer. A SPICE program is also available to run on an IBM PC or equivalent.

SPICE is a computer-aided simulation program—that is, the engineer designs the circuit and then inputs it into SPICE for simulation. This, of course, is a great aid to the designer, since the results of the program illustrate how the circuit will react to certain inputs. With computer simulation, it is not necessary to build and test a circuit before completing the design. We can change circuit components and find the results of the changes upon circuit performance. We can use additional approximations to speed up the design process and then let the SPICE program determine what effect the approximations have on the desired output.

The SPICE program was designed to determine the unknown parameters by using Kirchhoff's current equations (nodal analysis). Performance of this type of analysis requires the transistors and diodes to be characterized by an equivalent circuit. All other models for the transistors and diode are represented by using nonlinear exponential functions. For example, the BJT model used in SPICE is based upon the Ebers-Moll injection model with various high-injection effects defined by Gummell and Poon. The type of equivalent circuit to be used is built into the program and is determined by the type of transistor or diode specified in the program directions. Once this is accomplished, the program can be run.

The first operation the SPICE program performs is determining the dc operating point, or Q-point, by using the Newton-Raphson method of matrix solution. After this has been completed, the program considers the ac input and performs the necessary calculations for a single frequency. If solution for more than one frequency is required, the program continues for each frequency specified in the program directions. It repeats the analysis until all frequency points have been evaluated. The solution determined in the dc analysis provides the initial conditions for the transient analysis, which makes use of implicit numerical integration techniques for its solution. (These techniques are normally discussed as part of a study of numerical analysis. The understanding of the methods is not necessary for the SPICE user.) Since SPICE uses nodal analysis as the method of solution, it does possess some limitations, as follows:

1. Only voltage-controlled current sources can be used. All other sources must be converted to voltage-controlled sources, either internally or externally.
2. Since SPICE analysis is based upon a matrix operation using the admittance functions, a zero resistance cannot be included, or the matrix will have a zero determinant, and the solution cannot be found.
3. Multiterminal elements that have no admittance matrix (e.g., an ideal transformer) representation must be converted to allow an admittance matrix to exist.
4. Only voltage-controlled nonlinear resistors can be included in the circuit; items such as neon lamps and SCRs cannot be evaluated using nodal analysis.

Circuit behavior can be simulated with respect to time, frequency and voltage variations. This is accomplished by specifying how the SPICE program will analyze the circuit through the use of *analysis statements*. SPICE permits the following forms of analyses: nonlinear dc, nonlinear transient, and linear ac small signal. These analyses can be conducted at various specified temperatures.

A dc analysis determines the node voltages in the circuit with the inductors shorted and capacitors open. This analysis is accomplished with only dc power applied. The dc analysis is performed prior to transient or ac analysis. The dc analysis determines the initial conditions required for the transient analysis.

The dc analysis determines the linearized small signal models of the nonlinear devices for use in ac analysis. A dc analysis can also be used to determine the small signal value of the transfer function, the dc transfer curves, and the dc small signal sensitivities of specified output variables. The dc analysis options are specified by the .DC, .TF, .OP, and .SENS control statements.

We compute the voltage and current output variables as a function of time over a specified time interval using a transient analysis. All sources that are not time-dependent are set to their dc values. A Fourier analysis of the output waveform can be specified to obtain the frequency-domain Fourier coefficients for large-signal sinusoidal simulations. The transient time interval and Fourier analysis options are defined by the .TRAN and .FOURIER control statements.

We compute the voltage and current variables as a function of frequency using an ac small-signal analysis. The designer specifies the range of frequencies for which this analysis is to be conducted. The output of the ac analysis is a transfer function (e.g., voltage gain, transimpedance). If the circuit has only one ac input, it is convenient to set the input to unity magnitude and zero phase. In this manner, the output variables have the same value as the transfer function of the output variable with respect to the input. The ac analysis can also be used to analyze the noise generated by the resistors and semiconductor devices and the distortion characteristics of the circuit in the small signal mode. The ac, noise, and distortion options are specified by the .AC, .NOISE, and .DISTO control statements.

Once the circuit file is created by statements describing the circuit and the type of analysis of the circuit is defined, the simulation of the circuit can be accomplished. The results of the simulation can be displayed in either tabular or graphic form.

A.1   Programming Information

Each computer has a unique set of instructions for edit programs. These instructions must be known before attempting to input circuit simulations into the program. In this appendix, we describe circuits that contain resistors, capacitors, inductors, independent voltage and current sources, four types of dependent sources, and the four most common semiconductor devices: diodes, BJTs, JFETs, and MOSFETs.

Many of the parameters of the Gummel-Poon model for transistors are not needed in the simple evaluation of circuit performance. The SPICE program sets values for the parameters not defined by the user in the model statements for the transistor. These default values should be available for review in the instructions for the particular version of the SPICE program being used. The five programming areas are introduced in the following sequence:

1. Element description
2. Source description
3. Subcircuits
4. Analysis request
5. Output request

A.1.1   *Format*

SPICE uses a free format for inputs. Data fields are separated by one or more delimiters (a block, a comma, an equal sign, or a left or right parenthesis). A statement may be continued by entering a plus sign in column 1 of the line immediately following the statement line to be continued. A name field must begin with a letter and must not contain any delimiters. Only the first eight characters of the name are used for identification. A number field may contain an integer (e.g., 2, −35, 77), a floating-point number (e.g., 3.1416, 5.3), either an integer or floating-point number followed by an integer exponent (1E3, 3.2E-4), or either an integer or a floating point number followed by one of the scale factors presented next.

Scale Factors

MIL	= 2.54E-6	M =	1E-3
K	= 1E3	U =	1E-6
MEG	= 1E6	N =	1E-9
G	= 1E9	P =	1E-12
T	= 1E12	F =	1E-15

Letters immediately following a number (that are not scale factors) are ignored and letters immediately following a scale factor are ignored. Hence, 10, 10V, 10 VOLTS and 10 HZ all represent the same number. In addition, M, MA, MSEC, and MMHOS all represent the same scale factor, 10^{-3}. A comment statement may be indicated by entering an asterisk in the first column.

A.1.2   *Circuit Description*

Each element in the circuit to be analyzed must be defined by node numbers. All nodes in the circuit are numbered. Node numbers need not be consecutive. The 0 node is the ground or reference node. The circuit is described to SPICE by a file of element statements, which define the circuit topology and element values, and a set of control statements, which define the model parameters and the run controls. The first statement in the file must be a title statement and the last must be the end statement (.END). Statements in between, except for continuations, may be in any order. Each element in the circuit is specified by an element statement that contains the element name, the circuit nodes to which the element is connected, and the values of the parameters that determine the electrical characteristics of the element. The first letter in the element name specifies the element type. The strings xxxxxxx and yyyyyy denote a user-specified alphanumeric reference name for the applicable element. For example, a resistor, capacitor, and inductor may be defined as RLOAD, C3ST1, and L3ST2, respectively. Data fields enclosed in < > are optional. The element nodes must be nonnegative integers, which need not be numbered sequentially, and the ground node must always be numbered 0. Every node must have at least two connections and a dc path to ground when capacitors open and inductors short. With respect to branch voltages and currents, SPICE uses sink reference (i.e., current flows in the direction of voltage drop).

A.2 Input Data

In this section, we define how the input data are formatted to be accepted by the SPICE program.

A.2.1 Element Description

Each element requires a definition of the characteristics of the device so that the SPICE program can properly analyze the circuit.

A.2.1.1 Passive Elements   The element descriptions and the associated formats are shown in the following table:

Type	Format			
Resistor	Rxxxxxxx	n1	n2	value
Capacitor	Cxxxxxxx	n+	n−	value
Inductor	Lxxxxxxx	n+	n−	value
Diode	Dxxxxxxx	n+	n−	value

The element designations are shown in Figure A.1. The resistance dependence upon temperature is given by adding TC1 and TC2 to the value. (TC = 0.001, 0.013). The diode junction potential, reverse breakdown voltage, and ohmic resistance values are reset to applicable values by using the MODEL statement. A model name (MODNAME) is entered to reference the corresponding MODEL

Figure A.1
Element designations.

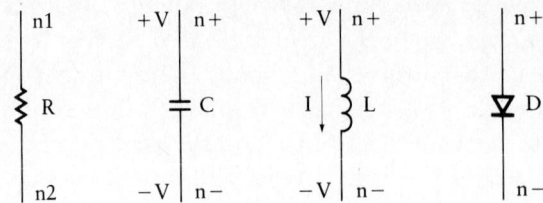

Figure A.2
Example of circuit
with passive
components.

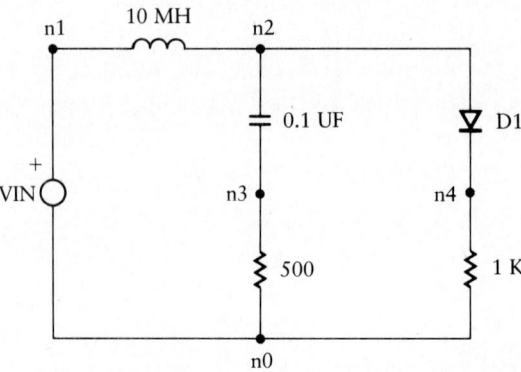

statement. (Refer to Subsection A.2.1.3 for MODEL statements and typical diode default values.)

We illustrate the procedure for an example of a passive circuit, as shown in Figure A.2. Note that the nodes have been numbered n0 to n4. The format used for entering the element descriptions for SPICE evaluation is shown as follows (we are printing element names without subscripts since that is how they appear in computers. Thus, for example, L_{in} is listed as LIN):

```
RCL SET UP
*ELEMENT DESCRIPTION
R1            3         0         500
RD            4         0         1K
LIN           1         2         10MH
CBATTERY   2         3         .1UF
D1            2         4         MOD1
.MODEL     MOD1     D         (VJ = 0.7)
*SOURCE DESCRIPTION
VIN           1         0 DC   5
.END
```

A.2.1.2 Active Components   The identification of the transistor in the format for active devices is as follows: The collector (or drain) comes first, the

Figure A.3
Active element
designations.

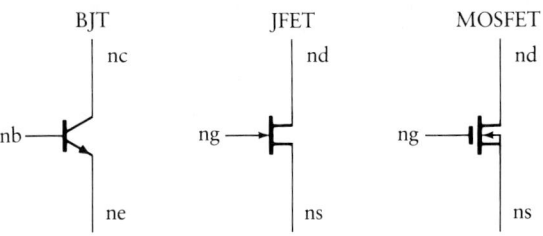

Figure A.4
Example of transistor
amplifier.

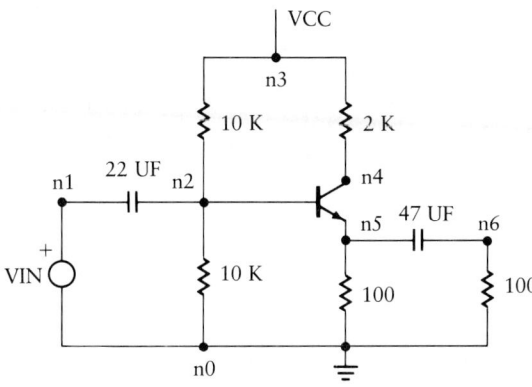

base (or gate) is second, and the emitter (or source) is last. This is illustrated as follows:

Type	Format				
BJT	Qxxxxxxx	nc	nb	ne	modname
JFET	Jxxxxxxx	nd	ng	ns	modname
MOSFET	Mxxxxxxx	nd	ng	ns	modname

Active element designations are shown in Figure A.3. A model name is entered along with the corresponding MODEL statement to specify the type of transistor (*npn*, *pnp*, *n*-channel or *p*-channel). The MODEL statement may also be used to reset the maximum value of beta, the reverse early voltage, or the base-emitter breakdown voltage of the BJT and to reset the threshold voltage or transconductance of the FET devices. There are other parameters that can be reset, depending upon what type of analysis is to be conducted. (Refer to Subsection A.2.1.3 for the MODEL statements and typical transistor default values.)

An example of a transistor amplifier is shown in Figure A.4. Note that the nodes have been numbered n0 to n6. The format used for entering the element descriptions for SPICE evaluation is shown next:

EMITTER FOLLOWER SET UP
*ELEMENT DESCRIPTION

R1	2	0	10K
R2	2	3	10K
RC	3	4	2K
RE	5	0	100
RL	6	0	100
CIN	2	1	22UF
C0	5	6	47UF
Q1	4	2	5 EFAM1

•MODEL EFAM1 NPN (BF = 75)
*SOURCE DESCRIPTION

VCC	3	0	DC 12
VIN	1	0	AC

.END

A.2.1.3 Semiconductor Devices   There are many parameters that can be defined in the SPICE MODEL statements—approximately 40 parameters for BJTs, 12 for JFETs, and 38 for MOSFETs. The particular version of the SPICE program instructions identifies the parameters that can be used and the typical default values assigned by that program. The MODEL statement abbreviations are shown next.

MODEL FORMAT

.MODEL modname type <pname1 = pvalue1 pname2 = pvalue2 pname3 = pvalue3>

Type	Applicable Device
NPN	*npn* BJT
PNP	*pnp* BJT
D	Diode
NJF	*n*-channel JFET
PJF	*p*-channel JFET
NMOS	*n*-channel MOSFET
PMOS	*p*-channel MOSFET

MODEL PARAMETER OPTIONS LIST (major parameters)

Parameter	pname	MODEL	pvalue DEFAULT
Junction potential	VJ	Diode	1V
Reverse breakdown voltage	BV	Diode	Infinite
Ohmic resistance	RS	Diode	0 ohms
Reverse early voltage	VAR	BJT	Infinite
Max forward beta	BF	BJT	100

Parameter	pname	MODEL	pvalue DEFAULT
Base-emitter voltage	VJE	BJT	.75 V
Base-collector capacitance	CJC	BJT	0
Base-emitter capacitance	CJE	BJT	0
Forward transit time	TF	BJT	0
Threshold voltage	VTO	JFET	-2
Transconductance	BETA	JFET	$1\text{E-}4 \text{ A/V}^2$
G-S junction capacitance	CGS	JFET	0
G-D junction capacitance	CGD	JFET	0
Threshold voltage	VTO	MOSFET	0
Transconductance	KP	MOSFET	2 A/V^2
Substrate-D J. Capacitance	CBD	MOSFET	0
Substrate-S J. Capacitance	CBS	MOSFET	0

The model name (modname) included in the MODEL statement corresponds to the model name specified in the active component and diode description statements. One MODEL statement may be used to reference all devices with the same model name provided the device specifications are identical. For example, the MODEL statements for the circuit shown in Figure A.5 are presented below.

Figure A.5
Use of MODEL
statements.

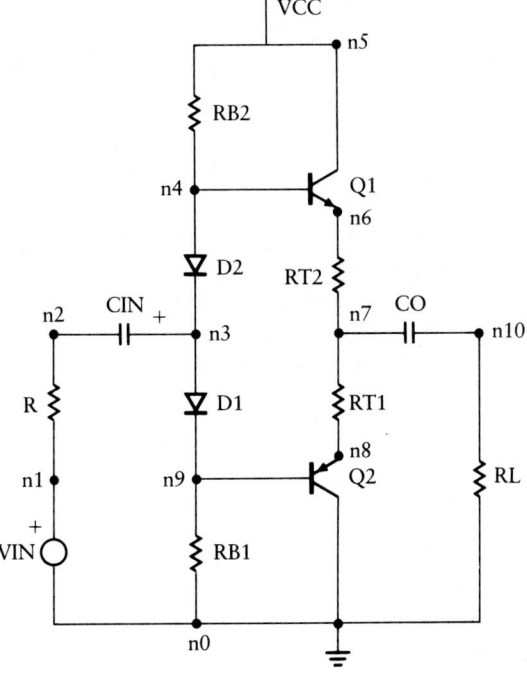

```
CSDC SET UP
*ELEMENT DESCRIPTION
RI          2    1     50
RT1         7    8     1
RT2         6    7     1
RB1         9    0     700
RB2         4    5     700
CIN         3    2     327U
C0          7    10    995U
D1          3    9     MOD1
D2          4    3     MOD1
Q1          5    4     6 MODTOP
Q2          0    9     8 MODBOT
.MODEL      MOD1       D(VJ = .7 RS = 10)
.MODEL      MODTOP     NPN(BF = 75 VJE = .7)
.MODEL      MODBOT     PNP(BF = 75 VJE = .7)
*SOURCE DESCRIPTION
VCC         5    0     DC 12
VIN         1    0     AC    .1M 90 DEGREES
.END
```

A.2.2   *Source Description*

The sources that we encounter in electronic circuits are voltage and current sources. We now discuss how both linear independent and dependent voltage and current sources are entered into the SPICE program.

A.2.2.1 Dependent Linear Sources   The four dependent type voltage and current sources are listed below.

Source Type	Format
Voltage-controlled current source	Gxxxxxxx n+ n− nc+ nc− value
Voltage-controlled voltage source	Exxxxxxx n+ n− nc+ nc− value
Current-controlled current source	Fxxxxxxx n+ n− vname value
Current-controlled voltage source	Hxxxxxxx n+ n− vname value

The source control is defined by the controlling voltage nodes (nc+ and nc−) or the name of the voltage sources through which the controlling current is flowing (vname). If no voltage source is contained within the controlling current loop, a dc source with a value of zero can be used to measure the controlling current. The direction of positive controlling current flow is from the positive node, through the source, and to the negative node of the applicable voltage source. A current source of positive value forces current to flow from the positive node, through the source, to the negative node. The output values

Figure A.6
Example of dependent current source.

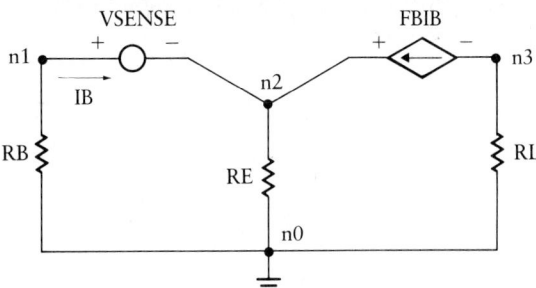

refer to the transconductance, voltage gain, current gain, or transresistance, respectively. We use the circuit of Figure A.6 as an example of how a dependent current source is formatted for input to SPICE. The input format is as shown next:

```
DEPENDENT SOURCE SET UP
RB          1      0    20K
RE          2      0    100
RL          3      0    2K
FBIB        3      2    VSENSE 100
VSENSE      1      2
.END
```

A.2.2.2 Independent Linear Sources   There are two linear sources, voltage and current, which are either ac or dc. The format for these sources is shown as follows:

Source Type	Source Input
Voltage	Vxxxxxxx n+ n− <<DC> d/t><AC mag <phase>>
Current	Ixxxxxxx n+ n− <<DC> d/t><AC mag <phase>>

An independent source is assigned an ac magnitude and phase (mag, phase), which is excited only during ac analysis, dc value (d/t) for determining the small signal bias solution for ac and transient analysis, and/or a time-dependent function (d/t) for transient and dc (using time-zero value) analysis. If the ac magnitude is omitted following the keyword AC, a value of unity is assumed. If the ac phase is omitted, a value of zero is assumed. The time-dependent functions may be sinusoidal or pulse trains. Positive current is assumed to flow from the positive node, through the source, to the negative node. A current source of positive value forces current out of the positive node, through the source, and into the negative node. Voltage sources, in addition to exciting the circuit, may be used as ammeters for SPICE. That is, a zero-value voltage source may be inserted for the purpose of measuring current.

Following are examples of the format for time dependent and pulse sources.

SINUSOIDAL FORMAT

SIN (vo va freq td theta)

Parameter	Default Values
vo (offset)	0
va (amplitude)	1
freq (frequency)	1/tstop
td (delay time)	0
theta (damping factor)	0

PULSE FORMAT

PULSE (v1 v2 td tr tf pw period)

Parameter	Default Values
v1 (initial value)	—
v2 (pulsed value)	—
td (delay time)	0
tr (rise time)	tstep
tf (fall time)	tstep
pw (pulse width)	tstop
period	tstop

The term *tstep* is defined as the printing increment and *tstop* is the final time of print. For a detailed explanation of tstep and tstop, refer to Subsection A.2.4.3.

A.2.3   *Subcircuits*

Complicated circuits may be reduced by defining subcircuits and then inter-connecting them with the main circuit in as many locations as needed. The subcircuit description must be placed between a SUBCKT statement and an ENDS statement. Subcircuits may be nested within other subcircuits. All sub-circuit element nodes not included in the SUBCKT statement are strictly local to that subcircuit, with the exception of node 0 (ground), which is global. All device models are also local to the applicable subcircuit. The element nodes defined in the SUBCKT and CALL statement must not be labeled zero (ground). Control statements (those statements defined in the analysis request and output request sections) must not appear within the subcircuit description. The definition and CALL formats are as follows:

DEFINITION FORMAT

.SUBCKT   subname n1   <n2   n3 ....>
                                subcircuit description
.ENDS   <subname>

The subcircuit name (subname) is only required for the ENDS statement where subcircuits are nested within subcircuits.

CALL FORMAT

Xyyyyyyy   n1   <n2   n3.....>   subname

The external nodes (n1 <n2   n3.....>) are the main circuit nodes, which correspond directly to the specified subcircuit nodes. Refer to the example of Section A.3.4 for demonstration of the use of subcircuits.

A.2.4   *Analysis Request*

Since we now have finished discussing techniques for describing the circuit, we are ready to use the program for analysis. Three types of analysis are used, as follows: dc analysis, ac analysis, and transient analysis. We discuss each of these individually.

A.2.4.1 dc Analysis   The dc analysis statement defines a dc voltage or current range to an existing INDEPENDENT, ac or dc, voltage or current source (srcname). The circuit is then analyzed at every increment (incr) within the specified dc voltage or current range (start stop). Optionally, a second source (src2) may be specified with associated sweep parameters. In this case, the first source is swept over its range for each value of the second source. This analysis request is useful for obtaining semiconductor-device output characteristics. The statement, .OP, must be inserted if only dc analysis is being performed. This type of analysis request forces SPICE to determine the dc operating point for the specified input dc voltage with the capacitors open and the inductors shorted. Prior to transient analysis, a dc operating-point analysis is automatically performed in order to determine the initial conditions. The dc analysis is also performed prior to an ac small-signal analysis to determine the linearized, small-signal models for nonlinear devices. To obtain the dc small-signal value of the transfer function (output/input, input resistance, and output resistance), we use the .TF analysis. This is summarized as follows:

DC FORMAT

.DC   srcname   start stop inc <src2 start2 stop2 incr2>
.OP
.TF   V (n1,n2) VIN
.TF   I(VLOAD) VIN

A.2.4.2 ac Analysis   The ac statement is used to perform a circuit analysis over a specified frequency range. The PLOT output statement produces a Bode plot. The frequency scale may be calibrated in decades (DEC), octaves (OCT), or linear (LIN). Before the ac analysis is performed, a small-signal bias solution is automatically performed to determine the linearized small-signal models for nonlinear devices. To make this analysis meaningful, at least one independent source must be specified with an ac value. The starting and stopping points need to be defined for this analysis. The resultant circuit is then analyzed at a number of points per decade (nd), octave (no), or linear (np) over the specified frequency range (fstart fstop). The ac analysis is insensitive to rail voltages. Therefore, to simplify work, a unity voltage or current source is used so that the output becomes the same as the transfer function. That is,

$$H(S) = OUTPUT(S)/INPUT(S) = OUTPUT(S)/1$$
$$H(S) = OUTPUT(S)$$

AC FORMAT

.AC	DEC	nd	fstart	fstop
.AC	OCT	no	fstart	fstop
.AC	LIN	np	fstart	fstop

A.2.4.3 Transient Analysis   The transient analysis portion of SPICE is used to compute the transient output variables as a function of time over a specified time interval (tstop <tstart>). A small-signal bias solution is automatically performed first, using the time-zero value for time dependent sources. Then the circuit is analyzed at each increment (tstep) within the specified time range. When tstart is omitted, it is assumed to be zero. Transient analysis is sensitive to rail voltages, and clipping therefore occurs when supply voltages are exceeded. Symbols for transient analysis are as follows:

TRANSIENT ANALYSIS
.TRAN   tstep   tstop   <tstart>

A.2.5   *Output Request*

After SPICE accomplishes the analysis, we record the data to be analyzed or stored for future use. This is accomplished by having the SPICE program either print or plot on a printer, using the PRINT or PLOT statements.

A.2.5.1 Print   The PRINT statement produces a tabular listing of the specified output variables (0V1 <0V2....0V8>), a current flowing through an INDE-PENDENT voltage source, or a specified voltage to be printed. The type of analysis to be printed (prtype) (ac, dc, noise, distortion, or transient) must also be defined with the following:

PRINT FORMAT

.PRINT   prtype   ov1   <ov2...ov8>

OUTPUT VARIABLE FORMAT

Parameter	Format
Voltage	V (n+ <,n−>)
Current	I (vname)

If the negative node of the output voltage is not indicated, ground is assumed. The direction of positive current flow is from the positive node, through the source, to the negative node of the applicable voltage source (vname). A maximum of eight output variables may be defined in one PRINT statement, but there is no limit to the number of PRINT statements for each type of analysis.

The various ac output variable parameters that may be defined are as follows:

AC OV FORMAT

Parameter	Voltage	Current
Real part	VR (n+ <,n−>)	IR (vname)
Imaginary part	VI (n+ <,n−>)	II (vname)
Magnitude	VM (n+ <,n−>)	IM (vname)
Phase	VP (n+ <,n−>)	IP (vname)
Decibels	VDB (N+ <,n−>)	IDB (vname)

Example Formats

.PRINT AC VM(1)   VP(1)
.PRINT TRAN I(VIN) V(3.4)
.PRINT DC   V(1,2)

In the example formats, the first PRINT example statement prints the ac magnitude and phase values of the voltage at node 1 with respect to ground. The next statement prints the transient values of the current through the INDE-PENDENT voltage source VIN and the voltage between nodes 3 and 4. The last statement prints the dc values for the voltage between nodes 1 and 2.

A.2.5.2 Plot   The PLOT statement causes the value of the defined output variables (0V1, 0V2...0V8) to be plotted. The plot type (pltype) is either AC, DC, or TRANSIENT. The PLOT statement output variable syntax and sign conventions are the same as those for the PRINT statement with the exception of optional upper- and lower-bound limits (plo, phi). All output variables to the left of the limits are plotted using the specified scale. Without the optional limits, SPICE automatically determines the minimum and maximum values of all output variables and scales the plot to fit. Multiple scaled plots and a legend are produced when appropriate. When more than one output variable appears on the same plot, the first output variables are printed as well as plotted. Two or more output variables with approximately the same value are indicated by an X on the plot. The plot format is as follows:

PLOT FORMAT

.PLOT   pltype ov1 <(pl01,phi1)>   <ov2 <(plo2,phi2)>..ov8>

A.2.5.3 Options Statement   User-defined model parameters may be suppressed (NOMOD) and/or the node (NODE) can be printed using OPTIONS statements, as follows:

OPTIONS FORMAT

.OPTIONS   <NOMOD>   <NODE>

A.3   Examples of Programs

In this section, we provide examples of circuits that show the listing of the input data and output of each example.

A.3.1   *CE Amplifier*

A CE amplifier, as shown in Figure A.7, is analyzed over the frequency range of 1 kHz to 100 kHz. The voltage source, VSENSOR, is used as an ammeter to measure the output current. You should study the printout and verify the following results:

Figure A.7
CE amplifier.

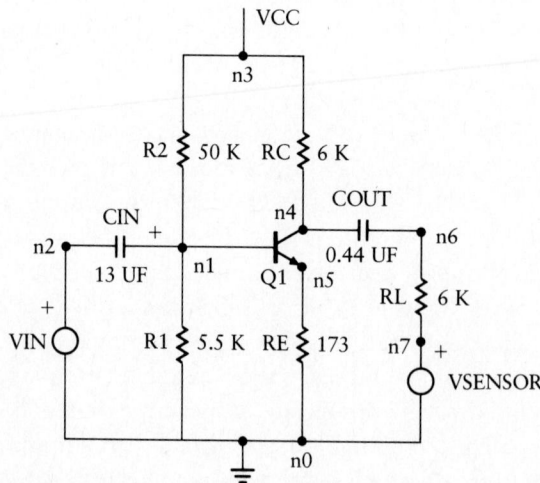

$$A_v \quad = 24 \text{ dB}$$
$$A_i \quad = 10.5$$
$$f(\text{break}) = 30 \text{ Hz}$$
$$R_{in} \quad = 4 \text{ k}\Omega$$

The listing is shown.

```
FFIND,SPICE,PROJ1
1******* 86/04/30.  *******  SPICE 2G.5 (10AUG81)  ******* 18.40.37.*****

0*  COMMON EMITTER

0****    INPUT LISTING               TEMPERATURE =   27.000 DEG C

0*****************************************************************************



*  ELEMENT DESCRIPTION

RC   3   4   6K
RL   6   7   6K
RE   5   0   173
R1   1   0   5.5K
R2   3   1   50K
CIN  2   1   13U
COUT 6   4   .44U
Q1   4   1   5  M2N2222A
.MODEL M2N2222A NPN (VJE=.7,CJE=25PF,CJC=8PF,TF=2.5NS,RB=100,RC=10,BF=100)

*  SOURCE DESCRIPTION

VCC    3   0   12
VIN    2   0   AC
VSENSOR 7  0

*  ANALYSIS REQUEST

.AC DEC   5   1   100MEGHZ

.OPTIONS NODE

*  OUTPUT REQUESTS

.PLOT  AC  I(VSENSOR)   I(VIN)
.PLOT  AC  VDB(6)

.END
1************* 86/04/30. ********************* SPICE 2G.5 (10AUG81) ******************** 18.40.37.**************

0*  COMMON EMITTER
0****               ELEMENT NODE TABLE               TEMPERATURE =   27.000 DEG C

0****************************************************************************************************************
```

```
0    0    RE      R1      VCC     VIN     VSENSOR  Q1
0    1    R1      R2      CIN     Q1
0    2    CIN     VIN
0    3    RC      R2      VCC
0    4    RC      COUT    Q1
0    5    RE      Q1
0    6    RL      COUT
0    7    RL      VSENSOR
```

1************** 86/04/30. ********************** SPICE 2G.5 (10AUG81) ****************** 18.40.37.***************

0* COMMON EMITTER
0****   BJT MODEL PARAMETERS   TEMPERATURE =   27.000 DEG C

0**

```
          M2N2222A
0TYPE     NPN
0IS       1.00E-16
0BF       100.000
0NF         1.000
0BR         1.000
0NR         1.000
0RB       100.000
0RC        10.000
0CJE      2.50E-11
0VJE        .700
0TF       2.50E-09
0CJC      8.00E-12
```

1************** 86/04/30. ********************** SPICE 2G.5 (10AUG81) ****************** 18.40.37.***************

0* COMMON EMITTER
0****   SMALL SIGNAL BIAS SOLUTION   TEMPERATURE =   27.000 DEG C

0**

```
NODE   VOLTAGE    NODE   VOLTAGE    NODE   VOLTAGE    NODE   VOLTAGE    NODE   VOLTAGE    NODE   VOLTAGE    NODE   VOLTAGE

( 1)   1.1012    ( 2)   0.0000    ( 3)  12.0000    ( 4)   1.3433    ( 5)    .3103    ( 6)   0.0000    ( 7)   0.0000
```

     VOLTAGE SOURCE CURRENTS

     NAME   CURRENT

     VCC   -1.994E-03

     VIN   0.

     VSENSOR   0.

     TOTAL POWER DISSIPATION   2.39E-02 WATTS
1************** 86/04/30. ********************** SPICE 2G.5 (10AUG81) ****************** 18.40.37.***************

0* COMMON EMITTER
0****   OPERATING POINT INFORMATION   TEMPERATURE =   27.000 DEG C

0**

```
0
0**** BIPOLAR JUNCTION TRANSISTORS


0          Q1
0MODEL     M2N2222A
 IB        1.78E-05
 IC        1.78E-03
 VBE        .791
 VBC       -.242
 VCE       1.033
 BETADC    100.000
 GM        6.87E-02
 RPI       1.46E+03
 RX        1.00E+02
 RO        1.00E+12
 CPI       2.16E-10
 CMU       7.33E-12
 CBX       0.
 CCS       0.
 BETAAC    100.000
 FT        4.89E+07
1*************** 86/04/30. ********************** SPICE 2G.5 (10AUG81) ******************** 18.40.37.***************

0*  COMMON EMITTER
0****                  AC ANALYSIS                      TEMPERATURE =   27.000 DEG C


0*****************************************************************************************************************


0LEGEND:

 *: I(VSENSOR)
 +: I(VIN)

     FREQ      I(VSENSOR)

 (*+)-------------  1.000E-05        1.000E-04        1.000E-03        1.000E-02        1.000E-01
                   - - - - - - - - - - - - - - - - - - - - - - - - - - - - - - - - - - - - - - - - -
 1.000E+00  2.664E-05    .        *        +    .              .                .                .
 1.585E+00  6.258E-05    .             *      . +              .                .                .
 2.512E+00  1.370E-04    .                 .  * +              .                .                .
 3.981E+00  2.710E-04    .                    +  *             .                .                .
 6.310E+00  4.827E-04    .                    .  +        *    .                .                .
 1.000E+01  7.899E-04    .                    .  +           * .                .                .
 1.585E+01  1.200E-03    .                    .  +             . *              .                .
 2.512E+01  1.669E-03    .                    .  +             .   *            .                .
 3.981E+01  2.088E-03    .                    .  +             .      *         .                .
 6.310E+01  2.368E-03    .                    .  +             .        *       .                .
 1.000E+02  2.514E-03    .                    .  +             .         *      .                .
 1.585E+02  2.581E-03    .                    .  +             .          *     .                .
 2.512E+02  2.609E-03    .                    .  +             .          *     .                .
 3.981E+02  2.620E-03    .                    .  +             .          *     .                .
 6.310E+02  2.624E-03    .                    .  +             .          *     .                .
 1.000E+03  2.626E-03    .                    .  +             .          *     .                .
 1.585E+03  2.627E-03    .                    .  +             .          *     .                .
 2.512E+03  2.627E-03    .                    .  +             .          *     .                .
 3.981E+03  2.627E-03    .                    .  +             .          *     .                .
 6.310E+03  2.627E-03    .                    .  +             .          *     .                .
 1.000E+04  2.627E-03    .                    .  +             .          *     .                .
```

```
1.585E+04    2.627E-03   .              .        +            .          x               .
2.512E+04    2.627E-03   .              .       +             .          x               .
3.981E+04    2.627E-03   .              .       +             .          x               .
6.310E+04    2.627E-03   .              .       +             .          x               .
1.000E+05    2.627E-03   .              .        +            .          x               .
1.585E+05    2.626E-03   .              .         +           .          x               .
2.512E+05    2.623E-03   .              .          +          .          x               .
3.981E+05    2.617E-03   .              .           +         .          x               .
6.310E+05    2.601E-03   .              .            +        .          x               .
1.000E+06    2.563E-03   .              .             +       .          x               .
1.585E+06    2.473E-03   .              .              +      .       x                   .
2.512E+06    2.284E-03   .              .               .    +x                           .
3.981E+06    1.951E-03   .              .                .   x  +                          .
6.310E+06    1.507E-03   .              .              x      .        +                  .
1.000E+07    1.064E-03   .              .            .x       .           +               .
1.585E+07    7.110E-04   .              .          x          .             +             .
2.512E+07    4.653E-04   .              .        x            .              +            .
3.981E+07    3.066E-04   .              .      x              .              +            .
6.310E+07    2.098E-04   .              .    x                .              +            .
1.000E+08    1.548E-04   .              .  x                  .              +            .
```
                         -

```
Y
1***************** 86/04/30.  ********************** SPICE 2G.5 (10AUG81)  ********************** 18.40.37.*************

0*  COMMON EMITTER
0*****                   AC ANALYSIS                            TEMPERATURE =   27.000 DEG C

0***************************************************************************************************************************
```

```
     FREQ      VDB(6)

                  -2.000E+01          0.           2.000E+01        4.000E+01        6.000E+01
                  - - - - - - - - - - - - - - - - - - - - - - - - - - - - - - - - - - - - -
    1.000E+00    -1.593E+01   .    x        .             .                .                .
    1.585E+00    -8.509E+00   .         x      .          .                .                .
    2.512E+00    -1.703E+00   .             x  .          .                .                .
    3.981E+00     4.222E+00   .             .  x          .                .                .
    6.310E+00     9.237E+00   .             .      x      .                .                .
    1.000E+01     1.351E+01   .             .        x    .                .                .
    1.585E+01     1.715E+01   .             .          x  .                .                .
    2.512E+01     2.001E+01   .             .            x.                .                .
    3.981E+01     2.196E+01   .             .            .x                .                .
    6.310E+01     2.305E+01   .             .            . x               .                .
    1.000E+02     2.357E+01   .             .            . x               .                .
    1.585E+02     2.380E+01   .             .            .  x              .                .
    2.512E+02     2.389E+01   .             .            .  x              .                .
    3.981E+02     2.393E+01   .             .            .  x              .                .
    6.310E+02     2.394E+01   .             .            .  x              .                .
    1.000E+03     2.395E+01   .             .            .  x              .                .
    1.585E+03     2.395E+01   .             .            .  x              .                .
    2.512E+03     2.395E+01   .             .            .  x              .                .
    3.981E+03     2.395E+01   .             .            .  x              .                .
    6.310E+03     2.395E+01   .             .            .  x              .                .
    1.000E+04     2.395E+01   .             .            .  x              .                .
    1.585E+04     2.395E+01   .             .            .  x              .                .
    2.512E+04     2.395E+01   .             .            .  x              .                .
    3.981E+04     2.395E+01   .             .            .  x              .                .
    6.310E+04     2.395E+01   .             .            .  x              .                .
    1.000E+05     2.395E+01   .             .            .  x              .                .
    1.585E+05     2.395E+01   .             .            .  x              .                .
```

```
2,512E+05   2,394E+01  ,            ,            ,      I        ,          ,
3,981E+05   2,392E+01  ,            ,            ,      I        ,          ,
6,310E+05   2,387E+01  ,            ,            ,      I        ,          ,
1,000E+06   2,374E+01  ,            ,            ,      I        ,          ,
1,585E+06   2,343E+01  ,            ,            ,    I          ,          ,
2,512E+06   2,274E+01  ,            ,            ,  , I          ,          ,
3,981E+06   2,137E+01  ,            ,            , I            ,          ,
6,310E+06   1,913E+01  ,            ,        I,                 ,          ,
1,000E+07   1,610E+01  ,            ,      I                    ,          ,
1,585E+07   1,260E+01  ,            ,    I                      ,          ,
2,512E+07   8,917E+00  ,            ,  I                        ,          ,
3,981E+07   5,295E+00  ,          I                            ,          ,
6,310E+07   2,000E+00  ,       , I                             ,          ,
1,000E+08  -6,438E-01  ,    I,                                 ,          ,
                       - - - - - - - - - - - - - - - - - - - - - - - - - -
```

```
Y
0
        JOB CONCLUDED
0         TOTAL JOB TIME        1,63
$REVERT, SPICE COMPLETED
/
```

A.3.2   *CS Amplifier*

An *n*-channel JFET is used as a CS amplifier, as shown in Figure A.8. The
input impedance is calculated by dividing the input voltage, VM(2), by unity.
You should verify that the current gain is approximately 70 and the corner
frequency is 1 Hz. The listings of the computer inputs and outputs are shown
next.

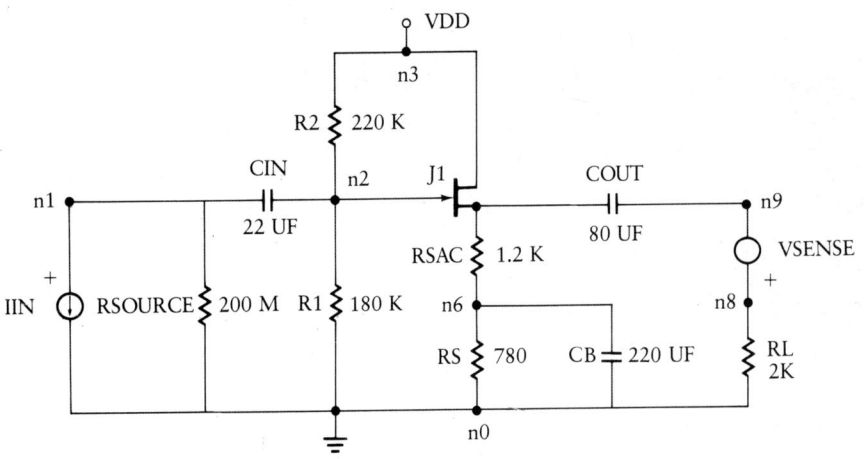

Figure A.8   CS amplifier.

```
FFIND,SPICE,PROJ2
1******* 86/04/30. ******* SPICE 2G.5 (10AUG81) ******* 19.25.47.*****

0* COMMON SOURCE

0****    INPUT LISTING                  TEMPERATURE =   27.000 DEG C

0********************************************************************

  * ELEMENT DESCRIPTION

  R1   2   0   180K
  R2   2   3   220K
  RSOURCE  1  0   200MEG
  RS   6   0   780
  RSAC 5   6   1.2K
  RL   8   0   2K
  CIN  1   2   22U
  COUT 5   9   80U
  CB   6   0   220U
  J1   3   2   5   M2N5951
  .MODEL M2N5951 NJF  (VTO=3, BETA=4.75M, RD=250, CGS=6PF, CGD=2PF)

  * SOURCE DESCRIPTION

  VDD  3   0   20
  IIN  1   0   AC
  VSENSE  8   9

  * ANALYSIS REQUESTS

  .AC  DEC   5   .01  1.0E11

  * OUTPUT REQUESTS

  .PLOT AC  VM(2)    (98940, 98955)  IM(VSENSE)
  .PLOT AC  VM(8)
  .END
1************** 86/04/30. ******************** SPICE 2G.5 (10AUG81) ******************** 19.25.47.***************

0* COMMON SOURCE
0****                JFET MODEL PARAMETERS                  TEMPERATURE =   27.000 DEG C

0**************************************************************************************************************

          M2N5951
0TYPE     NJF
0VTO       3.000
0BETA     4.75E-03
0RD       250.000
0CGS      6.00E-12
0CGD      2.00E-12
1************** 86/04/30. ******************** SPICE 2G.5 (10AUG81) ******************** 19.25.47.***************

0* COMMON SOURCE
0****                SMALL SIGNAL BIAS SOLUTION             TEMPERATURE =   27.000 DEG C

0**************************************************************************************************************
```

NODE	VOLTAGE	NODE	VOLTAGE	NODE	VOLTAGE	NODE	VOLTAGE	NODE	VOLTAGE	NODE	VOLTAGE	NODE	VOLTAGE
(1)	0.0000	(2)	.7557	(3)	20.0000	(5)	.1649	(6)	.0650	(8)	0.0000	(9)	0.0000

```
    VOLTAGE SOURCE CURRENTS
    NAME     CURRENT


    VDD     -8.747E-05
    VSENSE   0.


    TOTAL POWER DISSIPATION   1.75E-03  WATTS
1**************** 86/04/30. ********************** SPICE 2G.5 (10AUG81) ********************** 19.25.47.***************

0*  COMMON SOURCE
0****            OPERATING POINT INFORMATION              TEMPERATURE =   27.000 DEG C


0*************************************************************************************************************

0
0**** JFETS


0        J1
0MODEL    M2N5951
 ID      3.85E-11
 VGS     .591
 VDS     19.835
 GM      0.
 GDS     0.
 CGS     9.26E-12
 CGD     4.45E-13
1**************** 86/04/30. ********************** SPICE 2G.5 (10AUG81) ********************** 19.25.47.***************

0*  COMMON SOURCE
0****            AC ANALYSIS                              TEMPERATURE =   27.000 DEG C


0*************************************************************************************************************


0LEGEND:

*: VM(2)
+: IM(VSENSE)

    FREQ     VM(2)

(*)----------------- 9.894E+04        9.895E+04        9.895E+04        9.896E+04        9.896E+04
                     - - - - - - - - - - - - - - - - - - - - - - - - - - - - - - - - - - - - - - -

(+)----------------- 1.000E-03        1.000E-02        1.000E-01        1.000E+00        1.000E+01
                     - - - - - - - - - - - - - - - - - - - - - - - - - - - - - - - - - - - - - - -

 1.000E-02  2.238E+03  .           +               .               .               .
 1.585E-02  2.238E+03  :           .    +          .               .               .
 2.512E-02  2.236E+03  .           .         +     .               .               .
 3.981E-02  2.232E+03  .           .            +  .               .               .
 6.310E-02  2.221E+03  .           .              + .              .               .
 1.000E-01  2.195E+03  .           .               +.             .               .
 1.585E-01  2.136E+03  .           .               .  +           .               .
 2.512E-01  2.013E+03  .           .               .      +       .               .
 3.981E-01  1.806E+03  .           .               .         +    .               .
 6.310E-01  1.551E+03  .           .               .           +  .               .
 1.000E+00  1.330E+03  .           .               .            + .               .
 1.585E+00  1.187E+03  .           .               .             +.               .
 2.512E+00  1.111E+03  .           .               .             + .               .
 3.981E+00  1.075E+03  .           .               .             + .               .
```

```
 6.310E+00   1.060E+03  .                    .                    .              +                    .                                        .
 1.000E+01   1.054E+03  .                    .                    .              +                    .                                        .
 1.585E+01   1.051E+03  .                    .                    .              +                    .                                        .
 2.512E+01   1.050E+03  .                    .                    .              +                    .                                        .
 3.981E+01   1.050E+03  .                    .                    .              +                    .                                        .
 6.310E+01   1.049E+03  .                    .                    .              +                    .                                        .
 1.000E+02   1.049E+03  .                    .                    .              +                    .                                        .
 1.585E+02   1.049E+03  .                    .                    .              +                    .                                        .
 2.512E+02   1.049E+03  .                    .                    .              +                    .                                        .
 3.981E+02   1.049E+03  .                    .                    .              +                    .                                        .
 6.310E+02   1.049E+03  .                    .                    .              +                    .                                        .
 1.000E+03   1.049E+03  .                    .                    .              +                    .                                        .
 1.585E+03   1.049E+03  .                    .                    .              +                    .                                        .
 2.512E+03   1.049E+03  .                    .                    .              +                    .                                        .
 3.981E+03   1.049E+03  .                    .                    .              +                    .                                        .
 6.310E+03   1.049E+03  .                    .                    .              +                    .                                        .
 1.000E+04   1.049E+03  .                    .                    .              +                    .                                        .
 1.585E+04   1.049E+03  .                    .                    .              +                    .                                        .
 2.512E+04   1.049E+03  .                    .                    .              +                    .                                        .
 3.981E+04   1.049E+03  .                    .                    .              +                    .                                        .
 6.310E+04   1.049E+03  .                    .                    .              +                    .                                        .
 1.000E+05   1.049E+03  .                    .                    .              +                    .                                        .
 1.585E+05   1.049E+03  .                    .                    .              +                    .                                        .
 2.512E+05   1.049E+03  .                    .                    .              +                    .                                        .
 3.981E+05   1.049E+03  .                    .                    .              +                    .                                        .
 6.310E+05   1.049E+03  .                    .                    .              +                    .                                        .
 1.000E+06   1.049E+03  .                    .                    .              +                    .                                        .
 1.585E+06   1.049E+03  .                    .                    .              +                    .                                        .
 2.512E+06   1.049E+03  .                    .                    .              +                    .                                        .
 3.981E+06   1.048E+03  .                    .                    .              +                    .                                        .
 6.310E+06   1.045E+03  .                    .                    .              +                    .                                        .
 1.000E+07   1.039E+03  .                    .                    .              +                    .                                        .
 1.585E+07   1.024E+03  .                    .                    .              +                    .                                        .
 2.512E+07   9.925E+02  .                    .                    .              +                    .                                        .
 3.981E+07   9.341E+02  .                    .                    .              +                    .                                        .
 6.310E+07   8.523E+02  .                    .                    .             +                     .                                        .
 1.000E+08   7.684E+02  .                    .                    .          +                        .                                        .
 1.585E+08   6.933E+02  .                    .                    .        +                          .                                        .
 2.512E+08   6.124E+02  .                    .                    .     +                             .                                        .
 3.981E+08   5.107E+02  .                    .                    .   +                               .                                        .
 6.310E+08   3.993E+02  .                    .                    . +                                 .                                        .
 1.000E+09   3.061E+02  .                    .                    +                                   .                                        .
 1.585E+09   2.454E+02  .                    .                  +.                                    .                                        .
 2.512E+09   2.131E+02  .                    .                 .+                                     .                                        .
 3.981E+09   1.980E+02  .                    .                +                                       .                                        .
 6.310E+09   1.916E+02  .                    .                +                                       .                                        .
 1.000E+10   1.889E+02  .                    .              +.                                        .                                        .
 1.585E+10   1.879E+02  .                    .              +.                                        .                                        .
 2.512E+10   1.874E+02  .                    .              +.                                        .                                        .
 3.981E+10   1.873E+02  .                    .              +.                                        .                                        .
 6.310E+10   1.872E+02  .                    .              +.                                        .                                        .
 1.000E+11   1.872E+02  .                    .              +.                                        .                                        .
                       - - - - - - - - - - - - - - - - - - - - - - - - - - - - - - - - - - - - - - - - - - - - - - - - - - - - -
```

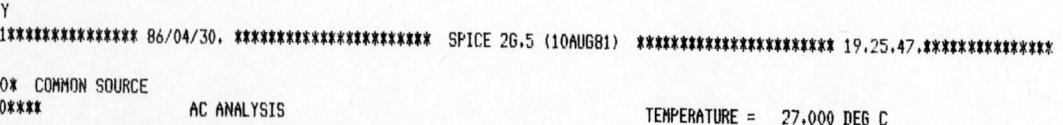

```
Y
1*************** 86/04/30.  ****************** SPICE 2G.5 (10AUG81)  ****************** 19.25.47.***************

0*  COMMON SOURCE
0****              AC ANALYSIS                                    TEMPERATURE =   27.000 DEG C

0**************************************************************************************************************
```

FREQ VH(8)

		1.000E+01	3.162E+01	1.000E+02	3.162E+02	1.000E+03
1.000E-02	1.945E+01					
1.585E-02	3.081E+01					
2.512E-02	4.878E+01					
3.981E-02	7.712E+01					
6.310E-02	1.214E+02					
1.000E-01	1.894E+02					
1.585E-01	2.891E+02					
2.512E-01	4.211E+02					
3.981E-01	5.650E+02					
6.310E-01	6.805E+02					
1.000E+00	7.417E+02					
1.585E+00	7.580E+02					
2.512E+00	7.545E+02					
3.981E+00	7.486E+02					
6.310E+00	7.450E+02					
1.000E+01	7.433E+02					
1.585E+01	7.425E+02					
2.512E+01	7.422E+02					
3.981E+01	7.421E+02					
6.310E+01	7.421E+02					
1.000E+02	7.421E+02					
1.585E+02	7.421E+02					
2.512E+02	7.420E+02					
3.981E+02	7.420E+02					
6.310E+02	7.420E+02					
1.000E+03	7.420E+02					
1.585E+03	7.420E+02					
2.512E+03	7.420E+02					
3.981E+03	7.420E+02					
6.310E+03	7.420E+02					
1.000E+04	7.420E+02					
1.585E+04	7.420E+02					
2.512E+04	7.420E+02					
3.981E+04	7.420E+02					
6.310E+04	7.420E+02					
1.000E+05	7.420E+02					
1.585E+05	7.420E+02					
2.512E+05	7.420E+02					
3.981E+05	7.420E+02					
6.310E+05	7.420E+02					
1.000E+06	7.420E+02					
1.585E+06	7.420E+02					
2.512E+06	7.420E+02					
3.981E+06	7.418E+02					
6.310E+06	7.414E+02					
1.000E+07	7.406E+02					
1.585E+07	7.385E+02					
2.512E+07	7.339E+02					
3.981E+07	7.252E+02					
6.310E+07	7.116E+02					
1.000E+08	6.916E+02					
1.585E+08	6.584E+02					
2.512E+08	5.987E+02					
3.981E+08	5.059E+02					
6.310E+08	3.978E+02					
1.000E+09	3.056E+02					

```
1.585E+09    2.453E+02    ,              ,              ,              ,            *    ,                    ,
2.512E+09    2.130E+02    ,              ,              ,              ,           *    ,                    ,
3.981E+09    1.980E+02    ,              ,              ,              ,          *    ,                     ,
6.310E+09    1.916E+02    ,              ,              ,              ,          *    ,                     ,
1.000E+10    1.889E+02    ,              ,              ,              ,          *    ,                     ,
1.585E+10    1.879E+02    ,              ,              ,              ,          *    ,                     ,
2.512E+10    1.874E+02    ,              ,              ,              ,          *    ,                     ,
3.981E+10    1.873E+02    ,              ,              ,              ,          *    ,                     ,
6.310E+10    1.872E+02    ,              ,              ,              ,          *    ,                     ,
1.000E+11    1.872E+02    ,              ,              ,              ,          *    ,                     ,
```

```
Y
0
            JOB CONCLUDED
0           TOTAL JOB TIME         1.94
$REVERT, SPICE COMPLETED
/
```

A.3.3   *Full-Wave Rectifier*

A full-wave rectifier, which is shown in Figure A.9, is designed using an op-amp subcircuit. The op-amp subcircuit, which is shown in Figure A.10, has a dependent voltage source that is a function of the differential input voltage, VIN. Two resistors of high value, RCM1 and RCM2, are used to maintain a dc path to ground. The circuit is analyzed to produce a dc transfer curve within the defined range of −5 to +5 V dc. The transient waveform is then plotted over one period. The computer inputs and outputs are shown next.

Figure A.9
Full-wave rectifier.

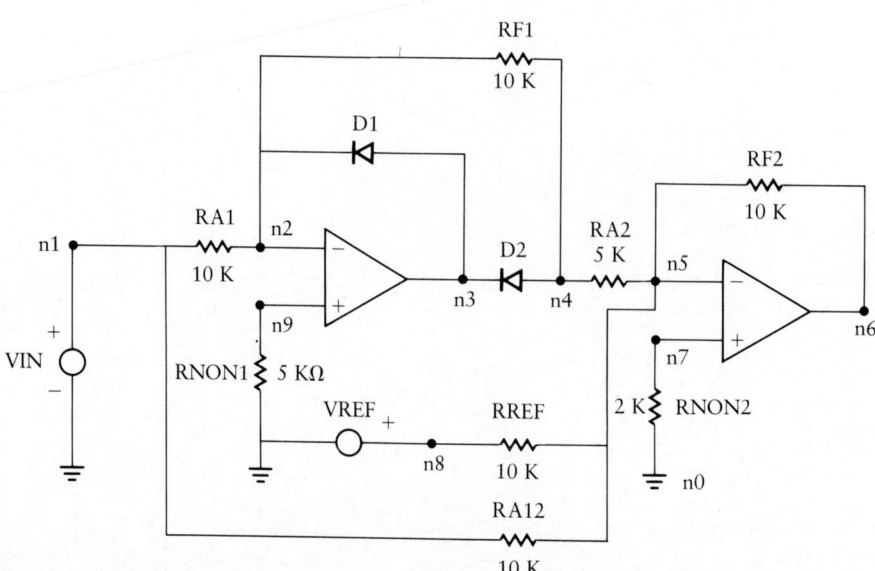

Figure A.10
Op-amp subcircuit.

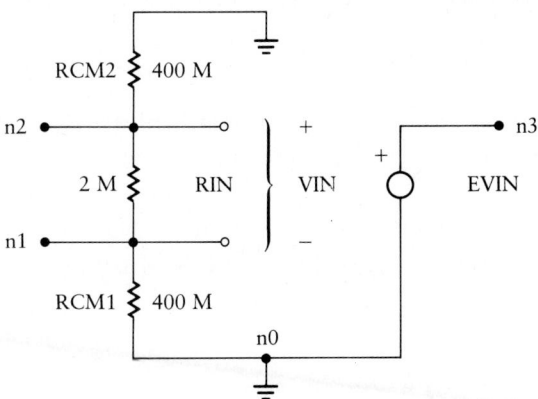

```
FFIND,SPICE,PROJ4
1******* 86/04/30, ******* SPICE 2G,5 (10AUG81)  ******* 18,56,41,*****

0*  FULLWAVE RECTIFIER

0****    INPUT LISTING           TEMPERATURE =   27,000 DEG C

0***************************************************************************

*  SUBCIRCUIT DESCRIPTION
,SUBCKT  OPAMP  1  2  3
RIN   1  2  2MEG
RCM1  1  0  400MEG
RCM2  2  0  400MEG
EVIN  3  0  2  1  10E5
,ENDS  OPAMP
*  MAIN CIRCUIT ELEMENT DESCRIPTION
RA1   1  2  10K
RF1   4  2  10K
D1    3  2  MOD1
D2    4  3  MOD1
RA12  1  5  10K
RA2   4  5  5K
RF2   6  5  10K
RREF  8  5  10K
RNON1 9  0  5K
RNON2 7  0  2K
,MODEL  MOD1  D  (VJ=,7)
*  MAIN CIRCUIT SOURCE DESCRIPTION
VREF  8  0  2
VIN   1  0  SIN (0  10  60)
*  CALL SUBCIRCUIT OPAMP
X1  2  9  3  OPAMP
X2  5  7  6  OPAMP
*  ANALYSIS REQUESTS
,TRAN  ,5M  16,5M
,DC  VIN  -5  5  ,5
*  OUTPUT REQUESTS
,PLOT  TRAN  V(6)
,PLOT  DC    V(6)
,END
```

```
1*************** 86/04/30. ********************** SPICE 2G.5 (10AUG81) ********************** 18.56.41.***************

0* FULLWAVE RECTIFIER
0****              DIODE MODEL PARAMETERS                          TEMPERATURE =   27.000 DEG C

0*******************************************************************************************************************


          MOD1
0IS    1.00E-14
0VJ       .700
1*************** 86/04/30. ********************** SPICE 2G.5 (10AUG81) ********************** 18.56.41.***************

0* FULLWAVE RECTIFIER
0****              DC TRANSFER CURVES                              TEMPERATURE =   27.000 DEG C

0*******************************************************************************************************************


   VIN       V(6)

            -2.000E+00         0.          2.000E+00        4.000E+00         6.000E+00
-5.000E+00   3.000E+00    .                .                .        *        .                .
-4.500E+00   2.500E+00    .                .                .      *         .                .
-4.000E+00   2.000E+00    .                .                *               .                .
-3.500E+00   1.500E+00    .                .          *                    .                .
-3.000E+00   1.000E+00    .                .      *                        .                .
-2.500E+00   5.000E-01    .                .  *                            .                .
-2.000E+00   4.058E-07    .             *                                  .                .
-1.500E+00  -5.000E-01    .          *                                     .                .
-1.000E+00  -1.000E+00    .      *                                         .                .
-5.000E-01  -1.500E+00    .  *                                             .                .
-2.842E-14  -2.000E+00    *                                                .                .
 5.000E-01  -1.500E+00    .  *                                             .                .
 1.000E+00  -1.000E+00    .      *                                         .                .
 1.500E+00  -5.000E-01    .          *                                     .                .
 2.000E+00  -1.067E-05    .             *                                  .                .
 2.500E+00   5.000E-01    .                .  *                            .                .
 3.000E+00   1.000E+00    .                .      *                        .                .
 3.500E+00   1.500E+00    .                .          *                    .                .
 4.000E+00   2.000E+00    .                .                *               .                .
 4.500E+00   2.500E+00    .                .                  *            .                .
 5.000E+00   3.000E+00    .                .                .        *      .                .
Y
1*************** 86/04/30. ********************** SPICE 2G.5 (10AUG81) ********************** 18.56.41.***************

0* FULLWAVE RECTIFIER
0****              INITIAL TRANSIENT SOLUTION                      TEMPERATURE =   27.000 DEG C

0*******************************************************************************************************************


 NODE   VOLTAGE    NODE   VOLTAGE    NODE   VOLTAGE    NODE   VOLTAGE    NODE   VOLTAGE    NODE   VOLTAGE    NODE   VOLTAGE

 (  1)   0.0000   (  2)    .0000   (  3)   -.2636   (  4)    .0000   (  5)    .0000   (  6)  -2.0000   (  7)    .0000

 (  8)   2.0000   (  9)    .0000
```

```
       VOLTAGE SOURCE CURRENTS

       NAME     CURRENT


       VREF     -2.000E-04

       VIN       2.266E-10



       TOTAL POWER DISSIPATION   4.00E-04  WATTS
1*************** 86/04/30, ********************** SPICE 2G.5 (10AUG81)  ********************** 18.56.41.***************

0* FULLWAVE RECTIFIER
0****              OPERATING POINT INFORMATION              TEMPERATURE =   27.000 DEG C


0*******************************************************************************************************************


0
0**** VOLTAGE-CONTROLLED VOLTAGE SOURCES


0          EVIN.X1   EVIN.X2
 V-SOURCE    -.264    -2.000
 I-SOURCE  2.67E-10  2.00E-04
0
0**** DIODES


0          D1        D2
0MODEL     MOD1      MOD1
  ID      -2.74E-13  2.68E-10
  VD       -.264      .264
1*************** 86/04/30. ********************** SPICE 2G.5 (10AUG81)  ********************** 18.56.41.***************

0* FULLWAVE RECTIFIER
0****              TRANSIENT ANALYSIS                        TEMPERATURE =   27.000 DEG C


0*******************************************************************************************************************



       TIME     V(6)

                       -5.000E+00          0.          5.000E+00          1.000E+01          1.500E+01
                       - - - - - - - - - - - - - - - - - - - - - - - - - - - - - - - - - - - - - - - - -
   0.        -2.000E+00   .         *        .             .                  .                  .
   5.000E-04 -1.291E-01   .                  *.            .                  .                  .
   1.000E-03  1.676E+00   .                  .    *        .                  .                  .
   1.500E-03  3.350E+00   .                  .        *    .                  .                  .
   2.000E-03  4.837E+00   .                  .             *.                 .                  .
   2.500E-03  6.077E+00   .                  .             .    *             .                  .
   3.000E-03  7.038E+00   .                  .             .         *        .                  .
   3.500E-03  7.669E+00   .                  .             .            *     .                  .
   4.000E-03  7.970E+00   .                  .             .              *   .                  .
   4.500E-03  7.903E+00   .                  .             .              *   .                  .
   5.000E-03  7.502E+00   .                  .             .            *     .                  .
   5.500E-03  6.747E+00   .                  .             .        *         .                  .
   6.000E-03  5.700E+00   .                  .             .  *               .                  .
```

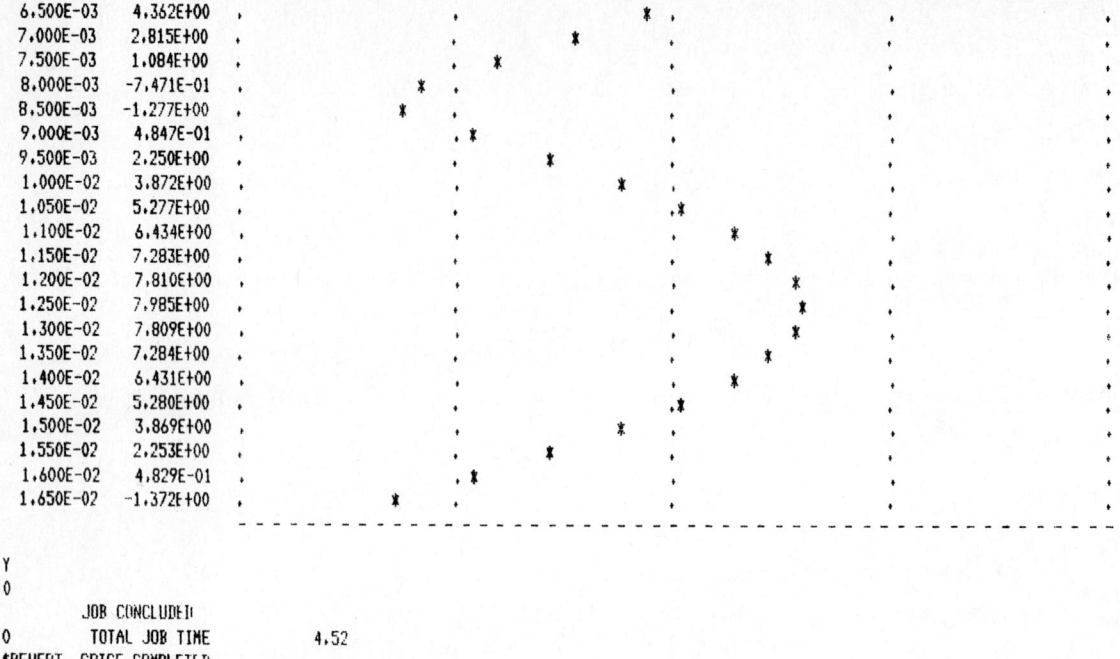

```
6.500E-03    4.362E+00   .                       .              *  .                    .           .
7.000E-03    2.815E+00   .                       .         *       .                    .           .
7.500E-03    1.084E+00   .                       .     *           .                    .           .
8.000E-03   -7.471E-01   .               *       .                 .                    .           .
8.500E-03   -1.277E+00   .            *          .                 .                    .           .
9.000E-03    4.847E-01   .                   . *  .                .                    .           .
9.500E-03    2.250E+00   .                       .    *            .                    .           .
1.000E-02    3.872E+00   .                       .         *       .                    .           .
1.050E-02    5.277E+00   .                       .              .*                      .           .
1.100E-02    6.434E+00   .                       .                    *                 .           .
1.150E-02    7.283E+00   .                       .                      *               .           .
1.200E-02    7.810E+00   .                       .                        *             .           .
1.250E-02    7.985E+00   .                       .                         *            .           .
1.300E-02    7.809E+00   .                       .                        *             .           .
1.350E-02    7.284E+00   .                       .                      *               .           .
1.400E-02    6.431E+00   .                       .                  *                   .           .
1.450E-02    5.280E+00   .                       .              .*                      .           .
1.500E-02    3.869E+00   .                       .        *        .                    .           .
1.550E-02    2.253E+00   .                       .    *            .                    .           .
1.600E-02    4.829E-01   .                   . *  .                .                    .           .
1.650E-02   -1.372E+00   .            *          .                 .                    .           .
```

```
Y
0
         JOB CONCLUDED
0        TOTAL JOB TIME        4.52
$REVERT, SPICE COMPLETED
/
```

A.3.4 *Fourth-Order Chebyshev Low-Pass Filter*

The filter shown in Figure A.11 is designed to have a 3 dB pass-band ripple, 3 dB cutoff of 1 kHz, and a maximum pass-band gain of 1. The printouts of the computer inputs and outputs are shown next.

Figure A.11
Chebyshev low-pass filter.

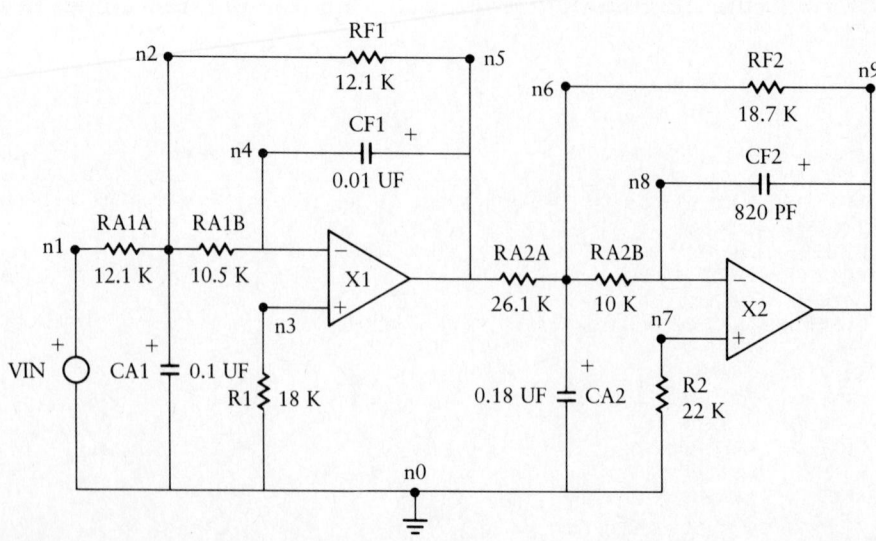

```
    PPROJ5
1******* 86/04/30. ******* SPICE 2G.5 (10AUG81)  ******* 18.54.35.*****


0*  FOURTH ORDER CHEBYSHEV LPF


0****    INPUT LISTING                TEMPERATURE =   27.000 DEG C


0************************************************************************


  *  SUBCIRCUIT OPAMP DESCRIPTION
  .SUBCKT  OPAMP  1  2  3
  RIN   1   2   2MEG
  RCM1  1   0   400MEG
  RCM2  2   0   400MEG
  EVIN  3   0   2   1   10E5
  .ENDS OPAMP


  *  MAIN CIRCUIT ELEMENT DESCRIPTION
  RA1A   1   2   12.1K
  RA1B   2   4   10.5K
  RF1    2   5   12.1K
  R1     3   0   18.0K
  CA1    2   0   .1U
  CF1    5   4   .01U
  RA2A   5   6   26.1K
  RA2B   6   8   10.0K
  RF2    6   9   18.7K
  R2     7   0   22.0K
  CA2    6   0   .18U
  CF2    9   8   820P


  *  CALL SUBCIRCUIT OPAMP
  X1   4   3   5   OPAMP
  X2   8   7   9   OPAMP


  *  SOURCE DESCRIPTION

  VIN  1   0   AC


  *  ANALYSIS REQUESTS

  .AC  DEC  15  100  2K


  *  OUTPUT REQUEST
  .PLOT  AC  VDB(9)  VDB(5)  VDB(9,5)
  .END
1**************** 86/04/30. ********************** SPICE 2G.5 (10AUG81)  ********************** 18.54.35.**************


0*  FOURTH ORDER CHEBYSHEV LPF
0****                 SMALL SIGNAL BIAS SOLUTION            TEMPERATURE =   27.000 DEG C


0*******************************************************************************************************************


    NODE   VOLTAGE    NODE   VOLTAGE    NODE   VOLTAGE    NODE   VOLTAGE    NODE   VOLTAGE    NODE   VOLTAGE    NODE   VOLTAGE

  ( 1)    0.0000    ( 2)    0.0000    ( 3)    0.0000    ( 4)    0.0000    ( 5)    0.0000    ( 6)    0.0000    ( 7)    0.0000

  ( 8)    0.0000    ( 9)    0.0000
```

```
   VOLTAGE SOURCE CURRENTS

   NAME      CURRENT

   VIN       0.


   TOTAL POWER DISSIPATION   0.      WATTS
1**************** 86/04/30. ******************** SPICE 2G.5 (10AUG81) ******************** 18.54.35.**************

0*  FOURTH ORDER CHEBYSHEV LPF
0****                   OPERATING POINT INFORMATION              TEMPERATURE =   27.000 DEG C


0****************************************************************************************************************


0
0**** VOLTAGE-CONTROLLED VOLTAGE SOURCES


0          EVIN.X1   EVIN.X2
 V-SOURCE    0.000     0.000
 I-SOURCE    0.        0.
1**************** 86/04/30. ******************** SPICE 2G.5 (10AUG81) ******************** 18.54.35.**************

0*  FOURTH ORDER CHEBYSHEV LPF
0****                   AC ANALYSIS                              TEMPERATURE =   27.000 DEG C


0****************************************************************************************************************

0LEGEND:

 *: VDB(9)
 +: VDB(5)
 =: VDB(9,5)

    FREQ      VDB(9)

(*)---------------- -6.000E+01        -4.000E+01        -2.000E+01         0.               2.000E+01
                    ------------------------------------------------------------------------------------
(+=)--------------- -3.000E+01        -2.000E+01        -1.000E+01         0.               1.000E+01
                    - - - - - - - - - - - - - - - - - - - - - - - - - - - - - - - - - - - - - - - - - -
 1.000E+02  -2.559E+00  .              .                 .              *  .+           =             .
 1.166E+02  -2.440E+00  .              .                 .              *  .+           =             .
 1.359E+02  -2.280E+00  .              .                 .              *  .+           =             .
 1.585E+02  -2.067E+00  .              .                 .              *  .+            =            .
 1.848E+02  -1.786E+00  .              .                 .              *  .+            =            .
 2.154E+02  -1.426E+00  .              .                 .               *  .  +          =           .
 2.512E+02  -9.811E-01  .              .                 .               *.   +           =           .
 2.929E+02  -4.832E-01  .              .                 .               *.   +            =          .
 3.415E+02  -4.241E-02  .              .                 .                *    +            =         .
 3.981E+02   9.777E-02  .              .                 .                *    +            =         .
 4.642E+02  -3.499E-01  .              .                 .                *+             =            .
 5.412E+02  -1.372E+00  .              .                 .                *+          =               .
 6.310E+02  -2.474E+00  .              .                 .            +  *  .       =                 .
 7.356E+02  -2.837E+00  .              .                 .        +       * .    =                    .
 8.577E+02  -1.168E+00  .              .                 .    +           *   . =                     .
 1.000E+03  -2.255E+00  .              .                 .  +           *.  =                          .
 1.166E+03  -1.333E+01  .              .           =.       +          *                               .
 1.359E+03  -2.210E+01  .          =           .  +       *                                            .
 1.585E+03  -2.944E+01  .              =       .  +   *                                                .
 1.848E+03  -3.605E+01  .       =    +          *                                                      .
 2.154E+03  -4.223E+01  . =    +           *                                                           .
```

```
Y
0
        JOB CONCLUDED
0       TOTAL JOB TIME          1.51
$REVERT. SPICE COMPLETED
/
```

A.3.5   *Two-Input NAND Gate*

Figure A.12 illustrates a two-input NAND gate. The circuit is designed to provide a high current output. This is done to provide more current to discharge and charge any parasitic capacitance that may be associated with the load.

This high current operation decreases the transition time required to turn the device on and off. The printout of the computer inputs and outputs is shown next.

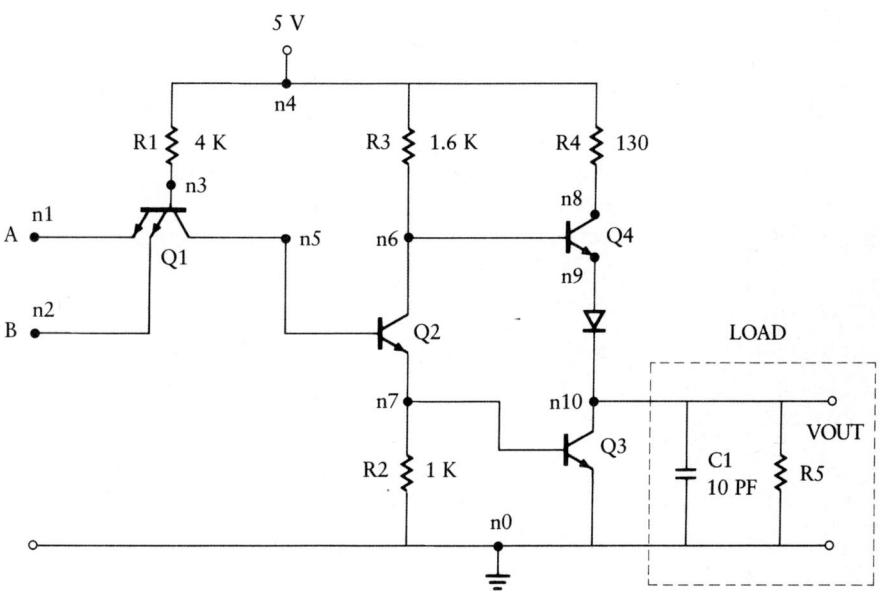

Figure A.12
Two-input NAND gate.

```
1.700E-02   3.778E-02   .*              REWIND,*
 9 FILES PROCESSED,
/FIND,SPICE,TEST
1******* B6/07/78, ******* SPICE 26.5 (10AUG81) ******* 16.53.57.*****

0NAND GATE

0****    INPUT LISTING           TEMPERATURE =   27.000 DEG C

0*******************************************************************************

C1 10  0 10P
R5 10  0 2000
R1 3 4 4K
R2 0 7 1K
```

```
R3 4 6 1.6K
R4 4 8 130
Q1 5 3 1 MOD1
Q1A 5 3 2 MOD1
Q2 6 5 7 MOD1
Q3 10 7 0 MOD1
Q4 8 6 9 MOD1
D1 9 10 MOD2
VA 1 0 PULSE (0 5 10M 5M 5M 20M 50M)
VB 2 0 DC 5
VCC 4 0 DC 5
.MODEL MOD1 NPN (VJE=.7 BF=30 BR=.3)
.MODEL MOD2 D (VJ=.7)
*ANALYSIS REQUEST
.TRAN 1M 50M
*OUTPUT REQUEST
.PLOT TRAN V(10)
.END
```

```
1************* 86/07/28, ********************* SPICE 26.5 (10AUG81) ********************* 16.53.57.**************

0NAND GATE
0****            DIODE MODEL PARAMETERS                          TEMPERATURE =  27.000 DEG C


0***********************************************************************************************************************



          MOD2
0IS     1,00E-14
0V.1       .700
1************* 86/07/28, ********************* SPICE 26.5 (10AUG81) ********************* 16.53.57.**************

0NAND GATE
0****            BJI MODEL PARAMETERS                            TEMPERATURE =  27.000 DEG C


0***********************************************************************************************************************



          MOD1
0TYPE     NPN
0IS     1.00E-16
08F     30.000
0NF      1.000
0BR       .300
0NR      1.000
0VJE      .700
1************* 86/07/28, ********************* SPICE 26.5 (10AUG81) ********************* 16.53.57.**************

0NAND GATE
0****            INITIAL TRANSIENT SOLUTION                      TEMPERATURE =  27.000 DEG C


0 **********************************************************************************************************************
```

NODE	VOLTAGE	NODE	VOLTAGE	NODE	VOLTAGE	NODE	VOLTAGE	NODE	VOLTAGE	NODE	VOLTAGE	NODE	VOLTAGE
(1)	0.0000	(2)	5.0000	(3)	.7813	(4)	5.0000	(5)	.0559	(6)	4.9109	(7)	.0000
(8)	4.7827	(9)	4.1234	(10)	3.4541								

```
     VOLTAGE SOURCE CURRENTS

     NAME      CURRENT


     VA        1.206E-03

     VB       -1.516E-04

     VCC      -2.782E=-03


   TOTAL POWER DISSIPATION  1.47E-02  WATTS
1*************** 86/07/28. ******************** SPICE 2G.5 (10AUG81) ******************** 16.53.57.***************

0NAND GATE
0****              OPERATING POINT INFORMATION              TEMPERATURE =  27.000 DEG C

0 ****************************************************************************************************************


0
0**** DIODES



0         D1
0MODEL    MOD2
 ID       1.73E-03
 VO        .669
0
0**** BIPOLAR JUNCTION TRANSISTORS


0         Q1       Q1A      Q2       Q3       Q4
0MODEL    MOD1     MOD1     MOD1     MOD1     MOD1
 IB       5.49E-04 5.05E-04 -1.62E-11 -1,15E-11 5.57E-05
 IC       6.57E-04 -6.56E-04 2.11E-11 1.50E-11 1.67E-03
 V3E       .781    -4.219    .056     .000     .737
 VBC       .725     .725    -4.855   -3.454    .128
 VCE       .056    -4.944   4.911    3.454     .659
 BETADC   1.196    -1.300   -1.304   -1.300    30.000
1*************** 86/07/28, ******************** SPICE 2G.5 (10AUG81) ******************** 15.52.57.***************

0NAND GATE
0****              TRANSIENT ANALYSIS                        TEMPERATURE =  27.000 DEG C
0 ****************************************************************************************************************



     TIME     V(10)

              0.           1.000E+00    2.000E+00    2.000E+00    4.000E+00
           - - - - - - - - - - - - - - - - - - - - - - - - - - - - - - - -
0.         3.454E+00 .          .            .            .         *        .
1.000E-03  3.454E+00 .          .            .            .         *        .
2.000E-03  3.454E+00 .          .            .            .         *        .
3.000E-03  3.454E+00 .          .            .            .         *        .
4.000E-03  3.454E+00 .          .            .            .         *        .
5.000E-03  3.454E+00 .          .            .            .         *        .
```

```
6.000E-03    3.454E+00    .                    .                    .                    .                    ✻                    .
7.000E-03    3.454E+00    .                    .                    .                    .                    ✻                    .
8.000E-03    3.454E+00    .                    .                    .                    .                    ✻                    .
9.000E-03    3.454E+00    .                    .                    .                    .                    ✻                    .
1.000E-02    3.454E+00    .                    .                    .                    .                    ✻                    .
1.100E-02    2.888E+00    .                    .                    .                    ✻    .                                    .
1.200E-02    3.778E-02    .✻                   .                    .                    .                                         .
1.300E-02    3.778E-02    .✻                   .                    .                    .                                         .
1.400E-02    3.778E-09    .✻                   .                    .                    .                                         .
1.500E-02    3.778E-02    .✻                   .                    .                    .                                         .
1.600E-02    3.778E-02    .✻                   .                    .                    .                                         .
1.700E-02    3.778E-02    .✻                   .                    .                    .                                         .
1.800E-02    3.778E-02    .✻                   .                    .                    .                                         .
1.900E-02    3.778E-02    .✻                   .                    .                    .                                         .
2.000E-02    3.779E-02    .✻                   .                    .                    .                                         .
2.100E-02    3.778E-02    .✻                   .                    .                    .                                         .
2.200E-02    3.778E-02    .✻                   .                    .                    .                                         .
2.300E-02    3.778E-02    .✻                   .                    .                    .                                         .
2.400E-02    3.779E-02    .✻                   .                    .                    .                                         .
2.500E-02    3.778E-02    .✻                   .                    .                    .                                         .
2.600E-02    3.778E-02    .✻                   .                    .                    .                                         .
2.700E-02    3.778E-02    .✻                   .                    .                    .                                         .
2.800E-02    3.778E-02    .✻                   .                    .                    .                                         .
2.900E-02    3.778E-02    .✻                   .                    .                    .                                         .
3.000E-02    3.778E-02    .✻                   .                    .                    .                                         .
3.100E-02    3.778E-02    .✻                   .                    .                    .                                         .
3.200E-02    3.778E-02    .✻                   .                    .                    .                                         .
3.300E-02    3.778E-02    .✻                   .                    .                    .                                         .
3.400E-02    3.778E-02    .✻                   .                    .                    .                                         .
3.500E-02    3.778E-02    .✻                   .                    .                    .                                         .
3.600E-02    3.778E-02    .✻                   .                    .                    .                                         .
3.700E-02    3.778E-02    .✻                   .                    .                    .                                         .
3.800E-02    3.778E-02    .✻                   .                    .                    .                                         .
3.900E-02    2.984E+00    .                    .                    .                    ✻    .                                    .
4.000E-02    3.454E+00    .                    .                    .                    .                    ✻                    .
4.100E-02    3.454E+00    .                    .                    .                    .                    ✻                    .
4.200E-02    3.454E+00    .                    .                    .                    .                    ✻                    .
4.300E-02    3.454E+00    .                    .                    .                    .                    ✻                    .
4.400E-02    3.454E+00    .                    .                    .                    .                    ✻                    .
4.500E-02    3.454E+00    .                    .                    .                    .                    ✻                    .
4.600E-02    3.454E+00    .                    .                    .                    .                    ✻                    .
4.700E-02    3.454E+00    .                    .                    .                    .                    ✻                    .
4.800E-02    3.454E+00    .                    .                    .                    .                    ✻                    .
4.900E-02    3.454E+00    .                    .                    .                    .                    ✻                    .
5.000E-02    3.454E+00    .                    .                    .                    .                    ✻                    .
             - - - - - - - - - - - - - - - - - - - - - - - - - - - - - - - - - - - - - - - - - - - - - - - -
```

```
Y
0
         JOB CONCLUDED
0        TOTAL JOB TIME        7.85
$REVERT. SPICE COMPLETED
/
```

B PRINCIPLES OF SEMICONDUCTOR PHYSICS

This appendix quantitatively treats some basic physical principles of electronic materials. Carrier concentrations in intrinsic and extrinsic semiconductors, electric currents due to drift and to diffusion, and the definition of the Fermi-level are discussed. The basic diode equation is derived.

B.1 Intrinsic Semiconductors

As discussed in Chapter 1, semiconductors are materials where there exists a forbidden energy gap: a gap in the energy levels where no electrons can exist. The valence electrons of the atoms of a semiconductor are not free to move throughout the volume of the material. Instead they participate in the covalent bonds that hold the assembly of atoms together in a periodic crystalline structure. Semiconductors belong to the fourth column in the table of Mendeljev and these elements tend to form covalent bonds.

Figure B.1 shows the crystal structure of silicon. Other semiconductors, such as germanium, have this same crystal structure. From now on we will focus our attention on silicon. Most of what is said here will also apply to other semiconductors.

Figure B.1
The diamond crystal
structure.

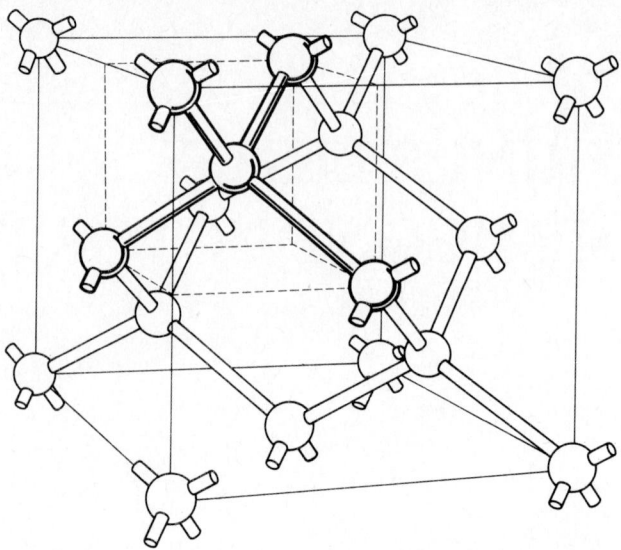

Silicon (Si) is by far the most extensively used semiconductor. Germanium is used only in very specialized applications. Another semiconductor that has been receiving attention is gallium-arsenide (GaAs). GaAs is relatively expensive and difficult to process, but it is much faster than silicon.

In the diamond lattice structure, every atom has four nearest neighbors and shares its valence electrons with those neighbors. The atoms are in the center of a tetrahedron. The lattice constant spacing of silicon is 5.4 Å. The connecting rods between the atoms in Figure B.1 can be thought of as indicating the spatial location of the valence electrons, making up the covalent bonds.

At 0° K all electrons are constrained to their covalent bonds. No free electrons are available and no conduction is possible. The material behaves as an insulator. In a semiconductor at room temperature, some covalent bonds will be broken. These broken bonds result from the random thermal vibration of the atoms and of the valence electrons. A few electrons acquire enough energy to "shake loose" from the bonds and become free. The energy required to break a covalent bond at room temperature is about 1.1 eV for silicon. The number of broken bonds is quite low—about $10^{11}/cm^3$ at room temperature. With about 10^{23} atoms per cm^3, only one out of every trillion atoms has a broken bond.

By comparison, diamond, which has the same crystalline structure, requires much higher energy to break a bond, and only 10^8 atoms per cm^3 have broken bonds at room temperature. Diamond is thus an insulator.

Due to the principle of covalent broken bonds, there are two independent groups of charge carriers: conduction electrons and holes. When a bond is

$$I = JA = \frac{\sigma AL\epsilon}{L} = \frac{\sigma AV}{L} = \frac{V}{R}$$

which is recognized as Ohm's law.

For holes and electrons in silicon we can now write

$$J_h = qp\mu_h\epsilon \qquad J_e = qn\mu_e\epsilon$$

so the total drift current is

$$J = q(p\mu_h + n\mu_e)\epsilon$$

Example B.2

Find the average drift velocity in a silicon semiconductor dop[ed with phos]phorus. Assume a doping density of 1 per million, a cross se[ction of] 10^{-4} m², and a current of 4 A.

SOLUTION   From Example B.1 we know the concentration [of atoms] in a silicon crystal

$$n_{Si} = 4.97 \times 10^{28} \text{ atoms/m}^3$$

With 1 per million phosphorus atoms and $n = N_d$ we have [...] electrons/m³ and a negligible density of holes.

$$v_e = \frac{J_e}{nq} = \frac{\frac{I}{A}}{nq} = \frac{4 \times 10^4}{(4.97 \times 10^{22})(1.609 \times 10^{-19})} = 5[...]$$

The average drift velocity is thus orders of magnitude lowe[r than the] thermal velocity.

Example B.3

What is the resistivity of intrinsic silicon at room temp[erature? The] resistivity of silicon doped with 1/million boron or [phosphorus at room] temperature?

SOLUTION   For intrinsic material:

---

broken, an electron is free to move through the crystal. As the negatively charged electron moves away, a positive charge remains, because the lattice was, and still is, electrically neutral. The broken bond remains behind and is positively charged. Since this bond will try to restore itself to its normal completed state, it attempts to capture an electron. The captured electron does not have to be a free electron. Even though the bound valence electrons are not free to move around through the crystal, it is possible for them to move from one bond to another provided that this destination bond is incomplete. The net result is that the broken bond still exists but has now moved in the opposite direction from that of the valence electron, moving between the two bonds. A mobile positive charge, referred to as a *hole*, results. Through quantum physics principles it can be proven that a hole has similar properties to those of a free electron (e.g., mass, mobility, lifetime), but has exactly the opposite charge. A hole will behave as a classical particle. We would not be able to describe the movement of the positive charge through the movement of the bound valence electrons with classical mechanics.

In a pure (intrinsic) semiconductor, the number of holes is equal to the number of free electrons. This is true since the generating processes create both a hole and an electron. Hole-electron pairs can be generated by thermal agitation or by other means of injecting energy into the material (e.g., light).

Hole-electron pairs can also disappear. This process is called *recombination*. Recombination takes place when a free electron moves too close to a hole and gets recaptured in the broken bond. At that point the electron ceases to be free and again becomes part of a covalent bond. Both a conduction electron and a hole disappear at that point.

Since generation and recombination affect holes and electrons as pairs, the hole concentration (p) must equal the electron concentration (n).

$$n = p = n_i \tag{B.1}$$

n_i is called the *intrinsic concentration*.

Since there are no broken bonds at 0° K and 10^{11}/cm³ at room temperature, the intrinsic concentration n_i is a function of temperature. This relationship is shown in Figure B.2. The formula for the temperature dependence is

$$np = n_i^2 = AT^3 e^{-E_G/kT} \tag{B.2}$$

A is a proportionality constant, T is the absolute temperature, k is Boltzmann's constant (1.38066×10^{-23} J/K), q is the electronic charge (1.602×10^{-19} C) and E_G is the bandgap energy—the minimum energy required to break a covalent bond (1.12 eV for silicon at room temperature). For silicon the constant A equals 5.06×10^{43} m^{-6}K^{-3}.

Figure B.4
Carrier flow in a conducting wire.

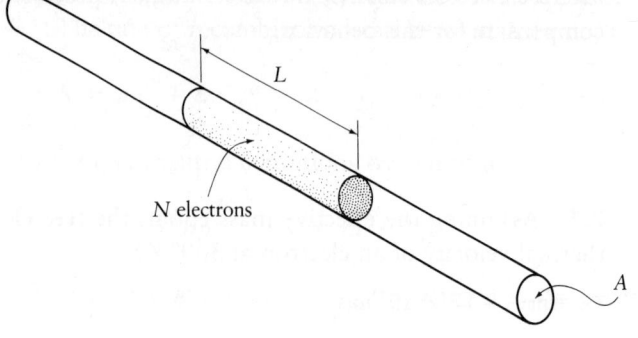

Si atom, or a doping atom, will get scattered, changing direction tering process depends on the temperature (the amount of energy tering atoms or ions) and on the amount of ions (doping).

The electric current associated with the drift is calculated in t way. Assume there are N electrons contained in a length L of co Figure B.4), and it takes an electron T seconds to travel a distanc in the conductor. The total number of electrons passing throu section of wire in a unit of time is N/T. By definition, the curren

$$I \equiv \left[\frac{N}{T}\right] q = \frac{Nq}{T} = \frac{Nq\left[\frac{L}{T}\right]}{L} = \frac{Nqv}{L}$$

Also, by definition, the current density, J [A/m^2], is

$$J \equiv \frac{I}{A} = \frac{Nqv}{LA}$$

With $\dfrac{N}{LA}$ being the electron concentration, n [electrons/m^3],

$$J = nqv$$

It should be noted that this derivation is independent of the ducting medium.

Interestingly, using formula (B.15), we get:

$$J = nqv = nq\mu\epsilon = \sigma\epsilon$$

where $\sigma \equiv nq\mu$ is the conductivity in $(\Omega\cdot m)^{-1}$. Combini gives

$$\int_a^b u \, dv = uv \Big|_a^b - \int_a^b v \, du$$

(C.6)

where the following substitutions are made:

$$u = e^{-st} \qquad du = -se^{-st} dt$$
$$dv = \left(\frac{dy}{dt}\right) dt \qquad v = y(t)$$

(C.7)

The integral is now evaluated as follows:

$$\mathcal{L}\,[dy/dt] = y(t)e^{-st}\Big|_0^\infty + s\int_0^\infty y(t)e^{-st}\, dt$$

(C.8)

Since the last integral in equation (C.8) is the Laplace transform of $y(t)$, that is,

$$\mathcal{L}\,[y(t)] = Y(s) = \int_0^\infty y(t)e^{-st}\, dt$$

(C.9)

and since $y(t)e^{-st}$ is zero at the upper limit provided that the real part of s is greater than zero, we obtain the result

$$\mathcal{L}\left[\frac{dy}{dt}\right] = -y(0) + sY(s)$$

(C.10)

In a similar fashion, the Laplace transform of higher derivatives can be found:

$$\mathcal{L}\left[\frac{d^2y}{dt^2}\right] = s^2 Y(s) - sy(0) - \frac{dy}{dt}\Big|_{t=0}$$
$$\mathcal{L}\left[\frac{d^n y}{dt^n}\right] = s^n Y(s) - s^{n-1}y(0) - s^{n-2}\frac{dy}{dt}\Big|_{t=0}$$
$$- \cdots - \frac{d^{n-1}y}{dt^{n-1}}\Big|_{t=0}$$

(C.11)

(C.12)

For the case of zero initial conditions, this last equation reduces to

$$\mathcal{L}\left[\frac{d^n y}{dt^n}\right] = s^n Y(s)$$

(C.13)

Hence, provided that initial conditions are equal to zero, finding the Laplace

$$\frac{(s + s_i)A(s)}{B(s)} = K_1 \frac{s + s_i}{s + s_1} + K_2 \frac{s + s_i}{s + s_2}$$

$$+ \cdots + K_i \frac{s + s_i}{s + s_i} + \cdots + K_q \frac{s + s_i}{s + s_q} \qquad (C.37)$$

Since $s + s_i$ is a factor in $B(s)$, it is divided out. When s is set equal to $-s_i$, the term on the left of the equal sign becomes a constant. All terms on the right reduce to zero except K_i. Hence, each constant can be evaluated from the equation,

$$K_i = \frac{A(s)(s + s_i)}{B(s)} \bigg|_{s = -s_i} \qquad (C.38)$$

The procedure is unaltered if one of the roots is located at the origin. The constant K_o is evaluated similarly:

$$K_o = \frac{sA(s)}{B(s)} \qquad (C.39)$$

When complex conjugate roots, $(s + \alpha)^2 + \beta^2$, exist, the procedure is similar:

$$K_{j1} = \frac{(s + \alpha + j\beta)A(s)}{B(s)} \bigg|_{s = -\alpha - j\beta} \qquad (C.40)$$

and

$$K_{j2} = \frac{(s + \alpha - j\beta)A(s)}{B(s)} \bigg|_{s = -\alpha + j\beta} \qquad (C.41)$$

Since K_{j1} and K_{j2} are complex conjugate, the sum of the imaginary parts is zero and the sum of the real parts is twice the real part of either constant. The two terms

$$\frac{K_{j1}}{s + \alpha + j\beta} \quad \text{and} \quad \frac{K_{j2}}{s + \alpha - j\beta} \qquad (C.42)$$

combine into a single term, which inverse-transforms into an exponentially decaying sinusoid.

2. $B(s)$ contains multiple-order roots: If the denominator of $Y(s)$ has multiple-order zeros, the procedure of the preceding section must be altered. For example, if

$$\frac{A(s)}{B(s)} = \frac{1}{(s + s_1)(s + s_2)^2} \tag{C.43}$$

the partial-fraction expansion must include a second-order term.

$$\frac{1}{(s + s_1)(s + s_2)^2} = \frac{K_1}{s + s_1} + \frac{K_{12}}{s + s_2} + \frac{K_{22}}{(s + s_2)^2} \tag{C.44}$$

In general, an nth-order root is expanded as follows:

$$\frac{1}{(s + s_1) \cdots (s + s_i)^n} = \frac{K_1}{s + s_1} + \cdots + \frac{K_{ni}}{(s + s_i)^n}$$
$$+ \frac{K_{(n-1)i}}{(s + s_i)^{n-1}} + \cdots + \frac{K_{1i}}{s + s_i} \tag{C.45}$$

The constants K_i associated with first-order roots are evaluated as above. The constant associated with the highest power, K_{ni}, is evaluated in a manner that is the same as that used for a simple pole. That is, we multiply both sides of equation (C.45) by $(s + s_i)^n$ and let $s = -s_i$. All terms on the right side are zero except the K_{ni} term. The left side reduces to a number. K_{ni} is evaluated as follows:

$$K_{ni} = \left. \frac{(s + s_i)^n A(s)}{B(s)} \right|_{s = -s_i} \tag{C.46}$$

The procedure used for simple roots and to evaluate the constant associated with the highest power, K_{ni}, is insufficient to evaluate any of the other coefficients. These constants are evaluated using differentiation. Both sides of equation (C.45) are multiplied by $(s + s_i)^n$. The resulting equation is differentiated once with respect to s:

$$\frac{d}{ds} \frac{(s + s_i)^n A(s)}{B(s)} = \frac{d}{ds} \frac{(s + s_i)^n}{s + s_1} K_1 + \cdots + K_{(n-1)i} + 2(s + s_i)K_{(n-2)i}$$
$$+ \cdots + (n - 1)(s + s_i)^{n-2} K_{1i} \tag{C.47}$$

By letting $s = -s_i$, all terms on the right except $K_{(n-1)i}$ vanish:

$$K_{(n-1)i} = \frac{1}{(n - 1)!} \frac{d}{ds} \left[\frac{(s + s_i)^n A(s)}{B(s)} \right] \Bigg|_{s = -s_i} \tag{C.48}$$

The process of differentiating and then setting $s = -s_i$ can be repeated until all the unknown constants are determined.

As an example, consider the partial-fraction expansion of the following transfer function:

$$\frac{A(s)}{B(s)} = \frac{4s^3 + s^2 - 22s + 16}{s(s + 2)(s - 2)^2} \tag{C.49}$$

The fraction is broken up as follows:

$$\frac{4s^3 + s^2 - 22s + 16}{s(s + 2)(s - 2)^2} = \frac{K_1}{s} + \frac{K_2}{s + 2} + \frac{K_{13}}{s - 2} + \frac{K_{23}}{(s - 2)^2} \tag{C.50}$$

The constants corresponding to the simple poles are found first:

$$K_1 = \left. \frac{s(4s^3 + s^2 - 22s + 16)}{s(s + 2)(s - 2)^2} \right|_{s=0} = 2$$

$$K_2 = \left. \frac{(s + 2)(4s^3 + s^2 - 22s + 16)}{s(s + 2)(s - 2)^2} \right|_{s=-2} = -1 \tag{C.51}$$

K_{23} is found in a similar manner:

$$K_{23} = \left. \frac{(s - 2)^2(4s^3 + s^2 - 22s + 16)}{s(s + 2)(s - 2)^2} \right|_{s=2} = 1 \tag{C.52}$$

K_{13} is found by multiplying equation (C.50) by $(s - 2)^2$ and then differentiating with respect to s:

$$\frac{d}{ds}\left[\frac{4s^3 + s^2 - 22s + 16}{s(s + 2)} \right] = \left. \frac{d}{ds}\left[\left(\frac{K_1}{s} + \frac{K_2}{s + 2} \right)(s - 2)^2 \right] \right|_{s=2}$$

$$+ \frac{d}{ds}(s - 2)K_{13} + \frac{d}{ds}K_{23} \tag{C.53}$$

which reduces to

$$K_{13} = \frac{d}{ds}\left[\frac{4s^3 + s^2 - 22s + 16}{s^2 + 2s} \right]$$

$$= \left. \frac{(s^2 + 2s)(12s^2 + 2s - 22) - (4s^3 + s^2 - 22s + 16)(2s + 2)}{(s^2 + 2s)^2} \right|_{s=2}$$

$$= 3 \tag{C.54}$$

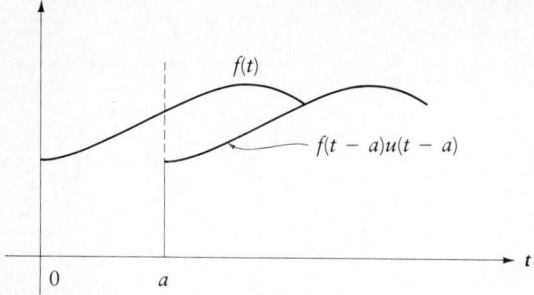

Figure C.2
Shifted function.

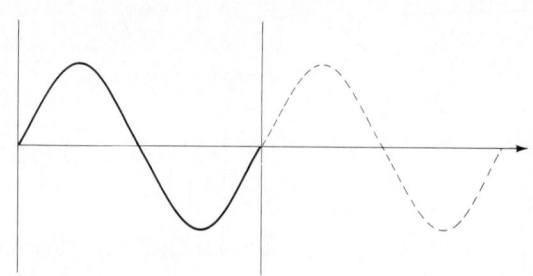

Figure C.3
Truncated sinusoid.

Hence the partial-fraction expansion of equation (C.49) is written as

$$\frac{A(s)}{B(s)} = \frac{2}{s} - \frac{1}{s+2} + \frac{1}{(s-2)^2} + \frac{3}{s-2} \tag{C.55}$$

C.5 Additional Properties of the Laplace Transform

Some important relationships involving the Laplace transformation are included in this section.

C.5.1 *Real Translation*

If $F(s)$ is the Laplace transform of $f(t)$, then

$$\mathscr{L}\left[f(t-a)u(t-a)\right] = e^{-as}F(s) \tag{C.56}$$

Multiplication by e^{-as} in the complex frequency plane (s-plane) results in translation in the time domain. The function $f(t-a)u(t-a)$ is shown shifted in Figure C.2. As an example of the use of this theorem, suppose it is necessary to find the Laplace transform of a truncated sinusoid representing one period of a sine wave, as shown in Figure C.3. The time function can be formed by taking the difference between a sine wave and another sinusoid that has been shifted in time by $2\pi/\omega$. This is written as

$$f(t) = A \sin \omega t\, u(t) - A \sin \omega\left(t - \frac{2\pi}{\omega}\right)u\left(t - \frac{2\pi}{\omega}\right) \tag{C.57}$$

These terms are transformed as follows:

$$\mathscr{L}\,[f(t)] = \frac{A\omega}{s^2 + \omega^2} - \frac{A\omega}{s^2 + \omega^2}\, e^{-(2\pi/\omega)s}$$

$$= \frac{A\omega}{s^2 + \omega^2}\, (1 - e^{-(2\pi/\omega)s}) \tag{C.58}$$

C.5.2   *Second Independent Variable*

If $F(s, a)$ is the transform of $f(t, a)$, the following relation holds:

$$\mathscr{L}_t \left[\lim_{a \to a_0} f(t, a) \right] = \lim_{a \to a_0} F(s, a) \tag{C.59}$$

where $\mathscr{L}_t$ means the Laplace transform with respect to time. As an example of the use of this equation, consider the transform pair

$$\mathscr{L}_t[e^{-at} \sin \omega t] = \frac{\omega}{(s + a)^2 + \omega^2} \tag{C.60}$$

given in Table C.1. By taking the limit as a approaches zero, a second pair results:

$$\mathscr{L}\,[\sin \omega t] = \frac{\omega}{s^2 + \omega^2} \tag{C.61}$$

In a similar fashion, differentiation with respect to the quantity a is permissible, yielding

$$\mathscr{L}_t \left[\frac{df(t, a)}{da} \right] = \frac{dF}{da}\, (s, a) \tag{C.62}$$

As an example, we differentiate the transform pair

$$\mathscr{L}_t\, [e^{-at}] = \frac{1}{s + a} \tag{C.63}$$

and obtain another pair,

$$\mathscr{L}_t\, [te^{-at}] = \frac{1}{(s + a)^2} \tag{C.64}$$

C.5.3   *Final Value and Initial Value Theorems*

The final value and initial value theorems are valuable and unique, since they permit finding a time function at either $t = 0$ or $t \to \infty$ directly from the transform without inverting the transformed equation.

The *final value theorem* states:

$$\lim_{t \to \infty} y(t) = \lim_{s \to 0} sY(s) \tag{C.65}$$

provided $y(t)$ is stable (i.e., all poles of $sY(s)$ are in the left half-plane).

The *initial value theorem* states:

$$\lim_{t \to 0} y(t) = \lim_{s \to \infty} sY(s) \tag{C.66}$$

provided the limit exists.

C.5.4   *The Convolution Theorem*

The *convolution theorem* is expressed as follows: If $F_1(s)$ is the Laplace transform of $f_1(t)$ and $F_2(s)$ is the Laplace transform of $f_2(t)$, then

$$\mathcal{L}\left[\int_0^t f_1(\tau)f_2(t - \tau)\, d\tau \right] = F_1(s)F_2(s) \tag{C.67}$$

The integral on the left is called the *convolution integral*. Thus, the Laplace transform of the convolution of two-time functions is the product of the individual Laplace transforms.

Convolution is extremely important in system analysis since the output of a linear system is the convolution of the input with the system's response to an impulse. Thus, if $h(t)$ is the system's response to an impulse and $f(t)$ is the input to the system, the output, $g(t)$, is given by

$$g(t) = \int_0^t h(t - \tau)f(\tau)\, d\tau \tag{C.68}$$

The Laplace transform of equation (C.69) yields the important result

$$G(s) = H(s)F(s) \tag{C.69}$$

Hence the Laplace transform of the output of a linear system is the product of the Laplace transform of the input, $F(s)$, with the Laplace transform of the impulse response, $H(s)$.

D MANUFACTURERS' DATA SHEETS

This appendix contains copies of representative data sheets for diodes, transistors, voltage regulators, voltage comparators, optical devices, and op-amps. The information is extracted from the manufacturers' data books. In some cases, only selected information is presented in order to give a sampling of the available data.

The appendix is not meant as a substitute for owning the appropriate data books. We once again strongly urge you to obtain copies of these books. We present only a very brief assortment of those sheets you will need to solve the problems within this text.

Contents

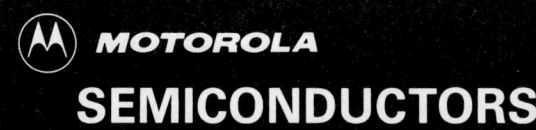

MOTOROLA

SEMICONDUCTORS

P.O. BOX 20912 • PHOENIX, ARIZONA 85036

Designers'Data Sheet

**1N4001
thru
1N4007**

**LEAD MOUNTED
SILICON RECTIFIERS**

**50-1000 VOLTS
DIFFUSED JUNCTION**

"SURMETIC"▲ RECTIFIERS

. . . subminiature size, axial lead mounted rectifiers for general-purpose low-power applications.

Designers Data for "Worst Case" Conditions

The Designers▲ Data Sheets permit the design of most circuits entirely from the information presented. Limit curves — representing boundaries on device characteristics — are given to facilitate "worst case" design.

*MAXIMUM RATINGS

Rating	Symbol	1N4001	1N4002	1N4003	1N4004	1N4005	1N4006	1N4007	Unit
Peak Repetitive Reverse Voltage Working Peak Reverse Voltage DC Blocking Voltage	V_{RRM} V_{RWM} V_R	50	100	200	400	600	800	1000	Volts
Non-Repetitive Peak Reverse Voltage (halfwave, single phase, 60 Hz)	V_{RSM}	60	120	240	480	720	1000	1200	Volts
RMS Reverse Voltage	$V_{R(RMS)}$	35	70	140	280	420	560	700	Volts
Average Rectified Forward Current (single phase, resistive load, 60 Hz, see Figure 8, $T_A = 75^\circ$C)	I_O	1.0							Amp
Non-Repetitive Peak Surge Current (surge applied at rated load conditions, see Figure 2)	I_{FSM}	30 (for 1 cycle)							Amp
Operating and Storage Junction Temperature Range	T_J, T_{stg}	–65 to +175							°C

*ELECTRICAL CHARACTERISTICS

Characteristic and Conditions	Symbol	Typ	Max	Unit
Maximum Instantaneous Forward Voltage Drop (i_F = 1.0 Amp, T_J = 25°C) Figure 1	v_F	0.93	1.1	Volts
Maximum Full-Cycle Average Forward Voltage Drop (I_O = 1.0 Amp, T_L = 75°C, 1 inch leads)	$V_{F(AV)}$	–	0.8	Volts
Maximum Reverse Current (rated dc voltage) T_J = 25°C T_J = 100°C	I_R	0.05 1.0	10 50	μA
Maximum Full-Cycle Average Reverse Current (I_O = 1.0 Amp, T_L = 75°C, 1 inch leads	$I_{R(AV)}$	–	30	μA

*Indicates JEDEC Registered Data.

MECHANICAL CHARACTERISTICS

CASE: Transfer Molded Plastic
MAXIMUM LEAD TEMPERATURE FOR SOLDERING PURPOSES: 350°C, 3/8" from case for 10 seconds at 5 lbs. tension
FINISH: All external surfaces are corrosion-resistant, leads are readily solderable
POLARITY: Cathode indicated by color band
WEIGHT: 0.40 Grams (approximately)

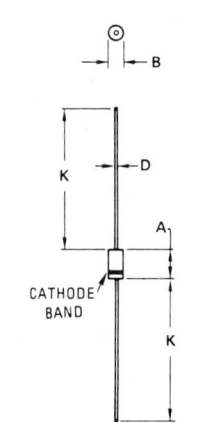

CATHODE
BAND

DIM	MILLIMETERS		INCHES	
	MIN	MAX	MIN	MAX
A	5.97	6.60	0.235	0.260
B	2.79	3.05	0.110	0.120
D	0.76	0.86	0.030	0.034
K	27.94	–	1.100	–

CASE 59-04
Does Not Conform to DO-41 Outline.

1N4001 THRU 1N4007

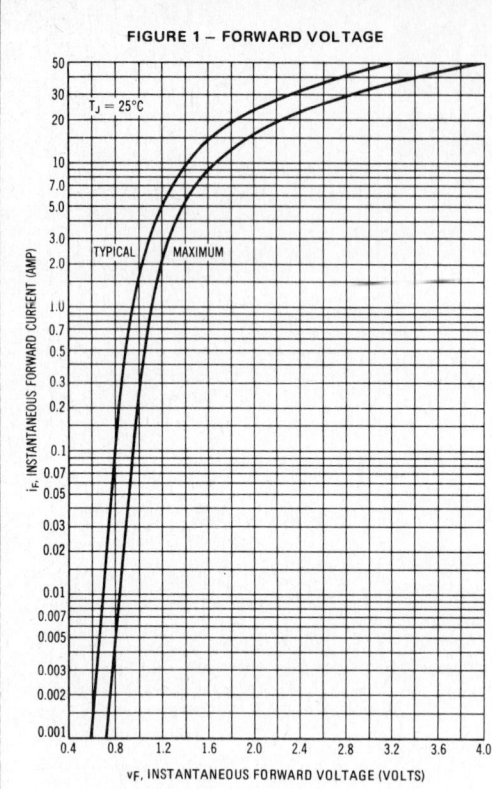

FIGURE 1 – FORWARD VOLTAGE

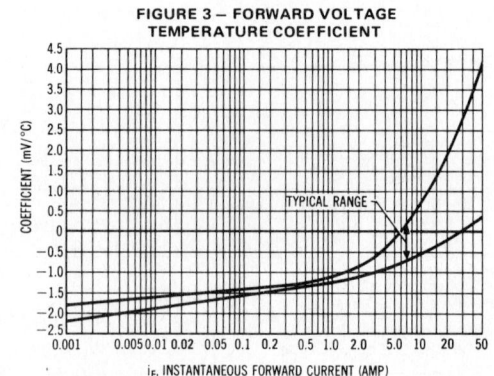

FIGURE 2 – NON-REPETITIVE SURGE CAPABILITY

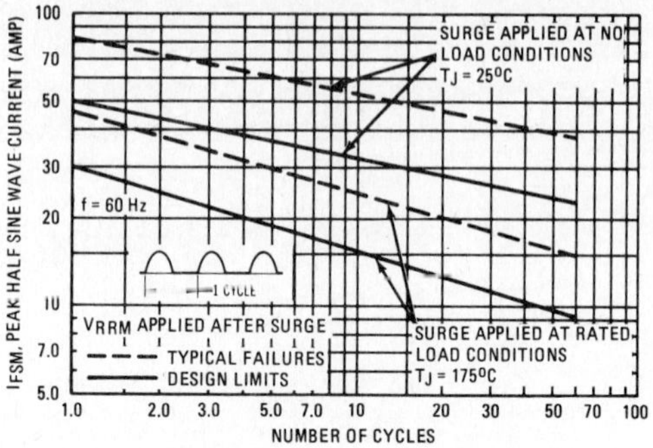

FIGURE 3 – FORWARD VOLTAGE
TEMPERATURE COEFFICIENT

FIGURE 4 – TYPICAL TRANSIENT THERMAL RESISTANCE

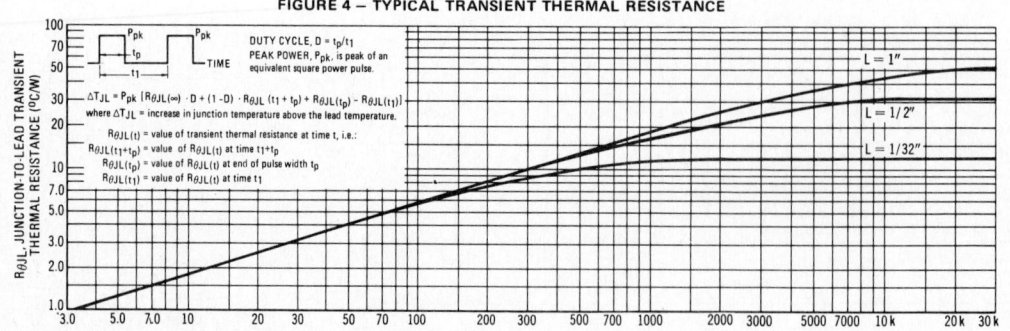

The temperature of the lead should be measured using a thermocouple placed on the lead as close as possible to the tie point. The thermal mass connected to the tie point is normally large enough so that it will not significantly respond to heat surges generated in the diode as a result of pulsed operation once steady-state conditions are achieved. Using the measured value of T_L, the junction temperature may be determined by:

$$T_J = T_L + \triangle T_{JL}.$$

 MOTOROLA *Semiconductor Products Inc.*

1N4001 THRU 1N4007

CURRENT DERATING DATA

FIGURE 5 — FORWARD POWER DISSIPATION

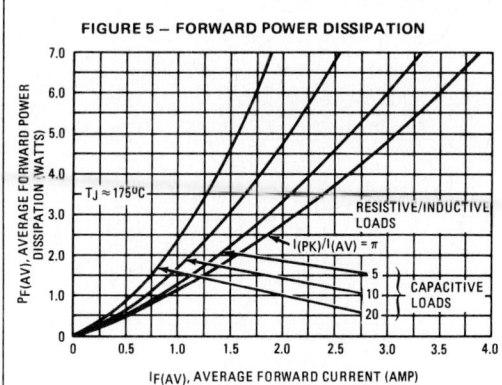

FIGURE 6 — EFFECT OF LEAD LENGTHS, RESISTIVE LOAD

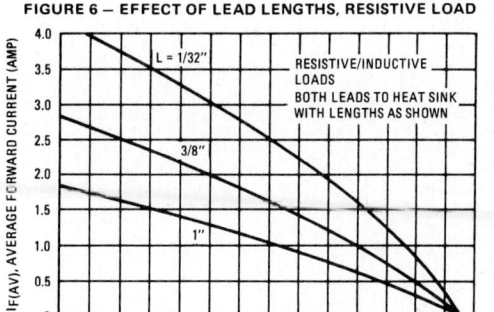

FIGURE 7 — 3/8'' LEAD LENGTH, VARIOUS LOADS

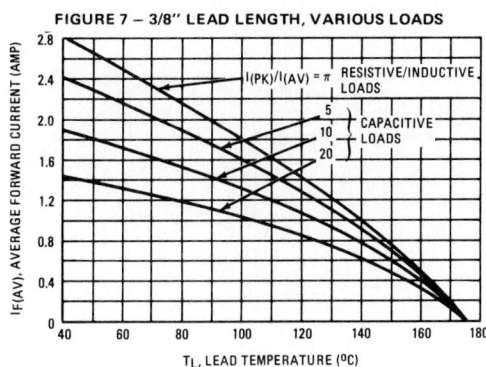

FIGURE 8 — PRINTED CIRCUIT BOARD MOUNTING — VARIOUS LOADS

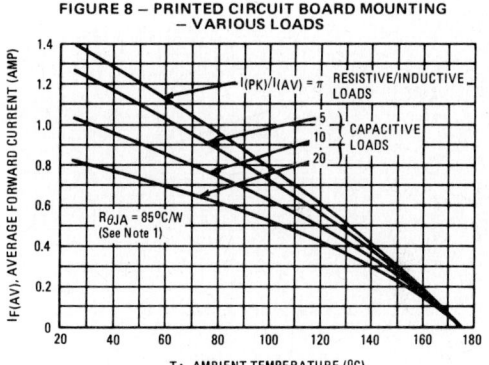

FIGURE 9 — STEADY-STATE THERMAL RESISTANCE

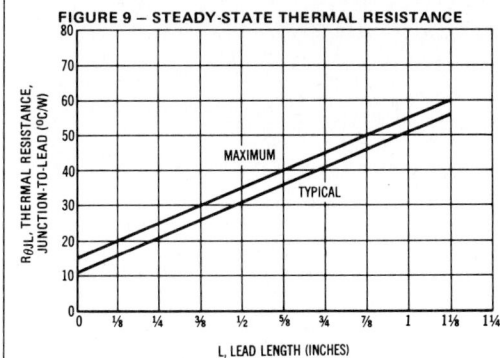

NOTE 1

Data shown for thermal resistance junction-to-ambient ($R_{\theta JA}$) for the mountings shown is to be used as typical guide-line values for preliminary engineering or in case the tie point temperature cannot be measured

TYPICAL VALUES FOR $R_{\theta JA}$ IN STILL AIR

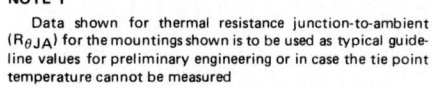

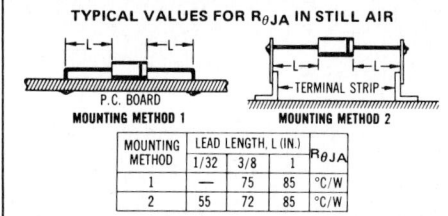

MOUNTING METHOD	LEAD LENGTH, L (IN.)			$R_{\theta JA}$
	1/32	3/8	1	
1	—	75	85	°C/W
2	55	72	85	°C/W

 MOTOROLA *Semiconductor Products Inc.*

1N4001 THRU 1N4007

TYPICAL DYNAMIC CHARACTERISTICS

FIGURE 10 — FORWARD RECOVERY TIME

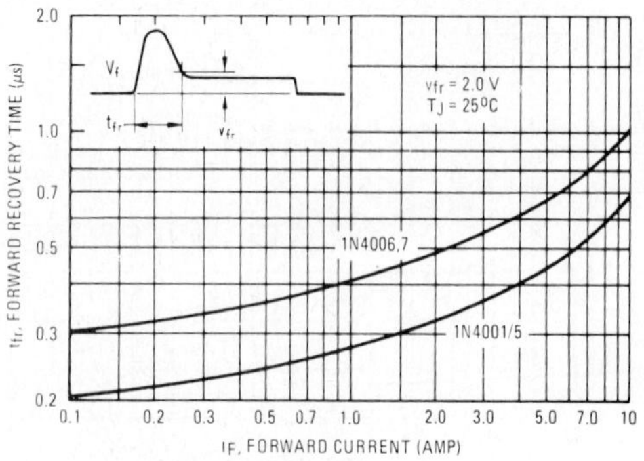

FIGURE 11 — REVERSE RECOVERY TIME

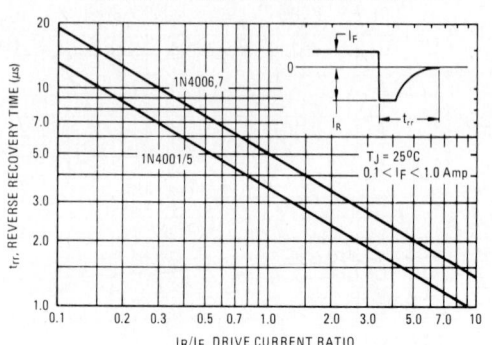

FIGURE 12 — JUNCTION CAPACITANCE

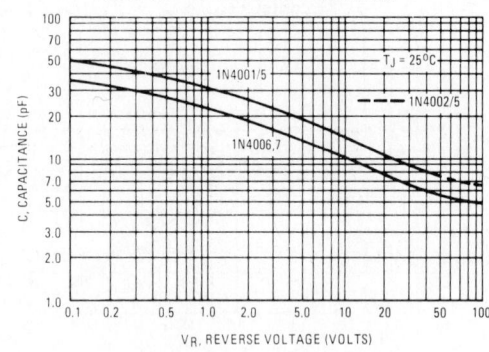

FIGURE 13 — RECTIFICATION WAVEFORM EFFICIENCY FOR SINE WAVE

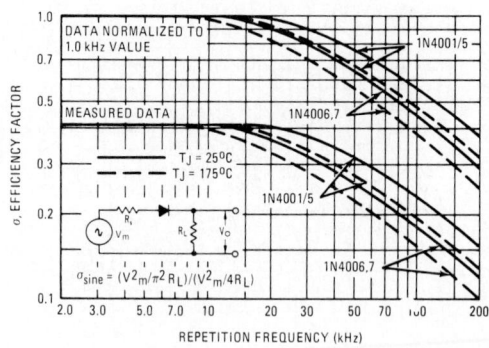

FIGURE 14 — RECTIFICATION WAVEFORM EFFICIENCY FOR SQUARE WAVE

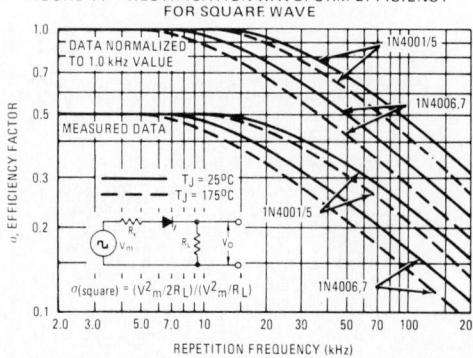

RECTIFIER EFFICIENCY NOTE

The rectification efficiency factor σ shown in Figures 13 and 14 was calculated using the formula:

$$\sigma = \frac{P_{dc}}{P_{rms}} = \frac{\dfrac{V^2_{O(dc)}}{R_L}}{\dfrac{V^2_{O(rms)}}{R_L}} \bullet 100\% = \frac{V^2_{O(dc)}}{V^2_{O(ac)} + V^2_{O(dc)}} \bullet 100\% \quad (1)$$

For a sine wave input $V_m \sin(\omega t)$ to the diode, assumed lossless, the maximum theoretical efficiency factor becomes 40%; for a square wave input of amplitude V_m, the efficiency factor becomes 50%. (A full wave circuit has twice these efficiencies).

As the frequency of the input signal is increased, the reverse recovery time of the diode (Figure 11) becomes significant, resulting in an increasing ac voltage component across R_L which is opposite in polarity to the forward current thereby reducing the value of the efficiency factor σ, as shown in Figures 13 and 14.

It should be emphasized that Figures 13 and 14 show waveform efficiency only; they do not account for diode losses. Data was obtained by measuring the ac component of V_O with a true rms voltmeter and the dc component with a dc voltmeter. The data was used in Equation 1 to obtain points for the Figures.

MOTOROLA *Semiconductor Products Inc.*

BOX 20912 • PHOENIX, ARIZONA 85036 • A SUBSIDIARY OF MOTOROLA INC.

MOTOROLA

SEMICONDUCTORS

P.O. BOX 20912 • PHOENIX, ARIZONA 85036

Designers Data Sheet

1N746
thru
1N759

1N957A
thru
1N986A

1N4370
thru
1N4372

500-MILLIWATT HERMETICALLY SEALED GLASS SILICON ZENER DIODES

- Complete Voltage Range — 2.4 to 110 Volts
- DO-35 Package — Smaller than Conventional DO-7 Package
- Double Slug Type Construction
- Metallurgically Bonded Construction
- Nitride Passivated Die

Designer's Data for "Worst Case" Conditions

The Designer's Data sheets permit the design of most circuits entirely from the information presented. Limit curves — representing boundaries on device characteristics — are given to facilitate "worst case" design.

GLASS ZENER DIODES
500 MILLIWATTS
2.4–110 VOLTS

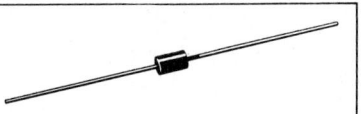

MAXIMUM RATINGS

Rating	Symbol	Value	Unit
DC Power Dissipation @ $T_L \leq 50^oC$, Lead Length = 3/8''	P_D		
*JEDEC Registration		400	mW
*Derate above T_L = 50°C		3.2	mW/°C
Motorola Device Ratings		500	mW
Derate above T_L = 50°C		3.33	mW/°C
Operating and Storage Junction Temperature Range	T_J, T_{stg}		°C
*JEDEC Registration		–65 to +175	
Motorola Device Ratings		–65 to +200	

*Indicates JEDEC Registered Data.

MECHANICAL CHARACTERISTICS

MAXIMUM LEAD TEMPERATURE FOR SOLDERING PURPOSES: 230°C, 1/16'' from case for 10 seconds

FINISH: All external surfaces are corrosion resistant with readily solderable leads.

POLARITY: Cathode indicated by color band. When operated in zener mode, cathode will be positive with respect to anode.

MOUNTING POSITION: Any

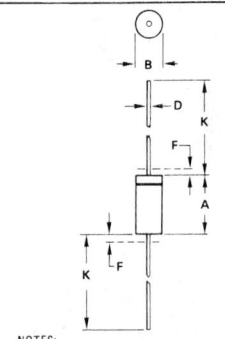

NOTES:
1. PACKAGE CONTOUR OPTIONAL WITHIN A AND B. HEAT SLUGS, IF ANY, SHALL BE INCLUDED WITHIN THIS CYLINDER, BUT NOT SUBJECT TO THE MINIMUM LIMIT OF B.
2. LEAD DIAMETER NOT CONTROLLED IN ZONE F TO ALLOW FOR FLASH, LEAD FINISH BUILDUP AND MINOR IRREGU-LARITIES OTHER THAN HEAT SLUGS.
3. POLARITY DENOTED BY CATHODE BAND.
4. DIMENSIONING AND TOLERANCING PER ANSI Y14.5, 1973.

DIM	MILLIMETERS		INCHES	
	MIN	MAX	MIN	MAX
A	3.05	5 08	0.120	0.200
B	1.52	2.29	0.060	0.090
D	0.46	0.56	0.018	0.022
F	—	1.27	—	0.050
K	25.40	38.10	1.000	1.500

All JEDEC dimensions and notes apply.

CASE 299-02
DO-204AH
(DO-35)

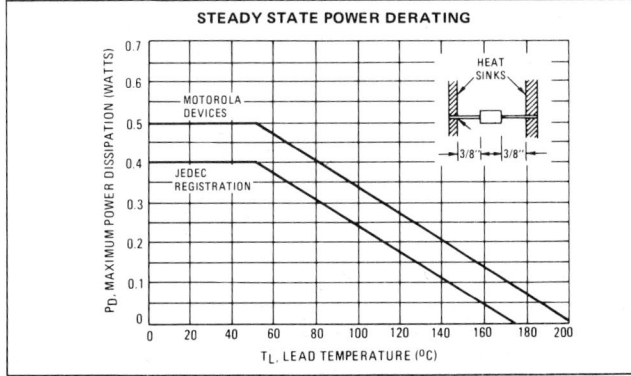

STEADY STATE POWER DERATING

P_D, MAXIMUM POWER DISSIPATION (WATTS)

MOTOROLA DEVICES

JEDEC REGISTRATION

HEAT SINKS

←3/8''→|←3/8''→

T_L, LEAD TEMPERATURE (°C)

Designer's is a trademark of Motorola Inc.

© MOTOROLA INC., 1982   DS 7021R3

ELECTRICAL CHARACTERISTICS ($T_A = 25^{\circ}C$, $V_F = 1.5$ V max at 200 mA for all types)

Type Number (Note 1)	Nominal Zener Voltage V_Z @ I_{ZT} (Note 2) Volts	Test Current I_{ZT} mA	Maximum Zener Impedance Z_{ZT} @ I_{ZT} (Note 3) Ohms	*Maximum DC Zener Current I_{ZM} (Note 4) mA		Maximum Reverse Leakage Current	
						$T_A = 25^{\circ}C$ I_R @ $V_R = 1$ V µA	$T_A = 150^{\circ}C$ I_R @ $V_R = 1$ V µA
1N4370	2.4	20	30	150	190	100	200
1N4371	2.7	20	30	135	165	75	150
1N4372	3.0	20	29	120	150	50	100
1N746	3.3	20	28	110	135	10	30
1N747	3.6	20	24	100	125	10	30
1N748	3.9	20	23	95	115	10	30
1N749	4.3	20	22	85	105	2	30
1N750	4.7	20	19	75	95	2	30
1N751	5.1	20	17	70	85	1	20
1N752	5.6	20	11	65	80	1	20
1N753	6.2	20	7	60	70	0.1	20
1N754	6.8	20	5	55	65	0.1	20
1N755	7.5	20	6	50	60	0.1	20
1N756	8.2	20	8	45	55	0.1	20
1N757	9.1	20	10	40	50	0.1	20
1N758	10	20	17	35	45	0.1	20
1N759	12	20	30	30	35	0.1	20

Type Number (Note 1)	Nominal Zener Voltage V_Z (Note 2) Volts	Test Current I_{ZT} mA	Maximum Zener Impedance (Note 3) Z_{ZT} @ I_{ZT} Ohms	Z_{ZK} @ I_{ZK} Ohms	I_{ZK} mA	*Maximum DC Zener Current I_{ZM} (Note 4) mA		Maximum Reverse Current		
								I_R Maximum µA	Test Voltage Vdc 5% V_R 10%	
1N957A	6.8	18.5	4.5	700	1.0	47	61	150	5.2	4.9
1N958A	7.5	16.5	5.5	700	0.5	42	55	75	5.7	5.4
1N959A	8.2	15	6.5	700	0.5	38	50	50	6.2	5.9
1N960A	9.1	14	7.5	700	0.5	35	45	25	6.9	6.6
1N961A	10	12.5	8.5	700	0.25	32	41	10	7.6	7.2
1N962A	11	11.5	9.5	700	0.25	28	37	5	8.4	8.0
1N963A	12	10.5	11.5	700	0.25	26	34	5	9.1	8.6
1N964A	13	9.5	13	700	0.25	24	32	5	9.9	9.4
1N965A	15	8.5	16	700	0.25	21	27	5	11.4	10.8
1N966A	16	7.8	17	700	0.25	19	37	5	12.2	11.5
1N967A	18	7.0	21	750	0.25	17	23	5	13.7	13.0
1N968A	20	6.2	25	750	0.25	15	20	5	15.2	14.4
1N969A	22	5.6	29	750	0.25	14	18	5	16.7	15.8
1N970A	24	5.2	33	750	0.25	13	17	5	18.2	17.3
1N971A	27	4.6	41	750	0.25	11	15	5	20.6	19.4
1N972A	30	4.2	49	1000	0.25	10	13	5	22.8	21.6
1N973A	33	3.8	58	1000	0.25	9.2	12	5	25.1	23.8
1N974A	36	3.4	70	1000	0.25	8.5	11	5	27.4	25.9
1N975A	39	3.2	80	1000	0.25	7.8	10	5	29.7	28.1
1N976A	43	3.0	93	1500	0.25	7.0	9.6	5	32.7	31.0
1N977A	47	2.7	105	1500	0.25	6.4	8.8	5	35.8	33.8
1N978A	51	2.5	125	1500	0.25	5.9	8.1	5	38.8	36.7
1N979A	56	2.2	150	2000	0.25	5.4	7.4	5	42.6	40.3
1N980A	62	2.0	185	2000	0.25	4.9	6.7	5	47.1	44.6
1N981A	68	1.8	230	2000	0.25	4.5	6.1	5	51.7	49.0
1N982A	75	1.7	270	2000	0.25	1.0	5.5	5	56.0	54.0
1N983A	82	1.5	330	3000	0.25	3.7	5.0	5	62.2	59.0
1N984A	91	1.4	400	3000	0.25	3.3	4.5	5	69.2	65.5
1N985A	100	1.3	500	3000	0.25	3.0	4.5	5	76	72
1N986A	110	1.1	750	4000	0.25	2.7	4.1	5	83.6	79.2

NOTE 1. TOLERANCE AND VOLTAGE DESIGNATION

Tolerance Designation

The type numbers shown have tolerance designations as follows:

1N4370 series: ±10%, suffix A for ±5% units.

1N746 series: ±10%, suffix A for ±5% units.

1N957 series: suffix A for ±10% units,
                  suffix B for ±5% units.

Voltage Designation

To designate units with zener voltages other than those listed, the Motorola type number should be modified as shown below. Unless otherwise specified, the electrical characteristics other than the nominal voltage (V_Z) and test voltage for leakage current will conform to the characteristics of the next higher voltage type shown in the table.

EXAMPLE: 1N746 series, 1N4370 series variations

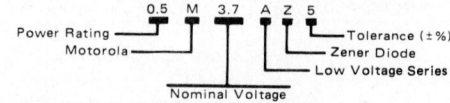

EXAMPLE: 1N957 series variations

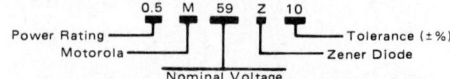

Matched Sets for Closer Tolerances or Higher Voltages

Series matched sets make zener voltages in excess of 100 volts or tolerances of less than 5% possible as well as providing lower temperature coefficients, lower dynamic impedance and greater power handling ability.

For Matched Sets or other special circuit requirements, contact your Motorola Sales Representative.

Ⓜ MOTOROLA *Semiconductor Products Inc.*

NOTE 2. ZENER VOLTAGE (V_Z) MEASUREMENT

Nominal zener voltage is measured with the device junction in thermal equilibrium at the lead temperature of 30°C ±1°C and 3/8" lead length.

NOTE 3. ZENER IMPEDANCE (Z_Z) DERIVATION

Z_{ZT} and Z_{ZK} are measured by dividing the ac voltage drop across the device by the ac current applied. The specified limits are for $I_Z(ac) = 0.1\ I_Z(dc)$ with the ac frequency = 60 Hz.

NOTE 4. MAXIMUM ZENER CURRENT RATINGS (I_{ZM})

Maximum zener current ratings are based on the maximum voltage of a 10% 1N746 type unit or a 20% 1N957 type unit. For closer tolerance units (10% or 5%) or units where the actual zener voltage (V_Z) is known at the operating point, the maximum zener current may be increased and is limited by the derating curve.

APPLICATION NOTE

Since the actual voltage available from a given zener diode is temperature dependent, it is necessary to determine junction temperature under any set of operating conditions in order to calculate its value. The following procedure is recommended:

Lead Temperature, T_L, should be determined from:

$$T_L = \theta_{LA} P_D + T_A$$

θ_{LA} is the lead-to-ambient thermal resistance (°C/W) and P_D is the power dissipation. The value for θ_{LA} will vary and depends on the device mounting method. θ_{LA} is generally 30–40°C/W for the various clips and tie points in common use and for printed circuit board wiring.

The temperature of the lead can also be measured using a thermocouple placed on the lead as close as possible to the tie point. The thermal mass connected to the tie point is normally large enough so that it will not significantly respond to heat surges generated in the diode as a result of pulsed operation once steady-state conditions are achieved. Using the measured value of T_L, the junction temperature may be determined by:

$$T_J = T_L + \Delta T_{JL}$$

ΔT_{JL} is the increase in junction temperature above the lead temperature and may be found from Figure 1 for dc power.

$$\Delta T_{JL} = \theta_{JL} P_D$$

For worst-case design, using expected limits of I_Z, limits of P_D and the extremes of $T_J(\Delta T_J)$ may be estimated. Changes in voltage, V_Z, can then be found from:

$$\Delta V = \theta_{VZ} \Delta T_J$$

θ_{VZ}, the zener voltage temperature coefficient, is found from Figures 3 and 4.

Under high power-pulse operation, the zener voltage will vary with time and may also be affected significantly by the zener resistance. For best regulation, keep current excursions as low as possible.

Surge limitations are given in Figure 6. They are lower than would be expected by considering only junction temperature, as current crowding effects cause temperatures to be extremely high in small spots, resulting in device degradation should the limits of Figure 6 be exceeded.

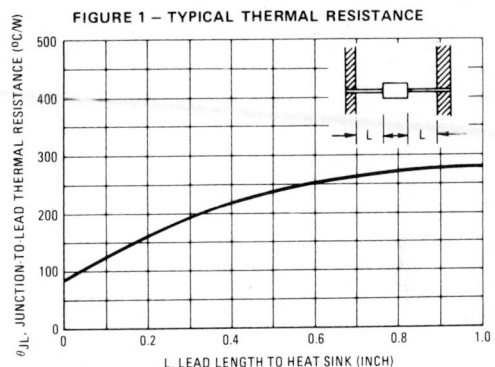

FIGURE 1 — TYPICAL THERMAL RESISTANCE

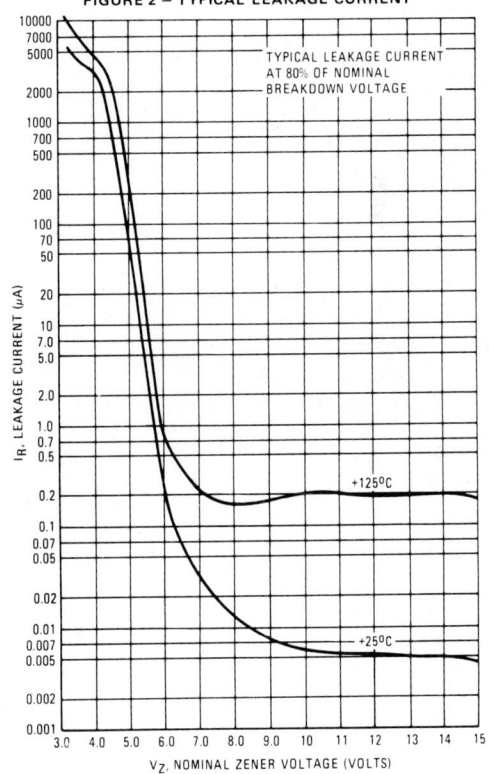

FIGURE 2 — TYPICAL LEAKAGE CURRENT

 MOTOROLA *Semiconductor Products Inc.*

1N746–1N759 • 1N957–1N986A • 1N4370–1N4372

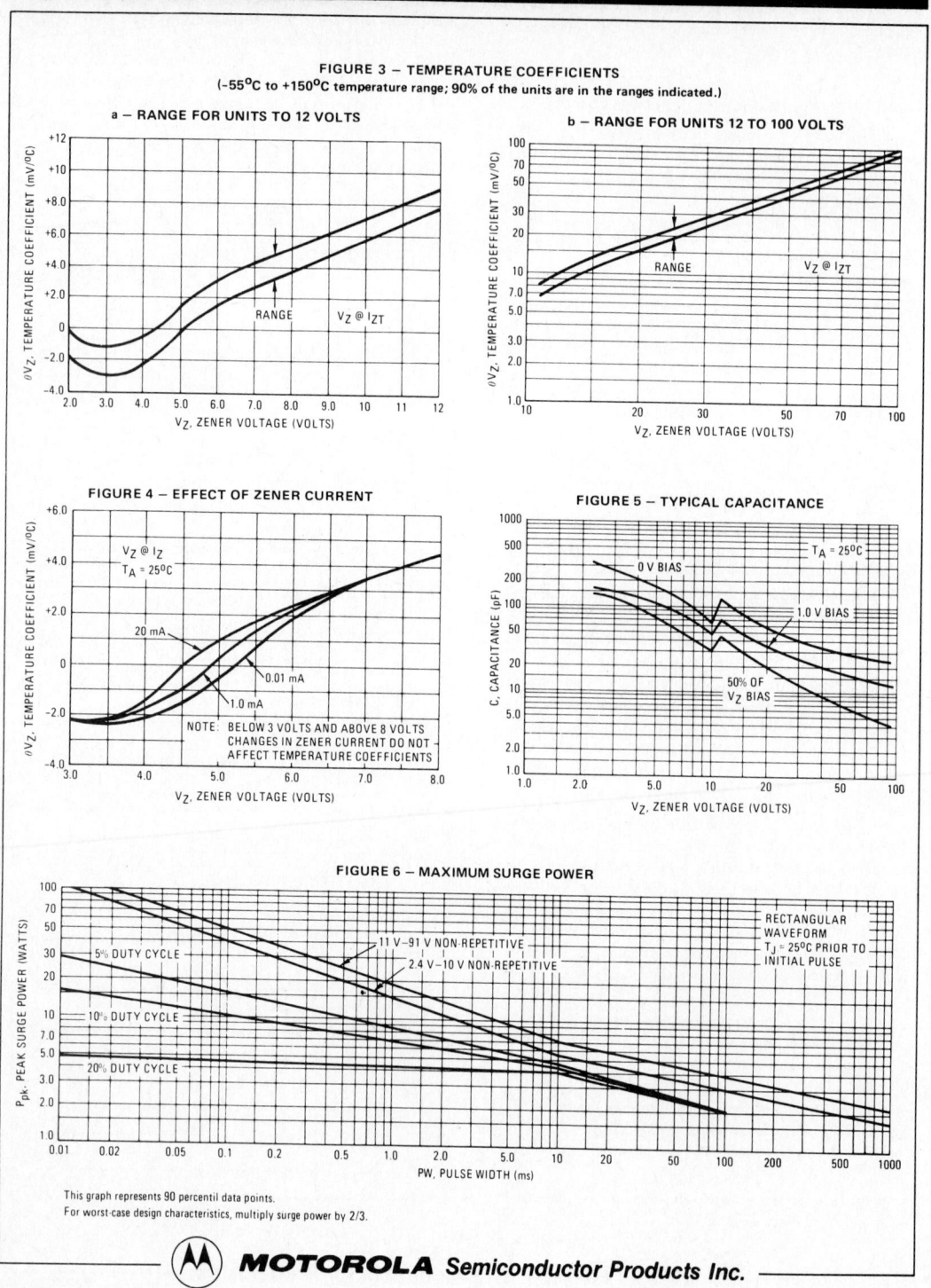

FIGURE 3 – TEMPERATURE COEFFICIENTS
(–55°C to +150°C temperature range; 90% of the units are in the ranges indicated.)

a – RANGE FOR UNITS TO 12 VOLTS

b – RANGE FOR UNITS 12 TO 100 VOLTS

FIGURE 4 – EFFECT OF ZENER CURRENT

FIGURE 5 – TYPICAL CAPACITANCE

FIGURE 6 – MAXIMUM SURGE POWER

This graph represents 90 percentil data points.
For worst-case design characteristics, multiply surge power by 2/3.

MOTOROLA *Semiconductor Products Inc.*

1N746–1N759 • 1N957–1N986A • 1N4370–1N4372

FIGURE 7 — EFFECT OF ZENER CURRENT ON ZENER IMPEDANCE

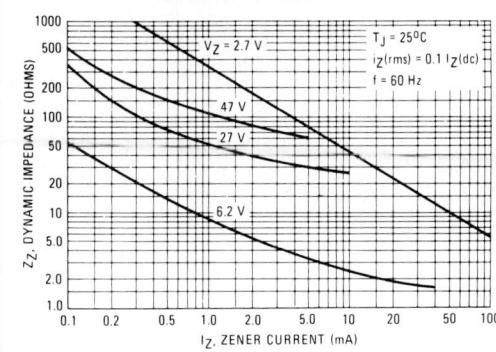

FIGURE 8 — EFFECT OF ZENER VOLTAGE ON ZENER IMPEDANCE

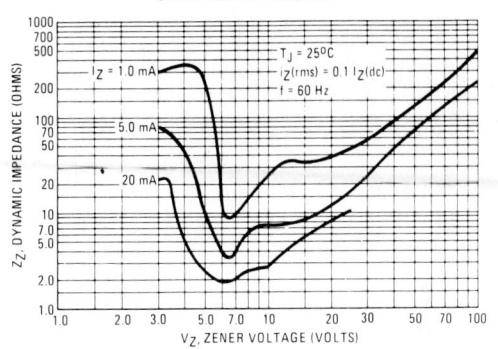

FIGURE 9 — TYPICAL NOISE DENSITY

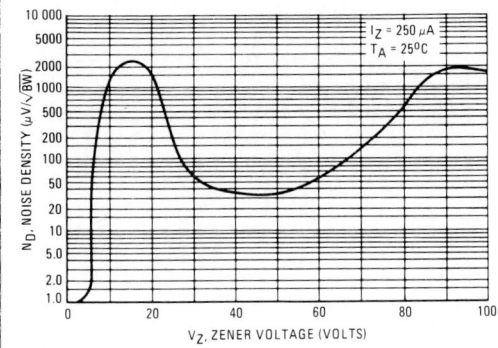

FIGURE 10 — NOISE DENSITY MEASUREMENT METHOD

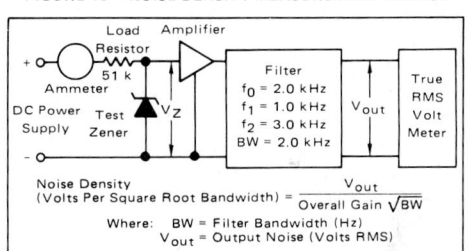

$$\text{Noise Density} \text{(Volts Per Square Root Bandwidth)} = \frac{V_{out}}{\text{Overall Gain} \sqrt{BW}}$$

Where: BW = Filter Bandwidth (Hz)
V_{out} = Output Noise (Volts RMS)

The input voltage and load resistance are high so that the zener diode is driven from a constant current source. The amplifier is low noise so that the amplifier noise is negligible compared to that of the test zener. The filter bandpass is known so that the noise density can be calculated from the formula shown.

FIGURE 11 — TYPICAL FORWARD CHARACTERISTICS

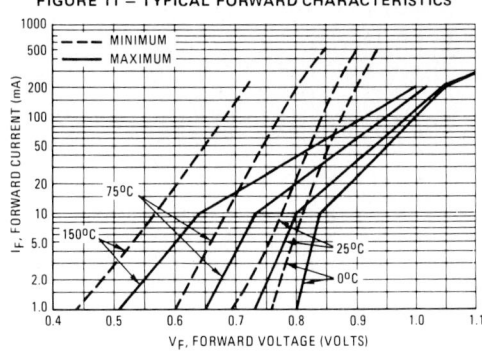

Motorola reserves the right to make changes to any products herein to improve reliability, function or design. Motorola does not assume any liability arising out of the application or use of any product or circuit described herein; neither does it convey any license under its patent rights nor the rights of others.

 MOTOROLA *Semiconductor Products Inc.*

1N746–1N759 • 1N957–1N986A • 1N4370–1N4372

FIGURE 12 — ZENER VOLTAGE versus ZENER CURRENT — V$_Z$ = 1 THRU 16 VOLTS

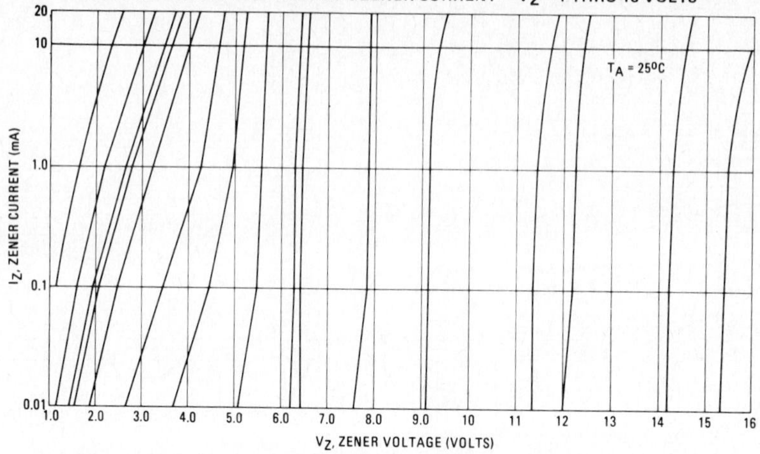

$T_A = 25^0C$

I_Z, ZENER CURRENT (mA)

V$_Z$, ZENER VOLTAGE (VOLTS)

FIGURE 13 — ZENER VOLTAGE versus ZENER CURRENT — V$_Z$ = 15 THRU 30 VOLTS

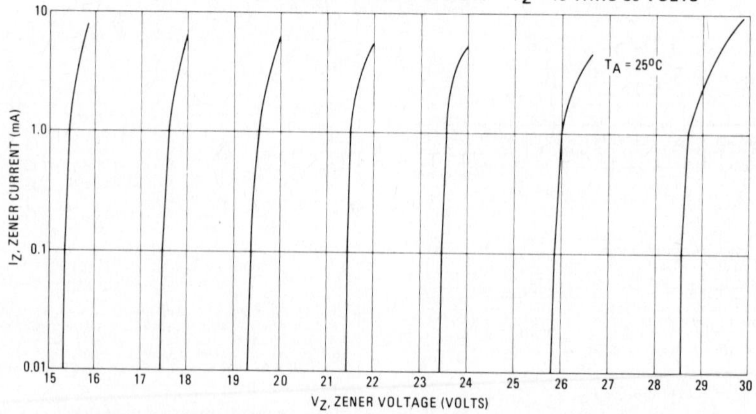

$T_A = 25^0C$

I_Z, ZENER CURRENT (mA)

V$_Z$, ZENER VOLTAGE (VOLTS)

FIGURE 14 — ZENER VOLTAGE versus ZENER CURRENT — V$_Z$ = 30 THRU 105 VOLTS

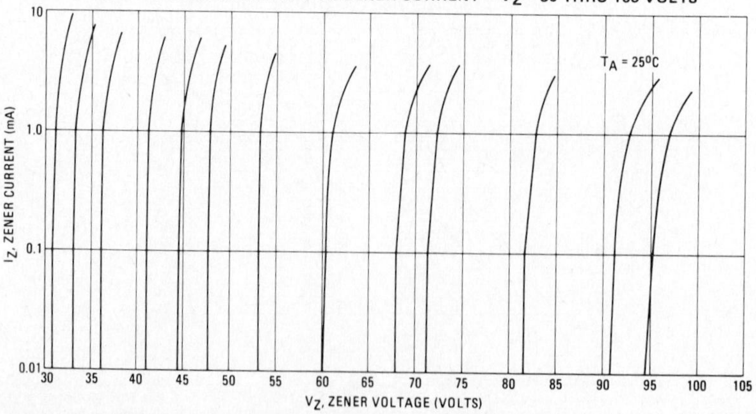

$T_A = 25^0C$

I_Z, ZENER CURRENT (mA)

V$_Z$, ZENER VOLTAGE (VOLTS)

 MOTOROLA *Semiconductor Products Inc.*

BOX 20912 • PHOENIX, ARIZONA 85036 • A SUBSIDIARY OF MOTOROLA INC.

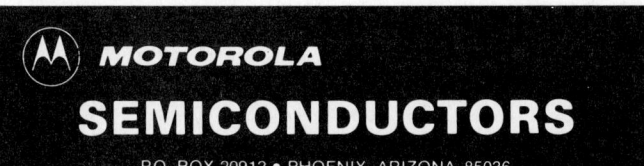

MOTOROLA

SEMICONDUCTORS

P.O. BOX 20912 • PHOENIX, ARIZONA 85036

2N3903
2N3904

NPN SILICON ANNULAR TRANSISTORS

... designed for general purpose switching and amplifier applications and for complementary circuitry with types 2N3905 and 2N3906.

- High Voltage Ratings — $V_{(BR)CEO}$ = 40 Volts (Min)
- Current Gain Specified from 100 μA to 100 mA
- Complete Switching and Amplifier Specifications
- Low Capacitance — C_{ob} = 4.0 pF (Max)

**NPN SILICON
SWITCHING & AMPLIFIER
TRANSISTORS**

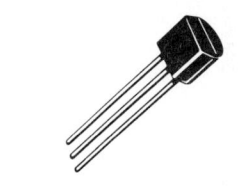

MAXIMUM RATINGS

Rating	Symbol	Value	Unit
*Collector-Emitter Voltage	V_{CEO}	40	Vdc
*Collector-Base Voltage	V_{CBO}	60	Vdc
*Emitter-Base Voltage	V_{EBO}	6.0	Vdc
*Collector Current — Continuous	I_C	200	mAdc
**Total Device Dissipation @ T_A = 25°C Derate above 25°C	P_D	625 5.0	mW mW/°C
Total Power Dissipation @ T_A = 60°C	P_D	450	mW
**Total Device Dissipation @ T_C = 25°C Derate above 25°C	P_D	1.5 12	Watts mW/°C
**Operating and Storage Junction Temperature Range	T_J, T_{stg}	−55 to 150	°C

THERMAL CHARACTERISTICS

Characteristic	Symbol	Max	Unit
Thermal Resistance, Junction to Case	$R_{\theta JC}$	83.3	°C/W
Thermal Resistance, Junction to Ambient	$R_{\theta JA}$	200	°C/W

*Indicates JEDEC Registered Data.
**Motorola guarantees this data in addition to the JEDEC Registered Data.

EQUIVALENT SWITCHING TIME TEST CIRCUITS

FIGURE 1 — TURN-ON TIME

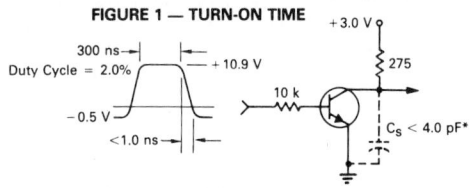

FIGURE 2 — TURN-OFF TIME

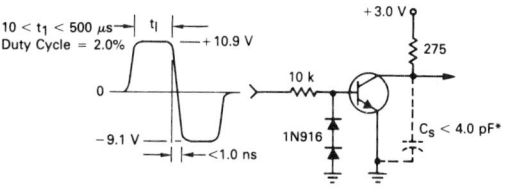

*Total shunt capacitance of test jig and connectors

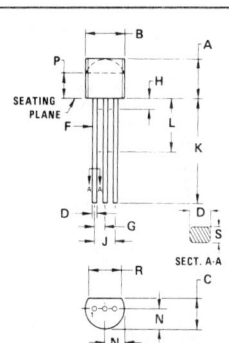

NOTES:
1. CONTOUR OF PACKAGE BEYOND ZONE "P" IS UNCONTROLLED.
2. DIM "F" APPLIES BETWEEN "H" AND "L". DIM "D" & "S" APPLIES BETWEEN "L" & 12.70 mm (0.5") FROM SEATING PLANE. LEAD DIM IS UNCONTROLLED IN "H" & BEYOND 12.70 mm (0.5") FROM SEATING PLANE.

	MILLIMETERS		INCHES	
DIM	MIN	MAX	MIN	MAX
A	4.32	5.33	0.170	0.210
B	4.44	5.21	0.175	0.205
C	3.18	4.19	0.125	0.165
D	0.41	0.56	0.016	0.022
F	0.41	0.48	0.016	0.019
G	1.14	1.40	0.045	0.055
H	–	2.54	–	0.100
J	2.41	2.67	0.095	0.105
K	12.70	–	0.500	–
L	6.35	–	0.250	–
N	2.03	2.67	0.080	0.105
P	2.92	–	0.115	–
R	3.43	–	0.135	–
S	0.36	0.41	0.014	0.016

All JEDEC dimensions and notes apply.

**CASE 29-02
(TO-226AA)**

DS5127 R2

ELECTRICAL CHARACTERISTICS (T_A = 25°C unless otherwise noted.)

Characteristic		Symbol	Min	Max	Unit
OFF CHARACTERISTICS					
Collector-Emitter Breakdown Voltage[1] (I_C = 1.0 mAdc, I_B = 0)		$V_{(BR)CEO}$	40	—	Vdc
Collector-Base Breakdown Voltage (I_C = 10 μAdc, I_E = 0)		$V_{(BR)CBO}$	60	—	Vdc
Emitter-Base Breakdown Voltage (I_E = 10 μAdc, I_C = 0)		$V_{(BR)EBO}$	6.0	—	Vdc
Collector Cutoff Current (V_{CE} = 30 Vdc, $V_{EB(off)}$ = 3.0 Vdc)		I_{CEX}	—	50	nAdc
Base Cutoff Current (V_{CE} = 30 Vdc, $V_{EB(off)}$ = 3.0 Vdc)		I_{BL}	—	50	nAdc
ON CHARACTERISTICS[1]					
DC Current Gain		h_{FE}			—
(I_C = 0.1 mAdc, V_{CE} = 1.0 Vdc)	2N3903		20	—	
	2N3904		40	—	
(I_C = 1.0 mAdc, V_{CE} = 1.0 Vdc)	2N3903		35	—	
	2N3904		70	—	
(I_C = 10 mAdc, V_{CE} = 1.0 Vdc)	2N3903		50	150	
	2N3904		100	300	
(I_C = 50 mAdc, V_{CE} = 1.0 Vdc)	2N3903		30	—	
	2N3904		60	—	
(I_C = 100 mAdc, V_{CE} = 1.0 Vdc)	2N3903		15	—	
	2N3904		30	—	
Collector-Emitter Saturation Voltage		$V_{CE(sat)}$			Vdc
(I_C = 10 mAdc, I_B = 1.0 mAdc)			—	0.2	
(I_C = 50 mAdc, I_B = 5.0 mAdc)			—	0.3	
Base-Emitter Saturation Voltage		$V_{BE(sat)}$			Vdc
(I_C = 10 mAdc, I_B = 1.0 mAdc)			0.65	0.85	
(I_C = 50 mAdc, I_B = 5.0 mAdc)			—	1.0	
SMALL-SIGNAL CHARACTERISTICS					
Current-Gain — Bandwidth Product		f_T			MHz
(I_C = 10 mAdc, V_{CE} = 20 Vdc, f = 100 MHz)	2N3903		150	—	
	2N3904		200	—	
Output Capacitance (V_{CB} = 5.0 Vdc, I_E = 0, f = 100 kHz)		C_{obo}	—	4.0	pF
Input Capacitance (V_{BE} = 0.5 Vdc, I_C = 0, f = 100 kHz)		C_{ibo}	—	8.0	pF
Input Impedance		h_{ie}			kΩ
(I_C = 1.0 mAdc, V_{CE} = 10 Vdc, f = 1.0 kHz)	2N3903		0.5	8.0	
	2N3904		1.0	10	
Voltage Feedback Ratio		h_{re}			$\times 10^{-4}$
(I_C = 1.0 mAdc, V_{CE} = 10 Vdc, f = 1.0 kHz)	2N3903		0.1	5.0	
	2N3904		0.5	8.0	
Small-Signal Current Gain		h_{fe}			—
(I_C = 1.0 mAdc, V_{CE} = 10 Vdc, f = 1.0 kHz)	2N3903		50	200	
	2N3904		100	400	
Output Admittance (I_C = 1.0 mAdc, V_{CE} = 10 Vdc, f = 1.0 kHz)		h_{oe}	1.0	40	μmhos
Noise Figure		NF			dB
(I_C = 100 μAdc, V_{CE} = 5.0 Vdc, R_S = 1.0 kΩ, f = 10 Hz to 15.7 kHz)	2N3903		—	6.0	
	2N3904		—	5.0	
SWITCHING CHARACTERISTICS					
Delay Time	(V_{CC} = 3.0 Vdc, $V_{BE(off)}$ = 0.5 Vdc, I_C = 10 mAdc, I_{B1} = 1.0 mAdc)	t_d	—	35	ns
Rise Time		t_r	—	50	ns
Storage Time	2N3903	t_s	—	800	ns
	2N3904 (V_{CC} = 3.0 Vdc, I_C = 10 mAdc,		—	900	
Fall Time	I_{B1} = I_{B2} = 1.0 mAdc)	t_f	—	90	ns

(1) Pulse Test: Pulse Width ≤ 300 μs, Duty Cycle ≤ 2.0%.

 MOTOROLA Semiconductor Products Inc.

2N3903 • 2N3904

TYPICAL NOISE CHARACTERISTICS
(V_{CE} = 5.0 Vdc, T_A = 25°C)

FIGURE 3 — NOISE VOLTAGE

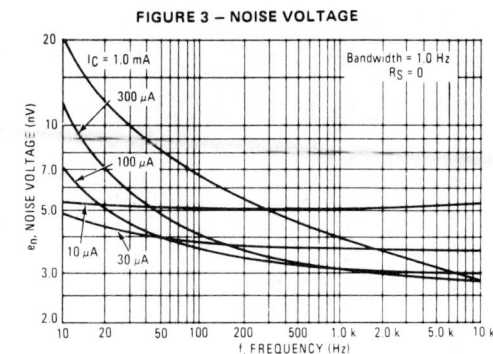

FIGURE 4 — NOISE CURRENT

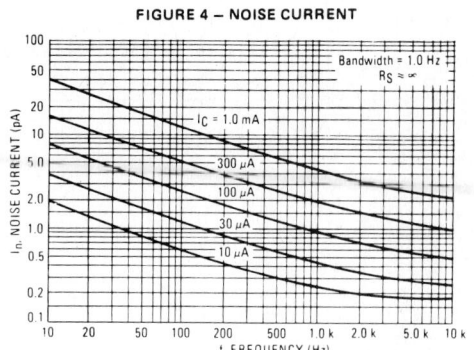

NOISE FIGURE CONTOURS
(V_{CE} = 5.0 Vdc, T_A = 25°C)

FIGURE 5 — NARROW BAND, 100 Hz

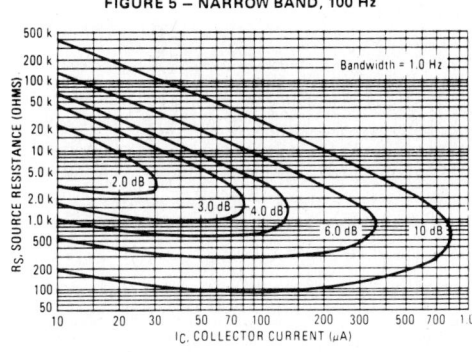

FIGURE 6 — NARROW BAND, 1.0 kHz

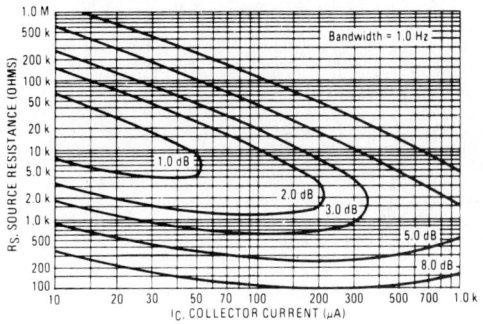

FIGURE 7 — WIDEBAND

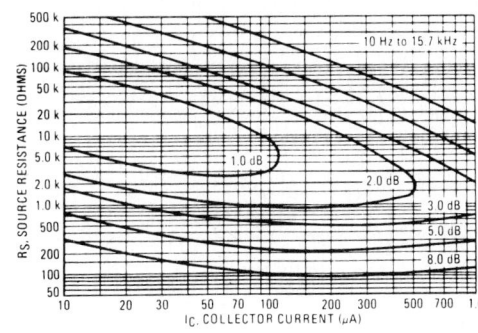

Noise Figure is Defined as:

$$NF = 20 \log_{10} \left(\frac{e_n{}^2 + 4KTR_S + I_n{}^2 R_S{}^2}{4KTR_S} \right)^{1/2}$$

e_n = Noise Voltage of the Transistor referred to the input (Figure 3)

I_n = Noise Current of the transistor referred to the input (Figure 4)

K = Boltzman's Constant (1.38 x 10^{-23} j/°K)

T = Temperature of the Source Resistance (°K)

R_S = Source Resistance (Ohms)

 MOTOROLA *Semiconductor Products Inc.*

2N3903 ● 2N3904

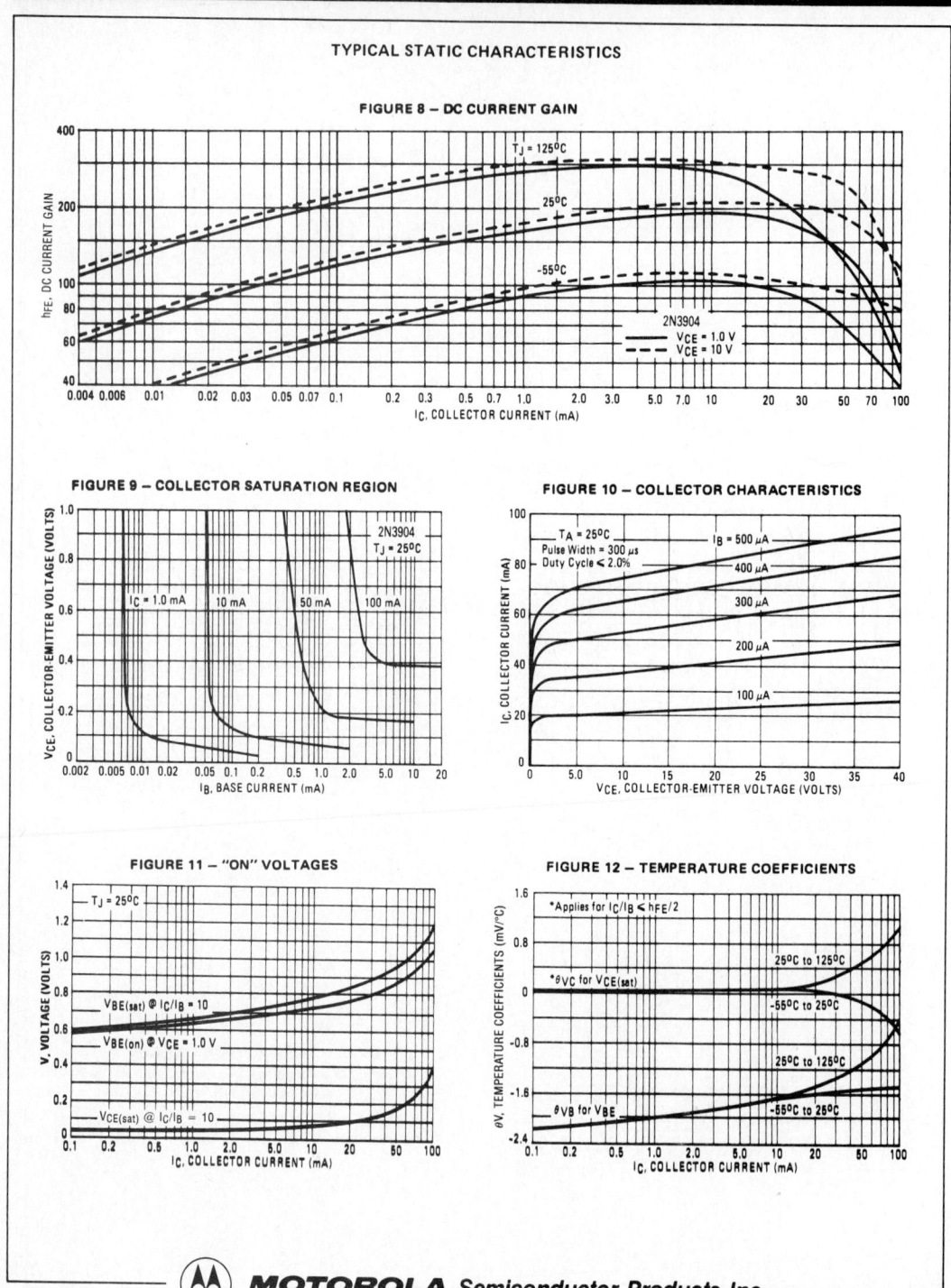

TYPICAL STATIC CHARACTERISTICS

FIGURE 8 — DC CURRENT GAIN

FIGURE 9 — COLLECTOR SATURATION REGION

FIGURE 10 — COLLECTOR CHARACTERISTICS

FIGURE 11 — "ON" VOLTAGES

FIGURE 12 — TEMPERATURE COEFFICIENTS

(M) MOTOROLA *Semiconductor Products Inc.*

2N3903 ● 2N3904

TYPICAL DYNAMIC CHARACTERISTICS

FIGURE 13 — TURN-ON TIME

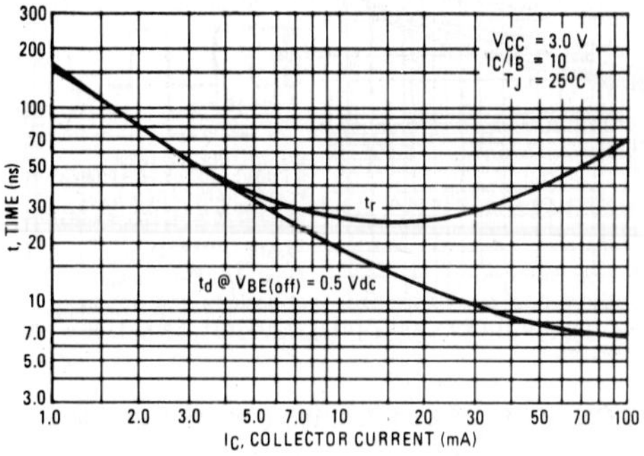

$V_{CC} = 3.0$ V
$I_C/I_B = 10$
$T_J = 25^oC$

t_r

t_d @ $V_{BE(off)} = 0.5$ Vdc

t, TIME (ns) vs. I_C, COLLECTOR CURRENT (mA)

FIGURE 14 — TURN-OFF TIME

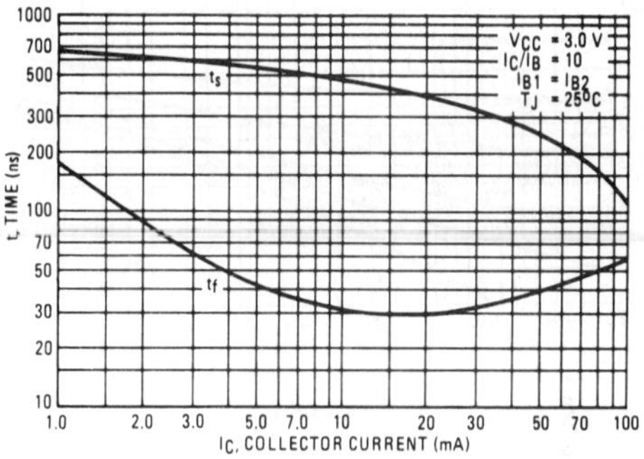

$V_{CC} = 3.0$ V
$I_C/I_B = 10$
$I_{B1} = I_{B2}$
$T_J = 25^oC$

t_s

t_f

t, TIME (ns) vs. I_C, COLLECTOR CURRENT (mA)

FIGURE 15 — CURRENT-GAIN — BANDWIDTH PRODUCT

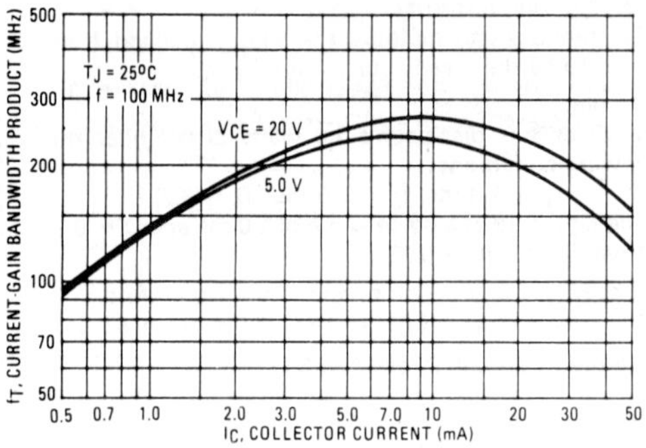

$T_J = 25^oC$
$f = 100$ MHz

$V_{CE} = 20$ V

5.0 V

f_T, CURRENT-GAIN BANDWIDTH PRODUCT (MHz) vs. I_C, COLLECTOR CURRENT (mA)

FIGURE 16 — CAPACITANCE

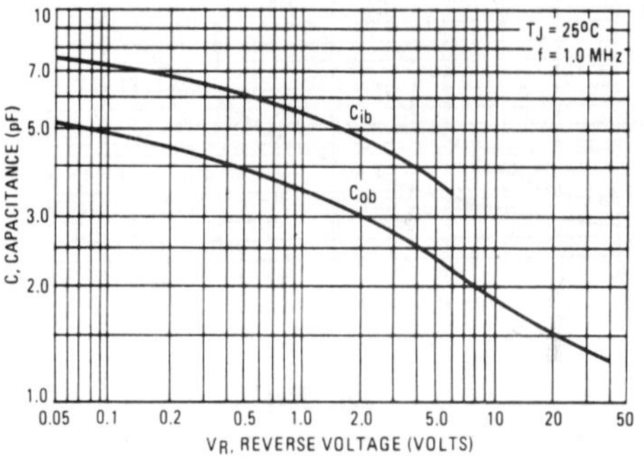

$T_J = 25^oC$
$f = 1.0$ MHz

C_{ib}

C_{ob}

C, CAPACITANCE (pF) vs. V_R, REVERSE VOLTAGE (VOLTS)

FIGURE 17 — INPUT IMPEDANCE

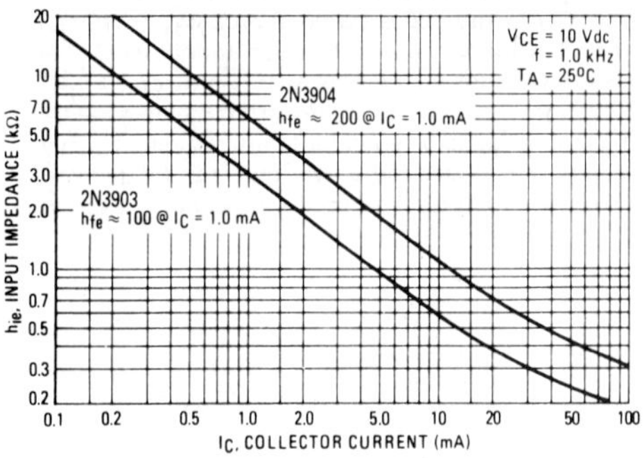

$V_{CE} = 10$ Vdc
$f = 1.0$ kHz
$T_A = 25^oC$

2N3904
$h_{fe} \approx 200$ @ $I_C = 1.0$ mA

2N3903
$h_{fe} \approx 100$ @ $I_C = 1.0$ mA

h_{ie}, INPUT IMPEDANCE (kΩ) vs. I_C, COLLECTOR CURRENT (mA)

FIGURE 18 — OUTPUT ADMITTANCE

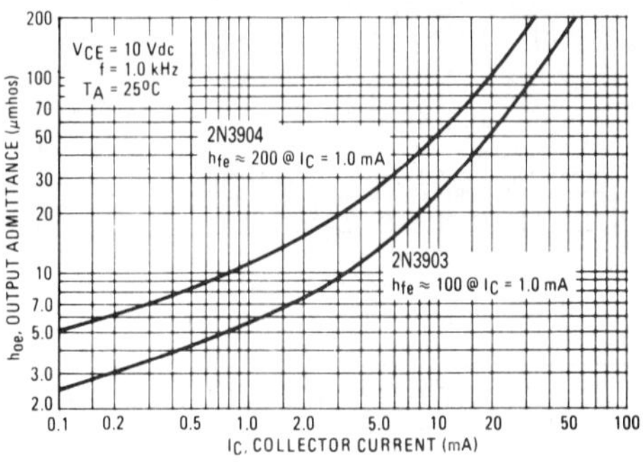

$V_{CE} = 10$ Vdc
$f = 1.0$ kHz
$T_A = 25^oC$

2N3904
$h_{fe} \approx 200$ @ $I_C = 1.0$ mA

2N3903
$h_{fe} \approx 100$ @ $I_C = 1.0$ mA

h_{oe}, OUTPUT ADMITTANCE (μmhos) vs. I_C, COLLECTOR CURRENT (mA)

 MOTOROLA *Semiconductor Products Inc.*

3N128

*ELECTRICAL CHARACTERISTICS (T_A = 25°C unless otherwise noted)

Characteristic	Symbol	Min	Max	Unit
OFF CHARACTERISTICS				
Gate-Source Breakdown Voltage (1) (I_G = –10 μAdc, V_{DS} = 0)	$V_{(BR)GSS}$	–50	—	Vdc
Gate-Source Cutoff Voltage (V_{DS} = 15 Vdc, I_D = 50 μAdc)	$V_{GS(off)}$	–0.5	–8.0	Vdc
Gate Reverse Current (V_{GS} = –8.0 Vdc, V_{DS} = 0) (V_{GS} = –8.0 Vdc, V_{DS} = 0, T_A = 125°C)	I_{GSS}	— —	0.05 5.0	nAdc
ON CHARACTERISTICS				
Zero-Gate-Voltage Drain Current (2) (V_{DS} = 15 Vdc, V_{GS} = 0)	I_{DSS}	5.0	25	mAdc
SMALL-SIGNAL CHARACTERISTICS				
Forward Transadmittance (V_{DS} = 15 Vdc, I_D = 5.0 mAdc, f = 1.0 kHz)	$|y_{fs}|$	5000	12,000	μmhos
Forward Transconductance (V_{DS} = 15 Vdc, I_D = 5.0 mAdc, f = 200 MHz)	$Re(y_{fs})$	5000	—	μmhos
Output Conductance (V_{DS} = 15 Vdc, I_D = 5.0 mAdc, f = 200 MHz)	$Re(y_{os})$	—	500	μmhos
Input Conductance (V_{DS} = 15 Vdc, I_D = 5.0 mAdc, f = 200 MHz)	$Re(y_{is})$	—	800	μmhos
Input Capacitance (V_{DS} = 15 Vdc, I_D = 5.0 mAdc, f = 1.0 MHz)	C_{iss}	—	7.0	pF
Reverse Transfer Capacitance (V_{DS} = 15 Vdc, I_D = 5.0 mAdc, f = 1.0 MHz)	C_{rss}	0.05	0.35	pF
Noise Figure (V_{DS} = 15 Vdc, I_D = 5.0 mAdc, f = 200 MHz)	NF	—	5.0	dB
Power Gain (V_{DS} = 15 Vdc, I_D = 5.0 mAdc, f = 200 MHz)	P_G	13.5	23	dB

*Indicates JEDEC Registered Data.
(1) Caution Destructive Test, can damage gate oxide beyond operation.
(2) Pulse Test: Pulse Width = 300 μs, Duty Cycle = 2.0%.

TYPICAL CHARACTERISTICS
(T_A = 25°C)

FIGURE 1 — DRAIN CHARACTERISTICS

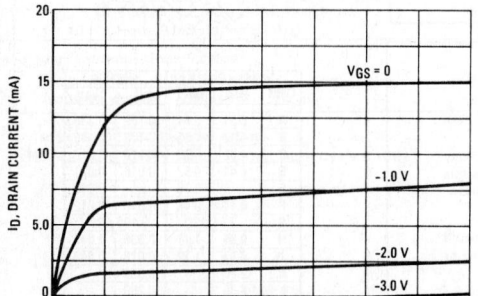

FIGURE 2 — TRANSFER CHARACTERISTICS

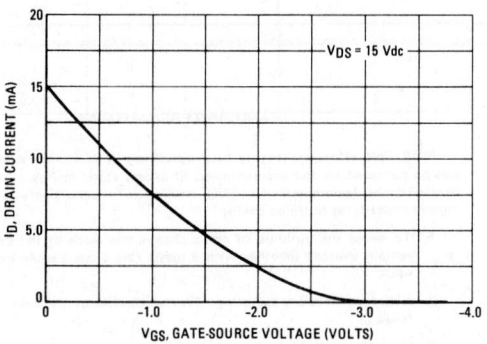

 MOTOROLA *Semiconductor Products Inc.*

MOTOROLA

SEMICONDUCTORS

P.O. BOX 20912 • PHOENIX, ARIZONA 85036

MC7800 Series

THREE-TERMINAL POSITIVE VOLTAGE REGULATORS

These voltage regulators are monolithic integrated circuits designed as fixed-voltage regulators for a wide variety of applications including local, on-card regulation. These regulators employ internal current limiting, thermal shutdown, and safe-area compensation. With adequate heatsinking they can deliver output currents in excess of 1.0 ampere. Although designed primarily as a fixed voltage regulator, these devices can be used with external components to obtain adjustable voltages and currents.

- Output Current in Excess of 1.0 Ampere
- No External Components Required
- Internal Thermal Overload Protection
- Internal Short-Circuit Current Limiting
- Output Transistor Safe-Area Compensation
- Output Voltage Offered in 2% and 4% Tolerance

THREE-TERMINAL POSITIVE FIXED VOLTAGE REGULATORS

SILICON MONOLITHIC INTEGRATED CIRCUITS

K SUFFIX
METAL PACKAGE
CASE 1-03
TO-204AA
(TO-3)

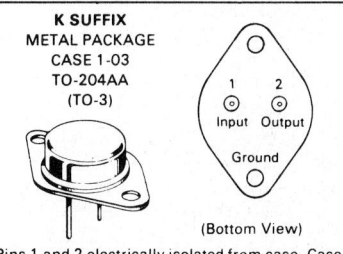

Pins 1 and 2 electrically isolated from case. Case is third electrical connection.

T SUFFIX
PLASTIC PACKAGE
CASE 221A
TO-220AB

Pin 1. Input
   2. Ground
   3. Output

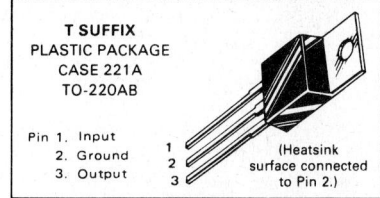

(Heatsink surface connected to Pin 2.)

EQUIVALENT SCHEMATIC DIAGRAM

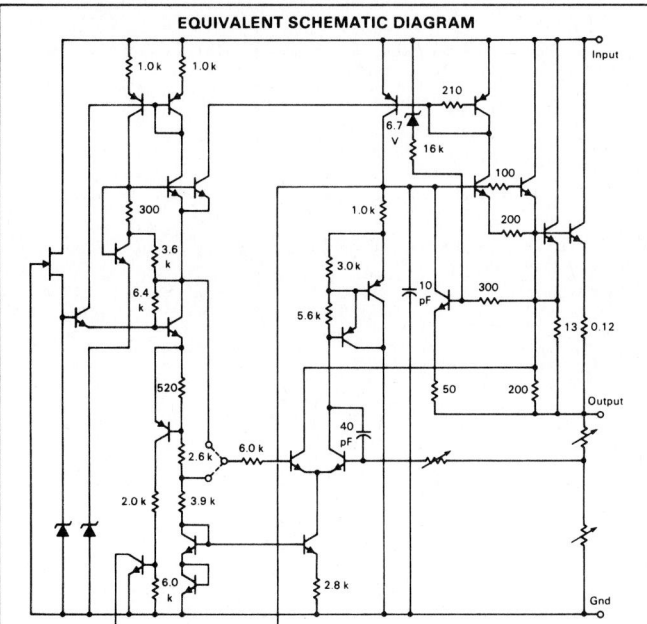

STANDARD APPLICATION

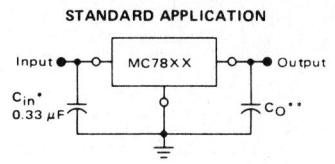

A common ground is required between the input and the output voltages. The input voltage must remain typically 2.0 V above the output voltage even during the low point on the input ripple voltage.

XX = these two digits of the type number indicate voltage.

* = C_{in} is required if regulator is located an appreciable distance from power supply filter.

** = C_O is not needed for stability; however, it does improve transient response.

XX indicates nominal voltage

ORDERING INFORMATION

Device	Output Voltage Tolerance	Temperature Range	Package
MC78XXK MC78XXAK	4% 2%	–55 to +150°C	Metal Power
MC78XXBK	4%	–40 to +125°C	
MC78XXCK MC78XXACK	4% 2%	0 to +125°C	
MC78XXCT MC78XXACT	4% 2%		Plastic Power
MC78XXBT	4%	–40 to +125°C	

TYPE NO /VOLTAGE			
MC7805	5.0 Volts	MC7815	15 Volts
MC7806	6.0 Volts	MC7818	18 Volts
MC7808	8.0 Volts	MC7824	24 Volts
MC7812	12 Volts		

     DS9557R1

MC7800 Series

MC7800 Series MAXIMUM RATINGS (T$_A$ = +25°C unless otherwise noted.)

Rating	Symbol	Value	Unit
Input Voltage (5.0 V – 18 V)	V$_{in}$	35	Vdc
(24 V)		40	
Power Dissipation and Thermal Characteristics			
Plastic Package			
T$_A$ = +25°C	P$_D$	Internally Limited	Watts
Derate above T$_A$ = +25°C	1/θ$_{JA}$	15.4	mW/°C
Thermal Resistance, Junction to Air	θ$_{JA}$	65	°C/W
T$_C$ = +25°C	P$_D$	Internally Limited	Watts
Derate above T$_C$ = +75°C (See Figure 1)	1/θ$_{JC}$	200	mW/°C
Thermal Resistance, Junction to Case	θ$_{JC}$	5.0	°C/W
Metal Package			
T$_A$ = +25°C	P$_D$	Internally Limited	Watts
Derate above T$_A$ = +25°C	1/θ$_{JA}$	22.5	mW/°C
Thermal Resistance, Junction to Air	θ$_{JA}$	45	°C/W
T$_C$ = +25°C	P$_D$	Internally Limited	Watts
Derate above T$_C$ = +65°C (See Figure 2)	1/θ$_{JC}$	182	mW/°C
Thermal Resistance, Junction to Case	θ$_{JC}$	5.5	°C/W
Storage Junction Temperature Range	T$_{stg}$	–65 to +150	°C
Operating Junction Temperature Range	T$_J$		°C
MC7800, A		–55 to +150	
MC7800C, AC		0 to +150	
MC7800, B		–40 to +150	

DEFINITIONS

Line Regulation — The change in output voltage for a change in the input voltage. The measurement is made under conditions of low dissipation or by using pulse techniques such that the average chip temperature is not significantly affected.

Load Regulation — The change in output voltage for a change in load current at constant chip temperature.

Maximum Power Dissipation — The maximum total device dissipation for which the regulator will operate within specifications.

Quiescent Current — That part of the input current that is not delivered to the load.

Output Noise Voltage — The rms ac voltage at the output, with constant load and no input ripple, measured over a specified frequency range.

Long Term Stability — Output voltage stability under accelerated life test conditions with the maximum rated voltage listed in the devices' electrical characteristics and maximum power dissipation.

OUTLINE DIMENSIONS

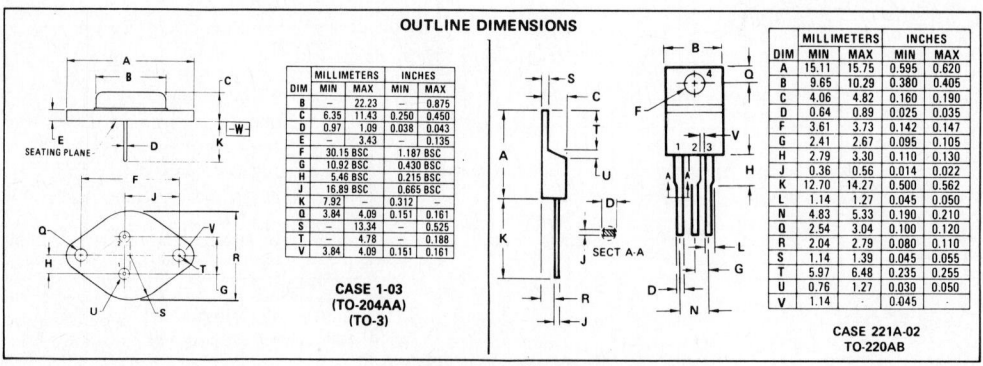

DIM	MILLIMETERS		INCHES	
	MIN	MAX	MIN	MAX
B	–	22.23	–	0.875
C	6.35	11.43	0.250	0.450
D	0.97	1.09	0.038	0.043
E	–	3.43	–	0.135
F	30.15 BSC		1.187 BSC	
G	10.92 BSC		0.430 BSC	
H	5.46 BSC		0.215 BSC	
J	16.89 BSC		0.665 BSC	
K	7.92	–	0.312	–
Q	3.84	4.09	0.151	0.161
S	–	13.34	–	0.525
T	–	4.78	–	0.188
V	3.84	4.09	0.151	0.161

CASE 1-03
(TO-204AA)
(TO-3)

DIM	MILLIMETERS		INCHES	
	MIN	MAX	MIN	MAX
A	15.11	15.75	0.595	0.620
B	9.65	10.29	0.380	0.405
C	4.06	4.82	0.160	0.190
D	0.64	0.89	0.025	0.035
F	3.61	3.73	0.142	0.147
G	2.41	2.67	0.095	0.105
H	2.79	3.30	0.110	0.130
J	0.36	0.56	0.014	0.022
K	12.70	14.27	0.500	0.562
L	1.14	1.27	0.045	0.050
N	4.83	5.33	0.190	0.210
Q	2.54	3.04	0.100	0.120
R	2.04	2.79	0.080	0.110
S	1.14	1.39	0.045	0.055
T	5.97	6.48	0.235	0.255
U	0.76	1.27	0.030	0.050
V	1.14	·	0.045	–

CASE 221A-02
TO-220AB

THERMAL INFORMATION

The maximum power consumption an integrated circuit can tolerate at a given operating ambient temperature, can be found from the equation:

$$P_{D(T_A)} = \frac{T_{J(max)} - T_A}{R_{\theta JA}(Typ)} \geq V_I I_S - V_O I_O$$

Where: $P_{D(T_A)}$ = Power Dissipation allowable at a given operating ambient temperature.

$T_{J(max)}$ = Maximum Operating Junction Temperature as listed in the Maximum Ratings Section

T_A = Maximum Desired Operating Ambient Temperature

$R_{\theta JA}(Typ)$ = Typical Thermal Resistance Junction to Ambient

I_S = Total Supply Current

 MOTOROLA *Semiconductor Products Inc.*

MC7808, B, C
ELECTRICAL CHARACTERISTICS (V_{in} = 14 V, I_O = 500 mA, T_J = T_{low} to T_{high} [Note 1] unless otherwise noted).

Characteristic	Symbol	MC7808			MC7808B			MC7808C			Unit
		Min	Typ	Max	Min	Typ	Max	Min	Typ	Max	
Output Voltage (T_J = +25°C)	V_O	7.7	8.0	8.3	7.7	8.0	8.3	7.7	8.0	8.3	Vdc
Output Voltage (5.0 mA ≤ I_O ≤ 1.0 A, P_O ≤ 15 W)	V_O										Vdc
10.5 Vdc ≤ V_{in} ≤ 23 Vdc		—	—	—	—	—	—	7.6	8.0	8.4	
11.5 Vdc ≤ V_{in} ≤ 23 Vdc		7.6	8.0	8.4	7.6	8.0	8.4	—	—	—	
Line Regulation (T_J = +25°C, Note 2)	Reg_{line}										mV
10.5 Vdc ≤ V_{in} ≤ 25 Vdc		—	3.0	80	—	12	160	—	12	160	
11 Vdc ≤ V_{in} ≤ 17 Vdc		—	2.0	40	—	5.0	80	—	5.0	80	
Load Regulation (T_J = +25°C, Note 2)	Reg_{load}										mV
5.0 mA ≤ I_O ≤ 1.5 A		—	28	100	—	45	160	—	45	160	
250 mA ≤ I_O ≤ 750 mA		—	9.0	40	—	16	80	—	16	80	
Quiescent Current (T_J = +25°C)	I_B	—	3.2	6.0	—	4.3	8.0	—	4.3	8.0	mA
Quiescent Current Change	ΔI_B										mA
10.5 Vdc ≤ V_{in} ≤ 25 Vdc		—	—	—	—	—	—	—	—	1.0	
11.5 Vdc ≤ V_{in} ≤ 25 Vdc		—	0.3	0.8	—	—	1.0	—	—	—	
5.0 mA ≤ I_O ≤ 1.0 A		—	0.04	0.5	—	—	0.5	—	—	0.5	
Ripple Rejection 11.5 Vdc ≤ V_{in} ≤ 21.5 Vdc, f = 120 Hz	RR	62	70	—	—	62	—	—	62	—	dB
Dropout Voltage (I_O = 1.0 A, T_J = +25°C)	V_{in} - V_O	—	2.0	2.5	—	2.0	—	—	2.0	—	Vdc
Output Noise Voltage (T_A = +25°C) 10 Hz ≤ f ≤ 100 kHz	V_n	—	10	40	—	10	—	—	10	—	μV/V_O
Output Resistance f = 1.0 kHz	r_O	—	18	—	—	18	—	—	18	—	mΩ
Short-Circuit Current Limit (T_A = +25°C) V_{in} = 35 Vdc	I_{sc}	—	0.2	1.2	—	0.2	—	—	0.2	—	A
Peak Output Current (T_J = +25°C)	I_{max}	1.3	2.5	3.3	—	2.2	—	—	2.2	—	A
Average Temperature Coefficient of Output Voltage	TCV_O	—	±1.0	—	—	-0.8	—	—	-0.8	—	mV/°C

MC7808A, AC
ELECTRICAL CHARACTERISTICS (V_{in} = 14 V, I_O = 1.0 A, T_J = T_{low} to T_{high} [Note 1] unless otherwise noted)

Characteristics	Symbol	MC7808A			MC7808AC			Unit
		Min	Typ	Max	Min	Typ	Max	
Output Voltage (T_J = +25°C)	V_O	7.84	8.0	8.16	7.84	8.0	8.16	Vdc
Output Voltage (5.0 mA ≤ I_O ≤ 1.0 A, P_O ≤ 15 W) 10.6 Vdc ≤ V_{in} ≤ 23 Vdc	V_O	7.7	8.0	8.3	7.7	8.0	8.3	Vdc
Line Regulation (Note 2)	Reg_{line}							mV
10.6 Vdc ≤ V_{in} ≤ 25 Vdc, I_O = 500 mA		—	4.0	13	—	12	80	
11 Vdc ≤ V_{in} ≤ 17 Vdc		—	6.0	20	—	15	80	
11 Vdc ≤ V_{in} ≤ 17 Vdc, T_J = +25°C		—	2.0	6.0	—	5.0	40	
10.4 Vdc ≤ V_{in} ≤ 23 Vdc, T_J = +25°C		—	4.0	13	—	12	80	
Load Regulation (Note 2)	Reg_{load}							mV
5.0 mA ≤ I_O ≤ 1.5 A, T_J = +25°C		—	2.0	25	—	45	100	
5.0 mA ≤ I_O ≤ 1.0 A		—	2.0	25	—	45	100	
250 mA ≤ I_O ≤ 750mA, T_J = +25°C		—	1.0	15	—	—	—	
250 mA ≤ I_O ≤ 750 mA		—	1.0	25	—	16	50	
Quiescent Current	I_B							mA
		—	—	5.0	—	—	6.0	
T_J = +25°C		—	3.2	4.0	—	4.3	6.0	
Quiescent Current Change	ΔI_B							mA
11 Vdc ≤ V_{in} ≤ 25 Vdc, I_O = 500 mA		—	0.3	0.5	—	—	0.8	
10.6 Vdc ≤ V_{in} ≤ 23 Vdc, T_J = +25°C		—	0.2	0.5	—	—	0.8	
5.0 mA ≤ I_O ≤ 1.0 A		—	0.04	0.2	—	—	0.5	
Ripple Rejection	RR							dB
11.5 Vdc ≤ V_{in} ≤ 21.5 Vdc, f = 120 Hz, T_J = +25°C		62	70	—	—	—	—	
11.5 Vdc ≤ V_{in} ≤ 21.5 Vdc, f = 120 Hz, I_O = 500 mA		62	70	—	—	62	—	
Dropout Voltage (I_O = 1.0 A, T_J = +25°C)	V_{in} - V_O	—	2.0	2.5	—	2.0	—	Vdc
Output Noise Voltage (T_A = +25°C) 10 Hz ≤ f ≤ 100 kHz	V_n	—	10	40	—	10	—	μV/V_O
Output Resistance (f = 1.0 kHz)	r_O	—	2.0	—	—	18	—	mΩ
Short-Circuit Current Limit (T_A = +25°C) V_{in} = 35 Vdc	I_{sc}	—	0.2	1.2	—	0.2	—	A
Peak Output Current (T_J = +25°C)	I_{max}	1.3	2.5	3.3	—	2.2	—	A
Average Temperature Coefficient of Output Voltage	TCV_O	—	±1.0	—	—	-0.8	—	mV/°C

NOTES: 1. T_{low} = -55°C for MC78XX, A T_{high} = +150°C for MC78XX, A
        = 0° for MC78XXC, AC   = +125°C for MC78XXC, AC, B
        = -40°C for MC78XXB
     2. Load and line regulation are specified at constant junction temperature. Changes in V_O due to heating effects must be taken into account
        separately. Pulse testing with low duty cycle is used.

 MOTOROLA *Semiconductor Products Inc.*

MC7812, B, C
ELECTRICAL CHARACTERISTICS (V_{in} = 19 V, I_O = 500 mA, T_J = T_{low} to T_{high} [Note 1] unless otherwise noted).

Characteristic	Symbol	MC7812			MC7812B			MC7812C			Unit
		Min	Typ	Max	Min	Typ	Max	Min	Typ	Max	
Output Voltage (T_J = +25°C)	V_O	11.5	12	12.5	11.5	12	12.5	11.5	12	12.5	Vdc
Output Voltage (5.0 mA ≤ I_O ≤ 1.0 A, P_O ≤ 15 W)	V_O										Vdc
14.5 Vdc ≤ V_{in} ≤ 27 Vdc		—	—	—	—	—	—	11.4	12	12.6	
15.5 Vdc ≤ V_{in} ≤ 27 Vdc		11.4	12	12.6	11.4	12	12.6	—	—	—	
Line Regulation (T_J = +25°C, Note 2)	Reg_{line}										mV
14.5 Vdc ≤ V_{in} ≤ 30 Vdc		—	5.0	120	—	13	240	—	13	240	
16 Vdc ≤ V_{in} ≤ 22 Vdc		—	3.0	60	—	6.0	120	—	6.0	120	
Load Regulation (T_J = +25°C, Note 2)	Reg_{load}										mV
5.0 mA ≤ I_O ≤ 1.5 A		—	30	120	—	46	240	—	46	240	
250 mA ≤ I_O ≤ 750 mA		—	10	60	—	17	120	—	17	120	
Quiescent Current (T_J = +25°C)	I_B	—	3.4	6.0	—	4.4	8.0	—	4.4	8.0	mA
Quiescent Current Change	ΔI_B										mA
14.5 Vdc ≤ V_{in} ≤ 30 Vdc		—	—	—	—	—	—	—	—	1.0	
15 Vdc ≤ V_{in} ≤ 30 Vdc		—	0.3	0.8	—	—	1.0	—	—	—	
5.0 mA ≤ I_O ≤ 1.0 A		—	0.04	0.5	—	—	0.5	—	—	0.5	
Ripple Rejection 15 Vdc ≤ V_{in} ≤ 25 Vdc, f = 120 Hz	RR	61	68	—	—	60	—	—	60	—	dB
Dropout Voltage (I_O = 1.0 A, T_J = +25°C)	V_{in} - V_O	—	2.0	2.5	—	2.0	—	—	2.0	—	Vdc
Output Noise Voltage (T_A = +25°C) 10 Hz ≤ f ≤ 100 kHz	V_n	—	10	40	—	10	—	—	10	—	µV/V_O
Output Resistance f = 1.0 kHz	r_O	—	18	—	—	18	—	—	18	—	mΩ
Short-Circuit Current Limit (T_A = +25°C) V_{in} = 35 Vdc	I_{sc}	—	0.2	1.2	—	0.2	—	—	0.2	—	A
Peak Output Current (T_J = +25°C)	I_{max}	1.3	2.5	3.3	—	2.2	—	—	2.2	—	A
Average Temperature Coefficient of Output Voltage	TCV_O	—	±1.5	—	—	-1.0	—	—	-1.0	—	mV/°C

MC7812A, AC
ELECTRICAL CHARACTERISTICS (V_{in} = 19 V, I_O = 1.0 A, T_J = T_{low} to T_{high} [Note 1] unless otherwise noted)

Characteristics	Symbol	MC7812A			MC7812AC			Unit
		Min	Typ	Max	Min	Typ	Max	
Output Voltage (T_J = +25°C)	V_O	11.75	12	12.25	11.75	12	12.25	Vdc
Output Voltage (5.0 mA ≤ I_O ≤ 1.0 A, P_O ≤ 15 W) 14.8 Vdc ≤ V_{in} ≤ 27 Vdc	V_O	11.5	12	12.5	11.5	12	12.5	Vdc
Line Regulation (Note 2)	Reg_{line}							mV
14.8 Vdc ≤ V_{in} ≤ 30 Vdc, I_O = 500 mA		—	5.0	18	—	13	120	
16 Vdc ≤ V_{in} ≤ 22 Vdc		—	8.0	30	—	16	120	
16 Vdc ≤ V_{in} ≤ 22 Vdc, T_J = +25°C		—	3.0	9.0	—	6.0	60	
14.5 Vdc ≤ V_{in} ≤ 27 Vdc, T_J = +25°C		—	5.0	18	—	13	120	
Load Regulation (Note 2)	Reg_{load}							mV
5.0 mA ≤ I_O ≤ 1.5 A, T_J = +25°C		—	2.0	25	—	46	100	
5.0 mA ≤ I_O ≤ 1.0 A		—	2.0	25	—	46	100	
250 mA ≤ I_O ≤ 750mA, T_J = +25°C		—	1.0	15	—	—	—	
250 mA ≤ I_O ≤ 750 mA		—	1.0	25	—	17	50	
Quiescent Current T_J = +25°C	I_B	—	—	5.0	—	—	6.0	mA
		—	3.4	4.0	—	4.4	6.0	
Quiescent Current Change	ΔI_B							mA
15 Vdc ≤ V_{in} ≤ 30 Vdc, I_O = 500 mA		—	0.3	0.5	—	—	0.8	
14.8 Vdc ≤ V_{in} ≤ 27 Vdc, T_J = +25°C		—	0.2	0.5	—	—	0.8	
5.0 mA ≤ I_O ≤ 1.0 A		—	0.04	0.2	—	—	0.5	
Ripple Rejection 15 Vdc ≤ V_{in} ≤ 25 Vdc, f = 120 Hz, T_J = +25°C	RR	61	68	—	—	—	—	dB
15 Vdc ≤ V_{in} ≤ 25 Vdc, f = 120 Hz, I_O = 500 mA		61	68	—	—	60	—	
Dropout Voltage (I_O = 1.0 A, T_J = +25°C)	V_{in} - V_O	—	2.0	2.5	—	2.0	—	Vdc
Output Noise Voltage (T_A = +25°C) 10 Hz ≤ f ≤ 100 kHz	V_n	—	10	40	—	10	—	µV/V_O
Output Resistance (f = 1.0 kHz)	r_O	—	2.0	—	—	18	—	mΩ
Short-Circuit Current Limit (T_A = +25°C) V_{in} = 35 Vdc	I_{sc}	—	0.2	1.2	—	0.2	—	A
Peak Output Current (T_J = +25°C)	I_{max}	1.3	2.5	3.3	—	2.2	—	A
Average Temperature Coefficient of Output Voltage	TCV_O	—	±1.5	—	—	-1.0	—	mV/°C

NOTES: 1. T_{low} = -55°C for MC78XX, A T_{high} = +150°C for MC78XX, A
   = 0° for MC78XXC, AC   = +125°C for MC78XXC, AC, B
   = -40°C for MC78XXB

2. Load and line regulation are specified at constant junction temperature. Changes in V_O due to heating effects must be taken into account separately. Pulse testing with low duty cycle is used.

 MOTOROLA *Semiconductor Products Inc.*

MC7800 Series

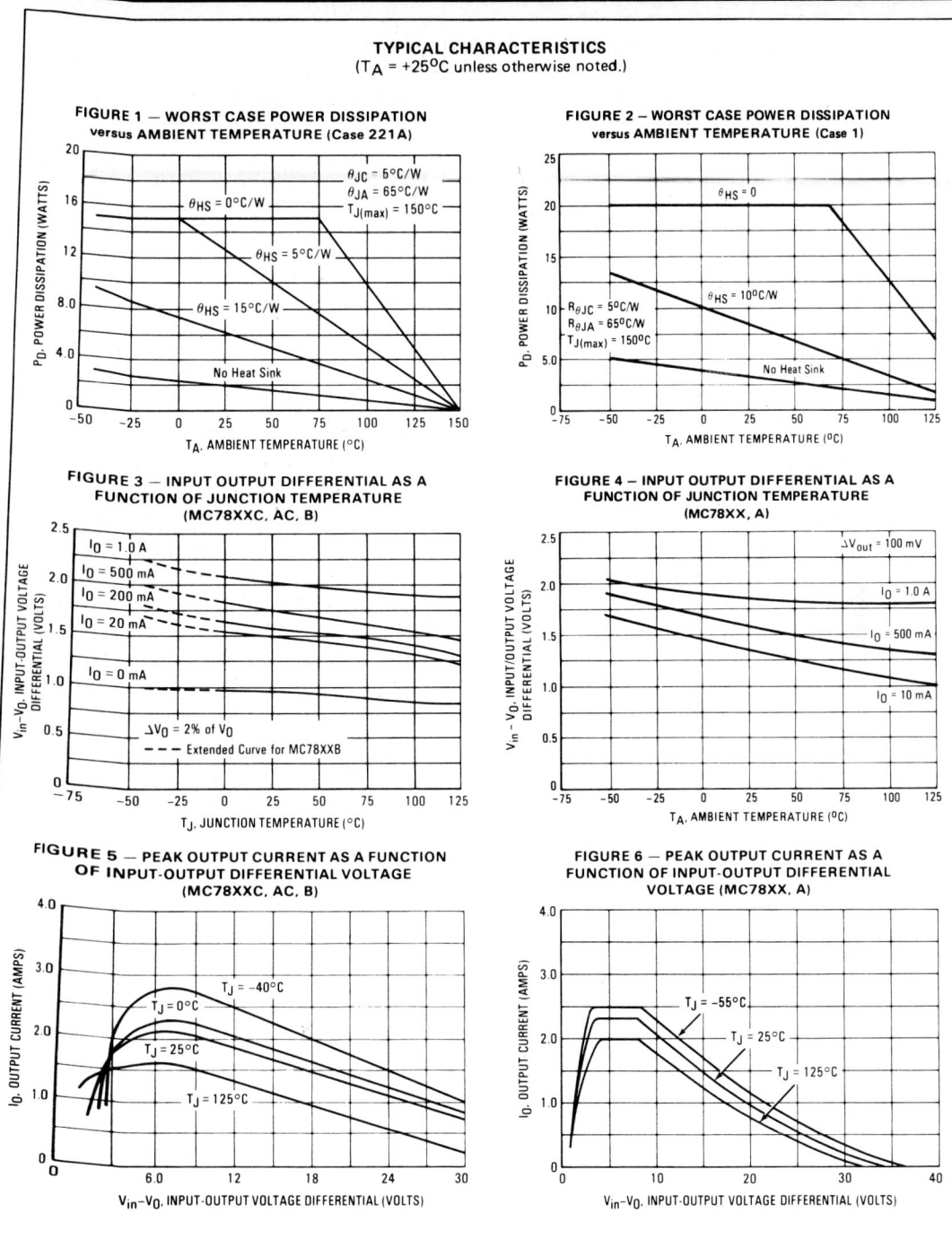

TYPICAL CHARACTERISTICS
(T_A = +25°C unless otherwise noted.)

FIGURE 1 — WORST CASE POWER DISSIPATION versus AMBIENT TEMPERATURE (Case 221A)

FIGURE 2 — WORST CASE POWER DISSIPATION versus AMBIENT TEMPERATURE (Case 1)

FIGURE 3 — INPUT OUTPUT DIFFERENTIAL AS A FUNCTION OF JUNCTION TEMPERATURE (MC78XXC, AC, B)

FIGURE 4 — INPUT OUTPUT DIFFERENTIAL AS A FUNCTION OF JUNCTION TEMPERATURE (MC78XX, A)

FIGURE 5 — PEAK OUTPUT CURRENT AS A FUNCTION OF INPUT-OUTPUT DIFFERENTIAL VOLTAGE (MC78XXC, AC, B)

FIGURE 6 — PEAK OUTPUT CURRENT AS A FUNCTION OF INPUT-OUTPUT DIFFERENTIAL VOLTAGE (MC78XX, A)

MOTOROLA *Semiconductor Products Inc.*

National Semiconductor

Voltage Comparators

LM139/239/339, LM139A/239A/339A, LM2901, LM3302
Low Power Low Offset Voltage Quad Comparators

General Description

The LM139 series consists of four independent precision voltage comparators with an offset voltage specification as low as 2 mV max for all four comparators. These were designed specifically to operate from a single power supply over a wide range of voltages. Operation from split power supplies is also possible and the low power supply current drain is independent of the magnitude of the power supply voltage. These comparators also have a unique characteristic in that the input common-mode voltage range includes ground, even though operated from a single power supply voltage.

Application areas include limit comparators, simple analog to digital converters; pulse, squarewave and time delay generators; wide range VCO; MOS clock timers; multivibrators and high voltage digital logic gates. The LM139 series was designed to directly interface with TTL and CMOS. When operated from both plus and minus power supplies, they will directly interface with MOS logic— where the low power drain of the LM339 is a distinct advantage over standard comparators.

Advantages

- High precision comparators
- Reduced V_{OS} drift over temperature

- Eliminates need for dual supplies
- Allows sensing near gnd
- Compatible with all forms of logic
- Power drain suitable for battery operation

Features

- Wide single supply voltage range or dual supplies
  LM139 series,   2 V_{DC} to 36 V_{DC} or
  LM139A series, LM2901 ±1 V_{DC} to ±18 V_{DC}
  LM3302   2 V_{DC} to 28 V_{DC}
                              or ±1 V_{DC} to ±14 V_{DC}
- Very low supply current drain (0.8 mA) — independent of supply voltage (2 mW/comparator at +5 V_{DC})
- Low input biasing current   25 nA
- Low input offset current   ±5 nA
  and offset voltage   ±3 mV
- Input common-mode voltage range includes gnd
- Differential input voltage range equal to the power supply voltage
- Low output   250 mV at 4 mA
  saturation voltage
- Output voltage compatible with TTL, DTL, ECL, MOS and CMOS logic systems

Schematic and Connection Diagrams

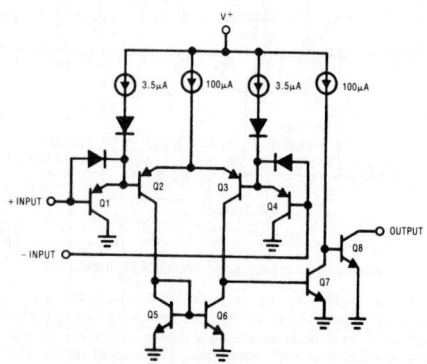

Dual-In-Line and Flat Package

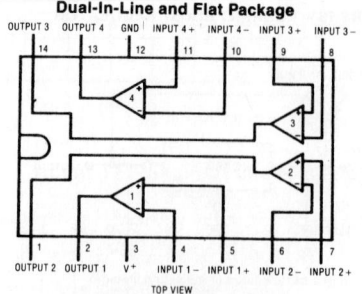

TOP VIEW

Order Number LM139J, LM139AJ, LM239J, LM239AJ, LM339J, LM339AJ, LM2901J or LM3302J
See NS Package J14A

Order Number LM339N, LM339AN, LM2901N or LM3302N
See NS Package N14A

Typical Applications (V^+ = 5.0 V_{DC})

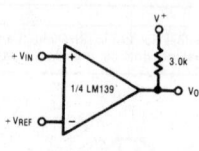

Basic Comparator

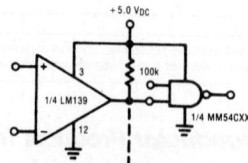

Driving CMOS

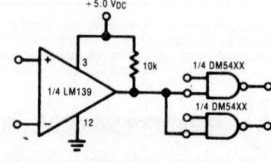

Driving TTL

Absolute Maximum Ratings

	LM139/LM239/LM339 LM139A/LM239A/LM339A LM2901	LM3302
Supply Voltage, V+	36 VDC or ±18 VDC	28 VDC or ±14 VDC
Differential Input Voltage	36 VDC	28 VDC
Input Voltage	−0.3 VDC to +36 VDC	−0.3 VDC to +28 VDC
Power Dissipation (Note 1)		
Molded DIP	570 mW	570 mW
Cavity DIP	900 mW	
Flat Pack	800 mW	
Output Short-Circuit to GND, (Note 2)	Continuous	Continuous
Input Current (V$_{IN}$ < −0.3 V$_{DC}$), (Note 3)	50 mA	50 mA
Operating Temperature Range		
LM339A	0°C to +70°C	−40°C to +85°C
LM239A	−25°C to +85°C	
LM2901	−40°C to +85°C	
LM139A	−55°C to +125°C	
Storage Temperature Range	−55°C to +150°C	−65°C to +150°C
Lead Temperature (Soldering, 10 seconds)	300°C	300°C

Electrical Characteristics (V+ = 5 VDC, Note 4)

PARAMETER	CONDITIONS	LM139A			LM239A, LM339A			LM139			LM239, LM339			LM2901			LM3302			UNITS
		MIN	TYP	MAX	MIN	TYP	MAX	MIN	TYP	MAX	MIN	TYP	MAX	MIN	TYP	MAX	MIN	TYP	MAX	
Input Offset Voltage	T$_A$ = 25°C, (Note 9)		±1.0	±2.0		±1.0	±2.0		±2.0	±5.0		±2.0	±5.0		±2.0	±7.0		±3	±20	mVDC
Input Bias Current	I$_{IN(+)}$ or I$_{IN(-)}$ with Output in Linear Range, T$_A$ = 25°C, (Note 5)		25	100		25	250		25	100		25	250		25	250		25	500	nADC
Input Offset Current	I$_{IN(+)}$ − I$_{IN(-)}$, T$_A$ = 25°C		±3.0	±25		±5.0	±50		±3.0	±25		±5.0	±50		±5	±50		±3	±100	nADC
Input Common-Mode Voltage Range	T$_A$ = 25°C, (Note 6)	0		V+−1.5	0		V+−1.5	0		V+−1.5	0		V+−1.5	0		V+−1.5	0		V+−1.5	VDC
Supply Current	R$_L$ = ∞ on all Comparators, T$_A$ = 25°C R$_L$ = ∞, V+ = 30V, T$_A$ = 25°C		0.8	2.0		0.8	2.0		0.8	2.0		0.8	2.0		0.8 / 1	2.0 / 2.5		0.8	2	mADC mADC
Voltage Gain	R$_L$ ≥ 15 kΩ, V+ = 15 V$_{DC}$ (To Support Large V$_O$ Swing), T$_A$ = 25°C	50	200		50	200			200			200		25	100		2	30		V/mV
Large Signal Response Time	V$_{IN}$ = TTL Logic Swing, V$_{REF}$ = 1.4 V$_{DC}$, V$_{RL}$ = 5 V$_{DC}$, R$_L$ = 5.1 kΩ, T$_A$ = 25°C		300			300			300			300			300			300		ns
Response Time	V$_{RL}$ = 5 V$_{DC}$, R$_L$ = 5.1 kΩ, T$_A$ = 25°C, (Note 7)		1.3			1.3			1.3			1.3			1.3			1.3		µs
Output Sink Current	V$_{IN(-)}$ ≥ 1 V$_{DC}$, V$_{IN(+)}$ = 0, V$_O$ ≤ 1.5 V$_{DC}$, T$_A$ = 25°C	6.0	16		6.0	16		6.0	16		6.0	16		6.0	16		6.0	16		mADC
Saturation Voltage	V$_{IN(-)}$ ≥ 1 V$_{DC}$, V$_{IN(+)}$ = 0, I$_{SINK}$ ≤ 4 mA, T$_A$ = 25°C		250	400		250	400		250	400		250	400		250	400		250	500	mVDC
Output Leakage Current	V$_{IN(+)}$ ≥ 1 V$_{DC}$, V$_{IN(-)}$ = 0, V$_O$ = 5 V$_{DC}$, T$_A$ = 25°C		0.1			0.1			0.1			0.1			0.1			0.1		nADC

Electrical Characteristics (Continued)

PARAMETER	CONDITIONS	LM139A			LM239A, LM339A			LM139			LM239, LM339			LM2901			LM3302			UNITS
		MIN	TYP	MAX	MIN	TYP	MAX	MIN	TYP	MAX	MIN	TYP	MAX	MIN	TYP	MAX	MIN	TYP	MAX	
Input Offset Voltage	(Note 9)			4.0			4.0			9.0			9.0		9	15			40	mV_{DC}
Input Offset Current	$I_{IN(+)} - I_{IN(-)}$			±100			±150			±100			±150		50	200			300	nA_{DC}
Input Bias Current	$I_{IN(+)}$ or $I_{IN(-)}$ with Output in Linear Range			300			400			300			400		200	500			1000	nA_{DC}
Input Common-Mode Voltage Range		0		$V^+{-}2.0$	0		$V^+{-}2.0$	0		$V^+{-}2.0$	0		$V^+{-}2.0$	0		$V^+{-}2.0$	0		$V^+{-}2.0$	V_{DC}
Saturation Voltage	$V_{IN(-)} \geq 1$ V_{DC}, $V_{IN(+)} = 0$, $I_{SINK} \leq 4$ mA			700			700			700			700		400	700			700	mV_{DC}
Output Leakage Current	$V_{IN(+)} \geq 1$ V_{DC}, $V_{IN(-)} = 0$, $V_O = 30$ V_{DC}			1.0			1.0			1.0			1.0			1.0			1.0	μA_{DC}
Differential Input Voltage	Keep all V_{IN}'s ≥ 0 V_{DC} (or V^- if used), (Note 8)			36			36			36			36			36			28	V_{DC}

Note 1: For operating at high temperatures, the LM339/LM339A, LM239A, LM2901, LM3302 must be derated based on a 125°C maximum junction temperature and a thermal resistance of 175°C/W which applies for the device soldered in a printed circuit board, operating in a still air ambient. The LM239 and LM139 must be derated based on a 150°C maximum junction temperature. The low bias dissipation and the "ON-OFF" characteristic of the outputs keeps the chip dissipation very small ($P_D \leq 100$ mW), provided the output transistors are allowed to saturate.

Note 2: Short circuits from the output to V^+ can cause excessive heating and eventual destruction. The maximum output current is approximately 20 mA independent of the magnitude of V^+.

Note 3: This input current will only exist when the voltage at any of the input leads is driven negative. It is due to the collector-base junction of the input PNP transistors becoming forward biased and thereby acting as input diode clamps. In addition to this diode action, there is also lateral NPN parasitic transistor action on the IC chip. This transistor action can cause the output voltages of the comparators to go to the V^+ voltage level (or to ground for a large overdrive) for the time duration that an input is driven negative. This is not destructive and normal output states will re-establish when the input voltage, which was negative, again returns to a value greater than -0.3 V_{DC} (at 25°C).

Note 4: These specifications apply for $V^+ = 5$ V_{DC} and $-55°C \leq T_A \leq +125°C$, unless otherwise stated. With the LM239/LM239A, all temperature specifications are limited to $-25°C \leq T_A \leq +85°C$, the LM339/LM339A temperature specifications are limited to $0°C \leq T_A \leq +70°C$, and the LM2901, LM3302 temperature range is $-40° \leq T_A \leq +85°C$.

Note 5: The direction of the input current is out of the IC due to the PNP input stage. This current is essentially constant, independent of the state of the output so no loading change exists on the reference or input lines.

Note 6: The input common-mode voltage or either input signal voltage should not be allowed to go negative by more than 0.3V. The upper end of the common-mode voltage range is V^+ -1.5V, but either or both inputs can go to $+30$ V_{DC} without damage (25V for LM3302).

Note 7: The response time specified is a 100 mV input step with 5 mV overdrive. For larger overdrive signals 300 ns can be obtained, see typical performance characteristics section.

Note 8: Positive excursions of input voltage may exceed the power supply level. As long as the other voltage remains within the common-mode range, the comparator will provide a proper output state. The low input voltage state must not be less than -0.3 V_{DC} (or 0.3 V_{DC} below the magnitude of the negative power supply, if used) (at 25°C).

Note 9: At output switch point, $V_O \cong 1.4$ V_{DC}. $R_S = 0\Omega$ with V^+ from 5 V_{DC}; and over the full input common-mode range (0 V_{DC} to V^+ -1.5 V_{DC}).

µA741
FREQUENCY-COMPENSATED OPERATIONAL AMPLIFIER
FAIRCHILD LINEAR INTEGRATED CIRCUITS

GENERAL DESCRIPTION — The µA741 is a high performance monolithic Operational Amplifier constructed using the Fairchild Planar* epitaxial process. It is intended for a wide range of analog applications. High common mode voltage range and absence of latch-up tendencies make the µA741 ideal for use as a voltage follower. The high gain and wide range of operating voltage provides superior performance in integrator, summing amplifier, and general feedback applications.

- **NO FREQUENCY COMPENSATION REQUIRED**
- **SHORT CIRCUIT PROTECTION**
- **OFFSET VOLTAGE NULL CAPABILITY**
- **LARGE COMMON MODE AND DIFFERENTIAL VOLTAGE RANGES**
- **LOW POWER CONSUMPTION**
- **NO LATCH-UP**

ABSOLUTE MAXIMUM RATINGS

Supply Voltage	
µA741A, µA741, µA741E	±22 V
µA741C	±18 V
Internal Power Dissipation (Note 1)	
Metal Can	500 mW
Molded and Hermetic DIP	670 mW
Mini DIP	310 mW
Flatpak	570 mW
Differential Input Voltage	±30 V
Input Voltage (Note 2)	±15 V
Storage Temperature Range	
Metal Can, Hermetic DIP, and Flatpak	−65°C to +150°C
Mini DIP, Molded DIP	−55°C to +125°C
Operating Temperature Range	
Military (µA741A, µA741)	−55°C to +125°C
Commercial (µA741E, µA741C)	0°C to +70°C
Pin Temperature (Soldering)	
Metal Can, Hermetic DIPs, and Flatpak (60 s)	300°C
Molded DIPs (10 s)	260°C
Output Short Circuit Duration (Note 3)	Indefinite

CONNECTION DIAGRAMS

8-PIN METAL CAN
(TOP VIEW)
PACKAGE OUTLINE 5B
PACKAGE CODE H

Note: Pin 4 connected to case

ORDER INFORMATION

TYPE	PART NO.
µA741A	µA741AHM
µA741	µA741HM
µA741E	µA741EHC
µA741C	µA741HC

14-PIN DIP
(TOP VIEW)
PACKAGE OUTLINES 6A, 9A
PACKAGE CODES D P

ORDER INFORMATION

TYPE	PART NO.
µA741A	µA741ADM
µA741	µA741DM
µA741E	µA741EDC
µA741C	µA741DC
µA741C	µA741PC

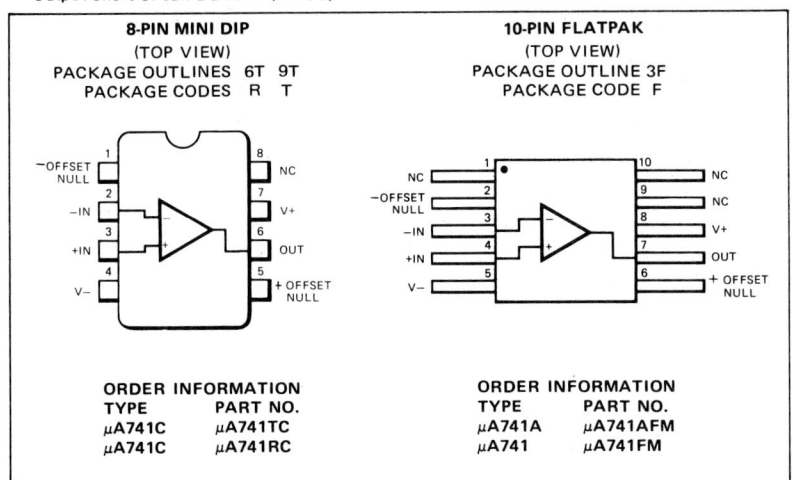

8-PIN MINI DIP
(TOP VIEW)
PACKAGE OUTLINES 6T 9T
PACKAGE CODES R T

10-PIN FLATPAK
(TOP VIEW)
PACKAGE OUTLINE 3F
PACKAGE CODE F

ORDER INFORMATION

TYPE	PART NO.
µA741C	µA741TC
µA741C	µA741RC

ORDER INFORMATION

TYPE	PART NO.
µA741A	µA741AFM
µA741	µA741FM

*Planar is a patented Fairchild process.

FAIRCHILD • μA741

μA741E

ELECTRICAL CHARACTERISTICS: $V_S = \pm 15$ V, $T_A = 25°C$ unless otherwise specified.

CHARACTERISTICS (see definitions)		CONDITIONS	MIN	TYP	MAX	UNITS
Input Offset Voltage		$R_S \leqslant 50\Omega$		0.8	3.0	mV
Average Input Offset Voltage Drift					15	μV/°C
Input Offset Current				3.0	30	nA
Average Input Offset Current Drift					0.5	nA/°C
Input Bias Current				30	80	nA
Power Supply Rejection Ratio		$V_S = +10, -20; V_S = +20, -10V, R_S = 50\Omega$		15	50	μV/V
Output Short Circuit Current			10	25	40	mA
Power Dissipation		$V_S = \pm 20V$		80	150	mW
Input Impedance		$V_S = \pm 20V$	1.0	6.0		MΩ
Large Signal Voltage Gain		$V_S = \pm 20V, R_L = 2k\Omega, V_{OUT} = \pm 15V$	50			V/mV
Transient Response	Rise Time			0.25	0.8	μs
(Unity Gain)	Overshoot			6.0	20	%
Bandwidth (Note 4)			.437	1.5		MHz
Slew Rate (Unity Gain)		$V_{IN} = \pm 10V$	0.3	0.7		V/μs
The following specifications apply for $0°C \leqslant T_A \leqslant 70°C$						
Input Offset Voltage					4.0	mV
Input Offset Current					70	nA
Input Bias Current					210	nA
Common Mode Rejection Ratio		$V_S = \pm 20V, V_{IN} = \pm 15V, R_S = 50\Omega$	80	95		dB
Adjustment For Input Offset Voltage		$V_S = \pm 20V$	10			mV
Output Short Circuit Current			10		40	mA
Power Dissipation		$V_S = \pm 20V$			150	mW
Input Impedance		$V_S = \pm 20V$	0.5			MΩ
Output Voltage Swing		$V_S = \pm 20V$, $R_L = 10k\Omega$	±16			V
		$R_L = 2k\Omega$	±15			V
Large Signal Voltage Gain		$V_S = \pm 20V, R_L = 2k\Omega, V_{OUT} = \pm 15V$	32			V/mV
		$V_S = \pm 5V, R_L = 2k\Omega, V_{OUT} = \pm 2$ V	10			V/mV

EQUIVALENT CIRCUIT

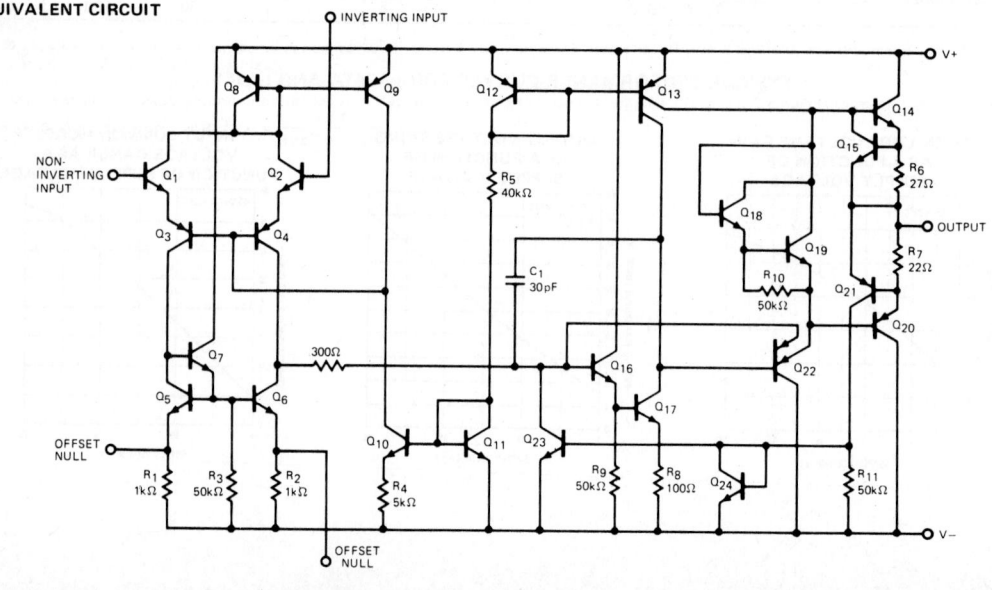

FAIRCHILD • µA741

µA741C

ELECTRICAL CHARACTERISTICS: $V_S = \pm 15$ V, $T_A = 25°$C unless otherwise specified.

CHARACTERISTICS (see definitions)	CONDITIONS	MIN	TYP	MAX	UNITS
Input Offset Voltage	$R_S \leqslant 10$ kΩ		2.0	6.0	mV
Input Offset Current			20	200	nA
Input Bias Current			80	500	nA
Input Resistance		0.3	2.0		MΩ
Input Capacitance			1.4		pF
Offset Voltage Adjustment Range			±15		mV
Input Voltage Range		±12	±13		V
Common Mode Rejection Ratio	$R_S \leqslant 10$ kΩ	70	90		dB
Supply Voltage Rejection Ratio	$R_S \leqslant 10$ kΩ		30	150	µV/V
Large Signal Voltage Gain	$R_L \geqslant 2$ kΩ, $V_{OUT} = \pm 10$ V	20,000	200,000		
Output Voltage Swing	$R_L \geqslant 10$ kΩ	±12	±14		V
	$R_L \geqslant 2$ kΩ	±10	±13		V
Output Resistance			75		Ω
Output Short Circuit Current			25		mA
Supply Current			1.7	2.8	mA
Power Consumption			50	85	mW
Transient Response (Unity Gain) — Rise time	$V_{IN} = 20$ mV, $R_L = 2$ kΩ, $C_L \leqslant 100$ pF		0.3		µs
Transient Response (Unity Gain) — Overshoot			5.0		%
Slew Rate	$R_L \geqslant 2$ kΩ		0.5		V/µs

The following specifications apply for $0°$C $\leqslant T_A \leqslant +70°$C:

CHARACTERISTICS	CONDITIONS	MIN	TYP	MAX	UNITS
Input Offset Voltage				7.5	mV
Input Offset Current				300	nA
Input Bias Current				800	nA
Large Signal Voltage Gain	$R_L \geqslant 2$ kΩ, $V_{OUT} = \pm 10$ V	15,000			
Output Voltage Swing	$R_L \geqslant 2$ kΩ	±10	±13		V

TYPICAL PERFORMANCE CURVES FOR µA741E AND µA741C

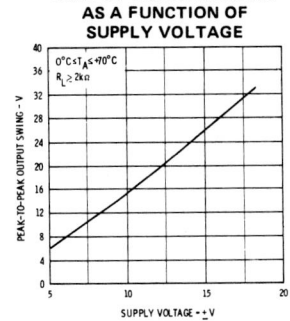

OPEN LOOP VOLTAGE GAIN AS A FUNCTION OF SUPPLY VOLTAGE

OUTPUT VOLTAGE SWING AS A FUNCTION OF SUPPLY VOLTAGE

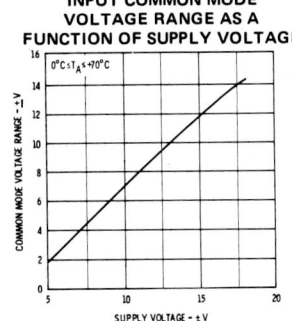

INPUT COMMON MODE VOLTAGE RANGE AS A FUNCTION OF SUPPLY VOLTAGE

FAIRCHILD • μA741

TYPICAL PERFORMANCE CURVES FOR μA741A, μA741, μA741E AND μA741C

POWER CONSUMPTION AS A FUNCTION OF SUPPLY VOLTAGE

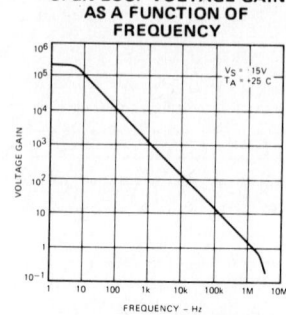

OPEN LOOP VOLTAGE GAIN AS A FUNCTION OF FREQUENCY

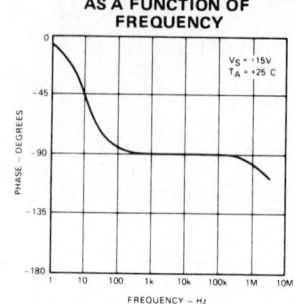

OPEN LOOP PHASE RESPONSE AS A FUNCTION OF FREQUENCY

INPUT OFFSET CURRENT AS A FUNCTION OF SUPPLY VOLTAGE

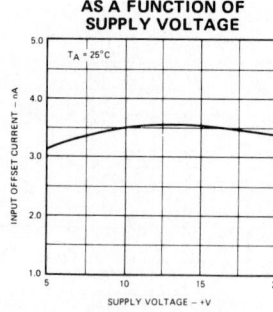

INPUT RESISTANCE AND INPUT CAPACITANCE AS A FUNCTION OF FREQUENCY

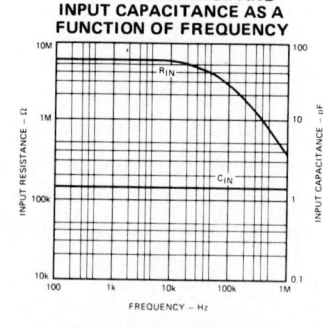

OUTPUT RESISTANCE AS A FUNCTION OF FREQUENCY

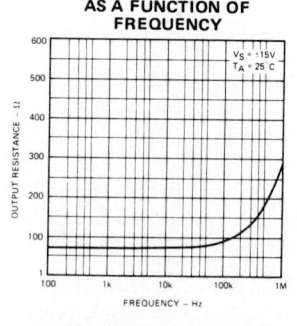

OUTPUT VOLTAGE SWING AS A FUNCTION OF LOAD RESISTANCE

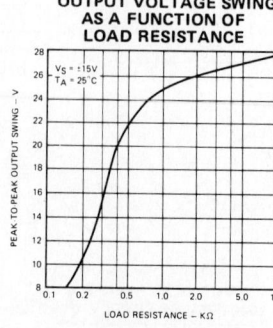

OUTPUT VOLTAGE SWING AS A FUNCTION OF FREQUENCY

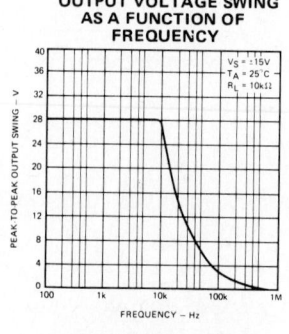

ABSOLUTE MAXIMUM POWER DISSIPATION AS A FUNCTION OF AMBIENT TEMPERATURE

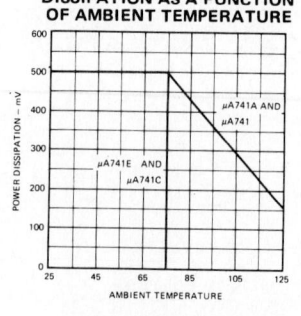

INPUT NOISE VOLTAGE AS A FUNCTION OF FREQUENCY

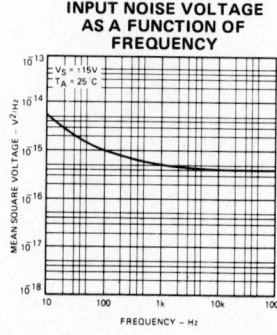

INPUT NOISE CURRENT AS A FUNCTION OF FREQUENCY

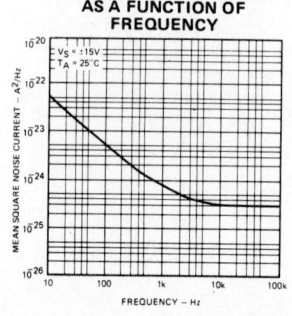

BROADBAND NOISE FOR VARIOUS BANDWIDTHS

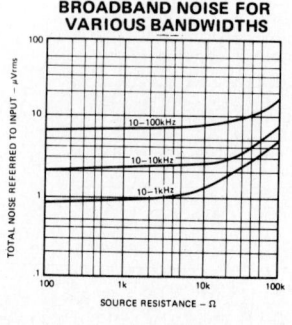

TYPICAL PERFORMANCE CURVES FOR μA741A AND μA741

INPUT BIAS CURRENT AS A FUNCTION OF AMBIENT TEMPERATURE

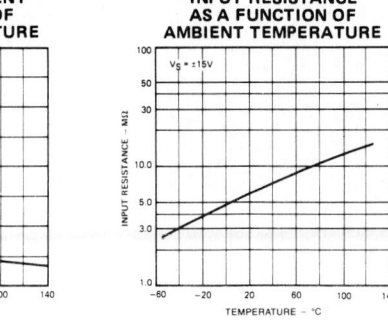

INPUT RESISTANCE AS A FUNCTION OF AMBIENT TEMPERATURE

OUTPUT SHORT-CIRCUIT CURRENT AS A FUNCTION OF AMBIENT TEMPERATURE

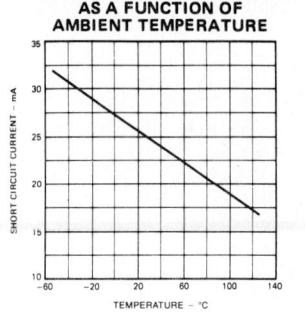

INPUT OFFSET CURRENT AS A FUNCTION OF AMBIENT TEMPERATURE

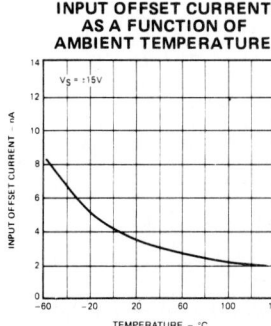

POWER CONSUMPTION AS A FUNCTION OF AMBIENT TEMPERATURE

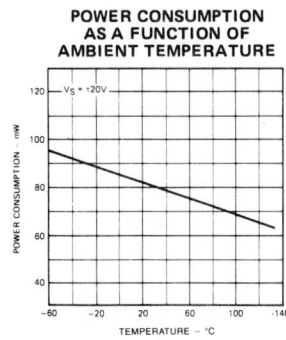

FREQUENCY CHARACTERISTICS AS A FUNCTION OF AMBIENT TEMPERATURE

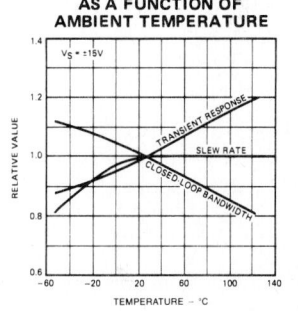

TYPICAL PERFORMANCE CURVES FOR μA741E AND μA741C

INPUT BIAS CURRENT AS A FUNCTION OF AMBIENT TEMPERATURE

INPUT RESISTANCE AS A FUNCTION OF AMBIENT TEMPERATURE

INPUT OFFSET CURRENT AS A FUNCTION OF AMBIENT TEMPERATURE

POWER CONSUMPTION AS A FUNCTION OF AMBIENT TEMPERATURE

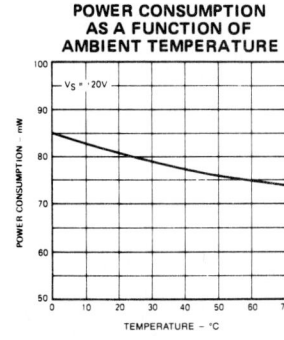

OUTPUT SHORT CIRCUIT CURRENT AS A FUNCTION OF AMBIENT TEMPERATURE

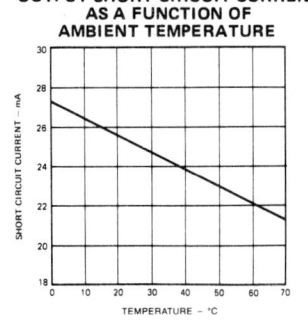

FREQUENCY CHARACTERISTICS AS A FUNCTION OF AMBIENT TEMPERATURE

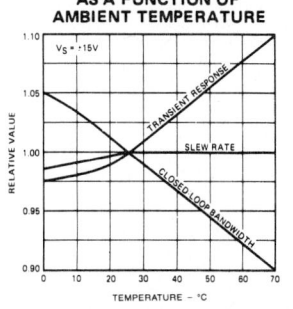

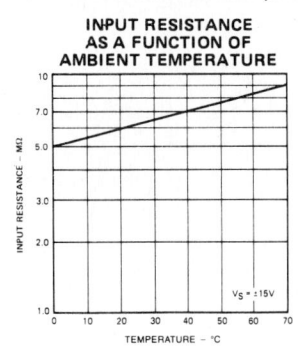
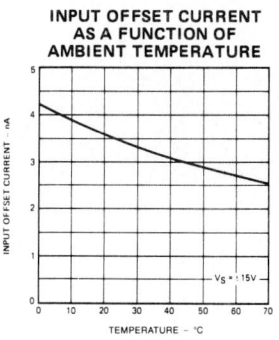

TRANSIENT RESPONSE

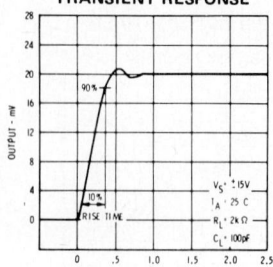

TRANSIENT RESPONSE TEST CIRCUIT

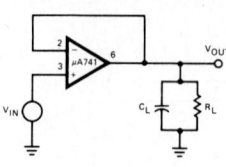

COMMON MODE REJECTION RATIO AS A FUNCTION OF FREQUENCY

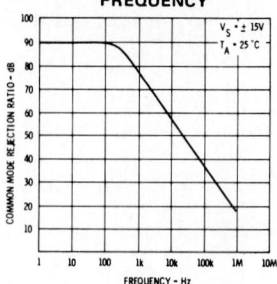

FREQUENCY CHARACTERISTICS AS A FUNCTION OF SUPPLY VOLTAGE

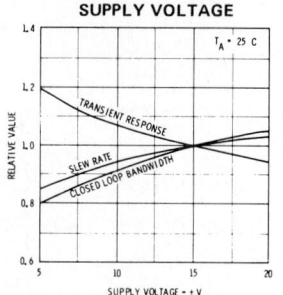

VOLTAGE OFFSET NULL CIRCUIT

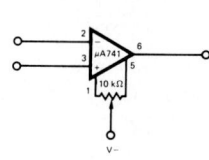

VOLTAGE FOLLOWER LARGE SIGNAL PULSE RESPONSE

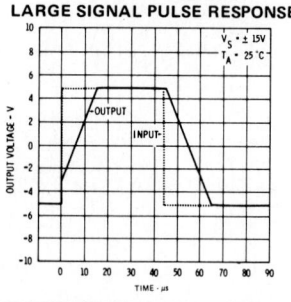

TYPICAL APPLICATIONS

UNITY-GAIN VOLTAGE FOLLOWER

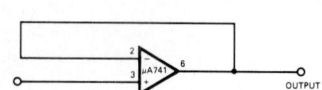

R_{IN} = 400 MΩ

C_{IN} = 1 pF

$R_{OUT} << 1$ Ω

B.W. = 1 MHz

NON-INVERTING AMPLIFIER

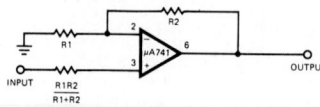

GAIN	R1	R2	B W	R_{IN}
10	1 kΩ	9 kΩ	100 kHz	400 MΩ
100	100 Ω	9.9 kΩ	10 kHz	280 MΩ
1000	100 Ω	99.9 kΩ	1 kHz	80 MΩ

INVERTING AMPLIFIER

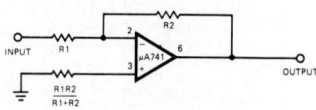

GAIN	R1	R2	B W	R_{IN}
1	10 kΩ	10 kΩ	1 MHz	10 kΩ
10	1 kΩ	10 kΩ	100 kHz	1 kΩ
100	1 kΩ	100 kΩ	10 kHz	1 kΩ
1000	100 Ω	100 kΩ	1 kHz	100 Ω

CLIPPING AMPLIFIER

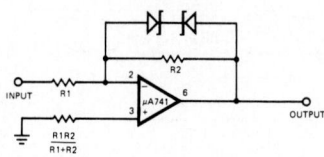

$$\frac{E_{OUT}}{E_{IN}} = \frac{R2}{R1} \text{ if } |E_{OUT}| \leqslant V_Z + 0.7 \text{ V}$$

where V_Z = Zener breakdown voltage

TYPICAL APPLICATIONS (Cont'd)

SIMPLE INTEGRATOR

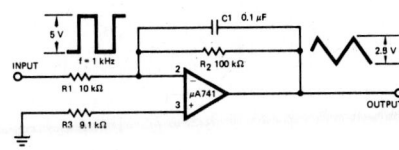

$$E_{OUT} = - \frac{1}{R_1 C_1} \int E_{IN} dt$$

SIMPLE DIFFERENTIATOR

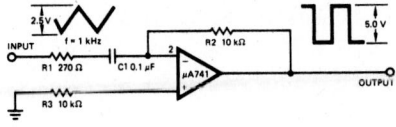

$$E_{OUT} = - R2C \frac{dE_{IN}}{dt}$$

LOW DRIFT LOW NOISE AMPLIFIER

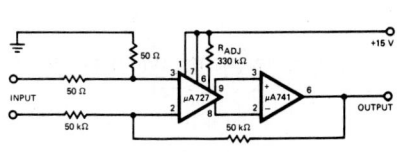

Voltage Gain = 10^3
Input Offset Voltage Drift = 0.6 µV/°C
Input Offset Current Drift = 2.0 pA/°C

HIGH SLEW RATE POWER AMPLIFIER

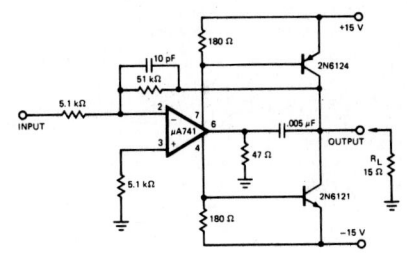

NOTCH FILTER USING THE µA741 AS A GYRATOR

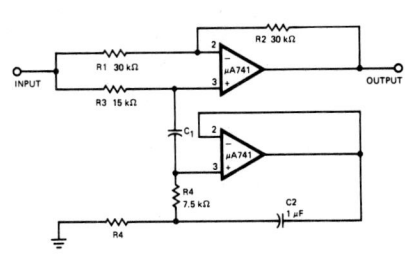

Trim R3 such that

$$\frac{R1}{R2} = \frac{R3}{2\,R4}$$

NOTCH FREQUENCY AS A FUNCTION C¹

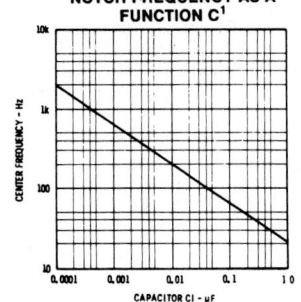

 **National Semiconductor**

Operational Amplifiers/Buffers

LM101A/LM201A/LM301A Operational Amplifiers

General Description

The LM101A series are general purpose operational amplifiers which feature improved performance over industry standards like the LM709. Advanced processing techniques make possible an order of magnitude reduction in input currents, and a redesign of the biasing circuitry reduces the temperature drift of input current. Improved specifications include:

- Offset voltage 3 mV maximum over temperature (LM101A/LM201A)
- Input current 100 nA maximum over temperature (LM101A/LM201A)
- Offset current 20 nA maximum over temperature (LM101A/LM201A)
- Guaranteed drift characteristics
- Offsets guaranteed over entire common mode and supply voltage ranges
- Slew rate of 10V/μs as a summing amplifier

This amplifier offers many features which make its application nearly foolproof: overload protection on the input and output, no latch-up when the common mode range is exceeded, freedom from oscillations and compensation with a single 30 pF capacitor. It has advantages over internally compensated amplifiers in that the frequency compensation can be tailored to the particular application. For example, in low frequency circuits it can be overcompensated for increased stability margin. Or the compensation can be optimized to give more than a factor of ten improvement in high frequency performance for most applications.

In addition, the device provides better accuracy and lower noise in high impedance circuitry. The low input currents also make it particularly well suited for long interval integrators or timers, sample and hold circuits and low frequency waveform generators. Further, replacing circuits where matched transistor pairs buffer the inputs of conventional IC op amps, it can give lower offset voltage and drift at a lower cost.

The LM101A is guaranteed over a temperature range of −55°C to +125°C, the LM201A from −25°C to +85°C, and the LM301A from 0°C to 70°C.

Schematic** and Connection Diagrams (Top Views)

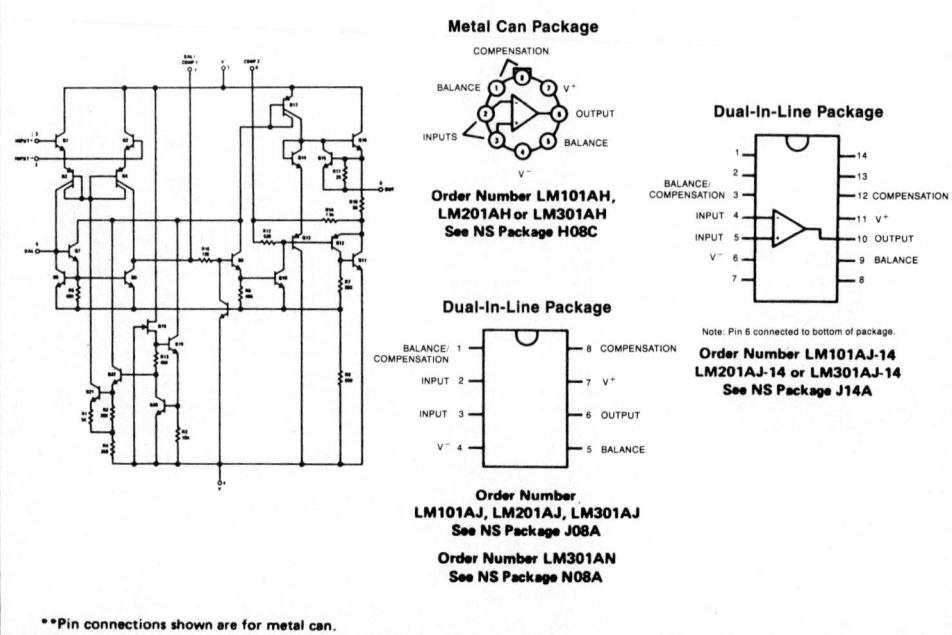

Metal Can Package

Order Number LM101AH, LM201AH or LM301AH
See NS Package H08C

Dual-In-Line Package

Note: Pin 6 connected to bottom of package.
Order Number LM101AJ-14
LM201AJ-14 or LM301AJ-14
See NS Package J14A

Dual-In-Line Package

Order Number LM101AJ, LM201AJ, LM301AJ
See NS Package J08A

Order Number LM301AN
See NS Package N08A

**Pin connections shown are for metal can.

Absolute Maximum Ratings

	LM101A/LM201A	LM301A
Supply Voltage	±22V	±18V
Power Dissipation (Note 1)	500 mW	500 mW
Differential Input Voltage	±30V	±30V
Input Voltage (Note 2)	±15V	±15V
Output Short Circuit Duration (Note 3)	Indefinite	Indefinite
Operating Temperature Range	$-55°C$ to $+125°C$ (LM101A)	
	$-25°C$ to $+85°C$ (LM201A)	$0°C$ to $+70°C$
Storage Temperature Range	$-65°C$ to $+150°C$	$-65°C$ to $+150°C$
Lead Temperature (Soldering, 10 seconds)	$300°C$	$300°C$

Electrical Characteristics (Note 4)

PARAMETER	CONDITIONS	LM101A/LM201A			LM301A			UNITS
		MIN	TYP	MAX	MIN	TYP	MAX	
Input Offset Voltage LM101A, LM201A, LM301A	$T_A = 25°C$, $R_S \leq 50\,k\Omega$		0.7	2.0		2.0	7.5	mV
Input Offset Current	$T_A = 25°C$		1.5	10		3.0	50	nA
Input Bias Current	$T_A = 25°C$		30	75		70	250	nA
Input Resistance	$T_A = 25°C$	1.5	4.0		0.5	2.0		$M\Omega$
Supply Current	$T_A = 25°C$, $V_S = \pm20V$		1.8	3.0				mA
	$V_S = \pm15V$					1.8	3.0	mA
Large Signal Voltage Gain	$T_A = 25°C$, $V_S = \pm15V$ $V_{OUT} = \pm10V$, $R_L \geq 2\,k\Omega$	50	160		25	160		V/mV
Input Offset Voltage	$R_S \leq 50\,k\Omega$			3.0			10	mV
	$R_S \leq 10\,k\Omega$							mV
Average Temperature Coefficient of Input Offset Voltage	$R_S \leq 50\,k\Omega$		3.0	15		6.0	30	$\mu V/°C$
	$R_S \leq 10\,k\Omega$							$\mu V/°C$
Input Offset Current				20			70	nA
	$T_A = T_{MAX}$							nA
	$T_A = T_{MIN}$							nA
Average Temperature Coefficient of Input Offset Current	$25°C \leq T_A \leq T_{MAX}$		0.01	0.1		0.01	0.3	nA/°C
	$T_{MIN} \leq T_A \leq 25°C$		0.02	0.2		0.02	0.6	nA/°C
Input Bias Current				0.1			0.3	μA
Supply Current	$T_A = T_{MAX}$, $V_S = \pm20V$		1.2	2.5				mA
Large Signal Voltage Gain	$V_S = \pm15V$, $V_{OUT} = \pm10V$, $R_L \geq 2k$	25			15			V/mV
Output Voltage Swing	$V_S = \pm15V$ $R_L = 10\,k\Omega$	±12	±14		±12	±14		V
	$R_L = 2\,k\Omega$	±10	±13		±10	±13		V
Input Voltage Range	$V_S = \pm20V$	±15						V
	$V_S = \pm15V$		+15, −13		±12	+15, −13		V
Common-Mode Rejection Ratio	$R_S \leq 50\,k\Omega$	80	96		70	90		dB
	$R_S \leq 10\,k\Omega$							dB
Supply Voltage Rejection Ratio	$R_S \leq 50\,k\Omega$	80	96		70	96		dB
	$R_S \leq 10\,k\Omega$							dB

Note 1: The maximum junction temperature of the LM101A is 150°C, and that of the LM201A/LM301A is 100°C. For operating at elevated temperatures, devices in the TO-5 package must be derated based on a thermal resistance of 150°C/W, junction to ambient, or 45°C/W, junction to case. The thermal resistance of the dual-in-line package is 187°C/W, junction to ambient.

Note 2: For supply voltages less than ±15V, the absolute maximum input voltage is equal to the supply voltage.

Note 3: Continuous short circuit is allowed for case temperatures to 125°C and ambient temperatures to 75°C for LM101A/LM201A, and 70°C and 55°C respectively for LM301A.

Note 4: Unless otherwise specified, these specifications apply for C1 ≈ 30 pF, ±5V ≤ V_S ≤ ±20V and −55°C ≤ T_A ≤ +125°C (LM101A), ±5V ≤ V_S ≤ ±20V and −25°C ≤ T_A ≤ +85°C (LM201A), ±5V ≤ V_S ≤ ±15V and 0°C ≤ T_A ≤ +70°C (LM301A).

Guaranteed Performance Characteristics LM101A/LM201A

Input Voltage Range

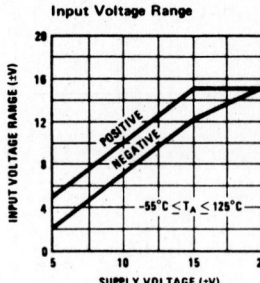

Output Swing

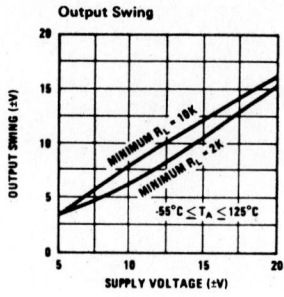

Voltage Gain

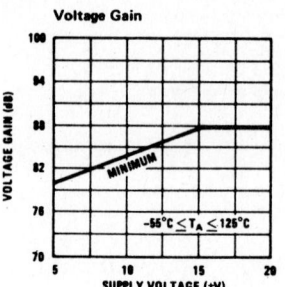

Guaranteed Performance Characteristics LM301A

Input Voltage Range

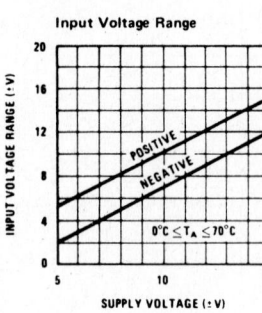

Output Swing

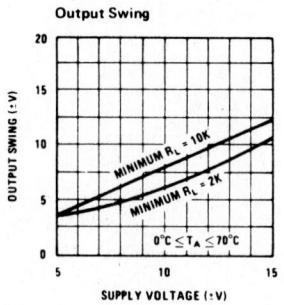

Voltage Gain

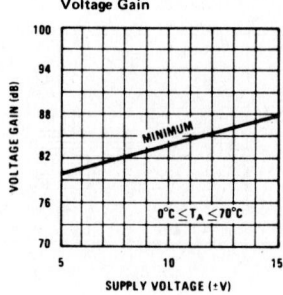

Typical Performance Characteristics

Supply Current

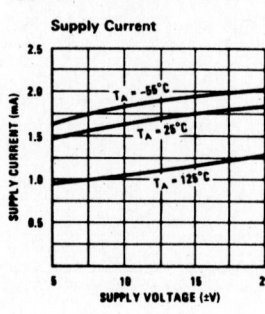

Voltage Gain

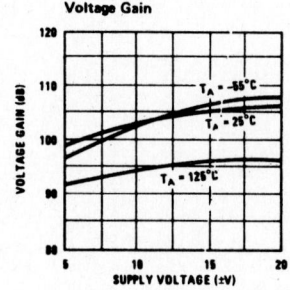

Maximum Power Dissipation

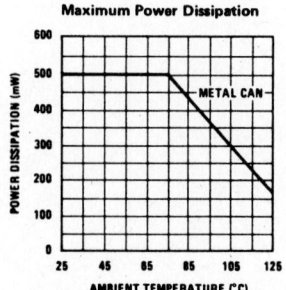

Typical Performance Characteristics (Continued)

Input Current, LM101A/LM201A/LM301A

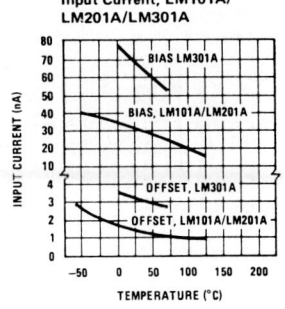

Current Limiting

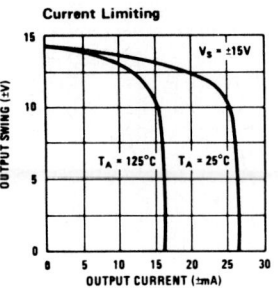

Input Noise Voltage

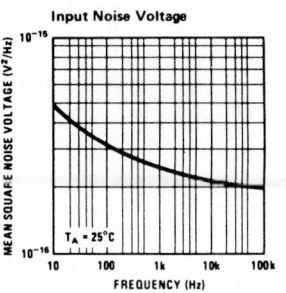

Input Noise Current

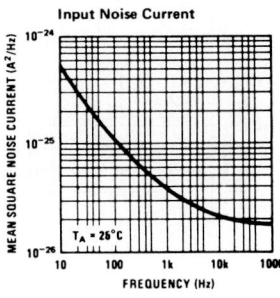

Common Mode Rejection

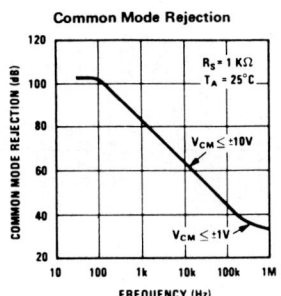

Power Supply Rejection

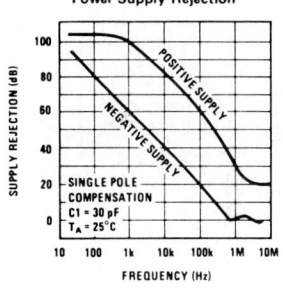

Closed Loop Output Impedance

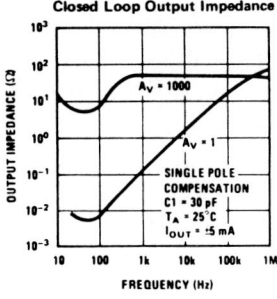

Typical Performance Characteristics for Various Compensation Circuits**

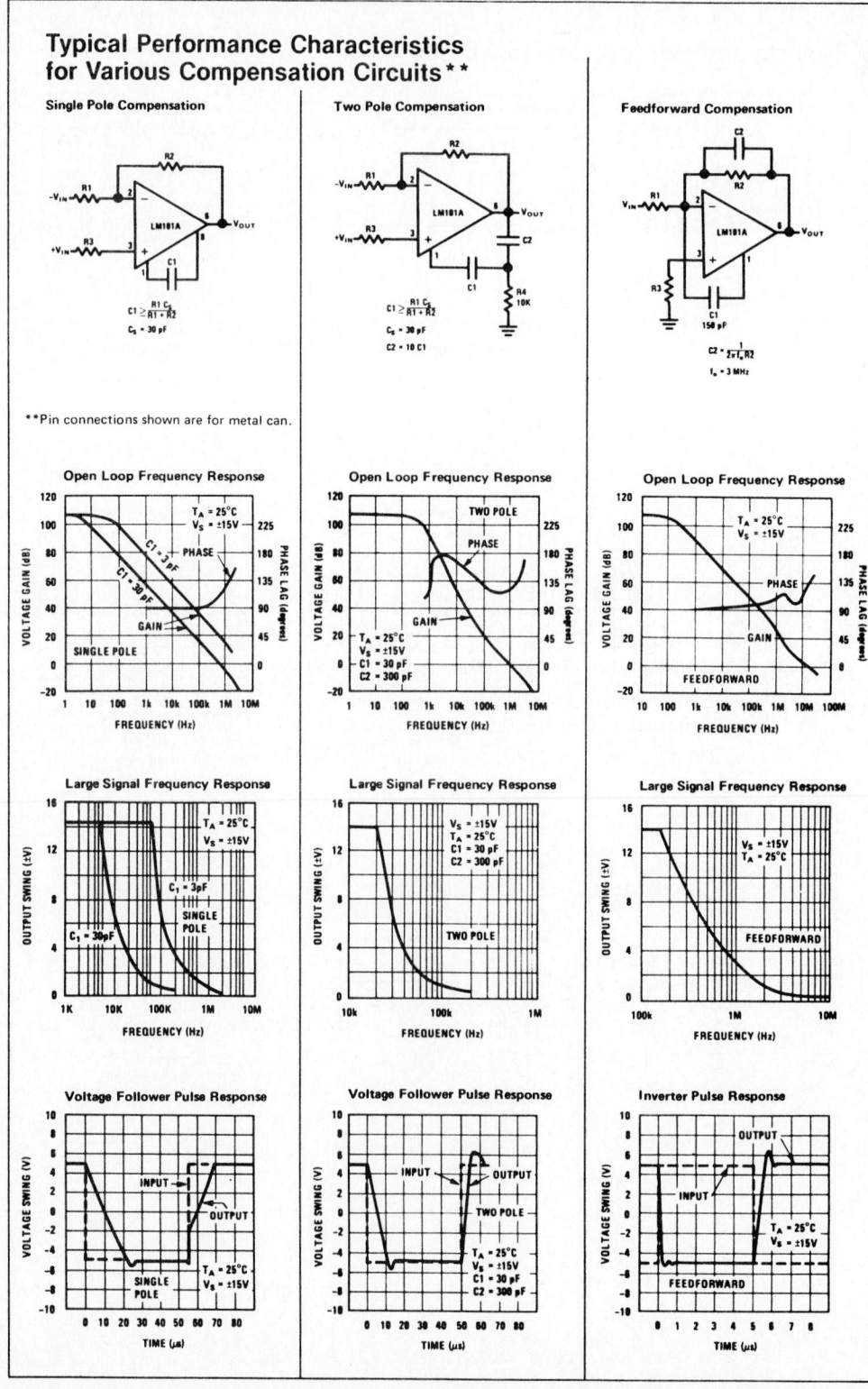

**Pin connections shown are for metal can.

E STANDARD COMPONENT VALUES

E.0 Introduction

In this appendix we list the standard component values to aid in the selection of resistor and capacitor values when designing an electronic system. There is some variation in these tabulated values from one manufacturer to another. Therefore, the tables should be considered as typical.

E.1 Resistors

Ten-percent tolerance carbon resistors are available in the following power ratings: $\frac{1}{4}$, $\frac{1}{2}$, 1, and 2 W. These resistors are manufactured in the sizes shown in Table E.1. Thus, for example, if your design called for a 675 Ω resistor, you would actually choose a 680 Ω resistor. If this is a 10% tolerance resistance, the manufacturer is guaranteeing the actual value to be between 612 Ω and 748 Ω.

Table E.1 Standard resistance values

2.7	3.3	3.9	4.7	Each of these values is multiplied
5.6	6.8	8.2	10.0	by 10^n, where n = 0, 1, 2, 3, 4,
12.0	15.0	18.0	22.0	5, ...

E.2   **Capacitors**

In Table E.2, we present the typical capacitor values from one manufacturer. These are 10% tolerance capacitors, and the values in the table are in microfarads.

Table E.2

Ceramic-disk capacitors

3.3	30	200	560	2200
5	39	220	600	2500
6	47	240	680	2700
6.8	50	250	750	3000
7.5	51	270	800	3300
8	56	300	820	3900
10	68	330	910	4000
12	75	350	1000	4300
15	82	360	1200	4700
18	91	390	1300	5000
20	100	400	1500	5600
22	120	470	1600	6800
24	130	500	1800	7500
25	150	510	2000	8200
27	180			

Tantalum capacitors

0.0047	0.010	0.022
0.0056	0.012	0.027
0.0068	0.015	0.033
0.0082	0.018	0.039

all $\times\ 10^n$, where n = 0, 1, 2, 3, 4, 5 (to 330 μF)

Electrolytic capacitors

250	2000
500	3000
1000	4000
1500	5000

F NOISE IN ELECTRONIC SYSTEMS

F.0 Introduction

In practically every electronic system, we find it necessary to measure small signals. This task is usually limited in precision and detectability due to noise. Noise limits measurement precision and signal detectability. In this appendix, we discuss some of the problems of noise and describe techniques for improving the situation.

The term *noise* includes any voltages and currents that accompany the desired signal and tend to contaminate it. Many different types of noise sources exist in electronic systems. Some of this noise is generated internally, as in resistors, diodes, and amplifiers. Other noise is generated externally, such as that generated in interconnective wiring and circuit-generated noise.

The environmental noise problem can be greatly reduced by following common sense engineering practice. This includes proper grounding and shielding procedures. Further improvement can be realized by considering the electronic noise (thermal noise and amplifier noise), its characteristics, and the effects of this noise.

$$\overline{i_f^2} = KI_{DC}\frac{f_2 - f_1}{f} \tag{F.3}$$

where

$$I_{DC} = \text{the average junction current in amps}$$
$$f_2 - f_1 = \text{bandwidth}$$
$$K = \text{a constant of the semiconductor device}$$

F.1.3   Diode Noise

The mean-square noise current, $\overline{i_D}^2$, in a diode is a combination of shot noise and flicker noise. This current is due to the series resistance of the silicon material. The mean-square value of the noise generated in a diode is given by the equation

$$\overline{i_D}^2 = \left(2q + \frac{K}{f}\right)I_{DC}(f_2 - f_1) \tag{F.4}$$

Equation (F.4) represents the sum of the shot noise and the flicker noise.

F.1.4   BJT Noise

Since we now know the types of noise voltages and currents, we can develop an equivalent circuit for a single-stage BJT. We use the simplified π-model from Chapter 10 and add the noise sources as shown in Figure F.2. For the midband frequency, flicker ($1/f$) noise can be ignored. We make the assumption that the noise sources are uncorrelated, with the result that we can find the total mean-square noise voltage by adding the individual mean-square noise voltages.

The noise voltage and current generators in Figure F.2 are summarized as follows:

$$\overline{v_{bb'}}^2 = 4kTr_{bb'}(f_2 - f_1) \tag{F.5a}$$
$$\overline{i_b}^2 = 2qI_B(f_2 - f_1) \tag{F.5b}$$
$$\overline{i_c}^2 = 2qI_C(f_2 - f_1) \tag{F.5c}$$

We find the output noise voltage for each of these noise sources separately. Then, using the fact that the sources are assumed to be uncorrelated, we can use superposition and obtain the total output noise voltage by adding each

Figure F.2
Equivalent noise cir-
cuit for a BJT.

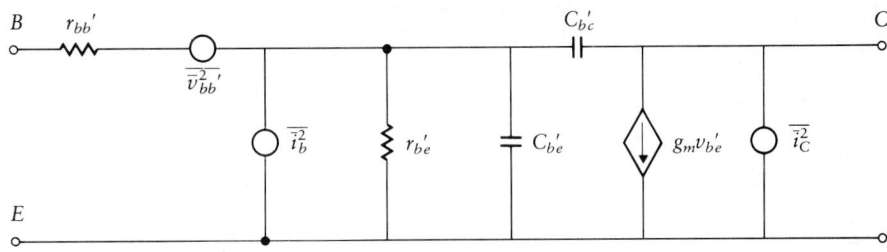

Figure F.3
Equivalent noise cir-
cuit for FET.

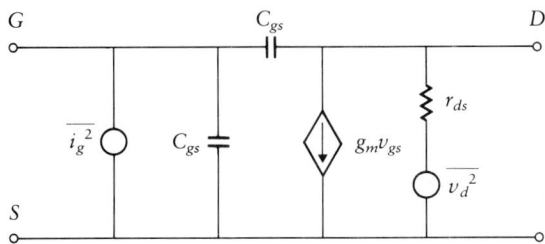

(mean-square) component of output noise voltage. Note that $r_{b'e}$ has no noise source associated with it since it is not a physical resistance.

F.1.5   *FET Noise*

The approach for noise analysis of FETs is similar to that of BJTs. We use the equivalent circuit for the FET, found in Figure 10.29(b), and add to it the noise sources, as shown in Figure F.3. These sources are summarized as follows:

$$\overline{i_g^2} = 2qI_G(f_2 - f_1) \tag{F.6a}$$

$$\overline{v_d^2} = 4kTr_{ds}(f_2 - f_1) \tag{F.6b}$$

Again, we find the total output noise voltage by superposition. That is, we add together the output mean-square voltage for each of the noise sources. The noise voltage at the output of a FET amplifier is much smaller than that for a BJT amplifier. This improved noise performance results because of the infinite input impedance of a FET.

The noise at the input to the first stage of a multistage amplifier is the most important to consider. This is true since the noise component at the input to the amplifier is multiplied by the voltage gain of the entire amplifier, whereas the noise voltage at the input to the second and later stages is amplified by a smaller gain.

F.2   Noise in Op-Amps

We now consider the important problem of applying the previously discussed noise sources to an op-amp system. (See [25] for further details on this topic.) We represent a noisy amplifier as a *noiseless* amplifier with a voltage-noise generator plus a current-noise generator connected to the input, as shown in Figure F.4. In this figure, we define the variables as follows:

$\overline{E_s^2}$ = mean-square signal source voltage

$\overline{e_s^2} = 4kTR_s(f_2 - f_1)$

R_s = noiseless source resistance

$\overline{e_n^2}$ = equivalent amplifier noise mean-square voltage generator

$\overline{i_n^2}$ = equivalent amplifier noise mean-square current generator

The low-pass RC filter at the output of the amplifier is used to reduce the white noise above the corner frequency. The resistor, R, is noiseless. The dimensions of the noise generators are as follows:

e_n is in volts(rms)/hertz$^{1/2}$

i_n is in amps(rms)/hertz$^{1/2}$

We again assume that the noise sources are uncorrelated so that the individual mean-square voltages can be added together. Hence, the total rms noise voltage is the square root of the sum of the squares of each noise source output.

We wish to find the total noise voltage output for the amplifier of Figure

Figure F.4
Equivalent noise circuit for an amplifier.

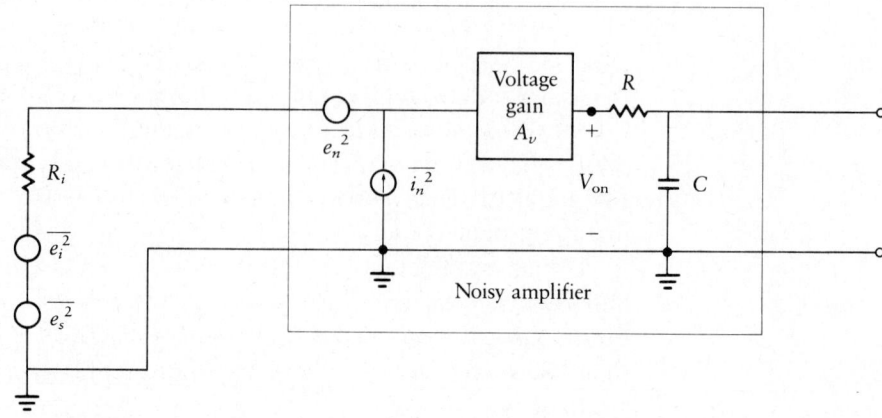

F.4. We add together all the noise sources and multiply them by the amplifier gain, A_v, with the result

$$V_{\text{on}} = \{[4kTR_i + \overline{e_n^2} + \overline{(i_n R_i)^2}] \, (f_2 - f_1)\}^{1/2} \, A_{vm} \tag{F.7}$$

The dimensions of the expression in equation (F.7) are volts (rms), and A_{vm} is the mid-range voltage gain of the amplifier.

F.2.1 *Signal-to-Noise Ratio*

We can rate the "goodness" of an amplifier by its ratio of signal output voltage to noise output voltage. The signal to noise voltage ratio at the output is represented by the symbol $(\text{SNR})_o$. We find $(\text{SNR})_o$ for the circuit of Figure F.4 by first calculating the signal voltage at the output, which is given by the equation

$$v_{os} = e_s A_{vm} \tag{F.8}$$

Hence, the output signal-to-noise voltage ratio, $(\text{SNR})_o$, is found by dividing equation (F.8) by equation (F.7), with the result

$$(\text{SNR})_o = \frac{e_s}{[4kTR_i + \overline{e_n^2} + \overline{(i_n R_i)^2}]^{1/2} \, (f_2 - f_1)^{1/2}} \tag{F.9}$$

The larger the $(\text{SNR})_o$ value, the better the amplifier. Note that the equivalent noise voltage, referred to the input of the amplifier, can be found by dividing equation (F.7) by the amplifier gain, A_{vm}. It is not possible to measure this voltage by placing a voltmeter across the amplifier input.

At this point, we observe that the $(\text{SNR})_o$ can be increased if we can eliminate any term from the denominator of equation (F.9). For example, we maximize the $(\text{SNR})_o$ by driving the amplifier with a zero source resistance, i.e., $R_i = 0$. We can further increase the $(\text{SNR})_o$ by limiting the bandwidth of the amplifier. We select the RC time constant of the low-pass filter in Figure F.4 to cut off any unnecessary frequencies, and in this manner, we increase the $(\text{SNR})_o$. The amplifier $(\text{SNR})_o$ can be further increased by using a higher-order filter, as discussed in Chapter 13.

F.2.2 *Noise Figure*

Noise figure is used to classify the noise performance of the amplifier. The noise figure is expressed in decibels and is derived from Figure F.4. We define the noise figure (NF) as follows:

$$NF = 20 \log_{10} \left[\frac{\text{input voltage SNR (amplifier disconnected)}}{\text{voltage SNR at amplifier output}} \right] \qquad (F.10)$$

We use Figure F.4 and substitute into equation (F.10), with the result

$$NF = 10 \log_{10} \left[\frac{\overline{e_s^2}/[4kTR_i(f_2 - f_1)]}{\overline{e_s^2}/[4kTR_i + \overline{e_n^2} + \overline{(i_n R_i)^2}] (f_2 - f_1)} \right] \qquad (F.11)$$

Equation (F.11) is further simplified to the following:

$$NF = 10 \log_{10} \left[1 + \frac{\overline{e_n^2} + \overline{(i_n R_i)^2}}{4kTR_i} \right] \qquad (F.12)$$

A noiseless amplifier, with $\overline{e_n^2} = \overline{i_n^2} = 0$, has a noise figure of 0 dB. For a fixed R_i, the least noisy amplifier has the smallest noise figure. As the input resistance approaches zero, the noise figure increases without limit.

F.2.3   *Noise-Reduction Considerations*

In this section, we consider optimizing the source resistance so that we can minimize the noise figure. The optimum source resistance, R_{iop}, is found by differentiating equation (F.12) as follows:

$$\frac{\partial NF}{\partial R_i} = 0 = \frac{4kT \ [2\overline{(i_n R_i)^2} - \overline{e_n^2} - \overline{(i_n R_i)^2}]}{\text{denominator in } R_i} \qquad (F.13)$$

with the result that

$$R_{iop} = \frac{e_n}{i_n} \qquad (F.14)$$

The minimum noise figure is found by substituting equation (F.14) into equation (F.12), with the result

$$NF_{min} = 10 \log_{10} \left[1 + \frac{e_n i_n}{4kT} \right] \qquad (F.15)$$

The optimum input resistance, which is the ratio of e_n to i_n, causes a minimum noise figure, as shown in equation (F.15). We can achieve a significant improvement in signal-to-noise ratio by matching the source resistance, R_i, to the R_{iop} of equation (F.14). This can be accomplished with a matching transformer.

We summarize the steps necessary to maximize the signal-to-noise ratio as follows:

1. Match the input resistance, R_i, to R_{iop}.
2. Use a filter to limit the system bandwidth, thus reducing the noise while permitting a tolerable signal distortion.
3. Use a high-input resistance amplifier with a low e_n and i_n. FETs should be used at the input to amplifiers.
4. Reduce source shot noise.
5. Reduce the input lead lengths as much as possible.

G   ANSWERS TO SELECTED PROBLEMS

In this appendix, we present answers to selected end-of-chapter problems. The more complex the problem, the less likely you will find the answer here. For example, the design problems in the later text chapters are intended to be *projects* involving many trade-off decisions. In most cases, there is more than one correct answer. To give one solution, and imply that you have achieved success if your answer agrees with ours, would be counterproductive.

The solutions to problems have been obtained using a calculator set for three significant digits. As such, rounding has occurred during complex mathematical operations.

1.3 Output waveshape as shown in Figure 1.21 with a 0 to peak amplitude of 45.5 V
1.6 0.0106 μF   **1.9** 3 mA; 13.9Ω   **1.12** 1.33Ω; 48 W; 60 W   **1.16** 2.62Ω   **1.25** Waveform clamped to zero—Waveform entirely negative

2.1 1.5 mA; 6.85 V New location: 2.73 mA; 4.27 V   **2.4** 8.74 mA   **2.7** (a) 139 mW; (b) 4.76 mW; 47.6 mW; 5.24 mW; 26.2 mW; (c) 55.4 mW   **2.10** (a) 2.34 kΩ; 13.8 kΩ (b) 6 V; (c) V_{CEQ} = 15 V; V'_{CC} = 18 V; I_{CM} = 60 mA   **2.12** (a) 2.9 kΩ; 6.45 kΩ; (b) 15 V; (c) V_{CEQ} = 7.5 V; V'_{CC} = 15 V; I_{CM} = 50 mA   **2.16** 1863 Ω; 5.97 V   **2.19** (a) 34.5 kΩ; (b) V_{CEQ} = 12 V; V'_{CC} = 18 V; I_{CM} = 18 mA; (c) 12 V; (d) 72 mW; 9 mW   **2.23** (a) −18.6 V; −2.12 mA; (b) V'_{CC} = 22.9 V; I_{CM} = −11.5 mA; (c) 4.24 V; (d) V'_{CC} would decrease, but output remains the same.   **2.26** I_{CQ} = 10 mA; v_o = 8 V maximum symmetrical swing; V_{CEQ} = 4 V; P_{trans} = 40 mW; P_o = 16 mW

3.2 (a) 4.88 kΩ; −5; −4.88; (b) 4.76 kΩ; −5; −4.76; (c) 3.44 kΩ; −4.55; −3.13   **3.5** −400   **3.11** −5.39; −20.5; 4.18 kΩ   **3.15** Graph starts out low and approaches 5 kΩ at infinite β. **3.18** I_{CQ} = -2.5 mA; R_E = 150 Ω since h_{ib} < $0.1R_E$; R_B = 3 kΩ; V_{BB} = -1.11 V; R_1 = 3.31 kΩ; R_2 = 32.4 kΩ; A_i =-9.1; v_o = 6.75 V undistorted symmetrical swing; R_{in} = 2.73 kΩ **3.22** I_{CQ} = 1.56 mA; R_E = 83 Ω; R_B = 6.67 kΩ; V_{BB} = 0.882 V; R_1 = 7.2 kΩ; R_2 = 91 kΩ; A_i = -25; v_o = 7.02 V **3.25** I_{CQ} = 20 mA; R_B = 16.67 kΩ; V_{BB} = 12.4 V; R_1 = 96.2 kΩ; R_2 = 20.2 kΩ; R_{in} = 12.5 kΩ; v_o = 9.0 V maximum symmetrical swing **3.28** I_{CQ} = 7.11 mA; R_B = 10.7 kΩ; V_{BB} = 11.8 V; R_1 = 40.8 kΩ; R_2 = 14.5 kΩ; A_i = 6.66; v_o = 9.6 V maximum symmetrical swing **3.31** I_{CQ} = 2.57 mA; R_B = 990 Ω; V_{BB} = 2.01 V; R_1 = 1.11 kΩ; R_2 = 8.87 kΩ; v_o = 9.25 V maximum symmetrical swing. **3.34** 0.2; 90.9; 4.55 kΩ **3.38** 2 V; 7.4 V; 8.1 V; 5.7 V **3.40** 206.7; 683.5

4.1 (a) -0.84 V; (b) 10 V; (c) 7.5 V; (d) 109 kΩ; 1.2 MΩ **4.4** R_D = 1.3 kΩ; R_S = 130 Ω; V_{GG} = 3.91 V; R_1 = 18.7 kΩ; R_2 = 76.7 kΩ; A_i = -15 **4.7** R_D = 2 kΩ; R_{Sdc} = 1 kΩ; R_{Sac} = 36 Ω; R_G = 20 kΩ; P_{trans} = 12 mW. **4.9** V_{GSQ} = 1.76 V; g_m = 1.18 mS; R_o = 3.3 kΩ; R_{Sdc} = 704 Ω; R_{Sac} = 146 Ω; R_o = 3.3 kΩ; R_G = 50 kΩ; P_{trans} = 25 mW **4.12** R_{S1} = 2.5 kΩ; R_{S2} = 1.5 kΩ; R_G = 20.2 kΩ; A_i = -3.1; A_v = -1.24 **4.15** V_{GSQ} = -0.94 V; I_{DQ} = 4.7 mA; g_m = 3.06 mS; A_v = -3.67; A_i = -612 **4.18** (a) -8.33; (b) -11.5; (c) -14.3 **4.20** R_D = 4.81 kΩ; R_S = 187 Ω; R_G = 8 kΩ; R_1 = 10.2 kΩ; R_2 = 36.5 kΩ **4.24** R_S = 1.43 kΩ; R_{Sac} = 820 Ω; R_1 = 18.5 kΩ; R_2 = 34.2 kΩ; A_v = 0.42 **4.27** R_S = 1.6 kΩ; R_{S1} = 200 Ω; R_{S2} = 1.4 kΩ; R_G = 2.44 kΩ; A_i = 1.17; A_v = 0.78

5.2 I_{CQ} = 6.15 mA; R_B = 217 kΩ; Circuit cannot be designed to have β independent of circuit operation; the circuit will saturate. **5.5** I_{CQ} = 2.05 mA; v_o = 6.98 **5.8** 7.42 V **5.11** 11.8 V **5.14** 10.1 V **5.17** 11.2 V

6.3 I_{CQ} = 13.6 mA; R_B = 287 Ω; R_1 = 334 Ω; R_2 = 2.05 kΩ **6.5** R_S = 15 kΩ; I_{CQ} = 8.57 mA; R_1 = 25.6 kΩ; R_2 = 36.1 kΩ; P_{trans} = 88.1 mW; P_L = 29.7 mW **6.8** (b) 2.25 W; (c) 63.4 Ω; 480 Ω; 199 μF; (d) 160 Ω **6.11** (a) I_{CM} = 354 mA; (b) 1.48 W; (c) 559 Ω; 398 μF; 24.3; 197 Ω **6.13** (a) 0.456 W; (b) 419 Ω; 151 Ω; 199 μF; (c) 18.1 **6.15** R_B = 6 kΩ; I_{CQ} = 0.8 A; C_1 = 15.9 μF; P_o = 0.648 W; R_1 = 40 kΩ; R_2 = 7.06 kΩ

7.2 -137.4; -0.5 **7.5** 0.6 V; 0.053 V **7.8** -5.075 V; -4.925 V **7.11** 0.227; -436; 65.7 dB **7.14** R_{C1} = 7.67 kΩ; A_c = 0.018; A_d = 6278; CMRR = 45 dB **7.18** I_{C1} = 0.732 mA; R_2 = 11.2 kΩ **7.21** From Spec. Sheet at 500 μA range, h_o = 6 μS or r_o = 167 kΩ; R_{TH} = 8.3 MΩ **7.24** R_E = 510 Ω; R'_E = 1.33 kΩ; R_1 = 48.4 kΩ; R_2 = 18.3 kΩ

8.3 1/121 **8.6** $-0.2v_1 - 2v_2 - 0.4 v_3$ **8.9** $-v_1 + 2v_2$ **8.12** (a) $-10v_1 - 3.66v_2$ **8.15** Example #1 Type: R_F = 96 kΩ; R_1 = 16 kΩ; R_2 = 12 kΩ; R_x = 48 kΩ; R_a = 32 kΩ; R_b = 8 kΩ; Example #2 Type: R_F = 128 kΩ; R_1 = 21.3 kΩ; R_2 = 16 kΩ; R_a = 42.7 kΩ; R_b = 10.7 kΩ; R_x = 64 kΩ **8.18** R = 100 kΩ **8.21** R_1 = R_3 = 5 kΩ; R_2 = 50 kΩ; C = 10 μF; R_S = 100 kΩ. Can use any logical values to meet requirements of equation. **8.24** $-j15/\omega$ **8.27** v_o = $0.66(1 - R/R_x)v_i$

9.2 (a) 20.5 mV; (b) 20.5 mV; (c) 12.8 mV   **9.5** All inputs into negative terminal.
R_F = 200 kΩ; R_1 = 20 kΩ; R_2 = 40 kΩ; R_3 = 50 kΩ; R_x = 10 kΩ;
$R_{in}(V_1)$ = 20 kΩ; $R_{in}(V_2)$ = 40 kΩ; $R_{in}(V_3)$ = 50 kΩ; R_o = 15 mΩ;
BW = 50 kHz. **9.8** Input Amplifier—Unity Gain Buffer—Two Stages. Output
Amplifier: R_F = 5 kΩ; R_A = 50 kΩ; R_1 = 770 kΩ; R_x = 1 kΩ   **9.11** Two stages—
Input amplifier—v_2 to plus terminal. R_1 = 9.8 kΩ; R_A = 10 kΩ; R_F = 490 kΩ.
Output Amplifier—First amplifier to negative terminal. v_1 into positive terminal.
R_1 = 9 kΩ; R_A = 500 kΩ; R_F = 10 kΩ.   **9.14** Three stages—Stage for v_1 and stage
for v_2 into an output summer stage. v_1 stage: R_1 = 10 kΩ = R_F (Unity Gain
buffer). v_2 stage: R_2 = 9.5 kΩ; R_A = 10 kΩ; R_F = 190 kΩ (Gain of +20).
Output stage: R_1 = 10 kΩ; R_2 = 350 kΩ; R_A = 10 kΩ; R_F = 350 kΩ;
R_o = 0.027 Ω; R_{in} ≈ 400 MΩ; BW = 27.8 kHz.   **9.21** 4 stages—3 unity gain buffers to obtain high input impedance and output amplifier to sum input. Output
stage: R_1 = 20 kΩ; R_2 = 42 kΩ; R_3 = 30 kΩ; R_F = 12.6 kΩ; R_A = 36 kΩ;
R_o ≈ 1 mΩ; BW = 740 kHz   **9.24** Use 3 pF since amplifier has gain above 10.
R_F = 1200 kΩ; R_A = 100 kΩ; R_y = 12.5 kΩ; R_1 = 10 kΩ; v_1 into R_1 and
+ terminal; v_2 into R_A and − terminal. $R_{in}(V_1)$ ≈ 200 MΩ; $R_{in}(V_2)$ = 100 kΩ;
BW = 1 MHz; R_o = 0.01 Ω

10.3 Amplitude plot starts at 40 dB and zero slope. First break point at 1 rad/s where
slope becomes − 20 dB/dec. Second break point at 10 rad/s where slope again
becomes zero at gain of 20 dB. Phase plot starts at 0° with slope of − 45°/dec. At 1
rad/sec, slope changes to zero at − 45°. At 10 rad/s, slope increases to 45°/dec. Slope
again becomes zero at 100 rad/s and 0°.   **10.6** Magnitude plot starts with slope of
− 20 dB/dec until 1 rad/s, at which point slope changes to zero at 0 dB. At 10 rad/s,
slope changes back to − 20 dB/dec. Phase starts with slope of + 45°/dec until it
reaches − 45° at 1 rad/s. Slope is then zero until 10 rad/s where it becomes − 45°/dec.
Slope changes to zero at 100 rad/s and a shift of − 90°.   **10.17** I_{CQ} = 0.75 mA;
R_B = 17.6 kΩ; R_1 = 19.5 kΩ; R_2 = 185 kΩ; (a) C_1 = 0.2 µF; C_2 = 2.7 µF;
(b) f_c = 25.8 Hz; C_1 = 0.31 µF; C_2 = 0.41 µF; (c) C = 0.33 µF; f_1 = 24 Hz;
f_2 = 32 Hz   **10.21** V_{GSQ} = − 2 V; (a) R_D = 1.25 kΩ; R_{Sdc} = 1 kΩ; R_{Sac} = 241 Ω;
(b) C_1 = 10.2 µF; C_2 = 57 µF; C_3 = 3.18 µF.   **10.23** R_D = 13.5 kΩ; R_S = 506 Ω;
No C_2 required; C_1 = 0.24 µF; C_3 = 1.59 µF   **10.26** I_{CQ} = 0.877 mA;
R_{in} = 1.26 kΩ; A_v = − 38.5; f_1 = 79.6 kHz; f_2 = 9.04 kHz; C_M = 178 pF;
f_h = 2.37 MHz. Bode plot starts at slope of 40 dB/dec until 79 Hz, then drops to
20 dB/dec until 9 kHz (0 dB), then becomes flat until 2.37 MHz and drop at
− 20 dB/dec.   **10.27** 412 kHz   **10.30** C_{gd} = 1.11 pF; C_{oss} = 1.27 pF;
C_{ds} = 0.163 pF **10.33** (a) High frequency: A_v = − 11.9; A_v (stage) = − 11.34;
C_{in} = 35.8 pF; C_o = 24 pF; f_1 = 93.6 kHz; f_2 = 1.4 MHz; (b) Low frequency:
f_1 = 83.3 Hz; f_2 = 0.53 Hz; f_3 = 3.18 Hz; f_4 = 1.5 Hz. Frequency response
is 83.3 Hz to 93.6 kHz.

11.1 − 500; 370 Ω; − 92.6   **11.3** − 500; 399 Ω; − 99.8   **11.6** A_v = − 500;
A_i = − 100   **11.12** Magnitude plot starts at slope of − 20 dB/dec, with first break at
10 rad/s and − 20 dB. Slope changes to − 40 dB/dec. Phase curve starts at − 90° and
slope of 0. Slope changes to − 45°/dec at 1 rad/s, and then back to zero slope at 100
rad/s and − 180° shift.   **11.25** Magnitude plot starts at slope of − 40 dB/dec until
break at 1 rad/s and value of − 40 dB. Slope then changes to − 20 dB/dec until 10
rad/s where it changes back to a slope of − 40 dB/dec. Phase plot starts at slope of
45°/dec until 1 rad/s and shift of − 135°. At that point, slope changes to − 45°/dec

until 10 rad/s, where slope changes to $-90°$/dec. At 100 rad/s and shift of $-270°$, slope changes to zero. **11.28** $C = 325$ pF; $C_{eq} = 0.101$ μF; $R_D = 12.5$ kΩ. If $C_1 = 0.2$ μF, then $C_2 = 0.205$ μF. **11.30** Let $R_F = 100$ kΩ, then $R_A = 50$ kΩ. If $R = 10$ kΩ then $C = 0.159$ pF.

12.5 Table 12.1 (Basic Negative Output, Inverting) and summer/inverter using negative terminal to invert and add a reference voltage. Rectifier Amp: $R_F = 10$ kΩ; $R_A = 10$ kΩ; $R_x = 5$ kΩ. Summer/invertor: $R_F = 10$ kΩ; $R_{A1} = 10$ kΩ; $R_{A2} = 20$ kΩ with input of negative 10 V reference voltage. **12.11** Table 12.3 (Upper and lower limiter) Balanced: $R_A = 10$ kΩ; $R_F = 20$ kΩ; $R_1 = 15.8$ kΩ; $R_2 = 4.87$ kΩ; $R_x = 6.67$ kΩ **12.20** Balanced limiter: For v_1 input, $R_A = 10$ kΩ; $R_F = 10$ kΩ. For v_2 input, $R_A = 20$ kΩ. Assume slope $= 1/20$, then $R_1 = 579$ Ω and $R_2 = 341$ Ω. **12.27** Balanced limiting comparator with axis shift: $R_A = 10$ kΩ; $R_1 = 896$ Ω; $R_2 = 360$ Ω using 1/20 as slope. Place -10 V into 1 kΩ/1 kΩ divider network to reduce voltage to -5 V into a 10 kΩ resistor in parallel with R_A.

13.1 Standard integrator. If $C = 1$ μF then $R = 100$ kΩ. **13.7** Invertor/summer with $Z_F = 1/sC$. If $C = 10$ μF, then $R_1 = 100$ kΩ, $R_2 = 10$ kΩ and $R_3 = 189$ kΩ. **13.14** Figure 13.12. If $C = 0.01$ μF, then $R = 159$ kΩ; $R_A = R_F = R_1 = R_2 = 10$ kΩ. Use 1 kΩ fixed resistor and 9 kΩ potentiometer. **13.22** Fig. 13.11(c). If $C = 0.001$ μF, then $R_1 = 8$ kΩ; $R_2 = 80$ kΩ. **13.28** Fig. 13.15. $R_A = 10$ kΩ; $R_F = 100$ kΩ; $R_1 = 10$ kΩ; $R_2 = 100$ kΩ; When $C = 0.01$ μF then $R = 80$ kΩ. Use a 1 kΩ fixed resistor and a 1 kΩ potentiometer. **13.34** Use 4th order. $C_1 = 0.35$ μF; $C_2 = 0.30$ μF; $C_3 = 0.84$ μF; $C_4 = 0.12$ μF and $R = 1$ kΩ. **13.37** If $C = 0.01$ μF, then $R_1 = 9.08$ kΩ; $R_2 = 11.76$ kΩ; $R_3 = 37.8$ kΩ; $R_4 = 4.92$ kΩ; $R_5 = 51.5$ kΩ.

14.1 See Figure 14.7(b) of text, with $V_1 = 4.15$ V, $V_2 = 0.86$ V. **14.6** See Figure 14.7(b) of text with $V_1 = 0.459$ V, $V_2 = 0$ V, $V_3 = -4.51$ V, $V_4 = -0.855$ V **14.8** See Figure 14.7(b) of text with $V_1 = 0.496$ V, $V_2 = 0.395$ V, $V_3 = -4.11$ V, $V_4 = -4.01$ V **14.10** See Figure 14.25 of text with $R_1 = 1$ kΩ, $R_2 = 6.7$ kΩ, and the capacitance between pin #2 and ground is switchable between 0.001 μF, 0.01 μF and 0.1 μF **14.12** See Figure 14.25 of text with R_1 as a series combination of a 9.6 kΩ fixed resistor and a 2.4 kΩ to 139.2 kΩ potentiometer, $R_2 = 2.4$ kΩ and the capacitance between pin #2 and ground is switchable between 0.01 μF, 0.1 μF and 1 μF. **14.18** Result is a pulse train with the widths of the pulses increasing with time.

15.2 $D = \overline{A} \cdot B \cdot \overline{C}$; $E = A \cdot B \cdot \overline{C}$

A	$\overline{A}$	B	C	$\overline{C}$	D	E	Y
0	1	0	0	1	0	0	0
0	1	0	1	0	0	0	0
0	1	1	0	1	1	0	1
0	1	1	1	0	0	0	0
1	0	0	0	1	0	0	0
1	0	0	1	0	0	0	0
1	0	1	0	1	0	1	1
1	0	1	1	0	0	0	0

15.6

A	B	C	A + B + C	Y
0	0	0	0	1
0	0	1	1	0
0	1	0	1	0
0	1	1	1	0
1	0	0	1	0
1	0	1	1	0
1	1	0	1	0
1	1	1	1	0

15.9 $Y = A \cdot B + B \cdot C$ **15.11** LUNCH SPEC = HAMBURGER$\cdot$(SOUP$\oplus$SALAD)
15.14 RENTED APART = COUPLE $\oplus$ SINGLE   **15.17** MUST ATTEND = (DAY OF CONF)$\cdot$(NIGHT + AFTERNOON)   **15.19** GAME = 1$\cdot$2$\cdot$3$\cdot$4

15.20

D	H	K	ALARM
0	0	0	0
0	0	1	0
0	1	0	0
0	1	1	0
1	0	0	0
1	0	1	1
1	1	0	1
1	1	1	1

15.23 Alarm is armed with a key operated switch, located in the fender. Once alarm is armed and burglars open door, trigger pulse activates 555 monostable. This timer provides 10 min pulse. Pulse enables astable 555 for 10 min, with output amplified by 2N2222 transistor, driving speaker located under hood.

15.30

A	B	Q_1	Q_2	Q_3	Q_4	Y
0	0	N	F	F	N	1
0	1	N	F	F	N	1
1	0	N	F	F	N	1
1	1	F	N	N	F	0

15.33

A	B	1	2	3	4	5	6	7	8	Y
0	0	N	N	F	F	F	N	N	F	1
0	1	N	F	F	N	F	N	N	F	1
1	0	F	N	N	F	F	N	N	F	1
1	1	F	F	N	N	N	F	N	N	0

15.35 See Figure 14.25 of text, with R_1 = 1 kΩ, R_2 is a series combination of a 1 kΩ fixed resistor and a 25 kΩ plot, the capacitance between pin #2 and ground is 0.01 µF, the capacitance between pin #5 and ground is 0.1 µF, and pin #3 feeds the LED display.

16.2	CMOS	TTL
	74C150	74150
SUPPLY V	3–15 V	7 V
Speed	120–250 ns	8–15 ns
Power Diss	20 mW	200 mW

16.7 For a base frequency, f_o of 10 kHz, C_{ext} = 0.05 µF. Output frequency range is 5.5 kHz to 11.3 kHz.   **16.9** Output Q_1 is connected to the clock B input and the counter is reset when the count reaches 10. When the outputs are 1010 the output of the AND gate is high and the zero set inputs are high. This clears the counter.
16.12 Use the 555 astable to develop a frequency that is twice the required frequency. This signal passes through a JK flip-flop which toggles on the rising edge of the pulse. The JK divides the frequency by 2 and maintains a duty cycle of 1.
16.13 A 555 astable is set to operate at 1 kHz with a duty cycle of 20 so the output at pin 3 is suitable to trigger the 555 monostable. It is a good design practice to use a fixed resistor for R_1 and a 10 kΩ ten turn potentiometer for R_2 so the frequency can be adjusted to 1 kHz. The variable duty cycle is achieved with a 555 monostable.

16.16 A 1 kHz 555 astable is used to clock a ÷N counter. The counter is enabled by pressing a button signifying a roll of the dice. The start signal is debounced before enabling the counter. A decoder circuit is designed using logic gates. The decoder outputs are fed into a 7-segment display.   **16.17** The rpm meter accepts the TTL compatible pulses and ANDs them with the window from a 555 astable. The output of the AND gate is input to three decade counters (74160), three latches (74175), three decoders (7447) and to the three 7-segment displays.

17.2 A 555 astable IC is designed to output pulses at a frequency of 1 kHz. These pulses are divided down until the output is 1 pulse per 5 s. This output clocks a 7493 binary counter. The outputs of the counter are used as select lines to a 16 to 1 multiplexer. The output of a 74150 MUX is active low. If a lamp is good, the output of the MUX is LOW, and if a lamp is faulty, the MUX output is HIGH. The MUX output is ANDed with the 1 kHz clock. The clock pulse triggers the 555 monostable IC which is designed to output a 5 s pulse.   **17.3** The approach to this problem is to determine the conditions necessary to reject a box. If sensor A is ON, the box is at least 4″ in height and too tall. If sensor B is not ON then the box is too short. And sensor C must be ON if a box is on the assembly line. The output is then $Y = (\bar{A}BC)'$, and can be produced with a 3-input NAND gate and one inverter. **17.5** We want to use a down counter since 9 represents full and 0 represents empty. Preset a 74193 UP/DOWN binary counter to 15 by connecting the transmitted pulse (inverted) to the load of the counter. Also use the transmitted pulse to trigger a monostable 555 IC to output a window pulse of 170 ms. This window pulse is ANDed with a 10 ms pulse train from a 555 astable IC. This gate, when enabled, begins the counter which counts down from 15. After 6 counts, the display will read 9, and after 16 counts, it will read 0. The received pulse latches the display and clears the counters. If the countdown does not reach 9 or goes past 0, the tank is either over 90% full or under 10% empty, and the alarm sounds.   **17.13** Use a 555 astable IC, designed to output one pulse per minute, as the circuit clock. Two cascaded 74190 decade counters are clocked by the 555 IC. To output the room number simultaneously, a 7493 binary counter is clocked and used to address a 16 to 1, 74150 multiplexer. After counting to 14, each counting system is synchronously cleared. Each room's TV set is monitored by the multiplexer for one minute every 14 minutes to determine if it is on or off. The output of the multiplexer is connected through a resistor to an LED to display whether a TV is on or off.   **17.24** The design requires an UP/DOWN counter to keep track of the number of cars in the garage. Initially (at the beginning of a workday), the counters must be cleared to zero. Every time a car enters, the counter counts up and every time a car leaves, the counter counts down. Since the pulse output from the entrance and exit gates is held high until a car passes through, the 74193 UP/DOWN BCD counters are ideally suited. Pin 4 and 5 of these counters are used to count down and up. The count can only occur if the pin not being clocked is held high, thus fitting the design specifications. The gate pulses need to be conditioned with an RC circuit to trigger the counters. Let the RC time constant equal 1 s. When the most significant counter reaches 3 (300 is the full count for the garage), display the word "FULL" on the LED display.

REFERENCES AND SOURCES FOR FURTHER STUDY

1. *AIM 65 Microcomputer User's Guide*. Anaheim, Calif.: Rockwell International, 1978.

2. Alley, C. L., and K. W. Atwood. *Microelectronics*. Englewood Cliffs, N.J.: Prentice Hall, Inc., 1986.

3. Allison, John. *Electronic Engineering Materials and Devices*. London: McGraw-Hill, 1971.

4. Ankrum, P. D. *Semiconductor Electronics*. Englewood Cliffs, N.J.: Prentice Hall, Inc., 1971.

5. Bekey, G. A., and M. D. Schwartz. *Hospital Information Systems*. New York: Marcel Dekker, Inc., 1972.

6. Boylestad, Robert, and Louis Nashelsky. *Electronic Devices and Circuit Theory*. Englewood Cliffs, N.J.: Prentice Hall, Inc., 1982.

7. Casasent, David. *Electronic Circuits*. New York: Quantum, 1973.

8. Clayton, David. *Operational Amplifiers*. London: Newnes-Butterworths, 1979.

9. *CMOS Databook*. Santa Clara, Calif.: National Semiconductor Corp., 1984.

10. Coblenz, A., and H. L. Owens. *Transistor Theory and Operation*. New York: McGraw-Hill, 1955.

11. Comer, D. J. *Modern Electronic Circuit Design*. Reading, Mass.: Addison-Wesley, 1976.

12. Cundy, K. R., and William Ball. *Infection Control in Health Care Facilities: Microbiological Surveillance*. Baltimore, Md.: University Park Press, 1977.

13. Ghausi, Mohammed S. *Electronic Devices and Circuits*. New York: Holt, Rinehart and Winston, 1985.

14. Gray, P. R., and R. G. Meyer. *Analysis and Design of Analog Integrated Circuits*. New York: John Wiley, 1984.

15. Grinich, V. H., and H. G. Jackson. *Introduction to Integrated Circuits*. New York: McGraw-Hill, 1975.

16. Gummel, H. K., and H. C. Poon. "An Integrated Charge Control Model of Bipolar Transistor." *Bell System Technical Journal* 49, no. 5 (1970): 827–852.

17. Hamilton, D. J., and W. G. Howard. *Basic Integrated Circuit Engineering*. New York: McGraw-Hill, 1975.

18. Horowitz, Paul, and Winfield Hill. *The Art of Electronics*. New York: Cambridge University Press, 1975.

19. Irvine, R. G. *Operational Amplifier Characteristics and Applications*. Englewood Cliffs, N.J.: Prentice-Hall, Inc., 1981.

20. Jacob, J. M. *Application and Design with Integrated Circuits*. Reston, Va.: Reston Publishing Co., 1982.

21. Jung, W. *IC Op-Amp Cookbook*. Indianapolis, Ind.: Howard Sams and Co., 1980.

22. Kiver, Milton. *Transistors*. New York: McGraw-Hill, 1962.

23. Lancaster, Don. *TTL Cookbook*. Indianapolis, Ind.: Howard Sams and Co., 1974.

24. Lancaster, Don. *CMOS Cookbook*. Indianapolis, Ind.: Howard Sams and Co., 1978.

25. Letzter, S., and N. Webster. "Noise in Amplifiers." *IEEE Spectrum* (August, 1970).

26. *Linear and Data Acquisition Products*. Melbourne, Fla.: Harris Semiconductor Products Division, 1983.

27. *Linear Databook*. Santa Clara, Calif.: National Semiconductor Corp., 1984.

28. Luciano, J. R. *Air Contamination Control in Hospitals*. New York: Plenum Press, 1977.

29. Mano, M. M. *Digital Design*. Englewood Cliffs, N.J.: Prentice Hall, Inc., 1984.

30. *Master Selection Guide*. Phoenix, Ariz.: Motorola Semiconductor Products, Inc.

31. *MECL System Design Handbook*. Mesa, Ariz.: Motorola Semiconductor Products, Inc., 1971.

32. Millman, J., and C. Halkias. *Electronic Fundamentals and Applications*. New York: McGraw-Hill, 1976.

33. Millman, J., and C. Halkias. *Integrated Electronics*. New York: McGraw-Hill, 1972.

34. Millman, J. *Microelectronics*. New York: McGraw-Hill, 1979.

35. Millman, J., and H. Taub. *Pulse, Digital and Switching Waveforms*. New York: McGraw-Hill, 1965.

36. Milnes, A. G. *Semiconductor Devices and Integrated Circuits*. New York: Van Nostrand-Reinhold, 1980.

37. Moll, J. *Physics of Semiconductors*. New York: McGraw-Hill, 1964.

38. Morris, H. M. "Pressure Measurement: A Wide View of a Wider Subject." *Controls Engineering* (May 1978): 57–60.

39. *MOS/CCD Databook*. Mountain View, Calif.: Fairchild Camera and Instrument Corp, 1975.

40. "Opto Electronics." Power Electronics Semiconductor Dept., General Electric Co., 1986.

41. Peatman, J. B. *The Design of Digital Systems*. New York: McGraw-Hill, 1972.

42. Peatman, J. B. *Digital Hardware Design*. New York: McGraw-Hill, 1980.

43. Peatman, J. B. *Microcomputer-Based Design*. New York: McGraw-Hill, 1977.

44. Pierret, J., and G. W. Neudeck. *Semiconductor Fundamentals*. Reading, Mass.: Addison-Wesley, 1983.

45. *Precision Monolithics 1977–1978 Linear & Conversion IC Products*. Santa Clara, Calif.: Precision Monolithics, Inc., 1977.

46. *Resistance Temperature Detectors and Systems*. Santa Fe Springs, Calif.: Hy-Cal Engineering, 1979.

47. Ruthowski, G. B. *Solid State Electronics*. Indianapolis, Ind.: Bobbs-Merrill, 1980.

48. Sah, C. T., R. N. Noyce, and W. Shockley. "Carrier Generation and Recombination in P-N Junction Characteristics." *Proc. IRE* (1957): 1228.

49. Sedra, A. S., and K. C. Smith. *Microelectronic Circuits*. New York: Holt, Rinehart and Winston, 1982.

50. Senturia, S. A., and B. D. Wedlock. *Electronic Circuits and Applications*. New York: John Wiley, 1974.

51. Shilling, D. L., and Charles Belove. *Electronic Circuits, Discrete and Integrated*. New York: McGraw-Hill, 1979.

52. *Schottky & Low Power Schottky Data Book*. Sunnyvale, Calif.: Advanced Micro Devices, Inc., 1975.

53. Streetman, B. G. *Solid State Electronic Devices*. Englewood Cliffs, N.J.: Prentice Hall, Inc., 1980.

54. Taub, H., and D. Schilling. *Digital Integrated Electronics*. New York: McGraw-Hill, 1977.

55. *Temperature Measurement Handbook*. Stamford, Conn.: Omega Engineering, Inc., 1979.

56. Timko, M. P. "A Two-Terminal IC Temperature Transducer." *IEEE Journal Solid State Circuits*. SC-11 (December 1976): 784–788.

57. Tocci, R. J. *Fundamentals of Electronic Devices*. Columbus, Ohio: Merrill, 1982.

58. *TTL Databook for Design Engineers*. Dallas: Texas Instruments, Inc., 1976.

59. U. S. Department of Health, Education, and Welfare. *Minimum Requirements of Construction and Equipment for Hospitals and Medical Facilities*. HEW Publication No. (HRA) 74-4000, 1974.

60. *Validyne Engineering Corporation Products and Capabilities Catalog*. Northridge, Calif.: Validyne Engineering Corporation, 1979.

61. Van der Ziel, A. *Solid State Physical Electronics*. Englewood Cliffs, N.J.: Prentice-Hall, Inc., 1968.

62. Van Valkenburg, M. E. *Network Analysis*. Englewood Cliffs, N.J.: Prentice-Hall, Inc., 1974.

63. Widlar, R. S. "Some Circuit Design Techniques for Linear Integrated Circuits." *IEEE Transactions on Circuit Theory*. CT-12 (1968).

64. Williams, A. B. *Electronic Filter Design Handbook*. New York: McGraw-Hill, 1981.

65. Wilson, G. R. "A Monolithic Junction FET-NPN Operational Amplifier." *IEEE Journal of Solid State Devices*. SC-2 (December 1968).

66. Young, Thomas. *Linear Integrated Circuits*. New York: John Wiley, 1981.

INDEX

ABOUT THE AUTHORS

C. J. SAVANT, JR. is a dedicated engineering educator. He received his Ph.D. *cum laude* from California Institute of Technology and has taught in the California State University system at both the Long Beach and the Los Angeles campuses. Dr. Savant is the recipient of the California State University "Outstanding Professor Award" and has consistently been voted the Most Loved Professor in the Electrical Engineering Department at California State University, Los Angeles, by his students. In addition to his teaching, Professor Savant has completed considerable research and has headed up his own engineering firm.

MARTIN S. RODEN is the Chairman of the Department of Electrical and Computer Engineering at California State University, Los Angeles. Dr. Roden received his BSEE *summa cum laude* from Polytechnic Institute of Brooklyn, and then went on to spend five years doing research at Bell Labs, the birthplace of the transistor. His interest in teaching led him back to academia, where he has gone on to hold positions as Department Chair, Associate Dean, Dean and Associate Vice President at various times. However, Professor Roden's first love remains teaching, for which he was awarded the University's Outstanding Professor Award. He is very active in IEEE, has earned the IEEE's Outstanding Adviser Award, and is a Fellow of the Institute for the Advancement of Engineering.

GORDON CARPENTER retired with the rank of Lt. Colonel from the U.S. Air Force, where he had over twenty years of experience in the design and development of high technology USAF equipment. This experience has made Professor Carpenter very realistic in his approach to the education of future engineers. In his Air Force career as an R&D manager, he trained new engineers to develop hardware specifications from system requirements, and to insure that hardware could be built to meet those specifications. Colonel Carpenter is a strong proponent of design-oriented education, and his practical experience is essential to this text.

Standard Notation

Component	Symbol	Subscript	Example
dc or average value	Upper-case	Upper-case	V_{CB}, I_C
s domain ω domain rms quantities	Upper-case	Lower-case	V_{cb}, I_c
Total (dc + time-varying component)	Lower-case	Upper-case	v_{CB}, i_C
Instantaneous value of time-varying component	Lower-case	Lower-case	v_{cb}, i_c
Bias supply voltage	Upper-case	Double, upper-case	V_{BB}, V_{CC}
Amplitude of a sinusoid	Upper-case	no subscript	I

Examples of Other Variables

V_{rms}	Root-mean-square voltage	R_o, Z_o	Output resistance, output impedance
$v_{(p\text{-}p)}$ or $v_{peak\text{-}to\text{-}peak}$	Peak-to-peak voltage of a time-varying signal (equals twice the signal amplitude)	P_o	Output power
V_{TH}, R_{TH}	Thevenin equivalent voltage and resistance	$I_{max}(I_{min})$	Maximum (minimum) current that can exist under given circuit conditions
V_i, v_i	Input voltage	$V_{max}(V_{min})$	Maximum (minimum) voltage that can exist under given circuit conditions
I_{in}, i_{in}	Input current		
R_{in}, Z_{in}	Input resistance, input impedance	$P_{max}(P_{min})$	Maximum (minimum) power that can exist under given circuit conditions
V_o, v_o	Output voltage		
I_o, i_o	Output current	$i_p (v_p)$	Peak value of current (voltage)